FIFTH EDITION

HANDEL'S NATIONAL DIRECTORY

FOR

THE PERFORMING ARTS

VOLUME ONE

ORGANIZATIONS AND FACILITIES

The 5th edition of Handel's NATIONAL DIRECTORY FOR THE PERFORMING ARTS was prepared by
R.R. Bowker's Data Base Publishing Group.

Marion Sader, Publisher

Dean Hollister, Director, Data Base Planning
Andrew Grabois, Editorial Director
Elizabeth A. Onaran, Managing Editor
Kimberly A. Willard, Senior Editor
April Messina, Carole J. Rafferty, Stacy A. Stanford, Pu Xiang; Associate Editors
Kimberley B. Jenkins, M. Michelle Mahlstadt, Erica Milowitz; Assistant Editors

Judy Redel, Director, Research
Tanya Hurst, Senior Editor, Research

Peter Simon, Vice President, Data Base Publishing Group

FIFTH EDITION

HANDEL'S NATIONAL DIRECTORY

FOR

THE PERFORMING ARTS

VOLUME ONE

ORGANIZATIONS AND FACILITIES

R.R.BOWKER®

Published by R.R. Bowker, a Reed Reference Publishing Company

International Standard Book Numbers:
2 Vol Set: 0-8352-3250-6
Volume 1:   0-8352-3327-8
Volume 2:   0-8352-3328-6
Library of Congress Catalog Card Number: 73-646635
Printed and bound in the United States of America

ISBN 0 - 8352 - 3250 - 6

9 780835 232500

TABLE OF CONTENTS

VOLUME ONE: ORGANIZATIONS & FACILITIES

VOLUME TWO: EDUCATIONAL INSTITUTIONS

ORGANIZATIONS & FACILITIES - STATE INDEX

PREFACE

Handel's National Directory for the Performing Arts was first published in 1973 as a result of the vision and energy of Beatrice Handel, who perceived that the explosive growth of the performing arts in all sections of the United States required an authoritative directory to document and encourage that development. From the beginning, the directory's mission has been to "serve as a major and comprehensive resource document for and about the performing arts industry, assisting individuals and organizations in their search for specific information that is qualitative and quantitative relative to their industry." *Handel's* is unique in providing information on both performing arts organizations and facilities as well as information on educational institutions that offer courses and degree programs in the performing arts.

This fifth edition is the first since 1988 and the first to be published by R.R. Bowker, a Reed Reference Publishing Company, a major publisher of directories worldwide. Like its predecessors, it provides current, authoritative information on the status of the performing arts in the United States. Reflecting the continued growth of the field, this edition features more than 900 new organizations and facilities and over 300 new educational programs.

Compilation

Methods used in the compilation of this edition included mail and telephone surveys, updating of fourth edition listings and analysis of published and unpublished sources. More than a year was spent compiling lists of organizations, educational institutions and facilities, retrieving the information needed, and verifying that information. The same process also confirmed the demise or inactivity of organizations, educational institutions and facilities. Information given in response to these requests has been edited to conform to the entry format.

Organization and Contents

Handel's is organized in two volumes, the first covering organizations and facilities, the second educational institutions. The performing arts areas covered in *Volume One* are Dance, Instrumental and Vocal Music, Theatre, and Performing Series. Organizations that do not fit into a specific arts area, such as festivals, sponsoring organizations, historical dramas and community concerts, are included under the general heading Performing Series.

Volume One is arranged alphabetically by state, city within each state, and then arts area. Organization listings contain the names, addresses and phone numbers of the organizations, names of artistic and administrative management, board members, numbers of staff, budget and attendance statistics, founding dates and performance facilities. The Facility listings include the types of facilities and stages, construction and remodeling costs, architects, resident groups, stage dimensions, seating capacities and information on rental availability.

The educational institutions in the second volume are listed alphabetically within the states and contain specific information on their Dance, Music and Theatre departments. Courses, degrees, department heads, numbers of faculty and students, technical training and financial assistance are detailed. Information is also included on each institution's performing groups and series, guest and resident artists, and facilities.

Indexing

Volume One contains separate indices to the Dance, Instrumental Music, Vocal Music, Theatre, and Performing Series organizations as well as a separate index to the Facilities. Additionally, there is a General Index which lists all organizations and facilities alphabetically by name. Similarly, *Volume Two* has separate indices to the Dance, Music and Theatre programs as well as the General Institution Index which lists educational institutions alphabetically by name.

Acknowledgments

The editors wish to thank Bea Handel for her suggestions and guidance for this edition. We are also grateful to all the organizations that took the time to submit information for this directory. Without their help, such an undertaking would not be possible. Comments and suggestions for future editions are always welcome.

AFFILIATIONS

AAA	American Arts Alliance
AACT	American Association of Community Theatres
AAM	American Association of Museums
AATA	American Alliance for Theatre Arts
AATE	American Association of Theatre Educators
AATY	Association of American Theatre for Youth
ACA	American Council for the Arts
ACDA	American Choral Directors Association
ACDFA	American Colleges Dance Festival Association
ACTA	American Community Theatre Association
ACTF	American College Theatre Festival
ACU-I	Association of College Unions - International
ADMA	Alliance for Dance and Movement Arts
ADTA	American Dinner Theatre Association
ADTI	American Dinner Theatre Institute
AEA	Actors' Equity Association
AFM	American Federation of Musicians of the United States and Canada
AFTRA	American Federation of Television and Radio Artists
AGMA	American Guild of Musical Artists
AGO	American Guild of Organists
AGVA	American Guild of Variety Artists
AHA	Association of Hispanic Arts
AMC	American Music Conference
APAC	American Performing Arts Center
APAP	Association of Performing Arts Presenters
ART/NY	Alliance of Resident Theatres/New York
ASCAP	American Society of Composers, Authors and Publishers
ASOL	American Symphony Orchestra League
ASSITEJ	Association Internationale du Theatre pour l'Enfance et de la Jeunesse (International Association of Theatre for Children and Youth)
ATHE	Association for Theatre in Higher Education
BMI	Broadcast Music, Inc.
BOMI	Box Office Management International
CA	Chorus America
CMA	Chamber Music America
CORST	Council of Resident Summer Theatres
COS	Central Opera Service
COST	Council of Stock Theatres
CTAA	Children's Theatre Association of America
DGA	Directors Guild of America
DTW	Dance Theatre Workshop
ECTC	East Coast Theatre Conference
EMA	Early Music America
FACT	Festival of American Community Theatre
FEDAPT	Foundation for the Extension and Development of American Professional Theatre
FIDOF	Federation Internationale des Organisateurs de Festivals (International Federation of Festival Organizations)
GALA Choruses	Gay and Lesbian Association of Choruses
GFA	Guitar Foundation of America
IAAM	International Association of Auditorium Managers
IADMS	International Association for Dance Medicine and Science
IAJE	International Association of Jazz Educators
IATSE	International Alliance of Theatrical Stage Employees and Moving Picture Machine Operators of the United States and Canada
ISPAA	International Society of Performing Arts Administrators

AFFILIATIONS

ITI	International Theatre Institute
LATA	Los Angeles Theatre Alliance
LATP	League of American Theatres and Producers
LCT	League of Chicago Theatres
LMDA	Literary Managers and Dramaturges of America
LOFT	League of Fringe Theatres
LORT	League of Resident Theatres
MAAA	Mid-America Arts Alliance
MENC	Music Educators National Conference
MESA	Middle East Studies Association
MOMA	Museum of Modern Art
NAAO	National Association of Artists Organizations
NACA	National Association for Campus Activities
NALAA	National Association of Local Arts Agencies
NARB	National Association for Regional Ballet
NASAA	National Assembly of State Arts Agencies
NASD	National Association of Schools of Dance
NAST	National Association of Schools of Theatre
NDA	National Dance Association
NDTA	National Dinner Theatre Association
NEA	National Endowment for the Arts
NEAT	New England Area Theatres
NEP	National Education Program
NETC	New England Theatre Conference
NGCSA	National Guild of Community Schools of the Arts, Inc.
NIMT	National Institute for Music Theater
NMTA	National Movement Theatre Association
NOA	National Opera Association
NPN	National Performance Network
NSOA	National Symphony Orchestra Association
NSOL	National Symphony Orchestra League
OA	Opera America
OGI	Opera Guild International
PNWAP	Pacific Northwest Arts Performers
PRBA	Pacific Regional Ballet Association
RDA	Regional Dance America
ROOTS	Rural Organization of Theatres South
SAF	Southern Arts Federation
SEM	Society for Ethno-Musicology
SERBA	Southeast Regional Ballet Association
SETC	Southeastern Theatre Conference
SPEBSQSA	Society for the Preservation and Encouragement of Barbershop Quartets Singing in America, Inc.
SPTA	Small Professional Theatre Association
SSDC	Society for Stage Directors and Choreographers
SWRBA	Southwest Regional Ballet Association
TAAC	The Association for Artists of Color
TCG	Theatre Communications Group
TOG	The Opera Guild
TYA	Theatre for Young Audiences
U/RTA	University/Resident Theatre Association
UNIMA	United International Marionette Association
USA	United Scenic Arts
USITT	United States Institute for Theatre Technology, Inc.
WAAA	Western Alliance of Arts Administrators
WSAF	Western States Arts Federation

ALABAMA

Andalusia

FACILITY

DIXON CENTER FOR THE PERFORMING ARTS
PO Box 1418, Andalusia, AL 36420
(205) 222-6591
FAX: (205) 222-6567
Founded: 1982
Type of Facility: Theatre Complex; Concert Hall; Auditorium; Studio Performance; Performance Center; Theatre House; Room; Loft
Type of Stage: Proscenium
Stage Dimensions: 42'x30' **Orchestra Pit**
Seating Capacity: 500
Year Built: 1982 **Architect:** Pearson, Humphries, Jones & Associates, Inc. **Cost:** $900,000
Acoustical Consultant: Electronic Engineers, Inc.
Contact for Rental: Jerry Padgett; (205) 222-6591, ext. 238
Resident Groups: Junior College Music and Drama Classes

Anniston

THEATRE

ANNISTON COMMUNITY THEATER
PO Box 1454, Anniston, AL 36202
(205) 236-8342
Founded: 1927
Arts Area: Professional; Community
Status: Semi-Professional; Non-Profit
Type: Performing; Resident; Educational
Purpose: To promote dramatic art and culture in the community
Management: Josephine E. Ayers, Producing Artistic Director; Dena Kirkland, Administrative Director
Officers: James Nolen, President; Margaret McNaron, Treasurer; Michael Cassidy, Secretary
Paid Staff: 2 **Volunteer Staff:** 50
Paid Artists: 10 **Non-Paid Artists:** 40
Budget: $50,000 - $100,000
Income Sources: Private Foundations/Grants/Endowments; Business/Corporate Donations; Box Office; Government Grants; Individual Donations
Season: 52 Weeks **Annual Attendance:** 6,000
Performance Facilities: ACT Playhouse

Birmingham

DANCE

SOUTHERN DANCEWORKS
2829 Second Avenue South, Suite 301, Birmingham, AL 35233
(205) 322-6483
Founded: 1963
Arts Area: Modern; Jazz
Status: Professional; Non-Profit; Commercial
Type: Performing; Educational; Sponsoring
Purpose: To promote performances and the teaching of contemporary dance by local and professional touring artists; to provide a climate where local dancers, teachers, choreographers and artists may realize creative potential; to encourage dance in public education
Management: Joanna Fuller, Director of Development; Mary Foshee, Artistic Director
Officers: Paulette ZanMatre, Chairman of the Board
Paid Staff: 2 **Volunteer Staff:** 16
Paid Artists: 6 **Non-Paid Artists:** 6
Utilizes: Guest Artists
Budget: $100,000 - $500,000
Income Sources: Private Foundations/Grants/Endowments; Business/Corporate Donations; Box Office; Government Grants; Individual Donations
Annual Attendance: 6,000

THE STATE OF ALABAMA BALLET/BALLET SOUTH
2001 Park Place North, Birmingham, AL 35203
(205) 252-2475
FAX: (205) 252-2476
Founded: 1981
Arts Area: Ballet
Status: Professional
Type: Performing; Touring
Purpose: To offer professional ballet performances to the Southeast
Management: Catherine Gilmore, Managing Director; Dame Sonia Arova, Artistic Director; Carol H. Cotton, Administrative Assistant; Gail L. Vaughn
Officers: George G. Lynn, Chair; Mrs. Lee Walls, President; Dr. Morgan Eland, Vice President; Mrs. Harvey Gotlieb, Secretary; Steven Christian, Treasurer
Paid Staff: 3   **Volunteer Staff:** 25
Paid Artists: 22   **Non-Paid Artists:** 20
Utilizes: Guest Artists; Guest Choreographers
Budget: $500,000 - $1,000,000
Income Sources: Private Foundations/Grants/Endowments; Business/Corporate Donations; Box Office; Individual Donations
Season: August - April   **Annual Attendance:** 20,000
Performance Facilities: Civic Center Theatre and Concert Hall

INSTRUMENTAL MUSIC

ALABAMA SYMPHONY ORCHESTRA
2001 Park Place North, Birmingham, AL 35203
(205) 326-0100
FAX: (205) 521-9069
Founded: 1933
Arts Area: Symphony; Orchestra
Status: Non-Profit
Type: Performing
Purpose: To promote, foster and encourage symphonic music and the art of music generally
Management: Mark Walker, Executive Director
Officers: Michael Warren, Chairman of the Board; Harold Apolinsky, President; Marvin Engel, Vice President; Peggy Werdehoff, Secretary
Paid Staff: 15
Paid Artists: 80
Utilizes: Guest Conductors; Guest Artists
Budget: $1,000,000 - $5,000,000
Income Sources: Private Foundations/Grants/Endowments; Business/Corporate Donations; Government Grants; Individual Donations
Season: September - May   **Annual Attendance:** 144,000
Affiliations: ASOL; AFM
Performance Facilities: Birmingham-Jefferson Civic Center Concert Hall

VOCAL MUSIC

BIRMINGHAM OPERA THEATER
2027 First Avenue North, Commerce Center, Suite 1, Birmingham, AL 35203
(205) 322-6737
FAX: (205) 251-6870
Founded: 1957
Arts Area: Grand Opera; Lyric Opera
Status: Professional; Non-Profit
Type: Performing; Touring; Educational
Purpose: To promote opera and American musical dramas through world-class productions and educational tours
Management: Zane Bradford, Executive Office Administrator
Officers: J. Ernest Hill, President
Paid Staff: 2   **Volunteer Staff:** 4
Paid Artists: 24   **Non-Paid Artists:** 25
Utilizes: Special Technical Talent; Guest Conductors; Guest Artists; Guest Directors
Budget: $100,000 - $500,000
Income Sources: Private Foundations/Grants/Endowments; Business/Corporate Donations; Box Office; Government Grants; Individual Donations
Season: September - May   **Annual Attendance:** 25,000

Affiliations: Alabama Shakespeare Festival; Atlanta Symphony
Performance Facilities: Birmingham Jefferson Civic Center

THEATRE

BIRMINGHAM CHILDREN'S THEATRE
3 Civic Center Plaza, Birmingham, AL 35203
(205) 324-0470
Founded: 1947
Arts Area: Professional; Theatrical Group
Status: Professional; Non-Profit
Type: Performing; Touring; Resident; Educational; Sponsoring
Purpose: The Birmingham Children's Theatre is a professional company providing quality theatre for young people which incorporates literature, art, music and drama into a medium that is both entertaining and culturally enriching.
Management: James W. Rye, Jr., Managing Director
Officers: Charles D. Perry Jr., President; Barnett Earles, First Vice President; James Moylan, Second Vice President; Felix Drennen III, Third Vice President; Betty H. Pewitt, Secretary; Jean P. Pierce, Treasurer
Paid Staff: 21   **Volunteer Staff:** 80
Paid Artists: 55
Utilizes: Special Technical Talent; Guest Artists; Guest Directors
Budget: $500,000 - $1,000,000
Income Sources: Private Foundations/Grants/Endowments; Business/Corporate Donations; Box Office; Government Grants; Individual Donations
Season: August - May
Annual Attendance: 520,000
Performance Facilities: Civic Center Theatre

TOWN AND GOWN THEATER
1116 South 26th Street, Birmingham, AL 35205
(205) 934-5088
Founded: 1950
Arts Area: Musical; Community; Theatrical Group
Status: Non-Profit
Type: Performing; Touring; Educational
Management: Gary Robertson, Director; Joyce Whitten, Administrative Assistant
Paid Staff: 17   **Volunteer Staff:** 50
Non-Paid Artists: 75
Utilizes: Special Technical Talent; Guest Artists; Guest Directors
Budget: $100,000 - $500,000
Income Sources: Private Foundations/Grants/Endowments; Business/Corporate Donations; Box Office; Individual Donations
Season: October - June   **Annual Attendance:** 33,000
Affiliations: AATA; SETC
Performance Facilities: Clark Memorial Theater

PERFORMING SERIES

BIRMINGHAM FESTIVAL OF ARTS ASSOCIATION
Commerce Center, 2027 First Avenue North, Suite 910, Birmingham, AL 35203
(205) 252-7652
FAX: (205) 252-7656
Founded: 1951
Arts Area: Dance; Vocal Music; Instrumental Music; Theater
Status: Non-Profit
Type: Performing; Educational; Sponsoring
Purpose: A voluntary, non-commercial endeavor to increase international and human understanding by bringing local ethnic groups and foreign citizens together to exhibit the cultural achievements of other nations and peoples
Management: Sara C. Crowder, Executive Director
Officers: Carole Staats, Chairman; David Carder, President
Paid Staff: 2
Utilizes: Special Technical Talent; Guest Conductors; Guest Artists; Guest Directors
Budget: $100,000 - $500,000
Income Sources: Business/Corporate Donations; Box Office; Individual Donations
Season: April - May   **Annual Attendance:** 150,000

FACILITY

BIRMINGHAM-JEFFERSON CIVIC CENTER
1 Civic Center Plaza, Birmingham, AL 35203
(205) 458-8400
FAX: (205) 458-8437
    Type of Facility: Civic Center
    Year Built: 1976   **Architect:** Geddes, Brecher, Qualls & Cunningham   **Cost:** $65,000,000
    Acoustical Consultant: Bolt, Beranek & Newman
    Contact for Rental: George Pierce;   (205) 458-8434
    Contains the Coliseum, Concert Hall, Theatre and Exhibition Hall. See separate listings for additional information.

BIRMINGHAM-JEFFERSON CIVIC CENTER - COLISEUM
1 Civic Center Plaza, PO Box 13347, Birmingham, AL 35202-3347
(205) 458-8400
FAX: (205) 458-8437
    Type of Facility: Civic Center; Arena
    Type of Stage: Flexible; Platform
    Seating Capacity: 16,750
    Year Built: 1976
    Contact for Rental: George Pierce;   (205) 458-8434
    Resident Groups: Birmingham Bulls (Ice Hockey)

BIRMINGHAM-JEFFERSON CIVIC CENTER - CONCERT HALL
1 Civic Center Plaza, PO Box 13347, Birmingham, AL 35202-3347
(205) 458-8400
FAX: (205) 458-8437
    Type of Facility: Concert Hall; Civic Center
    Type of Stage: Thrust; Proscenium
    Stage Dimensions: 88'Wx84'Dx26'H   **Orchestra Pit**
    Seating Capacity: 3,000
    Year Built: 1974
    Contact for Rental: George Pierce;   (205) 458-8434
    Resident Groups: Alabama Symphony Orchestra

BIRMINGHAM-JEFFERSON CIVIC CENTER - EXHIBITION HALL
1 Civic Center Plaza, PO Box 13347, Birmingham, AL 35202-3347
(205) 458-8400
FAX: (205) 458-8437
    Type of Facility: Civic Center; Exhibition Hall
    Type of Stage: Flexible
    Year Built: 1972
    Contact for Rental: George Pierce;   (205) 458-8434
    220,000 square feet of exhibition space; 70,000 square feet of meeting rooms

BIRMINGHAM-JEFFERSON CIVIC CENTER - THEATRE
1 Civic Center Plaza, PO Box 13347, Birmingham, AL 35202-3347
(205) 458-8400
FAX: (205) 458-8437
    Type of Facility: Theatre House; Civic Center
    Type of Stage: Thrust; Flexible; Proscenium
    Stage Dimensions: 70'Wx46'Dx27'H   **Orchestra Pit**
    Seating Capacity: 1000
    Year Built: 1974
    Contact for Rental: George Pierce;   (205) 458-8434
    Resident Groups: Birmingham Children's Theater

BIRMINGHAM-SOUTHERN COLLEGE THEATRE
900 Arkadelphia Road, Birmingham, AL 35254
(205) 226-4782
    Type of Facility: Theatre Complex
    Type of Stage: Thrust; Flexible; Proscenium; Arena
    Orchestra Pit
    Seating Capacity: 390
    Year Built: 1968   **Cost:** $1,500,000
    Contact for Rental: Matthew Mielke;   (205) 226-4785

Decatur

FACILITY

PRINCESS THEATRE
112 Second Avenue, NE, Decatur, AL 35601
(205) 350-1745
  Type of Facility: Performance Center
  Facility Originally: Stable
  Type of Stage: Proscenium
  Stage Dimensions: 34'Wx25'D; 34'Wx16'H proscenium opening   **Orchestra Pit**
  Seating Capacity: 677
  Year Built: 1887
  Year Remodeled: 1983   **Architect:** Frank Neville   **Cost:** $750,000
  Contact for Rental: Manager;   (205) 350-1745
  Resident Groups: Bank Street Players; Professional Series; Travelog Series
  Became Princess Theatre in 1919, remodeled in Art Deco in 1941

Dothan

THEATRE

SOUTHEAST ALABAMA COMMUNITY THEATRE
PO Box 6065, Dothan, AL 36303
(205) 794-0400
  Founded: 1974
  Arts Area: Summer Stock; Community
  Status: Non-Professional; Non-Profit
  Type: Performing
  Purpose: To bring performing theatre to southeast Alabama
  Management: Connie Miller, Business Manager; Marge Wein, General Manager
  Officers: Danny Richards, President; Nancy Robinson, Vice President; Jane Long, Secretary; Connie Miller, Treasurer
  Paid Staff: 2   **Volunteer Staff:** 200
  Budget: $100,000 - $500,000
  Income Sources: Box Office
  Season: 52 Weeks   **Annual Attendance:** 10,000
  Performance Facilities: Dothan Opera House

FACILITY

DOTHAN CIVIC CENTER
North St. Andrews Street, Dothan, AL 36303
(205) 793-0126
  Type of Facility: Auditorium
  Type of Stage: Proscenium
  Stage Dimensions: 54'Wx44'Dx28'H   **Orchestra Pit**
  Seating Capacity: 3100
  Year Built: 1974   **Architect:** Waid & Holmes   **Cost:** $7,000,000
  Contact for Rental: Betty Ellsworth;   (205) 793-0126
  Resident Groups: Southeast Alabama Community Theatre; Community Concerts

---

Huntsville

DANCE

HUNTSVILLE CIVIC BALLET
620 St. Claire Avenue SW, PO Box 373, Huntsville, AL 35801
(205) 539-0961
  Founded: 1967
  Arts Area: Modern; Ballet; Jazz
  Status: Semi-Professional; Non-Profit
  Type: Touring; Resident
  Purpose: To provide and educate people in Huntsville with dance; to promote arts with master classes
  Management: Floyd Tygett, Artistic Director; David Harriott, Assistant Director
  Officers: Joan May, President; Mrs. T. Craig, First Vice President; Lita Smith, Second Vice President; Betty Soule, Board Member
  Non-Paid Artists: 25

Utilizes: Guest Artists
Budget: $50,000 - $100,000
Income Sources: Private Foundations/Grants/Endowments; Business/Corporate Donations; Box Office; Government Grants; Individual Donations
Season: 52 Weeks

INSTRUMENTAL MUSIC

HUNTSVILLE SYMPHONY ORCHESTRA
PO Box 2400, Huntsville, AL 35804
(205) 539-4818
FAX: (205) 539-4819
Founded: 1953
Arts Area: Symphony
Status: Non-Professional; Non-Profit; Commercial
Type: Performing; Educational; Sponsoring
Purpose: To provide locally-generated, live orchestral music to the community
Management: Gloria Holdman, Executive Director; Taavo Virkhaus, Musical Director
Non-Paid Artists: 75
Utilizes: Guest Conductors; Guest Artists
Budget: $500,000 - $1,000,000
Income Sources: Business/Corporate Donations; Box Office; Government Grants; Individual Donations; Fund-raising
Season: October - May   **Annual Attendance:** 21,000
Affiliations: ASOL
Performance Facilities: Von Braun Civic Center Concert Hall

HUNTSVILLE YOUTH ORCHESTRA
607 Airport Road SW, Huntsville, AL 35802
(205) 882-0774
Founded: 1962
Arts Area: Orchestra; Chamber; Ensemble
Status: Non-Professional; Non-Profit
Type: Performing; Touring; Educational; Sponsoring
Purpose: To provide a rewarding and challenging experience for its members by means of an active participation in the performance of good music; to awaken interest in symphonic literature in young people by giving them an opportunity to play good music and train those young people having outstanding talent for future participation in the performance of good music
Management: Gary Parks, Music Director/Conductor; Johnny Brewer, Administrative Director; Kay Jones, Administrative Assistant
Paid Staff: 4   **Volunteer Staff:** 100
Non-Paid Artists: 270
Utilizes: Guest Conductors; Guest Artists
Budget: $50,000 - $100,000
Income Sources: Private Foundations/Grants/Endowments; Business/Corporate Donations; Box Office; Government Grants; Individual Donations
Season: October - May   **Annual Attendance:** 5,000
Affiliations: ASOL (Youth Orchestra Division); Alabama Federation of Music; Alabama Arts Council
Performance Facilities: Von Braun Civic Center

VOCAL MUSIC

HUNTSVILLE OPERA THEATER
8802 Willow Hills Drive, Huntsville, AL 35802
(205) 881-4796
Founded: 1981
Arts Area: Grand Opera
Status: Non-Profit
Type: Performing
Purpose: To foster the development of young singers, dancers and technicians
Management: Helen Bargetzi, Artistic Director
Officers: Kevin R. Alspaugh, President; Joseph Galloway, Vice President; Jeanne Marlow, Secretary/Treasurer
Budget: $1,000 - $50,000
Income Sources: Private Foundations/Grants/Endowments; Business/Corporate Donations; Box Office; Individual Donations
Season: October - July
Performance Facilities: Von Braun Civic Center Playhouse

THEATRE

HUNTSVILLE LITTLE THEATRE
700 Monroe Street, Huntsville, AL 35801
(205) 533-6565
> **Founded:** 1949
> **Arts Area:** Musical; Community; Theatrical Group
> **Status:** Non-Professional; Non-Profit
> **Type:** Performing
> **Purpose:** To develop, encourage and promote community interest in dramatic arts and to provide a means by which members may broaden and improve their knowledge and proficiency in theatre arts
> **Officers:** Patricia Blackman, President; Elaine Hubbard, Vice President; Ray Cooper, Secretary; Rene Sevigny, Treasurer
> **Volunteer Staff:** 60
> **Non-Paid Artists:** 50
> **Utilizes:** Special Technical Talent; Guest Artists
> **Budget:** $1,000 - $50,000
> **Income Sources:** Private Foundations/Grants/Endowments; Business/Corporate Donations; Box Office; Government Grants; Individual Donations
> **Season:** September - June **Annual Attendance:** 7,000
> **Affiliations:** Alabama Theatre Conference
> **Performance Facilities:** Von Braun Civic Center

FACILITY

VON BRAUN CIVIC CENTER
700 Monroe Street SW, Huntsville, AL 35801
(205) 533-1953
FAX: (205) 551-2203
> **Founded:** 1975
> **Type of Facility:** Theatre Complex; Concert Hall; Civic Center; Multi-Purpose
> **Type of Stage:** Thrust; Flexible; Proscenium; Platform
> **Seating Capacity:** Arena - 10,106; Playhouse - 502; Concert Hall - 2,171
> **Year Built:** 1975 **Architect:** Smith, Kranert, Tomblin & Associates **Cost:** $15,500,000
> **Acoustical Consultant:** C.P. Boner & Associates
> **Contact for Rental:** Ronald D. Evans, Executive Director; (205) 533-1953
> *The Civic Center contains the Arena, Concert Hall, Exhibit Hall and Playhouse. See separate listings for additional information.*

VON BRAUN CIVIC CENTER - ARENA
700 Monroe Street SW, Huntsville, AL 35801
(205) 533-1953
FAX: (205) 551-2203
> **Founded:** 1975
> **Type of Facility:** Arena
> **Type of Stage:** Arena
> **Seating Capacity:** 10,106
> **Year Built:** 1975 **Architect:** Smith, Kranert, Tomblin & Associates **Cost:** $15,500,000
> **Contact for Rental:** Ronald D. Evans, Executive Director; (205) 533-1953

VON BRAUN CIVIC CENTER - CONCERT HALL
700 Monroe Street SW, Huntsville, AL 35801
(205) 533-1953
FAX: (205) 551-2203
> **Type of Facility:** Concert Hall
> **Type of Stage:** Proscenium
> **Stage Dimensions:** 54'W **Orchestra Pit**
> **Seating Capacity:** 2,171
> **Year Built:** 1975
> **Contact for Rental:** Ronald Evans; (205) 553-1953
> **Resident Groups:** Huntsville Symphony

VON BRAUN CIVIC CENTER - EXHIBIT HALL
700 Monroe Street SW, Huntsville, AL 35801
(205) 533-1953
FAX: (205) 551-2203
> **Founded:** 1975
> **Type of Facility:** Exhibition Hall

Type of Stage: Flexible; Platform
Seating Capacity: 2,000
Year Built: 1975
Contact for Rental: Ronald Evans;   (205) 553-1953
Seats 2,000 banquet-style

VON BRAUN CIVIC CENTER - PLAYHOUSE
700 Monroe Street SW, Huntsville, AL 35801
(205) 533-1953
FAX: (205) 551-2203
    Type of Facility: Theatre House
    Type of Stage: Thrust; Flexible; Proscenium
    Stage Dimensions: 32'W
    Seating Capacity: 502, 348, 232
    Year Built: 1975
    Contact for Rental: Ronald Evans;   (205) 553-1953
    Resident Groups: Huntsville Little Theater; Fantasy Playhouse; Twinchenham Repertory Company; University Players; Tennessee Opera Association; Huntsville Literary Association

Mobile

VOCAL MUSIC

MOBILE OPERA
PO Box 8366, Mobile, AL 36689
(205) 460-2900
    Founded: 1946
    Arts Area: Grand Opera
    Status: Non-Profit
    Type: Performing; Touring; Educational
    Purpose: To educate youth and culturally enrich the metropolitan community
    Management: Pelham G. Pearce, Jr., General Manager; Ted Taylor, Music Director
    Officers: J.B. Horst, President; Wade B. Perry, Vice President
    Paid Staff: 5   **Volunteer Staff:** 40
    Paid Artists: 20
    Utilizes: Special Technical Talent; Guest Artists; Guest Directors
    Budget: $100,000 - $500,000
    Income Sources: Private Foundations/Grants/Endowments; Business/Corporate Donations; Box Office; Government Grants; Individual Donations
    Season: October - March
    Annual Attendance: 15,000
    Affiliations: OA
    Performance Facilities: Mobile Civic Center Theatre

THEATRE

MOBILE THEATRE GUILD
PO Box 1265, Mobile, AL 36633
(205) 433-7513
    Founded: 1950
    Arts Area: Community; Theatrical Group
    Status: Non-Professional
    Type: Performing; Educational
    Purpose: Community theater specializing in off-Broadway shows
    Management: Michael McKee, Director
    Officers: Reenie Aldes, President; Barbara Baughman, Vice President/Treasurer; Anne Scott, Secretary
    Paid Staff: 1
    Budget: $50,000 - $100,000
    Income Sources: Private Foundations/Grants/Endowments; Business/Corporate Donations; Box Office; Government Grants; Individual Donations
    Season: August - May   **Annual Attendance:** 3,500
    Affiliations: FACT

FACILITY

MOBILE CIVIC CENTER
Civic Center Drive, Mobile, AL 36602
(205) 434-7261
FAX: (205) 434-7551
Type of Facility: Civic Center
Year Built: 1964   **Architect:** Slater & Slater   **Cost:** $12,000,000
Contact for Rental: Rick Linio;   (205) 434-7261
Resident Groups: Greater Symphonic Concerts of Mobile; Mobile Municipal Theatre Performing Arts Series;
Mobile Symphonic Pops Orchestra; Mobile Opera; Mobile Ballet
Complex contains the Arena, Exposition Hall and Theatre. See separate listings for additional information.

MOBILE CIVIC CENTER - ARENA
401 Civic Center Drive, Mobile, AL 36602
(205) 434-7261
FAX: (205) 434-7551
Type of Facility: Arena
Type of Stage: Proscenium
Stage Dimensions: 88'Wx40'D
Seating Capacity: 10,680
Year Built: 1964
Contact for Rental: Rick Linio;   (205) 434-7261

MOBILE CIVIC CENTER - EXPOSITION HALL
401 Civic Center Drive, Mobile, AL 33602
(205) 434-7261
FAX: (205) 434-7551
Type of Facility: Exhibition Hall
Type of Stage: Flexible
Year Built: 1964
Contact for Rental: Rick Linio;   (205) 434-7261
Exposition Hall contains 30,000 square feet

MOBILE CIVIC CENTER - THEATRE
410 Civic Center Drive, Mobile, AL 33602
(205) 434-7261
FAX: (205) 435-7551
Type of Facility: Concert Hall; Theatre House
Type of Stage: Proscenium
Stage Dimensions: 42'Wx51'D   **Orchestra Pit**
Seating Capacity: 1,950
Year Built: 1964
Contact for Rental: Rick Linio;   (205) 434-7261

MOBILE THEATRE GUILD
14 North Lafayette Street, Mobile, AL 36607
(205) 433-7513
Type of Facility: Theatre House
Type of Stage: Thrust; Proscenium
Stage Dimensions: 10'x30'x50'
Seating Capacity: 150
Year Built: 1955
Contact for Rental: Mike McKee;   (205) 471-1795

Montgomery

DANCE

MONTGOMERY BALLET
4050 Troy Highway, Montgomery, AL 36116
(205) 288-3110
Founded: 1960
Arts Area: Ballet
Status: Semi-Professional; Non-Profit
Type: Performing; Educational
Purpose: To foster quality ballet in the community, state and region

Management: Don Steffy, Artistic Director; Marylou Hume, Associate Director
Officers: David Kahn, President; Dottye Hannan, President Elect
Paid Staff: 37
Paid Artists: 5
Utilizes: Guest Artists
Budget: $100,000 - $500,000
Income Sources: Private Foundations/Grants/Endowments; Box Office; Government Grants; Individual Donations
Season: 52 Weeks
Affiliations: SERBA
Performance Facilities: Davis Theatre; Alabama Shakespeare Festival; Carolyn Blount Theatre

INSTRUMENTAL MUSIC

MONTGOMERY SYMPHONY ORCHESTRA
220 North Hull Street, Montgomery, AL 36104
(205) 262-5182
Founded: 1976
Arts Area: Symphony; Orchestra
Status: Semi-Professional
Type: Performing; Educational
Purpose: To provide a symphony orchestra in the capital city
Management: Thomas Hinds, Musical Director/Conductor
Officers: Phil Murkett, President, Montgomery Symphony Association
Paid Staff: 2   **Volunteer Staff:** 3
Utilizes: Guest Artists
Budget: $100,000 - $500,000
Income Sources: Private Foundations/Grants/Endowments; Business/Corporate Donations; Box Office; Individual Donations
Season: October - June   **Annual Attendance:** 15,000
Affiliations: ASOL
Performance Facilities: Daves Theater

PERFORMING SERIES

ALABAMA SHAKESPEARE FESTIVAL
One Festival Drive, Montgomery, AL 36117
(205) 272-1640
Arts Area: Dance; Vocal Music; Instrumental Music; Theater; Festivals
Status: Professional; Non-Profit
Type: Performing; Touring; Resident; Educational; Sponsoring
Purpose: To present the classics as a living and exciting part of our dramatic literature; through the classics, we put a mirror up to other distant times and, by doing so, shed light on our times and the problems of our lives in the twentieth century
Management: E. Timothy Langan, Managing Director; Kent Thompson, Artistic Director
Paid Staff: 200
Paid Artists: 47
Utilizes: Special Technical Talent; Guest Artists; Guest Directors
Budget: $1,000,000 - $5,000,000
Income Sources: Private Foundations/Grants/Endowments; Business/Corporate Donations; Box Office; Government Grants; Individual Donations
Season: 52 Weeks   **Annual Attendance:** 130,000
Performance Facilities: Alabama Shakespeare Festival

FACILITY

ALABAMA SHAKESPEARE FESTIVAL
One Festival Drive, Montgomery, AL 36117
(205) 272-1640
FAX: (205) 271-5348
Type of Facility: Performance Center
Year Built: 1985   **Architect:** Tom Blount   **Cost:** $21,500,000
Acoustical Consultant: ARTEC
Contact for Rental: Beau Williams, General Manager;   (205) 271-5300
Resident Groups: Alabama Shakespeare Festival

ALABAMA SHAKESPEARE FESTIVAL - FESTIVAL STAGE
One Festival Drive, Montgomery, AL 36117
(205) 272-1640
FAX: (205) 271-5348
> **Type of Facility:** Theatre House
> **Type of Stage:** Proscenium; Modified Thrust
> **Stage Dimensions:** 95'7"Wx69'1"D; 60'3"Wx33'3"H proscenium opening   **Orchestra Pit**
> **Seating Capacity:** 750
> **Year Built:** 1985
> **Contact for Rental:** Beau Williams;   (205) 271-5300
> **Resident Groups:** Alabama Shakespeare Festival

ALABAMA SHAKESPEARE FESTIVAL - OCTAGON
One Festival Drive, Montgomery, AL 36117
(205) 272-1640
FAX: (205) 271-5348
> **Type of Facility:** Black Box
> **Type of Stage:** Flexible; Octagonal
> **Stage Dimensions:** 22'7"N, 28'3"NE, 22'7"E, 28'3"SE, 22'7"S, 28'3"SW, 22'7"W, 28'3"NW
> **Seating Capacity:** 225
> **Year Built:** 1985
> **Contact for Rental:** Beau Williams, General Manager;   (205) 271-5300
> **Manager:** Beau Williams;   (205) 271-5300
> **Resident Groups:** Alabama Shakespeare Festival
> *Stage dimensions are interior wall lengths of the octagonal space referenced by compass point directions*

Tuscaloosa

THEATRE

NEW PLAYWRIGHTS' PROGRAM - UNIVERSITY OF ALABAMA
PO Box 870239, Tuscaloosa, AL 35487
(205) 348-9032
> **Founded:** 1982
> **Arts Area:** Theatrical Group
> **Status:** Professional; Non-Profit
> **Type:** Touring; Resident; Educational
> **Purpose:** To develop new plays for production and workshops
> **Management:** Dr. Paul Castagno, Director
> **Officers:** Dr. Ed Williams, Department Chair
> **Paid Staff:** 2
> **Paid Artists:** 11
> **Utilizes:** Guest Artists; Guest Directors; Playwrights
> **Budget:** $50,000 - $100,000
> **Income Sources:** Private Foundations/Grants/Endowments; Box Office
> **Season:** August - April
> **Affiliations:** SETC; ATHE; NAST; LMDA; Dramatist Guild

FACILITY

BAMA THEATRE PERFORMING ARTS CENTER
600 Greensboro Avenue, Tuscaloosa, AL 35401
(205) 758-5195
> **Type of Facility:** Concert Hall; Theatre House; Opera House
> **Facility Originally:** Vaudeville; Movie House
> **Type of Stage:** Modified Apron Proscenium
> **Stage Dimensions:** 48'Wx30'D; 32'10"Wx24'H proscenium opening
> **Seating Capacity:** 1,100
> **Year Built:** 1938   **Architect:** WPA   **Cost:** $150,000
> **Year Remodeled:** 1985   **Architect:** Fitts & White Architects   **Cost:** $450,000
> **Contact for Rental:** Gail Skidmore or Danny Smalley;   (205) 758-5195
> **Manager:** Danny Smalley;   (205) 758-8083
> **Resident Groups:** Theatre Tuscaloosa; Punch & Judy Players; Tuscaloosa Children's Theatre; Tuscaloosa Community
> Dancers; Tuscaloosa Civic Chorus; Tuscaloosa Chapter, SPEBSQSA
> *The Center is a National Historic Landmark. Renovation began in 1976 and was completed in 1985.*

UNIVERSITY OF ALABAMA - CONCERT HALL
Frank Moody Music Building, PO Box 2876, Tuscaloosa, AL 35487-2876
(205) 348-7110
   Type of Facility: Concert Hall
   Type of Stage: Concert Stage
   Stage Dimensions: 36'x56'x54'   **Orchestra Pit**
   Seating Capacity: 1000
   Year Built: 1987   **Architect:** Woolen, Molzan & Partners and Fitts & White, Associated Architects   **Cost:** $2,000,000
   Acoustical Consultant: R. Lawrence Kirkegaard & Associates
   Contact for Rental: John Martin;   (205) 348-1471
   Resident Groups: School of Music Ensembles and University Symphony

UNIVERSITY OF ALABAMA - GALLAWAY THEATRE
Department of Theatre and Dance, PO Box 870239, Tuscaloosa, AL 35487-0239
(205) 348-5283
   Type of Facility: Theatre House
   Type of Stage: Proscenium
   Stage Dimensions: 30'Wx30'D; 30'Wx18'D proscenium opening   **Orchestra Pit**
   Seating Capacity: 338
   Year Built: 1956   **Architect:** Van Keuren, Davis & Company   **Cost:** $750,000
   Resident Groups: University Theatre; Dance Alabama

UNIVERSITY OF ALABAMA - HUEY RECITAL HALL
Frank Moody Music Building, PO Box 2876, Tuscaloosa, AL 35487-2876
(205) 348-7110
   Type of Facility: Recital Hall
   Type of Stage: Concert Stage
   Stage Dimensions: 15'x24'x26'
   Seating Capacity: 140
   Year Built: 1987   **Architect:** Woolen, Molzan & Partners and Fitts & White, Associated Architects
   Cost: $360,000
   Acoustical Consultant: R. Lawrence Kirkegaard & Associates
   Contact for Rental: John Martin;   (205) 348-1471
   Resident Groups: Student Recitals

UNIVERSITY OF ALABAMA - MORGAN AUDITORIUM
Department of Theater and Dance, PO Box 870239, Tuscaloosa, AL 35487
(205) 348-5283
   Type of Facility: Auditorium
   Type of Stage: Proscenium
   Stage Dimensions: 30'x29'x50'   **Orchestra Pit**
   Seating Capacity: 716
   Year Built: 1911
   Year Remodeled: 1976   **Cost:** $35,000
   Manager: Edie Barnes, Director
   Resident Groups: Dance Alabama

Tuscumbia

THEATRE

IVY GREEN THEATER
300 West North Commons, Tuscumbia, AL 35674
(205) 383-4066
   Founded: 1961
   Arts Area: Theatrical Group
   Status: Non-Profit
   Type: Performing; Sponsoring
   Purpose: To sponsor an outdoor production of William Gibson's "The Miracle Worker" at the birthplace of Helen Keller in Tuscumbia each summer
   Management: Sue Pilkilton, Manager
   Officers: Rea Mills, Chairman; Lurline Cook, Treasurer
   Paid Staff: 4   **Volunteer Staff:** 36
   Non-Paid Artists: 14
   Utilizes: Guest Directors
   Budget: $1,000 - $50,000
   Income Sources: Box Office
   Season: Mid-June - July   **Annual Attendance:** 5,350

ALASKA

Anchorage

DANCE

ANCHORAGE CONCERT ASSOCIATION INC.
524 West Fourth Avenue, Suite 208, Anchorage, AK 99501
(907) 272-1471
FAX: (907) 272-2519
    Arts Area: Modern; Mime; Ballet; Jazz; Ethnic; Folk; Classical
    Status: Non-Profit
    Type: Presenting
    Purpose: To be Alaska's premiere presenter of the arts
    Management: Ira Perman, Executive Director
    Officers: Tom Gallagher, President of the Board
    Budget: $1,000,000 - $5,000,000
    Income Sources: Private Foundations/Grants/Endowments; Business/Corporate Donations; Box Office; Government Grants; Individual Donations
    Season: 52 Weeks
    Performance Facilities: Anchorage Center for Performing Arts

ANCHORAGE FOLK DANCE CONSORTIUM
c/o Shirley Hauck, 2440 East Tudor Road, #342, Anchorage, AK 99507
(907) 345-2699
    Founded: 1975
    Arts Area: Folk
    Status: Non-Professional; Non-Profit
    Type: Performing; Educational
    Purpose: To teach, perform and promote interest in folk dance, especially dances of Eastern Europe and the Balkans
    Management: Shirley Hauck, Ph.D, Teacher and Choreographer
    Officers: Barbara Meyer, President; Ahmad Amer, Treasurer; Chris Maack, Member-at-Large
    Volunteer Staff: 10
    Non-Paid Artists: 10
    Budget: $1,000 - $50,000
    Income Sources: Private Foundations/Grants/Endowments; Government Grants; Individual Donations
    Season: 52 Weeks   **Annual Attendance:** 1,000

BALLET ALASKA
3605 Arctic Boulevard, Suite 267, Anchorage, AK 99503
(907) 346-3200
    Founded: 1960
    Arts Area: Ballet
    Status: Non-Profit
    Type: Performing; Educational
    Purpose: To bring quality dance to all Alaskans and to provide any Alaskan the opportunity to partake of dance
    Management: Lynda Lorimer, Founding Artistic Director; Kathy Fernandez, Executive Director; Earl Sterling, Technical Director
    Officers: Karl Thoennes, President
    Paid Staff: 5   **Volunteer Staff:** 40
    Utilizes: Guest Artists; Guest Directors; Guest Choreographers
    Budget: $50,000 - $100,000
    Income Sources: Private Foundations/Grants/Endowments; Business/Corporate Donations; Box Office; Government Grants; Individual Donations
    Season: September - June   **Annual Attendance:** 7,000
    Performance Facilities: Alaska Center for the Arts

INSTRUMENTAL MUSIC

ANCHORAGE SYMPHONY ORCHESTRA
524 West Fourth Avenue, Suite 205, Anchorage, AK 99501
(907) 274-8668
FAX: (907) 272-2519
    Founded: 1946
    Arts Area: Symphony; Orchestra; Chamber; Ensemble
    Status: Non-Profit
    Type: Performing; Educational

Purpose: To contribute to the quality of life by providing high-caliber orchestral music for an expanding audience
Management: Sherri Reddick, Executive Director; Stephen Stein, Music Director/Conductor; Wendy Long, Administrative Assistant
Paid Staff: 3   **Volunteer Staff:** 215
Paid Artists: 75
Utilizes: Guest Conductors; Guest Artists
Budget: $100,000 - $500,000
Income Sources: Business/Corporate Donations; Box Office; Government Grants; Individual Donations
Season: October - May   **Annual Attendance:** 15,000
Affiliations: ASOL
Performance Facilities: Anchorage Community College Performing Arts Center

ANCHORAGE YOUTH SYMPHONY
PO Box 240541, Anchorage, AK 99524-0541
(907) 243-1207
Founded: 1965
Arts Area: Symphony; Orchestra
Status: Non-Professional; Non-Profit
Type: Performing; Touring; Educational
Purpose: To rehearse and perform symphonic music of the masters; to tour
Management: Linn Weeda, Music Director/Conductor
Officers: Alan Persons, President
Paid Staff: 1   **Volunteer Staff:** 250
Non-Paid Artists: 210
Utilizes: Guest Artists
Budget: $50,000 - $100,000
Income Sources: Private Foundations/Grants/Endowments; Business/Corporate Donations; Box Office; Individual Donations; Fund-raising
Season: September - May   **Annual Attendance:** 4,000
Affiliations: ASOL (Youth Orchestra Division)
Performance Facilities: West High Auditorium

VOCAL MUSIC

ALASKA LIGHT OPERA THEATRE
639 West International Airport Road, #34, Anchorage, AK 99502
(907) 345-2568
FAX: (907) 561-7515
Founded: 1984
Arts Area: Light Opera
Status: Professional; Non-Profit
Type: Performing; Resident; Educational
Purpose: To produce professional-quality musical theatre; to produce musical-theatre education programs for Alaska school children; to provide professional development to aspiring Alaskan musical-theatre performers through the Resident Artists Program
Management: Gloria Marinacci Allen, General Director; Judy O'Neal, Administrative Assistant
Officers: James Feeney, President; Duane Heyman, Vice President; Frank Danner, Treasurer; Jacquie Turpin, Secretary
Paid Staff: 2   **Volunteer Staff:** 100
Paid Artists: 150
Utilizes: Special Technical Talent; Guest Conductors; Guest Artists; Guest Directors
Budget: $500,000 - $1,000,000
Income Sources: Private Foundations/Grants/Endowments; Business/Corporate Donations; Box Office; Government Grants; Individual Donations
Season: July - September   **Annual Attendance:** 12,000
Performance Facilities: Fourth Avenue Theatre

ANCHORAGE CONCERT CHORUS
PO Box 103738, Anchorage, AK 99510-3738
(907) 274-7464; (907) 561-8000
FAX: (907) 563-5980
Founded: 1947
Arts Area: Choral
Status: Non-Profit
Type: Performing
Purpose: To provide the community with the opportunity to participate in the performance of quality music
Officers: John Brower, President of the Board
Paid Staff: 3
Non-Paid Artists: 160
Utilizes: Guest Conductors

Budget: $50,000 - $100,000
Income Sources: Private Foundations/Grants/Endowments; Business/Corporate Donations; Box Office; Government Grants; Individual Donations
Season: September - April   **Annual Attendance:** 4,000
Affiliations: Anchorage Community College
Performance Facilities: Alaska Center for the Performing Arts

ANCHORAGE OPERA COMPANY
1507 Spar Avenue, Anchorage, AK 99501
(907) 270-2557
FAX: (907) 279-7798
    Founded: 1976
    Arts Area: Grand Opera; Lyric Opera; Light Opera; Operetta
    Status: Professional; Non-Profit
    Type: Performing; Resident; Educational
    Purpose: To produce professional opera
    Management: Margaret Wood, General Manager; Ian D. Hoak, Business Manager; H.E. Hollibaugh, Technical Director; Lisa D. Lind, Administrative Assistant
    Officers: Michael F.G. Williams, President
    Paid Staff: 4
    Paid Artists: 325
    Utilizes: Guest Conductors; Guest Artists; Guest Directors
    Budget: $500,000 - $1,000,000
    Income Sources: Private Foundations/Grants/Endowments; Business/Corporate Donations; Box Office; Government Grants; Individual Donations
    Season: September - March; April   **Annual Attendance:** 8,000
    Affiliations: OA
    Performance Facilities: Discovery Theatre; Alaska Center for the Performing Arts

THEATRE

OUT NORTH THEATRE COMPANY
PO Box 100140, Anchorage, AK 99510
(907) 279-8099
    Founded: 1985
    Arts Area: Theatrical Group
    Status: Semi-Professional
    Type: Performing; Educational
    Purpose: To be an alternative theatre company producing small-scale productions of contemporary plays and new interpretations of classics
    Management: Jay Brause, Managing Director; Gene Dugan, Artistic Director
    Paid Staff: 2
    Paid Artists: 40
    Budget: $100,000 - $500,000
    Income Sources: Private Foundations/Grants/Endowments; Business/Corporate Donations; Box Office; Government Grants; Individual Donations; Special Events; Gaming Permit
    Season: September - May
    Annual Attendance: 5,000
    Affiliations: League of Fringe Theatres

PERFORMING SERIES

ANCHORAGE FESTIVAL OF MUSIC
524 West Fourth Avenue, PO Box 10325, Suite 204A, Anchorage, AK 99501
(907) 276-2465
    Founded: 1976
    Arts Area: Vocal Music; Instrumental Music; Festivals
    Status: Professional; Non-Profit
    Type: Performing
    Purpose: To engage in educational, musical and charitable activities; to plan, coordinate, promote and develop cultural activities in the Anchorage area
    Management: David Hagen, General Director
    Paid Staff: 1   **Volunteer Staff:** 30
    Paid Artists: 50   **Non-Paid Artists:** 30
    Utilizes: Guest Conductors; Guest Artists
    Budget: $100,000 - $500,000
    Income Sources: Private Foundations/Grants/Endowments; Business/Corporate Donations; Box Office; Government Grants; Individual Donations
    Season: June - July   **Annual Attendance:** 2,000

SITKA SUMMER MUSIC FESTIVAL
PO Box 201988, Anchorage, AK 99520
(907) 747-6774
>**Founded:** 1972
>**Arts Area:** Instrumental Music; Festivals
>**Status:** Professional; Non-Profit
>**Type:** Performing; Touring
>**Purpose:** To present professional chamber music throughout the state of Alaska
>**Management:** Paul Rosenthal, Music Director; Wendy Kamrass, Administrative Director
>**Officers:** Thad Paulson, President; Charles Bovee, Vice President; Trish White, Secretary; Lowell Tornquist, Treasurer
>**Paid Staff:** 3
>**Paid Artists:** 12 **Non-Paid Artists:** 20
>**Utilizes:** Guest Artists
>**Budget:** $100,000 - $500,000
>**Income Sources:** Private Foundations/Grants/Endowments; Business/Corporate Donations; Box Office; Government Grants; Individual Donations
>**Season:** June, September, February
>**Annual Attendance:** 7,000
>**Affiliations:** CMA
>**Performance Facilities:** Centennial Building; Grant Hall Auditorium

FACILITY

ALASKA CENTER FOR THE PERFORMING ARTS
621 West Sixth Avenue, Anchorage, AK 99501
(907) 263-2900
FAX: (907) 263-2927
>**Founded:** 1988
>**Type of Facility:** Theatre Complex; Concert Hall; Auditorium; Performance Center; Theatre House
>**Type of Stage:** Proscenium
>**Stage Dimensions:** Three theatres: two at 50'x90'; one at 28'x90'
>**Orchestra Pit**
>**Seating Capacity:** 2,000; 702; 350
>**Year Built:** 1988 **Architect:** Hardy, Holzman and Pfeiffer Associates **Cost:** $70,000,000
>**Acoustical Consultant:** Jaffe
>**Contact for Rental:** Mark Seward; (907) 263-2918
>**Resident Groups:** Anchorage Concert Association; Anchorage Opera; Anchorage Symphony Orchestra; Anchorage Festival of Music; Alaska Junior Theatre; Alaska Stage Company; Anchorage Community Chorus

WILLIAM A. EGAN CIVIC AND CONVENTION CENTER
555 West Fifth Avenue, Anchorage, AK 99501
(907) 263-2800
>**Type of Facility:** Civic Center
>**Year Built:** 1984 **Cost:** $27,000,000
>**Contact for Rental:** (907) 263-2800
>*Contains Explorers Hall and Summit Hall. See separate listings for additional information.*

WILLIAM A. EGAN CIVIC AND CONVENTION CENTER - EXPLORERS HALL
555 West Fifth Avenue, Anchorage, AK 99501
(907) 263-2800
>**Type of Facility:** Concert Hall; Auditorium
>**Type of Stage:** Flexible; Platform
>**Seating Capacity:** 2,400
>**Year Built:** 1984
>**Contact for Rental:** (907) 263-2800

WILLIAM A. EGAN CIVIC AND CONVENTION CENTER - SUMMIT HALL
555 West Fifth Avenue, Anchorage, AK 99501
(907) 263-2800
>**Type of Facility:** Concert Hall; Auditorium
>**Type of Stage:** Flexible; Platform
>**Seating Capacity:** 1,100
>**Year Built:** 1984
>**Contact for Rental:** (907) 263-2800

Douglas

DANCE

JUNEAU FOLK ENSEMBLE
PO Box 241031, Douglas, AK 99824
(907) 364-2334
> **Founded:** 1980
> **Arts Area:** Ethnic; Folk
> **Status:** Non-Professional; Non-Profit
> **Type:** Performing; Touring; Sponsoring
> **Purpose:** To bring folk dance and related arts to the people of the region (Alaska and the Yukon)
> **Management:** Judy Jones, Artistic Director; Bruce Botelho, Business Manager
> **Volunteer Staff:** 5
> **Non-Paid Artists:** 45
> **Utilizes:** Guest Artists; Guest Directors
> **Budget:** $1,000 - $50,000
> **Income Sources:** Private Foundations/Grants/Endowments; Business/Corporate Donations; Box Office; Government Grants; Individual Donations
> **Season:** 52 Weeks **Annual Attendance:** 5,000

THEATRE

PERSEVERANCE THEATRE
914 Third Street, Douglas, AK 99824
(907) 364-2421
> **Founded:** 1979
> **Arts Area:** Professional; Theatrical Group
> **Status:** Professional; Non-Profit
> **Type:** Performing; Touring; Resident; Educational
> **Purpose:** To produce quality professional theatre which is by, for and about Alaskans; to train and develop Alaskan actors, directors, designers and playwrights
> **Management:** Molly D. Smith, Artistic Director; Lynette Turner, Producing Director; Vikki Benner, Luan Schooler, Art Rotch, Artistic Team; Rahz Brown, Community Exchange Coordinator; Kate Bowns,Company Manager; Tom Linklater, Outreach Coordinator; Jamie McLean, Training Director; Merry Ellefson, Development Director; Toby Clark, Producing Manager; Nancy Schaufelberger, Office Manager
> **Officers:** Molly D. Smith, Board President
> **Paid Staff:** 12 **Volunteer Staff:** 300
> **Paid Artists:** 277 **Non-Paid Artists:** 279
> **Utilizes:** Guest Artists; Guest Directors
> **Budget:** $1,000,000 - $5,000,000
> **Income Sources:** Private Foundations/Grants/Endowments; Business/Corporate Donations; Box Office; Government Grants; Individual Donations
> **Season:** 52 Weeks **Annual Attendance:** 19,000
> **Affiliations:** TCG; AAA; WAAA; Alaska Alliance on the Arts
> **Performance Facilities:** Mainstage; Voices Stage; Phoenix Stage

---
Fairbanks

DANCE

NORTH STAR DANCE FOUNDATION
PO Box 73486, Fairbanks, AK 99707
(907) 451-8800
> **Founded:** 1984
> **Arts Area:** Ballet
> **Status:** Non-Professional; Non-Profit
> **Type:** Performing; Touring; Resident; Educational
> **Purpose:** To promote the art of dance in Alaska through education and performance
> **Management:** Norman Shelburne, Artistic Director; Iris Lindsey, Administrative Director
> **Officers:** Paul Kennedy, Board President; Bruce Gordon, Vice President; Freddie Black, Secretary
> **Paid Staff:** 3 **Volunteer Staff:** 4
> **Non-Paid Artists:** 26
> **Utilizes:** Special Technical Talent; Guest Artists; Guest Choreographers; Guest Composers
> **Budget:** $100,000 - $500,000
> **Income Sources:** Private Foundations/Grants/Endowments; Business/Corporate Donations; Box Office; Government Grants; Individual Donations

Season: September - May   **Annual Attendance:** 7,000
Performance Facilities: Hering Auditorium

INSTRUMENTAL MUSIC

FAIRBANKS SYMPHONY ASSOCIATION
PO Box 82104, Fairbanks, AK 99708
(907) 479-3407
FAX: (907) 474-6420
   Founded: 1969
   Arts Area: Symphony; Orchestra; Chamber
   Status: Non-Profit
   Type: Performing; Touring; Resident; Educational; Sponsoring
   Purpose: To support an active and vital symphony orchestra; to promote instrumental music in the schools, a youth orchestra program, orchestra village tours and other related events
   Management: Jane Aspnes, General Manager; Dr. Madeline Schatz, Musical Director
   Officers: Dietrich Strohmaier, President; Charlotte Barker, Vice President; Ed Peebles, Secretary; Bruce Foote, Treasurer
   Paid Staff: 4
   Paid Artists: 6
   Utilizes: Guest Conductors; Guest Artists
   Budget: $100,000 - $500,000
   Income Sources: Private Foundations/Grants/Endowments; Business/Corporate Donations; Box Office; Government Grants; Individual Donations
   Season: September - May   **Annual Attendance:** 12,000
   Affiliations: ASOL; Alaska Alliance on the Arts
   Performance Facilities: Charles W. Davis Concert Hall

RED HACKLE PIPE BAND
PO Box 82782, Fairbanks, AK 99708-2782
(907) 479-5826
   Founded: 1974
   Arts Area: Ethnic; Band
   Status: Non-Profit
   Type: Performing; Educational
   Purpose: To offer Scottish music (bagpipe) and Highland dance performances and instruction
   Management: Bob White, Pipe Master; Dennis Stephens, Assistant Pipe Master; Arthur L. Robson, Lead Drummer
   Officers: John Myers, President; Jennifer Johnston, Vice President; Sandra E. White, Secretary/Treasurer
   Volunteer Staff: 30
   Non-Paid Artists: 20
   Utilizes: Guest Artists
   Budget: $1,000 - $50,000
   Income Sources: Private Foundations/Grants/Endowments; Business/Corporate Donations; Box Office; Government Grants; Individual Donations
   Season: 52 Weeks

VOCAL MUSIC

FAIRBANKS CHORAL SOCIETY, CHILDREN'S CHOIR AND CHORUS!
University of Alaska-Fairbanks, PO Box 900174, Fairbanks, AK 99775
(907) 456-1144
FAX: (907) 456-7464
   Founded: 1984
   Arts Area: Choral
   Status: Non-Professional; Non-Profit
   Type: Performing; Educational; Sponsoring
   Purpose: To sponsor the Fairbanks Children's Choir, CHORUS! and Sing-It-Yourself Messiah
   Management: Dr. Suzanne Summerville, Music Director
   Officers: Dr. Carol Diehl, President
   Paid Staff: 6
   Utilizes: Special Technical Talent; Guest Conductors; Guest Artists; Guest Directors
   Income Sources: Private Foundations/Grants/Endowments; Business/Corporate Donations; Box Office; Government Grants; Individual Donations
   Season: September - April   **Annual Attendance:** 3,000
   Performance Facilities: University of Alaska-Fairbanks Concert Hall; Alaskaland

FAIRBANKS LIGHT OPERA THEATRE
PO Box 72787, Fairbanks, AK 99707
(907) 456-3568
> **Founded:** 1969
> **Arts Area:** Light Opera
> **Status:** Non-Professional; Non-Profit
> **Type:** Performing; Touring
> **Purpose:** To bring light opera and musical theatre to our community
> **Officers:** Rusty Gieson, President; Diane Egley, Vice President; Theresa Reed, Vice President; Dot Moravec, Treasurer; Helen Burrell, Corresponding Secretary; Francis Gloria, Recording Secretary
> **Paid Staff:** 1   **Volunteer Staff:** 350
> **Budget:** $100,000 - $500,000
> **Income Sources:** Box Office; Government Grants; Individual Donations
> **Season:** September - March   **Annual Attendance:** 10,000
> **Performance Facilities:** Hering Auditorium; Alaskaland Civic Center

PERFORMING SERIES

FAIRBANKS SUMMER ARTS FESTIVAL
PO Box 80845, Fairbanks, AK 99708
(907) 479-6778
FAX: (907) 479-4329
> **Founded:** 1980
> **Arts Area:** Dance; Vocal Music; Instrumental Music; Theater; Festivals; Grand Opera; Ice Skating; Visual Art
> **Status:** Professional; Semi-Professional; Non-Professional; Non-Profit
> **Type:** Performing; Educational
> **Purpose:** To present a study/performance festival with 56 prestigious guest artists in residence for two weeks
> **Management:** Jo Ryman Scott, Producing Director/Founder; Fred Buda, Artistic Director; Myron Romanul, Music Director
> **Officers:** Jo Scott, Chair; Dick Scott, Vice Chair; Diane Egley, Secretary; Dave Stephenson, Treasurer; Randy Clapp, Jean Mackin, Jo Scotts Center for the Cultural Development, Inc.
> **Volunteer Staff:** 70
> **Paid Artists:** 58
> **Utilizes:** Special Technical Talent; Guest Conductors; Guest Artists; Guest Directors
> **Budget:** $100,000 - $500,000
> **Income Sources:** Business/Corporate Donations; Box Office; Government Grants; Individual Donations; Fundraisers; Registration Fees
> **Season:** July - August   **Annual Attendance:** 12,000
> **Performance Facilities:** University of Alaska at Fairbanks

FACILITY

ALASKALAND CIVIC CENTER
Airport Way and Peger Road, Fairbanks, AK 99701
(907) 452-4244
> **Type of Facility:** Concert Hall; Theatre House; Civic Center; Multi-Purpose; Art Gallery
> **Type of Stage:** Proscenium
> **Stage Dimensions:** 20'x30'x29'   **Orchestra Pit**
> **Seating Capacity:** 354 Fixed, 384 Maximum
> **Year Built:** 1967   **Architect:** Don Stetson   **Cost:** $250,000
> **Year Remodeled:** 1981   **Architect:** Ellerbe
> **Contact for Rental:** Bob Peterson
> **Resident Groups:** Fairbanks Arts Association; Fairbanks Drama Association

UNIVERSITY OF ALASKA - CHARLES W. DAVIS CONCERT HALL
University of Alaska, Fairbanks, AK 99775-1220
(907) 474-7555
> **Type of Facility:** Concert Hall
> **Type of Stage:** Proscenium
> **Seating Capacity:** 1957
> **Year Built:** 1972   **Architect:** Gray, Rogers, Morgan
> **Acoustical Consultant:** Bolt, Beranek & Newman
> **Contact for Rental:** Music Department;   (907) 474-7555
> **Manager:** University of Alaska Music Department

Haines

THEATRE

LYNN CANAL COMMUNITY PLAYERS
PO Box 75, Haines, AK 99827
(907) 766-2425
> **Founded:** 1957
> **Arts Area:** Musical; Community
> **Status:** Non-Professional
> **Type:** Performing
> **Purpose:** To perform in and sponsor all types of theatre; to host the Alaska Community Theatre Festival's biennial, a state-wide drama festival held the spring of odd-numbered years
> **Officers:** Mimi G. Gregg, President; Gail L. Gregg, Vice President; Joanna Egolf, Secretary; Raymond R. Menaker, Treasurer
> **Utilizes:** Special Technical Talent; Guest Artists; Guest Directors
> **Budget:** $1,000 - $50,000
> **Income Sources:** Box Office; Individual Donations
> **Season:** 52 Weeks
> **Annual Attendance:** 1,500
> **Affiliations:** Arts Southeast
> **Performance Facilities:** Chilkat Center for the Arts

PERFORMING SERIES

HAINES ARTS COUNCIL
PO Box 505, Haines, AK 99827
(907) 766-2791
> **Founded:** 1983
> **Arts Area:** Dance; Vocal Music; Instrumental Music; Theater; Festivals; Lyric Opera
> **Status:** Non-Professional; Non-Profit
> **Type:** Performing; Touring; Resident; Educational; Sponsoring
> **Purpose:** To provide an umbrella-type organization for local performing and visual artists; to organize a concert season; to sponsor local festivals
> **Management:** Dr. Suzanne Summerville, Music Director
> **Officers:** John Hunt, President; Heather Lende, Vice President; Mimi Gregg, Secretary; Maisie Jones, Treasurer
> **Volunteer Staff:** 4
> **Utilizes:** Special Technical Talent; Guest Conductors; Guest Artists
> **Budget:** $1,000 - $50,000
> **Income Sources:** Private Foundations/Grants/Endowments; Business/Corporate Donations; Box Office; Government Grants; Individual Donations; Fund-raisers
> **Season:** September - May
> **Annual Attendance:** 2,500
> **Affiliations:** Lynn Community Players; KHNS FM 102;
> **Performance Facilities:** Chilkat Center for the Arts

FACILITY

CHILKAT CENTER FOR THE ARTS
Tower Road and Theatre Lane, Haines, AK 99827
(907) 766-2160, ext. 2162
FAX: (907) 766-2160
> **Type of Facility:** Theatre Complex; Concert Hall; Auditorium; Studio Performance; Performance Center; Civic Center; Multi-Purpose; Room
> **Type of Stage:** Thrust; Flexible; Proscenium; Platform
> **Stage Dimensions:** 22'x36'x40'
> **Orchestra Pit**
> **Seating Capacity:** 300
> **Year Built:** 1901
> **Year Remodeled:** 1982   **Architect:** Wade Hampton   **Cost:** $1,500,000
> **Contact for Rental:** Lee Heinmiller;   (907) 766-2160, ext. 2162
> **Resident Groups:** Chilkat Dancers; KHNS Radio; Lynn Canal Community Players; Haines Schools; Haines Borough; Haines Chamber of Commerce

---
Homer

THEATRE

PIER ONE THEATRE
PO Box 894, Homer, AK 99603
(907) 235-7333
    Founded: 1973
    Arts Area: Musical; Dinner; Community; Theatrical Group
    Status: Semi-Professional; Non-Profit
    Type: Performing; Touring; Resident; Sponsoring
    Purpose: To produce and promote the performing arts
    Management: Lance Petersen, Artistic Director; Joan Evans, Office Manager; Barbara Petersen, Company Manager
    Officers: William Bell, President; Jean McMaster, Vice President; Gwen Neal, Secretary
    Paid Staff: 8 **Volunteer Staff:** 16
    Paid Artists: 250 **Non-Paid Artists:** 100
    Budget: $50,000 - $100,000
    Income Sources: Private Foundations/Grants/Endowments; Business/Corporate Donations; Box Office; Government Grants; Individual Donations
    Season: 52 Weeks **Annual Attendance:** 6,000
    Performance Facilities: Pier One Theatre; Mariner Theatre

FACILITY

PIER ONE THEATRE
PO Box 894, Homer, AK 99603
(907) 235-7333
    Founded: 1973
    Type of Facility: Theatre House
    Facility Originally: Warehouse
    Type of Stage: Flexible; Proscenium; Platform
    Stage Dimensions: 36'x30'
    Seating Capacity: 120
    Year Built: 1955
    Year Remodeled: 1986 **Cost:** $10,000
    Contact for Rental: Lance Petersen; (907) 235-7333
    Live Performances

Juneau

PERFORMING SERIES

JUNEAU JAZZ AND CLASSICS
PO Box 22152, Juneau, AK 99802
(907) 364-2801
FAX: (907) 586-1938
    Founded: 1987
    Arts Area: Vocal Music; Instrumental Music; Festivals
    Status: Professional; Non-Profit
    Type: Educational; Sponsoring
    Purpose: To present a music festival featuring world-class jazz and classical artists in Juneau each year
    Management: Kitty Sessions, Administrator; Linda Rosenthal, Artistic Director
    Paid Staff: 1 **Volunteer Staff:** 1
    Paid Artists: 20
    Utilizes: Guest Artists
    Budget: $50,000 - $100,000
    Income Sources: Private Foundations/Grants/Endowments; Business/Corporate Donations; Box Office; Government Grants; Individual Donations
    Season: May **Annual Attendance:** 3,000

FACILITY

CENTENNIAL HALL CONVENTION CENTER
101 Egan Drive, Juneau, AK 99801
(907) 586-5283
FAX: (907) 586-1135
    Type of Facility: Concert Hall; Auditorium; Civic Center

Type of Stage: Flexible
Seating Capacity: 1,200
Year Built: 1983
Contact for Rental: Dayle Tennison;   (907) 586-5283

Ketchikan

DANCE

KETCHIKAN THEATRE BALLET SCHOOL
400 Mission, PO Box 6118, Ketchikan, AK 99901
(907) 225-9311
Founded: 1965
Arts Area: Ballet; Jazz
Status: Semi-Professional; Non-Profit
Type: Performing; Touring; Resident; Educational
Purpose: To encourage and promote the serious dance student striving to become a professional
Management: Board of Directors
Officers: Lynn Jorgensen, Penny Luse, Co-Presidents; Elaine Olsen, Secretary; Marcia Lapinski, Treasurer
Paid Staff: 2   **Volunteer Staff:** 4
Utilizes: Guest Artists
Budget: $1,000 - $50,000
Income Sources: Private Foundations/Grants/Endowments; Business/Corporate Donations; Box Office; Government Grants; Individual Donations
Season: September - May   **Annual Attendance:** 2,000
Performance Facilities: Ketchikan High School Auditorium

Kodiak

FACILITY

KODIAK ARTS COUNCIL
PO Box 1792, Kodiak, AK 99615
(907) 486-9251
FAX: (907) 486-6162
Founded: 1963
Type of Facility: Theatre Complex
Type of Stage: Proscenium
Stage Dimensions: 32'x40'   **Orchestra Pit**
Seating Capacity: 750
Year Built: 1985   **Architect:** Sundberg & Associates   **Cost:** $10,500,000
Acoustical Consultant: Gerald C. Wilson
Resident Groups: Kodiak Arts Council; Kodiak Community Theater

Palmer

PERFORMING SERIES

VALLEY PERFORMING ARTS
PO Box 1230, Palmer, AK 99645
(907) 745-2484
Arts Area: Theater
Status: Non-Profit
Type: Performing; Touring; Educational; Sponsoring
Purpose: To provide social and cultural enrichment to the residents of the Matanuska and Susitna Valleys by producing plays which are of the highest artistic excellence
Management: Dean Phipps, Artistic Director
Officers: Grant Olson, President; John Fairfield, Vice President; Larry Bottjen, Treasurer
Volunteer Staff: 20
Paid Artists: 5   **Non-Paid Artists:** 100
Utilizes: Guest Artists; Guest Directors
Budget: $50,000 - $100,000
Income Sources: Private Foundations/Grants/Endowments; Business/Corporate Donations; Box Office; Government Grants; Individual Donations
Season: September - May   **Annual Attendance:** 5,000
Performance Facilities: Colony Theater

Petersburg

THEATRE

MITKOF MUMMERS
PO Box 624, Petersburg, AK 99833
(907) 772-4859
Founded: 1971
Arts Area: Musical; Community; Theatrical Group
Status: Non-Profit
Type: Performing; Resident; Sponsoring
Purpose: To provide local actors and actresses an opportunity to perform; to provide the community an opportunity to see live theatre performances
Management: Vara Wright, Director
Officers: Penny Baird, President; Peggie Morrison, Secretary/Treasurer; Vara Wright, Historian
Budget: $1,000 - $50,000
Income Sources: Box Office; Individual Donations
Season: September - June   **Annual Attendance:** 1,000
Affiliations: Petersburg Arts Councils; Little Norway Festival Committee
Performance Facilities: High School Auditorium

Sitka

FACILITY

SITKA CENTENNIAL BUILDING
330 Harbor Drive, Sitka, AK 99835
(907) 747-3225
Type of Facility: Concert Hall; Auditorium; Performance Center; Civic Center; Multi-Purpose; Room
Type of Stage: Proscenium; Platform
Stage Dimensions: 40'W x 20'D
Seating Capacity: 500, Dinner 350
Year Built: 1967   **Architect:** Allen McDonald   **Cost:** $1,295,188
Contact for Rental: Don Kluting;   (907) 747-3225
Resident Groups: Theatre Guild; New Archangel Dancers; Summer Music Festival; Sitka Film Society; Sheldon Jackson College Theater Department

ARIZONA

Carefree

PERFORMING SERIES

DESERT FOOTHILLS MUSIC FEST
PO Box 5254, Carefree, AZ 85377
(602) 488-0806
Founded: 1992
Arts Area: Festivals
Status: Professional; Non-Profit
Type: Performing; Educational
Purpose: To assist in making the Arizona High Desert area a major winter cultural center
Management: Paul Perry, Music Director/Conductor; Chet Goldberg, Chairman Cultural Division - Foothills Community Foundation; Ed Spack, Executive Director - Foothills Community Foundation
Paid Staff: 2   **Volunteer Staff:** 150
Paid Artists: 22
Utilizes: Guest Artists
Budget: $50,000 - $100,000
Income Sources: Private Foundations/Grants/Endowments; Business/Corporate Donations; Box Office; Individual Donations; Fund-raising
Season: January   **Annual Attendance:** 1,500
Performance Facilities: Cactus Shadows Fine Arts Center

Chandler

FACILITY

CHANDLER CENTER FOR THE ARTS
250 North Arizona Avenue, Chandler, AZ 85224
(602) 786-2996
FAX: (602) 814-0442
Founded: 1989
Type of Facility: Theatre Complex
Type of Stage: Proscenium
Stage Dimensions: 60'x40'   **Orchestra Pit**
Year Built: 1989
Architect: Wendell Rossman
Cost: $16,000,000
Contact for Rental: Katrina Mueller;   (602) 782-3996

Decatur

PERFORMING SERIES

PRINCESS THEATRE
112 Second Avenue, Decatur, AZ 35601
(205) 350-1745
Founded: 1983
Arts Area: Dance; Vocal Music; Instrumental Music; Theater
Status: Non-Profit
Type: Performing; Educational
Purpose: To present and promote a variety of performing-arts events
Management: Lindy Ashwander, Manager
Paid Staff: 3   **Volunteer Staff:** 400
Budget: $100,000 - $500,000
Income Sources: Private Foundations/Grants/Endowments; Business/Corporate Donations; Box Office; Government Grants; Individual Donations
Season: 52 Weeks   **Annual Attendance:** 50,000
Affiliations: APAP; League of Historic American Theatres
Performance Facilities: Princess Theatre

Flagstaff

INSTRUMENTAL MUSIC

FLAGSTAFF SYMPHONY ORCHESTRA
PO Box 122, Flagstaff, AZ 86002
(602) 774-5107
FAX: (602) 774-5109
Founded: 1950
Arts Area: Symphony; Orchestra; Chamber; Ensemble
Status: Semi-Professional; Non-Profit
Type: Performing; Touring; Resident; Educational; Sponsoring
Purpose: To provide a wide-range of symphonic programs for people of all ages in northern Arizona
Management: Harold Weller, Music Director/General Manager; Christine Dicob, Executive Secretary; Erin Murphy, Public Relations Director
Officers: Rita Rose, President, Flagstaff Symphony Association
Paid Staff: 8 **Volunteer Staff:** 1
Paid Artists: 120
Utilizes: Special Technical Talent; Guest Conductors; Guest Artists
Budget: $100,000 - $500,000
Income Sources: Private Foundations/Grants/Endowments; Business/Corporate Donations; Box Office; Government Grants; Individual Donations
Season: 52 Weeks **Annual Attendance:** 20,000
Affiliations: ASOL; Arizona Commission on the Arts; Flagstaff Arts Council; Arizonans for Cultural Development
Performance Facilities: Ardrey Memorial Auditorium, Northern Arizona University; Poco Diable Resort; Embry Riddle Aeronautical University; Yavapai College Auditorium

PERFORMING SERIES

FLAGSTAFF FESTIVAL OF THE ARTS
PO Box 1607, Flagstaff, AZ 86002
(800) 266-7740; (800) 266-7750
FAX: (602) 774-2600
Founded: 1966
Arts Area: Dance; Vocal Music; Instrumental Music; Theater; Festivals
Status: Professional; Semi-Professional; Non-Profit
Type: Performing; Educational
Purpose: To present professionally-produced, culturally diverse arts programs featuring the finest local, state, national and international artists
Management: Larry Reid, Managing Director; Irwin Hoffman, Orchestra Conductor; Tal Russell, Theatre Artistic Director
Officers: Pat Loven, President; Jose Colchado, Vice President; Red Miles, Secretary; Earl Briggs, Treasurer
Paid Staff: 2 **Volunteer Staff:** 12
Paid Artists: 125
Utilizes: Special Technical Talent; Guest Conductors; Guest Artists; Guest Directors
Budget: $100,000 - $500,000
Income Sources: Private Foundations/Grants/Endowments; Business/Corporate Donations; Box Office; Government Grants; Individual Donations; Fund-raising
Season: July - August **Annual Attendance:** 20,000
Affiliations: Northern Arizona University
Performance Facilities: Ardrey Auditorium; Creative Arts Theatre; Ashurst Auditorium

FACILITY

COCONINO CENTER FOR THE ARTS
2300 North Fort Valley Road, PO Box 296, Flagstaff, AZ 86002
(602) 779-6921
Type of Facility: Amphitheater
Type of Stage: 3/4 Arena
Seating Capacity: 200
Year Built: 1981
Contact for Rental: Kim O'Meally; (602) 779-6921

NORTHERN ARIZONA AUDITORIUM - ARDREY MEMORIAL AUDITORIUM
PO Box 6040, Flagstaff, AZ 86011
(602) 523-4120
Type of Facility: Concert Hall; Auditorium; Performance Center; Opera House; Multi-Purpose
Type of Stage: Proscenium
Stage Dimensions: 54'Wx50'D; 54'Wx26'H proscenium opening **Orchestra Pit**

Seating Capacity: 1,550
Year Built: 1974   **Architect:** T. Atkinson   **Cost:** $3,200,000
Acoustical Consultant: Vern Knudson
Contact for Rental: Jean A. Anderson;   (602) 523-4120
Resident Groups: Flagstaff Symphony; Flagstaff Festival of the Arts; Performing Arts Series

Glendale

FACILITY

GLENDALE COMMUNITY COLLEGE PERFORMING ARTS CENTER
6000 West Olive Avenue, Glendale, AZ 85302
(602) 435-3709
   Type of Facility: Theatre Complex; Concert Hall; Auditorium; Studio Performance; Performance Center; Theatre House
   Type of Stage: Proscenium
   Stage Dimensions: 58'Wx40'D   **Orchestra Pit**
   Seating Capacity: 328
   Year Built: 1977   **Architect:** Varney, Sutton & Sydnor   **Cost:** $3,000,000
   Acoustical Consultant: George Thomas Associates
   Contact for Rental: Jeff Glemba;   (602) 435-3529
   Manager: Virginia Ludders
   Resident Groups: Glendale Community College Theatre Arts and Music Departments
   Available for rent to small productions only. Please contact rental office for details concerning large productions.

Grand Canyon

INSTRUMENTAL MUSIC

GRAND CANYON CHAMBER MUSIC FESTIVAL
PO Box 1332, Grand Canyon, AZ 86023
(602) 638-9215
   Founded: 1984
   Arts Area: Chamber; Ensemble
   Status: Non-Profit
   Type: Presenting
   Purpose: To present a series of concerts in Grand Canyon National Park each September, maintaining high musical standards and diversity of programming; to commission new chamber music from American composers; to give a public service tour to schools in northern Arizona
   Management: Robert Bonfiglio, Festival Director; Clare Hoffman, Artistic Director; Beth Seely, Business Manager
   Officers: Kenneth Bacher, President of the Board; Clare Hoffman, Vice President/Secretary
   Paid Staff: 4   **Volunteer Staff:** 2
   Paid Artists: 18
   Utilizes: Guest Artists
   Budget: $100,000 - $500,000
   Income Sources: Private Foundations/Grants/Endowments; Business/Corporate Donations; Box Office; Government Grants; Individual Donations; Poster Sales
   Season: September - October   **Annual Attendance:** 3,600
   Performance Facilities: Shrine of the Ages; Grand Canyon National Park

Mesa

FACILITY

MESA COMMUNITY CENTER
201 North Center Street, Mesa, AZ 85201
(602) 644-2178
   Type of Facility: Civic Center
   Year Built: 1979   **Architect:** Taliesen West   **Cost:** $2,300,000
   Acoustical Consultant: George Thomas and Associates
   Contact for Rental: Brenda Gravatt;   (602) 644-2178

Manager: Ray Pittman
The Mesa Community Center contains Amphitheatre, Centennial Hall and Conference Center. See separate listings for additional information.

MESA COMMUNITY CENTER - AMPHITHEATRE
201 North Center Street, Mesa, AZ 85201
(602) 644-2178
FAX: (602) 644-2617
    Type of Facility: Outdoor (Concert); Amphitheater
    Type of Stage: Environmental
    Seating Capacity: 4,200
    Year Built: 1979
    Contact for Rental: Brenda Gravatt;   (602) 644-2178
    Manager: Ray Pittman

MESA COMMUNITY CENTER - CENTENNIAL HALL
201 North Center Street, Mesa, AZ 85201
(602) 644-2178
FAX: (602) 644-2617
    Type of Facility: Concert Hall
    Type of Stage: Flexible; Platform
    Stage Dimensions: 24'x40'
    Seating Capacity: 1,832
    Year Built: 1978
    Contact for Rental: Brenda Gravatt;   (602) 644-2178
    Manager: Ray Pittman
    Resident Groups: Mesa Symphony Orchestra

MESA COMMUNITY CENTER - CONFERENCE CENTER
201 North Center Street, Mesa, AZ 85201
(602) 644-2178
FAX: (602) 644-2617
    Type of Facility: Room; Film & Lecture Hall
    Type of Stage: Flexible; Platform
    Seating Capacity: Conference Theater - 100; Palo Verde Ballroom - 450
    Year Remodeled: 1984   **Architect:** CSA Architects   **Cost:** $2,000,000
    Acoustical Consultant: George Thomas and Associates
    Contact for Rental: Brenda Gravatt;   (602) 644-2178
    Manager: Ray Pittman;   (602) 644-2667

Phoenix

DANCE

BALLET ARIZONA
3645 East Indian School Road, Phoenix, AZ 85018
(602) 230-1140
    Founded: 1979
    Arts Area: Ballet
    Status: Professional; Non-Profit
    Type: Performing; Touring; Resident; Educational
    Purpose: To educate through entertainment by exposing audiences to professional dance
    Management: Michael Uthoff, Artistic Director; Julie Dalgleish, Managing Director; Richard Wade, Business Director
    Officers: Allen Rosenberg, Chairman; Sharon Ulrich, President
    Paid Staff: 4   **Volunteer Staff:** 2
    Paid Artists: 45   **Non-Paid Artists:** 5
    Utilizes: Guest Conductors; Guest Artists; Guest Directors
    Budget: $500,000 - $1,000,000
    Income Sources: Private Foundations/Grants/Endowments; Business/Corporate Donations; Box Office; Government Grants; Individual Donations
    Season: 52 Weeks   **Annual Attendance:** 95,000
    Affiliations: Dance USA; Arts in Mesa

PHOENIX DANCE THEATRE
1528 1/2 East Clarendon, Phoenix, AZ 85014
(602) 266-7131
    Founded: 1970

Arts Area: Modern; Ballet; Jazz; Ethnic
Status: Non-Profit
Type: Performing; Educational
Purpose: To entertain and educate
Management: Jean Campbell, Director/Choreographer
Volunteer Staff: 4
Paid Artists: 10 **Non-Paid Artists:** 12
Utilizes: Special Technical Talent; Guest Artists
Budget: $1,000 - $50,000
Income Sources: Individual Donations
Season: 52 Weeks
Affiliations: Royal Academy of Dancing

INSTRUMENTAL MUSIC

PHOENIX CHAMBER MUSIC SOCIETY
PO Box 34235, Phoenix, AZ 85067
(602) 266-3524
Founded: 1959
Arts Area: Chamber
Status: Non-Profit
Type: Sponsoring
Purpose: To bring the finest chamber music ensembles in the world to the Phoenix area
Management: Carol Olsen, Executive Director
Paid Staff: 1
Utilizes: Guest Artists
Budget: $50,000 - $100,000
Income Sources: Private Foundations/Grants/Endowments; Box Office; Individual Donations
Season: Fall - Spring **Annual Attendance:** 8,000
Performance Facilities: Scottsdale Center for the Arts

PHOENIX SYMPHONY
3707 North Seventh Street, Suite 107, Phoenix, AZ 85014
(602) 277-7291
FAX: (602) 277-7517
Founded: 1947
Arts Area: Symphony; Orchestra; Chamber; Ensemble
Status: Professional; Non-Profit
Type: Performing; Touring; Educational
Purpose: To foster and promote the knowledge and appreciation of music by the public; to establish, maintain, and operate a symphonic performing group in the Phoenix metropolitan area
Management: Howard McCrady, President/Chief Executive Officer; James Sedares, Music Director
Officers: Richard Hill, Chairman, Board of Directors
Paid Staff: 24 **Volunteer Staff:** 972
Paid Artists: 84
Utilizes: Special Technical Talent; Guest Conductors; Guest Artists
Budget: $1,000,000 - $5,000,000
Income Sources: Private Foundations/Grants/Endowments; Business/Corporate Donations; Box Office; Government Grants; Individual Donations
Season: September - June **Annual Attendance:** 204,000
Affiliations: ASOL
Performance Facilities: Phoenix Symphony Hall; Scottsdale Center for the Arts; Pointe Hilton at Tapatio Cliffs

PHOENIX SYMPHONY YOUTH ORCHESTRA
PO Box 15150, Phoenix, AZ 85060
(602) 820-3310; (602) 902-2356
FAX: (602) 831-1264
Founded: 1952
Arts Area: Symphony; Orchestra
Status: Non-Professional; Non-Profit
Type: Performing; Educational; Sponsoring
Purpose: To stimulate and create a challenge for talented young musicians and an appreciation of good music by participation in the Youth Orchestra, Symphonette Orchestra and the Junior Strings; to select orchestra members by audition
Management: Judy Begun, Director of Orchestral Training; Mark Russell Smith, Conductor, Youth Orchestra; Dr. Walter Temme, Conductor, Symphonette; Dr. Cynthia La Blanc, Conductor, Symphonic Wind Ensemble; Martha Hughes, Conductor, String Orchestra
Officers: Pat Sosnow, President, Phoenix Symphony Guild
Volunteer Staff: 8

> **Non-Paid Artists:** 140
> **Budget:** $1,000 - $50,000
> **Season:** September - May
> **Annual Attendance:** 15,000
> **Affiliations:** ASOL (Youth Orchestra Division)
> **Performance Facilities:** Phoenix Symphony Hall

VOCAL MUSIC

ORPHEUS MALE CHORUS OF PHOENIX
PO Box 217, Phoenix, AZ 85001
(602) 271-9396
> **Founded:** 1929
> **Arts Area:** Choral
> **Status:** Non-Professional; Non-Profit
> **Type:** Performing; Touring
> **Purpose:** To give a singing outlet to men who love to sing; to use music as a means of furthering international and intercultural goodwill
> **Management:** Lloyd Weberg, President; Paul Morrow, Assistant Musical Director
> **Paid Staff:** 2   **Volunteer Staff:** 1
> **Non-Paid Artists:** 112
> **Utilizes:** Special Technical Talent; Guest Artists
> **Budget:** $1,000 - $50,000
> **Income Sources:** Box Office; Individual Donations
> **Season:** September - June
> **Annual Attendance:** 8,000

PHOENIX BOYS CHOIR ASSOCIATION
4621 North 16th Street, Suite B-210, Phoenix, AZ 85016
(602) 264-5328
FAX: (602) 264-6778
> **Founded:** 1949
> **Arts Area:** Choral
> **Status:** Professional; Non-Professional; Non-Profit
> **Type:** Performing; Touring; Educational; Sponsoring
> **Purpose:** To maintain the historic tradition of singing boys; to contribute to local cultural life; to serve as musical ambassadors
> **Officers:** Harvey K. Smith, Artistic Director; Beverly Blanton, Executive Director
> **Paid Staff:** 10   **Volunteer Staff:** 5
> **Paid Artists:** 6   **Non-Paid Artists:** 120
> **Utilizes:** Special Technical Talent; Guest Artists; Guest Directors
> **Budget:** $100,000 - $500,000
> **Income Sources:** Private Foundations/Grants/Endowments; Business/Corporate Donations; Box Office; Government Grants; Individual Donations; Tuition; Fee Engagements
> **Season:** September - June
> **Annual Attendance:** 40,000
> **Affiliations:** CA; ACDA

THEATRE

ACTORS THEATRE OF PHOENIX
815 North First Avenue, # 3W, Phoenix, AZ 85020
(602) 253-6701
> **Founded:** 1985
> **Arts Area:** Professional; Theatrical Group
> **Status:** Professional; Non-Profit
> **Type:** Performing
> **Purpose:** To bring fine professional theatre to Phoenix; to exclusively employ local actors; to build a resident company and a training program
> **Management:** Judith Rollings, Artistic Director; James Pinkerton, Managing Director; Sheila O'Keefe, Marketing Director; Joe Onofrio, Director of Development; Monica Jay Burgess, Production Manager
> **Officers:** Rosemarie Christofalo, Board President; Peter Gerstman, Vice President; George Cohen, Treasurer
> **Paid Staff:** 7
> **Paid Artists:** 40

Utilizes: Special Technical Talent; Guest Artists; Guest Directors
Budget: $100,000 - $500,000
Income Sources: Private Foundations/Grants/Endowments; Business/Corporate Donations; Box Office; Government Grants; Individual Donations; Tuition
Season: September - May   **Annual Attendance:** 14,000
Affiliations: TCG
Performance Facilities: Herberger Theater Center; Stage West

BLACK THEATRE TROUPE
333 East Portland Street, Phoenix, AZ 85004
(602) 258-8128
Founded: 1970
Arts Area: Community
Status: Non-Professional; Non-Profit
Type: Performing; Touring; Resident
Purpose: To make significant contributions to fostering the artistic and theatrical development of the state; to enhance the cultural and artistic nature of the community by providing exposure to Black culture and ideology
Management: Helen Mason, Founder; Joel Coleman, Artistic Director; Brenda Williams, Managing Director
Utilizes: Guest Artists; Guest Directors
Budget: $500,000 - $1,000,000
Income Sources: Private Foundations/Grants/Endowments; Business/Corporate Donations; Box Office; Government Grants; Individual Donations
Season: October - June

PHOENIX LITTLE THEATRE
25 East Coronado Road, Phoenix, AZ 85004
(602) 258-1974
Founded: 1920
Arts Area: Community
Status: Semi-Professional; Non-Professional
Type: Performing; Resident
Purpose: To provide top-quality theatre using the best local talent serving the Phoenix metropolitan area
Management: Chris Swartz, Marketing/Publicity; Peter J. Hill, Producing Director
Paid Staff: 14   **Volunteer Staff:** 200
Paid Artists: 100   **Non-Paid Artists:** 100
Utilizes: Special Technical Talent; Guest Conductors; Guest Artists; Guest Directors
Budget: $500,000 - $1,000,000
Income Sources: Business/Corporate Donations; Box Office; Government Grants; Individual Donations
Season: September - July   **Annual Attendance:** 70,000

FACILITY

JOHN PAUL THEATRE
1202 West Thomas, Phoenix College, Phoenix, AZ 85013
(602) 264-2492
FAX: (602) 285-7700
Type of Facility: Theatre House
Facility Originally: Performing Arts Center
Type of Stage: Thrust
Stage Dimensions: 48'W x 45'D
Seating Capacity: 305
Year Built: 1976   **Architect:** Oberg, Hunt, Gilleland   **Cost:** $1,500,000
Manager: Gary Imel;   (602) 285-7301
Resident Groups: Phoenix College Dramas; Arizona Theatre Company

PHOENIX CIVIC PLAZA
225 East Adams, Phoenix, AZ 85004
(602) 262-6225
Type of Facility: Civic Center
Year Built: 1972   **Architect:** GSAS Architect Planners; Howard, Needles, Tammen & Burgendoff   **Cost:** $28,000,000
Year Remodeled: 1985   **Architect:** GSAS Architect Planners; Howard, Needles, Tammen & Burgendoff
Cost: $55,000,000
Contact for Rental: Maura McCarty, Booking Coordinator;   (602) 262-6225
The Phoenix Civic Center contains Convention Center and Symphony Hall, Exhibition Halls and Grand Ballroom. See separate listings for additional information.

PHOENIX CIVIC PLAZA - CONVENTION CENTER AND SYMPHONY HALL
225 East Adams, Phoenix, AZ 85004
(602) 262-6225
FAX: (602) 495-3608
> **Founded:** 1972
> **Type of Facility:** Concert Hall; Auditorium; Outdoor (Concert); Performance Center; Off Broadway; Theatre House; Opera House; Civic Center; Multi-Purpose; Room
> **Type of Stage:** Flexible; Proscenium; Platform
> **Stage Dimensions:** Symphony Hall and Ballroom - 60'x100' each **Orchestra Pit**
> **Seating Capacity:** Symphony Hall - 2,599; Ballroom - 3,800; other rooms vary
> **Year Built:** 1972 **Architect:** Charles Luckman & Associates **Cost:** $28,000,000
> **Year Remodeled:** 1985 **Architect:** GSAS Architect Planners, Inc. with Needles Tammen & Bergendoff
> **Cost:** $55,000,000
> **Acoustical Consultant:** Vern Knudson - original; Howard Smith - expansion
> **Contact for Rental:** Ann Hastings, Maura McCarty, Marilynn Leathers or Kim Gilbert; (602) 262-6225
> **Manager:** Eric Jones, General Manager; (602) 262-6225
> **Resident Groups:** Phoenix Symphony; Arizona Opera; Ballet Arizona
> *Tucson Room - 16,380 square feet; Yuma Room - 17,000 square feet; Phoenix Room - 10,500 square feet; Flagstaff Room - 5,000 square feet; Prescott Room - 3,750 square feet. Seating capacities in meeting rooms can vary from 10 to 2,600 people, depending on configuration.*

PHOENIX CIVIC PLAZA - EXHIBITION HALLS
225 East Adams, Phoenix, AZ 85004
(602) 262-6225
FAX: (602) 495-3608
> **Founded:** 1972
> **Type of Facility:** Concert Hall; Civic Center; Exhibition Hall
> **Type of Stage:** Flexible; Proscenium; Platform
> **Stage Dimensions:** Poscenium opening 76'Wx32'H **Orchestra Pit**
> **Year Built:** 1972
> **Year Remodeled:** 1985
> **Contact for Rental:** Maura McCarty, Sales Manager; (602) 262-6225
> *Five halls contain 223,000 square feet*

PHOENIX CIVIC PLAZA - GRAND BALLROOM
225 East Adams, Phoenix, AZ 85004
(602) 262-6225
> **Type of Facility:** Concert Hall; Auditorium; Multi-Purpose
> **Type of Stage:** Proscenium
> **Stage Dimensions:** 72'Wx32'H proscenium opening
> **Seating Capacity:** Theater Style - 3,700; Banquet - 2,000
> **Year Remodeled:** 1985
> **Contact for Rental:** Maura McCarty, Booking Coordinator; (602) 262-6225

Prescott

INSTRUMENTAL MUSIC

YAVAPI SYMPHONY ASSOCIATION
PO Box 2333, Prescott, AZ 86301
(602) 778-0184
> **Founded:** 1966
> **Arts Area:** Symphony
> **Status:** Non-Profit
> **Type:** Sponsoring
> **Purpose:** To provide quality music for the area of Prescott
> **Management:** Lori Bogart, Office
> **Officers:** John B. Schuyler Jr., President; Dana Wingate, A.J. Wilson, Kristi Edwards, Donna Fagan, Officers
> **Utilizes:** Guest Artists
> **Budget:** $1,000 - $50,000
> **Income Sources:** Business/Corporate Donations; Box Office; Government Grants; Individual Donations
> **Season:** September - March **Annual Attendance:** 3,000
> **Performance Facilities:** Hendrix Auditorium; Yavapi College Community Theatre

---
Scottsdale

INSTRUMENTAL MUSIC

SCOTTSDALE SYMPHONY ORCHESTRA
PO Box 664, Scottsdale, AZ 85252
(602) 945-8071
> **Founded:** 1972
> **Arts Area:** Symphony; Orchestra
> **Status:** Professional; Semi-Professional; Non-Profit
> **Type:** Performing
> **Purpose:** To provide symphonic music to the Scottsdale community
> **Management:** K. Dona Roberson, Business Manager; Irving Fleming, Music Director; Judy Vagis, Financial Director
> **Paid Staff:** 2
> **Non-Paid Artists:** 70
> **Utilizes:** Guest Conductors; Guest Artists
> **Budget:** $100,000 - $500,000
> **Income Sources:** Business/Corporate Donations; Box Office; Individual Donations; Fund-raising
> **Season:** November - June
> **Annual Attendance:** 10,000
> **Affiliations:** ASOL; Scottsdale Chamber of Commerce
> **Performance Facilities:** Scottsdale Center for the Arts

THEATRE

ACTORS LAB ARIZONA
7120 East Fourth Street, Scottsdale, AZ 85251
(602) 990-1731; (602) 990-7898
FAX: (602) 990-0013
> **Founded:** 1980
> **Arts Area:** Theatrical Group
> **Status:** Professional; Non-Profit
> **Type:** Performing; Touring
> **Purpose:** To advance an appreciation of legitimate theater through diverse programming that includes a two-theater complex, educational outreach programs to schools and communities throughout the state, and a school for the performing arts
> **Management:** Jan Rothman-Sickler, Artistic Director; Jerry A. Sickler, Producing Director
> **Paid Staff:** 4
> **Utilizes:** Special Technical Talent; Guest Artists; Guest Directors
> **Budget:** $100,000 - $500,000
> **Income Sources:** Private Foundations/Grants/Endowments; Business/Corporate Donations; Box Office; Government Grants; Individual Donations
> **Season:** October - August
> **Affiliations:** AEA; SPTA
> **Performance Facilities:** Actors Lab

PERFORMING SERIES

DETROIT CONCERT BAND, INC.
7443 East Butherus, Suite 100, Scottsdale, AZ 85260
(602) 948-9870
> **Founded:** 1949
> **Arts Area:** Instrumental Music
> **Status:** Professional; Non-Profit
> **Type:** Performing; Touring
> **Purpose:** To perform concerts
> **Officers:** Leonard B. Smith, President/Executive Director
> **Paid Artists:** 60
> **Utilizes:** Special Technical Talent
> **Budget:** $50,000 - $100,000
> **Income Sources:** Box Office; Individual Donations; Concert Performances
> **Season:** 52 Weeks
> **Affiliations:** AF of M

FACILITY

SCOTTSDALE CENTER FOR THE ARTS
7383 Scottsdale Mall, Scottsdale, AZ 85251
(602) 994-2301
FAX: (602) 994-7728
> **Type of Facility:** Concert Hall; Theatre House; Civic Center; Exhibition Galleries
> **Type of Stage:** Thrust; Flexible
> **Stage Dimensions:** 40'Wx48'D   **Orchestra Pit**
> **Seating Capacity:** 860
> **Year Built:** 1975   **Architect:** Bennie Gonzales   **Cost:** $8,500,000
> **Year Remodeled:** 1986   **Cost:** $500,000
> **Acoustical Consultant:** AIRO-London; Jaffe Acoustics
> **Contact for Rental:** Dan Bercovich;   (602) 994-2301
> *The Scottsdale Center for the Arts includes the Cinema and Theatre. See separate listings for more information.*

SCOTTSDALE CENTER FOR THE ARTS - CINEMA
7383 Scottsdale Mall, Scottsdale, AZ 85251
(602) 994-2301
FAX: (602) 994-7728
> **Type of Facility:** Film Theatre; Experimental Theatre
> **Seating Capacity:** 175
> **Year Built:** 1975
> **Contact for Rental:** Dan Bercovich;   (602) 994-2301
> **Manager:** Kathy Hotchner;   (602) 994-2301

SCOTTSDALE CENTER FOR THE ARTS - THEATER
7383 Scottsdale Mall, Scottsdale, AZ 85251
(602) 994-2301
FAX: (602) 994-7728
> **Type of Facility:** Theatre House
> **Type of Stage:** Modified Apron Proscenium   **Orchestra Pit**
> **Seating Capacity:** 800
> **Year Built:** 1975
> **Acoustical Consultant:** Jaffe Acoustics
> **Contact for Rental:** Dan Berkovich;   (602) 994-2301
> **Manager:** Kathy Hotchner;   (602) 994-2301
> **Resident Groups:** Scottsdale Symphony; Phoenix Symphony

Sedona

PERFORMING SERIES

SEDONA JAZZ ON THE ROCKS
PO Box 889, Sedona, AZ 86336-0889
(602) 282-1985
> **Founded:** 1982
> **Arts Area:** Festivals
> **Status:** Non-Profit
> **Type:** Performing; Sponsoring
> **Purpose:** To sponsor an annual jazz festival; to support education in the area of jazz music
> **Management:** Ann Briggs, Festival Administrator
> **Officers:** Ken Fisher, President; Marion Herrman, Vice President; Paula Erwin, Secretary; Chris Frish, Treasurer
> **Paid Staff:** 1   **Volunteer Staff:** 300
> **Paid Artists:** 6
> **Utilizes:** Guest Artists
> **Budget:** $1,000,000 - $5,000,000
> **Income Sources:** Private Foundations/Grants/Endowments; Business/Corporate Donations; Box Office; Government Grants; Individual Donations
> **Season:** September   **Annual Attendance:** 5,000
> **Performance Facilities:** Hamilton Warren Ampitheatre

Sun City

INSTRUMENTAL MUSIC

SUN CITIES CHAMBER MUSIC SOCIETY
PO Box 1043, Sun City, AZ 85351
(602) 972-0478
Founded: 1976
Arts Area: Chamber; Ensemble
Status: Non-Profit
Type: Sponsoring
Purpose: To present the finest in solo and chamber music and related arts
Officers: Mary Ellen Danley, President; Quillian Ditto, Rebecca O. Johnson, Vice Presidents
Paid Staff: 1
Budget: $50,000 - $100,000
Income Sources: Private Foundations/Grants/Endowments; Business/Corporate Donations; Box Office; Government Grants; Individual Donations
Season: November - April   **Annual Attendance:** 9,500
Affiliations: WAAA; CMA
Performance Facilities: Sundial Auditorium

Sun City West

FACILITY

ARIZONA STATE UNIVERSITY - SUNDOME CENTER FOR THE PERFORMING ARTS
19403 R.H. Johnson Boulevard, Sun City West, AZ 85375
(602) 584-3118
Type of Facility: Performance Center
Type of Stage: Thrust; Proscenium
Stage Dimensions: Thrust/Apron: 67'Wx24'D
Seating Capacity: 7,169
Year Built: 1980   **Architect:** Hawkins, Lindsey, Wilson Associates   **Cost:** $9,600,000
Acoustical Consultant: Coffeen, Anderson & Associates
Contact for Rental: Pat Edwards;   (602) 584-3118
Resident Groups: Sun Cities Symphony

Tempe

DANCE

DESERT DANCE THEATRE
PO Box 25332, Tempe, AZ 85285-5332
(602) 968-4498
Founded: 1979
Arts Area: Modern; Contemporary Dance Theatre
Status: Professional; Non-Profit
Type: Performing; Touring; Educational
Purpose: To develop, promote and present contemporary concert dance through the operation of a contemporary dance company
Management: Lisa R. Chow, Associate Artistic Director/Company Manager; Marion Kirk Jones, Artistic Director; Renee Davis, Rehearsal Director
Officers: Larry Davis, President; Marion Kirk Jones, Vice President; Kay Williams, Secretary; Pat Gosmon, Treasurer
Paid Staff: 2   **Volunteer Staff:** 10
Paid Artists: 10
Utilizes: Special Technical Talent; Guest Artists; Guest Choreographers
Budget: $1,000 - $50,000
Income Sources: Private Foundations/Grants/Endowments; Business/Corporate Donations; Box Office; Government Grants; Individual Donations
Season: September - May   **Annual Attendance:** 10,000
Affiliations: Arizona Commission on the Arts

FACILITY

ARIZONA STATE UNIVERSITY - GAMMAGE CENTER
Tempe, AZ 85287
(602) 965-5062
> **Type of Facility:** Concert Hall; Auditorium; Performance Center; Theatre House
> **Type of Stage:** Proscenium   **Orchestra Pit**
> **Seating Capacity:** 3,029
> **Year Built:** 1964   **Architect:** Frank Lloyd Wright   **Cost:** $3,400,000
> **Acoustical Consultant:** Vern Knudsen
> **Contact for Rental:** Carole Vogt, Scheduling Coordinator;   (602) 965-5602

ARIZONA STATE UNIVERSITY - UNIVERSITY ACTIVITY CENTER
Tempe, AZ 85287-0205
(602) 965-5062
FAX: (602) 965-7663
> **Founded:** 1885
> **Type of Facility:** Arena
> **Type of Stage:** Arena
> **Seating Capacity:** 14,000-15,000
> **Year Built:** 1974   **Cost:** $8,000,000
> **Contact for Rental:** Carole Vogt, Scheduling Coordinator;   (602) 965-5062
> **Manager:** Colleen Jennings-Roggensack, Director;   (602) 965-5062

Tucson

INSTRUMENTAL MUSIC

TUCSON JAZZ SOCIETY, INC.
PO Box 44163, Tucson, AZ 85733
(602) 743-7347
> **Founded:** 1978
> **Status:** Professional; Non-Profit
> **Type:** Sponsoring
> **Purpose:** To promote and present jazz
> **Management:** Yvonne Ervin, Executive Director; Gloria Butler, Volunteer Coordinator; Ben Nead, Technical Director
> **Paid Staff:** 1   **Volunteer Staff:** 2
> **Paid Artists:** 19
> **Utilizes:** Guest Artists; Guest Directors
> **Budget:** $100,000 - $500,000
> **Income Sources:** Private Foundations/Grants/Endowments; Business/Corporate Donations; Box Office; Government Grants; Individual Donations
> **Season:** 52 Weeks   **Annual Attendance:** 25,000
> **Affiliations:** National Jazz Service Organization; International Association of Jazz Educators

TUCSON SYMPHONY ORCHESTRA
443 South Stone, Tucson, AZ 85701
(602) 792-9155
FAX: (602) 792-9314
> **Founded:** 1928
> **Arts Area:** Symphony; Orchestra; Chamber; Ensemble
> **Status:** Professional
> **Type:** Performing; Touring; Educational
> **Purpose:** To present classical, pops, family, chamber, ensemble and educational concerts
> **Management:** Eric Meyer, General Manager; Robert Bernhardt, Music Director
> **Paid Staff:** 11   **Volunteer Staff:** 10
> **Paid Artists:** 86
> **Utilizes:** Guest Conductors; Guest Artists
> **Budget:** $500,000 - $1,000,000
> **Income Sources:** Private Foundations/Grants/Endowments; Business/Corporate Donations; Box Office; Government Grants
> **Season:** September - May   **Annual Attendance:** 45,000
> **Affiliations:** ASOL
> **Performance Facilities:** Tucson Community Center Music Hall

VOCAL MUSIC

ARIZONA OPERA COMPANY
3501 North Mountain Avenue, Tucson, AZ 85719
(602) 293-4336
FAX: (602) 293-5097
>**Founded:** 1972
>**Arts Area:** Grand Opera
>**Status:** Professional; Non-Profit
>**Type:** Performing
>**Purpose:** To present grand opera in Arizona
>**Management:** Glynn Ross, General Director
>**Officers:** Louis Lagomarsino, President; Robert Mueller, Vice President
>**Paid Staff:** 14　**Volunteer Staff:** 4
>**Paid Artists:** 60　**Non-Paid Artists:** 3
>**Utilizes:** Special Technical Talent; Guest Conductors; Guest Artists; Guest Directors
>**Budget:** $1,000,000 - $5,000,000
>**Income Sources:** Private Foundations/Grants/Endowments; Business/Corporate Donations; Box Office; Individual Donations
>**Season:** October - March　**Annual Attendance:** 35,000
>**Affiliations:** Tucson Opera Dames; Arizona Opera League; Southern Arizona Opera Guild
>**Performance Facilities:** Tucson Community Center Music Hall; Phoenix Symphony Hall

TUCSON ARIZONA BOYS CHORUS
5770 East Pima, Tucson, AZ 85732
(602) 296-6277
FAX: (602) 296-6751
>**Founded:** 1939
>**Arts Area:** Choral
>**Status:** Professional; Non-Profit
>**Type:** Performing; Touring; Educational
>**Purpose:** To educate and maintain a porfessional boys choir; to tour and perform
>**Management:** Dr. Julien Ackerley, Director; Robin Jablonski-Bryan, Managing Director
>**Officers:** Don Haskell, President of the Board; Bates Butler, Vice President; Mark Cowley, Treasurer; Judy Morriss, Secretary
>**Paid Staff:** 4　**Volunteer Staff:** 2
>**Paid Artists:** 4　**Non-Paid Artists:** 153
>**Utilizes:** Guest Conductors; Guest Artists
>**Budget:** $100,000 - $500,000
>**Income Sources:** Private Foundations/Grants/Endowments; Business/Corporate Donations; Box Office; Government Grants; Individual Donations
>**Season:** September - May　**Annual Attendance:** 35,000

UP WITH PEOPLE
3103 North Campbell Avenue, Tucson, AZ 85719
(602) 327-7351
FAX: (602) 325-3716
>**Founded:** 1968
>**Arts Area:** Popular Music with Choreography
>**Status:** Professional; Non-Professional; Non-Profit
>**Type:** Performing; Touring; Educational
>**Purpose:** To encourage understanding among people of all nations through an international educational program involving young men and women from many countries who travel for a year and learn from the people and places they visit while staging a musical show
>**Management:** Bruce L. Erley, Vice President of Scheduling; Glen Shepherd, Vice President of Admissions and Education; Reed W. Thompson, Vice President of Production Services; Jeffrey Stegenga, Chief Financial Officer
>**Officers:** J. Blanton Belk, Founder/Chairman of the Executive Committee; Steven W. Woods, Chairman of the Board/Chief Executive Officer; Dale M. Penny, President/Chief Operating Officer; Hans Chr. Magnus, President, Up With People/Europe; James E. MacLennan, Executive Vice President/Director of Planning
>**Paid Staff:** 204
>**Non-Paid Artists:** 560
>**Utilizes:** Special Technical Talent; Selected Students
>**Budget:** Over 10,000,000
>**Income Sources:** Private Foundations/Grants/Endowments; Business/Corporate Donations; Box Office; Individual Donations; Student Fees; Recordings
>**Season:** August - July　**Annual Attendance:** 1,500,000 (live)

THEATRE

ARIZONA THEATRE COMPANY
PO Box 1631, Tucson, AZ 85702
(602) 884-8210
FAX: (602) 628-9129
   Founded: 1967
   Arts Area: Professional; Theatrical Group
   Status: Professional; Non-Profit
   Type: Resident
   Purpose: To create professional theatre of the highest artistic quality for Arizona that impacts locally and throughout the nation
   Management: Ralph Alpaugh, Managing Director; David Ira Goldstein, Artistic Director; Rob Sweibel, Marketing Director; John Tabor, Development Director/Tucson; Douglas Richards, Development Director/Phoenix
   Officers: Jon R. Young, President; Dorothy Finley, Vice President/Tucson; Everett L. King, Vice President/Phoenix; Mary K. Sterling, Chairman; William Hawgood II, Secretary; David Ogilvy, Treasurer
   Paid Staff: 40
   Paid Artists: 60
   Utilizes: Special Technical Talent; Guest Artists; Guest Directors
   Budget: $1,000,000 - $5,000,000
   Income Sources: Private Foundations/Grants/Endowments; Business/Corporate Donations; Box Office; Government Grants; Individual Donations
   Season: October - June   **Annual Attendance:** 126,000
   Affiliations: LORT; TCG; AEA; SSDC
   Performance Facilities: Temple of Music and Art; Herberger Theater Center

BORDERLANDS THEATER/TEATRO FRONTERIZO
166 West Alameda, Tucson, AZ 85701
(602) 882-8607
   Founded: 1984
   Arts Area: Theatrical Group
   Status: Professional; Non-Profit
   Type: Performing; Touring; Educational
   Purpose: To produce plays that reflect the cultural diversity of the border region; to be an important voice in the region
   Management: Debra J.T. Padilla, Managing Director; Barclay Goldsmith, Artistic/Producing Director
   Paid Staff: 2   **Volunteer Staff:** 5
   Paid Artists: 20
   Utilizes: Guest Artists; Guest Directors
   Budget: $100,000 - $500,000
   Income Sources: Private Foundations/Grants/Endowments; Business/Corporate Donations; Box Office; Government Grants; Individual Donations
   Season: 52 Weeks
   Annual Attendance: 6,500
   Performance Facilities: Pima Community College Center for the Arts

INVISIBLE THEATRE
1400 North First Avenue, Tucson, AZ 85719
(602) 882-9721
   Founded: 1971
   Arts Area: Theatrical Group
   Status: Semi-Professional
   Type: Performing
   Purpose: To perform adaptations of classics, recent off-Broadway plays and musicals; to encourage new playwrights through full productions and staged readings
   Management: Susan Classen, Managing Artistic Director; James Blair, Associate Artistic Director; Deborah Dickey, Literary Manager/Associate Producer; Caroline Reed, Director of Public Relations; Diane Hamra, Business Manager; Gail Fitzhugh, Associate Director; MaryAnn Trombino, Artistic Associate
   Officers: Garry Bryant, Franki Levin, Co-Chairs; Ginny Burginger, Secretary; Joan Shillito, Treasurer
   Paid Staff: 5   **Volunteer Staff:** 20
   Paid Artists: 20
   Utilizes: Guest Artists; Guest Directors
   Budget: $50,000 - $100,000
   Income Sources: Private Foundations/Grants/Endowments; Business/Corporate Donations; Box Office; Government Grants; Individual Donations
   Season: September - June
   Annual Attendance: 10,000
   Affiliations: TCG

NKYIMKYIM STORY THEATRE
2004 East Irvington, #132, Tucson, AZ 85713
(602) 884-7951; (602) 623-9133
Founded: 1980
Arts Area: Professional; Community; Folk
Status: Professional
Type: Performing; Touring; Resident; Educational; Sponsoring
Purpose: To promote the art of storytelling as a means of cultural awareness and exchange
Management: Gloria Myers, Director
Paid Staff: 1
Paid Artists: 1
Utilizes: Special Technical Talent; Guest Artists; Guest Directors
Budget: $1,000 - $50,000
Income Sources: Private Foundations/Grants/Endowments; Business/Corporate Donations; Box Office; Individual Donations
Season: 52 Weeks **Annual Attendance:** 5,000

PERFORMING SERIES

ARIZONA MINI-CONCERTS
2540 Camino La Zorrela, Tucson, AZ 85718
(602) 299-2399
Founded: 1979
Arts Area: Dance; Instrumental Music; Theater; Lyric Opera; Grand Opera
Status: Professional; Non-Profit
Type: Sponsoring
Purpose: To bring high-quality professional concert experiences to outreach audience environments; to showcase local professionals when possible
Management: Louise Spizizen, Artistic Director; Mia Gay, Pat Watrous, Publicity
Officers: Louise Spizizen, President; David Lopez, Secretary; Elaine Baker, Treasurer
Volunteer Staff: 11
Utilizes: Guest Artists
Budget: $1,000 - $50,000
Income Sources: Private Foundations/Grants/Endowments; Business/Corporate Donations; Government Grants
Season: September - June **Annual Attendance:** 5,000
Performance Facilities: El Con Mall; Foothills Mall

TUCSON FESTIVAL SOCIETY
425 West Paseo Redondo, Tucson, AZ 85701
(602) 622-6911
FAX: (602) 622-8838
Founded: 1950
Arts Area: Festivals
Status: Professional; Non-Profit
Type: Performing; Educational; Sponsoring
Purpose: To celebrate and promote Tucson's Native American and Anglo-American cultures and their historic influences on the area through the production of special events
Management: Annette Wallenmeyer, Executive Director; Susan P. Lispron, Assistant to Director
Paid Staff: 4 **Volunteer Staff:** 3,000
Paid Artists: 150
Utilizes: Special Technical Talent; Guest Artists
Budget: $100,000 - $500,000
Income Sources: Private Foundations/Grants/Endowments; Business/Corporate Donations; Government Grants; Individual Donations
Season: April **Annual Attendance:** 200,000
Affiliations: International Festivals Association
Performance Facilities: El Presidio Neighborhood; Fort Lowell Park

FACILITY

TUCSON CONVENTION CENTER
260 South Church Avenue, Tucson, AZ 85701
(602) 791-4101
FAX: (602) 791-5572
Type of Facility: Theatre Complex; Concert Hall; Auditorium; Performance Center; Off Broadway; Opera House; Civic Center; Arena; Multi-Purpose
Type of Stage: Flexible; Platform
Year Built: 1971 **Architect:** Friedman & Jobusch

Year Remodeled: 1987   **Architect:** Anderson, DeBartolo & Pan
Contact for Rental: Joe Rzonca;   (602) 791-4101
Resident Groups: Tucson Symphony Orchestra; Arizona Opera Company; Southern Arizona Light Opera Company; Arizona Dance Company; Ballet Arizona
Contains the Arena, Exhibition Hall, Little Theatre, Music Hall and Theatre. See separate listings for additional information.

TUCSON CONVENTION CENTER - ARENA
260 South Church Avenue, Tucson, AZ 85701
(602) 791-4101
FAX: (602) 791-5572
  Type of Facility: Arena
  Type of Stage: Flexible; Platform; Arena
  Seating Capacity: 9,550
  Contact for Rental: Joe Rzonca;   (602) 791-4101

TUCSON CONVENTION CENTER - EXHIBITION HALL
260 South Church Avenue, Tucson, AZ 85701
(602) 791-4101
FAX: (602) 791-5572
  Type of Facility: Exhibition Hall
  Type of Stage: Flexible; Platform
  Contact for Rental: Joe Rzonca;   (602) 791-4101
  Contains 23,800 square feet of exhibition space

TUCSON CONVENTION CENTER - LITTLE THEATRE
260 South Church Avenue, Tucson, AZ 85701
(602) 791-4101
FAX: (602) 791-5572
  Type of Facility: Theatre House
  Type of Stage: Thrust; 3/4 Arena
  Stage Dimensions: 48'Wx45'D
  Seating Capacity: 526
  Year Built: 1972
  Contact for Rental: Joe Rzonca;   (602) 791-4101

TUCSON CONVENTION CENTER - MUSIC HALL
260 South Church Avenue, Tucson, AZ 85701
(602) 791-4101
FAX: (602) 791-5572
  Type of Facility: Concert Hall; Opera House
  Type of Stage: Proscenium
  Stage Dimensions: 128'Wx49'6"D   **Orchestra Pit**
  Seating Capacity: 2,280
  Contact for Rental: Joe Rzonca;   (602) 791-4101
  Resident Groups: Tucson Symphony Orchestra; Arizona Opera Company; Southern Arizona Light Opera Company; Ballet Arizona

TUCSON CONVENTION CENTER - THEATRE
260 South Church Avenue, Tucson, AZ 85701
(602) 791-4101
FAX: (602) 791-5572
  Type of Facility: Theatre House
  Type of Stage: Thrust
  Stage Dimensions: 130'Wx40'D
  Seating Capacity: 525
  Contact for Rental: Larry Lahaie;   (602) 791-4101

UNIVERSITY OF ARIZONA - CENTENNIAL HALL
Centennial Hall, Building 29, Tucson, AZ 85721
(602) 621-1249
  Type of Facility: Auditorium; Performance Center; Multi-Purpose
  Type of Stage: Proscenium
  Stage Dimensions: 58'Wx46'D   **Orchestra Pit**
  Seating Capacity: 2,454
  Year Built: 1935   **Architect:** Ray Place   **Cost:** $234,260
  Year Remodeled: 1986   **Architect:** John Mascarella & Associates   **Cost:** $4,300,000
  Acoustical Consultant: Initial - Bolt, Beranek & Newman; Sound Renovation - Paoletti Associates

Contact for Rental: Marg Hemmings, Director of Operations;   (602) 621-1249
Resident Groups: University of Arizona Series; University of Arizona Cultural Affairs

UNIVERSITY OF ARIZONA - CROWDER HALL
School of Music, Tucson, AZ 85721
(602) 621-1655
> **Type of Facility:** Concert Hall
> **Type of Stage:** Proscenium
> **Stage Dimensions:** 21'x50'x26'   **Orchestra Pit**
> **Seating Capacity:** 478
> **Year Built:** 1956   **Architect:** Place and Place
> **Contact for Rental:** Dr. Dorothy Payne;   (602) 621-7023
> **Resident Groups:** School of Music

Yuma

DANCE

YUMA BALLET THEATRE
PO Box 1275, Yuma, AZ 85366
(602) 341-1925
> **Founded:** 1979
> **Arts Area:** Ballet
> **Status:** Non-Professional; Non-Profit; Regional Honor Company
> **Type:** Performing; Educational
> **Purpose:** To create, perform and enhance the art of dance within the community
> **Management:** Jon Cristofori, Kathleen Sinclair, Artistic Directors; Carmen Feriend, Business Manager; David Campbell, Technical Director; Stephanie Jones, Costume; Tom French, Sound
> **Paid Staff:** 4
> **Paid Artists:** 2   **Non-Paid Artists:** 40
> **Utilizes:** Special Technical Talent; Guest Artists; Guest Choreographers
> **Budget:** $50,000 - $100,000
> **Income Sources:** Private Foundations/Grants/Endowments; Business/Corporate Donations; Box Office; Government Grants; Individual Donations; Fund-raising
> **Season:** September - May   **Annual Attendance:** 6,000
> **Affiliations:** Regional Dance America; Honor Company
> **Performance Facilities:** Snider Auditorium

FACILITY

YUMA CIVIC AND CONVENTION CENTER - YUMA ROOM
1440 Desert Hills Drive, PO Box 6468, Yuma, AZ 85364
(602) 344-3800
FAX: (602) 344-9121
> **Founded:** 1973
> **Type of Facility:** Concert Hall; Civic Center; Room
> **Facility Originally:** Meeting Hall
> **Type of Stage:** Flexible; Platform
> **Seating Capacity:** 2,000
> **Year Built:** 1973   **Architect:** Benham-Blair & Ditzler   **Cost:** $1,500,000
> **Acoustical Consultant:** Coffeen & Associates
> **Contact for Rental:** Suzanne Murray, Director;   (602) 344-3800
> **Manager:** Suzanne Murray

ARKANSAS

Arkadelphia

FACILITY

OUACHITA BAPTIST UNIVERSITY - DEPARTMENT OF THEATRE & ARTS
Arkadelphia, AR 71998-0001
(501) 245-5000
> **Type of Facility:** Theatre Complex; Theatre House
> **Type of Stage:** Thrust; Proscenium
> **Stage Dimensions:** 28'Wx36'Hx48'D
> **Seating Capacity:** 230
> **Year Built:** 1967   **Architect:** Bruce Anderson   **Cost:** $300,000
> **Contact for Rental:** Scott Holsclaw;   (501) 245-5561
> **Resident Groups:** Ouachita Baptist University Drama Department

Dumas

THEATRE

DUMAS AREA ARTS COUNCIL, INC.
North Main Street, Dumas, AR 71639
(501) 382-6074
> **Founded:** 1979
> **Arts Area:** Musical; Dinner; Community; Theatrical Group
> **Status:** Non-Professional; Non-Profit
> **Type:** Performing; Resident; Educational
> **Purpose:** To provide theatre, music, dance and visual arts to interested performers and attentive audiences
> **Officers:** Brian Payne, President; Sue Gill, Vice President; Tonya Tucker, Secretary; Jimmy Locke, Treasurer
> **Volunteer Staff:** 50
> **Non-Paid Artists:** 100
> **Budget:** $1,000 - $50,000
> **Income Sources:** Private Foundations/Grants/Endowments; Business/Corporate Donations; Box Office; Government Grants; Individual Donations
> **Season:** 52 Weeks   **Annual Attendance:** 1,200
> **Performance Facilities:** Tanenbaum Theatre

FACILITY

DUMAS AREA ARTS COUNCIL, INC.
North Main Street, PO Box 493, Dumas, AR 71639
(501) 382-6713
> **Type of Facility:** Theatre Complex; Multi-Purpose
> **Facility Originally:** Business Facility
> **Type of Stage:** Flexible
> **Seating Capacity:** 200
> **Year Remodeled:** 1986   **Cost:** $50,000
> **Contact for Rental:** Brian Payne;   (501) 382-6836
> **Resident Groups:** Dumas Area Arts Council
> *Rental to Arts-Council sponsored organizations only*

El Dorado

INSTRUMENTAL MUSIC

SOUTH ARKANSAS SYMPHONY
315 East Oak, #206, El Dorado, AR 71730
(501) 862-0521
> **Founded:** 1956
> **Arts Area:** Symphony
> **Status:** Non-Profit
> **Type:** Performing; Educational
> **Purpose:** To provide the highest quality symphonic programs and educational benefits to the largest possible number of people in the South Arkansas Area
> **Management:** Allan Burdick, Executive Director/Music Director & Conductor; Virginia Matthews, Executive Secretary

Officers: Andy Allen, President; John Talpas, First Vice President; Janis Lovell, Second Vice President; Virginia Ray Ellzey, Treasurer; Victoria Harden, Secretary
Paid Staff: 2   **Volunteer Staff:** 35
Paid Artists: 60
Utilizes: Guest Conductors; Guest Artists
Budget: $50,000 - $100,000
Income Sources: Private Foundations/Grants/Endowments; Business/Corporate Donations; Box Office; Government Grants; Individual Donations
Season: September - May   **Annual Attendance:** 3,000
Affiliations: ASOL
Performance Facilities: El Dorado Municipal Auditorium; Harton Theatre

FACILITY

EL DORADO MUNICIPAL AUDITORIUM
100 West Eighth Street, El Dorado, AR 71730
(501) 862-1387
Type of Facility: Auditorium
Type of Stage: Proscenium
Stage Dimensions: 86'Wx35'D   **Orchestra Pit**
Seating Capacity: 1872
Year Built: 1959   **Architect:** Herbert Voelcker   **Cost:** $750,000
Acoustical Consultant: Dr. Joe G. Robbins
Contact for Rental: John R. Alley;   (501) 862-1387
Resident Groups: South Arkansas Symphony Association; The South Arkansas Ballet Association; South Arkansas Jubilee

SOUTH ARKANSAS ARTS CENTER
110 East Fifth Street, El Dorado, AR 71730
(501) 862-5474
Type of Facility: Civic Center; Multi-Purpose
Facility Originally: National Guard Armory
Type of Stage: Proscenium
Stage Dimensions: 20'x36'x46'
Seating Capacity: 207
Year Built: 1965   **Architect:** John Abbott   **Cost:** $165,000
Year Remodeled: 1975   **Architect:** John Abbott   **Cost:** $65,000
Contact for Rental: Executive Director;   (501) 862-5474
Manager: Reuben Murray
Resident Groups: South Arkansas Arts Center Theatre; South Arkansas Arts Center Secondstage

Eureka Springs

THEATRE

ELNA M. SMITH FOUNDATION
PO Box 471, Eureka Springs, AR 72632
(501) 253-9200
Founded: 1964
Arts Area: Theatrical Group
Status: Professional; Non-Profit
Type: Performing; Sponsoring
Purpose: To present "The Great Passion Play," an outdoor drama dealing with the life and times of Christ and his passion
Management: Ken Smith, Production Vice President; Don Berrigan, Director
Officers: Robert C. Foster, Executive Director; D. Smith, Recording Secretary; Don Robe, Chairman of the Board
Paid Staff: 14
Paid Artists: 200
Budget: $1,000,000 - $5,000,000
Income Sources: Box Office; Individual Donations
Season: May - October   **Annual Attendance:** 275,000
Performance Facilities: Amphitheater

PERFORMING SERIES

INSPIRATION POINT FINE ARTS COLONY
Route 2, PO Box 127, Eureka Springs, AR 73632
(501) 253-8595
Founded: 1950

Arts Area: Instrumental Music; Lyric Opera; Grand Opera
Status: Non-Professional; Non-Profit
Type: Performing; Educational; Sponsoring
Purpose: To give students the opportunity to experience the real-life opera stage
Officers: James H. Swiggart, General Manager; Carroll Freeman, Artistic Director
Paid Staff: 3
Paid Artists: 28 **Non-Paid Artists:** 50
Utilizes: Special Technical Talent; Guest Conductors; Guest Artists; Guest Directors
Budget: $100,000 - $500,000
Income Sources: Private Foundations/Grants/Endowments; Box Office; Individual Donations
Season: June - July   **Annual Attendance:** 5,500
Affiliations: National Federation of Music Clubs
Performance Facilities: Inspiration Point Fine Arts Colony

Fayetteville

INSTRUMENTAL MUSIC

SYMPHONY SOCIETY OF NORTH ARKANSAS
201 North East Street, Fayetteville, AR 72701
(501) 521-4166
Founded: 1954
Arts Area: Symphony; Orchestra; Chamber; Music Festival
Status: Semi-Professional; Non-Profit
Type: Performing; Educational
Purpose: To offer northwest Arkansas classical and pops concerts in four communities and give educational concerts in the same area
Management: Constance L. Hendrix-Kral, Executive Director
Officers: Mary Nusser, President; Jack Byrd, Vice President; Mitzi Springborn, Secretary; Darlyn Speight, Treasurer
Paid Staff: 3 **Volunteer Staff:** 1
Paid Artists: 52 **Non-Paid Artists:** 23
Utilizes: Guest Conductors; Guest Artists
Budget: $100,000 - $500,000
Income Sources: Private Foundations/Grants/Endowments; Business/Corporate Donations; Box Office; Government Grants; Individual Donations
Season: September - June   **Annual Attendance:** 14,000
Affiliations: University of Arkansas
Performance Facilities: Walton Arts Center

PERFORMING SERIES

MUSIC FESTIVAL OF ARKANSAS
PO Box 1243, Fayetteville, AR 72702
(501) 521-4166
Founded: 1982
Arts Area: Vocal Music; Instrumental Music; Lyric Opera
Status: Professional; Non-Profit
Type: Educational; Sponsoring
Management: Carlton R. Woods, Director; Shea Crain, Festival Manager
Officers: Mary Nusser, President; Jack Byrd, Vice President; Mitzi Springborn, Secretary; Darlyn Speight, Treasurer
Paid Staff: 2
Utilizes: Special Technical Talent; Guest Conductors; Guest Artists
Budget: $50,000 - $100,000
Income Sources: Business/Corporate Donations; Box Office; Government Grants; Individual Donations
Season: June
Performance Facilities: Walton Arts Center

FACILITY

FINE ARTS CONCERT HALL
University of Arkansas, Fayetteville, AR 72701
(501) 575-4175
Type of Facility: Concert Hall
Type of Stage: Thrust
Seating Capacity: 200
Year Built: 1950
Year Remodeled: 1992

Contact for Rental: Dr. C. Johnson; (501) 521-8644
Resident Groups: University of Arkansas Orchestra; Choir; Student and Faculty Recitals

Fort Smith

INSTRUMENTAL MUSIC

FORT SMITH SYMPHONY
405 Central Mall, PO Box 3151, Fort Smith, AR 72913
(501) 452-7575
FAX: (501) 452-8985
Founded: 1923
Arts Area: Symphony; Orchestra; Chamber
Status: Non-Profit
Type: Performing; Resident; Educational
Purpose: To enhance the cultural life in the community
Management: Carol Sue Wooten, Executive Director; John A. Thellman, Music Director/Conductor
Officers: Dr. Benny Gooden, President; Brian McAlpin, First Vice President; John Lange, Second Vice President
Paid Staff: 4
Paid Artists: 60   **Non-Paid Artists:** 2
Utilizes: Guest Artists
Budget: $100,000 - $500,000
Income Sources: Private Foundations/Grants/Endowments; Business/Corporate Donations; Box Office; Government Grants; Individual Donations
Season: September - May   **Annual Attendance:** 6,000
Affiliations: ASOL
Performance Facilities: Southside Auditorium and Civic Center

THEATRE

FORT SMITH LITTLE THEATRE
PO Box 3752, Fort Smith, AR 72913
(501) 783-2966
Founded: 1947
Arts Area: Theatrical Group
Status: Non-Profit
Type: Performing
Volunteer Staff: 15
Non-Paid Artists: 200
Budget: $1,000 - $50,000
Income Sources: Box Office
Season: 52 Weeks   **Annual Attendance:** 10,000
Affiliations: SWTC
Performance Facilities: Fort Smith Little Theatre

FACILITY

FORT SMITH CIVIC CENTER
55 South Seventh Street, Fort Smith, AR 72901
(501) 785-2495
Type of Facility: Civic Center
Year Built: 1966
Acoustical Consultant: Charlie Long
Contact for Rental: Bobbie Sheperd; (501) 785-2495
Manager: Joan Stratmann
One building houses both the exhibition hall and theatre, see separate listing for more information.

FORT SMITH CIVIC CENTER - EXHIBITION HALL
55 South Seventh Street, Fort Smith, AR 72901
(501) 785-2495
Type of Facility: Exhibition Hall
Seating Capacity: 1,000-1,200
Year Built: 1966
Contact for Rental: Bobbie Shepherd; (501) 785-2495

FORT SMITH CIVIC CENTER - THEATER
55 South Seventh Street, Fort Smith, AR 72901
(501) 785-2495
Type of Facility: Concert Hall; Auditorium; Performance Center; Civic Center
Type of Stage: Proscenium
Stage Dimensions: 100'x42'   **Orchestra Pit**
Seating Capacity: 1,552
Year Built: 1966
Contact for Rental: Bobbie Shepherd;   (501) 785-2495
Manager: Joan Stratmann;   (501) 785-2495
One building houses both the theatre and exhibition hall

FORT SMITH LITTLE THEATRE
401 North Sixth Street, Fort Smith, AR 72901
(501) 783-2966
Type of Facility: Theatre House
Type of Stage: 3/4 Arena
Stage Dimensions: 35'Wx20'D
Seating Capacity: 193
Year Built: 1986   **Architect:** Mott, Mobley and McGowan   **Cost:** $415,000
Contact for Rental: Manager;   (501) 783-2966

WESTARK COMMUNITY COLLEGE - BREEDLOVE AUDITORIUM
PO Box 3649, Fort Smith, AR 72913
(501) 785-7000, ext. 257
Type of Facility: Auditorium
Type of Stage: Flexible
Stage Dimensions: 18'x40'x28'   **Orchestra Pit**
Seating Capacity: 440
Year Built: 1976   **Architect:** Ken Cockram   **Cost:** $1,500,000
Manager: Stacy Jones;   (501) 785-7198
Resident Groups: Fort Smith Symphony

Harrison

PERFORMING SERIES

NORTH CENTRAL ARKANSAS CONCERT ASSOCIATION
PO Box 2117, Harrison, AR 72601
(501) 741-7858
Founded: 1969
Arts Area: Dance; Vocal Music; Instrumental Music; Theater
Status: Non-Profit
Type: Sponsoring
Purpose: To promote culture and education
Officers: Mike Braken, President; Glenna Ragan, Vice President; Betty Shinall, Secretary; Rosalie O'Brien, Treasurer
Paid Staff: 1
Budget: $1,000 - $50,000
Income Sources: Private Foundations/Grants/Endowments; Business/Corporate Donations; Box Office; Government Grants; Individual Donations
Season: October - April   **Annual Attendance:** 1,500
Affiliations: Arkansas Arts Council; MAAA
Performance Facilities: Harrison High School Auditorium

Hot Springs

FACILITY

HOT SPRINGS CONVENTION AND VISITORS' BUREAU
PO Box K, Hot Springs, AR 71902
(501) 321-1706
Type of Facility: Auditorium; Civic Center
Type of Stage: Proscenium
Stage Dimensions: 18'x77'x39'   **Orchestra Pit**
Seating Capacity: 3,700
Year Built: 1965   **Architect:** I. Granger McDaniel   **Cost:** $2,500,000
Contact for Rental: Brenda Bates, Convention Services Manager;   (501) 321-2835

Jonesboro

FACILITY

THE FORUM
115 East Monroe, Jonesboro, AR 72401
(501) 935-2726
Founded: 1978
Type of Facility: Concert Hall; Auditorium; Performance Center; Theatre House; Civic Center
Facility Originally: Movie House
Type of Stage: Proscenium   **Orchestra Pit**
Seating Capacity: 690
Year Built: 1926
Year Remodeled: 1978
Contact for Rental: Lynda Bowen;   (501) 935-2726

Little Rock

DANCE

BALLET ARKANSAS
120 Tanglewood, PO Box 7574, Little Rock, AR 72217
(501) 666-4445
Founded: 1978
Arts Area: Ballet
Status: Semi-Professional; Non-Profit
Type: Performing; Touring; Educational; Sponsoring
Purpose: Ballet Arkansas was founded with the objective to provide for and promote the art of dance throughout the state of Arkansas.
Management: Philip Quick, Executive Director; Kirt Hathaway, Artistic Director
Paid Staff: 4   **Volunteer Staff:** 200
Paid Artists: 11   **Non-Paid Artists:** 13
Utilizes: Special Technical Talent; Guest Conductors; Guest Artists; Guest Directors
Budget: $100,000 - $500,000
Income Sources: Private Foundations/Grants/Endowments; Business/Corporate Donations; Box Office; Government Grants; Individual Donations
Annual Attendance: 20,000
Affiliations: SWRBA; NARB
Performance Facilities: Robinson Center Music Hall

INSTRUMENTAL MUSIC

ARKANSAS SYMPHONY ORCHESTRA SOCIETY
PO Box 7328, Little Rock, AR 72217
(501) 666-1761
FAX: (501) 666-3193
Founded: 1966
Arts Area: Symphony; Orchestra; Chamber
Status: Professional; Non-Profit
Type: Performing; Touring; Educational
Purpose: To provide the finest symphonic music to the people of the area
Management: Jo Ann Greene, Executive Director
Officers: George Mitchell, President; John Steari, Vice President; Philip Tappan, Secretary; George Worthen, Treasurer
Paid Staff: 7   **Volunteer Staff:** 3
Paid Artists: 85
Utilizes: Special Technical Talent; Guest Conductors; Guest Artists
Budget: $1,000,000 - $5,000,000
Income Sources: Private Foundations/Grants/Endowments; Business/Corporate Donations; Box Office; Government Grants; Individual Donations
Season: September - July   **Annual Attendance:** 60,000
Affiliations: ASOL; ASCAP
Performance Facilities: Robinson Center Music Hall

VOCAL MUSIC

OPERA THEATRE AT WILDWOOD PARK FOR THE PERFORMING ARTS
PO Box 25202, Little Rock, AR 72221
(501) 821-7275
FAX: (501) 821-7280
> **Arts Area:** Lyric Opera; Light Opera; Operetta; Musical Theatre
> **Status:** Professional; Non-Profit
> **Type:** Performing; Resident
> **Purpose:** To present operas done in English from standard repertoires as well as world premieres
> **Management:** Dr. Ann Chotaro, Founder/Artistic Director; Rod Gideons, Education/Tour Director & Artistic Administrator
> **Officers:** Dr. Aluah Nelson III, President of the Board
> **Budget:** $500,000 - $1,000,000
> **Income Sources:** Private Foundations/Grants/Endowments; Business/Corporate Donations; Box Office; Government Grants; Individual Donations
> **Season:** 52 Weeks
> **Performance Facilities:** Studio Theatre at Wildwood Park

THEATRE

THE ARKANSAS ARTS CENTER CHILDREN'S THEATER
PO Box 2137, Little Rock, AR 72203
(501) 372-4000
> **Founded:** 1979
> **Arts Area:** Professional; Theatrical Group
> **Status:** Professional; Non-Profit
> **Type:** Performing; Touring
> **Purpose:** Family theater
> **Management:** Bradley D. Anderson, Artistic Director; P.J. Powers, Administrative Manager
> **Officers:** Curt F. Bradbury, Board President
> **Paid Staff:** 15
> **Utilizes:** Special Technical Talent; Guest Artists; Guest Directors
> **Budget:** $100,000 - $500,000
> **Income Sources:** Private Foundations/Grants/Endowments; Business/Corporate Donations; Box Office; Government Grants; Individual Donations
> **Season:** October - May   **Annual Attendance:** 124,000
> **Affiliations:** TCG; ASSITEJ
> **Performance Facilities:** Arkansas Art Center Theater

ARKANSAS REPERTORY THEATRE
601 Main Street, PO Box 110, Little Rock, AR 72203
(501) 378-0445
FAX: (501) 378-0012
> **Founded:** 1976
> **Arts Area:** Professional; Theatrical Group
> **Status:** Professional; Non-Profit
> **Type:** Performing; Touring; Resident; Educational; Sponsoring
> **Management:** Andrew C. Gaupp, Managing Director; Cliff Fannin Baker, Artistic Director; Lynn Frazier, Business Manager; Susan Nichols, Development Associate
> **Officers:** Maurice Mitchell, Chairman; Don Steely, President; Phil Sutphin, Treasurer; Sandra Cotter, Secretary
> **Paid Staff:** 25
> **Paid Artists:** 50
> **Utilizes:** Special Technical Talent; Guest Artists; Guest Directors; Guest Designers
> **Budget:** $500,000 - $1,000,000
> **Income Sources:** Private Foundations/Grants/Endowments; Business/Corporate Donations; Box Office; Government Grants; Individual Donations
> **Season:** 52 Weeks   **Annual Attendance:** 50,000
> **Affiliations:** TCG; FEDAPT; SWTC; SETC
> **Performance Facilities:** Arkansas Repertory Theatre

FACILITY

ARKANSAS ARTS CENTER
PO Box 2137, Little Rock, AR 72203
(501) 372-4000
FAX: (501) 375-8053
> **Type of Facility:** Auditorium; Studio Performance; Theatre House

Type of Stage: Proscenium
Stage Dimensions: 63'Wx42'D   **Orchestra Pit**
Seating Capacity: 389
Year Built: 1962   **Architect:** Cromwell, Neyland, Truemper Millett & Gatchell
Acoustical Consultant: Bolt, Beranek & Newman
Contact for Rental: Ellen Becker;   (501) 372-4000
Manager: Townsend Wolfe
Resident Groups: Arkansas Arts Center Children's Theatre; Arkansas Repertory Theatre

ARKANSAS REPERTORY THEATRE
601 Main Street, Little Rock, AR 72201
(501) 378-0405
Type of Facility: Theatre Complex; Auditorium; Multi-Purpose; Black Box
Facility Originally: Retail Department Store
Type of Stage: Proscenium; Environmental; Modified Apron Proscenium
Stage Dimensions: 42'x23'x41'; 42'x33'x41'with apron   **Orchestra Pit**
Seating Capacity: Auditorium - 362; Black Box - 99
Year Built: 1910   **Architect:** Charles Thompson
Year Remodeled: 1987   **Architect:** Witsell, Evans and Rasco, P.A.   **Cost:** $2,200,000
Acoustical Consultant: Mitchell Kurtz Designs
Contact for Rental: Guy Couch;   (501) 378-0405
Resident Groups: Arkansas Repertory Theatre

ROBINSON CENTER MUSIC HALL
Markham and Broadway, Little Rock, AR 72201
(501) 376-4781
FAX: (501) 374-2255
Type of Facility: Concert Hall; Auditorium; Theatre House; Civic Center; Multi-Purpose
Type of Stage: Proscenium
Stage Dimensions: 35'x60'x40'   **Orchestra Pit**
Seating Capacity: 2,641
Year Built: 1939   **Architect:** WPA Project
Year Remodeled: 1972   **Architect:** Wittenburg, Deloney & Davidson   **Cost:** $3,800,000
Contact for Rental: Phyllis Lucas;   (501) 376-4781
Resident Groups: Arkansas Symphony Orchestra; Ballet Arkansas; Little Rock Community Concerts

UNIVERSITY OF ARKANSAS-LITTLE ROCK - STELLA BOYLE SMITH CONCERT HALL
2801 South University, Little Rock, AR 72204
(501) 569-3296
Type of Stage: Proscenium
Seating Capacity: 719
Year Built: 1965   **Architect:** Cromwell Associates   **Cost:** $350,000
Manager: Dr. Jess Anthony

Mena

THEATRE

OUACHITA LITTLE THEATRE
PO Box 1217, Mena, AR 71953
(501) 394-4436
Founded: 1979
Arts Area: Community; Theatrical Group
Status: Non-Professional; Non-Profit
Type: Performing; Educational
Purpose: Promote theatrical arts, produce plays (dramas, comedies, musicals, children's, educational and community theatre)
Officers: Leda S. Benson, Founder/Coordinator/Past President; Rudy Timmerman, President
Volunteer Staff: 9
Utilizes: Special Technical Talent
Budget: $1,000 - $50,000
Income Sources: Private Foundations/Grants/Endowments; Box Office; Individual Donations
Season: 52 Weeks   **Annual Attendance:** 2,000

Mountain Home

THEATRE

TWIN LAKES PLAYHOUSE
PO Box 482, Mountain Home, AR 72653
(501) 431-5594
> **Founded:** 1971
> **Arts Area:** Community
> **Status:** Semi-Professional; Non-Professional; Non-Profit
> **Type:** Performing
> **Purpose:** To provide live theater productions for the area
> **Officers:** Karin Floyd, Chairman; Glenn Payne, Vice Chairman; Shirley Spitzer, Secretary; Jennifer Baker, Treasurer
> **Volunteer Staff:** 8
> **Non-Paid Artists:** 40
> **Budget:** $1,000 - $50,000
> **Income Sources:** Business/Corporate Donations; Box Office; Individual Donations
> **Season:** Spring - Fall **Annual Attendance:** 1,000

North Little Rock

DANCE

MIRANA MIDDLE EASTERN DANCE COMPANY
257 Plainview Circle, North Little Rock, AR 72116-8913
(501) 753-5122
> **Founded:** 1985
> **Arts Area:** Ethnic
> **Status:** Professional; Non-Profit
> **Type:** Performing; Educational
> **Purpose:** To present classic and traditional forms of Middle Eastern dance to the public for education and understanding of the Middle Eastern cultural heritage
> **Management:** Mirana Thompson, Artistic Director
> **Officers:** David Martinous, President; Willie Oates, Vice President; Peggy Bowles, Secretary/Treasurer
> **Paid Artists:** 10 **Non-Paid Artists:** 10
> **Utilizes:** Special Technical Talent; Guest Artists
> **Budget:** $1,000 - $50,000
> **Income Sources:** Private Foundations/Grants/Endowments; Box Office; Individual Donations

Pine Bluff

FACILITY

ARTS AND SCIENCE CENTER OF SOUTHEAST ARKANSAS
220 Martin Street, Pine Bluff, AR 71601
(501) 536-3375
> **Type of Facility:** Civic Center
> **Type of Stage:** Proscenium
> **Stage Dimensions:** 12' x 38' x 24' **Orchestra Pit**
> **Seating Capacity:** 191
> **Year Built:** 1968 **Architect:** Edward Durell Stone
> **Contact for Rental:** Galen Colbert; (501) 536-3375
> **Resident Groups:** Center Stage Players

PINE BLUFF CONVENTION CENTER
500 East Eighth Street, Pine Bluff, AR 71601
(501) 536-7600
> **Type of Facility:** Civic Center
> **Type of Stage:** Arena
> **Year Built:** 1976 **Architect:** Reed, Willis & Burke **Cost:** $8,000,000
> **Contact for Rental:** Michael A. Nordine; (501) 536-7600

PINE BLUFF CONVENTION CENTER - ARENA
500 East Eighth Street, Pine Bluff, AR 71601
(501) 536-7600
> **Type of Facility:** Arena; Multi-Purpose

Type of Stage: Arena
Seating Capacity: 8,000
Year Built: 1976
Contact for Rental: Michael A. Nordine;   (501) 536-7600
Stage area contains 2,300 square feet

PINE BLUFF CONVENTION CENTER - AUDITORIUM
500 East Eighth Street, Pine Bluff, AR 71601
(501) 536-7600
   Type of Facility: Concert Hall; Auditorium; Theatre House; Opera House
   Type of Stage: Proscenium
   Stage Dimensions: 63'Wx93'D; 63'Wx25'H proscenium opening
   Orchestra Pit
   Seating Capacity: 2,027
   Year Built: 1976
   Contact for Rental: Michael A. Nordine;   (501) 536-7600

Russellville

FACILITY

ARKANSAS RIVER VALLEY ARTS CENTER
PO Box 2112, Russellville, AR 72801
(501) 968-2452
   Founded: 1990
   Type of Facility: Auditorium
   Facility Originally: School
   Type of Stage: Platform
   Seating Capacity: 300 ·

ARKANSAS TECH UNIVERSITY - WITHERSPOON ARTS AND HUMANITIES BUILDING
Russellville, AR 72801
(501) 968-0274
   Type of Facility: Auditorium
   Type of Stage: Flexible   **Orchestra Pit**
   Seating Capacity: 746
   Year Built: 1972   **Architect:** Dan Cowling & Associates
   Acoustical Consultant: C.P. Boner & Associates
   Contact for Rental: Jimmy Ferguson;   (501) 968-0239
   Resident Groups: University Music Department; Little Theatre; Russellville Community Concerts; small group programs

---

Searcy

FACILITY

BENSON AUDITORIUM
900 East Center Street, Searcy, AR 72149-0001
(501) 279-4557
   Founded: 1980
   Type of Facility: Auditorium
   Facility Originally: Auditorium for Harding University
   Type of Stage: Proscenium
   Stage Dimensions: 80'x40'   **Orchestra Pit**
   Seating Capacity: 3,111
   Year Built: 1980

Springdale

FACILITY

ARTS CENTER OF THE OZARKS
214 South Main, Springdale, AR 72765
(501) 751-5441
   Type of Facility: Theatre Complex; Multi-Purpose
   Facility Originally: Church
   Type of Stage: Flexible; Proscenium

Stage Dimensions: 40'Wx25'D
Seating Capacity: 350
Year Built: 1978
Contact for Rental: Harry Blundell;   (501) 751-5441
Resident Groups: In-house productions

Stuttgart

PERFORMING SERIES

GRAND PRAIRIE FESTIVAL OF THE ARTS
PO Box 65, Stuttgart, AR 72160
(501) 673-1781; (501) 673-7278
   Founded: 1956
   Arts Area: Vocal Music; Instrumental Music; Theater
   Status: Professional; Non-Professional
   Type: Educational; Sponsoring
   Purpose: To promote all of the cultural arts in the Grand Prairie area
   Officers: Marianne Maynard, Co-Chairperson; Linda Fischer, Co-Chairperson
   Volunteer Staff: 25
   Utilizes: Guest Artists; Guest Directors
   Budget: $1,000 - $50,000
   Income Sources: Business/Corporate Donations; Box Office; Government Grants; Individual Donations
   Season: September   **Annual Attendance:** 5,000
   Affiliations: Grand Prairie Arts Council
   Performance Facilities: Grand Prairie War Memorial Auditorium, Grand Prairie Arts Center

FACILITY

GRAND PRAIRIE WAR MEMORIAL AUDITORIUM
600 West 20th, Stuttgart, AR 72160
(501) 673-8585
   Type of Facility: Auditorium
   Type of Stage: Proscenium
   Seating Capacity: 1,000
   Contact for Rental: Jo Rowe;   (501) 673-8585
   Manager: Ronnie Simmons;   (501) 673-8585

CALIFORNIA

Anaheim

DANCE

XIPE TOTEC AZTEC DANCERS/VIRGINIA CARMELO
1757 Gardenaire Lane, Anaheim, CA 92804
(714) 491-7510
Founded: 1979
Arts Area: Traditional Aztec
Status: Semi-Professional
Type: Performing; Touring; Educational
Purpose: To retain cultural ties
Management: Virginia Carmelo
Budget: $1,000 - $50,000
Income Sources: Box Office

FACILITY

ANAHEIM CONVENTION CENTER
800 West Katella Avenue, Anaheim, CA 92802
(714) 999-8950
FAX: (714) 999-8965
Type of Facility: Multi-Purpose
Year Built: 1967   **Architect:** Adrian Wilson & Associates   **Cost:** $6,100,000
Year Remodeled: 1982   **Architect:** Howard Needles Tammen & Bergendoff   **Cost:** $17,785,000
Contact for Rental: Lynn Thompson;   (714) 999-8950
The Anaheim Convention Center contains the Anaheim Room and the Arena. See separate listings for additional information.

ANAHEIM CONVENTION CENTER - ANAHEIM ROOM
800 West Katella Avenue, Anaheim, CA 92802
(714) 999-8950
FAX: (714) 999-8965
Type of Facility: Multi-Purpose; Room
Type of Stage: Proscenium
Stage Dimensions: 40'Wx28'D
Seating Capacity: 1,600
Contact for Rental: Lynn Thompson;   (714) 999-8950

ANAHEIM CONVENTION CENTER - ARENA
800 West Katella Avenue, Anaheim, CA 92802
(714) 999-8950
FAX: (714) 999-8965
Type of Facility: Arena
Type of Stage: Arena
Seating Capacity: 8,900
Contact for Rental: Lynn Thompson;   (714) 999-8950

ANAHEIM CULTURAL ARTS CENTER
931 North Harbor Boulevard, Anaheim, CA 92805
(714) 533-3460
Type of Facility: Concert Hall; Auditorium; Studio Performance; Performance Center; Room
Facility Originally: School
Type of Stage: Proscenium
Stage Dimensions: 30'x40'x26'
Seating Capacity: 300
Year Built: 1931   **Cost:** $85,000
Year Remodeled: 1972   **Architect:** Dan Rowland & Associates
Contact for Rental: Sylvia Bula;   (714) 533-3460
Resident Groups: Anaheim Arts Association; Ana-Modjeska Players; Searchers Gem & Mineral Society; Scandinavian Dancers; Strathleven Scottish Country Dancers; Changing Visions Dance Theatre Company

Aptos

DANCE

CRASH, BURN AND DIE DANCE COMPANY
259 Rio Del Mar Boulevard, Aptos, CA 95003
(408) 688-3371
>   **Founded:** 1982
>   **Arts Area:** Modern
>   **Status:** Professional; Non-Profit
>   **Type:** Performing; Touring
>   **Purpose:** At or over the edge since 1982
>   **Management:** Leslie Swaha, Artistic Director
>   **Utilizes:** Guest Artists
>   **Income Sources:** Private Foundations/Grants/Endowments; Box Office; Individual Donations
>   **Season:** 52 Weeks

PERFORMING SERIES

CABRILLO MUSIC FESTIVAL
9053 Soquel, Aptos, CA 95003
(408) 662-2701
>   **Founded:** 1963
>   **Arts Area:** Vocal Music; Instrumental Music; Festivals
>   **Status:** Professional; Non-Profit
>   **Type:** Performing; Sponsoring
>   **Purpose:** To present the music of living composers, primarily American, to ever-widening audiences
>   **Management:** Tom Fredericks, Executive Director; Marin Alsop, Music Director
>   **Officers:** Celia Hartman, President
>   **Paid Staff:** 2   **Volunteer Staff:** 100
>   **Paid Artists:** 70
>   **Utilizes:** Guest Conductors; Guest Artists
>   **Budget:** $100,000 - $500,000
>   **Income Sources:** Private Foundations/Grants/Endowments; Business/Corporate Donations; Box Office; Government Grants; Individual Donations
>   **Annual Attendance:** 7,500
>   **Performance Facilities:** Santa Cruz Civic Auditorium; Mission San Juan Bautista

FACILITY

CABRILLO COLLEGE THEATER
6500 Soquel Drive, Aptos, CA 95003
(408) 479-6364
FAX: (408) 464-8382
>   **Type of Facility:** Theatre House
>   **Type of Stage:** Proscenium
>   **Stage Dimensions:** 48'Wx40'D; 48'Wx16'H proscenium opening
>   **Seating Capacity:** 527
>   **Year Built:** 1962   **Architect:** Kump Maston Hurd   **Cost:** $1,000,000
>   **Contact for Rental:** Bonnie Durham, Facilities Coordinator;   (408) 479-6331
>   **Manager:** John Mauceri

Arcata

FACILITY

HUMBOLDT STATE UNIVERSITY
Center Arts, Arcata, CA 95521
(707) 826-4411
>   **Type of Facility:** Performance Center
>   **Contact for Rental:** Center Arts Production Coordinator;   (707) 826-4411
>   *Contains East Gymnasium, Fulkerson Recital Hall, John Van Duzer Theatre and Kate Buchanon Room. See separate listings for additional information.*

HUMBOLDT STATE UNIVERSITY - EAST GYMNASIUM
Center Arts, Arcata, CA 95521
(707) 826-4411
 Type of Facility: Basketball Gymnasium
 Type of Stage: Platform
 Stage Dimensions: 20'x40'
 Seating Capacity: 1,800
 Contact for Rental: Center Arts Production Coordinator; (707) 826-4411
 Resident Groups: Center Arts

HUMBOLDT STATE UNIVERSITY - FULKERSON RECITAL HALL
Center Arts, Arcata, CA 95521
(707) 826-4411
 Type of Facility: Recital Hall
 Type of Stage: Proscenium **Orchestra Pit**
 Seating Capacity: 200
 Contact for Rental: Center Arts Production Coordinator; (707) 826-4411
 Resident Groups: University Music Department; Center Arts

HUMBOLDT STATE UNIVERSITY - JOHN VAN DUZER THEATRE
Center Arts, Arcata, CA 95521
(707) 826-4411
 Type of Facility: Theatre House
 Type of Stage: Proscenium **Orchestra Pit**
 Seating Capacity: 750
 Contact for Rental: Center Arts Production Coordinator; (707) 826-4411
 Resident Groups: Theater Arts Department; Music Department; Center Arts

HUMBOLDT STATE UNIVERSITY - KATE BUCHANAN ROOM
Center Arts, Arcata, CA 95521
(707) 826-4411
 Type of Facility: Multi-Purpose; Room
 Type of Stage: Platform
 Stage Dimensions: 8'x12'
 Seating Capacity: 260
 Contact for Rental: Center Arts Production Coordinator; (707) 826-4411
 Resident Groups: Center Arts

Bakersfield

INSTRUMENTAL MUSIC

BAKERSFIELD SYMPHONY ORCHESTRA
1401 19th Street, Suite 130, Bakersfield, CA 93301
(805) 323-7928
FAX: (805) 323-7331
 Founded: 1946
 Arts Area: Symphony
 Status: Professional
 Type: Performing
 Purpose: To present classical music, educational programs, ballet and pop concerts
 Management: A.H. Stanley, Manager
 Officers: Donald R. Lindsey, President
 Paid Staff: 5 **Volunteer Staff:** 100
 Paid Artists: 90
 Utilizes: Guest Conductors; Guest Artists
 Budget: $100,000 - $500,000
 Income Sources: Private Foundations/Grants/Endowments; Business/Corporate Donations; Box Office; Government Grants; Individual Donations
 Season: September - May **Annual Attendance:** 18,500
 Affiliations: ASOL; Association of California Symphony Orchestras
 Performance Facilities: Bakersfield Civic Auditorium

FACILITY

BAKERSFIELD CIVIC AUDITORIUM
1001 Truxton Avenue, Bakersfield, CA 93301
(805) 327-7553
FAX: (805) 861-9904
Type of Facility: Concert Hall; Theatre House; Arena; Multi-Purpose
Type of Stage: Proscenium
Stage Dimensions: 140'Wx52'D, 25'W proscenium opening   **Orchestra Pit**
Seating Capacity: Concert Hall 3,041; Festival 6,000
Year Built: 1962   **Architect:** Wright Metcalf & Parsons   **Cost:** $5,000,000
Acoustical Consultant: Vern Knudsen
Contact for Rental: Lee Anderson;   (805) 327-7553

DORE THEATRE - CALIFORNIA STATE UNIVERSITY, BAKERSFIELD
9001 Stockdale Highway, Bakersfield, CA 93311
(805) 664-2221
Type of Facility: Theatre Complex; Studio Performance
Type of Stage: Proscenium   **Orchestra Pit**
Seating Capacity: 492
Year Built: 1979
Contact for Rental: Dean of School of Arts and Sciences;   (805) 664-2221
Resident Groups: California State University, Bakersfield - Fine Arts Department

Bear Valley

PERFORMING SERIES

MUSIC FROM BEAR VALLEY
PO Box 5068, Bear Valley Road, Bear Valley, CA 95223
(209) 753-2574
FAX: (209) 753-2336
Founded: 1969
Arts Area: Instrumental Music; Festivals; Grand Opera
Status: Professional; Non-Profit
Type: Performing; Resident
Purpose: To present a sixteen day music fesitval of opera, symphony, pop, and chamber music concerts;
to present children's concerts and recitals
Management: Katherine L. Bort, Executive Director; Stewart Comer, General Manager
Officers: Ann Hicks, President; Daniel P. Hogan, Vice President; Linda Koenig, Secretary; Evelyn Bautista, Treasurer
Paid Staff: 16   **Volunteer Staff:** 25
Paid Artists: 110   **Non-Paid Artists:** 38
Utilizes: Special Technical Talent; Guest Artists
Budget: $100,000 - $500,000
Income Sources: Private Foundations/Grants/Endowments; Business/Corporate Donations; Box Office; Government
Grants; Individual Donations; Auction; Raffle; Product Sales
Season: July - August   **Annual Attendance:** 10,000
Affiliations: Association of California Symphony Orchestras

Belvedere

DANCE

THE DANCE ASSOCIATION/RUTH LANGRIDGE DANCE COMPANY
PO Box 692, Belvedere, CA 94920
(415) 435-2771
Founded: 1979
Arts Area: Modern; Ballet
Status: Professional; Non-Profit
Type: Performing; Touring; Resident; Educational
Purpose: To provide innovative, contemporary dance performances for the community and on tour; to provide
high-quality dance training and educational-outreach programs
Officers: Ruth Langridge, Artistic Director
Paid Staff: 3   **Volunteer Staff:** 25
Paid Artists: 8
Utilizes: Guest Artists; Guest Choreographers
Budget: $100,000 - $500,000

Income Sources: Private Foundations/Grants/Endowments; Business/Corporate Donations; Box Office; Government Grants; Individual Donations; Tuition; Fund-raising
Season: 52 Weeks
Performance Facilities: New Peformance Gallery

Berkeley

DANCE

BAY AREA REPERTORY DANCE THEATRE (BARD)
c/o David Wood, Department of Dramatic Arts, Berkeley, CA 94720
(510) 642-1677
    Founded: 1970
    Arts Area: Modern
    Status: Non-Professional; Non-Profit
    Type: Performing; Educational
    Purpose: To offer young dancers an opportunity to gain performance experience; to serve the community in various projects coordinated with educational programs in the arts
    Management: Carol Egan, Company Manager; David Wood, Artistic Director; Marni Thomas, General Manager; Barbara Codd, Stage Manager
    Paid Staff: 3   **Volunteer Staff:** 2
    Non-Paid Artists: 15
    Utilizes: Special Technical Talent; Guest Artists
    Budget: $1,000 - $50,000
    Income Sources: Private Foundations/Grants/Endowments; Box Office; Individual Donations
    Season: November - April

BERKELEY CITY BALLET
1800 Dwight Way, Berkeley, CA 94703
(510) 841-8913
    Founded: 1974
    Arts Area: Ballet
    Status: Non-Profit
    Type: Performing; Educational
    Purpose: To promote and foster dance in the Bay Area by providing training and presenting quality performances
    Management: Grace Doty, Artistic Director
    Officers: Jim Simonetti, President; Jack Johannes, First Vice President
    Paid Staff: 9
    Utilizes: Guest Artists; Guest Choreographers
    Budget: $100,000 - $500,000
    Income Sources: Private Foundations/Grants/Endowments; Business/Corporate Donations; Individual Donations
    Season: Spring - Winter   **Annual Attendance:** 15,000
    Performance Facilities: Zellerbach Hall; Berkeley Community Theater

WENDY ROGERS/CHOREOGRAPHICS
1187 Shattuck Avenue, Berkeley, CA 94707
(510) 524-8254
    Arts Area: Modern
    Status: Professional; Non-Profit
    Type: Performing; Touring; Resident
    Management: Wendy Rogers, Artistic Director
    Paid Artists: 5
    Utilizes: Guest Artists; Guest Choreographers; Collaborating Artists
    Budget: $50,000 - $100,000
    Income Sources: Private Foundations/Grants/Endowments; Business/Corporate Donations; Box Office; Government Grants; Individual Donations
    Season: 52 Weeks

INSTRUMENTAL MUSIC

BERKELEY SYMPHONY ORCHESTRA
2322 Shattuck Avenue, Berkeley, CA 94704
(510) 841-2800
FAX: (510) 644-2596
    Founded: 1969
    Arts Area: Symphony; Orchestra

Status: Semi-Professional
Type: Performing
Purpose: To perform contemporary and traditional symphony literature
Management: Kelly Johnson, Executive Director; Elisabeth Beaird, Development Director; Shohei Sawada, Bookeeper/Data Manager; Recardo Antoni, Administrative Assistant; Elizabeth Gibson, Personnel Manager
Officers: Jeffrey Shattuck Leiter, President; John E. Danielsen, Ruth Dorman, Vice Presidents; Janet Maestro, Secretary; Kirk Misaka, Treasurer
Paid Staff: 4   Volunteer Staff: 1
Paid Artists: 48   Non-Paid Artists: 37
Utilizes: Special Technical Talent; Guest Conductors; Guest Artists
Budget: $500,000 - $1,000,000
Income Sources: Private Foundations/Grants/Endowments; Business/Corporate Donations; Box Office; Government Grants; Individual Donations; Bingo
Season: August - June   Annual Attendance: 9,000
Performance Facilities: Zellerbach Hall, University of California at Berkeley

CONCERTO AMABILE
c/o San Francisco Early Music Society, PO Box 10151, Berkeley, CA 94709
(510) 528-1725
Arts Area: Chamber; Ensemble; Instrumental Group
Status: Professional; Non-Profit
Type: Performing; Touring
Purpose: To play the best baroque repertoires, especially of lesser-known composers
Management: Kathleen Kraft, Artistic Director
Officers: Kathleen Kraft, President
Budget: $1,000 - $50,000
Income Sources: Private Foundations/Grants/Endowments; Business/Corporate Donations; Box Office; Government Grants; Individual Donations

SAN FRANCISCO EARLY MUSIC SOCIETY
PO Box 10151, Berkeley, CA 94709
(510) 528-1725
Arts Area: Chamber; Ensemble; Ethnic; Folk
Status: Non-Profit
Type: Educational; Sponsoring
Purpose: To serve as an umbrella organization for early music activities in northern California
Management: John Dornenburg, President; Robert Jackson, Executive Director
Budget: $100,000 - $500,000
Income Sources: Private Foundations/Grants/Endowments; Business/Corporate Donations; Box Office; Government Grants; Individual Donations
Season: 52 Weeks
Performance Facilities: First Congregational Church, Berkeley

VOCAL MUSIC

BERKELEY OPERA
715 Arlington, Berkeley, CA 94707
(510) 524-5256
Founded: 1979
Arts Area: Lyric Opera
Status: Semi-Professional
Type: Performing
Purpose: To present opera
Management: Richard Goodman, General Director; Jane Rateaver, Audition Secretary; Bonnie Lockett, Orchestra Manager
Officers: Richard Goodman, President/Treasurer; Jane Rateaver, Vice President; Sue Goodman, Secretary; Edgar Braun, Board Chairman
Volunteer Staff: 20
Paid Artists: 75   Non-Paid Artists: 20
Utilizes: Local Talent
Budget: $100,000 - $500,000
Income Sources: Private Foundations/Grants/Endowments; Business/Corporate Donations; Box Office; Government Grants; Individual Donations
Season: February - August   Annual Attendance: 5,000
Affiliations: Theater Bay Area
Performance Facilities: Julia Morgan Theater; Hillside Club Theater

THEATRE

BERKELEY COMMUNITY THEATRE
1930 Allston Way, Berkeley, CA 94704
(510) 644-6863
FAX: (510) 845-9674
Founded: 1950
Arts Area: Professional; Musical; Community; Theatrical Group
Status: Professional; Non-Professional
Type: Performing; Touring; Educational
Purpose: To provide the community with a professional theatre available for rent to professional, community, and non-profit organizations
Management: Judson H. Owens, Theatre Manager; Lance C. James, Assistant Manager
Paid Staff: 14 **Volunteer Staff:** 70
Utilizes: Special Technical Talent; Guest Conductors; Guest Artists; Guest Directors
Budget: $100,000 - $500,000
Income Sources: Box Office; Government Grants
Season: 52 Weeks **Annual Attendance:** 200,000

BERKELEY REPERTORY THEATRE
2025 Addison Street, Berkeley, CA 94704
(510) 204-8901
FAX: (510) 841-7711
Founded: 1968
Arts Area: Professional; Theatrical Group
Status: Professional; Non-Profit
Type: Performing; Touring; Resident; Educational
Purpose: To present classical and contemporary plays of major stature, nurturing and stimulating the art form while at the same time stimulating our community
Management: Sharon Ott, Artistic Director; Susan Medak, Managing Director
Officers: Robert W. Burt, President; Edwin C. Shiver, Vice President; Dale Affonso, Secretary; Rick Messman, Treasurer
Paid Staff: 50 **Volunteer Staff:** 20
Paid Artists: 50
Utilizes: Special Technical Talent; Guest Artists; Guest Directors
Budget: $1,000,000 - $5,000,000
Income Sources: Private Foundations/Grants/Endowments; Business/Corporate Donations; Box Office; Government Grants; Individual Donations
Season: September - June **Annual Attendance:** 160,000
Affiliations: TCG; LORT; AAA; California Confederation of the Arts; California Theatre Council
Performance Facilities: Berkeley Repertory Theatre

BLACK REPERTORY GROUP INC.
3201 Adeline Street, Berkeley, CA 94703
(510) 652-2120
Founded: 1964
Arts Area: Community; Theatrical Group
Status: Non-Professional; Non-Profit
Type: Resident
Purpose: To give youth the opportunity to use drama as a means of discipline and building self-esteem
Management: Nora B. Vaughn, Executive Director
Utilizes: Special Technical Talent; Guest Artists; Guest Directors
Budget: $50,000 - $100,000
Income Sources: Private Foundations/Grants/Endowments; Business/Corporate Donations; Box Office; Government Grants; Individual Donations
Season: November - June

FLORENCE SCHWIMLEY LITTLE THEATRE
2246 Milvia Street, Berkeley, CA 94704
(510) 644-6863
Founded: 1948
Arts Area: Professional; Musical; Community; Theatrical Group
Status: Professional; Non-Professional
Type: Performing; Touring; Educational
Purpose: To provide the community with a professional theatre available for rent to professional, community and non-profit organizations
Management: Judson H. Owens, Theatre Manager; Lance C. James, Assistant Manager
Paid Staff: 3 **Volunteer Staff:** 20

Utilizes: Special Technical Talent; Guest Artists; Guest Directors
Budget: $100,000 - $500,000
Income Sources: Box Office; Government Grants
Season: 52 Weeks   **Annual Attendance:** 20,000

PERFORMING SERIES

BERKELEY SHAKESPEARE FESTIVAL
2531 Ninth Street, Berkeley, CA 94710
(510) 548-3422; (415) 861-3101
Founded: 1973
Arts Area: Theater
Status: Professional; Non-Profit
Type: Performing; Touring; Educational
Purpose: Committed to innovative productions of Shakespearean plays
Management: Maria A. O'Dea, Managing Director; Michael Addison, Artistic Director; Lauren Brown, Development Director; Scott Stuart, Production Manager; Carla Befera, Press Contact
Officers: David Bond, Board President
Paid Staff: 5   **Volunteer Staff:** 90
Paid Artists: 64
Utilizes: Special Technical Talent; Guest Artists; Guest Directors
Budget: $500,000 - $1,000,000
Income Sources: Private Foundations/Grants/Endowments; Business/Corporate Donations; Box Office; Government Grants; Individual Donations
Season: July - November   **Annual Attendance:** 35,000
Affiliations: Theatre/Bay Area; California Arts Council; TCG
Performance Facilities: John Hinkel Park Outdoor Amphitheatre

LA PENA CULTURAL CENTER
3105 Shattuck Avenue, Berkeley, CA 94705
(510) 849-2568
FAX: (510) 849-9397
Founded: 1975
Arts Area: Vocal Music; Instrumental Music
Status: Non-Profit
Type: Educational; Sponsoring
Purpose: To present cultural and educational programs which increase understanding of different cultures and support efforts to build a just society
Management: Paul Chin, Vanessa Whang, Co-Directors; Earthlyn Mannd, Development Director
Officers: Paul Chin, President of the Board
Paid Staff: 7
Utilizes: Special Technical Talent; Guest Artists
Budget: $100,000 - $500,000
Income Sources: Private Foundations/Grants/Endowments; Business/Corporate Donations; Box Office; Government Grants; Individual Donations
Season: 52 Weeks
Annual Attendance: 20,000

UNIVERSITY OF CALIFORNIA - BERKELEY CALIFORNIA PERFORMANCES
101 Zellerbach Hall, Berkeley, CA 94720
(510) 642-0212
FAX: (510) 643-6707
Founded: 1904
Arts Area: Dance; Vocal Music; Instrumental Music; Theater; Classical Music
Status: Non-Profit
Type: Educational; Sponsoring
Purpose: To offer performances at the highest level of content and execution, giving the student an opportunity to form his taste in the arts on a sound foundation
Management: Robert W. Cole, Director
Paid Staff: 25
Budget: $1,000,000 - $5,000,000
Income Sources: Private Foundations/Grants/Endowments; Box Office; Government Grants; Individual Donations
Season: July - June
Affiliations: APAP; ISPAA; WAAA
Performance Facilities: Zellerbach Auditorium, University of California at Berkeley; Zellerbach Playhouse, University of California at Berkeley; Wheeler Auditorium; Hearst Greek Theatre

FACILITY

BERKELEY COMMUNITY THEATRE
1930 Allston Way, Berkeley, CA 94704
(510) 644-6863
> **Type of Facility:** Theatre Complex; Auditorium; Studio Performance; Theatre House; Civic Center
> **Type of Stage:** Proscenium
> **Orchestra Pit**
> **Seating Capacity:** 3,491
> **Year Built:** 1950   **Architect:** Will Corlett/Henry Gutterson   **Cost:** $3,000,000
> **Contact for Rental:** Judson H. Owens;   (510) 644-6863

BERKELEY REPERTORY THEATRE
2025 Addison Street, Berkeley, CA 94704
(510) 204-8901
FAX: (510) 841-7711
> **Founded:** 1968
> **Type of Facility:** Theatre House
> **Type of Stage:** Thrust
> **Stage Dimensions:** Trapezoidal 25'x15'x20'x30'
> **Seating Capacity:** 401
> **Year Built:** 1980   **Architect:** Angell, Lockwood & Associates   **Cost:** $2,000,000
> **Acoustical Consultant:** James LeBrecht
> **Resident Groups:** Berkeley Repertory Theatre

UNIVERSITY OF CALIFORNIA-BERKELEY - ALFRED HERTZ MEMORIAL HALL
Department of Music, Berkeley, CA 94720
(510) 642-4864
> **Type of Facility:** Concert Hall
> **Type of Stage:** Platform
> **Stage Dimensions:** 68'x26'
> **Seating Capacity:** 714
> **Year Built:** 1958   **Architect:** Gardner Dailey   **Cost:** $1,000,000
> **Acoustical Consultant:** Vern Knudsen
> **Manager:** David Whitman
> **Resident Groups:** University musical organizations

UNIVERSITY OF CALIFORNIA-BERKELEY - HEARST GREEK THEATRE
c/o Cal Performances, 101 Zellerbach Hall, Berkeley, CA 94720
(510) 642-0212
> **Type of Facility:** Outdoor (Concert); Amphitheater
> **Type of Stage:** Greek
> **Stage Dimensions:** 135'x28'   **Orchestra Pit**
> **Seating Capacity:** 9,000
> **Year Built:** 1903   **Architect:** John Galen Howard   **Cost:** $40,000
> **Year Remodeled:** 1957   **Architect:** Ernest Born Associates
> **Contact for Rental:** David Hillbrand;   (510) 642-0212

UNIVERSITY OF CALIFORNIA-BERKELEY - ZELLERBACH HALL
Berkeley, CA 94720
(510) 642-0212
> **Type of Facility:** Theatre Complex; Auditorium; Theatre House; Multi-Purpose
> **Type of Stage:** Proscenium
> **Stage Dimensions:** 30'x63'x50'   **Orchestra Pit**
> **Seating Capacity:** 2,015
> **Year Built:** 1968   **Architect:** Vernon DeMars   **Cost:** $7,000,000
> **Acoustical Consultant:** Vern Knudsen & W.W. Soroka
> **Contact for Rental:** Ella Baff or David Hillbrand;   (510) 642-0212
> **Manager:** Robert Cole;   (510) 642-0212
> **Resident Groups:** Cal Performances

UNIVERSITY OF CALIFORNIA-BERKELEY - ZELLERBACH PLAYHOUSE
c/o Cal Performances, 101 Zellerbach Hall, Berkeley, CA 94720
(510) 642-0212
> **Type of Facility:** Theatre Complex; Auditorium; Studio Performance; Theatre House; Arena
> **Type of Stage:** Thrust; Flexible; Proscenium; Platform; 3/4 Arena; Arena
> **Stage Dimensions:** 20'x60'x36'   **Orchestra Pit**
> **Seating Capacity:** 500

Year Built: 1968   **Architect:** Vernon DeMars   **Cost:** $7,000,000
Acoustical Consultant: Vern Knudsen & W.W. Soroka
Contact for Rental: David Hillbrand;   (510) 642-0212
Resident Groups: University Theatre; University Dance; Department of Dramatic Art

Beverly Hills

INSTRUMENTAL MUSIC

BEVERLY HILLS SYMPHONY
PO Box 5429, Beverly Hills, CA 90210
(310) 276-8385
Founded: 1983
Arts Area: Symphony; Orchestra; Chamber; Ensemble
Status: Professional; Non-Profit
Type: Performing; Educational; Sponsoring
Purpose: To be a cultural entity of Beverly Hills, an organization of the highest quality producing first-rate concerts; to further the cultural pursuits of Beverly Hills and enhance the activities of other organizations in the community with our music
Management: Bogidar Avramov, Music Director/Conductor; Razdan Kuymijian, Orchestra Manager
Officers: Debbie Grossman, President
Volunteer Staff: 50
Paid Artists: 65
Utilizes: Guest Artists
Budget: $100,000 - $500,000
Income Sources: Private Foundations/Grants/Endowments; Business/Corporate Donations; Box Office; Government Grants; Individual Donations
Season: 52 Weeks   **Annual Attendance:** 10,000
Affiliations: ASOL; Association of California Symphony Orchestras

LOS ANGELES DOCTORS SYMPHONY
521 North Maple Drive, Beverly Hills, CA 90210
(310) 550-0691
Founded: 1953
Arts Area: Symphony; Orchestra
Status: Non-Professional
Type: Performing
Purpose: To present concert performances to benefit medical charitable organizations locally and internationally
Officers: Simon Gamer DDS, President; Geri Freeland-Soper PhD, Vice President; Nora Graham, Secretary; Harry Dapeer, Treasurer
Paid Staff: 1
Paid Artists: 1   **Non-Paid Artists:** 2
Utilizes: Guest Conductors; Guest Artists
Budget: $1,000 - $50,000
Income Sources: Individual Donations; Charity Organization Donations
Season: September - June   **Annual Attendance:** 3,000

VOCAL MUSIC

LOS ANGELES CONCERT OPERA ASSOCIATION
2250 Gloaming Way, Beverly Hills, CA 90210
(310) 276-2731
Founded: 1987
Arts Area: Lyric Opera
Status: Non-Profit
Type: Performing
Purpose: To give young semiprofessional singers an opportunity to perform
Management: Dr. Loren L. Zachary, General Director
Officers: Richard C. Wulliger, President
Volunteer Staff: 20
Paid Artists: 50
Utilizes: Guest Conductors
Budget: $1,000 - $50,000
Income Sources: Box Office; Individual Donations
Season: January   **Annual Attendance:** 1,200
Performance Facilities: Ambassador Auditorium

THEATRE

THEATRE 40
PO Box 5401, Beverly Hills, CA 90210
(310) 277-4221
FAX: (213) 876-0227
Founded: 1964
Arts Area: Professional; Theatrical Group
Status: Professional
Type: Performing; Educational
Purpose: A professional equity company committed to performing classical and contemporary plays
Management: Charles Arthur, Artistic Director; Lee Ann Holfelder, Business Manager; Diana Hale, Publicity Director
Paid Staff: 4
Utilizes: Guest Directors
Budget: $50,000 - $100,000
Income Sources: Business/Corporate Donations; Box Office; Individual Donations
Season: July - June **Annual Attendance:** 8,000
Affiliations: Los Angeles Theatre Alliance; League of Producers and Theatres of Greater Los Angeles
Performance Facilities: Theatre 40

PERFORMING SERIES

INTERNATIONAL CONCERTS EXCHANGE
1124 Summit Drive, Beverly Hills, CA 90210
(213) 272-5539
FAX: (213) 272-5539
Founded: 1942
Arts Area: Festivals
Status: Professional; Semi-Professional; Non-Professional; Non-Profit
Type: Performing; Educational
Management: Dr. Irwin Paones, Producer/Managing Director
Paid Staff: 2
Utilizes: Special Technical Talent; Guest Artists
Income Sources: Box Office

PLAYBOY JAZZ FESTIVAL
9242 Beverly Boulevard, Beverly Hills, CA 90210
(310) 246-4000
FAX: (310) 246-4077
Founded: 1979
Arts Area: Vocal Music; Instrumental Music
Status: Professional
Type: Sponsoring
Purpose: To provide a community service; to enable Los Angeles residents to enjoy jazz music
Utilizes: Guest Artists
Budget: $500,000 - $1,000,000
Income Sources: Box Office
Season: June **Annual Attendance:** 35,000
Performance Facilities: Hollywood Bowl

FACILITY

BEVERLY HILLS PLAYHOUSE
254 South Robertson Boulevard, Beverly Hills, CA 90211
(310) 855-1556
Type of Facility: Theatre House
Type of Stage: Proscenium
Stage Dimensions: 23'Wx18'6"D; 23'Wx12'H proscenium opening
Seating Capacity: 99
Year Built: 1940
Year Remodeled: 1982
Contact for Rental: Adrienne Woody; (213) 855-1556

Big Bear Lake

FACILITY

BIG BEAR LAKE PERFORMING ARTS CENTER
39707 Big Bear Boulevard, PO Box 2800, Big Bear Lake, CA 92315
(909) 866-5831
FAX: (909) 866-6766
  Founded: 1988
  Type of Facility: Concert Hall; Auditorium; Performance Center; Civic Center
  Type of Stage: Proscenium
  Stage Dimensions: 40'x42'   **Orchestra Pit**
  Seating Capacity: 400
  Year Built: 1977   **Architect:** Wolff, Lang, Christopher and Associates   **Cost:** $5,500,000
  Acoustical Consultant: John von Szelski (theatre)
  Contact for Rental: Colleen J. McBride;   (909) 866-5831

Blue Lake

THEATRE

DELL' ARTE PLAYERS COMPANY
131 H Street, PO Box 816, Blue Lake, CA 95525
(707) 668-5663
  Founded: 1971
  Arts Area: Professional; Theatrical Group
  Status: Professional; Non-Profit
  Type: Performing; Touring
  Purpose: To give artists a chance to live and work in a rural area
  Management: Michael Fields, Managing Director; Donald Forrest, Joan Schirle, Co-Artistic Directors
  Officers: Michael Fields, President; Bobbi Ricca, Secretary/Treasurer
  Paid Staff: 3
  Paid Artists: 5
  Budget: $100,000 - $500,000
  Income Sources: Private Foundations/Grants/Endowments; Business/Corporate Donations; Box Office; Government Grants; Individual Donations
  Season: 52 Weeks
  Affiliations: Humboldt Arts Council; California Theater Council
  Performance Facilities: Dell' Arte Theatre

Brea

FACILITY

CURTIS THEATRE
1 Civic Center Circle, Brea, CA 92621
(714) 990-7722
FAX: (714) 990-2258
  Founded: 1980
  Type of Facility: Theatre House
  Type of Stage: Proscenium
  Stage Dimensions: 50'Wx40'D
  Seating Capacity: 199
  Year Built: 1980   **Cost:** $5,000,000
  Contact for Rental: D. Scott Riordan;   (714) 990-7723
  Resident Groups: Brea's Youth Theatre; Brea Civic Light Opera; Brea Theatre League

Burbank

INSTRUMENTAL MUSIC

BURBANK SYMPHONY ASSOCIATION
PO Box 4141, Burbank, CA 91502
(818) 846-5981
  Founded: 1944
  Arts Area: Symphony; Orchestra

Status: Non-Profit
Type: Sponsoring
Purpose: To provide symphonic music for the community
Management: Victor Vener, Conductor/Music Director; Sabina Vener, Orchestra Manager
Officers: Walter Mears, President; Evan Binn, Vice President; Veronica Chavour, Treasurer
Volunteer Staff: 27
Paid Artists: 70
Utilizes: Guest Conductors; Guest Artists
Budget: $1,000 - $50,000
Income Sources: Private Foundations/Grants/Endowments; Business/Corporate Donations; Box Office; Government Grants; Individual Donations
Season: 52 Weeks   **Annual Attendance:** 5,000
Performance Facilities: Hall of Liberty, Forest Lawn; Starlight Amphitheatre

THEATRE

ACME PERFORMANCE GROUP, INC.
1212A North San Fernando, #119, Burbank, CA 91504
Founded: 1991
Arts Area: Professional; Theatrical Group
Status: Professional; Non-Profit
Type: Performing
Purpose: To produce new and unusual American theatrical works
Management: Lee Wochner, Managing Director; Gary Guidinger, Artistic Director; Julie Briggs, Eve Baker, Joe Stafford, Administrative Directors
Paid Staff: 2   **Volunteer Staff:** 5
Paid Artists: 12
Utilizes: Guest Artists; Guest Directors
Budget: $1,000 - $50,000
Income Sources: Private Foundations/Grants/Endowments; Business/Corporate Donations; Box Office; Government Grants; Individual Donations
Season: 52 Weeks

VICTORY THEATRE
3324-26 West Victory, Burbank, CA 91505
(818) 843-9253
Founded: 1979
Arts Area: Professional; Theatrical Group
Status: Professional; Non-Profit
Type: Performing; Educational
Purpose: To encourage the growth of American playwrights; to present original plays
Management: Maria Gobetti, Tom Ormeny, Artistic Directors
Utilizes: Special Technical Talent; Guest Artists; Guest Directors
Budget: $50,000 - $100,000
Income Sources: Private Foundations/Grants/Endowments; Box Office; Individual Donations
Season: 52 Weeks
Affiliations: Los Angeles Theatre Alliance; AEA
Performance Facilities: Victory Theatre

Calabasas

DANCE

KARPATOK HUNGARIAN FOLK ENSEMBLE
4377 Park Carona, Calabasas, CA 91302
(818) 363-2219; (818) 222-2704
FAX: (818) 363-1349
Founded: 1965
Arts Area: Folk
Status: Professional; Non-Profit
Type: Performing; Touring; Educational
Purpose: To contribute to the multi-ethnic American cultural landscape through the perpetuation of the performing arts of the Hungarian people
Management: Mary Beth Treen, Artists' Managment
Officers: Laszlo G. Heredy, President; Dennis Frigyes-Fredricks, Vice President; Marianne Toghia, Secretary; Rosemary Heredy, Treasurer
Paid Staff: 3   **Volunteer Staff:** 2
Paid Artists: 35

Utilizes: Guest Artists; Guest Directors; Guest Choreographers
Budget: $50,000 - $100,000
Income Sources: Private Foundations/Grants/Endowments; Business/Corporate Donations; Government Grants; Individual Donations
Season: 52 Weeks

Canoga Park

DANCE

JAZZ DANCERS, INC.
20314 Lorne Street, Canoga Park, CA 91306
(818) 709-7542
Founded: 1979
Arts Area: Jazz
Status: Professional; Non-Profit
Type: Performing; Touring; Educational
Purpose: To present and preserve the traditions of American jazz dance on a concert level
Management: Dennon Rawles, Managing Director; Nela Fry, Administrative Director
Officers: Charles Hardie CPA, President; Victoria Cashion, Secretary; Thomas Stevens, Treasurer
Paid Staff: 2   **Volunteer Staff:** 2
Paid Artists: 12
Utilizes: Guest Artists; Guest Choreographers; Commissioned Composers
Budget: $1,000 - $50,000
Income Sources: Business/Corporate Donations; Box Office; Government Grants; Individual Donations
Season: 52 Weeks   **Annual Attendance:** 2,000
Performance Facilities: Japan America Theatre

INSTRUMENTAL MUSIC

WEST VALLEY SYMPHONY, DIVISION OF THE LOS ANGELES CIVIC ORCHESTRA
20210 Haynes Street, Canoga Park, CA 91306
(818) 883-6283
Arts Area: Symphony; Orchestra; Chamber; Ethnic
Status: Professional; Semi-Professional; Non-Profit
Type: Performing; Touring; Resident; Educational; Sponsoring
Purpose: To showcase new composers, conductors and soloists; to build classical-music appreciation via affordable and/or free concerts
Management: James Elza Domine, Music Director; Nancy Ross, Associate Conductor
Officers: Jonathan Laurie, President; Leon Wood, Vice President
Paid Staff: 1   **Volunteer Staff:** 12
Paid Artists: 60
Utilizes: Special Technical Talent; Guest Conductors; Guest Artists
Budget: $50,000 - $100,000
Income Sources: Business/Corporate Donations; Box Office; Government Grants; Individual Donations
Season: September - July   **Annual Attendance:** 8,000
Affiliations: Association of California Symphony Orchestras; San Fernando Valley Arts Council
Performance Facilities: Main Stage Theater, Pierce College - Soka Campus

Carmel

INSTRUMENTAL MUSIC

CHAMBER MUSIC SOCIETY OF THE MONTEREY PENISULA
PO Box 6283, Carmel, CA 93921
(408) 625-2212
Founded: 1967
Arts Area: Chamber
Status: Non-Profit
Type: Sponsoring
Purpose: To present high-quality chamber music at a minimum cost; to sponsor an annual competition for young musicians
Officers: Jerry Foote, President; DeForest Sweeney, Vice President; Berenis Tomlinson, Secretary; Harry Handler, Treasurer
Volunteer Staff: 20
Utilizes: Guest Artists
Budget: $1,000 - $50,000

Income Sources: Private Foundations/Grants/Endowments; Business/Corporate Donations; Box Office; Individual Donations
Season: October - May **Annual Attendance:** 3,000

PERFORMING SERIES

CARMEL BACH FESTIVAL
San Carlos & Ninth, Room 11, PO Box 575, Carmel, CA 93921
(408) 624-1521
Founded: 1935
Arts Area: Vocal Music; Instrumental Music; Festivals; Lyric Opera
Status: Professional; Non-Profit
Type: Performing; Educational
Purpose: To perform the music of Johann Sebastian Bach, his predecessors, contemporaries, and successors
Management: Nana Faridany, Executive Director; Bruno Weil, Music Director/Conductor
Officers: Davis Factor, President; Roberta Bialek, Vice President; Lee Rosen, Treasurer
Paid Staff: 4 **Volunteer Staff:** 150
Paid Artists: 100 **Non-Paid Artists:** 35
Utilizes: Guest Conductors; Guest Artists
Budget: $500,000 - $1,000,000
Income Sources: Private Foundations/Grants/Endowments; Business/Corporate Donations; Box Office; Government Grants; Individual Donations
Season: July - August **Annual Attendance:** 17,000
Performance Facilities: Sunset Cultural Center

FACILITY

SUNSET CENTER THEATRE
PO Box 5066, Carmel, CA 93921
(408) 624-3996
Type of Facility: Theatre House
Type of Stage: Proscenium
Stage Dimensions: 40'x28'x35' **Orchestra Pit**
Seating Capacity: 732
Year Built: 1930
Contact for Rental: Manager; (408) 624-3996
Manager: Brian Donaghue, Director
Resident Groups: Carmel Bach Festival; Monterey County Symphony Orchestra; Carmel Music Society; Chamber Music Society; Performance Carmel

Carmel-by-the-Sea

INSTRUMENTAL MUSIC

MONTEREY COUNTY SYMPHONY
PO Box 3965, Carmel-by-the-Sea, CA 93921
(408) 624-8511
FAX: (408) 624-3837
Founded: 1946
Arts Area: Symphony; Orchestra; Chamber; Ensemble
Status: Professional; Non-Profit
Type: Performing
Purpose: To produce high-quality classical music for the people of Monterey County
Management: Joseph Truskot, Executive Director; Joan DeVisser, Director of Operations; Celia Perez Martinez, Director of Marketing/Development
Officers: Sherrie McCullough, President; Susan Schlen, Jeff Craig, Dick Zahm, Vice Presidents; Diane Kelley, Treasurer
Paid Staff: 5
Paid Artists: 100
Utilizes: Special Technical Talent; Guest Conductors; Guest Artists
Budget: $500,000 - $1,000,000
Income Sources: Private Foundations/Grants/Endowments; Business/Corporate Donations; Box Office; Government Grants; Individual Donations
Season: September - August **Annual Attendance:** 12,500
Affiliations: Association of California Symphony Orchestras; ASOL
Performance Facilities: Sunset Theater; Sherwood Hall

Carson
FACILITY

CALIFORNIA STATE UNIVERSITY-DOMINGUEZ HILLS - CONCERT HALL
1000 East Victoria Street, Carson, CA 90747
(310) 516-3543
    Type of Facility: Concert Hall
    Type of Stage: Flexible
    Seating Capacity: 200
    Year Built: 1972
    Contact for Rental: David Champion, Music Department, Chairman;   (310) 516-3543
    Manager: Quincy Jones

CALIFORNIA STATE UNIVERSITY-DOMINGUEZ HILLS - UNIVERSITY THEATRE
1000 East Victoria Street, Carson, CA 90747
(310) 516-3588
    Type of Facility: Theatre House
    Type of Stage: Proscenium
    Stage Dimensions: 65'x80'x40'   **Orchestra Pit**
    Seating Capacity: 467
    Year Built: 1977   **Architect:** Daniel Dworsky   **Cost:** $2,200,000
    Contact for Rental: Stewart Christie;   (310) 516-3898
    Manager: Peter Rodney
    Resident Groups: Theatre Arts Department

Claremont
FACILITY

THE CLAREMONT COLLEGES - GARRISON THEATRE
Tenth and Dartmouth, Claremont, CA 91711
(714) 621-8000, ext. 3800
    Type of Facility: Auditorium; Multi-Purpose
    Type of Stage: Proscenium
    Stage Dimensions: 35'Wx30'D; 35'Wx18'H proscenium opening   **Orchestra Pit**
    Seating Capacity: 690
    Year Built: 1963   **Architect:** Sheets
    Contact for Rental: Theatre Manager;   (714) 621-8000, ext. 3800
    Resident Groups: Pomona College Theatre Department; Claremont Travel Film Series

THE CLAREMONT COLLEGES - MABEL SHAW BRIDGES AUDITORIUM
Fourth Street and College Way, Claremont, CA 91711
(714) 621-8031; (714) 621-8032
FAX: (714) 621-8484
    Type of Facility: Concert Hall; Auditorium; Performance Center; Theatre House; Opera House
    Type of Stage: Proscenium
    Stage Dimensions: 62'Wx38'3"D; 62'Wx36'H proscenium opening   **Orchestra Pit**
    Seating Capacity: 2,483
    Year Built: 1977   **Architect:** William Templeton Johnson   **Cost:** $600,000
    Year Remodeled: 1977   **Architect:** H. Wendell Mounce & Associates   **Cost:** $1,600,000
    Acoustical Consultant: Abe Metzler
    Contact for Rental: Paula Thatcher;   (714) 621-8031

Columbia
FACILITY

FALLON HOUSE THEATRE
Columbia State Historic Park, PO Box 1079, Columbia, CA 95310
(209) 532-4644
    Type of Facility: Theatre Complex; Theatre House
    Facility Originally: Meeting Hall; Vaudeville; Movie House; Warehouse
    Type of Stage: Proscenium
    Stage Dimensions: 42'Wx46'D; 30'Wx9'6"H proscenium opening
    Seating Capacity: 277

Year Built: 1862
Year Remodeled: 1983   **Cost:** $1,500,000
Contact for Rental: David G. Purdy;   (209) 532-4644
Manager: Sally Farrington
Resident Groups: Columbia Actors' Repertory
An 1862 Period Theatre, Fallon House Theatre was restored between 1981 and 1983 by the California State Office of Historic Preservation.

Compton

THEATRE

LYNWOOD PERFORMING ARTS
PO Box 4393, Compton, CA 90224
(310) 631-5027
    Arts Area: Community
    Status: Non-Profit
    Type: Performing
    Management: Perry Brents, Director
    Volunteer Staff: 3
    Non-Paid Artists: 60
    Utilizes: Guest Artists
    Budget: $1,000 - $50,000
    Income Sources: Individual Donations
    Season: September - July
    Performance Facilities: Lynwood Civic Center

Concord

THEATRE

CITIARTS THEATRE
1950 Parkside Drive, Concord, CA 94519
(510) 671-3065
FAX: (510) 671-3375
    Founded: 1974
    Arts Area: Professional
    Status: Professional; Non-Profit
    Type: Performing; Resident; Educational
    Purpose: CitiArts Theatre is a small professional theatre committed to producing small musicals and plays as well as rarely produced classics
    Management: Richard H. Elliott, Artistic Director; Andrew F. Holtz, Managing Director; George Evano, Marketing Director; Leslye Asera, Development Director
    Officers: Don Fitzgerald, President; Karen Huckeby, Vice President/Treasurer; Trinna Sheley, Secretary
    Paid Staff: 18   **Volunteer Staff:** 1
    Paid Artists: 178
    Utilizes: Guest Artists; Guest Directors; Designers; Composers; Writers
    Budget: $1,000,000 - $5,000,000
    Income Sources: Private Foundations/Grants/Endowments; Business/Corporate Donations; Box Office; Government Grants; Individual Donations; Tuition; Merchandise Sales
    Season: 52 Weeks
    Affiliations: TCG; Theatre Bay Area; AEA
    Performance Facilities: Willows Theatre; Gasoline Alley Theatre; Centre Concord

FACILITY

CONCORD PAVILION
2000 Kirker Pass Road, Concord, CA 94524
(510) 676-8742
FAX: (510) 676-7262
    Mailing Address: PO Box 6166, Concord, CA 95424
    Type of Facility: Amphitheater
    Type of Stage: Flexible
    Stage Dimensions: 63'Wx60'D   **Orchestra Pit**
    Seating Capacity: 9,019
    Year Built: 1975   **Architect:** Frank O. Gehry   **Cost:** $6,600,000
    Acoustical Consultant: Jaffe Acoustics

Contact for Rental: Doug Warrick, Assistant General Manager; (510) 798-3318
Manager: John Toffoli, Jr.; (510) 671-3275

WILLOWS THEATRE
1975 Diamond Boulevard, Concord, CA 94520
(510) 671-3065
Type of Facility: Studio Performance; Performance Center; Theatre House; Multi-Purpose
Type of Stage: Proscenium
Stage Dimensions: 40'Wx24'D **Orchestra Pit**
Seating Capacity: 203
Year Built: 1977
Contact for Rental: Bob Webb; (510) 671-3387
Resident Groups: CitiArts Theatre Company

Costa Mesa

DANCE

THE BALLET MONTMARTRE
2632 Santa Ana Avenue, Costa Mesa, CA 92627
(714) 646-7688
Founded: 1972
Arts Area: Modern; Ballet; Jazz
Status: Semi-Professional; Non-Profit
Type: Performing; Resident
Management: Stela Viorica, Artistic Director
Paid Artists: 6 **Non-Paid Artists:** 18
Utilizes: Guest Artists; Guest Choreographers
Budget: $1,000 - $50,000
Income Sources: Private Foundations/Grants/Endowments; Business/Corporate Donations; Box Office;
Individual Donations
Season: 52 Weeks

VOCAL MUSIC

MASTER CHORALE OF ORANGE COUNTY
PO Box 2156, Costa Mesa, CA 92628
(714) 556-6262
FAX: (714) 556-6341
Founded: 1956
Arts Area: Choral
Status: Non-Profit
Type: Performing
Management: Dr. William D. Hall, Music Director; Dr. Thomas Sheets, Associate Music Director; Sheri Sheperd,
Administrative Director; Jean Updegraff, Administrative Assistant
Officers: Dr. Philip Winsor, Chairman; Robert W. Guyett, President; Julia Rappaport, Executive Vice President; Robert J.
Reyes, Vice President Finance; Kenneth Roehrs, Corresponding Secretary
Paid Staff: 5 **Volunteer Staff:** 10
Paid Artists: 10 **Non-Paid Artists:** 140
Utilizes: Guest Artists
Budget: $100,000 - $500,000
Income Sources: Private Foundations/Grants/Endowments; Business/Corporate Donations; Box Office; Government
Grants; Individual Donations
Season: September - May **Annual Attendance:** 10,000
Performance Facilities: Orange County Performing Arts Center

OPERA PACIFIC
650 Town Center Drive, Suite 400, Costa Mesa, CA 92626
(714) 546-7372
FAX: (714) 662-2796
Founded: 1986
Arts Area: Grand Opera; Light Opera; Musical Theatre
Status: Professional; Non-Profit
Type: Performing; Touring; Resident; Educational
Purpose: To present a broad repertoire of opera and American musicals with the highest artistic standards; to provide op-
portunities for emerging opera talent; to reach out to area communities with educational and performance opportunities
which will stimulate and develop new audiences

Management: Dr. David DiChiera, General Director; Richard H. Owens, Managing Director of Development and Administration; Lori Burrill, Managing Director of Production and Financial Planning
Officers: William H. Roberts, Chairman; Richard G. Engel, President; Michael D. Rubin, Secretary; Robert A. Huber, Treasurer
Paid Staff: 23   **Volunteer Staff:** 60
Paid Artists: 450
Utilizes: Special Technical Talent; Guest Conductors; Guest Artists; Guest Directors
Budget: $1,000,000 - $5,000,000
Income Sources: Private Foundations/Grants/Endowments; Business/Corporate Donations; Box Office; Government Grants; Individual Donations
Season: September - April   **Annual Attendance:** 60,000
Affiliations: OA
Performance Facilities: Orange County Performing Arts Center

THEATRE

PACIFIC AMPHITHEATRE
100 Fair Drive, Costa Mesa, CA 92626
(714) 546-4875
FAX: (714) 850-1157
>   **Founded:** 1983
>   **Arts Area:** Professional; Musical
>   **Status:** Commercial
>   **Type:** Performing
>   **Purpose:** To maintain an outdoor concert venue open May-October
>   **Management:** Susan Rosenbluth, General Manager; Mike Garcia, Theatre Manager; Jo-Ann Armstrong, Operating Manager
>   **Utilizes:** Special Technical Talent; Guest Artists
>   **Income Sources:** Box Office
>   **Season:** May - October

SOUTH COAST REPERTORY
655 Town Center Drive, Costa Mesa, CA 92626
(714) 957-2602
FAX: (714) 545-0391
>   **Founded:** 1964
>   **Arts Area:** Professional
>   **Status:** Professional; Non-Profit
>   **Type:** Performing; Touring; Resident; Educational
>   **Purpose:** To serve the art of theatre and Orange County audiences in a manner socially relevant and theatrically inventive
>   **Management:** David Emmes, Producing Artistic Director; Martin Benson, Artistic Director; Paula Tomei, Business Director; Paul Hammond, Production Director; Louise Cummings, Director of Development; John Mouledoux, Director of Marketing
>   **Officers:** Thomas Sutton, President; Lydia Wang Himes, James Henwood, Vice Presidents; Maryann Finley, Secretary; Donald Kennedy, Treasurer
>   **Paid Staff:** 51   **Volunteer Staff:** 237
>   **Paid Artists:** 150   **Non-Paid Artists:** 15
>   **Utilizes:** Guest Artists; Guest Directors
>   **Budget:** $1,000,000 - $5,000,000
>   **Income Sources:** Private Foundations/Grants/Endowments; Business/Corporate Donations; Box Office; Government Grants; Individual Donations
>   **Season:** September - June   **Annual Attendance:** 250,000
>   **Affiliations:** LORT; TCG
>   **Performance Facilities:** South Coast Repertory Theatre

PERFORMING SERIES

ORANGE COAST COLLEGE
2701 Fairview Road, PO Box 5005, Costa Mesa, CA 92628
(714) 432-5880
FAX: (714) 432-5902
>   **Founded:** 1947
>   **Arts Area:** Band
>   **Status:** Semi-Professional
>   **Type:** Performing; Touring; Educational
>   **Purpose:** To offer a comprehensive performing-arts season
>   **Management:** George Blanc, Dean of Community Services
>   **Paid Staff:** 8
>   **Paid Artists:** 50

Paid Artists: 50
Utilizes: Guest Artists
Budget: $100,000 - $500,000
Income Sources: Individual Donations
Season: September - June   **Annual Attendance:** 46,000
Affiliations: Orange Coast College
Performance Facilities: Robert B. Moore Theatre; Fine Arts Recital Hall

FACILITY

ORANGE COUNTY PERFORMING ARTS CENTER
600 Town Center Drive, Costa Mesa, CA 92626
(714) 556-2121
FAX: (714) 556-0156
Founded: 1986
Type of Facility: Theatre Complex; Concert Hall; Performance Center; Multi-Purpose
Type of Stage: Proscenium   **Orchestra Pit**
Year Built: 1986   **Architect:** The Blurock Partnership; CRS   **Cost:** $71,000,000
Acoustical Consultant: Jerald Hyde; A. Harold Marshall; Taoletti Lewitz Associates
Contact for Rental: Judith O'Dea Morr, General Manager;   (714) 556-2121
Manager: Judith O'Dea Morr;   (714) 556-2121
Resident Groups: Pacific Symphony; Opera Pacific; Orange County Philharmonic Society; Pacific Chorale;
Master Chorale of Orange County
Orange County Performing Arts Center contains Founders Hall and Segerstrom Hall. See separate listings for additional information.

ORANGE COUNTY PERFORMING ARTS CENTER - FOUNDERS HALL
600 Town Center Drive, Costa Mesa, CA 92626
(714) 556-2121
Type of Facility: Studio Performance; Black Box
Type of Stage: Flexible
Stage Dimensions: 50'Wx66'L
Seating Capacity: 300
Year Built: 1986
Contact for Rental: Judith O'Dea Morr, General Manager;   (714) 556-2121
Manager: Judith O'Dea Morr

ORANGE COUNTY PERFORMING ARTS CENTER - SEGERSTROM HALL
600 Town Center Drive, Costa Mesa, CA 92626
(714) 556-2121
Type of Facility: Concert Hall; Auditorium; Theatre House; Opera House
Type of Stage: Modified Apron Proscenium
Stage Dimensions: 124'10"Wx64'3"D; 68'Wx42'H proscenium opening   **Orchestra Pit**
Seating Capacity: 2,994
Year Built: 1986
Contact for Rental: Judith O'Dea Morr, General Manager;   (714) 556-2121
Manager: Judith O'Dea Morr
Orchestra pit is two separate screw-jack lifts. Lift A adds 8' and lift B adds 7' to stage depth for a total of 15' when both lifts are at stage level. Each may be used independently for varied stage configurations.

SOUTH COAST REPERTORY
655 Town Center Drive, Costa Mesa, CA 92626
(714) 957-2602
Founded: 1964
Type of Facility: Theatre Complex; Performance Center
Year Built: 1978   **Architect:** Stewart Woodard   **Cost:** $3,000,000
Year Remodeled: 1987   **Architect:** Stewart Woodard   **Cost:** $1,500,000
Acoustical Consultant: Purcell Noppe & Associates
Resident Groups: South Coast Repertory
South Coast Repertory contains Second Stage and Mainstage (Segerstrom Auditorium). See individual listings for additional information.

SOUTH COAST REPERTORY - SECOND STAGE
655 Town Center Drive, Costa Mesa, CA 92626
(714) 957-2603
Founded: 1964
Type of Facility: Theatre House
Type of Stage: 3/4 Arena

Stage Dimensions: 18'Wx29'D
Seating Capacity: 161
Year Built: 1978
Year Remodeled: 1987
Available for rent

SOUTH COAST REPERTORY - SEGERSTROM AUDITORIUM, MAINSTAGE
655 Town Center Drive, Costa Mesa, CA 92626
(714) 957-2603
Founded: 1964
Type of Facility: Auditorium; Theatre House
Type of Stage: Thrust; Proscenium
Stage Dimensions: 85'Wx41'D; 47'W proscenium opening
Seating Capacity: 507
Year Built: 1978   **Architect:** Stewart Woodard
Year Remodeled: 1987   **Architect:** Stewart Woodard
Contact for Rental: Paul Hammond, Director of Theatre Operations;   (714) 957-2602

Culver City

FACILITY

VETERAN'S MEMORIAL AUDITORIUM
4117 Overland Avenue, Culver City, CA 90230
(310) 837-5211
FAX: (310) 839-6106
Type of Facility: Auditorium
Type of Stage: Proscenium
Stage Dimensions: 50'x60'x30'
Seating Capacity: 1,600
Contact for Rental: Pamela Robinson;   (310) 202-5688
Manager: Kenneth D. Good

Cupertino

DANCE

ABHINAYA DANCE COMPANY
11445 Charsan Lane, Cupertino, CA 95014
(408) 725-2951
FAX: (408) 446-0433
Founded: 1981
Arts Area: Ethnic; Indian
Type: Performing
Purpose: To present classical Indian dance
Management: Mythili Kumar, Artistic Director/Choreographer
Season: 52 Weeks

PERFORMING SERIES

FLINT CENTER FOR THE PERFORMING ARTS
21250 Stevens Creek Boulevard, Cupertino, CA 95050
(408) 864-8820
Founded: 1971
Arts Area: Dance; Vocal Music; Instrumental Music; Theater; Lyric Opera; Popular Artists
Status: Professional; Semi-Professional; Non-Professional; Non-Profit; Commercial
Type: Performing; Touring; Educational; Sponsoring
Purpose: To present and sponsor internationally-renowned artists as well as non-professional performers
Management: Dr. Vicky K. O'Brien, Executive Director; Jaynos Szablya, Operations Manager
Paid Staff: 6
Utilizes: Special Technical Talent; Guest Artists
Budget: $500,000 - $1,000,000
Income Sources: Private Foundations/Grants/Endowments; Business/Corporate Donations; Box Office; Individual Donations
Season: 52 Weeks   **Annual Attendance:** 200,000
Affiliations: WAAA; APAP
Performance Facilities: Flint Center for the Performing Arts

FACILITY

DE ANZA COLLEGE - FLINT CENTER FOR THE PERFORMING ARTS
21250 Stevens Creek Boulevard, Cupertino, CA 95014
(408) 864-8820
Type of Facility: Concert Hall; Theatre House
Type of Stage: Proscenium
Stage Dimensions: 52'Wx32'Hx39'D   **Orchestra Pit**
Seating Capacity: 2,571
Year Built: 1971
Contact for Rental: Dr. Vicky K. O'Brien

Davis

PERFORMING SERIES

UNIVERSITY OF CALIFORNIA-DAVIS - UC DAVIS PRESENTS
University Cultural Programs, Davis, CA 95616
(916) 757-3488
FAX: (916) 757-6815
Founded: 1954
Arts Area: Dance; Vocal Music; Instrumental Music; Theater; Festivals; Grand Opera
Status: Non-Profit
Type: Touring; Educational; Sponsoring
Purpose: To present a broad range of quality performing arts for the Davis campus and the immediate geographical region
Management: James Wockenfuss, Director
Paid Staff: 11   **Volunteer Staff:** 50
Paid Artists: 25
Utilizes: Guest Artists
Budget: $500,000 - $1,000,000
Income Sources: Private Foundations/Grants/Endowments; Business/Corporate Donations; Box Office; Government Grants; Individual Donations
Season: October - June
Annual Attendance: 30,000
Affiliations: APAP; California Confederation of the Arts; California Presenters
Performance Facilities: Kleiber Hall; Freeborn Hall; Main Theater; Sacramento Convention Center Theater

FACILITY

DAVIS ART CENTER
1919 F Street, Davis, CA 95616
(916) 756-4100
Type of Facility: Multi-Purpose
Type of Stage: Platform
Stage Dimensions: 30'x30'
Seating Capacity: 100
Year Built: 1987   **Architect:** Ken LaGrone/Tandem

VETERANS' MEMORIAL THEATRE
203 East 14th Street, Davis, CA 95616
(916) 758-7839
Type of Facility: Concert Hall; Auditorium; Theatre House
Type of Stage: Thrust; Proscenium
Stage Dimensions: 29'x30'x40'   **Orchestra Pit**
Seating Capacity: 325
Year Built: 1974   **Architect:** Dean F. Unger   **Cost:** $400,000
Contact for Rental: Michael Gerell;   (916) 758-7839
Resident Groups: Davis Comic Opera; Black Repertoire Dance Troupe; Nexus Modern Dance Collective; The Davis Ballet; Davis Art Center

---
Downey

INSTRUMENTAL MUSIC

DOWNEY SYMPHONIC SOCIETY
PO Box 763, Downey, CA 90241
(310) 869-3323
Founded: 1958
Arts Area: Orchestra
Status: Semi-Professional; Non-Profit
Type: Performing
Management: Robert Armer, Music Director
Officers: Lorine Parks, President; Loren DeWind, Vice President; Ruth Hillecke, Secretary; C. Richard Holmes, Treasurer
Paid Staff: 1   **Volunteer Staff:** 22
Paid Artists: 20   **Non-Paid Artists:** 40
Utilizes: Guest Artists
Budget: $1,000 - $50,000
Income Sources: Private Foundations/Grants/Endowments; Business/Corporate Donations; Government Grants; Individual Donations
Season: November - May   **Annual Attendance:** 1,600
Performance Facilities: Downey Community Theater

YOUTH SYMPHONY WEST
7609 Calmcrest Drive, Downey, CA 90240
(310) 927-9455
Founded: 1974
Arts Area: Orchestra
Status: Non-Professional; Non-Profit
Type: Educational
Purpose: To afford young musicians an opportunity to perform orchestral literature in a full symphonic setting
Management: Art Mautner, Conductor; Steve Kerstein, Assistant Conductor
Officers: Mickey Fruchter, University Liaison
Paid Staff: 1   **Volunteer Staff:** 3
Utilizes: Special Technical Talent
Budget: $1,000 - $50,000
Income Sources: Individual Donations
Season: October - July
Affiliations: California State University at Los Angeles; Conservatory of Music
Performance Facilities: California State University at Los Angeles

---
El Cajon

DANCE

SAMAHAN PHILIPPINE DANCE COMPANY
1441 Hillsmont Drive, El Cajon, CA 92020
(619) 444-7528
Founded: 1974
Arts Area: Ethnic; Folk
Status: Semi-Professional; Non-Profit
Type: Performing; Touring; Educational; Sponsoring
Purpose: To preserve, develop and present the cultural performing arts of the Philippines
Management: Lolita D. Carter PhD, Executive Director; Ruby Pearl B. Chiong, Company Manager; George Ragaza, Artistic Director; Juanita Caccam, Music Coordinator
Officers: Tessie Porciuncula, President; Carlos Linayao, Vice President; Estela Garcia, Secretary; Dina Ellorin, Treasurer
Paid Staff: 3   **Volunteer Staff:** 3
Paid Artists: 16   **Non-Paid Artists:** 8
Utilizes: Guest Artists
Budget: $50,000 - $100,000
Income Sources: Private Foundations/Grants/Endowments; Box Office; Government Grants; Individual Donations; Fund-raising
Season: 52 Weeks   **Annual Attendance:** 10,000
Affiliations: San Diego Culture and Dance Alliance

FACILITY

EAST COUNTY PERFORMING ARTS CENTER - THEATRE EAST
210 East Main Street, El Cajon, CA 92020
(619) 440-2277
    Type of Facility: Concert Hall; Performance Center; Theatre House
    Type of Stage: Thrust; Proscenium
    Stage Dimensions: 70'Wx26'D; 70'Wx19'6"H proscenium opening   **Orchestra Pit**
    Seating Capacity: 1,200
    Year Built: 1977   **Architect:** William Blurock and Art Decker
    Contact for Rental: Jane Bender;   (619) 440-0372
    Manager: R.M.D. Childs;   (619) 440-0372
    Resident Groups: Grossmont Community College

El Granada

PERFORMING SERIES

BACH DANCING AND DYNAMITE SOCIETY GROUP
PO Box 302, El Granada, CA 94018
(415) 726-4143
    Founded: 1964
    Arts Area: Vocal Music; Instrumental Music; Headliner; Jazz
    Status: Professional; Non-Profit
    Type: Presenting
    Purpose: To present all forms of jazz and classical chamber music
    Management: Pete Douglas, Concert Manager
    Officers: Bennett Kilpack, President; Tom Morrison, Vice President; Sylvia Way, Secretary/Treasurer
    Paid Staff: 3
    Utilizes: Guest Artists
    Budget: $100,000 - $500,000
    Income Sources: Business/Corporate Donations; Government Grants; Individual Donations
    Season: February - December   **Annual Attendance:** 10,000
    Affiliations: Half Moon Bay
    Performance Facilities: Douglass Beach House

Emeryville

DANCE

NANCY KARP AND DANCERS
4250 Horton Street, Studio 6, Emeryville, CA 94608
(510) 653-1195
FAX: (510) 652-0898
    Founded: 1976
    Arts Area: Modern
    Status: Professional; Non-Profit
    Type: Performing; Touring
    Management: Nancy Karp, Artistic Director
    Officers: Laura Kline, President
    Paid Staff: 2   **Volunteer Staff:** 2
    Paid Artists: 10
    Utilizes: Special Technical Talent; Guest Artists
    Budget: $50,000 - $100,000
    Income Sources: Private Foundations/Grants/Endowments; Business/Corporate Donations; Box Office; Government Grants; Individual Donations
    Season: April - October
    Performance Facilities: Zellerbach Playhouse, University of California at Berkeley; Laney College Theatre; Theater Artaud

THEATRE

THE BMT THEATER
3617 San Pablo Avenue, #118, Emeryville, CA 94608
(510) 843-7519
FAX: (415) 822-7898
    Founded: 1988

Arts Area: Theatrical Group
Status: Semi-Professional; Non-Profit
Type: Performing; Touring; Educational
Management: Ed Bullins, Producing Director
Budget: $1,000 - $50,000
Income Sources: Private Foundations/Grants/Endowments; Box Office; Individual Donations
Season: 52 Weeks

Englewood

DANCE

HANNAH KAHN DANCE COMPANY
4685 South Ogden Street, Englewood, CA 80110
(303) 789-4181
Founded: 1992
Arts Area: Modern
Status: Professional
Type: Performing; Touring
Purpose: To perform the works of Hannah Kahn
Management: Hannah Kahn, Artistic Director
Officers: Hannah Kahn, President; Arthur Best, Secretary
Volunteer Staff: 2
Paid Artists: 8   **Non-Paid Artists:** 1
Budget: $1,000 - $50,000   **Income Sources:** Box Office; Government Grants; Individual Donations

Escondido

THEATRE

LAWRENCE WELK RESORT THEATRE
8860 Lawrence Welk Drive, Escondido, CA 92026
(619) 749-3000
FAX: (619) 749-6182
Arts Area: Professional; Dinner
Status: Professional; Commercial
Type: Performing
Management: Frank Wayne, Artistic Director
Officers: Bud Desantis, Executive Producer
Paid Staff: 33
Paid Artists: 18
Utilizes: Guest Artists
Budget: $500,000 - $1,000,000
Income Sources: Box Office
Season: 52 Weeks
Affiliations: AEA

Ferndale

THEATRE

FERNDALE REPERTORY THEATRE
447 Main Street, PO Box 892, Ferndale, CA 95536
(707) 725-4636
Founded: 1971
Arts Area: Community
Status: Semi-Professional; Non-Profit
Type: Performing
Purpose: To provide North Coast residents and visitors theatrical performances of the highest quality
Management: Clinton Rebik, Artistic Director
Officers: Judith Anderson, President; Robert Tait, Vice President; Janet Frost, Secretary; Dominique Jackson, Treasurer
Paid Staff: 7
Paid Artists: 20   **Non-Paid Artists:** 200
Utilizes: Special Technical Talent; Guest Artists; Guest Directors
Budget: $100,000 - $500,000

Income Sources: Private Foundations/Grants/Endowments; Business/Corporate Donations; Box Office; Government Grants; Individual Donations; Memberships
Season: 52 Weeks   **Annual Attendance:** 16,000
Performance Facilities: Ferndale Repertory Theatre

Fontana

FACILITY

FONTANA PERFORMING ARTS CENTER
9460 Sierra Avenue, Fontana, CA 92335
(909) 350-6741; (909) 350-6734
    Type of Facility: Auditorium; Performance Center; Room
    Facility Originally: Meeting Hall
    Type of Stage: Proscenium
    Stage Dimensions: 20'x40'
    Seating Capacity: 990
    Year Built: 1956   **Architect:** Herman Ruhraw
    Year Remodeled: 1985   **Cost:** $310,000
    Contact for Rental: Larry Watson;   (714) 350-6741

Fremont

INSTRUMENTAL MUSIC

FREMONT-NEWARK PHILHARMONIC
PO Box 104, Fremont, CA 94537
(510) 794-1652
    Founded: 1963
    Arts Area: Symphony; Orchestra; Ensemble
    Status: Professional; Semi-Professional
    Type: Performing; Educational
    Purpose: To perform orchestra and chamber concerts
    Management: Timothy Zerlang, Executive Director; David Sloss, Music Director
    Officers: Eva Maria Tisdale, President; Art Kimber, Treasurer
    Paid Staff: 2   **Volunteer Staff:** 30
    Paid Artists: 60   **Non-Paid Artists:** 2
    Utilizes: Special Technical Talent; Guest Artists
    Budget: $100,000 - $500,000
    Income Sources: Private Foundations/Grants/Endowments; Business/Corporate Donations; Box Office; Government Grants; Individual Donations
    Season: October - May   **Annual Attendance:** 3,500

Fresno

DANCE

FRESNO BALLET
1432 Fulton Street, Fresno, CA 93721
(209) 233-2623
FAX: (209) 233-2670
    Founded: 1967
    Arts Area: Modern; Ballet; Ethnic
    Status: Professional; Non-Profit
    Type: Performing; Touring; Educational; Sponsoring
    Purpose: To enrich the arts environment of central California through the production and presentation of dance
    Management: Donald Bradburn, Artistic Director; Chris Moad, Executive Director
    Paid Artists: 20   **Non-Paid Artists:** 30
    Utilizes: Special Technical Talent; Guest Conductors; Guest Artists; Guest Directors; Guest Choreographers
    Budget: $100,000 - $500,000
    Income Sources: Private Foundations/Grants/Endowments; Business/Corporate Donations; Box Office; Government Grants; Individual Donations
    Season: December - May; Summer Festival   **Annual Attendance:** 20,000
    Performance Facilities: William Saroyan Theatre

JOHN CHOOKASIAN FOLK ENSEMBLE - KING TUT REVUE BELLY DANCE
2511 West Browning, Fresno, CA 93711
(209) 449-1777
> **Founded:** 1962
> **Arts Area:** Ethnic; Folk
> **Status:** Professional; Non-Profit
> **Type:** Performing; Touring; Educational
> **Purpose:** To introduce people to the folk music, folk dance and folk instruments of the Middle East, including Armenian, Greek and Persian
> **Management:** John Chookasian, Artistic Director
> **Paid Staff:** 1
> **Paid Artists:** 8
> **Utilizes:** Guest Artists
> **Budget:** $1,000 - $50,000
> **Income Sources:** Private Foundations/Grants/Endowments; Box Office
> **Season:** 52 Weeks

INSTRUMENTAL MUSIC

FRESNO PHILHARMONIC ASSOCIATION
2610 West Shaw Avenue, Suite 103, Fresno, CA 93711-3332
(209) 261-0600
FAX: (209) 261-0700
> **Arts Area:** Symphony; Orchestra
> **Status:** Professional; Non-Profit
> **Type:** Performing; Educational
> **Purpose:** To provide quality orchestral music to central California
> **Management:** Andrew Massey, Music Director; Irene Klug-Nielson, General Manager
> **Officers:** Dr. Charles Mittman, President
> **Budget:** $500,000 - $1,000,000
> **Income Sources:** Private Foundations/Grants/Endowments; Business/Corporate Donations; Box Office; Government Grants; Individual Donations
> **Performance Facilities:** William Saroyan Theatre

FRESNO PHILHARMONIC ORCHESTRA
1300 North Fresno Street, #201-B, Fresno, CA 93703
(209) 485-3020
> **Founded:** 1954
> **Arts Area:** Symphony; Orchestra
> **Status:** Professional; Non-Profit
> **Type:** Performing; Touring; Resident
> **Management:** Andrew Massey, Principal Guest Conductor/Artistic Advisor; Irene Klug Nielsen, General Manager
> **Officers:** Parker Powell, President, Board of Directors; Larry Balakian, First Vice President; William M. Lyles, Second Vice President; John Dodson, Treasurer; Richardson Herrinton, Assistant Treasurer
> **Paid Staff:** 5   **Volunteer Staff:** 25
> **Paid Artists:** 65
> **Utilizes:** Guest Conductors; Guest Artists
> **Budget:** $500,000 - $1,000,000
> **Income Sources:** Private Foundations/Grants/Endowments; Business/Corporate Donations; Box Office; Government Grants; Individual Donations
> **Season:** October - May   **Annual Attendance:** 37,000
> **Affiliations:** ASOL; Association of California Symphony Orchestras
> **Performance Facilities:** Saroyan Theatre

THEATRE

GOOD COMPANY PLAYERS
833 East Fern, Fresno, CA 93728
(209) 266-0211
> **Founded:** 1973
> **Arts Area:** Community; Theatrical Group
> **Status:** Non-Professional; Commercial
> **Type:** Performing; Touring; Educational
> **Purpose:** To perform original works at local schools, Roger Rocka's Music Hall and the Second Theatre
> **Management:** Dan Pessano, Managing Director; Linda Thayer, Business Manager
> **Officers:** Dan Pessano, President; Laurie Pessano, Vice President; Linda Thayer, Secretary/Treasurer
> **Paid Staff:** 11   **Volunteer Staff:** 40
> **Utilizes:** Guest Directors

Budget: $1,000 - $50,000
Income Sources: Box Office
Season: 52 Weeks   **Annual Attendance:** 85,000
Affiliations: AACT
Performance Facilities: Roger Rocka's Music Hall; Good Company Players' Second Theatre

FACILITY

CALIFORNIA STATE UNIVERSITY-FRESNO - JOHN WRIGHT THEATRE
5201 North Maple, Fresno, CA 93740
(209) 278-2216
    Type of Facility: Theatre House; Arena
    Type of Stage: Proscenium   **Seating Capacity:** 180
    Year Built: 1960   **Cost:** $1,000,000
    Year Remodeled: 1991   **Cost:** $2,100,000
    Contact for Rental: Pam Dyer;   (209) 278-2216
    Resident Groups: Portable Dance Troupe

CALIFORNIA STATE UNIVERSITY-FRESNO - WAHLBERG RECITAL HALL
2380 East Keats, Fresno, CA 93740-0077
(209) 294-2654
    Type of Facility: Concert Hall
    Facility Originally: School
    Type of Stage: Platform
    Stage Dimensions: 16'x18'
    Seating Capacity: 180
    Year Built: 1960
    Contact for Rental: Beverly Noell;   (209) 294-2654
    Resident Groups: CSUF Faculty String Quartet; CSUF Graduate String Quartet; Opera Workshop; University Wind Ensemble; University Jazz Bands; Presidents Quintet; California Woodwind Quintet; Concert Choir; University Orchestra

FRESNO CONVENTION CENTER THEATRE
700 M Street, Fresno, CA 93721
(209) 498-1511
FAX: (209) 488-4643
    Type of Facility: Theatre House
    Type of Stage: Proscenium
    Stage Dimensions: 30'x52'x52'   **Orchestra Pit**
    Seating Capacity: 2,359
    Year Built: 1966   **Architect:** Robert Stevens Associates   **Cost:** $10,000,000
    Contact for Rental: Karen Thurber;   (209) 498-1511
    Manager: Michael J. Sweeney;   (209) 498-1511

TOWER THEATRE FOR THE PERFORMING ARTS
815 East Olive, Fresno, CA 93728
(209) 485-9050
FAX: (209) 485-3941
    Founded: 1990
    Type of Facility: Concert Hall
    Facility Originally: Movie House
    Type of Stage: Thrust
    Stage Dimensions: 30'Dx40'W
    Seating Capacity: 761
    Year Built: 1939   **Architect:** S. Charles Lee
    Year Remodeled: 1990   **Architect:** Kennedy Lutz Architecture, Inc.   **Cost:** $1,500,000
    Contact for Rental: Ronald D. Eichman;   (209) 485-9050

WARNOR'S THEATER
1400 Fulton Street, Fresno, CA 93721
(209) 233-1157
    Type of Facility: Concert Hall; Performance Center; Theatre House; Opera House
    Type of Stage: Proscenium
    Stage Dimensions: 47'10"Wx30'D   **Orchestra Pit**
    Seating Capacity: 2,164
    Year Built: 1927   **Architect:** B. Marcus Priteca
    Contact for Rental: Marty Schnepp;   (209) 233-1157

Fullerton

DANCE

DANCE REPERTORY THEATRE
California State University, Fullerton, CA 92634
(714) 773-2689
Founded: 1981
Arts Area: Modern; Ballet
Status: Professional; Non-Profit
Type: Performing; Touring; Resident; Educational
Purpose: A professional adjunct to the dance program of California State University at Fullerton, Dance Repertory Theatre provides professional opportunities for graduating dance majors.
Management: Barbara Arms, Artistic Director
Paid Staff: 3
Paid Artists: 9   **Non-Paid Artists:** 1
Budget: $1,000 - $50,000
Income Sources: Box Office; Individual Donations
Season: February - October
Affiliations: California State University at Fullerton

VOCAL MUSIC

FULLERTON CIVIC LIGHT OPERA
218 West Commonwealth, Fullerton, CA 92632
(714) 526-3832
Founded: 1972
Arts Area: Light Opera; Operetta; Musical Theatre
Status: Semi-Professional; Non-Profit
Type: Performing; Resident
Purpose: To provide entertainment at affordable prices
Management: Griff Duncan, General Manager; Jan Duncan, Artistic Director; Donna Parsons, Production Manager
Officers: Jack Bedell, President; Karen Gallio, Vice-President; Cecil Ricks, Secretary; David MacKain, Treasurer
Paid Staff: 50   **Volunteer Staff:** 50
Paid Artists: 40   **Non-Paid Artists:** 90
Utilizes: Special Technical Talent; Guest Conductors; Guest Artists; Guest Directors
Budget: $500,000 - $1,000,000
Income Sources: Private Foundations/Grants/Endowments; Business/Corporate Donations; Box Office; Government Grants; Individual Donations; Costume and Scenery Rentals
Season: October - May   **Annual Attendance:** 33,000
Performance Facilities: Plummer Auditorium

FACILITY

MUCKENTHALER CULTURAL CENTER
1201 West Malvern Avenue, Fullerton, CA 92633
(714) 738-6595
FAX: (714) 738-6366
Type of Facility: Outdoor (Concert); Studio Performance; Amphitheater; Civic Center; Multi-Purpose
Type of Stage: Platform
Stage Dimensions: 20'x40'
Seating Capacity: 264
Year Built: 1924
Year Remodeled: 1984   **Cost:** $750,000
Contact for Rental: Denise Watson;   (714) 738-6595
Resident Groups: Theatre-on-the-Green

PLUMMER AUDITORIUM
201 East Chapman Avenue, Fullerton, CA 92632
(714) 870-3739
FAX: (714) 870-3768
Type of Facility: Concert Hall; Auditorium; Theatre House
Type of Stage: Proscenium
Stage Dimensions: 35'9"x21'9"   **Orchestra Pit**
Seating Capacity: 1,334
Year Built: 1930   **Architect:** Carlton Monroe Winslow   **Cost:** $295,541
Year Remodeled: 1972   **Architect:** Frick, Frick & Jette
Contact for Rental: Walt De Jong, Theatre Manager;   (714) 870-3739

Manager: Walt De Jong
Resident Groups: Community Concerts; Fullerton Civic Light Opera; California State University - Fullerton Pair Series

Garden Grove

INSTRUMENTAL MUSIC

ORANGE COUNTY SYMPHONY
12866 Main Street, Suite 106, Garden Grove, CA 92640
(714) 534-1103
FAX: (714) 537-9652
Founded: 1985
Arts Area: Symphony
Status: Professional
Type: Performing; Resident; Educational
Management: Yaakov Dvir-Djerassi, General Manager
Officers: Richard H. Hain, President; Marion Silverberg, Vice President; Emma Daugherty, Secretary;
Ian Darley, Treasurer
Paid Staff: 3   **Volunteer Staff:** 10
Paid Artists: 85
Utilizes: Guest Conductors; Guest Artists; Guest Directors
Budget: $100,000 - $500,000
Income Sources: Private Foundations/Grants/Endowments; Business/Corporate Donations; Box Office; Government
Grants; Individual Donations; Fund-raising
Season: September - June   **Annual Attendance:** 15,000
Performance Facilities: Don Wash Auditorium

THEATRE

GROVE SHAKESPEARE
12852 Main Street, Garden Grove, CA 92640
(714) 636-7213
FAX: (714) 539-2651
Founded: 1979
Arts Area: Professional; Musical; Classical
Status: Professional; Non-Profit
Type: Performing
Purpose: To present classical works from the World Theatre; to present a Shakespeare Festival in summer
Management: W. Stuart McDowell, Artistic Director; Charles Johanson, Office Manager
Paid Staff: 8
Paid Artists: 250
Utilizes: Special Technical Talent; Guest Artists; Guest Directors
Budget: $100,000 - $500,000
Income Sources: Private Foundations/Grants/Endowments; Business/Corporate Donations; Box Office; Government
Grants; Individual Donations
Season: 52 Weeks   **Annual Attendance:** 30,000
Affiliations: TCG; California Theater Council; Orange County Theater Alliance
Performance Facilities: Gem Theatre; The Festival Amphitheatre

PERFORMING SERIES

THE GROVE SHAKESPEARE FESTIVAL
12852 Main Street, Garden Grove, CA 92640
(714) 636-7213
FAX: (714) 539-2651
Founded: 1979
Arts Area: Theater
Status: Professional; Non-Profit
Type: Performing; Resident; Educational
Management: W. Stuart McDowell, Artistic Director; Barbara G. Hammerman, Managing Director
Paid Staff: 9
Paid Artists: 15
Utilizes: Special Technical Talent; Guest Artists; Guest Directors
Budget: $500,000 - $1,000,000
Income Sources: Box Office; Government Grants; Individual Donations
Season: June - September   **Annual Attendance:** 8,000
Performance Facilities: The Festival Amphitheatre; Gem Theater

---

Glendale

INSTRUMENTAL MUSIC

GLENDALE SYMPHONY
401 North Brand Boulevard, Suite 520, Glendale, CA 91203
(818) 500-8720
Founded: 1924
Arts Area: Symphony; Orchestra
Status: Professional; Non-Profit
Type: Performing; Educational
Purpose: To educate youth and to bring high-quality familiar classical and light classical music to the community
Management: Shirley Seely, Administrator
Paid Staff: 1   **Volunteer Staff:** 3
Paid Artists: 95
Utilizes: Guest Conductors; Guest Artists
Budget: $100,000 - $500,000
Income Sources: Business/Corporate Donations; Box Office; Government Grants; Individual Donations
Season: October - April   **Annual Attendance:** 30,000
Affiliations: ASOL
Performance Facilities: Dorothy Chandler Pavilion

Glendora

FACILITY

HAUGH PERFORMING ARTS CENTER
1000 West Foothill, Glendora, CA 91740
(818) 914-8845
FAX: (818) 335-4715
Type of Facility: Theatre House
Type of Stage: Proscenium
Stage Dimensions: 28'x54'x70'; grid height 78'   **Orchestra Pit**
Seating Capacity: 1,451
Year Built: 1971   **Architect:** Neptune & Thomas   **Cost:** $2,300,000
Contact for Rental: Greg Hinrichsen, Director of Performing Arts;   (818) 914-8847
Manager: Greg Hinrichsen
Resident Groups: Evenings at Eight/Narrated Film Series; Citrus Singers

---

Guerneville

PERFORMING SERIES

RUSSIAN RIVER JAZZ FESTIVAL, INC.
16342 Third Street, Guerneville, CA 95446
(707) 869-3940
FAX: (707) 869-0147
Founded: 1976
Arts Area: Vocal Music; Instrumental Music; Festivals
Status: Non-Profit
Type: Performing
Purpose: To bring top name performers in jazz and related musical genres to an outdoor venue to benefit local, community and youth music programs
Management: Kathryn Marceau, Office Manager
Officers: Paul Neel, President; Debbie Padilla, Secretary; Dan Cool, John Hughes, Paul Larkin, Directors
Paid Staff: 1   **Volunteer Staff:** 60
Paid Artists: 14   **Non-Paid Artists:** 5
Utilizes: Special Technical Talent; Guest Artists
Budget: $100,000 - $500,000
Income Sources: Private Foundations/Grants/Endowments; Box Office; Government Grants
Season: June - September   **Annual Attendance:** 8,000

Hayward

FACILITY

CALIFORNIA STATE UNIVERSITY-HAYWARD - MAIN THEATRE
Carlos Bee Boulevard, Hayward, CA 94542
(510) 881-3374
> **Type of Facility:** Theatre House
> **Type of Stage:** Proscenium
> **Stage Dimensions:** 36'Wx40'D; 36'Wx22'H proscenium opening   **Orchestra Pit**
> **Seating Capacity:** 480
> **Year Built:** 1972   **Architect:** Niell Smith & Associates; Anderson Simons Dusel & Campini   **Cost:** $1,500,000
> **Contact for Rental:** Facilities Reservations;   (510) 881-3548
> **Resident Groups:** Theatre Arts Department

CHABOT COLLEGE PERFORMING ARTS CENTER
25555 Hesperian Boulevard, Hayward, CA 94545-2447
(510) 786-6976
FAX: (510) 782-9315
> **Type of Facility:** Theatre Complex; Concert Hall; Auditorium; Performance Center; Black Box
> **Type of Stage:** Flexible; Proscenium
> **Stage Dimensions:** Main Theatre - 46'Wx35'D; Little Theatre - Flexible   **Orchestra Pit**
> **Seating Capacity:** Main Theatre - 1,482; Little Theatre - 208
> **Year Built:** 1968   **Architect:** Johnson, Poole & Storm   **Cost:** $1,869,290
> **Contact for Rental:** Elliott Charnow, Chairman, Humanities Division;   (510) 786-6828
> **Manager:** Roger Noyes;   (510) 786-6976

Hemet

PERFORMING SERIES

RAMONA HILLSIDE PLAYERS
27402 Ramona Bowl Road, Hemet, CA 92544
(909) 658-3111
FAX: (909) 658-2695
> **Founded:** 1941
> **Arts Area:** Vocal Music; Instrumental Music; Theater
> **Status:** Non-Professional; Non-Profit
> **Type:** Performing; Resident; Educational
> **Purpose:** To present quality entertainment and train individuals in all phases of theatre
> **Management:** Peggy L. McQuown, Contact Person
> **Utilizes:** Guest Directors
> **Budget:** $1,000 - $50,000
> **Income Sources:** Box Office; Individual Donations
> **Season:** 52 Weeks   **Annual Attendance:** 5,500
> **Performance Facilities:** Ramona Hillside Playhouse

RAMONA PAGEANT ASSOCIATION
27400 Ramona Bowl Road, Hemet, CA 92544
(909) 658-3111
FAX: (909) 658-2695
> **Founded:** 1923
> **Arts Area:** Dance; Vocal Music; Theater; Community
> **Status:** Professional; Non-Professional; Non-Profit
> **Type:** Performing; Resident; Educational
> **Purpose:** To portray early California history - the coming of white men and its effect on the Spanish and Indian cultures
> **Management:** Roland C. Parker, Executive Director
> **Officers:** Michael McIntyre, President; Daniel T. Donnelly, Vice President; W.P. Ryan, Secretary; J. Robert Eichinger, Treasurer
> **Paid Staff:** 4
> **Paid Artists:** 2   **Non-Paid Artists:** 350
> **Utilizes:** Guest Artists; Guest Directors
> **Budget:** $100,000 - $500,000
> **Income Sources:** Box Office
> **Season:** April - May   **Annual Attendance:** 39,000

Affiliations: Institute of Outdoor Dramas
Performance Facilities: Ramona Bowl Outdoor Theatre

FACILITY

RAMONA BOWL
27400 Ramona Bowl Road, Hemet, CA 92544
(909) 658-3111
FAX: (909) 658-2695
    Type of Facility: Amphitheater
    Type of Stage: Environmental
    Seating Capacity: 6,662
    Contact for Rental: R.C. Parker;   (909) 658-3111
    Manager: W.R. Rose

Hollywood

THEATRE

AMERICAN LIVING HISTORY THEATER
PO Box 2677, Hollywood, CA 90078
(213) 876-2202
    Founded: 1975
    Arts Area: Professional
    Status: Professional; Non-Profit
    Type: Performing; Touring; Resident; Educational
    Purpose: To present theatre productions on American historical and literary characters and events
    Management: Dorene Ludwig, Artistic Director/President
    Income Sources: Business/Corporate Donations; Box Office; Government Grants; Individual Donations
    Season: 52 Weeks

THE CAST THEATRE/THE CAST-AT-THE-CIRCLE
804 North El Centro, Hollywood, CA 90038
(213) 462-0265; (213) 462-9872
    Founded: 1974
    Arts Area: Theatrical Group
    Status: Non-Profit
    Type: Performing; Touring
    Purpose: To encourage playwrights; to produce new American plays
    Management: R.T. Schmitt, Producing Artistic Director; Diana Gibson, Associate Artistic Director
    Officers: Doris Koenig, President; Stanley Handman, Secretary
    Paid Staff: 6   **Volunteer Staff:** 5
    Paid Artists: 40
    Utilizes: Special Technical Talent; Guest Artists; Guest Directors
    Budget: $50,000 - $100,000
    Income Sources: Private Foundations/Grants/Endowments; Business/Corporate Donations; Box Office; Government Grants; Individual Donations
    Season: 52 Weeks   **Annual Attendance:** 12,000
    Affiliations: TCG; Los Angeles Theatre Alliance; California Theatre Council
    Performance Facilities: The Cast Theatre; The Cast-at-the-Circle Theatre

FRIENDS AND ARTISTS THEATRE ENSEMBLE
1761 North Vermont Avenue, Hollywood, CA 90027
(213) 664-0680
    Founded: 1986
    Arts Area: Professional; Musical; Theatrical Group
    Status: Professional; Semi-Professional; Non-Profit
    Type: Performing; Touring; Resident; Educational
    Purpose: To produce and develop original works; to revive great works of literature
    Management: Pauli Dewitt, Administrative Director; Liz Hipwell, Production Coordinator; Tony Miller, Stage Manager; Steven Ingrassia, Technical Director
    Officers: Sal Romeo, Artistic Director; Laurie Wemdorf, Maria Simpson, Marc Handler, Vice Presidents; Bob Zemtis, Secretary; Michael Mehring, Treasurer
    Paid Staff: 5   **Volunteer Staff:** 50
    Paid Artists: 100   **Non-Paid Artists:** 100
    Utilizes: Special Technical Talent; Guest Conductors; Guest Artists; Guest Directors
    Budget: $50,000 - $100,000

Income Sources: Private Foundations/Grants/Endowments; Business/Corporate Donations; Box Office; Government Grants; Individual Donations
Season: 52 Weeks **Annual Attendance:** 10,000

MCCADDEN PLACE THEATRE
1157 North McCadden Place, Hollywood, CA 90038
(213) 856-0665
> **Founded:** 1981
> **Arts Area:** Professional; Theatrical Group
> **Status:** Professional; Non-Profit
> **Type:** Performing; Educational
> **Management:** Joy Rinaldi, Jay Donohue, Artistic Directors
> **Utilizes:** Special Technical Talent; Guest Artists; Guest Directors
> **Budget:** $1,000 - $50,000
> **Income Sources:** Box Office; Individual Donations
> **Season:** 52 Weeks
> **Affiliations:** AEA
> **Performance Facilities:** McCadden Theatre (scheduled to reopen in 1993)

STAGES THEATRE
1540 North McCadden Place, Hollywood, CA 90028
(213) 465-1010
FAX: (213) 462-2176
> **Founded:** 1981
> **Arts Area:** Professional
> **Status:** Professional; Non-Profit
> **Type:** Performing
> **Purpose:** To expose new or unfamiliar works or styles of theater to Los Angeles audiences; to host unique artists-in-residence who utilize distinctive theatrical styles, such as Theater of the Absurd and Commedia del' Arte
> **Management:** Paul Verdier, Artistic Director; Sonia Lloveras, Managing Director
> **Officers:** Pompea Smith, Chair; Sonia Lloveras, Treasurer
> **Paid Staff:** 1 **Volunteer Staff:** 8
> **Paid Artists:** 3 **Non-Paid Artists:** 3
> **Utilizes:** Guest Artists; Guest Directors
> **Budget:** $50,000 - $100,000
> **Income Sources:** Box Office; Government Grants; Individual Donations
> **Season:** October - September **Annual Attendance:** 6,000
> **Affiliations:** TCG
> **Performance Facilities:** Stages Theatre

THEATRE RAPPORT/HOLLYWOOD THEATRE CLUB
8128 Gould Avenue, Hollywood, CA 90046
(213) 660-0433
> **Founded:** 1967
> **Arts Area:** Theatrical Group
> **Status:** Professional
> **Type:** Performing
> **Purpose:** To present West Coast premieres of contemporary plays to an aware, adventurous audience
> **Management:** Crane Jackson, Artistic Director/Producer
> **Volunteer Staff:** 8
> **Non-Paid Artists:** 30
> **Utilizes:** Guest Directors
> **Budget:** $1,000 - $50,000
> **Income Sources:** Box Office; Individual Donations

UNICORN PLAYERS INC.
1743 North Hudson Avenue, Hollywood, CA 90028
(213) 464-8738
> **Founded:** 1973
> **Status:** Semi-Professional; Non-Profit
> **Type:** Touring
> **Purpose:** To expose as many children as possible to exciting theatrical experiences and examples of their literary heritage
> **Management:** Shirley Adams, General Manager; James Hays, Artistic Director
> **Officers:** James Hays, President; Beth Collier, Secretary
> **Volunteer Staff:** 2
> **Paid Artists:** 5
> **Utilizes:** Special Technical Talent
> **Budget:** $50,000 - $100,000
> **Income Sources:** Touring Fees

Season: October - June   **Annual Attendance:** 100,000
Affiliations: Los Angeles Theatre Alliance

FACILITY

THE COMPLEX
6476 Santa Monica Boulevard, Hollywood, CA 90038
(213) 465-0383
  Type of Facility: Theatre Complex
  Type of Stage: Proscenium
  Seating Capacity: 55 in each of five theatres
  Contact for Rental: Matt Chait;   (213) 465-0383
  Resident Groups: Theatre 6470; The Blueline Theatre Group
  1960's conversion to five theatre spaces

HOLLYWOOD BOWL
2301 North Highland Avenue, Hollywood, CA 90078
(213) 850-2000
  Type of Facility: Outdoor (Concert); Amphitheater
  Type of Stage: Proscenium; Arena
  Stage Dimensions: 106'x55'x48'
  Seating Capacity: 17,906
  Year Built: 1922
  Acoustical Consultant: Elizabeth Cohen
  Contact for Rental: Mark Ferber;   (213) 850-2080
  Manager: Anne Parsons;   (213) 850-2095
  Resident Groups: Los Angeles Philharmonic Association; Hollywood Bowl Orchestra

HOLLYWOOD PALLADIUM
6215 Sunset Boulevard, Hollywood, CA 90028
(213) 962-7600
  Type of Facility: Concert Hall; Multi-Purpose; Room
  Facility Originally: Ballroom
  Type of Stage: Thrust
  Stage Dimensions: 25'x65' with 4'x8' extensions
  Seating Capacity: Theater-style - 2,400; Festival-style - 4,400
  Year Built: 1940   **Architect:** McClellan and Cruz
  Contact for Rental: Mark Midgley;   (213) 962-7600

JAMES A. DOOLITTLE THEATRE
1615 North Vine Street, Hollywood, CA 90028
(213) 462-6666
FAX: (213) 926-2936
  Type of Facility: Theatre House
  Type of Stage: Proscenium
  Stage Dimensions: 74'10"Wx34'D; 38'Wx25'2"H proscenium opening   **Orchestra Pit**
  Seating Capacity: 1,019
  Year Built: 1926
  Year Remodeled: 1985   **Architect:** Brian Murphy   **Cost:** $650,000
  Acoustical Consultant: Bolt, Beranek & Newman
  Contact for Rental: Phil Lipman, UCLA;   (213) 825-9159
  Rental limited to equity only

Huntington Beach

THEATRE

HUNTINGTON BEACH PLAYHOUSE
PO Box 451, Huntington Beach, CA 92648
(714) 832-1405
  Founded: 1963
  Arts Area: Musical; Community; Theatrical Group
  Status: Non-Professional; Non-Profit
  Type: Performing
  Purpose: As a non-profit organization dedicated to community educational and cultural enrichment in dramatic arts, Huntington Beach Playhouse presents dramatic productions, sponsors student scholarships and offers stagecraft workshops.
  Management: Phil de Barros, President; Martin G. Eckmann, Technical Director

Officers: Phil de Barros, President; Lana Campbell, Vice President; Orvil Dart, Treasurer; Patricia Powers, Business Manager
Volunteer Staff: 25
Non-Paid Artists: 50
Utilizes: Special Technical Talent; Guest Directors
Budget: $50,000 - $100,000
Income Sources: Business/Corporate Donations; Box Office; Individual Donations
Season: October - August   **Annual Attendance:** 7,000
Affiliations: Huntington Beach Chamber of Commerce
Performance Facilities: Gisler Intermediate School; Huntington Beach Central Library

FACILITY

GOLDEN WEST COLLEGE - MAINSTAGE THEATRE
15744 Golden West Street, Huntington Beach, CA 92647
(714) 895-8772
Type of Facility: Theatre House
Type of Stage: Proscenium
Stage Dimensions: 72'Wx33'D   **Orchestra Pit**
Seating Capacity: 340
Year Built: 1971   **Architect:** William Pereira and Associates   **Cost:** $3,500,000
Year Remodeled: 1992   **Cost:** $85,000
Acoustical Consultant: William Pereira and Associates
Contact for Rental: David Anthony;   (714) 895-8772

Huntington Park

THEATRE

HUNTINGTON PARK CIVIC THEATRE
6952 Salt Lake Avenue, Huntington Park, CA 90255
(213) 584-6215
FAX: (213) 588-4577
Founded: 1947
Arts Area: Musical; Community
Status: Non-Profit
Type: Performing; Resident
Purpose: To develop an interest for drama in the community; to provide a recreational outlet for community members
Management: Board of Directors
Officers: Eileen Gerardi, President; Anne Parks, Vice President; Dorothy Fitzel, Secretary; Esther Hennes, Treasurer
Volunteer Staff: 15
Non-Paid Artists: 40
Utilizes: Guest Artists; Guest Directors
Budget: $1,000 - $50,000
Income Sources: Box Office; Individual Donations
Season: 52 Weeks   **Annual Attendance:** 1,500
Affiliations: Recreation Department
Performance Facilities: Bonelli Center

Idyllwild

PERFORMING SERIES

IDYLLWILD SCHOOL OF MUSIC AND THE ARTS
52500 Temecula Drive, Idyllwild, CA 90210
(909) 659-2171
Founded: 1950
Arts Area: Dance; Vocal Music; Instrumental Music; Theater; Festivals
Status: Professional; Non-Professional; Non-Profit
Type: Performing; Educational
Purpose: To make the arts and arts education available to all people
Management: Steven Fraider Summer, Program Director; William Lowman, Executive Director
Income Sources: Private Foundations/Grants/Endowments; Business/Corporate Donations; Box Office; Government Grants; Individual Donations
Season: June - August
Performance Facilities: Idyllwild Arts Foundation Theatre; Holmes Amphitheatre

---

Inglewood

FACILITY

THE GREAT WESTERN FORUM
3900 West Manchester Boulevard, Inglewood, CA 90306
(310) 419-3182
FAX: (310) 419-3234
  Type of Facility: Arena
  Type of Stage: Flexible; Arena
  Stage Dimensions: 48'x40'
  Seating Capacity: 18,679
  Year Built: 1967 **Architect:** Charles Luckman Associates
  Contact for Rental: Claire L. Rothman; (213) 419-3182

Irvine

INSTRUMENTAL MUSIC

ORANGE COUNTY PHILHARMONIC SOCIETY
2082 Business Center Drive, Suite 100, Irvine, CA 92715
(714) 553-2422
FAX: (714) 553-2421
  Founded: 1953
  Arts Area: Symphony; Orchestra; Chamber; Ensemble; Ethnic; Folk; Instrumental Group
  Status: Professional; Non-Profit
  Type: Educational; Sponsoring
  Purpose: To present the finest classical music; to provide a nationally-recognized network of educational outreach programs for Orange County youth, coordinated and funded in part by the 1,700 members of the Orange County Philharmonic Society's Women's Committees
  Management: Erich A. Vollmer, Executive Director; Rebecca A. Menes, Marketing/Communications Manager
  Officers: Susan S. Beechner, Chairman of the Board; Steven A. Lupinacci, President
  Utilizes: Special Technical Talent; Guest Conductors; Guest Artists; Guest Directors
  Budget: $1,000,000 - $5,000,000
  Income Sources: Private Foundations/Grants/Endowments; Business/Corporate Donations; Box Office; Government Grants; Individual Donations
  Season: September - May
  Affiliations: California Arts Council
  Performance Facilities: Orange County Performing Arts Center; Irvine Barclay Theatre

PACIFIC SYMPHONY ASSOCIATION
2151 Michelson Drive, Suite 216, Irvine, CA 92715
(714) 474-2109
FAX: (714) 474-2256
  Arts Area: Symphony; Orchestra
  Status: Professional; Non-Profit
  Type: Performing; Educational
  Purpose: To provide the Orange County region with symphonic performances of the highest quality through development and maintenance of a nationally-recognized orchestra; to broaden the appreciation of great music by exposing new and diverse audiences to the orchestra's performances
  Management: Carl St. Clair, Music Director; Louis G. Spisto, Executive Director
  Officers: G. Randolph Johnson, Chairman of the Board; Janice Johnson, President
  Budget: $5,000,000 - $10,000,000
  Income Sources: Private Foundations/Grants/Endowments; Business/Corporate Donations; Box Office; Government Grants; Individual Donations
  Performance Facilities: Orange County Performing Arts Center

VOCAL MUSIC

PACIFIC CHORALE
18218 East McDurmotte, Suite B-1, Irvine, CA 92714
(714) 252-1234
FAX: (714) 252-1885
  Arts Area: Choral
  Status: Semi-Professional; Non-Profit
  Type: Performing; Touring; Educational
  Purpose: To provide the finest classical choral performances for Orange County and beyond

Management: John Alexander, Artistic Director/Conductor; Bonnie McClain, Executive Director
Officers: Jay St. Clair, President of the Board
Budget: $500,000 - $1,000,000
Income Sources: Private Foundations/Grants/Endowments; Business/Corporate Donations; Box Office; Government Grants; Individual Donations
Performance Facilities: Orange County Performing Arts Center

PERFORMING SERIES

UCI CULTURAL EVENTS
320 University Tower, University of California, Irvine, CA 92717-5185
(714) 856-5589
FAX: (714) 725-2201
Founded: 1965
Arts Area: Dance; Instrumental Music; Theater
Status: Professional; Non-Profit
Type: Educational; Sponsoring; Presenting
Purpose: To present professional performing artists to the campus and community
Management: Desiree Mallory, Manager of Cultural Events
Paid Staff: 7
Utilizes: Guest Artists
Budget: $100,000 - $500,000
Income Sources: Private Foundations/Grants/Endowments; Business/Corporate Donations; Box Office; Government Grants; Individual Donations
Season: October - June
Performance Facilities: Irvine Barclay Theatre; Bren Events Center; University of California at Irvine Student Center

FACILITY

BREN EVENTS CENTER
University of California, Irvine, CA 92717-1500
(714) 856-5050
FAX: (714) 856-5097
Founded: 1987
Type of Facility: Arena
Type of Stage: Flexible; Platform; 3/4 Arena; Arena
Stage Dimensions: 60'Wx40'D
Seating Capacity: 5,400
Year Built: 1986   **Architect:** Parkin Architects   **Cost:** $17,000,000
Acoustical Consultant: Poaletti/Lewitz/Associates
Contact for Rental: Steven H. Neal;   (714) 856-5050

UNIVERSITY OF CALIFORNIA-IRVINE - VILLAGE THEATRE
University of California, Irvine, CA 92717
(714) 856-4901
Type of Facility: Theatre House
Type of Stage: Proscenium
Stage Dimensions: 60'x120'x40'   **Orchestra Pit**
Seating Capacity: 420
Year Built: 1970   **Architect:** William Pereira and Associates   **Cost:** $1,500,000
Acoustical Consultant: Del Sano
Manager: Production Manager;   (714) 856-4901

Kentfield

INSTRUMENTAL MUSIC

MARIN COMMUNITY COLLEGE SYMPHONY
Kentfield, CA 94904
(415) 485-9460
Founded: 1960
Arts Area: Symphony; Orchestra; Chamber; Instrumental Group
Status: Non-Professional; Non-Profit
Type: Performing; Educational
Purpose: To promote cultural advancement
Management: Norman Masonson, Music Director/Conductor
Paid Staff: 4   **Volunteer Staff:** 60
Utilizes: Special Technical Talent; Guest Artists

Budget: $1,000 - $50,000
Income Sources: Government Grants; Individual Donations
Season: August - December; January - May   **Annual Attendance:** 400
Performance Facilities: Fine Arts Theatre

La Jolla

INSTRUMENTAL MUSIC

LA JOLLA CHAMBER MUSIC SOCIETY
7949 Ivanhoe Street, Suite 319, La Jolla, CA 92037
(619) 459-3724
> **Mailing Address:** PO Box 2168, La Jolla, CA 92038
> **Founded:** 1968
> **Arts Area:** Symphony; Chamber; Ensemble
> **Status:** Professional; Non-Profit
> **Type:** Performing
> **Purpose:** To offer San Diego County audiences classical chamber music of the highest quality through concerts and recitals
> **Management:** Neale Perl, Executive Director
> **Officers:** Robert Edmunds, President
> **Paid Staff:** 3
> **Paid Artists:** 35
> **Utilizes:** Guest Artists
> **Budget:** $500,000 - $1,000,000
> **Income Sources:** Private Foundations/Grants/Endowments; Business/Corporate Donations; Box Office; Government Grants; Individual Donations
> **Season:** August - June   **Annual Attendance:** 50,000
> **Affiliations:** Association of California Symphony Orchestras; Combined Arts Council of San Diego County
> **Performance Facilities:** Sherwood Auditorium; Civic Theatre

THEATRE

LA JOLLA PLAYHOUSE
PO Box 12039, La Jolla, CA 92039
(619) 534-6760; (619) 534-3960
FAX: (619) 534-7870
> **Founded:** 1948
> **Arts Area:** Professional
> **Status:** Professional; Non-Profit
> **Type:** Touring; Resident; Educational; Produce
> **Purpose:** To produce bold and innovative theater of adventurous intent; to provide a summer home for the leading theater artists in America
> **Management:** Des McAnuff, Artistic Director; Terrance Dwyer, Managing Director; Robert Blacker, Associate Artistic Director; Sidney Baker, Director of Development; Patricia Nicholson, Marketing Director; Constance Harvey, Press Representative; Lisa Peterson, Associate Director
> **Officers:** Willard VanderLann, Board President
> **Paid Staff:** 18
> **Paid Artists:** 75
> **Utilizes:** Special Technical Talent; Guest Artists; Guest Directors
> **Budget:** $1,000,000 - $5,000,000
> **Income Sources:** Private Foundations/Grants/Endowments; Business/Corporate Donations; Box Office; Government Grants; Individual Donations
> **Season:** May - November   **Annual Attendance:** 120,000
> **Affiliations:** AEA; LORT; TCG
> **Performance Facilities:** La Jolla Playhouse; Mandell Weiss Performing Arts Center

PERFORMING SERIES

UNIVERSITY OF CALIFORNIA-SAN DIEGO - UNIVERSITY EVENTS OFFICE
9500 Gilman Drive, La Jolla, CA 92093-0078
(619) 534-4090
FAX: (619) 534-1505
> **Founded:** 1965
> **Arts Area:** Dance; Instrumental Music; Theater
> **Status:** Professional; Non-Profit
> **Type:** Educational; Sponsoring
> **Purpose:** To provide events and entertainment for the University and community

Management: Lynne Peterson, Director
Paid Staff: 8   **Volunteer Staff:** 60
Paid Artists: 60
Budget: $100,000 - $500,000
Income Sources: Box Office; Government Grants; Individual Donations
Season: October - June
Annual Attendance: 30,000
Affiliations: WAAA; APAP; California Confederation of the Arts; California Presenters
Performance Facilities: Mandeville Auditorium, University of California at San Diego

FACILITY

MANDELL WEISS PERFORMING ARTS CENTER
2910 La Jolla Village Drive, La Jolla, CA 92037
(619) 534-3791
FAX: (619) 534-1080
Type of Facility: Theatre Complex; Theatre House
Type of Stage: Thrust; Flexible; Proscenium; Three Stages
Stage Dimensions: 80'Wx40'D; 40'Wx24'H proscenium opening   **Orchestra Pit**
Seating Capacity: Forum - 400; Theatre - 500; Forum Studio - 120
Year Built: 1982   **Architect:** Forum-Antoine Predock
Acoustical Consultant: Bolt, Beranek & Newman
Contact for Rental: Mark Loigman
Resident Groups: La Jolla Playhouse (May-September); University of California at San Diego Theatre Department
(October-April)
The Mandel Weiss Performing Arts Center contains the Mandell Weiss Forum, the Mandell Weiss Theatre and the Mandell Weiss Forum Studio. For information concerning the Mandell Weiss Performing Arts Center, contact La Jolla Playhouse at (619) 534-6760 or University of California, San Diego at (619) 534-2062.

SHERWOOD AUDITORIUM
Museum of Contemporary Art- San Diego, 700 Prospect Street, La Jolla, CA 92037
(619) 454-3541
Type of Facility: Auditorium
Type of Stage: Proscenium
Stage Dimensions: 40'Wx26'D
Seating Capacity: 500
Year Built: 1959   **Architect:** Mosher & Drew
Contact for Rental: Gwen Fowler;   (619) 454-3541

UNIVERSITY OF CALIFORNIA-SAN DIEGO - MANDEVILLE AUDITORIUM
Mandeville Center for the Performing Arts, La Jolla, CA 92093
(619) 534-2380
Type of Facility: Concert Hall; Auditorium; Theatre House
Type of Stage: Proscenium
Stage Dimensions: 100'Wx40'D   **Orchestra Pit**
Seating Capacity: 788
Year Built: 1975   **Architect:** Quincy Jones
Acoustical Consultant: Dr. Gerald Strang
Contact for Rental: Shirley Pyykko;   (619) 534-2380
The Mandeville Auditorium also includes the 150-seat Recital Hall. Rental is limited to university departments and nonprofit organizations.

La Mesa

PERFORMING SERIES

GROSSMONT COMMUNITY CONCERTS
4900 Rosehedge Drive, Unit 213, La Mesa, CA 91941
(619) 465-7545
Founded: 1947
Arts Area: Dance; Vocal Music; Instrumental Music; Lyric Opera
Status: Professional; Non-Profit
Type: Performing
Purpose: To provide excellent concerts for our area at minimal cost
Management: Columbia Artists
Officers: Barbara Oppenheimer, President; Betty Coleman, First Vice President
Paid Staff: 1
Utilizes: Guest Artists

Budget: $1,000 - $50,000
Income Sources: Individual Donations
Season: October - May
Affiliations: Community Concert Association
Performance Facilities: East County Performing Arts Center

La Mirada

THEATRE

LA MIRADA THEATRE FOR THE PERFORMING ARTS
14900 La Mirada Boulevard, La Mirada, CA 90638
(714) 994-6150
Founded: 1977
Arts Area: Professional; Community
Status: Professional; Non-Profit
Type: Performing; Sponsoring
Purpose: To present theatre, music and dance in southern California
Management: Thomas C. Mitze, Executive Director
Paid Staff: 20   **Volunteer Staff:** 100
Paid Artists: 100   **Non-Paid Artists:** 500
Utilizes: Special Technical Talent; Guest Conductors; Guest Artists; Guest Directors
Budget: $1,000,000 - $5,000,000
Income Sources: Box Office; Government Grants
Season: 52 Weeks   **Annual Attendance:** 250,000
Performance Facilities: La Mirada Theatre For the Performing Arts

FACILITY

LA MIRADA THEATRE FOR THE PERFORMING ARTS
14900 La Mirada Boulevard, La Mirada, CA 90638
(714) 994-6150
Type of Facility: Theatre House
Facility Originally: Movie House
Type of Stage: Proscenium
Stage Dimensions: 80'Wx40'D   **Orchestra Pit**
Seating Capacity: 1,310
Year Built: 1977   **Architect:** Anthony & Langford   **Cost:** $3,500,000
Acoustical Consultant: Howard Smith
Contact for Rental: Thomas Mitze;   (714) 994-6150
Resident Groups: Broadway Season; La Mirada Playhouse; La Mirada Symphony; Whittier-La Mirada Musical Theatre; Golden State Children's Theatre

---

Laguna Beach

DANCE

BALLET PACIFICA
PO Box 626, Laguna Beach, CA 92652
(714) 642-9275
FAX: (714) 642-9277
Founded: 1962
Arts Area: Ballet
Status: Professional; Non-Profit
Type: Performing; Touring; Resident
Purpose: To provide entertainment for all ages
Management: Molly Lynch, Artistic Director
Officers: Barbara Stuart, Chairman
Paid Artists: 10   **Non-Paid Artists:** 16
Utilizes: Guest Artists
Budget: $100,000 - $500,000
Income Sources: Private Foundations/Grants/Endowments; Business/Corporate Donations; Box Office; Government Grants; Individual Donations
Season: 52 Weeks
Affiliations: Forum Theatre
Performance Facilities: Laguna Moulton Playhouse; The Forum; Irvine Barclay Theatre

INSTRUMENTAL MUSIC

LAGUNA CHAMBER MUSIC SOCIETY
PO Box 385, Laguna Beach, CA 92652
>**Founded:** 1959
>**Arts Area:** Chamber
>**Status:** Non-Profit
>**Type:** Sponsoring
>**Purpose:** To encourage an interest in classical music by presenting and promoting high-quality chamber music in the community
>**Management:** Glenda Vander Zaag, Executive Director
>**Officers:** Ray Hendrickson, President; Brenda Agren, Vice President; Jacqueline Hanson, Secretary; Curt Blankenbiller, Treasurer
>**Utilizes:** Guest Artists
>**Budget:** $50,000 - $100,000
>**Income Sources:** Private Foundations/Grants/Endowments; Business/Corporate Donations; Box Office; Government Grants; Individual Donations
>**Season:** September - May   **Annual Attendance:** 4,500
>**Affiliations:** Orange County Philharmonic Society
>**Performance Facilities:** Irvine Barclay Theatre

THEATRE

LAGUNA PLAYHOUSE
606 Laguna Canyon Road, Laguna Beach, CA 92651
(714) 494-8022
>**Founded:** 1920
>**Arts Area:** Community; Children's Theatre
>**Status:** Non-Professional; Non-Profit
>**Type:** Performing; Educational
>**Purpose:** Dedicated to excellence in the production of professional-quality theatre
>**Management:** Richard Stein, Executive Director; Andrew Barnicle, Artistic Director
>**Officers:** Joan McGillis, President; Don Crevier, Terry Neptune, Vice Presidents; James Gardiner, Secretary; Carl E. Schwab, Treasurer; Michael C. Miller, Parliamentarian
>**Paid Staff:** 12   **Volunteer Staff:** 50
>**Paid Artists:** 30   **Non-Paid Artists:** 150
>**Utilizes:** Guest Artists
>**Budget:** $1,000,000 - $5,000,000
>**Income Sources:** Private Foundations/Grants/Endowments; Business/Corporate Donations; Box Office; Government Grants; Individual Donations
>**Season:** September - June   **Annual Attendance:** 65,000
>**Affiliations:** Inter-theatre Institute; AATE
>**Performance Facilities:** Moulton Theater

FACILITY

LAGUNA PLAYHOUSE
606 Laguna Canyon Road, Laguna Beach, CA 92651
(714) 494-8022
>**Type of Facility:** Theatre House
>**Type of Stage:** Thrust; Proscenium
>**Seating Capacity:** 418
>**Year Built:** 1969   **Architect:** William Pereira and Associates   **Cost:** $500,000
>**Year Remodeled:** 1985   **Architect:** Thola Productions   **Cost:** $450,000
>**Contact for Rental:** Richard Stein;   (714) 494-8022
>**Resident Groups:** Laguna Playhouse

Long Beach

DANCE

LOS ANGELES CLASSICAL BALLET
1122 Wardlow Road, Long Beach, CA 90807
(310) 424-8498
FAX: (310) 426-2622
>**Arts Area:** Ballet
>**Status:** Professional; Non-Profit
>**Type:** Performing; Touring; Resident

Management: David Wilcox, Artistic Director/Chief Executive Officer
Utilizes: Guest Artists; Guest Choreographers
Income Sources: Private Foundations/Grants/Endowments; Business/Corporate Donations; Box Office; Government Grants; Individual Donations
Season: 52 Weeks
Performance Facilities: Terrace Theater; Long Beach Convention Center

INSTRUMENTAL MUSIC

LONG BEACH SYMPHONY ORCHESTRA
555 East Ocean Boulevard, Suite 106, Long Beach, CA 90892
(310) 436-3203
FAX: (310) 491-3599
Founded: 1935
Arts Area: Symphony; Orchestra
Status: Non-Profit
Type: Performing
Purpose: To present symphonic music
Management: Mary E. Newkirk, Executive Director
Paid Staff: 6   **Volunteer Staff:** 2
Paid Artists: 86
Budget: $1,000,000 - $5,000,000
Income Sources: Private Foundations/Grants/Endowments; Business/Corporate Donations; Box Office; Government Grants; Individual Donations
Annual Attendance: 40,000
Performance Facilities: Terrace Theater

VOCAL MUSIC

LONG BEACH CIVIC LIGHT OPERA
PO Box 20280, Long Beach, CA 90801
(310) 435-7605
Founded: 1950
Arts Area: Light Opera; Operetta
Status: Professional; Non-Profit
Type: Performing
Purpose: To maintain artistic excellence in the presentation and performance of professional musical theatre; to train pre-professionals and youth in musical theatre
Management: Pegge Logefeil, Managing Director; Martin Wiviott, Producer
Officers: James C. Barggren, President, Board of Directors
Paid Staff: 9
Utilizes: Special Technical Talent; Guest Conductors; Guest Artists; Guest Directors
Income Sources: Private Foundations/Grants/Endowments; Business/Corporate Donations; Box Office; Government Grants; Individual Donations
Season: October - August   **Annual Attendance:** 150,000
Performance Facilities: Terrace Theater

LONG BEACH OPERA
6372 Pacific Coast Hwy., Long Beach, CA 90803
(310) 596-5556
FAX: (310) 596-8380
Founded: 1978
Arts Area: Grand Opera; Lyric Opera
Status: Professional; Non-Profit
Type: Performing; Educational
Purpose: To present professional opera productions to southern California audiences; to instill in children a love for opera and the performing arts
Management: Michael Milenski, General Director
Officers: Joseph Sheridan, President, Board of Directors
Volunteer Staff: 10
Paid Artists: 250   **Non-Paid Artists:** 25
Utilizes: Special Technical Talent; Guest Conductors; Guest Artists; Guest Directors
Budget: $500,000 - $1,000,000
Income Sources: Private Foundations/Grants/Endowments; Business/Corporate Donations; Box Office; Government Grants; Individual Donations
Season: October - May   **Annual Attendance:** 25,000
Performance Facilities: Center Theater; Terrace Theater

THEATRE

THE FOUND THEATRE
251 East Seventh Street, Long Beach, CA 90813
(310) 433-3363
> **Founded:** 1974
> **Arts Area:** Theatrical Group
> **Status:** Professional; Non-Profit
> **Type:** Performing
> **Purpose:** To provide professional-quality alternative theatre to the community as inexpensively as possible; to provide a place for actors, directors, and technicians to experiment, refine their craft, and grow as artists
> **Management:** Cynthia Galles, Artistic Managing Director; Virginia DeMoss, Literary Director; Alice Secrist, Music Director
> **Paid Staff:** 1
> **Budget:** $1,000 - $50,000
> **Income Sources:** Private Foundations/Grants/Endowments; Business/Corporate Donations; Box Office; Government Grants; Individual Donations
> **Season:** 52 Weeks   **Annual Attendance:** 2,000
> **Performance Facilities:** The Found Theatre

LONG BEACH JEWISH COMMUNITY CENTER YOUTH SUMMER STOCK
3801 East Willow Street, Long Beach, CA 90815
(310) 426-7601
FAX: (310) 424-3915
> **Founded:** 1949
> **Arts Area:** Summer Stock; Community; Theatrical Group
> **Status:** Non-Profit
> **Type:** Performing
> **Management:** Lynne Rosenstein, Assistant Executive Director
> **Paid Staff:** 3
> **Non-Paid Artists:** 80
> **Utilizes:** Guest Directors; Guest Choreographers
> **Budget:** $1,000 - $50,000
> **Income Sources:** Private Foundations/Grants/Endowments; Box Office
> **Annual Attendance:** 2,000
> **Affiliations:** United Way; Jewish Welfare Board
> **Performance Facilities:** Jewish Community Center

FACILITY

JORDAN THEATRE
6500 Atlantic Avenue, Long Beach, CA 90805
(310) 423-1471, ext. 2150
> **Type of Facility:** Auditorium; Loft
> **Facility Originally:** School
> **Type of Stage:** Proscenium
> **Stage Dimensions:** 125'Wx49'D; 49'Wx26'H proscenium opening   **Orchestra Pit**
> **Seating Capacity:** 1,700
> **Year Built:** 1952   **Cost:** $750,000
> **Year Remodeled:** 1971   **Cost:** $500,000
> **Acoustical Consultant:** David Barclift, Unlimited Production Services
> **Contact for Rental:** Dave Barclift;   (213) 423-1471, ext. x2150

LONG BEACH COMMUNITY PLAYHOUSE - STAGE
5021 East Anaheim Street, Long Beach, CA 90804
(310) 494-1014
> **Type of Facility:** Theatre House
> **Type of Stage:** 3/4 Arena
> **Stage Dimensions:** 40'Wx16'D thrust with 8'D behind proscenium
> **Seating Capacity:** 200
> **Year Built:** 1951
> **Year Remodeled:** 1965
> **Manager:** Elaine Herman, Managing Director

LONG BEACH CONVENTION AND ENTERTAINMENT CENTER
300 East Ocean Boulevard, Long Beach, CA 90802
(310) 436-3636
FAX: (310) 436-9491
   Type of Facility: Theatre Complex
   Type of Stage: Thrust; Proscenium; Arena
   Stage Dimensions: 65'x88'
   Orchestra Pit
   Seating Capacity: Arena - 14,500; Terrace Theater - 3,141; Center Theater - 362
   Year Built: 1962   **Architect:** Kenneth Wing   **Cost:** $8,500,000
   Acoustical Consultant: Jonathan Deans
   Contact for Rental: Tracy Begerow, Booking Manager;   (310) 436-3636
   Resident Groups: Long Beach Symphony; Long Beach Opera; Long Beach Ballet; Long Beach Civic Light Opera

LONG BEACH PLAYHOUSE - MAINSTAGE THEATRE
5021 East Anaheim Street, Long Beach, CA 90804
(213) 494-1014
   Founded: 1929
   Type of Facility: Theatre Complex; Theatre House; Exhibition Gallery
   Type of Stage: Proscenium; 3/4 Arena; Combination
   Stage Dimensions: 19'Wx8'D proscenium opening; 16'x40' thrust (3/4 arena)
   Seating Capacity: 200
   Year Built: 1951   **Architect:** Hugh Gibbs   **Cost:** $125,000
   Year Remodeled: 1965   **Architect:** Francis Huesel   **Cost:** $200,000
   Manager: Elaine Herman, Managing Director;   (213) 494-1014
   1992 marks the 64th year of continuous operation for Long Beach Community Playhouse. The Playhouse contains the Stage and Studio Theatre. See individual listings for additional information.

LONG BEACH PLAYHOUSE - STUDIO THEATRE
5021 East Anaheim Street, Long Beach, CA 90804
(213) 494-1014
   Founded: 1929
   Type of Facility: Theatre Complex; Theatre House
   Type of Stage: Modified Apron Proscenium
   Stage Dimensions: 20'Wx20'D with 30'Wx8'D apron
   Seating Capacity: 99
   Year Built: 1951
   Year Remodeled: 1967
   Manager: Elaine Herman, Managing Director;   (310) 494-1014

WOODROW WILSON HIGH SCHOOL
4400 East Tenth Street, Long Beach, CA 90804
(310) 433-0481
   Type of Facility: Concert Hall; Auditorium
   Facility Originally: School
   Type of Stage: Proscenium
   Stage Dimensions: 22'x44'x36'   **Orchestra Pit**
   Seating Capacity: 1,652
   Year Built: 1926   **Architect:** W. Horace Austin
   Year Remodeled: 1937   **Architect:** W. Horace Austin
   Acoustical Consultant: Glen Clancy/Continental Sound & Acoustics
   Contact for Rental: Ronald W. Mahan;   (310) 433-0481
   Resident Groups: Rainbow Playhouse Players

Los Altos Hills

FACILITY

ROBERT C. SMITHWICK THEATRE
12345 El Monte Road, Los Altos Hills, CA 94022-2921
(415) 949-7252
FAX: (415) 949-7375
   Founded: 1961
   Type of Facility: Auditorium
   Facility Originally: College Theatre
   Type of Stage: Proscenium
   Stage Dimensions: 39'6"Wx15'5"H proscenium opening   **Orchestra Pit**

Seating Capacity: 952
Year Built: 1961   **Architect:** Ernest J. Krump and Maston & Hurd Associated Architects
Contact for Rental: Duncan Graham;   (415) 949-7252
Resident Groups: College Performance Arts Groups

Los Angeles

DANCE

AMAN INTERNATIONAL MUSIC AND DANCE COMPANY
PO Box 5820, Los Angeles, CA 90055-0820
(213) 629-8387
FAX: (213) 629-8396
    Founded: 1964
    Arts Area: Ethnic; Folk
    Status: Professional; Non-Profit
    Type: Performing; Touring; Educational
    Purpose: To preserve and present America's multicultural heritage as it is found in music, song and dance
    Management: Timothy Ney, Managing Director; Barry Glass, Artistic Director
    Officers: Hon. William Huss, Chairman
    Paid Staff: 5   **Volunteer Staff:** 3
    Paid Artists: 36
    Utilizes: Special Technical Talent; Guest Directors
    Budget: $100,000 - $500,000
    Income Sources: Private Foundations/Grants/Endowments; Business/Corporate Donations; Box Office; Government Grants; Individual Donations
    Season: September - June   **Annual Attendance:** 100,000
    Affiliations: Dance California; Dance USA

BETHUNE THEATREDANSE
8033 Sunset Boulevard, Suite 221, Los Angeles, CA 90046
(213) 874-0481
FAX: (213) 851-2078
    Founded: 1980
    Arts Area: Modern; Ballet
    Status: Professional; Non-Profit
    Type: Performing; Touring; Resident; Educational
    Purpose: To combine multimedia and dramatic dance to create contemporary theatre art; to utilize stories drawn from screen plays, the literary world and television scripts, involving a broad range of multimedia art forms
    Management: Libi Warren, Administrative Director; Zina Bethune, Artistic Director; Rachel Cohen, Booking Contact; Paula Graber, Producer
    Officers: Richard Sigler, President; Zita Rahbar, Vice President; Ida Meyers, Secretary; Henry Schiffer, Treasurer
    Paid Staff: 3   **Volunteer Staff:** 10
    Paid Artists: 20   **Non-Paid Artists:** 8
    Utilizes: Special Technical Talent; Guest Artists; Guest Choreographers
    Budget: $100,000 - $500,000
    Income Sources: Private Foundations/Grants/Endowments; Business/Corporate Donations; Box Office; Government Grants; Individual Donations
    Season: September - July   **Annual Attendance:** 10,000
    Affiliations: Dance Resource Center; Chamber of Commerce

JAZZ TAP ENSEMBLE
1416 Westwood Boulevard, Suite 206, Los Angeles, CA 90024
(310) 475-4412
    Season: 52 Weeks

LACE/LOS ANGELES CONTEMPORARY EXHIBITIONS
1804 Industrial Street, Los Angeles, CA 90021
(213) 624-5650
FAX: (213) 624-6679
    Founded: 1977
    Arts Area: Modern
    Status: Professional; Semi-Professional; Non-Profit
    Type: Performing
    Purpose: To present art and ideas; to serve as a forum for artists and audiences
    Management: Gwen Darien, Executive Director; Tom Dennison, Performance Coordinator
    Officers: Coleen Sterritt, Chair; Karen Carson, Vice Chair; Richard Duardo, Secretary; Catherine B. Chester, Treasurer
    Paid Staff: 7

Budget: $500,000 - $1,000,000
Income Sources: Private Foundations/Grants/Endowments; Box Office; Government Grants; Individual Donations
Season: April - June

LEWITZKY DANCE COMPANY
700 South Flower Street, Suite 2000, Los Angeles, CA 90017-4207
(213) 627-5555
FAX: (213) 627-9249
Founded: 1966
Arts Area: Modern
Status: Professional; Non-Profit
Type: Performing; Touring; Educational
Purpose: To maintain Lewitzky repertoire, choreograph new works and develop existing and new audiences for dance
Management: Darlene Neel, Company Manager; Bella Lewitzky, Artistic Director; Ruth L. Eliel, Managing Director; Edson Womble, Production Manager
Officers: Douglas L. Dodds, Chairperson of the Board
Paid Staff: 7
Paid Artists: 14
Utilizes: Guest Artists
Budget: $500,000 - $1,000,000
Income Sources: Private Foundations/Grants/Endowments; Business/Corporate Donations; Government Grants; Individual Donations
Season: Mid-August - Mid-July   **Annual Attendance:** 35,000

LOLA MONTES AND HER SPANISH DANCERS
1529 North Commonwealth Avenue, Los Angeles, CA 90027
(213) 664-3288
Founded: 1955
Arts Area: Ethnic
Status: Professional
Type: Performing; Touring; Educational
Purpose: To keep alive Hispanic heritage; to maintain a professional company of high standards; to develop young artists
Management: Lola Montes Foundation for Dances of Spain and the Americas
Officers: Lola Montes, President; Patricia Tashma, Vice President; Caroline Hicks, Secretary/Treasurer
Volunteer Staff: 5
Paid Artists: 10
Utilizes: Special Technical Talent; Guest Artists
Budget: $1,000 - $50,000
Income Sources: Private Foundations/Grants/Endowments; Government Grants; Individual Donations
Season: 52 Weeks   **Annual Attendance:** 50,000
Affiliations: WAAA; California Confederation of the Arts

LORETTA LIVINGSTON AND DANCERS
870 North Occidental Boulevard, #2, Los Angeles, CA 90026
(213) 484-9888
FAX: (213) 484-9888
Founded: 1984
Arts Area: Modern
Status: Professional; Non-Profit
Type: Performing; Touring; Educational
Purpose: To produce Loretta Livingston's choreography and maintain a touring dance company; to provide outreach and educational programs
Management: David Plettner, Managing Director; Loretta Livingston, Artistic Director; Madeline Sogun, Marketing Associate
Paid Staff: 3
Paid Artists: 6
Budget: $100,000 - $500,000
Income Sources: Private Foundations/Grants/Endowments; Business/Corporate Donations; Box Office; Government Grants; Individual Donations
Season: 52 Weeks   **Annual Attendance:** 10,000
Affiliations: Dance/USA
Performance Facilities: Japan America Theatre; UCLA Center for Performing Arts

LOS ANGELES CHAMBER BALLET
503 1/2 North Norton Avenue, Los Angeles, CA 90040
(310) 453-4952
Arts Area: Ballet
Status: Professional; Non-Profit

Type: Performing; Touring; Resident
Management: Victoria Koenig, Raiford Rogers, Artistic Directors
Income Sources: Private Foundations/Grants/Endowments; Business/Corporate Donations; Box Office; Government Grants; Individual Donations

LOS ANGELES CHOREOGRAPHERS AND DANCERS
1807 North Rodney Drive, Los Angeles, CA 90027
(213) 665-5628
Founded: 1979
Arts Area: Modern; Tap
Status: Professional; Non-Profit
Type: Performing; Touring
Purpose: To create performance opportunities for Los Angeles and expand and educate a dance audience; to present the work of Louise Reichlin and Alfred Desio
Management: Louise Reichlin, Artistic/Managing Director
Paid Staff: 10   **Volunteer Staff:** 25
Paid Artists: 15
Utilizes: Special Technical Talent
Budget: $50,000 - $100,000
Income Sources: Private Foundations/Grants/Endowments; Business/Corporate Donations; Box Office; Government Grants; Individual Donations
Season: 52 Weeks   **Annual Attendance:** 27,000
Affiliations: Dance Resource Center; WAAA
Performance Facilities: Bing Theatre at USC; Japan America Theatre

LULA WASHINGTON CONTEMPORARY DANCE FOUNDATION
5179 1/2 West Adams Boulevard, Los Angeles, CA 90016
(213) 936-6591
FAX: (310) 671-4572
Founded: 1980
Arts Area: Modern; Jazz; Ethnic
Status: Professional; Non-Profit
Type: Performing; Touring; Educational; Sponsoring
Purpose: To explore the Black experience through high-quality dance
Management: Lula Washington, Artistic Director; Erwin Washington, Executive Director
Officers: Nina Shaw, Board President; Robert Johnson, Vice President
Paid Staff: 6   **Volunteer Staff:** 1
Paid Artists: 10
Utilizes: Guest Choreographers
Budget: $100,000 - $500,000
Income Sources: Private Foundations/Grants/Endowments; Business/Corporate Donations; Box Office; Government Grants; Individual Donations
Season: 52 Weeks   **Annual Attendance:** 5,000
Affiliations: Black Dance Companies Association

RHAPSODY IN TAPS
1558 North Hoover Street, Los Angeles, CA 90027
(213) 661-2172; (714) 838-3318
FAX: (714) 838-4660
Founded: 1981
Arts Area: Rhythm Tap with Live Jazz
Status: Non-Profit
Type: Performing; Touring
Purpose: To promote and perform the act of rhythm tap dance while exploring new choreographic directions
Management: Kay L. Davis, Administrative Director; Marci Jurls, Administrative Assistant; Anne W. Smith, Development Consultant
Officers: Linda Sohl-Donnell, Persident; Marilyn Gatto, Secretary; O.T. Gatto, Treasurer
Paid Staff: 3   **Volunteer Staff:** 16
Paid Artists: 10
Utilizes: Special Technical Talent; Guest Artists; Guest Choreographers
Budget: $50,000 - $100,000
Income Sources: Private Foundations/Grants/Endowments; Business/Corporate Donations; Box Office; Government Grants; Individual Donations

RUDY PEREZ PERFORMANCE ENSEMBLE
PO Box 36614, Los Angeles, CA 90036
(213) 931-3604
Founded: 1970

Arts Area: Modern
Status: Professional; Non-Profit
Type: Performing; Touring
Purpose: To present and produce experimental dance works
Management: Rudy Perez, Artistic Director/Choreographer
Paid Artists: 5
Utilizes: Special Technical Talent
Budget: $50,000 - $100,000
Income Sources: Private Foundations/Grants/Endowments; Business/Corporate Donations; Box Office; Government Grants; Individual Donations
Season: 52 Weeks

RUTH ST. DENIS FOUNDATION
618 South Sycamore, Los Angeles, CA 90036
(213) 934-8643
Founded: 1948
Arts Area: Modern; Ethnic
Status: Professional; Non-Profit
Type: Performing; Touring; Resident; Educational
Purpose: To teach, perform, and continue the works of Ruth St. Denis and Michio Ito
Management: Karoun Tootikian, Artistic Director; Ronny Cothron, Secretary
Officers: Karoun Tootikian, President; Lonny Cothron, Secretary; Lalla Lezli, Treasurer; Wendy Uyeda, Program Coordinator
Volunteer Staff: 4
Paid Artists: 8
Budget: $1,000 - $50,000
Income Sources: Box Office; Individual Donations
Season: 52 Weeks

TNR-MOEBIUS
4091 West Eighth Street, Los Angeles, CA 90005
(213) 389-4088
FAX: (213) 388-3618
Founded: 1972
Arts Area: Modern
Status: Professional; Non-Profit
Type: Performing; Touring; Resident
Purpose: To create works of ceremony and rituals
Management: Yen Lu Wong, Artistic Director
Paid Staff: 2
Paid Artists: 30   **Non-Paid Artists:** 200
Utilizes: Guest Artists
Budget: $50,000 - $100,000
Income Sources: Private Foundations/Grants/Endowments; Business/Corporate Donations; Box Office; Government Grants; Individual Donations
Season: 52 Weeks

VALENTINA OUMANSKY DRAMATIC DANCE FOUNDATION
3433 Cahuenga Boulevard West, Los Angeles, CA 90068
(213) 850-9497
Founded: 1973
Arts Area: Ballet
Status: Non-Profit
Type: Performing; Touring; Resident; Educational
Management: Valentina Oumansky, Artistic Director
Officers: Robert Y. Takagi, President; Betsy Ross Lueke, Vice President; Marilyn Carter, Treasurer/Secretary
Utilizes: Guest Artists
Budget: $1,000 - $50,000
Income Sources: Private Foundations/Grants/Endowments; Business/Corporate Donations; Individual Donations
Season: 52 Weeks
Performance Facilities: Studio Theatre

ZAPPED TAPS/ALFRED DESIO
1807 North Rodney Drive, Los Angeles, CA 90027
(213) 665-5628
Founded: 1979
Arts Area: Tap
Status: Professional; Non-Profit

Type: Performing; Touring
Purpose: To create and perform new solo tap works, both traditional and using Alfred Desio's invention "Tap-Tronics"
Management: Louise Reichlin, Managing Director
Paid Staff: 1 **Volunteer Staff:** 25
Paid Artists: 7
Utilizes: Special Technical Talent
Budget: $1,000 - $50,000
Income Sources: Private Foundations/Grants/Endowments; Business/Corporate Donations; Box Office; Government Grants; Individual Donations
Season: 52 Weeks
Annual Attendance: 27,000
Affiliations: Dance Resource Center

INSTRUMENTAL MUSIC

CALIFORNIA E.A.R. UNIT FOUNDATION
PO Box 86374, Los Angeles, CA 90086-0734
(213) 488-9788
FAX: (213) 488-9788
Arts Area: Chamber; Electronic & Live Electronic
Status: Professional; Non-Profit
Type: Performing; Touring; Resident; Educational
Purpose: To promote and perform the music of our time
Management: Amy Knoles, Booking Manager; Dorothy Stone, Director
Budget: $50,000 - $100,000
Income Sources: Private Foundations/Grants/Endowments; Business/Corporate Donations; Box Office; Government Grants; Individual Donations
Performance Facilities: Los Angeles County Museum of Art

THE INTERNATIONAL ASSOCIATION OF JAZZ APPRECIATION
PO Box 48146, Los Angeles, CA 90048
(310) 673-7541
FAX: (310) 673-0757
Founded: 1982
Arts Area: Orchestra; Ensemble; Band
Status: Non-Profit
Type: Performing; Educational
Purpose: To preserve jazz music through education and presentation
Officers: Wm. J. Coffey MD, Founder/President
Paid Staff: 2 **Volunteer Staff:** 7
Paid Artists: 100
Utilizes: Guest Artists
Budget: $100,000 - $500,000
Income Sources: Private Foundations/Grants/Endowments; Business/Corporate Donations; Box Office; Government Grants; Individual Donations
Season: 52 Weeks

"KOROYAR" FOLKLORE ENSEMBLE
PO Box 27873, Los Feliz Station, Los Angeles, CA 90027
(909) 627-7150
Founded: 1969
Arts Area: Ethnic; Folk; Instrumental Group
Status: Non-Profit
Type: Performing; Educational
Purpose: To present the music and dance of southeast Europe and the Near East in an entertaining, authentic and educational manner; to reveal and explore other aesthetics
Management: Richard Unciano, Executive Director; Loren Lichty, Administrative Director; Ron Muller, Music Director; Jim Dimitroff, Associate Director
Officers: Richard Unciano, President; Ron Muller, Vice President; Karen Bassett, Secretary
Volunteer Staff: 5
Non-Paid Artists: 14
Utilizes: Guest Artists
Budget: $1,000 - $50,000
Income Sources: Box Office
Season: 52 Weeks
Annual Attendance: 6,000
Affiliations: Folk Dance Federation of California

LOS ANGELES CHAMBER ORCHESTRA
315 West Ninth Street, Suite 801, Los Angeles, CA 90015
(213) 622-7001
FAX: (213) 955-2071
> **Founded:** 1968
> **Arts Area:** Orchestra; Chamber
> **Status:** Professional; Non-Profit
> **Type:** Performing; Touring; Resident
> **Purpose:** To perform literature of the chamber orchestra repertoire; to foster an appreciation of chamber music within the community
> **Management:** Deborah Rutter, Executive Director; Welz Kauffman, General Manager; Robert McMullin, Development Director; George Sebastian, Marketing Director; Gloria Sanchez, Finance Director
> **Officers:** Jennifer Diener, President; David Gersh, Chairman; Douglas Brengal, Ed Zolla, Robert Davidson, Vice Presidents
> **Paid Staff:** 11
> **Paid Artists:** 40
> **Utilizes:** Guest Conductors; Guest Artists; Guest Directors
> **Budget:** $1,000,000 - $5,000,000
> **Income Sources:** Private Foundations/Grants/Endowments; Business/Corporate Donations; Box Office; Government Grants; Individual Donations; Fundraising
> **Season:** October - May
> **Annual Attendance:** 55,000
> **Affiliations:** ASOL; Association of California Symphony Orchestras; AAA; California Arts Alliance
> **Performance Facilities:** Ambassador Auditorium; Royce Hall, UCLA; Japan America Theatre

LOS ANGELES PHILHARMONIC ASSOCIATION
135 North Grand Avenue, Los Angeles, CA 90012
(213) 972-7300
FAX: (213) 617-3065
> **Founded:** 1919
> **Arts Area:** Symphony; Orchestra; Chamber; Ensemble
> **Status:** Professional; Non-Profit
> **Type:** Performing; Touring; Educational; Sponsoring
> **Purpose:** To present symphonic music concerts and other music events; to promote an appreciation of symphonic music in our community
> **Management:** Ernest Fleischmann, Executive Vice President; Bennett McClellan, General Manager; Gene Pasquarelli, Finance Director
> **Officers:** Stanley Beyer, Chairman of the Board; C. Joseph LaBonte, President; Dennis Kent, Treasurer
> **Utilizes:** Special Technical Talent; Guest Conductors; Guest Artists
> **Budget:** Over 10,000,000
> **Income Sources:** Private Foundations/Grants/Endowments; Business/Corporate Donations; Box Office; Government Grants; Individual Donations
> **Season:** 52 Weeks
> **Annual Attendance:** 1,000,000
> **Performance Facilities:** Dorothy Chandler Pavilion; Hollywood Bowl

VIKLARBO CHAMBER EMSEMBLE
7969 West Fourth Street, Los Angeles, CA 90048
(213) 653-3330
> **Founded:** 1978
> **Arts Area:** Chamber; Ensemble; Instrumental Group; New Music
> **Status:** Professional; Non-Profit
> **Type:** Performing; Touring; Educational
> **Purpose:** To perform standard and contemporary works using an ensemble of flexible instrumentation including violin, viola, clarinet, cello and piano
> **Management:** Wendy Prober, Managing Director
> **Officers:** Michael Arlen, Kenneth Hertz, Board Members; Maria Newman, President; Wendy Prober, Chairman; Larry Kohorn, Secretary/Treasurer
> **Paid Staff:** 1   **Volunteer Staff:** 4
> **Paid Artists:** 4
> **Utilizes:** Guest Artists
> **Budget:** $1,000 - $50,000
> **Income Sources:** Private Foundations/Grants/Endowments; Box Office; Government Grants; Individual Donations
> **Season:** 52 Weeks
> **Annual Attendance:** 1,200
> **Affiliations:** CMA; AMC
> **Performance Facilities:** Murphy Hall, Loyola Marymount University; Hancock Auditorium, University of Southern California

VOCAL MUSIC

GUILD OPERA COMPANY, INC.
6425 Hollywood Boulevard, Los Angeles, CA 90028
(213) 463-6593
Founded: 1949
Arts Area: Grand Opera; Lyric Opera; Light Opera
Status: Professional; Non-Profit
Type: Performing; Touring; Educational
Purpose: To provide professional opera, fully staged with orchestra, for young audiences
Management: Gayle Blankenburg, Managing Director; Heinz Blankenburg, Artistic Director
Officers: Steven Siskin, President; Peter Ulrich, Vice President of Administration; Clarke Morrow, Vice President of Education; Carolyn Novin, Secretary; Tess Macaraya, Treasurer
Paid Staff: 2   **Volunteer Staff:** 8
Paid Artists: 50
Utilizes: Special Technical Talent; Guest Artists
Budget: $100,000 - $500,000
Income Sources: Private Foundations/Grants/Endowments; Business/Corporate Donations; Box Office; Government Grants; Individual Donations
Season: March - May   **Annual Attendance:** 16,000
Performance Facilities: Royce Hall, UCLA ; Marsee Auditorium; Glendale High School Auditorium

LOS ANGELES MASTER CHORALE ASSOCIATION
135 North Grand Avenue, Los Angeles, CA 90012
(213) 972-7282
FAX: (213) 972-7312
Arts Area: Choral
Status: Professional
Type: Performing; Resident; Educational
Purpose: To educate the public in the art of choral singing and to foster an appreciation of the art form
Management: Paul Salamunovich, Music Director; Roger Wagner, Founder/Music Director Laureate; Maurice Staples, General Manager; Mark Praigg, Assistant to General Manager
Officers: Marshall A. Rutter, Chairman; Clifford A. Miller, Executive Committee Chairman; Edward J. McAniss, President
Paid Staff: 6   **Volunteer Staff:** 1
Paid Artists: 75   **Non-Paid Artists:** 37
Utilizes: Guest Conductors; Guest Artists
Budget: $1,000,000 - $5,000,000
Income Sources: Private Foundations/Grants/Endowments; Business/Corporate Donations; Box Office; Government Grants; Individual Donations
Season: November - April
Annual Attendance: 52,900
Affiliations: CA
Performance Facilities: Dorothy Chandler Pavilion

LOS ANGELES MUSIC CENTER OPERA
135 North Grand Avenue, Los Angeles, CA 90012
(213) 972-7219
FAX: (213) 687-3490
Founded: 1986
Arts Area: Grand Opera
Status: Professional; Non-Profit
Type: Performing; Resident; Educational
Purpose: To present opera at its highest professional standard with international guest artists and a resident company
Management: Peter Hemmings, General Director; Placido Domingo, Artistic Consultant; Patricia Mitchell, Deputy General Director
Paid Staff: 32
Paid Artists: 300
Utilizes: Guest Conductors; Guest Artists; Guest Directors; Guest Designers
Budget: Over 10,000,000
Income Sources: Private Foundations/Grants/Endowments; Business/Corporate Donations; Box Office; Government Grants; Individual Donations
Season: September - June   **Annual Attendance:** 120,000
Affiliations: OA
Performance Facilities: Dorothy Chandler Pavilion

UNIVERSITY OF SOUTHERN CALIFORNIA OPERA
Ramo Hall, #208B, University Park, Los Angeles, CA 90089-0851
(213) 740-3109
FAX: (213) 740-3217
Founded: 1940
Arts Area: Grand Opera; Lyric Opera; Light Opera; Operetta
Status: Semi-Professional; Non-Profit
Type: Performing; Touring; Educational
Purpose: To provide a training ground and performance possibilities for aspiring young singers in all areas of performance; to present two full operas and various single scenes
Management: William Williams, Opera Manager/Professor; William Vendice, Resident Director/Conductor; Frans Boerlage, Stage Director
Paid Staff: 7
Non-Paid Artists: 25
Budget: $1,000 - $50,000
Income Sources: University
Season: September - May   **Annual Attendance:** 3,000
Affiliations: University of Southern California
Performance Facilities: Bing Theater

THEATRE

ACTORS FOR THEMSELVES
Matrix Theatre, 7657 Melrose Avenue, Los Angeles, CA 90048
(213) 852-1445
Founded: 1974
Arts Area: Professional; Theatrical Group
Status: Professional; Non-Profit
Type: Performing; Resident; Educational
Purpose: To give actors a chance to practice their craft and the opportunity to control the full process of theater production
Management: Joe Stern, Artistic Director
Paid Staff: 2
Utilizes: Special Technical Talent; Guest Artists; Guest Directors
Budget: $100,000 - $500,000
Income Sources: Private Foundations/Grants/Endowments; Business/Corporate Donations; Box Office; Government Grants; Individual Donations
Season: 52 Weeks
Performance Facilities: Matrix Theatre

ATTIC THEATRE
6562 1/2 Santa Monica Boulevard, Los Angeles, CA 90038
(213) 462-9720
Founded: 1987
Arts Area: Professional; Theatrical Group
Status: Semi-Professional; Commercial
Type: Performing; Resident; Sponsoring
Purpose: To maintain a small commercial theatre with a resident company; to rent the facility to outside productions
Management: James Carey, Artistic Director; Denise Ragan, Business Manager
Paid Staff: 2   **Volunteer Staff:** 7
Utilizes: Special Technical Talent; Guest Directors
Budget: $1,000 - $50,000
Income Sources: Box Office; Individual Donations
Season: February - December
Affiliations: Theatre Los Angeles

BILINGUAL FOUNDATION OF THE ARTS
421 North Avenue 19, Los Angeles, CA 90031
(213) 225-4044
FAX: (213) 225-1250
Founded: 1973
Arts Area: Professional; Theatrical Group
Status: Professional; Non-Profit
Type: Performing; Touring; Educational
Purpose: To celebrate the diversity and the richness of the Hispanic Theater tradition by producing and directing in both the English and the Spanish language
Management: Carmen Zapata, Producing Director; Margarita Galban, Artistic Director; Estela Scar, Los Angeles Theatre Alliance, Production Director; Jim Payne, Managing Director
Officers: Al Mejia, Chairman; Carmen Zapata, President

Paid Staff: 7　**Volunteer Staff:** 40
Paid Artists: 120
Utilizes: Guest Artists; Guest Directors
Budget: $500,000 - $1,000,000
Income Sources: Private Foundations/Grants/Endowments; Business/Corporate Donations; Government Grants; Individual Donations
Season: 52 Weeks　**Annual Attendance:** 80,000
Affiliations: AAA; TCG; California Confederation of the Arts
Performance Facilities: The Bilingual Foundation of the Arts

BOB BAKER PRODUCTIONS
1345 West First Street, Los Angeles, CA 90026
(213) 250-9995
Founded: 1963
Arts Area: Professional; Puppet
Status: Professional
Type: Resident
Purpose: To produce marionette productions, shop tours and birthday parties
Management: Bob Baker, Director; Tina Gainsboro, Theatre Manager
Paid Staff: 20
Budget: $100,000 - $500,000
Income Sources: Box Office
Season: 52 Weeks
Annual Attendance: 100,000

BURBAGE THEATRE ENSEMBLE
2330 Sawtelle Boulevard, Los Angeles, CA 90064
(310) 478-0897
Founded: 1969
Arts Area: Professional
Status: Professional; Non-Profit
Type: Performing; Touring
Purpose: To stimulate the creative growth of the arts in our community
Management: Ivan Spiegel, Andy Griggs, Co-Artistic Directors; Lucas McClure, Production Manager
Officers: Andy Griggs, President; William Mohr, Secretary; Ivan Spiegel, Treasurer
Paid Staff: 4　**Volunteer Staff:** 8
Paid Artists: 25　**Non-Paid Artists:** 15
Budget: $100,000 - $500,000
Income Sources: Private Foundations/Grants/Endowments; Business/Corporate Donations; Box Office; Government Grants; Individual Donations
Season: 52 Weeks
Annual Attendance: 20,000
Affiliations: TCG
Performance Facilities: Burbage Theatre

CELEBRATION THEATRE
4470-107 Sunset Boulevard, #353, Los Angeles, CA 90027
(213) 957-1884
Founded: 1982
Arts Area: Professional
Status: Professional; Non-Profit
Type: Resident; Educational
Purpose: To produce gay and lesbian plays exclusively; to celebrate the positive aspects of gay and lesbian culture
Management: Paul Borden, Executive Director; Ron Edwards, Artistic Director
Volunteer Staff: 12
Non-Paid Artists: 10
Utilizes: Special Technical Talent; Guest Artists; Guest Directors
Budget: $1,000 - $50,000
Income Sources: Box Office; Individual Donations
Season: 52 Weeks
Annual Attendance: 6,000
Affiliations: Los Angeles Theatre Alliance; Gay and Lesbian Theatre Alliance
Performance Facilities: Celebration Theatre

CO-REAL ARTISTS
1811 West 45th Street, Los Angeles, CA 90062
(310) 827-1353
Founded: 1969
Arts Area: Musical; Drama; Dance

Status: Semi-Professional; Non-Profit
Type: Performing; Touring; Educational
Purpose: To prepare and present undiscovered talent through workshops and quality community theater productions
Management: Genie Jackson, Founder/Executive Director
Officers: Genie Jackson, Chairman; Rena Gist, President; Lynn Blount, Administrative Assistant
Paid Staff: 1 **Volunteer Staff:** 13
Paid Artists: 15 **Non-Paid Artists:** 4
Budget: $1,000 - $50,000
Income Sources: Business/Corporate Donations; Box Office; Government Grants; Individual Donations
Annual Attendance: 25,000
Affiliations: California Confederation of the Arts

COLONY THEATRE COMPANY
1944 Riverside Drive, Los Angeles, CA 90039
(213) 665-3011
   Founded: 1975
   Arts Area: Theatrical Group
   Status: Semi-Professional; Non-Profit
   Type: Performing; Resident
   Management: Barbara Beckley, Producing Director
   Officers: Barbara Beckley, President; Michael Wadler, Vice President; Robert Canning, Secretary; Rosser Cole, Treasurer
   Utilizes: Special Technical Talent; Guest Artists; Guest Directors
   Budget: $50,000 - $100,000
   Income Sources: Business/Corporate Donations; Box Office; Government Grants; Individual Donations
   Season: July - June
   Annual Attendance: 15,000
   Affiliations: Equity-Waiver; TCG; California Theatre Council; Glendale Arts Council; AEA
   Performance Facilities: Studio Theatre Play House

THE COMPLEX
6476 Santa Monica Boulevard, Los Angeles, CA 90038
(213) 465-0383
   Founded: 1990
   Arts Area: Professional; Theatrical Group
   Status: Semi-Professional; Non-Professional
   Type: Performing
   Management: Matt Chait, Owner; John Bergantine, Assistant
   Paid Staff: 1
   Utilizes: Special Technical Talent
   Budget: $1,000 - $50,000
   Income Sources: Box Office; Individual Donations
   Season: 52 Weeks

DILLON STREET PLAYERS
802 North Dillon Street, Los Angeles, CA 90026
(213) 663-1664
FAX: (213) 663-1664
   Arts Area: Professional; Repertory
   Status: Professional
   Management: Scott Crawford, Artistic Director
   Volunteer Staff: 6
   Non-Paid Artists: 20
   Utilizes: Guest Artists; Guest Directors
   Budget: $100,000 - $500,000
   Income Sources: Private Foundations/Grants/Endowments; Business/Corporate Donations; Box Office; Individual Donations
   Affiliations: AEA

EAST WEST PLAYERS
4424 Santa Monica Boulevard, Los Angeles, CA 90029
(213) 660-0366
   Founded: 1965
   Arts Area: Professional
   Status: Professional; Non-Profit
   Type: Performing; Touring; Resident; Educational
   Purpose: To foster the creation of an Asian-American aesthetic point of view and theatre; to support the development of artists possessing outstanding talent and of new works which address this mission
   Management: Nobu McCarty, Artistic Director; Tom Donaldson, General Producer; Lisa Lee, Administrative Director

Officers: Toshizaku Terasawa, Chairman; Jeff Smith, President; John Kobara, Wenda Fong, Vice Presidents; Janie Gates, Secretary
Paid Staff: 8
Paid Artists: 100
Utilizes: Special Technical Talent; Guest Artists; Guest Directors
Budget: $100,000 - $500,000
Income Sources: Private Foundations/Grants/Endowments; Business/Corporate Donations; Box Office; Government Grants; Individual Donations
Season: October - July   **Annual Attendance:** 40,000
Affiliations: TCG; Los Angeles Theatre Alliance; California Confederation of the Arts
Performance Facilities: East West Players Theater

EBONY SHOWCASE THEATRE
4720 West Washington Boulevard, Los Angeles, CA 90016
(213) 936-1107
Founded: 1950
Arts Area: Theatrical Group
Status: Semi-Professional; Non-Profit
Type: Performing; Resident
Purpose: To educate; to foster artistic and cultural enrichment through entertainment
Management: Nick and Edna Stewart, Founders/Managing Directors
Utilizes: Guest Artists; Guest Directors
Budget: $1,000 - $50,000
Income Sources: Box Office; Individual Donations
Season: 52 Weeks
Performance Facilities: Ebony Showcase Theatre

GENE DYNARSKI THEATER ENSEMBLE
5600 Sunset Boulevard, Los Angeles, CA 90028
(213) 465-5600
Founded: 1977
Arts Area: Theater Group
Status: Professional; Non-Profit
Type: Performing
Purpose: To provide high-quality theater directed in an experimental and educational manner
Management: Gene Dynarski, Artistic/Administrative Director
Season: 52 Weeks
Performance Facilities: Gene Dynarski Theater

THE GROUNDLING THEATRE
7307 Melrose Avenue, Los Angeles, CA 90046
(213) 934-4747
Founded: 1972
Arts Area: Theatrical Group
Status: Non-Profit
Type: Performing; Resident
Purpose: To create new comedy talent and new comedy productions
Management: John Gidcomb, Theatre Manager
Paid Staff: 30
Budget: $100,000 - $500,000
Income Sources: Private Foundations/Grants/Endowments; Business/Corporate Donations; Box Office; Government Grants; Individual Donations
Season: 52 Weeks   **Annual Attendance:** 26,000
Performance Facilities: The Groundling Theatre

LOS ANGELES CIVIC LIGHT OPERA
6233 Hollywood Boulevard, Los Angeles, CA 90028
(213) 972-7550
Founded: 1936
Arts Area: Musical Theatre
Status: Non-Profit
Type: Performing
Purpose: To make available top-quality musical theatre in southern California by presenting revivals and originating new productions
Management: James M. Nederlander, Chairman of the Board; Stan Seiden, President; Neil Papiano, Treasurer
Paid Staff: 40
Utilizes: Special Technical Talent; Guest Conductors; Guest Artists; Guest Directors
Budget: $500,000 - $1,000,000
Income Sources: Box Office

Season: May - September   **Annual Attendance:** 130,000
Performance Facilities: Pantages Theatre

THE LOS ANGELES THEATRE ACADEMY
Los Angeles City College, 855 North Vermont Avenue, Los Angeles, CA 90029
(213) 963-4336
> **Founded:** 1929
> **Arts Area:** Theatrical Group
> **Status:** Non-Profit
> **Type:** Performing; Educational
> **Purpose:** To provide a professional training program to students in all areas of theatre arts and to support this training with professional-level productions
> **Management:** Winston Butler, Department Chairperson; Dena M. Paponis, Theatre Manager
> **Officers:** Greg Sexton, President; Louise Ksoot-Haukkes, Vice President; William Mohr, Secretary; Ivan Spiegel, Treasurer
> **Paid Staff:** 19
> **Non-Paid Artists:** 100
> **Utilizes:** Special Technical Talent; Guest Artists
> **Budget:** $100,000 - $500,000
> **Income Sources:** Box Office
> **Season:** September - June   **Annual Attendance:** 10,000
> **Affiliations:** Equity-Waiver; Los Angeles Theatre Alliance; SCETA; American College Theatre Festival

LOS ANGELES THEATRE CENTER
514 South Spring Street, Los Angeles, CA 90013
(213) 627-6500
FAX: (213) 624-6096
> **Founded:** 1975
> **Arts Area:** Professional
> **Status:** Professional; Non-Profit
> **Type:** Touring; Educational
> **Purpose:** To faciliate the production of performance pieces of all disciplines that further communication between multiethnic communities
> **Management:** Lee Sweet, Business Manager; Laural Meade, Rental Contact; David MacMurtry, Technical Director
> **Paid Staff:** 85   **Volunteer Staff:** 500
> **Paid Artists:** 65
> **Utilizes:** Special Technical Talent; Guest Artists
> **Budget:** $1,000,000 - $5,000,000
> **Income Sources:** Private Foundations/Grants/Endowments; Business/Corporate Donations; Box Office; Government Grants; Individual Donations
> **Season:** 52 Weeks   **Annual Attendance:** 250,000

MELROSE THEATRE ASSOCIATION
733 Seward Street, Los Angeles, CA 90038
(213) 465-1885
> **Founded:** 1964
> **Arts Area:** Professional; Theatrical Group
> **Status:** Professional; Non-Profit
> **Type:** Performing; Educational
> **Purpose:** To provide an extension of the learning process for professional actors; to offer beginning acting classes
> **Management:** Paul Kent, Artistic Director; Jomarie Ward, Administrator
> **Volunteer Staff:** 6
> **Non-Paid Artists:** 20
> **Utilizes:** Special Technical Talent; Guest Artists; Guest Directors
> **Budget:** $1,000 - $50,000
> **Income Sources:** Business/Corporate Donations; Box Office; Individual Donations
> **Season:** 52 Weeks   **Annual Attendance:** 8,000
> **Affiliations:** Los Angeles Theatre Alliance
> **Performance Facilities:** Melrose Theatre

NINE O'CLOCK PLAYERS
1367 North St. Andrews Place, Los Angeles, CA 90028
(213) 469-1973
> **Founded:** 1929
> **Arts Area:** Musical; Theatrical Group; Musical Theatre
> **Status:** Semi-Professional; Non-Profit
> **Type:** Performing; Touring

Purpose: To provide free musical theater for culturally and physically disadvantaged children as well as paid performances for all children of southern California; to donate proceeds to the services of the Assistance League of Southern California
Management: Assistance League of Southern California
Officers: Ottilie Laybourne, Chairman; Linnette Temple, First Vice Chairman; Doretta Lee, Second Vice Chairman; Suzanna Royse, Third Vice Chairman/Production
Volunteer Staff: 65
Utilizes: Guest Directors
Income Sources: Private Foundations/Grants/Endowments; Business/Corporate Donations; Box Office; Individual Donations
Season: September - May
Annual Attendance: 13,000
Performance Facilities: ALSC Playhouse

ODYSSEY THEATRE ENSEMBLE
2055 South Sepulveda Boulevard, Los Angeles, CA 90025
(310) 477-2055
FAX: (310) 444-0455
Founded: 1969
Arts Area: Professional; Musical; Theatrical Group
Status: Professional; Non-Profit
Type: Performing; Resident; Sponsoring
Purpose: To create an alternative, experimental theatre centre housing an ensemble company; to work towards the creation of an international theatre center
Management: Ron Sossi, Artistic Director; Jason Loewith, Production Manager
Officers: Lynn Miller, President of the Board
Paid Staff: 7   **Volunteer Staff:** 150
Paid Artists: 15   **Non-Paid Artists:** 35
Utilizes: Special Technical Talent; Guest Artists; Guest Directors
Budget: $100,000 - $500,000
Income Sources: Private Foundations/Grants/Endowments; Business/Corporate Donations; Box Office; Government Grants; Individual Donations
Season: 52 Weeks
Annual Attendance: 17,500
Affiliations: Theatre Consortium (Los Angeles Theatre Pass), League of Producers and Theatres of Los Angeles; Los Angeles Theatre Alliance; TCG; California Confederation of the Arts
Performance Facilities: Odyssey Theatre

PADUA HILLS PLAYWRIGHTS WORKSHOP
PO Box 461450, Los Angeles, CA 90046
(213) 913-2636
Arts Area: Professional
Status: Professional; Non-Profit
Type: Performing; Resident; Educational
Purpose: The workshop is a seven-week conference taught by 12 master playwrights. The concurrent Padua Hills Playwrights Festival annually produces premiere works written and directed by resident playwrights and performed by Padua's resident professional acting company.
Management: Murray Mednick, Artistic Director; Cheryl Slean, Managing Director
Officers: Barry Opper, President of the Board
Budget: $50,000 - $100,000
Income Sources: Private Foundations/Grants/Endowments; Box Office; Government Grants; Individual Donations
Season: 52 Weeks

PIPELINE, INC.
11901 Santa Monica Boulevard, #497, Los Angeles, CA 90025
(310) 207-4380
Founded: 1982
Arts Area: Professional
Status: Professional; Non-Profit
Type: Performing; Touring; Resident; Educational
Purpose: To provide innovative and socially relevant theatre using entertainment as a vehicle for education and communication for the audiences and artists of Los Angeles
Management: Scott Kelman, Artistic Director; Aaron Slavin, Executive Director
Officers: Aaron Slavin, Chairman; Isabel Holt, Rob Seltzen, Vice Chairmen
Paid Staff: 5
Paid Artists: 25
Utilizes: Special Technical Talent; Guest Artists; Guest Directors
Budget: $1,000 - $50,000

Income Sources: Private Foundations/Grants/Endowments; Business/Corporate Donations; Box Office; Government Grants; Individual Donations
Season: 52 Weeks   **Annual Attendance:** 20,000

STAGES THEATRE CENTER
1540 North McCadden Place, Los Angeles, CA 90028
(213) 463-5356; (213) 465-1010
FAX: (213) 462-3176
Founded: 1980
Arts Area: Professional
Status: Non-Profit
Type: Performing
Purpose: To present and promote uncelebrated multicultural theatrical works, in English and other languages, at a modest admission, devised, selected and presented by informed and gifted theatre practitioners
Management: Paul Verdier, Artistic Director; Kay Tornborg, Managing Director
Officers: Sonia Lloveras, Board President; Pompea Smith, Board Chair; Hilma Carter, Secretary; Sonia Lloveras, Treasurer
Paid Staff: 4
Utilizes: Guest Directors; Artists-in-Residence
Budget: $100,000 - $500,000
Income Sources: Private Foundations/Grants/Endowments; Business/Corporate Donations; Box Office; Government Grants; Individual Donations
Season: 52 Weeks   **Annual Attendance:** 6,000

THEATRE WEST
3333 Cahuenga Boulevard West, Los Angeles, CA 90068
(213) 851-4839
Founded: 1962
Arts Area: Theatrical Group
Status: Professional; Non-Profit
Type: Performing; Resident; Educational
Purpose: Theatre West conducts weekly theater workshops, produces several plays a year and strives to be a cultural force in the community.
Management: Douglas Marney, Managing Director; Mary Van Arsdel, Administrative Assistant; Norman Cohen, Artistic Moderator
Officers: Timothy J. Noyes, Chairman; Valeri Jackson, Vice Chairperson; Kevin West, Secretary
Paid Staff: 3   **Volunteer Staff:** 7
Paid Artists: 60
Utilizes: Guest Directors
Budget: $100,000 - $500,000
Income Sources: Private Foundations/Grants/Endowments; Business/Corporate Donations; Box Office; Government Grants; Individual Donations
Season: 40 weeks   **Annual Attendance:** 10,000
Affiliations: AEA
Performance Facilities: Theatre West

THE WESTWOOD PLAYHOUSE
10886 Le Conte Avenue, Los Angeles, CA 90024
(310) 208-5454
Founded: 1974
Arts Area: Professional; Musical
Status: Professional; Commercial
Type: Performing; Resident
Purpose: To produce quality theatre in a broad range of presentations of many moods and characters; to present comedy, drama, musicals, new plays, revivals, classics, experimental children's theatre, special events, multimedia
Management: Eric Krebs, Executive Directors
Officers: Paul Morer, General Manager
Utilizes: Special Technical Talent; Guest Artists; Guest Directors
Budget: $100,000 - $500,000
Income Sources: Box Office
Season: 52 Weeks   **Annual Attendance:** 90,000
Performance Facilities: The Westwood Playhouse

THE WORLD'S FIRST INNER-MUSICAL THEATRE
1743 East 122nd Street, Los Angeles, CA 90059
(213) 636-7733
Founded: 1986
Arts Area: Musical; Community; Theatrical Group
Status: Non-Profit

Type: Performing; Touring; Educational
Purpose: To perform theatrical plays, using the inner-music or emotion-mastery acting technique involving expression of emotional punctuation symbols (a new art form)
Management: J.L. Sherman, Director
Officers: J.L. Sherman, President
Volunteer Staff: 3
Non-Paid Artists: 35
Utilizes: Special Technical Talent; Guest Artists; Guest Directors
Budget: $1,000 - $50,000
Income Sources: Box Office; Individual Donations
Season: 52 Weeks
Affiliations: Emotion Mastery Seminars

ZEPHYR THEATRE
7456 Melrose Avenue, Los Angeles, CA 90046
(213) 653-4667
Founded: 1977
Arts Area: Professional
Status: Professional; Commercial
Type: Performing
Purpose: To produce new work
Management: Stephen Barber, General Manager; Lee Sankowicz, Artistic Director
Paid Staff: 5
Paid Artists: 100
Utilizes: Guest Artists; Guest Directors
Budget: $50,000 - $100,000
Income Sources: Box Office
Season: 52 Weeks   **Annual Attendance:** 20,000
Affiliations: Los Angeles League of Theaters and Producers
Performance Facilities: Zephyr Theatre

PERFORMING SERIES

BING CONCERTS
5905 Wilshire Boulevard, Los Angeles, CA 90036
(213) 857-6000
Founded: 1965
Arts Area: Vocal Music; Instrumental Music
Status: Professional; Non-Profit
Type: Performing
Purpose: To present programs as a special benefit for members of the Los Angeles County Museum of Art
Management: Dorrance Stalvey, Director of Music Programs
Paid Staff: 1
Utilizes: Guest Conductors; Guest Artists
Budget: $1,000 - $50,000
Income Sources: Private Foundations/Grants/Endowments; Box Office
Season: July - June   **Annual Attendance:** 5,000
Affiliations: Los Angeles County Museum of Art
Performance Facilities: Leo S. Bing Theatre, Los Angeles County Museum of Art

CHAMBER MUSIC/LA FESTIVAL
3264 Primera Place, Los Angeles, CA 90068
(213) 850-8064
Founded: 1985
Arts Area: Instrumental Music; Festivals
Status: Professional
Type: Performing
Purpose: To promote appreciation and understanding of chamber music
Management: Susanne Glass, Executive Director; Yukiko Kamei, Artistic Director
Officers: James Arkatov, President; Josh Livingston, Vice President; Manya Schaff, Secretary; Mary Archibald, Treasurer
Paid Staff: 2   **Volunteer Staff:** 5
Paid Artists: 20
Utilizes: Guest Artists
Budget: $100,000 - $500,000
Income Sources: Private Foundations/Grants/Endowments; Business/Corporate Donations; Box Office; Government Grants; Individual Donations

Season: May **Annual Attendance:** 5,000
Performance Facilities: Japan America Theatre

CITY OF LOS ANGELES CULTURAL AFFAIRS DEPARTMENT
433 South Spring Street, 10th Floor, Los Angeles, CA 90013
(213) 485-2433
FAX: (213) 485-6835
Founded: 1980
Arts Area: Dance; Vocal Music; Instrumental Music; Theater; Festivals
Status: Non-Profit
Type: Performing
Purpose: To bring cultural events, both visual and performance-related, to the people of Los Angeles
Management: Adolfo Nodal, General Manager; Rodney Punt, Ann Giagmi, Assistant General Managers
Officers: David Smith, President; Julie A. Sgarzi, Vice President
Paid Staff: 60
Paid Artists: 125
Utilizes: Special Technical Talent; Guest Conductors; Guest Artists; Guest Directors
Budget: $1,000,000 - $5,000,000
Season: 52 Weeks
Annual Attendance: 25,000

FESTIVAL PLAYERS OF CALIFORNIA
3809 DeLongpre Avenue, Los Angeles, CA 90027
(213) 665-6444
Founded: 1957
Arts Area: Dance; Vocal Music; Instrumental Music; Theater; Festivals
Status: Professional; Non-Profit
Type: Performing; Touring; Educational; Sponsoring
Purpose: To present a full spectrum of performing and visual arts experiences, geared to meet the multicultural needs of the southern California community
Management: Dr. Dorye Roettger, Founder/Director; Margaret Bonadurer, Associate Director
Officers: Marion E. Rutger, President; Lewis I. Williams, Vice President; Caryl Warner, Secretary/Treasurer
Utilizes: Special Technical Talent; Guest Artists; Guest Directors
Budget: $1,000 - $50,000
Income Sources: Private Foundations/Grants/Endowments; Business/Corporate Donations; Government Grants; Individual Donations
Season: 52 Weeks

GREEK THEATRE
2700 North Vermont Avenue, Los Angeles, CA 90027
(213) 665-1927
Founded: 1930
Arts Area: Dance; Vocal Music; Instrumental Music; Theater
Status: Commercial
Type: Performing
Purpose: To present a variety of contemporary entertainment including concerts, Broadway plays, and comedy
Management: Susan Rosenbluth, General Manager
Utilizes: Special Technical Talent; Guest Artists
Income Sources: Box Office
Season: May - October
Performance Facilities: Greek Theatre

HOLLYWOOD BOWL SUMMER FESTIVAL
c/o Los Angeles Philharmonic Association, 135 North Grand Avenue, Los Angeles, CA 90012
(213) 972-7300
FAX: (213) 617-3065
Arts Area: Dance; Vocal Music; Instrumental Music; Festivals; Recitals; Jazz
Status: Professional; Non-Profit
Type: Performing; Touring; Resident; Educational; Sponsoring
Purpose: To provide a summer home for the Los Angeles Philharmonic and the Hollywood Bowl Orchestra; to present a summer festival featuring artists in the classical, pop, and jazz fields
Management: Anne Parsons, General Manager; Kathy Henkel, Publicity Assistant; Ernest Fleischmann, Executive Vice President/Managing Director; Esa-Pekka Salonen, Music Director of the Los Angeles Philharmonic; John Mauceri, Conductor of the Hollywood Bowl Orchestra
Officers: Stanley Beyer, Chairman of the Board; C. Joseph LaBonte, President of the Board, Los Angeles Philharmonic
Budget: Over 10,000,000
Season: June - September

Affiliations: Los Angeles Philharmonic
Performance Facilities: Hollywood Bowl

INNER CITY CULTURAL CENTER
North Hyland Avenue, Suite 200, Los Angeles, CA 90028
(213) 962-2102
FAX: (213) 962-2403
    Founded: 1966
    Arts Area: Dance; Theater
    Status: Professional; Non-Profit
    Type: Performing; Educational; Sponsoring
    Purpose: Through an extensive program of professionally-produced plays, concerts, exhibits and events, we attempt to explore and develop interest in the arts of all people. The Center maintains a multiracial policy in all aspects of its operation.
    Management: C. Bernard Jackson, Executive Director
    Officers: C. Bernard Jackson, Executive Vice President
    Paid Staff: 15
    Utilizes: Special Technical Talent; Guest Artists
    Budget: $100,000 - $500,000
    Income Sources: Business/Corporate Donations; Box Office; Government Grants; Individual Donations
    Season: September - June

LOS ANGELES COUNTY MUSEUM OF ART: MUSIC PROGRAMS
5905 Wilshire Boulevard, Los Angeles, CA 90036
(213) 857-6115
FAX: (213) 931-7347
    Founded: 1939
    Arts Area: Vocal Music; Instrumental Music
    Status: Professional; Non-Profit
    Type: Performing
    Purpose: To produce concerts of chamber music and Jazz
    Management: Dorrance Stalvey, Director of Music Programs; Cheryl Tiano, Administration/Promotion
    Paid Staff: 2
    Utilizes: Special Technical Talent; Guest Conductors; Guest Artists
    Budget: $100,000 - $500,000
    Income Sources: Private Foundations/Grants/Endowments; Business/Corporate Donations; Box Office; Government Grants; Individual Donations
    Season: 52 Weeks   **Annual Attendance:** 28,000
    Affiliations: Los Angeles County Museum of Art
    Performance Facilities: Leo S. Bing Theater

LOS ANGELES FESTIVAL
PO Box 5210, Los Angeles, CA 90055
(213) 689-8800
    Founded: 1985
    Arts Area: Dance; Vocal Music; Instrumental Music; Theater; Festivals; Lyric Opera; Grand Opera; Media; Literary; Visual
    Status: Professional; Non-Profit
    Type: Performing; Sponsoring
    Purpose: To present an international festival of the performing arts
    Management: Peter Sellars, Artistic Director; Allison Sampson, Executive Director
    Officers: Maureen A. Kindel, Chairman of the Board
    Utilizes: Special Technical Talent; Guest Conductors; Guest Artists; Guest Directors
    Budget: $1,000,000 - $5,000,000
    Income Sources: Private Foundations/Grants/Endowments; Business/Corporate Donations; Box Office; Government Grants; Individual Donations
    Season: September (biannually)   **Annual Attendance:** 150,000

THE MUSIC CENTER OF LOS ANGELES COUNTY
135 North Grand Avenue, Los Angeles, CA 90012
(213) 972-7570
    Founded: 1964
    Arts Area: Dance; Vocal Music; Instrumental Music; Theater; Festivals; Grand Opera
    Status: Professional; Non-Profit
    Type: Performing; Resident; Educational; Sponsoring
    Purpose: To sponsor educational outreach programs; to provide fund-raising support for the resident performing companies of the Los Angeles County Music Center

Officers: James A. Thomas, Chairman; Esther Watchell, President; Lyle Marshall, Vice President of Finance/Administration; Susan Pearce, Vice President of the Music Center Unified Fund; Louise Otis, Vice President of Donor Relations; Larry Landre, Vice President of Marketing and Communications; Joan Boyett, Vice President of Education
Paid Staff: 65   **Volunteer Staff:** 1,000
Budget: Over 10,000,000
Income Sources: Private Foundations/Grants/Endowments; Business/Corporate Donations; Box Office; Government Grants; Individual Donations; Retail; Travel Operations
Season: 52 Weeks   **Annual Attendance:** 2,000,000
Affiliations: Los Angeles Philharmonic Association; Center Theatre Group; Music Center Opera Association; Los Angeles Master Chorale Association; Music Center Operating Company; Music Center Education Division

OCCIDENTAL COLLEGE ARTIST SERIES
1600 Campus Road, Los Angeles, CA 90041
(213) 259-2737; (213) 259-2922
FAX: (213) 341-4987
    Founded: 1887
    Arts Area: Dance; Vocal Music; Instrumental Music; Theater; World Music
    Status: Non-Profit
    Type: Sponsoring
    Management: Sandy Robertson, Marketing Consultant; Terri Gens, Technical Director for Theatres
    Paid Staff: 2
    Season: October - April
    Performance Facilities: Thorne Hall; Keck Theater

FACILITY

BOB BAKER MARIONETTE THEATER
1345 West First Street, Los Angeles, CA 90026
(213) 250-9995
    Founded: 1963
    Type of Facility: Theatre House; Room
    Facility Originally: Warehouse
    Type of Stage: Proscenium; 3/4 Arena
    Seating Capacity: 245
    Year Built: 1930
    Year Remodeled: 1963
    Contact for Rental: Tina Gainsboro;   (213) 250-9995
    Resident Groups: Bob Baker Marionette Theater

CALIFORNIA PLAZA
300 South Grand Avenue, Suite 3200, Los Angeles, CA 90071
(213) 687-2190
FAX: (213) 687-2191
    Founded: 1987
    Type of Facility: Outdoor (Concert); Environmental; Amphitheater
    Type of Stage: Thrust; Flexible; Greek; Environmental
    Stage Dimensions: 1 at 40'x60'; 2 at 26' diameter
    Seating Capacity: 350; 550; 1,000
    Year Built: 1985   **Architect:** Arthur Erickson
    Year Remodeled: 1992   **Architect:** Arthur Erickson
    Contact for Rental: Melissa Schwartz;   (213) 687-2190

CALIFORNIA STATE UNIVERSITY-LOS ANGELES - MUSIC HALL
5151 State University Drive, Los Angeles, CA 90032
(213) 224-3348
    Type of Facility: Concert Hall
    Type of Stage: Proscenium
    Stage Dimensions: 18'x45'x24'   **Orchestra Pit**
    Seating Capacity: 195
    Year Built: 1957   **Architect:** Architecture Department, State of California   **Cost:** $2,500,000
    Contact for Rental: Mickey Fruchter;   (213) 224-3348
    Resident Groups: California State University Music Department

CALIFORNIA STATE UNIVERSITY-LOS ANGELES - PLAYHOUSE
5151 State University Drive, Los Angeles, CA 90032
(213) 224-3345
    Type of Facility: Theatre House
    Type of Stage: Proscenium

Stage Dimensions: 52'x84'x35'   **Orchestra Pit**
Seating Capacity: 422
Year Built: 1958   **Architect:** Architecture Department, State of California   **Cost:** $2,500,000
Contact for Rental: Ellen Ketchum;   (213) 224-3344
Resident Groups: Theatre Department

CELEBRATION THEATRE
7051B Santa Monica Boulevard, Los Angeles, CA 90028
(213) 957-1884
Type of Facility: Theatre House
Facility Originally: Business Facility
Type of Stage: Arena
Stage Dimensions: 15'x30'x20'
Seating Capacity: 50
Year Built: 1970   **Cost:** $4,000
Year Remodeled: 1983   **Cost:** $10,000
Contact for Rental: Chuck Rowland;   (213) 876-4257
Resident Groups: Celebration Theatre

EAST WEST PLAYERS
4424 Santa Monica Boulevard, Los Angeles, CA 90029
(213) 660-0366
FAX: (213) 666-1929
Founded: 1967
Type of Facility: Theatre House
Facility Originally: Ceramics Factory
Type of Stage: Flexible; Proscenium
Seating Capacity: 99
Year Remodeled: 1972   **Architect:** Rae Creevey   **Cost:** $5,000
Manager: Nobu McCarthy, Artistic Director

GREEK THEATRE
2700 North Vermont Avenue, Los Angeles, CA 90027
(213) 480-3232
Type of Facility: Outdoor (Concert); Performance Center; Theatre House; Amphitheater
Type of Stage: Proscenium
Stage Dimensions: 54'Wx23'H proscenium opening; 42'Dx60'W   **Orchestra Pit**
Seating Capacity: 6,187
Year Built: 1930
Year Remodeled: 1983   **Architect:** McClellan Cruz Glaylord & Associates   **Cost:** $1,000,000
Contact for Rental: Susan Rosenbluth;   (213) 665-5857

JAPAN AMERICA THEATER
244 South San Pedro Street, Los Angeles, CA 90012
(213) 680-3700
FAX: (213) 617-8576
Type of Facility: Theatre Complex; Concert Hall
Type of Stage: Thrust; Proscenium; Apron - 5' Deep
Stage Dimensions: 48'Wx36.5'Dx22.5'H   **Orchestra Pit**
Seating Capacity: 841
Year Built: 1983   **Architect:** Kajima Architecture
Contact for Rental: Teusa Koiwai;   (213) 680-3700

LOS ANGELES COUNTY MUSEUM OF ART - LEO S. BING THEATER
5905 Wilshire Boulevard, Los Angeles, CA 90036
(213) 857-6031
FAX: (213) 931-7347
Type of Facility: Concert Hall; Performance Center; Theatre House; Multi-Purpose
Type of Stage: Proscenium
Stage Dimensions: 36'Wx26'Dx18'H
Seating Capacity: 603
Year Built: 1965

LOS ANGELES THEATRE CENTER
514 South Spring Street, Los Angeles, CA 90013
(213) 627-6500
FAX: (213) 624-6096
Type of Facility: Theatre Complex; Performance Center

Facility Originally: Bank
Type of Stage: Thrust; Flexible; Proscenium; Modified Thrust (35'x35')
Stage Dimensions: 40'x45'; 30'x40'; 40'x28'
Seating Capacity: 498; 296; 323; 99
Year Built: 1916   **Architect:** John Parkinson
Year Remodeled: 1985   **Architect:** John Sergio Fisher   **Cost:** $16,000,000
Acoustical Consultant: John Sergio Fisher
Contact for Rental: Chaz McEwan, Laurel Meade;   (213) 627-6500
Contained within the Theatre Center are Theatre 2, Theatre 3, Theatre 4 and Tom Bradley Theatre. See separate listings for additional information.

LOS ANGELES THEATRE CENTER - THEATRE 2
514 South Spring Street, Los Angeles, CA 90013
(213) 627-6500
Type of Facility: Auditorium
Type of Stage: Proscenium
Stage Dimensions: 53'Wx25'D   **Orchestra Pit**
Seating Capacity: 296
Contact for Rental: Laurel Meade;   (213) 627-6500

LOS ANGELES THEATRE CENTER - THEATRE 3
514 South Spring Street, Los Angeles, CA 90013
(213) 627-6500
Type of Facility: Concert Hall
Type of Stage: Greek
Stage Dimensions: 40'Wx32'D
Seating Capacity: 323
Contact for Rental: Laurel Meade;   (213) 627-6500

LOS ANGELES THEATRE CENTER - THEATRE 4
514 South Spring Street, Los Angeles, CA 90013
(213) 627-6500
Type of Facility: Multi-Purpose; Room
Type of Stage: Flexible
Stage Dimensions: 44'Wx25'D, size of entire room
Seating Capacity: 99 maximum
Contact for Rental: Laurel Meade;   (213) 627-6500

LOS ANGELES THEATRE CENTER - TOM BRADLEY THEATRE
514 South Spring Street, Los Angeles, CA 90013
(213) 627-6500
Type of Facility: Theatre House
Type of Stage: Thrust
Stage Dimensions: 38'Wx44'D
Seating Capacity: 503
Contact for Rental: Chaz McEwan;   (213) 627-6500

MUNICIPAL ART GALLERY - GALLERY THEATER
Barnsdall Art Park, 4804 Hollywood Boulevard, Los Angeles, CA 90027
(213) 485-2460
Type of Facility: Theatre House
Type of Stage: Proscenium; Modified Apron Proscenium
Stage Dimensions: 50'Wx26'D; 29'Wx15'3"H proscenium opening
Seating Capacity: 295
Contact for Rental: Maxene Wolf;   (213) 485-2460

THE MUSIC CENTER OF LOS ANGELES COUNTY
135 North Grand Avenue, Los Angeles, CA 90012
(213) 972-7211
FAX: (213) 972-7474
Type of Facility: Theatre Complex; Performance Center
Year Built: 1967   **Architect:** Welton Beckett   **Cost:** $34,500,000
Acoustical Consultant: R. Lawrence Kirkegaard; Abraham Meltzer
Contact for Rental: Gordon Jenkins, Booking Manager;   (213) 972-7489
Resident Groups: Los Angeles Master Chorale; Glendale Symphony Orchestra
Contained within the Music Center are the Ahmanson Theater, Dorothy Chandler Pavilion and Mark Taper Forum. See individual listings for additional information.

THE MUSIC CENTER OF LOS ANGELES COUNTY - AHMANSON THEATER
135 North Grand Avenue, Los Angeles, CA 90012
(213) 972-7211
FAX: (213) 972-7474
    Type of Facility: Theatre House
    Type of Stage: Proscenium
    Stage Dimensions: 109'6"Wx47'Dx67'H; 40'Wx28'6"H proscenium opening   **Orchestra Pit**
    Seating Capacity: 2,071
    Year Built: 1967
    Contact for Rental: Gordon Jenkins, Booking Manager;   (213) 972-7479
    Resident Groups: Center Theater Group

THE MUSIC CENTER OF LOS ANGELES COUNTY - DOROTHY CHANDLER PAVILION
135 North Grand Avenue, Los Angeles, CA 90012
(213) 972-7211
FAX: (213) 972-7474
    Type of Facility: Concert Hall
    Type of Stage: Proscenium
    Stage Dimensions: 121'Wx60'Dx95'H; 58'Wx30'H proscenium opening   **Orchestra Pit**
    Seating Capacity: 3,197
    Year Built: 1967
    Contact for Rental: Gordon Jenkins, Booking Manager;   (213) 972-7489

THE MUSIC CENTER OF LOS ANGELES COUNTY - MARK TAPER FORUM
135 North Grand Avenue, Los Angeles, CA 90012
(213) 972-7211
FAX: (213) 972-7474
    Type of Facility: Theatre House
    Type of Stage: Thrust
    Stage Dimensions: 36'2"Wx30'D
    Seating Capacity: 737
    Year Built: 1967   **Architect:** Welton Beckett
    Acoustical Consultant: R. Lawrence Kirkegaard; Abraham Meltzer
    Contact for Rental: Gordon Jenkins, Booking Manager;   (213) 972-7489
    Resident Groups: Center Theater Group; Los Angeles Master Chorale; Los Angeles Philharmonic Orchestra; Music Center Opera, Education Division

OCCIDENTAL COLLEGE - THORNE HALL
1600 Campus Road, Los Angeles, CA 90041
(213) 259-2737
    Type of Facility: Auditorium
    Type of Stage: Proscenium   **Orchestra Pit**
    Seating Capacity: 960
    Year Built: 1938
    Year Remodeled: 1989
    Contact for Rental: Terri Gens;   (213) 259-2737

SHRINE AUDITORIUM AND EXPOSITION CENTER
649 West Jefferson Boulevard, Los Angeles, CA 90007
(213) 748-5116
FAX: (213) 742-9922
    Type of Facility: Theatre Complex; Concert Hall; Auditorium; Theatre House; Opera House; Civic Center; Multi-Purpose
    Type of Stage: Proscenium   **Orchestra Pit**
    Seating Capacity: 6,300
    Year Built: 1925   **Architect:** John C. Austin
    Year Remodeled: 1986   **Architect:** William D. Coffey & Associates
    Contact for Rental: Douglas Worthington;   (213) 748-5116
    Resident Groups: Soul Train Music Awards; American Music Awards; Ballet Folkloreico De Mexico; Comedy Awards

SHUBERT THEATRE
2020 Avenue of the Stars, Los Angeles, CA 90067
(310) 201-1500; (800) 233-3123
FAX: (310) 201-1585
    Type of Facility: Theatre House
    Type of Stage: Proscenium
    Stage Dimensions: 80'H deck to grid, ; 53'Wx30'H proscenium opening   **Orchestra Pit**
    Seating Capacity: 1,829
    Year Built: 1971   **Architect:** Henry George Greene, AIA

Contact for Rental: Lawrence K. O'Conner; (213) 201-1500
Manager: Alisa Fishbach

UNIVERSITY OF CALIFORNIA-LOS ANGELES - ROYCE HALL
405 Hilgard Avenue, Los Angeles, CA 90024
(310) 825-8981
    Type of Facility: Theatre House
    Type of Stage: Proscenium
    Stage Dimensions: 80'Wx35'D **Orchestra Pit**
    Seating Capacity: 1,843
    Year Built: 1929
    Year Remodeled: 1984 **Architect:** Carl Werniche Associates **Cost:** $10,000,000
    Acoustical Consultant: Bolt, Beranek & Newman
    Contact for Rental: UCLA Center for Performing Arts; (310) 206-8745
    Manager: James Bates, Technical Director
    Resident Groups: Los Angeles Philharmonic; American Youth Symphony; UCLA Dance Company; Los Angeles Chamber Orchestra
    Cultural Events; Film; Lectures

UNIVERSITY OF CALIFORNIA-LOS ANGELES - WADSWORTH THEATER
405 Hilgard Avenue, Los Angeles, CA 90024
(310) 206-8745
    Type of Facility: Theatre House
    Type of Stage: Proscenium
    Seating Capacity: 1,400
    Year Built: 1951
    Year Remodeled: 1983 **Architect:** Brian Murphy Associates
    Contact for Rental: UCLA Center for Performing Arts; (310) 206-8745
    Manager: James Bates, Technical Director

UNIVERSITY OF SOUTHERN CALIFORNIA - BOVARD AUDITORIUM
Los Angeles, CA 90089
(213) 740-2311
    Type of Facility: Auditorium
    Type of Stage: Thrust; Proscenium
    Seating Capacity: 1,600
    Year Built: 1921
    Year Remodeled: 1980
    Contact for Rental: Joe Singer; (213) 740-2514
    Resident Groups: University of Southern California Department of Music
    Rental limited to university-sponsored events and time availability

Malibu

INSTRUMENTAL MUSIC

SEAVER COLLEGE COMMUNITY SYMPHONY
c/o Music Department, Malibu, CA 90263
(310) 456-4503
    Founded: 1983
    Arts Area: Symphony
    Status: Semi-Professional
    Type: Performing
    Purpose: To train our students; to provide a good symphonic experience for our audience which includes students and people from the community
    Management: Thomas Osborn, Music Director/Conductor
    Paid Staff: 1 **Volunteer Staff:** 2
    Paid Artists: 27 **Non-Paid Artists:** 38
    Utilizes: Guest Artists
    Budget: $1,000 - $50,000
    Season: October - May
    Annual Attendance: 15,000
    Performance Facilities: Smothers Theatre, Pepperdine University; Railt Recital Hall

FACILITY

PEPPERDINE UNIVERSITY - AMPHITHEATRE, FINE ARTS DIVISION
24255 Pacific Coast Highway, Malibu, CA 90263-9605
(310) 456-4264
    Type of Facility: Amphitheater
    Type of Stage: Flexible
    Stage Dimensions: Open 32'x32'
    Seating Capacity: 400
    Year Built: 1972 **Architect:** William Periera and Associates
    Contact for Rental: Director of Auxiliary Services; (310) 456-4264

PEPPERDINE UNIVERSITY - MINI-THEATRE, FINE ARTS DIVISION
24255 Pacific Coast Highway, Malibu, CA 90263-9605
(310) 456-4264
    Type of Facility: Mini-theatre
    Facility Originally: School
    Type of Stage: Proscenium
    Stage Dimensions: 9'x24'x11'
    Seating Capacity: 48
    Year Built: 1972 **Architect:** William Periera and Associates
    Year Remodeled: 1977 **Cost:** $3,000
    Contact for Rental: Director of Auxiliary Services; (310) 456-4264
    Manager: Dr. Jerry Henderson

PEPPERDINE UNIVERSITY - SMOTHERS THEATRE
24255 Pacific Coast Highway, Malibu, CA 90263-4522
(213) 456-4558
    Type of Facility: Theatre Complex
    Type of Stage: Proscenium
    Stage Dimensions: 80'x30' **Orchestra Pit**
    Seating Capacity: 515
    Year Built: 1980 **Architect:** Neptune & Thomas **Cost:** $3,500,000
    Acoustical Consultant: Purcell & Noppe
    Contact for Rental: Marnie Duke-Mitze, Managing Director; (213) 456-4558
    Resident Groups: University Theatre and Music Departments

Mendocino

DANCE

MENDOCINO DANCE SERIES
PO Box 453, Mendocino, CA 95460
(707) 937-5611
    Founded: 1982
    Arts Area: Modern; Ballet; Jazz; Ethnic; Folk; Tap
    Status: Non-Profit
    Type: Presenting
    Management: Rhoda Teplow, Executive Director
    Paid Staff: 10 **Volunteer Staff:** 30
    Paid Artists: 100
    Utilizes: Special Technical Talent; Guest Artists; Guest Directors; Guest Choreographers
    Budget: $50,000 - $100,000
    Income Sources: Private Foundations/Grants/Endowments; Business/Corporate Donations; Box Office; Government Grants; Individual Donations
    Season: November - June **Annual Attendance:** 3,000
    Affiliations: WAAA; AAA; California Presenters
    Performance Facilities: Cotton Auditorium

PERFORMING SERIES

MENDOCINO MUSIC FESTIVAL ASSOCIATION
PO Box 1808, Mendocino, CA 95460
(707) 937-2044
    Founded: 1986
    Arts Area: Vocal Music; Instrumental Music
    Status: Professional; Non-Profit
    Type: Performing

Purpose: To blend the best of several orchestras - music history in the making
Management: Allan Pollack, Musical Director; Carolyn Steinbuck, Executive Manager; Walter Green, Artistic Advisor/Orchestra Manager
Paid Staff: 10
Paid Artists: 45   **Non-Paid Artists:** 22
Utilizes: Special Technical Talent; Guest Artists
Budget: $100,000 - $500,000
Income Sources: Business/Corporate Donations; Box Office; Individual Donations
Season: July - August   **Annual Attendance:** 4,200
Performance Facilities: The Grounds of the Ford House

FACILITY

MENDOCINO ART CENTER - HELEN SCHOENI THEATER
45200 Little Lake Road, Mendocino, CA 95460
(707) 937-4477
Type of Facility: Theatre House
Type of Stage: Proscenium
Stage Dimensions: 30'x20'
Seating Capacity: 81
Year Built: 1970   **Cost:** $58,000
Contact for Rental: Diana DeWees, Marjorie Eseppi;   (707) 937-4477
Resident Groups: Mendocino Theatre Company

Mill Valley

INSTRUMENTAL MUSIC

MILL VALLEY CHAMBER MUSIC SOCIETY
PO Box 5121, Mill Valley, CA 94942
(415) 383-7359
Founded: 1974
Arts Area: Chamber; Ensemble; Instrumental Group
Status: Non-Profit
Type: Educational; Sponsoring
Purpose: To present an annual subscription series that includes five concerts each season
Officers: Nelson N. Foote, President; Robert Glasson, Treasurer
Volunteer Staff: 17
Paid Artists: 20
Utilizes: Guest Artists
Budget: $1,000 - $50,000
Income Sources: Private Foundations/Grants/Endowments; Business/Corporate Donations; Box Office; Government Grants; Individual Donations
Season: October - May   **Annual Attendance:** 1,600

THEATRE

MARIN THEATRE COMPANY
397 Miller Avenue, Mill Valley, CA 94941
(415) 388-5200
FAX: (415) 381-3724
Founded: 1966
Arts Area: Professional; Theatrical Group
Status: Professional; Non-Profit
Type: Performing; Resident; Educational; Sponsoring
Purpose: To present a season of theatrical performances; to foster development of new plays; to provide theatrical training and present other art forms
Management: Joanne Williams, Public Relations; Lee Sankowich, Artistic Director; Regina Lickteig, Managing Director; Katherine Boneti, Development Director
Officers: Herb Boyer, Board President
Paid Staff: 4
Utilizes: Special Technical Talent; Guest Artists; Guest Directors
Budget: $1,000,000 - $5,000,000
Income Sources: Private Foundations/Grants/Endowments; Business/Corporate Donations; Box Office; Government Grants; Individual Donations
Season: September - June
Affiliations: TCG
Performance Facilities: Marin Theatre Company

Mission Hills

THEATRE

LITTLE BROADWAY PRODUCTIONS, INC.
PO Box 5008, Mission Hills, CA 91395-0008
(818) 894-4222; (800) 527-8747
FAX: (818) 891-1813
Arts Area: Musical; Musical Theatre for Children
Status: Professional; Non-Profit
Type: Performing; Touring
Purpose: To present quality main-stage musical theatre to young audiences
Management: Jill Shawn Adereth, Executive Producer; Marily Weitz, Artistic Director; Cathy Kelleher, Office/Tour Manager; Michael Benson, Technical Director
Officers: Jill Shawn Adereth, Chairman/Treasurer; Marilyn Weitz, President; Mary Jane Evans, John Kelleher, Frank Barneburg, Members; Marty Sokup, Secretary
Paid Staff: 4 **Volunteer Staff:** 2
Paid Artists: 9
Utilizes: Special Technical Talent; Guest Artists
Budget: $100,000 - $500,000
Income Sources: Private Foundations/Grants/Endowments; Business/Corporate Donations; Box Office; Government Grants
Season: October - February   **Annual Attendance:** 80,000
Affiliations: WAAA; Theatre Los Angeles; California Booking Exchange; SCETA; AATE; California Educational Theatre Association

Modesto

DANCE

MODESTO CIVIC BALLET THEATRE
1328 H Street, PO Box 22, Modesto, CA 95353
(209) 522-6879
Arts Area: Ballet
Status: Professional; Non-Profit
Type: Performing; Touring
Management: Mavis Dell Seeman, Artistic Director; Carla Fletcher, Assistant Artistic Director
Paid Artists: 25
Income Sources: Box Office; Individual Donations
Performance Facilities: Central Valley Performing Arts Center

INSTRUMENTAL MUSIC

MODESTO SYMPHONY
1700 McHenry Village Way, Suite 10A, Modesto, CA 95350
(209) 523-4156
Founded: 1931
Arts Area: Symphony
Status: Professional; Non-Profit
Type: Performing; Educational
Purpose: To provide high-quality symphonic performances; to promote educational opportunities
Management: Michael Royer, General Manager
Officers: Ken Berns, President; Dawn Berg, First Vice President; Richard Fisher, Second Vice President; James Beard, Treasurer
Paid Staff: 5 **Volunteer Staff:** 55
Paid Artists: 90
Utilizes: Special Technical Talent; Guest Artists
Budget: $500,000 - $1,000,000
Income Sources: Private Foundations/Grants/Endowments; Business/Corporate Donations; Box Office; Individual Donations
Season: September - May   **Annual Attendance:** 3,000
Affiliations: Association of California Symphony Orchestras; City of Modesto
Performance Facilities: Modesto Junior College Auditorium

VOCAL MUSIC

TOWNSEND OPERA PLAYERS
1502 Maywood Drive, Modesto, CA 95350
(209) 523-6426
FAX: (209) 579-0532
>**Founded:** 1982
>**Arts Area:** Grand Opera; Lyric Opera; Light Opera; Operetta
>**Status:** Professional; Non-Profit
>**Type:** Performing; Touring; Educational
>**Purpose:** To perform great opera and American musical theatre classics by and for the San Joaquin Valley and beyond
>**Management:** Erik Buck Townsend, Founder/General Director; Erika Townsend, Office Manager
>**Officers:** Alfred Hodder, Board President; Judy Schmidt, Secretary; Lynn Dooley, Treasurer
>**Paid Staff:** 4 **Volunteer Staff:** 210
>**Paid Artists:** 45 **Non-Paid Artists:** 50
>**Utilizes:** Special Technical Talent; Guest Conductors; Guest Artists; Guest Directors
>**Budget:** $100,000 - $500,000
>**Income Sources:** Private Foundations/Grants/Endowments; Business/Corporate Donations; Box Office; Government Grants; Individual Donations
>**Season:** 52 Weeks **Annual Attendance:** 30,000
>**Affiliations:** OA

FACILITY

MODESTO JUNIOR COLLEGE CABARET
Blue Gum Avenue, Modesto, CA 95350
(209) 523-4156
>**Type of Facility:** Theatre House
>**Facility Originally:** Warehouse
>**Type of Stage:** Flexible
>**Stage Dimensions:** 60'x60'
>**Seating Capacity:** 300
>**Year Built:** 1940
>**Year Remodeled:** 1976 **Architect:** James Shade **Cost:** $435,000
>**Contact for Rental:** Mrs. D. King, Facilities Coordinator; (209) 575-6020
>**Manager:** Steve Collins

Montclair

PERFORMING SERIES

STARLITE PATIO THEATER SUMMER SERIES
Montclair Civic Center, Benito and Fremont, Montclair, CA 91763
(909) 626-8571
>**Founded:** 1963
>**Arts Area:** Dance; Theater
>**Status:** Non-Profit
>**Type:** Performing
>**Purpose:** To offer admission-free summer cultural entertainment and special programs every Tuesday
>**Management:** Harve Edwards, Manager/Program Director
>**Budget:** $1,000 - $50,000
>**Annual Attendance:** 2,400
>**Performance Facilities:** The Starlite Patio Theater

FACILITY

MONTCLAIR CIVIC CENTER - STARLITE PATIO THEATRE
Montclair Civic Center, Montclair, CA 91763
(909) 626-8571
>**Type of Facility:** Outdoor (Concert); Civic Center
>**Type of Stage:** Flexible
>**Stage Dimensions:** 12'x24'x20'
>**Seating Capacity:** 350
>**Year Built:** 1957
>**Year Remodeled:** 1977
>**Contact for Rental:** Angie Antonelli, Recreation Director; (909) 626-8571

Manager: Harve Edwards;   (909) 986-4321
Resident Groups: Recreation Department Groups; Starlite Summer Series

---

Monterey

PERFORMING SERIES

MONTEREY JAZZ FESTIVAL
PO Box Jazz, Monterey, CA 93942
(408) 373-3366
FAX: (408) 373-0244
   Founded: 1958
   Arts Area: Dance; Vocal Music; Instrumental Music; Festivals
   Status: Non-Profit
   Type: Performing
   Purpose: To present jazz artists in an ideal setting
   Management: Stella Lepine, Education Coordinator; Jan Plunkett, Executive Secretary
   Paid Staff: 3
   Utilizes: Special Technical Talent; Guest Conductors; Guest Artists; Guest Directors
   Budget: $500,000 - $1,000,000
   Income Sources: Box Office; Individual Donations
   Season: 52 Weeks
   Performance Facilities: Monterey County Fairgrounds

Napa

INSTRUMENTAL MUSIC

NAPA VALLEY SYMPHONY
2407 California Boulevard, Napa, CA 94558
(707) 226-6872
FAX: (707) 226-3046
   Founded: 1933
   Arts Area: Symphony
   Status: Non-Profit
   Type: Performing; Educational
   Purpose: To provide symphonic music performances at high standards to the Napa Valley and serve youth with music education programs
   Management: Jay Goetting, General Manager; Anne Collett, Development Director; Jeanette Doxsee, Marketing Coordinator; Sandra Tront, Administrative Assistant; Asher Raboy, Music Director/Conductor
   Officers: Elaine John, President; Terry Robinson, Linda McClimans, Vice Presidents; Frank Takahashi, Treasurer
   Volunteer Staff: 35
   Paid Artists: 65   **Non-Paid Artists:** 10
   Utilizes: Special Technical Talent; Guest Artists
   Budget: $500,000 - $1,000,000
   Income Sources: Private Foundations/Grants/Endowments; Business/Corporate Donations; Box Office; Government Grants; Individual Donations
   Season: October - May   **Annual Attendance:** 21,500
   Affiliations: ASOL; Napa Valley Chamber of Commerce; Napa County Arts Council; Association of California Orchestras
   Performance Facilities: Lincoln Theatre, Yountville

FACILITY

NAPA VALLEY OPERA HOUSE
PO Box 6297, Napa, CA 94581
(707) 226-7372
   Type of Facility: Opera House
   Type of Stage: Proscenium
   Seating Capacity: 500
   Year Built: 1879   **Architect:** Samuel Newsom; Joseph Cather Newsom
   The Opera House, currently closed for renovations, is a member of the League of Historic American Theatres.

National City

THEATRE

THE LAMB'S PLAYERS THEATRE
PO Box 26, National City, CA 91951
(619) 474-3385
FAX: (619) 474-6156
Founded: 1973
Arts Area: Professional; Theatrical Group
Status: Professional; Non-Profit
Type: Performing; Touring; Resident; Educational
Purpose: To present a wide variety of theatrical productions which not only entertain but confront values and perspectives of our culture; to present the hope of the historic world viewed through the varied use of the dramatic arts
Management: W. Robert Smyth, Producing Artistic Director; Kerry Meads, Deborah Smyth, Associate Directors
Paid Staff: 3
Utilizes: Special Technical Talent; Guest Artists; Guest Directors
Budget: $500,000 - $1,000,000
Income Sources: Private Foundations/Grants/Endowments; Business/Corporate Donations; Box Office; Individual Donations
Season: February - November
Affiliations: TCG; California Theatre Council

Nevada City

PERFORMING SERIES

MUSIC IN THE MOUNTAINS
401 Spring Street, #101, Nevada City, CA 95959
(916) 265-6124
FAX: (916) 265-3170
Founded: 1981
Arts Area: Vocal Music; Instrumental Music; Festivals
Status: Professional; Non-Profit
Type: Performing; Resident; Educational; Sponsoring
Purpose: To present high-quality classical, pop and Broadway music at affordable prices
Management: Terry M. Brown, Executive Director; Paul Perry, Artistic Director/Conductor
Officers: Marguerite Blickenstaff, President; Marian Gallaher MD, First Vice President; Helen Daggett, Second Vice President; John van der Veen, Treasurer; Mike Hill, Secretary
Paid Staff: 6   **Volunteer Staff:** 315
Paid Artists: 62   **Non-Paid Artists:** 130
Utilizes: Guest Conductors; Guest Artists
Budget: $100,000 - $500,000
Income Sources: Private Foundations/Grants/Endowments; Business/Corporate Donations; Box Office; Government Grants; Individual Donations
Season: 52 Weeks   **Annual Attendance:** 13,150
Performance Facilities: Don Baggett Theatre; St. Joseph's Hall; Nevada County Fairgrounds

North Hollywood

VOCAL MUSIC

MUSICAL AMERICA
North Hollywood High School, 5231 Colfax Avenue, North Hollywood, CA 91607
(818) 769-8510, ext. 308
Founded: 1969
Arts Area: Choral
Status: Semi-Professional; Non-Professional
Type: Performing; Touring; Educational
Purpose: To educate with fine choral music; to provide entertainment for the community
Management: Cornelia Korney, Director
Paid Staff: 1   **Volunteer Staff:** 20
Utilizes: Special Technical Talent; Guest Conductors; Guest Artists
Budget: $1,000 - $50,000
Income Sources: Private Foundations/Grants/Endowments; Business/Corporate Donations; Government Grants; Individual Donations
Season: November - June

Affiliations: Los Angeles Unified School District
Performance Facilities: North Hollywood High School

THEATRE

ACTORS ALLEY REPERTORY THEATER
12135 Riverside Drive, North Hollywood, CA 91607
(818) 986-2278
Founded: 1971
Arts Area: Professional
Status: Professional; Non-Profit
Type: Performing; Resident
Purpose: The challenge of a true regional theater is to create and enhance the development of all facets of theater arts within the community in which it lives. Actors Alley Repertory Theater is dedicated to meeting that challenge.
Management: Jeremiah Morris, Artistic Director; Robert Caine, Managing Director
Officers: Thomas H. Cole, President; Carol Rowen, Vice President; Sunny Caine, Secretary
Paid Staff: 6 **Volunteer Staff:** 75
Non-Paid Artists: 65
Utilizes: Special Technical Talent; Guest Directors
Budget: $100,000 - $500,000
Income Sources: Private Foundations/Grants/Endowments; Business/Corporate Donations; Box Office; Individual Donations
Season: 52 Weeks **Annual Attendance:** 12,000
Affiliations: Los Angeles Theatre Alliance; California Theater Council
Performance Facilities: Actors Alley Repertory Theater

BARRIO PLAYERS - ACTORES DEL BARRIO
12443 Huston Street, North Hollywood, CA 91607
(818) 766-1066
Founded: 1977
Arts Area: Theatrical Group
Status: Semi-Professional; Non-Profit
Type: Performing
Purpose: To find and develop promising young actors and writers in the barrio
Management: Joseph (Pepe) Arciga, Playwright/Founder
Officers: Helen Lopez; Bernadette Cologne; Ruben Garfias
Volunteer Staff: 5
Non-Paid Artists: 10
Budget: $1,000 - $50,000
Income Sources: Box Office; Individual Donations
Annual Attendance: 1,500
Affiliations: Los Angeles Theater Center

GROUP REPERTORY THEATRE
10900 Burbank Boulevard, North Hollywood, CA 91601
(818) 769-7529
Founded: 1973
Arts Area: Theatrical Group
Status: Professional; Non-Profit
Type: Performing
Purpose: To stage five-six productions each year emphasizing new works by playwrights and young actors; to work with the Los Angeles Unified School District to produce theatrical presentations for those learning English as a second language
Management: Lonny Chapman, Artistic Director; Burt Rosario, Assistant Artistic Director
Officers: Larry Eisenberg, President; Geraldine Allen, Treasurer
Budget: $50,000 - $100,000
Income Sources: Business/Corporate Donations; Box Office; Individual Donations
Season: 52 Weeks **Annual Attendance:** 4,000
Affiliations: Valley Arts Council
Performance Facilities: Group Repertory Theatre

SYNTHAXIS THEATRE COMPANY
6310 Whitsett Avenue, North Hollywood, CA 91607
(213) 877-4726
Founded: 1972
Arts Area: Theatrical Group
Status: Professional; Non-Profit
Type: Performing; Touring; Resident; Educational
Purpose: To present new works and lesser-known material by renowned authors with particular attention to works by women; to present children's shows and benefit performances

Management: Estelle Bush, Executive Director
Paid Staff: 2
Paid Artists: 15
Budget: $1,000 - $50,000
Income Sources: Private Foundations/Grants/Endowments; Business/Corporate Donations; Box Office; Government Grants; Individual Donations
Season: 52 Weeks
Annual Attendance: 10,000
Affiliations: Los Angeles Theatre Alliance; San Fernando Valley Arts Council

THEATRE EXCHANGE
11855 Hart Street, North Hollywood, CA 91605
(818) 765-9005
Founded: 1975
Arts Area: Theatrical Group
Status: Professional
Type: Performing; Educational
Purpose: To seek out and produce the best in American and European drama with a current emphasis on new American full-length plays
Management: Rob Zapple, Managing Director; Matthew Faison, Artistic Director; Alison Evans, Box Office Manager; Carol Monroe, Treasurer
Volunteer Staff: 50
Non-Paid Artists: 50
Utilizes: Guest Directors
Budget: $1,000 - $50,000
Income Sources: Business/Corporate Donations; Box Office; Individual Donations
Season: 52 Weeks
Affiliations: Los Angeles Theatre Alliance

Northridge

PERFORMING SERIES

MULTI-CULTURAL MUSIC AND ART FOUNDATION OF NORTHRIDGE
PO Box 101, Northridge, CA 91328
(818) 349-3400; (818) 349-3431
FAX: (818) 349-0716
Founded: 1990
Arts Area: Dance; Vocal Music; Instrumental Music; Festivals
Status: Non-Profit
Type: Performing; Educational
Purpose: To promote multicultural music, art and dance
Management: Grace Wan Kien Lee, Program Coordinator; Jonathan Green, Music
Paid Staff: 2   **Volunteer Staff:** 5
Utilizes: Special Technical Talent; Guest Artists
Budget: $1,000 - $50,000
Income Sources: Private Foundations/Grants/Endowments; Business/Corporate Donations; Box Office
Season: January; March - April; December
Annual Attendance: 1,000
Performance Facilities: McMafn Theatre

FACILITY

CALIFORNIA STATE UNIVERSITY-NORTHRIDGE - CAMPUS THEATRE
18111 Nordhoff Street, Northridge, CA 91330
(818) 885-3086
Type of Facility: Theatre Complex; Theatre House
Type of Stage: Proscenium
Stage Dimensions: 21'x40'x36'
Orchestra Pit
Seating Capacity: 400
Year Built: 1960
Contact for Rental: Jeffrey Levy;   (818) 885-3091
Resident Groups: Department of Theatre, California State University at Northridge

CALIFORNIA STATE UNIVERSITY-NORTHRIDGE - LITTLE THEATRE
18111 Nordhoff Street, Northridge, CA 91330
(818) 885-3086
    Type of Facility: Theatre Complex; Theatre House
    Type of Stage: Proscenium
    Stage Dimensions: 16'x20'x24'9"
    Orchestra Pit
    Seating Capacity: 210
    Year Built: 1960
    Contact for Rental: Jeffrey Levy;   (818) 885-3091
    Resident Groups: Department of Theatre, California State University at Northridge

CALIFORNIA STATE UNIVERSITY-NORTHRIDGE - STUDIO THEATRE
18111 Nordhoff Street, Northridge, CA 91330
(818) 885-3086
    Type of Facility: Theatre Complex; Studio Performance; Environmental; Theatre House; Arena; Multi-Purpose; Room
    Type of Stage: Flexible; Environmental; Arena
    Stage Dimensions: 46'5"x50'10"
    Seating Capacity: 90-120
    Year Built: 1960
    Contact for Rental: Jeffrey Levy;   (818) 885-3091
    Resident Groups: Department of Theatre, California State University at Northridge

---

Oakland

DANCE

DANCE BRIGADE
1515 Webster, Oakland, CA 94612
(510) 465-3686
    Founded: 1986
    Arts Area: Modern; Ethnic
    Status: Professional
    Type: Performing; Touring; Resident; Sponsoring
    Purpose: To present socially-relevant dance to the widest possible audience
    Management: Raquel Lopez, Managing Director; Nina Finchter, Krissy Keefer, Artistic Directors
    Officers: Jerry Atkin, President; Robert Hanamura; James Orgala
    Paid Staff: 3   **Volunteer Staff:** 5
    Paid Artists: 6
    Utilizes: Special Technical Talent; Guest Conductors; Guest Artists; Guest Choreographers
    Budget: $100,000 - $500,000
    Income Sources: Private Foundations/Grants/Endowments; Box Office; Government Grants; Individual Donations; Concessions; Performance Fees
    Annual Attendance: 15,000

DIMENSIONS DANCE THEATER
606 60th Street, Oakland, CA 94609-1420
(510) 428-2466
FAX: (510) 428-2910
    Founded: 1972
    Arts Area: Modern; Jazz; Ethnic
    Status: Professional; Non-Profit
    Type: Performing; Touring; Resident; Educational
    Purpose: To promote and perpetuate the knowledge and appreciation of African and African-derived dance
    Management: Mlinzi Majigiza, Executive Director; Jim Dees, Shirley Bucher, Agents - J. Dees Presents
    Officers: Deborah Stevenson, Chairperson; Paul Johnson, Secretary
    Paid Staff: 2
    Paid Artists: 17
    Utilizes: Special Technical Talent; Guest Artists; Guest Choreographers
    Budget: $100,000 - $500,000
    Income Sources: Private Foundations/Grants/Endowments; Business/Corporate Donations; Box Office; Government Grants; Individual Donations
    Season: October - August
    Annual Attendance: 2,200
    Affiliations: International Association of Blacks in Dance; Dance Bay Area
    Performance Facilities: Scottish Rite Theater Center

ELLEN WEBB DANCE FOUNDATION
2822-A Union Street, Oakland, CA 94608-4426
(510) 452-5919
> **Founded:** 1987
> **Arts Area:** Modern
> **Status:** Professional; Non-Profit
> **Type:** Performing; Touring
> **Purpose:** To change the way people see the world; to tie together three seperate projects—the Ellen Webb Dance Company, the Talking Dance Porject and the Ellen Webb Dance Studio
> **Management:** Ellen Webb, Artistic Director
> **Budget:** $50,000 - $100,000
> **Income Sources:** Private Foundations/Grants/Endowments; Business/Corporate Donations; Box Office; Government Grants; Individual Donations
> **Annual Attendance:** 6,000

OAKLAND BALLET
2025 Broadway, Oakland, CA 94612
(510) 452-9288
> **Founded:** 1965
> **Arts Area:** Ballet
> **Status:** Professional; Non-Profit
> **Type:** Performing; Touring
> **Purpose:** To reconstruct, preserve and present ballets from the Diaghilev era, ballets by American choreogrphers and those by contemporary choreographers
> **Management:** Laird Rodet, General Manager; Todd Perreira, Marketing Director; Carol Tanenbaum, Development Director; Robin Hovis James, Operations Director
> **Officers:** Ronn Guidi, Artistic Director; Ron Thiele, Associate Artistic Director
> **Paid Staff:** 14   **Volunteer Staff:** 25
> **Paid Artists:** 35
> **Utilizes:** Guest Conductors; Guest Artists; Guest Choreographers
> **Budget:** $1,000,000 - $5,000,000
> **Income Sources:** Private Foundations/Grants/Endowments; Business/Corporate Donations; Box Office; Government Grants; Individual Donations; Rentals; Boutique
> **Season:** September - March
> **Performance Facilities:** Paramount Theatre

VOCAL MUSIC

KITKA
1201 Martin Luther King Jr. Way, Oakland, CA 94612
(510) 444-0323
> **Founded:** 1979
> **Arts Area:** Choral; Ethnic
> **Status:** Professional
> **Type:** Performing; Touring
> **Management:** Russ Jennings, Administrative Director
> **Officers:** Bon Brown, Artistic Director
> **Paid Staff:** 2
> **Paid Artists:** 11
> **Utilizes:** Guest Artists
> **Budget:** $100,000 - $500,000
> **Income Sources:** Private Foundations/Grants/Endowments; Box Office; Government Grants; Individual Donations; Performing Fees
> **Season:** 52 Weeks

OAKLAND YOUTH CHORUS
2619 Broadway, Oakland, CA 94612
(510) 832-6080
FAX: (510) 832-2211
> **Founded:** 1974
> **Arts Area:** Choral
> **Status:** Professional; Non-Profit
> **Type:** Performing; Touring; Sponsoring
> **Purpose:** To provide multicultural youth ages 14-21 with professionally-directed training that advances the choral art form
> **Management:** Diana Freeland, General Manager

Officers: Trente Morant, Artistic Director; Elizabeth Min, Conductor
Paid Staff: 6   **Volunteer Staff:** 15
Paid Artists: 26   **Non-Paid Artists:** 80
Utilizes: Guest Conductors; Guest Artists; Guest Directors
Budget: $100,000 - $500,000
Income Sources: Private Foundations/Grants/Endowments; Business/Corporate Donations; Box Office; Government Grants; Individual Donations
Season: September - June
Annual Attendance: 6,000
Performance Facilities: First Presbyterian Church; Calvin Simmons Theater; Paramount Theater

THEATRE

OAKLAND CIVIC THEATRE
1520 Lakeside Drive, Oakland, CA 94612
(510) 452-2909
FAX: (510) 238-2224
Founded: 1968
Arts Area: Community; Theatrical Group
Status: Non-Profit
Type: Performing; Touring; Resident
Purpose: To provide quality entertainment for, and by, the community
Management: Ted Smalley, Director
Paid Staff: 1   **Volunteer Staff:** 90
Utilizes: Special Technical Talent
Budget: $1,000 - $50,000
Income Sources: Private Foundations/Grants/Endowments; Business/Corporate Donations; Box Office; Government Grants; Individual Donations
Season: October - September
Annual Attendance: 4,000
Affiliations: AACT
Performance Facilities: Lakeside Park Garden

OAKLAND ENSEMBLE THEATRE
1428 Alice Street, Suite 289, Oakland, CA 94612
(510) 763-7774
Founded: 1974
Arts Area: Professional; Theatrical Group
Status: Professional; Non-Profit; Commercial
Type: Performing; Touring; Resident
Purpose: To provide insightful and engaging works of contemporary theatre shaped by the sensitivities and sensibilities of African-Americans
Management: Sharon Walton, Producing Director; Kim Euell, Managing Director
Utilizes: Special Technical Talent; Guest Artists; Guest Directors
Budget: $100,000 - $500,000
Income Sources: Box Office; Individual Donations
Season: 52 Weeks

OAKLAND SUMMER THEATRE
1520 Lakeside Drive, Oakland, CA 94612
(510) 658-2085
Founded: 1975
Arts Area: Community
Status: Non-Profit
Type: Performing
Purpose: To provide a performing-arts experience during the summer months for youth and adults
Management: Oakland Office of Parks and Recreation (Drama Section); Ted Smalley, Director
Officers: Rosemary Thomas, President; Theresa Denham, Secretary; James Thomas, Treasurer
Paid Staff: 12   **Volunteer Staff:** 20
Paid Artists: 4   **Non-Paid Artists:** 8
Utilizes: Special Technical Talent
Budget: $1,000 - $50,000
Income Sources: Private Foundations/Grants/Endowments; Box Office
Season: June - August
Annual Attendance: 20,000
Performance Facilities: Laney College Theatre

PERFORMING SERIES

OAKLAND JAZZ ALLIANCE
1330 Broadway, #1030, Oakland, CA 94612
(510) 839-2440
FAX: (510) 268-9065
Founded: 1987
Arts Area: Vocal Music; Instrumental Music; Festivals
Status: Non-Profit
Type: Performing; Educational
Purpose: To preserve, develop and express jazz music; to develop serious young artists
Management: Charla Montgomery, Executive Director
Officers: Buddy Montgomery, President; David Montgomery, Vice President; Majors Harrison, Secretary;
Dr. Alan Werblin, Treasurer
Paid Staff: 1   **Volunteer Staff:** 2
Non-Paid Artists: 1
Utilizes: Guest Artists
Budget: $1,000 - $50,000
Income Sources: Private Foundations/Grants/Endowments; Business/Corporate Donations; Box Office; Government
Grants; Individual Donations; Charter Memberships
Season: 52 Weeks   **Annual Attendance:** 800

FACILITY

HENRY J. KAISER CONVENTION CENTER
10 Tenth Street, Oakland, CA 94607
(510) 839-7500
Type of Facility: Civic Center
Year Built: 1914   **Architect:** John J. Donovan & W.J. Matthews   **Cost:** $7,000,000
Year Remodeled: 1984   **Cost:** $15,000,000
Contact for Rental: Oakland Convention Center Management;   (415) 839-7500
Resident Groups: Oakland Opera
*The Convention Center contains the Arena and Calvin Simmons Theatre. See separate listings for additional
information.*

HENRY J. KAISER CONVENTION CENTER - ARENA
10 Tenth Street, Oakland, CA 94607
(510) 839-7500
Type of Facility: Auditorium; Arena; Multi-Purpose; Room
Type of Stage: Flexible; Arena
Stage Dimensions: portable stage of 124 sections, each 4'x8'
Seating Capacity: 6,200
Year Built: 1914
Year Remodeled: 1984
Contact for Rental: Oakland Convention Center Management;   (510) 839-7500

HENRY J. KAISER CONVENTION CENTER - CALVIN SIMMONS THEATRE
10 Tenth Street, Oakland, CA 94611
(510) 839-7500
FAX: (510) 839-0356
Type of Facility: Theatre House
Type of Stage: Proscenium
Stage Dimensions: 65'x65'x40'   **Orchestra Pit**
Seating Capacity: 1,924
Year Built: 1914
Year Remodeled: 1984
Contact for Rental: Oakland Convention Center Management;   (510) 839-7500
Manager: Charles J. Pattersen;   (510) 839-7509
Resident Groups: Oakland Chamber Orchestra; Oakland Opera; Oakland Eastbay Symphony

LANEY COLLEGE THEATRE
900 Fallon Street, Oakland, CA 94607
(510) 464-3230
Type of Facility: Theatre House
Type of Stage: Proscenium
Stage Dimensions: 43'Wx35'D with additional wing space   **Orchestra Pit**
Seating Capacity: 325
Year Built: 1975   **Architect:** Skidmore Owings & Merrill   **Cost:** $5,000,000

Contact for Rental: David Hartenstein;   (510) 464-3230
Resident Groups: Bay Area Dance Series

MILLS COLLEGE CONCERT HALL
5000 MacArthur Boulevard, Oakland, CA 94613
(510) 430-2171
    Type of Facility: Concert Hall
    Type of Stage: Proscenium
    Orchestra Pit
    Seating Capacity: 540
    Year Built: 1928   **Architect:** Walter H. Ratcliff
    Contact for Rental: Karen Maggio
    Resident Groups: Mills College Music Department; Mills College Center for Contemporary Music; Mills Chamber Ensemble

PARAMOUNT THEATRE
2025 Broadway, Oakland, CA 94612
(510) 893-2300
    Type of Facility: Theatre House
    Facility Originally: Movie House
    Type of Stage: Proscenium
    Stage Dimensions: 66'Wx35'D (angles); 24'D SR; 37'D SL; 66'Wx30'H proscenium opening
    Orchestra Pit
    Seating Capacity: 2,998
    Year Built: 1931   **Architect:** Timothy Pflueger   **Cost:** $3,000,000
    Year Remodeled: 1973   **Cost:** $1,000,000
    Acoustical Consultant: Jaffe Acoustics
    Contact for Rental: Peter J. Botto;   (510) 893-2300
    Resident Groups: Oakland Ballet; Paramount Organ Pops Series; Paramount Movie Classics

Ojai

PERFORMING SERIES

OJAI FESTIVALS
201 South Signal Street, Ojai, CA 93023
(805) 646-2094
FAX: (805) 646-6037
    Founded: 1947
    Arts Area: Vocal Music; Instrumental Music
    Status: Professional; Non-Profit
    Type: Educational; Sponsoring
    Purpose: To emphasize contemporary repertoire
    Management: Lawrence Morton, Artistic Director Emeritus; Ara Guzelimian, Artistic Director
    Officers: Joan Kemper, President; Dee Palmer, First Vice President; Rick Gould, Second Vice President; Gwen Erickson, Secretary; Al Urban, Treasurer
    Paid Staff: 3   **Volunteer Staff:** 4
    Paid Artists: 140
    Utilizes: Guest Conductors; Guest Artists
    Budget: $100,000 - $500,000
    Income Sources: Private Foundations/Grants/Endowments; Business/Corporate Donations; Box Office; Government Grants; Individual Donations
    Season: May - June   **Annual Attendance:** 5,000
    Affiliations: ASOL; California Confederation of the Arts
    Performance Facilities: Ojai Festival Bowl

FACILITY

OJAI FESTIVAL BOWL
Libbey Park, Ojai, CA 93023
(805) 646-2094
    Type of Facility: Amphitheater
    Type of Stage: Proscenium
    Seating Capacity: 1,000
    Year Built: 1956

Orinda

INSTRUMENTAL MUSIC

EARPLAY
32 Scenic Drive, Orinda, CA 94563
(510) 253-0357
Founded: 1985
Arts Area: Chamber
Status: Professional; Non-Profit
Type: Performing
Purpose: To provide excellent performances of new works by American composers
Officers: Robert Festinger, President; Rachel Winheld, Executive Director
Paid Staff: 1   **Volunteer Staff:** 5
Paid Artists: 8
Utilizes: Guest Conductors; Guest Artists
Budget: $1,000 - $50,000
Income Sources: Private Foundations/Grants/Endowments; Box Office; Government Grants; Individual Donations
Season: October - May   **Annual Attendance:** 1,000
Performance Facilities: Cowell Theater; Fort Mason Center for the Arts

Oroville

FACILITY

OROVILLE STATE THEATER
1489 Myers Street, Oroville, CA 95965
(916) 538-2470
FAX: (916) 538-2426
Type of Facility: Performance Center
Facility Originally: Vaudeville; Movie House
Type of Stage: Proscenium
Stage Dimensions: 39'10"Wx24'D   **Orchestra Pit**
Seating Capacity: 612
Year Built: 1927   **Architect:** Timothy L. Pflueger
Year Remodeled: 1986   **Cost:** $680,000
Acoustical Consultant: Vorin Dornan
Contact for Rental: Amelia Jennings;   (916) 538-2470
Resident Groups: Performings Arts & Family Series; Lecture Series; Travelogue Series; Community Concert Series; Annual Musical

Oxnard

FACILITY

OXNARD CIVIC AUDITORIUM
800 Hobson Way, Oxnard, CA 93030
(805) 486-2424
Type of Facility: Concert Hall; Auditorium; Theatre House; Multi-Purpose
Type of Stage: Proscenium
Stage Dimensions: 52'Wx45'D; 52'Wx25'H proscenium opening   **Orchestra Pit**
Seating Capacity: 1,604
Year Built: 1968   **Architect:** Adrian Wilson & Associates   **Cost:** $2,600,000
Acoustical Consultant: Hughes Sound
Contact for Rental: Jack C. Lavin;   (805) 486-2424
Resident Groups: Ventura County Symphony; Oxnard Community Concert Association; Cabrillo Music Theater

Pacific Palisades

INSTRUMENTAL MUSIC

PALISADES SYMPHONY ORCHESTRA
1081 Palisair Place, Pacific Palisades, CA 90272
(310) 454-8040
Founded: 1966
Arts Area: Symphony; Orchestra

Status: Non-Professional; Non-Profit
Type: Performing; Resident; Educational; Sponsoring
Purpose: To bring high-quality orchestra performances to the community without charge, including major choral works; to give singers and orchestra musicians performance experience; to encourage young musicians at annual young artist concert
Management: Eva Holberg, Manager; Joel Lish, Conductor/Music Director; Sigrid Hofer, Fund Chairman
Officers: Eva Holberg, President; Sigrid Hofer, First Vice President; Francis Murray, Secretary; Melissa Leicester, Treasurer
Utilizes: Guest Artists
Budget: $1,000 - $50,000
Income Sources: Private Foundations/Grants/Endowments; Business/Corporate Donations; Individual Donations
Season: September - June   **Annual Attendance:** 3,000
Affiliations: ASOL; Association of California Symphony Orchestras

Palm Desert

VOCAL MUSIC

WEST COAST OPERA THEATRE
PO Box 166, Palm Desert, CA 92661
(619) 779-0061
Founded: 1962
Arts Area: Grand Opera; Light Opera; Operetta; Musical Theatre
Status: Professional; Non-Profit
Type: Performing; Educational
Purpose: To keep opera and its allied educational opportunities open to young audiences; to provide a training ground for young, aspiring artists
Management: Josephine Lombardo, General Manager/Artistic Director
Officers: Mary Stewart, President; Anita Slater, Vice President; Ron Powers, Secretary
Volunteer Staff: 10
Paid Artists: 150
Utilizes: Special Technical Talent; Guest Conductors; Guest Artists; Guest Directors
Budget: $50,000 - $100,000
Income Sources: Box Office; Individual Donations; Fundraising
Season: November - May   **Annual Attendance:** 3,000
Affiliations: COS
Performance Facilities: Annenberg Theater; McAllum Theatre; Bob Hope Cultural Center

FACILITY

BOB HOPE CULTURAL CENTER - MCALLUM THEATRE
73000 Fred Waring Drive, Palm Desert, CA 92260
(619) 346-6505
FAX: (619) 341-9508
Type of Facility: Theatre House
Type of Stage: Modified Apron Proscenium
Stage Dimensions: 50'Wx40'D with 6'D apron; 50'Wx30'H proscenium   **Orchestra Pit**
Seating Capacity: 1,127
Year Built: 1988   **Architect:** Anthony and Langford   **Cost:** $20,000,000
Acoustical Consultant: Smith Fause Associates
Contact for Rental: Charles Giora, Director of Operations;   (619) 346-6505
Manager: Nancy Dolensek, Executive Director;   (619) 346-6505
Resident Groups: Bob Hope Cultural Center - McAllum Theatre

Palm Springs

VOCAL MUSIC

PALM SPRINGS OPERA GUILD OF THE DESERT
PO Box 1378, Palm Springs, CA 92263
(619) 325-6107
Founded: 1968
Arts Area: Grand Opera; Light Opera
Status: Professional; Non-Profit
Type: Performing; Educational; Sponsoring
Purpose: To present high-quality opera and musical theatre productions to the Palm Springs area
Officers: Robert James, President; Tony Rose, Opera Vice President; Hendrik de Boer, Executive Vice President

Volunteer Staff: 635
Utilizes: Special Technical Talent
Budget: $50,000 - $100,000
Income Sources: Box Office; Individual Donations
Season: September - April   **Annual Attendance:** 2,400
Affiliations: COS
Performance Facilities: McAllum Theatre

FACILITY

PALM SPRINGS DESERT MUSEUM/ANNENBERG THEATER
101 Museum Drive, Palm Springs, CA 92262
(619) 325-7186
FAX: (619) 327-5069
Founded: 1938
Type of Facility: Concert Hall; Studio Performance; Performance Center; Theatre House; Multi-Purpose; Movie House
Type of Stage: Proscenium
Stage Dimensions: 50'4"Wx31'Dx18'H proscenium opening
Seating Capacity: 450
Year Built: 1976   **Architect:** E. Stewart Williams   **Cost:** $9,000,000
Stage Renovated: 1991   **Architect:** Theatre Products International   **Cost:** $460,000
Acoustical Consultant: Theatre Products International
Contact for Rental: Dr. Dale Hearth;   (619) 325-7186

Palmdale

VOCAL MUSIC

DESERT OPERA THEATRE
PO Box 900434, Palmdale, CA 93590-0434
(805) 947-9442
Founded: 1971
Arts Area: Grand Opera; Lyric Opera; Light Opera; Operetta; Musical Theatre
Status: Semi-Professional; Non-Profit
Type: Performing; Resident; Educational
Purpose: To bring musical theatre to the Antelope Valley showcasing local talent
Management: David Milligan, General/Artistic Director; Dorothy Lewellin, Business Manager
Paid Staff: 9   **Volunteer Staff:** 50
Paid Artists: 25   **Non-Paid Artists:** 20
Utilizes: Special Technical Talent; Guest Artists; Guest Directors
Budget: $1,000 - $50,000
Income Sources: Private Foundations/Grants/Endowments; Business/Corporate Donations; Box Office; Government Grants; Individual Donations
Season: 52 Weeks   **Annual Attendance:** 4,000
Affiliations: California Confederation of the Arts; Antelope Valley Arts Council
Performance Facilities: Palmdale Cultural Center

Palo Alto

INSTRUMENTAL MUSIC

CALIFORNIA YOUTH SYMPHONY
PO Box 1441, Palo Alto, CA 94302
(415) 325-6666
Founded: 1952
Arts Area: Symphony
Status: Non-Professional; Non-Profit
Type: Performing; Educational
Purpose: To provide an opportunity for young musicians to perform in a high quality symphony orchestra
Management: James Hogan, Executive Director; Ruby Seto, Executive Secretary; Leo Eylar, Music Director
Officers: Greg Wheelwright, President
Paid Staff: 4   **Volunteer Staff:** 50
Paid Artists: 7   **Non-Paid Artists:** 300
Budget: $100,000 - $500,000
Income Sources: Private Foundations/Grants/Endowments; Business/Corporate Donations; Box Office; Government Grants; Individual Donations
Season: November - June   **Annual Attendance:** 6,000

Affiliations: ASOL (Youth Orchestra Division); Association of California Symphony Orchestras
Performance Facilities: Flint Center for the Performing Arts; San Mateo Performing Arts Center

VOCAL MUSIC

WEST BAY OPERA
PO Box 1714, Palo Alto, CA 94302
(415) 321-3471
Founded: 1955
Arts Area: Grand Opera; Lyric Opera; Light Opera
Status: Semi-Professional; Non-Profit
Type: Performing; Educational
Purpose: To provide high quality opera performances and opportunities for community participation; to provide training for aspiring opera performers
Management: Maria Holt, General Director
Officers: Ben DeBolt, Business Manager; Matthew Gilmartin, Development Officer; Michele Sullivan, Production Manager
Paid Staff: 4   **Volunteer Staff:** 1
Paid Artists: 12   **Non-Paid Artists:** 40
Utilizes: Guest Conductors; Guest Artists; Guest Directors
Budget: $100,000 - $500,000
Income Sources: Private Foundations/Grants/Endowments; Business/Corporate Donations; Box Office; Government Grants; Individual Donations
Season: October - May   **Annual Attendance:** 10,000
Performance Facilities: Lucie Stern Theatre

THEATRE

PALO ALTO CHILDREN'S THEATRE
1305 Middlefield Road, Palo Alto, CA 94301
(415) 329-2216
Founded: 1932
Arts Area: Musical; Theatrical Group
Status: Non-Professional; Non-Profit
Type: Performing; Educational
Management: Patricia Briggs, Director; Michael Litfin, Assistant Director; Andy Hayes, Technical Director/Designer; Alison Williams, Costume Supervisor; Sandy Rankin, Program Assistant
Paid Staff: 20   **Volunteer Staff:** 50
Utilizes: Special Technical Talent; Guest Artists; Guest Directors; Instructors
Budget: $100,000 - $500,000
Income Sources: Private Foundations/Grants/Endowments; Business/Corporate Donations; Government Grants; Individual Donations; Part of City Department
Season: 52 Weeks   **Annual Attendance:** 50,000
Performance Facilities: Palo Alto Children's Theatre

THEATREWORKS
1305 Middlefield Road, Palo Alto, CA 94301
(415) 323-8311
FAX: (415) 323-3311
Founded: 1970
Arts Area: Professional; Musical; Theatrical Group
Status: Semi-Professional; Non-Profit
Type: Performing
Management: Robert Kelley, Artistic Director; Randy Adams, Managing Director
Paid Staff: 9   **Volunteer Staff:** 15
Paid Artists: 350
Utilizes: Special Technical Talent; Guest Artists; Guest Directors
Budget: $1,000,000 - $5,000,000
Income Sources: Private Foundations/Grants/Endowments; Business/Corporate Donations; Box Office; Government Grants; Individual Donations
Season: June - May
Annual Attendance: 58,000
Affiliations: TCG
Performance Facilities: The Lucy Stern Theatre; The Mountain View Center for the Performing Arts; Cubberley Stage II

FACILITY

GUNN HIGH SCHOOL - SPANGENBERG THEATRE
780 Arastradero, Palo Alto, CA 94306
(415) 354-8220
  Type of Facility: Theatre House
  Type of Stage: Proscenium
  Stage Dimensions: 18'x44'x35' **Orchestra Pit**
  Seating Capacity: 1,000
  Contact for Rental: Jorgen Wedseltoft, Manager; (415) 354-8220
  Manager: Jorgen Wedseltoft
  Resident Groups: Palo Alto Chamber Orchestra; Peninsula Youth Theatre; Korean-American Musical Society Association

Paradise

PERFORMING SERIES

PARADISE AREA ARTS COUNCIL
6686 Brook Way, Paradise, CA 95969
(916) 877-8360
  Founded: 1980
  Arts Area: Dance; Vocal Music; Theater; Festivals
  Status: Semi-Professional; Non-Profit
  Type: Performing; Educational; Sponsoring
  Purpose: To support the arts in the Paradise area; to be a liaison to local town government
  Officers: Thomas E. Wilson, President; Wayne Angel, Vice President; Joan Anderson Hayes, Secretary; Trudi Angel, Treasurer
  Paid Staff: 1
  Utilizes: Guest Artists
  Budget: $1,000 - $50,000
  Income Sources: Business/Corporate Donations; Individual Donations
  Season: June
  Affiliations: National Music Council

Pasadena

DANCE

PASADENA CIVIC BALLET
25 South Sierra Madre Boulevard, Pasadena, CA 91107
(818) 792-0873
  Founded: 1980
  Arts Area: Modern; Mime; Ballet; Jazz; Ethnic
  Status: Semi-Professional; Non-Profit
  Type: Performing; Educational
  Purpose: To provide a semi-professional ballet experience, assist those who dance as an avocation, give young dancers performance opportunities and provide them with a chance to study abroad to enhance dance in our community
  Management: Elly-Charlotte Van Dijk, Artistic Director; Diane DeFranco, Associate Artistic Director
  Officers: Holly Davis, President; Dr. John Houseman, Treasurer; Kathy Moscarello, Secretary
  Volunteer Staff: 15
  Paid Artists: 4 **Non-Paid Artists:** 46
  Utilizes: Guest Artists; Guest Choreographers
  Budget: $1,000 - $50,000
  Income Sources: Business/Corporate Donations; Box Office; Individual Donations
  Season: September - June **Annual Attendance:** 6,000
  Affiliations: Pasadena Arts Council
  Performance Facilities: San Gabriel Civic Auditorium

TERRI LEWIS DANCE ENSEMBLE
787 Merrett Drive, Pasadena, CA 91104
(818) 798-9853
  Founded: 1986
  Arts Area: Ballet
  Status: Professional; Semi-Professional; Non-Profit
  Type: Performing; Touring; Educational
  Purpose: To perform contemporary chamber ballet in conjunction with residencies in smaller communities
  Management: Terri Lewis, Artistic Director; Aletheia Zaremba, Managing Director

Paid Staff: 2
Paid Artists: 10
Utilizes: Guest Choreographers
Budget: $1,000 - $50,000
Income Sources: Business/Corporate Donations; Box Office; Government Grants; Individual Donations
Season: September - June

INSTRUMENTAL MUSIC

COLEMAN CHAMBER MUSIC ASSOCIATION
202 South Lake Avenue, Suite 201, Pasadena, CA 91101
(818) 793-4191
Founded: 1904
Arts Area: Chamber
Status: Non-Profit
Type: Sponsoring
Purpose: To present the finest international chamber ensembles, both established and emerging
Management: Kathy R. Freeland, Manager
Officers: Dr. Robert Wark, President; Robert Zurbach, First Vice President; Carol Bressler, Second Vice President; Mrs. David Grether, Secretary; Chistopher Harcourt, Treasurer
Paid Staff: 2   **Volunteer Staff:** 50
Utilizes: Guest Artists
Budget: $100,000 - $500,000
Income Sources: Private Foundations/Grants/Endowments; Business/Corporate Donations; Box Office; Government Grants; Individual Donations
Season: October - May   **Annual Attendance:** 4,500
Affiliations: APAP; WAAA; CMA
Performance Facilities: Beckman Auditorium, California Institute of Technology

PASADENA SYMPHONY
117 East Colorado Boulevard, #375, Pasadena, CA 91105
(818) 793-7172
FAX: (818) 793-7180
Founded: 1928
Arts Area: Symphony; Orchestra
Status: Professional
Type: Performing
Purpose: To provide the highest quality symphonic music and educational programs to the people of Pasadena and the greater Los Angeles area
Management: Wayne Shilkret, Executive Director; Gloria Smith, Director of Operations
Officers: Stephen J.M. Morris, President; Robert Zurbach, Executive Vice President; Marvin Schultz, Treasurer; Mary Kay Driscoll, Recording Secretary
Paid Staff: 4
Paid Artists: 100
Utilizes: Guest Artists
Budget: $500,000 - $1,000,000
Income Sources: Private Foundations/Grants/Endowments; Business/Corporate Donations; Box Office; Government Grants; Individual Donations
Season: October - May
Annual Attendance: 2,300
Performance Facilities: Pasadena Civic Auditorium

PERFORMING SERIES

OFFICE OF PUBLIC EVENTS
California Institute of Technology, 1201 East California Boulevard, Pasadena, CA 91125
(818) 356-3834
Founded: 1963
Arts Area: Dance; Instrumental Music; Theater
Status: Non-Profit
Type: Educational; Sponsoring
Purpose: To serve as a performing arts presentation center for Cal. Tech and the surrounding community
Management: Jerry Willis, Public Events Manager
Officers: Dr. Samuel Epstein, Chairman, COIP
Paid Staff: 15
Utilizes: Guest Artists
Budget: $100,000 - $500,000
Income Sources: Box Office
Season: October - May   **Annual Attendance:** 70,000

Affiliations: APAP; IAAM; WAAA; California Presenters
Performance Facilities: Beckman Auditorium; Ramo Auditorium

FACILITY

CALIFORNIA INSTITUTE OF TECHNOLOGY - BECKMAN AUDITORIUM
Office of Public Events, 1201 East California Boulevard, Pasadena, CA 91125
(818) 356-3834
   Type of Facility: Auditorium
   Type of Stage: Thrust
   Stage Dimensions: 43'Wx17'H, depth varies from 12'6" to 21'6"
   Seating Capacity: 1,165
   Year Built: 1964   **Architect:** Edward Durell Stone   **Cost:** $1,300,000
   Year Remodeled: 1966   **Cost:** $500,000
   Acoustical Consultant: Vern Knudsen
   Manager: Jerry Willis;   (818) 356-4638
   Resident Groups: Coleman Chamber Music Association

CALIFORNIA INSTITUTE OF TECHNOLOGY - RAMO AUDITORIUM
Office of Public Events, Cal Tech, 332-92, Pasadena, CA 91125
(818) 356-3834
FAX: (818) 577-0130
   Type of Facility: Concert Hall
   Type of Stage: Proscenium
   Stage Dimensions: 32'Wx24'D; 32'Wx13'H proscenium opening
   Seating Capacity: 423
   Year Built: 1971   **Architect:** Robert E. Alexander   **Cost:** $600,000
   Acoustical Consultant: Paul S. Veneklasen & Associates
   Resident Groups: Conejo Symphony Association

PASADENA CIVIC AUDITORIUM
300 East Green Street, Pasadena, CA 91101
(818) 793-2122
FAX: (818) 793-8014
   Founded: 1931
   Type of Facility: Concert Hall; Auditorium; Theatre House; Opera House; Multi-Purpose
   Type of Stage: Proscenium
   Stage Dimensions: 110'Wx42'D; 47'Wx32'H proscenium opening   **Orchestra Pit**
   Seating Capacity: 2,965; 98 removable pit seats
   Year Built: 1931   **Architect:** Bergstrom, Bennett, Haskell   **Cost:** $1,350,000
   Year Remodeled: 1979   **Cost:** $500,000
   Contact for Rental: Auditorium Manager;   (818) 793-2122
   Resident Groups: Pasadena Symphony

PASADENA PLAYHOUSE - BALCONY THEATRE
39 South El Molino Avenue, Pasadena, CA 91101
(818) 792-8672
FAX: (818) 792-7343
   Type of Facility: Theatre House
   Type of Stage: Thrust
   Seating Capacity: 99
   Year Built: 1937
   Contact for Rental: Lars Hansen, Executive Director;   (818) 792-8672
   Resident Groups: Pasadena Playhouse

PASADENA PLAYHOUSE - MAINSTAGE THEATRE
39 South El Molino Avenue, Pasadena, CA 91101
(818) 792-8672
FAX: (818) 792-7343
   Type of Facility: Theatre House
   Type of Stage: Proscenium
   Stage Dimensions: 32'6"x43'   **Orchestra Pit**
   Seating Capacity: 699
   Year Built: 1924
   Year Remodeled: 1984   **Architect:** Richard McCann
   Contact for Rental: Lars Hansen, Executive Director;   (818) 792-8672
   Resident Groups: Pasadena Playhouse

Pomona

FACILITY

CALIFORNIA POLYTECHNIC UNIVERSITY-POMONA - THEATRE
3801 West Temple Avenue, Pomona, CA 91768
(909) 869-7659
   Type of Facility: Auditorium; Theatre House
   Type of Stage: Proscenium
   Stage Dimensions: 50'x96'x38'   **Orchestra Pit**
   Seating Capacity: 500
   Year Built: 1964   **Cost:** $1,900,000
   Contact for Rental: Dennis A. Logan;   (909) 598-4547

Rancho Santa Fe

INSTRUMENTAL MUSIC

SAN DIEGO CHAMBER ORCHESTRA
PO Box 3333, Rancho Santa Fe, CA 92067
(619) 753-6402
FAX: (619) 753-2089
   Founded: 1984
   Arts Area: Symphony; Orchestra; Chamber
   Status: Professional; Non-Profit
   Type: Performing
   Purpose: To present chamber orchestra concerts of the highest artistic quality with fine soloists throughout San Diego
County
   Management: Donald Barra, Music Director; Tamra Saylor, General Manager
   Officers: Charles Dierenfield, President; D. Frederick Shefte, Vice President; Frances Pope, Secretary;
O. Rea Mowery, Treasurer
   Paid Staff: 4
   Paid Artists: 36
   Utilizes: Guest Conductors; Guest Artists
   Budget: $100,000 - $500,000
   Income Sources: Private Foundations/Grants/Endowments; Business/Corporate Donations; Box Office; Government
Grants; Individual Donations
   Season: October - May   **Annual Attendance:** 56,000
   Affiliations: ASOL; Association of California Symphony Orchestras
   Performance Facilities: Sherwood Hall; Fairbanks Ranch

Redding

INSTRUMENTAL MUSIC

SHASTA SYMPHONY
1065 North Old Oregon Trail, Redding, CA 96099
(916) 241-3523
   Founded: 1950
   Arts Area: Symphony; Orchestra; Ensemble
   Status: Non-Professional; Non-Profit
   Type: Performing; Touring; Resident; Educational
   Purpose: Shasta Symphony is a college and community orchestra. It serves an educational and entertainment function for
the college and community.
   Management: Bob Davis, Fine Arts Chairman
   Officers: Harry Blaesing, Orchestra President; Pat Chipps, Orchestra Vice President; Mary Farruggia,
Orchestra League President
   Paid Staff: 2   **Volunteer Staff:** 30
   Paid Artists: 2   **Non-Paid Artists:** 65
   Utilizes: Guest Conductors; Guest Artists; Guest Directors
   Budget: $1,000 - $50,000
   Income Sources: Business/Corporate Donations; Box Office; Individual Donations
   Season: September - June   **Annual Attendance:** 5,000
   Affiliations: Shasta College
   Performance Facilities: Shasta College Fine Arts Theatre

FACILITY

REDDING CIVIC AUDITORIUM - TRADE AND CONVENTION CENTER
700 Auditorium Drive, Redding, CA 96099
(916) 225-4130
FAX: (916) 225-4354
Founded: 1970
Type of Facility: Auditorium; Multi-Purpose
Type of Stage: Proscenium
Stage Dimensions: 85'x40'
Seating Capacity: 2,082
Year Built: 1970 **Architect:** Van Bourg/Nakamoura, Smart and Claybough **Cost:** $3,200,000
Contact for Rental: Pat Foruria; (916) 225-4130
Manager: John Gorman; (916) 225-4100
Resident Groups: Shasta Symphony; Community Concerts; Travel Films

SHASTA COLLEGE - FINE ARTS THEATRE
PO Box 6006, Redding, CA 96001
(916) 225-4610
Type of Facility: Theatre Complex; Concert Hall; Theatre House; Amphitheater
Type of Stage: Thrust; Proscenium
Stage Dimensions: 47'Wx50'D **Orchestra Pit**
Seating Capacity: 471
Year Built: 1968 **Architect:** Woodward/Nicols
Contact for Rental: Dan Howard, Fine Arts Events Coordinator; (916) 225-4610
Manager: Dan Howard; (916) 225-4610
Resident Groups: Shasta College Theatre Arts Department; Shasta College Music Department

Redlands

PERFORMING SERIES

REDLANDS BOWL SUMMER MUSIC FESTIVAL
PO Box 466, Redlands, CA 92373
(909) 793-7316
Founded: 1923
Arts Area: Dance; Vocal Music; Instrumental Music; Lyric Opera; Grand Opera
Status: Professional; Non-Profit
Type: Performing; Sponsoring
Purpose: Provide admission-free symphonies, ballets, operas, musicals and recitals
Officers: Conant K. Halsey, President; Florence Beeler, Vice President/Program Director; David B. Raff,
Chief Financial Officer; Janet M. Weder, Corporate Secretary
Paid Staff: 4 **Volunteer Staff:** 25
Budget: $100,000 - $500,000
Income Sources: Private Foundations/Grants/Endowments; Business/Corporate Donations; Individual Donations
Season: July - August **Annual Attendance:** 80,000
Performance Facilities: Open-air Amphitheatre

REDLANDS SYMPHONY ASSOCIATION
1200 East Colton, PO Box 3080, Redlands, CA 92373-0999
(909) 793-2121
FAX: (909) 793-2029
Founded: 1958
Arts Area: Vocal Music; Instrumental Music
Status: Professional; Non-Profit
Type: Performing; Educational
Purpose: To create and maintain a high-quality symphony orchestra with an annual concert series; to coordinate outreach
programs
Management: James Keays, Orchestra Manager; Bruce Anderson, Personnel Contractor; Jon Robertson, Conductor/Music Director; Viola Slade, Office Manager
Officers: Barbara Wormser, President; Una Hellyer, Vice President; Helen Nies, Secretary; Phillip Doolittle, Treasurer;
Carol Robinson, President Emeritus; Sam Dickey, Controller
Paid Staff: 4 **Volunteer Staff:** 20
Paid Artists: 66 **Non-Paid Artists:** 15
Utilizes: Guest Conductors; Guest Artists
Budget: $100,000 - $500,000
Income Sources: Private Foundations/Grants/Endowments; Business/Corporate Donations; Box Office; Government
Grants; Individual Donations

Season: September - May
Annual Attendance: 8,500
Affiliations: ASOL; Association of California Symphony Orchestras
Performance Facilities: Memorial Chapel, University of Redlands

FACILITY

REDLANDS COMMUNITY MUSIC ASSOCIATION, INC.
PO Box 466, 25 Grant Street, Redlands, CA 92373
(909) 793-7316
Founded: 1923
Type of Facility: Amphitheater
Facility Originally: Park
Type of Stage: Proscenium   **Seating Capacity:** 3,750
Year Built: 1930   **Architect:** Herbert J. Powell
Contact for Rental: City of Redlands;   (714) 798-7528
Resident Groups: Redlands Bowl Summer Music Festival

Redondo Beach

INSTRUMENTAL MUSIC

BEACH CITIES SYMPHONY
PO Box 248, Redondo Beach, CA 90277
(310) 541-2877
Founded: 1951
Arts Area: Symphony
Status: Semi-Professional; Non-Profit
Type: Performing
Purpose: To present an annual season of great masterworks for orchestra in the South Bay at no charge to the audience
Management: Margaret Kendziorek, Orchestra Manager; Theodora Hilley, Librarian
Officers: Margaret M. McWilliams, President; Hans Wohlwill, Chairman of the Board
Paid Staff: 2   **Volunteer Staff:** 12
Paid Artists: 3
Utilizes: Guest Artists
Budget: $1,000 - $50,000
Income Sources: Business/Corporate Donations; Government Grants; Individual Donations
Season: Fall - Spring
Annual Attendance: 6,000
Affiliations: ASOL; Symphony League of Los Angeles County
Performance Facilities: Marsee Auditorium, El Camino College

Redway

PERFORMING SERIES

MATEEL COMMUNITY CENTER, INC.
PO Box 1910, Redway, CA 95489
(707) 923-3368
FAX: (707) 923-4660
Founded: 1979
Arts Area: Dance; Vocal Music; Instrumental Music; Theater; Festivals
Status: Non-Profit
Type: Sponsoring
Purpose: To create a facility for the cultural and educational enhancement of the South Humboldt and
North Mendocino area
Management: Carol Bruno, Events Coordinator; Doug Green, Public Relations; Paul Bassis, Hall Manager; Susan
Manttila, Bookkeeper; Charity Green, Office Manager
Officers: Gary Chapman, President; Doug Green, Vice President; Jane Gund, Secretary; Jimmy Dangler, Treasurer
Paid Staff: 3
Utilizes: Guest Artists
Budget: $500,000 - $1,000,000
Income Sources: Private Foundations/Grants/Endowments; Business/Corporate Donations; Box Office; Government
Grants; Individual Donations
Season: 52 Weeks
Annual Attendance: 20,000

Richmond

FACILITY

RICHMOND MEMORIAL CONVENTION CENTER
PO Box 4046, Richmond, CA 94804
(510) 620-6789
FAX: (510) 620-6583
> **Type of Facility:** Theatre Complex; Concert Hall; Auditorium; Studio Performance; Performance Center; Theatre House; Opera House; Civic Center; Arena; Multi-Purpose
> **Facility Originally:** Meeting Hall
> **Type of Stage:** Proscenium; Arena
> **Stage Dimensions:** 140'Wx60'Dx40'H   **Orchestra Pit**
> **Seating Capacity:** 3,756
> **Year Built:** 1951   **Architect:** Milton Pflueger   **Cost:** $1,250,000
> **Contact for Rental:** Bill Allums, Manager;   (510) 620-6789
> **Resident Groups:** Community Concerts; Power Pak Productions; Farr Entertainment; Nyarit Promociones; WRA Productions
> *Facilities for a host of entertainment programs*

Riverside

DANCE

RIVERSIDE BALLET THEATRE
3840 Lemon Street, Riverside, CA 92501
(909) 787-7850
FAX: (909) 683-1284
> **Founded:** 1968
> **Arts Area:** Modern; Ballet
> **Status:** Professional; Non-Profit
> **Type:** Performing; Educational; Sponsoring
> **Purpose:** To give the young dancers the opportunity to perform in a professional atmosphere and provide high-calibre productions to the community
> **Management:** Moira Kamgar, Chief Officer; Fred Arens, Office Manager
> **Officers:** Glend Carhart-Hensly, Director
> **Volunteer Staff:** 10
> **Paid Artists:** 5   **Non-Paid Artists:** 75
> **Utilizes:** Special Technical Talent; Guest Artists
> **Budget:** $50,000 - $100,000
> **Income Sources:** Private Foundations/Grants/Endowments; Business/Corporate Donations; Box Office; Government Grants; Individual Donations
> **Season:** September - May   **Annual Attendance:** 8,000
> **Performance Facilities:** Landis Auditorium

INSTRUMENTAL MUSIC

RIVERSIDE COUNTY PHILHARMONIC
PO Box 1601, Riverside, CA 92502
(909) 787-0251
> **Founded:** 1958
> **Arts Area:** Symphony; Orchestra
> **Status:** Professional; Non-Profit
> **Type:** Performing
> **Purpose:** To provide the Inland area with symphonic music to the general public and for education
> **Management:** Helen Norton, General Manager; Patrick Flynn, Musical Director/Conductor
> **Paid Staff:** 1   **Volunteer Staff:** 10
> **Paid Artists:** 55
> **Budget:** $1,000,000 - $5,000,000
> **Income Sources:** Private Foundations/Grants/Endowments; Business/Corporate Donations; Box Office; Government Grants; Individual Donations
> **Season:** November - May   **Annual Attendance:** 5,000

Affiliations: ASOL
Performance Facilities: Municipal Auditorium

PERFORMING SERIES

PERFORMING ARTS PRESENTATIONS
University of California, Riverside, CA 92521
(909) 787-4629
FAX: (909) 787-2221
Founded: 1973
Arts Area: Dance; Vocal Music; Instrumental Music; Theater
Status: Professional; Non-Profit
Type: Sponsoring
Purpose: To be a cultural and educational resource to the campus and community
Management: Marnie Duke, Manager
Paid Staff: 3   **Volunteer Staff:** 1
Utilizes: Guest Artists
Budget: $100,000 - $500,000
Income Sources: Private Foundations/Grants/Endowments; Business/Corporate Donations; Box Office; Government
Grants; Individual Donations; University Resources
Season: October - May
Annual Attendance: 10,000
Affiliations: WAAA; APAP; California Presenters
Performance Facilities: University Theatre

FACILITY

RIVERSIDE CONVENTION CENTER AT RAINCROSS SQUARE
3443 Orange Street, Riverside, CA 92506
(909) 787-7950
FAX: (909) 787-4940
Founded: 1975
Type of Facility: Concert Hall; Auditorium; Outdoor (Concert); Civic Center; Arena; Multi-Purpose; Room
Type of Stage: Flexible
Stage Dimensions: 40'x26'D; 40'x32'
Seating Capacity: 2,700
Year Built: 1975   **Architect:** Brown & Rawdon   **Cost:** $7,000,000
Acoustical Consultant: Paul Richardson, House Technician
Contact for Rental: Lisa Snider, Event Services/Catering Manager;   (909) 787-7950
Manager: Joseph Prevratil, President/CEO

RIVERSIDE MUNICIPAL AUDITORIUM
3485 7th Street, Riverside, CA 92501
(909) 787-7950
FAX: (909) 787-4940
Type of Facility: Auditorium
Facility Originally: Meeting Hall; Ballroom; Movie House
Type of Stage: Proscenium
Stage Dimensions: 70'Wx40'D; 40'Wx26'H proscenium opening
Seating Capacity: 1,642
Year Built: 1929   **Architect:** Arthur Benton & Stanley Wilson
Contact for Rental: Bill Harper;   (909) 787-7678

UNIVERSITY OF CALIFORNIA-RIVERSIDE - UNIVERSITY THEATRE
900 University Avenue, PO Box 112, Riverside, CA 92521
(909) 787-3319
Type of Facility: Theatre House
Type of Stage: Proscenium
Stage Dimensions: 60'x62'x47'   **Orchestra Pit**
Seating Capacity: 496
Year Built: 1962   **Architect:** George V. Russel   **Cost:** $1,500,000
Year Remodeled: 1977   **Architect:** Donald O'Neill   **Cost:** $250,000
Contact for Rental: David E. Kellstrand, Facilities Director;   (909) 787-3319

Rolling Hills Estate

FACILITY

NORRIS THEATRE FOR THE PERFORMING ARTS
27570 Crossfield Drive, Rolling Hills Estate, CA 90274
(310) 544-0403
FAX: (310) 544-2473
    Founded: 1983
    Type of Facility: Auditorium; Performance Center; Theatre House
    Type of Stage: Proscenium
    Stage Dimensions: 44'x38' **Orchestra Pit**
    Seating Capacity: 450
    Year Built: 1983 **Architect:** Anthony - Langford Architects **Cost:** $6,000,000
    Contact for Rental: Ellen Rodney; (310) 544-0403
    Resident Groups: Chamber Orchestra

Sacramento

DANCE

DALE SCHOLL DANCE ART
PO Box 162432, Sacramento, CA 95816
(916) 364-8721; (916) 483-4017
    Founded: 1982
    Arts Area: Modern; Ballet; Jazz; Theatre; Storytelling
    Status: Professional; Non-Profit
    Type: Performing; Resident
    Purpose: To offer an eclectic mix of dance and theatre
    Management: Joan Liddicoat, Manager; Dale Scholl, Artistic Director
    Paid Staff: 2
    Paid Artists: 7
    Utilizes: Guest Artists; Guest Choreographers
    Budget: $1,000 - $50,000
    Income Sources: Private Foundations/Grants/Endowments; Business/Corporate Donations; Box Office; Government Grants; Individual Donations
    Season: September - April
    Affiliations: Sacramento Area Dance Alliance
    Performance Facilities: 24th Street Theatre

SACRAMENTO BALLET
2791 24th Street, #16, Sacramento, CA 95818
(916) 736-2860
FAX: (916) 452-3445
    Founded: 1956
    Arts Area: Ballet
    Status: Professional; Non-Profit
    Type: Performing; Touring; Resident
    Purpose: To present professional performances of a wide range of standard and contemporary ballets in the classical mode to diverse audiences
    Management: Ernest Phinney, Executive Director; Ron Cunningham, Artistic Director
    Officers: Richard N. Frey, President; Claudia Cummings, First Vice President; Dave Molit, Treasurer; Lisa Wright, Secretary
    Paid Staff: 10 **Volunteer Staff:** 5
    Paid Artists: 18 **Non-Paid Artists:** 40
    Utilizes: Special Technical Talent; Guest Conductors; Guest Artists
    Budget: $1,000,000 - $5,000,000
    Income Sources: Private Foundations/Grants/Endowments; Business/Corporate Donations; Box Office; Government Grants; Individual Donations
    Season: August - April **Annual Attendance:** 75,000
    Affiliations: Dance USA; NSFRE; Regional Dance Pacific America
    Performance Facilities: Sacramento Community Center Theatre

INSTRUMENTAL MUSIC

CAMELLIA SYMPHONY
PO Box 19786, Sacramento, CA 95819
(916) 344-5844
>**Founded:** 1963
>**Arts Area:** Symphony
>**Status:** Semi-Professional; Non-Profit
>**Type:** Performing
>**Purpose:** To expand the musical growth of the Sacramento area by providing unique repertoire, opportunities for area musicians and composers, and performances at reasonable prices
>**Management:** Lauren Russel, General Manager; Nan Washburn, Music Director/Conductor
>**Officers:** Donald Houser, President; Mary Schneider, Vice President; Margaret Thompson, Secretary; Carl Van Der Camp, Treasurer
>**Paid Staff:** 7
>**Paid Artists:** 6   **Non-Paid Artists:** 73
>**Utilizes:** Guest Conductors; Guest Artists
>**Budget:** $50,000 - $100,000
>**Income Sources:** Private Foundations/Grants/Endowments; Business/Corporate Donations; Box Office; Government Grants; Individual Donations
>**Season:** October - May   **Annual Attendance:** 5,000
>**Affiliations:** ASOL; Association of California Symphony Orchestras
>**Performance Facilities:** Hiram Johnson High School Auditorium

SACRAMENTO SYMPHONY ASSOCIATION
77 Cadillac Drive, #B1, Sacramento, CA 95825
(916) 649-0300
FAX: (916) 641-0830
>**Founded:** 1948
>**Arts Area:** Symphony; Orchestra; Chamber; Ensemble
>**Status:** Professional; Non-Profit
>**Type:** Performing; Touring; Educational; Sponsoring
>**Management:** Robert Walker, Executive Director; Alasdair Neale, Music Director; Tracy Davis, Orchestra Manager
>**Officers:** Ernist Lewis, President
>**Paid Staff:** 22
>**Paid Artists:** 39
>**Utilizes:** Guest Conductors; Guest Artists
>**Budget:** $1,000,000 - $5,000,000
>**Income Sources:** Private Foundations/Grants/Endowments; Business/Corporate Donations; Box Office; Government Grants; Individual Donations
>**Season:** September - May   **Annual Attendance:** 250,000
>**Affiliations:** ASOL
>**Performance Facilities:** Sacramento Community Center Theater

VOCAL MUSIC

SACRAMENTO MEN'S CHORUS
PO Box 188726, Sacramento, CA 95818
(916) 444-5213
>**Founded:** 1985
>**Arts Area:** Choral
>**Status:** Non-Professional; Non-Profit
>**Type:** Performing; Touring
>**Management:** Frank Lawler, Business Manager
>**Paid Staff:** 2
>**Non-Paid Artists:** 30
>**Budget:** $1,000 - $50,000
>**Income Sources:** Box Office; Individual Donations
>**Season:** September - June   **Annual Attendance:** 3,000
>**Performance Facilities:** First United Methodist

SACRAMENTO OPERA
2131 Capital Avenue, Sacramento, CA 95816
(916) 442-4224
FAX: (916) 442-4254
>**Founded:** 1947
>**Arts Area:** Grand Opera
>**Status:** Professional; Non-Profit

Type: Performing; Educational
Purpose: To produce opera of the highest level to the Sacramento community
Management: Marianne H. Oaks, General Director; Gene Sirois, Marketing Director
Officers: Randall Yim, President
Paid Staff: 4 **Volunteer Staff:** 2
Utilizes: Special Technical Talent; Guest Conductors; Guest Artists; Guest Directors
Budget: $500,000 - $1,000,000
Income Sources: Private Foundations/Grants/Endowments; Business/Corporate Donations; Box Office; Government Grants; Individual Donations
Season: September - March **Annual Attendance:** 22,000
Affiliations: OA
Performance Facilities: Sacramento Community Center Theatre

THEATRE

SACRAMENTO MUSIC CIRCUS
1510 J Street, Suite 100, Sacramento, CA 95814
(916) 446-5880; (916) 557-1999
FAX: (916) 446-1370
> **Founded:** 1951
> **Arts Area:** Musical; Theatrical Group
> **Status:** Professional; Non-Profit
> **Type:** Performing; Resident
> **Purpose:** To present a week of musical summer stock in Sacramento, as well as national tours
> **Management:** Russell Lewis, President; Leland Ball, Producing Director; Richard Lewis, Marlene Shire, Managing Directors
> **Paid Staff:** 110 **Volunteer Staff:** 3
> **Paid Artists:** 40 **Non-Paid Artists:** 10
> **Utilizes:** Special Technical Talent; Guest Artists
> **Budget:** $5,000,000 - $10,000,000
> **Income Sources:** Box Office
> **Season:** July - Labor Day
> **Affiliations:** Resident Musical Theatre Association

SACRAMENTO THEATRE COMPANY
1419 H Street, Sacramento, CA 95814
(916) 446-7501
FAX: (916) 446-4066
> **Founded:** 1942
> **Arts Area:** Theatrical Group
> **Status:** Semi-Professional; Non-Profit
> **Type:** Performing; Resident
> **Purpose:** The Sacramento Theatre Company produces 10 productions on its two stages between September and May
> **Management:** Mark Cuddy, Artistic Director
> **Officers:** Susan Peters, President; Barry Kohn, Vice President; Michael Moy, Treasurer; Diane Hazelroth, Secretary
> **Paid Staff:** 17
> **Paid Artists:** 6
> **Utilizes:** Guest Artists; Guest Directors
> **Budget:** $1,000,000 - $5,000,000
> **Income Sources:** Private Foundations/Grants/Endowments; Business/Corporate Donations; Box Office; Government Grants; Individual Donations
> **Season:** September - May
> **Annual Attendance:** 40,000
> **Affiliations:** TCG
> **Performance Facilities:** McClatchey Mainstage and Stage Two

PERFORMING SERIES

CROCKER ART MUSEUM
216 O Street, Sacramento, CA 95814
(916) 264-5423
> **Founded:** 1885
> **Arts Area:** Dance; Vocal Music; Instrumental Music; Theater
> **Status:** Non-Profit
> **Type:** Sponsoring
> **Purpose:** To offer opportunity for artists to perform in a museum—a small and intimate setting
> **Management:** Barbara Gibbs, Museum Director
> **Officers:** Jane Lamb, Music Board Chairman
> **Paid Staff:** 23

Utilizes: Guest Artists
Budget: $500,000 - $1,000,000
Income Sources: Private Foundations/Grants/Endowments; Business/Corporate Donations; Government Grants; Individual Donations
Season: September - June
Annual Attendance: 4,500
Performance Facilities: Crocker Art Museum Ballroom

FESTIVAL OF NEW AMERICAN MUSIC
c/o Music Dept., CSU-Sacramento, 6000 J Street, Sacramento, CA 95819
(916) 278-6514
FAX: (916) 278-7217
Arts Area: Vocal Music; Instrumental Music; Festivals; Chamber Music
Status: Non-Profit
Type: Performing; Educational; Sponsoring
Purpose: To perform works written by American composers from the last ten years
Management: Gene Savage, Festival Director
Budget: $100,000 - $500,000
Income Sources: Private Foundations/Grants/Endowments; Business/Corporate Donations; Government Grants; Individual Donations
Performance Facilities: Music Recital Hall

FINEST ASIAN PERFORMING ARTS, INC.
PO Box 162163, Sacramento, CA 95816
(916) 924-1212; (415) 566-1252
FAX: (916) 924-7212; (415) 566-6005
Alternate Mailing Address: PO Box 22668, San Francisco, CA 94122
Founded: 1988
Arts Area: Dance; Vocal Music; Instrumental Music; Festivals
Status: Professional; Semi-Professional
Type: Performing; Sponsoring
Purpose: To promote Eastern culture through performing arts to the Western world and community
Management: Anna Y. Mayo, Executive Director; Lucy Nemac, Secretary; Yan Zhang, Music Director/Advisor
Officers: Anna Y. Mayo, President; William Ku, Finance Officer; Lucy Nemac, Secretary; Jesse Kaplan, Legal Officer; Cheung Fong DDS, Vice President
Paid Staff: 2   **Volunteer Staff:** 30
Paid Artists: 10   **Non-Paid Artists:** 12
Utilizes: Special Technical Talent; Guest Artists
Budget: $50,000 - $100,000
Income Sources: Private Foundations/Grants/Endowments; Business/Corporate Donations; Government Grants; Individual Donations
Season: August - November   **Annual Attendance:** 5,000
Affiliations: Finest Asian Music Festival

FACILITY

SACRAMENTO COMMUNITY CENTER EXHIBITION HALL
1100 14th Street, Sacramento, CA 95814
(916) 264-5291
FAX: (916) 264-7687
Type of Facility: Exhibition Hall
Type of Stage: Flexible
Seating Capacity: 7,000
Year Built: 1974
Contact for Rental: Michael Stauffer;   (916) 264-5291
Manager: Sam Burns;   (916) 264-5291

SACRAMENTO COMMUNITY CENTER THEATER
1301 L Street, Sacramento, CA 95814
(916) 264-5181
Type of Facility: Theatre House
Type of Stage: Proscenium
Stage Dimensions: 70'x85'x46'3"   **Orchestra Pit**
Seating Capacity: 2,436
Year Built: 1974
Contact for Rental: (916) 264-5291
Manager: Sam Burns;   (916) 264-5291

SACRAMENTO COMMUNITY CONVENTION CENTER
1100 14th Street, Sacramento, CA 95814
(916) 449-5291
FAX: (916) 264-7687
    Administrative Offices: 1030 15th Street, Suite 250, Sacramento, CA 95814
    Type of Facility: Civic Center
    Year Built: 1974 **Architect:** Sacramento Architects Collaboration **Cost:** $19,100,000
    Acoustical Consultant: Bolt, Beranek & Newman
    Contact for Rental: Michael Stauffer; (916) 264-5291
    Manager: Sam Burns; (916) 264-5291
    Resident Groups: Sacramento Symphony; Sacramento Ballet; Sacramento Opera

San Anselmo

DANCE

CHHANDAM CHITRESH DAS DANCE COMPANY
PO Box 716, San Anselmo, CA 94979
(415) 453-4305
    Founded: 1980
    Arts Area: Ethnic
    Status: Professional; Non-Profit
    Type: Performing; Touring; Resident; Educational; Sponsoring
    Purpose: To establish Kathak dance in the United States through teaching, performing and community outreach
    Management: Chitresh Das, Artistic Director; Michele Zonka, Manager
    Officers: Chitresh Das, Executive Director; Dr. Surjit Singh, President; Shamim Formosa; Doug Flegal
    Paid Staff: 2 **Volunteer Staff:** 2
    Paid Artists: 10 **Non-Paid Artists:** 5
    Budget: $50,000 - $100,000
    Income Sources: Private Foundations/Grants/Endowments; Box Office; Government Grants; Individual Donations
    Season: September - June

San Bernardino

INSTRUMENTAL MUSIC

INLAND EMPIRE SYMPHONY ASSOCIATION
362 West Court Street, San Bernardino, CA 92401
(909) 381-5388
    Founded: 1960
    Arts Area: Symphony; Orchestra; Chamber; Ensemble
    Status: Professional; Non-Profit
    Type: Performing; Touring; Educational; Sponsoring
    Management: Susan Feller, Executive Director; Arlette Cardenes, Operations Manager
    Officers: Allen Gresham, President; Brian Tomkins, Treasurer; Marilyn Bidney, Secretary; Mary Schnepp, Guild President
    Paid Staff: 4 **Volunteer Staff:** 15
    Paid Artists: 75
    Utilizes: Guest Conductors; Guest Artists
    Budget: $500,000 - $1,000,000
    Income Sources: Private Foundations/Grants/Endowments; Business/Corporate Donations; Box Office; Government Grants; Individual Donations
    Season: September - April **Annual Attendance:** 80,000
    Affiliations: ASOL; Association of California Symphony Orchestras; APAP
    Performance Facilities: The California Theatre of Performing Arts

VOCAL MUSIC

SAN BERNARDINO CIVIC LIGHT OPERA ASSOCIATION
1398 North E Street, PO Box 606, San Bernardino, CA 92402
(909) 386-7353
FAX: (909) 386-7358
    Founded: 1947
    Arts Area: Light Opera; MUSICAL THEATRE
    Status: Professional; Non-Profit
    Type: Performing; Educational
    Purpose: The presentation of live musical theatre with opportunities for professional and non-professionals; educational theatre

Management: C. Dale Jenks, General Manager/Producer/Treasurer
Officers: Evlyn Wilcox, President; Walter Shaidnagle, Carl H. Reitz, Vice Presidents
Utilizes: Special Technical Talent; Guest Conductors; Guest Artists; Guest Directors
Income Sources: Private Foundations/Grants/Endowments; Business/Corporate Donations; Box Office;
Government Grants; Individual Donations
Season: 52 Weeks
Affiliations: AEA
Performance Facilities: The California Theatre of Performing Arts

FACILITY

CALIFORNIA STATE UNIVERSITY - CREATIVE ARTS BUILDING
5500 University Parkway, San Bernardino, CA 92407
(909) 887-7452
Type of Facility: Performance Center
Type of Stage: Thrust
Seating Capacity: 143
Year Built: 1977 **Architect:** Carl Maston **Cost:** $2,500,000
Acoustical Consultant: Gerald Strang

THE CALIFORNIA THEATRE OF PERFORMING ARTS
562 West Fourth Street, San Bernardino, CA 92402
(909) 386-7361
Type of Facility: Auditorium; Theatre House; Opera House
Facility Originally: Vaudeville
Type of Stage: Proscenium
Stage Dimensions: 60'x60'x30'
Orchestra Pit
Seating Capacity: 1,760
Year Built: 1928 **Architect:** Thomas Lamb
Contact for Rental: C. Dale Jenks
Resident Groups: San Bernardino Civic Light Opera Association; San Bernardino Valley Community Concert
Association; Inland Empire Symphony Orchestra

San Diego

DANCE

CALIFORNIA BALLET COMPANY
8276 Ronson Road, San Diego, CA 92111
(619) 560-5676
Founded: 1967
Arts Area: Ballet
Status: Semi-Professional; Non-Profit
Type: Performing; Touring; Resident
Management: Maxine Mahon, Director; Matt Bean, Production Manager
Paid Staff: 6 **Volunteer Staff:** 20
Utilizes: Guest Artists
Budget: $500,000 - $1,000,000
Income Sources: Private Foundations/Grants/Endowments; Business/Corporate Donations; Box Office; Government
Grants; Individual Donations

MALASHOCK DANCE AND COMPANY
438 Camino del Rio South, #213, San Diego, CA 92108
(619) 298-3304
FAX: (619) 291-6652
Founded: 1988
Arts Area: Modern
Status: Professional
Type: Performing; Touring
Purpose: To create, produce and perform modern dance choreographed by John Malashock
Management: John Malashock, Artistic Director; Victoria Saunders, Managing Director
Paid Staff: 2
Paid Artists: 5
Utilizes: Special Technical Talent; Guest Artists; Guest Choreographers

Budget: $100,000 - $500,000
Income Sources: Private Foundations/Grants/Endowments; Business/Corporate Donations; Box Office; Government Grants; Individual Donations
Season: April - November   **Annual Attendance:** 3,000
Performance Facilities: Old Globe Theatre

SAN DIEGO FOUNDATION FOR THE PERFORMING ARTS
625 Broadway, Suite 1006, San Diego, CA 92101
(619) 234-5853
FAX: (619) 234-0521
Founded: 1982
Arts Area: Modern; Ballet; Ethnic
Status: Professional; Non-Profit
Type: Educational; Presenter
Purpose: To act as a catalyst in the development of an appreciation for dance in San Diego
Management: Fred Colby, Executive Director; Nadine Buchner, Development Director; Albert Rodewald, Public Affairs Director; William Conrow, Project Director
Officers: Danah Fayman, President; Jean Hellerich, Vice President; Bob Levy, Secretary
Paid Staff: 9   **Volunteer Staff:** 2
Paid Artists: 20   **Non-Paid Artists:** 250
Utilizes: Guest Artists; Guest Choreographers
Budget: $1,000,000 - $5,000,000
Income Sources: Private Foundations/Grants/Endowments; Business/Corporate Donations; Box Office; Government Grants; Individual Donations
Season: September - June
Annual Attendance: 28,000
Affiliations: APAP: California Presenters; WAAA
Performance Facilities: Spreduls Theatre; Civic Center

SUSHI PERFORMANCE AND VISUAL ART
852 Eighth Avenue, San Diego, CA 92101
(619) 235-8466
FAX: (619) 235-8466
Founded: 1980
Arts Area: Modern
Status: Professional; Non-Profit
Type: Performing; Touring; Educational
Purpose: Sushi is a presenter of contemporary performance and dance by those artists working in experimental and meaningful form and content and whose vision embodies the diversity of our rich cultural, ethnic, sexual and personal backgrounds
Management: Lynn Schurhe, Executive Director; Vicki Wolf, Managing Director
Paid Staff: 5   **Volunteer Staff:** 5
Paid Artists: 75
Utilizes: Guest Artists
Budget: $100,000 - $500,000
Income Sources: Private Foundations/Grants/Endowments; Business/Corporate Donations; Government Grants; Individual Donations; Admissions; Membership
Season: September - June
Annual Attendance: 6,000

INSTRUMENTAL MUSIC

ARIOSO WIND QUARTET
San Diego State University, Department of Music, San Diego, CA 92182
(619) 594-6031
FAX: (619) 594-1692
Arts Area: Chamber; Ensemble; Instrumental Group
Status: Professional; Non-Profit
Type: Performing; Touring; Resident; Educational
Purpose: To increase the number and diversity of chamber music enthusiasts; to perform high-caliber concerts featuring works selected for a specific audience; to educate performers, teachers and audiences now and in the future; to sponsor educational outreach programs and adult multi-cultural concerts locally and in conjunction with touring engagements
Management: Marian Liebowitz, Artistic Director; Constance Mullin, Booking Agent
Budget: $1,000 - $50,000
Income Sources: Private Foundations/Grants/Endowments; Business/Corporate Donations; Government Grants; Individual Donations

SAN DIEGO SYMPHONY ORCHESTRA
1245 Seventh Avenue, San Diego, CA 92101
(619) 699-4200
FAX: (619) 699-4237
Founded: 1910
Arts Area: Symphony; Orchestra
Status: Professional; Non-Profit
Type: Performing; Educational; Sponsoring
Purpose: To present the highest quality performances of classical music and build a superior organization within the San Diego arts community
Management: Wesley Brustad, Executive Director; Yoav Talmi, Music Director; Lynn Hallbacka, General Manager
Paid Staff: 25   **Volunteer Staff:** 500
Paid Artists: 81
Utilizes: Guest Conductors; Guest Artists
Budget: $5,000,000 - $10,000,000
Income Sources: Business/Corporate Donations; Box Office; Individual Donations
Season: October - May   **Annual Attendance:** 125,000
Affiliations: ASOL; Association of California Symphony Orchestras
Performance Facilities: Copley Symphony Hall

SAN DIEGO YOUTH SYMPHONY
Casa Del Prado, Balboa Park, San Diego, CA 92101
(619) 233-3232
Founded: 1945
Arts Area: Symphony; Orchestra; Chamber; Ensemble
Status: Non-Professional; Non-Profit
Type: Performing; Touring; Educational
Purpose: To enhance the music in youthful musicians in San Diego County and to provide educational and performance opportunities for youthful musicians
Management: Louis Campiglia, Music Director/Conductor
Officers: Kristine Henyer, President
Volunteer Staff: 12
Non-Paid Artists: 75
Utilizes: Guest Artists
Budget: $100,000 - $500,000
Income Sources: Private Foundations/Grants/Endowments; Business/Corporate Donations; Box Office; Government Grants; Individual Donations; Fundraising
Season: September - July
Annual Attendance: 7,000
Affiliations: ASOL (Youth Orchestra Division); Association of California Symphony Orchestras
Performance Facilities: Balboa Park Club; Westgate Hotel

VOCAL MUSIC

SAN DIEGO COMIC OPERA
526 Market Street, San Diego, CA 92101
(619) 231-5714
FAX: (619) 231-0662
Founded: 1980
Arts Area: Light Opera; Operetta; Musical Theater
Status: Professional; Semi-Professional; Non-Profit
Type: Performing; Touring; Resident; Educational
Purpose: To produce musical theater that provides creative employment for local professional artists and a proving ground for young artists moving toward a professional career
Management: Leon Nataker, Artistic Director; Kathleen Switzer, Managing Director
Officers: John Lasher, President; Bonnie Cogan, Treasurer; Patti Goodwin, Secretary
Paid Staff: 4   **Volunteer Staff:** 100
Paid Artists: 150
Utilizes: Special Technical Talent; Guest Conductors; Guest Directors
Budget: $100,000 - $500,000
Income Sources: Private Foundations/Grants/Endowments; Business/Corporate Donations; Box Office; Government Grants; Individual Donations
Season: March - October
Annual Attendance: 9,000
Affiliations: San Diego Theatre League; OA; San Diego Arts and Culture Coalition; Central City Association
Performance Facilities: Casa del Prado

SAN DIEGO MEN'S CHORUS
PO Box 33825, San Diego, CA 92163
(619) 296-7664
>**Founded:** 1985
>**Arts Area:** Choral
>**Status:** Non-Professional; Non-Profit
>**Type:** Performing; Touring
>**Purpose:** To sing, to unite in song and to share our music and unity
>**Officers:** Del Garrett, Secretary
>**Paid Staff:** 3   **Volunteer Staff:** 7
>**Non-Paid Artists:** 50
>**Utilizes:** Guest Artists
>**Budget:** $50,000 - $100,000
>**Income Sources:** Box Office; Individual Donations; Fund-raising
>**Season:** September - July   **Annual Attendance:** 5,000

SAN DIEGO OPERA ASSOCIATION
PO Box 988, San Diego, CA 92112
(619) 232-7636
FAX: (619) 231-6915
>**Founded:** 1965
>**Arts Area:** Grand Opera; Operetta
>**Status:** Professional; Non-Profit
>**Type:** Performing; Touring; Resident; Educational
>**Purpose:** To present professional opera, concerts, recitals and educational programs
>**Management:** Ian D. Campbell, General Director; Marianne Flettner, Artistic Administrator
>**Officers:** Lee Goldberg, President
>**Paid Staff:** 22   **Volunteer Staff:** 150
>**Paid Artists:** 350
>**Utilizes:** Special Technical Talent; Guest Conductors; Guest Artists; Guest Directors
>**Budget:** $5,000,000 - $10,000,000
>**Income Sources:** Private Foundations/Grants/Endowments; Business/Corporate Donations; Box Office; Government Grants; Individual Donations
>**Season:** October - May   **Annual Attendance:** 58,000
>**Performance Facilities:** Civic Theater

STARLIGHT MUSICAL THEATRE/SAN DIEGO CIVIC LIGHT OPERA ASSOCIATION
1549 El Prado - Balboa Park, San Diego, CA 92101
(619) 544-7800
FAX: (619) 544-0496
>**Founded:** 1946
>**Arts Area:** Light Opera; Musical Theatre
>**Status:** Professional; Non-Profit
>**Type:** Performing; Educational
>**Purpose:** To promote and preserve musical theatre as an art form
>**Management:** C.E. "Bud" Farnks, Executive Director; Don and Bonnie Ward, Producing Artistic Directors
>**Officers:** James Bowers, President of the Board of Directors
>**Paid Staff:** 19   **Volunteer Staff:** 1
>**Paid Artists:** 249
>**Utilizes:** Special Technical Talent; Guest Conductors; Guest Directors
>**Budget:** $1,000,000 - $5,000,000
>**Income Sources:** Private Foundations/Grants/Endowments; Business/Corporate Donations; Box Office; Government Grants; Individual Donations; Memberships
>**Season:** May - September; October-April   **Annual Attendance:** 130,000
>**Performance Facilities:** Starlight Bowl; Civic Theatre; Spreckles Theatre

THEATRE

BLACKFRIARS THEATRE
PO Box 126957, San Diego, CA 92112
(619) 232-4088
>**Founded:** 1982
>**Arts Area:** Professional
>**Status:** Professional; Non-Profit
>**Type:** Performing; Resident; Co-Produce Community Projects
>**Purpose:** To entertain and challange audiences with plays that speak to the American experience, plays whose impact is enhanced by the intimacy of our small theatre space, and whose content is most powerfully communicated by honest, meticulously-crafted performances

Management: Ralph Elias, Artistic Director; Allison Brennan, Executive Producer; Dan C. Campbell, Marketing/Communications Manager
Officers: Ronald L. Styn, President; Terrence L. Bingman, Vice President; Stephen H. Streifer, Treasurer; Linda G. Hack, Secretary
Paid Staff: 5   **Volunteer Staff:** 85
Paid Artists: 50
Utilizes: Guest Artists; Guest Directors; Local Artists and Directors
Budget: $100,000 - $500,000
Income Sources: Private Foundations/Grants/Endowments; Business/Corporate Donations; Box Office; Government Grants; Individual Donations
Season: September - June   **Annual Attendance:** 16,000
Affiliations: AEA; San Diego Theatre League
Performance Facilities: Bristol Court Playhouse; Blackfriars Theatre

GASLAMP QUARTER THEATRE
436 Fourth Avenue, San Diego, CA 92101
(619) 232-9608
Founded: 1980
Arts Area: Professional; Musical; Theatrical Group
Status: Professional; Non-Profit
Type: Performing; Educational; Sponsoring
Purpose: To present professional productions of contemporary off-Broadway type plays, most of which San Diego premiers; to present works which tackle the most pressing social issues in American society with a focus on urban issues
Management: Steve Bevans, Managing Director; Kit Goldman, Adleane Hunter, Will Roberson, Rosina Widdowsen-Reynolds, Artistic Associates
Paid Staff: 8   **Volunteer Staff:** 100
Paid Artists: 50
Utilizes: Guest Artists; Guest Directors
Budget: $500,000 - $1,000,000
Income Sources: Private Foundations/Grants/Endowments; Business/Corporate Donations; Box Office; Government Grants; Individual Donations
Season: September - June   **Annual Attendance:** 40,000
Affiliations: San Diego Theatre League
Performance Facilities: Hahn Cosmopolitan Theatre

INSTITUTE FOR READERS THEATRE
PO Box 178333, San Diego, CA 92117
(619) 276-1948
Founded: 1972
Arts Area: Professional
Status: Commercial
Type: Performing; Touring; Resident; Educational
Purpose: To promote all aspects of Readers Theatre, the fastest-growing innovation in art and education
Management: Dr. William Adams, Director; Rosemary Adams, Assistant Director; William Franklin Smith, Business Manager; Flossie Smith, Technician; Thomas Graves, Manager, Readers Theatre Script Service
Paid Staff: 14
Utilizes: Special Technical Talent; Guest Artists; Guest Directors
Budget: $100,000 - $500,000
Income Sources: Business/Corporate Donations
Affiliations: University of Central Florida

OLD GLOBE THEATRE
1363 Old Globe Way, San Diego, CA 92101
(619) 231-1941
FAX: (619) 231-5879
Mailing Address: PO Box 2171, San Diego, CA 92112
Founded: 1937
Arts Area: Professional; Theatrical Group
Status: Professional; Non-Profit
Type: Performing; Educational; Sponsoring
Purpose: To affirm its commitment to its survival in maintaining the integrity of theatre by producing the highest quality professional theatre; to undertake a wide spectrum of theatrical enterprises with continued emphasis on Shakespeare as well as other world classics and contemporary and new works; to provide theatrical professionals with a challenging and supportive environment condusive to individual and collective artistic growth; to establish a training program which will afford the intern direct involvement in all aspects of the professional theatre; to serve and involve the community in a manner that delights, stimulates, and instructs; to develop audiences through educational, outreach, and touring programs; to provide a forum for promoting an understanding of the unique character of this region; to achieve local, regional and national recognition by a commitment to an American classical standard
Management: Thomas Hall, Managing Director; Craig Noel, Executive Producer; Jack O'Brien, Artistic Director

Officers: Bobbie Quick, President, Board of Directors
Paid Staff: 120
Paid Artists: 150
Utilizes: Special Technical Talent; Guest Artists; Guest Directors
Budget: $5,000,000 - $10,000,000
Income Sources: Private Foundations/Grants/Endowments; Business/Corporate Donations; Box Office; Government Grants; Individual Donations
Season: December - October   **Annual Attendance:** 275,000
Affiliations: TCG; LORT; AAA
Performance Facilities: Old Globe Theatre; Cassius Carter Centre Stage; Lowell Davies Festival Theatre

SAN DIEGO JUNIOR THEATRE
Casa del Prado, #208, Balboa Park, San Diego, CA 92101
(619) 239-1311
Founded: 1948
Arts Area: Theatrical Group
Status: Non-Professional; Non-Profit
Type: Performing; Educational
Purpose: To instruct youth, ages 8-18, in theatre arts for their benefit and enjoyment
Management: Pat Rogers, Executive Director; Michael Erickson, Artistic Director; Jennifer Nash, Education Director; Deborah Sims, Marketing/Public Relations
Officers: Roseanne Luth, President, Board of Directors; Carol Windham, Secretary; Kathy Haber, Treasurer
Paid Staff: 8   **Volunteer Staff:** 15
Paid Artists: 15   **Non-Paid Artists:** 300
Utilizes: Guest Artists; Guest Directors
Budget: $100,000 - $500,000
Income Sources: Private Foundations/Grants/Endowments; Business/Corporate Donations; Box Office; Government Grants; Individual Donations; Tuition
Season: November - August   **Annual Attendance:** 25,000
Affiliations: SCETA; San Diego Theatre League
Performance Facilities: Casa del Prado Theater

SAN DIEGO REPERTORY THEATRE
79 Horton Plaza, San Diego, CA 92101
(619) 231-3586
FAX: (619) 235-0939
Founded: 1976
Arts Area: Professional
Status: Professional; Non-Profit
Type: Performing; Touring; Educational; Sponsoring
Management: Sam Woodhouse, Producing Director; Doug Jacobs, Artistic Director; John Redman, General Manager
Paid Staff: 30
Paid Artists: 60
Utilizes: Guest Directors
Budget: $1,000,000 - $5,000,000
Income Sources: Private Foundations/Grants/Endowments; Business/Corporate Donations; Box Office; Government Grants; Individual Donations
Season: April - January   **Annual Attendance:** 500,000
Affiliations: TCG
Performance Facilities: The Lyceum Theatre

SOUTHEAST COMMUNITY THEATRE
5140 Solola Avenue, San Diego, CA 92114
(619) 262-2817; (619) 264-0698
Founded: 1976
Arts Area: Community; Theatrical Group
Status: Semi-Professional; Non-Profit
Type: Performing; Resident; Sponsoring
Purpose: To mount theatrical productions that promote the works of African-American playwrights by utilizing and showcasing the talent of amateur, semi-professional and professional artists
Management: Floyd Gaffney, Artistic Director; Bonnie J. Ward, Production Manager; Rufus DeWitt, Business Manager
Officers: Kathleen Harmon, President; Henry McClaron, Vice President; Yvette McClaron, Secretary; Robert Matthews, Treasurer
Paid Staff: 3   **Volunteer Staff:** 10
Utilizes: Guest Artists; Guest Directors
Budget: $50,000 - $100,000
Income Sources: Private Foundations/Grants/Endowments; Business/Corporate Donations; Box Office; Government Grants; Individual Donations
Season: September - June   **Annual Attendance:** 8,000

Affiliations: AACT
Performance Facilities: Educational Cultural Complex Performing Arts Theater; Lyceum Space Theatre

PERFORMING SERIES

STARLIGHT-SAN DIEGO CIVIC LIGHT OPERA ASSOCIATION
Balboa Park, 1549 El Drado, #11, San Diego, CA 92101
(619) 544-7800
FAX: (619) 544-0496
Founded: 1946
Arts Area: Theater
Status: Professional; Non-Profit
Type: Performing; Touring; Resident; Educational
Purpose: To present and further the American musical theatre through productions for residents and visitors to the San Diego area in the unique setting of the 4,324-seat Starlight Bowl in Balboa Park
Management: C. E. "Bud" Franks, Executive Director; Don and Bonnie Ward, Co-Artistic Directors
Officers: James L. Bowers, President/Board of Directors; Kent C. Thompson, Secretary; Michael J. Howard, Treasurer
Paid Staff: 23
Paid Artists: 300
Utilizes: Guest Artists; Guest Directors
Budget: $1,000,000 - $5,000,000
Income Sources: Private Foundations/Grants/Endowments; Business/Corporate Donations; Box Office; Government Grants; Individual Donations
Season: June - September
Annual Attendance: 150,000
Performance Facilities: Starlight Bowl/Balboa Park

FACILITY

BLACKFRIARS THEATRE
1057 First Avenue, San Diego, CA 92101
(619) 232-4088
Type of Facility: Theatre House; Room
Facility Originally: Ballroom; Hotel & Meeting Rooms
Type of Stage: Thrust; 3/4 Arena
Stage Dimensions: 25'Wx18'D
Seating Capacity: 99
Year Remodeled: 1985   **Architect:** Kim McCallum   **Cost:** $5,000
Contact for Rental: Dan Campbell;   (619) 232-4088
Resident Groups: The Bowery Theatre
Originally built in the 1920's

CAFE DEL REY MORO
House of Hospitality, 1549 El Prado, San Diego, CA 92101
(619) 234-8511
Type of Facility: Auditorium; Theatre House; Multi-Purpose; Room
Facility Originally: Exhibition Facility Of The 1914 Panama C
Type of Stage: Proscenium
Stage Dimensions: 41'9"Wx18'D
Seating Capacity: 400
Year Built: 1914
Year Remodeled: 1935
Contact for Rental: Cafe del Rey Moro;   (619) 234-8511
Originally the 1914 Foreign Arts Building, the building was remodeled in 1935 for the California Pacific International Exposition.

CASA DEL PRADO THEATRE
Village Place, Balboa Park, San Diego, CA 92101
(619) 235-1105
FAX: (619) 235-1112
Type of Facility: Theatre House
Facility Originally: Meeting Hall; Movie House
Type of Stage: Proscenium
Stage Dimensions: 48'Wx36'D   **Orchestra Pit**
Seating Capacity: 682
Year Built: 1971   **Architect:** Wheeler   **Cost:** $2,500,000
Year Remodeled: 1981   **Cost:** $500,000
Contact for Rental: Inge Dickens;   (619) 235-1105

Resident Groups: San Diego Junior Theatre; San Diego Youth Ballet; San Diego Comic Opera Company; San Diego Parks and Recreation Dance Productions
Rental available on a limited basis only.

COPLEY SYMPHONY HALL
1245 Seventh Avenue, San Diego, CA 92101
(619) 699-4200
FAX: (619) 699-4237
    Founded: 1929
    Type of Facility: Concert Hall; Performance Center; Theatre House; Multi-Purpose
    Facility Originally: Vaudeville
    Type of Stage: Proscenium
    Stage Dimensions: 50'Wx40'D   **Orchestra Pit**
    Seating Capacity: 2,250
    Year Built: 1929   **Architect:** Weeks & Day   **Cost:** $2,500,000
    Year Remodeled: 1985   **Architect:** Deemes/Lewis & Partners   **Cost:** $6,900,000
    Acoustical Consultant: ARTEC
    Contact for Rental: Nina Doggrell;   (619) 699-4200
    Resident Groups: San Diego Symphony Orchestra

GASLAMP QUARTER THEATRE
444 Fourth Avenue, San Diego, CA 92101
(619) 232-9608
    Type of Facility: Theatre House
    Facility Originally: Paper Box Factory
    Type of Stage: Proscenium
    Stage Dimensions: 30'Wx22'6"D, 30'Wx18'H proscenium opening
    Seating Capacity: 250
    Year Remodeled: 1986   **Architect:** Robert Earl   **Cost:** $3,300,000
    Contact for Rental: Ginger Beraha;   (619) 232-9608
    Manager: Mark Loigman
    Resident Groups: Gaslamp Quarter Theatre Company

THE MARIE HITCHCOCK PUPPET THEATRE IN BALBOA PARK
c/o Balboa Park Management Office, San Diego, CA 92101
(619) 296-5504
FAX: (619) 235-1100
    Type of Facility: Puppet Theatre
    Facility Originally: Exhibition facility of the 1935 California International Exhibition
    Type of Stage: Proscenium
    Stage Dimensions: 18'Dx44'W downstage, 24'W upstage
    Seating Capacity: 254
    Year Built: 1935
    Year Remodeled: 1948
    Contact for Rental: Balboa Park Management Office;   (619) 235-1100
    Resident Groups: San Diego Guild of Puppetry
    Originally the Palisades Building (Hollywood Hall of Fame), converted to a theatre in 1948

THE RECITAL HALL - BALBOA PARK
2130 Pan American Road West, San Diego, CA 92101
(619) 235-1100
    Type of Facility: Recital Hall
    Facility Originally: Exhibition facility of the 1935 California International Exhibition
    Type of Stage: Proscenium
    Stage Dimensions: 60'Wx22'D
    Seating Capacity: 250
    Year Built: 1935
    Contact for Rental: Balboa Park Management Office;   (619) 235-1100

SAN DIEGO CONCOURSE
202 C Street, San Diego, CA 92101
(619) 236-6500
    Type of Facility: Theatre Complex; Civic Center
    Year Built: 1964   **Architect:** Frank Hope Jr.   **Cost:** $21,000,000
    Acoustical Consultant: Purcell & Knoppe

Contact for Rental: Marika Nieratko; (619) 236-6500
Manager: Donald Telford
Resident Groups: San Diego Opera; San Diego Playgoers; California Ballet; San Diego Foundation for the Performing Arts
The Concourse contains the Civic Theatre and Golden Hall. See separate listings for additional information.

SAN DIEGO CONCOURSE - CIVIC THEATRE
202 C Street, San Diego, CA 92101
(619) 236-6500
> **Type of Facility:** Concert Hall; Theatre House
> **Type of Stage:** Proscenium
> **Stage Dimensions:** 129'Wx55'D; 56'Wx29'6"H proscenium opening   **Orchestra Pit**
> **Seating Capacity:** 3,000
> **Year Built:** 1965   **Architect:** Frank Hope Jr.   **Cost:** $4,500,000
> **Acoustical Consultant:** Purcell & Knoppe
> **Contact for Rental:** Marika Nieratko; (619) 236-6500
> **Manager:** Donald Telford; (619) 236-6500
> **Resident Groups:** San Diego Opera; San Diego Playgoers; California Ballet; San Diego Foundation for Performing Arts
> *The Concourse also includes Golden Hall. See separate listing for additional information.*

SAN DIEGO CONCOURSE - GOLDEN HALL
202 C Street, San Diego, CA 92101
(619) 236-6500
> **Type of Facility:** Auditorium; Arena; Multi-Purpose
> **Type of Stage:** Hydraulic Lift Stage
> **Stage Dimensions:** 37'6"Wx19'6"D
> **Seating Capacity:** 4,337
> **Year Built:** 1964   **Architect:** Frank Hope Jr.
> **Acoustical Consultant:** Purcell & Knoppe
> **Contact for Rental:** Marika Nieratko; (619) 236-6500
> *The Concourse also includes Civic Theatre. See separate listing for additional information.*

SIMON EDISON CENTER FOR THE PERFORMING ARTS
Balboa Park, PO Box 2171, San Diego, CA 92112-2171
(619) 231-1941
FAX: (619) 231-5879
> **Type of Facility:** Theatre Complex
> **Contact for Rental:** Thomas Hall; (619) 231-1941
> *The Performing Arts Center contains the Cassius Carter Centre Stage, Lowell Davies Festival Theatre and Old Globe Theatre. See separate listings for additional information.*

SIMON EDISON CENTER FOR THE PERFORMING ARTS - CASSIUS CARTER CENTRE STAGE
Balboa Park, PO Box 2171, San Diego, CA 92112
(619) 231-1941
FAX: (619) 231-5879
> **Type of Facility:** Studio Performance; Arena
> **Facility Originally:** Restaurant for the 1935 California Pacific International Exhibition
> **Type of Stage:** Arena
> **Stage Dimensions:** 21'x23'
> **Seating Capacity:** 225
> **Year Built:** 1935
> **Year Remodeled:** 1969   **Architect:** Victor Wulff   **Cost:** $350,000
> **Contact for Rental:** Thomas Hall; (619) 231-1941

SIMON EDISON CENTER FOR THE PERFORMING ARTS - LOWELL DAVIES FESTIVAL THEATRE
Balboa Park, PO Box 2171, San Diego, CA 92112-2171
(619) 231-1941
FAX: (619) 231-5879
> **Type of Facility:** Amphitheater
> **Type of Stage:** Platform; Environmental
> **Stage Dimensions:** 50'Wx50'D
> **Seating Capacity:** 612
> **Year Built:** 1978   **Architect:** Leibhardt, Weston & Associates   **Cost:** $550,000
> **Year Remodeled:** 1985   **Architect:** Leibhardt, Weston & Associates   **Cost:** $2,300,000
> **Contact for Rental:** Thomas Hall; (619) 231-1941
> *Original structure burned in 1984, was rebuilt and reopened in 1985.*

SIMON EDISON CENTER FOR THE PERFORMING ARTS - OLD GLOBE THEATRE
Balboa Park, PO Box 2171, San Diego, CA 92112-2171
(619) 231-1941
FAX: (619) 231-5879
Type of Facility: Theatre House
Facility Originally: Exhibition facility of the 1935 California International Exhibition
Type of Stage: Modified Stage
Stage Dimensions: 45'W to 96'W, 48'D
Seating Capacity: 581
Year Built: 1935   **Architect:** Thomas Wood Steven
Year Remodeled: 1982
Contact for Rental: Thomas Hall;   (619) 231-1941
Original Theatre burned in 1978, was rebuilt and reopened in 1982.

SPRECKELS ORGAN PAVILION
Balboa Park Administration Building, 2125 Park Boulevard, San Diego, CA 92101-4792
(619) 235-1100
FAX: (619) 235-1112
Type of Facility: Amphitheater
Type of Stage: Proscenium
Stage Dimensions: 69'Wx38'D
Seating Capacity: 2,400
Year Built: 1915   **Architect:** Harrison Albright
Year Remodeled: 1986
Contact for Rental: Ann-Marie Vavak;   (619) 235-1103
Pavilion houses a large pipe organ with free performances every Sunday.

STARLIGHT BOWL
Balboa Park, PO Box 3519, San Diego, CA 92163
(619) 544-STAR
Type of Facility: Environmental; Amphitheater
Facility Originally: Exhibition facility of the 1935 California International Exhibition
Type of Stage: Proscenium
Stage Dimensions: 50'Wx40'D; 50'Wx24'H proscenium opening   **Orchestra Pit**
Seating Capacity: 4,324
Year Built: 1935
Year Remodeled: 1985   **Architect:** Gerald Garapich
Contact for Rental: Pat Stallard;   (619) 544-7827
Manager: Bud Franks
Resident Groups: Starlight - San Diego Civic Light Opera Association
$1,200,000 has been expended since 1980 in ongoing improvements. Since Starlight Bowl is in the flight path of San Diego International Airport, performances are often interrupted by approaching aircraft. Using a stoplight system, a spotter halts performances as planes approach and gives a green light when they have passed.

San Francisco

DANCE

ASIAN AMERICAN DANCE PERFORMANCES
2403 16th Street, San Francisco, CA 94103-4210
(415) 552-8980
Founded: 1975
Arts Area: Modern
Status: Professional; Non-Profit
Type: Performing; Touring; Resident; Educational
Purpose: To express experiences of Asians in America.
Management: Anna Sun, Artistic Director; Gayle T. Nishikawa, General Manager
Officers: Lena Chang, President
Paid Artists: 7
Utilizes: Guest Artists; Guest Choreographers
Budget: $1,000 - $50,000
Income Sources: Private Foundations/Grants/Endowments; Box Office; Government Grants; Individual Donations
Season: June - October
Affiliations: Ethnic Dance Festival

BAILES FLAMENCOS
267 Teresita Boulevard, San Francisco, CA 94127
(415) 824-1960
FAX: (415) 824-1960
> **Arts Area:** Ethnic
> **Status:** Professional; Non-Profit
> **Type:** Performing; Touring; Resident; Educational
> **Purpose:** To advance understanding of the culture and art of Spain in particular the performing arts of flamenco and classical Spanish dance and music
> **Management:** Melanie B. Rainey, Executive Director; Rosa Montoya, Artistic Director
> **Officers:** Carmen Torrico, President of the Board
> **Budget:** $100,000 - $500,000
> **Income Sources:** Private Foundations/Grants/Endowments; Business/Corporate Donations; Box Office; Government Grants; Individual Donations
> **Performance Facilities:** Herbst Theater

CITY CELEBRATION, INC.
Building A, Fort Mason Center, San Francisco, CA 94123
(415) 474-3914
FAX: (415) 474-3922
> **Founded:** 1978
> **Arts Area:** Ethnic; Folk
> **Status:** Non-Profit
> **Type:** Performing; Resident; Educational; Sponsoring
> **Purpose:** To present, promote and celebrate the diverse performing arts of the Bay Area
> **Management:** Robert R. Allen, Executive Director; Joann Knecht, Associate Director; Lily Kharrazi, Program Coordinator; Yasmen Sorab Mehta, Production Coordinator
> **Officers:** Mara Brazer, President; Michael Huerta, Norma Garcia-Kennedy and Larry Giddings, Vice Presidents; Christine Stokes, Treasurer; Susan Tibbons, Secretary
> **Paid Staff:** 7
> **Paid Artists:** 1,000
> **Utilizes:** Guest Artists
> **Budget:** $500,000 - $1,000,000
> **Income Sources:** Private Foundations/Grants/Endowments; Box Office; Government Grants; Individual Donations
> **Annual Attendance:** 18,000
> **Affiliations:** Dance Bay Area; APAP; Dance USA; California Presenters
> **Performance Facilities:** Palace of Fine Arts; Cowell Theater; Golden Gate Bandshell

CONTRABAND
499 Alabama Street, #120, San Francisco, CA 94110
(415) 558-8821
FAX: (415) 864-5437
> **Founded:** 1985
> **Arts Area:** Modern; Contact Improvisation
> **Status:** Professional; Non-Profit
> **Type:** Performing; Touring; Educational
> **Purpose:** Contraband is a team of dancers, artists and musicians committed to the exploration of live theatre forms
> **Management:** Sara Shelton Mann, Artistic Director; Karen Schiller, Administrative Coordinator; Jess Curtis, Production Manager
> **Officers:** Sara Shelton Mann, President
> **Paid Staff:** 3 **Volunteer Staff:** 5
> **Paid Artists:** 8
> **Budget:** $100,000 - $500,000
> **Income Sources:** Private Foundations/Grants/Endowments; Box Office; Government Grants; Individual Donations
> **Season:** September - June
> **Annual Attendance:** 3,000
> **Affiliations:** Dance Bay Area

DANCERS' GROUP
3221 22nd Street, San Francisco, CA 94110
(415) 824-5044
FAX: (415) 824-2873
> **Founded:** 1982
> **Arts Area:** Modern; Performance Art
> **Status:** Professional; Semi-Professional; Non-Professional; Non-Profit
> **Type:** Performing; Educational; Sponsoring
> **Purpose:** To educate the community in dance and the performing arts
> **Management:** Wayne Hazzard, Director; Michael Jones, Manager; Rebecca Lowe, Assistant Manager

Paid Staff: 7   **Volunteer Staff:** 2
Paid Artists: 15
Utilizes: Guest Artists
Budget: $100,000 - $500,000
Income Sources: Private Foundations/Grants/Endowments; Business/Corporate Donations; Box Office; Government Grants; Individual Donations
Season: 52 Weeks   **Annual Attendance:** 5,000
Affiliations: Dance Bay Area

DEBORAH SLATER AND COMPANY
c/o Art of the Matter, 100 Putnam Street, San Francisco, CA 94110
(415) 824-2464
Arts Area: Dance Theater; Experimental
Status: Professional; Non-Profit
Type: Performing; Touring; Resident; Educational
Purpose: To attempt to find meaning in the human experience through dance and theater
Management: Deborah Slater, Director
Officers: Barbara Slotnik, Board President
Budget: $1,000 - $50,000
Income Sources: Private Foundations/Grants/Endowments; Business/Corporate Donations; Box Office; Government Grants; Individual Donations
Performance Facilities: Studio 210

DELLA DAVIDSON DANCE COMPANY
223 Mississippi, San Francisco, CA 94107
(415) 861-5797
Founded: 1976
Arts Area: Modern
Status: Professional; Non-Profit
Type: Performing; Touring
Purpose: Produce the original dance theatre work of Della Davidson
Management: Della Davidson, Artistic Director; John Rush, Executive Director
Officers: Nancy Barlet, President; Derek Dean, Secretary; Suzanne Mayor, Treasurer
Paid Staff: 3   **Volunteer Staff:** 25
Paid Artists: 7
Utilizes: Special Technical Talent; Guest Conductors; Guest Artists; Guest Directors
Budget: $100,000 - $500,000
Income Sources: Private Foundations/Grants/Endowments; Business/Corporate Donations; Box Office; Government Grants; Individual Donations; Tuition; Commissions
Season: September - May   **Annual Attendance:** 20,000
Affiliations: Theatre Artaud
Performance Facilities: Theatre Artaud

ISADORA DUNCAN DANCE CENTER
741 Lakeview Avenue, San Francisco, CA 94112
Founded: 1989
Arts Area: Modern; Historical
Status: Semi-Professional
Type: Performing; Touring; Educational
Officers: Maria Villazana-Ruiz, Director; Madelyn Szepesi, Teacher
Paid Staff: 2   **Volunteer Staff:** 4
Paid Artists: 2   **Non-Paid Artists:** 4
Utilizes: Guest Artists
Budget: $1,000 - $50,000
Income Sources: Box Office; Individual Donations
Season: Spring - Fall   **Annual Attendance:** 2,000
Performance Facilities: Isadora Duncan Dance Center

KHADRA INTERNATIONAL FOLK BALLET
1182 Market Street, Suite 217, San Francisco, CA 94102
(415) 626-7360
FAX: (415) 824-1599
Arts Area: Ethnic; Folk
Status: Semi-Professional; Non-Profit
Type: Performing; Touring; Resident; Educational; Sponsoring
Purpose: To make a unique artistic statement by drawing on traditional folk music and dance; to capture the essence of national character in theatrical presentations
Management: Mari Nijessen, Art; Tricia Dell, General Manager
Officers: F.J. Dale, Chairman of the Board

Budget: $100,000 - $500,000
Income Sources: Private Foundations/Grants/Endowments; Business/Corporate Donations; Box Office; Government Grants; Individual Donations

MARGARET JENKINS DANCE COMPANY
3153 17th Street, San Francisco, CA 94110
(415) 863-1173
Founded: 1972
Arts Area: Modern
Status: Professional; Non-Profit
Type: Performing; Touring; Resident; Educational
Purpose: To perform the work of Artistic Director and choreographer Margaret Jenkins
Management: Steve Jordan, Producing Director
Officers: Margaret Jenkins, President
Paid Staff: 10 **Volunteer Staff:** 10
Paid Artists: 10
Budget: $500,000 - $1,000,000
Income Sources: Private Foundations/Grants/Endowments; Business/Corporate Donations; Box Office; Government Grants; Individual Donations
Annual Attendance: 15,000
Affiliations: California Confederation of the Arts; AAA; Dance USA; Dance California; San Francisco Bay Area Dance Coalition
Performance Facilities: New Performance Gallery; Herbst Theatre; Theatre Arts Auditorium

NEVA RUSSIAN DANCE ENSEMBLE
2450 Sutter Street, San Francisco, CA 94110
(415) 563-7362
Founded: 1983
Arts Area: Ethnic; Folk
Status: Professional; Non-Profit
Type: Performing; Touring; Resident; Educational
Purpose: To present and preserve character/folk dances of northern Russia, Ukraine, Romania and Moldova
Management: Vladimir Riazantsev, Artistic Director; Michal Myers, Business Manager
Officers: Stuart Platt, President of the Board; Nadine Howard, Marie Bergstedt, Board Members; Bob Dettmer, Treasurer
Paid Staff: 1 **Volunteer Staff:** 4
Paid Artists: 2 **Non-Paid Artists:** 2
Utilizes: Special Technical Talent; Guest Artists
Budget: $1,000 - $50,000
Income Sources: Private Foundations/Grants/Endowments; Government Grants; Individual Donations
Performance Facilities: Russian Center of San Francisco

ODC/SAN FRANCISCO
3153 17th Street, San Francisco, CA 94110
(415) 863-6606
FAX: (415) 863-9833
Founded: 1971
Arts Area: Modern
Status: Professional; Non-Profit
Type: Performing; Touring; Resident; Educational
Purpose: To create and perform modern dance
Management: Susan Davis Cushing, Executive Director
Paid Staff: 5
Paid Artists: 12
Utilizes: Special Technical Talent; Guest Conductors; Guest Artists
Budget: $500,000 - $1,000,000
Income Sources: Private Foundations/Grants/Endowments; Business/Corporate Donations; Box Office; Government Grants; Individual Donations
Season: 52 Weeks **Annual Attendance:** 50,000
Affiliations: Dance USA; San Francisco Bay Area Dance Coalition

SAN FRANCISCO BALLET ASSOCIATION
455 Franklin Street, San Francisco, CA 94102
(415) 861-5600
Founded: 1933
Arts Area: Ballet
Status: Professional; Non-Profit
Type: Performing; Touring; Educational
Purpose: To provide a repertoire of classical and contemporary ballet; provide educational opportunities for the professional training of dancers and choreographers; and excel in ballet, artistic direction and administration

Management: Joyce A. Moffatt, Vice President/General Manager; Helgi Tomasson, Artistic Director; Bonita Borne, Ballet Mistress/Assistant Artistic Director
Officers: Mrs. F. Warren Hellman, Chairman of the Board; Susan S. Briggs, Secretary
Paid Staff: 60   **Volunteer Staff:** 100
Paid Artists: 57
Utilizes: Special Technical Talent; Guest Choreographers
Budget: Over 10,000,000
Income Sources: Private Foundations/Grants/Endowments; Business/Corporate Donations; Box Office; Government Grants; Individual Donations
Season: December - May   **Annual Attendance:** 250,000
Affiliations: California Dance Coalition; San Francisco Chamber of Commerce
Performance Facilities: War Memorial Opera House

SAN FRANCISCO JAZZ DANCE COMPANY
PO Box 22336, San Francisco, CA 94122
(415) 456-8053
Founded: 1980
Arts Area: Jazz
Status: Professional; Non-Profit
Type: Performing; Touring; Resident; Educational
Purpose: To perform, preserve and promote the American art form of jazz dance
Management: Allen Habel, Business Manager
Officers: Wendy Ballard, President; Deborah Adams, Vice President; Allen Habel, Secretary; Robert Yastacek, Treasurer
Paid Staff: 1   **Volunteer Staff:** 15
Paid Artists: 9   **Non-Paid Artists:** 2
Utilizes: Guest Artists
Budget: $1,000 - $50,000
Income Sources: Box Office; Individual Donations
Season: September - May   **Annual Attendance:** 1,750
Affiliations: WAAA; San Francisco Bay Area Dance Coalition

SAN FRANCISCO PERFORMANCES
500 Sutter Street, Suite 710, San Francisco, CA 94102
(415) 398-6449
FAX: (415) 398-6439
Founded: 1979
Arts Area: Modern; Ethnic
Status: Professional
Type: Sponsoring
Purpose: To present outstanding national, international and emerging artists; to introduce innovative programs; to build new and diversified audiences for the arts
Management: Ruth A. Felt, President/Executive Director; Marian Kohlstedt, Diretor of Public Relations; Nancy Petrisko, Director of Operations/Tickets; Cindy Rasicot, Director of Development
Officers: Amy McCombs, Chair; Clifford Orent, Vice Chair; Dr. Yanek Chiu, Secretary; Barbara Kokesh, Treasurer
Paid Staff: 7   **Volunteer Staff:** 3
Utilizes: Guest Artists
Budget: $1,000,000 - $5,000,000
Income Sources: Private Foundations/Grants/Endowments; Business/Corporate Donations; Box Office; Government Grants; Individual Donations
Season: October - May   **Annual Attendance:** 7,100
Affiliations: Dance Bay Area; APAP; ISPAA
Performance Facilities: Herbst Theatre; Cowell Theater at Fort Mason; Palace of Fine Arts Theatre

SAN FRANCISCO'S BALLET CELESTE INTERNATIONAL
25 Taylor Street, Suite 200, San Francisco, CA 94102
(415) 567-0988
FAX: (415) 567-0547
Founded: 1949
Arts Area: Ballet; Jazz; Ethnic; Folk
Status: Non-Professional; Non-Profit
Type: Performing; Touring; Resident
Purpose: To provide a unique performing experience to young artists founded on classical tradition; to present inexpensive concerts for the public
Management: Merriem Lanova, Director; Barbara Owen, Touring Director; John Bischof, Music
Officers: Merriem Lanova, Chief Executive Officer; Stephen Kopel, Secretary; Barbara Owen, Finances; William Holsman, Legal
Paid Staff: 1   **Volunteer Staff:** 30
Non-Paid Artists: 25
Utilizes: Special Technical Talent; Guest Artists; Guest Choreographers

Budget: $50,000 - $100,000
Income Sources: Private Foundations/Grants/Endowments; Business/Corporate Donations; Box Office; Government Grants; Individual Donations
Season: July - August; November-December   **Annual Attendance:** 160,000

TANCE DANZ
347 Dolores Street, #243, San Francisco, CA 94110
(415) 968-5959
Founded: 1980
Arts Area: Modern; Ballet
Status: Professional; Non-Profit
Type: Performing; Touring
Purpose: To extend the horizons of dance through arts interaction - multimedia artists of many disciplines with dance
Management: Tance Johnson, Artistic Director; Carl Sitton, Music Director; Cheryl Elliot, Public Relations
Officers: Margo Sims, President; Wendy Pappas, Vice President; Maggie Merrill, Secretary; Carl Sitton, Treasurer
Paid Staff: 3   **Volunteer Staff:** 10
Paid Artists: 12   **Non-Paid Artists:** 5
Utilizes: Guest Choreographers
Budget: $50,000 - $100,000
Income Sources: Private Foundations/Grants/Endowments; Business/Corporate Donations; Box Office; Government Grants; Individual Donations
Season: 28 Weeks
Affiliations: Dance Action, Inc.; Dance Bay Area

THEATER ARTAUD
2403 16th Street, San Francisco, CA 94103
(415) 621-7641
FAX: (415) 621-7647
Arts Area: Modern; Mime; Ballet; Jazz; Ethnic; Folk; Contemporary Work
Status: Professional
Type: Performing
Purpose: To perform a variety of disciplines; to provide professional technical and administrative services to performing arts companies; to present, produce and collaborate on productions and provide an expansive alternative performance space
Management: Dean Beck-Stewart, Executive Director; Jack Carpenter, Technical Director; Elouise Burrell, Business Manager; Noreen Cooper, Administrative Assistant; Lyndie Riemann, Technical Assistant; Kathleen O'Hara, House Manager; Jennifer Ross, House Manager; Jonny McPhee, Box Office Manager; Janet Adams, Box Office Assistant
Officers: Benjamin Young, President; Sigrid Rupp, Secretary/Treasurer; Dean Beck-Stewart, Executive Director; Melanie Grondel, Elizabeth Spicuzza, Bob Taxin
Paid Staff: 10   **Volunteer Staff:** 2
Paid Artists: 70
Utilizes: Special Technical Talent; Guest Conductors; Guest Artists; Guest Directors; Guest Choreographers
Budget: $500,000 - $1,000,000
Income Sources: Private Foundations/Grants/Endowments; Business/Corporate Donations; Box Office; Government Grants; Individual Donations
Season: 52 Weeks   **Annual Attendance:** 20,000
Affiliations: NPN; California Presenters

THE THEATRE BALLET OF SAN FRANCISCO
25 Taylor Street, Suite 200, San Francisco, CA 94102
(415) 567-0988
FAX: (415) 567-0547
Founded: 1949
Arts Area: Modern; Ballet; Ethnic; Folk
Status: Professional; Semi-Professional; Non-Profit
Type: Performing; Touring
Purpose: To provide as much employment as possible; provide good theater at modest prices; to keep classic traditions alive for both artists and audiences alike
Management: Merriem Lanova, Director; Barbara Owen, Tour Director; John Bischof, Music Librarian
Officers: Merriem Lanova, Chief Executive Officer; Stephan Kopel, Secretary; Barbara Owen, Finances; William Holsman, Attorney
Paid Staff: 10   **Volunteer Staff:** 10
Paid Artists: 45   **Non-Paid Artists:** 20
Utilizes: Special Technical Talent; Guest Conductors; Guest Artists; Guest Choreographers
Budget: $100,000 - $500,000
Income Sources: Private Foundations/Grants/Endowments; Business/Corporate Donations; Box Office; Individual Donations
Season: October - December   **Annual Attendance:** 40,000

INSTRUMENTAL MUSIC

CHAMBER MUSIC WEST FESTIVAL
San Francisco Conservatory of Music, 1201 Ortega Street, San Francisco, CA 94122
(415) 564-8086
FAX: (415) 759-3499
Arts Area: Chamber
Status: Professional; Non-Profit
Type: Performing; Educational
Purpose: To provide advanced students and faculty with the opportunity to perform with outstanding guest artists, continuing the tradition of master artists and gifted young apprentices; To offer Bay Area audiences concerts featuring highly imaginative programming and less cautious, nontraditional interpretations of both traditional and newer repertoire
Management: Colin Murdoch, Artistic Director; Timothy Bach, Festival Coordinator
Officers: Colin Murdoch, Pres. of Conservatory; Michael J. Savage, Chairman of the Board of Conservatory
Budget: $50,000 - $100,000
Income Sources: Private Foundations/Grants/Endowments; Business/Corporate Donations; Box Office; Government Grants; Individual Donations
Season: 52 Weeks
Performance Facilities: Hellman Hall

INTERNATIONAL CREATIVE MUSIC ORCHESTRA
c/o Rova Saxophone Quartet, 332 12th Street, San Francisco, CA 94103
(510) 644-3112; (415) 648-9164
FAX: (510) 704-8350
Arts Area: Jazz Ensemble
Status: Professional; Non-Profit
Type: Performing; Touring
Purpose: An ensemble of musicians from Europe, the US and Canada performing music inspired by jazz and world music
Management: Larry Ochs, Artistic Director; Lawrence Butch Morris, Conductor
Budget: $1,000 - $50,000
Income Sources: Box Office
Season: 52 Weeks

KRONOS QUARTET
1235-A Ninth Avenue, San Francisco, CA 94122
(415) 731-3533
Founded: 1973
Arts Area: Chamber; Ensemble
Status: Professional; Non-Profit
Type: Performing; Touring; Sponsoring
Purpose: To perform and commission new music
Management: Janet Cowperthwaite, Managing Director
Paid Staff: 3   **Volunteer Staff:** 20
Paid Artists: 4
Utilizes: Special Technical Talent; Guest Directors
Budget: $100,000 - $500,000
Income Sources: Private Foundations/Grants/Endowments; Business/Corporate Donations; Box Office; Government Grants; Individual Donations
Season: 52 Weeks

PHILHARMONIA BAROQUE ORCHESTRA
57 Post Street, Suite 705, San Francisco, CA 94104
(415) 391-5252
FAX: (415) 391-3737
Founded: 1981
Arts Area: Orchestra; Historical Performance
Status: Professional; Non-Profit
Type: Performing; Touring
Purpose: To perform 17th and 18th century music on instruments of the period
Management: Nicholas McGegan, Music Director; George Gellas, Executive Director
Utilizes: Guest Conductors; Guest Artists
Budget: $1,000,000 - $5,000,000
Income Sources: Private Foundations/Grants/Endowments; Business/Corporate Donations; Box Office; Government Grants; Individual Donations
Season: September - April
Performance Facilities: Herbst Theatre

SAN FRANCISCO CONSERVATORY OF MUSIC
1201 Ortega Street, San Francisco, CA 94122
(415) 564-8086
FAX: (415) 759-3499
Founded: 1917
Arts Area: Orchestra; Chamber; Ensemble; Electronic & Live Electronic
Status: Non-Profit
Type: Performing; Educational
Purpose: To train classical musicians for professional careers as performers, composers, conductor and teachers
Management: Colin Murdoch, President; Timothy Bach, Acting Dean; Patricia Berkowitz, Director of Administration
Officers: Michael J. Savage, Chairman of the Board
Paid Staff: 35
Utilizes: Special Technical Talent; Guest Conductors; Guest Artists
Budget: $5,000,000 - $10,000,000
Income Sources: Private Foundations/Grants/Endowments; Business/Corporate Donations; Box Office; Government Grants; Individual Donations; Tuition
Season: 52 Weeks
Annual Attendance: 30,000
Performance Facilities: Hellman Hall

SAN FRANCISCO CONTEMPORARY MUSIC PLAYERS
44 Page Street, Suite 604A, San Francisco, CA 94102
(415) 252-6235
FAX: (415) 621-2533
Founded: 1975
Arts Area: Chamber; Ensemble
Status: Professional; Non-Profit
Type: Performing; Touring
Purpose: To professionally perform contemporary chamber music using a mixed ensemble
Management: Stephen L. Mosco, Music Director; Adam L. Frey, Administrator
Officers: Paul Griffin, President; Roy C. Johns, Vice President; T. William Melis, Treasurer
Paid Staff: 3   **Volunteer Staff:** 5
Paid Artists: 12
Budget: $100,000 - $500,000
Income Sources: Private Foundations/Grants/Endowments; Business/Corporate Donations; Box Office; Government Grants; Individual Donations
Season: September - May   **Annual Attendance:** 1,800
Affiliations: CMA
Performance Facilities: Veterans Building

SAN FRANCISCO SYMPHONY ORCHESTRA
Louise M. Davies Symphony Hall, San Francisco, CA 94102
(415) 552-8000
Founded: 1911
Arts Area: Symphony; Orchestra
Status: Professional; Non-Profit
Type: Performing; Touring; Resident; Educational
Purpose: The goals of the San Francisco Symphony Orchestra are: to be a great orchestra; to be recognized as a great orchestra, and to serve the community. These goals are subject to achieving the appropriate balances of financial and organizational strength.
Management: Peter Pastreich, Executive Director; Herbert Blomstedt, Music Director/Conductor; Andrew Massey, Associate Conductor; Leif Bjaland, Exxon Arts Endowment Conductor/Assistant Conductor; Don Roth, General Manager
Paid Staff: 152   **Volunteer Staff:** 1,500
Paid Artists: 105
Utilizes: Guest Conductors; Guest Artists
Budget: Over 10,000,000
Income Sources: Private Foundations/Grants/Endowments; Business/Corporate Donations; Box Office; Government Grants; Individual Donations
Season: September - May
Annual Attendance: 622,000
Affiliations: ASOL; Association of California Symphony Orchestras
Performance Facilities: Louise M. Davies Symphony Hall; Flint Center for the Performing Arts; Stern Grove

SAN FRANCISCO SYMPHONY YOUTH ORCHESTRA
Louise M. Davies Symphony Hall, San Francisco, CA 94102
(415) 552-8000
FAX: (415) 431-6857
Founded: 1981

Arts Area: Symphony; Orchestra
Status: Non-Professional; Non-Profit
Type: Performing; Touring; Resident; Educational; Sponsoring
Purpose: To present the best pre-professional, performance training program for Bay Area, young musicians
Management: Richard L. Bains, Director of Education Programs/Youth Orchestra; Alasdair Neale,
Music Director/Conductor
Paid Staff: 3
Non-Paid Artists: 110
Utilizes: Guest Conductors; Guest Artists
Budget: $100,000 - $500,000
Income Sources: Private Foundations/Grants/Endowments; Business/Corporate Donations; Box Office; Government
Grants; Individual Donations
Season: September - June   **Annual Attendance:** 9,500
Affiliations: ASOL (Youth Orchestra Division)
Performance Facilities: Louise M. Davies Symphony Hall

THE. ART. RE. GRÜP, INC./THE LAB
1807 Divisadero Street, San Francisco, CA 94115
(415) 346-4063
FAX: (415) 346-4567
Arts Area: Chamber; Electronic & Live Electronic; Avant Garde
Status: Professional; Non-Profit
Type: Presenting
Purpose: To support the development of new work in performance, literature, media, visual arts and new music
Management: Laura Brun, Artistic Director; Keesje Fischer, Administrative Director
Officers: Richard Pinegar, Chairman of the Board
Budget: $100,000 - $500,000
Income Sources: Private Foundations/Grants/Endowments; Business/Corporate Donations; Box Office; Government
Grants; Individual Donations
Performance Facilities: The Lab

WOMEN'S PHILHARMONIC
330 Townsend Street, Suite 218, San Francisco, CA 94107
(415) 543-2297
FAX: (415) 543-3244
Founded: 1980
Arts Area: Orchestra; Chamber; Ensemble
Status: Professional; Non-Profit
Type: Performing; Touring; Resident; Educational
Purpose: To promote women composers, conductors and performers through the performance of orchestral and chamber
works, serving as a national resource center for women composers
Management: Miriam Abrams, Executive Director; JoAnn Falletta, Music Director
Officers: Julia Bloomfield, President; Lorraine Gnecco, Vice President; Carol Pierson, Treasurer;
Peggy Bennington, Secretary
Paid Staff: 3   **Volunteer Staff:** 10
Paid Artists: 65
Utilizes: Guest Conductors; Guest Artists
Budget: $100,000 - $500,000
Income Sources: Private Foundations/Grants/Endowments; Business/Corporate Donations; Box Office; Government
Grants; Individual Donations
Season: October - May   **Annual Attendance:** 4,000
Affiliations: ASOL; Association of California Symphony Orchestras; AMC; ASCAP;
League of Women Composers
Performance Facilities: First Congregational Church

VOCAL MUSIC

LAMPLIGHTERS/OPERA WEST FOUNDATION
2350 Turk Boulevard, San Francisco, CA 94118
(415) 752-9813
FAX: (415) 752-9818
Founded: 1952
Arts Area: Light Opera; Operetta
Status: Semi-Professional; Non-Profit
Type: Performing
Purpose: To perform light opera and operettas, especially Gilbert and Sullivan, Lehar, Kalman and Strauss;
to further careers of young singers, designers and musicians
Management: John J. Alecca, General Director; Baker Peeles, Artistic Director

Officers: John Vlahos, President; Nick Tarlson, Treasurer
Paid Staff: 6 **Volunteer Staff:** 180
Paid Artists: 22 **Non-Paid Artists:** 180
Utilizes: Special Technical Talent; Guest Conductors; Guest Artists; Guest Directors
Budget: $500,000 - $1,000,000
Income Sources: Private Foundations/Grants/Endowments; Business/Corporate Donations; Box Office; Government Grants; Individual Donations
Season: March - December
Annual Attendance: 42,000
Affiliations: AFM; California Confederation of the Arts; Theatre Bay Area; California Theatre Council
Performance Facilities: Presentation Theatre

MEROLA OPERA PROGRAM
War Memorial Opera House, San Francisco, CA 94102
(415) 565-6427; (415) 861-4008
FAX: (415) 255-6774
Founded: 1954
Arts Area: Grand Opera; Lyric Opera
Status: Non-Profit
Type: Educational; Sponsoring
Purpose: To discover and develop young professional opera singers; to sponsor the San Francisco Opera Center auditions and the Merola Opera Program at the San Francisco Opera
Management: Rachel Malan, Administrator
Officers: Dr. Jess Shenson, President of the Board
Paid Staff: 16
Utilizes: Special Technical Talent; Guest Conductors; Guest Directors
Budget: $500,000 - $1,000,000
Income Sources: Private Foundations/Grants/Endowments; Business/Corporate Donations; Government Grants; Individual Donations; Fund-raising
Season: June - Mid-August
Annual Attendance: 35,000
Affiliations: COS
Performance Facilities: War Memorial Opera House

PAUL DRESHER ENSEMBLE
c/o Musical Traditions Inc., 235 Surrey Street, San Francisco, CA 94131
(415) 333-4994
FAX: (510) 843-4057
Arts Area: Avant Garde; Electronic Opera
Status: Professional; Non-Profit
Type: Performing; Touring; Educational
Purpose: To create dynamic multi-disciplined musical theatre engaging in varied issues arising from contemporary American life to produce works that range in scale from stage concerts to full-scale productions, becoming a meeting place for art and technology
Management: Paul Dresher, Artistic Director; Robin Kirck, Executive Director
Officers: Paul Dresher, President; Robin Kirck, Vice President
Budget: $100,000 - $500,000
Income Sources: Private Foundations/Grants/Endowments; Business/Corporate Donations; Box Office; Government Grants; Individual Donations; Performance Fees; Sales
Performance Facilities: Theater Artaud; Cowell Theater at Fort Mason

SAN FRANCISCO CHANTICLEER, INC.
650 Fifth Street, Suite 311, San Francisco, CA 94107
(415) 896-5866
FAX: (415) 896-1660
Arts Area: Choral
Status: Professional; Non-Profit
Type: Performing; Touring; Resident; Educational
Purpose: A full-time professional a cappella vocal ensemble of 12 men committed to elevating the standards of choral music through a unique ensemble sound utilizing the full male vocal range from counter-tenor to bass
Management: Louis Botto, Artistic Director; Susan Duncan, Executive Director
Officers: Dr. Richard E. LeBlond Jr., President of the Board
Budget: $1,000,000 - $5,000,000
Income Sources: Private Foundations/Grants/Endowments; Business/Corporate Donations; Box Office; Government Grants; Individual Donations; Recordings
Performance Facilities: Mission Dolores Basilica; Calvary Presbyterian Church; Saint Ignatius Church; Mission Santa Clara

SAN FRANCISCO CHILDREN'S OPERA ASSOCIATION
245 Tenth Avenue, San Francisco, CA 94118
(415) 386-9622
> **Founded:** 1952
> **Arts Area:** Light Opera
> **Status:** Semi-Professional; Non-Profit
> **Type:** Performing; Educational
> **Purpose:** Development of children's enjoyment of music, drama and dance
> **Management:** Dr. Norbert Gingold, Director; Venetia Gingold, Co-Director
> **Officers:** Natalie Stryks, President; Raoul Epling, Vice President; Dr. Linda Angin, Secretary; Raoul Epling, Treasurer
> **Paid Staff:** 12 **Volunteer Staff:** 26
> **Paid Artists:** 16
> **Budget:** $1,000 - $50,000
> **Income Sources:** Private Foundations/Grants/Endowments; Box Office; Individual Donations
> **Season:** November - April
> **Annual Attendance:** 5,000
> **Performance Facilities:** Herbst Theatre

SAN FRANCISCO CHORAL ARTISTS
601 Van Ness Avenue, Suite E 3344, San Francisco, CA 94102
(415) 979-5779
> **Arts Area:** Choral
> **Status:** Professional; Non-Profit
> **Type:** Performing
> **Purpose:** To develop and maintain an outstanding performing choral ensemble dedicated to the art of modern classical music
> **Management:** Claire Giovannetti, Music Director; Doug Wyatt, Associate Conductor; Teresa Byrne, Development Manager; Audrey Wong, Publicity
> **Officers:** Maureen Stone, President of the Board
> **Budget:** $1,000 - $50,000
> **Income Sources:** Private Foundations/Grants/Endowments; Business/Corporate Donations; Box Office; Government Grants; Individual Donations
> **Performance Facilities:** Calvary Presbyterian Church; St. Mark's Episcopal Church, Berkeley; First Presbyterian Church, Palo Alto

SAN FRANCISCO GIRLS CHORAL ASSOCIATION
1100 Ellis Street, San Francisco, CA 94109
(415) 673-1511
FAX: (415) 673-0639
> **Founded:** 1978
> **Arts Area:** Choral
> **Status:** Professional; Non-Professional; Non-Profit
> **Type:** Performing; Touring; Resident; Educational; Sponsoring
> **Purpose:** To make excellent music with young female voices; to provide leadership in the emerging art form of girls choral music
> **Management:** June Wiley, Executive Director; Janet Garvin, Development/Public Relations Director
> **Officers:** Frank Spiller, President; Arthur Perkins, Vice President Finance; James Warren, Vice President Fund-raising; Anne Smith, Vice President Marketing; Emily Mugge, Treasurer; Margaret Haldeman, Secretary
> **Paid Staff:** 6 **Volunteer Staff:** 100
> **Paid Artists:** 16 **Non-Paid Artists:** 200
> **Utilizes:** Guest Artists
> **Budget:** $500,000 - $1,000,000
> **Income Sources:** Private Foundations/Grants/Endowments; Business/Corporate Donations; Box Office; Government Grants; Individual Donations; Tuition; Fees
> **Season:** September - June
> **Annual Attendance:** 106,000
> **Affiliations:** San Francisco Opera

SAN FRANCISCO OPERA ASSOCIATION
301 Van Ness Avenue, San Francisco, CA 94102
(415) 861-4008
FAX: (415) 621-7508
> **Founded:** 1923
> **Arts Area:** Grand Opera
> **Status:** Professional; Non-Profit
> **Type:** Performing; Touring; Resident; Educational; Sponsoring
> **Purpose:** To present international opera performances of the highest quality; to enhance the operatic art form by developing artists, new works and the widest possible audiences

Management: Lotfi Mansouri, General Director; Donald Runnicles, Music Director; Russ Walton, Comapany Manager
Officers: Reid W. Dennis, Chairman; Thomas Tilton, President
Paid Staff: 63
Paid Artists: 340
Utilizes: Special Technical Talent; Guest Conductors; Guest Artists; Guest Directors
Budget: Over 10,000,000
Income Sources: Private Foundations/Grants/Endowments; Business/Corporate Donations; Box Office; Government Grants; Individual Donations
Affiliations: OA; AAA; California Confederation of the Arts
Performance Facilities: War Memorial Opera House

SAN FRANCISCO OPERA CENTER
War Memorial Opera House, 301 Van Ness Avenue, San Francisco, CA 94102
(415) 565-6491; (415) 565-6435
FAX: (415) 255-6774
Founded: 1982
Arts Area: Grand Opera; Lyric Opera; Light Opera; Operetta
Status: Professional; Non-Profit
Type: Performing; Touring; Resident; Educational; Sponsoring
Purpose: To utilize the various affiliate components of the San Francisco Opera Association in a comprehensive and unique professional training program for artists
Management: Christine Bullin, Director; Robin A. Hodgkin, Sales and Marketing Manager/Touring
Paid Staff: 12   **Volunteer Staff:** 20
Paid Artists: 125
Utilizes: Special Technical Talent; Guest Conductors; Guest Artists; Guest Directors; Guest Choreographers
Budget: $1,000,000 - $5,000,000
Income Sources: Private Foundations/Grants/Endowments; Business/Corporate Donations; Box Office; Government Grants; Individual Donations
Season: 52 Weeks   **Annual Attendance:** 400,000
Affiliations: San Francisco Opera Association; San Francisco Opera; APAP; Metropolitan Opera Guild; WAAA; CAC; WSAF
Performance Facilities: Theatre Artaud; Herbst Theater

SAN FRANCISCO POCKET OPERA
333 Kearny Street, Suite 703, San Francisco, CA 94108
(415) 989-1853
Founded: 1977
Arts Area: Grand Opera; Lyric Opera; Light Opera; Operetta
Status: Professional; Non-Profit
Type: Performing; Touring; Resident
Purpose: Pocket Opera was created to address the need to preserve and promote accessibility of the broad range of operatic literature for English-speaking audiences at affordable ticket prices.
Management: Donald Pippin, Artistic Director; Judith Whitney, General Manager
Officers: Mel Bachmeier, President; Jim Erhart, Bob Shomler, Vice Presidents
Paid Staff: 4   **Volunteer Staff:** 20
Paid Artists: 90
Utilizes: Guest Artists
Budget: $100,000 - $500,000
Income Sources: Private Foundations/Grants/Endowments; Business/Corporate Donations; Box Office; Government Grants; Individual Donations
Season: 52 Weeks
Annual Attendance: 150,000
Affiliations: COS

SAN FRANCISCO SYMPHONY CHORUS
c/o San Francisco Symphony, Louise M. Davies Symphony Hall, San Francisco, CA 94102
(415) 552-8000
FAX: (415) 431-6857
Arts Area: Symphonic
Status: Professional; Non-Profit
Type: Performing
Purpose: To be a world-class chorus; to perform a varied repertoire of great music under the world's leading conductors
Management: Vance George, Chorus Director; Gregory Boals, Chorus Administrator
Budget: $100,000 - $500,000
Income Sources: Private Foundations/Grants/Endowments; Business/Corporate Donations; Box Office; Government Grants
Performance Facilities: Louise M. Davies Symphony Hall

THEATRE

AFRICAN AMERICAN DRAMA COMPANY
394 5th Avenue, San Francisco, CA 94118
(415) 386-2832
>**Founded:** 1977
>**Arts Area:** Theatrical Group
>**Status:** Professional
>**Type:** Touring
>**Purpose:** To perform African and Black history plays for American audiences
>**Management:** Phillip E. Walker, Ethel Pitts Walker, Executive Directors
>**Paid Staff:** 2
>**Paid Artists:** 5
>**Utilizes:** Guest Directors
>**Budget:** $1,000 - $50,000
>**Income Sources:** Box Office
>**Season:** August - June   **Annual Attendance:** 100,000

AMERICAN CONSERVATORY THEATRE
450 Geary Street, San Francisco, CA 94102
(415) 749-2200
FAX: (415) 771-4859
>**Founded:** 1967
>**Arts Area:** Professional
>**Status:** Professional; Non-Profit
>**Type:** Performing; Resident; Educational
>**Purpose:** To perform classical and contemporary plays concurrently with theatre training
>**Management:** Carey Perloff, Artistic Director; John Sullivan, Managing Director; Susan Stauter, Conservatory Director
>**Officers:** Patrick F. Flannery, President; Shepard P. Pollack, Vice President; Keith B. Williams, Treasurer; Marijke Donat, Secretary
>**Paid Staff:** 52   **Volunteer Staff:** 100
>**Paid Artists:** 60
>**Utilizes:** Special Technical Talent; Guest Artists; Guest Directors
>**Budget:** $5,000,000 - $10,000,000
>**Income Sources:** Private Foundations/Grants/Endowments; Business/Corporate Donations; Box Office; Government Grants; Individual Donations
>**Season:** October - June
>**Annual Attendance:** 250,000
>**Affiliations:** LORT; TCG; AAA; California Confederation of the Arts; National Corporation Theatre Fund
>**Performance Facilities:** Stage Door Theatre; Marines Memorial Theatre; Orpheum Theatre

EL TEATRO DE LA ESPERANZA
PO Box 40578, San Francisco, CA 94140
(415) 255-2320
>**Arts Area:** Theatrical Group
>**Status:** Professional; Non-Profit
>**Type:** Touring; Resident
>**Purpose:** To enhance the theatre movement through the Chicano community with bilingual and bi-cultural plays
>**Management:** Rodrigo Durte Clark, Artistic Director; Eve Donovan, General Manager
>**Officers:** Ruben Castro, President of the Board
>**Budget:** $100,000 - $500,000
>**Income Sources:** Private Foundations/Grants/Endowments; Business/Corporate Donations; Box Office; Government Grants; Individual Donations
>**Performance Facilities:** Mission Culture Center

EUREKA THEATRE COMPANY
340 Townsend Street, #519, San Francisco, CA 94107-1607
(415) 243-9899
>**Founded:** 1972
>**Arts Area:** Professional; Theatrical Group
>**Status:** Professional; Non-Profit
>**Type:** Performing; Resident; Educational
>**Purpose:** To produce contemporary plays that focus directly on political and social issues
>**Officers:** Paul Fagin, Board President
>**Paid Staff:** 10

Utilizes: Special Technical Talent; Guest Artists; Guest Directors
Budget: $100,000 - $500,000
Income Sources: Private Foundations/Grants/Endowments; Business/Corporate Donations; Box Office; Government Grants; Individual Donations
Season: October - June
Affiliations: AEA; Coalition of Bay Area Theatres
Performance Facilities: Eureka Theatre

GEORGE COATES PERFORMANCE WORKS
110 McAllister Street, San Francisco, CA 94102
(415) 863-8520
FAX: (415) 863-7939
Founded: 1977
Arts Area: New Music Theatre
Status: Non-Profit
Type: Performing; Touring; Resident
Purpose: To broaden the boundaries of contemporary performances and the creative experience itself; to explore new relationships between performer and audience; to develop new alliances between arts ensembles, individuals and emerging technology industries; emphasis on contemporary vocal expression and multimedia
Management: George Coates, Artistic Director; Beau Takahara, Executive Director; David Hurd, General Manager; Dan Corr, Production Manager
Officers: Lee Bendekgey, President; Larry Batiste, Vice President; Cookie Marenco, Secretary; Michael McDonell, Treasurer
Paid Staff: 5   **Volunteer Staff:** 10
Paid Artists: 27   **Non-Paid Artists:** 4
Utilizes: Special Technical Talent; Guest Artists; Multimedia
Budget: $500,000 - $1,000,000
Income Sources: Private Foundations/Grants/Endowments; Business/Corporate Donations; Box Office; Government Grants; Individual Donations
Season: September - June
Annual Attendance: 19,000
Performance Facilities: Performance Works

ILLUSTRATED STAGE COMPANY
PO Box 640063, San Francisco, CA 94164
(415) 861-6655
Founded: 1979
Arts Area: Professional; Theatrical Group
Status: Professional; Non-Profit
Type: Performing; Resident
Management: Barbara Malinowski, General Manager
Paid Staff: 2   **Volunteer Staff:** 7
Paid Artists: 4   **Non-Paid Artists:** 1
Utilizes: Guest Artists; Guest Directors
Budget: $100,000 - $500,000
Income Sources: Business/Corporate Donations; Box Office; Individual Donations
Season: 52 Weeks
Annual Attendance: 52,000
Performance Facilities: Alcazar Theatre

THE JULIAN THEATRE
777 Valencia, San Francisco, CA 94110
(415) 626-8986
Founded: 1965
Arts Area: Professional; Theatrical Group
Status: Professional; Non-Profit
Type: Performing; Touring; Resident; Educational; Sponsoring
Purpose: To maintain interest in works that have a social or political sense of the times; multi-cultural theater working with new plays
Management: Richard Reineccius, Artistic/General Director; Veronica Masterson, Library Manager; Jackie Hayes, Development Director; Michael Dingle, Production Manager
Officers: George Crowe, Board Chairman
Paid Staff: 3
Utilizes: Special Technical Talent; Guest Artists; Guest Directors
Budget: $50,000 - $100,000
Income Sources: Box Office; Government Grants
Season: September - June
Affiliations: AEA

LORRAINE HANSBERRY THEATER
500 Sutter Street, Suite 511, San Francisco, CA 94102-1115
(415) 433-9115
FAX: (415) 288-0326
Arts Area: Professional
Status: Professional; Non-Profit
Type: Performing; Educational
Purpose: To produce plays by America's and the world's leading Black writers; to foster the development of new Black writers through the ongoing activities of the playwrights' workshop
Management: Stanley Williams, Artistic Director; Quentin Easter, Executive Director
Budget: $100,000 - $500,000
Income Sources: Private Foundations/Grants/Endowments; Business/Corporate Donations; Box Office; Government Grants; Individual Donations
Performance Facilities: Lorraine Hansberry Theater

MAGIC THEATRE
Fort Mason Center, Building D, San Francisco, CA 94123
(415) 441-8001; (415) 441-8822
FAX: (415) 771-5505
Founded: 1967
Arts Area: Professional; Theatrical Group
Status: Professional; Non-Profit
Type: Performing; Resident; Sponsoring
Purpose: Devoted exclusively to the development of new plays and playwrights; operates two professional theaters
Management: Jeff Rowlings, General Manager
Officers: John St. John, Board Chairman
Paid Staff: 7   **Volunteer Staff:** 8
Paid Artists: 130   **Non-Paid Artists:** 20
Utilizes: Special Technical Talent; Guest Artists; Guest Directors
Budget: $500,000 - $1,000,000
Income Sources: Private Foundations/Grants/Endowments; Business/Corporate Donations; Box Office; Government Grants; Individual Donations
Season: October - June   **Annual Attendance:** 25,000
Affiliations: AEA
Performance Facilities: Northside Theatre; Southside Theatre

MAKE A CIRCUS
Fort Mason Center, Building C, San Francisco, CA 94123
(415) 776-8477
Arts Area: Musical; Community; Circus
Status: Non-Profit
Type: Performing; Touring; Educational; Participatory
Purpose: To bring social issues to the arts through participatory circus theater; to perform free in the parks—especially in low-income areas where theater is not accessible; to reach out to high-risk teens by providing them with summer employment
Management: Peggy Ford, Artistic Director; Mary Anne Cook, Managing Director
Officers: Jane Herzog, President of the Board
Budget: $100,000 - $500,000
Income Sources: Private Foundations/Grants/Endowments; Business/Corporate Donations; Government Grants; Individual Donations

MUSICAL TRADITIONS INC.
235 Surrey Street, San Francisco, CA 94131
(415) 333-4994
FAX: (510) 843-4057
Arts Area: Professional
Status: Professional; Non-Profit
Type: Performing; Touring; Educational
Management: Carrie Boram, Business Manager
Budget: $100,000 - $500,000

THE NEW CONSERVATORY CHILDRENS THEATRE COMPANY AND SCHOOL
25 Van Ness, Lower Lobby, San Francisco, CA 94102
(415) 861-4914
FAX: (415) 861-6988
Founded: 1981
Arts Area: Professional; Musical; Community; Children's Theatre
Status: Non-Profit

Type: Performing; Touring; Educational
Purpose: As a professional theatre arts school and performing arts company, we strive to make a positive contribution to our community and to serve as a model for educational theatres across the country.
Management: Ed Decker, Executive Director; Carol Majenski, Executive Assistant; Susan Glenn, Business Manager; Irene Cooper-Basch, Development Associate
Officers: A. Hess, Chairperson; Ed Decker, President; Brad Pence, Treasurer; Wendell Rickets, Secretary
Paid Staff: 14   **Volunteer Staff:** 1
Paid Artists: 16   **Non-Paid Artists:** 1
Utilizes: Guest Directors; Guest Musical Directors
Budget: $100,000 - $500,000
Income Sources: Private Foundations/Grants/Endowments; Business/Corporate Donations; Box Office; Government Grants; Individual Donations; Tuition
Season: October - May   **Annual Attendance:** 2,000
Performance Facilities: The New Conservatory Theatre Center

PERSONA GRATA PRODUCTIONS, INC.
355 15th Avenue, #6, San Francisco, CA 94118
(415) 387-7898
Founded: 1982
Arts Area: Professional; Theatrical Group; Puppet
Status: Professional; Non-Profit
Type: Performing; Educational
Purpose: Cross-cultural and educational
Management: Paul Kwan, Executive Director; Arnold Iger, Artistic Director
Paid Staff: 2
Paid Artists: 8   **Non-Paid Artists:** 4
Utilizes: Special Technical Talent; Guest Artists
Budget: $100,000 - $500,000
Income Sources: Private Foundations/Grants/Endowments; Box Office; Government Grants; Individual Donations

PICKLE FAMILY CIRCUS AND PICKLE FAMILY CIRCUS SCHOOL
400 Missouri Street, San Francisco, CA 94107
(415) 826-0747
FAX: (415) 826-1711
Founded: 1974
Arts Area: Professional; Theatrical Group
Status: Professional; Non-Profit
Type: Performing; Touring; Educational
Purpose: One ring circus, no hype, no animals, just great family entertainment, often works as a fund-raiser for other non-profit organizations. The school teaches both beginning and recreational circus skills and professional level classes, students begin at age 4
Management: Ann Vermel, Executive Director; Lu Yi, Associate Director; Tandy Beal, Artistic Director
Officers: Marc Snyder, Chairman; Jon Carroll, Nancy Pietrafesa, Vice Chairmans
Paid Staff: 6   **Volunteer Staff:** 2
Paid Artists: 20
Utilizes: Special Technical Talent; Guest Artists; Guest Directors
Budget: $1,000,000 - $5,000,000
Income Sources: Private Foundations/Grants/Endowments; Business/Corporate Donations; Box Office; Government Grants; Individual Donations
Season: October - April   **Annual Attendance:** 180,000

SAN FRANCISCO MIME TROUPE
855 Treat Avenue, San Francisco, CA 94110
(415) 285-1717
FAX: (415) 285-1290
Founded: 1959
Arts Area: Professional
Status: Professional; Non-Profit
Type: Performing; Touring; Educational
Purpose: To create socially-relevant, original musical theatre of the highest professional quality; to perform before the broadest possible audience
Management: Patrick L. Osbon, General Manager; Peggy Rose, Financial Manager; Barbara A. Jeppesen, Publicist; Ellen Callas, Production Manager
Paid Staff: 4
Paid Artists: 16
Utilizes: Special Technical Talent; Guest Artists
Budget: $500,000 - $1,000,000

Income Sources: Private Foundations/Grants/Endowments; Business/Corporate Donations; Box Office; Government Grants; Individual Donations
Annual Attendance: 100,000

SOON 3 THEATER
231 Franklin Street, Suite 1, San Francisco, CA 94102
(415) 558-8575
Founded: 1972
Arts Area: Professional; Theatrical Group; Interdisciplinary Experimental
Status: Professional; Non-Profit
Type: Performing
Purpose: To develop innovative forms for presenting theatrical works of social significance
Management: Liz Sizensky, Executive Director
Officers: Alan Finneran, President; John Lion, Vice President; Laurey Finneran, Secretary/Treasurer
Paid Staff: 2   **Volunteer Staff:** 3
Paid Artists: 7
Utilizes: Special Technical Talent; Guest Artists; Guest Directors; Composers; Filmmakers
Budget: $100,000 - $500,000
Income Sources: Private Foundations/Grants/Endowments; Box Office; Government Grants; Individual Donations
Season: May - June   **Annual Attendance:** 4,000
Affiliations: Theater Bay Area

STEVE SILVER PRODUCTIONS
678 Green Street, San Francisco, CA 94133
(415) 421-4284
Founded: 1974
Arts Area: Professional; Musical
Status: Professional; Commercial
Type: Performing; Resident
Management: Steve Silver, Producer/Director/Designer
Officers: Steve Silver, President
Paid Staff: 85
Paid Artists: 30
Income Sources: Box Office
Season: 52 Weeks   **Annual Attendance:** 160,000
Affiliations: San Francisco and California Chambers of Commerce; Theater Bay Area
Performance Facilities: Club Fugazi

THEATER RHINOCERUS, INC.
2926 16th Street, San Francisco, CA 94103
(415) 522-4100
Founded: 1977
Arts Area: Theatrical Group
Status: Professional; Non-Profit
Type: Performing; Resident
Purpose: To present Gay and Lesbian theatre
Management: Adele Prandini, Artistic Director; Judie Ghidinelli, Managing Director; Doug Holsclaw, Associate Artistic Director
Officers: Linda Schneider, Board President
Utilizes: Guest Directors
Budget: $100,000 - $500,000
Income Sources: Private Foundations/Grants/Endowments; Business/Corporate Donations; Box Office; Government Grants; Individual Donations
Season: September - June   **Annual Attendance:** 25,000
Affiliations: TCG; Theatre Bay Area
Performance Facilities: Main Stage; Studio Theater

THEATRE ON THE SQUARE
450 Post Street, San Francisco, CA 94102
(415) 433-6461
FAX: (415) 433-2910
Founded: 1981
Arts Area: Professional; Musical
Status: Professional; Commercial
Type: Performing; Touring
Purpose: To present both original and touring plays
Management: Jonathan Reinis, Owner; Joe Watson, Theatre Manager; Gillian Roth, Treasurer; Judy Karwan, House Manager
Officers: Jonathan Reinis, Owner

Paid Staff: 10
Utilizes: Guest Artists; Guest Directors
Budget: $100,000 - $500,000
Income Sources: Box Office
Season: 52 Weeks   **Annual Attendance:** 75,000
Performance Facilities: Theatre on the Square

THE THESPIAN THEATRICAL CLUB
1750 Clay Street, San Francisco, CA 94109
(415) 474-3516
Founded: 1932
Arts Area: Professional; Musical; Community; Theatrical Group
Status: Non-Profit
Type: Performing; Resident
Management: Rex Waldron, Manager
Officers: Jose Ulloa, Vice President; Jenny Scheck, Recording Secretary; Cynthia Powell, Treasurer; Leone Johns, Finance
Volunteer Staff: 8
Budget: $1,000 - $50,000
Season: 52 Weeks

A TRAVELING JEWISH THEATRE
PO Box 421985, San Francisco, CA 94142-1985
(415) 861-4880
Founded: 1978
Arts Area: Professional; Theatrical Group
Status: Professional; Non-Profit
Type: Performing; Touring; Educational
Purpose: An experimental theatre creating original works of universal concern through the specifics of Jewish experience
Management: Corey Fischer, Albert Greenberg, Naomi Newman, Helen Stoltzfus, Artistic Ensemble; Anna Becker, Managing Director
Officers: Evan Mendelson, Board President; Corey Fischer, Vice President; Mark Jansen, Treasurer; Ursula Sherman, Secretary
Paid Staff: 3
Paid Artists: 4
Utilizes: Special Technical Talent; Guest Artists; Guest Directors
Budget: $100,000 - $500,000
Income Sources: Private Foundations/Grants/Endowments; Box Office; Government Grants; Individual Donations
Annual Attendance: 10,000
Affiliations: TCG

VEERA WIBAUX MIME THEATRE
1536 18th Street, San Francisco, CA 94107
(415) 621-6002
Founded: 1969
Arts Area: Professional
Status: Professional; Non-Profit
Type: Performing; Touring; Resident; Educational
Purpose: Touring performances, workshops, lecture demonstrations
Management: Bert Houle, Veera Wibaux, Artistic Directors
Officers: Bert Houle, President; Veera Wibaux, Vice President
Paid Staff: 2
Paid Artists: 2
Utilizes: Special Technical Talent
Budget: $1,000 - $50,000
Income Sources: Private Foundations/Grants/Endowments; Box Office; Government Grants; Individual Donations
Season: 52 Weeks

PERFORMING SERIES

CITY CELEBRATION ARTS
Fort Mason, Building A, San Francisco, CA 94123
(415) 474-3914
Founded: 1979
Arts Area: Dance; Vocal Music; Instrumental Music; Theater
Status: Professional; Non-Profit
Type: Performing; Sponsoring
Purpose: To present, promote and celebrate the diverse performing arts of the Bay Area
Management: Robert Allen, Executive Director
Officers: Mara Brazer, President

Utilizes: Guest Artists
Income Sources: Private Foundations/Grants/Endowments; Business/Corporate Donations; Box Office; Government Grants; Individual Donations
Season: June - October

MIDSUMMER MOZART
World Trade Center, #280, San Francisco, CA 94111
(415) 781-5931
FAX: (415) 781-6329
Founded: 1975
Arts Area: Instrumental Music; Festivals
Status: Professional; Non-Profit
Type: Performing
Purpose: To present orchestral/chamber music of Mozart
Management: William L. Denton, Executive Director; Marilyn Shaw, Development Director; Jeff Phillips, Administrative Assistant
Officers: James M. Rockett, Chairman; Wendell Rider, President; Richard Heath, Treasurer
Paid Staff: 3
Paid Artists: 40
Utilizes: Guest Artists
Budget: $500,000 - $1,000,000
Income Sources: Private Foundations/Grants/Endowments; Business/Corporate Donations; Box Office; Government Grants; Individual Donations
Season: July - August
Annual Attendance: 40,000
Affiliations: ASOL; California Confederation of the Arts; Association of California Symphony Orchestras

SAN FRANCISCO ARTS COMMISSION
25 Van Ness Avenue, Suite 240, San Francisco, CA 94102
(415) 554-9671
FAX: (415) 621-3868
Founded: 1932
Arts Area: Vocal Music; Instrumental Music
Status: Professional
Type: Performing; Educational; Sponsoring
Purpose: To support and advocate for the visual arts and artists of the Bay Area
Management: Joanne Chow Winship, Director of Cultural Affairs; Maya Rath, Assistant Director
Paid Staff: 17   **Volunteer Staff:** 8
Paid Artists: 8   **Non-Paid Artists:** 4
Utilizes: Special Technical Talent; Guest Conductors; Guest Artists
Budget: $1,000,000 - $5,000,000
Income Sources: Private Foundations/Grants/Endowments; Business/Corporate Donations; Box Office; Government Grants; Individual Donations
Season: 52 Weeks
Annual Attendance: 500,000
Affiliations: NALAA; CAC

SAN FRANCISCO JAZZ FESTIVAL
c/o Jazz in the City, 141 Tenth Street, San Francisco, CA 94103
(415) 864-5449
FAX: (415) 863-9462
Founded: 1983
Arts Area: Dance; Vocal Music; Instrumental Music; Festivals; Jazz
Status: Professional; Non-Profit
Type: Performing; Resident; Educational
Purpose: Featuring the best of national and Bay Area jazz artists, the San Francisco Jazz Festival performs in venues throughout San Francisco.
Management: Randall Kline, Director; Shirley Kline, Associate Producer; Ann Dyer, Publicist; Dmitri Matheny, Development Director; Cynthia Taylor, Administrative Production Assistant
Officers: Kim Fowler, Chairman of the Board; Tom Noonan, President; James P. Mayer, Treasurer; Shirley Kline, Secretary
Utilizes: Guest Artists
Budget: $100,000 - $500,000
Income Sources: Private Foundations/Grants/Endowments; Business/Corporate Donations; Box Office; Government Grants; Individual Donations
Season: October - November
Annual Attendance: 25,000

STERN GROVE FESTIVAL ASSOCIATION
44 Page Street, Suite 604D, San Francisco, CA 94102
(415) 252-6252
> **Founded:** 1937
> **Arts Area:** Dance; Vocal Music; Instrumental Music; Theater; Festivals; Lyric Opera; Grand Opera
> **Status:** Professional; Non-Profit
> **Type:** Sponsoring
> **Purpose:** To present free events each summer on Sundays in outdoor Sigmund Stern Grove featuring the finest dance, musical theater, instrumental music, vocal music and jazz
> **Management:** Patricia Kristof Moy, Executive Director; Don O'Brien, Artistic Coordinator
> **Officers:** Mrs. Richard N. Goldman, Chairman; Al H. Nathe, Finance Chairman; Mrs. Robilee Fredrick Deane, Program Chairman
> **Paid Staff:** 20   **Volunteer Staff:** 150
> **Paid Artists:** 500
> **Utilizes:** Guest Conductors; Guest Artists; Guest Directors
> **Budget:** $100,000 - $500,000
> **Income Sources:** Private Foundations/Grants/Endowments; Business/Corporate Donations; Government Grants; Individual Donations
> **Season:** June - August   **Annual Attendance:** 150,000
> **Performance Facilities:** Sigmund Stern Grove

FACILITY

THE ALCAZAR THEATRE
650 Geary, San Francisco, CA 94102
(415) 861-6655
> **Type of Facility:** Theatre House
> **Facility Originally:** Shrine Temple
> **Type of Stage:** Thrust
> **Stage Dimensions:** 15'x30'x40'
> **Seating Capacity:** 499
> **Year Built:** 1917
> **Year Remodeled:** 1976   **Architect:** John Gerrity   **Cost:** $91,000
> **Contact for Rental:** Steve Dobbins;   (415) 861-6655
> **Manager:** Joseph Perrotti

BAYVIEW OPERA HOUSE
4705 Third Street, San Francisco, CA 94124
(415) 824-0386
> **Type of Facility:** Theatre Complex; Concert Hall; Auditorium; Outdoor (Concert); Performance Center; Theatre House; Opera House; Multi-Purpose; Room
> **Type of Stage:** Proscenium
> **Stage Dimensions:** 30'Wx15'D
> **Seating Capacity:** 350
> **Year Built:** 1888
> **Year Remodeled:** 1965
> **Contact for Rental:** Fred McKenzie-Acting Director;   (415) 824-0386
> **Resident Groups:** San Francisco Senior Community Choir; Four Visions Theater Company; Bayview Opera House Community Choir
> *The oldest theater in San Francisco*

CENTER FOR AFRICAN AND AFRICAN AMERICAN ART AND CULTURE
762 Fulton Street, San Francisco, CA 94102
(415) 928-8546
> **Founded:** 1990
> **Type of Facility:** Theatre Complex; Concert Hall; Auditorium; Outdoor (Concert); Studio Performance; Performance Center; Off Broadway; Theatre House; Opera House; Civic Center; Multi-Purpose; Room; Loft
> **Facility Originally:** Garage; Business Facility; Warehouse
> **Type of Stage:** Thrust; Platform; 3/4 Arena
> **Stage Dimensions:** 36'x26'x12'
> **Seating Capacity:** 240
> **Year Built:** 1935
> **Year Remodeled:** 1984   **Architect:** Rose Kraus & Broder   **Cost:** $500,000
> **Acoustical Consultant:** Community Design Center of UC Berkeley, Chuck Turner
> **Contact for Rental:** Kola Thomas;   (415) 928-8546
> **Resident Groups:** Wajumbe Cultural Institution; GO Productions; Cultural Odyssey; BES Children's Educational Theatre; San Francisco African American Historical & Cultural Society
> *Performances; workshops; seminars; classes; rehearsals; conferences; films*

COMMUNITY MUSIC CENTER
544 Capp Street, San Francisco, CA 94110
(415) 647-6015
Founded: 1921
Type of Facility: Concert Hall
Type of Stage: Proscenium
Stage Dimensions: 40'Wx20'D
Seating Capacity: 125
Year Built: 1926
Year Remodeled: 1985   **Architect:** Robert Hersey   **Cost:** $150,000
Contact for Rental: Claire Harmon;   (415) 647-6015
Recitals, auditions, rehearsals

CURRAN THEATRE
445 Geary Street, San Francisco, CA 94102
(415) 474-3800
Type of Facility: Theatre House
Type of Stage: Proscenium
Orchestra Pit
Seating Capacity: 1,740
Year Built: 1922   **Architect:** Homer Curran
Manager: Shorenstein Hays Nederlander Organizatio

FLORENCE GOULD THEATRE IN THE CALIFORNIA PALACE OF THE LEGION OF HONOR
Lincoln Park, San Francisco, CA 94121
(415) 750-3600
Type of Facility: Concert Hall; Theatre House
Type of Stage: Thrust; Proscenium
Stage Dimensions: 25'Wx13'Hx31'D, includes 5' thrust beyond proscenium
Seating Capacity: 332
Year Built: 1924   **Architect:** George Applegarth
Year Remodeled: 1987   **Architect:** Rosekrans & Broder   **Cost:** $1,000,000
Acoustical Consultant: Wilson, Ihrig & Associates
The theatre will be closed for seismic upgrade and renovation through January 1995. No rental inquiries can be accepted until fall 1994.

FORT MASON CENTER - COWELL THEATRE
Fort Mason Center Building A, San Francisco, CA 94123
(415) 941-5706
Founded: 1989
Type of Facility: Theatre Complex; Performance Center; Multi-Purpose
Facility Originally: Army Base
Type of Stage: Proscenium
Stage Dimensions: 41'x30'
Seating Capacity: 440
Year Built: 1989   **Architect:** Robinson, Mills and Williams   **Cost:** $2,500,000
Contact for Rental: Robert Martin;   (415) 941-5706

GOLDEN GATE THEATRE
#1 at Taylor and Market Street, San Francisco, CA 94102
(415) 776-9211
Type of Facility: Theatre House
Type of Stage: Proscenium
Stage Dimensions: 50'Wx33'D   **Orchestra Pit**
Seating Capacity: 2,350
Year Built: 1922   **Architect:** G. Albert Lansburg   **Cost:** $2,000,000
Year Remodeled: 1979   **Architect:** G. Albert Lansburg   **Cost:** $7,000,000
Contact for Rental: Nederlander Organization;   (212) 262-2400

MUSIC AND ARTS INSTITUTE
2622 Jackson Street, San Francisco, CA 94115
(415) 567-1445
Type of Facility: Studio Performance; Room
Facility Originally: School; Ballroom
Type of Stage: Flexible
Seating Capacity: 100
Year Built: 1894   **Architect:** Willis Polk
Contact for Rental: (415) 567-1445

NEW PERFORMANCE GALLERY OF SAN FRANCISCO
3153 17th Street, San Francisco, CA 94110
(415) 626-6745
    Type of Facility: Studio Performance
    Facility Originally: Warehouse
    Type of Stage: Flexible; Loft
    Stage Dimensions: 40'x40'
    Seating Capacity: 200
    Year Remodeled: 1980 **Architect:** Peter Van Dyne
    Contact for Rental: K.T. Nelson; (415) 626-6745
    Resident Groups: Oberlin Dance Company - San Francisco; Margaret Jenkins Dance Company

NOB HILL MASONIC CENTER
1111 California Street, San Francisco, CA 94108
(415) 776-4702
    Type of Facility: Concert Hall; Auditorium; Exhibit Hall
    Facility Originally: Masonic Meeting House
    Type of Stage: Thrust
    Stage Dimensions: 30'Wx50'D
    Seating Capacity: 3,165
    Year Built: 1956 **Architect:** Isaiah Roller
    Contact for Rental: Ray W. Ward, CFE; (415) 776-4702
    Exhibit Hall is 16,500 square feet.

ORPHEUM THEATER
1192 Market Street, San Francisco, CA 94102
(415) 474-3800
FAX: (415) 775-0309
    Type of Facility: Theatre House
    Facility Originally: Vaudeville; Movie House
    Type of Stage: Proscenium **Orchestra Pit**
    Seating Capacity: 2,500
    Year Built: 1926 **Architect:** B. Marcus Priteca **Cost:** $800,000
    Year Remodeled: 1977 **Cost:** $2,000,000
    Acoustical Consultant: Tim Purcell
    Contact for Rental: Pat Heagy; (415) 673-6400
    Manager: Shorenstein Hays Nederlander Organization; (415) 673-6400

PALACE OF FINE ARTS
3301 Lyon Street, San Francisco, CA 94123
(415) 563-6504
    Type of Facility: Performance Center; Multi-Purpose
    Facility Originally: Exhibition Facility Of The 1915 Panama P
    Year Built: 1913 **Architect:** Bernard Maybeck **Cost:** $580,000
    Year Remodeled: 1967 **Architect:** Hans Gerson **Cost:** $7,500,000
    Contact for Rental: Kevin J. O'Brien, Executive Director; (415) 563-6504
    The building houses the Palace of Fine Arts Theatre. See separate listing for additional information.

PALACE OF FINE ARTS THEATRE
3301 Lyon Street, San Francisco, CA 94123
(415) 563-6504
FAX: (415) 567-4062
    Founded: 1970
    Type of Facility: Theatre House; Multi-Purpose
    Facility Originally: Exhibit Hall
    Type of Stage: Proscenium
    Stage Dimensions: 73'Wx52'Dx24'H **Orchestra Pit**
    Seating Capacity: 1,000
    Year Built: 1970 **Architect:** Vincent Raney **Cost:** $750,000
    Acoustical Consultant: Dennis Paoletti
    Contact for Rental: Kevin J. O'Brien, Executive Director; (415) 563-6504
    Theatre was added to Palace of Fine Arts in 1970.

SAN FRANCISCO CIVIC AUDITORIUM
99 Grove Street, San Francisco, CA 94102
(415) 974-4000
FAX: (415) 974-4084
    Type of Facility: Concert Hall; Auditorium

Type of Stage: Platform
Seating Capacity: 7,000
Year Built: 1915
Contact for Rental: Melody Lendaro;   (415) 974-4000
Manager: John Adams;   (415) 974-4000

SAN FRANCISCO COUNTY FAIR BUILDING
9th & Lincoln, San Francisco, CA 94122
(415) 753-7090
Type of Facility: Auditorium; Multi-Purpose
Type of Stage: Regular
Stage Dimensions: 12'x20'x20'
Seating Capacity: 400
Year Built: 1961   **Cost:** $800,000
Contact for Rental: Elaine Calderon, Reservation Secretary;   (415) 753-7090
Manager: Walden R. Valen;   (415) 753-7090

SAN FRANCISCO WAR MEMORIAL AND PERFORMING ARTS CENTER
401 Van Ness Avenue, Suite 110, San Francisco, CA 94102
(415) 621-6600
Orchestra Pit
Year Built: 1931   **Architect:** Arthur Brown, Jr.   **Cost:** $6,000,000
Contact for Rental: Margo Cowan;   (415) 621-6600
Resident Groups: San Francisco Symphony; San Francisco Opera; San Francisco Ballet
The facility contains the Green Room, Herbst Theatre, Louise M. Davies Symphony Hall and War Memorial Opera House. See separate listings for additional information.

SAN FRANCISCO WAR MEMORIAL AND PERFORMING ARTS CENTER - GREEN ROOM
401 Van Ness Avenue, Suite 110, San Francisco, CA 94102
(415) 621-6600
FAX: (415) 621-5091
Founded: 1932
Type of Facility: Concert Hall; Performance Center; Civic Center; Room
Facility Originally: Library; Lounge
Type of Stage: Platform
Seating Capacity: 350
Year Built: 1931   **Architect:** Arthur Brown Jr.
Contact for Rental: Elizabeth Glaze;   (415) 621-6600
Manager: Thelma Shelley
Resident Groups: San Francisco Contemporary Music Players; Composers, Inc.; D'Addario Foundation for the Performing Arts - Guitar Series; Avedis; ARTEA Chamber Orchestra; Pacific Mozart Ensemble

SAN FRANCISCO WAR MEMORIAL AND PERFORMING ARTS CENTER - HERBST THEATRE
401 Van Ness Avenue, Suite 110, San Francisco, CA 94102
(415) 621-6600
FAX: (415) 621-5091
Founded: 1932
Type of Facility: Concert Hall; Auditorium; Performance Center; Theatre House; Opera House; Civic Center
Facility Originally: Meeting Hall; Ballroom; Movie House
Type of Stage: Proscenium
Stage Dimensions: 49'1"Wx33'10"D stage; 33'11"Wx24'H proscenium opening
Orchestra Pit
Seating Capacity: 928
Year Built: 1931   **Architect:** Arthur Brown Jr.   **Cost:** $1,000,000
Year Remodeled: 1976   **Architect:** Skidmore Owings Merrill   **Cost:** $10,000,000
Contact for Rental: Margo Cowan;   (415) 621-6600
Manager: Thelma Shelley
Resident Groups: San Francisco Performances; City Arts and Lectures; San Francisco Children's Opera; Midsummer Mozart; Chamber Symphony San Francisco; ODC; Today's Artists; Golden Gate Geographic; San Francisco Museum of Modern Art

SAN FRANCISCO WAR MEMORIAL AND PERFORMING ARTS CENTER - LOUISE M. DAVIES SYMPHONY HALL
201 Van Ness Avenue, Suite 110, San Francisco, CA 94102
(415) 621-6600
FAX: (415) 621-5091
Founded: 1980
Type of Facility: Concert Hall; Auditorium; Performance Center; Civic Center
Type of Stage: 3/4 Arena

Orchestra Pit
Seating Capacity: 2743
Year Built: 1980   **Architect:** Skidmore Owings Merrill   **Cost:** $36,000,000
Year Remodeled: 1992   **Architect:** Skidmore Owings Merrill   **Cost:** $10,000,000
Contact for Rental: Margo Cowan;   (415) 621-6600
Manager: Thelma Shelley
Resident Groups: San Francisco Symphony

SAN FRANCISCO WAR MEMORIAL AND PERFORMING ARTS CENTER - WAR MEMORIAL OPERA HOUSE
301 Van Ness Avenue, Suite 110, San Francisco, CA 94102
(415) 621-6600
FAX: (415) 621-5091
Founded: 1932
Type of Facility: Concert Hall; Performance Center; Opera House; Civic Center
Type of Stage: Proscenium
Stage Dimensions: 134'Wx84'6"D stage; 52'Wx51'H proscenium opening   **Orchestra Pit**
Seating Capacity: 3,252
Year Built: 1931   **Architect:** Arthur Brown Jr.   **Cost:** $2,500,000
Year Remodeled: 1976   **Architect:** Skidmore Owings Merrill   **Cost:** $6,000,000
Contact for Rental: Margo Cowan;   (415) 621-6600
Manager: Thelma Shelley;   (415) 621-6600
Resident Groups: San Francisco Opera; San Francisco Ballet; Merola Opera

TRUSTEES AUDITORIUM - ASIAN ART MUSEUM
Golden Gate Park, San Francisco, CA 94118
(415) 668-6314
Type of Facility: Auditorium
Type of Stage: Platform
Stage Dimensions: 25'x25'x10'
Seating Capacity: 390
Year Built: 1950
Contact for Rental: Alexandra Morgan;   (415) 668-6314
Manager: Preston Ni

San Gabriel

FACILITY

SAN GABRIEL CIVIC AUDITORIUM
320 South Mission Drive, San Gabriel, CA 91776
(818) 308-2865
Type of Facility: Auditorium; Performance Center; Theatre House; Multi-Purpose
Type of Stage: Proscenium
Stage Dimensions: 100'Wx75'D; 58'Wx29'6"H proscenium opening   **Orchestra Pit**
Seating Capacity: 1,488
Year Built: 1927
Contact for Rental: William D. Shaw;   (818) 308-2865
Resident Groups: San Gabriel Valley Civic Light Opera

San Jose

DANCE

SAN JOSE CLEVELAND BALLET
PO Box 1666, San Jose, CA 95109
(408) 993-9531
Founded: 1985
Arts Area: Ballet
Status: Professional; Non-Profit
Type: Performing
Management: Dennis Nahat, Artistic Director
Officers: Carole Minton, President
Paid Staff: 6
Paid Artists: 40
Utilizes: Guest Artists
Budget: $1,000,000 - $5,000,000

Income Sources: Private Foundations/Grants/Endowments; Business/Corporate Donations; Box Office; Individual Donations
Season: October - May
Affiliations: Cleveland Ballet
Performance Facilities: San Jose Center for the Performing Arts

SAN JOSE DANCE THEATRE
753 North 9th Street, Suite 234, San Jose, CA 95112
(408) 293-5665
FAX: (408) 293-0852
Founded: 1965
Arts Area: Ballet
Status: Semi-Professional; Non-Profit
Type: Performing; Touring; Resident; Educational
Purpose: A professional organization that develops the performing arts for young dancers
Management: Paul E. Curtis Jr., Artistic Director
Officers: Carolyne Hui, President; Bob Chortek, First Vice President; Clare Noonan, Secretary; Michael Dertro, Treasurer
Paid Staff: 1   **Volunteer Staff:** 18
Paid Artists: 5   **Non-Paid Artists:** 28
Utilizes: Guest Conductors; Guest Artists
Budget: $500,000 - $1,000,000
Income Sources: Private Foundations/Grants/Endowments; Business/Corporate Donations; Box Office; Government Grants; Individual Donations
Season: September - May   **Annual Attendance:** 15,000
Affiliations: PRBA
Performance Facilities: San Jose Center for the Performing Arts

INSTRUMENTAL MUSIC

SAN JOSE SYMPHONY
99 Almaden Boulevard, #400, San Jose, CA 95113
(408) 287-7383
Founded: 1879
Arts Area: Symphony; Orchestra; Ensemble
Status: Professional; Non-Profit
Type: Performing; Educational
Management: Leonid Grin, Music Director/Conductor
Officers: M. Cathy Peek, Chairman of the Board; Douglas McLendon, President
Paid Staff: 18
Paid Artists: 87
Utilizes: Guest Conductors; Guest Artists
Budget: $1,000,000 - $5,000,000
Income Sources: Private Foundations/Grants/Endowments; Business/Corporate Donations; Box Office; Government Grants; Individual Donations
Season: September - June
Annual Attendance: 50,000
Affiliations: ASOL; Association of California Symphony Orchestras
Performance Facilities: Center for Performing Arts; Flint Center

SAN JOSE TAIKO GROUP
PO Box 26895, San Jose, CA 95159
(408) 293-9344
FAX: (408) 293-9366
Founded: 1973
Arts Area: Ethnic; Instrumental Group
Status: Professional; Semi-Professional; Non-Profit
Type: Performing; Touring; Educational
Purpose: To perform using the taiko (Japanese drum) as the principle instrument in a contemporary performing arts form
Management: Mariko Miho, General Manager; Roy Hirabayashi, Artistic Director
Officers: Jean Shimoguchi, Chairperson; Sharon Noguchi, Secretary; Todd Hirozawa, Treasurer
Paid Staff: 3
Paid Artists: 5   **Non-Paid Artists:** 15
Utilizes: Special Technical Talent; Guest Artists
Budget: $100,000 - $500,000
Income Sources: Private Foundations/Grants/Endowments; Business/Corporate Donations; Box Office; Government Grants; Individual Donations
Season: 52 Weeks

VOCAL MUSIC

OPERA SAN JOSE
12 South First Street, #207, San Jose, CA 95113-2404
(408) 283-4880
Founded: 1984
Arts Area: Lyric Opera; Operetta
Status: Professional; Non-Profit
Type: Performing; Touring; Educational; Sponsoring
Purpose: To maintain and enhance a professional opera company of artistic excellence; to provide principally in opera of all periods and secondarily in operetta; to provide opera singers with professional development and performance opportunities; to develop, educate and entertain
Management: Irene Dalis, General/Artistic Director; David Rohrbaugh, Musical Director
Officers: Kitty Spaulding, Chairman; Michael Kalkstein, President
Paid Staff: 8
Paid Artists: 149
Utilizes: Special Technical Talent; Guest Directors
Budget: $1,000,000 - $5,000,000
Income Sources: Private Foundations/Grants/Endowments; Business/Corporate Donations; Box Office; Government Grants; Individual Donations
Season: October - June   **Annual Attendance:** 235,000
Affiliations: OA; COS; Theatre Bay Area
Performance Facilities: Montgomery Theater

SAN JOSE CIVIC LIGHT OPERA ASSOCIATION INC.
4 North Second Street, Suite 100, San Jose, CA 95113
(408) 297-8811
FAX: (408) 971-4046
Arts Area: Light Opera; Musical Theater
Status: Semi-Professional; Non-Profit
Type: Performing; Resident
Purpose: Our full-scale, musical-theater production company is one of the largest subscribed musical theater companies on the West Coast.
Management: Dianna Shuster; Stewart Slater, Executive Producer
Officers: Sunny Claggett, President of the Board
Income Sources: Private Foundations/Grants/Endowments; Business/Corporate Donations; Box Office; Government Grants; Individual Donations
Performance Facilities: San Jose Center of the Performing Arts

THEATRE

THE NORTHSIDE THEATRE COMPANY
848 East William Street, San Jose, CA 95008
(408) 288-7820
Arts Area: Theatrical Group
Status: Non-Profit
Type: Performing; Touring; Resident; Educational
Purpose: To provide high quality, theatrical opportunities for youth, regardless of economic, educational, cultural or physical limitations
Management: Richard T. Orlando, Artistic Director; Stu Richel, Development Director; Chriss Zaida, Director of Theater Education; Sandra Winslow, Office Manager; Alice Willoughby, Administrative Associate
Officers: Al Reuter, Chairman of the Board; Kathy Harwood, Secretary; Richard Desmond, Vice Chairman; Bev Laflamme, Marketing Chair; Jon Rensen, Treasurer
Paid Staff: 7   **Volunteer Staff:** 4
Paid Artists: 1   **Non-Paid Artists:** 10
Utilizes: Special Technical Talent; Guest Artists
Budget: $100,000 - $500,000
Income Sources: Private Foundations/Grants/Endowments; Business/Corporate Donations; Box Office; Government Grants; Individual Donations
Season: October - June   **Annual Attendance:** 6,500
Affiliations: San Jose Civic Light Opera

SAN JOSE REPERTORY THEATRE
1 North First Street, Suite 1, San Jose, CA 95113
(408) 291-2266; (408) 291-2255
FAX: (408) 995-0737
Mailing Address: PO Box 2399, San Jose, CA 95109
Founded: 1980

Arts Area: Professional; Theatrical Group
Status: Professional; Non-Profit
Type: Performing; Resident; Educational
Management: Timothy Near, Artistic Director; Alexandra Boisvert, Managing Director
Officers: Jane Decker, Board President
Paid Staff: 35
Paid Artists: 70
Utilizes: Guest Artists; Guest Directors
Budget: $1,000,000 - $5,000,000
Income Sources: Private Foundations/Grants/Endowments; Business/Corporate Donations; Box Office; Government Grants; Individual Donations
Season: November - August   **Annual Attendance:** 90,000
Affiliations: LORT; TCG
Performance Facilities: Montgomery Theater

TEATRO VISION
271 South 20th Street, San Jose, CA 95116
   Founded: 1984
   Arts Area: Theatrical Group; Chicano Theatre
   Status: Semi-Professional; Non-Profit
   Type: Performing; Touring
   Purpose: To produce and perform plays with themes that address the Chicano experience
   Management: Elisa Marina Gonzalez, Production Manager; Denis Marks, Technical Director
   Officers: Norma Ruiz, Board Chair; Elisa Marina Gonzalez, Vice Chair; Jaime Alvarado, Secretary; Rose Mendoza, Treasurer
   Volunteer Staff: 25
   Utilizes: Guest Artists; Guest Directors
   Budget: $50,000 - $100,000
   Income Sources: Private Foundations/Grants/Endowments; Business/Corporate Donations; Box Office; Government Grants; Individual Donations
   Season: May - December   **Annual Attendance:** 3,000
   Affiliations: Movimiento de Arte y Cultura Latinoamericana; Theatre Bay Area

FACILITY

SAN JOSE CITY COLLEGE
2100 Moorpark Avenue, San Jose, CA 95128
(408) 288-3785
   Type of Facility: Theatre House
   Type of Stage: Proscenium
   Stage Dimensions: 16'x32'x36'   **Orchestra Pit**
   Seating Capacity: 332
   Year Built: 1963   **Architect:** Higgins & Root   **Cost:** $800,000
   Contact for Rental: Antoinette Rodriguez;   (408) 288-3756
   Manager: Bill Kester;   (408) 288-3785
   Resident Groups: San Jose City College Drama Department

SAN JOSE CONVENTION AND CULTURAL FACILITIES
408 Almaden Avenue, San Jose, CA 95110
(408) 277-3925
FAX: (408) 277-3525
   Type of Facility: Performance Center
   Year Built: 1972   **Architect:** Frank Lloyd Wright   **Cost:** $13,000,000
   Contact for Rental: Robin Merriam;   (408) 277-3925
   Manager: Ellen Oppenheim
   The Convention and Cultural Facilities include the Center for Performing Arts, Civic Auditorium and Montgomery Theater. See separate listings for additional information.

SAN JOSE CONVENTION AND CULTURAL FACILITIES - CENTER FOR THE PERFORMING ARTS
PO Box 90250, San Jose, CA 95109
(408) 277-3925
FAX: (408) 277-3535
   Type of Facility: Concert Hall; Opera House
   Type of Stage: Proscenium
   Stage Dimensions: 144'Wx40'6"D; 60'Wx34'H proscenium opening   **Orchestra Pit**
   Seating Capacity: 2,701
   Year Built: 1972
   Contact for Rental: Robin Merriam;   (408) 277-3925

Manager: Ellen Oppenheim
Resident Groups: San Jose Symphony Association; San Jose Civic Light Opera; San Jose Cleveland Ballet

SAN JOSE CONVENTION AND CULTURAL FACILITIES - CIVIC AUDITORIUM
PO Box 90250, San Jose, CA 95109
(408) 277-3925
FAX: (408) 277-3535
Type of Facility: Auditorium
Type of Stage: Proscenium
Stage Dimensions: 116'Wx36'Dx65'H; 49'9"Wx30'H proscenium opening   **Orchestra Pit**
Seating Capacity: 3,060
Year Built: 1972
Contact for Rental: Robin Merriam;   (408) 277-3925
Manager: Ellen Oppenheim

SAN JOSE CONVENTION AND CULTURAL FACILITIES - MONTGOMERY THEATER
PO Box 90250, San Jose, CA 95109
(408) 277-3925
FAX: (408) 277-3535
Type of Facility: Theatre House; Opera House
Type of Stage: Proscenium
Stage Dimensions: 50'Wx30'D; 26'Wx14'H proscenium opening
Seating Capacity: 537
Year Built: 1972
Contact for Rental: Robin Merriam;   (408) 277-3925
Manager: Ellen Oppenheim, Director
Resident Groups: San Jose Repertory Theatre; Gilbert and Sullivan Society of San Jose; San Jose Children's Musical Theatre; Opera San Jose

SAN JOSE STATE UNIVERSITY - CONCERT HALL
Washington Square, San Jose, CA 95192-0095
(408) 924-4673
FAX: (408) 924-4773
Type of Facility: Concert Hall
Type of Stage: Platform
Seating Capacity: 527
Year Built: 1953   **Architect:** Architecture Department, State of California
Contact for Rental: Wanda Butts;   (408) 924-4709
Resident Groups: San Jose State University Orchestra; San Jose State University Symphonic Band
Available for rental to non-profit organizations and student groups

SAN JOSE STATE UNIVERSITY - UNIVERSITY THEATRE
One Washington Square, San Jose, CA 95192-0098
(408) 924-4530
FAX: (408) 924-1018
Type of Facility: Theatre Complex; Theatre House
Type of Stage: Flexible; Proscenium
Stage Dimensions: 60'Wx33'D   **Orchestra Pit**
Seating Capacity: 393
Year Built: 1955
Contact for Rental: James Culley;   (408) 924-4552
Manager: Buddy Butler;   (408) 924-4584

San Juan Bautista

THEATRE

EL TEATRO CAMPESINO
PO Box 1240, San Juan Bautista, CA 95045
(408) 623-2444
FAX: (408) 623-4127
Arts Area: Professional; Theatrical Group
Status: Professional; Non-Profit
Type: Touring; Resident; Educational; Sponsoring
Purpose: To be one of the nation's pre-eminent Latino/Chicano theaters
Management: Phillip Esparza, Managing Director; Rosa Maria Escalante, Education/Workdhop Director; Luis Valdez, Artistic Director

Officers: Luis Valdez, Chairman of the Board
Budget: $1,000,000 - $5,000,000
Income Sources: Private Foundations/Grants/Endowments; Business/Corporate Donations; Box Office; Government Grants; Individual Donations
Performance Facilities: El Teatro

San Luis Obispo

INSTRUMENTAL MUSIC

SAN LUIS OBISPO COUNTY SYMPHONY
1160 Marsh, San Luis Obispo, CA 93401
(805) 543-3533
Founded: 1950
Arts Area: Symphony; Chamber
Status: Non-Profit
Type: Performing
Management: Cricket Handler, Executive Director; Michael Nowak, Conductor; Sandy Bear, Marketing Director
Officers: Frank St. Denis, President; Patrick Perry, Chairman of Development
Paid Staff: 3 **Volunteer Staff:** 150
Utilizes: Guest Conductors; Guest Artists
Budget: $100,000 - $500,000
Income Sources: Private Foundations/Grants/Endowments; Business/Corporate Donations; Box Office; Government Grants; Individual Donations
Season: September - May **Annual Attendance:** 4,500
Affiliations: ASOL; Association of California Symphony Orchestras
Performance Facilities: Church of the Nazarene

PERFORMING SERIES

SAN LUIS OBISPO MOZART FESITVAL
1160 Marsh Street, Suite 310, San Luis Obispo, CA 93401
(805) 543-4580
FAX: (805) 541-5425
Founded: 1970
Arts Area: Vocal Music; Instrumental Music; Festivals; Lyric Opera
Status: Professional; Non-Profit
Type: Performing; Educational
Purpose: To present a classical music festival highlighting Mozart and other classical and contemporary composers
Management: Clifton Swanson, Music Director; Patricia Martin, Executive Director; Jean Ciampi, Public Relations Director
Officers: Jeffrey Kahane, Associate Conductor
Paid Staff: 4 **Volunteer Staff:** 300
Paid Artists: 100
Utilizes: Guest Conductors; Guest Artists; Guest Directors; Guest Lecturers
Budget: $100,000 - $500,000
Income Sources: Private Foundations/Grants/Endowments; Business/Corporate Donations; Box Office; Government Grants; Individual Donations
Season: July - August **Annual Attendance:** 8,000

FACILITY

CUESTA COLLEGE AUDITORIUM
Cuesta College Campus, PO Box 8106, San Luis Obispo, CA 93403
(805) 546-3100
Type of Facility: Auditorium; Theatre House
Facility Originally: Recreation Hall/gymnasium
Type of Stage: Proscenium
Stage Dimensions: 42'Wx17'6"H
Seating Capacity: 810
Year Built: 1942 **Acoustical Consultant:** Ron McKay of Bolt, Beranek & Newman
Contact for Rental: Community Services; (805) 544-2943
Resident Groups: San Luis Obispo County Symphony; Pacific Ballet; Pat Jackson's American Dancers
Only rented to non-profit organizations

San Mateo

DANCE

PENINSULA BALLET THEATRE
333 South B Street, San Mateo, CA 94401
(415) 343-8485
> **Founded:** 1967
> **Arts Area:** Ballet
> **Status:** Professional; Non-Profit
> **Type:** Performing; Resident
> **Purpose:** To provide the community with the educational and cultural advantages of a resident ballet company of the highest quality and varied repertoire and to give the artists the enjoyment of community roots not available in touring companies
> **Management:** Anne Bena, Artistic Director; Mary Dahlquist, Company Coordinator
> **Paid Staff:** 2   **Volunteer Staff:** 25
> **Paid Artists:** 30   **Non-Paid Artists:** 15
> **Utilizes:** Special Technical Talent; Guest Conductors; Guest Choreographers
> **Budget:** $100,000 - $500,000
> **Income Sources:** Private Foundations/Grants/Endowments; Business/Corporate Donations; Box Office; Government Grants; Individual Donations
> **Season:** November - June   **Annual Attendance:** 12,000
> **Performance Facilities:** San Mateo Performing Arts Center

FACILITY

SAN MATEO PERFORMING ARTS CENTER
600 North Delaware, San Mateo, CA 94401
(415) 348-8243
> **Type of Facility:** Concert Hall; Performance Center; Theatre House; Opera House
> **Type of Stage:** Proscenium
> **Stage Dimensions:** 100'Wx50'D; 50'W proscenium opening   **Orchestra Pit**
> **Seating Capacity:** 1,600
> **Year Built:** 1953   **Cost:** $800,000
> **Contact for Rental:** Dave LeBlanc;   (415) 348-8243

San Pedro

FACILITY

ANGELS GATE CULTURAL CENTER
3601 South Gaffey Street, PO Box 1471, San Pedro, CA 90731
(310) 519-1874
> **Type of Facility:** Outdoor (Concert); Amphitheater; Multi-Purpose
> **Facility Originally:** Military Base
> **Type of Stage:** 3/4 Arena
> **Stage Dimensions:** 60'x120'
> **Seating Capacity:** 135
> **Year Built:** 1924
> **Year Remodeled:** 1984   **Architect:** Kenneth Darling   **Cost:** $18,000
> **Acoustical Consultant:** David Lamb
> **Contact for Rental:** Besty Lohrer

San Rafael

DANCE

THE MARIN BALLET
100 Elm Street, San Rafael, CA 94901
(415) 453-6705
FAX: (415) 453-5894
> **Founded:** 1963
> **Arts Area:** Modern; Ballet; Jazz; Tap
> **Status:** Non-Profit; Pre-Professional Training
> **Type:** Educational
> **Purpose:** To provide the highest quality dance training in all disciplines at all levels as well as providing performance opportunities to extend the students' experience

Management: Barbara Steele, Business Manager; Margaret Swarthout, Artistic Director
Officers: Nancy Alvarez, President; Diane Parker and Elizabeth Cooper, Vice Presidents; Trish Prokop, Secretary
Paid Staff: 5   **Volunteer Staff:** 30
Paid Artists: 30
Utilizes: Special Technical Talent; Guest Artists; Guest Choreographers
Budget: $500,000 - $1,000,000
Income Sources: Private Foundations/Grants/Endowments; Business/Corporate Donations; Box Office; Individual Donations; Tuition
Season: 52 Weeks   **Annual Attendance:** 20,000
Affiliations: NASD
Performance Facilities: Civic Center

INSTRUMENTAL MUSIC

MARIN SYMPHONY ASSOCIATION
4340 Redwood Highway, Suite 409, San Rafael, CA 94903
(415) 479-8100
FAX: (415) 479-8110
Arts Area: Symphony; Orchestra
Status: Non-Profit
Type: Performing; Educational
Purpose: To provide high-quality musical performances in Marin County; to provide performance opportunities for young people
Management: Jennifer Duston, Executive Director; Gary Sheldon, Music Director
Officers: Howard Creighton, President, Board of Directors
Paid Staff: 8
Utilizes: Guest Artists
Budget: $500,000 - $1,000,000
Income Sources: Private Foundations/Grants/Endowments; Business/Corporate Donations; Box Office; Government Grants; Individual Donations
Season: November - April
Affiliations: California Arts Council; Marin Arts Council; ASOL; Association of California Symphony Orchestras
Performance Facilities: Marin Veterans Memorial Auditorium

MARIN SYMPHONY YOUTH ORCHESTRA
4340 Redwood Highway, Suite 409, San Rafael, CA 94903
(415) 479-8100
Founded: 1954
Arts Area: Symphony; Orchestra; Chamber
Status: Non-Professional; Non-Profit
Type: Performing; Touring; Educational; Sponsoring
Purpose: To provide quality musical training, education and scholarship opportunities for young people in the community
Management: Leslie Stewart, Conductor/Director of MSY Programs
Paid Staff: 11   **Volunteer Staff:** 1
Non-Paid Artists: 40
Budget: $50,000 - $100,000
Income Sources: Private Foundations/Grants/Endowments; Business/Corporate Donations; Box Office; Individual Donations; Fund-raising
Season: September - May   **Annual Attendance:** 6,300
Affiliations: ASOL (Youth Orchestra Division)
Performance Facilities: San Rafael High School Auditorium

THEATRE

BLAKE STREET HAWKEYES
37 Sirard Lane, San Rafael, CA 94901
(415) 456-4384
Arts Area: Professional
Status: Non-Profit
Type: Performing; Touring; Resident; Educational
Purpose: To promote and create new theater on the edge; to promote new and experimental theater at the grass roots level
Management: Robert Ernst, Jim Cave, Co-Artistic Directors
Budget: $1,000 - $50,000
Income Sources: Private Foundations/Grants/Endowments; Government Grants

FACILITY

DOMINICAN COLLEGE - AUDITORIUM
50 Acacia, San Rafael, CA 94901
(415) 457-4440
Type of Facility: Concert Hall; Auditorium
Type of Stage: Thrust; Proscenium
Stage Dimensions: 20'x36'x22'   **Orchestra Pit**
Seating Capacity: 700
Year Built: 1922
Contact for Rental: Manager of College Facilities;   (415) 457-4440
Manager: Martin Frick
Resident Groups: College Orchestra and Chorus

MARIN CENTER
Avenue of the Flags, San Rafael, CA 94903
(415) 499-6396
FAX: (415) 499-3700
Type of Facility: Civic Center
Year Built: 1971   **Architect:** Frank Lloyd Wright
Acoustical Consultant: George Izenour
Contact for Rental: Jim Farley;   (415) 499-6396
Marin Center contains the Showcase Theatre and Veterans Memorial Auditorium. See separate listings for additional information.

MARIN CENTER - SHOWCASE THEATRE
Avenue of the Flags, San Rafael, CA 94903
(415) 499-6396
FAX: (415) 499-3700
Type of Facility: Theatre House
Type of Stage: Proscenium
Stage Dimensions: 39"9"Wx30'D; 39'9"Wx12'H proscenium opening
Seating Capacity: 309
Year Built: 1976   **Architect:** Frank Lloyd Wright Foundation
Contact for Rental: Jim Farley;   (415) 499-6396

MARIN CENTER - VETERANS MEMORIAL AUDITORIUM
Avenue of the Flags, San Rafael, CA 94903
(415) 499-6396
FAX: (415) 499-3700
Type of Facility: Auditorium
Type of Stage: Proscenium
Stage Dimensions: 60'Wx30'D; 60'Wx21'H proscenium opening   **Orchestra Pit**
Seating Capacity: 2,086
Year Built: 1971   **Architect:** Frank Lloyd Wright Foundation
Acoustical Consultant: George Izenour
Contact for Rental: Jim Farley;   (415) 499-6396

Santa Ana

INSTRUMENTAL MUSIC

SOUTH COAST SYMPHONY
1631 Sunflower Avenue, Suite C-45, Santa Ana, CA 92704
(714) 662-7220
FAX: (714) 641-3898
Founded: 1973
Arts Area: Symphony; Orchestra; Chamber
Status: Professional; Non-Profit
Type: Performing
Purpose: To serve the diverse musical needs of the southern California coastal area
Management: Doreen Hardy, Executive Director
Officers: Arlene Schafer, President; William Crosby, Vice President; Leslie Santana, Recording Secretary; Lorraine Lambeth, Treasurer
Paid Staff: 3   **Volunteer Staff:** 70
Paid Artists: 125
Utilizes: Special Technical Talent; Guest Conductors; Guest Artists

Budget: $100,000 - $500,000
Income Sources: Private Foundations/Grants/Endowments; Business/Corporate Donations; Box Office; Government Grants; Individual Donations
Season: September - May; July - September   **Annual Attendance:** 15,750
Affiliations: ASOL; Association of California Symphony Orchestras
Performance Facilities: Irvine Barclay Theatre; Fairview Park

THEATRE

STOP-GAP
523 North Grand, Santa Ana, CA 92701
(714) 648-0135
FAX: (714) 835-5087
Founded: 1978
Arts Area: Professional; Theatrical Group
Status: Professional; Non-Profit
Type: Performing; Touring; Educational
Purpose: We use theater to build bridges between generations thereby reintegrating families and communities. We use drama as a therapeutic tool to improve impaired physical, mental, emotional and social functioning.
Management: Don Laffoon, Executive Director; Victoria Bryan, Managing Director
Paid Staff: 4   **Volunteer Staff:** 10
Paid Artists: 8
Budget: $100,000 - $500,000
Income Sources: Private Foundations/Grants/Endowments; Business/Corporate Donations; Box Office; Government Grants; Individual Donations
Season: 52 Weeks

Santa Barbara

INSTRUMENTAL MUSIC

MUSIC ACADEMY OF THE WEST
1070 Fairway Road, Santa Barbara, CA 93108
(805) 969-4726
FAX: (805) 969-0686
Founded: 1945
Arts Area: Symphony; Chamber; Ensemble
Status: Professional; Non-Professional; Non-Profit
Type: Performing; Educational; Sponsoring
Purpose: To maintain a pre-professional instrumental company with vocal instruction
Management: Robert W. Holmes, President; Carleen Landes, Artistic Manager; Brian Stenfors, Development Director; Ven Holbrook, Marketing Director; Diane Lyytikainen, Controller
Officers: Mrs. Frank R. Miller, Chairman; Marsha Wayne, First Vice Chairman; Mrs. A. Stevens Halsted, Treasurer; Raymond C. Freeman Jr., Vice Chairman
Paid Staff: 10   **Volunteer Staff:** 3
Paid Artists: 33   **Non-Paid Artists:** 145
Utilizes: Guest Conductors; Guest Artists; Guest Directors
Budget: $1,000,000 - $5,000,000
Income Sources: Private Foundations/Grants/Endowments; Business/Corporate Donations; Box Office; Government Grants; Individual Donations
Season: June - August   **Annual Attendance:** 5,400
Performance Facilities: Lobero Theatre; Abravanel Hall

SANTA BARBARA SYMPHONY ORCHESTRA
214 East Victoria Street, Santa Barbara, CA 93101
(805) 965-6596
FAX: (805) 963-3510
Founded: 1954
Arts Area: Symphony; Orchestra; Ethnic
Status: Professional; Non-Profit
Type: Performing; Educational
Purpose: To provide classical music and music education
Management: Varujan Kojian, Music Director; James Wright, General Manager
Officers: Norman Sosner, Board President
Utilizes: Guest Artists
Budget: $1,000,000 - $5,000,000
Income Sources: Private Foundations/Grants/Endowments; Business/Corporate Donations; Box Office; Government Grants; Individual Donations

Season: October - May   **Annual Attendance:** 25,000
Affiliations: ASOL; Association of California Symphony Orchestras
Performance Facilities: Arlington Theatre

WEST COAST CHAMBER ORCHESTRA
1812 La Coronilla Drive, Santa Barbara, CA 93109
(805) 962-6609
      Founded: 1966
      Arts Area: Symphony; Orchestra; Chamber
      Status: Professional; Non-Profit
      Type: Performing
      Purpose: To provide the finest music at the best price; to employ the finest local musicians available
      Management: Storyland Productions; Cielo Foundation for the Performing Arts; P.W. Productions
      Officers: Christopher Story VI, President
      Volunteer Staff: 5
      Paid Artists: 60   **Non-Paid Artists:** 20
      Utilizes: Guest Conductors; Guest Artists
      Budget: $50,000 - $100,000
      Income Sources: Private Foundations/Grants/Endowments; Business/Corporate Donations; Box Office; Government Grants; Individual Donations
      Season: October - August   **Annual Attendance:** 4,000
      Affiliations: Old Spanish Days Fiesta
      Performance Facilities: Courthouse; Sunken Gardens; Lobero Theater; Goleta Valley Community Center

WEST COAST SYMPHONY
1812 La Coronilla Drive, Santa Barbara, CA 93109
(805) 962-6609
      Founded: 1966
      Arts Area: Symphony; Orchestra; Chamber
      Status: Professional; Semi-Professional; Non-Profit
      Type: Performing
      Purpose: To provide the finest music at the best price and employ the finest local musicians available
      Management: Storyland Concerts; Cielo Foundation for the Performing Arts; Piw Productions
      Officers: Christopher Story VI, President; Jacqueline Sturgeon, Vice President; Lawrence F. Hilton, Secretary; Gary Gray CPA, Treasurer
      Volunteer Staff: 5
      Paid Artists: 60   **Non-Paid Artists:** 20
      Utilizes: Guest Conductors; Guest Artists
      Budget: $50,000 - $100,000
      Income Sources: Private Foundations/Grants/Endowments; Business/Corporate Donations; Box Office; Government Grants; Individual Donations
      Season: October - August   **Annual Attendance:** 4,000
      Affiliations: Old Spanish Days Fiesta
      Performance Facilities: Courthouse; Sunken Gardens; Lobero Theatre; Goleta Valley Community Center

THEATRE

SANTA BARBARA CHILDREN'S THEATRE
PO Box 4445, Santa Barbara, CA 93140
(805) 965-8313
      Founded: 1976
      Arts Area: Theatrical Group
      Status: Non-Professional; Non-Profit
      Type: Performing; Touring; Educational
      Purpose: We are dedicated to the development of theatrical experiences for youth through theater for children by children ages 4-16.
      Management: Jan Carter, Artistic Director
      Officers: Janice Gaines, President
      Paid Staff: 1   **Volunteer Staff:** 150
      Non-Paid Artists: 600
      Utilizes: Special Technical Talent; Guest Directors
      Budget: $1,000 - $50,000
      Income Sources: Private Foundations/Grants/Endowments; Business/Corporate Donations; Box Office; Government Grants; Individual Donations; Fund-raising
      Season: 52 Weeks   **Annual Attendance:** 3,000
      Affiliations: Southern California Educational Theatre Association
      Performance Facilities: La Colina Junior High

PERFORMING SERIES

COMMUNITY ARTS AND MUSIC ASSOCIATION OF SANTA BARBARA
924 Anacapa Street, Suite B-1E, Santa Barbara, CA 93101
(805) 966-4324
Founded: 1919
Arts Area: Instrumental Music
Status: Non-Profit
Type: Sponsoring
Purpose: To provide the best symphonic music available to Santa Barbara
Management: Cathy Oliverson, Manager
Officers: James H. Hurley Jr., President; Melville H. Haskell Jr. MD, First Vice President; Mrs. Max E. Meyer, Second Vice President; Frank F. Reed, Treasurer; Ray K. Person Jr., Secretary
Paid Staff: 2   **Volunteer Staff:** 20
Utilizes: Guest Conductors; Guest Artists
Budget: $100,000 - $500,000
Income Sources: Private Foundations/Grants/Endowments; Box Office; Individual Donations
Season: October - May   **Annual Attendance:** 12,000
Performance Facilities: Arlington Center for the Performing Arts

UNIVERSITY OF CALIFORNIA AT SANTA BARBARA ARTS & LECTURES
University of California, Santa Barbara, CA 93106
(805) 893-2080
Founded: 1959
Arts Area: Dance; Vocal Music; Instrumental Music; Theater
Status: Professional; Non-Profit
Type: Performing; Educational; Presenting
Purpose: To present a wide variety of professional touring artists and ensembles in dance, theater, classical music, ethnic and traditional arts, film and literature for campus and community audiences
Management: Janet Oetinger, Director
Paid Staff: 11
Budget: $500,000 - $1,000,000
Income Sources: Private Foundations/Grants/Endowments; Box Office; Government Grants; University
Season: October - May   **Annual Attendance:** 90,000
Affiliations: WAAA; Arts Presenters; California Presenters
Performance Facilities: Campbell Hall

FACILITY

ARLINGTON CENTER FOR THE PERFORMING ARTS
1317 State Street, Santa Barbara, CA 93101
(805) 963-9589
FAX: (805) 966-4688
Type of Facility: Concert Hall; Performance Center; Theatre House
Facility Originally: Vaudeville; Movie House
Type of Stage: Proscenium
Stage Dimensions: 50'Wx38'Dx27'H   **Orchestra Pit**
Seating Capacity: 2,018
Year Built: 1931   **Architect:** Plunkett and Edwards   **Cost:** $2,000,000
Year Remodeled: 1976   **Architect:** Grant, Peterson and Phillips   **Cost:** $500,000
Acoustical Consultant: Paul Veneklasen
Contact for Rental: Karen Spotten;   (805) 963-9589

LOBERO THEATRE
33 East Canon Perdido Street, Santa Barbara, CA 93101
(805) 963-0761
Type of Facility: Concert Hall; Theatre House
Type of Stage: Proscenium
Stage Dimensions: 73'Wx38'D; 36'W proscenium opening   **Orchestra Pit**
Seating Capacity: 680
Year Built: 1873   **Architect:** Jose Lobero
Year Remodeled: 1924   **Architect:** George Washington Smith, Lutah Maria Riggs   **Cost:** $300,000
Acoustical Consultant: Paul Veneklasen
Contact for Rental: Annette deKnijf;   (805) 963-0761

Santa Clara

DANCE

SANTA CLARA BALLET
3123 Millar Avenue, Santa Clara, CA 95051
(408) 247-9178
Founded: 1973
Arts Area: Ballet; Jazz
Status: Semi-Professional; Non-Profit
Type: Performing; Touring; Resident
Management: Benjamin Reyes, Josefa Villanueva, Co-Artistic Directors; Josefa Reyes, Company Manager
Officers: Dennis Mullen, President; Susan Kaplan, Vice President; Maryanne Santos, Secretary/Treasurer
Paid Staff: 2   **Volunteer Staff:** 10
Paid Artists: 2   **Non-Paid Artists:** 10
Utilizes: Guest Artists
Budget: $50,000 - $100,000
Income Sources: Private Foundations/Grants/Endowments; Business/Corporate Donations; Box Office; Government Grants; Individual Donations; Fund-raising
Season: Winter - Summer   **Annual Attendance:** 16,000
Affiliations: Foothill College Performing Arts Alliance

Santa Cruz

DANCE

TANDY BEAL AND COMPANY
500 Seabright Avenue, Suite 101, PO Box 633, Santa Cruz, CA 95061
(408) 429-1324
Founded: 1974
Arts Area: Modern
Status: Professional; Non-Profit
Type: Performing; Touring
Purpose: To perform and produce the choreography of Tandy Beal
Management: Tandy Beal, Artistic Director; Michael Stamp, Managing Director
Paid Staff: 5
Paid Artists: 12
Utilizes: Guest Artists
Budget: $100,000 - $500,000
Income Sources: Private Foundations/Grants/Endowments; Business/Corporate Donations; Box Office; Government Grants; Individual Donations
Season: 52 Weeks
Affiliations: Dance USA; ACA
Performance Facilities: Cabrillo College Theatre

INSTRUMENTAL MUSIC

SANTA CRUZ BRASS QUINTET
216 Alhambra Avenue, Suite C, Santa Cruz, CA 95062
(408) 423-7360
Founded: 1981
Arts Area: Instrumental Group
Status: Semi-Professional; Commercial
Type: Performing; Touring
Purpose: To perform jazz, ragtime, Dixieland, baroque, comtemporary and Renaissance music for audience enjoyment, the quintet plays in various locations including the UC Santa Cruz Arts Festival and the Santa Cruz Summer Arts Concert Series
Management: Scott Harris, Director
Paid Artists: 5
Utilizes: Guest Artists
Budget: $1,000 - $50,000
Income Sources: Box Office
Season: 52 Weeks   **Annual Attendance:** 20,000
Affiliations: AFM; International Trombone Association

SANTA CRUZ COUNTY SYMPHONY
200 Seventh Avenue, Suite 225, Santa Cruz, CA 95062
(408) 462-0553
Founded: 1957
Arts Area: Symphony; Orchestra; Chamber
Status: Professional; Non-Profit
Type: Performing; Educational
Purpose: The mission of the Santa Cruz County Symphony is to serve the diverse Santa Cruz County as a leading musical performing arts group, which fulfills its cultural role by providing a wide variety of fine classical music, entertainment and educational services
Management: John Larry Granger, Music Director/Conductor
Officers: Nancy Hendee, President
Paid Staff: 4   **Volunteer Staff:** 100
Paid Artists: 80
Utilizes: Guest Conductors; Guest Artists
Budget: $100,000 - $500,000
Income Sources: Private Foundations/Grants/Endowments; Business/Corporate Donations; Box Office; Government Grants; Individual Donations
Season: October - May   **Annual Attendance:** 10,000
Affiliations: ASOL; Association of California Symphony Orchestras; California Confederation of the Arts
Performance Facilities: Santa Cruz Civic Auditorium

THE SCOTT HARRIS BIG BAND
216 Alhambra Avenue, Suite C, Santa Cruz, CA 95062
(408) 423-7360
Founded: 1980
Arts Area: Instrumental Group; Band
Status: Professional; Commercial
Type: Performing; Touring
Purpose: To present Big Band music of the 1920's-40's purely for audience entertainment
Management: Scott Harris, Director
Paid Artists: 14
Utilizes: Guest Artists
Budget: $1,000 - $50,000
Income Sources: Box Office
Season: 52 Weeks   **Annual Attendance:** 15,000

PERFORMING SERIES

SANTA CRUZ BAROQUE FESTIVAL
PO Box 482, Santa Cruz, CA 95061
(408) 336-5731
FAX: (408) 336-2464
Founded: 1974
Arts Area: Festivals
Status: Professional; Non-Profit
Type: Performing; Sponsoring
Purpose: To provide a series of spring concerts featuring early music
Management: Linda K. Fawcett, General Manager; Linda Burman-Hall, Artistic Director
Officers: Charles J. Sutton, President; Jan Jaffe, Vice President; Charles Hall, Treasurer/Secretary
Paid Staff: 2   **Volunteer Staff:** 30
Paid Artists: 28
Utilizes: Guest Artists
Budget: $50,000 - $100,000
Income Sources: Private Foundations/Grants/Endowments; Business/Corporate Donations; Box Office; Government Grants; Individual Donations; Program Ads
Season: February - May   **Annual Attendance:** 1,700

FACILITY

KUUMBWA JAZZ CENTER
320-2 Cedar Street, Santa Cruz, CA 95060
(408) 427-2227
Type of Facility: Performance Center
Facility Originally: Business Facility
Type of Stage: Platform
Seating Capacity: 140
Year Remodeled: 1977

Contact for Rental: Tim Jackson;   (408) 427-2227
Resident Groups: Kuumbwa Jazz Center

SANTA CRUZ CIVIC AUDITORIUM
307 Church Street, Santa Cruz, CA 95060
(408) 429-3779
FAX: (408) 458-0455
Founded: 1939
Type of Facility: Theatre Complex; Concert Hall; Auditorium; Performance Center; Civic Center; Arena; Multi-Purpose
Type of Stage: Proscenium; Arena
Stage Dimensions: 32'x40'
Seating Capacity: 1,957
Year Built: 1939   **Architect:** Mark Daniels   **Cost:** $285,000
Contact for Rental: Eddie Scher;   (408) 429-3779

UNIVERSITY OF CALIFORNIA-SANTA CRUZ - PERFORMING ARTS CENTER
Santa Cruz, CA 95064
(408) 459-2147
Type of Facility: Theatre House
Type of Stage: Thrust
Stage Dimensions: 35'x23'
Seating Capacity: 537
Year Built: 1971   **Architect:** Ralph Rapson   **Cost:** $2,700,000
Contact for Rental: Scott Anderson;   (408) 459-2147
Resident Groups: Theatre Arts Board of Studies; Arts and Lectures Program

Santa Maria

INSTRUMENTAL MUSIC

SANTA MARIA SYMPHONY SOCIETY
110 South Pine Street, Suite 103-B-386, Santa Maria, CA 93454
(805) 937-7652
Founded: 1961
Arts Area: Symphony
Status: Non-Profit
Type: Performing
Purpose: Professional imports for concerts
Management: Karen Breitinger, Executive Director
Officers: Ron Williams, President of Symphony Society
Budget: $1,000 - $50,000
Income Sources: Private Foundations/Grants/Endowments; Business/Corporate Donations; Box Office; Individual Donations
Season: November - June   **Annual Attendance:** 1,500
Performance Facilities: First Assembly of God Church

THEATRE

PCPA THEATERFEST
PO Box 1700, Santa Maria, CA 93456
(805) 928-7731
FAX: (805) 928-7506
Founded: 1964
Arts Area: Professional; Theatrical Group
Status: Professional; Semi-Professional; Non-Professional; Non-Profit
Type: Performing; Resident; Educational
Purpose: Professional theater training program (Acting and Technician) and resident professional theater company
Management: Jack Shouse, Managing Artistic Director; Paul Barnes, Conservatory Director/Associate Artistic Director
Officers: Michael O. Brady, Chairman; Linda Kastner, Vice Chairman
Paid Staff: 35
Paid Artists: 6
Utilizes: Special Technical Talent; Guest Artists; Guest Directors
Budget: $1,000,000 - $5,000,000
Income Sources: Private Foundations/Grants/Endowments; Business/Corporate Donations; Box Office; Government Grants; Individual Donations
Season: October - September   **Annual Attendance:** 90,000
Affiliations: TCG; AEA; U/RTA
Performance Facilities: Festival Theatre; Marian Theatre; Interim Theater

SOLVANG THEATERFEST
PO Box 1700, Santa Maria, CA 93456
Founded: 1974
Arts Area: Professional; Summer Stock; Musical; Community; Theatrical Group
Status: Professional; Non-Profit
Type: Performing; Resident; Educational
Purpose: Solvang Theaterfest is a unique collaboration of artistic, professional and educational talent.
Management: Jack Shouse, Artistic Director; Paul Barnes, Associate Artistic Director/Conservatory Director
Officers: Mike Brady, Chairman of the Board
Utilizes: Special Technical Talent; Guest Artists; Guest Directors
Budget: $100,000 - $500,000
Income Sources: Private Foundations/Grants/Endowments; Business/Corporate Donations; Box Office; Government Grants; Individual Donations
Season: 52 Weeks
Performance Facilities: Solvang Festival Theatre; Backstage Theater; Marian Performance Theater; Severson Theater

FACILITY

PACIFIC CONSERVATORY OF THE PERFORMING ARTS
800 South College Drive, Santa Maria, CA 93454
(805) 928-7731
Type of Facility: Theatre Complex
Type of Stage: Thrust
Stage Dimensions: 29'x29'
Seating Capacity: 450
Year Built: 1967   **Architect:** Stewart Kerr   **Cost:** $900,000
Contact for Rental: Jack Shouse;   (805) 928-7731
Resident Groups: Pacific Conservatory of the Performing Arts

Santa Monica

THEATRE

ACTORS REPERTORY THEATRE & SANTA MONICA GROUP THEATRE
1211 Fourth Street, Santa Monica, CA 90401
(310) 394-9779
FAX: (310) 393-5573
Founded: 1962
Arts Area: Professional; Summer Stock; Musical; Theatrical Group; Family Theatre (Children's)
Status: Professional; Non-Profit
Type: Performing; Touring; Resident; Educational
Purpose: New plays, touring, educational workshops, young professionals company, resident acting company, international touring
Management: Evelyn Rudie, Artistic Director; Chris De Carlo, Artistic/Managing Director; Elynmarie Kazle, Resident Producer; Cheryl Moffatt, Director of Education/International touring
Paid Staff: 12   **Volunteer Staff:** 3
Non-Paid Artists: 50
Utilizes: Special Technical Talent; Guest Artists
Budget: $100,000 - $500,000
Income Sources: Private Foundations/Grants/Endowments; Business/Corporate Donations; Box Office; Individual Donations
Season: 52 Weeks   **Annual Attendance:** 35,000
Affiliations: TCG; AEA; Theatre Los Angeles
Performance Facilities: Santa Monica Playhouse

SANTA MONICA PLAYHOUSE AND GROUP THEATRE
1211 Fourth Street, Suite E, Santa Monica, CA 90401-1391
(310) 394-9779
Founded: 1962
Arts Area: Professional
Status: Professional; Non-Profit
Type: Performing; Touring; Resident; Educational
Purpose: To provide an alternative for today's television audience
Management: Evelyn Rudie, Chris DeCarlo, Artistic Directors
Paid Staff: 5
Utilizes: Special Technical Talent; Guest Artists; Guest Directors
Budget: $50,000 - $100,000

Income Sources: Private Foundations/Grants/Endowments; Business/Corporate Donations; Box Office; Government Grants; Individual Donations
Season: 52 Weeks   **Annual Attendance:** 40,000
Affiliations: ACTA
Performance Facilities: Santa Monica Playhouse

FACILITY

MORGAN-WIXSON THEATRE
2627 Pico Boulevard, Santa Monica, CA 90405
(310) 828-7519
  Type of Facility: Concert Hall; Auditorium; Theatre House
  Type of Stage: Proscenium
  Stage Dimensions: 30'Wx35'D
  Seating Capacity: 201
  Year Built: 1964
  Contact for Rental: Woodrow Coleman;   (213) 450-4763
  Resident Groups: Santa Monica Theatre Guild

SANTA MONICA CIVIC AUDITORIUM
1855 Main Street, Santa Monica, CA 90401
(213) 393-9962
  Type of Facility: Auditorium; Theatre House; Opera House; Civic Center; Arena; Multi-Purpose; Room
  Type of Stage: Flexible; Proscenium; Arena
  Stage Dimensions: 70'x120'x42'   **Orchestra Pit**
  Seating Capacity: 3,000 seated; 4,500 festival
  Year Built: 1958   **Architect:** Welton Becket   **Cost:** $3,000,000
  Contact for Rental: Ellen French, Carole Curtin;   (310) 458-8551

Santa Rosa

INSTRUMENTAL MUSIC

SANTA ROSA SYMPHONY
50 Mark West Springs Road, Santa Rosa, CA 95403
(707) 546-8742
  Founded: 1927
  Arts Area: Symphony; Orchestra; Chamber; Ensemble
  Status: Non-Profit
  Type: Performing; Resident; Educational
  Purpose: Provide symphonic music to Sonoma County and the Northern Bay Area; to conduct educational projects, youth orchestras, music center in-school demonstrations and youth concerts
  Management: Pauline Fisher, Manager; Sarah Obuchowski, Development/Public Relations/Marketing
  Paid Staff: 7   **Volunteer Staff:** 40
  Paid Artists: 100   **Non-Paid Artists:** 3
  Utilizes: Guest Conductors; Guest Artists
  Budget: $500,000 - $1,000,000
  Income Sources: Private Foundations/Grants/Endowments; Business/Corporate Donations; Box Office; Government Grants; Individual Donations
  Season: October - May
  Performance Facilities: Luther Burbank Center for the Arts

FACILITY

LUTHER BURBANK CENTER FOR THE ARTS
50 Mark West Springs Road, Santa Rosa, CA 95403
(707) 527-7006
  Type of Facility: Performance Center
  Facility Originally: Church
  Year Built: 1972
  Contact for Rental: Scheduling Administrator;   (707) 527-7006

Resident Groups: Baroque Sinfonia; Redwood Empire Lyric Theater; Redwood Empire Theater; Santa Rosa Symphony; Sonoma County Folk Society
The Center contains the Concert Chamber, East Auditorium, Gold Room and Ruth Finley Person Memorial Theatre.
See separate listings for additional information.

LUTHER BURBANK CENTER FOR THE ARTS - CONCERT CHAMBER
50 Mark West Springs Road, Santa Rosa, CA 95403
(707) 527-7006
FAX: (707) 545-0518
 Type of Facility: Concert Hall; Performance Center; Theatre House
 Facility Originally: Church
 Type of Stage: Platform
 Stage Dimensions: 16'x35'
 Seating Capacity: 325
 Year Built: 1972
 Contact for Rental: Scheduling Administrator; (707) 527-7006
 Resident Groups: Baroque Sinfonia; Redwood Empire Lyric Theater; Redwood Empire Theater; Santa Rosa Symphony; Sonoma County Folk Society

LUTHER BURBANK CENTER FOR THE ARTS - EAST AUDITORIUM
50 Mark West Springs Road, Santa Rosa, CA 95403
(707) 527-7006
FAX: (707) 545-0518
 Type of Facility: Auditorium
 Facility Originally: Church
 Type of Stage: Platform
 Stage Dimensions: 18'Wx15'D
 Seating Capacity: 425
 Contact for Rental: Scheduling Administrator; (707) 527-7006
 Resident Groups: Baroque Sinfonia; Redwood Empire Lyric Theater; Redwood Empire Theater; Santa Rosa Symphony; Sonoma County Folk Society

LUTHER BURBANK CENTER FOR THE ARTS - GOLD ROOM
50 Mark West Springs Road, Santa Rosa, CA 95403
(707) 527-7006
FAX: (707) 545-0518
 Type of Facility: Room; Dinner Theatre
 Facility Originally: Church
 Type of Stage: Flexible
 Seating Capacity: 100
 Year Built: 1972
 Contact for Rental: Scheduling Administrator; (707) 527-7006
 Resident Groups: Baroque Sinfonia; Redwood Empire Lyric Theater; Redwood Empire Theater; Santa Rosa Symphony; Sonoma County Folk Society

LUTHER BURBANK CENTER FOR THE ARTS - RUTH FINLEY PERSON MEMORIAL THEATRE
50 Mark West Springs Road, Santa Rosa, CA 95403
(707) 527-7006
FAX: (707) 545-0518
 Type of Facility: Performance Center; Theatre House
 Facility Originally: Church
 Type of Stage: Thrust
 Stage Dimensions: 61'Wx40'D
 Seating Capacity: 1,500
 Year Built: 1972
 Contact for Rental: Scheduling Administrator; (707) 527-7006
 Resident Groups: Baroque Sinfonia; Redwood Empire Lyric Theater; Redwood Empire Theater; Santa Rosa Symphony; Sonoma County Folk Society

Saratoga

PERFORMING SERIES

PAUL MASSON SUMMER SERIES
PO Box 2279, Saratoga, CA 95070
(408) 741-5181; (408) 741-5182
 Founded: 1957

Arts Area: Vocal Music; Instrumental Music; Theater
Status: Professional; Non-Profit
Type: Performing; Sponsoring
Purpose: To enhance the cultural atmosphere of the San Francisco Bay Area and generate publicity for Paul Masson Vineyards
Management: Bruce Zabadie, Director of Series; Pat Sjcklocha, Assistant Director
Paid Staff: 2
Utilizes: Special Technical Talent; Guest Artists; Guest Directors
Budget: $1,000,000 - $5,000,000
Income Sources: Business/Corporate Donations; Box Office
Season: June - September
Performance Facilities: Paul Masson Mountain Winery

VILLA MONTALVO CENTER FOR THE ARTS
PO Box 158, Saratoga, CA 95071
(408) 741-3421
Founded: 1930
Arts Area: Dance; Vocal Music; Instrumental Music; Theater; Festivals; Lyric Opera; Grand Opera
Status: Non-Profit
Type: Resident; Educational; Sponsoring
Purpose: To provide cultural and recreational activities for promising students, artists, and the public; to instill an appreciation of the arts and the environment
Management: Elisbeth Challener, Executive Director; Sam Nuccio, Program Director
Officers: J. Michael Patterson, President; Sally Lucas, Vice President; Leigh Weimers, Secretary; Joseph Maglione, Treasurer
Paid Staff: 12 **Volunteer Staff:** 100
Utilizes: Special Technical Talent; Guest Conductors; Guest Artists; Guest Directors
Budget: $500,000 - $1,000,000
Income Sources: Private Foundations/Grants/Endowments; Business/Corporate Donations; Box Office; Government Grants; Individual Donations; Facilities Rentals
Season: April - September **Annual Attendance:** 26,000
Affiliations: California Connection; APAP
Performance Facilities: Carriage House Theatre; Lilian Fontaine Garden Theatre

FACILITY

VILLA MONTALVO CENTER FOR THE ARTS
PO Box 158, Saratoga, CA 95071
(408) 741-3421
Type of Facility: Outdoor (Concert); Environmental; Performance Center; Theatre House; Amphitheater; Multi-Purpose
Year Built: 1912 **Architect:** Curlett & Son
Contact for Rental: Executive Director; (408) 741-3421
The Center contains the Carriage House Theatre and Lilian Fontaine Garden Theatre. See individual listings for additional information.

VILLA MONTALVO CENTER FOR THE ARTS - CARRIAGE HOUSE THEATRE
PO Box 158, Saratoga, CA 95071
(408) 741-3421
Type of Facility: Theatre House; Black Box
Facility Originally: Garage
Type of Stage: Thrust; Proscenium
Stage Dimensions: 20'x20'
Seating Capacity: 275
Year Built: 1912
Year Remodeled: 1960 **Architect:** Higgins & Root
Contact for Rental: Executive Director; (408) 741-3421

VILLA MONTALVO CENTER FOR THE ARTS - LILIAN FONTAINE GARDEN THEATRE
PO Box 158, Saratoga, CA 95071
(408) 741-3421
Type of Facility: Outdoor (Concert); Environmental; Amphitheater
Type of Stage: Thrust; Environmental
Stage Dimensions: 40'x60' **Orchestra Pit**
Seating Capacity: 800
Year Built: 1960
Year Remodeled: 1987 **Architect:** Design Professionals
Contact for Rental: Executive Director; (408) 741-3421

Sausalito

THEATRE

ANTENNA THEATER
PO Box 176, Sausalito, CA 94966
(415) 322-4862
FAX: (415) 332-4870
Founded: 1980
Arts Area: Theatrical Group
Status: Professional; Non-Profit
Type: Performing; Touring
Purpose: To stretch the boundaries of contemporary theater by inventing new formats involving nontraditional technologies such as Walkmen, infrared-transmitted sound, 3-D projections, prefabricated environments and audience interaction
Management: Chris Hardman, Artistic Director; Christine Murray, Administrative Director
Paid Staff: 6
Utilizes: Special Technical Talent
Budget: $100,000 - $500,000
Income Sources: Private Foundations/Grants/Endowments; Box Office; Government Grants
Season: 52 Weeks
Affiliations: TCG; California Confederation of the Arts; Theatre Bay Area

Solana Beach

THEATRE

NORTH COAST REPERTORY THEATRE
PO Box 389, Solana Beach, CA 92075
(619) 481-1055
Founded: 1982
Arts Area: Musical; Theatrical Group
Status: Non-Professional; Non-Profit
Type: Performing
Purpose: To educate the public in an appreciation of the theatre arts through stage productions of consistent quality; to provide opportunities for actors and theatre professionals to develop their artistic skills; to evolve into a professional, regional theatre
Management: Olive Blakistone, Artistic Director; Mary Hagan, Operations Manager; Bonnie Barrett, Marketing Manager; John Guth, Box Office Manager; Tom Blakistone, Managing Director; Leslee Baren, Technical Director; Kate King, Development Director
Officers: Edward George, President; Joan Glatthorn, Vice President; Jean Schlinger, Treasurer; Tom Blakistone, Secretary
Paid Staff: 6   **Volunteer Staff:** 120
Non-Paid Artists: 60
Utilizes: Special Technical Talent; Guest Directors
Budget: $100,000 - $500,000
Income Sources: Private Foundations/Grants/Endowments; Business/Corporate Donations; Box Office; Government Grants; Individual Donations
Season: 52 Weeks   **Annual Attendance:** 21,000
Affiliations: San Diego Theatre League; CAC
Performance Facilities: Lomas Santa Fe Plaza

South Pasadena

DANCE

AVAZ INTERNATIONAL DANCE THEATRE
1801 Fair Oaks, Suite 209, South Pasadena, CA 91030
(818) 441-1630; (818) 622-6646
Founded: 1977
Arts Area: Folk
Status: Professional; Non-Profit
Type: Performing; Touring; Educational
Purpose: To preserve and perform the traditional dances and music of the Middle East, North Africa and Central Asia
Management: J. Dees Presents
Officers: Conrad Von Bibra, President of the Board; Anthony Shay, Vice President; Keihan Marefat, Treasurer; Bonita Edelberg, Secretary; Boualim Bousouloub, Assistant Treasurer
Paid Staff: 1   **Volunteer Staff:** 4
Paid Artists: 28

Utilizes: Guest Choreographers
Budget: $100,000 - $500,000
Income Sources: Private Foundations/Grants/Endowments; Business/Corporate Donations; Box Office; Government Grants; Individual Donations
Season: 52 Weeks
Annual Attendance: 50,000
Affiliations: Dance/USA; Los Angeles Dance Resource Center

PASADENA DANCE THEATRE
100 West Villa, South Pasadena, CA 91103
(818) 792-4616
FAX: (818) 792-4893
Founded: 1963
Arts Area: Ballet
Status: Semi-Professional; Non-Profit
Type: Performing; Touring; Resident
Management: Phillip Fuller, Artistic Director
Volunteer Staff: 3
Paid Artists: 3   **Non-Paid Artists:** 12
Utilizes: Guest Artists
Budget: $100,000 - $500,000
Income Sources: Private Foundations/Grants/Endowments; Box Office; Government Grants
Season: September - June
Affiliations: NARB

Spring Valley

THEATRE

SAN DIEGO GUILD OF PUPPETRY
3002 Helix Street, Spring Valley, CA 92077
(619) 466-7128
Founded: 1948
Arts Area: Puppet
Status: Professional; Non-Profit
Type: Performing; Resident; Educational
Purpose: To produce shows year-round using hand puppets, rod puppets and marionettes with three shows each Saturday and Sunday; to further the art of puppetry
Management: Marie Hitchcock, Public Relations Director, Guild Coordinator
Volunteer Staff: 7
Non-Paid Artists: 6
Income Sources: Box Office
Season: 52 Weeks
Annual Attendance: 63,000
Affiliations: Puppeteers of America; San Diego Parks & Recreation Department
Performance Facilities: The Marie Hitchcock Puppet Theatre in Balboa Park

Stanford

PERFORMING SERIES

THE LIVELY ARTS AT STANFORD UNIVERSITY
Press Courtyard, Santa Teresa Street, Stanford, CA 94305
(415) 723-2551
FAX: (415) 723-8231
Arts Area: Dance; Vocal Music; Instrumental Music; Theater
Status: Professional; Non-Profit
Type: Resident; Educational; Sponsoring
Purpose: To provide outstanding quality performances for the education and enjoyment of Stanford students, faculty, staff and the surrounding community
Management: Lois Wagner, Director
Paid Staff: 5   **Volunteer Staff:** 30
Paid Artists: 30
Utilizes: Guest Artists
Budget: $500,000 - $1,000,000
Income Sources: Private Foundations/Grants/Endowments; Business/Corporate Donations; Box Office; Government Grants; Individual Donations

Season: October - May   **Annual Attendance:** 40,000
Affiliations: APAP; WAAA; California Confederation of the Arts; ACA
Performance Facilities: Dinkelspiel Auditorium; Memorial Auditorium; Memorial Church; Frost Amphitheater

FACILITY

STANFORD UNIVERSITY - ANNENBURG AUDITORIUM
Press Courtyard, Santa Theresa Street, Stanford, CA 94305-2250
(415) 723-2551
Type of Facility: Studio Performance; Multi-Purpose; Room
Type of Stage: Platform
Stage Dimensions: 25'Wx12'D
Seating Capacity: 350
Year Built: 1969   **Architect:** Warnecke & Associates

STANFORD UNIVERSITY - BRAUN RECITAL HALL
Press Courtyard, Santa Theresa Street, Stanford, CA 94305-2250
(415) 723-2551
Type of Facility: Studio Performance; Room; Recital Hall
Seating Capacity: 200
Year Built: 1984   **Architect:** Braun & Associates

STANFORD UNIVERSITY - CAMBLE RECITAL HALL
Press Courtyard, Santa Theresa Street, Stanford, CA 94305-2250
(415) 723-2551
Type of Facility: Auditorium; Recital Hall
Type of Stage: Proscenium   **Seating Capacity:** 225
Year Built: 1985   **Architect:** Marquis & Associates

STANFORD UNIVERSITY - COVERLY AUDITORIUM
Press Courtyard, Santa Theresa Street, Stanford, CA 94305-2250
(415) 723-2551
Type of Facility: Auditorium
Type of Stage: Proscenium
Stage Dimensions: 30'Wx15'D
Seating Capacity: 400
Year Built: 1938
Architect: Bakerwell and Brown

STANFORD UNIVERSITY - DINKELSPIEL AUDITORIUM
Press Courtyard, Santa Theresa Street, Stanford, CA 94305-2250
(415) 723-2551
Type of Facility: Auditorium
Type of Stage: Thrust; Proscenium
Stage Dimensions: 40'Wx40'D   **Orchestra Pit**
Seating Capacity: 720
Year Built: 1957   **Architect:** Milton F. Pflueger

STANFORD UNIVERSITY - MEMORIAL AUDITORIUM
Press Courtyard, Santa Theresa Street, Stanford, CA 94305-2250
(415) 723-2551
Type of Facility: Auditorium; Performance Center; Theatre House; Multi-Purpose
Type of Stage: Proscenium   **Orchestra Pit**
Seating Capacity: 1,714
Year Built: 1937   **Architect:** Bakerwell and Brown

Stockton

INSTRUMENTAL MUSIC

STOCKTON SYMPHONY ASSOCIATION
37 West Yokuts, Suite C-4, Stockton, CA 95207
(209) 951-0196
FAX: (209) 951-1050
Founded: 1926
Arts Area: Symphony; Orchestra
Status: Professional; Non-Profit

Type: Performing; Educational
Management: Kyung-Soo Won, Music Director/Conductor; George A. Sinclair, Executive Director
Officers: Nancy Schneider, President
Paid Staff: 3   **Volunteer Staff:** 125
Paid Artists: 70
Utilizes: Special Technical Talent; Guest Conductors; Guest Artists
Budget: $500,000 - $1,000,000
Income Sources: Private Foundations/Grants/Endowments; Business/Corporate Donations; Box Office; Government Grants; Individual Donations; Fund-raising
Season: September - May   **Annual Attendance:** 18,000
Affiliations: ASOL; Association of California Symphony Orchestras
Performance Facilities: San Joaquin Delta College

THEATRE

STOCKTON CIVIC THEATRE
2312 Rose Marie Lane, Stockton, CA 95207
(209) 473-2400
FAX: (209) 473-1502
Founded: 1951
Arts Area: Musical; Community; Theatrical Group
Status: Non-Professional; Non-Profit
Type: Performing; Resident
Purpose: To provide quality theatre to the community
Management: Helen Kastner, Executive Director
Officers: George Royston, President; Marge Breezee, Vice President; Frank Whitney, Vice President/Operations
Paid Staff: 1
Utilizes: Guest Artists; Guest Directors
Budget: $100,000 - $500,000
Income Sources: Private Foundations/Grants/Endowments; Business/Corporate Donations; Box Office; Government Grants; Individual Donations
Season: September - May

FACILITY

ATHERTON AUDITORIUM
5151 Pacific Avenue, Stockton, CA 95207
(209) 474-5051
Type of Facility: Theatre Complex; Concert Hall; Auditorium
Type of Stage: Proscenium
Stage Dimensions: 89'x102'x45'   **Orchestra Pit**
Seating Capacity: 1,456
Year Built: 1977   **Architect:** E.J. Kump Associates; Gwathmey Sellier Crosby   **Cost:** $4,700,000
Contact for Rental: Dr. Don Bennett;   (209) 474-5209

UNIVERSITY OF THE PACIFIC - DE MARCUS BROWN STUDIO THEATRE
Stockton, CA 95211
(209) 946-2116
Type of Facility: Studio Performance; Room
Facility Originally: School; Tractor Shop
Type of Stage: Flexible
Stage Dimensions: 38'x42'
Seating Capacity: 110
Year Built: 1977
Resident Groups: University of the Pacific Drama and Dance Department

UNIVERSITY OF THE PACIFIC - FAYE SPANOS CONCERT HALL
Stockton, CA 95211
(209) 946-2415
Type of Facility: Concert Hall; Auditorium
Type of Stage: Proscenium
Orchestra Pit
Seating Capacity: 950
Year Built: 1924   **Architect:** Davis Heller & Pierce
Year Remodeled: 1987   **Architect:** Dean Unger   **Cost:** $1,500,000
Contact for Rental: Joanne Paine;   (209) 946-2415

UNIVERSITY OF THE PACIFIC - LONG THEATRE
Stockton, CA 95211
(209) 946-2116
Type of Facility: Auditorium
Type of Stage: Proscenium; Concentric Arch
Stage Dimensions: 40'Wx24'D   **Orchestra Pit**
Seating Capacity: 400 fixed seating
Year Built: 1959   **Architect:** Clowdsley & Whipple
Year Remodeled: 1979   **Cost:** $210,000
Acoustical Consultant: Edwin W. Wilson
Contact for Rental: Jack Pratt;   (209) 946-2054
Resident Groups: University of the Pacific Drama And Dance Department

UNIVERSITY OF THE PACIFIC - RECITAL HALL
Conservatory of Music, Stockton, CA 95211
(209) 946-2415
Type of Facility: Recital Hall
Type of Stage: Platform
Stage Dimensions: 18'Wx18'D
Seating Capacity: 119
Year Built: 1986   **Architect:** Radcliff Associates
Contact for Rental: Joanne Paine;   (209) 946-2415

Studio City

THEATRE

HOLLYWOOD THEATER COMPANY
12838 Kling Street, Studio City, CA 91604-1127
(310) 984-1867
Founded: 1972
Arts Area: Professional; Summer Stock; Dinner
Status: Professional; Non-Profit
Type: Performing; Touring
Purpose: To perform revivals and new plays for diversified Black actors, and on occassion, an integrated entity
Management: Rai Tasco, Artistic Director; J. Christopher Sullivan, PhD, Co-Manager; Patricia Bell, Production Manager
Volunteer Staff: 8
Non-Paid Artists: 16
Utilizes: Special Technical Talent; Guest Artists; Guest Directors
Budget: $1,000 - $50,000
Income Sources: Box Office
Season: 52 Weeks

THEATRE EAST
17655 Ventura Boulevard, Studio City, CA 91604
(818) 760-4160
Founded: 1967
Arts Area: Theatrical Group
Status: Professional
Type: Resident
Purpose: Actors Gymnasium
Officers: Elaine Welton Hill, Acting President; John Gowans, Secretary; Suzanne Hunt, Treasurer
Volunteer Staff: 20
Non-Paid Artists: 125
Income Sources: Individual Donations

FACILITY

THEATRE EAST
12655 Ventura Boulevard, Studio City, CA 91604
(818) 760-4160
Type of Facility: Theatre House
Type of Stage: Proscenium
Seating Capacity: 99
Year Built: 1967

Sunnyvale

VOCAL MUSIC

SILICON VALLEY GAY MEN'S CHORUS OF SAN JOSE
PO Box 62151, Sunnyvale, CA 94088
(408) 275-6344
Founded: 1983
Arts Area: Choral
Status: Non-Professional; Non-Profit
Type: Performing
Management: Bob Welton, President; Lynne McLaughlin, Director; Don Giberson, Assistant Director; Doug McGrath, Accompanist
Paid Staff: 3   **Volunteer Staff:** 7
Non-Paid Artists: 18
Utilizes: Guest Conductors; Guest Artists
Budget: $1,000 - $50,000
Income Sources: Box Office; Individual Donations
Season: September - June   **Annual Attendance:** 1,500
Affiliations: Gay And Lesbian Association Choruses
Performance Facilities: Christ the Good Shepherd Lutheran Church

THEATRE

CALIFORNIA THEATRE CENTER
PO Box 2007, Sunnyvale, CA 94087
(408) 245-2978
FAX: (408) 245-0235
Founded: 1975
Arts Area: Professional; Theatrical Group
Status: Professional; Non-Profit
Type: Performing; Touring
Purpose: To provide quality theater for children and families
Management: Gayle Cornelison, General Director; Will Huddleston, Resident Director; Lynn Pace, Production Director; Mary Farrow, Production Manager
Paid Staff: 25
Utilizes: Special Technical Talent; Guest Artists; Guest Directors
Budget: $500,000 - $1,000,000
Income Sources: Private Foundations/Grants/Endowments; Business/Corporate Donations; Box Office; Government Grants; Individual Donations
Season: October - August
Affiliations: AEA
Performance Facilities: The Performing Arts Center

Thousand Oaks

INSTRUMENTAL MUSIC

CONEJO SYMPHONY ORCHESTRA
PO Box 1045, Thousand Oaks, CA 91358
(805) 498-7092
Founded: 1961
Arts Area: Symphony; Chamber
Status: Semi-Professional; Non-Profit
Type: Performing
Purpose: To maintain a non-profit corporation for the education and stimulation of the musical, cultural and social interests of the community, through the medium of a symphony orchestra
Management: Everett Ascher, Executive Director; Susan Ward, Office Manager; Elmer Ramsey, Music Director; Carol Alexander, Conductor, Youth Symphony; Bonnie Boss, Personnel Manager
Officers: James Thompson, President; Cate Brown, Vice President; Daryl Hill, Secretary; John McLaine, Treasurer
Paid Staff: 5   **Volunteer Staff:** 12
Paid Artists: 50   **Non-Paid Artists:** 37
Utilizes: Special Technical Talent; Guest Conductors; Guest Artists
Budget: $100,000 - $500,000
Income Sources: Private Foundations/Grants/Endowments; Business/Corporate Donations; Box Office; Individual Donations
Season: June - May   **Annual Attendance:** 7,200

Affiliations: ASOL
Performance Facilities: Preus-Brandt Forum, California Lutheran University

FACILITY

CALIFORNIA LUTHERAN UNIVERSITY - PREUS-BRANDT FORUM
60 West Olsen Road, Thousand Oaks, CA 91360-2787
(805) 493-3195
FAX: (805) 493-3513
    Type of Facility: Auditorium; Multi-Purpose
    Facility Originally: School
    Type of Stage: Proscenium
    Stage Dimensions: 14'6"x45'x22'
    Seating Capacity: 700
    Year Built: 1962
    Contact for Rental: Dennis Bryant; (805) 493-3195

Topanga Canyon

THEATRE

THE WILL GEER THEATRICUM BOTANICUM
1419 North Topanga Canyon Boulevard, Topanga Canyon, CA 90290
(310) 455-2322
    Founded: 1973
    Arts Area: Theatrical Group
    Status: Professional; Non-Profit
    Type: Performing; Resident; Educational
    Purpose: The Will Geer Theatricum Botanicum is dedicated to the belief that theatre, music and education are integral and necessary parts of life for all individuals to experience on a regular and inexpensive basis.
    Management: Kathy Schutzer, General Manager; Ellen Geer, Artistic Director
    Paid Staff: 4
    Paid Artists: 40
    Budget: $100,000 - $500,000
    Income Sources: Private Foundations/Grants/Endowments; Business/Corporate Donations; Box Office; Government Grants; Individual Donations
    Season: May - October   **Annual Attendance:** 40,000
    Performance Facilities: Will Geer Theatricum Botanicum

Torrance

INSTRUMENTAL MUSIC

EL CAMINO COLLEGE - COMMUNITY ORCHESTRA
16007 South Crenshaw Boulevard, Torrance, CA 90506
(310) 532-3670
    Founded: 1949
    Arts Area: Orchestra
    Status: Non-Professional; Non-Profit
    Type: Performing; Educational
    Purpose: To train college musicians and provide for community musicians to read and perform a greater variety of music than in other local groups
    Management: James E. Mack, Music Director/Conductor
    Paid Staff: 1
    Non-Paid Artists: 50
    Utilizes: Guest Artists
    Budget: $1,000 - $50,000
    Season: September - June   **Annual Attendance:** 2,000
    Performance Facilities: Marsee Auditorium

VOCAL MUSIC

LA MARCA AMERICAN VARIETY SINGERS
2424 West Sepulueda Boulevard, Torrance, CA 90501
(310) 325-8708
    Founded: 1974
    Arts Area: Lyric Opera; Light Opera; Choral; Folk; Show Choirs

Status: Professional; Non-Profit; Commercial
Type: Performing; Touring; Resident; Educational
Purpose: To entertain, educate and promote the arts and the American spirit
Management: Priscilla LaMarca, Director/Manager
Officers: Priscilla LaMarca, President; E. Scottie Brown, Secretary; Barbara Barnes, Treasurer
Volunteer Staff: 4
Utilizes: Special Technical Talent; Original Music
Budget: $1,000 - $50,000
Income Sources: Business/Corporate Donations; Box Office; Individual Donations; Performance Fees; Sponsoring
Season: 52 Weeks   **Annual Attendance:** 10,000
Affiliations: FIDOF

THEATRE

TORRANCE COMMUNITY THEATRE
1522 Cravens Avenue, Torrance, CA 90501
(310) 533-0576
Founded: 1950
Arts Area: Musical; Community; Theatrical Group; Puppet
Status: Non-Profit
Type: Performing
Purpose: To produce live theatre
Officers: Linda Green, President; Jack Drake, Vice President; Shirley Bluman, Secretary
Paid Staff: 2   **Volunteer Staff:** 70
Income Sources: Business/Corporate Donations; Box Office; Individual Donations
Season: 52 Weeks   **Annual Attendance:** 6,000
Performance Facilities: Torrance Community Theatre

PERFORMING SERIES

TORRANCE CULTURAL ARTS CENTER
3330 Civic Center Drive, Torrance, CA 90503
(310) 781-7150
FAX: (310) 781-7199
Founded: 1991
Arts Area: Dance; Vocal Music; Instrumental Music; Theater; Children's Activities
Status: Non-Profit
Type: Sponsoring
Purpose: To enhance community offerings and build audiences; to provide a rental hall for the community
Management: Bob Stewart, Manager
Paid Staff: 26   **Volunteer Staff:** 20
Income Sources: Private Foundations/Grants/Endowments; Business/Corporate Donations; Box Office; Government Grants; Individual Donations
Season: September - June
Affiliations: IAAM; APAP; WAAA
Performance Facilities: Armstrong Theatre

FACILITY

EL CAMINO COLLEGE - SOUTH BAY CENTER FOR THE ARTS
16007 South Crenshaw Boulevard, Torrance, CA 90506
(310) 532-3670
Type of Facility: Auditorium
Type of Stage: Proscenium   **Orchestra Pit**
Seating Capacity: 2,054
Year Built: 1968   **Architect:** Morgridge   **Cost:** $2,500,000
Contact for Rental: Arlene Cabalo;   (310) 715-3485

Turlock

FACILITY

CALIFORNIA STATE UNIVERSITY-STANISLAUS - MAINSTAGE THEATRE
801 West Monte Vista Avenue, Turlock, CA 95380
(209) 667-3451
Type of Facility: Auditorium; Theatre House
Type of Stage: Proscenium
Stage Dimensions: 60'x40'x60'   **Orchestra Pit**

Seating Capacity: 300
Year Built: 1970   **Cost:** $2,500,000
Acoustical Consultant: Landry, Bogen
Contact for Rental: Connie Bratten;   (209) 667-3207
Resident Groups: Drama and Music Departments

Ukiah

THEATRE

UKIAH PLAYERS THEATRE
1041 Low Gap Road, Ukiah, CA 95482
(707) 462-1210
 Founded: 1977
 Arts Area: Musical; Community; Theatrical Group
 Status: Semi-Professional; Non-Profit
 Type: Performing; Touring; Resident; Educational; Sponsoring
 Purpose: To provide the general community with a wide range of theatre experiences; to encourage and educate future
 theatre artists; to serve as a cultural venue
 Management: Ellen Weed, Artistic Director; Dudley Folks, General Manager; Doug Hundley, Production Manager;
 Kate Magruder, Associate Director; David Hayes, Associate Technical Director; Dan Hibshman, Publicity Manager
 Officers: Jeanine Bauman, Board President; Todd Evans, Board Vice President; Christine Webb, Board Secretary;
 Judy Waterman, Board Treasurer
 Paid Staff: 7   **Volunteer Staff:** 40
 Paid Artists: 7   **Non-Paid Artists:** 70
 Utilizes: Special Technical Talent; Guest Conductors; Guest Artists; Guest Directors
 Budget: $100,000 - $500,000
 Income Sources: Private Foundations/Grants/Endowments; Business/Corporate Donations; Box Office; Government
 Grants; Individual Donations
 Season: 52 Weeks   **Annual Attendance:** 10,000
 Affiliations: Theatre Bay Area

Upland

DANCE

CONCERT DANCE THEATRE
2315 West Foothill Boulevard, #7, Upland, CA 91786
(909) 949-4166
 Founded: 1968
 Arts Area: Ballet; Jazz
 Status: Semi-Professional; Non-Profit
 Type: Performing; Educational
 Purpose: To educate the community in classical ballet, other types of dance and culture
 Officers: Mark Amendola, President; Bill Hemphill, Vice President; Frances Maginn, Secretary; Patti Coleman, Treasurer;
 JoAnn Warner, Artistic Director
 Paid Staff: 1   **Volunteer Staff:** 5
 Paid Artists: 12   **Non-Paid Artists:** 40
 Utilizes: Special Technical Talent; Guest Artists
 Budget: $1,000 - $50,000
 Income Sources: Private Foundations/Grants/Endowments; Box Office; Individual Donations
 Season: March - December   **Annual Attendance:** 3,200

Valencia

INSTRUMENTAL MUSIC

NEW CENTURY PLAYERS
c/o California Institute of the Arts, 24700 McBean Park, Valencia, CA 91355
(805) 253-7817
FAX: (805) 254-8352
 Arts Area: Symphony; Orchestra; Chamber; Ensemble; Ethnic; Folk; Instrumental Group; Electronic &
 Live Electronic; Band
 Status: Professional; Non-Profit
 Type: Resident

Purpose: The ensemble is comprised of accomplished and versatile musicians who merge high-quality performance with skillfull teaching methods and present concerts versed in traditional chamber music combining performance with commentary.
Management: David Rosenboom, Dean, School of Music/Artistic Director
Budget: $1,000 - $50,000
Income Sources: Private Foundations/Grants/Endowments; Box Office; Government Grants; Individual Donations
Performance Facilities: Roy Disney Music Hall

PERFORMING SERIES

SPRING MUSIC FESTIVAL
c/o California Institute of the Arts, School of Music, 24700 McBean Pkwy, Valencia, CA 91355
(805) 253-7816
FAX: (805) 254-8352
    Status: Professional; Non-Profit
    Type: Performing; Educational
    Purpose: To present the latest in contemporary direction of music and allied arts with a global style and cultural perspectives
    Management: David Rosenboom, Dean, School of Music; Bob Clendenen, Production Manager
    Budget: $1,000 - $50,000
    Income Sources: Private Foundations/Grants/Endowments; Business/Corporate Donations; Government Grants
    Performance Facilities: California Institute of the Arts; Japan American Theater

Van Nuys

DANCE

THE FRANCISCO MARTINEZ DANCETHEATRE
6723 Matilija Avenue, Van Nuys, CA 91405
(818) 988-2192
FAX: (310) 821-1163
    Founded: 1981
    Arts Area: Modern; Ballet
    Status: Professional
    Type: Performing; Touring; Educational
    Purpose: To perform an eclectic repertory for broad audiences and special programs for schools
    Officers: David Allen Jones, Executive Director; Lyn Profant, Administrative Assistant; Francisco Martinez, Artistic Director
    Volunteer Staff: 15
    Paid Artists: 7
    Budget: $1,000 - $50,000
    Income Sources: Private Foundations/Grants/Endowments; Business/Corporate Donations; Box Office; Government Grants; Individual Donations
    Season: September - June   **Annual Attendance:** 5,000
    Affiliations: WAAA; Bay Area Dance; Dance Resource Center
    Performance Facilities: Plaza de la Raza

THEATRE

PASSAGE THEATRE
6650 Havenhurst Street, Van Nuys, CA 91406
(818) 904-0838
    Founded: 1981
    Arts Area: Professional
    Status: Professional; Non-Profit
    Type: Performing; Touring; Educational
    Purpose: The purposes of the Passage Theatre are to produce classical plays, to establish a repertory theatre of national importance, and to take performances of the classics to those who might otherwise not have the opportunity to see them.
    Management: Scott Guy, Artistic Director; Margaret Scott, Managing Director
    Paid Staff: 2
    Paid Artists: 50
    Utilizes: Special Technical Talent; Guest Directors
    Budget: $1,000 - $50,000
    Income Sources: Business/Corporate Donations; Box Office; Government Grants; Individual Donations
    Season: 52 Weeks   **Annual Attendance:** 21,000
    Affiliations: LCT

Venice

THEATRE

HUDSON THEATRE
225 Howland Canal, Venice, CA 90291
(310) 306-1310
> **Founded:** 1975
> **Arts Area:** Professional
> **Status:** Professional; Non-Profit
> **Type:** Producing In House
> **Management:** Gary Blumsack and Elizabeth Reilly, Artistic Directors
> **Volunteer Staff:** 12
> **Utilizes:** Special Technical Talent; Guest Artists; Guest Directors
> **Budget:** $1,000 - $50,000
> **Income Sources:** Box Office
> **Season:** 52 Weeks
> **Performance Facilities:** Hudson Theatre; Husdon Backstage

LOS ANGELES THEATRE WORKS
681 Venice Boulevard, Venice, CA 90291
(310) 827-0808
FAX: (310) 827-4949
> **Founded:** 1974
> **Arts Area:** Professional
> **Status:** Professional; Non-Profit
> **Type:** Touring; Producing
> **Purpose:** Los Angeles Theatre Works, a pioneering lab for playwrights, directors and other theatre artists, is committed to the exploration of contemporary work in theatre.
> **Management:** Susan Albert-Loewenberg, Producing Director
> **Officers:** Doug Jaffe, President; Robert Talcott, Vice President; Genie Shapiro, Secretary; Alan Finkel, Treasurer
> **Budget:** $100,000 - $500,000
> **Income Sources:** Private Foundations/Grants/Endowments; Business/Corporate Donations; Box Office; Government Grants; Individual Donations
> **Season:** 52 Weeks   **Annual Attendance:** 25,000
> **Affiliations:** TCG; Los Angeles Theatre Alliance; California Confederation of the Arts; California Theatre Council

---
Ventura

INSTRUMENTAL MUSIC

VENTURA COUNTY SYMPHONY ASSOCIATION
PO Box 1088, Ventura, CA 93002
(805) 643-8646
> **Founded:** 1962
> **Arts Area:** Symphony; Chamber; Ensemble
> **Status:** Professional; Non-Profit
> **Type:** Performing
> **Purpose:** To present concerts of classical music for the community; to foster and promote an increased public knowledge and appreciation of concert music
> **Management:** Ila G. Winterbourne, General Manager; Frank Salazar, Music Director/Conductor; Karine Beesley, Executive Director; Boris Brott, Music Director
> **Officers:** Gregory Smith, President
> **Paid Staff:** 6   **Volunteer Staff:** 1
> **Paid Artists:** 15
> **Utilizes:** Guest Conductors; Guest Artists
> **Budget:** $100,000 - $500,000
> **Income Sources:** Private Foundations/Grants/Endowments; Business/Corporate Donations; Box Office; Government Grants; Individual Donations
> **Season:** October - June
> **Annual Attendance:** 10,000
> **Performance Facilities:** Oxnard Civic Auditorium, Ojai Libbey Bowl

---

Victorville

FACILITY

VICTOR VALLEY COLLEGE PERFORMING ARTS CENTER
18422 Bear Valley Road, Victorville, CA 92392
(619) 245-4271
FAX: (619) 245-9744
Type of Facility: Concert Hall; Auditorium; Performance Center; Theatre House; Multi-Purpose
Type of Stage: Proscenium
Stage Dimensions: 40'Hx42'D proscenium opening   **Orchestra Pit**
Seating Capacity: 493
Year Built: 1981   **Architect:** Howard H. Morgridge & Associates   **Cost:** $2,600,000
Acoustical Consultant: Howard G. Smith Associates
Contact for Rental: Margie Lough;   (619) 245-4271, ext. 251

Visalia

INSTRUMENTAL MUSIC

TULARE COUNTY SYMPHONY ORCHESTRA
PO Box 1201, Visalia, CA 93279
(209) 732-8600
Founded: 1960
Arts Area: Symphony; Orchestra
Status: Professional; Non-Profit
Type: Performing; Resident; Educational
Purpose: To promote and foster the appreciation of all matters of music; to further adult participation in creative musical activity; to promote the education and development of young musicians
Management: David Andre, Music Director/Conductor; Anne R. Bernardo, General Manager
Officers: Thomas A. Akin M.D., President; Pat Finger, Vice President; Christine Richards, Recording Secretary; Martin V. Clevenger, Treasurer
Paid Staff: 3
Paid Artists: 75
Utilizes: Guest Conductors; Guest Artists
Budget: $100,000 - $500,000
Income Sources: Private Foundations/Grants/Endowments; Business/Corporate Donations; Box Office; Government Grants; Individual Donations
Season: September - May
Annual Attendance: 21,000
Affiliations: Association of California Symphony Orchestras
Performance Facilities: L.J. Williams Theatre

FACILITY

VISALIA CONVENTION CENTER - EXHIBIT HALL
303 East Acequia Street, Visalia, CA 93291
(209) 738-3386
FAX: (209) 738-3579
Type of Facility: Concert Hall; Auditorium; Multi-Purpose; Exhibition Hall
Seating Capacity: 2,200
Year Built: 1972   **Architect:** Moring and Hayslett   **Cost:** $4,000,000
Contact for Rental: Mimi McKell;   (209) 738-3386

VISALIA CONVENTION CENTER - L.J. WILLIAMS THEATRE
1001 West Main, Visalia, CA 93291
(209) 738-3386
FAX: (209) 738-3574
Type of Facility: Theatre House
Facility Originally: School
Type of Stage: Modified Apron Proscenium
Stage Dimensions: 65'Wx48'D; 38'Wx21'H proscenium opening   **Orchestra Pit**
Seating Capacity: 1,268
Year Built: 1940
Year Remodeled: 1972   **Architect:** Walter Vogel   **Cost:** $1,000,000
Contact for Rental: Mimi McKell;   (209) 738-3386
Resident Groups: Tulare County Symphony

VISALIA CONVENTION CENTER - ROTARY THEATRE
330 South Dollner, Visalia, CA 93291
(209) 738-3386
FAX: (209) 738-3386
Type of Facility: Theatre House
Facility Originally: School
Type of Stage: Thrust; Flexible; Proscenium
Stage Dimensions: 38'Wx18'D; 32'Wx16'D de-mountable thrust
Seating Capacity: 328
Year Built: 1939
Year Remodeled: 1987   **Architect:** Ray Schlick   **Cost:** $400,000
Contact for Rental: Mimi McKell;   (209) 738-3386

Walnut

DANCE

ANJANI'S KATHAK DANCE OF INDIA
1934 Peaceful Hills Road, Walnut, CA 91789
(909) 595-8934
Founded: 1983
Arts Area: Ethnic
Status: Professional
Type: Performing; Touring
Purpose: To enlighten audiences all over with the unique traditional classical dance of India-Kathak
Paid Artists: 8
Utilizes: Guest Choreographers
Budget: $50,000 - $100,000
Income Sources: Private Foundations/Grants/Endowments; Box Office; Government Grants
Season: 52 Weeks
Annual Attendance: 4,000

Walnut Creek

INSTRUMENTAL MUSIC

THE DIABLO SYMPHONY ORCHESTRA
PO Box 2222, Walnut Creek, CA 94595
(510) 935-7764
Founded: 1969
Arts Area: Symphony; Orchestra
Status: Professional; Non-Profit
Type: Performing; Sponsoring
Management: Joyce Johnson-Hamilton, Music Director/Conductor
Officers: Mary-Margaret Scobey, President, Diablo Symphony Association
Paid Staff: 4   **Volunteer Staff:** 24
Non-Paid Artists: 60
Utilizes: Guest Artists
Budget: $1,000 - $50,000
Income Sources: Private Foundations/Grants/Endowments; Business/Corporate Donations; Individual Donations
Season: September - July   **Annual Attendance:** 9,000
Affiliations: ASOL; Association of California Symphony Orchestras
Performance Facilities: Regional Arts Center

YOUNG ARTISTS SYMPHONY ORCHESTRA
PO Box 4849, Walnut Creek, CA 94596
(510) 486-4398
Founded: 1980
Arts Area: Symphony; Orchestra
Status: Non-Professional; Non-Profit
Type: Performing; Touring; Educational; Sponsoring
Purpose: To offer young musicians in Contra Costa and neighboring counties musical education in a teaching and performing group and to participate in a symphony orchestra; to provide social activities; to participate in a biennial tour; to sponsor an annual concerto competition
Management: H.T. Payne, Music Director/Conductor
Officers: Caroline Oliver, President; Dellyn Pacilio, Manager
Paid Staff: 2   **Volunteer Staff:** 20

Non-Paid Artists: 70
Budget: $1,000 - $50,000
Income Sources: Private Foundations/Grants/Endowments; Business/Corporate Donations; Individual Donations; Fund-raising
Season: September - May **Annual Attendance:** 1,000
Affiliations: ASOL (Youth Orchestra Division)

VOCAL MUSIC

DIABLO LIGHT OPERA COMPANY
PO Box 5034, Walnut Creek, CA 94596
(510) 939-6161; (510) 376-8887
Founded: 1960
Arts Area: Light Opera; Operetta; Musical Theatre
Status: Non-Professional; Non-Profit
Type: Performing; Educational
Purpose: Diablo Light Opera Company (DLOC) is a non-profit community theatre dedicated to providing quality musical and light opera, and to enhancing the lives of our members, audiences and the community.
Management: Rhoda Klitsner, Artistic Advisor; Grete Egan, Producer
Officers: Bobbi Bach, President
Volunteer Staff: 40
Non-Paid Artists: 50
Utilizes: Special Technical Talent; Guest Conductors; Guest Directors; Guest Choreographers; Guest Choreographers
Budget: $100,000 - $500,000
Income Sources: Private Foundations/Grants/Endowments; Business/Corporate Donations; Box Office; Individual Donations
Season: September - June
Annual Attendance: 30,000
Performance Facilities: Regional Center for the Arts

PERFORMING SERIES

REGIONAL CENTER FOR THE ARTS
1601 Civic Drive, Walnut Creek, CA 94596
(510) 295-1400
FAX: (510) 943-7222
Founded: 1965
Arts Area: Dance; Vocal Music; Theater
Status: Non-Profit
Type: Performing
Purpose: Main stage is used for musical theatre; drama, jazz, ballet and films, Stage II is used for drama, lectures and reviews
Management: Scott Denison, Arts Center Manager
Officers: Gary Schaub, Director of Cultural Services
Paid Staff: 12 **Volunteer Staff:** 23
Utilizes: Guest Artists; Guest Directors
Budget: $500,000 - $1,000,000
Income Sources: Government Grants
Season: 52 Weeks **Annual Attendance:** 100,000
Performance Facilities: Hoffmann Theatre; Dean Lefher Theatre

Weed

FACILITY

COLLEGE OF THE SISKIYOUS - THEATRE
800 College Avenue, Weed, CA 96094
(916) 938-5257
FAX: (916) 938-5227
Type of Facility: Theatre House
Type of Stage: Proscenium
Stage Dimensions: 15'6"x36'6"x24'6" plus apron
Orchestra Pit
Seating Capacity: 604
Year Built: 1969 **Architect:** Allyn Martin **Cost:** $750,000
Contact for Rental: Carol Kramm; (916) 938-5206
Manager: Keith Ronee; (916) 938-5257
Resident Groups: College Drama and Music Departments

West Los Angeles

INSTRUMENTAL MUSIC

AMERICAN YOUTH SYMPHONY
321 Tilden Avenue, West Los Angeles, CA 90049
(310) 476-2825
Founded: 1964
Arts Area: Symphony; Orchestra
Status: Non-Professional; Non-Profit
Type: Performing; Educational
Purpose: To educate tomorrow's professional musicians and to provide free concerts for the community of Los Angeles
Management: Bonnie McClain, Manager; Mehli Mehta, Music Director/Conductor
Paid Staff: 3   **Volunteer Staff:** 50
Non-Paid Artists: 110
Utilizes: Guest Artists
Budget: $100,000 - $500,000
Income Sources: Private Foundations/Grants/Endowments; Business/Corporate Donations; Government Grants; Individual Donations
Season: October - June   **Annual Attendance:** 14,000
Affiliations: ASOL (Youth Orchestra Division)
Performance Facilities: Royce Hall, UCLA

Whittier

INSTRUMENTAL MUSIC

RIO HONDO SYMPHONY ASSOCIATION
PO Box 495, Whittier, CA 90608
(310) 695-1102
Founded: 1933
Arts Area: Symphony; Orchestra
Status: Non-Profit
Type: Performing; Resident
Purpose: To provide free concerts of symphonic music to all residents of Whittier and surrounding cities known as the Rio Hondo Area; to encourage young talented musicians through Young Artist Auditions
Management: Wayne Rienecke, Conductor
Officers: Louis Galindo, President
Paid Staff: 5   **Volunteer Staff:** 20
Paid Artists: 60   **Non-Paid Artists:** 25
Utilizes: Guest Artists
Budget: $1,000 - $50,000
Income Sources: Private Foundations/Grants/Endowments; Business/Corporate Donations; Government Grants; Individual Donations
Annual Attendance: 6,000
Affiliations: Rio Hondo Symphony Guild
Performance Facilities: Whittier Union High School Auditorium

THEATRE

WHITTIER JUNIOR THEATRE
7630 South Washington Avenue, Whittier, CA 90602
(310) 945-8207
Founded: 1962
Arts Area: Theatrical Group
Status: Non-Professional; Non-Profit
Type: Performing; Touring; Educational
Purpose: Whittier Junior Theatre is composed of children 9-18 years of age and presents three childrens' theatre productions per year.
Management: Pamela Franklin Bradac, Managing Supervisor
Paid Staff: 10   **Volunteer Staff:** 4
Non-Paid Artists: 150
Utilizes: Guest Directors
Budget: $50,000 - $100,000
Income Sources: Box Office; Individual Donations
Annual Attendance: 3,000
Affiliations: CAC; City of Whittier
Performance Facilities: The Center Theatre

FACILITY

RIO HONDO COLLEGE - MERTON WRAY THEATRE
3600 Workman Mill Road, Whittier, CA 90601
(310) 692-0921
> **Type of Facility:** Concert Hall; Auditorium; Theatre House
> **Type of Stage:** Proscenium
> **Stage Dimensions:** 40'W proscenium opening   **Orchestra Pit**
> **Seating Capacity:** 320
> **Year Built:** 1967   **Architect:** Powell, Morgridge, Richards & Goghlan   **Cost:** $2,000,000
> **Contact for Rental:** Rachel Esqueda;   (310) 908-3426, ext. 301
> **Manager:** Perry Sites
> **Resident Groups:** College Student Performing Groups

Woodland

FACILITY

WOODLAND OPERA HOUSE
340 Second Street, Woodland, CA 95695
(916) 666-9617
> **Founded:** 1895
> **Type of Facility:** Concert Hall; Auditorium; Performance Center; Theatre House; Opera House; Civic Center; Multi-Purpose
> **Type of Stage:** Proscenium
> **Stage Dimensions:** 25'x25' playing area   **Orchestra Pit**
> **Seating Capacity:** 530
> **Year Built:** 1895
> **Year Restored:** 1988   **Architect:** Brocchini & Associates   **Cost:** $2,300,000
> **Contact for Rental:** Elaine Edstrom, General Manager;   (916) 666-9617
> **Resident Groups:** Theatre Company

Woodland Hills

INSTRUMENTAL MUSIC

THE WEST VALLEY CHAMBER ORCHESTRA
Pierce College Music Department, 6201 Winnetka Avenue, Woodland Hills, CA 91371
(818) 347-0551
> **Founded:** 1972
> **Arts Area:** Orchestra
> **Status:** Non-Professional; Non-Profit
> **Type:** Performing; Resident; Educational
> **Purpose:** To offer free concerts to the community year-round
> **Management:** Rowan Taylor, Conductor; Timothy J. Durand, Assistant Director
> **Paid Staff:** 1   **Volunteer Staff:** 2
> **Non-Paid Artists:** 15
> **Utilizes:** Special Technical Talent; Guest Conductors; Guest Artists
> **Budget:** $1,000 - $50,000   **Season:** August - June

THEATRE

SHOWBOAT TROUPE
19817 Ventura Boulevard, Woodland Hills, CA 91364
(818) 884-7461
> **Founded:** 1979
> **Arts Area:** Musical; Dinner
> **Status:** Professional; Non-Profit
> **Type:** Performing; Educational
> **Purpose:** To provide the only legitimate theatre in the west end of the San Fernando Valley
> **Management:** Mike Monahan, Managing Director; Cynthia Orme, Business Manager; Ann Mahan, Choreographer/Secretary
> **Volunteer Staff:** 7
> **Non-Paid Artists:** 100
> **Budget:** $50,000 - $100,000
> **Income Sources:** Box Office

Season: 52 Weeks   **Annual Attendance:** 12,000
Performance Facilities: Showboat Dinner Theatre

Yreka

FACILITY

YREKA COMMUNITY THEATRE CENTER
810 North Oregon Street, Yreka, CA 96097
(916) 842-2355
FAX: (916) 842-3628
Founded: 1976
Type of Facility: Auditorium; Multi-Purpose
Type of Stage: Proscenium
Stage Dimensions: 38'x22'
Seating Capacity: 307
Year Built: 1978   **Architect:** Asefth, Jacobs & Schmitz   **Cost:** $1,600,000
Contact for Rental: Bob Marshall;   (916) 842-2355

COLORADO

Arvada

INSTRUMENTAL MUSIC

ROCKY MOUNTAIN BRASSWORKS
6974 Teller Court, Arvada, CO 80003
(303) 420-6452
Founded: 1980
Arts Area: Band
Status: Non-Professional; Non-Profit
Type: Performing; Educational
Purpose: To give the opportunity for the performer and listener to hear the great wealth of brass band music
Management: Stephen Asheim, Conductor; Rick Argotsinger, Associate Conductor
Officers: Rick Argostinger, Chairman; Ken Anderson, Vice Chairman; David Ciancio, Treasurer
Volunteer Staff: 5
Non-Paid Artists: 38
Budget: $1,000 - $50,000
Income Sources: Private Foundations/Grants/Endowments; Business/Corporate Donations; Individual Donations
Season: September - July   **Annual Attendance:** 3,500

FACILITY

ARVADA CENTER FOR THE ARTS AND HUMANITIES
6901 Wadsworth Boulevard, Arvada, CO 80003
(303) 431-3080
Type of Facility: Theatre Complex; Concert Hall; Outdoor (Concert); Studio Performance; Performance Center; Amphitheater; Civic Center; Multi-Purpose
Type of Stage: Thrust
Seating Capacity: 500
Year Built: 1976   **Architect:** Syracuse Lawylor   **Cost:** $3,600,000
Available for rent.

Aspen

DANCE

DANCE ASPEN
210 AABC, Suite NN, PO Box 8745, Aspen, CO 81611
(303) 925-7718
FAX: (303) 925-3041
Founded: 1981
Arts Area: Modern; Ballet; Ethnic
Status: Non-Profit
Type: Sponsoring
Purpose: To present a summer dance festival featuring professional dance companies from the United States and South America
Management: Jeffrey J. Bentley, Director
Officers: Andrew V. Hecht, President
Paid Staff: 5
Budget: $1,000,000 - $5,000,000
Income Sources: Private Foundations/Grants/Endowments; Business/Corporate Donations; Box Office; Government Grants; Individual Donations
Season: July - August   **Annual Attendance:** 9,000
Affiliations: APAP

PERFORMING SERIES

ASPEN MUSIC FESTIVAL AND SCHOOL
PO Box AA, Aspen, CO 81612
(303) 925-3254
FAX: (303) 925-3802
Founded: 1949
Arts Area: Vocal Music; Instrumental Music; Festivals; Lyric Opera; Grand Opera
Status: Professional; Semi-Professional; Non-Profit

Type: Performing; Resident; Educational
Purpose: To provide the finest supplemental classical music education possible for professionally-oriented students; to produce high-quality concerts for the public
Management: Robert Harth, President/Dean; Lawrence Foster, Music Director; Tom Eirman, General Manager; Martin Verdrager, Artistic Administrator; Debra Ayers, Director of Publicity; Edward Sweeney, Director of Operations
Officers: Fredric Benedict, Chairman; Les Anderson, Vice Chairman; Charles Paterson, Secretary; Noel Congdon, Treasurer
Paid Staff: 400 **Volunteer Staff:** 250
Paid Artists: 200 **Non-Paid Artists:** 965
Utilizes: Special Technical Talent; Guest Conductors; Guest Artists; Guest Directors
Budget: $1,000,000 - $5,000,000
Income Sources: Private Foundations/Grants/Endowments; Business/Corporate Donations; Box Office; Government Grants; Individual Donations
Season: June - August **Annual Attendance:** 80,000
Performance Facilities: Festival Music Tent

THE DANCE ASPEN FESTIVAL
PO Box 8745, Aspen, CO 81612
(303) 925-7718
Founded: 1981
Arts Area: Ballet
Status: Professional; Non-Profit
Type: Sponsoring
Purpose: To present the finest professional dance companies available in this part of the United States
Management: Jeffrey Bentley, Executive Producing Director
Officers: Andrew V. Hecht, President
Utilizes: Guest Artists
Budget: $500,000 - $1,000,000
Income Sources: Private Foundations/Grants/Endowments; Business/Corporate Donations
Season: July - August **Annual Attendance:** 11,000
Affiliations: Aspen/Snowmass Arts Council
Performance Facilities: Aspen High School; Performing Arts Center

WHEELER OPERA HOUSE ASSOCIATION
320 East Hyman Avenue, Aspen, CO 81611
(303) 920-2268
FAX: (303) 930-5197
Founded: 1985
Arts Area: Dance; Vocal Music; Instrumental Music; Theatre
Status: Non-Profit
Type: Sponsoring
Management: Heather Tharp, Secretary
Officers: Joyce Semple, President; Denise Jurgens, Treasurer; Robert Murray, Secretary; King Woodward, Treasurer
Utilizes: Special Technical Talent; Guest Artists; Guest Directors
Budget: $100,000 - $500,000
Income Sources: Private Foundations/Grants/Endowments; Business/Corporate Donations; Box Office; Government Grants; Individual Donations
Season: 52 Weeks
Affiliations: APAP
Performance Facilities: Wheeler Opera House

FACILITY

MUSIC TENT
980 North Third Street, Aspen, CO 81611
(303) 925-3254
Type of Facility: Amphitheater; Tent-covered Amphitheatre
Type of Stage: 3/4 Arena
Stage Dimensions: 75'x100'
Seating Capacity: 1731
Year Built: 1949 **Architect:** Eero Saarinen
Year Remodeled: 1965 **Architect:** Herbert Baer
Contact for Rental Director of Operations; (303) 925-3254
Resident Groups: Aspen Chamber Symphony; Aspen Festival Orchestra; Aspen Concert Orchestra; Sinfonia
Limited availability

WHEELER OPERA HOUSE
320 East Hyman Avenue, Aspen, CO 81611
(303) 925-2750
> **Type of Facility:** Theatre House
> **Type of Stage:** Thrust; Proscenium
> **Stage Dimensions:** 27'11"Wx27'10"D; 27'11"Wx17'3"H proscenium opening   **Orchestra Pit**
> **Seating Capacity:** 502
> **Year Built:** 1889   **Architect:** Edbrook
> **Year Remodeled:** 1984   **Architect:** William Kessler and Associates   **Cost:** $4,500,000
> **Contact for Rental** Robert Murray, Executive Director;   (303) 920-2268
> **Manager:** Leslie Shor
> **Resident Groups:** Aspen Music Festival and School
> *The Wheeler Opera house is a member of the League of Historic American Theatres.*

Aurora

DANCE

AURORA DANCE ARTS
3054 South Laredo Street, Aurora, CO 80013
(303) 699-3911
> **Founded:** 1973
> **Arts Area:** Ballet; Jazz; Tap
> **Status:** Non-Professional
> **Type:** Performing; Resident; Educational
> **Purpose:** To provide instruction in ballet, tap, jazz and pointe for all ages and ability levels and to provide a chance to perform for an audience
> **Management:** Julie Martin, Director; Pam Ziedman, Joy Hines, Office; 13 Dance Instructors
> **Paid Staff:** 16   **Volunteer Staff:** 150
> **Non-Paid Artists:** 50
> **Utilizes:** Special Technical Talent; Guest Artists
> **Budget:** $50,000 - $100,000
> **Income Sources:** Box Office; Government Grants; Individual Donations
> **Season:** 52 Weeks   **Annual Attendance:** 30,000
> **Affiliations:** City of Aurora
> **Performance Facilities:** Central High School; Aurora Fox Arts Center

JAN JUSTIS DANCE COMPANY
11787 East Atlantic Place, Aurora, CO 80014-1106
(302) 369-8687
> **Founded:** 1984
> **Arts Area:** Modern
> **Status:** Professional; Non-Profit
> **Type:** Performing; Touring; Educational
> **Purpose:** To further an appreciation of dance as an art form through cultural and educational programs, concerts, and experimental work, including collaborations with other artists
> **Management:** Jan Justis, Artistic Director/Manager; Rosanne Sterne, Director of Development
> **Officers:** Stephanie Reineke, President; Mark Overmeyer, Vice President; Robin Schaffer, Secretary
> **Paid Staff:** 1   **Volunteer Staff:** 1
> **Paid Artists:** 12
> **Utilizes:** Special Technical Talent; Guest Artists; Guest Choreographers; Composers; Visual Arts
> **Budget:** $1,000 - $50,000
> **Income Sources:** Private Foundations/Grants/Endowments; Business/Corporate Donations; Box Office; Government Grants; Individual Donations
> **Season:** 52 Weeks   **Annual Attendance:** 4,500
> **Affiliations:** Colorado Dance Alliance; Colorado Council on the Arts; Young Audiences of Denver

INSTRUMENTAL MUSIC

AURORA SYMPHONY
9900 East Colfax Avenue, Aurora, CO 80010
(303) 361-2908
> **Founded:** 1979
> **Arts Area:** Symphony
> **Status:** Non-Professional
> **Type:** Performing; Resident
> **Purpose:** To provide Aurora residents a chance to share their musical talents with an audience
> **Management:** Richard Molzer, Conductor/Musical Director; Alice Lee Main, Cultural Arts Administrator

Paid Staff: 1   **Volunteer Staff:** 65
Paid Artists: 4   **Non-Paid Artists:** 65
Utilizes: Guest Artists
Budget: $1,000 - $50,000
Income Sources: Business/Corporate Donations; Box Office; Government Grants; Individual Donations
Season: September - May   **Annual Attendance:** 1,200
Affiliations: City of Aurora
Performance Facilities: Aurora Fox Arts Center

VOCAL MUSIC

AURORA SINGERS
PO Box 9, Fox Arts Center, Aurora, CO 80040
(303) 361-2910; (303) 361-2908
FAX: (303) 361-2952
Founded: 1977
Arts Area: Choral
Status: Non-Professional
Type: Performing; Resident
Purpose: To provide Aurora residents a chance to share their vocal music skills with an audience
Management: Ken Johnson, Conductor/Music Director; Alice Lee Main, Cultural Arts Administrator
Paid Staff: 1   **Volunteer Staff:** 50
Non-Paid Artists: 50
Utilizes: Guest Directors
Budget: $1,000 - $50,000
Income Sources: Business/Corporate Donations; Box Office; Government Grants; Individual Donations
Season: September - May   **Annual Attendance:** 1,600
Affiliations: City of Aurora
Performance Facilities: Aurora Fox Arts Center

THEATRE

AURORA CHILDREN'S THEATRE COMPANY
9900 East Colfax Avenue, Aurora, CO 80010
(303) 361-2910
Founded: 1979
Arts Area: Community
Status: Non-Professional
Type: Performing; Resident; Educational
Purpose: To provide children an opportunity to learn acting skills and perform for an audience
Management: Alice Lee Main, Cultural Arts Administrator; Kim Smith, Theatre Producer; Robert Salisbury, Art Center Director
Paid Staff: 1   **Volunteer Staff:** 400
Non-Paid Artists: 200
Utilizes: Special Technical Talent; Guest Directors
Budget: $1,000 - $50,000
Income Sources: Business/Corporate Donations; Box Office; Government Grants
Season: September - August   **Annual Attendance:** 5,000
Affiliations: City of Aurora
Performance Facilities: Aurora Fox Arts Center

AURORA THEATRE COMPANY
9900 East Colfax Avenue, Aurora, CO 80010
(303) 361-2910
Founded: 1973
Arts Area: Theatrical Group
Status: Non-Professional
Type: Performing; Resident; Educational
Purpose: To provide actors and actresses an opportunity to advance their skills and entertain audiences
Management: Alice Lee Main, Cultural Arts Administrator; Liz Jury, Theatre Producer; Robert Salisbury, Art Center Director
Utilizes: Special Technical Talent; Guest Directors
Budget: $1,000 - $50,000
Income Sources: Business/Corporate Donations; Box Office; Government Grants; Individual Donations
Season: September - May   **Annual Attendance:** 7,000
Affiliations: City of Aurora
Performance Facilities: Aurora Fox Arts Center

FACILITY

AURORA FOX ARTS CENTER
9900 East Colfax, Aurora, CO 80010
(303) 695-7538
> **Founded:** 1985
> **Type of Facility:** Performance Center
> **Facility Originally:** Movie House
> **Type of Stage:** Proscenium
> **Stage Dimensions:** 29'x29' with 10' apron
> **Seating Capacity:** 251 + 4 wheelchair
> **Year Built:** 1946   **Cost:** $100,000
> **Year Remodeled:** 1985   **Architect:** Baer & Hickman Architects   **Cost:** $800,000
> **Acoustical Consultant:** Howard McGregor-Engineering Dynamics
> **Contact for Rental** Robert Salisbury;   (303) 695-7538
> **Resident Groups:** Aurora Theatre Company; Aurora Children's Theatre Company; Aurora Symphony; Aurora Singers; Aurora Dance Arts

BICENTENNIAL ART CENTER
13655 East Alameda, Aurora, CO 80012
(303) 344-1776
> **Type of Facility:** Visual Arts Center
> **Facility Originally:** Military Base
> **Year Built:** 1940
> **Year Remodeled:** 1978   **Cost:** $134,000
> **Resident Groups:** Aurora Potter's Guild
> *Owned by City of Aurora*

Boulder

INSTRUMENTAL MUSIC

BOULDER PHILHARMONIC ORCHESTRA
1722 14th Street, Suite 100, Boulder, CO 80302
(303) 449-1343
FAX: (303) 443-9203
> **Founded:** 1956
> **Arts Area:** Symphony; Orchestra
> **Status:** Non-Professional; Non-Profit
> **Type:** Performing; Sponsoring
> **Purpose:** To provide quality symphonic music to the people of Boulder County and the surrounding region; to take a leadership role in enhancing the cultural environment of Boulder County; to develop an understanding and interest among area residents for fine artistic expression
> **Management:** William Lightfoot, Executive Director; Oswald Lehnert, Conductor/Musical Director
> **Paid Staff:** 3
> **Non-Paid Artists:** 60
> **Utilizes:** Guest Artists
> **Budget:** $100,000 - $500,000
> **Income Sources:** Private Foundations/Grants/Endowments; Business/Corporate Donations; Box Office; Individual Donations
> **Season:** September - April   **Annual Attendance:** 12,000
> **Affiliations:** ASOL; WAAA
> **Performance Facilities:** Macky Auditorium Concert Hall

THEATRE

THE BOULDER REPERTORY COMPANY
3850 Norwood Court, Boulder, CO 80304
(303) 449-7258
> **Founded:** 1975
> **Arts Area:** Theatrical Group
> **Status:** Non-Profit
> **Type:** Performing
> **Purpose:** To perform plays of quality, either classics or the best of contemporary writers, studying people in depth or life in society today; to introduce contemporary plays to the Rocky Mountain region
> **Management:** Frank Georgianna, Artistic Director; Ernestine Georgianna, Administrative Director
> **Officers:** Frank Georgianna, President; Patricia Fitzgerald, Vice President; Susan D'Autremont, Secretary; Ernestine Georgianna, Treasurer

Volunteer Staff: 2
Paid Artists: 15
Utilizes: Special Technical Talent; Guest Artists
Budget: $1,000 - $50,000
Income Sources: Private Foundations/Grants/Endowments; Box Office; Government Grants; Individual Donations
Season: Summer   **Annual Attendance:** 3,000
Performance Facilities: Guild Theatre, Boulder

PERFORMING SERIES

BOULDER FOLK AND BLUEGRASS ASSOCIATION
2888 Bluff, #492, Boulder, CO 80301
(303) 753-3261
Founded: 1983
Arts Area: Festivals
Status: Non-Profit
Type: Sponsoring
Purpose: Boulder Folk and Bluegrass Association puts on a one-day folk festival annually in September; daytime events are generally free to the public
Management: John Sirkis, Festival Director
Volunteer Staff: 5
Utilizes: Guest Artists
Budget: $1,000 - $50,000
Income Sources: Private Foundations/Grants/Endowments; Business/Corporate Donations; Box Office; Government Grants; Individual Donations
Season: September
Annual Attendance: 5,000

COLORADO DANCE FESTIVAL
PO Box 356, Boulder, CO 80306
(303) 442-7666
Founded: 1979
Arts Area: Dance
Status: Professional; Non-Profit
Type: Performing; Touring; Resident; Educational; Sponsoring
Purpose: To develop new ideas in the arts through innovative dance and arts presentations, research, and education; to be an incubator for the research and development of new work in the area; to present programming of the highest quality that is inspiring and provocative; to respond to the changing needs of emerging artists
Management: Marda Kirn, Artistic Director; Felicia Dryden, Managing Director
Officers: Noel Hefty, President
Paid Staff: 23   **Volunteer Staff:** 3
Paid Artists: 40
Utilizes: Guest Artists
Budget: $100,000 - $500,000
Income Sources: Private Foundations/Grants/Endowments; Business/Corporate Donations; Box Office; Government Grants; Individual Donations
Season: June - July
Annual Attendance: 5,000
Affiliations: University of Colorado

COLORADO MUSIC FESTIVAL
1035 Pearl Street, Suite 303, Boulder, CO 80302
(303) 449-1397
FAX: (303) 449-0071
Founded: 1977
Arts Area: Instrumental Music
Status: Professional; Non-Profit
Type: Performing
Purpose: To develop and promote an appreciation and love for the musical arts through the operation of an international professional orchestra; to present traditional symphonic literature; to challenge audiences with new or contemporary compositions; to stimulate an intellectual experience
Management: Giora Bernstein, Musical Director; Michael A. Smith, Executive Director
Officers: Carol Kassoy, President; Richard Collins, President - Elect; Robert Bunting, Henry Beer, Timothy Schoecmle, William Phillips, Arthur Smoot, Vice Presidents; Francine Scchauer, Treasurer; Alan Shapely, Secretary
Paid Staff: 10   **Volunteer Staff:** 20
Paid Artists: 85

Utilizes: Guest Conductors; Guest Artists
Budget: $500,000 - $1,000,000
Income Sources: Private Foundations/Grants/Endowments; Business/Corporate Donations; Box Office; Government Grants; Individual Donations
Season: June - August
Annual Attendance: 30,000
Affiliations: ASOL
Performance Facilities: Chautauqua Auditorium

COLORADO SHAKESPEARE FESTIVAL
University of Colorado, Campus Box 261, Boulder, CO 80309-0261
(303) 492-0554; (303) 492-1527
Founded: 1958
Arts Area: Theater
Status: Professional; Non-Profit
Type: Performing
Purpose: To present four full-scale Shakespearean or classical productions in repertory June - August; to promote an appreciation of Shakespeare
Management: Richard M. Devin, Artistic Director; Patricia B. McFerran, Director of Publicity and Public Relations; Ann Watson, General Manager
Paid Staff: 50
Paid Artists: 75   **Non-Paid Artists:** 5
Utilizes: Special Technical Talent; Guest Artists; Guest Directors
Budget: $100,000 - $500,000
Income Sources: Private Foundations/Grants/Endowments; Box Office; Individual Donations
Season: June - August
Annual Attendance: 30,000
Performance Facilities: Outdoor theatre; University Theatre

FACILITY

BOULDER ART CENTER
1750 13th, Boulder, CO 80302
(303) 443-2122
Type of Facility: Gallery
Facility Originally: Warehouse
Type of Stage: Floor space only
Seating Capacity: 125
Contact for Rental Angie Lee;   (303) 443-2122

THE NAROPA INSTITUTE
2130 Arapahoe Avenue, Boulder, CO 80302
(303) 444-0202
FAX: (303) 444-0410
Type of Facility: Studio Performance; Environmental; Performance Center; Visual And Performing Arts Classroom
Facility Originally: Recreation Hall/Gymnasium
Type of Stage: Environmental
Year Built: 1920
Contact for Rental Rebecca Zepp; Phil Jacobson;   (303) 444-0202

UNIVERSITY OF COLORADO - MACKY AUDITORIUM CONCERT HALL
Box 285, Boulder, CO 80309
(303) 492-8423
FAX: (303) 492-5105
Type of Facility: Concert Hall; Multi-Purpose
Type of Stage: Proscenium
Stage Dimensions: 39'Wx27'D
Orchestra Pit
Seating Capacity: 2,047
Year Built: 1910   **Architect:** Gove and Walsh   **Cost:** $300,000
Year Remodeled: 1986   **Architect:** Midyette/Seieroe & Associates   **Cost:** $2,800,000
Acoustical Consultant: Lawrence Kirkegaard and Associates
Contact for Rental Kristin Anderson;   (303) 492-8423
Resident Groups: The Artist Series; The Boulder Philharmonic Orchestra; University of Colorado College of Music Orchestra; Symphonic Band and Choral Groups

Breckenridge

THEATRE

BACKSTAGE THEATRE COMPANY
PO Box 297, Breckenridge, CO 80424
(303) 453-0199
Founded: 1974
Arts Area: Musical; Community; Theatrical Group
Status: Semi-Professional; Non-Profit
Type: Performing; Educational
Purpose: To present a wide range of cultural events centered on theatre
Management: Bob and Wendy Moore
Paid Staff: 2   **Volunteer Staff:** 4
Paid Artists: 8
Utilizes: Guest Artists; Guest Directors
Budget: $50,000 - $100,000
Income Sources: Private Foundations/Grants/Endowments; Business/Corporate Donations; Box Office; Government Grants; Individual Donations
Season: Winter; Summer   **Annual Attendance:** 4,500
Affiliations: Rocky Mountain Theatre Guild
Performance Facilities: Backstage Theatre

PERFORMING SERIES

BRECKENRIDGE MUSIC INSTITUTE
130 Ski Hill Road, PO Box 1254, Breckenridge, CO 80424
(303) 453-9142
FAX: (303) 453-1423
Founded: 1980
Arts Area: Vocal Music; Instrumental Music; Festivals
Status: Professional; Non-Profit
Type: Performing; Educational
Purpose: To provide cultural and educational growth and enrichment in music for Summit County residents and visitors
Management: Pamela G. Miller, Executive Director; Peter Bay, Music Advisor; Daniel Schmidt, Festival Administrator; Allison Rouse, Administrative Assistant
Officers: R.H. VanDenburg, President; Charles Simpson, Vice President; James Robertson, Secretary; Richard L. Thomas, Treasurer
Paid Staff: 64   **Volunteer Staff:** 250
Paid Artists: 55
Utilizes: Guest Conductors; Guest Artists
Budget: $100,000 - $500,000
Income Sources: Private Foundations/Grants/Endowments; Business/Corporate Donations; Box Office; Government Grants; Individual Donations
Season: July - August   **Annual Attendance:** 16,000
Performance Facilities: Breckenridge Event Tent

FACILITY

BACKSTAGE THEATRE
PO Box 297, Breckenridge, CO 80424
(303) 453-0199
Type of Facility: Theatre House
Type of Stage: Proscenium
Stage Dimensions: 22'Wx16'D
Seating Capacity: 98
Year Built: 1980   **Architect:** Jon Gunson, AIA
Resident Groups: Backstage Theatre Company

Central City

FACILITY

CENTRAL CITY OPERA HOUSE
Central City, CO 80427
(303) 623-7167
Mailing Address: 621 17th Street, Suite 1601, Denver, CO 80293

Type of Facility: Theatre House; Opera House
Type of Stage: Proscenium
Stage Dimensions: 40'Wx50'D **Orchestra Pit**
Seating Capacity: 756
Year Built: 1878 **Architect:** Robert Roeschlaub **Cost:** $23,000
Year Remodeled: 1987 **Architect:** Grammar of Ornament **Cost:** $80,000
Contact for Rental Daniel Rule; (303) 623-7167
Resident Groups: Central City Opera
The Opera House has been designated a National Historic Landmark.

Colorado Springs

DANCE

COLORADO SPRINGS DANCE THEATRE
7 East Bijou, Suite 213, Colorado Springs, CO 80903
(719) 630-7434
Founded: 1977
Arts Area: Modern; Ballet; Jazz; Ethnic; Folk; Other Types
Status: Non-Profit
Type: Sponsoring
Purpose: To educate and entertain through dance
Management: Joan Bliss-Pollock, Executive Director; Esther Geoffrey, Artistic Consultant
Officers: Kevin McTernan, President; Maureen Christopher, Vice President; David Parker, Secretary; Mary Pat
Sweetman, Treasurer
Paid Staff: 3 **Volunteer Staff:** 2
Utilizes: Guest Artists; Guest Choreographers
Budget: $50,000 - $100,000
Income Sources: Private Foundations/Grants/Endowments; Business/Corporate Donations; Box Office; Government
Grants; Individual Donations
Season: September - May **Annual Attendance:** 7,000
Performance Facilities: Pikes Peak Center; Armstrong Theatre

INSTRUMENTAL MUSIC

COLORADO SPRINGS SYMPHONY ORCHESTRA
PO Box 1692, Colorado Springs, CO 80901
(719) 633-4611
FAX: (719) 633-6699
Founded: 1922
Arts Area: Symphony; Orchestra; Chamber
Status: Professional; Non-Profit
Type: Performing; Educational; Sponsoring
Purpose: To present symphonic music; to sponsor other performing-arts productions and music education in the schools
Management: Daniel J. Hart, Executive Director; Christopher Wilkins, Conductor/Music Director; Douglas Ismail, Direc-
tor of Marketing and Development
Officers: Richard Nagl, President; Phillip Kendall, Ralph Schauer, Vice Presidents; Susan S. Greene, Secretary; Bruce
Kopper, Treasurer
Paid Staff: 16 **Volunteer Staff:** 25
Paid Artists: 87
Utilizes: Guest Conductors; Guest Artists
Budget: $1,000,000 - $5,000,000
Income Sources: Private Foundations/Grants/Endowments; Business/Corporate Donations; Box Office; Government
Grants; Individual Donations
Season: September - July **Annual Attendance:** 256,000
Affiliations: NEA; ASOL; Colorado Council on Humanities
Performance Facilities: Pikes Peak Center

DA VINCI QUARTET
c/o DVC Association, PO Box 7150, Colorado Springs, CO 80923
(719) 593-3331
FAX: (719) 593-3362
Arts Area: Chamber
Status: Professional; Non-Profit
Type: Performing; Touring; Resident; Educational
Purpose: To promote the work of American and women composers as well as the standard repertoire; to maintain a strong
educational focus
Management: Madeline Jenkins Millard, Operations Manager

Officers: Brooke Bower, President; Kent Bortes, Vice President
Budget: $50,000 - $100,000
Income Sources: Private Foundations/Grants/Endowments; Business/Corporate Donations; Box Office; Government Grants; Individual Donations
Performance Facilities: Colorado Springs Fine Arts Centre

SOUNDSCAPES
608 Bennett Avenue, Colorado Springs, CO 80909
(719) 634-7470
Arts Area: Chamber; Instrumental Group
Status: Professional; Non-Profit
Type: Performing
Purpose: To bring 20th-century music to the Rocky Mountain area
Management: Sandy Craddock, Artistic Director
Officers: Kathleen Collins, Chairman of the Board
Budget: $1,000 - $50,000
Income Sources: Private Foundations/Grants/Endowments; Government Grants; Individual Donations

VOCAL MUSIC

COLORADO SPRINGS CHORALE
27 South Tejon, PO Box 2304, Colorado Springs, CO 80903
(719) 634-3737
Founded: 1956
Arts Area: Choral
Status: Non-Professional; Non-Profit
Type: Performing; Resident
Purpose: A fully-auditioned community chorus of 130 voices, dedicated to the well-rehearsed performance of great works from the symphonic-choral literature
Management: Jan Boothroyd, General Manager
Officers: Ken Myers, Chairman; Sylvia Hutson, Vice Chairman; Myrtis Thompson, Secretary; James Price, Treasurer
Paid Staff: 2　**Volunteer Staff:** 20
Paid Artists: 2　**Non-Paid Artists:** 130
Utilizes: Guest Conductors; Guest Artists
Budget: $50,000 - $100,000
Income Sources: Private Foundations/Grants/Endowments; Business/Corporate Donations; Box Office; Individual Donations
Season: Fall - Spring　**Annual Attendance:** 10,000
Affiliations: CA
Performance Facilities: Pikes Peak Center

MOSAIC
27 South Tejon, PO Box 2304, Colorado Springs, CO 80903
(719) 634-3737
Founded: 1990
Arts Area: Choral
Status: Non-Professional; Non-Profit
Type: Performing; Resident; Educational
Purpose: A representative ensemble of the Colorado Springs Chorale, performing a repertoire of diverse musical styles, performing in schools, service clubs, retirement homes and businesses, and private and public functions
Management: Carolyn Schwartz, Manager
Officers: Ken Myers, Chairman; Sylvia Hutson, Vice Chairman; Myrtis Thompson, Secretary; James Price, Treasurer
Paid Staff: 1　**Volunteer Staff:** 2
Paid Artists: 1　**Non-Paid Artists:** 12
Budget: $1,000 - $50,000
Income Sources: Private Foundations/Grants/Endowments; Business/Corporate Donations; Individual Donations
Season: 52 Weeks

PERFORMING SERIES

COLORADO OPERA FESTIVAL
PO Box 1484, Colorado Springs, CO 80901
(719) 473-0073
Founded: 1971
Arts Area: Grand Opera
Status: Professional; Non-Profit
Type: Performing; Resident
Purpose: To promote and develop the art of opera and knowledge and enjoyment of opera by the public; to carry out public education programs with respect to opera and the commissioning of new works

Management: Elizabeth Lilly, Executive Director; Donald Jenkins, General Director
Officers: Charles Shay, President; Carla Peperzak, Vice President; Penny Sayre, Treasurer
Paid Staff: 4 **Volunteer Staff:** 25
Paid Artists: 20
Utilizes: Special Technical Talent; Guest Conductors; Guest Artists; Guest Directors
Budget: $100,000 - $500,000
Income Sources: Private Foundations/Grants/Endowments; Business/Corporate Donations; Box Office; Government Grants; Individual Donations
Season: July - August **Annual Attendance:** 6,000
Performance Facilities: Pikes Peak Center

FACILITY

ARNOLD HALL THEATER - UNITED STATES AIR FORCE ACADEMY
HQ/USAFA - CWXRXX, 2302 Cadet Drive, Colorado Springs, CO 80840-5454
(719) 472-4497
FAX: (719) 472-4597
Founded: 1957
Type of Facility: Concert Hall
Type of Stage: Proscenium
Stage Dimensions: 110'Wx44'D
Orchestra Pit
Seating Capacity: 2,808
Year Built: 1958 **Architect:** Skidmore, Owings & Merrill **Cost:** $2,000,000
Year Remodeled: 1980 **Cost:** $200,000
Acoustical Consultant: Skidmore, Owings & Merrill
Manager: Paula Stamps; (719) 472-4497
Resident Groups: Academy Band; Blue Bird Cadets

CITY AUDITORIUM
221 East Kiowa Street, Colorado Springs, CO 80903
(719) 578-6652; (719) 578-6640
FAX: (719) 578-6934
Type of Facility: Auditorium; Arena
Type of Stage: Proscenium
Stage Dimensions: 42'x52'x32'; Lon Chaney Theatre - 25'x20'x12'
Seating Capacity: 2,500; Lon Chaney Theatre - 225
Year Built: 1923 **Architect:** Lamar Kelsey **Cost:** $1,000,000
Year Remodeled: 1975 **Cost:** $142,000
Contact for Rental Michael S. Garcia; (719) 578-6652
Resident Groups: Star Bar Players

COLORADO COLLEGE - PACKARD HALL
Colorado Springs, CO 80903
(719) 389-6545, ext. X545
FAX: (719) 389-6862
Type of Facility: Concert Hall; Music Performance Hall
Type of Stage: Platform
Stage Dimensions: 30'x25'x15'
Seating Capacity: 350
Year Built: 1976 **Architect:** Edward Larabee Barnes **Cost:** $3,000,000
Manager: Lyn Doyon; (719) 389-6545
Resident Groups: Colorado College Music Department

COLORADO SPRINGS FINE ARTS CENTER THEATRE
30 West Dale Street, Colorado Springs, CO 80903
(719) 634-5581
Type of Facility: Civic Center; Multi-Purpose
Type of Stage: Proscenium
Stage Dimensions: 30'x30'x38'
Orchestra Pit
Seating Capacity: 450
Year Built: 1936 **Architect:** John Gaw Meem
Year Remodeled: 1984 **Architect:** Wallace/Nakata **Cost:** $1,100,000
Contact for Rental Kenneth M. Wohlford, Director of Performing Arts; (719) 634-5581

PIKES PEAK CENTER
190 South Cascade, Colorado Springs, CO 80903
(719) 520-7453
FAX: (719) 520-7462
    Type of Facility: Theatre Complex; Concert Hall; Auditorium; Studio Performance; Environmental; Theatre House; Opera House; Civic Center; Multi-Purpose
    Type of Stage: Flexible; Proscenium
    Stage Dimensions: 50'x100' **Orchestra Pit**
    Seating Capacity: 2,000
    Year Built: 1982 **Architect:** John James Wallace & Associates **Cost:** $13,400,000
    Acoustical Consultant: ARTEC
    Contact for Rental Cindy Ballard; (719) 520-7453
    Manager: Steve Martin; (719) 520-7453
    Resident Groups: Colorado Springs Symphony; Colorado Opera Festival; Colorado Springs Chorale; Center Attractions

Creede

THEATRE

CREEDE REPERTORY THEATRE
PO Box 269, Creede, CO 81130
(719) 658-2541
FAX: (719) 658-2343
    Founded: 1966
    Arts Area: Professional; Summer Stock; Musical; Theatrical Group
    Status: Professional; Non-Profit
    Type: Performing; Touring; Educational; Sponsoring
    Purpose: To produce five plays in summer in repertory; to promote greater understanding of the performing arts; to raise standards and practice; to make performing arts more accessible to the public
    Management: Richard Baxter, Producing Director; Kay Wyley, Administrative Director; Ken Burt, Business Manager; Julie Purcell, Financial Director
    Officers: Mike Rierson, Chairman of Board; Nell Wyley, Vice President; Dr. Carl Koch, Secretary/Treasurer
    Paid Staff: 3 **Volunteer Staff:** 30
    Paid Artists: 31
    Utilizes: Special Technical Talent; Guest Artists; Guest Directors
    Budget: $100,000 - $500,000
    Income Sources: Private Foundations/Grants/Endowments; Business/Corporate Donations; Box Office; Government Grants; Individual Donations
    Season: Memorial Day - Labor Day **Annual Attendance:** 15,000
    Performance Facilities: Creede Repertory Theatre

FACILITY

CREEDE REPERTORY THEATRE
PO Box 269, Creede, CO 81130
(719) 658-2541
FAX: (719) 658-2343
    Founded: 1966
    Type of Facility: Performance Center; Theatre House
    Facility Originally: Movie House
    Type of Stage: Proscenium
    Stage Dimensions: 25'x20'
    Seating Capacity: 242
    Year Built: 1935
    Year Remodeled: 1992 **Architect:** Long-Hoeft **Cost:** $1,100,000
    Manager: Richard Baxter, Producing/Art Director; (719) 658-2541

Crested Butte

DANCE

DANSWINTER/DANSUMMER
PO Box 506, Crested Butte, CO 81224
(303) 349-6707
    Founded: 1984

Arts Area: Ballet; Jazz; Tap
Status: Semi-Professional; Non-Professional
Type: Resident; Sponsoring
Purpose: To bring dance, enjoyment, technique and style to beginners and intermediates
Management: Heidi Coe DuVal, Artistic Director; Bobbie Reinhardt, Administrative Director
Paid Staff: 2
Paid Artists: 2
Utilizes: Guest Artists
Budget: $1,000 - $50,000
Income Sources: Individual Donations; Tuition
Season: January - February; June-August
Affiliations: Chamber of Commerce; Crested Butte Society for the Arts
Performance Facilities: Indoor Stage; Outdoor Stage

FACILITY

CRESTED BUTTE MOUNTAIN THEATRE
Second and Elk, PO Box 611, Crested Butte, CO 81224
(303) 349-5418
    Type of Facility: Performance Center; Theatre House
    Facility Originally: Meeting Hall; Movie House
    Type of Stage: Flexible
    Stage Dimensions: 12'x20'x14'
    Seating Capacity: 100
    Year Built: 1883 **Architect:** James Kuziak **Cost:** $25,000
    Year Remodeled: 1976
    Contact for Rental Cindy Valian; (303) 349-5418
    Manager: Gloria Wojtalik

Cripple Creek

THEATRE

IMPERIAL PLAYERS
123 North Third Street, Cripple Creek, CO 80813
(719) 689-2922
FAX: (719) 689-2922
    Founded: 1948
    Arts Area: Professional; Musical; Dinner
    Status: Professional
    Type: Performing; Resident
    Purpose: To professionally produce 19th-century melodramas with authentic scripts dating from 1850 to 1900
    Management: Imperial Hotel and Casino
    Paid Staff: 3
    Paid Artists: 14
    Utilizes: Special Technical Talent
    Budget: $50,000 - $100,000
    Income Sources: Box Office
    Season: June - September **Annual Attendance:** 33,000
    Affiliations: SWTC
    Performance Facilities: Gold Bar Room Theatre

FACILITY

GOLD BAR ROOM THEATRE, IMPERIAL HOTEL
123 North Third Street, PO Box 1003, Cripple Creek, CO 80813
(719) 689-7777
    Type of Facility: Multi-Purpose; Historic Hotel & Theatre
    Facility Originally: Hotel & Meeting Rooms
    Type of Stage: Open 2 Sides
    Stage Dimensions: 16'x14'
    Seating Capacity: 280
    Year Remodeled: 1981
    Contact for Rental Imperial Hotel; (303) 689-2307
    Resident Groups: Imperial Players
    Opened as a theatre in 1948; remodeled in 1955, 1978 and 1981

Denver

DANCE

ACADEMY OF CREATIVE DANCE AND ELIZABETH MANDEVILLE DANCE COMPANY
3875 Tennyson Street, Denver, CO 80212
(303) 480-1162
> **Founded:** 1975
> **Arts Area:** Modern; Jazz
> **Status:** Commercial
> **Type:** Performing; Educational
> **Purpose:** To train dancers safely and to educate people in dance-injury prevention; to build an interest in modern dance
> **Management:** Elizabeth Mandeville, Director; Lisa Wood, Administrator
> **Paid Staff:** 3
> **Non-Paid Artists:** 6
> **Utilizes:** Special Technical Talent
> **Budget:** $1,000 - $50,000
> **Income Sources:** Box Office
> **Annual Attendance:** 600
> **Performance Facilities:** Shwayder Theatre

BALLET DENVER
3955 Tennyson Street, Denver, CO 80212
(303) 455-4974
> **Founded:** 1973
> **Arts Area:** Modern; Ballet; Folk
> **Status:** Professional; Non-Profit
> **Type:** Performing; Touring; Educational
> **Purpose:** To present an introduction to ballet consisting of classical, romantic, character and modern works; to bring the art of ballet to communities not visited by full companies
> **Management:** Rieke Maria Love, Director; Brian Slota, Company Manager; Janet Hirschfield, Ballet Mistress; Kereen Happe, Rehearsal Regisseur; Barbara Hirschfield, Wardrobe Mistress; Scott Bagley, Light Design Technician; Cindy Rowell, Set Design Technician
> **Officers:** Rieke Maria Love, President; Janet Hirschfield, Vice President; Barbara Hirschfield, Secretary/Treasurer
> **Paid Staff:** 1   **Volunteer Staff:** 3
> **Paid Artists:** 7
> **Budget:** $1,000 - $50,000
> **Income Sources:** Box Office; Government Grants; Individual Donations
> **Annual Attendance:** 5,000

CLEO PARKER ROBINSON DANCE ENSEMBLE
119 Park Avenue West, Denver, CO 80205
(303) 295-1759
FAX: (303) 295-1328
> **Founded:** 1972
> **Arts Area:** Modern; Jazz
> **Status:** Professional; Non-Profit
> **Type:** Performing; Touring; Resident; Educational
> **Management:** Cleo Parker Robinson, Executive Artistic Director; Thomas E. Robinson, Business Manager; Sharon Baumgarten, Development Director; Reina Silva, Booking Manager/Operations Director; Keith W. Rice, Technical Director
> **Officers:** Cleo Parker Robinson, Chairman of the Board; Thomas E. Robinson, Secretary
> **Paid Staff:** 4   **Volunteer Staff:** 4
> **Paid Artists:** 35
> **Utilizes:** Guest Artists; Guest Choreographers
> **Budget:** $100,000 - $500,000
> **Income Sources:** Private Foundations/Grants/Endowments; Box Office; Government Grants; Individual Donations
> **Season:** September - June   **Annual Attendance:** 35,000
> **Performance Facilities:** The Cleo Parker Robinson Dance Theatre

COLORADO BALLET
999 18th Street, Suite 1645, Denver, CO 80202
(303) 298-0677
FAX: (303) 298-9104
> **Founded:** 1961
> **Arts Area:** Ballet
> **Status:** Professional; Non-Profit
> **Type:** Performing; Touring; Resident; Sponsoring

Purpose: To perform, present, tour and educate classical and contemporary ballet
Management: Jim Harvey, General Manager; Martin Freedmann, Artistic Director; Leanna Clark, Director of Communication
Officers: Colleen Reed, President
Paid Staff: 8
Paid Artists: 18
Utilizes: Special Technical Talent; Guest Artists; Guest Directors
Budget: $500,000 - $1,000,000
Income Sources: Private Foundations/Grants/Endowments; Business/Corporate Donations; Box Office; Government Grants; Individual Donations
Season: October - March   **Annual Attendance:** 50,000
Performance Facilities: Denver Auditorium Theatre; Temple Hoyne Buell Theatre

FLAMENCO FANTASY DANCE THEATRE/GYPSY PRODUCTIONS INC.
600 South Emerson Street, Denver, CO 80209
(303) 722-0054
Founded: 1983
Arts Area: Ethnic; Folk
Status: Professional; Commercial
Type: Performing; Touring; Resident; Educational
Purpose: To further the knowledge and educate the American public about Spanish music and dance
Management: Gypsy Productions, Inc.
Officers: Rene Meredia, Director; Candace Bevior
Paid Staff: 1
Paid Artists: 3   **Non-Paid Artists:** 7
Utilizes: Special Technical Talent; Guest Artists; Guest Choreographers
Budget: $1,000 - $50,000
Income Sources: Box Office
Season: 52 Weeks

INSTRUMENTAL MUSIC

COLORADO SYMPHONY ORCHESTRA
1031 13th Street, Denver, CO 80204
(303) 595-4915
FAX: (303) 595-4935
Founded: 1922
Arts Area: Symphony; Orchestra
Status: Professional; Non-Profit
Type: Performing; Touring; Resident; Educational; Sponsoring
Purpose: To be Colorado's premier full-time professional symphonic music resource
Management: James Copenhaver, Executive Director; David Abosch, Artistic Director; Sandy Lasky, Marketing Director
Paid Staff: 13   **Volunteer Staff:** 35
Utilizes: Guest Conductors; Guest Artists
Budget: $5,000,000 - $10,000,000
Income Sources: Private Foundations/Grants/Endowments; Business/Corporate Donations; Box Office; Government Grants; Individual Donations
Season: 52 Weeks   **Annual Attendance:** 225,000
Performance Facilities: Boettcher Concert Hall

DENVER CHAMBER ORCHESTRA
1616 Glenarm Place, Suite 1360, Denver, CO 80202
(303) 825-4911
Founded: 1968
Arts Area: Orchestra; Chamber
Status: Professional; Non-Profit
Type: Performing; Touring; Educational
Purpose: To provide the highest quality chamber orchestra music to Denver and tour the orchestra throughout the Rocky Mountain Region
Management: Paul Lustiq Dunkel, Music Director/Conductor
Officers: John C. Graff, President; Allan Marter, Treasurer
Paid Staff: 2   **Volunteer Staff:** 50
Paid Artists: 35
Utilizes: Guest Conductors; Guest Artists
Budget: $100,000 - $500,000
Income Sources: Private Foundations/Grants/Endowments; Business/Corporate Donations; Box Office; Government Grants; Individual Donations
Season: September - May   **Annual Attendance:** 20,000
Performance Facilities: Trinity Methodist Church; Paramount Theatre

DENVER MUNICIPAL BAND
3372 South Magnolia Street, Denver, CO 80224
(303) 756-0151
Founded: 1891
Arts Area: Band
Status: Professional
Type: Performing
Purpose: To present free summer concerts in Denver parks
Management: Ed Lenicheck, Conductor; Gerald Endsley, Manager
Officers: Ed Lenicheck, President; Gerald Endsley, Vice President
Paid Staff: 2
Paid Artists: 44
Utilizes: Guest Artists
Budget: $50,000 - $100,000
Income Sources: Private Foundations/Grants/Endowments; Business/Corporate Donations; Government Grants; Individual Donations; Denver Musicians Association
Season: July - August   **Annual Attendance:** 30,000
Affiliations: Association of Concert Bands

FRIENDS OF CHAMBER MUSIC
PO Box 6089, Cherry Creek Station, Denver, CO 80206
Arts Area: Chamber
Status: Non-Profit
Type: Presenting
Purpose: To present five chamber-music concerts annually and sponsor outreach activity including workshops and master classes
Officers: Rosemarie P. Murane, President Board of Directors; Chet Sterne, Vice President; John Lebsack, Treasurer
Volunteer Staff: 15
Utilizes: Guest Artists
Budget: $1,000 - $50,000
Income Sources: Private Foundations/Grants/Endowments; Business/Corporate Donations; Box Office; Individual Donations
Season: October - April   **Annual Attendance:** 2,500

NATIONAL REPERTORY ORCHESTRA
899 Logan Street, Suite 510, Denver, CO 80203
(303) 831-8480
Founded: 1960
Arts Area: Symphony; Orchestra
Status: Professional; Non-Profit
Type: Performing; Touring; Resident
Purpose: To provide an intensive professional internship to musicians, 18-28 years of age, from around the country
Management: Elisa Zimmerman, Director of Development; Edward Birdwell, Orchestra Manager
Officers: Edward Haligman, President of the Board; Richard F. Zellner, President
Paid Staff: 14
Non-Paid Artists: 90
Utilizes: Special Technical Talent; Guest Conductors; Guest Artists
Budget: $100,000 - $500,000
Income Sources: Private Foundations/Grants/Endowments; Business/Corporate Donations; Box Office; Government Grants; Individual Donations
Season: June - August   **Annual Attendance:** 65,000
Affiliations: ASCAP; ASOL; Colorado Council of the Arts; Colorado Music Alliance
Performance Facilities: Keystone Resort; Colorado Front Range Cities

VOCAL MUSIC

CENTRAL CITY OPERA
621 17th Street, Suite 1601, Denver, CO 80293
(303) 292-6500
FAX: (303) 292-4958
Founded: 1932
Arts Area: Grand Opera; Operetta
Status: Professional; Non-Profit
Type: Performing; Educational
Management: John Moriarty, Artistic Director, Administrative/Training Program; Daniel Rule, General Manager
Officers: Nancy Parker, President of the Board
Paid Staff: 8
Paid Artists: 300

Utilizes: Special Technical Talent; Guest Conductors; Guest Artists; Guest Directors
Budget: $1,000,000 - $5,000,000
Income Sources: Private Foundations/Grants/Endowments; Business/Corporate Donations; Box Office; Government Grants; Individual Donations
Season: July - August **Annual Attendance:** 20,000
Affiliations: OA; Metro Denver Arts Alliance
Performance Facilities: Central City Opera House, Central City

COLORADO CHILDREN'S CHORALE
910 15th Street, Suite 1020, Denver, CO 80202
(303) 892-5600
FAX: (303) 892-0828
> **Founded:** 1974
> **Arts Area:** Choral
> **Status:** Professional; Non-Profit
> **Type:** Performing; Touring; Educational
> **Purpose:** To provide the nation a performing-arts group with children as its medium and excellence as its goal
> **Management:** Duain Wolfe, Artistic Director
> **Officers:** Stephan Clarke, Chairman; Gregory Glissmann, Vice Chairman; Corry Doty, Treasurer
> **Paid Staff:** 17 **Volunteer Staff:** 100
> **Paid Artists:** 10 **Non-Paid Artists:** 350
> **Utilizes:** Guest Conductors; Guest Artists
> **Budget:** $500,000 - $1,000,000
> **Income Sources:** Private Foundations/Grants/Endowments; Business/Corporate Donations; Box Office; Government Grants; Individual Donations
> **Season:** August - July **Annual Attendance:** 50,000

THE DENVER CHAMBER CHOIR
12312 West Mississippi Avenue, Denver, CO 80228
(303) 986-7893
> **Founded:** 1977
> **Arts Area:** Choral
> **Status:** Semi-Professional; Non-Profit
> **Type:** Performing; Resident; Educational
> **Purpose:** To perform advanced choral repertory from all periods of music history
> **Management:** Dr. William Jones, Director; Carol Luft, Projects Coordinator
> **Officers:** Robert Miller, Counsel; Nina Rockley, Secretary
> **Volunteer Staff:** 2
> **Paid Artists:** 1 **Non-Paid Artists:** 24
> **Utilizes:** Guest Artists
> **Budget:** $1,000 - $50,000
> **Income Sources:** Private Foundations/Grants/Endowments; Business/Corporate Donations; Government Grants; Individual Donations
> **Season:** September - July **Annual Attendance:** 3,500
> **Affiliations:** CA; ACDA

OPERA COLORADO
695 South Colorado Boulevard, Suite 20, Denver, CO 80222
(303) 778-1500
> **Founded:** 1981
> **Arts Area:** Grand Opera
> **Status:** Professional; Non-Profit
> **Type:** Performing; Resident; Educational
> **Purpose:** To produce international quality grand opera in-the-round and to develop appreciation and understanding of opera throughout the community
> **Management:** Nathaniel Merrill, General Director; William Dickinson, Director of Development
> **Officers:** Eleanor Caulkins, Chairman of the Board
> **Paid Staff:** 10 **Volunteer Staff:** 100
> **Paid Artists:** 250 **Non-Paid Artists:** 75
> **Utilizes:** Special Technical Talent; Guest Conductors; Guest Artists
> **Budget:** $1,000,000 - $5,000,000
> **Income Sources:** Private Foundations/Grants/Endowments; Business/Corporate Donations; Box Office; Government Grants; Individual Donations
> **Season:** May
> **Annual Attendance:** 21,000
> **Affiliations:** OA
> **Performance Facilities:** Boettcher Concert Hall

THEATRE

CHANGING SCENE THEATER
1527 1/2 Champa Street, Denver, CO 80202
(303) 893-5775
>**Founded:** 1968
>**Arts Area:** Theatrical Group
>**Status:** Non-Profit
>**Type:** Performing; Resident; Educational; Sponsoring
>**Purpose:** To provide a performing space and experience for young artists
>**Management:** Alfred Brooks, President; Maxine Munt, Vice President
>**Volunteer Staff:** 2
>**Utilizes:** Guest Artists; Guest Directors
>**Budget:** $1,000 - $50,000
>**Income Sources:** Box Office; Government Grants; Individual Donations
>**Season:** 52 Weeks

DENVER CENTER THEATER COMPANY
1050 13th Street, Denver, CO 80204
(303) 893-4200
>**Founded:** 1980
>**Arts Area:** Professional; Musical; Theatrical Group
>**Status:** Professional; Non-Profit
>**Type:** Performing; Touring; Resident; Educational
>**Purpose:** We are dedicated to presenting the best of the performing arts to the Rocky Mountain Region
>**Management:** Donovan Markey, Artistic Director; Kevin Maifeld, Executive Director; Barbara Sellers, Producing Director; Tony Church, Dean of the Conservatory
>**Paid Staff:** 30 **Volunteer Staff:** 300
>**Paid Artists:** 275
>**Utilizes:** Special Technical Talent; Guest Artists; Guest Directors
>**Budget:** $5,000,000 - $10,000,000
>**Income Sources:** Private Foundations/Grants/Endowments; Business/Corporate Donations; Box Office; Government Grants; Individual Donations
>**Season:** September - June **Annual Attendance:** 150,000
>**Affiliations:** The Denver Center; TCG; LORT
>**Performance Facilities:** Denver Center Theatre

EL CENTRO SU TEATRO
4725 High Street, Denver, CO 80216
(303) 296-0219
>**Founded:** 1971
>**Arts Area:** Professional; Musical; Community; Folk; Theatrical Group
>**Status:** Semi-Professional; Non-Profit
>**Type:** Performing; Touring; Resident; Educational; Sponsoring
>**Management:** Anthony J. Garcia, Artistic Director; Rodolfo W. Bustos, Managing Director; Debra Gallegos, Development Director
>**Officers:** Anthony J. Garcia, President; Sherry Candelaria, Secretary
>**Paid Staff:** 2 **Volunteer Staff:** 10
>**Paid Artists:** 8 **Non-Paid Artists:** 12
>**Utilizes:** Guest Artists
>**Budget:** $100,000 - $500,000
>**Income Sources:** Private Foundations/Grants/Endowments; Business/Corporate Donations; Box Office; Government Grants; Individual Donations; Concessions
>**Season:** September - May **Annual Attendance:** 8,300
>**Affiliations:** Teatro Nacional de Aztlan (TENAZ)

GERMINAL STAGE DENVER
2450 West 44th Avenue, Denver, CO 80211
(303) 455-7108
>**Founded:** 1974
>**Arts Area:** Professional; Theatrical Group
>**Status:** Professional; Non-Profit
>**Type:** Performing
>**Management:** Ed Baierlein, Director/Manager
>**Officers:** Ed Baierlein, President; Ginger Valone, Vice President; Sallie D. Baierlein, Secretary; John C. Seifert, Treasurer
>**Paid Staff:** 2
>**Paid Artists:** 50
>**Budget:** $50,000 - $100,000
>**Income Sources:** Business/Corporate Donations; Box Office; Government Grants

Season: October - August   **Annual Attendance:** 12,000
Affiliations: TCG; Colorado Producers Guild
Performance Facilities: Germinal Stage Denver

STUDIO E THEATRE ENSEMBLE
2715 Welton Street, Denver, CO 80205
(303) 297-9812
Founded: 1982
Arts Area: Theatrical Group
Status: Semi-Professional; Non-Profit
Type: Performing; Touring; Resident; Educational; Sponsoring
Purpose: To perform plays written exclusively by Black playwrights
Management: Jo Bunton Keel, Executive Director
Paid Staff: 2   **Volunteer Staff:** 60
Paid Artists: 100   **Non-Paid Artists:** 30
Budget: $100,000 - $500,000
Income Sources: Private Foundations/Grants/Endowments; Business/Corporate Donations; Box Office; Individual
Donations
Season: March - December   **Annual Attendance:** 65,000

SU TEATRO, INC.
4725 High Street, Denver, CO 80216
(303) 296-0219
Arts Area: Community; Theatrical Group
Status: Semi-Professional; Non-Profit
Type: Performing; Touring; Educational; Sponsoring
Purpose: To carry the message of the struggles of the Southwestern barrios; to preserve and perpetuate the
Chicano language and culture
Management: Anthony J. Garcia, Artistic Director; Rudolfo W. Bustos, Managing Director; Debra Gallegos, Develop-
ment Director
Officers: Debra Gallegos, Board Member
Budget: $100,000 - $500,000
Income Sources: Private Foundations/Grants/Endowments; Business/Corporate Donations; Box Office; Government
Grants; Individual Donations; Touring Fees
Performance Facilities: El Centro Su Teatro

VICTORIAN THEATRE
4201 Hooker Street, Denver, CO 80211
(303) 433-4343
Founded: 1911
Arts Area: Community; Theatrical Group
Status: Semi-Professional; Non-Profit; Commercial
Type: Performing; Sponsoring
Purpose: To present a five-production season of plays with a variety of drama and comedy
Officers: Michael Hughes, President; Michelle Serries, Vice President; Richard Thompson, Treasurer; Gail Medland
Roberts, Secretary
Volunteer Staff: 50
Non-Paid Artists: 30
Utilizes: Guest Artists; Guest Directors
Budget: $1,000 - $50,000
Income Sources: Private Foundations/Grants/Endowments; Business/Corporate Donations; Box Office; Government
Grants; Individual Donations
Season: 52 Weeks   **Annual Attendance:** 6,000

PERFORMING SERIES

COLORADO COUNCIL ON THE ARTS
750 Pennsylvania Street, Denver, CO 80203-3699
(303) 894-2617
FAX: (303) 894-2615
Founded: 1967
Arts Area: Dance; Vocal Music; Instrumental Music; Theater; Festivals; Lyric Opera; Grand Opera
Status: Professional; Non-Profit; State Agency
Type: Sponsoring; Grant Making
Purpose: To stimulate arts development in the state; to assist and encourage artists and arts organizations
Management: Barbara Neal, Executive Director; Jim Thompson, Program Director Arts Organizations; Maryo Ewell, Pro-
gram Director, Community Programs; Daniel Salazar, Program Director, Individual Artists
Officers: Jerry Wartgow, Chair
Paid Staff: 12

Budget: $1,000,000 - $5,000,000
Income Sources: Government Grants
Affiliations: NEA; WSAF; NALAA

FACILITY

AUDITORIUM THEATER - DENVER PERFORMING ARTS COMPLEX
950 13th Street, Denver, CO 80204
(303) 640-2862
FAX: (303) 640-2397
   Founded: 1908
   Type of Facility: Theatre House
   Type of Stage: Proscenium
   Stage Dimensions: 107'Wx48"D; 58'W proscenium opening
   Orchestra Pit
   Seating Capacity: 2,089
   Year Built: 1908   **Architect:** Robert L. Willison   **Cost:** $590,000
   Year Remodeled: 1950   **Architect:** Musik & Musik   **Cost:** $2,000,000
   Contact for Rental Bobbie McFarland, Drew Armstrong;   (303) 640-2862
   Manager: James P. Thompson, Manager;   (303) 640-2862
   Resident Groups: Colorado Contemporary Dance; Colorado Ballet; Robert Garner/Center Attractions

BOETTCHER CONCERT HALL - DENVER PERFORMING ARTS COMPLEX
950 13th Street, Denver, CO 80204
(303) 640-2862
FAX: (303) 640-2397
   Founded: 1978
   Type of Facility: Concert Hall; Opera House
   Type of Stage: In-the-round Capability
   Stage Dimensions: 75'Wx50'D
   Orchestra Pit
   Seating Capacity: 2,629
   Year Built: 1978   **Architect:** Hardy Holtzman Pfieffer   **Cost:** $13,000,000
   Acoustical Consultant: Christopher Jaffe Associates
   Contact for Rental Bobbie McFarland, Drew Armstrong;   (303) 640-2637
   Manager: James P. Thompson;   (303) 640-2862
   Resident Groups: Colorado Symphony Orchestra; Opera Colorado

CHANGING SCENE THEATER
1527 1/2 Champa Street, Denver, CO 80202
(303) 893-5775
   Type of Facility: Off Broadway; Loft
   Facility Originally: Meeting Hall; Movie House
   Type of Stage: Flexible
   Stage Dimensions: 30'x24'
   Seating Capacity: 76
   Year Built: 1900
   Year Remodeled: 1968   **Architect:** John Lucas   **Cost:** $10,000
   Acoustical Consultant: Wesley Wada

DENVER AUDITORIUM - ARENA
1323 Champa Street, Denver, CO 80204
(303) 575-2637
   Type of Facility: Auditorium; Civic Center; Arena; Multi-Purpose
   Type of Stage: Arena
   Stage Dimensions: 20,000 square feet of usable floor area
   Seating Capacity: 7,000
   Year Built: 1952   **Architect:** G. Meredith Musick   **Cost:** $1,200,000
   Contact for Rental Bobbi Niles or Gary Lane;   (303) 575-2637

DENVER AUDITORIUM - CURRIGAN EXHIBITION HALL
1324 Champa Street, Denver, CO 80204
(303) 640-3856
   Type of Facility: Multi-Purpose; Exhibition Hall
   Seating Capacity: 14000
   Year Built: 1969   **Cost:** $7,500,000
   Contact for Rental Bobbi Niles or Gary Lane
   100,800 square feet of space, new hall planned with 300,000 square feet

DENVER AUDITORIUM - MCNICHOLS SPORTS ARENA
1635 Bryant Street, Denver, CO 80204
(303) 572-4700
FAX: (303) 572-4709
  Founded: 1975
  Type of Facility: Arena
  Type of Stage: Arena
  Seating Capacity: 19,000
  Year Built: 1975 **Architect:** Sink-Combs **Cost:** $10,000,000
  Contact for Rental Bobbie McFarland or Gary Lane; (303) 575-2637
  Arena has 20,000 square feet of usable floor area.

DENVER AUDITORIUM - THEATRE
14th and Curtis, Denver, CO 80204
(303) 575-2637
  Type of Facility: Auditorium; Performance Center; Civic Center
  Type of Stage: Proscenium
  Stage Dimensions: 58'x44'
  Seating Capacity: 2,100
  Year Built: 1905 **Architect:** Robert Willison **Cost:** $545,000
  Year Remodeled: 1955 **Architect:** G. Meredith Musick
  Contact for Rental Bobbi Niles or Gary Lane; (303) 575-2637

DENVER COLISEUM
4600 Humboldt Street, Denver, CO 80216
(303) 575-2637
  Founded: 1951
  Type of Facility: Arena
  Type of Stage: Arena
  Seating Capacity: 11,500
  Year Built: 1951 **Cost:** $3,000,000
  Acoustical Consultant: David Adams & Associates
  Contact for Rental Bobbi Niles or Drew Armstrong; (303) 640-2637
  Manager: Bud Quinn; (303) 295-4444
  Coliseum has 25,000 square feet of usable floor area.

DENVER PERFORMING ARTS COMPLEX - BUELL THEATRE
950 13th Street, Denver, CO 80204
(303) 640-2862
FAX: (303) 640-2397
  Type of Facility: Theatre House; Exhibition Hall
  Facility Originally: Arena
  Type of Stage: Flexible; Proscenium
  Stage Dimensions: 115'Wx52'D; 67'-50'Wx41'-30'H proscenium opening **Orchestra Pit**
  Seating Capacity: 2,830
  Year Built: 1991 **Architect:** Van Dijk Johnson - Beyer Blinder Belle **Cost:** $27,500,000
  Acoustical Consultant: Kirkkegaard and Associates
  Contact for Rental Bobbi McFarland, Drew Armstrong; (303) 640-2637
  Manager: James P. Thompson; (303) 640-2862
  Resident Groups: Robert Garner/Center Attractions; Colorado Ballet; Colorado Symphony; Opera Colorado

GERMINAL STAGE DENVER
2450 West 44th Avenue, Denver, CO 80211
(303) 455-7108
  Type of Facility: Theatre House
  Facility Originally: Business Facility
  Type of Stage: 3/4 Arena
  Stage Dimensions: 20'x15'
  Seating Capacity: 100
  Year Built: 1925
  Year Remodeled: 1987 **Architect:** Ron Rinker **Cost:** $60,000
  Resident Groups: Germinal Stage Denver

HOUSTON FINE ARTS CENTER
7111 Montview Boulevard, Denver, CO 80220
(303) 871-6404
FAX: (303) 871-6411
  Type of Facility: Concert Hall; Auditorium; Arena

Facility Originally: School
Type of Stage: Proscenium
Stage Dimensions: 38'x32'
Orchestra Pit
Seating Capacity: 690
Year Built: 1967
Contact for Rental: (303) 871-6873

MAY BONFILS STANTON CENTER FOR THE PERFORMING ARTS
3001 South Federal Boulevard, Denver, CO 80110
(303) 936-8441
Type of Facility: Performance Center
Year Built: 1890
Contact for Rental Rich Harris;   (303) 936-8441
The Center, whose original structure was built in 1890, consists of Little Auditorium, Proscenium Theatre and Stage 2. Additions and remodelings have occurred in 1963 and 1984. See separate listings for additional information.

MAY BONFILS STANTON CENTER FOR THE PERFORMING ARTS - LITTLE AUDITORIUM
3001 South Federal Boulevard, Denver, CO 80110
(303) 936-8441
Type of Facility: Auditorium
Type of Stage: Platform
Seating Capacity: 400
Year Built: 1890
Contact for Rental Rich Harris;   (303) 936-8441

MAY BONFILS STANTON CENTER FOR THE PERFORMING ARTS - PROSCENIUM THEATRE
3001 South Federal Boulevard, Denver, CO 80110
(303) 936-8441
Type of Facility: Theatre House
Type of Stage: Proscenium
Stage Dimensions: 60'Wx40'D
Orchestra Pit
Seating Capacity: 999
Year Built: 1963
Contact for Rental Rich Harris;   (303) 936-8441

MAY BONFILS STANTON CENTER FOR THE PERFORMING ARTS - STAGE 2
3001 South Federal Boulevard, Denver, CO 80110
(303) 936-8441
Type of Facility: Theatre House; Black Box
Type of Stage: Flexible
Stage Dimensions: 48'x60'
Seating Capacity: 180
Year Built: 1984
Contact for Rental Rich Harris;   (303) 936-8441

RED ROCKS AMPHITHEATRE - MORRISON COLORADO
c/o 1380 Lawrence Street, Suite 790, Denver, CO 80204
(303) 640-2637
Type of Facility: Outdoor (Concert); Amphitheater
Type of Stage: Greek
Stage Dimensions: 60'x40' concrete slab
Seating Capacity: 9,000
Year Built: 1941   **Architect:** Burnham Hoyt   **Cost:** $175,000
Year Remodeled: 1958
Contact for Rental Bibbi McFarland or Drew Armstrong;   (303) 640-2637
This 1941 CCC Project turned a small valley into an amphitheater.

VICTORIAN THEATRE
4201 Hooker Street, Denver, CO 80211
(303) 433-4343
Founded: 1911
Type of Facility: Theatre House
Type of Stage: Thrust; Proscenium
Stage Dimensions: 20'Wx16'D
Seating Capacity: 99
Year Built: 1911   **Architect:** George Swartz

Contact for Rental: (303) 433-4343
Manager: Pamela Clifton
Presentation of one-set dramas

Durango

VOCAL MUSIC

DURANGO CHORAL SOCIETY
780 Main Avenue, Suite 214, Durango, CO 81301
(303) 259-3457
> **Founded:** 1961
> **Arts Area:** Choral
> **Status:** Semi-Professional
> **Type:** Performing; Touring; Resident; Educational; Sponsoring
> **Purpose:** DCS exists for the purpose of providing quality choral and orchestral music for the audience and performers of the four-corners region.
> **Management:** Diane Vandenberg, Executive Director/Music Director
> **Officers:** Steven C. Harris, President; Sally Morrissey, Secretary
> **Paid Staff:** 3
> **Non-Paid Artists:** 45
> **Utilizes:** Special Technical Talent; Guest Artists
> **Budget:** $1,000 - $50,000
> **Income Sources:** Private Foundations/Grants/Endowments; Business/Corporate Donations; Box Office; Government Grants; Individual Donations
> **Season:** 52 Weeks   **Annual Attendance:** 3,200
> **Affiliations:** American Choral Directors Association

PERFORMING SERIES

MUSIC IN THE MOUNTAINS, FESTIVAL OF MUSIC AT PURGATORY
PO Box 2082, Durango, CO 81302
(303) 247-9000, ext. 3030
FAX: (303) 385-2107
> **Founded:** 1986
> **Arts Area:** Instrumental Music; Festivals
> **Status:** Professional; Non-Profit
> **Type:** Performing; Educational
> **Purpose:** To provide live classical music of the highest quality to the Four Corners of Colorado, New Mexico, Utah and Arizona
> **Management:** Misha Semanitzky, Music Director; Georg Ann Beauparlant, Festival Coordinator
> **Officers:** Mary Jane Clark, President
> **Paid Staff:** 5   **Volunteer Staff:** 20
> **Paid Artists:** 40
> **Budget:** $100,000 - $500,000
> **Income Sources:** Private Foundations/Grants/Endowments; Business/Corporate Donations; Box Office; Government Grants; Individual Donations
> **Season:** July - August   **Annual Attendance:** 3,000

Englewood

VOCAL MUSIC

CHERRY CREEK CHORALE
c/o 10093 East Weaver Avenue, Englewood, CO 80111
(303) 694-9587
> **Founded:** 1980
> **Arts Area:** Choral
> **Status:** Non-Profit
> **Type:** Performing
> **Purpose:** To provide adults an opportunity to perform varied choral literature; to increase their knowledge and skill
> **Management:** Richard Larson, Executive Director
> **Officers:** Richard Krening, President; John Arenson, Vice President; Lorraine Cooper, Secretary; Elaine Gilley, Treasurer
> **Paid Staff:** 2   **Volunteer Staff:** 60
> **Utilizes:** Special Technical Talent
> **Budget:** $1,000 - $50,000

Income Sources: Private Foundations/Grants/Endowments; Business/Corporate Donations; Box Office; Government Grants; Individual Donations
Season: September - June **Annual Attendance:** 1,500
Affiliations: Colorado Arts; Metro Denver Arts Alliance

THEATRE

COUNTRY DINNER PLAYHOUSE
6875 South Clinton, Englewood, CO 80112
(303) 790-9311
FAX: (303) 790-2615
Founded: 1970
Arts Area: Professional; Musical; Dinner
Status: Professional
Type: Performing
Management: Bill McHale, Executive Producer/Director
Paid Staff: 24
Paid Artists: 20
Utilizes: Special Technical Talent
Budget: $100,000 - $500,000
Income Sources: Box Office
Season: 52 Weeks

Estes Park

PERFORMING SERIES

ROCKY RIDGE MUSIC CENTER
465 Long's Peak Route, Estes Park, CO 80517
Winter Address: PO Box 81727, Lincoln, NE 68501-1727; (402) 486-4363
Founded: 1942
Arts Area: Instrumental Music; Festivals
Status: Non-Profit
Type: Performing; Educational
Purpose: To offer summer programs of conservatory-level music training for young people, with emphasis on Youth Orchestra, young pianists, chamber music and composition; to offer this program simultaneously with the summer concert series "Music in the Mountains"
Management: Patrick B. Gaines, Executive Director; Jack J. Rinke, Executive Secretary; Gregory Dubinsky, Music in the Mountains Coordinator
Officers: Beth Miller Harrod, Founder/Musical Director; Dr. John Hajdu Heyer, President; Miriam Reitz Baer, Vice President; F.M. Tuttle, Treasurer
Paid Staff: 7 **Volunteer Staff:** 3
Paid Artists: 23 **Non-Paid Artists:** 4
Utilizes: Guest Artists; Guest Conductors
Budget: $50,000 - $100,000
Income Sources: Private Foundations/Grants/Endowments; Box Office; Individual Donations
Season: June - August **Annual Attendance:** 730

Evergreen

FACILITY

CENTER STAGE AT EVERGREEN
27608 Fireweed Drive, Evergreen, CO 80439
(303) 674-4002
Founded: 1990
Type of Facility: Concert Hall; Auditorium; Performance Center; Theatre House; Opera House; Multi-Purpose
Facility Originally: Church; Meeting Hall
Type of Stage: Thrust; Proscenium
Stage Dimensions: 24'x30'
Seating Capacity: 200
Year Built: 1924
Year Remodeled: 1992 **Architect:** Jack Dysart, AIA **Cost:** $100,000
Contact for Rental Marcia Phelps; (303) 674-4002
Resident Groups: Evergreen Chorale, Inc.

Fort Collins

DANCE

THE DANCE CONNECTION
PO Box 2014, Fort Collins, CO 80522
(303) 484-6518
Founded: 1980
Arts Area: Modern
Status: Professional; Non-Profit
Type: Performing; Touring; Educational
Purpose: To communicate the energy and excitement of contemporary dance through quality performances
Management: Linda Green, Business Manager; Eleanor Van Dusen, Sharon Wilson, Co-Artistic Directors
Officers: Roslyn Ruppert, President Board of Directors
Paid Staff: 2   **Volunteer Staff:** 1
Paid Artists: 4
Utilizes: Special Technical Talent; Guest Artists; Guest Choreographers
Budget: $1,000 - $50,000
Income Sources: Private Foundations/Grants/Endowments; Business/Corporate Donations; Box Office; Government Grants; Individual Donations
Season: October - August   **Annual Attendance:** 4,000
Performance Facilities: Lincoln Center

INSTRUMENTAL MUSIC

FORT COLLINS SYMPHONY ORCHESTRA
PO Box 1963, Fort Collins, CO 80522
(303) 482-4823
FAX: (303) 482-4858
Founded: 1949
Arts Area: Symphony; Orchestra
Status: Non-Profit
Type: Performing; Educational
Purpose: To further serious music appreciation and general cultural growth in this and neighboring communities
Management: Michael Klesert, General Manager; Merrilee Pouliot, Office Manager; Willfred Schwarz, Conductor
Officers: Kathryn Quan, President; John Clark Pratt, Vice President; Alvin J. Kruckten, Treasurer; Frank Johnson Jr., Secretary
Paid Staff: 4
Paid Artists: 85
Utilizes: Guest Conductors; Guest Artists
Budget: $100,000 - $500,000
Income Sources: Private Foundations/Grants/Endowments; Business/Corporate Donations; Box Office; Government Grants; Individual Donations
Season: September - July   **Annual Attendance:** 20,000
Affiliations: ASOL; Fort Collins Chamber of Commerce
Performance Facilities: Lincoln Center

VOCAL MUSIC

THE LARIMER CHORAL SOCIETY
PO Box 884, Fort Collins, CO 80522
(303) 223-2059
Founded: 1978
Arts Area: Choral; Ethnic; Folk; Musicals
Status: Non-Profit
Type: Performing; Resident; Educational
Purpose: To perform the great choral music of the world and to educate the community about choral music
Paid Staff: 3   **Volunteer Staff:** 10
Paid Artists: 10
Utilizes: Guest Artists
Budget: $100,000 - $500,000
Income Sources: Private Foundations/Grants/Endowments; Business/Corporate Donations; Box Office; Individual Donations
Season: August - April   **Annual Attendance:** 2,100
Performance Facilities: Lincoln Center

THEATRE

OPENSTAGE THEATRE AND COMPANY, INC.
PO Box 617, 201 South College Avenue, Fort Collins, CO 80522
(303) 484-5237
Founded: 1973
Arts Area: Theatrical Group
Status: Semi-Professional; Non-Profit
Type: Performing
Management: Bruce K. Freestone, Executive Producer; Peter Anthony, Artistic Director; Lisa Rosenhagen, Office Manager
Officers: Mollie Smilie, Chair; Joannah Lyn Merriman, Vice Chair; Neil Petrie, Treasurer; Toni Farquhar, Secretary
Paid Staff: 3
Paid Artists: 60 **Non-Paid Artists:** 25
Utilizes: Special Technical Talent
Budget: $100,000 - $500,000
Income Sources: Business/Corporate Donations; Box Office; Government Grants; Individual Donations
Season: September - June **Annual Attendance:** 10,000
Affiliations: AACT; Colorado Theatre Producers Guild; Fort Collins Convention and Visitors Bureau; Fort Collins Chamber of Commerce
Performance Facilities: Lincoln Center Mini-Theatre

PERFORMING SERIES

COLORADO STATE UNIVERSITY - OFFICE OF CULTURAL PROGRAMS
Lory Student Center, Fort Collins, CO 80523
(303) 491-6626
FAX: (303) 491-6423
Founded: 1962
Arts Area: Dance; Vocal Music; Instrumental Music; Theater
Status: Non-Profit
Type: Educational; Sponsoring
Purpose: To coordinate the cultural programs for Colorado State University
Management: Mims Harris, Associate Director, Programs; Barb Kistler, Assistant Director, Programs; David Laughlin, Technical Coordinator
Paid Staff: 4 **Volunteer Staff:** 4
Utilizes: Guest Artists
Budget: $50,000 - $100,000
Income Sources: Private Foundations/Grants/Endowments; Box Office
Season: September - May **Annual Attendance:** 2,000
Affiliations: WSAF; NACA; ACU-I; APAP; WAAA;
Performance Facilities: 670 Theatre

FACILITY

COLORADO STATE UNIVERSITY - UNIVERSITY THEATRE
Fort Collins, CO 80523
(303) 491-5116
Type of Facility: Environmental; Theatre House
Facility Originally: Ballroom; University Student Center
Type of Stage: Proscenium; Environmental
Stage Dimensions: 35'x37'with 14' forestage
Seating Capacity: 320
Year Built: 1937
Year Remodeled: 1964

LINCOLN CENTER
417 West Magnolia, Fort Collins, CO 80521
(303) 221-6735
FAX: (303) 484-0424
Type of Facility: Theatre Complex; Concert Hall; Civic Center; Multi-Purpose
Type of Stage: Thrust; Proscenium
Stage Dimensions: 40'x60'
Orchestra Pit
Seating Capacity: 1180
Year Built: 1978 **Architect:** Stearns-Rogers **Cost:** $3,000,000
Acoustical Consultant: Jaffe Acoustics
Contact for Rental David Siever, Director; (303) 221-6733

Resident Groups: Larimer Chorale; Fort Collins Symphony; Openstage Theatre; Fort Collins Civic Theatre
The original structure, a school facility built prior to 1978, became Lincoln Center with new construction and renovations that were completed in 1978.

Golden

INSTRUMENTAL MUSIC

JEFFERSON SYMPHONY ORCHESTRA
1204 1/2 Washington Avenue, Golden, CO 80401
(303) 278-4237
> **Founded:** 1953
> **Arts Area:** Symphony; Orchestra; Ensemble
> **Status:** Semi-Professional; Non-Profit
> **Type:** Performing
> **Purpose:** To provide performing opportunities for serious musicians; to provide good symphonic music; to maintain a position which educates the public of all ages to the pleasure of classical and light classical music
> **Management:** M. Liane McHardy, Office Manager; Eileen Billings, Bookkeeper; Julie Stolt, Fundraiser; Glen DiConstanza, Stage Manager; Jackie Shaffer, Orchestra Personnel Manager; T. Gordon Parks, Music Director/Conductor
> **Officers:** Jack Galland, President; Rod Johnson, Vice President Finance; Helen Leith, Vice President Activities; Joan Havercroft, Vice President Performance; Jean Olhoeft, Secretary; Eileen Beaudrie, Treasurer; Doris McGowan, Vice President Marketing
> **Paid Staff:** 6   **Volunteer Staff:** 50
> **Paid Artists:** 10   **Non-Paid Artists:** 60
> **Utilizes:** Special Technical Talent; Guest Conductors; Guest Artists
> **Budget:** $100,000 - $500,000
> **Income Sources:** Private Foundations/Grants/Endowments; Business/Corporate Donations; Box Office; Government Grants; Individual Donations
> **Season:** October - May   **Annual Attendance:** 8,000
> **Affiliations:** Chamber of Commerces
> **Performance Facilities:** Green Centre, Colorado School of Mines

THEATRE

HERITAGE SQUARE MUSIC HALL
5 Heritage Square, Golden, CO 80401
(303) 279-7800
> **Arts Area:** Professional; Musical; Dinner
> **Status:** Professional; Commercial
> **Type:** Performing; Resident
> **Management:** C.J. Helsley, President; T.J. Mullin, Vice President
> **Paid Staff:** 100
> **Paid Artists:** 15
> **Income Sources:** Box Office
> **Season:** Feburary - December

Grand Junction

INSTRUMENTAL MUSIC

GRAND JUNCTION MUSICAL ARTS ASSOCIATION
130 North Fourth Street, #100, Grand Junction, CO 81501
(303) 243-6787
> **Founded:** 1977
> **Arts Area:** Symphony; Orchestra; Band
> **Status:** Non-Profit
> **Type:** Performing; Touring; Educational; Sponsoring
> **Purpose:** To bring quality classical music to western Colorado
> **Management:** Naomi Shepherd, Manager; Kirk Gustafson, Music Director
> **Officers:** Gudrun Rice, President; John Halvorson, First Vice President; Jack Roberts, Second Vice President; Charles Jones, Secretary; Linda Tice, Treasurer
> **Paid Staff:** 4
> **Paid Artists:** 68
> **Utilizes:** Guest Artists
> **Budget:** $100,000 - $500,000
> **Income Sources:** Private Foundations/Grants/Endowments; Business/Corporate Donations; Box Office; Individual Donations

Season: September - May   **Annual Attendance:** 13,500
Performance Facilities: Grand Junction High School Auditorium

FACILITY

MESA COLLEGE - WALTER WALKER AUDITORIUM
PO Box 2647, Grand Junction, CO 81502
(303) 248-1504
  Type of Facility: Auditorium
  Type of Stage: Thrust
  Orchestra Pit
  Seating Capacity: 469, (627 with loges)
  Year Built: 1969   **Architect:** Van Deusen   **Cost:** $800,000
  Contact for Rental Lorene Sanford, Building Coordinator;   (303) 248-1788
  Resident Groups: Mesa College Music Choir; Chamber Choir; Concert Band; Jazz Combos; Mesa College Theatre Department; Mesa College Dance Repertory

Greeley

VOCAL MUSIC

THE GREELEY CHORALE
PO Box 5098, Greeley, CO 80621
(303) 330-1769
  Founded: 1964
  Arts Area: Operetta; Choral; Ethnic; Folk
  Status: Non-Professional; Non-Profit
  Type: Performing; Educational; Sponsoring
  Purpose: To present a variety of quality choral music for public performance
  Management: Bill Howe, Administrator; Carl Gerbrandt, Conductor
  Officers: Ken Whitney, President; Stan Peek, Secretary; Sue Varrel, Vice President; Jerry Crews, Treasurer
  Paid Staff: 4
  Utilizes: Guest Artists
  Budget: $50,000 - $100,000
  Income Sources: Private Foundations/Grants/Endowments; Business/Corporate Donations; Box Office; Government Grants; Individual Donations
  Season: September - May   **Annual Attendance:** 3,000
  Performance Facilities: Union Colony Civic Center

THEATRE

ALBUNDEGUS ALL-STARS
709 13th Street, Greeley, CO 80631
  Founded: 1989
  Arts Area: Theatrical Group
  Status: Non-Profit
  Type: Performing; Workshops; Readings
  Purpose: To develop new and original work, expecially works by Colorado playwrights
  Management: Michael Baczuk, Artistic Director; David Keyon, Associate Director; Christopher Caldwell, Treasurer
  Volunteer Staff: 3
  Utilizes: Community Talent
  Budget: $1,000 - $50,000
  Income Sources: Box Office; Individual Donations
  Season: September - May
  Performance Facilities: Evans City Hall Auditorium

FACILITY

UNION COLONY CIVIC CENTER
701 Tenth Avenue, Greeley, CO 80631
(303) 350-9450
FAX: (303) 350-9475
  Founded: 1988
  Type of Facility: Concert Hall; Auditorium; Performance Center; Civic Center
  Type of Stage: Proscenium
  Stage Dimensions: 50'x60'   **Orchestra Pit**
  Seating Capacity: 1,667; 220
  Year Built: 1988   **Architect:** ARIX - Bob Shreve   **Cost:** $9,200,000

Acoustical Consultant: Dave Adams & Associates
Contact for Rental: Joyce Jasurda;   (303) 350-9449

UNIVERSITY OF NORTHERN COLORADO - HELEN LANGWORTHY THEATRE
Frazier Hall, Greeley, CO 80639
(303) 351-2454
FAX: (303) 351-1923
Type of Facility: Theatre House
Type of Stage: Proscenium
Stage Dimensions: 62'Wx32"D   **Orchestra Pit**
Seating Capacity: 614
Year Built: 1954   **Architect:** F.W. Ireland   **Cost:** $140,000
Year Remodeled: 1987
Acoustical Consultant: Mead and Mount
Contact for Rental Bill VanLoo;   (303) 351-2454
Resident Groups: Little Theatre of the Rockies; UNC Opera Theatre; UNC Dance Theatre; UNC Performing Arts

La Junta

THEATRE

PICKETWIRE PLAYERS
Eighth and San Juan, La Junta, CO 81050
(719) 384-8320
Founded: 1968
Arts Area: Community; Theatrical Group
Status: Non-Professional; Non-Profit
Type: Performing
Purpose: To provide a good theatre showcase for regional talent in Southeastern Colorado
Management: Board of Directors
Officers: Todd Hilstad, President; Rebecca Goodwin, Vice President; Deanna Brown, Secretary; Lindy Nelson, Treasurer
Volunteer Staff: 9
Utilizes: Guest Conductors; Guest Artists; Guest Directors
Budget: $1,000 - $50,000
Income Sources: Box Office; Individual Donations
Season: October - July   **Annual Attendance:** 3,600
Affiliations: La Junta Chamber of Commerce; Colorado Community Theater Coalition
Performance Facilities: Picketwire Center for the Performing and Visual Arts

FACILITY

OTERO JUNIOR COLLEGE - HUMANITIES CENTER THEATRE
1802 Colorado, La Junta, CO 81050
(719) 384-6870
Type of Facility: Performance Center
Type of Stage: Proscenium
Stage Dimensions: 18'x40'x36'   **Orchestra Pit**
Seating Capacity: 518
Year Built: 1971   **Architect:** Joseph Wilson
Contact for Rental Ed Stafford;   (719) 384-6870
Resident Groups: Otero Players

PICKETWIRE PLAYERS AND COMMUNITY THEATRE
802 San Juan, La Junta, CO 81050
(719) 384-8320
Type of Facility: Theatre House
Facility Originally: School
Type of Stage: Thrust
Stage Dimensions: 25'x30'   **Orchestra Pit**
Seating Capacity: 400
Year Built: 1934
Year Remodeled: 1976   **Cost:** $84,000
Contact for Rental John Spencer, President
Resident Groups: Picketwire Players

Littleton

DANCE

DAVID TAYLOR DANCE THEATRE
2539 West Main Street, Littleton, CO 80210
(303) 797-6944
Founded: 1980
Arts Area: Modern; Ballet
Status: Professional; Non-Profit
Type: Performing; Touring; Resident; Educational
Purpose: Professional performing contemporary ballet company and school
Management: Gary Lindsey, Artist Services
Officers: Art Binkley, Chairman of Board; Dan Winter, Vice Chairman
Paid Staff: 13 **Volunteer Staff:** 100
Paid Artists: 15 **Non-Paid Artists:** 25
Utilizes: Special Technical Talent; Guest Artists; Guest Choreographers
Budget: $100,000 - $500,000
Income Sources: Private Foundations/Grants/Endowments; Business/Corporate Donations; Box Office; Government Grants; Individual Donations
Season: 52 Weeks
Annual Attendance: 30,000

Longmont

FACILITY

DICKENS OPERA HOUSE
302 Main Street, Longmont, CO 80501
(303) 772-5167
Type of Facility: Studio Performance; Performance Center; Opera House; Multi-Purpose; Room
Type of Stage: Thrust; Proscenium
Stage Dimensions: 44'Wx16'D, thrust 23'6"Wx9'9"D
Seating Capacity: Theater style - 283; Cabaret style - 184
Year Built: 1881 **Architect:** William Dickens
Year Remodeled: 1986 **Architect:** Roger Burton **Cost:** $500,000
Contact for Rental Dickens Opera House Association; (303) 772-5167

Pueblo

DANCE

PUEBLO BALLET
431 East Pitkin, Pueblo, CO 81004
(719) 543-7362
Founded: 1974
Arts Area: Ballet
Status: Non-Profit
Type: Performing; Touring; Educational
Purpose: To provide high-quality performance and dance education for Pueblo and southern Colorado
Management: Sharon Conders, Executive Director
Officers: Phyllis Crawford, President; Mary Swearinger, Secretary; Darryl Gurule, Treasurer
Paid Staff: 6 **Volunteer Staff:** 100
Paid Artists: 6 **Non-Paid Artists:** 10
Utilizes: Special Technical Talent; Guest Artists
Budget: $50,000 - $100,000
Income Sources: Private Foundations/Grants/Endowments; Business/Corporate Donations; Box Office; Government Grants; Individual Donations
Season: 52 Weeks **Annual Attendance:** 5,000
Affiliations: NARB; Colorado Dance Alliance
Performance Facilities: Memorial Hall; Sangre de Cristo Arts and Conference Center

INSTRUMENTAL MUSIC

PUEBLO SYMPHONY ORCHESTRA
503 Noth Main, Thatcher Building, Suite 414, Pueblo, CO 81003
(719) 546-0333
Founded: 1966
Arts Area: Orchestra
Status: Non-Profit
Type: Performing
Management: Tom Christner, Executive Director; Jacob Chi, Musical Director/Conductor
Officers: Richard Moran, President/Executive Board
Paid Staff: 5 **Volunteer Staff:** 4
Paid Artists: 70
Utilizes: Guest Conductors; Guest Artists
Budget: $100,000 - $500,000
Income Sources: Private Foundations/Grants/Endowments; Business/Corporate Donations; Box Office; Individual Donations; Fund-raising
Season: September - May
Affiliations: ASOL
Performance Facilities: Memorial Hall; Hoag Hall, University of Southern Colorado

THEATRE

BROADWAY THEATRE LEAGUE OF PUEBLO
PO Box 3145, Pueblo, CO 81005
(719) 545-4721
FAX: (719) 543-0134
Founded: 1960
Arts Area: Professional
Status: Professional; Non-Profit
Type: Performing; Touring; Sponsoring
Purpose: To bring to the community the opportunity to see professional theatre
Management: Maggie Divelbiss, Manager; David Zupancic, Assistant Manager; Susan Velasco, Administrative Assistant; Cheryl Califano, Box Office Manager
Paid Staff: 2 **Volunteer Staff:** 20
Utilizes: Special Technical Talent
Budget: $100,000 - $500,000
Income Sources: Private Foundations/Grants/Endowments; Business/Corporate Donations; Box Office; Individual Donations
Season: 52 Weeks **Annual Attendance:** 4,500
Performance Facilities: Pueblo Memorial Hall

THE IMPOSSIBLE PLAYERS
PO Box 1005, Pueblo, CO 81002
(719) 542-6969
Founded: 1966
Arts Area: Community; Theatrical Group
Status: Non-Professional; Non-Profit
Type: Performing; Resident; Educational
Purpose: To promote the enjoyment of the performing arts by the public; to further the education of both members and the public in the skills of those arts; to give people an opportunity to perform for the public
Officers: Marlene Schmidt, President; Bill Mattoon, Vice President; Carol Martin, Secretary; Don Warren, Treasurer
Paid Staff: 1
Budget: $1,000 - $50,000
Income Sources: Private Foundations/Grants/Endowments; Business/Corporate Donations; Box Office; Individual Donations
Season: October - April **Annual Attendance:** 28,000
Performance Facilities: Public Community College - The Hoag Theater

PERFORMING SERIES

SANGRE DE CRISTO ARTS AND CONFERENCE CENTER
210 North Santa Fe Avenue, Pueblo, CO 81003
(719) 543-0130
Founded: 1972
Arts Area: Dance; Vocal Music; Instrumental Music; Theater; Festivals; Lyric Opera
Status: Professional; Non-Profit
Type: Performing; Touring; Resident; Educational; Sponsoring

Purpose: To foster and promote the performing and visual arts in a nineteen-county region of southeastern Colorado
Management: Maggie Divelbiss, Director; David Zupancic, Associate Director; Timothy F. Gately, Technical Director
Officers: Assege Abebe, Chairman, Board of Trustees; Keith Lovin, Vice Chairman; Lalonna Meoska, Secretary; Charles Ready, Treasurer
Paid Staff: 50   **Volunteer Staff:** 80
Paid Artists: 10   **Non-Paid Artists:** 75
Utilizes: Special Technical Talent; Guest Artists
Budget: $500,000 - $1,000,000
Income Sources: Private Foundations/Grants/Endowments; Business/Corporate Donations; Box Office; Government Grants; Individual Donations
Season: 52 Weeks   **Annual Attendance:** 250,000
Affiliations: APAP; WAAA; Rocky Mountain Theatre Guild
Performance Facilities: Sangre de Cristo Arts and Conference Center

FACILITY

SANGRE DE CRISTO ARTS AND CONFERENCE CENTER
210 North Santa Fe Avenue, Pueblo, CO 81003
(719) 543-0130
FAX: (719) 543-0134
Founded: 1972
Type of Facility: Arts Center
Type of Stage: Thrust
Orchestra Pit
Seating Capacity: 500
Year Built: 1972   **Architect:** Hurtig, Gardner, Froelich   **Cost:** $1,300,000
Contact for Rental Jeff Giadone;   (719) 543-0130
Resident Groups: Danspectra; Southern Colorado Repertory Theatre (SCRT)

Steamboat Springs

PERFORMING SERIES

STRINGS IN THE MOUNTAINS
PO Box 774627, Steamboat Springs, CO 80477
(303) 879-5056
FAX: (303) 879-5057
Founded: 1988
Arts Area: Vocal Music; Instrumental Music; Festivals
Status: Professional; Non-Profit
Type: Performing
Purpose: To present the finest chamber possible in the inspirational setting of Steamboat Springs
Management: John Sant'Ambrogio, Music Director; Belse Grassby, Executive Director; Kay Clagett, Development Director
Officers: Art Smith, Chairman; Candyce Wither, Treasurer
Paid Staff: 4   **Volunteer Staff:** 25
Paid Artists: 63
Utilizes: Guest Conductors; Guest Artists
Budget: $100,000 - $500,000
Income Sources: Private Foundations/Grants/Endowments; Business/Corporate Donations; Box Office; Government Grants; Individual Donations
Season: July - August   **Annual Attendance:** 10,000
Affiliations: ASOL; CMA

Sterling

FACILITY

NORTHEASTERN JUNIOR COLLEGE THEATRE
Northeastern Junior College, Sterling, CO 80751
(303) 522-6600, ext. 666
Type of Facility: Performance Center; Theatre House
Type of Stage: Proscenium; Black Box   **Orchestra Pit**
Seating Capacity: 566
Year Built: 1968   **Architect:** Murrin, Kasch, Konn   **Cost:** $1,000,000
Contact for Rental Dave Grams;   (303) 522-6600
Resident Groups: Northeastern Junior College Players

Telluride

PERFORMING SERIES

TELLURIDE JAZZ CELEBRATION
PO Box 279, Telluride, CO 81435
(303) 728-7009
Founded: 1975
Arts Area: Vocal Music; Instrumental Music; Festivals
Status: Professional; Non-Profit
Type: Sponsoring
Purpose: To keep the Telluride Jazz Festival alive
Management: Paul Machado, Producer/Executive Director
Paid Staff: 25   **Volunteer Staff:** 225
Paid Artists: 10
Utilizes: Special Technical Talent; Guest Artists
Budget: $100,000 - $500,000
Income Sources: Business/Corporate Donations; Box Office; Government Grants; Individual Donations
Season: July
Annual Attendance: 5,500
Performance Facilities: Sheridan Opera House; Telluride Town Park

FACILITY

SHERIDAN OPERA HOUSE
110 North Oak Street, PO Box 2680, Telluride, CO 81435
(303) 728-5182
FAX: (303) 728-6966
Type of Facility: Theatre House; Amphitheater; Civic Center
Type of Stage: Proscenium
Stage Dimensions: 28'Wx12'D; 20'W
Seating Capacity: 240
Year Built: 1914
Year Remodeled: 1985   **Architect:** Johnson-Nimmer   **Cost:** $450,000
Contact for Rental Steven Anderson;   (303) 784-6363
Manager: R.J. White
Resident Groups: Telluride Film Festival; Telluride Jazz Festival; Blue Grass Festival; Mountain Film; Telluride Chamber Music Ensemble; Telluride Institute; Telluride Council for Arts and Humanities
The Sheridan Opera House is on the National Register of Historic Places.

Vail

INSTRUMENTAL MUSIC

BRAVO! COLORADO MUSIC FESTIVAL AT VAIL-BEAVER CREEK
953 South Frontage Road, #104, Vail, CO 81657
(303) 476-0206
FAX: (303) 479-0559
Founded: 1988
Arts Area: Symphony; Orchestra; Chamber; Ethnic
Status: Professional
Type: Performing; Educational
Management: John W. Giovando, Executive Director; Ida Kavafian, Music Director
Paid Staff: 6   **Volunteer Staff:** 125
Paid Artists: 47
Utilizes: Guest Conductors; Guest Artists
Budget: $1,000,000 - $5,000,000
Income Sources: Private Foundations/Grants/Endowments; Business/Corporate Donations; Box Office; Government Grants; Individual Donations
Season: July - August   **Annual Attendance:** 17,100

Westminster

PERFORMING SERIES

WESTMINSTER COMMUNITY ARTIST SERIES
7380 Lowell Boulevard, Westminster, CO 80030
(303) 429-1999
Founded: 1983
Arts Area: Dance; Vocal Music; Instrumental Music; Grand Opera
Status: Non-Profit
Type: Performing
Purpose: To present the finest performing and visual artists from across the nation to Westminster Area audiences
Officers: JoAnne Groff, President; Jeanie Beck, Vice President; Diane Schmidt, Treasurer; William Christopher, Development Director; Wilbur Flachman, Chairman of the Board
Paid Staff: 2   **Volunteer Staff:** 15
Utilizes: Special Technical Talent; Guest Artists
Income Sources: Private Foundations/Grants/Endowments; Business/Corporate Donations; Box Office; Individual Donations
Season: January - December   **Annual Attendance:** 17,000

CONNECTICUT

Avon

VOCAL MUSIC

THE HARTFORD CHORALE, INC.
16 Bridgestone Lane, Avon, CT 06001
(203) 673-1341
Founded: 1971
Arts Area: Choral
Status: Non-Professional; Non-Profit
Type: Performing
Purpose: To reach the broadest possible audience with major choral-orchestral literature
Management: Henley Denmead, Music Director
Officers: Dougla Pyrke, President
Paid Staff: 2 **Volunteer Staff:** 14
Non-Paid Artists: 150
Utilizes: Guest Artists
Budget: $50,000 - $100,000
Income Sources: Private Foundations/Grants/Endowments; Business/Corporate Donations; Box Office; Government Grants; Individual Donations
Season: September - July **Annual Attendance:** 9,000
Performance Facilities: Horace Bushnell Memorial Hall

Bloomfield

INSTRUMENTAL MUSIC

HARTFORD JAZZ SOCIETY
116 Cottage Grove Road, Room 204, Bloomfield, CT 06002
(203) 242-6688
Founded: 1960
Arts Area: Jazz
Status: Professional
Type: Sponsoring
Purpose: To promote and keep alive jazz music in this area, we present seven to 11 concerts a year in Hartford, as well as offer community programs on jazz
Management: Betty Ector, President; Bill Sullivan, Program Director
Volunteer Staff: 20
Utilizes: Guest Artists
Budget: $50,000 - $100,000
Income Sources: Private Foundations/Grants/Endowments; Business/Corporate Donations; Box Office; Individual Donations
Season: 52 Weeks **Annual Attendance:** 2,000
Performance Facilities: Hartford Holiday Inn

Bridgeport

INSTRUMENTAL MUSIC

BRIDGEPORT CIVIC ORCHESTRA
Arnold Bernhard Center, University of Bridgeport, Bridgeport, CT 06602
(203) 576-4404
Founded: 1947
Arts Area: Symphony; Orchestra
Status: Non-Professional; Non-Profit
Type: Performing
Purpose: To perform fine orchestral music, bringing together the forces and talents of students, faculty and community members
Management: Daniel D'Addio, Conductor
Paid Staff: 1
Performance Facilities: Arnold Bernhard Center

GREATER BRIDGEPORT SYMPHONY
446 University Avenue, Bridgeport, CT 06604
(203) 576-0263
FAX: (203) 367-0064
Founded: 1945
Arts Area: Symphony; Orchestra; Chamber; Ensemble
Status: Professional; Non-Profit
Type: Performing; Educational
Purpose: To present symphonic and chamber music concerts as well as educational music programs
Management: Jena Maric, General Manager; Glenn Mortimer, Operations Manager
Officers: Nancy Johmann, President; Robert S. Tellalian, Chairman of the Board
Paid Staff: 5 **Volunteer Staff:** 50
Paid Artists: 80
Utilizes: Guest Conductors; Guest Artists
Budget: $100,000 - $500,000
Income Sources: Private Foundations/Grants/Endowments; Business/Corporate Donations; Box Office; Government Grants; Individual Donations
Season: September - June **Annual Attendance:** 10,000
Affiliations: ASOL
Performance Facilities: Klein Memorial Auditorium

FACILITY

DOWNTOWN CABARET THEATRE
263 Golden Hill Street, Bridgeport, CT 06604
(203) 576-1634
Type of Facility: Cabaret
Facility Originally: YWCA All-purpose Room
Type of Stage: Proscenium **Stage Dimensions:** 30'x19'
Seating Capacity: 294
Year Built: 1944
Year Remodeled: 1975
Contact for Rental: Bert Bernardi; (203) 576-1634
Resident Groups: Downtown Cabaret Theatre and Cabaret Children's Company

KLEIN MEMORIAL AUDITORIUM
910 Fairfield Avenue, Bridgeport, CT 06605
(203) 576-8115
Founded: 1940
Type of Facility: Auditorium; Theatre House
Type of Stage: Proscenium
Stage Dimensions: 60'x36'x36' **Orchestra Pit**
Seating Capacity: 1,500
Year Built: 1940 **Architect:** Leonard Asheim **Cost:** $500,000
Contact for Rental: Len Alexander, Management Consultants for the Arts, Inc.; (203) 661-3003
Manager: Len Alexander; (203) 661-3003
Resident Groups: Connecticut Grand Opera; Connecticut Ballet Theatre

UNIVERSITY OF BRIDGEPORT - BERNHARD CENTER
84 Iranistan Avenue, Bridgeport, CT 06601
(203) 576-4925
Type of Facility: Theatre Complex; Concert Hall; Auditorium; Performance Center
Type of Stage: Proscenium
Stage Dimensions: 40'Wx18'Hx30'D **Orchestra Pit**
Seating Capacity: 900
Year Built: 1972 **Architect:** Lyons Mater & Lechner **Cost:** $7,000,000
Contact for Rental: Helen Conlon; (203) 576-4925
Resident Groups: University of Bridgeport Theatre and Music Departments; Bernhard Center Arts Calendar Events

Cheshire

DANCE

SILO CONCERT DANCERS
855 North Brooksvale Road, Cheshire, CT 06410
(203) 272-9377
Founded: 1985

Arts Area: Modern
Status: Professional; Non-Profit
Type: Performing; Educational
Purpose: To maintain a professional performing company dedicated to presenting the works of Doris Humphrey and preserving their artistic integrity
Management: Ernestine Stodelle, Artistic Director; Gail Corbin, Associate Artistic Director
Paid Staff: 2
Paid Artists: 14
Utilizes: Special Technical Talent; Guest Artists
Budget: $1,000 - $50,000
Income Sources: Box Office; Individual Donations

THEATRE

CHESHIRE COMMUNITY THEATRE
PO Box 149, Cheshire, CT 06410
(203) 271-2903
Founded: 1953
Arts Area: Musical; Community; Theatrical Group
Status: Non-Professional; Non-Profit
Type: Performing; Resident
Officers: Pat Murphy, President
Volunteer Staff: 25
Budget: $1,000 - $50,000
Income Sources: Business/Corporate Donations; Box Office
Season: September - June   **Annual Attendance:** 3,000
Affiliations: New Haven Council of the Arts
Performance Facilities: Cheshire High School

Chester

THEATRE

GOODSPEED-AT-CHESTER/THE NORMA TERRIS THEATRE
North Main Street, Chester, CT 06423
(203) 873-8664
Founded: 1984
Arts Area: Musical
Status: Professional; Non-Profit
Type: Performing; Equity Theater
Purpose: The satellite theatre of the Goodspeed Opera House, Goodspeed-At-Chester/The Norma Terris Theatre is dedicated to developing new works of musical theatre, producing several musicals-in-progress each season.
Management: Michael P. Price, Executive Director; Sue Frost, Producing Associate; Warren Pincus, Casting Director; Michael Sande, Public Relations Director
Officers: Norwood R.G. Goodspeed, Chairman of the Board; Richard Schneller, President
Utilizes: Guest Artists; Guest Directors
Income Sources: Private Foundations/Grants/Endowments; Business/Corporate Donations; Box Office; Government Grants; Individual Donations
Season: May - November   **Annual Attendance:** 20,000

THE NATIONAL THEATRE OF THE DEAF
The Hazel E. Stark Center, Chester, CT 06412
(203) 526-4971
FAX: (203) 526-9732
Founded: 1967
Arts Area: Professional; Theatrical Group
Status: Professional; Non-Profit
Type: Performing; Touring; Educational
Purpose: A professional, international touring company whose productions combine Sign Language and the spoken word
Management: David Hays, Founding Artistic Director; Julianna Fjeld, Co-Artistic Director; Liane Dyer, Director of Public Relations
Paid Staff: 15   **Volunteer Staff:** 2
Paid Artists: 15
Utilizes: Special Technical Talent; Guest Artists; Guest Directors
Budget: $1,000,000 - $5,000,000
Income Sources: Private Foundations/Grants/Endowments; Business/Corporate Donations; Box Office; Government Grants; Individual Donations
Season: 52 Weeks   **Annual Attendance:** 100,000

FACILITY

GOODSPEED-AT-CHESTER/THE NORMA TERRIS THEATRE
North Main Street, Chester, CT 06423
(203) 873-8664
> **Founded:** 1984
> **Type of Facility:** Theatre House
> **Facility Originally:** Factory
> **Type of Stage:** Proscenium
> **Stage Dimensions:** 31'Wx22'6"D   Orchestra Pit
> **Seating Capacity:** 200
> **Year Remodeled:** 1984

Danbury

INSTRUMENTAL MUSIC

ASTON MAGNA FOUNDATION FOR MUSIC AND THE HUMANITIES, INC.
PO Box 310, Danbury, CT 06813
(203) 792-4662
FAX: (203) 744-7244
> **Founded:** 1972
> **Arts Area:** Chamber; Early Music
> **Status:** Professional; Non-Profit
> **Type:** Performing; Touring; Educational; Sponsoring
> **Purpose:** To perform baroque and classical music on period instruments; to sponsor educational programs that connect the music with the society and culture in which it was written
> **Management:** Ronnie Boriskin, Executive Director; Daniel Stepner, Artistic Director; Raymond Erickson, Academy/Outreach Director; Amy Poliakoff, Festival Administrator; Constance Baldwin, Academy/Outreach Administrator; Florence Lynch, Business Manager
> **Officers:** Robert B. Strassler, Chairman; Edwin E. McAmis, Treasurer; Richard Bodig, Secretary; Bernard Krainis, Clerk; Dominick Attanasio, Raymond Erickson, Nina Korda, Christopher H. Murray and Sarah Pinchot, Directors
> **Utilizes:** Guest Artists
> **Budget:** $100,000 - $500,000
> **Income Sources:** Private Foundations/Grants/Endowments; Business/Corporate Donations; Box Office; Government Grants; Individual Donations
> **Season:** 52 Weeks
> **Performance Facilities:** St. James Church Festival, Great Barrington, MA

DANBURY MUSIC CENTRE, INC.
256 Main Street, Danbury, CT 06810
(203) 748-1716
> **Founded:** 1935
> **Arts Area:** Symphony; Orchestra; Chamber; Ensemble; Folk
> **Status:** Semi-Professional; Non-Professional; Non-Profit
> **Type:** Performing; Educational; Sponsoring
> **Purpose:** A community organization dedicated to the performance of classical music free to the public
> **Management:** Nancy F. Sudik, Executive Director; James Humphreville, Musical Director, Orchestra; Richard Brooks, Orchestra; Charles Matz, Chorus; Edith Schwab, Symphonette; Julianne LaFond, Nutcracker Director
> **Officers:** James Tegolotti, President; Karen Mattscheck, Vice President; Kris Meier, Secretary; Betsy McIlvaine, Treasurer
> **Paid Staff:** 11   **Volunteer Staff:** 30
> **Paid Artists:** 20   **Non-Paid Artists:** 250
> **Utilizes:** Guest Artists
> **Budget:** $50,000 - $100,000
> **Income Sources:** Private Foundations/Grants/Endowments; Business/Corporate Donations; Individual Donations
> **Season:** September - June   **Annual Attendance:** 8,000

FACILITY

CHARLES IVES CENTER - PAVILION
PO Box 2957, Danbury, CT 06813
(203) 797-4002
FAX: (203) 731-2807
> **Type of Facility:** Environmental; Amphitheater
> **Type of Stage:** Platform; Environmental; Octagonal

Stage Dimensions: 62' diameter octagon with 55'x40' usable stage area
Seating Capacity: 5000
Year Built: 1985
Architect: Kosinsky Associates
Cost: $600,000
Acoustical Consultant: Jaffe Acoustics

Darien

THEATRE

CONNECTICUT'S BROADWAY THEATRE, DARIEN
65 Tokeneke Road, Darien, CT 06820
(203) 655-6812
FAX: (203) 655-9619
Founded: 1977
Arts Area: Professional; Musical; Dinner
Status: Professional; Commercial
Type: Performing; Resident
Purpose: To present professional musical theatre - revivals of vintage pieces and just-released musicals
Management: Jane Bergere, Producer; Donne Shaw, Assistant to the Producer; Paul Squire, Controller
Officers: Phillip Molstre, President
Paid Staff: 50
Paid Artists: 35
Utilizes: Special Technical Talent; Guest Conductors; Guest Artists; Guest Directors
Budget: $100,000 - $500,000
Income Sources: Box Office
Season: 52 Weeks   **Annual Attendance:** 104,000
Affiliations: AEA; SSDC; IATSE; AFM; ADTI

East Haddam

THEATRE

GOODSPEED OPERA HOUSE
Route 82, East Haddam, CT 06423
(203) 873-8664; (203) 873-8668
FAX: (203) 873-2329
Founded: 1963
Arts Area: Musical
Status: Professional; Non-Profit
Type: Performing; Equity Theater
Purpose: The Goodspeed Opera House is one of the only theatres in America dedicated to the heritage of the American musical and the development of new works to add to the repertoire.
Management: Michael P. Price, Executive Director; Sue Frost, Producing Associate; Warren Pincus, Casting Director; Michael Sande, Public Relations Director
Officers: Norwood R.G. Goodspeed, Chairman of the Board; Richard Schneller, President
Utilizes: Guest Artists; Guest Directors
Income Sources: Private Foundations/Grants/Endowments; Business/Corporate Donations; Box Office; Government Grants; Individual Donations
Season: April - December   **Annual Attendance:** 110,000

FACILITY

GOODSPEED OPERA HOUSE
Route 82, East Haddam, CT 06423
(203) 873-8664
Type of Facility: Theatre House; Opera House
Type of Stage: Proscenium
Stage Dimensions: 27'Wx18'D
Orchestra Pit
Seating Capacity: 398
Year Built: 1876   **Architect:** William H. Goodspeed
Year Remodeled: 1962   **Architect:** Frederic Palmer, Henry Sage Goodwin
Manager: Edward Blaschik

East Windsor

THEATRE

COACHLIGHT DINNER THEATRE
266 Main Street, East Windsor, CT 06088
(203) 623-8227
Founded: 1972
Arts Area: Dinner
Status: Professional; Commercial
Type: Performing
Management: Samuel Belkin, Janis Belkin, Ruth Belkin, Producers

---

Fairfield

INSTRUMENTAL MUSIC

GREATER BRIDGEPORT SYMPHONY YOUTH ORCHESTRA
PO Box 645, Fairfield, CT 06430
(203) 576-0263
Founded: 1970
Arts Area: Symphony; Orchestra
Status: Non-Professional
Type: Performing; Educational
Purpose: To provide a quality orchestral experience for young musicians in the Greater Bridgeport Area
Officers: Beth Harris, President
Paid Staff: 5
Budget: $1,000 - $50,000
Income Sources: Private Foundations/Grants/Endowments; Box Office; Individual Donations
Season: September - May   **Annual Attendance:** 2,000
Performance Facilities: Fairfield High School

Falls Village

PERFORMING SERIES

MUSIC MOUNTAIN
Falls Village, CT 06031
(203) 438-8868
FAX: (203) 438-1769
Founded: 1930
Arts Area: Vocal Music; Instrumental Music
Status: Professional; Non-Profit
Type: Performing; Educational; Sponsoring
Purpose: To bring Connecticut the finest in chamber music; to present the Summer Chamber Music Festival; to broadcast concerts to 200 radio stations
Officers: Nicholas Gordon, President; Jack Amster, Executive Vice President; Louise King, Secretary; Anne Stewart, Treasurer
Paid Staff: 2   **Volunteer Staff:** 15
Paid Artists: 30
Utilizes: Guest Artists
Budget: $50,000 - $100,000
Income Sources: Private Foundations/Grants/Endowments; Business/Corporate Donations; Box Office; Government Grants; Individual Donations
Season: June - September   **Annual Attendance:** 6,000
Performance Facilities: Gordon Hall

Greenwich

INSTRUMENTAL MUSIC

GREENWICH SYMPHONY ORCHESTRA
PO Box 35, Greenwich, CT 06836
(203) 869-2664
Founded: 1958
Arts Area: Symphony

Status: Professional
Type: Performing
Purpose: To present symphonic music performances and a Youth Concert Series for all Greenwich school children in grades 2-7, free of charge
Management: Mrs. Richard W. Radcliffe, President
Officers: Mrs. Richard W. Radcliffe, President; Richard Slagle, First Vice President/Secretary; Harriet Aberle, Publicity; Richard W. Radcliffe, Treasurer
Paid Staff: 3 **Volunteer Staff:** 40
Paid Artists: 95 **Non-Paid Artists:** 2
Utilizes: Guest Artists
Budget: $100,000 - $500,000
Income Sources: Private Foundations/Grants/Endowments; Business/Corporate Donations; Box Office; Individual Donations
Season: October - June **Annual Attendance:** 12,000
Affiliations: ASOL
Performance Facilities: Greenwich High School

VOCAL MUSIC

GREENWICH CHORAL SOCIETY
PO Box 5, Greenwich, CT 06836
(203) 622-5136
Founded: 1925
Arts Area: Choral
Status: Non-Profit
Type: Performing
Purpose: To make a broad range of choral music available to audiences for their entertainment and education
Management: Wendy Ann Dunkle, Business Administrator
Officers: Curt Carlson, President; Betsy Lawrence, Executive Vice President; Nancy Pierson, Vice President Administration; Susan Deal, Vice President Communications; Tom Casper, Vice President Concert; Roy Pfeil, Vice President Funding; Suzanne Warner, Secretary; Don Lewis, Treasurer
Paid Staff: 1
Utilizes: Guest Artists
Budget: $100,000 - $500,000
Income Sources: Private Foundations/Grants/Endowments; Business/Corporate Donations; Individual Donations
Season: 52 Weeks **Annual Attendance:** 9,000
Performance Facilities: State University of New York at Purchase

Groton

THEATRE

THE AVERY POINT PLAYERS
University of Connecticut at Avery Point, Groton, CT 06340
(203) 446-1020
FAX: (203) 445-3498
Founded: 1972
Arts Area: Theatrical Group
Status: Non-Professional
Type: Performing; Touring; Educational; Sponsoring
Purpose: To develop programs, performers, leaders and audiences for and in theatre, by and for youth
Management: K.E. Janney, Associate Professor/Producer/Director
Paid Staff: 1
Utilizes: Guest Artists; Guest Directors
Budget: $1,000 - $50,000
Income Sources: Box Office; Individual Donations
Season: September - June **Annual Attendance:** 2,500

Guilford

INSTRUMENTAL MUSIC

EASTERN BRASS QUINTET
33 Kenneth Circle, Guilford, CT 06437
(203) 481-9226
Founded: 1970
Arts Area: Chamber; Ensemble; Instrumental Group

Status: Professional
Type: Performing; Touring; Educational
Purpose: To perform the best in brass chamber music to a wide variety of audiences
Management: Lisa Sapinkopf, Artist Manager
Officers: Richard Green, Director
Paid Artists: 5
Budget: $50,000 - $100,000
Income Sources: Private Foundations/Grants/Endowments; Individual Donations
Season: 52 Weeks

Hartford

DANCE

ALBANO BALLET COMPANY
15 Girard Avenue, Hartford, CT 06105
(203) 232-8898
Founded: 1972
Arts Area: Modern; Ballet
Status: Professional; Non-Profit
Type: Performing; Touring; Educational
Purpose: To bring quality ballet to the Connecticut area through training and performance
Management: Joseph Albano, Artistic Director
Officers: Julius E. Scheir, President; Herbert Deming, Treasurer; Mrs. Herman Hiebert, Secretary
Utilizes: Guest Artists
Budget: $100,000 - $500,000
Income Sources: Private Foundations/Grants/Endowments; Box Office; Government Grants; Individual Donations
Season: September - May
Affiliations: University of Central Connecticut

HARTFORD BALLET
226 Farmington Avenue, Hartford, CT 06105
(203) 525-9396
FAX: (203) 249-8116
Founded: 1960
Arts Area: Modern; Ballet
Status: Professional; Non-Profit
Type: Performing; Touring; Resident; Educational; Sponsoring
Purpose: To maintain a full-time resident professional dance company and a school for the training of dance teachers and performers
Management: John Simone, Executive Director; Enid Lynn, Director of the School
Officers: Wayne Hauge, President; Robin Pearson, Joan Brown, Vice Presidents
Paid Artists: 22 **Non-Paid Artists:** 12
Utilizes: Special Technical Talent; Guest Artists; Designers
Budget: $1,000,000 - $5,000,000
Income Sources: Private Foundations/Grants/Endowments; Business/Corporate Donations; Box Office; Government Grants; Individual Donations; Tour Fees
Season: August - May **Annual Attendance:** 80,000
Affiliations: School of the Hartford Ballet
Performance Facilities: The Bushnell Hall

INSTRUMENTAL MUSIC

THE HARTFORD SYMPHONY ORCHESTRA INC.
228 Farmington Road, Hartford, CT 06105
(203) 246-8742
FAX: (203) 247-1720
Arts Area: Symphony; Orchestra; Chamber; Ensemble
Status: Professional; Non-Profit
Type: Performing; Educational
Purpose: To provide the highest quality musical performances to the widest possible audience
Management: Michael Lankester, Music Director; Paul K. Reuter, Executive Director
Officers: Peter S. Burgess, President of the Board
Budget: $1,000,000 - $5,000,000
Income Sources: Private Foundations/Grants/Endowments; Business/Corporate Donations; Box Office; Government Grants; Individual Donations
Performance Facilities: The Bushnell

VOCAL MUSIC

CONNECTICUT OPERA
226 Farmington Avenue, Hartford, CT 06105
(203) 527-0713
FAX: (203) 293-1715
Founded: 1942
Arts Area: Grand Opera; Light Opera; Operetta
Status: Professional
Type: Performing; Touring; Resident; Educational; Sponsoring
Purpose: To present high-quality, professional opera, musical theater and educational services
Management: George D. Osborne, General Director
Officers: John G. Ewen, Chairman; Thomas K. Standish, Vice Chairman; Calvin S. Price, President
Paid Staff: 15 **Volunteer Staff:** 5
Paid Artists: 500 **Non-Paid Artists:** 50
Utilizes: Special Technical Talent; Guest Conductors; Guest Artists; Guest Directors
Budget: $1,000,000 - $5,000,000
Income Sources: Private Foundations/Grants/Endowments; Business/Corporate Donations; Box Office; Government Grants; Individual Donations
Season: September - May
Annual Attendance: 100,000
Affiliations: OA
Performance Facilities: Horace Bushnell Memorial Hall

THEATRE

ARTISTS COLLECTIVE
35 Clark Street, Hartford, CT 06120
(203) 527-3205
Founded: 1970
Arts Area: Theatrical Group
Status: Non-Professional; Non-Profit
Type: Resident
Management: Dollie McLean, Executive Director; Jackie McLean, Creative Consultant
Utilizes: Special Technical Talent; Guest Artists; Guest Directors
Budget: $100,000 - $500,000
Income Sources: Private Foundations/Grants/Endowments; Business/Corporate Donations; Box Office; Government Grants; Individual Donations
Season: September - June

COMPANY ONE
30 Arbor Street, Hartford, CT 06106
(203) 233-4588
FAX: (203) 233-2941
Founded: 1983
Arts Area: Theatrical Group
Status: Professional; Non-Profit
Type: Performing; Touring; Resident; Educational
Purpose: To present evening and matinee performances of full-length plays, staged script readings of new full-length plays (Script Teas), and radio drama (RadioPlaying); to produce new works by emerging artists and developing regional and local artists; to create educational programs which weave theater into the fabric of everyday life
Management: Juanita Rockwell, Artistic Director; Elizabeth Bermel, Managing Director
Officers: Ed Hogan, Board President; Terry O'Conner, First Vice President; Nancy Wolfe, Second Vice President; Jackie Porter, Treasurer; Frederica Brenneman, Secretary
Paid Staff: 5 **Volunteer Staff:** 3
Paid Artists: 50
Utilizes: Special Technical Talent; Guest Artists; Guest Directors
Budget: $50,000 - $100,000
Income Sources: Private Foundations/Grants/Endowments; Business/Corporate Donations; Box Office; Government Grants; Individual Donations
Season: 52 Weeks
Annual Attendance: 7,000
Affiliations: TCG; AEA; New Dramatists Guild
Performance Facilities: The Aetna Theatre at the Wadsworth Atheneum

HARTFORD STAGE COMPANY
50 Church Street, Hartford, CT 06103
(203) 525-5601
FAX: (203) 525-4420
  Founded: 1964
  Arts Area: Professional
  Status: Professional; Non-Profit
  Type: Performing; Resident
  Purpose: To reinterpret the classics; to discover provocative new plays
  Management: Mark Lamos, Artistic Director; David Hawkanson, Managing Director; Michael Ross, Business Manager
  Officers: Elliot Gerson, President, Board of Directors
  Utilizes: Guest Artists; Guest Directors
  Budget: $1,000,000 - $5,000,000
  Income Sources: Private Foundations/Grants/Endowments; Business/Corporate Donations; Box Office; Government Grants; Individual Donations
  Season: October - June   **Annual Attendance:** 105,000
  Affiliations: LORT; TCG; AAA
  Performance Facilities: John W. Huntington Theatre

PERFORMING SERIES

AMERICAN MUSIC THEATRE GROUP
487 Main Street, Suite 6, Hartford, CT 06103
(203) 527-2944
  Founded: 1978
  Arts Area: Vocal Music; Instrumental Music; Lyric Opera
  Status: Professional; Non-Profit
  Type: Performing; Touring; Educational; Sponsoring
  Purpose: To perform American music of all styles and periods
  Management: Phillis Bruce, Booking Agent/Program Development Coordinator
  Officers: Neely Bruce, President/Artistic Director
  Volunteer Staff: 1
  Paid Artists: 12
  Utilizes: Special Technical Talent; Guest Conductors; Guest Artists; Guest Directors
  Budget: $50,000 - $100,000
  Income Sources: Private Foundations/Grants/Endowments; Business/Corporate Donations; Box Office; Government Grants; Individual Donations
  Season: 52 Weeks   **Annual Attendance:** 3,000
  Affiliations: CA
  Performance Facilities: Horace Bushnell Memorial Hall

FIRST NIGHT HARTFORD, INC.
c/o Hartford Downtown Council, 250 Constitution Avenue, Hartford, CT 06103
(203) 728-3089
FAX: (203) 527-9696
  Founded: 1988
  Arts Area: Dance; Vocal Music; Instrumental Music; Theater; Festivals; Lyric Opera; Grand Opera; Major Arts Event
  Status: Non-Profit
  Type: Performing
  Purpose: To provide a New Year's Eve celebration at 25 locations in downtown Hartford
  Management: Hartford Downtown Council - Maureen Connolly, Events Manager
  Officers: Mayor Perry, President; Christine Austin, Vice President; Anthony Caruso, Secretary; Peter Shapiro, Treasurer
  Paid Staff: 2   **Volunteer Staff:** 150
  Paid Artists: 250
  Utilizes: Special Technical Talent
  Budget: $100,000 - $500,000
  Income Sources: Private Foundations/Grants/Endowments; Business/Corporate Donations; Individual Donations; Button Sales
  Season: New Year's Eve   **Annual Attendance:** 18,000

FACILITY

ALBANO BALLET AND PERFORMING ARTS CENTER
15 Girard Avenue, Hartford, CT 06105
(203) 232-8898
  Type of Facility: Performance Center
  Type of Stage: Flexible
  Stage Dimensions: 12'x30'x25'

Seating Capacity: 185
Year Built: 1900   **Cost:** $125,000
Year Remodeled: 1976   **Cost:** $20,000
Contact for Rental: Joseph Albano;   (303) 232-8898

HARTFORD CIVIC CENTER
One Civic Center Plaza, Hartford, CT 06103
(203) 249-6333
   Type of Facility: Concert Hall; Auditorium; Civic Center; Arena; Multi-Purpose
   Type of Stage: Flexible; Platform; Arena
   Seating Capacity: 16,200
   Year Built: 1975   **Architect:** Vincent Kling   **Cost:** $31,000,000
   Year Remodeled: 1980   **Cost:** $27,000,000
   Contact for Rental: Kathy Martin;   (203) 249-6333
   Manager: Gerald Peterson

HARTFORD STAGE COMPANY
50 Church Street, Hartford, CT 06103
(203) 525-5601
   Type of Facility: Theatre House
   Type of Stage: Thrust
   Stage Dimensions: 40'x90'x90'
   Seating Capacity: 489
   Year Built: 1977   **Architect:** Venturi and Rauch   **Cost:** $2,500,000
   Contact for Rental: Candice Chirgotis, Production Manager;   (203) 525-5601
   Resident Groups: Hartford Stage Company

HORACE BUSHNELL MEMORIAL HALL
166 Capitol Avenue, Hartford, CT 06106
(203) 527-3123
FAX: (203) 527-4142
   Founded: 1928
   Type of Facility: Concert Hall; Studio Performance; Performance Center; Opera House; Multi-Purpose; Room
   Type of Stage: Thrust; Proscenium
   Stage Dimensions: 30'x55'x40'   **Orchestra Pit**
   Seating Capacity: 2,819
   Year Built: 1930   **Architect:** Helmle, Corbett and Harrison
   Year Remodeled: 1974   **Architect:** Venturi and Rauch   **Cost:** $940,000
   Contact for Rental: Andrea Rynn;   (203) 527-3123
   Manager: Douglas C. Evans;   (203) 527-3123
   Resident Groups: Hartford Symphony Orchestra; Connecticut Opera; Hartford Ballet

---

Manchester

DANCE

CONNECTICUT CONCERT BALLET
280 Garden Grove, Manchester, CT 06040
(203) 643-4796
   Founded: 1973
   Arts Area: Ballet
   Status: Semi-Professional; Non-Profit
   Type: Performing; Touring; Resident; Educational; Sponsoring
   Purpose: To provide classical training for young dancers and adults
   Management: Joyce Karpiej, Director; Dave Fairbanks, Stage Director; Judy McCue, Costume Mistress; Cindy Fair-banks, Production Assistant
   Officers: Joyce Karpiej, President; Judy McCue, Vice President; Linda Fraleigh, Secretary; Rosemary Rae, Treasurer
   Paid Staff: 4
   Paid Artists: 6
   Utilizes: Guest Artists; Guest Directors
   Budget: $1,000 - $50,000
   Income Sources: Private Foundations/Grants/Endowments; Business/Corporate Donations; Box Office; Individual Donations
   Season: September - May

INSTRUMENTAL MUSIC

MANCHESTER SYMPHONY ORCHESTRA/CHORALE
PO Box 861, Manchester, CT 06040
(203) 659-8260
> **Founded:** 1960
> **Arts Area:** Symphony; Orchestra; Chorale
> **Status:** Non-Professional; Non-Profit; Volunteer; Community
> **Type:** Performing; Resident
> **Purpose:** To provide a place for talented volunteers to perform; to bring good classical music to the community
> **Management:** Betsy Henderson, Managing Director; Kim Sirois, Publicist
> **Officers:** Charles Morse, President; Ruby Bechtold, Vice President; Nick Mason, Treasurer; Christine Mantie, Secretary
> **Paid Staff:** 2   **Volunteer Staff:** 25
> **Paid Artists:** 4   **Non-Paid Artists:** 150
> **Utilizes:** Guest Conductors; Guest Artists
> **Budget:** $1,000 - $50,000
> **Income Sources:** Private Foundations/Grants/Endowments; Business/Corporate Donations; Box Office; Individual Donations
> **Season:** September - June   **Annual Attendance:** 2,500
> **Affiliations:** Artist-in-Residence Manchester High School
> **Performance Facilities:** Manchester High School

THEATRE

MANCHESTER MUSICAL PLAYERS
PO Box 626, Manchester, CT 06045
(203) 649-9065
> **Founded:** 1947
> **Arts Area:** Musical
> **Status:** Semi-Professional; Non-Profit
> **Type:** Performing
> **Purpose:** To produce and present quality musical theatre at reasonable prices and to provide a forum in which our members can perfect and perform their skills
> **Management:** Board of Directors
> **Officers:** Christopher Stone, President; Dianna Burnham, Secretary; William Bengraff, Treasurer; Gail Stone, Fundraising Chairman; Jill Kemp, Publicity Chairman
> **Volunteer Staff:** 33
> **Non-Paid Artists:** 50
> **Utilizes:** Special Technical Talent; Guest Conductors; Guest Directors
> **Budget:** $1,000 - $50,000
> **Income Sources:** Private Foundations/Grants/Endowments; Business/Corporate Donations; Box Office; Individual Donations
> **Season:** April - December   **Annual Attendance:** 4,000
> **Affiliations:** East of the River Tourism District
> **Performance Facilities:** Cheney Hall

Middletown

DANCE

DANCES FOR 2
6 Glynn Avenue, Middletown, CT 06457
(203) 346-2210
> **Founded:** 1979
> **Arts Area:** Modern; Ballroom; Ragtime
> **Status:** Professional
> **Type:** Performing; Touring; Educational
> **Purpose:** To perform duet concerts of modern and ballroom choreography using American composers and master teachers of modern technique, composition and ballroom dance
> **Management:** Willie Feuer, Susan Matheke, Artistic Directors
> **Paid Artists:** 2
> **Utilizes:** Guest Artists; Guest Choreographers
> **Budget:** $1,000 - $50,000
> **Income Sources:** Box Office; Individual Donations
> **Season:** 52 Weeks   **Annual Attendance:** 1,000
> **Affiliations:** Educational Center for the Arts, Wesleyan University
> **Performance Facilities:** Arts Hall, Wesleyan University

PERFORMING SERIES

WESLEYAN UNIVERSITY CENTER FOR THE ARTS
Wesleyan University, Middletown, CT 06459-0442
(203) 347-9411, ext. 2563
FAX: (203) 344-7948
Founded: 1973
Arts Area: Dance; Vocal Music; Instrumental Music; Theater; Exhibitions
Status: Professional; Non-Profit
Type: Performing; Educational; Sponsoring
Purpose: To provide education in the arts through direct involvement in the artistic process; to enrich and extend the cultural resources of central Connecticut
Management: Jean Shaw, Director
Officers: William M. Chase, President; Raymond Denworth, Chairman, Board of Trustees
Paid Staff: 10 **Volunteer Staff:** 15
Paid Artists: 30
Utilizes: Guest Artists; Guest Directors
Budget: $100,000 - $500,000
Income Sources: Private Foundations/Grants/Endowments; Business/Corporate Donations; Box Office; Government Grants; Individual Donations
Season: September - May **Annual Attendance:** 25,000
Performance Facilities: Wesleyan University Center for the Arts

FACILITY

WESLEYAN UNIVERSITY CENTER FOR THE ARTS
Wesleyan University, Middletown, CT 06459-0442
(203) 347-9411
FAX: (203) 344-7948
Founded: 1973
Type of Facility: Theatre Complex; Concert Hall; Studio Performance; Performance Center; Multi-Purpose; Visual & Performing Arts Classrooms
Year Built: 1970 **Architect:** Roche Dinkeloo Associates **Cost:** $11,900,000
Acoustical Consultant: Bolt, Beranek & Newman
Contact for Rental: University Coordinator; (203) 347-9411, ext. 2593
Manager: Jean Shaw, Director; (203) 347-9411, ext. 2563
The Center for the Arts is available for rental only on a very limited basis. The 11-building complex is on 6.5 acres and includes the Cinema, Crowell Concert Hall, Theater and World Music Hall. See individual listings for details.

WESLEYAN UNIVERSITY CENTER FOR THE ARTS - CINEMA
Wesleyan University, Middletown, CT 06459-0442
(203) 347-9411, ext. 2563
FAX: (203) 344-7948
Type of Facility: Film & Lecture Hall
Seating Capacity: 265
Contact for Rental: University Coordinator; (203) 347-9411, ext. 2593
Manager: Jean Shaw, Director; (203) 347-9411, ext. 2563
Capability for 16mm, 35mm and slides

WESLEYAN UNIVERSITY CENTER FOR THE ARTS - CROWELL CONCERT HALL
Wesleyan University, Middletown, CT 06459-0442
(203) 347-9411, ext. 2563
FAX: (203) 344-7948
Type of Facility: Concert Hall
Type of Stage: Platform
Stage Dimensions: 48'x23'
Seating Capacity: 400
Contact for Rental: University Coordinator; (203) 347-9411, ext. 2593
Manager: Jean Shaw, Director; (203) 347-9411, ext. 2563

WESLEYAN UNIVERSITY CENTER FOR THE ARTS - THEATER
Wesleyan University, Middletown, CT 06459-0442
(203) 347-9411, ext. 2563
FAX: (203) 344-7948
Type of Facility: Theatre House
Type of Stage: Thrust; Flexible; Proscenium; In-the-round Capability
Stage Dimensions: 42'x54'x55'
Orchestra Pit

Seating Capacity: 400-525
Contact for Rental: University Coordinator;   (203) 347-9411, ext. 2593
Manager: Jean Shaw, Director;   (203) 347-9411, ext. 2563

WESLEYAN UNIVERSITY CENTER FOR THE ARTS - WORLD MUSIC HALL
Wesleyan University, Middletown, CT 06459-0442
(203) 347-9411, ext. 2563
FAX: (203) 344-7948
Type of Facility: Concert Hall
Type of Stage: Platform; Carpeted Risers
Seating Capacity: 175
Contact for Rental: University Coordinator;   (203) 347-9411, ext. 2593
Manager: Jean Shaw, Director;   (203) 347-9411, ext. 2563
Originally built to house a Javanese Gamelan Orchestra

New Britain

INSTRUMENTAL MUSIC

NEW BRITAIN SYMPHONY ORCHESTRA
PO Box 1253, New Britain, CT 06050
(203) 621-0316
Founded: 1947
Arts Area: Symphony; Orchestra
Status: Non-Profit
Type: Performing
Management: Jerome Laszloffy, Conductor
Utilizes: Guest Artists
Income Sources: Private Foundations/Grants/Endowments; Business/Corporate Donations; Box Office; Individual Donations
Performance Facilities: Vincent Sala Auditorium, New Britain High School

VOCAL MUSIC

CONNECTICUT CHORALARTISTS, INC.
90 Main Street, New Britain, CT 06051
(603) 224-7500
Founded: 1974
Arts Area: Choral
Status: Professional; Non-Profit
Type: Performing; Touring; Resident; Educational
Purpose: To perform the finest choral music in a professional manner
Management: Catherine Stockuar, Executive Director
Officers: Ray Gialitto, President
Paid Staff: 1   Volunteer Staff: 4
Paid Artists: 50
Utilizes: Guest Conductors
Budget: $100,000 - $500,000
Income Sources: Private Foundations/Grants/Endowments; Business/Corporate Donations; Box Office; Government Grants; Individual Donations
Season: September - June   Annual Attendance: 5,000

GREATER NEW BRITAIN OPERA ASSOCIATION
PO Box 664, New Britain, CT 06050
(203) 223-7557
Founded: 1976
Arts Area: Grand Opera
Status: Professional; Non-Profit
Type: Performing; Resident
Purpose: To showcase young artists in principal roles; to introduce opera to Connecticut youth via work-study programs and class experience
Management: Kenneth A. Larson, General Manager
Officers: Kenneth A. Larson, President; George Zenoble, Vice President; Ursula Gaudette, Secretary; Joseph Geraci, Finance
Volunteer Staff: 40
Paid Artists: 80
Utilizes: Special Technical Talent; Guest Conductors; Guest Directors
Budget: $1,000 - $50,000

Income Sources: Private Foundations/Grants/Endowments; Business/Corporate Donations; Box Office; Government Grants; Individual Donations
Season: September - June

THEATRE

HOLE IN THE WALL THEATRE
10 Harvard Street, New Britain, CT 06051
(203) 229-3049
>**Founded:** 1972
>**Arts Area:** Professional; Musical; Community; Theatrical Group
>**Status:** Professional; Non-Profit
>**Type:** Performing; Resident
>**Purpose:** To bring live theatre to everyone regardless of their ability to pay, donations only at the door
>**Budget:** $1,000 - $50,000
>**Income Sources:** Box Office; Government Grants; Individual Donations
>**Season:** 52 Weeks   **Annual Attendance:** 7,000

New Canaan

INSTRUMENTAL MUSIC

THE FAIRFIELD ORCHESTRA
191 Main Street, New Canaan, CT 06840
(203) 972-7400
FAX: (203) 972-7042
>**Founded:** 1981
>**Arts Area:** Orchestra
>**Status:** Professional; Non-Profit
>**Type:** Performing
>**Purpose:** To create, support and develop a classical music orchestra and related ensembles in Fairfield County, Connecticut to be among the finest in the greater New York area; to bring renowned guest artists, modern instrument players and period players to the county; to appeal to all segments of society
>**Management:** Thomas Crawford, Music Director; Amanda C. Fry, Executive Director; Claire Sommers, Production Manager; Andrea Flaks, Box Office Coordinator
>**Officers:** Lawrence D. Pearson, President; Robert E. Enslein, Vice President; John Bartlett, Secretary
>**Paid Staff:** 4   **Volunteer Staff:** 4
>**Paid Artists:** 60
>**Utilizes:** Guest Artists
>**Budget:** $100,000 - $500,000
>**Income Sources:** Private Foundations/Grants/Endowments; Business/Corporate Donations; Box Office; Government Grants; Individual Donations
>**Season:** October - May   **Annual Attendance:** 9,000
>**Performance Facilities:** Norwalk Concert Hall

New Fairfield

THEATRE

CANDLEWOOD PLAYHOUSE
Junction of Routes 37 & 39, PO Box 8209, New Fairfield, CT 06812
(203) 746-6557
FAX: (203) 746-6550
>**Founded:** 1983
>**Arts Area:** Professional; Summer Stock; Musical; Theatrical Group
>**Status:** Professional; Non-Profit
>**Type:** Performing; Touring; Resident; Educational
>**Purpose:** To present the finest in musical theatre; to create and develop new works to add to the repertoire
>**Management:** Rick Belzer, Producer
>**Officers:** Rick Belzer, President
>**Paid Staff:** 20   **Volunteer Staff:** 5
>**Paid Artists:** 250   **Non-Paid Artists:** 20
>**Utilizes:** Special Technical Talent; Guest Conductors; Guest Artists; Guest Directors
>**Budget:** $5,000,000 - $10,000,000
>**Income Sources:** Private Foundations/Grants/Endowments; Business/Corporate Donations; Box Office; Individual Donations
>**Season:** June - September   **Annual Attendance:** 200,000

New Haven

DANCE

AJDE! FOLK DANCE ENSEMBLE
36 Everit Street, New Haven, CT 06511
(203) 776-2210
> **Founded:** 1965
> **Arts Area:** Folk
> **Status:** Non-Professional; Non-Profit
> **Type:** Performing; Touring
> **Purpose:** To perform traditional European folk dances in authentic costumes
> **Management:** Fred Linton
> **Non-Paid Artists:** 8
> **Budget:** $1,000 - $50,000
> **Income Sources:** Private Foundations/Grants/Endowments
> **Season:** September - June   **Annual Attendance:** 1,500
> **Affiliations:** Arts Council of Greater New Haven

BARBARA FELDMAN AND DANCERS
PO Box 3060, New Haven, CT 06515
(203) 387-0774
> **Founded:** 1981
> **Arts Area:** Modern
> **Status:** Professional
> **Type:** Performing; Touring; Resident; Educational
> **Purpose:** With an emphasis on spirited ensemble dancing and collaborations with composers, BF & D strives to bring innovative modern dance to our audience.
> **Management:** Barbara Feldman, Artistic Director; Tom Haskell, Suzanne Service and Barbara Feldman, Directors
> **Officers:** Barbara Feldman, President; Suzanne Serviss, Secretary
> **Paid Staff:** 2   **Volunteer Staff:** 6
> **Paid Artists:** 6
> **Utilizes:** Special Technical Talent; Guest Artists
> **Budget:** $1,000 - $50,000
> **Income Sources:** Private Foundations/Grants/Endowments; Business/Corporate Donations; Box Office; Government Grants; Individual Donations
> **Affiliations:** Arts Council of Greater New Haven; Connecticut Touring Program; Connecticut Commission on the Arts
> **Performance Facilities:** Educational Center for the Arts; Artspace

INSTRUMENTAL MUSIC

BRASS RING
320 Blatchley Avenue, New Haven, CT 06513
(203) 562-7477
> **Founded:** 1983
> **Arts Area:** Chamber
> **Status:** Professional; Non-Profit
> **Type:** Performing; Touring; Resident; Educational
> **Purpose:** To perform and promote brass chamber music
> **Management:** Hillyer International, New York City - Vincent Wagner
> **Paid Artists:** 5
> **Utilizes:** Guest Artists
> **Budget:** $50,000 - $100,000
> **Income Sources:** Private Foundations/Grants/Endowments; Business/Corporate Donations; Box Office; Government Grants; Individual Donations
> **Season:** September - July   **Annual Attendance:** 5,000
> **Affiliations:** Hartt School of Music; University of Bridgeport

NEW HAVEN CIVIC ORCHESTRA
PO Box 2015, New Haven, CT 06521
(203) 562-0253
> **Founded:** 1940
> **Arts Area:** Symphony; Orchestra; Instrumental Group
> **Status:** Non-Professional; Non-Profit
> **Type:** Performing

Purpose: To give amateur musicians the opportunity to practice and perform good music at a near professional level; to serve the New Haven area with standard, and decidedly non-standard, symphonic repertoire through free concerts
Management: Gordon Emerson, Music Director
Paid Staff: 1
Utilizes: Guest Artists
Budget: $1,000 - $50,000
Income Sources: Private Foundations/Grants/Endowments; Business/Corporate Donations; Individual Donations
Season: September - May
Performance Facilities: Yale University

NEW HAVEN SYMPHONY ORCHESTRA
33 Whitney Avenue, New Haven, CT 06510
(203) 865-0831
FAX: (203) 789-8907
Founded: 1894
Arts Area: Symphony; Orchestra; Ensemble
Status: Professional; Non-Profit
Type: Performing; Touring; Educational; Sponsoring
Purpose: To provide orchestral music to all ages
Management: Catherine Weiskel, General Manager; Michael Palmer, Music Director
Officers: Patrick McFadden, President; John Collaran, Treasurer
Paid Staff: 9   **Volunteer Staff:** 450
Paid Artists: 70
Utilizes: Guest Artists
Budget: $1,000,000 - $5,000,000
Income Sources: Private Foundations/Grants/Endowments; Business/Corporate Donations; Box Office; Government Grants; Individual Donations
Season: October - July
Annual Attendance: 100,000
Performance Facilities: Woolsey Hall

ORCHESTRA NEW ENGLAND
1124 Campbell Avenue, New Haven, CT 06516-2005
(203) 934-8863
FAX: (203) 934-8379
Founded: 1975
Arts Area: Orchestra
Status: Professional; Non-Profit
Type: Performing; Touring
Purpose: To perform the highest quality of music for as many people as possible
Management: James Sinclair, Music Director/Conductor; John McDonald, General Manager
Officers: Walter R. Miller, Chairman; Edward B. Chansky, President
Paid Staff: 3
Budget: $100,000 - $500,000
Income Sources: Private Foundations/Grants/Endowments; Business/Corporate Donations; Box Office; Government Grants; Individual Donations
Season: 52 Weeks
Annual Attendance: 10,000
Affiliations: ASOL
Performance Facilities: Battell Chapel, Yale University

YALE SYMPHONY ORCHESTRA
165 Elm Street, New Haven, CT 06520
(203) 432-4140
Founded: 1965
Arts Area: Symphony; Orchestra
Status: Non-Profit
Type: Performing; Touring; Educational
Purpose: To provide the Yale community a chance both to play and to hear quality classical music
Management: Deborah Gaulrap, Manager; James Russ, Conductor
Paid Staff: 1
Paid Artists: 1   **Non-Paid Artists:** 90
Utilizes: Guest Artists
Budget: $1,000 - $50,000
Season: September - April
Annual Attendance: 12,000
Affiliations: Yale University
Performance Facilities: Woolsey Hall

THEATRE

LONG WHARF THEATRE
222 Sargent Drive, New Haven, CT 06511
(203) 787-4284
FAX: (203) 776-2287
Founded: 1965
Arts Area: Professional
Status: Professional; Non-Profit
Type: Touring; Resident; Educational; Producing
Management: Arvin Brown, Artistic Director; M. Edgar Rosenblum, Executive Director
Officers: G. Newton Schenck, Chairman of Board; Ruth Lord, President; Betty Kubler, Vice President; Patricia Pierce, Treasurer
Paid Staff: 60
Utilizes: Special Technical Talent; Guest Artists; Guest Directors
Budget: $1,000,000 - $5,000,000
Season: October - June
Affiliations: LORT; TCG; Connecticut Commission on the Arts; AEA
Performance Facilities: Long Wharf Theatre

RENAISSANCE THEATER COMPANY
217 Greenwich Avenue, New Haven, CT 06519
(203) 772-2557
Founded: 1978
Arts Area: Theatrical Group
Status: Professional; Non-Profit
Type: Performing; Touring; Educational
Purpose: To produce work of the highest artistic caliber, while promoting understanding, tolerance and friendship among different cultures, races, nationalities and faiths
Management: Dana Sachs, Artistic Director
Officers: Salvatore Pace, President; Alida Engel, Vice President; Kris Sainsbury, Secretary; Dana Sachs, Treasurer
Paid Staff: 2   **Volunteer Staff:** 5
Paid Artists: 6
Utilizes: Guest Artists
Budget: $1,000 - $50,000
Income Sources: Private Foundations/Grants/Endowments; Business/Corporate Donations; Government Grants; Individual Donations
Season: 52 Weeks   **Annual Attendance:** 30,000
Affiliations: New England Foundation for the Arts

YALE REPERTORY THEATRE
222 York Street, New Haven, CT 06520
(203) 432-1515
Founded: 1966
Arts Area: Professional; Theatrical Group
Status: Professional; Non-Profit
Type: Performing; Resident; Educational
Purpose: To produce new American plays, neglected works of the past and classics reviewed through contemporary metaphors
Management: Stan Wojewodski Jr., Artistic Director; Benjamin Mordecai, Managing Director
Utilizes: Guest Artists; Guest Directors
Budget: $1,000,000 - $5,000,000
Income Sources: Private Foundations/Grants/Endowments; Business/Corporate Donations; Box Office; Government Grants; Individual Donations
Season: October - May   **Annual Attendance:** 75,000
Affiliations: AEA; TCG; AAA; LORT; Connecticut Advocates for the Arts
Performance Facilities: Yale Repertory Theatre; University Theatre

FACILITY

LONG WHARF THEATRE
222 Sargent Drive, New Haven, CT 06511
(203) 787-4284
FAX: (203) 776-2287
Type of Facility: Theatre House
Facility Originally: Meat and Produce Terminal
Type of Stage: Thrust; 3/4 Arena
Stage Dimensions: Mainstage - 66'Wx17'D; Thrust - 24'Wx20'Dx18'H

Seating Capacity: 484
Year Remodeled: 1975   **Architect:** Roth and Moore   **Cost:** $100,000
Contact for Rental: Janice Muirhead;   (203) 787-4284

LONG WHARF THEATRE - STAGE II
222 Sargent Drive, New Haven, CT 06511
(203) 787-4284
Type of Facility: Black Box
Type of Stage: Flexible
Stage Dimensions: 50'x50'x16'
Seating Capacity: 200
Year Built: 1978
Manager: Janice Muirhead

PALACE THEATRE
246-248 College Street, New Haven, CT 06510
(203) 777-3071
Type of Facility: Concert Hall; Performance Center
Facility Originally: Vaudeville
Type of Stage: Thrust; Proscenium
Stage Dimensions: 40'x60'
Orchestra Pit
Seating Capacity: 2,000
Year Remodeled: 1984
Acoustical Consultant: Greg Cocco T.D.
Contact for Rental: (203) 777-3071

SHUBERT PERFORMING ARTS CENTER
247 College Street, New Haven, CT 06510
(203) 624-1825
FAX: (203) 789-2286
Type of Facility: Theatre House
Type of Stage: Proscenium
Stage Dimensions: 91'Wx38'D; 40'Wx30'H proscenium opening
Orchestra Pit
Seating Capacity: 1,629
Year Built: 1914
Year Remodeled: 1984   **Architect:** Bob Wendler   **Cost:** $6,000,000
Acoustical Consultant: Jaffe Acoustics
Contact for Rental: Morton Langbord;   (203) 624-1825
Manager: Judith Lisi;   (203) 624-1825

YALE REPERTORY THEATRE
222 York Street, New Haven, CT 06520
(203) 432-1515
FAX: (203) 432-1550
Type of Facility: Theatre House
Facility Originally: Church
Type of Stage: Thrust; Proscenium
Stage Dimensions: 26'Hx39'Wx20'6"D plus alcove 22'Hx26'Wx18'6"D
Seating Capacity: 487
Year Built: 1872
Year Remodeled: 1975   **Architect:** Patricia Tetrault   **Cost:** $500,000
Manager: Benjamin Mordcar
Resident Groups: Yale Repertory Theatre Company

New London

INSTRUMENTAL MUSIC

EASTERN CONNECTICUT SYMPHONY
26 Meridian Street, New London, CT 06320
(203) 443-2876
Founded: 1946
Arts Area: Symphony; Orchestra; Ensemble
Status: Professional
Type: Performing; Educational

Purpose: To provide high-quality musical performances, especially orchestral concerts, to the people of eastern Connecticut
Management: Isabelle G. Singer, Executive Director; Judith Azzinaro, Assistant to the Executive Director; Iris Lampert, Bookkeeper
Officers: Dorothy Askelson, President; Debra Salomonson, Vice President; Tom Castle, Secretary; John Bysko, Treasurer
Paid Staff: 3 **Volunteer Staff:** 6
Utilizes: Special Technical Talent; Guest Conductors; Guest Artists
Budget: $100,000 - $500,000
Income Sources: Private Foundations/Grants/Endowments; Business/Corporate Donations; Box Office; Government Grants; Individual Donations
Season: October - May **Annual Attendance:** 5,000
Performance Facilities: Garde Arts Center

PERFORMING SERIES

CONNECTICUT EARLY MUSIC FESTIVAL
PO Box 329, New London, CT 06320
(203) 444-2419
Founded: 1983
Arts Area: Dance; Vocal Music; Instrumental Music; Festivals
Status: Professional; Non-Profit
Type: Performing
Purpose: To present an annual fesitval of music from the 1500s to the 1800s, performed on period instruments
Management: Igor Kipnis, John Slocum, Artistic Directors; Richard Wyton, Executive Director
Utilizes: Guest Conductors; Guest Artists
Income Sources: Private Foundations/Grants/Endowments; Business/Corporate Donations; Box Office; Government Grants; Individual Donations
Season: June **Annual Attendance:** 3,000

CONNETICUT COLLEGE CONCERT AND ARTIST SERIES
PO Box 5331, 270 Mohegan Avenue, New London, CT 06320
Founded: 1939
Arts Area: Dance; Vocal Music; Instrumental Music; Theater; Grand Opera
Status: Professional; Non-Profit
Type: Performing; Presenting
Purpose: To present a varied annual series of the world's great performing artists thereby enriching and enhancing the cultural life of our community
Management: Peggy Middleton, Concert Manager
Officers: John P. Anthony, Chairman Concerts Committee
Paid Staff: 4
Utilizes: Guest Artists
Budget: $100,000 - $500,000
Income Sources: Box Office; Individual Donations; College Subsidy
Season: September - May **Annual Attendance:** 9,000
Affiliations: APAP; NEP
Performance Facilities: Palmer Auditorium

SUMMER MUSIC, INC.
300 Captain's Walk, Suite 503, New London, CT 06320
(203) 442-9199
FAX: (203) 442-9290
Founded: 1984
Arts Area: Vocal Music; Instrumental Music; Festivals
Status: Non-Profit
Type: Performing
Purpose: To enrich and expand the musical experience of southeastern Connecticut by developing and conducting a summer festival of primarily classical music
Management: Cynde Iverson, Executive Director; Peter Sacco, Music Director; Betsy Carr, General Manager; Keirsten Jenkins, Office Manager; Anne Folino, Box Office Manager
Officers: Jon Kodama, Chairperson; Dr. Lynda Smith, Vice Chairperson; Gail Hamsher, Secretary; Dr. Daniel E. Moalli, Treasurer; Gerald Ceniglio, Executive Committee
Paid Staff: 40 **Volunteer Staff:** 35
Paid Artists: 110
Utilizes: Special Technical Talent; Guest Artists
Budget: $500,000 - $1,000,000
Income Sources: Private Foundations/Grants/Endowments; Business/Corporate Donations; Box Office; Government Grants; Individual Donations
Season: July - August **Annual Attendance:** 35,000

Affiliations: The Connecticut Orchestra
Performance Facilities: Harkness Park

FACILITY

CONNECTICUT COLLEGE - PALMER AUDITORIUM
270 Mohegan Avenue, PO Box 5331, New London, CT 06320
(203) 439-2787
FAX: (203) 439-2700
    Type of Facility: Concert Hall; Auditorium; Theatre House
    Type of Stage: Proscenium
    Stage Dimensions: 40'x74'x29'   **Orchestra Pit**
    Seating Capacity: 1,298
    Year Built: 1939
    Contact for Rental: Patricia Johnson;   (203) 439-2836
    Manager: Peggy Middleton;   (203) 439-2708
    Resident Groups: Concert and Artist Series; Theatre One

GARDE ARTS CENTER
325 State Street, New London, CT 06320
(203) 444-6766
FAX: (203) 447-0503
    Founded: 1985
    Type of Facility: Concert Hall; Auditorium; Performance Center; Art Galleries; Office Space
    Facility Originally: Vaudeville; Movie House
    Type of Stage: Proscenium
    Stage Dimensions: 41'x36'   **Orchestra Pit**
    Seating Capacity: 1,545
    Year Built: 1926   **Architect:** Arland Johnson   **Cost:** $750,000
    Year Remodeled: 1992   **Architect:** Daniel P. Coffey   **Cost:** $10,000,000
    Acoustical Consultant: Jaffe Acoustics
    Contact for Rental: Steve Siegel;   (203) 444-6766
    Resident Groups: Eastern Connecticut Symphony Orchestra

New Milford

DANCE

CHILDREN'S DANCE THEATRE OF NEW MILFORD
79 West Street, New Milford, CT 06776
(203) 354-2978
    Founded: 1985
    Arts Area: Modern; Ballet
    Status: Non-Professional; Non-Profit
    Type: Performing; Touring; Educational
    Purpose: To provide performance experience for young dancers; to educate the public; to provide pre-professional training
    Management: Julianne LaFond, Artistic Director; Alexi Tchernichov, Assistant Artistic Director
    Officers: Julianne LaFond, President
    Volunteer Staff: 5
    Non-Paid Artists: 18
    Utilizes: Guest Artists
    Budget: $1,000 - $50,000
    Income Sources: Box Office; Individual Donations
    Season: September - August   **Annual Attendance:** 1,000
    Affiliations: LaFond School of Ballet

Newington

THEATRE

NEWINGTON CHILDREN'S THEATRE
131 Cedar Street, Newington, CT 06111
(203) 666-4661
    Founded: 1963
    Arts Area: Musical; Theatrical Group
    Status: Non-Professional; Non-Profit
    Type: Performing; Touring

Purpose: To provide quality theater productions for children by children
Management: Barbara Bianci, Assistant Superintendent of Parks and Recreation
Paid Staff: 3
Non-Paid Artists: 30
Budget: $1,000 - $50,000
Season: February - June   **Annual Attendance:** 2,000
Performance Facilities: Newington Auditorium

Norfolk

PERFORMING SERIES

NORFOLK CHAMBER MUSIC FESTIVAL - YALE SUMMER SCHOOL OF MUSIC
Ellen Battell Stoeckel Estate, Norfolk, CT 06058
(203) 542-5537; (203) 432-1966
Founded: 1941
Arts Area: Festivals
Status: Professional; Non-Profit
Type: Performing; Educational
Purpose: To provide chamber-music performances and professional training
Management: Joan Panetti, Executive Director; Michael Geller, Festival Manager
Paid Staff: 10   **Volunteer Staff:** 5
Paid Artists: 45   **Non-Paid Artists:** 5
Budget: $500,000 - $1,000,000
Income Sources: Private Foundations/Grants/Endowments; Business/Corporate Donations; Box Office; Government Grants; Individual Donations; Student Fees
Season: June - August   **Annual Attendance:** 12,000
Affiliations: Yale University
Performance Facilities: The Music Shed

Norwalk

INSTRUMENTAL MUSIC

NORWALK SYMPHONY SOCIETY
83 East Avenue, Suite 304, Norwalk, CT 06851
(203) 866-2455
Founded: 1939
Arts Area: Symphony
Status: Semi-Professional; Non-Profit
Type: Performing; Resident
Purpose: To bring quality musical experiences to audiences in southern Connecticut
Management: Rosemary Cook, Executive Director; Jesse Levine, Music Director/Conductor
Officers: J. Robert Flagg, President; Thomas C. Hofstetter, Executive Vice President
Paid Staff: 2   **Volunteer Staff:** 34
Paid Artists: 25   **Non-Paid Artists:** 40
Utilizes: Guest Artists
Budget: $100,000 - $500,000
Income Sources: Private Foundations/Grants/Endowments; Business/Corporate Donations; Box Office; Government Grants; Individual Donations
Season: October - May   **Annual Attendance:** 2,500
Affiliations: ASOL
Performance Facilities: Norwalk Concert Hall

NORWALK YOUTH SYMPHONY
PO Box 73, Norwalk, CT 06856-0073
(203) 226-6562
FAX: (203) 227-9494
Founded: 1956
Arts Area: Symphony; Orchestra; Chamber
Status: Non-Profit
Type: Performing; Educational
Purpose: To provide the finest possible orchestral training and performing opportunities for the young people of Fairfield County and surrounding area
Management: Carolyn Monk, Manager
Officers: James Welsch, Chairman; Janet Canning, Eric Lundgren, Vice Chairmen; Sharon Gilbert, Secretary; Maureen Sheehen, Treasurer

Paid Staff: 4   **Volunteer Staff:** 24
Non-Paid Artists: 160
Utilizes: Guest Artists
Budget: $1,000 - $50,000
Income Sources: Private Foundations/Grants/Endowments; Business/Corporate Donations; Box Office; Government Grants; Individual Donations
Season: September - May   **Annual Attendance:** 2,500
Affiliations: ASOL
Performance Facilities: Brien McMahon High School

PERFORMING SERIES

SONO ARTS CELEBRATION, INC.
PO Box 2222, Norwalk, CT 06852
(203) 866-7916
   Founded: 1976
   Arts Area: Dance; Vocal Music; Instrumental Music; Theater; Festivals
   Status: Non-Profit
   Type: Performing; Educational
   Purpose: To present high-calibre performing and visual arts free to the public; to teach and inspire
   Officers: Kathryn Hebert, President; Melissa Pisani, Larry Pisani, Fenn Harvey, Brec Morgan, Marsha Kjoller, Lisa Kohanek, Board Members
   Volunteer Staff: 400
   Paid Artists: 30
   Utilizes: Special Technical Talent; Guest Artists
   Budget: $50,000 - $100,000
   Income Sources: Private Foundations/Grants/Endowments; Business/Corporate Donations; Individual Donations
   Season: August   **Annual Attendance:** 70,000

Oakville

THEATRE

CLOCKWORK REPERTORY THEATRE
133 Main Street, Oakville, CT 06779
(203) 274-7247
   Founded: 1977
   Arts Area: Theatrical Group
   Status: Semi-Professional; Non-Profit
   Type: Performing; Resident
   Purpose: To produce plays with an emphasis on new American plays depicting controversial events
   Management: Harold J. Pantely, Producer; Susan P. Pantely, Artistic Director
   Paid Staff: 4   **Volunteer Staff:** 8
   Utilizes: Guest Artists; Guest Directors
   Budget: $50,000 - $100,000
   Income Sources: Private Foundations/Grants/Endowments; Business/Corporate Donations; Box Office; Government Grants; Individual Donations
   Season: November - May   **Annual Attendance:** 6,000
   Affiliations: NETC

Ridgefield

INSTRUMENTAL MUSIC

RIDGEFIELD SYMPHONY ORCHESTRA
PO Box 613, Ridgefield, CT 06877
(203) 438-3208
   Founded: 1964
   Arts Area: Symphony
   Status: Professional; Non-Profit
   Type: Performing
   Management: Beatrice Brown, Music Director/Conductor
   Officers: Jeanne Cooke, President; William Stopper, Vice President; Frank T. Gellinek, Treasurer
   Paid Artists: 68
   Utilizes: Guest Conductors; Guest Artists
   Budget: $50,000 - $100,000

Income Sources: Private Foundations/Grants/Endowments; Business/Corporate Donations; Box Office; Individual Donations
Season: September - April   **Annual Attendance:** 3,600
Affiliations: ASOL; BMI; ASCAP

Salisbury

PERFORMING SERIES

BERKSHIRE HILLS MUSIC AND DANCE ASSOCIATION
PO Box 351, Salisbury, CT 06068
(203) 435-2442
Founded: 1970
Arts Area: Dance; Vocal Music; Instrumental Music
Status: Non-Profit
Type: Sponsoring
Purpose: To foster appreciation of the performing arts through the presentation of concerts, recitals and dance attractions of superior quality
Officers: Albert C. Sly, President; Dorothy Massey, Vice President; Heather Schaufele, Secretary; John Estabrook, Treasurer
Utilizes: Guest Artists
Budget: $1,000 - $50,000
Income Sources: Private Foundations/Grants/Endowments; Box Office; Individual Donations
Season: September - April   **Annual Attendance:** 1,500

Sharon

THEATRE

EAST-WEST FUSION THEATRE
PO Box 145, Sharon, CT 06069
(203) 364-5220
Founded: 1975
Arts Area: Theatrical Group; Puppet
Status: Professional; Non-Profit
Type: Performing; Touring; Resident; Educational; Sponsoring
Purpose: To bring together artists and scholars from around the world to create a truly international theatre inspired by Asian and other non-Western performing arts and devoted to fusion of the arts
Management: Teviot Fairservis Pourchot, Artistic Director; Dr. Walter A. Fairservis Jr., Producing Director; Amy Schindler, Assistant to the Artistic Director
Officers: Jano Bell Fairservis, President
Paid Staff: 2   **Volunteer Staff:** 50
Paid Artists: 5
Utilizes: Special Technical Talent; Guest Conductors; Guest Artists; Guest Directors
Budget: $50,000 - $100,000
Income Sources: Private Foundations/Grants/Endowments; Business/Corporate Donations; Box Office; Government Grants; Individual Donations
Season: June - August   **Annual Attendance:** 8,000
Affiliations: ASSITEJ; ART/NY; DTW
Performance Facilities: Center for East-West Studies

Sherman

THEATRE

SHERMAN PLAYERS
PO Box 404, Sherman, CT 06784
(203) 354-3622
Founded: 1925
Arts Area: Musical; Community; Theatrical Group
Status: Non-Professional; Non-Profit
Type: Performing; Sponsoring
Purpose: To bring high-quality community theatre productions to the area
Officers: George H. Sutton, President; Larry Buoy, Terry Johanesen, Vice Presidents; Betsy Scholze, Treasurer
Utilizes: Special Technical Talent; Guest Directors
Budget: $1,000 - $50,000

Income Sources: Business/Corporate Donations; Box Office; Individual Donations
Season: April - November   **Annual Attendance:** 7,000
Performance Facilities: Sherman Playhouse

FACILITY

SHERMAN PLAYHOUSE
PO Box 471, Sherman, CT 06776
(203) 354-3622
Founded: 1926
Type of Facility: Theatre House
Facility Originally: Church
Type of Stage: Proscenium
Seating Capacity: 120
Year Built: 1832
Year Remodeled: 1974
Resident Groups: Sherman Players

South Windsor

INSTRUMENTAL MUSIC

MANCHESTER PIPE BAND
35 Breezy Hill Road, South Windsor, CT 06074
(203) 644-2709
Founded: 1914
Arts Area: Ethnic; Band
Status: Semi-Professional; Non-Profit
Type: Performing
Purpose: To perform Scottish Pipe Band Music at the highest level of proficiency; to perpetuate this music form
Management: S. Yeomans, President; M. Brannick, Vice President; J. Jones, Secretary; F. Yeomans, Treasurer
Officers: C. Murdoch, Pipe Major; D. Ritchie, Pipe Sargeant; S. Yeomans, Drum Sargeant; D. Ewen, Drum Major
Volunteer Staff: 8
Non-Paid Artists: 20
Budget: $1,000 - $50,000
Income Sources: Business/Corporate Donations; Box Office
Season: 52 Weeks
Affiliations: Eastern U.S. Pipe Band Association

Southington

FACILITY

SOUTHINGTON COMMUNITY THEATRE
PO Box 411, Southington, CT 06489
(203) 621-0071
Type of Facility: Auditorium
Type of Stage: Platform

Stamford

DANCE

CONNECTICUT BALLET THEATRE
PO Box 127, Stamford, CT 06904
(203) 259-3930
Founded: 1981
Arts Area: Modern; Ballet
Status: Professional
Type: Performing; Touring; Educational
Purpose: Classical and contemporary ballet repertory company serving Connecticut and New England
Management: Brett Raphael, Artistic Director
Officers: Ishier Jacobson, Chairman; Brett Raphael, President
Paid Staff: 3   **Volunteer Staff:** 10
Paid Artists: 18

Utilizes: Guest Artists; Guest Choreographers
Budget: $500,000 - $1,000,000
Income Sources: Private Foundations/Grants/Endowments; Business/Corporate Donations; Box Office; Individual Donations
Season: November - May   **Annual Attendance:** 25,000
Performance Facilities: Palace Theatre of the Arts

INSTRUMENTAL MUSIC

STAMFORD SYMPHONY ORCHESTRA
400 Main Street, Stamford, CT 06903
(203) 325-1407
FAX: (203) 325-8762
Founded: 1968
Arts Area: Symphony; Orchestra; Ensemble
Status: Professional; Non-Profit
Type: Performing; Resident; Educational
Purpose: To perform the finest symphony music in the Fairfield County area
Management: Barbara J. Soroca, Executive Director
Officers: Clifford N. Angers, President
Paid Staff: 5   **Volunteer Staff:** 30
Paid Artists: 10
Utilizes: Guest Artists
Budget: $100,000 - $500,000
Income Sources: Private Foundations/Grants/Endowments; Business/Corporate Donations; Box Office; Government Grants; Individual Donations
Season: October - May   **Annual Attendance:** 11,000
Performance Facilities: Palace Theatre of the Arts

THE YOUNG ARTISTS PHILHARMONIC
Ridgeway Station, PO Box 3301, Stamford, CT 06905
(203) 323-0899
Founded: 1960
Arts Area: Orchestra
Status: Non-Professional; Non-Profit
Type: Performing; Educational
Purpose: To develop musical excellence among talented young artists in the area through membership in Young String Ensemble (Elementary), Young People's Orchestra (Middle School) and Young Artists Philharmonic (High School); membership is by audition
Management: Frances Lourie, Manager; Salvatore Princiotti, Musical Director
Paid Staff: 5   **Volunteer Staff:** 30
Non-Paid Artists: 150
Utilizes: Guest Artists
Budget: $1,000 - $50,000
Income Sources: Private Foundations/Grants/Endowments; Business/Corporate Donations; Box Office; Government Grants; Individual Donations
Season: September - May
Performance Facilities: Stamford High School

VOCAL MUSIC

CONNECTICUT GRAND OPERA
61 Atlantic Street, Stamford, CT 06901
(203) 327-2867; (203) 359-0009
Founded: 1978
Arts Area: Grand Opera
Status: Professional
Type: Performing; Resident
Purpose: To develop a permanent professional opera company of international standards in southwestern Connecticut
Management: John Hiddlestone, General Manager
Officers: Sheldon G. Gilgore, Chairman; Frank D. Rich Jr., President; Charles L. Fry, Secretary; Lloyd F. Pierce, Treasurer
Paid Staff: 4
Paid Artists: 120
Utilizes: Special Technical Talent; Guest Conductors; Guest Artists; Guest Directors
Budget: $500,000 - $1,000,000
Income Sources: Private Foundations/Grants/Endowments; Business/Corporate Donations; Box Office; Government Grants; Individual Donations
Season: September - May

Affiliations: AGMA; IATSE
Performance Facilities: Palace Theatre of the Arts; Klein Auditorium

NEW ENGLAND LYRIC OPERETTA
84 West Park Place, Stamford, CT 06901
(203) 324-0240
FAX: (203) 655-0566
    Founded: 1986
    Status: Professional; Non-Profit
    Type: Performing; Resident
    Purpose: To perform the full range of European and American operetta
    Management: Esme J. Ingledew, General Manager; William H. Edgerton, Artistic Director; Stephen Sulich, Music Director/Conductor; Robert G. Waring, Resident Stage Director
    Officers: Ralph L. Rossi, Chairman of the Board; Stephen Pierson, Vice Chairman; William Edgerton, Treasurer
    Paid Staff: 3 **Volunteer Staff:** 5
    Paid Artists: 75
    Utilizes: Special Technical Talent; Guest Artists
    Budget: $100,000 - $500,000
    Income Sources: Private Foundations/Grants/Endowments; Business/Corporate Donations; Box Office; Government Grants; Individual Donations
    Season: September - May **Annual Attendance:** 6,000
    Performance Facilities: Palace Theatre

PRO ARTE CHAMBER SINGERS OF CONNECTICUT
PO Box 3635, Stamford, CT 06905
(203) 323-7955
    Founded: 1974
    Arts Area: Choral
    Status: Professional
    Type: Performing; Touring
    Purpose: To present the range of choral repertoire, from medieval to contemporary times
    Management: Cynthia King, Managing Director
    Officers: Arthur Congdon, Chairman
    Paid Staff: 2 **Volunteer Staff:** 20
    Paid Artists: 32
    Utilizes: Special Technical Talent
    Budget: $50,000 - $100,000
    Income Sources: Private Foundations/Grants/Endowments; Business/Corporate Donations; Box Office; Government Grants; Individual Donations
    Season: September - June **Annual Attendance:** 1,500
    Performance Facilities: First Presbyterian Church

THEATRE

PALACE THEATRE OF THE ARTS
61 Atlantic Street, Stamford, CT 06901
(203) 325-4466
    Founded: 1983
    Arts Area: Professional; Musical; Theatrical Group
    Status: Professional; Commercial
    Type: Sponsoring
    Management: John Hiddlestone, Facilities Manager; Nancy Koffin, Marketing Director; Vicki Kieffer, House Manager
    Paid Staff: 6
    Budget: $100,000 - $500,000
    Income Sources: Box Office
    Season: 52 Weeks
    Affiliations: IATSE
    Performance Facilities: Palace Theatre

STAMFORD THEATRE WORKS
95 Atlantic Street, Stamford, CT 06901
(203) 359-4414
FAX: (203) 356-1846
    Founded: 1988
    Arts Area: Professional
    Status: Professional; Non-Profit
    Type: Performing

Purpose: To produce plays of cultural and social signifigance for the benefit of the greater Stamford area; to build a theatre of regional and national prominence, acclaimed for its innovative productions of contemporary and classical plays
Management: Steve Karp, Artistic/Managing Director; Richard B. Kelley, General Manager; Jane Desy, Literary Manager; Roberta Cohen, Press/Marketing Director
Officers: Steve Karp, President; Robert M. Karp, Vice President; Miriam Burdock Shaw, Secretary/Treasurer; Thomas G. Finck, Chairman of the Board
Paid Staff: 4 **Volunteer Staff:** 10
Paid Artists: 40
Utilizes: Special Technical Talent; Guest Artists; Guest Directors
Budget: $100,000 - $500,000
Income Sources: Private Foundations/Grants/Endowments; Business/Corporate Donations; Box Office; Government Grants; Individual Donations
Season: September - May **Annual Attendance:** 8,000
Affiliations: AEA; SSDC

FACILITY

PALACE THEATRE - STAMFORD CENTER FOR THE ARTS
61 Atlantic Street, Stamford, CT 06901
(203) 358-0288
Type of Facility: Concert Hall; Theatre House; Opera House
Facility Originally: Vaudeville
Type of Stage: Proscenium
Stage Dimensions: 46'Wx24'D **Orchestra Pit**
Seating Capacity: 1584
Year Built: 1927 **Architect:** Thomas Lamb
Year Remodeled: 1983 **Architect:** Roger Lang **Cost:** $2,000,000
Contact for Rental: George Murdock; (203) 325-0288
Resident Groups: Connecticut Grand Opera; Stamford Symphony Orchestra

Stony Creek

THEATRE

PUPPET HOUSE THEATRE
PO Box 3081, Stony Creek, CT 06405
(203) 488-5752
Founded: 1972
Arts Area: Professional; Summer Stock; Community; Folk; Puppet
Status: Semi-Professional; Non-Professional; Non-Profit
Type: Performing; Touring; Sponsoring
Purpose: To present theatrical programs of community and small professional groups
Management: Barry Fritz, James Weil
Volunteer Staff: 10
Paid Artists: 25 **Non-Paid Artists:** 75
Utilizes: Special Technical Talent; Guest Artists; Guest Directors
Budget: $1,000 - $50,000
Income Sources: Private Foundations/Grants/Endowments; Box Office; Individual Donations
Season: April - December **Annual Attendance:** 10,000

Storrs

FACILITY

UNIVERSITY OF CONNECTICUT - HARRIET S. JORGENSEN THEATRE
U-127, 802 Bolton Road, Storrs, CT 06269-1127
(203) 486-4025
Type of Facility: Theatre House
Type of Stage: Proscenium
Stage Dimensions: 18'x32'x33' **Orchestra Pit**
Seating Capacity: 494
Year Built: 1955 **Architect:** Teich **Cost:** $1,000,000
Acoustical Consultant: Ed Cole
Manager: David R. Kanter, Department Head
Resident Groups: Nutmeg Summer Theatre

UNIVERSITY OF CONNECTICUT - STUDIO THEATRE
Fine Arts Center, Storrs, CT 06269-1127
(203) 486-4025
> **Type of Facility:** Theatre Complex; Studio Performance; Theatre House
> **Type of Stage:** Proscenium
> **Stage Dimensions:** 14'x26'x20'
> **Seating Capacity:** 120
> **Year Built:** 1959   **Architect:** Golden-Storrs Associates
> **Manager:** David R. Kanter, Department Head

Stratford

INSTRUMENTAL MUSIC

THE CLARION BRASS QUINTET
199 College Street, Stratford, CT 06497
(203) 380-2485
> **Founded:** 1976
> **Arts Area:** Chamber; Ensemble; Instrumental Group
> **Status:** Semi-Professional
> **Type:** Performing; Educational
> **Purpose:** To cultivate a deep love of brass music and the desire to bring this music to the people of Connecticut
> **Management:** R. Russell Phillips, Corinne Zanetti, Co-Founders
> **Volunteer Staff:** 5
> **Paid Artists:** 5
> **Utilizes:** Special Technical Talent; Guest Artists
> **Budget:** $1,000 - $50,000
> **Income Sources:** Private Foundations/Grants/Endowments; Business/Corporate Donations; Box Office; Individual Donations
> **Season:** 52 Weeks   **Annual Attendance:** 2,000
> **Affiliations:** Connecticut Touring Program
> **Performance Facilities:** Recital Hall

Torrington

DANCE

NUTMEG BALLET COMPANY
21 Water Street, Torrington, CT 06790
(203) 482-4413
> **Founded:** 1971
> **Arts Area:** Ballet
> **Status:** Semi-Professional; Non-Profit
> **Type:** Performing; Touring; Resident; Educational; Sponsoring
> **Purpose:** To train and provide students with exceptional performance opportunities leading to professional careers in dance and related disciplines
> **Management:** Sharon E. Dante, Artistic Director
> **Officers:** Robert Calabrese, Chairman
> **Paid Staff:** 10   **Volunteer Staff:** 40
> **Paid Artists:** 15   **Non-Paid Artists:** 25
> **Utilizes:** Special Technical Talent; Guest Conductors; Guest Artists; Guest Directors
> **Budget:** $100,000 - $500,000
> **Income Sources:** Private Foundations/Grants/Endowments; Business/Corporate Donations; Box Office; Government Grants; Individual Donations
> **Season:** September - June   **Annual Attendance:** 10,000
> **Performance Facilities:** Warner Theatre/Studio

THEATRE

TORRINGTON CIVIC THEATRE
PO Box 22, Torrington, CT 6790
(203) 482-0073
> **Founded:** 1962
> **Arts Area:** Musical; Community; Theatrical Group
> **Status:** Non-Professional; Non-Profit
> **Type:** Performing
> **Officers:** Chuck Carlin, President

Budget: $1,000 - $50,000
Income Sources: Business/Corporate Donations; Box Office; Individual Donations
Season: November - May   **Annual Attendance:** 1,500
Affiliations: Theatre Guild of Northwest Connecticut
Performance Facilities: Coe Park Civic Center

FACILITY

COE PARK CIVIC CENTER
101 Litchfield Street, Torrington, CT 06790
(203) 489-2274
    Type of Facility: Auditorium; Civic Center
    Type of Stage: Proscenium
    Stage Dimensions: 39'Wx21'D
    Seating Capacity: 250
    Year Built: 1975   **Architect:** Tom Babbitt   **Cost:** $450,000
    Contact for Rental: John Timm;   (203) 489-2274
    Resident Groups: Torrington Civic Theatre; T.A.S.S. Theater Group; Rainbow Summer Theater; Torrington
Symphony

Wallingford

INSTRUMENTAL MUSIC

WALLINGFORD SYMPHONY ORCHESTRA
333 Christian Street, Wallingford, CT 06492
(203) 269-2699
    Founded: 1976
    Arts Area: Symphony; Orchestra
    Status: Professional; Non-Profit
    Type: Performing
    Purpose: To provide musical enjoyment for the people of the greater Wallingford area
    Officers: Sandra Ulbricht, President
    Utilizes: Special Technical Talent; Guest Artists
    Budget: $50,000 - $100,000
    Income Sources: Private Foundations/Grants/Endowments; Business/Corporate Donations; Box Office; Government
Grants; Individual Donations
    Season: September - May   **Annual Attendance:** 15,000
    Affiliations: Affiliate Artist Program
    Performance Facilities: Paul Mellon Arts Center

FACILITY

OAKDALE THEATRE
95 South Turnpike Road, Wallingford, CT 06492
(203) 269-8721
    Type of Facility: Concert Hall
    Facility Originally: Tent
    Type of Stage: In-the-Round
    Stage Dimensions: 40'Wx28'D
    Seating Capacity: 3184
    Year Built: 1953
    Year Remodeled: 1973
    Contact for Rental: Beau Segal;   (203) 269-8721
    A wooden dome was constructed over the seating in 1973. No seat in the theatre is more than 70' from the stage.

PAUL MELLON ARTS CENTER
Christian Street, Wallingford, CT 06492
(203) 269-1113
    Type of Facility: Concert Hall; Performance Center; Theatre House; Multi-Purpose
    Type of Stage: Thrust; Flexible; Proscenium
    Stage Dimensions: 90'Wx30'D; 48'Wx36'H proscenium opening   **Orchestra Pit**
    Seating Capacity: 850
    Year Built: 1972   **Architect:** I.M. Pei and Partners   **Cost:** $4,700,000

Manager: Terrence Ortwein
The Paul Mellon Arts Center is used by both the Choate School and Rosemary Hall.

Washington

THEATRE

DRAMALITES
PO Box 1117, Washington, CT 06793
    Arts Area: Community
    Status: Non-Professional; Non-Profit
    Type: Performing
    Purpose: To promote community theatre
    Officers: Larry Friedman, President; Mary Adams Childs, Vice President; Phyllis McBride, Secretary; Henry W. Kunhardt, Treasurer
    Budget: $1,000 - $50,000
    Income Sources: Box Office; Individual Donations
    Season: July - August   **Annual Attendance:** 1,000
    Performance Facilities: Shepaug Valley Regional School Auditorium

---

Washington Depot

DANCE

PILOBOLUS DANCE THEATRE
PO Box 388, Washington Depot, CT 06794
(203) 868-0538
    Founded: 1971
    Arts Area: Modern
    Status: Professional; Non-Profit
    Type: Performing; Touring; Resident
    Management: Susan Mandler, Manager; Robby Barnett, Alison Chase, Moses Pendleton, Michael Tracy, Artistic Directors; Jonathan Wolken, Executive Director/Artistic Director
    Paid Staff: 7
    Paid Artists: 5
    Utilizes: Special Technical Talent; Guest Artists
    Budget: $500,000 - $1,000,000
    Income Sources: Private Foundations/Grants/Endowments; Business/Corporate Donations; Box Office; Government Grants; Individual Donations
    Season: September - July
    Performance Facilities: Stamford Center for the Performing Arts

PERFORMING SERIES

ARMSTRONG CHAMBER CONCERTS, INC.
86 Church Hill Road, Washington Depot, CT 06794
(203) 868-0522
    Founded: 1983
    Arts Area: Instrumental Music
    Status: Professional; Non-Profit
    Type: Performing; Touring; Resident; Educational
    Purpose: To perform chamber music of the highest quality, thus broadening the public's understanding of this special kind of music
    Officers: Helen Armstrong, President/Treasurer; Ajit Hutheesing, Vice President; Marvin Ginsky, Secretary
    Paid Staff: 1   **Volunteer Staff:** 4
    Paid Artists: 6
    Utilizes: Guest Artists
    Budget: $1,000 - $50,000
    Income Sources: Private Foundations/Grants/Endowments; Business/Corporate Donations; Box Office; Government Grants; Individual Donations
    Season: October - June   **Annual Attendance:** 1,000

Waterbury

INSTRUMENTAL MUSIC

WATERBURY SYMPHONY ORCHESTRA
PO Box 1762, Waterbury, CT 06721
(203) 574-4283
FAX: (203) 756-3507
Founded: 1938
Arts Area: Symphony; Orchestra
Status: Professional
Type: Performing
Purpose: To provide symphonic concerts for the greater Waterbury area
Management: Carol C. Gilbert, Administrative Director
Officers: Direk Barhudt, President; Robert Nocera, Vice President; Robert Griffin, Second Vice President
Paid Staff: 2 **Volunteer Staff:** 100
Paid Artists: 70
Utilizes: Guest Artists
Budget: $100,000 - $500,000
Income Sources: Private Foundations/Grants/Endowments; Business/Corporate Donations; Box Office; Government Grants; Individual Donations
Season: October - May **Annual Attendance:** 6,000
Performance Facilities: Fine Arts Center, Kennedy High School

---

Waterford

THEATRE

O'NEILL THEATER CENTER
305 Great Neck Road, Waterford, CT 06385
(203) 443-5378
Founded: 1964
Arts Area: Professional; Theatrical Group
Status: Professional; Non-Profit
Type: Performing; Educational; Sponsoring
Management: Sylvia F. Traeger, Manager; Boyd Richards, Artistic Director, National Playwrights Conference
Officers: George C. White, President and Founder
Paid Staff: 30 **Volunteer Staff:** 50
Paid Artists: 75
Utilizes: Guest Artists; Guest Directors
Budget: $1,000,000 - $5,000,000
Income Sources: Private Foundations/Grants/Endowments; Business/Corporate Donations; Box Office; Government Grants; Individual Donations
Season: July - September **Annual Attendance:** 13,000
Affiliations: LORT
Performance Facilities: O'Neill Theater Center

West Cornwall

DANCE

LOTTE GOSLAR AND COMPANY
39 Town Street, West Cornwall, CT 06796
(203) 672-6042
Arts Area: Modern; Mime; Ballet
Status: Professional; Non-Profit
Type: Performing
Purpose: To perform at colleges, universities and communities; to teach master classes at universities and wherever asked; to give children's concerts and teach children's classes
Officers: Lotte Goslar, Director
Paid Staff: 12
Utilizes: Special Technical Talent
Budget: $100,000 - $500,000
Income Sources: Government Grants
Season: 52 Weeks
Affiliations: NEA Dance Touring Program

West Hartford

INSTRUMENTAL MUSIC

CONNECTICUT STRING ORCHESTRA, INC.
19 Sunset Terrace, West Hartford, CT 06107
(203) 246-9503
Founded: 1968
Arts Area: Orchestra
Status: Non-Professional; Non-Profit
Type: Performing; Resident
Purpose: Community string orchestra
Officers: Thomas P. Kugelman, Librarian; David McMullen, President
Paid Artists: 2   **Non-Paid Artists:** 50
Utilizes: Guest Conductors; Guest Artists
Budget: $1,000 - $50,000
Income Sources: Private Foundations/Grants/Endowments; Business/Corporate Donations; Government Grants; Individual Donations
Season: September - June   **Annual Attendance:** 1,000
Performance Facilities: Asylum Hill Congregational Church

PERFORMING SERIES

HARTT SUMMER YOUTH MUSIC FESTIVAL
Hartt School of Music, 200 Bloomfield Avenue, West Hartford, CT 06117
(203) 243-4421
Arts Area: Vocal Music; Instrumental Music
Status: Professional; Non-Profit
Type: Educational; Sponsoring
Purpose: To provide residents of the greater Hartford area with the highest quality musical performances
Management: Neal Smith, Director
Paid Staff: 1
Utilizes: Special Technical Talent; Guest Conductors; Guest Artists
Budget: $50,000 - $100,000
Income Sources: Box Office
Season: June - July
Performance Facilities: Fuller Music Center

FACILITY

LINCOLN THEATER
200 Bloomfield Avenue, West Hartford, CT 06117
(203) 768-4536
FAX: (203) 768-4229
Founded: 1978
Type of Facility: Theatre House
Type of Stage: Thrust; Flexible
Stage Dimensions: 60'x57'   **Orchestra Pit**
Seating Capacity: 1,100
Year Built: 1978
Contact for Rental: Raffaella De Gruttola;   (203) 768-4536

ROBERTS CENTER THEATRE
170 Kingswood Road, West Hartford, CT 06119
(203) 233-9631
FAX: (203) 232-3843
Type of Facility: Theatre House
Type of Stage: Proscenium
Orchestra Pit
Seating Capacity: 600
Year Built: 1972   **Architect:** Theatre Tech   **Cost:** $3,000,000
Contact for Rental: Thomas Burke Jr., Business Manager;   (203) 233-9631

Westport

THEATRE

THE FAIRFIELD COUNTY STAGE COMPANY
25 Powers Court, Westport, CT 06880
(203) 227-1072; (203) 227-1290
Founded: 1981
Arts Area: Professional; Theatrical Group
Status: Professional
Type: Performing; Resident
Purpose: Professional regional theatre operating under the Letter of Agreement/LORT "D" Contract with Actors' Equity Association
Management: Burry Fredrick, Artistic Director; Marilyn Hersey, Managing Director; Christopher Cull, Associate Director; Susan Haggstrom, Technical Director
Officers: Rita Fredricks, Board Chairman; Marilyn Hersey, President; Christopher Cull, Secretary; Burry Fredrik, Treasurer
Paid Staff: 11
Paid Artists: 70   **Non-Paid Artists:** 8
Utilizes: Guest Directors
Budget: $500,000 - $1,000,000
Income Sources: Private Foundations/Grants/Endowments; Business/Corporate Donations; Box Office; Government Grants; Individual Donations
Season: October - May
Annual Attendance: 18,000
Affiliations: AEA; SSDC; TCG

WESTPORT COMMUNITY THEATRE
Town Hall, 110 Myrtle Avenue, Westport, CT 06880
(203) 226-1983
Founded: 1956
Arts Area: Community; Theatrical Group
Status: Non-Professional; Non-Profit
Type: Performing
Purpose: To provide entertainment and instruction in the performing art of theatre to the community; to develop an appreciation of theatre amongst our audience
Management: H. Edward Spires, Artistic Manager
Officers: Glenna Kean, Chairman
Paid Staff: 1
Utilizes: Guest Conductors; Guest Directors
Budget: $1,000 - $50,000
Income Sources: Box Office; Individual Donations
Season: 52 Weeks
Annual Attendance: 6,000

WESTPORT COUNTRY PLAYHOUSE
25 Powers Court, PO Box 629, Westport, CT 06880
(203) 227-5137
FAX: (203) 221-7482
Founded: 1930
Arts Area: Professional; Summer Stock
Status: Professional; Non-Profit
Type: Performing; Resident
Purpose: To develop professional theatre in Connecticut
Management: James B. McKenzie, Executive Producer; Julie Monahan, General Manager
Officers: Janet Plotkin, President; Freda Welsh, Vice President; Sharon Giese, Secretary; Wally Meyer, Treasurer
Paid Staff: 50   **Volunteer Staff:** 100
Paid Artists: 100
Utilizes: Guest Artists; Guest Directors
Budget: $1,000,000 - $5,000,000
Income Sources: Private Foundations/Grants/Endowments; Box Office; Individual Donations
Season: June - September
Annual Attendance: 60,000
Affiliations: COST
Performance Facilities: Westport Country Playhouse

PERFORMING SERIES

LEVITT PAVILION FOR THE PERFOMING ARTS
Town Hall, 110 Myrtle Avenue, Westport, CT 06880
(203) 226-7600
FAX: (203) 222-7541
   Founded: 1973
   Arts Area: Dance; Vocal Music; Instrumental Music; Theater; Lyric Opera
   Status: Non-Profit
   Type: Performing; Educational
   Purpose: To provide 50 nights of high quality entertainment at no admission to audiences of all ages
   Management: Michele M. Orris, Managing Director
   Officers: Diane Mangano-Cohen, Chairman; Patricia Blaufuss, Vice Chairman; Robert Wettach, Treasurer
   Paid Staff: 1   **Volunteer Staff:** 50
   Utilizes: Special Technical Talent
   Budget: $50,000 - $100,000
   Income Sources: Private Foundations/Grants/Endowments; Business/Corporate Donations; Box Office; Government Grants; Individual Donations; Membership; Civic Organizations
   Season: June - August   **Annual Attendance:** 50,000
   Performance Facilities: Levitt Pavilion for the Performing Arts

FACILITY

LEVITT PAVILION FOR THE PERFORMING ARTS
Off Jesup Road, behind New Westport Library, Westport, CT 06880
(203) 226-7600
FAX: (203) 222-7541
   Mailing Address: c/o Westport Town Hall, 110 Myrtle Avenue, Westport, CT 06880
   Founded: 1973
   Type of Facility: Outdoor (Concert); Outdoor Performance Stage; Bandshell
   Seating Capacity: 2,500 lawn seating
   Year Built: 1973   **Architect:** Bruce Campbell Graham
   Year Remodeled: 1992   **Architect:** Bruce Campbell Graham

WESTPORT COMMUNITY THEATRE
110 Myrtle Avenue, Westport, CT 06880
(203) 226-1983
   Type of Facility: Auditorium; Environmental
   Facility Originally: School
   Type of Stage: 3/4 Arena
   Stage Dimensions: 26'x23'
   Seating Capacity: 185
   Year Remodeled: 1978   **Architect:** H. Edward Spires   **Cost:** $65,000
   Resident Groups: Westport Community Theatre

WESTPORT COUNTRY PLAYHOUSE
25 Powers Court, PO Box 629, Westport, CT 06880
(203) 227-5137
FAX: (203) 221-7482
   Founded: 1931
   Type of Facility: Theatre House
   Facility Originally: Business Facility; Tanning Factory
   Type of Stage: Proscenium
   Stage Dimensions: 16'x30'x26'
   Seating Capacity: 706
   Year Built: 1930   **Architect:** Throckmortan   **Cost:** $400,000
   Contact for Rental: Julie Monahan;   (203) 227-5137
   Manager: James B. McKenzie;   (202) 227-5137

Wilton

THEATRE

THE WILTON PLAYSHOP
15 Lovers Lane, Wilton, CT 06897
(203) 762-7629
   Founded: 1937

Arts Area: Theatrical Group
Status: Non-Professional
Type: Performing; Educational
Purpose: To provide fine theatre at reasonable prices; to educate and train members so that quality continues
Management: Carol Albert, President, Board of Directors; Jane Kelly, Business Manager; Pat Gould, Secretary
Officers: Kay Strakosh, President, Board of Trustees; Sigh Schneid, Secretary; Carole Harris, Business Manager
Volunteer Staff: 50
Non-Paid Artists: 300
Utilizes: Guest Artists; Guest Directors
Budget: $1,000 - $50,000
Income Sources: Private Foundations/Grants/Endowments; Business/Corporate Donations; Box Office; Individual Donations
Season: 52 Weeks

DELAWARE

Bear

VOCAL MUSIC

DIAMOND STATE CHORUS OF SWEET ADELINES INTERNATIONAL
42 Craig Road, Bear, DE 19701
(302) 322-6445
FAX: (302) 378-0935
Founded: 1978
Arts Area: Choral
Status: Semi-Professional; Non-Profit
Type: Performing; Educational
Purpose: To entertain and educate the public in the American art form of barber shop harmony
Management: Becky Diamond, Chorus Manager
Officers: Emily Pinder, President; Louisa Leipold, Vice President; Sylvia Taggart, Secretary; Celia Renai, Treasurer
Paid Staff: 1   **Volunteer Staff:** 12
Non-Paid Artists: 50
Utilizes: Special Technical Talent; Guest Artists
Budget: $1,000 - $50,000
Income Sources: Box Office
Season: 52 Weeks

Dover

DANCE

DELAWARE REGIONAL BALLET
1071 Governors Avenue, PO Box 160, Dover, DE 19901
(302) 674-1020
Founded: 1973
Arts Area: Ballet; Jazz
Status: Non-Professional; Non-Profit
Type: Performing
Management: Tatjana Akinfieva-Smith, Artistic Director; Marion Tracy, Administration Director
Officers: Ellie Boone, President
Non-Paid Artists: 35
Utilizes: Guest Artists; Guest Choreographers
Budget: $1,000 - $50,000
Income Sources: Private Foundations/Grants/Endowments; Business/Corporate Donations; Box Office; Individual Donations
Season: September - May

Georgetown

THEATRE

POSSUM POINT PLAYERS
Old Laurel Highway, PO Box 96, Georgetown, DE 19947
(302) 856-3460
Founded: 1973
Arts Area: Musical; Dinner; Community; Theatrical Group
Status: Non-Professional; Non-Profit
Type: Performing; Educational
Purpose: To produce and perform high-quality theatrical productions in Sussex County, Delaware
Management: Andre Beaumont, Executive Director; Mary Cahill, Adminstrative Assistant
Officers: Nina Galerstein, President; Anne Maloney, Vice President; Rhonda Sharman, Secretary; William Thompson, Treasurer
Paid Staff: 1   **Volunteer Staff:** 2
Non-Paid Artists: 50
Utilizes: Guest Directors
Budget: $50,000 - $100,000
Income Sources: Private Foundations/Grants/Endowments; Business/Corporate Donations; Box Office; Government Grants; Individual Donations

Season: 52 Weeks **Annual Attendance:** 3,800
Affiliations: Delaware Theater Association
Performance Facilities: Possum Hall; Delaware Tech Theater; Millsboro Civic Center

---

Newark

DANCE

THE DANCE NETWORK
East Delaware Avenue and Haines Street, Newark, DE 19711
(302) 368-0365
Founded: 1980
Arts Area: Modern
Status: Semi-Professional; Non-Profit
Type: Performing; Touring; Resident; Educational; Sponsoring
Management: Linda Moores, Director; Dave Fardig, Assistant
Utilizes: Special Technical Talent; Guest Artists; Guest Directors; Guest Choreographers
Budget: $1,000 - $50,000
Income Sources: Private Foundations/Grants/Endowments; Business/Corporate Donations; Box Office; Government Grants; Individual Donations

DELAWARE DANCE COMPANY
22 Prestbury Square Building, Newark, DE 19713
(302) 731-9615
Founded: 1982
Arts Area: Modern; Ballet
Status: Professional; Non-Profit
Type: Performing; Touring; Educational
Purpose: To provide quality dance performances throughout Delaware, Maryland and Pennsylvania while providing a venue for emerging artists (dancers, choreographers and musicians) to hone their professional skills
Management: Priscilla R. Payson, Director; Anne Horgan and Catherine Samardza, Ballet Mistresses; Rick Webster, General Manager; Camille Izard, Artistic Advisor
Officers: Priscilla R. Payson, President; Janan Crouse, Secretary; Jennifer Reynolds, Treasurer
Paid Staff: 2 **Volunteer Staff:** 10
Paid Artists: 6 **Non-Paid Artists:** 30
Utilizes: Special Technical Talent; Guest Artists; Guest Choreographers
Budget: $50,000 - $100,000
Income Sources: Box Office; Individual Donations
Season: September - June **Annual Attendance:** 10,000
Performance Facilities: Dickinson Theatre; Delaware Theatre Company

INSTRUMENTAL MUSIC

NEWARK SYMPHONY ORCHESTRA
PO Box 7775, Newark, DE 19714
(302) 366-8491
FAX: (302) 368-4419
Founded: 1966
Arts Area: Symphony
Status: Non-Professional; Non-Profit
Type: Performing
Purpose: To provide volunteer musicians the opportunity to play symphonic literature and the community to hear live performances
Officers: Vernon Vernier, President, Board of Directors; Jean Unrun, Vice President; Frank Mazlewski, Treasurer; Carolyn Fuhrman, Secretary
Paid Staff: 3
Paid Artists: 15 **Non-Paid Artists:** 80
Utilizes: Guest Artists
Budget: $1,000 - $50,000
Income Sources: Private Foundations/Grants/Endowments; Business/Corporate Donations; Box Office; Government Grants; Individual Donations
Season: October - May **Annual Attendance:** 3,500
Affiliations: University of Delaware
Performance Facilities: University of Delaware

Wilmington

INSTRUMENTAL MUSIC

DELAWARE SYMPHONY ASSOCIATION
PO Box 1870, Wilmington, DE 19899
(302) 656-7374
Founded: 1929
Arts Area: Symphony; Orchestra; Chamber; Ensemble; Instrumental Group
Status: Professional; Non-Profit
Type: Performing; Educational
Purpose: To present quality symphonic music which educates, inspires, challenges and entertains a diverse and expanding range of individuals
Management: Curtis Long, Executive Director
Officers: Bernard Lochtenberg, Chairman; Robert B. Rickards, President
Paid Staff: 8
Paid Artists: 85
Utilizes: Guest Conductors; Guest Artists
Budget: $1,000,000 - $5,000,000
Income Sources: Private Foundations/Grants/Endowments; Business/Corporate Donations; Box Office; Government Grants; Individual Donations
Season: September - May   **Annual Attendance:** 60,000
Affiliations: ASOL
Performance Facilities: Grand Opera House

DICKINSON THEATRE ORGAN SOCIETY
1801 Milltown Road, Wilmington, DE 19808
(302) 995-2603
Founded: 1970
Status: Professional; Semi-Professional; Non-Profit
Type: Sponsoring
Purpose: To present theatre organ concerts on the theatre pipe organ in the Dickinson High School Auditorium
Management: Connie Mead, Chairman of Publicity
Officers: Robert E. Dilworth, President; Paul Pringle, Vice President; Karl Keller, Secretary; Rad Mead, Treasurer
Volunteer Staff: 30
Paid Artists: 8
Utilizes: Guest Artists
Budget: $1,000 - $50,000
Income Sources: Private Foundations/Grants/Endowments; Business/Corporate Donations; Box Office; Individual Donations
Season: September - June   **Annual Attendance:** 5,000
Performance Facilities: Dickinson High School Auditorium

VOCAL MUSIC

THE DELAWARE SINGERS
1715 Sycamore Street, Wilmington, DE 19805
(302) 652-2977
Founded: 1984
Arts Area: Choral
Status: Professional
Type: Performing; Touring; Resident; Educational
Purpose: To establish and maintain a standard of choral excellence; to expand awareness of the scope and character of choral music; to encourage the pursuit of professional choral singing
Management: Jean Scalessa, Artistic Director/Founder; Raymond Egan, Music Director/Conductor
Officers: F.L. Peter Stone Esq., President; Sandra Curley-Edstrom, Vice President; Denise Ross, Recording Secretary; Elizabeth Joyce, Treasurer; Joyce Adams, Correspondence
Paid Staff: 2   **Volunteer Staff:** 4
Paid Artists: 16   **Non-Paid Artists:** 24
Utilizes: Guest Conductors; Guest Artists
Budget: $1,000 - $50,000
Income Sources: Private Foundations/Grants/Endowments; Business/Corporate Donations; Box Office; Government Grants; Individual Donations
Season: September - June   **Annual Attendance:** 2,000
Affiliations: CA

MADRIGAL SINGERS OF WILMINGTON
Faith Presbyterian Church, 720 Marsh Road, Wilmington, DE 19803
(215) 358-0946
FAX: (215) 358-5789
Founded: 1959
Arts Area: Choral
Status: Semi-Professional; Non-Profit
Type: Performing; Touring; Educational
Purpose: To present Renaissance and other chamber music, a capella and accompanied, by singers and musicians in period costumes, for the enrichment of the community
Management: Virginia Vaalburg, Director
Officers: Barbara Tilton, President of Board; Carolyn Zoldos-Crowell, Secretary of Board; Brian Hanson, Treasurer of Board
Paid Staff: 1   **Volunteer Staff:** 6
Non-Paid Artists: 20
Utilizes: Guest Artists   **Budget:** $1,000 - $50,000
Income Sources: Private Foundations/Grants/Endowments; Box Office; Government Grants; Individual Donations
Season: 52 Weeks   **Annual Attendance:** 2,000

NORTHERN DELAWARE ORATORIO SOCIETY
2603 Pike Creek Road, Wilmington, DE 19808
(302) 737-1082
Founded: 1970
Arts Area: Choral
Status: Non-Professional; Non-Profit
Type: Performing; Resident; Educational
Purpose: To provide a learning experience for our members; to present reasonably priced, high-level concerts for our audiences
Management: Jean Mosteller, Business Manager; Sheila and Calvin Bourgeault, Artistic Directors
Officers: Robert Mahr, President
Paid Staff: 2   **Volunteer Staff:** 12
Paid Artists: 6   **Non-Paid Artists:** 100
Utilizes: Guest Artists
Budget: $1,000 - $50,000
Income Sources: Box Office; Government Grants; Individual Donations
Season: September - May   **Annual Attendance:** 1,000
Performance Facilities: Grace United Methodist Church

OPERA DELAWARE
St. Andrews Episcopal Church, 719 North Shipley Street, Wilmington, DE 19801-1726
(302) 658-8063
Founded: 1948
Arts Area: Grand Opera
Status: Semi-Professional
Type: Performing; Educational
Purpose: To perform professional grand opera with full orchestra
Management: Eric W. Kjellmark, General Director; Leland Kimball, Artistic Director; Donna Shopa, Public Relations
Officers: Ann Houseman, President; Harry Glaze, Vice President; David Nayes, Treasurer; Geneve Yates, Secretary
Paid Staff: 1   **Volunteer Staff:** 15
Paid Artists: 130   **Non-Paid Artists:** 90
Utilizes: Special Technical Talent; Guest Conductors; Guest Artists; Guest Directors
Budget: $500,000 - $1,000,000
Income Sources: Private Foundations/Grants/Endowments; Business/Corporate Donations; Box Office; Government Grants; Individual Donations
Season: November - May   **Annual Attendance:** 9,000
Affiliations: OA; COS; AAA
Performance Facilities: Grand Opera House

THEATRE

ARTISTS THEATRE ASSOCIATION
PO Box 7258, Wilmington, DE 19803
(302) 798-8775
Founded: 1968
Arts Area: Musical; Community; Theatrical Group
Status: Non-Professional; Non-Profit
Type: Performing

Purpose: To promote the dramatic arts; to encourage the writing of new plays; to present workshop presentations with high school student participation
Officers: Michelle Fay, President; Kathy Bratton, Vice President; Thomas M. Marshall, Treasurer; Barbara Bradbury, Secretary
Volunteer Staff: 100
Non-Paid Artists: 100
Utilizes: Guest Conductors; Guest Directors
Budget: $1,000 - $50,000
Income Sources: Business/Corporate Donations; Box Office; Individual Donations
Season: February - October   **Annual Attendance:** 2,000
Affiliations: Delaware Theatre Association; Delaware Alliance for Arts Education

DELAWARE THEATRE COMPANY
200 Water Street, Wilmington, DE 19801
(302) 594-1104
FAX: (302) 594-1107
Founded: 1978
Arts Area: Professional; Musical; Theatrical Group
Status: Professional; Non-Profit
Type: Performing; Educational
Purpose: The DTC is a cultural, educational, and community service organization whose purpose is to create theatre of the highest professional quality in Delaware.
Management: Cleveland Morris, Artistic Director; David Edelman, Managing Director
Officers: John S. Garrett, Jr., Chairman of the Board; Peter H. Flint, President; Robert C. Forney, Treasurer; Susan Townsend, Secretary
Paid Staff: 10   **Volunteer Staff:** 100
Paid Artists: 35
Utilizes: Guest Artists; Guest Directors
Budget: $1,000,000 - $5,000,000
Income Sources: Private Foundations/Grants/Endowments; Business/Corporate Donations; Box Office; Government Grants; Individual Donations
Season: October - April   **Annual Attendance:** 26,084
Performance Facilities: The Delaware Theatre Company

SHOESTRING PRODUCTIONS, LIMITED
214 West 18th Street, Wilmington, DE 19802
(302) 655-0299
Founded: 1978
Arts Area: Musical; Theatrical Group
Status: Professional
Type: Performing; Touring; Educational
Purpose: To create, produce and tour original musicals for young audiences that entertain and educate
Management: Deborah Dehart, Artistic Director
Officers: Deborah Dehart, President; Charles Conway, Vice President; Judith Conway, Corresponding Secretary; Joseph Kinsolving, Recording Secretary; Susan Zaleski, Treasurer
Volunteer Staff: 3
Paid Artists: 10
Utilizes: New Productions
Budget: $1,000 - $50,000
Income Sources: Private Foundations/Grants/Endowments; Box Office
Season: 52 Weeks   **Annual Attendance:** 22,000

WILMINGTON DRAMA LEAGUE
PO Box 504, Wilmington, DE 19899
(302) 764-1172
Founded: 1933
Arts Area: Community; Theatrical Group
Status: Non-Professional; Non-Profit
Type: Performing; Educational
Purpose: To provide low-cost, quality theatre, theatrical activities, and education to the city of Wilmington and surrounding communities
Management: Laurie Bailey, Ray Jackson, Richard Kane, Judy Marsey, Jack Murphy, Directors at Large; David Reynolds, George Spillane, Ruby Stanley, Bob Winters, Directors at Large; Barbara Reynold, Office Manager
Officers: Bob Evans, President; Jeff Williams, Greg Tigani, Steve Robinson, Rob Tietze, Vice Presidents; Helen Rolph, Bill Rolph, Charles Houghton, Curtis King, Sue Webster, Vice Presidents; Dennis Williams, Treasurer; Sally Waslick, Secretary
Paid Staff: 1
Utilizes: Special Technical Talent
Budget: $50,000 - $100,000

Income Sources: Private Foundations/Grants/Endowments; Business/Corporate Donations; Box Office; Government Grants; Individual Donations
Season: September - June   **Annual Attendance:** 10,500
Affiliations: Delaware Arts Council; Delaware Theatre Association; AACT

PERFORMING SERIES

GRAND OPERA HOUSE
818 Market Street, Wilmington, DE 19801
(302) 658-7897
  Founded: 1973
  Arts Area: Dance; Vocal Music; Instrumental Music; Theater; Lyric Opera; Grand Opera
  Status: Professional; Non-Profit
  Type: Performing; Educational; Sponsoring
  Purpose: To present top-quality international performing artists and showcase local professional performers
  Management: David W. Fleming, Executive Director
  Officers: Alexander F. Giacco, Chairman of the Board; Philip Syng Reese, President; H. Rodney Sharp III, Vice President; Marilyn R. Hayward, Secretary; Basil L. Anderson, Treasurer
  Paid Staff: 23   **Volunteer Staff:** 200
  Utilizes: Special Technical Talent; Guest Artists
  Budget: $1,000,000 - $5,000,000
  Income Sources: Private Foundations/Grants/Endowments; Business/Corporate Donations; Box Office; Government Grants; Individual Donations
  Season: September - July   **Annual Attendance:** 75,000
  Affiliations: APAP; League of Historic American Theatres
  Performance Facilities: Grand Opera House

FACILITY

GRAND OPERA HOUSE
818 Market Street, Wilmington, DE 19801
(302) 658-7897
  Type of Facility: Concert Hall; Opera House
  Type of Stage: Thrust; Proscenium
  Stage Dimensions: 70'Wx40'D (12'D thrust); 38'Wx25'H proscenium opening   **Orchestra Pit**
  Seating Capacity: 1,110
  Year Built: 1871   **Architect:** Charles Carson, Thomas Dickson   **Cost:** $125,300
  Year Remodeled: 1976   **Architect:** Armstrong Child & Grieves   **Cost:** $6,500,000
  Acoustical Consultant: Roger Morgan
  Contact for Rental: Marilyn Bacon;   (302) 658-7897
  Resident Groups: Opera Delaware; Delaware Symphony
  The Opera House is a member of the League of Historic American Theatres.

THE PLAYHOUSE THEATRE
Tenth and Market Streets, DuPont Building, Wilmington, DE 19801
(302) 656-4401
FAX: (302) 656-2145
  Type of Facility: Theatre House
  Type of Stage: Proscenium
  Orchestra Pit
  Seating Capacity: 1,250
  Year Built: 1913
  Contact for Rental: Patricia Dill;   (302) 656-4401

DISTRICT OF COLUMBIA

Washington

DANCE

AFRICAN DANCE FESTIVAL FOR KANKOURAN WEST AFRICAN DANCE CO.
c/o Kankouran, 1709 Lang Place NE, Washington, DC 20002
(202) 737-4941; (202) 396-0841
Arts Area: Ethnic
Status: Professional; Non-Profit
Type: Performing
Purpose: To perpetuate and preserve African culture
Management: Assane Konte, Artistic Director; Abbou Kounta, Music Director
Budget: $100,000 - $500,000
Income Sources: Private Foundations/Grants/Endowments; Business/Corporate Donations; Box Office; Government Grants; Individual Donations
Performance Facilities: Stables Art Center

CAPITOL BALLET COMPANY
1200 Delafield Place NW, Washington, DC 20011
(202) 882-4039
Founded: 1961
Arts Area: Ballet
Status: Professional; Non-Profit
Type: Resident
Officers: Audrey Dickerson, President; Shirley Massengale, Vice President
Non-Paid Artists: 12
Utilizes: Special Technical Talent; Guest Artists; Guest Choreographers
Budget: $1,000 - $50,000
Income Sources: Private Foundations/Grants/Endowments; Business/Corporate Donations; Box Office; Individual Donations
Season: September - May

D.C. CONTEMPORARY DANCE THEATRE
1410 Eighth NW, 3rd Floor, Washington, DC 20004
(202) 783-7126
FAX: (202) 393-0156
Founded: 1984
Arts Area: Modern; Ballet; Jazz
Status: Professional; Non-Profit
Type: Performing; Touring; Resident
Purpose: To maintain a multiracial, cross-cultural repertory company perpetuating contemporary American choreography
Management: Miya Hisaka, Artistic Director
Paid Staff: 4
Paid Artists: 10
Utilizes: Guest Artists; Guest Choreographers
Budget: $100,000 - $500,000
Income Sources: Private Foundations/Grants/Endowments; Business/Corporate Donations; Box Office; Government Grants; Individual Donations
Season: September - June

DANCE EXCHANGE
1746-B Kalorama NW, Washington, DC 20009
(202) 232-0833
FAX: (202) 745-7077
Arts Area: Modern
Status: Professional; Non-Profit
Type: Performing; Touring; Resident; Educational
Purpose: An intergenerational dance company, promoting the idea that dance is for everyone
Management: Liz Lerman, Artistic Director; Kimberli Boyd, Associate Artistic Director; Bob Fogelgren, General Manager
Officers: Ronald Eichner, Chairman
Budget: $100,000 - $500,000
Income Sources: Private Foundations/Grants/Endowments; Business/Corporate Donations; Box Office; Government Grants; Individual Donations

DANCE PLACE
3225 Eighth Street NE, Washington, DC 20017
(202) 269-1600
>**Founded:** 1980
>**Arts Area:** Modern; Ethnic
>**Status:** Professional; Non-Profit
>**Type:** Performing; Touring; Resident; Educational; Sponsoring
>**Purpose:** To improve social conditions through educational and cultural programs of contemporary and ethnic dance and arts forms
>**Management:** Carla Perlo, Executive/Artistic Director; Lesa McLaughlin, Associate Artistic Director; Deborah Riley, Public Relations; Sharon Mansur, Development/Box Office; Stefan Johnson, Technical Director; Daniel Burkholder, Associate Technical Director
>**Officers:** Richard Pilkinton, Chairman; David Sparkman, Vice Chairman; Carla Perlo, Secretary; Steve Bloom, President; Phil Schonberger, Capital Campaign Chair
>**Paid Staff:** 7 **Volunteer Staff:** 35
>**Utilizes:** Guest Artists; Guest Choreographers
>**Budget:** $100,000 - $500,000
>**Income Sources:** Private Foundations/Grants/Endowments; Business/Corporate Donations; Box Office; Government Grants; Individual Donations
>**Season:** 52 Weeks

LIZ LERMAN EXCHANGE
1746 Kalorara Road NW, Washington, DC 20009
(202) 232-0833
>**Founded:** 1976
>**Arts Area:** Modern
>**Status:** Professional; Non-Profit
>**Type:** Performing; Touring; Resident; Educational
>**Purpose:** Dance Exchange is based on the belief that the skills, discipline, expression, and beauty of dance can be a part of everyone's life. Two companies, Liz Lerman and the Dance Exchange and The Dancers of the Third Age, have performed at a wide variety of locations in the United States and Europe.
>**Management:** Liz Lerman, Artistic Director; Robert Fogelgren, General Manager; Barbara Greenfield, Executive Director; Kimberli Boyd, Associate Director
>**Officers:** Ronald Eichner, Chairman of the Board
>**Paid Staff:** 5 **Volunteer Staff:** 4
>**Paid Artists:** 19
>**Utilizes:** Special Technical Talent; Guest Choreographers
>**Budget:** $100,000 - $500,000
>**Income Sources:** Private Foundations/Grants/Endowments; Business/Corporate Donations; Box Office; Government Grants; Individual Donations
>**Season:** 52 Weeks **Annual Attendance:** 100,000
>**Affiliations:** Dance USA; Cultural Alliance of Greater Washington

MICHELLE AVA AND COMPANY
3000 Connecticut Avenue NW, Washington, DC 20008
(202) 328-8092
>**Founded:** 1976
>**Arts Area:** Modern; Jazz
>**Status:** Professional; Non-Profit
>**Type:** Performing; Touring; Educational
>**Purpose:** To promote movement as a healing art
>**Management:** Michelle Ava, Artistic Director
>**Utilizes:** Guest Artists; Guest Choreographers
>**Budget:** $50,000 - $100,000
>**Income Sources:** Private Foundations/Grants/Endowments; Box Office; Individual Donations
>**Season:** September - June
>**Performance Facilities:** Joy of Motion Dance Center

THE WASHINGTON BALLET
3515 Wisconsin Avenue NW, Washington, DC 20016
(202) 362-3606; (202) 362-1683
FAX: (202) 362-1311
>**Founded:** 1976
>**Arts Area:** Ballet
>**Status:** Professional
>**Type:** Performing; Touring
>**Purpose:** To present a unique blend of classical and contemporary ballet

Management: Mary Day, Founder/Artistic Director; Elvi Moore, General Director; Kevin McKenzie,
Lupe Serrano, Artistic Associates
Officers: Frank E. Loy, President
Paid Staff: 18 **Volunteer Staff:** 4
Utilizes: Special Technical Talent; Guest Conductors
Budget: $1,000,000 - $5,000,000
Income Sources: Private Foundations/Grants/Endowments; Business/Corporate Donations; Box Office; Government
Grants; Individual Donations
Season: September - June
Performance Facilities: John F. Kennedy Center for the Performing Arts

INSTRUMENTAL MUSIC

AMERICAN SYMPHONY ORCHESTRA LEAGUE
777 14th Street NW, Suite 500, Washington, DC 20005
(202) 628-0099
FAX: (202) 783-7228
Founded: 1942
Arts Area: Symphony; Orchestra; Chamber
Status: Professional; Non-Profit
Type: Educational; Sponsoring
Purpose: A national service organization serving symphony and chamber orchestras, working to ensure artistic excellence
and administrative effectiveness for large and small orchestras, the ASOL offers a variety of training programs and other
necessary services.
Management: Catherine French, Chief Executive Officer; Donald Thulean, Vice President of Orchestra Services
Officers: Mrs. Ben M. Birkhead
Paid Staff: 38
Budget: $1,000,000 - $5,000,000
Income Sources: Private Foundations/Grants/Endowments; Business/Corporate Donations; Government Grants;
Individual Donations **Season:** 52 Weeks

CHARLIN JAZZ SOCIETY, INC.
2025 I Street NW, Suite 501, Washington, DC 20006
(202) 331-9404
Founded: 1979
Arts Area: Orchestra; Ensemble; Instrumental Group; Band
Status: Professional; Non-Profit
Type: Performing; Touring; Resident; Educational
Purpose: To nourish jazz as a national treasure
Management: Linda S. Wernick-Cassell, Director
Officers: Charles I. Cassell, President; Julie Van Blarcom, Secretary; Glenn Williams, Treasurer
Paid Staff: 3 **Volunteer Staff:** 3
Utilizes: Guest Artists; Guest Directors
Budget: $100,000 - $500,000
Income Sources: Private Foundations/Grants/Endowments; Business/Corporate Donations; Box Office; Government
Grants; Individual Donations
Season: 52 Weeks **Annual Attendance:** 10,500
Affiliations: Washington Performing Arts Society; Ellington School of the Arts; WCDU-FM;
George Washington University
Performance Facilities: John F. Kennedy Center for the Performing Arts, Lissner Auditorium;
Ellington School of the Arts

CONTEMPORARY MUSIC FORUM
1690 36th Street NW, Suite 408, Washington, DC 20007
(202) 333-4529
Founded: 1973
Arts Area: Chamber
Status: Non-Profit
Type: Performing; Resident
Purpose: To present contemporary music to the greater Washington area
Management: Helmut Braunlich, Personnel Director; Tony Stark, Program Director
Officers: James McKay, Chairman; Penny Farley, Vice Chairman; Ann Stansbury, Secretary
Paid Staff: 1 **Volunteer Staff:** 20
Paid Artists: 10
Utilizes: Guest Artists **Budget:** $1,000 - $50,000
Income Sources: Private Foundations/Grants/Endowments; Business/Corporate Donations; Box Office; Government
Grants; Individual Donations
Season: September - May **Annual Attendance:** 200
Performance Facilities: Armand Hammes Auditorium; Corcoran Gallery

D.C. YOUTH ORCHESTRA PROGRAM, INC.
PO Box 56198, Brightwood Station, Washington, DC 20011
(202) 723-1612
> **Founded:** 1960
> **Arts Area:** Symphony; Orchestra; Chamber
> **Status:** Non-Profit
> **Type:** Performing; Touring; Educational
> **Purpose:** To maintain an instrumental music training center for children ages 5-19
> **Management:** Lyn McLain, Director; Carol Rende, Assistant Director for Administration; Erika Schulte, Assistant Director for Music; Wing-Chi Chan, Director of Development
> **Officers:** Nsia Opare, President; Patricia Silvey, Vice President; Patricia R. Johnson, Treasurer; Lyn McLain, Executive Secretary Ex-Officio; Ed Arnold APR; Stuart L. Graham
> **Utilizes:** Guest Artists
> **Budget:** $1,000,000 - $5,000,000
> **Income Sources:** Private Foundations/Grants/Endowments; Business/Corporate Donations; Box Office; Government Grants; Individual Donations; Fundraising
> **Annual Attendance:** 5,000
> **Affiliations:** ASOL Youth Orchestra Division

NATIONAL GALLERY ORCHESTRA
National Gallery of Art, Washington, DC 20565
(202) 737-4215
FAX: (202) 842-2407
> **Founded:** 1941
> **Arts Area:** Symphony; Orchestra; Chamber; Ensemble
> **Status:** Non-Profit
> **Type:** Performing
> **Purpose:** To provide free concerts for the public at the National Gallery of Art
> **Management:** George Manos, Music Director
> **Paid Staff:** 4
> **Paid Artists:** 55
> **Utilizes:** Guest Artists
> **Income Sources:** Private Foundations/Grants/Endowments; Business/Corporate Donations
> **Season:** October - June **Annual Attendance:** 6,000
> **Performance Facilities:** Museum Garden Courts, National Gallery

NATIONAL MUSICAL ARTS
2101 Constitution Avenue NW, Washington, DC 20016
(301) 946-0355
> **Founded:** 1980
> **Arts Area:** Chamber; Ensemble
> **Status:** Professional; Non-Profit
> **Type:** Performing; Touring; Resident
> **Purpose:** To present rarely-heard chamber music masterpieces in the context of the traditional repertoire with emphasis on little-known works and composers of American origin; to collaborate with foreign embassies to present music of specific countries
> **Officers:** Dr. Charles Cleland, Chairman of the Board; Dr. Patricia Gray, President; James Tavares, Secretary; Chris Griner, Treasurer
> **Volunteer Staff:** 15
> **Paid Artists:** 10
> **Utilizes:** Special Technical Talent; Guest Conductors; Guest Artists
> **Budget:** $50,000 - $100,000
> **Income Sources:** Private Foundations/Grants/Endowments; Business/Corporate Donations; Government Grants; Individual Donations
> **Season:** September - May **Annual Attendance:** 3,500
> **Affiliations:** CMA
> **Performance Facilities:** National Academy of Sciences Auditorium

NATIONAL SYMPHONY ORCHESTRA ASSOCIATION
John F. Kennedy Center for the Performing Arts, Washington, DC 20566
(202) 416-8100
> **Founded:** 1930
> **Arts Area:** Symphony; Orchestra; Chamber
> **Status:** Non-Profit
> **Type:** Performing; Touring
> **Purpose:** To foster, promote and increase the musical knowledge and appreciation of the public by organizing and presenting performances of symphonic and other music

Management: Mstislav Rostropovich, Music Director; Stephen Klein, Executive Director
Officers: Albert J. Beveridge III, President; Daniel K. Mayers, Immediate Past President; F. David Fowler, Vice President; Samuel Lehrman, Treasurer/Chairman of Finance Committee; Mrs. John E. Chapoton, Secretary
Paid Staff: 12
Paid Artists: 106
Utilizes: Guest Conductors; Guest Artists
Budget: Over 10,000,000
Income Sources: Private Foundations/Grants/Endowments; Business/Corporate Donations; Box Office; Government Grants; Individual Donations
Season: 52 Weeks
Annual Attendance: 1,000,000
Affiliations: ASOL; John F. Kennedy Center for the Performing Arts
Performance Facilities: John F. Kennedy Center for the Performing Arts - Concert Hall; Wolf Trap Farm Park for the Performing Arts; West Lawn, United States Capitol

THEATER CHAMBER PLAYERS OF THE KENNEDY CENTER
John F. Kennedy Center for the Performing Arts, Washington, DC 20566
(202) 667-4470; (202) 338-3102
Founded: 1968
Arts Area: Chamber
Status: Professional
Type: Performing; Touring; Resident; Educational
Purpose: Presenting outstanding music of the 20th century in relation to the music of the past, the philosophy is that, in our time, new music is best appreciated when heard in company with music of other periods, illustrating lines of continuity between the past and the present.
Management: Leon Fleisher, Dina Koston, Directors; Anita Leong, General Manager
Paid Staff: 1   **Volunteer Staff:** 10
Paid Artists: 27
Season: October - May
Affiliations: CMA; Cultural Alliance of Greater Washington
Performance Facilities: John F. Kennedy Center for the Performing Arts - Terrace Theater

THE UNITED STATES AIR FORCE BAND
Bolling Air Force Base, Washington, DC 20332-6458
(202) 767-4224
FAX: (202) 767-0686
Founded: 1941
Arts Area: Symphony; Orchestra; Chamber; Ensemble; Instrumental Group; Electronic & Live Electronic; Band
Status: Professional; Non-Profit
Type: Performing; Touring
Purpose: The United States Air Force Band performs national and international concert tours to support Air Force and Department of Defense public awareness, community relations objectives and international understanding.
Management: Lieutenant Colonel Alan L. Bonner, Commander/Conductor; Capt. Mark R. Peterson, Vice Commander; Allan P. Waite Jr., The Singing Sergeants Director; Capt. Kevin D. Smith, The Air Force Strings Director; Capt. Robert A. Pouliot, Executive Officer
Paid Staff: 35
Paid Artists: 186
Utilizes: Special Technical Talent; Guest Artists
Season: 52 Weeks
Annual Attendance: 1,800,000
Affiliations: ASOL; MENC; National Bandmasters Association; American Bandmasters Association
Performance Facilities: DAR Constitution Hall

WASHINGTON CHAMBER SYMPHONY
1099 22nd Street NW, #602, Washington, DC 20037
(202) 452-1321
FAX: (202) 728-1134
Arts Area: Symphony; Chamber
Status: Professional; Non-Profit
Type: Performing; Touring; Resident; Educational; Sponsoring
Purpose: To promote classical music; to educate a new generation of audience
Management: Bonnie Ward Simon, Executive Director; Stephen Simon, Music Director/Conductor
Officers: Kathryn Donaldson Baker, Chairman of the Board
Budget: $500,000 - $1,000,000
Income Sources: Private Foundations/Grants/Endowments; Business/Corporate Donations; Box Office; Government Grants; Individual Donations
Performance Facilities: John F. Kennedy Center for the Performing Arts

VOCAL MUSIC

CHORAL ARTS SOCIETY OF WASHINGTON
4321 Wisconsin Avenue NW, Washington, DC 20016
(202) 244-3669
FAX: (202) 244-4244
> **Founded:** 1965
> **Arts Area:** Choral
> **Status:** Non-Professional; Non-Profit
> **Type:** Performing; Resident
> **Purpose:** The Choral Arts Society is dedicated to the highest ideals of excellence in choral programming and performance
> **Management:** Norman Scribner, Music Director; Judith Brophy, Executive Director; Johnnye Egnot, Director of Operations; Robert Schiller, Director of Public Relations and Marketing
> **Officers:** Lou Durden, Chairman; Albert Beveridge, Mrs. Morris C. Hover Jr., Barbara Rossotti, Vice Chairmen; Anne B. Keiser, Secretary; G. Bradford Cook, Treasurer
> **Paid Staff:** 4   **Volunteer Staff:** 2
> **Paid Artists:** 1
> **Utilizes:** Special Technical Talent; Guest Conductors; Guest Artists
> **Budget:** $500,000 - $1,000,000
> **Income Sources:** Private Foundations/Grants/Endowments; Business/Corporate Donations; Box Office; Government Grants; Individual Donations
> **Season:** October - May   **Annual Attendance:** 15,000
> **Performance Facilities:** John F. Kennedy Center for the Performing Arts

DISTRICT CURATORS, INC.
PO Box 14197, Washington, DC 20044
(202) 783-0360
FAX: (202) 783-4185
> **Arts Area:** Ethnic
> **Status:** Non-Profit
> **Type:** Presenting
> **Purpose:** To present the finest of the new performing arts to audiences in Washington, DC and the mid-Atlantic region; to advance cultural opportunities for artists and audiences worldwide
> **Management:** Bill Warrell, Executive Director; Katea Stitt, Producer
> **Officers:** Byrne Murphy, Chairman of the Board
> **Budget:** $100,000 - $500,000
> **Income Sources:** Private Foundations/Grants/Endowments; Business/Corporate Donations; Box Office; Government Grants; Individual Donations

NATIONAL LYRIC OPERA COMPANY
5332 Sherrier Place NW, Washington, DC 20016
(202) 244-5041
> **Founded:** 1978
> **Arts Area:** Grand Opera; Lyric Opera; Operetta; Choral
> **Status:** Semi-Professional; Non-Profit
> **Type:** Performing
> **Purpose:** To provide performances to the general public at reasonable prices; to provide a showcase for up-and-coming artists
> **Management:** Nikita Wells, General Manager/Artistic Director; Ruben Vartanyan, Conductor/Music Director; Sidney Yudain, Chairman of the Board
> **Officers:** Armaud Weiss, Business Manager; Michael Reilly, Secretary
> **Volunteer Staff:** 10
> **Paid Artists:** 10   **Non-Paid Artists:** 60
> **Utilizes:** Guest Artists
> **Budget:** $1,000 - $50,000
> **Income Sources:** Private Foundations/Grants/Endowments; Business/Corporate Donations; Box Office; Government Grants; Individual Donations
> **Season:** October - June   **Annual Attendance:** 3,000
> **Performance Facilities:** Lisner Auditorium; Warner Theatre

THE PAUL HILL CHORALE/THE WASHINGTON SINGERS
5630 Connecticut Avenue NW, #200, Washington, DC 20015
(202) 364-4321
FAX: (202) 362-2453
> **Founded:** 1967
> **Arts Area:** Choral
> **Status:** Professional; Semi-Professional; Non-Profit
> **Type:** Performing

Purpose: To present choral music concerts
Management: Lunette Arledge, Managing Director; Felicia Burrey, Director of Public Relations; Dennis Martin, Stage Manager/Director of Development; Kathryn Hartzler, Director of Group Sales; Marcia Milleville, Accountant
Officers: John H. Buchanan Jr., Chairman; Robert G. Heiss, President; Jean M. Riddell, Edith W. Seashore, Vice Presidents; Raymond J. Kimball, Secretary; Janene S. Mitchell, Treasurer
Volunteer Staff: 6
Paid Artists: 18 **Non-Paid Artists:** 140
Utilizes: Guest Artists
Budget: $100,000 - $500,000
Income Sources: Private Foundations/Grants/Endowments; Business/Corporate Donations; Box Office; Government Grants; Individual Donations; Events
Season: September - June
Annual Attendance: 14,000
Performance Facilities: John F. Kennedy Center for the Performing Arts - Concert Hall

SUMMER OPERA THEATRE COMPANY
620 Michigan Avenue NE, Washington, DC 20064
(202) 526-1669
Founded: 1978
Arts Area: Grand Opera; Lyric Opera; Operetta
Status: Professional; Non-Profit
Type: Performing; Resident; Educational
Management: Elaine R. Walter PhD, Founder/General Manager
Officers: Constance Donohoe, Chairman of the Board; Thomas L. Helinsk Jr., Vice Chairman; Edith Shubert, Chairman-Emeritus; Dena C. Feeney Esq., Secretary/Treasurer
Paid Staff: 2 **Volunteer Staff:** 2
Paid Artists: 150
Utilizes: Special Technical Talent; Guest Conductors; Guest Artists
Budget: $100,000 - $500,000
Income Sources: Private Foundations/Grants/Endowments; Business/Corporate Donations; Box Office; Government Grants; Individual Donations
Season: July - August
Affiliations: The Catholic University of America
Performance Facilities: Harthe Theatre

WASHINGTON BACH CONSORT
1690 36th Street NW, Washington, DC 20007
(202) 337-1202
FAX: (202) 337-2268
Founded: 1977
Arts Area: Choral; Orchestral
Status: Professional; Non-Profit
Type: Performing; Touring; Educational
Purpose: To present the highest quality performances of the music of J.S. Bach to both national and international audiences; to contribute to the music education of school children
Management: Jane E. Arenberg, General Manager
Officers: Ann Meier, President; Robert Inglis, Treasurer; Craig Hosmer, Secretary
Paid Staff: 2 **Volunteer Staff:** 10
Paid Artists: 66
Utilizes: Guest Artists
Budget: $100,000 - $500,000
Income Sources: Private Foundations/Grants/Endowments; Business/Corporate Donations; Box Office; Government Grants; Individual Donations
Season: October - June **Annual Attendance:** 5,000

WASHINGTON OPERA
John F. Kennedy Center for the Performing Arts, Washington, DC 20566
(202) 416-7890; (202) 416-7800
FAX: (202) 416-7857
Founded: 1956
Arts Area: Grand Opera; Lyric Opera; Light Opera; Operetta
Status: Professional; Non-Profit
Type: Performing; Resident; Educational
Purpose: To produce opera of the highest standard in the nation's capitol
Management: Martin Feinstein, General Director; Edward Turrington, Administrative Director
Officers: Paul Dragoumis, President; Mrs. Eugene V. Casey, Chairperson, Board of Trustees
Paid Staff: 34 **Volunteer Staff:** 20
Paid Artists: 75
Utilizes: Special Technical Talent; Guest Conductors; Guest Artists; Guest Directors

Budget: Over 10,000,000
Income Sources: Private Foundations/Grants/Endowments; Business/Corporate Donations; Box Office; Government Grants; Individual Donations
Season: November - March   **Annual Attendance:** 97,000
Affiliations: Washington Opera Guild/Educational
Performance Facilities: John F. Kennedy Center for the Performing Arts

WASHINGTON SINGERS
c/o National Choral Foundation, 5630 Connecticut Avenue NW, Suite 200, Washington, DC 20015
(202) 364-4321
FAX: (202) 362-2453
Arts Area: Choral
Status: Professional; Non-Profit
Type: Performing
Purpose: To present the full range of repertoire for chamber chorus, specializing in 20th-century music
Management: Paul Hill, Conductor; Lunette Arledge, Managing Director
Officers: Robert G. Heiss, President of the Board
Budget: $100,000 - $500,000
Income Sources: Private Foundations/Grants/Endowments; Business/Corporate Donations; Box Office; Government Grants; Individual Donations

THEATRE

ARENA STAGE
Sixth and Maine Avenue SW, Washington, DC 20024
(202) 554-9066
FAX: (202) 488-4056
Founded: 1950
Arts Area: Professional
Status: Professional; Non-Profit
Type: Performing; Educational
Purpose: To perform the best theatre for Washingtonians
Management: Douglas C. Wager, Artistic Director; Stephen Richard, Executive Director; Guy Bergquist, General Manager; Regan Byrne, Director of Communications
Officers: Denie S. Weil, President; Carlton D. Lewis, Stephen Richard, Jaan Whitehead, Vice Presidents; Jonathan M. Weisgall, Secretary; Bert I. Helfinstein, Treasurer
Paid Staff: 150
Paid Artists: 17
Utilizes: Guest Directors
Budget: $5,000,000 - $10,000,000
Income Sources: Private Foundations/Grants/Endowments; Business/Corporate Donations; Box Office; Government Grants; Individual Donations
Season: September - June   **Annual Attendance:** 250,000
Affiliations: AEA; SSDC
Performance Facilities: Arena Stage: Arena Theater, Kreeger Theater, Old Vat Theatre

FORD'S THEATRE SOCIETY
511 Tenth Street NW, Washington, DC 20004
(202) 638-2941
FAX: (202) 347-6269
Founded: 1968
Arts Area: Professional; Musical
Status: Professional; Non-Profit
Type: Performing; Educational
Purpose: To present live theatre productions as a tribute to Abraham Lincoln's love of the performing arts
Management: Frankie Hewitt, Executive Producer
Officers: William McSweeny, Chairman
Paid Staff: 20
Budget: $1,000,000 - $5,000,000
Income Sources: Private Foundations/Grants/Endowments; Business/Corporate Donations; Box Office; Government Grants; Individual Donations
Season: 52 Weeks
Performance Facilities: Ford's Theatre

GALA HISPANIC THEATRE
PO Box 43209, Washington, DC 20010
(202) 234-7174
Arts Area: Theatrical Group

Status: Professional; Non-Profit
Type: Resident; Educational
Purpose: To expand and promote Hispanic culture in the United States
Management: Hugo Medrano, Artistic Producing Director; Abel Lopez, Associate Producing Director
Budget: $100,000 - $500,000
Income Sources: Private Foundations/Grants/Endowments; Business/Corporate Donations; Box Office; Government Grants; Individual Donations
Performance Facilities: GALA Hispanic Theatre

HORIZONS THEATRE
PO Box 50204, Washington, DC 20091
(202) 265-6574
Founded: 1976
Arts Area: Theatrical Group
Status: Professional; Non-Profit
Type: Performing; Touring; Resident; Educational
Purpose: To give women artists a forum; to provide women playwrights a broader audience; to offer audiences professional theatre conceived and performed from a woman's viewpoint
Management: Ginger Moss, General Manager; Leslie Jacobson, Artistic Director; Nancy Tartt, Associate Art Director; Marian DiJulio, Literary Manager
Officers: Pat Hawkins, Chairman; Ida Prosky, Vice Chairman; Eda Edgerton, Treasurer
Paid Staff: 3   **Volunteer Staff:** 3
Utilizes: Special Technical Talent; Guest Directors
Budget: $50,000 - $100,000
Income Sources: Private Foundations/Grants/Endowments; Business/Corporate Donations; Box Office; Government Grants; Individual Donations
Season: 52 Weeks   **Annual Attendance:** 7,600
Affiliations: League of Washington Theatres; Cultural Alliance of Washington, DC

LIVING STAGE
Sixth Street and Maine Avenue SW, Washington, DC 20024
(202) 554-9066
Founded: 1966
Arts Area: Theatrical Group
Status: Professional; Non-Profit
Type: Resident
Purpose: To bring the art of theatre to people who do not normally have access to the arts
Management: Robert Alexander, Artistic Director; Catherine Irwin, Managing Director
Budget: $100,000 - $500,000
Income Sources: Private Foundations/Grants/Endowments; Business/Corporate Donations; Box Office; Government Grants; Individual Donations
Season: December - June
Performance Facilities: The Living Stage Theatre

NATIONAL THEATRE
1321 Pennsylvania Avenue NW, Washington, DC 20004
(202) 783-6854
Founded: 1835
Arts Area: Professional; Musical; Community; Folk; Puppet
Status: Professional; Non-Profit; Commercial
Type: Educational; Sponsoring
Purpose: To preserve the historic playhouse; to present Class-A legitimate touring productions; to showcase non-professional and professional groups in second stage
Management: Donn B. Murphy, Executive Director; Harry Teter Jr., General Manager
Officers: Donn B. Murphy, President; Jay Adams, Chair
Paid Staff: 10   **Volunteer Staff:** 5
Paid Artists: 500   **Non-Paid Artists:** 100
Utilizes: Special Technical Talent; Guest Artists
Budget: $500,000 - $1,000,000
Income Sources: Private Foundations/Grants/Endowments; Business/Corporate Donations; Box Office; Individual Donations
Season: 52 Weeks   **Annual Attendance:** 40,000
Affiliations: AEA; IATSE; The Shubert Organization

THE SHAKESPEARE THEATRE
450 Seventh Street NW, Washington, DC 20004
(202) 547-3230; (202) 393-2700
FAX: (202) 547-0226
Founded: 1970

Arts Area: Professional; Theatrical Group
Status: Professional; Non-Profit
Type: Performing; Resident
Purpose: To present quality classical and Shakespearean productions in an intimate 447-seat theatre
Management: Michael Kahn, Artistic Director; Jessica Andrews, Managing Director; Beth Hauptle,
Director of Public Relations and Marketing
Officers: Lawrence A. Hugh, Chairman; Daniel W. Toohey, Vice Chairman; Emily Malino Scheuer, Secretary;
James B. Adler, Treasurer
Paid Staff: 50
Utilizes: Special Technical Talent; Guest Artists; Guest Directors
Budget: $5,000,000 - $10,000,000
Income Sources: Private Foundations/Grants/Endowments; Business/Corporate Donations; Box Office; Government
Grants; Individual Donations
Season: October - June   **Annual Attendance:** 60,000
Affiliations: League of Washington Theatres; Cultural Alliance of Greater Washington
Performance Facilities: The Shakespeare Theatre at the Lansburgh

SOURCE THEATRE COMPANY
1835 17th Street NW, Washington, DC 20009
(202) 462-1073
FAX: (202) 462-0676
Founded: 1977
Arts Area: Professional; Theatrical Group
Status: Professional; Non-Profit
Type: Performing; Touring; Resident
Purpose: To provide the community with exciting and innovative productions of new plays as well as contemporary plays
that are particularly relevant to our community; to reinterpret the classics
Management: Pat Murphy Sheehy, Producing Artistic Director; Keith Parker, Literary Manager
Officers: Michael Winston, Chairman; Ted Gay, Vice Chairman; Malcolm Smith, Treasurer; Virginia Knight, Secretary
Paid Staff: 9   **Volunteer Staff:** 26
Paid Artists: 120   **Non-Paid Artists:** 320
Utilizes: Special Technical Talent; Guest Artists; Guest Directors; Guest Designers
Budget: $100,000 - $500,000
Income Sources: Private Foundations/Grants/Endowments; Business/Corporate Donations; Box Office; Government
Grants; Individual Donations
Season: 52 Weeks   **Annual Attendance:** 15,000
Affiliations: TCG; AEA

THE STUDIO THEATRE
1333 P Street NW, Washington, DC 20005
(202) 232-7267
Founded: 1975
Arts Area: Professional; Theatrical Group
Status: Professional; Non-Profit
Type: Performing; Educational; Sponsoring
Purpose: The Studio Theatre is committed to creating the best in contemporary theatre—area premieres of American and
European works, revivals, and solo performance art. The Studio Theatre is an energetic, eclectic urban theatre focused on
the primacy of performance, intimacy between actor and audience, and high production values. The Studio Theatre Second-
stage nutures emerging artists by providing a creative home for them, free of commercial consideration. The Studio Thea-
tre Acting Conservatory trains actors to their fullest potential.
Management: Joy Zinoman, Artistic Director/Managing Director/Founder; Keith Allan Baker,
Associate Managing Director/Artistic Director of Secondstage
Officers: Nancy Linn Patton, Chairperson; Ronald V. McGowan, Vice Chairperson; Irene Harriet Blum,
Chairperson Emeritus
Paid Staff: 20   **Volunteer Staff:** 250
Paid Artists: 250
Utilizes: Guest Artists; Guest Directors
Budget: $1,000,000 - $5,000,000
Income Sources: Private Foundations/Grants/Endowments; Business/Corporate Donations; Box Office; Government
Grants; Individual Donations; Special Events; Tuition
Season: September - June   **Annual Attendance:** 50,000
Affiliations: TCG; Cultural Alliance of Greater Washington; League of Washington Theatres
Performance Facilities: The Studio Theatre; The Secondstage

THE WASHINGTON STAGE GUILD
4048 Seventh Street NE, #4, Washington, DC 20017-1939
Founded: 1986
Arts Area: Professional; Theatrical Group
Status: Professional; Non-Profit

Type: Performing; Resident; Educational
Purpose: To perform plays that are often overlooked, including lesser-known works of famous playwrights, classics, and new plays of merit
Management: John MacDonald, Producing Artistic Director; Ann Norton, Executive Director; William Largess, Dramaturge
Paid Staff: 5   **Volunteer Staff:** 10
Paid Artists: 50
Utilizes: Special Technical Talent
Budget: $100,000 - $500,000
Income Sources: Private Foundations/Grants/Endowments; Business/Corporate Donations; Box Office; Government Grants; Individual Donations
Season: September - June   **Annual Attendance:** 8,000
Affiliations: AEA; League of Washington Theatres; Cultural Arts Alliance of DC
Performance Facilities: Carroll Hall

WOOLLY MAMMOTH THEATRE COMPANY
1401 Church Street NW, Washington, DC 20005
(202) 393-3939
Founded: 1980
Arts Area: Professional; Musical; Theatrical Group
Status: Professional; Non-Profit
Type: Performing; Resident; Educational
Purpose: To present the most daring and experimental plays in the Washington, DC area.
Management: Howard Shalwitz, Artistic Director; Molly White, Associate Director; Nancy Turner Hensley, Producing Associate
Officers: John Mendonca, President; Sunny Jung Scully, Vice President; Jeffrey B. Stern, Secretary; Sheldon Repp, Treasurer
Paid Staff: 6   **Volunteer Staff:** 400
Paid Artists: 5   **Non-Paid Artists:** 65
Utilizes: Special Technical Talent; Guest Artists; Guest Directors
Budget: $500,000 - $1,000,000
Income Sources: Private Foundations/Grants/Endowments; Business/Corporate Donations; Box Office; Government Grants; Individual Donations
Season: October - July
Annual Attendance: 15,000
Affiliations: TCG
Performance Facilities: Woolly Mammoth Theatre

PERFORMING SERIES

DUMBARTON CONCERT SERIES
3133 Dumbarton Street NW, Washington, DC 20007
(202) 965-2000
FAX: (202) 338-9008
Arts Area: Instrumental Music
Status: Non-Profit
Type: Presenting
Purpose: To present Washinton's best performers in the beautiful historic environment of Dumbarton Church; to promote an extensive outreach program in the community called LIVE MUSIC NOW!
Management: Connie Zimmer, Executive Director; Katy O'Keefe, Producer; Susan Osburn, Associate Producer
Budget: $50,000 - $100,000
Income Sources: Private Foundations/Grants/Endowments; Business/Corporate Donations; Box Office; Government Grants; Individual Donations
Performance Facilities: Dumbarton Church

JOHN F. KENNEDY CENTER FOR THE PERFORMING ARTS
2700 F Street NW, Washington, DC 20566
(202) 872-0466
Authorized: 1958   **Opened:** 1971
Arts Area: Dance; Theater; Grand Opera; Vocal Music; Instrumental Music; Lyric Opera; Musical Theater
Status: Non-Profit; Professional
Purpose: The John F. Kennedy Center for the Performing Arts was authorized by an Act of Congress in 1958 as the National Cultural Center. Since opening its doors in 1971, the Center has operated seven days a week, 365 days a year, and welcomed more than 60 million visitors from all parts of the United States and the world. The Center attracts the most talented national and international stars of dance, theater and music, and entertains, educates and serves millions of Americans across the country through television programs, its touring productions and its education and public service programs.

Board of Trustees: Under the terms of the National Cultural Act of 1958 (as amended in 1964), the Kennedy Center is administered by a Board of Trustees as a separate, independent and self-sustaining bureau of the Smithsonian Institution. This 45-member Board of Trustees is composed of 30 Presidential appointees who serve 10-year overlapping terms. The 15 remaining members are legislatively designated, serving by virtue of their specific public office. The present members of the Board the Board of Trustees are:
Honorary Chairmen: Mrs. George Bush; Mrs. Ronald Reagan; Mrs. Jimmy Carter; Mrs. Gerald R. Ford; Mrs. Richard M. Nixon; Mrs. Lyndon B. Johnson; Mrs. Aristotle Onassis
Officers: James D. Wolfensohn, Chairman; James. H. Evans, Vice Chairman; Leonard L. Silverstein, Vice Chairman; Lawrence J. Wilker, Managing Director; Jean Kennedy Smith, Secretary; Charlotte Woolard, Assistant Secretary; Paul G. Stern, Treasurer; Henry Strong, Assistant Treasurer; Kenneth M. Kaufman, General Counsel; William Becker, Associate Counsel
Members Appointed by the President: Philip F. Anschutz; Mrs. Bennett Archambault; Mrs. Howard H. Baker, Jr.; Mrs. William Cafritz; Ralph P. Davidson; Kenneth Duberstein; James H. Evans; Mrs. Max M. Fisher; Robert Fryer; Mrs. Joseph B. Gildenhorn; Lionel Hampton; Mrs. William Lee Hanley, Jr.; Dina Merrill Hartley; Helen Joan Holt; Caroline Rose Hunt; Mrs. Earle M. Jorgensen; Donald M. Koll; Melvin R. Laird; Mrs. J. Willard Marriott; James A. McClure; Mrs. Abraham A. Ribicoff; Joy A. Silverman; Leonard L. Silverstein; Jean Kennedy Smith; Roger B. Smith; Dennis Stanfill; Roger L. Stevens; Jerry Weintraub; Charles Z. Wick; James D. Wolfensohn
Members Ex-Officio Designated by Act of Congress: Louis Sullivan; Lamar Alexander; Henry E. Catto; Senator Edward M. Kennedy; Senator George J. Mitchell; Senator Mark O. Hatfield; Representative Joseph M. McDade; Representative Charles Wilson; Representative Sidney R. Yates; Sharon Pratt Kelly; Robert McC. Adams; James H. Billington; J. Carter Brown; James M. Ridenour
Utilizes: Special Technical Talent; Guest Conductors; Guest Artists; Guest Directors
Budget: Over $50,000,000
Income Sources: Private Foundations/Grants/Endowments; Business/Corporate Donations; Box Office; Government Grants; Individual Donations
Season: 52 Weeks   **Annual Attendance:** 1,460,507
Since 1971, the Kennedy Center has presented a varied and comprehensive array of programming in dance, drama, musical theater, classical and contemporary music and opera. These performances have been sponsored by the Kennedy Center or by its affiliated constituent (the National Symphony Orchestra) and associated constituents (Washington Opera, American Film Institute and the Washington Performing Arts Society) and independent producers and sponsors.
Affiliations: National Symphony Orchestra; Washington Opera; American Film Institute; Washington Performing Arts Society
Performance Facility: John F. Kennedy Center for the Performing Arts: Concert Hall, Eisenhower Theater, American Film Institute, Opera House; Terrace Theater, Theater Lab. In addition to the performance facilities listed, the Performing Arts Library, a joint undertaking with the Library of Congress, provides video computer access to the nation's most comprehensive collections of films, books recordings and other materials on the performing arts.

NATIONAL GALLERY OF ART/CONCERT SERIES
National Gallery of Art, Washington, DC 20565
(202) 737-4215
Founded: 1941
Arts Area: Vocal Music; Instrumental Music
Status: Non-Profit
Type: Performing
Management: George Manos, Music Director
Season: October - June
Performance Facilities: Museum Garden Courts

SMITHSONIAN INSTITUTION RESIDENT ASSOCIATE PROGRAM
1100 Jefferson Drive SW, Washington, DC 20560
(202) 357-3030
FAX: (202) 786-2034
Arts Area: Dance; Vocal Music; Instrumental Music; Theater
Status: Professional; Non-Profit
Type: Educational; Sponsoring
Purpose: To involve the residents of the Washington metropolitan area in the ongoing activities of the Smithsonian Institution
Management: Janet W. Solinger, Director/RAP (Resident Associate Program); Penelope P. Dann, Program Coordinator; Joan Cole, Public Affairs
Officers: The Board of Regents of the Smithsonian Institution
Paid Staff: 47
Paid Artists: 150
Utilizes: Guest Artists
Budget: $1,000,000 - $5,000,000
Income Sources: Box Office; Memberships
Season: 52 Weeks
Annual Attendance: 22,000
Performance Facilities: Hirshhorn Museum Auditorium; Baird Auditorium; Carmichael Auditorium

WASHINGTON PERFORMING ARTS SOCIETY
2000 L Street NW, #810, Washington, DC 20036
(202) 833-9800
FAX: (202) 331-7678
>**Founded:** 1966
>**Arts Area:** Dance; Vocal Music; Instrumental Music; Festivals
>**Status:** Professional; Non-Profit
>**Type:** Educational; Sponsoring
>**Purpose:** To present the world's finest artists in the nation's capital; to present over 100 concerts annually on the major stages, as well as over 800 concerts each year in the schools of the metropolitan Washington area using resident artists
>**Management:** Douglas H. Wheeler, Managing Director; Craig M. Hosmer, General Manager; Patrick Hayes, Managing Director Emeritus; Linda Coleman Soma, Director of Public Relations and Marketing
>**Officers:** Lydia Marshall, President
>**Paid Staff:** 23   **Volunteer Staff:** 10
>**Utilizes:** Guest Conductors; Guest Artists; Guest Directors
>**Budget:** $1,000,000 - $5,000,000
>**Income Sources:** Private Foundations/Grants/Endowments; Business/Corporate Donations; Box Office; Government Grants; Individual Donations
>**Season:** 52 Weeks   **Annual Attendance:** 250,000
>**Affiliations:** ISPAA
>**Performance Facilities:** John F. Kennedy Center for the Performing Arts; DAR Constitution Hall; Lisner Auditorium; George Washington University; Warner Theatre

FACILITY

THE AMERICAN UNIVERSITY - MCDONALD RECITAL HALL
4400 Massachusetts Avenue NW, Washington, DC 20016
(202) 885-3420
FAX: (202) 885-1092
>**Type of Facility:** Concert Hall; Studio Performance
>**Type of Stage:** Proscenium
>**Stage Dimensions:** 40'Wx20'D
>**Seating Capacity:** 200
>**Year Built:** 1966
>**Contact for Rental:** Susan Boyd;   (202) 885-3420

THE AMERICAN UNIVERSITY - NEW LECTURE HALL THEATRE
4400 Massachusetts Avenue NW, Washington, DC 20016
(202) 885-3420
FAX: (202) 885-1092
>**Type of Facility:** Theatre Complex; Studio Performance; Black Box
>**Facility Originally:** Lecture Hall
>**Type of Stage:** Flexible
>**Seating Capacity:** 200
>**Year Remodeled:** 1985
>**Contact for Rental:** Susan Boyd;   (202) 885-3420

ARENA STAGE - FICHANDLER THEATER
Sixth and Maine Avenue SW, Washington, DC 20024
(202) 554-9066
FAX: (202) 488-4056
>**Founded:** 1950
>**Type of Facility:** Theatre House
>**Type of Stage:** Arena
>**Seating Capacity:** 800
>**Year Built:** 1960   **Architect:** Harry Weese & Associates   **Cost:** $1,000,000
>**Contact for Rental:** Production Office;   (202) 554-9066
>**Resident Groups:** Arena Stage Resident Company

ARENA STAGE - KREEGER THEATER
Sixth and Maine Avenue SW, Washington, DC 20024
(202) 554-9066
FAX: (202) 488-4056
>**Founded:** 1950
>**Type of Facility:** Theatre House
>**Type of Stage:** Thrust; Proscenium; End Stage
>**Stage Dimensions:** 32'x40'x32'
>**Seating Capacity:** 500

Year Built: 1970   **Architect:** Harry Weese & Associates   **Cost:** $1,500,000
Contact for Rental: Production Office;   (202) 554-9066
Resident Groups: Arena Stage Resident Company

ARENA STAGE - OLD VAT THEATER
Sixth and Maine Avenue SW, Washington, DC 20024
(202) 554-9066
FAX: (202) 488-4056
   Founded: 1950
   Type of Facility: Theatre House
   Facility Originally: Restaurant
   Type of Stage: Flexible; Cabaret-style
   Seating Capacity: 165
   Year Remodeled: 1976   **Cost:** $21,000
   Contact for Rental: Production Office;   (202) 554-9066
   Resident Groups: Arena Stage Resident Company

CONSTITUTION HALL
18th and D Streets NW, Washington, DC 20006
(202) 628-4780
   Type of Facility: Concert Hall; Auditorium; Multi-Purpose
   Type of Stage: Thrust
   Stage Dimensions: 52'Wx33'D
   Seating Capacity: 3,746
   Year Built: 1920   **Architect:** John Russel Pope   **Cost:** $2,000,000
   Contact for Rental: George Brooks or Rose Magruder;   (202) 628-4780
   Manager: George Brooks;   (202) 628-4780

FORD'S THEATRE
511 Tenth Street NW, Washington, DC 20004
(202) 638-2941
FAX: (202) 347-6269
   Founded: 1968
   Type of Facility: Theatre House
   Facility Originally: Warehouse
   Type of Stage: Proscenium
   Orchestra Pit
   Seating Capacity: 699
   Year Built: 1863   **Architect:** James J. Gifford   **Cost:** $75,000
   Year Remodeled: 1968   **Cost:** $2,073,600
   Manager: Michael Gennaro, Managing Director;   (202) 638-2941
   Ford's Theatre was restored to its original appearance after an extensive study. The theatre is available for rent on a very limited basis.

GASTON HALL
37th and "O" Streets NW, Washington, DC 20057
(202) 687-4081
   Founded: 1879
   Type of Facility: Concert Hall; Auditorium
   Facility Originally: Lecture/Concert/Convocation Hall
   Stage Dimensions: 50'x20'
   Seating Capacity: 734
   Year Built: 1879
   Contact for Rental: Facilities Coordinator;   (202) 687-4081
   Resident Groups: Georgetown Symphony; Cantate Chamber Singers

GEORGE WASHINGTON UNIVERSITY - LISNER AUDITORIUM
730 21st Street NW, Washington, DC 20052
(202) 994-6800
   Type of Facility: Concert Hall; Auditorium; Theatre House
   Type of Stage: Proscenium
   Stage Dimensions: 55'W x 36'D   **Orchestra Pit**
   Seating Capacity: 1,495 plus wheelchairs
   Year Built: 1945   **Architect:** Waldron Faulkner
   Year Remodeled: 1992   **Cost:** $400,000
   Acoustical Consultant: Phil Fox, Stage Manager
   Contact for Rental: Sylvia L. Kohrn;   (202) 994-6800

Manager: Rosanna Ruscetti, Director;   (202) 994-9120
Resident Groups: The Washington Concert Opera; Masterworks Chorus; Kan-Kouran West African Dance Company

HALL OF NATIONS BLACK BOX THEATRE
1221 36th Street NW, Washington, DC 20057
(202) 687-4081
    Founded: 1988
    Type of Stage: Flexible
    Seating Capacity: 200
    Year Built: 1955
    Year Remodeled: 1988
    Contact for Rental: Facilities Coordinator;   (202) 687-4081
    Resident Groups: Student Performance Organizations

JOHN F. KENNEDY CENTER FOR THE PERFORMING ARTS
2700 F Street NW, Washington, DC 20566
(202) 416-8000
    Type of Facility: National Cultural Center
    Year Built: 1971   **Architect:** Edward Durell Stone   **Cost:** $71,000,000
    Acoustical Consultant: Dr. Cyril Harris
    Contact for Rental: Helen Hamm, Scheduling Coordinator;   (202) 416-8050
    The National Park Service maintains the Kennedy Center as a presidential memorial and is responsible for its security. See individual listings for the American Film Institute, Concert Hall, Eisenhower Theater, Opera House, Terrace Theater and Theater Lab. Under the terms of the National Cultural Center Act of 1958 (as amended in 1964), the Kennedy Center is administered by a Board of Trustees as a separate, independent and self-sustaining bureau of the Smithsonian Institution. This 45-member Board of Trustees is composed of 30 Presidential appointees who serve 10-year overlapping terms. The 15 remaining members are legislatively designated, serving by virtue of their specific public office. For further information reference the Performing Series listing for John F. Kennedy Center for the Performing Arts.

JOHN F. KENNEDY CENTER FOR THE PERFORMING ARTS - AMERICAN FILM INSTITUTE THEATER
2700 F Street NW, Washington, DC 20566
(202) 416-8000
    Type of Facility: Film Theater/experimental Theater
    Type of Stage: Flexible
    Seating Capacity: 224
    Year Built: 1973   **Architect:** Lisa Parks
    Acoustical Consultant: Dr. Cyril Harris
    Contact for Rental: Helen Hamm, Scheduling Coordinator;   (202) 416-8050

JOHN F. KENNEDY CENTER FOR THE PERFORMING ARTS - CONCERT HALL
2700 F Street NW, Washington, DC 20566
(202) 416-8000
    Type of Facility: Concert Hall
    Type of Stage: Concert Platform
    Seating Capacity: 2,759
    Year Built: 1971   **Architect:** Edward Durell Stone
    Acoustical Consultant: Dr. Cyril Harris
    Contact for Rental: Helen Hamm, Scheduling Coordinator;   (202) 416-8050
    Manager: Paul D. Simmerman

JOHN F. KENNEDY CENTER FOR THE PERFORMING ARTS - EISENHOWER THEATER
2700 F Street NW, Washington, DC 20566
(202) 416-8200
FAX: (202) 416-8205
    Type of Facility: Theatre House
    Type of Stage: Proscenium
    Stage Dimensions: 75'Wx55'D   **Orchestra Pit**
    Seating Capacity: 1,142
    Year Built: 1971   **Architect:** Edward Durell Stone
    Acoustical Consultant: Dr. Cyril Harris
    Contact for Rental: Elizabeth Thomas, Scheduling Coordinator;   (202) 416-8032
    Manager: Ed Blacker;   (202) 416-8250

JOHN F. KENNEDY CENTER FOR THE PERFORMING ARTS - OPERA HOUSE
2700 F Street NW, Washington, DC 20566
(202) 872-0466
    Type of Facility: Opera House
    Type of Stage: Proscenium

Stage Dimensions: 100'Wx65'D   **Orchestra Pit**
Seating Capacity: 2,318
Year Built: 1971   Architect: Edward Durell Stone
Acoustical Consultant: Dr. Cyril Harris
Contact for Rental: Max A. Woodward, General Manager;   (202) 416-8200
Manager: Richard W. Kidwell;   (202) 416-8159

JOHN F. KENNEDY CENTER FOR THE PERFORMING ARTS - TERRACE THEATER
2700 F Street NW, Washington, DC 20566
(202) 416-8000
Type of Facility: Chamber Hall
Type of Stage: Proscenium
Stage Dimensions: 34'11"Wx17'10 3/4"D
Seating Capacity: 500
Year Built: 1979   Architect: Philip Johnson, Associates
Acoustical Consultant: Dr. Cyril Harris
Contact for Rental: Helen Hamm, Scheduling Coordinator
Manager: Ed Blacker

JOHN F. KENNEDY CENTER FOR THE PERFORMING ARTS - THEATER LAB
2700 F Street NW, Washington, DC 20566
(202) 416-8000
Type of Facility: Multipurpose
Type of Stage: Flexible
Seating Capacity: 100
Year Built: 1971   Architect: Edward Durell Stone
Acoustical Consultant: Dr. Cyril Harris
Contact for Rental: Helen Hamm, Scheduling Coordinator;   (202) 416-8050
Manager: Carole Sullivan

LIBRARY OF CONGRESS
10 First Street SE, Washington, DC 20540
(202) 707-5000
Founded: 1800
Type of Facility: Concert Hall
Type of Stage: Proscenium   **Orchestra Pit**
Seating Capacity: 500
Year Built: 1925
Year Remodeled: 1992

MASK AND BAUBLE DRAMATIC SOCIETY THEATER
The Leavey Center, Room 316, Washington, DC 20057-1074
(202) 687-3838
Type of Facility: Environmental; Theatre House; Room; Black Box
Facility Originally: Lecture Hall
Type of Stage: Flexible; Environmental
Stage Dimensions: 64'x30'x11'6"
Seating Capacity: 110
Year Built: 1948   Architect: Georgetown University
Year Remodeled: 1976   Architect: Georgetown University
Resident Groups: Mask and Bauble Dramatic Society

NATIONAL THEATRE
1321 Pennsylvania Avenue NW, Washington, DC 20004
(202) 783-6854
Type of Facility: Theatre House
Type of Stage: Modified Apron Proscenium
Stage Dimensions: 80'Wx36'6"D; 39'8"Wx28'H proscenium opening   **Orchestra Pit**
Seating Capacity: 1,679
Year Remodeled: 1984   Cost: $6,000,000
Contact for Rental: Harry Teter;   (202) 628-6161
Original 1835 construction was destroyed by fire. Renovated in 1984 by Pennsylvania Avenue Foundation

THE SHAKESPEARE THEATRE
450 Seventh Street NW, Washington, DC 20004
(202) 547-3230
Type of Facility: Theatre House
Facility Originally: Department Store

Type of Stage: Proscenium
Stage Dimensions: 36'Wx21'Hx46'D
Seating Capacity: 447
Year Built: 1991   **Architect:** Graham Gund
Contact for Rental: Randy Engels;   (202) 547-3230
Resident Groups: The Shakespeare Theatre

SMITHSONIAN INSTITUTION - BAIRD AUDITORIUM
Tenth and Constitution Avenue NW, Washington, DC 20560
(202) 357-1300
Type of Facility: Auditorium
Seating Capacity: 560
Year Built: 1910   **Architect:** Hornblower and Marshall

SMITHSONIAN INSTITUTION - CARMICHAEL AUDITORIUM
14th and Constitution Avenue NW, Washington, DC 20560
(202) 357-1300
Type of Facility: Auditorium
Seating Capacity: 281
Year Built: 1964   **Architect:** McKim, Meade and White

WARNER THEATRE
PO Box 27280, Washington, DC 20003-7280
(202) 628-1818
FAX: (202) 783-0204
Type of Facility: Concert Hall; Theatre House; Multipurpose
Facility Originally: Vaudeville
Type of Stage: Proscenium
Stage Dimensions: 40'Wx30'D   **Orchestra Pit**
Seating Capacity: 1,987
Year Built: 1924   **Architect:** C. Howard Crane
Year Remodeled: 1992   **Architect:** Shalom Baranes Associates   **Cost:** $8,000,000
Contact for Rental: Jane Podgurski, General Manager;   (202) 628-1818

FLORIDA

Anna Maria

THEATRE

ISLAND PLAYERS
PO Box 2059, Anna Maria, FL 34216
(813) 778-5755
> **Founded:** 1948
> **Arts Area:** Community
> **Status:** Non-Professional; Non-Profit
> **Type:** Performing
> **Purpose:** To provide high-quality community theatre productions for the cultural environment of the area
> **Officers:** Geoffrey Todd, President; Jane Adam, First Vice President; Ruth Stevens, Second Vice President; Patricia Rohrer, Treasurer
> **Paid Staff:** 5
> **Utilizes:** Special Technical Talent; Guest Directors
> **Budget:** $1,000 - $50,000
> **Income Sources:** Private Foundations/Grants/Endowments; Box Office; Individual Donations
> **Season:** October - May   **Annual Attendance:** 11,000
> **Performance Facilities:** Island Players Theatre

FACILITY

ISLAND PLAYERS THEATRE
PO Box 2059, Anna Maria, FL 34216
(813) 778-5755
> **Type of Facility:** Theatre House
> **Type of Stage:** Proscenium
> **Seating Capacity:** 137
> **Year Built:** 1900
> **Year Remodeled:** 1974   **Architect:** John Piercy   **Cost:** $30,000
> **Resident Groups:** Island Players

Belle Glade

FACILITY

DOLLY HAND CULTURAL ARTS CENTER
1977 College Drive, Belle Glade, FL 33430
(407) 992-6160
FAX: (407) 992-6179
> **Founded:** 1992
> **Type of Facility:** Concert Hall; Auditorium; Performance Center; Off Broadway; Theatre House; Multi-Purpose
> **Type of Stage:** Proscenium
> **Stage Dimensions:** 40'Wx16'Hx36'10 1/2"D proscenium opening
> **Seating Capacity:** 468
> **Year Built:** 1982
> **Contact for Rental:** Monika M. Potter;   (407) 992-6160

Boca Raton

VOCAL MUSIC

PICCOLO OPERA COMPANY
24 Del Rio Boulevard, Boca Raton, FL 33432
(800) 282-3161
> **Founded:** 1962
> **Arts Area:** Grand Opera; Lyric Opera; Light Opera; Operetta
> **Status:** Professional; Non-Profit
> **Type:** Performing; Touring; Educational
> **Purpose:** To perform professional operas in English, for adults and children
> **Management:** Lee Jon Associates
> **Officers:** Marjorie Gordon, President; Jack Bean, Vice President; Merry Silber, Secretary; Milton J. Miller, Treasurer

Utilizes: Special Technical Talent; Guest Conductors; Guest Artists; Guest Directors
Budget: $1,000 - $50,000
Income Sources: Performance Sponsors
Season: 52 Weeks
Affiliations: NOA; COS

THEATRE

CALDWELL THEATRE COMPANY
7873 North Federal Highway, Boca Raton, FL 33487
(407) 241-7380
FAX: (407) 997-6917
Founded: 1980
Arts Area: Professional; Theatrical Group
Status: Professional; Non-Profit
Type: Performing; Touring; Resident
Purpose: To present regional professional theater
Management: Michael Hall, Executive Director; Patricia Burdett, Company Manager; Kathy Walton, Marketing Director; Joe Ancker, Director of Development; Chip Latimer, Technical Director
Officers: Donald Giancola, President
Paid Staff: 20
Paid Artists: 15
Utilizes: Guest Artists; Guest Directors; Equity Actors
Budget: $1,000,000 - $5,000,000
Income Sources: Private Foundations/Grants/Endowments; Business/Corporate Donations; Box Office; Government Grants; Individual Donations
Season: 52 Weeks   **Annual Attendance:** 80,000
Affiliations: TCG; Florida Professional Theatre Association

FACILITY

UNIVERSITY CENTER AUDITORIUM
500 NW 20th Street, Boca Raton, FL 33432
(407) 367-3730
FAX: (407) 367-2740
Founded: 1982
Type of Facility: Auditorium; General Purpose Center (fixed seating)
Type of Stage: Thrust
Stage Dimensions: 38'Hx66'W; 24'8" radius
Seating Capacity: 2,400
Year Built: 1982   **Architect:** Stewart Richmond Associates   **Cost:** $2,100,000
Year Remodeled: 1991   **Architect:** Giller and Associates   **Cost:** $250,000
Contact for Rental: Matt Hollander;   (407) 367-3730
Resident Groups: Boca Raton Symphonic Pops; Florida Philharmonic Orchestra; Concert Showcase of Florida

---

Boynton Beach

INSTRUMENTAL MUSIC

THE JAMES E. BUFFAN GOLD COAST BAND
Freedom Hall Community Center, 128 East Ocean, Boynton Beach, FL 33435
(407) 738-7444
Founded: 1976
Arts Area: Band
Status: Non-Profit
Type: Performing
Purpose: To provide cultural programming for the entire community and promote an opportunity for the development of players. These adult volunteer musicians have played professionally and nonprofessionally.
Management: Devere Fader, Band Director; Debby Banks, Supervisor (Boynton Beach Recreation & Parks Department)
Officers: Al Miller, Arthur Chargois, Marilyn Wilson, Leone Buffan, Band Committee
Paid Staff: 1
Non-Paid Artists: 70
Utilizes: Guest Artists
Budget: $1,000 - $50,000
Income Sources: Individual Donations
Season: October - May   **Annual Attendance:** 4,000
Affiliations: Palm Beach County Council of the Arts
Performance Facilities: Boynton Beach Freedom Hall Community Center

Bradenton

THEATRE

MANATEE PLAYERS/RIVERFRONT THEATRE
102 Old Main Street, Bradenton, FL 33505
(813) 748-0111
Founded: 1948
Arts Area: Community
Status: Non-Profit
Type: Performing; Educational
Purpose: To improve the educational and cultural climate of the community by providing quality live theatre
Management: Nan Alderson, Managing Director; Peter Massey, Artistic Director; Dan Yerman, Technical Director
Officers: Catherine Bonner, President; Bud Douglas, Vice President; Margaret Newsome, Secretary; Ruth Nielson-Rice, Treasurer
Paid Staff: 4   **Volunteer Staff:** 100
Non-Paid Artists: 100
Utilizes: Special Technical Talent; Guest Artists; Guest Directors
Budget: $100,000 - $500,000
Income Sources: Private Foundations/Grants/Endowments; Business/Corporate Donations; Box Office; Government Grants; Individual Donations; Fund-raising Events
Season: 52 Weeks
Affiliations: FACT; AACT; Manatee County Cultural Alliance
Performance Facilities: Riverfront Theatre

Clearwater

DANCE

HIS IMAGE, SACRED DANCE
2037 Edgewater Drive, #4, Clearwater, FL 34615
(813) 443-2133
Founded: 1981
Arts Area: Modern; Ballet
Status: Non-Profit
Type: Performing; Educational
Purpose: Image has sponsored many workshops with professional instructors and performed for the dance-in-school program to stimulate the interest in dance and to help educate and promote modern dance in the Pinellas County Area.
Management: Janet East Beyer, Director
Volunteer Staff: 6
Non-Paid Artists: 8
Utilizes: Guest Artists; Guest Directors
Budget: $1,000 - $50,000
Income Sources: Individual Donations
Season: 52 Weeks   **Annual Attendance:** 200
Performance Facilities: Ruth Eckerd Hall, Saint Petersburg Junior College

THEATRE

CITY PLAYERS
Clearwater Parks and Recreation, PO Box 4748, Clearwater, FL 34618
(813) 462-6035
Founded: 1971
Arts Area: Community; Theatrical Group
Status: Non-Professional; Non-Profit
Type: Performing; Educational
Purpose: To bring quality theatre (and education of same) to the public of all ages at very nominal fees
Management: Margo Walbolt, Cultural Arts Supervisor; Phillip Terry, Technical Director; B.J. Pucci, Musical Director
Paid Staff: 4
Paid Artists: 3   **Non-Paid Artists:** 4
Utilizes: Guest Artists
Budget: $1,000 - $50,000

Season: September - August   **Annual Attendance:** 8,000
Performance Facilities: Ruth Eckerd Hall; Saint Petersburg Junior College

SHOWBOAT DINNER THEATRE
3405 Ulmerton Road, Clearwater, FL 34622
(813) 573-3777
FAX: (813) 573-2735
Founded: 1967
Arts Area: Professional; Dinner
Status: Professional; Commercial
Type: Performing
Management: Virginia Sherwood, Owner/President/Producer
Paid Staff: 12
Utilizes: Special Technical Talent; Guest Artists; Guest Directors
Income Sources: Box Office
Season: 52 Weeks

PERFORMING SERIES

PACT-RUTH ECKERD HALL AT THE BAUMGARDNER PERFORMING ARTS CENTER
1111 McMullen Booth Road, Clearwater, FL 34619
(813) 791-7060
FAX: (813) 791-6020
Founded: 1978
Arts Area: Dance; Vocal Music; Instrumental Music; Theater
Status: Non-Profit
Type: Performing; Educational; Sponsoring
Purpose: To present major national and international artists and attractions year-round in a fine acoustic hall; to present educational programming, visual arts exhibits and senior citizen programs
Management: Elissa Getto, Executive Director; Diane Eliades, House Manager; Jan Hickin, Director of Marketing/Publicity
Paid Staff: 40   **Volunteer Staff:** 900
Income Sources: Private Foundations/Grants/Endowments; Business/Corporate Donations; Box Office; Government Grants; Individual Donations
Season: 52 Weeks   **Annual Attendance:** 500,000
Affiliations: APAP; ISPAA
Performance Facilities: Ruth Eckerd Hall

Coconut Creek

FACILITY

OMNI AUDITORIUM - BROWARD COMMUNITY COLLEGE
1000 Coconut Boulevard, Coconut Creek, FL 33066
(305) 973-2233
Type of Facility: Concert Hall; Auditorium; Theatre House; Opera House
Type of Stage: Proscenium
Stage Dimensions: 75'Wx40'D
Seating Capacity: 2,008
Year Built: 1980   **Architect:** Louis Wolffe and Associates
Contact for Rental: Susan Berlin;   (305) 973-2233
Resident Groups: Gold Coast Opera

WYNMOOR RECITAL HALL
1300 Avenue of the Stars, Coconut Creek, FL 33066
(305) 974-2627
Founded: 1974
Type of Facility: Concert Hall
Type of Stage: Thrust
Stage Dimensions: 39'x29'
Seating Capacity: 950
Year Built: 1979   **Cost:** $3,000,000

Coral Gables

DANCE

FREDDICK BRATCHER AND COMPANY
PO Box 140099, Coral Gables, FL 33114-0099
(305) 448-2021
FAX: (305) 445-1412
Founded: 1980
Arts Area: Modern; Jazz
Status: Professional; Non-Profit
Type: Performing; Touring; Educational
Purpose: To provide South Florida with high-quality and innovative contemporary dance theater
Management: Maria Lemus, Managing Director
Officers: Jolie Cummings, President; Aaron Morris, Chairman of the Board; Freddick Bratcher, Artistic
Director/Choreographer
Paid Staff: 1 **Volunteer Staff:** 12
Paid Artists: 11
Utilizes: Special Technical Talent; Guest Choreographers
Budget: $50,000 - $100,000
Income Sources: Private Foundations/Grants/Endowments; Business/Corporate Donations; Box Office; Government
Grants; Individual Donations
Season: September - June **Annual Attendance:** 10,000
Performance Facilities: Gusman Center for the Performing Arts; Colony Theater; James L. Knight Center

THEATRE

NEW THEATRE
65 Almeria Avenue, Coral Gables, FL 33134
(305) 443-5909
Founded: 1986
Arts Area: Professional; Theatrical Group
Status: Professional
Type: Performing
Purpose: To present the best of world theatre to South Florida
Management: Rafael DeAcha, Executive Artistic Director; Kimberly Daniel, Company Manager; Maggie Gonzalez,
House Manager
Officers: Dianne Joyce, Chairman
Paid Staff: 3
Utilizes: Special Technical Talent; Guest Artists; Guest Directors
Budget: $100,000 - $500,000
Income Sources: Private Foundations/Grants/Endowments; Business/Corporate Donations; Box Office; Government
Grants; Individual Donations
Season: 52 Weeks **Annual Attendance:** 9,000

PERFORMING SERIES

FLORIDA SHAKESPEARE FESTIVAL
232 Minora Avenue, Coral Gables, FL 33134
(305) 446-1116
FAX: (305) 445-8645
Founded: 1979
Arts Area: Theater; Festivals
Status: Professional; Non-Profit
Type: Performing; Touring; Resident; Educational
Purpose: To popularize Shakespeare and other classical dramatist's works in Florida; to educate young audiences to
Shakespeare's works
Management: Gail Deschamps, Artistic Director
Officers: Jeanine Goodstein, Chairman of the Board
Paid Staff: 20 **Volunteer Staff:** 100
Paid Artists: 65 **Non-Paid Artists:** 10
Utilizes: Special Technical Talent; Guest Artists; Guest Directors
Budget: $500,000 - $1,000,000
Income Sources: Private Foundations/Grants/Endowments; Business/Corporate Donations; Box Office; Individual
Donations
Season: October - May **Annual Attendance:** 40,000
Performance Facilities: Minora Playhouse

Daytona Beach

INSTRUMENTAL MUSIC

DAYTONA BEACH SYMPHONY SOCIETY
230 South Beach Street, Daytona Beach, FL 32115
(904) 253-2901
FAX: (904) 253-0068
Founded: 1952
Arts Area: Symphony; Orchestra; Chamber
Status: Non-Profit
Type: Sponsoring
Management: Bill Lazarus, Managing Director
Officers: Dorothy Bradley, President; James Finn, First Vice President; Rod Resta, Second Vice President; Dr. Jim Woodward, Third Vice President
Paid Staff: 1   **Volunteer Staff:** 50
Paid Artists: 8
Utilizes: Guest Conductors; Guest Artists; Guest Directors
Budget: $100,000 - $500,000
Income Sources: Private Foundations/Grants/Endowments; Business/Corporate Donations; Box Office; Government Grants; Individual Donations
Season: November - April
Annual Attendance: 10,000
Performance Facilities: Peabody Auditorium

THEATRE

DAYTONA PLAYHOUSE
100 Jessamine Boulevard, Daytona Beach, FL 32118
(904) 255-2431
Founded: 1947
Arts Area: Community
Status: Non-Profit
Type: Performing; Resident
Purpose: Pleasure
Management: James F. Sturgell, Artistic Director
Officers: Dick Vaughan, President; Dave Koch, Treasurer; Louise Murray, Secretary
Paid Staff: 1
Utilizes: Community Volunteers
Budget: $50,000 - $100,000
Income Sources: Box Office; Individual Donations
Season: September - July
Annual Attendance: 10,000
Performance Facilities: Daytona Playhouse

SEASIDE MUSIC THEATER
PO Box 2835, Daytona Beach, FL 32120
(904) 252-3394; (904) 252-6200
FAX: (904) 252-8991
Founded: 1977
Arts Area: Professional; Musical; Dinner; Theatrical Group
Status: Professional; Non-Profit
Type: Performing; Touring; Educational
Purpose: To produce a variety of the best examples of musical theater, operetta and opera in repertory
Management: Lester Malizig, General Manager; Lisa Brooks, Director of Marketing and Sales; Nona Lloyd, Production Manager; Tippen Davidson, Artistic Director/Producer
Paid Staff: 30   **Volunteer Staff:** 25
Paid Artists: 50   **Non-Paid Artists:** 5
Utilizes: Guest Conductors; Guest Artists; Guest Directors
Budget: $1,000,000 - $5,000,000
Income Sources: Private Foundations/Grants/Endowments; Business/Corporate Donations; Box Office; Government Grants; Individual Donations
Season: May - August
Annual Attendance: 35,000
Affiliations: Florida Professional Theatre Association; USITT; SETC
Performance Facilities: Daytona Beach Community College Theatre

PERFORMING SERIES

CENTRAL FLORIDA CULTURAL ENDEAVORS
PO Box 1310, Daytona Beach, FL 32015
(904) 252-1511, ext. 410
Founded: 1982
Arts Area: Dance; Vocal Music; Instrumental Music; Theater; Festivals
Status: Professional; Non-Profit
Type: Sponsoring
Purpose: To provide residents in this area the opportunity to hear quality music by the world's greatest orchestras and chamber groups
Management: Dewey Anderson, General Manager
Officers: Tippen Davidson, President; Georgia Kaney, Treasurer; Nancy Spence, Accountant
Paid Staff: 4
Utilizes: Guest Conductors; Guest Artists
Budget: $500,000 - $1,000,000
Income Sources: Business/Corporate Donations; Box Office; Government Grants
Performance Facilities: Peabody Auditorium

FLORIDA INTERNATIONAL FESITVAL
PO Box 1310, Daytona Beach, FL 32115
(904) 257-7790
FAX: (904) 238-1663
Founded: 1966
Arts Area: Dance; Vocal Music; Instrumental Music; Festivals
Status: Professional
Type: Performing; Educational; Sponsoring
Purpose: To present a biennial festival featuring the London Symphony Orchestra and many other types of performances
Management: Tippen Davidson, Founder and Director; Dewey Anderson, General Manager; Pam Stipsits, Marketing Director
Officers: Tippen Davidson, President
Paid Staff: 15   **Volunteer Staff:** 60
Paid Artists: 150
Utilizes: Guest Conductors; Guest Artists
Budget: $1,000,000 - $5,000,000
Income Sources: Private Foundations/Grants/Endowments; Business/Corporate Donations; Box Office; Government Grants; Individual Donations; Advertising; Souvenirs
Season: July - August   **Annual Attendance:** 35,000
Affiliations: APAP; Florida Arts Presenters
Performance Facilities: Peabody Auditorium; Ocean Center; Ormond Beach PAC

FACILITY

DAYTONA BEACH COMMUNITY COLLEGE - THEATRE CENTER
1200 Volusia Avenue, Daytona Beach, FL 32115
(904) 254-3000
FAX: (904) 254-3044
Type of Facility: Theatre Complex; Auditorium; Performance Center; Theatre House
Type of Stage: Proscenium
Stage Dimensions: 36'W arch; 28' plaster to wall   **Orchestra Pit**
Seating Capacity: 508

DAYTONA PLAYHOUSE
100 Jessamine Boulevard, Daytona Beach, FL 32118
(904) 255-2431
Type of Facility: Theatre House
Type of Stage: Proscenium
Stage Dimensions: 40'x28'x35'   **Orchestra Pit**
Year Built: 1947
Manager: Jim Sturgell

OCEAN CENTER
101 North Atlantic, Daytona Beach, FL 32118
(904) 254-4500
Type of Facility: Civic Center
Year Built: 1985   **Architect:** Ellerbe Builders   **Cost:** $37,000,000
Contact for Rental: Rick Hamilton;   (904) 254-4500
Contains the Conference Center and Arena. See separate listings

OCEAN CENTER - ARENA
101 North Atlantic, Daytona Beach, FL 32118
(904) 254-4500
> **Type of Facility:** Arena; Multi-Purpose
> **Type of Stage:** Flexible; Platform
> **Seating Capacity:** 10,000
> **Year Built:** 1985   **Architect:** Ellerbe Builders
> **Contact for Rental:** Rick Hamilton;   (904) 254-4500

OCEAN CENTER - CONFERENCE CENTER
101 North Atlantic, Daytona Beach, FL 32118
(904) 254-4500
> **Type of Facility:** Multi-Purpose
> **Type of Stage:** Flexible; Platform
> **Year Built:** 1985   **Architect:** Ellerbe Builders
> **Contact for Rental:** Rick Hamilton;   (904) 254-4500
> *Conference Center contains 14,000 square feet*

PEABODY AUDITORIUM
600 Auditorium, PO Box 551, Daytona Beach, FL 32015
(904) 258-3169
> **Type of Facility:** Auditorium
> **Type of Stage:** Proscenium
> **Stage Dimensions:** 22'x80'x39'
> **Orchestra Pit**
> **Seating Capacity:** 2,560
> **Year Built:** 1948   **Architect:** Francis Walton   **Cost:** $750,000
> **Year Remodeled:** 1986   **Cost:** $900,000
> **Contact for Rental:** Janet Ford, Assistant Manager;   (904) 258-3169
> **Manager:** Owen Davidson;   (904) 258-3169

Delray Beach

THEATRE

DELRAY BEACH PLAYHOUSE
950 NW Ninth Street, PO Box 1056, Delray Beach, FL 33444
(407) 272-1281
> **Founded:** 1948
> **Arts Area:** Summer Stock; Community
> **Status:** Non-Professional; Non-Profit
> **Type:** Performing; Educational
> **Purpose:** To provide involvement in performing arts to members of the community
> **Management:** Randolph del Lago, Artistic Director; Joyce Lunsford, Box Office Manager; Chuck Tisdale, Technical Director; Ann Cadaret, Scenic Director
> **Officers:** Harvey Brown Jr., President; Ernest G. Simon, Vice President; Yvonne Gugel, Secretary; Jerry McDaniel, Treasurer
> **Paid Staff:** 4   **Volunteer Staff:** 40
> **Non-Paid Artists:** 100
> **Utilizes:** Guest Artists
> **Budget:** $100,000 - $500,000
> **Income Sources:** Business/Corporate Donations; Box Office; Individual Donations
> **Season:** October - June   **Annual Attendance:** 35,000
> **Affiliations:** Florida Theatre Conference
> **Performance Facilities:** Delray Beach Playhouse

FACILITY

DELRAY BEACH PLAYHOUSE
950 NW Ninth Street, PO Box 1056, Delray Beach, FL 33444
(305) 272-1281
> **Type of Facility:** Auditorium
> **Type of Stage:** Proscenium
> **Stage Dimensions:** 16'x34'x26'   **Orchestra Pit**
> **Seating Capacity:** 238
> **Year Built:** 1948   **Cost:** $50,000
> **Year Remodeled:** 1978   **Architect:** James Whilden Jr.   **Cost:** $75,000
> **Resident Groups:** Delray Beach Playhouse

Eustis

THEATRE

BAY STREET PLAYERS
PO Box 1405, Eustis, FL 32726
(904) 357-7777
Founded: 1975
Arts Area: Musical; Community; Theatrical Group
Status: Non-Professional; Non-Profit
Type: Performing; Touring; Educational
Purpose: To develop all aspects of positions in theatre through practical experience gained by doing
Management: Dale R. Carpenter, Executive Director; Deborah Carpenter, Lou Tally, Directors; Michael Lake, Managing Director
Officers: Deborah J. Carpenter, President; Charlie Smith, Secretary; Lou Tally, Comptroller; Timi Lake, Treasurer
Paid Staff: 4 **Volunteer Staff:** 12
Utilizes: Special Technical Talent; Guest Directors
Budget: $50,000 - $100,000
Income Sources: Business/Corporate Donations; Box Office; Individual Donations
Season: 52 Weeks **Annual Attendance:** 15,000
Performance Facilities: State Theatre

Fort Lauderdale

INSTRUMENTAL MUSIC

PHILHARMONIC ORCHESTRA OF FLORIDA
3401 NW Ninth Avenue, Suite 1, Fort Lauderdale, FL 33309
(305) 561-2997
FAX: (305) 561-1390
Founded: 1949
Arts Area: Symphony
Status: Professional; Non-Profit
Type: Performing; Touring; Resident; Educational
Purpose: To maintain a symphony orchestra for cultural and educational purposes to serve South Florida
Management: John E. Graham, Executive Director; Melinda Hipp, Orchestra Manager; Barbara Fead, Director of Development; Bonnie Arnold, Public Relations; Ed Cambron, Marketing
Officers: John B. Deinhardt, Chairman of the Board; Stanley Marks, President Ft. Lauderdale Symphony Orchestra Foundation; Donald Lyman, President, Boca Raton Board of Trustees; Malcolm Farrel JR., President, Broward Board of Trustees; Mrs. Bobbi Litt and Mrs. Christa Paul Co-Presidents, Dade Board of Trustees; Robert Gunn Esq., President, Palm Beaches Board of Trustees; Melvin T. Goldberger, Treasurer
Paid Staff: 10 **Volunteer Staff:** 1
Paid Artists: 85
Utilizes: Special Technical Talent; Guest Conductors; Guest Artists
Budget: $1,000,000 - $5,000,000
Income Sources: Private Foundations/Grants/Endowments; Business/Corporate Donations; Box Office; Government Grants
Season: October - May **Annual Attendance:** 200,000
Performance Facilities: War Memorial Auditorium; Florida Atlantic University Auditorium

VOCAL MUSIC

FORT LAUDERDALE OPERA
333 SW Second Street, Fort Lauderdale, FL 33312
Founded: 1945
Arts Area: Grand Opera
Status: Professional; Non-Profit
Type: Performing; Educational; Sponsoring
Management: William H. Martin, General Manager; Marvin David Levy, Artistic Director; G. David Black, Assistant General Manager
Officers: Theodore K. Friedt, President; Bernice Schwenke, First Vice President; Norman F. Codo, Second Vice President; Michael Bienes, Treasurer; Patricia Helmus, Secretary
Paid Staff: 3 **Volunteer Staff:** 350
Utilizes: Special Technical Talent; Guest Conductors; Guest Artists; Guest Directors
Budget: $1,000,000 - $5,000,000
Income Sources: Private Foundations/Grants/Endowments; Business/Corporate Donations; Box Office; Government Grants; Individual Donations

Season: October - May   **Annual Attendance:** 10,400
Performance Facilities: Broward Center for the Perfroming Arts

OPERA GUILD
333 SW Second Street, Fort Lauderdale, FL 33312
(305) 728-9700
FAX: (305) 728-9702
>**Founded:** 1944
>**Arts Area:** Grand Opera
>**Status:** Non-Profit
>**Type:** Touring
>**Purpose:** To promote opera and the new performing arts
>**Management:** William H. Martin, General Manager
>**Paid Staff:** 3
>**Utilizes:** Guest Conductors; Guest Artists; Guest Directors
>**Budget:** $100,000 - $500,000
>**Income Sources:** Private Foundations/Grants/Endowments; Business/Corporate Donations; Box Office; Government Grants; Individual Donations
>**Season:** January - April   **Affiliations:** Junior Opera Guild/Children's
>**Performance Facilities:** Broward Center for the Performing Arts

THEATRE

FORT LAUDERDALE CHILDREN'S THEATRE
640 North Andrews Avenue, Fort Lauderdale, FL 33311
(305) 763-6882
>**Founded:** 1959
>**Arts Area:** Community; Theatrical Group
>**Status:** Non-Profit
>**Type:** Performing; Touring; Educational
>**Purpose:** To provide educational courses in theatre arts for area youth; to present performances for children, by children
>**Management:** Carol Ries, Executive Director; Darlene J. Lentz, Education Director; Carol Fretwell, Administrative Director
>**Officers:** Melinda Hord, President; Susan Wedwaldt, First Vice President; Valerie Bailey, Second Vice President; Jill Keesler, Registrar; Louise Roth, Secretary; Michael Roth, Treasurer
>**Paid Staff:** 3   **Volunteer Staff:** 60
>**Paid Artists:** 12   **Non-Paid Artists:** 10
>**Utilizes:** Special Technical Talent; Guest Artists; Guest Directors
>**Budget:** $100,000 - $500,000
>**Income Sources:** Private Foundations/Grants/Endowments; Business/Corporate Donations; Box Office; Government Grants; Individual Donations
>**Season:** 52 Weeks   **Annual Attendance:** 25,000
>**Affiliations:** SETC; Florida Theatre Conference; ASSITEJ; American Association of Theatre Educators
>**Performance Facilities:** The Studio; Main Library Theatre

ONE WAY PUPPETS
PO Box 5346, Fort Lauderdale, FL 33310
(305) 491-4221; (305) 444-8842
>**Founded:** 1971
>**Arts Area:** Theatrical Group; Puppet
>**Status:** Professional
>**Type:** Performing; Educational
>**Purpose:** To entertain and educate through the art of puppetry
>**Management:** Bob Dolan, Director
>**Paid Staff:** 2
>**Paid Artists:** 2
>**Budget:** $1,000 - $50,000
>**Income Sources:** Private Foundations/Grants/Endowments; Individual Donations   **Season:** 52 Weeks

PERFORMING SERIES

PTG-FLORIDA, INC./PARKER PLAYHOUSE
707 NE Eighth Street, Fort Lauderdale, FL 33304
(305) 764-1441
FAX: (305) 764-0708
>**Founded:** 1967
>**Arts Area:** Dance; Vocal Music; Instrumental Music; Theater
>**Status:** Professional; Semi-Professional; Non-Professional; Non-Profit; Commercial

Type: Performing; Touring
Purpose: To promote a Broadway series; to make the theatre available to other local and professional promoters
Management: Ronald Stokes, Manager; Sheila Turkiewicz, Director of Theatre Operations; Carol Crolla, Box Office Treasurer; Beverly Sapp, Box Office Manager
Paid Staff: 12
Income Sources: Box Office
Season: November - April   **Annual Attendance:** 75,000
Affiliations: Pace Theatrical
Performance Facilities: Broadway Series

FACILITY

BAILEY HALL
3501 SW Davie Road, Fort Lauderdale, FL 33314
(305) 475-6880
FAX: (305) 424-3154
    Founded: 1979
    Type of Facility: Theatre Complex; Concert Hall; Theatre House
    Type of Stage: Proscenium
    Stage Dimensions: 110'Wx40'D   **Orchestra Pit**
    Seating Capacity: 1,201
    Year Built: 1979   **Architect:** William Crawford   **Cost:** $6,000,000
    Year Remodeled: 1986   **Architect:** Southeast Contractors   **Cost:** $20,000
    Contact for Rental: Cindy Garren;   (305) 475-6880
    Resident Groups: Gold Coast Opera; Miami City Ballet; Florida Philharmonic; Broward Friends of Chamber Music

BROWARD CENTER FOR THE PERFORMING ARTS
201 SW Fifth Avenue, Fort Lauderdale, FL 33312
(305) 463-3290
FAX: (305) 462-3541
    Type of Facility: Theatre Complex
    Type of Stage: Proscenium
    Stage Dimensions: 60'x20'; 45'x80'   **Orchestra Pit**
    Seating Capacity: 2,700; 600
    Year Built: 1991   **Architect:** Benjamin Thompson & Associates   **Cost:** $60,000,000
    Acoustical Consultant: Kirkegaard
    Contact for Rental: John D. Vogt;   (305) 468-3290
    Resident Groups: Florida Philharmonic Orchestra; Sinfonia Virtuosi; Greater Miami Opera; Ft. Lauderdale Opera Guild; Miami City Ballet; Concert Association of Florida; Ft. Lauderdale Broadway Series

PARKER PLAYHOUSE
707 NE Eighth Street, PO Box 4603, Fort Lauderdale, FL 33304
(305) 764-1441
    Type of Facility: Theatre Complex; Concert Hall; Auditorium; Off Broadway; Theatre House
    Type of Stage: Proscenium
    Stage Dimensions: 40'Wx33'D; 40'Wx19'H proscenium opening
    Orchestra Pit
    Seating Capacity: 1,200
    Year Built: 1966   **Architect:** John Volk
    Acoustical Consultant: Robert Haskins
    Contact for Rental: Ronald Stokes;   (305) 764-1442
    Resident Groups: Story Theatre Productions; Ft. Lauderdale Broadway Series
    Rentals from late April until mid-December; December - April as available

WAR MEMORIAL AUDITORIUM
800 NE Eighth Street, Fort Lauderdale, FL 33304
(305) 761-5380
    Type of Facility: Theatre Complex; Concert Hall; Auditorium; Theatre House; Opera House; Multi-Purpose; Exhibition Hall
    Type of Stage: Proscenium
    Stage Dimensions: 93'Wx42'D
    Orchestra Pit
    Seating Capacity: 2,110
    Year Built: 1950   **Architect:** Gilroy-Gamble   **Cost:** $650,000
    Year Remodeled: 1983
    Contact for Rental: Robert Stried;   (305) 761-5380

Fort Myers

DANCE

GULFCOAST DANCE
2265 Peck Street, Fort Myers, FL 33902-1593
(813) 334-3274
Founded: 1976
Arts Area: Modern; Ballet; Jazz
Status: Non-Profit
Type: Performing
Purpose: To offer performance opportunities for southwest Florida dancers under professional direction
Management: Jeanne Bochette, Director
Officers: Jeanne Bochette, President; Marc Platt, Vice President; Carol Thagard, Secretary/Treasurer
Non-Paid Artists: 3
Utilizes: Special Technical Talent; Guest Artists
Budget: $1,000 - $50,000
Income Sources: Private Foundations/Grants/Endowments; Business/Corporate Donations; Box Office; Government Grants; Individual Donations
Season: 52 Weeks   **Annual Attendance:** 31,000
Affiliations: State Dance Association of Florida
Performance Facilities: Mann Hall

THEATRE

PENINSULA PLAYERS
1436 Rosada Way, Fort Myers, FL 33901
(813) 334-0780
Founded: 1978
Arts Area: Dinner; Community; Theatrical Group
Status: Non-Profit
Type: Performing
Purpose: To provide the highest quality theatre possible to the people of southwestern Florida
Management: Al Richter, Dan Perry, Directors; Martha Richter, Director/Producer
Budget: $1,000 - $50,000
Income Sources: Box Office
Season: September - June   **Annual Attendance:** 5,000
Affiliations: Lee County Alliance of Arts
Performance Facilities: Peninsula Playhouse

FACILITY

BARBARA B. MANN PERFORMING ARTS HALL
8099 College Parkway SW, Fort Myers, FL 33906
(813) 489-3033
FAX: (813) 481-4849
Founded: 1985
Type of Facility: Concert Hall; Performance Center; Off Broadway; Theatre House; Opera House; Multi-Purpose
Type of Stage: Proscenium
Stage Dimensions: 57'Wx54'D proscenium opening   **Orchestra Pit**
Seating Capacity: 1,776
Year Built: 1985
Acoustical Consultant: Joe Gleason
Contact for Rental: Kevin Frederick;   (813) 489-3033

FORT MYERS HARBORSIDE 3 BUILDINGS
1375 Monroe Street, Fort Myers, FL 33901
(813) 334-6683
FAX: (813) 332-6683
Founded: 1990
Type of Facility: Concert Hall; Auditorium; Civic Center; Arena; Multi-Purpose
Type of Stage: Thrust; Flexible; Proscenium; Platform; Arena
Stage Dimensions: 40'x68'
Seating Capacity: Conv. Hall - 3,088; Exhibit Hall - 1,400; Hall of 50 States - 400
Year Built: 1991   **Architect:** Spillis Camilla and Partners
Contact for Rental: Theresa Joiner;   (813) 334-2073
Multi-purpose facility

Fort Pierce

FACILITY

SAINT LUCIE COUNTY CIVIC CENTER
2300 Virginia Avenue, Fort Pierce, FL 34982
(407) 468-1526
FAX: (407) 468-2132
> **Type of Facility:** Civic Center
> **Year Built:** 1977
> **Architect:** Hank Riegler
> **Contact for Rental:** Rosemary Kelley or Harold Wheeler;   (407) 468-1526
> **Manager:** Rosemary Kelley;   (407) 468-1526
> *Contains the Auditorium and Theater. See separate listings*

SAINT LUCIE COUNTY CIVIC CENTER - AUDITORIUM
2300 Virginia Avenue, Fort Pierce, FL 34982
(407) 468-1526
FAX: (407) 268-2132
> **Type of Facility:** Auditorium
> **Type of Stage:** Flexible; Platform
> **Seating Capacity:** 4,000
> **Year Built:** 1977
> **Architect:** Hank Riegler
> **Contact for Rental:** Rosemary Kelley or Harold Wheeler;   (407) 468-1526
> **Manager:** Rosemary Kelley;   (407) 468-1526

SAINT LUCIE COUNTY CIVIC CENTER - THEATER
2300 Virginia Avenue, Fort Pierce, FL 34982
(407) 468-1526
FAX: (407) 468-3132
> **Type of Facility:** Concert Hall; Theatre House; Opera House
> **Type of Stage:** Platform
> **Stage Dimensions:** 40'Wx32'D
> **Seating Capacity:** 2,200
> **Year Built:** 1977   **Architect:** Hank Riegler
> **Contact for Rental:** Rosemary Kelley or Harold Wheeler;   (407) 468-1526
> **Manager:** Rosemary Kelley;   (407) 468-1526
> **Resident Groups:** Treasure Coast Opera; Treasure Coast Concert Association

---
Fort Walton Beach

DANCE

NORTHWEST FLORIDA BALLET
101 Chicago Avenue, Fort Walton Beach, FL 32548
(904) 664-7787
> **Founded:** 1969
> **Arts Area:** Modern; Ballet; Jazz
> **Status:** Professional; Semi-Professional; Non-Profit
> **Type:** Performing; Touring; Resident; Educational; Sponsoring
> **Purpose:** To perform; to educate the public as well as dancers; to enrich the cultural environment
> **Management:** Bernadette Clements, Director; Fiona Fairrie, Ballet Mistress
> **Paid Staff:** 2
> **Paid Artists:** 6   **Non-Paid Artists:** 12
> **Utilizes:** Guest Artists; Guest Choreographers
> **Budget:** $100,000 - $500,000
> **Income Sources:** Private Foundations/Grants/Endowments; Business/Corporate Donations; Box Office; Government Grants; Individual Donations
> **Season:** September - July
> **Annual Attendance:** 10,000
> **Affiliations:** Florida Dance Association
> **Performance Facilities:** Pensacola-Saenger Theatre; Panama City Marina Civic Center; Fort Walton Beach High Auditorium

Gainesville

DANCE

DANCE ALIVE!
1325 NW Second Street, Gainesville, FL 32601
(904) 371-2986
Founded: 1966
Arts Area: Modern; Ballet; Jazz
Status: Professional; Non-Profit
Type: Performing; Touring; Resident; Educational
Purpose: To present and perform as a professional dance company; to offer artist residencies and arts-in-education residencies; to utilize the work of resident choreographers as well as old masters
Management: Kim Tuttle, Artistic Director; Judy Skinner, Executive Director; Elaine Funk, Development Director; Ric Rose, Production Director
Officers: Allen Edgar, President; Carl Schwait, President Elect; Linda Sexton, Secretary; Bill Zetrouer, Treasurer; Sheila Bilak, Past President
Paid Staff: 5   **Volunteer Staff:** 5
Paid Artists: 10   **Non-Paid Artists:** 20
Utilizes: Special Technical Talent; Guest Conductors; Guest Artists; Guest Choreographers
Budget: $100,000 - $500,000
Income Sources: Private Foundations/Grants/Endowments; Business/Corporate Donations; Box Office; Government Grants; Individual Donations
Season: September - May
Annual Attendance: 20,000
Affiliations: Siegel Artists Management
Performance Facilities: Center for the Performing Arts

THEATRE

HIPPODROME STATE THEATRE
25 SE Second Place, Gainesville, FL 32601
(904) 373-5968; (904) 375-4477
Founded: 1973
Arts Area: Professional; Theatrical Group
Status: Professional; Non-Profit
Type: Performing; Touring; Resident; Educational; Sponsoring
Purpose: To present the best contemporary theatre possible, and when doing the classics, to reexamine them under our present standards
Management: Mary Hausch, Producing Director; Carlos Asse, Associate Producing Director
Paid Staff: 23
Paid Artists: 30
Utilizes: Guest Artists; Guest Directors
Budget: $500,000 - $1,000,000
Income Sources: Private Foundations/Grants/Endowments; Business/Corporate Donations; Box Office; Government Grants; Individual Donations
Season: 52 Weeks
Annual Attendance: 50,000
Affiliations: TCG; LORT; AAA
Performance Facilities: Hippodrome

FACILITY

HIPPODROME
25 SE Second Place, Gainesville, FL 32601
(904) 373-5968
Type of Facility: Theatre Complex
Facility Originally: Post Office
Type of Stage: Thrust; 3/4 Arena
Seating Capacity: 266
Year Built: 1909   **Architect:** Al Dompe   **Cost:** $2,000,000
Year Remodeled: 1980
Acoustical Consultant: University of Florida
Contact for Rental: Shirley Lasseter;   (904) 373-5968

Hialeah

DANCE

BALLET ETUDES
415 West 51st Place, Hialeah, FL 33012
(305) 557-1142
> **Founded:** 1981
> **Arts Area:** Ballet
> **Status:** Semi-Professional; Non-Profit
> **Type:** Performing; Touring; Educational
> **Purpose:** To perform classical and new classical ballet in southeastern Florida
> **Management:** Susana Prieto, Artistic Director
> **Volunteer Staff:** 10
> **Paid Artists:** 15
> **Utilizes:** Guest Artists; Guest Choreographers
> **Budget:** $1,000 - $50,000
> **Income Sources:** Box Office; Individual Donations
> **Season:** September - June
> **Affiliations:** Dance Educators of America
> **Performance Facilities:** Jackie Gleason Theater

Hollywood

THEATRE

THE GOLDEN THESPIANS
900 Tyler Street, Hollywood, FL 33019
(305) 920-5492
> **Founded:** 1965
> **Arts Area:** Musical; Community; Folk; Theatrical Group
> **Status:** Non-Profit
> **Type:** Performing
> **Purpose:** To bring together a senior group of men and women who were professional musicians, singers and dancers in their younger days to perform one-hour vaudeville shows in nursing homes, hospitals and at community affairs
> **Management:** Ellen Bush, President/Director of Shows
> **Officers:** Ellen Bush, President; Gloria Williams, Vice President; Virginia Godfrey, Treasurer; Madeline Barauskas, Secretary
> **Volunteer Staff:** 25
> **Non-Paid Artists:** 25
> **Utilizes:** Guest Artists
> **Season:** September - June
> **Annual Attendance:** 224
> **Affiliations:** President's Council
> **Performance Facilities:** Recreation Center

HOLLYWOOD PLAYHOUSE
2640 Washington Street, Hollywood, FL 33020
(305) 922-0404
> **Founded:** 1948
> **Arts Area:** Musical; Community; Theatrical Group
> **Status:** Semi-Professional; Non-Profit
> **Type:** Performing
> **Purpose:** To bring culture to the community through theatre
> **Management:** Marianne Mavrides, Executive Director; Elaine Trell, Executive Secretary
> **Officers:** Arnold Ilovitch, President; Howard Greenfield, Vice President; Andy Weinman, Treasurer; Abby Frank, Secretary
> **Paid Staff:** 2   **Volunteer Staff:** 80
> **Utilizes:** Guest Conductors
> **Income Sources:** Box Office; Individual Donations
> **Season:** October - July   **Annual Attendance:** 30,000
> **Affiliations:** Florida Theatre Conference

FACILITY

BEACH THEATRE UNDER THE STARS
Johnson Street and Hollywood Beach Boardwalk, Hollywood, FL 33020
(305) 921-3399
FAX: (305) 921-3233
   Type of Facility: Outdoor (Concert); Amphitheater
   Type of Stage: Proscenium
   Stage Dimensions: 30'x20'
   Seating Capacity: 900
   Year Built: 1965
   Contact for Rental: Jerry Estep;   (305) 921-3404

YOUNG CIRCLE PARK AND BANDSHELL
US Highway 1 and Hollywood Boulevard, Hollywood, FL 33020
(305) 921-3399
FAX: (305) 921-3233
   Type of Facility: Outdoor (Concert); Amphitheater
   Type of Stage: Proscenium
   Stage Dimensions: 60'Wx30'D   **Orchestra Pit**
   Seating Capacity: 2,400
   Year Built: 1952   **Architect:** Ken Spry
   Contact for Rental: Irene Devin;   (305) 921-3404
   Resident Groups: Greater Hollywood Philharmonic Orchestra

Homestead

THEATRE

ACTORS COMMUNITY THEATRE SHOWCASE
8851 SW 107th Avenue, Homestead, FL 33030
(305) 246-0704
   Founded: 1983
   Arts Area: Dinner; Community; Theatrical Group
   Status: Non-Profit
   Type: Performing; Touring; Resident; Educational
   Purpose: To let non-professionals in the community be involved in drama; to bring "live" performances to areas that do not normally have the opportunity to see these presentations
   Management: David Arisco, Artistic Director; Barbara Stein, Executive Director; Gerald Brow, Director of Development
   Officers: Lawrence Stein, President
   Volunteer Staff: 10
   Non-Paid Artists: 10
   Utilizes: Guest Artists; Guest Directors
   Budget: $1,000 - $50,000
   Income Sources: Business/Corporate Donations; Box Office; Individual Donations
   Season: October - May   **Annual Attendance:** 2,000
   Affiliations: Homestead Center for the Arts

Indialantic

INSTRUMENTAL MUSIC

MELBOURNE CHAMBER MUSIC SOCIETY
PO Box 33403, Indialantic, FL 32903
(407) 729-3278
FAX: (407) 725-6406
   Founded: 1978
   Arts Area: Chamber; Ensemble; Instrumental Group
   Status: Non-Profit
   Type: Sponsoring
   Purpose: To bring outstanding professional chamber music to members and the community
   Officers: Tom Kabaservice, President; Andy Pavlakos, Vice President; Madeline Herczog, Programs; Roger Uhlhorn, Treasurer
   Volunteer Staff: 10
   Paid Artists: 20
   Utilizes: Guest Artists
   Budget: $1,000 - $50,000

Income Sources: Business/Corporate Donations; Box Office; Individual Donations
Season: November - March
Annual Attendance: 750
Performance Facilities: Ascension Luthern Church, Indian Harbor Beach

Jacksonville

DANCE

FLORIDA BALLET AT JACKSONVILLE
123 East Forsyth Street, Jacksonville, FL 32202
(904) 353-7518
Founded: 1978
Arts Area: Ballet; Guest Choreographers
Status: Professional; Non-Profit
Type: Performing; Touring; Resident
Purpose: To take a contemporary approach to performance of classical ballet
Management: Laurie Picinich-Byrd, Michael F. Byrd, Artistic Directors
Paid Staff: 5
Paid Artists: 11
Utilizes: Guest Choreographers
Budget: $50,000 - $100,000
Income Sources: Private Foundations/Grants/Endowments; Business/Corporate Donations; Box Office; Government Grants; Individual Donations
Season: September - May
Performance Facilities: Florida Theatre Performing Arts Center

JACKSONVILLE BALLET THEATRE
5516 Keystone Drive South, Jacksonville, FL 32207
(904) 396-5893
Founded: 1970
Arts Area: Modern; Ballet; Jazz
Status: Semi-Professional; Non-Profit
Type: Performing; Educational
Purpose: To further talent in the community by performing and improving technique, acting abilities and audience awareness
Management: Dulce Anaya, Artistic Director
Volunteer Staff: 16
Utilizes: Guest Artists
Income Sources: Private Foundations/Grants/Endowments; Box Office; Individual Donations
Season: September - August
Performance Facilities: Civic Auditorium

INSTRUMENTAL MUSIC

JACKSONVILLE SYMPHONY ORCHESTRA
33 South Hogan Street, Suite 400, Jacksonville, FL 32202
(904) 354-5479
Founded: 1949
Arts Area: Symphony; Orchestra; Chamber
Status: Professional; Non-Profit
Type: Performing; Touring; Educational
Purpose: To provide performances of high artistic quality designed to reach the broadest possible audience; to strive to not only inspire and challenge its audience with classical music, but also provide educational and public service programs
Management: Roger Nierenberg, Music Director/Conductor; David L. Pierson, Executive Director
Officers: Robert T. Shircliff, President; Robert Purcifull, Vice President; Isabelle Davis, Secretary; G. Kennedy Thompson, Treasurer
Paid Staff: 13
Paid Artists: 90
Utilizes: Special Technical Talent; Guest Conductors; Guest Artists
Budget: $1,000,000 - $5,000,000
Income Sources: Private Foundations/Grants/Endowments; Business/Corporate Donations; Box Office; Government Grants; Individual Donations; Fund-raising
Season: September - May   **Annual Attendance:** 250,000
Affiliations: ASOL; Florida Arts Council; Arts Assembly of Jacksonville
Performance Facilities: Florida Theatre Performing Arts Center; Civic Auditorium

THEATRE

ALHAMBRA DINNER THEATRE
12000 Beach Boulevard, Jacksonville, FL 32216
(904) 641-1212
FAX: (904) 642-3505
Founded: 1967
Arts Area: Professional; Dinner
Status: Professional; Commercial
Type: Performing
Purpose: To produce the finest in professional theatrical productions
Management: Tod Booth, Executive Producer
Officers: Tod Booth, President
Paid Staff: 75
Paid Artists: 25
Utilizes: Guest Artists
Budget: $1,000,000 - $5,000,000
Income Sources: Box Office
Season: 52 Weeks   **Annual Attendance:** 130,000
Affiliations: AEA; ADTI; SSDC; AFM
Performance Facilities: Alhambra Dinner Theatre

FACILITY

ALHAMBRA DINNER THEATRE
12000 Beach Boulevard, Jacksonville, FL 32216
(904) 641-1212
FAX: (904) 642-3505
Type of Facility: Theatre House
Type of Stage: Thrust
Stage Dimensions: 18'x22'
Seating Capacity: 388
Year Built: 1967
Contact for Rental: Jack Booth;   (904) 641-1212

FLORIDA NATIONAL PAVILION
1410 East Adams Street, Jacksonville, FL 32202
(904) 630-0837
Type of Facility: Outdoor (Concert)
Type of Stage: Environmental
Stage Dimensions: 97'x47'
Seating Capacity: Concert - 58,000; Theater - 1,875
Year Built: 1983 **Cost:** $3,000,000
Contact for Rental: Sharon Brown;   (904) 630-0837
Manager: Dewitt Gibbs
Resident Groups: Saint John's River City Band; Jacksonville Symphony Orchestra

FLORIDA THEATRE PERFORMING ARTS CENTER
128 East Forsyth Street, Suite 300, Jacksonville, FL 32202
(904) 355-5661
FAX: (904) 358-1874
Type of Facility: Concert Hall; Theatre House
Facility Originally: Vaudeville; Movie House
Type of Stage: Proscenium
Stage Dimensions: 40'Wx28'H proscenium opening
Orchestra Pit
Seating Capacity: 1,978
Year Built: 1927 **Architect:** Hall & Benjamin
Year Remodeled: 1983 **Architect:** Herschel Shepard   **Cost:** $5,700,000
Contact for Rental: Sondra Floyd;   (904) 355-5661
Manager: J. Erik Hart;   (904) 355-5661
Resident Groups: Jacksonville Symphony

JACKSONVILLE CIVIC AUDITORIUM
300 West Water Street, Jacksonville, FL 32202
(904) 630-0701
Type of Facility: Auditorium
Type of Stage: Proscenium

Stage Dimensions: 55'Wx30'H proscenium opening
Orchestra Pit
Seating Capacity: 3,200
Year Built: 1962
Contact for Rental: Pat Craig
Contains the Little Theater and Exhibition Hall. See separate listings

JACKSONVILLE CIVIC AUDITORIUM - EXHIBITION HALL
300 West Water Street, Jacksonville, FL 32202
(904) 630-0701
Type of Facility: Exhibition Hall
Year Built: 1962
Contact for Rental: Pat Craig
The Exhibition Hall contains 21,500 square feet

JACKSONVILLE CIVIC AUDITORIUM - LITTLE THEATER
300 West Water Street, Jacksonville, FL 32202
(904) 630-0701
Type of Facility: Theatre House
Type of Stage: Proscenium
Stage Dimensions: 30'Wx28'H proscenium opening
Orchestra Pit
Seating Capacity: 609
Year Built: 1962
Contact for Rental: Pat Craig

Jupiter

THEATRE

COASTAL PLAYERS/JUPITER CIVIC THEATRE
PO Box 1641, Jupiter, FL 33468-1641
(305) 746-6303
Founded: 1964
Arts Area: Community
Status: Non-Professional; Non-Profit
Type: Performing
Purpose: To encourage interest and participation in live theatre; to cultivate community appreciation and support of the theatre
Officers: Don Blaney, President; Royce Emley, Vice President; Jean Menilla, Treasurer; Anna Bell, Secretary
Volunteer Staff: 9
Budget: $1,000 - $50,000
Income Sources: Box Office; Individual Donations
Season: November - March
Annual Attendance: 2,000
Performance Facilities: Jupiter Community Theatre

Key West

THEATRE

KEY WEST PLAYERS
Wall Street Waterfront Playhouse, PO Box 724, Key West, FL 33041
(305) 294-5015
Founded: 1940
Arts Area: Community; Theatrical Group
Status: Non-Profit
Type: Performing; Educational
Purpose: To present live entertainment featuring professional and amateur artists; to provide a teaching experience; to teach all aspects of theater
Officers: Nancy Holt Kamp, President; George Gugleotti, First Vice President; David Bird, Second Vice President; Florence Recher, Treasurer
Volunteer Staff: 20
Utilizes: Special Technical Talent; Guest Artists; Guest Directors
Budget: $50,000 - $100,000
Income Sources: Box Office; Individual Donations
Season: October - May **Annual Attendance:** 10,000

RED BARN THEATRE
319 Duval Street, Rear Box 707, Key West, FL 33040
(305) 296-9911
    Founded: 1979
    Arts Area: Professional; Musical; Theatrical Group
    Status: Professional; Non-Profit
    Type: Performing; Resident; Educational
    Management: Joy Hawkins, Co-Artistic Director; Mimi McDonald, Business Manager
    Paid Staff: 5
    Paid Artists: 60
    Utilizes: Guest Artists; Guest Directors
    Budget: $100,000 - $500,000
    Income Sources: Private Foundations/Grants/Endowments; Business/Corporate Donations; Box Office; Government Grants; Individual Donations
    Season: November - June
    Annual Attendance: 13,500 ·
    Affiliations: TCG
    Performance Facilities: Red Barn Theatre

PERFORMING SERIES

TENNESSEE WILLIAMS FINE ARTS CENTER
5901 West College Road, Key West, FL 33040
(305) 296-9081, ext. 299
FAX: (305) 292-5155
    Founded: 1977
    Arts Area: Dance; Vocal Music; Instrumental Music; Theater; Festivals; Lyric Opera; Grand Opera
    Status: Non-Profit
    Type: Performing; Sponsoring
    Purpose: To expose tourists and residents to a varied program of the arts through in-house productions and sponsored touring productions
    Management: Ken Bryant, Theatre Director; Florida Keys Community College Fine Arts Department
    Paid Staff: 5
    Paid Artists: 400   **Non-Paid Artists:** 100
    Utilizes: Guest Conductors; Guest Artists; Guest Directors
    Season: October - June
    Annual Attendance: 19,000
    Affiliations: Florida Keys Community College
    Performance Facilities: Tennessee Williams Fine Arts Center

FACILITY

FLORIDA KEYS COMMUNITY COLLEGE - TENNESSEE WILLIAMS THEATRE
Tennessee Williams Fine Arts Center, 5901 West College Road, Key West, FL 33040
(305) 296-1520
    Type of Facility: Concert Hall; Theatre House; Opera House
    Type of Stage: Proscenium; Hydraulic Lift Stage
    Stage Dimensions: 40'Wx20'D;- 40'Wx20'H proscenium opening
    Orchestra Pit
    Seating Capacity: 490
    Year Built: 1977   **Architect:** Carr Smith and Associates
    Contact for Rental: Ken Bryant; (305) 296-9081, ext. 299
    Resident Groups: Tennessee Williams Fine Arts Center Presenting Series
    Southernmost performance facility in the continental United States

RED BARN THEATRE
319 Duval Street, Rear Box 707, Key West, FL 33040
(305) 296-9911
    Type of Facility: Theatre House
    Facility Originally: Barn
    Type of Stage: Platform
    Seating Capacity: 99
    Year Remodeled: 1980
    Contact for Rental: Joy Hawkins, Mimi McDonald; (305) 296-9911
    Resident Groups: Red Barn Theatre

Kissimmee

THEATRE

OSCEOLA PLAYERS
PO Box 451088, Kissimmee, FL 34745
(407) 846-6257
Founded: 1960
Arts Area: Theatrical Group
Status: Non-Professional; Non-Profit
Type: Performing
Purpose: To promote and foster an interest in the dramatic arts as evidenced through presentations of theatrical works
Officers: Robin DuBois-Borden, President; Sharon Sikorski, Vice President; Terrilea Myers, Vice President; Bob Jones, Treasurer
Volunteer Staff: 15
Non-Paid Artists: 50
Utilizes: Special Technical Talent; Guest Directors
Budget: $1,000 - $50,000
Income Sources: Box Office; Individual Donations
Season: September - May   **Annual Attendance:** 10,000
Affiliations: Florida Theatre Conference
Performance Facilities: Osceola Center for the Arts

FACILITY

OSCEOLA CENTER FOR THE ARTS
PO Box 1195, Kissimmee, FL 32742
(407) 846-6257
Founded: 1966
Type of Facility: Theatre Complex; Multi-Purpose; Art Gallery & Classroom; Music Wing
Type of Stage: Proscenium; C.H. Parsons
Stage Dimensions: 50'Dx30'W   **Orchestra Pit**
Seating Capacity: 249
Year Built: 1968   **Cost:** $85,000
Year Remodeled: 1975   **Architect:** C. H. Parsons   **Cost:** $105,000
Contact for Rental: Pete Edwards, Executive Director;   (407) 846-6257
Resident Groups: Osceola Players; Osceola Choral Society; Osceola Historical Society; Osceola Creative Arts League
All but religious or political events

Lake Worth

FACILITY

PALM BEACH COMMUNITY COLLEGE - WATSON B. DUNCAN III, THEATRE
4200 Congress, Lake Worth, FL 33461
(305) 439-8244
Type of Facility: Theatre Complex; Recital Hall
Type of Stage: Thrust; Proscenium; Hydraulic Lift Stage
Stage Dimensions: 36'dx54'W; 19'Hx42'W proscenium opening   **Orchestra Pit**
Seating Capacity: Main House - 720, Recital Hall - 130
Year Built: 1960
Year Remodeled: 1986   **Architect:** Schwabb & Twitty   **Cost:** $3,100,000
Contact for Rental: W. Lee Bell, Manager;   (305) 439-8244

Lakeland

INSTRUMENTAL MUSIC

IMPERIAL SYMPHONY
217 South Tennessee Avenue, Lakeland, FL 33801
(813) 688-3743
Founded: 1965
Arts Area: Symphony
Status: Non-Profit
Type: Performing; Resident; Educational

Purpose: To provide quality musical experiences to listeners of all ages in Lakeland and audiences in other parts of the area; to enhance the music programs in public schools by providing performance opportunities for advanced students and faculty
Management: Larry Collison, Conductor; Beth Mason, Director
Officers: Susan Cruz, President; Jean Palm, Treasurer
Volunteer Staff: 6
Non-Paid Artists: 65
Utilizes: Guest Artists
Budget: $100,000 - $500,000
Income Sources: Private Foundations/Grants/Endowments; Business/Corporate Donations; Box Office; Government Grants; Individual Donations
Season: September - May
Annual Attendance: 10,000
Affiliations: ASOL
Performance Facilities: Lakeland Civic Center

FACILITY

BRANSCOMB MEMORIAL AUDITORIUM
Florida Southern College, 111 Lake Hollingsworth Drive, Lakeland, FL 33801-5698
(813) 680-4295
FAX: (813) 680-3758
Founded: 1964
Type of Facility: Concert Hall; Auditorium; Performance Center; Theatre House; Opera House
Type of Stage: Proscenium
Stage Dimensions: 40'x28'
Orchestra Pit
Seating Capacity: 1,809
Year Built: 1964   **Architect:** Nils Schweitzer   **Cost:** $1,000,000
Contact for Rental: Anthony C. Harris;   (813) 680-4295
Resident Groups: Robert McDonald, Pianist; Beverly Wolff, Mezzo Soprano; The Clarion Brass; The Hollingsworth Trio; Florida Southern College: Symphony Band; Concert Chorale; Jazz Ensemble; Opera Theatre

FLORIDA SOUTHERN COLLEGE - BUCKNER THEATRE
Lakeland, FL 33801-5986
(813) 680-4226
Type of Facility: Theatre House
Type of Stage: Thrust
Stage Dimensions: 22'x28'x41'
Seating Capacity: 336
Year Built: 1970
Architect: Nils Schweizer   **Cost:** $750,000
Contact for Rental: Richard LeVene, Manager;   (813) 680-4184
Manager: Richard LeVene;   (813) 680-4184
Resident Groups: Florida Southern College Vagabonds

LAKELAND CIVIC CENTER
700 West Lemon Street, Lakeland, FL 33802
(813) 499-8100
FAX: (813) 499-8101
Founded: 1974
Type of Facility: Theatre Complex; Civic Center
Type of Stage: Thrust
Stage Dimensions: 78'x47'
Orchestra Pit
Seating Capacity: 2,282
Year Built: 1972   **Architect:** Wade Setliff   **Cost:** $12,000,000
Contact for Rental: Allen Johnson;   (813) 499-8100

LAKELAND CIVIC CENTER - ARENA
700 West Lemon Street, Lakeland, FL 33802
(813) 686-7126
Type of Facility: Concert Hall; Arena
Type of Stage: Flexible; Platform
Seating Capacity: 10,000
Year Built: 1974
Contact for Rental: Allen Johnson;   (813) 499-8100

LAKELAND CIVIC CENTER - EXHIBITION HALL
700 West Lemon Street, Lakeland, FL 33802
(813) 499-8100
FAX: (813) 499-8101
   Type of Facility: Exhibition Hall
   Type of Stage: Flexible; Platform
   Year Built: 1974
   Contact for Rental: Allen Johnson;   (813) 499-8100
   Contains 34,000 square feet of exhibit space

LAKELAND CIVIC CENTER - THEATRE
700 West Lemmon Street, Lakeland, FL 33802
(813) 686-7126
   Type of Facility: Concert Hall; Theatre House
   Type of Stage: Proscenium
   Stage Dimensions: 87'Wx47'D   **Orchestra Pit**
   Seating Capacity: 2,282
   Year Built: 1974
   Contact for Rental: Allen Johnson;   (813) 499-8100
   Resident Groups: Imperial Symphony Orchestra

Longboat Key

INSTRUMENTAL MUSIC

SARASOTA-MANATEE COMMUNITY ORCHESTRA
PO Box 8754, Longboat Key, FL 34228
(813) 383-0734
   Founded: 1975
   Arts Area: Orchestra
   Status: Non-Professional; Non-Profit
   Type: Performing; Resident
   Purpose: To give all those who wish to express themselves musically an opportunity to play in a quality orchestra
   Management: Patricia Stenberg, Conductor; Catherine Miller, Librarian
   Officers: Carleton Brower, President; Mary Jane Meyer, Corresponding Secretary; C. Vincent Wright, Treasurer; Elizabeth Baritaud, Recording Secretary
   Paid Staff: 2   **Volunteer Staff:** 5
   Paid Artists: 8   **Non-Paid Artists:** 85
   Utilizes: Guest Artists
   Budget: $50,000 - $100,000
   Income Sources: Private Foundations/Grants/Endowments; Box Office; Individual Donations
   Season: October - April   **Annual Attendance:** 7,500
   Affiliations: ASOL
   Performance Facilities: Van Wezel Performing Arts Hall

Lynn Haven

THEATRE

KALEIDOSCOPE THEATRE
207 East 24th Street, Lynn Haven, FL 32444
(904) 265-3226; (904) 265-3757
   Founded: 1972
   Arts Area: Musical; Dinner; Community
   Status: Non-Professional; Non-Profit
   Type: Performing; Educational
   Purpose: To enhance the presentational and educational aspects of live theatre for cultural enrichment
   Management: Board of Directors: Lois Carter; David Garcia; Inia J. Plumb; Bill Lanier; Barry Brunetti; Blonza Layfield; Martha Laniel; Kerrie Casey; Sue Webb
   Officers: Charles Wilson, President; Gail Salsman, Vice President; Drew Casey, Secretary; Nancy Parsons, Treasurer
   Volunteer Staff: 20
   Non-Paid Artists: 300
   Utilizes: Special Technical Talent; Guest Artists; Guest Directors
   Budget: $1,000 - $50,000
   Income Sources: Private Foundations/Grants/Endowments; Business/Corporate Donations; Box Office; Government Grants; Individual Donations

Season: September - June
Annual Attendance: 6,000
Performance Facilities: Kaleidoscope Theatre

Manalapan

THEATRE

THEATRE CLUB OF THE PALM BEACHES
262 South Ocean Boulevard, Manalapan, FL 33462
(407) 585-3404
FAX: (407) 585-4708
    Arts Area: Professional; Theatrical Group
    Status: Professional
    Type: Performing
    Purpose: To present the best new works by young American playwrights
    Management: Louis Tyrrell, Producing Director; Nancy Barnett, Company Manager; Caroline Breder, Office Manager; Cheryl Dun, Marketing Director; Alison Pruitt, Development Director
    Officers: Richard Rampell, President; David Freese, Mary Montgomery, Vice Presidents; Dan Hall, Treasurer; William Bone, Secretary
    Paid Staff: 14   **Volunteer Staff:** 200
    Paid Artists: 30
    Utilizes: Guest Directors; AEA Actors
    Budget: Over 10,000,000
    Income Sources: Private Foundations/Grants/Endowments; Business/Corporate Donations; Box Office; Government Grants; Individual Donations
    Season: 52 Weeks
    Annual Attendance: 40,000
    Affiliations: AEA; SSDC

Marathon

THEATRE

MARATHON COMMUNITY THEATRE
PO Box 124, Marathon, FL 33050
(305) 743-5277
    Founded: 1957
    Arts Area: Musical; Dinner; Community; Theatrical Group; Puppet
    Status: Non-Profit
    Type: Performing; Sponsoring
    Purpose: To produce quality theatre events for the adult community; to present cultural programs in the local school system
    Officers: Ray Dimarco, President; Joyce Zwart, Vice President; Bud Kreh, Treasurer; Judi Gorman, Secretary
    Non-Paid Artists: 60
    Utilizes: Special Technical Talent; Guest Conductors; Guest Artists; Guest Directors
    Budget: $1,000 - $50,000
    Income Sources: Private Foundations/Grants/Endowments; Business/Corporate Donations; Box Office; Government Grants; Individual Donations
    Season: 52 Weeks
    Annual Attendance: 10,000

Margate

INSTRUMENTAL MUSIC

NORTHWEST SYMPHONIC POPS ORCHESTRA
6009 NW Tenth Street, Margate, FL 33063
(305) 977-9505
    Founded: 1982
    Arts Area: Orchestra
    Status: Non-Professional; Non-Profit
    Type: Performing; Resident
    Purpose: To promote music appreciation and fund-raising through the Seniors Foundation of Northwest Broward County
    Management: Tony Pandy, Music Director/Conductor
    Officers: Anne Oller, President; Henry Katz, Vice President; Joseph Goldstein, Treasurer; Natalie Shrage, Secretary

Volunteer Staff: 100
Paid Artists: 10   **Non-Paid Artists:** 60
Utilizes: Guest Artists
Budget: $1,000 - $50,000
Income Sources: Private Foundations/Grants/Endowments; Business/Corporate Donations; Box Office; Individual Donations
Season: October - March   **Annual Attendance:** 6,000
Performance Facilities: Broward Community College, North Campus

Melbourne

THEATRE

MELBOURNE CIVIC THEATRE
625 East New Haven Avenue, Melbourne, FL 32901
(305) 723-6935
Founded: 1952
Arts Area: Community; Theatrical Group
Status: Non-Professional; Non-Profit
Type: Performing; Educational
Purpose: To entertain, educate and enrich the community in the theatre arts
Management: David B. Beyer, Artistic Director; Fran S. Delisle, Business Manager; Patricia England, Technical Director
Officers: John Warwick, President; Joseph Langlois, Vice President; Darcia Jones-Francey, Secretary; Greg Pollock, Treasurer
Paid Staff: 3   **Volunteer Staff:** 25
Non-Paid Artists: 250
Budget: $100,000 - $500,000
Income Sources: Business/Corporate Donations; Box Office; Government Grants
Season: September - June   **Annual Attendance:** 19,000
Affiliations: Florida Theatre Conference; ACT; SETC
Performance Facilities: Henegar Center

FACILITY

MAXWELL C. KING CENTER FOR THE PERFORMING ARTS
3865 North Wickham Road, Melbourne, FL 32935
(407) 254-0305, ext. 5100
FAX: (407) 242-2730
Type of Facility: Theatre Complex
Type of Stage: Proscenium
Stage Dimensions: 120'x45'   **Orchestra Pit**
Seating Capacity: 1,993
Year Built: 1988   **Architect:** Spillas & Candella   **Cost:** $12,300,000
Acoustical Consultant: George Eisenhour
Contact for Rental: Ron McCown;   (407) 254-0305

MELBOURNE AUDITORIUM
625 East Hibiscus Boulevard, Melbourne, FL 32901
(407) 722-6000
Type of Facility: Auditorium; Multi-Purpose
Type of Stage: Proscenium
Stage Dimensions: 60'Wx40'D; 60'Wx17'H proscenium opening
Seating Capacity: 1,400
Year Built: 1965   **Cost:** $365,000
Contact for Rental: Wendi Moon;   (407) 722-6000

Miami

DANCE

BALLET CONCERTO COMPANY OF MIAMI
3410 Coral Way, Miami, FL 33145
(305) 446-7922
Founded: 1966
Arts Area: Modern; Ballet; Jazz; Folk
Status: Semi-Professional; Non-Profit
Type: Performing; Educational

Purpose: To present dance in all its forms and shapes in performances of the highest quality
Management: Sonia Diaz, Martha Del Pino, Co-Artistic Directors; Vera Dubson, Executive Director
Officers: Nina Saun, Secretary; Noel Puig, Accountant; Mirita Saun, Treasurer
Volunteer Staff: 4
Paid Artists: 15
Utilizes: Guest Artists
Budget: $50,000 - $100,000
Income Sources: Private Foundations/Grants/Endowments; Business/Corporate Donations; Box Office; Government Grants; Individual Donations
Season: October - May   **Annual Attendance:** 30,000
Affiliations: SERBA; Dance Umbrella

BALLET SPECTACULAR/INTERNATIONAL CULTURAL EXCHANGE, INC.
59 NW 25th Avenue, Miami, FL 33125
(305) 642-8000
Founded: 1948
Arts Area: Modern; Mime; Ballet; Jazz; Ethnic; Folk
Status: Professional
Type: Performing; Touring; Resident; Educational; Sponsoring
Management: Francis Mayville, Managing Director; Herschell Munoz, Associate Director; Camilo Giraldo, Director of Public Relations
Paid Staff: 3   **Volunteer Staff:** 10
Paid Artists: 30
Utilizes: Special Technical Talent; Guest Conductors; Guest Artists; Guest Directors; Guest Choreographers
Budget: $100,000 - $500,000
Income Sources: Box Office
Season: January - June
Affiliations: Hungarian Church of Reformation
Performance Facilities: Gusman Center; Jackie Gleason Theatre of the Performing Arts

FLORIDA DANCE ASSOCIATION INC.
300 Northeast Second Avenue, Suite 1412, Miami, FL 33132-2204
(305) 237-3413
FAX: (305) 237-3645
Founded: 1974
Arts Area: Modern; Ballet; Jazz; Ethnic; Folk
Status: Professional; Non-Profit
Type: Educational; Sponsoring; Service
Management: Rebecca Terrell, Executive Director; Thomas E. Thielen, Associate Director
Officers: Toya Dubin, President; Kip Watson, President Elect; Daniel Lewis, Treasurer; Kathryn Cashin, Secretary
Paid Staff: 2
Utilizes: Guest Artists; Guest Choreographers
Budget: $100,000 - $500,000
Income Sources: Private Foundations/Grants/Endowments; Business/Corporate Donations; Box Office; Government Grants; Individual Donations; Technical Assistance Projects

MIAMI DANCE THEATRE
12205 SW 133rd Court, Miami, FL 33165
(305) 238-4362
Founded: 1980
Arts Area: Ballet
Status: Non-Profit
Type: Performing
Purpose: To maintain a classical ballet company for serious students ages 9 through 18
Management: Judith Newman, Mariana Alvarez-Brake, Co-Artistic Directors
Officers: Lana Brown, President; Marcia Stone, Treasurer; Linda Chastine, Secretary
Paid Staff: 3   **Volunteer Staff:** 5
Non-Paid Artists: 27
Utilizes: Special Technical Talent
Budget: $1,000 - $50,000
Income Sources: Private Foundations/Grants/Endowments; Business/Corporate Donations; Box Office; Government Grants; Individual Donations
Season: September - June
Affiliations: SERBA; Dance Umbrella

MOMENTUM DANCE COMPANY
174 East Flagler Street, Miami, FL 33156
(305) 530-8332
Founded: 1982

Arts Area: Modern; Ballet; Jazz
Status: Professional; Non-Profit
Type: Performing; Touring; Resident; Educational
Purpose: To focus on producing new works as well as reconstructing works of historical significance; to act as a modern dance resource for the community though educational programs
Management: Delma Iles, Artistic Director; Diane Guida, Company Manager
Officers: Dr. Michael Newman, President; Delma Iles, Vice President; Laurel Kalser, Secretary/Treasurer
Paid Staff: 2   **Volunteer Staff:** 3
Paid Artists: 11
Utilizes: Special Technical Talent; Guest Artists; Guest Choreographers
Budget: $100,000 - $500,000
Income Sources: Private Foundations/Grants/Endowments; Business/Corporate Donations; Box Office; Government Grants; Individual Donations
Season: September - May   **Annual Attendance:** 15,000
Affiliations: Dance Umbrella; State Dance Association of Florida
Performance Facilities: James L. Knight Center Auditorium

INSTRUMENTAL MUSIC

GREATER MIAMI MERRY MUMMERS STRING BAND
1261 NE 112th Street, Miami, FL 33161
   Founded: 1965
   Arts Area: Orchestra; Band
   Status: Non-Professional; Non-Profit
   Type: Performing
   Purpose: To do charity work in our community, teach interested folks to play string instruments and bring cheer wherever we go
   Officers: George Helker, President; Rhoda Samuels, Vice President; Joe Keilson, Treasurer; Barb Vlugt, Secretary; Joey Dean, Captain; Bob Vlugt, Music Director
   Non-Paid Artists: 32
   Budget: $1,000 - $50,000
   Income Sources: Individual Donations
   Season: 52 Weeks   **Annual Attendance:** 25
   Affiliations: Philadelphia Mummers Association
   Performance Facilities: North Miami Beach Senior High School

MIAMI CHAMBER SYMPHONY
5690 North Kendall Drive, Miami, FL 33156
(305) 662-6600
   Founded: 1981
   Arts Area: Symphony; Chamber
   Status: Professional; Non-Profit
   Type: Performing
   Purpose: To perform a subscription season of chamber orchestra concerts with famous international artists as well as a series of student concerts
   Management: Burton Dines, Music Director/Manager; Jean Bailly, Office Manager
   Officers: Patrick R. Sullivan, President; Norris Siert, Vice President; Douglas Archbold, Treasurer
   Paid Staff: 2   **Volunteer Staff:** 2
   Paid Artists: 40
   Utilizes: Guest Conductors; Guest Artists; Guild Activities
   Budget: $100,000 - $500,000
   Income Sources: Private Foundations/Grants/Endowments; Business/Corporate Donations; Box Office; Government Grants; Individual Donations
   Season: October - May   **Annual Attendance:** 4,000
   Affiliations: ASOL
   Performance Facilities: Gusman Concert Hall

SOUTH FLORIDA YOUTH SYMPHONY
555 NW 152nd Street, Miami, FL 33169
(305) 238-2706
FAX: (305) 252-9876
   Founded: 1964
   Arts Area: Orchestra; Chamber; Ensemble
   Status: Non-Profit
   Type: Performing; Educational
   Purpose: To broaden the horizons of young talented musicians in the area of symphonic music; to train them in the performance of this music, in conducting and for solos; to offer a junior string training program for beginning students
   Officers: Marcia Hencinski, President; Al Babcock, First Vice President; Helaine Clein, Second Vice President
   Paid Staff: 2   **Volunteer Staff:** 3

Non-Paid Artists: 3
Utilizes: Guest Artists
Budget: $100,000 - $500,000
Income Sources: Private Foundations/Grants/Endowments; Business/Corporate Donations; Individual Donations
Season: September - June   **Annual Attendance:** 7,300
Affiliations: ASOL; Dade Partners; Barry University Early Credit Program

VOCAL MUSIC

THE GREATER MIAMI OPERA ASSOCIATION
1200 Coral Way, Miami, FL 33145
(305) 854-1643
FAX: (305) 856-1042
Founded: 1941
Arts Area: Grand Opera; Lyric Opera
Status: Professional; Non-Profit
Type: Performing; Touring; Resident; Educational
Management: Robert M. Heuer, General Manager; Willie Anthony Waters, Artistic Director; Paul Lapinski, Assistant General Manager/Production Director
Paid Staff: 26
Utilizes: Special Technical Talent; Guest Conductors; Guest Artists; Guest Directors
Budget: $5,000,000 - $10,000,000
Income Sources: Private Foundations/Grants/Endowments; Business/Corporate Donations; Box Office; Government Grants; Individual Donations
Season: January - May   **Annual Attendance:** 220,000
Performance Facilities: Dade County Auditorium

THEATRE

COCONUT GROVE PLAYHOUSE
3500 Main Highway, PO Box 616, Miami, FL 33133
(305) 442-2662
FAX: (305) 444-6437
Founded: 1956
Arts Area: Professional; Theatrical Group
Status: Professional; Non-Profit
Type: Performing; Touring; Educational
Purpose: To bring good theater to the community; to attempt to expand the knowledge of theater in the community
Management: Arnold Mittelman, Producing Artistic Director; Lynne Peyser, Associate Producer; Mark Sylvester, Director of Marketing; Judith Delgado, Director of Education; Savannah Whaley, Public Relations Manager; Lisa Pearson, Development Director
Paid Staff: 35
Paid Artists: 50
Utilizes: Guest Artists; Guest Directors
Income Sources: Business/Corporate Donations; Box Office; Individual Donations
Season: October - May   **Annual Attendance:** 11,000
Affiliations: TCG
Performance Facilities: Coconut Grove Playhouse

LAS MASCARAS THEATRE
2833 NW Seventh Street, Miami, FL 33125
(305) 649-5301
Founded: 1968
Arts Area: Professional; Summer Stock; Musical; Theatrical Group
Status: Professional; Non-Profit
Type: Performing
Purpose: To perform plays in Spanish by local and international authors
Management: Alfonso Cremata, Salvador Ugarte, Artistic Directors/Lead Actors
Officers: Delia Carballo, President; Consuelo Otero, Vice President; Nina Saun, Secretary
Paid Staff: 4   **Volunteer Staff:** 10
Paid Artists: 20
Utilizes: Guest Artists
Budget: $50,000 - $100,000
Income Sources: Box Office
Season: 52 Weeks   **Annual Attendance:** 25,000
Performance Facilities: Las Mascaras Theatre #1; Las Mascaras Theatre #2

TEATRO AVANTE
742 SW Eighth Street, Miami, FL 33130
(305) 858-4155
FAX: (305) 854-5445
>**Founded:** 1979
>**Arts Area:** Professional; Summer Stock; Theatrical Group
>**Status:** Professional; Non-Profit
>**Type:** Performing; Touring; Educational
>**Purpose:** To promote Hispanic theatre
>**Management:** Mario Ernesto Sanchez, Producing Artistic Director; Rolando Moreno, Resident Director/Designer; Manelo Mina, Technical Coordinator
>**Officers:** Maris Ernest Sanches, President; Edna Schwab, Treasurer; Marilyn Barrot, Secretary
>**Paid Staff:** 5   **Volunteer Staff:** 10
>**Paid Artists:** 30
>**Utilizes:** Special Technical Talent; Guest Artists; Guest Directors
>**Budget:** $100,000 - $500,000
>**Income Sources:** Private Foundations/Grants/Endowments; Business/Corporate Donations; Box Office; Government Grants; Individual Donations
>**Season:** 52 Weeks
>**Annual Attendance:** 25,000
>**Performance Facilities:** El Carruse Theatre

FACILITY

DADE COUNTY AUDITORIUM
2901 West Flagler Street, Miami, FL 33135
(305) 547-5414
FAX: (305) 541-7782
>**Type of Facility:** Auditorium
>**Type of Stage:** Proscenium
>**Stage Dimensions:** 60'Wx40'D; 60'Wx30'H proscenium opening
>**Orchestra Pit**
>**Seating Capacity:** 2,498
>**Year Built:** 1950   **Architect:** Stewart and Skinner   **Cost:** $1,500,000
>**Year Remodeled:** 1989   **Architect:** Tilton and Tachi   **Cost:** $1,500,000
>**Acoustical Consultant:** Edmunds & Mulgreen
>**Contact for Rental:** Barry Steinman;   (305) 547-5414

GUSMAN CENTER FOR THE PERFORMING ARTS
174 East Flagler Street, Miami, FL 33131
(305) 374-2444
FAX: (305) 374-0303
>**Founded:** 1926
>**Type of Facility:** Theatre House; Multi-Purpose
>**Facility Originally:** Movie House
>**Type of Stage:** Proscenium
>**Stage Dimensions:** 41'4"Wx29'H proscenium opening; 66'1"Wx31'D overall; 52' stage depth
>**Orchestra Pit**
>**Seating Capacity:** 1,739
>**Year Built:** 1926   **Architect:** John Eberson   **Cost:** $1,500,000
>**Year Remodeled:** 1972   **Architect:** Morris Lapidus Jr.
>**Contact for Rental:** Jeannie Piazza-Zuniga;   (305) 374-2444

JAMES L. KNIGHT CENTER
400 SE Second Avenue, Miami, FL 33131
(305) 372-0277
FAX: (305) 372-2919
>**Founded:** 1982
>**Type of Facility:** Multi-Purpose
>**Type of Stage:** Arena; Portable Staging - 16,000 square feet
>**Stage Dimensions:** 56'x36'
>**Seating Capacity:** 5,000
>**Year Built:** 1982   **Cost:** $96,000,000
>**Acoustical Consultant:** Jerry McDonald, Director of Operations
>**Contact for Rental:** Manny Fernandez;   (305) 372-0277

Miami Beach

DANCE

MIAMI CITY BALLET
905 Lincoln Road, Miami Beach, FL 33139
(305) 532-4880
> **Founded:** 1985
> **Arts Area:** Ballet
> **Status:** Professional; Non-Profit
> **Type:** Performing; Touring; Resident
> **Purpose:** To maintain Florida's first fully-professional, major, resident ballet company; to provide a variety of performances and outreach services statewide
> **Management:** Edward Villeua, Executive Director; Pam Millor, General Manager
> **Officers:** Rhoda Levitt, President
> **Paid Staff:** 7
> **Paid Artists:** 23
> **Utilizes:** Special Technical Talent; Guest Conductors; Guest Choreographers
> **Budget:** $1,000,000 - $5,000,000
> **Income Sources:** Private Foundations/Grants/Endowments; Business/Corporate Donations; Box Office; Government Grants; Individual Donations
> **Season:** August - May   **Annual Attendance:** 30,000
> **Affiliations:** Dance USA; State Dance Association of Florida
> **Performance Facilities:** Dade County Auditorium

INSTRUMENTAL MUSIC

BROWARD SYMPHONY ORCHESTRA
5225 La Gorce Drive, Miami Beach, FL 33140
(305) 864-7984
FAX: (305) 868-3623
> **Founded:** 1965
> **Arts Area:** Symphony; Orchestra; Chamber; Ensemble; Instrumental Group
> **Status:** Professional; Semi-Professional; Non-Profit
> **Type:** Performing; Touring; Resident; Educational; Sponsoring
> **Purpose:** To provide professional cultural community education
> **Management:** Laurence Gordon Siegel, Music Director
> **Paid Staff:** 1   **Volunteer Staff:** 6
> **Paid Artists:** 6
> **Utilizes:** Guest Conductors; Guest Artists; Guest Directors
> **Budget:** $1,000 - $50,000
> **Income Sources:** Private Foundations/Grants/Endowments; Business/Corporate Donations; Box Office; Individual Donations
> **Season:** October - June
> **Annual Attendance:** 6,000

NEW WORLD SYMPHONY
541 Lincoln Road, Miami Beach, FL 33139
(305) 673-3330
FAX: (305) 673-6749
> **Founded:** 1987
> **Arts Area:** Symphony; Orchestra; Chamber
> **Status:** Professional; Non-Profit
> **Type:** Performing; Touring
> **Purpose:** To maintain a national advanced-training program that prepares gifted young orchestral musicians (ages 21-30) for full-time professional music careers and provides participants the opportunity to study and perform with distinguished conductors and solo artists
> **Management:** Christopher T. Dunworth, Executive Director; John Duffy, Vice President of Operations; Michael Tilson-Thomas, Artistic Advisor/Conductor
> **Officers:** Sherwood Weiser, Chairman; Sheldon Schneider, Treasurer; Diane Sepler, Secretary
> **Paid Staff:** 8
> **Paid Artists:** 75
> **Utilizes:** Guest Conductors
> **Budget:** $1,000,000 - $5,000,000
> **Income Sources:** Private Foundations/Grants/Endowments; Business/Corporate Donations; Box Office; Government Grants; Individual Donations; Fund-raising
> **Season:** October - March   **Affiliations:** ASOL
> **Performance Facilities:** Gusman Center for the Performing Arts

VOCAL MUSIC

PAN-AMERICAN SOCIETY OF ARTISTS INC.
5225 La Gorce Drive, Miami Beach, FL 33140
(305) 864-7984
Founded: 1990
Arts Area: Grand Opera; Lyric Opera; Light Opera; Operetta; Choral; Ethnic; Folk; Symphony; Ballet
Status: Professional; Semi-Professional; Non-Profit
Type: Performing; Touring; Resident; Educational; Sponsoring; Cultural Exchange
Management: Dr. P. Melendez, Development; Maxey Melendez, Public Relations; Lawrence G. Siegel, Music Director
Officers: Luz Morales, President; Dr. F. E. Reyes, Vice President; Mariem Leuiem, Secretary/Treasurer
Paid Staff: 3 **Volunteer Staff:** 10
Paid Artists: 1
Utilizes: Special Technical Talent; Guest Conductors; Guest Artists; Guest Directors
Budget: $50,000 - $100,000
Income Sources: Private Foundations/Grants/Endowments; Business/Corporate Donations; Box Office; Government Grants; Individual Donations
Season: 52 Weeks **Annual Attendance:** 10,000

THEATRE

GOLD COAST MIME COMPANY
345 West 37th Street, Miami Beach, FL 33140
(305) 538-5500
Founded: 1982
Arts Area: Theatrical Group; Mime
Status: Professional
Type: Performing; Touring; Educational
Purpose: To bring professionalism to mime in South Florida; to extend the limits of creativity
Management: Jude Parry, Director
Paid Staff: 1
Paid Artists: 3
Utilizes: Special Technical Talent
Budget: $1,000 - $50,000
Income Sources: Business/Corporate Donations; Box Office
Season: November - May **Annual Attendance:** 100,000

FACILITY

JACKIE GLEASON THEATER
1700 Washington Avenue, Miami Beach, FL 33139
(305) 673-7311
FAX: (305) 673-7435
Type of Facility: Concert Hall; Theatre House
Type of Stage: Proscenium
Stage Dimensions: 58'Wx110'D **Orchestra Pit**
Seating Capacity: 3,023
Year Built: 1950 **Cost:** $2,000,000
Year Remodeled: 1976 **Architect:** Morris Lapidus, Jr. **Cost:** $7,100,000
Acoustical Consultant: C.P. Boner
Contact for Rental: Steve Clark; (305) 673-7311
Manager: Norman Litz

Monticello

FACILITY

MONTICELLO OPERA HOUSE
Courthouse Square, PO Box 518, Monticello, FL 32344
(904) 997-4242
Founded: 1890
Type of Facility: Performance Center; Opera House; Ballroom; Meeting Rooms
Facility Originally: Business Facility
Type of Stage: Proscenium
Stage Dimensions: 27'x27'
Orchestra Pit
Seating Capacity: Main Auditorium - 380; Lower Level Bays/Ballroom - 250
Year Built: 1890 **Architect:** John Perkins

Year Remodeled: 1992 **Architect:** Barnett Fronczak Architects **Cost:** $1,000,000
Contact for Rental: Helen Rouse; (904) 997-4242
Manager: Camilla Augustine, Program Manager; (904) 997-7142
Performance season consisting of 8-12 scheduled performances runs from October to April; other special events are held throughout the year.

New Port Richey

VOCAL MUSIC

JUBILLEE MENS CHORUS
5936 Grand Boulevard, New Port Richey, FL 34652
(813) 848-6969
>**Founded:** 1980
>**Arts Area:** Light Opera; Operetta; Choral; Ethnic; Folk
>**Status:** Semi-Professional; Non-Profit
>**Type:** Performing
>**Purpose:** To encourage the trained singer to remain an active participant in musical performances
>**Management:** Dolores K. Long, Director
>**Paid Staff:** 2 **Volunteer Staff:** 2
>**Paid Artists:** 4 **Non-Paid Artists:** 2
>**Utilizes:** Guest Artists
>**Budget:** $1,000 - $50,000
>**Income Sources:** Box Office; Individual Donations
>**Season:** October - June
>**Annual Attendance:** 1,000

THE THURSDAY MUSICALE
5936 Grand Boulevard, New Port Richey, FL 34652
(813) 848-6969
>**Founded:** 1947
>**Arts Area:** Grand Opera; Lyric Opera; Light Opera; Operetta; Choral; Ethnic; Folk
>**Status:** Semi-Professional; Non-Profit
>**Type:** Performing; Touring; Sponsoring
>**Purpose:** To present monthly performances of chorus featuring guest artists; to award two musical scholarships per year, with recipients featured in performances
>**Management:** Dolores K. Long, Director
>**Officers:** Lynn Pfieffer, President; Billie Helm, Vice President; Norma Douglass, Secretary; Mildred Ferrari, Treasurer
>**Paid Staff:** 2 **Volunteer Staff:** 10
>**Paid Artists:** 8 **Non-Paid Artists:** 1
>**Utilizes:** Special Technical Talent; Guest Artists
>**Budget:** $1,000 - $50,000
>**Income Sources:** Box Office; Individual Donations
>**Season:** September - June
>**Annual Attendance:** 6,000
>**Performance Facilities:** First Baptist Church

New Smyrna Beach

PERFORMING SERIES

ATLANTIC CENTER FOR THE ARTS
1414 Art Center Avenue, New Smyrna Beach, FL 32168
(904) 427-6975
FAX: (904) 427-5669
>**Arts Area:** Dance; Vocal Music; Instrumental Music; Theater; Performance Art; Installations
>**Status:** Non-Profit
>**Type:** Performing
>**Purpose:** To provide an interdisciplinary artists' community in which master artists and associates collaborate during a three-week project-based or process-based residency
>**Management:** Ted Potter, Executive Director; James Murphy, Program Director; Suzanne Fetscher, Assistant Program Director; Jenni Mac Innes, Education Coordinator
>**Officers:** Board of Trustees
>**Paid Staff:** 10 **Volunteer Staff:** 45
>**Paid Artists:** 20 **Non-Paid Artists:** 100
>**Utilizes:** Guest Artists; Master Artists in Residence
>**Budget:** $500,000 - $1,000,000

Income Sources: Private Foundations/Grants/Endowments; Business/Corporate Donations; Government Grants; Individual Donations; Auction
Season: 52 Weeks
Affiliations: University of Central Florida

North Fort Myers

FACILITY

LEE CIVIC CENTER
11831 Bayshore Road, North Fort Myers, FL 33917
(813) 543-8368
    Type of Facility: Civic Center
    Year Built: 1978
    Contact for Rental: Glenda Dunlap;   (813) 543-8368
    Contains the Arena and Small Theater. See separate listings

LEE CIVIC CENTER - ARENA
11831 Bayshore Road, North Fort Myers, FL 33917
(813) 543-8368
    Type of Facility: Arena
    Type of Stage: Flexible; Platform
    Stage Dimensions: 40'x48'
    Seating Capacity: 8,063
    Contact for Rental: Glenda Dunlap;   (813) 543-8368

LEE CIVIC CENTER - SMALL THEATER
11831 Bayshore Road, North Fort Myers, FL 33917
(813) 543-8368
    Type of Facility: Theatre House
    Type of Stage: Flexible; Platform
    Stage Dimensions: 40'x48'
    Seating Capacity: 3,763
    Contact for Rental: Glenda Dunlap;   (813) 543-8368

North Miami Beach

FACILITY

VICTORY PARK AUDITORIUM
17011 NE 19th Avenue, North Miami Beach, FL 33162
(305) 948-2957
    Type of Facility: Auditorium; Multi-Purpose
    Facility Originally: Recreation Hall; Gymnasium
    Type of Stage: Proscenium
    Stage Dimensions: 28'x35'
    Seating Capacity: 1,394
    Year Built: 1963
    Contact for Rental: North Miami Beach Parks and Recreation Department;   (305) 948-2957
    Manager: Peter S. Kadish
    Resident Groups: North Miami Beach Symphony; South Florida Youth Symphony; Pro Show; Barry University Basketball; Miami Christian College Basketball; Saint Thomas University Basketball

North Palm Beach

THEATRE

THE VILLAGE PLAYERS
501 US Highway 1, North Palm Beach, FL 33408-4906
(407) 626-5310
    Founded: 1980
    Arts Area: Community; Theatrical Group
    Status: Non-Professional; Non-Profit
    Type: Performing; Resident
    Purpose: To provide clean, low cost, quality entertainment for the community; to provide an outlet for talented amateurs
    Management: Roma Smith, Business Manager; Alice Bachman, Liason; Dick Norton, Technical Director

Officers: Caroline Breder, President; Lee Greco, First Vice President; Marilyn Causa, Second Vice President; Roseanne Wolf, Secretary; Terry Elliott, Treasurer
Utilizes: Special Technical Talent; Guest Artists; Guest Directors
Budget: $1,000 - $50,000
Income Sources: Box Office; Individual Donations
Season: August - June
Affiliations: North Palm Beach Recreation
Performance Facilities: North Palm Beach Community Center

Ocala

FACILITY

CENTRAL FLORIDA COMMUNITY COLLEGE - FINE ARTS AUDITORIUM
College Road, PO Box 1388, Ocala, FL 32678
(904) 237-2111, ext. 348
Founded: 1968
Type of Facility: Auditorium
Type of Stage: Proscenium
Orchestra Pit
Seating Capacity: 379
Year Built: 1968   **Architect:** Vance Duncan   **Cost:** $300,000
Year Remodeled: 1991   **Cost:** $500,000
Contact for Rental: Daryl Harrison;   (904) 237-2111, ext. 348

Orange Park

THEATRE

ORANGE PARK COMMUNITY THEATRE
2900 Moody Avenue, PO Box 391, Orange Park, FL 32065
(904) 276-2599
Founded: 1968
Arts Area: Musical; Community
Status: Non-Professional; Non-Profit
Type: Performing; Educational
Purpose: To perpetuate live theatre in Clay County
Officers: Emma Lee Carpenter, President; Virginia Bell, Vice President; Irving Norton, Secretary; Ray Patterson, Treasurer
Volunteer Staff: 200
Income Sources: Business/Corporate Donations; Box Office; Individual Donations
Season: January - June
Performance Facilities: Lions Club

Orlando

DANCE

SOUTHERN BALLET THEATRE
1111 North Orange Avenue, Orlando, FL 32804
(407) 426-1733
FAX: (407) 426-1734
Founded: 1974
Arts Area: Modern; Ballet; Jazz
Status: Professional; Non-Profit
Type: Performing; Touring; Sponsoring
Purpose: To deliver dance to every corner of the community, from the schools to the theatres - we want our audiences to feel the power and the joy of dance
Management: Kip Watson, General Manager; Barbara Riggins, Artistic Director
Officers: Rosemary O' Shea, President; Pat Anyell, Tony Conway, Candido Seganna, Maria Motes, Michael Brogan, Nancy Jacobson, Vice Presidents; Susan Stucker, President-Elect; Dr. Harry Eisenberg, Secretary; Jim Hutcheson, Treasurer
Paid Staff: 12
Paid Artists: 16
Utilizes: Special Technical Talent; Guest Artists; Guest Choreographers
Budget: $1,000,000 - $5,000,000

Income Sources: Private Foundations/Grants/Endowments; Business/Corporate Donations; Box Office; Government Grants; Individual Donations
Season: September - May   **Annual Attendance:** 40,000
Affiliations: State Dance Association of Florida
Performance Facilities: Bob Carr Performing Arts Center

INSTRUMENTAL MUSIC

FLORIDA SYMPHONY ORCHESTRA
1900 North Mills Avenue, #3, Orlando, FL 32803
(407) 896-0331
FAX: (407) 896-2373
Founded: 1950
Arts Area: Symphony; Orchestra; Chamber
Status: Professional; Non-Profit
Type: Performing; Educational
Purpose: To give concerts; to promote musical education and greater public appreciation of music; to assist in the education of young musicians
Management: Benjamin Greene, Executive Vice President; Kevin Hagen, General Manager; Joseph Silverstein, Music Advisor
Officers: Ann Smith, President; Harvey Massey, President-Elect
Paid Staff: 13
Paid Artists: 72
Utilizes: Guest Conductors; Guest Artists
Budget: $1,000,000 - $5,000,000
Income Sources: Private Foundations/Grants/Endowments; Business/Corporate Donations; Box Office; Government Grants; Individual Donations
Season: September - May   **Annual Attendance:** 150,000
Affiliations: ASOL
Performance Facilities: Bob Carr Performing Arts Center

VOCAL MUSIC

ORLANDO OPERA
1100 North Orange Avenue, PO Box 426-1700, Orlando, FL 32804
(407) 426-1717
FAX: (407) 426-1705
Founded: 1958
Arts Area: Grand Opera
Status: Professional
Type: Performing
Management: Robert Swedberg, General Manager; Barbara Battersby, Director of Development; Alden Brun, Marketing and Advertising
Officers: L.C. Grammer, President; Leyton Yates, President-Elect
Paid Staff: 8   **Volunteer Staff:** 15
Utilizes: Special Technical Talent; Guest Conductors; Guest Artists; Guest Directors
Budget: $100,000 - $500,000
Income Sources: Private Foundations/Grants/Endowments; Business/Corporate Donations; Box Office; Government Grants; Individual Donations
Season: November - April   **Annual Attendance:** 24,000
Affiliations: OA
Performance Facilities: Bob Carr Performing Arts Center

THEATRE

CIVIC THEATRE OF CENTRAL FLORIDA
1001 East Princeton Street, Orlando, FL 32803
(407) 896-7365
FAX: (407) 897-3284
Founded: 1926
Arts Area: Musical; Community; Theatrical Group; Semi-Professional
Status: Semi-Professional; Non-Professional; Non-Profit
Type: Performing; Touring; Educational
Purpose: To serve the community by entertaining, informing, stimulating, educating and providing a forum for artistic expression through live theatre and classroom experiences

Management: Mary Ann Dean, General Manager; Michael Fortner, Artistic Director; Jill Hardester, Theatre for Young People/Second Stage Producer; Julie Bailey, Marketing Director; Ryszard Lukaszewicz, Technical Director
Officers: Ruby Homayssi, President; Jonathan Rich, Linda Santieri, Michael Harding, Vice Presidents; John Holloway, Secretary; Janet Ziomek, Treasurer
Paid Staff: 15
Non-Paid Artists: 1
Utilizes: Special Technical Talent; Guest Conductors; Guest Artists; Guest Directors
Budget: $1,000,000 - $5,000,000
Income Sources: Private Foundations/Grants/Endowments; Business/Corporate Donations; Box Office; Government Grants; Individual Donations
Season: September - June
Annual Attendance: 150,000
Affiliations: AACT; Florida Theatre Conference; United Arts
Performance Facilities: Civic Theatre Complex

MARK TWO DINNER THEATER
3376 Edgewater Drive, Orlando, FL 32804
(407) 843-6275
FAX: (407) 843-1510
Founded: 1986
Arts Area: Professional; Dinner
Status: Professional
Type: Performing
Purpose: To provide Orlando with the best theater and dining possible
Management: Mark Howard, Executive Producer/Director; Scott A. Reeds, General Manager
Officers: Mark Howard, President
Paid Staff: 54
Paid Artists: 10
Utilizes: Guest Artists
Budget: $100,000 - $500,000
Income Sources: Box Office
Season: 52 Weeks
Affiliations: AEA; American Dinner Theatre Association
Performance Facilities: Mark Two Dinner Theater

THEATRE-IN-THE-WORKS
PO Box 532016, Orlando, FL 32853
(407) 365-7235
Founded: 1984
Arts Area: Professional; Theatrical Group
Status: Professional; Non-Profit
Purpose: To develop original plays, musicals and operas witten primarily by Florida authors
Management: Edward Dilks, Producing Director
Paid Staff: 1   **Volunteer Staff:** 6
Utilizes: Guest Artists
Budget: $1,000 - $50,000
Income Sources: Private Foundations/Grants/Endowments; Business/Corporate Donations; Box Office; Government Grants; Individual Donations
Season: March - October

FACILITY

BOB CARR PERFORMING ARTS CENTER
401 West Livingston Street, Orlando, FL 32801
(305) 849-2562
Type of Facility: Concert Hall; Auditorium; Performance Center; Theatre House; Opera House
Type of Stage: Proscenium; Hydraulic Lift Stage
Stage Dimensions: 50'x34'
Orchestra Pit
Seating Capacity: 2,534
Year Built: 1926   **Cost:** $250,000
Year Remodeled: 1978   **Architect:** Don Duer/Tom Price   **Cost:** $3,700,000
Acoustical Consultant: George Izenour
Contact for Rental: Robin Handlin or Bill Becker;   (305) 849-2562
Resident Groups: Florida Symphony Orchestra; Southern Ballet; Orlando Opera; Orlando Broadway Series

ORANGE COUNTY CIVIC CENTER
9800 International Drive, Orlando, FL 32819
(407) 345-9800
FAX: (407) 345-9876
    Type of Facility: Civic Center
    Type of Stage: Platform
    Seating Capacity: 11,000
    Year Built: 1983   **Architect:** Hellman Hurley Charvatt & Peabody   **Cost:** $50,000,000
    Contact for Rental: Elizabeth Forsythe; (407) 345-9800

VALENCIA COMMUNITY COLLEGE - BLACK BOX THEATRE
701 North Econlockhatchee Trail, Orlando, FL 32825
(407) 299-5000
    Type of Facility: Black Box
    Type of Stage: Flexible
    Stage Dimensions: 50'x50' space
    Seating Capacity: 100-200
    Year Built: 1981
    Contact for Rental: Richard Rietveld; (407) 299-5000, ext. 2285
    Manager: Que Throm; (407) 299-5000, ext. 2340

VALENCIA COMMUNITY COLLEGE - PERFORMING ARTS CENTER
701 North Econlockhatchee Trail, Orlando, FL 32817
(407) 299-5000, ext. 2285
    Type of Facility: Theatre Complex
    Type of Stage: Proscenium; Environmental
    Stage Dimensions: 50'x50'; 40'W proscenium opening   **Orchestra Pit**
    Seating Capacity: 588
    Year Built: 1981
    Contact for Rental: Richard Rietveld; (407) 299-5000, ext. 2285
    Resident Groups: Valencia Character Company

Palm Beach

INSTRUMENTAL MUSIC

GREATER PALM BEACH SYMPHONY
139 North County Road, Palm Beach, FL 33480
(407) 655-2657
FAX: (407) 655-9113
    Founded: 1974
    Arts Area: Symphony
    Status: Professional
    Type: Performing
    Management: Timothy Gilligan, General Manager
    Officers: Ethel S. Stone, Chairman
    Paid Staff: 4   **Volunteer Staff:** 5
    Utilizes: Guest Conductors; Guest Artists
    Budget: $500,000 - $1,000,000
    Income Sources: Private Foundations/Grants/Endowments; Business/Corporate Donations; Box Office; Government Grants; Individual Donations
    Season: November - April
    Performance Facilities: Royal Poinciana Playhouse

FACILITY

THE SOCIETY OF THE FOUR ARTS GALLERY - THEATER
Four Arts Plaza, Palm Beach, FL 33480
(407) 655-7226
FAX: (407) 655-7233
    Founded: 1936
    Type of Facility: Auditorium; Multi-Purpose; Exhibition Galleries
    Facility Originally: Private Club
    Type of Stage: Proscenium
    Stage Dimensions: 25'D, 32'W downstage, 40'W upstage
    Seating Capacity: 718
    Year Built: 1936   **Architect:** Addison Mizner

Year Remodeled: 1947
Two-building complex includes the Gallery Building and Library Building; Auditorium added 1947

Palm Beach Garden

VOCAL MUSIC

THE CHORAL SOCIETY OF THE PALM BEACHES, INC.
PO Box 30831, Palm Beach Garden, FL 33410-7831
(407) 546-7867
> **Founded:** 1963
> **Arts Area:** Choral
> **Status:** Non-Professional; Non-Profit
> **Type:** Performing
> **Purpose:** To strive to meet presentation excellence, public accessability, musical opportunity and public awareness of significant choral literature in Palm Beach County
> **Management:** Calvin Gage, Music Director
> **Officers:** Robert Beaulieu, President
> **Paid Artists:** 2   **Non-Paid Artists:** 45
> **Utilizes:** Guest Artists
> **Budget:** $1,000 - $50,000
> **Income Sources:** Private Foundations/Grants/Endowments; Box Office; Individual Donations
> **Season:** September - May   **Annual Attendance:** 1,500

Pensacola

DANCE

KALEIDOSCOPE DANCE THEATRE BALLET
400 South Jefferson Street, Pensacola, FL 32501
(904) 432-9546
> **Founded:** 1978
> **Arts Area:** Modern; Ballet
> **Status:** Non-Professional; Non-Profit
> **Type:** Performing; Resident; Educational
> **Purpose:** To provide quality training and performing opportunities in classical ballet and modern dance from elementary school through high school
> **Management:** Judy Gomez, Debbie Parrish, Artistic Directors; Patsy Hill, Nannette Whidby, Associate Directors
> **Officers:** Hilda Jones, President; Emily Hill, Vice President; Peggy Nunning, Treasurer; Cane Duch, Secretary
> **Paid Staff:** 7   **Volunteer Staff:** 25
> **Utilizes:** Special Technical Talent; Guest Artists
> **Budget:** $1,000 - $50,000
> **Income Sources:** Private Foundations/Grants/Endowments; Business/Corporate Donations; Box Office; Individual Donations
> **Season:** September - June   **Annual Attendance:** 1,500
> **Affiliations:** Pensacola Dance Alliance

INSTRUMENTAL MUSIC

PENSACOLA SYMPHONY ORCHESTRA
PO Box 1705, Pensacola, FL 32518
(904) 435-2533
FAX: (904) 469-0786
> **Founded:** 1926
> **Arts Area:** Symphony; Orchestra; Chamber
> **Status:** Professional
> **Type:** Performing; Resident; Educational; Sponsoring
> **Purpose:** To provide quality entertainment and assist in educating young minds to appreciate fine music
> **Management:** Brenda Pitts, General Manager; Grier Williams, Music Director; Barbara Gabriel, Personnel Manager
> **Officers:** Dr. Bill Philip Payne, President; John Dunworth, President-Elect; Carlton Proctor, First Vice President; Donna Bloomer, Treasurer
> **Volunteer Staff:** 30
> **Paid Artists:** 72
> **Utilizes:** Special Technical Talent; Guest Conductors; Guest Artists
> **Budget:** $100,000 - $500,000
> **Income Sources:** Private Foundations/Grants/Endowments; Business/Corporate Donations; Box Office; Government Grants; Individual Donations

Season: October - April **Annual Attendance:** 20,000
Affiliations: ASOL
Performance Facilities: Saenger Theatre

VOCAL MUSIC

CHORAL SOCIETY OF PENSACOLA
1000 College Boulevard, Pensacola, FL 32504
(904) 476-5410, ext. 1800
    Founded: 1935
    Arts Area: Choral
    Status: Semi-Professional; Non-Profit
    Type: Performing; Resident
    Purpose: To perform choral literature
    Management: William Clarke, Conductor/Musical Director
    Officers: Melba Powell, President; Dan Geem Vice President; Ann Cowan, Recording Secretary; Myrna Martin, Corresponding Secretary; John Layman, Treasurer
    Paid Staff: 1 **Volunteer Staff:** 15
    Paid Artists: 50 **Non-Paid Artists:** 82
    Utilizes: Guest Artists
    Budget: $1,000 - $50,000
    Income Sources: Private Foundations/Grants/Endowments; Business/Corporate Donations; Box Office; Government Grants; Individual Donations
    Season: September - May
    Annual Attendance: 2,500
    Affiliations: Arts Council of North West Florida; CA; Florida Cultural Action Alliance
    Performance Facilities: Saenger Theatre; Cokesbury United Methodist Church

THEATRE

PENSACOLA LITTLE THEATRE
PO Box 415, Pensacola, FL 32592
(904) 432-8621; (904) 432-2042
    Founded: 1936
    Arts Area: Community; Children's Theatre
    Status: Non-Professional; Non-Profit
    Type: Performing; Educational; Sponsoring
    Purpose: To stimulate an interest in the performing arts and offer members of the community an opportunity to participate in all phases of live theatre
    Management: Herman Fischer, General Manager
    Officers: Brian K. Spencer, President; Renee C. Ard, Vice President; Jan C. McLendon, Treasurer; Jane Switzer, Secretary
    Paid Staff: 2 **Volunteer Staff:** 30
    Non-Paid Artists: 100
    Budget: $50,000 - $100,000
    Income Sources: Business/Corporate Donations; Box Office; Individual Donations; Season Subscriptions
    Season: 52 Weeks
    Annual Attendance: 15,000
    Affiliations: Florida Theatre Conference; AACT; SETC
    Performance Facilities: Pensacola Little Theatre

PERFORMING SERIES

MUSIC HALL ARTIST SERIES
11000 University Parkway, Pensacola, FL 32514
(904) 474-2147
    Founded: 1969
    Status: Professional
    Type: Sponsoring
    Purpose: To provide the community with high-quality chamber music programs of professional touring groups
    Management: Grier Williams, Chairman
    Paid Staff: 2 **Volunteer Staff:** 3
    Paid Artists: 30
    Utilizes: Guest Artists
    Budget: $1,000 - $50,000
    Income Sources: Private Foundations/Grants/Endowments; Box Office; Government Grants
    Season: October - April
    Annual Attendance: 1,000
    Affiliations: University of West Florida
    Performance Facilities: New Music Hall

FACILITY

PENSACOLA CIVIC CENTER
201 East Gregory Street, Pensacola, FL 32501
(904) 432-0800
    Type of Facility: Civic Center; Arena; Multi-Purpose
    Type of Stage: Flexible
    Seating Capacity: Permanent - 8,200; Floor - 2,300 extra
    Year Built: 1985   **Architect:** Sverdrup Architects   **Cost:** $24,000,000
    Acoustical Consultant: E.D.I.
    Contact for Rental: Carol Pollock; (904) 432-0800

PENSACOLA JUNIOR COLLEGE, MUSIC AND DRAMA DEPARTMENT
1000 College Boulevard, Pensacola, FL 32504-8998
(904) 484-1800
FAX: (904) 484-1826
    Founded: 1948
    Type of Facility: Concert Hall; Auditorium
    Facility Originally: School
    Type of Stage: Proscenium
    Orchestra Pit
    Seating Capacity: 315
    Year Built: 1958
    Year Remodeled: 1990

SAENGER THEATRE
118 Palafox Place, Pensacola, FL 32501
(904) 444-7699
FAX: (904) 444-7684
    Founded: 1925
    Type of Facility: Auditorium; Theatre House
    Facility Originally: Vaudeville; Movie House
    Type of Stage: Proscenium
    Orchestra Pit
    Seating Capacity: 1,790
    Year Built: 1925   **Cost:** $300,000
    Year Remodeled: 1981   **Architect:** Bullock-Graves   **Cost:** $1,600,000
    Contact for Rental: Douglas Lee; (904) 444-7699

UNIVERSITY OF WEST FLORIDA CENTER FOR THE PERFORMING ARTS
11000 University Parkway, Pensacola, FL 32514
(904) 474-2938
FAX: (904) 474-3166
    Founded: 1967
    Type of Facility: Theatre Complex; Concert Hall; Outdoor (Concert); Studio Performance; Off Broadway; Theatre House; Amphitheater; Multi-Purpose
    Type of Stage: Platform
    Stage Dimensions: 84'x43'
    Orchestra Pit
    Seating Capacity: Theatre - 500; Music Hall - 300
    Year Built: 1991   **Architect:** Barrett Daffin and Carlan   **Cost:** $8,000,000

Plantation

INSTRUMENTAL MUSIC

BROWARD'S FRIENDS OF CHAMBER MUSIC, INC.
7950 Northwest Fourth Place, Plantation, FL 33324-1950
(305) 473-2353
FAX: (305) 474-1392
    Founded: 1980
    Arts Area: Chamber
    Status: Non-Profit
    Type: Performing; Educational
    Purpose: To bring chamber groups of international reputation to the community
    Officers: Leila G. Winton, President of Board; Robert Hoffman, Vice President of Board; Matthew Carole, Secretary of Board; Aviva Weiss Baer, Board Member; Harold M. Wilton, Treasurer of Board

Volunteer Staff: 4
Paid Artists: 7
Income Sources: Private Foundations/Grants/Endowments; Business/Corporate Donations; Box Office; Government Grants; Individual Donations
Season: December - April   **Annual Attendance:** 5,000
Performance Facilities: Bailey Concert Hall; Broward Community College

THEATRE

PLANTATION THEATRE COMPANY
1829 North Pineland Road, Plantation, FL 33317
(305) 472-6873
Founded: 1975
Arts Area: Musical; Community
Status: Semi-Professional; Non-Professional; Non-Profit
Type: Performing; Educational
Purpose: To afford the community an opportunity to become involved in the performing arts either by participation or by affordable audience participation
Paid Staff: 1   **Volunteer Staff:** 2
Utilizes: Special Technical Talent
Budget: $1,000 - $50,000
Season: 52 Weeks
Performance Facilities: Diecke Auditorium

Pompano Beach

VOCAL MUSIC

GOLD COAST OPERA
1000 Coconut Creek Boulevard, Pompano Beach, FL 33066
(305) 973-2323
FAX: (305) 973-2389
Founded: 1980
Arts Area: Operetta; Muiscal Theatre
Status: Professional; Non-Profit
Type: Performing; Touring; Educational
Purpose: To provide high-quality, fully-staged musical works including musical theatre, comic opera and other operatic productions to Pompano Beach and surrounding communities
Management: Dr. Thomas Cavendish, General Director
Paid Staff: 5
Paid Artists: 40   **Non-Paid Artists:** 20
Utilizes: Special Technical Talent; Guest Artists; Guest Directors
Budget: $100,000 - $500,000
Income Sources: Private Foundations/Grants/Endowments; Business/Corporate Donations; Box Office; Government Grants; Individual Donations
Season: November - April   **Annual Attendance:** 13,000
Affiliations: OA
Performance Facilities: Omni Auditorium; Bailey Hall; Coral Springs Civic Center

THEATRE

POMPANO PLAYERS, INC.
PO Box 2045, Pompano Beach, FL 33061
(305) 946-4646
Founded: 1956
Arts Area: Musical; Community; Theatrical Group
Status: Semi-Professional; Non-Profit
Type: Performing; Resident; Educational
Purpose: To provide live theatre to the community
Management: Penny Manwell, Box Office; David Stockton, Technical; Jerry Sullivan, Technical
Officers: Al Edick, President; Baynor Crane, Vice-President; Don Walters, Treasurer; Dale Petrie, Recording Secretary; Fred Leers, Corresponding Secretary
Paid Staff: 3   **Volunteer Staff:** 8
Utilizes: Special Technical Talent; Guest Artists; Guest Directors
Budget: $50,000 - $100,000
Income Sources: Private Foundations/Grants/Endowments; Business/Corporate Donations; Box Office; Government Grants; Individual Donations
Season: September - May   **Annual Attendance:** 10,400

Affiliations: Florida Theatre Conference
Performance Facilities: Pompano Players Theatre

Port Charlotte
THEATRE

CHARLOTTE PLAYERS
PO Box 2187, Port Charlotte, FL 33949
(813) 743-3229; (813) 627-5393
Founded: 1960
Arts Area: Community; Theatrical Group
Status: Non-Professional; Non-Profit
Type: Performing
Purpose: To provide live, community theater to a growing retirement community; to encourage young people to enjoy theater
Officers: Mark Weiser, President; Rich Schmith, Vice President; Janet Castro, Recording Secretary; Dawn Stuart, Treasurer
Paid Staff: 1
Budget: $50,000 - $100,000
Income Sources: Box Office; Individual Donations
Season: October - June   **Annual Attendance:** 10,000
Performance Facilities: Cultural Center Theater

Punta Gorda
FACILITY

CHARLOTTE COUNTY MEMORIAL AUDITORIUM
75 Taylor Street, Punta Gorda, FL 33950
(813) 639-5833; (800) 329-9988
FAX: (813) 639-3814
Type of Facility: Auditorium
Type of Stage: Proscenium
Stage Dimensions: 119'x126'
Seating Capacity: 1,416
Year Built: 1968   **Architect:** Ray Griffith   **Cost:** $500,000
Contact for Rental: James Morrison

Saint Augustine
THEATRE

LIMELIGHT DINNER THEATRE
Monson Resort, On The Bayfront, 32 Avenida Menendez, Saint Augustine, FL 32084
(904) 829-2277
FAX: (904) 824-4754
Founded: 1980
Arts Area: Professional; Dinner; Theatrical Group
Status: Professional
Type: Performing
Purpose: To provide professional entertainment to visitors to the Saint Augustine area
Management: Jean Rahner, Anne Kraft, Co-Producers
Paid Staff: 5
Paid Artists: 3
Budget: $1,000 - $50,000
Income Sources: Box Office
Season: 52 Weeks   **Annual Attendance:** 4,000
Performance Facilities: Monson Resort

PERFORMING SERIES

FLORIDA'S CROSS AND SWORD
Saint Augustine Amphitheatre, Saint Augustine, FL 32084
(904) 471-1965
Founded: 1965

Arts Area: Theater
Status: Non-Profit
Type: Performing
Purpose: To present an historical drama depicting the founding of Saint Augustine by Don Pedro Manendez de Aviles in 1565
Management: T. Wayne Sims, General Manager
Officers: Dave Judkins, President; Bud Harriss, Vice President; Edward V. Calhoun, Treasurer
Paid Staff: 9
Paid Artists: 75
Budget: $100,000 - $500,000
Income Sources: Private Foundations/Grants/Endowments; Business/Corporate Donations; Box Office; Government Grants; Individual Donations
Season: June - August   **Annual Attendance:** 20,000
Performance Facilities: Saint Augustine Amphitheatre

FACILITY

CROSS AND SWORD AMPHITHEATRE
1340 A1A South, PO Box 1965, Saint Augustine, FL 32085
(904) 471-1965
Founded: 1965
Type of Facility: Amphitheater
Type of Stage: Platform
Stage Dimensions: 75'x55'
Seating Capacity: 2,000
Year Built: 1964   **Architect:** Walker/Parker   **Cost:** $1,000,000
Contact for Rental: T. Wayne Sims, Executive Vice President;   (904) 471-1965
Resident Groups: Florida's Cross and Sword

Saint Petersburg

VOCAL MUSIC

FLORIDA LYRIC OPERA
1183 D, 85th Terrace North, Saint Petersburg, FL 33702
(813) 578-1657
Founded: 1978
Arts Area: Grand Opera; Lyric Opera; Light Opera; Operetta
Status: Professional
Type: Performing; Educational
Purpose: To promote area talent; to direct, train and/or discover talent in every phase of musical performance
Management: Rosalia Maresca, General Manager
Officers: Dr. Walter Afield, President; Marie Hillman, Vice President, Rena Laurenti, Secretary; Rosalia Maresca, Treasurer
Paid Staff: 1
Utilizes: Guest Conductors; Guest Artists; Guest Directors
Budget: $1,000 - $50,000
Income Sources: Box Office; Individual Donations
Annual Attendance: 5,000

THEATRE

AMERICAN STAGE COMPANY
211 Third Street South, PO Box 1560, Saint Petersburg, FL 33731
(813) 823-1600
FAX: (813) 823-7529
Founded: 1979
Arts Area: Professional; Theatrical Group
Status: Professional; Non-Profit
Type: Performing; Touring; Resident; Educational
Purpose: To present and develop the best in theatrical literature, both contemporary and classical
Management: Victoria Holloway, Artistic Director; John A. Berglund, Executive Producer
Officers: Susan Hough, President; Martin Normile, Vice President; Enez Hart, Secretary; Joseph Wheeler, Treasurer
Paid Staff: 9   **Volunteer Staff:** 125
Paid Artists: 105
Utilizes: Special Technical Talent; Guest Directors
Budget: $1,000,000 - $5,000,000
Income Sources: Business/Corporate Donations; Box Office; Government Grants; Individual Donations

Season: November - June
Annual Attendance: 36,100
Affiliations: AEA; TCG; Florida Professional Theatre Association; Pinellas County Arts Council
Performance Facilities: American Stage Company Theatre

VAUDEVILLE PALACE
7951 Ninth Street North, Saint Petersburg, FL 33702
(813) 557-5515
FAX: (813) 578-1024
Founded: 1991
Arts Area: Professional; Dinner; Vaudeville
Status: Professional; Commercial
Type: Performing; Resident
Purpose: To provide amusing entertainment
Management: Buddy Graf, Producer/Director; Carol Graf, General Manager; Skip Lewis, Box Office Manager
Income Sources: Box Office
Season: 52 Weeks   **Annual Attendance:** 36,000
Performance Facilities: Vaudeville Palace

FACILITY

BAYFRONT CENTER COMPLEX
400 First Street South, Saint Petersburg, FL 33701
(813) 892-5798
FAX: (813) 892-5858
Type of Facility: Civic Center
Seating Capacity: Auditorium - 2250; Arena - 8200; Al Lang Stadium - 8,000
Year Built: 1965
Architect: Connell Pierce Garland & Friedman
Cost: $6,300,000
Contact for Rental: Jeff Forman;   (813) 892-5798
Resident Groups: The Florida Orchestra

Sanibel Island

THEATRE

PIRATE PLAYHOUSE
2200 Periwinkle Way, Sanibel Island, FL 33957
(813) 472-0006
Founded: 1985
Arts Area: Professional; Theatrical Group
Status: Professional; Non-Profit
Type: Performing; Touring; Resident; Educational; Sponsoring
Purpose: To present live, professional theatre in Southwest Florida
Management: Carrie Lund, Producing Director; Robert Cacioppo, Artistic Director; Todd Bakerian, Technical Director; Dena Allen, Production Stage Manager; Ricki Cooper, Assistant to the Producers
Officers: John McTavish, President; Jerald Melum, Vice President; Al Leonard, Treasurer; Lois Kessler, Secretary
Paid Staff: 8   **Volunteer Staff:** 150
Paid Artists: 30   **Non-Paid Artists:** 8
Utilizes: Special Technical Talent; Guest Artists; Guest Directors
Budget: $100,000 - $500,000
Income Sources: Private Foundations/Grants/Endowments; Business/Corporate Donations; Box Office; Individual Donations
Season: 52 Weeks
Annual Attendance: 26,000
Performance Facilities: Pirate Playhouse

Sarasota

INSTRUMENTAL MUSIC

FLORIDA BRASS QUINTET
709 North Tamiami Trail, Sarasota, FL 33577
(813) 955-4562
Founded: 1986
Arts Area: Chamber; Ensemble

Status: Professional; Non-Profit
Type: Performing; Touring; Resident; Educational
Purpose: To share the talent of the Florida West Coast Symphony's brass section with residents throughout the community and state
Paid Staff: 14
Paid Artists: 5
Utilizes: Guest Artists
Budget: $50,000 - $100,000
Income Sources: Private Foundations/Grants/Endowments; Business/Corporate Donations; Box Office; Government Grants; Individual Donations
Season: October - May   **Annual Attendance:** 4,000
Affiliations: Florida West Coast Symphony

FLORIDA WEST COAST CHAMBER ORCHESTRA
709 North Tamiami Trail, Sarasota, FL 33577
(813) 953-4562
Founded: 1961
Arts Area: Orchestra; Chamber
Status: Professional; Non-Profit
Type: Performing
Purpose: To provide chamber orchestra programs of the finest quality in the local area, particularly in Manatee and Sarasota counties
Management: Gretchen Serrie, Executive Director; Trevor Cramer, General Manager; Janet Petrecca, Business Manager
Officers: Neil Moody, President; Beatrice Friedman, Vice President; Ernest Rice, Treasurer; Elaine Barnett, Secretary
Paid Staff: 14
Paid Artists: 30
Budget: $1,000 - $50,000
Income Sources: Private Foundations/Grants/Endowments; Business/Corporate Donations; Box Office; Government Grants; Individual Donations
Season: November - January
Annual Attendance: 2,500
Affiliations: Florida West Coast Symphony, Inc.
Performance Facilities: Van Wezel Performing Arts Hall; Lota Mundy Hall

FLORIDA WEST COAST SYMPHONY ORCHESTRA
709 North Tamiami Trail, Sarasota, FL 33577
(813) 953-4252
Founded: 1949
Arts Area: Symphony
Status: Professional; Non-Profit
Type: Performing; Resident
Purpose: To present fine music and musicians to the community, particularly in Manatee and Sarasota counties
Management: Gretchen Serrie, Executive Director; Trevor Cramer, General Manager; Janet Petrecca, Business Manager
Officers: Neil Moody, President; Beatrice Friedman, Vice President; Ernest Rice, Treasurer; Elaine Barnett, Secretary
Paid Staff: 14
Paid Artists: 80
Utilizes: Guest Conductors; Guest Artists
Budget: $1,000,000 - $5,000,000
Income Sources: Private Foundations/Grants/Endowments; Business/Corporate Donations; Box Office; Government Grants; Individual Donations
Season: November - April
Annual Attendance: 20,000
Affiliations: ASOL; Florida West Coast Symphony Inc.
Performance Facilities: Van Wezel Performing Arts Hall

FLORIDA WEST COAST YOUTH ORCHESTRAS
709 North Tamiami Trail, Sarasota, FL 34236
(813) 955-4562
Founded: 1956
Arts Area: Symphony; Orchestra
Status: Non-Professional; Non-Profit
Type: Performing; Educational
Purpose: To provide the finest possible music education and to help create performers and audiences for the future
Management: Chris Confessore, Youth Program Director
Paid Staff: 14
Utilizes: Guest Conductors; Guest Artists

Income Sources: Private Foundations/Grants/Endowments; Business/Corporate Donations; Government Grants; Individual Donations
Season: 52 Weeks
Annual Attendance: 5,000
Affiliations: Florida West Coast Music
Performance Facilities: Florida West Coast Music Center

FLORIDA WIND QUINTET
709 North Tamiami Trail, Sarasota, FL 33577
(813) 955-4562
FAX: (813) 953-3059
Founded: 1985
Arts Area: Ensemble
Status: Professional; Non-Profit
Type: Performing; Resident
Purpose: The resident wind quintet of the Florida West Coast Symphony performs in concert to share its expertise with the community.
Paid Staff: 14
Paid Artists: 5
Utilizes: Guest Artists
Budget: $50,000 - $100,000
Income Sources: Private Foundations/Grants/Endowments; Business/Corporate Donations; Box Office; Government Grants; Individual Donations
Season: October - May
Annual Attendance: 4,000
Affiliations: Florida West Coast Music
Performance Facilities: Florida West Coast Music Center

NEW ARTISTS PIANO QUARTET
709 North Tamiami Trail, Sarasota, FL 33577
(813) 955-4562
Founded: 1991
Arts Area: Ensemble
Status: Professional; Non-Profit
Type: Performing; Resident
Purpose: To showcase new, young pianists from the Florida West Coast Symphony
Management: Trevor Cramer, General Manager, Florida West Coast Symphony
Paid Staff: 14
Paid Artists: 4
Utilizes: Guest Artists
Budget: $50,000 - $100,000
Income Sources: Private Foundations/Grants/Endowments; Business/Corporate Donations; Box Office; Government Grants; Individual Donations
Season: October - May
Annual Attendance: 3,000
Affiliations: Florida West Coast Symphony
Performance Facilities: Florida West Coast Symphony Center

NEW ARTISTS STRING QUARTET
709 North Tamiami Trail, Sarasota, FL 33577
(813) 955-4562
Founded: 1986
Arts Area: Ensemble
Status: Professional; Non-Profit
Type: Performing; Touring; Resident
Purpose: To showcase new, young string players in the Florida West Coast Symphony
Management: Gretchen Seirie, Executive Director; Trevor Cramer, General Manager Florida West Coast Symphony
Officers: Neil Moody, President
Paid Staff: 14
Paid Artists: 4
Utilizes: Guest Artists
Budget: $50,000 - $100,000
Income Sources: Private Foundations/Grants/Endowments; Business/Corporate Donations; Box Office; Government Grants; Individual Donations
Season: October - May
Annual Attendance: 4,000
Affiliations: Florida West Coast Symphony Inc.
Performance Facilities: Van Wezel Performing Arts Hall; Holley Hall; Florida West Coast Symphony Center

VOCAL MUSIC

SARASOTA OPERA ASSOCIATION
61 North Pineapple Avenue, Sarasota, FL 34236
(813) 366-8450
FAX: (813) 955-5571
Founded: 1979
Arts Area: Grand Opera
Status: Professional; Non-Profit
Type: Performing; Educational; Sponsoring
Purpose: To continue to bring quality opera to our community and to showcase it in our own opera house; to educate the general community in an appreciation of opera and send our outreach programs into the schools of both Manatee and Sarasota counties; to offer statewide touring programs
Management: Victor De Renzi, Artistic Director; Deane C. Allyn, Executive Director; Libby Smith, Public Relations; Laurie Clark, House Manager
Officers: Leo M. Rogers and David Pomier, Co-Chairmen; Margaret Wise, President
Paid Staff: 17   **Volunteer Staff:** 225
Paid Artists: 75   **Non-Paid Artists:** 50
Utilizes: Special Technical Talent; Guest Conductors; Guest Artists; Guest Directors
Budget: $1,000,000 - $5,000,000
Income Sources: Private Foundations/Grants/Endowments; Business/Corporate Donations; Box Office; Government Grants; Individual Donations
Season: February - March   **Annual Attendance:** 32,000
Affiliations: OA; COS; AGMA
Performance Facilities: Sarasota Opera House

THEATRE

ASOLO CENTER FOR THE PERFORMING ARTS
5555 North Tamiami Trail, Sarasota, FL 34243
(813) 351-9010
FAX: (813) 351-5796
Founded: 1960
Arts Area: Professional; Musical; Theatrical Group
Status: Professional; Non-Profit
Type: Performing; Educational
Purpose: To foster an appreciation for the performing arts in the community, state and country by utilizing live performances as well as television and film; to educate students by placing them with professional actors with whom they may learn the theatrical trade
Management: Margaret Booker, Artistic Director; Lee Warner, Executive Director
Officers: Elizabeth Lindsay, Board President
Paid Staff: 82   **Volunteer Staff:** 567
Paid Artists: 72
Utilizes: Special Technical Talent; Guest Artists; Guest Directors
Budget: $1,000,000 - $5,000,000
Income Sources: Private Foundations/Grants/Endowments; Business/Corporate Donations; Box Office; Government Grants; Individual Donations
Season: September - July   **Annual Attendance:** 14,000
Affiliations: TCG; AAA; AEA; LORT
Performance Facilities: Asolo Theater

FLORIDA STUDIO THEATRE
1241 North Palm Avenue, Sarasota, FL 33577
(813) 366-9017
FAX: (813) 955-4137
Founded: 1973
Arts Area: Professional; Theatrical Group
Status: Professional; Non-Profit
Type: Performing; Resident; Educational
Purpose: To produce contemporary theatre with an emphasis on new plays and regional premieres
Officers: Dennis McGillicuddy, Board President
Paid Staff: 10
Paid Artists: 30
Utilizes: Special Technical Talent; Guest Artists; Guest Directors
Budget: $500,000 - $1,000,000

Income Sources: Private Foundations/Grants/Endowments; Business/Corporate Donations; Box Office; Government Grants; Individual Donations
Season: December - July   **Annual Attendance:** 93,000
Affiliations: SPTA; AEA
Performance Facilities: Florida Studio Theatre

GOLDEN APPLE DINNER THEATRE
25 North Pineapple Avenue, Sarasota, FL 34236
(813) 366-2646
FAX: (813) 364-9100
Founded: 1971
Arts Area: Professional; Musical; Dinner
Status: Professional; Commercial
Type: Sponsoring
Purpose: To educate, entertain and enlighten
Management: Robert Turoff, Producer/Director/General Manager
Paid Staff: 30
Paid Artists: 50
Utilizes: Special Technical Talent; Guest Conductors; Guest Artists
Budget: $100,000 - $500,000
Income Sources: Box Office
Season: 52 Weeks   **Annual Attendance:** 65,000
Affiliations: AEA
Performance Facilities: Golden Apple Dinner Theatre

THE PLAYERS OF SARASOTA
838 North Tamiami Trail, Sarasota, FL 34236
(813) 365-2494
Founded: 1930
Arts Area: Musical; Community; Theatrical Group; Puppet
Status: Non-Professional; Non-Profit
Type: Performing; Touring; Educational
Purpose: To be the first and only community theatre in Sarasota offering live entertainment, full orchestra, professional direction and children's theatre
Management: Elizabeth J. DeVivo, Executive Director; Peter Strader, Artistic Director
Officers: Maryann Shorin, President; Barry Miller, Vice President; Ray Suplee, Teasurer; Charlene Knopp, Secretary
Paid Staff: 7   **Volunteer Staff:** 250
Paid Artists: 5   **Non-Paid Artists:** 215
Utilizes: Special Technical Talent; Guest Conductors; Guest Artists; Guest Directors
Budget: $100,000 - $500,000
Income Sources: Private Foundations/Grants/Endowments; Business/Corporate Donations; Box Office; Government Grants; Individual Donations
Season: September - June   **Annual Attendance:** 35,000

PERFORMING SERIES

FLORIDA WEST COAST SYMPHONY
709 North Tamiami Trail, Sarasota, FL 33577
(813) 955-4562
Founded: 1949
Arts Area: Instrumental Music; Festivals
Status: Professional; Non-Profit
Type: Performing; Resident; Educational; Sponsoring
Purpose: To present the Florida West Coast Symphony, Sarasota Music Festival, Florida String Quartet, Florida Wind Quintet, Florida Brass Quintet, New Artists String Quartet, Florida West Coast Chamber Orchestra and Florida West Coast Youth Orchestras
Management: Paul Wolfe, Conductor/Music Director; Gretchen Serrie, Executive Director; Jeff Seloeika, Business Manager; JoAanne Klemart, Marketing Director; Trevor Cramer, General Manager
Officers: Neil Moody, President; Beatrice Friedman, Ruth Robbins, Lionel Williams, Vice Presidents; Elaine Barnett, Secretary; Ernest Rice, Treasurer
Paid Staff: 14
Paid Artists: 80
Utilizes: Guest Conductors; Guest Artists
Budget: $1,000,000 - $5,000,000
Income Sources: Private Foundations/Grants/Endowments; Business/Corporate Donations; Box Office; Government Grants; Individual Donations
Season: September - June   **Annual Attendance:** 50,000
Performance Facilities: Van Wezel Auditorium

SARASOTA MUSIC FESTIVAL
709 North Tamiami Trail, Sarasota, FL 34236
(813) 952-9634
FAX: (813) 953-3059
Founded: 1965
Arts Area: Festivals
Status: Professional; Non-Profit
Type: Performing; Educational
Purpose: To present a teaching and performing festival which will enhance the professional training of young musicians and provide the finest in chamber music performances
Management: Trevor Cramer, Administrative Director
Officers: Neil V. Moody, President; Beatrice Friedman, Lionel Willens, Ruth Robbins, Vice-Presidents; Elaine Barnett, Secretary; Ernest Rice, Treasurer
Paid Staff: 14   **Volunteer Staff:** 50
Paid Artists: 35
Utilizes: Guest Artists
Budget: $100,000 - $500,000
Income Sources: Private Foundations/Grants/Endowments; Business/Corporate Donations; Box Office; Government Grants; Individual Donations
Season: June
Annual Attendance: 10,500
Affiliations: CMA
Performance Facilities: Van Wezel Auditorium; Holley Hall

FACILITY

FLORIDA STUDIO THEATRE
1241 North Palm Avenue, Sarasota, FL 33577
(813) 366-9017
Type of Facility: Theatre House; Black Box
Facility Originally: Meeting Hall; Movie House
Stage Dimensions: Black Box space 30'x35'x25'
Seating Capacity: 165
Year Built: 1913
Year Remodeled: 1987
Contact for Rental: Jayne Dowd;   (813) 366-9017
Resident Groups: Florida Studio Theatre

THE PLAYERS OF SARASOTA THEATRE
838 North Tamiami Trail, Sarasota, FL 34236
(813) 365-2494
Type of Facility: Theatre Complex; Concert Hall; Auditorium; Studio Performance; Performance Center; Off Broadway; Theatre House; Multi-Purpose
Type of Stage: Proscenium
Orchestra Pit
Seating Capacity: 507
Year Built: 1974   **Architect:** Erwin Gremli, II   **Cost:** $550,000
Acoustical Consultant: Davidson and Son
Contact for Rental: Elizabeth De Vivo;   (813) 365-2494

SARASOTA OPERA HOUSE
61 North Pineapple Avenue, Sarasota, FL 34236
(813) 366-8450
FAX: (813) 955-5571
Founded: 1926
Type of Facility: Theatre Complex; Concert Hall; Performance Center; Opera House; Multi-Purpose
Facility Originally: Vaudeville; Movie House
Type of Stage: Flexible; Proscenium; Pit may be covered for additional 10'3"
Stage Dimensions: 36'2"x37'8" stage; 11'6"x30' stage left; 20'3"x30' stage right   **Orchestra Pit**
Seating Capacity: 1,033
Year Built: 1926   **Architect:** Lloyd A. Benjamin   **Cost:** $350,000
Year Remodeled: 1984   **Cost:** $3,000,000
Contact for Rental: Laurie Clark, Manager;   (813) 366-8450
Originally the Edwards Theatre, the Sarasota Opera House is on the National Register of Historic Places. Education in Youth Opera; Radio Reading for the Blind; Music Archive

VAN WEZEL AUDITORIUM
777 North Tamiami Trail, Sarasota, FL 33577
(813) 955-7332
FAX: (813) 951-1449
  Type of Facility: Auditorium
  Type of Stage: Flexible   **Orchestra Pit**
  Seating Capacity: 1,779
  Year Built: 1970   **Architect:** Taliesin   **Cost:** $2,527,000
  Acoustical Consultant: Vern Knudsen
  Contact for Rental: John D. Wikes

Seminole

DANCE

GRUPO FOLKLORICO MEXICANA
11698 Walker Avenue, Seminole, FL 34642
(813) 393-3107 '
  Founded: 1979
  Arts Area: Ethnic; Folk; Mexican
  Status: Semi-Professional
  Type: Performing; Educational
  Purpose: To promote the rich Mexican culture through ethnic folkloric dance, colorful costumes and lively music
  Management: Elena Tellone, Director
  Non-Paid Artists: 10
  Utilizes: Guest Artists
  Budget: $1,000 - $50,000
  Income Sources: Box Office; Individual Donations
  Season: 52 Weeks
  Affiliations: Mexican-American Club; Pinellas County Arts Council; State Dance Association of Florida
  Performance Facilities: Saint Petersburg International Folk Fair

South Miami

DANCE

MIAMI BALLET COMPANY
5818 SW 73rd Street, South Miami, FL 33143
(305) 667-5985
  Founded: 1951
  Arts Area: Ballet
  Status: Non-Professional; Non-Profit
  Type: Performing; Resident
  Purpose: To help young people enjoy and learn ballet before professional experience
  Management: Thomas Armour, Artistic Director
  Non-Paid Artists: 30
  Utilizes: Guest Choreographers
  Budget: $100,000 - $500,000
  Income Sources: Private Foundations/Grants/Endowments; Box Office; Individual Donations
  Season: September - May
  Performance Facilities: Dade County Auditorium

Spring Hill

FACILITY

THE SPRINGSTEAD THEATRE
3300 Mariner Boulevard, Spring Hill, FL 34609
(904) 683-2843
  Founded: 1990
  Type of Facility: Concert Hall; Auditorium; Performance Center; Off Broadway; Theatre House; Opera House; Civic Center
  Type of Stage: Proscenium
  Stage Dimensions: 50'x31'
  Seating Capacity: 606

Year Built: 1990
Architect: Harvard, Jolly and Marcet   **Cost:** $2,200,000
Contact for Rental: Tizzy Schoelles;   (904) 683-2843
Resident Groups: The Repertory Theatre Company; The Winding Waters Dance Ensemble; The Nature Coast Light Opera; The Hernando Symphony Orchestra

Tallahassee

DANCE

TALLAHASSEE BALLET COMPANY
PO Box 772, Tallahassee, FL 32302
(904) 222-1287
Founded: 1972
Arts Area: Modern; Ballet; Jazz
Status: Semi-Professional; Non-Profit
Type: Performing; Resident; Educational
Purpose: To serve as a training ground for professionals; to educate the citizens of Tallahassee and surrounding areas in the dance arts
Management: Joyce Straub, Artistic Director; Kathryn Cashin, Artistic Associate; Helen Earl, Ballet Mistress
Officers: Jan Williams, President; Jan Keshen, Vice President; Deborah Stephens, Treasurer; Nancy Floyd, Secretary
Paid Staff: 5   **Volunteer Staff:** 62
Paid Artists: 15   **Non-Paid Artists:** 45
Utilizes: Special Technical Talent; Guest Artists; Guest Directors; Guest Choreographers
Budget: $100,000 - $500,000
Income Sources: Private Foundations/Grants/Endowments; Business/Corporate Donations; Box Office; Government Grants; Individual Donations
Season: September - May
Annual Attendance: 7,000
Affiliations: Florida Dance Association
Performance Facilities: Ruby Diamond Auditorium; Florida State University; Turner Auditorium; Tallahassee Community College

INSTRUMENTAL MUSIC

TALLAHASSEE SYMPHONY ORCHESTRA
203 North Gadsden Street, Suite 3, Tallahassee, FL 32301
(904) 224-0461
Founded: 1981
Arts Area: Symphony
Status: Semi-Professional; Non-Profit
Type: Performing; Resident
Purpose: To maintain a high-quality symphony orchestra in Tallahassee dedicated to superior quality and to furthering cultural opportunities in the community
Management: Anne Robinson Hodges, General Manager; Julie Maisel, Assistant Manager
Officers: Dot P. Hinson, Chairman; Dr. Robert Glidden, Vice Chairman; Chris Roady, President; W.R. Lindquist, Immediate Past Chairman; Lou Kellenberger, Immediate Past President; John Fons, Treasurer
Paid Staff: 2   **Volunteer Staff:** 3
Paid Artists: 80   **Non-Paid Artists:** 2
Utilizes: Guest Artists
Budget: $100,000 - $500,000
Income Sources: Private Foundations/Grants/Endowments; Business/Corporate Donations; Box Office; Government Grants; Individual Donations
Season: October - April
Annual Attendance: 8,500
Affiliations: ASOL
Performance Facilities: Ruby Diamond Auditorium

VOCAL MUSIC

FLORIDA STATE OPERA AT FLORIDA STATE UNIVERSITY
School of Music, 002 HMU, Tallahassee, FL 32306
(904) 644-5248
FAX: (904) 644-6100
Founded: 1963
Arts Area: Grand Opera; Lyric Opera; Operetta

Status: Semi-Professional; Non-Profit
Type: Performing
Purpose: To provide training for Florida State University students and serve as a cultural resource for the capital and state
Management: Lincoln Clark, Director of Opera
Officers: Dale Nick, President, Florida State University; Jon Piersol, Interim Dean, School of Music
Paid Staff: 6   **Volunteer Staff:** 68
Paid Artists: 5   **Non-Paid Artists:** 200
Utilizes: Special Technical Talent; Guest Conductors; Guest Artists; Guest Directors
Budget: $50,000 - $100,000
Income Sources: Private Foundations/Grants/Endowments; Business/Corporate Donations; Box Office; Government Grants; Individual Donations
Season: November - June
Annual Attendance: 19,000
Affiliations: NOA; COS; TOG
Performance Facilities: Ruby Diamond Auditorium; Opperman Music Hall

THEATRE

YOUNG ACTORS THEATRE
609 Glenview Drive, Tallahassee, FL 32303
(904) 386-6602
Founded: 1975
Arts Area: Musical; Community; Theatrical Group
Status: Semi-Professional; Non-Profit
Type: Performing; Touring; Educational
Purpose: To educate youth in theatre arts and performance
Management: Cristina Williams, Director; Alison Grimes, Musical Director; Alison Busby, Dance Director
Officers: Terry Mara, President; Thomas Walden, Treasurer; David Van Leuven, Vice President; Tina Williams, Executive Director
Paid Staff: 9   **Volunteer Staff:** 125
Paid Artists: 10   **Non-Paid Artists:** 335
Utilizes: Special Technical Talent; Guest Artists; Guest Directors
Budget: $50,000 - $100,000
Income Sources: Private Foundations/Grants/Endowments; Business/Corporate Donations; Box Office; Government Grants; Individual Donations
Season: December - August
Annual Attendance: 5,000
Affiliations: SETC; American Association of Theatre Educators
Performance Facilities: Young Actors Theatre

FACILITY

FLORIDA A&M UNIVERSITY - CHARLES WINTER WOOD THEATRE
Tallahassee, FL 32307
(904) 599-3394
Type of Facility: Theatre House
Type of Stage: Proscenium
Stage Dimensions: 87'x50'x50'   **Orchestra Pit**
Seating Capacity: 647
Year Built: 1956   **Cost:** $1,000,000
Year Remodeled: 1977   **Architect:** Rowe & Holmes
Contact for Rental: Ronald O. Davis, Phd.;   (904) 599-3394
Resident Groups: Florida A&M University/Essential Theatre

TALLAHASSEE-LEON COUNTY CIVIC CENTER
505 West Pensacola Street, Tallahassee, FL 32302
(904) 487-1691
FAX: (904) 222-6947
Type of Facility: Civic Center; Arena; Multi-Purpose
Type of Stage: Flexible; Arena
Stage Dimensions: 6'x8' portable sections, adjustable in height
Seating Capacity: 3,500-14,000
Year Built: 1981   **Architect:** Barrett Daffin & Carlan   **Cost:** $33,400,000
Acoustical Consultant: Bolt, Beranek & Newman
Contact for Rental: Ron Spencer;   (904) 487-1691

Tampa

INSTRUMENTAL MUSIC

THE FLORIDA ORCHESTRA
1211 North Westshore Boulevard, #512, Tampa, FL 33607
(813) 286-1170
FAX: (813) 286-2316
> **Founded:** 1968
> **Arts Area:** Symphony; Orchestra
> **Status:** Professional; Non-Profit
> **Type:** Performing; Touring; Resident; Educational
> **Purpose:** To serve the Tampa Bay Area and the state of Florida with high-quality symphonic music
> **Management:** Jerry Ferrara, Director of Marketing; Julia Ann Fleming, Director of Development; Donny Rye, Controller; Alan Hopper, Orchestra Manager; John Hyer, President/Chief Executive Officer; Kathryn Holm, Associate Director
> **Officers:** F. Wallace Popc Jr. Esq., Chairman; Jane Peppard, Vice President; Michael J. Lagorac Jr., Vice Chairman; Gerald R. Wicker, Treasurer; Ernie A. Reiner M.D., Secretary
> **Paid Staff:** 19   **Volunteer Staff:** 40
> **Paid Artists:** 110
> **Utilizes:** Guest Conductors; Guest Artists
> **Budget:** $1,000,000 - $5,000,000
> **Income Sources:** Private Foundations/Grants/Endowments; Business/Corporate Donations; Box Office; Government Grants; Individual Donations
> **Season:** September - May   **Annual Attendance:** 300,000
> **Affiliations:** ASOL
> **Performance Facilities:** Tampa Bay Performing Arts Center; Ruth Eckerd Hall, Bayfront Center

TAMPA BAY CHAMBER ORCHESTRA
PO Box 10353, Tampa, FL 33679
(813) 874-8367
> **Founded:** 1983
> **Arts Area:** Orchestra; Chamber; Ensemble
> **Status:** Professional; Non-Profit
> **Type:** Performing
> **Purpose:** To provide chamber music and works for chamber orchestra to Florida's west coast
> **Management:** Dennis Herron, Music Director/Conductor; Sally Olsson, Executive Director; David Dillingham, Personnel Manager
> **Officers:** Renate K. Hartman, Chairman; Victor E. Palmer, Vice Chairman; Sheila Seig Griffin Esq., Secretary; W. Haskell Gates, Treasurer
> **Paid Staff:** 2
> **Paid Artists:** 35
> **Utilizes:** Guest Artists
> **Budget:** $1,000 - $50,000
> **Income Sources:** Private Foundations/Grants/Endowments; Business/Corporate Donations; Box Office; Government Grants; Individual Donations
> **Season:** September - June   **Annual Attendance:** 1,500
> **Affiliations:** ASOL
> **Performance Facilities:** Tampa Museum of Art

THEATRE

BITS 'N PIECES GIANT PUPPET THEATRE
PO Box 368, Tampa, FL 33601
(813) 228-0702
> **Founded:** 1976
> **Arts Area:** Professional; Puppet
> **Status:** Professional; Non-Profit
> **Type:** Performing; Touring; Resident; Educational
> **Purpose:** To present original, educational musicals with unique nine-foot tall puppets
> **Management:** Jerry Bickel, Executive Director; Holli Rubin, Artistic Director; Jackie Hiendlmayr, Business Director
> **Paid Staff:** 3   **Volunteer Staff:** 3
> **Paid Artists:** 8   **Non-Paid Artists:** 6
> **Utilizes:** Special Technical Talent; Guest Artists
> **Budget:** $100,000 - $500,000
> **Income Sources:** Private Foundations/Grants/Endowments; Business/Corporate Donations; Box Office; Government Grants
> **Season:** 52 Weeks   **Annual Attendance:** 175,000

FLORIDA SUNCOAST PUPPET GUILD
7107 North Howard Avenue, Tampa, FL 33604
(813) 932-9252
 Founded: 1973
 Arts Area: Puppet
 Status: Non-Profit
 Type: Educational; Sponsoring
 Purpose: To promote the art of puppetry through shows, workshops, lectures, demonstrations, meetings and festivals
 Management: Norma Bigler, Festival Director
 Officers: Jody Wren, President; Priscilla LaKus, Secretary/Treasurer; Bill Weber, Vice President/Program; Celine Mac-Donald, Historian
 Volunteer Staff: 4
 Paid Artists: 19
 Utilizes: Special Technical Talent; Guest Artists
 Budget: $1,000 - $50,000
 Income Sources: Private Foundations/Grants/Endowments; Box Office; Memberships; Special Festivals
 Season: 52 Weeks
 Annual Attendance: 12,000
 Affiliations: Puppeteers of America

PLAYMAKERS
PO Box 5745, Tampa, FL 33675
(813) 248-6933
 Founded: 1981
 Arts Area: Professional
 Status: Professional; Non-Profit
 Type: Resident
 Purpose: To provide stimulating, thought-provoking, contemporary theatre that explores the human condition
 Management: John Owens, Producing Director
 Officers: Steve Bragin, Board Member
 Paid Staff: 8 **Volunteer Staff:** 100
 Utilizes: Guest Artists; Guest Directors
 Budget: $100,000 - $500,000
 Income Sources: Private Foundations/Grants/Endowments; Business/Corporate Donations; Box Office; Government Grants; Individual Donations
 Season: 52 Weeks
 Annual Attendance: 25,000
 Affiliations: AEA; TCG; SETC; Florida Professional Theatre Association

SPANISH LYRIC THEATRE
1032 Coral Street, Tampa, FL 33602
(813) 223-7341
 Founded: 1959
 Arts Area: Musical; Theatrical Group
 Status: Semi-Professional; Non-Profit
 Type: Performing
 Purpose: To further production of Spanish musicals (Zarzuelas); to provide lyric theatre in both Spanish and English
 Management: Rene J. Gonzalez, Founder and Artistic Director
 Officers: Joel Phillips, Chairman; Armando Dorta Jr., Vice President; Martin A. Favata, Secretary; Oscar Bonis Jr., Treasurer
 Paid Staff: 3 **Volunteer Staff:** 5
 Paid Artists: 40 **Non-Paid Artists:** 20
 Utilizes: Special Technical Talent; Guest Artists
 Budget: $100,000 - $500,000
 Income Sources: Private Foundations/Grants/Endowments; Box Office; Government Grants; Individual Donations
 Season: September - May
 Performance Facilities: Tampa Bay Performing Arts Center

THE TAMPA PLAYERS
601 South Florida Avenue, Tampa, FL 33602
(813) 229-1505
 Founded: 1926
 Arts Area: Professional; Theatrical Group
 Status: Professional; Non-Profit
 Type: Performing
 Management: Bill Leldach, Managing and Artistic Director
 Paid Staff: 4 **Volunteer Staff:** 50
 Paid Artists: 60

Utilizes: Special Technical Talent; Guest Artists; Guest Directors
Budget: $100,000 - $500,000
Income Sources: Private Foundations/Grants/Endowments; Business/Corporate Donations; Box Office; Government Grants; Individual Donations
Season: September - May
Annual Attendance: 13,500

FACILITY

TAMPA BAY PERFORMING ARTS CENTER
1010 North MacInnes Place, Tampa, FL 33602
(813) 222-1000
FAX: (813) 222-1057
    Founded: 1987
    Type of Facility: Performance Center
    Type of Stage: Flexible; Proscenium; Three-Hall Complex
    Stage Dimensions: Festival Hall - 60'x40'; Playhouse - 40'x30'; Jaeb - 24'x40' **Orchestra Pit**
    Seating Capacity: Festival Hall - 2,493; Playhouse - 960; Jaeb - 299
    Year Built: 1987 **Cost:** $57,000,000
    Acoustical Consultant: Artec
    Contact for Rental: Lorrin Shepard; (813) 222-1017
    Resident Groups: The Florida Orchestra; Spanish Lyric Theater

TAMPA BAY PERFORMING ARTS CENTER - FESTIVAL HALL
1010 North MacInnes Place, Tampa, FL 33602
(813) 229-7827
FAX: (813) 222-1057
    Type of Facility: Concert Hall
    Type of Stage: Proscenium
    Stage Dimensions: 60'Wx40'Hx65'D **Orchestra Pit**
    Seating Capacity: 2,400
    Year Built: 1987
    Contact for Rental: Mrs. Bobbi Warnick; (813) 222-1017
    Resident Groups: Florida Orchestra

TAMPA BAY PERFORMING ARTS CENTER - JAEB THEATER
1010 North MacInnes Place, Tampa, FL 33602
(813) 229-7827
    Type of Facility: Theatre House; Black Box
    Type of Stage: Proscenium
    Stage Dimensions: 42'Wx24'D **Orchestra Pit**
    Seating Capacity: 300
    Year Built: 1987
    Contact for Rental: Mrs. Bobbi Warnick; (813) 222-1017
    Resident Groups: The Playmakers

TAMPA BAY PERFORMING ARTS CENTER - PLAYHOUSE
1010 North MacInnes Place, Tampa, FL 33602
(813) 229-7827
    Type of Facility: Theatre House
    Type of Stage: Proscenium
    Stage Dimensions: 40'Wx50'Dx30'H **Orchestra Pit**
    Seating Capacity: 900
    Year Built: 1987
    Contact for Rental: Mrs. Bobbi Warnick; (813) 222-1017
    Resident Groups: Tampa Ballet

TAMPA THEATRE
711 Franklin Street Mall, Tampa, FL 33602
(813) 223-8286
    Type of Facility: Theatre House
    Facility Originally: Vaudeville; Movie House
    Type of Stage: Thrust
    Stage Dimensions: 46'6" Wx25'3"D
    Seating Capacity: 1,446
    Year Built: 1926 **Architect:** John Eberson **Cost:** $1,250,000
    Year Remodeled: 1977 **Architect:** Joseph Dixon **Cost:** $1,000,000
    Contact for Rental: John Bell; (813) 223-8286

UNIVERSITY OF SOUTH FLORIDA - STUDIO THEATRE
TAR 230, Tampa, FL 33620-7450
(813) 974-2701
    Type of Facility: Theatre House; Arena
    Type of Stage: Flexible; Arena
    Seating Capacity: 120
    Year Built: 1968 **Architect:** Jim Green **Cost:** $668,389
    Manager: Dr. Dennis Calandra

UNIVERSITY OF SOUTH FLORIDA - THEATRE I
TAR 230, Tampa, FL 33620
(813) 974-2701
    Type of Facility: Theatre House
    Type of Stage: Proscenium
    Orchestra Pit
    Seating Capacity: 552
    Year Built: 1961 **Architect:** Gamble Pinell & Gilroy **Cost:** $537,314
    Acoustical Consultant: George Izenour
    Contact for Rental: Dr. Dennis Calandra
    Occasionally available for rent

UNIVERSITY OF SOUTH FLORIDA - THEATRE II
TAR 230, Tampa, FL 33620-7450
(813) 974-2701
    Type of Facility: Black Box
    Stage Dimensions: Black Box 70'x70'
    Seating Capacity: 150-300
    Year Built: 1984 **Architect:** Randolph Wedding Associates **Cost:** $1,800,000
    Acoustical Consultant: Russell Johnson Associates; ARTEC
    Contact for Rental: Dr. Dennis Calandra
    Occasionally available for rent

Tequesta

THEATRE

BURT REYNOLDS INSTITUTE FOR THEATRE TRAINING
304 Tequesta Drive, Tequesta, FL 33469
(407) 746-8887
FAX: (407) 743-7452
    Founded: 1979
    Arts Area: Theatrical Group
    Status: Professional; Non-Profit
    Type: Performing; Educational
    Purpose: To provide professional theatre training for developing artists
    Management: Richard Valentine, Executive Director
    Officers: Burt Reynolds, Chairman of the Board
    Volunteer Staff: 22
    Paid Artists: 8 **Non-Paid Artists:** 10
    Utilizes: Guest Artists; Guest Directors
    Budget: $500,000 - $1,000,000
    Income Sources: Private Foundations/Grants/Endowments; Business/Corporate Donations; Box Office; Individual Donations
    Season: 52 Weeks
    Annual Attendance: 14,500
    Affiliations: AEA
    Performance Facilities: Burt Reynolds Institute Theatre

Venice

THEATRE

THE VENICE LITTLE THEATRE
140 West Tampa Avenue, Venice, FL 34285
(813) 488-2419
    Founded: 1950
    Arts Area: Community

Status: Non-Professional; Non-Profit
Type: Performing
Purpose: To present intellectual and instructive entertainment in the performing arts
Management: Lee Linkous, Managing Director
Income Sources: Box Office

FACILITY

VENICE COMMUNITY CENTER
326 South Nokomis Avenue, Venice, FL 34285
(813) 485-6196
    Type of Facility: Civic Center
    Type of Stage: Platform
    Stage Dimensions: 54'x28'
    Seating Capacity: 750
    Year Built: 1976
    Contact for Rental: Diana Finnegan;   (813) 485-6196

Vero Beach

THEATRE

THE ACTING COMPANY OF RIVERSIDE THEATRE
3250 Riverside Park Drive, Vero Beach, FL 32963
(407) 231-5860
FAX: (407) 234-5298
    Founded: 1985
    Arts Area: Professional; Theatrical Group
    Status: Professional; Non-Profit
    Type: Performing
    Purpose: To provide audiences of this region with productions that are relevant either by nature of their importance within a particular genre or as socially vital within the changing environment of our culture
    Management: Allen D. Cornell, Artistic Director; Brian Spitler, Production Manager; Ida Spada, Business Manager; Lynn Potter, Development Director; Michael Kint, Director of Education
    Officers: Marilyn Chenault, Board President; Pat Trimble, Board Vice President; Rebecca Allen, Board Treasurer; Judy Balph, Board Secretary
    Paid Staff: 19   **Volunteer Staff:** 2
    Paid Artists: 83   **Non-Paid Artists:** 10
    Utilizes: Guest Artists; Guest Directors
    Budget: $1,000,000 - $5,000,000
    Income Sources: Private Foundations/Grants/Endowments; Business/Corporate Donations; Box Office; Government Grants; Individual Donations; Fund-raising
    Season: October - May   **Annual Attendance:** 50,000
    Affiliations: AEA; TCG; Florida Performing Theatre Association
    Performance Facilities: Riverside Theatre

VERO BEACH THEATRE GUILD
PO Box 1502, Vero Beach, FL 32961
(407) 562-8300
    Founded: 1958
    Arts Area: Community
    Status: Non-Professional; Non-Profit
    Type: Performing; Educational
    Purpose: To stimulate interest in dramatic and musical works through the means of community theater; to provide theatrical arts to the people of the Treasure Coast of Florida
    Management: Board of Directors
    Officers: Read Johnson, President; Tony Morely, Vice President; Edna Craven, Secretary; Albert Busck, Treasurer
    Volunteer Staff: 50
    Non-Paid Artists: 200
    Utilizes: Special Technical Talent
    Budget: $100,000 - $500,000
    Income Sources: Private Foundations/Grants/Endowments; Business/Corporate Donations; Box Office; Individual Donations
    Season: September - May   **Annual Attendance:** 11,000
    Performance Facilities: Riverside Theatre

FACILITY

RIVERSIDE THEATRE
3250 Riverside Park Drive, Vero Beach, FL 32963
(407) 231-5860
Mailing Address: PO Box 3788, Vero Beach, FL 32964
Type of Facility: Theatre House
Type of Stage: Proscenium
Stage Dimensions: 25'x50'x25'
Seating Capacity: 609
Year Built: 1972

West Palm Beach

DANCE

BALLET FLORIDA
500 Fern Street, West Palm Beach, FL 33401
(407) 659-1212
FAX: (407) 659-2222
Founded: 1973
Arts Area: Ballet
Status: Professional; Non-Profit
Type: Performing; Touring; Resident; Educational
Purpose: To achieve a dynamic synthesis of the aspiration of dancers, choreographers, and audiences by challenging all three
Management: Marie Hale, Artistic Director; A. Harrison Cromer Jr., Executive Director
Paid Artists: 20
Utilizes: Guest Artists; Guest Choreographers
Budget: $1,000,000 - $5,000,000
Income Sources: Private Foundations/Grants/Endowments; Business/Corporate Donations; Box Office; Individual Donations
Season: November - April
Annual Attendance: 50,000
Affiliations: Dance/USA

VOCAL MUSIC

PALM BEACH OPERA
415 South Olive Avenue, West Palm Beach, FL 33401
(407) 833-7888
FAX: (407) 833-8294
Founded: 1961
Arts Area: Grand Opera
Status: Professional; Non-Profit
Type: Performing; Touring; Resident; Educational
Purpose: To produce operas and allied musical performances
Management: Anton Guadagno, Artistic Director; Herbert Benn, General Director
Paid Staff: 4   **Volunteer Staff:** 8
Paid Artists: 55
Utilizes: Guest Artists
Budget: $1,000,000 - $5,000,000
Income Sources: Private Foundations/Grants/Endowments; Business/Corporate Donations; Box Office; Government Grants; Individual Donations
Season: December - March
Annual Attendance: 15,000
Performance Facilities: Kravis Center for the Performing Arts

PERFORMING SERIES

SUNFEST OF PALM BEACH COUNTY, INC.
319 Clematis Street, Suite 701, West Palm Beach, FL 33401
(407) 659-5980
FAX: (407) 659-3567
Founded: 1982
Arts Area: Festivals
Status: Non-Profit

Type: Resident
Purpose: Sunfest, Florida's largest jazz, art and water-events festival, is held annually the first weekend in May in West Palm Beach
Management: Sue A. Twyford, Executive Director; Paul Jamieson, Event Manager; Doreen Poreba, Public Relations Manager; Tamra McCraw, Marketing Manager; Sharvell Becton, Pin Program Coordinator
Officers: Dennis Grady, President; J. Kenneth Brower, President Elect; Dari Bowman, Past President; Robert L. Broadway, Thomas G. Burns Vice Presidents ·
Paid Staff: 8   **Volunteer Staff:** 3,000
Utilizes: Guest Artists; Guest Visual Artists
Budget: $1,000,000 - $5,000,000
Income Sources: Private Foundations/Grants/Endowments; Business/Corporate Donations; Admission Fees; Concessions
Season: May
Annual Attendance: 345,000
Affiliations: International Festival Association
Performance Facilities: Along the Intracoastal Waterway, Flagler Drive, West Palm Beach

FACILITY

WEST PALM BEACH AUDITORIUM
1610 Palm Beach Lakes, West Palm Beach, FL 33401
(407) 683-6010
FAX: (407) 687-1687
Founded: 1967
Type of Facility: Multi-Purpose
Type of Stage: Flexible; Proscenium; Platform; Arena
Stage Dimensions: 56'Wx38'D on stage; 88'Wx40'D off stage
Orchestra Pit
Seating Capacity: 6,098
Year Built: 1967
Architect: Bertrand Goldberg
Year Remodeled: 1991
Contact for Rental: Bob Burdett;   (407) 683-6010

White Springs

FACILITY

STEPHEN FOSTER STATE FOLK CULTURE CENTER - AMPHITHEATRE
US 41 North, PO Drawer G, White Springs, FL 32096
(904) 397-2733
Type of Facility: Outdoor (Concert); Amphitheater
Type of Stage: Environmental
Seating Capacity: 5,000
Year Built: 1953
Year Remodeled: 1975   **Architect:** Arthur Rude   **Cost:** $100,000
Contact for Rental: Darrell Krause, Park Office;   (904) 397-2733
Manager: Darrell Krause;   (904) 397-2733
Resident Groups: Florida Folk Life Programs

Winter Haven

THEATRE

THEATRE WINTER HAVEN
210 Cypress Gardens Boulevard, PO Drawer 1230, Winter Haven, FL 33882
(813) 299-2672
Founded: 1970
Arts Area: Community; Theatrical Group
Status: Non-Professional; Non-Profit
Type: Performing; Educational
Purpose: To nurture the cultural growth of the community by providing top-quality live theatre through presentation, participation and training
Management: Norman M. Small, Producing Director; Kim N. Siedentopf, General Manager; Bob Campbell, Technical Director
Paid Staff: 4   **Volunteer Staff:** 300
Paid Artists: 14   **Non-Paid Artists:** 9
Utilizes: Special Technical Talent; Guest Conductors; Guest Artists; Guest Directors

Budget: $100,000 - $500,000
Income Sources: Private Foundations/Grants/Endowments; Business/Corporate Donations; Box Office; Government Grants; Individual Donations
Season: 52 Weeks
Annual Attendance: 18,000
Affiliations: AACT

Winter Park

THEATRE

ANNIE RUSSELL THEATRE
Rollins College, 1000 Holt Avenue - 2735, Winter Park, FL 32789
(407) 646-2145
FAX: (407) 646-2600
  Founded: 1931
  Arts Area: Musical; Theatrical Group; Academic Theatre Program
  Status: Semi-Professional; Non-Professional; Non-Profit; Commercial
  Type: Performing; Resident; Educational; Sponsoring
  Purpose: To provide educational theatre; to book touring events
  Management: S. Joseph Nassif, Director
  Paid Staff: 9   **Volunteer Staff:** 12
  Utilizes: Guest Artists; Guest Directors
  Budget: $100,000 - $500,000
  Income Sources: Private Foundations/Grants/Endowments; Business/Corporate Donations; Box Office; Government Grants; Individual Donations
  Season: 52 Weeks   **Annual Attendance:** 20,000
  Affiliations: APAP; SETC; Florida Theatre Conference
  Performance Facilities: Annie Russell Theatre

FACILITY

ROLLINS COLLEGE - ANNIE RUSSELL THEATRE
1000 Holt Avenue - 2735, Winter Park, FL 32789
(407) 646-2145
FAX: (407) 646-2600
  Type of Facility: Theatre Complex
  Type of Stage: Proscenium
  Stage Dimensions: 27'Wx30'D   **Orchestra Pit**
  Seating Capacity: 375
  Year Built: 1931   **Cost:** $500,000
  Year Remodeled: 1978   **Cost:** $200,000
  Manager: Theatre Department
  Resident Groups: Rollins Players

GEORGIA

Albany

INSTRUMENTAL MUSIC

ALBANY SYMPHONY ASSOCIATION, INC.
PO Box 70065, Albany, GA 31707
(912) 888-8799
> **Founded:** 1964
> **Arts Area:** Symphony; Orchestra; Chamber; Ensemble
> **Status:** Professional
> **Type:** Performing; Educational
> **Purpose:** To provide and promote quality symphonic music for southwest Georgia through the organization of a symphony orchestra and related educational activities
> **Management:** Daphne Burt, General Manager; Claire Fox Hillard, Music Director
> **Officers:** James B. Ligon, President Elect; Mitch Everett, First Vice President; Marilyn Malphurs, Second Vice President; Merrel Callaway, Treasurer; Janet Woods, Secretary
> **Paid Staff:** 3   **Volunteer Staff:** 175
> **Paid Artists:** 75
> **Utilizes:** Guest Artists
> **Budget:** $100,000 - $500,000
> **Income Sources:** Private Foundations/Grants/Endowments; Business/Corporate Donations; Box Office; Government Grants; Individual Donations
> **Season:** September - April   **Annual Attendance:** 13,000
> **Affiliations:** ASOL; Albany Arts Council
> **Performance Facilities:** Municipal Auditorium, Albany

THEATRE

THEATRE ALBANY
514 Pine Avenue, Albany, GA 31702
(912) 439-7193
> **Founded:** 1932
> **Arts Area:** Musical; Community; Theatrical Group
> **Status:** Non-Professional; Non-Profit
> **Type:** Performing; Educational
> **Purpose:** To foster live theatre in the community
> **Management:** Mark Costello, Artistic/Managing Director; Walter Thompson, Technical Director; Yvette Foster, Business Manager
> **Officers:** Miriam Gilberg, President; Vic Sullivan III, Vice President; Charles Hancock, Treasurer; Mary Morrison, Recording Secretary
> **Paid Staff:** 5   **Volunteer Staff:** 200
> **Paid Artists:** 6   **Non-Paid Artists:** 60
> **Utilizes:** Guest Directors
> **Budget:** $100,000 - $500,000
> **Income Sources:** Private Foundations/Grants/Endowments; Business/Corporate Donations; Box Office; Individual Donations
> **Season:** October - June   **Annual Attendance:** 125,000
> **Affiliations:** AACT; SETC; Georgia Theatre Conference
> **Performance Facilities:** Theatre Albany

FACILITY

ALBANY JAMES H. GRAY SR., CIVIC CENTER
100 West Oglethorpe Boulevard, Albany, GA 31702
(912) 430-5200
FAX: (912) 430-5163
> **Type of Facility:** Civic Center
> **Year Built:** 1983   **Architect:** Taylor and Mathis
> **Contact for Rental:** Matty Goddard;   (912) 430-5200
> *Civic Center contains Arena and Ballroom. See separate listings for additional information.*

ALBANY JAMES H. GRAY SR., CIVIC CENTER - ARENA
100 West Oglethorpe Boulevard, Albany, GA 31702
(912) 430-5163
FAX: (912) 430-5163
        Type of Facility: Concert Hall; Arena
        Type of Stage: Platform
        Seating Capacity: 10,240
        Year Built: 1983
        Contact for Rental: Matty Goddard;   (912) 430-5200

ALBANY JAMES H. GRAY SR., CIVIC CENTER - BALLROOM
100 West Oglethorpe Boulevard, Albany, GA 31702
(912) 430-5200
FAX: (912) 430-5163
        Type of Facility: Multi-Purpose; Room
        Type of Stage: Platform
        Seating Capacity: Theatre style - 900; Banquet style - 450
        Year Built: 1983
        Contact for Rental: Matty Goddard;   (912) 430-5200

THEATRE ALBANY
514 Pine Avenue, Albany, GA 31702
(912) 439-7193
        Type of Facility: Theatre House
        Facility Originally: Private Residence
        Type of Stage: Flexible; Proscenium
        Orchestra Pit
        Seating Capacity: 314
        Year Built: 1853
        Year Remodeled: 1965
        Contact for Rental: Managing Director;   (912) 439-7193
        Resident Groups: Theatre Albany

Athens

DANCE

ATHENS BALLET
126 Barrington Drive, Athens, GA 30605
(706) 353-2082
        Founded: 1973
        Arts Area: Ballet
        Status: Non-Profit
        Type: Performing
        Purpose: To promote the opportunity to perform and learn
        Management: Mary Ann Hale, Artistic Director
        Officers: Ted Baumgartner, President; Randy Kemphouse, Vice President; Kathy Whitaker, Treasurer
        Non-Paid Artists: 23
        Budget: $1,000 - $50,000
        Income Sources: Business/Corporate Donations; Box Office; Individual Donations
        Season: September - May
        Affiliations: Georgia Council of the Arts
        Performance Facilities: Athens School of Ballet

THEATRE

ATHENS PUPPET THEATRE COMPANY
525 West Cloverhurst Avenue, Athens, GA 30606
(706) 354-1860
        Founded: 1972
        Arts Area: Puppet
        Status: Professional; Non-Profit
        Type: Performing; Touring; Educational
        Purpose: To provide a permanent, professional puppet troupe to tour Northeast Georgia and train puppeteers and encourage puppet skills development in our area
        Management: Amburn H. Power, Artistic Director; Karen Gilmore, Business Manager
        Officers: Ronnie Norton, President of Board of Directors

Paid Staff: 2   **Volunteer Staff:** 25
Paid Artists: 12
Budget: $1,000 - $50,000
Income Sources: Private Foundations/Grants/Endowments; Business/Corporate Donations; Box Office; Government Grants; Individual Donations
Season: October - April   **Annual Attendance:** 20,000
Affiliations: Puppeteers of America; Georgia Theatre Conference

GABBIES PUPPETS
367 Lexington Heights, Athens, GA 30605
(706) 353-2785
Founded: 1975
Arts Area: Puppet
Status: Professional
Type: Performing; Educational
Purpose: To present and teach language communication skills through the arts of puppets, storytelling, and creative dramatics
Management: Carolyn S. Gabb, Director
Paid Staff: 1
Paid Artists: 1
Utilizes: Special Technical Talent; Guest Artists
Budget: $1,000 - $50,000
Income Sources: Private Foundations/Grants/Endowments
Season: 52 Weeks

Atlanta

DANCE

THE ATLANTA BALLET
477 Peachtree Street NE, Atlanta, GA 30308
(404) 873-5811
FAX: (404) 874-7905
Founded: 1929
Arts Area: Ballet
Status: Professional; Non-Profit
Type: Performing; Touring; Resident
Purpose: To provide professional ballet performances for the people of metropolitan Atlanta and the surrounding area
Management: Chuck Johnston, Executive Director; Robert Barnett, Artistic Director
Officers: Lynda Courts, Chairman of the Board
Paid Staff: 28
Paid Artists: 29
Utilizes: Special Technical Talent; Guest Artists; Guest Directors
Budget: $1,000,000 - $5,000,000
Income Sources: Private Foundations/Grants/Endowments; Business/Corporate Donations; Box Office; Government Grants; Individual Donations
Season: September - May
Affiliations: Dance USA; NARB
Performance Facilities: Atlanta Civic Center

THE RUTH MITCHELL DANCE COMPANY
3509 Northside Parkway, Atlanta, GA 30327
(404) 237-2477
Founded: 1956
Arts Area: Modern; Ballet; Jazz
Status: Professional; Non-Profit
Type: Performing; Touring
Purpose: To provide the community with a small, eclectic company which can perform in places not suited for large ballet companies
Management: Ruth Mitchell, Artistic Director; Courtney Kennedy, Production Manager
Officers: Sandra Ratchford, President, Board of Trustees; Courtney Kennedy, Vice President; Carmen Dillard, Treasurer; Judy Freeman, President of the Guild
Paid Staff: 2   **Volunteer Staff:** 2
Paid Artists: 8
Utilizes: Guest Artists; Guest Choreographers
Budget: $100,000 - $500,000
Income Sources: Private Foundations/Grants/Endowments; Business/Corporate Donations; Box Office; Government Grants; Individual Donations

Season: August - May   **Annual Attendance:** 40,000
Affiliations: NARB; Dance Coalition of Atlanta; Young Audiences of Atlanta
Performance Facilities: 14th Street Playhouse; Cobb Civic Center; Pace Fine Arts

INSTRUMENTAL MUSIC

ATLANTA CHAMBER PLAYERS
68 GSU-Georgia State University, PO Box 4038, Atlanta, GA 30302
(404) 651-1228
Arts Area: Chamber
Status: Professional; Non-Profit
Type: Performing; Touring; Resident; Educational
Purpose: Atlanta Chamber Players is a professional ensemble of musicians dedicated to providing audiences with world class traditional and contemporary masterpieces as well as commissioned new works
Management: Paula Peace, Artistic Director; Ed Trafford, Business Manager
Officers: Cherry Emerson, President of the Board
Budget: $50,000 - $100,000
Income Sources: Private Foundations/Grants/Endowments; Business/Corporate Donations; Box Office; Government Grants; Individual Donations
Performance Facilities: Georgia State University Recital Hall

ATLANTA POPS ORCHESTRA
PO Box 723172-0172, Atlanta, GA 31139-0172
(404) 435-1222
Founded: 1945
Arts Area: Orchestra; Pops; Popular Selections
Status: Professional; Non-Profit
Type: Performing; Touring
Purpose: To provide a showcase for amateur guest talent; to give them a chance to grow musically in public performances
Management: Lorne Coleman, Manager; Albert Coleman, Originator/Director/Conductor
Officers: Albert Coleman, President; Charles Wills, Vice President; Betty Fitz, Administrative Assistant; Nancy Holland, Publicist
Paid Staff: 3
Paid Artists: 55
Utilizes: Guest Artists
Budget: $100,000 - $500,000
Income Sources: Private Foundations/Grants/Endowments; Business/Corporate Donations; Performance Fees
Season: 52 Weeks   **Annual Attendance:** 40,000
Performance Facilities: Chastain Park; Stone Mountain; McIntosh Amphitheatre

ATLANTA SYMPHONY ORCHESTRA
1293 Peachtree Street NE, Suite 300, Atlanta, GA 30309
(404) 898-1182
FAX: (404) 898-9557
Founded: 1945
Arts Area: Symphony; Orchestra; Chamber
Status: Professional; Non-Profit
Type: Performing
Purpose: To present symphonic concerts for the enjoyment of Atlanta area audiences
Management: J. Thomas Bacchetti, Executive Director; Robert Shaw, Music Director Emeritus/Conductor Laureate; Yoel Levy, Music Director; George Hanson, Resident Conductor
Officers: Jay Levine, President; J. Thomas Bacchetti, Vice President
Paid Staff: 54   **Volunteer Staff:** 1,000
Paid Artists: 94
Utilizes: Guest Conductors; Guest Artists
Budget: Over 10,000,000
Income Sources: Private Foundations/Grants/Endowments; Business/Corporate Donations; Box Office; Government Grants; Individual Donations
Season: 52 Weeks   **Annual Attendance:** 600,000
Affiliations: ASOL
Performance Facilities: Symphony Hall; Chastain Park Amphitheatre

ATLANTA SYMPHONY YOUTH ORCHESTRA
1293 Peachtree Street NE, Atlanta, GA 30309
(404) 898-1182; (404) 898-9572
FAX: (404) 898-9557
Founded: 1973
Arts Area: Symphony; Orchestra

Status: Non-Professional; Non-Profit
Type: Performing; Educational
Management: Cynthia Thomas, Director of Education; Jere Flint, Conductor
Paid Staff: 4
Non-Paid Artists: 110
Utilizes: Guest Conductors
Income Sources: Business/Corporate Donations; Box Office; Individual Donations
Season: September - May   **Annual Attendance:** 5,200
Affiliations: ASOL (Youth Orchestra Division); Atlanta Symphony Orchestra
Performance Facilities: Symphony Hall, Robert W. Woodruff Arts Center

VOCAL MUSIC

ATLANTA BACH CHOIR
1026 Ponce de Leon Avenue, Atlanta, GA 30306
(404) 872-2224
Founded: 1980
Arts Area: Choral
Status: Professional; Non-Profit
Type: Performing; Touring; Resident
Purpose: Performance of cantatas, orchestral, chamber and major works of J.S. Bach
Management: Porter Remington, Conductor
Officers: Sue McConner, President; David Miller, Vice President; Deborah Hildebrand, Treasurer
Paid Staff: 1   **Volunteer Staff:** 15
Paid Artists: 102   **Non-Paid Artists:** 33
Utilizes: Guest Artists
Budget: $1,000 - $50,000
Income Sources: Private Foundations/Grants/Endowments; Business/Corporate Donations; Box Office; Government Grants; Individual Donations
Season: September - July   **Annual Attendance:** 3,000

THE ATLANTA OPERA
1800 Peachtree Street NW, Suite 620, Atlanta, GA 30309
(404) 355-3311
Founded: 1979
Arts Area: Grand Opera; Lyric Opera
Status: Professional; Non-Profit
Type: Performing; Educational
Purpose: The company is committed to establishing itself as a major artistic presence in the Southeast by combining quality mainstage productions with programs designed to serve community, cultural and educational needs.
Management: William Fred Scott, Artistic Director; Alfred D. Kennedy, General Manager
Officers: Mrs. Shepard B. Ansley, Chairman; Robert Fischer, President
Paid Staff: 7   **Volunteer Staff:** 15
Paid Artists: 6
Utilizes: Special Technical Talent; Guest Conductors; Guest Artists
Budget: $500,000 - $1,000,000
Income Sources: Private Foundations/Grants/Endowments; Business/Corporate Donations; Box Office; Government Grants; Individual Donations
Season: June - August   **Annual Attendance:** 15,000
Affiliations: Alliance Theatre
Performance Facilities: Alliance Theatre; Symphony Hall

ATLANTA SYMPHONY CHORUS
c/o Robert W. Woodruff Arts Center, 1292 Peachtree Street NE, Atlanta, GA 30309
(404) 898-1182
FAX: (404) 898-9557
Arts Area: Grand Opera; Operetta; Arias
Status: Non-Professional; Non-Profit; Volunteer
Type: Performing; Touring
Management: Robert Shaw, Conductor; Nola Frank, Choral Administrator
Budget: $50,000 - $100,000
Income Sources: Private Foundations/Grants/Endowments; Business/Corporate Donations; Box Office; Government Grants; Individual Donations
Performance Facilities: Robert W. Woodruff Arts Center Symphony Hall

CHORAL GUILD OF ATLANTA
PO Box 7872, Atlanta, GA 30357
(404) 435-6563
Arts Area: Choral

Status: Semi-Professional; Non-Profit
Type: Performing; Touring
Purpose: To be the pre-eminent large civic chorus in metro Atlanta performing major choral works from the non-standard repertoire while becoming increasingly financially solvent
Management: William Noll, Conductor/Director
Officers: C. William Moody, Chairman of the Board
Budget: $50,000 - $100,000
Income Sources: Business/Corporate Donations; Box Office; Government Grants; Individual Donations

THEATRE

ACADEMY THEATRE
PO Box 191306, Atlanta, GA 31119
(404) 365-8088
Founded: 1956
Arts Area: Professional
Status: Professional; Non-Profit
Type: Performing; Touring; Resident; Educational; Sponsoring
Purpose: To foster an atmosphere that assists the individual in discovering creative resources that will lead to artistic expression of individual feelings and insights and be a forum for ideas, a place to question values, a means to entertain and enhance life
Management: Frank Wittow, Founder/Producing Artistic Director; Lorenne Fey, Managing Director
Officers: Sue L. Symons, Chairman of the Board; Frank Wittow, President
Paid Staff: 5 **Volunteer Staff:** 35
Paid Artists: 40 **Non-Paid Artists:** 30
Utilizes: Special Technical Talent; Guest Conductors; Guest Artists; Guest Directors
Budget: $100,000 - $500,000
Income Sources: Private Foundations/Grants/Endowments; Business/Corporate Donations; Box Office; Government Grants; Individual Donations
Season: 52 Weeks **Annual Attendance:** 130,000
Affiliations: TCG; Atlanta Theatre Coalition; Atlanta Chamber of Commerce; AATA; ASSITEJ; Georgia Citizens for the Arts

ALLIANCE THEATRE COMPANY
1280 Peachtree Street NE, Atlanta, GA 30309
(404) 898-1132
Founded: 1969
Arts Area: Professional; Theatrical Group
Status: Professional; Non-Profit
Type: Performing; Touring; Resident; Educational
Purpose: To create an environment in which to achieve the highest quality theatre nationally as well as regionally
Management: Edith H. Love, Managing Director; Kenny Leon, Artistic Director; T. Jane Bishop, General Manager
Officers: Robert E. Reiser, President; Kenneth Bernhardt, First Vice President; Chuck Frew, Teasurer
Paid Staff: 203 **Volunteer Staff:** 750
Paid Artists: 200
Utilizes: Special Technical Talent; Guest Artists; Guest Directors
Budget: $5,000,000 - $10,000,000
Income Sources: Private Foundations/Grants/Endowments; Business/Corporate Donations; Box Office; Government Grants; Individual Donations
Season: August - June **Annual Attendance:** 290,000
Affiliations: AEA; SSDC; LORT; USA
Performance Facilities: Alliance Theatre

ATLANTA SHAKESPEARE COMPANY
PO Box 5436, Atlanta, GA 30307
(404) 874-9219
Founded: 1979
Arts Area: Professional; Theatrical Group
Status: Professional; Non-Profit
Type: Performing; Touring
Purpose: To reinstate the popular appeal inherent, not only in the works of William Shakespeare, but of all living theater
Management: Jeffrey Watkins, Artistic Director; Tony Wright, Marketing Director; Cindy Kearns, Stage Manager
Officers: Jeffrey Watkins, President
Paid Staff: 2 **Volunteer Staff:** 6
Paid Artists: 26
Utilizes: Special Technical Talent; Guest Conductors; Guest Artists; Guest Directors
Budget: $100,000 - $500,000
Income Sources: Business/Corporate Donations; Box Office; Government Grants; Individual Donations

Annual Attendance: 8,000
Affiliations: Atlanta Coalition of Theatres

ATLANTA STREET THEATRE
1660 Moores Mill Road, Atlanta, GA 30327
(404) 355-0020
Founded: 1976
Arts Area: Professional
Status: Professional; Non-Profit
Type: Performing; Touring; Educational
Purpose: To provide relevant theatre to underprivileged youth; to maintain an interracial group at all levels; to use theatre educationally
Management: Michele McNichols, Executive Artistic Director
Officers: Donna Watts-Nunn, Chairman of the Board; John Coleman, Treasurer; Brenda Webb, Secretary
Paid Staff: 1   **Volunteer Staff:** 3
Paid Artists: 10
Budget: $1,000 - $50,000
Income Sources: Private Foundations/Grants/Endowments; Business/Corporate Donations
Season: 52 Weeks   **Annual Attendance:** 5,000

CENTER FOR PUPPETRY ARTS
1404 Spring Street NW, Atlanta, GA 30309
(404) 873-3089; (404) 873-3391
FAX: (404) 873-9907
Founded: 1978
Arts Area: Professional; Puppet
Status: Professional; Non-Profit
Type: Performing; Touring; Resident; Educational; Sponsoring
Purpose: Dedicated to expanding the public's awareness of puppetry as a fine art and to expose people to the global aspects of the art form
Management: Vincent Anthony, Executive Director
Officers: Barbara Wylly, Chairman, Board of Trustees
Paid Staff: 22   **Volunteer Staff:** 20
Paid Artists: 30
Utilizes: Special Technical Talent; Guest Artists; Guest Directors
Budget: $1,000,000 - $5,000,000
Income Sources: Private Foundations/Grants/Endowments; Business/Corporate Donations; Box Office; Government Grants; Individual Donations
Season: 52 Weeks   **Annual Attendance:** 250,000
Affiliations: TCG; UNIMA; Puppeteers of America; Georgia Citizens for the Arts; Metro Arts
Performance Facilities: Mainstage Theater; Downstairs Theater; Museum Mini Theater; Theater III

GATEWAY PERFORMANCE PRODUCTIONS
PO Box 8062, Atlanta, GA 30306
(404) 222-9884
Founded: 1974
Arts Area: Theatrical Group; MIME
Status: Professional; Non-Profit
Type: Performing; Touring; Resident; Educational
Purpose: To explore and expand the parameters of the art of mime and related movement theatre
Management: Sandra Hughes, Artistic Director; Michael E. Hickey, Company Coordinator
Officers: H. Lamar Mixson, Chairman; Sandra Hughes, President; Michael E. Hickey, Treasurer; Dorothy Sussman, Secretary
Paid Staff: 2
Utilizes: Special Technical Talent; Guest Artists
Budget: $50,000 - $100,000
Income Sources: Private Foundations/Grants/Endowments; Business/Corporate Donations
Season: 52 Weeks

JOMANDI PRODUCTIONS
1444 Mayson Street, Atlanta, GA 30324
(404) 876-6346
Founded: 1978
Arts Area: Theatrical Group
Status: Professional; Non-Profit
Type: Performing; Touring; Resident
Purpose: To nurture the development of new works about the African-American experience and to provide a vehicle for theatre artists to train and perform
Management: Tom Jones, Marsha Jackson, Artistic Directors; Geri Blanchet, Public Relations Director

Officers: Clifton Barber, Chairperson; Herman Reese, Vice Chair; Diana Stevens, Secretary; Andrea Fuller, Treasurer
Utilizes: Special Technical Talent; Guest Artists; Guest Directors
Budget: $50,000 - $100,000
Income Sources: Private Foundations/Grants/Endowments; Business/Corporate Donations; Box Office; Government Grants; Individual Donations
Season: October - June
Performance Facilities: Academy Theatre

JUST US THEATER COMPANY
PO Box 42271, Atlanta, GA 30311-4271
(404) 753-2399
　　　　Founded: 1976
　　　　Arts Area: Theatrical Group
　　　　Status: Professional
　　　　Type: Performing; Touring; Resident; Educational
　　　　Purpose: Just Us Theater Company is a Black professional company dedicated to the development of minority artists and the presentation of quality arts programs that reflect the diversity of our community; focus on sexism and racism
　　　　Management: Pearl Cleage, Artistic Director; Zaron Burnett Jr., Producing Director
　　　　Officers: Walter R. Huntley, Board President; Pearle Cleage, Treasurer; Zaron W. Burnett Jr., Secretary
　　　　Paid Staff: 4　**Volunteer Staff:** 25
　　　　Paid Artists: 70
　　　　Utilizes: Special Technical Talent; Guest Artists; Guest Directors
　　　　Budget: $100,000 - $500,000
　　　　Income Sources: Private Foundations/Grants/Endowments; Business/Corporate Donations; Box Office; Government Grants; Individual Donations
　　　　Season: 52 Weeks　**Annual Attendance:** 10,000

OMILAMI PRODUCTIONS/PEOPLE'S SURVIVAL THEATRE
8 East Lake Drive NE, Atlanta, GA 30317
(404) 377-6434
FAX: (404) 584-9166
　　　　Founded: 1977
　　　　Arts Area: Community; Theatrical Group
　　　　Status: Semi-Professional; Non-Profit
　　　　Type: Performing; Touring; Educational
　　　　Purpose: To produce, provide and encourage arts programming for impoverished areas that are not serviced by traditional groups; to stimulate and encourage new playwrights and directors to write and direct for the inner city and rural areas
　　　　Management: Elizabeth and Afemo Omilami, Co-Artistic Directors
　　　　Paid Staff: 2　**Volunteer Staff:** 3
　　　　Paid Artists: 12　**Non-Paid Artists:** 8
　　　　Utilizes: Special Technical Talent; Guest Artists; Guest Directors
　　　　Budget: $100,000 - $500,000
　　　　Income Sources: Private Foundations/Grants/Endowments; Business/Corporate Donations; Box Office; Government Grants; Individual Donations
　　　　Season: 52 Weeks　**Annual Attendance:** 10,000

SEVEN STAGES
430 Moreland Avenue NE, Atlanta, GA 30307
(404) 522-0911
FAX: (404) 522-0913
　　　　Founded: 1978
　　　　Arts Area: Professional; Musical; Community; Theatrical Group
　　　　Status: Professional; Non-Profit
　　　　Type: Performing; Resident
　　　　Purpose: To produce new plays which might not otherwise be seen and produce reinterpretations of classics and contemporary theatre
　　　　Management: Del Hamilton, Artistic Director; Faye Allen, Producing Director; Lisa Mount, Managing Director; Linda Burgess, Technical Director
　　　　Paid Staff: 4　**Volunteer Staff:** 40
　　　　Paid Artists: 75
　　　　Utilizes: Special Technical Talent; Guest Artists; Guest Directors
　　　　Budget: $100,000 - $500,000
　　　　Income Sources: Private Foundations/Grants/Endowments; Business/Corporate Donations; Box Office; Government Grants; Individual Donations
　　　　Season: 52 Weeks　**Annual Attendance:** 10,000
　　　　Affiliations: TCG; Alternate Roots
　　　　Performance Facilities: Seven Stages

THE SOUTHEASTERN SAVOYARDS
3270 Ivanhoe Drive, Atlanta, GA 30327
(404) 233-7002
> **Founded:** 1980
> **Arts Area:** Musical Theatre
> **Status:** Professional; Non-Profit
> **Type:** Theatrical Group
> **Purpose:** Gilbert & Sullivan repertory company
> **Management:** John H. Stevens, Executive Producer; J. Lynn Thompson, Artistic/Music Director
> **Officers:** John H. Stevens, President; Robert B. Langdon, Vice President; Fern M. Stevens, Treasurer; Marcia Lane, Secretary
> **Paid Staff:** 4 **Volunteer Staff:** 20
> **Paid Artists:** 43
> **Utilizes:** Special Technical Talent; Guest Artists; Guest Directors
> **Budget:** $100,000 - $500,000
> **Income Sources:** Private Foundations/Grants/Endowments; Business/Corporate Donations; Box Office; Government Grants; Individual Donations
> **Season:** October - May **Annual Attendance:** 10,000
> **Performance Facilities:** Center Stage Theater Atlanta

THEATRE GAEL
PO Box 77156, Atlanta, GA 30357
(404) 876-1138
FAX: (404) 892-0355
> **Founded:** 1982
> **Arts Area:** Professional; Theatrical Group; Children's Theatre
> **Status:** Professional; Non-Profit
> **Type:** Performing
> **Purpose:** To perform the plays of Ireland, Scotland and Wales
> **Management:** Aimee Chubb, Managing Director; John Stephens, Artistic Director
> **Paid Staff:** 4 **Volunteer Staff:** 25
> **Paid Artists:** 100 **Non-Paid Artists:** 25
> **Utilizes:** Special Technical Talent; Guest Artists; Guest Directors
> **Budget:** $100,000 - $500,000
> **Income Sources:** Private Foundations/Grants/Endowments; Business/Corporate Donations; Box Office; Government Grants; Individual Donations
> **Season:** 52 Weeks **Annual Attendance:** 60,000
> **Affiliations:** AATA; Alternate ROOTS
> **Performance Facilities:** 14th Street Playhouse

THEATRICAL OUTFIT
1012 Peachtree Street, PO Box 7098, Atlanta, GA 30357
(404) 872-0665
FAX: (404) 872-1164
> **Founded:** 1978
> **Arts Area:** Professional; Musical
> **Status:** Professional; Non-Profit
> **Type:** Performing; Educational
> **Purpose:** Georgia's only theatre that produces new work with music, new musicals, and new adaptations with music
> **Management:** Phillip DePoy, Artistic Director; Robert Hill, General Manager; Robert Teverino, Production Manager; Lori Youngers, Director of Marketing; Chris Cofrin, Volunteer Director of Development
> **Officers:** David Cofrin, Board President
> **Paid Staff:** 4 **Volunteer Staff:** 4
> **Utilizes:** Special Technical Talent; Guest Artists; Guest Directors
> **Budget:** $100,000 - $500,000
> **Income Sources:** Private Foundations/Grants/Endowments; Business/Corporate Donations; Box Office; Government Grants; Individual Donations
> **Season:** 52 Weeks **Annual Attendance:** 30,000
> **Affiliations:** AEA; TCG

PERFORMING SERIES

ATLANTA JAZZ FESTIVAL
c/o Atlanta Bureau of Cultural Affairs, 675 Ponce de Leon, Atlanta, GA 30308
(404) 653-7160
FAX: (404) 658-6945
> **Arts Area:** Dance; Vocal Music; Instrumental Music
> **Status:** Professional; Non-Profit

Type: Performing; Educational
Purpose: To provide an opportunity to showcase local and national talent; to expose the citizens of Atlanta to jazz music
Management: Barbara Bowser, Bureau Director; Jackie Davis, Festivals Manager
Budget: $100,000 - $500,000
Income Sources: Private Foundations/Grants/Endowments; Business/Corporate Donations; Box Office; Government Grants; Individual Donations
Performance Facilities: Grant Park

GEORGIA SHAKESPEARE FESTIVAL
4484 Peachtree Road NE, Atlanta, GA 30319
(404) 264-0020
Founded: 1985
Arts Area: Theater; Festivals
Status: Professional; Non-Profit
Type: Performing; Resident
Purpose: To produce an annual summer Shakespeare festival
Management: Richard Garner, Artistic/Producing Director; Margaret Dickson, Managing Director
Officers: Bruce Callner, President; Eric Bitterman, Treasurer; Barbara Stanton, Secretary
Paid Staff: 3 **Volunteer Staff:** 3
Paid Artists: 20 **Non-Paid Artists:** 7
Utilizes: Guest Artists; Guest Directors
Budget: $100,000 - $500,000
Income Sources: Private Foundations/Grants/Endowments; Business/Corporate Donations; Box Office; Government Grants; Individual Donations
Season: July - August **Annual Attendance:** 6,100
Affiliations: SETC; Atlanta Theatre Coalition

MONTREUX ATLANTA MUSIC FESTIVAL
c/o Atlanta Bureau of Cultural Affairs, 675 Ponce de Leon, Atlanta, GA 30308
(404) 653-7160
FAX: (404) 658-6945
Arts Area: Vocal Music; Instrumental Music
Status: Professional; Non-Profit
Type: Performing; Educational
Purpose: To expose the citizens of Atlanta to a variety of musical categories including gospel, country, blues, jazz, pop, rhythm and blues and world music; the festival is part of a musical exchange between the cities of Atlanta and Montreux, Switzerland and is a counterpart of the Montreux Jazz Festival
Management: Barbara Bowser, Bureau Director; Jackie Davis, Festivals Manager
Budget: $100,000 - $500,000
Income Sources: Private Foundations/Grants/Endowments; Business/Corporate Donations; Box Office; Government Grants; Individual Donations
Performance Facilities: Piedmont Park

NATIONAL BLACK ARTS FESTIVAL
236 Forsyth Street SW, Suite 400, Atlanta, GA 30303
(404) 730-7315
FAX: (404) 730-7104
Founded: 1987
Arts Area: Dance; Vocal Music; Instrumental Music; Theater; Festivals
Status: Non-Profit
Type: Presenting
Purpose: To showcase and celebrate the works of artists of African descent in eight artistic disciplines
Management: Myrna Anderson-Fuller, Managing Director; Stephanie Hughley, Artistic Director
Officers: Michael Lomax, Chairman of the Board; Nancy Boxill, Vice Chairperson; Milford McGuirt, Treasurer; Sandra Baccus, Secretary
Paid Staff: 8
Paid Artists: 964 **Non-Paid Artists:** 135
Utilizes: Special Technical Talent; Guest Conductors; Guest Artists; Guest Directors; Curators, Choreographers
Budget: $1,000,000 - $5,000,000
Income Sources: Private Foundations/Grants/Endowments; Business/Corporate Donations; Box Office; Government Grants; Individual Donations
Season: August **Annual Attendance:** 600,000
Affiliations: Fulton County Arts Council

THEATER OF THE STARS
PO Box 11748, Atlanta, GA 30355
(404) 252-8960
Founded: 1953

Arts Area: Dance; Vocal Music; Instrumental Music; Musicals; Plays
Status: Professional; Non-Profit
Type: Performing; Touring; Sponsoring
Management: Christopher Manos, Producer
Paid Staff: 6
Utilizes: Special Technical Talent; Guest Artists; Guest Directors
Income Sources: Business/Corporate Donations; Box Office; Government Grants; Individual Donations
Season: July - August

FACILITY

ACADEMY THEATRE - FIRST STAGE
PO Box 191306, Atlanta, GA 31119
(404) 365-8088
Type of Facility: Black Box
Type of Stage: Flexible
Stage Dimensions: 50'Wx50'Dx16'H
Seating Capacity: 175
Year Built: 1987
Contact for Rental: (404) 365-8088

ACADEMY THEATRE - LAB
173 14th Street, PO Box 191306, Atlanta, GA 31119
(404) 365-8088
Type of Facility: Multi-Purpose; Room
Type of Stage: Flexible
Stage Dimensions: 25'Wx50'D
Seating Capacity: 50
Year Built: 1987
Contact for Rental: (404) 365-8088

ACADEMY THEATRE - PHOEBE THEATRE
PO Box 191306, Atlanta, GA 31119
(404) 365-8088
Type of Facility: Theatre House
Type of Stage: Modified Thrust
Stage Dimensions: 40'Wx44'D
Seating Capacity: 375
Year Built: 1987
Contact for Rental: (404) 365-8088

ATLANTA CIVIC CENTER
395 Piedmont Avenue NE, Atlanta, GA 30308
(404) 523-6275
FAX: (404) 525-4634
Type of Facility: Civic Center
Year Built: 1968   **Architect:** Roberts and Company   **Cost:** $21,000,000
Contact for Rental: Walt Elder;   (404) 523-6275
The Civic Center contains Room 104 and Theater Auditorium. See separate listings for additional information.

ATLANTA CIVIC CENTER - ROOM 104
395 Piedmont Avenue NE, Atlanta, GA 30308
(404) 523-6275
FAX: (404) 525-4634
Type of Facility: Multi-Purpose; Room
Type of Stage: Flexible
Seating Capacity: 800
Year Built: 1968   **Architect:** Roberts and Company
Contact for Rental: Walt Elder;   (404) 523-6275
Resident Groups: Club Zebra

ATLANTA CIVIC CENTER - THEATER AUDITORIUM
395 Piedmont Avenue NE, Atlanta, GA 30308
(404) 523-6275
FAX: (404) 525-4634
Type of Facility: Concert Hall; Auditorium; Theatre House
Type of Stage: Proscenium
Stage Dimensions: 121'8"Wx57'6"D; 86'W proscenium opening   **Orchestra Pit**

Seating Capacity: 4,600
Year Built: 1968   **Architect:** Roberts and Company
Contact for Rental: Walt Elder;   (404) 523-6275
Resident Groups: Atlanta Ballet

14TH STREET PLAYHOUSE
173 14th Street, Atlanta, GA 30309
(404) 892-0103
FAX: (404) 892-0355
Type of Facility: Theatre Complex; Performance Center
Type of Stage: Thrust; Flexible; Proscenium; Three stages
Stage Dimensions: Secondstage - thrust; Stage 3 - flexible; Mainstage - proscenium
Seating Capacity: Mainstage - 400; Secondstage - 200; Stage Three - 100
Year Built: 1987   **Architect:** IA Group   **Cost:** $4,500,000
Acoustical Consultant: Michael Stauffer
Contact for Rental: Robert Putnam;   (404) 892-0103
Resident Groups: Carl Ratcliff Dance Theatre; Jomandi Productions; Theatre Gael; Ruth Mitchell Dance; S.A.M.E.
Performance spaces within the 14th Street Playhouse are Mainstage, Secondstage and Stage 3. See separate listings for additional information.

FOX THEATRE
660 Peachtree Street NE, Atlanta, GA 30365
(404) 881-2100
Type of Facility: Concert Hall; Theatre House; Opera House
Facility Originally: Shrine Temple
Type of Stage: Modified Thrust
Stage Dimensions: 135'Wx39'D; add 19'6"D with 3 hydraulic lift pits at stage level   **Orchestra Pit**
Seating Capacity: 4,518
Year Built: 1929   **Architect:** Mayre Alger Vinour   **Cost:** $3,500,000
Year Remodeled: 1993   **Architect:** Rosser Fabrap International   **Cost:** $8,000,000
Contact for Rental: Edgar Neiss;   (404) 881-2100
The Fox Theatre was originally built to house Yaraab Temple of the Ancient Arabic Order of the Nobles of the Mystic Shrine. A National Historic Landmark, restoration began in 1975. Completion is projected for 1995 with the building remaining open and fully functional during restoration.

GLENN MEMORIAL AUDITORIUM
1652 North Decatur Road NE, Atlanta, GA 30307-1010
(404) 727-6691
FAX: (404) 634-3936
Founded: 1931
Type of Facility: Concert Hall; Auditorium; Multi-Purpose; Church
Facility Originally: Church
Type of Stage: Platform
Stage Dimensions: 44'x40' with extensions
Seating Capacity: 1,250
Year Built: 1931   **Architect:** Hentz, Adler & Shultz   **Cost:** $160,000
Year Remodeled: 1960   **Architect:** Newcomb & Boyd   **Cost:** $300,000
Resident Groups: Emory Music Department

ROBERT W. WOODRUFF ARTS CENTER
1280 Peachtree Street, Atlanta, GA 30309
(404) 892-3600
Type of Facility: Performance Center; Civic Center
Year Built: 1967   **Architect:** Toombs Amisano & Wells; Stevenson & Wilkerson   **Cost:** $13,000,000
Acoustical Consultant: Vern Knudsen
The Arts Center consists of the Alliance Theatre-Main Stage, Alliance Theatre-Studio Theatre, Richard H. Rich Auditorium and Symphony Hall. See separate listings for additional information.

ROBERT W. WOODRUFF ARTS CENTER - ALLIANCE THEATRE-MAIN STAGE
1280 Peachtree Street, Atlanta, GA 30309
(404) 898-1132
FAX: (404) 898-9576
Founded: 1968
Type of Facility: Performance Center; Theatre House
Type of Stage: Proscenium
Stage Dimensions: 94'Wx40'D; 40'Wx28'H proscenium opening   **Orchestra Pit**
Seating Capacity: 784
Year Built: 1967

Acoustical Consultant: Jaffe Acoustics
Contact for Rental: Tom Semans;   (404) 898-1133
Resident Groups: Alliance Theatre Company

ROBERT W. WOODRUFF ARTS CENTER - ALLIANCE THEATRE-STUDIO THEATRE
1280 Peachtree Street, Atlanta, GA 30309
(404) 892-3600
Type of Facility: Black Box
Type of Stage: Flexible
Seating Capacity: 200
Year Built: 1969
Contact for Rental: Tom Semans;   (404) 898-1133

ROBERT W. WOODRUFF ARTS CENTER - RICHARD H. RICH AUDITORIUM
1280 Peachtree Street, Atlanta, GA 30309
(404) 892-3600
Type of Facility: Auditorium
Type of Stage: Proscenium
Stage Dimensions: 35'Wx16'D
Seating Capacity: 437
Year Built: 1967
Contact for Rental: Larry Ahern;   (404) 892-3600, ext. 104

ROBERT W. WOODRUFF ARTS CENTER - SYMPHONY HALL
1280 Peachtree Street, Atlanta, GA 30309
(404) 892-3600
Founded: 1967
Type of Facility: Concert Hall; Theatre House
Type of Stage: Proscenium; Modified Apron Proscenium
Stage Dimensions: 122'6"Wx53'7"D; 65'Wx37'H proscenium opening   **Orchestra Pit**
Seating Capacity: 1,762
Year Built: 1967
Contact for Rental: Maria Williamson;   (404) 898-1182
Resident Groups: Atlanta Symphony Orchestra
Hydraulic lift pit can be raised to stage level. Add 11'D to stage with lift at stage level.

SEVEN STAGES
1105 Euclid Avenue, Atlanta, GA 30307
(404) 522-0911
Type of Facility: Theatre House
Facility Originally: Business Facility
Type of Stage: L-shaped
Stage Dimensions: 30'x30'
Seating Capacity: 96
Year Remodeled: 1983   **Architect:** Community Design Center   **Cost:** $40,000
Acoustical Consultant: Margaret Lemon
Contact for Rental: Del Hamilton;   (404) 523-7647

Augusta

DANCE

AUGUSTA BALLET COMPANY
PO Box 3448, Augusta, GA 30904
(706) 733-5511
Founded: 1964
Arts Area: Ballet; Jazz
Status: Semi-Professional; Non-Profit
Type: Performing; Touring; Resident
Purpose: To present quality dance
Management: Ron Colton, Zanne Beaufort, Artistic Directors
Paid Artists: 20
Utilizes: Guest Artists; Guest Choreographers
Budget: $1,000,000 - $5,000,000
Income Sources: Box Office; Individual Donations
Season: September - May
Performance Facilities: Imperial Community Theater

INSTRUMENTAL MUSIC

AUGUSTA SYMPHONY ORCHESTRA
PO Box 579, Augusta, GA 30903
(706) 826-4705
FAX: (706) 826-4735
Founded: 1945
Arts Area: Symphony
Status: Non-Profit
Type: Performing
Management: Pat Finch, Executive Director; Donald Portnoy, Music Director
Paid Staff: 3
Paid Artists: 75
Utilizes: Guest Conductors; Guest Artists; Guest Directors
Budget: $100,000 - $500,000
Income Sources: Private Foundations/Grants/Endowments; Business/Corporate Donations; Box Office; Government Grants; Individual Donations
Season: September - April   **Annual Attendance:** 5,000
Performance Facilities: Augusta College Performing Arts Theater

VOCAL MUSIC

AUGUSTA OPERA ASSOCIATION
PO Box 3865, Hill Station, Augusta, GA 30904
(706) 826-4710
FAX: (706) 826-4732
Founded: 1967
Arts Area: Grand Opera; Lyric Opera; Light Opera; Operetta
Status: Professional
Type: Performing; Resident; Educational
Purpose: To present operas of young American artists to be performed in English
Management: Edward Bradberry, General Director; Cynthia Hunsucker, Director of Devlopment; Thomas Turner, Director of Marketing; Nancy Gleason, Administrative Assistant
Officers: Dennis G. Sodomka, President; Robert D. Huntley Jr., Treasurer; Stan Marinoff, Secretary
Paid Staff: 4
Paid Artists: 35   **Non-Paid Artists:** 35
Utilizes: Special Technical Talent; Guest Conductors; Guest Artists; Guest Directors
Budget: $500,000 - $1,000,000
Income Sources: Private Foundations/Grants/Endowments; Business/Corporate Donations; Box Office; Government Grants; Individual Donations
Season: September - May   **Annual Attendance:** 21,000
Affiliations: Augusta Symphony and Ballet
Performance Facilities: Imperial Theater

THEATRE

AUGUSTA PLAYERS
PO Box 3541, Augusta, GA 30914
(706) 826-4707
Founded: 1945
Arts Area: Theatrical Group
Status: Non-Professional; Non-Profit
Type: Performing; Educational
Management: Jay Willis, Executive Director
Officers: Helen Symms, President, Board of Trustees, Business and Professional Alliance; Ingrid Titus, President, Board of Directors, Theatre Guild
Paid Staff: 3   **Volunteer Staff:** 30
Non-Paid Artists: 400
Utilizes: Special Technical Talent
Budget: $100,000 - $500,000
Income Sources: Private Foundations/Grants/Endowments; Business/Corporate Donations; Box Office; Government Grants; Individual Donations
Season: 52 Weeks   **Annual Attendance:** 7,000
Affiliations: Georgia Theatre Conference; SETC

FACILITY

AUGUSTA/RICHMOND COUNTY CIVIC CENTER COMPLEX - ARENA
601 Seventh Street, Augusta, GA 30901
(706) 722-3521
Type of Facility: Civic Center; Arena
Type of Stage: Flexible; Platform
Seating Capacity: 8,500
Year Built: 1979   **Architect:** I.M. Pei and Partners   **Cost:** $13,700,000
Contact for Rental: Larry Rogers
The Complex also contains a 14,070 square foot Exhibit Hall & Meeting Rooms

IMPERIAL THEATRE
745 Broad Street, Augusta, GA 30903
(706) 722-8290
Founded: 1990
Type of Facility: Concert Hall; Auditorium; Theatre House
Facility Originally: Vaudeville; Movie House
Type of Stage: Proscenium; Orchestra Pit holds 30 and percussion
Stage Dimensions: 36'Wx39'D   **Orchestra Pit**
Seating Capacity: 860
Year Built: 1917   **Architect:** Lloyd Preacher and Howard
Contact for Rental: M.S. Easterbrook;   (706) 722-8293

Cedartown

FACILITY

CEDARTOWN CIVIC AUDITORIUM
205 East Avenue, Cedartown, GA 30125
(706) 748-3220
FAX: (706) 748-8962
Founded: 1974
Type of Facility: Auditorium
Type of Stage: Thrust; Proscenium
Stage Dimensions: 58'9"Wx36'2"Dx40'W'; 11'6" thrust
Seating Capacity: 1,012
Year Built: 1974
Contact for Rental: Kristy R. Hughes;   (706) 748-3220

Columbus

INSTRUMENTAL MUSIC

COLUMBUS SYMPHONY ORCHESTRA
PO Box 5361, Columbus, GA 31906
(706) 323-5059
Founded: 1855
Arts Area: Symphony
Status: Semi-Professional
Type: Performing; Touring; Resident; Educational; Sponsoring
Purpose: To provide good music to this area
Management: Susan Lagg, Executive Director
Officers: David C. Colby, Board President
Paid Staff: 7
Paid Artists: 75   **Non-Paid Artists:** 1
Utilizes: Guest Conductors; Guest Artists
Budget: $100,000 - $500,000
Income Sources: Private Foundations/Grants/Endowments; Business/Corporate Donations; Box Office; Government Grants; Individual Donations
Season: October - May   **Annual Attendance:** 50,000
Affiliations: ASOL
Performance Facilities: Three Arts Theatre

THEATRE

SPRINGER OPERA HOUSE/THE STATE THEATER OF GEORGIA
103 Tenth Street, Columbus, GA 31902
(706) 324-1100
>   **Founded:** 1961
>   **Arts Area:** Community; Theatrical Group
>   **Status:** Semi-Professional; Non-Profit
>   **Type:** Performing; Touring; Producing
>   **Purpose:** To offer high quality productions to the Southeast United States as the Official State Theatre of Georgia
>   **Management:** Paul R. Pierce, Managing & Artistic Director
>   **Officers:** Tom Austin, President of Board
>   **Paid Staff:** 4   **Volunteer Staff:** 200
>   **Paid Artists:** 6   **Non-Paid Artists:** 4
>   **Utilizes:** Special Technical Talent; Guest Artists; Guest Directors
>   **Budget:** $100,000 - $500,000
>   **Income Sources:** Private Foundations/Grants/Endowments; Business/Corporate Donations; Box Office; Individual Donations
>   **Season:** September - June   **Annual Attendance:** 20,000
>   **Affiliations:** Georgia Theatre Conference; SETC; League of Historic American Theatres
>   **Performance Facilities:** Springer Opera House

PERFORMING SERIES

SOUTHEASTERN MUSIC CENTER
PO Box 8348, Columbus, GA 31908-8348
(706) 568-2465
>   **Founded:** 1983
>   **Arts Area:** Instrumental Music
>   **Status:** Non-Profit
>   **Type:** Performing; Resident; Educational
>   **Purpose:** To present a four week chamber and orchestra music festival where students study with leading artists in their field
>   **Management:** William Bullock, Executive Director; Sharon Faust, Administrative Director; Diana Mann, Administrative Assistant
>   **Officers:** James Sigmund, Chairman; Pam White, Vice Chairman
>   **Paid Staff:** 3
>   **Paid Artists:** 14
>   **Utilizes:** Guest Conductors; Guest Artists
>   **Budget:** $50,000 - $100,000
>   **Income Sources:** Private Foundations/Grants/Endowments; Business/Corporate Donations; Box Office; Government Grants; Individual Donations
>   **Season:** July   **Annual Attendance:** 1,500

FACILITY

COLUMBUS MUNICIPAL AUDITORIUM
PO Box 1340, Columbus, GA 31902
(706) 571-5890
>   **Type of Facility:** Amphitheater
>   **Type of Stage:** Proscenium
>   **Contact for Rental:** Tony Ford;   (706) 571-5889

SPRINGER OPERA HOUSE - THE STATE THEATRE OF GEORGIA
103 Tenth Street, Columbus, GA 31902
(706) 324-5714
>   **Type of Facility:** Theatre House
>   **Facility Originally:** Hotel & Meeting Rooms
>   **Type of Stage:** Proscenium
>   **Stage Dimensions:** 32'Wx50'D   **Orchestra Pit**
>   **Seating Capacity:** 749
>   **Year Built:** 1871   **Architect:** Daniel Matthew Foley
>   **Year Remodeled:** 1965   **Architect:** Edward Neal   **Cost:** $1,300,000
>   **Acoustical Consultant:** Abe Feder
>   **Contact for Rental:** Deborah Arnette;   (706) 324-5714
>   **Manager:** Paul R. Pierce, Managing Art Director

Resident Groups: Springer Opera House; Springer Children's Theatre; Columbus Jazz Society; Springer Guild; Columbus Symphony Chamber Orchestra
The Opera House is listed on the National Register of Historic Places, a National Historic Landmark, a member of the League of Historic American Theatres and is the Official State Theater of Georgia.

THREE ARTS THEATRE
1020 Talbotton Road, Columbus, GA 31901
(706) 571-5893
> **Type of Facility:** Theatre House
> **Type of Stage:** Proscenium
> **Orchestra Pit**
> **Seating Capacity:** 1,668
> **Year Built:** 1925
> **Contact for Rental:** Steve Jackson;   (404) 571-5889

Decatur

DANCE

BEACON DANCE COMPANY
411 West Trinity Place, Decatur, GA 30030
(404) 377-6927
> **Founded:** 1952
> **Arts Area:** Modern; Ballet; Jazz
> **Status:** Semi-Professional; Non-Profit
> **Type:** Performing; Educational
> **Management:** D. Patton White, Artistic Director
> **Officers:** J. Mitchell Bowling Jr., President; Ellen Rosenthal, Secretary; Gregory N. Pierce, Treasurer
> **Paid Staff:** 1   **Volunteer Staff:** 10
> **Paid Artists:** 8   **Non-Paid Artists:** 14
> **Utilizes:** Special Technical Talent; Guest Artists
> **Budget:** $1,000 - $50,000
> **Income Sources:** Private Foundations/Grants/Endowments; Business/Corporate Donations; Box Office; Government Grants; Individual Donations
> **Season:** September - May

VOCAL MUSIC

YOUNG SINGERS OF CALLANWOLDE, INC.
315 West Ponce de Leon Avenue, Suite 915, Decatur, GA 30030
(404) 377-6081
> **Founded:** 1975
> **Arts Area:** Choral
> **Status:** Non-Profit
> **Type:** Performing; Touring; Educational
> **Purpose:** To provide an auditioned children's choir (grades 3-9) based on sound musicianship, vocal training and personal development; credo is "service and growth through singing"
> **Management:** Stephen J. Ortlip, Founder/Musical Director; Jo Ivey, Executive Director; William E. Krape, Accompanist; Doris Ortlip, Instructor; Ellis McIntyre, Financial Secretary
> **Officers:** Leamon R. Scott, President of Board of Directors; Dona Drake, Secretary Board of Directors; Alvin H. Hart, Treasurer Board of Directors
> **Paid Staff:** 5   **Volunteer Staff:** 100
> **Utilizes:** Guest Artists
> **Budget:** $100,000 - $500,000
> **Income Sources:** Private Foundations/Grants/Endowments; Business/Corporate Donations; Box Office; Government Grants; Individual Donations; Tuition
> **Season:** September - May   **Annual Attendance:** 50,000
> **Affiliations:** School of Music, Georgia State University

THEATRE

NEIGHBORHOOD PLAYHOUSE
430 West Trinity Place, Decatur, GA 30030
(404) 373-3904; (404) 373-5311
> **Founded:** 1980
> **Arts Area:** Professional; Theatrical Group
> **Status:** Semi-Professional; Non-Profit
> **Type:** Performing

Purpose: To provide professional quality theatre designed to entertain, educate and challenge our community
Management: Sondra A. Nelson, Artistic/Executive Director; Ken Anderson, Marketing Director; John David Williams, Operations Manager
Officers: Cary Jackson, Secretary; Barry West, Treasurer
Paid Staff: 3   **Volunteer Staff:** 50
Paid Artists: 200
Utilizes: Special Technical Talent; Guest Artists; Guest Directors
Budget: $100,000 - $500,000
Income Sources: Private Foundations/Grants/Endowments; Business/Corporate Donations; Box Office; Government Grants; Individual Donations
Season: 52 Weeks   **Annual Attendance:** 25,000
Affiliations: SETC; Atlanta Theatre Coalition; Atlanta Chamber of Commerce; Decatur Business Association; DeKalb Chamber of Commerce

THE PICCADILLY PUPPETS COMPANY
621 Densley Drive, Decatur, GA 30033
(404) 636-0022
Founded: 1970
Arts Area: Professional; Puppet
Status: Professional
Type: Performing; Touring; Educational
Purpose: Puppet theatre for children, mostly educational programs
Management: Carol Daniel, Manager
Officers: Dr. Pat Penn, President; Carol Daniel, Secretary/Treasurer
Paid Staff: 1   **Volunteer Staff:** 2
Paid Artists: 5
Budget: $50,000 - $100,000
Income Sources: Private Foundations/Grants/Endowments; Government Grants; Individual Donations
Season: 52 Weeks   **Annual Attendance:** 75,000

FACILITY

GAINES CHAPEL - AGNES SCOTT COLLEGE
Agnes Scott College, Decatur, GA 30030
(404) 371-6000
FAX: (404) 371-6177
Founded: 1889
Type of Facility: Concert Hall; Auditorium; Theatre House
Type of Stage: Proscenium
Stage Dimensions: 32'x28'
Seating Capacity: 825
Year Built: 1940   **Cost:** $275,000
Year Remodeled: 1989
Contact for Rental: Campus Events and Conferences;   (404) 371-6408

Gainesville

DANCE

THE GAINESVILLE BALLET
PO Box 1663, Gainesville, GA 30503
(706) 532-4241
Founded: 1974
Arts Area: Modern; Ballet; Jazz
Status: Non-Professional; Non-Profit
Type: Performing; Educational; Sponsoring
Purpose: To further the cause of dance artistry in northeast Georgia through productions of classical, neoclassical, jazz and modern dance
Management: Diane Callahan, Artistic Director; Victoria Burke, Managing Director
Officers: Anne Gress, President
Paid Staff: 5   **Volunteer Staff:** 30
Paid Artists: 8   **Non-Paid Artists:** 35
Utilizes: Special Technical Talent; Guest Artists
Budget: $100,000 - $500,000
Income Sources: Private Foundations/Grants/Endowments; Business/Corporate Donations; Box Office; Government Grants; Individual Donations
Season: August - May   **Annual Attendance:** 7,000

Affiliations: Dance Coalition of Metro Atlanta; SERBA
Performance Facilities: Pearce Auditorium

INSTRUMENTAL MUSIC

THE GAINESVILLE SYMPHONY ORCHESTRA
PO Box 162, Gainesville, GA 30503
(706) 532-5727
    Founded: 1982
    Arts Area: Symphony
    Status: Semi-Professional; Non-Profit
    Type: Performing
    Purpose: To provide performances of orchestral music in the Northeast Georgia Area
    Management: Nancy Jacob, Executive Director; Mary Alice Swope, Personnel Manager
    Paid Staff: 1 **Volunteer Staff:** 2
    Paid Artists: 50 **Non-Paid Artists:** 5
    Budget: $50,000 - $100,000
    Income Sources: Private Foundations/Grants/Endowments; Business/Corporate Donations; Box Office; Government Grants; Individual Donations
    Season: November - April **Annual Attendance:** 1,300
    Affiliations: ASOL
    Performance Facilities: Pearce Auditorium, Brenau College

Jekyll Island

FACILITY

JEKYLL ISLAND AMPHITHEATER
Stable Road, Jekyll Island, GA 31527
(912) 333-5820
    Type of Facility: Amphitheater
    Type of Stage: Proscenium
    Stage Dimensions: 100'Wx40'D
    Seating Capacity: 1,600
    Year Built: 1972 **Architect:** Bull & Kinney **Cost:** $250,000
    Contact for Rental: Jekyll Island Authority; (912) 635-2236
    Resident Groups: Jekyll Island Musical Theatre Festival

Macon

INSTRUMENTAL MUSIC

MACON SYMPHONY ORCHESTRA, INCORPORATED
PO Box 5700, Macon, GA 31208
(912) 474-5700
FAX: (912) 477-6146
    Arts Area: Orchestra
    Status: Professional; Non-Profit
    Type: Performing; Resident; Educational
    Purpose: To provide live quality classical music for the enjoyment of the community; to encourage the appreciation of music through educational programs
    Management: Doris Wood, Development Director; Brenda Lipman, General Manager; Adrian Gnam, Music Director/Conductor
    Officers: Ted S. Alexander, President of the Board
    Budget: $100,000 - $500,000
    Income Sources: Private Foundations/Grants/Endowments; Business/Corporate Donations; Box Office; Government Grants; Individual Donations
    Performance Facilities: Porter Auditorium, Wesleyan College

FACILITY

GRAND OPERA HOUSE
651 Mulberry Street, Macon, GA 31201
(912) 749-6580
    Type of Facility: Opera House
    Type of Stage: Proscenium
    Stage Dimensions: 90'Wx58'D; 37'W proscenium opening **Orchestra Pit**

Seating Capacity: 1057
Year Built: 1884   **Cost:** $75,000
Year Remodeled: 1970   **Architect:** Ella Mae Ellis League   **Cost:** $300,000
Contact for Rental: Bill Preissner;   (912) 749-6580
National Register of Historic Places; charter member, League of Historic American Theatres

WESLEYAN COLLEGE - PORTER AUDITORIUM
4760 Forsyth Road, Macon, GA 31297
(912) 477-1110
FAX: (912) 477-7572
    Type of Facility: Theatre Complex; Concert Hall; Auditorium; Theatre House
    Type of Stage: Proscenium
    Stage Dimensions: 40'Wx27'5"D   **Orchestra Pit**
    Seating Capacity: 1,124
    Year Built: 1955
    Contact for Rental: Frances Van Horn;   (912) 477-1110

Madison

FACILITY

MADISON - MORGAN CULTURAL CENTER
434 South Main Street, Madison, GA 30650
(706) 342-4743
    Founded: 1976
    Type of Facility: Auditorium
    Facility Originally: School
    Type of Stage: Proscenium
    Stage Dimensions: 26'x25' stage; 72'x67' auditorium
    Seating Capacity: 395
    Year Built: 1895   **Cost:** $15,000
    Year Remodeled: 1975   **Cost:** $450,000
    Acoustical Consultant: Magnum Companies
    Contact for Rental: Office;   (706) 342-4745

Marietta

DANCE

JAZZ DANCE THEATRE SOUTH
3218 Rimrock Drive, Marietta, GA 30066
(404) 425-1208; (404) 971-1109
    Founded: 1986
    Arts Area: Jazz
    Status: Professional
    Type: Performing; Touring; Resident; Educational
    Purpose: To educate in jazz dance through performances, classes and lecture demonstrations
    Management: Marcus R. Alford, Artistic Director
    Paid Staff: 1   **Volunteer Staff:** 3
    Paid Artists: 7
    Utilizes: Special Technical Talent; Guest Choreographers
    Budget: $100,000 - $500,000
    Income Sources: Private Foundations/Grants/Endowments; Box Office
    Season: 52 Weeks
    Performance Facilities: Cobb County Civic Center

THEATRE

PARENTHESIS THEATRE CLUB
4336 Highborne Drive, Marietta, GA 30066
(404) 977-8340
    Founded: 1991
    Arts Area: Dinner; Theatrical Group
    Status: Semi-Professional
    Type: Performing; Resident
    Purpose: To produce socially relevant ten minute plays and one acts with emphasis on original work
    Management: Gregory Blum, Artistic Director; Darrell Wofford, Producing Director

Paid Staff: 9
Paid Artists: 9
Utilizes: Guest Artists
Budget: $1,000 - $50,000
Income Sources: Box Office
Season: 52 Weeks   **Annual Attendance:** 4,000
Performance Facilities: Cabaret Space

THEATRE IN THE SQUARE
11 Whitlock Avenue, Marietta, GA 30064
(404) 422-8369
Founded: 1982
Arts Area: Theatrical Group
Status: Professional
Type: Performing; Touring
Purpose: To present a full variety of live theatre, and provide exciting material and good conditions for theatre professionals to work
Management: Michael W. Horne, Producing Director; Palmer D. Wells, Managing Director
Officers: Cherry Spencer-Stark, Chair
Paid Staff: 5   **Volunteer Staff:** 30
Utilizes: Special Technical Talent; Guest Artists; Guest Directors
Budget: $100,000 - $500,000
Income Sources: Private Foundations/Grants/Endowments; Business/Corporate Donations; Box Office; Government Grants; Individual Donations
Season: 52 Weeks   **Annual Attendance:** 40,000
Performance Facilities: Theatre in the Square

FACILITY

COBB COUNTY CIVIC CENTER
548 South Marietta Parkway, Marietta, GA 30060
(404) 528-8450
FAX: (404) 528-8457
Type of Facility: Civic Center
Year Built: 1975   **Architect:** Cleveland Cail & William Tapp   **Cost:** $3,500,000
Contact for Rental: Bob Ash;   (404) 528-8450
Manager: Liz Fields
The Cobb County Civic Center contains the Jennie T. Anderson Theater and Romeo Hudgins Memorial Hall. See individual listings for more information.

COBB COUNTY CIVIC CENTER - JENNIE T. ANDERSON THEATER
548 South Marietta Parkway, Marietta, GA 30060
(404) 528-8450
FAX: (404) 528-8457
Type of Facility: Concert Hall; Theatre House
Type of Stage: Proscenium; Modified Apron Proscenium
Stage Dimensions: 84'Wx35'D; 50'Wx22'H proscenium opening   **Orchestra Pit**
Seating Capacity: 570
Year Built: 1975
Contact for Rental: Bob Ash;   (404) 404-5280
Manager: Liz Fields

COBB COUNTY CIVIC CENTER - ROMEO HUDGINS MEMORIAL HALL
548 South Marietta Parkway, Marietta, GA 30060
(404) 528-8450
FAX: (404) 528-8457
Type of Facility: Auditorium; Civic Center; Arena; Multi-Purpose
Type of Stage: Flexible
Stage Dimensions: 42'x32'x20'
Seating Capacity: 3,700
Year Built: 1975
Year Remodeled: 1977   **Cost:** $24,000
Contact for Rental: Bob Ash;   (404) 528-8450
Manager: Liz Field

THEATRE IN THE SQUARE
11 Whitlock Avenue, Marietta, GA 30064
(404) 422-8369
FAX: (404) 424-2637
Type of Facility: Theatre House
Facility Originally: Warehouse
Type of Stage: Proscenium
Stage Dimensions: 32'Wx21'D
Seating Capacity: 160
Year Built: 1930
Year Remodeled: 1982   **Architect:** Bill Chegmidden   **Cost:** $65,000
Acoustical Consultant: Warren Short
Contact for Rental: Michael Horne or Palmer Wells;   (404) 422-8369
Resident Groups: Theatre in the Square
Dance recitals; chamber music; comedy; one-person shows

Perry

THEATRE

PERRY PLAYERS, INC.
PO Box 143, Perry, GA 31069
(912) 987-5354
Founded: 1982
Arts Area: Musical; Community; Theatrical Group
Status: Non-Professional; Non-Profit
Purpose: We offer high-quality entertainment and cultural activities to the citizens of middle Georgia; individuals who enjoy acting, singing, dancing and producing cultural entertainment share and improve these skills in a welcoming environment of cooperation and enthusiasm
Officers: Dennis Hooper, President; D. Shawn Kitrell, Vice President; Carol Howard, Secretary; Cathy Stanley, Treasurer
Volunteer Staff: 15
Non-Paid Artists: 30
Utilizes: Special Technical Talent; Guest Artists; Guest Directors
Budget: $1,000 - $50,000
Income Sources: Private Foundations/Grants/Endowments; Business/Corporate Donations; Box Office; Government Grants; Individual Donations
Season: 52 Weeks   **Annual Attendance:** 2,500
Affiliations: Houston County Arts Alliance; Macon Arts Alliance; Perry Chamber of Commerce

Rome

FACILITY

ROME CITY AUDITORIUM
601 Broad Street, Rome, GA 30161
(706) 236-4416
FAX: (706) 236-4549
Type of Facility: Auditorium; Theatre House; Opera House
Type of Stage: Proscenium
Stage Dimensions: 34'8"Dx54'3"L total size including wings; 35'11"x28'4" stage only
Seating Capacity: 1,112
Year Built: 1916   **Architect:** A. Ted Eych Brown   **Cost:** $140,000
Year Remodeled: 1989   **Architect:** Jack McGuffie   **Cost:** $1,200,000
Contact for Rental: Linda Davis;   (706) 236-4416

Savannah

INSTRUMENTAL MUSIC

SAVANNAH SYMPHONY
PO Box 9505, Savannah, GA 31412
(706) 236-9536
Founded: 1953
Arts Area: Symphony; Orchestra; Chamber; Ensemble
Status: Professional; Non-Profit
Type: Performing

Purpose: To provide a wide range of orchestra repertoire in high-quality performances to all segments of our market area; to provide a wide range of educational activities for school-aged and adult members of the community
Management: Gregg Gustafson, General Manager; Katie O'Grady, Marketing Director; Phillip Greenberg, Music Director/Conductor; Laura Hibberts, Development Director; George Council, Operations Manager
Officers: Barbara Murphy, President; Pamela H. Young, Secretary
Paid Staff: 10   **Volunteer Staff:** 500
Paid Artists: 75
Utilizes: Guest Artists
Budget: $500,000 - $1,000,000
Income Sources: Private Foundations/Grants/Endowments; Business/Corporate Donations; Box Office; Government Grants; Individual Donations
Season: September - May   **Annual Attendance:** 50,000
Affiliations: ASOL
Performance Facilities: Savannah Civic Center Theatre

FACILITY

ARMSTRONG STATE COLLEGE FINE ARTS AUDITORIUM
11935 Abercorn Street, Savannah, GA 31419
(912) 927-5329
FAX: (912) 921-5472
Founded: 1975
Type of Facility: Auditorium
Type of Stage: Thrust; Proscenium
Stage Dimensions: 60'x40'
Seating Capacity: 998
Year Built: 1975   **Cost:** $1,800,000
Contact for Rental: Judy Grizzard;   (912) 927-5329
Resident Groups: Armstrong State College: Chorus; Jazz Band; Community Orchestra

SAVANNAH CIVIC CENTER
Montgomery at Liberty, PO Box 726, Savannah, GA 31402
(912) 651-6550
FAX: (912) 651-6552
Type of Facility: Theatre House; Civic Center; Arena; Multi-Purpose
Seating Capacity: 9,600; 2,566
Year Built: 1971   **Cost:** $10,000,000
Acoustical Consultant: Jaffe Acoustics
Contact for Rental: Cynthia Brinson;   (912) 651-6553
Manager: John Lutz, Manager;   (912) 651-6551
Resident Groups: Savannah Symphony Orchestra; Ballet South
The Savannah Civic Center contains the Arena and Theatre. See separate listings for additional information.

SAVANNAH CIVIC CENTER - ARENA
Montgomery at Liberty, PO Box 726, Savannah, GA 31402
(912) 651-6550
FAX: (912) 651-6552
Type of Facility: Arena
Type of Stage: Arena
Seating Capacity: 9,600
Year Built: 1971
Contact for Rental: Cynthia Brinson or John Lutz;   (912) 651-6553
Manager: John Lutz;   (912) 651-6551

SAVANNAH CIVIC CENTER - THEATRE
Montgomery at Liberty, PO Box 726, Savannah, GA 31402
(912) 651-6550
FAX: (912) 651-6552
Type of Facility: Theatre House
Type of Stage: Proscenium
Stage Dimensions: 60'Wx30'D   **Orchestra Pit**
Seating Capacity: 2,566
Year Built: 1971
Contact for Rental: Cynthia Brinson or John Lutz;   (912) 651-6553
Manager: John Lutz;   (912) 651-6551

Sea Island

PERFORMING SERIES

GOLDEN ISLES CHAMBER MUSIC FESTIVAL, INC.
PO Box 1202, Sea Island, GA 31561
(706) 663-4631
Founded: 1988
Arts Area: Instrumental Music
Status: Professional
Type: Performing; Educational
Purpose: To perform the highest quality chamber music
Officers: Susan L. Walters, Musical Director; Jeffrey Moore, Artistic Director
Volunteer Staff: 5
Paid Artists: 13
Utilizes: Guest Artists
Budget: $1,000 - $50,000
Income Sources: Private Foundations/Grants/Endowments; Business/Corporate Donations; Box Office; Government Grants; Individual Donations
Season: May   **Annual Attendance:** 500

Statesboro

FACILITY

GEORGIA SOUTHERN UNIVERSITY - FOY FINE ARTS RECITAL HALL
Department of Music - LB8052, Statesboro, GA 30460
(912) 681-5396
Type of Facility: Concert Hall; Performance Center
Type of Stage: Proscenium
Seating Capacity: 340
Year Built: 1967   **Architect:** Aeck & Associates   **Cost:** $1,250,000
Acoustical Consultant: Bolt, Beranek & Newman
Contact for Rental: Lissa Addington;   (912) 681-5396
Resident Groups: GSU/Music Department

GEORGIA SOUTHERN UNIVERSITY - PUPPET THEATRE
PO Box 8124, Statesboro, GA 30460
(912) 681-5138
Type of Facility: Theatre House
Facility Originally: Skating Rink
Type of Stage: Flexible
Seating Capacity: 100
Year Built: 1972
Year Remodeled: 1985
Contact for Rental: Facilities Office;   (912) 681-5666
Resident Groups: Statesboro/GSU Puppetry Guild

Thomaston

PERFORMING SERIES

THOMASTON-UPSON ARTS COUNCIL
201 South Center Street, PO Box 211, Thomaston, GA 30286
(706) 647-1605
Founded: 1986
Arts Area: Dance; Vocal Music; Instrumental Music; Theater
Status: Non-Profit
Type: Performing; Educational; Sponsoring
Paid Staff: 2
Budget: $50,000 - $100,000
Income Sources: Private Foundations/Grants/Endowments; Business/Corporate Donations; Box Office; Government Grants; Individual Donations

---
Thomasville

FACILITY

THOMASVILLE CULTURAL CENTER AUDITORIUM
c/o Thomasville Entertainment Foundation, 600 East Washington Street, Thomasville, GA 31792
(706) 226-0588
  Type of Facility: Auditorium
  Facility Originally: School
  Type of Stage: Proscenium
  Seating Capacity: 550
  Year Built: 1915   **Architect:** Frank Galliher   **Cost:** $50,000
  Year Remodeled: 1986   **Architect:** Sibley Jennings   **Cost:** $3,300,000
  Contact for Rental: (912) 226-0588

Toccoa

INSTRUMENTAL MUSIC

TOCCOA SYMPHONY ORCHESTRA GUILD
PO Box 532, Toccoa, GA 30577
(706) 886-6551
  Founded: 1977
  Arts Area: Symphony
  Status: Semi-Professional; Non-Profit
  Type: Performing; Educational
  Purpose: To promote good symphonic music in our community; to educate our youth to perform with artists
  Management: Dr. Archie Sharretts, Conductor; Mrs. Pinkie Ware, Personnel Manager; Bob Tresly, General Manager
  Officers: Dr. Paul Nichols, President; Toccoa Symphony Orchestra Guild, Board of Managers
  Paid Staff: 25   **Volunteer Staff:** 45
  Paid Artists: 25   **Non-Paid Artists:** 45
  Utilizes: Guest Conductors; Guest Artists; Guest Directors
  Budget: $1,000 - $50,000
  Income Sources: Private Foundations/Grants/Endowments; Business/Corporate Donations; Box Office; Government Grants; Individual Donations
  Season: December - April   **Annual Attendance:** 1,500
  Affiliations: Georgia Arts Council
  Performance Facilities: Georgia Baptist Assembly and Theater

---
Valdosta

THEATRE

JEKYLL ISLAND MUSICAL THEATRE FESTIVAL
Department of Communication Arts, Valdosta, GA 31698
(912) 333-5820
FAX: (912) 333-7408
  Founded: 1990
  Arts Area: Professional; Summer Stock; Musical
  Status: Professional; Non-Profit
  Type: Performing; Touring
  Purpose: To provide high-quality musical theatre for residents of and visitors to Georgia's Golden Isles; to provide professional training to college interns
  Management: Victoria Pennington, Production Supervisor; Robert B. Welch, Dean, School of the Arts
  Officers: Paul Salter, Chairman
  Paid Staff: 14
  Paid Artists: 44
  Utilizes: Special Technical Talent; Guest Directors; Guest Designers
  Budget: $100,000 - $500,000
  Income Sources: Private Foundations/Grants/Endowments; Business/Corporate Donations; Box Office; Government Grants; Individual Donations
  Season: June - August   **Annual Attendance:** 20,000
  Affiliations: Valdosta State College
  Performance Facilities: Jekyll Island Amphitheater

FACILITY

VALDOSTA STATE COLLEGE - SAWYER THEATRE
Fine Arts Building, Valdosta, GA 31698
(912) 333-5820
       Type of Facility: Theatre House
       Type of Stage: Proscenium
       Seating Capacity: 250
       Year Built: 1969 **Architect:** Zeb Lackey
       Contact for Rental: (912) 333-5820
       Manager: Dr. Robert B. Welch

VALDOSTA STATE COLLEGE - WHITEHEAD AUDITORIUM
Fine Arts Building, Valdosta, GA 31698
(912) 333-5816
       Type of Facility: Theatre Complex; Concert Hall; Auditorium; Outdoor (Concert); Theatre House; Amphitheater
       Type of Stage: Proscenium
       Stage Dimensions: 60'Wx40'D **Orchestra Pit**
       Seating Capacity: 900
       Year Built: 1969 **Architect:** Zeb Lackey **Cost:** $2,500,000
       Contact for Rental: Dr. Robert B. Welch; (912) 333-2150

HAWAII

Fort Shafter

THEATRE

ARMY ENTERTAINMENT PROGRAM
USASCH, DPCA, CRD, CSDAB, Entertainment Section, Fort Shafter, HI 96858-5000
(808) 438-1980
FAX: (808) 438-1980
>**Founded:** 1949
>**Arts Area:** Musical; Community; Theatrical Group
>**Status:** Non-Professional; Non-Profit
>**Type:** Performing; Resident; Educational
>**Purpose:** The goals of the Army Entertainment Program are to provide interested individuals with a constructive outlet for talents, to maintain a high level of morals and to promote good cultural relations with the local civilian community.
>**Management:** Vanita Rae Smith, Chief, Army Entertainment; Tom Giza, Technical Director
>**Paid Staff:** 2 **Volunteer Staff:** 2
>**Non-Paid Artists:** 30
>**Utilizes:** Special Technical Talent; Guest Conductors; Guest Directors
>**Budget:** $100,000 - $500,000
>**Income Sources:** Private Foundations/Grants/Endowments; Business/Corporate Donations; Box Office; Government Grants; Individual Donations
>**Season:** 52 Weeks
>**Affiliations:** AACT; Hawaii State Theatre Council
>**Performance Facilities:** Richardson Performing Arts Center

Hilo

INSTRUMENTAL MUSIC

HAWAII CONCERT SOCIETY
PO Box 233, Hilo, HI 96721
(808) 935-5831
>**Founded:** 1956
>**Arts Area:** Symphony; Orchestra; Chamber; Ensemble; Instrumental Group
>**Status:** Non-Profit
>**Type:** Sponsoring
>**Purpose:** To provide quality classical music to east Hawaii (the Island of Hawaii), performed by professional musicians
>**Officers:** Tom Geballe, President; Ray Boyea, First Vice President; Judith Wakely, Second Vice President; Bob Fuhrel, Secretary; Emily Spargo-Guerrero, Treasurer
>**Volunteer Staff:** 14
>**Utilizes:** Guest Artists
>**Budget:** $1,000 - $50,000
>**Income Sources:** Business/Corporate Donations; Box Office; Government Grants; Individual Donations
>**Season:** September - April **Annual Attendance:** 2,500
>**Affiliations:** Hawaii Association of Music Societies
>**Performance Facilities:** Hilo Theatre, University of Hawaii

THEATRE

HILO COMMUNITY PLAYERS
141 Kalakaua Street, Hilo, HI 96720
(808) 935-9155
>**Mailing Address:** PO Box 46, Hilo, HI 96721
>**Founded:** 1938
>**Arts Area:** Community; Theatrical Group
>**Status:** Non-Professional; Non-Profit
>**Type:** Performing; Educational
>**Purpose:** To organize, promote and conduct an educational program of amateur dramatics on the Island of Hawaii
>**Management:** Paul M. Clark, Business Manager; Peter Schickler, Equipment Manager; Sarah Hilliard, Costume Manager
>**Officers:** Michael Moore, President; Carl Moon, Treasurer
>**Paid Staff:** 3
>**Paid Artists:** 1 **Non-Paid Artists:** 100
>**Utilizes:** Guest Artists; Guest Directors
>**Budget:** $1,000 - $50,000

Income Sources: Private Foundations/Grants/Endowments; Box Office; Government Grants; Individual Donations
Season: 52 Weeks   **Annual Attendance:** 2,500

FACILITY

UNIVERSITY OF HAWAII - HILO THEATRE
523 West Lanikaula Street, Hilo, HI 96720-4091
(808) 933-3310
Type of Facility: Auditorium
Type of Stage: Proscenium
Stage Dimensions: 40'Wx27'D; 40'Wx20'H proscenium opening   **Orchestra Pit**
Seating Capacity: 600
Year Built: 1972   **Architect:** Roehrig Oncdera Kinder
Year Remodeled: 1977   **Architect:** Team Pacific
Contact for Rental: Larry Joseph;   (808) 933-3310
Resident Groups: University of Hawaii at Hilo Performing Arts (Drama/Dance/Music)

Honolulu

DANCE

DANCES WE DANCE
PO Box 22657, Honolulu, HI 96823-2657
(808) 537-2152
FAX: (808) 537-2152
Founded: 1971
Arts Area: Modern; Ballet
Status: Professional; Non-Profit
Type: Performing; Touring; Resident; Educational; Sponsoring
Purpose: To further the appreciation and understanding of dance through cultural and educational services, which include sponsoring performances, Artists-in-the-Schools programs, workshops, professional training, and video projects
Management: Betty Jones, Executive Director; Fritz Ludin, Artistic Director
Officers: Betty Ona, President; Lou Ann Guanson, Vice President; Mary Jo Freshley, Secretary; Denise Miyahana, Treasurer
Paid Staff: 2
Paid Artists: 2
Utilizes: Special Technical Talent; Guest Artists; Guest Choreographers
Budget: $50,000 - $100,000
Income Sources: Private Foundations/Grants/Endowments; Box Office; Government Grants; Individual Donations
Season: 52 Weeks   **Annual Attendance:** 10,000
Affiliations: Artists-in-the-Schools; Hawaii Alliance for Arts in Education
Performance Facilities: Dance Studio

HAWAII STATE BALLET
1418 Copulani Boulevard, Honolulu, HI 96814
(808) 947-2755
Arts Area: Ballet
Status: Professional; Non-Profit
Type: Touring; Resident
Management: John Landovsky, Artistic Director; Gina Surles, Company Manager
Paid Artists: 8
Income Sources: Box Office; Individual Donations

INSTRUMENTAL MUSIC

CHAMBER MUSIC HAWAII
PO Box 61939, Honolulu, HI 96839
(808) 947-1975
FAX: (808) 947-2047
Arts Area: Chamber; Ensemble
Status: Professional; Non-Profit
Type: Presenting
Purpose: To support resident chamber music ensembles and thereby provide chamber music to the people of Hawaii
Management: Amy Walters, Executive Director
Officers: Emery Grantham, Chairman of the Board
Budget: $100,000 - $500,000

Income Sources: Private Foundations/Grants/Endowments; Business/Corporate Donations; Box Office; Government Grants; Individual Donations

HAWAII CHAMBER ORCHESTRA

3810 Maunaloa Avenue, Honolulu, HI 98616

(808) 734-0397

Founded: 1967
Arts Area: Chamber; Ensemble; Opera
Status: Professional; Non-Profit
Type: Performing; Educational
Purpose: To interest the audience in classical music
Management: Herbert Ward, Music Director; Jacqueline Ward, General Manager/Opera Director
Officers: Dorothy Buscemi, President; Henry Klein, Secretary/Treasurer
Budget: $1,000 - $50,000
Season: 52 Weeks

HAWAII YOUTH SYMPHONY ASSOCIATION

1100 University Avenue, Suite 202, Honolulu, HI 96826

(808) 941-9706

FAX: (808) 941-4995

Founded: 1968
Arts Area: Symphony; Orchestra
Status: Non-Profit
Type: Performing; Educational
Purpose: To encourage educational and artistic development of student musicians
Management: Henry Miyamura, Music Director; Michael Nakasone, Director, Concert Orchestra; Louise Ching, Director, String Classes
Officers: F. Robert Springer, President; Leslie Murata, Vice President; Alan Emura, Secretary; Lanny Williams, Treasurer
Paid Staff: 7   **Volunteer Staff:** 50
Paid Artists: 4
Utilizes: Special Technical Talent; Guest Artists
Budget: $100,000 - $500,000
Income Sources: Private Foundations/Grants/Endowments; Business/Corporate Donations; Box Office; Government Grants; Individual Donations
Season: September - May   **Annual Attendance:** 12,500
Performance Facilities: Neal S. Blaisdell Center Concert Hall

HONOLULU SYMPHONY SOCIETY

1441 Kapiolani Boulevard, Suite 1515, Honolulu, HI 96814

(808) 942-2200

Founded: 1901
Arts Area: Symphony; Orchestra; Ensemble
Status: Professional; Non-Profit
Type: Performing; Touring; Resident; Educational
Purpose: To bring music in concert to the citizens of Hawaii
Management: Tony H. Bechario, Executive Director
Officers: Richard Hicks, Chairman
Utilizes: Special Technical Talent; Guest Conductors; Guest Artists
Budget: $1,000,000 - $5,000,000
Income Sources: Private Foundations/Grants/Endowments; Business/Corporate Donations; Box Office; Government Grants; Individual Donations
Season: August - April
Affiliations: ASOL
Performance Facilities: Neal S. Blaisdell Center - Concert Hall; Waikiki Shell

MUSIC PROJECTS HONOLULU

905 Spencer Street, #404, Honolulu, HI 96822

(808) 531-6617

FAX: (808) 537-1818

Founded: 1979
Arts Area: Symphony; Orchestra; Chamber; Ensemble; Instrumental Group; Band
Status: Professional; Non-Profit
Type: Performing; Touring; Resident; Educational; Sponsoring
Purpose: To support and present concerts and educational programs by the musicians of the Honolulu Symphony
Management: Amy Walters, Manager; Dianne Wachsman, Publicity
Officers: Paul Barrett, President; Marsha Schweitzer, Vice President/Treasurer; Jean Harling, Secretary
Paid Staff: 2   **Volunteer Staff:** 10
Paid Artists: 60

Utilizes: Guest Conductors; Guest Artists
Budget: $50,000 - $100,000
Income Sources: Private Foundations/Grants/Endowments; Business/Corporate Donations; Box Office; Government Grants; Individual Donations; Benefits; Product Sales
Season: 52 Weeks   **Annual Attendance:** 1,000
Affiliations: Honolulu Symphony Musicians

SPRING WIND QUARTET
905 Spencer Street, #404, Honolulu, HI 96822
(808) 531-6617
Founded: 1974
Arts Area: Chamber; Ensemble; Instrumental Group
Status: Professional
Type: Performing; Touring; Resident; Educational
Purpose: To meet the performer's need to play chamber music; to provide a resident wind quartet to Hawaii
Management: Marsha Schweitzer, Bassoonist
Paid Staff: 1
Paid Artists: 5
Utilizes: Guest Artists
Budget: $1,000 - $50,000
Income Sources: Private Foundations/Grants/Endowments; Business/Corporate Donations; Box Office; Government Grants; Individual Donations
Season: August - May   **Annual Attendance:** 6,000
Affiliations: Chamber Music Hawaii
Performance Facilities: Luthern Church; Honolulu Academy of Arts

UNIVERSITY OF HAWAII AT MANOA,
COLLEGE OF CONTINUING EDUCATION AND COMMUNITY SERVICE
2530 Dole Street, Honolulu, HI 96822
(808) 956-2042
FAX: (808) 956-3364
Founded: 1907
Arts Area: Chamber; Ensemble; Ethnic; Instrumental Group; Solo
Status: Professional
Type: Sponsoring
Purpose: To present quality musical, dance, theater and special attractions throughout Hawaii, including the Honolulu Chamber Music Series
Management: Barbara Furstenberg, Director; Cheryl Kohashi, Marketing/Production Coordinator; Suzanne Shoemaker, Program Specialist; Susan Yokouchi, Secretary
Paid Staff: 4
Utilizes: Guest Artists
Budget: $100,000 - $500,000
Income Sources: Private Foundations/Grants/Endowments; Box Office; Government Grants
Season: September - May   **Annual Attendance:** 30,000
Affiliations: WAAA; APAP
Performance Facilities: Blaisdell Concert Hall; Orvis Auditorium; Kennedy Theatre

VOCAL MUSIC

HAWAII ECUMENICAL CHORALE
3752 Old Pali Road, Honolulu, HI 96817
(808) 595-3447
Founded: 1979
Arts Area: Grand Opera; Choral; Ethnic; Folk
Status: Semi-Professional; Non-Profit
Type: Performing; Resident; Educational
Purpose: To provide an opportunity for local singers to participate in more challenging music than average choirs offer; to sponsor a local choral composition contest to encourage indigenous choral work
Management: Eileen Lum, Artistic Director
Volunteer Staff: 20
Paid Artists: 4   **Non-Paid Artists:** 4
Utilizes: Special Technical Talent; Guest Conductors; Guest Artists; Guest Directors
Budget: $1,000 - $50,000
Income Sources: Private Foundations/Grants/Endowments; Government Grants; Individual Donations
Season: September - June
Affiliations: State Foundation on Culture and the Arts

HAWAII OPERA THEATRE
987 Waimanu Street, Honolulu, HI 96814
(808) 521-6537
>**Founded:** 1962
>**Arts Area:** Grand Opera
>**Status:** Professional; Non-Profit
>**Type:** Performing; Touring; Resident; Educational
>**Purpose:** To produce opera in Hawaii
>**Management:** J. Mario Ramos, General Director
>**Officers:** Peter A. Lee, President; Galen C.K. Leong, Vice President; Michael J. Meagher MD, Treasurer; Charles R. Wade, Recording Secretary; Evelyn Lance, Corresponding Secretary
>**Paid Staff:** 7   **Volunteer Staff:** 250
>**Utilizes:** Guest Conductors; Guest Artists; Guest Directors
>**Budget:** $1,000,000 - $5,000,000
>**Income Sources:** Private Foundations/Grants/Endowments; Business/Corporate Donations; Box Office; Government Grants; Individual Donations
>**Season:** January - March   **Annual Attendance:** 20,000
>**Affiliations:** OA; COS
>**Performance Facilities:** Neal S. Blaisdell Center - Concert Hall

HONOLULU CHILDREN'S OPERA CHORUS
PO Box 22304, Honolulu, HI 96822
(808) 521-2982
>**Founded:** 1961
>**Arts Area:** Grand Opera; Light Opera; Choral; Ethnic
>**Status:** Non-Profit
>**Type:** Performing; Educational
>**Purpose:** To nurture, foster and develop the performing arts through the medium of choral music; to serve as an educational and artistic resource for the state of Hawaii
>**Management:** Nola A. Nahulu, Music Director; Malla Ka'ai, Business Manager; Wendy Chang, Accompanist
>**Officers:** Diane Kurz, President; Frances Goo, First Vice President; Melody Actouka, Second Vice President; Melvin Ah Yo, Treasurer; Donna Tanimura, Recording Secretary; Kela Holt, Corresponding Secretary
>**Budget:** $1,000 - $50,000
>**Income Sources:** Private Foundations/Grants/Endowments; Individual Donations
>**Season:** September - June

THEATRE

DIAMOND HEAD THEATRE
520 Makapuu Avenue, Honolulu, HI 96816
(808) 734-8763; (808) 734-8763
FAX: (808) 735-1250
>**Founded:** 1915
>**Arts Area:** Professional; Musical; Community; Theatrical Group
>**Status:** Non-Professional; Non-Profit
>**Type:** Performing; Educational
>**Purpose:** To present plays and musicals to the community; to hold classes and workshops in acting for all ages; to offer opportunities for all persons interested to participate both on stage and backstage in theatre
>**Management:** Jim Hutchison, Artistic Director; Stan Michaels, Managing Director; Gordon Svec, Technical Director
>**Officers:** Michael Linos, Chairman of the Board; Ed Cassidy, President; Bob Brown, Secretary; David Powell, Treasurer
>**Paid Staff:** 20   **Volunteer Staff:** 350
>**Paid Artists:** 15   **Non-Paid Artists:** 400
>**Utilizes:** Guest Artists; Guest Directors
>**Budget:** $1,000,000 - $5,000,000
>**Income Sources:** Private Foundations/Grants/Endowments; Business/Corporate Donations; Box Office; Government Grants; Individual Donations
>**Season:** 52 Weeks   **Annual Attendance:** 50,000
>**Affiliations:** ACTA; USITT; Hawaii State Theatre Council
>**Performance Facilities:** Diamond Head Theatre

HONOLULU THEATRE FOR YOUTH
2846 Ualena Street, Honolulu, HI 96819-1910
(808) 839-9885
FAX: (808) 839-7018
>**Founded:** 1955
>**Arts Area:** Professional; Theatrical Group
>**Status:** Professional; Non-Profit

Type: Performing; Touring; Resident; Educational
Purpose: To produce professional theatre for a wide range of audiences in the state of Hawaii, specializing in theatre for young audiences
Management: Jane Campbell, Managing Director; Pam Sterling, Artistic Director
Officers: David M. Taylor, President, Board of Trustees; William A. Bonnet, Neil J. Hannahs, Vice Presidents; Nancy Williamson, Corporate Secretary; G. Stephen Holaday, Treasurer
Paid Staff: 19   **Volunteer Staff:** 1
Paid Artists: 24
Utilizes: Special Technical Talent; Guest Artists; Guest Directors
Budget: $1,000,000 - $5,000,000
Income Sources: Private Foundations/Grants/Endowments; Business/Corporate Donations; Box Office; Government Grants; Individual Donations
Season: 52 Weeks   **Annual Attendance:** 140,000
Affiliations: TCG; ASSITEJ; AATY

FACILITY

NEAL S. BLAISDELL CENTER
777 Ward Avenue, Honolulu, HI 96814
(808) 527-5400
   Type of Facility: Concert Hall; Auditorium; Outdoor (Concert); Studio Performance; Arena; Multi-Purpose; Room
   Year Built: 1963   **Architect:** Adrian Wilson & Associates; Merrill Simms & Roehrig   **Cost:** $8,375,600
   Acoustical Consultant: Vern Knudsen
   Contact for Rental: Carla W. Coray, Director;   (808) 527-5400
   Resident Groups: Honolulu Symphony Society; Hawaii Opera Theatre
   Blaisdell Center contains the Arena, Concert Hall and Waikiki Shell. See separate listings for additional information.

NEAL S. BLAISDELL CENTER - ARENA
777 Ward Avenue, Honolulu, HI 96814
(808) 527-5400
   Type of Facility: Arena
   Type of Stage: Arena
   Stage Dimensions: 64'Wx27'D
   Orchestra Pit
   Seating Capacity: 8,805
   Year Built: 1963
   Contact for Rental: Carla W. Coray, Director;   (808) 527-5400

NEAL S. BLAISDELL CENTER - CONCERT HALL
777 Ward Avenue, Honolulu, HI 96814
(808) 527-5400
   Type of Facility: Concert Hall
   Type of Stage: Concert Stage
   Stage Dimensions: 80'Wx40'D
   Orchestra Pit
   Seating Capacity: 2,107
   Year Built: 1963
   Contact for Rental: Carla W. Coray, Director;   (808) 527-5400

NEAL S. BLAISDELL CENTER - WAIKIKI SHELL
777 Ward Avenue, Honolulu, HI 96814
(808) 527-5400
   Type of Facility: Outdoor (Concert)
   Type of Stage: Greek
   Stage Dimensions: 88'Wx58'D
   Seating Capacity: 8,404
   Year Built: 1963   **Cost:** $8,375,600
   Contact for Rental: Carla W. Coray, Director;   (808) 527-5400

OLD FORT RUGER THEATRE
520 Makapu Avenue, Honolulu, HI 96816
(808) 734-8763
FAX: (808) 735-1250
   Type of Facility: Theatre House
   Facility Originally: Movie House; Military
   Type of Stage: Proscenium
   Stage Dimensions: 70'Wx30'D; 70'Wx30'H proscenium opening
   Seating Capacity: 500

Year Built: 1940   **Architect:** United States Army   **Cost:** $13,000
Year Remodeled: 1981
Contact for Rental: Stan Michaels, Managing Director;   (808) 734-8763
Resident Groups: Diamond Head Theatre
The theater is also known as Diamond Head Theatre

SAINT LOUIS CENTER FOR THE PERFORMING ARTS - THE MAMIYA THEATRE
3142 Waialae Avenue, Honolulu, HI 96816
(808) 739-7777
FAX: (808) 739-4853
>**Type of Facility:** Theatre Complex
>**Type of Stage:** Proscenium
>**Stage Dimensions:** 35'Wx14'5"D   **Orchestra Pit**
>**Seating Capacity:** 500
>**Year Built:** 1986   **Architect:** LMLI Architects   **Cost:** $38,000,000
>**Acoustical Consultant:** James K.C. Chang, PE
>**Contact for Rental:** David Lewis, Manager;   (808) 739-7777, ext. 821

Kahului

THEATRE

MAUI ACADEMY OF PERFORMING ARTS
107A Wahi Hoola Ha, Kahului, HI 96732
(808) 244-8760
FAX: (808) 244-8762
>**Founded:** 1974
>**Arts Area:** Community; Youth
>**Status:** Non-Profit
>**Type:** Performing; Touring; Educational
>**Purpose:** To present educational performing arts for youths and adults
>**Management:** Frances A. von Tempsky, Managing Director; David C. Johnston, Artistic Director; Stephanie Sheppard, Director of Development
>**Officers:** Joel E. August, President; Alan Yoshioka, Vice President; Linda Howlett, Secretary; Thomas Seif Ph.D., Treasurer
>**Paid Staff:** 10   **Volunteer Staff:** 250
>**Paid Artists:** 8   **Non-Paid Artists:** 200
>**Utilizes:** Guest Artists; Guest Directors
>**Budget:** $100,000 - $500,000
>**Income Sources:** Private Foundations/Grants/Endowments; Business/Corporate Donations; Box Office; Government Grants; Individual Donations
>**Season:** 52 Weeks

Kailua

THEATRE

WINDWARD THEATRE GUILD
PO Box 624, Kailua, HI 96734
(808) 254-1721
>**Founded:** 1956
>**Arts Area:** Musical; Dinner; Community; Theatrical Group
>**Status:** Non-Profit
>**Type:** Performing; Educational
>**Purpose:** To enhance and promote theatrical excellence in all phases of production
>**Management:** Charles Brockman, Manager
>**Officers:** Phil Haff, President; Alex Nishimura, Vice President; Valerie Stubblefield, Treasurer; Margaret Cox, Secretary
>**Volunteer Staff:** 110
>**Non-Paid Artists:** 60
>**Utilizes:** Special Technical Talent; Guest Artists; Guest Directors
>**Budget:** $50,000 - $100,000
>**Income Sources:** Private Foundations/Grants/Endowments; Business/Corporate Donations; Box Office; Government Grants; Individual Donations
>**Season:** October - June   **Annual Attendance:** 9,000
>**Affiliations:** Hawaii State Theatre Council; State Foundation for Culture and the Arts; Alliance for Drama Education
>**Performance Facilities:** Boondocker Theatre; Kaneohe Marine Corps Air Station

Kamuela

THEATRE

KAHILU THEATRE
Mamalahoa Highway, Parker Ranch Shopping Center, Kamuela, HI 96743
(808) 885-6017
FAX: (808) 885-0546
  Founded: 1980
  Status: Professional; Non-Profit
  Type: Performing; Sponsoring
  Purpose: To maintain a performing arts center designed to present high-quality national and international artists/groups; to produce two plays annually using local talent under the direction of a professional director
  Management: Virginia Pfaff, Managing Director
  Officers: Richard P. Smart, President; Warren Gunderson, Vice President/Treasurer; Richard Hendrick, Vice President/Secretary
  Paid Staff: 3   **Volunteer Staff:** 54
  Paid Artists: 15
  Utilizes: Guest Artists; Guest Directors
  Budget: $100,000 - $500,000
  Income Sources: Business/Corporate Donations; Box Office; Government Grants; Individual Donations
  Season: September - May   **Annual Attendance:** 10,000
  Affiliations: WAAA; APAP; ISPAA

WAIMEA COMMUNITY THEATRE
PO Box 1387, Kamuela, HI 96743
  Founded: 1965
  Arts Area: Musical; Dinner; Community; Theatrical Group
  Status: Non-Professional; Non-Profit
  Type: Performing; Educational
  Purpose: To provide quality theatrical entertainment to the north Hawaii area; to provide educational and community support services in areas related to theatrical performance
  Officers: Jay West, President; Andy Kunellis, Vice President; Kim Finke, Secretary; Michael Bray, Treasurer
  Volunteer Staff: 20
  Non-Paid Artists: 50
  Utilizes: Special Technical Talent; Guest Artists; Guest Directors
  Budget: $1,000 - $50,000
  Income Sources: Box Office; Government Grants; Individual Donations
  Season: August - June   **Annual Attendance:** 5,000
  Affiliations: Hawaii State Theatre Council
  Performance Facilities: Parker School Auditorium

Laie

FACILITY

MCKAY AUDITORIUM AT BRIGHAM YOUNG UNIVERSITY HAWAII
Brigham Young University, Laie, HI 96762
(808) 293-3903
  Founded: 1959
  Type of Facility: Auditorium
  Type of Stage: Thrust; Proscenium
  Stage Dimensions: 33'x20'x20' proscenium opening   **Orchestra Pit**
  Seating Capacity: 655
  Year Built: 1959   **Architect:** Carl Burton
  Contact for Rental: Craig Ferre;   (808) 293-3903

Wailuku

INSTRUMENTAL MUSIC

MAUI SYMPHONY ORCHESTRA
95 Mahalani Street, PO Box 788, Wailuku, HI 96793
(808) 244-5439
FAX: (808) 242-0812
  Founded: 1979
  Arts Area: Symphony; Orchestra; Ethnic

Status: Semi-Professional; Non-Profit
Type: Performing
Purpose: To give native musicians an opportunity to perform; to provide the Maui community with a permanent resident orchestra; to provide an opportunity for local performers and choreographers to display their talents through association with the orchestra; to premiere original works
Management: James French, Music Director/Conductor
Officers: Frank Blackwell, President
Paid Staff: 1   **Volunteer Staff:** 40
Paid Artists: 20   **Non-Paid Artists:** 40
Utilizes: Special Technical Talent; Guest Conductors; Guest Artists
Budget: $50,000 - $100,000
Income Sources: Private Foundations/Grants/Endowments; Business/Corporate Donations; Box Office; Government Grants; Individual Donations
Season: September - April   **Annual Attendance:** 15,000
Affiliations: ASOL; Maui Community Arts Council
Performance Facilities: Baldwin Auditorium, Wailuku

IDAHO

Boise

DANCE

AMERICAN FESTIVAL BALLET
Esther Simplot Performing Arts Academy, 516 North Ninth Street, Boise, ID 83702
(208) 343-0556
Founded: 1971
Arts Area: Modern; Ballet; Jazz
Status: Professional
Type: Performing; Touring; Resident; Educational; Sponsoring
Management: Esther B. Simplot, Executive Director; Betty Sinow, Assistant Executive Director
Paid Staff: 5 **Volunteer Staff:** 40
Paid Artists: 16
Utilizes: Guest Artists
Budget: $100,000 - $500,000
Income Sources: Private Foundations/Grants/Endowments; Business/Corporate Donations; Box Office; Government Grants; Individual Donations
Season: October - March **Annual Attendance:** 30,000
Performance Facilities: Morrison Center for the Performing Arts

OINKARI BASQUE DANCERS
2418 Pendleton, PO Box 1675, Boise, ID 83705
(208) 336-8219
Arts Area: Ethnic; Folk
Status: Non-Profit
Type: Performing; Touring; Educational
Purpose: To promote and enhance our culture through dance, song, language and education
Management: John Kirtland, Business Manager; Dan Ansotegui, Boys Dance Director; Toni Ansotegui, Girls Dance Director; Julie Achabal, Historian; Ron Lemmon, Sergeant-at-Arms
Officers: Lisa Achurra, President
Paid Staff: 1 **Volunteer Staff:** 7
Paid Artists: 1 **Non-Paid Artists:** 70
Utilizes: Special Technical Talent; Guest Artists; Guest Directors
Budget: $1,000 - $50,000
Income Sources: Private Foundations/Grants/Endowments; Business/Corporate Donations; Individual Donations
Season: 52 Weeks **Annual Attendance:** 25,000
Affiliations: Euskaldunak
Performance Facilities: Boise Basque Center

INSTRUMENTAL MUSIC

BOISE PHILHARMONIC
205 North Tenth, Suite 617, Boise, ID 83702
(208) 344-7849
Founded: 1887
Arts Area: Symphony; Chamber
Status: Professional; Non-Profit
Type: Performing; Educational
Purpose: The purpose of the Boise Philharmonic is to maintain a symphony orchestra as a high-quality artistic resource for the Treasure Valley. To insure this mission, the association is committed to the highest performance quality and widest community service that finances will allow.
Management: James Ogle, Artistic Director/Conductor; Margie Stoy Smith, General Manager
Officers: Richard Roller, President
Paid Staff: 9
Paid Artists: 70
Utilizes: Guest Conductors; Guest Artists
Budget: $500,000 - $1,000,000
Income Sources: Private Foundations/Grants/Endowments; Business/Corporate Donations; Box Office; Government Grants; Individual Donations
Season: September - May **Annual Attendance:** 50,000
Affiliations: ASOL
Performance Facilities: Morrison Center for the Performing Arts, Boise; Brandt Auditorium, Nampa Civic Center

VOCAL MUSIC

BOISE MASTER CHORALE
6925 Copper Drive, Boise, ID 83704
(208) 375-2948
Arts Area: Choral
Status: Professional; Semi-Professional; Non-Profit
Type: Performing
Purpose: To provide the community with fine choral music and enable people in the community to sing in an outstanding choral group
Management: Carson Wong, Conductor; Randall Pierson, Stage Manager
Officers: Shari Cutshall, President; Katherine Sullivan, Secretary; Emily Riley, Treasurer
Paid Staff: 10   **Volunteer Staff:** 10
Non-Paid Artists: 125
Budget: $1,000 - $50,000
Income Sources: Private Foundations/Grants/Endowments; Business/Corporate Donations; Box Office; Government Grants; Individual Donations
Season: September - May   **Annual Attendance:** 4,000
Performance Facilities: Saint John's Cathedral; Morrison Center for the Performing Arts

BOISE OPERA
516 South Ninth, Boise, ID 83702
(208) 345-3531
Founded: 1972
Arts Area: Grand Opera; Music Theatre
Status: Professional; Non-Profit
Type: Performing; Educational
Management: Michael Winter, Executive Director
Paid Staff: 1
Utilizes: Special Technical Talent; Guest Conductors; Guest Artists; Guest Directors
Budget: $100,000 - $500,000
Income Sources: Private Foundations/Grants/Endowments; Business/Corporate Donations; Box Office; Individual Donations
Season: September - March   **Annual Attendance:** 2,300
Performance Facilities: Morrison Center for the Performing Arts

THEATRE

IDAHO THEATER FOR YOUTH
Eighth Street Market Place, Suite 232, Boise, ID 83702
(208) 345-0060
FAX: (208) 336-6731
Mailing Address: PO Box 7926, Boise, ID 83707
Founded: 1981
Arts Area: Professional; Theatrical Group
Status: Professional; Non-Profit
Type: Performing; Touring; Educational
Purpose: To provide live, professional theater for the cultural enrichment and theater-arts education of children, young adults and their families at a cost which makes the programs easily accessible to all
Management: Cynthia Gaede, Managing Director; David Lee-Painter, Artistic Director; Terri April Dillion, Marketing Director; Dan Peterson, Associate Artistic Director; Jane Baker, Business Manager
Officers: Dale Smith, President; David Nevin, Vice President; Gwen Engle, Secretary; Nial Bradshaw, Treasurer
Paid Staff: 5
Paid Artists: 12
Utilizes: Special Technical Talent; Guest Artists; Guest Directors
Budget: $100,000 - $500,000
Income Sources: Private Foundations/Grants/Endowments; Business/Corporate Donations; Box Office; Government Grants; Individual Donations
Season: September - May   **Annual Attendance:** 100,000
Performance Facilities: Morrison Center for the Performing Arts

PERFORMING SERIES

IDAHO SHAKESPEARE FESTIVAL
412 South Ninth St., PO Box 9365, Boise, ID 83707
(208) 336-9221
FAX: (208) 336-6731
Founded: 1976

Arts Area: Theater
Status: Professional; Non-Profit
Type: Performing; Touring; Educational
Management: Charles Fee, Artistic, Director; Vangie Osborn, General Manager
Officers: Charles Davis, President, Board of Trustees
Paid Staff: 4   **Volunteer Staff:** 10
Paid Artists: 12   **Non-Paid Artists:** 10
Utilizes: Guest Artists; Guest Directors
Budget: $100,000 - $500,000
Income Sources: Private Foundations/Grants/Endowments; Business/Corporate Donations; Box Office; Individual Donations
Season: May - September   **Annual Attendance:** 20,000

FACILITY

BOISE STATE UNIVERSITY - MORRISON CENTER FOR THE PERFORMING ARTS
1910 University Drive, Boise, ID 83725
(208) 385-1609
FAX: (208) 385-3021
Type of Facility: Concert Hall; Performance Center; Theatre House; Multi-Purpose
Type of Stage: Proscenium
Stage Dimensions: 120'Wx52'D; 60'Wx30'H proscenium opening   **Orchestra Pit**
Seating Capacity: 2,030
Year Built: 1984   **Architect:** Lombard/Conrad   **Cost:** $18,500,000
Acoustical Consultant: Paeoletti & Levitz
Contact for Rental: Frank Heise;   (208) 385-1609
Resident Groups: Boise Opera; Boise Philharmonic; American Festival Ballet

Caldwell

PERFORMING SERIES

CALDWELL FINE ARTS SERIES
2112 Cleveland Boulevard, Caldwell, ID 83605
(208) 454-1376
FAX: (208) 459-2077
Founded: 1961
Arts Area: Dance; Vocal Music; Instrumental Music; Theater; Grand Opera
Status: Non-Profit
Type: Educational; Sponsoring
Purpose: To present quality performances in all disciplines; to provide educational services for schools in the area; to assist other arts organizations
Management: Sylvia Hunt, Manager
Officers: Beverly Hopper, President; Shirley Marmon, Vice President; Jeanne Skyrm, Secretary; Hanni Hinkle, Treasurer
Paid Staff: 1   **Volunteer Staff:** 40
Paid Artists: 100
Utilizes: Guest Artists
Budget: $50,000 - $100,000
Income Sources: Private Foundations/Grants/Endowments; Business/Corporate Donations; Box Office; Government Grants; Individual Donations
Season: October - April   **Annual Attendance:** 7,500
Affiliations: Pacific Northwest Presenters
Performance Facilities: Jewett Auditorium

Idaho Falls

INSTRUMENTAL MUSIC

IDAHO FALLS SYMPHONY
545 Shoup Avenue, #101, Idaho Falls, ID 83402
(208) 529-1080
Founded: 1955
Arts Area: Symphony; Orchestra
Status: Semi-Professional; Non-Profit
Type: Performing; Resident; Educational
Management: John LoPiccolo, Conductor/Music Director; Linda Waugh, Business Manager
Utilizes: Guest Artists

Budget: $100,000 - $500,000
Income Sources: Business/Corporate Donations; Box Office; Government Grants; Individual Donations
Season: October - May   **Annual Attendance:** 10,000
Affiliations: ASOL
Performance Facilities: Civic Auditorium

FACILITY

CIVIC AUDITORIUM
501 South Holmes, Idaho Falls, ID 83401
(208) 529-1396
    Type of Facility: Concert Hall; Auditorium; Performance Center; Opera House; Civic Center; Multi-Purpose
    Type of Stage: Proscenium
    Stage Dimensions: 84'Wx35'D   **Orchestra Pit**
    Seating Capacity: 1,902
    Year Built: 1951   **Architect:** Fetzer & Fetzer   **Cost:** $1,000,000
    Acoustical Consultant: C.P. Boner & Associates
    Contact for Rental: Roger T. Ralphs;   (208) 529-1396
    Resident Groups: Idaho Falls Symphony; Idaho Falls Opera Theatre; Sounds Choir; Idaho Falls Symphony Chorale; Ballet Society; Idaho Falls Music Club; Community Concerts

Moscow

INSTRUMENTAL MUSIC

WASHINGTON IDAHO SYMPHONY
PO Box 9185, Moscow, ID 83843
(208) 882-6555
    Founded: 1972
    Arts Area: Symphony; Ensemble
    Status: Non-Professional; Non-Profit
    Type: Performing; Resident; Educational
    Purpose: To bring the pleasure of fine music to adults and children while allowing area musicians to participate in an orchestra or chorus
    Management: Cecelia Lund, Executive Director
    Officers: Samuel H. Butterfield, President; Dr. William Cone, First Vice President; Day Bassett, Second Vice President; Bruce Wollenberg, Secretary/Treasurer
    Paid Staff: 8   **Volunteer Staff:** 309
    Paid Artists: 55   **Non-Paid Artists:** 40
    Utilizes: Guest Artists
    Budget: $50,000 - $100,000
    Income Sources: Private Foundations/Grants/Endowments; Business/Corporate Donations; Box Office; Government Grants; Individual Donations
    Season: September - April   **Annual Attendance:** 3,812
    Affiliations: ASOL

THEATRE

IDAHO REPERTORY THEATRE COMPANY
University of Idaho, Moscow, ID 83843
(208) 885-6465
    Founded: 1950
    Arts Area: Professional; Theatrical Group
    Status: Semi-Professional; Non-Profit
    Type: Performing; Educational
    Purpose: To provide high-quality summer theatre for the state of Idaho
    Management: Bruce C. Brockman, Producing Director
    Paid Staff: 3
    Paid Artists: 27
    Utilizes: Special Technical Talent; Guest Artists; Guest Directors
    Budget: $1,000 - $50,000
    Income Sources: Private Foundations/Grants/Endowments; Business/Corporate Donations; Box Office; Government Grants; Individual Donations
    Season: June - August   **Annual Attendance:** 10,000
    Performance Facilities: Hartung Theatre

PERFORMING SERIES

FESTIVAL DANCE AND PERFORMING ARTS
University of Idaho, Moscow, ID 83843
(208) 883-3267
Founded: 1989
Arts Area: Dance; Musical Theatre
Status: Professional; Non-Profit
Type: Performing; Educational; Sponsoring
Purpose: To bring the best of the performing arts to the Inland Northwest through performances, education and outreach programs
Management: Joann Muneta, Executive Director
Officers: Jeff Helbling, Chairman; Paul Smith, Vice Chairman
Paid Staff: 2
Paid Artists: 3
Utilizes: Guest Artists; Guest Companies
Budget: $100,000 - $500,000
Income Sources: Private Foundations/Grants/Endowments; Business/Corporate Donations; Box Office; Government Grants; Individual Donations
Season: 52 Weeks   **Annual Attendance:** 10,000
Affiliations: WAAA; Pacific Northwest Arts Performers
Performance Facilities: Beasly Performing Arts Coliseum, Washington State University

LIONEL HAMPTON, CHEVRON JAZZ FESTIVAL
University of Idaho, Hampton School of Music, Moscow, ID 83843
(208) 835-6765
FAX: (208) 885-6513
Founded: 1968
Arts Area: Festivals
Status: Non-Profit
Type: Performing; Educational; Sponsoring
Purpose: To promote jazz music among the youth of America
Management: Dr. Lynn J. Skinner, Executive Director
Paid Staff: 3   **Volunteer Staff:** 200
Paid Artists: 50
Utilizes: Special Technical Talent; Guest Artists
Budget: $100,000 - $500,000
Income Sources: Private Foundations/Grants/Endowments; Business/Corporate Donations; Box Office; Government Grants; Individual Donations
Season: February - March
Annual Attendance: 45,000

Mountain Home

PERFORMING SERIES

PERFORMING ARTS SERIES OF MOUNTAIN HOME
935 North 12 East, Mountain Home, ID 83647
(208) 587-4821
Arts Area: Dance; Vocal Music; Instrumental Music; Theater
Status: Non-Professional
Type: Performing; Educational
Purpose: To bring culturally enriching performances to our rural community and surrounding areas
Management: Laurie Unrein, Executive Director
Officers: Sher Sellman, President; Tom Bennick, Vice President; Karen Bird, Treasurer; Lorretta Olmstead, Secretary
Paid Staff: 1   **Volunteer Staff:** 12
Utilizes: Guest Artists
Budget: $1,000 - $50,000
Income Sources: Private Foundations/Grants/Endowments; Business/Corporate Donations; Box Office; Government Grants; Individual Donations
Season: September - May
Annual Attendance: 1,400

Pocatello

FACILITY

IDAHO STATE UNIVERSITY - FRAZIER AUDITORIUM
Eighth Street, Pocatello, ID 83209
(208) 236-3695
> **Type of Facility:** Theatre Complex; Auditorium
> **Type of Stage:** Proscenium
> **Stage Dimensions:** 42'Wx20'D   **Orchestra Pit**
> **Seating Capacity:** 750
> **Year Built:** 1924
> **Contact for Rental:** Reed Turner, Theater Director;   (208) 236-2925

IDAHO STATE UNIVERSITY - GORANSON HALL
Department of Music, PO Box 8099, Pocatello, ID 83209
(208) 236-3636
> **Type of Facility:** Concert Hall
> **Type of Stage:** Proscenium
> **Seating Capacity:** 475
> **Year Built:** 1967   **Cost:** $2,000,000
> **Contact for Rental:** Music Department Secretary;   (208) 236-3636
> **Resident Groups:** Idaho State Civic Symphony; University Music Organizations

IDAHO STATE UNIVERSITY - POWELL LITTLE THEATRE
Eighth Street, Pocatello, ID 83209
(208) 236-3695
> **Type of Facility:** Arena; Multi-Purpose; Visual And Performing Classrooms
> **Facility Originally:** Library
> **Type of Stage:** Arena
> **Stage Dimensions:** 20'x30'
> **Seating Capacity:** 150
> **Year Built:** 1924
> **Contact for Rental:** Reed Turner, Theater Director;   (208) 236-2925

Rexburg

FACILITY

ELIZA R. SNOW PERFORMING ARTS CENTER
Rexburg, ID 83460-1210
(208) 356-1260
FAX: (208) 356-2390
> **Type of Facility:** Theatre Complex; Concert Hall
> **Type of Stage:** Platform
> **Stage Dimensions:** Drama Theater - 42'x45'; Concert Hall - 54'x30'
> **Orchestra Pit**
> **Seating Capacity:** 700
> **Year Built:** 1980   **Architect:** Collard and Call
> **Acoustical Consultant:** Rein Pirn
> **Contact for Rental:** Ken Howell;   (208) 356-1149

Sandpoint

THEATRE

PANIDA THEATER
300 North First Avenue, PO Box 1981, Sandpoint, ID 83864
(208) 263-9191
> **Founded:** 1985
> **Arts Area:** Professional; Musical; Community; Folk; Theatrical Group; Puppet; Dance; Film
> **Status:** Non-Profit
> **Type:** Performing; Resident; Educational; Sponsoring
> **Purpose:** To provide a beautiful and versatile space for organizations and sponsors to present quality performances; to continue efforts to revitalize downtown Sandpoint
> **Management:** Karen Bowers, Manager/Executive Director; Bill Lewis, Technical Director

Officers: Michael Merrell, President; Bruce Millard, Vice President; Barbara Shaver, Secretary/Treasurer; Phyllis Marks, Facilities Chair
Paid Staff: 2 **Volunteer Staff:** 30
Paid Artists: 100 **Non-Paid Artists:** 725
Utilizes: Special Technical Talent; Guest Artists
Budget: $50,000 - $100,000
Income Sources: Private Foundations/Grants/Endowments; Business/Corporate Donations; Box Office; Government Grants; Individual Donations; Theatre Rental
Season: 52 Weeks **Annual Attendance:** 24,500

PERFORMING SERIES

FESTIVAL AT SANDPOINT
c/o Festival at Sandpoint Inc., PO Box 695, Sandpoint, ID 83864
(208) 265-4554
FAX: (208) 263-9466
Arts Area: Vocal Music; Instrumental Music; Children's Programs
Status: Professional; Commercial
Type: Performing; Educational; Sponsoring
Purpose: To present high-quality musical performances including classical, symphonic, Big Band, ragtime, jazz, country and western, pops, and children's programming; to advance musical education through the Schweitzer Institute of Music
Management: Gunther Schuller, Artistic Director; Constance Berghan, Executive Director
Officers: Bobbie Huguenin, President
Budget: $500,000 - $1,000,000
Income Sources: Private Foundations/Grants/Endowments; Business/Corporate Donations; Box Office; Government Grants; Individual Donations
Performance Facilities: Festival Tent

Sun Valley

PERFORMING SERIES

ELKHORN MUSIC FESTIVAL, INC.
PO Box 1914, Sun Valley, ID 83353
(208) 622-5607
Founded: 1985
Arts Area: Vocal Music; Instrumental Music; Festivals
Status: Professional; Non-Profit
Type: Performing; Educational
Purpose: To present 20 free concerts by Idaho's first and only professional chamber orchestra
Management: Carl Eberl, Music Director/Conductor; Julianne Eberl, Executive Director; Craig Knutson, Stage Manager; Isabel Thompson, Administrative Assistant
Officers: Carl Eberl, President; Rickie Orchin Brady, Vice President; James Hancock, Treasurer; Julianne Eberl, Secretary
Paid Staff: 4
Paid Artists: 40
Utilizes: Guest Artists
Budget: $100,000 - $500,000
Income Sources: Private Foundations/Grants/Endowments; Business/Corporate Donations; Government Grants; Individual Donations; Sale of Specialty Items
Season: August **Annual Attendance:** 8,000
Affiliations: Sun Valley Chamber of Commerce
Performance Facilities: Elkhorn Plaza Tent

SUN VALLEY CENTER FOR THE ARTS AND HUMANITIES
PO Box 656, Sun Valley, ID 83353
(208) 726-9491
FAX: (208) 726-2344
Arts Area: Dance; Vocal Music; Instrumental Music; Theater
Type: Presenting
Purpose: To present programs highlighting music (classical, chamber, opera, jazz, folk, ethnic and popular), theatre, and dance
Management: Kate Wright, Director of Performing Arts
Budget: $100,000 - $500,000
Season: 52 Weeks
Performance Facilities: Sun Valley Center for the Arts and Humanities

---
Twin Falls

INSTRUMENTAL MUSIC

MAGIC VALLEY SYMPHONY
PO Box 1805, Twin Falls, ID 83303
(208) 733-1079
Founded: 1959
Arts Area: Symphony; Orchestra
Status: Non-Professional; Non-Profit
Type: Performing
Purpose: To enhance the cultural life of the community and provide an outlet for performers
Management: Theodore A. Hadley, Conductor; Edna Thorsen, Business Manager
Officers: Kevin Howard, President; Ernest Moss, Vice President; Judy Call, Secretary
Utilizes: Guest Artists
Budget: $1,000 - $50,000
Income Sources: Business/Corporate Donations; Box Office; Individual Donations
Season: September - May   **Annual Attendance:** 1,800
Affiliations: ASOL; BMI; ASCAP
Performance Facilities: College of Southern Idaho Fine Arts Auditorium

---
Wallace

THEATRE

VALLEY COMMUNITY THEATER
PO Box 866, Wallace, ID 83873
(208) 753-5792
Founded: 1966
Arts Area: Musical; Community
Status: Non-Professional; Non-Profit
Type: Performing; Sponsoring
Purpose: Valley Community Theater was founded and is supported by members of the community seriously interested in the performing arts
Officers: Debbie Morris, President; Mary Rae Faraca, Vice President; Ann Wilson, Secretary
Volunteer Staff: 15
Non-Paid Artists: 15
Budget: $1,000 - $50,000

Weiser

FACILITY

INTERMOUNTAIN CULTURAL CENTER AND MUSEUM
2295 Paddock Avenue, Weiser, ID 83672
(208) 549-0205
Type of Facility: Auditorium
Facility Originally: School
Type of Stage: Platform
Seating Capacity: 296
Year Built: 1923
Year Remodeled: 1980
Contact for Rental: Intermountain Cultural Center and Museum;   (208) 549-0205

ILLINOIS

Alton

INSTRUMENTAL MUSIC

ALTON SYMPHONY ORCHESTRA
PO Box 1205, Alton, IL 62002-1205
(618) 462-3184
> **Founded:** 1946
> **Arts Area:** Symphony
> **Status:** Non-Professional; Non-Profit
> **Type:** Performing
> **Purpose:** To provide a medium for the further development of instrumental abilities of area musicians; to build an interest in orchestral music; and to present concerts for the public
> **Management:** Dr. Frank M. Boals, Manager
> **Officers:** James S. Reeves, President; Henry B. Lenhardt, Vice President; Jill Zitnick, Secretary; Abby Davison, Treasurer
> **Paid Artists:** 4
> **Utilizes:** Guest Artists
> **Budget:** $1,000 - $50,000
> **Income Sources:** Private Foundations/Grants/Endowments; Business/Corporate Donations; Box Office; Government Grants; Individual Donations
> **Season:** September - May   **Annual Attendance:** 3,000
> **Affiliations:** Illinois Council of Orchestras
> **Performance Facilities:** Hatheway Hall, Lewis and Clark Community College

Argonne

PERFORMING SERIES

ARTS AT ARGONNE
Argonne National Laboratory, 221-D244, Argonne, IL 60439
(708) 252-7160
FAX: (708) 252-5986
> **Founded:** 1988
> **Arts Area:** Instrumental Music
> **Status:** Non-Professional
> **Type:** Sponsoring
> **Purpose:** To enrich the cultural climate at the laboratory by presenting a program of cultural manifestation of the highest artistic quality
> **Officers:** Dr. Hans Kaper, Chairman
> **Volunteer Staff:** 15
> **Utilizes:** Guest Artists
> **Budget:** $1,000 - $50,000
> **Income Sources:** Private Foundations/Grants/Endowments; Box Office
> **Season:** October - May   **Annual Attendance:** 1,500
> **Affiliations:** Chicago Music Alliance
> **Performance Facilities:** Building 362 Auditorium

Aurora

FACILITY

PARAMOUNT ARTS CENTRE
23 East Galena Boulevard, Aurora, IL 60506
(708) 896-7676
> **Type of Facility:** Theatre House
> **Type of Stage:** Proscenium
> **Stage Dimensions:** 48'9"Wx40'Dx30'H   **Orchestra Pit**
> **Seating Capacity:** 1,888
> **Year Built:** 1931   **Architect:** Jules J. Rubens
> **Year Remodeled:** 1976   **Architect:** Prisco & Duffy   **Cost:** $2,950,000
> **Contact for Rental:** James Kampert, Assistant Manager;   (708) 896-7676
> *In 1980, the Paramount Arts Centre was placed on the National Register of Historic Places.*

Batavia

PERFORMING SERIES

FERMILAB ARTS SERIES
Pine Street and Kirk Road, Batavia, IL 60647
(708) 840-2059
FAX: (708) 840-2939
> **Arts Area:** Dance; Instrumental Music; Theater; Comedy; Jazz
> **Status:** Non-Profit
> **Type:** Sponsoring
> **Purpose:** To provide quality arts presentations to Fermilab and surrounding communities
> **Management:** Janet Mac Kay, Arts Coordinator; Colleen Choy, Box Office Manager
> **Officers:** Morris Binkley, Chairman Auditorium Committee
> **Paid Staff:** 2 **Volunteer Staff:** 30
> **Paid Artists:** 12 **Non-Paid Artists:** 3
> **Utilizes:** Guest Artists
> **Income Sources:** Box Office
> **Season:** 52 Weeks **Annual Attendance:** 9,960
> **Affiliations:** Fermi National Accel Laboratories
> **Performance Facilities:** Ramsey Auditorium

Belleville

INSTRUMENTAL MUSIC

BELLEVILLE PHILHARMONIC
116 North Jackson, Belleville, IL 62220
(618) 235-5600
> **Founded:** 1866
> **Arts Area:** Symphony; Orchestra; Instrumental Group
> **Status:** Non-Professional; Non-Profit
> **Type:** Performing; Educational
> **Purpose:** To serve the interests of music and musicians in Greater Belleville
> **Management:** Kathleen J. AuBuchon, Administrator; Kathly Albers, Office Manager
> **Officers:** Audrey Mudd, President; Bill Kniesly, Vice President; Mary Durnell, Secretary; Steve Gondek, Treasurer
> **Paid Staff:** 3 **Volunteer Staff:** 2
> **Paid Artists:** 10 **Non-Paid Artists:** 100
> **Utilizes:** Guest Artists
> **Budget:** $50,000 - $100,000
> **Income Sources:** Business/Corporate Donations; Box Office; Government Grants; Individual Donations
> **Season:** September - May **Annual Attendance:** 5,000

Bloomington

INSTRUMENTAL MUSIC

BLOOMINGTON-NORMAL SYMPHONY SOCIETY
106 West Monroe, Bloomington, IL 61702-0375
(309) 828-2882
FAX: (309) 827-2726
> **Founded:** 1944
> **Arts Area:** Symphony; Orchestra; Chamber
> **Status:** Semi-Professional; Non-Profit
> **Type:** Performing; Touring; Resident
> **Purpose:** To support a symphony orchestra for the purpose of producing high-quality symphonic music for the Bloomington-Normal area.
> **Management:** Carole M. Ringer, General Manager; Alice D. Morris, Administrative Secretary
> **Officers:** Susan Smart, President; John Killian, Dr. David Skillrud, Vice Presidents; Kyle C. Sessions, Secretary; Richard Lenahan, Treasurer
> **Paid Staff:** 2
> **Paid Artists:** 100
> **Utilizes:** Guest Conductors; Guest Artists
> **Budget:** $100,000 - $500,000
> **Income Sources:** Private Foundations/Grants/Endowments; Business/Corporate Donations; Box Office; Government Grants; Individual Donations
> **Season:** September - May **Annual Attendance:** 7,500

Affiliations: Illinois Council of Orchestras; ASOL
Performance Facilities: Braden Auditorium, Illinois State University

FACILITY

ILLINOIS WESLEYAN SCHOOL OF DRAMA - MCPHERSON HALL
302 East Graham, Bloomington, IL 61702
(309) 556-3011
Type of Facility: Theatre Complex; Auditorium; Theatre House
Type of Stage: Flexible
Stage Dimensions: 18'x36'x50'   **Orchestra Pit**
Seating Capacity: 279
Year Built: 1962   **Architect:** Shafter Wilson Evans   **Cost:** $500,000
Manager: Dr. Jared Brown, Director

ILLINOIS WESLEYAN UNIVERSITY - WESTBROOK AUDITORIUM
Presser Hall, School of Music, Bloomington, IL 61702
(309) 556-3061
Type of Facility: Auditorium
Type of Stage: Proscenium
Orchestra Pit
Seating Capacity: 574
Year Built: 1929   **Architect:** Pillsbury
Year Remodeled: 1970   **Architect:** Evans Associates   **Cost:** $129,000
Manager: Dr. Robert A. Kvam
Rental is only on a limited basis.

Champaign

INSTRUMENTAL MUSIC

CHAMPAIGN-URBANA SYMPHONY
44 East Main Street, Room 414, Champaign, IL 61824
(217) 351-9139
FAX: (217) 351-1698
Founded: 1959
Arts Area: Symphony
Status: Professional; Non-Profit
Type: Performing
Management: Paul Vermel, Conductor; Terry I. Benson, Symphony Manager
Utilizes: Guest Artists
Season: September - May
Performance Facilities: Foellinger Great Hall

PERFORMING SERIES

ASSEMBLY HALL
University of Illinois, Champaign, IL 61820
(217) 333-2923
Founded: 1963
Arts Area: Dance; Vocal Music; Instrumental Music; Theater
Status: Professional; Non-Profit
Type: Sponsoring
Purpose: Entertainment and cultural events for university students, the community and the area
Management: Wayne N. Hecht, Director
Paid Staff: 5
Budget: $100,000 - $500,000
Income Sources: Box Office
Affiliations: IAAM; ISPAA; APAP; Big Ten Concert Managers
Performance Facilities: Assembly Hall

THE GREAT AMERICAN PEOPLE SHOW
Station A, Box 2178, Champaign, IL 61820
(217) 367-1900
Founded: 1975
Arts Area: Theater
Status: Non-Profit
Type: Performing; Touring

Purpose: To create historical theatrical pieces using primary materials (letters, diaries, newspaper accounts, poems, and commentary) written or spoken about or by Americans. TGAPS currently produces three historical dramas at Lincoln's New Salem Historical Site.
Management: John Ahart and Rose Buckner Ahart, Co-Artistic Directors; Donna Buzicky, Office Manager
Officers: John Ahart, President; Professor Robert Johannson, Chairman of the Board
Paid Staff: 7   **Volunteer Staff:** 20
Paid Artists: 35
Utilizes: Special Technical Talent; Guest Conductors; Guest Artists
Budget: $100,000 - $500,000
Income Sources: Private Foundations/Grants/Endowments; Box Office; Government Grants; Individual Donations
Season: June - August   **Annual Attendance:** 10,000
Affiliations: Illinois Historic Preservation Agency
Performance Facilities: Lincoln's New Salem

Chicago

DANCE

AKASHA AND COMPANY
1016 North Dearborn, Chicago, IL 60657
(312) 266-0039
Founded: 1979
Arts Area: Modern
Status: Professional; Non-Profit
Type: Performing; Touring
Purpose: Akasha: "Spirit Leaping Forth"
Management: Laura Wade, Artistic Director; Jeanne Knowles, General Manager
Paid Staff: 2
Paid Artists: 6
Utilizes: Guest Artists; Guest Choreographers
Budget: $50,000 - $100,000
Income Sources: Private Foundations/Grants/Endowments; Business/Corporate Donations; Box Office; Government Grants; Individual Donations
Season: 52 Weeks

BALLET CHICAGO
222 South Riverside Plaza, Suite 865, Chicago, IL 60606
(312) 993-7575
FAX: (312) 993-1974
Arts Area: Ballet
Status: Professional; Non-Profit
Type: Performing; Touring; Educational
Purpose: To provide metropolitan Chicago and its environs with the finest classical ballet; to develop a diverse repetoire; to educate and develop audiences of all ages and backgrounds
Management: Daniel Duell, Artistic Director; Patricia Blair, Assistant Artistic Director; Gordon Pierce Schmidt, Resident Choreographer
Officers: John C. Staley, Chairman; Peggy Fowler, President
Budget: $1,000,000 - $5,000,000
Income Sources: Private Foundations/Grants/Endowments; Business/Corporate Donations; Box Office; Government Grants; Individual Donations

CHICAGO DANCE COALITION
67 East Madison, Suite 2112, Chicago, IL 60603
(312) 410-8384
Founded: 1981
Status: Professional; Non-Profit
Type: Sponsoring; Service
Purpose: To serve and promote dance in Chicago through publications, hotline, library, seminars, Ruth Page Awards and member services
Management: Lisa Tylke, Executive Director; Lisa Abigai Crampton, Program Coordinator; Valerie Baxley, Membership Services Coordinator
Paid Staff: 3   **Volunteer Staff:** 5
Budget: $100,000 - $500,000
Income Sources: Private Foundations/Grants/Endowments; Business/Corporate Donations; Government Grants; Individual Donations

CHICAGO MOVING COMPANY
1225 West School Street, Chicago, IL 60057
(312) 880-5002
>**Founded:** 1972
>**Arts Area:** Modern
>**Status:** Professional; Non-Profit
>**Type:** Performing; Touring; Educational
>**Purpose:** We believe that art should speak to life; we touch the spirit of the audience, engage them in feeling and reflections, and entertain them
>**Management:** Nana Shineflug, Artistic Director; Dennis Wise, Managing Director
>**Officers:** Bill Gilmore, President; Larry Blust, Vice President
>**Paid Staff:** 1   **Volunteer Staff:** 3
>**Paid Artists:** 10
>**Utilizes:** Special Technical Talent
>**Budget:** $50,000 - $100,000
>**Income Sources:** Private Foundations/Grants/Endowments; Business/Corporate Donations; Box Office; Government Grants; Individual Donations
>**Season:** September - June   **Annual Attendance:** 26,000
>**Performance Facilities:** Columbia Dance Center

THE DANCE CENTER OF COLUMBIA COLLEGE
4730 North Sheridan Road, Chicago, IL 60640
(312) 271-7804
FAX: (312) 271-7046
>**Arts Area:** Modern; Ballet; Jazz; Ethnic; Choreography; Improvisation
>**Status:** Professional; Non-Profit
>**Type:** Performing; Educational
>**Purpose:** To provide dance instruction to a variety of people from culturally diverse backgrounds
>**Management:** Shirley Mordine, Artistic Director
>**Paid Staff:** 18   **Volunteer Staff:** 4
>**Utilizes:** Guest Choreographers
>**Budget:** $500,000 - $1,000,000
>**Income Sources:** Private Foundations/Grants/Endowments; Business/Corporate Donations; Box Office; Government Grants; Individual Donations
>**Season:** August - June   **Annual Attendance:** 24,000
>**Affiliations:** Chicago Dance Coalition; Donors Forum; League of Chicago Theatres
>**Performance Facilities:** Dance Center; Medina Temple; Harold Washington Library Theatre

HUBBARD STREET DANCE COMPANY
218 South Wabash Avenue, Chicago, IL 60604
(312) 663-0853
FAX: (312) 663-9095
>**Founded:** 1977
>**Arts Area:** Ballet-Based Contemporary
>**Status:** Professional
>**Type:** Performing; Touring; Resident; Educational
>**Purpose:** To present the finest of professional dance to our home audiences and on tour
>**Management:** David Foster, John Luckacovic, Columbia Artists Management
>**Officers:** James Peponis, Chairman; William Wood Prince, President; Donald H. Ratner, Treasurer; Jo Hopkins Deutsch, Secretary
>**Paid Staff:** 17   **Volunteer Staff:** 25
>**Paid Artists:** 22
>**Utilizes:** Special Technical Talent; Guest Choreographers; Scenic Designers; Composers
>**Budget:** $5,000,000 - $10,000,000
>**Income Sources:** Private Foundations/Grants/Endowments; Business/Corporate Donations; Box Office; Government Grants; Individual Donations; Merchandise Income
>**Season:** 52 Weeks   **Annual Attendance:** 75,000
>**Affiliations:** Dance USA; APAP; Illinois Arts Alliance; Chicago Dance Coalition; WAAA; NAPAMA; Ohio Regional Association of Concert and Lecture Enterprises; ISPAA
>**Performance Facilities:** Civic Opera House; Ravinia Festival

JAN ERKERT AND COMPANY
2121 West Webster, Chicago, IL 60647
(312) 252-6557
>**Founded:** 1979
>**Arts Area:** Modern
>**Status:** Professional; Non-Profit
>**Type:** Performing; Touring; Resident

Purpose: To make modern dance accessible to a wide audience
Management: Jan Erkert, Artistic Director; Bernt Lewy, Executive Director
Paid Staff: 4
Paid Artists: 8
Utilizes: Guest Artists; Guest Choreographers
Budget: $100,000 - $500,000
Income Sources: Private Foundations/Grants/Endowments; Business/Corporate Donations; Box Office; Government Grants; Individual Donations
Season: September - June

JOEL HALL DANCERS
1225 West School, Chicago, IL 60657
(312) 880-1002
Founded: 1974
Arts Area: Jazz
Status: Professional; Non-Profit
Type: Performing; Touring; Resident; Educational
Management: Joel Hall, Artistic Director; Joseph Ehrenberg, Managing Director
Paid Artists: 12
Utilizes: Guest Artists; Guest Choreographers
Budget: $100,000 - $500,000
Income Sources: Private Foundations/Grants/Endowments; Business/Corporate Donations; Box Office; Government Grants; Individual Donations
Season: 52 Weeks

JOSEPH HOLMES CHICAGO DANCE THEATRE
1935 South Halsted, Chicago, IL 60608
(312) 942-0065
FAX: (312) 942-0815
Founded: 1974
Arts Area: Modern; Jazz
Status: Professional; Non-Profit
Type: Performing; Touring; Educational
Purpose: Chance to Dance Program: to present original choreography to make dance accessible to a large audience
Management: Randy Duncan, Artistic Director; Harriet Ross, Associate Artistic Director; Gary Lindsey, Artist Services; Mary F. Webster, Managing Director; Betsy Whipple, Director of Development
Officers: Kenneth R. Kimbrough, Chairman; Michael S. Kesner, Executive Vice President; Cheryl M. McWorter, Vice President Artistic; Carol Slater, Vice President Special Events
Paid Staff: 4   **Volunteer Staff:** 5
Paid Artists: 14
Utilizes: Guest Artists; Guest Choreographers
Budget: $500,000 - $1,000,000
Income Sources: Private Foundations/Grants/Endowments; Business/Corporate Donations; Box Office; Government Grants; Individual Donations
Season: 52 Weeks
Affiliations: NEA; Chicago Dance Coalition; Arts Midwest; Illinois Arts Alliance
Performance Facilities: Civic Opera House

KAST AND COMPANY
5320 South University Avenue, Chicago, IL 60615
(312) 643-8916
Founded: 1988
Arts Area: Modern; Liturgical
Status: Professional; Non-Profit
Type: Performing
Purpose: To present innovative modern dance as well as dance for worship, schools and community centers
Management: Maggie Kast, Director
Officers: James Jana, President; Jane Siarny, Maggie Kast, Directors
Volunteer Staff: 1
Paid Artists: 3   **Non-Paid Artists:** 1
Budget: $1,000 - $50,000
Income Sources: Box Office; Government Grants; Individual Donations
Annual Attendance: 3,000
Affiliations: Chicago Dance Coalition; Sacred Dance Guild; Phoenix Power and Light

LE BALLET PETIT GUILD
4630 North Francisco, Chicago, IL 60625-3729
(312) 463-3385
Founded: 1962

Arts Area: Mime; Ballet; Jazz; Ethnic; Tap
Status: Non-Professional; Non-Profit
Type: Performing; Resident; Educational
Purpose: To produce traditional and contemporary ballet performance for student participation, and establish and maintain a training facility and a program of scholarship funding
Management: Ida Velez, Director/Choreographer; Delores Schleser, Business Manager
Officers: Margie Dunne, President; Nancy Mason, Secretary; Faith Wilk, Treasurer
Paid Staff: 11   **Volunteer Staff:** 25
Non-Paid Artists: 210
Utilizes: Special Technical Talent; Guest Artists; Guest Choreographers
Budget: $1,000 - $50,000
Income Sources: Box Office; Government Grants; Individual Donations
Season: September - July   **Annual Attendance:** 2,000
Performance Facilities: St. Scholastica Theater

MORDINE AND COMPANY DANCE THEATRE
4730 North Sheridan Road, Chicago, IL 60640
(312) 271-7804
FAX: (312) 271-7046
Founded: 1968
Arts Area: Modern
Status: Professional; Non-Profit
Type: Performing; Resident; Educational
Purpose: To perform the works of artistic director, Shirley Mordine; to perform experimental, expansive, architectural and humorous works
Management: Shirley Mordine, Artistic Director; Michael McStraw, General Manager; Elizabeth Hutar, Development Director
Officers: Stephen Marcus, Chairman; Joan Erdman, Vice President; Doe Thornburg, Secretary
Paid Staff: 3
Paid Artists: 7
Utilizes: Special Technical Talent; Guest Artists; Guest Choreographers; Visual Designers; Composers
Budget: $100,000 - $500,000
Income Sources: Private Foundations/Grants/Endowments; Business/Corporate Donations; Box Office; Government Grants; Teaching
Season: October - June   **Annual Attendance:** 5,000
Affiliations: APAP; Dance USA; Chicago Dance Coalition
Performance Facilities: The Dance Center of Columbia College

MUNTU DANCE THEATRE
6800 South Wentworth, Suite 3E96, Chicago, IL 60621
(312) 602-1135
FAX: (312) 962-9116
Arts Area: Ethnic
Status: Professional; Non-Profit
Type: Performing; Touring; Resident
Purpose: To perform traditional and contemporary African and African-American dance, music and folklore
Management: Amaniyea Payne, Artistic Director; Mignon McPherson, Administrative Assistant; David K. Smith, Manager of Marketing/Production; Patricia Johnson, Development Officer; Atiba Walker, Assistant Artistic Director
Officers: Joan Gray, President
Budget: $100,000 - $500,000
Income Sources: Private Foundations/Grants/Endowments; Business/Corporate Donations; Box Office; Government Grants; Individual Donations
Performance Facilities: Katherine Dunham Theater, Kennedy-King College

NAJWA DANCE CORPS
1900 West Van Buren, Room 0505, Chicago, IL 60612
(312) 664-7943; (312) 921-4722
Founded: 1975
Arts Area: Modern; Jazz; Ethnic
Status: Professional; Non-Profit
Type: Performing; Touring; Educational
Purpose: The preservation of dance styles and techniques; to dance and entertain with dances of different areas in a historical context
Management: Celeste Harrell, Business Manager; Najwa I, Artistic Director
Officers: Annice Lillard, Jack Ward, Presidents; Sheila Wilkens, Treasurer
Paid Staff: 6
Paid Artists: 15
Utilizes: Special Technical Talent; Guest Artists; Guest Choreographers
Budget: $100,000 - $500,000

Income Sources: Private Foundations/Grants/Endowments; Business/Corporate Donations; Box Office; Government Grants; Individual Donations
Season: 52 Weeks **Annual Attendance:** 30,000
Affiliations: Chicago Dance Art Coalition; African-American Arts Alliance

INSTRUMENTAL MUSIC

BLACK MUSIC REPERTORY ENSEMBLE
Center for Black Music Research, Columbia College, 600 South Michigan, Chicago, IL 60605-1996
(312) 663-1600, ext. 559
FAX: (213) 663-9019
Founded: 1988
Arts Area: Chamber; Ensemble; Ethnic
Status: Professional; Non-Profit
Type: Performing; Touring
Purpose: To perfrom works by black composers from 1700 to present
Management: Morris A. Phipps, Coordinator of Programs and Services Center for Black Music Research
Officers: Dominique-Rene de Lerma, Director - Center for Black Music Reasearch; Samuel A. Floyd Jr., Artistic Director
Paid Artists: 15
Budget: $100,000 - $500,000
Income Sources: Private Foundations/Grants/Endowments; Business/Corporate Donations; Box Office; Government Grants; Individual Donations
Affiliations: Columbia College, Chicago

CHICAGO BAR ASSOCIATION SYMPHONY ORCHESTRA
321 South Plymouth Court, Chicago, IL 60604
(312) 554-2000
Founded: 1986
Arts Area: Symphony; Orchestra; Chamber
Status: Non-Professional; Non-Profit
Type: Performing; Touring
Purpose: To provide quality orchestral performance experience for legal professionals in the Chicago area
Management: David Katz, Music Director; Julia Nowicki, Founder; Susan Chernoff, Founder; Todd Wiener, Chairman
Paid Staff: 1 **Volunteer Staff:** 3
Paid Artists: 1 **Non-Paid Artists:** 40
Utilizes: Guest Conductors; Guest Artists
Budget: $1,000 - $50,000
Income Sources: Private Foundations/Grants/Endowments; Business/Corporate Donations; Box Office; Individual Donations
Season: September - June **Annual Attendance:** 1,000
Affiliations: ASOL; Illinois Council of Orchestras

CHICAGO BRASS QUINTET
PO Box 31917, Chicago, IL 60631-0917
(312) 696-1449; (800) 582-7913
FAX: (312) 696-1937
Founded: 1962
Arts Area: Chamber; Ensemble; Instrumental Group
Status: Professional; Non-Profit
Type: Performing; Touring; Resident; Educational; Sponsoring
Purpose: To promote brass chamber music through performance, recordings, broadcasts, educational workshops and commissioning
Management: Diane Dillavou, Artist Manager
Officers: James Mattern, President; Ross Beacraft, Treasurer; Diane Dillavou, Secretary
Paid Staff: 1
Paid Artists: 5
Utilizes: Guest Artists
Budget: $100,000 - $500,000
Income Sources: Private Foundations/Grants/Endowments; Business/Corporate Donations; Box Office; Government Grants; Individual Donations
Season: 52 Weeks

THE CHICAGO CHAMBER ORCHESTRA
410 South Michigan Avenue, Suite 631, Chicago, IL 60605
(312) 922-5570
FAX: (312) 922-5508
Founded: 1952
Arts Area: Orchestra; Chamber

Status: Professional; Non-Profit
Type: Performing
Purpose: To provide regularly scheduled, admission-free performances of great music on a year-round basis and to show-case each distinctive programming through national and international touring
Management: Dr. Dieter Kober, Music Director; Magdalene Lorenz, General Manager; Dorothy Marchi, Secretary
Officers: Frank Williams, President; William Mitchel, Vice President; Sharon Peterson, Treasurer
Paid Staff: 4   **Volunteer Staff:** 15
Paid Artists: 140
Utilizes: Guest Artists
Budget: $100,000 - $500,000
Income Sources: Private Foundations/Grants/Endowments; Business/Corporate Donations; Government Grants; Individual Donations
Season: September - June   **Annual Attendance:** 20,000
Affiliations: ASOL; Illinois Council of Orchestras; CMA

CHICAGO PHILHARMONIA
5528 South Hyde Park Boulevard, Suite 1002, Chicago, IL 60637
(312) 493-1915
FAX: (312) 324-6650
Founded: 1985
Arts Area: Symphony; Chamber; Ensemble
Status: Professional; Non-Profit
Type: Performing
Purpose: To present symphonic works for the enjoyment of Chicago area residents
Management: George W. Flynn, Music Administrator; Farobag Homi Cooper, Music Director/Conductor; John Albert, Director of Advertising
Volunteer Staff: 35
Paid Artists: 65
Utilizes: Guest Artists
Budget: $100,000 - $500,000
Income Sources: Private Foundations/Grants/Endowments; Business/Corporate Donations; Box Office; Individual Donations
Season: October - June   **Annual Attendance:** 10,000
Performance Facilities: Mandel Hall

CHICAGO STRING ENSEMBLE
3524 West Belmont Avenue, Chicago, IL 60618
(312) 332-0567
FAX: (708) 869-3925
Founded: 1977
Arts Area: Orchestra; Chamber; Ensemble; Instrumental Group
Status: Professional; Non-Profit
Type: Performing; Touring; Educational
Purpose: To develop string orchestra repertoire to its highest level; to bring to Chicago this body of music literature spanning three centuries
Management: Alan Heatherington, Music Director; Mary Jo Deysach, General Manager
Officers: Carl LaMell, President; Art Vallette, James Vogler, Vice Presidents
Utilizes: Guest Artists
Budget: $100,000 - $500,000
Income Sources: Private Foundations/Grants/Endowments; Business/Corporate Donations; Box Office; Government Grants; Individual Donations
Season: September - May
Affiliations: Chicago Music Alliance; ASOL; Illinois Council of Orchestras; Chicago Chamber Consortium
Performance Facilities: Saint Paul's Church; Unitarian Church, Evanston; Elmhurst College

CHICAGO SYMPHONY ORCHESTRA
220 South Michigan Avenue, Chicago, IL 60604
(312) 435-8122
FAX: (312) 786-1207
Founded: 1890
Arts Area: Symphony; Orchestra
Status: Non-Profit
Type: Performing
Management: Henry Fogel, Executive Director; Vanessa Moss, Manager; Martha Gilmer, Artistic Administrator; Joyce Idema, Director of Marketing and Public Relations; Tom Hallett, Director of Finance
Officers: Thomas Eyerman, Vice President for Development
Utilizes: Guest Conductors; Guest Artists

Budget: Over 10,000,000
Income Sources: Private Foundations/Grants/Endowments; Business/Corporate Donations; Box Office; Government Grants; Individual Donations
Season: 52 Weeks
Affiliations: ASOL

CHICAGO YOUTH SYMPHONY
410 South Michigan Avenue, Suite 922, Chicago, IL 60605
(312) 939-2207
Founded: 1946
Arts Area: Symphony; Orchestra; Chamber; Ensemble
Status: Non-Profit
Type: Performing; Touring; Sponsoring
Purpose: To provide the finest quality orchestral training and performance opportunities for Midwestern high school students in a central Chicago location
Management: Jeannette Kreston, Executive Director; Michael Morgan, Music Director/Conductor
Paid Staff: 5   **Volunteer Staff:** 15
Non-Paid Artists: 115
Utilizes: Guest Conductors; Guest Artists; Guest Directors
Budget: $100,000 - $500,000
Income Sources: Private Foundations/Grants/Endowments; Business/Corporate Donations; Box Office; Government Grants; Individual Donations; Tuition
Season: September - May   **Annual Attendance:** 13,000
Affiliations: ASOL (Youth Symphony Division); Chicago Music Alliance
Performance Facilities: Orchestra Hall

CIVIC ORCHESTRA OF CHICAGO
220 South Michigan Avenue, Chicago, IL 60604
(312) 435-8159
Founded: 1919
Arts Area: Symphony; Orchestra; Chamber; Ensemble
Status: Non-Professional; Non-Profit
Type: Performing; Educational
Purpose: To train musicians to be professional symphony orchestra members within the environment of a first-rate symphony orchestra such as the Chicago Symphony Orchestra
Management: Henry Fogel, Executive Director; Jeffrey Heggem, Manager
Officers: Henry Fogel, Executive Vice President
Paid Staff: 3
Non-Paid Artists: 110
Utilizes: Guest Conductors; Guest Artists
Budget: $500,000 - $1,000,000
Income Sources: Private Foundations/Grants/Endowments; Business/Corporate Donations; Government Grants; Individual Donations
Season: October - May
Annual Attendance: 16,000
Performance Facilities: Orchestra Hall

MUSIC OF THE BAROQUE
343 South Dearborn, Suite 1716, Chicago, IL 60604
(312) 663-1900; (312) 986-3236
FAX: (312) 347-1490
Founded: 1972
Arts Area: Orchestra; Chamber; Ensemble; Chorus
Status: Professional; Non-Profit
Type: Performing; Educational
Purpose: To provide a chorus and orchestra specializing in music of the 16th through 18th centuries
Management: Kathleen Butera, Executive Director; Thomas Wikman, Music Director
Officers: Jay A. Baylin, Chairman
Paid Staff: 9
Paid Artists: 65
Utilizes: Special Technical Talent; Guest Artists
Budget: $1,000,000 - $5,000,000
Income Sources: Private Foundations/Grants/Endowments; Business/Corporate Donations; Box Office; Government Grants; Individual Donations; Merchandise; Recordings
Season: October - June
Annual Attendance: 13,000
Affiliations: ASOL; CA; Chicago Music Alliance

PERFORMING ARTS CHICAGO
410 South Michigan Avenue, #911, Chicago, IL 60605
(312) 663-1628
FAX: (312) 663-1043
Founded: 1960
Arts Area: Chamber
Status: Professional; Non-Profit
Type: Performing; Resident; Educational; Sponsoring
Purpose: To present artists who explore the creative tension between tradition and innovation, to nurture an environment for and bring to performance new works and new performers, and to remain accountable to its community, furthering support for local artists, engagement and education, not only for its direct audience, but for society at large
Management: Susan Lipman, Executive Director; Heidi Feldman, Director of Marketing and Public Relations
Officers: Lewis Duberman, President; James Peponis, First Vice President of Fund-raising; Drucilla Handy Redinger, Second Vice President of Marketing; Averill Leviton, Third Vice President of Special Events; Norma Stone, Secretary; David Ellis, Treasurer
Utilizes: Guest Artists
Budget: $100,000 - $500,000
Income Sources: Private Foundations/Grants/Endowments; Business/Corporate Donations; Box Office; Government Grants; Individual Donations
Season: September - June   **Annual Attendance:** 9,280
Performance Facilities: The Civic Theatre

STREET MINSTRELS JAZZ SOCIETY
4339 South Berkeley, Chicago, IL 60653
(312) 483-2802
Founded: 1986
Arts Area: Ethnic; Instrumental Group
Status: Non-Professional; Non-Profit
Type: Educational; Sponsoring
Purpose: To capture on film and video local Afro-American jazz musicians performing original works
Management: Edward E. Mead, Founder/Business Manager; Sudan Mahmoud, Public Relations/Media Liason; Edward Rebb, Talent Coordinator
Volunteer Staff: 6
Utilizes: Local Unknown Artists
Budget: $1,000 - $50,000
Income Sources: Individual Donations
Season: June - September   **Annual Attendance:** 300
Affiliations: Arts Midwest
Performance Facilities: Twenty-First Century Bookstore

VOCAL MUSIC

CHAMBER OPERA CHICAGO
500 North Orleans, Chicago, IL 60610
(312) 822-0770
Founded: 1982
Arts Area: Grand Opera; Lyric Opera
Status: Professional; Non-Profit
Type: Performing
Purpose: To present quality opera in English; to provide talented young singers with opportunities to sing major roles
Management: Barre Seid, General Director; Carl Ratner, Artistic Director; Lawrence Rapchak, Administrative/Musical Director
Officers: Barre Seid, President/Treasurer; Lawrence Rapchak, Secretary; Carl Ratner, Arlene Dunn, Kenneth Recu, Directors
Paid Staff: 4
Paid Artists: 100
Budget: $100,000 - $500,000
Income Sources: Private Foundations/Grants/Endowments; Business/Corporate Donations; Box Office; Government Grants; Individual Donations
Season: April - May   **Annual Attendance:** 3,500
Performance Facilities: Ruth Page Auditorium

CHICAGO CHILDREN'S CHOIR
1720 East 54th Street, Chicago, IL 60615
(312) 324-8300
FAX: (312) 324-8333
Founded: 1956
Arts Area: Choral; Folk

Status: Semi-Professional
Type: Performing; Touring; Educational
Purpose: To develop and maintain a high-quality choral training and performance program for children and young people from a variety of cultural, religious, racial and ethnic backgrounds
Management: Nancy Carstedt, Executive Director; Martha O. Swisher, Music Director; Mary E. Adams, Business Manager
Paid Staff: 20
Non-Paid Artists: 110
Utilizes: Guest Artists
Budget: $100,000 - $500,000
Income Sources: Private Foundations/Grants/Endowments; Business/Corporate Donations; Box Office; Government Grants; Individual Donations
Season: September - June   **Annual Attendance:** 55,000
Affiliations: CA

CHICAGO OPERA THEATER
20 East Jackson, Chicago, IL 60604
(312) 663-0555
FAX: (312) 986-3999
Founded: 1974
Arts Area: Lyric Opera
Status: Professional; Non-Profit
Type: Performing; Touring; Educational
Purpose: To make outstanding performances of a broad repertory accessible to the broadest possible audience by offering all operas in English, in an intimate environment, with tickets at reasonable prices
Management: Alan Stone, Artistic Director; Jean Perkins, Managing Director; Tom DeWalle, Director of Development; Lex Poppens, Director of Marketing; Michelle Anderson, Director of Operations
Officers: Marilyn Arado, Chairman; Oreste Boscia, President
Paid Staff: 12   **Volunteer Staff:** 150
Paid Artists: 300
Utilizes: Special Technical Talent; Guest Conductors; Guest Artists; Guest Directors
Budget: $1,000,000 - $5,000,000
Income Sources: Private Foundations/Grants/Endowments; Business/Corporate Donations; Box Office; Individual Donations
Season: mid-February - mid-May   **Annual Attendance:** 20,000
Affiliations: OA; Chicago Music Alliance
Performance Facilities: Athenaeum Theatre

CHICAGO SYMPHONY CHORUS
Orchestra Hall, 220 South Michigan Avenue, Chicago, IL 60604
(312) 435-8712
FAX: (312) 435-0914
Founded: 1957
Arts Area: Choral
Status: Professional; Semi-Professional; Non-Profit
Type: Performing; Touring; Educational
Purpose: To perform with a major symphony orchestra
Management: Joseph Fabbioli, Manager; Margaret Hillis, Founder/Director Artistic Leadership
Paid Staff: 3
Paid Artists: 130   **Non-Paid Artists:** 60
Utilizes: Guest Conductors; Guest Artists; Guest Directors
Income Sources: Private Foundations/Grants/Endowments; Business/Corporate Donations; Box Office; Government Grants; Individual Donations
Season: 52 Weeks   **Annual Attendance:** 100,000
Affiliations: ASOL; CA
Performance Facilities: Orchestra Hall; Ravinia Festival

HUNGARIAN OPERA WORKSHOP
1014 South Michigan Avenue, Chicago, IL 60605
(312) 427-6267
FAX: (312) 427-6677
Founded: 1970
Arts Area: Light Opera; Operetta; Ethnic; Folk
Status: Professional; Non-Profit
Type: Performing; Touring; Resident; Educational
Purpose: To preserve and produce works in their original languages of Hungarian, German or French as well as works translated into English; to present productions to audiences at no charge
Management: Maria D'Albert, Instructor; Susan Kincaid, Executive Director of the Conservatory

Utilizes: Guest Artists
Budget: $1,000 - $50,000
Income Sources: Individual Donations
Season: 52 Weeks   **Annual Attendance:** 600
Performance Facilities: Sherwood Conservatory

LINCOLN OPERA
2456 North Surrey Court, Chicago, IL 60614
(312) 549-3249
Founded: 1983
Arts Area: Grand Opera
Status: Professional; Non-Profit
Type: Performing; Touring; Resident; Educational
Purpose: To perform standard repertoire for all ages at affordable prices; resident company
Management: Norma M. Williams, Artistic Director; Charles Rich, President; Dianna Marks, Executive Consultant; Kevin McMahon, Conductor; Heidi Mayer, Music Director
Officers: Charles Rich, President; Mark Richardson, Treasurer; Babs Lieberman, Director of Education; Louise Biga, Secretary
Paid Staff: 1   **Volunteer Staff:** 42
Paid Artists: 95
Utilizes: Special Technical Talent; Guest Directors
Budget: $100,000 - $500,000
Income Sources: Private Foundations/Grants/Endowments; Business/Corporate Donations; Box Office; Government Grants; Individual Donations
Season: 52 Weeks
Annual Attendance: 20,000

LYRIC OPERA CENTER FOR AMERICAN ARTISTS
20 North Wacker Drive, Chicago, IL 60606
(312) 332-2244
Founded: 1974
Arts Area: Grand Opera; Lyric Opera; Light Opera
Status: Professional; Non-Profit
Type: Performing; Educational
Purpose: To provide final stepping stone for young singers to bridge the transition to a professional career
Management: Andrew Foldi, Director
Officers: Brena Freeman, Chairman of Board; Kip Kelley, President of Board; Irene Antoniov, Vice President of Board; Samuel Budwig Jr., Treasurer of Board
Paid Staff: 4
Paid Artists: 15
Utilizes: Special Technical Talent; Guest Directors
Budget: $500,000 - $1,000,000
Income Sources: Private Foundations/Grants/Endowments; Business/Corporate Donations; Government Grants; Individual Donations
Season: February - August
Affiliations: Lyric Opera of Chicago

LYRIC OPERA OF CHICAGO
20 North Wacker Drive, Chicago, IL 60606
(312) 332-2244
FAX: (312) 419-8345
Founded: 1954
Arts Area: Grand Opera
Status: Professional; Non-Profit
Type: Performing; Sponsoring
Purpose: To bring quality opera to the Chicago area
Management: Ardis Krainik, General Manager
Officers: James Cozad, President/Chief Executive Officer
Paid Staff: 46
Utilizes: Special Technical Talent; Guest Conductors; Guest Artists; Guest Directors
Budget: Over 10,000,000
Income Sources: Private Foundations/Grants/Endowments; Business/Corporate Donations; Box Office; Government Grants; Individual Donations
Season: September - January
Annual Attendance: 240,000
Affiliations: Lyric Opera Center for American Artists
Performance Facilities: Civic Opera House

THE OPERA FACTORY
6161 North Hamilton Avenue, Chicago, IL 60659
(312) 761-1334
FAX: (312) 338-8331
> **Founded:** 1979
> **Arts Area:** Light Opera; Ethnic
> **Status:** Professional; Non-Profit
> **Type:** Performing; Touring; Educational
> **Purpose:** To present Spanish zarazuela, Hispanic song and dance, and plays by Spanish and Hispanic authors with music and dance
> **Management:** Blanche Artis Lewis, Executive Director; Donna Sadlicka, Administrative Assistant; Alex Boas, Director of Development; Roberto Sapier, Artistic Director; Gloria Maria Cruz, Director of Publicity
> **Officers:** Peter Pagratis, Chairman; Terrence Healy, Vice President/Treasurer; Donna Sadlicka, Secretary
> **Paid Staff:** 1   **Volunteer Staff:** 12
> **Utilizes:** Guest Conductors; Guest Artists; Guest Directors
> **Budget:** $1,000 - $50,000
> **Income Sources:** Private Foundations/Grants/Endowments; Business/Corporate Donations; Box Office; Government Grants; Individual Donations; Government of Spain
> **Season:** June   **Annual Attendance:** 800
> **Affiliations:** OA; Chicago Music Alliance
> **Performance Facilities:** Angel Guardian; Northeastern Illinois University

THEATRE

AMERICAN BLUES THEATRE
1225 West Belmont, Chicago, IL 60657
(312) 929-1031
> **Founded:** 1985
> **Arts Area:** Professional
> **Status:** Professional; Non-Profit
> **Type:** Performing
> **Purpose:** To develop and produce new plays by and for the people of the Midwest
> **Management:** Jim Leaming, Kate Buddeke, Co-Artistic Directors
> **Officers:** Doug Laux, Board President
> **Volunteer Staff:** 7
> **Paid Artists:** 50   **Non-Paid Artists:** 125
> **Budget:** $1,000 - $50,000
> **Income Sources:** Business/Corporate Donations; Box Office; Government Grants; Individual Donations
> **Season:** 52 Weeks
> **Affiliations:** League of Chicago Theatres

APOLLO THEATER CENTER
2540 North Lincoln Avenue, Chicago, IL 60614
(312) 935-6100
> **Founded:** 1978
> **Arts Area:** Professional
> **Status:** Professional; Commercial
> **Type:** Sponsoring; Presenting
> **Purpose:** Present local productions of Broadway and off-Broadway shows and serve as a transfer house for smaller off-loop theaters
> **Management:** Leavitt Fox Theatricals
> **Paid Staff:** 12
> **Budget:** $100,000 - $500,000
> **Income Sources:** Box Office
> **Season:** 52 Weeks   **Annual Attendance:** 139,000
> **Affiliations:** League of Chicago Theatres

BAILIWICK REPERTORY
1225 West Belmont, Chicago, IL 60657
(312) 883-1090; (312) 327-5252
FAX: (312) 327-1404
> **Founded:** 1982
> **Arts Area:** Theatrical Group
> **Status:** Professional; Non-Profit
> **Type:** Performing; Sponsoring
> **Purpose:** To provide contemporary theater with a classical core; to produce vivid productions of the greatest dramatists of all times, alongside great works from our time; to serve as host or co-producer for other productions or attractions with similar artistic aims; to present festivals of one act plays; to showcase new directors and gay and lesbian plays

Management: David Zak, Executive Director
Paid Staff: 2   **Volunteer Staff:** 125
Paid Artists: 250
Utilizes: Guest Artists; Guest Directors
Budget: $100,000 - $500,000
Income Sources: Private Foundations/Grants/Endowments; Business/Corporate Donations; Box Office; Government Grants; Individual Donations
Season: 52 Weeks   **Annual Attendance:** 50,000
Affiliations: League of Chicago Theatres; TCG; Illinois Theater Association
Performance Facilities: Theatre Building

BLACK ENSEMBLE THEATER
4520 North Beacon, Chicago, IL 60640
(312) 769-5516
   Founded: 1975
   Arts Area: Professional; Theatrical Group
   Status: Professional; Non-Profit
   Type: Performing; Touring; Resident; Educational
   Purpose: To supply continual employment in the theater for the Black artist and adhere to our philosophy of excellence in the art form of professional theater
   Management: Jackie Taylor, Artistic Director/Producer; Ben Morgan, Stage Manager
   Officers: Andrea Lyon, President; Bill Gillmore, Vice President; Allen Daniels, Secretary; Jackie Taylor, Treasurer
   Paid Staff: 9   **Volunteer Staff:** 5
   Paid Artists: 9
   Utilizes: Guest Artists; Guest Directors
   Budget: $100,000 - $500,000
   Income Sources: Private Foundations/Grants/Endowments; Business/Corporate Donations; Box Office; Government Grants; Individual Donations
   Season: September - August   **Annual Attendance:** 20,000
   Affiliations: Black Theater Alliance
   Performance Facilities: Leo Lerner Theater

BLIND PARROT PRODUCTIONS
1446 West Berteau, Chicago, IL 60613
(312) 549-3991
   Founded: 1983
   Arts Area: Theatrical Group
   Status: Non-Professional
   Type: Performing
   Purpose: To produce innovative, intelligent, thought-provoking writing for the stage with a focus on scripts which test the limits of theatrical form; to introduce new concepts; to pursue new relationships between artists and the audience
   Management: Clare Nolan-Long and David Perkins, Co-Artistic Directors; Jane Molnar, Executive Director
   Officers: Fred Hachmeister, President; Sheri Jones, Secretary; Frank Tourangeau, Treasurer
   Volunteer Staff: 4
   Non-Paid Artists: 20
   Utilizes: Guest Artists; Guest Directors
   Budget: $1,000 - $50,000
   Income Sources: Private Foundations/Grants/Endowments; Business/Corporate Donations; Box Office; Government Grants; Individual Donations
   Season: October - June   **Annual Attendance:** 3,500
   Affiliations: League of Chicago Theatres

BODY POLITIC THEATRE
2261 North Lincoln Avenue, Chicago, IL 60614
(312) 348-7901
   Founded: 1966
   Arts Area: Professional
   Status: Professional; Non-Profit
   Type: Performing; Touring; Resident; Educational
   Purpose: The Body Politic Theatre, Chicago's oldest off-loop theatre, provides an intimate forum for the best of classic and contemporary dramatic literature through thought-provoking and entertaining productions.
   Management: Albert Pertalion, Artistic Director; Kim Patrick Bitz, Administrative Director; Rick Sheingold, Business Director
   Officers: Richard Wier, President
   Paid Staff: 4   **Volunteer Staff:** 2
   Paid Artists: 40   **Non-Paid Artists:** 10
   Utilizes: Guest Directors
   Budget: $500,000 - $1,000,000

Income Sources: Private Foundations/Grants/Endowments; Business/Corporate Donations; Box Office; Government Grants; Individual Donations
Season: September - June   Annual Attendance: 20,000
Affiliations: AEA; USA; League of Chicago Theatres; TCG; Producers Association of Chicago Area Theatres

CENTER THEATER AND THE TRAINING CENTER
1346 West Devon, Chicago, IL 60660
(312) 508-0200; (312) 508-5422
Founded: 1984
Arts Area: Theatrical Group
Status: Professional; Non-Profit
Type: Performing; Touring; Resident; Educational
Purpose: To educate, inspire and cultivate theatre audiences; professional theater and ongoing training program for actors
Management: Dan LaMorte, Artistic Director; R.J. Coleman, General Manager
Officers: Jerry Proffit, Board President; Diane Tuscher-Ancede, Vice President; Michael A. Africk, Treasurer; Alisa Levy, Secretary
Paid Staff: 26   Volunteer Staff: 20
Paid Artists: 20   Non-Paid Artists: 10
Utilizes: Guest Artists; Guest Directors
Budget: $500,000 - $1,000,000
Income Sources: Private Foundations/Grants/Endowments; Business/Corporate Donations; Box Office; Government Grants; Individual Donations; Tuitions
Season: September - June   Annual Attendance: 10,000
Affiliations: TCG; ASSITEJ
Performance Facilities: Center Theater

CHICAGO ACTORS ENSEMBLE
941 West Lawrence Avenue, 5th Floor, Chicago, IL 60642
(312) 275-4463
Founded: 1984
Arts Area: Professional
Status: Professional; Non-Profit
Type: Performing; Touring; Resident
Management: Richard Helweg, Artistic Director
Officers: Kit Carson, President
Utilizes: Special Technical Talent; Guest Directors
Budget: $1,000 - $50,000
Income Sources: Private Foundations/Grants/Endowments; Business/Corporate Donations; Box Office; Individual Donations
Season: October - April   Annual Attendance: 1,000
Affiliations: League of Chicago Theatres

CHICAGO CITY THEATRE COMPANY
1225 West School Street, Chicago, IL 60657
(312) 880-1002
Founded: 1974
Arts Area: Professional
Status: Professional; Semi-Professional; Non-Profit
Type: Performing; Touring; Resident; Educational; Sponsoring
Purpose: Theatre (Chicago City Theatre), dance (Joel Hall Dancers) and training (New School North), which are multiracial, professional, national and international in scope
Management: Joseph Ehrenberg and Joel Hall, Co-Directors; Florence Martin, Studio Manager
Officers: Thomas A. Hajjar, President; David S. Mann, Secretary; Albert D. Beedie, Jr., Treasurer
Paid Staff: 3   Volunteer Staff: 30
Paid Artists: 25
Utilizes: Special Technical Talent; Guest Artists; Guest Directors
Budget: $100,000 - $500,000
Income Sources: Private Foundations/Grants/Endowments; Business/Corporate Donations; Box Office; Government Grants; Individual Donations
Season: September - June   Annual Attendance: 25,000
Affiliations: League of Chicago Theatres

CHICAGO DRAMATISTS WORKSHOP
1105 West Chicago Avenue, Chicago, IL 60657
(312) 633-0630
Founded: 1979
Arts Area: Professional; Theatrical Group
Status: Professional; Non-Profit
Type: Performing

Purpose: The Chicago Dramatists Workshop is a professional, non-profit theatre, dedicated to the development of promising, Chicago-area playwrights.
Management: Russ Tutterow, Director; Anita-Joyce Barnes, General Manager
Officers: Gene Jones, Vice President; Gary Brichetto, Treasurer
Paid Staff: 2 **Volunteer Staff:** 5
Utilizes: Guest Artists; Guest Directors
Budget: $1,000 - $50,000
Income Sources: Private Foundations/Grants/Endowments; Business/Corporate Donations; Box Office; Government Grants; Individual Donations
Season: September - August **Annual Attendance:** 5,000
Affiliations: League of Chicago Theatres

THE CHICAGO MEDIEVAL PLAYERS
International House, 1414 East 59th Street, Chicago, IL 60637
(312) 935-0742
Founded: 1985
Arts Area: Professional; Theatrical Group
Status: Professional; Non-Profit
Type: Performing; Touring
Purpose: The production of Medieval and Renaissance theatre
Management: Ann Faulkner, Artistic Director
Officers: Sheila Chapman, President; Robert Schmidt, Frank Underbriuk, Vice Presidents; Peter Christensen, Secretary
Paid Staff: 2 **Volunteer Staff:** 10
Paid Artists: 20
Utilizes: Guest Artists; Guest Directors
Budget: $1,000 - $50,000
Income Sources: Private Foundations/Grants/Endowments; Box Office; Government Grants; Individual Donations
Season: 52 Weeks
Affiliations: AEA; Societe International pour L'etudier du Theatre Medieval

THE CHICAGO THEATRE COMPANY
500 East 67th Street, Chicago, IL 60637
(312) 493-0901
Founded: 1984
Arts Area: Professional
Status: Professional; Non-Profit
Type: Performing; Resident
Purpose: To provide a professional and creative environment in which local artists may develop their talents, broaden the public's theatrical options, improve economic opportunities for minority artists, and enhance the cultural environment of the inner-city neighborhoods
Management: Douglas Alan Mann, Artistic Director
Officers: Stephanie Davenport, President; Hilton Clark, Vice President; Delia Coy, Treasurer; Marcie Creque, Secretary
Paid Staff: 1
Utilizes: Guest Artists; Guest Directors
Budget: $100,000 - $500,000
Income Sources: Private Foundations/Grants/Endowments; Business/Corporate Donations; Box Office; Government Grants; Individual Donations
Season: September - June
Affiliations: League of Chicago Theatres
Performance Facilities: Parkway Playhouse

CHILD'S PLAY TOURING THEATRE
2650 West Belden, Chicago, IL 60647
(312) 235-8911
FAX: (312) 235-5478
Founded: 1978
Arts Area: Professional; Theatrical Group
Status: Professional; Non-Profit
Type: Performing; Touring; Educational
Purpose: Child's Play Touring Theatre performs only original literature written by children. Its mission is to share, encourage and validate the creative writing of children.
Management: Victor Podagrosi, Artistic Director; June Podagrosi, Executive Director; Valerie Hogan, General Manager
Officers: Joan Mazzonelli, President; June Podagrosi, Mary Bryant, Vice Presidents; Susan Darby, Treasurer; Marie Donovan, Secretary
Paid Staff: 14
Paid Artists: 10
Budget: $50,000 - $100,000

Income Sources: Private Foundations/Grants/Endowments; Business/Corporate Donations; Government Grants; Individual Donations; Touring Fees
Season: September - July **Annual Attendance:** 175,000

CITY LIT THEATER COMPANY
4753 North Broadway, #618, Chicago, IL 60640
(312) 271-1100
    Founded: 1979
    Arts Area: Professional
    Status: Professional; Non-Profit
    Type: Performing; Touring; Resident; Educational
    Purpose: City Lit Theater Company's purpose is to adapt literary material for the stage.
    Management: Arnold Aprill, Artistic Director; Charles Twichell, General Manager
    Officers: Paul Pribbenow, President
    Paid Staff: 4
    Paid Artists: 20
    Budget: $100,000 - $500,000
    Income Sources: Private Foundations/Grants/Endowments; Business/Corporate Donations; Box Office; Government Grants; Individual Donations
    Season: 52 Weeks **Annual Attendance:** 38,000
    Affiliations: League of Chicago Theatres

CLASSICS ON STAGE! LTD
PO Box 25365, Chicago, IL 60625
(312) 989-0532
    Founded: 1982
    Arts Area: Professional; Musical; Theatrical Group
    Status: Professional; Commercial
    Type: Performing; Resident; Educational
    Purpose: To provide quality professional live theatre experiences for young audiences in order to develop and sustain live audiences for the future of legitimate theatre for all audiences
    Management: Robert D. Boburka, Managing Director; Michele L. Vacca, Artistic Director
    Officers: Robert D. Boburka, President and Treasurer; Michele L. Vacca, Vice President and Secretary
    Paid Staff: 8
    Paid Artists: 14
    Utilizes: Special Technical Talent; Guest Artists
    Budget: $50,000 - $100,000
    Income Sources: Box Office
    Season: October - June
    Annual Attendance: 50,000
    Affiliations: AEA; AATY; League of Chicago Theatres

COURT THEATRE
5535 South Ellis Avenue, Chicago, IL 60637
(312) 702-7005
FAX: (312) 702-5814
    Founded: 1954
    Arts Area: Professional
    Status: Professional; Non-Profit
    Type: Performing; Educational
    Purpose: To make high quality productions of the world's classic plays available to the people of Chicago and, due to the theatre's association with the University of Chicago, to educate its adult and high school audiences regarding each play
    Management: Nicholas Rudall, Executive Director; Sandra Karuschak, Managing Director
    Officers: William O'Connor, Chair; Robert McDermott, Vice Chair
    Paid Staff: 24
    Paid Artists: 70
    Utilizes: Special Technical Talent; Guest Artists; Guest Directors
    Budget: $1,000,000 - $5,000,000
    Income Sources: Private Foundations/Grants/Endowments; Business/Corporate Donations; Box Office; Government Grants; Individual Donations
    Season: September - May **Annual Attendance:** 45,000
    Affiliations: AEA; League of Chicago Theatres; TCG; Producers Association of Chicago Area Theatres
    Performance Facilities: Court Theatre

DREISKE PERFORMANCE COMPANY
1517 West Fullerton Avenue, Chicago, IL 60614
(312) 281-9075
    Founded: 1975

Arts Area: Professional; Theatrical Group
Status: Professional; Non-Profit
Type: Performing; Touring; Resident; Educational
Purpose: Professional touring ensemble, many of whose productions were developed in historic and on-location projects; "The Book of Lear" in the Sahara Desert, "Macondo" in Columbia, South America; currently developing new theater works for performance for international TV and tours
Management: Nicole Dreiske, Artistic Director; Milos Stehlik, Managing Director; Catherine Berkenstein, Literary Manager; John Dreiske, General Manager
Officers: David Edelberg, Chair; Emilye Hunterfields, Secretary
Paid Staff: 18
Paid Artists: 12
Utilizes: Special Technical Talent; Guest Directors
Budget: $500,000 - $1,000,000
Income Sources: Private Foundations/Grants/Endowments; Business/Corporate Donations; Box Office; Government Grants; Individual Donations
Season: February - December
Affiliations: ATHE; ITI; League of Chicago Theatres
Performance Facilities: International Performance Studio

ENSEMBLE ESPANOL
5500 North Saint Louis Avenue, Chicago, IL 60625
(312) 583-4050
Founded: 1976
Arts Area: Professional; Musical; Community; Folk
Status: Professional; Non-Profit
Type: Performing; Touring; Resident; Educational; Sponsoring
Purpose: To share the rich tradition of dance, music, literature, and culture of Spain with all the communities of the United States and to be a center which encourages new artistic creativity
Management: Libby Komaiko Fleming, Director; Jorge D. Perez, Administrative Assistant; Jeanette Lukaszow, Executive Secretary; Flor Dumblao, Accountant
Officers: Dr. Robert Komaiko, President; Angelina Pedroso, Vice President; Janie S. Petersen, Secretary; Edward Garcia, Treasurer
Paid Staff: 4 **Volunteer Staff:** 5
Paid Artists: 20
Utilizes: Guest Artists; Guest Directors
Budget: $100,000 - $500,000
Income Sources: Private Foundations/Grants/Endowments; Business/Corporate Donations; Box Office; Government Grants; Individual Donations
Season: September - August
Annual Attendance: 10,000
Performance Facilities: Northeastern Illinois University, Chicago

ETA CREATIVE ARTS FOUNDATION
7558 So. South Chicago Avenue, Chicago, IL 60619
(312) 752-3955
FAX: (312) 752-8727
Founded: 1971
Arts Area: Professional
Status: Professional; Non-Profit
Type: Performing; Touring; Resident; Educational
Purpose: ETA provides training in the performing and technical aspects of the arts, encouraging the development and employment primarily of Black artists. ETA also works to encourage the development and propagation of the works of Black writers through its productions of original works.
Management: Abena Joan P. Brown, President/Producer; Runako Jahi, Artistic Director; Jerome A. Adams, Director of Development; Teresa A. White, Business Manager; Kenneth Simmons, Building Manager; Darryl Goodman, Technical Director
Officers: Milton Davis, Chairman of the Board; Abena Joan Brown, President; Velma Wilson, Secretary/Treasurer; Wiley Moore, Finance
Paid Staff: 14 **Volunteer Staff:** 450
Paid Artists: 150
Utilizes: Guest Artists; Guest Directors
Budget: $500,000 - $1,000,000
Income Sources: Private Foundations/Grants/Endowments; Business/Corporate Donations; Box Office; Government Grants; Individual Donations
Season: September - July
Annual Attendance: 63,000
Affiliations: Afro-American Arts Alliance; Department of Cultural Affairs; League of Chicago Theatres
Performance Facilities: ETA Square

FREE STREET THEATER
441 West North Avenue, Chicago, IL 60610
(312) 642-1234
Founded: 1969
Arts Area: Professional; Theatrical Group
Status: Professional; Non-Profit
Type: Performing; Touring
Management: David Stein, Artistic Director; Patricia Patton, Marketing Director; Julie Mittman-Glazer, Managing Director
Paid Staff: 3
Paid Artists: 50
Budget: $100,000 - $500,000
Income Sources: Private Foundations/Grants/Endowments; Business/Corporate Donations; Box Office; Government Grants; Individual Donations
Season: 52 Weeks   **Annual Attendance:** 50,000
Affiliations: TCG; Illinois Arts Alliance

GOODMAN THEATRE
200 South Columbus Drive, Chicago, IL 60603
(312) 443-3811
FAX: (312) 263-6004
Founded: 1925
Arts Area: Professional; Musical
Status: Professional; Non-Profit
Type: Performing; Educational; Sponsoring
Purpose: To provide the highest quality professional theatre, both classical and contemporary
Management: Roche Schulfer, Producing Director; Robert Falls, Artistic Director
Paid Staff: 70
Non-Paid Artists: 11
Utilizes: Special Technical Talent; Guest Artists; Guest Directors
Budget: $1,000,000 - $5,000,000
Income Sources: Private Foundations/Grants/Endowments; Business/Corporate Donations; Box Office; Government Grants; Individual Donations
Season: September - July
Affiliations: TCG

IMAGINATION THEATER
1801 West Bryon, Studio 2S, Chicago, IL 60613
(312) 929-4100
Founded: 1966
Arts Area: Professional
Status: Professional; Non-Profit
Type: Performing; Touring; Educational
Purpose: Committed to the value of creative drama as a tool for learning through two basic programs: participatory theater for children, the elderly, and the disabled; and Child Sexual Abuse Prevention Program, a comprehensive program for teachers, parents and students
Management: Warren W. Baumgart Jr., Artistic Director
Paid Staff: 6
Paid Artists: 12
Budget: $100,000 - $500,000
Income Sources: Private Foundations/Grants/Endowments; Business/Corporate Donations; Box Office; Government Grants; Individual Donations
Season: 52 Weeks   **Annual Attendance:** 225,000

LIFELINE THEATRE
6912 North Glenwood, Chicago, IL 60660
(312) 761-4477
Founded: 1982
Arts Area: Theatre Group
Status: Professional; Non-Profit
Type: Performing
Purpose: We at Lifeline believe it is vital to offer an art form that reaffirms the underlying humanity and sense of connection that is essential to all our lives.
Management: Suzanne Plunkett, Managing Director
Officers: Randy Snyder, President; Christina Calvit, Treasurer; Meryl Friedman, Secretary
Paid Staff: 5   **Volunteer Staff:** 10
Paid Artists: 12
Budget: $50,000 - $100,000

Income Sources: Private Foundations/Grants/Endowments; Business/Corporate Donations; Box Office; Government Grants; Individual Donations
Season: September - June   **Annual Attendance:** 10,000
Affiliations: League of Chicago Theatres
Performance Facilities: Lifeline Theatre

MAYFAIR THEATRE/"SHEAR MADNESS"
636 South Michigan Avenue, Chicago, IL 60605
(312) 786-9317
Founded: 1982
Arts Area: Theatrical Group
Status: Professional; Commercial
Type: Performing
Purpose: Mayfair Theatre presents "Shear Madness," the comedy whodunit that lets the audience play armchair detective. "Shear Madness" is the longest running play in the history of Chicago theatre.
Management: Deborah Gordon, Company Manager; Marilyn Abrams and Bruce Jordan, Producers
Paid Staff: 10
Paid Artists: 9
Utilizes: Guest Artists
Budget: $500,000 - $1,000,000
Income Sources: Box Office
Season: 52 Weeks   **Annual Attendance:** 100,000
Affiliations: League of Chicago Theatres
Performance Facilities: Mayfair Theatre

NEW TUNERS THEATRE
c/o Performance Community, 1225 West Belmont, Chicago, IL 60657
(312) 929-7367
FAX: (312) 327-1404
Arts Area: Professional; Musical
Status: Professional; Non-Profit
Type: Performing; Resident
Purpose: To give new musicals exposure; to support up-and-coming artists of the Chicago area
Management: Ruth Higgins, Joan Mazzonelli, Co-Producers; Alan Chambers, Casting/Drama Director
Officers: Howard Walker, Chairman of the Board
Paid Staff: 10   **Volunteer Staff:** 35
Budget: $500,000 - $1,000,000
Income Sources: Private Foundations/Grants/Endowments; Business/Corporate Donations; Box Office; Government Grants; Individual Donations
Season: 52 Weeks
Affiliations: League of Chicago Theatres; TCG; National Alliance of Theatre Producers
Performance Facilities: New Tuners Theatre Building

ORGANIC THEATER COMPANY
3319 North Clark Street, Chicago, IL 60657
(312) 327-5588
FAX: (312) 327-8947
Founded: 1969
Arts Area: Professional
Status: Professional; Non-Professional; Non-Profit
Type: Performing; Educational
Purpose: To develop and produce new works of theatre and to nurture the artists involved in that process; interested in adventurous, challanging scripts that truly explore the theatrical medium and its possibilities
Management: Richard Fire, Producing Artistic Director; Jeff Neal, General Manager; Sarah Tucker, Literary Manager/Intern Coordinator
Officers: Kathleen B. Gillig, President; Barry Gomberg, Vice President/Secretary; Carl LaMell, Treasurer
Paid Staff: 10   **Volunteer Staff:** 12
Utilizes: Guest Artists; Guest Directors
Budget: $500,000 - $1,000,000
Income Sources: Private Foundations/Grants/Endowments; Business/Corporate Donations; Box Office; Government Grants; Individual Donations
Season: 52 Weeks   **Annual Attendance:** 40,000
Affiliations: League of Chicago Theatres; TCG

PEGASUS PLAYERS
Truman College, 1145 West Wilson, Chicago, IL 60640
(312) 878-9761
Founded: 1979

Arts Area: Theatrical Group
Status: Professional; Non-Profit
Type: Performing
Purpose: To provide professional, top-quality theater to the people of Chicago, especially the Uptown Area, at affordable prices and to serve the community with outreach, touring, and educational programs
Management: Arlene Crewdson, Artistic Director; Alan Salzenstein, Managing Director
Paid Staff: 5   **Volunteer Staff:** 5
Paid Artists: 150
Utilizes: Special Technical Talent; Guest Artists; Guest Directors
Budget: $500,000 - $1,000,000
Income Sources: Private Foundations/Grants/Endowments; Business/Corporate Donations; Box Office; Government Grants; Individual Donations
Season: September - August   **Annual Attendance:** 11,000
Affiliations: League of Chicago Theatres
Performance Facilities: O'Rourke Center

PLAYWRIGHTS' CENTER
1222 West Wilson, Chicago, IL 60640
(312) 334-9981
Founded: 1958
Arts Area: THEATRE GROUP
Status: Semi-Professional; Non-Profit
Type: Educational
Purpose: To offer a place where a playwright may have a workshop reading and critique of his/her play, followed by a staged reading and a possible production
Management: James McDowell, Artistic Director; B.L. Robbins, Executive Director
Budget: $1,000 - $50,000
Income Sources: Private Foundations/Grants/Endowments; Business/Corporate Donations; Government Grants; Individual Donations
Performance Facilities: Playwrights' Center

RAVEN THEATRE COMPANY
6931 North Clark Street, Chicago, IL 60626
(312) 338-2177
Founded: 1983
Arts Area: Professional; Theatrical Group
Status: Professional; Non-Profit
Type: Performing; Resident
Purpose: To provide professional theatre affordable and accessible to the broadest cross-section of the people of Chicagoland and to provide the opportunity for local theatre artists to develop a showcase for their talents
Management: Michael Menendian, Executive/Artistic Director; John Munson, Technical Director; Joni Gatz, Production Manager
Officers: John Munson, President; Barbara King, Vice President; Joni Gatz, Secretary; Ed Bray, Treasurer
Volunteer Staff: 4
Paid Artists: 30   **Non-Paid Artists:** 30
Utilizes: Special Technical Talent; Guest Artists; Guest Directors
Budget: $50,000 - $100,000
Income Sources: Private Foundations/Grants/Endowments; Business/Corporate Donations; Box Office; Government Grants; Individual Donations
Season: 52 Weeks   **Annual Attendance:** 6,000
Affiliations: League of Chicago Theatres

REMAINS THEATRE
1800 North Clybourn Avenue, Chicago, IL 60614
(312) 335-9595; (312) 335-9800
FAX: (312) 335-0626
Founded: 1979
Arts Area: Professional
Status: Professional; Non-Profit
Type: Performing; Touring; Educational
Purpose: The purpose of Remains Theatre is to establish and maintain a theatre company dedicated to presenting work focused in three areas: 1) ensemble-developed original works; 2) provocative contemporary plays; and 3) lesser-known works by eminent writers.
Management: Larry Sloan, Artistic Director; R.P. Sekon, Producing Director; Janis Post, General Manager
Officers: Valerie Hoffman, President; David Harvey, Vice President; Elizabeth Hubbard, Secretary
Paid Staff: 9
Paid Artists: 20
Utilizes: Special Technical Talent; Guest Artists; Guest Directors
Budget: $500,000 - $1,000,000

Income Sources: Private Foundations/Grants/Endowments; Business/Corporate Donations; Box Office; Government Grants; Individual Donations
Season: September - July   **Annual Attendance:** 25,000
Affiliations: TCG; League of Chicago Theatres
Performance Facilities: Remains Theatre

SAINT SEBASTIAN PLAYERS
1641 West Diversey, Chicago, IL 60614
(312) 404-7922
FAX: (312) 728-0496
Founded: 1982
Arts Area: Musical; Community; Theatrical Group
Status: Non-Profit
Type: Performing
Purpose: To enrich the life of the parish community of Saint Bonaventure, as well as that of our surrounding neighborhood
Officers: Chris Andrews, President; Jill Chukerman, Vice President/Secretary; Jim Masini, Treasurer
Volunteer Staff: 10
Non-Paid Artists: 10
Utilizes: Special Technical Talent
Budget: $1,000 - $50,000
Income Sources: Box Office; Individual Donations
Season: May - November   **Annual Attendance:** 750
Affiliations: League of Chicago Theatres
Performance Facilities: Saint Bonaventure Hall

THE SECOND CITY
1616 North Wells, Chicago, IL 60614
(312) 337-3992
FAX: (312) 664-9837
Founded: 1959
Arts Area: Professional
Status: Professional; Commercial
Type: Performing; Touring; Resident; Educational
Purpose: Satirical revue
Management: Andrew Alexander, Executive Producer; Kelly Leonard, Associate Producer
Paid Staff: 43
Paid Artists: 30
Income Sources: Box Office
Season: 52 Weeks
Performance Facilities: Second City; Second City, Etc.

SHAKESPEARE REPERTORY
2140 Lincoln Park West, Suite 1001, Chicago, IL 60614
(312) 281-2101
FAX: (312) 642-8817
Arts Area: Professional; Theatrical Group
Status: Professional; Non-Profit
Type: Performing; Touring; Resident; Educational; Sponsoring
Purpose: To bring accessible Shakespearean productions to Chicago audiences
Management: Barbara Gaines, Artistic Director; Criss Henderson, Producing Director
Officers: Katherine Updike, President of the Board; Sheila Penrose, Executive Vice President of the Board
Budget: $500,000 - $1,000,000
Income Sources: Private Foundations/Grants/Endowments; Business/Corporate Donations; Box Office; Government Grants; Individual Donations
Performance Facilities: Ruth Page Theatre

SHATTERED GLOBE THEATER
2856 North Halsted, Chicago, IL 60657
(312) 404-1237
Founded: 1990
Arts Area: Theatrical Group
Status: Semi-Professional; Commercial
Type: Performing; Resident; Educational
Purpose: The foundation of the Shattered Globe is a core of actors, directors, playwrights, designers and teachers working together as the result of having received similar training in the Sanford Meisner technique.
Management: Brian Pudil, General Manager; Roger Smart, Artistic Director; Joe Forbrich, Associate Director
Officers: Brian Pudil, President; Joe Forbrich, Vice President; Leigh Horsley, Secretary; Linda Reiter, Treasurer
Volunteer Staff: 3

Non-Paid Artists: 15
Utilizes: Special Technical Talent; Guest Artists; Guest Directors; Performance Artists
Budget: $1,000 - $50,000
Income Sources: Box Office; Individual Donations
Season: September - June **Annual Attendance:** 6,000
Affiliations: League of Chicago Theatres
Performance Facilities: Chicago Actors Project

STAGE LEFT THEATRE
3244 North Clark Street, Chicago, IL 60657
(312) 883-8830
Founded: 1982
Arts Area: Professional; Theatrical Group
Status: Professional; Non-Profit
Type: Performing; Touring; Educational
Purpose: To produce plays that raise the level of debate on political and social issues
Management: Mike Troccoli, Sandra Jean Verthein, Co-Artistic Directors; Drew Martin, Managing Director
Officers: Jay Tarshis, Chairman of the Board; Jeff Cory, Vice Chairman; Sandra Jean Verthein, Secretary; Drew Martin, Treasurer
Volunteer Staff: 10
Paid Artists: 46 **Non-Paid Artists:** 25
Utilizes: Guest Artists; Guest Directors
Budget: $50,000 - $100,000
Income Sources: Private Foundations/Grants/Endowments; Business/Corporate Donations; Box Office; Government Grants; Individual Donations
Season: 52 Weeks
Affiliations: League of Chicago Theatres

STEPPENWOLF THEATRE COMPANY
1650 North Halstead, Chicago, IL 60614
(312) 335-1888
FAX: (312) 335-0440
Founded: 1976
Arts Area: Professional
Status: Professional; Non-Profit
Type: Performing; Resident; Educational
Purpose: The Steppenwolf Theatre Company is comprised of twenty-three actors dedicated to the ensemble approach of dramatic art.
Management: Randall Arney, Artistic Director; Stephen Eich, Managing Director
Paid Staff: 20
Paid Artists: 23
Utilizes: Special Technical Talent; Guest Artists; Guest Directors
Budget: $1,000,000 - $5,000,000
Income Sources: Private Foundations/Grants/Endowments; Business/Corporate Donations; Box Office; Government Grants; Individual Donations
Season: September - July **Annual Attendance:** 60,000
Affiliations: TCG; AEA; Producers Association of Chicago Theatres
Performance Facilities: Steppenwolf Theater

THEATRE FIRST
6656 Sioux Avenue, Chicago, IL 60646
(312) 792-2226
Founded: 1952
Arts Area: Theatrical Group
Status: Non-Professional
Type: Performing
Management: Joanne Notz, Executive Producer; William Mages, Business Manager
Officers: Edwarc Cavaliere, Chairman of the Board; Dale Marach, Comptroller; Jeaniane Benton, Secretary
Volunteer Staff: 12
Utilizes: Guest Conductors
Budget: $1,000 - $50,000
Income Sources: Private Foundations/Grants/Endowments; Business/Corporate Donations; Box Office; Government Grants; Individual Donations
Season: September - April
Annual Attendance: 10,000
Affiliations: League of Chicago Theatres
Performance Facilities: Athenaeum Theatre

THEATRE II COMPANY
3700 West 103rd Street, Chicago, IL 60655
(312) 779-3300, ext. 475
Founded: 1978
Arts Area: Theatrical Group
Status: Professional; Non-Profit
Type: Performing
Purpose: Theatre II's primary objective is to provide quality live theater to the Southwest Chicago community.
Management: Steve Micotto, Artistic Director; JoAnne Fleming, Managing Director
Paid Staff: 8 **Volunteer Staff:** 8
Paid Artists: 30
Utilizes: Special Technical Talent
Budget: $50,000 - $100,000
Income Sources: Business/Corporate Donations; Box Office; Government Grants; Individual Donations
Season: September - June **Annual Attendance:** 5,000
Affiliations: League of Chicago Theatres; Saint Xavier University
Performance Facilities: McGuire Hall

VICTORY GARDENS THEATER
2257 North Lincoln Avenue, Chicago, IL 60614
(312) 549-5788
Founded: 1974
Arts Area: Professional; Theatrical Group
Status: Professional
Type: Performing; Touring; Resident; Educational
Purpose: Development of Chicago theatre artists, with special emphasis on playwrights
Management: John Walker, Managing Director; Dennis Zacek, Artistic Director; Allyn Pokraka, Administrative Director
Officers: Nancy Breseke, President
Paid Staff: 20
Paid Artists: 20
Utilizes: Special Technical Talent; Guest Artists; Guest Directors
Budget: $1,000,000 - $5,000,000
Income Sources: Private Foundations/Grants/Endowments; Business/Corporate Donations; Box Office; Government Grants; Individual Donations
Season: September - July

WISDOM BRIDGE THEATRE
1559 West Howard Street, Chicago, IL 60626
(312) 743-0486
FAX: (312) 743-1614
Founded: 1974
Arts Area: Professional
Status: Professional; Non-Profit
Type: Performing; Touring; Educational
Purpose: Wisdom Bridge Theatre exists to explore classic literature and address new works within a context of risk-taking and enlightenment.
Management: Jefferey Ortmann, Producing Director; Karl Sullivan, Producing Manager; Sharon Phillips, Director of Program Administration; Terry McCabe, Resident Director
Officers: John Conlon, Jack Johnson, Co-Chairs; Louise Sunderland, Secretary; Ellen Baras, Treasurer
Paid Staff: 12
Utilizes: Special Technical Talent; Guest Artists; Guest Directors
Budget: $1,000,000 - $5,000,000
Income Sources: Private Foundations/Grants/Endowments; Business/Corporate Donations; Box Office; Government Grants; Individual Donations
Season: September - July **Annual Attendance:** 35,000
Affiliations: AEA; League of Chicago Theatres; TCG
Performance Facilities: Wisdom Bridge Theatre

PERFORMING SERIES

AUDITORIUM THEATRE COUNCIL
50 East Congress Parkway, Chicago, IL 60605
(312) 922-4046
Founded: 1960
Arts Area: Dance; Vocal Music; Theater
Status: Professional; Non-Profit
Type: Resident; Educational; Sponsoring

Purpose: To restore the Auditorium Theatre to its original architectural splendor and present dance, music and theatre programs for their cultural and educational value
Management: Robert A. Alsaker, Executive Director; Morton Zolotow, Theatre Manager; Barbara V. Corrigan, Director of Marketing and Group Sales
Utilizes: Special Technical Talent; Guest Conductors; Guest Artists
Performance Facilities: Auditorium Theatre

CRYSTAL BALLROOM CONCERT ASSOCIATION
410 South Michigan Avenue, #521, Chicago, IL 60605
(312) 481-2370
Founded: 1984
Arts Area: Dance; Vocal Music; Instrumental Music; Festivals
Status: Professional; Non-Profit
Type: Performing; Educational; Sponsoring
Purpose: To present nationally and internationally known and young local artists in concert; To promote first world premieres of commissioned works
Management: Beverly DeFries-D'Albert, Executive Secretary/Program Director
Officers: Dr. Francois D'Albert, President; Leslie Kondorossy, Vice President; Beverly DeFries-D'Albert, Treasurer
Volunteer Staff: 10
Paid Artists: 150 **Non-Paid Artists:** 50
Utilizes: Guest Artists
Budget: $1,000 - $50,000
Income Sources: Private Foundations/Grants/Endowments; Box Office; Individual Donations
Season: 52 Weeks
Affiliations: Zoltan Kodaly Academy and Institute
Performance Facilities: Crystal Ballroom

14TH ANNUAL CHICAGO JAZZ FESTIVAL
Mayor's Office of Special Events, 121 North LaSalle Street, Chicago, IL 60602
(312) 744-0576
FAX: (312) 744-8523
Founded: 1979
Arts Area: Vocal Music; Instrumental Music; Jazz
Status: Professional
Type: Performing
Purpose: To present a festival, free to the public featuring jazz in all of its forms
Management: Mayor's Office of Special Events, Producer; Jazz Institute of Chicago, Programmer
Officers: Penny Tyler, Coordinator
Paid Staff: 60 **Paid Artists:** 250
Utilizes: Guest Artists
Budget: $100,000 - $500,000
Income Sources: Business/Corporate Donations
Season: Labor Day Weekend **Annual Attendance:** 360,000
Performance Facilities: Symphony Music Shell; Petrillo Music Shell

GRANT PARK MUSIC FESTIVAL
425 East McFetridge Drive, Chicago, IL 60605
(312) 294-2420
Founded: 1934
Arts Area: Instrumental Music
Status: Professional; Non-Profit
Type: Performing; Resident; Educational
Purpose: Providing professional symphonic concerts without charge to the people of Chicago
Management: Catherine M. Cahill, General Manager/Artistic Director
Officers: Robert A. Podesta, President; Lucille Burrus, Vice President
Paid Staff: 5 **Volunteer Staff:** 3
Paid Artists: 200 **Non-Paid Artists:** 100
Utilizes: Guest Conductors; Guest Artists
Budget: $1,000,000 - $5,000,000
Income Sources: Government Grants
Season: June - August **Annual Attendance:** 1,000,000
Performance Facilities: James C. Petrillo Music Shell

FACILITY

ARIE CROWN THEATRE
McCormick Place, Chicago, IL 60616
(312) 791-6516
Type of Facility: Theatre Complex; Theatre House

Type of Stage: Proscenium; Hydraulic Lift Stage
Stage Dimensions: 90'Wx77'D   **Orchestra Pit**
Seating Capacity: 4,319
Year Built: 1971   **Architect:** Gene Summers   **Cost:** $11,000,000
Acoustical Consultant: Klepper Marshall & King
Contact for Rental: Jacqueline A. Huels;   (312) 791-6516

ATHENAEUM THEATRE
2936 North Southport Avenue, Chicago, IL 60657
(312) 935-6860
  Type of Facility: Theatre House
  Type of Stage: Proscenium
  Stage Dimensions: 44'Wx32'Dx20'H plus loft   **Orchestra Pit**
  Seating Capacity: 925
  Year Built: 1911   **Architect:** Hermann Gaul
  Contact for Rental: Clyde Foster;   (312) 935-6860
  Resident Groups: Athenaeum Theatre Company; Chicago Opera Theatre

AUDITORIUM THEATRE
50 East Congress Parkway, Chicago, IL 60605
(312) 922-2110
FAX: (312) 922-0347
  Type of Facility: Auditorium
  Type of Stage: Proscenium
  Stage Dimensions: 99'Wx63'D   **Orchestra Pit**
  Seating Capacity: 4,000
  Year Built: 1889   **Architect:** Dankmar Adler & Louis Sullivan   **Cost:** $3,145,291
  Year Remodeled: 1967   **Architect:** Harry M. Weese & Associates   **Cost:** $3,175,000
  Contact for Rental: Marie Cali;   (312) 922-4046
  Manager: Dolcie Gilmore
  Our purpose is to restore the Auditorium Theatre, a National Historic Landmark, to its original splendor

BEVERLY ART CENTER
2153 West 111th Street, Chicago, IL 60643
(312) 445-3838
  Founded: 1969
  Type of Facility: Visual and Performing Arts Center
  Type of Stage: Proscenium
  Stage Dimensions: 45'x45'
  Seating Capacity: 425
  Year Built: 1969   **Architect:** Fugard and Orth Associates   **Cost:** $800,000
  Acoustical Consultant: Dan Richardson
  Contact for Rental: Rita Moster;   (312) 881-6705
  Resident Groups: Beverly Dance Ensemble; Beverly Theatre Guild; Pitt Players; Beverly Hills University Club

CIVIC STAGES CHICAGO
20 North Wacker Drive, Chicago, IL 60606
(312) 346-0270
FAX: (312) 704-6051
  Type of Facility: Theatre Complex; Auditorium; Studio Performance; Performance Center; Theatre House; Opera House; Multi-Purpose
  Year Built: 1929   **Architect:** Graham Anderson Probst White
  Contact for Rental: Fred Solari;   (312) 346-0270
  Manager: Randall L. Green
  Resident Groups: Lyric Opera of Chicago
  The Civic Center contains the Civic Theatre and Opera House. See individual listings for additional information.

CIVIC STAGES CHICAGO - CIVIC THEATRE
20 North Wacker Drive, Chicago, IL 60606
(312) 346-0270
FAX: (312) 704-6051
  Type of Facility: Theatre House
  Type of Stage: Proscenium
  Stage Dimensions: 72'Wx31'D   **Orchestra Pit**
  Seating Capacity: 906
  Year Built: 1929
  Contact for Rental: Fred Solari;   (312) 346-0270
  Manager: Randall L. Green

CIVIC STAGES CHICAGO - OPERA HOUSE
20 North Wacker Drive, Chicago, IL 60606
(312) 346-0270
FAX: (312) 704-6051
> **Type of Facility:** Opera House
> **Type of Stage:** Proscenium
> **Stage Dimensions:** 115'Wx75'D
> **Orchestra Pit**
> **Seating Capacity:** 3,486
> **Year Built:** 1929
> **Contact for Rental:** Fred Solari;   (312) 346-0270
> **Manager:** Randall L. Green

CURTISS HALL
410 South Michigan, Chicago, IL 60605
(312) 939-3380
> **Type of Facility:** Concert Hall; Auditorium; Studio Performance; Multi-Purpose; Room
> **Facility Originally:** Recital Hall
> **Type of Stage:** Proscenium
> **Stage Dimensions:** 15'x30'
> **Seating Capacity:** 200
> **Year Built:** 1885   **Architect:** Solon S. Beman
> **Contact for Rental:** Lee Newcomer;   (312) 939-3380

DE PAUL UNIVERSITY - BLACKSTONE THEATRE
60 East Balbo Drive, Chicago, IL 60605
(312) 362-8455
> **Type of Facility:** Theatre House
> **Type of Stage:** Proscenium
> **Stage Dimensions:** 60'6"Wx34'D; 37'10"Wx32'H proscenium opening
> **Orchestra Pit**
> **Seating Capacity:** 1,424
> **Contact for Rental:** Peter Entin;   (212) 944-3700
> **Manager:** The Shubert Organization
> *Limited availability for rental.*

JAMES C. PETRILLO MUSIC SHELL
c/o Grant Park Music Hall, 425 East McSetridge, Chicago, IL 60605
(312) 294-2420
> **Type of Facility:** Outdoor (Concert); Amphitheater
> **Type of Stage:** Concert Shell (outdoor)
> **Seating Capacity:** 5,000 fixed seats, unlimited lawn seating
> **Year Built:** 1978
> **Acoustical Consultant:** Klepper Marshall King Associates, Ltd.
> **Contact for Rental:**
> **Manager:** Catherine Cahill
> **Resident Groups:** Grant Park Symphony Orchestra and Chorus
> *Available for rental on a limited basis to charity and civic organizations*

ORCHESTRA HALL
220 South Michigan Avenue, Chicago, IL 60604
(312) 435-8122
> **Type of Facility:** Concert Hall
> **Type of Stage:** Concert Stage
> **Stage Dimensions:** 73'Wx40'D
> **Seating Capacity:** 2,566
> **Year Built:** 1904   **Architect:** Daniel H. Burnham   **Cost:** $750,000
> **Year Remodeled:** 1981   **Architect:** Skidmore Owings & Merrill   **Cost:** $3,400,000
> **Acoustical Consultant:** R. Lawrence Kirkegaard & Associates
> **Contact for Rental:** Michael Mach;   (312) 435-8122, ext. 8141
> **Resident Groups:** Chicago Symphony Orchestra; Allied Arts Association; Chicago Symphony Chorus; Civic Orchestra of Chicago

PARKWAY PLAYHOUSE
500 East 67th Street, Chicago, IL 60637
(312) 493-0901
> **Type of Facility:** Performance Center; Multi-Purpose

Type of Stage: Thrust
Stage Dimensions: 20'Wx20'D
Seating Capacity: 100
Contact for Rental: Elizabeth Murphy;   (312) 493-0901
Resident Groups: The Chicago Theatre Company

PETRILLO MUSIC SHELL
Columbus Drive and Jackson Boulevard, Chicago, IL 60603
(312) 294-2420
FAX: (312) 616-3719
Mailing Address: Grant Park Music Festival, 425 East McFetridge Drive, Chicago, IL 60605
Founded: 1935
Type of Facility: Outdoor (Concert)
Type of Stage: Pavilion
Stage Dimensions: 96'x53'
Seating Capacity: 5,000
Year Built: 1978
Acoustical Consultant: Christopher Jaffe
Contact for Rental: Marge Frantz;   (312) 294-4772
Resident Groups: Grant Park Symphony Orchestra and Chorus

PLAYWRIGHTS' CENTER OF CHICAGO
1222 West Wilson Avenue, Chicago, IL 60640
(312) 334-9981
Type of Facility: Studio Performance; Multi-Purpose; Room
Facility Originally: Business Facility
Type of Stage: Flexible
Stage Dimensions: 24'x14'
Seating Capacity: 50
Year Remodeled: 1986   **Architect:** S. Bruce   **Cost:** $1,000
Acoustical Consultant: S. Bruce
Contact for Rental: B.L. Robbins;   (312) 975-7711
Resident Groups: Playwrights' Center
Suitable for auditions, studio performances, meetings, classes

ROOSEVELT UNIVERSITY - PATRICK L. O'MALLEY THEATRE
430 South Michigan Avenue, Chicago, IL 60605
(312) 341-3719
FAX: (312) 341-3655
Type of Facility: Theatre House; Multi-Purpose
Type of Stage: Thrust
Stage Dimensions: 26'x32'
Seating Capacity: 336
Year Built: 1899   **Architect:** Dankmar Adler & Louis Sullivan
Year Remodeled: 1973   **Architect:** Marion Gutnayer   **Cost:** $140,000
Resident Groups: Roosevelt University Theatre and Music Theatre Programs

SHUBERT THEATRE
22 West Monroe Street, Chicago, IL 60603
(312) 977-1700
FAX: (312) 977-1740
Founded: 1906
Type of Facility: Theatre House
Facility Originally: Vaudeville
Type of Stage: Proscenium
Orchestra Pit
Seating Capacity: 2,008
Year Built: 1906   **Architect:** E.R. Krause
Contact for Rental: Ken Shaw;   (312) 977-1700

THEATRE BUILDING
1225 West Belmont Avenue, Chicago, IL 60657
(312) 929-7367
FAX: (312) 327-1404
Founded: 1968

Type of Facility: Theatre Complex; Performance Center; Multi-purpose Room
Facility Originally: Warehouse
Type of Stage: Thrust; Flexible; Proscenium
Seating Capacity: 148 in each of three theatres
Year Remodeled: 1977
Contact for Rental: Joan Mazzonelli; (312) 929-7367
Resident Groups: New Tuners Theatre; Illinois Theatre Association; Bailiwick Repertory; American Blues Theatre
Building contains three separate stages

TRUMAN COLLEGE - O'ROURKE CENTER FOR THE PERFORMING ARTS
1145 West Wilson, Chicago, IL 60640
(312) 878-9761
FAX: (312) 271-8057
Type of Facility: Theatre Complex
Type of Stage: Thrust; Proscenium
Stage Dimensions: 38'x34'
Orchestra Pit
Seating Capacity: 250
Year Built: 1980   **Cost:** $4,000,000
Manager: Arlene Crewdson
Resident Groups: Pegasus Players
Has modest performing arts series

VICTORY GARDENS THEATER
2257 North Lincoln Avenue, Chicago, IL 60614
(312) 549-5788
Type of Facility: Theatre Complex
Facility Originally: Cannery
Type of Stage: Thrust
Seating Capacity: 195
Year Remodeled: 1981   **Architect:** Sakal & Hood
Acoustical Consultant: R. Lawrence Kirkegaard & Associates
Contact for Rental: John Walker; (312) 549-5788
Resident Groups: Victory Gardens Theater; Body Politic Theatre

---

Crystal Lake

INSTRUMENTAL MUSIC

MCHENRY COUNTY YOUTH ORCHESTRA
46 South Walkup Avenue, Crystal Lake, IL 60014
(815) 477-4676
Founded: 1980
Arts Area: Symphony; Orchestra; Chamber; Ensemble
Status: Non-Professional; Non-Profit
Type: Performing; Educational; Sponsoring
Purpose: To foster educational, cultural, and musical activities; to support orchestras; to contribute to the cultural life of the community by performances of the orchestras, ensemble and students; to provide private and class instruction in orchestral instruments, piano and voice
Management: Marie Ann Vos, Executive Director
Officers: Tim Warnecke, President; Cathy Braun, First Vice President; Greg Baron, Second Vice President; Joyce Wright, Third Vice President; Cindy Charoenying, Recording Secretary; Deb Rosulek, Corresponding Secretary; N. Landon Hoyt, Treasurer
Paid Staff: 1
Paid Artists: 10   **Non-Paid Artists:** 135
Utilizes: Guest Artists
Budget: $100,000 - $500,000
Income Sources: Private Foundations/Grants/Endowments; Business/Corporate Donations; Box Office; Government Grants; Individual Donations
Season: September - May
Annual Attendance: 1,200
Affiliations: ASOL; Illinois Council of Orchestras; Illinois Arts Alliance; National Guild Community School of the Arts; Barrington Area Arts Council; Suzuki Association of the Americas; Greater Crystal Lake Chamber of Commerce and Industry

---
Danville

INSTRUMENTAL MUSIC

DANVILLE SYMPHONY ORCHESTRA
205 1/2 North Walnut Street, Danville, IL 61832
(217) 443-5300
>**Founded:** 1967
>**Arts Area:** Symphony; Orchestra; Chamber
>**Status:** Semi-Professional; Non-Profit
>**Type:** Performing; Educational
>**Purpose:** To provide quality, educational performances to a five-county, two-state area, bringing in top talent and utilizing top local talent
>**Management:** Connie Anderson, Administrative Director; Jeremy A. Swerling, Music Director; Kelly Talsma, Orchestra Manager
>**Officers:** Richard Doyle, President; Steve Foster, Vice President; Dick Cheney, Secretary; M.E. Cary, Treasurer
>**Paid Staff:** 6 **Volunteer Staff:** 25
>**Paid Artists:** 76
>**Utilizes:** Guest Artists
>**Budget:** $50,000 - $100,000
>**Income Sources:** Private Foundations/Grants/Endowments; Business/Corporate Donations; Box Office; Individual Donations
>**Season:** September - March
>**Annual Attendance:** 5,500
>**Affiliations:** Illinois Council of Orchestras; Illinois Presenters Network
>**Performance Facilities:** High School Auditorium; David Palmer Civic Center

---
De Kalb

DANCE

EMERGENCE DANCE THEATRE
804 1/2 Market Street, PO Box 186, De Kalb, IL 60115
(815) 758-6613
>**Founded:** 1984
>**Arts Area:** Modern; Media
>**Status:** Professional; Non-Profit
>**Type:** Performing; Touring; Educational
>**Purpose:** To promote quality professional dance and media performance in the northern Illinois area
>**Management:** Sandra Schramel, Artistic Director; John Schmitz, Executive Director
>**Paid Artists:** 7
>**Utilizes:** Guest Artists; Guest Choreographers
>**Budget:** $50,000 - $100,000
>**Income Sources:** Private Foundations/Grants/Endowments; Business/Corporate Donations; Box Office; Government Grants; Individual Donations
>**Season:** 52 Weeks
>**Annual Attendance:** 1,200
>**Performance Facilities:** Northern Illinois University Concert Hall

FACILITY

EGYPTIAN THEATRE
135 North Second Street, DeKalb, IL 60115
(815) 758-1215
>**Founded:** 1929
>**Type of Facility:** Concert Hall; Auditorium; Performance Center; Off Broadway; Theatre House
>**Facility Originally:** Vaudeville; Movie House
>**Type of Stage:** Thrust; Proscenium
>**Stage Dimensions:** 30'Dx75'W, including wing space 35' opening
>**Orchestra Pit**
>**Seating Capacity:** 1,483
>**Year Built:** 1929 **Architect:** Elmer F. Behrens **Cost:** $300,000
>**Year Remodeled:** 1983 **Architect:** Roland Killian of AEC Group, Inc. **Cost:** $2,125,000
>**Contact for Rental:** Barbara Kummerfeldt, Executive Director; (815) 758-1215
>**Resident Groups:** Kishwaukee Symphony; Children's Community Theatre; NIU Fine Arts Series
>*Preservation of the Egyptian Theatre (PET) is an all-volunteer organization formed in 1978 to preserve and operate this historic theatre.*

Decatur

VOCAL MUSIC

MILLIKIN UNIVERSITY OPERA THEATRE
1184 West Main Street, Decatur, IL 62522
(217) 424-6209
Founded: 1955
Arts Area: Grand Opera; Lyric Opera; Operetta
Status: Non-Profit
Type: Educational
Purpose: To provide performance opportunities for university students and audiences participation for students and community
Management: Stephen Fiol, General Director; Dr. Wesley Tower, Dean of School of Music
Officers: Maria Klott, Assistant to the Director
Paid Staff: 9   **Volunteer Staff:** 10
Non-Paid Artists: 55
Utilizes: Guest Directors
Budget: $1,000 - $50,000
Season: November - May   **Annual Attendance:** 12,000
Affiliations: COS; NOA; OA
Performance Facilities: Kirkland Theater

FACILITY

DECATUR CIVIC CENTER
1 Civic Center Plaza, Decatur, IL 62523
(217) 422-7300
Type of Facility: Civic Center
Year Built: 1980   **Architect:** Hellmuth Obata & Kassabaum   **Cost:** $13,800,000
Acoustical Consultant: Ned Lustig
Contact for Rental:
Manager: Ann Brunson
The Civic Center contains the Arena and Theater. See separate listings for additional information.

DECATUR CIVIC CENTER - ARENA
1 Civic Center Plaza, Decatur, IL 62523
(217) 422-7300
Type of Facility: Arena
Type of Stage: Flexible; Platform
Stage Dimensions: 32'x40'
Seating Capacity: Bleachers - 1,200; Portable Seating - 1,800
Year Built: 1980
Contact for Rental:
Manager: Ann Brunson

DECATUR CIVIC CENTER - THEATER
1 Civic Center Plaza, Decatur, IL 62523
(217) 422-7300
Type of Facility: Concert Hall; Theatre House
Type of Stage: Proscenium
Stage Dimensions: 40'Wx16'H   **Orchestra Pit**
Seating Capacity: 460
Year Built: 1980
Contact for Rental:
Manager: Ann Brunson

KIRKLAND FINE ARTS CENTER
1184 West Main Street, Decatur, IL 62522
(217) 424-6253
FAX: (217) 424-3993
Type of Facility: Performance Center; Fine Arts Center
Type of Stage: Proscenium   **Orchestra Pit**
Seating Capacity: 1,944
Year Built: 1970   **Architect:** Perkins and Will   **Cost:** $3,500,000
Acoustical Consultant: Bolt, Beranek & Newman
Contact for Rental: Ken Foster, Managing Director;   (217) 424-6253

Des Plaines

INSTRUMENTAL MUSIC

NORTHWEST SYMPHONY ORCHESTRA
1603 Thacker Street, Des Plaines, IL 60016
(708) 824-1279
> **Founded:** 1951
> **Arts Area:** Symphony; Orchestra; Chamber
> **Status:** Non-Profit
> **Type:** Performing; Educational
> **Purpose:** To provide musical training and a full scale performing symphony for Northwest Suburban Chicago residents
> **Officers:** Sherry Kujala, President; Ann Butler, Treasurer
> **Volunteer Staff:** 15
> **Paid Artists:** 1   **Non-Paid Artists:** 100
> **Utilizes:** Guest Artists
> **Budget:** $1,000 - $50,000
> **Income Sources:** Private Foundations/Grants/Endowments; Business/Corporate Donations; Box Office; Government Grants; Individual Donations
> **Season:** September - June   **Annual Attendance:** 2,000
> **Affiliations:** Maine-Oakton-Niles Adult Evening Education Program
> **Performance Facilities:** Maine West High School

THEATRE

DES PLAINES THEATRE GUILD
620 Lee Street, Des Plaines, IL 60016
(708) 296-1211
> **Founded:** 1946
> **Arts Area:** Community; Theatrical Group
> **Status:** Non-Professional; Non-Profit
> **Type:** Performing
> **Purpose:** To produce professional quality community theatre that will educate and entertain the Northwest Suburban Chicago Area
> **Officers:** Carol Kempiak, President; Marilyn Collignon, Financial Vice President; Jane Berman, Production Vice President; Donald Collignon, Administrative Vice President
> **Volunteer Staff:** 12
> **Utilizes:** Guest Directors
> **Budget:** $50,000 - $100,000
> **Income Sources:** Private Foundations/Grants/Endowments; Business/Corporate Donations; Box Office; Individual Donations
> **Season:** September - June   **Annual Attendance:** 15,000
> **Performance Facilities:** Prairie Lake Community Center

Downers Grove

PERFORMING SERIES

DOWNERS GROVE CONCERT ASSOCIATION
731 59th Street, Downers Grove, IL 60516
(708) 252-7160
FAX: (708) 252-5986
> **Founded:** 1947
> **Arts Area:** Dance; Instrumental Music
> **Status:** Non-Professional
> **Type:** Sponsoring
> **Purpose:** To promote public interest in the performing arts in and about the area of Downers Grove by presenting outstanding professional talent in the sphere of music and dance
> **Officers:** Ellen L. Webb, President; Chris Saricks, Vice President; Robert Durnberger, Secretary; Steven C. Pieper, Treasurer; Hans G. Kaper, Concert Impresario
> **Volunteer Staff:** 20
> **Utilizes:** Guest Artists
> **Budget:** $1,000 - $50,000
> **Income Sources:** Business/Corporate Donations; Box Office; Individual Donations
> **Season:** September - April   **Annual Attendance:** 1,400
> **Affiliations:** Chicago Music Alliance
> **Performance Facilities:** Downers Grove North High School Auditorium

---
Edwardsville

PERFORMING SERIES

SOUTHERN ILLINOIS UNIVERSITY-EDWARDSVILLE
Campus Box 1083, Edwardsville, IL 62026
(618) 692-2626
> **Arts Area:** Dance; Instrumental Music; Theater
> **Status:** Non-Profit
> **Type:** Educational; Sponsoring
> **Purpose:** The Arts and Issues series provides speakers and performance events to the University community to complement the academic programs at the University
> **Management:** Rich Walker, Series Coordinator
> **Officers:** Earl Lazerson, President
> **Paid Staff:** 5
> **Paid Artists:** 32
> **Utilizes:** Guest Artists
> **Budget:** $100,000 - $500,000
> **Income Sources:** Private Foundations/Grants/Endowments; Business/Corporate Donations; Box Office; Government Grants
> **Season:** September - June   **Annual Attendance:** 3,500
> **Affiliations:** APAP
> **Performance Facilities:** University Center and Communications Theater

---
Elgin

INSTRUMENTAL MUSIC

ELGIN AREA YOUTH ORCHESTRA
1700 Spartan Drive, Elgin, IL 60123
(708) 888-7389
FAX: (708) 888-7995
> **Founded:** 1976
> **Arts Area:** Symphony; Orchestra
> **Status:** Non-Professional; Non-Profit
> **Type:** Performing; Educational
> **Purpose:** Provide the finest orchestral performance opportunity to young musicians from schools throughout Illinois' Northern Fox Valley
> **Management:** Elizabeth Prieslozny, Music Director; Martha Henrikson, Assistant Conductor
> **Officers:** Cherie Lee Lewis, President/Elgin Symphony Board; Florence Jacobsen, President/Elgin Symphony League
> **Paid Staff:** 3   **Volunteer Staff:** 3
> **Paid Artists:** 2   **Non-Paid Artists:** 100
> **Utilizes:** Guest Conductors; Guest Artists
> **Budget:** $1,000 - $50,000
> **Income Sources:** Private Foundations/Grants/Endowments; Business/Corporate Donations; Box Office; Government Grants; Individual Donations
> **Season:** September - May   **Annual Attendance:** 3,500
> **Affiliations:** ASOL; MENC; NSOL
> **Performance Facilities:** Hemmens Auditorium

ELGIN SYMPHONY ORCHESTRA
1700 Spartan Drive, Elgin, IL 60123
(708) 888-7389
FAX: (708) 888-7995
> **Founded:** 1950
> **Arts Area:** Symphony; Orchestra
> **Status:** Professional
> **Type:** Performing; Educational
> **Purpose:** To create and provide the finest possible orchestral music serving educational and culttural needs to our entire regional community
> **Management:** Marcene Linstrom, Executive Director; Edith Fitts, Marketing Manager; James Hegarty, Operations Manager; Robert Hanson, Music Director
> **Officers:** Mark Seigle, President of Board; David McClintock, Secretary; Len Rempert, Treasurer; John Snow, Financial Development
> **Paid Staff:** 8
> **Paid Artists:** 69
> **Utilizes:** Guest Conductors; Guest Artists
> **Budget:** $500,000 - $1,000,000

Income Sources: Private Foundations/Grants/Endowments; Business/Corporate Donations; Box Office; Government Grants; Individual Donations
Season: October - May   **Annual Attendance:** 1,100
Performance Facilities: Hemmens Auditorium

Evanston

DANCE

GUS GIORDANO JAZZ DANCE CHICAGO
614 Davis Street, Evanston, IL 60201
(708) 866-6779
Founded: 1968
Arts Area: Modern; Ballet; Jazz
Status: Professional
Type: Performing; Touring; Educational
Purpose: The purpose of Gus Giordano Jazz Dance Chicago is to get audiences excited about dance in general, specifically jazz dance. Contributions will be used for the continued existence and growth of GGJDC so that jazz can continue to be a major art form.
Management: Nan Giordano, Associate Director; Gardner Arts Network, New York City
Officers: Hilary Pender, President; Lloyd Culbertson, Randy Mehrberg, Vice Presidents; A. Steven Crown, Treasurer; William Madden, Secretary
Paid Staff: 2   **Volunteer Staff:** 5
Paid Artists: 12   **Non-Paid Artists:** 3
Utilizes: Special Technical Talent; Guest Artists; Guest Choreographers
Budget: $100,000 - $500,000
Income Sources: Private Foundations/Grants/Endowments; Business/Corporate Donations; Box Office; Government Grants; Individual Donations; Benefits
Season: September - May   **Annual Attendance:** 7,000
Affiliations: Chicago Dance Arts Coalition; Illinois Arts Council; Evanston Arts Council

VOCAL MUSIC

HIS MAJESTIE'S CLERKES
PO Box 1001, Evanston, IL 60204
(708) 866-7464
Arts Area: Choral
Status: Semi-Professional; Non-Profit
Type: Performing
Purpose: To present historically-informed performances of Renaissance masterworks as well as works of the 19th and 20th centuries
Management: Anne Heider, Executive/Art/Music Director
Officers: R. Stephen Warner, President of the Board
Budget: $50,000 - $100,000
Income Sources: Private Foundations/Grants/Endowments; Business/Corporate Donations; Box Office; Government Grants; Individual Donations
Season: 52 Weeks

LIGHT OPERA WORKS
927 Noyes Street, Evanston, IL 60201
(708) 869-6300
FAX: (708) 869-6302
Founded: 1980
Arts Area: Light Opera; Operetta; Musical Comedy
Status: Professional; Non-Profit
Type: Performing
Purpose: Professional production of light opera
Management: Bridget McDonough, Managing Director; Philip A. Kraus, Artistic Director; Tim Pleiman, Business Manager
Officers: Harry Clamor, President; John Auwaerter, Treasurer; Philip A. Kraus, Secretary
Paid Staff: 3   **Volunteer Staff:** 2
Paid Artists: 200
Utilizes: Guest Conductors; Guest Directors
Budget: $100,000 - $500,000
Income Sources: Private Foundations/Grants/Endowments; Business/Corporate Donations; Box Office; Government Grants; Individual Donations
Season: June - December   **Annual Attendance:** 12,000

Affiliations: NOA; OA; League of Chicago Theatres; Chicago Music Alliance
Performance Facilities: Cahn Auditorium

THEATRE

LIVE THEATRE
1234 Sherman Avenue, Evanston, IL 60201
(708) 475-2570
Founded: 1983
Arts Area: Professional
Status: Professional; Non-Profit
Type: Performing
Purpose: "The Focus of Live Theatre," says Artistic Director A.C. Thomas, "is to create a nourishing and challenging environment for our actors and artists in our continued exploration of the human condition."
Management: A.C. Thomas, Artistic Director; Marcia Riegel, Executive Director; Marjorie Cohn, Managing Director; Richard O'Connell and Michael E. Myers, Directors
Officers: Kimberly A. Zeitlin, President; Marcia Riegel, Treasurer
Paid Staff: 4
Paid Artists: 6
Budget: $1,000 - $50,000
Income Sources: Business/Corporate Donations; Box Office; Individual Donations
Season: September - July   **Annual Attendance:** 500
Affiliations: League of Chicago Theatres; Evanston Arts Council
Performance Facilities: Live Theatre

NEXT THEATRE COMPANY
927 Noyes, Evanston, IL 60201
(708) 475-6763
FAX: (708) 475-6767
Founded: 1981
Arts Area: Professional
Status: Professional; Non-Profit
Type: Performing; Resident
Purpose: We believe theatre is a powerful tool for moving, entertaining and provoking people in a positive way. Therefore, the Next Theatre Company devotes itself to producing plays about current social concerns.
Management: Harriet Spizziri, Artistic Director; Jim Keister, Managing Director; Tim Engle, Production Manager; Dexter Bullard, Matt DeCaro, Artistic Associates
Officers: Kate Saccany, President; Alan Leib, Vice President; Charlotte Leib, Secretary; Irwin Noparstak, Treasurer
Paid Staff: 11   **Volunteer Staff:** 20
Paid Artists: 15
Utilizes: Special Technical Talent; Guest Artists; Guest Directors
Budget: $100,000 - $500,000
Income Sources: Private Foundations/Grants/Endowments; Business/Corporate Donations; Box Office; Government Grants; Individual Donations
Season: September - April   **Annual Attendance:** 16,000
Affiliations: AEA; TCG; League of Chicago Theatres; Producers Association of Chicago Area Theatres
Performance Facilities: Noyes Cultural Arts Center

NORTHLIGHT THEATRE AT THE CORONET
817 Chicago Avenue, Evanston, IL 60202
(708) 869-7732; (708) 869-7278
FAX: (708) 869-9445
Founded: 1974
Arts Area: Professional
Status: Professional; Non-Profit
Type: Resident; Producing
Purpose: The theatre's objective is to challenge, as well as entertain, its audiences with a focus to produce compelling new interpretations of contemporary plays drawn from an international repertoire and to create stage adaptions inspired by the full spectrum of artistic disciplines.
Management: Russell Vandenbroucke, Artistic Director; Kimberly C. Sleight, Managing Director
Paid Staff: 15
Paid Artists: 75
Budget: $1,000,000 - $5,000,000
Income Sources: Private Foundations/Grants/Endowments; Business/Corporate Donations; Box Office; Government Grants; Individual Donations
Season: August - May   **Annual Attendance:** 70,000
Affiliations: TCG; LORT; AAA
Performance Facilities: Northlight Theatre at the Coronet

PIVEN THEATRE WORKSHOP
927 Noyes Street, Evanston, IL 60201
(708) 866-6597
> **Founded:** 1974
> **Arts Area:** Theatrical Group
> **Status:** Professional; Non-Profit
> **Type:** Performing; Educational
> **Purpose:** A center for training in the performing arts for the child and adult, the novice and the professional, these classes may be ends in themselves or serve to prepare the student for the professional theatre; share work with the public
> **Management:** Joyce and Byrne Piven, Artistic Directors; Janie Weisenberg, Administrative Director
> **Officers:** Steve Goranson, President; Bonnie Wilson, Vice President; Ron Saiet, Treasurer
> **Paid Staff:** 12
> **Paid Artists:** 8
> **Budget:** $100,000 - $500,000
> **Income Sources:** Private Foundations/Grants/Endowments; Business/Corporate Donations; Box Office; Government Grants; Individual Donations
> **Season:** 52 Weeks   **Annual Attendance:** 10,000
> **Affiliations:** Illinois Arts Alliance; Evanston Arts Alliance
> **Performance Facilities:** Noyes Cultural Arts Center

TRINITY SQUARE ENSEMBLE
PO Box 1798, Evanston, IL 60204
(708) 328-0330
> **Founded:** 1981
> **Arts Area:** Professional
> **Status:** Professional
> **Type:** Performing; Touring; Educational
> **Management:** Deborah Stewart, Managing Director; Karen L. Erickson, Artistic Director
> **Officers:** Carl Wesselman, President; Tom Gahlon, Vice President; Glen Rippie, Secretary
> **Paid Staff:** 1   **Volunteer Staff:** 5
> **Paid Artists:** 6   **Non-Paid Artists:** 8
> **Utilizes:** Guest Artists; Guest Directors
> **Budget:** $50,000 - $100,000
> **Income Sources:** Private Foundations/Grants/Endowments; Business/Corporate Donations; Box Office; Government Grants; Individual Donations
> **Season:** 52 Weeks   **Annual Attendance:** 3,000
> **Affiliations:** League of Chicago Theatres

FACILITY

NATIONAL - LOUIS UNIVERSITY'S WEINSTEIN CENTER FOR THE PERFORMING ARTS
2840 North Sheridan Road, Evanston, IL 60201
(708) 256-5150, ext. 2593
FAX: (708) 256-1047
> **Type of Facility:** Auditorium; Performance Center
> **Facility Originally:** Gymnasium
> **Type of Stage:** Proscenium; Partial Thrust
> **Stage Dimensions:** 45'Dx60'W, 10' curved apron thrust; 52'x18' proscenium opening
> **Seating Capacity:** 634
> **Year Built:** 1925
> **Year Remodeled:** 1972   **Architect:** Perkins and Will   **Cost:** $100,000
> **Contact for Rental:** Karin L. Lewis, Director;   (708) 256-5150, ext. 2273

PICK - STAIGER CONCERT HALL
1977 Sheridan Road, Evanston, IL 60208
(708) 332-2373
FAX: (708) 467-1831
> **Founded:** 1975
> **Type of Facility:** Concert Hall
> **Type of Stage:** Thrust
> **Stage Dimensions:** 57'x38'
> **Seating Capacity:** 1,003
> **Year Built:** 1975   **Architect:** Edward D. Dart   **Cost:** $4,000,000
> **Acoustical Consultant:** Bolt, Beranek and Newman
> **Contact for Rental:** Jeff Cech;   (708) 491-5441
> **Resident Groups:** Northwestern University School of Music Performing Organizations

---

Galesburg

INSTRUMENTAL MUSIC

KNOX GALESBURG SYMPHONY
Knox College, PO Box 31, Galesburg, IL 61401
(309) 343-0112, ext. 268
    Founded: 1951
    Arts Area: Symphony; Orchestra
    Status: Non-Profit
    Type: Performing
    Purpose: To provide symphonic music for the community; to educate
    Management: Ruth Ann Baughman, Manager; Bruce Polay, Conductor
    Officers: Jim Jackson, President
    Paid Staff: 1
    Paid Artists: 5
    Utilizes: Guest Artists
    Budget: $100,000 - $500,000
    Income Sources: Private Foundations/Grants/Endowments; Business/Corporate Donations; Box Office; Government Grants; Individual Donations
    Season: October - June **Annual Attendance:** 4,000
    Performance Facilities: Orpheum Theatre

THEATRE

PRAIRIE PLAYERS CIVIC THEATRE
60 South Kellogg Street, Galesburg, IL 61401
(309) 342-2299
    Founded: 1915
    Arts Area: Musical; Dinner; Community
    Status: Non-Profit
    Type: Performing; Touring; Educational
    Purpose: As the main community theatre in the Galesburg Area, PPCT provides volunteers and audiences the opportunity to actively participate in, learn about and enjoy all aspects of the theatre arts.
    Management: Kathleen Bashem, Youth Theatre Director
    Officers: Patricia Conolly, Executive Director
    Paid Staff: 2 **Volunteer Staff:** 15
    Non-Paid Artists: 50
    Budget: $100,000 - $500,000
    Income Sources: Private Foundations/Grants/Endowments; Business/Corporate Donations; Box Office; Individual Donations
    Season: September - August **Annual Attendance:** 24,000
    Affiliations: Illinois Arts Council

FACILITY

KNOX COLLEGE - ELEANOR ABBOTT FORD CENTER FOR THE FINE ARTS
2 East South Street, Galesburg, IL 61401-4999
(309) 343-0112, ext. X408
    Type of Facility: Theatre Complex; Concert Hall; Auditorium; Studio Performance; Theatre House; Multi-Purpose
    Type of Stage: Thrust; Flexible; Proscenium; Turntable
    Stage Dimensions: 65'Wx45'D **Orchestra Pit**
    Seating Capacity: Proscenium-598; Thrust-450
    Year Built: 1965 **Architect:** Perkins and Will **Cost:** $3,500,000
    Acoustical Consultant: Bolt, Beranek & Newman
    Contact for Rental: Ivan H. Davidson; (309) 343-0112, ext. x408
    Resident Groups: Knox College Theatre; Knox-Galesburg Symphony; Nova Singers; Collegium Musicum

---

Glen Ellyn

INSTRUMENTAL MUSIC

DUPAGE SYMPHONY
PO Box 488, Glen Ellyn, IL 60137
(708) 858-4042
    Founded: 1954
    Arts Area: Symphony; Orchestra; Chamber; Ensemble
    Status: Non-Professional; Non-Profit

Type: Performing; Touring
Purpose: To give citizens of the area the opportunity to hear live music and musicians a chance to play it
Management: Barbara Schubert, Musical Director/Conductor; Doris Purdie, Business Manager
Officers: Wayne Thomas, President; James Kaduk, Vice President; Beri Noble, Secretary; James Swackhamer, Treasurer
Paid Staff: 2
Paid Artists: 1 **Non-Paid Artists:** 65
Utilizes: Guest Conductors; Guest Artists
Budget: $1,000 - $50,000
Income Sources: Business/Corporate Donations; Box Office; Individual Donations
Season: September - August **Annual Attendance:** 2,000
Affiliations: Illinois Council of Orchestras
Performance Facilities: Dupage County Auditorium

VOCAL MUSIC

GLEN ELLYN CHILDREN'S CHORUS
586 Duane Street, Suite 102, Glen Ellyn, IL 60137
(708) 858-2471
FAX: (708) 858-2476
Arts Area: Choral; Children's
Status: Non-Professional; Non-Profit
Type: Performing; Touring; Educational
Purpose: To provide a music education program for children; to strengthen abilities through performance; to provide an outreach program to sections of the community that would not be able to participate otherwise
Management: Sandra Prodan, Music Director; Linda Madura, Manager
Officers: Thomas Drovin, President of the Board
Budget: $50,000 - $100,000
Income Sources: Private Foundations/Grants/Endowments; Business/Corporate Donations; Box Office; Government Grants; Individual Donations; Tuition
Season: 52 Weeks

FACILITY

COLLEGE OF DUPAGE ARTS CENTER
22nd Street and Park Boulevard, Glen Ellyn, IL 60137-6599
(708) 858-2800, ext. 3008
FAX: (708) 790-9806
Type of Facility: Theatre Complex; Performance Center
Year Built: 1986 **Architect:** Wight and Company **Cost:** $14,400,000
Acoustical Consultant: Lyle F. Yerges
Contact for Rental: Pat Polonus; (312) 858-2800, ext. 3009
Manager: Richard Holgate
Resident Groups: New Philharmonic Orchestra; New Classic Singers; Jazz Ensemble; Buffalo Theatre Ensemble
The Arts Center contains the Auditorium, Mainstage, Studio Theatre and Theatre 2. See individual listings for additional information.

COLLEGE OF DUPAGE ARTS CENTER - AUDITORIUM
22nd Street and Park Boulevard, Glen Ellyn, IL 60137-6599
(708) 858-2800, ext. 3008
FAX: (708) 790-9806
Type of Facility: Auditorium
Type of Stage: Proscenium
Seating Capacity: 500
Year Built: 1986
Contact for Rental: Pat Polonus; (708) 858-2800, ext. 3009
Manager: Richard Holgate
Resident Groups: New Philharmonic Orchestra; New Classic Singers; Jazz Ensemble; Buffalo Theatre Ensemble

COLLEGE OF DUPAGE ARTS CENTER - MAINSTAGE
22nd Street and Park Boulevard, Glen Ellyn, IL 60137-6599
(708) 858-2800, ext. 3008
FAX: (708) 790-9806
Type of Facility: Concert Hall; Theatre House
Type of Stage: Modified Apron Proscenium
Stage Dimensions: 49'Wx25'Hx50'D; add 10'D for hydraulic pit at stage level **Orchestra Pit**
Seating Capacity: 800
Year Built: 1986

Contact for Rental: Pat Polonus; (708) 858-2800, ext. 3009
Manager: Richard Holgate

COLLEGE OF DUPAGE ARTS CENTER - STUDIO THEATRE
22nd Street and Park Boulevard, Glen Ellyn, IL 60137-6599
(708) 858-2800, ext. 3008
FAX: (708) 858-9806
    Type of Facility: Studio Performance; Black Box
    Type of Stage: Flexible
    Year Built: 1986
    Contact for Rental: Pat Polonus; (708) 858-2800, ext. 3009
    Manager: Richard Holgate

COLLEGE OF DUPAGE ARTS CENTER - THEATRE 2
22nd Street and Park Boulevard, Glen Ellyn, IL 60137-6599
(708) 858-2800, ext. 3008
FAX: (708) 790-9806
    Type of Facility: Theatre House
    Type of Stage: Thrust
    Stage Dimensions: 30'x30'
    Seating Capacity: 200
    Year Built: 1986
    Contact for Rental: Pat Polonus; (708) 858-2800, ext. 3009
    Manager: Richard Holgate

Glencoe

DANCE

MARGOT GRIMMER AMERICAN DANCE COMPANY
970 Vernon Avenue, Glencoe, IL 60022
(708) 835-2556
    Founded: 1971
    Arts Area: Modern; Ballet; Jazz
    Status: Professional; Non-Profit
    Type: Performing; Touring
    Management: Margot Grimmer, Artistic Director
    Paid Staff: 1
    Paid Artists: 7
    Utilizes: Special Technical Talent; Guest Artists
    Budget: $100,000 - $500,000
    Income Sources: Private Foundations/Grants/Endowments; Box Office; Individual Donations
    Season: August - June

Goodfield

THEATRE

CONKLIN PLAYERS DINNER THEATRE
PO Box 301, Conklin Court, Goodfield, IL 61742
(309) 965-2545
    Arts Area: Professional; Dinner; Children's Theatre
    Status: Professional; Commercial
    Type: Performing; Resident
    Purpose: To entertain, educate and spread the word about live performance
    Management: Chaunce Conklin, Owner/Producer/Director; Mary Simon, Manager
    Officers: Conklin Players Inc.; Chaunce Conklin, President; Mary Simon, Secretary/Treasurer
    Paid Staff: 35
    Paid Artists: 15
    Utilizes: Actors; Singers; Dancers
    Budget: $500,000 - $1,000,000
    Income Sources: Box Office
    Season: January - December   **Annual Attendance:** 70,000

Grayslake

VOCAL MUSIC

LIBERTY FREMONT CHAMBER SINGERS
32600 East Lane, Grayslake, IL 60030
(708) 546-2050
>**Founded:** 1973
>**Arts Area:** Choral
>**Status:** Semi-Professional; Non-Profit
>**Type:** Performing
>**Purpose:** Provide performance opportunities and cultural outreach through fine music
>**Management:** Edwin Kramer, Music Director
>**Paid Staff:** 1 **Volunteer Staff:** 15
>**Paid Artists:** 5 **Non-Paid Artists:** 50
>**Utilizes:** Guest Conductors; Guest Artists; Guest Directors
>**Budget:** $1,000 - $50,000
>**Income Sources:** Private Foundations/Grants/Endowments; Business/Corporate Donations; Box Office; Government Grants; Individual Donations
>**Season:** October - May **Annual Attendance:** 2,500

Highland Park

THEATRE

THE APPLE TREE THEATRE COMPANY
595 Elm Place, Highland Park, IL 60035
(708) 432-4335
>**Founded:** 1982
>**Arts Area:** Professional; Theatrical Group
>**Status:** Professional; Non-Profit
>**Type:** Performing; Educational
>**Purpose:** To allow new directors, projects and actors a forum in which to perform in a fully professional environment in Chicago
>**Management:** Eileen Boevers, Artistic Director; Scott Slein, General Manager
>**Officers:** Sue Thompson, President; Bryan Gamson, Vice President; June Carrol, Secretary; Diane Rochester, Treasurer
>**Paid Staff:** 3
>**Utilizes:** Guest Artists; Guest Directors
>**Budget:** $100,000 - $500,000
>**Income Sources:** Private Foundations/Grants/Endowments; Business/Corporate Donations; Box Office; Government Grants; Individual Donations
>**Season:** September - May
>**Affiliations:** League of Chicago Theatres

PERFORMING SERIES

RAVINIA FESTIVAL
1575 Oakwood Avenue, Highland Park, IL 60035
(708) 433-8800
>**Founded:** 1935
>**Arts Area:** Dance; Vocal Music; Instrumental Music
>**Status:** Professional; Non-Profit
>**Type:** Performing; Educational
>**Purpose:** Present, at cost, the best music (classical jazz, folk and pop) to the public
>**Utilizes:** Guest Conductors; Guest Artists

FACILITY

APPLE TREE THEATRE
595 Elm Place, Suite 210, Highland Park, IL 60035
(708) 432-4335; (708) 432-8223
>**Type of Facility:** Theatre House
>**Facility Originally:** School
>**Type of Stage:** Thrust
>**Seating Capacity:** 200
>**Year Built:** 1970
>**Manager:** Scott Slein
>**Resident Groups:** The Apple Tree Theatre Company; The Eileen Boevers Performing Arts Workshop

Joliet

FACILITY

RIALTO SQUARE THEATRE
15 East Van Buren Street, Joliet, IL 60431
(815) 726-7171
FAX: (815) 726-0352
    Founded: 1926
    Type of Facility: Concert Hall; Performance Center; Theatre House
    Facility Originally: Vaudeville; Movie House
    Type of Stage: Proscenium
    Stage Dimensions: 52'Wx23'6"H proscenium opening   **Orchestra Pit**
    Seating Capacity: 1,920
    Year Built: 1926   **Architect:** C.W. And George Rapp   **Cost:** $3,000,000
    Year Remodeled: 1981   **Architect:** Conrad Schmitt Studios   **Cost:** $7,000,000
    Contact for Rental: Mary Beth Perros;   (815) 726-7171

Lake Forest

INSTRUMENTAL MUSIC

LAKE FOREST SYMPHONY ASSOCIATION, INC.
225 East Deerpath, Suite 138, Lake Forest, IL 60045
(708) 295-2135
FAX: (708) 295-2747
    Arts Area: Orchestra; Ensemble
    Status: Professional; Non-Profit
    Type: Performing
    Purpose: To provide artistically enriching, diverse music programs such as family-oriented concerts, youth programs and classical series that are tailored to suit the cultural needs of the northern Illinois community
    Management: Paul Anthony McRae, Music Director; Fran Chaloupka, Director of Marketing/Operations
    Officers: Jean Beck, President of the Board
    Budget: $500,000 - $1,000,000
    Income Sources: Private Foundations/Grants/Endowments; Business/Corporate Donations; Box Office; Government Grants; Individual Donations
    Performance Facilities: Rhoades Auditorium, Chicago

Libertyville

FACILITY

DAVID ADLER CULTURAL CENTER
1700 North Milwaukee Avenue, Libertyville, IL 60048
(708) 367-0707
FAX: (708) 367-0804
    Founded: 1980
    Type of Facility: Concert Hall; Studio Performance; Performance Center; Civic Center; Multi-Purpose
    Facility Originally: Historic Home
    Type of Stage: Flexible; Platform   **Stage Dimensions:** 5'x14'
    Year Built: 1917   **Architect:** David Adler
    Year Remodeled: 1980
    Acoustical Consultant: Stuart Rosenberg
    Contact for Rental: Stuart Rosenberg;   (708) 367-0707
    Resident Groups: The Adler Enseble
    The Adler Center provides a variety of art workshops, concerts and exhibits.

Lincolnshire

THEATRE

MARRIOTT'S LINCOLNSHIRE THEATRE
10 Marriott Drive, Lincolnshire, IL 60069
(708) 634-0200
    Founded: 1975
    Arts Area: Musical

Status: Professional; Commercial
Type: Performing; Resident
Purpose: To present five productions each year including classic musicals, seldom-seen musicals, and premiere productions of new works
Management: Dyann Earley, Artistic Director; Kary Walker, Producer; Lauren Johnson, Director of Marketing
Paid Staff: 50
Utilizes: Guest Artists
Budget: $1,000,000 - $5,000,000
Income Sources: Box Office
Season: 52 Weeks   **Annual Attendance:** 300,000
Affiliations: League of Chicago Theatres; ADTI
Performance Facilities: Marriott's Lincolnshire Theatre

Litchfield

THEATRE

ENCORE PLAYERS
222 East Sargent, Litchfield, IL 62056
(217) 326-4414
Founded: 1968
Arts Area: Musical; Dinner; Community; Theatrical Group
Status: Non-Professional; Non-Profit
Type: Performing
Purpose: Promotion of art and development of artistic abilities and other skills in the field of theatrical arts; encouragement of public appreciation of all theatrical arts
Management: Mae Morton, Dennis Plozizka, David Lewey, Tim Price, Directors
Officers: James Wreath, President; David Parsons, Vice President; Teresa Donahoe, Secretary/Treasurer
Volunteer Staff: 30
Utilizes: Guest Directors
Budget: $1,000 - $50,000
Income Sources: Box Office; Individual Donations
Season: 52 Weeks   **Annual Attendance:** 900
Performance Facilities: Community Center

Macomb

THEATRE

SUMMER MUSIC THEATRE
Western Illinois University, Theatre Dep., Brown Hall, Macomb, IL 61455
(309) 298-1543
FAX: (309) 298-2695
Founded: 1972
Arts Area: Summer Stock; Musical
Status: Non-Profit
Type: Performing; Resident; Educational
Purpose: To provide musical theatre for the community and serve as a training ground for students
Management: David Patrick, Managing Director
Paid Staff: 8
Paid Artists: 25
Utilizes: Special Technical Talent; Guest Artists; Guest Directors
Budget: $1,000 - $50,000
Income Sources: Box Office; Individual Donations
Season: June - August   **Annual Attendance:** 6,000
Affiliations: U/RTA
Performance Facilities: Hainline Theatre

FACILITY

WESTERN ILLINOIS UNIVERSITY - HAINLINE THEATRE
Macomb, IL 61455
(309) 298-1543
FAX: (309) 298-2695
Type of Facility: Theatre House
Type of Stage: Proscenium
Stage Dimensions: 64'Wx30'D; 40'Wx16'H proscenium opening   **Orchestra Pit**

Seating Capacity: 387
Year Built: 1957   **Architect:** Lankton-Fregele-Terry
Year Remodeled: 1987   **Architect:** Phillips Swager Associates   **Cost:** $1,200,000
Resident Groups: Summer Music Theatre; University Theatre; Department of Music groups

---

Marengo

THEATRE

SHADY LANE THEATER
24803 West Grant, Business 20, Marengo, IL 60152
(815) 568-7219
>**Founded:** 1940
>**Arts Area:** Professional; Dinner
>**Status:** Professional; Commercial
>**Type:** Resident
>**Management:** Donna Zeffery, General Manager; Sandra Smith, Artistic Director
>**Paid Staff:** 12
>**Paid Artists:** 75
>**Utilizes:** Special Technical Talent; Guest Artists; Guest Directors
>**Budget:** $100,000 - $500,000
>**Income Sources:** Box Office
>**Season:** March - January   **Annual Attendance:** 40,000
>**Performance Facilities:** Shady Lane Playhouse

Marion

FACILITY

MARION CULTURAL AND CIVIC CENTER
700 Tower Square Plaza, Marion, IL 62959
(618) 997-4030
>**Founded:** 1974
>**Type of Facility:** Concert Hall; Auditorium; Performance Center; Theatre House; Opera House; Civic Center; Multi-Purpose
>**Facility Originally:** Vaudeville; Movie House
>**Type of Stage:** Proscenium
>**Stage Dimensions:** 35'x35'
>**Seating Capacity:** 938
>**Year Built:** 1920
>**Year Remodeled:** 1973   **Cost:** $150,000
>**Contact for Rental:** Ray Reynolds;   (618) 997-4030
>**Resident Groups:** Paradise Alley Players; Volunteers to the Arts

---

Maywood

THEATRE

COLEMAN PUPPET THEATRE
1516 South Second Avenue, Maywood, IL 60153
(708) 344-2920
>**Founded:** 1947
>**Arts Area:** Puppet
>**Status:** Professional
>**Type:** Performing; Touring
>**Purpose:** To help keep alive classic and modern stories by dramatizing them with puppets
>**Management:** F.R. Coleman, Barbara Coleman, Directors
>**Paid Staff:** 2
>**Budget:** $1,000 - $50,000
>**Income Sources:** Box Office; Private/Corporate Functions
>**Affiliations:** Puppeteers of America; Chicagoland Puppetry Guild; Puppeteers of America

Mendota

THEATRE

MENDOTA COMMUNITY THEATRE
Box 304, Mendota, IL 61342
(312) 344-2920
   Founded: 1953
   Arts Area: Community; Theatrical Group
   Status: Non-Professional; Non-Profit
   Type: Performing; Resident; Educational
   Purpose: To provide and promote theatre and theatre activities in the Tri-County Area
   Management: George Likeness, Treasurer/Business Manager; Rosemary Reger, Audience Relations
   Officers: Darla Cocanour, President; Lori Bieschke, Recording Secretary; Alberta Katthoefer, Corresponding Secretary; George Likeness, Treasurer
   Volunteer Staff: 50
   Non-Paid Artists: 50
   Budget: $1,000 - $50,000   **Income Sources:** Box Office
   Season: September - May   **Annual Attendance:** 2,500
   Performance Facilities: Mendota High School Auditorium

Moline

VOCAL MUSIC

THE MOLINE BOYS CHOIR
3406 54th Street, Moline, IL 61265
(309) 764-3109
   Founded: 1948
   Arts Area: Choral
   Status: Semi-Professional; Non-Profit
   Type: Performing; Touring; Educational
   Purpose: To perform choral literature of a variety of styles; to provide vocal/choral training to boys of talent, interest and ability
   Management: Kermit Wells, Director; Margaret Mangelsdorf, Manager
   Officers: William Barrett, President of Board
   Paid Staff: 5   **Volunteer Staff:** 13
   Non-Paid Artists: 150
   Budget: $50,000 - $100,000
   Income Sources: Business/Corporate Donations; Box Office; Individual Donations
   Season: September - July

Mount Vernon

INSTRUMENTAL MUSIC

CEDARHURST CHAMBER MUSIC
Richview Road, PO Box 907, Mount Vernon, IL 62864
(618) 244-5871
FAX: (618) 244-5871
   Founded: 1979
   Arts Area: Orchestra; Chamber; Ensemble; Ethnic
   Status: Professional; Non-Profit
   Type: Sponsoring
   Purpose: To present a series of chamber music concerts for the broad southern Illinois audience, featuring performers from Illinois, the rest of the United States and overseas
   Management: Carl L. Schweinfurth, Director
   Officers: Catherina Suttle, Operations Manager; Sharon Bradham, Chairman; Joann Nelson, Co-Chair
   Volunteer Staff: 18
   Paid Artists: 50
   Utilizes: Guest Artists
   Budget: $1,000 - $50,000
   Income Sources: Private Foundations/Grants/Endowments; Business/Corporate Donations; Box Office; Government Grants; Individual Donations
   Season: September - May   **Annual Attendance:** 1,600
   Affiliations: CMA; Illinois Presenters Network
   Performance Facilities: Main Gallery, Mitchell Art Museum

Naperville

PERFORMING SERIES

NAPERVILLE-NORTH CENTRAL COLLEGE PERFORMING ARTS ASSOCIATION
30 North Brainard Street, Naperville, IL 60566
(312) 420-3309
> **Founded:** 1974
> **Arts Area:** Dance; Vocal Music; Instrumental Music; Theater
> **Status:** Non-Professional; Non-Profit
> **Type:** Sponsoring
> **Management:** James R. Doody, VP Operations
> **Officers:** Norma Ladley, President; James R. Doody, Vice President Operations; Don Hennessy, Secretary; Olive S. Frantz, Treasurer
> **Volunteer Staff:** 33
> **Utilizes:** Guest Artists
> **Budget:** $50,000 - $100,000
> **Income Sources:** Private Foundations/Grants/Endowments; Business/Corporate Donations; Box Office; Government Grants; Individual Donations
> **Season:** September - May   **Annual Attendance:** 5,000
> **Affiliations:** North Central College
> **Performance Facilities:** Pfeiffer Hall

Normal

PERFORMING SERIES

ILLINOIS SHAKESPEARE FESTIVAL
Illinois State University, Box 6901, Normal, IL 61761-6901
(309) 438-2535
FAX: (309) 438-8318
> **Founded:** 1978
> **Arts Area:** Festivals
> **Status:** Non-Profit
> **Type:** Performing; Educational
> **Management:** Barbara Funk, Executive Director; John Sipes, Artistic Director; Peter Guither, General Manager; John Stefano, Managing Director
> **Paid Staff:** 12
> **Paid Artists:** 60
> **Utilizes:** Guest Artists; Guest Directors
> **Budget:** $100,000 - $500,000
> **Income Sources:** Private Foundations/Grants/Endowments; Business/Corporate Donations; Box Office; Government Grants; Individual Donations
> **Season:** June - August   **Annual Attendance:** 12,000
> **Performance Facilities:** Ewing Manor

Northbrook

FACILITY

SHEELY CENTER FOR THE PERFORMING ARTS
2300 Shermer Road, Northbrook, IL 60062
(708) 272-6400, ext. X298
FAX: (708) 272-4330
> **Type of Facility:** Concert Hall; Auditorium
> **Type of Stage:** Proscenium
> **Stage Dimensions:** 55'Wx39'D   **Orchestra Pit**
> **Seating Capacity:** 1,500
> **Year Built:** 1979   **Architect:** Otis Associates   **Cost:** $4,000,000
> **Acoustical Consultant:** Jerit Boies; Bolt, Beranek & Newman

Contact for Rental: Joel A. Monaghan;   (708) 272-6400, ext. x298
Resident Groups: Northbrook Symphony

Oak Park

DANCE

OAK PARK CIVIC BALLET COMPANY
136 North Marion, Oak Park, IL 60301
(708) 383-0361
Founded: 1978
Arts Area: Modern; Ballet
Status: Professional; Non-Profit
Type: Performing; Touring; Resident
Purpose: To bring the great ballets to the public and improve the skills of the performers through constant performances
Management: Eva Lorraine, Artistic Director; Carole Bessler, Len Petrulis, Marketing
Officers: James Bagley, Chairman; Eva Lorraine, President; Geoff Obrzut, Vice President
Paid Staff: 4
Paid Artists: 24
Utilizes: Special Technical Talent; Guest Artists
Budget: $50,000 - $100,000
Income Sources: Box Office; Individual Donations
Season: October - May   **Annual Attendance:** 5,000

THEATRE

OAK PARK FESTIVAL THEATRE
PO Box 4114, Oak Park, IL 60303
(708) 524-2050
Founded: 1975
Arts Area: Professional; Summer Stock
Status: Professional; Non-Profit
Type: Performing
Management: David Darlow, Artistic Director; Susan Levine-Kelley, Managing Director
Paid Staff: 10
Paid Artists: 21
Utilizes: Special Technical Talent; Guest Artists; Guest Directors
Budget: $50,000 - $100,000
Income Sources: Private Foundations/Grants/Endowments; Business/Corporate Donations; Box Office; Individual Donations
Season: July - August   **Annual Attendance:** 5,000
Affiliations: League of Chicago Theatres
Performance Facilities: Austin Gardens

VILLAGE PLAYERS (OAK PARK-RIVER FOREST CIVIC THEATRE, INC.)
1010 Madison Street, Oak Park, IL 60304
(708) 524-1892; (708) 383-9829
Founded: 1961
Arts Area: Community; Theatrical Group
Status: Non-Professional; Non-Profit
Type: Performing; Resident; Educational
Purpose: To promote interest and involvement of the community in the cultural arts and develop their theatrical abilities through education and public performances
Management: Rita Krysko-Harrington, Business Administrator
Officers: Dr. Peter Baker, Chairman; Jerry Le Beda, Vice Chairman; Barbara Hemminger, Secretary; Cathy Madden, Treasurer; Jeff Carey, Charles Cichler, Marcia Mrazek, Board Members
Paid Staff: 1   **Volunteer Staff:** 50
Paid Artists: 10   **Non-Paid Artists:** 90
Utilizes: Special Technical Talent; Guest Artists; Guest Directors
Budget: $100,000 - $500,000
Income Sources: Private Foundations/Grants/Endowments; Business/Corporate Donations; Box Office; Government Grants; Individual Donations
Season: July - June   **Annual Attendance:** 30,000

Oakbrook Terrace

THEATRE

DRURY LANE OAKBROOK TERRACE
100 Drury Lane, Oakbrook Terrace, IL 60181
(708) 530-8300
    Founded: 1984
    Arts Area: Professional; Musical; Dinner
    Status: Professional; Non-Professional; Commercial
    Type: Performing; Touring
    Purpose: The Drury Lane Oakbrook Terrace presents large-scale musicals as well as comedies that boast some of the top names in theatre both on and off stage.
    Management: Diane Van Lente, Managing Director; Hugh Cassidy, General Manager
    Paid Staff: 250
    Paid Artists: 50
    Budget: Over $10,000,000
    Income Sources: Box Office
    Season: 52 Weeks   **Annual Attendance:** 250,000
    Affiliations: ADTA
    Performance Facilities: Drury Lane Theater

Park Forest

INSTRUMENTAL MUSIC

ILLINOIS PHILHARMONIC ORCHESTRA ASSOCIATION
210 Illinois Street, Park Forest, IL 60466
(708) 481-6046
    Arts Area: Orchestra; Chamber
    Status: Professional; Non-Profit
    Type: Performing; Educational
    Purpose: To provide the citizens of Illinois, particularly the south suburban region, with professional orchestral music
    Management: Carmen DeLeone, Music/Artistic Director
    Officers: Marilynn Tannebaum, Board President
    Budget: $500,000 - $1,000,000
    Income Sources: Private Foundations/Grants/Endowments; Business/Corporate Donations; Box Office; Government Grants; Individual Donations
    Performance Facilities: Bloom High School Workman Auditorium

THEATRE

ILLINOIS THEATRE CENTER
400A Lakewood Boulevard, Park Forest, IL 60466
(708) 481-3510
    Founded: 1976
    Arts Area: Professional; Theatrical Group
    Status: Professional; Non-Profit
    Type: Performing; Touring; Resident; Educational
    Purpose: To bring professional, equity productions of new and award winning plays and musicals to residents of the Southland and surrounding communities; to provide a full season of seven productions, each running one month, and two summer productions
    Management: Etel Billig, Administrative Director; Steve S. Billig, Artistic Director; Jonathan Roark, Musical Director; Wayne Adams, Assistant Artistic and Technical Director
    Officers: Donna Jemilo, Board President
    Paid Staff: 12   **Volunteer Staff:** 2
    Paid Artists: 48
    Utilizes: Special Technical Talent; Guest Artists; Guest Directors
    Budget: $100,000 - $500,000
    Income Sources: Private Foundations/Grants/Endowments; Business/Corporate Donations; Box Office; Government Grants; Individual Donations
    Season: September - August   **Annual Attendance:** 56,000
    Affiliations: AEA; TCG; League of Chicago Theatres
    Performance Facilities: Illinois Theatre Center

FACILITY

FREEDOM HALL, NATHAN MANILOW THEATRE
410 Lakewood Boulevard, Park Forest, IL 60466
(708) 747-0580
FAX: (708) 503-7713
Founded: 1976
Type of Facility: Theatre House
Type of Stage: Proscenium
Stage Dimensions: 40'x23'x60'
Seating Capacity: 330
Year Built: 1976
Contact for Rental: Naomi Fell;   (708) 747-0580

ILLINOIS THEATRE CENTER
400A Lakewood Boulevard, Park Forest, IL 60466
(708) 481-3510
Type of Facility: Theatre House
Facility Originally: Library
Type of Stage: Thrust
Stage Dimensions: 33'Wx18'D
Seating Capacity: 187
Year Built: 1958   **Architect:** R.H. Norton
Year Remodeled: 1969   **Architect:** R.H. Norton
Manager: Ms. Etel Billig;   (708) 481-3510
Resident Groups: Illinois Theatre Center

Peoria

DANCE

PEORIA CIVIC BALLET
Central College Performing Arts Center, Peoria, IL 61635
(309) 694-5106
Arts Area: Ballet
Status: Professional; Non-Profit
Type: Performing; Touring; Resident
Management: Shirley Shear, Artistic Director
Officers: Steve Staff, President
Paid Artists: 20
Income Sources: Box Office; Individual Donations

INSTRUMENTAL MUSIC

PEORIA SYMPHONY ORCHESTRA
105 East Arcadia, Peoria, IL 61603
(309) 682-6069
Founded: 1897
Arts Area: Symphony; Orchestra
Status: Semi-Professional
Type: Performing; Resident
Purpose: The performance of symphonic music for the enjoyment of residents of Central Illinois
Management: Judy Furniss, Manager; William Wilsen, Music Director/Conductor; Janice N. Hellman, Office Manager
Officers: Karl Kuppler, President; Stanley Butler, Vice President; Thomas Romanowski, Treasurer; Ann Rullman, Secretary
Paid Staff: 9
Paid Artists: 85
Utilizes: Special Technical Talent; Guest Conductors; Guest Artists
Budget: $100,000 - $500,000
Income Sources: Business/Corporate Donations; Box Office; Government Grants; Individual Donations
Season: 52 Weeks   **Annual Attendance:** 20,000
Affiliations: ASOL
Performance Facilities: Peoria Civic Center

VOCAL MUSIC

PEORIA CIVIC OPERA
PO Box 120198, Peoria, IL 61604
(309) 673-0864
Founded: 1973
Arts Area: Grand Opera; Light Opera; Musical Theatre
Status: Professional; Non-Profit
Type: Performing; Educational
Management: Dr. Fiora Contino, Artistic Director/Conductor
Paid Staff: 1 **Volunteer Staff:** 32
Paid Artists: 150 **Non-Paid Artists:** 200
Utilizes: Guest Conductors; Guest Artists; Guest Directors
Budget: $100,000 - $500,000
Income Sources: Private Foundations/Grants/Endowments; Business/Corporate Donations; Box Office; Government Grants; Individual Donations
Season: September - April **Annual Attendance:** 6,000
Performance Facilities: Civic Center Theatre

THEATRE

PEORIA PLAYERS THEATRE
4300 North University, Peoria, IL 61614
(309) 688-4473
Founded: 1919
Arts Area: Community
Status: Non-Professional; Non-Profit
Type: Performing; Resident; Educational
Purpose: The presentation of plays and the study of theatre for and by the community
Management: Rebecca Canty, Theatre Manager
Officers: Arno Loeffler, President; Tom Broderick, Vice President; Gail Anderson, Secretary; Gene Pratt, Treasurer
Paid Staff: 4 **Volunteer Staff:** 300
Budget: $50,000 - $100,000
Income Sources: Private Foundations/Grants/Endowments; Business/Corporate Donations; Box Office; Individual Donations
Season: September - May **Annual Attendance:** 24,000
Affiliations: AACT; Illinois Theatre Association
Performance Facilities: Peoria Players Theatre

PERFORMING SERIES

AMATEUR MUSICAL CLUB OF PEORIA, INC.
416 Hamilton Boulevard, Box 666, Peoria, IL 61652
(309) 674-6516
Founded: 1906
Arts Area: Dance; Vocal Music; Instrumental Music
Status: Professional; Non-Profit
Type: Educational; Sponsoring
Purpose: To offer an annual series of world-class artists
Management: Natalie Casper, Office Manager
Officers: Thomas F. Broderick, President; Tim Bertschy, Vice President; Louise Mueller, Treasurer; Nancy Morgan, Secretary
Paid Staff: 1
Paid Artists: 150 **Non-Paid Artists:** 75
Utilizes: Guest Conductors; Guest Artists; Dance Companies
Budget: $100,000 - $500,000
Income Sources: Private Foundations/Grants/Endowments; Business/Corporate Donations; Box Office; Government Grants; Individual Donations
Season: September - April **Annual Attendance:** 10,000
Affiliations: APAP; Arts Midwest
Performance Facilities: Peoria Civic Center Theatre

FACILITY

PEORIA CIVIC CENTER
201 SW Jefferson Street, Peoria, IL 61602-1448
(309) 673-8900
Type of Facility: Civic Center
Year Built: 1982 **Architect:** Philip Johnson & John Burgee **Cost:** $64,300,000

Acoustical Consultant: Jaffe Acoustics
Contact for Rental: Debbie Ritschell, Booking Manager;   (309) 673-8900
Peoria Civic Center contains the Arena, Exhibition Hall and Theatre. See individual listings for additional information.

PEORIA CIVIC CENTER - ARENA
201 Southwest Jefferson Street, Peoria, IL 61602-1448
(309) 673-8900
Type of Facility: Concert Hall; Arena
Type of Stage: Flexible
Stage Dimensions: 60'x40'
Seating Capacity: 12,400
Year Built: 1982
Contact for Rental: Debbie Ritschell, Booking Manager;   (309) 673-8900

PEORIA CIVIC CENTER - EXHIBITION HALL
201 SW Jefferson Street, Peoria, IL 61602
(309) 673-8900
Type of Facility: Exhibition Hall
Type of Stage: Flexible; Platform
Year Built: 1982
Contact for Rental: Debbie Ritschell, Booking Manager;   (309) 673-8900
Exhibition Hall contains 33,000 square feet

PEORIA CIVIC CENTER - THEATRE
201 SW Jefferson Street, Peoria, IL 61602
(309) 673-8900
Type of Facility: Concert Hall; Theatre House; Opera House
Type of Stage: Thrust; Proscenium
Stage Dimensions: 50'Wx26'3"D   **Orchestra Pit**
Seating Capacity: 2,187
Year Built: 1982
Contact for Rental: Debbie Ritschell, Booking Manager;   (309) 673-8900
Manager: Jon Smock, Stage Manager;   (309) 673-8900, ext. 240
Resident Groups: Peoria Civic Opera; Peoria Symphony Orchestra; Peoria Civic Ballet; Peoria Area Civic Chorale; Amateur Musical Club; Broadway Theater Series; YouTHeater

PEORIA PLAYERS THEATRE
4300 North University, Peoria, IL 61614
(309) 688-4473
Type of Facility: Auditorium; Theatre House
Type of Stage: Proscenium
Stage Dimensions: 15'x36'x40'
Seating Capacity: 390
Year Built: 1956   **Architect:** Leslie Keynon   **Cost:** $225,000
Contact for Rental: Rebecca Canty, Manager;   (309) 688-4473
Manager: Rebecca Canty
Resident Groups: Peoria Players Theatre
Musical, dance, lectures

Quincy

INSTRUMENTAL MUSIC

QUINCY SYMPHONY ORCHESTRA
428 Main, Quincy, IL 62301
(217) 222-2856
Founded: 1947
Arts Area: Symphony; Orchestra; Chamber
Status: Non-Professional; Non-Profit
Type: Performing; Resident; Educational
Purpose: To bring fine orchestral music to the area, providing local musicians the opportunity to perform; to provide educational programs
Management: Douglas W. Reeve, General Manager; Vivian Langellier, Executive Secretary
Officers: Fr. Harry Speakman o.f.m., President
Paid Staff: 7
Paid Artists: 25   **Non-Paid Artists:** 45
Utilizes: Guest Artists
Budget: $50,000 - $100,000

Income Sources: Private Foundations/Grants/Endowments; Business/Corporate Donations; Box Office; Government Grants; Individual Donations
Season: October - May   **Annual Attendance:** 9,000
Affiliations: ASOL; Illinois Council of Orchestras
Performance Facilities: Quincy Junior High School Auditorium

River Forest

INSTRUMENTAL MUSIC

CHICAGO SINFONIETTA
7900 West Division Street, River Forest, IL 60305
(708) 366-1062
FAX: (708) 366-5419
Founded: 1987
Arts Area: Symphony; Orchestra; Chamber; Ethnic
Status: Professional; Non-Profit
Type: Performing; Touring; Educational
Purpose: To present classical music in original orchestration; to promote ethnic diversity in the concert hall
Management: Camille McGinley, General Manager; Margaret Burk, Director of Development; Derek Scruggs, Operations Coordinator
Officers: Paul Freeman, President; Jim Paglia, Executive Vice President; Bill Kashul and Bettiann Gardner, Vice Presidents; Howard Shapiro, Treasurer; Roger Wilson, Secretary
Paid Staff: 7
Utilizes: Guest Conductors; Guest Artists
Budget: $500,000 - $1,000,000
Income Sources: Private Foundations/Grants/Endowments; Business/Corporate Donations; Box Office; Government Grants; Individual Donations
Season: September - June   **Annual Attendance:** 9,000
Affiliations: Chicago Music Alliance
Performance Facilities: Lund Auditorium, Rosary College

River Grove

FACILITY

RICHARD BURTON PERFORMING ARTS CENTER TRITON COLLEGE
2000 Fifth Avenue, River Grove, IL 60171
(708) 456-0300, ext. 375
FAX: (708) 456-0049
Founded: 1967
Type of Facility: Concert Hall; Auditorium; Performance Center; Theatre House; Multi-Purpose
Facility Originally: Meeting Hall
Type of Stage: Proscenium
Stage Dimensions: 44'Wx20'D proscenium opening   **Orchestra Pit**
Seating Capacity: 412
Year Built: 1981
Year Remodeled: 1982
Contact for Rental: Steven Ginley;   (708) 456-0300, ext. 375; 804
Resident Groups: Triton College Fine Arts Department; AlphaBet Soup Children's Theatre Company

---

Rock Island

THEATRE

CIRCA '21 DINNER PLAYHOUSE
1828 Third Avenue, Rock Island, IL 61201
(309) 786-2667
FAX: (309) 786-4119
Founded: 1976
Arts Area: Professional; Dinner
Status: Professional; Commercial
Type: Performing; Touring; Resident
Purpose: To provide year-round professional plays and musicals along with high-quality fine dining
Management: Dennis Hitchcock, Producer
Paid Staff: 70

Utilizes: Special Technical Talent; Guest Directors
Budget: $1,000,000 - $5,000,000
Income Sources: Box Office
Season: 52 Weeks   **Annual Attendance:** 75,000

PERFORMING SERIES

QUAD CITY ARTS
1715 Second Avenue, Rock Island, IL 61201
(309) 793-1213
FAX: (309) 793-1265
   Founded: 1988
   Arts Area: Dance; Vocal Music; Instrumental Music; Theater
   Status: Non-Profit
   Type: Performing; Educational
   Purpose: To present 400 community concerts by professional perfroming artists througout a 100 mile radius of the area; to maintain local and regional visual exhibitions
   Management: Diane Sulg, Executive Director; Holly Richard, Director of Visiting Artist Series; Lloyd Schoeneman, Director of Programs; Steve Fors, Gallery Manager
   Paid Staff: 14   **Volunteer Staff:** 3
   Paid Artists: 50
   Utilizes: Guest Artists
   Budget: $1,000,000 - $5,000,000
   Income Sources: Private Foundations/Grants/Endowments; Business/Corporate Donations; Government Grants; Individual Donations
   Season: 52 Weeks   **Annual Attendance:** 150,000
   Affiliations: APAP

FACILITY

AUGUSTANA COLLEGE - CENTENNIAL HALL
639 38th Street, Rock Island, IL 61201
(309) 794-7306
FAX: (309) 794-7431
   Type of Facility: Auditorium
   Type of Stage: Proscenium
   Seating Capacity: 1,620
   Year Built: 1959   **Cost:** $1,150,000
   Manager: Dan Urton, Director
   Resident Groups: Augustana Choir; Augustana Concert Band; Augustana Symphony Orchestra; Handel Oratorio Society; Quad-City Symphony Orchestra

---
Rockford

DANCE

ROCKFORD DANCE COMPANY
711 North Main Street, Rockford, IL 61103
(815) 963-3341
   Founded: 1972
   Arts Area: Modern; Ballet; Jazz
   Status: Semi-Professional; Non-Profit
   Type: Performing; Resident; Educational; Sponsoring
   Purpose: To serve as an arts resource in dance through presentations, performances and education
   Management: Melissa Teske, Executive Director; Joy Xu, Artistic Director
   Officers: Grace Wilson, President; L. Paul Harnois, Vice President/Finance; John Holevas, Vice President/Administration; Joyce Lombardozzi, Treasurer; Gail Barton, Secretary
   Paid Staff: 3
   Paid Artists: 6   **Non-Paid Artists:** 15
   Utilizes: Guest Artists; Guest Choreographers
   Budget: $100,000 - $500,000

Income Sources: Private Foundations/Grants/Endowments; Business/Corporate Donations; Box Office; Government Grants; Individual Donations
Season: September - May

INSTRUMENTAL MUSIC

ROCKFORD SYMPHONY ORCHESTRA
711 North Main, Rockford, IL 61103
(815) 965-0049
FAX: (815) 965-0042
Arts Area: Symphony
Status: Professional; Non-Profit
Type: Performing
Purpose: To provide symphonic music
Management: Steven Larsen, Music Director; Camille Day, Executive Director
Officers: Robert Fredrickson, President; LoRayne Logan, Vice President; Eugene Engrav, Treasurer; Scott Sullivan, Secretary
Paid Staff: 3
Utilizes: Guest Conductors; Guest Artists
Budget: $100,000 - $500,000
Income Sources: Private Foundations/Grants/Endowments; Business/Corporate Donations; Box Office; Government Grants; Individual Donations
Season: October - May   **Annual Attendance:** 6,000
Affiliations: ASOL
Performance Facilities: Midway Theater; Coronado Theater

THEATRE

NEW AMERICAN THEATER
118 North Main, Rockford, IL 61101
(815) 963-9454
FAX: (815) 963-7215
Founded: 1972
Arts Area: Professional; Theatrical Group
Status: Professional; Non-Profit
Type: Performing; Touring; Resident; Educational
Purpose: To present classic, modern and new work
Management: J.R. Sullivan, Producing Director
Officers: John Pick, President; David Bippus, Vice President of Operations; Mark Murphy, Vice President of Development; Dewayne Fellows, Treasurer
Paid Staff: 14   **Volunteer Staff:** 25
Paid Artists: 10   **Non-Paid Artists:** 20
Utilizes: Special Technical Talent; Guest Artists; Guest Directors
Budget: $1,000,000 - $5,000,000
Income Sources: Private Foundations/Grants/Endowments; Business/Corporate Donations; Box Office; Government Grants; Individual Donations
Season: September - June   **Annual Attendance:** 37,000
Affiliations: TCG
Performance Facilities: New American Theater

FACILITY

MIDWAY THEATRE
721 East State Street, Rockford, IL 61104
(815) 965-2511
FAX: (815) 964-8378
Founded: 1918
Type of Facility: Concert Hall; Auditorium
Facility Originally: Movie House
Type of Stage: Thrust
Stage Dimensions: 40'x90'
Seating Capacity: 1,500
Year Built: 1918   **Architect:** J.E.O. Pridmore
Year Remodeled: 1981   **Architect:** Gary Anderson
Contact for Rental: Mary S. Campbell;   (815) 965-2511
Resident Groups: Rockford Symphony Orchestra

Saint Charles

INSTRUMENTAL MUSIC

ILLINOIS CHAMBER SYMPHONY
12 South First Avenue, Saint Charles, IL 60174
(708) 377-6423
FAX: (708) 377-3105
Founded: 1983
Arts Area: Orchestra; Chamber
Status: Professional; Non-Profit
Type: Performing
Purpose: To promote live classical music of the highest artistic caliber and foster cultural growth in the state of Illinois
Management: Stephen Squires, Music Director; Robert Murphy, Marketing Director; Catherine Squires, Executive Director; Tim Juergensen, Librarian; Amy Scarlato, Personnel Manager
Officers: Charles Brown, President; Jeffrey Hunt, Vice President; William Simmons, Secretary/Treasurer
Paid Staff: 5   **Volunteer Staff:** 2
Paid Artists: 35
Utilizes: Guest Artists
Budget: $50,000 - $100,000
Income Sources: Private Foundations/Grants/Endowments; Business/Corporate Donations; Box Office; Government Grants; Individual Donations
Season: October - May   **Annual Attendance:** 5,000
Affiliations: ICO; Kane County Tourism Association; ASOL; Fox Valley Arts Council
Performance Facilities: Norris Cultural Arts Center; Baker Methodist Church

THEATRE

PHEASANT RUN THEATRE
PO Box 64, Saint Charles, IL 60174
(708) 584-6342
Founded: 1964
Arts Area: Professional; Dinner
Status: Professional; Commercial
Type: Performing
Management: Diana Martinez, Producer/Director
Paid Staff: 12
Paid Artists: 16
Utilizes: Guest Directors
Budget: $100,000 - $500,000
Income Sources: Box Office
Season: 52 Weeks   **Annual Attendance:** 60,000

FACILITY

NORRIS CULTURAL ARTS CENTER
1040 Dunham Road, Saint Charles, IL 60174
(708) 584-9599
FAX: (708) 513-5392
Founded: 1978
Type of Facility: Concert Hall; Performance Center; Theatre House; Gallery
Type of Stage: Proscenium
Stage Dimensions: 40'D (wing space 24'x40'); 30'x50' proscenium opening   **Orchestra Pit**
Seating Capacity: 1,000
Year Built: 1978   **Architect:** Ron Gerritis
Contact for Rental: Patti Harmon-Lind;   (708) 584-9599
Resident Groups: No Center Aisle Theatre Company

Skokie

DANCE

PASCUAL OLIVERA AND ANGELA DEL MORAL'S CELEBRATION OF SPANISH DANCE
7017 Lorel, Skokie, IL 60077
(708) 675-7456
Founded: 1977
Arts Area: Ethnic

Status: Professional
Type: Performing; Touring; Resident; Educational
Purpose: To romantically celebrate Spanish dance from the classical, to the folk, to the Flamenco
Management: Siegel Artist Management
Officers: Ethel Siegel, Liz Silverstein, Jane Curtiss, Co-Directors; Pascual Olivera, Angela Del Moral, Directors
Paid Staff: 2
Paid Artists: 5
Utilizes: Special Technical Talent
Budget: $50,000 - $100,000
Income Sources: Box Office; Touring Fees
Season: 52 Weeks

THEATRE

CENTRE EAST
7701A Lincoln Avenue, Skokie, IL 60077
(708) 673-6305
Founded: 1979
Arts Area: Professional; Musical
Status: Non-Profit
Type: Performing
Purpose: To present and provide the best in the performing arts
Officers: Dorothy S. Litwin, Executive Director
Paid Staff: 10   **Volunteer Staff:** 150
Utilizes: Guest Artists
Budget: $1,000,000 - $5,000,000
Income Sources: Private Foundations/Grants/Endowments; Business/Corporate Donations; Box Office; Government Grants; Individual Donations
Season: September - June

FACILITY

CENTRE EAST
7701A Lincoln Avenue, Skokie, IL 60077
(708) 673-6305
FAX: (708) 673-6327
Founded: 1979
Type of Facility: Theatre Complex; Concert Hall; Auditorium
Facility Originally: School
Type of Stage: Proscenium
Stage Dimensions: 80'Wx40'D   **Orchestra Pit**
Seating Capacity: 1,310
Year Built: 1963
Contact for Rental: Jula Radom;   (708) 673-6305
Manager: Dorothy Litwin;   (708) 673-6305
Resident Groups: Skokie Valley Symphony Orchestra

Springfield

DANCE

SPRINGFIELD BALLET COMPANY
2820 South MacArthur, Springfield, IL 62704
(217) 544-1967
Founded: 1975
Arts Area: Modern; Ballet; Jazz; Folk
Status: Non-Professional; Non-Profit
Type: Performing; Touring; Educational; Sponsoring
Purpose: To foster and promote dance in central Illinois
Management: Grace Luttrell Nanavati, Artistic Director; Julienne Guttas, Ballet Mistress/Manager
Paid Staff: 3   **Volunteer Staff:** 20
Non-Paid Artists: 30
Utilizes: Special Technical Talent; Guest Artists; Guest Directors
Budget: $100,000 - $500,000
Income Sources: Private Foundations/Grants/Endowments; Business/Corporate Donations; Box Office; Government Grants; Individual Donations
Season: June - May   **Annual Attendance:** 17,000
Performance Facilities: Sangamon State University

INSTRUMENTAL MUSIC

SPRINGFIELD SYMPHONY ORCHESTRA
524 1/2 East Capitol Avenue, Springfield, IL 62701
(217) 522-2838
FAX: (217) 522-7374
>**Founded:** 1921
>**Arts Area:** Symphony; Orchestra; Chamber; Ensemble
>**Status:** Professional; Non-Profit
>**Type:** Performing; Touring; Resident; Educational
>**Purpose:** To sponsor, promote and assist in the presentation of symphonic concerts; encourage and develop a desire for symphonic music; instruct, assist and develop musical abilities; assist in training and education; provide concerts, musical programs and other entertainment
>**Management:** Linda G. Moore, General Manager; Kenneth Kiesler, Music Director/Conductor; Judith Lampert, Orchestra Manager
>**Paid Staff:** 4   **Volunteer Staff:** 3
>**Paid Artists:** 100
>**Utilizes:** Guest Artists
>**Budget:** $500,000 - $1,000,000
>**Income Sources:** Private Foundations/Grants/Endowments; Business/Corporate Donations; Box Office; Government Grants; Individual Donations; Touring Fees
>**Season:** September - April   **Annual Attendance:** 35,000
>**Affiliations:** ASOL; CMA; Illinois Arts Alliance
>**Performance Facilities:** Braden Auditorium-Illinois State University; Sangamon State University Auditorium

FACILITY

SANGAMON STATE UNIVERSITY AUDITORIUM
Sangamon State University, Springfield, IL 62794-9243
(217) 786-6150
FAX: (217) 786-7279
>**Founded:** 1981
>**Type of Facility:** Auditorium
>**Type of Stage:** Proscenium
>**Stage Dimensions:** 120'x44'   **Orchestra Pit**
>**Seating Capacity:** 1,951; 60 additional in pit
>**Year Built:** 1980   **Architect:** Ferry & Henderson   **Cost:** $18,000,000
>**Acoustical Consultant:** Kirkegaard
>**Contact for Rental:** Ann Schleyhann;   (217) 786-6150

SPRINGFIELD COLLEGE - MUSIC HALL
1500 North Fifth Street, Springfield, IL 62702
(217) 525-1420
>**Type of Facility:** Concert Hall; Studio Performance
>**Type of Stage:** Proscenium
>**Stage Dimensions:** 26'x26'
>**Seating Capacity:** 250
>**Year Built:** 1910
>**Contact for Rental:** Fred Greenwald;   (217) 525-1420, ext. 33

Summit

THEATRE

CANDLELIGHT DINNER PLAYHOUSE AND FORUM THEATRE
5620 South Harlem, Summit, IL 60501
(708) 496-3000
>**Founded:** 1959
>**Arts Area:** Professional; Musical; Dinner
>**Status:** Professional; Commercial
>**Type:** Performing; Resident
>**Purpose:** America's first dinner theatre prides itself on presenting first-class Broadway musicals year round.
>**Management:** William Pullinsi, Producer/Director; Anthony D'Angelo, Producer/Designer
>**Officers:** William Pullinsi, President
>**Paid Staff:** 150
>**Paid Artists:** 30
>**Utilizes:** Special Technical Talent

Income Sources: Box Office
Season: 52 Weeks
Performance Facilities: Forum Theatre

Urbana

FACILITY

KRANNERT CENTER FOR THE PERFORMING ARTS
500 South Goodwin Avenue, Urbana, IL 61801
(217) 333-6700
FAX: (217) 244-0810
    Type of Facility: Theatre Complex; Performance Center
    Year Built: 1969   **Architect:** Max Abramovitz   **Cost:** $21,000,000
    Acoustical Consultant: Dr. Cyril M. Harris
    Contact for Rental: Janet Taylor;   (217) 333-6703
    Manager: Terrence D. Jones
    Resident Groups: Illinois Repertory Theatre; Illinois Opera Theatre; Illinois Dance Theatre; Champaign-Urbana Symphony; Sinfonia da Camera
    The Performing Arts Center contains Colwell Playhouse, Festival Theatre, Foellinger Great Hall and Studio Theatre. See individual listings for additional information.

KRANNERT CENTER FOR THE PERFORMING ARTS - COLWELL PLAYHOUSE
500 South Goodwin Avenue, Urbana, IL 61801
(217) 333-6700
FAX: (217) 244-0810
    Type of Facility: Concert Hall; Theatre House
    Type of Stage: Proscenium; Hydraulic Lift Stage
    Stage Dimensions: 38'Wx33'D, 18'D added with lifts at stage level   **Orchestra Pit**
    Seating Capacity: 675, continental seating
    Contact for Rental: Janet Taylor;   (217) 333-6703
    Manager: Terrence D. Jones
    Resident Groups: Illinois Repertory Theatre; Illinois Dance Theatre

KRANNERT CENTER FOR THE PERFORMING ARTS - FESTIVAL THEATRE
500 South Goodwin Avenue, Urbana, IL 61801
(217) 333-6700
FAX: (217) 244-0810
    Type of Facility: Concert Hall; Theatre House
    Type of Stage: Proscenium; Hydraulic Lift Stage
    Stage Dimensions: 40'Wx35'D, 16'D added with lifts at stage level
    Orchestra Pit
    Seating Capacity: 1,000
    Contact for Rental: Terrence D, Jones, Manager;   (217) 333-6703
    Manager: Terrence D. Jones;   (216) 333-6703
    Resident Groups: Illinois Opera Theatre; Illinois Dance Theatre; Kabuki Theatre with Shozo Sato
    Two hydraulic lifts: 6'Dx40'W and 8'Dx40'W, each operates independently

KRANNERT CENTER FOR THE PERFORMING ARTS - FOELLINGER GREAT HALL
500 South Goodwin Avenue, Urbana, IL 61801
(217) 333-6700
FAX: (217) 244-0810
    Type of Facility: Concert Hall
    Type of Stage: Concert Stage
    Stage Dimensions: 60'Wx48'D, 8'D added with lift at stage level   **Orchestra Pit**
    Seating Capacity: 2,100
    Contact for Rental: Janet Taylor;   (217) 333-6703
    Resident Groups: Champaign-Urbana Symphony; Sinfonia da Camera
    One hydraulic lift, 8'Dx60'W

KRANNERT CENTER FOR THE PERFORMING ARTS - STUDIO THEATRE
500 South Goodwin Avenue, Urbana, IL 61801
(217) 333-6700
FAX: (217) 244-0810
    Type of Facility: Studio Performance; Black Box
    Type of Stage: Flexible
    Stage Dimensions: 45'x55' Black Box with 15'H Grid

Seating Capacity: 200
Contact for Rental: Janet Taylor;   (217) 333-6703
Resident Groups: Illinois Repertory Theatre; Illinois Dance Theatre

---
Waukegan

FACILITY

GOODFELLOW HALL (JACK BENNY CENTER FOR THE ARTS)
39 Jack Benny Drive, Waukegan, IL 60087
(708) 360-4741
FAX: (708) 244-8270
    Founded: 1987
    Type of Facility: Auditorium; Studio Performance; Performance Center; Theatre House; Opera House
    Facility Originally: Meeting Hall; Ballroom
    Type of Stage: Lecture; Recital
    Stage Dimensions: 18'Dx23"W
    Seating Capacity: 100
    Year Built: 1922   **Architect:** Hull House   **Cost:** $1,200
    Year Remodeled: 1987   **Architect:** Waukegan Park District   **Cost:** $18,000
    Contact for Rental: Lynn Schornick;   (708) 360-4741
    Resident Groups: Bowen Park Opera Company; Bowen Park Theatre Company

---
Western Springs

THEATRE

THEATRE OF WESTERN SPRINGS
4384 Hampton Avenue, Western Springs, IL 60558
(708) 246-4043
    Founded: 1929
    Arts Area: Community; Theatrical Group; Children's Theatre
    Status: Non-Professional; Non-Profit
    Type: Performing; Educational; Sponsoring
    Purpose: To promote, develop and maintain a community theatre producing plays of significance and interest; to provide an open forum for the arts
    Management: Ronn Toebaas, Artistic Director; Jeanne Hopson, Children's Theatre Director
    Officers: Jon Mills, Chairperson
    Paid Staff: 3
    Non-Paid Artists: 250
    Utilizes: Guest Directors
    Budget: $100,000 - $500,000
    Income Sources: Business/Corporate Donations; Box Office; Individual Donations
    Season: September - July
    Affiliations: AACT

Wheaton

INSTRUMENTAL MUSIC

WHEATON SYMPHONY ORCHESTRA
1600 East Roosevelt Road, Wheaton, IL 60187
(708) 668-8585
    Founded: 1959
    Arts Area: Symphony
    Status: Non-Professional
    Type: Performing
    Purpose: To perform the music of 19th and 20th-century composers, composed for large orchestras
    Management: Dr. Donald C. Mattison, General Manager
    Volunteer Staff: 2
    Non-Paid Artists: 2
    Budget: $1,000 - $50,000
    Income Sources: Box Office; Individual Donations
    Season: June - August

Affiliations: ASOL
Performance Facilities: Edman Chapel, Wheaton College

FACILITY

WHEATON COLLEGE - ARENA THEATER
501 East College Avenue, Wheaton, IL 60187
(708) 260-5000
> **Type of Facility:** Black Box
> **Facility Originally:** Recreation Hall/gymnasium
> **Type of Stage:** Flexible
> **Stage Dimensions:** 60'Wx39'D
> **Seating Capacity:** 180
> **Year Built:** 1984
> **Contact for Rental:** Virginia Kolb
> **Resident Groups:** Wheaton College Opera Theatre; Wheaton College Players

WHEATON COLLEGE - EDMAN CHAPEL
501 East College Avenue, Wheaton, IL 60187
(708) 752-5000
> **Type of Facility:** Concert Hall; Auditorium
> **Facility Originally:** Chapel
> **Type of Stage:** Proscenium
> **Stage Dimensions:** 52'x71'x26'
> **Seating Capacity:** 2,383
> **Year Built:** 1961   **Architect:** J. Emil Anderson & Son   **Cost:** $1,525,000
> **Contact for Rental:** Virginia Kolb
> **Resident Groups:** Wheaton College Concert Choir; Wheaton College Men's Glee Club; Wheaton College Women's Chorale; Wheaton College Wind Ensemble; Wheaton College Symphony Orchestra

Winnetka

THEATRE

T. DANIEL MIME/MOVEMENT THEATRE
1047 Gage, Winnetka, IL 60093
(708) 441-0183
> **Founded:** 1971
> **Arts Area:** Professional; Theatrical Group
> **Status:** Professional
> **Type:** Performing
> **Purpose:** To create and present on tour programs on mime and theatre for adults, families and children
> **Paid Staff:** 1   **Volunteer Staff:** 1
> **Paid Artists:** 2
> **Budget:** $1,000 - $50,000
> **Income Sources:** Box Office; Government Grants
> **Season:** 52 Weeks   **Annual Attendance:** 100,000

FACILITY

DILLER STREET THEATER
310 Greenbay Road, Winnetka, IL 60093
(708) 446-1978
> **Founded:** 1980
> **Type of Facility:** Concert Hall; Auditorium; Theatre House; Multi-Purpose
> **Type of Stage:** Proscenium
> **Stage Dimensions:** 40'x30'   **Seating Capacity:** 471
> **Year Built:** 1926   **Architect:** Edwin Clark
> **Year Remodeled:** 1991   **Architect:** Schuler and Shook, Consultants
> **Contact for Rental:** Lisa Tomoleoni;   (312) 446-1978
> **Resident Groups:** Chicago Children's Theater; North Shore Country Day School

Woodridge

INSTRUMENTAL MUSIC

THE CHINESE CLASSICAL ORCHESTRA
Chinese Music Society of North America, One Heritage Plaza PO Box 5275, Woodridge, IL 60517-0275
(708) 910-1551
FAX: (708) 910-1561
Founded: 1976
Arts Area: Orchestra; Ensemble; Ethnic; Folk
Status: Professional; Non-Profit
Type: Performing; Touring
Purpose: To create music of the 21st century; to perform using the tonal groups of reeded wind, percussion, plucked string and bowed string; to employ just intervals; to tour internationally and in North America year round
Management: Dr. Yuan-Yuan Lee, Director
Officers: Dr. Sin-yan Shen, Music Director; Dr. Yuan-Yuan Lee, Director of Concert and Lecture; Kerry Leung, Production Manager; Billie J. Jefferson, Artistic Administrator
Paid Staff: 10   **Volunteer Staff:** 12
Paid Artists: 28
Utilizes: Special Technical Talent; Guest Conductors; Guest Artists; Guest Directors
Budget: $500,000 - $1,000,000
Income Sources: Private Foundations/Grants/Endowments; Business/Corporate Donations; Box Office; Government Grants; Individual Donations
Season: 52 Weeks
Annual Attendance: 500,000

CHINESE MUSIC EDUCATIONAL PROGRAM
Chinese Music Society of North America, One Heritage Plaza, PO Box 5275, Woodridge, IL 60517-0275
(708) 910-1551
FAX: (708) 910-1561
Founded: 1986
Status: Professional; Non-Profit
Type: Performing; Touring; Educational
Purpose: To provide a national educational program on Chinese music and music of the world, using methods based on musical psychology, thereby eliminating cultural barriers; to provide programs internationally
Management: Dr. Yuan-Yuan Lee, Director Concert and Lecture Department
Officers: Dr. Sin-yan Shen, Music Director; Dr.Yuan-Yuan Lee, Director of Concert and Lecture; Billie J. Jefferson, Artistic Administrator; Scott Conover, Program Manager
Paid Staff: 4   **Volunteer Staff:** 12
Paid Artists: 28
Utilizes: Special Technical Talent; Guest Conductors; Guest Artists; Guest Directors
Budget: $500,000 - $1,000,000
Income Sources: Private Foundations/Grants/Endowments; Business/Corporate Donations; Box Office; Government Grants; Individual Donations
Season: 52 Weeks
Annual Attendance: 500,000

CHINESE MUSIC SOCIETY OF NORTH AMERICA
One Heritage Plaza, PO Box 5275, Woodridge, IL 60517-0275
(708) 910-1551
FAX: (708) 910-1561
Founded: 1976
Arts Area: Symphony; Orchestra; Chamber; Ensemble; Ethnic; Folk; Instrumental Group; Electronic & Live Electronic
Status: Professional; Non-Profit
Type: Performing; Touring; Resident; Educational; Sponsoring
Purpose: The largest Chinese music educational service institution in North America; publishes the Chinese Music Monograph Series, the international journal Chinese Music, and educational material on music and acoustics, and recordings and videos
Management: Dr. Yuan-Yuan Lee, Director Concert and Lecture Department
Officers: Dr. Sin-yan Shen, President; Kok-Koon Ng, Vice President
Paid Staff: 11   **Volunteer Staff:** 30
Paid Artists: 28
Utilizes: Special Technical Talent; Guest Conductors; Guest Artists; Guest Directors
Budget: $500,000 - $1,000,000
Income Sources: Private Foundations/Grants/Endowments; Business/Corporate Donations; Box Office; Government Grants; Individual Donations

Season: 52 Weeks
Annual Attendance: 500,000

THE SILK AND BAMBOO ENSEMBLE
Chinese Music Society of North America, One Heritage Plaza, PO Box 5275, Woodridge, IL 60517-0275
(708) 910-1551
FAX: (708) 910-1561
Founded: 1981
Arts Area: Chamber; Ensemble; Ethnic; Instrumental Group
Status: Professional; Non-Profit
Type: Performing; Touring; Educational
Purpose: To create chamber music of the 21st century; to perform works utilizing silk and bamboo instrumentation and just intervals; to tour internationally and in the U.S. year round
Management: Dr. Yuan-Yuan Lee, Director Concert and Lecture Department
Officers: Dr. Sin-yan Shen, Music Director
Paid Staff: 4 **Volunteer Staff:** 6
Paid Artists: 5
Utilizes: Special Technical Talent; Guest Conductors; Guest Artists; Guest Directors
Budget: $500,000 - $1,000,000
Income Sources: Private Foundations/Grants/Endowments; Business/Corporate Donations; Box Office; Government Grants; Individual Donations
Season: 52 Weeks
Annual Attendance: 500,000

Woodstock

PERFORMING SERIES

WOODSTOCK OPERA HOUSE
121 Van Buren Street, Woodstock, IL 60098
(815) 338-4212
Founded: 1977
Arts Area: Dance; Vocal Music; Instrumental Music; Theater; Festivals
Status: Non-Profit
Type: Performing; Resident; Educational; Sponsoring
Purpose: To be a cultural center for McHenry County, Illinois, highlighting Illinois, American and international artists; to work closely with the Woodstock community
Management: John Scharres, Executive Director
Paid Staff: 6 **Volunteer Staff:** 200
Paid Artists: 50 **Non-Paid Artists:** 50
Utilizes: Special Technical Talent; Guest Conductors; Guest Artists; Guest Directors
Budget: $500,000 - $1,000,000
Income Sources: Private Foundations/Grants/Endowments; Business/Corporate Donations; Box Office; Government Grants; Individual Donations
Season: 52 Weeks **Annual Attendance:** 70,000
Affiliations: ISPAA; APAP
Performance Facilities: Woodstock Opera House

FACILITY

WOODSTOCK OPERA HOUSE
121 Van Buren Street, Woodstock, IL 60098
(815) 338-4212
Type of Facility: Opera House
Type of Stage: Proscenium
Stage Dimensions: 24'x15'x26'
Seating Capacity: 429
Year Built: 1890 **Architect:** Smith Hoag **Cost:** $25,000
Year Remodeled: 1977 **Architect:** John Vincent Anderson **Cost:** $500,000
Contact for Rental: Manager; (815) 338-4212
Resident Groups: Townsquare Players; Judith Svalander Dance Theatre; Woodstock Musical Theatre Company
Woodstock Opera House is a National Historic Landmark

Zion

THEATRE

ZION PASSION PLAY
2500 Dowie Memorial Drive, Zion, IL 60099-2594
(708) 746-2221
FAX: (708) 746-1452
Founded: 1935
Arts Area: Musical; Community
Status: Non-Professional; Non-Profit
Type: Performing; Resident; Educational
Purpose: Biblical production of the life of Christ
Management: Board of Trustees
Officers: Rev. Roger Ottersen, President; Calvin Weese, Secretary/Treasurer
Paid Staff: 3 **Volunteer Staff:** 15
Non-Paid Artists: 200
Utilizes: Special Technical Talent
Budget: $1,000 - $50,000
Income Sources: Box Office; Individual Donations
Season: Good Friday - May **Annual Attendance:** 5,200
Affiliations: Christian Catholic Church
Performance Facilities: Christian Arts Auditorium

FACILITY

CHRISTIAN ARTS AUDITORIUM
Dowie Memorial Drive, Zion, IL 60099
(708) 746-2221
Type of Facility: Theatre Complex; Concert Hall; Auditorium
Facility Originally: Amphitheatre
Type of Stage: Proscenium
Stage Dimensions: 90'Wx51'D
Seating Capacity: 552
Year Built: 1980 **Architect:** Rehder Rothermel Pekkarin **Cost:** $994,087
Acoustical Consultant: Sound, Incorporated
Resident Groups: Zion Passion Play; Zion Chamber Orchestra; Zion Concert Band; Christian Catholic Church Vesper Service

INDIANA

Anderson

INSTRUMENTAL MUSIC

ANDERSON SYMPHONY ORCHESTRA
PO Box 741, Anderson, IN 46015
(317) 641-4545
 Founded: 1978
 Arts Area: Symphony
 Status: Semi-Professional; Non-Profit
 Type: Performing; Resident
 Purpose: The production of music and the development of musical culture
 Management: Pam Coletti, Manager
 Officers: Marion Hovermale, President; John Kane, Treasurer
 Paid Staff: 1 **Volunteer Staff:** 5
 Paid Artists: 52 **Non-Paid Artists:** 11
 Utilizes: Guest Conductors; Guest Artists
 Budget: $50,000 - $100,000
 Income Sources: Private Foundations/Grants/Endowments; Business/Corporate Donations; Box Office; Government Grants; Individual Donations
 Season: October - May **Annual Attendance:** 9,000
 Affiliations: Women's Guild
 Performance Facilities: Reardon Auditorium

FACILITY

REARDON AUDITORIUM
1015 East Fifth Street, Anderson, IN 46012
(317) 641-4143
FAX: (317) 641-3851
 Founded: 1983
 Type of Facility: Auditorium
 Type of Stage: Proscenium
 Stage Dimensions: 54'x72' **Orchestra Pit**
 Seating Capacity: 2,211
 Year Built: 1983 **Architect:** Kent Montgomery **Cost:** $5,500,000
 Contact for Rental: Roger Byrd; (317) 641-4144

Bedford

THEATRE

BEDFORD LITTLE THEATRE
PO Box 142, Bedford, IN 47421
(812) 279-3009
 Founded: 1960
 Arts Area: Musical; Community; Theatrical Group
 Status: Non-Profit
 Type: Performing
 Purpose: To provide an opportunity for volunteer performers and directors to entertain our community with theatrical productions
 Management: Board of Directors, Executive Committee
 Officers: Richard Hahn, President; Jack May, Vice President; Judith Jacobs, Treasurer; Lisa Hardwick, Secretary
 Volunteer Staff: 8
 Non-Paid Artists: 150
 Budget: $1,000 - $50,000
 Income Sources: Box Office; Individual Donations
 Season: September - June **Annual Attendance:** 700
 Performance Facilities: Little Theatre

Bloomington

INSTRUMENTAL MUSIC

BLOOMINGTON SYMPHONY ORCHESTRA
PO Box 1823, Bloomington, IN 47402
(812) 331-2320
Founded: 1969
Arts Area: Symphony; Orchestra
Status: Non-Profit
Type: Performing; Touring; Educational
Purpose: To present quality performances of orchestra literature to the community of Bloomington and its surrounding areas, fulfilling a function not met by the Indiana University symphonies
Management: Faythe Freese, General Manager; David Pickett, Music Director; Pat Kinzer, Personnel Manager
Officers: Judy Schmid, President; Rodney Young, Vice President; Pat Fell Barker, Treasurer
Volunteer Staff: 14
Non-Paid Artists: 6
Utilizes: Guest Artists
Budget: $50,000 - $100,000
Income Sources: Private Foundations/Grants/Endowments; Business/Corporate Donations; Box Office; Government Grants; Individual Donations
Season: September - May   **Annual Attendance:** 5,000
Affiliations: ASOL
Performance Facilities: St. Mark's Methodist Church

PERFORMING SERIES

INDIANA UNIVERSITY PERFORMING ARTS SERIES
Indiana University Auditorium, Bloomington, IN 47405-5501
(812) 855-9528
FAX: (812) 855-4244
Founded: 1820
Arts Area: Dance; Instrumental Music; Theater
Status: Professional; Non-Profit
Type: Educational; Sponsoring
Purpose: To present to the University community the best available professional performing arts programs
Management: James Holland, Director
Paid Staff: 13   **Volunteer Staff:** 150
Budget: $100,000 - $500,000
Income Sources: Private Foundations/Grants/Endowments; Box Office; Government Grants
Season: September - April
Affiliations: IAAM; APAP
Performance Facilities: Indiana University Auditorium

FACILITY

INDIANA UNIVERSITY AUDITORIUM
Indiana University, Bloomington, IN 47405-5501
(812) 855-9528
FAX: (812) 855-4244
Type of Facility: Concert Hall; Auditorium; Performance Center; Theatre House; Opera House
Type of Stage: Proscenium
Stage Dimensions: 104'Wx40'D   **Orchestra Pit**
Seating Capacity: 3,760
Year Built: 1939   **Architect:** Eggers & Higgins   **Cost:** $1,125,000
Acoustical Consultant: John Ditamore
Contact for Rental: Elise Kushigian;   (812) 855-0170
Manager: James C. Holland, Director;   (812) 855-9528
Our purpose is to present the finest in the performing arts

INDIANA UNIVERSITY MUSICAL ARTS CENTER
Indiana University, School of Music, Bloomington, IN 47405
(812) 335-9053
Type of Facility: Concert Hall; Opera House
Type of Stage: Flexible; Proscenium
Stage Dimensions: 90'Wx60'D   **Orchestra Pit**
Seating Capacity: 1,460
Year Built: 1971   **Architect:** Woolen Associates   **Cost:** $11,300,000

Acoustical Consultant: Bolt, Beranek & Newman
Resident Groups: Indiana University Orchestras; Indiana University Opera Theater; Indiana University Ballet Theater

INDIANA UNIVERSITY THEATRE
Theatre 200, Indiana University, Bloomington, IN 47405
(812) 855-4535
FAX: (812) 855-4704
    Type of Facility: Theatre House; Black Box
    Type of Stage: Flexible; Proscenium
    Orchestra Pit
    Seating Capacity: Mainstage - 383; Black Box - 66
    Year Built: 1941   **Architect:** Strauss Eggers & Higgins
    Acoustical Consultant: Lee Simonson
    Manager: R. Keith Michael, Chairman

Brazil

THEATRE

COMMUNITY THEATRE OF CLAY COUNTY
8 East National, Brazil, IN 47834
(812) 443-8012
    Founded: 1983
    Arts Area: Musical; Dinner; Community; Theatrical Group
    Status: Non-Professional; Non-Profit
    Type: Performing; Educational
    Purpose: To provide opportunities for involvement in the arts in Clay County for all ages, by presenting dinner theatre, musicals, children's workshops, senior citizens programs, and sponsoring drama scholarships
    Officers: Susan M. Bradbury, President; John Berry, Vice President; Lois Myers, Secretary/Treasurer
    Volunteer Staff: 11
    Non-Paid Artists: 200
    Utilizes: Special Technical Talent; Guest Conductors; Guest Artists; Guest Directors
    Budget: $1,000 - $50,000
    Income Sources: Private Foundations/Grants/Endowments; Business/Corporate Donations; Box Office; Individual Donations
    Season: 52 Weeks   **Annual Attendance:** 2,000
    Affiliations: Arts Illiana; ITA

Bristol

THEATRE

ELKHART CIVIC THEATRE
Bristol Opera House, 210 East Vistula, PO Box 252, Bristol, IN 46507
(219) 848-4116
    Founded: 1946
    Arts Area: Musical; Community; Theatrical Group
    Status: Non-Professional; Non-Profit
    Type: Performing; Resident; Educational
    Purpose: To provide a high quality theatre experience to audience and participants, including eight major productions per year plus workshops in acting, voice, dance and technical theatre
    Management: Frank F. Brush, Manager; Leslie K. Torok, Artistic Director
    Officers: William Lavery, President; Kevin Egelsky, Vice President; Brad Gilbert, Treasurer; Frank Brush, Secretary
    Paid Staff: 2   **Volunteer Staff:** 10
    Non-Paid Artists: 80
    Utilizes: Guest Directors
    Budget: $100,000 - $500,000
    Income Sources: Private Foundations/Grants/Endowments; Business/Corporate Donations; Box Office; Government Grants; Individual Donations
    Season: 52 Weeks   **Annual Attendance:** 14,000
    Affiliations: Indiana Community Theatre Association; AACT
    Performance Facilities: The Bristol Opera House

Brownstown
THEATRE

JACKSON COUNTY COMMUNITY THEATRE
121 West Walnut Street, PO Box 65, Brownstown, IN 47220
(812) 358-2812
> **Founded:** 1971
> **Arts Area:** Dinner; Community; Theatrical Group
> **Status:** Non-Professional; Non-Profit
> **Type:** Performing; Educational
> **Purpose:** Produce live plays and bring cultural programs to the community
> **Management:** Marianne Green, Artistic Director
> **Officers:** Fred Lewis, President; Mark Coggeshall, Vice President; John Lewis, Secretary; Sarah McGill, Treasurer
> **Utilizes:** Guest Artists; Guest Directors
> **Budget:** $1,000 - $50,000
> **Income Sources:** Business/Corporate Donations; Government Grants; Individual Donations
> **Season:** September - May **Annual Attendance:** 2,000
> **Affiliations:** Indiana Theatre Association
> **Performance Facilities:** Royal Office Square Theatre

Clarksville
THEATRE

DERBY DINNER PLAYHOUSE
525 Marriott Drive, Clarksville, IN 47129
(812) 288-2632
FAX: (812) 288-2636
> **Founded:** 1975
> **Arts Area:** Dinner
> **Status:** Professional; Commercial
> **Type:** Performing
> **Purpose:** Professional dinner entertainment
> **Management:** Bekki Jo Schneider, Producer; Carolyn Lamb, General Manager
> **Paid Staff:** 50
> **Utilizes:** Special Technical Talent; Guest Artists; Guest Directors
> **Budget:** $100,000 - $500,000
> **Income Sources:** Business/Corporate Donations; Box Office; Individual Donations
> **Season:** 52 Weeks
> **Performance Facilities:** Derby Dinner Playhouse

Columbus
INSTRUMENTAL MUSIC

COLUMBUS PRO MUSICA
302 Washington Street, Columbus, IN 47201
(812) 376-2638
FAX: (812) 376-2567
> **Founded:** 1971
> **Arts Area:** Symphony
> **Status:** Semi-Professional; Non-Profit
> **Type:** Performing; Educational; Sponsoring
> **Purpose:** To promote and encourage an active interest in music; to promote and facilitate instruction, study and performing of instrumental music; to work toward providing necessary facilities and equipment; to widen the availability of music instruction; sponsor and present performances
> **Management:** Alice O. Jolly, Manager; Kaye Ellen Connor, Administrative Assistant; David Bowden, Music Director
> **Officers:** Robert S. Kasper, President; Nancy Morris, Vice President; Richard A. Stenner, Treasurer; Lori Phillips, Secretary
> **Paid Staff:** 3
> **Utilizes:** Guest Artists
> **Budget:** $100,000 - $500,000
> **Income Sources:** Private Foundations/Grants/Endowments; Business/Corporate Donations; Box Office; Government Grants; Individual Donations
> **Season:** September - June **Annual Attendance:** 15,000
> **Affiliations:** ASOL; Indiana Orchestra Consort; Indiana Arts Commission; Columbus Area Arts Council

---
Cromwell

THEATRE

ENCHANTED HILLS PLAYHOUSE
9358 East Wizard of Oz Way, PO Box 41, Cromwell, IN 46732
(219) 856-2328
Founded: 1960
Arts Area: Professional; Summer Stock; Musical
Status: Professional; Non-Profit
Type: Performing; Touring; Resident; Educational
Purpose: The mission of Enchanted Hills Playhouse is to produce quality theatre in Kosciusko County and serve as the cultural leader in the area and to provide positive influences on the community.
Management: Robert O. Decker, Executive Producer; Jerry O'Boyle, Associate Producer
Paid Staff: 21   **Volunteer Staff:** 3
Paid Artists: 25
Utilizes: Guest Artists; Guest Directors
Budget: $100,000 - $500,000
Income Sources: Private Foundations/Grants/Endowments; Business/Corporate Donations; Box Office; Government Grants; Individual Donations
Season: June - August   **Annual Attendance:** 15,000
Affiliations: Indiana Theatre Association; Ohio Theatre Alliance; Michigan Theatre Association; Michigan Arts and Sciences Council Inc.
Performance Facilities: Enchanted Hills Playhouse

East Chicago

DANCE

BALLET FOLKLORICO OF EAST CHICAGO, INDIANA
210 East Columbus Drive, East Chicago, IN 46312
(219) 391-4122
FAX: (219) 391-4155
Arts Area: Ballet; Ethnic; Folk
Status: Non-Profit
Type: Performing; Educational
Purpose: To depict the various dances and music of Mexico
Management: Dr. Jose Arredondo, Assistant Superintendent/Director
Paid Artists: 1
Budget: $1,000 - $50,000
Income Sources: Private Foundations/Grants/Endowments; Business/Corporate Donations
Season: 52 Weeks   **Annual Attendance:** 3,000
Performance Facilities: Central High School

Elkhard

PERFORMING SERIES

ELKHART CONCERT CLUB
53336 Old Farm Road, Elkhard, IN 46514
Founded: 1952
Arts Area: Dance; Vocal Music; Theater; Grand Opera
Status: Professional
Type: Performing; Educational
Volunteer Staff: 30
Utilizes: Guest Artists
Budget: $50,000 - $100,000
Income Sources: Private Foundations/Grants/Endowments; Business/Corporate Donations; Box Office; Individual Donations
Season: September - May   **Annual Attendance:** 5,000

Evansville

DANCE

EVANSVILLE DANCE THEATRE
333-E North Plaza East Boulevard, Evansville, IN 47715
(812) 473-8937
Founded: 1981
Arts Area: Ballet
Status: Professional; Non-Profit
Type: Performing; Touring; Resident; Educational
Management: Myron Taylor, Director; David Keener, Deena Laska, Artistic Directors; Patty Muenchen, General Director
Officers: Terry Haynie, President
Paid Artists: 7   **Non-Paid Artists:** 13
Utilizes: Guest Artists; Guest Choreographers
Budget: $1,000 - $50,000
Income Sources: Business/Corporate Donations
Season: September - May

INSTRUMENTAL MUSIC

EVANSVILLE PHILHARMONIC ORCHESTRA
318 Main Street, Suite 218, Evansville, IN 47708
(812) 425-5050
FAX: (812) 426-7008
Founded: 1934
Arts Area: Symphony; Orchestra; Chamber; Ensemble
Status: Professional
Type: Performing; Educational
Purpose: To provide symphonic music of the highest quality for the Tri-State Area of Southern Indiana, Illinois and Kentucky, both for adult audiences and students in the school systems
Management: James W. Palermi, General Manager
Officers: Nancy Hartley Gaunt, President; Thomas H. Bryan, President-Elect; Joan David, Vice President; Charles Schuger, Secretary; Jay Hargis, Treasurer
Paid Staff: 7   **Volunteer Staff:** 200
Paid Artists: 80
Utilizes: Guest Conductors; Guest Artists
Budget: $500,000 - $1,000,000
Income Sources: Private Foundations/Grants/Endowments; Business/Corporate Donations; Box Office; Government Grants; Individual Donations
Season: September - May   **Annual Attendance:** 23,400
Affiliations: ASOL; IOC; Evansville Arts and Education Council
Performance Facilities: Vanderburgh Auditorium

THEATRE

REPERTORY PEOPLE OF EVANSVILLE
Old Courthouse Building, Room 200, PO Box 3555, Evansville, IN 47708
(812) 423-2060
Founded: 1975
Arts Area: Theatrical Group
Status: Non-Professional; Non-Profit
Type: Performing; Resident
Purpose: Majority of plays are serious American dramas with occasional comedies
Management: Jim Jackson, Artistic Director; Tom Angermeier, Executive Producer
Paid Staff: 2   **Volunteer Staff:** 15
Budget: $1,000 - $50,000
Income Sources: Private Foundations/Grants/Endowments; Business/Corporate Donations; Box Office; Government Grants; Individual Donations
Season: September - June   **Annual Attendance:** 6,000

PERFORMING SERIES

EVANSVILLE ARTIST EDUCATION COUNCIL
123 NW Fourth Street, Suite 312, Evansville, IN 47708
(812) 422-2111
Founded: 1969
Arts Area: Festivals

Status: Professional; Non-Profit
Type: Educational; Sponsoring
Purpose: To promote development of the arts to arts audiences
Management: Lorie Clouser, Executive Director; Kim Setzer, Program Coordinator
Officers: Joe Meyer, President; Tom Fitzsimmons, Vice President; Danny Bateman, Treasurer; Mary Schepper, Secretary
Paid Staff: 4
Utilizes: Special Technical Talent; Guest Artists
Income Sources: Private Foundations/Grants/Endowments; Business/Corporate Donations; Box Office; Government Grants; Individual Donations
Season: 52 Weeks
Affiliations: NALAA; ACA; Alliance for Arts Education

FACILITY

VANDERBURGH AUDITORIUM CONVENTION CENTER
715 Locust Street, Evansville, IN 47708
(812) 426-2270
Type of Facility: Auditorium; Multi-Purpose
Type of Stage: Proscenium
Stage Dimensions: 102'Wx46'Dx22'H Orchestra Pit
Seating Capacity: 2,001
Year Built: 1967 Architect: Virgil Miller Cost: $2,500,000
Manager: Sandra Toton
Resident Groups: Evansville Philharmonic Orchestra

Fort Wayne

DANCE

FORT WAYNE BALLET
324 Penn, Fort Wayne, IN 46805
(219) 484-9646
FAX: (219) 484-9647
Founded: 1955
Arts Area: Modern; Ballet; Jazz
Status: Semi-Professional; Non-Profit
Type: Performing; Educational
Purpose: Fort Wayne Ballet is both a teaching and performing company.
Management: Michael Tevlin, Artistic Director
Officers: Ron Cassidente, President
Paid Staff: 14 Volunteer Staff: 135
Paid Artists: 5 Non-Paid Artists: 17
Utilizes: Special Technical Talent; Guest Artists; Guest Directors
Budget: $100,000 - $500,000
Income Sources: Private Foundations/Grants/Endowments; Business/Corporate Donations; Box Office; Individual Donations
Season: October - May
Affiliations: IAC; Fine Arts Foundation; Mid States Regional Ballet
Performance Facilities: Performing Arts Center

FORT WAYNE DANCE COLLECTIVE
437 East Berry Street, Fort Wayne, IN 46802
(219) 424-6574
Founded: 1979
Arts Area: Modern
Status: Professional; Non-Profit
Type: Performing; Educational; Sponsoring; Video Producer for Public Access
Purpose: To create an interest and appreciation for the art of modern dance
Management: Liz Monnier, Artistic Director
Officers: John H. Brandt, President; James Prickett, Vice President; Lois Schmidt, Secretary; Lisa Isenberger, Treasurer
Paid Staff: 9 Volunteer Staff: 15
Paid Artists: 4 Non-Paid Artists: 3
Utilizes: Guest Artists; Guest Choreographers
Budget: $100,000 - $500,000
Income Sources: Private Foundations/Grants/Endowments; Business/Corporate Donations; Box Office; Government Grants; Individual Donations
Season: September - June Annual Attendance: 1,400

Affiliations: Chicago Dance Art Coalition; Arts United of Greater Fort Wayne
Performance Facilities: Performing Arts Center

INSTRUMENTAL MUSIC

FORT WAYNE PHILHARMONIC ORCHESTRA
2340 Fairfield Avenue, Fort Wayne, IN 46807
(219) 744-1700
> **Founded:** 1943
> **Arts Area:** Symphony; Orchestra; Chamber; Ensemble
> **Status:** Professional; Non-Profit
> **Type:** Performing; Touring; Resident; Educational
> **Purpose:** To present music of the master composers and significant music of our time in Fort Wayne and Northern Indiana
> **Management:** Christopher D. Guerin, General Manager; Ronald Ondrejka, Music Director; David Crowe, Assistant Conductor
> **Officers:** Leonard M. Goldstein, President; Michael McCollum, Vice President; William C. Lee, Secretary; David A. Haist, Treasurer
> **Paid Staff:** 12   **Volunteer Staff:** 300
> **Paid Artists:** 92
> **Utilizes:** Guest Conductors; Guest Artists; Guest Directors
> **Budget:** $1,000,000 - $5,000,000
> **Income Sources:** Private Foundations/Grants/Endowments; Business/Corporate Donations; Box Office; Government Grants; Individual Donations
> **Season:** September - May   **Annual Attendance:** 36,000
> **Affiliations:** ASOL; MOMA; Fine Arts Foundation
> **Performance Facilities:** Embassy Theatre

THEATRE

ARENA DINNER THEATRE
7820 Schwartz Road, Fort Wayne, IN 46835
(219) 493-1384
> **Founded:** 1974
> **Arts Area:** Dinner; Community
> **Status:** Non-Professional
> **Type:** Performing
> **Purpose:** To give another option for theatre-goers and actors in the community
> **Officers:** Darrell Monroe, President; Brad Beauchamp, Vice President; Marlene Niccum, Treasurer; Stan Volz, Secretary
> **Paid Staff:** 1   **Volunteer Staff:** 20
> **Non-Paid Artists:** 50
> **Budget:** $50,000 - $100,000
> **Income Sources:** Private Foundations/Grants/Endowments; Business/Corporate Donations; Box Office; Government Grants; Individual Donations
> **Season:** September - May   **Annual Attendance:** 4,200
> **Affiliations:** IAC; Fine Arts Foundation; ITA

FIRST PRESBYTERIAN THEATER
300 West Wayne Street, Fort Wayne, IN 46802
(219) 422-6329
> **Founded:** 1968
> **Arts Area:** Dinner; Community
> **Status:** Non-Profit
> **Type:** Performing; Educational
> **Purpose:** To provide supportive group atmosphere for participants in production of classical and provocative contemporary drama
> **Management:** Mary Yarnelle, Director/Theatre Manager
> **Officers:** Myra McFarland, Church Drama Committee Chairman
> **Paid Staff:** 3   **Volunteer Staff:** 100
> **Paid Artists:** 2   **Non-Paid Artists:** 100
> **Utilizes:** Guest Directors
> **Budget:** $1,000 - $50,000
> **Income Sources:** Private Foundations/Grants/Endowments; Box Office; Individual Donations
> **Season:** September - May   **Annual Attendance:** 6,400
> **Affiliations:** Fort Wayne Community Arts Council

FORT WAYNE CIVIC THEATRE
303 East Main Street, Fort Wayne, IN 46802
(219) 422-8641
> **Arts Area:** Community

Status: Non-Professional; Non-Profit
Type: Resident
Purpose: Dedicated to strengthening itself as a significant cultural force in the Fort Wayne area through excellence in programming, theatre education and development of talent in the disciplines of theatre and the related performing arts
Management: Michael Mitchell, Executive Director; Mickie Martin, Business Manager
Officers: Michael McMath, President; Carolyn Pictor, Vice President; Chuck Schimper, Treasurer; Denise Lapsley, Secretary
Utilizes: Guest Directors; Guest Designers
Budget: $500,000 - $1,000,000
Income Sources: Private Foundations/Grants/Endowments; Business/Corporate Donations; Box Office; Individual Donations
Season: 52 Weeks   **Annual Attendance:** 45,000
Performance Facilities: The Performing Arts Center

FACILITY

EMBASSY THEATRE
1107 South Harrison Street, Fort Wayne, IN 46802
(219) 424-6287
Type of Facility: Theatre House
Facility Originally: Show Palace
Type of Stage: Proscenium
Stage Dimensions: 55'Wx26'D; 55'Wx29'6"H proscenium opening   **Orchestra Pit**
Seating Capacity: 2,750
Year Built: 1928   **Architect:** A.M. Strauss   **Cost:** $1,500,000
Year Remodeled: 1987   **Cost:** $1,000,000
Contact for Rental: Doris Stovall, Manager;   (219) 424-6287
Manager: Doris Stovall
Original Page Pipe Organ is in facility. Remodeling is in progress.

FOELLINGER THEATER IN FRANKE PARK
705 East State Boulevard, Fort Wayne, IN 46805
(219) 483-0057
Type of Facility: Theatre Complex; Concert Hall; Auditorium; Outdoor (Concert); Theatre House; Amphitheater; Opera House
Type of Stage: Proscenium
Stage Dimensions: 27'x56'x55'   **Orchestra Pit**
Seating Capacity: 2,715
Year Built: 1949   **Architect:** Shoaff   **Cost:** $100,000
Year Remodeled: 1976   **Architect:** Grinsfelder   **Cost:** $300,000
Acoustical Consultant: K.L.F.
Contact for Rental: Betty Khan;   (219) 483-0057
Resident Groups: Foellinger Theatre Group
Summer theater only, June 1 through September 30

PERFORMING ARTS CENTER
303 East Main Street, Fort Wayne, IN 46802
(219) 423-4349
Type of Facility: Theatre House
Type of Stage: Proscenium
Stage Dimensions: 28'x60'x42'   **Orchestra Pit**
Seating Capacity: 682
Year Built: 1973   **Architect:** Louis Kahn   **Cost:** $4,500,000
Acoustical Consultant: George C. Izenour
Contact for Rental: Janet McCauley;   (219) 423-4349
Resident Groups: Civic Theatre; Fort Wayne Ballet; Philharmonic Orchestra; Youth Theatre
John Wainwright, Technical Director

SCOTTISH RITE AUDITORIUM
431 West Berry Street, Fort Wayne, IN 46802
(219) 423-2593
FAX: (219) 426-4126
Type of Facility: Auditorium; Theatre House
Type of Stage: Thrust; Flexible; Proscenium
Stage Dimensions: 65'x65'x35'   **Orchestra Pit**
Seating Capacity: 2,197
Year Built: 1925
Year Remodeled: 1958
Contact for Rental: James De Monde;   (219) 423-2593

Manager: James De Mond
Resident Groups: Ancient Accepted Scottish Rite of Freemasonry
Family entertainment only

French Lick

THEATRE

FLS ENTERTAINMENT
French Lick Springs Resort, French Lick, IN 47432
(812) 936-9300, ext. 1003
Founded: 1992
Arts Area: Professional; Musical; Theatrical Group
Status: Professional
Type: Performing; Resident; Educational
Purpose: To present original theatre to the populus and cultivate new talent
Management: Chris Bundy, Director of Entertainment; Steve Gorman, Assistant Director of Entertainment
Paid Staff: 2
Paid Artists: 15
Utilizes: Special Technical Talent; Guest Artists
Income Sources: Private Foundations/Grants/Endowments; Business/Corporate Donations; Box Office; Individual Donations
Season: 52 Weeks

Gary

PERFORMING SERIES

I.U. DONS, INC.
PO Box M622, Gary, IN 46401
(219) 887-2041
Founded: 1969
Arts Area: Dance; Vocal Music; Theater
Status: Non-Profit
Type: Educational; Sponsoring
Purpose: To promote educational attainment
Officers: Dr. Vernon G. Smith, President
Volunteer Staff: 20
Utilizes: Guest Artists
Budget: $1,000 - $50,000
Income Sources: Private Foundations/Grants/Endowments; Individual Donations
Season: September - December   **Annual Attendance:** 2,000

Goshen

THEATRE

THE BRIDGEWORK THEATER
113 1/2 East Lincoln Avenue, Goshen, IN 46526
(219) 534-1085
Founded: 1979
Arts Area: Theatrical Group
Status: Professional; Non-Profit
Type: Performing; Touring
Purpose: To create and perform issue-oriented plays for children in the Great Lakes Region
Management: Donald C. Yost, Director
Officers: Ruth Hollinger, Board President; Shirley Lint, Vice President; Cheryl Cooper, Treasurer; Lynn Miller, Secretary
Paid Staff: 4
Paid Artists: 12
Utilizes: Guest Directors
Budget: $100,000 - $500,000
Income Sources: Private Foundations/Grants/Endowments; Business/Corporate Donations; Box Office; Government Grants; Individual Donations; Royalty Income
Season: September - May   **Annual Attendance:** 45,000
Affiliations: ITA

FACILITY

GOSHEN COLLEGE - JOHN S. UMBLE CENTER
1700 South Main, Goshen, IN 46526
(219) 533-3161
> **Type of Facility:** Theatre House
> **Type of Stage:** Thrust; Flexible; Proscenium
> **Stage Dimensions:** 60'Wx47'6"Dx29'H
> **Seating Capacity:** 410
> **Year Built:** 1977   **Architect:** Weldon Pries   **Cost:** $1,400,000
> **Acoustical Consultant:** William Cavanaugh
> **Contact for Rental:** Judy Hollar;   (219) 533-3161
> **Manager:** Lauren Friesen, Director
> *Very limited rental use*

Hagerstown

THEATRE

NETTLE CREEK PLAYERS
98 East Main Street, PO Box 23, Hagerstown, IN 47346
(317) 489-5214
> **Founded:** 1971
> **Arts Area:** Summer Stock; Musical; Community; Theatrical Group
> **Status:** Semi-Professional; Non-Professional; Non-Profit
> **Type:** Performing
> **Purpose:** Summer stock season also consists of training program in musical theatre for ten resident performers
> **Management:** Alan Montgomery, Artistic Director
> **Officers:** W.E. Stackhouse, Jr., President
> **Paid Staff:** 2   **Volunteer Staff:** 1
> **Paid Artists:** 21   **Non-Paid Artists:** 40
> **Utilizes:** Guest Directors
> **Budget:** $50,000 - $100,000
> **Income Sources:** Private Foundations/Grants/Endowments; Business/Corporate Donations; Box Office; Government Grants; Individual Donations
> **Season:** June - August   **Annual Attendance:** 10,000
> **Affiliations:** ITA; SETC
> **Performance Facilities:** Nettle Creek Playhouse

Highland

THEATRE

MAIN SQUARE PLAYERS
8749 Idlewild, Highland, IN 46322
(219) 838-1052
> **Founded:** 1980
> **Arts Area:** Professional; Musical
> **Status:** Semi-Professional; Non-Profit
> **Type:** Performing; Educational
> **Purpose:** To introduce new forms of theatre as far as nonconventional space and multi-age backgrounds
> **Management:** Gregory J. Ladd, Director/Producer
> **Paid Staff:** 3   **Volunteer Staff:** 8
> **Paid Artists:** 2   **Non-Paid Artists:** 50
> **Utilizes:** Special Technical Talent
> **Budget:** $1,000 - $50,000
> **Income Sources:** Business/Corporate Donations; Box Office; Individual Donations
> **Season:** 52 Weeks
> **Affiliations:** LCT
> **Performance Facilities:** Saint Thomas More Church, Westminster Presbyterian Church

Indianapolis

DANCE

DANCE KALEIDOSCOPE
429 Vermont Street, Indianapolis, IN 46202
(317) 634-8484
   Founded: 1972
   Arts Area: Modern; Contemporary
   Status: Professional; Non-Profit
   Type: Performing; Touring; Resident
   Management: David Hochoy, Artistic Director
   Officers: Gerda Fogle, President
   Paid Staff: 10
   Paid Artists: 8
   Utilizes: Guest Artists; Guest Choreographers
   Budget: $100,000 - $500,000
   Income Sources: Private Foundations/Grants/Endowments; Business/Corporate Donations; Box Office; Individual Donations
   Season: August - June
   Performance Facilities: Indiana Repertory Theatre; Civic Theatre

INDIANAPOLIS BALLET THEATRE
411 East Michigan Street, Indianapolis, IN 46204
(317) 637-8979
   Founded: 1973
   Arts Area: Modern; Ballet; Jazz
   Status: Professional
   Type: Performing; Touring; Resident; Educational; Sponsoring
   Purpose: To present a total theatrical experience, offer a variety of styles, bring the medium of dance to a wider range of audiences and develop future audiences and artists through school performances; features guest musicians, composers, vocalists and choreographers
   Management: Kathryn Stephenson, Executive Director; Dace Dindonis, Artistic Director; Barbara Turner, Development Director; Tim Moore, Public Relations/Marketing Director; Tim Hubbard, Tour Director; Michele Hankins, Costume Mistress; Nancy Baney, Accounting Manager; Doris Hartman, Administrative Assistant; Michael Stephenson, Assistant Artistic Director; Dale Shield, Repetiteur
   Officers: Frederick W. Ruebeck, President; Mrs. Evan L. Noyes, Past President; Mrs. W. Taylor Wilson, Robert G. Risk, Larry K. Pitts and Mary Gallagher, Vice Presidents; Myra Selby, Secretary; Robert Rawlings, Treasurer
   Paid Staff: 12
   Paid Artists: 20   **Non-Paid Artists:** 2
   Utilizes: Guest Conductors; Guest Artists; Guest Choreographers
   Budget: $500,000 - $1,000,000
   Income Sources: Private Foundations/Grants/Endowments; Business/Corporate Donations; Box Office; Government Grants; Individual Donations
   Season: July - May   **Annual Attendance:** 160,000
   Affiliations: APAP; Arts Midwest; ASOL; IPN; ISPAA; Indiana Advocates for the Arts
   Performance Facilities: Clowes Memorial Hall, Butler University; Warren Performing Arts Center

INSTRUMENTAL MUSIC

THE ENSEMBLE MUSIC SOCIETY
PO Box 40188, Indianapolis, IN 46240-0188
(317) 254-8915
   Founded: 1944
   Arts Area: Chamber
   Status: Professional; Non-Profit
   Type: Sponsoring
   Purpose: To present nationally and internationally known chamber music groups to adult and student audiences
   Management: Pamela Steele, Administrative Chief; Julie Marks, Artistic Director; Judith Moore, Production Manager
   Officers: Pamela Steele, President; Julie Marks, Vice President; Sylvia Peacock, Secretary; Richard Parker, Treasurer
   Volunteer Staff: 6
   Paid Artists: 30
   Utilizes: Guest Artists
   Budget: $1,000 - $50,000
   Income Sources: Private Foundations/Grants/Endowments; Business/Corporate Donations; Box Office; Government Grants; Individual Donations

Season: October - April   **Annual Attendance:** 1,700
Affiliations: CMA
Performance Facilities: Lilly Theatre at Children's Muesum

INDIANA JAZZ
PO Box 39013, Indianapolis, IN 46239
(317) 862-4479
Founded: 1984
Arts Area: Jazz
Status: Non-Profit
Type: Performing; Educational
Purpose: To promote Indiana music and musicians both in the state and out-of-state
Management: Kathryn Stephenson, Executive Director; George C. Verdak, Artistic Director; Roberta Donahue, Business Manager; Jason Smith, Development Director; Mary Bashaw, Public Relations/Marketing Director; Claire Braswell, Tour Director
Officers: James A. Clark, President; Josephine Weathers, Secretary; Reginald A. DuValle, Treasurer
Volunteer Staff: 20
Utilizes: Guest Conductors; Guest Writers
Budget: $1,000 - $50,000
Income Sources: Private Foundations/Grants/Endowments; Business/Corporate Donations; Box Office; Government Grants; Individual Donations

INDIANAPOLIS SYMPHONY ORCHESTRA
45 Monument Circle, Indianapolis, IN 46204-2919
(317) 262-1100
FAX: (317) 637-1917
Founded: 1930
Arts Area: Symphony; Orchestra; Chamber; Ensemble
Status: Professional; Non-Profit
Type: Performing; Touring; Resident; Educational
Purpose: To provide the finest musical performances to audiences locally, nationally, and internationally
Management: Robert C. Jones, President; Thomas R. Ramsey, Vice President/General Manager; Herbert L. Jones, Vice President for Development; Susan L. Prenatt, Director of Finance/Administration; Robert Bruce Gold, Director of Marketing; Thomas N. Akins, Director of Public Relations; Paul Hogle, Director of Development
Officers: Rolla E. McAdams, Chairman of the Board; Mrs. Vaughn D. Bryson, Richard C. Notebaert, Vice Chairmans; Robert C. Jones, President; Mrs. Boris E. Meditch, Secretary; Steven A. Wagner, Treasurer; Dr. Arthur G. Hanson, Immediate Past Chairman
Paid Staff: 40   **Volunteer Staff:** 3,400
Paid Artists: 100
Utilizes: Special Technical Talent; Guest Conductors; Guest Artists
Budget: Over 10,000,000
Income Sources: Private Foundations/Grants/Endowments; Business/Corporate Donations; Box Office; Government Grants; Individual Donations
Season: 52 Weeks   **Annual Attendance:** 425,000
Affiliations: ASOL
Performance Facilities: Circle Theatre

PHILHARMONIC ORCHESTRA OF INDIANAPOLIS
PO Box 503, Indianapolis, IN 46206
(317) 283-5242
Founded: 1940
Arts Area: Symphony; Orchestra; Chamber
Status: Non-Professional; Non-Profit
Type: Performing; Resident; Educational
Purpose: Community symphony offering concerts at low prices, performed by volunteer musicians, some of whom are soloists from time to time, and/or paid soloists
Management: Carl Henn Jr., General Manager; Allan Dennis, Music Director
Officers: Edward Staubach, President; Lorelei Faxlow, Vice President; Marty Frank, Treasurer; Bill Bryan, Secretary
Paid Staff: 2   **Volunteer Staff:** 4
Non-Paid Artists: 65
Utilizes: Guest Conductors; Guest Artists
Budget: $1,000 - $50,000
Income Sources: Private Foundations/Grants/Endowments; Business/Corporate Donations; Box Office; Government Grants; Individual Donations
Season: September - June
Annual Attendance: 4,000
Performance Facilities: Caleb Mills Hall

VOCAL MUSIC

INDIANAPOLIS OPERA
250 East 38th Street, Indianapolis, IN 46205
(317) 283-3531
FAX: (317) 923-5611
Arts Area: Grand Opera; Lyric Opera; Light Opera; Operetta
Status: Professional; Non-Profit
Type: Performing; Touring; Resident; Educational; Sponsoring
Management: Durand L. Pope, General Director; James H. Coraher, Acting Artistic Director
Officers: Mrs. Thomas Reilly, President; Mr. Rob Knapp, Executive Vice President
Paid Staff: 9 **Volunteer Staff:** 170
Paid Artists: 250
Utilizes: Special Technical Talent; Guest Conductors; Guest Artists; Guest Directors
Budget: $1,000,000 - $5,000,000
Income Sources: Private Foundations/Grants/Endowments; Business/Corporate Donations; Box Office; Government Grants; Individual Donations
Affiliations: Opera America
Performance Facilities: Clowes Memorial Hall, Butler University

MACALLISTER
PO Box 1941, Indianapolis, IN 46206
(317) 636-7372
FAX: (317) 543-0310
Founded: 1980
Arts Area: Grand Opera; Lyric Opera; Light Opera; Operetta; Competition
Status: Professional; Non-Profit
Type: Performing; Touring; Sponsoring
Purpose: To provide opera opportunities for young artists through opera productions and sponsorship of the MacAllister Awards, the largest sponsored, nonrestricted opera competition on the continent; to provide, through productions, training for young artists, both artistic and technical; Affiliate Artist program will include young conductors and stage directors
Management: Elaine Bookwalter, General Director; P.E. MacAllister, President, Board of Directors
Officers: P.E. MacAllister, President; Melvin Carroway, Vice President; Dawn Smith, Treasurer; Greg Jordan, Secretary
Paid Staff: 1 **Volunteer Staff:** 3
Utilizes: Special Technical Talent; Guest Conductors; Guest Artists; Guest Directors
Budget: $100,000 - $500,000
Income Sources: Private Foundations/Grants/Endowments; Business/Corporate Donations; Box Office; Government Grants; Individual Donations
Season: August **Annual Attendance:** 6,000
Affiliations: COS; Butler University Romantic Festival
Performance Facilities: Frederic M. Ayers Auditorium

THEATRE

BEEF AND BOARDS DINNER THEATRE
9301 North Michigan Road, Indianapolis, IN 46268
(317) 872-9664
Founded: 1971
Arts Area: Professional; Dinner
Status: Professional
Type: Performing
Management: Robert Zehr, Managing Director; Douglas Stark, Artistic Director
Officers: Robert Zehr, President; Douglas Stark, Secretary/Treasurer
Paid Staff: 80
Paid Artists: 15
Income Sources: Box Office
Season: 52 Weeks **Annual Attendance:** 160,000
Affiliations: NDTA; ADTI
Performance Facilities: Beef and Boards Dinner Theatre

INDIANA REPERTORY THEATRE
140 West Washington, Indianapolis, IN 46204
(317) 635-5277
FAX: (317) 236-0767
Founded: 1971
Arts Area: Professional
Status: Professional; Non-Profit
Type: Performing; Resident; Educational

Purpose: Through innovative productions of classic and contemporary plays, the Indiana Repertory Theatre creates high quality, professional theatre of consistent artistic and cultural significance; the theatre offers student programs that enables students the opportunity to experience live theatre as a performing art form
Management: Victoria Nolan, Managing Director; Libby Appel, Artistic Director; Janet Allen, Associate Artistic Director
Officers: Robert A. Anker, Chairman of the Board; David H. Kleiman, President; Michael M. Sample, Vice President; Jack R. Shaw, Vice President; Lorene Burkhart, Secretary; R. Brentson Smith, Treasurer
Paid Staff: 65   **Volunteer Staff:** 500
Paid Artists: 90
Utilizes: Special Technical Talent; Guest Artists; Guest Directors
Budget: $1,000,000 - $5,000,000
Income Sources: Private Foundations/Grants/Endowments; Business/Corporate Donations; Box Office; Government Grants; Individual Donations
Season: October - May   **Annual Attendance:** 110,000
Affiliations: LORT
Performance Facilities: Indiana Theatre

PHOENIX THEATRE
749 North Park Avenue, Indianapolis, IN 46202
(317) 635-7529
FAX: (317) 635-7529
Founded: 1983
Arts Area: Community; Theatrical Group
Status: Semi-Professional; Non-Profit
Type: Performing
Purpose: To nurture the professional growth and development of local actors, directors, playwrights and other theatre artists
Management: Bryan D. Fonseca, Artistic Director; Karen E. Farley, Business Manager
Officers: Betty LaClare, Board Chairman
Paid Staff: 4   **Volunteer Staff:** 3
Utilizes: Special Technical Talent; Guest Artists; Guest Directors
Budget: $100,000 - $500,000
Income Sources: Private Foundations/Grants/Endowments; Business/Corporate Donations; Box Office; Government Grants; Individual Donations
Season: 52 Weeks   **Annual Attendance:** 10,000
Affiliations: AATA; ITA

PERFORMING SERIES

CLOWES MEMORIAL HALL
Butler University, 4600 Sunset Avenue, Indianapolis, IN 46208
(317) 283-9696
Founded: 1963
Arts Area: Dance; Vocal Music; Instrumental Music; Theater; Festivals
Status: Non-Profit
Type: Touring; Educational; Sponsoring
Purpose: Booking and presenting cultural and entertainment attractions in the Indianapolis area
Management: Michael Sells, General Manager/Dean of Jordan College of Fine Arts, Butler University
Officers: Board of Trustees, Butler University; Kathryn Betley, Chair of Clowes Memorial Hall Committee
Paid Staff: 9   **Volunteer Staff:** 300
Utilizes: Guest Artists
Budget: $100,000 - $500,000
Income Sources: Private Foundations/Grants/Endowments; Business/Corporate Donations; Box Office; Individual Donations
Season: September - June
Affiliations: Butler University
Performance Facilities: Clowes Memorial Hall, Butler University

FACILITY

CLOWES MEMORIAL HALL OF BUTLER UNIVERSITY
4600 Sunset Avenue, Indianapolis, IN 46208
(317) 283-9696
FAX: (317) 283-9820
Founded: 1963
Type of Facility: Theatre House; Opera House; Multi-Purpose
Type of Stage: Proscenium
Stage Dimensions: 52'Wx60'Dx35'H; 80' grid   **Orchestra Pit**
Seating Capacity: 2,182
Year Built: 1963   **Architect:** John Johanson and Evans Woollen   **Cost:** $3,500,000

Acoustical Consultant: Bolt Beranek and Newman, Inc.
Contact for Rental: Linda Neal, Business Manager;   (317) 283-9696
Manager: Tom McTamney, Manager;   (317) 283-9696
Resident Groups: Jordan College of Fine Arts; Indianapolis Opera Company; Indianapolis Ballet Theatre; Indianapolis Chamber Orchestra; INB Broadway Series; Kiwanis Travelogues; Town Hall Lectures
Presents a subscription series of 13-15 events annually

WARREN PERFORMING ARTS CENTER
9301 East 18th Street, Indianapolis, IN 46229
(317) 898-8061
   Type of Facility: Performance Center
   Year Built: 1983   **Architect:** Daverman Associates   **Cost:** $5,500,000
   Acoustical Consultant: Bureky & Brennen
   Contact for Rental: Penny Mitchell;   (317) 898-8061
   Contains Esch Auditorium and Studio Theater. See separate listings

WARREN PERFORMING ARTS CENTER - ESCH AUDITORIUM
9301 East 18th Street, Indianapolis, IN 46229
(317) 898-8061
   Type of Facility: Concert Hall; Auditorium
   Type of Stage: Proscenium
   Stage Dimensions: 48'Wx59'10"D; 48'Wx25'H proscenium opening   **Orchestra Pit**
   Seating Capacity: 1,033
   Year Built: 1983
   Contact for Rental: Penny Mitchell
   Resident Groups: Warren Central High School Music and Theater Departments

WARREN PERFORMING ARTS CENTER - STUDIO THEATER
9301 East 18th Street, Indianapolis, IN 46229
(317) 898-8061
   Type of Facility: Room; Rehearsal Studio
   Type of Stage: Flexible; Platform
   Seating Capacity: 120
   Year Built: 1983
   Contact for Rental: Penny Mitchell
   Resident Groups: Warren High School Theater Department

Jasper

FACILITY

JASPER CIVIC AUDITORIUM
951 College Avenue, Jasper, IN 47546
(812) 482-3070
   Founded: 1977
   Type of Facility: Concert Hall; Auditorium; Studio Performance; Civic Center; Multi-Purpose; Room; Dance Studio; Art Gallery; Meeting Rooms
   Type of Stage: Proscenium
   Stage Dimensions: 40'W proscenium; 50' wood; 40'D   **Orchestra Pit**
   Seating Capacity: 700
   Year Built: 1977   **Architect:** Wayne Seufert   **Cost:** $1,000,000
   Year Remodeled: 1982   **Architect:** Wayne Seufert   **Cost:** $100,000
   Acoustical Consultant: Bolt, Baranek and Newman
   Contact for Rental: Doreen Lechner;   (812) 482-3070
   Resident Groups: Jasper Community Players; Dubois County Art Guild; Strings in Jasper

Kokomo

INSTRUMENTAL MUSIC

KOKOMO SYMPHONY
PO Box 6115, Kokomo, IN 46902
(317) 455-1659
   Founded: 1971
   Arts Area: Symphony; Orchestra; Chamber
   Status: Non-Profit
   Type: Performing; Touring; Resident; Educational; Sponsoring

Purpose: To provide the highest quality of music performed by our local orchestra under the direction of a capable conductor; to maintain an orchestra, chorus and youth orchestra
Management: Barbara M. Cassis, Executive Director
Paid Staff: 2   **Volunteer Staff:** 300
Paid Artists: 20   **Non-Paid Artists:** 40
Utilizes: Guest Artists
Budget: $100,000 - $500,000
Income Sources: Private Foundations/Grants/Endowments; Business/Corporate Donations; Box Office; Government Grants; Individual Donations
Season: September - May   **Annual Attendance:** 650
Affiliations: ASOL; IOC; Indiana Advocates for the Arts
Performance Facilities: Havens Auditorium

Lafayette

INSTRUMENTAL MUSIC

LAFAYETTE SYMPHONY
111 North Sixth, PO Box 52, Lafayette, IN 47902
(317) 742-6463
Founded: 1951
Arts Area: Symphony; Orchestra
Status: Semi-Professional; Non-Profit
Type: Performing; Educational
Purpose: To provide symphonic literature for the enjoyment and education of the Greater Lafayette Area
Management: Michael Cunningham, General Manager
Officers: Bill Bonsignore, President
Paid Staff: 4
Paid Artists: 65
Utilizes: Guest Conductors; Guest Artists
Budget: $100,000 - $500,000
Income Sources: Private Foundations/Grants/Endowments; Business/Corporate Donations; Box Office; Government Grants; Individual Donations
Season: September - May   **Annual Attendance:** 8,000
Affiliations: ASOL; IOC
Performance Facilities: Long Center for the Performing Arts

FACILITY

LONG CENTER FOR THE PERFORMING ARTS
111 North Sixth Street, Lafayette, IN 47905
(317) 742-5664
Founded: 1978
Type of Facility: Theatre Complex; Performance Center; Theatre House; Loft
Facility Originally: Vaudeville; Movie House
Type of Stage: Proscenium
Stage Dimensions: 38'Wx37'D
Seating Capacity: 1,200
Year Built: 1921   **Architect:** Scholer Architects
Year Remodeled: 1978   **Architect:** Scholer Architects   **Cost:** $900,000
Contact for Rental: C.H. Copeland;   (317) 742-5664
Resident Groups: Lafayette Symphony Orchestra

Lawrenceburg

THEATRE

RIVERTOWN PLAYERS
PO Box 454, Lawrenceburg, IN 47025
(812) 537-0751
FAX: (812) 537-5618
Founded: 1982
Arts Area: Community; Theatrical Group
Status: Non-Professional; Non-Profit
Type: Performing
Purpose: To promote, encourage, and develop the enjoyment, appreciation, and participation in theatre through production and performance of plays and musicals

Management: Janice Hizer, Production Manager
Budget: $1,000 - $50,000
Income Sources: Box Office; Individual Donations
Season: 52 Weeks   **Annual Attendance:** 3,000
Affiliations: Indiana Theatre Association
Performance Facilities: Lawrenceburg High School Auditorium

Marion

INSTRUMENTAL MUSIC

MARION PHILHARMONIC ORCHESTRA
215 South Adams, PO Box 272, Marion, IN 46952
(317) 662-0012
FAX: (317) 668-5443
Founded: 1969
Arts Area: Orchestra
Status: Non-Profit
Type: Performing
Purpose: To further the cultural and educational development of the Grant County area
Management: Sue Wanninger, Business Manager; Neal Gittleman, Music Director/Conductor
Officers: Jerry Albrecht, President; Jim Fordham, Vice President; Susan Munn, Secretary; Bob Hogan, Treasurer
Paid Staff: 2
Paid Artists: 50
Utilizes: Guest Conductors; Guest Artists
Budget: $100,000 - $500,000
Income Sources: Private Foundations/Grants/Endowments; Business/Corporate Donations; Box Office; Government Grants; Individual Donations
Season: September - May   **Annual Attendance:** 5,000
Performance Facilities: Marion High School Auditorium

Muncie

INSTRUMENTAL MUSIC

MUNCIE SYMPHONY ORCHESTRA
310 North McKinley Avenue, Muncie, IN 47306
(317) 285-5531
Founded: 1948
Arts Area: Symphony
Status: Semi-Professional; Non-Profit
Type: Performing; Educational
Purpose: To encourage the performance, development, and appreciation of fine music in east central Indiana by means of combined university and community support of the Muncie Symphony Orchestra
Management: Joan McKee, Business Manager
Officers: Thomas Sargent, President; Julie Skinner, Vice President; Robert Gibiser, Treasurer; Nanette Rushton, Secretary
Paid Staff: 4   **Volunteer Staff:** 1
Paid Artists: 85
Utilizes: Guest Conductors; Guest Artists
Budget: $100,000 - $500,000
Income Sources: Private Foundations/Grants/Endowments; Business/Corporate Donations; Box Office; Government Grants; Individual Donations
Season: September - June   **Annual Attendance:** 18,000
Affiliations: ASOL; ASCAP; BMI; IOC; ACA; Indiana Advocates for the Arts
Performance Facilities: Emens Auditorium

Munster

INSTRUMENTAL MUSIC

NORTHWEST INDIANA SYMPHONY SOCIETY
1040 Ridge Road, Munster, IN 46321
(219) 836-0525
Founded: 1941
Arts Area: Symphony; Orchestra; Chamber; Ensemble
Status: Professional; Non-Profit

Type: Performing; Resident; Educational
Purpose: Presentation of subscription, special, and children's concerts and maintenance of Youth Orchestra and Chorus
Management: Richard Scharf, General Manager; Robert Vodnoy, Music Director; Kevin McMahon, Youth Orchestra Conductor; Joe Burt, Chorus Director
Officers: Michael Schrage, President; Richard Combs, Vice Presidents; Barbara Haas, Secretary; Joseph F. Glotzbach, Treasurer
Paid Staff: 4
Paid Artists: 75
Utilizes: Special Technical Talent; Guest Conductors; Guest Artists
Budget: $500,000 - $1,000,000
Income Sources: Private Foundations/Grants/Endowments; Business/Corporate Donations; Box Office; Government Grants; Individual Donations
Season: October - May   **Annual Attendance:** 35,000
Affiliations: ASOL; IOC; Chicago Music Alliance
Performance Facilities: Star Plaza Theatre, Merrillville

North Manchester

FACILITY

MANCHESTER COLLEGE - CORDIER AUDITORIUM
604 College Avenue, North Manchester, IN 46962
(219) 982-5247
FAX: (219) 982-6868
  Founded: 1978
  Type of Facility: Concert Hall; Auditorium; Performance Center; Multi-Purpose
  Type of Stage: Proscenium
  Stage Dimensions: 60'Wx39'Dx21'H   **Orchestra Pit**
  Seating Capacity: 1,300
  Year Built: 1978   **Architect:** The Maguire and Shook Corporation
  Contact for Rental: Karl F. Merritt;   (219) 982-5247

Peru

THEATRE

OLE OLSEN MEMORIAL THEATRE
8 Wallace Row, PO Box 580, Peru, IN 46970
(317) 473-9937
  Founded: 1963
  Arts Area: Community; Theatrical Group
  Status: Non-Professional; Non-Profit
  Type: Performing
  Purpose: Purpose of this organization shall be to promote and encourage interest in the theatrical arts on a non-profit basis
  Officers: Bonnie Chilcatt, President; Lynn Bockover, Executive Vice President; William Gornto, First Vice President; Kurt Krauskopf, Second Vice President; Ann Hubbard, Third Vice President; TyAnn Snyder, Secretary; Bob Radel, Treasurer
  Budget: $1,000 - $50,000
  Income Sources: Box Office; Individual Donations
  Season: October - June   **Annual Attendance:** 1,500
  Affiliations: Indiana Community Theatre League; Division of Indiana Theaters
  Performance Facilities: High School Auditorium

Richmond

INSTRUMENTAL MUSIC

CHANTICLEER STRING QUARTET
944 Woods Road, Richmond, IN 47374
(317) 966-6214
  Founded: 1977

Arts Area: Chamber
Status: Professional; Non-Profit
Type: Performing; Touring; Educational
Purpose: To share in creative ways the beauty of chamber music with people in all walks of life and of all ages
Management: Caroline Klemperer Green, Founder/Violinist/Agent
Paid Staff: 1
Paid Artists: 6
Utilizes: Guest Artists
Budget: $1,000 - $50,000
Income Sources: Private Foundations/Grants/Endowments; Business/Corporate Donations; Government Grants; Individual Donations
Annual Attendance: 15,000

RICHMOND SYMPHONY ORCHESTRA
300 Hub Etchison Parkway, PO Box 982, Richmond, IN 47375
(317) 966-5181
FAX: (317) 962-9723
Founded: 1908
Arts Area: Symphony; Orchestra; Chamber; Ensemble
Status: Professional; Non-Profit
Type: Performing; Resident; Educational
Purpose: To present a full repertoire of symphonic literature; to present educational programs; to present performance opportunities to area musicians
Management: William Perrin, Executive Director; Daniel Graves, Choral Conductor; Evelyn Woolard, Personnel Manager; Cynthia Jackson, Office Manager
Officers: Lynn Mayer, President; Nancy Mulick, Maxine Hampton, Vice Presidents; Daniel Braewley, Treasurer; Karen Niersbach, Secretary
Paid Staff: 3   **Volunteer Staff:** 6
Utilizes: Special Technical Talent; Guest Artists
Budget: $100,000 - $500,000
Income Sources: Private Foundations/Grants/Endowments; Business/Corporate Donations; Box Office; Government Grants; Individual Donations
Season: October - May
Annual Attendance: 5,000
Affiliations: ASOL; IOC
Performance Facilities: Civic Auditorium

VOCAL MUSIC

WHITEWATER OPERA COMPANY
805 Promenade, PO Box 633, Richmond, IN 47375
(317) 962-7106
Founded: 1972
Arts Area: Grand Opera; Lyric Opera; Light Opera; Operetta
Status: Professional; Non-Profit
Type: Performing; Touring; Educational
Purpose: To present full-length and one-act operas, locally and on tour, and to present educational operatic programs for schools and organizations
Management: Charles Combopiano, General Manager/Artistic Director; Elsie Klute, Administrative Assistant; Claire Combodiano, Interim Development/Marketing Director; Beverly Senese, Bookkeeper
Officers: Gail Toedebusch, President; James Miller, Vice President; Elsie Klute, Secretary; Beverly Senese, Treasurer
Paid Staff: 3   **Volunteer Staff:** 54
Paid Artists: 175
Utilizes: Special Technical Talent; Guest Conductors; Guest Artists; Guest Directors
Budget: $100,000 - $500,000
Income Sources: Private Foundations/Grants/Endowments; Business/Corporate Donations; Box Office; Government Grants; Individual Donations; Rentals
Season: October - June
Annual Attendance: 4,500
Affiliations: OA; NOA; IPN; Sorg Opera Company
Performance Facilities: Don Kehoe Performing Arts Center; Sorg Opera House

FACILITY

RICHMOND CIVIC THEATRE
1003 East Main Street, Richmond, IN 47374
(317) 962-1816
Type of Facility: Auditorium; Theatre House

Facility Originally: Vaudeville
Type of Stage: Proscenium
Stage Dimensions: 39'6"Wx27'6"D
Orchestra Pit
Seating Capacity: 610
Year Built: 1909   **Architect:** Fred Elliot   **Cost:** $40,000
Year Remodeled: 1987   **Architect:** Phil Uhl   **Cost:** $150,000
Resident Groups: Richmond Civic Theatre; Richmond Junior Players

South Bend

INSTRUMENTAL MUSIC

SOUTH BEND SYMPHONY
120 West LaSalle, Suite 602, South Bend, IN 46601
(219) 232-6343
FAX: (219) 232-6343
Founded: 1933
Arts Area: Symphony; Chamber; Ensemble; Pops
Status: Non-Profit
Type: Performing; Educational
Management: Lee Ellen Hveem, General Manager
Officers: Mrs. Judd Leighton, Chairman of the Board; Donald A. Dake, Vice Chairman of the Board; Thomas P. Bergin, President
Paid Staff: 4   **Volunteer Staff:** 1
Paid Artists: 100   **Non-Paid Artists:** 120
Utilizes: Guest Conductors; Guest Artists
Budget: $500,000 - $1,000,000
Income Sources: Private Foundations/Grants/Endowments; Business/Corporate Donations; Box Office; Government Grants; Individual Donations
Season: September - May
Annual Attendance: 12,500
Affiliations: ASOL
Performance Facilities: Morris Civic Auditorium

PERFORMING SERIES

FIREFLY FESTIVAL FOR THE PERFORMING ARTS
202 South Michigan, Suite 845, South Bend, IN 46601-2012
(219) 288-3472
Founded: 1981
Arts Area: Dance; Vocal Music; Instrumental Music; Theater; Festivals
Status: Professional; Semi-Professional; Non-Professional; Non-Profit
Type: Performing; Educational
Purpose: To present outstanding music, dance and theatre in an outdoor setting; to promote the performing arts and enrich the cultural scene in Michigan
Management: Carol Weiss Rosenberg, Executive Director; Carol B. Privette, Administrative Assistant; David Homann, Office Assistant; Bill Soderberg, Production Manager; Loretta Baker, House Manger
Officers: Helen V. Hepler, President; Michael B. Watkins, First Vice President; Pam Jarrett, Second Vice President; Candace Butler, Secretary; John M. Schmitt, Treasurer
Paid Staff: 5   **Volunteer Staff:** 392
Paid Artists: 124   **Non-Paid Artists:** 87
Utilizes: Special Technical Talent; Guest Conductors; Guest Artists; Guest Directors
Budget: $100,000 - $500,000
Income Sources: Private Foundations/Grants/Endowments; Business/Corporate Donations; Box Office; Individual Donations
Season: June - August
Annual Attendance: 23,000
Affiliations: APAP; Indiana Arts Commission; Indiana Presenters Network
Performance Facilities: Robert J. Fischgrund Center for the Performing Arts

FACILITY

CENTURY CENTER
120 South St. Joseph Street, South Bend, IN 46601
(219) 235-9711
FAX: (219) 235-9185
Type of Facility: Civic Center

Year Built: 1977   **Architect:** Philip Johnson and John Burgee
Contact for Rental: Sandy Lee, Director of Sales

CENTURY CENTER - BENDIX THEATRE
120 South St. Joseph Street, South Bend, IN 46601
(219) 235-9711
  Type of Facility: Theatre House
  Type of Stage: Thrust
  Stage Dimensions: 32'Wx39'10"D
  Seating Capacity: 694
  Year Built: 1977
  Contact for Rental: Sandra Lee, Director of Sales;   (219) 235-9711

CENTURY CENTER - CONVENTION HALL
120 South St. Joseph Street, South Bend, IN 46601
(219) 235-9711
  Type of Facility: Multi-Purpose; Room; Exhibition Hall
  Type of Stage: Flexible; Platform
  Seating Capacity: 3,000
  Year Built: 1977   **Architect:** Philip Johnson; John Burgee
  Contact for Rental: Sandra Lee, Director of Sales;   (219) 235-9711

CENTURY CENTER - RECITAL HALL
120 South St. Joseph Street, South Bend, IN 46601
(219) 235-9711
  Type of Facility: Concert Hall; Recital Hall
  Type of Stage: Thrust
  Stage Dimensions: 25'5"Wx16'1"D
  Seating Capacity: 166
  Year Built: 1977
  Contact for Rental: Sandra Lee, Director of Sales;   (219) 235-9711

MORRIS CIVIC AUDITORIUM
211 North Michigan, South Bend, IN 46601
(219) 284-9198
FAX: (219) 284-9892
  Founded: 1922
  Type of Facility: Theatre House
  Facility Originally: Vaudeville
  Type of Stage: Proscenium
  Stage Dimensions: 54'Wx27'Dx25'H
  Seating Capacity: 2,468
  Year Built: 1922   **Architect:** Jacob Aroner   **Cost:** $1,150,000
  Acoustical Consultant: Kirkegard
  Contact for Rental: Dale Balsbaugh;   (219) 284-9198
  Resident Groups: South Bend Symphony; Broadway Theatre League

Terre Haute

INSTRUMENTAL MUSIC

TERRE HAUTE SYMPHONY ORCHESTRA
25 North Sixth Street, Terre Haute, IN 47807
(812) 234-6060
  Founded: 1926
  Arts Area: Symphony; Orchestra; Ensemble
  Status: Semi-Professional
  Type: Performing; Educational; Run-Outs
  Purpose: To maintain an orchestra dedicated to excellent performances of symphonic literature for the enjoyment and cultural enrichment of audiences from the Wabash Valley area
  Management: Susan E. Bunce, General Manager; Shelley Criss, Personnel Manager and Administrative Assistant; Dan Powers, Librarian

Officers: Barbara Passmore, President; Martin Morrow, Vice President for Development; Joyce Keenan, Vice President for Marketing; James Colligan, Vice President for Long Range Planning; Susan Brattain, Secretary; Don Schillson, Treasurer; Marian Pettus, Member at Large
Paid Staff: 4   **Volunteer Staff:** 3
Paid Artists: 85
Utilizes: Guest Conductors; Guest Artists
Budget: $100,000 - $500,000
Income Sources: Private Foundations/Grants/Endowments; Business/Corporate Donations; Box Office; Government Grants; Individual Donations; Indiana State University
Season: September - May
Annual Attendance: 15,000
Affiliations: Indiana State University
Performance Facilities: Tilson Auditorium, Indiana State University

FACILITY

COMMUNITY THEATRE OF TERRE HAUTE
1431 South 25th Street, Terre Haute, IN 47803
(812) 232-7172
Type of Facility: Theatre Complex; Auditorium; Performance Center; Theatre House; Multi-Purpose
Type of Stage: Thrust; Proscenium; Platform
Stage Dimensions: 61'Wx35'D; 25'Wx15'H proscenium opening
Seating Capacity: 375
Year Built: 1940
Year Remodeled: 1954
Resident Groups: Terre Haute International Film Series; Community Theatre

Vincennes

THEATRE

VINCENNES UNIVERSITY SUMMER THEATRE
1002 North First, Vincennes, IN 47591
(812) 885-4256
FAX: (812) 885-5868
Founded: 1968
Arts Area: Summer Stock; Musical
Status: Semi-Professional; Non-Profit
Type: Performing; Resident; Educational
Purpose: To provide quality theatrical entertainment for Vincennes and the surrounding area during the summer months
Management: James J. Spurrier, PhD, Managing/Artistic Director
Officers: Phillip M. Summers, PhD, President, Vincennes University
Utilizes: Special Technical Talent; Guest Artists
Budget: $50,000 - $100,000
Income Sources: Private Foundations/Grants/Endowments; Business/Corporate Donations; Box Office; Government Grants; Individual Donations
Season: June - August
Annual Attendance: 5,400
Performance Facilities: Shircliff Theatre

West Lafayette

THEATRE

PURDUE PROFESSIONAL SUMMER THEATRE
1376 Stewart Center, Room 85, West Lafayette, IN 47907
(317) 494-3082
FAX: (317) 494-3660
Founded: 1958

Status: Professional; Non-Profit
Type: Performing
Purpose: Interested in newer American plays both comedic and dramatic
Management: Jim O'Connor, Division of Theater
Paid Staff: 20   **Volunteer Staff:** 10
Paid Artists: 20
Utilizes: Special Technical Talent; Guest Directors
Budget: $1,000 - $50,000
Income Sources: Box Office
Season: June - August   **Annual Attendance:** 5,000
Affiliations: Purdue University
Performance Facilities: Experimental Theater

FACILITY

ELLIOTT HALL OF MUSIC
Purdue University, West Lafayette, IN 47906
(317) 494-3920
FAX: (317) 494-6621
Founded: 1940
Type of Facility: Concert Hall; Auditorium; Theatre House
Type of Stage: Proscenium
Stage Dimensions: 100'Wx35'D   **Orchestra Pit**
Seating Capacity: 6,027
Year Built: 1940   **Architect:** Walter Scholer and Associates   **Cost:** $1,200,000
Year Remodeled: 1991   **Cost:** $1,200,000
Contact for Rental: Stephen D. Hall;   (317) 494-3937

IOWA

Ames

DANCE

CO'MOTION DANCE THEATER
129 East Seventh Street, Ames, IA 50010
(515) 232-7374
FAX: (515) 232-7374
Founded: 1978
Arts Area: Modern
Status: Professional; Non-Profit
Type: Performing; Touring; Resident; Educational
Purpose: Co'Motion Dance exists to bring high-caliber professional dance to Midwestern sponsors at affordable prices and to offer the highest quality in dance education to its students.
Management: Valerie Williams, Director; J. Thomas Kidd, General Manager
Officers: Dana Schumacher, President; Deb Felton, Vice President; J. Thomas Kidd, Secretary/Treasurer
Paid Staff: 1
Paid Artists: 4
Utilizes: Special Technical Talent; Guest Artists; Guest Choreographers
Budget: $50,000 - $100,000
Income Sources: Private Foundations/Grants/Endowments; Box Office; Government Grants; Individual Donations; Presenter Fees
Season: September - May

INSTRUMENTAL MUSIC

AMES TOWN AND GOWN CHAMBER MUSIC ASSOCIATION
c/o Art Staniforth, 1634 Crestwood Circle, Ames, IA 50010
Founded: 1950
Arts Area: Chamber; Ensemble; Instrumental Group
Status: Non-Profit
Type: Sponsoring
Purpose: To present four to six chamber music concerts per year
Officers: Art Staniforth, President; Paula Helmath, Vice President; Herbert T. David, Secretary; George Karas, Treasurer
Volunteer Staff: 17
Utilizes: Guest Artists
Budget: $1,000 - $50,000
Income Sources: Private Foundations/Grants/Endowments; Business/Corporate Donations; Box Office; Government Grants; Individual Donations; Fundraising
Season: September - May   **Annual Attendance:** 1,400
Affiliations: Iowa State University Music Department
Performance Facilities: Iowa State University Music Hall Recital Hall; Ames City Hall Auditorium

PERFORMING SERIES

AMES INTERNATIONAL ORCHESTRA FESTIVAL ASSOCIATION
PO Box 1243, Ames, IA 50010
(515) 294-3213
Founded: 1969
Arts Area: Dance; Vocal Music; Instrumental Music; Theater; Festivals
Status: Non-Professional; Non-Profit
Type: Educational; Sponsoring
Purpose: To promote, assist and encourage the presentation of symphony orchestras, national and international, and associated events in a festival setting
Management: Robert E. Maxham, Executive Director
Officers: E. Douglas Brown, President; Thomas Griswold, President-Elect; Norman Riis, First Vice President; George Hinshaw, Second Vice President; Carol Torrents, Secretary; Ken Anderson, Treasurer
Paid Staff: 1
Utilizes: Guest Conductors; Guest Artists; Guest Directors
Budget: $100,000 - $500,000
Income Sources: Private Foundations/Grants/Endowments; Business/Corporate Donations; Box Office; Individual Donations
Season: September - May

Affiliations: ASOL
Performance Facilities: C.Y. Stephens Auditorium, Iowa State University

FACILITY

IOWA STATE UNIVERSITY-IOWA STATE CENTER
Suite 4, Scheman Building, Ames, IA 50011-1112
(515) 294-3347
FAX: (515) 294-3349
    Type of Facility: Concert Hall; Auditorium; Theatre House; Arena; Multi-Purpose
    Type of Stage: Proscenium; 3/4 Arena; Arena **Orchestra Pit**
    Seating Capacity: Variable
    Year Built: 1975
    Contact for Rental: Beth A. Lindquist; (515) 294-3347
    Manager: Joseph Romano
    Resident Groups: Iowa State University Theatre
    Iowa State Center contains Benton Auditorium, C.Y. Stephens Auditorium, Hilton Coliseum and J.W. Fisher Auditorium.
    See separate listings for additional information.

IOWA STATE UNIVERSITY-IOWA STATE CENTER - BENTON AUDITORIUM
Suite 4, Scheman Building, Ames, IA 50011
(515) 294-3347
    Type of Facility: Auditorium
    Type of Stage: Platform
    Stage Dimensions: 38'x20'
    Seating Capacity: 464
    Year Built: 1975 **Architect:** Crites & McConnell; Brooks Borg & Skiles
    Manager: Joe Romano, Director

IOWA STATE UNIVERSITY-IOWA STATE CENTER - C.Y. STEPHENS AUDITORIUM
Suite 4, Scheman Building, Ames, IA 50011
(515) 294-3347
    Type of Facility: Auditorium
    Type of Stage: Proscenium
    Stage Dimensions: 80'Wx56'D; 80'Wx30'H proscenium opening **Orchestra Pit**
    Seating Capacity: 2,749
    Year Built: 1972
    Architect: Crites & McConnell; Brooks Borg & Skiles
    Cost: $4,925,000
    Contact for Rental: David M. Olson; (515) 294-3347
    Manager: Joe Romano

IOWA STATE UNIVERSITY-IOWA STATE CENTER - HILTON COLISEUM
Suite 4, Scheman Building, Ames, IA 50011
(515) 294-3347
    Type of Facility: Arena; Multi-Purpose
    Type of Stage: Flexible; Platform
    Stage Dimensions: 40'x60'
    Seating Capacity: 14,000
    Year Built: 1971
    Architect: Crites & McConnell; Brooks Borg & Skiles
    Cost: $8,165,000
    Acoustical Consultant: Paul S. Veneklasen
    Contact for Rental: David M. Olson; (515) 294-3347
    Manager: Joe Romano

IOWA STATE UNIVERSITY -IOWA STATE CENTER - J.W. FISHER AUDITORIUM
Suite 4, Scheman Building, Ames, IA 50011
(515) 294-3347
    Type of Facility: Theatre House
    Type of Stage: Proscenium
    Stage Dimensions: 36'x18'x36' **Orchestra Pit**
    Seating Capacity: 454
    Year Built: 1974 **Architect:** Crites & McConnell; Brooks Borg & Skiles **Cost:** $900,000
    Contact for Rental: David M. Olson; (515) 294-3347

Manager: Joe Romano
Resident Groups: Iowa State Theatre

Bettendorf

FACILITY

LINCOLN CENTER FOR THE CULTURAL ARTS
951 27th Street, Bettendorf, IA 52722
(319) 355-8626
> **Type of Facility:** Performance Center; Multi-Purpose; Cultural Arts
> **Facility Originally:** School
> **Type of Stage:** Thrust; Proscenium
> **Stage Dimensions:** 40'x35'
> **Seating Capacity:** 350
> **Year Built:** 1920
> **Year Remodeled:** 1954
> **Contact for Rental:** Nancy Sann;   (319) 355-8626

Cedar Falls

FACILITY

UNIVERSITY OF NORTHERN IOWA - OLD AUDITORIUM
Cedar Falls, IA 50614-0358
(319) 273-2725
FAX: (319) 273-2731
> **Mailing Address:** Artists Series Committee, University of Northern Iowa, CAC 269, Cedar Falls, IA 50614-0358
> **Type of Facility:** Auditorium
> **Type of Stage:** Proscenium
> **Stage Dimensions:** 34'x32'
> **Seating Capacity:** 1,025
> **Year Built:** 1900
> **Year Remodeled:** 1987
> **Contact for Rental:** Maucker Union Office;   (319) 273-2257

UNIVERSITY OF NORTHERN IOWA - RUSSELL HALL
Cedar Falls, IA 50614
(319) 273-2024
> **Type of Facility:** Concert Hall
> **Type of Stage:** Proscenium   **Orchestra Pit**
> **Seating Capacity:** 600
> **Year Built:** 1960   **Architect:** Thorson
> **Manager:** Robert Byrnes, Administrative Assistant
> **Resident Groups:** UNI/Music Groups

UNIVERSITY OF NORTHERN IOWA - STRAYER-WOOD THEATRE
Cedar Falls, IA 50614-0371
(319) 273-6386
> **Type of Facility:** Theatre Complex
> **Year Built:** 1978   **Architect:** Thorson-Brom   **Cost:** $2,000,000
> **Acoustical Consultant:** Bolt, Beranek & Newman
> **Contact for Rental:** Greta Berghammer;   (319) 273-6386
> **Resident Groups:** Theatre UNI
> *Strayer-Wood Theatre contains Black Box and Main Stage. See separate listings for additional information.*

UNIVERSITY OF NORTHERN IOWA - STRAYER-WOOD THEATRE-BLACK BOX
Cedar Falls, IA 50614-0371
(319) 273-6386
FAX: (319) 273-2731
> **Type of Facility:** Theatre Complex; Studio Performance; Black Box
> **Type of Stage:** Flexible   **Orchestra Pit**
> **Seating Capacity:** 500
> **Year Built:** 1978
> **Contact for Rental:** Gretta Berghammer;   (319) 273-6386
> **Manager:** Paul Sannerud;   (319) 273-2500

UNIVERSITY OF NORTHERN IOWA - STRAYER-WOOD THEATRE-MAIN STAGE
Cedar Falls, IA 50614-0371
(319) 273-6386
Type of Facility: Theatre House
Type of Stage: Proscenium
Stage Dimensions: 22'x84'x39' **Orchestra Pit**
Seating Capacity: 508
Year Built: 1978
Contact for Rental: Greta Berghammer;   (319) 273-6386

Cedar Rapids

INSTRUMENTAL MUSIC

CEDAR RAPIDS SYMPHONY ORCHESTRA
205 Second Avenue SE, Cedar Rapids, IA 52401
(319) 366-8203
FAX: (319) 366-5206
Founded: 1922
Arts Area: Symphony; Orchestra; Chamber; Ensemble
Status: Professional; Non-Profit
Type: Performing; Educational
Management: Marc D. Levy, Executive Director; Christian Tiemeyer, Music Director/Conductor
Officers: John Smith, President; Thomas Pitner, Vice President/President Elect; Lynn Olsen, Secretary; David McIrvin, Treasurer
Paid Staff: 7
Paid Artists: 85
Utilizes: Guest Artists
Budget: $1,000,000 - $5,000,000
Income Sources: Private Foundations/Grants/Endowments; Business/Corporate Donations; Box Office; Government Grants; Individual Donations
Season: September - May
Affiliations: ASOL
Performance Facilities: Paramount Theatre

PERFORMING SERIES

THE DRAWING LEGION
1103 Third Street SE, Cedar Rapids, IA 52401
(319) 364-1580
FAX: (319) 365-7502
Founded: 1981
Arts Area: Dance; Instrumental Music; Theater
Status: Semi-Professional; Non-Profit
Type: Performing; Touring; Sponsoring
Purpose: To serve as a progressive, multidisciplinary company, producing original performance art and running CSPS, an alternative gallery and performance space
Management: Mel Andringa, Artistic Director; F. John Herbert, Project Director
Paid Staff: 2   **Volunteer Staff:** 3
Utilizes: Guest Artists
Budget: $50,000 - $100,000
Income Sources: Private Foundations/Grants/Endowments; Business/Corporate Donations; Box Office; Government Grants; Individual Donations
Season: 52 Weeks
Affiliations: APAP; NAAO

FACILITY

FIVE SEASONS CENTER ARENA
370 First Avenue NE, Cedar Rapids, IA 52401
(319) 398-5211
FAX: (319) 362-2102
Type of Facility: Concert Hall; Arena; Multi-Purpose
Type of Stage: Flexible; Platform
Seating Capacity: 10,000
Year Built: 1979   **Architect:** Leo Peiffer Associates

Contact for Rental: Sharon Cummins, Chris Werner;   (319) 398-5211
Manager: Ann Larson;   (319) 398-5211

PARAMOUNT THEATRE FOR THE PERFORMING ARTS
370 First Avenue NE, Cedar Rapids, IA 52401
(319) 398-5211
FAX: (319) 362-2102
  Type of Facility: Concert Hall; Off Broadway; Theatre House
  Type of Stage: Proscenium
  Stage Dimensions: 44'Wx27'H proscenium opening   **Orchestra Pit**
  Seating Capacity: 1,913
  Year Built: 1928   **Architect:** Peacock and Frank
  Year Remodeled: 1987   **Architect:** Leo Peiffer & Associates
  Contact for Rental: Sharon Cummins, Chris Werner;   (319) 398-5211
  Manager: Ann Larson;   (319) 398-5211
  Resident Groups: Cedar Rapids Symphony Orchestra; Community Concerts Association; The Cedar Rapids Theater Organ Society

---

Council Bluffs

THEATRE

CHANTICLEER
PO Box 363, Council Bluffs, IA 51502
(712) 323-9955; (712) 322-9751
  Founded: 1952
  Arts Area: Community
  Status: Non-Profit
  Type: Performing
  Purpose: To promote and educate theatrical performers and performances
  Management: Kay Esancy, Office Manager; Joyce Sheehan, Business Manager; Dixie Price, House Manager
  Officers: John Myers, President/Vice President; Kay Esancy, Secretary/Treasurer
  Paid Staff: 3
  Utilizes: Special Technical Talent; Guest Directors
  Budget: $50,000 - $100,000
  Income Sources: Private Foundations/Grants/Endowments; Business/Corporate Donations; Box Office; Individual Donations
  Season: September - June   **Annual Attendance:** 8,000

Davenport

INSTRUMENTAL MUSIC

QUAD CITY SYMPHONY ORCHESTRA
PO Box 1144, Davenport, IA 52805
(319) 322-0931
FAX: (319) 322-6864
  Founded: 1915
  Arts Area: Symphony; Orchestra
  Status: Professional; Non-Profit
  Type: Performing; Educational
  Purpose: To support symphonic performances and to foster, stimulate and encourage orchestral ensemble and other music through developmental programs and scholarships for talented persons
  Management: Lance O. Willett, Executive Director; Dennis Loftin, Operations Manager; James Dixon, Music Director/Conductor
  Officers: Joyce Bawden, President; John Kindschuk, Executive Vice President; June Stimac, Secretary; Charles Brooke, Treasurer; Elsie von Maur, Honorary Chairman
  Paid Staff: 7   **Volunteer Staff:** 350
  Paid Artists: 95
  Utilizes: Guest Artists
  Budget: $500,000 - $1,000,000
  Income Sources: Private Foundations/Grants/Endowments; Business/Corporate Donations; Box Office; Government Grants; Individual Donations
  Season: September - May   **Annual Attendance:** 56,000
  Affiliations: ASOL; Illinois Council of Orchestras
  Performance Facilities: Centennial Hall, Rock Island; Adler Theater, Davenport

QUAD CITY YOUTH SYMPHONY ORCHESTRA
PO Box 1144, Davenport, IA 52805
(319) 322-0931
   Founded: 1958
   Arts Area: Symphony; Orchestra; Chamber; Ensemble
   Status: Non-Professional; Non-Profit
   Type: Performing; Educational
   Management: Daniel Culver, Music Director/Conductor
   Officers: Eloise Smit, Chairperson
   Non-Paid Artists: 82
   Utilizes: Guest Artists
   Budget: $1,000 - $50,000
   Income Sources: Box Office; Individual Donations
   Season: September - June   **Annual Attendance:** 5,000
   Affiliations: ASOL(Youth Symphony Division); Quad City Symphony Orchestra
   Performance Facilities: Centennial Hall, Rock Island; Masonic Temple Auditorium

THEATRE

JUNIOR THEATRE
2822 Eastern Avenue, PO Box 130, Davenport, IA 52803
(319) 326-7862
   Founded: 1953
   Arts Area: Community; Puppet
   Status: Non-Profit
   Type: Performing; Touring; Educational
   Purpose: Classes in creative drama and play production for students five years old through high school. All students perform each semester and do technical work. Five major productions, 28 touring productions
   Management: Parks and Recreation Department of City of Davenport; Bonnie F. Guenther, Cultural Arts Supervisor
   Officers: Marlene Miller, President; Carole Kucharo, Vice President; Beverly Rosenbohm, Secretary; Carol Jorgensen, Treasurer
   Paid Staff: 12   **Volunteer Staff:** 30
   Budget: $50,000 - $100,000
   Income Sources: Business/Corporate Donations; Government Grants; City of Davenport Funding
   Season: September - August   **Annual Attendance:** 40,000
   Affiliations: Iowa Community Theatres; AATE
   Performance Facilities: Mary Fluhrer Nighswander Junior Theatre

PERFORMING SERIES

BROADWAY THEATRE LEAGUE OF THE QUAD-CITIES
PO Box 130, Davenport, IA 52805
(319) 326-1916
   Founded: 1960
   Status: Non-Profit
   Type: Sponsoring
   Purpose: To sponsor touring New York productions, bus and truck companies, of major Broadway Shows
   Officers: Norman J. Kelinson, President & Manager; Leone Bredbeck, Vice President; Suzie Lewis, Secretary; Jim Victor, Treasurer
   Paid Staff: 1   **Volunteer Staff:** 35
   Utilizes: Guest Artists
   Budget: $100,000 - $500,000
   Income Sources: Box Office
   Season: September - May   **Annual Attendance:** 40,000
   Performance Facilities: Adler Theatre

SAINT AMBROSE COLLEGE - GALVIN FINE ARTS CENTER
518 West Locust, Davenport, IA 52803
(319) 383-8878
   Founded: 1969
   Arts Area: Dance; Vocal Music; Instrumental Music; Theater; Festivals
   Status: Non-Profit
   Type: Performing; Touring; Educational; Sponsoring
   Purpose: To present quality cultural programs for the college and community; to create a positive educational arts experience
   Management: Nancy Cerny, Marketing Coordinator; Lance Sadlek, Director
   Paid Staff: 32
   Utilizes: Special Technical Talent; Guest Conductors; Guest Artists; Guest Directors
   Budget: $100,000 - $500,000

Income Sources: Box Office; Government Grants
Season: 52 Weeks   **Annual Attendance:** 60,000
Affiliations: APAP; USITT; Iowa Arts Council; Illinois Arts Council

FACILITY

MARYCREST COLLEGE - UPHAM AUDITORIUM
1607 West 12th Street, Davenport, IA 52804
(319) 326-9343
    Type of Facility: Concert Hall; Auditorium
    Facility Originally: School
    Type of Stage: Proscenium; 50' Foot Thrust
    Stage Dimensions: 26'Wx16'D
    Seating Capacity: 300
    Year Built: 1942
    Contact for Rental: Communication, Fine and Performing Arts Division;   (319) 326-9221
    Resident Groups: Marycrest Performing Arts Scrics

SAINT AMBROSE COLLEGE - ALLAERT HALL
Galvin Fine Arts Center, 518 West Locust Street, Davenport, IA 52803
(319) 383-8878
FAX: (319) 383-8791
    Type of Facility: Auditorium; Performance Center; Theatre House
    Type of Stage: Proscenium
    Stage Dimensions: 64'x70'   **Orchestra Pit**
    Seating Capacity: 1,236
    Year Built: 1969   **Architect:** Braecke-Hayes-Miller   **Cost:** $1,500,000
    Acoustical Consultant: Wess Ling Beling Engineering Company
    Contact for Rental: Lance Sadler;   (319) 383-8878
    Manager: Terry Miller;   (319) 383-8878
    Resident Groups: Children's Theatre Company

Decorah

VOCAL MUSIC

DORIAN OPERA THEATRE
Decorah, IA 52101
(319) 382-3389
    Founded: 1985
    Arts Area: Lyric Opera; Light Opera; Operetta
    Status: Semi-Professional; Non-Profit
    Type: Touring; Resident; Educational
    Purpose: To offer performance experience for young professionals and student artists
    Management: David Greedy, Douglas Meyer, Co-Directors
    Officers: Karen Gray, President; Vicki Donhowe, Vice President; Jack Nelson, Secretary/Treasurer
    Paid Staff: 12   **Volunteer Staff:** 12
    Paid Artists: 4   **Non-Paid Artists:** 25
    Utilizes: Special Technical Talent; Guest Artists
    Budget: $50,000 - $100,000
    Income Sources: Private Foundations/Grants/Endowments; Business/Corporate Donations; Box Office; Government Grants; Individual Donations
    Season: June - July   **Annual Attendance:** 4,000
    Performance Facilities: Luther College Center for Faith and Life

PERFORMING SERIES

DECORAH COMMUNITY CONCERT ASSOCIATION
123 West Water Street, Decorah, IA 52101
(319) 382-2665; (319) 382-4504
    Founded: 1941
    Arts Area: Dance; Vocal Music; Instrumental Music; Lyric Opera; Ballet
    Status: Non-Profit
    Type: Performing; Educational
    Purpose: To provide opportunities to the community to hear and see the best in music and entertainment
    Officers: W.G. Linnevold, President; Mrs. F. Peterson, Secretary/Campaign Supervisor; John Hess, Treasurer
    Utilizes: Guest Artists
    Budget: $1,000 - $50,000

Season: September - May   Annual Attendance: 3,500
Affiliations: CCA
Performance Facilities: Center for Faith and Life, Luther College

Des Moines

DANCE

IOWA DANCE THEATRE
6720 Hickman Road, Des Moines, IA 50322
(515) 276-2694
Founded: 1983
Arts Area: Modern; Ballet; Jazz
Status: Semi-Professional; Non-Profit
Type: Performing; Touring; Educational
Purpose: To support a company of dancers who will perform and promote dance as an art form
Management: Mary Joyce Lind, Artistic Director; Janice Baker-Haines, Robert Thomas, Co-Directors
Volunteer Staff: 10
Utilizes: Guest Artists
Budget: $1,000 - $50,000
Income Sources: Individual Donations
Annual Attendance: 1,400
Performance Facilities: Performing Arts Hall, Drake University

INSTRUMENTAL MUSIC

DES MOINES SYMPHONY
530 42nd Street, Des Moines, IA 50312
(515) 255-2343
Founded: 1937
Arts Area: Symphony; Orchestra; Chamber; Ensemble
Status: Professional; Non-Profit
Type: Performing; Educational
Management: Paul Ferrone, Executive Director; Joseph Giunta, Music Director and Conductor
Paid Staff: 5
Paid Artists: 84
Utilizes: Guest Conductors; Guest Artists
Budget: $500,000 - $1,000,000
Income Sources: Private Foundations/Grants/Endowments; Business/Corporate Donations; Box Office; Government Grants; Individual Donations; Fund-raising
Season: September - May   Annual Attendance: 30,000
Affiliations: ASOL
Performance Facilities: Civic Center of Greater Des Moines

FACILITY

CIVIC CENTER OF GREATER DES MOINES
221 Walnut, Des Moines, IA 50309
(515) 243-0766
FAX: (515) 243-1179
Type of Facility: Concert Hall; Auditorium; Studio Performance; Performance Center; Off Broadway; Theatre House; Opera House; Black Box
Type of Stage: Flexible; Proscenium; Stoner Studio Theatre
Stage Dimensions: 76'Wx30'D; 76'Wx28'H proscenium opening   Orchestra Pit
Seating Capacity: 2,735; Stoner Studio Theatre - 200
Year Built: 1979   Architect: Charles Herbert & Associates   Cost: $9,500,000
Acoustical Consultant: Paul Veneklasen
Contact for Rental: David Olson;   (515) 243-0766
Manager: Gordon D. Smith, Manager
Resident Groups: Des Moines Symphony; Ballet Iowa; Civic Music Association; Drama Workshop
Rental available for all types of musical, theatrical, dance and seminar events

DES MOINES WOMEN'S CLUB
Hoyt Sherman Place, 1501 Woodland, Des Moines, IA 50309
(515) 243-0913
Type of Facility: Concert Hall; Auditorium; Studio Performance; Theatre House
Type of Stage: Proscenium
Stage Dimensions: 35'Wx20'D   Orchestra Pit

Seating Capacity: 1,400
Year Built: 1922
Year Remodeled: 1950
Contact for Rental: A.B. Wonders;   (515) 243-0913
Dramas, concerts, seminars, speakers (no rock)

DRAKE UNIVERSITY - HALL OF PERFORMING ARTS, HARMON FINE ARTS CENTER
26th Street & Carpenter Avenue, Des Moines, IA 50311
(515) 271-2018
FAX: (515) 271-3977
   Founded: 1881
   Type of Facility: Concert Hall; Performance Center
   Type of Stage: Proscenium
   Stage Dimensions: 40'Wx32'D   **Orchestra Pit**
   Seating Capacity: 460
   Year Built: 1972   **Architect:** Harry Weese & Associates
   Year Remodeled: 1992   **Architect:** RDG Bussard/Dikis Associates Ltd.   **Cost:** $100,000
   Contact for Rental: Myron Marty;   (515) 271-3939
   Resident Groups: Drake University Theatre Arts and Music Departments

DRAKE UNIVERISTY - OLD MAIN AUDITORIUM
Des Moines, IA 50311
(515) 271-3939
FAX: (515) 271-3977
   Founded: 1881
   Type of Facility: Concert Hall; Auditorium
   Facility Originally: Chapel; Auditorium
   Type of Stage: Platform
   Stage Dimensions: 36'W at front; 30'W at rear; 32'D
   Seating Capacity: 775
   Year Built: 1900   **Cost:** $20,000
   Year Remodeled: 1992   **Architect:** Baldwin Clause Architects PC   **Cost:** $3,800,000
   Acoustical Consultant: Talaske
   Contact for Rental: Myron Marty;   (515) 271-3939
   Resident Groups: Drake University Music Department

Dubuque

INSTRUMENTAL MUSIC

DUBUQUE SYMPHONY ORCHESTRA
1072 Locust Street, PO Box 881, Dubuque, IA 52004-0881
(319) 557-1677
   Founded: 1959
   Arts Area: Symphony; Orchestra; Chamber; Ensemble
   Status: Semi-Professional; Non-Profit
   Type: Performing; Resident; Educational; Sponsoring
   Purpose: To present quality performances and educational programs in the field of classical music
   Management: Robert A. Birman, General Manager; Mary Ellen Rogers, Operations Manager; Tracey Rush, Librarian
   Officers: David Howell, President; Jean Dunn, Secretary; William Skemp, Treasurer
   Paid Staff: 2
   Paid Artists: 4
   Utilizes: Guest Artists
   Budget: $100,000 - $500,000
   Income Sources: Private Foundations/Grants/Endowments; Business/Corporate Donations; Box Office; Government Grants; Individual Donations
   Season: August - May   **Annual Attendance:** 15,000
   Affiliations: Symphony League
   Performance Facilities: Five Flags Center - Theatre

THEATRE

BARN COMMUNITY THEATRE
135 Eighth Street, Dubuque, IA 52001
(319) 588-1305
   Founded: 1971
   Arts Area: Musical; Community
   Status: Non-Professional; Non-Profit

Type: Performing; Educational
Purpose: To provide quality entertainment through live performances and educational experiences thus contributing to the cultural and economic growth of the community
Management: Sue Riedel, Theatre Manager; Helen Johnston, Office Manager
Officers: Dave Grable, President; Daryl Barklow, Vice President; Sue Reilly, Secretary; Melanie Olson, Treasurer
Paid Staff: 8   **Volunteer Staff:** 600
Paid Artists: 45   **Non-Paid Artists:** 200
Utilizes: Guest Artists; Guest Directors
Budget: $100,000 - $500,000
Income Sources: Private Foundations/Grants/Endowments; Business/Corporate Donations; Box Office; Government Grants; Individual Donations
Season: 52 Weeks
Affiliations: ACT; Iowa Community Theatre Association; Dubuque Arts Alliance; Dubuque Area, Galena and Dyersville Area Chambers of Commerce
Performance Facilities: Grand Opera House

FACILITY

FIVE FLAGS CENTER
Fourth and Main Streets, PO Box 628, Dubuque, IA 52001
(319) 556-4369
>   **Type of Facility:** Civic Center
>   **Year Built:** 1979
>   **Contact for Rental:** Carole Barry;   (319) 589-4254
>   *Five Flags Center contains the Arena and Theatre. See separate listings for additional information.*

FIVE FLAGS CENTER - ARENA
Fourth and Main Streets, PO Box 628, Dubuque, IA 52001
(319) 556-4369
>   **Type of Facility:** Concert Hall; Arena
>   **Type of Stage:** Flexible; Platform
>   **Stage Dimensions:** 85'x40'
>   **Seating Capacity:** 5,200
>   **Year Built:** 1979
>   **Contact for Rental:** Carole Barry;   (319) 589-4254
>   *The arena is also used for ice hockey*

FIVE FLAGS CENTER - THEATRE
Fourth and Main Streets, PO Box 628, Dubuque, IA 52001
(319) 556-4369
>   **Type of Facility:** Concert Hall; Theatre House
>   **Type of Stage:** Proscenium
>   **Stage Dimensions:** 32'Wx27'5"D; 32'Wx29'H proscenium opening   **Orchestra Pit**
>   **Seating Capacity:** 717
>   **Year Built:** 1910   **Architect:** Rapp & Rapp
>   **Year Remodeled:** 1976   **Cost:** $1,000,000
>   **Contact for Rental:** Carole Barry;   (319) 589-4254

Forest City

PERFORMING SERIES

WALDORF COMMUNITY ARTISTS SERIES
Waldorf College, 106 South Sixth Street, Forest City, IA 50436
(515) 582-8177
FAX: (515) 582-8111
>   **Founded:** 1988
>   **Arts Area:** Dance; Vocal Music; Instrumental Music; Theater; Lyric Opera; Grand Opera
>   **Status:** Non-Profit
>   **Type:** Sponsoring
>   **Purpose:** To bring high quality performing arts to Waldorf and Forest City
>   **Management:** Steven B. Thompson, Chair Waldorf Community Artist Series
>   **Paid Staff:** 2   **Volunteer Staff:** 12
>   **Utilizes:** Guest Artists
>   **Budget:** $1,000 - $50,000
>   **Income Sources:** Private Foundations/Grants/Endowments; Business/Corporate Donations; Box Office; Government Grants

Season: September - April   **Annual Attendance:** 5,000
Affiliations: Waldorf College

Fort Dodge

INSTRUMENTAL MUSIC

FORT DODGE AREA SYMPHONY ORCHESTRA
Box 1291, Fort Dodge, IA 50501
(515) 573-4224
    Arts Area: Symphony
    Status: Non-Profit
    Type: Performing
    Purpose: To provide live classical music to the community
    Management: Ardella Hein, Personnel Manager
    Officers: Laurel Mors, President; Doris Porter, Vice President; John Mors, Treasurer; Judy Gunderson, Secretary
    Paid Staff: 1   **Volunteer Staff:** 21
    Paid Artists: 3
    Utilizes: Guest Artists
    Budget: $1,000 - $50,000
    Income Sources: Private Foundations/Grants/Endowments; Business/Corporate Donations; Box Office; Government Grants; Individual Donations
    Season: October - April
    Annual Attendance: 3,000
    Performance Facilities: Phillips Middle School Auditorium

---

Garrison

THEATRE

THE OLD CREAMERY THEATRE COMPANY
PO Box 160, Garrison, IA 52229
(319) 477-3925
    Founded: 1971
    Arts Area: Professional; Theatrical Group
    Status: Professional; Non-Profit
    Type: Performing; Touring; Resident; Educational
    Purpose: To bring live theater to as many people as possible in rural Iowa
    Management: Thomas Peter Johnson, Producing Director; Blaine Stephens, Associate Artistic Director
    Officers: Rod Geist, Board President
    Paid Staff: 6
    Utilizes: Special Technical Talent; Guest Artists; Guest Directors
    Budget: $100,000 - $500,000
    Income Sources: Private Foundations/Grants/Endowments; Business/Corporate Donations; Box Office; Government Grants; Individual Donations
    Season: May - December
    Annual Attendance: 40,000
    Affiliations: AEA; TCG
    Performance Facilities: The Old Creamery Theatre (Garrison and Amana)
    Also located at the Amana Colonies Visitors Center, Amana, Iowa

FACILITY

THE OLD CREAMERY THEATRE
PO Box 160, Garrison, IA 52229
(319) 477-3925
    Type of Facility: Theatre Complex; Studio Performance; Theatre House
    Type of Stage: Thrust; Flexible
    Stage Dimensions: 32'Wx22'D
    Seating Capacity: 262
    Year Built: 1899
    Year Remodeled: 1976   **Cost:** $15,000
    Contact for Rental: Thomas P. Johnson; (319) 477-3925
    Resident Groups: The Old Creamery Theatre Company
    Brenton Stage - studio theatre added in 1981 - seats 135, flexible stage

Indianola

VOCAL MUSIC

DES MOINES METRO OPERA
106 West Boston, Indianola, IA 50125
(515) 961-6221
FAX: (515) 961-2994
    Founded: 1973
    Arts Area: Grand Opera; Lyric Opera
    Status: Professional; Non-Profit
    Type: Performing; Touring; Resident; Educational
    Purpose: To provide a stage for young American artists, produce high quality performances and educate audiences to opera in the Midwest
    Management: Robert L. Larsen, Artistic Director; Jerilee M. Mace, Managing Director
    Officers: Don Easter, President; Cherie Shreck, Vice President/President-Elect; Richard Calkins, Vice President/Development; LaDonna Mathes, Secretary; Charles Farr, Treasurer
    Paid Staff: 6
    Paid Artists: 20   **Non-Paid Artists:** 45
    Budget: $1,000,000 - $5,000,000
    Income Sources: Private Foundations/Grants/Endowments; Business/Corporate Donations; Box Office; Government Grants; Individual Donations
    Season: June - July
    Affiliations: OA
    Performance Facilities: Blank Performing Arts Center

Iowa City

THEATRE

RIVERSIDE THEATRE
PO Box 1651, Iowa City, IA 52244
(319) 338-7672
    Founded: 1981
    Arts Area: Theatrical Group
    Status: Semi-Professional; Non-Profit
    Type: Performing; Touring; Resident; Educational; Sponsoring
    Purpose: To provide a season of shows ranging from the classics to premieres of new plays; to sponsor other theatre groups; to provide education and a touring season throughout the Midwest
    Management: Jody Hovland, Managing Director; Ron Clark, Artistic Director
    Officers: Janice Wilson, Chairman; Tom Walsh, Vice Chairman
    Paid Staff: 1
    Utilizes: Special Technical Talent; Guest Artists; Guest Directors
    Budget: $100,000 - $500,000
    Income Sources: Business/Corporate Donations; Box Office; Government Grants; Individual Donations
    Season: September - March   **Annual Attendance:** 3,000
    Performance Facilities: Riverside Theatre

FACILITY

THE UNIVERSITY OF IOWA - HANCHER AUDITORIUM
Iowa City, IA 52242
(319) 335-1160
    Type of Facility: Auditorium
    Type of Stage: Proscenium
    Stage Dimensions: 170'Wx85'Hx55'D   **Orchestra Pit**
    Seating Capacity: 2,684
    Year Built: 1972   **Architect:** Max Abramovitz   **Cost:** $7,000,000
    Acoustical Consultant: Paul Veneklasen
    Contact for Rental: Wally Chappel

Mason City

FACILITY

NORTH IOWA COMMUNITY AUDITORIUM
500 College Drive, Mason City, IA 50401
(515) 421-4240
> **Type of Facility:** Theatre Complex; Concert Hall; Auditorium; Theatre House
> **Type of Stage:** Thrust; Proscenium
> **Orchestra Pit**
> **Seating Capacity:** 1,167
> **Year Built:** 1980   **Architect:** Tom Wagner   **Cost:** $1,800,000
> **Contact for Rental:** Robert A. Davis;   (515) 421-4241

Mount Pleasant

INSTRUMENTAL MUSIC

SOUTHEAST IOWA SYMPHONY ORCHESTRA
601 North Main, Mount Pleasant, IA 52641
(319) 385-6352
FAX: (319) 385-6296
> **Founded:** 1950
> **Arts Area:** Symphony; Orchestra
> **Status:** Non-Professional; Non-Profit
> **Type:** Performing
> **Purpose:** To educate, encourage and perform orchestral music in southeast Iowa
> **Management:** Robert McConnell, Conductor/Music Director; Joy Rayman Anderson, Manager
> **Officers:** Judy Blommer, President; Elaine Cederquist, Vice President; Bobby K. Wilson, Secretary; Ruth Sein, Treasurer
> **Paid Staff:** 4   **Volunteer Staff:** 50
> **Paid Artists:** 20   **Non-Paid Artists:** 40
> **Utilizes:** Guest Artists
> **Budget:** $50,000 - $100,000
> **Income Sources:** Private Foundations/Grants/Endowments; Business/Corporate Donations; Box Office; Government Grants; Individual Donations
> **Season:** September - March   **Annual Attendance:** 5,000
> **Affiliations:** ASOL; BMI; ASCAP
> **Performance Facilities:** James Madison Auditorium; Iowa Wesleyan Chapel Auditorium; Saint John Auditorium

Orange City

FACILITY

NORTHWESTERN COLLEGE
101 Seventh Street SW, Orange City, IA 51041
(712) 737-4821
FAX: (712) 737-8847
> **Type of Facility:** Theatre House; Multi-Purpose
> **Facility Originally:** Church
> **Type of Stage:** Thrust; Proscenium; Two Spaces
> **Seating Capacity:** 224; 175
> **Year Built:** 1925
> **Contact for Rental:** Tres Jacobsma;   (712) 737-4821

Sioux City

DANCE

SIOUXLAND CIVIC DANCE ASSOCIATION
813 Pearl Street, Sioux City, IA 51101
(712) 255-0972
> **Founded:** 1971
> **Arts Area:** Ballet; Jazz
> **Status:** Non-Profit
> **Type:** Performing; Touring; Sponsoring

Officers: Jan King, President; Marge Herbold, Vice President; Karen Eberle, Secretary; Hess Roorda, Treasurer; Shirley Dill, Artistic Director
Volunteer Staff: 20
Non-Paid Artists: 50
Utilizes: Guest Artists; Guest Choreographers
Budget: $1,000 - $50,000
Income Sources: Private Foundations/Grants/Endowments; Business/Corporate Donations; Box Office; Government Grants; Individual Donations
Season: September - May **Annual Attendance:** 5,000

INSTRUMENTAL MUSIC

SIOUX CITY SYMPHONY ORCHESTRA
258 Orpheum Building, PO Box 754, Sioux City, IA 51102
(712) 277-2111
FAX: (712) 252-0224
Founded: 1923
Arts Area: Symphony; Orchestra; Ensemble
Status: Professional; Non-Profit
Type: Performing; Resident; Educational
Purpose: To perform at concerts
Management: Dr. John E. Luebke, Executive Director; Dr. Alan L. Arnold, Operations Manager/Office Manager; Sandra Lehmberg, Marketing Assistant
Officers: Michael Zimmerman, President; Thomas Borchert, Dr. Jeffrey Williams, Vice Presidents; David Silverberg, CFP, Treasurer; Linda Bowden, Secretary
Paid Staff: 4
Paid Artists: 85
Utilizes: Guest Conductors; Guest Artists
Budget: $100,000 - $500,000
Income Sources: Private Foundations/Grants/Endowments; Business/Corporate Donations; Box Office; Government Grants; Individual Donations
Season: October - April **Annual Attendance:** 15,000
Affiliations: ASOL
Performance Facilities: Eppley Auditorium

THEATRE

SIOUX CITY COMMUNITY THEATRE
PO Box 512, Sioux City, IA 51102
(712) 233-2719
Founded: 1948
Arts Area: Community; Theatrical Group
Status: Non-Professional
Type: Performing
Purpose: Outlet for those interested in producing theatrical productions and educational tool in teaching theatre crafts
Management: Tom Peterson, General Manager; C. Ann Falkenberg, Operations Manager
Officers: Gregg Galloway, President; A. Frank Baron, Vice President; Keith Roeper, Treasurer; Kristi Quinn, Secretary
Paid Staff: 1
Budget: $50,000 - $100,000
Income Sources: Private Foundations/Grants/Endowments; Business/Corporate Donations; Box Office; Individual Donations
Season: October - June **Annual Attendance:** 1,500
Affiliations: ACT: Iowa Community Theatre Association
Performance Facilities: Shore Acres

Spirit Lake

FACILITY

OKOBOJI SUMMER THEATRE
PO Box 341, Spirit Lake, IA 51360
(712) 332-7277
Type of Facility: Theatre House
Facility Originally: Airplane Hangar
Type of Stage: Proscenium
Stage Dimensions: 120'Wx120'D
Seating Capacity: 450
Year Built: 1930

Year Remodeled: 1965   **Architect:** Chin   **Cost:** $20,000
Manager: Addison Myers;   (314) 876-7193

Waterloo

INSTRUMENTAL MUSIC

WATERLOO-CEDAR FALLS SYMPHONY ORCHESTRA
225 Commercial Street, Waterloo, IA 50702
(319) 235-6331
FAX: (319) 235-6332
   Founded: 1930
   Arts Area: Symphony; Orchestra; Chamber; Ensemble
   Status: Non-Profit
   Type: Performing
   Purpose: To meet the musical needs of the Northeast Iowa community
   Management: Kevin S. Taylor, General Manager; Joseph Giunta, Conductor Laureate
   Officers: Joani Hollen, President; Wes Heitzman, Vice President; Louis Fettkether, Treasurer; Joan Diamond, Secretary
   Paid Staff: 3   **Volunteer Staff:** 500
   Paid Artists: 80
   Utilizes: Guest Conductors; Guest Artists
   Budget: $100,000 - $500,000
   Income Sources: Private Foundations/Grants/Endowments; Business/Corporate Donations; Box Office; Government Grants; Individual Donations
   Season: September - May
   Affiliations: ASOL; ASCAP; BMI
   Performance Facilities: Kersenbrock Auditorium

THEATRE

WATERLOO COMMUNITY PLAYHOUSE/BLACK HAWK CHILDREN'S THEATRE
225 Cedar Street, Waterloo, IA 50701
(319) 235-0367
   Founded: 1916
   Arts Area: Musical; Community
   Status: Non-Professional; Non-Profit
   Type: Performing; Educational; Sponsoring
   Purpose: To provide high quality theatre productions and education for the cultural and creative growth of the northeast Iowa community
   Management: Charles Stilwill, Managing Director; Roger Crimmins, Development Director; Mark Rockwell, Business Manager; Thomas Ballmer, Children's Theatre Director
   Officers: Thomas Lauglas, President; Betty Steege, President-Elect; David Richter, Treasurer; Linda Schipper, Secretary
   Paid Staff: 15   **Volunteer Staff:** 475
   Paid Artists: 10   **Non-Paid Artists:** 175
   Utilizes: Special Technical Talent; Guest Conductors; Guest Artists; Guest Directors
   Budget: $100,000 - $500,000
   Income Sources: Private Foundations/Grants/Endowments; Business/Corporate Donations; Box Office; Government Grants; Individual Donations
   Season: 52 Weeks   **Annual Attendance:** 40,000
   Affiliations: ACT; AATY; Waterloo, Cedar Falls and Waverly Chambers of Commerce; Iowa Community Theatre Association; Cedar Arts Forum
   Performance Facilities: Hope Martin Theatre

FACILITY

HOPE MARTIN THEATRE
225 Commercial, Waterloo, IA 50701
(319) 291-4494
   Type of Facility: Performance Center
   Type of Stage: Proscenium
   Stage Dimensions: 14'x32'x28'   **Orchestra Pit**
   Seating Capacity: 368
   Year Built: 1965   **Architect:** Thorson, Brom & Broshar   **Cost:** $100,000
   Year Remodeled: 1976   **Architect:** Thorson, Brom & Broshar   **Cost:** $2,500
   Contact for Rental: Marlene Ackerman;   (319) 291-4491
   Resident Groups: Waterloo Community Playhouse; Black Hawk Children's Theatre; Metro Dance Theatre

---

Waverly

PERFORMING SERIES

WARTBURG COLLEGE ARTISTS SERIES
222 Ninth Street NW, PO Box 1003, Waverly, IA 50677
(319) 352-8328
    Arts Area: Dance; Vocal Music; Instrumental Music; Theater; Lyric Opera; Grand Opera
    Status: Non-Profit; College
    Type: Sponsoring
    Purpose: To present the arts for educational uses and community service
    Management: Franklin E. Williams, Director; Tony Lutz, Technical Director
    Paid Staff: 1
    Utilizes: Guest Artists
    Budget: $50,000 - $100,000
    Income Sources: Box Office; College Support
    Season: September - April
    Performance Facilities: Neumann Auditorium

FACILITY

WARTBURG COLLEGE - NEUMANN AUDITORIUM
222 Ninth Street NW, PO Box 1003, Waverly, IA 50677
(319) 352-8286
FAX: (319) 352-8394
    Type of Facility: Auditorium
    Facility Originally: Church
    Type of Stage: Flexible; Proscenium
    Stage Dimensions: 42'Wx18'Hx25'D; 35' from edge to back wall   **Orchestra Pit**
    Seating Capacity: 1343
    Year Built: 1959   **Architect:** Woodburn & O'Neil   **Cost:** $342,996
    Year Remodeled: 1985   **Architect:** Thorson, Brom, Broshar, Snyder   **Cost:** $152,788
    Acoustical Consultant: Woodburn & O'Neil
    Contact for Rental: Karen Funk;   (319) 352-8286
    Manager: Tom Lutz;   (319) 352-8216
    Resident Groups: Wartburg Community Symphony Orchestra; Wartburg Choral Groups and Bands; Wartburg College Artist Series
    Programs by educational and cultural organizations on and off campus

---

West Des Moines

DANCE

BALLET IOWA
2020 Grand Avenue, West Des Moines, IA 50265
(515) 222-0698
    Founded: 1966
    Arts Area: Ballet
    Status: Professional; Non-Profit
    Type: Performing; Touring; Resident; Educational; Sponsoring
    Management: Konstantin Uralsky, Artistic Director
    Paid Staff: 10
    Paid Artists: 20
    Utilizes: Special Technical Talent; Guest Artists
    Budget: $500,000 - $1,000,000
    Income Sources: Private Foundations/Grants/Endowments; Business/Corporate Donations; Box Office; Government Grants; Individual Donations
    Season: August - April   **Annual Attendance:** 15,000
    Performance Facilities: Civic Center of Greater Des Moines; Stephens Auditorium

BALLET IOWA ASSOCIATION
2020 Grand Avenue, West Des Moines, IA 50265
(515) 222-0698
    Founded: 1966
    Arts Area: Ballet
    Status: Professional; Non-Profit
    Type: Performing; Touring; Resident; Educational

Purpose: To support and promote through education and performance a high quality school of dance and professional company

Management: Konstantin Uralsky, Artistic Director; Lynn Lavin, Education Director; Steven Crick, Production Director

Officers: Cynthia Lidgett, President; Chuck Johnson, President-Elect

Paid Staff: 10

Paid Artists: 18

Utilizes: Special Technical Talent; Guest Conductors; Guest Artists; Guest Choreographers

Budget: $500,000 - $1,000,000

Income Sources: Private Foundations/Grants/Endowments; Business/Corporate Donations; Box Office; Government Grants; Individual Donations

Season: October - June   **Annual Attendance:** 20,000

Performance Facilities: Civic Center of Greater Des Moines

KANSAS

Chanute

THEATRE

CHANUTE COMMUNITY THEATRE
PO Box 371, Chanute, KS 66720
(316) 431-3213
Founded: 1978
Arts Area: Musical; Dinner; Community; Theatrical Group
Status: Non-Professional; Non-Profit
Type: Performing; Resident; Educational
Purpose: To provide wide-based theatrical entertainment to the community
Officers: Rick Bushnell, President; Bruce LaRue, Vice President; Cindy Crowl, Treasurer; Cindy Fairchild, Secretary
Volunteer Staff: 12
Budget: $1,000 - $50,000
Income Sources: Private Foundations/Grants/Endowments; Business/Corporate Donations; Box Office; Government Grants; Individual Donations
Season: August - May   **Annual Attendance:** 2,000
Affiliations: Association of Kansas Theatres
Performance Facilities: Memorial Auditorium; Chanute Country Club

FACILITY

MEMORIAL AUDITORIUM
First and Lincoln, Chanute, KS 66720
(316) 431-3213; (316) 431-5200
Type of Facility: Auditorium
Type of Stage: Proscenium
Stage Dimensions: 60'Wx40'D   **Orchestra Pit**
Seating Capacity: 1,800
Year Remodeled: 1978
Contact for Rental: City of Chanute;   (316) 431-9300
Resident Groups: Chanute Community Theatre

Coffeyville

THEATRE

COFFEYVILLE COMMUNITY THEATRE
PO Box 317, Coffeyville, KS 67337
(316) 251-1164
Founded: 1945
Arts Area: Musical; Dinner; Community; Theatrical Group
Status: Non-Professional; Non-Profit
Type: Performing
Purpose: To provide live theatre entertainment to the community
Officers: Sally Kimball, President; Andy Medford, Vice President; Lois Hendrix, Treasurer; Nancy Reinecker, Secretary
Paid Staff: 3   **Volunteer Staff:** 40
Non-Paid Artists: 35
Utilizes: Guest Artists
Budget: $1,000 - $50,000
Income Sources: Private Foundations/Grants/Endowments; Business/Corporate Donations; Box Office; Individual Donations
Season: 52 Weeks   **Annual Attendance:** 1,000
Affiliations: Association of Kansas Theatres; Kansas Arts Council
Performance Facilities: Floral Hall

FACILITY

FLORAL HALL
PO Box 1629, Coffeyville, KS 67337
(316) 252-6108
Type of Facility: Theatre House
Type of Stage: Proscenium; Platform

Stage Dimensions: 50'Wx30'D
Seating Capacity: 150
Contact for Rental: City of Coffeyville;   (316) 252-6108
Manager: Mike Maier, Parks Director
Resident Groups: Coffeyville Community Theatre

Concordia

THEATRE

BROWN GRAND THEATRE
310 West Sixth, PO Box 341, Concordia, KS 66901-0341
(913) 243-2553
Founded: 1907
Arts Area: Professional; Musical; Community; Folk; Theatrical Group; Puppet
Status: Non-Profit
Type: Performing; Educational; Sponsoring
Purpose: To maintain the historic Brown Grand Theatre; to enrich the cultural lives of area residents by providing quality live theatre and other entertainment
Management: Susan Haver, Theatre Manager
Officers: Susan Sutton, President; Robert Boardman, Vice President; Everett Miller, Secretary; Wonda Brunkow, Treasurer
Paid Staff: 4   Volunteer Staff: 8
Utilizes: Special Technical Talent; Guest Conductors; Guest Artists; Guest Directors
Budget: $50,000 - $100,000
Income Sources: Private Foundations/Grants/Endowments; Business/Corporate Donations; Box Office; Government Grants; Individual Donations
Season: September - May   Annual Attendance: 11,900
Affiliations: MAAA

Dodge City

FACILITY

DODGE CITY CIVIC CENTER
705 First Avenue, Dodge City, KS 67801
(316) 225-8150
Type of Facility: Theatre Complex; Auditorium; Off Broadway; Multi-Purpose; Exhibit Space
Type of Stage: Proscenium
Stage Dimensions: 60'x43'; 30' ceiling
Seating Capacity: 3,178
Year Built: 1954
Contact for Rental: Jim Bowlin, Director;   (316) 225-8150
Resident Groups: Junior College Basketball

Garden City

THEATRE

THE ARTS PROGRAM, GARDEN CITY RECREATION COMMISSION
PO Box 637, 1101 Kansas Plaza, Garden City, KS 67846
(316) 276-1200
Founded: 1976
Arts Area: Community
Status: Non-Profit; Community
Type: Resident
Purpose: To provide community arts and theatre for the Garden City community and southwest Kansas
Management: Mark Hays, Arts Program Director
Paid Staff: 1
Utilizes: Community Volunteers
Budget: $1,000 - $50,000
Income Sources: Box Office; User Fees; Class Fees
Season: June - August
Affiliations: Association of Community Arts Agencies of Kansas
Performance Facilities: Garden City Community College Fine Arts Theatre

---

Hays

INSTRUMENTAL MUSIC

HAYS SYMPHONY ORCHESTRA
Fort Hays State University, Hays, KS 67601
(913) 628-5360
FAX: (913) 628-4096
Founded: 1920
Arts Area: Symphony; Orchestra
Status: Non-Profit
Type: Performing; Educational
Purpose: To provide western Kansas with musical and culture activities; to provide music students with educational and artistic opportunities
Management: Christine Webber, Conductor/Music Director
Officers: Lyle Dilley, President; Esther Halling, Past President; Ann Pflughoft, Vice President; William Miller, Treasurer; Connie Wilson, Secretary
Paid Staff: 1   **Volunteer Staff:** 20
Paid Artists: 2   **Non-Paid Artists:** 2
Utilizes: Special Technical Talent; Guest Artists
Budget: $1,000 - $50,000
Income Sources: Business/Corporate Donations; Box Office; Government Grants; Individual Donations
Season: September - May   **Annual Attendance:** 2,500
Affiliations: ASCAP; ASOL
Performance Facilities: Beach/Schmidt Performing Arts Center

FACILITY

FORT HAYS STATE UNIVERSITY-FELTON - START THEATRE
600 Park Street, Hays, KS 67601-4099
(913) 628-5365
Type of Facility: Theatre Complex
Type of Stage: Proscenium; Modified Apron Proscenium
Stage Dimensions: 40'Wx40'D, 15'D apron; 40'Wx17'H proscenium opening   **Orchestra Pit**
Seating Capacity: 316
Year Built: 1965   **Architect:** Woods & Starr
Year Remodeled: 1983
Contact for Rental: Tomme Williams;   (913) 628-5365
Resident Groups: Fort Hays State Players; Hays Symphony Orchestra; Encore Series; Fort Hayes Singers; Fort Hayes Concert Choir

---

Hesston

PERFORMING SERIES

HESSTON PERFORMING ARTS SERIES
PO Box 3000, Hesston, KS 67062
(316) 327-8206
Founded: 1982
Arts Area: Vocal Music; Instrumental Music
Status: Non-Profit
Type: Sponsoring
Management: Kathy Goering, Secretary to Hesston Performing Arts Community
Volunteer Staff: 25
Paid Artists: 5
Utilizes: Guest Artists
Budget: $1,000 - $50,000
Income Sources: Business/Corporate Donations; Box Office; Government Grants; Individual Donations
Annual Attendance: 4,500
Performance Facilities: Yost Center, Hesston College

Hutchinson

INSTRUMENTAL MUSIC

HUTCHINSON SYMPHONY
PO Box 1241, Hutchinson, KS 67504
(316) 663-8000
Founded: 1948
Arts Area: Symphony; Chamber
Status: Semi-Professional; Non-Profit
Type: Performing
Purpose: To present concerts locally
Management: Terry L. David, General Manager; Dr. Leon Buske III, Conductor/Musical Director
Officers: Amy Carcy, President; Peg Stephens, Vice President; Linda Dillon, Secretary
Paid Staff: 2
Paid Artists: 60
Utilizes: Guest Conductors; Guest Artists
Budget: $50,000 - $100,000
Income Sources: Private Foundations/Grants/Endowments; Business/Corporate Donations; Box Office; Government Grants; Individual Donations
Season: October - April   **Annual Attendance:** 3,500
Performance Facilities: Hutchinson Fine Arts Center

FACILITY

KANSAS STATE FAIR - GRANDSTAND
2000 North Poplar, Hutchinson, KS 67502
(316) 669-3600
Type of Facility: Outdoor (Concert)
Type of Stage: Platform
Stage Dimensions: 40'Dx60'Wx6'H
Seating Capacity: 10,550
Year Built: 1928
Contact for Rental: Kansas State Fair;   (316) 669-3600
Remodeling completed; dirt race track adjacent

Iola

FACILITY

BOWLUS FINE ARTS CENTER
205 East Madison, Iola, KS 66749
(316) 365-6101
Type of Facility: Auditorium; Performance Center; Multi-Purpose
Type of Stage: Proscenium
Stage Dimensions: 42'Wx37'D
Seating Capacity: 752
Year Built: 1964   **Architect:** Brink & Dunwoody   **Cost:** $1,250,000
Contact for Rental: Manager/Director;   (316) 365-6101
Resident Groups: Iola Community Theatre; Iola Area Symphony; Iola City Band; Southeast Shavers
Non-profit, educational entertainment

Kingman

THEATRE

PRAIRIE PLAYERS, INC.
233 North Main, PO Box 291, Kingman, KS 67068-0291
(316) 532-3321
Founded: 1974
Arts Area: Dinner; Community; Theatrical Group; Puppet
Status: Non-Professional; Non-Profit; Community Theatre
Type: Performing; Resident
Purpose: To maintain live theatre arts within a rural setting
Management: Dennis Lee Hoppes, Trustee
Officers: Rob Monk, President; Sandre Pearson, Vice President; Dennis Lee Hoppes, Secretary/Treasurer; Elizabeth Sheldon; Julie Page

Volunteer Staff: 50
Utilizes: Special Technical Talent; Guest Artists; Guest Directors
Budget: $1,000 - $50,000
Income Sources: Private Foundations/Grants/Endowments; Business/Corporate Donations; Box Office; Government Grants; Individual Donations
Season: April-May; September - October
Affiliations: Association of Kansas Theatres

Lawrence

INSTRUMENTAL MUSIC

KANSAS UNIVERSITY SYMPHONY ORCHESTRA
Murphy Hall, University of Kansas, Lawrence, KS 66045
(913) 864-3436
Founded: 1935
Arts Area: Symphony; Orchestra
Status: Non-Profit
Type: Performing; Educational; Sponsoring
Purpose: To present orchestral performances for the community; to provide orchestral training for advanced students
Management: Brian Priestman, Conductor
Paid Staff: 3
Paid Artists: 1   **Non-Paid Artists:** 4
Utilizes: Guest Conductors; Guest Artists
Budget: $1,000 - $50,000
Season: September - May   **Annual Attendance:** 4,000
Affiliations: University of Kansas
Performance Facilities: Crafton-Preyer Theatre, University of Kansas

FACILITY

UNIVERSITY OF KANSAS - CRAFTON-PREYER THEATRE
Lawrence, KS 66045
(913) 864-3469
Type of Facility: Concert Hall; Theatre House
Type of Stage: Proscenium; Turntable
Stage Dimensions: 40'Wx70'D; 40'Wx20'H proscenium opening; 40'Wx10'D hydraulic lift pit   **Orchestra Pit**
Seating Capacity: 1,188
Year Built: 1957
Contact for Rental: Jack Wright;   (913) 864-3381
Resident Groups: Kansas University Theatre; Kansas University Theatre for Young People

Leavenworth

FACILITY

SAINT MARY COLLEGE - XAVIER HALL THEATRE
Leavenworth, KS 66048
(913) 682-5151
Type of Facility: Studio Performance; Theatre House; Multi-Purpose
Type of Stage: Proscenium
Stage Dimensions: 28'x30'
Seating Capacity: 440
Year Built: 1923
Year Remodeled: 1985
Contact for Rental: Van Ibsen;   (913) 682-5151

Lindsborg

PERFORMING SERIES

MESSIAH FESTIVAL OF MUSIC
Bethany College, 421 North First Street, Lindsborg, KS 67456-1897
(913) 227-3311
Founded: 1882

Arts Area: Vocal Music; Instrumental Music
Status: Non-Profit
Type: Performing; Sponsoring
Management: Gregory Aune, Conductor; A. John Pearson, Public Relations and Information
Utilizes: Guest Artists
Income Sources: Box Office
Season: Palm Sunday - Easter
Annual Attendance: 8,000
Affiliations: Bethany College
Performance Facilities: Presser Hall Auditorium

FACILITY

BETHANY COLLEGE - BURNETT CENTER FOR PERFORMING ARTS
Lindsborg, KS 67456
(913) 227-3311, ext. X257
  Type of Facility: Auditorium; Performance Center
  Type of Stage: Thrust
  Stage Dimensions: 36'x40'
  Seating Capacity: 243
  Year Built: 1973   **Architect:** The Shaver Partnership   **Cost:** $300,519
  Contact for Rental: Tricia Hawk, Special Programs;   (913) 227-3311, ext. 132
  Manager: Norman E. Schroder;   (913) 227-3311, ext. 257
  Resident Groups: Bethany College Theatre Program

Manhattan

PERFORMING SERIES

MANHATTAN ARTS COUNCIL
PO Box 74, Manhattan, KS 66502
(913) 539-3276
  Founded: 1972
  Arts Area: Vocal Music; Instrumental Music; Theater; Festivals
  Status: Non-Profit
  Type: Educational; Sponsoring
  Purpose: To foster and support the knowledge, appreciation, and practice of the arts in the community via education, programming, and funding for arts programs
  Management: John Biggs, Executive Director; Dale Clore, Administrative Assistant
  Paid Staff: 2   **Volunteer Staff:** 50
  Utilizes: Guest Artists
  Budget: $50,000 - $100,000
  Income Sources: Private Foundations/Grants/Endowments; Business/Corporate Donations; Government Grants; Individual Donations
  Season: 52 Weeks
  Affiliations: Association of Community Arts Agencies of Kansas

FACILITY

KANSAS STATE UNIVERSITY - MCCAIN AUDITORIUM
Manhattan, KS 66506
(913) 532-6425
FAX: (913) 532-7114
  Type of Facility: Performance Center
  Type of Stage: Flexible
  Stage Dimensions: 60'Wx36'D   **Orchestra Pit**
  Seating Capacity: 1,800
  Year Built: 1970   **Architect:** Canole & Hale; Wolfenbarger & McCulley
  Cost: $3,035,933
  Acoustical Consultant: Bolt, Beranek & Newman
  Contact for Rental: Richard P. Martin;   (913) 532-6425

McPherson

FACILITY

MCPHERSON COLLEGE - BROWN AUDITORIUM
1600 East Euclid, McPherson, KS 67460
(316) 241-0731
FAX: (316) 241-0731
Type of Facility: Concert Hall; Auditorium; Studio Performance; Theatre House
Type of Stage: Proscenium
Stage Dimensions: 40'Wx14'Dx19'H   **Orchestra Pit**
Seating Capacity: 1,224
Year Built: 1960   **Architect:** Mann & Company
Contact for Rental: Rick Tyler;   (316) 241-0731
Resident Groups: McPherson College Choir
Used for band concerts, theatre, community orchestras and convocations

Neodesha

FACILITY

NEODESHA ARTS ASSOCIATION
200 North Fifth Street, PO Box 65, Neodesha, KS 66757
(316) 325-3422
Founded: 1973
Type of Facility: Performance Center
Facility Originally: Church
Type of Stage: Proscenium
Seating Capacity: 150
Year Built: 1914
Year Remodeled: 1973
Manager: Zanada Overpeck, Director;   (316) 325-4322

Ottawa

FACILITY

OTTAWA MUNICIPAL AUDITORIUM
PO Box 452, Ottawa, KS 66067
(913) 242-8810
Type of Facility: Concert Hall; Auditorium; Performance Center; Theatre House; Multi-Purpose
Facility Originally: Opera House
Type of Stage: Proscenium
Stage Dimensions: 65'x40'   **Orchestra Pit**
Seating Capacity: 839
Year Built: 1919
Year Remodeled: 1978   **Architect:** Earl DeVore   **Cost:** $750,000
Contact for Rental: Dick Smith;   (913) 242-8810

Overland Park

DANCE

AMERICAN YOUTH BALLET
11728 Quivira Road, Shawnee Mission Area, Overland Park, KS 66210
(913) 451-9292
Founded: 1979
Arts Area: Modern; Mime; Ballet; Ethnic
Status: Non-Professional; Non-Profit
Type: Performing; Touring; Educational
Purpose: To establish an outlet for aspiring young dancers to learn, practice, and perform all forms of dance in a professional atmosphere
Management: Kathy and Dennis Landsman, Artistic Directors
Officers: Kathy Landsman, President; Dennis Landsman, Vice President; Linda Smith, Secretary; Elizabeth Eike, Treasurer
Paid Staff: 2   **Volunteer Staff:** 20

Non-Paid Artists: 27
Utilizes: Guest Artists; Guest Choreographers
Budget: $1,000 - $50,000
Income Sources: Private Foundations/Grants/Endowments; Business/Corporate Donations; Box Office; Individual Donations
Season: September - May   **Annual Attendance:** 6,000
Performance Facilities: Johnson County Community College Cultural Education Center

THEATRE

THE NEW THEATER COMPANY
9229 Foster, Overland Park, KS 66202
(913) 649-0103
Founded: 1992
Arts Area: Professional; Dinner
Status: Professional
Type: Performing
Management: Dennis D. Hennessy, Richard Carrothers, Executive Producers; Jay Kingwill, Associate Producer
Officers: Donn Miller, Vice President of Operations; Mary Hay, Vice President of Marketing; Cindy Beatty, Company Comptroller
Paid Staff: 10
Utilizes: Guest Artists
Budget: $1,000,000 - $5,000,000
Income Sources: Box Office
Season: 52 Weeks   **Annual Attendance:** 120,000
Performance Facilities: The New Theater Company

Pittsburg

FACILITY

MEMORIAL AUDITORIUM AND CONVENTION CENTER
503 North Pine, Pittsburg, KS 66762
(316) 231-7827
Type of Facility: Concert Hall; Auditorium; Theatre House; Civic Center; Multi-Purpose; Exhibition Hall
Type of Stage: Proscenium
Stage Dimensions: 90'Wx37'D   **Orchestra Pit**
Seating Capacity: 1,588
Year Built: 1925   **Architect:** Thomas W. Williamson   **Cost:** $262,450
Year Remodeled: 1983   **Architect:** Seidler, Owsley & Associates   **Cost:** $3,400,000
Acoustical Consultant: Coffeen, Anderson, Fricke & Associates
Contact for Rental: Pat Ashmore, Mariann David;   (316) 231-7827
Manager: Pat Ashmore, Supervisor
Resident Groups: Pittsburg Arts Council; Pittsburg Community Theater
Professional performances; art exhibits; meetings; and conventions

Prairie Village

INSTRUMENTAL MUSIC

YOUTH SYMPHONY OF KANSAS CITY
5209 West 83rd Street, Prairie Village, KS 66208
(913) 642-7141
FAX: (913) 642-6183
Founded: 1958
Arts Area: Symphony; Orchestra
Status: Non-Professional; Non-Profit
Type: Performing; Touring; Educational; Sponsoring
Purpose: To give talented young musicians of the Kansas City area an opportunity to perform standard symphonic literature; to encourage students to broaden the horizons of their own musicianship and to help them and their audiences to become truly appreciative listeners
Management: Carolyn Holtman, Business Manager; Dr. Glenn A. Block, Music Director/Conductor
Officers: John Schramm, President; Jan Ericson, Vice President; Marian Reeves, Secretary; Elaine Minden, Treasurer
Paid Staff: 4   **Volunteer Staff:** 40
Non-Paid Artists: 183
Utilizes: Guest Conductors; Guest Artists; Guest Directors
Budget: $50,000 - $100,000

Income Sources: Private Foundations/Grants/Endowments; Business/Corporate Donations; Box Office; Government Grants; Individual Donations
Season: November - May   **Annual Attendance:** 4,000
Affiliations: ASOL (Youth Orchestra Division); Missouri Citizens for the Arts
Performance Facilities: White Recital Hall, University of Missouri-Kansas City; Conservatory of Music

Salina

THEATRE

SALINA COMMUNITY THEATRE
303 East Iron, PO Box 2305, Salina, KS 67402
(913) 827-6126
Founded: 1960
Arts Area: Musical; Community; Theatrical Group
Status: Non-Professional; Non-Profit
Type: Performing; Sponsoring
Purpose: To provide entertainment for the community and recreation for volunteers who like to participate
Management: Charles Kephart, Managing Director
Officers: Jamie Hall, President; Jerry Hinrikus, Vice President; Pat Sampson, Treasurer
Paid Staff: 3   **Volunteer Staff:** 200
Non-Paid Artists: 50
Utilizes: Guest Artists; Guest Directors
Budget: $100,000 - $500,000
Income Sources: Private Foundations/Grants/Endowments; Business/Corporate Donations; Box Office; Government Grants; Individual Donations
Season: October - July   **Annual Attendance:** 12,000

FACILITY

SALINA BICENTENNIAL CENTER
PO Box 1727, Salina, KS 67402-1727
(913) 826-7200
FAX: (913) 826-7207
Type of Facility: Auditorium; Civic Center; Arena; Multi-Purpose
Type of Stage: Flexible; 3/4 Arena; Arena
Stage Dimensions: Flexible varies to 60'x40'
Seating Capacity: 8,000
Year Built: 1979   **Architect:** Bucher Willis & Ratliff   **Cost:** $6,500,000
Acoustical Consultant: McClellan Sound
Contact for Rental: Karen Fallis;   (913) 826-7200
Manager: Phil Shamoff;   (913) 826-7200

Shawnee Mission

THEATRE

THE BARN PLAYERS THEATRE
PO Box 12767, Shawnee Mission, KS 66282-2767
(913) 381-4004
Founded: 1956
Arts Area: Community; Theatrical Group
Status: Non-Profit
Type: Performing
Purpose: To promote artistic excellence through theatre; to produce community theatre productions; to encourage participation by interested persons; to promote theatre interest in the community
Management: Margaret Godfrey, Managing Director; Max Beatty, Artistic Director
Officers: Margaret Godfrey, President; Shirley Wagner, Vice President; Martha Coulter, Secretary
Volunteer Staff: 50
Utilizes: Special Technical Talent
Budget: $1,000 - $50,000
Income Sources: Business/Corporate Donations; Box Office; Individual Donations
Season: August - September   **Annual Attendance:** 1,000

Affiliations: Association of Kansas Theatres; AACT
Performance Facilities: Overland Theatre

THE SENIOR BARN PLAYERS
PO Box 12767, Shawnee Mission, KS 66212-2767
(913) 381-4004; (913) 681-8446
    Founded: 1977
    Arts Area: Community; Theatrical Group; One-Act Comedies
    Status: Non-Professional; Non-Profit
    Type: Performing; Touring
    Purpose: To perform one-act comedies from a repertoire of six plays as well as a variety show; to provide theatre opportunities for persons 55 or older
    Officers: Martha Coulter, Chairman; Russ Shepherd, Vice Chairman; Eleanor Tarson, Treasurer; Monte Woodruff, Secretary; Francis Moore, Manager of Office Volunteers
    Volunteer Staff: 20
    Non-Paid Artists: 45
    Utilizes: Volunteer Directors/Actors
    Budget: $1,000 - $50,000
    Income Sources: Private Foundations/Grants/Endowments; Booking Donations
    Season: September - June   **Annual Attendance:** 15,000

Topeka

INSTRUMENTAL MUSIC

TOPEKA JAZZ WORKSHOP
1725 South West Gage, Topeka, KS 66604
(913) 273-0186
    Founded: 1968
    Arts Area: Orchestra; Instrumental Group; Band
    Status: Non-Profit
    Type: Performing; Educational
    Purpose: To promote interest in jazz through sponsorship of concerts, clinics and scholarships
    Officers: James A. Monroe, President; Gerald L. Goodell, Secretary; Jim Parker, Treasurer
    Volunteer Staff: 18
    Paid Artists: 32   **Non-Paid Artists:** 57
    Utilizes: Guest Artists; Guest Directors
    Budget: $1,000 - $50,000
    Income Sources: Box Office
    Season: August - April   **Annual Attendance:** 2,000
    Performance Facilities: Topeka Civic Theatre

THEATRE

TOPEKA CIVIC THEATRE
534 1/2 North Kansas Avenue, Topeka, KS 66608
(913) 357-5213
FAX: (913) 357-0719
    Founded: 1936
    Arts Area: Musical; Dinner; Community
    Status: Non-Professional; Non-Profit
    Type: Performing
    Purpose: To stimulate, entertain, educate and serve our community; to provide opportunities for performance and development of theatrical skills
    Management: Michael Wainstein, Producing Artistic Director; Brett Landow, Business Manager; Donna Jenks, Box Office Manager
    Paid Staff: 5   **Volunteer Staff:** 200
    Non-Paid Artists: 100
    Utilizes: Guest Conductors; Guest Directors
    Budget: $500,000 - $1,000,000
    Income Sources: Business/Corporate Donations; Box Office; Individual Donations
    Season: 52 Weeks   **Annual Attendance:** 25,000
    Affiliations: AACT; Association of Kansas Theatres; Kansas Community Theatre Conference
    Performance Facilities: Topeka Civic Theatre

FACILITY

TOPEKA PERFORMING ARTS CENTER
214 East Eighth, Topeka, KS 66603
(913) 234-2787
FAX: (913) 295-3752
Founded: 1987
Type of Facility: Theatre Complex; Concert Hall; Performance Center; Civic Center; Multi-Purpose
Facility Originally: Arena
Type of Stage: Thrust; Proscenium
Stage Dimensions: 50'x35'; 50'x61' with Thrust   **Orchestra Pit**
Seating Capacity: 2,600
Year Built: 1939   **Architect:** Grist & Co.   **Cost:** $2,000,000
Year Remodeled: 1987   **Architect:** Bradley   **Cost:** $10,000,000
Acoustical Consultant: Coffeen
Contact for Rental: Morey Sullivan;   (913) 234-2787

Waterville

THEATRE

WATERVILLE SUMMER THEATRE CORPORATION
Waterville, KS 66548
(913) 785-2323
Founded: 1973
Arts Area: Community; Theatrical Group
Status: Non-Professional; Non-Profit
Type: Performing
Purpose: To bring live theater to a small Kansas community
Officers: Yvonne Larson, President; Eunice Larson, Secretary/Treasurer
Budget: $1,000 - $50,000
Income Sources: Private Foundations/Grants/Endowments; Box Office
Season: May - September   **Annual Attendance:** 2,500
Affiliations: Association of Kansas Theatres
Performance Facilities: Waterville Opera House

FACILITY

WATERVILLE OPERA HOUSE
204 East Front Street, Waterville, KS 66548
(913) 785-2766
Type of Facility: Opera House
Type of Stage: Platform
Stage Dimensions: 22'x36'   **Orchestra Pit**
Seating Capacity: 340
Year Built: 1903   **Cost:** $7,000
Contact for Rental: City of Waterville;   (913) 785-2367
Manager: Beverly Roepke;   (913) 785-2766
Resident Groups: Waterville Summer Theatre Corporation
Owned by the city of Waterville

Wichita

INSTRUMENTAL MUSIC

WICHITA SYMPHONY
Century II Concert Hall, 225 West Douglas, Wichita, KS 67202
(316) 267-5259
FAX: (316) 267-1937
Founded: 1944
Arts Area: Symphony; Orchestra; Chamber
Status: Professional; Non-Profit
Type: Performing; Touring; Educational; Sponsoring
Management: Mitchell Berman, General Manager; Meistro Zouhuang Chen, Music Director/Conductor
Paid Staff: 10   **Volunteer Staff:** 400

Paid Artists: 86
Utilizes: Guest Artists
Income Sources: Private Foundations/Grants/Endowments; Business/Corporate Donations; Box Office; Government Grants; Individual Donations
Season: October - April   Annual Attendance: 250,000
Affiliations: ASOL; Wichita Arts Council; Kansas Arts Council
Performance Facilities: Century II Concert Hall

WICHITA YOUTH ORCHESTRA
Century II Concert Hall, 225 West Douglas, Wichita, KS 67202
(316) 267-5259
Founded: 1947
Arts Area: Symphony; Orchestra; Ensemble
Status: Non-Professional; Non-Profit
Type: Performing; Educational
Management: Ann Trechak, Manager; Steve Luttrell, Conductor of Youth Symphony; Gary Burrow, Conductor of Repertory Orchestra
Paid Staff: 6
Non-Paid Artists: 200
Season: November - March   Annual Attendance: 3,000
Affiliations: Wichita Symphony; ASOL (Youth Orchestra Division)
Performance Facilities: Century II Concert Hall

THEATRE

WICHITA COMMUNITY THEATRE
258 North Fountain, Wichita, KS 67208
(316) 686-1282
Founded: 1946
Arts Area: Theatrical Group
Status: Non-Professional; Non-Profit
Type: Performing
Purpose: To provide a wide variety of theatrical entertainment to the community; to provide opportunities for theatre performers and technicians at the amateur level
Management: Scott Marshall, Business Manager
Officers: Dr. R.L. Sifford, President; Betty Johnston, Vice President; Ed Francis, Treasurer
Paid Staff: 2   Volunteer Staff: 1
Paid Artists: 1
Utilizes: Guest Artists
Budget: $50,000 - $100,000
Income Sources: Private Foundations/Grants/Endowments; Business/Corporate Donations; Box Office; Individual Donations
Season: 52 Weeks   Annual Attendance: 12,000
Affiliations: Association of Kansas Theatres
Performance Facilities: Century II Civic Center; Workshop

PERFORMING SERIES

MUSIC THEATRE OF WICHITA
225 West Douglas, Suite 202, Wichita, KS 67202
(316) 265-3253
FAX: (316) 265-8708
Founded: 1971
Arts Area: Theater
Status: Professional; Non-Profit
Type: Performing; Educational
Management: Wayne Bryan, Producing Director
Paid Staff: 3   Volunteer Staff: 150
Paid Artists: 160   Non-Paid Artists: 50
Budget: $500,000 - $1,000,000
Income Sources: Private Foundations/Grants/Endowments; Business/Corporate Donations; Box Office; Government Grants; Individual Donations
Season: June - August   Annual Attendance: 54,000
Affiliations: Association of Kansas Theatres; Kansas Arts Council
Performance Facilities: Century II Concert Hall

FACILITY

CENTURY II CIVIC CENTER
225 West Douglas Avenue, Wichita, KS 67202
(316) 264-9121
Founded: 1969
Type of Facility: Theatre Complex; Concert Hall; Theatre House; Civic Center; Multi-Purpose
Type of Stage: Proscenium
Seating Capacity: See separate listings
Year Built: 1969   **Architect:** Varenhorst   **Cost:** $15,000,000
Acoustical Consultant: Coffeen & Associates
Contact for Rental: Judy Eggleston;   (316) 264-9121
Resident Groups: Wichita Symphony; Music Theatre of Wichita; Wichita Community Theatre; Wichita Children's Theatre; Music Theatre for Young People; Metro Ballet
The Century II Civic Center contains the Concert Hall, Convention Hall, Exhibition Hall and Theatre. See separate listings for further information.

CENTURY II CIVIC CENTER - CONCERT HALL
225 West Douglas Avenue, Wichita, KS 67202
(316) 264-9121
Type of Facility: Concert Hall; Civic Center
Type of Stage: Proscenium
Stage Dimensions: 60'Wx29'Hx49'D   **Orchestra Pit**
Seating Capacity: 2,187
Year Built: 1969
Acoustical Consultant: Coffeen & Associates
Contact for Rental: Judy Eggleston;   (316) 264-9121
Manager: James Hess;   (316) 264-9121
Resident Groups: Wichita Symphony; Music Theatre of Wichita; Metropolitan Ballet

CENTURY II CIVIC CENTER - CONVENTION HALL
225 West Douglas Avenue, Wichita, KS 67202
(316) 264-9121
Type of Facility: Auditorium; Civic Center
Type of Stage: Proscenium
Stage Dimensions: 60'Wx29'Hx33'D
Seating Capacity: 5,244
Year Built: 1969
Acoustical Consultant: Coffeen & Associates
Contact for Rental: Judy Eggleston;   (316) 264-9121
Manager: James Hess;   (316) 264-9121

CENTURY II CIVIC CENTER - EXHIBITION HALL
225 West Douglas Avenue, Wichita, KS 67202
(316) 264-9121
Type of Facility: Civic Center; Exhibition Hall
Type of Stage: Platform
Stage Dimensions: 60'Wx30'D
Seating Capacity: Banquet style - 2,400
Year Built: 1986   **Architect:** Schaeffer & Associates
Contact for Rental: Judy Eggleston;   (316) 264-9121
Manager: James Hess;   (316) 264-9121
Resident Groups: Wichita Theatre Organ

CENTURY II CIVIC CENTER - THEATRE
225 West Douglas Avenue, Wichita, KS 67202
(316) 264-9121
Type of Facility: Theatre House
Type of Stage: Proscenium
Stage Dimensions: 72'Wx40'Dx30'H   **Orchestra Pit**
Seating Capacity: 661
Year Built: 1969
Acoustical Consultant: Coffeen & Associates
Contact for Rental: Judy Eggleston;   (316) 264-9121
Resident Groups: Wichita Community Theatre; Wichita Children's Theatre; Music Theatre for Young People

KENTUCKY

Anchorage

THEATRE

ANCHOR THEATRE
PO Box 23545, Anchorage, KY 40223
(502) 245-4327
> **Founded:** 1984
> **Arts Area:** Community; Theatrical Group
> **Status:** Non-Professional; Non-Profit
> **Type:** Performing; Sponsoring
> **Purpose:** To produce non-musical plays in the theatre; to tour with small casts to local nursing homes and country clubs; to sponsor the Producer's Review
> **Officers:** William J. Aiken, President; Anne Rives, Vice President
> **Volunteer Staff:** 11
> **Non-Paid Artists:** 59
> **Utilizes:** Special Technical Talent; Guest Directors
> **Budget:** $1,000 - $50,000
> **Income Sources:** Private Foundations/Grants/Endowments; Business/Corporate Donations; Box Office; Government Grants; Individual Donations
> **Season:** August - December   **Annual Attendance:** 4,000

Ashland

FACILITY

PARAMOUNT ARTS CENTER
1300 Winchester Avenue, Ashland, KY 41101
(606) 324-3175
> **Founded:** 1972
> **Type of Facility:** Performance Center
> **Facility Originally:** Movie House
> **Type of Stage:** Thrust; Proscenium
> **Stage Dimensions:** 45'x22'
> **Seating Capacity:** 1,308
> **Year Built:** 1931   **Cost:** $450,000
> **Year Remodeled:** 1976   **Architect:** Alan Schatz
> **Acoustical Consultant:** David Portugal
> **Contact for Rental:** Panda Powell;   (606) 324-3175
> **Manager:** Kathleen L. Timmons, Executive Director;   (606) 324-2441
> **Resident Groups:** Ashland Youth Ballet; Backstage Players

Bardstown

PERFORMING SERIES

STEPHEN FOSTER DRAMA ASSOCIATION
US 150 East, PO Box 546, Bardstown, KY 40004
(502) 348-5971; (800) 626-1563
> **Founded:** 1959
> **Arts Area:** Dance; Vocal Music; Theater
> **Status:** Professional; Semi-Professional; Non-Profit
> **Type:** Performing
> **Purpose:** To foster cultural activities in the area
> **Management:** Carlene Offutt, General Manager; Scott Ray, Director/Choreographer; David Brown, Musical Director
> **Officers:** John S. Kelley, Chairman; Donald Busick, Vice Chairman
> **Paid Staff:** 76   **Volunteer Staff:** 50
> **Paid Artists:** 53
> **Utilizes:** Special Technical Talent; Guest Artists
> **Budget:** $500,000 - $1,000,000
> **Income Sources:** Box Office
> **Season:** June - September   **Annual Attendance:** 75,000
> **Performance Facilities:** J. Dan Talbott Amphitheatre

Berea

FACILITY

PHELPS - STOKES AUDITORIUM
Berea College Campus, Berea, KY 40404
(606) 986-9341
> **Founded:** 1904
> **Type of Facility:** Concert Hall; Auditorium; Multi-Purpose
> **Type of Stage:** Platform
> **Stage Dimensions:** 16'6"x36'10"
> **Seating Capacity:** 1,585
> **Year Built:** 1904
> **Contact for Rental:** Office of Special Programs;   (606) 986-9341, ext. 6830

Bowling Green

INSTRUMENTAL MUSIC

BOWLING GREEN-WESTERN SYMPHONY ORCHESTRA
416 East Main Street, Bowling Green, KY 42101
(502) 745-3751
> **Founded:** 1982
> **Arts Area:** Symphony; Orchestra; Chamber
> **Status:** Semi-Professional; Non-Profit
> **Type:** Performing; Resident; Educational
> **Purpose:** To provide classical music for the people of southern Kentucky
> **Management:** Christopher Norton, Music Director/Conductor
> **Officers:** Jack Haberkorn, President
> **Volunteer Staff:** 25
> **Paid Artists:** 22   **Non-Paid Artists:** 35
> **Utilizes:** Guest Artists
> **Budget:** $1,000 - $50,000
> **Income Sources:** Private Foundations/Grants/Endowments; Business/Corporate Donations; Box Office; Government Grants; Individual Donations
> **Season:** September - April   **Annual Attendance:** 3,500
> **Affiliations:** ASOL
> **Performance Facilities:** Van Meter Auditorium

THEATRE

FOUNTAIN SQUARE PLAYERS
416 East Main Street, Bowling Green, KY 42101
(502) 782-2787
> **Founded:** 1978
> **Arts Area:** Community; Theatrical Group
> **Status:** Non-Professional; Non-Profit
> **Type:** Performing
> **Purpose:** To provide for the production, appreciation and enjoyment of all phases of the theatre outside of and in addition to that provided by our school systems
> **Officers:** Jerry Wallace, President; Whit Crawford, Secretary; William B. Russell, Treasurer; Pat Sprouse, Membership
> **Volunteer Staff:** 50
> **Non-Paid Artists:** 150
> **Budget:** $1,000 - $50,000
> **Income Sources:** Box Office; Individual Donations; Program Advertisements
> **Season:** October - August   **Annual Attendance:** 7,000
> **Affiliations:** AAA
> **Performance Facilities:** Capitol Arts Center

PERFORMING SERIES

BG-WC ARTS COMMISSION
416 East Main, Bowling Green, KY 42101
(502) 782-2787
FAX: (502) 782-2804
> **Founded:** 1979
> **Arts Area:** Dance; Vocal Music; Instrumental Music; Theater; Festivals

Status: Non-Profit
Type: Educational; Sponsoring; Rental
Purpose: To provide a regional arts center for the performing and visual arts
Management: Martha A. Hills, Executive Director; Ginger Cleary, Marketing Director; Stephanie Stottman, Program Director; Ace Raymond, Technical Director; Janice Renusch, Office Manager
Officers: Jeane Robertson, President; Michael Bachmann, Vice President; John Grider, Treasurer; Regina Newell, Secretary; Jerry Martin, Parliamentarian
Paid Staff: 6 **Volunteer Staff:** 22
Utilizes: Guest Artists
Budget: $500,000 - $1,000,000
Income Sources: Private Foundations/Grants/Endowments; Business/Corporate Donations; Box Office; Government Grants; Individual Donations
Season: September - May **Annual Attendance:** 7,800
Performance Facilities: Capitol Arts Center

FACILITY

CAPITOL ARTS CENTER
416 East Main Street, Bowling Green, KY 42101
(502) 782-2787
FAX: (502) 782-2804
Type of Facility: Performance Center
Facility Originally: Vaudeville
Type of Stage: Proscenium
Stage Dimensions: 45'2"Wx37'8"D; 29'3"Wx20'H proscenium opening **Orchestra Pit**
Seating Capacity: 850
Year Built: 1900
Year Remodeled: 1981 **Architect:** William G. Moore Jr. **Cost:** $1,300,000
Contact for Rental: Janice Renusch; (502) 782-2787
Resident Groups: Fountain Square Players

Danville

THEATRE

PIONEER PLAYHOUSE OF KENTUCKY
Danville, KY 40422
(606) 236-2747
Founded: 1950
Arts Area: Professional; Summer Stock; Musical; Dinner
Status: Professional; Non-Profit
Type: Performing; Resident; Educational
Purpose: To maintain an arts center for vocational training using professionals as teachers and performers
Management: Colonel Eben Henson, Founder/Producer
Officers: Colonel Eben Henson, President; Charlotte Henson, Vice President/Secretary
Paid Staff: 10 **Volunteer Staff:** 20
Paid Artists: 25 **Non-Paid Artists:** 30
Budget: $100,000 - $500,000
Income Sources: Box Office; Government Grants
Season: 52 Weeks
Affiliations: SETC; Kentucky Theatre Association
Performance Facilities: Colonel Eben Henson Amphitheatre

FACILITY

NORTON CENTER FOR THE ARTS
Centre College, Danville, KY 40422
(606) 236-4692
FAX: (606) 236-9610
Founded: 1973
Type of Facility: Theatre Complex; Auditorium
Type of Stage: Thrust; Proscenium
Stage Dimensions: 50'x40' proscenium; 30'x30' thrust **Orchestra Pit**
Seating Capacity: 1,440; 360
Year Built: 1973 **Architect:** William Wesley Peters **Cost:** $8,000,000
Acoustical Consultant: Vern O. Knudson
Contact for Rental: Alice Davis; (606) 236-4692
Resident Groups: Centre College Music and Theatre Performing Groups

---

Falmouth

THEATRE

KINCAID REGIONAL THEATRE
211 West Shelby Street, PO Box 208, Falmouth, KY 41040
(800) 647-7409; (606) 654-2636
FAX: (606) 654-6143
   Founded: 1983
   Arts Area: Professional; Musical; Theatrical Group
   Status: Professional; Non-Profit
   Type: Performing; Resident; Educational; Sponsoring
   Purpose: To offer quality entertainment and employ talented actors and technicians from the region (northern Kentucky, southwestern Ohio and southeastern Indiana)
   Management: Charles Kondek, Artistic Director; Terry Lee Stump, Production Manager; Bob Myers, Musical Director; Linda Dietrich, Public Relations
   Officers: Patsy Hampton, Chairman; Julia McClanahan, Vice Chairman; Clifford Wallace, Secretary/Treasurer
   Paid Staff: 30   **Volunteer Staff:** 100
   Paid Artists: 50
   Utilizes: Special Technical Talent; Guest Conductors; Guest Artists; Guest Directors
   Budget: $100,000 - $500,000
   Income Sources: Private Foundations/Grants/Endowments; Business/Corporate Donations; Box Office; Government Grants; Individual Donations
   Season: June - September   **Annual Attendance:** 14,000
   Affiliations: SETC
   Performance Facilities: Falmouth Auditorium

Georgetown

THEATRE

GEORGETOWN CHILDREN'S THEATRE
Georgetown College, PO Box 258, Georgetown, KY 40324
(502) 863-8162
   Founded: 1985
   Arts Area: Theatrical Group
   Status: Non-Profit
   Type: Performing
   Purpose: To promote interest in drama and opportunities to participate in theatre to local children
   Officers: George J. McGee Jr., President; Margaret Greynolds, Vice President; Cathy McGee, Secretary
   Volunteer Staff: 10
   Paid Artists: 3   **Non-Paid Artists:** 30
   Budget: $1,000 - $50,000
   Income Sources: Private Foundations/Grants/Endowments; Box Office; Government Grants
   Annual Attendance: 4,000
   Affiliations: SETC
   Performance Facilities: Hill Chapel

Glasgow

THEATRE

THE FAR-OFF BROADWAY PLAYERS
2110 Hall Street, Glasgow, KY 42141
(502) 651-8612
   Founded: 1980
   Arts Area: Community; Theatrical Group
   Status: Non-Professional; Non-Profit
   Type: Performing; Resident
   Purpose: To study and perform amateur drama
   Officers: Eve Harris, President; Louise Bachelor, Vice President; Pat Hazelip, Secretary; Phillip Patton, Treasurer
   Non-Paid Artists: 40
   Income Sources: Business/Corporate Donations; Box Office; Individual Donations

---

Greenville

THEATRE

MUHLENBERG COMMUNITY THEATRE
PO Box 505, Greenville, KY 42345
(502) 754-1935
Founded: 1980
Arts Area: Professional; Musical; Dinner; Community; Theatrical Group
Status: Semi-Professional; Non-Profit
Type: Performing; Touring; Resident; Educational
Purpose: To provide and promote the theatrical arts
Management: Karen Willis, Managing Director
Officers: Larry Willis, President; David Eplett, Vice President; Karen Willis, Secretary; Terry Jessup, Treasurer
Volunteer Staff: 10
Non-Paid Artists: 20
Utilizes: Special Technical Talent; Guest Conductors; Guest Directors
Budget: $1,000 - $50,000
Income Sources: Business/Corporate Donations; Box Office; Government Grants; Individual Donations
Season: 52 Weeks **Annual Attendance:** 1,600
Affiliations: AACT
Performance Facilities: Palace Theatre

Hopkinsville

THEATRE

COMMUNITY PLAYERS
30-B Pennyrile, Hopkinsville, KY 42240
(502) 886-5455
Founded: 1977
Arts Area: Community; Theatrical Group
Status: Non-Professional; Non-Profit
Type: Performing
Purpose: To bring current Broadway shows to the Hopkinsville community
Management: Paulette Stamps, Director; Shirley Shelton, Assistant Director
Officers: Linda Torain Pearson, NingPing Brooks, Sarah Nance, James Jordon, Hugh Northington, Thelma Moore, Lillian Boyd, Board Members
Volunteer Staff: 36
Non-Paid Artists: 36
Utilizes: Guest Directors
Budget: $1,000 - $50,000
Income Sources: Private Foundations/Grants/Endowments; Government Grants
Season: Fall - Spring **Annual Attendance:** 400
Performance Facilities: Alhambra Theatre

PENNYRILE PLAYERS
2007 South Main, Hopkinsville, KY 42240
(502) 885-2401
Founded: 1972
Arts Area: Musical; Dinner; Community; Theatrical Group; Puppet
Status: Non-Profit
Type: Performing; Touring; Resident; Educational; Sponsoring
Purpose: To provide live theatrical entertainment while helping to develop and promote the talents of an ever-growing group of participants in theatre arts
Management: Marjanna J. Frising, Producer; Juanita Peacock, Artistic Director; Tim Meredith, Building Security; Rhea Kidd, Technical Director
Officers: Kat Peterson, President; Connie Sloan, Vice President; Marjanna J. Frising, Secretary/Treasurer
Volunteer Staff: 5
Utilizes: Special Technical Talent; Guest Artists; Guest Directors
Budget: $1,000 - $50,000
Income Sources: Private Foundations/Grants/Endowments; Business/Corporate Donations; Box Office; Government Grants; Individual Donations
Season: 52 Weeks
Affiliations: Kentucky Arts Council

Horse Cave

THEATRE

HORSE CAVE THEATRE
107-109 Main Street, PO Box 215, Horse Cave, KY 42749
(502) 786-1200; (800) 342-2177
    Founded: 1977
    Arts Area: Professional; Theatrical Group
    Status: Professional; Non-Profit
    Type: Performing; Touring; Resident; Educational
    Purpose: To be the only resident professional theater outside of metropolitan Louisville that provides a forum for Kentucky writers to produce their works; to present an annual Shakespeare production that assists in meeting the needs of students where schools cannot
    Management: Warren Hammack, Director; Pamela White, Associate Director
    Officers: Carol Glaser, Board President
    Paid Staff: 5
    Paid Artists: 25
    Utilizes: Special Technical Talent; Guest Artists; Guest Directors
    Budget: $100,000 - $500,000
    Income Sources: Private Foundations/Grants/Endowments; Business/Corporate Donations; Box Office; Government Grants; Individual Donations
    Season: July - August   **Annual Attendance:** 14,000
    Affiliations: AEA; TCG; Kentucky Arts Council
    Performance Facilities: Horse Cave Theatre

Lexington

DANCE

LEXINGTON BALLET
161 North Mill Street, Lexington, KY 40507
(606) 233-3925; (606) 257-4929
FAX: (606) 255-2787
    Founded: 1974
    Arts Area: Ballet
    Status: Semi-Professional; Non-Profit
    Type: Performing; Resident
    Purpose: To offer a variety of presentations in contemporary and classical dance; to educate with a strong emphasis on classical ballet
    Management: Karl Kaufman, Artistic Director; Rosemary Miles, Associate Artistic Director; Sylvia Grace, Executive Director
    Officers: David Smith Jr., President, Board of Directors
    Paid Artists: 2   **Non-Paid Artists:** 16
    Utilizes: Guest Artists; Guest Choreographers
    Budget: $100,000 - $500,000
    Income Sources: Private Foundations/Grants/Endowments; Business/Corporate Donations; Box Office; Individual Donations
    Season: October - May
    Performance Facilities: The Opera House

INSTRUMENTAL MUSIC

LEXINGTON PHILHARMONIC SOCIETY
161 North Mill Street, Lexington, KY 40507
(606) 233-4226
    Arts Area: Symphony; Chamber; Ensemble
    Status: Non-Profit
    Type: Performing
    Purpose: To provide entertainment for the local community
    Management: George Zack, Music Director; Barry Auman, Executive Director
    Income Sources: Private Foundations/Grants/Endowments; Business/Corporate Donations; Box Office; Government Grants; Individual Donations
    Performance Facilities: Singletary Center for the Arts

THEATRE

LEXINGTON CHILDREN'S THEATRE
161 North Mill Street, Lexington, KY 40507
(606) 254-4546
Founded: 1938
Arts Area: Professional; Theatrical Group
Status: Professional; Non-Profit
Type: Performing; Touring; Resident; Educational
Purpose: To provide professional-quality theatrical experiences and education to the young people of Kentucky at affordable prices
Management: Larry E. Snipes, Producing Director; Ronald K. Shull, General Manager; Vivian Robin Snipes, Production Manager
Officers: Michelle Gardner, President; Lorie Morgan, President Elect; Kim Knight, Secretary; Tracy Rivette, Treasurer
Paid Staff: 6
Paid Artists: 19
Utilizes: Guest Artists; Guest Directors
Budget: $100,000 - $500,000
Income Sources: Private Foundations/Grants/Endowments; Business/Corporate Donations; Box Office; Government Grants; Individual Donations; Tuition
Season: September - May   **Annual Attendance:** 40,000
Affiliations: AATY; SETC; Kentucky Theatre Association
Performance Facilities: Lexington Opera House; Arts Place

FACILITY

LEXINGTON OPERA HOUSE
c/o Lexington Center, 430 West Vine, Lexington, KY 40507
(606) 233-4567
Founded: 1886
Type of Facility: Theatre House; Opera House
Type of Stage: Proscenium
Stage Dimensions: 45'x37'x30'   **Orchestra Pit**
Seating Capacity: 1,100
Year Built: 1887   **Architect:** Cobb of Chicago
Year Remodeled: 1976   **Architect:** James Ross
Contact for Rental: Manager;   (606) 233-4567
Resident Groups: Lexington Ballet; Lexington Children's Theatre; Lexington Musical Theatre

OTIS A. SINGLETARY CENTER FOR THE ARTS
University of Kentucky, Lexington, KY 40502-0241
(606) 257-1706
FAX: (606) 257-1433
Founded: 1979
Type of Facility: Concert Hall; Performance Center; Recital Hall
Type of Stage: Proscenium
Stage Dimensions: 74'x50'   **Orchestra Pit**
Seating Capacity: Concert Hall - 1,500; Recital Hall - 392
Year Built: 1979   **Architect:** Johnson/Romanowitz Architect   **Cost:** $6,300,000
Acoustical Consultant: Paul S. Veneklasen
Contact for Rental: Holly Salisbury;   (606) 257-1706
Resident Groups: Lexington Philharmonic Orchestra; Central Kentucky Youth Orchestra; University of Kentucky School of Music Ensembles; Chamber Music Society; The Guitar Society; The Lexington Singers

TRANSYLVANIA UNIVERSITY
300 North Broadway, Lexington, KY 40508
(606) 233-8141
Type of Facility: Auditorium; Performance Center
Type of Stage: Thrust; Proscenium
Stage Dimensions: Haggin Auditorium & Carrick Theatre - 87'x32'; Coleman Recital Hall - 35'x18'
Seating Capacity: Haggin Auditorium - 1,050; Carrick Theatre - 300; Coleman Recital Hall - 172
Year Built: 1969   **Architect:** John T. Gillig   **Cost:** $2,800,000
Contact for Rental: Devon Query;   (606) 233-8141
Includes Haggin Auditorium, Carrick Theatre and Coleman Recital Hall

London

PERFORMING SERIES

SUE BENNETT COLLEGE, APPALACHIAN FOLK FESTIVAL
151 College Street, London, KY 40741
(606) 864-2238
FAX: (606) 864-8475
    Founded: 1973
    Arts Area: Vocal Music; Festivals
    Status: Non-Profit
    Type: Performing; Educational
    Purpose: To preserve Appalachian cultural heritage, music, folklore and arts and crafts
    Management: Madge Chestnut, Chairperson
    Officers: Linda Mathies, Jan Mayes, Co-Chairs, Arts and Crafts Show
    Volunteer Staff: 20
    Paid Artists: 12
    Utilizes: Guest Artists
    Budget: $1,000 - $50,000
    Income Sources: Private Foundations/Grants/Endowments; Sue Bennett College
    Season: April   **Annual Attendance:** 3,000
    Performance Facilities: Sue Bennett College Auditorium

Louisville

DANCE

GENESIS ARTS/KENTUCKY INC.
3726 West Broadway, Louisville, KY 40211
(502) 776-5715
    Founded: 1984
    Arts Area: Modern; Ballet; Jazz; Ethnic; Tap
    Status: Professional; Non-Profit
    Type: Performing; Resident; Educational; Sponsoring
    Purpose: To promote cultural enterprises presented by minorities; to provide disadvantaged children and youth with an avenue to artistic expression and dance through theatre arts, creative writing, boys choir and art
    Management: Dolores White, Executive Director
    Officers: Vadra Henderson, President; Patricia E. Tobin, Secretary; Susan Post; Richard Beal
    Volunteer Staff: 3
    Paid Artists: 4   **Non-Paid Artists:** 3
    Utilizes: Special Technical Talent; Guest Artists; Guest Choreographers
    Budget: $1,000 - $50,000
    Income Sources: Private Foundations/Grants/Endowments; Business/Corporate Donations; Box Office; Government Grants; Individual Donations
    Season: 52 Weeks   **Annual Attendance:** 900
    Performance Facilities: First Unitarian Church; Kathrine Spalding Auditorium; R.E. Jones United Methodist Church

LOUISVILLE BALLET
1300 Bardstown Road, Louisville, KY 40204
(502) 456-4520
    Founded: 1952
    Arts Area: Modern; Ballet; Jazz
    Status: Professional; Non-Profit
    Type: Performing; Touring; Resident; Educational; Sponsoring
    Purpose: To bring high-quality professional dance to a broad audience
    Management: Debra Humes Hoffer, Executive Director; Alan Jones, Artistic Director
    Paid Staff: 8 **Volunteer Staff:** 200
    Paid Artists: 40   **Non-Paid Artists:** 120
    Utilizes: Special Technical Talent; Guest Conductors; Guest Artists; Guest Directors
    Budget: $1,000,000 - $5,000,000
    Income Sources: Private Foundations/Grants/Endowments; Business/Corporate Donations; Box Office; Government Grants; Individual Donations
    Season: August - May   **Annual Attendance:** 65,000
    Affiliations: Dance USA; SERBA
    Performance Facilities: Kentucky Center For The Arts

INSTRUMENTAL MUSIC

KENTUCKY CENTER CHAMBER PLAYERS
c/o Kentucky Center For The Arts, 5 Riverfront Plaza, Louisville, KY 40202
(502) 584-7777; (502) 893-0052
Founded: 1984
Arts Area: Chamber
Status: Professional; Non-Profit
Type: Performing; Touring
Purpose: To present a mixed instrumental ensemble performing traditional and unusual works
Management: Kentucky Center For The Arts
Officers: Joanna Goldstein, President
Utilizes: Guest Artists
Budget: $1,000 - $50,000
Income Sources: Private Foundations/Grants/Endowments; Business/Corporate Donations; Box Office; Individual Donations
Season: September - April   **Annual Attendance:** 1,000
Performance Facilities: University of Louisville; Kentucky Center For The Arts

LOUISVILLE BACH SOCIETY
4607 Hanford Lane, Louisville, KY 40207
(502) 893-7954
Founded: 1964
Arts Area: Orchestra; Choral
Status: Non-Profit
Type: Performing; Touring; Resident; Educational
Purpose: To perform choral and orchestral music of Bach, with other baroque, modern, classical and romantic composers also emphasized
Management: Melvin Dickinson, Musical Director
Officers: Michele Wiggins, President; Tom Diener, Vice President; Robert Myers, Secretary; Milton Moore, Treasurer
Paid Staff: 4   **Volunteer Staff:** 80
Paid Artists: 12   **Non-Paid Artists:** 80
Utilizes: Guest Artists
Budget: $50,000 - $100,000
Income Sources: Private Foundations/Grants/Endowments; Business/Corporate Donations; Box Office; Government Grants; Individual Donations
Season: October - June   **Annual Attendance:** 10,000
Affiliations: Kentucky Arts Council; Greater Louisville Fund for the Arts; AFM
Performance Facilities: University of Louisville

THE LOUISVILLE ORCHESTRA
611 West Main Street, Louisville, KY 40202
(502) 587-8681
FAX: (502) 589-7870
Founded: 1937
Arts Area: Symphony; Orchestra; Chamber
Status: Professional; Non-Profit
Type: Performing; Touring; Educational; Sponsoring
Purpose: To bring the finest orchestral music to our region; to provide an educational resource; to maintain our own recording company that commissions, performs and records new music for our time
Management: Wayne S. Brown, Executive Director; Nora Steinschulte, Director of Public Affairs; Lawrence Leighton Smith, Music Director/Conductor; Albert George, Resident Conductor
Paid Staff: 15   **Volunteer Staff:** 600
Paid Artists: 90
Utilizes: Special Technical Talent; Guest Conductors; Guest Artists
Budget: $1,000,000 - $5,000,000
Income Sources: Private Foundations/Grants/Endowments; Business/Corporate Donations; Box Office; Government Grants; Individual Donations
Season: September - May; June - July   **Annual Attendance:** 180,000
Affiliations: ASOL; AAA; Greater Louisville Fund for the Arts
Performance Facilities: Whitney Hall; Macauley Auditorium; Louisville Gardens; Louisville Zoo

LOUISVILLE YOUTH ORCHESTRA
623 West Main, Louisville, KY 40208
(502) 582-0135
FAX: (502) 582-0149
Founded: 1958
Arts Area: Orchestra

Status: Non-Profit
Type: Performing; Educational
Purpose: To offer a high-quality musical experience to youngsters ages 8-21
Management: Daniel Spurlock, Music Director; Melody Welsh, Executive Director
Officers: Paul Shoemaker, President; Ken Weissteck, Vice President; Jerri Barnsteable, Secretary; Rodney Henderson, Treasurer
Paid Staff: 7   **Volunteer Staff:** 30
Utilizes: Guest Conductors; Guest Artists
Budget: $50,000 - $100,000
Income Sources: Private Foundations/Grants/Endowments; Business/Corporate Donations; Box Office; Government Grants; Individual Donations
Season: September - May   **Annual Attendance:** 10,000
Affiliations: Greater Louisville Fund for the Arts; Youth Performing Arts Council
Performance Facilities: Youth Performing Arts Center

VOCAL MUSIC

KENTUCKY OPERA
631 South Fifth Street, Louisville, KY 40202
(502) 584-4500
FAX: (502) 584-7484
Founded: 1952
Arts Area: Grand Opera; Lyric Opera; Light Opera; Operetta
Status: Professional; Non-Profit
Type: Performing; Touring; Educational
Purpose: To provide quality opera
Management: Thomson Smillie, General Director; Mary Ann Krebs, Executive Director
Officers: Mrs. Charles C. Boyer, Chairman of the Board; John Bridgendall, President; Ronald J. Murphy, Stephen T. Bow, Vice Presidents; Mrs. John Holtman, Secretary; Garrison Cox, Treasurer
Paid Staff: 17   **Volunteer Staff:** 300
Paid Artists: 600   **Non-Paid Artists:** 200
Utilizes: Special Technical Talent; Guest Conductors; Guest Artists; Guest Directors
Budget: $1,000,000 - $5,000,000
Income Sources: Private Foundations/Grants/Endowments; Business/Corporate Donations; Box Office; Government Grants; Individual Donations; Fundraising
Season: October - May   **Annual Attendance:** 25,000
Affiliations: OA
Performance Facilities: Kentucky Center for the Arts; Macauley Theatre

THE LOUISVILLE CHORUS
204 Breckinridge Lane, Louisville, KY 40207
(502) 895-7070
Founded: 1939
Arts Area: Choral
Status: Semi-Professional; Non-Profit
Type: Performing; Touring; Educational; Sponsoring
Purpose: To foster the art of vocal music; to provide a high-quality musical experience, representing a wide variety of styles from the Renaissance to the present
Management: Daniel Spurlock, Music Director; Therese Davis, Managing Director
Officers: Lester Blank, President Board of Directors; Rebecca Greenwell, Secretary; Jena Tippin, Treasurer
Paid Staff: 2   **Volunteer Staff:** 3
Utilizes: Guest Conductors; Guest Artists
Income Sources: Private Foundations/Grants/Endowments; Business/Corporate Donations; Box Office; Individual Donations; Guest Appearances
Season: August - June   **Annual Attendance:** 90,000
Affiliations: Community and State Arts Councils
Performance Facilities: Kentucky Center for the Arts

THEATRE

ACTORS THEATRE OF LOUISVILLE
316-320 West Main Street, Louisville, KY 40202-4218
(502) 584-1265
FAX: (502) 561-3300
Founded: 1964
Arts Area: Professional
Status: Professional; Non-Profit
Type: Performing; Resident

Purpose: To present top-quality professional entertainment to as wide an audience as possible at reasonable prices and at the same time operate in a fiscally responsible manner
Management: Jon Jory, Producing Director; Alexander Speer, Executive Director; Marilee Hebert-Slater, Associate Director
Officers: Caldwell R. Willig, President; Neville Blakemore Jr., Vice President; David W. Hughes, Treasurer; Rande Nortof Swann, Secretary
Paid Staff: 45
Paid Artists: 90
Utilizes: Special Technical Talent; Guest Artists; Guest Directors
Budget: $1,000,000 - $5,000,000
Income Sources: Private Foundations/Grants/Endowments; Business/Corporate Donations; Box Office; Government Grants; Individual Donations
Season: October - May   **Annual Attendance:** 190,000
Affiliations: LORT

STAGE ONE THE LOUISVILLE CHILDREN'S THEATRE
425 West Market Street, Louisville, KY 40202
(502) 589-5946
FAX: (502) 589-5779
Founded: 1946
Arts Area: Professional; Theatrical Group
Status: Professional
Type: Performing; Touring; Educational
Purpose: To provide high-quality, professional live theatre for young people and their families
Management: Moses Goldberg, Producing Director; G. Jane Jarrett, Managing Director
Officers: Mary Michael Steele, President; Sam Corbett, Vice President of Fund-raising; William T. Tyrrell, Vice President of Administration; Mike Keene, Treasurer
Paid Staff: 32   **Volunteer Staff:** 55
Paid Artists: 23   **Non-Paid Artists:** 1
Utilizes: Special Technical Talent; Guest Artists; Guest Directors
Budget: $500,000 - $1,000,000
Income Sources: Private Foundations/Grants/Endowments; Business/Corporate Donations; Box Office; Government Grants; Individual Donations
Season: September - May   **Annual Attendance:** 124,000
Affiliations: AEA
Performance Facilities: Kentucky Center for the Arts; Louisville Gardens

PERFORMING SERIES

SHAKESPEARE IN CENTRAL PARK - KENTUCKY SHAKESPEARE FESTIVAL
520 West Magnolia, Louisville, KY 40208
(502) 634-8237
Founded: 1960
Arts Area: Theater; Festivals
Status: Professional; Non-Profit
Type: Performing; Educational
Purpose: To keep the works of William Shakespeare alive and meaningful for all, regardless of their ability to pay; to remain a dynamic statewide educational resource for Elizabethan studies
Management: Curt L. Tostelend, Producing Director
Officers: Lee Davis, President of the Board
Paid Staff: 3   **Volunteer Staff:** 20
Paid Artists: 30   **Non-Paid Artists:** 10
Utilizes: Special Technical Talent; Guest Artists; Guest Directors
Budget: $100,000 - $500,000
Income Sources: Private Foundations/Grants/Endowments; Business/Corporate Donations; Government Grants; Individual Donations
Season: June - August   **Annual Attendance:** 25,000
Affiliations: AEA

FACILITY

KENTUCKY CENTER FOR THE ARTS
5 Riverfront Plaza, Louisville, KY 40202
(502) 562-0100
Type of Facility: Theatre Complex; Concert Hall; Performance Center; Theatre House; Opera House; Multi-Purpose
Year Built: 1983   **Architect:** Caudill Rowlett Scott   **Cost:** $33,500,000
Acoustical Consultant: Jaffe & Associates
Contact for Rental: Thomas Roberts;   (502) 562-0100

Resident Groups: Louisville Ballet; The Louisville Orchestra; Kentucky Opera; Broadway Series (Louisville Theatrical Association); Stage One; Louisville Children's Theatre
The Center contains the Bomhard Theater, Boyd Martin Experimental Theater and Whitney Hall. See individual listings for additional information.

KENTUCKY CENTER FOR THE ARTS - BOMHARD THEATER
5 Riverfront Plaza, Louisville, KY 40202
(502) 562-0100
    Type of Facility: Theatre House; Opera House
    Type of Stage: Modified Thrust
    Stage Dimensions: 120'Wx30'D; 36'Wx20'H proscenium opening   **Orchestra Pit**
    Seating Capacity: 626
    Contact for Rental: Thomas Roberts; (502) 562-0100

KENTUCKY CENTER FOR THE ARTS - BOYD MARTIN EXPERIMENTAL THEATER
5 Riverfront Plaza, Louisville, KY 40202
(502) 562-0100
    Type of Facility: Multi-Purpose; Black Box
    Type of Stage: Flexible
    Stage Dimensions: 42'6"x37'x15'6"H
    Seating Capacity: 135
    Year Remodeled: 1987 **Architect:** Steve Barry **Cost:** $277,000
    Contact for Rental: Thomas Roberts; (502) 562-0100
    Resident Groups: Boathouse Troupe; Necessary Theater; Walden Theater; Kentucky Playwrights Theater; Creation Theater
    Technical Director - Keith Kimmel

KENTUCKY CENTER FOR THE ARTS - WHITNEY HALL
5 Riverfront Plaza, Louisville, KY 40202
(502) 562-0100
    Type of Facility: Concert Hall; Theatre House; Opera House
    Type of Stage: Modified Thrust
    Stage Dimensions: 160'Wx60'D; 56'Wx30'H proscenium opening   **Orchestra Pit**
    Seating Capacity: 2,400
    Contact for Rental: Thomas Roberts; (502) 562-0100

LOUISVILLE MEMORIAL AUDITORIUM
970 South Fourth Street, Louisville, KY 40203
(502) 584-4911
FAX: (502) 625-4130
    Type of Facility: Auditorium
    Type of Stage: Proscenium
    Stage Dimensions: 85'Wx39'D; 85'Wx36'H proscenium opening   **Orchestra Pit**
    Seating Capacity: 2,000
    Year Built: 1929 **Cost:** $2,000,000
    Year Remodeled: 1986 **Cost:** $800,000
    Contact for Rental: Basil P. Caummisar; (502) 584-4911
    Manager: Dale Royer; (502) 584-4911
    Auditorium has the world's largest Pilcher Organ with 588 pipes.

MACAULEY THEATRE
315 West Broadway, Louisville, KY 40202
(502) 562-0194
FAX: (502) 562-0188
    Type of Facility: Theatre House
    Type of Stage: Proscenium
    Stage Dimensions: 90'Wx38'D **Orchestra Pit**
    Seating Capacity: 1,453
    Year Built: 1925 **Architect:** Preston-Bradshaw
    Year Remodeled: 1972
    Contact for Rental: Jonathan Smillie; (502) 562-0194
    Resident Groups: Theater Workshop of Louisville; Louisville Orhcestra

SOUTHERN BAPTIST THEOLOGICAL SEMINARY - ALUMNI MEMORIAL CHAPEL
2825 Lexington Road, Louisville, KY 40206
(502) 897-4115
    Type of Facility: Auditorium
    Type of Stage: Flexible

Seating Capacity: 1,600
Year Built: 1950   **Architect:** Joseph Kolbrook   **Cost:** $1,500,000
Acoustical Consultant: Bolt, Beranek & Newman
Manager: Dr. Milburn Price
Resident Groups: Seminary Oratorio Chorus and Orchestra; Male Chorale; Seminary Choir; Collegium Musicum

SOUTHERN BAPTIST THEOLOGICAL SEMINARY - HEEREN RECITAL HALL
2825 Lexington Road, Louisville, KY 40280
(502) 897-4115
Type of Facility: Concert Hall
Type of Stage: Thrust
Seating Capacity: 255
Year Built: 1971   **Architect:** John Grossman   **Cost:** $250,000
Acoustical Consultant: Bolt, Beranek & Newman
Manager: Dr. Milburn Price

Murray

PERFORMING SERIES

MURRAY CIVIC MUSIC ASSOCIATION
College of Fine Arts and Communication, University Station, Murray, KY 42071
(502) 762-6339, ext. 4669
Founded: 1959
Arts Area: Dance; Vocal Music; Instrumental Music; Theater; Lyric Opera; Grand Opera
Status: Non-Profit
Type: Sponsoring
Purpose: To bring outstanding performing arts attractions to the region
Officers: Roger E. Reichmuth, President
Volunteer Staff: 18
Paid Artists: 94
Utilizes: Guest Artists
Budget: $1,000 - $50,000
Income Sources: Business/Corporate Donations; Box Office; Government Grants; Individual Donations
Season: September - May   **Annual Attendance:** 6,000
Performance Facilities: Lovett Auditorium, Murray State University

FACILITY

MURRAY STATE UNIVERSITY - LOVETT AUDITORIUM
College of Fine Arts and Communication, Murray, KY 42071
(502) 762-4516
FAX: (502) 762-6335
Type of Facility: Auditorium
Facility Originally: Recreation Hall; Gymnasium
Type of Stage: Proscenium
Stage Dimensions: 79'6"Wx53'Dx20'H
Seating Capacity: 2,100
Year Built: 1934
Year Remodeled: 1938
Contact for Rental: Gary Hunt;   (502) 762-4516

Owensboro

INSTRUMENTAL MUSIC

OWENSBORO SYMPHONY ORCHESTRA
122 East Eighteenth Street, Owensboro, KY 42301
(502) 684-0661
Founded: 1966
Arts Area: Symphony; Orchestra
Status: Professional; Non-Profit
Type: Performing; Touring; Resident; Educational
Purpose: The Owensboro Symphony Orchestra performs symphonic music to enhance the cultural environment of western Kentucky.
Management: G. Dan Griffith, General Manager; Michael Luxner, Music Director; Paula Hudson, Office Manager
Paid Staff: 7   **Volunteer Staff:** 3

Paid Artists: 90   **Non-Paid Artists:** 2
Utilizes: Guest Conductors; Guest Artists
Budget: $100,000 - $500,000
Income Sources: Private Foundations/Grants/Endowments; Business/Corporate Donations; Box Office; Government Grants; Individual Donations
Season: September - April   **Annual Attendance:** 14,000
Affiliations: ASOL
Performance Facilities: River Park Center

THEATRE

THEATRE WORKSHOP OF OWENSBORO
407 West Fifth Street, PO Box 170, Owensboro, KY 42302
(502) 683-5003
Founded: 1955
Arts Area: Musical; Community; Theatrical Group; Youth Theatre
Status: Non-Professional; Non-Profit
Type: Performing; Resident
Purpose: To provide the Owensboro area with high-quality amateur theatre; to provide an outlet for area performers and technicians to practice their craft
Management: Nestra McFarland, Office Manager
Officers: Robert Wagner, President Board of Directors; Betty Taylor, Vice President; Mary Martin, Secretary; Terry Walker, Treasurer
Paid Staff: 2   **Volunteer Staff:** 75
Utilizes: Guest Conductors; Guest Directors
Budget: $50,000 - $100,000
Income Sources: Business/Corporate Donations; Box Office; Government Grants; Individual Donations
Season: 52 Weeks   **Annual Attendance:** 5,500
Affiliations: AACT; Kentucky Theatre Association
Performance Facilities: Old Trinity Centre; River Park Center

Paducah

THEATRE

MARKET HOUSE THEATRE
141 Kentucky Avenue, Paducah, KY 42003
(502) 444-6828
Founded: 1964
Arts Area: Community
Status: Non-Professional; Non-Profit
Type: Performing; Touring; Educational
Purpose: To enrich the community's cultural and artistic life through the production of a diverse season as well as educational and touring programs
Management: April S. Cochran, Artistic/Executive Director; Michael L. Cochran, Technical Director
Officers: Martha Emmons, President; Sherry Shadle, Vice President; Lana Sirk, Secretary; Lars Blythe, Treasurer
Paid Staff: 4
Non-Paid Artists: 120
Utilizes: Special Technical Talent; Guest Artists; Guest Directors
Budget: $100,000 - $500,000
Income Sources: Private Foundations/Grants/Endowments; Business/Corporate Donations; Box Office; Government Grants; Individual Donations
Season: 52 Weeks   **Annual Attendance:** 12,000
Performance Facilities: Market House Theatre

Radcliff

THEATRE

HARDIN COUNTY PLAYHOUSE
PO Box 394, Radcliff, KY 40160
(502) 351-0577
Founded: 1969
Arts Area: Musical; Community; Theatrical Group
Status: Semi-Professional; Non-Professional; Non-Profit
Type: Performing
Purpose: To present performing arts to the community

Management: Hardin County Playhouse Board of Directors
Officers: Deborah Hibberd, President; Duane Clug, Vice President; Christine Reich, Secretary; Michael Laughlin, Treasurer
Volunteer Staff: 100
Utilizes: Special Technical Talent; Guest Artists; Guest Directors
Budget: $1,000 - $50,000
Income Sources: Private Foundations/Grants/Endowments; Business/Corporate Donations; Box Office; Individual Donations
Season: 52 Weeks   **Annual Attendance:** 1,800
Performance Facilities: Hardin County Playhouse

Richmond

THEATRE

RICHMOND CHILDREN'S THEATRE
321 North Second Street, Richmond, KY 40475
(606) 623-8753
Founded: 1978
Arts Area: Musical; Community; Theatrical Group
Status: Non-Professional; Non-Profit
Type: Performing; Touring; Educational
Purpose: To offer to all youth, ages 8-18, the opportunity to participate in the theatre arts through the avenues of workshops, performances, stagecraft and crew
Officers: Kathie Bettler, President; Jo Wernegreen, Vice President Finance; Jeanette Duncan, Secretary; Sandy Johnstone, Treasurer
Volunteer Staff: 30
Paid Artists: 5
Utilizes: Special Technical Talent; Guest Directors
Budget: $1,000 - $50,000
Income Sources: Business/Corporate Donations; Box Office; Government Grants; Individual Donations
Season: September - May   **Annual Attendance:** 1,500
Affiliations: Richmond Parks and Recreation Department
Performance Facilities: Eastern Kentucky University Campus Theatre

Whitesburg

THEATRE

ROADSIDE THEATER
306 Madison Street, Whitesburg, KY 41858
(606) 633-0108
Founded: 1975
Arts Area: Professional; Theatrical Group
Status: Professional; Non-Profit
Type: Performing; Touring; Educational
Purpose: To create original plays about central Appalachia and its people
Management: Dudley Cocke, Director; Donna Porterfield, Managing Director; Ron Short, Artistic Director; Valeria Craft, Marketing Director
Paid Staff: 7
Utilizes: Special Technical Talent; Guest Artists; Guest Directors
Budget: $100,000 - $500,000
Income Sources: Private Foundations/Grants/Endowments; Business/Corporate Donations; Box Office; Government Grants; Individual Donations
Season: 52 Weeks
Affiliations: TCG; Alternate ROOTS
Performance Facilities: Appalshop Theatre

LOUISIANA

Baton Rouge

DANCE

BATON ROUGE BALLET THEATRE
301 Main Street, Baton Rouge, LA 70801
(504) 336-0544
Arts Area: Ballet
Status: Professional; Non-Profit
Type: Performing; Touring; Resident
Management: Sharon Mathews, Molly Boehmann, Artistic Directors
Paid Artists: 25
Income Sources: Box Office; Individual Donations
Performance Facilities: Centroplex Theater for the Performing Arts

INSTRUMENTAL MUSIC

BATON ROUGE SYMPHONY ORCHESTRA
1 America Place, Suite 620, Baton Rouge, LA 70825
(504) 387-2776
FAX: (504) 387-5445
Founded: 1947
Arts Area: Symphony; Orchestra; Chamber; Ensemble
Status: Non-Profit
Type: Performing
Purpose: To provide professional quality orchestral performance in symphony and related arts
Management: Douglas Gerhert, Executive Director
Officers: George Ballars, President; Charles Lamar, Vice President; Sharon Rochford, Treasurer; Robert Hawthorne, Secretary; Beth Fuller, Immediate Past President
Paid Staff: 4   **Volunteer Staff:** 150
Paid Artists: 80
Utilizes: Guest Artists
Budget: $500,000 - $1,000,000
Income Sources: Private Foundations/Grants/Endowments; Business/Corporate Donations; Box Office; Government Grants; Individual Donations
Season: September - May   **Annual Attendance:** 16,000
Performance Facilities: Riverside/Centroplex Theatre for Performing Arts

VOCAL MUSIC

BATON ROUGE GILBERT AND SULLIVAN SOCIETY
PO Box 80099, Baton Rouge, LA 70898
(504) 291-7236
Founded: 1975
Arts Area: Operetta
Status: Non-Professional; Non-Profit
Type: Performing
Purpose: To perform in full, and in excerpts, the operettas of W.S. Gilbert and Arthur Sullivan
Officers: Lance Parker, President
Volunteer Staff: 11
Paid Artists: 5   **Non-Paid Artists:** 35
Utilizes: Guest Conductors; Guest Directors
Budget: $1,000 - $50,000
Income Sources: Private Foundations/Grants/Endowments; Business/Corporate Donations; Box Office; Government Grants; Individual Donations
Annual Attendance: 1,400
Performance Facilities: Baton Rouge Little Theatre

BATON ROUGE OPERA
PO Box 2269, Baton Rouge, LA 70821
(504) 922-9936
Founded: 1982
Arts Area: Grand Opera; Light Opera
Status: Professional; Non-Profit
Type: Performing; Educational

Management: Marioara Trifan, Artistic Director; Samuel Gray, General Director; Lynn Allen, Office Manager
Officers: Marlene Weyand, President; William Newman, Vice President; Don DeVille, Treasurer; Ellen Hill, Secretary
Paid Staff: 3
Paid Artists: 76   **Non-Paid Artists:** 12
Utilizes: Special Technical Talent; Guest Conductors; Guest Artists; Guest Directors
Budget: $100,000 - $500,000
Income Sources: Private Foundations/Grants/Endowments; Business/Corporate Donations; Box Office; Government Grants; Individual Donations
Season: October - June   **Annual Attendance:** 7,500
Affiliations: Arts and Humanities Council of Baton Rouge; OA
Performance Facilities: Union Theatre, Louisiana State University

THEATRE

BATON ROUGE LITTLE THEATRE
7155 Florida Boulevard, Baton Rouge, LA 70806
(504) 924-6496
Founded: 1946
Arts Area: Musical; Community
Status: Non-Professional; Non-Profit
Type: Performing; Educational
Purpose: To entertain, educate and provide an artistic outlet
Management: Henry Avery, Managing/Artistic Director
Paid Staff: 7   **Volunteer Staff:** 100
Paid Artists: 40   **Non-Paid Artists:** 100
Utilizes: Guest Conductors; Guest Directors
Budget: $100,000 - $500,000
Income Sources: Private Foundations/Grants/Endowments; Box Office; Individual Donations
Season: October - May; July   **Annual Attendance:** 25,000

FACILITY

LSU UNION THEATER
Highland Road, LSU Campus, Baton Rouge, LA 70894
(504) 388-5728
FAX: (504) 388-4329
Founded: 1964
Type of Facility: Theatre Complex; Concert Hall; Auditorium; Off Broadway; Theatre House; Opera House
Type of Stage: Proscenium
Stage Dimensions: 44'Wx30'Dx22'H proscenium opening   **Orchestra Pit**
Seating Capacity: 1,262
Year Built: 1964   **Architect:** John Desmond Associates   **Cost:** $3,500,000
Contact for Rental: Michael R. Derr, Director;   (504) 388-5782
Resident Groups: Baton Rouge Opera; LSU Symphony Orchestra

RIVERSIDE CENTROPLEX
PO Box 4047, Baton Rouge, LA 70821
(504) 389-3030
Type of Facility: Civic Center
Year Built: 1977   **Architect:** Bradley Mermont   **Cost:** $25,000,000
Contact for Rental: Mike Pierce, Executive Director;   (504) 389-3030
The Centroplex contains an Arena, Exhibition Hall and Theatre. See separate listings for further information.

RIVERSIDE CENTROPLEX - ARENA
PO Box 4047, Baton Rouge, LA 70821
(504) 389-3030
FAX: (504) 389-4954
Type of Facility: Concert Hall; Arena
Type of Stage: Flexible; Platform
Seating Capacity: 12,813
Year Built: 1977
Contact for Rental: Mike Pierce, Executive Director;   (504) 389-3030

RIVERSIDE CENTROPLEX - EXHIBITION HALL
PO Box 4047, Baton Rouge, LA 70821
(504) 389-3030
FAX: (504) 389-4954
Type of Facility: Exhibition Hall

Type of Stage: Flexible; Platform
Year Built: 1977
Contact for Rental: Mike Pierce, Executive Director;   (504) 389-3030

RIVERSIDE CENTROPLEX - THEATRE FOR PERFORMING ARTS
PO Box 4047, Baton Rouge, LA 70821
(504) 389-3030
FAX: (504) 389-4954
Type of Facility: Concert Hall; Theatre House; Opera House
Type of Stage: Proscenium
Stage Dimensions: 57'9"Wx47'D; 57'9"Wx28'H proscenium opening; 20' wings left and right   **Orchestra Pit**
Seating Capacity: 2,011
Year Built: 1980
Contact for Rental: Mike Pierce, Executive Director;   (504) 389-3030
Resident Groups: Baton Rouge Symphony Orchestra; Baton Rouge Ballet; Baton Rouge Opera

Eunice

THEATRE

EUNICE PLAYERS THEATRE
PO Box 306, Eunice, LA 70535
(318) 457-3330
Founded: 1969
Arts Area: Musical; Community
Status: Non-Professional; Non-Profit
Type: Performing
Purpose: To continue to provide quality live theater to Eunice and the surrounding area
Officers: John Cobb, President; Jody Powell, Secretary; Joan Kerstein, Treasurer
Volunteer Staff: 16
Non-Paid Artists: 100
Budget: $1,000 - $50,000
Income Sources: Business/Corporate Donations; Box Office; Individual Donations
Season: 52 Weeks   **Annual Attendance:** 1,800
Affiliations: Acadiana Arts Council; Saint Landry Arts Association; Eunice Chamber of Commerce

FACILITY

EUNICE PLAYERS THEATRE
PO Box 306, Eunice, LA 70535
(318) 457-3330
Type of Facility: Studio Performance
Facility Originally: Business Facility
Type of Stage: Proscenium
Stage Dimensions: 22'x20'
Seating Capacity: 112
Year Remodeled: 1970
Contact for Rental: Joanie Kurstein;   (318) 457-3330
Resident Groups: Eunice Players Theatre

Hammond

FACILITY

SOUTHEASTERN LOUISIANA UNIVERSITY - VONNIE BORDEN THEATRE
Hammond, LA 70402
(504) 549-2105
Type of Facility: Theatre House
Type of Stage: Proscenium
Stage Dimensions: 40'x80'

Seating Capacity: 450
Year Built: 1971 **Architect:** Oliver-Frantz, AIA **Cost:** $2,000,000

Lafayette

INSTRUMENTAL MUSIC

LAFAYETTE CONCERT BAND
PO Box 53762, Lafayette, LA 70505
(318) 233-7060
Founded: 1982
Arts Area: Band
Status: Semi-Professional; Non-Profit
Type: Performing; Touring; Resident; Educational; Sponsoring
Purpose: To provide a competent, well-rehearsed organization which would introduce the unique repertoire for wind ensemble to the people of Southwest Louisiana and to provide a performance outlet for the musical talents of band instrumentalists
Management: Dr. George Sparks, Music Director
Volunteer Staff: 5
Non-Paid Artists: 65
Utilizes: Special Technical Talent; Guest Conductors; Guest Artists
Budget: $1,000 - $50,000
Income Sources: Private Foundations/Grants/Endowments; Business/Corporate Donations; Box Office; Government Grants; Individual Donations
Season: 52 Weeks **Annual Attendance:** 8,000
Affiliations: National Association of Concert Bands

THEATRE

LAFAYETTE COMMUNITY THEATRE
504 Plaza Village, Lafayette, LA 70506
(318) 235-1532
Founded: 1981
Arts Area: Community; Theatrical Group
Status: Non-Professional; Non-Profit
Type: Performing; Touring; Resident
Purpose: To produce quality drama for local citizens; to encourage participation in all activities by interested residents; to educate citizens regarding theatre and train them in theatre arts
Management: Jack Reedy, Business Manager; John Fiero, Artistic Director; Charles Manns, Technical Director
Officers: Roma Hepburn, President; Maureen Brennan, Vice President; Alozia St. Julien, Secretary; Jack Reedy, Treasurer
Budget: $1,000 - $50,000
Income Sources: Private Foundations/Grants/Endowments; Business/Corporate Donations; Box Office; Individual Donations
Season: 52 Weeks **Annual Attendance:** 5,000

FACILITY

HEYMANN PERFORMING ARTS AND CONVENTION CENTER
1373 South College Road, Lafayette, LA 70503
(318) 268-5540
FAX: (318) 268-5580
Founded: 1960
Type of Facility: Performance Center; Convention Center
Type of Stage: Proscenium
Stage Dimensions: 107'x49' **Orchestra Pit**
Seating Capacity: 2,230
Year Built: 1960 **Architect:** Hayes Town **Cost:** $1,200,000
Year Remodeled: 1989 **Architect:** Wayne Corme **Cost:** $3,500,000
Acoustical Consultant: Dave Nieblieu
Contact for Rental: Frank Bradshaw; (318) 268-5540

LAFAYETTE COMMUNITY THEATRE
529 Jefferson Street, Lafayette, LA 70501
(318) 235-1532
Type of Facility: Theatre House
Facility Originally: Business Facility
Type of Stage: Flexible; Proscenium
Stage Dimensions: 40'Wx18'Dx15'H

Seating Capacity: 90
Year Remodeled: 1986   **Architect:** Bob Bennet   **Cost:** $25,000
Contact for Rental: John Fiero;   (318) 234-8210
Resident Groups: Lafayette Community Theatre

Lake Charles

DANCE

LAKE CHARLES BALLET SOCIETY
PO Box 5515, Lake Charles, LA 70606
(318) 436-0160
Founded: 1963
Arts Area: Ballet; Jazz
Status: Non-Professional; Non-Profit
Type: Performing; Resident; Educational; Sponsoring
Purpose: To provide Southwest Louisiana with the highest quality of dance programs, concert series, resident performing companies, dance in schools, and the sponsorship of professional dance companies
Management: Ida Clarke, Artistic Director; Cissie Clarke, Assistant Director/Ballet Mistress
Officers: Marie McCreedy, President; Maureen Cannon, Vice President, Membership; Janet Postell, Secretary; Zippy Scott, Treasurer
Volunteer Staff: 25
Paid Artists: 2   **Non-Paid Artists:** 16
Utilizes: Guest Artists
Budget: $50,000 - $100,000
Income Sources: Private Foundations/Grants/Endowments; Business/Corporate Donations; Box Office; Individual Donations
Season: October - April
Performance Facilities: Lake Charles Civic Center

LAKE CHARLES SOCIETY FOR BALLET JOYEUX
140 West 18th Street, Lake Charles, LA 70601
(318) 436-5217
Founded: 1963
Arts Area: Ballet
Status: Non-Professional; Non-Profit
Type: Performing; Touring; Resident
Management: Cissie Clark, Acting Director
Non-Paid Artists: 20
Utilizes: Guest Artists; Guest Choreographers
Budget: $50,000 - $100,000
Income Sources: Private Foundations/Grants/Endowments; Business/Corporate Donations; Box Office; Individual Donations
Season: September - June
Performance Facilities: Lake Charles Civic Center

THEATRE

ARTISTS CIVIC THEATRE AND STUDIO
One Reid Street, PO Box 278, Lake Charles, LA 70602
(318) 433-2287
Founded: 1966
Arts Area: Musical; Dinner; Community; Theatrical Group; Children's
Status: Non-Professional; Non-Profit
Type: Performing; Touring; Resident; Educational
Purpose: To give local talent a place to work under the direction of a trained professional director where production values are maintained at a high level; to offer formal classes in various aspects of theatre
Management: Marc Pettaway, Executive Director
Officers: Dr. Charles Woodard, President
Paid Staff: 2   **Volunteer Staff:** 40
Paid Artists: 2   **Non-Paid Artists:** 70
Utilizes: Special Technical Talent
Budget: $50,000 - $100,000
Income Sources: Box Office
Season: 52 Weeks   **Annual Attendance:** 8,000
Affiliations: SWTC
Performance Facilities: ACTS' One Reid Street Theatre

PERFORMING SERIES

LAKE CHARLES LITTLE THEATRE
813 Enterprise Boulevard, Lake Charles, LA 70601
(318) 433-7988
> **Founded:** 1926
> **Arts Area:** Theater
> **Status:** Non-Professional; Non-Profit
> **Type:** Performing
> **Management:** Adley Cormier, Artistic Director; Paul Draughn and John Hogan, Board Members
> **Officers:** Bob Michael, President; James Johnson, Vice President; Mathilde Gano, Secretary; Waverlyn Bayard, Treasurer
> **Paid Staff:** 1
> **Utilizes:** Guest Directors
> **Budget:** $1,000 - $50,000
> **Income Sources:** Private Foundations/Grants/Endowments; Business/Corporate Donations; Box Office; Individual Donations
> **Season:** September - May   **Annual Attendance:** 3,500

FACILITY

LAKE CHARLES CIVIC CENTER
900 Lakeshore Drive, PO Box 900, Lake Charles, LA 70602
(318) 491-1256
FAX: (318) 491-1534
> **Type of Facility:** Civic Center
> **Year Built:** 1972   **Architect:** J.T. Platt   **Cost:** $16,000,000
> **Contact for Rental:** Al Harris;   (318) 491-1256
> *Civic Center contains the Coliseum, Exhibition Hall and Rosa Hart Theatre. See separate listings for further information.*

LAKE CHARLES CIVIC CENTER - COLISEUM
900 Lakeshore Drive, PO Box 900, Lake Charles, LA 70602
(318) 491-1256
FAX: (318) 491-1534
> **Type of Facility:** Concert Hall; Arena
> **Type of Stage:** Flexible; Platform
> **Seating Capacity:** 8,000
> **Year Built:** 1972   **Architect:** J.T. Platt
> **Contact for Rental:** Al Harris;   (318) 491-1256

LAKE CHARLES CIVIC CENTER - EXHIBITION HALL
900 Lakeshore Drive, PO Box 900, Lake Charles, LA 70602
(318) 491-1256
FAX: (318) 491-1534
> **Type of Facility:** Exhibition Hall
> **Type of Stage:** Flexible
> **Year Built:** 1972   **Architect:** J.T. Platt
> **Contact for Rental:** Al Harris;   (318) 491-1256
> *18,000 square feet of hall space*

LAKE CHARLES CIVIC CENTER - ROSA HART THEATRE
900 Lakeshore Drive, PO Box 900, Lake Charles, LA 70602
(318) 491-1256
FAX: (318) 491-1534
> **Type of Facility:** Concert Hall; Theatre House
> **Type of Stage:** Proscenium
> **Stage Dimensions:** 65'3"Wx28'Hx60'D   **Orchestra Pit**
> **Seating Capacity:** 2,704
> **Year Built:** 1972   **Architect:** J.T. Platt
> **Contact for Rental:** Al Harris;   (318) 491-1256
> **Resident Groups:** Lake Charles Symphony; Lake Charles Civic Ballet; Southwest Louisiana Concert Association

ONE REID STREET THEATRE
One Reid Street, PO Box 278, Lake Charles, LA 70602
(318) 433-2287
> **Type of Facility:** Theatre Complex
> **Type of Stage:** Proscenium
> **Stage Dimensions:** 44'x25'
> **Seating Capacity:** 200

Year Remodeled: 1987   **Architect:** Gus Quinn; Blair Stoker
Contact for Rental: Marc Pettaway;   (318) 433-2287
Resident Groups: Artists Civic Theatre & Studio

Mamou

PERFORMING SERIES

MAMOU CAJUN MUSIC FESTIVAL ASSOCIATION
420 East Street, Apt. 1, Mamou, LA 70554
(318) 468-2258
  Founded: 1972
  Arts Area: Vocal Music; Festivals
  Status: Non-Profit
  Type: Performing; Resident; Educational
  Purpose: To promote authentic and traditional cajun music, food and games
  Officers: Eric Fontenot, President; Donald Landreneau, Vice President; Roy Chamberlin, Secretary; Norris Fontenot, Treasurer
  Volunteer Staff: 65
  Paid Artists: 40
  Utilizes: Special Technical Talent; Guest Artists; Paid Performers
  Budget: $1,000 - $50,000
  Income Sources: Private Foundations/Grants/Endowments; Box Office; Concessions
  Season: June   **Annual Attendance:** 15,000

Metairie

DANCE

CRESCENT BALLET COMPANY
3211 Taft Park, Metairie, LA 70002
(504) 885-2352
  Founded: 1970
  Arts Area: Ballet
  Status: Non-Professional; Non-Profit
  Type: Performing; Resident
  Management: Patricia LeClercq, Director
  Non-Paid Artists: 20
  Utilizes: Guest Artists; Guest Choreographers
  Budget: $1,000 - $50,000
  Income Sources: Private Foundations/Grants/Endowments; Business/Corporate Donations; Box Office; Individual Donations
  Season: September - June

DELTA FESTIVAL BALLET
3850 North Causeway Boulevard, Metairie, LA 70003
(504) 836-7166
  Founded: 1969
  Arts Area: Ballet
  Status: Professional; Non-Profit
  Type: Performing; Touring; Resident; Educational
  Purpose: To promote the art of dance through professional performance, education, cultural outreach and community involvement
  Management: Joseph and Maria Giacobbe, Artistic Directors; Christines Hodgins, Administrative Director
  Officers: Dr. R. V. Hamsa, President; Thomas Bernard, Vice President; John Bruno, Secretary; Terri Fishbein, Treasurer
  Paid Staff: 7   **Volunteer Staff:** 20
  Paid Artists: 20   **Non-Paid Artists:** 15
  Utilizes: Special Technical Talent; Guest Conductors; Guest Artists; Guest Directors
  Budget: $100,000 - $500,000
  Income Sources: Private Foundations/Grants/Endowments; Business/Corporate Donations; Box Office; Government Grants; Individual Donations
  Season: September - May   **Annual Attendance:** 100,000
  Affiliations: NARB

PERFORMING SERIES

JEFFERSON PERFORMING ARTS SOCIETY
PO Box 704, Metairie, LA 70004
(504) 834-5727
FAX: (504) 834-5741
>**Founded:** 1978
>**Arts Area:** Dance; Vocal Music; Instrumental Music; Theater; Festivals; Grand Opera
>**Status:** Professional; Semi-Professional; Non-Professional; Non-Profit
>**Type:** Performing; Educational
>**Purpose:** To create a better community through high-quality art education (especially youth), performance and competitions; to develop schools for the arts in the parish
>**Management:** Dennis G. Assaf Founder/Executive Director/Artistic Director; Carol Artery, Development Association
>**Officers:** Hannah Cunningham, Chairman; Teresa Guzzutta, President; John Brooks, Vice President; Dean Wilson, Secretary
>**Paid Staff:** 4 **Volunteer Staff:** 8
>**Paid Artists:** 35 **Non-Paid Artists:** 100
>**Budget:** $500,000 - $1,000,000
>**Income Sources:** Business/Corporate Donations; Box Office; Government Grants; Individual Donations
>**Season:** September - May
>**Affiliations:** CA

Monroe

INSTRUMENTAL MUSIC

MONROE SYMPHONY ORCHESTRA
PO Box 4353, Monroe, LA 71211-4353
(318) 329-8085
>**Founded:** 1971
>**Arts Area:** Symphony; Orchestra; Chamber; Ensemble
>**Status:** Semi-Professional; Non-Profit
>**Type:** Performing; Educational
>**Purpose:** To present cultural music to the community and to educate students through a program of music in the schools
>**Management:** Dr. Doug Baer, Business Manager
>**Officers:** Chris Cheshier, President; K. Katz, Past President; John Kelly, First Vice President
>**Paid Staff:** 1 **Volunteer Staff:** 8
>**Paid Artists:** 60
>**Utilizes:** Guest Conductors; Guest Artists
>**Budget:** $50,000 - $100,000
>**Income Sources:** Business/Corporate Donations; Box Office; Government Grants
>**Annual Attendance:** 2,000
>**Performance Facilities:** Monroe Civic Center

PERFORMING SERIES

NORTHEAST LOUISIANA UNIVERSITY CONCERTS
Northeast Louisiana University, Monroe, LA 71209
(318) 342-1000
FAX: (318) 342-1034
>**Arts Area:** Dance; Vocal Music; Instrumental Music; Theater
>**Status:** Non-Profit
>**Type:** Performing; Sponsoring
>**Purpose:** To bring to students and townspeople the best in professional cultural entertainment
>**Management:** Jerry D. Holmes, Chairman
>**Paid Staff:** 1 **Volunteer Staff:** 2
>**Utilizes:** Guest Artists
>**Budget:** $50,000 - $100,000
>**Income Sources:** Private Foundations/Grants/Endowments; Box Office
>**Season:** October - April **Annual Attendance:** 2,200
>**Performance Facilities:** Civic Center Theater; Brown Auditorium

FACILITY

MONROE CIVIC CENTER
401 Lea Joyner Boulevard, PO Box 1853, Monroe, LA 71210
(318) 329-2225
FAX: (318) 329-2548
    Type of Facility: Civic Center
    Year Built: 1967   **Architect:** Johns & Neel   **Cost:** $13,000,000
    Acoustical Consultant: Tracor
    Contact for Rental: Obie Webser, Stan Lockridge;   (318) 329-2225
    Civic Center contains the Arena, Theater, and Conference Hall. See separate listings for further information.

MONROE CIVIC CENTER - ARENA
401 Lea Joyner Boulevard, PO Box 1853, Monroe, LA 71210
(318) 329-2225
FAX: (318) 329-2548
    Type of Facility: Arena
    Type of Stage: Proscenium; Platform
    Stage Dimensions: 48'x72'
    Seating Capacity: 8,000
    Year Built: 1967
    Contact for Rental: Obie Webser, Stan Lockridge;   (318) 329-2225

MONROE CIVIC CENTER - THEATER
401 Lea Joyner Boulevard, PO Box 300, Monroe, LA 71201
(318) 329-2225
    Type of Facility: Theatre House
    Type of Stage: Proscenium; Platform
    Stage Dimensions: 56'x72'   **Orchestra Pit**
    Seating Capacity: 2,250
    Year Built: 1967
    Contact for Rental: Obie Webster;   (318) 329-2225
    Manager: Stan Lockridge;   (318) 329-2225

New Orleans

DANCE

NEW ORLEANS BALLET ASSOCIATION
821 Gravier Street, Suite 610, New Orleans, LA 70112
(504) 522-0996
FAX: (504) 595-8454
    Founded: 1971
    Arts Area: Modern; Ballet; Jazz
    Status: Non-Profit
    Type: Sponsoring; Presenting
    Purpose: To present professional dance in the greater New Orleans area
    Management: Jon H. Teeuwissen, Executive Director
    Officers: Phyllis Taylor, President; John Reidy, Vice President; Elizabeth Ryan, Secretary; Curt Queyrouze, Treasurer
    Paid Staff: 7   **Volunteer Staff:** 200
    Paid Artists: 12
    Utilizes: Guest Artists; Guest Choreographers; Guest Companies
    Budget: $500,000 - $1,000,000
    Income Sources: Private Foundations/Grants/Endowments; Business/Corporate Donations; Box Office; Government Grants; Individual Donations
    Season: September - April   **Annual Attendance:** 28,000
    Affiliations: Dance USA
    Performance Facilities: Theatre for the Perfroming Arts; Saenger Theatre; Orpheum Theatre; St. Bernard Cultural Center

INSTRUMENTAL MUSIC

LOUISIANA JAZZ FEDERATION
333 Saint Charles Avenue, Suite 613, New Orleans, LA 70130
(504) 522-3154
FAX: (504) 522-3154
    Founded: 1980
    Arts Area: Ensemble; Ethnic; Band

Status: Semi-Professional; Non-Profit
Type: Performing; Educational; Sponsoring
Purpose: To promote the development and unification of the jazz community in Louisiana
Management: Jason Patterson, Executive Director; Patrice Fisher, Development Director; Amber Wallace, JAM Coordinator
Officers: Tim Green, President; Harold Battiste, Vice President; Lorraine Farr, Secretary; Eric Glaser, Treasurer
Paid Staff: 3   **Volunteer Staff:** 18
Paid Artists: 120
Utilizes: Guest Artists
Budget: $50,000 - $100,000
Income Sources: Private Foundations/Grants/Endowments; Business/Corporate Donations; Box Office; Government Grants; Individual Donations
Season: 52 Weeks   **Annual Attendance:** 12,000

NEW ORLEANS CONCERT BAND
2200 Lake Oaks Parkway, New Orleans, LA 70122
(504) 282-8609
Founded: 1974
Arts Area: Band
Status: Professional; Non-Professional
Type: Resident
Management: Milton Bush, Conductor/Manager; Ed Barnhart, Property Manager
Officers: Lisa McDonald, President; John Risey, Vice President; Maureen Haney, Secretary; Nicholas Woolverton, Treasurer
Volunteer Staff: 10
Non-Paid Artists: 65
Budget: $1,000 - $50,000
Income Sources: Private Foundations/Grants/Endowments; Individual Donations
Season: September - July   **Annual Attendance:** 4,000
Performance Facilities: Saint Charles Avenue Baptist Church

NEW ORLEANS FRIENDS OF MUSIC
1035 Eleanore Street, New Orleans, LA 70115
(504) 897-3491; (504) 895-0690
Founded: 1956
Arts Area: Chamber
Status: Non-Profit
Type: Sponsoring
Purpose: To bring the best chamber music possible to the people of New Orleans at a reasonable ticket price
Management: Marcie Scheurmann, Subscription Manager
Officers: Dr. Stuart D. Farber, President; Lawrence M. Lehmann, Vice President; Dr. Teal F. Bennett, Secretary; Dr. Anne S. Bradburn, Treasurer
Volunteer Staff: 30
Utilizes: Guest Artists
Budget: $1,000 - $50,000
Income Sources: Private Foundations/Grants/Endowments; Business/Corporate Donations; Box Office; Individual Donations
Season: September - April   **Annual Attendance:** 5,000
Performance Facilities: Dixon Hall

VOCAL MUSIC

THE B SHARP MUSIC CLUB OF NEW ORLEANS
2724 Mexico Street, New Orleans, LA 70122
(504) 288-0959
Founded: 1917
Arts Area: Light Opera; Operetta
Status: Non-Profit
Type: Performing; Sponsoring
Purpose: To foster the preservation of music from including classical, Negro spirituals and contemporary pieces; to encourage youthful talent by giving scholarship aid and providing the opportunity for youth to perform; to develop followship among music patrons and musicians
Management: Lillian D. Perry, Volunteer Director
Officers: Audrey C. Robertson, President; Lillian Dunn Perry, President Emeritus; Elise Dunn Cain, Vice President; Sylvia N. Oliver, Corresponding Secretary; Leona H. Dawson, Financial Secretary; Sharon Auguillard, Recording Secretary; Junealee Populus, Treasurer

Budget: $1,000 - $50,000
Income Sources: Individual Donations
Season: October - June
Affiliations: National Association of Negro Musicians

NEW ORLEANS OPERA ASSOCIATION
333 Saint Charles Avenue, #907, New Orleans, LA 70130
(504) 529-2278; (504) 524-1018
FAX: (504) 529-7668
Founded: 1943
Arts Area: Grand Opera
Status: Professional; Non-Profit
Type: Performing; Resident; Educational
Purpose: To produce and present the finest in grand opera to Louisiana and the surrounding area
Management: Arthur G. Cosenza, General Director; Garold Whisler, Music Administrator/Chorus Master; Mollie B. Anderson, Senior Studio Administrator
Officers: Joseph Young Jr., President; H. Lloyd Hawkins Jr., Executive Vice President; John G. Panzeca, Treasurer; Owen Q. Niehaus, Secretary
Paid Staff: 10
Paid Artists: 300
Utilizes: Special Technical Talent; Guest Conductors; Guest Artists; Guest Directors
Budget: $1,000,000 - $5,000,000
Income Sources: Private Foundations/Grants/Endowments; Business/Corporate Donations; Box Office; Government Grants; Individual Donations
Season: October - March   **Annual Attendance:** 30,000
Performance Facilities: New Orleans Theatre of Performing Arts

WOMEN'S GUILD OF THE NEW ORLEANS OPERA ASSOCIATION
2504 Prytania Street, New Orleans, LA 70130
(504) 899-1945
Founded: 1942
Status: Professional; Non-Profit
Type: Educational; Sponsoring
Purpose: To support the New Orleans Opera Association through fund-raising; to educate
Officers: Veronica Porteous Scheinuk, President
Paid Staff: 1   **Volunteer Staff:** 10
Utilizes: Special Technical Talent; Guest Conductors; Guest Artists; Guest Directors
Budget: $100,000 - $500,000
Income Sources: Private Foundations/Grants/Endowments; Business/Corporate Donations; Box Office
Season: 52 Weeks

THEATRE

CONTEMPORARY ART CENTER
900 Camp Street, PO Box 30498, New Orleans, LA 70130
(504) 523-1216
FAX: (504) 528-3828
Founded: 1977
Arts Area: Professional; Theatrical Group
Status: Professional; Non-Profit
Type: Performing; Touring; Educational
Purpose: Contemporary Arts Center serves contemporary visual and performing artists and their audiences and provides exhibitions, performances, facilities, education and promotes development for artists in the community
Management: Annette Dimeo Carlozzi, Executive Director
Officers: Martha Jane Murray, President; Jan Gilbert, Vice President-Arts Policy; Thomas Mann, Vice President-Building; Bob Scott, Vice President-Corporate and Foundation Relations; Patricia Chandler, Vice President-Marketing; Nannette Smith-Goins, Vice President-Membership; Suzanne Mestayer, Treasurer; Barbara Lemann, Secretary
Paid Staff: 26   **Volunteer Staff:** 150
Paid Artists: 100
Utilizes: Guest Artists; Guest Directors
Budget: $500,000 - $1,000,000
Income Sources: Private Foundations/Grants/Endowments; Business/Corporate Donations; Box Office; Government Grants; Individual Donations
Season: 52 Weeks   **Annual Attendance:** 50,000
Affiliations: Arts Council of New Orleans
Performance Facilities: Contemporary Arts Center

JUNEBUG PRODUCTIONS INC.
1061 Camp Street, Suite D, New Orleans, LA 70130
(504) 524-8257
FAX: (504) 529-5403
> **Founded:** 1980
> **Arts Area:** Professional
> **Status:** Professional; Non-Profit
> **Type:** Performing; Touring; Educational; Sponsoring
> **Purpose:** To support and inspire efforts to end the exploitation of people and the environment
> **Management:** John O'Neal, Artistic Director; James B. Borders, Managing Director
> **Officers:** Wallace Young, Chairman; John O'Neal, President; Lolis Elie, Vice President; Theresa Holden, Treasurer; John T. Scott, Secretary
> **Paid Staff:** 4
> **Paid Artists:** 4
> **Utilizes:** Special Technical Talent; Guest Artists; Guest Directors; Guest Composers
> **Budget:** $100,000 - $500,000
> **Income Sources:** Private Foundations/Grants/Endowments; Business/Corporate Donations; Box Office; Government Grants; Individual Donations
> **Season:** 52 Weeks   **Annual Attendance:** 40,000
> **Affiliations:** Alternate ROOTS

UNIVERSITY OF NEW ORLEANS RESIDENT ACTING COMPANY
Lakefront, New Orleans, LA 70148
(504) 286-6317
FAX: (504) 286-6098
> **Founded:** 1969
> **Arts Area:** Professional
> **Status:** Professional; Non-Profit
> **Type:** Performing; Resident; Educational
> **Purpose:** Create an ensemble theatrical, television and film performance group to assist in instruction of classes as well as represent the university in the community
> **Management:** Phil Karnell, Managing Director
> **Officers:** Dr. Kevin L. Graves, Chairman
> **Paid Staff:** 3
> **Paid Artists:** 7
> **Utilizes:** Special Technical Talent; Guest Artists; Guest Directors
> **Budget:** $1,000 - $50,000
> **Income Sources:** Private Foundations/Grants/Endowments; Government Grants
> **Season:** August - May   **Annual Attendance:** 8,000
> **Performance Facilities:** University of New Orleans Performing Arts Center

PERFORMING SERIES

NEW ORLEANS JAZZ AND HERITAGE FESTIVAL
142 North Alexander Street, New Orleans, LA 70119
(504) 522-4786
FAX: (504) 522-5456
> **Founded:** 1970
> **Arts Area:** Festivals
> **Status:** Non-Profit
> **Type:** Performing
> **Purpose:** To present and preserve Louisiana music and culture
> **Management:** Quint Davis, Producer/Director
> **Paid Staff:** 50
> **Paid Artists:** 7,000
> **Budget:** $1,000,000 - $5,000,000
> **Income Sources:** Business/Corporate Donations; Box Office; Concession Sales; Sponsorship
> **Season:** April - May   **Annual Attendance:** 300,000

FACILITY

LE PETIT THEATRE DU VIEUX CARRE
616 St. Peter Street, New Orleans, LA 70116
(504) 522-9958
> **Type of Facility:** Theatre House
> **Type of Stage:** Proscenium
> **Seating Capacity:** 460
> **Year Built:** 1797

LOYOLA UNIVERSITY - LOUIS J. ROUSSEL PERFORMANCE HALL
6363 St. Charles Avenue, New Orleans, LA 70118
(504) 865-2148 ·
> **Type of Facility:** Concert Hall
> **Type of Stage:** Flexible
> **Stage Dimensions:** 50'x36'   **Orchestra Pit**
> **Seating Capacity:** 592
> **Year Built:** 1985   **Architect:** The Mathes Group
> **Acoustical Consultant:** C.P. Boner and Associates
> **Contact for Rental:** Stewart Becnel;   (504) 865-2148

LOYOLA UNIVERSITY - MARQUETTE THEATRE
6363 St. Charles Avenue, New Orleans, LA 70118
(504) 865-2170
> **Type of Facility:** Theatre House
> **Type of Stage:** Proscenium
> **Seating Capacity:** 155
> **Contact for Rental:** Ernest Ferlita, SJ

NEW ORLEANS MUNICIPAL AUDITORIUM
1201 St. Peter Street, New Orleans, LA 70016
(504) 565-7470
> **Type of Facility:** Auditorium
> **Year Built:** 1929   **Architect:** Mathes Bergman & Associates

NEW ORLEANS THEATRE OF THE PERFORMING ARTS
801 North Rampart, New Orleans, LA 70116
(504) 522-0592
> **Type of Facility:** Theatre House
> **Type of Stage:** Proscenium
> **Stage Dimensions:** 32'x60'x80'   **Orchestra Pit**
> **Seating Capacity:** 2,316
> **Year Built:** 1973   **Architect:** William Bergman   **Cost:** $7,000,000
> **Acoustical Consultant:** Bolt, Beranek & Newman
> **Contact for Rental:** Sharon Sheridan
> **Resident Groups:** New Orleans Philharmonic Symphony

ORPHEUM THEATER
129 University Place, New Orleans, LA 70112
(504) 524-3285
FAX: (504) 524-3286
> **Type of Facility:** Concert Hall; Multi-Purpose
> **Type of Stage:** Proscenium
> **Stage Dimensions:** 77'Wx45'D; 45'Wx27'H proscenium opening   **Orchestra Pit**
> **Seating Capacity:** 1,925
> **Year Built:** 1921   **Architect:** G. Albert Landsburgh; Samuel Stone   **Cost:** $600,000
> **Year Remodeled:** 1982   **Architect:** Jack Stewart   **Cost:** $3,100,000
> **Acoustical Consultant:** Jaffe Acoustics
> **Contact for Rental:** Jeff Montalbano, General Manager;   (504) 524-3285
> **Manager:** Peter Pfeil;   (504) 524-3288
> **Resident Groups:** Louisiana Philharmonic Orchestra
> *Listed on the National Register of Historic Places, the Orpheum has the largest expanse of polychrome terra cotta on its facade in the city of New Orleans.*

SAENGER PERFORMING ARTS CENTER
143 North Rampart, New Orleans, LA 70112
(504) 525-1052
FAX: (504) 569-1533
> **Type of Facility:** Performance Center; Theatre House
> **Type of Stage:** Proscenium
> **Stage Dimensions:** 81'9"Wx36'3"D; 51'9"Wx36'3"D proscenium opening   **Orchestra Pit**
> **Seating Capacity:** 3,000
> **Year Built:** 1927   **Architect:** Emil Weil
> **Year Remodeled:** 1980   **Cost:** $1,500,000

Contact for Rental: Dale Harris;   (504) 525-1052
Manager: Marks Chowning;   (504) 525-1052

TULANE UNIVERSITY - ALBERT I. LUPIN MEMORIAL EXPERIMENTAL THEATRE
Brandt V.B. Dixon Performing Arts Center, New Orleans, LA 70118
(504) 865-5360
    Type of Facility: Theatre Complex; Studio Performance; Arena; Multi-Purpose
    Type of Stage: Flexible
    Seating Capacity: 150
    Year Built: 1984   **Architect:** George Leake & David Leake   **Cost:** $500,000
    Acoustical Consultant: David Leake
    Resident Groups: Tulane University Theatre; Center Stage at Tulane

UNIVERSITY OF NEW ORLEANS PERFORMING ARTS CENTER
Lakefront, New Orleans, LA 70148
(504) 286-6317
    Type of Facility: Theatre Complex; Concert Hall; Studio Performance; Performance Center; Theatre House; Arena; Multi-Purpose
    Type of Stage: Thrust; Flexible; Proscenium; Arena
    Seating Capacity: 180
    Year Built: 1972   **Architect:** Custis & Davis   **Cost:** $3,000,000
    Resident Groups: UNO Video; Opera Workshop; Resident Acting Company; UNO Department of Music; UNO Department of Drama and Communications

---

Reserve

THEATRE

ST. JOHN THEATRE
103-205 West Fourth Street, Reserve, LA 70084
(504) 536-2410
    Founded: 1931
    Arts Area: Musical; Community
    Status: Non-Professional; Non-Profit; Community
    Type: Performing; Educational
    Purpose: To provide live theatre to our community, especially to our schools and students
    Management: Jack S. Snowdy, Managing Director
    Officers: Lucien Cambre, President; Sterling Snowdy, Vice President; Donna Laurent, Secretary; Richard Oubre, Treasurer
    Paid Staff: 2   **Volunteer Staff:** 10
    Non-Paid Artists: 50
    Utilizes: Special Technical Talent; Guest Artists; Guest Directors; High School Drama Departments
    Budget: $1,000 - $50,000
    Income Sources: Private Foundations/Grants/Endowments; Business/Corporate Donations; Box Office; Individual Donations
    Season: 52 Weeks   **Annual Attendance:** 8,000
    Performance Facilities: St. John Theatre Stage

Ruston

FACILITY

LOUISIANA TECH - HOWARD AUDITORIUM CENTER FOR THE PERFORMING ARTS
Arizona & Adams, PO Box 3033 T.S., Ruston, LA 71272
(318) 257-4109
    Founded: 1945
    Type of Facility: Auditorium; Performance Center; Theatre House; Opera House; Multi-Purpose
    Type of Stage: Proscenium   **Orchestra Pit**
    Seating Capacity: 1,126
    Year Remodeled: 1982
    Contact for Rental: David Wylie, Director;   (318) 257-4109

Shreveport

DANCE

SHREVEPORT METROPOLITAN BALLET
6040 Fairfield Avenue, Shreveport, LA 71106
(318) 865-8242
>**Founded:** 1973
>**Arts Area:** Ballet
>**Status:** Non-Professional; Non-Profit
>**Type:** Performing; Resident; Educational
>**Purpose:** An educational vehicle for area young people to learn and perform ballet
>**Management:** Marion Mills, Artistic Director
>**Non-Paid Artists:** 30
>**Utilizes:** Guest Artists; Guest Choreographers
>**Budget:** $1,000 - $50,000
>**Income Sources:** Private Foundations/Grants/Endowments; Business/Corporate Donations; Box Office; Government Grants; Individual Donations
>**Season:** September - June
>**Performance Facilities:** The Shreveport Civic Theatre

INSTRUMENTAL MUSIC

SHREVEPORT SYMPHONY ORCHESTRA
619 Louisiana Avenue, Suite 400, Shreveport, LA 71101
(318) 222-7496
FAX: (318) 222-7490
>**Founded:** 1947
>**Arts Area:** Symphony; Orchestra; Chamber; Ensemble
>**Status:** Professional; Non-Profit
>**Type:** Performing; Touring; Educational
>**Purpose:** To supply the three-state area with the highest possible quality musical performances
>**Management:** Cornelia Mason, General Manager; Jean Ellis, Director of Development; Peter Leonard, Music Director
>**Officers:** Sybil Patten, President; Robert Neff, Treasurer; Dr. Kathy Upham, Secretary
>**Paid Staff:** 8   **Volunteer Staff:** 130
>**Paid Artists:** 65
>**Utilizes:** Guest Conductors; Guest Artists
>**Budget:** $1,000,000 - $5,000,000
>**Income Sources:** Private Foundations/Grants/Endowments; Business/Corporate Donations; Box Office; Government Grants; Individual Donations
>**Season:** 52 Weeks   **Annual Attendance:** 150,000
>**Affiliations:** ASOL
>**Performance Facilities:** Civic Theatre

VOCAL MUSIC

SHREVEPORT OPERA
212 Texas Street, Suite 101, Shreveport, LA 71101-3249
(318) 227-9503
>**Founded:** 1949
>**Arts Area:** Grand Opera; Lyric Opera; Light Opera; Operetta
>**Status:** Professional; Non-Profit
>**Type:** Performing; Touring; Resident; Educational
>**Purpose:** To provide professional music theatre to the region
>**Management:** Robert Murray, General Director
>**Officers:** Merritt B. Chastain Jr., President
>**Paid Staff:** 1   **Volunteer Staff:** 200
>**Paid Artists:** 423   **Non-Paid Artists:** 735
>**Utilizes:** Special Technical Talent; Guest Conductors; Guest Artists; Guest Directors
>**Budget:** $100,000 - $500,000
>**Income Sources:** Private Foundations/Grants/Endowments; Business/Corporate Donations; Box Office; Government Grants; Individual Donations; Guild Projects
>**Season:** Fall - Spring
>**Affiliations:** OA; NOA; Shreveport, Bossier Chambers of Commerce
>**Performance Facilities:** Shreveport Civic Theatre; Strand Theatre

THEATRE

THE GAS LIGHT PLAYERS
PO Box 271, Shreveport, LA 71162
(318) 635-8273
> **Founded:** 1959
> **Arts Area:** Theatrical Group
> **Status:** Non-Profit
> **Type:** Performing
> **Purpose:** Community theater whose primary performances will be early melodrama or original works of melodrama style
> **Officers:** C. Marvin Cox, President; George Sewell, Vice President; Nita Renshaw, Treasurer; Anna Aslin, Secretary
> **Volunteer Staff:** 15
> **Budget:** $1,000 - $50,000
> **Income Sources:** Private Foundations/Grants/Endowments; Business/Corporate Donations; Box Office; Individual Donations
> **Season:** June - October **Annual Attendance:** 11,000

SHREVEPORT LITTLE THEATRE
812 Margaret Place, Shreveport, LA 71101
(318) 424-4439
> **Founded:** 1921
> **Arts Area:** Community
> **Status:** Non-Professional; Non-Profit
> **Type:** Performing; Touring
> **Purpose:** Committed to produce a variety of quality live theatre with predominantly volunteer participation from the community, with the guidance of trained artistic and managerial leadership, for entertainment, enlightenment and growth of audience awareness and pride
> **Management:** John C. Mitchell, Managing Director
> **Officers:** Paul Jordan, President
> **Paid Staff:** 1 **Volunteer Staff:** 30
> **Utilizes:** Guest Directors
> **Budget:** $100,000 - $500,000
> **Income Sources:** Private Foundations/Grants/Endowments; Business/Corporate Donations; Box Office; Individual Donations
> **Season:** September - July **Annual Attendance:** 8,000

PERFORMING SERIES

THEATRE OF THE PERFORMING ARTS
400 North Dale Avenue, Shreveport, LA 71101
(318) 221-7964
> **Founded:** 1975
> **Arts Area:** Dance; Vocal Music; Instrumental Music; Theater; Festivals
> **Status:** Professional; Non-Profit
> **Type:** Performing; Touring; Sponsoring
> **Purpose:** Multi-discipline organization whose mission is to foster the culture of Afro-America
> **Management:** Gloria J. Christopher Gibson, Artistic Director/Founder
> **Officers:** Willie B. Meyers, President
> **Paid Staff:** 3
> **Utilizes:** Special Technical Talent; Guest Conductors; Guest Artists; Guest Directors
> **Budget:** $50,000 - $100,000
> **Income Sources:** Private Foundations/Grants/Endowments; Business/Corporate Donations; Box Office; Government Grants; Individual Donations
> **Season:** 52 Weeks
> **Affiliations:** Louisiana Black Culture Commission

FACILITY

CENTENARY COLLEGE - RECITAL HALL
Hurley School of Music, Shreveport, LA 71134
(318) 869-5235
> **Type of Facility:** Concert Hall
> **Type of Stage:** Proscenium
> **Seating Capacity:** 315
> **Year Built:** 1964
> **Resident Groups:** Camerata; Opera Theater; Symphony Orchestra; Wind Ensemble; Jazz Band

HIRSCH MEMORIAL COLISEUM
Louisiana State Fair, PO Box 9100, Shreveport, LA 71139-9100
(318) 635-1361
FAX: (318) 631-4909
    Type of Facility: Arena
    Type of Stage: Platform; Arena
    Stage Dimensions: 60'x40'
    Seating Capacity: 10,200
    Year Built: 1954   **Architect:** E.M. Freeman & Associates
    Contact for Rental: Cecil M. Faries; (318) 635-1361

SHREVEPORT CIVIC THEATRE
400 Clyde Fant Parkway, Shreveport, LA 71101
(318) 673-5100
FAX: (318) 673-5100
    Type of Facility: Theatre House
    Facility Originally: Meeting Hall; Movie House
    Type of Stage: Proscenium
    Stage Dimensions: 49'8"Wx23'5"D **Orchestra Pit**
    Seating Capacity: 1,737
    Year Built: 1965   **Architect:** Somdal, Sorenson, Smitherman & Associates
    Acoustical Consultant: Local 298 IATSE
    Contact for Rental: Sharron Killen; (318) 673-5100
    Manager: James B. Hobbs Jr.; (318) 673-5100
    Resident Groups: Shreveport Metropolitan Ballet; Shreveport Symphony; Shreveport Opera

SHREVEPORT MUNICIPAL AUDITORIUM
705 Grand Avenue, Shreveport, LA 71101
(318) 673-5100
FAX: (318) 673-5100
    Founded: 1929
    Type of Facility: Theatre Complex; Auditorium; Off Broadway; Theatre House; Opera House; Arena; Multi-Purpose
    Facility Originally: Meeting Hall
    Type of Stage: Proscenium
    Stage Dimensions: 58'5"Wx37'5"D
    Seating Capacity: 3,293
    Year Built: 1928   **Architect:** Weiner
    Acoustical Consultant: Local 298 IATSE
    Contact for Rental: Sharron Killen; (318) 673-5100
    Manager: James B. Hobbs Jr.; (318) 673-5100

STRAND THEATRE
619 Louisiana Avenue, PO Box 1547, Shreveport, LA 71165-1547
(318) 226-2924
    Type of Facility: Concert Hall; Theatre House
    Type of Stage: Proscenium
    Stage Dimensions: 35'Dx80'W; 44'Wx27'H proscenium opening **Orchestra Pit**
    Seating Capacity: 1,640
    Year Built: 1925   **Architect:** Emil Weil **Cost:** $850,000
    Year Remodeled: 1984   **Architect:** Haas & Massey Architects **Cost:** $4,300,000
    Acoustical Consultant: C.P. Boner & Associates
    Contact for Rental: Craig Young; (318) 226-1481
    Resident Groups: Shreveport Symphony

MAINE

Augusta

INSTRUMENTAL MUSIC

AUGUSTA SYMPHONY
PO Box 481, Augusta, ME 04330
(207) 622-5998
Founded: 1920
Arts Area: Symphony; Band
Status: Non-Professional; Non-Profit
Type: Performing
Purpose: To present concerts; to hold rehearsals
Officers: Lynne Burney, President; Timothy Paulin, Vice President; Joan Passle, Secretary; Robert McGuire, Treasurer
Volunteer Staff: 24
Paid Artists: 1   **Non-Paid Artists:** 180
Budget: $1,000 - $50,000
Income Sources: Box Office; Individual Donations
Season: September - June   **Annual Attendance:** 4,000

PERFORMING SERIES

NEW MUSIK DIRECTIONS
67 Green Street, Augusta, ME 04330
(207) 623-1941
Founded: 1981
Arts Area: Festivals
Status: Professional; Commercial
Type: Performing; Educational; Sponsoring
Purpose: To provide a vehicle for the performance of new music, film and video
Management: Joseph Baltar, Director
Paid Staff: 1
Utilizes: Guest Artists
Budget: $1,000 - $50,000
Income Sources: Private Foundations/Grants/Endowments; Business/Corporate Donations; Box Office; Government Grants; Individual Donations
Season: 52 Weeks   **Annual Attendance:** 500

FACILITY

AUGUSTA CIVIC CENTER
Community Drive, Augusta, ME 04330
(207) 626-2405
FAX: (207) 626-5968
Type of Facility: Civic Center; Multi-Purpose
Year Built: 1973   **Architect:** Bunker & Savage   **Cost:** $4,000,000
Year Remodeled: 1978   **Cost:** $3,500,000
Acoustical Consultant: Canfield
Contact for Rental: Bob Howard;   (207) 626-2405
The Civic Center contains the Arena and North Hall, a 1978 addition to the Center. See individual listings for additional information.

AUGUSTA CIVIC CENTER - ARENA
Community Drive, Augusta, ME 04330
(207) 626-2405
FAX: (207) 626-5968
Founded: 1973
Type of Facility: Arena
Type of Stage: Flexible; Platform
Stage Dimensions: 40'x60'
Seating Capacity: Full House - 6,800; Half House - 3,000
Year Built: 1973
Contact for Rental: Bob Howard;   (207) 626-2405

AUGUSTA CIVIC CENTER - NORTH HALL
Community Drive, Augusta, ME 04330
(207) 626-2405
FAX: (207) 626-5968
  Type of Facility: Multi-Purpose; Room
  Type of Stage: Platform
  Stage Dimensions: 20'x20'
  Seating Capacity: 500
  Year Remodeled: 1978   **Cost:** $3,500,000
  Contact for Rental: Bob Howard;   (207) 626-2405

Bangor

INSTRUMENTAL MUSIC

BANGOR SYMPHONY ORCHESTRA
PO Box 1441, Bangor, ME 04401
(207) 942-5555
FAX: (207) 942-9278
  Founded: 1896
  Arts Area: Symphony; Orchestra; Chamber; Ensemble
  Status: Professional; Non-Profit
  Type: Performing; Touring; Resident; Sponsoring
  Purpose: As the oldest community orchestra in the United States offering continuous service at the community level, the Bangor Symphony Orchestra performs for local audiences as well as on tour.
  Management: Robert Bahr, General Manager; Werner Torkanowsky, Music Director/Conductor
  Paid Staff: 3   **Volunteer Staff:** 200
  Paid Artists: 80   **Non-Paid Artists:** 2
  Utilizes: Guest Conductors; Guest Artists; Guest Directors
  Budget: $100,000 - $500,000
  Income Sources: Private Foundations/Grants/Endowments; Business/Corporate Donations; Box Office; Government Grants; Individual Donations
  Season: September - May
  Affiliations: ASOL; Greater Bangor Arts Council
  Performance Facilities: Bangor Opera House

THEATRE

PENOBSCOT THEATRE COMPANY
183 Main Street, Bangor, ME 04401
(207) 942-3333
  Founded: 1974
  Arts Area: Professional
  Status: Professional; Non-Profit
  Type: Performing; Touring; Resident; Sponsoring
  Purpose: To provide a resident regional theatre for the Bangor Area; to host and support local arts organizations; to broaden the area's cultural life and activities
  Management: Mark Torres, Producing/Artistic Director
  Paid Staff: 4   **Volunteer Staff:** 4
  Paid Artists: 8   **Non-Paid Artists:** 8
  Utilizes: Special Technical Talent; Guest Artists; Guest Directors
  Budget: $50,000 - $100,000
  Income Sources: Business/Corporate Donations; Box Office; Government Grants; Individual Donations
  Season: October - March   **Annual Attendance:** 10,000

FACILITY

BANGOR AUDITORIUM
100 Dutton Street, Bangor, ME 04401
(207) 942-9000
FAX: (207) 947-5105
  Type of Facility: Auditorium; Arena
  Type of Stage: Arena
  Stage Dimensions: 40'x60'; sound wings available
  Seating Capacity: 7,000
  Year Built: 1953   **Architect:** Eaton/Tarbell   **Cost:** $1,400,000
  Contact for Rental: Kurt Rogerson;   (207) 942-9000

BANGOR CIVIC CENTER
100 Dutton Street, Bangor, ME 04401
(207) 942-9000
FAX: (207) 947-5105
Type of Facility: Civic Center
Type of Stage: Flexible; Platform
Stage Dimensions: 40'x60'; sound wings available
Seating Capacity: 1,600
Year Built: 1978 **Architect:** Eaton/Tarbell **Cost:** $1,225,000
Contact for Rental: Kurt Rogerson; (207) 942-9000

Bar Harbor

PERFORMING SERIES

ARCADY MUSIC SOCIETY
PO Box 780, Bar Harbor, ME 04609
(207) 288-3151
Founded: 1981
Arts Area: Vocal Music; Instrumental Music; Festivals
Status: Professional; Non-Profit
Type: Performing; Educational; Sponsoring
Purpose: To bring high-quality classical and contemporary music to central, northern, and Downeast Maine through live performances, with an emphasis on chamber music and programs for young people
Management: Masanobu Ikemiya, Artistic Director; Melba Wilson, Executive Director
Officers: Etel Thomas, President; Marie Nolb, First Vice President; John Hoelter, Secretary; Richard Fox, Treasurer
Paid Staff: 4 **Volunteer Staff:** 50
Utilizes: Guest Conductors; Guest Artists
Budget: $100,000 - $500,000
Income Sources: Private Foundations/Grants/Endowments; Business/Corporate Donations; Box Office; Government Grants; Individual Donations
Season: 52 Weeks **Annual Attendance:** 3,000
Affiliations: CMA

BAR HARBOR MUSIC FESTIVAL
The Rodick Building, 59 Cottage Street, Bar Harbor, ME 04609
(207) 288-5744
Founded: 1967
Arts Area: Vocal Music; Instrumental Music; Festivals; New Composers
Status: Professional; Non-Profit
Type: Performing; Touring; Resident; Educational; Sponsoring
Purpose: To create performance opportunities for young artists through an annual summer festival and tours
Management: Francis Fortier, Artistic Director
Officers: Francis Fortier, President; J. Philip Benkard, Vice President
Paid Staff: 6 **Volunteer Staff:** 10
Paid Artists: 30
Utilizes: Special Technical Talent; Guest Conductors; Guest Artists
Budget: $100,000 - $500,000
Income Sources: Private Foundations/Grants/Endowments; Business/Corporate Donations; Box Office; Government Grants; Individual Donations
Season: July - August **Annual Attendance:** 10,000
Performance Facilities: Congregational Church; Kebo Valley Golf Club Auditorium

Brunswick

THEATRE

MAINE STATE MUSIC THEATER
PO Box 656, Brunswick, ME 04011
(207) 725-8769
FAX: (207) 725-1199
Founded: 1959
Arts Area: Professional; Summer Stock; Musical
Status: Professional; Non-Profit
Type: Performing; Resident; Educational

Purpose: To educate young theatre professionals; to present quality musical theatre; to preserve the American musical
Management: Chuck Abbott, Artistic Director; Billings Lapierre, General Manager
Officers: Janet Wilk, President; Thomas Pierce, Vice President; Sara McMahan, Secretary; Peter Chandler, Treasurer
Paid Staff: 50 **Volunteer Staff:** 35
Paid Artists: 25 **Non-Paid Artists:** 15
Utilizes: Special Technical Talent; Guest Artists; Guest Directors
Budget: $500,000 - $1,000,000
Income Sources: Box Office; Individual Donations
Season: June - August **Annual Attendance:** 45,000
Affiliations: AEA

FACILITY

PICKARD THEATRE
Memorial Hall, Bowdoin College, Brunswick, ME 04011
(207) 725-3000; (207) 725-1199
Type of Facility: Theatre House
Facility Originally: School
Type of Stage: Proscenium
Stage Dimensions: 52'Wx35'D **Orchestra Pit**
Seating Capacity: 600
Year Built: 1865 **Architect:** Stanford White
Year Remodeled: 1955
Resident Groups: Brunswick Summer Music Theater; Maine State Music Theater

Camden

PERFORMING SERIES

BAY CHAMBER CONCERTS
PO Box 191, Camden, ME 04843
(207) 236-2823
Founded: 1960
Arts Area: Instrumental Music
Status: Professional
Type: Performing
Purpose: To encourage the appreciation of music, especially chamber music, in the state of Maine
Management: Thomas Wolf, Artistic Director; Jean Freedman, Administrative Director
Officers: Marvin Garner, President; Bill May, Vice President; Carroll Roberts Jr., Secretary; Steve McAllister, Treasurer
Paid Staff: 2
Utilizes: Guest Artists
Budget: $50,000 - $100,000
Income Sources: Private Foundations/Grants/Endowments; Business/Corporate Donations; Box Office; Government Grants; Individual Donations
Season: July - May **Annual Attendance:** 5,700
Performance Facilities: Rockport Opera House

FACILITY

CAMDEN OPERA HOUSE
29 Elm Street, Camden, ME 04843
(207) 236-3353
Type of Facility: Concert Hall
Type of Stage: Proscenium
Stage Dimensions: 25'x20'x15' **Orchestra Pit**
Seating Capacity: 550
Year Built: 1893 **Cost:** $40,000
Year Remodeled: 1930
Contact for Rental: Nancy Hayes; (207) 236-3353
Resident Groups: Camden Civic Theatre

Freeport
THEATRE

FIGURES OF SPEECH THEATRE
Rural Route 4, PO Box 4277, Freeport, ME 05032
(207) 865-6355
> **Management:** Carol Llewelyn
> **Season:** 52 Weeks

Hancock
PERFORMING SERIES

THE PIERRE MONTEUX SCHOOL
Route 1, PO Box 157, Hancock, ME 04640
(207) 422-3931
FAX: (207) 422-9122
> **Founded:** 1943
> **Arts Area:** Instrumental Music; Symphony
> **Status:** Professional; Non-Profit
> **Type:** Performing; Educational
> **Purpose:** To acquaint young conductors and future orchestra musicians with the full symphonic repertoire
> **Management:** Nancie Monteux-Barendse, Administrative President; Michael Jinbo, Marc David, Assistant Conductors; Charles Bruck, Director/Maestro
> **Paid Staff:** 2
> **Budget:** $50,000 - $100,000
> **Income Sources:** Private Foundations/Grants/Endowments; Business/Corporate Donations; Government Grants; Individual Donations
> **Season:** June - July **Annual Attendance:** 1,200

Lewiston
PERFORMING SERIES

BATES DANCE FESTIVAL
Lane Hall, Bates College, Lewiston, ME
(207) 786-6077
FAX: (207) 786-6123
> **Founded:** 1982
> **Arts Area:** Dance
> **Status:** Professional
> **Type:** Resident; Educational; Sponsoring
> **Purpose:** To support education, performance and the creation of new works by providing a non-competitive, high-quality dance program
> **Management:** Laura Faure, Director; Larissa Vigue, Administrative Assistant; Linda Stimpson, Development Assistant
> **Paid Staff:** 4 **Volunteer Staff:** 8
> **Paid Artists:** 40
> **Utilizes:** Special Technical Talent; Guest Artists; Guest Choreographers
> **Budget:** $100,000 - $500,000
> **Income Sources:** Private Foundations/Grants/Endowments; Business/Corporate Donations; Box Office; Government Grants; Individual Donations
> **Season:** July - August **Annual Attendance:** 3,000
> **Performance Facilities:** Schaeffer Theatre

LA ARTS
234 Lisbon Street, Lewiston, ME 04210
(207) 782-7228
> **Founded:** 1973
> **Arts Area:** Dance; Vocal Music; Instrumental Music; Theater; Festivals
> **Status:** Professional; Non-Profit
> **Type:** Performing; Educational; Sponsoring
> **Purpose:** To integrate the arts into the fabric of everyday life in central Maine
> **Management:** Katherine Knowles, Executive Director
> **Paid Staff:** 4
> **Paid Artists:** 40

Budget: $100,000 - $500,000
Income Sources: Private Foundations/Grants/Endowments; Business/Corporate Donations; Box Office; Government Grants; Individual Donations
Season: September - June   **Annual Attendance:** 12,000
Affiliations: APAP; Maine Arts Sponsor Association

FACILITY

BATES COLLEGE - CONCERT HALL
Olin Arts Center, Lewiston, ME 04240
(207) 786-6255
Type of Facility: Concert Hall
Type of Stage: Semicircular
Stage Dimensions: 40'Wx24'D
Seating Capacity: 300
Manager: Mark Howard;   (207) 786-6135

BATES COLLEGE - OLIN ARTS CENTER
Lewiston, ME 04240
(207) 786-6255
Type of Facility: Studio Performance; Performance Center; Multi-Purpose
Year Built: 1986   **Architect:** The Architects Collaborative   **Cost:** $4,300,000
Acoustical Consultant: Cavanaugh Tocci Associates
Manager: Mark Howard;   (207) 786-6135
Resident Groups: Bates College activities

Machias

PERFORMING SERIES

MACHIAS BAY CHAMBER CONCERTS, INC.
PO Box 332, Machias, ME 04654
Founded: 1969
Arts Area: Instrumental Music
Status: Professional; Non-Profit
Type: Sponsoring
Purpose: To present chamber music concerts; to encourage music appreciation; to perform in schools and the community
Officers: Dorothy Day, President; Mrs. Wallace Greenwood, Vice President; Mrs. Hollis Ingalls, Secretary; Richard Shaw, Treasurer
Volunteer Staff: 20
Utilizes: Guest Artists
Income Sources: Private Foundations/Grants/Endowments; Business/Corporate Donations; Box Office; Government Grants; Individual Donations
Season: July - August   **Annual Attendance:** 1,000
Affiliations: Maine Art Sponsors Association

STAGE FRONT: THE ARTS DOWNEAST
University of Maine, O'Brien Avenue, Machias, ME 04654
(207) 255-3313
FAX: (207) 255-4864
Founded: 1969
Arts Area: Dance; Vocal Music; Instrumental Music; Theater; Festivals; Children's Program
Status: Non-Profit
Type: Performing; Educational; Sponsoring
Purpose: Stage Front is the arts organization of the University of Maine at Machias. It presents all areas of the visual and performing arts.
Management: Joan Chamberlain, Program Coordinator for Performing Arts
Paid Staff: 2   **Volunteer Staff:** 25
Utilizes: Special Technical Talent; Guest Artists
Budget: $1,000 - $50,000
Income Sources: Business/Corporate Donations; Box Office; Government Grants; Individual Donations
Season: September - May   **Annual Attendance:** 5,000
Affiliations: Maine Arts Sponsors; New Brunswick Arts Council
Performance Facilities: Powers Hall/Performing Arts Center

FACILITY

UNIVERSITY OF MAINE AT MACHIAS - STAGE FRONT
The Arts Downeast, #9 O'Brien Avenue, Machias, ME 04654
(207) 255-3313
> **Type of Facility:** Concert Hall; Auditorium; Performance Center; Theatre House
> **Facility Originally:** Recreation Hall; Gymnasium
> **Type of Stage:** Thrust; Proscenium
> **Stage Dimensions:** Proscenium - 40'x17'; Thrust - 40'x18'
> **Seating Capacity:** 400
> **Year Built:** 1936   **Architect:** Bunker & Savage
> **Year Remodeled:** 1982   **Architect:** Alonzo J. Harriman   **Cost:** $125,000
> **Acoustical Consultant:** Alonzo J. Harriman & Associates
> **Manager:** Joan Chamberlain, Director;   (207) 255-3314
> **Resident Groups:** The Bad Little Falls Players

Monmouth

THEATRE

THE THEATER AT MONMOUTH
Main Street, PO Box 385, Monmouth, ME 04259
(207) 933-2952
> **Founded:** 1969
> **Arts Area:** Professional; Summer Stock; Theatrical Group
> **Status:** Professional; Non-Profit
> **Type:** Performing; Touring; Resident; Educational
> **Purpose:** To offer a classical repertory season; to present educational productions utilizing the plays of Shakespeare during the school year; to sponsor special events and children's productions
> **Management:** Richard C. Sewell, Artistic Director; M. George Carlson, Managing Director; Christopher Rock, Associate Artistic Director
> **Officers:** Edward N. Hersley, President; Ralph Conant, Vice President; Jeff Smith, Treasurer; Robert V. Schauer, Executive Producer
> **Paid Staff:** 40   **Volunteer Staff:** 20
> **Paid Artists:** 20   **Non-Paid Artists:** 5
> **Utilizes:** Special Technical Talent; Guest Artists; Guest Directors
> **Budget:** $100,000 - $500,000
> **Income Sources:** Private Foundations/Grants/Endowments; Business/Corporate Donations; Box Office; Government Grants; Individual Donations
> **Season:** June - August   **Annual Attendance:** 12,000
> **Affiliations:** TCG; NETC; Maine Arts Sponsors Association
> **Performance Facilities:** Cumston Hall

FACILITY

CUMSTON HALL
Main Street, PO Box 385, Monmouth, ME 04259
(207) 933-2952
> **Type of Facility:** Theatre House; Opera House
> **Facility Originally:** Library; Meeting Hall; Theater; Town Office
> **Type of Stage:** Thrust; Proscenium
> **Seating Capacity:** 275
> **Year Built:** 1900   **Architect:** Harry Cochrane
> **Resident Groups:** The Theater at Monmouth
> *Available for rent in winter only*

Northeast Harbor

PERFORMING SERIES

MOUNT DESERT FESTIVAL OF CHAMBER MUSIC
Neighborhood House, PO Box 862, Northeast Harbor, ME 04662
(212) 362-1870
> **Founded:** 1963
> **Arts Area:** Festivals
> **Status:** Professional
> **Type:** Resident

Purpose: To present a series of five Tuesday-evening concerts using the Composers String Quartet as a nucleus and guest artists
Paid Staff: 2
Paid Artists: 28
Utilizes: Guest Artists
Budget: $1,000 - $50,000
Income Sources: Box Office; Individual Donations
Season: July - August   **Annual Attendance:** 1,500
Performance Facilities: Neighborhood House

Ogunquit-by-the-Sea

THEATRE

OGUNQUIT PLAYHOUSE
PO Box 915, Ogunquit-by-the-Sea, ME 03907
(207) 646-2402
Founded: 1933
Arts Area: Professional
Status: Professional; Commercial
Type: Sponsoring
Management: John Lane, Producer
Paid Staff: 30
Paid Artists: 150
Income Sources: Box Office
Season: June - September   **Annual Attendance:** 55,000
Performance Facilities: Ogunquit Playhouse

FACILITY

OGUNQUIT PLAYHOUSE
PO Box 915, Ogunquit-by-the-Sea, ME 03907
(207) 646-2402
Type of Facility: Theatre House
Type of Stage: Proscenium
Stage Dimensions: 18'x34'x50'   **Orchestra Pit**
Seating Capacity: 750
Year Built: 1932   **Architect:** Wycoft   **Cost:** $100,000

Orono

THEATRE

MARSH ISLAND STAGE
37 Penobscot Street, Orono, ME 04473
(207) 866-5647
Founded: 1984
Arts Area: Theatrical Group
Status: Non-Profit
Type: Performing
Purpose: To bring contemporary playwrights' works to Maine
Management: Christopher Bates, Artistic Director; Susan Camp, Graphic Arts
Officers: Dick Brucher, Carlene Hirsch, Chris Luthin, Board of Directors
Volunteer Staff: 12
Utilizes: Guest Directors
Budget: $1,000 - $50,000
Income Sources: Box Office; Individual Donations
Season: September - June   **Annual Attendance:** 1,000
Performance Facilities: The Ram's Horn

THEATRE OF THE ENCHANTED FOREST
PO Box 336, Orono, ME 04473
(207) 945-0800
Founded: 1974
Arts Area: Professional; Theatrical Group; Family
Status: Professional; Non-Profit
Type: Performing; Touring; Resident; Educational; Sponsoring

Purpose: To bring Maine families the very best that live theatre has to offer; to respect the intelligence and integrity of all audience members, no matter what age; to provide theatre that is not simple-minded nor condescending, but poses plausible dilemmas
Management: Christopher E. Rock, Artistic Director; Sandra Zuk Cyrus, Producing Director; Bronwyn W. Kortge, Associate Producer
Officers: Carol Woodcock, President; Adrian Humphreys, Vice President; Nancy Grover, Secretary; Sandy Ervin, Treasurer
Paid Staff: 3
Paid Artists: 15
Utilizes: Special Technical Talent; Guest Artists; Guest Directors
Budget: $50,000 - $100,000
Income Sources: Business/Corporate Donations; Box Office; Government Grants; Individual Donations
Season: November - July   **Annual Attendance:** 2,500
Performance Facilities: Pavilion Theatre, University of Maine at Orono

FACILITY

UNIVERSITY OF MAINE - MAINE CENTER FOR THE ARTS
Orono, ME 04469
(207) 581-1805
Type of Facility: Concert Hall; Auditorium; Performance Center; Theatre House; Opera House
Type of Stage: Flexible; Proscenium
Stage Dimensions: 70'x30'   **Orchestra Pit**
Seating Capacity: 1,628
Year Built: 1986   **Architect:** Eaton W. Tarbell   **Cost:** $7,500,000
Acoustical Consultant: Bolt, Beranek & Newman
Contact for Rental: John I. Patches;   (207) 581-1805

Portland

DANCE

RAM ISLAND DANCE
25A Forest Avenue, Portland, ME 04101
(207) 773-2562
Arts Area: Modern; Ballet; Inter-arts
Status: Non-Profit
Type: Performing; Touring; Resident; Educational
Purpose: To promote contemporary dance; to support artists living and working in the region
Management: Daniel McCusker, Artistic Director/Choreographer; Linda Pervier, Managing Director
Officers: Sandra I. Lovell, Board President
Budget: $1,000 - $50,000
Income Sources: Private Foundations/Grants/Endowments; Business/Corporate Donations; Box Office; Government Grants; Individual Donations

INSTRUMENTAL MUSIC

LARK SOCIETY FOR CHAMBER MUSIC
PO Box 11, Portland, ME 04112
(207) 761-1522
Arts Area: Chamber; Ensemble
Status: Professional
Type: Performing; Touring; Resident; Educational
Purpose: To support and present a Portland concert series as well as educational presentations by the Portland String Quartet
Management: Barbara Duff Management
Officers: Nancy Aldrich, Executive Director
Paid Staff: 1
Paid Artists: 4
Utilizes: Guest Artists
Budget: $50,000 - $100,000
Income Sources: Private Foundations/Grants/Endowments; Business/Corporate Donations; Box Office; Government Grants; Individual Donations

Season: 52 Weeks
Affiliations: CMA

PORTLAND SYMPHONY ORCHESTRA
30 Myrtle Street, Portland, ME 04111
(207) 773-8191
FAX: (207) 773-6089
Founded: 1924
Arts Area: Symphony; Orchestra
Status: Non-Profit
Type: Performing
Management: Jane E. Hunter, Executive Director
Paid Staff: 10
Utilizes: Guest Artists
Budget: $1,000,000 - $5,000,000
Income Sources: Private Foundations/Grants/Endowments; Business/Corporate Donations; Box Office; Government Grants; Individual Donations
Season: October - April; July
Performance Facilities: Portland City Hall Auditorium

THEATRE

PORTLAND STAGE COMPANY
25A Forest Avenue, Box 1458, Portland, ME 04104
(207) 774-1043
FAX: (207) 774-0576
Founded: 1974
Arts Area: Professional; Theatrical Group
Status: Professional; Non-Profit
Type: Performing; Resident; Educational
Purpose: To produce and develop high-quality work and programs that explore basic human issues and concerns, the purpose of which is to entertain, educate, and engage the audience
Management: Greg Leaming, Artistic Director; William Chance, Managing Director
Officers: Peggy Siegle, President; Margaret Pusch, Vice President of Administration; A. Leroy Greason, Vice President of Development; Deborah Locke, Secretary; Robert F. Wade, Treasurer
Paid Staff: 26 **Volunteer Staff:** 150
Paid Artists: 45
Utilizes: Special Technical Talent; Guest Artists; Guest Directors
Budget: $500,000 - $1,000,000
Income Sources: Private Foundations/Grants/Endowments; Business/Corporate Donations; Box Office; Government Grants; Individual Donations
Season: November - May **Annual Attendance:** 42,000
Affiliations: LORT; TCG
Performance Facilities: Portland Performing Arts Center

PERFORMING SERIES

THE MAINE FESTIVAL
582 Congers Street, Portland, ME 04101
(207) 772-9012
FAX: (207) 772-3995
Founded: 1977
Arts Area: Dance; Vocal Music; Instrumental Music; Theater; Festivals
Status: Professional; Non-Profit
Type: Sponsoring
Purpose: To provide artistic opportunities and to encourage the advancement of the performing and the visual arts in Maine through the presentation of a public program of services to artists
Management: Burl Hash, Artistic Director; Diane Briggs, Fund-raising Coordinator; Bruce Hazard, Executive Director
Paid Staff: 7 **Volunteer Staff:** 300
Paid Artists: 1,000
Utilizes: Guest Artists
Budget: $500,000 - $1,000,000
Income Sources: Private Foundations/Grants/Endowments; Business/Corporate Donations; Box Office; Government Grants; Individual Donations
Season: August - September **Annual Attendance:** 30,000
Affiliations: Bowdoin College; APAP
Performance Facilities: Portland Performing Arts Center; Thomas Point Beach

PORTLAND PERFORMING ARTS CENTER, INC.
25A Forest Avenue, Portland, ME 04101
(207) 761-0591
FAX: (207) 761-0576
  Arts Area: Vocal Music; Instrumental Music
  Status: Professional; Non-Profit
  Type: Performing
  Purpose: To support alternative artists, primarily traditional and ethnic performers but also international artists
  Management: Phyllis O'Neill, Executive Director; Bau Graves, Artistic Director
  Officers: Everett Ingalls, Chairman
  Budget: $100,000 - $500,000
  Income Sources: Private Foundations/Grants/Endowments; Business/Corporate Donations; Box Office; Government Grants; Individual Donations
  Performance Facilities: Portland Performing Arts Center

FACILITY

CUMBERLAND COUNTY CIVIC CENTER
1 Civic Center Square, Portland, ME 04101
(207) 775-3481
FAX: (207) 828-1920
  Type of Facility: Civic Center; Arena
  Type of Stage: Arena
  Seating Capacity: 9,500
  Year Built: 1977   **Architect:** Eduardo Catalano   **Cost:** $6,000,000
  Contact for Rental: Steven Rosenblatt;   (207) 775-3481

PORTLAND EXPOSITION BUILDING
239 Park Avenue, Portland, ME 04102
(207) 874-8200
FAX: (207) 874-8130
  Type of Facility: Arena
  Type of Stage: Arena
  Seating Capacity: 3,000
  Year Built: 1915   **Cost:** $3,000,000
  Year Remodeled: 1983   **Cost:** $300,000
  Acoustical Consultant: Bolt, Beranek & Newman
  Contact for Rental: Frank P. LaTorre;   (207) 874-8200
  Concerts, ballet, theatre, environmental

PORTLAND PERFORMING ARTS CENTER
25A Forest Avenue, Portland, ME 04101
(207) 761-0591
  Type of Facility: Theatre Complex; Studio Performance; Performance Center; Theatre House
  Facility Originally: Meeting Hall; Movie House
  Type of Stage: Thrust; Proscenium
  Stage Dimensions: 31'x21'
  Seating Capacity: 290
  Year Remodeled: 1983   **Architect:** Winton Scott Associates
  Contact for Rental: Manager;   (207) 761-0591

Rockport

FACILITY

ROCKPORT OPERA HOUSE - TOWN OF ROCKPORT
Central Street, PO Box 10, Rockport, ME 04856
(207) 236-9648
  Type of Facility: Concert Hall; Auditorium; Theatre House; Opera House
  Type of Stage: Proscenium
  Stage Dimensions: 22'x24'
  Seating Capacity: 400
  Year Built: 1891
  Year Remodeled: 1972
  Contact for Rental: Nancy Dowling;   (207) 236-9648, ext. 22
  Resident Groups: Bay Chamber Concerts Inc.; Rockport Folk Festival

---
South Paris

FACILITY

CELEBRATION BARN THEATER
RD 1, PO Box 236, Stockfarm Road, South Paris, ME 04281
(207) 743-8452
Founded: 1972
Type of Facility: Theatre Complex; Outdoor (Concert); Studio Performance; Theater School
Type of Stage: Proscenium
Seating Capacity: 100-125
Year Built: 1902
Year Remodeled: 1989
Contact for Rental: Carolyn Brett;   (207) 743-8452
The theater is used primarily for workshops and other theater-related activities as well as small conferences.

Waterville

FACILITY

COLBY COLLEGE - GIVEN AUDITORIUM
Waterville, ME 04901
(207) 872-3000
FAX: (207) 872-3555
Type of Facility: Auditorium
Type of Stage: Proscenium
Seating Capacity: 397
Year Built: 1950
Resident Groups: Colby College musical organizations

MARYLAND

Annapolis

DANCE

BALLET THEATRE OF ANNAPOLIS
PO Box 3311, Annapolis, MD 21403
(410) 263-2909
Founded: 1978
Arts Area: Ballet
Status: Professional; Non-Profit
Type: Touring; Resident
Management: Edward Stewart, Artistic Director; Deboran H. Harris, General Manager
Paid Artists: 14   **Non-Paid Artists:** 27
Utilizes: Guest Artists; Guest Choreographers
Budget: $1,000,000 - $5,000,000
Income Sources: Box Office; Individual Donations
Season: December - January; April - May
Performance Facilities: Maryland Hall for the Creative Arts

VOCAL MUSIC

ANNAPOLIS OPERA
PO Box 24, Annapolis, MD 21404
(410) 267-8135
Founded: 1973
Arts Area: Grand Opera; Light Opera; Operetta
Status: Professional; Non-Professional; Non-Profit
Type: Performing; Educational
Purpose: To present light and grand opera, thus contributing to the educational, cultural and artistic development of the community
Officers: Harry Lindauer, President; Jean Jackson, Vice President; Marie Hampton, Recording Secretary
Volunteer Staff: 10
Paid Artists: 40   **Non-Paid Artists:** 30
Utilizes: Guest Conductors; Guest Artists; Guest Directors
Budget: $100,000 - $500,000
Income Sources: Private Foundations/Grants/Endowments; Business/Corporate Donations; Box Office; Government Grants; Individual Donations
Season: September - May   **Annual Attendance:** 4,500
Performance Facilities: Annapolis Senior High School; Maryland Hall

FACILITY

FRANCIS SCOTT KEY AUDITORIUM
60 College Avenue, Annapolis, MD 21401
(410) 626-2547
FAX: (410) 263-4828
Type of Facility: Theatre Complex; Auditorium
Seating Capacity: 600
Year Built: 1960
Year Remodeled: 1989
Contact for Rental: Jeanette Hoffman;   (410) 626-2547

MARYLAND HALL FOR THE CREATIVE ARTS
801 Chase Street, Annapolis, MD 21401
(410) 263-5544
FAX: (410) 263-5114
Founded: 1979
Type of Facility: Auditorium; Multi-Purpose; Recital Halls; Meeting Space; Galleries
Facility Originally: School
Type of Stage: Proscenium
Stage Dimensions: 30'x40'
Seating Capacity: 855
Year Built: 1932
Year Remodeled: 1980   **Architect:** Riggs Architecture   **Cost:** $3,500,000
Acoustical Consultant: Bolt, Beranek & Newman

Contact for Rental: Denise Bailey-Jackson; (410) 263-5544
Resident Groups: Maryland Hall Story Theatre; Ballet Theatre of Annapolis; Annapolis Symphony Orchestra; Annapolis Chorale

Arnold

INSTRUMENTAL MUSIC

BRASS CHAMBER MUSIC SOCIETY OF ANNAPOLIS
PO Box 161, Arnold, MD 21012
(410) 235-4302
FAX: (410) 235-4302
Founded: 1980
Arts Area: Chamber; Ensemble; Instrumental Group
Status: Non-Profit
Type: Performing; Educational; Sponsoring
Purpose: To promote brass chamber music through concert series and educational outreach programs
Officers: George Rinehart, Chair; Joan Machinchick, Secretary; Maria Coughlin, Treasurer; Robert Posten, Artistic Director
Volunteer Staff: 8
Utilizes: Guest Artists
Budget: $1,000 - $50,000
Income Sources: Private Foundations/Grants/Endowments; Business/Corporate Donations; Box Office; Government Grants; Individual Donations
Season: October - May   **Annual Attendance:** 1,460
Performance Facilities: Anne Arundel Community College

Baltimore

DANCE

BALTIMORE DANCE THEATRE
c/o Auty Associates, 15 Charles Plaza, Suite 306, Baltimore, MD 21201
(410) 685-1313
FAX: (410) 997-3899
Founded: 1975
Arts Area: Modern
Status: Professional; Commercial
Type: Performing; Touring
Purpose: The Baltimore Dance Theatre, the performing group of the Eva Anderson Dancers, sponsors a professional dance company presenting modern ballets.
Management: Auty Associates; Eva Anderson, Artistic Director
Paid Staff: 1
Paid Artists: 8
Utilizes: Guest Artists; Guest Choreographers
Budget: $100,000 - $500,000
Income Sources: Private Foundations/Grants/Endowments; Business/Corporate Donations; Box Office; Government Grants; Individual Donations
Season: 52 Weeks

DOWNTOWN DANCE COMPANY
TSU 8000 York Road, Baltimore, MD 21204-7083
(410) 830-3369
Founded: 1986
Arts Area: Modern; Ballet
Status: Professional; Non-Profit
Type: Sponsoring
Purpose: To present the best new work being created in the modern, ballet and movement theatre genres
Management: Claire Braswell, Managing Director
Officers: Bryon Mollica, Chairman
Paid Staff: 2   **Volunteer Staff:** 20
Budget: $50,000 - $100,000
Income Sources: Private Foundations/Grants/Endowments; Business/Corporate Donations; Box Office; Government Grants; Individual Donations; Program Advertisements
Season: September - May   **Annual Attendance:** 4,000
Affiliations: Baltimore Area Contemporary Arts Presenters
Performance Facilities: Stephens Hall Theatre

THE MARYLAND BALLET
PO Box 26150, Baltimore, MD 21210
(410) 467-8495
Founded: 1986
Arts Area: Ballet
Status: Professional; Non-Profit
Type: Performing; Touring; Resident; Educational; Sponsoring
Purpose: To present the finest in classical ballet as the resident professional ballet company of Maryland
Management: Phillip B. Carman, Artistic Director; Daniel J. Kane, Executive Director
Paid Staff: 4 **Volunteer Staff:** 13
Paid Artists: 28 **Non-Paid Artists:** 4
Utilizes: Special Technical Talent; Guest Conductors; Guest Artists; Guest Choreographers
Budget: $100,000 - $500,000
Income Sources: Private Foundations/Grants/Endowments; Business/Corporate Donations; Box Office; Government Grants; Individual Donations
Season: 52 Weeks **Annual Attendance:** 35,000
Performance Facilities: The Lyric Opera House

INSTRUMENTAL MUSIC

BALTIMORE SYMPHONY ORCHESTRA
1212 Cathedral Street, Baltimore, MD 21201
(410) 783-8100
FAX: (410) 783-8077; (410) 783-8078
Founded: 1916
Arts Area: Symphony
Status: Professional
Type: Performing
Management: John Gidwitz, Executive Director; George Alexsovich, General Manager; Patricia Purcell, Director of Development and Community Affairs; Paul Dupree, Director of Marketing and Publications; Thomas D. May, Finance Director
Officers: Geaorge V. McGowan, Chairman of the Board; Calman J. Zamoisky, President/Chief Executive Officer
Paid Staff: 32 **Volunteer Staff:** 100
Paid Artists: 100
Utilizes: Guest Conductors; Guest Artists
Budget: Over 10,000,000
Income Sources: Private Foundations/Grants/Endowments; Business/Corporate Donations; Box Office; Government Grants; Individual Donations
Season: 52 Weeks **Annual Attendance:** 350,000
Affiliations: ASOL; AAA
Performance Facilities: Joseph Meyerhoff Symphony Hall

CHAMBER MUSIC SOCIETY OF BALTIMORE
2909 Woodvalley Drive, Baltimore, MD 21208
(410) 486-1140
Founded: 1949
Arts Area: Chamber; Ensemble; Electronic & Live Electronic
Status: Professional; Non-Profit
Type: Performing; Educational; Sponsoring
Purpose: To present the finest chamber artists performing a mixture of standard repertory and new work, concentrating on contemporary American pieces
Management: Anthony Stark, Managing Director; Robert Hall Lewis, Music Director
Officers: Randolph S. Rothschild, President; Gordon Cyr, Vice President
Paid Staff: 1 **Volunteer Staff:** 20
Non-Paid Artists: 1
Utilizes: Guest Artists
Budget: $1,000 - $50,000
Income Sources: Private Foundations/Grants/Endowments; Business/Corporate Donations; Box Office; Government Grants; Individual Donations
Season: Autumn - Spring **Annual Attendance:** 2,000
Performance Facilities: Baltimore Museum of Art; Joseph Meyerhoff Symphony Hall

GETTYSBURG SYMPHONY ORCHESTRA
4707 Renwick Avenue, Baltimore, MD 21206
(410) 458-4011
Founded: 1958
Arts Area: Symphony; Orchestra
Status: Professional; Non-Profit

Type: Performing; Educational
Purpose: To produce educational concerts for youth as well as full symphonic performances for adults
Management: Raphael Faraco, Conductor/Music Director and Manager
Officers: John Renneberg, President; Daniel S. Sullivan Jr., Treasurer/Secretary; Charles A. Bodie Jr.; Z. John Levay MD
Budget: $1,000 - $50,000
Income Sources: Private Foundations/Grants/Endowments
Performance Facilities: Loch Raven Senior High School Auditorium

VOCAL MUSIC

BALTIMORE CHORAL ARTS SOCIETY
1316 Park Avenue, Baltimore, MD 21217
(410) 523-7070
Founded: 1966
Arts Area: Choral
Status: Semi-Professional; Non-Profit
Type: Performing; Touring; Educational; Sponsoring
Purpose: To present classical and choral music at the highest professional level
Management: Tom Hall, Music Director; Mary Schretlen, Executive Director; Nancy Hall, Development Director
Officers: John H. Laporte, President; Anita Kreeger, Vice President; Wes Poling, Treasurer; M. Carter Warren, Secretary
Paid Staff: 4   **Volunteer Staff:** 2
Paid Artists: 60   **Non-Paid Artists:** 70
Utilizes: Guest Conductors; Guest Artists; Guest Emsembles
Budget: $100,000 - $500,000
Income Sources: Private Foundations/Grants/Endowments; Business/Corporate Donations; Box Office; Government Grants; Individual Donations; Run Outs
Season: October - May   **Annual Attendance:** 9,000
Performance Facilities: Joseph Meyerhoff Symphony Hall; Kraushaar Auditorium

BALTIMORE MEN'S CHORUS
1 East Pratt Street, Baltimore, MD 21202
(410) 547-8610
Founded: 1984
Arts Area: Choral
Status: Non-Profit
Type: Performing
Management: William Garrison, Music Director
Officers: George Rogers, President; Robert Greenfield, Vice President; Stephen Phillips, Secretary; Alan Baumgarten, Treasurer
Volunteer Staff: 5
Non-Paid Artists: 33
Utilizes: Special Technical Talent; Guest Artists
Budget: $1,000 - $50,000
Income Sources: Individual Donations
Season: September - June   **Annual Attendance:** 2,000

BALTIMORE OPERA COMPANY
101 West Read Street, Suite 605, Baltimore, MD 21201
(410) 727-0592
FAX: (410) 727-7854
Founded: 1950
Arts Area: Grand Opera; Lyric Opera
Status: Professional; Non-Profit
Type: Performing; Touring; Educational
Purpose: To produce the highest level of artistic performance within our economic means; to educate the public, particularly the youth
Management: Michael Harrison, General Manager; Patricia Elizabeth McMahon, Director of Public Relations and Marketing; William Yannuzzi, Music Director
Officers: Lowell R. Bowen, Chairman; John R. Young, President
Paid Staff: 15   **Volunteer Staff:** 125
Paid Artists: 400
Utilizes: Special Technical Talent; Guest Conductors; Guest Artists; Guest Directors
Budget: $1,000,000 - $5,000,000
Income Sources: Private Foundations/Grants/Endowments; Business/Corporate Donations; Box Office; Government Grants; Individual Donations
Season: October - April   **Annual Attendance:** 21,000

Affiliations: OA
Performance Facilities: Lyric Opera House

BALTIMORE SYMPHONY CHORUS
c/o Baltimore Symphony Orchestra Inc., 1212 Cathedral Street, Baltimore, MD 21201
(410) 783-8100
FAX: (410) 783-8077
Arts Area: Choral
Status: Non-Profit; Volunteer
Type: Performing
Purpose: The choir is the choral arm of the Baltimore Symphony and performs when the Symphony needs singers.
Management: Edward Polochick, Director; Felice Homann, Manager
Officers: Richard Holland, Chorus Representative
Budget: $50,000 - $100,000
Income Sources: Private Foundations/Grants/Endowments; Business/Corporate Donations; Box Office; Government Grants; Individual Donations
Performance Facilities: Joseph Meyerhoff Symphony Hall

THEATRE

ARENA PLAYERS
801 McCulloh Street, Baltimore, MD 21201
(410) 728-6500
FAX: (410) 728-6515
Founded: 1953
Arts Area: Community; Theatrical Group
Status: Non-Professional; Non-Profit
Type: Performing; Touring; Educational
Purpose: To discover, foster and showcase talent from the community
Management: Samuel H. Wilson, Artistic Director; Gerald Catus, Managing Director; Catherine B. Orange, Youth Program Director
Officers: Quentin Lawson, Chairman of the Board; Dr. Hilbert Stanley, Vice Chairman, Advisory Board
Utilizes: Guest Artists; Guest Directors
Income Sources: Private Foundations/Grants/Endowments; Business/Corporate Donations; Box Office; Government Grants; Individual Donations
Season: September - August
Affiliations: NEA; Maryland State Arts Council; Mayor's Committee

BALTIMORE ACTORS' THEATRE, INC.
The Dumbarton House, 300 Dumbarton Road, Baltimore, MD 21212
(410) 337-8519
Founded: 1959
Arts Area: Musical; Dinner; Theatrical Group; Children's
Status: Semi-Professional; Non-Profit
Type: Performing; Touring; Educational
Purpose: To teach and perform the arts on a professional level
Management: Helen M. Grigal, Artistic Director; Walter E. Anderson, Executive Director
Officers: Helen M. Grigal, President; Walter E. Anderson, Vice President; Victor L. Grigal, Secretary/Treasurer
Paid Staff: 20   **Volunteer Staff:** 100
Budget: $100,000 - $500,000
Income Sources: Private Foundations/Grants/Endowments; Box Office; Individual Donations
Season: 52 Weeks

CENTER STAGE
700 North Calvert Street, Baltimore, MD 21202
(410) 685-3200
FAX: (410) 539-3912
Founded: 1963
Arts Area: Professional; Theatrical Group
Status: Professional; Non-Profit
Type: Performing; Resident; Educational
Purpose: Center Stage is the official theatrical company of Maryland
Management: Peter Culman, Managing Director; Irene Lewis, Artistic Director
Paid Staff: 40   **Volunteer Staff:** 100
Paid Artists: 54
Utilizes: Guest Artists; Guest Directors
Budget: $1,000,000 - $5,000,000

Income Sources: Private Foundations/Grants/Endowments; Business/Corporate Donations; Box Office; Government Grants; Individual Donations
Season: September - June   **Annual Attendance:** 80,023
Performance Facilities: Center Stage

CHILDREN'S THEATER ASSOCIATION
121 McMechen Street, Baltimore, MD 21217
(410) 225-0052
Founded: 1943
Arts Area: Children's Theatre
Status: Professional; Non-Profit
Type: Performing; Touring; Educational
Purpose: To stimulate the creativity of young minds through theatre performances and creative drama classes
Management: Kevin R. Daly, Managing Director; Roz Byus, Administrative Assistant
Officers: Linda Dalsimer, President; Clarence Shelley, Vice President of Special Events; Marley Willard, Vice President of Education; Dorothy Potts, Vice President of Finance; Deborah Dickerson, Secretary; Jeffrey Collier, Treasurer
Paid Staff: 3
Paid Artists: 27   **Non-Paid Artists:** 200
Budget: $100,000 - $500,000
Income Sources: Private Foundations/Grants/Endowments; Business/Corporate Donations; Box Office; Government Grants; Individual Donations
Season: October - June   **Annual Attendance:** 110,000

THEATRE PROJECT
45 West Preston Street, Baltimore, MD 21201
(410) 539-3091
Founded: 1971
Arts Area: Musical; Theatrical Group; Puppet
Status: Professional; Non-Profit
Type: Sponsoring
Purpose: To support national and international new works and innovative forms of expression; to continue as the entry point for international performing companies; to further promote new performance opportunities for them throughout North America
Management: Philip Arnoult, Director
Paid Staff: 5   **Volunteer Staff:** 100
Paid Artists: 100
Utilizes: Guest Artists
Budget: $100,000 - $500,000
Income Sources: Private Foundations/Grants/Endowments; Business/Corporate Donations; Box Office; Government Grants; Individual Donations
Season: September - May   **Annual Attendance:** 23,500
Affiliations: TCG; International Theatre Institute; Towson State University
Performance Facilities: Theatre Project

PERFORMING SERIES

YOUNG AUDIENCES OF MARYLAND
927 North Calvert Street, Baltimore, MD 21202
(410) 837-7577
Founded: 1950
Arts Area: Dance; Vocal Music; Instrumental Music; Theater; Lyric Opera
Status: Professional; Non-Profit
Type: Performing; Educational; Sponsoring
Purpose: To present performing arts-in-education programs in schools and elsewhere throughout the community to both children and adults—Young Audiences of Maryland presents 1,100 programs to 300,000 people annually
Management: Patricia M. Thomas, Executive Director
Officers: Dr. Michael L. Mark, President; E. Scott Johnson, Donna Hamilton, Vice Presidents; Helen M. Schlossberg Cohen, Secretary; Eric M. Pripstein, Treasurer
Paid Staff: 5   **Volunteer Staff:** 20
Paid Artists: 98
Utilizes: Guest Artists
Budget: $100,000 - $500,000
Income Sources: Private Foundations/Grants/Endowments; Business/Corporate Donations; Government Grants; Individual Donations
Season: 52 Weeks   **Annual Attendance:** 300,000
Affiliations: Maryland Alliance for Arts Education; National Young Audiences

FACILITY

ARENA PLAYERS
801 McCulloh Street, Baltimore, MD 21201
(410) 728-6500
FAX: (410) 728-6515
     Type of Facility: Auditorium; Theatre House; Arena; Multi-Purpose
     Facility Originally: Warehouse
     Type of Stage: Thrust; Platform; Arena
     Seating Capacity: 300
     Year Remodeled: 1973   **Architect:** Bridges & Trionfo   **Cost:** $10,000
     Contact for Rental: Gerard W. Catus; (410) 728-6500
     Resident Groups: Arena Players; Youtheater; Main Stage Performers; Studio 801; The Road Company

BALTIMORE MUSEUM OF ART - AUDITORIUM
Art Museum Drive, Baltimore, MD 21218
(410) 396-7100
FAX: (410) 396-6562
     Type of Facility: Auditorium; Multi-Purpose
     Type of Stage: Proscenium
     Stage Dimensions: 36'Wx33'D
     Seating Capacity: 375
     Year Remodeled: 1982   **Architect:** Bower Lewis & Thrower
     Acoustical Consultant: Frink & Beuchat
     Contact for Rental: Deborah Tunney; (410) 396-6314
     Resident Groups: Baltimore Film Forum; Pro Musica Rara; Chamber Music Society of Baltimore
     The Auditorium was built as part of the 1982 expansion/renovation program of the museum. Total cost of this project was $13,500,000.

CENTER STAGE
700 North Calvert Street, Baltimore, MD 21202
(410) 685-3200
FAX: (410) 539-3912
     Founded: 1963
     Type of Facility: Theatre House
     Facility Originally: School
     Type of Stage: Thrust; Flexible; Proscenium; Flexible Stage & Seating in Head Theater
     Stage Dimensions: 54'Wx11'D, add 6'D for thrust
     Orchestra Pit
     Seating Capacity: 541 - Flexible
     Year Built: 1866
     Year Remodeled: 1975   **Architect:** James Grieves, Roger Morgan   **Cost:** $1,800,000
     Year of Head Theatre Renovation: 1991   **Architect:** Ziger, Hoopes & Snead
     Contact for Rental: Joe Rooney; (301) 685-3200
     Resident Groups: Center Stage, The State Theatre of Maryland
     Two stages - Pearlstone and Head Theaters

DUNBAR PERFORMING ARTS CENTER
1400 Orleans Street, Baltimore, MD 21231
(410) 396-9474
     Type of Facility: Concert Hall; Performance Center; Theatre House
     Seating Capacity: 800
     Year Built: 1974   **Architect:** Cochran Stephenson Donkervoert
     Contact for Rental: Charlotte Dunbar, Principal, Dunbar High School; (410) 396-9478
     Resident Groups: Urban Services Cultural Arts Program

THE JOHNS HOPKINS UNIVERSITY - THE MERRICK BARN
3400 North Charles Street, Baltimore, MD 21218
(410) 516-7159
     Type of Facility: Theatre House
     Facility Originally: Barn
     Type of Stage: Proscenium
     Stage Dimensions: 14'x28'
     Seating Capacity: 106
     Year Built: 1803
     Year Remodeled: 1982
     Resident Groups: Theatre Hopkins
     Redesigned as a theatre in the 1920's

LYRIC INC./LYRIC OPERA HOUSE
1404 Maryland Avenue, Baltimore, MD 21201
(410) 685-5086
FAX: (410) 332-8234
> **Founded:** 1894
> **Type of Facility:** Concert Hall; Auditorium; Performance Center; Off Broadway; Opera House
> **Type of Stage:** Proscenium
> **Stage Dimensions:** 30'x50'x36'   **Orchestra Pit**
> **Seating Capacity:** 2,564
> **Year Built:** 1894   **Architect:** Griffin & Randall
> **Year Remodeled:** 1992   **Architect:** Richter Cornbrooks Gribble, Inc.   **Cost:** $22,500,000
> **Contact for Rental:** Robert M. Pomory, President;   (410) 685-5087
> **Manager:** John T. Kroneberger;   (410) 685-5086
> **Resident Groups:** Baltimore Opera Company

THEATRE PROJECT
45 West Preston Street, Baltimore, MD 21201
(410) 539-3091
FAX: (410) 539-2137
> **Type of Facility:** Performance Center
> **Facility Originally:** Meeting Hall; Movie House
> **Type of Stage:** Flexible
> **Stage Dimensions:** 37'Wx37'Dx21'H
> **Seating Capacity:** 157
> **Year Built:** 1896
> **Year Remodeled:** 1984   **Architect:** Gould Associates   **Cost:** $2,000,000
> **Contact for Rental:** Robert Mrozek;   (410) 539-3091
> *Short-term rentals only, not available for long-run productions*

Bowie

FACILITY

BOWIE STATE COLLEGE - MARTIN LUTHER KING JR., COMMUNICATION ARTS CENTER
Bowie, MD 20715
(301) 464-3441
> **Founded:** 1865
> **Type of Facility:** Auditorium
> **Type of Stage:** Proscenium
> **Orchestra Pit**
> **Seating Capacity:** 1,000
> **Year Built:** 1973   **Architect:** Anthony Johns   **Cost:** $5,200,000
> **Contact for Rental:** Dr. Amos White IV, Department of Humanities & Fine Arts;   (301) 464-7286

Chevy Chase

VOCAL MUSIC

CHILDREN'S OPERA THEATER
3203 Pickwick Lane, Chevy Chase, MD 20815
(301) 656-2442
> **Founded:** 1976
> **Arts Area:** Light Opera; Choral
> **Status:** Professional; Non-Profit
> **Type:** Touring; Educational
> **Purpose:** To introduce and involve young people in opera; to provide employment opportunities for artists in the transitional phase of their careers from apprentice to professional
> **Management:** Michael Kaye, Artistic Director
> **Paid Staff:** 6
> **Paid Artists:** 20
> **Budget:** $50,000 - $100,000
> **Income Sources:** Private Foundations/Grants/Endowments; Business/Corporate Donations; Individual Donations
> **Season:** 52 Weeks   **Annual Attendance:** 20,000

College Park

PERFORMING SERIES

MARYLAND HANDEL FESTIVAL
University of Maryland, College Park, MD 20742
(301) 405-5571
> **Founded:** 1981
> **Arts Area:** Vocal Music; Instrumental Music; Theater; Festivals
> **Status:** Non-Profit
> **Type:** Performing; Educational
> **Purpose:** To focus on the music of Handel; to foster research into Handel and 18th-century topics; to practice performing in the style of that period
> **Management:** Jesse Parker, General Manager/Artistic Staff; Paul Traver, Artistic Director; Howard Serwer, Associate Director
> **Season:** 52 Weeks

UNIVERSITY OF MARYLAND INTERNATIONAL PIANO FESTIVAL AND WILLIAM KAPELL COMPETITION
Summer Programs, University of Maryland, College Park, MD 20740
(301) 454-5276
FAX: (301) 314-9572
> **Founded:** 1971
> **Arts Area:** Instrumental Music; Festivals
> **Status:** Non-Profit
> **Type:** Educational; Sponsoring
> **Purpose:** To sponsor a major biennial international festival featuring master classes, lecture-recitals, recitals, symposia and the William Kapell Piano Competition
> **Management:** George Moquin, Executive Director
> **Utilizes:** Guest Artists
> **Budget:** $100,000 - $500,000
> **Income Sources:** Private Foundations/Grants/Endowments; Business/Corporate Donations; Box Office; Individual Donations
> **Season:** July
> **Affiliations:** University of Maryland
> **Performance Facilities:** Tawes Fine Arts Center

Columbia

DANCE

EVA ANDERSON DANCERS LTD.
5452 High Tor Hill, Columbia, MD 21045
(410) 997-3899
FAX: (410) 730-7411
> **Founded:** 1974
> **Arts Area:** Modern; Ethnic
> **Status:** Professional
> **Type:** Performing; Touring; Educational
> **Purpose:** To create dance based on the American experience with special emphasis on African-American experiences
> **Management:** Eva Anderson, Artistic Director; Yvette Shipley, Assistant Artistic Director
> **Officers:** Doris Williams, President; Ernest Miller, Vice President; Yvette Shipley, Secretary; Troy Burman, Treasurer
> **Paid Staff:** 2 **Volunteer Staff:** 5
> **Paid Artists:** 10
> **Utilizes:** Special Technical Talent; Guest Artists; Guest Choreographers
> **Budget:** $50,000 - $100,000
> **Income Sources:** Private Foundations/Grants/Endowments; Business/Corporate Donations; Box Office; Government Grants; Individual Donations
> **Season:** September - July

PERFORMING SERIES

CANDLELIGHT CONCERT SOCIETY, INC.
5829 Banneker Road, Columbia, MD 21044
(410) 720-1027; (301) 596-6203
> **Founded:** 1974
> **Arts Area:** Vocal Music; Instrumental Music; Chamber Music; Children
> **Status:** Professional; Non-Profit

Type: Performing; Sponsoring
Purpose: To present the finest chamber music artists available to audiences of central Maryland
Management: Bonita J. Bush, Managing Director
Officers: Charles E. Thomas, Acting President of the Board; Will Cook, Secretary of the Board
Paid Staff: 1   **Volunteer Staff:** 150
Utilizes: Guest Artists
Budget: $100,000 - $500,000
Income Sources: Private Foundations/Grants/Endowments; Business/Corporate Donations; Box Office; Government Grants; Individual Donations
Season: October - May   **Annual Attendance:** 15,000
Affiliations: CMA
Performance Facilities: Smith Theatre, Howard Community College

COLUMBIA FESTIVAL, INC.
9861 Broken Land Parkway, Suite 300, Columbia, MD 21117
(410) 381-0520
FAX: (401) 381-4530
Founded: 1988
Arts Area: Dance; Vocal Music; Instrumental Music; Theater; Festivals
Status: Non-Profit
Type: Presenting
Purpose: To present a variety of art forms and to make these accessible to the public
Management: Lynne Nemeth, Managing Director; Donald Hicken, Artistic Director; Alexandria Lippincott, Assistant Managing Director
Officers: Padraic M. Kennedy, President; Jean F. Moon, Vice President; Lynne Nemeth, Secretary; Richard G. McCauley Esq., Treasurer; Harvey B. Steinman Esq., Counsel
Paid Staff: 17   **Volunteer Staff:** 400
Paid Artists: 450
Utilizes: Special Technical Talent; Guest Artists
Budget: $500,000 - $1,000,000
Income Sources: Private Foundations/Grants/Endowments; Business/Corporate Donations; Box Office; Government Grants; Individual Donations
Season: June - July   **Annual Attendance:** 30,000
Performance Facilities: Merriweather Post Pavilion

FACILITY

TOBY'S DINNER THEATRE
PO Box 1003, Columbia, MD 21044
(410) 730-8311
Type of Facility: Dinner Theatre
Type of Stage: Arena
Stage Dimensions: 20'x20'   **Orchestra Pit**
Seating Capacity: 360
Year Built: 1968
Year Remodeled: 1981

Fort Washington

FACILITY

JOHN ADDISON CONCERT HALL
Harmony Hall Regional Center, 10701 Livingston Road, Fort Washington, MD 20744
(301) 292-8331
FAX: (301) 292-7856
Founded: 1989
Type of Facility: Concert Hall; Performance Center; Multi-Purpose
Facility Originally: School
Type of Stage: Proscenium
Stage Dimensions: 37'x41'
Seating Capacity: 209
Year Built: 1965
Year Remodeled: 1989   **Cost:** $1,900,000

Contact for Rental: Dr. Carolyn Bock;   (301) 292-8331
Resident Groups: Stratford Chamber Players; Monumental Brass Quintet; Heritage Singers

---

Hagerstown

INSTRUMENTAL MUSIC

MARYLAND SYMPHONY ORCHESTRA
12 Rochester Place, Hagerstown, MD 21740
(301) 797-4000
>**Founded:** 1982
>**Arts Area:** Symphony
>**Status:** Professional
>**Type:** Performing
>**Management:** Cassandra Wantz, Managing Director; Carolyn Bryant, Operations Manager; Barbara Wetzel, Marketing Director; Kathleen Dayhoff, Secretary
>**Paid Staff:** 4
>**Paid Artists:** 150
>**Utilizes:** Special Technical Talent; Guest Conductors; Guest Artists
>**Budget:** $500,000 - $1,000,000
>**Income Sources:** Private Foundations/Grants/Endowments; Business/Corporate Donations; Box Office; Government Grants; Individual Donations
>**Season:** October - March   **Annual Attendance:** 45,000
>**Affiliations:** ASOL
>**Performance Facilities:** Maryland Theatre

THEATRE

MARYLAND THEATRE
21 South Potomac Street, Hagerstown, MD 21740-5512
(301) 790-3500
FAX: (301) 791-6114
>**Founded:** 1976
>**Arts Area:** Professional; Musical; Community; Theatrical Group
>**Status:** Non-Profit
>**Type:** Performing; Touring; Sponsoring
>**Purpose:** To restore and maintain this historic structure and present the performing arts
>**Management:** Paul A. Frank III, Executive Director; Barbara L. Cushwa, Box Office Manager; Donna DeWitt, Administrative Assistant; Michael J. Snabley, Stage Manager
>**Officers:** Susan Elliot, President; Mary Dabbwa, Vice President of Programming; Suzanne Kass, Secretary; Jim Baker, Treasurer
>**Paid Staff:** 4   **Volunteer Staff:** 100
>**Utilizes:** Special Technical Talent; Guest Artists
>**Budget:** $500,000 - $1,000,000
>**Income Sources:** Private Foundations/Grants/Endowments; Business/Corporate Donations; Box Office; Government Grants; Individual Donations
>**Season:** 52 Weeks   **Annual Attendance:** 70,000
>**Performance Facilities:** The Maryland Theatre

FACILITY

MARYLAND THEATRE
21 South Potomac Street, Hagerstown, MD 21740-5512
(301) 790-3500
FAX: (301) 791-6114
>**Type of Facility:** Theatre House
>**Facility Originally:** Vaudeville
>**Type of Stage:** Modified Apron Proscenium
>**Stage Dimensions:** 66'Wx39'D with 15'D apron; 33'9"Wx25'H proscenium opening   **Orchestra Pit**
>**Seating Capacity:** 1,403
>**Year Built:** 1915   **Architect:** Thomas Lamb   **Cost:** $200,000
>**Year Remodeled:** 1976   **Cost:** $1,500,000
>**Contact for Rental:** Paul Frank;   (301) 790-3500
>**Resident Groups:** Maryland Symphony Orchestra; Miss Maryland Scholarship Pageant; Community Concerts
>*The Maryland Theatre has been designated a National Historic Landmark.*

Laurel

THEATRE

PETRUCCI'S DINNER THEATRE
312 Main Street, Laurel, MD 20707
(301) 725-5226
Founded: 1977
Arts Area: Dinner
Status: Commercial
Type: Performing
Management: C. David Petrucci, Angela Jo Leonard, Producers
Paid Staff: 7
Paid Artists: 20
Budget: $1,000 - $50,000
Income Sources: Box Office
Season: 52 Weeks   **Annual Attendance:** 40,000
Affiliations: NDTA

Mt. Rainier

DANCE

THE FIDDLE PUPPET DANCERS
PO Box 207, Mt. Rainier, MD 20712
(301) 277-5915
FAX: (301) 277-5915
Founded: 1979
Arts Area: Percussive Dance
Status: Professional
Type: Performing
Purpose: To perform percussive dances including tap, step dancing and clogging, in the U.S. and abroad
Management: Laura Lewis, Manager; Eileen Carson, Artistic Director; New Music Times - Agent
Paid Staff: 2
Paid Artists: 7
Utilizes: Special Technical Talent; Guest Artists
Budget: $50,000 - $100,000
Income Sources: Private Foundations/Grants/Endowments; Box Office; Individual Donations
Season: March - November   **Annual Attendance:** 500,000

Ocean City

FACILITY

OCEAN CITY CONVENTION CENTER
4001 Coastal Highway, Ocean City, MD 21863
(410) 289-8311
Type of Facility: Auditorium; Civic Center; Arena; Multi-Purpose; Room
Facility Originally: Meeting Hall; Movie House
Type of Stage: Proscenium
Stage Dimensions: 40'x60'
Seating Capacity: 3600
Year Built: 1969   **Cost:** $3,000,000
Contact for Rental: Bob Rothermel;   (410) 289-8311

Olney

THEATRE

OLNEY THEATRE/NATIONAL PLAYERS
2001 Olney-Sandy Spring Road, Olney, MD 20832
(301) 924-4485
Founded: 1952
Arts Area: Professional; Summer Stock
Status: Professional; Non-Profit
Type: Performing; Touring; Educational

Management: James A. Petosh, General Manager; Bill Graham Jr., Managing Director
Officers: William H. Graham, President; Harry Teter, Vice President; William P. Roche, Secretary/Treasurer
Paid Staff: 30   **Volunteer Staff:** 120
Paid Artists: 70
Budget: $1,000,000 - $5,000,000
Income Sources: Private Foundations/Grants/Endowments; Business/Corporate Donations; Box Office; Government Grants; Individual Donations
Season: May - November   **Annual Attendance:** 70,000
Affiliations: AEA; SSDC
Performance Facilities: Olney Theatre

Rockville

INSTRUMENTAL MUSIC

NATIONAL CHAMBER ORCHESTRA SOCIETY, INC.
15209 Frederick Road, Suite 207, Rockville, MD 20850
(301) 762-8580
   Arts Area: Orchestra; Chamber
   Status: Professional; Non-Profit
   Type: Resident
   Purpose: To cultivate an appreciation for great classical music through concerts and programs
   Management: Wing Chi-Chan, Executive Director; Piotr Ghaewski, Conductor/Music Director
   Officers: Robert Bourne, President of the Board
   Budget: $100,000 - $500,000
   Income Sources: Private Foundations/Grants/Endowments; Business/Corporate Donations; Box Office; Government Grants; Individual Donations
   Performance Facilities: Duke Ellington School of the Arts; F. Scott Theatre

FACILITY

KREEGER FINE ARTS AUDITORIUM
6125 Montrose Road, Rockville, MD 20852
(301) 881-0100
   Type of Facility: Auditorium
   Type of Stage: Proscenium
   Stage Dimensions: 35'Wx30'Dx30'H; 30'Wx16'H proscenium opening
   Seating Capacity: 300
   Year Built: 1969
   Contact for Rental: Felice Kornberg;   (301) 881-0100
   Resident Groups: Jewish Community Center Orchestra; Center Dance Ensemble; Kinor Dance Troup; Washington Jewish Theatre

Salisbury

FACILITY

WICOMICO YOUTH AND CIVIC CENTER
500 Glen Avenue, Salisbury, MD 21801
(410) 548-4906
FAX: (410) 546-0490
   Type of Facility: Civic Center; Arena; Multi-Purpose
   Type of Stage: Arena
   Seating Capacity: 6,800
   Year Built: 1980   **Cost:** $13,000,000
   Contact for Rental: Robert C. Wagoner;   (410) 548-4906

Silver Spring

DANCE

AMERICAN YOUTH BALLET COMPANY
10111 Colesville Road, Suite 112, Silver Spring, MD 20901
(301) 587-7807
   Founded: 1991
   Arts Area: Ballet

Status: Non-Professional; Non-Profit
Type: Performing; Resident
Management: Lauri Dickmann, Artistic Director
Non-Paid Artists: 30
Utilizes: Guest Artists; Guest Choreographers
Budget: $1,000 - $50,000
Income Sources: Private Foundations/Grants/Endowments; Box Office; Individual Donations
Season: September - July

THEATRE

ROUND HOUSE THEATRE
12210 Bushey Drive, Silver Spring, MD 20902
(301) 217-6770
FAX: (301) 217-6819
Founded: 1978
Arts Area: Professional; Theatrical Group
Status: Professional; Non-Profit
Type: Performing; Touring; Resident; Educational
Purpose: To engage and envolve the community by addressing contemporary social issues through a wide range of entertaining and provocative theatre experiences; to offer audiences, students and professionals rewarding experiences in live theatre and related educational activities
Management: Tony Elliot, Producing Associate; Barbara Payne, Production Office Manager; Jerry B. Whiddon, Artistic Director; Frank Kirby, Box Office Manager; Geri Olsen, Director of Public Relations
Officers: Jeff Davis, President; Andy Zvara, Vice President; Nancee Simonson, Treasurer
Paid Staff: 12   **Volunteer Staff:** 150
Paid Artists: 45
Utilizes: Special Technical Talent; Guest Artists; Guest Directors
Budget: $500,000 - $1,000,000
Income Sources: Private Foundations/Grants/Endowments; Business/Corporate Donations; Government Grants; Individual Donations
Season: September - June
Affiliations: AEA; SPT
Performance Facilities: Round House Theatre

Stevenson

FACILITY

VILLA JULIA COLLEGE - INSCAPE THEATRE
(410) 486-7000
Type of Facility: Theatre Complex; Studio Performance; Arena; Multi-Purpose; Video Studio
Type of Stage: Thrust; Flexible; 3/4 Arena; Arena
Stage Dimensions: 22'x22'
Seating Capacity: 150
Year Built: 1970   **Architect:** Carl Buck
Contact for Rental: Sally Harris;   (410) 486-7000

Towson

DANCE

DANCE ON THE EDGE
8000 York Road, Stephen Annex, Towson, MD 21204
(410) 830-3369
Arts Area: Modern
Status: Non-Profit
Type: Sponsoring
Purpose: To present new and innovative dance, stretching the boundaries of ballet, modern and contemporary work
Officers: Bryon Mollica, President
Budget: $50,000 - $100,000
Income Sources: Private Foundations/Grants/Endowments; Business/Corporate Donations; Box Office; Government Grants; Individual Donations
Performance Facilities: Stephen Hall Theatre

FACILITY

TOWSON STATE UNIVERSITY - STEPHENS AUDITORIUM
Towson, MD 21204
(410) 830-3289
> **Type of Facility:** Auditorium
> **Type of Stage:** Proscenium   **Orchestra Pit**
> **Seating Capacity:** 701
> **Year Built:** 1925   **Architect:** Fenten Lichtig
> **Resident Groups:** University Opera Workshop; University Dance Company; Towson Ensemble Dancers; Dance on The Edge

TOWSON STATE UNIVERSITY FINE ARTS CENTER
Towson, MD 21204
(410) 830-3289
> **Type of Facility:** Theatre Complex; Concert Hall; Studio Performance; Theatre House; Black Box
> **Seating Capacity:** Concert Hall - 518; Mainstage Theatre - 348; Black Box - 121
> **Year Built:** 1973   **Architect:** Fenten Lichtig   **Cost:** $7,000,000
> **Contact for Rental:** Events & Conference Services;   (410) 830-2244
> **Manager:** Gilbert Brungardt
> **Resident Groups:** Towson State University Departments of Dance, Art, Music and Theatre Arts
> *The Fine Arts Center contains the Concert Hall, Main Stage and Studio Theatre. See individual listings for additional information.*

TOWSON STATE UNIVERSITY FINE ARTS CENTER - CONCERT HALL
Towson, MD 21204
(410) 830-3289
> **Type of Facility:** Concert Hall; Recital Hall
> **Type of Stage:** Platform
> **Stage Dimensions:** 25'x56'
> **Seating Capacity:** 504
> **Year Built:** 1973
> **Contact for Rental:** Events & Conference Services;   (410) 830-2244

TOWSON STATE UNIVERSITY FINE ARTS CENTER - MAIN STAGE
Towson, MD 21204
(410) 830-3289
> **Type of Facility:** Concert Hall; Theatre House
> **Type of Stage:** Modified Apron Proscenium
> **Stage Dimensions:** 46'Wx40'D   **Orchestra Pit**
> **Year Built:** 1973
> **Contact for Rental:** Events & Conference Services;   (410) 830-2244

TOWSON STATE UNIVERSITY FINE ARTS CENTER - STUDIO THEATRE
Towson, MD 21204
(410) 830-3289
> **Type of Facility:** Studio Performance; Black Box
> **Type of Stage:** Flexible
> **Stage Dimensions:** 25'x25'
> **Year Built:** 1973   **Architect:** Fenten Lichtig
> **Contact for Rental:** Events & Conference Services;   (410) 830-2244

MASSACHUSETTS

Allston

THEATRE

DOUBLE EDGE THEATRE PRODUCTIONS INC.
5 Saint Luke's Road, Allston, MA 02134
(617) 254-4228
FAX: (617) 547-7032
    Arts Area: Theatrical Group
    Status: Professional; Non-Profit
    Type: Touring; Resident
    Purpose: The Double Edge Theatre, founded in 1982, is a laboratory theatre composed of directors, actors, musicians, designers, scholars and technicians from Israel, Poland, Indonesia and the U.S., committed to the development of a "living culture" in this country.
    Management: Stacy Klein, Artistic Director; David Flaxman, Managing Director
    Budget: $50,000 - $100,000
    Income Sources: Private Foundations/Grants/Endowments; Business/Corporate Donations; Box Office; Government Grants; Individual Donations
    Performance Facilities: Double

Amherst

DANCE

AMHERST BALLET THEATRE COMPANY
29 Strong Street, Amherst, MA 01002
(413) 549-1555
    Founded: 1977
    Arts Area: Modern; Ballet; Jazz; Ethnic
    Status: Non-Professional; Non-Profit
    Type: Performing; Touring; Educational
    Purpose: To train young people to perform for young people bringing an awareness of diversity and art through dance to educate young audiences
    Management: Therese Brady Donohue, Artistic Director; Kira Lamb, School Director
    Officers: Louis Raboin, President; Gladys Martin, Secretary; Sandra Sacco, Treasurer
    Paid Staff: 2   **Volunteer Staff:** 12
    Non-Paid Artists: 21
    Utilizes: Special Technical Talent; Guest Choreographers
    Budget: $1,000 - $50,000
    Income Sources: Private Foundations/Grants/Endowments; Business/Corporate Donations; Box Office; Government Grants; Individual Donations
    Season: September - June   **Annual Attendance:** 3,000
    Performance Facilities: Bowker Auditorium; Fine Arts Center; Concert Hall; University of Massachusetts

VOCAL MUSIC

VALLEY LIGHT OPERA
PO Box 2143, Amherst, MA 01004
(413) 549-1098
    Founded: 1975
    Arts Area: Light Opera
    Status: Non-Professional; Non-Profit
    Type: Performing
    Purpose: To prepare and produce light opera for the enjoyment of both participants and audiences
    Management: Sally Venman, Bill Venman, General Managers
    Officers: Carol Flandowgh, President; Louis Mold, Vice President; Melton Miller, Treasurer; Lucy Robinson, Clerk
    Non-Paid Artists: 100
    Budget: $1,000 - $50,000
    Income Sources: Box Office; Government Grants; Individual Donations
    Season: November - February   **Annual Attendance:** 4,000
    Performance Facilities: Amherst High School Auditorium

THEATRE

MOLE END PUPPETRY PRODUCTIONS INC.
45 Ward Street, Amherst, MA 01002
(413) 256-0453
    Arts Area: Puppet
    Status: Professional; Non-Profit
    Type: Educational; Sponsoring; Presenting
    Purpose: To present storytelling arts in the western Massachusetts area
    Management: Steve Stoia, Executive Director
    Officers: John Morrison, Chair
    Budget: $100,000 - $500,000
    Income Sources: Private Foundations/Grants/Endowments; Business/Corporate Donations; Box Office; Government Grants; Individual Donations
    Performance Facilities: Paramount Theater

FACILITY

UNIVERSITY OF MASSACHUSETTS - BOWKER AUDITORIUM
Stockbridge Hall, Amherst, MA 01003
(413) 545-0190
    Type of Facility: Auditorium
    Type of Stage: Proscenium
    Stage Dimensions: 35'Wx20'D
    Seating Capacity: 700
    Year Built: 1914
    Year Remodeled: 1985
    Manager: Barbara Aldrich
    Resident Groups: Music and Dance Departments; Concert Series

UNIVERSITY OF MASSACHUSETTS - CONCERT HALL
205 Hasbrouck Lab, Amherst, MA 01003
(413) 545-0190
FAX: (413) 545-0132
    Founded: 1975
    Type of Facility: Theatre Complex; Concert Hall; Performance Center; Multi-Purpose
    Type of Stage: Proscenium
    Stage Dimensions: 58'Wx41'D   **Orchestra Pit**
    Seating Capacity: 2,000
    Year Built: 1974   **Architect:** Roche Dinkeloo Associates   **Cost:** $16,000,000
    Acoustical Consultant: Bolt, Beranek & Newman
    Contact for Rental: Barbara Aldrich;   (413) 545-0190

Arlington

THEATRE

UNDERGROUND RAILWAY THEATER
41 Foster Street, Arlington, MA 02174
(617) 643-6916
    Founded: 1976
    Arts Area: Professional; Musical; Puppet
    Status: Professional; Non-Profit
    Type: Performing; Touring; Educational
    Purpose: Combining puppets, actors and music, URT creates and tours new works including political cabaret, family theatre, and spectacles for symphony orchestras.
    Management: Mara Youdelman, General Manager; Debra Wise, Executive Director; Wes Sanders, Artistic Director; Carl Wieting, Technical Director
    Officers: Downing Cless, President
    Paid Staff: 4   **Volunteer Staff:** 8
    Paid Artists: 4   **Non-Paid Artists:** 4
    Utilizes: Guest Artists
    Budget: $100,000 - $500,000

Income Sources: Private Foundations/Grants/Endowments; Business/Corporate Donations; Box Office; Government Grants; Individual Donations
Season: 52 Weeks

Becket

DANCE

JACOB'S PILLOW DANCE FESTIVAL
George Carter Road, Becket, MA 01223
(413) 637-1322
    Founded: 1932
    Arts Area: Modern; Mime; Ballet; Jazz; Ethnic
    Status: Professional; Non-Profit
    Type: Performing; Resident; Educational; Sponsoring
    Purpose: To encourage, support, nurture and sustain the art and artists of dance
    Management: Samuel A. Miller, Executive Director; William C. Yehle, General Manager
    Paid Staff: 25   **Volunteer Staff:** 25
    Paid Artists: 100
    Utilizes: Special Technical Talent; Guest Artists
    Budget: $1,000,000 - $5,000,000
    Income Sources: Private Foundations/Grants/Endowments; Business/Corporate Donations; Box Office; Government Grants; Individual Donations
    Season: June - September   **Annual Attendance:** 35,000
    Affiliations: Dance USA
    Performance Facilities: Ted Shawn Theatre

Belmont

THEATRE

BELMONT CHILDREN'S THEATRE
226 Beech Street, Belmont, MA 02178
(617) 489-4380
    Founded: 1982
    Arts Area: Musical; Community
    Status: Non-Professional
    Type: Performing; Educational
    Purpose: To provide a stimulating educational experience for young people who have an interest in theatre
    Management: Laura Kalo, Artistic Director
    Officers: Jacqueline Rossi, Faculty; Keith Kirkpatrick, Musician
    Paid Staff: 1
    Paid Artists: 2
    Utilizes: Special Technical Talent
    Budget: $1,000 - $50,000
    Income Sources: Private Foundations/Grants/Endowments; Business/Corporate Donations; Box Office; Government Grants
    Season: September - June   **Annual Attendance:** 1,000

BELMONT DRAMATIC CLUB
58 Harriet Avenue, Belmont, MA 02178
(617) 484-9174
    Founded: 1903
    Arts Area: Musical; Community; Theatrical Group
    Status: Non-Professional; Non-Profit
    Type: Performing
    Purpose: To bring good drama to the community
    Officers: Stephanie Cloutier, President; Cornie Bosse, Carolyn Hickok, Vice Presidents; Willa Rockett, Correspondence Secretary; Marcus Hatch, Treasurer
    Utilizes: Guest Directors
    Income Sources: Business/Corporate Donations; Box Office; Individual Donations
    Season: September - May   **Annual Attendance:** 900
    Performance Facilities: Belmont Town Hall, Hendall School

Beverly

THEATRE

NORTH SHORE MUSIC THEATRE
Dunham Road, PO Box 62, Beverly, MA 01915
(508) 922-8500
FAX: (508) 921-0793
Founded: 1955
Arts Area: Professional; Musical; Theatrical Group
Status: Professional; Non-Profit
Type: Performing; Touring; Educational
Purpose: North Shore Music Theatre presents the art of musical theatre to the greater Boston community and, in so doing, contributes to the cultural and educational lives of audiences, theatre artists and students.
Management: Jon Kimbell, Executive Producer; James K. Polese, General Manager; Jim Alberghini, Production Manager; David James, Marketing Director
Officers: John P. Drislane, President; Donald J. Short, Vice President; Wendell P. Wood, Treasurer
Paid Staff: 20   **Volunteer Staff:** 150
Paid Artists: 200
Utilizes: Guest Artists; Guest Directors
Budget: $1,000,000 - $5,000,000
Income Sources: Private Foundations/Grants/Endowments; Business/Corporate Donations; Box Office; Government Grants; Individual Donations
Season: 52 Weeks   **Annual Attendance:** 310,000
Affiliations: COST; Massachusetts Cultural Alliance
Performance Facilities: North Shore Music Theatre

FACILITY

NORTH SHORE MUSIC THEATRE
Dunham Road, PO Box 62, Beverly, MA 01915
(508) 922-8220
FAX: (508) 921-0793
Type of Facility: Theatre House; Arena
Type of Stage: Arena   **Orchestra Pit**
Seating Capacity: 1,790
Year Built: 1955   **Architect:** Irving Salsberg & Ralph LeBlanc
Contact for Rental: James K. Polese, General Manager/John Kimbell, Executive Producer;   (617) 922-8220
Manager: James K. Polese, General Manager
Resident Groups: North Shore Music Theatre

Boston

DANCE

BOSTON BALLET COMPANY
19 Clarendon Street, Boston, MA 02116
(617) 695-6950
FAX: (617) 695-6995
Founded: 1963
Arts Area: Ballet
Status: Professional; Non-Profit
Type: Performing
Purpose: Professional ballet company
Management: Bruce Marks, Artistic Director; Bruce Wells, Associate Director; D. David Brown, General Manager
Officers: John W. Humphrey, Chairman; Jill Goldweitz, Morris Hamilburg, Richard Pollard, Vice Presidents
Paid Staff: 39
Paid Artists: 83
Utilizes: Special Technical Talent; Guest Artists
Budget: $1,000,000 - $5,000,000
Income Sources: Private Foundations/Grants/Endowments; Business/Corporate Donations; Box Office; Government Grants; Individual Donations

Season: September - May **Annual Attendance:** 300,000
Performance Facilities: The Wang Center for the Performing Arts

BOSTON BALLET II
19 Clarendon Street, Boston, MA 02116
(617) 695-6950
FAX: (617) 695-6995
Founded: 1980
Arts Area: Ballet
Status: Professional; Non-Profit
Type: Performing; Touring; Educational
Purpose: To educate audiences and young professional dancers through community outreach and children's programming
Management: Susan Larson, Compnay Manager; Laura Young, Director
Paid Staff: 4
Paid Artists: 15
Utilizes: Guest Choreographers
Budget: $100,000 - $500,000
Income Sources: Private Foundations/Grants/Endowments; Business/Corporate Donations; Box Office; Individual Donations
Season: 32 Weeks

DANCE PROJECTS INC./BETH SOLL AND COMPANY
PO Box 825, Prudential Station, Boston, MA 02199
(617) 547-8771
Arts Area: Modern
Status: Professional; Non-Profit
Type: Performing; Touring; Educational
Purpose: To embody the inventive and compelling choreographic style of Beth Soll
Management: Sally Fabens, Managing Director; Beth Soll, Artistic Director
Officers: Lawrence Kunz, President of the Board
Budget: $50,000 - $100,000
Income Sources: Private Foundations/Grants/Endowments; Business/Corporate Donations; Box Office; Government Grants; Individual Donations
Season: 52 Weeks

MARCUS SCHULKIND DANCE COMPANY
352 West Newton Street, #3, Boston, MA 02116
(617) 536-2962
Founded: 1975
Arts Area: Modern
Status: Professional
Type: Performing; Touring; Resident; Educational
Management: Maria Schwartz, Co-Manager; Marcus Schulkind, Artistic Director
Paid Staff: 1 **Volunteer Staff:** 4
Paid Artists: 6 **Non-Paid Artists:** 2
Utilizes: Guest Choreographers
Budget: $1,000 - $50,000
Income Sources: Private Foundations/Grants/Endowments; Business/Corporate Donations; Box Office; Government Grants; Individual Donations
Season: July - October **Annual Attendance:** 5,000

MJT DANCE COMPANY
Studio: Boston Center For The Arts, Boston, MA 02116
(617) 482-0351
Founded: 1974
Arts Area: Modern
Status: Professional; Non-Profit
Type: Performing; Touring; Educational
Purpose: To educate and enrich through modern dance people of all ages through performances, classes, and outreach
Management: Margie J. Topf, Artistic Director; Brenda Lee Tracey, Business Manager
Officers: Kube Thurston, Board Chairman; Stuart M. Rose, Treasurer
Paid Staff: 5 **Volunteer Staff:** 20
Paid Artists: 15 **Non-Paid Artists:** 10
Utilizes: Guest Artists
Budget: $50,000 - $100,000
Income Sources: Private Foundations/Grants/Endowments; Business/Corporate Donations; Box Office; Individual Donations
Season: September - June **Annual Attendance:** 5,000

SPANISH DANCE THEATRE
791 Tremont Street, Boston, MA 02118
(619) 266-2120
 Arts Area: Ethnic
 Status: Professional; Non-Profit
 Type: Performing; Touring; Resident; Educational
 Purpose: To promote the enjoyment and understanding of Flamenco Dance technique through performance and education
 Management: Ramon de los Reyes, Artistic Director; Clara Ramona, Chief Choreographer
 Budget: $50,000 - $100,000
 Income Sources: Private Foundations/Grants/Endowments; Business/Corporate Donations; Box Office; Government Grants; Individual Donations

INSTRUMENTAL MUSIC

ALEA III
855 Commonwealth Avenue, Boston, MA 02215
(617) 353-3340
FAX: (617) 353-9551
 Founded: 1979
 Arts Area: Chamber; Ensemble; Electronic & Live Electronic
 Status: Professional; Non-Profit
 Type: Performing; Resident
 Purpose: To play and promote twentieth century classical music and to support the work of contemporary composers
 Management: Synneve Carlino, Executive Administrator; Theodore Antoniou, Music Director
 Officers: Keith Botsford, Chairman; George and Ellen Demeter, Co-Presidents; Electra Cardona, Treasurer
 Paid Staff: 3
 Utilizes: Guest Conductors; Guest Artists; Guest Directors; Guest Speakers
 Budget: $50,000 - $100,000
 Income Sources: Private Foundations/Grants/Endowments; Business/Corporate Donations; Box Office; Government Grants; Individual Donations; University Monies
 Season: September - May **Annual Attendance:** 700
 Affiliations: Boston University
 Performance Facilities: Tsai Performance Center

BOSTON CLASSICAL ORCHESTRA
551 Tremont Street, Boston, MA 02116
(617) 426-2387
 Founded: 1978
 Arts Area: Symphony; Orchestra; Chamber
 Status: Professional; Non-Profit
 Type: Performing
 Purpose: To perform the classics and music rooted in the classic tradition
 Management: Robert Brink, Executive Secretary; Quindara Dodge, Manager; Harry Ellis Dickson, Music Director
 Officers: Dorothy Bearak, President; Robert M. Leavy, Treasurer; Peter B. Finn, Secretary
 Paid Staff: 1 **Volunteer Staff:** 8
 Paid Artists: 30
 Utilizes: Guest Artists
 Budget: $50,000 - $100,000
 Income Sources: Private Foundations/Grants/Endowments; Business/Corporate Donations; Box Office; Government Grants; Individual Donations
 Season: October - June **Annual Attendance:** 6,000
 Performance Facilities: Faneuil Hall

BOSTON MUSICA VIVA
25 Huntington Avenue, Suite 612, Boston, MA 02116-5713
(617) 353-0556
FAX: (617) 353-0893
 Founded: 1969
 Arts Area: Chamber; New Music
 Status: Professional
 Type: Performing; Touring; Educational
 Purpose: To champion the work of living American composers along with comtemporary classics
 Management: Hilary Field, General Manager
 Officers: Richard Pittman, Music Director
 Paid Staff: 1 **Volunteer Staff:** 20
 Paid Artists: 6
 Utilizes: Guest Artists; Multi-Media Collaborations
 Budget: $100,000 - $500,000

Income Sources: Private Foundations/Grants/Endowments; Business/Corporate Donations; Box Office; Government Grants; Individual Donations
Season: September - May
Annual Attendance: 4,000
Performance Facilities: Edward Pickman Hall; Blackman Auditorium; Tsai Center

BOSTON POPS
Symphony Hall, 301 Massachusetts Avenue, Boston, MA 02115
(617) 266-1492
FAX: (617) 638-9223
    Arts Area: Orchestra; Pops; Popular Selections
    Status: Professional; Non-Profit
    Type: Performing; Touring
    Management: John Williams, Conductor
    Performance Facilities: Symphony Hall

BOSTON SYMPHONY CHAMBER PLAYERS
Symphony Hall, 301 Massachusetts Avenue, Boston, MA 02115
(617) 266-1492
    Founded: 1964
    Arts Area: Chamber; Ensemble
    Status: Professional; Commercial
    Type: Performing; Touring
    Purpose: The Chamber Players comprise the 12 first-chair players of the Boston Symphony Orchestra. They present programs of standard and contemporary literature not only in Boston and at Tanglewood, but on tour throughout this country and abroad, especially to audiences in locations which would not ordinarily be able to hear the Boston Symphony Orchestra in person.
    Management: Daniel R. Gustin, Manager; Richard Ortner, Assistant Manager
    Paid Staff: 2
    Paid Artists: 12
    Utilizes: Guest Artists
    Budget: $100,000 - $500,000
    Income Sources: Box Office
    Season: Winter; - Spring
    Affiliations: Boston Symphony Orchestra
    Performance Facilities: Jordan Hall; Tanglewood

BOSTON SYMPHONY ORCHESTRA
Symphony Hall, 301 Massachusetts Avenue, Boston, MA 02115
(617) 266-1492
    Founded: 1881
    Arts Area: Symphony; Orchestra; Chamber; Ensemble
    Status: Professional; Non-Profit
    Type: Performing; Touring; Resident; Educational
    Purpose: To bring great music to the widest possible audience; the Boston Symphony Orchestra, Inc. is the parent organization of the Boston Symphony Orchestra, the Boston Pops, the Boston Symphony Chamber Players, Tanglewood and the Tanglewood Music Center
    Management: Kenneth Haas, Managing Director; Daniel R. Gustin, Assistant Managing Director/Manager of Tanglewood; Michael G. McDonough, Director of Finance and Business Affairs; Evans Mirageas, Artistic Administrator; Caroline Smedvig, Director of Public Relations and Marketing; Josiah Stevenson, Director of Development; Ray F. Wellbaum, Orchestra Manager
    Officers: Nelson J. Darling Jr., Chairman Emeritus; J.P. Barger, Chairman; Mrs. Lewis S. Dabney, Mrs. John H. Fitzpatrick, Vice Chairmans; George H. Kidder, President; Archie C. Epps, Vice Chairman; William J. Poorvu, Vice Chairman/Treasurer
    Utilizes: Special Technical Talent; Guest Conductors; Guest Artists
    Budget: Over $10,000,000
    Income Sources: Private Foundations/Grants/Endowments; Business/Corporate Donations; Box Office; Government Grants; Individual Donations
    Season: 52 Weeks
    Performance Facilities: Symphony Hall

DINOSAUR ANNEX MUSIC ENSEMBLE
PO Box 5824, Boston, MA 02114
(617) 643-6627
    Arts Area: Orchestra; Chamber; Ensemble; Instrumental Group; Electronic & Live Electronic
    Status: Professional; Non-Profit
    Type: Performing
    Purpose: To play the best in contemporary music for chamber ensemble
    Management: Scott Wheeler, Artistic Director

Officers: Vance Koven, Chairman of the Board
Budget: $1,000 - $50,000
Income Sources: Private Foundations/Grants/Endowments; Business/Corporate Donations; Box Office; Government Grants; Individual Donations
Performance Facilities: First and Second Church, Boston

GREATER BOSTON YOUTH SYMPHONY ORCHESTRAS
855 Commonwealth Avenue, Boston, MA 02215
(617) 353-3348
FAX: (617) 353-2053
Founded: 1958
Arts Area: Symphony; Orchestra; Chamber
Status: Non-Professional; Non-Profit
Type: Performing; Touring; Resident; Educational
Purpose: To provide quality music education programs; to bring the music of young performers before a wide audience
Management: Parker Monroe, Executive Director; David Commanday, Music Director; Cathy Cotton, Orchestra Manager; Charles Sumner, Director of Public Relations
Officers: Tom Draper, President
Paid Staff: 7
Non-Paid Artists: 250
Budget: $100,000 - $500,000
Income Sources: Private Foundations/Grants/Endowments; Business/Corporate Donations; Box Office; Government Grants; Individual Donations
Season: September - June
Affiliations: Boston University

HANDEL AND HAYDN SOCIETY
300 Massachusetts Avenue, Boston, MA 02115
(617) 266-3605
FAX: (617) 266-4217
Founded: 1815
Arts Area: Chamber; Ensemble; Choral
Status: Professional; Non-Profit
Type: Performing; Touring; Educational; Sponsoring
Purpose: To promote the performance, study, composition and appreciation of music
Management: Christopher Hogwood, Artistic Director; Mary Deissler, Executive Director
Utilizes: Guest Conductors; Guest Artists; Guest Directors
Budget: $500,000 - $1,000,000
Income Sources: Private Foundations/Grants/Endowments; Business/Corporate Donations; Box Office; Government Grants; Individual Donations
Season: September - May   **Annual Attendance:** 55,000
Performance Facilities: Symphony Hall; Jordan Hall

MASSACHUSETTS YOUTH WIND ENSEMBLE
290 Huntington Avenue, Boston, MA 02115
(617) 262-1120, ext. 350
Founded: 1970
Arts Area: Chamber; Ensemble; Instrumental Group; Band
Status: Non-Profit
Type: Performing; Touring; Educational
Purpose: To offer exceptionally talented high school musicians an opportunity to study and perform the quality literature written for wind, brass, and percussion instruments
Management: Daniel J. Riley, Music Director/Conductor; Mark Churchill, Extension Division Director, New England Conservatory
Paid Staff: 14   **Volunteer Staff:** 5
Utilizes: Special Technical Talent; Guest Conductors; Guest Artists; Guest Directors
Budget: $1,000 - $50,000
Income Sources: Business/Corporate Donations; Individual Donations
Season: September - May   **Annual Attendance:** 5,000
Affiliations: New England Conservatory
Performance Facilities: Jordon Hall

SHIRIM KLEZMER ORCHESTRA
15 Perkins Square, #7, Boston, MA 02130
(617) 247-1606
FAX: (617) 524-5425
Founded: 1982
Arts Area: Ethnic; Folk

Status: Professional; Commercial
Type: Performing; Touring; Educational
Purpose: To perform music in the traditions of Eastern European Klezmer, Yiddish Theatre and Yiddish Folk Music
Management: Margaret Pash, Vintage Entertainment
Officers: Glenn Dickson, Owner
Paid Staff: 1
Paid Artists: 8
Budget: $50,000 - $100,000
Income Sources: Box Office; Individual Donations
Season: 52 Weeks

VOCAL MUSIC

BOSTON LYRIC OPERA COMPANY
114 State Street, Boston, MA 02109
(617) 248-8811; (617) 248-8660
FAX: (617) 248-8810
Founded: 1976
Arts Area: Lyric Opera
Status: Professional
Type: Performing
Purpose: To present a varied reportoire of works accessible to a broad segment of the community, productions featuring both young American artists of promise and the most highly-regarded figures in the world of opera
Management: Jan Del Sesto, Managing Director; Thomas Dreeze, Artistic Administrator; David Coolidge, Director of Finance; Laurie Way, Box Office Manager
Officers: Horace H. Irvine II, Chairman Board of Directors; Randolph Fuller, President; Akiba Herman, Treasurer; Michael Lytton, Clerk
Paid Staff: 7 **Volunteer Staff:** 2
Paid Artists: 100
Utilizes: Special Technical Talent; Guest Conductors; Guest Artists; Guest Directors
Budget: $1,000,000 - $5,000,000
Income Sources: Private Foundations/Grants/Endowments; Business/Corporate Donations; Box Office; Government Grants; Individual Donations
Season: September - March **Annual Attendance:** 11,000
Affiliations: OA
Performance Facilities: Emerson Majestic Theatre

BOSTON OPERA ASSOCIATION
Four Copley Place, Suite 140, Boston, MA 02116
(617) 437-1316
Founded: 1937
Arts Area: Grand Opera; Lyric Opera; Light Opera; Operetta
Status: Professional; Non-Profit
Type: Performing; Educational; Sponsoring
Purpose: To bring opera and operatic performances of high quality to the Boston and New England community that would not otherwise be available
Management: John W. Brewer, Administrator
Officers: William I. Cowin Esq., President
Paid Staff: 1 **Volunteer Staff:** 75
Utilizes: Guest Conductors; Guest Artists
Budget: $500,000 - $1,000,000
Income Sources: Private Foundations/Grants/Endowments; Business/Corporate Donations; Box Office; Individual Donations
Season: September - May **Annual Attendance:** 20,000
Performance Facilities: The Wang Center for The Performing Arts and Symphony Hall

OPERA COMPANY OF BOSTON
539 Washington Street, PO Box 50, Boston, MA 02112
(617) 426-5300
Founded: 1958
Arts Area: Grand Opera
Status: Professional
Type: Performing; Educational
Purpose: Opera Company of Boston is a professional, performing opera company. Opera New England is the touring arm of Opera Company of Boston.
Management: Sarah Caldwell, Artistic Director; Clifford Brooks, Manager
Paid Staff: 15 **Volunteer Staff:** 10
Utilizes: Special Technical Talent; Guest Conductors; Guest Artists; Guest Directors

Budget: $1,000,000 - $5,000,000
Income Sources: Private Foundations/Grants/Endowments; Business/Corporate Donations; Box Office; Government Grants; Individual Donations
Season: January - June   **Annual Attendance:** 52,000
Performance Facilities: Boston Opera House

OPERA NEW ENGLAND
539 Washington Street, Boston, MA 02111
(617) 426-5300
Founded: 1973
Arts Area: Grand Opera
Status: Professional; Non-Profit
Type: Performing; Touring; Educational
Purpose: As the touring arm of Opera Company of Boston, Opera New England disseminates opera through productions on tour.
Management: Sarah Caldwell, Artistic Director; Clifford Brooks, Manager
Officers: Helen Closson, President; Lucille Johnson, Vice President; Linda Cabot Black, Second Vice President; Demetre Steffon, Treasurer
Paid Staff: 2   **Volunteer Staff:** 18
Utilizes: Guest Conductors; Guest Artists; Guest Directors
Budget: $100,000 - $500,000
Income Sources: Private Foundations/Grants/Endowments; Business/Corporate Donations; Box Office; Government Grants; Individual Donations
Season: October - May   **Annual Attendance:** 18,000
Affiliations: OA

THEATRE

BOSTON CHILDREN'S THEATRE
93 Massachusetts Avenue, Boston, MA 02115
(617) 424-6634
Founded: 1951
Arts Area: Professional; Theatrical Group
Status: Professional; Non-Profit
Type: Performing
Purpose: To promote live theatre for children, by children; "Enchanted Forest," hosted at the Franklin Park Zoo in October
Management: Patricia M. Gleeson, Executive Director
Paid Staff: 2
Paid Artists: 8   **Non-Paid Artists:** 20
Utilizes: Special Technical Talent; Guest Artists; Guest Directors
Budget: $100,000 - $500,000
Income Sources: Private Foundations/Grants/Endowments; Business/Corporate Donations; Box Office; Government Grants; Individual Donations
Season: November - May   **Annual Attendance:** 21,000
Affiliations: NETC; AATY; Massachusetts Cultural Alliance
Performance Facilities: New England Life Hall

CITY STAGE COMPANY
539 Tremont Street, Boston, MA 02116
(617) 542-2291
FAX: (617) 426-5336
Founded: 1974
Arts Area: Professional; Theatrical Group
Status: Professional
Type: Performing; Touring; Educational
Purpose: To bring innovative theater and educational programs to specifically defined groups and audiences
Management: Tom Roulston, Susan Gassett, Artistic Co-Directors; Larry Coen, Associate Director
Officers: Richard Warren, Chairman; Tom Roulston, President; Susan Gassett, Secretary/Treasurer
Paid Staff: 3
Paid Artists: 100
Utilizes: Special Technical Talent
Budget: $100,000 - $500,000
Income Sources: Private Foundations/Grants/Endowments; Business/Corporate Donations; Box Office; Government Grants; Individual Donations
Season: 52 Weeks   **Annual Attendance:** 100,000
Affiliations: Massachusetts Cultural Alliance

HUNTINGTON THEATRE COMPANY
252 Huntington Avenue, Boston, MA 02115
(617) 353-3320
> **Founded:** 1982
> **Arts Area:** Professional; Theatrical Group
> **Status:** Professional; Non-Profit
> **Type:** Performing; Resident
> **Purpose:** Presenting classic works in their true spirit, and to respond to today's issues and emotions by presenting literate, trenchant, contemporary plays new to Boston
> **Management:** Michael Maso, Managing Director; Peter Altman, Producing Director
> **Officers:** Gerald J. Gross, President; Charles W. Smith, Treasurer
> **Paid Staff:** 25
> **Paid Artists:** 100
> **Utilizes:** Special Technical Talent; Guest Conductors; Guest Artists; Guest Directors
> **Budget:** $1,000,000 - $5,000,000
> **Income Sources:** Private Foundations/Grants/Endowments; Business/Corporate Donations; Box Office; Government Grants; Individual Donations
> **Season:** September - June   **Annual Attendance:** 100,000
> **Affiliations:** Boston University
> **Performance Facilities:** Boston University Theatre

LYRIC STAGE
140 Clarendon Street, Boston, MA 02116
(617) 437-7172
> **Founded:** 1973
> **Arts Area:** Professional; Theatrical Group
> **Status:** Professional; Non-Profit
> **Type:** Performing
> **Purpose:** To present high-quality, professional theatre at low-cost prices to audiences who would otherwise never have known their theatrical heritage
> **Management:** Ron Ritchell, Artistic Director; Polly Ritchell, Producer; James Denietolis, Subscription/Box Office Manager; Carolyn Ridgway, Marketing/Public Relations; Anne Fletcher, Group Sales
> **Officers:** S. Michael Bates, President; Frick Jones, Vice President; Jane Salloway, Treasurer; Kathleen Bates, Clerk
> **Paid Staff:** 6   **Volunteer Staff:** 10
> **Paid Artists:** 50
> **Utilizes:** Special Technical Talent; Guest Directors
> **Budget:** $100,000 - $500,000
> **Income Sources:** Private Foundations/Grants/Endowments; Business/Corporate Donations; Box Office; Individual Donations
> **Season:** September - June   **Annual Attendance:** 25,000
> **Affiliations:** AEA; New England Area Theatres

NEW THEATRE
755 Boyleston, Boston, MA 02116
> **Founded:** 1980
> **Arts Area:** Professional; Theatrical Group
> **Status:** Semi-Professional; Non-Profit
> **Type:** Performing; Resident; Educational
> **Purpose:** To develop new plays, new interpretations of plays and Massachusetts theatre artists
> **Management:** Richard W. Freeman, Artistic Director; John Hennessy, General Manager; Ruth Polleys, Production Manager; Deborah Scaglione, Development Director; Kathleen Canzano, Business Manager; David J. Lima, Box Office
> **Paid Staff:** 6   **Volunteer Staff:** 15
> **Paid Artists:** 80   **Non-Paid Artists:** 7
> **Budget:** $100,000 - $500,000
> **Income Sources:** Private Foundations/Grants/Endowments; Business/Corporate Donations; Box Office; Government Grants; Individual Donations
> **Season:** September - June   **Annual Attendance:** 15,000
> **Affiliations:** Boston Regional Theatre Association

THE PUBLICK THEATRE
11 Ridgemont Street, Boston, MA 02134
(617) 782-5425
> **Founded:** 1970
> **Arts Area:** Professional; Musical; Theatrical Group
> **Status:** Professional; Non-Profit
> **Type:** Performing; Touring; Resident; Sponsoring
> **Purpose:** To discover, develop and showcase Boston-area theatrical talent in programs of professional quality that are accessible to a diverse audience
> **Management:** Spiro Veloudos, Artistic Director; Deborah Schoenberg, Marketing/Development Director

Officers: Michael McDermott, President; Randall Filer, Treasurer
Paid Staff: 7   Volunteer Staff: 7
Paid Artists: 50
Utilizes: Guest Artists; Guest Directors
Budget: $100,000 - $500,000
Income Sources: Private Foundations/Grants/Endowments; Business/Corporate Donations; Box Office; Government Grants; Individual Donations
Season: June - Labor Day
Annual Attendance: 10,000
Performance Facilities: The Publick Theatre

PERFORMING SERIES

BOSTON EARLY MUSIC FESTIVAL AND EXHIBITION, INC.
729 Boylston Street, Suite 600, Boston, MA 02116
(617) 661-1812; (617) 262-0650
FAX: (617) 267-6539
Founded: 1980
Arts Area: Dance; Vocal Music; Instrumental Music; Festivals; Lyric Opera; Grand Opera; Early Music Festival
Status: Non-Profit
Type: Performing; Touring; Educational; Sponsoring
Purpose: To discover and reproduce, insofar as possible, the way early music originally sounded to a composer and his audience; to produce a biennial international festival in Boston; to educate youth
Management: Kathleen Fay, Executive Director
Officers: E.S. Whitney Thompson, President; Richard Hester, Vice President; Howard V. Wagner, Treasurer; Richard Portars, Clerk
Paid Staff: 2   Volunteer Staff: 200
Paid Artists: 250
Utilizes: Special Technical Talent; Guest Conductors; Guest Artists; Guest Directors
Budget: $500,000 - $1,000,000
Income Sources: Private Foundations/Grants/Endowments; Business/Corporate Donations; Box Office; Government Grants; Individual Donations
Season: 52 Weeks
Annual Attendance: 11,000

CELEBRITY SERIES OF BOSTON, INC.
20 Park Plaza, Suite 832, Boston, MA 02116
(617) 482-2595
FAX: (617) 482-3208
Founded: 1938
Arts Area: Dance; Vocal Music; Instrumental Music; Theater
Status: Non-Profit
Type: Presenting
Purpose: To bring Boston the world's greatest performing artists
Management: Walter Pierce, Executive Director; Martha Jones, General Manager; Kathleen Panoff, Development Director; Michael Botte, Comptroller
Officers: Arnold Zetcher, President; Joop Spanjaard, Chairman Finance
Paid Staff: 12   Volunteer Staff: 60
Paid Artists: 200
Utilizes: Guest Artists
Budget: $1,000,000 - $5,000,000
Income Sources: Private Foundations/Grants/Endowments; Business/Corporate Donations
Season: September - May
Annual Attendance: 150,000
Affiliations: ISPAA
Performance Facilities: Symphony Hall; Wang Center; Jordan Hall

FIRST NIGHT, INC.
20 Park Plaza, Suite 927, Boston, MA 02116
(617) 542-1399
FAX: (617) 426-9531
Founded: 1976
Arts Area: Dance; Vocal Music; Theater
Status: Non-Profit
Type: Art Presenter
Purpose: To broaden and deepen the public's appreciation for the visual and performing arts

Management: Zeren Earls, President; Deborah Kittredge, General Manager
Officers: Sam Frankenheim, Chairman; Rosamond Vaule, Vice Chair; Zeren Earls, President; Rina Spence, Treasurer; Randi Ingerman, Clerk
Paid Staff: 10   **Volunteer Staff:** 800
Paid Artists: 1,000
Utilizes: Guest Conductors; Guest Artists; Guest Directors
Budget: $500,000 - $1,000,000
Income Sources: Private Foundations/Grants/Endowments; Government Grants; Buttons; Admissions
Season: New Year's Eve   **Annual Attendance:** 600,000

ISABELLA STEWART GARDNER MUSEUM
280 The Fenway, Boston, MA 02115
(617) 566-1401
FAX: (617) 232-8039
Founded: 1900
Arts Area: Vocal Music; Instrumental Music; Theater; Lyric Opera
Status: Non-Profit
Type: Sponsoring
Purpose: Art Museum
Management: Anne Hawley, Director; Susan Davy, Director of Operations & Finance; Hilliard Goldfarb, Curator
Paid Staff: 85   **Volunteer Staff:** 12
Paid Artists: 75
Utilizes: Guest Conductors; Guest Artists
Budget: $1,000 - $50,000
Income Sources: Private Foundations/Grants/Endowments; Business/Corporate Donations; Box Office; Government Grants; Individual Donations
Season: September - June
Annual Attendance: 130,000
Performance Facilities: Isabella Stewart Gardner Museum

KING'S CHAPEL CONCERT SERIES
58 Tremont Street, Boston, MA 02108
(617) 876-8375
Founded: 1958
Arts Area: Vocal Music; Instrumental Music
Status: Professional
Type: Performing
Purpose: To present chamber works and works for small chorus, especially baroque and contemporary selections
Management: Daniel Pinkham, Music Director
Paid Staff: 1   **Volunteer Staff:** 8
Paid Artists: 30
Utilizes: Special Technical Talent; Guest Artists
Budget: $1,000 - $50,000
Income Sources: Individual Donations
Season: September - February
Performance Facilities: King's Chapel

TANGLEWOOD FESTIVAL
c/o Boston Symphony Orchestra Inc., 301 Massachusetts Avenue, Boston, MA 02115
(617) 266-1492
FAX: (617) 638-9288
Arts Area: Vocal Music; Instrumental Music; Festivals; Orchestral
Status: Professional; Non-Profit
Type: Performing; Educational
Purpose: Tanglewood is the summer home of the Boston Symphony Orchestra and is one of the world's preeminent summer music schools.
Management: Seiji Ozawa, Music Director; Kenneth Haas, Managing Director; Daniel Gustin, Assistant Managing Director of Boston Symphony and Tanglewood
Officers: J.P. Barger, Chairman of the Board; George Kidder, President of the Board
Paid Staff: 100   **Volunteer Staff:** 1,000
Utilizes: Special Technical Talent; Guest Conductors; Guest Artists
Budget: $5,000,000 - $10,000,000
Income Sources: Private Foundations/Grants/Endowments; Business/Corporate Donations; Box Office; Government Grants; Individual Donations
Season: June - August
Annual Attendance: 300,000
Performance Facilities: Tanglewood

FACILITY

BOSTON CENTER FOR THE ARTS - CYCLORAMA
539 Tremont Street, Boston, MA 02116
(617) 426-5000
FAX: (617) 426-5336
Type of Facility: Multi-Purpose; Exhibition Hall
Facility Originally: Cyclorama
Type of Stage: Rotunda
Stage Dimensions: 125' diameter brick floor
Year Built: 1884   **Architect:** Cummings & Sears
Year Remodeled: 1923   **Cost:** $80,000
Contact for Rental: Harlan Jones;   (617) 426-5000

BOSTON CENTER FOR THE ARTS - THE NATIONAL THEATRE
539 Tremont Street, Boston, MA 02116
(617) 426-5000
FAX: (617) 426-5336
Type of Facility: Concert Hall; Performance Center; Theatre House; Opera House
Facility Originally: Opera House
Type of Stage: Thrust; Proscenium
Stage Dimensions: 40'Wx25'D   **Orchestra Pit**
Seating Capacity: 2,500
Year Built: 1911   **Architect:** Clarence Howard Blackall
Year Remodeled: 1986   **Architect:** Hidell-Eyster & Associates   **Cost:** $3,500,000
Contact for Rental: Harlan Jones;   (617) 426-5000

BOSTON OPERA HOUSE
539 Washington Street, Boston, MA 02111
(617) 426-5300
Type of Facility: Concert Hall; Theatre House; Opera House
Facility Originally: Vaudeville
Type of Stage: Modified Apron Proscenium   **Orchestra Pit**
Seating Capacity: 2,600
Year Built: 1928   **Architect:** Charles Lamb
Year Remodeled: 1977
Contact for Rental: Jim DeVeer or Nancy Talbot;   (617) 426-5300
Resident Groups: Opera Company of Boston

BOSTON UNIVERSITY SCHOOL FOR THE ARTS - CONCERT HALL
855 Commonwealth Avenue, Boston, MA 02115
(617) 353-3385
Type of Facility: Concert Hall
Type of Stage: Platform; Concert Stage
Stage Dimensions: 1,507 square feet
Seating Capacity: 450
Year Built: 1957   **Architect:** George Sherwood
Acoustical Consultant: Bolt, Beranek & Newman
Contact for Rental: David Cross;   (617) 353-3831

BOSTON UNIVERSITY THEATRE
264 Huntington Avenue, Boston, MA 02115
(617) 266-7900
FAX: (617) 363-8300
Type of Facility: Theatre Complex
Type of Stage: Proscenium   **Orchestra Pit**
Seating Capacity: 850
Year Built: 1926   **Architect:** J. William Beal & Sons   **Cost:** $1,000,000
Year Remodeled: 1973   **Architect:** Harry Weese & Associates   **Cost:** $500,000
Contact for Rental: Roger Meeker;   (617) 266-7900
Resident Groups: Huntington Theatre Company; School of Theatre Arts; School of Music (Opera Workshop)
Boston University Theatre contains the Main Stage and Studio 210. See individual listings for additional information.

BOSTON UNIVERSITY THEATRE - MAIN STAGE
264 Huntington Avenue, Boston, MA 02115
(617) 266-7900
FAX: (617) 363-8300
Type of Facility: Auditorium; Theatre House

Type of Stage: Proscenium
Stage Dimensions: 76'Wx33'D; 36'Wx24'H proscenium opening   **Orchestra Pit**
Seating Capacity: 856
Year Built: 1926
Year Remodeled: 1973
Contact for Rental: Roger Meeker;   (617) 266-7900
Resident Groups: Huntington Theatre Company; School of Theatre Arts; School of Music (Opera Workshop)

BOSTON UNIVERSITY THEATRE - STUDIO 210
264 Huntington Avenue, Boston, MA 02115
(617) 266-7900
FAX: (617) 363-8300
Type of Facility: Studio Performance; Black Box
Type of Stage: Flexible
Stage Dimensions: 35'Wx75'Lx14'H
Seating Capacity: 100
Year Built: 1926
Year Remodeled: 1973
Contact for Rental: Roger Meeker;   (617) 266-7900
Resident Groups: Huntington Theatre Company; School of Theatre Arts

EMERSON MAJESTIC THEATRE
219 Tremont Street, Boston, MA 02116
(617) 578-8727
FAX: (617) 578-8725
Type of Facility: Theatre House
Type of Stage: Proscenium
Stage Dimensions: 38'Wx35'D   **Orchestra Pit**
Seating Capacity: 850
Year Built: 1903   **Architect:** John Galen Howard   **Cost:** $135,000
Year Remodeled: 1988
Contact for Rental: (617) 578-8727

ISABELLA STEWART GARDNER MUSEUM
280 The Fenway, Boston, MA 02115
(617) 566-1401
FAX: (617) 232-8039
Type of Facility: Multi-Purpose; Room; Museum Gallery
Type of Stage: Flexible; Platform
Seating Capacity: 325
Year Built: 1900
Manager: Scott Nickrenz, Music Director;   (617) 566-1401

JORDAN HALL AT NEW ENGLAND CONSERVATORY
30 Gainsboro Street, Boston, MA 02115
(617) 262-1120
FAX: (617) 262-0500
Founded: 1903
Type of Facility: Concert Hall; Auditorium
Type of Stage: Proscenium
Stage Dimensions: 40'Wx29'D
Seating Capacity: 1,019
Year Built: 1903
Year Remodeled: 1938
Contact for Rental: Jon Wulp;   (617) 262-1120, ext. 268
Resident Groups: New England Conservatory Performers

ORPHEUM THEATRE
Hamilton Place, Boston, MA 02108
(617) 482-0651
Type of Facility: Theatre House
Type of Stage: Proscenium
Stage Dimensions: 44'Wx39'D
Seating Capacity: 2,763
Year Built: 1900   **Architect:** Charles Lamb
Contact for Rental: Bruce Montgomery;   (617) 482-0651

SHUBERT THEATRE
265 Tremont Street, Boston, MA 02116
(617) 426-4520
   Type of Facility: Theatre House
   Type of Stage: Proscenium
   Stage Dimensions: 78'Wx42'6'D; 40'Wx30'H proscenium opening   **Orchestra Pit**
   Seating Capacity: 1,696
   Contact for Rental: Peter Entin;   (212) 944-3700
   Manager: The Shubert Organization;   (212) 944-3700
   Limited availability for rental

SYMPHONY HALL
301 Massachusetts Avenue, Boston, MA 02115
(617) 266-1492
   Type of Facility: Concert Hall
   Type of Stage: Proscenium
   Stage Dimensions: 50'x36'x34'
   Seating Capacity: 2,625
   Year Built: 1900   **Architect:** McKim, Meade, White
   Acoustical Consultant: Wallace Sabine
   Contact for Rental: Functions Manager;   (617) 266-1492
   Manager: James Whitaker;   (413) 637-1600
   Resident Groups: Boston Symphony Orchestra; Boston Pops Orchestra

THE WANG CENTER FOR THE PERFORMING ARTS
270 Tremont Street, Boston, MA 02116
(617) 482-9393
   Type of Facility: Concert Hall; Auditorium; Performance Center; Theatre House; Opera House
   Facility Originally: Vaudeville
   Type of Stage: Proscenium
   Stage Dimensions: 60'3"Wx36'1"Hx60'D   **Orchestra Pit**
   Seating Capacity: 4,000
   Year Built: 1927
   Year Remodeled: 1980
   Contact for Rental: Sandy Chapiro;   (617) 482-9393
   Resident Groups: Boston Ballet

Braintree

VOCAL MUSIC

BRAINTREE CHORAL SOCIETY
263 West Street, Braintree, MA 02184
(617) 848-0084
   Founded: 1923
   Arts Area: Choral
   Status: Non-Professional; Non-Profit
   Type: Performing
   Purpose: To promote interest and participation in choral music in the community
   Management: Steven Young, Director; Blanche Blazo, Membership Chairman
   Paid Staff: 1   **Volunteer Staff:** 10
   Paid Artists: 6   **Non-Paid Artists:** 4
   Utilizes: Special Technical Talent; Guest Artists
   Budget: $1,000 - $50,000
   Income Sources: Business/Corporate Donations; Box Office; Government Grants; Individual Donations
   Season: September - May   **Annual Attendance:** 200

Brookline

THEATRE

PUPPET SHOWPLACE THEATRE
32 Station Street, Brookline, MA 02146
(617) 731-6400
   Founded: 1974
   Arts Area: Puppet
   Status: Professional; Non-Profit

Type: Performing; Touring; Resident; Sponsoring
Management: Mary Churchill, Executive Director; Paul Vincent-Davis, Artistic Director
Officers: Claire Dilleo, President; Margaret Keiley, Treasurer; Julie Kronenberg, Clerk
Paid Staff: 4
Paid Artists: 21
Utilizes: Guest Artists
Budget: $100,000 - $500,000
Income Sources: Private Foundations/Grants/Endowments; Box Office
Season: 52 Weeks   **Annual Attendance:** 15,000
Affiliations: Puppeteers of America; UNIMA

Brookline Village

INSTRUMENTAL MUSIC

JAZZ COMPOSERS ALLIANCE
PO Box 752, Brookline Village, MA 02147
(617) 964-5471
Founded: 1986
Arts Area: Ensemble; Band; Jazz
Status: Professional; Non-Profit
Type: Performing; Sponsoring
Purpose: To advance the art of jazz composition by featuring the work of established and emerging composers
Officers: Darrell Katz, Director; Duane Johnson, Treasurer; Susan Calkins, Art Work; Bob Pilkington, Secretary
Paid Artists: 25
Utilizes: Special Technical Talent; Guest Artists
Budget: $1,000 - $50,000
Income Sources: Private Foundations/Grants/Endowments; Business/Corporate Donations; Box Office; Government Grants; Individual Donations; Advertising
Season: September - June   **Annual Attendance:** 1,000

Burlington

INSTRUMENTAL MUSIC

CAMBRIDGE FOLK ORCHESTRA
6 Tami Lane, Burlington, MA 01803
(617) 272-0396
Founded: 1966
Arts Area: Orchestra; Ensemble; Ethnic; Folk; Instrumental Group; Band
Status: Professional; Semi-Professional; Commercial
Type: Performing; Resident; Educational
Purpose: The orchestra plays for folk dances, parties, workshops, festivals, weddings and social events with most of the selections being ethnic dance music from many countries.
Management: Calvin R. Howard, Business Manager; Aubry Jaffer, Orchestra Leader
Paid Artists: 9   **Non-Paid Artists:** 9
Utilizes: Guest Artists
Budget: $1,000 - $50,000
Income Sources: Box Office; Individual Donations
Season: 52 Weeks

Cambridge

DANCE

BOSTON FLAMENCO BALLET
79 Rice Street, Cambridge, MA 02140
(617) 354-8608; (800) 435-8687
Founded: 1973
Arts Area: Mime; Ballet; Ethnic; Folk
Status: Professional; Non-Profit
Type: Performing; Touring; Educational
Purpose: To educate students and adults about Spanish and Hispanic culture and history through dance and music

Management: Simon Blasco, Artistic Director
Officers: Heda Skiotis, President; Jose Alcaraz, Treasurer; Maria E. Calderon, Clerk
Paid Staff: 2   **Volunteer Staff:** 1
Paid Artists: 15
Utilizes: Special Technical Talent; Guest Artists
Budget: $100,000 - $500,000
Income Sources: Box Office
Season: September - December; February-April   **Annual Attendance:** 50,000

DANCE UMBRELLA, BOSTON, INC.
380 Green Street, Cambridge, MA 02139
(617) 492-7578
FAX: (617) 354-1603
Founded: 1979
Arts Area: Modern; Mime; Ballet; Jazz; Ethnic; Folk; Performance Art; Dance Theatre
Status: Professional; Non-Profit
Type: Performing; Resident; Educational; Presenting
Purpose: To present the best contemporary and culturally diverse artists from around the world; to nurture dance by commissioning new work; to provide educational programs for the public; to provide services to the local dance community
Management: Jeremy Alliger, Executive Director/Producer; Kara Keller, General Manager
Officers: Gordon Orloff Esq., Chairman of the Board; Libby Chiu, President
Paid Staff: 11
Utilizes: Guest Artists; Guest Choreographers
Budget: $1,000,000 - $5,000,000
Income Sources: Private Foundations/Grants/Endowments; Business/Corporate Donations; Box Office; Government Grants; Individual Donations
Season: October - June
Annual Attendance: 30,000
Affiliations: National Performance Network; APAP; Dance USA

HARVARD SUMMER DANCE CENTER
51 Brattle Street, Cambridge, MA 02138
(617) 495-5535
FAX: (617) 495-9176
Founded: 1973
Arts Area: Modern; Ballet; Jazz; Tap
Status: Non-Profit
Type: Educational
Purpose: To bring together students and a distinguished faculty of teacher/artists in a six-week program of classics and performances, films and lectures on the world of dance
Management: Iris Fanger, Director; Regina Boyland, Coordinator
Paid Staff: 8
Paid Artists: 20
Utilizes: Special Technical Talent; Guest Artists
Budget: $100,000 - $500,000
Income Sources: Private Foundations/Grants/Endowments; Business/Corporate Donations; Box Office; Government Grants; Individual Donations
Annual Attendance: 2,400

MANDALA FOLK DANCE ENSEMBLE
PO Box 246, Cambridge, MA 02139
(617) 868-3641
Founded: 1965
Arts Area: Ethnic; Folk
Status: Professional; Semi-Professional; Non-Profit
Type: Performing; Touring; Resident; Educational
Purpose: To research, preserve and perform traditional folk dance and music from around the world; to broaden cross-cultural awareness; to introduce accessible dance to a broad audience
Paid Staff: 3   **Volunteer Staff:** 10
Non-Paid Artists: 35
Utilizes: Special Technical Talent; Guest Choreographers
Budget: $100,000 - $500,000
Income Sources: Private Foundations/Grants/Endowments; Business/Corporate Donations; Box Office; Government Grants; Individual Donations
Season: November - July   **Annual Attendance:** 30,000
Affiliations: Massachusetts Council on the Arts; New England Foundation Tour Program; NEA Dance Program
Performance Facilities: John Hancock Hall

INSTRUMENTAL MUSIC

BOSTON BAROQUE
PO Box 380190, Cambridge, MA 02238
(617) 641-1310
FAX: (617) 641-1322
Founded: 1973
Arts Area: Orchestra; Chorus
Status: Professional; Non-Profit
Type: Performing; Touring; Resident
Purpose: To perform Baroque and classical music using period instruments and chorus
Management: Martin Pearlman, Music Director; Carole Friedman, Executive Director
Officers: Marshall Goldman, President; Charles Christenson, Vice President; Thomas R. Kolb, Clerk; John A. Gunnarson, Treasurer
Paid Staff: 4
Paid Artists: 50
Utilizes: Guest Artists
Budget: $100,000 - $500,000
Income Sources: Private Foundations/Grants/Endowments; Business/Corporate Donations; Box Office; Government Grants; Individual Donations
Season: October - June   **Annual Attendance:** 10,000
Performance Facilities: Jordan Hall

BOSTON PHILHARMONIC
PO Box 3000, Cambridge, MA 02218
(617) 861-8530
FAX: (617) 861-8530
Founded: 1979
Arts Area: Symphony; Orchestra
Status: Professional; Semi-Professional; Non-Profit
Type: Performing; Touring
Management: Benjamin Zander, Music Director/Conductor; Mary S. Jaffee, Manager
Officers: Seymour Rothchild, President; Urs Gauchat, Vice President; Gary Seligson, Treasurer; Ira Deitsch, Clerk
Paid Staff: 3   **Volunteer Staff:** 4
Paid Artists: 30   **Non-Paid Artists:** 55
Utilizes: Guest Artists
Budget: $100,000 - $500,000
Income Sources: Private Foundations/Grants/Endowments; Business/Corporate Donations; Box Office; Government Grants; Individual Donations; Fund-raising
Season: November - May   **Annual Attendance:** 10,000
Affiliations: Arts Boston
Performance Facilities: Jordan Hall; Sanders Theater; Symphony Hall

KLEZMER CONSERVATORY BAND
83 Inman, Cambridge, MA 02139
(617) 354-2884
Founded: 1980
Arts Area: Ethnic; Folk; Band
Status: Professional
Type: Performing; Touring
Purpose: Yiddish instrumental and vocal music with many influences (Jazz, Dixieland, Ragtime, Broadway, Latin)
Management: Aaron Concert Management, Boston Mass.; James Guttmann, Business Manager
Officers: Hankus Netsky, President
Paid Staff: 2
Paid Artists: 15
Income Sources: Box Office
Season: September - June

NEW ENGLAND PHILHARMONIC
1972 Massachusetts Avenue, 4th Floor, Cambridge, MA 02140
(617) 868-1222
Founded: 1976
Arts Area: Orchestra
Status: Non-Professional
Type: Performing; Resident
Purpose: To foster and encourage enjoyment and appreciation of new and unusual orchestral music; to perform standard orchestral literature in community locations
Management: Elisa Birdseye, Executive Director; Jeffrey Rink, Music Director; Dick Yoder, Personnel Manager

Officers: Nancy Hawkins, President; Constance Wark, Vice President; Susan Browse, Treasurer
Volunteer Staff: 3
Paid Artists: 3   **Non-Paid Artists:** 65
Utilizes: Guest Artists; Composer-in-Residence
Budget: $1,000 - $50,000
Income Sources: Private Foundations/Grants/Endowments; Business/Corporate Donations; Box Office; Government Grants; Individual Donations
Season: September - May
Annual Attendance: 2,000
Affiliations: ASOL
Performance Facilities: Sanders Theatre, Cambridge; Dwight Hall, Framingham

PRO ARTE CHAMBER ORCHESTRA
1950 Massachusetts Aveneue, Cambridge, MA 02140
(617) 661-7067
FAX: (617) 661-7067
Founded: 1978
Arts Area: Orchestra; Chamber
Status: Professional; Non-Profit
Type: Performing
Purpose: To perform a self-produced yearly series of orchestral works, classical and contemporary, for chamber orchestra
Management: Evelyn Dueck, General Manager
Officers: William Moyer, President; W. Easley Hamner, Secretary; John Porter, Treasurer
Paid Staff: 2   **Volunteer Staff:** 20
Paid Artists: 40
Utilizes: Guest Conductors; Guest Artists; Guest Directors
Budget: $100,000 - $500,000
Income Sources: Private Foundations/Grants/Endowments; Business/Corporate Donations; Box Office; Government Grants; Individual Donations
Season: September - May   **Annual Attendance:** 6,000
Affiliations: Harvard University
Performance Facilities: Sanders Theater

WATER MUSIC
12 Arrow Street, Cambridge, MA 02138
(617) 876-8742
FAX: (617) 876-6036
Founded: 1971
Arts Area: Ensemble; Instrumental Group
Status: Professional; Commercial
Type: Sponsoring
Purpose: To produce music cruises, concerts and special events
Management: Fenton Hollander, Program and Publicity Director
Officers: Fenton Hollander, President
Paid Staff: 5
Paid Artists: 350
Utilizes: Special Technical Talent; Guest Artists
Budget: $100,000 - $500,000
Income Sources: Box Office
Season: 52 Weeks   **Annual Attendance:** 28,000

VOCAL MUSIC

OPERA NEW ENGLAND
5 Hilliard Place, Cambridge, MA 02138
(617) 354-0451
Founded: 1973
Arts Area: Lyric Opera; Light Opera
Status: Professional; Non-Profit
Type: Educational; Sponsoring
Purpose: To present seasons of opera for children and for general audiences. As the regional development program of The Opera Company of Boston, we present productions prepared by The Opera Company of Boston. Since 1983, our chapter has presented only productions for children.
Management: Linda C. Black, Founder
Officers: Linda C. Black, President; Barbara Barclay, Hagnette Cumitz, Norma Peterson, Sonya Schopick, Vice Presidents; Anne Chemiavsky, Secretary; Robert W. Burmester, Treasurer
Volunteer Staff: 1
Paid Artists: 2
Budget: $1,000 - $50,000

Income Sources: Private Foundations/Grants/Endowments; Business/Corporate Donations; Box Office; Government Grants; Individual Donations
Season: September - November   **Annual Attendance:** 8,000
Affiliations: Opera Company of Boston

REVELS INC.
One Kendall Square, Building 600, Cambridge, MA 02139
(617) 621-0505
FAX: (617) 621-1709
Founded: 1971
Arts Area: Musical Theatre
Status: Non-Profit
Type: Performing; Educational
Purpose: To promote education, understanding and appreciation of traditional music, songs, rituals and customs through the mediums of performance and recordings
Management: Gayle Rich, Executive Director; John Langstaff, Artistic Director; Alan Casso, General Manager; William Scheick, Business Manager
Officers: David Mortensen, President; Paul Rahmeier, Vice President; Joseph H. Bragden, Treasurer
Paid Staff: 6   **Volunteer Staff:** 35
Paid Artists: 20   **Non-Paid Artists:** 60
Utilizes: Guest Artists
Budget: $500,000 - $1,000,000
Income Sources: Private Foundations/Grants/Endowments; Business/Corporate Donations; Box Office; Government Grants; Individual Donations
Season: December   **Annual Attendance:** 18,500
Performance Facilities: Sanders Theatre, Harvard University

THEATRE

AMERICAN REPERTORY THEATRE
Harvard University, 64 Brattle Street, Cambridge, MA 02138
(617) 495-2668
FAX: (617) 495-1705
Founded: 1980
Arts Area: Professional
Status: Professional; Non-Profit
Type: Performing; Touring; Resident; Educational
Purpose: The American Repertory Theatre is a separately incorporated not-for-profit organization chartered to provide a service to the widest possible public in the Boston/Cambridge community and to the theatre world in general.
Management: Robert Brustein, Artistic Director; Robert J. Orchard, Managing Director; Ron Daniels, Associate Artistic Director
Paid Staff: 249   **Volunteer Staff:** 458
Paid Artists: 203   **Non-Paid Artists:** 7
Utilizes: Guest Directors
Budget: $5,000,000 - $10,000,000
Income Sources: Private Foundations/Grants/Endowments; Business/Corporate Donations; Box Office; Government Grants; Individual Donations
Annual Attendance: 130,610
Affiliations: AEA; LORT
Performance Facilities: Loeb Drama Center

FACILITY

LOEB DRAMA CENTER
64 Brattle Street, Cambridge, MA 02138
(617) 495-2668
FAX: (617) 495-1705
Type of Facility: Theatre House
Type of Stage: Thrust; Flexible; Proscenium
Orchestra Pit
Seating Capacity: 556
Year Built: 1960   **Architect:** Hugh Stubbins   **Cost:** $1,700,000
Acoustical Consultant: Bolt, Beranek & Newman
Contact for Rental: Production Manager;   (617) 495-2668

Manager: Robert J. Orchard
Resident Groups: American Repertory Theatre; Harvard/Radcliffe Dramatic Club

RADCLIFFE COLLEGE - AGASSIZ THEATER
10 Garden Street, Cambridge, MA 02138
(617) 495-8676
Type of Facility: Theatre House
Facility Originally: Meeting Hall; Movie House
Type of Stage: Proscenium   **Orchestra Pit**
Seating Capacity: 350
Year Built: 1902   **Architect:** A.W. Longfellow   **Cost:** $200,000
Year Remodeled: 1983   **Architect:** Goody, Clancey & Associates   **Cost:** $2,000,000
Acoustical Consultant: Cavanaugh & Jucci
Rental is for Harvard and Radcliffe groups only.

RADCLIFFE COLLEGE - LYMAN COMMON ROOM
10 Garden Street, Cambridge, MA 02138
(617) 495-8676
Type of Facility: Room
Facility Originally: Ballroom
Type of Stage: Flexible
Seating Capacity: 150
Year Built: 1902   **Architect:** A.W. Longfellow   **Cost:** $200,000
Year Remodeled: 1983   **Architect:** Goody, Clancey & Associates   **Cost:** $2,000,000
Rental is for Harvard and Radcliffe groups only.

SANDERS THEATRE
Quincy and Kirkland Streets, Cambridge, MA 02138
(617) 495-4968
FAX: (617) 495-2420
Mailing Address: Harvard Real Estate, 1350 Massachusetts Avenue, Cambridge, MA 02138
Founded: 1876
Type of Facility: Concert Hall; Auditorium; Performance Center
Type of Stage: Semi-Proscenium, no curtain
Stage Dimensions: 59'x27'
Seating Capacity: 1,224
Year Built: 1876   **Architect:** Ware and Van Brunt
Contact for Rental: Ann Dumaresq;   (617) 495-4968
Resident Groups: Boston Philharmonic; Pro Arte Chamber Orchestra; The Boston Chamber Music Society

---

Charlestown

THEATRE

CHARLESTOWN WORKING THEATER
442 Bunker Hill Street, Charlestown, MA 02129
(617) 242-3534
Founded: 1972
Arts Area: Professional; Summer Stock; Community; Theatrical Group; Puppet
Status: Professional; Semi-Professional; Non-Professional; Non-Profit
Type: Performing; Touring; Resident; Educational; Sponsoring
Purpose: To produce a quality of life that can be felt and understood through the artistic process involving a community of people participating in a world of their own making
Management: Kristen Johnson, Managing Director
Officers: Randall Warren, President; John McKelway, Vice President; Christopher Burnett, Secretary
Paid Staff: 1   **Volunteer Staff:** 60
Utilizes: Special Technical Talent; Guest Artists; Guest Directors
Budget: $1,000 - $50,000
Income Sources: Private Foundations/Grants/Endowments; Business/Corporate Donations; Box Office; Government Grants; Individual Donations
Season: October - May
Affiliations: Massachusetts Council on the Arts and Humanities

Chilmark

FACILITY

BARN THEATRE
PO Box 405, Chilmark, MA 02535
(508) 645-9662
> **Type of Facility:** Theatre Complex; Performance Center; Multi-Purpose
> **Facility Originally:** Barn
> **Type of Stage:** Modified Apron Proscenium
> **Stage Dimensions:** 36'Wx27'D
> **Seating Capacity:** 100
> **Year Remodeled:** 1983   **Architect:** Ben Moore
> **Contact for Rental:** John Dodson;   (508) 645-9662
> **Resident Groups:** The Yard

Concord

INSTRUMENTAL MUSIC

THE CONCORD BAND
PO Box 302, Concord, MA 01742
> **Founded:** 1959
> **Arts Area:** Band
> **Status:** Non-Professional; Non-Profit
> **Type:** Performing
> **Management:** Wilheim Toland, Music Director; J. Kemson, Manager/Librarian; L. Matson, Fundraising
> **Officers:** B. P. Troup, President; J. Grace, Treasurer
> **Paid Staff:** 2   **Volunteer Staff:** 7
> **Paid Artists:** 1   **Non-Paid Artists:** 70
> **Utilizes:** Guest Conductors; Guest Artists
> **Budget:** $1,000 - $50,000
> **Income Sources:** Private Foundations/Grants/Endowments; Business/Corporate Donations; Box Office; Government Grants; Individual Donations
> **Season:** September - August
> **Affiliations:** Association of Concert Bands
> **Performance Facilities:** 51 Walden

CONCORD ORCHESTRA
PO Box 381, Concord, MA 01742
(508) 369-4967
> **Founded:** 1952
> **Arts Area:** Symphony; Orchestra
> **Status:** Non-Professional; Non-Profit
> **Type:** Performing
> **Purpose:** Amateur orchestra dedicated to enjoyment of playing music by its members and providing good music to the community
> **Management:** Richard Pittman, Conductor
> **Officers:** Fan-Chia Tao, President; Nancy McCarthy, Vice President; Priscilla Derananian, Secretary; David Powell, Treasurer
> **Paid Staff:** 1   **Volunteer Staff:** 8
> **Paid Artists:** 2   **Non-Paid Artists:** 70
> **Utilizes:** Guest Artists
> **Budget:** $1,000 - $50,000
> **Income Sources:** Box Office; Government Grants; Individual Donations
> **Season:** September - May   **Annual Attendance:** 3,600
> **Affiliations:** ASOL

FACILITY

THE FRIENDS OF THE PERFORMING ARTS IN CONCORD - 51 WALDEN
51 Walden Street, PO Box 251, Concord, MA 01742
(508) 369-7911
> **Type of Facility:** Theatre Complex; Concert Hall; Auditorium
> **Facility Originally:** Meeting Hall; Movie House
> **Type of Stage:** Flexible; Proscenium
> **Stage Dimensions:** 26'x24'
> **Seating Capacity:** 400

Year Built: 1885
Year Remodeled: 1974   **Architect:** Joseph Schiffer   **Cost:** $300,000
Acoustical Consultant: G. Anderson
Contact for Rental: Kathleen Chick;   (508) 369-7911
Resident Groups: The Concord Players; The Concord Orchestra; The Concord Band

Deerfield

INSTRUMENTAL MUSIC

MUSIC IN DEERFIELD
PO Box 264, Deerfield, MA 01342
(413) 772-0241, ext. 3327
FAX: (413) 774-6629
Founded: 1979
Arts Area: Chamber; Ensemble; Instrumental Group
Status: Semi-Professional; Non-Profit
Type: Sponsoring
Purpose: To bring to Franklin County the finest chamber music artists of national and international reputation
Management: David C. Howell, President; Priscilla Butterworth, Treasurer
Volunteer Staff: 18
Paid Artists: 15
Utilizes: Guest Artists
Budget: $50,000 - $100,000
Income Sources: Private Foundations/Grants/Endowments; Business/Corporate Donations; Box Office; Government Grants; Individual Donations
Season: September - May   **Annual Attendance:** 1,500
Affiliations: CMA; New England Presenters
Performance Facilities: Brick Church Meeting House

Dennis

THEATRE

CAPE PLAYHOUSE OF THE RAYMOND MOORE FOUNDATION
Route 6A, Dennis, MA 02638
(508) 385-3838
FAX: (508) 385-8162
Founded: 1927
Arts Area: Professional; Summer Stock
Status: Professional; Non-Profit
Type: Performing
Purpose: Established by the Raymond Moore Foundation and chartered by the Commonwealth of Massachusetts in 1948, Cape Playhouse operates for educational and charitable purposes as well as presenting top summer entertainment with stars of stage, screen and television.
Management: Carleton Davis, Managing Director
Officers: Emily Levine, President; James Julian, Vice President; J. Lee Marchildon, Treasurer; Avard Craig, Secretary
Paid Staff: 45   **Volunteer Staff:** 8
Paid Artists: 90
Budget: $500,000 - $1,000,000
Income Sources: Private Foundations/Grants/Endowments; Box Office
Season: June - September   **Annual Attendance:** 50,000
Performance Facilities: Cape Playhouse

FACILITY

CAPE PLAYHOUSE
Route 6A, Dennis, MA 02638
(508) 385-3838
Founded: 1927
Type of Facility: Theatre House
Facility Originally: Church; Meeting Hall; Movie House
Type of Stage: Proscenium
Stage Dimensions: 80'Wx50'D
Seating Capacity: 607
Year Built: 1820
Year Remodeled: 1927   **Architect:** Cleon Throckmorton

Dorchester

INSTRUMENTAL MUSIC

ASHMONT HILL CHAMBER MUSIC
67 Ocean Street, Dorchester, MA 02124
(617) 288-3697
FAX: (617) 825-9789
> **Founded:** 1985
> **Arts Area:** Chamber
> **Status:** Professional
> **Type:** Performing; Touring
> **Purpose:** To perfrom high quality chamber music concerts from a repertoire that spans the centuries; to combine seldom heard and classical works; to educate new audiences about chamber music
> **Officers:** Rachel Goodwin, Artistic Director; Andrea Dietrich, Treasurer; Cetta DiCara, Secretary
> **Volunteer Staff:** 5
> **Non-Paid Artists:** 13
> **Utilizes:** Guest Artists
> **Budget:** $1,000 - $50,000
> **Income Sources:** Private Foundations/Grants/Endowments; Box Office; Government Grants; Individual Donations
> **Season:** September - May   **Annual Attendance:** 600
> **Affiliations:** CMA
> **Performance Facilities:** Peabody Hall; All Saints Church

THEATRE

BOSTON THEATER GROUP
26 Eastman Street, Dorchester, MA 02125
(617) 288-3085
> **Founded:** 1978
> **Arts Area:** Professional; Theatrical Group
> **Status:** Semi-Professional; Non-Profit
> **Type:** Performing; Touring; Educational
> **Purpose:** Founded by a small core of actors to create original works for the stage, each piece evolves through the collective work of the actors together with the director, writers, designers and musicians.
> **Management:** Thomas C. Henry, Artistic Director and Administrative Co-Director; Karen S. Henry, Administrative Co-Director; Cornelia Boniface, Booking Manager
> **Officers:** John Hoffman, Chairman, Karen S. Henry, President; Eleanor Shay, Treasurer
> **Paid Staff:** 3   **Volunteer Staff:** 10
> **Paid Artists:** 5
> **Budget:** $1,000 - $50,000
> **Income Sources:** Private Foundations/Grants/Endowments; Business/Corporate Donations; Box Office; Government Grants; Individual Donations
> **Season:** September - June   **Annual Attendance:** 5,000

Dover

PERFORMING SERIES

CHARLES RIVER CREATIVE ARTS PROGRAM
56 Centre Street, Box 339, Dover, MA 02054
(508) 785-1260
> **Founded:** 1970
> **Arts Area:** Dance; Vocal Music; Instrumental Music; Theater; Festivals
> **Status:** Non-Professional; Non-Profit
> **Type:** Performing; Resident; Educational; Sponsoring
> **Purpose:** To promote dance, drama, music, art and media among boys and girls ages 8-15, both as creators and performers; to sponsor two 4-week sessions each summer, producing two Arts Festivals
> **Management:** Talbot Dewey, Jr., Director; Liz Callahan, Theatre Director; Bob Ingari, Music Director; Peter D. Dewey, Technical Director; Mary Tsiongas, Art Director; Anne Carey, Dance Director; Anna Jones, Director of the Charles River School; Priscilla B. Dewey, Arts Consultant
> **Officers:** Frank Sola, Chairman of the Board
> **Paid Staff:** 58
> **Paid Artists:** 40
> **Utilizes:** Special Technical Talent; Guest Artists; Guest Directors
> **Budget:** $100,000 - $500,000
> **Income Sources:** Private Foundations/Grants/Endowments; Business/Corporate Donations; Box Office; Government Grants; Individual Donations

Season: June - August   **Annual Attendance:** 2,000
Affiliations: NETC; Charles River School
Performance Facilities: Festival Theatre

FACILITY

FESTIVAL THEATRE
56 Centre Street, Dover, MA 02030
(508) 785-1260
    Type of Facility: Outdoor (Concert); Multi-Purpose
    Type of Stage: Thrust; Environmental; Elizabethan
    Stage Dimensions: 17'x34'x20'   **Orchestra Pit**
    Seating Capacity: 500
    Year Built: 1977   **Architect:** Dan Veaner   **Cost:** $7,000
    Year Remodeled: 1992   **Cost:** $50,000
    Acoustical Consultant: Peter D. Dewey
    Contact for Rental: Talbot Dewey, Jr.;   (617) 785-1260
    Resident Groups: Charles River Creative Arts Program; Freelance Players
    Occasionally available for rental

East Wareham

THEATRE

THE GATEWAY PLAYERS
PO Box 369, East Wareham, MA 02538
(617) 295-6768
    Founded: 1972
    Arts Area: Theatrical Group
    Status: Semi-Professional; Non-Profit
    Type: Performing; Touring; Resident; Educational
    Purpose: To provide theater on a year-round basis to the people in Southeastern Massachusetts
    Management: Robin Vontura, Directors
    Officers: George Hayden, Chairman; Raymond David Cardoza, Vice Chairman; Paul Arthur Wirth, Recording Secretary; Irene Zook, Corresponding Secretary; Dolores Rinko, Treasurer
    Paid Staff: 1   **Volunteer Staff:** 3
    Paid Artists: 3   **Non-Paid Artists:** 28
    Utilizes: Special Technical Talent; Guest Conductors; Guest Artists; Guest Directors
    Budget: $1,000 - $50,000
    Income Sources: Private Foundations/Grants/Endowments; Business/Corporate Donations; Box Office; Government Grants; Individual Donations
    Season: 52 Weeks   **Annual Attendance:** 6,000

Fall River

INSTRUMENTAL MUSIC

GREATER FALL RIVER SYMPHONY SOCIETY
PO Box 2101, Fall River, MA 02722
(508) 673-2022
    Founded: 1925
    Arts Area: Symphony
    Status: Professional; Non-Professional; Non-Profit
    Type: Performing
    Purpose: Cultural resource for over sixty years
    Management: Faust D. Fiore, Music Conductor
    Officers: Bruce E. Rex, President; Hazel L. Costa, Vice President; Loretta Pacheco, Secretary
    Volunteer Staff: 4
    Paid Artists: 2   **Non-Paid Artists:** 2
    Utilizes: Guest Artists
    Budget: $1,000 - $50,000
    Income Sources: Private Foundations/Grants/Endowments; Business/Corporate Donations; Box Office; Government Grants; Individual Donations
    Season: September - April   **Annual Attendance:** 1,500

Falmouth

VOCAL MUSIC

COLLEGE LIGHT OPERA COMPANY
PO Drawer F, Falmouth, MA 02541
(508) 548-0668; (508) 774-8485
>**Founded:** 1969
>**Arts Area:** Light Opera; Operetta; Musical Theatre
>**Status:** Non-Professional; Non-Profit
>**Type:** Performing; Resident; Educational
>**Management:** Robert A. Haslun, Producer/General Manager; Ursula R. Haslun, Producer/Business Manager
>**Officers:** DeWitt C. Jones III, President; Robert A. Haslun, Treasurer; Ursula R. Haslun, Secretary
>**Paid Staff:** 10   **Volunteer Staff:** 5
>**Non-Paid Artists:** 55
>**Utilizes:** Guest Conductors; Guest Directors
>**Budget:** $100,000 - $500,000
>**Income Sources:** Private Foundations/Grants/Endowments; Business/Corporate Donations; Box Office; Individual Donations
>**Season:** July - September   **Annual Attendance:** 15,000
>**Performance Facilities:** Highfield Theatre

FACILITY

HIGHFIELD THEATRE
PO Drawer F, Falmouth, MA 02541
(508) 548-2211
>**Type of Facility:** Theatre House
>**Facility Originally:** Barn
>**Type of Stage:** Proscenium
>**Stage Dimensions:** 20'x30'x15'   **Orchestra Pit**
>**Seating Capacity:** 302
>**Year Built:** 1890
>**Year Remodeled:** 1948   **Cost:** $38,000
>**Manager:** Robert Haslun;   (508) 548-2211
>**Resident Groups:** The Falmouth Theatre Guild; The College Light Opera Company

---
Gloucester

THEATRE

GLOUCESTER STAGE COMPANY
267 East Main Street, Gloucester, MA 01930
(508) 281-4099
FAX: (508) 283-5150
>**Founded:** 1979
>**Arts Area:** Professional; Theatrical Group
>**Status:** Professional; Non-Profit
>**Type:** Performing; Resident; Educational; Sponsoring; Producing
>**Purpose:** Through support and performance of drama by contemporary playwrights, Gloucester Stage Company does staged readings of new works-in-process and fun productions of new and important plays.
>**Management:** Mary John Boylan, Business Director; Heidi J. Dallin, Publicity Director; Janet Howes, Production Stage Manager; Israel Horovitz, Artistic Director; Keri Ellis Cahill, Production Coordinator; Robbie Chasitz, Assistant Artistic Director; Rob Duggan, Technical Director
>**Officers:** Barry Y. Wainer Esq., President; Thomas S. Grilk Esq., Vice President; James Dunne, Treasurer; Elaine Conway, Secretary
>**Paid Staff:** 6   **Volunteer Staff:** 30
>**Paid Artists:** 40
>**Utilizes:** Special Technical Talent; Guest Artists; Guest Directors
>**Budget:** $100,000 - $500,000
>**Income Sources:** Private Foundations/Grants/Endowments; Business/Corporate Donations; Box Office; Government Grants; Individual Donations
>**Season:** 40 weeks   **Annual Attendance:** 20,000

Great Barrington

DANCE

OLGA DUNN DANCE COMPANY
321 Main Street, PO Box 157, Great Barrington, MA 01230
(413) 528-9674
Founded: 1978
Arts Area: Modern; Ballet; Jazz
Status: Semi-Professional; Non-Profit
Type: Performing; Touring; Educational; Sponsoring
Purpose: To promote dance through outreach programs, school lecture demonstrations and full-length concerts; to train professional-level dancers; to develop original choreography in collaboration with music and theater; to feature local and guest talent
Management: Joan Nikitas, Business Manager; Brian Burke, Development Director; Cora Portnoff, Booking/Travel Coordinator; Marie Care, Administrative Assistant
Officers: Olga Dunn, President; Merrill Sanderson, Secretary; Diana Moxon, Treasurer
Paid Staff: 6   **Volunteer Staff:** 32
Paid Artists: 4   **Non-Paid Artists:** 7
Utilizes: Guest Artists; Guest Choreographers
Budget: $1,000 - $50,000
Income Sources: Private Foundations/Grants/Endowments; Business/Corporate Donations; Box Office; Government Grants; Individual Donations
Season: 52 Weeks   **Annual Attendance:** 5,000
Affiliations: Mahaiwe Theater
Performance Facilities: Mahaiwe Theater

Greenfield

THEATRE

ARENA CIVIC THEATRE
Shea Theatre, Avenue A, PO Box 744, Greenfield, MA 01302
(413) 774-5898
Founded: 1971
Arts Area: Community; Theatrical Group
Status: Non-Professional; Non-Profit
Type: Performing
Purpose: Arena Civic Theatre is a volunteer community organization which recognizes the unique spiritual fulfillment and opportunity for personal growth that theatre provides its participants.
Officers: Kimberley Morin, President; Alan Maynard, Vice President; Sondra Radosh, Treasurer; Wendy Fydenkevez, Secretary
Volunteer Staff: 15
Non-Paid Artists: 70
Utilizes: Special Technical Talent; Guest Directors
Budget: $1,000 - $50,000
Income Sources: Business/Corporate Donations; Box Office; Government Grants; Individual Donations
Season: 52 Weeks   **Annual Attendance:** 7,500
Affiliations: NALAA; Mohawk Trail Association
Performance Facilities: Shea Theater, Turner Falls, MA

Groton

FACILITY

LAWRENCE ACADEMY THEATRE
Powderhouse Road, Groton, MA 01450
(508) 448-6535
Type of Facility: Theatre House
Type of Stage: Proscenium
Stage Dimensions: 30'x30'
Seating Capacity: 400
Year Built: 1965
Contact for Rental: Donna Tyrrell;   (508) 448-6535

Hingham

THEATRE

HINGHAM CIVIC MUSIC THEATRE
Box 50, Hingham, MA 02043
(617) 749-0934
FAX: (617) 426-3180
Founded: 1935
Arts Area: Musical; Dinner; Community; Theatrical Group
Status: Non-Professional; Non-Profit
Type: Performing; Resident; Educational
Purpose: To foster and promote educational and practical aspects of music and theatre arts in the community
Utilizes: Special Technical Talent; Guest Conductors; Guest Directors
Budget: $1,000 - $50,000
Income Sources: Box Office
Season: September - June   **Annual Attendance:** 4,000
Performance Facilities: Hingham High School Auditorium

FACILITY

HINGHAM HIGH SCHOOL - AUDITORIUM
41 Pleasant Street, Hingham, MA 02043
(617) 749-2160
Type of Facility: Auditorium
Type of Stage: Proscenium
Seating Capacity: 750
Year Built: 1940
Contact for Rental: Nancy Stinson;   (617) 749-2160
Resident Groups: Hingham Civic Music Theatre; Hingham Civic Orchestra

Holliston

DANCE

LITHUANIAN FOLK DANCE GROUP OF BOSTON
24 Mitchell Road, Holliston, MA 01746
(508) 429-7567
FAX: (508) 429-3298
Founded: 1937
Arts Area: Ethnic; Folk
Status: Non-Profit
Type: Performing
Purpose: To preserve and promote Lithuanian culture
Management: Ruta Mickunas, Instructor/Choreographer; Gema Phillips, Administrator
Officers: Gema Phillips, Chairman of the Board
Volunteer Staff: 6
Non-Paid Artists: 40
Budget: $1,000 - $50,000
Income Sources: Individual Donations
Season: October - July

Ipswich

PERFORMING SERIES

CASTLE HILL FESTIVAL
Castle Hill Foundation, PO Box 563, Ipswich, MA 01938
(508) 356-4351
FAX: (508) 356-2143
Founded: 1951
Arts Area: Vocal Music; Instrumental Music; Festivals
Status: Professional; Non-Profit
Type: Performing; Educational; Sponsoring
Purpose: Presentation of the performing arts in a historic location, the R.T. Crane Estate
Management: Elizabeth Ann Hathaway, Public Programs Manager

Officers: Glenn Dickson, President; Jim LaFitte, Treasurer
Paid Staff: 7   **Volunteer Staff:** 200
Paid Artists: 121
Utilizes: Special Technical Talent; Guest Conductors; Guest Artists
Budget: $100,000 - $500,000
Income Sources: Private Foundations/Grants/Endowments; Business/Corporate Donations; Box Office; Government Grants; Individual Donations
Season: July - August   **Annual Attendance:** 16,000
Affiliations: APAP; Massachusetts Cultural Alliance
Performance Facilities: Crane Memorial Reservation

Jamaica Plain

THEATRE

THE FOOTLIGHT CLUB
Eliot Hall, PO Box 114, Jamaica Plain, MA 02130
(617) 524-6506
Founded: 1877
Arts Area: Community; Theatrical Group
Status: Non-Professional; Non-Profit
Type: Performing; Resident
Purpose: To provide quality theatre as an integral component of a vital arts community and to offer involvement to anyone interested in theatre
Officers: John Thomann, President; Jane Yoffe, Vice President; Patti Darssigny, Secretary; Lisa Macmillan, Treasurer
Volunteer Staff: 200
Non-Paid Artists: 200
Budget: $1,000 - $50,000
Income Sources: Business/Corporate Donations; Box Office; Individual Donations
Season: 52 Weeks   **Annual Attendance:** 3,000
Performance Facilities: Eliot Hall

Lee

VOCAL MUSIC

BERKSHIRE OPERA COMPANY, INC.
17 Main Street, Box 598, Lee, MA 01238
(413) 243-1343
Founded: 1985
Arts Area: Lyric Opera; Chamber Opera
Status: Professional; Non-Profit
Type: Performing; Touring; Resident; Educational
Purpose: To provide opera fully staged in English to residents and tourists in the Berkshires
Management: Rex Hearn, General Director; Joseph Bascetta, Artistic Director; Joel Revzen, Music Director; Barbara Martin, Administrator
Officers: L.D. Cohen MD, Chairman; R.A. Hearn, President
Paid Staff: 4   **Volunteer Staff:** 12
Paid Artists: 60
Utilizes: Special Technical Talent; Guest Artists; Guest Directors
Budget: $100,000 - $500,000
Income Sources: Private Foundations/Grants/Endowments; Business/Corporate Donations; Box Office; Individual Donations; Program Advertising
Season: July - August   **Annual Attendance:** 4,000
Affiliations: Berkshire Hills Visitors Bureau
Performance Facilities: Cranwell Opera House

Lexington

VOCAL MUSIC

THE MASTER SINGERS
PO Box 172, Lexington, MA 02173
(617) 275-8498
Founded: 1967
Arts Area: Choral

Status: Non-Profit
Type: Performing; Touring
Purpose: To present the chamber chorus repertoire of all eras in an intimate setting aimed at maximum enjoyment for both singers and listeners
Management: James Oleson, Music Director
Officers: Sarah Getty, President; Shaylor Lindsay, Treasurer; Virginia Fitzgerald, Secretary
Volunteer Staff: 6
Paid Artists: 2 **Non-Paid Artists:** 30
Utilizes: Guest Artists
Budget: $1,000 - $50,000
Income Sources: Private Foundations/Grants/Endowments; Business/Corporate Donations; Box Office; Government Grants; Individual Donations
Season: September - June **Annual Attendance:** 1,000
Affiliations: Massachusetts Cultural Alliance
Performance Facilities: First Parish Church, Lexington

Lowell

THEATRE

MERRIMACK REPERTORY THEATRE
Liberty Hall, 50 East Merrimack, Lowell, MA 01852
(508) 454-6324
Founded: 1979
Arts Area: Professional; Theatrical Group
Status: Professional; Non-Profit
Type: Performing; Resident
Purpose: To engage our audience in a theatrically vital process of communication; to enjoy, together, the resonance of romantic arts
Management: David G. Kent, Artistic Director
Officers: Jack O'Conner, Board President
Paid Staff: 16
Utilizes: Special Technical Talent; Guest Directors
Budget: $500,000 - $1,000,000
Income Sources: Private Foundations/Grants/Endowments; Business/Corporate Donations; Box Office; Government Grants; Individual Donations
Season: November - May
Affiliations: AEA; LORT
Performance Facilities: Liberty Hall

FACILITY

UNIVERSITY OF LOWELL - CENTER FOR THE ARTS
One University Avenue, Lowell, MA 01854
(508) 452-5000
Type of Facility: Performance Center
Type of Stage: Proscenium
Stage Dimensions: 37'Dx40'H proscenium opening **Orchestra Pit**
Seating Capacity: Theater - 970; Recital Hall - 200
Contact for Rental: Oliver Chamberlain; (508) 934-4444

Lynn

FACILITY

LYNN CITY HALL MEMORIAL AUDITORIUM
3 City Hall Square, Lynn, MA 01901
(617) 598-4000, ext. 133
FAX: (617) 592-9411
Type of Facility: Auditorium
Type of Stage: Proscenium
Stage Dimensions: 84'Wx31'D **Orchestra Pit**
Seating Capacity: 2,072
Year Built: 1947 **Architect:** M.A. Dyer Company
Contact for Rental: James I. Starratt, Building Commissioner; (617) 598-4000

Mansfield

FACILITY

GREAT WOODS CENTER FOR THE PERFORMING ARTS
PO Box 810, Mansfield, MA 02048
(508) 339-2331
    Type of Facility: Amphitheater
    Type of Stage: Environmental
    Seating Capacity: Permanent - 7,000; Lawn Seating- 8,000
    Year Built: 1986
    Contact for Rental: Bruce Montgomery, General Manager; (508) 339-2331
    Resident Groups: Summer Home of the Pittsburg Symphony Orchestra

---
Marblehead

INSTRUMENTAL MUSIC

NORTH SHORE PHILHARMONIC ORCHESTRA
PO Box 1131, Marblehead, MA 01945
(617) 631-6513
    Founded: 1948
    Arts Area: Symphony; Orchestra
    Status: Semi-Professional; Non-Profit
    Type: Performing; Resident
    Purpose: To present quality affordable music performances at the local level to a broad cross-section of audiences
    Management: Herbert A. Cohen, Manager; Max Hobart, Music Director
    Officers: Robert Marra, President; Janine M. Grillo, Secretary; Donald Melino, Treasurer
    Volunteer Staff: 10
    Paid Artists: 40 **Non-Paid Artists:** 35
    Utilizes: Guest Artists
    Budget: $1,000 - $50,000
    Income Sources: Private Foundations/Grants/Endowments; Business/Corporate Donations; Box Office; Government Grants; Individual Donations
    Season: September - May **Annual Attendance:** 10,000

Marlboro

THEATRE

MARLBORO CULTURAL AFFAIRS
255 Main Street, Marlboro, MA 01752
(508) 481-8104
FAX: (508) 624-6397
    Founded: 1978
    Arts Area: Musical; Dinner; Community; Puppet
    Status: Non-Profit
    Type: Performing; Sponsoring
    Purpose: To provide professional leadership in promoting, educating and creating awareness of quality cultural activities in the greater Marlboro area
    Officers: Cecile Sharon, Chairman of the Board
    Paid Staff: 5 **Volunteer Staff:** 75
    Paid Artists: 30 **Non-Paid Artists:** 10
    Utilizes: Special Technical Talent; Guest Conductors; Guest Artists; Guest Directors
    Budget: $100,000 - $500,000
    Income Sources: Private Foundations/Grants/Endowments; Business/Corporate Donations; Box Office; Government Grants; Individual Donations
    Season: 52 Weeks **Annual Attendance:** 80,000
    Performance Facilities: Johnson Auditorium

Medford

THEATRE

THE MAGIC CIRCLE THEATER
Tufts University, Balch Arena Theater, Medford, MA 02155
(617) 627-3493
Founded: 1944
Arts Area: Summer Stock; Theatrical Group
Status: Non-Profit; Children, Ages 11-15
Type: Performing; Resident; Educational
Purpose: To entertain and educate
Management: Paula Samson, Artistic Director; Sherwood Collins, Executive Director; Joanne Barnett, Business Manager
Paid Staff: 25   **Volunteer Staff:** 9
Paid Artists: 15
Utilizes: Guest Directors
Budget: $1,000 - $50,000
Income Sources: Box Office
Season: June - August
Affiliations: Tufts University
Performance Facilities: Arena Theatre

FACILITY

TUFTS UNIVERSITY - BALCH ARENA THEATER
Medford, MA 02155
(617) 627-3493
Type of Facility: Theatre House
Type of Stage: Arena
Stage Dimensions: 18'x23'
Seating Capacity: 211
Year Built: 1991   **Architect:** CBT
Manager: Joanne Barnett
Resident Groups: Tufts University Theater; Magic Circle Children's Theater; Pen, Paint and Pretzels

Melrose

INSTRUMENTAL MUSIC

MELROSE ORCHESTRAL ASSOCIATION
PO Box 175, Melrose, MA 02176
(617) 662-0641
Founded: 1918
Arts Area: Symphony; Orchestra
Status: Non-Profit
Type: Performing
Purpose: To provide classical music to the community and provide a place for community individuals and students to perform
Officers: Millie Rich, President/CEO; Anne Fremont-Smith, First Vice President; Alice C. Gross, Second Vice President; Caroline Soule, Secretary; Albert J. Traveis, Treasurer
Volunteer Staff: 20
Paid Artists: 1   **Non-Paid Artists:** 72
Utilizes: Guest Artists
Budget: $1,000 - $50,000
Income Sources: Private Foundations/Grants/Endowments; Business/Corporate Donations; Box Office; Government Grants; Individual Donations
Season: September - May   **Annual Attendance:** 2,500
Performance Facilities: Memorial Building, Melrose

Milton

INSTRUMENTAL MUSIC

ROSALIE GERUT AND FRIENDS
15 Parkway Crescent, Milton, MA 02186
(617) 698-9806
Founded: 1985

Arts Area: Chamber; Ethnic; Folk; Instrumental Group
Status: Professional
Type: Performing; Touring; Educational
Purpose: To present authentic concerts of Jewish music drawing on folk, Yiddish theater, Klezmer, Hebrew and original music; to preserve this culture by means of recording this music; Rosalie Gerut is the daughter of a folk musician from Lithuania and learned folk music of the Jewish tradition from him
Management: Steve Netsky, Boston Agent; Jewish Lecture Bureau, New York Agent
Officers: Rosalie Gerut, Director/Composer/Singer; Cam Sawzin, Cellist; Robin Miller, Flute/Recorders; Jim Guttman, Upright Bass; Jeff Warschauer, Guitar/Mandolin
Paid Staff: 2
Paid Artists: 5
Budget: $1,000 - $50,000
Season: 52 Weeks
Affiliations: ASCAP

Nantucket

THEATRE

ACTORS THEATRE OF NANTUCKET
18 Hinckley Lane, Nantucket, MA 02554
(508) 228-6325
Founded: 1985
Arts Area: Professional; Musical; Theatrical Group; Children's Theatre
Status: Professional; Non-Profit; Non-Equity
Type: Performing; Resident; Educational; Sponsoring
Purpose: To provide professional theatre for Nantucket Island
Management: Richard Cary, Producing Artistic Director; Tori Haring-Smith, Associate Director
Officers: Bill Hourihan, President; Bob Lang, Vice President; Roger Seitz, Secretary; Richard Cary, Treasurer
Paid Staff: 8   Volunteer Staff: 2
Paid Artists: 15
Utilizes: Special Technical Talent; Guest Artists; Guest Directors; Resident Professionals
Budget: $100,000 - $500,000
Income Sources: Private Foundations/Grants/Endowments; Business/Corporate Donations; Box Office; Government Grants; Individual Donations
Season: June - October   Annual Attendance: 8,000

THE THEATRE WORKSHOP OF NANTUCKET, INC.
2 Twin Street, PO Box 1297, Nantucket, MA 02554
(508) 228-4655; (508) 228-4305
Founded: 1956
Arts Area: Community
Status: Non-Professional; Non-Profit
Type: Performing; Educational
Purpose: To bring theatrical stage entertainment to the community using local talent; to offer year-round productions
Management: Edgar A. Anderson, Business Manager; S. Warren Krebs, Artistic Director
Officers: Elizabeth Gilbert, President; Marie Giffin, Treasurer
Volunteer Staff: 6
Non-Paid Artists: 25
Utilizes: Guest Directors
Budget: $50,000 - $100,000
Income Sources: Private Foundations/Grants/Endowments; Business/Corporate Donations; Box Office; Individual Donations
Annual Attendance: 6,000
Performance Facilities: Bennett Hall

New Bedford

THEATRE

ZEITERION THEATRE
684 Purchase Street, PO Box 4084, New Bedford, MA 02741
(508) 997-5664
FAX: (508) 999-5956
Founded: 1982
Arts Area: Professional
Status: Professional; Non-Profit

Type: Performing; Touring; Sponsoring
Purpose: To present a broad range of quality performing arts programs for the community
Management: Alan C. Liddell, Executive Director
Officers: Philip M. Carney, President; Ben Baker, Vice President; Doug Rodrigues, Treasurer
Paid Staff: 12 **Volunteer Staff:** 100
Budget: $500,000 - $1,000,000
Income Sources: Private Foundations/Grants/Endowments; Business/Corporate Donations; Box Office; Government Grants; Individual Donations
Season: 52 Weeks **Annual Attendance:** 65,000
Affiliations: New England Presenters
Performance Facilities: Zeiterion Theatre

FACILITY

ZEITERION THEATRE
684 Purchase Street, PO Box 4084, New Bedford, MA 02741
(508) 997-5664
FAX: (508) 999-5956
 Type of Facility: Concert Hall; Performance Center; Theatre House
 Facility Originally: Vaudeville
 Type of Stage: Proscenium
 Stage Dimensions: 80'Wx27'D **Orchestra Pit**
 Seating Capacity: 1,267
 Year Built: 1923 **Architect:** Leary & Walker **Cost:** $800,000
 Year Remodeled: 1982 **Architect:** Dyer & Brown Associates **Cost:** $1,300,000
 Contact for Rental: Christopher LeBlanc; (508) 997-5664
 Resident Groups: New Bedford Symphony; Miss Massachusetts Pageant; New Bedford Festival Theatre

Newburyport

DANCE

JOPPA JAZZ DANCE COMPANY
"The Tannery", 12 Federal Street, Newburyport, MA 01950
(508) 465-1485
 Founded: 1983
 Arts Area: Jazz
 Status: Non-Profit
 Type: Performing; Educational
 Purpose: To provide performance experience for aspiring dancers, and to educate the public on the beauty and benefits of dance
 Management: Irene L. Weiss, Artistic Director
 Officers: Carole Wagan, President; Claudia Stein, Secretary; Donn Kerrjan, Treasurer
 Volunteer Staff: 2
 Non-Paid Artists: 15
 Utilizes: Special Technical Talent; Guest Artists; Guest Choreographers
 Budget: $1,000 - $50,000
 Income Sources: Private Foundations/Grants/Endowments; Box Office; Government Grants; Individual Donations
 Season: 52 Weeks **Annual Attendance:** 1,000

PERFORMING SERIES

NEWBURYPORT FAMILY YMCA
76 State, Newburyport, MA 01950
(508) 462-6711
 Founded: 1874
 Arts Area: Dance; Theater; Festivals
 Status: Non-Professional; Non-Profit
 Type: Performing; Educational; Sponsoring
 Purpose: To enrich the lives of the citizens in this area through physical, cultural and academic means
 Management: Jane P. Breaker, Executive Director; Kurt Anderson, Program Director
 Officers: Chip Wyser, President; Mae Bradshaw, Vice President; James Hughes, Treasurer
 Paid Staff: 6 **Volunteer Staff:** 5
 Utilizes: Special Technical Talent; Guest Artists; Guest Directors
 Budget: $50,000 - $100,000
 Income Sources: Private Foundations/Grants/Endowments; Business/Corporate Donations; Individual Donations
 Season: 52 Weeks

Newton

INSTRUMENTAL MUSIC

NEWTON SYMPHONY ORCHESTRA
PO Box 124, Newton, MA 02168
(617) 965-2555
> **Founded:** 1965
> **Arts Area:** Symphony; Orchestra
> **Status:** Non-Profit; Community
> **Type:** Performing
> **Purpose:** To provide outstanding music experience and perform a program from a broad repertoire at affordable prices
> **Management:** Constance G. Kantar, General Manager; Adrienne Hartzell, Personnel Manager/Librarian; Ronald Knudsen, Music Director/Conductor
> **Officers:** Judith Abrams, President; Linda Clarke, Vice President; Sally Baker, Secretary; George Hughes, Treasurer
> **Paid Staff:** 4   **Volunteer Staff:** 25
> **Paid Artists:** 21   **Non-Paid Artists:** 70
> **Utilizes:** Guest Artists
> **Budget:** $50,000 - $100,000
> **Income Sources:** Private Foundations/Grants/Endowments; Business/Corporate Donations; Box Office; Government Grants; Individual Donations
> **Season:** November - May   **Annual Attendance:** 3,600
> **Affiliations:** Newton Public Schools
> **Performance Facilities:** Aquinas College

VOCAL MUSIC

MASTERWORKS CHORALE
PO Box 620692, Newton, MA 02162
> **Founded:** 1940
> **Arts Area:** Choral
> **Status:** Semi-Professional; Non-Profit
> **Type:** Performing; Touring
> **Purpose:** To perform major choral works
> **Management:** Maria D. Hagigeorges, General Manager
> **Officers:** Julia Fox, President; Keivan Towfigh, Vice President; Doreen Fairbairn, Treasurer
> **Paid Staff:** 6   **Volunteer Staff:** 25
> **Paid Artists:** 2   **Non-Paid Artists:** 120
> **Budget:** $100,000 - $500,000
> **Income Sources:** Private Foundations/Grants/Endowments; Business/Corporate Donations; Box Office; Government Grants; Individual Donations; Performance Fees; Member Dues
> **Season:** October - May   **Annual Attendance:** 10,000
> **Performance Facilities:** Sanders Theatre, Harvard University

---
Newton Centre

ZAMIR CHORALE OF BOSTON
PO Box 126, Newton Centre, MA 02159
(617) 965-6522
> **Founded:** 1969
> **Arts Area:** Choral; Ethnic
> **Status:** Non-Professional; Non-Profit
> **Type:** Performing; Touring; Resident; Educational
> **Purpose:** To perfrom and preserve music arising from the Jewish people and tradition
> **Management:** Mark Miller, Manager; Joshua Jacobson, Music Director; Karen Harvey, Accompanist
> **Officers:** Jules Rosenberg, President; Jeffrey Levine, Vice President; Michael Haselkorn, Treasurer
> **Paid Staff:** 1   **Volunteer Staff:** 10
> **Paid Artists:** 2   **Non-Paid Artists:** 45
> **Utilizes:** Guest Artists
> **Budget:** $50,000 - $100,000
> **Income Sources:** Box Office; Government Grants; Individual Donations
> **Season:** September - July   **Annual Attendance:** 5,000
> **Affiliations:** CA

North Falmouth

THEATRE

FALMOUTH PLAYHOUSE
Off Boxberry Hill Road, PO Box 350, North Falmouth, MA 02556
(508) 563-5922
FAX: (508) 564-4546
> **Founded:** 1949
> **Arts Area:** Professional; Musical; Theatrical Group
> **Status:** Professional; Commercial
> **Type:** Touring; Educational; Producing
> **Purpose:** To produce quality musical theatre, assist in offering young people professional experience, and be profit-making
> **Management:** Jade Curtain Ltd., Hubert Fryman, Producer
> **Paid Staff:** 50   **Volunteer Staff:** 30
> **Paid Artists:** 250
> **Utilizes:** Guest Directors
> **Budget:** $50,000 - $100,000
> **Income Sources:** Box Office
> **Season:** June - October
> **Performance Facilities:** Falmouth Playhouse

FACILITY

FALMOUTH PLAYHOUSE
Off Route 151, PO Box 350, North Falmouth, MA 02556
(508) 563-5922
> **Type of Facility:** Theatre House; Multi-Purpose
> **Facility Originally:** Private Club
> **Type of Stage:** Proscenium
> **Orchestra Pit**
> **Seating Capacity:** 564
> **Year Built:** 1932   **Architect:** E. Gunnar Peterson
> **Year Remodeled:** 1949
> **Contact for Rental:** Hubert Fryman;   (508) 564-4546
> **Manager:** Robert Zeida
> *A restaurant and bar are attached to the theater.*

Northampton

VOCAL MUSIC

COMMONWEALTH OPERA
160 Main Street, Northampton, MA 01060
(413) 586-5026
> **Founded:** 1977
> **Arts Area:** Grand Opera; Lyric Opera
> **Status:** Semi-Professional
> **Type:** Performing; Touring
> **Purpose:** To further the enjoyment and professional opportunities of grand opera regionally
> **Management:** Richard R. Rescia, Artistic Director
> **Officers:** Nancy Gregg, President; Robert Reed, Vice President; Allan Smith, Treasurer; Helen K. Gallivan, Guild President
> **Volunteer Staff:** 10
> **Budget:** $50,000 - $100,000
> **Income Sources:** Private Foundations/Grants/Endowments; Business/Corporate Donations; Box Office; Government Grants; Individual Donations
> **Season:** September - May
> **Performance Facilities:** Academy of Music; Congden Auditorium

THEATRE

NO THEATRE
c/o Available Potential Enterprises, Thornes Market, 150 Main Street, Northampton, MA 01060
(413) 586-5553
> **Arts Area:** Professional; Theatrical Group
> **Status:** Professional; Non-Profit

Type: Touring; Resident; Sponsoring
Purpose: To create original works for the stage using the vocabulary of various media
Management: Gordon G. Thorne, Executive Director; Roy Faudree, Artistic Director of NO Theatre
Officers: Gordon G. Thorne, President
Budget: $100,000 - $500,000
Income Sources: Private Foundations/Grants/Endowments; Business/Corporate Donations; Box Office; Government Grants; Individual Donations
Performance Facilities: Third Floor Thornes

Orleans

THEATRE

ACADEMY OF PERFORMING ARTS, INC.
120 Main Street, PO Box 1843, Orleans, MA 02653
(508) 255-5510; (508) 255-1963
    Founded: 1975
    Arts Area: Musical; Community; Theatrical Group
    Status: Professional; Semi-Professional; Non-Professional; Non-Profit
    Type: Performing; Touring; Educational; Sponsoring
    Purpose: School for the arts as well as a community theatre offering year-round opportunities in education and performance
    Management: Gail Meyers Sharman, Managing Director
    Officers: Patricia N. Silverman, President; Ann-Marie Litchfield, Vice President; C. Page McMahan, Treasurer
    Paid Staff: 22   **Volunteer Staff:** 20
    Non-Paid Artists: 100
    Utilizes: Special Technical Talent; Guest Conductors; Guest Artists; Guest Directors
    Budget: $100,000 - $500,000
    Income Sources: Private Foundations/Grants/Endowments; Business/Corporate Donations; Box Office; Government Grants; Individual Donations
    Season: 52 Weeks   **Annual Attendance:** 17,000
    Performance Facilities: Academy Playhouse

PERFORMING SERIES

THE CAPE AND ISLANDS CHAMBER MUSIC FESTIVAL
PO Box 2721, Orleans, MA 02653
(508) 349-7709
    Founded: 1979
    Arts Area: Festivals
    Status: Professional; Non-Profit
    Type: Performing; Educational
    Purpose: To produce a three-week chamber music festival presenting world-famous artists and rising young stars; to offer master classes and open rehearsals; to present new works by composers-in-residence each season
    Management: Samuel Sanders and Brian Zeger, Co-Artistic Directors; Joan Stevens, Administrative Director
    Officers: Robert Wright, President/Treasurer
    Paid Staff: 3
    Utilizes: Guest Artists
    Budget: $50,000 - $100,000
    Income Sources: Private Foundations/Grants/Endowments; Business/Corporate Donations; Box Office; Government Grants; Individual Donations
    Season: July - August   **Annual Attendance:** 2,000

FACILITY

ACADEMY PLAYHOUSE
120 Main Street, Orleans, MA 02653
(508) 255-1963
    Type of Facility: Theatre House
    Facility Originally: Town Hall
    Type of Stage: Flexible
    Seating Capacity: 172
    Year Built: 1873
    Year Remodeled: 1955
    Manager: Gail Meyers Sharman
    Available for rent

Osterville

INSTRUMENTAL MUSIC

CAPE COD SYMPHONY ORCHESTRA
1080 Main Street, Osterville, MA 02655
(508) 428-3577
Founded: 1961
Arts Area: Symphony; Orchestra
Status: Semi-Professional
Type: Performing
Purpose: To foster, promote and increase music knowledge and appreciation
Management: Wesley DeLacy, Executive Director; Christine Wells, Production/Promotion; Royston Nash, Music Director/Conductor
Officers: Fredrick Plumb, President; Gardiner Bridge, Leona Penn, Vice Presidents; Marjorie Burling, Secretary; Robert Barnet, Treasurer
Paid Staff: 4   **Volunteer Staff:** 1
Paid Artists: 70   **Non-Paid Artists:** 25
Utilizes: Guest Artists
Budget: $100,000 - $500,000
Income Sources: Private Foundations/Grants/Endowments; Business/Corporate Donations; Box Office; Government Grants; Individual Donations
Season: October - May   **Annual Attendance:** 30,000
Affiliations: ASOL
Performance Facilities: Mattacheese School, West Yarmouth

Pittsfield

VOCAL MUSIC

BERKSHIRE LYRIC THEATRE
PO Box 347, Pittsfield, MA 01202
(413) 499-8233
Founded: 1964
Arts Area: Light Opera; Choral
Status: Non-Profit
Type: Performing
Purpose: Light opera and choral concerts
Officers: Donald Phipps, President; Sharyl Noroian, Tom Sherer, Vice Presidents; Sue Burke, Secretary; Kathleen Kelley, Treasurer
Volunteer Staff: 50
Paid Artists: 20   **Non-Paid Artists:** 40
Utilizes: Special Technical Talent; Guest Artists
Budget: $1,000 - $50,000
Income Sources: Private Foundations/Grants/Endowments; Business/Corporate Donations; Box Office; Government Grants; Individual Donations
Season: September - June   **Annual Attendance:** 2,000

THEATRE

THE BERKSHIRE PUBLIC THEATRE COMPANY
30 Union Street, PO Box 860, Pittsfield, MA 01202
(413) 445-4631
FAX: (413) 445-4640
Founded: 1976
Arts Area: Professional; Theatrical Group
Status: Professional; Non-Profit
Type: Performing; Resident
Purpose: To provide affordable access to the performing arts, including theatre, music and dance for the Berkshire audience year round
Management: Frank Besell, Artistic Director; Iris Besell, Managing Director
Officers: Maria Caccaviello, Board President
Paid Staff: 10   **Volunteer Staff:** 200
Paid Artists: 50   **Non-Paid Artists:** 50
Utilizes: Guest Artists; Guest Directors
Budget: $100,000 - $500,000
Income Sources: Private Foundations/Grants/Endowments; Business/Corporate Donations; Box Office; Government Grants; Individual Donations

Season: 52 Weeks   Annual Attendance: 40,000
Affiliations: TCG
Performance Facilities: The Berkshire Public Theatre

PERFORMING SERIES

SOUTH MOUNTAIN ASSOCIATION
PO Box 23, Pittsfield, MA 01202
(413) 442-2106
Founded: 1918
Arts Area: Instrumental Music
Status: Non-Profit
Type: Sponsoring
Purpose: Sponsor of chamber music concerts
Management: Lou R. Steigler, Director
Paid Staff: 1
Paid Artists: 20
Utilizes: Guest Artists
Budget: $50,000 - $100,000
Income Sources: Private Foundations/Grants/Endowments; Business/Corporate Donations; Box Office; Individual Donations
Season: August - October   Annual Attendance: 1,900
Performance Facilities: Concert Hall

FACILITY

BERKSHIRE COMMUNITY COLLEGE - KOUSSEVITZKY ARTS CENTER
1350 West Street, Pittsfield, MA 01201
(413) 499-0886
Type of Facility: Theatre House
Type of Stage: Thrust; Proscenium; Arena
Stage Dimensions: 40'Wx46'Dx64'H   Orchestra Pit
Seating Capacity: 510
Year Built: 1970   Cost: $2,500,000
Contact for Rental: Sam Slack;   (413) 499-0886
Resident Groups: Pittsfield Town Players; Berkshire Ballet

Plymouth

INSTRUMENTAL MUSIC

PLYMOUTH PHILHARMONIC ORCHESTRA
130 Court Street, Plymouth, MA 02361
(508) 746-8008
FAX: (508) 746-0115
Founded: 1913
Arts Area: Symphony; Orchestra; Chamber; Ensemble
Status: Professional; Semi-Professional; Non-Profit
Type: Performing; Educational; Sponsoring
Purpose: To perform symphonic music for southeastern Massachusetts audiences
Management: Roberta J. Otto, Managing Director; Susan Lawrenson, Administrative Assistant
Officers: Marcella Stanton, President; Robert Dawley, Judith Ingram, Vice Presidents; Diane Hilker, Secretary/Clerk; Ronald Orleans, Treasurer
Paid Staff: 3
Paid Artists: 68   Non-Paid Artists: 7
Utilizes: Special Technical Talent; Guest Artists
Budget: $100,000 - $500,000
Income Sources: Private Foundations/Grants/Endowments; Business/Corporate Donations; Box Office; Government Grants; Individual Donations; Benefit Events
Season: October - May   Annual Attendance: 8,000
Affiliations: ASOL; Plymouth County Development Council; Plymouth Area Chamber of Commerce
Performance Facilities: Memorial Hall

Richmond

THEATRE

ROBBINS - ZUST FAMILY MARIONETTES
East Road, Richmond, MA 01254
(413) 698-2591
Founded: 1971
Arts Area: Professional; Theatrical Group; Puppet
Status: Professional
Type: Performing; Touring
Purpose: To share our classic, richly-traditional tales and stories with new audiences and to develop and train those new audiences
Officers: Richard L Robbins, President; Maia Robbins-Zust, Vice President; Genie Zust, Secretary/Treasurer
Paid Staff: 6
Paid Artists: 6
Utilizes: Special Technical Talent; Guest Artists; Guest Directors
Budget: $1,000 - $50,000
Income Sources: Private Foundations/Grants/Endowments; Box Office; Individual Donations
Season: 52 Weeks   **Annual Attendance:** 10,000
Performance Facilities: Berkshire Public Theatre

Rockport

INSTRUMENTAL MUSIC

ROCKPORT CHAMBER MUSIC FESTIVAL
PO Box 312, Rockport, MA 01966
(508) 546-7391; (212) 533-2429
Arts Area: Chamber
Status: Professional; Non-Profit
Type: Presenting
Purpose: To present eight chamber ensembles performing alone and in collaboration in a 16-concert series in June
Management: Lila Deis, Artistic Director
Officers: Warren Salinger, President of the Board
Budget: $50,000 - $100,000
Income Sources: Private Foundations/Grants/Endowments; Business/Corporate Donations; Government Grants; Individual Donations; Advertising/ Product Sales
Season: June
Performance Facilities: Rockport Art Association

Roslindale

THEATRE

POOBLEY GREEGY PUPPET THEATRE
106 Kittredge Street, Roslindale, MA 02131
(617) 325-5620
Founded: 1974
Arts Area: Puppet
Status: Professional; Non-Profit
Type: Performing; Touring; Educational
Purpose: To apply the art of puppetry to nonfictional subjects like dinosaurs, whaling, Ancient Egypt and elephants
Management: Janice and Stephen Babcock
Officers: Stephen Babcock, President; Janice Babcock, Treasurer
Paid Staff: 2
Paid Artists: 2
Utilizes: Special Technical Talent
Budget: $1,000 - $50,000
Income Sources: Private Foundations/Grants/Endowments; Box Office
Season: 52 Weeks   **Annual Attendance:** 30,000
Affiliations: Arts Institute; New England Foundation for the Arts

Salem

VOCAL MUSIC

PAUL MADORE CHORALE
PO Box 992, Salem, MA 01970
(508) 774-7981
> **Founded:** 1966
> **Arts Area:** Lyric Opera; Choral; American Music
> **Status:** Semi-Professional; Non-Profit
> **Type:** Performing
> **Purpose:** To perform choral masterpieces toward the cultural pleasure and advancement of music throughout the North Shore and Boston areas
> **Management:** Paul Madore, Director
> **Officers:** Jacqueline Opie, President; Pauline Maher, Vice President; Roger Dugas, Treasurer; Ann Michaud, Recording Secretary; Nadine Sippel, Cooresponding Secretary; Josephine Kennedy, Librarian
> **Paid Staff:** 1   **Volunteer Staff:** 10
> **Paid Artists:** 12   **Non-Paid Artists:** 6
> **Budget:** $1,000 - $50,000
> **Income Sources:** Private Foundations/Grants/Endowments; Box Office; Individual Donations
> **Season:** September - June   **Annual Attendance:** 2,000
> **Affiliations:** Salem Chamber of Commerce; Nash-Patterson Opera Guild

Sharon

THEATRE

SHARON COMMUNITY THEATRE, INC.
53 High Street, Sharon, MA 02067
(617) 784-3721
> **Founded:** 1975
> **Arts Area:** Community; Theatrical Group
> **Status:** Non-Profit
> **Type:** Performing; Educational
> **Purpose:** Produce high quality, family-oriented, local entertainment (mainly play productions) at reasonable prices in the South Shore area
> **Management:** Tina Koppel, Business Manager; Dick Leemon, Publicity
> **Officers:** Eric Kahn, President; Mark Anderson, Vice President; Janet Abrahamson, Secretary; Jo Zagieboylo, Treasurer; Leon Saperstein, Past President; Ed Bolster, Historian
> **Volunteer Staff:** 65
> **Non-Paid Artists:** 60
> **Utilizes:** Special Technical Talent; Guest Directors
> **Budget:** $1,000 - $50,000
> **Income Sources:** Private Foundations/Grants/Endowments; Business/Corporate Donations; Box Office; Government Grants; Individual Donations
> **Season:** September - June   **Annual Attendance:** 1,000
> **Affiliations:** NETC
> **Performance Facilities:** Sharon Recreation Department Mini-Theatre

Sheffield

VOCAL MUSIC

BERKSHIRE CHORAL INSTITUTE
Berkshire School, 245 North Undermountain Road, Sheffield, MA 01257
(413) 229-8526
> **Founded:** 1982
> **Arts Area:** Choral
> **Status:** Non-Profit
> **Type:** Performing
> **Purpose:** To provide a summer workshop for amateur choral singers devoted to preparing and performing great choral works
> **Management:** Richard P. Unsworth, Executive Director; Linda Dufault, Business Manager
> **Officers:** John Hoyt Stookey, Founder/President
> **Utilizes:** Guest Conductors; Guest Artists
> **Season:** July - August

Shelburne

PERFORMING SERIES

MOHAWK TRAIL CONCERTS
PO Box 75, Shelburne, MA 01370
(413) 625-9511
>**Founded:** 1970
>**Arts Area:** Vocal Music; Instrumental Music; Festivals
>**Status:** Professional; Non-Profit
>**Type:** Performing; Touring; Resident; Educational; Sponsoring
>**Purpose:** To provide outstanding chamber music in our summer/fall concert series in the Berkshires and our in-school music programs
>**Management:** Cynthia Stetson, Office Manager; Arnold Black, Artistic Director
>**Officers:** Helen Spencer, President; Frederick Purnell, Treasurer
>**Paid Staff:** 1   **Volunteer Staff:** 150
>**Paid Artists:** 200
>**Utilizes:** Guest Artists
>**Budget:** $50,000 - $100,000
>**Income Sources:** Private Foundations/Grants/Endowments; Business/Corporate Donations; Box Office; Government Grants; Individual Donations
>**Season:** July - August
>**Performance Facilities:** Federated Church

Sherborn

INSTRUMENTAL MUSIC

STAN MCDONALD'S BLUE HORIZON JAZZ BAND
25 Farm Road, Sherborn, MA 01770
(508) 653-7247
>**Founded:** 1981
>**Arts Area:** Ensemble; Instrumental Group; Band
>**Status:** Professional
>**Type:** Performing; Touring
>**Purpose:** To preserve, in spirited performance, America's original contribution to the performing arts: the blues, jazz standards, pop tunes, ballads and rags of the early 1900's (especially the 1920's and 1930's)
>**Management:** Stan McDonald, Leader; Ellen McDonald, Manager
>**Paid Staff:** 1
>**Paid Artists:** 7
>**Utilizes:** Guest Artists
>**Income Sources:** Fees
>**Season:** 52 Weeks
>**Affiliations:** Cape Cod Jazz Society; Potomac River Jazz Society; Jazz Appreciation Society of Syracuse; Greater Boston Convention and Visitors Bureau

Somerville

DANCE

ART OF BLACK DANCE AND MUSIC
PO Box 362, Somerville, MA 02144
(617) 666-1859
>**Founded:** 1975
>**Arts Area:** Ethnic
>**Status:** Professional; Non-Profit
>**Type:** Performing; Touring; Resident; Educational
>**Purpose:** To teach the common history of mankind through dance, music and folklore to educate and entertain audiences using the culturally diverse expressions of our African heritage
>**Management:** De Ama Battle, Executive Director
>**Officers:** William Taylor; Roberta Jackson
>**Paid Staff:** 2   **Volunteer Staff:** 1
>**Paid Artists:** 8
>**Utilizes:** Special Technical Talent; Guest Artists; Guest Choreographers
>**Budget:** $50,000 - $100,000
>**Income Sources:** Private Foundations/Grants/Endowments; Business/Corporate Donations; Box Office; Individual Donations; Tuition

Season: September - June   **Annual Attendance:** 30,000
Affiliations: Cambridge Multicultural Arts Center; Boston Cultural Partnership

THEATRE

STUDEBAKER MOVEMENT THEATER COMPANY
1 Fitchburg Street, B450, Somerville, MA 02143
(617) 666-1819
>   **Founded:** 1978
>   **Arts Area:** Professional; Theatrical Group; Performance
>   **Status:** Professional
>   **Type:** Performing; Touring; Resident; Sponsoring
>   **Purpose:** To create new works in performance
>   **Management:** John Bay, Tour Manager
>   **Officers:** M.B, Flanders, President; Caroline D'Agincourt, Treasurer
>   **Paid Staff:** 2   **Volunteer Staff:** 6
>   **Paid Artists:** 6   **Non-Paid Artists:** 10
>   **Utilizes:** Special Technical Talent; Guest Artists; Guest Directors
>   **Budget:** $1,000 - $50,000
>   **Income Sources:** Private Foundations/Grants/Endowments; Business/Corporate Donations; Box Office; Government Grants; Individual Donations
>   **Season:** September - May   **Annual Attendance:** 6,000
>   **Affiliations:** NMTA
>   **Performance Facilities:** Performance Place

South Hadley

PERFORMING SERIES

THE MUSICORDA SUMMER STRING PROGRAM AND FESTIVAL
PO Box 557, South Hadley, MA 01075
(413) 532-0607
FAX: (413) 538-2828
>   **Arts Area:** Instrumental Music
>   **Status:** Professional; Non-Profit
>   **Type:** Performing; Touring; Resident; Educational
>   **Purpose:** To provide advanced training and performance experience for gifted string students; to sponsor a performing festival in western Massachusetts
>   **Management:** Leopold Teraspulsky, Artistic Director; Jacqueline Melnick, Administrative Director
>   **Budget:** $100,000 - $500,000
>   **Income Sources:** Private Foundations/Grants/Endowments; Business/Corporate Donations; Box Office; Government Grants; Individual Donations
>   **Performance Facilities:** Chapin Auditorium, Mount Holyoke College

South Lancaster

INSTRUMENTAL MUSIC

THAYER SYMPHONY ORCHESTRA
PO Box 271, Main Street, South Lancaster, MA 01561
(508) 368-0041
FAX: (508) 368-0041
>   **Founded:** 1973
>   **Arts Area:** Symphony
>   **Status:** Semi-Professional; Non-Profit
>   **Type:** Performing; Educational
>   **Purpose:** To provide musical concerts for the residents of Eastern Massachusetts
>   **Management:** Francis Wada, General Manager
>   **Officers:** Ron Ansin, President; Linda Esposito, Vice President; John Davis, Second Vice President; William Jacobson, Clerk
>   **Paid Staff:** 1   **Volunteer Staff:** 120
>   **Paid Artists:** 40   **Non-Paid Artists:** 20
>   **Utilizes:** Guest Conductors; Guest Artists
>   **Budget:** $100,000 - $500,000
>   **Income Sources:** Private Foundations/Grants/Endowments; Business/Corporate Donations; Box Office; Government Grants; Individual Donations
>   **Season:** October - June   **Annual Attendance:** 9,500

Affiliations: ASOL; North Central Massachusetts Chamber of Commerce
Performance Facilities: Machlan Auditorium, Atlantic Union College

South Weymouth

VOCAL MUSIC

FINE ARTS CHORALE
779 Main Street, South Weymouth, MA 02190
(617) 337-3023
>**Founded:** 1966
>**Arts Area:** Choral
>**Status:** Non-Professional; Non-Profit
>**Type:** Performing
>**Purpose:** The authentic performances of sacred choral masterworks using professional orchestra and soloists; no dues required
>**Management:** Peter L. Edwards, Musical Director/Founder
>**Officers:** Deborah Kohl, President; Kate Lacatell, Vice President; Eleanor MacDonald, Secretary; Louise Bacon, Treasurer
>**Paid Staff:** 1   **Volunteer Staff:** 26
>**Paid Artists:** 100   **Non-Paid Artists:** 130
>**Utilizes:** Guest Artists
>**Budget:** $1,000 - $50,000
>**Income Sources:** Private Foundations/Grants/Endowments; Business/Corporate Donations; Box Office; Government Grants; Individual Donations
>**Season:** September - May   **Annual Attendance:** 2,000

Springfield

INSTRUMENTAL MUSIC

SPRINGFIELD ORCHESTRA ASSOCIATION
1391 Main Street, Suite 1006, Springfield, MA 01103
(413) 733-0636
FAX: (413) 781-4129
>**Arts Area:** Symphony
>**Status:** Professional; Non-Profit
>**Type:** Performing; Touring; Educational
>**Purpose:** To foster among the residents of western Massachusetts an appreciation for symphonic music and to provide this and other musical entertainment
>**Management:** Raymond Harvey, Music Director; Robert Stiles, Executive Director
>**Officers:** Peter Carando, President of the Board
>**Budget:** $1,000,000 - $5,000,000
>**Income Sources:** Private Foundations/Grants/Endowments; Business/Corporate Donations; Box Office; Government Grants; Individual Donations
>**Performance Facilities:** Springfield Symphony Hall

WESTERN MASSACHUSETTS YOUNG PEOPLE'S SYMPHONY/PHILHARMONIA
1391 Main Street, Suite 1006, Springfield, MA 01103
(413) 733-0636
FAX: (413) 781-4129
>**Founded:** 1944
>**Arts Area:** Symphony; Orchestra
>**Status:** Non-Professional; Non-Profit
>**Type:** Performing; Educational; Sponsoring
>**Purpose:** To give aspiring and talented young musicians of western Massachusetts and northern Connecticut the opportunity to perform symphonic repertoire, especially important to those whose schools have no formal symphony orchestras or orchestral programs; to cultivate excellence in performance through active participation in a continuous, weekly experience
>**Management:** Elel Thomas, Youth Orchestras Coordinator
>**Officers:** Yek Cheng, Mely Cheng, Co-Presidents; Judy Mish, Vice President; Daniel Dress, Treasurer; Mayme Lajoie, Historian
>**Paid Staff:** 2
>**Non-Paid Artists:** 110
>**Utilizes:** Guest Conductors
>**Budget:** $1,000 - $50,000
>**Income Sources:** Box Office; Government Grants; Individual Donations
>**Season:** September - May   **Annual Attendance:** 1,500
>**Performance Facilities:** Springfield Symphony Hall

THEATRE

STAGEWEST
One Columbus Center, Springfield, MA 01103
(413) 781-4470
FAX: (413) 781-3741
Founded: 1967
Arts Area: Professional
Status: Professional; Non-Profit
Type: Performing; Resident; Educational
Purpose: Professional resident theatre education and outreach research and development of new work and revitalized classics
Management: Eric Hill, Artistic Director; Martha Richards, Managing Director; Catherine Mandel, Artistic Administrator; Rebecca Strang, Marketing/Public Relations
Officers: Rand Gesing, President; Marie Stebbins, Vice President; Malcolm George, Secretary; Barbara Wallace, Treasurer
Paid Staff: 50   **Volunteer Staff:** 10
Paid Artists: 35   **Non-Paid Artists:** 10
Utilizes: Special Technical Talent; Guest Conductors; Guest Artists; Guest Directors
Budget: $1,000,000 - $5,000,000
Income Sources: Private Foundations/Grants/Endowments; Business/Corporate Donations; Box Office; Government Grants; Individual Donations
Season: October - April
Annual Attendance: 95,000
Affiliations: TCG; AAA; LORT
Performance Facilities: S. Prestley Blake Theatre; Winifred Arms Studio Theatre

FACILITY

SPRAGUE - GRISWOLD CULTURAL ART CENTER
American International College, 1000 State Street, Springfield, MA 01109
(413) 747-6393; (413) 747-6394
FAX: (413) 737-2803
Founded: 1885
Type of Facility: Theatre Complex; Performance Center
Type of Stage: Platform
Stage Dimensions: 24'x40'
Seating Capacity: 504
Year Built: 1984   **Architect:** Studio One/Alvin Paige   **Cost:** $2,000,000
Contact for Rental: Alvin Paige;   (413) 747-6393
Resident Groups: Berkshire Ballet; Community Music School

SPRINGFIELD CIVIC CENTER
1277 Main Street, Springfield, MA 01103
(413) 787-6610
FAX: (413) 787-6645
Founded: 1972
Type of Facility: Concert Hall; Civic Center; Arena; Multi-Purpose
Type of Stage: Flexible; Arena
Seating Capacity: 10,000
Year Built: 1972   **Architect:** Edwardo Catalano   **Cost:** $10,200,000
Contact for Rental: Michael J. Graney;   (413) 787-6610, ext. 224
Resident Groups: Springfield Indians Hockey Club (AHL)

SPRINGFIELD SYMPHONY HALL
Court Square, Springfield, MA 01103
(413) 787-6610
Type of Facility: Theatre Complex; Concert Hall; Auditorium; Opera House
Type of Stage: Proscenium
Stage Dimensions: 36'x63'x57'   **Orchestra Pit**
Seating Capacity: 2,589
Year Built: 1913
Year Remodeled: 1980   **Architect:** Reinhardt Associates   **Cost:** $1,000,000
Contact for Rental: Michael J. Graney, Executive Director;   (413) 787-6610
Resident Groups: Springfield Symphony Orchestra

Stockbridge

PERFORMING SERIES

BERKSHIRE THEATRE FESTIVAL
East Main Street, PO Box 797, Stockbridge, MA 01262
(413) 298-5536
>**Founded:** 1928
>**Arts Area:** Theater; Festivals
>**Status:** Professional; Non-Profit
>**Type:** Performing; Resident; Educational; Sponsoring
>**Purpose:** To provide thought-provoking summer entertainment
>**Management:** Dick Dunlop, Artistic Director; Chuck Still, Managing Director
>**Officers:** Jane Fitzpatrick, President; Fredric Rutburg, Secretary; DeKay Palmer, Treasurer
>**Paid Staff:** 7 **Volunteer Staff:** 25
>**Paid Artists:** 22 **Non-Paid Artists:** 12
>**Utilizes:** Special Technical Talent; Guest Artists; Guest Directors
>**Budget:** $500,000 - $1,000,000
>**Income Sources:** Private Foundations/Grants/Endowments; Business/Corporate Donations; Box Office; Government Grants; Individual Donations
>**Season:** June - August **Annual Attendance:** 30,000
>**Affiliations:** AEA; CORST

STOCKBRIDGE CHAMBER CONCERTS
Box 164, Stockbridge, MA 01262
(413) 442-7711
>**Founded:** 1975
>**Arts Area:** Vocal Music; Instrumental Music; Festivals
>**Status:** Professional; Non-Profit
>**Type:** Performing; Touring; Resident; Educational; Sponsoring
>**Purpose:** For the exclusively charitable and educational purposes of supporting the art of music by sponsoring concerts, lectures and recitals to encourage the cultural education of the public and individual students of music alike
>**Management:** Elizabeth A. Hagenah, Artistic Director
>**Officers:** Elizabeth A. Hagenah, President; Jean MacGaffey, First Vice President; Elizabeth C. Erston, Second Vice President; Patricia Webber, Clerk; Ruth Beers, Treasurer; Jean MacGaffey, Jane Shanahan, Assistant Treasurers; Norma Thompson, Chsirman of Gala Receptions
>**Volunteer Staff:** 12
>**Paid Artists:** 17
>**Utilizes:** Guest Artists
>**Budget:** $1,000 - $50,000
>**Income Sources:** Private Foundations/Grants/Endowments; Business/Corporate Donations; Box Office; Individual Donations
>**Annual Attendance:** 1,000
>**Affiliations:** CMA

FACILITY

BERKSHIRE THEATRE FESTIVAL
East Main Street, PO Box 797, Stockbridge, MA 01262
(413) 298-5536
>**Type of Facility:** Theatre Complex
>**Facility Originally:** Private Club
>**Type of Stage:** Proscenium
>**Seating Capacity:** 915
>**Year Built:** 1887 **Architect:** Stamford White
>**Contact for Rental:**
>**Resident Groups:** Berkshire Theatre Festival; Unicorn Acting Company
>*To present revivals, new plays and musicals*

Tisbury

FACILITY

KATHARINE CORNELL MEMORIAL THEATRE
21 Spring Street, PO Box 1239, Tisbury, MA 02568
(508) 696-4200
>**Type of Facility:** Concert Hall; Theatre House
>**Facility Originally:** Church

Type of Stage: Thrust
Stage Dimensions: 40'x100'
Seating Capacity: 195
Year Built: 1844
Year Remodeled: 1971   **Architect:** William Katzenbach   **Cost:** $250,000
Contact for Rental: Aase Jones, Secretary;   (617) 693-4200

Waltham

INSTRUMENTAL MUSIC

BRANDEIS UNIVERSITY DEPARTMENT OF MUSIC
South Street, PO Box 9110, Waltham, MA 02254-9110
(617) 736-3331
> **Founded:** 1940
> **Arts Area:** Orchestra; Chamber; Ensemble; Instrumental Group; Electronic & Live Electronic
> **Status:** Professional; Non-Professional; Non-Profit
> **Type:** Performing; Resident
> **Purpose:** University concert series including Professional Series, Concerts at Noon and student performances
> **Officers:** Sarah Mead, Concert Coordinator/Artist in Residence; Lydrian String Quartet, Ensemble in Residence
> **Paid Staff:** 1
> **Utilizes:** Guest Conductors; Guest Artists
> **Budget:** $1,000 - $50,000
> **Income Sources:** Private Foundations/Grants/Endowments
> **Season:** September - May
> **Performance Facilities:** Slosberg Recital Hall

PERFORMING SERIES

BRANDEIS SUMMER MUSIC FESTIVAL
Sydeman Hall, Room 108, Brandeis University, Waltham, MA 02254
(617) 736-3424
> **Founded:** 1989
> **Arts Area:** Instrumental Music
> **Status:** Professional; Non-Professional
> **Type:** Performing; Resident; Educational
> **Purpose:** To present a concert series by the Lydian Quartet and a three-week chamber music course for young professional musicians
> **Officers:** Rhonda Rider and Sanford Lotter, Directors; Gwenn Smaxwill, Administrator
> **Paid Staff:** 7   **Volunteer Staff:** 10
> **Paid Artists:** 6
> **Utilizes:** Guest Artists
> **Budget:** $1,000 - $50,000
> **Income Sources:** Private Foundations/Grants/Endowments; Box Office; Individual Donations
> **Season:** June   **Annual Attendance:** 400
> **Performance Facilities:** Slosberg Hall, Brandeis University

SPINGOLD THEATER CENTER
Brandeis University, PO Box 9110, Waltham, MA 02254-9110
(617) 736-3400
FAX: (617) 736-3389
> **Founded:** 1964
> **Arts Area:** Theater
> **Status:** Professional; Non-Profit
> **Type:** Performing; Educational
> **Purpose:** To blend an educational program with resident professionals and booked programming; to make as broad a training program as possible
> **Management:** John-Edward Hill, General Manager; Michael Murray, Director of the Theatre Arts Program
> **Officers:** Brandeis University Board of Trustees
> **Paid Staff:** 4
> **Utilizes:** Guest Artists; Guest Directors
> **Budget:** $100,000 - $500,000
> **Income Sources:** Private Foundations/Grants/Endowments; Box Office; Individual Donations
> **Season:** October - May   **Annual Attendance:** 28,000
> **Affiliations:** NETC; Massachusetts Cultural Alliance
> **Performance Facilities:** Spingold Theater Center

FACILITY

BRANDEIS UNIVERSITY - SPINGOLD THEATER CENTER
Waltham, MA 02254
(617) 736-3400
FAX: (617) 736-3389
Founded: 1966
Type of Facility: Theatre House
Type of Stage: Proscenium
Stage Dimensions: 36'Wx40'L   **Orchestra Pit**
Seating Capacity: 747
Year Built: 1964   **Architect:** Max Abramowitz
Contact for Rental: John Edward Hill;   (617) 736-3400
Resident Groups: Theatre Arts Department; Brandeis Gilbert and Sullivan Society

Watertown

THEATRE

HISTORY MAKING PRODUCTIONS
100 Summer, Suite 3-6, Watertown, MA 02172
(617) 924-4430
Founded: 1976
Arts Area: Professional; Theatrical Group
Status: Professional; Non-Profit
Type: Performing; Touring; Educational
Purpose: To tour live, professional plays which dramatize historical events and people; to bring literature to life; to spark critical thinking and thoughtful discussion on gender, race, social diversity and social change in our adult and youth audiences
Management: Linda Myer, Director
Officers: Lisa Gregory, Board Chairwoman; Judith Einach, Secretary Clerk; Richard Freedberg, Treasurer
Paid Staff: 1   **Volunteer Staff:** 5
Paid Artists: 4
Utilizes: Special Technical Talent; Guest Directors
Budget: $1,000 - $50,000
Income Sources: Business/Corporate Donations; Box Office; Individual Donations
Season: August - June   **Annual Attendance:** 18,000
Affiliations: Massachusetts Advocates for Arts, Sciences and Humanities; Stage Source

West Newton

VOCAL MUSIC

YOUTH PRO MUSICA
1075 Washington Street, West Newton, MA 02165
(617) 965-5899
Founded: 1970
Arts Area: Choral
Status: Non-Professional; Non-Profit
Type: Performing; Educational
Purpose: An hundred-member organization divided into three choruses providing choral experience of professional quality to promising young singers and exposing them to a wide variety of choral literature
Management: Roberta Humez, Music Director; Tom Anderson, Administrator
Officers: Margo Connoe, President; Peter Witt, Vice President/Clerk
Paid Staff: 3   **Volunteer Staff:** 4
Paid Artists: 2
Utilizes: Guest Conductors
Budget: $1,000 - $50,000
Income Sources: Private Foundations/Grants/Endowments; Business/Corporate Donations; Government Grants; Individual Donations
Season: September - June   **Annual Attendance:** 10,000
Affiliations: Massachusetts Cultural Alliance; American Boychoir Federation

West Springfield

FACILITY

HORACE A. MOSES BUILDING
1305 Memorial Avenue, West Springfield, MA 01089
(413) 737-2443
Type of Facility: Theatre House
Facility Originally: 4-H Dormitory and Auditorium
Year Built: 1925
Year Remodeled: 1967   **Cost:** $40,000
Contact for Rental: Susan Lavoie;   (413) 737-2443
Resident Groups: StageWest
Located on Eastern States Exposition Grounds; used as a 4-H and FFA participants' dormitory during the Big E each September

Weston

PERFORMING SERIES

CONCERTS-AT-THE-COMMON (HARVARD UNITARIAN CHURCH)
c/o Bernard J. Fine, 32 Coburn Road, Weston, MA 02193
(617) 899-7331
Founded: 1979
Arts Area: Vocal Music; Instrumental Music
Status: Non-Profit
Type: Sponsoring
Purpose: To present community concerts
Officers: Bernard J. Fine, Concert Series Director
Volunteer Staff: 1
Utilizes: Guest Artists
Budget: $1,000 - $50,000
Income Sources: Business/Corporate Donations; Box Office; Individual Donations
Annual Attendance: 750

Whitehorse Beach

FACILITY

PRISCILLA BEACH THEATER SCHOOL
PO Box 424, Whitehorse Beach, MA 02381
(508) 224-4888
Type of Facility: Theatre Complex; Studio Performance; Performance Center; Theatre House; Multi-Purpose
Facility Originally: Private Residence
Type of Stage: Thrust; Visual And Performing Arts Classrooms
Stage Dimensions: 30'x40'   **Orchestra Pit**
Seating Capacity: 300
Year Built: 1850
Year Remodeled: 1932   **Architect:** Dr. Franklin Trask   **Cost:** $50,000
Anne Joelle, Producer
Resident Groups: American Association of Dramatic Arts
It is the first and oldest barn theatre in America

Williamstown

INSTRUMENTAL MUSIC

BERKSHIRE SYMPHONY
Williams College, Williamstown, MA 01267
(413) 597-2127
Founded: 1944
Arts Area: Symphony; Orchestra
Status: Professional; Non-Professional; Non-Profit; Student
Type: Performing; Resident; Educational
Purpose: To encourage participation in and enjoyment of old and new symphonic literature
Management: Kristine Johnson, Concert Manager

Paid Staff: 2
Paid Artists: 35   **Non-Paid Artists:** 40
Utilizes: Special Technical Talent; Guest Artists
Budget: $1,000 - $50,000
Income Sources: Private Foundations/Grants/Endowments; Business/Corporate Donations; Box Office; Individual Donations
Season: October - May
Affiliations: ASOL
Performance Facilities: Chapin Hall, Williams College

THE WILLIAMS TRIO
Williams College, Williamstown, MA 01267
(413) 597-2127
Founded: 1970
Arts Area: Chamber
Status: Professional; Non-Profit
Type: Performing; Touring; Resident
Purpose: To bring high-quality performance of piano trio repertoire to Williams students and the community-at-large at home and on tour
Management: Douglas Moore, Manager
Paid Artists: 3
Utilizes: Guest Artists
Budget: $1,000 - $50,000
Season: 52 Weeks
Performance Facilities: Brooks-Rogers Recital Hall; Bernhard Music Center

THEATRE

THE NEW PHOENIX
42 Cold Spring Road, Williamstown, MA 01267
(413) 458-5235
Founded: 1975
Arts Area: Theatrical Group
Status: Professional; Semi-Professional; Non-Profit
Type: Performing; Touring; Educational; Sponsoring
Purpose: To produce a diversity of small-cast, transportable theatre pieces; special interest in Samuel Beckett, mono dramas, psychological thrillers and black comedies
Management: Ralph Hammann, Artistic Director/Producer; Ed DiNicola, Douglas Bradburd, Associate Director
Officers: Ralph Hamman, President; Dana Swanson, Vice President
Paid Staff: 1
Paid Artists: 3
Utilizes: Guest Artists; Guest Directors
Budget: $1,000 - $50,000
Income Sources: Box Office; Individual Donations

WILLIAMSTOWN THEATRE FESTIVAL
PO Box 517, Williamstown, MA 01267
(413) 597-3377; (413) 458-3200
FAX: (413) 458-3147
Founded: 1955
Arts Area: Professional; Musical; Theatrical Group
Status: Professional; Non-Profit
Type: Performing
Purpose: Outstanding production of modern classics on the main stage and development of new writing, acting, and musical talent at large
Management: William Stewart, Managing Director; Christopher Boll, Production Manager; Peter Hunt, Artistic Director; Steven Lawson, Rachel Davidson Associate Artistic Directors
Officers: Dr. William Everett, President; Ralph Renzi, Vice President; Fred A. Windover, Secretary; Henry N. Flynt, Jr., Treasurer
Paid Staff: 35   **Volunteer Staff:** 70
Paid Artists: 50
Utilizes: Special Technical Talent; Guest Artists; Guest Directors
Budget: $1,000,000 - $5,000,000
Income Sources: Private Foundations/Grants/Endowments; Business/Corporate Donations; Box Office; Government Grants; Individual Donations
Season: June - August   **Annual Attendance:** 23,000
Affiliations: AEA
Performance Facilities: Adams Memorial Theater; The Other Stage

FACILITY

WILLIAMS COLLEGE - CHAPIN HALL
Williamstown, MA 01267
(413) 597-2127
> **Type of Facility:** Concert Hall
> **Type of Stage:** Proscenium
> **Seating Capacity:** 1,050
> **Resident Groups:** Berkshire Symphony; Williams College Jazz Ensemble

Worcester

THEATRE

WORCESTER CHILDREN'S THEATRE
6 Chatman Street, Worcester, MA 01609
(508) 752-7537
> **Founded:** 1968
> **Arts Area:** Children's Theatre
> **Status:** Professional; Semi-Professional; Non-Profit
> **Type:** Performing; Touring; Educational
> **Purpose:** To teach children about theatre through performance and educational programming
> **Management:** Mary Pantano, Director of Programs and Development; Liz Humphreys, Managing Director; Steven Braddock, Artistic Director
> **Officers:** Angeles Baldanza, President; Kristine Johnson, Donna Clough, Vice Presidents; Ann Shea, Secretary; Mark Edoff, Treasurer; Mayo Morgan, Assistant Treasurer
> **Paid Staff:** 3
> **Utilizes:** Guest Artists; Guest Directors
> **Budget:** $100,000 - $500,000
> **Income Sources:** Private Foundations/Grants/Endowments; Business/Corporate Donations; Box Office; Government Grants; Individual Donations
> **Annual Attendance:** 6,000
> **Performance Facilities:** Worcester State College, Administration Building Theatre

WORCESTER FOOTHILLS THEATRE COMPANY
74 Worcester Center, 100 Front Street, Worcester, MA 01608
(508) 754-4018
> **Founded:** 1974
> **Arts Area:** Professional; Theatrical Group
> **Status:** Professional; Non-Profit
> **Type:** Performing
> **Purpose:** To provide professional regional theatre for Worcester and the Central New England Region and serve the region by providing many ancillary services including a theatre conservatory, intern/apprentice programs, youth services, services for the communicatively and physically disabled and more
> **Management:** Marc P. Smith, Executive Producer/Artistic Director; Doug Landrum, Associate Producer, Production; Susan L. Smith, Associate Producer/Public Relations & Marketing
> **Officers:** Dr. Tamara A. Bethel, President; James F. Goulet, Treasurer; Hon. Mel Greenberg, Clerk
> **Paid Staff:** 40 **Volunteer Staff:** 180
> **Paid Artists:** 50
> **Utilizes:** Special Technical Talent; Guest Artists; Guest Directors
> **Budget:** $500,000 - $1,000,000
> **Income Sources:** Private Foundations/Grants/Endowments; Business/Corporate Donations; Box Office; Government Grants; Individual Donations
> **Season:** October - May **Annual Attendance:** 52,000
> **Affiliations:** AEA
> **Performance Facilities:** Worcester Foothills Theatre

FACILITY

MECHANICS HALL
321 Main Street, Worcester, MA 06108
(508) 752-5608
FAX: (508) 752-4408
> **Type of Facility:** Concert Hall; Multi-Purpose
> **Facility Originally:** Meeting Hall
> **Stage Dimensions:** 46'8"Wx16'9"D (can be extended to 54'Wx28'9"D)
> **Seating Capacity:** 1,500
> **Year Built:** 1857 **Architect:** Eldridge Boyden **Cost:** $101,000

Year Remodeled: 1976   **Architect:** Anderson, Notter & Feingold Inc.   **Cost:** $5,000,000
Acoustical Consultant: Cavanaugh, Tocci Associates
Contact for Rental: Norma J. Sandison, Director;   (508) 752-5608
Resident Groups: Worcester County Music Association; International Artists Series

WORCESTER MEMORIAL AUDITORIUM
Lincoln Square, Worcester, MA 06108
(508) 755-6600

Type of Facility: Concert Hall; Auditorium
Type of Stage: Proscenium
Stage Dimensions: 67'Wx44'D   **Orchestra Pit**
Seating Capacity: 3,000
Year Built: 1933   **Architect:** Lucius Briggs & Frederick Hirons   **Cost:** $2,000,000
Contact for Rental: Gregg Tassone;   (508) 755-6600

Worthington

PERFORMING SERIES

SEVENARS CONCERTS
South Worthington Academy, Worthington, MA 01098
(413) 238-5854

Winter Address: 3A, 30 East End Avenue, New York, NY 10028
Arts Area: Vocal Music; Instrumental Music; Festivals
Status: Professional; Non-Profit
Type: Performing; Educational
Purpose: To develop classical-music artists and audiences
Utilizes: Guest Artists; Guest Conductors
Budget: $1,000 - $50,000
Income Sources: Private Foundations; Business/Corporate Donations; Box Office; Government Grants; Individual Donations
Season: July - August   **Annual Attendance:** 2,400

MICHIGAN

Adrian

INSTRUMENTAL MUSIC

ADRIAN SYMPHONY ORCHESTRA
110 South Madison Street, Adrian, MI 49221
(517) 264-3121
FAX: (517) 264-3331
Founded: 1981
Arts Area: Symphony; Orchestra; Chamber; Ensemble
Status: Professional; Non-Profit
Type: Performing; Touring; Resident; Educational
Purpose: To remain Lenawee County's premiere musical ensemble and Adrian College's professional orchestra-in-residence; to perform classical, family, holiday, pops, chamber and young peoples' concerts
Management: David Katz, Music Director/Principal Conductor; Susan Hoffman, Executive Director; Nancy Wagner, Administrative Assistant
Officers: Muriel Bell, President; Hon. Henry Newlin, Vice President; Dr. Roger Fechner, Past President
Paid Staff: 5   **Volunteer Staff:** 10
Paid Artists: 65   **Non-Paid Artists:** 5
Utilizes: Guest Conductors; Guest Artists
Budget: $100,000 - $500,000
Income Sources: Private Foundations/Grants/Endowments; Business/Corporate Donations; Box Office; Government Grants; Individual Donations
Season: September - May   **Annual Attendance:** 10,000
Affiliations: ASOL; Michigan Orchestra Association
Performance Facilities: Dawson Auditorium

VOCAL MUSIC

FRIEDRICH SCHORR MEMORIAL PERFORMANCE PRIZE IN VOICE
110 South Madison Street, Adrian, MI 49221
(517) 264-3121
FAX: (517) 264-3331
Founded: 1989
Arts Area: Grand Opera; Lyric Opera; Operetta
Status: Professional; Non-Profit
Type: Sponsoring; Vocal Competition
Purpose: To sponsor an annual international competition which awards performance prizes and stipends in excess of $10,000 annually
Management: David Katz, Robert Soller, Artistic Directors
Officers: Charles Nelson Reilly, Honorary Chairman; Mrs. Friedrich Schorr, Founder
Paid Staff: 4   **Volunteer Staff:** 4
Paid Artists: 10
Utilizes: Guest Artists
Budget: $50,000 - $100,000
Income Sources: Private Foundations/Grants/Endowments; Business/Corporate Donations; Box Office; Individual Donations
Season: October - April   **Annual Attendance:** 5,000
Affiliations: NOA; OA
Performance Facilities: Croswell Opera House

OPERA! LEWANEE
110 South Madison Street, Adrian, MI 49221
(517) 264-3121
FAX: (517) 264-3331
Founded: 1989
Arts Area: Grand Opera; Lyric Opera; Operetta
Status: Professional; Non-Profit
Type: Performing; Resident; Educational
Purpose: To create grand opera performances for the citizens of Lenawee County, Michigan; to sponsor the Friedrich Schorr Memorial Performance Prize in Voice; to collaborate between the Adrian Symphony and the Croswell Opera House
Management: David Katz, Music Director; Robert Soller, Stage Director; Susan Hoffman, Jimmy Hilburger, Producers
Officers: Robert and Muriel Bell, Co-Chairs
Paid Staff: 8   **Volunteer Staff:** 15

Paid Artists: 50
Utilizes: Special Technical Talent; Guest Artists
Budget: $100,000 - $500,000
Income Sources: Private Foundations/Grants/Endowments; Business/Corporate Donations; Box Office; Individual Donations
Season: October - April   **Annual Attendance:** 5,000
Affiliations: NOA; OA
Performance Facilities: Croswell Opera House

FACILITY

ADRIAN COLLEGE
110 South Madison, Rush Union, Adrian, MI 49221
(517) 264-3156
FAX: (517) 264-3331
Founded: 1859
Type of Facility: Theatre Complex; Concert Hall; Auditorium; Theatre House
Facility Originally: Auditorium
Type of Stage: Proscenium
Seating Capacity: 1,185
Year Built: 1964
Contact for Rental: Office of Conferences and Campus Programs;   (517) 264-3156

Alpena

THEATRE

THUNDER BAY THEATRE
400 North Second Avenue, Alpena, MI 49707
(517) 354-2267
Founded: 1977
Arts Area: Professional; Summer Stock; Musical; Theatrical Group
Status: Professional; Non-Profit; Non-Equity
Type: Performing; Resident; Educational
Purpose: To signify and positively affect the cultural climate of northeast Michigan
Management: David P. Drobot, Artistic Director; Jodi Prahler, Assistant Artistic Director; Ann M. Seymour, Administrative Assistant
Officers: Robert E. Haltiner, President; Carol Witherbee, Vice President; Grace Bachwich, Secretary; Jerry Lamb, Treasurer
Paid Staff: 6   **Volunteer Staff:** 25
Paid Artists: 30
Utilizes: Special Technical Talent; Guest Directors
Budget: $100,000 - $500,000
Income Sources: Private Foundations/Grants/Endowments; Business/Corporate Donations; Box Office; Government Grants; Individual Donations
Season: 52 Weeks   **Annual Attendance:** 10,000
Performance Facilities: Thunder Bay Theatre

PERFORMING SERIES

THUNDER BAY ARTS COUNCIL
312 East Chisholm Street, Alpena, MI 49766
(517) 356-6678
Founded: 1967
Arts Area: Dance; Vocal Music; Instrumental Music; Theater; Lyric Opera
Status: Professional; Non-Profit
Type: Educational; Sponsoring
Purpose: To foster, encourage, and promote cultural arts; to serve as a coordinating agency in scheduling area presentations by other art groups; to enhance the quality of life
Management: Thunder Bay Arts Council Board of Directors
Officers: Peggy Kusler, President; Adelaide Ammon, First Vice President; Elaine Mandenberg, Second Vice President; Alice Silver, Secretary; Nathalie Szczukowski, Treasurer
Paid Staff: 1   **Volunteer Staff:** 27
Utilizes: Special Technical Talent; Guest Conductors; Guest Artists; Guest Directors
Budget: $1,000 - $50,000
Income Sources: Private Foundations/Grants/Endowments; Business/Corporate Donations; Box Office; Government Grants; Individual Donations

Season: 52 Weeks   **Annual Attendance:** 21,000
Performance Facilities: High School Auditorium; Alpena Fine Arts Shell

---

Ann Arbor

DANCE

ANN ARBOR BALLET THEATRE
548 Church Street, Ann Arbor, MI 48104
(313) 662-2942
  Founded: 1980
  Arts Area: Ballet; Guest Choreographers
  Status: Semi-Professional; Non-Profit
  Type: Performing; Touring; Educational
  Purpose: To promote local interest and appreciation of classical Russian ballet, combined with live music and theatre
  Management: Carol A. Sharp-Radovic, Artistic Director; Kathryn E. Sharp, Assistant Director; Gail Etter, Gen. Manager
  Volunteer Staff: 6
  Non-Paid Artists: 35
  Utilizes: Special Technical Talent; Guest Conductors; Guest Artists; Guest Choreographers
  Budget: $1,000 - $50,000
  Income Sources: Private Foundations/Grants/Endowments; Business/Corporate Donations; Box Office; Government Grants; Individual Donations
  Season: September - June   **Annual Attendance:** 6,000
  Affiliations: Michigan Dance Association; Washtenaw Council for the Arts; Washtenaw Dance Association
  Performance Facilities: Power Center for Performing Arts; Michigan Theatre; Lydia Mendelssohn

ANN ARBOR CIVIC BALLET
525 East Liberty Street, Ann Arbor, MI 48103
(313) 668-8066
  Founded: 1958
  Arts Area: Ballet
  Status: Non-Profit
  Type: Performing; Resident; Educational
  Purpose: To encourage young people in the area of dance; to bring guest performers to the community
  Management: Sylvia Hamer, Founder; Lee Ann King, Director
  Officers: Wanda Dawson, President; Kathleen Smith, Vice President; Debra Haas, Secretary; Wanda King, Treasurer
  Volunteer Staff: 15
  Non-Paid Artists: 25
  Utilizes: Special Technical Talent; Guest Artists
  Budget: $1,000 - $50,000
  Income Sources: Private Foundations/Grants/Endowments; Business/Corporate Donations; Box Office; Individual Donations
  Season: September - July   **Annual Attendance:** 2,500

DANCE GALLERY COMPANY
111 Third Street, Ann Arbor, MI 48103
(313) 761-2728
  Founded: 1981
  Arts Area: Modern; Ballet; Jazz
  Status: Professional; Non-Profit
  Type: Performing; Touring; Resident; Educational
  Purpose: To bring quality modern dance to audiences; to promote and supply quality modern dance training
  Management: Noonie Anderson, Studio Manager; Diane Black, Rental Coordinator
  Officers: Linda Greene, President; Robin Cooper, Treasurer; Nancy Baker Fate Heers, Secretary; Stuart Tsubota, Jane Stanton, Harry Gable, Ron Miller, Board Members
  Paid Staff: 2   **Volunteer Staff:** 2
  Paid Artists: 8
  Budget: $1,000 - $50,000
  Income Sources: Private Foundations/Grants/Endowments; Business/Corporate Donations; Box Office; Government Grants; Individual Donations
  Season: 52 Weeks   **Annual Attendance:** 2,000
  Affiliations: Michigan Council for Arts and Cultural Affairs; Washtenaw Council of Arts

MALINI'S DANCES OF INDIA
1355 Wynnstone Drive, Ann Arbor, MI 48105
(313) 994-3167
  Arts Area: Ethnic
  Status: Non-Profit

Type: Performing; Touring; Resident; Educational; Sponsoring
Purpose: To promote East Indian classical and folk dances through performances, lecture demonstrations, workshops and residencies
Officers: Malini Srirama, Artistic Director; Vijaya Sarathy, President
Volunteer Staff: 30
Non-Paid Artists: 140
Utilizes: Special Technical Talent; Guest Artists
Budget: $1,000 - $50,000
Income Sources: Box Office; Government Grants; Individual Donations
Season: 52 Weeks   **Annual Attendance:** 4,000

INSTRUMENTAL MUSIC

ANN ARBOR SYMPHONY ORCHESTRA
PO Box 1412, Ann Arbor, MI 48106
(313) 994-4801
FAX: (313) 994-3949
Founded: 1928
Arts Area: Symphony; Orchestra
Status: Professional
Type: Performing; Educational
Management: Anne Glendon, Executive Director; Kay Rowe, Personnel Manager; Kristin Reynolds, Librarian; Everett Armstrong, Operations Manager; Samuel Wong, Music Director
Officers: William W. Boddie, President; Roger Bookwalter, Vice President; Forrest Alter, Secretary; John Dale, Treasurer
Paid Staff: 4   **Volunteer Staff:** 10
Paid Artists: 75   **Non-Paid Artists:** 11
Utilizes: Guest Conductors; Guest Artists
Budget: $500,000 - $1,000,000
Income Sources: Private Foundations/Grants/Endowments; Business/Corporate Donations; Box Office; Government Grants; Individual Donations; Special Events
Season: September - May   **Annual Attendance:** 6,000
Performance Facilities: Michigan Theater

VOCAL MUSIC

COMIC OPERA GUILD
PO Box 1922, Ann Arbor, MI 48106
(313) 973-3264
Founded: 1973
Arts Area: Operetta
Status: Professional; Semi-Professional; Non-Profit
Type: Performing; Touring; Resident
Purpose: The Comic Opera Guild was formed for the purpose of creating and developing interest in comic opera as a separate theatrical form. The touring approach is fundamental to this purpose because of the potential in reaching large numbers of people unacquainted with comic opera.
Management: Thomas Petiet, Managing Director
Officers: Nancy Kerner, President Board of Directors; Thomas Skylis, Secretary
Paid Staff: 8   **Volunteer Staff:** 10
Paid Artists: 40   **Non-Paid Artists:** 40
Utilizes: Special Technical Talent; Guest Conductors; Guest Artists; Guest Directors
Budget: $1,000 - $50,000
Income Sources: Private Foundations/Grants/Endowments; Box Office; Government Grants; Individual Donations
Season: October - March   **Annual Attendance:** 6,000
Affiliations: COS; Washtenaw Council for the Arts
Performance Facilities: Michigan Theater

UNIVERSITY OF MICHIGAN CHORAL UNION
University Musical Society, Burton Memorial Tower, Ann Arbor, MI 48109
(313) 764-2538
FAX: (313) 747-1171
Founded: 1879
Arts Area: Choral
Status: Non-Professional; Non-Profit
Type: Performing; Touring; Resident; Educational
Purpose: To provide an enterprise which offers the community a chance to be in an oratorio society
Management: Sara Billmann, Chorus Manager; Thomas Hilbish, Conductor
Officers: Norman G. Herbert, President, Board of Directors
Paid Staff: 2
Non-Paid Artists: 250

Utilizes: Guest Conductors; Guest Artists
Budget: $1,000 - $50,000
Income Sources: Box Office
Season: September - May   **Annual Attendance:** 18,000
Affiliations: University Musical Society
Performance Facilities: Hill Auditorium, University of Michigan

UNIVERSITY OF MICHIGAN GILBERT AND SULLIVAN SOCIETY
The Michigan League Building, 911 North University, Ann Arbor, MI 48109-1265
(313) 761-7855; (313) 764-0446
Founded: 1946
Arts Area: Operetta
Status: Non-Professional; Non-Profit
Type: Performing; Resident; Educational
Volunteer Staff: 20
Non-Paid Artists: 40
Budget: $50,000 - $100,000
Income Sources: Box Office; Individual Donations
Season: December - April   **Annual Attendance:** 12,000
Performance Facilities: Mendelssohn Theatre, University of Michigan

THEATRE

UNIVERSITY OF MICHIGAN, UNIVERSITY PRODUCTIONS
911 North University, Ann Arbor, MI 48109-1265
(313) 763-5213
FAX: (313) 747-2282
Founded: 1973
Arts Area: Professional; Musical; University
Status: Professional; Non-Profit; University
Type: Performing; Educational
Purpose: Producing unit for the University of Michigan departments of Dance, Musical Theatre, Opera and Theatre, creating 10 productions per year
Management: Jeffrey Kuras, Managing Director; Paul Boylan, Dean, School of Music
Paid Staff: 29
Non-Paid Artists: 200
Utilizes: Guest Directors;   Guest Designers
Budget: $1,000,000 - $5,000,000
Income Sources: Box Office; Government Grants
Season: September - April   **Annual Attendance:** 30,000
Performance Facilities: Power Center for Performing Arts; Trueblood Theatre; Mendelssohn Theatre

PERFORMING SERIES

ANN ARBOR SUMMER FESTIVAL
PO Box 4070, Ann Arbor, MI 48106
(313) 747-2278
FAX: (313) 936-3393
Founded: 1978
Arts Area: Dance; Theater; Festivals
Status: Professional; Non-Profit
Type: Performing; Sponsoring
Purpose: To present a wide variety of performing arts including free and ticketed events for a diverse audience
Management: Susan Pollay, Festival Director; Amy Harris, Develoment Director; Nancy Possley, Business Manager; Jamie Mistry, Program Assistant; Henry Reynolds, Production Manager
Officers: Ruth Whitaker, Chairman; Ronald Cresswell, President
Paid Staff: 34   **Volunteer Staff:** 20
Paid Artists: 50
Utilizes: Guest Artists
Budget: $500,000 - $1,000,000
Income Sources: Private Foundations/Grants/Endowments; Business/Corporate Donations; Box Office; Government Grants; Individual Donations
Season: June - July   **Annual Attendance:** 90,000
Affiliations: University of Michigan
Performance Facilities: Power Center; Lydia Mendelssohn; Top of the Park

UNIVERSITY MUSICAL SOCIETY OF THE UNIVERSITY OF MICHIGAN
Burton Memorial Tower, #100, Ann Arbor, MI 48109-1270
(313) 764-2538; (313) 747-1171
  Founded: 1879
  Arts Area: Dance; Vocal Music; Instrumental Music; Theater; Festivals; Grand Opera
  Status: Professional; Non-Profit
  Type: Performing; Educational
  Purpose: To present music, dance and theatre of high quality to the University and southeastern Michigan communities
  Management: Kenneth C. Fischer, Executive Director; John Kennard, Administrative Manager; Catherine Arcure, Director of Development; Robin Stephenson, Director of Marketing
  Officers: Norman Herbert, President; Lois Stegeman, Vice President; Rebecca McGowen, Secretary; Carl Braver, Treasurer
  Paid Staff: 16   **Volunteer Staff:** 300
  Paid Artists: 1,600   **Non-Paid Artists:** 250
  Budget: $1,000,000 - $5,000,000
  Income Sources: Private Foundations/Grants/Endowments; Business/Corporate Donations; Box Office; Government Grants; Individual Donations
  Season: September - May   **Annual Attendance:** 85,000
  Affiliations: APAP; CMA; ISPAA
  Performance Facilities: Hill Auditorium; Power Center; Rackham Auditorium

FACILITY

MICHIGAN THEATER
603 East Liberty, Ann Arbor, MI 48104
(313) 668-8397; (313) 668-8405
FAX: (313) 668-8397
  Founded: 1928
  Type of Facility: Concert Hall; Auditorium; Theatre House
  Facility Originally: Vaudeville; Movie House
  Type of Stage: Proscenium
  Stage Dimensions: 34'9"x25'8"; 24'6" proscenium opening   **Orchestra Pit**
  Seating Capacity: 1,710
  Year Built: 1928   **Architect:** Maurice Finkel   **Cost:** $600,000
  Year Remodeled: 1986   **Architect:** Osler/Milling and Quinn Evans   **Cost:** $1,500,000
  Contact for Rental: Debra Polich-Swain;   (313) 668-8397
  Resident Groups: Ann Arbor Symphony; Ann Arbor Film Festival; Ann Arbor Ballet Theatre

POWER CENTER FOR THE PERFORMING ARTS
Fletcher Street at East Huron, Ann Arbor, MI 48109
(313) 747-3327
FAX: (313) 747-2282
  Type of Facility: Theatre Complex; Concert Hall; Performance Center; Theatre House; Opera House
  Type of Stage: Flexible
  Stage Dimensions: 42'Dx28'Hx56'W   **Orchestra Pit**
  Seating Capacity: 1,412
  Year Built: 1971   **Architect:** John Dinkaloo & Kevin Roche
  Contact for Rental: Amanda Mengden;   (313) 747-3327
  Resident Groups: University Productions; University Musical Society; Office of Major Events

UNIVERSITY OF MICHIGAN - MENDELSSOHN THEATRE
911 North University, Ann Arbor, MI 48109
(313) 747-3327
FAX: (313) 747-2282
  Type of Facility: Theatre House
  Type of Stage: Proscenium
  Stage Dimensions: 30'Wx24'Dx17'6"   **Orchestra Pit**
  Seating Capacity: 658
  Year Built: 1928   **Cost:** $200,000
  Year Remodeled: 1976
  Contact for Rental: Amanda Mengden;   (313) 747-3327
  Manager: Jeffrey Kuras
  Resident Groups: University Productions, Office of Major Events

UNIVERSITY OF MICHIGAN - TRUEBLOOD THEATRE
State Street at Washington, Ann Arbor, MI 48109
(313) 763-0950
  Type of Facility: Theatre House

Facility Originally: School; High School Auditorium
Type of Stage: 3/4 Arena; Arena
Stage Dimensions: Arena - 35'Wx35'D; 3/4 arena - 35'Wx55'D
Seating Capacity: 200
Year Built: 1906
Year Remodeled: 1981   **Architect:** Engineering Services
Contact for Rental: Mark Sullivan;   (313) 763-0950
Resident Groups: University Players

Augusta

THEATRE

BARN THEATRE
13351 West Michigan 96, Augusta, MI 49012
(616) 731-4545
FAX: (616) 731-2306
Founded: 1946
Arts Area: Professional; Summer Stock; Musical
Status: Professional; Commercial
Type: Performing; Resident
Purpose: To produce high-quality commercial summer theatre for the southwestern Michigan region
Management: Jack P. Ragotzy, Founder/Producer; Betty Ebert Ragotzy, Dusty Reeds, Associate Producers; Howard McBride, General Manager; James B. Knox, Resident Manager; Brendan Ragotzy, Assistant to the Producer
Paid Staff: 25
Paid Artists: 25
Utilizes: Guest Artists; Equity Actors
Budget: $100,000 - $500,000
Income Sources: Box Office; Concessions
Season: June - September   **Annual Attendance:** 40,000
Affiliations: AEA

Battle Creek

INSTRUMENTAL MUSIC

BATTLE CREEK SYMPHONY ORCHESTRA
PO Box 1319, Battle Creek, MI 49016
(616) 962-2518
Founded: 1899
Arts Area: Symphony; Orchestra; Chamber
Status: Professional; Non-Profit
Type: Performing; Educational
Purpose: To perform classical and pops concerts
Management: Matthew Hazelwood, Music Director; Pamela Starrett, Executive Director
Officers: Arthur Learmonth, President
Paid Staff: 4   **Volunteer Staff:** 1
Paid Artists: 90
Utilizes: Guest Conductors; Guest Artists
Budget: $100,000 - $500,000
Income Sources: Private Foundations/Grants/Endowments; Business/Corporate Donations; Box Office; Government Grants; Individual Donations
Season: September - May   **Annual Attendance:** 10,000
Affiliations: MOA; ASOL
Performance Facilities: W.K. Kellogg Auditorium

FACILITY

BATTLE CREEK CIVIC THEATRE
PO Box 519, Battle Creek, MI 49106-0519
(616) 968-8131
Type of Facility: Theatre House
Type of Stage: 3/4 Arena
Seating Capacity: 160
Year Built: 1992
Contact for Rental: Kevin Schulz;   (616) 968-5752
Resident Groups: Battle Creek Civic Theatre; Battle Creek United Arts Council

KELLOGG CENTER ARENA
36 Hamblin Avenue, Battle Creek, MI 49017
(616) 963-4800
FAX: (616) 968-8840
     Type of Facility: Concert Hall; Civic Center; Arena; Multi-Purpose
     Type of Stage: Flexible; Platform; Arena
     Stage Dimensions: 60'x40'
     Seating Capacity: 6,083
     Year Built: 1981   **Cost:** $6,000,000
     Contact for Rental: Jim Walczak; (616) 963-4800

Bay City

THEATRE

BAY CITY PLAYERS
1214 Columbus Avenue, Bay City, MI 48708
(517) 893-5555
     Mailing Address: PO Box 1, Bay City, MI 48707
     Founded: 1918
     Arts Area: Musical; Community; Theatrical Group
     Status: Non-Profit
     Type: Performing
     Purpose: To present quality theatrical productions to our area
     Management: Kenneth Arnett, Manager
     Officers: Tina Sills, President; Susan Craves, First Vice President; Dorothy Arnett, Second Vice President; Shari Neimann, Treasurer
     Paid Staff: 1   **Volunteer Staff:** 200
     Non-Paid Artists: 50
     Budget: $100,000 - $500,000
     Income Sources: Private Foundations/Grants/Endowments; Box Office; Individual Donations
     Season: September - May   **Annual Attendance:** 13,000
     Affiliations: Community Theatre Association of Michigan

Bay View

PERFORMING SERIES

BAY VIEW MUSIC FESITVAL
21 Encampment Drive, Bay View, MI 48801
(616) 347-4210
     Founded: 1886
     Arts Area: Vocal Music; Instrumental Music; Theater; Lyric Opera
     Status: Professional; Non-Profit; Conservatory
     Type: Performing; Educational
     Purpose: To present musical concerts for the northern Michigan community
     Management: Will Nichols, Director; Irving Prescott, Assistant Director; Rod Slocum, Executive Director
     Paid Staff: 3   **Volunteer Staff:** 15
     Paid Artists: 25
     Utilizes: Guest Artists
     Budget: $100,000 - $500,000
     Income Sources: Private Foundations/Grants/Endowments; Box Office; Individual Donations
     Season: June - August   **Annual Attendance:** 15,000
     Affiliations: United Methodist Church
     Performance Facilities: John M. Hall Auditorium

Birmingham

INSTRUMENTAL MUSIC

BIRMINGHAM-BLOOMFIELD SYMPHONY
1592 Buckingham, Birmingham, MI 48009
(313) 645-2276
     Founded: 1975
     Arts Area: Symphony; Orchestra; Ensemble
     Status: Professional; Non-Profit

Type: Performing; Educational
Purpose: To promote an appreciation of the musical arts
Management: Carla Lamphere, Executive Director; Jon Boyd, Personnel Manager; Eldonna May, Librarian; Joe Labuta, Administrative Assistant
Officers: Barbara Diles-Zobl, Chairman of the Board; Ken Eaton, President; Ken Zorn, Vice President; Bill Estes, Treasurer; Lagratta Mitchell, Secretary
Paid Staff: 3 **Volunteer Staff:** 5
Paid Artists: 80
Utilizes: Guest Conductors; Guest Artists
Budget: $100,000 - $500,000
Income Sources: Private Foundations/Grants/Endowments; Business/Corporate Donations; Box Office; Government Grants; Individual Donations
Season: October - June **Annual Attendance:** 5,000
Affiliations: ASCAP; MOA; Michigan Orchestra Volunteer Association
Performance Facilities: Temple Beth El

PERFORMING SERIES

MICHIGAN RENAISSANCE FESTIVAL
700 East Maple, Birmingham, MI 48011
(313) 645-9640
FAX: (313) 645-5351
Founded: 1980
Arts Area: Dance; Vocal Music; Instrumental Music; Theater; Festivals
Status: Professional; Commercial
Type: Performing
Purpose: To promote the Renaissance and bring the pageantry, excitement and romance of the 16th century to the southeastern Michigan area
Management: Mary Mann, General Manager
Paid Staff: 13
Paid Artists: 220 **Non-Paid Artists:** 30
Utilizes: Guest Artists
Season: August - September **Annual Attendance:** 206,000
Performance Facilities: Hollygrove, Holly

Bloomfield Hills

PERFORMING SERIES

AMERICAN ARTISTS SERIES
435 Goodhue Road, Bloomfield Hills, MI 48304
(313) 547-2230
FAX: (313) 547-1525
Founded: 1970
Arts Area: Instrumental Music; Theater; Chamber Music
Status: Professional; Non-Profit
Type: Performing; Touring; Sponsoring
Purpose: To present a series of five diverse performing-arts events featuring native musicians and invited guest artists
Management: Joann Freeman, Artistic Director; Leonard Mazern, Executive Director; Morton Malitz, Business Manager
Volunteer Staff: 35
Paid Artists: 30
Utilizes: Guest Artists; Detroit Symphony Orchestra
Budget: $50,000 - $100,000
Income Sources: Private Foundations/Grants/Endowments; Business/Corporate Donations; Box Office; Government Grants; Individual Donations
Season: November - May **Annual Attendance:** 2,000
Performance Facilities: Kingswood Auditorium

Cadillac

PERFORMING SERIES

GOPHERWOOD MUSIC SOCIETY
10212 East 48 Road, Cadillac, MI 49601
(616) 825-2113
Founded: 1984
Arts Area: Dance; Vocal Music; Instrumental Music

Status: Non-Profit
Type: Sponsoring
Purpose: To sponsor traditional music and dance concerts as well as children's concerts
Officers: Shelley Youngman, President; Janice Hever, Vice President; Rita Meech, Treasurer; Frank Youngman, Secretary
Utilizes: Guest Artists
Budget: $1,000 - $50,000
Income Sources: Box Office; Government Grants; Individual Donations
Season: September - April

Calumet

THEATRE

CALUMET THEATRE COMPANY
340 Sixth Street, Calumet, MI 49913
(906) 337-2610
Founded: 1900
Arts Area: Professional; Musical; Dinner; Community; Folk; Theatrical Group
Status: Professional; Non-Profit
Type: Educational; Sponsoring
Purpose: A historic theatre and rural arts education center, the theatre both hosts and sponsors performing events
Management: James F. O'Brien, III, Executive Director; James Jacobson, Technical Director
Officers: Harry Cobb, Chairperson; Edward Burger, Vice Chairperson; Nancy Pintar, Secretary/Treasurer
Paid Staff: 5   **Volunteer Staff:** 120
Budget: $100,000 - $500,000
Income Sources: Private Foundations/Grants/Endowments; Business/Corporate Donations; Box Office; Government Grants; Individual Donations
Season: 52 Weeks   **Annual Attendance:** 26,000
Affiliations: Michigan Association of Community Arts Agencies

Cass City

PERFORMING SERIES

VILLAGE BACH FESTIVAL
PO Box 27, Cass City, MI 48726
(517) 872-3465
FAX: (517) 872-2301
Founded: 1979
Arts Area: Vocal Music; Instrumental Music; Festivals
Status: Professional; Non-Profit
Type: Performing
Purpose: To bring quality, professional musical performance to the Thumb Area of Michigan and to encourage the establishment of a tradition
Officers: Holly Althaver, Chairman; Celia House, Treasurer; L. E. Althaver, Business Manager
Volunteer Staff: 25
Paid Artists: 30
Utilizes: Guest Artists
Budget: $1,000 - $50,000
Income Sources: Private Foundations/Grants/Endowments; Business/Corporate Donations; Box Office; Government Grants; Individual Donations
Season: November   **Annual Attendance:** 1,000

Cheboygan

PERFORMING SERIES

CHEBOYGAN AREA ARTS COUNCIL
PO Box 95, Cheboygan, MI 49721
(616) 627-5432
Founded: 1972
Arts Area: Dance; Vocal Music; Instrumental Music; Theater; Festivals; Lyric Opera
Status: Non-Profit
Type: Educational; Sponsoring
Purpose: To operate with its facility, the Opera House, as a regional arts center with quality programming and arts education for the northern Michigan area

Management: Joann P. Leal, Executive Director; Jerry Bronson, Stage Technician
Officers: Jeannette Bronson, President; Michael Stack, Vice President; John Woodruff, Treasurer; Celeste Spencer, Secretary
Paid Staff: 4 **Volunteer Staff:** 160
Utilizes: Special Technical Talent; Guest Artists
Budget: $100,000 - $500,000
Income Sources: Private Foundations/Grants/Endowments; Business/Corporate Donations; Box Office; Government Grants; Individual Donations
Season: 52 Weeks **Annual Attendance:** 10,000
Affiliations: Michigan Association of Community Arts Agencies; APAP
Performance Facilities: Opera House

FACILITY

CHEBOYGAN OPERA HOUSE - CITY HALL
403 North Huron, PO Box 95, Cheboygan, MI 49721
(616) 627-5432
Founded: 1877
Type of Facility: Performance Center; Theatre House; Opera House; Visual And Performing Arts Classrooms
Type of Stage: Proscenium
Stage Dimensions: 34'x20'; extended backstage - 40'D **Orchestra Pit**
Seating Capacity: 581
Year Built: 1888 **Cost:** $35,000
Year Remodeled: 1984 **Architect:** Wolf & Nichols **Cost:** $2,500,000
Contact for Rental: Joann P. Leal, Executive Director; (616) 627-5432
Performing Arts and Arts Center, classes and performances

Coldwater

PERFORMING SERIES

TIBBITS OPERA AND ARTS COUNCIL
14 South Hanchett Street, Coldwater, MI 49036
(517) 278-6029
Founded: 1964
Arts Area: Dance; Vocal Music; Instrumental Music; Theater; Festivals; Lyric Opera
Status: Professional; Semi-Professional; Non-Professional; Non-Profit
Type: Performing; Touring; Resident; Educational; Sponsoring
Purpose: To restore and operate the historic Tibbits Opera House and provide facilities, programming classes, and arts service to a wide segment of the community
Management: Donald F Hebert, Executive Director
Officers: John Shea, President; Barry Case, Vice President; Kristina Gerlach, Correspondence Secretary; Rae Kleindirst, Recording Secretary; Caroline Lowe, Treasurer
Paid Staff: 6 **Volunteer Staff:** 35
Paid Artists: 40
Utilizes: Special Technical Talent; Guest Artists; Guest Directors
Budget: $100,000 - $500,000
Income Sources: Private Foundations/Grants/Endowments; Business/Corporate Donations; Box Office; Government Grants; Individual Donations
Season: 52 Weeks
Affiliations: APAP; Michigan Association of Community Arts Agencies
Performance Facilities: Tibbits Opera House

FACILITY

TIBBITS OPERA HOUSE
14 South Hanchett Street, Coldwater, MI 49036
(517) 278-6029; (800) 444-6029
Type of Facility: Theatre Complex; Concert Hall; Auditorium; Theatre House; Opera House; Civic Center; Multi-Purpose
Type of Stage: Proscenium
Orchestra Pit
Seating Capacity: 571
Year Built: 1882 **Architect:** Mortimer Smith **Cost:** $25,000
Contact for Rental: John Shea; (517) 278-6029
Manager: Donald F. Hebert
Resident Groups: Tibbits Summer Theatre; Coldwater Community Theatre; Tibbits Theatre for Young Audiences; Tibbtis Opera Foundation
To serve as a cultural center for our broadly-based constituency

---
Dearborn

PERFORMING SERIES

MICHIGAN BACH FESTIVAL
400 Town Center Drive, Suite 300, Dearborn, MI 48126
(313) 271-1939
FAX: (313) 593-5604
    Founded: 1982
    Arts Area: Vocal Music; Instrumental Music; Festivals
    Status: Professional; Non-Profit
    Type: Performing; Touring; Educational
    Purpose: To present a series of concerts
    Officers: Curtis J. Posuniak, General Director; Dr. Ronald Dobrzynski, Chairman of the Board; Dr. Shirley Harbin, Vice Chairman; V.C. Madias, Vice President; Carl Misiak, Treasurer; Judith Modelski, Secretary; Waltraud Prechter, Assistant Secretary
    Paid Staff: 3
    Paid Artists: 150
    Utilizes: Guest Conductors; Guest Artists
    Budget: $1,000 - $50,000
    Income Sources: Private Foundations/Grants/Endowments; Business/Corporate Donations; Government Grants; Individual Donations
    Season: March   **Annual Attendance:** 4,000

Detroit

DANCE

MADAME CADILLAC DANCE THEATRE
15 East Kirby, #903, Detroit, MI 48202
(313) 875-6354
FAX: (313) 832-4290
    Founded: 1982
    Arts Area: Ethnic; Folk; Historical
    Status: Semi-Professional; Non-Profit
    Type: Performing; Touring; Educational
    Purpose: To perform 18th-century dance and music of the court and country to tell the story of the American-French Colonial Period
    Management: Harriet Berg, Artistic Director; Matt Stockard, Business Manager; Callt Kypros, Booking Agent
    Paid Staff: 3   **Volunteer Staff:** 2
    Paid Artists: 10
    Utilizes: Special Technical Talent; Guest Artists
    Budget: $1,000 - $50,000
    Income Sources: Private Foundations/Grants/Endowments; Business/Corporate Donations; Box Office; Government Grants; Individual Donations
    Season: 52 Weeks

RENAISSANCE DANCE COMPANY OF DETROIT
15 East Kirby, #903, Detroit, MI 48202
(313) 875-6354
FAX: (313) 832-4290
    Founded: 1969
    Arts Area: Ethnic; Folk; Historical
    Status: Semi-Professional; Non-Profit
    Type: Performing; Touring; Educational
    Purpose: To perform 16th-century court and country dances of the Elizabethan age
    Management: Harriet Berg, Artistic Director; Matt Stockard, Business Manager
    Paid Staff: 2   **Volunteer Staff:** 2
    Paid Artists: 10
    Utilizes: Special Technical Talent; Guest Artists
    Budget: $1,000 - $50,000
    Income Sources: Private Foundations/Grants/Endowments; Business/Corporate Donations; Box Office; Government Grants; Individual Donations
    Season: 52 Weeks
    Performance Facilities: Detroit Institute of Arts

INSTRUMENTAL MUSIC

DETROIT JAZZ ORCHESTRA
1428 Broadway, #212, Detroit, MI 48226
(313) 393-5299
> **Founded:** 1981
> **Arts Area:** Orchestra; Ensemble; Ethnic; Instrumental Group
> **Status:** Professional; Non-Profit
> **Type:** Performing; Touring; Resident; Educational; Sponsoring
> **Purpose:** To preserve the history, evolve the art of, and improve the socio-economic conditions of jazz and its practitioners
> **Management:** Marsha Walden, Administrator; Linnette Phillips, Business Manager; Oliver Ragsdale, Administrative Assistant
> **Officers:** Donald Walden, Executive/Artistic Director; Reuben A. Munday, President; Marsha Walden, Vice President
> **Paid Staff:** 3   **Volunteer Staff:** 10
> **Paid Artists:** 35
> **Utilizes:** Guest Conductors; Guest Artists; Guest Directors
> **Budget:** $50,000 - $100,000
> **Income Sources:** Business/Corporate Donations; Box Office; Government Grants; Individual Donations
> **Season:** 52 Weeks   **Annual Attendance:** 7,000
> **Performance Facilities:** New World Stage

DETROIT SYMPHONY ORCHESTRA
400 Buhl Building, Detroit, MI 48226
(313) 962-1000
FAX: (313) 962-9107
> **Founded:** 1914
> **Arts Area:** Symphony; Orchestra
> **Status:** Professional; Non-Profit
> **Type:** Performing; Touring; Resident; Educational; Sponsoring
> **Purpose:** To perform and educate
> **Management:** Neeme Jarvi, Music Director; Mark Volpe, Executive Director; Willa Rovder, Artistic Administrator
> **Officers:** Alfred R. Glancy III, Chairman of the Board of Directors
> **Paid Staff:** 59   **Volunteer Staff:** 600
> **Paid Artists:** 105
> **Utilizes:** Guest Conductors; Guest Artists
> **Budget:** Over 10,000,000
> **Income Sources:** Private Foundations/Grants/Endowments; Business/Corporate Donations; Box Office; Government Grants; Individual Donations
> **Season:** September - August   **Annual Attendance:** 300,000
> **Performance Facilities:** Orchestra Hall; Meadow Brook Music Festival

VOCAL MUSIC

MICHIGAN OPERA THEATRE
6519 Second Avenue, Detroit, MI 48214
(313) 874-7850
> **Founded:** 1971
> **Arts Area:** Grand Opera; Operetta
> **Status:** Professional; Non-Profit
> **Type:** Performing; Touring
> **Purpose:** To present the highest quality opera possible in Michigan
> **Management:** Dr. David DiChiera, General Director
> **Officers:** Robert Dewar, Chairman
> **Paid Staff:** 28
> **Utilizes:** Special Technical Talent; Guest Conductors; Guest Artists; Guest Directors
> **Budget:** $1,000,000 - $5,000,000
> **Income Sources:** Private Foundations/Grants/Endowments; Business/Corporate Donations; Box Office; Government Grants; Individual Donations
> **Season:** Fall - Spring

OPERA LITE
PO Box 405, Dearborn, Detroit, MI 48121
(517) 482-3096
> **Founded:** 1986
> **Arts Area:** Light Opera
> **Type:** Performing; Touring; Resident
> **Management:** David Pulice, Managing Director; Amy Kutt, Assistant Director
> **Officers:** David Pulice, President

Paid Staff: 3 **Volunteer Staff:** 15
Paid Artists: 130
Utilizes: Guest Conductors; Guest Artists; Guest Directors
Income Sources: Business/Corporate Donations; Box Office; Individual Donations
Season: September - June

THEATRE

AFRO-AMERICAN STUDIO THEATRE
3944 Chalmers, Detroit, MI 48205
(313) 885-5222
Founded: 1982
Arts Area: Professional; Dinner; Community; Theatrical Group
Status: Professional; Semi-Professional; Non-Professional; Non-Profit
Type: Performing; Touring; Educational; Sponsoring
Purpose: To promote the development and exposure of dramatic works depicting and extolling the African-American experience while also giving Black artists a forum in which to perform and grow
Management: James Reed Faulkner, Artistic Director/Founder
Officers: Gail L. Faulkner, President of the Board; Carol Wilkerson, Secretary; Octavius Sapp, Treasurer; Nehemiah Pitts, Fundraising
Paid Staff: 6 **Volunteer Staff:** 7
Paid Artists: 9 **Non-Paid Artists:** 12
Utilizes: Special Technical Talent; Guest Artists; Guest Directors
Budget: $50,000 - $100,000
Income Sources: Private Foundations/Grants/Endowments; Business/Corporate Donations; Box Office; Individual Donations
Season: 52 Weeks **Annual Attendance:** 8,000

ATTIC/NEW CENTER THEATRE
2990 West Grand Boulevard, Suite 308, Detroit, MI 48202-8285
(313) 875-8285
Founded: 1975
Arts Area: Professional; Musical; Theatrical Group
Status: Professional; Non-Profit
Type: Performing; Touring; Resident; Educational
Purpose: Attic/New Center Theatre is a resident, professional theatre company committed to the development of actors, directors, playwrights, and technicians as craftsmen in the art of theatre. It exists to create new works and to present new and challenging plays by contemporary playwrights.
Management: Lavinia Moyer, Artistic Director; Jim Moran, Managing Director
Officers: Andy Soffel, Chairman; Lavinia Moyer, President; Peter C. Gray, Treasurer; Paul R. Retenbach, Secretary
Paid Staff: 15 **Volunteer Staff:** 75
Paid Artists: 65
Utilizes: Special Technical Talent; Guest Artists; Guest Directors
Budget: $1,000,000 - $5,000,000
Income Sources: Private Foundations/Grants/Endowments; Business/Corporate Donations; Box Office; Government Grants; Individual Donations
Season: 52 Weeks
Annual Attendance: 36,000
Affiliations: TCG; FEDAPT
Performance Facilities: The New Center Theatre

CONCEPT EAST II
1144 Pengree, Detroit, MI 48202
(313) 972-1030
Founded: 1986
Arts Area: Professional; Theatrical Group
Status: Professional
Type: Performing; Touring; Educational; Sponsoring
Purpose: To preserve the art of Black cinema and theater
Management: James Wheeler, Founder/Artistic Director
Paid Staff: 4
Utilizes: Special Technical Talent; Guest Artists; Guest Directors
Budget: $1,000 - $50,000
Income Sources: Private Foundations/Grants/Endowments; Box Office; Government Grants; Individual Donations
Season: 52 Weeks
Performance Facilities: Concept East II

DETROIT REPERTORY THEATRE
13103 Woodrow Wilson, Detroit, MI 48238
(313) 868-1347
FAX: (313) 868-1705
    Founded: 1956
    Arts Area: Professional
    Status: Professional; Non-Profit
    Type: Performing
    Management: Bruce E. Millan, Artistic Director/Managing Director
    Officers: Hope Byrd, Chair, Advisory Board
    Paid Staff: 7   **Volunteer Staff:** 4
    Paid Artists: 12
    Budget: $100,000 - $500,000
    Income Sources: Private Foundations/Grants/Endowments; Business/Corporate Donations; Box Office; Government Grants; Individual Donations
    Season: November - June   **Annual Attendance:** 30,000
    Performance Facilities: Detroit Repertory Theatre

PLOWSHARES THEATRE
PO Box 11399, Detroit, MI 48211
(313) 353-5591
    Founded: 1989
    Arts Area: Professional; Theatrical Group
    Status: Professional; Non-Profit
    Type: Performing; Touring
    Purpose: To produce engaging theatre that reflects the cultural diversity of the Detroit area
    Management: Gary Anderson, Micahel Garza, Artistic Directors
    Officers: Gary Anderson, President; Michael Garza, Chairman; Addell Austin Anderson, Secretary/Treasurer
    Paid Staff: 2   **Volunteer Staff:** 10
    Utilizes: Guest Artists; Guest Directors
    Budget: $1,000 - $50,000
    Income Sources: Private Foundations/Grants/Endowments; Box Office; Individual Donations
    Season: September - May
    Annual Attendance: 6,600

THEATER GROTTESCO
PO Box 32658, Detroit, MI 48232
(313) 961-5880
    Founded: 1983
    Arts Area: Professional; Theatrical Group
    Status: Professional; Non-Profit
    Type: Performing; Touring; Educational
    Purpose: To create modern original plays and conduct training workshops and master classes
    Management: John Flax, Elizabeth Wiseman, Co-Artistic Directors
    Officers: Mary A. Zatina, President; Eric Dueweke, Vice President; Sandra Abmrozy, Treasurer; Gerald Conway, Secretary
    Paid Staff: 2
    Paid Artists: 4
    Budget: $100,000 - $500,000
    Income Sources: Private Foundations/Grants/Endowments; Business/Corporate Donations; Box Office; Government Grants; Individual Donations
    Season: 52 Weeks
    Affiliations: APAP; TCG; Arts Midwest; NACA

WAYNE STATE UNIVERSITY HILBERRY AND BONSTELLE THEATRES
95 West Hancock, Detroit, MI 48092
(313) 577-3511
FAX: (313) 577-0935
    Founded: 1963
    Arts Area: Musical; Theatrical Group
    Status: Non-Professional; Non-Profit
    Type: Performing; Touring; Resident; Educational; Sponsoring
    Purpose: The Bonstelle is the house of the undergraduate theatre program; the Hilberry houses our graduate repertory company
    Management: Robert T. Hazzard, Chair/Director; Anthony B. Schmitt, Thomas Schraeder, Associate Directors; Robert E. McGill, Assistant Chair
    Paid Staff: 20

Paid Artists: 48
Utilizes: Special Technical Talent; Guest Artists; Guest Directors
Budget: $1,000,000 - $5,000,000
Income Sources: Private Foundations/Grants/Endowments; Business/Corporate Donations; Box Office; Individual Donations; University Budget
Season: October - May   **Annual Attendance:** 90,000
Affiliations: ATHE; U/RTA; TCG; NAST
Performance Facilities: Bonstelle Theatre; Hilberry Theatre

PERFORMING SERIES

CASA DE UNIDAS
1920 Scotten, Detroit, MI 48209
(313) 843-9598
   Founded: 1981
   Arts Area: Dance; Vocal Music; Instrumental Music; Theater
   Status: Non-Profit
   Type: Performing; Touring; Educational; Sponsoring
   Purpose: To present community-based, arts and media presentations serving predominantly Hispanic communities
   Management: Marta Lagos, Program Coordinator/Community Relations
   Officers: Delores Gonzalez, President; Violo Chakmakian, Vice President
   Paid Staff: 4   **Volunteer Staff:** 10
   Paid Artists: 15   **Non-Paid Artists:** 10
   Utilizes: Special Technical Talent; Guest Artists; Guest Directors
   Budget: $50,000 - $100,000
   Income Sources: Private Foundations/Grants/Endowments; Business/Corporate Donations; Box Office; Government Grants; Individual Donations
   Season: June - October
   Performance Facilities: Clark Park Theatre

MONTREUX DETROIT JAZZ FESTIVAL - DETROIT RENAISSANCE FOUNDATION
100 Renaissance Center, Suite 1760, Detroit, MI 48243-1066
(313) 259-5400
FAX: (313) 567-8355
   Founded: 1980
   Arts Area: Vocal Music; Instrumental Music; Festivals
   Status: Non-Profit
   Type: Performing; Sponsoring
   Purpose: To preseve, promote and maintain the understanding of jazz music
   Management: Eric R. Dueweke, Director of Operations; Beryl J. Javery, Director of Administrative Services; Keith Kaminski, Director of Media Relations; Glenn Lapin, Director of Site Development; Kathleen M. McNamara, Managing Director; Michael D. Samueloff, Fireworks Director; Diane Taylor, Director of Event Services
   Officers: Robert E. McCabe, President; Edward Fleischmann, Secretary/Treasurer
   Paid Staff: 38   **Volunteer Staff:** 200
   Income Sources: Private Foundations/Grants/Endowments
   Season: September

UNITED BLACK ARTISTS, USA, INC.
7661 LaSalle Boulevard, Detroit, MI 48206
(313) 898-5574; (313) 363-0369
   Founded: 1987
   Arts Area: Instrumental Music; Theater
   Status: Non-Profit
   Type: Educational; Sponsoring
   Purpose: To promote cultural and literary growth thereby stimulating the quality of life among blacks
   Management: Dr. Daphne W. Ntiri, Management Staff
   Officers: Roderick E. Warren, President/Treasurer; Verona Morton, Vice President
   Paid Staff: 2   **Volunteer Staff:** 6
   Paid Artists: 15   **Non-Paid Artists:** 20
   Utilizes: Guest Artists
   Budget: $1,000 - $50,000
   Income Sources: Private Foundations/Grants/Endowments; Business/Corporate Donations; Government Grants; Individual Donations; City and Local Contributions
   Season: 52 Weeks
   Annual Attendance: 750
   Affiliations: Harmony Park Playhouse

FACILITY

COBO ARENA
301 Civic Center Drive, Detroit, MI 48226
(313) 567-6000
>**Type of Facility:** Theatre House; Arena; Multi-Purpose
>**Type of Stage:** Flexible; Arena
>**Seating Capacity:** Arena - 12,191; 3/4 Arena - 7,000
>**Year Built:** 1960 **Architect:** Giffels & Rossetti **Cost:** $55,000,000
>**Contact for Rental:** Allan Vella; (313) 567-6000
>*Cost reflects convention center construction*

DETROIT CENTER FOR THE PERFORMING ARTS
8041 Harper, Detroit, MI 48213
(313) 925-7138
>**Type of Facility:** Theatre Complex; Concert Hall; Auditorium; Studio Performance; Performance Center; Off Broadway; Multi-Purpose
>**Type of Stage:** Proscenium
>**Stage Dimensions:** 36'x40' **Orchestra Pit**
>**Seating Capacity:** 2,983
>**Year Built:** 1930
>**Year Remodeled:** 1980 **Architect:** Dietrich & Cassavaugh **Cost:** $200,000
>**Contact for Rental:** Bruce E. Nilsson; (313) 925-7138
>**Manager:** Nancy Engel
>**Resident Groups:** Detroit Center for the Performing Arts

DETROIT SYMPHONY ORCHESTRA HALL
3711 Woodward, Detroit, MI 48201
(313) 833-3362
>**Type of Facility:** Concert Hall
>**Type of Stage:** Proscenium
>**Stage Dimensions:** 40'x40'
>**Seating Capacity:** 2,038
>**Year Built:** 1919 **Architect:** C. Howard Crane **Cost:** $700,000
>**Year Remodeled:** 1990 **Architect:** Diohl and Diohl Architects **Cost:** $5,500,000
>**Acoustical Consultant:** Jaffe Acoustics
>**Contact for Rental:** Stanley Hobbs, Lori Boccia; (313) 833-3362
>**Resident Groups:** Detroit Symphony Orchestra; Chamber Music Society of Detroit; Detroit Symphony Chamber Orchestra

FOX THEATRE
2211 Woodward Avenue, Detroit, MI 48201
(313) 965-7100
>**Type of Facility:** Theatre House
>**Facility Originally:** Show Palace
>**Seating Capacity:** 5,600
>**Year Built:** 1928 **Architect:** C. Howard Crane **Cost:** $12,000,000
>**Contact for Rental:** Stu Mayer; (313) 965-7100
>**Manager:** Greg Bellamy

JOE LOUIS ARENA
600 Civic Center Drive, Detroit, MI 48226
(313) 567-6000
>**Type of Facility:** Theatre House; Arena; Multi-Purpose
>**Type of Stage:** Flexible; Arena
>**Seating Capacity:** End Stage - 19,868; Floor Stage - 20,666
>**Year Built:** 1979 **Architect:** Smith Hinchman & Grylls **Cost:** $29,700,000
>**Year Remodeled:** 1982 **Cost:** $4,000,000
>**Contact for Rental:** John Pettit, Operations Manager; (313) 567-7444

MUSIC HALL CENTER FOR THE PERFORMING ARTS
350 Madison Avenue, Detroit, MI 48226
(313) 963-7622
FAX: (313) 963-2466
>**Type of Facility:** Theatre House
>**Type of Stage:** Proscenium
>**Stage Dimensions:** 41'9"x44'x38; 40'x40' proscenium opening **Orchestra Pit**
>**Seating Capacity:** 1,790

Year Built: 1928 **Architect:** Smith Hinchman & Grylls
Contact for Rental: Karen Wright; (313) 963-7622

Farmington Hills

FACILITY

THE COMMUNITY CENTER FARMINGTON - FARMINGTON HILLS
24705 Farmington, Farmington Hills, MI 48336
(313) 477-8404
Founded: 1969
Type of Facility: Outdoor (Concert); Amphitheater; Civic Center; Multi-Purpose; Room
Facility Originally: Family Mansion
Type of Stage: Proscenium; Platform
Stage Dimensions: 40'x20'
Seating Capacity: Indoor - 100; Outdoor - 300
Year Built: 1869
Year Remodeled: 1920 **Architect:** Marcus Burrowes
Contact for Rental: Bobbi Gelman; (313) 477-8404
Resident Groups: Men's Club; Farmington Area Community Women; Ridge Writers

---
Ferndale

VOCAL MUSIC

CANTATA ACADEMY
2441 Pinecrest, Ferndale, MI 48220
(313) 546-0420
Founded: 1961
Arts Area: Choral
Status: Semi-Professional; Non-Profit
Type: Performing; Touring
Purpose: To perform fine choral music
Management: Phillip O'Jibway, Manager; Frederick Bellinger, Musical Director/Conductor
Officers: Ellen Boyes, President; Robert Branch, Vice President; Jenny Meisel, Secretary; Bonnie Hart, Treasurer
Paid Staff: 3
Paid Artists: 50
Budget: $1,000 - $50,000
Income Sources: Private Foundations/Grants/Endowments; Business/Corporate Donations; Box Office; Government Grants; Individual Donations
Season: September - June **Annual Attendance:** 4,000
Affiliations: CA

Flint

INSTRUMENTAL MUSIC

FLINT SYMPHONY ORCHESTRA
Flint Institute of Music, 1025 East Kearsley Street, Flint, MI 48503
(313) 238-9651
FAX: (313) 238-6385
Founded: 1917
Arts Area: Symphony; Orchestra
Status: Professional; Non-Profit
Type: Performing; Resident; Educational
Management: Thomas Gerdon, Executive Director
Utilizes: Guest Conductors; Guest Artists
Income Sources: Private Foundations/Grants/Endowments; Business/Corporate Donations; Box Office; Government Grants; Individual Donations
Performance Facilities: James H. Whiting Auditorium

PERFORMING SERIES

THE FLINT INSTITUTE OF MUSIC
1025 East Kearsley Street, Flint, MI 48503
(313) 238-9651
>**Founded:** 1966
>**Arts Area:** Dance; Vocal Music; Instrumental Music
>**Status:** Professional; Non-Profit
>**Type:** Performing; Touring; Educational; Sponsoring
>**Purpose:** To foster, promote and increase the musical knowledge and appreciation of the public through educational activities and the organization and presentation of performances of music and dance
>**Management:** Thomas Gerdom, Executive Director; Paul Torre, Director, Flint School of Performing Arts; Claudia J. Ferguson, Director of Development
>**Officers:** John D. Mott, Chairman; Gloria Van Duyne, Chairman-Elect; Edward P. Abbott, John R. Wilson, Vice Chairmen; Bruce J. Boss, Secretary; John E. Birky, Treasurer
>**Paid Staff:** 36
>**Paid Artists:** 87
>**Utilizes:** Special Technical Talent; Guest Conductors; Guest Artists
>**Budget:** $1,000,000 - $5,000,000
>**Income Sources:** Private Foundations/Grants/Endowments; Business/Corporate Donations; Box Office; Government Grants; Individual Donations
>**Season:** 52 Weeks
>**Affiliations:** ASOL; APAP; MOA; BOMI; NARB
>**Performance Facilities:** MacArthur Recital Hall; University of Michigan-Flint; Whiting Auditorium

FACILITY

THE FLINT INSTITUTE OF MUSIC
1025 East Kearsley Street, Flint, MI 48503
(313) 238-9651
>**Type of Facility:** Auditorium; Performance Center; Multi-Purpose
>**Type of Stage:** Proscenium
>**Stage Dimensions:** 45'x24'   **Seating Capacity:** 270
>**Year Built:** 1970   **Architect:** Ellis Arndt and Truesdale   **Cost:** $1,500,000
>**Contact for Rental:** Paul Torre;   (313) 238-9651
>**Resident Groups:** Ensembles of the Flint School of the Performing Arts; Ballet Michigan; Ensembles of the Flint Symphony Orchestra

JAMES H. WHITING AUDITORIUM
1241 East Kearsley Street, Flint, MI 48503
(313) 760-1138
>**Type of Facility:** Auditorium

Garden City

FACILITY

MAPLEWOOD COMMUNITY CENTER
31735 Maplewood, Garden City, MI 48135
(313) 525-8846
>**Type of Facility:** Multi-Purpose; Room
>**Facility Originally:** School
>**Type of Stage:** Platform
>**Seating Capacity:** 160
>**Resident Groups:** Ann Arbor Goodtime Players; Crossroads Productions
>*Available for rent*

Grand Haven

FACILITY

CITY OF GRAND HAVEN COMMUNITY CENTER
421 Columbus, Grand Haven, MI 49417
(616) 842-2550
FAX: (616) 842-0085
>**Type of Facility:** Auditorium
>**Type of Stage:** Proscenium

Stage Dimensions: 16'x22'x20'
Seating Capacity: 200
Year Built: 1967   **Architect:** Jickling & Lyman
Contact for Rental: Bill Kool;   (616) 842-2550
Resident Groups: Central Park Players Community Theater
Performing Arts events, conferences

Grand Rapids

DANCE

THE GRAND RAPIDS BALLET
233 East Fulton, Suite 8, Grand Rapids, MI 49503
(616) 454-4771
Founded: 1973
Arts Area: Ballet
Status: Non-Professional; Non-Profit
Type: Performing; Touring; Educational; Sponsoring
Purpose: To present programs of professional and amateur dancers; to give ballet training to students of the area
Management: Charthel Arthur, Artistic Director
Officers: Susan Meyers, President; Judy Freeman, First Vice President; Deb Meadows, Second Vice President; Dale Iverson, Secretary; Mary Nell Baldwin, Treasurer
Paid Staff: 3   **Volunteer Staff:** 50
Non-Paid Artists: 55
Utilizes: Special Technical Talent; Guest Conductors; Guest Artists; Guest Choreographers
Budget: $100,000 - $500,000
Income Sources: Private Foundations/Grants/Endowments; Business/Corporate Donations; Box Office; Government Grants; Individual Donations
Season: December - June   **Annual Attendance:** 20,000
Affiliations: Arts Council of Greater Grand Rapids; NARB
Performance Facilities: DeVos Hall

INSTRUMENTAL MUSIC

THE CHAMBER MUSIC SOCIETY OF GRAND RAPIDS, INC.
c/o St. Cecilia Music Society, 24 Ransom Avenue Northeast, Grand Rapids, MI 49503
(616) 459-2224
Founded: 1980
Arts Area: Chamber
Status: Non-Profit
Type: Sponsoring
Purpose: To promote and support chamber music performance in western Michigan, specifically Grand Rapids
Management: LeAnn Arkema, Administrator of Saint Cecilia Music Society
Officers: Mary Barr, President; Lance Jones and Kathy Bissell, Vice Presidents; Jan Candler, Secretary; Sue Meyer, Treasurer
Paid Staff: 2   **Volunteer Staff:** 17
Utilizes: Guest Artists
Budget: $1,000 - $50,000
Income Sources: Business/Corporate Donations; Box Office; Individual Donations
Season: September - May   **Annual Attendance:** 250
Performance Facilities: Royce Auditorium; Saint Cecilia Music Society

GRAND RAPIDS SYMPHONY ORCHESTRA
220 Lyon Street NW, Suite 415, Grand Rapids, MI 49503
(616) 454-9451
FAX: (616) 454-7477
Founded: 1929
Arts Area: Symphony; Orchestra; Chamber; Ensemble
Status: Non-Profit
Type: Performing; Touring; Resident; Educational
Purpose: The purpose of the Grand Rapids Symphony Society is to provide concerts of orchestral and chamber music and educational programs of the highest quality to the widest possible audience.
Management: Peter W. Smith, Executive Director/General Manager
Paid Staff: 10   **Volunteer Staff:** 100
Utilizes: Guest Conductors; Guest Artists; Guest Directors
Budget: $1,000,000 - $5,000,000
Income Sources: Private Foundations/Grants/Endowments; Business/Corporate Donations; Box Office; Government Grants; Individual Donations

Season: September - May   **Annual Attendance:** 65,000
Affiliations: ASOL; MOA
Performance Facilities: DeVos Hall

GRAND RAPIDS YOUTH SYMPHONY
220 Lyon Street NW, Suite 415, Grand Rapids, MI 49503
(616) 454-9451
Founded: 1959
Arts Area: Symphony; Orchestra
Status: Non-Professional; Non-Profit
Type: Performing; Educational
Purpose: The Grand Rapids Youth Symphony provides an opportunity for talented students to perform with other musicians of their caliber, to broaden their musical experience and to provide an invaluable training ground for the professional musicians of the future.
Management: John Varineau, Conductor; Pam French, Outreach Director
Paid Staff: 2
Non-Paid Artists: 80
Season: September - June   **Annual Attendance:** 1,000
Affiliations: ASOL (Youth Orchestra Division); Grand Rapids Symphony
Performance Facilities: Forest Hills Northern High School Auditorium

VOCAL MUSIC

OPERA GRAND RAPIDS
161 Ottawa NW, Suite 205B, Grand Rapids, MI 49503
(616) 451-2741
FAX: (616) 451-4587
Founded: 1967
Arts Area: Grand Opera; Musical Theatre
Status: Professional; Non-Profit
Type: Performing; Educational; Sponsoring
Purpose: To enhance the quality of life in the Grand Rapids area and western Michigan by providing professional-quality operatic/musical theater productions; to raise the level of appreciation and understanding of opera in all residents
Management: Robert Lyall, General Director; Andrea Creswick, Business Manager; Jody Parraguez, Public Relations/Marketing Director
Paid Staff: 6   **Volunteer Staff:** 4
Paid Artists: 100   **Non-Paid Artists:** 12
Utilizes: Special Technical Talent; Guest Conductors; Guest Artists; Guest Directors
Budget: $100,000 - $500,000
Income Sources: Private Foundations/Grants/Endowments; Business/Corporate Donations; Box Office; Government Grants; Individual Donations
Season: October - April   **Annual Attendance:** 8,500
Affiliations: OA
Performance Facilities: DeVos Hall

PERFORMING SERIES

FESTIVAL OF THE ARTS
207 Waters Building, Grand Rapids, MI 49503
(616) 459-2787
Founded: 1970
Arts Area: Dance; Vocal Music; Instrumental Music; Theater; Festivals
Status: Professional; Non-Profit
Type: Sponsoring
Purpose: To support the arts and artists of the Greater Grand Rapids Community; to promote and support the arts financially and through technical assistance to organizations or individuals; to promote experiences for participants and observers from within the general public
Management: Jacqueline Udell, Office Manager
Officers: Patricia Duthler, President; Norma Van Kuiken, Vice President; Johanne Neu, Secretary; Michael Julien, Treasurer
Paid Staff: 2   **Volunteer Staff:** 2,500
Non-Paid Artists: 3,000
Utilizes: Guest Artists
Budget: $50,000 - $100,000
Income Sources: Business/Corporate Donations; Individual Donations
Season: June   **Annual Attendance:** 600,000
Performance Facilities: Calder Plaza

FACILITY

CALVIN COLLEGE FINE ARTS CENTER
3201 Burton Street SE, Grand Rapids, MI 49546
(616) 957-6280
FAX: (616) 957-6469
    Type of Facility: Theatre Complex; Concert Hall; Auditorium; Performance Center; Multi-Purpose
    Type of Stage: Thrust; Proscenium
    Stage Dimensions: 60'Wx40'D
    Orchestra Pit
    Seating Capacity: 1,200
    Year Built: 1966 **Architect:** Daverman Associates **Cost:** $2,500,000
    Acoustical Consultant: Bolt, Beranek & Newman
    Contact for Rental: Jeff Stob; (616) 957-6280

FOUNTAIN STREET CHURCH
24 Fountain Street NE, Grand Rapids, MI 49503
(616) 459-8386
    Facility Originally: Church
    Type of Stage: Platform
    Stage Dimensions: 24'x24'
    Seating Capacity: 1,600
    Contact for Rental: Lisa Hill; (616) 459-8386
    Resident Groups: Fountain Street Church Choir
    Only rented to non-profit groups

GRAND CENTER - AUDITORIUM
245 Monroe Avenue NW, Grand Rapids, MI 49503
(616) 456-3922
    Type of Facility: Auditorium; Civic Center
    Type of Stage: Flexible; Proscenium
    Seating Capacity: 4,300
    Year Built: 1933 **Architect:** Robinson-Campau **Cost:** $1,500,000
    Year Remodeled: 1985 **Architect:** Daverman Associates **Cost:** $6,000,000
    Contact for Rental: Robert Hodge, Maryanne McIntyre; (616) 456-3922
    Manager: Robert Hodge
    Remodeling and additions done in 1985 to the Welsh Auditorium

GRAND CENTER - DEVOS HALL
245 Monroe Avenue NW, Grand Rapids, MI 49503
(616) 456-3922
FAX: (616) 456-3995
    Type of Facility: Performance Center; Off Broadway; Theatre House; Multi-Purpose
    Type of Stage: Proscenium
    Stage Dimensions: 58'Wx43'D; 58'Wx35'H proscenium opening **Orchestra Pit**
    Seating Capacity: 2,446
    Year Built: 1981
    Contact for Rental: Robert Hodge; (616) 456-3922
    Resident Groups: Grand Rapids Symphony; Grand Rapids Ballet; Opera Grand Rapids
    Part of the 1981 addition to Grand Center

Grosse Pointe Farms

VOCAL MUSIC

RACKHAM SYMPHONY CHOIR
165 Hillcrest Lane, Grosse Pointe Farms, MI 48236
(313) 882-1285; (313) 886-1821
    Founded: 1949
    Arts Area: Choral
    Status: Non-Profit
    Type: Performing; Educational
    Purpose: To provide the metropolitan Detroit area with choral symphonic performances of the classical masters
    Management: D. Frederic DeHaven, Music Director; Shari Fiori, Assistant Director
    Officers: Lance J. Kronzer, President of the Board; Anne Weston, Vice President; Luanne Offer, Treasurer; Janet Oakes, Secretary
    Paid Staff: 3 **Volunteer Staff:** 14

Non-Paid Artists: 60
Utilizes: Guest Artists
Budget: $50,000 - $100,000
Income Sources: Private Foundations/Grants/Endowments; Business/Corporate Donations; Box Office; Government Grants; Individual Donations
Season: September - June   **Annual Attendance:** 4,000

PERFORMING SERIES

GROSSE POINTE SUMMER FESTIVAL
181 Beaupre Avenue, Grosse Pointe Farms, MI 48236-3448
(313) 558-6370; (313) 885-0793
FAX: (313) 573-4806
Founded: 1957
Arts Area: Vocal Music; Instrumental Music; Theater; Festivals; Lyric Opera
Status: Professional; Non-Profit
Type: Performing; Touring; Resident
Purpose: To present outdoor concerts for community enrichment in summer
Management: Alexander C. Suczek, Founder/Artistic Director
Officers: Mrs. Barbara Denler, Program Director; Mrs. Johanna Gilber, General Chairman
Paid Staff: 10   **Volunteer Staff:** 20
Paid Artists: 5
Utilizes: Special Technical Talent; Guest Conductors; Guest Artists
Budget: $100,000 - $500,000
Income Sources: Private Foundations/Grants/Endowments; Business/Corporate Donations; Box Office; Individual Donations
Annual Attendance: 5,000
Performance Facilities: Terrace of Alger House

PRO MUSICA, INC.
181 Beaupre Avenue, Grosse Pointe Farms, MI 48236-3448
(313) 558-6370; (313) 885-0793
FAX: (313) 573-4806
Founded: 1976
Arts Area: Vocal Music; Instrumental Music; Composers' New Works
Status: Professional; Non-Profit
Type: Performing
Purpose: To present emerging world-class artists in debut recitals in Detroit; to present composers in connection with performances of their music
Management: Alexander C. Suczek, President
Officers: Alice Haidostian, First Vice President; Dr. Hershel Sandberg, Second Vice President; Ann Kondak, Secretary; James Diamond, Treasurer
Paid Staff: 1
Paid Artists: 3
Utilizes: Guest Artists
Budget: $1,000 - $50,000
Income Sources: Private Foundations/Grants/Endowments; Business/Corporate Donations; Box Office; Individual Donations
Season: October - May   **Annual Attendance:** 1,000
Affiliations: Detroit Institute of the Arts
Performance Facilities: Recital Hall of the Detroit Institute of the Arts

Holland

INSTRUMENTAL MUSIC

HOPE COLLEGE ORCHESTRA AND SYMPHONETTE
Music Department, Holland, MI 49423
(616) 392-5111
Founded: 1949
Arts Area: Orchestra; Chamber
Status: Non-Professional; Non-Profit
Type: Performing; Touring; Resident; Educational
Purpose: To present concerts on campus and in other cities
Management: Robert Ritsema, Conductor
Paid Staff: 1
Non-Paid Artists: 60
Utilizes: Guest Conductors; Guest Artists; Guest Directors

Budget: $1,000 - $50,000
Season: September - May   **Annual Attendance:** 7,000
Affiliations: ASOL; MOA
Performance Facilities: Dimnent Chapel

FACILITY

HOPE COLLEGE THEATRE DEPARTMENT
Holland, MI 49423
(616) 392-5111
Founded: 1968
Type of Facility: Theatre Complex
Type of Stage: Thrust; Flexible; Proscenium
Stage Dimensions: 40'Wx20'Hx35'D   **Orchestra Pit**
Seating Capacity: 494
Year Built: 1971   **Architect:** Casler
Year Remodeled: 1983
Contact for Rental: Perry Landes;   (616) 394-7597

Interlochen

PERFORMING SERIES

INTERLOCHEN ARTS CAMP
Interlochen Center for the Arts, Interlochen, MI 49643
(616) 276-9221
FAX: (616) 276-6321
Founded: 1928
Arts Area: Dance; Vocal Music; Instrumental Music; Theater; Festivals; Visual Arts
Status: Non-Professional; Non-Profit
Type: Performing; Touring; Educational; Sponsoring
Purpose: To sponsor an eight-week summer program for talented boys and girls ages eight through college
Management: Edward J. Downing, Director of Arts Camp
Officers: Dean Boal, President
Paid Staff: 1
Utilizes: Guest Conductors; Guest Artists; Guest Directors
Budget: $5,000,000 - $10,000,000
Income Sources: Private Foundations/Grants/Endowments; Business/Corporate Donations; Box Office; Government Grants; Individual Donations
Season: June - August
Annual Attendance: 250,000
Performance Facilities: Corson Auditorium; Kresge Auditorium

INTERLOCHEN ARTS FESTIVAL
Interlochen Center for the Arts, Interlochen, MI 49643
(616) 276-9221
Founded: 1928
Arts Area: Dance; Vocal Music; Instrumental Music; Theater
Status: Semi-Professional; Non-Profit
Type: Performing; Educational
Purpose: To offer an eight-week extension of the National Music Camp
Officers: Edward Downing, Vice President
Paid Staff: 1,000
Utilizes: Special Technical Talent; Guest Artists; Guest Directors
Budget: $100,000 - $500,000
Income Sources: Private Foundations/Grants/Endowments; Business/Corporate Donations; Box Office; Government Grants; Individual Donations
Season: June - August
Performance Facilities: Kresge Auditorium; Corson Auditorium; Dendirnos Recital Hall

FACILITY

INTERLOCHEN CENTER FOR THE ARTS - CORSON AUDITORIUM
M-199, Interlochen, MI 49643
(616) 276-9221
Type of Facility: Concert Hall; Auditorium
Type of Stage: Proscenium
Stage Dimensions: 60'Wx28'Hx42'D   **Orchestra Pit**

Seating Capacity: 1,000
Year Built: 1975   **Architect:** Dow and Associates   **Cost:** $2,100,000
Acoustical Consultant: Jaffe Acoustics
Resident Groups: All on-campus groups and guest artists
On-campus concerts

INTERLOCHEN CENTER FOR THE ARTS - DENDRINOS CHAPEL/RECITAL HALL
M-199, Interlochen, MI 49643
(616) 276-9221
Type of Facility: Concert Hall
Type of Stage: Platform
Stage Dimensions: 40'Wx40'Hx22'D
Seating Capacity: 230
Year Built: 1981   **Architect:** Dow, Howell, Gilmore & Associates   **Cost:** $800,000
Acoustical Consultant: Jaffe Acoustics
Resident Groups: Selected on-campus groups and selected guest artists
On-campus concerts

INTERLOCHEN CENTER FOR THE ARTS - KRESGE AUDITORIUM
M-199, Interlochen, MI 49643
(616) 276-9221
Type of Facility: Concert Hall; Auditorium; Outdoor (Concert)
Type of Stage: Proscenium
Stage Dimensions: 60'Wx25'Hx40'D
Orchestra Pit
Seating Capacity: 4,000
Year Built: 1948
Year Remodeled: 1964   **Architect:** Dow and Associates
Acoustical Consultant: Bolt, Beranek & Newman
Resident Groups: All on-campus groups and guest artists
On-campus groups, primarily for music

Ironwood

FACILITY

HISTORIC IRONWOOD THEATRE
113 East Aurora, Ironwood, MI 49938
(906) 932-0618
FAX: (906) 932-4660
Founded: 1928
Type of Facility: Theatre Complex; Concert Hall; Performance Center; Off Broadway; Theatre House; Opera House; Multi-Purpose; Sponsorship
Facility Originally: Vaudeville; Movie House
Type of Stage: Proscenium
Stage Dimensions: 28'4"Wx30'H   **Orchestra Pit**
Seating Capacity: Main Floor - 438
Year Built: 1928   **Architect:** Albert Nelson   **Cost:** $160,000
Contact for Rental: Joan Borcherdt;   (906) 932-0618
Resident Groups: Gogebic Range Players Productions
The theatre is available for art exhibitions, area school and college productions, second-run movies and as rental space for conventions and organizations.

Kalamazoo

DANCE

KALAMAZOO BALLET COMPANY
326 West Kalamazoo Avenue, Kalamazoo, MI 49007
(616) 343-3027
Founded: 1969
Arts Area: Modern; Ballet; Ethnic; Folk
Status: Semi-Professional; Non-Professional; Non-Profit
Type: Performing; Touring; Educational
Purpose: To give dancers the opportunity of experiencing professional rehearsals and performances while in Kalamazoo; to serve as a stepping stone to professional companies
Management: Birgitte Scheele, Business Manager; Therese Bullard, Artistic Director

Officers: Sherman Smith, President; Shirley Topp, Pat Middleton and Terry Bullard, Board Members
Paid Staff: 2   **Volunteer Staff:** 6
Paid Artists: 5   **Non-Paid Artists:** 50
Utilizes: Special Technical Talent; Guest Conductors; Guest Artists; Guest Choreographers
Budget: $1,000 - $50,000
Income Sources: Private Foundations/Grants/Endowments; Business/Corporate Donations; Box Office; Government Grants; Individual Donations
Season: September - June   **Annual Attendance:** 40,000
Affiliations: NARB; Mid-State Regional Dance America
Performance Facilities: Civic Auditorium; Miller Auditorium

INSTRUMENTAL MUSIC

THE KALAMAZOO JUNIOR SYMPHONY SOCIETY
714 South Westnedge Avenue, Room 344, Kalamazoo, MI 49007
(616) 349-7557
Founded: 1939
Arts Area: Symphony; Orchestra
Status: Non-Profit
Type: Performing; Touring; Educational
Purpose: To encourage and develop artistic excellence among young musicians in the southwest area of Michigan by providing a diversity of quality orchestral experiences; to enhance the cultural environment of the families and communities we serve
Management: Lee Fletcher, Business Manager; Dr. Robert Ritsema, Conductor, Kalamazoo Junior Symphony Society; Mary Hinderliter, Conductor, Prep String
Officers: Andrew Tang, President; Sandra J. Zegerius, Vice President; Ruth Tomlinson, Secretary; Stuart Eddy, Treasurer
Paid Staff: 3
Paid Artists: 2   **Non-Paid Artists:** 1
Budget: $1,000 - $50,000
Income Sources: Private Foundations/Grants/Endowments; Business/Corporate Donations; Box Office; Individual Donations
Season: September - May   **Annual Attendance:** 1,800
Performance Facilities: Chenery Auditorium

KALAMAZOO SYMPHONY ORCHESTRA
426 South Park Street, Kalamazoo, MI 49007
(616) 349-7759
FAX: (616) 349-9229
Founded: 1921
Arts Area: Symphony; Orchestra; Chamber; Ensemble
Status: Professional; Non-Profit
Type: Performing; Educational
Purpose: To support a professional symphony orchestra and staff; to present concerts of symphonic music and related programs of the highest possible artistic level; to support effective regional music education; to serve and involve the people of the greater Kalamazoo area in the Symphony Society
Management: Yoshimi Takeda, Music Director/Conductor; John Forsyte, General Manager; Paul Helfrich, Assistant Manager
Officers: Jacob Stucki, President
Paid Staff: 6   **Volunteer Staff:** 300
Paid Artists: 86
Utilizes: Guest Conductors; Guest Artists
Budget: $500,000 - $1,000,000
Income Sources: Private Foundations/Grants/Endowments; Business/Corporate Donations; Box Office; Government Grants; Individual Donations
Season: September - April   **Annual Attendance:** 20,000
Affiliations: ASOL; MOA; Kalamazoo Chamber of Commerce
Performance Facilities: Miller Auditorium

THEATRE

KALAMAZOO CIVIC PLAYERS
329 South Park Street, Kalamazoo, MI 49007
(616) 343-1313
FAX: (616) 343-0532
Founded: 1929
Arts Area: Theatrical Group
Status: Non-Profit
Type: Performing
Purpose: To provide the area with the best possible dramatic experience

Management: James C. Carver, Managing Director
Officers: John Bernhard, President; Priscilla Cronley, Vice President; Gersteen Sherrod, Secretary; Richard Groh, Treasurer
Paid Staff: 19   **Volunteer Staff:** 800
Paid Artists: 25   **Non-Paid Artists:** 250
Utilizes: Guest Directors
Budget: $100,000 - $500,000
Income Sources: Private Foundations/Grants/Endowments; Business/Corporate Donations; Box Office; Government Grants; Individual Donations
Season: 52 Weeks   **Annual Attendance:** 60,000
Affiliations: AACT; Community Theatre Association of Michigan
Performance Facilities: Civic Auditorium; Carver Center

THE MAD HATTERS EDUCATIONAL THEATRE
c/o Gilmore's, 143 South Kalamazoo Mall, Kalamazoo, MI 49007
(616) 385-5871
Founded: 1979
Status: Professional; Non-Profit
Type: Performing; Touring; Educational
Purpose: To foster full integration into society and greater understanding of people with special needs or disabilities
Management: Roberta Robinson, Executive Director; Kathleen McGookey, Fund and Program Manager/Program Facilitator; Timothy Hayden, Production Manager; Beatrice Olsen, Public Relations/Financial/Office Manager; Randy Seaman, Computer Manager
Officers: Harold H. Holland, President, Board of Trustees; James Avery Smith, Karl Sandelin, Vice Presidents; Donna Lambert, Secretary; Donald Vanderkooy, Treasurer
Paid Staff: 11
Paid Artists: 7
Utilizes: Contract Actors
Budget: $100,000 - $500,000
Income Sources: Private Foundations/Grants/Endowments; Business/Corporate Donations; Government Grants; Individual Donations
Season: 52 Weeks   **Annual Attendance:** 10,000
Affiliations: Arts Council of Greater Kalamazoo

WHOLE ART THEATER
326 West Kalamazoo, Kalamazoo, MI 49007
(616) 344-0182
Founded: 1976
Arts Area: Professional; Theatrical Group
Status: Professional; Non-Profit
Type: Performing; Touring; Educational
Purpose: To provide experimental theater for all ages and tour such theater to schools, theaters and other locales in the Midwest
Management: Sniedze Rungis, Artistic Director; Daniel Runyan, Educational Director; Francis Bilancio, Managing Director; Matthew Clysdale, Office Manager
Officers: Dr. Irene S. Vasquez, President; Francis P. Bilancio, Vice President; Carol Manstrom, Secretary; John Hircsh, Treasurer
Paid Staff: 4
Paid Artists: 5
Utilizes: Guest Artists; Guest Directors
Budget: $50,000 - $100,000
Income Sources: Private Foundations/Grants/Endowments; Business/Corporate Donations; Box Office; Government Grants; Individual Donations
Season: 52 Weeks   **Annual Attendance:** 15,000
Affiliations: Great Lakes Performing Arts Association

PERFORMING SERIES

FONTANA CONCERT SOCIETY
821 West South Street, Kalamazoo, MI 49007
(616) 382-0826
Founded: 1980
Arts Area: Vocal Music; Instrumental Music; Festivals
Status: Professional; Non-Profit
Type: Performing; Sponsoring
Purpose: To present high quality and diverse programs of chamber music in a rural and relaxed setting
Management: I Fu Wang, Robert Humiston, Interim Co-Directors; Janet Karpus, General Manager
Officers: Janlee Rothman, Ann Meade Sanders, Administrative Assistants
Paid Staff: 5   **Volunteer Staff:** 20

Paid Artists: 40
Utilizes: Guest Artists
Budget: $100,000 - $500,000
Income Sources: Private Foundations/Grants/Endowments; Business/Corporate Donations; Box Office; Individual Donations
Season: July - August   **Annual Attendance:** 5,000
Performance Facilities: The Art Emporium

IRVING S. GILMORE INTERNATIONAL KEYBOARD FESTIVAL
100 West Michigan Avenue, Kalamazoo, MI 49007
(616) 342-1166
FAX: (616) 342-0968
Founded: 1989
Arts Area: Festivals
Status: Non-Profit
Purpose: To identify and support concert pianists; to produce a biennial festival
Management: David Hook, Executive Director; David Pocock, Artistic Director; Sandra Wolfinbarger, Assistant Director; Julie Cook, Director of Public Relations and Marketing; Shannon Rininger, Box Office Manager/Secretary
Officers: Gayl Werme, President; James Westin, Vice President/Treasurer; Robert Luscombe, Secretary
Paid Staff: 5   **Volunteer Staff:** 500
Paid Artists: 185
Utilizes: Guest Artists
Budget: $1,000,000 - $5,000,000
Income Sources: Private Foundations/Grants/Endowments; Business/Corporate Donations; Box Office; Government Grants
Season: April - May   **Annual Attendance:** 45,000
Affiliations: APAP
Performance Facilities: Miller Auditorium; Dalton Center Recital Hall; State Theatre; Sturges-Young Auditorium

NEW YEAR'S FEST
128 North Kalamazoo Mall, Kalamazoo, MI 49002
(616) 381-4003
Founded: 1986
Arts Area: Dance; Vocal Music; Instrumental Music; Theater; Festivals; Lyric Opera
Status: Non-Profit
Type: Festival
Purpose: To present an annual New Year's Eve non-alcoholic celebration of performing arts in downtown Kalamazoo
Management: Jan Dancer, Executive Director
Officers: Jack Ullrey, President; Gordon Brown, Vice President; Marty Ream, Treasurer; Barb Chester, Secretary
Paid Staff: 1   **Volunteer Staff:** 13
Paid Artists: 40
Utilizes: Guest Artists
Budget: $100,000 - $500,000
Income Sources: Private Foundations/Grants/Endowments; Business/Corporate Donations; Box Office; Individual Donations
Season: New Year's Eve   **Annual Attendance:** 10,000

FACILITY

KALAMAZOO CIVIC AUDITORIUM
329 South Park Street, Kalamazoo, MI 49006
(616) 343-1313
FAX: (616) 343-0532
Type of Facility: Auditorium
Type of Stage: Proscenium   **Orchestra Pit**
Seating Capacity: 536
Year Built: 1931   **Architect:** Emery
Acoustical Consultant: Bolt, Beranek and Newman
Contact for Rental: Manager;   (616) 343-1313
Resident Groups: Kalamazoo Civic Players; Kalamazoo Chamber Orchestra

KALAMAZOO COLLEGE
1200 Academy Street, Kalamazoo, MI 49006
(616) 383-8511
Type of Facility: Theatre Complex; Concert Hall; Auditorium
Type of Stage: Thrust; Proscenium   **Orchestra Pit**
Seating Capacity: Thrust - 300; Proscenium - 400

Year Built: 1958
Contact for Rental: Carol Kennedy;   (616) 337-7047
Resident Groups: Festival Theatre Summer Company

WESTERN MICHIGAN UNIVERSITY - JAMES W. MILLER AUDITORIUM
Kalamazoo, MI 49008
(800) 228-9858; (616) 387-2300
Type of Facility: Auditorium
Type of Stage: Proscenium
Stage Dimensions: 150'x150'; 68' Proscenium
Seating Capacity: 3,527
Year Built: 1967   **Architect:** O'Dell, Hewlett & Luckenbach   **Cost:** $6,000,000
Acoustical Consultant: Bolt, Beranek & Newman
Contact for Rental: Ron Newhouse;   (616) 387-2311
Manager: Kenneth Farrance
Resident Groups: Kalamazoo Symphony Orchestra

WESTERN MICHIGAN UNIVERSITY - LAURA V. SHAW THEATRE
Kalamazoo, MI 49008
(616) 387-3224
Type of Facility: Theatre Complex
Type of Stage: Proscenium; Arena
Stage Dimensions: Arena - 40'x40"; 35'x30' proscenium opening   **Orchestra Pit**
Seating Capacity: 571
Year Built: 1968
Contact for Rental: Tery Williams;   (616) 387-3224

Lansing

INSTRUMENTAL MUSIC

GREATER LANSING SYMPHONY ORCHESTRA
230 North Washington Square, Suite 315, Lansing, MI 48933
(517) 487-5001
Founded: 1930
Arts Area: Symphony; Orchestra; Chamber; Ensemble
Status: Professional; Non-Profit
Type: Performing; Educational
Purpose: To provide the greater Lansing area with the finest quality symphonic music and educational services as is possible
Management: Sandra Sutton Gaffe', GeneralManager; Judith Kopeloff-Moore, Operations Manager; Bernie Geaham, Office Manager; Geoffrey Day, Personnel Manager
Officers: Ronald Pengescost, President; James Miller, President-Elect; Carol Fitzgerald, Treasurer
Paid Staff: 6   **Volunteer Staff:** 400
Paid Artists: 95
Utilizes: Guest Conductors; Guest Artists
Budget: $100,000 - $500,000
Income Sources: Private Foundations/Grants/Endowments; Business/Corporate Donations; Box Office; Government Grants; Individual Donations
Season: October - May   **Annual Attendance:** 60,000
Affiliations: ASOL; MOA; Arts Council of Greater Lansing
Performance Facilities: Wharton Center for Performing Arts

VOCAL MUSIC

OPERA COMPANY OF MID-MICHIGAN
300 South Washington, Suite 410, Lansing, MI 48933
(517) 482-1431
Founded: 1973
Arts Area: Grand Opera; Light Opera; Operetta
Status: Professional; Non-Profit
Type: Performing; Educational
Purpose: To bring to the mid-Michigan area operatic performances, augmented by an education program designed to enhance the understanding of opera and to aid in the development of future audiences
Management: Theresa Weller, Executive Director
Officers: Gina King, President; Sherwood Berman, President-Elect; Glenda Seiuphuis, Secretary; Kristina Arundel, Treasurer
Paid Staff: 1   **Volunteer Staff:** 6

Utilizes: Special Technical Talent; Guest Conductors; Guest Artists; Guest Directors
Budget: $100,000 - $500,000
Income Sources: Private Foundations/Grants/Endowments; Business/Corporate Donations; Box Office; Government Grants; Individual Donations
Annual Attendance: 2,100
Performance Facilities: Wharton Center for the Performing Arts

THEATRE

BOARSHEAD: MICHIGAN PUBLIC THEATER
425 South Grand Avenue, Lansing, MI 48933
(517) 484-7800
Founded: 1966
Arts Area: Professional
Status: Professional
Type: Performing; Touring; Resident; Educational; Sponsoring
Purpose: Top present a season featuring a collection of plays ranging from fresh productions of familiar theater works to the introduction of new and innovative plays and playwrights, as well as plays for children and families
Management: John Peakes, Founding Artistic Director; Judith Gentry, Managing Director; Romy Fitschen, Business Manager; Constance Peakes, Director of Public Relations/Marketing
Officers: Joseph Schwinger, Chairperson; Ute von der Heyden, Vice Chairperson; Doris Anderson, Secretary; William P. Weiner, Treasurer
Paid Staff: 18   **Volunteer Staff:** 100
Utilizes: Guest Artists; Guest Directors
Budget: $500,000 - $1,000,000
Income Sources: Private Foundations/Grants/Endowments; Business/Corporate Donations; Box Office; Government Grants; Individual Donations; Fund-raising
Season: October - May   **Annual Attendance:** 24,000
Affiliations: TCG; AEA; IATSE; Lansing Chamber of Commerce
Performance Facilities: Lansing Center for the Arts

FACILITY

LANSING CIVIC ARENA
505 West Allegan Street, Lansing, MI 48933
(517) 483-7425
FAX: (517) 483-7440
Founded: 1956
Type of Facility: Auditorium; Civic Center; Arena; Multi-Purpose
Type of Stage: Proscenium
Stage Dimensions: 48'x48'
Seating Capacity: 5,400
Year Built: 1955   **Cost:** $3,500,000
Year Remodeled: 1977   **Architect:** Duncan Black   **Cost:** $3,000,000
Contact for Rental: Executive Director;   (517) 483-7425

Midland

INSTRUMENTAL MUSIC

MIDLAND SYMPHONY ORCHESTRA
1801 West St. Andrews Road, Midland, MI 48640
(517) 631-4234
FAX: (517) 631-7890
Founded: 1936
Arts Area: Symphony; Orchestra; Chamber; Ensemble; Instrumental Group
Status: Professional; Semi-Professional; Non-Professional; Non-Profit
Type: Performing; Touring; Educational; Sponsoring
Purpose: To encourage and support the Midland Symphony Orchestra in the pursuit of artistic excellence in its presentations
Management: Judyth L. Peterson, General Manager
Officers: James Kimball, Vice Chairman; Mary Van Cleve, Chairman
Paid Staff: 6   **Volunteer Staff:** 166
Paid Artists: 75
Utilizes: Guest Conductors; Guest Artists
Budget: $100,000 - $500,000
Income Sources: Private Foundations/Grants/Endowments; Business/Corporate Donations; Box Office; Government Grants; Individual Donations

Season: October - April   **Annual Attendance:** 7,000
Affiliations: MOA; ASOL
Performance Facilities: Midland Center for the Arts

MUSIC SOCIETY, MIDLAND CENTER FOR THE ARTS
1801 West St. Andrews, Midland, MI 48640
(517) 631-1072
> **Founded:** 1943
> **Arts Area:** Orchestra; Chamber; Ensemble; Folk; Instrumental Group; Band
> **Status:** Non-Profit
> **Type:** Performing; Educational; Sponsoring
> **Purpose:** To provide performing and educational opportunities that would not otherwise exist
> **Management:** Dr. Victor A. Klimash, Artistic Director
> **Officers:** George Callaghan, Chairman
> **Paid Staff:** 8   **Volunteer Staff:** 1,000
> **Non-Paid Artists:** 2,000
> **Utilizes:** Special Technical Talent; Guest Conductors; Guest Artists; Guest Directors
> **Budget:** $500,000 - $1,000,000
> **Income Sources:** Private Foundations/Grants/Endowments; Business/Corporate Donations; Box Office; Government Grants; Individual Donations
> **Season:** September - August   **Annual Attendance:** 52,254
> **Performance Facilities:** Midland Center for the Arts

NORTHWOOD ORCHESTRA
Northwood Institute, 3225 Cook Road, Midland, MI 48640-2398
(517) 837-4364
FAX: (517) 832-7744
> **Founded:** 1979
> **Arts Area:** Symphony; Orchestra; Chamber
> **Status:** Professional; Non-Profit
> **Type:** Performing; Touring; Resident
> **Purpose:** The Northwood Orchestra is a professional chamber ensemble which tours nationally, presents an annual summer festival in northern Michigan and performs on the campuses of Northwood as artists-in-residence.
> **Management:** Christine R. Goedert, Executive Director; Don T. Jaeger, Music Director/Conductor; Dana L. Zietz, Special Projects Coordinator
> **Officers:** Macauley Whiting, Chairman
> **Paid Staff:** 3
> **Paid Artists:** 48
> **Utilizes:** Special Technical Talent; Guest Artists
> **Budget:** $100,000 - $500,000
> **Income Sources:** Private Foundations/Grants/Endowments; Business/Corporate Donations; Box Office; Individual Donations
> **Season:** March; July - August   **Annual Attendance:** 10,000

PERFORMING SERIES

MIDLAND COMMUNITY CONCERT SOCIETY
1801 West St. Andrews Road, Midland, MI 48640
(517) 631-5930
> **Arts Area:** Vocal Music; Instrumental Music
> **Status:** Non-Profit
> **Type:** Educational; Sponsoring
> **Purpose:** To build and maintain a permanent concert audience on a membership basis; to provide opportunities for students to attend professional performances
> **Officers:** Mrs. James B. Arnold, Chairman
> **Utilizes:** Guest Artists; Guest Directors
> **Income Sources:** Box Office

FACILITY

MIDLAND CENTER FOR THE ARTS
1801 West St. Andrews Road, Midland, MI 48640
(517) 631-5930
> **Type of Facility:** Auditorium; Theatre House
> **Type of Stage:** Proscenium
> **Stage Dimensions:** 70'x50'; 40'x40'   **Orchestra Pit**
> **Seating Capacity:** Auditorium - 1,538; Theatre - 426; Lecture - 94
> **Year Built:** 1971   **Architect:** Alden B. Dow & Associates   **Cost:** $8,600,000
> **Acoustical Consultant:** Bolt, Beranek & Newman

Contact for Rental: Tina Siegmund; (517) 631-4573
Resident Groups: Midland Symphony Orchestra; Midland Theatre Guild; Midland Music Society; Midland Art Council; Midland County Historical Society; Hall of Ideas; Matrix: Midland Festival

---

Mt. Clemens

FACILITY

MACOMB CENTER FOR THE PERFORMING ARTS
44575 Garfield, Mt. Clemens, MI 48038
(313) 286-2141
FAX: (313) 286-2272
Founded: 1982
Type of Facility: Concert Hall; Auditorium; Performance Center; Theatre House; Opera House
Type of Stage: Proscenium
Stage Dimensions: 40'x40'   **Orchestra Pit**
Seating Capacity: 1,244
Year Built: 1982   **Architect:** TMP Associates   **Cost:** $8,000,000
Acoustical Consultant: Kirkegard and Associates
Contact for Rental: Operations Manager; (313) 286-2183

Muskegon

INSTRUMENTAL MUSIC

WEST SHORE SYMPHONY
406 Frauenthal Center, Muskegon, MI 49440
(616) 726-3231
Founded: 1940
Arts Area: Symphony; Orchestra; Chamber
Status: Professional; Non-Profit
Type: Performing
Purpose: To bring fine live music to the west Michigan area
Management: Murray Gross, Music Director; Janet L. Smith, General Manager; Dr Lee Copenhaver, Youth Symphony Conductor
Officers: Thomas L. Jones, President; Meckie Tyson, Vice President; Stephan Patoprsty, Secretary; Timothy D. Arter, Treasurer
Paid Staff: 11
Paid Artists: 65
Utilizes: Guest Conductors; Guest Artists
Budget: $100,000 - $500,000
Income Sources: Private Foundations/Grants/Endowments; Business/Corporate Donations; Box Office; Government Grants; Individual Donations
Season: September - June   **Annual Attendance:** 18,000
Affiliations: MOA; ASOL; Concerned Citizens for the Arts in Michigan
Performance Facilities: Frauenthal Theater

WEST SHORE YOUTH SYMPHONY ORCHESTRA
425 West Western, Suite 406, Muskegon, MI 49440
(616) 726-3231
FAX: (616) 722-6913
Founded: 1966
Arts Area: Symphony; Orchestra
Status: Non-Professional; Non-Profit
Type: Performing; Educational; Sponsoring
Management: Susan Tindall, Manager; Dr. Lee Copenhaver, Conductor
Non-Paid Artists: 65
Utilizes: Guest Artists; Guest Directors
Season: September - May   **Annual Attendance:** 1,600
Affiliations: ASOL (Youth Orchestra Division); West Shore Symphony Orchestra
Performance Facilities: Frauenthal Center for the Performing Arts

THEATRE

CHERRY COUNTY PLAYHOUSE
411 West Western, Muskegon, MI 49440
(616) 727-8888
FAX: (616) 722-0549
Founded: 1955
Arts Area: Summer Stock
Status: Professional; Commercial
Type: Performing
Management: Neil Rosen, Producer/Owner
Paid Staff: 15   **Volunteer Staff:** 15
Paid Artists: 50
Budget: $100,000 - $500,000
Income Sources: Box Office
Season: July - September
Affiliations: COST

COMMUNITY THEATRE ASSOCIATION OF MICHIGAN
3985 Grand Haven Road, 103A, Muskegon, MI 49441
(616) 798-7477
Founded: 1952
Arts Area: Community
Status: Non-Profit
Type: Service Organization
Purpose: To promote communication and cooperation among community theatre groups in Michigan; to provide educational programs
Management: Barbara L. Elliott, Executive Secretary; Barbara Beckers, Secretary
Officers: Joanne Berry, President; Beverly Hellus, Vice-President; Mr. F. Merrill Wyble, Treasurer
Paid Staff: 1
Budget: $1,000 - $50,000
Income Sources: Government Grants; Individual Donations

PERFORMING SERIES

FRAUENTHAL CENTER FOR THE PERFORMING ARTS
425 West Western Avenue, Suite 304, Muskegon, MI 49440
(616) 722-4538
FAX: (616) 722-4616
Founded: 1976
Arts Area: Dance; Vocal Music; Instrumental Music; Theater
Status: Professional; Non-Professional; Non-Profit
Type: Performing; Resident; Educational; Sponsoring; Presenter
Purpose: To foster the growth, appreciation and development of the performing arts and film in western Michigan audiences
Management: Tom Harryman, Managing Director
Officers: Patricia B. Johnson, President
Paid Staff: 13   **Volunteer Staff:** 200
Utilizes: Guest Artists
Budget: $100,000 - $500,000
Income Sources: Private Foundations/Grants/Endowments; Business/Corporate Donations; Box Office; Government Grants; Individual Donations; Rental Income
Season: 52 Weeks   **Annual Attendance:** 130,000
Affiliations: League of Historic American Theatres
Performance Facilities: Frauenthal Theatre; Beardsley Theatre

FACILITY

FRAUENTHAL FOUNDATION FINE ARTS CENTER
221 South Quarterline Road, Muskegon, MI 49442
(616) 777-0324
Type of Facility: Theatre House; Multi-Purpose
Type of Stage: Proscenium
Stage Dimensions: 24'x59'x26'
Year Built: 1968   **Architect:** Alden B. Dow & Associates   **Cost:** $1,000,000
Contact for Rental: Lornella Faucher, MCC Business Office;   (616) 777-0319
Resident Groups: Muskegon Community College Creative and Performing Arts Department

---
Omena

PERFORMING SERIES

CHAMBER ARTS NORTH
PO Box 2, Omena, MI 49674
(616) 386-5529
>**Founded:** 1982
>**Arts Area:** Dance; Instrumental Music; Theater; Lyric Opera
>**Status:** Non-Profit
>**Type:** Sponsoring
>**Purpose:** To sponsor arts programs in Teelanan County
>**Officers:** Daniel Viskochil, President; Jim Keeler, Vice President; Debbie Freed, Treasurer; Dick Sheppard, Tita Coleman
>**Budget:** $1,000 - $50,000
>**Income Sources:** Box Office; Individual Donations
>**Season:** September - June   **Annual Attendance:** 1,500

Petoskey

PERFORMING SERIES

CROOKED TREE ARTS COUNCIL
461 East Mitchell Street, Petoskey, MI 49770
(616) 347-4337
>**Founded:** 1972
>**Arts Area:** Dance; Vocal Music; Instrumental Music; Festivals
>**Status:** Non-Profit
>**Type:** Performing; Educational; Sponsoring
>**Purpose:** To sponsor and encourage cultural and educational activities in the fine arts for Charlevoix and Emmet Counties
>**Management:** Sean Ley, Executive Director
>**Officers:** Mary Fink, President; Valavra Nibblelink, Vice President for Volunteers; John Nicholson, Vice President for Finance; Otis Hardy, Secretary
>**Paid Staff:** 5   **Volunteer Staff:** 42
>**Paid Artists:** 3   **Non-Paid Artists:** 10
>**Utilizes:** Guest Conductors; Guest Artists
>**Budget:** $100,000 - $500,000
>**Income Sources:** Private Foundations/Grants/Endowments; Business/Corporate Donations; Box Office; Government Grants; Individual Donations
>**Season:** 52 Weeks   **Annual Attendance:** 22,000
>**Affiliations:** NGCSA; Michigan Association of Community Arts Agencies; Michigan Council on the Arts
>**Performance Facilities:** Virginia McCune Arts Center

Pontiac

INSTRUMENTAL MUSIC

PONTIAC-OAKLAND SYMPHONY
PO Box 431174, Pontiac, MI 48343
(313) 334-6024
>**Founded:** 1954
>**Arts Area:** Symphony; Orchestra; Chamber; Ensemble; Instrumental Group
>**Status:** Semi-Professional; Non-Profit
>**Type:** Performing; Touring; Educational; Sponsoring
>**Purpose:** To present concerts of orchestral and chamber music
>**Management:** Sheila Ashcraft, Consultant; David Daniels, Conductor; Peter Geiger, Personnel Manager
>**Officers:** David Downing, President; Adrian Spinks, Vice President; Jan Roberts, Secretary
>**Paid Staff:** 1   **Volunteer Staff:** 42
>**Paid Artists:** 35   **Non-Paid Artists:** 25
>**Utilizes:** Special Technical Talent; Guest Conductors; Guest Artists; Guest Directors
>**Budget:** $50,000 - $100,000
>**Income Sources:** Private Foundations/Grants/Endowments; Business/Corporate Donations; Box Office; Individual Donations
>**Season:** September - April   **Annual Attendance:** 3,000
>**Affiliations:** ASOL; MOA

THEATRE

ATTIC/STRAND THEATRE
12 North Saginaw, Pontiac, MI 48058
(313) 335-8100
> **Arts Area:** Professional; Musical; Theatrical Group
> **Status:** Professional; Non-Profit
> **Type:** Performing; Touring; Resident; Educational
> **Purpose:** To develop actors, directors, playwrights and technicians as craftsmen in the art of theatre; to create new works and to present new and challenging plays by contemporary playwrights
> **Management:** Lavinia Moyer, Artistic Director; ¨ Moran, Managing Director
> **Officers:** Andy Soffel, Chairman; Lavinia Moyer President; Peter C. Gray, Treasurer; Paul R. Rentenbach, Secretary
> **Paid Staff:** 15   **Volunteer Staff:** 75
> **Paid Artists:** 65
> **Utilizes:** Special Technical Talent; Guest Artists; Guest Directors
> **Budget:** $1,000,000 - $5,000,000
> **Income Sources:** Private Foundations/Grants/Endowments; Business/Corporate Donations; Box Office; Government Grants; Individual Donations
> **Season:** 52 Weeks
> **Affiliations:** TCG; FEDAPT
> **Performance Facilities:** Stand Theatre

Port Huron

INSTRUMENTAL MUSIC

INTERNATIONAL SYMPHONY ORCHESTRA OF SARNIA AND PORT HURON
PO Box 610242, Port Huron, MI 48060
(519) 337-7775; (313) 984-8857
> **Alternate Address:** 774 London Road, Sarnia, Ontario, Canada N7T 4Y1; (519) 337-7775
> **Founded:** 1956
> **Arts Area:** Symphony; Orchestra; Chamber
> **Status:** Non-Profit
> **Type:** Performing; Resident; Educational
> **Purpose:** To provide the communities of Port Huron, Michigan and Sarnia, Ontario with excellent symphonic and choral performances; to continue our committment to our "youth initiative" programs
> **Management:** Anne M. Brown, Executive Director; Zdzislaw Kopac, Music Director
> **Officers:** Bill Barill, President; Allan Peattie, Vice President; Nancy Corbett, Treasurer; Robert Fraser-Lee, Past President
> **Paid Staff:** 3
> **Paid Artists:** 5   **Non-Paid Artists:** 45
> **Utilizes:** Guest Conductors; Guest Artists
> **Budget:** $100,000 - $500,000
> **Income Sources:** Private Foundations/Grants/Endowments; Business/Corporate Donations; Box Office; Government Grants; Individual Donations; Fund-raising
> **Season:** September - May
> **Annual Attendance:** 16,000
> **Affiliations:** ASOL; MOA; Association of Canadian Orchestras; Ontario Federation of Symphony Orchestras
> **Performance Facilities:** McMorran Auditorium; SCITS Auditorium

THEATRE

PORT HURON CIVIC THEATRE
731 Griswold Street, PO Box 821, Port Huron, MI 48060
(313) 984-4014
> **Founded:** 1957
> **Arts Area:** Community; Theatrical Group
> **Status:** Semi-Professional; Non-Profit
> **Type:** Performing; Educational
> **Purpose:** To present a season of theatre each year; to educate and train; to further theatre arts
> **Officers:** Pamela Leslie, President; Nancy Osborn, Micki Lepla, Vice Presidents; Cindy Osgood, Treasurer; Viola Barr, Secretary
> **Volunteer Staff:** 150
> **Paid Artists:** 4   **Non-Paid Artists:** 200
> **Utilizes:** Guest Directors
> **Budget:** $50,000 - $100,000
> **Income Sources:** Private Foundations/Grants/Endowments; Business/Corporate Donations; Box Office; Government Grants; Individual Donations

Season: October - May
Annual Attendance: 12,000
Affiliations: Saint Clair County Community College
Performance Facilities: McMorran Place Theatre

FACILITY

MCMORRAN PLACE
701 McMorran Boulevard, Port Huron, MI 48060
(313) 985-6166
FAX: (313) 985-3358
Type of Facility: Theatre Complex; Arena; Multi-Purpose
Type of Stage: Thrust; Proscenium
Stage Dimensions: 50'Wx32'D
Orchestra Pit
Seating Capacity: 1,169
Year Built: 1959   **Architect:** Alden B. Dow & Associates
Contact for Rental: Morris Snider;   (313) 985-6166

Rochester

THEATRE

MEADOW BROOK THEATRE
Oakland University, Rochester, MI 48309-4401
(313) 370-3310
FAX: (313) 370-3108
Founded: 1967
Arts Area: Professional; Theatrical Group
Status: Professional; Non-Profit
Type: Performing; Touring
Purpose: To perform a wide variety of high-quality live theatre, from the classics to current works; to perform seven plays per season
Management: Terence Kilburn, Artistic Director; Gregg Bloomfield, Acting Managing Director; Jane Mosher, Director of Community Relations
Officers: Shirley Wells, President; Nancy Golick, Vice President; Brenda Hare, Recording Secretary; Kathie Eastman, Corresponding Secretary; Claudia Goss, Financial Secretary; Anne Parsons, Parliamentarian
Paid Staff: 42   **Volunteer Staff:** 120
Paid Artists: 70
Utilizes: Special Technical Talent; Guest Artists; Guest Directors
Budget: $1,000,000 - $5,000,000
Income Sources: Private Foundations/Grants/Endowments; Business/Corporate Donations; Box Office; Government Grants; Individual Donations
Season: October - May   **Annual Attendance:** 13,000
Affiliations: Oakland University; Concerned Citizens for the Arts in Michigan

PERFORMING SERIES

MEADOW BROOK MUSIC FESTIVAL
Oakland University, Rochester, MI 48309
(313) 370-3100
Founded: 1964
Arts Area: Dance; Vocal Music; Instrumental Music; Theater; Festivals
Status: Professional; Non-Profit
Type: Performing; Resident; Sponsoring
Purpose: To promote quality cultural and popular entertainment in the metropolitan Detroit area; summer home of the Detroit Symphony Orchestra
Paid Staff: 15   **Volunteer Staff:** 100
Paid Artists: 200
Utilizes: Special Technical Talent; Guest Conductors; Guest Artists
Budget: $1,000,000 - $5,000,000
Income Sources: Private Foundations/Grants/Endowments; Business/Corporate Donations; Box Office; Government Grants; Individual Donations
Season: June - September   **Annual Attendance:** 225,000
Performance Facilities: Howard C. Baldwin Memorial Pavilion

Rochester Hills

DANCE

OAKLAND FESTIVAL BALLET COMPANY
6841 North Rochester Road, Rochester Hills, MI 48309
(313) 652-3117
    Arts Area: Ballet
    Status: Professional; Non-Profit
    Type: Performing; Resident
    Income Sources: Box Office; Individual Donations

Saginaw

DANCE

BALLET CULTURAL AZTECA
2725 Brandon Place, Saginaw, MI 48603
(517) 793-6384
    Founded: 1978
    Arts Area: Ethnic; Folk
    Status: Professional; Non-Profit
    Type: Performing; Touring; Educational
    Purpose: Our organization is dedicated to the research, preservation, presentation and education of our Mexican culture and heritage, through the realms of dance, music and art.
    Management: Mary Lee Orozco, Artistic Director
    Officers: Linda Banda, Bookkeeper; Ida Rocha, Secretary
    Paid Staff: 3   **Volunteer Staff:** 15
    Paid Artists: 16   **Non-Paid Artists:** 2
    Utilizes: Special Technical Talent; Guest Artists; Guest Directors
    Budget: $1,000 - $50,000
    Income Sources: Box Office; Government Grants; Individual Donations
    Season: 52 Weeks   **Annual Attendance:** 11,900

INSTRUMENTAL MUSIC

SAGINAW SYMPHONY ORCHESTRA
PO Box 415, Saginaw, MI 48606
(517) 755-6471
    Founded: 1935
    Arts Area: Symphony; Orchestra
    Status: Professional; Non-Profit
    Type: Performing; Educational
    Purpose: Believing that great music can enrich the quality of life, the association will sustain an orchestra of the highest quality possible to serve audiences in the Saginaw and Bay counties. It will offer a full range of concerts and performances of music of artistic excellence.
    Management: Leo Najar, Musical Director/Conductor; Horace T. Maddux, General Manager
    Officers: Kristin Schmidt Maier, Administrative Assistant
    Paid Staff: 5   **Volunteer Staff:** 200
    Paid Artists: 80
    Utilizes: Guest Conductors; Guest Artists; Guest Directors
    Budget: $100,000 - $500,000
    Income Sources: Private Foundations/Grants/Endowments; Business/Corporate Donations; Box Office; Government Grants; Individual Donations
    Season: October - May   **Annual Attendance:** 10,000
    Affiliations: ASOL; MOA
    Performance Facilities: Heritage Theater, Saginaw Civic Center

SAGINAW SYMPHONY SCHOOL OF MUSIC AND YOUTH ORCHESTRA
PO Box 415, Saginaw, MI 48606
(517) 755-6471
    Founded: 1978
    Arts Area: Symphony; Orchestra; Chamber; Ensemble
    Status: Non-Professional; Non-Profit
    Type: Performing; Educational
    Purpose: To help area young people grow in their musical development and to help them develop an appreciation for the arts
    Management: Mrs. Toniann Amadio, Administrator

Paid Staff: 9
Non-Paid Artists: 35
Budget: $50,000 - $100,000
Income Sources: Private Foundations/Grants/Endowments; Business/Corporate Donations; Individual Donations
Season: September - May   Annual Attendance: 400
Affiliations: ASOL (Youth Orchestra Division); Saginaw Symphony Orchestra; Michigan School Band and Orchestra Association; National Guild of Community Schools of the Arts

THEATRE

TEMPLE THEATRE ORGAN CLUB
315 Court Street, Saginaw, MI 48602
(517) 793-8941; (517) 754-2575
FAX: (517) 793-7225
Founded: 1960
Status: Non-Profit
Type: Educational; Sponsoring; Historic Preservation
Purpose: To restore the Temple Theatre to its original splendor; to reestablish its prominence as a performing arts center
Management: Ken Wuepper, General Manager
Officers: Joanne Leach, President; Burt Castle, Vice President; Stanley Houser, Treasurer
Volunteer Staff: 300
Budget: $100,000 - $500,000
Income Sources: Private Foundations/Grants/Endowments; Business/Corporate Donations; Box Office; Individual Donations
Season: 52 Weeks   Annual Attendance: 100,000

FACILITY

SAGINAW CIVIC CENTER - HERITAGE THEATER
303 Johnson Street, Saginaw, MI 48607
(517) 759-1320
FAX: (517) 759-1322
Type of Facility: Theatre House
Type of Stage: Proscenium
Seating Capacity: 2,300
Year Built: 1972   Architect: Welton Becket & Associates   Cost: $11,500,000
Contact for Rental: A.C. Chapman;   (517) 759-1320
Manager: Clinton Walker;   (517) 759-1320
Resident Groups: Saginaw Symphony; Saginaw Choral Society; Town Hall

Saint Clair Shores

INSTRUMENTAL MUSIC

LAKE SAINT CLAIR SYMPHONY ORCHESTRA
21120 Benjamin, Saint Clair Shores, MI 48081
(313) 776-1012
Founded: 1961
Arts Area: Symphony; Orchestra
Status: Semi-Professional; Non-Profit
Type: Performing
Purpose: To provide the citizens of southeast Macomb County with live orchestral music programs designed to entertain our audience; to promote the artistic excellence of our constituents; to develop cultural awareness within the communities we serve
Management: Charlotte Zuraw, Executive Director
Paid Staff: 1   Volunteer Staff: 25
Paid Artists: 72
Utilizes: Guest Artists
Budget: $50,000 - $100,000
Income Sources: Private Foundations/Grants/Endowments; Business/Corporate Donations; Box Office; Government Grants; Individual Donations
Season: October - May   Annual Attendance: 6,500
Affiliations: ASOL; MOA

MACOMB CHAMBER MUSIC SOCIETY
28200 Ursuline, Saint Clair Shores, MI 48081
(313) 775-8138
Founded: 1984

Arts Area: Chamber
Status: Non-Professional; Non-Profit
Type: Sponsoring
Purpose: To present chamber music in an informal atmosphere; to provide an opportunity for musicians to perform
Officers: Thomas Ulrich, President; Jean Stanaitis, Secretary; Mae Dunn, Board Member
Utilizes: Guest Artists
Budget: $1,000 - $50,000
Income Sources: Business/Corporate Donations; Box Office; Government Grants; Individual Donations
Season: November - May   **Annual Attendance:** 200

Saint Joseph

INSTRUMENTAL MUSIC

SOUTHWEST MICHIGAN SYMPHONY ORCHESTRA
615 Broad Street, Saint Joseph, MI 49085
(616) 983-4334
Founded: 1950
Arts Area: Symphony; Orchestra
Status: Professional
Type: Performing; Educational
Purpose: To present concerts; to sponsor an orchestra as well as music educational activities
Management: Jeffrey G. White, General Manager; Robert Vodnoy, Music Director
Officers: Albert E. Vossler, President
Paid Staff: 6   **Volunteer Staff:** 1
Paid Artists: 60
Utilizes: Guest Artists
Budget: $100,000 - $500,000
Income Sources: Private Foundations/Grants/Endowments; Business/Corporate Donations; Box Office; Government Grants; Individual Donations
Season: September - June
Annual Attendance: 7,500
Performance Facilities: Mendel Center, Lake Michigan College

Southfield

INSTRUMENTAL MUSIC

LYRIC CHAMBER ENSEMBLE
3000 Town Center, Suite 1335, Southfield, MI 48075
(313) 357-1111
FAX: (313) 357-3607
Founded: 1980
Arts Area: Chamber; Ensemble
Status: Professional; Non-Profit
Type: Performing; Touring; Resident
Purpose: To provide innovative chamber music of the highest artistic quality that is accessible to all
Management: Fedora Horowitz, Artistic Director; Valerie Youa, Administrator
Officers: Tom Rhoads, Chairman; Sergio Sanchez, Vice Chairman
Paid Staff: 2   **Volunteer Staff:** 10
Paid Artists: 25
Utilizes: Guest Conductors; Guest Artists
Budget: $100,000 - $500,000
Income Sources: Private Foundations/Grants/Endowments; Business/Corporate Donations; Box Office; Government Grants; Individual Donations
Season: September - June
Annual Attendance: 9,000
Affiliations: CMA
Performance Facilities: Orchestra Hall; Music Hall; Gem Theatre; Grosse Pointe War Memorial

THEATRE

ACTORS ALLIANCE THEATRE COMPANY
30800 Evergreen Road, Southfield, MI 48076
(313) 642-1326
Founded: 1981
Arts Area: Professional; Theatrical Group

Status: Professional; Non-Profit
Type: Performing; Touring; Resident; Educational
Purpose: To nuture the human creative spirit through educational and cultural programs that encourage excellence in art and individual expression, thereby enriching the community it serves
Management: Jeffrey M. Nahan, Artistic/Executive Director; Annette DePetris, Managing Director; Lorraine Walker, Educational Coordinator
Officers: Al Sasson, Chairman
Paid Staff: 3
Paid Artists: 85
Utilizes: Guest Artists; Guest Directors
Budget: $100,000 - $500,000
Income Sources: Private Foundations/Grants/Endowments; Business/Corporate Donations; Box Office; Government Grants; Individual Donations
Season: 52 Weeks
Affiliations: TCG; AEA; Michigan Council on the Arts

Tecumseh

FACILITY

TECUMSEH CIVIC AUDITORIUM
400 North Maumee, Tecumseh, MI 49286
(517) 423-6617
Founded: 1981
Type of Facility: Theatre Complex; Concert Hall; Auditorium; Performance Center; Theatre House; Room
Type of Stage: Proscenium
Stage Dimensions: 40'Wx30'D   **Orchestra Pit**
Seating Capacity: 572
Year Built: 1981   **Architect:** Tony Marino   **Cost:** $1,750,000
Year Remodeled: 1986   **Cost:** $500,000
Contact for Rental: John S. Raeburn;   (517) 423-6617
Resident Groups: Tecumseh Youth Theatre; Tecumseh Players; Tecumseh Pops

Traverse City

INSTRUMENTAL MUSIC

TRAVERSE SYMPHONY ORCHESTRA
123 1/2 East Front Street, PO Box 1247, Traverse City, MI 49685
(616) 947-7120
Founded: 1951
Arts Area: Symphony; Orchestra; Chamber
Status: Professional
Type: Performing; Touring; Sponsoring
Management: Timothy Gunsolley, General Manager
Officers: Cheryl Knight, President
Paid Staff: 3   **Volunteer Staff:** 80
Paid Artists: 75
Utilizes: Special Technical Talent; Guest Conductors; Guest Artists
Budget: $100,000 - $500,000
Income Sources: Private Foundations/Grants/Endowments

THEATRE

OLD TOWN PLAYHOUSE
148 East Eighth, Traverse City, MI 49684
(616) 947-2210
Founded: 1959
Arts Area: Community
Status: Non-Professional; Non-Profit
Type: Performing; Educational
Purpose: To assist, encourage, promote and improve the cultural and literary development of the community through entertainment and education in the dramatic arts
Management: Mary Cassaday Jone, Executive Director; Michael Kay, Technical Director; Mary Lou Iavco-Bewley, Marketing
Officers: Cinder Conlon, President; Pat Ganter, Vice President; Larry Hains, Secretary; George Beeby, Treasurer
Paid Staff: 4   **Volunteer Staff:** 1,060

Paid Artists: 10   **Non-Paid Artists:** 1,060
Utilizes: Special Technical Talent; Guest Artists
Budget: $100,000 - $500,000
Income Sources: Private Foundations/Grants/Endowments; Business/Corporate Donations; Box Office; Government Grants; Individual Donations
Season: September - August   **Annual Attendance:** 17,000
Affiliations: Community Theatre Association of Michigan

FACILITY

DENNOS MUSEUM CENTER - MILLIKEN AUDITORIUM
1701 East Front Street, Traverse City, MI 49684
(616) 922-1055
FAX: (616) 922-1597
Type of Facility: Auditorium
Type of Stage: Open stage
Stage Dimensions: 50'x28'
Seating Capacity: 367
Year Built: 1991   **Architect:** Robert Holdeman, AIA   **Cost:** $5,200,000
Contact for Rental: Eugen Jenneman, Museum Director;   (616) 922-1572
Resident Groups: Michigan Ensemble Theatre

PARK PLACE HOTEL
300 East State Street, Traverse City, MI 49684
(616) 946-5000
Type of Facility: Multi-Purpose
Type of Stage: Platform; Arena
Seating Capacity: 729
Year Built: 1964   **Architect:** Dow Chemical Company
Resident Groups: Cherry County Playhouse
Available for rent

Troy

INSTRUMENTAL MUSIC

DETROIT CHAMBER WINDS
755 West Big Beaver, Suite 1900, Troy, MI 48082
(313) 362-2622
FAX: (313) 362-2628
Arts Area: Chamber
Status: Professional; Non-Profit
Type: Performing
Purpose: To perform works featuring between six and 20 winds
Management: H. Robert Reynolds, Artistic Advisor; Maury Okun, Executive Director
Budget: $1,000 - $50,000
Income Sources: Private Foundations/Grants/Endowments; Business/Corporate Donations; Box Office; Government Grants; Individual Donations

VOCAL MUSIC

DETROIT SYMPHONY CHORALE
2696 English Drive, Troy, MI 48098
(313) 879-9362
Arts Area: Choral
Status: Professional; Non-Profit
Type: Performing; Resident; Educational
Purpose: To serve as the main choral group of the Detroit Symphony, formerly known as the Kenneth Jewell Chorale
Management: Eric Freudigman, Director; Carol Petty, Personnel Manager
Paid Staff: 4
Paid Artists: 40
Budget: $100,000 - $500,000
Income Sources: Private Foundations/Grants/Endowments; Business/Corporate Donations; Box Office; Government Grants; Individual Donations
Season: 52 Weeks   **Annual Attendance:** 300,000
Affiliations: CA; Detroit Symphony; Detroit Symphony Chorus
Performance Facilities: Orchestra Hall

DETROIT SYMPHONY CHORUS
2696 English Drive, Troy, MI 48098
(313) 879-9362
 Arts Area: Choral
 Status: Professional; Non-Profit
 Type: Performing; Resident; Educational
 Purpose: The Detroit Symphony Chorus includes the 40-member Detroit Symphony Chorale
 Management: Eric Freudigman, Director; Carol Petty, Personnel Manager
 Paid Staff: 4
 Paid Artists: 100
 Budget: $100,000 - $500,000
 Income Sources: Private Foundations/Grants/Endowments; Business/Corporate Donations; Box Office; Government Grants; Individual Donations
 Season: 52 Weeks
 Affiliations: CA; Detroit Symphony
 Performance Facilities: Ford Auditorium; Orchestra Hall

Twin Lake

THEATRE

BLUE LAKE REPERTORY THEATRE
Route #2, Twin Lake, MI 49457
(616) 894-1966
FAX: (616) 893-5120
 Founded: 1966
 Arts Area: Summer Stock; Musical; Theatrical Group
 Status: Semi-Professional
 Type: Performing; Resident; Educational
 Purpose: To present quality summer-stock theatre for our community
 Management: Fritz Stansell, President; Reverend Walter Marek, Treasurer
 Paid Staff: 6
 Paid Artists: 14
 Budget: $50,000 - $100,000
 Income Sources: Business/Corporate Donations; Box Office; Individual Donations
 Season: July - August **Annual Attendance:** 5,000
 Affiliations: Blue Lake Fine Arts Camp
 Performance Facilities: Howmet Playhouse

Warren

INSTRUMENTAL MUSIC

WARREN SYMPHONY ORCHESTRA
4504 East Nine Mile Road, Warren, MI 48091
(313) 754-2950
FAX: (313) 755-5407
 Founded: 1972
 Arts Area: Symphony; Orchestra; Chamber; Ensemble
 Status: Semi-Professional
 Type: Performing; Resident; Educational
 Purpose: To present symphony concerts and chamber ensembles
 Management: David Daniels, Music Director
 Officers: Donald Chmura, President; Louise Anslow, Christine Bonkowski, Glen Musselman, Vice Presidents; John Ahern, Treasurer
 Paid Staff: 2 **Volunteer Staff:** 50
 Paid Artists: 45 **Non-Paid Artists:** 20
 Utilizes: Guest Artists
 Budget: $100,000 - $500,000
 Income Sources: Private Foundations/Grants/Endowments; Business/Corporate Donations; Box Office; Government Grants; Individual Donations
 Season: November - May **Annual Attendance:** 25,000
 Affiliations: ASOL; MOA
 Performance Facilities: Warren Woods Community Theater

Wyandotte

PERFORMING SERIES

DOWNRIVER COUNCIL FOR THE ARTS
2630 Biddle Avenue, Wyandotte, MI 48192
(313) 281-2787
FAX: (313) 281-0709
Founded: 1978
Arts Area: Dance; Vocal Music; Instrumental Music; Theater; Festivals
Status: Professional; Non-Profit
Type: Educational; Sponsoring
Purpose: To promote, stimulate and encourage the study and presentation of the performing and fine arts throughout the sixteen Downriver Communities
Management: Beth A. Stone, Executive Director
Officers: Raymond Lozano, Chairman of the Board; Dr. Donald F. Van Every, President
Paid Staff: 4   **Volunteer Staff:** 200
Paid Artists: 130   **Non-Paid Artists:** 35
Utilizes: Special Technical Talent; Guest Conductors; Guest Artists
Budget: $100,000 - $500,000
Income Sources: Private Foundations/Grants/Endowments; Business/Corporate Donations; Box Office; Government Grants; Individual Donations
Season: 52 Weeks

MINNESOTA

Albert Lea

FACILITY

ALBERT LEA CIVIC THEATER
147 North Broadway, Albert Lea, MN 56007
(507) 377-4371
FAX: (507) 377-4336
   Type of Facility: Concert Hall; Auditorium; Performance Center; Theatre House; Civic Center
   Facility Originally: Meeting Hall; Movie House
   Type of Stage: Proscenium
   Stage Dimensions: 28'x24'   **Orchestra Pit**
   Seating Capacity: 261
   Year Built: 1909
   Year Remodeled: 1981   **Architect:** Kilstofe   **Cost:** $650,000
   Contact for Rental: Anne Ehrhardt;   (507) 377-4372
   Resident Groups: Albert Lea Community Theatre; Minnesota Festival Theatre

Alexandria

INSTRUMENTAL MUSIC

ALEXANDRIA BIG BAND
Route 5, PO Box 92, Alexandria, MN 56308
(612) 762-2140; (612) 846-3273
   Founded: 1966
   Arts Area: Big Band; Swing
   Status: Non-Professional; Non-Profit; Commercial
   Type: Performing; Touring
   Purpose: Maintain the tradition of big band music of the past and present with an emphasis towards Glenn Miller and other big band leaders
   Officers: Bill Riggs, President; Rick Temple, Secretary; Bill Flaig, Treasurer
   Volunteer Staff: 17
   Non-Paid Artists: 17
   Budget: $1,000 - $50,000
   Income Sources: Individual Donations
   Annual Attendance: 2,000
   Affiliations: AFM

Austin

THEATRE

MATCHBOX CHILDREN'S THEATRE
PO Box 576, Austin, MN 55912
(507) 433-1931
   Arts Area: Musical; Community; Theatrical Group
   Status: Non-Profit
   Type: Performing; Resident
   Purpose: To provide quality theatre experiences for young audiences and families on a consistent basis
   Officers: Janet Anderson, President; Cynthia Dibble, Vice President; Cindy Bellrichard, Secretary; John Gray, Treasurer
   Volunteer Staff: 16
   Utilizes: Special Technical Talent; Guest Directors
   Budget: $1,000 - $50,000
   Income Sources: Private Foundations/Grants/Endowments; Business/Corporate Donations; Box Office; Government Grants; Individual Donations
   Season: September - April   **Annual Attendance:** 6,000
   Performance Facilities: Austin Community College Theatre

Bemidji

THEATRE

PAUL BUNYAN PLAYHOUSE
PO Box 752, Bemidji, MN 56601
(218) 751-7270
Founded: 1951
Arts Area: Professional; Summer Stock; Musical; Theatrical Group
Status: Professional; Non-Profit
Type: Performing; Educational
Purpose: The oldest professional summer theatre running in Minnesota, our goal is to produce the best possible theatre utilizing local and regional talent as well as interns from Bemidji State University.
Management: Jack Blanchard, Administrative Assistant Board of Directors; Michael Kissin, Artistic Director
Officers: Becky Lueben, President; Kristine Cannon, Vice President; Karen Moe, Treasurer; Sandy Johnson, Secretary
Paid Staff: 10   **Volunteer Staff:** 24
Paid Artists: 30   **Non-Paid Artists:** 15
Utilizes: Special Technical Talent; Guest Artists; Guest Directors
Budget: $100,000 - $500,000
Income Sources: Private Foundations/Grants/Endowments; Business/Corporate Donations; Box Office; Individual Donations
Season: June - August   **Annual Attendance:** 13,250
Performance Facilities: Paul Bunyan Playhouse, Old Chief Theatre

PERFORMING SERIES

HOBSON MEMORIAL UNION - PROGRAM BOARD
Bemidji State University, Bemidji, MN 56601
(218) 755-3760
FAX: (218) 755-4048
Arts Area: Dance; Vocal Music; Instrumental Music
Status: Non-Profit
Type: Performing; Sponsoring
Purpose: To provide social, cultural, and educational programs to Bemidji State University and the Bemidji Community
Paid Staff: 1
Utilizes: Guest Artists
Budget: $1,000 - $50,000
Income Sources: Private Foundations/Grants/Endowments; Student Fees
Season: September - May

FACILITY

BEMIDJI STATE UNIVERSITY - BANGSBERG FINE ARTS BUILDING
1500 Birchmont Drive NE, Bemidji, MN 56601
(218) 755-3990
FAX: (218) 755-4048
Type of Facility: Theatre Complex
Seating Capacity: Recital Hall - 250; Theatre - 300
Year Built: 1970   **Architect:** Grover Dimond   **Cost:** $3,000,000

Bloomington

FACILITY

ARTS IN THE PARKS - PORTABLE STAGE
2215 West Old Shakopee Road, Bloomington, MN 55431
(612) 887-9601, ext. 388
FAX: (612) 887-9695
Founded: 1978
Type of Facility: Auditorium; Outdoor (Concert)
Type of Stage: Platform; Portable; Showmobile
Stage Dimensions: 36'x36'
Seating Capacity: 425 - see notation
Auditorium space at the community college is used for indoor performances as part of the Arts in the Parks concert series.

Blue Earth

THEATRE

BLUE EARTH TOWN AND COUNTRY PLAYERS
PO Box 194, Blue Earth, MN 56013
(507) 526-2407
Founded: 1976
Arts Area: Musical; Community; Theatrical Group
Status: Non-Professional; Non-Profit
Type: Performing; Educational
Purpose: Creative enrichment and leisure activity for members and area community members
Officers: Mrs. Douglas Richards, President; Wayne Ankeny, Nancy Willette, Brian Roverud, Mike Ellingsen, Lil Robinson, Dr. Judith Edling
Volunteer Staff: 50
Budget: $1,000 - $50,000
Income Sources: Box Office; Individual Donations
Season: February - July   **Annual Attendance:** 2,500
Performance Facilities: Coleman Hall Auditorium

Brooklyn Center

FACILITY

BROOKLYN CENTER
6301 Shingle Creek Parkway, Brooklyn Center, MN 55430
(612) 561-5448
Type of Facility: Multi-Purpose
Year Built: 1986   **Cost:** $65,000
Summer concerts held on a weekly basis, free to the public

Chanhassen

THEATRE

CHANHASSEN DINNER THEATRE
501 West 78th, Chanhassen, MN 55417
(612) 934-1500
Founded: 1968
Arts Area: Professional; Dinner; Theatrical Group
Status: Professional
Type: Performing
Purpose: Present quality theatre and dining experience
Management: Solveig Huseth, Managing Director; Michael Brindisi, Artistic Director
Officers: Jim Jude, Chief Executive Officer; Marlin Schoep, Controller
Paid Staff: 50
Paid Artists: 40
Utilizes: Special Technical Talent; Guest Artists; Guest Directors
Budget: $5,000,000 - $10,000,000
Income Sources: Box Office
Season: 52 Weeks   **Annual Attendance:** 300,000
Affiliations: ADTI
Performance Facilities: Chanhassen Dinner Theatres

Detroit Lakes

THEATRE

PLAYHOUSE 412
PO Box 1112, Detroit Lakes, MN 56502
(612) 459-1874
Arts Area: Musical; Community; Theatrical Group
Status: Non-Profit
Type: Performing; Educational
Purpose: A community theater for the local and surrounding area; a readers theater troupe; entertainment

Officers: Sharon Santwire, President; Lind Henderson, Vice President; Gladys Holt, Secretary; Rick Pechmann, Treasurer; Shirley Gunderson; Jim Pearson; Lorren Steinhaus; Dorothy Erickson; Joyce Wieners
Volunteer Staff: 40
Utilizes: Guest Directors
Budget: $1,000 - $50,000
Income Sources: Private Foundations/Grants/Endowments; Box Office; Government Grants; Individual Donations
Season: 52 Weeks   **Annual Attendance:** 1,000

Duluth

DANCE

THE DULUTH BALLET
506 West Michigan Street, Duluth, MN 55802
(218) 722-2314; (218) 722-2904
FAX: (218) 727-8025
Founded: 1965
Arts Area: Ballet; Jazz
Status: Professional; Non-Profit
Type: Performing; Touring; Resident; Educational; Sponsoring
Purpose: To maintain a high-quality school of ballet and a company of professional dancers; to present a regular series of performances
Management: Allen Fields, Artistic Director; Vicki Taruba, General Manager; Willy McManis, Secretary/Office Administration
Officers: Mary Gummerson, President
Paid Staff: 5   **Volunteer Staff:** 28
Paid Artists: 8   **Non-Paid Artists:** 2
Utilizes: Special Technical Talent; Guest Artists; Guest Directors
Budget: $100,000 - $500,000
Income Sources: Private Foundations/Grants/Endowments; Business/Corporate Donations; Box Office; Government Grants; Individual Donations
Season: September - March   **Annual Attendance:** 6,500
Affiliations: NARB
Performance Facilities: Depot Theater; Marshall Performing Arts Center; The Deck Arena

INSTRUMENTAL MUSIC

DULUTH-SUPERIOR SYMPHONY ORCHESTRA
506 West Michigan Street, Duluth, MN 55802
(218) 727-7429
Founded: 1934
Arts Area: Symphony; Orchestra; Chamber; Ensemble
Status: Professional; Non-Profit
Type: Performing; Educational
Purpose: To generate the requisite financial and artistic resources to maintain the finest possible symphony orchestra and related programs and services. The goals are to: 1) enhance the quality of life by providing audiences with symphonic music, 2) strengthen the artistic quality of the orchestra, 3) develop future musicians and audiences and 4) generate income necessary to fulfill program and service goals of the association.
Management: Gerard Gibbs, Interim Manager; Taavo Virkhaus, Music Director/Conductor
Paid Staff: 6
Paid Artists: 88
Utilizes: Guest Artists
Budget: $100,000 - $500,000
Income Sources: Private Foundations/Grants/Endowments; Box Office; Government Grants; Individual Donations
Season: September - May   **Annual Attendance:** 20,000
Affiliations: ASOL; Saint Louis County Heritage and Arts Center
Performance Facilities: Duluth Auditorium

DULUTH-SUPERIOR YOUTH ORCHESTRA AND SINFONIA
506 West Michigan Street, Duluth, MN 55802
(218) 727-7429
FAX: (218) 722-0351
Founded: 1940
Arts Area: Symphony; Orchestra; Chamber; Ensemble
Status: Non-Professional; Non-Profit
Type: Performing; Educational
Purpose: To offer a learning and performing experience for students in the Youth Orchestra (high school) and Sinfonia (junior and senior high school)

Management: Gerard Gibbs, Interim General Manager; Jeanne Doty, Director of Sinfonia; Kevin Hoeschen, Director Youth Orchestra
Non-Paid Artists: 100
Income Sources: Box Office
Season: September - May   **Annual Attendance:** 3,000
Affiliations: ASOL (Youth Orchestra Division); Duluth-Superior Symphony Orchestra

THEATRE

COLDER BY THE LAKE
PO Box 452, Duluth, MN 55801
(218) 722-4192
> **Founded:** 1983
> **Arts Area:** Theatrical Group
> **Status:** Non-Profit
> **Type:** Performing; Touring
> **Purpose:** Colder by the Lake presents all original theater, specifically: satire, comedy and the offbeat.
> **Management:** Margaret Preus, Managing Director
> **Officers:** Harlan Quist, President; Mary Treuer, Vice President
> **Utilizes:** Guest Artists; Guest Directors
> **Budget:** $1,000 - $50,000
> **Income Sources:** Private Foundations/Grants/Endowments; Box Office
> **Season:** 52 Weeks   **Annual Attendance:** 4,000

FACILITY

THE DEPOT, ST. LOUIS CO. HERITAGE AND ARTS CENTER
506 West Michigan Street, Duluth, MN 55802
(218) 727-8025
FAX: (218) 727-8025
> **Founded:** 1979
> **Type of Facility:** Theatre Complex; Auditorium; Theatre House
> **Type of Stage:** Thrust; Proscenium
> **Stage Dimensions:** 32'x24'   **Orchestra Pit**
> **Seating Capacity:** 275
> **Year Built:** 1979
> **Contact for Rental:** Pat Shinn;   (218) 727-8025
> **Resident Groups:** Duluth Playhouse

DULUTH ENTERTAINMENT CONVENTION CENTER
350 Harbor Drive, Duluth, MN 55802
(218) 722-5573
> **Type of Facility:** Auditorium; Arena
> **Seating Capacity:** Arena - 5,600; Auditorium - 2,403
> **Year Built:** 1966   **Cost:** $6,000,000
> **Contact for Rental:** Manager;   (218) 722-5573
> **Manager:** Dan Russell, Executive Director
> **Resident Groups:** Duluth Ballet Company; Duluth-Superior Symphony Orchestra

Edina

THEATRE

CHILD'S PLAY THEATRE COMPANY
5701 Normandale Road, Room 343, Edina, MN 55424
(612) 925-5250
> **Founded:** 1984
> **Arts Area:** Musical; Theatrical Group
> **Status:** Semi-Professional; Non-Profit
> **Type:** Performing; Resident; Educational
> **Purpose:** To provide theatre education and entertainment for young people and families; premiere introductory theatre group for young people
> **Management:** Steve Barberio, Executive Director; Sandy Boren, Program Director; Bruce Wolen, Communications Director; Dave Hoaty, Production Manager; Alison Albrecht, Development Director
> **Officers:** Benjamin Auny, Chairman; Michelle Bergrud, Vice Chair; LeRona Redepenning, Secretary; David Mahler, Treasurer
> **Paid Staff:** 3   **Volunteer Staff:** 30
> **Paid Artists:** 8   **Non-Paid Artists:** 30

Utilizes: Special Technical Talent; Guest Directors
Budget: $50,000 - $100,000
Income Sources: Private Foundations/Grants/Endowments; Business/Corporate Donations; Box Office; Government Grants; Individual Donations
Season: August - July **Annual Attendance:** 15,000
Performance Facilities: Eisenhower Community Center, Hopkins

Excelsior

THEATRE

OLD LOG THEATER
5175 Meadville Street, PO Box 250, Excelsior, MN 55331
(612) 474-5951
FAX: (612) 474-1290
Founded: 1940
Arts Area: Professional; Dinner; Theatrical Group
Status: Professional
Type: Performing; Touring; Resident
Purpose: To entertain the public
Management: Don Stolz, Manager
Paid Staff: 20
Paid Artists: 20
Budget: $1,000,000 - $5,000,000
Income Sources: Box Office
Season: 52 Weeks
Performance Facilities: Old Log Theatre

Fairmont

FACILITY

THE FAIRMONT OPERA HOUSE
45 Downtown Plaza, PO Box 226, Fairmont, MN 56031
(507) 238-4900
Type of Facility: Concert Hall; Auditorium; Theatre House; Opera House
Facility Originally: Vaudeville
Type of Stage: Proscenium
Stage Dimensions: 36'6"Wx25'D
Seating Capacity: 489
Year Built: 1901 **Architect:** C.S. Dunham
Contact for Rental: Janet Roth;   (507) 238-1448
Resident Groups: Fairmont Civic Summer Theatre; Fairmont Children's Theatre

Fergus Falls

INSTRUMENTAL MUSIC

OTTER TAIL VALLEY COMMUNITY ORCHESTRA
1324 Linwood Court, Fergus Falls, MN 56537
(218) 736-3694
Founded: 1947
Arts Area: Orchestra
Status: Non-Professional; Non-Profit
Type: Performing
Purpose: To give the community the opportunity to perform or listen to orchestral music
Management: Roger Solie, Director
Officers: Duane Larson, Treasurer
Paid Staff: 1 **Volunteer Staff:** 1
Non-Paid Artists: 50
Utilizes: Guest Artists
Budget: $1,000 - $50,000
Income Sources: Box Office

Season: October - March   **Annual Attendance:** 400
Performance Facilities: Fergus Falls Community College Auditorium

THEATRE

FERGUS FALLS SUMMER COMMUNITY THEATRE
1414 College Way, Fergus Falls, MN 56537
(218) 739-7509
FAX: (218) 739-7475
Founded: 1972
Arts Area: Musical; Community; Theatrical Group
Status: Non-Professional; Non-Profit
Type: Performing; Resident; Educational
Purpose: Public-service project for local amateur performers and for area audiences
Management: James J. McDonald, Director; Geneva Eschweiler, Music Director
Paid Staff: 6   **Volunteer Staff:** 5
Paid Artists: 6   **Non-Paid Artists:** 50
Utilizes: Special Technical Talent; Guest Artists
Budget: $1,000 - $50,000
Income Sources: Business/Corporate Donations; Box Office; Government Grants; Individual Donations
Season: June - August   **Annual Attendance:** 3,000
Performance Facilities: Fergus Falls Community College Theatre

Grand Rapids

PERFORMING SERIES

THE REIF ARTS COUNCIL
800 Conifer Drive, PO Box 245, Grand Rapids, MN 55744
(218) 326-8215
Founded: 1969
Arts Area: Dance; Vocal Music; Instrumental Music; Theater
Status: Non-Profit
Type: Sponsoring
Purpose: Main project: Center Series, annual seven concerts covering theater, music and dance
Officers: Nancy Brierley, President; Caryl Kaler, Vice President; Mary Ives, Secretary; Dean Sing Sank, Treasurer
Budget: $1,000 - $50,000
Income Sources: Private Foundations/Grants/Endowments; Box Office; Government Grants
Season: October - April   **Annual Attendance:** 3,000
Performance Facilities: Reif Performing Arts Center

YOUNG ARTISTS SERIES
1851 East Highway 169, Grand Rapids, MN 55744
(218) 326-1639
Founded: 1978
Arts Area: Dance; Vocal Music; Instrumental Music
Status: Professional; Non-Profit
Type: Performing; Educational; Sponsoring
Purpose: To serve as a showcase for the emerging professional performer
Management: Ann Winberg, Director
Paid Staff: 1   **Volunteer Staff:** 4
Paid Artists: 5
Utilizes: Guest Artists
Budget: $1,000 - $50,000
Income Sources: Private Foundations/Grants/Endowments; Box Office; Government Grants
Season: September - April   **Annual Attendance:** 500
Performance Facilities: Davies Theatre

Hibbing

INSTRUMENTAL MUSIC

HIBBING COLLEGE - COMMUNITY BAND
1515 East 25th Street, Hibbing, MN 55746
(218) 262-6729
Founded: 1980
Arts Area: Band

Status: Non-Professional; Non-Profit
Type: Performing; Touring; Resident; Educational
Purpose: To rehearse and perform contemporary works for wind ensemble as well as traditional literature; to provide a social function for musicians
Management: Thomas Palmersheim, Director
Volunteer Staff: 1
Non-Paid Artists: 30
Utilizes: Guest Conductors; Guest Artists; Guest Directors
Budget: $1,000 - $50,000
Season: October - May
Performance Facilities: Hibbing Community College Auditorium

Luverne

THEATRE

GREEN EARTH PLAYERS
216 West Main Street, Luverne, MN 56156
(507) 283-9891
Founded: 1978
Arts Area: Musical; Community; Theatrical Group
Status: Non-Profit
Type: Performing
Purpose: Provide live theatre for the area
Officers: Jim Jelken, President; Dee Korthal, Vice President; Sally McFadden, Secretary; Doug Eisma, Treasurer
Volunteer Staff: 75
Paid Artists: 2
Utilizes: Guest Directors
Budget: $1,000 - $50,000
Income Sources: Business/Corporate Donations; Box Office; Government Grants; Individual Donations
Season: October - June   **Annual Attendance:** 2,500
Affiliations: ACT; Minnesota Arts Council; Southern Minnesota Arts and Humanities Council
Performance Facilities: Palace Theater

Mankato

INSTRUMENTAL MUSIC

MANKATO SYMPHONY ORCHESTRA
PO Box 645, Mankato, MN 56001
(507) 625-8880
Founded: 1952
Arts Area: Symphony; Orchestra
Status: Non-Professional; Non-Profit
Type: Performing; Resident; Educational
Purpose: To provide the regional Mankato area with fine public concerts at a minimal cost, expose students to high quality musical experiences and enrich the cultural climate of the area
Management: Mary Ann Holdrege, Executive Director
Officers: Kenneth Tate, President; Mary Ann Holdrege, Vice President/Executive Director; Jane Confer, Secretary; Dick Osborne, Treasurer
Paid Staff: 3   **Volunteer Staff:** 32
Paid Artists: 78
Utilizes: Special Technical Talent; Guest Artists
Budget: $100,000 - $500,000
Income Sources: Private Foundations/Grants/Endowments; Business/Corporate Donations; Box Office; Government Grants; Individual Donations
Season: October - May   **Annual Attendance:** 8,500
Performance Facilities: Mankato West High School Auditorium

FACILITY

MANKATO STATE UNIVERSITY - ELIAS J. HALLING RECITAL HALL
Mankato, MN 56001
Type of Facility: Concert Hall
Type of Stage: Proscenium
Seating Capacity: 352

Year Built: 1967   **Architect:** Czerny Associates   **Cost:** $2,000,000
Contact for Rental: William Lecklider

Minneapolis

DANCE

THE ETHNIC DANCE THEATRE
1940 Hennepin Avenue South, Minneapolis, MN 55403
(612) 872-0024
> **Founded:** 1974
> **Arts Area:** Ethnic
> **Status:** Semi-Professional; Non-Profit
> **Type:** Performing; Touring; Resident; Educational
> **Purpose:** The Ethnic Dance Theatre is a regional performing arts company dedicated to the artistic and dynamic traditions of ethnic dance and music. The EDT performs concerts and conducts residencies and public workshops.
> **Management:** Donald LaCourse, Jonathan Frey, Artistic Directors; Gordy Abel, Orchestra Director; Deborah Ingebretsen, Vocal Director; Sara Oxton, Company Manager
> **Officers:** Graham Thatcher, Chairman; Cindy Geiger, Vice Chairman; Jeanette Anderson, Secretary; Richard Van Puyvelde, Treasurer
> **Paid Staff:** 5
> **Paid Artists:** 26   **Non-Paid Artists:** 20
> **Utilizes:** Guest Artists; Guest Choreographers
> **Budget:** $100,000 - $500,000
> **Income Sources:** Private Foundations/Grants/Endowments; Business/Corporate Donations; Box Office; Government Grants; Individual Donations
> **Season:** October - July   **Annual Attendance:** 25,000

MINNESOTA DANCE THEATRE AND SCHOOL
528 Hennepin Avenue, Studio 5B, Minneapolis, MN 55403
(612) 338-0627
> **Founded:** 1962
> **Arts Area:** Modern; Ballet
> **Status:** Professional; Non-Profit
> **Type:** Performing; Touring; Resident; Educational
> **Purpose:** To present classical and contemporary ballet and dance school training to career-oriented performers and teachers as well as the general public
> **Management:** Loyce Houlton, Artistic Director/Founder
> **Officers:** Dr. William Houlton, President
> **Paid Staff:** 18
> **Paid Artists:** 50
> **Utilizes:** Special Technical Talent; Guest Artists
> **Budget:** $1,000,000 - $5,000,000
> **Income Sources:** Private Foundations/Grants/Endowments; Business/Corporate Donations; Box Office; Government Grants; Individual Donations
> **Season:** September - May   **Annual Attendance:** 53,000
> **Affiliations:** NARB; NASD
> **Performance Facilities:** State Theatre

NANCY HAUSER DANCE COMPANY AND SCHOOL
1940 Hennepin Avenue, Minneapolis, MN 55403
(612) 871-9077
FAX: (612) 870-0764
> **Founded:** 1961
> **Arts Area:** Modern
> **Status:** Professional; Non-Profit
> **Type:** Performing; Touring; Educational; Sponsoring
> **Purpose:** The Nancy Hauser Dance Company and School fosters, performs and teaches the constantly evolving Mary Wiginan/Hanya Holm/Nancy Hauser aesthetic of modern dance in Minnesota, the Central United States and abroad.
> **Management:** Heidi Jasmin, Artistic Director
> **Officers:** Charles Zimmerman, Chairman; Michael Tezla, Treasurer
> **Paid Staff:** 2   **Volunteer Staff:** 25
> **Paid Artists:** 10   **Non-Paid Artists:** 9
> **Utilizes:** Special Technical Talent; Guest Artists
> **Budget:** $100,000 - $500,000

Income Sources: Private Foundations/Grants/Endowments; Business/Corporate Donations; Box Office; Government Grants; Individual Donations
Season: September - June   **Annual Attendance:** 1,000
Affiliations: Minnesota Dance Alliance
Performance Facilities: Nancy Hauser Memorial Theater

NEW DANCE PERFORMANCE LAB
528 Hennepin Avenue, #205, Minneapolis, MN 55404-3
(612) 341-3050
Founded: 1981
Arts Area: Modern
Status: Professional; Non-Profit
Type: Performing; Resident; Educational
Purpose: The lab is a national resource for choreographers and other artists to investigate new ideas and develop new material.
Management: Linda Shapiro, Artistic Director
Paid Staff: 4
Paid Artists: 8
Utilizes: Guest Choreographers
Budget: $100,000 - $500,000
Income Sources: Private Foundations/Grants/Endowments; Business/Corporate Donations; Box Office; Government Grants; Individual Donations
Season: September - May   **Annual Attendance:** 8,000
Affiliations: Dance USA; Minnesota Dance Alliance
Performance Facilities: Hennepin Center for the Arts

ZENON DANCE COMPANY AND SCHOOL, INC.
528 Hennepin Avenue, Suite 400, Minneapolis, MN 55403
(612) 338-1101
Founded: 1983
Arts Area: Modern; Ballet; Jazz
Status: Professional; Non-Profit
Type: Performing; Touring; Resident; Educational
Purpose: To sustain an artistically excellent, professional dance company in the Twin Cities
Management: Linda Z. Andrews, Artistic Director; Dawn Barrett, Executive Director; Mary Jo Peloquin, Operations Manager
Officers: Diane Fridley Norman, President; Mary J. Atmore, Vice President; Cynthia A. Pickard, Treasurer; Patricia A. Timpane, Secretary
Paid Staff: 3   **Volunteer Staff:** 20
Paid Artists: 11
Utilizes: Guest Choreographers
Budget: $100,000 - $500,000
Income Sources: Private Foundations/Grants/Endowments; Business/Corporate Donations; Box Office; Government Grants; Individual Donations; Proceeds from School
Season: September - June   **Annual Attendance:** 15,000
Performance Facilities: Ordway McKnight Theatre

INSTRUMENTAL MUSIC

CONCENTUS MUSICUS
1219 University Avenue SE, Minneapolis, MN 55414
(612) 379-4463
Founded: 1966
Arts Area: Ensemble
Status: Professional; Non-Professional; Non-Profit
Type: Performing; Touring; Educational
Purpose: Concentus Musicus seeks to recreate the best works of Medieval and Renaissance music and related arts and foster an appreciation of this heritage in the community.
Management: Arthur Maud, Artistic Director; Mark Ellenberger, Administrative Director; Carole Broad, Associate Administrator
Officers: Allen Siedle, Chairman/Board of Directors; Charles Bathke, Vice Chairman
Paid Staff: 3   **Volunteer Staff:** 5
Paid Artists: 20   **Non-Paid Artists:** 30
Utilizes: Special Technical Talent
Budget: $1,000 - $50,000
Income Sources: Private Foundations/Grants/Endowments; Business/Corporate Donations; Box Office; Individual Donations
Season: September - May   **Annual Attendance:** 2,700

GREATER TWIN CITIES YOUTH SYMPHONIES
430 Oak Grove, Suite B-5, Minneapolis, MN 55403
(612) 870-7611
> **Founded:** 1972
> **Arts Area:** Symphony; Chamber; Ensemble
> **Status:** Non-Professional; Non-Profit
> **Type:** Performing; Touring; Educational
> **Purpose:** To provide the finest symphonic music experience to talented youth of the Greater Twin Cities Area in order that they might learn to grow artistically and socially, accomplished through the formation of ensembles that afford each student maximum opportunity commensurate with ability
> **Management:** Dr. William L. Jones, Music Director/Administrator; Mary Mueller, Jane Anfinson, Shantel Nelson, Administrative Assistants
> **Officers:** William Barber, Chairman of the Board; Fred Steiner, President; Kathy Cunningham, Vice President; Margaret Burchell, Treasurer
> **Paid Staff:** 10
> **Utilizes:** Special Technical Talent; Guest Artists
> **Budget:** $100,000 - $500,000
> **Income Sources:** Private Foundations/Grants/Endowments; Business/Corporate Donations; Box Office; Government Grants; Individual Donations
> **Season:** 52 Weeks **Annual Attendance:** 25,000
> **Affiliations:** ASOL; MENC
> **Performance Facilities:** Orchestra Hall; O'Shaughnessy Auditorium

THE KENWOOD CHAMBER ORCHESTRA
2020 West Lake of Theisles Parkway, Minneapolis, MN 55406
(612) 377-5095
> **Founded:** 1972
> **Arts Area:** Orchestra; Chamber
> **Status:** Non-Professional; Non-Profit
> **Type:** Performing; Touring; Educational
> **Purpose:** To give amateur musicians an opportunity to perform great music to serve the musical hunger of the Twin Cities Area
> **Officers:** Kady Stauss, President; Sarah Headley, Secretary
> **Paid Staff:** 1   **Volunteer Staff:** 8
> **Paid Artists:** 1   **Non-Paid Artists:** 44
> **Utilizes:** Guest Conductors; Guest Artists; Guest Directors
> **Budget:** $1,000 - $50,000
> **Income Sources:** Individual Donations
> **Season:** September - July   **Annual Attendance:** 4,000
> **Performance Facilities:** Walker Art Center, Minneapolis Institute of Art

MINNEAPOLIS CHAMBER SYMPHONY
100 North Sixth Street, Suite 935C, Minneapolis, MN 55403
(612) 339-0235
> **Founded:** 1978
> **Arts Area:** Orchestra; Chamber
> **Status:** Professional
> **Type:** Performing; Touring; Resident; Educational
> **Purpose:** To produce high quality, professional performances of music from the chamber orchestra repertoire
> **Management:** Jere Lantz, Music Director; Peter Dross, Executive Director; John Coughlin, General Manager
> **Officers:** John Schultz, Chair; Susan Finn, Vice Chair; Catherine Bernard, Treasurer; Angela Chicoine, Secretary
> **Paid Staff:** 4
> **Paid Artists:** 26
> **Utilizes:** Guest Artists
> **Budget:** $100,000 - $500,000
> **Income Sources:** Private Foundations/Grants/Endowments; Business/Corporate Donations; Box Office; Government Grants; Individual Donations
> **Performance Facilities:** World Theater; Walker Center

MINNEAPOLIS POPS ORCHESTRA
1611 West 32nd Street, Minneapolis, MN 55408
(612) 825-2922
> **Founded:** 1950
> **Arts Area:** Orchestra
> **Status:** Professional; Non-Profit
> **Type:** Performing
> **Purpose:** To provide free, outdoor Pops concerts for the public
> **Management:** Jere Lantz, Conductor; Cynthia Stokes, Manager; Marilyn Ford, Director of Development
> **Paid Staff:** 3

Paid Artists: 44
Utilizes: Guest Artists
Budget: $50,000 - $100,000
Income Sources: Private Foundations/Grants/Endowments; Business/Corporate Donations; Government Grants; Individual Donations
Season: June 27 - July 26   **Annual Attendance:** 30,000
Affiliations: Minneapolis Park Board; People for Minneapolis Parks Fund
Performance Facilities: Bandstand, Lake Harriet

MINNESOTA ORCHESTRAL ASSOCIATION
1111 Nicollet Mall, Minneapolis, MN 55403
(612) 371-5600
FAX: (612) 371-0838
Founded: 1903
Arts Area: Symphony; Orchestra; Chamber
Status: Professional; Non-Profit
Type: Performing; Touring; Resident; Educational; Sponsoring
Purpose: To sponsor a symphony orchestra of world renown and devote its efforts to the cultural enrichment of citizens of this region as well as national and international audiences
Management: Steve Ovitsky, General Manager; Mary Ellen Kuhi, Director of Development
Officers: Nicky Carpenter, Chairman of the Board; David Hyslop, President
Paid Staff: 67
Paid Artists: 99
Utilizes: Special Technical Talent; Guest Conductors; Guest Artists; Guest Directors
Budget: Over 10,000,000
Income Sources: Private Foundations/Grants/Endowments; Business/Corporate Donations; Box Office; Government Grants; Individual Donations
Season: 52 Weeks   **Annual Attendance:** 750,000
Affiliations: ASOL; Minnesota Orchestra, Rochester; Women's Association of the Minnesota Symphony; Young People's Symphony Concert Association; Young Audiences
Performance Facilities: Orchestra Hall; Ordway Music Theatre

MINNESOTA YOUTH SYMPHONIES
2619 Coon Rapids Boulevard, Suite 205, Minneapolis, MN 55433
(612) 755-3277
Founded: 1972
Arts Area: Symphony; Orchestra
Status: Non-Professional; Non-Profit
Type: Performing; Touring; Educational; Sponsoring
Purpose: To provide the highest possible level of musical training and experience for talented students through study, rehearsal and performance of literature
Management: Vicki Krueger, Manager; Claudette and Manny Laureno, Music Directors
Officers: Kyung Park, President; Craig Runde, Vice President; Bill Hjerpe, Treasurer; Karen Newell, Secretary
Paid Staff: 7   **Volunteer Staff:** 200
Non-Paid Artists: 300
Utilizes: Guest Conductors; Guest Artists; Guest Directors
Budget: $50,000 - $100,000
Income Sources: Private Foundations/Grants/Endowments; Business/Corporate Donations; Box Office; Individual Donations
Season: September - May   **Annual Attendance:** 10,000
Affiliations: ASOL (Youth Orchestra Division); Minnesota Citizens For The Arts; ASCAP

VOCAL MUSIC

DALE WARLAND SINGERS
120 North Fourth Street, Minneapolis, MN 55401
(612) 339-9707
FAX: (612) 339-9826
Arts Area: Grand Opera; Light Opera; Folk; Jazz; New Music
Status: Professional
Type: Performing; Touring; Educational
Purpose: To strive for the highest standards of vocal perfection; to support music of the 20th century in live and media performances and educational programs within the context of choral music; to foster the creation of new music
Management: Dale Warland, Artistic Director; Russ Bursch, Manager
Officers: Michael McCarthy, President of the Board
Budget: $500,000 - $1,000,000
Income Sources: Private Foundations/Grants/Endowments; Business/Corporate Donations; Box Office; Government Grants; Individual Donations

THE MINNESOTA CHORALE
528 Hennepin Avenue, Suite 211, Minneapolis, MN 55408
(612) 333-4866
Founded: 1972
Arts Area: Choral
Status: Semi-Professional; Non-Profit
Type: Performing
Purpose: To provide the orchestras of the Twin Cities with a symphonic chorus of the highest artistic calibre and to offer entertaining and educational concerts for area audiences
Management: Rebecca Scheele, Executive Director; Carolann Haley, Operations/Management Assistant
Officers: Joyce Gordon, President; Chris Trost, Vice President; Malcolm MacLean, Secretary; Ed Robinson, Treasurer
Paid Staff: 2   **Volunteer Staff:** 25
Paid Artists: 20   **Non-Paid Artists:** 130
Utilizes: Guest Artists
Budget: $100,000 - $500,000
Income Sources: Private Foundations/Grants/Endowments; Business/Corporate Donations; Box Office; Government Grants; Individual Donations
Season: September - June   **Annual Attendance:** 27,000
Affiliations: CA
Performance Facilities: Orchestra Hall; Ordway Music Theatre

THE MINNESOTA OPERA
620 North First Street, Minneapolis, MN 55401
(612) 221-0122
Founded: 1963
Arts Area: Lyric Opera; Light Opera; Operetta
Status: Professional; Non-Profit
Type: Performing; Touring
Purpose: The Minnesota Opera is a professional vocal/music/theater company dedicated to serving and developing audiences, artists, creators and, thus, providing the community with quality programs and creative productions of both standard and new works.
Management: Kevin H. Smith, President/General Director; Dale Johnson, Director of Artistic Planning; George Manahan, Principal Conductor
Officers: Karen Bachman, Chairperson of the Board; Philip G. Heasley, Vice President of the Board; Lucy Rosenberry Jones, Secretary; Timothy J. Admonius, Treasurer
Paid Staff: 14
Paid Artists: 50
Utilizes: Special Technical Talent; Guest Conductors; Guest Artists; Guest Directors
Budget: $1,000,000 - $5,000,000
Income Sources: Private Foundations/Grants/Endowments; Business/Corporate Donations; Box Office; Government Grants; Individual Donations
Season: October - July   **Annual Attendance:** 63,550
Affiliations: OA; Midwest Opera Theater; Minnesota Opera Association
Performance Facilities: Ordway Music Theatre

NATIONAL LUTHERAN CHOIR
3355 Hiawatha Avenue South, PO Box 6450, Minneapolis, MN 55406
(612) 722-2301
Founded: 1986
Arts Area: Choral
Status: Professional
Type: Performing
Purpose: To present sacred choral music
Management: Mark Junkert, Executive Director/General Manager
Paid Staff: 2
Paid Artists: 55   **Non-Paid Artists:** 1
Utilizes: Guest Conductors; Guest Artists
Budget: $100,000 - $500,000
Income Sources: Private Foundations/Grants/Endowments; Business/Corporate Donations; Box Office; Individual Donations
Season: September - June
Affiliations: ACA; American Lutheran Church Musicians; CA

TWIN CITIES GAY MEN'S CHORUS
528 Hennepin Avenue, Suite 701, Minneapolis, MN 55403
(612) 891-9130
Founded: 1981
Arts Area: Choral
Status: Non-Profit

Type: Performing
Officers: James Wilson, President
Paid Staff: 2   **Volunteer Staff:** 94
Non-Paid Artists: 75
Utilizes: Guest Conductors; Guest Artists
Budget: $50,000 - $100,000
Income Sources: Business/Corporate Donations; Box Office; Individual Donations
Season: September - July
Annual Attendance: 5,200
Affiliations: Hennepin Center for the Arts

THEATRE

THE CHILDREN'S THEATER COMPANY
2400 Third Avenue South, Minneapolis, MN 55404
(612) 874-0500
FAX: (612) 874-8119
Founded: 1965
Arts Area: Professional; Musical; Theatrical Group
Status: Professional
Type: Performing; Touring; Educational
Purpose: To produce significant theatre experiences for young people and their families through nuturing a creative ensemble of the highest professional quality
Management: Jon Cranney, Artistic Director; Paula Gottschalk, Executive Director
Officers: Earl Klein, Chairman; Jeff Stiefler, Carol O'Toole, Co-Vice Chairs; Caroline Loken, Secretary; Robert Scott, Treasurer
Paid Staff: 280
Utilizes: Special Technical Talent; Guest Artists; Guest Directors
Budget: $5,000,000 - $10,000,000
Income Sources: Private Foundations/Grants/Endowments; Business/Corporate Donations; Box Office; Government Grants; Individual Donations
Season: September - June
Annual Attendance: 250,000
Affiliations: TCG; ASSITEJ; AEA

COMMEDIA THEATER COMPANY
3040 Tenth Avenue South, Minneapolis, MN 55407
(612) 788-2157
Founded: 1975
Arts Area: Professional; Theatrical Group
Status: Professional
Type: Performing; Touring; Educational
Purpose: To bring direct audience contact, improvisational comedy, to communities that don't usually see live theater
Management: Linda Bruning, General Manager; Rudd Rayfield, Office and Booking Manager
Volunteer Staff: 2
Paid Artists: 6
Budget: $1,000 - $50,000
Income Sources: Private Foundations/Grants/Endowments; Box Office; Sponsors
Season: 52 Weeks

THE CRICKET THEATRE
1407 Nicollet Avenue, Minneapolis, MN 55403
(612) 871-3763
FAX: (612) 871-0291
Founded: 1971
Arts Area: Professional; Theatrical Group
Status: Professional; Non-Profit
Type: Performing; Touring; Resident; Educational; Sponsoring
Purpose: The Cricket Theatre is a fully professional theatre dedicated to the production of works by emerging playwrights.
Management: William Partlan, Artistic Director
Officers: Don Arbour, Chairman; William Partlan, President
Paid Staff: 5   **Volunteer Staff:** 3
Paid Artists: 50
Utilizes: Guest Artists; Guest Directors
Budget: $500,000 - $1,000,000
Income Sources: Private Foundations/Grants/Endowments; Business/Corporate Donations; Box Office; Government Grants; Individual Donations
Season: September - June

Annual Attendance: 20,000
Affiliations: The Network; TCG
Performance Facilities: The Cricket Theatre

THE GUTHRIE THEATRE
725 Vineland Place, Minneapolis, MN 55403
(612) 377-2224; (612) 347-1100
FAX: (612) 347-1188
    Founded: 1963
    Arts Area: Professional
    Status: Professional; Non-Profit
    Type: Performing; Touring; Resident
    Purpose: To present, in rotating repertory, classical plays—both ancient and modern—by a resident company of actors
    Management: Garland Wright, Artistic Director; Edward Martenson, Executive Director
    Officers: Ronald James, President; Mary Vaughan, Chairperson; DeWalt Ankeny Jr., Treasurer; Sarah Anderson, Secretary
    Paid Staff: 115 **Volunteer Staff:** 225
    Paid Artists: 231
    Utilizes: Special Technical Talent; Guest Artists; Guest Directors
    Budget: $5,000,000 - $10,000,000
    Income Sources: Private Foundations/Grants/Endowments; Business/Corporate Donations; Box Office; Government Grants; Individual Donations
    Season: June - March
    Annual Attendance: 400,000
    Affiliations: LORT
    Performance Facilities: The Guthrie Theater

ILLUSION THEATER
528 Hennepin Avenue, Suite 704, Minneapolis, MN 55403
(612) 339-4944
    Founded: 1974
    Arts Area: Professional; Theatrical Group
    Status: Professional; Non-Profit
    Type: Performing; Touring; Resident; Educational; Sponsoring
    Management: Michael Robins, Executive Director; Cordelia Anderson, Prevention Program Director; Bonnie Morris, Producing Director; John Montilino, Managing Director
    Officers: Cecily Hines, Board President
    Paid Staff: 5
    Utilizes: Special Technical Talent; Guest Artists; Guest Directors
    Income Sources: Private Foundations/Grants/Endowments; Business/Corporate Donations; Box Office; Government Grants; Individual Donations
    Season: February - July
    Affiliations: AEA; SPTA
    Performance Facilities: Hennepin Center For The Arts

IN THE HEART OF THE BEAST PUPPET AND MASK THEATRE
1500 East Lake Street, Minneapolis, MN 55407
(612) 721-2535
    Founded: 1973
    Arts Area: Professional; Theatrical Group; Puppet
    Status: Professional; Non-Profit
    Type: Performing; Touring; Resident; Educational; Sponsoring
    Purpose: To entertain and enrich audiences of all ages and cultures through puppetry and mask; to build a relationship between artist and audience; to be an active participant in the dialogue of our times
    Management: Sandy Spieler, Artistic Director; Beth Peterson, Outreach Director; Nadya Reubenova, Executive Director; Heather Baum, Development Director
    Officers: Judy Tilsen, Chair; Rosemary Williams, Vice Chair; Julie Stoneberg, Secretary; David Emerson, Treasurer
    Paid Staff: 13 **Volunteer Staff:** 300
    Paid Artists: 150
    Utilizes: Special Technical Talent; Guest Artists; Guest Directors
    Budget: $500,000 - $1,000,000
    Income Sources: Private Foundations/Grants/Endowments; Business/Corporate Donations; Box Office; Government Grants; Individual Donations
    Season: 52 Weeks
    Annual Attendance: 50,000
    Affiliations: Alliance for Cultural Democracy; Network; Minnesota Citizens for the Arts

JACKSON MARIONETTE PRODUCTIONS
2107 Perry Avenue North, Minneapolis, MN 55422
(612) 588-3629
Arts Area: Professional; Puppet
Status: Professional
Type: Performing; Touring
Management: Sara Jackson, Manager
Volunteer Staff: 1
Paid Artists: 1
Utilizes: Special Technical Talent
Budget: $1,000 - $50,000
Income Sources: Box Office
Season: 52 Weeks
Affiliations: Puppeteers of America; UNIMA; Twin City Puppeteers

MIXED BLOOD THEATRE COMPANY
1501 South Fourth Street, Minneapolis, MN 55454
(612) 338-6131
Founded: 1976
Arts Area: Theatrical Group
Status: Professional; Non-Profit
Type: Performing; Touring; Educational
Purpose: Professional, multiracial theatre ensemble utilizing "colorblind casting," dedicated to the spirit of Dr. King's dream
Management: Jack Reuler, Managing Artistic Director; Charlie Moore, Marketing Director; Kim Walton, Director of Development; Christine Nelson, Associate Producer
Paid Staff: 125
Paid Artists: 125
Utilizes: Guest Artists; Guest Directors
Budget: $100,000 - $500,000
Income Sources: Private Foundations/Grants/Endowments; Business/Corporate Donations; Box Office; Government Grants; Individual Donations
Season: September - May   **Annual Attendance:** 80,000
Affiliations: AEA; ASCAP

NEW MUSIC-THEATER ENSEMBLE
620 North First Street, Minneapolis, MN 55401
(612) 333-2700
FAX: (612) 333-0869
Arts Area: Professional
Status: Professional; Non-Profit
Type: Performing; Educational
Purpose: To develop and produce new musical theater works; to nurture the creative artist
Management: Ben Krywosz, Karen Miller, Co-Artistic Directors; Marge Betley, Managing Director
Budget: $100,000 - $500,000
Income Sources: Private Foundations/Grants/Endowments; Box Office; Government Grants

THE PLAYWRIGHTS' CENTER
2301 Franklin Avenue East, Minneapolis, MN 55406
(612) 332-7481
FAX: (612) 332-6037
Founded: 1971
Arts Area: Playwright Service Organization
Status: Non-Profit
Type: Touring; Educational; Sponsoring; Developmental Workshops; Reading
Purpose: To fuel the contemporary theatre by providing services that support the development and public appreciation of playwrights and playwriting
The Playwrights' Center fuels the contemporary theater by providing services that support the development and public appreciation of playwrights and playwriting.
Management: David Moore Jr., Executive Director
Officers: Emily Ann Staples, President, Board of Directors
Paid Staff: 8
Paid Artists: 200
Utilizes: Guest Artists; Guest Directors
Budget: $100,000 - $500,000
Income Sources: Private Foundations/Grants/Endowments; Business/Corporate Donations; Government Grants; Individual Donations

Season: 52 Weeks
Affiliations: AEA; TCG

RED EYE COLLABORATION
15 West 14th Street, Minneapolis, MN 55403
(612) 870-7531
Founded: 1983
Arts Area: Theatrical Group
Status: Professional; Non-Profit
Type: Performing; Touring; Resident; Educational
Purpose: An experimental theatre company committed to the development of multimedia theater productions
Management: Miriam Must, Managing Director; Steve Busa, Artistic Director; Karen Sauro, Marketing Director; Tim Heins, Production and Facility Manager
Officers: Peter Wold, President; David Kelley, Vice President; Terry Barczak, Secretary/Treasurer; Steve Busa, Andrea Fike, Lauren Marks, Miriam Must, Cheryl Rantala, Judy Thompson, Directors
Paid Staff: 4   **Volunteer Staff:** 2
Utilizes: Special Technical Talent; Guest Artists; Guest Directors
Budget: $100,000 - $500,000
Income Sources: Private Foundations/Grants/Endowments; Business/Corporate Donations; Box Office; Government Grants; Individual Donations
Season: January - November
Annual Attendance: 4,500
Affiliations: NEA; Dayton Hudson Foundation; Jerome Foundation; McKnight Foundation; United Artists; Metropolitan Regional Arts Council
Performance Facilities: Red Eye's 14th Street Theatre

THEATRE DE LA JEUNE LUNE
105 First Street North, Minneapolis, MN 55401
(612) 332-3968
Founded: 1978
Arts Area: Professional; Theatrical Group
Status: Non-Profit
Type: Performing; Touring
Purpose: To produce dynamic, energetic and immediate theatre through scripted material and company creations
Management: Robert Rosen, Barbra Berlovitz-Desbois, Dominique Serrand, Vincent Gracieux, Artistic Directors; Kit Waickman, Business Director; Jennifer Halcrow, Development Director; Steve Richardson, Marketing Director
Paid Staff: 3   **Volunteer Staff:** 4
Paid Artists: 7   **Non-Paid Artists:** 10
Budget: $500,000 - $1,000,000
Income Sources: Private Foundations/Grants/Endowments; Business/Corporate Donations; Box Office; Government Grants; Individual Donations
Season: September - May
Annual Attendance: 20,000
Affiliations: FEDAPT

THEATRE IN THE ROUND PLAYERS
245 Cedar Avenue, Minneapolis, MN 55454
(612) 333-3010
Founded: 1953
Arts Area: Community
Status: Non-Professional; Non-Profit
Type: Performing; Resident; Educational
Purpose: To serve as a bridge between amateur and professional theatre; to entertain and educate the community with quality drama
Management: Steve Antenucci, Managing Director
Officers: Jan Hilton, President; David Hancox, Vice President; Sheri Sheeks, Secretary; Lee Wilwerding, Treasurer
Paid Staff: 4   **Volunteer Staff:** 150
Paid Artists: 10   **Non-Paid Artists:** 250
Utilizes: Special Technical Talent; Guest Artists; Guest Directors
Budget: $100,000 - $500,000
Income Sources: Private Foundations/Grants/Endowments; Business/Corporate Donations; Box Office; Government Grants; Individual Donations
Season: 52 Weeks
Annual Attendance: 20,000
Affiliations: AACT; Minnesota Association of Community Theatres
Performance Facilities: Theatre-in-the-Round

TROUPE AMERICA INC.
528 Hennepin Avenue, Suite 206, Minneapolis, MN 55403
(612) 333-3302
FAX: (612) 333-4337
Founded: 1987
Arts Area: Professional; Musical; Theatrical Group
Status: Professional; Commercial
Type: Performing; Touring; Resident; Sponsoring
Purpose: To provide top quality theatrical experiences for our audiences, on the road and in the Twin Cities
Management: Curtis N. Wollan, Producing Director; John Tsafoxannis, Associate Producer; Thomas Hailey, Production Manager; Jane Allen, Office Manager
Officers: Curtis N. Wollan, President; Jane Wollan, Secretary/Treasurer
Paid Staff: 7
Paid Artists: 40
Utilizes: Special Technical Talent; Guest Artists; Guest Directors
Budget: $1,000,000 - $5,000,000
Income Sources: Box Office; Producing Fees; Booking Agents
Season: 52 Weeks   **Annual Attendance:** 540,000
Affiliations: SETC
Performance Facilities: Plymouth Playhouse, Minneapolis; Venetian Playhouse, St. Paul

WALKER ART CENTER
Vineland Place, Minneapolis, MN 55403
(612) 375-7600
FAX: (612) 375-7618
Arts Area: Professional
Status: Non-Profit
Type: Performing; Touring; Resident; Educational; Sponsoring; Exhibition
Purpose: To serve as an international and regional catalyst for new forms of expression while engaging the audience in the issues shaping the arts of our time
Management: Kathy Halbreich, Director
Officers: Gary Capen, President of the Board
Income Sources: Private Foundations/Grants/Endowments; Business/Corporate Donations; Box Office; Government Grants; Individual Donations
Season: 52 Weeks
Performance Facilities: Walker Art Center Auditorium

THE WORLD TREE PUPPET THEATER
3305 East Calhoun Parkway, Minneapolis, MN 55408
(612) 824-3112
Founded: 1982
Arts Area: Professional; Puppet
Status: Professional
Type: Performing; Touring; Resident
Purpose: To use the traditions of puppetry and adaptations of folklore to entertain families and children; to employ experimental uses of puppets, dolls and masks for adult theater
Management: Joan Mickelson, Director
Paid Staff: 1
Paid Artists: 4
Utilizes: Guest Artists
Budget: $1,000 - $50,000
Income Sources: Private Foundations/Grants/Endowments; Box Office; Government Grants; Individual Donations

PERFORMING SERIES

MACPHAIL CENTER FOR THE ARTS
1128 LaSalle Avenue, Minneapolis, MN 55403
(612) 627-4020
Founded: 1907
Arts Area: Vocal Music; Instrumental Music
Status: Semi-Professional; Non-Profit
Type: Educational
Purpose: MacPhail Center, a part of the continuing education program of, and an extension of, the University of Minnesota, is one of the nation's oldest and largest community music schools, offering lessons and classes in music to both adults and young people of all ages and levels.

Management: Joanna Cortright, Assistant Director
Paid Staff: 110   **Volunteer Staff:** 20
Utilizes: Guest Artists
Budget: $1,000,000 - $5,000,000
Income Sources: Private Foundations/Grants/Endowments; Business/Corporate Donations; Government Grants; Individual Donations
Season: 52 Weeks   **Annual Attendance:** 5,000
Affiliations: University of Minnesota; National Guild of Community Schools of Music

MINNESOTA ORCHESTRA
1111 Nicollet Mall, Minneapolis, MN 55403
(612) 371-5600
FAX: (612) 371-0838
Founded: 1903
Arts Area: Vocal Music; Instrumental Music; Festivals; Grand Opera
Status: Professional; Non-Profit
Type: Performing; Touring; Resident; Educational; Sponsoring
Purpose: To enrich and inspire the community through the highest quality performances of great music; provide the vision and leadership necessary to support, in a fiscally responsible manner a symphony orchestra internationally recognized for its artistic excellence and innovation
Management: David J. Hyslop, President; Steven A. Ovitsky, Vice President/General Manager; Mary Ellen Kuhi, Development Director; Edward Gill, Finance Director; Mary Loiselle, Director of Public Affairs; Helen Franczyk Roberts, Marketing Director; Asadour A. Santourian, Music Administrator
Officers: Nicky Carpenter, Chairman of the Board
Paid Staff: 800
Paid Artists: 250
Utilizes: Special Technical Talent; Guest Conductors; Guest Artists; Guest Directors
Budget: Over 10,000,000
Income Sources: Private Foundations/Grants/Endowments; Business/Corporate Donations; Box Office; Government Grants; Individual Donations
Season: 52 Weeks   **Annual Attendance:** 444,036

NORTHROP DANCE SERIES
84 Church Street SE, Minneapolis, MN 55455
(612) 625-6600
FAX: (612) 624-6369
Founded: 1919
Arts Area: Dance
Status: Professional
Type: Sponsoring
Purpose: To present a series of six to eight dance companies each year of the highest artistic quality
Management: Dale Schatzlein, Director
Paid Staff: 13   **Volunteer Staff:** 350
Utilizes: Touring Companies
Budget: $1,000,000 - $5,000,000
Income Sources: Private Foundations/Grants/Endowments; Business/Corporate Donations; Box Office; Government Grants; Individual Donations
Season: October - May
Affiliations: APAP; ISPAA
Performance Facilities: Northrop Memorial Auditorium

PLYMOUTH MUSIC SERIES OF MINNESOTA
1900 Nicollet Avenue, Minneapolis, MN 55403
(612) 870-0943
FAX: (612) 870-9962
Founded: 1969
Arts Area: Vocal Music
Status: Professional; Non-Profit
Type: Performing; Educational; Sponsoring
Purpose: To present choral/orchestral performances of newly commissioned and deserving but rarely heard works
Management: Philip Brunelle, Executive Director; Frank Stubbs, General Manager
Paid Staff: 8   **Volunteer Staff:** 3
Paid Artists: 80   **Non-Paid Artists:** 75
Utilizes: Guest Artists
Budget: $500,000 - $1,000,000
Income Sources: Private Foundations/Grants/Endowments; Business/Corporate Donations; Box Office; Government Grants; Individual Donations
Season: September - May   **Annual Attendance:** 15,000

FACILITY

THE CHILDREN'S THEATRE COMPANY
2400 Third Avenue South, Minneapolis, MN 55404
(612) 874-0500
FAX: (612) 874-8119
   Founded: 1965
   Type of Facility: Theatre House
   Type of Stage: Proscenium
   Stage Dimensions: 90'x90'x40'   **Orchestra Pit**
   Seating Capacity: 746
   Year Built: 1974   **Architect:** Kenzo Tange   **Cost:** $4,000,000
   Acoustical Consultant: Bolt, Beranek & Newman
   Contact for Rental: Donna Bachman;   (612) 874-0500
   Manager: Lynn Von Eschen
   Resident Groups: The Children's Theatre Company

THE GUTHRIE THEATER
725 Vineland Place, Minneapolis, MN 55403
(612) 347-1100
FAX: (612) 347-1188
   Type of Facility: Theatre Complex
   Type of Stage: Thrust; Flexible
   Stage Dimensions: 32'x36'
   Seating Capacity: 1,441
   Year Built: 1963   **Architect:** Ralph Rapson & Associates   **Cost:** $2,250,000
   Acoustical Consultant: Robert Lambert
   Contact for Rental: Sue McLean;   (612) 347-1161
   Resident Groups: Guthrie Theater Acting Company

HENNEPIN CENTER FOR THE ARTS
528 Hennepin Avenue, Minneapolis, MN 55403
(612) 332-4478
FAX: (612) 340-1255
   Founded: 1979
   Type of Facility: Theatre Complex; Auditorium; Studio Performance; Performance Center; Theatre House; Multi-Purpose; Room; Dance Studio
   Facility Originally: Ballroom; Mason Temple
   Stage Dimensions: 45'x35'
   Year Built: 1888   **Architect:** Long and Kees   **Cost:** $359,525
   Year Remodeled: 1979   **Architect:** Vern Svedberg   **Cost:** $5,500,000
   Acoustical Consultant: John Linnerson
   Contact for Rental: Doris Overby;   (612) 332-4478
   Temporary and permanent space for performing artists, dancers and writers/publishers; Audition and rehearsal space available; Video and filming accommodated; Classes offered

MACPHAIL CENTER FOR THE ARTS
1128 LaSalle Avenue, Minneapolis, MN 55403
(612) 627-4020
   Founded: 1907
   Type of Facility: Auditorium; No fixed seating
   Facility Originally: School
   Type of Stage: Proscenium
   Stage Dimensions: 32'Wx24'D
   Seating Capacity: 250
   Year Built: 1923   **Architect:** Magney & Associates
   Educational

ORCHESTRA HALL
1111 Nicollet Mall, Minneapolis, MN 55403
(612) 371-5600
   Type of Facility: Concert Hall
   Type of Stage: Proscenium
   Stage Dimensions: 45'x71'x32'
   Seating Capacity: 2,465
   Year Built: 1974   **Architect:** Hardy Holzman Pfeiffer Associates   **Cost:** $15,000,000
   Acoustical Consultant: Dr. Cyril Harris
   Contact for Rental: Susan Diffatte;   (612) 371-5633

Manager: Steven Ovitsky
Resident Groups: Minnesota Orchestra

THEATRE IN THE ROUND
245 Cedar Avenue, Minneapolis, MN 55454
(612) 333-3010
Type of Facility: Theatre House; Arena
Facility Originally: Warehouse
Type of Stage: Arena
Stage Dimensions: 20'x28'
Seating Capacity: 261
Year Remodeled: 1969   **Architect:** Ralph Rapson & Associates   **Cost:** $75,000
Contact for Rental: Steven Antenucci;   (612) 333-3010
Resident Groups: Theatre in the Round Players

Moorhead

PERFORMING SERIES

MOORHEAD STATE UNIVERSITY
1104 Seventh Avenue South, Moorhead, MN 56563
(218) 236-2764
FAX: (218) 236-2168
Arts Area: Dance; Vocal Music; Instrumental Music; Theater
Status: Professional; Non-Profit
Type: Performing; Educational; Sponsoring
Purpose: To provide cultural programming of the highest calibre to the community and campus audiences
Management: Kathy Friese, Director, Performing Arts Series
Paid Staff: 3
Paid Artists: 75
Utilizes: Guest Artists
Budget: $50,000 - $100,000
Income Sources: Private Foundations/Grants/Endowments; Box Office; Government Grants; Individual Donations
Season: September - May   **Annual Attendance:** 5,000
Performance Facilities: Center for the Arts Auditorium

New Hope

THEATRE

OFF-BROADWAY MUSICAL THEATRE
3243 Flag Avenue North, New Hope, MN 55427
(612) 544-3810
Founded: 1979
Arts Area: Community
Status: Non-Profit
Type: Performing
Purpose: To produce major musicals using local talent in varying degrees of proficiency at every age
Officers: Barb Nordberg, President; Joan Hastings, Vice President; Keith Struck, Secretary; Dan Nordberg, Treasurer
Volunteer Staff: 11
Utilizes: Special Technical Talent; Guest Conductors; Guest Directors
Budget: $1,000 - $50,000
Income Sources: Box Office
Season: 52 Weeks   **Annual Attendance:** 5,000
Affiliations: Minnesota State Arts Council
Performance Facilities: New Hope Outdoor Theatre; Brooklyn Center Civic Center

FACILITY

NEW HOPE OUTDOOR THEATRE
4401 Xylon Avenue North, New Hope, MN 55428
(612) 531-5153
Type of Facility: Outdoor (Concert)
Type of Stage: Thrust
Stage Dimensions: 36'x44'; Second Floor - 360 square feet   **Orchestra Pit**
Seating Capacity: 500
Year Built: 1986   **Architect:** Bernard Herman   **Cost:** $75,000

Resident Groups: Off-Broadway Musical Theatre
Performances of off-Broadway musical theatre; theatre classes

---

New Ulm

VOCAL MUSIC

THE CONCORD SINGERS OF NEW ULM
PO Box 492, New Ulm, MN 56073
(507) 354-8850
> **Founded:** 1931
> **Arts Area:** Choral; Ethnic
> **Status:** Non-Professional; Non-Profit
> **Type:** Performing; Sponsoring
> **Purpose:** Good singing, fellowship and good will extended to the enjoyment and culture of the people and development of the musical art and promotion of community relations for the city of New Ulm; to keep alive the German language through the songs we sing
> **Management:** Leo H. Berg, Manager; Bob Beusmann, Director
> **Officers:** Gary Kliunek, President; Wally Ebert, Vice President; Fremont Franta, Secretary; Phil Vareuerk, Treasurer
> **Utilizes:** Guest Artists
> **Budget:** $1,000 - $50,000
> **Income Sources:** Business/Corporate Donations; Box Office
> **Season:** 52 Weeks

Northfield

INSTRUMENTAL MUSIC

BACH SOCIETY OF MINNESOTA
1114 Lia Court, Northfield, MN 55057
(507) 645-5209
FAX: (507) 663-3549
> **Founded:** 1933
> **Arts Area:** Orchestra; Chamber; Ensemble
> **Status:** Semi-Professional; Non-Profit
> **Type:** Performing; Educational
> **Purpose:** The Bach Society of Minnesota is dedicated to studying and performing choral music with an emphasis on 18th century music and earlier; to pursue a committment to stylistic integrity and excellence as epitomized by Johanne Sebastian Bach
> **Management:** Paul Oakley, Music Director
> **Officers:** Pater Bolsted, Treasurer
> **Paid Staff:** 3
> **Paid Artists:** 7   **Non-Paid Artists:** 75
> **Utilizes:** Guest Artists
> **Budget:** $50,000 - $100,000
> **Income Sources:** Private Foundations/Grants/Endowments; Business/Corporate Donations; Box Office; Government Grants; Individual Donations
> **Season:** September - May   **Annual Attendance:** 5,000

PERFORMING SERIES

CARLETON COLLEGE CONCERT SERIES
One North College Street, Northfield, MN 55057
(507) 663-4354
FAX: (507) 633-4347
> **Founded:** 1945
> **Arts Area:** Vocal Music; Instrumental Music
> **Status:** Professional; Non-Profit
> **Type:** Educational; Sponsoring
> **Purpose:** To provide music excellently performed, as an important part of our educational program
> **Management:** Harry Nordstrom, Concert Manager
> **Paid Staff:** 1
> **Paid Artists:** 5
> **Utilizes:** Guest Artists
> **Budget:** $1,000 - $50,000
> **Season:** September - May 15   **Annual Attendance:** 2,000
> **Performance Facilities:** Carleton Concert Hall; Skinner Chapel

---

Owatonna

THEATRE

LITTLE THEATRE OF OWATONNA
Dunell Drive, PO Box 64, Owatonna, MN 55060
(507) 451-0764
Founded: 1966
Arts Area: Theatrical Group
Status: Non-Professional; Non-Profit
Type: Performing
Purpose: Bring performing arts to the community, especially theatre
Management: Sharon Stark, Executive Secretary
Officers: Matt Kottke, President; Lois Vranesh, Vice President; Gail Plathe, Secretary & Treasurer
Utilizes: Guest Directors
Budget: $1,000 - $50,000
Income Sources: Box Office; Individual Donations
Season: September - July   **Annual Attendance:** 8,000

Rochester

INSTRUMENTAL MUSIC

ROCHESTER CIVIC MUSIC
City Hall, Room 109, Rochester, MN 55902
(507) 281-6005
FAX: (507) 285-8256
Founded: 1869
Arts Area: Symphony; Orchestra; Chamber; Ensemble; Ethnic; Folk; Instrumental Group; Band
Status: Professional; Government Agency
Type: Performing; Touring; Resident; Educational; Sponsoring
Purpose: To provide a comprehensive and coordinated music program
Management: Steven Schmidt, General Manager
Officers: Richard Edwards, President; Ann Grooves, Vice President; Dan Kutzke, Treasurer; Martha Casey; Robert Pettit, Past President
Paid Staff: 5   **Volunteer Staff:** 25
Paid Artists: 150
Utilizes: Special Technical Talent; Guest Conductors; Guest Artists
Budget: $500,000 - $1,000,000
Income Sources: Private Foundations/Grants/Endowments; Business/Corporate Donations; Box Office; Government Grants; Individual Donations; Government Tax Levy
Season: 52 Weeks
Performance Facilities: Mayo Civic Center

ROCHESTER SYMPHONY ORCHESTRA
City Hall, Room 109, Rochester, MN 55902
(507) 281-6005
FAX: (507) 285-8256
Founded: 1869
Arts Area: Symphony; Orchestra; Chamber; Ensemble; Band
Status: Professional; Non-Professional; Non-Profit
Type: Performing; Touring; Resident; Educational
Management: Steven J. Schmidt, General Manager; Dr. Jere Lantz, Music Director
Officers: Richard Edwards, President
Paid Staff: 7   **Volunteer Staff:** 26
Paid Artists: 80
Utilizes: Special Technical Talent; Guest Conductors; Guest Artists; Guest Directors
Budget: $100,000 - $500,000
Income Sources: Private Foundations/Grants/Endowments; Business/Corporate Donations; Box Office; Government Grants; Individual Donations
Season: September - May   **Annual Attendance:** 45,000
Performance Facilities: Mayo Civic Auditorium

THEATRE

ROCHESTER CIVIC THEATRE
220 East Center Street, Rochester, MN 55904
(507) 282-8481
Founded: 1951
Arts Area: Community
Status: Non-Professional; Non-Profit
Type: Performing; Touring; Educational
Purpose: To promote interest in and enjoyment of the dramatic arts through educational and recreational programs and productions
Management: Russell Wiseman, Artistic/Executive Director
Officers: Glenna Wasko, President
Paid Staff: 6 **Volunteer Staff:** 300
Utilizes: Special Technical Talent; Guest Directors
Budget: $100,000 - $500,000
Income Sources: Private Foundations/Grants/Endowments; Business/Corporate Donations; Box Office; Government Grants; Individual Donations
Season: September - July **Annual Attendance:** 33,000
Affiliations: ACT; Minnesota Association of Community Theatres

FACILITY

MAYO CIVIC CENTER
30 Civic Center Drive SE, Rochester, MN 55904
(507) 281-6184
Type of Facility: Theatre Complex; Civic Center
Year Built: 1938 **Architect:** Ellerbe Architects **Cost:** $450,000
Year Remodeled: 1986 **Architect:** Ellerbe Architects **Cost:** $18,000,000
Acoustical Consultant: Bolt, Beranek & Newman
Contact for Rental: Director of Promotions; (507) 281-6184
Resident Groups: Rochester Symphony Orchestra; Minnesota Symphony
Mayo Civic Center contains the Arena, Auditorium and Theatre. See separate listings for additional information.

MAYO CIVIC CENTER - ARENA
30 Second Avenue SE, Rochester, MN 55904
(507) 281-6184
FAX: (507) 281-6277
Founded: 1938
Type of Facility: Auditorium
Type of Stage: Flexible
Orchestra Pit
Seating Capacity: 3,400
Year Built: 1938
Year Remodeled: 1986
Contact for Rental: Director of Promotions; (507) 281-6184
Resident Groups: Rochester Symphony Orchestra; Minnesota Orchestra

MAYO CIVIC CENTER - AUDITORIUM
30 Civic Center Drive SE, Rochester, MN 55904
(507) 281-6184
FAX: (507) 281-6277
Founded: 1938
Type of Facility: Auditorium
Type of Stage: Flexible; Hydraulic Lift Pit
Stage Dimensions: 80'Wx40'D **Orchestra Pit**
Seating Capacity: 3,400
Year Built: 1938
Year Remodeled: 1986
Contact for Rental: Director of Promotions; (507) 281-6184
Resident Groups: Rochester Symphony Orchestra; Minnesota Orchestra

MAYO CIVIC CENTER - THEATRE
30 Civic Center Drive SE, Rochester, MN 55904
(507) 281-6184
Type of Facility: Theatre House
Type of Stage: Proscenium
Stage Dimensions: 62'Wx25'D **Orchestra Pit**

Seating Capacity: 1,340
Year Built: 1938
Year Remodeled: 1986
Contact for Rental: Director of Promotions;   (507) 281-6184

Saint Cloud

INSTRUMENTAL MUSIC

CHAMBER MUSIC SOCIETY OF ST. CLOUD, INC.
PO Box 205, Saint Cloud, MN 56302
(612) 221-0382
Arts Area: Chamber
Status: Non-Profit
Type: Presenting
Purpose: To present high-quality chamber music concerts in central Minnesota
Management: Susan Dubin, Executive Director
Budget: $1,000 - $50,000
Income Sources: Private Foundations/Grants/Endowments; Business/Corporate Donations; Box Office; Government Grants; Individual Donations
Performance Facilities: Atonement Lutheran Church; First United Methodist Church

Saint Joseph

FACILITY

COLLEGE OF SAINT BENEDICT - BENEDICTA ARTS CENTER
Saint Joseph, MN 56374-2099
(612) 363-5777
Type of Facility: Theatre Complex; Multi-Purpose
Year Built: 1964   **Architect:** Hammel Green & Abrahamson   **Cost:** $2,750,000
Contact for Rental: Director of Fine Arts;   (612) 363-5777
The Arts Center hosts fine arts performances by regional presenting organizations

COLLEGE OF SAINT BENEDICT - BENEDICTA ARTS CENTER AUDITORIUM
Saint Joseph, MN 56374-2099
(612) 363-5777
Type of Facility: Auditorium
Type of Stage: Proscenium
Stage Dimensions: 50'Wx38'D   **Orchestra Pit**
Seating Capacity: 983
Year Built: 1964
Contact for Rental: Director of Fine Arts;   (612) 363-5777

COLLEGE OF SAINT BENEDICT - BENEDICTA ARTS CENTER FORUM
Saint Joseph, MN 56374-2099
(612) 363-5777
Type of Facility: Theatre House; Multi-Purpose
Type of Stage: Thrust; Flexible; 3/4 Arena
Stage Dimensions: 32'x8'
Seating Capacity: 292
Year Built: 1964
Contact for Rental: Director of Fine Arts;   (612) 363-5777

Saint Paul

DANCE

ANDAHAZY BALLET COMPANY
1680 Grand Avenue, Saint Paul, MN 55105
(612) 698-8786
Founded: 1937
Arts Area: Ballet
Status: Semi-Professional; Non-Profit
Type: Performing; Touring; Educational
Management: Marius Andahazy, Artistic Director; Lori Kartheiser, Business Manager

Paid Staff: 3
Utilizes: Special Technical Talent; Guest Artists
Budget: $1,000 - $50,000
Income Sources: Private Foundations/Grants/Endowments; Business/Corporate Donations; Box Office; Individual Donations

ESTYRE BRINDLE DANCE THEATRE
637 Ohio Street, Saint Paul, MN 55107
(612) 227-0027
Founded: 1930
Arts Area: Ballet; Jazz
Status: Non-Professional; Non-Profit; Commercial
Type: Performing; Educational
Purpose: Dance Education and Performance
Management: B.A. Brenny, Director

INSTRUMENTAL MUSIC

451ST ARMY BAND
Fort Snelling, Building 506, Saint Paul, MN 55111
(612) 725-5237
Founded: 1923
Arts Area: Ensemble; Ethnic; Folk; Band
Status: Professional; Non-Profit
Type: Performing; Touring; Educational
Purpose: To represent the 88th United States Army Reserve Command to the military and to the general public; to promote and encourage the performing arts
Management: CW4 Bruce J. Hedblom, Commander/Band Master; SSG Robert A. Lake, Assistant Conductor
Paid Staff: 45
Utilizes: Guest Conductors; Guest Artists; Guest Directors
Budget: $1,000 - $50,000
Income Sources: Government Grants
Season: 52 Weeks   **Annual Attendance:** 100,000

MINNESOTA STATE BAND
90 West Plato Boulevard, Saint Paul, MN 55107
(612) 296-1577
FAX: (612) 297-1056
Founded: 1898
Arts Area: Ensemble; Ethnic; Instrumental Group; Band
Status: Professional; Non-Profit
Type: Performing; Touring; Educational
Purpose: To continue the musical development and appreciation of America's concert band and wind ensemble movement and its appreciation by the public
Management: Joseph Komro, Conductor/Music Director; Neil Danielson, Public Relations; Adam Torres, Stage Manager; Helmut Kahlert, Concert Coordinator
Officers: Gordon Backlund, President
Paid Staff: 1   **Volunteer Staff:** 70
Non-Paid Artists: 70
Utilizes: Special Technical Talent; Guest Conductors; Guest Artists; Guest Directors
Budget: $100,000 - $500,000
Income Sources: Private Foundations/Grants/Endowments; Business/Corporate Donations; Box Office; Government Grants; Individual Donations
Season: 52 Weeks   **Annual Attendance:** 100,000
Affiliations: Association of Concert Bands

THE SAINT PAUL CHAMBER ORCHESTRA
Landmark Center, 75 West 5th Street, Saint Paul, MN 55102
(612) 292-3248
Founded: 1968
Arts Area: Orchestra; Chamber; Ensemble
Status: Professional; Non-Profit
Type: Performing; Touring; Resident; Educational
Purpose: To present a world-class professional chamber orchestra in the Twin Cities, dedicated to superior performance and artistic innovation, for the enrichment of community life and world audiences
Management: David Schillhammer, General Manager; David Feider, Public Relations Manager; William Vickery, President/Managing Director
Paid Staff: 29   **Volunteer Staff:** 15
Paid Artists: 36

Utilizes: Guest Conductors; Guest Artists
Budget: $1,000,000 - $5,000,000
Income Sources: Private Foundations/Grants/Endowments; Business/Corporate Donations; Box Office; Government Grants; Individual Donations
Season: September - June   **Annual Attendance:** 100,000
Affiliations: ASOL; APAP
Performance Facilities: Ordway Music Theater

VOCAL MUSIC

NORTH STAR OPERA
1863 Eleanor Avenue, Saint Paul, MN 55116
(612) 698-5386
Founded: 1980
Arts Area: Lyric Opera; Light Opera; Operetta
Status: Professional; Non-Profit
Type: Performing; Touring; Resident; Educational
Purpose: To develop and showcase highly-talented and well-qualified professional singers, musicians and stage personnel from the local and upper Midwest areas; to sponsor college internship programs
Management: Irma Wechtler, General Manager; Steven Stucki, Artistic Director
Officers: Irma Wechtler, President; Dr. Joyce Funke, Vice President; Don Machowicz, Treasurer; Florence Stephens, Secretary
Paid Staff: 1   **Volunteer Staff:** 8
Paid Artists: 65
Utilizes: Special Technical Talent; Guest Conductors; Guest Artists; Guest Directors
Budget: $100,000 - $500,000
Income Sources: Private Foundations/Grants/Endowments; Business/Corporate Donations; Box Office; Individual Donations
Season: October - July   **Annual Attendance:** 7,000
Performance Facilities: O'Shaughnessy Auditorium; Drew Fine Arts Theatre; Brady Auditorium

THEATRE

CLIMB THEATRE - CREATIVE LEARNING IDEAS FOR MIND AND BODY
500 North Robert Street, Suite 220, Saint Paul, MN 55101
(612) 227-9660; (800) 767-9660
FAX: (612) 227-9730
Founded: 1975
Arts Area: Professional; Theatrical Group
Status: Professional; Non-Profit
Type: Performing; Touring; Educational
Purpose: To harness and direct the creative power and artistic talents of its writers, directors, actors and educators to create and perform plays, classes and other creative works which communicate matters of social or educational significance to all citizens
Management: Peg Wetli, Executive Director; Peg Endres, Residency Company Manager; Susan Lund, Performance Company Sales Representative; Leigh Anne Adams, Performance Company Director
Officers: Peg Wetli, President; D. Joe Haller, Secretary; Greg Rybak, Treasurer
Paid Artists: 23
Utilizes: Special Technical Talent
Budget: $500,000 - $1,000,000
Income Sources: Private Foundations/Grants/Endowments; Business/Corporate Donations; Government Grants; Individual Donations; Performance Fees
Season: 52 Weeks   **Annual Attendance:** 200,000

GREAT AMERICAN HISTORY THEATRE
30 East Tenth Street, Saint Paul, MN 55101
(612) 292-4323
Founded: 1978
Arts Area: Professional; Musical; Folk; Theatrical Group
Status: Professional; Non-Profit
Type: Performing; Touring; Resident; Educational; Sponsoring
Purpose: To provide audiences with a mirror to the lives of the people of Minnesota and the Midwest and a window to other people and other times; to commission, produce and tour plays that dramatize the history, folklore and social issues of the region and other locales
Management: Lynn Lohr, Producer/Co-Artistic Director; Lance Belville, Co-Artistic Director/Playwright-in-Residence; Thomas H. Berger, General Manager/Tour Director; Carol Marget, Education/Group Director; Karen Kullman, Box Office Manager/Administrative Assistant
Paid Staff: 6
Utilizes: Special Technical Talent; Guest Artists; Guest Directors

Budget: $500,000 - $1,000,000
Income Sources: Private Foundations/Grants/Endowments; Business/Corporate Donations; Box Office; Government Grants; Individual Donations
Season: October - May
Affiliations: TCG
Performance Facilities: Crawford Livingston Theatre

GREAT NORTH AMERICAN HISTORY THEATRE
30 East Tenth Street, Saint Paul, MN 55101
(612) 227-1416
Founded: 1977
Arts Area: Professional; Theatrical Group
Status: Professional; Non-Profit
Type: Performing; Touring
Purpose: To develop and professionally produce new plays about the people, places, events of our home region and the great United States
Management: Lynnell M. Lohr, Producer; Thomas H. Berger, General Manager/Co-Artistic Director; Lance Belville, Playwright-in-Residence/Co-Artistic Director
Officers: David Byrd, President
Utilizes: Special Technical Talent
Budget: $100,000 - $500,000
Income Sources: Private Foundations/Grants/Endowments; Box Office; Individual Donations
Season: October - May   **Annual Attendance:** 20,000
Performance Facilities: Crawford Livingston Theater

PARK SQUARE THEATRE COMPANY
253 East Fourth Street, Saint Paul, MN 55101
(612) 291-7005
Founded: 1975
Arts Area: Theatrical Group
Status: Professional; Non-Profit
Type: Performing
Purpose: To entertain and enrich area audiences through the creation of high-quality productions of the classical repertory
Management: Richard G. Cook, Artistic Director; Steven Kent Lockwood, Managing Director
Officers: Melinda Urion, President; Mary E. Krell, Vice President; Brian J. Raney, Treasurer; Scott Peterson, Secretary
Paid Staff: 4
Paid Artists: 23
Budget: $100,000 - $500,000
Income Sources: Private Foundations/Grants/Endowments; Business/Corporate Donations; Box Office; Government Grants; Individual Donations
Season: September - June   **Annual Attendance:** 20,000
Affiliations: United Arts; TCG

PENUMBRA THEATRE COMPANY
270 North Kent, Saint Paul, MN 55102
(612) 224-4601
FAX: (612) 224-7074
Founded: 1976
Arts Area: Professional; Musical; Folk
Status: Professional; Non-Profit
Type: Performing; Touring; Educational
Purpose: To present artistically excellent theatre from the Pan African/American perspective
Management: Lou Bellamy, Artistic Director; Strider Hammer, Technical Director; Paula Sanders, Marketing Director
Paid Staff: 8   **Volunteer Staff:** 300
Utilizes: Guest Artists; Guest Directors
Budget: $500,000 - $1,000,000
Income Sources: Private Foundations/Grants/Endowments; Business/Corporate Donations; Box Office; Government Grants; Individual Donations
Season: August - May
Affiliations: AEA

RAINBO CHILDREN'S THEATRE COMPANY
688 Selby Avenue, Saint Paul, MN 55104
(612) 228-0854
Founded: 1979
Arts Area: Professional; Community; Folk; Theatrical Group
Status: Professional; Non-Profit
Type: Performing; Touring; Resident; Educational; Sponsoring

Purpose: Formed to bring children of different cultures together to learn about each other's cultures through the performing arts
Management: Merline Batiste Doty, Founder/Managing Artistic Director
Officers: Anne Waters, President; Fred B. Williams, First Vice President; Jonah Ogiamien, Treasurer; Denise LaBranch, Secretary
Paid Staff: 2 **Volunteer Staff:** 4
Paid Artists: 10 **Non-Paid Artists:** 10
Utilizes: Special Technical Talent; Guest Artists; Guest Directors
Budget: $50,000 - $100,000
Income Sources: Private Foundations/Grants/Endowments; Business/Corporate Donations; Box Office; Government Grants; Individual Donations
Season: 52 Weeks **Annual Attendance:** 10,000

FACILITY

COLLEGE OF SAINT CATHERINE - O'SHAUGHNESSY AUDITORIUM
2004 Randolph, Saint Paul, MN 55105
(612) 690-6701
FAX: (612) 690-6769
   Founded: 1970
   Type of Facility: Performance Center
   Type of Stage: Flexible; Proscenium
   Orchestra Pit
   Seating Capacity: 1,900
   Year Built: 1970 **Architect:** Hammel Green & Abrahamson **Cost:** $6,000,000
   Acoustical Consultant: George Izenour
   Contact for Rental: Susan Federbusch; (612) 690-6701

ORDWAY MUSIC THEATRE
345 Washington Street, Saint Paul, MN 55102
(612) 282-3000
FAX: (612) 224-5319
   Type of Facility: Concert Hall; Theatre House
   Year Built: 1985 **Architect:** Benjamin Thompson & Associates **Cost:** $45,000,000
   Acoustical Consultant: R. Lawrence Kirkegaard & Associates
   Contact for Rental: Marge Kazmierczak; (612) 282-3000
   Manager: James C. Sheeley, General Manager
   Contains McKnight Theatre and The Main Hall. See separate listings for additional information.

ORDWAY MUSIC THEATRE - THE MAIN HALL
345 Washington Street, Saint Paul, MN 55102
(612) 282-3000
FAX: (612) 224-5319
   Type of Facility: Concert Hall; Theatre House; Opera House
   Type of Stage: Proscenium
   Stage Dimensions: 136'Wx49'6"D; 64'Wx34'6"H proscenium opening **Orchestra Pit**
   Seating Capacity: 1,815
   Year Built: 1985
   Contact for Rental: Marge Kazmierczak; (612) 282-3000
   Manager: James C. Sheeley
   Resident Groups: The Minnesota Opera; The Saint Paul Chamber Orchestra; The Shubert Club

ORDWAY MUSIC THEATRE - MCKNIGHT THEATRE
345 Washington Street, Saint Paul, MN 55102
(612) 282-3000
FAX: (612) 224-5319
   Type of Facility: Theatre House
   Type of Stage: Proscenium
   Stage Dimensions: 40'3"Wx33'6"D; 40'3"Wx22'H proscenium opening
   Seating Capacity: 315
   Year Built: 1985
   Contact for Rental: Marge Kazmierczak; (612) 282-3000
   Manager: James C. Sheeeley, General Manager

SAINT PAUL CIVIC CENTER
143 West Fourth Street, Saint Paul, MN 55102
(612) 224-7361
   Type of Facility: Civic Center

Year Built: 1973   **Architect:** Convention Center Architects   **Cost:** $19,500,000
Year Remodeled: 1984   **Architect:** DWBR   **Cost:** $10,500,000
Contact for Rental: Barbara Chandler, Manager;   (612) 224-7361
Manager: Barbara Chandler
Saint Paul Civic Center contains the Arena and Auditorium. See separate listings for further information.

SAINT PAUL CIVIC CENTER - ARENA
143 West Fourth Street, Saint Paul, MN 55102
(612) 224-7361
FAX: (612) 224-1142
Type of Facility: Concert Hall; Arena
Type of Stage: Flexible; Platform
Seating Capacity: 17,700
Year Built: 1973
Year Remodeled: 1984
Contact for Rental: David Rosenwasser, Barbara Chandler;   (612) 224-7361
Manager: David Rosenwasser, Executive Director;   (612) 224-7361

SAINT PAUL CIVIC CENTER - AUDITORIUM
143 West Fourth Street, Saint Paul, MN 55102
(612) 224-7361
FAX: (612) 224-1142
Type of Facility: Concert Hall; Auditorium
Type of Stage: Flexible; Platform
Seating Capacity: 5,500
Year Built: 1973
Year Remodeled: 1984
Contact for Rental: Barbara Chandler, David Rosenwasser;   (612) 224-7361
Manager: Barbara Chandler, Managing Director;   (612) 224-7361

Saint Peter

FACILITY

GUSTAVUS ADOLPHUS COLLEGE - SCHAEFFER FINE ARTS COMPLEX
800 West College Avenue, Saint Peter, MN 56082
(507) 933-7363
Founded: 1862
Type of Facility: Performance Center
Year Built: 1971   **Architect:** Hammel Green & Abrahamson   **Cost:** $3,500,000
Acoustical Consultant: Hammel Green & Abrahamson
Contact for Rental: Al Behrends;   (507) 933-7363
Complex contains Evelyn E. Anderson Theatre and Jussi Bjorling Concert Hall. See separate listings for more information.

GUSTAVUS ADOLPHUS COLLEGE - SCHAEFFER FINE ARTS COMPLEX -
EVELYN E. ANDERSON THEATRE
800 West College Avenue, Saint Peter, MN 56082
(507) 933-7363
Founded: 1862
Type of Facility: Theatre House
Type of Stage: Thrust
Stage Dimensions: 30'Wx60'D
Seating Capacity: 275
Year Built: 1971
Contact for Rental: Al Behrends;   (507) 933-7363

GUSTAVUS ADOLPHUS COLLEGE - SCHAEFFER FINE ARTS COMPLEX -
JUSSI BJORLING CONCERT HALL
800 West College Avenue, Saint Peter, MN 56082
(507) 933-7363
Founded: 1862
Type of Facility: Concert Hall
Type of Stage: Concert Stage
Stage Dimensions: 43'Wx34'D
Seating Capacity: 510

Year Built: 1971
Contact for Rental: Al Behrends;   (507) 933-7363

White Bear Lake

THEATRE

LAKESHORE PLAYERS
4820 Stewart Avenue, PO Box 10562, White Bear Lake, MN 55110
(612) 426-3275
Founded: 1953
Arts Area: Musical; Theatrical Group
Status: Non-Profit
Type: Performing; Educational
Purpose: To bring entertainment to the community
Management: Sherrie Tarble, Business Manager
Officers: Kevin Chandler, President; Bill Collins, Vice President; Sue Riedinger, Secretary; Danette Olsen, Treasurer
Paid Staff: 4   **Volunteer Staff:** 14
Non-Paid Artists: 25
Utilizes: Special Technical Talent; Guest Directors
Budget: $50,000 - $100,000
Income Sources: Box Office; Individual Donations
Season: August - May   **Annual Attendance:** 15,000
Affiliations: ACT; Minnesota Association of Community Theatres
Performance Facilities: Lakeshore Playhouse

FACILITY

LAKESHORE PLAYHOUSE
4820 Steward Avenue, PO Box 10562, White Bear Lake, MN 55110
(612) 429-5674
Type of Facility: Theatre House
Facility Originally: Church
Seating Capacity: 210
Year Remodeled: 1970
Contact for Rental: Manager;   (612) 429-5674
Manager: Sherrie Tarble, Business Manager
Resident Groups: Lakeshore Players

Winona

INSTRUMENTAL MUSIC

JOHN PAULSON JAZZ QUARTET
725 37th Avenue, Winona, MN 55987
(507) 454-4948
Founded: 1980
Arts Area: Instrumental Group; Electronic & Live Electronic
Status: Professional
Type: Performing; Touring; Educational
Purpose: To perform high quality creative jazz music and help advance the jazz idiom through education
Management: Dr. John C. Paulson, Leader
Paid Artists: 4
Utilizes: Guest Artists
Budget: $1,000 - $50,000

MISSISSIPPI

Belzoni

FACILITY

DEPOT THEATRE
110 Magnolia Street, Belzoni, MS 39038
(601) 247-1343
    Type of Facility: Theatre House; Multi-Purpose
    Type of Stage: Proscenium
    Stage Dimensions: 26'Wx20'Dx8'H
    Seating Capacity: 250
    Year Remodeled: 1981
    Contact for Rental: Tom Turner Jr.;   (601) 247-1343

Biloxi

VOCAL MUSIC

GULF COAST OPERA THEATRE
1279 Father Ryan, Biloxi, MS 39530
(601) 432-5956
    Founded: 1973
    Arts Area: Grand Opera; Operetta; Musical Theatre
    Status: Semi-Professional; Non-Profit
    Type: Performing; Resident
    Purpose: To educate residents of the Mississippi Gulf Coast in the art forms of opera and musical theatre
    Management: Dr. Laurence Oden, Director; Shirley Heitzman, Chairman of Opera Workshop
    Officers: Charles Kremer, President, Board of Directors; Betty Kendall, President, Opera Salon
    Paid Staff: 7
    Paid Artists: 50 **Non-Paid Artists:** 40
    Budget: $100,000 - $500,000
    Income Sources: Box Office; Individual Donations
    Season: November - May **Annual Attendance:** 4,000
    Performance Facilities: Saenger Theatre for the Performing Arts

FACILITY

SAENGER THEATRE FOR THE PERFORMING ARTS
416 Reynoir Street, PO Box 775, Biloxi, MS 39533
(601) 435-6291
    Type of Facility: Performance Center; Theatre House
    Facility Originally: Vaudeville
    Type of Stage: Modified Apron Proscenium
    Stage Dimensions: 58'Wx23'7"D, 36'Wx20'H proscenium opening **Orchestra Pit**
    Seating Capacity: 1,190
    Year Built: 1929 **Architect:** Roy A. Benjamin **Cost:** $200,000
    Year Remodeled: 1984 **Architect:** Collins & Collins **Cost:** $100,000
    Contact for Rental: Tina Cowart; (601) 435-6294
    Manager: Benjamin Shelton; (601) 435-6291
    Resident Groups: Gulf Coast Opera Theatre; Gulf Coast Symphony; Riviera Productions; Kinetic Neoskeine; Walter Anderson Players
    Opened January 15, 1929, with one of the first sound films, "Interference"

Cleveland

FACILITY

WHISTLE STOP PLAYHOUSE
Cleveland Community Theatre, PO Box 44, Cleveland, MS 38732
(601) 843-3096
    Type of Facility: Theatre House
    Facility Originally: Train Station
    Type of Stage: Proscenium
    Stage Dimensions: 40'Wx40'Dx40'H **Orchestra Pit**

Seating Capacity: 150
Year Built: 1955
Contact for Rental: June McClendon;   (601) 843-3096
Resident Groups: Cleveland Community Theatre

Columbus

FACILITY

COLUMBUS CONVENTION AND CIVIC CENTER
Second Avenue North, Columbus, MS 39701
(601) 328-4164
    Type of Facility: Auditorium
    Type of Stage: Proscenium
    Stage Dimensions: 33'Wx31'Dx12'H
    Seating Capacity: 1,900
    Year Remodeled: 1987   **Architect:** Virden & Alexander, Ltd.
    Contact for Rental: Property Manager;   (601) 328-4164
    Manager: Frank Goodman

PRINCESS THEATER
Fifth Street South, Columbus, MS 39701
(601) 327-8665
    Type of Facility: Theatre House
    Facility Originally: Vaudeville
    Type of Stage: Proscenium
    Stage Dimensions: 75'Wx50'Dx30'H   **Orchestra Pit**
    Seating Capacity: 700
    Year Built: 1924
    Year Remodeled: 1986
    Contact for Rental: Mrs. Ed Kuykendall Sr.;   (601) 327-8665

Corinth

THEATRE

CORINTH THEATRE-ARTS
Fulton Drive, PO Box 127, Corinth, MS 38834
(601) 287-2995
    Founded: 1967
    Arts Area: Community
    Status: Non-Profit
    Type: Resident
    Management: Murray Chase, Resident Director
    Paid Staff: 1   **Volunteer Staff:** 85
    Budget: $1,000 - $50,000
    Income Sources: Business/Corporate Donations; Box Office; Individual Donations
    Season: 52 Weeks   **Annual Attendance:** 9,000
    Performance Facilities: Crossroads Playhouse; Coliseum Civic Center

FACILITY

COLISEUM CIVIC CENTER
404 Taylor Street, PO Box 723, Corinth, MS 38834
(601) 287-1328
FAX: (601) 286-0903
    Type of Facility: Concert Hall; Auditorium; Theatre House; Opera House; Civic Center
    Facility Originally: Vaudeville; Movie House
    Type of Stage: Proscenium
    Stage Dimensions: 28'Wx20'Dx20'H   **Orchestra Pit**
    Seating Capacity: 900
    Year Built: 1924   **Architect:** Benjamin F. Liddon
    Year Remodeled: 1982   **Architect:** Ledbetter Associates   **Cost:** $250,000
    Contact for Rental: Mrs. H.L. Williams Jr.;   (601) 287-1328
    Resident Groups: Northeast Mississippi Community Concert Association; Corinth Theatre-Arts; Corinth Symphony Orchestra

Greenwood

FACILITY

GREENWOOD LEFLORE CIVIC CENTER
Highway 7 North, Greenwood, MS 38930
(601) 453-4065
> **Type of Facility:** Civic Center; Arena
> **Type of Stage:** Proscenium
> **Stage Dimensions:** 60'Wx30'D
> **Seating Capacity:** 2,800
> **Year Built:** 1980   **Architect:** Bowman & Bowman, Ltd
> **Contact for Rental:** James Belk;   (601) 453-4065

Gulfport

INSTRUMENTAL MUSIC

GULF COAST SYMPHONY
PO Box 7294, Gulfport, MS 39506
(205) 666-9554
> **Founded:** 1963
> **Arts Area:** Symphony
> **Status:** Semi-Professional; Non-Profit
> **Type:** Performing; Touring; Educational
> **Purpose:** To present symphonic music to residents of the Gulf Coast
> **Officers:** Mrs. John Green, President of Board; Col. Sidney Lanier, Vice President; Elaine Martinolich, Publicity Chairman; Dr. Andrew Harper, Music Director
> **Volunteer Staff:** 25
> **Paid Artists:** 4
> **Utilizes:** Guest Artists
> **Budget:** $50,000 - $100,000
> **Income Sources:** Private Foundations/Grants/Endowments; Business/Corporate Donations; Box Office; Government Grants; Individual Donations
> **Season:** September - May   **Annual Attendance:** 4,000
> **Performance Facilities:** Saenger Theater, Hattiesburg

Hattiesburg

FACILITY

MANNONI PERFORMING ARTS CENTER
Southern Station, PO Box 5052, Hattiesburg, MS 39406-5052
(601) 266-4988
> **Type of Facility:** Performance Center; Theatre House
> **Type of Stage:** Proscenium
> **Stage Dimensions:** 43'6"Wx37'6"Dx29'H   **Orchestra Pit**
> **Seating Capacity:** 744
> **Year Built:** 1971
> **Contact for Rental:** Chris Zink;   (601) 266-4988
> **Resident Groups:** University of Southern Mississippi College of the Arts

SAENGER THEATRE
Forest & Front Streets, PO Box 1898, Hattiesburg, MS 39401
(601) 545-4580
> **Type of Facility:** Theatre House
> **Facility Originally:** Vaudeville
> **Type of Stage:** Proscenium
> **Stage Dimensions:** 32'Wx11'Dx22'H   **Orchestra Pit**
> **Seating Capacity:** 1,000
> **Year Built:** 1929
> **Year Remodeled:** 1976   **Architect:** David K. Hemeter
> **Contact for Rental:** Nan Wilson;   (601) 545-4580

Indianola

FACILITY

INDIANOLA LITTLE THEATRE
Main and Sunflower Avenue, Indianola, MS 38751
(601) 887-9920
> **Type of Facility:** Theatre House
> **Facility Originally:** Church
> **Type of Stage:** Proscenium
> **Stage Dimensions:** 30'Wx30'Dx20'H
> **Seating Capacity:** 160
> **Year Remodeled:** 1985
> **Contact for Rental:** D. Harold Manning;   (601) 887-1300

Jackson

DANCE

BALLET MISSISSIPPI
PO Box 1787, Jackson, MS 39215-1787
(601) 960-1560
> **Founded:** 1982
> **Arts Area:** Ballet
> **Status:** Professional; Non-Profit
> **Type:** Performing; Touring; Resident; Educational
> **Purpose:** To encourage and promote the study, understanding and appreciation of ballet and other forms of dance
> **Management:** Vladimir Juluhadze, Artistic Director; Joanna Hunt, Executive Director
> **Officers:** Dr. Michael Campbell, Chairman/President, Board of Directors
> **Paid Staff:** 11
> **Paid Artists:** 15
> **Utilizes:** Special Technical Talent; Guest Artists; Guest Choreographers
> **Budget:** $100,000 - $500,000
> **Income Sources:** Private Foundations/Grants/Endowments; Business/Corporate Donations; Box Office; Government Grants; Individual Donations
> **Season:** September - April   **Annual Attendance:** 8,500
> **Performance Facilities:** Jackson Municipal Auditorium

INSTRUMENTAL MUSIC

JACKSON SYMPHONY YOUTH ORCHESTRA
PO Box 2052, Jackson, MS 39225
(601) 960-1565
> **Arts Area:** Symphony; Orchestra
> **Status:** Non-Professional; Non-Profit
> **Type:** Performing; Touring; Educational
> **Purpose:** To promote education and appreciation of classical music through participation in the junior or senior youth orchestras
> **Management:** Philip Messner, Executive Director; Mark Hatchman, Assistant Manager; David Arnott, Conductor, Senior Youth Orchestra; Rebecca Ruttenberg, Conductor, Junior Youth Orchestra; Mark Hatch, Education Director
> **Paid Staff:** 3
> **Non-Paid Artists:** 70
> **Budget:** $1,000 - $50,000
> **Income Sources:** Fund-raising
> **Season:** September - May   **Annual Attendance:** 300
> **Affiliations:** ASOL(Youth Orchestra Division)
> **Performance Facilities:** Chastain Junior High School

MISSISSIPPI SYMPHONY ORCHESTRA
PO Box 2052, Jackson, MS 39225-2052
(601) 960-1565
> **Founded:** 1944
> **Arts Area:** Symphony; Orchestra; Chamber; Pops/Popular Selections
> **Status:** Professional; Non-Profit
> **Type:** Performing; Touring; Educational; Sponsoring
> **Management:** Phillip K. Messner, Executive Director; Guy Drake, Financial Director
> **Officers:** Jack Garner, Chairman/President, Board of Directors
> **Paid Staff:** 4   **Volunteer Staff:** 800

Paid Artists: 70
Budget: $500,000 - $1,000,000
Income Sources: Private Foundations/Grants/Endowments; Business/Corporate Donations; Box Office; Government Grants; Individual Donations
Season: September - May   **Annual Attendance:** 3,300
Affiliations: ASOL; Jackson Symphony Youth Orchestra
Performance Facilities: Jackson Municipal Auditorium; Briarwood Presbyterian Church

VOCAL MUSIC

MISSISSIPPI OPERA ASSOCIATION
PO Box 1551, Jackson, MS 39215
(601) 960-1528
FAX: (601) 960-1526
Founded: 1945
Arts Area: Grand Opera; Lyric Opera; Light Opera; Operetta; Musical Theatre
Status: Professional; Non-Profit
Type: Performing; Touring; Educational
Purpose: To promote and encourage the study, understanding and appreciation of opera; to develop opera talent
Management: Frank Marion Johnson, General Director
Officers: Monroe Wright, President; Ovida Bass Holland, Guild President
Paid Staff: 4   **Volunteer Staff:** 3
Paid Artists: 100   **Non-Paid Artists:** 50
Utilizes: Special Technical Talent; Guest Conductors; Guest Artists; Guest Directors
Budget: $500,000 - $1,000,000
Income Sources: Private Foundations/Grants/Endowments; Business/Corporate Donations; Box Office; Government Grants; Individual Donations
Season: 52 Weeks   **Annual Attendance:** 10,000
Affiliations: OA
Performance Facilities: Jackson Municipal Auditorium

THEATRE

NEW STAGE THEATRE
PO Box 4792, Jackson, MS 39296
(601) 948-3533
FAX: (601) 948-3538
Founded: 1965
Arts Area: Professional
Status: Professional; Non-Profit
Type: Resident; Educational; Producing
Management: Loyce Root, Business Manager; Janice Englehart, Managing Director
Officers: Carol Daily, Board President
Paid Staff: 7
Utilizes: Special Technical Talent; Guest Artists; Guest Directors
Budget: $100,000 - $500,000
Income Sources: Private Foundations/Grants/Endowments; Business/Corporate Donations; Box Office; Government Grants; Individual Donations
Season: September - May
Affiliations: AEA
Performance Facilities: New Stage Theatre

PUPPET ARTS THEATRE
1927 Springridge Drive, Jackson, MS 39211
(601) 956-3414
Founded: 1968
Arts Area: Puppet
Status: Professional; Commercial
Type: Performing; Touring
Purpose: To provide entertaining and educational shows in the Southeast featuring classical music and puppets
Management: Peter Zapletal, Artistic Director; Jarmila Zapletal, Business Manager
Paid Staff: 2
Paid Artists: 5
Budget: $1,000 - $50,000
Income Sources: Business/Corporate Donations; Box Office; Government Grants
Season: 52 Weeks   **Annual Attendance:** 15,000

PERFORMING SERIES

USA INTERNATIONAL BALLET COMPETITION
PO Box 55791, Jackson, MS 39216
(601) 355-9853
FAX: (601) 355-5253
Founded: 1979
Arts Area: Dance
Status: Semi-Professional; Non-Profit
Type: Performing
Purpose: The only world-class international dance event sanctioned by the ITT. This excellence-in-the-art competition is held every four years.
Management: Sue Lobrano, Executive Director; Norma Barnett, Public Relations Director
Paid Staff: 4
Utilizes: Special Technical Talent; Guest Artists
Income Sources: Private Foundations/Grants/Endowments; Business/Corporate Donations; Box Office; Government Grants; Individual Donations
Season: June - July
Performance Facilities: City Auditorium

FACILITY

GIRAULT AUDITORIUM
Belhaven College, 1500 Peachtree Street, Jackson, MS 39202-1789
(601) 968-8707
Founded: 1883
Type of Facility: Theatre Complex; Concert Hall; Auditorium; Performance Center; Theatre House; Opera House; Multi-Purpose
Type of Stage: Platform
Stage Dimensions: 36'Wx26'D   **Orchestra Pit**
Seating Capacity: 600
Year Built: 1949
Contact for Rental: Office of Student Affairs;   (619) 968-5916

JACKSON MUNICIPAL AUDITORIUM
255 East Pacagoula Street, Jackson, MS 39205
(601) 960-1537
FAX: (601) 960-1583
Founded: 1964
Type of Facility: Concert Hall; Auditorium; Performance Center; Off Broadway; Theatre House; Opera House
Type of Stage: Proscenium
Stage Dimensions: 104'Wx45'D; 60'W proscenium opening   **Orchestra Pit**
Seating Capacity: 2,510
Year Built: 1964
Year Remodeled: 1988
Contact for Rental: Herb Anderson;   (601) 960-1537
Resident Groups: Mississippi Symphony; Mississippi Ballet; Mississippi Opera

Mathiston

FACILITY

WOOD JUNIOR COLLEGE - THEATRE
Mathiston, MS 39752
(601) 263-5352
Type of Facility: Auditorium
Type of Stage: Proscenium
Stage Dimensions: 20'x34'x28'
Seating Capacity: 500
Year Built: 1966   **Cost:** $180,000
Contact for Rental: Shelby Oakes;   (601) 263-5352
Resident Groups: Wood Players

McComb

FACILITY

STATE THEATRE
220 State Street, PO Box 1141, McComb, MS 39648
(601) 684-5229
    Type of Facility: Theatre House
    Type of Stage: Proscenium; Modified Thrust
    Stage Dimensions: 76'Wx36'D; 44'Wx18'H proscenium opening   **Orchestra Pit**
    Seating Capacity: 438
    Year Built: 1924
    Year Remodeled: 1982   **Architect:** Ragland Watkins
    Contact for Rental: Loretta Easley;   (601) 684-5229
    Manager: Charles Schilling
    Resident Groups: Pike County Little Theatre; Pike County Arts Council, Inc.

Meridian

FACILITY

MERIDIAN COMMUNITY COLLEGE - THEATRE
5500 Highway 19 North, Meridian, MS 39301
(601) 483-8241
FAX: (601) 482-3936
    Type of Facility: Theatre Complex; Auditorium
    Type of Stage: Proscenium
    Stage Dimensions: 70'Wx35'D
    Seating Capacity: 600
    Year Built: 1964   **Architect:** Archer and Associates
    Year Remodeled: 1984
    Acoustical Consultant: Ronnie Miller
    Contact for Rental: Ronnie Miller;   (601) 484-8666

Mississippi State

FACILITY

LEE HALL AUDITORIUM
Mississippi State Univeristy, Lee Boulevard, PO Box HY, Mississippi State, MS 39762
(601) 325-3228
    Type of Facility: Concert Hall; Auditorium
    Type of Stage: Thrust; Proscenium
    Stage Dimensions: 23'x35'1/2"
    Seating Capacity: 1,200
    Year Built: 1920

Oxford

FACILITY

UNIVERSITY OF MISSISSIPPI - FULTON CHAPEL
Oxford, MS 38677
(601) 232-7411
    Type of Facility: Theatre House
    Type of Stage: Modified Apron Proscenium
    Stage Dimensions: 60'Wx28'D, 36'4"x18'H proscenium opening
    Orchestra Pit
    Seating Capacity: 917
    Year Built: 1927
    Year Remodeled: 1982   **Cost:** $160,000
    Contact for Rental: Jerry Kellum;   (601) 232-7411
    Originally built as a chapel with theatre capabilities

UNIVERSITY OF MISSISSIPPI - MEEK AUDITORIUM
Oxford, MS 38677
(601) 232-7411
    Type of Facility: Auditorium
    Type of Stage: Proscenium
    Stage Dimensions: 72'Wx40'D, 32'W proscenium opening
    Seating Capacity: 235
    Year Built: 1955
    Contact for Rental: Jerry Kellum;   (601) 232-7411

UNIVERSITY OF MISSISSIPPI - STUDIO THEATRE
Oxford, MS 38677
(601) 232-7411
    Type of Facility: Studio Performance; Theatre House
    Facility Originally: Library
    Type of Stage: Proscenium
    Stage Dimensions: 42'Wx25'D, 26'W proscenium opening
    Seating Capacity: 100
    Year Built: 1898
    Year Remodeled: 1960

Sardis

FACILITY

PANOLA PLAYHOUSE
Main Street, PO Box 43, Sardis, MS 38666
(601) 487-3451
    Type of Facility: Theatre House
    Type of Stage: Proscenium
    Stage Dimensions: 40'Wx30'Dx12'H
    Seating Capacity: 180
    Year Remodeled: 1964
    Manager: Hugh Rhoads

Tupelo

INSTRUMENTAL MUSIC

TUPELO SYMPHONY
PO Box 474, Tupelo, MS 38802
(601) 842-8433
    Founded: 1971
    Arts Area: Symphony; Orchestra
    Status: Professional
    Type: Performing; Touring
    Purpose: To perform symphonic works
    Management: Eric Knight, Music Director
    Officers: Doyce Deas, Chairman/Chief Executive Officer
    Paid Staff: 1
    Paid Artists: 80
    Utilizes: Guest Artists
    Budget: $50,000 - $100,000
    Income Sources: Private Foundations/Grants/Endowments; Business/Corporate Donations; Box Office; Government Grants; Individual Donations
    Season: October - April
    Annual Attendance: 4,000
    Affiliations: ASOL
    Performance Facilities: Civic Auditorium

Yazoo City

FACILITY

TRIANGLE CULTURAL CENTER
322 North Main, Yazoo City, MS 39194
(601) 746-2273
Type of Facility: Theatre House
Facility Originally: School
Type of Stage: Proscenium
Stage Dimensions: 28'Wx22'Dx19'H
Seating Capacity: 250
Year Built: 1904
Year Remodeled: 1977   **Architect:** John E. De Cell   **Cost:** $220,000
Contact for Rental: Sandra Younger;   (601) 746-2273

MISSOURI

Arrow Rock

THEATRE

LYCEUM REPERTORY COMPANY
Main Street, Arrow Rock, MO 65320
(816) 837-3311
>**Founded:** 1961
>**Arts Area:** Professional
>**Status:** Professional; Non-Profit
>**Type:** Performing; Touring; Resident
>**Purpose:** To touch, enrich and entertain human beings with live professional theatre
>**Management:** Michael Bollinger, Artistic Producing
>**Officers:** Janet Campbell, President; Eliz Kruse, Vice President; Winnie Davis, Secretary; Bob Bagby, Treasurer
>**Paid Staff:** 35 **Volunteer Staff:** 40
>**Paid Artists:** 20 **Non-Paid Artists:** 15
>**Utilizes:** Special Technical Talent; Guest Artists; Guest Directors
>**Budget:** $100,000 - $500,000
>**Income Sources:** Private Foundations/Grants/Endowments; Business/Corporate Donations; Box Office; Government Grants; Individual Donations
>**Season:** June - September **Annual Attendance:** 16,000
>**Affiliations:** AEA
>**Performance Facilities:** Lyceum Theatre

FACILITY

LYCEUM THEATRE
Main Street, Arrow Rock, MO 65320
(816) 837-3311
>**Founded:** 1961
>**Type of Facility:** Theatre House
>**Facility Originally:** Church
>**Type of Stage:** Proscenium
>**Stage Dimensions:** 23'9"Wx20'D; 23'9"Wx12'H proscenium opening
>**Seating Capacity:** 300
>**Year Built:** 1872
>**Year Remodeled:** 1968 **Architect:** Henry Swanson **Cost:** $37,000
>**Contact for Rental:** Michael Bollinger; (816) 837-3311
>**Resident Groups:** Lyceum Repertory Company
>*Converted into a theater in 1961 for $10,000.*

Boonville

PERFORMING SERIES

FRIENDS OF HISTORIC BOONVILLE
614 East Morgan, PO Box 1776, Boonville, MO 65233
(816) 882-7977
>**Founded:** 1971
>**Arts Area:** Dance; Vocal Music; Instrumental Music; Theater; Festivals; Lyric Opera; Grand Opera
>**Status:** Non-Profit
>**Type:** Performing; Educational; Sponsoring
>**Purpose:** To provide community arts program in our historic theatre, Thespian Hall
>**Management:** Judy Shields, Administrator
>**Officers:** Julie Thacher, President; Paul Davis, Second Vice President; Maxine Hughes, First Vice President; Jerry Smith, Secretary; Paul Sombart, Treasurer
>**Paid Staff:** 5 **Volunteer Staff:** 300
>**Budget:** $100,000 - $500,000
>**Income Sources:** Private Foundations/Grants/Endowments; Business/Corporate Donations; Box Office; Government Grants; Individual Donations
>**Season:** March - December **Annual Attendance:** 10,000
>**Performance Facilities:** Thespian Hall

Branson

THEATRE

TRI LAKES COMMUNITY THEATRE
PO Box 1301, Branson, MO 65616
(417) 335-4241
> **Founded:** 1983
> **Arts Area:** Musical; Community; Theatrical Group
> **Status:** Non-Profit
> **Type:** Performing
> **Purpose:** Promote the Performing Arts and to provide entertainment for our community
> **Officers:** Mark Weisz, President; Magellen Shock, Vice President; Jean Cantwell, Secretary; Ted Reed, Treasurer
> **Volunteer Staff:** 50
> **Paid Artists:** 3   **Non-Paid Artists:** 30
> **Utilizes:** Special Technical Talent
> **Budget:** $1,000 - $50,000
> **Income Sources:** Private Foundations/Grants/Endowments; Business/Corporate Donations; Box Office; Individual Donations
> **Season:** November - March   **Annual Attendance:** 2,000
> **Affiliations:** Missouri Arts Council

Cape Girardeau

PERFORMING SERIES

SOUTHEAST MISSOURI STATE UNIVERSITY - CULTURAL PROGRAMS
Southeast Missouri State University, Cape Girardeau, MO 63701
(314) 651-2154
FAX: (314) 651-2200
> **Founded:** 1873
> **Arts Area:** Dance; Vocal Music; Instrumental Music; Theater
> **Status:** Non-Profit
> **Type:** Educational; Sponsoring
> **Purpose:** To bring in attractions of a professional quality in the arts; to sponsor workshops where students may learn from visiting professionals
> **Management:** Dr. Martin Jones, Dean, College of Humanities; Dr. Ray G. Ewing, Chairperson, Speech Communications and Theatre Dept.
> **Volunteer Staff:** 4
> **Utilizes:** Guest Artists
> **Budget:** $1,000 - $50,000
> **Income Sources:** Box Office; Government Grants
> **Season:** September - May   **Annual Attendance:** 1,000
> **Affiliations:** Missouri Council on the Arts
> **Performance Facilities:** Academic Hall Auditorium

FACILITY

SOUTHEAST MISSOURI STATE UNIVERSITY - ACADEMIC HALL AUDITORIUM
1 University Plaza, Cape Girardeau, MO 63701
(314) 651-2000
> **Type of Facility:** Auditorium
> **Type of Stage:** Proscenium
> **Stage Dimensions:** 65'Wx40'H; 45'Wx20'H proscenium opening
> **Seating Capacity:** 1,200
> **Year Built:** 1906
> **Year Remodeled:** 1986   **Architect:** Tom Holzhauser and Associates   **Cost:** $350,000
> **Contact for Rental:** Facilities Scheduling;   (314) 651-2280

SOUTHEAST MISSOURI STATE UNIVERSITY - SHOW ME CENTER
1 University Plaza, Cape Girardeau, MO 63701
(314) 651-2297
> **Type of Facility:** Multi-Purpose
> **Type of Stage:** Flexible; 3/4 Arena; Arena
> **Seating Capacity:** Arena - 6,778; 3/4 Arena - 7,400
> **Year Built:** 1987   **Architect:** Hastings & Chivetta   **Cost:** $17,000,000

Contact for Rental: Facilities Scheduling;   (314) 651-2280
Manager: David Ross

Chesterfield

DANCE

ALEXANDRA BALLET COMPANY
68 East Four Seasons Center, Chesterfield, MO 63017
(314) 469-6222
Founded: 1984
Arts Area: Ballet
Status: Semi-Professional; Non-Profit
Type: Performing
Purpose: Training ground to produce dancers to go on to professional work
Management: Alexandra Zaharias, Artistic Director
Paid Artists: 1   **Non-Paid Artists:** 35
Utilizes: Guest Artists
Budget: $1,000 - $50,000
Income Sources: Private Foundations/Grants/Endowments; Business/Corporate Donations; Box Office; Government Grants; Individual Donations
Season: September - May   **Annual Attendance:** 2,000
Affiliations: NARB
Performance Facilities: Fontbonne College Theatre; Edison Theatre, Washington University

---

Columbia

INSTRUMENTAL MUSIC

MISSOURI SYMPHONY SOCIETY
203 South Ninth Street, PO Box 1121, Columbia, MO 65205
(314) 875-0600
Founded: 1971
Arts Area: Symphony; Orchestra; Chamber
Status: Professional; Non-Profit
Type: Performing; Touring; Educational; Sponsoring
Purpose: The Missouri Symphony Society is dedicated to the enhancement of the cultural environment through fine music, education and encouragment of young musicians.
Management: Hugo Vianello, Artistic Director/Conductor; Debra Sapp-Yarwood, General Manager
Officers: Arthur E. Rikli M.D., President; Kay Dinwiddie, Vice President-Membership; David Harrison, Vice President-Finance; Wiley Miller, Treasurer; Jackie Blanton, Secretary
Paid Staff: 4   **Volunteer Staff:** 65
Paid Artists: 45   **Non-Paid Artists:** 22
Utilizes: Guest Conductors; Guest Artists
Budget: $100,000 - $500,000
Income Sources: Private Foundations/Grants/Endowments; Business/Corporate Donations; Box Office; Government Grants; Individual Donations
Season: June - July   **Annual Attendance:** 12,000
Affiliations: Pops Orchestra; Chamber Orchestra Festival Symphony
Performance Facilities: Missouri Theatre

FACILITY

MISSOURI THEATRE
203 South Ninth Street, Columbia, MO 65205
(314) 875-0600
Founded: 1928
Type of Facility: Concert Hall; Auditorium; Historic
Facility Originally: Vaudeville; Movie House
Type of Stage: Proscenium
Stage Dimensions: 36'x24' proscenium opening; 9'x40' with apron
Seating Capacity: 1,184
Year Built: 1928
Year Remodeled: 1992   **Architect:** Luer and Associates

Contact for Rental: Debra Sapp-Yarnwood;   (314) 875-0600
Resident Groups: Missouri Symphony Society

UNIVERSITY OF MISSOURI- COLUMBIA - JESSE AUDITORIUM
311 Jesse Hall, Columbia, MO 65211
(314) 882-3753
Type of Facility: Concert Hall; Auditorium; Performance Center; Theatre House; Opera House
Type of Stage: Proscenium
Stage Dimensions: 75'Wx35H' proscenium opening   **Orchestra Pit**
Seating Capacity: 1,840
Year Built: 1953   **Architect:** Jamieson, Spearl, Hammond & Grolock   **Cost:** $2,000,000
Year Remodeled: 1986
Contact for Rental: Pat Higgins;   (314) 882-7254

Fulton

FACILITY

WESTMINSTER COLLEGE - WESTMINSTER CHAMP AUDITORIUM
Fulton, MO 65251
(314) 642-3361
Type of Facility: Auditorium
Type of Stage: Proscenium
Stage Dimensions: 20'x36'x28'   **Orchestra Pit**
Seating Capacity: 1,400
Year Built: 1967
Contact for Rental: Kerry Farnham;   (314) 642-3361

WESTMINSTER COLLEGE - WINSTON CHURCHILL MEMORIAL AND LIBRARY IN THE UNITED STATES
Seventh and Westminster, Fulton, MO 65251
(314) 642-3361
Type of Facility: Multi-Purpose
Facility Originally: Church
Type of Stage: Platform; Altar With Elevated Pulpit
Seating Capacity: 280
Year Built: 1676   **Architect:** Christopher Wren
Year Remodeled: 1969   **Architect:** Marshall Sisson & Frederick C. Sternberg   **Cost:** $3,000,000
Contact for Rental: Judith Pugh;   (314) 642-3361
The Church of Saint Mary the Virgin, Aldermanbury, was dismantled in London in 1965, shipped to Fulton, reassembled in its original form and rehallowed on May 7, 1969.

WILLIAM WOODS COLLEGE - CAMPUS CENTER
200 West 12th Street, Fulton, MO 65251
(314) 642-2251
Type of Facility: Auditorium
Type of Stage: Proscenium
Stage Dimensions: 100'Wx30'D; 46'Wx18'H proscenium opening
Orchestra Pit
Seating Capacity: 1,300
Year Built: 1976
Contact for Rental: Brenda Stafford;   (314) 642-2251

WILLIAM WOODS COLLEGE - DULANY AUDITORIUM
200 West 12th Street, Fulton, MO 65251
(314) 642-2251
Type of Facility: Concert Hall; Theatre House
Facility Originally: Church
Type of Stage: Thrust
Stage Dimensions: 40'Wx36'D
Seating Capacity: 315
Year Built: 1900

Year Remodeled: 1976
Contact for Rental: Brenda Stafford;   (314) 642-2251

Kansas City

DANCE

STATE BALLET OF MISSOURI
706 West 42nd Street, Kansas City, MO 64111
(816) 931-2232
Founded: 1980
Arts Area: Ballet
Status: Professional
Type: Performing; Touring
Purpose: To become the leading producer of world class ballet in the Midwest
Management: Todd Bolender, Artistic Director; Martin Cohen, General Manager
Officers: John Hunkele M.D., President; Randall Clark, Vice President/Finance; Roger Arwood, Vice President/Development; John Marvin, Secretary
Paid Staff: 11   **Volunteer Staff:** 40
Paid Artists: 26
Utilizes: Guest Conductors; Guest Choreographers
Budget: $1,000,000 - $5,000,000
Income Sources: Private Foundations/Grants/Endowments; Business/Corporate Donations; Box Office; Government Grants; Individual Donations
Season: September - May
Annual Attendance: 80,000
Performance Facilities: Midland Theatre

INSTRUMENTAL MUSIC

CHARLIE PARKER MEMORIAL FOUNDATION
4605 The Paseo, Kansas City, MO 64110
(816) 924-2200
FAX: (816) 924-8605
Arts Area: Instrumental Group; Voice; Dance; Theatre
Status: Non-Profit
Type: Performing; Educational; Sponsoring
Purpose: To foster the arts for underprivleged youth in the greater metropolitan area; to provide an opportunity for young people in humanizing programs
Management: Eddie Baker, Executive Director; Jack Lightfoot, Artistic Director
Officers: Kark J. Arterbery, Chairman
Budget: $50,000 - $100,000
Income Sources: Private Foundations/Grants/Endowments; Business/Corporate Donations; Box Office; Government Grants; Individual Donations
Performance Facilities: Charlie Parker

FRIENDS OF CHAMBER MUSIC KANSAS CITY
118 West 47th Street, Suite 201, Kansas City, MO 64112
(816) 561-9999
FAX: (816) 561-8810
Founded: 1976
Arts Area: Orchestra; Chamber; Ensemble; Ethnic
Status: Non-Profit
Type: Educational; Sponsoring
Purpose: To present the finest in chamber music possible
Management: Cynthia Siebert, Executive Director; Kathleen Markham, Marketing Director; Christy Peterson, Accountant
Officers: William Levi, President; Sally Rheinfrank, Vice President; David Steinhaus, Secretary; Betsey Hughes, Treasurer
Paid Staff: 5   **Volunteer Staff:** 30
Paid Artists: 112
Utilizes: Guest Artists
Budget: $500,000 - $1,000,000
Income Sources: Private Foundations/Grants/Endowments; Business/Corporate Donations; Box Office; Government Grants; Individual Donations; Fundraising; Merchandise Sales
Season: August - May

Annual Attendance: 15,000
Performance Facilities: Folly Theater

KANSAS CITY SYMPHONY
Lyric Theatre, 1020 Central, Kansas City, MO 64105-1672
(816) 471-1100
FAX: (816) 471-0976
Founded: 1982
Arts Area: Symphony; Orchestra
Status: Professional; Non-Profit
Type: Performing; Touring; Educational
Purpose: To present the widest range of symphonic music at the highest level with a special priority on its role as a major resource for the educational cultural development of citizens of all ages
Management: William McGlaughlin, Music Director/Conductor; Susan Franaho, Manager
Paid Staff: 11
Paid Artists: 79
Utilizes: Guest Conductors; Guest Artists
Budget: $1,000,000 - $5,000,000
Income Sources: Private Foundations/Grants/Endowments; Business/Corporate Donations; Box Office; Government Grants; Individual Donations
Season: August - May
Annual Attendance: 290,000
Affiliations: ASOL; Missouri Arts Council; Missouri Citizens for the Arts; MAAA
Performance Facilities: Lyric Theatre

VOCAL MUSIC

HEARTLAND MEN'S CHORUS
PO Box 32374, Kansas City, MO 64111
(816) 842-0399
Founded: 1986
Arts Area: Choral
Status: Non-Professional; Non-Profit
Type: Performing
Purpose: To maintain a chorus open to all men, age 18 and above, sensitive to community issues while serving the Kansas City community at large
Management: Reuben M. Reynolds, Artistic Director; Anthony Edwards, Accompanist
Officers: Randall L. Conradt, President/Treasurer; Brad Allen, Vice President; Lynn Reddick, Secretary
Paid Staff: 2   **Volunteer Staff:** 8
Non-Paid Artists: 46
Utilizes: Guest Artists
Budget: $1,000 - $50,000
Income Sources: Box Office; Government Grants; Individual Donations; Membership Dues
Season: 52 Weeks   **Annual Attendance:** 1,500
Affiliations: Gay and Lesbian Association of Choruses
Performance Facilities: The Granada Theater; The Folly Theater; St. Mark's Lutheran Church

LYRIC OPERA OF KANSAS CITY
Lyric Theatre, 1029 Central, Kansas City, MO 64105
(816) 471-4933
Founded: 1958
Arts Area: Grand Opera; Lyric Opera; Operetta
Status: Professional; Non-Profit
Type: Performing; Touring; Resident
Purpose: Opera theatre in English using American artists
Management: Russell Patterson, General Artistic Director; Evan R. Luskin, Managing Director
Officers: Richard Stern, Chairman; Stephen Hill, President
Paid Staff: 12
Paid Artists: 120
Utilizes: Special Technical Talent; Guest Conductors; Guest Artists; Guest Directors
Budget: $1,000,000 - $5,000,000
Income Sources: Private Foundations/Grants/Endowments; Business/Corporate Donations; Box Office; Government Grants; Individual Donations
Annual Attendance: 23,000
Affiliations: OA; AAA
Performance Facilities: Lyric Theatre

THEATRE

BLACK THEATER GUILD OF GREATER KANSAS CITY
411 East Armour Boulevard, Suite 206, Kansas City, MO 64109
(816) 531-4808
Founded: 1991
Arts Area: Professional; Community
Status: Professional; Semi-Professional; Non-Profit
Type: Performing; Educational; Sponsoring
Purpose: To develop both theatre and audiences in the inner city and among youth
Management: Elroy Reed, President; Demetrius Franklin, Vice President; Sammie Edwards, Legal Counsel
Officers: Elroy Reed, Chairman of the Board; Yvonne Wilson, Joan Johnson, Donna Gray, Rick Peters, Lillie Evans, Dianne Crump, Board of Directors
Volunteer Staff: 3
Paid Artists: 10 **Non-Paid Artists:** 15
Utilizes: Special Technical Talent; Guest Artists; Guest Directors
Budget: $1,000 - $50,000
Income Sources: Business/Corporate Donations; Box Office; Individual Donations
Season: 52 Weeks **Annual Attendance:** 15,000

THE COTERIE THEATRE
2450 Grand Avenue, Suite 144, Kansas City, MO 64108-2520
(816) 474-6785
Founded: 1979
Arts Area: Professional; Musical; Theatrical Group
Status: Professional; Non-Profit
Type: Performing; Touring; Resident; Educational
Purpose: To produce theatre relevant to young audiences; expand the horizons of our audiences by offering the best theatrical works and literature for young people; to present work which challanges traditional views of the theatre, stereotypes of all kinds, and which opens lines of communication between races, sexes, and generations
Management: Kim Ingels, Executive Director; Jeff Church, Artistic Director; Margaret Shelby, Marketing Manager; Daniel Epley, Office Manager; Joel Hoy, Box Office Manager; Laura Burkhart, Production Manager; Brad Shaw, Artist-in-Residence
Officers: Greg Vranicar, President; Martha Crider, Vice President; John Carey, Secretary
Paid Staff: 7
Paid Artists: 45
Utilizes: Guest Artists; Guest Directors
Budget: $100,000 - $500,000
Income Sources: Private Foundations/Grants/Endowments; Business/Corporate Donations; Box Office; Government Grants; Individual Donations
Season: January - December **Annual Attendance:** 47,239
Affiliations: TCG; ASSITEJ

EAGLE-REED AMERICAN THEATER
411 East Armour Boulevard, Suite 206, Kansas City, MO 64106
(816) 531-4808
Founded: 1987
Arts Area: Professional; Community
Status: Professional; Semi-Professional; Non-Profit
Type: Performing; Educational; Sponsoring
Purpose: To perform theatrical productions
Management: Elroy Reed, President; Demetrius Franklin, Promotional Director; Sammy Edwards, Legal Counsel
Volunteer Staff: 3
Utilizes: Special Technical Talent; Guest Artists; Guest Directors
Budget: $1,000 - $50,000
Income Sources: Business/Corporate Donations; Box Office; Individual Donations
Season: 52 Weeks **Annual Attendance:** 5,000

MISSOURI REPERTORY THEATRE
4949 Cherry Street, Kansas City, MO 64110
(816) 235-2727
Founded: 1964
Arts Area: Professional
Status: Professional; Non-Profit
Type: Performing; Resident; Educational
Purpose: To produce plays from classic and contemporary literature which have special significance to our company artists and our audiences
Management: James D. Costin, Executive Director; George Keathley, Artistic Director

Officers: Mark S. Gilman, President; William L. Bruning, Vice President For Planning; Nancy M. Hatch, Vice President for Development; Thomas R. Brous, Vice President for Finance/Treasurer; Robert D. Firnhaber, Vice President for Marketing; Mrs. Richard Ballentine, Vice President for Volunteer Services; Mrs. William A. Fay, Secretary; Joseph Appelt, Assistant Secretary/Assistant Treasurer; Laurie Petring Jarrett, Business Manager
Paid Staff: 25
Paid Artists: 75   **Non-Paid Artists:** 15
Utilizes: Special Technical Talent; Guest Artists; Guest Directors
Budget: $1,000,000 - $5,000,000
Income Sources: Private Foundations/Grants/Endowments; Business/Corporate Donations; Box Office; Government Grants; Individual Donations
Season: September - May   **Annual Attendance:** 100,000
Affiliations: TCG; LORT
Performance Facilities: Helen F. Spencer Theatre

UNICORN THEATRE
3820 Main Street, Kansas City, MO 64111
(816) 531-7529
Founded: 1974
Arts Area: Professional; Musical; Theatrical Group
Status: Professional
Type: Performing
Purpose: Contemporary off-Broadway and original productions
Management: Cynthia Levin, Artistic Director
Officers: Daniel C. Hall, Board Chairman
Paid Staff: 5   **Volunteer Staff:** 2
Paid Artists: 96   **Non-Paid Artists:** 14
Utilizes: Special Technical Talent; Guest Artists; Guest Directors
Budget: $100,000 - $500,000
Income Sources: Private Foundations/Grants/Endowments; Business/Corporate Donations; Box Office; Government Grants; Individual Donations
Season: 52 Weeks   **Annual Attendance:** 12,000
Affiliations: AEA; TCG
Performance Facilities: Unicorn Theatre

PERFORMING SERIES

KANSAS CITY JAZZ FESTIVAL COMMITTEE
PO Box 26264, Kansas City, MO 64196
(913) 722-4258
FAX: (913) 722-3121
Founded: 1983
Arts Area: Festivals
Status: Non-Profit
Type: Educational; Producing
Purpose: To produce annual blues and jazz festival
Management: Kathe Kaul, Executive Director
Officers: Tim Swinney, President; Jack Davis, Vice President; Daphne Moore, Secretary; Michael Moore, Treasurer
Paid Staff: 1   **Volunteer Staff:** 400
Paid Artists: 300
Utilizes: Guest Artists
Budget: $100,000 - $500,000
Income Sources: Private Foundations/Grants/Endowments; Business/Corporate Donations; Government Grants; Individual Donations; Concessions; Novelties
Season: July   **Annual Attendance:** 110,000
Performance Facilities: Penn Valley Park

12TH STREET JAZZ SERIES
c/o Performing Arts Foundation of Kansas City, 300 West 12th Street, Kansas City, MO 64105
(816) 842-5500
Arts Area: Instrumental Music; Jazz
Status: Professional; Non-Profit
Type: Sponsoring
Purpose: To broaden community awareness, support and use of the Folly Theater; to encourage tourism in the Kansas City area; to provide educational services and programs in the performing arts
Management: Robert Dustman
Budget: $100,000 - $500,000
Income Sources: Business/Corporate Donations; Box Office; Government Grants; Individual Donations

Season: 52 Weeks
Performance Facilities: Folly Theater

FACILITY

AVILA COLLEGE - GOPPERT THEATRE
11901 Wornall Road, Kansas City, MO 64145
(816) 942-8400, ext. 289
FAX: (816) 942-3362
    Founded: 1916
    Type of Facility: Concert Hall; Auditorium; Performance Center; Theatre House
    Type of Stage: Thrust; Modified Thrust
    Stage Dimensions: 43'x34'x15' **Orchestra Pit**
    Seating Capacity: 493
    Year Built: 1974 **Architect:** Palmer & Kuehn **Cost:** $1,000,000
    Acoustical Consultant: Coffeen Anderson & Associates
    Contact for Rental: Dr. Daniel Paul Larson; (816) 942-8400, ext. 289
    Resident Groups: Academic Theatre and Music Program

FOLLY
300 West 12th Street, Kansas City, MO 64105
(816) 842-5500
FAX: (816) 842-8709
    Founded: 1900
    Type of Facility: Concert Hall; Auditorium; Performance Center; Theatre House
    Facility Originally: Burlesque Hall
    Type of Stage: Proscenium
    Stage Dimensions: 34'x21' proscenium opening; 4' apron edge; 10' pit lift; 27' back wall **Orchestra Pit**
    Seating Capacity: 1,078
    Year Built: 1900 **Architect:** Louis B. Curtiss
    Year Remodeled: 1981 **Architect:** PENI **Cost:** $3,500,000
    Acoustical Consultant: Wenger
    Contact for Rental: Roselle Tyner; (816) 842-5500

KANSAS CITY MUNICIPAL AUDITORIUM
301 West 13th Street, Suite 100, Kansas City, MO 64105
(816) 871-3700
FAX: (816) 871-3710
    Type of Facility: Civic Center
    Year Built: 1936
    Year Remodeled: 1981
    Contact for Rental: Kathleen Lee; (816) 871-3700
    Manager: Bill Langley; (816) 871-3700
    Contains the Arena and Music Hall. See separate listings for additional information.

KANSAS CITY MUNICIPAL AUDITORIUM - ARENA
301 West 13th Street, Suite 100, Kansas City, MO 64105
(816) 871-3700
FAX: (816) 871-3710
    Type of Facility: Concert Hall; Arena
    Type of Stage: Flexible; Platform
    Seating Capacity: 8,100 permanent; 10,500 concert seating
    Year Built: 1936
    Contact for Rental: Kathleen Lee; (816) 871-3700
    Manager: Bill Langley; (816) 871-3700
    Resident Groups: UMKC Basketball

KANSAS CITY MUNICIPAL AUDITORIUM - MUSIC HALL
301 West 13th Street, Suite 100, Kansas City, MO 64105
(816) 871-3700
FAX: (816) 871-3710
    Type of Facility: Concert Hall
    Type of Stage: Proscenium
    Stage Dimensions: 85'6"Wx32'8"D; 46'Wx23'9"H proscenium opening **Orchestra Pit**
    Seating Capacity: 2,402
    Year Built: 1936
    Year Remodeled: 1981 **Cost:** $26,000,000
    Acoustical Consultant: Coffeen, Anderson & Associates

Contact for Rental: Kathleen Lee;   (816) 871-3700
Manager: Bill Langley;   (816) 871-3700
Resident Groups: State Ballet of Missouri; William Jewell College Fine Arts Series; Theatre League; Kansas City Symphony Pops Series

KEMPER ARENA
1800 Genessee, Kansas City, MO 64102
(816) 274-1900
FAX: (816) 274-0306
Type of Facility: Arena
Type of Stage: Platform
Seating Capacity: 17,500
Year Built: 1974
Contact for Rental: Carolyn Foxworthy;   (816) 274-6713
Resident Groups: Kansas City Blades Hockey Team; Kansas City Attack Soccer Club

LYRIC THEATRE
1029 Central, Kansas City, MO 64105
(816) 471-4933
Type of Facility: Theatre House
Facility Originally: Masonic Temple
Type of Stage: Proscenium
Stage Dimensions: 50'Wx45'Dx26'H   **Orchestra Pit**
Seating Capacity: 1,663
Year Built: 1930   **Architect:** Duncan Architects   **Cost:** $250,000
Year Remodeled: 1992   **Cost:** $300,000
Acoustical Consultant: Coffeen Anderson & Associates
Contact for Rental: Manager;   (816) 471-4933
Resident Groups: Lyric Opera of Kansas; Kansas City Symphony; State Ballet of Missouri

PARK COLLEGE - GRAHAM TYLER MEMORIAL CHAPEL
8700 River Park Drive, Kansas City, MO 64152
(816) 741-2000
Type of Facility: Concert Hall
Facility Originally: Church
Type of Stage: Platform
Stage Dimensions: 45'x35'
Seating Capacity: 600
Year Built: 1937
Year Remodeled: 1973   **Cost:** $20,000
Contact for Rental: Katy Goodwin;   (816) 741-2000, ext. 377
Resident Groups: Northland Symphony Orchestra; Parkville Chamber Players; Park College Band; Park College Choir
Rented on a very limited basis for serious musical events only

UNICORN THEATRE
3820 Main Street, Kansas City, MO 64111
(816) 531-7529
Type of Facility: Off Broadway
Facility Originally: Garage
Type of Stage: Thrust
Stage Dimensions: 30'x40'
Seating Capacity: 201
Year Built: 1926
Year Remodeled: 1986   **Architect:** Ralph Keyes   **Cost:** $200,000
Acoustical Consultant: Ralph Keyes
Contact for Rental: Jan Kohl;   (816) 531-7529
Manager: Cynthia Levin, Executive Artistic Dir.;   (816) 531-7529
Resident Groups: Unicorn Theatre

Marshall

INSTRUMENTAL MUSIC

MARSHALL PHILHARMONIC ORCHESTRA
1644 South Colby, Marshall, MO 65340
(816) 886-7044
Founded: 1963
Arts Area: Symphony

Status: Non-Professional; Non-Profit
Type: Performing; Educational
Purpose: To offer an opportunity to area amateur musicians to play
Management: Charles Ferguson, Conductor
Officers: Jane Huff, President; Buena Stolberg, Vice President; Marjorie Haggard, Secretary; Rodney Polson, Treasurer
Volunteer Staff: 4
Paid Artists: 3   **Non-Paid Artists:** 60
Utilizes: Guest Artists
Budget: $1,000 - $50,000
Income Sources: Business/Corporate Donations; Individual Donations
Season: October - April   **Annual Attendance:** 2,800
Affiliations: Missouri Arts Council
Performance Facilities: Harold L. Lickey Auditorium

Maryville

PERFORMING SERIES

NORTHWEST MISSOURI STATE UNIVERSITY PERFORMING ARTS SERIES
800 University Drive, Maryville, MO 64468-6001
(816) 562-1212
Arts Area: Vocal Music; Instrumental Music; Theater
Status: Non-Profit
Type: Educational; Sponsoring
Purpose: To provide a variety of performing arts and lectures to the University and the community
Management: David Gieseke, Chairman
Volunteer Staff: 10
Utilizes: Guest Artists
Budget: $1,000 - $50,000
Income Sources: Government Grants
Season: September - May
Affiliations: Missouri Arts Council
Performance Facilities: Charles Johnson Theatre, Mary Linn Performing Arts Center

FACILITY

NORTHWEST MISSOURI STATE UNIVERSITY - CHARLES JOHNSON THEATRE
Maryville, MO 64468
(816) 582-4500
Type of Facility: Auditorium
Type of Stage: Proscenium
Orchestra Pit
Seating Capacity: 1,095
Year Built: 1985
Resident Groups: University Theatre Department

NORTHWEST MISSOURI STATE UNIVERSITY - MARY LINN PERFORMING ARTS CENTER
Maryville, MO 64468
(816) 562-1176
Type of Facility: Auditorium; Studio Performance; Performance Center
Type of Stage: Proscenium
Stage Dimensions: 36'Wx30'D   **Orchestra Pit**
Seating Capacity: 1,100
Year Built: 1984   **Architect:** Architect Design Collaborative   **Cost:** $3,500,000
Contact for Rental: Dean Robert Sunkel;   (816) 562-1325
Resident Groups: Northwest Missouri State University Department of Theatre

Memphis

THEATRE

MEMPHIS COMMUNITY PLAYERS
125 South Main, Memphis, MO 63555
(816) 465-7770
Founded: 1974
Arts Area: Musical; Community; Theatrical Group
Status: Non-Professional; Non-Profit

Type: Performing; Resident; Educational
Purpose: To provide summer musical theatre for our area
Officers: Harlo L. Donelson, President; Rick Fischer, Vice President; Deb Seamster, Secretary; Ruth Kerr, Treasurer; Charles Harris, Board Member
Budget: $1,000 - $50,000
Income Sources: Box Office; Individual Donations
Season: June - August   **Annual Attendance:** 1,000
Performance Facilities: Memphis Cinema

Moberly

THEATRE

MOBERLY COMMUNITY THEATRE
212 Crest Drive, Moberly, MO 65270
(816) 263-3345
Founded: 1979
Arts Area: Musical; Dinner; Community
Status: Non-Profit
Type: Performing; Sponsoring
Purpose: Promote the performing arts, community working together
Management: Carolee Hazlet, Producer/Director
Volunteer Staff: 15
Non-Paid Artists: 50
Utilizes: Special Technical Talent; Guest Directors
Budget: $1,000 - $50,000
Income Sources: Business/Corporate Donations; Box Office; Individual Donations
Season: 52 Weeks   **Annual Attendance:** 1,500
Performance Facilities: Moberly Municipal Auditorium; Peppermint Loft

Parkville

FACILITY

PARK COLLEGE - ALUMNI HALL THEATRE
Park College, Parkville, MO 64152
(816) 741-2000
Type of Facility: Theatre Complex; Auditorium; Studio Performance; Theatre House; Black Box
Facility Originally: Movie House
Type of Stage: Proscenium
Stage Dimensions: 16'x22'x20'
Seating Capacity: 205
Year Built: 1950
Contact for Rental: S.L. Sartain, Dean of Students;   (816) 741-2000, ext. 379
Manager: Marsha M. Morgan, Theatre Dept. Chairman;   (816) 741-2000, ext. 450
Resident Groups: Park College Theatre Department

Point Lookout

FACILITY

COLLEGE OF THE OZARKS - JONES AUDITORIUM
Point Lookout, MO 65726
(417) 334-6411
Type of Facility: Auditorium
Type of Stage: Proscenium   **Orchestra Pit**
Seating Capacity: 980
Year Built: 1968
Contact for Rental: Dr. William Todd, President;   (417) 334-6411
Manager: Mark Young;   (417) 334-6411

Saint Ann

DANCE

GATEWAY BALLET OF SAINT LOUIS
10674 Saint Charles Rock Road, Saint Ann, MO 63074
(314) 423-1600
Founded: 1970
Arts Area: Mime; Ballet; Jazz
Status: Non-Professional; Non-Profit
Type: Performing; Educational
Purpose: To give young dancers from the metropolitan St. Louis area the opportunity to dance in a professional atmosphere with guest artists and choreographers; to provide high-quality dance performances at reasonable prices
Management: Norma Beutell Van Sickle, Artistic Director
Officers: Paul Stuart, President; Dan Francis, Vice President; Carol Wofsey, Secretary; John Niemann, Treasurer
Paid Staff: 3 **Volunteer Staff:** 15
Paid Artists: 3 **Non-Paid Artists:** 30
Utilizes: Special Technical Talent; Guest Artists; Guest Directors; Guest Choreographers
Budget: $1,000 - $50,000
Income Sources: Private Foundations/Grants/Endowments; Business/Corporate Donations; Box Office; Individual Donations
Season: September - June **Annual Attendance:** 6,000
Affiliations: Missouri Arts Council
Performance Facilities: Florissant Civic Center

Saint Joseph

INSTRUMENTAL MUSIC

THE SAINT JOSEPH SYMPHONY SOCIETY
120 South Eighth Street, Saint Joseph, MO 64501
(816) 233-7701
Founded: 1959
Arts Area: Symphony
Status: Professional; Non-Profit
Type: Performing; Educational
Purpose: To present symphonic concerts and educational activities for the citizens of northwest Missouri and eastern Kansas
Management: Judith A. McMurray, Managing Director
Officers: David W. Lewis Jr., President; Clay Whitehead M.D., Vice President; Pat Speiser, Treasurer; Dee Hurley, Secretary
Paid Staff: 6 **Volunteer Staff:** 200
Paid Artists: 61
Utilizes: Guest Artists
Budget: $100,000 - $500,000
Income Sources: Private Foundations/Grants/Endowments; Business/Corporate Donations; Box Office; Government Grants; Individual Donations
Season: September - May **Annual Attendance:** 3,000
Affiliations: ASOL; Missouri Citizens for the Arts
Performance Facilities: Missouri Theater

FACILITY

SAINT JOSEPH CIVIC CENTER
100 North Fourth Street, Saint Joseph, MO 64501
(816) 271-4717
FAX: (816) 232-9213
Type of Facility: Theatre Complex; Arena
Year Built: 1980 **Cost:** $5,250,000
Contact for Rental: (816) 271-4717
Contains the Arena and the Missouri Theatre. See separate listings for additional information.

SAINT JOSEPH CIVIC CENTER - ARENA
100 North Fourth Street, Saint Joseph, MO 64501
(816) 271-4717
FAX: (816) 232-9213
Type of Facility: Arena

Type of Stage: Platform
Stage Dimensions: 36'x48'
Seating Capacity: 5,000
Year Built: 1980
Contact for Rental: Kathy Brock, Bill France;   (816) 271-4717
Manager: Bill France;   (816) 271-4717

SAINT JOSEPH CIVIC CENTER - MISSOURI THEATRE
100 North Fourth Street, Saint Joseph, MO 64501
(816) 271-4717
FAX: (816) 232-9213
Type of Facility: Concert Hall; Performance Center; Opera House; Multi-Purpose
Type of Stage: Proscenium
Stage Dimensions: 42'Wx30'D; 42'Wx25'H proscenium opening   **Orchestra Pit**
Seating Capacity: 1,217
Year Built: 1927   **Architect:** Boller Brothers   **Cost:** $1,000,000
Year Remodeled: 1979   **Architect:** Brunner & Brunner   **Cost:** $1,500,000
Contact for Rental: Kerry Strahm, Bill France;   (816) 271-4628
Manager: Bill France;   (816) 271-4717
Resident Groups: Allied Arts, Robidoux; St. Joseph Symphony; Performing Arts Association; Creative Arts Productions

Saint Louis

DANCE

DANCE ST. LOUIS
634 North Grand Boulevard, Suite 1102, Saint Louis, MO 63103
(314) 534-5000, ext. 6622
FAX: (314) 534-5001
Founded: 1966
Arts Area: Modern; Mime; Ballet; Jazz; Ethnic; Folk
Status: Non-Profit
Type: Resident; Educational; Sponsoring
Purpose: To promote an interest in dance by providing varied professional dance concerts and related programs
Management: Bill Eastman, General Manager; Adam A. Pinsker, Executive Director; Laura Burkhart, Operation Manager
Officers: Peter J. Genovese, President
Paid Staff: 4
Utilizes: Special Technical Talent; Guest Artists
Budget: $1,000,000 - $5,000,000
Income Sources: Private Foundations/Grants/Endowments; Business/Corporate Donations; Box Office; Government Grants; Individual Donations
Season: 52 Weeks   **Annual Attendance:** 65,000
Affiliations: Dance USA
Performance Facilities: Kiel Opera House; Edison Theatre, Washington University; J.C. Penney Auditorium, University of Missouri-Saint Louis; Fox Theatre

MID AMERICA DANCE COMPANY
4440 Lindell Boulevard, Suite 1104, Saint Louis, MO 63108
(314) 367-3620
Founded: 1976
Arts Area: Modern
Status: Professional; Non-Profit
Type: Performing; Touring; Educational
Purpose: To produce the highest level of modern dance through teaching, concerts and workshops
Management: Ross Winter, Executive Director; David Kruger, Booking Agent
Officers: Carolyn Maymon, President; Susan Fay, Vice President; Lynn Mutch, Secretary; Lois Ladd, Treasurer
Paid Staff: 2   **Volunteer Staff:** 12
Paid Artists: 7
Utilizes: Special Technical Talent; Guest Conductors; Guest Artists; Guest Choreographers
Budget: $100,000 - $500,000
Income Sources: Private Foundations/Grants/Endowments; Business/Corporate Donations; Box Office; Government Grants; Individual Donations
Season: September - June   **Annual Attendance:** 15,000
Affiliations: Mid-America Dance Network; Dance St, Louis; Arts & Education Council of Greater St. Louis
Performance Facilities: Edison Theatre

SAINT LOUIS BALLET
634 North Grand Boulevard, Suite 10E, Saint Louis, MO 63103
(314) 652-7711
FAX: (314) 533-3345
Founded: 1985
Arts Area: Ballet
Status: Professional; Non-Profit
Type: Performing; Touring; Resident; Educational
Purpose: To provide St. Louis and surrounding areas with a permanent, professional resident ballet company capable of performing both classical and contemporary works in the Ballet Russe tradition
Management: Betty L. Jehle, General Director; Cynthia S. Peak, Assistant to the General Director; Ludmila Dokoudovsky and Antoni Zalewski, Artistic Directors
Officers: J. Kent McNeil, President; John M. Regan Jr., Vice President; Gwen Knight, Treasurer; James Whitener, Secretary
Paid Staff: 3   **Volunteer Staff:** 1
Paid Artists: 18
Utilizes: Special Technical Talent; Guest Artists; Guest Choreographers
Budget: $100,000 - $500,000
Income Sources: Private Foundations/Grants/Endowments; Business/Corporate Donations; Box Office; Government Grants; Individual Donations; Interest; Product Sales
Season: September - April   **Annual Attendance:** 25,000
Affiliations: Grand Center
Performance Facilities: Meramec Theatre; Edison Theatre; Orthwein Theatre

SAINT LOUIS CULTURAL FLAMENCO SOCIETY
PO Box 21818, Saint Louis, MO 63109
(314) 832-3911
Founded: 1983
Arts Area: Ballet
Status: Non-Profit
Type: Performing
Purpose: To promote the Spanish culture through classical, regional and Flamenco dances
Management: Marisel Weeks, Artistic Director; Alvaro Molano, Manager
Officers: Rosa Schwarz, President; Roberto Alvarez, Vice President; Alvaro Molano, Treasurer; Irma Martinez, Secretary
Volunteer Staff: 8
Non-Paid Artists: 7
Utilizes: Guest Artists; Guest Choreographers
Budget: $1,000 - $50,000
Income Sources: Private Foundations/Grants/Endowments; Business/Corporate Donations; Box Office; Government Grants
Season: 52 Weeks   **Annual Attendance:** 7,000
Affiliations: Dance St. Louis

INSTRUMENTAL MUSIC

METROPOLITAN ORCHESTRA OF SAINT LOUIS
8282 Big Ben Boulevard, Suite 206, Saint Louis, MO 63119
(314) 821-0119
Founded: 1967
Arts Area: Symphony; Orchestra; Ensemble
Status: Semi-Professional; Non-Profit
Type: Performing; Educational
Purpose: To provide and present a high quality symphony orchestra in the Greater Saint Louis Area in order to expand the cultural resources of communities and audiences not readily served by other various orchestras
Management: Allen Carl Larson, Music Director/Conductor; Jean Lovati, Executive Director; Carl Dettlebach, Director of Operations
Officers: Jean Lovati, President, Board of Directors
Utilizes: Guest Conductors; Guest Artists
Budget: $100,000 - $500,000
Income Sources: Private Foundations/Grants/Endowments; Business/Corporate Donations; Box Office; Government Grants; Individual Donations
Annual Attendance: 6,000
Performance Facilities: Loretto-Hilton Center for the Performing Arts, Webster University

NEW MUSIC CIRCLE
1110 Washington, 7th Floor, Saint Louis, MO 63101
(314) 567-5384
Arts Area: Electronic & Live Electronic; New Music, Avant Garde

Status: Professional; Non-Profit
Type: Presenting
Purpose: To serve as an advocate for new music; to commission new works and promote promising composers and ensembles
Management: Rich O'Donnell, Music Director
Officers: Nancy Kranzberg, President
Budget: $1,000 - $50,000
Income Sources: Private Foundations/Grants/Endowments; Business/Corporate Donations; Box Office; Government Grants; Individual Donations

THE SAINT LOUIS CLASSICAL GUITAR SOCIETY
PO Box 24153, Saint Louis, MO 63130
(314) 725-0739
Arts Area: Instrumental Group
Status: Non-Profit
Type: Sponsoring
Purpose: To promote an appreciation of music for the classical guitar and related fretted instruments
Management: Kathleen Ash, Program Director
Officers: William B. Ash, President
Budget: $50,000 - $100,000
Income Sources: Private Foundations/Grants/Endowments; Business/Corporate Donations; Box Office; Government Grants; Individual Donations
Performance Facilities: Ethical Society of Saint Louis

SAINT LOUIS PHILHARMONIC ORCHESTRA
PO Box 3858, Saint Louis, MO 63122
(314) 569-8520
Founded: 1860
Arts Area: Symphony
Status: Non-Professional; Non-Profit
Type: Performing
Purpose: To provide an opportunity to play good music under an able conductor
Officers: Marilyn K. Hamiston, President
Utilizes: Guest Conductors
Budget: $1,000 - $50,000
Income Sources: Private Foundations/Grants/Endowments; Government Grants; Individual Donations
Season: November - May
Performance Facilities: Scottish Rite Cathedral

SAINT LOUIS SYMPHONY CHAMBER ORCHESTRA
Powell Symphony Hall, 718 North Grand Boulevard, Saint Louis, MO 63103
(314) 533-2500
Founded: 1971
Arts Area: Chamber
Status: Professional; Non-Profit
Type: Performing; Resident
Utilizes: Guest Conductors; Guest Artists
Income Sources: Individual Donations
Season: October - May
Affiliations: Saint Louis Symphony Orchestra
Performance Facilities: Powell Symphony Hall at Grand Center

SAINT LOUIS SYMPHONY ORCHESTRA
Powell Symphony Hall, 718 North Grand Boulevard, Saint Louis, MO 63103
(314) 533-2500
Founded: 1879
Arts Area: Symphony
Status: Professional; Non-Profit
Type: Performing; Touring; Educational
Management: Bruce Coppock, Executive Director
Officers: Thomas H. Jacobsen, Chairman
Paid Staff: 73   **Volunteer Staff:** 2,500
Utilizes: Guest Conductors; Guest Artists
Budget: Over 10,000,000
Income Sources: Private Foundations/Grants/Endowments; Business/Corporate Donations; Box Office; Government Grants; Individual Donations
Season: September - August
Performance Facilities: Powell Symphony Hall at Grand Center

SAINT LOUIS SYMPHONY YOUTH ORCHESTRA
Powell Symphony Hall, 718 North Grand Boulevard, Saint Louis, MO 63103
(314) 533-2500
Founded: 1970
Arts Area: Symphony; Orchestra; Chamber
Status: Non-Professional; Non-Profit
Type: Performing; Touring; Educational; Sponsoring
Purpose: The Saint Louis Symphony Youth Orchestra was founded in 1970 by Leonard Slatkin to acquaint young instrumentalists with the atmosphere of a professional orchestra, to introduce them to the environment of the Saint Louis Symphony and to provide them with the opportunity of investigating and performing a wide spectrum of symphonic music.
Management: Margaret Neilson, Manager; David Loebel, Music Director; Leonard Slatkin, Music Advisor
Officers: Mrs. Matthew F. Mayer, Youth Orchestra Committee Chairman
Paid Staff: 2
Non-Paid Artists: 100
Utilizes: Guest Artists
Budget: $1,000 - $50,000
Income Sources: Private Foundations/Grants/Endowments; Business/Corporate Donations; Box Office; Individual Donations
Season: September - May   **Annual Attendance:** 3,500
Affiliations: ASOL (Youth Orchestra Division)
Performance Facilities: Powell Symphony Hall at Grand Center

SYNCHRONIA
PO Box 2937, Saint Louis, MO 63130
(314) 664-9313
Founded: 1985
Arts Area: Ensemble
Status: Professional; Non-Profit
Type: Performing; Touring; Educational
Purpose: To perform and promote recent art music with emphasis on the United States and living composers of the past 25 years
Officers: Timothy Vincent Clark, Music Director
Paid Staff: 1   **Volunteer Staff:** 1
Paid Artists: 6
Utilizes: Guest Artists
Budget: $50,000 - $100,000
Season: September - May   **Annual Attendance:** 1,000
Performance Facilities: Ethical Society

VOCAL MUSIC

OPERA THEATRE OF SAINT LOUIS
539 Garden Avenue, PO Box 19110, Saint Louis, MO 63119
(314) 961-0171
FAX: (314) 961-7463
Founded: 1964
Arts Area: Grand Opera; Lyric Opera; Light Opera; Operetta
Status: Non-Profit
Type: Performing; Touring; Educational
Purpose: To present opera in English affording career advancement of young American singers under direction of renowned directors and conductors
Management: Charles R. MacKay, General Director; Colin Graham, Artistic Director; Stephen Lord, Music Director; Jeff Thurston, Business Manager
Officers: Mrs. Monte Throdahl, Chairman; Donald Bryant Jr. and William B. McMillan Jr., Vice Chairmen; Robert L. Scharff Jr., Secretary; Reuben M. Morriss, III, Treasurer
Paid Staff: 15
Paid Artists: 90
Utilizes: Special Technical Talent; Guest Conductors; Guest Artists; Guest Directors
Budget: $1,000,000 - $5,000,000
Income Sources: Private Foundations/Grants/Endowments; Business/Corporate Donations; Box Office; Government Grants; Individual Donations
Season: May - June   **Annual Attendance:** 24,000
Performance Facilities: Loretto-Hilton Center for the Performing Arts; Webster University

SAINT LOUIS CHAMBER CHORUS
PO Box 11558, Saint Louis, MO 63105
(314) 458-4343
Founded: 1957

Arts Area: Choral
Status: Professional; Non-Profit
Type: Performing; Educational
Purpose: To present in concert choral works of unusual rarely performed music by outstanding composers, usually a cappela
Management: Board of Directors; Sally Jones, Executive Director; Philip Barnes, Music Director
Officers: Alfred O. Heitzmann, President; O.L. Lippard, Vice President; Barbara Boland, Secretary; M. Mark McCallum, Treasurer
Paid Staff: 2
Paid Artists: 40
Budget: $1,000 - $50,000
Income Sources: Private Foundations/Grants/Endowments; Business/Corporate Donations; Box Office; Government Grants; Individual Donations
Season: September - May   **Annual Attendance:** 1,500

SAINT LOUIS SYMPHONY CHORUS
718 North Grand Boulevard, Saint Louis, MO 63104
(314) 533-2500
FAX: (314) 533-6000
Founded: 1977
Arts Area: Choral
Status: Professional; Non-Professional; Non-Profit
Type: Performing; Touring; Educational
Purpose: To perform orchestral works involving chorus
Management: Richard Ashburner, Manager; Thomas Peck, Chorus Director; Alan Freed, Assistant Director; Barbara Liberman, Accompanist
Officers: Thomas H. Jacobsen, Chairman of the Board; Richard R. Hoffert, Acting Executive Director; Leon R. Strauss, Secretary; W.L. Hadley Griffin, Vice Chairman Development; Mrs. William W. Scott, Vice Chairman Affiliates and Artistic; Michale F. Neidorff, Vice Chairman Public Affairs
Paid Staff: 4
Paid Artists: 26   **Non-Paid Artists:** 114
Utilizes: Guest Conductors; Guest Artists
Budget: $100,000 - $500,000
Income Sources: Private Foundations/Grants/Endowments; Business/Corporate Donations; Box Office; Government Grants; Individual Donations
Season: September - May   **Annual Attendance:** 32,000
Affiliations: CA
Performance Facilities: Powell Symphony Hall
Income Sources: Private Foundations/Grants/Endowments; Business/Corporate Donations; Box Office; Government Grants; Individual Donations

THEATRE

CIRCUS ARTS FOUNDATION OF MISSOURI
634 North Grand Boulevard, Suite 1029, Saint Louis, MO 63103
(314) 531-6273
FAX: (314) 533-3345
Founded: 1988
Arts Area: Professional
Status: Non-Profit
Type: Performing; Touring; Educational
Purpose: To create and foster an artistic, enlightening and joyous circus
Management: Judy Pierson, Executive Director; Ivor David Balding, Artistic Director/Producer; Maria Atchison, Administrative Assistant; Jessica Hentoff, School Director
Officers: A.R. Naunheim, President; Harry Wuertenbaecher, Vice President; Eddie G. Davis, Treasurer; Judy C. Pierson, Secretary
Paid Staff: 3   **Volunteer Staff:** 3
Utilizes: Guest Artists
Budget: $500,000 - $1,000,000
Income Sources: Private Foundations/Grants/Endowments; Business/Corporate Donations; Box Office; Government Grants; Individual Donations
Season: May - October   **Annual Attendance:** 42,000
Performance Facilities: The Jewell Tent

METRO THEATER COMPANY/THE CENTER FOR CREATIVE ARTS
524 Trinity, Saint Louis, MO 63130
(314) 727-3552
Founded: 1973
Arts Area: Professional; Theatrical Group

Status: Professional; Non-Profit
Type: Performing; Touring; Resident; Educational
Purpose: To tour live theater for young people and families; to stimulate interest and participation in the creative arts
Management: Carol Evans, Producing Director; Kitty Daly, Marketing Director
Officers: Philip Moses, President; Mary Ellen Finch, Vice President; John Weil, Secretary/Treasurer
Paid Staff: 3
Paid Artists: 7
Utilizes: Guest Artists
Budget: $100,000 - $500,000
Income Sources: Private Foundations/Grants/Endowments; Business/Corporate Donations; Individual Donations
Season: October - June   **Annual Attendance:** 90,000
Affiliations: ASSITEJ; Missouri Citizens for the Arts

THE NEW THEATRE
634 North Grand Boulevard, Suite 10-C, Saint Louis, MO 63103
(314) 531-8330
FAX: (314) 533-3345
Founded: 1985
Arts Area: Professional; Theatrical Group
Status: Professional; Non-Profit
Type: Performing
Purpose: To provide innovative professional theatre in accessible locations for Saint Louis audiences
Management: Agnes Wilcox, Artistic Director; Amy Allen, Production Manager; Dean Minderman, Director of Public Relations and Marketing; Joan Duggan, Office Manager
Officers: DeLancey Smith, President; Suzanne Couch, Vice President; James F. O'Donnell, Treasurer; Agnes Wilcox, Secretary
Paid Staff: 4
Paid Artists: 75
Utilizes: Special Technical Talent; Guest Artists; Guest Directors
Budget: $100,000 - $500,000
Income Sources: Private Foundations/Grants/Endowments; Business/Corporate Donations; Box Office; Government Grants; Individual Donations
Season: October - July   **Annual Attendance:** 4,500
Affiliations: TCG; League of Saint Louis Theatres

THE REPERTORY THEATRE OF SAINT LOUIS
130 Edgar Road, Saint Louis, MO 63119
(314) 968-7340
Founded: 1966
Arts Area: Professional; Theatrical Group
Status: Professional
Type: Performing
Management: Steven Woolf, Artistic Director
Officers: Gretta Forrester, Board President
Paid Staff: 35
Paid Artists: 65
Utilizes: Special Technical Talent; Guest Artists; Guest Directors
Budget: $1,000,000 - $5,000,000
Income Sources: Private Foundations/Grants/Endowments; Business/Corporate Donations; Box Office; Government Grants; Individual Donations
Season: September - April   **Annual Attendance:** 100,000
Affiliations: AEA; SSDC; AFM; IATSE
Performance Facilities: Loretto-Hilton Center for the Performing Arts (Webster University)

SAINT LOUIS BLACK REPERTORY COMPANY
634 North Grand, Saint Louis, MO 63103
(314) 534-3807
FAX: (314) 533-3345
Founded: 1976
Arts Area: Professional; Musical; Community; Theatrical Group
Status: Professional; Non-Profit
Type: Performing; Touring; Educational; Sponsoring
Purpose: We are committed to providing quality Black Theatre to the Saint Louis area
Management: Ron Himes, Producing Director; Donna Adams, General Manager
Officers: Arthur D. Jordan, Chairman; Charles Polk, Vice Chairman; Stephen M. Coleman, Treasurer; Susan Corcoran, Secretary
Paid Staff: 9   **Volunteer Staff:** 5
Paid Artists: 55
Utilizes: Special Technical Talent; Guest Artists; Guest Directors

Budget: $500,000 - $1,000,000
Income Sources: Private Foundations/Grants/Endowments; Business/Corporate Donations; Box Office; Government Grants; Individual Donations
Season: September - June   **Annual Attendance:** 15,000
Affiliations: TCG; AEA
Performance Facilities: Grandel Square Theatre

THEATER FACTORY SAINT LOUIS
4265 Shaw Avenue, Saint Louis, MO 63110
(314) 773-8880
Founded: 1982
Arts Area: Professional; Summer Stock; Theatrical Group
Status: Professional
Type: Performing; Educational
Management: Earl D. Weaver, Managing Director; Hope Wurdack, Artistic Director; Cindy Vahle, Business Manager
Officers: William Leith, President; Marie Brauer, Vice President; Cathy Coughlin, Secretary; Karen Herman, Treasurer; Mary Pat Blake, Marketing
Paid Staff: 3
Utilizes: Special Technical Talent; Guest Conductors; Guest Artists; Guest Directors; Musical Directors
Budget: $100,000 - $500,000
Income Sources: Private Foundations/Grants/Endowments; Business/Corporate Donations; Box Office; Government Grants; Individual Donations
Season: June - September   **Annual Attendance:** 15,000
Affiliations: League of St. Louis Theatres

PERFORMING SERIES

BLACK MUSIC SOCIETY OF MISSOURI
3701 Grandel Square, Saint Louis, MO 63108
(314) 534-4344
Founded: 1984
Arts Area: Vocal Music; Instrumental Music; Festivals
Status: Professional; Semi-Professional; Non-Profit
Type: Performing; Touring; Resident; Educational; Sponsoring
Purpose: To preserve and promote Black America's musical heritage
Management: Prince A. Wells, Music Director
Officers: Prince A. Wells, III, President; Sheryl Jones, Vice President; Patricia Wilson, Secretary; Shirley Richardson, Treasurer
Paid Staff: 1   **Volunteer Staff:** 3
Paid Artists: 12
Utilizes: Guest Conductors; Guest Artists; Guest Directors
Budget: $1,000 - $50,000
Income Sources: Business/Corporate Donations; Box Office; Government Grants; Individual Donations
Season: 52 Weeks

CITICORP SUMMERFEST
Powell Symphony Hall, 718 North Grand Boulevard, Saint Louis, MO 63103
(314) 533-2500
Founded: 1984
Arts Area: Instrumental Music
Status: Professional; Non-Profit
Type: Performing
Management: Leonard Slatkin, Music Director/Conductor
Paid Staff: 15   **Volunteer Staff:** 50
Paid Artists: 101
Utilizes: Guest Conductors; Guest Artists
Income Sources: Business/Corporate Donations; Box Office; Government Grants; Individual Donations
Season: May - June   **Annual Attendance:** 8,000
Affiliations: Saint Louis Symphony Orchestra
Performance Facilities: Powell Symphony Hall At Grand Center

EDISON THEATRE AT WASHINGTON UNIVERSITY
Campus Box 1119, One Brookings Drive, Saint Louis, MO 63130
(314) 935-6518
FAX: (314) 935-7362
Founded: 1973
Arts Area: Dance; Vocal Music; Instrumental Music; Theater
Status: Professional; Non-Profit
Type: Performing; Touring; Educational; Sponsoring; Presenting

Purpose: To present three annual series of national and international artists and companies in dance, theatre, music and other arts
Management: Evy Warshawski, Managing Director; Charles Robin, Operations Manager
Paid Staff: 4 **Volunteer Staff:** 75
Utilizes: Guest Artists
Budget: $100,000 - $500,000
Income Sources: Private Foundations/Grants/Endowments; Business/Corporate Donations; Box Office; Government Grants; Individual Donations
Season: September - May
Annual Attendance: 45,000
Performance Facilities: Edison Theatre; Mallinckrodt Drama Studio

MUNICIPAL THEATER ASSOCIATION OF SAINT LOUIS
Forest Park, Saint Louis, MO 63112
(314) 361-1900
FAX: (314) 361-0009
Founded: 1919
Arts Area: Theater
Status: Professional; Non-Profit
Type: Performing; Educational
Purpose: THE MUNY, 'Alone in its Greatness,' is the largest musical theatre in the country performing self-produced and touring shows 7 nights a week, run on the star system.
Management: Dennis M. Reagan, General Manager/CEO
Utilizes: Special Technical Talent; Guest Conductors; Guest Artists; Guest Directors
Budget: $1,000,000 - $5,000,000
Income Sources: Business/Corporate Donations; Box Office; Individual Donations
Season: 52 Weeks
Affiliations: NAMTP; Arts & Education Council of Greater Saint Louis
Performance Facilities: THE MUNY, Forest Park

SAINT LOUIS SYMPHONY QUEENY POPS
Powell Symphony Hall, 718 North Grand Boulevard, Saint Louis, MO 63103
(314) 533-2500
FAX: (314) 533-6000
Founded: 1975
Arts Area: Vocal Music; Instrumental Music
Status: Professional; Non-Profit
Type: Performing
Management: Richard Hayman, McDonnell Douglas Principal Pops Conductor; Sam Dixon, Director of Artistic Planning
Paid Staff: 15 **Volunteer Staff:** 50
Paid Artists: 101
Utilizes: Guest Conductors; Guest Artists
Income Sources: Business/Corporate Donations; Box Office; Government Grants
Season: June - August
Annual Attendance: 8,000
Affiliations: Saint Louis Symphony Orchestra
Performance Facilities: Greensfelder Recreation Center in Queeny Park

FACILITY

AMERICAN THEATRE
416 North Ninth Street, Saint Louis, MO 63101-1470
(314) 231-7000
Type of Facility: Concert Hall; Theatre House
Facility Originally: Vaudeville
Type of Stage: Proscenium
Seating Capacity: 1,853
Year Built: 1918
Year Remodeled: 1985 **Cost:** $175,000
Contact for Rental: Karen McCrory; (314) 231-7000
Resident Groups: Municipal Theater Association of Saint Louis

ETHICAL SOCIETY AUDITORIUM
9001 Clayton Road, Saint Louis, MO 63117
(314) 991-0955
Type of Facility: Auditorium
Facility Originally: Lecture Hall
Type of Stage: Platform

Seating Capacity: 450
Year Built: 1960   **Architect:** Harris Armstrong
Contact for Rental: John Hoad, Leader;   (314) 991-0955

THE FABULOUS FOX THEATRE
Grand Center, 527 North Grand Boulevard, Saint Louis, MO 63103
(314) 534-1678
    Type of Facility: Performance Center; Theatre House
    Facility Originally: Movie House
    Type of Stage: Proscenium
    Stage Dimensions: 125'Wx35'5"D; 78'Wx32'H proscenium opening   **Orchestra Pit**
    Seating Capacity: 4,299
    Year Built: 1929   **Architect:** C. Howard Crane   **Cost:** $6,000,000
    Year Remodeled: 1982   **Cost:** $2,000,000
    Contact for Rental: Fox Productions;   (314) 534-1678
    Manager: David R. Fay
    Resident Groups: Fox Productions; Dance St. Louis
    Now listed on the National Register of Historic Places, the Fox Theatre was the second largest movie palace in the nation with 5,060 seats when it was built in 1929.

THE KIEL CENTER
100 North Broadway, Saint Louis, MO 63102
(314) 466-4649
FAX: (314) 466-4660
    Type of Facility: Performance Center; Multi-Purpose
    Year Built: 1932   **Cost:** $7,000,000
    Contact for Rental: Christine Cool;   (314) 466-4649
    Resident Groups: Dance Saint Louis; Saint Louis Philharmonic
    Contains Arena and Opera House. See separate listings for additional information.

THE KIEL CENTER - ARENA
100 North Broadway, Suite 820, Saint Louis, MO 63102
(314) 466-4649
FAX: (314) 466-4660
    Type of Facility: Concert Hall; Auditorium; Studio Performance; Arena; Multi-Purpose
    Type of Stage: Proscenium; Hydraulic Lift Stage
    Stage Dimensions: 95'Wx48'D; 67'W proscenium opening   **Orchestra Pit**
    Seating Capacity: 10,500
    Contact for Rental: Christine Cool;   (314) 466-4649
    12'Dx80'W Hydraulic Lift Pit

THE KIEL CENTER - OPERA HOUSE
100 North Broadway, Suite 820, Saint Louis, MO 63102
(314) 466-4649
FAX: (314) 466-4660
    Type of Facility: Concert Hall; Theatre House; Opera House
    Type of Stage: Thrust; Proscenium; Hydraulic Lift Stage
    Stage Dimensions: 63'Wx56'D; 63'W proscenium opening   **Orchestra Pit**
    Seating Capacity: 3,500
    Contact for Rental: Christine Cool;   (314) 466-4649
    Resident Groups: Saint Louis Philharmonic; Dance Saint Louis
    12'Dx63'W Hydraulic Lift Pit

THE MUNY
Forest Park, Saint Louis, MO 63112
(314) 361-1900
FAX: (314) 361-0009
    Type of Facility: Outdoor (Concert); Amphitheater
    Type of Stage: Proscenium; Environmental
    Stage Dimensions: 90'Wx60'D with a 48' diameter turntable   **Orchestra Pit**
    Seating Capacity: 12,000
    Year Built: 1917
    Resident Groups: Municipal Theater Association of Saint Louis

POWELL SYMPHONY HALL AT GRAND CENTER
718 North Grand Boulevard, Saint Louis, MO 63103
(314) 533-2500
    Type of Facility: Concert Hall

Facility Originally: Vaudeville
Type of Stage: Proscenium; Concert Shell
Stage Dimensions: 65'6"Wx43'4"D
Seating Capacity: 2,777
Year Built: 1920   **Architect:** Rapp & Rapp
Year Remodeled: 1963   **Architect:** Angelo Corrubia   **Cost:** $2,000,000
Acoustical Consultant: Dr. Cyril Harris
Contact for Rental: Christine Wagnon;   (314) 533-2500
Resident Groups: Saint Louis Symphony Orchestra; Saint Louis Youth Orchestra

SHELDON CONCERT HALL AND BALLROOM
3648 Washington Avenue, Saint Louis, MO 63108
(314) 533-9900
FAX: (314) 533-2958
Founded: 1912
Type of Facility: Concert Hall; Performance Center; Multi-Purpose; Room; Loft
Facility Originally: Meeting Hall
Type of Stage: Thrust; Flexible; Platform
Stage Dimensions: Concert Hall - 13'x24' expandable; Ballroom - 19'x19' proscenium open
Seating Capacity: Main Hall - ,850; Ballroom - 414
Year Built: 1912   **Architect:** Louis C. Spiering   **Cost:** $300,000
Year Remodeled: 1986   **Architect:** Walter F. Gunn, Supervisor   **Cost:** $1,600,000
Acoustical Consultant: Walter F. Gunn
Contact for Rental: Jane Teichman;   (314) 533-9900
Resident Groups: Opera Theater of St. Louis; Premier Performances; Washington University; New Music Circle; River
Styx; Endangered Arts Foundation

WASHINGTON UNIVERSITY - EDISON THEATRE
Mallinckrodt Center, Campus Box 1119, Saint Louis, MO 63130
(314) 935-6543
Type of Facility: Auditorium; Performance Center
Type of Stage: Flexible; Proscenium
Stage Dimensions: 32'Dx40'W upstage; 80'W downstage   **Orchestra Pit**
Seating Capacity: 656
Year Built: 1973   **Architect:** Robert Vickery; Smith & Entzeroth Architects
Acoustical Consultant: Ned Lustig, Theatre Consultant
Contact for Rental: Charlie Robin, Operations Director
Manager: Anne Yard
The Performing Arts Center of Washington University

WEBSTER UNIVERSITY-LORETTO - HILTON CENTER FOR THE PERFORMING ARTS
130 Edgar Road, Saint Louis, MO 63119
(314) 968-6933
Type of Facility: Theatre House
Type of Stage: Thrust
Orchestra Pit
Seating Capacity: 952
Year Built: 1965   **Architect:** Murphy & Mackey   **Cost:** $2,000,000
Acoustical Consultant: Bolt, Beranek & Newman; George C. Izenour Associates
Contact for Rental: Arthur L. Lueking, Director;   (314) 968-6933
Resident Groups: Repertory Theatre of Saint Louis; Opera Theatre of Saint Louis; Conservatory of Theatre Arts; Webster
University; Metropolitan Orchestra of Saint Louis

Sedalia

INSTRUMENTAL MUSIC

SCOTT JOPLIN RAGTIME FESTIVAL
113 East Fourth Street, Sedalia, MO 65301
(816) 826-2271
Founded: 1974
Arts Area: Orchestra; Ensemble; Instrumental Group; Electronic & Live Electronic; Band
Status: Non-Profit
Type: Performing; Educational
Purpose: To bring the historical and aesthetic value of Scott Joplin and ragtime music to a greater variety of people and to
enrich our understanding
Management: John Moore, Festival Coordinator; Julie Renberg, Executive Secretary
Officers: John Moore, President

Paid Staff: 2 **Volunteer Staff:** 30
Utilizes: Special Technical Talent; Guest Artists
Budget: $50,000 - $100,000
Income Sources: Private Foundations/Grants/Endowments; Business/Corporate Donations; Box Office; Individual Donations
Season: June 4 - June 7 **Annual Attendance:** 1,500

THEATRE

LIBERTY CENTER
111 West Fifth, Sedalia, MO 65301
(816) 827-3228
Founded: 1981
Arts Area: Professional; Musical; Dinner; Community; Folk; Theatrical Group; Puppet
Status: Professional; Non-Professional; Non-Profit
Type: Performing; Touring; Educational; Sponsoring
Purpose: To promote the Arts and activities which encourage the cultural growth of the community
Management: Patti McFatrich, Administrator
Officers: Don Buller, President; Carla Eding, Vice President; Debbie Klatt, Secretary; Chris Spangler, Treasurer
Paid Staff: 3 **Volunteer Staff:** 24
Paid Artists: 20 **Non-Paid Artists:** 100
Utilizes: Special Technical Talent; Guest Artists
Budget: $50,000 - $100,000
Income Sources: Business/Corporate Donations; Box Office; Government Grants; Individual Donations
Season: 52 Weeks **Annual Attendance:** 8,000
Performance Facilities: Liberty Center

Sikeston

THEATRE

SIKESTON LITTLE THEATRE
PO Box 126, Sikeston, MO 63801
(314) 471-6888
Founded: 1959
Arts Area: Musical; Community; Theatrical Group
Status: Non-Professional; Non-Profit
Type: Performing; Resident
Purpose: Promote theatrical arts for the Sikeston area and provide educational experience for students in theatre
Management: Lynn A. Colley, Administrator
Officers: Lynn A. Colley, President; Jim Wenneker, Vice President; Connie Thompson, Secretary; Electa O'Hara, Treasurer
Paid Staff: 1 **Volunteer Staff:** 15
Non-Paid Artists: 150
Budget: $1,000 - $50,000
Income Sources: Business/Corporate Donations; Box Office; Government Grants; Individual Donations
Season: July - June **Annual Attendance:** 3,000
Affiliations: Missouri Community Theatre Association
Performance Facilities: Chaney-Harris Cultural Center

Springfield

DANCE

SPRINGFIELD BALLET
305 East Walnut, Suite 301, Springfield, MO 65806-2300
(417) 862-1343
FAX: (417) 869-7815
Founded: 1976
Arts Area: Modern; Ballet; Jazz; Tap
Status: Non-Professional; Non-Profit
Type: Performing; Educational; Sponsoring
Purpose: To educate students and the public in techniques of dance; to perform at the highest possible level; to present guest dance companies
Management: Louis H. Schaeffer, Executive Director; Mark Rhodes, Artistic Director
Officers: J. Howard Schwartz, President; Brent Dunn, President Elect; Jack Weimer, Treasurer; Sherry Hopkins, Recording Secretary; Betty Luckie, Corresponding Secretary

Paid Staff: 9 **Volunteer Staff:** 8
Paid Artists: 43 **Non-Paid Artists:** 12
Utilizes: Special Technical Talent; Guest Artists; Guest Directors
Budget: $100,000 - $500,000
Income Sources: Private Foundations/Grants/Endowments; Business/Corporate Donations; Box Office; Government Grants; Individual Donations
Season: October - May **Annual Attendance:** 5,200
Performance Facilities: Landers Theatre, Vandivort Center; Hammons Hall for the Performing Arts

INSTRUMENTAL MUSIC

SPRINGFIELD SYMPHONY ASSOCIATION
1536 East Division, Springfield, MO 65803
(417) 864-6683
FAX: (417) 864-8967
Founded: 1934
Arts Area: Symphony
Status: Semi-Professional
Type: Performing
Purpose: To recreate, with the highest possible degree of artistic and historical integrity, the body of orchestral literature from 1700 to present
Management: Dana C. Randall, Executive Director; Charles Bontrager, Conductor
Officers: Patricia LeFevre, President; Barbara Brian, Secretary; John Owens, Treasurer
Paid Staff: 6 **Volunteer Staff:** 50
Paid Artists: 80
Utilizes: Special Technical Talent; Guest Conductors; Guest Artists; Guest Directors
Budget: $100,000 - $500,000
Income Sources: Private Foundations/Grants/Endowments; Business/Corporate Donations; Box Office; Government Grants; Individual Donations
Season: September - May **Annual Attendance:** 16,000
Affiliations: ASOL; Missouri Arts Council
Performance Facilities: Juanita K. Hammons Hall for the Performing Arts

VOCAL MUSIC

SPRINGFIELD REGIONAL OPERA
305 East Walnut, Springfield, MO 65806
(417) 869-1960
FAX: (417) 869-7815
Founded: 1979
Arts Area: Grand Opera; Lyric Opera; Light Opera; Operetta
Status: Professional; Non-Profit
Type: Performing
Purpose: To perform opera and musical theatre; to bring these performances to the southwest Missouri region; to offer young American singers an opportunity to perform and further their careers
Management: James Billings, Managing Artistic/Administrative Director
Paid Staff: 2
Paid Artists: 8 **Non-Paid Artists:** 8
Utilizes: Special Technical Talent; Guest Conductors; Guest Artists; Guest Directors
Budget: $50,000 - $100,000
Income Sources: Private Foundations/Grants/Endowments; Business/Corporate Donations; Box Office; Government Grants; Individual Donations
Season: October - March
Affiliations: OA

THEATRE

SPRINGFIELD LITTLE THEATRE
311 East Walnut, Springfield, MO 65806
(417) 869-3869
Founded: 1934
Arts Area: Musical; Dinner; Community; Theatrical Group; Puppet
Status: Non-Professional; Non-Profit
Type: Performing; Educational; Sponsoring
Purpose: To bring live performances to Southwest Missourians
Management: E. M. Denniston, Managing/Artistic Director; Kay Hamilton, Business Manager; Dorothy Lemmon, Education Director; Lisa Kristek, Development Director
Officers: Art Luebke, President; Steve Sheppard, Vice President; Dan Busch, Secretary; David Hayes, Treasurer
Paid Staff: 6 **Volunteer Staff:** 300

Paid Artists: 100   **Non-Paid Artists:** 200
Utilizes: Special Technical Talent; Guest Conductors; Guest Artists; Guest Directors
Budget: $100,000 - $500,000
Income Sources: Private Foundations/Grants/Endowments; Business/Corporate Donations; Box Office; Government Grants; Individual Donations
Season: September - July   **Annual Attendance:** 50,000
Performance Facilities: Landers Theatre

FACILITY

LANDERS THEATRE
311 East Walnut, Springfield, MO 65806
(417) 869-3869
Type of Facility: Auditorium; Theatre House; Opera House
Facility Originally: Vaudeville
Type of Stage: Proscenium
Orchestra Pit
Seating Capacity: 679
Year Built: 1909   **Architect:** Carl Boller   **Cost:** $100,000
Year Remodeled: 1985   **Architect:** Galen Pellham   **Cost:** $400,000
Acoustical Consultant: Sounds Great
Contact for Rental: E. M. Denniston;   (417) 869-3869
Resident Groups: Springfield Little Theatre

Tarkio

PERFORMING SERIES

MULE BARN THEATRE OF TARKIO COLLEGE
PO Box 114, 224 Main Street, Tarkio, MO 64491
(816) 736-4185
Founded: 1967
Arts Area: Theater
Status: Professional; Non-Profit
Type: Performing
Purpose: To provide cultural and educational enrichment for the area featuring the American musical and children's theatre, theatre for the area residents and training for young professionals in theatre
Paid Staff: 20
Paid Artists: 30   **Non-Paid Artists:** 15
Utilizes: Special Technical Talent; Guest Artists; Guest Directors
Budget: $100,000 - $500,000
Income Sources: Business/Corporate Donations; Box Office; Government Grants; Individual Donations
Season: June - August   **Annual Attendance:** 15,000
Performance Facilities: Mule Barn Theatre

FACILITY

MULE BARN THEATRE
224 Main, Tarkio, MO 64491
(816) 736-4185
Type of Facility: Theatre House
Facility Originally: Barn
Type of Stage: Thrust
Seating Capacity: 212
Year Built: 1892
Year Remodeled: 1967   **Cost:** $30,000
Manager: Wesley Van Tassel

Versailles

THEATRE

THE ROYAL ARTS COUNCIL
South Monroe Street, PO Box 273, Versailles, MO 65084
(314) 378-6226
Founded: 1984
Arts Area: Musical; Community; Theatrical Group

Status: Non-Professional; Non-Profit
Type: Performing; Educational; Sponsoring
Purpose: The performance, promotion, organization, and sponsorship of arts activities in the City of Versailles, Missouri
Management: Richard Elliott, Executive Director
Officers: Duane Miller, President; Emma Dornan, Vice President; David Baumgartner, Treasurer; Nancy Petersen, Secretary
Paid Staff: 1   **Volunteer Staff:** 5
Paid Artists: 3   **Non-Paid Artists:** 100
Utilizes: Special Technical Talent; Guest Artists; Guest Directors
Budget: $1,000 - $50,000
Income Sources: Private Foundations/Grants/Endowments; Business/Corporate Donations; Box Office; Government Grants; Individual Donations
Season: 52 Weeks   **Annual Attendance:** 4,000
Performance Facilities: Royal Theatre

MONTANA

Bigfork

FACILITY

BIGFORK CENTER FOR THE PERFORMING ARTS
PO Box 1230, Bigfork, MT 59911
(406) 837-4885
    Type of Facility: Concert Hall; Auditorium; Performance Center; Theatre House
    Type of Stage: Thrust; Proscenium
    Stage Dimensions: 28'x32' **Orchestra Pit**
    Seating Capacity: 435
    Year Built: 1988 **Architect:** Wayne Whitney **Cost:** $750,000
    Acoustical Consultant: Lee Irvine
    Contact for Rental: General Manager; (406) 837-4885

Billings

INSTRUMENTAL MUSIC

BILLINGS SYMPHONY SOCIETY
PO Box 7055, Billings, MT 59103
(406) 252-3610
    Founded: 1951
    Arts Area: Symphony; Orchestra
    Status: Semi-Professional; Non-Profit
    Type: Performing
    Purpose: To present live symphonic music to the community and the region
    Management: Dr. Uri Barnea, Music Director; Lynn Jordan, Chorale Director; Maxine Pihlaja, General Manager
    Officers: David Hummel, President
    Paid Staff: 4 **Volunteer Staff:** 1
    Paid Artists: 8
    Utilizes: Guest Conductors; Guest Artists
    Budget: $100,000 - $500,000
    Income Sources: Private Foundations/Grants/Endowments; Business/Corporate Donations; Box Office; Government Grants; Individual Donations
    Season: September - April **Annual Attendance:** 20,000
    Affiliations: ASOL; Montana Association of Symphony Orchestras
    Performance Facilities: The Alberta Bair Theater for the Performing Arts

YELLOWSTONE CHAMBER PLAYERS
1204 Rimhaven Way, Billings, MT 59102
(406) 248-2205
    Founded: 1980
    Arts Area: Chamber; Ensemble; Instrumental Group
    Status: Professional; Non-Profit
    Type: Performing; Touring; Resident
    Purpose: To perform a wide variety of chamber music, from string quartets and piano quintets to small ensembles employing clarinet, flute and guitar
    Management: Dr. Daniel Johnson, Publicity Manager; Elizabeth Adcock, Tour Director; Caron Schultz, Ticket Manager
    Officers: Caron Schultz, President; Mary LaMonaca, Vice President; Joanne Solberg, Secretary; Ramona Turnbull, Treasurer; Janet Keating, Mike Peterson, Board Members
    Volunteer Staff: 15
    Paid Artists: 14
    Budget: $1,000 - $50,000
    Income Sources: Private Foundations/Grants/Endowments; Business/Corporate Donations; Box Office; Government Grants; Individual Donations
    Season: 52 Weeks **Annual Attendance:** 2,000
    Affiliations: Yellowstone Art Center

FACILITY

THE ALBERTA BAIR THEATER FOR THE PERFORMING ARTS
PO Box 1556, Billings, MT 59103
(406) 256-8915
  Type of Facility: Theatre House
  Facility Originally: Vaudeville
  Type of Stage: Proscenium
  Stage Dimensions: 54'Wx30'D Orchestra Pit
  Seating Capacity: 1,416
  Year Built: 1931 **Architect:** Charles Renner
  Year Remodeled: 1986 **Architect:** Richard F. McCann **Cost:** $5,300,000
  Contact for Rental: Barry Bonifas; (406) 256-8915
  Resident Groups: Billings Symphony Orchestra

Bozeman

DANCE

MONTANA BALLET COMPANY
PO Box 6021, Bozeman, MT 59771-6021
(406) 587-7192
  Founded: 1983
  Arts Area: Modern; Ballet; Jazz
  Status: Professional; Non-Profit
  Type: Performing; Touring; Educational; Sponsoring
  Purpose: To provide affordable workshops and performance tours to rural communities throughout the western region; We offer New York Connection (NYCB dancers and teachers) and The Nutcracker annually.
  Management: Ann Bates, Artistic Director; Joan Chadwick, Business Manager
  Officers: Dianne Lorang, President; Susan Ledbetter, Vice President; Leslee Finck, Secretary
  Paid Staff: 2 **Volunteer Staff:** 100
  Paid Artists: 20 **Non-Paid Artists:** 6
  Utilizes: Guest Artists; Guest Choreographers; Guest Teachers
  Budget: $1,000 - $50,000
  Income Sources: Private Foundations/Grants/Endowments; Business/Corporate Donations; Box Office; Government Grants; Individual Donations
  Season: 52 Weeks **Annual Attendance:** 6,000
  Affiliations: Montana Ballet Studio
  Performance Facilities: Willson Auditorium

INSTRUMENTAL MUSIC

BOZEMAN SYMPHONY ORCHESTRA
104 East Main, #101, Bozeman, MT 59715
(406) 585-9774
FAX: (406) 585-5293
  Founded: 1968
  Arts Area: Symphony; Orchestra
  Status: Non-Professional; Non-Profit
  Type: Performing; Resident; Sponsoring
  Purpose: To support performance of symphonic and choral music by a resident orchestra and choir
  Management: Elizabeth Sellers, Music Director/Conductor; Patricia McNamer, Business Manager; Lowell Hickman, Choir Director
  Officers: Sharon Tudor, President; Robyn Erlenbush, Vice President; John E. Taylor, Secretary
  Paid Staff: 3
  Paid Artists: 2 **Non-Paid Artists:** 55
  Utilizes: Guest Conductors; Guest Artists
  Budget: $50,000 - $100,000
  Income Sources: Private Foundations/Grants/Endowments; Business/Corporate Donations; Box Office; Government Grants; Individual Donations
  Season: September - April **Annual Attendance:** 5,000
  Performance Facilities: Willson Auditorium

VOCAL MUSIC

INTERMOUNTAIN OPERA COMPANY
PO Box 37, Bozeman, MT 59715
(406) 587-1603; (406) 587-5589
>**Founded:** 1978
>**Arts Area:** Grand Opera; Light Opera
>**Status:** Professional; Non-Profit
>**Type:** Performing; Educational; Sponsoring
>**Purpose:** To introduce and involve young audiences of Montana in opera by producing operatic works and sponsoring education opportunities
>**Management:** Pablo Elvira, Artistic Director; Robert Stivanello, Producer
>**Officers:** Marilyn Hathaway, President
>**Volunteer Staff:** 12
>**Paid Artists:** 85
>**Utilizes:** Guest Artists
>**Budget:** $50,000 - $100,000
>**Income Sources:** Business/Corporate Donations; Box Office; Individual Donations
>**Season:** May   **Annual Attendance:** 2,000
>**Performance Facilities:** Willson Auditorium

THEATRE

VIGILANTE THEATRE COMPANY
PO Box 507, Bozeman, MT 59771-0507
(406) 994-5884
FAX: (406) 586-3732
>**Founded:** 1981
>**Arts Area:** Professional; Dinner; Theatrical Group
>**Status:** Professional; Non-Profit
>**Type:** Performing; Touring; Educational
>**Purpose:** To stimulate, cultivate and promote interest in theatre; to tour original, professional-quality theatre throughout the Northwest
>**Management:** John Hosking, Artistic Director; Joanne Eaton, Executive Director
>**Officers:** Jay Schuttler, President; Don McLaughlin, Vice President; Gwyn Ganjeau, Secretary/Treasurer
>**Paid Staff:** 2   **Volunteer Staff:** 10
>**Paid Artists:** 4
>**Utilizes:** Special Technical Talent
>**Budget:** $50,000 - $100,000
>**Income Sources:** Private Foundations/Grants/Endowments; Business/Corporate Donations; Box Office; Government Grants; Individual Donations
>**Season:** September - May   **Annual Attendance:** 10,000
>**Affiliations:** WESTAF; Montana State Theater Association; Pacific Northwest Arts Performers; Montana Performing Arts Council

Butte

INSTRUMENTAL MUSIC

BUTTE SYMPHONY ASSOCIATION
1009 Placer Street, Butte, MT 59701
(406) 782-2546
>**Founded:** 1950
>**Arts Area:** Symphony
>**Status:** Non-Profit
>**Type:** Performing
>**Purpose:** To provide fine concerts to the community and recreation for adults and teenagers in music
>**Officers:** Arthur Pascoe, President; Howard Wing, Vice President; Mrs. Warren Glover, Secretary; Dorothy Ann Honeychurch, Treasurer
>**Volunteer Staff:** 35
>**Non-Paid Artists:** 55
>**Utilizes:** Guest Artists
>**Budget:** $1,000 - $50,000
>**Income Sources:** Private Foundations/Grants/Endowments; Business/Corporate Donations; Box Office; Individual Donations
>**Season:** September - May   **Annual Attendance:** 2,400
>**Affiliations:** Montana Association of Symphonies
>**Performance Facilities:** Fox Theatre

Great Falls

INSTRUMENTAL MUSIC

GREAT FALLS SYMPHONY ASSOCIATION
Civic Center, PO Box 1078, Great Falls, MT 59403
(406) 453-4102
> **Founded:** 1959
> **Arts Area:** Symphony; Orchestra; Chamber; Ensemble
> **Status:** Professional; Non-Profit
> **Type:** Performing; Touring; Resident; Educational; Sponsoring
> **Purpose:** To serve as the primary source of cultural and educational service to north central Montana. Performances include the symphony orchestra with guest artists, choir, musical theatre, ballet, opera and resident string quartet recitals as well as public school demonstrations.
> **Management:** Carolyn Valacich, Executive Director; Gordon J. Johnson, Music Director/Conductor; Mary Moore, Choir Director
> **Paid Staff:** 5   **Volunteer Staff:** 10
> **Paid Artists:** 6   **Non-Paid Artists:** 135
> **Utilizes:** Special Technical Talent; Guest Conductors; Guest Artists
> **Budget:** $100,000 - $500,000
> **Income Sources:** Private Foundations/Grants/Endowments; Business/Corporate Donations; Box Office; Government Grants; Individual Donations
> **Season:** September - May   **Annual Attendance:** 25,000
> **Affiliations:** ASOL; Montana Association of Symphony Orchestras
> **Performance Facilities:** Great Falls Civic Center

VOCAL MUSIC

MONTANA CHORALE
PO Box 6083, Great Falls, MT 59406
(406) 771-7110
> **Founded:** 1976
> **Arts Area:** Choral
> **Status:** Professional; Non-Profit
> **Type:** Performing; Touring; Sponsoring
> **Purpose:** To inspire and develop the choral arts in Montana, provide continuing education and employment for professional singers in Montana and develop an artistic climate with international reputation in Montana
> **Management:** Linda Bottjer, General Manager
> **Officers:** Ann Cogswell, President; Lorrin Darby, Vice President; Sharon Knowles, Treasurer
> **Paid Staff:** 1
> **Paid Artists:** 24
> **Utilizes:** Guest Conductors; Guest Artists
> **Budget:** $1,000 - $50,000
> **Income Sources:** Private Foundations/Grants/Endowments; Business/Corporate Donations; Box Office; Government Grants; Individual Donations; Fund-raising
> **Season:** 52 Weeks   **Annual Attendance:** 7,000
> **Affiliations:** CA
> **Performance Facilities:** Great Falls Civic Center

FACILITY

GREAT FALLS CENTER FOR THE PERFORMING ARTS
600 First Avenue SW, Great Falls, MT 59404
(406) 727-2974
> **Type of Facility:** Theatre Complex; Auditorium; Studio Performance; Performance Center; Theatre House; Opera House; Multi-Purpose; Room
> **Facility Originally:** Library; Business Facility; Meeting Hall; School; Ballroom
> **Type of Stage:** Thrust; Flexible; Platform
> **Seating Capacity:** 225
> **Year Built:** 1940   **Architect:** Shanley and Van Teylingen
> **Year Remodeled:** 1988
> **Contact for Rental:** Great Falls Performing Arts Center;   (406) 727-2974
> **Resident Groups:** Theatre Company; Costume Shop; Dance School; Music Department; Baton Instruction

GREAT FALLS CIVIC CENTER THEATER
PO Box 5021, Great Falls, MT 59403
(406) 727-5881
> **Type of Facility:** Concert Hall; Theatre House; Civic Center

Type of Stage: Concert Shell
Stage Dimensions: 50'Wx33'D   **Orchestra Pit**
Seating Capacity: 1,857
Year Built: 1940   **Architect:** George H. Shanley & J. Van Teylingen   **Cost:** $665,000
Year Remodeled: 1987   **Architect:** Davidson & Cuhr
Acoustical Consultant: Towne Richards & Chaudiere
Contact for Rental: Parks & Recreation Department;   (406) 727-5881
Resident Groups: Great Falls Symphony Association; Community Concerts

Helena

INSTRUMENTAL MUSIC

HELENA SYMPHONY SOCIETY
Helena, MT 59601
(406) 442-1860
Founded: 1955
Arts Area: Symphony; Orchestra; Chamber; Ethnic
Status: Non-Profit
Type: Performing; Educational
Purpose: To present classical and popular symphony concerts, including choral and chamber concerts
Management: Sharon Nielsen, Business Manager; Dee Dawse, Development Director; Elizabeth Sellers, Music Director
Officers: Alton Hendrickson, President; Joe Schendel, Treasurer; Helen Ballinger, Secretary
Paid Staff: 3   **Volunteer Staff:** 22
Paid Artists: 12   **Non-Paid Artists:** 40
Utilizes: Guest Artists
Budget: $50,000 - $100,000
Income Sources: Private Foundations/Grants/Endowments; Business/Corporate Donations; Box Office; Individual Donations
Season: September - May   **Annual Attendance:** 5,000
Affiliations: ASCAP; BMI
Performance Facilities: Helena Civic Center

HOMEMADE JAM
526 Clarke Street, Helena, MT 59601
(406) 442-0535
Founded: 1980
Arts Area: Folk
Status: Professional
Type: Folk
Purpose: Performance of traditional Irish, American, and French-Canadian music in concert, in schools, and for dances
Officers: David Nimick, Angie Leprohon, Directors
Paid Artists: 4
Budget: $1,000 - $50,000
Income Sources: Box Office
Season: 52 Weeks

VOCAL MUSIC

HELENA YOUTH CHOIRS, INC.
PO Box 201, Helena, MT 59624
(406) 442-4877
Founded: 1982
Arts Area: Choral
Status: Non-Professional; Non-Profit
Type: Performing; Touring
Management: Dr. Melvin W. Roe, Choir Manager
Paid Staff: 4   **Volunteer Staff:** 20
Budget: $100,000 - $500,000
Income Sources: Private Foundations/Grants/Endowments; Business/Corporate Donations; Box Office; Individual Donations
Season: 52 Weeks

THEATRE

ALEPH MOVEMENT THEATRE
822 East Sixth Avenue, Helena, MT 59601
(406) 443-1274
Founded: 1985
Arts Area: Professional; Theatrical Group
Status: Professional; Non-Profit
Type: Performing; Touring; Educational
Purpose: Performance of movement theatre, to provide a vehicle for educational opportunities for individuals and organizations and cultural exchange between artists nationally and abroad
Management: Wally Bivins, Beck Newell
Officers: Peter Held, Vice President; Margaret Woo Showen, Secretary/Treasurer
Paid Staff: 2
Paid Artists: 2
Utilizes: Special Technical Talent; Guest Artists; Guest Directors
Budget: $1,000 - $50,000
Income Sources: Private Foundations/Grants/Endowments; Business/Corporate Donations; Box Office; Government Grants; Individual Donations
Season: 52 Weeks   **Annual Attendance:** 5,000
Affiliations: National Mime Association

PERFORMING SERIES

HELENA PRESENTS
15 North Ewing, Helena, MT 59601
(406) 443-0287
FAX: (406) 443-6620
Arts Area: Dance; Vocal Music; Instrumental Music; Theater; Festivals; Lyric Opera
Status: Non-Profit
Type: Performing; Touring; Resident; Educational; Sponsoring
Purpose: To sponsor programs in performing, literary, media and visual arts; to provide educational activities, humanities programs and grants to artists
Management: Arnie Melina, Executive Director
Officers: Dr. Robert Shepard, Chairman of the Board
Income Sources: Private Foundations/Grants/Endowments; Business/Corporate Donations; Box Office; Government Grants; Individual Donations
Performance Facilities: Myrna Loy Center; Helena Middle School; Helena Civic Center Auditorium

FACILITY

CARROLL COLLEGE - THEATRE
North Benton Avenue, Helena, MT 59625
(406) 442-3450
FAX: (406) 447-4533
Type of Facility: Performance Center; Theatre House
Facility Originally: Library
Type of Stage: Flexible; Proscenium
Seating Capacity: 100
Year Remodeled: 1959
Contact for Rental: Kim DeLong;   (406) 442-3450
Resident Groups: Carroll Theatre
For touring production/lectures on a limited scale

HELENA CIVIC CENTER
Neill and Park Avenue, Helena, MT 59601
(406) 447-8481
Type of Facility: Civic Center
Facility Originally: Shrine Temple
Year Built: 1920
Contact for Rental: Gery Carpenter, Diane Stavnes;   (406) 447-8481
The Civic Center contains the Auditorium and Ballroom. See separate listings for additional information.

HELENA CIVIC CENTER - AUDITORIUM
Neill and Park Avenue, Helena, MT 59601
(406) 447-8481
Type of Facility: Concert Hall; Auditorium; Theatre House; Opera House
Facility Originally: Shrine Temple

Type of Stage: Proscenium
Stage Dimensions: 45'Wx38'Dx19'6"H
Seating Capacity: 2,000
Year Built: 1920
Contact for Rental: Diane Stavnes, Gery Carpenter;   (406) 447-8481

HELENA CIVIC CENTER - BALLROOM
Neill and Park Avenue, Helena, MT 59601
(406) 447-8481
Type of Facility: Multi-Purpose; Room
Facility Originally: Shrine Temple
Type of Stage: Proscenium
Stage Dimensions: 25'Wx15'Dx12'H
Seating Capacity: 1,500
Year Built: 1920
Contact for Rental: Diane Stavnes, Gery Carpenter;   (406) 447-8481

Kalispell

DANCE

DANCE ART CENTER
1411 First Avenue West, Kalispell, MT 59901
(406) 755-0760
Founded: 1977
Arts Area: Modern; Ballet; Jazz; Tap
Status: Non-Profit; Commercial
Type: Performing; Touring; Resident; Educational; Sponsoring
Purpose: To enhance and educate the dance world in our small town; to run a small touring company
Management: Carol Jakes, Sole Proprietor; Kathy Barten, Kim Bristol, Janet Landon, Desiree Gravelle, Sherry Johns, Mary Jo Smith, Jazz Teachers
Paid Staff: 7
Non-Paid Artists: 5
Utilizes: Special Technical Talent; Guest Artists
Budget: $1,000 - $50,000
Income Sources: Business/Corporate Donations; Box Office; Individual Donations
Season: September - May; July   **Annual Attendance:** 1,000

INSTRUMENTAL MUSIC

GLACIER ORCHESTRA
140 First Avenue East, PO Box 2491, Kalispell, MT 59903
(406) 257-3241
FAX: (406) 257-3241
Founded: 1982
Arts Area: Symphony; Orchestra; Chamber; Chorus
Status: Non-Professional; Non-Profit
Type: Performing; Educational; Sponsoring
Purpose: To bring quality classical music to area audiences and provide an opportunity for local musicians to perform
Management: Robin Bailey, Executive Director; Gordon Johnson, Music Director; Shauneen Garner, Chorale Conductor/Children's Choir Conductor
Officers: Steve Cummings, President; Eric Kaplan, Vice President; Sally Murdock, Secretary; Diane Thompson, Treasurer
Paid Staff: 3   **Volunteer Staff:** 5
Paid Artists: 1   **Non-Paid Artists:** 100
Utilizes: Guest Conductors; Guest Artists
Budget: $50,000 - $100,000
Income Sources: Private Foundations/Grants/Endowments; Business/Corporate Donations; Box Office; Government Grants; Individual Donations
Season: September - May
Annual Attendance: 6,500
Affiliations: ASOL; Montana Association of Symphony Orchestras; Flathead Arts Council
Performance Facilities: Flathead High School Auditorium; Central School Auditorium

VOCAL MUSIC

GLACIER CHORALE
140 First Avenue East, Kalispell, MT 59901
(406) 257-3241
FAX: (406) 257-3241
>**Founded:** 1982
>**Arts Area:** Choral
>**Status:** Non-Professional; Non-Profit
>**Type:** Performing
>**Purpose:** To bring classical choral works to area audiences; to provide local choral performers with the opportunity to perform
>**Management:** Robin Bailey, Executive Director; Shauneen Garner, Chorale Conductor/Children's Choir Conductor; Gordon Johnson, Music Director
>**Officers:** Steve Cummings, President; Eric Kaplan, Vice President; Sally Murdock, Secretary; Diane Thompson, Treasurer
>**Paid Staff:** 3   **Volunteer Staff:** 5
>**Non-Paid Artists:** 55
>**Utilizes:** Guest Conductors; Guest Artists
>**Budget:** $50,000 - $100,000
>**Income Sources:** Private Foundations/Grants/Endowments; Business/Corporate Donations; Box Office; Government Grants; Individual Donations
>**Season:** September - May   **Annual Attendance:** 6,500
>**Affiliations:** ASOL; Montana Association of Symphony Orchestras; Glacier Orchestra
>**Performance Facilities:** Flathead High School Auditorium; Central School Auditorium

Missoula

INSTRUMENTAL MUSIC

MISSOULA SYMPHONY ASSOCIATION
131 South Higgins Avenue, Missoula, MT 59802
(406) 721-3194
>**Founded:** 1951
>**Arts Area:** Symphony
>**Status:** Non-Profit
>**Type:** Performing; Sponsoring
>**Purpose:** To present artistic programs of excellence to Missoula and the surrounding areas, provide an opportunity for young persons and develop an interest in the arts through concerts and master classes
>**Management:** Caralee Blair, General Manager
>**Officers:** Greg Davlin, President
>**Paid Staff:** 2
>**Paid Artists:** 18   **Non-Paid Artists:** 67
>**Utilizes:** Guest Artists
>**Budget:** $100,000 - $500,000
>**Income Sources:** Private Foundations/Grants/Endowments; Business/Corporate Donations; Box Office; Individual Donations
>**Season:** November - May   **Annual Attendance:** 6,000
>**Affiliations:** ASOL
>**Performance Facilities:** Wilma Theatre

STRING ORCHESTRA OF THE ROCKIES
PO Box 8265, Missoula, MT 59807
(406) 543-7803; (406) 549-0645
>**Founded:** 1984
>**Arts Area:** Symphony; Orchestra; Chamber; Ensemble
>**Status:** Professional; Non-Profit
>**Type:** Performing; Touring; Resident; Educational
>**Purpose:** To provide high quality classical music performances and educational programs to audiences in Montana and beyond
>**Officers:** Allison Justman, President; Fern Glassboyd, Orchestra Member
>**Paid Staff:** 2   **Volunteer Staff:** 1
>**Paid Artists:** 13
>**Utilizes:** Special Technical Talent; Guest Artists
>**Budget:** $1,000 - $50,000
>**Income Sources:** Business/Corporate Donations; Box Office; Government Grants; Individual Donations
>**Season:** 52 Weeks   **Annual Attendance:** 5,000

VOCAL MUSIC

MISSOULA MENDELSSOHN CLUB
University of Montana School of Music, Missoula, MT 59801
(406) 243-6880
Founded: 1944
Arts Area: Choral
Status: Non-Professional
Type: Performing; Touring; Sponsoring
Purpose: To provide an opportunity to express music; to increase the public's enjoyment of music
Management: Professor Donald Carey, Conductor
Officers: Frank A. Carter, President; Walt Kaostra, Secretary/Treasurer
Non-Paid Artists: 50
Budget: $1,000 - $50,000
Income Sources: Private Foundations/Grants/Endowments; Business/Corporate Donations; Box Office; Government Grants; Individual Donations
Season: October - May   **Annual Attendance:** 500
Performance Facilities: Music Recital Hall

THEATRE

THE MONTANA REP
Drama/Dance Department, University of Montana, Missoula, MT 59812
(406) 243-6809
Founded: 1967
Arts Area: Professional; Theatrical Group
Status: Professional; Non-Profit
Type: Performing; Touring; Resident; Educational
Purpose: To bring quality theatre and educational outreach to the West
Management: Arlynn Fishbaugh, Booking Manager
Officers: Greg Johnson, Artistic Director; Steve Wing, Production Coordinator
Paid Artists: 7   **Non-Paid Artists:** 8
Utilizes: Special Technical Talent; Guest Artists; Guest Directors; Student Interns
Budget: $100,000 - $500,000
Income Sources: Private Foundations/Grants/Endowments; Business/Corporate Donations; Box Office; Government Grants; Individual Donations
Season: September - June   **Annual Attendance:** 20,000
Affiliations: AEA; Uiversity of Montana
Performance Facilities: Montana Theatre, University of Montana

PERFORMING SERIES

YOUNG AUDIENCES OF WESTERN MONTANA
2920 Garfield, Missoula, MT 59801
(406) 721-5924
Founded: 1966
Arts Area: Dance; Vocal Music; Instrumental Music; Theater
Status: Professional; Non-Profit
Type: Performing; Touring; Educational
Purpose: To introduce school-age children to the live performing arts
Management: Dorothy Kinsley, Executive Director
Officers: Mark Thane, President; Barney White, Vice President; Susan Carlson, Secretary; Margaret Langel, Treasurer
Paid Staff: 1
Paid Artists: 30
Budget: $1,000 - $50,000
Income Sources: Private Foundations/Grants/Endowments; Business/Corporate Donations; Box Office; Government Grants; Individual Donations; Program Fees
Season: October - May   **Annual Attendance:** 21,000
Affiliations: National Young Audiences

FACILITY

UNIVERSITY OF MONTANA - MONTANA THEATRE
Department of Drama and Dance, Missoula, MT 59812
(406) 243-4970
Type of Facility: Theatre Complex
Type of Stage: Proscenium   **Orchestra Pit**
Seating Capacity: 499
Year Built: 1985   **Architect:** CTA   **Cost:** $8,500,000

Contact for Rental: Bryan Spellman, School of Fine Arts;   (406) 243-4970
Resident Groups: University of Montana Department of Drama and Dance; Montana Repertory Theatre

---

Red Lodge

PERFORMING SERIES

SCANDINAVIAN DANCERS
PO Box 691, Red Lodge, MT 59068
(406) 446-2657
Founded: 1970
Arts Area: Dance; Festivals
Status: Non-Professional; Non-Profit
Type: Performing
Purpose: To plan and perform the Scandinavian Day program during the Red Lodge Festival of Nations
Management: Bob Holmen, Dance Coordinator
Officers: Greta Bummer, President; John McCampbell, Vice President; Ken Firebaugh, Secretary; Jim Guimont, Treasurer
Volunteer Staff: 1
Non-Paid Artists: 24
Budget: $1,000 - $50,000
Income Sources: Fundraisers
Season: 52 Weeks   **Annual Attendance:** 2,500
Affiliations: Member of the Red Lodge Festival of Nations
Performance Facilities: Red Lodge Civic Center

Sheridan

PERFORMING SERIES

OLD TIMERS CONCERT
Sheridan High School, Sheridan, MT 59749
(406) 842-5226
Founded: 1974
Arts Area: Dance; Vocal Music; Instrumental Music; Theater; Festivals
Status: Semi-Professional; Non-Professional
Type: Performing; Resident
Purpose: To provide an opportunity to share talent with the community; to promote the arts in all fields of music; to raise money for school music programs and scholarships
Management: Sue Nottingham, Manager
Officers: Sue Nottingham, Treasurer
Volunteer Staff: 12
Non-Paid Artists: 50
Utilizes: Special Technical Talent; Guest Conductors; Guest Artists; Guest Directors
Budget: $1,000 - $50,000
Income Sources: Box Office; Individual Donations
Performance Facilities: Sheridan School Gym

Sidney

VOCAL MUSIC

SUGAR VALLEY CHAPTER OF SWEET ADELINES
PO Box 384, Sidney, MT 59270
(406) 842-1194
Founded: 1976
Arts Area: Choral
Status: Semi-Professional; Non-Profit
Type: Performing; Resident
Purpose: Sugar Valley Chapter of Sweet Adelines is united by a common interest in singing four-part harmony, barbershop style; to bring the joy of music to our community
Paid Staff: 2
Utilizes: Special Technical Talent; Guest Artists; Guest Directors

Budget: $1,000 - $50,000
Income Sources: Business/Corporate Donations

Twin Bridges

VOCAL MUSIC

RUBY VALLEY CHORALE
248 Bayers Lane, Twin Bridges, MT 59754
(406) 684-5465
Founded: 1976
Arts Area: Choral
Status: Non-Professional; Non-Profit
Type: Performing
Purpose: Entertainment for our small community; a means of expressing musically and vocally for those with talent in our community and an ecumenical effort of the churches
Management: Pauline Bayers, Director
Officers: Carolyn Carrol, Treasurer
Volunteer Staff: 3
Income Sources: Individual Donations
Season: September - April   **Annual Attendance:** 1,200
Performance Facilities: Church of the Valley; Bethel Methodist Church

Whitefish

PERFORMING SERIES

FLATHEAD FESTIVAL OF THE ARTS
PO Box 1780, Whitefish, MT 59937
(406) 862-1780
Founded: 1986
Arts Area: Vocal Music; Instrumental Music; Festivals; Lyric Opera
Status: Non-Profit
Type: Performing; Touring; Educational; Sponsoring
Management: Charles Buchwalter, Executive Director; Gordon Johnson, Artistic Director; Rebecca Grouse, Administrative Director
Officers: Carol Atkinson, President; Mike Bluk, Secretary; Rebecca Lyman, Treasurer
Paid Staff: 6   **Volunteer Staff:** 200
Paid Artists: 40
Utilizes: Guest Artists
Budget: $100,000 - $500,000
Income Sources: Private Foundations/Grants/Endowments; Business/Corporate Donations; Box Office; Government Grants; Individual Donations
Season: July   **Annual Attendance:** 2,000

NEBRASKA

Beatrice

FACILITY

COMMUNITY PLAYERS
412 Ella, PO Box 116, Beatrice, NE 68310
(402) 228-1801
    Type of Facility: Studio Performance; Arena
    Facility Originally: Garage; Warehouse
    Type of Stage: Flexible; Platform; Arena
    Stage Dimensions: 46'x63'
    Seating Capacity: 280
    Year Remodeled: 1982
    Contact for Rental: Marya Lucca-Thyberg;   (402) 228-1801
    Resident Groups: Community Players
    Performances; meetings; conventions

Bellevue

THEATRE

BELLEVUE LITTLE THEATRE
203 West Mission Avenue, PO Box 162, Bellevue, NE 68005
(402) 291-1554
    Founded: 1968
    Arts Area: Musical; Community; Theatrical Group; Puppet
    Status: Non-Professional; Non-Profit
    Type: Performing; Educational
    Purpose: To provide a Performing Arts Center for the community and the surrounding area
    Management: Board of Directors
    Officers: Edward B. Roche, President; Cheryl Bailey, Vice President; Paula Darnell, Secretary; George Rice, Treasurer
    Volunteer Staff: 100
    Non-Paid Artists: 275
    Utilizes: Special Technical Talent; Guest Artists; Guest Directors
    Budget: $50,000 - $100,000
    Income Sources: Private Foundations/Grants/Endowments; Business/Corporate Donations; Box Office; Government Grants; Individual Donations
    Season: 52 Weeks   **Annual Attendance:** 5,000

FACILITY

BELLEVUE LITTLE THEATRE
203 West Mission, Bellevue, NE 68005
(402) 291-1554
    Founded: 1968
    Type of Facility: Auditorium; Theatre House
    Type of Stage: Thrust; Platform
    Stage Dimensions: 35'Wx33'D (10" rise at 25')
    Seating Capacity: 244
    Year Built: 1948
    Year Remodeled: 1990   **Cost:** $32,000
    Contact for Rental: Bette Swanson;   (402) 292-1920
    Educational activities

Bladen

FACILITY

BLADEN OPERA HOUSE
Main Street, Bladen, NE 68928
    Type of Facility: Concert Hall; Studio Performance; Performance Center; Theatre House; Opera House
    Facility Originally: Meeting Hall; Vaudeville; Movie House
    Type of Stage: Thrust; Platform
    Stage Dimensions: Main - 21'x18'; Thrust - 18'x12'   **Orchestra Pit**

Seating Capacity: 250
Year Built: 1913   **Cost:** $15,000
For local and surrounding community groups

Chadron

FACILITY

CHADRON STATE COLLEGE - MEMORIAL HALL
10th and Main, Chadron, NE 69337
(308) 432-6316
FAX: (308) 432-3561
> **Type of Facility:** Auditorium
> **Type of Stage:** Proscenium
> **Orchestra Pit**
> **Seating Capacity:** 764
> **Year Built:** 1953   **Cost:** $750,000
> **Year Remodeled:** 1984   **Architect:** Hindl and Harrison   **Cost:** $990,000
> **Contact for Rental:** Dr. Charles J. Harrington;   (308) 432-6316

Gothenburg

THEATRE

GOTHENBURG COMMUNITY PLAYHOUSE
10th and D Street, PO Box 15, Gothenburg, NE 69138
(308) 537-7596
> **Founded:** 1967
> **Arts Area:** Dinner; Community
> **Status:** Non-Professional; Non-Profit
> **Type:** Performing; Resident; Sponsoring
> **Purpose:** To provide cultural, educational and literary opportunities to the members of the community and the surrounding region
> **Management:** LaVon Pape, Manager
> **Paid Staff:** 1
> **Utilizes:** Special Technical Talent; Guest Artists; Guest Directors
> **Budget:** $1,000 - $50,000
> **Income Sources:** Box Office; Individual Donations
> **Performance Facilities:** Sun Theatre

FACILITY

GOTHENBURG COMMUNITY PLAYHOUSE - SUN THEATRE
10th and D Street, PO Box 15, Gothenburg, NE 69138
(308) 537-3235
> **Type of Facility:** Theatre House
> **Type of Stage:** Platform
> **Seating Capacity:** 324
> **Contact for Rental:** LaVon Pape;   (308) 537-7596
> **Resident Groups:** Gothenburg Community Playhouse
> *To bring cultural and artistic entertainment to our community*

Hastings

INSTRUMENTAL MUSIC

HASTINGS SYMPHONY ORCHESTRA
Fuhr Hall, Ninth and Ash, Hastings, NE 68901
(402) 463-2402
FAX: (402) 463-3002
> **Founded:** 1926
> **Arts Area:** Symphony; Orchestra; Chamber
> **Status:** Non-Professional; Non-Profit
> **Type:** Performing; Touring; Resident; Educational
> **Purpose:** To promote the best possible performance of symphonic music and to provide an educational and performance outlet for the citizens of south central Nebraska

Management: Dr. James Johnson, Conductor/Music Director; Becky Pitman, Executive Secretary
Officers: Karen Doer, President; Ann Martin, President Elect; Mary Wright, Treasurer
Paid Staff: 2   **Volunteer Staff:** 24
Paid Artists: 4   **Non-Paid Artists:** 70
Utilizes: Guest Artists
Budget: $1,000 - $50,000
Income Sources: Private Foundations/Grants/Endowments; Business/Corporate Donations; Box Office; Government Grants; Individual Donations
Season: September - May   **Annual Attendance:** 5,000
Affiliations: ASOL
Performance Facilities: Hastings Masonic Temple

Hyannis

THEATRE

VILLAGE PLAYERS
PO Box 81, Hyannis, NE 69350
(308) 458-2701
Founded: 1980
Arts Area: Professional; Summer Stock; Musical; Dinner; Community; Theatrical Group
Status: Semi-Professional; Non-Profit; Commercial
Type: Performing; Touring; Sponsoring
Purpose: Presenting and sponsoring organization
Management: Al Davis, Artistic Director
Officers: Les Schreurs, President; John Glenn, Treasurer; Erik Johnson, Vice President; Fayann Blaylock, Secretary
Volunteer Staff: 13
Paid Artists: 20
Utilizes: Special Technical Talent; Guest Artists; Guest Directors
Budget: $100,000 - $500,000
Income Sources: Private Foundations/Grants/Endowments; Business/Corporate Donations; Box Office; Government Grants; Individual Donations
Season: 52 Weeks   **Annual Attendance:** 1,000

Kearney

THEATRE

KEARNEY COMMUNITY THEATRE
83 Plaza Boulevard, Kearney, NE 68847
(308) 234-1529
Founded: 1977
Arts Area: Musical; Dinner; Community; Theatrical Group
Status: Non-Professional; Non-Profit
Type: Performing; Educational; Sponsoring
Purpose: Perform five shows yearly plus summer workshop for children who do their own show
Management: Bradley J. Driml, Executive Director
Paid Staff: 3   **Volunteer Staff:** 300
Utilizes: Guest Directors
Budget: $100,000 - $500,000
Income Sources: Private Foundations/Grants/Endowments; Business/Corporate Donations; Box Office; Government Grants; Individual Donations; Fundraising
Season: 52 Weeks   **Annual Attendance:** 11,000
Affiliations: Nebraska Arts Council; Nebraska Association of Community Theatres; AACT
Performance Facilities: Kearney Community Theatre

FACILITY

KEARNEY COMMUNITY THEATRE
83 Plaza Boulevard, Kearney, NE 68847
(308) 234-1529
Type of Facility: Theatre Complex
Facility Originally: Church
Type of Stage: Platform
Seating Capacity: Theater - 165; Dinner Theater - 115
Year Built: 1890
Year Remodeled: 1984   **Architect:** Theatre Board

Contact for Rental: (308) 234-1529
Manager: Bradley Driml, Administrator

UNIVERSITY OF NEBRASKA - UNIVERSITY THEATRE
905 West 25th Street, Kearney, NE 68849
(308) 234-8406
    Type of Facility: Theatre Complex; Studio Performance; Theatre House; Amphitheater
    Type of Stage: Flexible; Proscenium
    Stage Dimensions: 39'6"Wx25'D
    Orchestra Pit
    Seating Capacity: 334
    Year Built: 1970
    Architect: Helleberg
    Cost: $1,775,000
    Manager: Charles Davies
    The building also contains a 500-seat recital hall.

Lincoln

DANCE

LINCOLN CITY BALLET COMPANY
PO Box 2441, Lincoln, NE 68502
(402) 489-7218
    Founded: 1979
    Arts Area: Modern; Ballet; Jazz; Folk
    Status: Non-Professional; Non-Profit
    Type: Performing; Resident; Educational; Sponsoring
    Purpose: To give gifted young dancers of our community an additional performing outlet; to expose more community members to various forms of dance
    Management: Betsy Bobenhouse, Director
    Officers: Linda Haase, President; Dee Churchill, First Vice President; Debbie Guenzel, Second Vice President; Jan Budde, Treasurer
    Paid Staff: 1   **Volunteer Staff:** 17
    Non-Paid Artists: 32
    Utilizes: Special Technical Talent; Guest Artists
    Budget: $1,000 - $50,000
    Income Sources: Private Foundations/Grants/Endowments; Business/Corporate Donations; Box Office; Individual Donations
    Season: September - May

LINCOLN MIDWEST BALLET COMPANY
PO Box 30126, Lincoln, NE 68503-0126
(402) 464-7737
    Founded: 1985
    Arts Area: Ballet
    Status: Non-Profit
    Type: Performing; Touring; Educational
    Purpose: To contonue to foster, promote and expand classical ballet training and its expression in various dance forms; to develop an audience for ballet; to promote and expand education of dance and the arts in Nebraska
    Management: Shari Shell-True, Artistic Director
    Officers: Joann Reirden, President; Bill Ford, President Elect; Cindy Ketner, Secretary; Joan Chopp, Treasurer
    Paid Staff: 1   **Volunteer Staff:** 10
    Paid Artists: 1   **Non-Paid Artists:** 30
    Utilizes: Special Technical Talent; Guest Artists; Guest Directors
    Budget: $1,000 - $50,000
    Income Sources: Private Foundations/Grants/Endowments; Business/Corporate Donations; Box Office; Individual Donations
    Annual Attendance: 2,000
    Affiliations: Nebraska Arts Council
    Performance Facilities: Cotner Center; Pershing Auditorium

INSTRUMENTAL MUSIC

LINCOLN CIVIC EXPERIENCE/LINCOLN CIVIC ORCHESTRA
3800 South 48th Street, Lincoln, NE 68506
(402) 488-2331
    Arts Area: Orchestra

Status: Non-Profit
Type: Resident
Purpose: To provide community members a chance to perform serious music
Officers: Carol Rees, President; Beth Friedline, Secretary; Barbara Mercier, Treasurer
Paid Artists: 20 **Non-Paid Artists:** 130
Utilizes: Special Technical Talent; Guest Artists
Budget: $1,000 - $50,000
Income Sources: Private Foundations/Grants/Endowments; Individual Donations
Season: September - May **Annual Attendance:** 4,000
Performance Facilities: Union College

LINCOLN SYMPHONY
1200 North Street, Lincoln, NE 68508
(402) 474-5610
FAX: (402) 434-1163
Founded: 1925
Arts Area: Symphony; Orchestra
Status: Professional; Non-Profit
Type: Performing; Sponsoring
Management: Richard Frevert, Manager; Robert Emile, Music Director/Conductor
Paid Staff: 5 **Volunteer Staff:** 40
Paid Artists: 75
Utilizes: Guest Artists
Budget: $100,000 - $500,000
Income Sources: Private Foundations/Grants/Endowments; Business/Corporate Donations; Box Office; Government Grants; Individual Donations
Season: October - April **Annual Attendance:** 8,000
Affiliations: ASOL
Performance Facilities: Kimball Hall; Lied Center

LINCOLN YOUTH SYMPHONY ORCHESTRA
Public School Administration Building, 5901 O Street, Lincoln, NE 68501
(402) 475-1081
Founded: 1953
Arts Area: Symphony; Orchestra
Status: Non-Professional; Non-Profit
Type: Performing; Touring; Educational; Sponsoring
Purpose: The Lincoln Youth Symphony Orchestra was organized to perform symphonic literature unable to be played within regular school instruction through participation in the Youth Orchestra or the Junior Youth Orchestra.
Management: Richard Scott, Administrator; Michael Swartz, Business Manager; Dr. Brian Moore, Music Director/Conductor
Officers: Joyce Glaesemann, President; Linda Maack, Secretary; Carl Olson, Treasurer
Paid Staff: 5 **Volunteer Staff:** 80
Non-Paid Artists: 76
Budget: $1,000 - $50,000
Income Sources: Business/Corporate Donations; Individual Donations
Season: October - May
Annual Attendance: 1,500
Affiliations: ASOL (Youth Orchestra Division); Lincoln Public Schools
Performance Facilities: Kimball Recital Hall, University of Nebraska

NEBRASKA CHAMBER ORCHESTRA
749 NBC Center, Lincoln, NE 68512
(402) 477-0366
FAX: (402) 476-6368
Founded: 1976
Arts Area: Chamber
Status: Professional; Non-Profit
Type: Performing; Touring; Educational
Purpose: To offer a variety of entertaining, provocative and challenging chamber orchestra programs through a subscription series, touring concerts and chamber ensembles
Management: Sherrie Geier, General Manager
Officers: Carl Rohman, President; Tyler Sutton, Michael Letheby, Vice Presidents; Emily Zimmer, Secretary/Treasurer
Paid Staff: 2 **Volunteer Staff:** 50
Paid Artists: 50
Utilizes: Guest Conductors; Guest Artists
Budget: $100,000 - $500,000

Income Sources: Private Foundations/Grants/Endowments; Business/Corporate Donations; Box Office; Government Grants; Individual Donations
Season: September - April   **Annual Attendance:** 3,000
Affiliations: ASOL

THEATRE

LINCOLN COMMUNITY PLAYHOUSE
2500 South 56th Street, Lincoln, NE 68506
(402) 489-9608
　Founded: 1946
　Arts Area: Community
　Status: Non-Profit
　Type: Performing
　Purpose: The mission of the Lincoln Community Playhouse is to provide quality theatrical experiences offering education participation and entertainment opportunities to the community.
　Management: Rod McCullough, Executive Director; Mark A. Adams, Artistic Director; Lenette Nelson Schwinn, Children's Theatre Director
　Officers: Linda Hoff, President; Ginny Parker, Secretary; Mary Ann Kochler, Treasurer; Tom Larson, President-Elect
　Paid Staff: 10
　Non-Paid Artists: 400
　Utilizes: Guest Artists; Guest Directors
　Budget: $100,000 - $500,000
　Income Sources: Private Foundations/Grants/Endowments; Business/Corporate Donations; Box Office; Government Grants; Individual Donations
　Season: September - June   **Annual Attendance:** 33,000
　Affiliations: AACT; Nebraska Association of Community Theatres
　Performance Facilities: Oliver T. Joy Mainstage; L.L. Coryell and Sons Children's Theatre; Lawrence A. Emerson Gallery Theatre

NEBRASKA REPERTORY THEATRE
215 Temple Building, 12th and R Streets, Lincoln, NE 68588-0201
(402) 472-2072
　Founded: 1968
　Arts Area: Professional; Theatrical Group
　Status: Semi-Professional; Non-Profit
　Type: Performing; Resident
　Management: Tice Miller, Executive Director; Robert Hall, Artistic Director; Patricia Overton, Theatre Manager
　Paid Staff: 10
　Utilizes: Special Technical Talent; Guest Artists; Guest Directors
　Budget: $100,000 - $500,000
　Income Sources: Box Office; Government Grants; Individual Donations
　Season: June - August   **Annual Attendance:** 10,000
　Affiliations: AEA; Guest Artist Contract
　Performance Facilities: Howell Theatre; Studio Theatre; Carson Theatre

PERFORMING SERIES

THE LIED CENTER FOR PERFORMING ARTS
301 North 12th, Lincoln, NE 68588
(402) 472-4700
FAX: (402) 472-4730
　Founded: 1972
　Arts Area: Dance; Vocal Music; Instrumental Music; Theater
　Status: Professional
　Type: Performing
　Purpose: To provide a top-quality series of performances during the school year; to provide the students with the opportunity to encounter these visiting artists in workshops and other learning situations
　Management: Bob Chumbley, Director
　Paid Staff: 7
　Utilizes: Guest Artists
　Budget: $100,000 - $500,000
　Income Sources: Private Foundations/Grants/Endowments; Box Office; Government Grants; Individual Donations
　Season: September - May   **Annual Attendance:** 16,000
　Performance Facilities: Lied Center

LINCOLN FRIENDS OF CHAMBER MUSIC
1935 A Street, Lincoln, NE 68502
(402) 475-0221
FAX: (402) 472-3574
Founded: 1965
Arts Area: Instrumental Music
Status: Non-Profit
Type: Sponsoring
Purpose: To present chamber music; to promote community interest in chamber music; to aid local chamber music talent
Officers: Bob Kuzelka, President
Volunteer Staff: 10
Utilizes: Guest Artists
Income Sources: Private Foundations/Grants/Endowments; Business/Corporate Donations; Box Office; Government Grants; Individual Donations
Season: October - April
Performance Facilities: Sheldon Art Gallery Auditorium

FACILITY

LIED CENTER FOR THE PERFORMING ARTS
301 North 12th Street, Lincoln, NE 68588
(402) 472-4700
FAX: (402) 472-4730
Founded: 1990
Type of Facility: Theatre Complex
Type of Stage: Flexible; Proscenium; Second Proscenium
Stage Dimensions: Varied
Orchestra Pit
Seating Capacity: 2278; 850; 300
Year Built: 1989   **Architect:** HDR and Associates   **Cost:** $30,000,000
Acoustical Consultant: Paul Venaklausen
Contact for Rental: Tim Bartholow;   (402) 472-4700
Resident Groups: Lincoln Symphony; Nebraska Chamber Orchestra; Nebraska Repertory Theater

PERSHING AUDITORIUM
226 Centennial Mall South, PO Box 81126, Lincoln, NE 68501-1126
(402) 471-7500
Type of Facility: Concert Hall; Auditorium; Theatre House; Arena; Multi-Purpose
Type of Stage: Proscenium
Stage Dimensions: 110'Wx40'D
Orchestra Pit
Seating Capacity: 7,691
Year Built: 1957   **Architect:** Davis & Wilson   **Cost:** $2,500,000
Year Remodeled: 1976   **Architect:** Morrow   **Cost:** $1,000,000
Contact for Rental: Douglas Kuhnel;   (402) 471-7500
Resident Groups: Lincoln Community Concert Association

UNIVERSITY OF NEBRASKA-LINCOLN - KIMBALL RECITAL HALL
11th & R Streets, Lincoln, NE 68588
(402) 472-2997
Type of Facility: Concert Hall
Type of Stage: Proscenium
Orchestra Pit
Seating Capacity: 849
Year Built: 1970   **Architect:** Robinson   **Cost:** $1,000,000
Acoustical Consultant: Bolt, Beranek & Newman
Manager: Ron Bowlin;   (402) 472-2997
Resident Groups: School of Music

McCook

PERFORMING SERIES

HERITAGE DAYS
PO Box 337, McCook, NE 69001
(308) 345-3200
Founded: 1969

Arts Area: Dance; Vocal Music; Instrumental Music; Arts and Crafts
Status: Non-Professional; Non-Profit
Type: Sponsoring
Paid Staff: 2
Budget: $1,000 - $50,000
Income Sources: Private Foundations/Grants/Endowments; Business/Corporate Donations; Box Office; Government Grants; Individual Donations
Season: June - August

Omaha

DANCE

OMAHA BALLET COMPANY AND SCHOOL
2655 Farnham Street, Omaha, NE 68131
(402) 346-7332; (402) 346-7394
FAX: (402) 422-0148
Founded: 1968
Arts Area: Modern; Ballet
Status: Professional; Non-Profit
Type: Performing; Touring; Educational
Purpose: To provide high-quality, professional classical and contemporary ballet that responds to the region's cultural and educational needs and enriches the cultural fabric of the region
Management: Robert Vickrey, Artistic Director; Sharon McGill, Ballet Mistress; Robin Welch, Program Director/Associate Ballet Mistress; Kathleen Sullivan, Executive Director
Officers: Roger Lewis, President; Warren Whithed, Vice President/President-Elect
Paid Staff: 9   **Volunteer Staff:** 15
Paid Artists: 14   **Non-Paid Artists:** 5
Utilizes: Special Technical Talent; Guest Conductors; Guest Artists; Guest Directors
Budget: $1,000,000 - $5,000,000
Season: September - May   **Annual Attendance:** 25,000
Affiliations: Nebraska Arts Council
Performance Facilities: Orpheum Theater

OMAHA MODERN DANCE COLLECTIVE
PO Box 1084, Omaha, NE 68101
(402) 551-7473
Founded: 1981
Arts Area: Modern
Status: Non-Profit
Type: Educational; Sponsoring
Purpose: To serve the community of modern dancers and choreographers by providing educational and performance opportunities; to promote public awareness of modern dance
Officers: Amy Matthews, President; Carl Ogden, Vice President; Susan Dickson Matsunami, Secretary; Taffy Howard, Treasurer
Non-Paid Artists: 12
Utilizes: Special Technical Talent; Guest Artists; Guest Choreographers
Budget: $1,000 - $50,000
Income Sources: Private Foundations/Grants/Endowments; Box Office; Government Grants; Individual Donations
Season: 52 Weeks

INSTRUMENTAL MUSIC

NEBRASKA WIND SYMPHONY
PO Box 24114, Omaha, NE 68124
(402) 391-6329
Founded: 1977
Arts Area: Band
Status: Semi-Professional; Non-Profit
Type: Performing
Purpose: To provide wind and percussion players with a performance group; to encourage the composition of new literature for bands by awarding commissions and programming premiere performances; to entertain
Management: Darwyn Snyder, Music Director
Officers: Diana Bee, President; Mark Foster, Vice President; Geneviere Holtz, Secretary/Treasurer; Linda Ashley, Corresponding Secretary
Paid Staff: 3
Paid Artists: 10   **Non-Paid Artists:** 85
Utilizes: Guest Conductors; Guest Artists

Budget: $1,000 - $50,000
Income Sources: Private Foundations/Grants/Endowments; Business/Corporate Donations; Box Office; Government Grants; Individual Donations
Season: September - June   **Annual Attendance:** 3,500
Performance Facilities: Strauss Performing Arts Center, University of Nebraska at Omaha

OMAHA AREA YOUTH ORCHESTRAS
PO Box 24813, Omaha, NE 68124
(402) 553-7655
Founded: 1958
Arts Area: Symphony; Orchestra; Chamber; Ensemble
Status: Non-Professional; Non-Profit
Type: Performing; Educational; Sponsoring
Purpose: To enhance the musical education of aspiring and talented young musicians through the medium of orchestral performance; to help them become appreciative listeners; and to build discipline, cooperation, and other skills necessary for a group accomplishment
Management: Stephen G. Hobson, Music Director; Susan Bogden, General Manager
Officers: Mary Ellen Wychulis, Chairman of the Board; Patty Deckel, Associate Chairman; Robley Garrigan, Secretary; Richard Jorgenson, Treasurer
Paid Staff: 3   **Volunteer Staff:** 70
Non-Paid Artists: 300
Utilizes: Guest Artists
Budget: $50,000 - $100,000
Income Sources: Private Foundations/Grants/Endowments; Business/Corporate Donations; Box Office; Government Grants; Individual Donations
Season: September - May   **Annual Attendance:** 8,000
Affiliations: ASOL; Omaha Symphony Guild; ASTA; MENC
Performance Facilities: University Recital Hall

OMAHA SYMPHONY ASSOCIATION
1615 Howard Street, Suite 310, Omaha, NE 68102
(402) 342-3836
FAX: (402) 342-3819
Founded: 1921
Arts Area: Symphony; Orchestra; Chamber; Ensemble
Status: Professional; Non-Profit
Type: Performing; Touring; Resident; Educational; Sponsoring
Management: Bruce Hangen, Music Director
Paid Staff: 14
Paid Artists: 36
Utilizes: Guest Conductors; Guest Artists
Budget: $1,000,000 - $5,000,000
Income Sources: Private Foundations/Grants/Endowments; Business/Corporate Donations; Box Office; Government Grants; Individual Donations
Annual Attendance: 72,000
Affiliations: ASOL; NEA; Nebraska Arts Council; United Arts Omaha

VOCAL MUSIC

CLARION CHAMBER CHORALE
PO Box 31366, Omaha, NE 68131
(402) 597-1240; (402) 330-5505
Founded: 1982
Arts Area: Choral
Status: Semi-Professional; Non-Profit
Type: Performing; Touring
Purpose: To present concerts to the general public that focus on choral literature suitable for chamber ensembles; 80% performed is sung a cappella, 20% is sung with instrumental accompaniment
Management: Clarion Choral Foundation; Stanley Schmidt, Artistic Director
Officers: Morgan Holmes, President; Karen Weber, Publicist
Volunteer Staff: 32
Utilizes: Guest Artists
Budget: $1,000 - $50,000
Income Sources: Private Foundations/Grants/Endowments; Business/Corporate Donations; Box Office; Individual Donations
Season: September - April
Affiliations: Clarion Choral Foundations
Performance Facilities: First United Methodist Church

DIE MEISTERSINGERS
PO Box 241281, Omaha, NE 68124
(402) 453-3719
   Founded: 1964
   Arts Area: Choral; Ethnic; Folk; Jazz
   Status: Semi-Professional
   Type: Performing; Touring; Educational
   Purpose: Committed to the promotion of excellence in choral music in Nebraska
   Management: Jim Elsberry, Artistic Director
   Officers: Paul Rooker, President
   Paid Staff: 1   **Volunteer Staff:** 24
   Utilizes: Special Technical Talent; Guest Artists
   Budget: $1,000 - $50,000
   Income Sources: Private Foundations/Grants/Endowments; Box Office; Individual Donations
   Season: Fall - Spring   **Annual Attendance:** 3,000
   Affiliations: United Arts Council; Omaha Arts Council
   Performance Facilities: University of Nebraska Performing Arts Center

OPERA/OMAHA
PO Box 807 DTS, Omaha, NE 68101
(402) 346-4398
   Founded: 1958
   Arts Area: Grand Opera; Lyric Opera; Light Opera; Musical Theatre
   Status: Professional; Non-Profit
   Type: Performing; Touring; Resident; Educational; Sponsoring
   Management: Mary Robert, General/Artistic Director; Keith Warner, Associate Artistic Director; Hal France, Music Director
   Paid Staff: 12   **Volunteer Staff:** 250
   Paid Artists: 420   **Non-Paid Artists:** 260
   Utilizes: Special Technical Talent; Guest Conductors; Guest Artists; Guest Directors
   Budget: $1,000,000 - $5,000,000
   Income Sources: Private Foundations/Grants/Endowments; Business/Corporate Donations; Box Office; Government Grants; Individual Donations; Fundraising
   Season: September - March   **Annual Attendance:** 35,000
   Affiliations: OA
   Performance Facilities: Orpheum Theater; Witherspoon Hall

THEATRE

CENTER STAGE
3010 R Street, Omaha, NE 68107
(402) 733-5777
   Founded: 1980
   Arts Area: Community; Theatrical Group
   Status: Non-Professional; Non-Profit
   Type: Performing
   Purpose: The only theater in Omaha that attempts to present ethnic performances
   Management: Linda Runice, Executive Director
   Officers: Roger Sayers, President; Susan Murphy, Vice President; Mark Grieb, Treasurer
   Paid Staff: 2   **Volunteer Staff:** 2
   Paid Artists: 60
   Utilizes: Special Technical Talent; Guest Artists; Guest Directors
   Budget: $50,000 - $100,000
   Income Sources: Private Foundations/Grants/Endowments; Business/Corporate Donations; Box Office; Government Grants; Individual Donations
   Season: August - July   **Annual Attendance:** 6,000
   Performance Facilities: LaFerne Williams Center

CIRCLE THEATRE, INC.
2015 South 60th Street, Omaha, NE 68106
(402) 553-4715
   Founded: 1983
   Arts Area: Dinner; Theatrical Group
   Status: Semi-Professional; Non-Profit
   Type: Performing; Touring; Resident
   Purpose: To develop and produce new works by Nebraska playwrights utilizing Nebraska artists
   Management: Laura Marr, Executive Director; Peg Gibbs, Bookkeeper; Doug Marr, Artistic Director; Robyn Munger, Technical Director

Officers: Ward Peters, President; Jane Erdenberger, Vice President; Dave D'Elia, Treasurer; Doug Paterson, Secretary
Paid Staff: 4   **Volunteer Staff:** 5
Paid Artists: 75   **Non-Paid Artists:** 10
Utilizes: Guest Artists; Guest Directors
Budget: $50,000 - $100,000
Income Sources: Private Foundations/Grants/Endowments; Business/Corporate Donations; Box Office; Government Grants; Individual Donations
Season: 52 Weeks
Annual Attendance: 6,000
Performance Facilities: Vidlak's Cafe

EMMY GIFFORD CHILDREN'S THEATER
3504 Center Street, Omaha, NE 68105
(402) 345-4852
Founded: 1949
Arts Area: Theatrical Group
Status: Professional; Non-Profit
Type: Performing; Touring; Resident; Educational
Purpose: To provide a quality theater experience for the children of Omaha and their families
Management: Mark Hoeger, Executive Director; James Larson, Artistic Director; Roberta Larson, Associate Director; Lisa Winton, Marketing
Officers: Susy Buffet, Board President
Paid Staff: 10
Paid Artists: 9
Utilizes: Special Technical Talent; Guest Artists; Guest Directors
Budget: $500,000 - $1,000,000
Income Sources: Private Foundations/Grants/Endowments; Business/Corporate Donations; Box Office; Government Grants; Individual Donations
Season: September - June
Annual Attendance: 101,403
Affiliations: TCG; ASSITEJ

FIREHOUSE THEATRE/NOODLES COMEDY CLUB
11th & Jackson, Omaha, NE 68102
(402) 346-6009
Founded: 1972
Arts Area: Professional; Musical; Dinner; Theatrical Group
Status: Professional; Commercial
Type: Performing
Purpose: To provide good theatre commercially
Management: Keith Allerton, General Manager, Firehouse Theatre; Howard Koffin, General Manager, Noodles Comedy Club
Paid Staff: 20
Paid Artists: 10
Utilizes: Special Technical Talent; Guest Conductors; Guest Artists; Guest Directors
Budget: $1,000,000 - $5,000,000
Income Sources: Box Office
Season: 52 Weeks
Annual Attendance: 100,000
Affiliations: ADTI; NDTA; AEA
Performance Facilities: Firehouse Dinner Theatre

GRANDE OLDE PLAYERS
2339 North 90th, Omaha, NE 68134
(402) 397-5262
Founded: 1983
Arts Area: Musical; Community; Theatrical Group
Status: Non-Professional; Non-Profit
Type: Performing; Touring; Educational
Purpose: To provide an artistic outlet and education in the arts for people over fifty-five or those advocates of fifty-five and better
Management: Mark J. Manhart, Artistic Director; Bonnie Gill Kusleika, Administrative Director
Officers: Mark J. Manhart, President
Volunteer Staff: 50
Non-Paid Artists: 36
Utilizes: Guest Directors
Budget: $1,000 - $50,000

Income Sources: Private Foundations/Grants/Endowments; Business/Corporate Donations; Box Office; Government Grants; Individual Donations
Season: 52 Weeks   **Annual Attendance:** 3,000

NEBRASKA THEATRE CARAVAN
6915 Cass Street, Omaha, NE 68132
(402) 553-4890
FAX: (402) 553-6288
Founded: 1976
Arts Area: Professional; Theatrical Group
Status: Professional; Non-Profit
Type: Performing; Touring; Resident; Educational
Purpose: To bring quality entertainment and educational opportunities to communities where distance, financial limitations, or lack of appropriate resources has hindered or prevented such activities
Management: Charles Jones, Artistic Director; Carolyn Rutherford, Managing Director; Kathy Wheeldon, Public Relations Director
Officers: Redd Thomas, Board President
Paid Staff: 2
Utilizes: Special Technical Talent; Guest Artists; Guest Directors
Budget: $500,000 - $1,000,000
Income Sources: Private Foundations/Grants/Endowments; Business/Corporate Donations; Box Office; Government Grants; Individual Donations
Season: September - May
Affiliations: TCG
Performance Facilities: Omaha Playhouse

OMAHA COMMUNITY PLAYHOUSE
6915 Cass Street, Omaha, NE 68132
(402) 553-4890
FAX: (402) 553-6288
Founded: 1924
Arts Area: Theatrical Group
Status: Professional; Non-Professional; Non-Profit
Type: Performing; Touring
Purpose: To offer the best possible theatre for our audiences and to offer those people who choose to pursue theatre as an avocation a place to perform
Management: Charles Jones, Executive Director; Ginny Winsor, General Manager; Carolyn Rutherford, Managing Director; Nebraska Theatre Caravan; Susan Long, Comptroller
Officers: L.B. Thomas, President, Board of Trustees; Sue Fegler, Executive Vice President; Dee Owen, Secretary; John Hancock, Treasurer
Paid Staff: 24   **Volunteer Staff:** 3,000
Paid Artists: 15
Utilizes: Special Technical Talent; Guest Artists; Guest Directors
Budget: $1,000,000 - $5,000,000
Income Sources: Private Foundations/Grants/Endowments; Business/Corporate Donations; Box Office; Government Grants; Individual Donations
Season: September - July   **Annual Attendance:** 120,000
Affiliations: AACT; TCG
Performance Facilities: Omaha Community Playhouse

OMAHA MAGIC THEATRE
1417 Farnam, Omaha, NE 68102
(402) 346-1227
Founded: 1968
Arts Area: Professional; Musical; Theatrical Group
Status: Professional; Non-Profit
Type: Performing; Touring
Purpose: Research, development, production and touring of new plays with music; training of theatre artists
Management: JoAnn Schmidman, Artistic Director
Officers: JoAnn Schmidman, President; Bette Schmidman, Vice President
Paid Staff: 15   **Volunteer Staff:** 25
Paid Artists: 60   **Non-Paid Artists:** 12
Utilizes: Special Technical Talent; Guest Artists; Guest Directors
Budget: $100,000 - $500,000
Income Sources: Private Foundations/Grants/Endowments; Business/Corporate Donations; Box Office; Government Grants; Individual Donations
Season: 52 Weeks   **Annual Attendance:** 15,000

PERFORMING SERIES

TUESDAY MUSICAL CONCERT SERIES
8543 Hickory, Omaha, NE 68124
(402) 391-4661
FAX: (402) 397-9510
> **Founded:** 1892
> **Arts Area:** Present Classical Recitals
> **Status:** Non-Professional; Non-Profit
> **Type:** Sponsoring
> **Purpose:** To present four or five concerts annually for the purpose of hearing fine performers play fine music
> **Officers:** Mrs. Thomas P.K. Lim, President; Mrs. James Keene III, Vice President; Mrs. Julian Rips, Secretary; Mrs. David Shrader, Treasurer
> **Volunteer Staff:** 36
> **Paid Artists:** 5
> **Utilizes:** Guest Artists
> **Budget:** $50,000 - $100,000
> **Income Sources:** Private Foundations/Grants/Endowments; Business/Corporate Donations; Box Office; Government Grants; Individual Donations
> **Season:** September - May   **Annual Attendance:** 5,000
> **Performance Facilities:** Josly Art Museum

FACILITY

FIREHOUSE DINNER THEATRE
11th & Jackson, Omaha, NE 68102
(402) 346-8833
> **Type of Facility:** Theatre House
> **Facility Originally:** Fire Station
> **Type of Stage:** Thrust
> **Stage Dimensions:** 26'x30'   **Orchestra Pit**
> **Seating Capacity:** 289
> **Year Built:** 1903
> **Year Remodeled:** 1986   **Architect:** Mueller & Mueller   **Cost:** $200,000
> **Contact for Rental:** Keith Allerton;   (402) 346-8833

OMAHA CIVIC AUDITORIUM - MUSIC HALL
1804 Capitol Avenue, Omaha, NE 68134
(402) 444-4750
> **Type of Facility:** Theatre Complex; Auditorium; Arena
> **Facility Originally:** Vaudeville
> **Type of Stage:** Proscenium
> **Stage Dimensions:** 114'Wx48'D   **Orchestra Pit**
> **Seating Capacity:** Theater 2,608 **Cost:** $1,800,000
> **Acoustical Consultant:** Coffeen and Associates
> **Contact for Rental:** Susan Busskohl;   (402) 444-4750
> **Manager:** Larry Foster;   (402) 444-4750
> **Resident Groups:** Omaha Symphony Association; Opera Omaha; Omaha Ballet
> *The building also contains an 11,500-seat arena with flexible staging.*

ORPHEUM THEATER
409 South 16th Street, Omaha, NE 68102
(402) 444-4750
> **Type of Facility:** Theatre House
> **Facility Originally:** Vaudeville
> **Type of Stage:** Proscenium
> **Stage Dimensions:** 54'Wx48'D
> **Orchestra Pit**
> **Seating Capacity:** 2,759
> **Year Built:** 1927
> **Year Remodeled:** 1975   **Architect:** Leo A. Daly   **Cost:** $2,000,000
> **Contact for Rental:** Susan Busskohl;   (402) 444-4750
> **Manager:** Larry Foster;   (402) 444-4750
> **Resident Groups:** Omaha Symphony Association; Omaha Ballet; Opera/Omaha

Papillion

DANCE

OMAHA INTERNATIONAL FOLK DANCERS
525 Cordes Drive, Papillion, NE 68046
(402) 339-4660
    Founded: 1979
    Arts Area: Ethnic; Folk
    Status: Non-Profit
    Type: Performing; Educational
    Purpose: To provide a cultural experience through folk dancing for both children and adults
    Officers: Alice Morris, Chairman of the Board
    Volunteer Staff: 20
    Utilizes: Special Technical Talent; Guest Artists
    Budget: $1,000 - $50,000
    Income Sources: Individual Donations
    Season: 52 Weeks

NEVADA

Carson City

THEATRE

BREWERY ARTS CENTER
449 West King, Carson City, NV 89703
(702) 883-1976
   Arts Area: Musical; Community; Folk; Theatrical Group
   Status: Non-Professional; Non-Profit
   Type: Performing; Sponsoring
   Purpose: To provide and promote arts and cultural opportunities in Carson City, Nevada
   Management: Carl Dahlen, Executive Director; Jean Murray, Program Director
   Paid Staff: 4   **Volunteer Staff:** 30
   Budget: $100,000 - $500,000
   Income Sources: Private Foundations/Grants/Endowments; Business/Corporate Donations; Box Office; Government Grants; Individual Donations
   Performance Facilities: Carson City Community Center; Brewery Arts Center

PROSCENIUM PLAYERS
PO Box 1165, Carson City, NV 89702
(702) 883-1976
   Arts Area: Community; Theatrical Group
   Status: Non-Professional; Non-Profit
   Type: Performing; Resident
   Purpose: To bring live theatre to the community; to give interested persons an opportunity to participate
   Officers: Carolyn Demar, President; Matt Rifley, Vice President; Carla Davis, Secretary; Jonni Moon, Treasurer; Pete Coates, Member-at-Large
   Volunteer Staff: 15
   Non-Paid Artists: 20
   Budget: $1,000 - $50,000
   Income Sources: Box Office; Individual Donations
   Season: September - June   **Annual Attendance:** 2,000
   Affiliations: Nevada Community Theatre Association; Brewery Arts Center; Carson City Chamber of Commerce
   Performance Facilities: Brewery Arts Center

Incline Village

INSTRUMENTAL MUSIC

NORTH LAKE TAHOE SYMPHONY ASSOCIATION
PO Box 4368, Incline Village, NV 89450
(702) 831-4024; (702) 831-4662
   Founded: 1972
   Arts Area: Symphony; Orchestra; Chamber; Instrumental Group
   Status: Professional; Non-Professional; Non-Profit
   Type: Resident; Sponsoring
   Purpose: To bring quality music to our community in an on-going series of free concerts
   Management: John Hays, President; Carl Robinson and Andrea Guthrie, Directors; Joy Miechel, Vice President
   Volunteer Staff: 25
   Paid Artists: 80
   Utilizes: Guest Conductors; Guest Artists; Guest Directors   **Budget:** $1,000 - $50,000
   Income Sources: Private Foundations/Grants/Endowments; Individual Donations; Membership Dues
   Season: 52 Weeks   **Annual Attendance:** 1,500
   Performance Facilities: The Chateau

Las Vegas

DANCE

BALLET COLBERT
4225 Spencer, #206, Las Vegas, NV 89119
(702) 893-9782
   Founded: 1980

Status: Semi-Professional; Non-Profit
Type: Performing; Educational
Officers: M.M. Colbert, Director
Utilizes: Visual Artists; Composers
Budget: $1,000 - $50,000
Income Sources: Business/Corporate Donations; Box Office; Government Grants; Individual Donations
Season: 52 Weeks

NEVADA DANCE THEATRE
4505 South Maryland Parkway, Las Vegas, NV 89154
(702) 739-3838
FAX: (702) 739-1355
Founded: 1972
Arts Area: Modern; Ballet; Ethnic
Status: Professional; Non-Profit
Type: Performing; Touring; Resident; Educational; Sponsoring
Purpose: To provide quality performance to the people of Nevada
Management: Norman Cain, Company Manager; Vassili Sulich, Artistic Director
Officers: Mrs. J.K. Houssels, Jr., Honorary Chairman of the Board
Paid Staff: 8   **Volunteer Staff:** 150
Paid Artists: 25   **Non-Paid Artists:** 12
Utilizes: Special Technical Talent; Guest Artists; Guest Choreographers
Budget: $500,000 - $1,000,000
Income Sources: Private Foundations/Grants/Endowments; Business/Corporate Donations; Box Office; Government Grants; Individual Donations
Season: 52 Weeks   **Annual Attendance:** 20,000
Affiliations: Academy of Nevada Dance Theatre; University of Nevada
Performance Facilities: Judy Bayley Theatre

INSTRUMENTAL MUSIC

CHAMBER MUSIC SOUTHWEST
UNLV Department of Music, 4505 Maryland Parkway, Las Vegas, NV 89154
(702) 739-3377
Founded: 1987
Arts Area: Chamber; Ensemble; Instrumental Group
Status: Professional; Non-Profit
Type: Performing; Touring; Educational
Purpose: To advance the cause of high quality chamber music in southern Nevada; to foster the growth of understanding of great music in Las Vegas
Officers: Richard L. Soule and Daniel Lewin, Directors
Volunteer Staff: 4
Paid Artists: 15   **Non-Paid Artists:** 8
Utilizes: Guest Artists
Budget: $1,000 - $50,000
Income Sources: Private Foundations/Grants/Endowments; Business/Corporate Donations; Box Office; Government Grants; Individual Donations
Season: October - May   **Annual Attendance:** 1,200
Affiliations: University of Nevada-Las Vegas; KNPR-FM
Performance Facilities: Artemus W. Ham Hall; Judy Bayley Theatre; Black Box Theatre

NEVADA SYMPHONY ORCHESTRA
4505 Maryland Parkway, Las Vegas, NV 89154
(702) 739-3420
FAX: (702) 739-3850
Founded: 1980
Arts Area: Symphony; Orchestra
Status: Professional; Non-Profit
Type: Performing; Educational
Management: Virko Baley, Music Director; Judith Markham, Executive Director; Timothy Bonenfant, Director of Operations
Officers: M. Rex Baird, President; Bruce B. Borgelt, Vice President; Colleen Schroeder, Secretary; B. Michl Lloyd, Treasurer/President Elect
Paid Staff: 4
Paid Artists: 60
Utilizes: Guest Conductors; Guest Artists
Budget: $500,000 - $1,000,000

Budget: $500,000 - $1,000,000
Income Sources: Private Foundations/Grants/Endowments; Business/Corporate Donations; Box Office; Government Grants; Individual Donations
Season: 52 Weeks   **Annual Attendance:** 20,000
Affiliations: ASOL; Las Vegas Symphonic and Chamber Music Association
Performance Facilities: Artemus Ham Hall, University of Nevada-Las Vegas

SIERRA WIND QUINTET
4505 Maryland Parkway, Las Vegas, NV 89154
(702) 739-3738
FAX: (702) 597-4194
Arts Area: Chamber; Ensemble; Ethnic; Instrumental Group
Status: Professional; Non-Profit
Type: Performing; Touring; Resident; Educational; Sponsoring
Purpose: To promote the highest standards of chamber music and education nationally and internationally
Management: Stephen Caplan, Executive Director
Officers: Patrick Gaffey, President
Budget: $1,000 - $50,000
Income Sources: Private Foundations/Grants/Endowments; Business/Corporate Donations; Box Office; Government Grants; Individual Donations
Performance Facilities: Artemus W. Ham Concert Hall

THEATRE

LAS VEGAS LITTLE THEATRE
2026 Western Avenue, Las Vegas, NV 89102
(702) 383-0021
Founded: 1974
Arts Area: Musical; Community; Theatrical Group
Status: Semi-Professional; Non-Profit
Type: Performing; Educational
Purpose: To educate and entertain the community while providing an hands-on training ground for interested artists
Management: Jack Bell, Executive Producer; Paul A. Thornton, Managing Director
Officers: Paul A. Thornton, President; Erin Breen, Vice President; Karl Johnson, Secretary; Rae Fell, Treasurer
Volunteer Staff: 12
Paid Artists: 2
Utilizes: Special Technical Talent; Guest Directors
Budget: $1,000 - $50,000
Income Sources: Private Foundations/Grants/Endowments; Business/Corporate Donations; Box Office; Government Grants; Individual Donations
Season: September - June   **Annual Attendance:** 5,000
Affiliations: Nevada Community Theatre Association; Allied Arts Council of Southern Nevada; AACT

PERFORMING SERIES

NEVADA SYMPHONY ORCHESTRA
4505 Maryland Parkway, Las Vegas, NV 89154
(702) 739-3420
FAX: (702) 736-6656
Founded: 1980
Arts Area: Vocal Music; Instrumental Music
Status: Professional; Non-Profit
Type: Performing; Educational; Sponsoring
Purpose: To offer performances, services and educational opportunities and add to the quality of life in Las Vegas through the Las Vegas Symphony Orchestra, Las Vegas Chamber Players and Las Vegas Opera Company
Management: Virko Baley, Artistic Director
Paid Staff: 2   **Volunteer Staff:** 100
Utilizes: Guest Artists
Budget: $100,000 - $500,000
Income Sources: Private Foundations/Grants/Endowments; Business/Corporate Donations; Box Office; Government Grants; Individual Donations

REED WHIPPLE CULTURAL ARTS CENTER
821 Las Vegas Boulevard North, Las Vegas, NV 89101
(702) 386-6211
Founded: 1961
Arts Area: Dance; Vocal Music; Instrumental Music; Theater
Status: Non-Profit

Type: Performing; Touring; Educational; Sponsoring
Purpose: Community arts developed through programming education, coordination and community involvement
Management: Patricia L. Harris, Center Coordinator; City of Las Vegas Department of Parks; And Leisure Activities; Cultural & Community Affairs Div.
Officers: David L.Kuiper, Department Director; Joanne L. Nivison, Division Chief; Jan L. Jones, Mayor; William Noonan, City Manager
Paid Staff: 5   **Volunteer Staff:** 10
Paid Artists: 20   **Non-Paid Artists:** 100
Utilizes: Special Technical Talent; Guest Artists; Guest Directors
Budget: $50,000 - $100,000
Income Sources: Private Foundations/Grants/Endowments; Business/Corporate Donations; Box Office; Government Grants; Individual Donations
Season: 52 Weeks
Affiliations: ACA; Nevada Recreation and Parks Society; Nevada Presenters Network

FACILITY

LAS VEGAS CONVENTION AND VISITORS AUTHORITY-CASHMAN'S FIELD CENTER
850 Las Vegas Boulevard North, Las Vegas, NV 89101
(702) 386-7100
Type of Facility: Concert Hall; Auditorium; Theatre House; Multi-Purpose; Room; Loft
Type of Stage: Proscenium
Seating Capacity: 1,938
Year Built: 1983
Architect: SC3 Associates
Cost: $26,000,000
Contact for Rental: Thomas A. Smith, General Manager;   (702) 386-7100
Manager: Thomas A. Smith

REED WHIPPLE CULTURAL ARTS CENTER
821 Las Vegas Boulevard North, Las Vegas, NV 89101
(702) 229-6211
FAX: (702) 383-6306
Type of Facility: Theatre Complex; Studio Performance; Multi-Purpose; Room
Facility Originally: LDS Church Stake Center
Type of Stage: Proscenium
Stage Dimensions: 18'x45'x24'   **Seating Capacity:** 300
Year Built: 1961
Year Remodeled: 1975
Contact for Rental: Patricia Harris;   (702) 229-6211
Resident Groups: Las Vegas Civic Symphony; The Rainbow Company; The Las Vegas Civic Ballet; Las Vegas Summer Orchestra; Las Vegas Youth Orchestra

UNIVERSITY OF NEVADA-LAS VEGAS - ARTEMUS HAM CONCERT HALL
4505 Maryland Parkway, Las Vegas, NV 89154
(702) 739-3737
Type of Facility: Concert Hall; Opera House
Type of Stage: End Stage
Stage Dimensions: 60'Wx40'D; downstage 60'W; Hydraulic lift   **Orchestra Pit**
Seating Capacity: 1,885
Year Built: 1976
Architect: James McDaniel
Cost: $4,000,000
Acoustical Consultant: Bolt, Beranek & Newman
Contact for Rental: Facilities Manager;   (702) 739-3737
Manager: Rick Romito
Resident Groups: Las Vegas Chamber Players; Las Vegas Symphony; Las Vegas Opera; Nevada School of the Arts

Reno

INSTRUMENTAL MUSIC

RENO CHAMBER ORCHESTRA
1595 Skyline Boulevard, Reno, NV 89509
(702) 826-0880
Founded: 1973
Arts Area: Orchestra
Status: Professional; Non-Profit

Type: Performing; Educational
Purpose: To present quality chamber orchestra music to the area
Management: Judith F. Simpson, Manager; Cathy Chapman, Assistant Manager
Officers: Doug Damon, President; Ralph Weiss, First Vice President; Neal Ferguson, Second Vice President; John Walker, Treasurer; Robbi Whipp, Secretary
Paid Staff: 3
Paid Artists: 45
Utilizes: Guest Conductors; Guest Artists; Guest Directors
Budget: $100,000 - $500,000
Income Sources: Private Foundations/Grants/Endowments; Business/Corporate Donations; Box Office; Government Grants; Individual Donations
Season: October - May
Annual Attendance: 3,500
Affiliations: ASOL
Performance Facilities: Nightingale Concert Hall

VOCAL MUSIC

NEVADA OPERA ASSOCIATION
150 South Virginia (rear), Reno, NV 89501
(702) 786-4046; (800) 992-2072
FAX: (702) 786-4063
Founded: 1968
Arts Area: Grand Opera; Lyric Opera; Light Opera; Operetta
Status: Professional; Non-Profit
Type: Performing; Resident
Purpose: To encourage and promote opera and musical theater in northern Nevada
Management: Ted Puffer, Artistic Director; Donna Picollo, Business Manager
Officers: Helen Buck, President
Paid Staff: 3   **Volunteer Staff:** 100
Paid Artists: 75
Utilizes: Special Technical Talent; Guest Conductors; Guest Artists
Budget: $500,000 - $1,000,000
Income Sources: Private Foundations/Grants/Endowments; Business/Corporate Donations; Box Office; Government Grants; Individual Donations
Season: October - April   **Annual Attendance:** 12,000
Affiliations: OA
Performance Facilities: Pioneer Theater

FACILITY

CENTENNIAL COLISEUM - RENO SPARKS CONVENTION AND VISITORS AUTHORITY
4590 South Virginia, Reno, NV 89502
(702) 827-7600
FAX: (702) 827-7646
Type of Facility: Auditorium
Type of Stage: Flexible
Seating Capacity: 7,500
Year Built: 1965   **Architect:** Richard J. Neutra   **Cost:** $5,000,000
Contact for Rental: Lindh Stednick;   (702) 827-7600

PIONEER CENTER FOR THE PERFROMING ARTS
100 South Virginia Street, Reno, NV 89501
(702) 786-5105
FAX: (702) 786-3086
Type of Facility: Auditorium; Theatre House; Multi-Purpose
Type of Stage: Proscenium
Stage Dimensions: 70'x100'x38'   **Orchestra Pit**
Seating Capacity: 1,434
Year Built: 1968   **Architect:** Bozalis, Dickinson, Roloff   **Cost:** $3,000,000
Contact for Rental: Kathi Baglin;   (702) 786-5105
Manager: John Shelton, Executive Director
Resident Groups: Nevada Opera Association; Reno Philharmonic Orchestra; UNR Performing Artists Series; Washoe County Community Concert Association; Nevada Festival Ballet

RENO LITTLE THEATER
690 North Sierra, PO Box 2088, Reno, NV 89505
(702) 329-0661
> **Type of Facility:** Theatre House
> **Facility Originally:** Meeting Hall; Movie House
> **Type of Stage:** Proscenium
> **Seating Capacity:** 289
> **Year Remodeled:** 1986   **Architect:** Graham Eskine   **Cost:** $260,000
> **Acoustical Consultant:** Phil Raglin
> **Contact for Rental:** Joan Long, Business Manager;   (702) 329-0661

UNIVERSITY OF NEVADA-RENO - CHURCH FINE ARTS CENTER
Reno, NV 89557
(702) 784-6659
> **Type of Facility:** Theatre Complex; Auditorium; Studio Performance; Performance Center; Theatre House
> **Year Built:** 1960   **Architect:** Richard J. Neutra   **Cost:** $1,250,000
> **Year Remodeled:** 1986   **Architect:** Vhay and Ferrari   **Cost:** $4,500,000
> **Contact for Rental:** Karren Garel;   (702) 784-6837
> **Resident Groups:** Nevada Repertory Company
> *Church Fine Arts Center contains the Experimental Theatre, Fine Arts Theatre and Nightingale Hall. See separate listings for additional information.*

UNIVERSITY OF NEVADA-RENO - CHURCH FINE ARTS CENTER - FINE ARTS THEATRE
Reno, NV 89557
(702) 784-6659
> **Type of Facility:** Theatre House
> **Type of Stage:** Proscenium
> **Stage Dimensions:** 30'x36'
> **Seating Capacity:** 270
> **Year Built:** 1960   **Architect:** Richard J. Neutra   **Cost:** $1,250,000
> **Contact for Rental:** Karren Garel;   (702) 784-6837
> **Manager:** James Bernardi

UNIVERSITY OF NEVADA-RENO - CHURCH FINE ARTS CENTER - NIGHTINGALE HALL
Reno, NV 89557
(702) 784-6659
> **Type of Facility:** Concert Hall
> **Type of Stage:** Proscenium
> **Stage Dimensions:** 48'x30'
> **Seating Capacity:** 650
> **Year Built:** 1986   **Architect:** Vhay and Ferrari   **Cost:** $3,000,000
> **Contact for Rental:** Karren Garel;   (702) 784-6837
> **Manager:** Music Department

UNIVERSITY OF NEVADA-RENO - CHURCH FINE ARTS CENTER, REDFIELD STUDIO THEATRE
Reno, NV 89557
(702) 784-6659
> **Type of Facility:** Studio Performance
> **Type of Stage:** Flexible
> **Stage Dimensions:** 50'x50'
> **Seating Capacity:** 200
> **Year Built:** 1986   **Architect:** Vhay and Ferrari   **Cost:** $1,000,000
> **Contact for Rental:** Karren Garel;   (702) 784-6837
> **Manager:** James Bernardi
> **Resident Groups:** The Nevada Repertory Company

UNIVERSITY OF NEVADA-RENO - LAWLOR EVENTS CENTER
Reno, NV 89557
(702) 784-4659
> **Type of Facility:** Arena; Multi-Purpose
> **Type of Stage:** Flexible
> **Seating Capacity:** 12,400
> **Year Built:** 1983   **Architect:** Crain Anderson   **Cost:** $26,000,000
> **Acoustical Consultant:** C.P. Boner & Associates
> **Contact for Rental:** Robert Stewart, Joseph Kerr;   (702) 784-4659
> **Manager:** Robert Stewart

Virginia City

FACILITY

PIPER'S OPERA HOUSE
Box 157, Virginia City, NV 89440
(702) 847-0433
  Type of Facility: Theatre House
  Type of Stage: Proscenium
  Stage Dimensions: 50'Wx35'D
  Seating Capacity: 500
  Year Built: 1867
  Year Remodeled: 1980
  Contact for Rental: Louise Driggs; (702) 847-0433

NEW HAMPSHIRE

Centre Harbor

PERFORMING SERIES

NEW HAMPSHIRE MUSIC FESTIVAL
PO Box 147, Centre Harbor, NH 03226
(603) 253-4331
Founded: 1952
Arts Area: Festivals; Classical & Chamber music
Status: Professional; Non-Profit
Type: Performing; Touring; Educational
Purpose: To promote appreciation and dissemination of classical music in the Lakes Region of New Hampshire
Management: David H. Graham, Executive Director
Officers: T. Holmes Moore, President; Lewis A. Aldrich, Treasurer
Paid Staff: 3 **Volunteer Staff:** 1
Paid Artists: 48
Utilizes: Guest Conductors; Guest Artists
Budget: $100,000 - $500,000
Income Sources: Private Foundations/Grants/Endowments; Business/Corporate Donations; Box Office; Government Grants; Individual Donations
Season: July - August **Annual Attendance:** 9,000
Affiliations: ASOL
Performance Facilities: Plymouth's Silver Hall; Gilford's Middle High School Auditorium

Claremont

FACILITY

CLAREMONT OPERA HOUSE
PO Box 664, Claremont, NH 03755
(603) 542-4433
Founded: 1897
Type of Facility: Theatre Complex; Concert Hall; Multi-Purpose
Facility Originally: Opera House
Type of Stage: Proscenium
Stage Dimensions: 34'Wx30'D
Seating Capacity: 787
Year Built: 1897 **Architect:** Charles Rich **Cost:** $62,000
Year Remodeled: 1977 **Architect:** Paul Mirski **Cost:** $1,000,000
Contact for Rental: John Goyette; (603) 542-4433

Concord

INSTRUMENTAL MUSIC

NEVERS' 2ND REGIMENT BAND
110 South State Street, Concord, NH 03301
(603) 225-2684
Founded: 1861
Arts Area: Band
Status: Semi-Professional; Non-Profit
Type: Performing
Purpose: To provide live band music to the residents of the Concord area and other areas throughout New Hampshire at no charge to the public
Management: Maryanne Sisk, Director; George M. West, Business Manager
Officers: Deborah G. Lincoln, Secretary; Elizabeth Densmore, Treasurer; Paul T. Giles, Historian
Paid Artists: 25
Utilizes: Guest Conductors; Guest Artists
Budget: $1,000 - $50,000
Income Sources: Private Foundations/Grants/Endowments; Individual Donations
Annual Attendance: 2,000

THEATRE

COMMUNITY PLAYERS OF CONCORD
PO Box 681, Concord, NH 03302
(603) 224-4905
   Founded: 1927
   Arts Area: Community; Theatrical Group
   Status: Non-Profit
   Type: Performing
   Purpose: To promote interest in all phases of community theater
   Officers: Sharon LaJoie, President; Betsy Stebbins, Vice President; Jeanne Bailey, Secretary; Fritz Sabbow, Treasurer
   Budget: $1,000 - $50,000
   Income Sources: Box Office; Individual Donations
   Season: November - May   **Annual Attendance:** 6,000
   Affiliations: New Hampshire Community Theater Association
   Performance Facilities: Concord City Auditorium

FACILITY

THE FRIENDS OF THE CONCORD CITY AUDITORIUM
PO Box 652, Concord, NH 03302-0652
(603) 225-8580
   Type of Facility: Concert Hall; Auditorium; Theatre House
   Type of Stage: Proscenium
   Stage Dimensions: 26'x26'   **Orchestra Pit**
   Seating Capacity: 792
   Year Built: 1904
   Architect: Barn Raising (Community Volunteers)
   Contact for Rental: Eugene Blake;   (603) 225-8580
   Resident Groups: Concord Community Players; Walker Lecture Series; Concord Community Concert Association
   Restoration and rehabilitation of building; Foster use of the facility to benefit community citizens

Durham

FACILITY

UNIVERSITY OF NEW HAMPSHIRE - DURHAM
Paul Creative Arts Center, Durham, NH 03824
(603) 862-3038
   Type of Facility: Theatre Complex; Multi-Purpose
   Year Built: 1960   **Architect:** Sheply Bulfinch Richardson Abbott   **Cost:** $2,100,000
   Year Remodeled: 1982   **Architect:** University Architects   **Cost:** $300,000
   Paul Creative Arts Center contains Bratton Recital Hall, Hennessy Theater and Johnson Theater. See separate listings for additional information.

UNIVERSITY OF NEW HAMPSHIRE-DURHAM - BRATTON RECITAL HALL
Paul Creative Arts Center, Durham, NH 03824
(603) 862-3038
   Type of Facility: Recital Hall
   Facility Originally: School
   Type of Stage: Flexible
   Seating Capacity: 150
   Year Built: 1960
   Year Remodeled: 1982
   Resident Groups: Music Department

UNIVERSITY OF NEW HAMPSHIRE-DURHAM - HENNESSY THEATER
Paul Creative Arts Center, Durham, NH 03824
(603) 862-3038
   Type of Facility: Studio Performance; Arena
   Type of Stage: Flexible; Arena
   Seating Capacity: 200
   Year Built: 1960
   Year Remodeled: 1982

UNIVERSITY OF NEW HAMPSHIRE-DURHAM - JOHNSON THEATER
Paul Creative Arts Center, Durham, NH 03824
(603) 862-3038
    Type of Facility: Concert Hall; Theatre House
    Type of Stage: Proscenium
    Stage Dimensions: 65'Wx60'D; 39'10"Wx20'H proscenium opening   **Orchestra Pit**
    Seating Capacity: 716
    Year Built: 1960
    Year Remodeled: 1990   **Cost:** $300,000

East Sullivan

INSTRUMENTAL MUSIC

APPLE HILL CENTER FOR CHAMBER MUSIC
Apple Hill Road, East Sullivan, NH 03445
(603) 847-3371
FAX: (603) 847-9972
    Founded: 1971
    Arts Area: Chamber; Ensemble
    Status: Professional; Semi-Professional; Non-Professional; Non-Profit
    Type: Performing; Resident; Educational; Sponsoring
    Purpose: The Apple Hill Chamber Players, a full-time, professional concert ensemble, joined by a distinguished guest faculty, coach students of all ages and at different levels in the interpretation of chamber music of all periods.
    Management: Eric Stumacher, Executive Director; Kathy Stumacher, Director of Administration; Susan King, Fiscal Manager; Harriet Feinberg, Recruiter/Music Librarian
    Officers: Julie Albright, President; Arthur Cohen, Vice President; Jeremiah Dolan, Secretary; David Ross, Treasurer
    Paid Staff: 5
    Paid Artists: 6
    Utilizes: Guest Artists
    Budget: $100,000 - $500,000
    Income Sources: Private Foundations/Grants/Endowments; Business/Corporate Donations; Box Office; Government Grants; Individual Donations
    Season: June - October   **Annual Attendance:** 1,500
    Performance Facilities: Louise Shonk Kelly Concert Barn

Franconia

DANCE

WHITE MOUNTAIN SUMMER DANCE FESTIVAL
PO Box 94, Franconia, NH 03580
(603) 444-2928
FAX: (603) 444-1258
    Winter Address: c/o Dance Base Inc., 162 West 21st Street, New York, NY 10011; (212) 929-5733;
    FAX: (203) 233-2941
    Founded: 1979
    Arts Area: Modern; Ballet
    Status: Professional; Semi-Professional; Non-Professional; Non-Profit
    Type: Performing; Educational; Resident
    Purpose: To provide dance training and movement-analysis education; to create performance opportunities for local and area communities through a three-week intensive summer program
    Management: Laura Glenn, Artistic Director; Rebecca Lazier, Festival Coordinator
    Officers: John Murphy, President; Jim Severyn, Vice President; Michael Valcourt, Secretary
    Paid Staff: 2   **Volunteer Staff:** 10
    Paid Artists: 13   **Non-Paid Artists:** 55
    Budget: $50,000 - $100,000
    Income Sources: Private Foundations/Grants/Endowments; Box Office; Individual Donations; Tuition
    Season: July - August (3 weeks)   **Annual Attendance:** 355
    Performance Facilities: White Mountain School, Littleton

INSTRUMENTAL

NORTH COUNTRY CHAMBER PLAYERS
PO Box 94, Franconia, NH 03580
(603) 869-3154
FAX: (603) 869-2660
Arts Area: Chamber
Status: Professional; Non-Profit
Type: Performing; Touring; Resident; Educational
Purpose: To bring classical music to northern New England
Management: Bonnie Bauch, Artistic Director
Officers: Kate Walsh, Chairman of the Board
Budget: $100,000 - $500,000
Income Sources: Private Foundations/Grants/Endowments; Business/Corporate Donations; Box Office; Government Grants; Individual Donations
Performance Facilities: Governor Adams Lodge, Lincoln; Sugar Hill Meeting House, Sugar Hill

Hampton

THEATRE

HAMPTON PLAYHOUSE
Winnacunnet Road, Hampton, NH 03842
(603) 926-3076
Founded: 1948
Arts Area: Professional; Summer Stock; Musical
Status: Professional; Commercial
Type: Performing; Resident; Educational
Management: Alfred Christie, Producing/Artistic Director; John Vari, Producer
Paid Staff: 10
Paid Artists: 35
Utilizes: Special Technical Talent; Guest Artists; Guest Directors
Budget: $100,000 - $500,000
Income Sources: Business/Corporate Donations; Box Office; Individual Donations
Season: June - September **Annual Attendance:** 30,000
Affiliations: AEA; SSDC; CORST
Performance Facilities: Hampton Playhouse Theatre Arts Workshop

FACILITY

HAMPTON PLAYHOUSE THEATRE ARTS WORKSHOP
357 Winnacunnet Road, Hampton, NH 03842
(603) 926-3073
Type of Facility: Auditorium
Facility Originally: Barn
Type of Stage: Proscenium
Seating Capacity: 500
Year Built: 1787
Manager: John Vari
Resident Groups: Hampton Playhouse Company

Hanover

PERFORMING SERIES

HOPKINS CENTER SUMMER
Hopkins Center, Dartmouth College, Hanover, NH 03755
(603) 646-2424
Founded: 1962
Arts Area: Dance; Vocal Music; Instrumental Music; Theater
Status: Professional; Non-Profit
Type: Educational; Sponsoring
Purpose: To present performing and visual arts as both a co-curricular component to the Dartmouth community and as a regional arts resource
Management: Lewis Crickard, Director
Utilizes: Guest Artists; Guest Directors
Budget: $1,000,000 - $5,000,000

Income Sources: Private Foundations/Grants/Endowments; Business/Corporate Donations; Box Office; Government Grants; Individual Donations
Season: July - August   **Annual Attendance:** 250,000
Affiliations: Dartmouth College
Performance Facilities: Hopkins Center

Keene

FACILITY

ARTS CENTER ON BRICKYARD POND - KEENE STATE COLLEGE
229 Main Street, Keene, NH 03431
(603) 358-2167
FAX: (603) 358-2257
    Founded: 1909
    Type of Facility: Theatre Complex
    Type of Stage: Thrust; Flexible; Proscenium; 3/4 Arena
    Stage Dimensions: 36'6"x35'
    Seating Capacity: Main Theatre - 572; Recital Hall - 360; Studio Theatre - 100
    Year Built: 1981
    Architect: Sheplley, Bullfinch
    Cost: $7,000,000
    Contact for Rental: Events Coordinator;   (603) 358-2167

Lincoln

PERFORMING SERIES

NORTH COUNTRY CENTER FOR THE ARTS
PO Box 1060, Lincoln, NH 03251
(603) 745-6032
    Founded: 1986
    Arts Area: Theater; Festivals
    Status: Professional; Non-Profit
    Type: Performing; Touring; Educational
    Purpose: To present both adult and childrens theatre, theatre education and special events
    Management: Van McLeod, Producing Director; Lesley Parker, Managing Director
    Officers: Peter E. Gould, Board Chairman
    Paid Staff: 2   **Volunteer Staff:** 60
    Paid Artists: 70   **Non-Paid Artists:** 30
    Utilizes: Guest Artists; Guest Directors
    Budget: $100,000 - $500,000
    Income Sources: Private Foundations/Grants/Endowments; Business/Corporate Donations; Box Office; Government Grants; Individual Donations
    Season: May - September   **Annual Attendance:** 17,000

Manchester

INSTRUMENTAL MUSIC

NEW HAMPSHIRE PHILHARMONIC ORCHESTRA
PO Box 4547, Manchester, NH 03108
(603) 666-9023
    Founded: 1959
    Arts Area: Symphony; Orchestra
    Status: Professional; Non-Professional; Non-Profit
    Type: Performing; Resident; Educational
    Purpose: To present classical concerts, enhance music education, and give non-professionals the opportunity to work with music professionals
    Management: Roxanne L. Turner, Executive Director; Darcy Scott, Director of Public Relations; Art Mirabile, Stage Manager
    Officers: Gregg Cunningham, President; Gary Turner, Vice President; Pat Cunningham, Secretary; Robert Consaga, Treasurer
    Paid Staff: 3   **Volunteer Staff:** 12
    Paid Artists: 5   **Non-Paid Artists:** 65
    Utilizes: Guest Artists

Budget: $100,000 - $500,000
Income Sources: Private Foundations/Grants/Endowments; Business/Corporate Donations; Box Office; Individual Donations
Season: September - May   **Annual Attendance:** 100,000
Affiliations: ASOL; Manchester Chamber of Commerce
Performance Facilities: Palace Theatre

NEW HAMPSHIRE SYMPHONY ORCHESTRA
PO Box 1298, Manchester, NH 03105-1298
(603) 669-3559
FAX: (603) 623-1195
Founded: 1973
Arts Area: Symphony; Orchestra
Status: Professional; Non-Profit
Type: Performing; Touring; Educational
Management: David A. Ball, Executive Director; Alan D. Jordan, Director of Operations; Marian Royal, Administrative Assistant; James Bolle, Music Director
Officers: Leonard Lacouture, President; Donald Gendron, Vice President, Development; Susan Monson, Vice President-Planning; John Graf, Secretary; Richard Hodgkinson, Treasurer
Paid Staff: 5
Utilizes: Guest Artists
Budget: $100,000 - $500,000
Income Sources: Private Foundations/Grants/Endowments; Business/Corporate Donations; Box Office; Government Grants; Individual Donations
Season: October - May   **Annual Attendance:** 7,954
Affiliations: ASOL
Performance Facilities: Palace Theatre

FACILITY

NEW HAMPSHIRE PERFORMING ARTS CENTER
80 Hanover Street, PO Box 3006, Manchester, NH 03105
(603) 669-8021
Type of Facility: Concert Hall; Performance Center; Theatre House; Opera House
Facility Originally: Vaudeville
Type of Stage: Proscenium
Stage Dimensions: 62'Wx33'D; 40'Wx26'H proscenium opening   **Orchestra Pit**
Seating Capacity: 893
Year Built: 1915   **Architect:** Leon Lempart
Year Remodeled: 1985   **Architect:** Fred Matuszewski   **Cost:** $650,000
Contact for Rental: Robert Shea;   (603) 669-8021
Resident Groups: New Hampshire Performing Arts Center; New Hampshire Symphony Orchestra; Opera League of New Hampshire

Milford

THEATRE

PEACOCK PLAYERS CHILDREN'S THEATRE
PO Box 225, Milford, NH 03055
(603) 673-4005
FAX: (603) 673-4792
Founded: 1980
Arts Area: Musical; Theatrical Group
Status: Non-Professional; Non-Profit
Type: Performing; Educational
Purpose: Education, Entertainment
Management: Lorraine Lanes, Managing Director; Blair Hundtertmark, Artistic Director
Paid Staff: 2
Utilizes: Guest Conductors; Guest Directors
Budget: $1,000 - $50,000
Income Sources: Private Foundations/Grants/Endowments; Business/Corporate Donations; Box Office; Individual Donations; Tuition - workshops
Season: September - August   **Annual Attendance:** 5,000

PERFORMING SERIES

AMERICAN STAGE FESTIVAL
PO Box 225, Milford, NH 03055
(603) 673-6896
FAX: (603) 673-4792
Founded: 1971
Arts Area: Theater; Festival
Status: Professional; Non-Profit
Type: Performing; Touring; Resident; Educational; Developmental
Purpose: To expand the spectrum of theatre by presenting entertaining, rewarding and challenging theatrical material, paying particular attention to pieces that reflect the concerns of southern New Hampshire
Management: Richard Rose, Producing Director; Robert Walsh, Associate Director; Blanche Risteen, Marketing/Education; Cynthia Marshall, Subscriptions; Blair Hundtermare, John Thichnor, Young Company
Officers: Mark Roberts, President; Lionel Bourasa, Vice President of Finance; Dora Weiner, Secretary
Paid Staff: 15
Paid Artists: 70 **Non-Paid Artists:** 30
Utilizes: Guest Conductors; Guest Artists; Guest Directors
Budget: $500,000 - $1,000,000
Income Sources: Private Foundations/Grants/Endowments; Business/Corporate Donations; Box Office; Government Grants; Individual Donations
Season: May - August
Affiliations: NETC; AEA; SSDC; TCG; New Hampshire Theatre Council; Souhegan Theatre Council
Performance Facilities: Souhegan Valley Theatre

FACILITY

SOUHEGAN VALLEY THEATRE
Mount Vernon Street, Milford, NH 03055
(603) 673-4005
FAX: (603) 673-4792
Founded: 1973
Type of Facility: Theatre House
Type of Stage: Proscenium
Orchestra Pit
Seating Capacity: 500
Year Built: 1975 **Architect:** Thomas Johnson **Cost:** $250,000
Contact for Rental: Richard Rose, Manager; (603) 673-4005
Manager: Richard Rose
Resident Groups: American Stage Festival

Nashua

PERFORMING SERIES

KIDS INTO DRAMA
14 Court Street, Nashua, NH 03060
(603) 883-1506
Founded: 1981
Arts Area: Theater
Status: Non-Profit
Type: Performing; Touring; Educational
Management: Robert W. Haven, Director; Michele Laliberty, Music Director
Volunteer Staff: 4
Budget: $1,000 - $50,000
Income Sources: Box Office; Individual Donations
Season: 52 Weeks **Annual Attendance:** 1,800
Performance Facilities: Arts and Science Center Theatre

FACILITY

ARTS AND SCIENCE CENTER THEATRE
14 Court Street, Nashua, NH 03060
(603) 883-1506
Type of Facility: Auditorium; Performance Center; Exhibition Galleries
Type of Stage: Proscenium
Stage Dimensions: 80'Wx40'D
Seating Capacity: 230

Year Built: 1974   **Architect:** Carter & Woodruff   **Cost:** $150,000
Contact for Rental: Debra Espersen;   (603) 883-1506
Manager: Robert Daniels
Resident Groups: Granite Statesmen

New London

THEATRE

NEW LONDON PLAYERS
Main Street, PO Box 285, New London, NH 03257
(603) 526-6710
    Founded: 1933
    Arts Area: Professional; Summer Stock; Musical; Theatrical Group
    Status: Professional; Commercial
    Type: Performing; Resident
    Purpose: To provide theatrical entertainment for summer visitors and summer residents of the Lake Sunapee Area
    Management: Norman M. Leger, Producer; Steve Mendelson, Associate Producer
    Paid Staff: 15
    Paid Artists: 25
    Utilizes: Special Technical Talent; Guest Artists; Guest Directors
    Budget: $100,000 - $500,000
    Income Sources: Box Office
    Season: June - Labor Day   **Annual Attendance:** 20,000
    Affiliations: NETC
    Performance Facilities: New London Barn Playhouse

PERFORMING SERIES

SUMMER MUSIC ASSOCIATES
PO Box 603, New London, NH 03257
(603) 526-2154
    Founded: 1974
    Arts Area: Vocal Music; Instrumental Music
    Status: Non-Profit
    Type: Sponsoring
    Purpose: To present a series of summer concerts for our knowledgeable audience by a dedicated volunteer board
    Management: Robert Fraley, Program Committee Chariman
    Officers: Beverly Wolf, President; Barbara Chase, Vice President; Andrew Supplee, Treasurer
    Volunteer Staff: 24
    Utilizes: Guest Artists
    Budget: $1,000 - $50,000
    Income Sources: Private Foundations/Grants/Endowments; Business/Corporate Donations; Box Office; Individual Donations
    Season: June - August   **Annual Attendance:** 2,500
    Performance Facilities: King Ridge Ski Lodge; Colby-Sawyer College

FACILITY

NEW LONDON BARN PLAYHOUSE
Main Street, PO Box 285, New London, NH 03257
(603) 526-4631
    Type of Facility: Theatre House
    Facility Originally: Barn
    Type of Stage: Proscenium
    Stage Dimensions: 12'x24'x20'   **Orchestra Pit**
    Seating Capacity: 325
    Year Built: 1820
    Year Remodeled: 1990   **Architect:** Mike English   **Cost:** $200,000
    Manager: Norman W. Leger;   (603) 526-6570
    Resident Groups: New London Players

North Conway

THEATRE

MOUNT WASHINGTON VALLEY THEATRE COMPANY
Main Street, North Conway, NH 03860
(603) 356-5776
>**Founded:** 1972
>**Arts Area:** Summer Stock; Musical
>**Status:** Professional; Non-Profit
>**Type:** Performing; Resident
>**Purpose:** To fill the summer evenings with the joy and excitement of live theatre while offering a training ground to young professionals
>**Officers:** Linda Pinkham, President; Olga Morrill, Vice President; Doris Levesgue, Secretary; Dorothy Lovering, Treasurer
>**Paid Staff:** 15 **Volunteer Staff:** 5
>**Paid Artists:** 20 **Non-Paid Artists:** 5
>**Utilizes:** Special Technical Talent; Guest Artists
>**Budget:** $50,000 - $100,000
>**Income Sources:** Private Foundations/Grants/Endowments; Business/Corporate Donations; Box Office; Government Grants; Individual Donations
>**Season:** June - September **Annual Attendance:** 7,000
>**Performance Facilities:** Eastern Slope Playhouse

FACILITY

EASTERN SLOPE PLAYHOUSE
Main Street, North Conway, NH 03860
(603) 356-5776 summer; (603) 356-5425
FAX: (603) 356-8357
>**Type of Facility:** Auditorium; Performance Center; Theatre House; Multi-Purpose
>**Type of Stage:** Thrust; Flexible; Proscenium
>**Stage Dimensions:** 20'x20'x29' **Orchestra Pit**
>**Seating Capacity:** 183
>**Year Built:** 1917
>**Year Remodeled:** 1986
>**Contact for Rental:** Linda Pinkham; (603) 356-5425
>**Resident Groups:** Mount Washington Valley Theatre Company

---
Peterborough

THEATRE

PETERBOROUGH PLAYERS
Middle Hancock Road, PO Box 1, Peterborough, NH 03458
(603) 924-7585
>**Founded:** 1933
>**Arts Area:** Professional; Theatrical Group
>**Status:** Professional; Non-Profit
>**Type:** Performing; Resident; Educational
>**Management:** Ellen Dinerstein, Producing Director
>**Officers:** Joan Brewster, Board President
>**Paid Staff:** 6
>**Utilizes:** Special Technical Talent; Guest Artists; Guest Directors
>**Budget:** $100,000 - $500,000
>**Income Sources:** Private Foundations/Grants/Endowments; Business/Corporate Donations; Box Office; Government Grants; Individual Donations
>**Season:** June - September
>**Affiliations:** AEA; CORST

PERFORMING SERIES

MONADNOCK MUSIC
PO Box 255, Peterborough, NH 03458
(603) 924-7610
FAX: (603) 924-9403
>**Founded:** 1966
>**Arts Area:** Vocal Music; Instrumental Music; Festivals; Lyric Opera

Status: Professional; Non-Profit
Type: Performing; Educational
Purpose: To present first-rate, professional performances of music representing as wide a repertory as possible; to maintain an atmosphere which is conducive to a close audience-performer relationship; to make these performances truly accessible to people in the Monadnock Region
Management: James Bolle, Director; Jocelyn Bolle, Executive Director
Officers: Edith Milton, President; Richard McAdoo, Vice President; Faith Hanson, Clerk; John Keefe, Treasurer
Paid Staff: 5   **Volunteer Staff:** 27
Paid Artists: 114
Utilizes: Guest Artists
Budget: $100,000 - $500,000
Income Sources: Private Foundations/Grants/Endowments; Business/Corporate Donations; Box Office; Government Grants; Individual Donations
Season: July - August   **Annual Attendance:** 7,500
Affiliations: Arts 1000; New Hampshire State Council on the Arts
Performance Facilities: Pine Hall Waldorf Auditorium; Old Meeting House

---

Plymouth

FACILITY

SILVER CULTURAL ARTS CENTER
Plymouth State College, Plymouth, NH 03264
(603) 536-5000
   Type of Facility: Theatre Complex; Concert Hall; Auditorium; Studio Performance; Performance Center; Theatre House
   Type of Stage: Thrust; Flexible; Proscenium; Three spaces
   Stage Dimensions: 52'Wx32'Dx24'H proscenium opening   **Orchestra Pit**
   Seating Capacity: Mainstage - 680; Recital Hall - 174; Studio Theatre - 150
   Year Built: 1992   **Architect:** Koetter Kim Associates   **Cost:** $9,500,000
   Acoustical Consultant: Carl Rosenberg, Accentech Inc.
   Contact for Rental: John Clark, Assistant to the President;   (603) 536-1550
   Resident Groups: Plymouth State College - Department of Music and Theatre; New Hampshire Music Festival; Plymouth Friends of the Arts

---

Portsmouth

THEATRE

PONTINE MOVEMENT THEATRE
135 McDonough Street, Portsmouth, NH 03801
(603) 436-6660
   Founded: 1977
   Arts Area: Professional
   Status: Professional; Non-Profit
   Type: Performing; Touring; Resident; Educational; Sponsoring
   Purpose: Dedicated to the cultural enhancements of its various publics, its performances and educational programs are offered to inform the public in the art of corporeal mime and to the preservation and development of this exciting theatrical form
   Management: Marguerite Mathews and Greg Gathers, Co-Artistic Directors
   Paid Staff: 3   **Volunteer Staff:** 30
   Paid Artists: 5
   Utilizes: Guest Artists
   Budget: $100,000 - $500,000
   Income Sources: Private Foundations/Grants/Endowments; Business/Corporate Donations; Box Office; Government Grants; Individual Donations
   Season: October - June   **Annual Attendance:** 6,500
   Affiliations: Arts 1000, National Mime Association; New Hampshire State Council on the Arts
   Performance Facilities: McDonough Street Theater

SEACOAST REPERTORY COMPANY
125 Bow Street, Portsmouth, NH 03801
(603) 433-4793
   Founded: 1986
   Arts Area: Professional; Summer Stock; Musical; Theatrical Group
   Status: Professional; Non-Profit
   Type: Performing; Resident; Educational
   Purpose: To provide a safe haven for all performances and audiences

Management: Roy Rogosin, Artistic Director; Eileen Rogosin, Associate Director; Jean Benda, Administrative Director; Maurice Richards, Administrative Assistant
Officers: Sanford Roberts Esq, President; Irja Ciluffo, Vice President; John Colliander, Secretary; Van Sweat, Treasurer
Paid Staff: 12   **Volunteer Staff:** 20
Paid Artists: 100   **Non-Paid Artists:** 25
Utilizes: Special Technical Talent; Guest Artists; Guest Directors; Guest Designers
Budget: $100,000 - $500,000
Income Sources: Private Foundations/Grants/Endowments; Business/Corporate Donations; Box Office; Individual Donations
Season: 52 Weeks   **Annual Attendance:** 15,000
Affiliations: TCG
Performance Facilities: Bow Street Theater

PERFORMING SERIES

PRESCOTT PARK ARTS FESTIVAL
PO Box 4370, 105 Marcy Street, Portsmouth, NH 03802
(603) 436-2748
Founded: 1974
Arts Area: Dance; Vocal Music; Theater; Festivals
Status: Non-Profit
Type: Performing; Touring; Resident; Educational; Sponsoring
Purpose: To provide a financially accessible, quality mutli-arts festival to a diverse audience
Management: Michael Greenblatt, Executive Director; Sue Bolduc, Festival Coordinator; Mark Vadney, Program Director
Officers: Timothy Phoenix, President; Susan Anderson, Secretary; Anita Freedman, Treasurer
Paid Staff: 3
Paid Artists: 250
Utilizes: Special Technical Talent; Guest Artists
Budget: $500,000 - $1,000,000
Income Sources: Private Foundations/Grants/Endowments; Business/Corporate Donations; Individual Donations
Season: July - August   **Annual Attendance:** 100,000
Performance Facilities: Prescott Park

FACILITY

THE MUSIC HALL
28 Chestnut Street, Portsmouth, NH 03801
(603) 433-3100
Founded: 1986
Type of Facility: Theatre House
Facility Originally: Theater
Type of Stage: Proscenium
Stage Dimensions: 30'x32'
Seating Capacity: 900
Year Built: 1978   **Architect:** William A. Ashe
Contact for Rental: Executive Director;   (603) 433-3100

Tamworth

THEATRE

THE BARNSTORMERS
Tamworth, NH 03886
(603) 323-8500
Founded: 1931
Arts Area: Professional; Summer Stock
Status: Professional; Non-Profit
Type: Performing; Resident
Purpose: To provide a summer theatre program featuring old—and some new—plays
Officers: Helen Steele, Secretary; Bob Lloyd, Treasurer; Kate Thompson, Dana Steele, Co-Chairs
Paid Staff: 12
Paid Artists: 12
Budget: $50,000 - $100,000
Income Sources: Box Office
Season: July - September
Affiliations: AEA
Performance Facilities: The Barnstormers Theatre

Waterville Valley

PERFORMING SERIES

WATERVILLE VALLEY FOUNDATION
Town Square, Waterville Valley, NH 03215
(603) 236-8311
  Founded: 1985
  Arts Area: Vocal Music; Instrumental Music; Festivals; Concerts
  Status: Non-Profit
  Type: Performing; Educational
  Purpose: To present an annual summer festival of the arts
  Management: Peter Adams, Festival Director; Thomas A. Corcoran, Director
  Officers: Howard Grimes, Chairman; Henry Stebbins, Secretary; Robert Ashton, Treasurer
  Paid Staff: 3
  Paid Artists: 87
  Utilizes: Special Technical Talent; Guest Artists
  Budget: $100,000 - $500,000
  Income Sources: Private Foundations/Grants/Endowments; Business/Corporate Donations; Box Office; Government Grants; Membership; Sponsorship
  Season: July - August   **Annual Attendance:** 25,000
  Performance Facilities: Town Square Concert Pavillion

Whitefield

THEATRE

WEATHERVANE THEATRE
55 Jefferson Road, Whitefield, NH 03598
(603) 837-9010
  Founded: 1965
  Arts Area: Professional; Summer Stock; Musical
  Status: Professional; Commercial
  Type: Performing
  Purpose: Resident alternating repertory theater company presenting 7-8 shows per season, including musicals
  Management: Gibbs Murray, Richard Portner, Producing Directors; Tom Barthel, Jacques Stewart, Associate Artists
  Paid Staff: 29   **Volunteer Staff:** 1
  Paid Artists: 15   **Non-Paid Artists:** 5
  Utilizes: Guest Artists; Guest Directors
  Budget: $100,000 - $500,000
  Income Sources: Private Foundations/Grants/Endowments; Box Office; Individual Donations
  Season: July - August   **Annual Attendance:** 12,000
  Performance Facilities: Barn Theatre

NEW JERSEY

Aberdeen

THEATRE

CREATIVE PRODUCTIONS
2 Beaver Place, Aberdeen, NJ 07747
(908) 566-6985
Founded: 1975
Arts Area: Musical; Theatrical Group
Status: Non-Profit
Type: Performing; Educational
Purpose: Non-Equity musical-theater performing company that features folks with disabilities in leading roles
Management: Walter L. Born, Director
Officers: Mary Born, Treasurer
Volunteer Staff: 8
Non-Paid Artists: 10
Utilizes: Special Technical Talent; Guest Artists
Budget: $1,000 - $50,000
Income Sources: Box Office; Government Grants; Individual Donations
Season: 52 Weeks   **Annual Attendance:** 2,000
Performance Facilities: Lloyd Road School, Aberdeen

Allenhurst

VOCAL MUSIC

METRO LYRIC OPERA
40 Ocean Avenue, PO Box 35, Allenhurst, NJ 07711
(908) 531-2378
Founded: 1959
Arts Area: Grand Opera; Operetta
Status: Professional
Type: Performing; Educational; Community Service
Purpose: To bring opera of a high standard to all people at popular prices; to create a professional outlet for deserving young artists as well as experienced professionals; to bring opera in English to public schools
Management: Mme. Fra Tognoli, Artistic/Executive Director; Vincent J. Rifici, Chairman of the Board/Business Advisor; Evelyn Axelrod, Vice President/Box Office Director; Lucious Zachary, Assistant Artistic Director
Officers: John Mullins, President; John Plunkett, Vice President; Joan Benoist, Secretary
Paid Staff: 2   **Volunteer Staff:** 6
Paid Artists: 20
Utilizes: Special Technical Talent; Guest Conductors; Guest Artists
Budget: $500,000 - $1,000,000
Income Sources: Private Foundations/Grants/Endowments; Business/Corporate Donations; Box Office; Government Grants; Individual Donations
Season: October - August   **Annual Attendance:** 6,000
Affiliations: Monmouth Opera Guild
Performance Facilities: Paramount Theatre, Asbury Park

Alpine

DANCE

THE AMERICAN DANCE MACHINE
PO Box 647, Alpine, NJ 07620
(201) 784-1617
Founded: 1978
Arts Area: Modern; Ballet; Jazz; Ethnic
Status: Professional; Non-Profit
Type: Performing; Touring; Resident
Purpose: Reconstruct original Broadway pieces to keep the choreography alive
Management: Robert Tucker, Artistic Director
Paid Artists: 20   **Non-Paid Artists:** 10
Utilizes: Guest Artists; Guest Choreographers
Budget: $500,000 - $1,000,000

Income Sources: Private Foundations/Grants/Endowments; Box Office; Individual Donations
Season: 52 Weeks

Beach Haven

THEATRE

SURFLIGHT THEATRE
Beach and Engleside, PO Box 1155, Beach Haven, NJ 08008
(609) 492-9477
FAX: (609) 492-4469
Founded: 1950
Arts Area: Summer Stock; Musical
Status: Semi-Professional
Type: Performing; Resident
Management: T. Scott Henderson, Executive Producer; Guil Fisher, Assistant Producer/Artistic Director
Officers: T. Scott Henderson, President/CEO; Jane A. Henderson, Vice President/Secretary
Paid Staff: 17   **Volunteer Staff:** 3
Paid Artists: 20
Utilizes: Guest Directors
Budget: $100,000 - $500,000
Income Sources: Box Office; Individual Donations
Season: June - September   **Annual Attendance:** 25,000

FACILITY

SURFLIGHT SUMMER THEATRE
PO Box 1155, Beach Haven, NJ 08008
(609) 492-9477; (609) 492-2639
Type of Facility: Theatre Complex; Theatre House
Type of Stage: Proscenium
Stage Dimensions: 40'Wx24'D
Seating Capacity: 450
Year Built: 1986   **Architect:** Tonge   **Cost:** $1,500,000
Acoustical Consultant: Josh Weitzman
Contact for Rental: T. Scott Henderson;   (609) 492-2639
Available for rental only in winter

Bloomfield

INSTRUMENTAL MUSIC

BLOOMFIELD SYMPHONY ORCHESTRA
84 Broad Street, Bloomfield, NJ 07003
(201) 743-9074
Founded: 1932
Arts Area: Symphony
Status: Non-Profit
Type: Performing
Purpose: A non-profit community orchestra sponsored by the Bloomfield Federation of Music
Management: Edward J. Napiwocki, Conductor
Officers: Stephen Lepp, President; Sig Harac, Vice President; Ruth Lepp, Corresponding Secretary; Phyllis Lax, Recording Secretary; Louis Cerrullo, Treasurer
Paid Staff: 1   **Volunteer Staff:** 6
Paid Artists: 8   **Non-Paid Artists:** 2
Utilizes: Special Technical Talent; Guest Artists
Income Sources: Private Foundations/Grants/Endowments; Business/Corporate Donations; Individual Donations
Season: November - May   **Annual Attendance:** 3,000
Affiliations: New Jersey Orchestra Association
Performance Facilities: North Junior High School

Caldwell

FACILITY

CALDWELL COLLEGE - STUDENT UNION BUILDING
9 Ryerson Avenue, Caldwell, NJ 07006
(201) 228-4424
FAX: (201) 228-3851
    Type of Facility: Studio Performance
    Type of Stage: Proscenium
    Seating Capacity: 1,500
    Year Built: 1968
    Contact for Rental: Marianne Streleck;   (201) 228-4424

Cape May

PERFORMING SERIES

MID-ATLANTIC CENTER FOR THE ARTS
1048 Washington Street, Cape May, NJ 08204-0340
(609) 884-5404
FAX: (609) 884-2006
    Founded: 1970
    Arts Area: Vocal Music; Instrumental Music; Theater
    Status: Professional; Non-Profit
    Type: Sponsoring
    Purpose: To promote awareness of the Victorian era and its customs; to promote the performing arts
    Management: B. Michael Zuckerman, Director; Mary Stewart, Sandra Allison, Assistant Directors; Stephen Rogers Radcliffe, Artistic Director Cape May Music Festival
    Officers: John Bailey, President; Tom Carroll, First Vice President; Fred Kuhner, Second Vice President; R. Norris Clark, Treasurer; Joan Wells, Secretary; R. Norris Clark, Cape May Music Festival Chairman
    Paid Staff: 35   **Volunteer Staff:** 200
    Paid Artists: 150
    Utilizes: Guest Conductors; Guest Artists; Guest Directors
    Budget: $1,000,000 - $5,000,000
    Income Sources: Private Foundations/Grants/Endowments; Business/Corporate Donations; Box Office; Government Grants; Individual Donations
    Season: May - June   **Annual Attendance:** 3,000
    Performance Facilities: Congress Hall Hotel

Chatham

INSTRUMENTAL MUSIC

SOLID BRASS
5 Sunset Drive, Chatham, NJ 07928
(201) 701-0674
FAX: (201) 701-0674
    Founded: 1982
    Arts Area: Chamber; Ensemble
    Status: Professional
    Type: Performing; Touring; Educational
    Purpose: To preserve and perpetuate brass chamber music through but not limited to performance, recording and composing
    Management: Paul Goldberg, Go Management
    Officers: Douglas Haislip, Carl Della Peruti, Managing Directors; Ted Wynant, President; Larry Hutton, Vice President; Linda Browner, Secretary
    Paid Staff: 2   **Volunteer Staff:** 10
    Paid Artists: 11
    Utilizes: Guest Composers; Arrangers
    Budget: $100,000 - $500,000
    Income Sources: Private Foundations/Grants/Endowments; Business/Corporate Donations; Box Office; Government Grants; Individual Donations; Touring Fees
    Season: 52 Weeks   **Annual Attendance:** 50,000

Cranford

THEATRE

CRANFORD DRAMATIC CLUB
78 Winans Avenue, PO Box 511, Cranford, NJ 07016
(908) 276-7611
>**Founded:** 1919
>**Arts Area:** Community
>**Status:** Non-Professional; Non-Profit
>**Type:** Performing
>**Purpose:** To stimulate community interest in theatre
>**Officers:** Kate Slavin, President; Carol Weltner, Business Vice President; Marilyn Court, Production Vice President; Barbara Heineman, Membership Vice President; Janet Peterson, Corresponding Secretary; Sue Chandler, Treasurer
>**Volunteer Staff:** 175
>**Budget:** $50,000 - $100,000
>**Income Sources:** Box Office
>**Season:** October - June   **Annual Attendance:** 9,000
>**Performance Facilities:** Cranford Dramatic Club

FACILITY

CRANFORD DRAMATIC CLUB THEATRE
78 Winans Avenue, PO Box 511, Cranford, NJ 07016
(908) 276-7611
>**Type of Facility:** Theatre House
>**Type of Stage:** Proscenium
>**Stage Dimensions:** 19'x30'x32'
>**Seating Capacity:** 300
>**Year Built:** 1957   **Cost:** $60,000
>**Year Remodeled:** 1992   **Architect:** Maurice Moran   **Cost:** $25,000
>**Resident Groups:** Cranford Dramatic Club

Dover

FACILITY

DOVER LITTLE THEATRE
Elliott Street, PO Box 82, Dover, NJ 07801
(201) 328-9202
>**Type of Facility:** Theatre House
>**Facility Originally:** Morgue
>**Type of Stage:** Proscenium
>**Stage Dimensions:** 8'6"x21'x17'
>**Seating Capacity:** 115
>**Year Remodeled:** 1933   **Cost:** $2,000
>**Manager:** Dover Little Theatre

East Orange

FACILITY

UPSALA COLLEGE - WORKSHOP 90 THEATER
East Orange, NJ 07019
(201) 266-7202; (201) 266-7200
>**Type of Facility:** Theatre House
>**Facility Originally:** Carriage House
>**Type of Stage:** Thrust
>**Stage Dimensions:** 31'x18'
>**Seating Capacity:** 140
>**Year Remodeled:** 1984
>**Contact for Rental:** Robert Marcazzo;   (201) 266-7202
>**Resident Groups:** Workshop 90 Theater Group
>*Rarely available for rent*

Elmer

PERFORMING SERIES

APPEL FARM ARTS AND MUSIC CENTER
PO Box 888, Elmer, NJ 08318
(609) 358-2472
FAX: (609) 358-6513
Founded: 1960
Arts Area: Dance; Vocal Music; Instrumental Music; Theater; Festivals
Status: Professional; Non-Profit
Type: Performing; Resident; Educational
Management: Mark E. Packer, Executive Director; Sean Timmons, Artistic Director; V. Susan Fisher, Development Director
Officers: Ronnie Cimprich VMD, President
Paid Staff: 14   **Volunteer Staff:** 200
Budget: $1,000,000 - $5,000,000
Income Sources: Private Foundations/Grants/Endowments; Business/Corporate Donations; Box Office; Government Grants; Individual Donations
Season: September - June   **Annual Attendance:** 16,000

FACILITY

APPEL FARM ARTS AND MUSIC CENTER
PO Box 888, Elmer, NJ 08318
(609) 358-2472
FAX: (609) 358-6513
Type of Facility: Outdoor (Concert); Studio Performance; Performance Center; Theatre House; Multi-Purpose; Room
Facility Originally: Farm
Type of Stage: Proscenium
Stage Dimensions: 40'x40'   **Orchestra Pit**
Seating Capacity: Theatre - 300; Outdoor Facility - 10,000
Year Built: 1960
Contact for Rental: Sean Timmons;   (609) 358-2472
Summer camp program available

Englewood

FACILITY

JOHN HARMS CENTER FOR THE ARTS
30 North Van Brunt Street, Englewood, NJ 07631
(201) 567-5797
FAX: (201) 567-7357
Founded: 1976
Type of Facility: Performance Center
Facility Originally: Vaudeville; Movie House
Type of Stage: Thrust; Proscenium
Stage Dimensions: 40'x29' stage; 33'W proscenium   **Orchestra Pit**
Seating Capacity: 1,246
Year Built: 1926
Year Remodeled: 1992   **Architect:** Ecoplan/Wells Associates   **Cost:** $6,000,000
Contact for Rental: Allison Perrine;   (201) 567-5797
Resident Groups: New Jersey Symphony

Fort Lee

VOCAL MUSIC

OPERA CLASSICS OF NEW JERSEY
One Bridge Plaza, Suite 400, Fort Lee, NJ 07024
(201) 592-5821; (212) 724-0989
Founded: 1963

Arts Area: Grand Opera
Status: Professional; Non-Profit
Type: Performing; Resident; Educational
Purpose: To present professional grand opera as well as build an audience from young people
Management: Giovanni Consiglio, Executive Director; Colin Ungaro, Assistant Director
Officers: Giovanni Consiglio, Presidnet; Colin Ungaro, Vice President; Marion Gambardella, Secretary; Peter Kerschhagel, Treasurer
Volunteer Staff: 50
Paid Artists: 100
Utilizes: Special Technical Talent; Guest Conductors; Guest Artists; Guest Directors
Budget: $100,000 - $500,000
Income Sources: Private Foundations/Grants/Endowments; Business/Corporate Donations; Box Office; Government Grants
Season: October - May
Annual Attendance: 7,000
Affiliations: AGMA; AFM
Performance Facilities: Orrie De Nooyer Auditorium, Hackensack

---

Glassboro

THEATRE

STAGEWORKS TOURING COMPANY
PO Box 922, Glassboro, NJ 08028
(609) 863-7150
FAX: (609) 863-6553
  Arts Area: Professional; Folk; Theatrical Group
  Status: Professional; Non-Equity
  Type: Performing; Touring; Resident
  Purpose: To create and tour plays based on regional history, folklore and oral history; to spotlight social issues and concerns of underserved segments of the local population
  Management: Carolyn O'Donnell, Producing Artistic Director; Victoria Ford, Michael Sharp, Miles Thompson and Ray Verna, Artistic Corp
  Officers: Carolyn O'Donnell, President; Bruce M. Bradway, Vice President; Carol N. Welsh, Treasurer; Polly K. Davis, Board Chairman
  Paid Staff: 6   **Volunteer Staff:** 2
  Paid Artists: 20
  Budget: $50,000 - $100,000
  Season: 52 Weeks   **Annual Attendance:** 33,577
  Affiliations: New Jersey Theater Association; Artpride, Inc.; Southern New Jersey Cultural Alliance; GPCA; Alternate ROOTS, Inc.
  Performance Facilities: Rowan College (formerly Glassboro)

PERFORMING SERIES

GLASSBORO CENTER FOR THE ARTS
Rowan College of New Jersey, Wilson Music Building, Room 211, Glassboro, NJ 08028
(609) 863-5167
FAX: (603) 863-5021
  Founded: 1989
  Arts Area: Dance; Vocal Music; Instrumental Music; Theater; Festivals; Lyric Opera; Grand Opera; Jazz
  Status: Professional
  Type: Performing; Touring; Resident; Educational; Sponsoring
  Purpose: To provide a variety of high-quality cultural events to the southern New Jersey general public
  Management: Dr. Michael J. Rose, Executive Director; Mark Fields, Managing Director
  Paid Staff: 6
  Utilizes: Special Technical Talent; Guest Conductors; Guest Artists; Guest Directors
  Budget: $100,000 - $500,000
  Income Sources: Private Foundations/Grants/Endowments; Business/Corporate Donations; Box Office; Government Grants; Individual Donations
  Season: October - May   **Annual Attendance:** 35,000
  Affiliations: APAP
  Performance Facilities: Wilson Concert Hall

Hackensack

PERFORMING SERIES

FEDERATED ARTS
185 Prospect Avenue 12M, Hackensack, NJ 07601
(201) 646-1061
 Arts Area: Instrumental Music; Festivals
 Status: Professional; Non-Profit
 Type: Performing
 Purpose: To present free musical programs
 Management: Isadore Freeman, Director
 Utilizes: Guest Artists
 Budget: $1,000 - $50,000
 Income Sources: Business/Corporate Donations; Individual Donations
 Season: July - September; December **Annual Attendance:** 30,000

FACILITY

ORRIE DE NOOYER AUDITORIUM
200 Hackensack Avenue, Hackensack, NJ 07601
(201) 343-6000, ext. 308
 Type of Facility: Concert Hall; Auditorium; Theatre House; Opera House
 Type of Stage: Thrust; Proscenium
 Stage Dimensions: 58'Wx45'D; 58'Wx20'H procenium opening **Orchestra Pit**
 Seating Capacity: 1201
 Year Built: 1966 **Architect:** Frank E. Johnson **Cost:** $3,000,000
 Year Remodeled: 1987 **Cost:** $25,000
 Contact for Rental: Steven Danieli, Technical Director; (201) 343-6000, ext. 308
 Resident Groups: The Fokine Ballet Company; Music, Music, Music Concert Productions

---
Haddonfield

INSTRUMENTAL MUSIC

HADDONFIELD SYMPHONY
30 Washington Avenue, PO Box 212, Haddonfield, NJ 08033
(609) 429-1880
FAX: (609) 428-5634
 Founded: 1952
 Arts Area: Symphony; Orchestra
 Status: Professional; Non-Profit
 Type: Performing; Educational
 Purpose: To enrich the musical lives of the citizens and residents of the state of New Jersey
 Management: Dorothy W. Rivers, Executive Director; Alan Gilbert, Music Director
 Utilizes: Special Technical Talent; Guest Conductors; Guest Artists; Guest Directors
 Budget: $100,000 - $500,000
 Income Sources: Private Foundations/Grants/Endowments; Business/Corporate Donations; Box Office; Government Grants; Individual Donations

---
Holmdel

FACILITY

GARDEN STATE ARTS CENTER
PO Box 116, Holmdel, NJ 07733
(908) 442-9200
 Type of Facility: Outdoor (Concert); Amphitheater
 Type of Stage: Thrust; Proscenium
 Stage Dimensions: 60'Wx30'H **Orchestra Pit**
 Seating Capacity: 5,163; addition lawn seating available
 Year Built: 1968 **Architect:** Edward Durell Stone **Cost:** $6,700,000
 Year Remodeled: 1986 **Cost:** $3,400,000
 Acoustical Consultant: Solstice Company
 Contact for Rental: Linda P. Crane; (908) 888-2030
 Available for rent on a limited basis only

Jersey City

DANCE

AVODAH DANCE ENSEMBLE
243 Fifth Street, #9, Jersey City, NJ 07302
(201) 659-7072
> **Alternate Address:** c/o HUC-JIR, One West Fourth Street, New York, NY 10012
> **Founded:** 1974
> **Arts Area:** Modern
> **Status:** Professional
> **Type:** Performing; Touring; Resident; Educational
> **Purpose:** To develop a repertory based on Jewish ritual, history and culture; to present multicultural and interfaith pieces and projects
> **Management:** JoAnne Tucker, Artistic Director
> **Officers:** Stephen Bayer, President; Emily Gardner, Vice President; Marianne Mendelson, Treasurer; JoAnne Tucker, Executive Vice President
> **Volunteer Staff:** 1
> **Paid Artists:** 7
> **Utilizes:** Special Technical Talent; Guest Artists; Guest Choreographers
> **Income Sources:** Private Foundations/Grants/Endowments; Individual Donations; Booking Fees
> **Annual Attendance:** 15,000

PERFORMING SERIES

FRIENDS OF MUSIC AND ART OF HUDSON COUNTY
880 Bergen Avenue, Jersey City, NJ 07306
(201) 963-4200
> **Founded:** 1972
> **Arts Area:** Vocal Music; Instrumental Music
> **Status:** Non-Profit
> **Type:** Performing
> **Purpose:** To encourage young gifted students to continue their work; to promote interest and support of music and art in Hudson County
> **Officers:** Jesse Moskowitz, President; Sol Seaith, Vice President; Hilda Feith, Recording Secretary; Sophie Filkner, Treasurer/Historian
> **Volunteer Staff:** 9
> **Paid Artists:** 7
> **Utilizes:** Guest Artists   **Budget:** $1,000 - $50,000
> **Income Sources:** Business/Corporate Donations; Individual Donations
> **Season:** September - May   **Annual Attendance:** 1,000
> **Performance Facilities:** Public Library Auditorium

FACILITY

MAJESTIC THEATRE
275 Grove Street, Jersey City, NJ 07303
(201) 433-7502
FAX: (201) 333-5948
> **Founded:** 1907
> **Type of Facility:** Concert Hall; Performance Center; Theatre House; Opera House; Multi-Purpose
> **Type of Stage:** Flexible; Proscenium
> **Stage Dimensions:** 85'Wx50'Dx90'H   **Orchestra Pit**
> **Seating Capacity:** 1,546
> **Year Built:** 1907   **Architect:** William McElfactrick   **Cost:** $700,000
> **Year Remodeled:** 1992   **Cost:** $50,000,000
> **Contact for Rental:** Albert Stinchcomb;   (201) 333-5948
> **Resident Groups:** Liberty Center for the Performing Arts

---

Lakewood

FACILITY

OCEAN COUNTY CENTER FOR THE ARTS - STRAND THEATRE
PO Box 315, Lakewood, NJ 08701-0315
(908) 367-6688
> **Type of Facility:** Concert Hall; Theatre House; Opera House

Facility Originally: Vaudeville
Type of Stage: Proscenium
Stage Dimensions: 40'Wx30'D
Seating Capacity: 1,000
Year Built: 1922   **Architect:** Thomas Lamb
Year Remodeled: 1987   **Architect:** Beyer Blinder & Belle   **Cost:** $3,000,000
Contact for Rental: Alan McCracken;   (201) 367-6688

Lawrenceville

FACILITY

RIDER COLLEGE - FINE ARTS THEATER
Rider College, PO Box 6400, Lawrenceville, NJ 08648
(609) 896-5168
Type of Facility: Auditorium
Type of Stage: Proscenium   **Orchestra Pit**
Seating Capacity: 490
Contact for Rental: Patrick Chmel;   (609) 896-5168

Madison

INSTRUMENTAL MUSIC

COLONIAL SYMPHONY
205 Madison Avenue, Madison, NJ 07940
(201) 377-1310
FAX: (201) 377-2337
Arts Area: Symphony
Status: Professional; Non-Profit
Type: Performing; Educational
Purpose: To nurture and sustain a superior orchestra emphasizing a balance of classical and contemporary music; to enhance the understanding of music through education
Management: Yehuda Gilad, Artistic Director/Conductor; Elizabeth Stockly, Executive Director
Officers: Myles J. Connor Jr., President
Budget: $100,000 - $500,000
Income Sources: Private Foundations/Grants/Endowments; Business/Corporate Donations; Box Office; Government Grants; Individual Donations
Performance Facilities: Madison Junior School

VOCAL MUSIC

OPERA AT FLORHAM
295 Madison Avenue, Madison, NJ 07940
(201) 593-8622
FAX: (201) 593-8510
Founded: 1982
Arts Area: Grand Opera; Lyric Opera
Status: Professional; Artists-In-Residence
Type: Performing; Resident
Purpose: To provide stage and music experience in productions for apprenticed young artists
Management: Dr. Charles F. Del Rosso, General Manager
Officers: German Bustos, Chairperson Board of Trustees; Edward Zamengo, First Vice Chair Board of Trustees
Paid Staff: 2   **Volunteer Staff:** 10
Paid Artists: 50
Utilizes: Special Technical Talent; Guest Artists; Guest Directors
Budget: $100,000 - $500,000
Income Sources: Private Foundations/Grants/Endowments; Business/Corporate Donations; Box Office; Individual Donations
Season: September - May   **Annual Attendance:** 2,000
Affiliations: Fairleigh Dickinson University
Performance Facilities: Dreyfuss Theater; Lengfell Hall

THEATRE

NEW JERSEY SHAKESPEARE FESTIVAL
Route 24, Madison, NJ 07940
(201) 408-3278
    Founded: 1963
    Arts Area: Professional; Theatrical Group
    Status: Professional; Non-Profit
    Type: Performing; Educational; Sponsoring
    Purpose: To present professional productions of Shakespearean and other plays, including classics and modern
    Management: Bonnie Jay Monte, Artistic Director; Michael Stotts, Managing Director
    Paid Staff: 15   **Volunteer Staff:** 80
    Paid Artists: 25   **Non-Paid Artists:** 80
    Utilizes: Special Technical Talent; Guest Artists; Guest Directors
    Budget: $500,000 - $1,000,000
    Income Sources: Private Foundations/Grants/Endowments; Business/Corporate Donations; Box Office; Government Grants; Individual Donations
    Season: June - October
    Affiliations: AEA; SSDC
    Performance Facilities: Bowne Theatre

FACILITY

DREW UNIVERSITY - BOWNE THEATRE
36 Madison Avenue, Madison, NJ 07940
(201) 408-3000
    Type of Facility: Concert Hall; Theatre House
    Facility Originally: Recreation Hall; Gymnasium
    Type of Stage: Thrust
    Seating Capacity: 238
    Year Built: 1910
    Year Remodeled: 1972
    Resident Groups: New Jersey Shakespeare Festival; Drew University Theatre Arts Department

Maplewood

DANCE

NEW JERSEY DANCE THEATRE
202 Maplewood Avenue, Maplewood, NJ 07040
(201) 762-3033
    Founded: 1982
    Arts Area: Ballet
    Status: Semi-Professional; Commercial
    Type: Resident
    Purpose: To acquaint the community with dance
    Management: Anne Krohley, Artistic Director; Brian Gestring, Business Manager
    Paid Artists: 15
    Utilizes: Guest Artists
    Budget: $1,000 - $50,000
    Income Sources: Box Office
    Season: September - June
    Performance Facilities: New Jersey Dance Theatre

Millburn

THEATRE

PAPER MILL PLAYHOUSE
Brookside Drive, Millburn, NJ 07041
(201) 379-3636
    Founded: 1934
    Arts Area: Professional; Musical
    Status: Professional; Non-Profit
    Type: Performing; Touring; Resident; Educational; Sponsoring
    Purpose: To produce and present a wide range of performing and visual arts, with emphasis on production, preservation and development of musical theatre work

Management: Angelo Del Rossi, Executive Producer; Robert Johanson, Artistic Director; Geoffrey Merrill Cohen, General Manager
Officers: C.E. Williams, Chairman; Maurice J. Ferris Jr., Vice-Chairman; Angelo Del Rossi, President
Paid Staff: 40
Paid Artists: 280
Utilizes: Special Technical Talent; Guest Conductors; Guest Artists; Guest Directors
Budget: Over 10,000,000
Income Sources: Private Foundations/Grants/Endowments; Business/Corporate Donations; Box Office; Government Grants; Individual Donations
Season: 52 Weeks   **Annual Attendance:** 400,000
Affiliations: AEA; COST; SSDC; AFM; IATSE; USA; ARTPRIDE, NJ
Performance Facilities: Paper Mill Playhouse

FACILITY

PAPER MILL PLAYHOUSE
Brookside Drive, Millburn, NJ 07041
(201) 379-3636
Type of Facility: Theatre Complex; Performance Center; Theatre House; Multi-Purpose; Room
Facility Originally: Paper Mill
Type of Stage: Proscenium
Stage Dimensions: 100'Wx47'Dx56'H; 40'Wx24'H proscenium opening   **Orchestra Pit**
Seating Capacity: 1,192
Year Built: 1795
Year Remodeled: 1982   **Architect:** Ashok Bhavnani   **Cost:** $5,500,000
Acoustical Consultant: Peter George Associates
Resident Groups: New Jersey Ballet; Paper Mill Playhouse
Original structure was built in 1795 and converted to a theatre in 1934. Original structure was destroyed by fire in 1980 and was rebuilt in 1982.

Montclair

DANCE

DANMARI LTD./YASS HAKOSHIMA MIME THEATRE
239 Midland Avenue, Montclair, NJ 07042
(201) 783-9845
FAX: (201) 783-0001
Founded: 1976
Arts Area: Mime
Status: Professional; Non-Profit
Type: Performing; Touring; Resident; Educational
Purpose: To present the highest form of the art of mime through performances, master classes, lecture demonstrations and workshops worldwide
Management: Lynn K. Palmer, Business Manager; Danmari Ltd.
Officers: Yass Hakoshima, Artistic Director; Renate A. Boue, Assistant Director
Paid Staff: 3   **Volunteer Staff:** 8
Paid Artists: 4
Budget: $50,000 - $100,000
Income Sources: Private Foundations/Grants/Endowments; Business/Corporate Donations; Government Grants; Individual Donations
Season: 52 Weeks   **Annual Attendance:** 35,000

RENATE BOUE DANCE COMPANY
239 Midland Avenue, Montclair, NJ 07042
(201) 783-9845
FAX: (201) 783-0001
Founded: 1972
Arts Area: Modern
Status: Professional; Semi-Professional
Type: Performing; Educational
Officers: Barbara Francett, Chairperson; Muriel Holub, Assistant Director; Renate Boue, Artistic Director
Paid Staff: 2   **Volunteer Staff:** 2
Paid Artists: 2   **Non-Paid Artists:** 4
Utilizes: Guest Artists
Income Sources: Box Office; Individual Donations

ST. JOHN'S RENAISSANCE DANCERS
239 Midland Avenue, Montclair, NJ 07042
(201) 783-9845
FAX: (201) 783-0001
Founded: 1979
Arts Area: Historic Dance
Status: Professional
Type: Performing; Touring; Educational
Purpose: To present high quality dance and music of the Renaissance, recreating the splendor of 15th and 16th-century Europe
Officers: Renate Boue, Artistic Director; Phyllis Workinger, Associate Director; Muriel Holub, Educational Director
Paid Staff: 1 **Volunteer Staff:** 1
Paid Artists: 10
Utilizes: Guest Musicians
Income Sources: Box Office; Individual Donations
Season: 52 Weeks

INSTRUMENTAL MUSIC

NEW JERSEY CHAMBER MUSIC SOCIETY
22 Valley Road, Montclair, NJ 07042
(201) 746-6068
FAX: (201) 746-0685
Founded: 1974
Arts Area: Chamber
Status: Professional; Non-Profit
Type: Performing; Touring; Resident; Educational
Management: Eileen Y. Sheldon, Executive Director; Peggy Scheeter and Bernice Silk, Artistic Directors; Jeremy V. Johnson, Director of Development
Officers: Richard Snyder, President; Martin McKerrow, Honey McGrath, Vice Presidents; Clarence Seniors, Secretary; Jack Nadler, Treasurer
Paid Staff: 3 **Volunteer Staff:** 4
Paid Artists: 19
Utilizes: Guest Artists
Budget: $100,000 - $500,000
Income Sources: Private Foundations/Grants/Endowments; Business/Corporate Donations; Box Office; Government Grants; Individual Donations
Season: October - May **Annual Attendance:** 7,000
Performance Facilities: Union Congregational Church, Montclair

THEATRE

BLOOMING GROVE THEATER ENSEMBLE, LTD.
544 Bloomfield Avenue, Montclair, NJ 07042
(201) 744-3004
FAX: (201) 744-6208
Founded: 1985
Arts Area: Professional; Musical; Theatrical Group
Status: Professional; Non-Profit
Type: Performing; Resident; Educational
Purpose: To provide a wide range of theatrical performances and educational programs to northern New Jersey and the New York metropolitan area
Management: Michael Huseman, Managing Director; Alberta Huseman, Artistic Director
Officers: Alberta Huseman, President; Michael Huseman, Vice President
Utilizes: Special Technical Talent
Budget: $50,000 - $100,000
Income Sources: Private Foundations/Grants/Endowments; Business/Corporate Donations; Box Office; Government Grants; Individual Donations
Season: 52 Weeks **Annual Attendance:** 32,000
Performance Facilities: Blooming Grove Theater

YASS HAKOSHIMA MIME THEATRE
239 Midland Avenue, Montclair, NJ 07042
(201) 783-9845
FAX: (201) 783-0001
Founded: 1976
Arts Area: Professional
Status: Professional; Non-Profit

Type: Performing; Touring; Resident; Educational
Purpose: To further the appreciation and understanding of the art of mime through performances, master classes and workshops
Management: Danmari Limited; Lynn K. Palmer, Business Manager; David VanZand, Assistant Manager
Officers: Yass Hakoshima, Artistic Director; Renate A. Boue, Assistant Director
Paid Staff: 3   **Volunteer Staff:** 5
Paid Artists: 3
Utilizes: Special Technical Talent; Guest Artists
Budget: $50,000 - $100,000
Income Sources: Private Foundations/Grants/Endowments; Business/Corporate Donations; Government Grants; Individual Donations; Performance Tours
Season: 52 Weeks   **Annual Attendance:** 30,000

PERFORMING SERIES

UNITY CONCERTS
22 Valley Road, Montclair, NJ 07042
(201) 744-6770
FAX: (201) 744-2169
Founded: 1920
Arts Area: Vocal Music; Instrumental Music; Classical
Status: Non-Profit
Type: Sponsoring
Purpose: To provide the finest classical music concerts to northern New Jersey
Management: Nancy P. Barry, Director; Kathy Schumacher, Assistant
Paid Staff: 4   **Volunteer Staff:** 24
Paid Artists: 100
Utilizes: Guest Conductors; Guest Artists
Budget: $100,000 - $500,000
Income Sources: Private Foundations/Grants/Endowments; Business/Corporate Donations; Box Office
Season: October - May   **Annual Attendance:** 11,700
Affiliations: APAP
Performance Facilities: Montclair Community Auditorium; Glenfield Auditorium

FACILITY

BLOOMING GROVE THEATRE
544 Bloomfield Avenue, Montclair, NJ 07042
(201) 744-3004
Type of Facility: Theatre House
Facility Originally: Bank
Type of Stage: Flexible
Stage Dimensions: 19'x44'x22'
Seating Capacity: 199
Year Remodeled: 1977
Cost: $156,000
Contact for Rental: Manager;   (201) 744-3004

Moorestown

INSTRUMENTAL MUSIC

WEST JERSEY CHAMBER MUSIC SOCIETY
PO Box 211, Moorestown, NJ 08057
(609) 778-1899
Founded: 1980
Arts Area: Orchestra; Chamber; Choral
Status: Professional; Non-Profit
Type: Performing; Touring
Utilizes: Guest Conductors; Guest Artists; Guest Directors
Season: October - June

Mount Laurel

DANCE

NATIONAL BALLET/NEW JERSEY
5113 Church Road, Mount Laurel, NJ 08054
(609) 235-5342
FAX: (609) 953-7212
Founded: 1974
Arts Area: Ballet; Contemporary
Status: Professional; Non-Profit
Type: Performing; Resident
Purpose: To foster quality dance in the state of New Jersey
Management: Kerina Connor, Assistant Director; Lorraine McAdams, Executive Artistic Director; Gayle Gardner, Manager
Paid Artists: 12
Utilizes: Guest Artists
Budget: $50,000 - $100,000
Income Sources: Private Foundations/Grants/Endowments; Business/Corporate Donations; Box Office; Government Grants
Season: October - May
Affiliations: NARB
Performance Facilities: The Grove

New Brunswick

DANCE

PRINCETON BALLET
80 Albany Street, New Brunswick, NJ 08901
(908) 249-1254
FAX: (908) 249-8475
Founded: 1978
Arts Area: Ballet
Status: Professional; Non-Profit
Type: Performing; Touring
Management: Judith Leviton, Director; Marjorie Nussman, Artistic Director
Paid Staff: 7
Paid Artists: 14
Utilizes: Guest Artists
Budget: $1,000,000 - $5,000,000
Income Sources: Private Foundations/Grants/Endowments; Business/Corporate Donations; Box Office; Government Grants; Individual Donations
Season: September - June
Affiliations: George Street Playhouse
Performance Facilities: McCarter Theatre, Princeton; State Theater, New Brunswick

THEATRE

CROSSROADS THEATRE COMPANY
7 Livingston Avenue, New Brunswick, NJ 08901
(908) 249-5581
FAX: (908) 249-1861
Founded: 1978
Arts Area: Professional; Theatrical Group; Afro-American Theatre Company
Status: Non-Profit
Type: Touring; Resident; Educational
Purpose: To provide a professional environment to encourage public interest of all backgrounds; to present honest portrayals and uphold the highest standard of artistic excellence of professional Black Theatre
Management: Rick Khan, Artistic Director/Producer; Paul Tetreault, General Manager; Marcia Wayand, Director of Development
Officers: Frank Bolden, Board President
Utilizes: Special Technical Talent; Guest Conductors; Guest Artists; Guest Directors
Budget: $500,000 - $1,000,000
Income Sources: Private Foundations/Grants/Endowments; Business/Corporate Donations; Box Office; Government Grants; Individual Donations

Season: September - May   **Annual Attendance:** 30,000
Affiliations: TCG; APAP

GEORGE STREET PLAYHOUSE
9 Livingston Avenue, New Brunswick, NJ 08901
(908) 846-2895
FAX: (908) 247-9151
> **Founded:** 1974
> **Arts Area:** Professional; Musical; Theatrical Group
> **Status:** Professional; Non-Profit
> **Type:** Performing; Touring; Resident; Producing
> **Purpose:** To produce world premieres and new musicals; to revitalize contemporary classics
> **Management:** Gregory Hurst, Production/Artistic Director; Diane Claussen, Managing Director; Wendy Liscow, Associate Artistic Director; Karen Price, Business Manager
> **Officers:** Al D'Augusta, President, Board of Directors
> **Paid Staff:** 35   **Volunteer Staff:** 70
> **Paid Artists:** 75
> **Utilizes:** Special Technical Talent; Guest Artists; Guest Directors
> **Budget:** $1,000,000 - $5,000,000
> **Income Sources:** Private Foundations/Grants/Endowments; Business/Corporate Donations; Box Office; Government Grants; Individual Donations
> **Season:** October - May   **Annual Attendance:** 73,000
> **Affiliations:** TCG
> **Performance Facilities:** George Street Playhouse

PERFORMING SERIES

NEW BRUNSWICK CULTURAL CENTER, INC.
19 Livingston Avenue, New Brunswick, NJ 08901
(908) 247-7200
FAX: (908) 247-5004
> **Founded:** 1983
> **Arts Area:** Presenting
> **Status:** Non-Profit
> **Type:** Performing; Educational; Sponsoring
> **Purpose:** To present the finest of the performing arts
> **Officers:** William Wright, President; Doug Hosner, Vice President
> **Budget:** $1,000,000 - $5,000,000
> **Income Sources:** Private Foundations/Grants/Endowments; Business/Corporate Donations; Box Office; Government Grants; Individual Donations
> **Season:** September - June   **Annual Attendance:** 150,000
> **Performance Facilities:** State Theatre

RUTGERS SUMMERFEST
106 Walters Hall, Rutgers Art Center, New Brunswick, NJ 08901-5056
(908) 932-7591
FAX: (908) 932-6973
> **Arts Area:** Dance; Vocal Music; Instrumental Music; Theater; Festivals
> **Status:** Non-Profit
> **Type:** Performing; Resident; Educational; Sponsoring
> **Purpose:** To celebrate music, dance, theatre and visual art
> **Management:** Lance Olson, Assistant Dean of Arts Programming; Charles Fessenden, Marketing Director; Ellen Saxon, Publicity Director; Kevin Coleman, Operations Manager; Jeanne Salzmann, Box Office Manager
> **Paid Staff:** 27   **Volunteer Staff:** 3
> **Paid Artists:** 250
> **Utilizes:** Special Technical Talent; Guest Artists; Guest Directors
> **Budget:** $100,000 - $500,000
> **Income Sources:** Private Foundations/Grants/Endowments; Business/Corporate Donations; Box Office; Government Grants; Individual Donations
> **Season:** June - August   **Annual Attendance:** 60,000
> **Performance Facilities:** Rutgers Arts Center

RUTGERS UNIVERSITY CONCERT SERIES
106 Walters Hall, New Brunswick, NJ 08907-5056
(908) 932-7591
FAX: (908) 932-6973
> **Founded:** 1917
> **Arts Area:** Instrumental Music

Status: Professional
Type: Presenting
Purpose: To present artists who shape art music today
Management: Lance Olson, Assistant Dean for Arts Programming; Charles Fessenden, Marketing Director; Ellen Saxon, Publicity Director; Kevin Coleman, Operations Manager; Jeanne Salzman, Box Office Manager
Utilizes: Guest Artists
Budget: $100,000 - $500,000
Income Sources: Private Foundations/Grants/Endowments; Business/Corporate Donations; Box Office; Government Grants; Individual Donations
Season: September - May   **Annual Attendance:** 3,500
Performance Facilities: Rutgers Art Center

FACILITY

RUTGERS ARTS CENTER
George Street & Route 18, New Brunswick, NJ 08903-5056
(908) 932-7591
Founded: 1916
Type of Facility: Theatre Complex; Concert Hall; Studio Performance; Performance Center; Theatre House; Multi-Purpose
Type of Stage: Thrust; Flexible; Proscenium; Concert Hall
Stage Dimensions: four stages - various dimensions   **Orchestra Pit**

Newark

DANCE

GARDEN STATE BALLET
45 Academy Street, Newark, NJ 07102
(201) 623-0267
FAX: (201) 623-8269
Founded: 1960
Arts Area: Ballet
Status: Professional; Non-Profit
Type: Performing; Touring; Resident; Educational
Purpose: To present a varied repertory of quality classical ballets that will stimulate artistic growth for dancers and audiences alike
Management: Bonnie Hyslop, General Manager; Peter Anastos, Artistic Director
Officers: Joel Sobo, President; Barry H. Smith, Rosemary Alito, Vice Presidents; Paul Holte, Treasurer; Lois Van Deusen, Secretary
Paid Staff: 5   **Volunteer Staff:** 25
Paid Artists: 25
Budget: $100,000 - $500,000
Income Sources: Private Foundations/Grants/Endowments; Business/Corporate Donations; Box Office; Government Grants; Individual Donations
Season: October - May   **Annual Attendance:** 45,000

INSTRUMENTAL MUSIC

CATHEDRAL CONCERT SERIES
89 Ridge Street, Newark, NJ 07104
(201) 484-2400
FAX: (201) 484-8773
Founded: 1983
Arts Area: Symphony; Orchestra; Chamber; Ensemble
Status: Professional; Non-Profit
Type: Performing; Resident; Sponsoring
Purpose: To bring quality musical programs to the Newark community
Management: Keith Clark, Music Director; Gloria Christ, Executive Director; Susan Zeigler, Associate Director
Officers: Donald Caste, Board Chairman; Joseph Honle, Finance Chairman; James Blanchard, Development Chairman
Paid Staff: 3   **Volunteer Staff:** 20
Paid Artists: 100
Utilizes: Guest Conductors; Guest Artists
Budget: $100,000 - $500,000
Income Sources: Private Foundations/Grants/Endowments; Business/Corporate Donations; Box Office; Government Grants; Individual Donations

Season: October - May   **Annual Attendance:** 10,000
Performance Facilities: Cathedral of the Sacred Heart

NEW JERSEY SYMPHONY ORCHESTRA
50 Park Place, 11th Floor, Newark, NJ 07101
(201) 624-3713
FAX: (201) 624-2115
Founded: 1922
Arts Area: Symphony; Orchestra; Chamber; Ensemble
Status: Professional; Non-Profit
Type: Performing
Purpose: To provide superior performances of music for symphonic orchestra and chamber orchestra and an exceptional educational program statewide
Management: Lawrence J. Tamburri, Executive Director; Karen Swanson, Orchestra Manager
Officers: Dr. Victor Parsonnet, Chairman of the Board; Robert C. Waggoner, Vice Chairman of the Board
Paid Staff: 25   **Volunteer Staff:** 2
Paid Artists: 85
Utilizes: Guest Conductors; Guest Artists
Budget: $5,000,000 - $10,000,000
Income Sources: Private Foundations/Grants/Endowments; Business/Corporate Donations; Box Office; Government Grants; Individual Donations
Season: October - August   **Annual Attendance:** 190,000
Performance Facilities: Newark Symphony Hall; John Harms Center for the Performing Arts; Count Basie Theatre, Redbank; War Mem. Theatre, Trenton; New Brunswick State Theatre

VOCAL MUSIC

NEW JERSEY STATE OPERA
1020 Broad Street, Newark, NJ 07102
(201) 623-5757
FAX: (201) 623-5761
Founded: 1966
Arts Area: Grand Opera
Status: Professional
Type: Performing
Management: Alfredo Silipigni, General Director; Gwen Hall, Executive Director; Brian Dallon, Director of Marketing
Officers: Robert B. O'Brien, Chairman; Luna Kaufman, President; William Mikesell, Treasurer
Paid Staff: 7   **Volunteer Staff:** 6
Paid Artists: 210   **Non-Paid Artists:** 50
Utilizes: Special Technical Talent; Guest Artists; Guest Directors
Budget: $500,000 - $1,000,000
Income Sources: Private Foundations/Grants/Endowments; Business/Corporate Donations; Box Office; Government Grants; Individual Donations
Season: November - May   **Annual Attendance:** 18,000
Affiliations: Essex County Arts Council; New Jersey State Arts Council
Performance Facilities: Newark Symphony Hall

NEWARK BOYS CHORUS
1016 Broad Street, Newark, NJ 07102
(201) 621-8900
Founded: 1967
Arts Area: Choral; Ethnic
Status: Professional; Non-Profit
Type: Performing; Touring; Educational
Budget: $100,000 - $500,000
Income Sources: Private Foundations/Grants/Endowments; Business/Corporate Donations; Government Grants; Individual Donations
Season: September - June

THEATRE

NEWARK PERFORMING ARTS CORPORATION/NEWARK SYMPHONY HALL
1030 Broad Street, Newark, NJ 07102
(201) 643-4550
FAX: (201) 643-6722
Founded: 1986
Arts Area: Professional; Musical; Community; Theatrical Group
Status: Professional; Non-Profit

Type: Performing; Presenting
Purpose: To enrich the cultural, educational and community life of the citizens of the greater Newark area by developing a program of the highest quality emphasizing theatrical works which reflect contemporary urban culture
Management: Leon Denmark, Executive Director; Elisabeth Stewart, General Manager; Midge Guerrera, Director of Arts Education; Marshall Jones, Director of Events
Officers: Harold Lucas, Chair; Mamie Hale, Vice Chair; Marie Villani, Vice Chair; Walter Molineux, Treasurer/Secretary
Paid Staff: 320
Paid Artists: 200
Budget: $500,000 - $1,000,000
Income Sources: Private Foundations/Grants/Endowments; Business/Corporate Donations; Box Office; Government Grants; Individual Donations
Season: 52 Weeks   **Annual Attendance:** 180,000
Affiliations: IATSE; AEA
Performance Facilities: Newark Symphony Hall

THEATRE OF UNIVERSAL IMAGES
360 Central Avenue, Newark, NJ 07103
(201) 645-6930
FAX: (201) 642-6013
Founded: 1970
Arts Area: Professional
Status: Professional; Non-Profit
Type: Performing; Touring; Resident
Purpose: Providing education in the performing arts and telecommunications to the Greater Newark Community, the priority of TUI is to increase opportunities and cultural enrichment of African Americans in Greater Essex County.
Management: Clarence C. Lilley, Executive Producer
Paid Staff: 7   **Volunteer Staff:** 20
Utilizes: Special Technical Talent; Guest Artists; Guest Directors
Budget: $100,000 - $500,000
Income Sources: Private Foundations/Grants/Endowments; Business/Corporate Donations; Box Office; Government Grants; Individual Donations
Season: October - June   **Annual Attendance:** 108,000
Affiliations: NEA; Dodge Foundation; Victoria Foundation; Black United Foundation
Performance Facilities: Theatre of Universal Images

FACILITY

NEWARK SYMPHONY HALL
1020 Broad Street, Newark, NJ 07102-2410
(201) 643-4550
Type of Facility: Concert Hall
Type of Stage: Proscenium
Stage Dimensions: 87'Wx42'Dx60'H; 63'4"Wx28'H proscenium opening   **Orchestra Pit**
Seating Capacity: 2,821
Year Built: 1925
Contact for Rental: Marshal Jones;   (201) 643-4550
Resident Groups: New Jersey State Opera; New Jersey Symphony Orchestra; Newark Boys Chorus

Paramus

VOCAL MUSIC

ARS MUSICA CHORALE AND ORCHESTRA
PO Box 525, Paramus, NJ 07653
(201) 599-2732
Founded: 1967
Arts Area: Grand Opera; Lyric Opera; Choral
Status: Professional; Semi-Professional; Non-Profit
Type: Performing; Touring
Purpose: To present performances of rarely heard works by masters including national premieres
Management: Diane Montemurro, Administration; Italo Marchini, Artistic Director
Officers: Linda Glasgal, President
Paid Staff: 2   **Volunteer Staff:** 50
Paid Artists: 45   **Non-Paid Artists:** 60
Utilizes: Special Technical Talent; Guest Artists
Budget: $50,000 - $100,000

Income Sources: Private Foundations/Grants/Endowments; Business/Corporate Donations; Box Office; Government Grants; Individual Donations
Season: September - May   **Annual Attendance:** 2,600
Affiliations: American Institute Verdi Studies; OA; ACDA
Performance Facilities: John Harmes; First Presbyterian Church, Englewood; Alice Tully Hall, Lincoln Center, New York City

---

Pitman

INSTRUMENTAL MUSIC

SOUTH JERSEY SYMPHONY ORCHESTRA
27 Columbia Avenue, Pitman, NJ 08071
(609) 582-2374
 Arts Area: Symphony; Orchestra
 Status: Professional; Non-Profit
 Type: Performing
 Purpose: To perform symphony orchestra repertoire in southern New Jersey
 Management: Samuel Muni, Music/Artistic Director
 Officers: Sharon Kewish, President
 Budget: $100,000 - $500,000
 Income Sources: Private Foundations/Grants/Endowments; Business/Corporate Donations; Box Office; Government Grants; Individual Donations
 Season: 52 Weeks

Pomona

FACILITY

STOCKTON STATE COLLEGE - PERFORMING ARTS CENTER
Jim Leeds Road, Pomona, NJ 08240
(609) 652-9000
FAX: (609) 748-5523
 Type of Facility: Concert Hall; Theatre House
 Type of Stage: Thrust; Proscenium
 Stage Dimensions: 48'Wx28'H proscenium opening   **Orchestra Pit**
 Seating Capacity: 550
 Year Built: 1976
 Contact for Rental: Michael Cool;   (609) 652-4607
 Resident Groups: Professional Guest Artists Series
 The Center also contains a 100-seat black box theatre

Princeton

VOCAL MUSIC

THE AMERICAN BOYCHOIR
The American Boychoir School, Lambert Drive, Princeton, NJ 08540
(609) 924-5858
FAX: (609) 924-5812
 Founded: 1937
 Arts Area: Choral
 Status: Professional; Non-Profit
 Type: Performing; Touring; Educational
 Purpose: The Boychoir includes choristers from throughout North America, who are students at the internationally-renowned boarding and day choir school (which offers a full academic program)
 Management: James H. Litton, Music Director; Columbia Artists Management, Sheldon Division
 Officers: Herbert W. Hobler, Board Chairman; John Ellis, President; James H. Litton, Music Director; Thomas E. Thompson, Headmaster
 Paid Staff: 35
 Paid Artists: 72
 Utilizes: Guest Conductors; Guest Artists
 Budget: $1,000,000 - $5,000,000

Income Sources: Private Foundations/Grants/Endowments; Business/Corporate Donations; Box Office; Government Grants; Individual Donations; Touring Fees
Season: September - June   **Annual Attendance:** 150,000

PRINCETON PRO MUSICA
20 Nassau Street, Suite 241, Princeton, NJ 08542
(609) 683-5122; (609) 683-1154
FAX: (609) 683-9676
Founded: 1979
Arts Area: Choral
Status: Non-Profit
Type: Performing
Purpose: To perform masterpieces of the choral repertoire with a professional orchestra and soloists
Management: Lee Franklin Milhous, General Manager; Sandy Clark, Administrative Assistant
Officers: Robert Jones, President; Isabel Griffith, Vice President; Patricia Paynter, Secretary; Bruce Bedient, Treasurer; Frances Slade, Music Director
Paid Staff: 2
Paid Artists: 16   **Non-Paid Artists:** 120
Utilizes: Guest Conductors; Guest Artists
Budget: $100,000 - $500,000
Income Sources: Private Foundations/Grants/Endowments; Business/Corporate Donations; Box Office; Government Grants; Individual Donations; Fundraisers; Benefits
Season: September - June   **Annual Attendance:** 10,000
Affiliations: CA; Art Pride
Performance Facilities: Richardson Auditorium, Princeton University; Nicholas Music Center, Rutgers University

THEATRE

CREATIVE THEATRE
102 Witherspoon Street, Princeton, NJ 08540
(609) 924-3489
Founded: 1969
Arts Area: Professional; Children's Theatre
Status: Professional; Non-Profit
Type: Performing; Touring; Resident; Educational
Purpose: To offer creative drama and theatre for children through participatory experiences
Management: Carly Tilton, Executive Director; Eloise Bruce, Artistic Director; Jean Prall, Education Director
Officers: Deborah Gwajda, President; Margee Greenberg, Vice President; Robert Solomon, Treasurer
Paid Staff: 5   **Volunteer Staff:** 15
Paid Artists: 20
Budget: $100,000 - $500,000
Income Sources: Private Foundations/Grants/Endowments; Business/Corporate Donations; Box Office; Government Grants; Individual Donations
Season: September - May; July   **Annual Attendance:** 40,000

FACILITY

MCCARTER THEATRE
91 University Place, Princeton, NJ 08540
(609) 683-9100
FAX: (609) 497-0369
Type of Facility: Theatre House
Type of Stage: Proscenium
Stage Dimensions: 22'x41'x39'   **Orchestra Pit**
Seating Capacity: 1,078
Year Built: 1929   **Architect:** D.K. Este Fisher   **Cost:** $430,000
Year Remodeled: 1985   **Architect:** James R. Grieves Associates   **Cost:** $4,300,000
Acoustical Consultant: KMK Associates
Contact for Rental: Kathleen Nolan, General Manager;   (609) 683-9100
Resident Groups: McCarter Theatre Company
Extremely limited rental - performing-arts events only

RICHARDSON AUDITORIUM IN ALEXANDER HALL
Princeton University, Princeton, NJ 08544
(609) 258-4239
FAX: (609) 258-6793
Type of Facility: Concert Hall; Auditorium
Type of Stage: Platform

Stage Dimensions: 50'Wx30'D   **Orchestra Pit**
Seating Capacity: 850
Year Built: 1894   **Architect:** William Appleton Potter
Year Remodeled: 1984   **Architect:** James R. Grieves Associates, Inc.
Acoustical Consultant: KMK Associates
Contact for Rental: Nathan A. Randall;   (609) 250-4239

Princeton Junction

PERFORMING SERIES

OPERA FESTIVAL OF NEW JERSEY
55 Princeton-Hightstown Rd., Suite 202, Princeton Junction, NJ 08550
(609) 936-1505
FAX: (609) 936-0008
Founded: 1983
Arts Area: Vocal Music; Lyric Opera; Grand Opera
Status: Professional; Non-Profit
Type: Performing; Resident; Sponsoring
Purpose: To present opera in English of new and unusual works as well as classical works intended for an intimate theater setting
Management: Deborah Sandler, Executive Director; Michael Pratt, Artistic Director
Paid Staff: 5   **Volunteer Staff:** 50
Paid Artists: 85   **Non-Paid Artists:** 2
Utilizes: Special Technical Talent; Guest Conductors; Guest Artists; Guest Directors
Budget: $500,000 - $1,000,000
Income Sources: Private Foundations/Grants/Endowments; Business/Corporate Donations; Box Office; Government Grants; Individual Donations
Season: June - July; February - March   **Annual Attendance:** 25,000
Affiliations: COS
Performance Facilities: Kirby Arts Center, Lawrenceville School

Rahway

FACILITY

UNION COUNTY ARTS CENTER
1601 Irving Street, Rahway, NJ 07065
(908) 499-0441
FAX: (908) 499-8227
Founded: 1928
Type of Facility: Concert Hall; Auditorium; Performance Center; Theatre House
Facility Originally: Vaudeville; Movie House
Type of Stage: Proscenium
Stage Dimensions: 48'Wx24'D   **Orchestra Pit**
Seating Capacity: 1,300
Year Built: 1928   **Architect:** Oltarsh
Year Remodeled: 1986   **Cost:** $1,200,000
Acoustical Consultant: Ed O'Conner
Contact for Rental: Bruce A. Conway;   (908) 499-0441

Red Bank

VOCAL MUSIC

MONMOUTH CIVIC CHORUS
PO Box 16, Red Bank, NJ 07701
(908) 747-0860
Founded: 1949
Arts Area: Light Opera; Choral
Status: Non-Professional; Non-Profit
Type: Performing; Touring
Purpose: To provide opportunities for community individuals to participate in the preparation and presentation of large choral works and staged musical productions all with orchestral accompaniment
Management: Mark Shapiro, Artistic Director/Conductor; Karin Moncrieff, Accompanist; Meredith Pennotti, Stage Director

Officers: Kathi Blinn, President; Laura Elliot, Vice President; Debbie Macock, Secretary; Tom Myers, Treasurer
Paid Staff: 3   **Volunteer Staff:** 60
Non-Paid Artists: 180
Utilizes: Special Technical Talent
Budget: $50,000 - $100,000
Income Sources: Private Foundations/Grants/Endowments; Business/Corporate Donations; Box Office; Government Grants; Individual Donations
Season: 52 Weeks   **Annual Attendance:** 7,000
Affiliations: Monmouth Arts Council
Performance Facilities: Count Basie Theatre

FACILITY

COUNT BASIE THEATRE
99 Monmouth Street, Red Bank, NJ 07701
(908) 842-9000
FAX: (908) 842-9323
   Type of Facility: Theatre House
   Facility Originally: Vaudeville
   Type of Stage: Thrust; Proscenium
   Stage Dimensions: 43'6"Wx27'Dx21'3"H
   Orchestra Pit
   Seating Capacity: 1,529
   Year Built: 1926   **Architect:** William Lehman
   Contact for Rental: Jerry Bakal;   (908) 842-9000
   Resident Groups: New Jersey Symphony Orchestra; Monmouth Civic Chorus; Garden State Ballet; Monmouth Conservatory of Music; Monmouth Symphony; Dance East; Company of Dance Arts

Ridgewood

DANCE

IRINE FOKINE BALLET COMPANY
33 Chestnut Street, Ridgewood, NJ 07450
(201) 652-9653
   Founded: 1956
   Arts Area: Ballet
   Status: Semi-Professional; Non-Profit
   Type: Performing; Touring; Educational
   Purpose: To bring ballet to young people in suburban communities and to give training to young dancers
   Management: Irine Fokine, Director; Margaret Dunworth, Secretary
   Paid Artists: 25
   Utilizes: Special Technical Talent; Guest Artists
   Season: 52 Weeks
   Performance Facilities: Bergen County Technical High School, Hackensack

INSTRUMENTAL MUSIC

RIDGEWOOD SYMPHONY ORCHESTRA
PO Box 176, Ridgewood, NJ 07675
(201) 612-0118
   Founded: 1939
   Arts Area: Symphony; Orchestra
   Status: Non-Profit
   Type: Performing
   Purpose: Performs orchestral concerts with playing opportunities for local musicians and provides music scholarships for high school and college students; to sponsor a childrens' series twice a year as well as the Ridgewood Symphony Orchestra Festival Strings for middle school youngsters
   Management: Dr. Sandra Dackow, Musical Director; Donna Denniston, Personnel Manager
   Officers: Jennifer McElrath, President
   Paid Staff: 1   **Volunteer Staff:** 7
   Paid Artists: 4   **Non-Paid Artists:** 75
   Utilizes: Guest Artists
   Budget: $1,000 - $50,000
   Income Sources: Private Foundations/Grants/Endowments; Business/Corporate Donations; Box Office; Individual Donations
   Season: September - May   **Annual Attendance:** 2,400
   Performance Facilities: Benjamin Franklin Middle School

VOCAL MUSIC

RIDGEWOOD GILBERT AND SULLIVAN OPERA COMPANY
975 East Ridgewood Avenue, Ridgewood, NJ 07450
(201) 385-9314
Founded: 1937
Arts Area: Light Opera
Status: Non-Professional; Non-Profit
Type: Performing; Touring
Purpose: To present the operas of Gilbert and Sullivan; to foster appreciation of music, drama, and production of the Gilbert and Sullivan operas
Management: Wilbur Watkin Lewis, Stage Director; Chester Wolfson, Music Director; Jack Strangfeld, Business Manager
Officers: Carol Ciancia, President; Welles Hotchkiss, Vice President; Phillip Sternenberg, Secretary; Rhonda Cooperstein, Treasurer
Paid Staff: 2   **Volunteer Staff:** 50
Non-Paid Artists: 50
Budget: $1,000 - $50,000
Income Sources: Box Office
Season: April - June; November - December   **Annual Attendance:** 8,000
Affiliations: AACT
Performance Facilities: Ben Franklin Middle School

Rutherford

FACILITY

WILLIAMS CENTER FOR THE ARTS - THE RIVOLI
One Williams Plaza, Rutherford, NJ 07070
(201) 939-6969
FAX: (201) 939-0843
Founded: 1979
Type of Facility: Theatre Complex; Concert Hall; Environmental; Multi-Purpose; Movie Theatre
Facility Originally: Vaudeville; Movie House
Type of Stage: Flexible; Proscenium; Platform; Three stages
Stage Dimensions: 12'x17'; 25'x40'; 30'D'x35'H proscenium opening
Seating Capacity: George W. Newman Theatre - 640; Marcus Recital Hall - 147; Oscar Theatre - 325
Year Built: 1922
Year Remodeled: 1992   **Architect:** John Leyman, Designer; John Capazzi, Architect   **Cost:** $500,000
Acoustical Consultant: Robert Hunsen Associates
Contact for Rental: John Leyman, Director of Operations
Resident Groups: Williams Center Repertory Theatre (WCRT); Dance Compass (modern dance); New Jersey Ballet; Vagabond Puppets
The Williams Center for the Arts contains the Marcus Recital Hall, the black box Oscar Theatre, and the mainstage George W. Newman Theatre.

Somers Point

THEATRE

SOUTH JERSEY REGIONAL THEATRE
Bay Avenue & Higbee Avenue, Somers Point, NJ 08244
(609) 653-0553
Founded: 1977
Arts Area: Professional; Theatrical Group
Status: Professional; Non-Profit
Type: Performing; Educational
Purpose: To produce the highest quality theatre entertainment for residents and visitors to this part of our state
Management: Thom Maslow, Executive Director; Joanna Papada, Artistic Director
Officers: George Kisby, Chairman
Paid Staff: 15   **Volunteer Staff:** 100
Paid Artists: 30
Utilizes: Special Technical Talent; Guest Artists; Guest Directors
Budget: $500,000 - $1,000,000
Income Sources: Private Foundations/Grants/Endowments; Business/Corporate Donations; Box Office; Government Grants; Individual Donations
Season: 52 Weeks   **Annual Attendance:** 40,000

Affiliations: LORT; AEA; GPCA; New Jersey Theatre Group
Performance Facilities: South Jersey Regional Theatre

Summit

INSTRUMENTAL MUSIC

SUMMIT SYMPHONY
5 Myrtle Avenue, Summit, NJ 07901
(908) 277-2932
    Founded: 1937
    Arts Area: Symphony
    Status: Non-Professional; Non-Profit
    Type: Performing
    Purpose: To provide orchestra music for Summit and surrounding communities; to provide an arena for non-professionals to perform major works
    Management: James Sadewhite, Music Director; Barry Davidson, Manager of Orchestra Personnel
    Officers: Carol Smith, President; Donald Hufnail, Vice President; Peter Boak, Treasurer
    Paid Staff: 1   **Volunteer Staff:** 16
    Paid Artists: 3
    Utilizes: Guest Artists
    Budget: $1,000 - $50,000
    Income Sources: Private Foundations/Grants/Endowments; Business/Corporate Donations; Individual Donations
    Season: September - May   **Annual Attendance:** 1,500
    Affiliations: Summit Board of Recreation; New Jersey Council on the Arts
    Performance Facilities: Summit Senior High School; Summit Middle School

VOCAL MUSIC

COMMUNITY OPERA, INCORPORATED
417 Morris Avenue #22, Summit, NJ 07901
(908) 277-1934
    Founded: 1981
    Arts Area: Grand Opera; Operetta
    Status: Professional
    Purpose: To provide a showcase for opera singers and composers of modern works
    Management: Edward Q. Watts, President
    Officers: Barbara Railo, Secretary/Treasurer
    Volunteer Staff: 2
    Paid Artists: 5
    Utilizes: Special Technical Talent; Guest Artists
    Income Sources: Private Foundations/Grants/Endowments; Business/Corporate Donations; Box Office; Individual Donations
    Season: September - June   **Annual Attendance:** 300
    Affiliations: Orpheus Society
    Performance Facilities: Hudson Guild; South Street Seaport - Fulton Center

Teaneck

THEATRE

AMERICAN STAGE COMPANY
892 River Road, Teaneck, NJ 07666
(201) 692-7744
    Founded: 1985
    Arts Area: Professional; Theatrical Group
    Status: Professional; Non-Profit
    Type: Performing; Resident; Educational
    Purpose: To present the best in dramatic art; to nurture recognizable talent in all aspects of theatre by providing a forum for established artists to hone their skills and for new artists to develop and expand their talents
    Management: James A. Vagias, Executive Producer
    Officers: Robert Lusko, President
    Paid Staff: 5   **Volunteer Staff:** 15
    Utilizes: Special Technical Talent; Guest Artists; Guest Directors
    Budget: $100,000 - $500,000
    Income Sources: Private Foundations/Grants/Endowments; Business/Corporate Donations; Box Office; Government Grants; Individual Donations

Season: October - May   **Annual Attendance:** 21,000
Affiliations: AEA; New Jersey Theatre Group; New Jersey Arts Council
Performance Facilities: Becton Theatre

Toms River

INSTRUMENTAL MUSIC

GARDEN STATE PHILHARMONIC SYMPHONY ORCHESTRA
PO Box 269, Toms River, NJ 08754
(908) 349-6277
   Founded: 1956
   Arts Area: Symphony; Orchestra
   Status: Semi-Professional; Non-Profit
   Type: Performing
   Purpose: To maintain a community orchestra in Ocean County, NJ that will give concerts of the highest cultural and educational value for the community; to provide both educational and training programs; to foster activities that encourage an interest and appreciation of music
   Management: Raymond Wojcik, Music Director/Conductor; JoAnn Montarelli, Administrator
   Officers: Estelle Brodkey, President; Norman Olsen, Jack Lamping, Sylvia Davis, Vice Presidents; Winifred Ewart, Treasurer
   Paid Staff: 2   **Volunteer Staff:** 150
   Paid Artists: 125   **Non-Paid Artists:** 50
   Utilizes: Guest Artists; New Jersey Composers
   Budget: $100,000 - $500,000
   Income Sources: Private Foundations/Grants/Endowments; Business/Corporate Donations; Box Office; Government Grants; Individual Donations
   Season: November - May   **Annual Attendance:** 10,000
   Affiliations: ASOL
   Performance Facilities: Toms River High School North

GARDEN STATE PHILHARMONIC YOUTH ORCHESTRA
PO Box 269, Toms River, NJ 08754
(908) 349-6277
   Founded: 1970
   Arts Area: Symphony
   Status: Non-Professional; Non-Profit
   Type: Performing; Educational
   Purpose: To provide musical training and orchestral performance experience for school-aged children
   Management: Don Spaulding, Conductor
   Officers: Morris Adler, Executive Vice President
   Non-Paid Artists: 70
   Budget: $1,000 - $50,000
   Income Sources: Private Foundations/Grants/Endowments; Business/Corporate Donations; Box Office; Government Grants; Individual Donations
   Season: September - May   **Annual Attendance:** 2,700
   Affiliations: Garden State Philharmonic Symphony Orchestra

VOCAL MUSIC

GARDEN STATE PHILHARMONIC CHORUS
PO Box 269, Toms River, NJ 08754
(908) 349-6277
   Founded: 1984
   Arts Area: Choral
   Status: Non-Professional; Non-Profit
   Type: Performing
   Management: Paul Chapin, Choral Director
   Paid Artists: 3   **Non-Paid Artists:** 100
   Utilizes: Guest Artists
   Season: November - May   **Annual Attendance:** 2,000
   Performance Facilities: Toms River High School North

Trenton

INSTRUMENTAL MUSIC

GREATER TRENTON SYMPHONY ORCHESTRA
28 West State Street, Trenton, NJ 08608
(609) 394-1338
> **Founded:** 1921
> **Arts Area:** Symphony; Orchestra
> **Status:** Professional; Non-Profit
> **Type:** Performing; Educational
> **Purpose:** To offer high-quality performances of classical music for orchestra to the residents of the greater Trenton area
> **Management:** John Peter Holly, Executive Director
> **Paid Staff:** 2 **Volunteer Staff:** 1
> **Paid Artists:** 100
> **Utilizes:** Local Artists **Budget:** $100,000 - $500,000
> **Income Sources:** Private Foundations/Grants/Endowments; Business/Corporate Donations; Box Office; Government Grants; Individual Donations
> **Season:** October - May **Annual Attendance:** 6,000
> **Performance Facilities:** War Memorial Theater

THEATRE

SHAKESPEARE '70
121 Grand Street, Trenton, NJ 08611
(609) 695-1955
> **Founded:** 1970
> **Arts Area:** Summer Stock; Musical; Theatrical Group
> **Status:** Semi-Professional; Non-Profit
> **Type:** Performing; Educational
> **Purpose:** To bring the works of William Shakespeare and other classical writers to the region; to perform musicals with a classical root and bring Shakespeare productions to New Jersey Cable TV and thus into the classrooms of schools and colleges
> **Management:** Gerald E. Guarnieri, Executive Director; John F. Erath, PhD, Director
> **Officers:** Gerald E. Guarnieri, Chief Executive Officer/President; John F. Erath, Vice President; Gail Erath, Secretary; Carol Rosenthal, Board Member; Bruce S. Bushman, Controller
> **Paid Staff:** 3 **Volunteer Staff:** 6
> **Paid Artists:** 4 **Non-Paid Artists:** 25
> **Utilizes:** Special Technical Talent; Guest Artists; Guest Directors
> **Budget:** $1,000 - $50,000
> **Income Sources:** Private Foundations/Grants/Endowments; Business/Corporate Donations; Box Office; Government Grants; Individual Donations
> **Season:** February - November **Annual Attendance:** 10,000
> **Affiliations:** New Jersey Theatre League
> **Performance Facilities:** Washington Crossing Open Air Theatre; Artists Showcase Theatre

FACILITY

NEW JERSEY STATE MUSEUM AUDITORIUM
205 West State Street, Trenton, NJ 08625
(609) 292-6308
FAX: (609) 599-4098
> **Type of Facility:** Auditorium
> **Type of Stage:** Proscenium
> **Seating Capacity:** 416
> **Year Built:** 1964 **Architect:** Frank Grad

Union

FACILITY

KEAN COLLEGE OF NEW JERSEY - WILKENS THEATRE
Morris Avenue, Union, NJ 07083
(908) 527-2088
FAX: (908) 527-8345
> **Founded:** 1965
> **Type of Facility:** Theatre House

Type of Stage: Thrust
Stage Dimensions: 40'x30'   **Orchestra Pit**
Seating Capacity: 956
Year Built: 1965   **Architect:** S,S&P
Contact for Rental: Performing Arts Office;   (908) 527-2088
Resident Groups: New Jersey Ballet; Chaison Dance Theatre Company; Garden State Orchestra; Kean Dance Theatre

Union City

THEATRE

PARK PERFORMING ARTS CENTER
560 32nd Street, Union City, NJ 07087
(201) 865-6980
Arts Area: Professional
Status: Professional; Non-Profit
Type: Performing
Purpose: To provide cultural enrichment and quality entertainment to all residents of New Jersey and the surrounding area
Management: Kevin P. Ashe, Executive Director; Eric Hafen, Artistic Director; Jorge Fernandez, Business Director; Pilar Suarez, Public Relations
Paid Staff: 25   **Volunteer Staff:** 35
Budget: $100,000 - $500,000
Income Sources: Private Foundations/Grants/Endowments; Business/Corporate Donations; Box Office; Government Grants; Individual Donations
Performance Facilities: Park Theatre Performing Arts Centre

FACILITY

PARK THEATRE PERFORMING ARTS CENTRE
560 32nd Street, Union City, NJ 07087
(201) 865-6980
Type of Facility: Performance Center
Type of Stage: Proscenium
Orchestra Pit
Year Built: 1931   **Architect:** Frank J. Ricker & Louis A. Axt
Contact for Rental: Sixto Perez;   (201) 865-6980
The Performing Arts Centre contains the Main Theatre. See separate listing for additional information.

PARK THEATRE PERFORMING ARTS CENTRE - MAIN THEATRE
560 32nd Street, Union City, NJ 07087
(201) 865-6980
FAX: (201) 865-5339
Type of Facility: Concert Hall; Theatre House
Facility Originally: Vaudeville
Type of Stage: Proscenium
Stage Dimensions: 44'Wx40'Dx70'H   **Orchestra Pit**
Seating Capacity: 1,350
Year Built: 1931
Contact for Rental: Sixto Perez;   (201) 865-6980
Resident Groups: Park Players

Upper Montclair

FACILITY

MONTCLAIR STATE COLLEGE - MEMORIAL AUDITORIUM
Upper Montclair, NJ 07043
(201) 893-4351
Type of Facility: Theatre Complex; Auditorium; Performance Center
Type of Stage: Thrust; Proscenium
Stage Dimensions: 40'x36'x18'   **Orchestra Pit**
Seating Capacity: 1,009

Year Built: 1958   **Architect:** Rigolo Associates
Contact for Rental: Gene Lotito;   (201) 893-4351
Resident Groups: Cultural Progress Dance Series; SummerFest; Student Organizations; Theatre Series

Warren

INSTRUMENTAL MUSIC

PHILHARMONIC ORCHESTRA OF NEW JERSEY
PO Box 4064, Warren, NJ 07059
(908) 356-6165
FAX: (908) 560-0881
Founded: 1987
Arts Area: Symphony; Orchestra
Status: Professional; Non-Profit
Type: Performing
Purpose: To present the highest quality symphonic concerts in Somerset and Hunterdon counties in New Jersey
Management: Marcia Blackstone, Managing Director
Officers: Judith-Ann Corrente, President; Patricia Hyer, Vice President; James Mersfelder, Treasurer
Paid Staff: 1   **Volunteer Staff:** 5
Paid Artists: 100
Utilizes: Guest Artists
Budget: $100,000 - $500,000
Income Sources: Private Foundations/Grants/Endowments; Business/Corporate Donations; Box Office; Government Grants; Individual Donations
Season: September - June   **Annual Attendance:** 3,000
Affiliations: ASOL
Performance Facilities: Pingry Auditorium, Pingry School, Martinsville

Waterloo

PERFORMING SERIES

WATERLOO MUSIC FESTIVAL
Waterloo Foundation for the Arts, Waterloo, NJ 07874
(201) 347-4700
FAX: (201) 347-0900
Founded: 1967
Arts Area: Dance; Vocal Music; Instrumental Music; Theater; Festivals; Grand Opera
Status: Professional; Non-Profit
Type: Performing; Sponsoring
Purpose: To combine history, music, art and architecture; to educate all persons in the state of New Jersey with appreciation of these arts forms; to aid in the rehabilitation of youth via the culinary arts, performing arts and maintenance—eventually leading to jobs in these fields
Management: Carole Delaire, Administrative Director; Samuel Lipman, Art Director; Gerard Schwarz, Principal Conductor
Officers: Percival Leach, President; Finn Casperson, Chariman
Paid Staff: 15   **Volunteer Staff:** 10
Paid Artists: 40
Utilizes: Guest Conductors; Guest Artists; Guest Directors
Budget: $1,000,000 - $5,000,000
Income Sources: Private Foundations/Grants/Endowments; Business/Corporate Donations; Box Office; Government Grants; Individual Donations
Season: May - October   **Annual Attendance:** 200,000
Affiliations: New Jersey State Council of the Arts; New Jersey Tourism Council
Performance Facilities: Waterloo Music Festival Tent

Wayne

INSTRUMENTAL MUSIC

FRIENDS OF MUSIC OF WAYNE, INC.
c/o Schuyler-Colfax JHS, 1500 Hamburg Turnpike, Wayne, NJ 07470
(201) 633-3021
FAX: (201) 628-8837
Founded: 1981

Arts Area: Symphony; Orchestra; Chamber; Ensemble; Ethnic; Folk; Instrumental Group; Electronic & Live Electronic; Band
Status: Non-Profit
Type: Educational; Sponsoring
Purpose: To support a high quality music program in our schools as an integral part of a balanced curriculum; to foster the appreciation of music
Management: Dr. Jacques Rizzo, Fine Arts Supervisor
Officers: Dee Herrmann, Matthew Paterno, Co-Presidents; Beverly Sullivan, First Vice President; Larry Silano, Second Vice President; Gwen Eckstein, Cooresponding Secretary; Laura Macey, Recording Secretary; Ruth Kotik, Treasurer
Volunteer Staff: 25
Utilizes: Guest Conductors; Guest Artists
Budget: $1,000 - $50,000
Income Sources: Private Foundations/Grants/Endowments; Business/Corporate Donations; Government Grants; Individual Donations
Season: September - June   **Annual Attendance:** 5,000
Affiliations: MENC
Performance Facilities: Wayne Valley High School; Wayne Hills High School; George Washington Junior High School; Schuyler-Colfax Junior High School

WAYNE CHAMBER ORCHESTRA
William Paterson College, 300 Pompton Road, Wayne, NJ 07470
(201) 595-2674
FAX: (201) 595-2460
Founded: 1986
Arts Area: Orchestra
Status: Professional
Type: Performing
Purpose: To present American music; to present works that are not frequently performed by chamber orchestras
Management: Murry Colosimo, Conductor; Martin Krivin, Executive Director; Sheri Newberger, Business Manager
Officers: Fletcher Fish, President; Erwin Knauer, Vice President; Ronald Hinchman, Treasurer; Mae Fish, Secretary
Paid Staff: 7   **Volunteer Staff:** 15
Paid Artists: 40   **Non-Paid Artists:** 8
Utilizes: Guest Artists
Budget: $100,000 - $500,000
Income Sources: Private Foundations/Grants/Endowments; Business/Corporate Donations; Box Office; Government Grants; Individual Donations
Season: October - May   **Annual Attendance:** 2,600
Performance Facilities: Shea Center for the Performing Arts, William Paterson College

PERFORMING SERIES

WILLIAM PATERSON COLLEGE - THE JAZZ ROOM SERIES
300 Pompton Road, Wayne, NJ 07470
(201) 595-2268
FAX: (201) 595-2460
Founded: 1978
Arts Area: Instrumental Music
Status: Professional
Type: Performing
Purpose: To present a complete spectrum of jazz music
Management: Martin Krivin, Producer; Rufus Reid, Artistic Advisor
Paid Staff: 2
Paid Artists: 38
Utilizes: Guest Artists
Budget: $1,000 - $50,000
Income Sources: Box Office; Government Grants
Season: October - March   **Annual Attendance:** 2,700
Performance Facilities: Shea Center for the Performing Arts, William Paterson College

WILLOWBROOK JAZZ FESTIVAL
William Paterson College, 300 Pompton Road, Wayne, NJ 07470
(201) 595-2268
FAX: (201) 595-2460
Arts Area: Jazz
Status: Professional; Non-Profit
Type: Performing
Purpose: To make jazz music as accessible to the public as possible by making it free and by locating it at a convenient time and place

Management: Dr. Martin Krivin, Special Projects Assistant to the President; Rufus Reid, Director of Jazz Program at William Paterson College
Budget: $50,000 - $100,000
Income Sources: Business/Corporate Donations; Government Grants
Season: April
Performance Facilities: Willowbrook Mall

West Orange

DANCE

NEW JERSEY BALLET COMPANY
270 Pleasant Valley Way, West Orange, NJ 07940
(201) 736-5940
FAX: (201) 736-5582
Founded: 1958
Arts Area: Ballet; Jazz
Status: Professional; Non-Profit
Type: Performing; Touring; Educational
Purpose: To maintain a highly regarded reperatory of standard classical pieces and audience attracting contemporary classical and jazz pieces which can be programmed to meet the needs of all presenters; to retain a roster of highly qualified dancers to perform the reperatory for all audiences
Management: Carolyn Clark, Executive/Artistic Director; Eleanor D'Antuono, Leonid Kozlov and Edward Villella, Artistic Advisors; Paul Sutherland, Ballet Master
Officers: David Farris, Chairman; Francis Mastro, President; Carolyn Clark, Executive Vice President
Paid Staff: 7 **Volunteer Staff:** 6
Paid Artists: 20
Utilizes: Guest Conductors; Guest Artists; Guest Directors; Guest Choreographers
Budget: $500,000 - $1,000,000
Income Sources: Private Foundations/Grants/Endowments; Business/Corporate Donations; Box Office; Government Grants; Individual Donations
Season: 32 Weeks **Annual Attendance:** 100,000
Performance Facilities: Paper Mill Playhouse; Newark Symphony Hall; John Harms Center for the Performing Arts; Kean College; Ocean City Music Pier

PERFORMING SERIES

JEWISH COMMUNITY CENTER OF METROPOLITAN NEW JERSEY
760 Northfield Avenue, West Orange, NJ 07052
(201) 736-3200
FAX: (201) 736-6871
Founded: 1877
Arts Area: Vocal Music; Instrumental Music; Theater; Festivals; Film Series
Status: Professional; Non-Professional; Non-Profit
Type: Performing; Educational; Sponsoring
Management: Jo Goldstien, Programming Supervisor; Marsha Fleisch, Program Assistant
Officers: Rhoda Goodman, Director YM-YWHA; Martha Cohen, Chairman of Committee of the Arts; Peter Leibman, Co-Chair of the Committee of the Arts
Paid Staff: 3 **Volunteer Staff:** 100
Paid Artists: 100
Utilizes: Special Technical Talent; Guest Artists
Budget: $100,000 - $500,000
Income Sources: Private Foundations/Grants/Endowments; Business/Corporate Donations; Box Office; Government Grants; Individual Donations
Season: September - May **Annual Attendance:** 15,000
Performance Facilities: Maurice Levin Theater

FACILITY

MAURICE LEVIN THEATER
760 Northfield Avenue, West Orange, NJ 07052
(201) 736-3200
FAX: (201) 736-6871
Type of Facility: Concert Hall
Type of Stage: Proscenium
Stage Dimensions: 38'x50' **Orchestra Pit**
Seating Capacity: 500
Year Built: 1966

Contact for Rental: Jo Goldstein;   (201) 736-3200
Resident Groups: Metropolitan Orchestra

Westfield

INSTRUMENTAL MUSIC

THE WESTFIELD SYMPHONY
321 Elm Street, PO Box 491, Westfield, NJ 07090
(908) 232-9400
FAX: (908) 232-2446
Founded: 1983
Arts Area: Symphony
Status: Professional
Type: Performing
Purpose: To bring the highest quality professional music to the central New Jersey area; to provide education programs for grades 1-12 in the area
Management: Kenneth W. Hopper, General Manager
Officers: Nancy W. Priest, President; Robert J. Edelman, Treasurer; M.J. Vincentsen, Vice President; Ellen I. Albertson, Secretary
Paid Staff: 3
Paid Artists: 70
Utilizes: Guest Artists
Budget: $100,000 - $500,000
Income Sources: Private Foundations/Grants/Endowments; Business/Corporate Donations; Box Office; Government Grants; Individual Donations
Season: October - April   **Annual Attendance:** 4,500

VOCAL MUSIC

THE CHORAL ART SOCIETY OF NEW JERSEY
PO Box 2036, Westfield, NJ 07091
(908) 232-2173
Founded: 1962
Arts Area: Choral
Status: Non-Professional
Type: Performing
Purpose: To study, perform and promote choral works
Management: Evelyn Bleeke, Musical Director
Officers: James Zgoda, President; Ted Schirm, Vice President; Linda Jacobey, Treasurer; Suzanne Beeny, Secretary
Paid Staff: 2   **Volunteer Staff:** 21
Paid Artists: 10
Utilizes: Guest Artists
Budget: $1,000 - $50,000
Income Sources: Private Foundations/Grants/Endowments; Business/Corporate Donations; Box Office; Government Grants; Individual Donations
Season: September - June   **Annual Attendance:** 1,000

Woodbridge

FACILITY

BARRON ARTS CENTER
582 Rahway Avenue, Woodbridge, NJ 07095
(908) 634-0413
Founded: 1977
Type of Facility: Concert Hall; Outdoor (Concert); Multi-Purpose
Facility Originally: Library
Type of Stage: Flexible
Seating Capacity: 100
Year Built: 1877   **Architect:** J. Cleveland Cadey   **Cost:** $19,000

NEW MEXICO

Alamogordo

FACILITY

FLICKINGER CENTER FOR THE PERFORMING ARTS
1110 New York Avenue, Alamogordo, NM 88310
(505) 437-2202
Founded: 1988
Type of Facility: Concert Hall; Auditorium; Performance Center; Theatre House; Multi-Purpose
Facility Originally: Movie House
Type of Stage: Proscenium
Stage Dimensions: 30'x40'
Orchestra Pit
Seating Capacity: 700
Year Built: 1956
Year Remodeled: 1992   **Architect:** Nolan and Associates   **Cost:** $380,000
Acoustical Consultant: Smith Electrical
Contact for Rental: Susie Hall;   (505) 437-2202
Resident Groups: Alamogordo Music Theater; Alamogordo Players Workshop

Albuquerque

DANCE

THE NEW MEXICO BALLET COMPANY
PO Box 21518, Albuquerque, NM 87154
(505) 292-4245
Founded: 1972
Arts Area: Ballet
Status: Non-Professional; Non-Profit
Type: Performing; Touring
Purpose: To promote the dance arts through education, training, and performances
Management: David Chavez, Artistic Director; Mildred Ness, Executive Director
Officers: June Leonard, Chairman
Paid Artists: 24   **Non-Paid Artists:** 40
Utilizes: Guest Artists; Guest Choreographers
Budget: $100,000 - $500,000
Income Sources: Private Foundations/Grants/Endowments; Business/Corporate Donations; Box Office; Individual Donations
Season: October - April
Performance Facilities: Popejoy Hall, University of New Mexico at Albuquerque

INSTRUMENTAL MUSIC

ALBUQUERQUE YOUTH SYMPHONY
220 Monroe SE, PO Box 25704, Albuquerque, NM 87104
(505) 345-5365, ext. 397
Founded: 1955
Arts Area: Symphony; Orchestra; Ensemble
Status: Non-Professional; Non-Profit
Type: Performing; Touring; Educational; Sponsoring
Purpose: To provide an outlet for talented students above and beyond their regular school musical programs through participation in one of four orchestras: Albuquerque Youth Symphony, Albuquerque Youth Orchestra, Albuquerque Junior Symphony or Albuquerque Junior Orchestra
Management: Dale E. Kempter, Conductor
Paid Staff: 4   **Volunteer Staff:** 200
Non-Paid Artists: 400
Income Sources: Fund-raising
Season: September - May   **Annual Attendance:** 15,000
Affiliations: ASOL (Youth Orchestra Division); ASCAP
Performance Facilities: Popejoy Hall, University of New Mexico

CHAMBER ORCHESTRA OF ALBUQUERQUE
PO Box 35081, Albuquerque, NM 87176-5081
(505) 881-0844
Founded: 1976
Arts Area: Orchestra
Status: Professional; Non-Profit
Type: Performing
Purpose: To provide a broad range of listening and participatory musical opportunities to the State of New Mexico; to maintain a professional orchestra whose work enriches the quality of community life
Management: David Oberg, Music Director/Conductor/General Manager; Diane V. Teare, Managing Assistant
Officers: Michael H. Smith, President; John T. Duff, Treasurer; Julia Cohen, Secretary
Paid Staff: 2   **Volunteer Staff:** 2
Paid Artists: 37
Utilizes: Guest Conductors; Guest Artists
Budget: $100,000 - $500,000
Income Sources: Private Foundations/Grants/Endowments; Business/Corporate Donations; Box Office; Government Grants; Individual Donations
Season: October - June
Annual Attendance: 9,000
Performance Facilities: St. John's United Methodist Church

MUSICA ANTIGUA DE ALBUQUERQUE
1017 Roma NE, Albuquerque, NM 87106
(505) 842-9613
Founded: 1978
Arts Area: Ensemble
Status: Professional; Non-Profit
Type: Performing; Touring; Educational
Purpose: To bring music of the Middle Ages, Renaissance and Baroque eras of music history to audiences through concert performances and lecture demonstrations
Officers: Art Sheinberg, President of the Executive Board; Allison Edwards, Vice President; Colleen Sheinberg, Secretary/Treasurer
Paid Staff: 1   **Volunteer Staff:** 1
Paid Artists: 6
Utilizes: Special Technical Talent; Guest Artists
Budget: $1,000 - $50,000
Income Sources: Business/Corporate Donations; Box Office; Government Grants; Individual Donations; Merchandise Sales
Season: September - May
Annual Attendance: 1,350
Affiliations: Early Music America; Albuquerque Arts Alliance
Performance Facilities: Central United Methodist Church; Loretto Chapel, Santa Fe

NEW MEXICO SYMPHONY ORCHESTRA
220 Gold Avenue SW, Albuquerque, NM 87102
(505) 843-7657
FAX: (505) 247-8422
Mailing Address: PO Box 769, Albuquerque, NM 87103
Founded: 1932
Arts Area: Symphony; Orchestra; Chamber; Ensemble
Status: Professional; Non-Profit
Type: Performing; Educational
Purpose: To present live concerts of music for small ensembles through full orchestra in both educational and concert settings
Management: Paul Bunker, Executive Director; Carl Johnston, Finance Director; Geoge Sampson, Development Director; Marge Navarro, Marketing Director
Officers: Herbert Koogle, President; Michael Bowlin, President-Elect; Derick Pasternak, Vice President; Michael Thompson, Vice President/Secretary; Mark Smith, Treasurer
Paid Staff: 13   **Volunteer Staff:** 2
Paid Artists: 78   **Non-Paid Artists:** 109
Utilizes: Special Technical Talent; Guest Conductors; Guest Artists; Guest Directors
Budget: $1,000,000 - $5,000,000
Income Sources: Private Foundations/Grants/Endowments; Business/Corporate Donations; Box Office; Government Grants; Individual Donations
Season: September - May
Annual Attendance: 120,000
Affiliations: ASOL; AAA
Performance Facilities: Popejoy Hall

VOCAL MUSIC

ALBUQUERQUE CIVIC LIGHT OPERA
4201 Ellison NE, Albuquerque, NM 87109
(505) 345-6577
> **Founded:** 1968
> **Arts Area:** Light Opera; Musical Theatre
> **Status:** Non-Profit
> **Type:** Performing
> **Purpose:** To present musical theatre with community based performers, musicians and crews
> **Management:** Linda McVey, Executive Director
> **Officers:** Nickey Prokapiak, President; John Wright, Vice President; Karen Lynch, Secretary; E. John Caruso, Treasurer
> **Paid Staff:** 10 **Volunteer Staff:** 200
> **Paid Artists:** 3 **Non-Paid Artists:** 500
> **Utilizes:** Guest Directors
> **Budget:** $500,000 - $1,000,000
> **Income Sources:** Private Foundations/Grants/Endowments; Business/Corporate Donations; Box Office; Individual Donations
> **Season:** March - December **Annual Attendance:** 12,000
> **Affiliations:** SWTC
> **Performance Facilities:** Popejoy Hall

ALBUQUERQUE OPERA THEATRE - OPERA SOUTHWEST
515 15th Street NW, Albuquerque, NM 87104
(505) 243-0591
> **Founded:** 1972
> **Arts Area:** Grand Opera; Lyric Opera; Light Opera; Operetta
> **Status:** Professional; Non-Profit
> **Type:** Performing; Educational
> **Purpose:** To present fully staged, costumed operas with accomplished musicians at the highest artistic level
> **Management:** Justine Tate-Opel, Production Manager/General Director
> **Officers:** Sheila Johnson, President, Board of Directors
> **Paid Staff:** 3 **Volunteer Staff:** 25
> **Paid Artists:** 20 **Non-Paid Artists:** 30
> **Utilizes:** Special Technical Talent; Guest Artists; Guest Directors
> **Budget:** $100,000 - $500,000
> **Income Sources:** Business/Corporate Donations; Box Office; Government Grants; Individual Donations
> **Season:** October - May **Annual Attendance:** 8,000
> **Affiliations:** COS
> **Performance Facilities:** KiMo Theatre

NEW MEXICO GAY MEN'S CHORUS
8640 Horacio Place NE, Albuquerque, NM 87111
(505) 296-9215
> **Founded:** 1981
> **Arts Area:** Choral
> **Status:** Non-Professional; Non-Profit
> **Type:** Performing; Resident; Educational
> **Management:** David Arenallenes, Conductor
> **Officers:** Alan Stringer, Manager
> **Paid Staff:** 1 **Volunteer Staff:** 5
> **Paid Artists:** 1 **Non-Paid Artists:** 30
> **Budget:** $1,000 - $50,000
> **Income Sources:** Business/Corporate Donations; Box Office; Individual Donations
> **Season:** December - June **Annual Attendance:** 500
> **Affiliations:** Common Bond
> **Performance Facilities:** First Unitarian Church

THEATRE

LA COMPANIA DE TEATRO DE ALBURQUERQUE
423 Central Avenue NE, PO Box 884, Albuquerque, NM 87103-0884
(505) 242-7929
> **Founded:** 1977
> **Arts Area:** Theatrical Group
> **Status:** Semi-Professional; Non-Profit
> **Type:** Performing; Touring; Resident; Educational
> **Purpose:** To reflect, preserve and empower the New Mexican society and culture through professional production; Southwest bilingual theatre

Management: Ramon A. Flores, Artistic Director; Jeannette Chavez, Administrative Aide
Officers: Dr. Joe Valles, President; Edward Benavidez Esq., Vice President; Patricia Romero CPA, Treasurer; Catherine Abeyta, Secretary
Paid Staff: 2 **Volunteer Staff:** 20
Paid Artists: 10 **Non-Paid Artists:** 30
Utilizes: Special Technical Talent
Budget: $100,000 - $500,000
Income Sources: Private Foundations/Grants/Endowments; Business/Corporate Donations; Box Office; Government Grants; Individual Donations; Touring Fees
Season: September - June **Annual Attendance:** 7,000
Performance Facilities: KiMo Theatre; South Broadway Cutural Center

NEW MEXICO REPERTORY THEATRE
PO Box 789, Albuquerque, NM 87103-0789
(505) 243-4577
Founded: 1983
Arts Area: Professional; Theatrical Group
Status: Professional; Non-Profit
Type: Performing; Touring; Resident; Educational
Purpose: To present the finest in contemporary and classical theatre to the residents of New Mexico
Management: Martin L. Platt, Artistic Director; Bob MacDonald, Managing Director
Paid Staff: 12 **Volunteer Staff:** 200
Paid Artists: 45
Utilizes: Special Technical Talent; Guest Artists; Guest Directors
Budget: $1,000,000 - $5,000,000
Income Sources: Private Foundations/Grants/Endowments; Business/Corporate Donations; Box Office; Government Grants; Individual Donations
Season: October - June **Annual Attendance:** 60,000
Affiliations: TCG
Performance Facilities: KiMo Theatre; New Mexico Repertory Theatre

PERFORMING SERIES

GUEST ARTIST SERIES
c/o New Mexico Jazz Workshop Inc., PO Box 1925, Albuquerque, NM 87103
(505) 255-9798
Arts Area: Jazz
Status: Professional; Non-Profit
Type: Performing; Touring
Purpose: To present major jazz artists January-May for performing and educational activities
Management: Jim Williams, Executive Director
Officers: George Sampson, President
Budget: $1,000 - $50,000
Income Sources: Private Foundations/Grants/Endowments; Business/Corporate Donations; Box Office; Government Grants; Individual Donations
Season: January - May
Performance Facilities: Albuquerque Little Theater; Kimo Theater; Sunshine Music Hall

FACILITY

ALBUQUERQUE CONVENTION CENTER
401 Second Street NW, Albuquerque, NM 87103
(505) 768-4575
FAX: (505) 768-3239
Type of Facility: Civic Center
Year Built: 1972 **Architect:** Flato Bryan and Moore **Cost:** $12,000,000
Contact for Rental: Dale Scott; (505) 768-4575
Albuquerque Convention Center contains the Ballroom and Kiva Auditorium. See separate listings for additional information.

ALBUQUERQUE CONVENTION CENTER - BALLROOM
401 Second Street NW, Albuquerque, NM 87103
(505) 768-4575
FAX: (505) 768-3239
Type of Facility: Multi-Purpose; Room
Type of Stage: Flexible; Platform

Seating Capacity: Banquet - 1,900; Theater - 2,400
Contact for Rental: Dale Scott;   (505) 768-4575

ALBUQUERQUE CONVENTION CENTER - KIVA AUDITORIUM
401 Second Street NW, Albuquerque, NM 87103
(505) 768-4575
FAX: (505) 768-3239
   Type of Facility: Concert Hall; Auditorium
   Type of Stage: Proscenium
   Stage Dimensions: 36'Wx24'D
   Seating Capacity: 2,300
   Contact for Rental: Dale Scott;   (505) 768-4575
   Resident Groups: Albuquerque Symphony

SOUTH BROADWAY CULTURAL CENTER
1025 Broadway SE, Albuquerque, NM 87102
(505) 848-1320
FAX: (505) 848-1329
   Founded: 1970
   Type of Facility: Multi-Purpose
   Facility Originally: Library; Storefront
   Type of Stage: Proscenium
   Stage Dimensions: 20'x40'
   Seating Capacity: 214
   Year Built: 1985
   Architect: City of Albuquerque
   Cost: $60,000
   Contact for Rental: Marge Armijo;   (505) 848-1320

UNIVERSITY OF NEW MEXICO - POPEJOY HALL
Albuquerque, NM 87131
(505) 277-3824
   Type of Facility: Concert Hall
   Type of Stage: Proscenium
   Stage Dimensions: 120'Wx68'Dx38'H   **Orchestra Pit**
   Seating Capacity: 2,002
   Year Built: 1956
   Architect: University of New Mexico
   Cost: $3,000,000
   Acoustical Consultant: Bolt, Beranek & Newman
   Contact for Rental: William Martin, Director;   (505) 277-3824
   Resident Groups: Albuquerque Civic Light Opera; New Mexico Symphony Orchestra; Albuquerque Children's Theatre

Angel Fire

INSTRUMENTAL MUSIC

MUSIC FROM ANGEL FIRE
PO Box 502, Angel Fire, NM 87710
(505) 989-4772
FAX: (505) 989-4773
   Founded: 1984
   Arts Area: Chamber
   Status: Professional; Non-Profit
   Type: Performing
   Management: John W. Giovando, Executive Director; Ida Kavafian, Music Director
   Paid Staff: 3   Volunteer Staff: 50
   Paid Artists: 30
   Budget: $100,000 - $500,000
   Income Sources: Private Foundations/Grants/Endowments; Business/Corporate Donations; Box Office; Government Grants; Individual Donations
   Season: August - September   Annual Attendance: 5,000
   Performance Facilities: Taos; Angel Fire; Raton

Farmington

FACILITY

FARMINGTON CIVIC CENTER
200 West Arrington, Farmington, NM 87401
(505) 599-1150
FAX: (505) 599-1146
Founded: 1976
Type of Facility: Civic Center
Type of Stage: Modified Thrust   **Orchestra Pit**
Seating Capacity: 1,200
Year Built: 1976   **Architect:** Schermer & Schafer   **Cost:** $3,800,000
Contact for Rental: Civic Center;   (505) 599-1145

Las Cruces

THEATRE

LAS CRUCES COMMUNITY THEATRE
313 North Downtown Mall, Las Cruces, NM 88004
(505) 523-1200
Founded: 1963
Arts Area: Theatrical Group
Status: Non-Professional; Non-Profit
Type: Performing
Management: Yvette Lyannas, Box Office
Officers: Dick Rundell, President
Volunteer Staff: 20
Utilizes: Special Technical Talent; Guest Conductors; Guest Artists; Guest Directors
Budget: $1,000 - $50,000
Income Sources: Private Foundations/Grants/Endowments; Business/Corporate Donations; Box Office; Government Grants; Individual Donations
Season: October - July   **Annual Attendance:** 8,000

FACILITY

NEW MEXICO STATE UNIVERSITY - AMERICAN SOUTHWEST THEATRE
PO Box 3072, Las Cruces, NM 88003
(505) 646-4517
Type of Facility: Studio Performance; Theatre House
Type of Stage: Greek
Seating Capacity: 386
Year Built: 1962   **Architect:** Walgamood   **Cost:** $750,000
Year Remodeled: 1984   **Architect:** Len Auerbach   **Cost:** $1,500,000
Acoustical Consultant: Len Auerbach
Manager: Hilda Olivas
Resident Groups: American Southwest Theatre Company
Available for rent

PAN AMERICAN CENTER
PO Box 3SE, Las Cruces, NM 88003
(505) 646-4413
Type of Facility: Arena
Type of Stage: Flexible; Platform
Stage Dimensions: 72'Wx40'D
Seating Capacity: 13,500
Year Built: 1967
Contact for Rental: Barbara Hubbard;   (505) 646-4413

Los Alamos
FACILITY

LOS ALAMOS CIVIC AUDITORIUM
1400 Diamond Drive, Los Alamos, NM 87544
(505) 662-3683, ext. 53
FAX: (505) 662-4141
    Founded: 1950
    Type of Facility: Auditorium
    Type of Stage: Proscenium
    Stage Dimensions: 40'W   **Orchestra Pit**
    Seating Capacity: 965
    Year Built: 1950
    Contact for Rental: Carol Rodriguez; (505) 662-3683, ext. 53
    Resident Groups: Los Alamos Light Opera

Roswell
FACILITY

PEARSON AUDITORIUM
New Mexico Military Institute, College of Main, Roswell, NM 88201
(505) 622-6250
    Type of Facility: Auditorium
    Type of Stage: Proscenium   **Orchestra Pit**
    Seating Capacity: 1,300
    Year Built: 1940   **Cost:** $500,000
    Contact for Rental: Colonel Taylor; (505) 622-6250

Santa Fe
DANCE

MARIA BENITEZ SPANISH DANCE COMPANY
914 Rio Vista, Santa Fe, NM 87501
(505) 983-8477
    Founded: 1972
    Arts Area: Ethnic
    Status: Professional; Non-Profit
    Type: Performing; Touring; Educational
    Purpose: To foster the development of a high level of excellence in Spanish dancing through national and international touring, educational programs, concerts and television programs
    Management: Maria Benitez, Artistic Director
    Paid Staff: 4
    Paid Artists: 9
    Utilizes: Guest Artists
    Income Sources: Private Foundations/Grants/Endowments; Business/Corporate Donations; Box Office; Government Grants; Individual Donations
    Season: 52 Weeks   **Annual Attendance:** 12,000
    Performance Facilities: Sheraton of Sante Fe; Joyce Theatre, New York

INSTRUMENTAL MUSIC

THE ENSEMBLE OF SANTA FE
PO Box 8427, Santa Fe, NM 87504-8427
(505) 984-2501
    Founded: 1980
    Arts Area: Chamber
    Status: Professional; Non-Profit
    Type: Performing; Touring; Resident; Educational
    Purpose: To present chamber music and promote understanding
    Management: Santa Fe World Music Agency
    Officers: Thomas O'Connor, President; William Kirschke, Vice President; Carol Redman, Secretary/Treasurer
    Paid Staff: 2
    Paid Artists: 20
    Utilizes: Special Technical Talent; Guest Artists

Budget: $50,000 - $100,000
Income Sources: Private Foundations/Grants/Endowments; Business/Corporate Donations; Box Office; Government Grants; Individual Donations; Contracted Services
Season: 52 Weeks   **Annual Attendance:** 8,000
Performance Facilities: Loretto Chapel

ORCHESTRA OF SANTA FE
PO Box 2091, Santa Fe, NM 87504
(505) 988-4640
Founded: 1972
Arts Area: Symphony; Orchestra; Chamber
Status: Professional; Non-Profit
Type: Performing; Touring; Educational
Purpose: To provide the highest quality chamber music possible and make youth concerts and educational lectures available to the public
Management: Jennifer Martin, Business Manager; William Kirschke, Conductor; Anne Beeson, Development Director
Officers: Nancy Long Garcia, Roger Miller, Past Presidents
Paid Staff: 2   **Volunteer Staff:** 50
Paid Artists: 35
Utilizes: Guest Artists
Budget: $100,000 - $500,000
Income Sources: Private Foundations/Grants/Endowments; Business/Corporate Donations; Box Office; Government Grants; Individual Donations
Season: September - May   **Annual Attendance:** 12,000
Affiliations: ASOL
Performance Facilities: Lensic Theatre

SANTA FE SYMPHONY
PO Box 9692, Santa Fe, NM 87504
(505) 983-3530
FAX: (505) 982-3888
Founded: 1984
Arts Area: Symphony; Orchestra; Chamber; Folk
Status: Professional; Non-Profit
Type: Performing; Resident; Educational; Sponsoring
Management: Lynn Case, General Manager; Stewart Robertson, Music Director
Paid Staff: 2   **Volunteer Staff:** 110
Paid Artists: 80   **Non-Paid Artists:** 60
Utilizes: Guest Conductors; Guest Artists
Budget: $100,000 - $500,000
Income Sources: Private Foundations/Grants/Endowments; Business/Corporate Donations; Box Office; Government Grants; Individual Donations
Season: August - May   **Annual Attendance:** 8,000
Affiliations: ASOL; ASCAP
Performance Facilities: Sweeney Center

VOCAL MUSIC

THE SANTA FE DESERT CHORALE
PO Box 2813, Santa Fe, NM 87504-2813
(505) 988-7505
FAX: (505) 988-7522
Founded: 1982
Arts Area: Choral
Status: Professional; Non-Profit
Type: Performing; Educational
Purpose: To perform music from the choral repertoire within the last five centuries, especially baroque and modern
Management: Lawrence Bandfield, Music Director; Thomas Maguire, Executive Director
Officers: Mary Ann Nelson, President
Paid Staff: 4   **Volunteer Staff:** 100
Paid Artists: 45
Utilizes: Guest Conductors; Guest Artists
Budget: $100,000 - $500,000
Income Sources: Private Foundations/Grants/Endowments; Business/Corporate Donations; Box Office; Government Grants; Individual Donations
Season: June - September   **Annual Attendance:** 6,500

Affiliations: CA
Performance Facilities: Santuario de Guadalupe; Loretto Chapel; Sunshine Music Hall

THE SANTA FE OPERA
PO Box 2408, Santa Fe, NM 87504
(505) 982-3851
FAX: (505) 989-7012
 Arts Area: Lyric Opera; Light Opera; Operetta
 Status: Professional; Non-Profit
 Type: Performing; Educational; Sponsoring
 Purpose: To bring the finest opera productions to the American public with a varied repertoire, paying special attention to new works
 Management: John Crosby, Founder/General Director; Thomas Morris, Operations Manager
 Volunteer Staff: 25
 Paid Artists: 40
 Utilizes: Special Technical Talent; Guest Conductors; Guest Artists; Guest Directors
 Budget: $5,000,000 - $10,000,000
 Income Sources: Private Foundations/Grants/Endowments; Business/Corporate Donations; Box Office; Government Grants; Individual Donations
 Season: July - August
 Annual Attendance: 70,000
 Affiliations: OA
 Performance Facilities: Santa Fe Opera Theatre

THEATRE

SANTA FE COMMUNITY THEATRE
142 East DeVargas, Santa Fe, NM 87501
(505) 988-4262
 Founded: 1919
 Arts Area: Professional; Theatrical Group
 Status: Non-Professional; Non-Profit
 Type: Performing; Touring; Educational
 Officers: Robert Sinn, President; Carol Couch, Vice President; Ted Mclaughlin, Recording Secretary
 Volunteer Staff: 500
 Non-Paid Artists: 60
 Utilizes: Guest Artists; Guest Directors
 Income Sources: Private Foundations/Grants/Endowments; Business/Corporate Donations; Box Office; Government Grants; Individual Donations
 Season: 52 Weeks **Annual Attendance:** 7,600
 Affiliations: AACT
 Performance Facilities: Santa Fe Community Theatre

PERFORMING SERIES

SANTA FE CHAMBER MUSIC FESTIVAL
640 Paseo de Peralta, Santa Fe, NM 87501
(505) 983-2075
FAX: (505) 986-0251
 Founded: 1973
 Arts Area: Chamber
 Status: Professional; Non-Profit
 Type: Performing; Touring; Resident; Educational
 Purpose: To produce innovative chamber music concerts and related educational programs of exceptional artistic quality; to serve as a chamber music center attracting American musicians, composers and audiences whose combined influence, stimulation and energy will benefit American culture
 Management: James E. McGarry, Executive Director; Heiichiro Ohyama, Artistic Director
 Officers: Gifford Phillips, Chairman, Board of Trustes; Jacqueline Hoefer, Vice-Chairman; Dode Kenney, Secretary; Terrence Melia, Treasurer
 Paid Staff: 12 **Volunteer Staff:** 150
 Paid Artists: 60
 Utilizes: Guest Conductors; Guest Artists
 Budget: $1,000,000 - $5,000,000
 Income Sources: Private Foundations/Grants/Endowments; Business/Corporate Donations; Box Office; Government Grants; Individual Donations
 Season: July - August **Annual Attendance:** 20,000
 Performance Facilities: Saint Francis Auditorium: Museum of Fine Arts

FACILITY

CENTER FOR CONTEMPORARY ARTS
291 East Barcelona, Santa Fe, NM 87504
(505) 982-1338
FAX: (505) 982-9854
Founded: 1979
Type of Facility: Concert Hall; Multi-Purpose
Type of Stage: Platform; Portable
Stage Dimensions: 20'Wx12'D
Seating Capacity: 140
Year Remodeled: 1985   **Architect:** Mike Freeman

GREER GARSON THEATRE CENTER - COLLEGE OF SANTA FE
1600 St. Michael's Drive, Santa Fe, NM 87501
(505) 473-6439
Type of Facility: Theatre House
Type of Stage: Proscenium; Modified Apron Proscenium
Stage Dimensions: 70'Wx32'Dx33'H; 40'Wx16'H proscenium opening   **Orchestra Pit**
Seating Capacity: 514
Year Built: 1965   **Architect:** Philippe Register   **Cost:** $1,000,000
Year Remodeled: 1987   **Architect:** Davis & Associates
Contact for Rental: Mary Ann Fellows;   (505) 473-6270
Resident Groups: College of Santa Fe Performing Arts Department

NEW MEXICO REP
1050 Old Pecos Trail, Santa Fe, NM 87501
(505) 983-2382
FAX: (505) 984-1296
Founded: 1984
Type of Facility: Theatre House; Multi-Purpose
Facility Originally: Armory
Type of Stage: Modified Thrust Proscenium
Stage Dimensions: 40'Wx30'D
Seating Capacity: 340
Year Built: 1971
Year Remodeled: 1976
Acoustical Consultant: Applied Acoustics Associates
Contact for Rental: Bob McDonald;   (505) 983-2382
Resident Groups: La Compania Working Classroom

SANTA FE CONVENTION AND VISITORS BUREAU AT SWEENEY CENTER
201 West Marcy, PO Box 909, Santa Fe, NM 87501-0909
(505) 984-6760; (800) 777-2489
FAX: (505) 984-6679
Type of Facility: Concert Hall; Civic Center; Multi-Purpose
Facility Originally: High School Gymnasium
Type of Stage: Platform
Stage Dimensions: 64'Wx38'D
Seating Capacity: Theater - 1500; Banquet - 600
Year Built: 1955
Year Remodeled: 1979   **Architect:** Clark Aarison Germanas, AIA
Contact for Rental: Roxanne Smyth;   (505) 984-6760
Resident Groups: Santa Fe Symphony; New Mexico Symphony

SANTUARIO DE GUADALUPE
100 Guadalupe Street, Santa Fe, NM 87501
(505) 988-2027
Type of Facility: Concert Hall; Theatre House
Facility Originally: Church
Type of Stage: Platform
Stage Dimensions: 22'Wx13'W
Seating Capacity: 250
Year Built: 1776   **Architect:** Franciscan Missionaries
Year Remodeled: 1976   **Architect:** Nathaniel Owings, Chairman, National Trust for Historic Preservation
Contact for Rental: Emilio I. Ortiz;   (505) 988-2027

Resident Groups: Santa Fe Desert Chorale; Sangre de Cristo Chorale; Santa Fe Chamber Music Festival; Gamelan Encantada; Ars Nova Chamber Singers
State of New Mexico Bicentennial Project; National Register of Historic Places

SWEENEY CONVENTION CENTER
201 West Marcy Street, Santa Fe, NM 87501
(505) 984-6760
FAX: (505) 984-6679
Founded: 1974
Type of Facility: Concert Hall; Auditorium; Performance Center; Civic Center; Multi-Purpose
Facility Originally: School
Type of Stage: Flexible
Stage Dimensions: 24'x64'
Seating Capacity: 1,500
Year Built: 1956
Year Remodeled: 1972
Contact for Rental: Kenny Tennyson;   (505) 984-6760

WECKESSER STUDIO THEATRE
Greer Garson Theatre Center, College of Santa Fe, 1600 St. Michael's Drive, Santa Fe, NM 87501
(505) 473-6439
Type of Facility: Black Box
Facility Originally: Lecture Hall
Type of Stage: Flexible
Stage Dimensions: 40'x39' with 40'x12' raised section at one end
Seating Capacity: 100
Year Built: 1965   **Architect:** Philippe Register
Year Remodeled: 1987   **Architect:** Davis & Associates
Contact for Rental: Mary Ann Fellows;   (505) 473-6270

Taos

PERFORMING SERIES

TAOS SCHOOL OF MUSIC, INC.
PO Box 1879, Taos, NM 87571
(505) 776-2388
Founded: 1963
Arts Area: Instrumental Music; Festivals
Status: Non-Profit
Type: Performing; Educational
Purpose: To further the understanding, enjoyment and performance of chamber music through the school and festival
Officers: Chilton Anderson, President/Treasurer; R. Jamesson Burns, Vice President; Grace M. Parr, Secretary
Utilizes: Special Technical Talent; Guest Artists
Budget: $50,000 - $100,000
Income Sources: Private Foundations/Grants/Endowments; Business/Corporate Donations; Individual Donations
Season: June - August   **Annual Attendance:** 2,500
Performance Facilities: Taos Community Auditorium; Hotel St. Bernard

NEW YORK

Albany

INSTRUMENTAL MUSIC

ALBANY SYMPHONY ORCHESTRA
19 Clinton Avenue, Albany, NY 12207
(518) 465-4755
FAX: (518) 465-3711
   Founded: 1931
   Arts Area: Symphony
   Status: Professional; Non-Profit
   Type: Performing
   Purpose: To give quality performances of classical music, with an emphasis on the establishment of an American symphonic repertoire, at the same time developing programs which bring new audiences to our concerts
   Management: David Alan Miller, Music Director/Conductor; Susan Filipp, Executive Director
   Officers: Peter R. Kermani, Chairman of the Board; Barry Richman, President; Anthony Esposito, Dennis L. Kemper, James E. Panton, Timothy D. White, Vice Presidents; E. Kristin Frederick, Secretary; John Lavaelle, Treasurer
   Paid Staff: 4
   Paid Artists: 76
   Utilizes: Guest Conductors; Guest Artists
   Budget: $500,000 - $1,000,000
   Income Sources: Private Foundations/Grants/Endowments; Business/Corporate Donations; Box Office; Government Grants; Individual Donations
   Season: September - May   **Annual Attendance:** 18,000
   Affiliations: ASOL
   Performance Facilities: Palace Theatre; Troy Music Hall

CAPITOL CHAMBER ARTISTS, INC.
263 Manning Boulevard, Albany, NY 12206
(518) 458-9231
FAX: (518) 458-9231
   Founded: 1969
   Arts Area: Chamber
   Status: Professional; Non-Profit
   Type: Performing; Touring; Resident; Educational
   Purpose: To perfrom the highest quality chamber music and to educate a new audience
   Management: Mary Lou Saetta, Director
   Officers: Mary Lou Saetta, President; Irvin E. Gilman, Vice President
   Paid Staff: 2   **Volunteer Staff:** 8
   Paid Artists: 21
   Utilizes: Guest Artists
   Budget: $50,000 - $100,000
   Income Sources: Private Foundations/Grants/Endowments; Business/Corporate Donations; Box Office; Government Grants; Individual Donations
   Season: 52 Weeks   **Annual Attendance:** 10,000

THEATRE

THE BLACK EXPERIENCE ENSEMBLE
5 Homestead Avenue, Albany, NY 12203
(518) 482-6683
   Founded: 1968
   Arts Area: Community; Theatrical Group
   Status: Professional; Non-Profit
   Type: Performing; Touring; Sponsoring
   Purpose: To provide cultural exposure and enrichment to the minority community through the performing arts
   Management: Mars Hill, President/Founder
   Volunteer Staff: 7
   Non-Paid Artists: 5
   Utilizes: Special Technical Talent; Guest Conductors; Guest Artists; Guest Directors
   Budget: $1,000 - $50,000
   Income Sources: Private Foundations/Grants/Endowments; Business/Corporate Donations; Box Office; Individual Donations

Season: 52 Weeks **Annual Attendance:** 15,000
Affiliations: Albany League of Arts

CAPITAL REPERTORY COMPANY
111 North Pearl Street, Box 399, Albany, NY 12207
(518) 462-4531
Founded: 1980
Arts Area: Professional; Theatrical Group
Status: Professional; Non-Profit
Type: Performing; Resident
Purpose: Capital Repertory Company is a theater in which language is as vital as image or actions. The characters' survival of their immediate circumstances is framed by the playwright within a particular social, moral or political issue of concern to a section of the human community.
Management: Bruce Bouchard, Producing Director
Officers: Lynn Pauquette, President, Board of Trustees
Paid Staff: 10 **Volunteer Staff:** 75
Paid Artists: 44
Utilizes: Guest Artists; Guest Directors
Budget: $500,000 - $1,000,000
Income Sources: Private Foundations/Grants/Endowments; Business/Corporate Donations; Box Office; Government Grants; Individual Donations
Season: October - June
Annual Attendance: 41,000
Performance Facilities: The Market Theatre

THE NEW YORK STATE THEATER INSTITUTE
c/o State University of New York- Albany, 1400 Washington Avenue, Albany, NY 12222
(518) 442-3995
FAX: (518) 443-5782
Founded: 1975
Arts Area: Professional; Musical; Theatrical Group
Status: Professional; Non-Profit
Type: Performing; Touring; Resident; Educational; Sponsoring
Purpose: We utilize a great deal of talent from New York City to achieve our principal objectives: new play development; exceptional arts in education programming; the mounting of high-quality theatre for adult and family audiences; and international touring and exchange.
Management: Patricia Snyder, Producing Director/Founder
Paid Staff: 55 **Volunteer Staff:** 300
Paid Artists: 15
Utilizes: Special Technical Talent; Guest Artists; Guest Directors
Budget: $1,000,000 - $5,000,000
Income Sources: Private Foundations/Grants/Endowments; Business/Corporate Donations; Box Office; Government Grants; Individual Donations
Season: September - June **Annual Attendance:** 90,000
Affiliations: TCG; Albany League of Arts; Friends of the Kennedy Center

PERFORMING SERIES

L'ENSEMBLE
11 North Pearl Street, Suite 508, Albany, NY 12207
(518) 436-5321
Founded: 1972
Arts Area: Vocal Music; Instrumental Music; Festivals
Status: Professional; Non-Profit
Type: Performing; Touring; Resident; Educational
Purpose: To present the highest quality performance of chamber music as well as related workshops
Management: Ida Faiella, Executive Artistic Director; Kristine DeFord, Promotion and Publicity Assistant; Andrea Meldrum, Financial and Operations Assistant; Jennifer Chadwick, Music Assistant
Officers: Jonathan C. Mills, Chairman; Frank Gilmore, President; Timothy Smith, Vice President of Finance; Beverly Wittner, Vice President of Marketing; David Barnert, Treasurer; Timothy Meigher, Secretary
Paid Staff: 4 **Volunteer Staff:** 20
Utilizes: Special Technical Talent; Guest Artists
Budget: $50,000 - $100,000
Income Sources: Private Foundations/Grants/Endowments; Business/Corporate Donations; Box Office; Government Grants; Individual Donations
Season: July - September; October-April **Annual Attendance:** 10,000
Affiliations: CMA; Albany League of Arts; Minnesota Composers Forum
Performance Facilities: City Arts Building; L'Ensemble Chamber Music Center

FACILITY

THE EMPIRE STATE PERFORMING ARTS CENTER
PO Box 2065, Albany, NY 12220
(518) 473-1061
> **Type of Facility:** Performance Center
> **Year Built:** 1978   **Architect:** Harrison & Abramowitz   **Cost:** $50,000,000
> **Contact for Rental:** Paul Fontane;   (518) 473-1061
> **Manager:** Paul Fontane, House Manager
> **Resident Groups:** Ellen Sinopoli Dance Company
> *The Empire State Performing Arts Center, also known as "The Egg" due to its elliptical shape, contains the Kitty Carlisle Hart Theater and the Lewis A. Swyer Theater. See separate listings for more information.*

THE EMPIRE STATE PERFORMING ARTS CENTER - KITTY CARLISLE HART THEATER
PO Box 2065, Albany, NY 12220
(518) 473-1061
> **Type of Facility:** Concert Hall; Theatre House
> **Type of Stage:** Thrust; Flexible
> **Stage Dimensions:** 39'2"Wx55'D   **Orchestra Pit**
> **Seating Capacity:** 956
> **Year Built:** 1978
> **Contact for Rental:** Paul Fontane, House Manager;   (518) 473-1061

THE EMPIRE STATE PERFORMING ARTS CENTER- LEWIS A. SWYER THEATER
PO Box 2065, Albany, NY 12220
(518) 473-1061
> **Type of Facility:** Theatre House; :
> **Type of Stage:** Thrust
> **Stage Dimensions:** 34'Wx23'D
> **Seating Capacity:** 450
> **Year Built:** 1978
> **Contact for Rental:** Paul Fontane, House Manager;   (518) 473-1061

PALACE THEATRE
19 Clinton Avenue, Albany, NY 12207
(518) 465-3334
> **Type of Facility:** Concert Hall
> **Facility Originally:** Vaudeville
> **Type of Stage:** Proscenium
> **Stage Dimensions:** 27'x64'x43'   **Orchestra Pit**
> **Seating Capacity:** 2,897
> **Year Built:** 1931   **Architect:** John Eberson
> **Year Remodeled:** 1960
> **Contact for Rental:** Robert C. Goebfert;   (518) 465-3334
> **Manager:** Maureen Salkin
> **Resident Groups:** Albany Symphony Orchestra

STATE UNIVERSITY OF NEW YORK-ALBANY - ALBANY PERFORMING ARTS CENTER
1400 Washington Avenue, Albany, NY 12222
(518) 442-3995
> **Type of Facility:** Performance Center
> **Year Built:** 1967   **Architect:** Edward Durell Stone
> **Acoustical Consultant:** Jean Rosenthal
> **Contact for Rental:** Alton McCloud;   (518) 442-3996
> *Albany Performing Arts Center contains the Arena, Laboratory Theatre, Main Theatre, Recital Hall and Studio Theatre. See separate listings for additional information.*

STATE UNIVERSITY OF NEW YORK-ALBANY - ARENA
Albany Performing Arts Center, 1400 Washington Avenue, Albany, NY 12222
(518) 442-3995
> **Type of Facility:** Arena
> **Type of Stage:** Arena; In-the-round Capability
> **Stage Dimensions:** 25' diameter
> **Seating Capacity:** 189
> **Year Built:** 1967
> **Contact for Rental:** Alton McCloud;   (518) 442-3996

STATE UNIVERSITY OF NEW YORK-ALBANY - MAIN THEATRE
Albany Performing Arts Center, 1400 Washington Avenue, Albany, NY 12222
(518) 442-3995
    Type of Facility: Concert Hall; Auditorium; Theatre House
    Type of Stage: Proscenium; Hydraulic Lift Stage
    Stage Dimensions: 48'Wx37'Dx20'H; add 8'6"D for orchestra pit **Orchestra Pit**
    Seating Capacity: 500
    Year Built: 1967
    Contact for Rental: Alton McCloud; (518) 442-3996
    Resident Groups: State University of New York-Albany Department of Music and Theatre

STATE UNIVERSITY OF NEW YORK-ALBANY - RECITAL HALL
Albany Performing Arts Center, 1400 Washington Avenue, Albany, NY 12222
(518) 442-3995
    Type of Facility: Concert Hall; Recital Hall
    Type of Stage: Proscenium
    Stage Dimensions: 21'Wx24'D
    Seating Capacity: 242
    Year Built: 1967
    Contact for Rental: Alton McCloud; (518) 442-3996
    Resident Groups: State Uiversity of New York-Albany Department of Music

Alfred

PERFORMING SERIES

ALFRED UNIVERSITY
PO Box 781, Alfred, NY 14802
(607) 871-2134
    Founded: 1836
    Arts Area: Dance; Instrumental Music; Theater
    Type: Performing; Educational; Sponsoring
    Purpose: To serve the southern tier of New York state by presenting quality professional performing artists
    Officers: Steven G. Johnson, Director of Arts Programming
    Paid Staff: 3
    Paid Artists: 10
    Utilizes: Guest Artists
    Budget: $50,000 - $100,000
    Income Sources: Private Foundations/Grants/Endowments; Government Grants
    Season: September - April

Amherst

FACILITY

DAEMEN COLLEGE - DAEMEN THEATRE
4380 Main Street, Amherst, NY 14226
(716) 839-3144
    Type of Facility: Theatre House
    Type of Stage: Flexible; Proscenium
    Stage Dimensions: 14'x32'x35'
    Seating Capacity: 120
    Year Built: 1949
    Year Remodeled: 1986 **Cost:** $200,000
    Contact for Rental: Rosalynd Cramer; (716) 839-3144
    Resident Groups: The New Ensemble

Astoria

INSTRUMENTAL MUSIC

GOLIARD CHAMBER SOLOISTS
c/o Goliard Concerts Inc., 21-65 41st Street, Astoria, NY 11105
(718) 728-8927
    Arts Area: Chamber
    Status: Professional; Non-Profit

Type: Performing; Touring; Presenting
Purpose: To perform eclectic chamber music in various vocal and instrumental combinations
Management: Patricia Handy, Artistic Director; Limor Tomer, Executive Director
Officers: Suzanne Gimbrere, President of the Board; Jacqueline Taylor, Vice President
Budget: $50,000 - $100,000
Income Sources: Private Foundations/Grants/Endowments; Business/Corporate Donations; Box Office; Government Grants; Individual Donations
Performance Facilities: Merkin Concert Hall at the Abrahman Goodman House; Steinway Reformed Church, Astoria

Auburn

THEATRE

THE AUBURN PLAYERS COMMUNITY THEATRE
PO Box 543, Auburn, NY 13021
(315) 252-6310
Founded: 1961
Arts Area: Community
Status: Non-Profit
Type: Performing
Purpose: To be a non-profit, educational and cultural organization; to present dramatic productions; to increase appreciation for the theatre
Management: Joseph and Eileen Daloia, Directors
Officers: Cindy Nangle, President
Volunteer Staff: 17
Non-Paid Artists: 100
Budget: $1,000 - $50,000
Income Sources: Private Foundations/Grants/Endowments; Box Office; Individual Donations
Season: July - June   **Annual Attendance:** 3,500

MERRY-GO-ROUND PLAYHOUSE
17 Williams Street, Box 506, Auburn, NY 13021
(315) 255-1305
Founded: 1958
Arts Area: Professional; Musical; Theatrical Group
Status: Professional; Non-Profit
Type: Performing; Touring; Educational
Purpose: To provide quality musical summer stock, experimental contemporary theater and alternative youth theater
Management: Edward Sayles, Producing Director; Karen Buttaro, Business Manager
Paid Staff: 12
Paid Artists: 50
Utilizes: Special Technical Talent; Guest Artists; Guest Directors
Budget: $100,000 - $500,000
Income Sources: Private Foundations/Grants/Endowments; Business/Corporate Donations; Box Office; Government Grants; Individual Donations
Season: June - April   **Annual Attendance:** 120,000
Affiliations: TCG
Performance Facilities: Merry-Go-Round Playhouse

Babylon

THEATRE

MOHAWK PLAYERS
PO Box 382, Babylon, NY 11702
(516) 669-7605
Founded: 1954
Arts Area: Community
Status: Non-Profit
Type: Performing; Touring
Purpose: To bring live theatre to various groups at library locations
Officers: Kathleen Ryerson, President
Paid Artists: 1   **Non-Paid Artists:** 10
Budget: $1,000 - $50,000
Income Sources: Box Office; Government Grants; Individual Donations

Season: 52 Weeks   **Annual Attendance:** 3,000
Affiliations: NYSCA

Bayside

VOCAL MUSIC

THE QUEENSBOROUGH CHORUS
c/o Music Department, Queensborough Community College, Bayside, NY 11364
(718) 631-6394
FAX: (718) 423-9620
    Founded: 1970
    Arts Area: Choral
    Status: Non-Professional; Non-Profit
    Type: Performing; Educational
    Purpose: To provide opportunities for performance of choral works of all eras to students and the community; to bring artistic performances to the community
    Management: R. John Specht, Director
    Paid Staff: 2   **Volunteer Staff:** 1
    Utilizes: Guest Artists
    Budget: $1,000 - $50,000
    Income Sources: Private Foundations/Grants/Endowments; Business/Corporate Donations; Box Office; Individual Donations
    Season: September - June   **Annual Attendance:** 1,200
    Performance Facilities: Queensborough Community College Theater

FACILITY

QUEENSBOROUGH COMMUNITY COLLEGE THEATER
222-05 56th Avenue near Springfield Boulevard, Bayside, NY 11364-1497
(718) 631-6311; (718) 631-6321
FAX: (718) 428-0802
    Type of Facility: Concert Hall; Auditorium; Studio Performance; Off-Broadway; Theatre House; Opera House; Multi-Purpose
    Type of Stage: Proscenium   **Orchestra Pit**
    Seating Capacity: 875
    Year Built: 1967
    Contact for Rental: Anthony Carobine;   (718) 631-6321

Bearsville

THEATRE

RIVER ARTS REPERTORY
Route 212, Bearsville, NY 12409
(914) 679-2100
FAX: (914) 679-9239
    Founded: 1979
    Arts Area: Professional; Summer Stock; Theatrical Group; Puppet
    Status: Professional; Non-Profit
    Type: Performing; Sponsoring
    Purpose: To present fresh interpretations of classic plays; to develop innovative new plays
    Management: Lawrence Sacharow, Michael Cristofer, Co-Artistic Directors; Albert Idhe, Managing Director
    Officers: Carol Ricken, Chairman of Board
    Paid Staff: 5   **Volunteer Staff:** 25
    Utilizes: Special Technical Talent; Guest Artists; Guest Directors
    Budget: $100,000 - $500,000
    Income Sources: Private Foundations/Grants/Endowments; Business/Corporate Donations; Box Office; Government Grants; Individual Donations
    Season: June - September   **Annual Attendance:** 5,000
    Affiliations: AEA; TCG
    Performance Facilities: Bearsville Theatre

Binghamton

INSTRUMENTAL MUSIC

B.C. POPS
1 Marine Midland Plaza, 6th Floor, West Tower, Binghamton, NY 13901
(607) 724-0007
FAX: (607) 777-0902
Founded: 1976
Arts Area: Orchestra; Pops/Popular Selections
Status: Professional; Non-Profit
Type: Performing
Management: W. Mack Richardson, Executive Director; David L. Agard, Conductor/Artistic Director
Officers: Edwin C. Gent, President, Board of Directors
Paid Staff: 5   **Volunteer Staff:** 5
Paid Artists: 65
Utilizes: Guest Artists
Income Sources: Private Foundations/Grants/Endowments; Business/Corporate Donations; Box Office; Government Grants; Individual Donations
Season: October - July
Affiliations: B.C. Pops Chorus
Performance Facilities: Forum Theatre

BINGHAMTON SYMPHONY ORCHESTRA AND CHORAL SOCIETY
315 Clinton Street, Binghamton, NY 13905
(607) 729-3444
FAX: (607) 797-6344
Founded: 1954
Arts Area: Symphony; Orchestra
Status: Professional; Semi-Professional; Non-Profit
Type: Performing; Touring; Educational
Purpose: To bring high quality symphonic orchestral music to this community and the surrounding area
Management: Nancy Marshall, Executive Director; John Covelli, Music Director/Conductor; Rosemary Henkle, Director of Subscriptions; Marilyn Sall, Director of Publicity; Susan Stanhope, Office Manager; Betty Warner, Director of Marketing
Officers: Lillian Levy Esq., President; Louise Akel, David Howard, Vice Presidents; Joseph Nishimura, Treasurer
Paid Staff: 7   **Volunteer Staff:** 200
Paid Artists: 80
Utilizes: Guest Artists
Budget: $100,000 - $500,000
Income Sources: Private Foundations/Grants/Endowments; Business/Corporate Donations; Box Office; Government Grants; Individual Donations
Season: September - May   **Annual Attendance:** 15,000
Affiliations: ASOL
Performance Facilities: The Forum Theatre

BINGHAMTON YOUTH SYMPHONY
26 Murray, Binghamton, NY 13905
(607) 722-7150
Founded: 1962
Arts Area: Symphony
Status: Non-Professional; Non-Profit
Type: Performing; Touring; Educational
Purpose: Offering music and performance opportunities not found in the regular music curriculum of Binghamton area schools, membership in the Senior and Junior Orchestras is determined by auditions held three times annually and draws musicians from 20 area schools.
Management: Bernard J, Shifrin, Music Director/Conductor; Russell Colton, Junior Orchestra Music Director
Officers: Leonard Hoover, President; Philip Westcott, Vice President; Dana Thurston, Treasurer
Paid Staff: 2   **Volunteer Staff:** 13
Non-Paid Artists: 160
Budget: $1,000 - $50,000
Income Sources: Private Foundations/Grants/Endowments; Business/Corporate Donations; Box Office; Individual Donations
Season: September - June   **Annual Attendance:** 10,000
Affiliations: Binghamton Symphony; Broome County Arts Council; B.C. Pops; Tri-Cities Opera; Binghampton Symphony
Performance Facilities: West Middle School

VOCAL MUSIC

TRI-CITIES OPERA COMPANY
315 Clinton Street, Binghamton, NY 13905
(607) 729-3444
FAX: (607) 797-6344
Founded: 1949
Arts Area: Grand Opera
Status: Professional; Non-Profit
Type: Performing; Resident; Educational
Management: Carmen Savoca, Peyton Hibbitt, Artistic Directors; Richard Hook, Interim Director
Officers: Chuck Ungraham, President; George Akel, First Vice President; Sandra Perkins, Second First President; John Westcott, Treasurer; Stephanie Franck, Secretary
Paid Staff: 13 **Volunteer Staff:** 25
Paid Artists: 30 **Non-Paid Artists:** 50
Utilizes: Guest Artists
Budget: $500,000 - $1,000,000
Income Sources: Private Foundations/Grants/Endowments; Business/Corporate Donations; Box Office; Government Grants; Individual Donations
Season: September - May **Annual Attendance:** 13,500
Affiliations: AGMA; AFM; IATSE
Performance Facilities: Broome County Forum

PERFORMING SERIES

BINGHAMTON SUMMER MUSIC FESTIVAL, INC.
PO Box 112 SVS, Binghamton, NY 13903
(607) 777-4777
FAX: (607) 777-4000
Founded: 1984
Arts Area: Dance; Vocal Music; Instrumental Music; Festivals
Status: Non-Profit
Type: Performing; Educational
Purpose: To provide an annual summer performing arts program for audiences in New York's Southern Tier
Management: David K. Patterson, Executive Director; Ethan Lercher, Assistant Director
Officers: Gary E. Lind, President; Thomas E. Bell, Vice President; Peter C. Cronk, Secretary; Donald H. Weber, Treasurer
Paid Staff: 2 **Volunteer Staff:** 30
Utilizes: Guest Conductors; Guest Artists
Budget: $100,000 - $500,000
Income Sources: Private Foundations/Grants/Endowments; Business/Corporate Donations; Box Office; Government Grants; Individual Donations
Season: July - August **Annual Attendance:** 12,000
Performance Facilities: Anderson Center for Performing Arts, SUNY Binghamton

FACILITY

BROOME CENTER FOR THE PRFORMING ARTS - THE FORUM
236 Washington Street, Binghamton, NY 13901
(607) 778-2480
FAX: (607) 778-6041
Founded: 1975
Type of Facility: Concert Hall; Theatre House; Opera House
Facility Originally: Vaudeville
Type of Stage: Proscenium
Stage Dimensions: 38'6"Wx24'6"H proscenium opening; 36'D includes 4" apron **Orchestra Pit**
Seating Capacity: 1,519
Year Built: 1919
Year Remodeled: 1974 **Architect:** Cummings and Pash
Contact for Rental: Christine A. Springer; (607) 778-2480
Resident Groups: Binghamton Symphony Orchestra; BC Pops Orchestra; Tri-Cities Opera; Broadway Theatre League of Binghampton

STATE UNIVERSITY OF NEW YORK-BINGHAMPTON - CHAMBER HALL
Anderson Center for the Arts, PO Box 6000, Binghamton, NY 13902-6000
(607) 777-6802
Type of Facility: Concert Hall; Theatre House
Type of Stage: Proscenium
Stage Dimensions: 62'Wx27'D **Orchestra Pit**

Seating Capacity: 430
Year Built: 1985   **Architect:** Hutchins Evans & Lefferts
Acoustical Consultant: Paul S. Veneklasen & Associates
Contact for Rental: Floyd Herzog;   (607) 777-6802

STATE UNIVERSITY OF NEW YORK-BINGHAMPTON - CONCERT THEATRE
Anderson Center for the Arts, PO Box 6000, Binghamton, NY 13902-6000
(607) 777-6802
Type of Facility: Theatre House; Amphitheater
Type of Stage: Proscenium
Stage Dimensions: 92'Wx38'6"D   **Orchestra Pit**
Seating Capacity: 1,200 with 24 wheelchair spaces
Year Built: 1985   **Architect:** Hutchins Evans & Lefferts
Acoustical Consultant: Paul S. Veneklasen & Associates
Contact for Rental: Floyd Herzog;   (607) 777-6802
Rear wall opens to provide outdoor audience space

Blue Mountain Lake

FACILITY

ADIRONDACK LAKES CENTER FOR THE ARTS
PO Box 101, Blue Mountain Lake, NY 12812
(518) 352-7715
Type of Facility: Concert Hall; Performance Center; Theatre House; Multi-Purpose; Room
Facility Originally: Garage
Type of Stage: Platform
Stage Dimensions: 25'x30'
Seating Capacity: 200
Year Built: 1936
Year Remodeled: 1967

Brentwood

FACILITY

SUFFOLK COUNTY COMMUNITY COLLEGE - SAQTIKOS THEATRE
Crooked Hill Road, Brentwood, NY 11717
(516) 451-4163
Type of Facility: Theatre House
Type of Stage: Proscenium
Stage Dimensions: 36'x40'   **Orchestra Pit**
Seating Capacity: 474
Year Built: 1989

Brockport

INSTRUMENTAL MUSIC

BROCKPORT SYMPHONY ORCHESTRA
PO Box 344, Brockport, NY 14420
(716) 637-2115
Founded: 1966
Arts Area: Symphony
Status: Semi-Professional; Non-Profit
Type: Performing
Purpose: To provide fine music for the Western Monroe County Area, at times in joint performances with the Greece Symphony and the Geneseo Chamber Symphony
Management: James Walker, Music Director; Mary Edwards, Business Manager
Paid Staff: 2   **Volunteer Staff:** 17
Paid Artists: 6   **Non-Paid Artists:** 45
Utilizes: Guest Artists
Budget: $1,000 - $50,000
Income Sources: Private Foundations/Grants/Endowments; Business/Corporate Donations; Box Office; Individual Donations
Season: September - May   **Annual Attendance:** 1,000

Affiliations: Arts For Greater Rochester
Performance Facilities: Tower Fine Arts Center, State University of New York-Brockport

FACILITY

STATE UNIVERSITY OF NEW YORK COLLEGE-BROCKPORT - TOWER FINE ARTS CENTER
Department of Dance, Brockport, NY 14420
(716) 395-2153
Type of Facility: Theatre House
Type of Stage: Proscenium
Stage Dimensions: 30'Wx35'L
Seating Capacity: 450
Year Remodeled: 1972
Contact for Rental: Chairman, Department of Dance;   (716) 395-2153
Resident Groups: Danscore; Brockport Dance Department; Brockport Symphony Orchestra

Bronx

INSTRUMENTAL MUSIC

BRONX ARTS ENSEMBLE INC.
c/o Golf House, Van Cortland Park, Bronx, NY 10471
(212) 601-7399
FAX: (212) 549-4008
Arts Area: Symphony; Chamber
Status: Professional; Non-Profit
Type: Performing; Resident; Educational
Purpose: To bring chamber music programs and chamber orchestras to a variety of locations in the Bronx at affordable prices
Management: William Scribner, Artistic Director
Officers: Gail McMillan, Chairman of the Board
Budget: $100,000 - $500,000
Income Sources: Private Foundations/Grants/Endowments; Business/Corporate Donations; Box Office; Government Grants; Individual Donations
Performance Facilities: Fordham University

VOCAL MUSIC

BRONX OPERA COMPANY
5 Minerva Place, Apt 2J, Bronx, NY 10468
(212) 365-4209
Founded: 1967
Arts Area: Grand Opera; Lyric Opera; Light Opera; Operetta
Status: Semi-Professional; Non-Profit
Type: Performing
Purpose: To bring high-quality, full opera productions, in English with an orchestra, to the community; to give excellent young performers the opportunity for experience and exposure
Management: Michael Spierman, Artistic Director
Non-Paid Artists: 120
Budget: $100,000 - $500,000
Income Sources: Private Foundations/Grants/Endowments; Business/Corporate Donations; Government Grants; Individual Donations
Season: September - June   Annual Attendance: 10,000
Performance Facilities: Lehman College Theatre; John Jay College Theatre

THEATRE

PREGONES THEATER
295 St. Ann's Avenue, Bronx, NY 10454
(212) 585-1202
FAX: (212) 585-1608
Founded: 1979
Arts Area: Theatrical Group
Status: Professional; Non-Profit
Type: Performing; Touring

Purpose: To provide bilingual theatre programming primarily for Latino audiences; to present a wide range of professional artists at the theatre
Management: Rosalba Rolon, Executive Director; Aluan Colon, Judith Rivera, Jorge Merced, Associate Directors
Officers: Harold A. Stella, Chairman of the Board; Ada Brinas, Treasurer; Sistuido Benitez, Vice Chairman; Elmer Sanchez, Secretary
Paid Staff: 7 **Volunteer Staff:** 9
Paid Artists: 11
Utilizes: Guest Artists; Guest Directors; Resident Artists
Budget: $100,000 - $500,000
Income Sources: Private Foundations/Grants/Endowments; Business/Corporate Donations; Box Office; Government Grants; Individual Donations; Contracted Tours
Season: September - May

Bronxville

DANCE

ELLEN KOGAN SOLO DANCE
14 McIntyre Street, Bronxville, NY 10708
(914) 337-6063
Status: Professional; Non-Profit
Type: Performing; Touring; Resident; Educational
Purpose: To promote and preserve solo dance as an integral part of the art of contemporary dance; to contribute to the heritage of modern dance by adding reconstructions of modern dance classics to the repertoire; to bring historic dances to life for contemporary audiences
Management: Kathryn Wolf, Manager; Mark Mongold, Technical Director
Budget: $1,000 - $50,000
Income Sources: Private Foundations/Grants/Endowments; Government Grants; Booking Fees

Brooklyn

DANCE

BEVERLY BLOSSOM AND COMPANY
311 Ocean Parkway, #125, Brooklyn, NY 11235
(718) 266-1286
Founded: 1981
Arts Area: Modern; Theater Dance
Status: Professional
Type: Performing; Touring
Management: Circum-Arts, Inc.
Officers: Beverly Blossom, Director
Paid Artists: 5
Budget: $1,000 - $50,000
Income Sources: Private Foundations/Grants/Endowments; Box Office; Government Grants; Individual Donations
Season: September - May
Affiliations: Circum-Arts, Inc.
Performance Facilities: Dance Theatre Workshop

BROOKLYN CENTER FOR THE PERFORMING ARTS AT BROOKLYN COLLEGE
c/o College Community Services Inc., PO Box 163, Brooklyn, NY 11210
(718) 258-5291
FAX: (718) 258-3475
Arts Area: Modern; Mime; Ballet; Jazz; Ethnic; Folk
Status: Non-Profit
Type: Educational; Sponsoring
Purpose: To provide world-famous artists and ensembles at affordable prices
Management: David Levenson, Managing Director; Richard Grossberg, General Manager
Officers: William Slapin, President of the Board
Budget: $1,000,000 - $5,000,000
Income Sources: Private Foundations/Grants/Endowments; Business/Corporate Donations; Box Office; Government Grants; Individual Donations

Season: 52 Weeks
Performance Facilities: Whitman Hall

CHARLES MOORE - DANCES AND DRUMS OF AFRICA
1043 President Street, Brooklyn, NY 11225
(718) 467-7127
Arts Area: Modern; Jazz; Ethnic
Status: Professional; Non-Profit
Type: Performing; Touring; Educational
Purpose: To promote the spiritual, social and physical welfare of individuals pursuing research and studies in the field of African and Afro-American dance and music
Management: Ella Thompson-Moore, Artistic Director; Pam Mitchell-Yarber, Executive Director; Marina Lynk, Company Director
Paid Staff: 3
Paid Artists: 20
Utilizes: Special Technical Talent; Guest Artists
Income Sources: Box Office; Government Grants
Affiliations: NEA; Brooklyn Arts and Culture Association; New York Division of the Humanities, Education Department
Performance Facilities: Charles Moore Center for Ethnic Studies

DANCEWAVE, INC. (THE DIANE JACOBOWITZ DANCE THEATER)
72 Seventh Avenue, Brooklyn, NY 11217
(718) 622-1810
Founded: 1979
Arts Area: Modern
Status: Professional
Type: Performing; Touring; Resident; Educational; Sponsoring
Paid Artists: 6
Utilizes: Special Technical Talent; Guest Artists; Guest Choreographers
Budget: $1,000 - $50,000
Income Sources: Private Foundations/Grants/Endowments; Business/Corporate Donations; Box Office; Government Grants; Individual Donations
Performance Facilities: Long Island University-Triangle Theater

JUBILATION DANCE COMPANY
PO Box 401804, Brooklyn, NY 11240-1804
(718) 237-0634
Founded: 1982
Arts Area: Modern; Ballet; Jazz; Ethnic
Status: Professional; Non-Profit
Type: Performing; Touring
Purpose: To support individuals in realizing their creative potential
Management: Laverne Jeff, Managing Director
Paid Staff: 2   Volunteer Staff: 5
Paid Artists: 11
Utilizes: Special Technical Talent; Guest Conductors; Guest Artists; Guest Directors
Budget: $100,000 - $500,000
Income Sources: Private Foundations/Grants/Endowments; Business/Corporate Donations; Box Office; Government Grants; Individual Donations
Season: October - November

MARTHA BOWERS' DANCE THEATRE
143 Bond Street, Brooklyn, NY 11217
(718) 858-0841
Founded: 1976
Arts Area: Modern
Status: Professional; Non-Profit
Type: Performing; Touring; Resident
Purpose: To perform contemporary dance theatre works
Management: Martha Bowers, Artistic Director
Paid Staff: 1
Paid Artists: 12
Utilizes: Guest Artists
Budget: $1,000 - $50,000
Income Sources: Private Foundations/Grants/Endowments; Box Office; Government Grants; Individual Donations
Season: 52 Weeks
Affiliations: Dancing in the Streets; Mayfair

INSTRUMENTAL MUSIC

THE BROOKLYN PHILHARMONIC
30 Lafayette Avenue, Brooklyn, NY 11217
(718) 622-1000
FAX: (718) 857-2021
Founded: 1954
Arts Area: Symphony; Orchestra; Chamber; Ensemble; Ethnic
Status: Professional; Non-Profit
Type: Performing; Educational
Purpose: To bring the best in standard and modern repertoire at the lowest possible prices and best performance level to the borough of Brooklyn and Greater New York, as well as free concerts to the general public in the parks and in the schools
Management: Vicki Margulies, Executive Director; Maurice Edwards, Artistic Director; Jana Strauss, Director of Development; Eric Klein, Operations Manager/Education Director
Officers: Stanley H. Kaplan, Chairman of the Board; Robert C. Rosenberg, President; I. Stanley Kriegel, Honorary Chairman; Richard Kane, Treasurer; Craig Matthews and John Tamberlane, Executive Vice Presidents
Paid Staff: 7   **Volunteer Staff:** 3
Paid Artists: 100
Utilizes: Guest Conductors; Guest Artists
Budget: $1,000,000 - $5,000,000
Income Sources: Private Foundations/Grants/Endowments; Business/Corporate Donations; Box Office; Government Grants; Individual Donations
Annual Attendance: 125,000
Affiliations: Brooklyn Academy of Music
Performance Facilities: Brooklyn Academy of Music

MANHATTAN MARIMBA QUARTET
160 North Fourth Street, Brooklyn, NY 11211
(201) 567-8108
Arts Area: Chamber; Ensemble
Status: Professional; Non-Profit
Type: Performing; Touring; Resident; Educational
Purpose: To perform music that spans eight centuries and many different styles, spotlighting the beauty, individuality and versatility of the marimba as a concert instrument
Management: Sheila Rizzo, Manager
Budget: $1,000 - $50,000
Income Sources: Private Foundations/Grants/Endowments; Business/Corporate Donations; Box Office; Government Grants; Individual Donations

S.E.M. ENSEMBLE
25 Columbia Place, Brooklyn, NY 11201
(718) 243-0964
FAX: (718) 243-0964
Arts Area: Orchestra; Chamber
Status: Professional
Type: Performing; Touring; Resident; Educational
Purpose: To perform new music; education in new music
Officers: William J. Buckley, President; John Maggiotto, Secretary; Petr Kotik, Artistic Director
Paid Staff: 2   **Volunteer Staff:** 3
Paid Artists: 30
Budget: $50,000 - $100,000
Income Sources: Private Foundations/Grants/Endowments; Business/Corporate Donations; Box Office; Government Grants; Individual Donations
Season: September - June   **Annual Attendance:** 1,500
Performance Facilities: Willow Place Auditorium

VOCAL MUSIC

IL PICCOLO TEATRO DELL'OPERA, INC.
118 Pierrepont Street, Brooklyn, NY 11201-2768
(718) 643-7775
FAX: (718) 855-4751
Founded: 1984
Arts Area: Grand Opera; Lyric Opera; Light Opera; Piccolo Teatro
Status: Professional
Type: Performing; Educational
Purpose: To develop new audiences for opera/theatre and nurture emerging careers

Management: Barbara Elliot, General Director/Artistic Director
Officers: Stephen Zelnick, Chairman; Barbara Elliot, President; Nancy Lowendahl, Secretary
Paid Staff: 3 **Volunteer Staff:** 10
Paid Artists: 100
Utilizes: Special Technical Talent; Guest Conductors; Guest Artists; Guest Directors
Budget: $100,000 - $500,000
Income Sources: Private Foundations/Grants/Endowments; Business/Corporate Donations; Box Office; Government Grants; Individual Donations
Season: 52 Weeks **Annual Attendance:** 25,000
Performance Facilities: Brooklyn Academy of Music

QUEENS OPERA ASSOCIATION
313 Bay 14th Street, Brooklyn, NY 11214
(718) 256-6045
FAX: (718) 837-8726
Founded: 1961
Arts Area: Grand Opera
Status: Professional; Non-Profit
Type: Performing; Touring; Resident
Purpose: To present opera and concerts to communities where it is not available; to discover new voices
Management: Joseph Messina, General Director
Officers: Jerry Cannon, President; Michael Callaghan, Vice President; Fran Callaghan, Secretary
Paid Staff: 2 **Volunteer Staff:** 10
Paid Artists: 60
Utilizes: Guest Conductors; Guest Artists
Budget: $100,000 - $500,000
Income Sources: Private Foundations/Grants/Endowments; Business/Corporate Donations; Box Office; Government Grants; Individual Donations
Season: October - July **Annual Attendance:** 14,000
Performance Facilities: Saint John's University Auditorium

REGINA OPERA COMPANY
1251 Tabor Court, Brooklyn, NY 11219
(718) 232-3555
FAX: (718) 232-3555
Founded: 1971
Arts Area: Grand Opera; Lyric Opera; Light Opera; Operetta
Status: Semi-Professional; Non-Profit
Type: Performing
Purpose: To provide a training ground for young porfessionals and showcase more experienced performers and directors
Officers: Marie Cantoni, President; Francine Garber-Cohen, Executive Vice President; Linda Cantoni, Vice President/Legal Advisor; Selma Tepper, Secretary
Utilizes: Guest Conductors; Guest Artists; Guest Directors
Budget: $1,000 - $50,000
Income Sources: Business/Corporate Donations; Box Office; Individual Donations; Brooklyn Arts Council
Season: September - June **Annual Attendance:** 4,000
Performance Facilities: Regina Hall

THEATRE

ADELPHIAN PLAYERS
8515 Ridge Boulevard, Brooklyn, NY 11209
(718) 238-3308
FAX: (718) 238-2894
Founded: 1964
Arts Area: Summer Stock; Theatrical Group
Status: Non-Professional
Type: Performing; Educational
Purpose: To bring theatre to the people of Brooklyn
Management: Russel Bonanno, Artistic Director; Philip Stone, Business Manager
Volunteer Staff: 10
Non-Paid Artists: 25
Utilizes: Guest Artists; Guest Directors
Budget: $1,000 - $50,000
Income Sources: Private Foundations/Grants/Endowments; Business/Corporate Donations; Box Office; Government Grants; Individual Donations
Season: June - August
Performance Facilities: Adelphi Academy

BILLIE HOLIDAY THEATRE
1368 Fulton Street, Brooklyn, NY 11216
(718) 636-0919
FAX: (718) 636-6956
Founded: 1972
Arts Area: Theatrical Group
Status: Professional; Non-Profit
Type: Performing; Resident
Purpose: To provide trained Black artists with a professional environment; to present theatre that educates and enlightens the community
Management: Marjorie Moon, Executive Director
Utilizes: Special Technical Talent; Guest Artists; Guest Directors
Budget: $100,000 - $500,000
Income Sources: Box Office; Government Grants; Individual Donations
Season: 52 Weeks

CONEY ISLAND, USA
1205-11 Boardwalk at West 12th Street, Brooklyn, NY 11224
(718) 372-5159
Founded: 1980
Arts Area: Professional; Musical; Theatrical Group
Status: Professional; Non-Profit
Type: Performing; Educational; Sponsoring
Purpose: To champion the honor of American popular art forms through innovative exhibitions and performances
Management: Dick D. Zigun, Artistic Director; Valerie Haller, Design Director
Officers: Dick D. Zigun, President
Paid Staff: 4 **Volunteer Staff:** 6
Paid Artists: 50 **Non-Paid Artists:** 100
Utilizes: Special Technical Talent; Guest Artists
Budget: $100,000 - $500,000
Income Sources: Private Foundations/Grants/Endowments; Business/Corporate Donations; Box Office; Government Grants; Individual Donations
Season: March - Decemer **Annual Attendance:** 100,000
Affiliations: ART/NY; TCG

INTERBOROUGH REPERTORY THEATER (IRT)
467 Pacific Street, #6, Brooklyn, NY 11217
(718) 522-2858
Founded: 1986
Arts Area: Musical; Theatrical Group
Status: Semi-Professional; Non-Profit; Non-AEA
Type: Performing; Touring; Educational
Purpose: To present issues of current interest or adaptions of literature/history to the disenfranchised audience; to showcase standard repertory to general audiences
Management: Luane Davis, Artistic Director; Jonathan Fluck, General Manager; Stephanie Trudeau, Publicity; Suan Mondzak, Fund-raising
Paid Staff: 2 **Volunteer Staff:** 3
Paid Artists: 30
Utilizes: Special Technical Talent; Guest Artists; Guest Directors
Budget: $100,000 - $500,000
Income Sources: Private Foundations/Grants/Endowments; Business/Corporate Donations; Box Office; Government Grants; Individual Donations; Performance Fees
Season: August - June **Annual Attendance:** 200,000
Affiliations: Brooklyn Arts and Cultural Association; AEA; Encore; Saturaday Theater for Children, Division of American Theater Wing

MARGOLIS BROWN ADAPTORS
397 Bridge Street, 2nd Floor, Brooklyn, NY 11201
(718) 797-3930
Founded: 1983
Arts Area: Professional; Theatrical Group; Multimedia Movement Theatre
Status: Professional; Non-Profit
Type: Performing; Touring; Resident; Educational; Sponsoring; Dramatic Movement School
Purpose: To create original multimedia movement theatre productions; to share video editing studio and facility with other artists at low cost
Management: Beverly Perlman, Touring/Performance Manager; Tony Brown, Artistic/Executive Director; Kari Margolis, Artistic/Executive Director
Officers: Olympia Dukakis; Ted Killmer; Lauren Farber; Anna Salmi; Luke Gordon

Paid Staff: 3   **Volunteer Staff:** 5
Paid Artists: 10
Utilizes: Special Technical Talent; Guest Artists
Budget: $100,000 - $500,000
Income Sources: Private Foundations/Grants/Endowments; Business/Corporate Donations; Box Office; Government Grants; Individual Donations; School; Video/Recording Studio
Season: 52 Weeks   **Annual Attendance:** 2,000
Affiliations: NMTA

RYAN REPERTORY COMPANY AT HARRY WARREN THEATRE
2445 Bath Avenue, Brooklyn, NY 11214
(718) 996-4800
Founded: 1972
Arts Area: Professional; Musical; Theatrical Group
Status: Professional; Non-Profit
Type: Performing; Resident
Purpose: To develop new musicals, and to work on new plays for playwrights' purposes
Management: Barbara Parisi, Executive Director; Jonathan Rosenblum, Producing Director; John Sannuto, Artistic Director
Volunteer Staff: 15
Paid Artists: 50   **Non-Paid Artists:** 150
Utilizes: Guest Artists; Guest Directors
Budget: $1,000 - $50,000
Income Sources: Private Foundations/Grants/Endowments; Business/Corporate Donations; Box Office; Government Grants; Individual Donations
Season: 52 Weeks   **Annual Attendance:** 5,000
Performance Facilities: Harry Warren Theatre

PERFORMING SERIES

BARGEMUSIC LTD.
Fulton Ferry Landing, Brooklyn, NY 11201
(718) 624-4061
FAX: (718) 596-7137
Founded: 1977
Arts Area: Instrumental Music
Status: Non-Profit
Type: Performing
Purpose: To present chamber music concerts throughout the year in concert space in a barge permantly moored in New York Harbor
Management: Olga Bloom, President; Ik-Hwan Bae, Artistic Director; Margaret Barclay, Executive Director
Paid Staff: 8
Paid Artists: 100
Budget: $500,000 - $1,000,000
Income Sources: Private Foundations/Grants/Endowments; Business/Corporate Donations; Box Office; Government Grants; Individual Donations
Season: 52 Weeks   **Annual Attendance:** 10,000
Affiliations: CMA

BROOKLYN ACADEMY OF MUSIC
30 Lafayette Avenue, Brooklyn, NY 11217-1486
(718) 636-4100
Founded: 1861
Arts Area: Dance; Vocal Music; Instrumental Music; Theater; Festivals
Status: Professional; Non-Profit
Type: Performing; Touring; Educational; Sponsoring
Purpose: BAM's programming policy involves a commitment to provide our audiences with quality performing arts, new and innovative theatre, and dance and music, both foreign and domestic, as well as diversified choices in all areas at affordable and accessible prices.
Management: Harvey Lichtenstein, Executive Producer; Judith E. Daykin, Managing Director; Karen Hopkins, Planning/Development; Richard Balzano, Finance; Doug Allan, Promotion/Marketing
Officers: Neil Chrisman, Chairman of the Board; Rita Hillman, Franklin Weissberg, I. Stanley Kriegel, Vice Chairmen; Harvey Lichtenstein, President; David Kleiser, Vice President; Judith E. Daykin, Executive Vice President; Richard Balzano, Treasurer
Paid Staff: 100
Paid Artists: 500
Utilizes: Special Technical Talent; Guest Conductors; Guest Artists; Guest Directors
Budget: $5,000,000 - $10,000,000

Income Sources: Private Foundations/Grants/Endowments; Business/Corporate Donations; Box Office; Government Grants; Individual Donations
Season: October - June **Annual Attendance:** 250,000
Affiliations: New York Department of Cultural Affairs
Performance Facilities: Brooklyn Academy of Music

CELEBRATE BROOKLYN FESTIVAL
16 Court Street, Suite 1400W, Brooklyn, NY 11241
(718) 855-7882
Founded: 1979
Arts Area: Dance; Vocal Music; Instrumental Music; Theater; Festivals
Status: Professional; Non-Profit
Type: Performing
Purpose: To identify and present professional music, theater and dance reflecting the international community of Brooklyn, and produce original music, dance and theatre
Management: Stacey Temple, Producer
Officers: Ninetta Rain, President
Paid Staff: 15
Paid Artists: 300
Budget: $100,000 - $500,000
Income Sources: Private Foundations/Grants/Endowments; Business/Corporate Donations; Box Office; Government Grants; Individual Donations
Annual Attendance: 100,000
Performance Facilities: Prospect Park Bandshell and Picnic House

FACILITY

BROOKLYN ACADEMY OF MUSIC
30 Lafayette Avenue, Brooklyn, NY 11217-1486
(718) 636-4100
FAX: (718) 857-2021
Type of Facility: Theatre Complex; School
Year Built: 1907 **Architect:** Herts & Tallant **Cost:** $1,500,000
Year Remodeled: 1975 **Architect:** Hardy Holzman Pfeiffer
Acoustical Consultant: Peter George; Christopher Jaffe
Contact for Rental: Lynn Moffat; (718) 636-4195
Manager: Laurie Sackler
Resident Groups: Brooklyn Philharmonic
Brooklyn Academy of Music contains Carey Playhouse, Lepercq Space and the Opera House. See separate listings for additional information.

BROOKLYN ACADEMY OF MUSIC - CAREY PLAYHOUSE
30 Lafayette Avenue, Brooklyn, NY 11217-1486
(718) 636-4100
FAX: (718) 857-2021
Type of Facility: Concert Hall; Theatre House
Type of Stage: Thrust; Proscenium
Stage Dimensions: 38'Wx31'D
Seating Capacity: 1,011
Year Built: 1907
Year Remodeled: 1975 **Architect:** Hardy Holzman Pfeiffer
Acoustical Consultant: Peter George; Christopher Jaffe
Contact for Rental: Lynn Moffat; (718) 636-4195
Manager: Laurie Sackler
Resident Groups: Brooklyn Philharmonic

BROOKLYN ACADEMY OF MUSIC - LEPERCQ SPACE
30 Lafayette Avenue, Brooklyn, NY 11217-1486
(718) 636-4100
FAX: (718) 857-2021
Type of Facility: Theatre House; Multi-Purpose
Facility Originally: Ballroom
Type of Stage: Flexible
Stage Dimensions: 125'Wx42'Dx35'H
Seating Capacity: 550
Year Built: 1907
Year Remodeled: 1973 **Architect:** Edward Knoles
Acoustical Consultant: Peter George

Contact for Rental: Lynn Moffat; (718) 636-4195
Manager: Laurie Sackler

BROOKLYN ACADEMY OF MUSIC - OPERA HOUSE
30 Lafayette Avenue, Brooklyn, NY 11217-1486
(718) 636-4100
FAX: (718) 857-2021
    Type of Facility: Opera House
    Type of Stage: Proscenium
    Stage Dimensions: 47'Wx47'D   **Orchestra Pit**
    Seating Capacity: 2,086
    Year Built: 1907
    Contact for Rental: Lynn Moffat; (718) 636-4195
    Manager: Laurie Sackler
    Resident Groups: Brooklyn Philharmonic

PRATT INSTITUTE - AUDITORIUM
200 Willoughby Avenue, Brooklyn, NY 11205
(718) 636-3422
    Type of Facility: Auditorium
    Type of Stage: Proscenium
    Seating Capacity: 555
    Contact for Rental: Jeff Kessler; (718) 636-3422

Buffalo

INSTRUMENTAL MUSIC

AMHERST SAXOPHONE QUARTET
PO Box 101, Buffalo, NY 14207-0101
(716) 832-7411
FAX: (716) 832-7411
    Founded: 1978
    Arts Area: Chamber; Ensemble; Instrumental Group
    Status: Professional; Non-Profit
    Type: Performing; Touring; Resident; Educational
    Purpose: To maintain an international touring quartet; to promote new music
    Management: Ethel Siegel, Siegel Artists Management; Stephen Rosenthal, Executive Director Amherst Saxophone Society, Inc.; Tom Gallant, Director
    Officers: Eleanor Millonzi, President; Harry R. Stainrook, Vice President; Michael Swart, Secretary; Felix Gramza, Treasurer
    Paid Staff: 1   **Volunteer Staff:** 18
    Paid Artists: 4
    Utilizes: Guest Artists
    Budget: $100,000 - $500,000
    Income Sources: Private Foundations/Grants/Endowments; Business/Corporate Donations; Box Office; Government Grants; Individual Donations; Touring Fees
    Season: 52 Weeks   **Annual Attendance:** 50,000
    Performance Facilities: Rockwell Hall

ARS NOVA MUSICIANS CHAMBER ORCHESTRA
136 Goethe Street, Buffalo, NY 14206
    Founded: 1974
    Status: Professional
    Type: Performing
    Purpose: To provide a 16-member chamber orchestra, most members belonging to the Buffalo Philharmonic
    Management: Marylouise Nanna, Music Director; Susan Willet, Managing Director

BUFFALO PHILHARMONIC ORCHESTRA
71 Symphony Circle, PO Box 905, Buffalo, NY 14222
(716) 885-0331
FAX: (716) 885-9372
    Founded: 1936
    Arts Area: Symphony; Orchestra; Chamber; Ethnic
    Status: Professional; Non-Profit
    Type: Performing; Touring; Educational

Purpose: To provide a resident, professional, major symphony orchestra of artistic excellence and integrity to enrich the quality of life in western New York through the presentation of live symphonic music and other music events which will educate and entertain the broadest audiences possible
Management: Michael Tiknis, Excutive Director; Maximiano Valdes, Music Director; Lynn Osmond, General Manager; Doc Severinsen, Principal Pops Conductor
Officers: Andrew Rudnick, Chairman
Paid Staff: 21   **Volunteer Staff:** 600
Paid Artists: 300
Utilizes: Special Technical Talent; Guest Conductors; Guest Artists; Guest Directors
Budget: $5,000,000 - $10,000,000
Income Sources: Private Foundations/Grants/Endowments; Business/Corporate Donations; Box Office; Government Grants; Individual Donations
Season: September - May   **Annual Attendance:** 500,000
Affiliations: ASOL
Performance Facilities: Kleinhaus Music Hall

MAELSTROM PERCUSSION ENSEMBLE, LTD.
PO Box 841, Buffalo, NY 14213-0841
(716) 668-4729
> **Founded:** 1982
> **Arts Area:** Chamber; Ensemble; Ethnic; Instrumental Group; Electronic & Live Electronic
> **Status:** Professional; Non-Profit
> **Type:** Performing; Touring; Resident; Educational
> **Purpose:** To perform existing works for percussion, original compositions and pieces written for or commissioned by the ensemble
> **Management:** Robert D. Accurso, Executive Director
> **Officers:** Robert B. Fleming Jr., President; Paul Musilli, Treasurer; Allan Hebeler, Secretary
> **Paid Staff:** 2
> **Paid Artists:** 4
> **Utilizes:** Guest Artists
> **Budget:** $50,000 - $100,000
> **Income Sources:** Private Foundations/Grants/Endowments; Business/Corporate Donations; Box Office; Government Grants
> **Season:** 52 Weeks   **Annual Attendance:** 30,000
> **Affiliations:** Artists-in-Residence, State University College at Buffalo

VOCAL MUSIC

GREATER BUFFALO OPERA COMPANY
24 Linwood Avenue, Buffalo, NY 14215
> **Founded:** 1987
> **Arts Area:** Grand Opera; Light Opera; Operetta; Ethnic
> **Status:** Professional
> **Type:** Performing; Resident; Educational
> **Purpose:** To produce and present grand and light opera at its finest and accessible to people of all backgrounds
> **Management:** Gary Burgess, Artistic Director; Dr. Judith G. Wolf, Executive Director
> **Officers:** Harry R. Stainrook, Chairman of Board of Trustees; Eugene M. Setel, President; Albert J. Meaney CPA, Treasurer
> **Paid Staff:** 5   **Volunteer Staff:** 10
> **Utilizes:** Special Technical Talent; Guest Conductors; Guest Artists; Guest Directors
> **Budget:** $500,000 - $1,000,000
> **Income Sources:** Private Foundations/Grants/Endowments; Business/Corporate Donations; Box Office; Government Grants; Individual Donations
> **Season:** September - April   **Annual Attendance:** 15,200
> **Performance Facilities:** Shea's Buffalo Theater

THEATRE

PAUL ROBESON THEATRE
350 Masten Avenue, Buffalo, NY 14209
(716) 884-2013
> **Founded:** 1958
> **Arts Area:** Theatrical Group
> **Status:** Semi-Professional; Non-Profit
> **Type:** Performing; Educational
> **Purpose:** To promote, sponsor, foster and develop in the Black community, particularly among Black youth, a taste and love of Black theatre
> **Management:** Agnes M. Bain, Executive Director

Officers: Darlene Badgett, Chairman; Emma Bassett, Vice Chairman; Paulette S. Counts, Treasurer; Gwendolyn Neal, Secretary
Paid Staff: 10   **Volunteer Staff:** 22
Utilizes: Special Technical Talent; Guest Artists; Guest Directors
Budget: $50,000 - $100,000
Income Sources: Private Foundations/Grants/Endowments; Box Office; Government Grants; Individual Donations
Season: 52 Weeks
Performance Facilities: Paul Robeson Theatre

STUDIO ARENA THEATRE
710 Main Street, Buffalo, NY 14202
(716) 856-8025
FAX: (716) 845-4123
Arts Area: Professional
Status: Professional; Non-Profit
Type: Performing; Educational
Purpose: To provide a varied season of plays, produced at the highest possible quality, for the western New York area
Management: Gavin Cameron-Webb, Artistic Director; Raymond Bonnard, Executive Director; Anne E. Hayes, Director of Development; Courtney Walsh, Director of Marketing
Officers: Frank J. Colantuono, President, Board of Trustees
Paid Staff: 73   **Volunteer Staff:** 7
Utilizes: Special Technical Talent; Guest Artists; Guest Directors
Budget: $1,000,000 - $5,000,000
Income Sources: Private Foundations/Grants/Endowments; Business/Corporate Donations; Box Office; Government Grants; Individual Donations
Season: October - June   **Annual Attendance:** 128,000
Affiliations: LORT; TCG; AEA

THEATRE OF YOUTH CO.
282 Franklin Street, Buffalo, NY 14202
Founded: 1972
Arts Area: Professional; Children's Theatre
Status: Professional; Non-Profit
Type: Performing; Touring; Educational
Management: Collen Maroney Fahey, Managing Director; Cathy Block, Business Manager; Sonya Swain, Box Office Manager/Bookkeeper; Cathy Schultz, Development Director; Meg Quinn, Marketing Director
Officers: Meg Rosters, Artistic Director; Pat Gorman, Technical Director; Greg Rapp, Stage Manager; David Bathrich, Costume Designer
Paid Staff: 5   **Volunteer Staff:** 2
Paid Artists: 7
Utilizes: Special Technical Talent; Guest Artists; Guest Directors
Budget: $50,000 - $100,000
Income Sources: Private Foundations/Grants/Endowments; Business/Corporate Donations; Box Office; Government Grants; Individual Donations
Season: September - May   **Annual Attendance:** 60,000

PERFORMING SERIES

AFRICAN-AMERICAN CULTURAL CENTER
350 Masten Avenue, Buffalo, NY 14209
(716) 884-2013
Founded: 1958
Arts Area: Dance; Theater
Status: Non-Profit
Type: Performing; Sponsoring
Purpose: To cultivate, promote, sponsor, foster and develop an appreciation, understanding, taste and love of the traditions of the arts of Africa through social and cultural activities
Management: Agnes M. Bain, Executive Director
Officers: Darlene Badgett, Chairman; Emma Bassett, Vice Chairman; Gwendolyn Neal, Secretary; Paulett S. Counts, Treasurer
Paid Staff: 9   **Volunteer Staff:** 8
Paid Artists: 8   **Non-Paid Artists:** 35
Utilizes: Guest Artists
Budget: $100,000 - $500,000
Income Sources: Private Foundations/Grants/Endowments; Box Office; Government Grants; Individual Donations
Season: January - December   **Annual Attendance:** 15,000
Performance Facilities: Paul Robeson Theatre

NORTH AMERICAN NEW MUSIC FESTIVAL
c/o State University of New York at Buffalo, Department of Music, 222 Baird Hall, Buffalo, NY 14260
(716) 636-2765
FAX: (716) 636-3821
   Arts Area: Instrumental Music; Festivals
   Status: Professional; Non-Profit
   Type: Performing
   Purpose: To promote the understanding and awareness of new music
   Management: Yvar Mikashoff, Artistic Director; Donald Metz, Assistant Artistic Director
   Budget: $1,000 - $50,000
   Income Sources: Private Foundations/Grants/Endowments; Box Office; Government Grants
   Performance Facilities: Slee Concert Hall; Albright-Knox Art Gallery; Hallwalls Art Gallery

QRS ARTS FOUNDATION
1026 Niagara Street, Buffalo, NY 14213
(716) 886-0067
FAX: (716) 885-7510
   Founded: 1973
   Arts Area: Dance; Vocal Music; Instrumental Music
   Status: Professional
   Type: Sponsoring
   Purpose: To present the highest quality artists in recital; to present a variety of dance from ballet to modern
   Management: Arlette Rosen, Director
   Officers: Mary Collins Demske, President; Ramsi P. Tick, Chairman
   Paid Staff: 3
   Paid Artists: 15
   Utilizes: Guest Artists
   Budget: $100,000 - $500,000
   Income Sources: Private Foundations/Grants/Endowments; Business/Corporate Donations; Box Office; Government Grants; Individual Donations
   Season: August - May   **Annual Attendance:** 15,000
   Affiliations: APAP
   Performance Facilities: Kleinhans Music Hall; Shea's Buffalo; Rockwell Hall Auditorium; Slee Hall

FACILITY

AFRICAN-AMERICAN CULTURAL CENTER - PAUL ROBESON THEATRE
350 Masten Avenue, Buffalo, NY 14209
(716) 884-2013
   Founded: 1958
   Type of Facility: Multi-Purpose
   Facility Originally: Welding Shop
   Type of Stage: Platform
   Stage Dimensions: 28'6"x16'3"
   Seating Capacity: 100
   Year Remodeled: 1958
   Contact for Rental: Agnes M. Bain;   (716) 884-2013

BUFFALO MEMORIAL AUDITORIUM
140 Main Street, Buffalo, NY 14202
(716) 851-5663
FAX: (716) 851-4269
   Type of Facility: Auditorium
   Type of Stage: Proscenium   **Orchestra Pit**
   Contact for Rental: Manager;   (716) 851-5663

BUFFALO STATE COLLEGE-PERFORMING ARTS CENTER - ROCKWELL HALL
1300 Elmwood Avenue, Buffalo, NY 14222
(716) 878-3032
FAX: (716) 878-6914
   Founded: 1987
   Type of Facility: Auditorium; Performance Center
   Type of Stage: Proscenium
   Stage Dimensions: 40'Wx20'H   **Orchestra Pit**
   Seating Capacity: 856
   Year Built: 1932
   Year Remodeled: 1987   **Cost:** $15,000,000
   Contact for Rental: J.V. Flanagan;   (716) 878-3032

KLEINHANS MUSIC HALL
Symphony Circle, Buffalo, NY 14201
(716) 883-3560
    Type of Facility: Concert Hall; Auditorium
    Type of Stage: Proscenium
    Stage Dimensions: 33'x68'x44' **Orchestra Pit**
    Seating Capacity: 2,839
    Year Built: 1940
    Architect: Eliel & Eero Saarinen
    Cost: $1,000,000
    Contact for Rental: Douglas J. Lengyel, Director; (716) 883-3560
    Resident Groups: Buffalo Philharmonic; QRS Arts Foundation; Buffalo Chamber Music Society

STATE UNIVERSITY OF NEW YORK-BUFFALO - DEPARTMENT OF THEATRE AND DANCE
201 Harriman Hall, Buffalo, NY 14214
(716) 829-3742
    Type of Facility: Studio Performance; Theatre House
    Facility Originally: Library; Vaudeville
    Type of Stage: Thrust; Flexible
    Seating Capacity: Thrust - 350; Flex - 150
    Year Built: 1920
    Year Remodeled: 1986 **Cost:** $250,000
    Contact for Rental: Jerry Kegler; (716) 645-2038
    Manager: Gary Casarella
    Resident Groups: State University of New York-Buffalo Department of Theatre and Dance

---

Cambridge

INSTRUMENTAL MUSIC

L'ENSEMBLE DU MUSIQUE
Content Farm Road, Cambridge, NY 12816
(518) 677-5455
    Arts Area: Chamber; Ensemble
    Status: Professional; Non-Profit
    Type: Performing; Touring; Resident; Educational
    Purpose: Dedicated to the performance of rarely heard works as well as works of living American composers
    Management: Ida Faiella, Artistic Director; Kristine DeFord, Assistant Artistic Director
    Officers: Jonathan C. Mills, Chairman; Frank Gilmore, President; Timothy D. Smith, Vice President Finance
    Budget: $100,000 - $500,000
    Income Sources: Private Foundations/Grants/Endowments; Business/Corporate Donations; Box Office; Government Grants; Individual Donations
    Performance Facilities: Albany City Arts Building

PERFORMING SERIES

MUSIC FROM SALEM
25 East Main Street, Cambridge, NY 12816
(518) 677-2495
    Founded: 1986
    Arts Area: Vocal Music; Instrumental Music
    Status: Professional
    Type: Performing; Resident
    Purpose: To provide a summer residency for European and American musicians presenting chamber music in a rural setting as a member of the larger community
    Officers: Judith Eissenberg, Lila Brown, Co-Directors
    Paid Staff: 1 **Volunteer Staff:** 8
    Paid Artists: 12
    Budget: $1,000 - $50,000
    Income Sources: Private Foundations/Grants/Endowments; Business/Corporate Donations; Government Grants; Individual Donations
    Season: July - August **Annual Attendance:** 600
    Performance Facilities: Hubbard Hall

Chautauqua

INSTRUMENTAL MUSIC

CHAUTAUQUA SYMPHONY ORCHESTRA
Chautauqua Institution, Chautauqua, NY 14722
(716) 357-6200
FAX: (716) 357-9014
Founded: 1874
Arts Area: Symphony; Orchestra
Status: Professional; Non-Profit
Type: Performing; Resident; Educational
Management: Daniel L. Bration, President; Marty Merkley, Program Director; James Stubbs, Personnel Manager
Paid Staff: 6
Paid Artists: 200
Utilizes: Guest Conductors; Guest Artists
Budget: $500,000 - $1,000,000
Income Sources: Private Foundations/Grants/Endowments; Business/Corporate Donations; Box Office; Government Grants; Individual Donations
Season: July - August   **Annual Attendance:** 80,000
Affiliations: ASOL
Performance Facilities: Amphitheater, Chautauqua Institution

VOCAL MUSIC

CHAUTAUQUA OPERA
Chautauqua, NY 14722
(716) 357-6200
FAX: (716) 357-9014
Founded: 1929
Arts Area: Grand Opera; Lyric Opera; Light Opera; Operetta
Status: Professional
Type: Performing; Resident; Educational
Purpose: To present opera sung in English by young, up-and-coming artists as well as run a training program for young singers
Management: Daniel Bratton, President; Linda Jackson, General Director
Paid Staff: 30
Paid Artists: 50
Utilizes: Special Technical Talent; Guest Conductors; Guest Artists; Guest Directors
Budget: $500,000 - $1,000,000
Income Sources: Private Foundations/Grants/Endowments; Business/Corporate Donations; Box Office; Government Grants; Individual Donations
Season: July - August   **Annual Attendance:** 12,500
Affiliations: OA
Performance Facilities: Norton Hall; Chautauqua Institution

PERFORMING SERIES

CHAUTAUQUA INSTITUTION
Chautauqua, NY 14722
(716) 357-6200
Founded: 1874
Arts Area: Dance; Vocal Music; Instrumental Music; Theater; Grand Opera
Status: Professional; Semi-Professional; Non-Professional; Non-Profit
Type: Performing; Resident; Educational; Sponsoring
Purpose: A superb interplay of the arts, education, religion and recreation, all available on a self-selecting basis within a Victorian community
Management: Marty Merkley, Program Director
Officers: Dr. Daniel L. Bratton, President
Paid Staff: 52   **Volunteer Staff:** 700
Paid Artists: 400   **Non-Paid Artists:** 300
Utilizes: Special Technical Talent; Guest Conductors; Guest Artists; Guest Directors
Budget: $5,000,000 - $10,000,000
Income Sources: Private Foundations/Grants/Endowments; Business/Corporate Donations; Box Office; Government Grants; Individual Donations
Season: June - August   **Annual Attendance:** 200,000
Affiliations: OA; ASOL; APAP; MENC; AAA
Performance Facilities: Amphitheater; Norton Hall

FACILITY

CHAUTAUQUA INSTITUTION - AMPHITHEATER
Chautauqua, NY 14722
(716) 357-6200
FAX: (716) 357-9014
Type of Facility: Concert Hall; Auditorium; Outdoor (Concert); Performance Center; Amphitheater; Arena; Multi-Purpose
Facility Originally: Meeting Hall; Movie House
Type of Stage: Thrust; Platform; 3/4 Arena; Arena
Stage Dimensions: 40'x60'
Seating Capacity: 6,000
Year Built: 1874
Year Remodeled: 1979   **Architect:** Lawson Pulver Knapp   **Cost:** $2,900,000
Acoustical Consultant: Farrell Becker
Contact for Rental: Ed Keating;   (716) 357-6264
Resident Groups: Chautauqua Symphony Orchestra; Chautauqua Dance Festival Company; Chautauqua Music Festival Orchestra; Chautauqua Lecture Series; Chautauqua Youth Orchestra

CHAUTAUQUA INSTITUTION - NORTON HALL
Chautauqua, NY 14722
(716) 357-6000
Type of Facility: Concert Hall; Theatre House; Opera House
Type of Stage: Proscenium
Stage Dimensions: 40'Wx30'D   **Orchestra Pit**
Seating Capacity: 1,367
Year Built: 1929
Year Remodeled: 1984   **Architect:** W. Thomas Smith   **Cost:** $500,000
Contact for Rental: Ed Keating;   (716) 357-6264
Resident Groups: Chautauqua Opera

Clinton

INSTRUMENTAL MUSIC

CHAMBER MUSIC SOCIETY OF UTICA INC.
Rural Route 4, PO Box 396, Clinton, NY 13323
(315) 330-4664
Arts Area: Chamber
Status: Non-Profit
Type: Presenting
Purpose: To present an annual series of high-quality chamber music concerts
Management: James Taylor, Trustee; Dr. Jon Magendanz, Head of Music Selection
Officers: Dorothy Deimel, President
Budget: $1,000 - $50,000
Income Sources: Private Foundations/Grants/Endowments; Business/Corporate Donations; Box Office; Government Grants; Individual Donations
Performance Facilities: Munson-Williams-Proctor Museum of Art Auditorium

FACILITY

HAMILTON COLLEGE - MINOR THEATRE
198 College Hill Road, Clinton, NY 13323
(315) 859-4205
Type of Facility: Theatre House
Facility Originally: Library
Type of Stage: Flexible
Stage Dimensions: 50'x26'x34'
Seating Capacity: 250
Year Built: 1890
Year Remodeled: 1963   **Architect:** Edward Durell Stone
Contact for Rental: Bill Burd;   (315) 859-4205
Resident Groups: Hamilton College Departments of Theatre and Dance

KIRKLAND ART CENTER
East Park Row, PO Box 213, Clinton, NY 13323
(315) 853-8871
Founded: 1960

Type of Facility: Multi-Purpose
Facility Originally: Church
Type of Stage: Platform
Stage Dimensions: 22'x14'
Seating Capacity: 130
Year Built: 1842
Year Remodeled: 1965
Contact for Rental: Dare Thompson;   (315) 853-8871

Cohoes

THEATRE

HERITAGE ARTISTS
PO Box 586, Cohoes, NY 12047
(518) 235-7909
Founded: 1982
Arts Area: Theatrical Group; Musical Theatre
Status: Professional; Non-Profit
Type: Performing
Purpose: To produce musical theatre works
Management: Robert Tolan, Producing Director; Sarah S. Burke, Public Relations Director; Joseph Abaldo, Casting Director
Officers: John P. Ryan, Board President
Paid Staff: 12
Utilizes: Special Technical Talent; Guest Artists; Guest Directors
Budget: $100,000 - $500,000
Income Sources: Private Foundations/Grants/Endowments; Business/Corporate Donations; Box Office; Government Grants; Individual Donations
Season: October - May
Affiliations: TCG

Cooperstown

PERFORMING SERIES

COOPERSTOWN CONCERT SERIES, INC.
PO Box 624, Cooperstown, NY 13326
(607) 293-6124
FAX: (617) 293-6130
Founded: 1970
Arts Area: Dance; Vocal Music; Instrumental Music; Theater
Status: Non-Profit
Type: Sponsoring
Purpose: To promote the cultural growth of our community by presenting live performances of high quality
Officers: Jane Johngren and Donna Thomson, Co-Directors; Lois Hopper, Treasurer; Dottie Leslie, Secretary
Volunteer Staff: 40
Paid Artists: 25
Budget: $1,000 - $50,000
Income Sources: Private Foundations/Grants/Endowments; Business/Corporate Donations; Box Office; Government Grants; Individual Donations; In-Kind; Program Advertising
Season: September - May   **Annual Attendance:** 1,500
Performance Facilities: Sterling Auditorium

GLIMMERGLASS OPERA
PO Box 191, Cooperstown, NY 13326
(607) 547-5704
Founded: 1975
Arts Area: Vocal Music; Lyric Opera; Grand Opera
Status: Professional; Non-Profit
Type: Performing
Purpose: To present opera with gifted young American professional talent and to introduce opera to new audiences
Management: Paul Kellogg, General Director; Stewart Robertson, Music Director
Paid Staff: 8   **Volunteer Staff:** 8
Paid Artists: 70   **Non-Paid Artists:** 32
Utilizes: Special Technical Talent; Guest Conductors; Guest Artists; Guest Directors
Budget: $500,000 - $1,000,000

Income Sources: Private Foundations/Grants/Endowments; Business/Corporate Donations; Box Office; Government Grants; Individual Donations
Season: July - August   **Annual Attendance:** 20,000
Affiliations: OA
Performance Facilities: Alice Busch Opera Theater

Corning

INSTRUMENTAL MUSIC

CORNING PHILHARMONIC SOCIETY
PO Box 113, Corning, NY 14830
(607) 962-8582
Founded: 1933
Arts Area: Symphony; Orchestra
Status: Professional; Non-Profit
Type: Performing; Educational; Sponsoring
Purpose: To provide high quality musical experiences at an affordable price
Management: Marietta Cheng, Music Director/Conductor; Fitzray Stewart, Conductor, Youth Orchestra; David Thurkins, Business Manager
Officers: Jane Fenn, President; John Jay, Vice President
Paid Staff: 3   **Volunteer Staff:** 30
Paid Artists: 45   **Non-Paid Artists:** 5
Utilizes: Guest Artists
Budget: $50,000 - $100,000
Income Sources: Private Foundations/Grants/Endowments; Business/Corporate Donations; Box Office; Government Grants; Individual Donations
Season: October - April   **Annual Attendance:** 3,500
Performance Facilities: Corning Glass Center Auditorium

PERFORMING SERIES

CORNING-PAINTED POST CIVIC MUSIC ASSOCIATION
PO Box 1402, Corning, NY 14830
(607) 962-5713
Founded: 1928
Arts Area: Dance; Vocal Music; Instrumental Music; Jazz; Classical Presentation
Status: Professional
Type: Performing
Purpose: To present the finest artists and talent at the lowest possible cost; subscription series
Officers: David Schirmer, President; Nancy Martin, First Vice President; Ginger Schirmer, Second Vice President; Evelyn Baum, Corresponding Secretary; Gaile Felli, Membersip Secretary; Virginia Wrench, Treasurer
Volunteer Staff: 36
Paid Artists: 5
Utilizes: Five Seasonal Concerts
Budget: $1,000 - $50,000
Income Sources: Private Foundations/Grants/Endowments; Business/Corporate Donations; Box Office; Government Grants; Individual Donations
Season: October - May   **Annual Attendance:** 5,000
Performance Facilities: Corning Glass Center Auditorium

FACILITY

CORNING GLASS CENTER
Centerway, Corning, NY 14831
(607) 974-8276
FAX: (607) 974-8310
Type of Facility: Concert Hall; Auditorium; Theatre House; Multi-Purpose
Type of Stage: Proscenium
Seating Capacity: 1,000
Year Built: 1951   **Architect:** Harrison & Abramovitz
Year Remodeled: 1972

Cortland

THEATRE

CORTLAND REPERTORY THEATRE
PO Box 783, Cortland, NY 13045
(607) 753-6161
 Founded: 1971
 Arts Area: Professional; Summer Stock; Musical
 Status: Non-Profit
 Type: Performing
 Purpose: To provide live theater for the region
 Management: Jana Mack, Managing Director; Marie Alyn King, Artistic Director
 Officers: Karl Blixt, President; Richard Fox, Vice President; Nancy Mann, Secretary; Edward Karsch, Treasurer
 Paid Staff: 6 **Volunteer Staff:** 30
 Paid Artists: 35 **Non-Paid Artists:** 30
 Utilizes: Special Technical Talent; Guest Artists; Guest Directors
 Budget: $100,000 - $500,000
 Income Sources: Private Foundations/Grants/Endowments; Business/Corporate Donations; Box Office; Individual Donations
 Season: June - August **Annual Attendance:** 11,000
 Performance Facilities: Pavilion Theatre

PERFORMING SERIES

STATE UNIVERSITY OF NEW YORK - CORTLAND CAMPUS ARTIST AND LECTURE SERIES
PO Box 2000, Cortland, NY 13045
(607) 753-2321
FAX: (607) 753-2807
 Founded: 1984
 Arts Area: Dance; Instrumental Music; Theater; Festivals
 Status: Professional; Non-Profit
 Type: Presenting
 Purpose: To enhance the cultural awareness of the Cortland College and general community
 Management: Donna Margine, Coordinator of Performing Arts Programs
 Paid Staff: 1
 Paid Artists: 7
 Budget: $1,000 - $50,000
 Income Sources: Private Foundations/Grants/Endowments
 Season: September - May
 Affiliations: APAP; Upstate New York Presenters
 Performance Facilities: Dowd Fine Arts Theatre

Craryville

PERFORMING SERIES

TOURING CONCERT OPERA CO. INC. - BERKSHIRE-HUDSON VALLEY FESTIVAL OF OPERA AND BALLET
PO Box 156A, Craryville, NY 12521
(518) 851-6778
 Founded: 1971
 Arts Area: Dance; Vocal Music; Instrumental Music; Theater; Lyric Opera; Grand Opera
 Status: Professional; Non-Profit
 Type: Performing; Touring
 Purpose: To bring live professional opera and dance to people who would not normally have access to productions on a regular basis; primarily serving Massachusetts, the Southern Berkshires and the Hudson Valley
 Management: Ramon Alsina, Artist Representative
 Officers: Alberto Figols, President; Glenn Wilder, Vice President; Priscilla Gordon, Secretary/Treasurer
 Paid Staff: 1 **Volunteer Staff:** 15
 Paid Artists: 8 **Non-Paid Artists:** 30
 Utilizes: Guest Conductors; Guest Artists; Guest Directors
 Budget: $1,000 - $50,000
 Income Sources: Private Foundations/Grants/Endowments; Business/Corporate Donations; Box Office; Government Grants; Individual Donations
 Season: 52 Weeks **Annual Attendance:** 6,000

Crompond

FACILITY

MARTHA GUINSBERG PAVILION
Baron De Hirsh Road, Crompond, NY 10517
(914) 528-1835
Type of Stage: Proscenium
Stage Dimensions: 22'x28'x20'
Seating Capacity: 800
Year Built: 1956
Contact for Rental: Manager;   (914) 528-1835

Delhi

FACILITY

STATE UNIVERSITY AGRICULTURAL AND TECHNICAL COLLEGE - LITTLE THEATRE
Delhi, NY 13753
(607) 746-4222
Type of Facility: Theatre Complex; Auditorium; Theatre House; Film & Lecture Hall
Type of Stage: Proscenium
Stage Dimensions: 36'Wx24'D   **Orchestra Pit**
Seating Capacity: 356
Year Built: 1967
Contact for Rental: William Campbell;   (607) 746-4222
Resident Groups: Delhi College Players

Dobbs Ferry

INSTRUMENTAL MUSIC

PHILHARMONIA VIRTUOSI CORPORATION
145 Palisade Street, Dobbs Ferry, NY 10522
(914) 693-5595
FAX: (914) 693-7040
Founded: 1974
Arts Area: Orchestra; Chamber
Status: Professional; Non-Profit
Type: Performing; Touring; Educational; Recording
Purpose: To perform an exceptionally broad spectrum of music from the 1600s to the present; to remain a flexible ensemble that performs orchestra concerts with up to 45 players and chamber music programs with as few as three
Management: Richard Kapp, Music Director
Budget: $500,000 - $1,000,000
Season: 52 Weeks

FACILITY

MERCY COLLEGE - LECTURE HALL
555 Broadway, Dobbs Ferry, NY 10566
(914) 693-4500
Type of Facility: Theatre House
Type of Stage: Proscenium
Seating Capacity: 230
Year Built: 1968
Contact for Rental: Anne Grow;   (914) 693-4500, ext. 228
Manager: Anthony Ivancich

Earlville

FACILITY

EARLVILLE OPERA HOUSE
West Main Street, Earlville, NY 13332
(315) 691-3500
Type of Facility: Auditorium; Opera House

Facility Originally: Vaudeville
Type of Stage: Proscenium
Stage Dimensions: 13'x19'x19'
Seating Capacity: 300
Year Built: 1892
Year Remodeled: 1975   **Architect:** A.H. Arnold
Contact for Rental: Director;   (315) 691-3550

East Farmingdale

THEATRE

ARENA PLAYERS REPERTORY COMPANY OF LONG ISLAND
296 Route 109, East Farmingdale, NY 11735
(516) 293-0674
    Founded: 1955
    Arts Area: Theatrical Group
    Status: Professional; Non-Profit
    Type: Performing; Touring
    Purpose: To develop and encourage appreciation of arena theatre, and to assist new playwrights in the development of original scripts.
    Management: Frederic De Feis, Artistic Director; Joanne Gobrick, Production Coordinator; George Snow, Administrative Assistant
    Officers: Frederic De Feis, President; Joanne Gobrick, Vice President; Frank Zummo, Secretary; George Anderson, Treasurer
    Paid Staff: 3   **Volunteer Staff:** 4
    Paid Artists: 7
    Utilizes: Guest Directors
    Budget: $100,000 - $500,000
    Income Sources: Private Foundations/Grants/Endowments; Business/Corporate Donations; Box Office; Government Grants; Individual Donations
    Season: 52 Weeks
    Annual Attendance: 55,000
    Affiliations: TCG
    Performance Facilities: Arena Players Repertory Theater

East Hampton

PERFORMING SERIES

THE JOHN DREW THEATER OF GUILD HALL
158 Main Street, East Hampton, NY 11937
(516) 324-4051
FAX: (516) 324-2722
    Founded: 1931
    Arts Area: Dance; Instrumental Music; Theater
    Status: Professional; Non-Profit
    Type: Performing; Educational
    Purpose: The John Drew Theater of Guild Hall operates under an educational/arts charter; dedicated to the presentation of the finest in the performing arts.
    Management: Joy Gordon, Executive Director; Pamela Calvert, Program Director
    Officers: Jo Raymond, Chairman of the Board
    Paid Staff: 15   **Volunteer Staff:** 10
    Paid Artists: 130   **Non-Paid Artists:** 50
    Utilizes: Special Technical Talent; Guest Artists; Guest Directors
    Budget: $100,000 - $500,000
    Income Sources: Private Foundations/Grants/Endowments; Business/Corporate Donations; Box Office; Government Grants; Individual Donations
    Season: 52 Weeks   **Annual Attendance:** 25,000
    Affiliations: AEA
    Performance Facilities: John Drew Theater

East Islip

PERFORMING SERIES

ISLIP ARTS COUNCIL
40 Irish Lane, East Islip, NY 11730
(516) 224-5420
FAX: (516) 224-5440
Founded: 1974
Arts Area: Vocal Music; Instrumental Music
Status: Professional; Non-Profit
Type: Performing
Purpose: To present a variety of disciplines ranging from fine classical music to young persons' programs to avant garde performance art; to enable exsisting and emerging art organizations to gain information and assistance from the Arts Council library and staff in applying for not-for-profit status, funding, computer services, publicity, mailing lists, etc; to publicize the activities of the arts organization around Long Island
Management: Lillian Barbash, Executive Director; Jodi Gianni, Dorothy Kalson, Co-Directors of Operations; Angela Wallace, Clerk Typist; Barbara Kreisler, Director of Marketing and Development
Officers: Helene Katz, President; Nicholas Wartella, Vice President; Jean Lipshie, Secretary; Edward E. Wankel, Treasurer
Paid Staff: 5 **Volunteer Staff:** 2
Paid Artists: 35
Utilizes: Special Technical Talent; Guest Artists
Budget: $100,000 - $500,000
Income Sources: Private Foundations/Grants/Endowments; Business/Corporate Donations; Box Office; Government Grants; Individual Donations
Season: January - December **Annual Attendance:** 60,000
Affiliations: Township of Islip; Suffolk County
Performance Facilities: Sayville Schools; Dowling College; Bayard Cutting Arboretum; Heckscher State Park

---
Elmira

INSTRUMENTAL MUSIC

ELMIRA SYMPHONY AND CHORAL SOCIETY
PO Box 22, Elmira, NY 14902
(607) 732-3011
Founded: 1903
Arts Area: Symphony; Chamber
Status: Professional
Type: Performing; Sponsoring
Purpose: To perform standard classical orchestral and choral music, with occasional popular concerts
Officers: Anita Kimball, President; Mark Fleisher, Vice President; Carol Balmer, Secretary; Donald Peterson, Treasurer
Paid Staff: 62 **Volunteer Staff:** 30
Paid Artists: 3
Utilizes: Guest Artists
Budget: $50,000 - $100,000
Income Sources: Private Foundations/Grants/Endowments; Business/Corporate Donations; Box Office; Individual Donations
Season: September - April **Annual Attendance:** 11,000

FACILITY

CLEMENS CENTER
Clemens Center Parkway and Gray Street, PO Box 1046, Elmira, NY 14902
(607) 733-5639
FAX: (607) 737-1162
Type of Facility: Performance Center
Facility Originally: Vaudeville
Type of Stage: Proscenium
Stage Dimensions: 48'Wx28'H **Orchestra Pit**
Seating Capacity: 1,615
Year Built: 1925
Year Remodeled: 1976 **Architect:** Haskell, Conner & Frost
Contact for Rental: Michael Kenna; (607) 733-5639
Manager: Thomas Weidemann; (607) 733-5639
Resident Groups: Elmira Little Theatre; Elmira Symphony and Choral Society

Elmsford

FACILITY

WESTCHESTER BROADWAY THEATRE
1 Broadway Plaza, Elmsford, NY 10523
(914) 592-2222
Type of Facility: Theatre House
Type of Stage: Thrust; Proscenium
Stage Dimensions: 20'x20'   **Orchestra Pit**
Seating Capacity: 449
Year Built: 1991   **Architect:** Judith Chafee
Cost: $4,500,000
Contact for Rental: Robert Funking;   (914) 592-2268

Fishkill

DANCE

MID HUDSON BALLET COMPANY
Route 9 North, Fishkill, NY 12524
(914) 897-2667
Founded: 1959
Arts Area: Ballet
Status: Non-Profit
Type: Performing; Educational
Management: Shirley Sedore, Company Manager; Estelle and Alfonso, Artistic Directors
Officers: Cheryl Kroll, President; Pat Holt, Secretary; Sue Maio, Treasurer
Paid Staff: 3   **Volunteer Staff:** 23
Utilizes: Guest Artists; Guest Directors
Budget: $50,000 - $100,000
Income Sources: Business/Corporate Donations; Box Office; Government Grants; Individual Donations
Season: September - August
Affiliations: Northeast Regional Ballet; Dutchess County Arts Council
Performance Facilities: Mid Hudson Civic Center

Flushing

FACILITY

COLDEN CENTER FOR THE PERFORMING ARTS
Queens College, Flushing, NY 11367
(718) 544-2996
FAX: (718) 261-7063
Founded: 1961
Type of Facility: Theatre Complex; Concert Hall; Auditorium
Type of Stage: Proscenium
Stage Dimensions: 76'Wx37'Dx20'H proscenium opening   **Orchestra Pit**
Seating Capacity: 2,143
Year Built: 1961
Acoustical Consultant: Peterheorge Associates
Contact for Rental: Stephen Mallalieu;   (718) 544-2996
Resident Groups: Queens Symphony Orchestra; Queen's College: Choral Society; Drama Department

QUEENS COLLEGE - COLDEN CENTER FOR THE PERFORMING ARTS
Flushing, NY 11367
(718) 544-2996
FAX: (718) 261-7063
Type of Facility: Concert Hall; Auditorium; Theatre House
Type of Stage: Proscenium
Stage Dimensions: 76'x37'   **Orchestra Pit**
Seating Capacity: 2,143
Year Built: 1961   **Architect:** Felheimer & Wagner
Contact for Rental: Steve Mallalieu;   (718) 544-2996
Resident Groups: Queens Symphony

Fredonia

INSTRUMENTAL MUSIC

FREDONIA CHAMBER PLAYERS
Mason Hall, State University College, Fredonia, NY 14063
(716) 673-3463
FAX: (716) 673-3397
    Founded: 1981
    Arts Area: Orchestra; Chamber
    Status: Professional; Non-Profit
    Type: Performing; Touring; Resident; Educational; Sponsoring
    Purpose: To present concerts throughout western New York, Pennsylvania and on tour; to sponsor a chamber orchestra and chamber music series; to sponsor an ensemble-in-residence at the State University of New York, Fredonia School of Music
    Management: James East, Executive Director; Grant Cooper, Music Director
    Officers: Gary Woodbury, President; Sue Evans, Vice President; Catherine Kilpatrick, Secretary; Hal Kwasniewski, Treasurer
    Paid Staff: 2 **Volunteer Staff:** 8
    Paid Artists: 45 **Non-Paid Artists:** 45
    Utilizes: Guest Conductors; Guest Artists
    Budget: $50,000 - $100,000
    Income Sources: Private Foundations/Grants/Endowments; Business/Corporate Donations; Box Office; Government Grants; Individual Donations
    Season: September - June **Annual Attendance:** 15,000
    Affiliations: Arts Council for Chautauqua County; Fund for the Arts in Chautauqua County
    Performance Facilities: King Concert Hall, State University of New York-Fredonia

FACILITY

STATE UNIVERSITY OF NEW YORK-FREDONIA - MICHAEL C. ROCKEFELLER ARTS CENTER
Michael C. Rockefeller Arts Center, Fredonia, NY 14063
(716) 673-3217
    Type of Facility: Theatre Complex; Concert Hall
    Type of Stage: Flexible; Proscenium
    Year Built: 1969 **Architect:** I. M. Pei
    Acoustical Consultant: Bolt, Beranek & Newman
    Contact for Rental: Jefferson Westwood; (716) 673-3217
    Resident Groups: Fredonia Chamber Players
    The Michael C. Rockefeller Arts Center contains the Concert Hall, Experimental Theatre and Proscenium Theatre. See separate listings for additional information.

STATE UNIVERSITY OF NEW YORK-FREDONIA - MICHAEL C. ROCKEFELLER ARTS CENTER - CONCERT HALL
Michael C. Rockefeller Arts Center, Fredonia, NY 14063
(716) 673-3217
    Type of Facility: Concert Hall
    Type of Stage: Proscenium
    Stage Dimensions: 60'x45'
    Seating Capacity: 1,200
    Year Built: 1969
    Contact for Rental: Jefferson Westwood; (716) 673-3217

STATE UNIVERSITY OF NEW YORK-FREDONIA - MICHAEL C. ROCKEFELLER ARTS CENTER - EXPERIMENTAL THEATRE
Michael C. Rockefeller Arts Center, Fredonia, NY 14063
(716) 673-3217
    Type of Facility: Multi-Purpose; Black Box
    Type of Stage: Flexible
    Seating Capacity: 150
    Year Built: 1969
    Contact for Rental: Jurgen Banse-Fay; (716) 673-3217

STATE UNIVERSITY OF NEW YORK-FREDONIA - MICHAEL C. ROCKEFELLER ARTS CENTER - THEATRE
Michael C. Rockefeller Arts Center, Fredonia, NY 14063
(716) 673-3217
    Type of Facility: Theatre House

Type of Stage: Proscenium
Seating Capacity: 400
Year Built: 1969
Contact for Rental: Jurgen Banse-Fay;   (716) 673-3217

Freeport

INSTRUMENTAL MUSIC

AMERICAN MUSICAL ROOTS ASSOCIATION
101 North Bergen Place, Freeport, NY 11520
(212) 850-6423
Founded: 1984
Arts Area: Ethnic; Folk
Status: Professional; Semi-Professional; Non-Profit
Type: Sponsoring
Purpose: Provide local musicians work opportunities, provide area residents with traditional culture, and expose both to the best national traditional groups
Officers: Larry Brittain, President; Billy Clockel, Treasurer
Paid Staff: 2   **Volunteer Staff:** 15
Utilizes: Guest Artists
Budget: $1,000 - $50,000
Income Sources: Private Foundations/Grants/Endowments; Business/Corporate Donations; Box Office; Government Grants; Individual Donations
Season: 52 Weeks   **Annual Attendance:** 10,000

Garden City

VOCAL MUSIC

NATIONAL GRAND OPERA
231 Washington Avenue, Garden City, NY 11530-1707
(516) 248-1040
Founded: 1983
Arts Area: Grand Opera
Status: Professional; Non-Profit
Type: Performing; Resident
Purpose: To bring the highest quality operatic entertainment to the residents of our area
Management: Linda Holgers, General Director; Eugene Brister, Artistic Director
Paid Staff: 2   **Volunteer Staff:** 20
Paid Artists: 175
Utilizes: Special Technical Talent; Guest Conductors; Guest Artists; Guest Directors
Budget: $100,000 - $500,000
Income Sources: Private Foundations/Grants/Endowments; Business/Corporate Donations; Box Office; Government Grants; Individual Donations
Season: October - July   **Annual Attendance:** 28,000
Affiliations: Long Island University
Performance Facilities: Tilles Center for the Performing Arts

---

Geneseo

INSTRUMENTAL MUSIC

FRIENDS OF MUSIC ORCHESTRA AT SAINT MICHAEL'S
Brodie Fine Arts Building, State University of New York - Geneseo, Geneseo, NY 14454
(716) 243-2958
Founded: 1970
Arts Area: Orchestra
Status: Professional; Profit
Type: Performing; Educational; Sponsoring
Purpose: To provide on a professional level a wide range of repertoire including emphasis on new music for chamber orchestra to the Geneseo Valley region
Management: James Walker, Musical Director
Officers: Dr. James Willey, President
Volunteer Staff: 6
Paid Artists: 27

Utilizes: Guest Artists
Budget: $1,000 - $50,000
Income Sources: Private Foundations/Grants/Endowments; Business/Corporate Donations; Box Office; Government Grants; Individual Donations
Season: September - May   **Annual Attendance:** 6,000
Performance Facilities: Saint Michael's Church

GENESEO CHAMBER SYMPHONY

Brodie Fine Arts Building, State University of New York-Geneseo, Geneseo, NY 14454
(716) 245-5824
Founded: 1970
Arts Area: Chamber
Status: Semi-Professional; Non-Profit
Type: Performing; Educational; Sponsoring
Purpose: To give younger performers an opportunity to interact with respected, established artists in both performance and educational environments
Management: James Walker, Musical Director
Paid Staff: 3
Paid Artists: 12   **Non-Paid Artists:** 39
Budget: $50,000 - $100,000
Income Sources: Private Foundations/Grants/Endowments; Government Grants
Season: September - May   **Annual Attendance:** 3,600
Performance Facilities: Wadsworth Auditorium

TREMONT STRING QUARTET, INC.

PO Box 396, Geneseo, NY 14454
(716) 243-4429
FAX: (716) 245-5005
Arts Area: Chamber
Status: Professional; Non-Profit
Type: Performing; Touring; Resident; Educational; Sponsoring
Purpose: To perform the best contemporary and standard chamber music repertory for venues throughout the world
Management: Richard Balkin, Artistic Director; James Kirkwood, Executive Director
Officers: James Walker, Mark Congdon, Board Members
Budget: $100,000 - $500,000
Income Sources: Private Foundations/Grants/Endowments; Business/Corporate Donations; Box Office; Government Grants; Individual Donations

FACILITY

WADSWORTH AUDITORIUM

State University of New York-Geneseo, 1 College Circle, Geneseo, NY 14454
(716) 245-5855
FAX: (716) 245-5400
Type of Facility: Concert Hall; Auditorium
Facility Originally: School
Type of Stage: Proscenium
Stage Dimensions: 46'Wx26'Dx32'8"H proscenium opening   **Orchestra Pit**
Seating Capacity: 942
Year Built: 1930

Geneva

PERFORMING SERIES

GENEVA CONCERTS, INC.

PO Box 709, Geneva, NY 14456
(315) 789-2310
FAX: (315) 787-2326
Founded: 1946
Arts Area: Dance; Vocal Music; Instrumental Music; Theater; Lyric Opera; Grand Opera
Status: Professional; Non-Profit
Type: Educational; Sponsoring
Purpose: To promote the arts in Geneva and the surrounding Finger Lakes community by presenting music, dance and vocal
Officers: Tony Shelton, President; Kim Hardy, First Vice President; Lee Thomas, Second Vice President; Ford Weiskittel, Secretary; Addie Heosler, Treasurer
Volunteer Staff: 21

Utilizes: Guest Conductors; Guest Artists; Guest Directors
Budget: $50,000 - $100,000
Income Sources: Private Foundations/Grants/Endowments; Business/Corporate Donations; Box Office; Government Grants; Individual Donations
Season: September - April   **Annual Attendance:** 3,500
Performance Facilities: Smith Opera House

FACILITY

SMITH OPERA HOUSE FOR THE PERFORMING ARTS
Finger Lakes Regional Arts Council, Inc., PO Box 58, Geneva, NY 14456
(315) 789-2221
Type of Facility: Performance Center; Theatre House; Opera House; Multi-Purpose; Film & Lecture Hall
Facility Originally: Vaudeville
Type of Stage: Thrust; Proscenium
Stage Dimensions: 43'10"Wx37'D, 43'10"Wx28'H proscenium opening   **Orchestra Pit**
Seating Capacity: 1,500
Year Built: 1892   **Architect:** Pierce & Bickford
Year Remodeled: 1927   **Architect:** Victor Ridgemont & Associates   **Cost:** $600,000
Contact for Rental: Richard Erwin, Executive Director;   (315) 789-2221
Resident Groups: Geneva Theatre Guild; Finger Lakes Symphony; Geneva Concerts

Glen Falls

PERFORMING SERIES

LAKE GEORGE OPERA FESTIVAL
13 South Street, PO Box 425, Glen Falls, NY 12801
(518) 793-3858
Founded: 1961
Arts Area: Vocal Music; Instrumental Music
Status: Professional; Non-Profit
Type: Performing
Purpose: To present opera in English with professional young American singers, and to perform a fully-staged season of opera and musical theater work repertory
Management: Brian Lingham, General Director; John Clark, Business Manager; Christopher Minnes, Director of Marketing; Theresa Riddell, Company Administrator; William Wyatt, Production Manager
Officers: Ross Masterman, President; Captain John K. Ryder, Treasurer
Paid Staff: 6   **Volunteer Staff:** 200
Paid Artists: 200   **Non-Paid Artists:** 25
Utilizes: Guest Conductors; Guest Artists; Guest Directors
Budget: $500,000 - $1,000,000
Income Sources: Private Foundations/Grants/Endowments; Business/Corporate Donations; Box Office; Government Grants; Individual Donations
Season: July - August
Affiliations: OA; Albany League of Arts
Performance Facilities: Queensbury High School

FACILITY

OPERA FESTIVAL AUDITORIUM
PO Box 2172, Glen Falls, NY 12801
(518) 793-3858
Type of Facility: Auditorium
Type of Stage: Thrust   **Orchestra Pit**
Seating Capacity: 876
Year Built: 1962

Greenfield Center

PERFORMING SERIES

FOUNDATION FOR BAROQUE MUSIC
165 Wilton Road, Greenfield Center, NY 12833
(518) 893-7527
Founded: 1959
Arts Area: Dance; Vocal Music; Instrumental Music; Festivals

Status: Professional; Non-Profit
Type: Performing; Resident; Educational
Purpose: To promote the music of the 17th and 18th centuries using historical instruments and performance practices
Management: Robert Conant, Artistic Director; Mark E. Baker, Administrative Director
Officers: Robert Conant, President; Eugene M. Krader, Vice President/Secretary
Paid Staff: 1   **Volunteer Staff:** 3
Paid Artists: 30
Utilizes: Guest Artists
Budget: $1,000 - $50,000
Income Sources: Private Foundations/Grants/Endowments; Business/Corporate Donations; Box Office; Government Grants; Individual Donations
Season: July - August   **Annual Attendance:** 1,000
Affiliations: Albany League of Arts; Saratoga County Arts Council; CMA; EMA
Performance Facilities: Baroque Festival Studio

FACILITY

BAROQUE FESTIVAL STUDIO
165 Wilton Road, Greenfield Center, NY 12833
(518) 893-7527
Type of Facility: Concert Hall; Recording Studio
Type of Stage: Flexible
Stage Dimensions: 25'x30'
Seating Capacity: 110
Year Built: 1973   **Architect:** Michael Curtis   **Cost:** $30,000
Acoustical Consultant: Michael Curtis
Contact for Rental: Robert Conant;   (518) 893-7527
Resident Groups: Festival of Baroque Music

Hamilton

PERFORMING SERIES

COLGATE UNIVERSITY CONCERT SERIES
Colgate University, Hamilton, NY 13346-1398
(315) 824-7642
FAX: (315) 824-7787
Arts Area: Dance; Vocal Music; Instrumental Music; Theater
Status: Non-Professional; Non-Profit
Type: Educational; Sponsoring
Purpose: To present concerts to the Colgate University student body and others
Officers: Joseph Swain, Chairperson; Roberta Healey, Concert Manager
Utilizes: Guest Artists
Budget: $1,000 - $50,000
Income Sources: Box Office; Government Grants
Season: 52 Weeks
Performance Facilities: Colgate Memorial Chapel

FACILITY

COLGATE UNIVERSITY - BREHMER THEATER
Dana Arts Center, 13 Oak Drive, Hamilton, NY 13346
(315) 824-1000
Type of Facility: Auditorium
Type of Stage: Proscenium
Stage Dimensions: 20'x30'x40'
Seating Capacity: 400
Year Built: 1966
Architect: Paul Rudolph
Manager: Garda M. Parker
Resident Groups: Colgate University Theater; Colgate Dance Theater

COLGATE UNIVERSITY - UNIVERSITY THEATER
Dana Arts Center, 13 Oak Drive, Hamilton, NY 13346
(315) 824-1000
Type of Facility: Auditorium
Type of Stage: Proscenium
Stage Dimensions: 20'x30'x40'

Seating Capacity: 400
Year Built: 1966   **Architect:** Paul Rudolph
Acoustical Consultant: W. G. Brown Sound

Hartsdale

INSTRUMENTAL MUSIC

THE NEW ORCHESTRA OF WESTCHESTER
111 North Central Avenue, Hartsdale, NY 10530
(914) 682-3707
FAX: (914) 682-3716
Founded: 1983
Arts Area: Symphony
Status: Professional; Non-Profit
Type: Performing; Educational
Purpose: The New Orchestra of Westchester is committed to bringing the highest quality music to the Westchester area with a goal of featuring music by living American composers as part of annual programming
Management: Mary Luehrsen-Young, Executive Director; Paul Lustig Dunkel, Music Director; Jonathan Taylor, Personnel Manager; Susan Hackel, Assistant Director; Peggy Levin, Development Director; Dan Johnsen, Box Office Manager; Karen Castopoulos, Administrative Manager
Officers: Michael Baun, Chairman; Tom Bezanson, Music Chair; Neal Gantchen, Secretary/Counsel
Paid Staff: 5   **Volunteer Staff:** 30
Paid Artists: 75
Utilizes: Guest Artists
Budget: $500,000 - $1,000,000
Income Sources: Private Foundations/Grants/Endowments; Business/Corporate Donations; Box Office; Government Grants; Individual Donations
Season: September - May   **Annual Attendance:** 9,000
Affiliations: Council for Arts Westchester
Performance Facilities: Performing Arts Center, State University of New York-Purchase

Hawthorne

INSTRUMENTAL MUSIC

WESTCHESTER ELEMENTARY ORCHESTRA
Westchester County Dept. of Parks and Recreation, 19 Bradhurst Avenue, Hawthorne, NY 10532
(914) 593-2626
Founded: 1983
Arts Area: Orchestra
Status: Non-Profit
Type: Performing; Educational
Purpose: To provide educational and performing experience for gifted young musicians, grades 4-6, from throughout Westchester County
Management: Arnold Gamson, Supervisor; Jacqueline Stern, Music Director
Officers: Park Allen, Chairman of the Board
Volunteer Staff: 3
Non-Paid Artists: 30
Utilizes: Special Technical Talent; Guest Artists
Budget: $1,000 - $50,000
Income Sources: Private Foundations/Grants/Endowments; Business/Corporate Donations; Government Grants; Individual Donations
Season: September - May   **Annual Attendance:** 1,500
Performance Facilities: Westchester Community College

WESTCHESTER JUNIOR STRING ORCHESTRA
Westchester County Dept. of Parks and Recreation, 19 Bradhurst Avenue, Hawthorne, NY 10532
(914) 593-2626
Founded: 1959
Arts Area: Orchestra
Status: Non-Professional; Non-Profit
Type: Performing; Touring; Educational
Purpose: To provide educational and performing experience for gifted young musicians, grades 7-9, from throughout Westchester County
Management: Arnold Gamson, Supervisor; Dale Lewis, Music Department
Officers: Park Allen, Chairman of the Board

Volunteer Staff: 6
Non-Paid Artists: 46
Utilizes: Special Technical Talent; Guest Artists
Budget: $1,000 - $50,000
Income Sources: Private Foundations/Grants/Endowments; Business/Corporate Donations; Government Grants; Individual Donations
Season: September - May
Annual Attendance: 4,000
Performance Facilities: Westchester Community College

WESTCHESTER YOUTH SYMPHONY
Westchester County Dept. of Parks and Recreation, 19 Bradhurst Avenue, Hawthorne, NY 10532
(914) 593-2626
Founded: 1959
Arts Area: Orchestra
Status: Non-Professional; Non-Profit
Type: Performing; Educational
Purpose: To provide educational and performing experience for gifted young musicians, grades 10-12, from throughout Westchester County
Management: Arnold Gamson, Supervisor; C. Vincent Lionti, Music Director
Officers: Park Allen, Chairman of the Board
Volunteer Staff: 6
Paid Artists: 3   **Non-Paid Artists:** 96
Utilizes: Special Technical Talent; Guest Artists
Budget: $1,000 - $50,000
Income Sources: Private Foundations/Grants/Endowments; Business/Corporate Donations; Government Grants; Individual Donations
Season: September - May
Annual Attendance: 8,500
Performance Facilities: Westchester Community College

PERFORMING SERIES

COUNTY OF WESTCHESTER - PARKS, RECREATION AND CONSERVATION - PERFORMING ARTS
19 Bradhurst Avenue, Hawthorne, NY 10532
(914) 593-2626
Arts Area: Dance; Instrumental Music; Theater
Status: Non-Profit
Type: Performing
Purpose: Production and presentation of concerts, ethnic events in parks and county facilities; and provision of training in performing arts to talented young people and amateurs
Management: Arnold Gamson, Supervisor Performing Arts
Officers: Andrew O'Rourke, County Executive; Barry C. Samuel, Commissioner of Parks Recreation and Conservation
Paid Staff: 60
Paid Artists: 50
Utilizes: Special Technical Talent; Guest Artists; Guest Directors
Budget: $100,000 - $500,000
Income Sources: Business/Corporate Donations; Box Office; Government Grants
Season: 52 Weeks
Annual Attendance: 40,000
Affiliations: Westchester County Department of Parks, Recreation and Conservation
Performance Facilities: Kensico Dam Plaza; Westchester County Center

---

Houghton

PERFORMING SERIES

HOUGHTON COLLEGE ARTIST SERIES
Houghton College, Houghton, NY 14744
(716) 567-2211
Founded: 1930
Arts Area: Vocal Music; Instrumental Music; Theater; Grand Opera
Status: Non-Profit
Type: Performing; Educational; Sponsoring
Purpose: Serious concert presentations
Management: Dr. Bruce Brown, Director
Paid Staff: 2   **Volunteer Staff:** 5
Paid Artists: 5

Utilizes: Guest Conductors; Guest Artists
Budget: $1,000 - $50,000
Income Sources: Private Foundations/Grants/Endowments; Box Office; Individual Donations
Season: September - May   **Annual Attendance:** 4,000
Affiliations: APAP
Performance Facilities: Wesley Chapel

FACILITY

HOUGHTON COLLEGE - WESLEY CHAPEL
Houghton College, Houghton, NY 14744
(716) 567-2211
   Type of Facility: Concert Hall; Auditorium
   Type of Stage: Concert Stage
   Stage Dimensions: 57'x35'
   Seating Capacity: 1,200

Ithaca

DANCE

ITHACA BALLET (BALLET GUILD OF ITHACA, INC.)
105 Sheldon Road, Ithaca, NY 14850
(607) 257-1967
   Founded: 1959
   Arts Area: Modern; Ballet
   Status: Semi-Professional; Non-Profit
   Type: Performing; Touring
   Purpose: To bring classical and contemporary ballet to areas of upstate New York and Pennsylvania
   Management: Lawrence Brantley, General Manager
   Officers: Elisabeth Thorn, President; Charlotte Fogel, Vice President; Elizabeth Schermerhorn, Secretary; Helene Wilmarth, Treasurer
   Paid Staff: 2   **Volunteer Staff:** 20
   Utilizes: Special Technical Talent
   Budget: $50,000 - $100,000
   Income Sources: Private Foundations/Grants/Endowments; Business/Corporate Donations; Box Office; Individual Donations
   Season: 52 Weeks   **Annual Attendance:** 6,000
   Performance Facilities: Statler Auditorium, Cornell University

VOCAL MUSIC

ITHACA OPERA ASSOCIATION
109 East Seneca Street, Ithaca, NY 14850
(607) 272-0168
   Founded: 1949
   Arts Area: Grand Opera; Lyric Opera; Light Opera; Operetta; Musical Theatre
   Status: Professional; Non-Profit
   Type: Performing; Touring; Educational
   Purpose: To bring quality entertainment to the Finger Lakes community through the use of local and regional talent
   Management: Edward Murray, Musical Director
   Officers: James P. Cassaro, President, Board of Directors
   Paid Staff: 1   **Volunteer Staff:** 75
   Paid Artists: 45   **Non-Paid Artists:** 20
   Utilizes: Special Technical Talent; Guest Conductors; Guest Artists; Guest Directors
   Budget: $50,000 - $100,000
   Income Sources: Private Foundations/Grants/Endowments; Business/Corporate Donations; Box Office; Government Grants; Individual Donations
   Affiliations: NYSCA
   Performance Facilities: Hangar Theatre; Statler Auditorium, Cornell University

THEATRE

THE HANGAR THEATRE
DeWitt Mall, PO Box 205, Ithaca, NY 14851
(607) 273-8588
   Founded: 1970
   Arts Area: Professional

Status: Professional; Non-Profit
Type: Performing; Educational
Purpose: To produce outstanding professional theatre for the benefit of our region and to provide hands-on educational opportunities for theatre artists through our directing fellowship, acting internship and acting training programs
Management: Robert Moss, Producing Director; Lynn Fitzpatrick, Managing Director
Officers: Andrea Fleck Clardy, President; John Alexander, Vice President; Susan Kaplan, Secretary; John A. Elliott, Treasurer
Paid Staff: 100   **Volunteer Staff:** 20
Paid Artists: 35   **Non-Paid Artists:** 15
Utilizes: Special Technical Talent; Guest Artists; Guest Directors
Budget: $100,000 - $500,000
Income Sources: Private Foundations/Grants/Endowments; Business/Corporate Donations; Box Office; Government Grants; Individual Donations
Season: June - September   **Annual Attendance:** 23,000
Affiliations: Finger Lakes Chamber of Commerce; Tompkins City Chamber of Commerce
Performance Facilities: Hangar Theatre, Cass Park

FACILITY

CORNELL UNIVERSITY - ALICE STATLER AUDITORIUM
Statler Hotel, Ithaca, NY 14853-7001
(607) 254-2604
FAX: (607) 257-6432
   Founded: 1989
   Type of Facility: Auditorium
   Type of Stage: Proscenium
   Stage Dimensions: 30'x36'   **Orchestra Pit**
   Seating Capacity: 921
   Contact for Rental: Carol Markwardt;   (607) 255-2331
   Resident Groups: Cornell Concert Series; Cornell Cinema; Cornell Lecture Series; Cornell Dance Club; Cornell Savoyards

HANGAR THEATRE
Cass Park, PO Box 205, Ithaca, NY 14851
(607) 273-8588
   Type of Facility: Performance Center; Theatre House
   Facility Originally: Airplane Hangar
   Type of Stage: Thrust; Platform; In-the-Round Capability
   Stage Dimensions: 28'x26'
   Seating Capacity: 380
   Year Built: 1934
   Year Remodeled: 1974   **Architect:** Robert Mueller   **Cost:** $125,000
   Contact for Rental: Lynn Fitzpatrick, Managing Director;   (607) 273-8588
   Resident Groups: Hangar Theatre Company; North Lobby Company
   Available for rent May and September only

ITHACA COLLEGE - DILLINGHAM CENTER FOR THE PERFORMING ARTS
Dillingham Center for the Performing Arts, Ithaca, NY 14850
(607) 274-3345
   Type of Facility: Theatre Complex; Performance Center
   Year Built: 1968   **Architect:** T.A. Canfield
   Contact for Rental: Special Events Office;   (607) 274-3313
   Resident Groups: Ithaca College Department of Theatre Arts
   The Performing Arts Center contains the Arena and Hoerner Auditorium. See separate listings for additional information.

ITHACA COLLEGE - DILLINGHAM CENTER FOR THE PERFORMING ARTS - ARENA
Dillingham Center for the Performing Arts, Ithaca, NY 14850
(607) 274-3345
   Type of Facility: Arena
   Type of Stage: Flexible; Arena
   Seating Capacity: 312
   Year Built: 1968
   Contact for Rental: Special Events Office;   (607) 274-3313

ITHACA COLLEGE - DILLINGHAM CENTER FOR THE PERFORMING ARTS - HOERNER AUDITORIUM
Dillingham Center for the Performing Arts, Ithaca, NY 14850
(607) 274-3345
   Type of Facility: Auditorium

Type of Stage: Proscenium
Stage Dimensions: 56'Wx39'D; 56'Wx22'H proscenium opening   **Orchestra Pit**
Seating Capacity: 535
Year Built: 1968
Contact for Rental: Special Events Office;   (607) 274-3313

Jackson Heights

THEATRE

YUEH LUNG SHADOW THEATRE
34-41 74th Street, Jackson Heights, NY 11372
(718) 478-6246
Founded: 1976
Arts Area: Professional; Folk; Puppet
Status: Professional; Non-Profit
Type: Performing; Touring; Educational
Purpose: To preserve and perpetuate the 2000-year-old Chinese art of shadow theatre
Management: Mrs. Joe Humphrey, Executive/Artistic Director; Sarah Jonker-Burke, Assistant Director
Officers: Samuel Magdoff, Chairman; Katharine McKelligott, Treasurer; David Sterling, Vice Chairman
Paid Staff: 3   **Volunteer Staff:** 5
Paid Artists: 9
Budget: $1,000 - $50,000
Income Sources: Private Foundations/Grants/Endowments; Business/Corporate Donations; Government Grants; Individual Donations; Performance Fees
Season: 52 Weeks   **Annual Attendance:** 10,000
Affiliations: ART/NY; UNIMA; Queens Council on Arts; Puppeteers of America; UNIMA

Jamaica

DANCE

DINIZULU AFRICAN DANCERS, DRUMMERS AND SINGERS
c/o Aims of Modzawe, 115-62 Sutphin Boulevard, Jamaica, NY 11434
(718) 843-6213
Arts Area: Ethnic
Status: Professional; Non-Profit
Type: Performing; Touring; Resident; Educational; Sponsoring
Purpose: To present the beauty and majesty of African culture through dance
Management: Alice Dinizulu, Executive Director; Esi-Ayisi Dinizulu, Artistic Director
Income Sources: Private Foundations/Grants/Endowments; Business/Corporate Donations; Box Office; Government Grants; Individual Donations

THEATRE

AFRIKAN POETRY THEATRE
176-03 Jamaica Avenue, Jamaica, NY 11432
(718) 523-3312
Founded: 1976
Arts Area: Professional; Musical; Community; Folk
Status: Professional; Non-Profit
Type: Performing; Touring; Educational; Sponsoring
Purpose: To provide cultural and educational classes and workshops, performances, exhibits and cultural reference sources for the benefit of the community
Management: John Watusi Branch, Executive Director; Byron W. Perry, Ronald Burwell, Administrative Assistants; Shadiyah Waliyaya, Program Director
Officers: Fred Abramson, President; Roger Burwell, Vice President; Willie E. Cooper, Secretary; Louise Adelokiki, Treasurer
Paid Staff: 3   **Volunteer Staff:** 12
Paid Artists: 5   **Non-Paid Artists:** 20
Utilizes: Guest Artists
Budget: $100,000 - $500,000
Income Sources: Private Foundations/Grants/Endowments; Business/Corporate Donations; Box Office; Government Grants; Individual Donations
Season: 52 Weeks   **Annual Attendance:** 15,000
Performance Facilities: Afrikan Poetry Theatre

FACILITY

JAMAICA ARTS CENTER
161-04 Jamaica Avenue, Jamaica, NY 11432
(718) 658-7400
    Type of Facility: Studio Performance; Performance Center; Multi-Purpose; Room
    Facility Originally: Business Facility
    Type of Stage: Platform
    Seating Capacity: 50
    Year Built: 1898   **Architect:** Geoffrey Freeman & Associates   **Cost:** $1,000,000
    Contact for Rental: Vevonique LeMelle, Executive Director
    Resident Groups: The Tribe Ensemble; New York Street Theater Caravan; Mimestrals; Jamaica Arts Center Jazz Ensemble; Jamaica Arts Center Co-Op
    Continuous renovations done on the New York City landmark; formerly Queens Hall of Records

SAINT JOHN'S UNIVERSITY
Grand Central and Utopia Parkways, Jamaica, NY 11439
(718) 990-6452
FAX: (718) 380-0353
    Type of Facility: Auditorium; Theatre House
    Type of Stage: Proscenium
    Stage Dimensions: 29'x35'x30'
    Seating Capacity: 400
    Manager: Ed Guinan; (718) 990-6452

Jamaica Estates

THEATRE

NEW YORK STREET THEATRE CARAVAN
8705 Chelsea Street, Jamaica Estates, NY 11432
(718) 657-8070
    Founded: 1968
    Arts Area: Theatrical Group
    Status: Professional
    Type: Performing
    Management: Marketa Kimbrell, Artistic Director of the Collective
    Paid Staff: 4
    Budget: $50,000 - $100,000
    Income Sources: Private Foundations/Grants/Endowments; Box Office

Jamestown

INSTRUMENTAL MUSIC

JAMESTOWN CONCERT ASSOCIATION
PO Box 747, Jamestown, NY 14702-0747
(716) 487-1522
FAX: (716) 484-2300
    Founded: 1932
    Arts Area: Symphony; Orchestra; Chamber; Ensemble; Ethnic; Instrumental Group; Band
    Status: Non-Profit
    Type: Educational; Sponsoring
    Purpose: To sponsor professional musicians in concert for our membership
    Management: Shirlea Roman, Executive Secretary
    Officers: R. Richard Corbin, President; Clayton Berlinghoff, Vice President; Katherine Kotsi, Treasurer
    Volunteer Staff: 30
    Utilizes: Guest Conductors; Guest Artists
    Budget: $1,000 - $50,000
    Income Sources: Private Foundations/Grants/Endowments; Business/Corporate Donations; Box Office; Government Grants; Individual Donations
    Season: 52 Weeks   **Annual Attendance:** 9,500
    Affiliations: Arts Association Chautauqua County
    Performance Facilities: Civic Center

FACILITY

LUCILLE BALL LITTLE THEATRE BUILDING
18-24 East Second Street, Jamestown, NY 14701
(716) 483-1095
> **Type of Facility:** Auditorium
> **Type of Stage:** Proscenium
> **Stage Dimensions:** 80'x40'x24'   **Orchestra Pit**
> **Seating Capacity:** 440
> **Year Built:** 1900
> **Year Remodeled:** 1969   **Cost:** $250,000
> **Contact for Rental:**   (716) 483-1095

Katonah

PERFORMING SERIES

CARAMOOR CENTER FOR MUSIC AND THE ARTS
Katonah, NY 10536
(914) 232-4206
> **Founded:** 1945
> **Arts Area:** Vocal Music; Instrumental Music; Festivals
> **Status:** Professional; Non-Profit
> **Type:** Performing; Educational; Sponsoring
> **Purpose:** To provide a center for music and the arts for the town of Bedford and the state of New York
> **Management:** Howard Herring, Executive Director
> **Officers:** Peter M. Gottsegen, Chairman
> **Paid Staff:** 35   **Volunteer Staff:** 90
> **Paid Artists:** 100
> **Utilizes:** Guest Conductors; Guest Artists; Guest Directors
> **Budget:** $1,000,000 - $5,000,000
> **Income Sources:** Private Foundations/Grants/Endowments; Business/Corporate Donations; Box Office; Government Grants; Individual Donations
> **Performance Facilities:** Museum Music Room Venetian Theatre; Spanish Courtyard

FACILITY

CARAMOOR CENTER FOR MUSIC AND THE ARTS
Girdle Ridge Road, Katonah, NY 10536
(914) 232-5035
FAX: (914) 232-5521
> **Founded:** 1945
> **Type of Facility:** Concert Hall; Outdoor (Concert); Multi-Purpose
> **Type of Stage:** Proscenium; Platform; Environmental
> **Stage Dimensions:** 35'x35'; 20'x24'
> **Contact for Rental:** Paul Rosenblum;   (914) 232-5035
> **Resident Groups:** Orchestra and Ensemble of St. Luke's; Cassatt String Quartet

VENETIAN THEATRE
Caramoor, Girdle Ridge Road, Katonah, NY 10536
(914) 232-5035
FAX: (914) 232-5521
> **Founded:** 1946
> **Type of Facility:** Concert Hall; Outdoor (Concert); Performance Center; Theatre House
> **Type of Stage:** Proscenium
> **Orchestra Pit**
> **Seating Capacity:** 1,650
> **Year Built:** 1957   **Architect:** Frederick Kiesler
> **Contact for Rental:** Paul Rosenblum;   (914) 232-5035
> **Resident Groups:** Orchestra of St. Luke's; Cossott String Quartet
> *Off-season (before mid-June and after mid-August)*

Kingston

THEATRE

COACH HOUSE PLAYERS
12 Augusta Street, PO Box 3481, Kingston, NY 12401
(914) 338-7097
Founded: 1950
Arts Area: Musical; Community; Theatrical Group
Status: Non-Profit
Type: Performing; Educational
Purpose: To present the best possible productions in all phases of theatre
Management: Kay Finn, Business Manager
Officers: Tom Tierney, President; Cate Tomlinson, Vice President; Pat Tonzi, Treasurer
Utilizes: Guest Directors
Budget: $1,000 - $50,000
Income Sources: Box Office; Individual Donations
Season: September - June   **Annual Attendance:** 5,000
Performance Facilities: J. Watson Bailey School

FACILITY

ULSTER PERFORMING ARTS CENTER
601 Broadway, Kingston, NY 12401
(914) 331-1613
FAX: (914) 339-3814
Founded: 1978
Type of Facility: Theatre Complex; Concert Hall; Studio Performance; Performance Center; Civic Center; Teaching Facility
Facility Originally: Vaudeville; Movie House
Type of Stage: Proscenium
Stage Dimensions: 37'Wx28'D   **Orchestra Pit**
Seating Capacity: 1,538
Year Built: 1927   **Architect:** Douglas Hall
Acoustical Consultant: Jaffe
Contact for Rental: Joan Roberts;   (914) 331-1613

Lafayette

THEATRE

CONTEMPORARY THEATRE OF SYRACUSE
2888 Eager Road, Lafayette, NY 13084
Founded: 1980
Arts Area: Theatrical Group
Status: Semi-Professional
Type: Performing
Purpose: To present contemporary drama, stage readings of works-in-progress, and programs in schools
Management: Kristi McKay, Producer; Jo Lynn Stressing, Summer Producer; David Feldman, New Plays Artistic Director; Shirley Myrls, New Plays Production Director
Officers: Mary Earle, President; Kitty McCarthy, Secretary
Paid Staff: 4   **Volunteer Staff:** 20
Paid Artists: 20   **Non-Paid Artists:** 35
Budget: $50,000 - $100,000
Income Sources: Private Foundations/Grants/Endowments; Business/Corporate Donations; Box Office; Government Grants; Individual Donations
Season: 52 Weeks   **Annual Attendance:** 1,500

Lake George

THEATRE

LAKE GEORGE DINNER THEATRE
Canada Street, Lake George, NY 12845
(518) 761-1092
FAX: (518) 798-0735
Mailing Address: PO Box 4623, Queensbury, NY 12804

Founded: 1967
Arts Area: Professional; Dinner; Theatrical Group
Status: Professional
Type: Performing
Management: Sharon Reynolds, General Manager
Officers: David Eastwood, Producer
Paid Staff: 2
Non-Paid Artists: 8
Budget: $50,000 - $100,000
Income Sources: Box Office
Season: June - October   **Annual Attendance:** 15,000

PERFORMING SERIES

LAKE GEORGE JAZZ WEEKEND
c/o Lake George Arts Project Inc., Canada Street, Lake George, NY 12845
(518) 668-2616
FAX: (518) 668-3788
    Arts Area: Instrumental Music; Jazz
    Status: Professional; Non-Profit
    Type: Performing; Touring
    Purpose: To sponsor a two-day festival held each September that features nationally acclaimed and emerging jazz artists
    Management: John Strong, Executive Director; Paul Pines, Music Director
    Officers: Theodore Zoli Jr., President of the Board
    Budget: $1,000 - $50,000
    Income Sources: Private Foundations/Grants/Endowments; Business/Corporate Donations; Government Grants; Individual Donations
    Performance Facilities: Shepard Park Bandstand

FACILITY

LAKE GEORGE DINNER THEATRE
PO Box 4623, Lake George, NY 12845
(518) 761-1092
    Type of Facility: Theatre House
    Facility Originally: Ballroom
    Type of Stage: 3/4 Arena
    Stage Dimensions: 14'x24'
    Seating Capacity: 166
    Manager: Sharon Reynolds

Lake Placid

PERFORMING SERIES

LAKE PLACID CENTER FOR THE ARTS
Saranac Avenue, Lake Placid, NY 12946
(518) 523-2512
    Founded: 1972
    Arts Area: Dance; Vocal Music; Theater; Festivals
    Status: Non-Profit
    Type: Performing; Resident; Sponsoring
    Purpose: To disseminate arts in a rural, sports-oriented community
    Management: Nadine Duhaime, Director
    Officers: Lesly Handler, President
    Paid Staff: 4   **Volunteer Staff:** 20
    Utilizes: Guest Artists; Guest Directors
    Income Sources: Private Foundations/Grants/Endowments; Business/Corporate Donations; Box Office; Government Grants; Individual Donations
    Season: 52 Weeks   **Annual Attendance:** 25,000
    Affiliations: Lyceum/Sinfonietta CTP Players

FACILITY

LAKE PLACID CENTER FOR THE ARTS - THEATER
Saranac Avenue, Lake Placid, NY 12946
(518) 523-2512
    Type of Facility: Concert Hall; Performance Center; Theatre House

Type of Stage: Proscenium
Stage Dimensions: 66'Wx35'D; 48'Wx15'H proscenium opening   **Orchestra Pit**
Seating Capacity: 353
Year Built: 1972
Architect: Frost/McConnell
Cost: $3,000,000
Contact for Rental: Robin Pell;   (518) 523-2512
The Center also contains an art gallery and studios.

Lancaster

FACILITY

LANCASTER NEW YORK OPERA HOUSE
21 Central Avenue, Lancaster, NY 14086
(716) 683-1776
>**Type of Facility:** Theatre House; Multi-Purpose
>**Type of Stage:** Proscenium
>**Stage Dimensions:** 18'Dx24'W
>**Seating Capacity:** 350
>**Year Built:** 1897   **Architect:** George J. Metzger
>**Year Remodeled:** 1981   **Architect:** William Shelgren   **Cost:** $700,000
>**Contact for Rental:** Executive Director;   (716) 683-1776

Lewiston

PERFORMING SERIES

ARTPARK
PO Box 371, Lewiston, NY 14092
(716) 754-9000
>**Founded:** 1974
>**Arts Area:** Dance; Vocal Music; Instrumental Music; Festivals; Grand Opera
>**Status:** Professional; Non-Profit
>**Type:** Performing; Resident; Sponsoring
>**Purpose:** Publicly-funded state park devoted to the visual and performing arts, intended to bridge the gap between the public and the arts
>**Management:** David Midland, Executive Director; Jennifer McDonough, Director of Development; Tracy Gibbons, Director of Finance; Dean Cohan, Director of Operations; Katherine Rooney, Director of Marketing
>**Officers:** David Midland, President
>**Paid Staff:** 18   **Volunteer Staff:** 500
>**Paid Artists:** 200
>**Utilizes:** Special Technical Talent; Guest Conductors; Guest Artists; Guest Directors
>**Budget:** $1,000,000 - $5,000,000
>**Income Sources:** Private Foundations/Grants/Endowments; Business/Corporate Donations; Box Office; Government Grants; Individual Donations
>**Season:** June - September   **Annual Attendance:** 840,000
>**Affiliations:** AEA; IATSE; AGMA; AFM

FACILITY

ARTPARK THEATER
PO Box 371, Lewiston, NY 14092
(716) 754-9000
FAX: (716) 754-2741
>**Founded:** 1974
>**Type of Facility:** Concert Hall; Auditorium; Outdoor (Concert); Performance Center; Theatre House; Opera House
>**Type of Stage:** Proscenium
>**Stage Dimensions:** 38'-50'Wx20'-30'H adjustable proscenium; 48'x39'x79'   **Orchestra Pit**
>**Seating Capacity:** Inside - 2,324; Outside - 1,500
>**Year Built:** 1972   **Architect:** Volmer Associates   **Cost:** $7,500,000

Lindenhurst

FACILITY

STUDIO THEATRE
141 South Wellwood Avenue, Lindenhurst, NY 11757
(516) 226-1833
Type of Facility: Theatre House
Facility Originally: Upstairs Loft
Type of Stage: Thrust
Stage Dimensions: 10'x60'x40'
Seating Capacity: 175
Converted into a theatre in 1972 for $5,000

Little Falls

FACILITY

MOHAWK VALLEY CENTER FOR THE ARTS
401 South Ann Street, Little Falls, NY 13365-0611
(315) 823-0808
Type of Facility: Room
Facility Originally: Meeting Hall; Movie House
Type of Stage: Proscenium
Stage Dimensions: 40'x32'
Seating Capacity: 300
Year Built: 1914   **Architect:** Smith   **Cost:** $40,000
Contact for Rental: Matt Mielnick;   (315) 823-0808

Locust Valley

INSTRUMENTAL MUSIC

LONG ISLAND BAROQUE ENSEMBLE
PO Box 7, Locust Valley, NY 11560
(516) 724-7386
Founded: 1970
Arts Area: Chamber; Ensemble
Status: Professional; Non-Profit
Type: Performing; Touring; Educational
Purpose: To perform early music on period instruments with vocal specialists
Officers: Edward Pressman, President; Michael Pressman, Treasurer; Dominic Buonanno, Secretary; Victor Fetter, Vice President
Paid Staff: 2   **Volunteer Staff:** 15
Paid Artists: 14
Utilizes: Guest Artists
Budget: $50,000 - $100,000
Income Sources: Private Foundations/Grants/Endowments; Business/Corporate Donations; Box Office; Government Grants; Individual Donations; Subscriptions
Season: September - April   **Annual Attendance:** 2,100
Performance Facilities: Coe Hall; Planting Fields Arboretum, Oyster Bay

PERFORMING SERIES

BEETHOVEN FESTIVAL
c/o Friends of the Arts Inc., PO Box 702, Locust Valley, NY 11560
(516) 922-0061
FAX: (516) 922-0770
Arts Area: Instrumental Music
Status: Professional; Non-Profit
Type: Performing
Purpose: To present Beethoven's lifetime of work in one spectacular weekend
Management: Theodora Bookman, Executive Director
Officers: Morton Weber Esq., Chairman of the Board
Budget: $1,000 - $50,000
Income Sources: Box Office; Government Grants; Individual Donations
Performance Facilities: Planting Fields Arboretum

Mamaroneck

FACILITY

THE EMELIN THEATRE FOR THE PERFORMING ARTS
Library Lane, Mamaroneck, NY 10543
(914) 698-3045; (914) 698-0098
FAX: (914) 698-1404
Type of Facility: Performance Center
Stage Dimensions: 22'x40'x18'
Seating Capacity: 280
Year Built: 1972 **Cost:** $350,000
Contact for Rental: Norman Kline; (914) 698-3045
Resident Groups: Emelin Trio
To present high-quality performing arts to Westchester County and the New York area

Melville

INSTRUMENTAL MUSIC

LONG ISLAND PHILHARMONIC
One Huntington Quadrangle, #LL-09, Melville, NY 11747
(516) 293-2222
FAX: (516) 293-2655
Founded: 1979
Arts Area: Symphony; Orchestra; Chamber
Status: Professional
Type: Performing; Resident; Educational
Management: Daniel C. Brown, General Manager; Kevin Barnes, Orchestra Manager; Robin Postiglione, Accounting Manager
Officers: Barry R. Shapio, Chairman; John J. Rusell, Robert M. Johnson, Vice Chairmen
Paid Staff: 8
Utilizes: Guest Artists
Budget: $1,000,000 - $5,000,000
Income Sources: Private Foundations/Grants/Endowments; Business/Corporate Donations; Box Office; Government Grants; Individual Donations
Season: October - May
Performance Facilities: Tilles Center; Staller Center

Monticello

THEATRE

PERIWINKLE NATIONAL THEATRE
19 Clinton Avenue, Monticello, NY 12701
(914) 794-1666
FAX: (914) 794-0304
Founded: 1963
Arts Area: Professional; Theatrical Group
Status: Professional; Non-Profit
Type: Performing; Touring; Educational
Purpose: To provide quality programming with a unique blend of preliminary materials, original productions and workshops designed to challenge students intellectually, imaginatively and artistically
Management: Sunna Rasch, Executive Director; Kathy Sharpe, Business Manager
Officers: Robert S. Kapito, President; Dr. Nellie McCaslin, Vice President; Alfred Christie, Secretary/Treasurer
Paid Staff: 4
Paid Artists: 15
Utilizes: Special Technical Talent
Budget: $100,000 - $500,000
Income Sources: Private Foundations/Grants/Endowments; Business/Corporate Donations; Government Grants; Individual Donations; Program Fees
Season: September-December; - January-May **Annual Attendance:** 100,000

Mount Vernon

INSTRUMENTAL MUSIC

BOWDOIN SUMMER MUSIC FESTIVAL
141 Rich Avenue, Mount Vernon, NY 10550
(207) 725-3322, ext. June-Aug; (914) 664-5957
> **Arts Area:** Chamber
> **Status:** Non-Profit
> **Type:** Educational; Presenting
> **Purpose:** To provide intensive training to pre-professional music students and professional concert presentations
> **Management:** Lewis Kaplan, Artistic Director; Mary Klibonoff, Administrator
> **Officers:** George S. Isaacson, President
> **Budget:** $100,000 - $500,000
> **Income Sources:** Private Foundations/Grants/Endowments; Business/Corporate Donations; Box Office; Government Grants; Individual Donations
> **Performance Facilities:** First Parish Church

Narrowsburg

VOCAL MUSIC

DELAWARE VALLEY OPERA
PO Box 188, Narrowsburg, NY 12764
(914) 252-3910
> **Founded:** 1986
> **Arts Area:** Light Opera; Operetta
> **Status:** Semi-Professional; Non-Profit
> **Type:** Performing; Educational
> **Management:** Gloria Krause, General Manager
> **Officers:** Sheldon Soffer, President; Lester Wallman, Vice President; Elizabeth Brown, Finance; Sharon Schroeder, Secretary; Gloria Krause, Treasurer
> **Paid Staff:** 2 **Volunteer Staff:** 15
> **Non-Paid Artists:** 40
> **Utilizes:** Special Technical Talent; Guest Artists
> **Budget:** $1,000 - $50,000
> **Income Sources:** Box Office; Government Grants; Individual Donations
> **Season:** May - December **Annual Attendance:** 2,000
> **Performance Facilities:** Tusten Theatre; Sullivan County Community College

---

New Berlin

INSTRUMENTAL MUSIC

DEL-SE-NANGO OLDE TYME FIDDLERS ASSOCIATION, INC.
RD #3, PO Box 233, New Berlin, NY 13411
(607) 847-8501
> **Founded:** 1978
> **Arts Area:** Folk
> **Status:** Non-Profit
> **Type:** Performing; Educational; Sponsoring
> **Purpose:** To preserve, promote and perpetuate the art of olde tyme fiddling, its music and dances
> **Officers:** Marjorie T. Crawford, President; Paul Krum, Vice President; Catherine Whitbeck, Secretary; Margaret Sherwood, Treasurer
> **Volunteer Staff:** 250
> **Non-Paid Artists:** 40
> **Utilizes:** Guest Artists
> **Budget:** $1,000 - $50,000
> **Income Sources:** Box Office; Individual Donations
> **Season:** April - December

New Paltz
THEATRE

NINETY MILES OFF BROADWAY
PO Box 565, New Paltz, NY 12651
> **Founded:** 1963
> **Arts Area:** Theatrical Group
> **Status:** Non-Profit
> **Type:** Performing
> **Officers:** Judy Eliott, President
> **Volunteer Staff:** 50
> **Budget:** $1,000 - $50,000
> **Income Sources:** Box Office; Individual Donations

New Windsor
DANCE

ORANGE COUNTY BALLET THEATRE
170 Windsor Highway, New Windsor, NY 12553
(914) 562-6750
> **Founded:** 1963
> **Arts Area:** Ballet
> **Status:** Non-Professional; Non-Profit
> **Type:** Resident
> **Management:** Regis Powers, Artistic Director
> **Non-Paid Artists:** 30
> **Utilizes:** Guest Choreographers
> **Budget:** $1,000 - $50,000
> **Income Sources:** Private Foundations/Grants/Endowments; Business/Corporate Donations; Box Office; Individual Donations
> **Season:** September - August

New York
DANCE

AGNES DE MILLE DANCE THEATER
25 East 9th Street, New York, NY 10003
(212) 473-3024
> **Founded:** 1953
> **Arts Area:** Ballet; Folk
> **Status:** Professional; Non-Profit
> **Type:** Performing; Touring; Educational
> **Purpose:** A ballet repertoire based on and stemming from the American Heritage
> **Management:** Agnes De Mille, Artistic Director
> **Officers:** Robert Whitehead, President; Beatrio Renfield, Vice President; Charles Hallerith, Secretary/Treasurer
> **Paid Staff:** 12 **Volunteer Staff:** 2
> **Paid Artists:** 28
> **Utilizes:** Guest Artists; Guest Directors
> **Budget:** $100,000 - $500,000
> **Income Sources:** Private Foundations/Grants/Endowments; Business/Corporate Donations; Box Office; Government Grants
> **Season:** October - November; March - April

ALLNATIONS DANCE COMPANY
Performing Arts Foundation, 500 Riverside Drive, New York, NY 10027
(212) 316-8430
> **Founded:** 1967
> **Arts Area:** Ethnic
> **Status:** Professional; Non-Profit
> **Type:** Performing; Touring; Educational
> **Purpose:** Different people from different parts of the world, can dance in harmony and peace and with mutual respect. "That Brotherhood May Prevail"
> **Management:** Chuck Golden, Artistic Director; Herman Rottenberg, Founder/Executive Director
> **Paid Artists:** 9

Utilizes: Special Technical Talent; Guest Choreographers
Budget: $100,000 - $500,000
Income Sources: Private Foundations/Grants/Endowments; Box Office
Season: September - June **Annual Attendance:** 100,000
Performance Facilities: International House

ALPHA-OMEGA THEATRICAL DANCE COMPANY
c/o Dolores Vanison-Blakely, 711 Amsterdam Avenue, #4E, New York, NY 10025
(212) 749-0095
Founded: 1972
Arts Area: Modern; Jazz
Status: Professional; Non-Profit
Type: Performing
Purpose: To promote knowledge and appreciation of artistic activities related to dance through schools, repertory emsembles and a professional company
Management: Dolores Vanison-Blakely, Executive Director; Martial Roumain, Artistic Director; Ettie Cooper, Fiscal/Bookings
Officers: Migdalia Rodriguez, President; Minnie Richardson, Secretary/Treasurer
Paid Staff: 4 **Volunteer Staff:** 6
Utilizes: Special Technical Talent; Guest Artists; Guest Choreographers
Budget: $1,000 - $50,000
Income Sources: Private Foundations/Grants/Endowments; Business/Corporate Donations; Box Office; Government Grants; Individual Donations
Annual Attendance: 2,000

ALVIN AILEY AMERICAN DANCE THEATER
211 West 61st Street, 3rd Floor, New York, NY 10023
(212) 767-0590
FAX: (212) 767-0625
Founded: 1958
Arts Area: Modern; Ballet; Jazz; Ethnic
Status: Professional; Non-Profit
Type: Performing; Touring; Educational
Purpose: A repertory company dedicated to the presentation and enrichment of the American modern dance heritage and the uniqueness of Black cultural expression; administered by Dance Theater Foundation; affiliated with the Alvin Ailey Repertory Ensemble, a junior company comprised of outstanding scholarship students and the Alvin Ailey American Dance Center, the official school
Management: Judith Jamison, Artistic Director; Masazumi Chaya, Associate Artistic Director; Bill Ferry, General Manager; Michael Kaiser, Executive Director; Sharon Luckman, Director of Development; Laura Beaumont, Director of Marketing; Paul Carlson, Finance Director; Kathleen Rose, Assistant Finance Director/Personnel Director; Sylvia Waters, Artistic Director/Alvin Ailey Dance Ensemble; Denise Jefferson, Director of the Ailey School; Donald Washington, Alvin Company Manager
Officers: Kenneth D. Brody, President; Eleanor Appleharte, Esq., Allan S. Gray, Alex J. Plinio, Vice Chairmen
Paid Staff: 50
Paid Artists: 30
Utilizes: Special Technical Talent; Guest Artists; Guest Choreographers
Budget: $5,000,000 - $10,000,000
Income Sources: Private Foundations/Grants/Endowments; Business/Corporate Donations; Box Office; Government Grants; Individual Donations
Season: 52 Weeks
Affiliations: AGMA; Dance USA
Performance Facilities: City Center Theatre

ALVIN AILEY REPERTORY ENSEMBLE
211 West 61st Street, New York, NY 10023
(212) 767-0590
FAX: (212) 767-0625
Founded: 1974
Arts Area: Modern; Ballet; Jazz; Ethnic
Status: Professional; Non-Profit
Type: Performing; Touring; Educational
Management: Sylvia Waters, Artistic Director; Judith Schray, Business Manager
Officers: Harold Levine, Chairman; Kenneth D. Brody, President
Paid Staff: 18
Paid Artists: 32
Utilizes: Special Technical Talent; Guest Artists; Guest Choreographers
Budget: $5,000,000 - $10,000,000
Income Sources: Private Foundations/Grants/Endowments; Business/Corporate Donations; Box Office; Government Grants; Individual Donations

Season: 52 Weeks
Affiliations: National Corporate Funds For Dance; Dance USA

AMERICAN AUTHENTIC JAZZ DANCE THEATRE
554 West 53rd Street, Suite 8-24, New York, NY 10019
(212) 265-4412
Founded: 1972
Arts Area: Jazz
Status: Non-Profit
Type: Resident; Educational
Management: Ludwig Sheppard, Administrator
Officers: Pepsi Bethel, Artistic Director
Paid Artists: 2
Utilizes: Special Technical Talent; Guest Artists; Guest Choreographers
Budget: $100,000 - $500,000
Income Sources: Private Foundations/Grants/Endowments; Business/Corporate Donations; Box Office; Government Grants; Individual Donations
Season: 52 Weeks

AMERICAN BALLET THEATRE
890 Broadway, 3rd Floor, New York, NY 10003
(212) 477-3030
FAX: (212) 254-5938
Founded: 1940
Arts Area: Ballet
Status: Professional
Type: Performing; Touring
Purpose: National touring annually, international bookings
Management: Les Schoof, General Manager
Paid Artists: 90
Budget: Over 10,000,000
Income Sources: Private Foundations/Grants/Endowments; Business/Corporate Donations; Box Office; Government Grants; Individual Donations
Season: 52 Weeks
Performance Facilities: The Metropolitan Opera House

AMERICAN BALLROOM THEATER COMPANY INC.
305 East 24th Street, #7T, New York, NY 10010
(212) 532-8091
FAX: (212) 532-8091
Arts Area: Ballroom
Status: Professional; Non-Profit
Type: Performing; Educational
Purpose: To preserve, develop and further the tradition of American ballroom dancing; to present it in a choreographed and theatrical form on the stage
Management: Pierre Dulaine, Yvonne Marceau, Co-Artistic Directors; Otto Cappel, Executive Director
Officers: Edward J. Ross, President of the Board
Budget: $500,000 - $1,000,000
Income Sources: Private Foundations/Grants/Endowments; Business/Corporate Donations; Box Office; Government Grants; Individual Donations; Performance Fees
Performance Facilities: St. Paul the Apostle Church, Manhattan

AMERICAN INTERNATIONAL DANCE THEATRE, INC.
375 Riverside Drive, Suite 13A, New York, NY 10025-2170
(212) 662-3468
FAX: (212) 489-9727
Founded: 1981
Arts Area: Ballet; Ethnic; Folk
Status: Professional
Type: Performing; Touring; Educational
Purpose: To present dance shows and concerts for theatres, colleges, municipalities and hotels
Management: Paulette Singer, Managing Director; Russell Miller, Art Director; Max Block, Musical Director
Officers: Paulette Singer, President; Andrew Miller, Secretary; Russell Miller, Treasurer
Paid Staff: 3
Paid Artists: 50
Utilizes: Special Technical Talent; Guest Conductors; Guest Artists; Guest Directors; Guest Choreographers
Budget: $100,000 - $500,000
Income Sources: Box Office

Season: 52 Weeks
Annual Attendance: 100,000
Affiliations: American International Lyric Theatre, Inc.

THE AMERICAN MIME THEATRE
123-40 83rd Avenue, New York, NY 10003
(212) 777-1710
Founded: 1952
Arts Area: Mime; American Mime
Status: Professional; Non-Profit
Type: Performing; Educational
Purpose: To perform and train artists in "American Mime," a form created by Paul J. Curtis, Director of the American Mime Theatre
Management: Paul J. Curtis, Founder/Director; Jean Barbour, Managing Director
Paid Staff: 1 **Volunteer Staff:** 4
Paid Artists: 10
Budget: $1,000 - $50,000
Income Sources: Private Foundations/Grants/Endowments; Business/Corporate Donations; Individual Donations
Season: September - July

ANNABELLA GONZALEZ DANCE THEATER, INC.
4 East 89th Street, #PH-C, New York, NY 10128
(212) 722-4128
Founded: 1976
Arts Area: Modern; Ethnic
Status: Non-Profit
Type: Performing; Touring; Educational
Purpose: To create excellent and original dances; to educate through art
Management: Sonia Miller, Management Consultant
Officers: Annabella Gonzalez, Director; Richard Grimm, Board Chairman; Claude M. Scales, Board Secretary; George Budabin, Carolyn Sanchez, Board Members
Paid Staff: 1 **Volunteer Staff:** 1
Paid Artists: 5 **Non-Paid Artists:** 2
Utilizes: Special Technical Talent; Guest Artists; Guest Choreographers
Budget: $1,000 - $50,000
Income Sources: Private Foundations/Grants/Endowments; Business/Corporate Donations; Box Office; Government Grants; Individual Donations; Class Fees
Season: 52 Weeks
Annual Attendance: 10,000
Affiliations: DTW; The American Dance Guild; The Association of Hispanic Arts

ART BRIDGMAN/MYRNA PACKER
c/o Foundation for Independent Artists, 104 Franklin, New York, NY 10013
(914) 268-9008
Arts Area: Contempory
Status: Professional; Non-Profit
Type: Performing; Touring; Resident; Educational
Purpose: To perform the works and choreography of Myrna Packer and Art Bridgman
Management: Art Bridgman, Myrna Packer, Co-Managers/Choreographers
Budget: $50,000 - $100,000
Income Sources: Business/Corporate Donations; Government Grants; Individual Donations; Touring Fees

ASIAN AMERICAN DANCE THEATRE
26 Bowery, New York, NY 10013
(212) 233-2154
Founded: 1974
Arts Area: Modern; Ethnic; Folk
Status: Professional; Non-Profit
Type: Performing; Touring; Educational
Purpose: Promote traditional Asian dance and its synthesis with traditional dance by performing and visual art programs, concerts, exhibitions, research center and a forum for critical exchange
Management: Eleanor Yung, Artistic Director; Ananya Chatterjea, Manager
Paid Staff: 3
Paid Artists: 25
Utilizes: Guest Artists; Guest Choreographers
Budget: $50,000 - $100,000
Income Sources: Box Office; Government Grants
Season: September - August

BALLET HISPANICO OF NEW YORK
167 West 89th Street, New York, NY 10024
(212) 362-6710
>**Founded:** 1970
>**Arts Area:** Modern; Ballet; Ethnic
>**Status:** Professional; Non-Profit
>**Type:** Performing; Touring; Educational
>**Purpose:** To provide performances and training in contemporary and traditional Hispanic-American dance
>**Management:** Tina Ramirez, Artistic Director; Verdery Roosevelt, Executive Director
>**Officers:** Dhuanne Tansill, President
>**Paid Staff:** 55   **Volunteer Staff:** 15
>**Paid Artists:** 33
>**Utilizes:** Guest Choreographers
>**Budget:** $1,000,000 - $5,000,000
>**Income Sources:** Private Foundations/Grants/Endowments; Business/Corporate Donations; Box Office; Government Grants; Individual Donations
>**Season:** 52 Weeks   **Annual Attendance:** 60,000
>**Affiliations:** Dance USA
>**Performance Facilities:** The Joyce Theater

BALLET MANHATTAN FOUNDATION, INC.
61 West 62nd Street, Suite 17M, New York, NY 10023
(212) 315-4478
FAX: (212) 272-6527
>**Founded:** 1985
>**Arts Area:** Modern; Ballet
>**Status:** Non-Profit
>**Type:** Performing; Touring
>**Purpose:** To perform eclectic works by contemporary choreographers to a wide audience throughout the world
>**Management:** Paul Croitoroo, Executive Director; Charla Genn, Artistic Director; Carollyn Philip, Development Director
>**Officers:** Charla Genn, Vice President; Lawrence C. Manson III; Paul Croitoroo
>**Paid Staff:** 1   **Volunteer Staff:** 2
>**Paid Artists:** 20
>**Utilizes:** Guest Choreographers
>**Budget:** $100,000 - $500,000
>**Income Sources:** Private Foundations/Grants/Endowments; Box Office; Individual Donations; Performance Fees
>**Annual Attendance:** 100,000

BATTERY DANCE COMPANY
380 Broadway, Fifth Floor, New York, NY 10013
(212) 219-3910
FAX: (212) 219-3911
>**Founded:** 1976
>**Arts Area:** Modern
>**Status:** Professional
>**Type:** Performing; Touring; Resident; Educational; Sponsoring
>**Management:** Jonathan Hollander, Artistic Director; Catherine Iannone, Company Manager; Audrey Ross, Press Representative
>**Officers:** Steven Field, Chairman; Robert Brodeegaard, Vice Chairman; Jonathan Hollander, President
>**Paid Staff:** 3   **Volunteer Staff:** 4
>**Paid Artists:** 15
>**Utilizes:** Guest Conductors
>**Budget:** $100,000 - $500,000
>**Income Sources:** Private Foundations/Grants/Endowments; Business/Corporate Donations; Box Office; Government Grants; Individual Donations
>**Season:** 52 Weeks   **Annual Attendance:** 25,000
>**Affiliations:** Pace University
>**Performance Facilities:** French Alliance; Florence Gould Hall

BEBE MILLER COMPANY
c/o Gotham Dance Inc., 54 West 21st Street, Suite 502, New York, NY 10010
(212) 242-6433
FAX: (212) 645-6317
>**Arts Area:** Modern
>**Status:** Professional; Non-Profit
>**Type:** Performing; Touring; Resident
>**Purpose:** To perform the works of Bebe Miller throughout the United States and abroad
>**Management:** Bebe Miller, Artistic Director; Tricia Pierson, Managing Director

Budget: $100,000 - $500,000
Income Sources: Private Foundations/Grants/Endowments; Business/Corporate Donations; Box Office; Government Grants; Individual Donations

BILL T. JONES/ARNIE ZANE AND COMPANY
853 Broadway, Suite 1706, New York, NY 10003
(212) 477-1850
Founded: 1979
Arts Area: Modern
Status: Professional; Non-Profit
Type: Performing; Touring
Purpose: To promote the works of choreographers Bill T. Jones and Arnie Zane
Management: Billena Briggs, Executive Director; Jodi Krizer, Associate Director; Bill T. Jones, Artistic Director
Paid Staff: 5
Paid Artists: 11
Budget: $500,000 - $1,000,000
Income Sources: Private Foundations/Grants/Endowments; Business/Corporate Donations; Box Office; Government Grants; Individual Donations
Season: 52 Weeks

BRUCE KING FOUNDATION FOR AMERICAN DANCE
160 West 73rd Street, New York, NY 10023
(212) 877-6700
Founded: 1959
Arts Area: Modern
Status: Professional; Non-Profit
Type: Performing; Educational
Management: Bruce King Foundation
Officers: Bruce King, President; R.E. Townsend, Secretary; Ron Rader, Treasurer
Volunteer Staff: 3
Paid Artists: 1
Utilizes: Special Technical Talent
Budget: $1,000 - $50,000
Income Sources: Box Office; Individual Donations
Affiliations: AEA; AFTRA

CARLOTA SANTANA SPANISH DANCE COMPANY
One University Place, New York, NY 10003
(212) 473-4605
Founded: 1983
Arts Area: Ethnic
Status: Professional; Non-Profit
Type: Performing; Touring; Resident; Educational
Purpose: To create new ways to work within the traditional Spanish dance vocabulary; to develop new Spanish dance music
Management: Cliff Scott, Downtown Art Company
Officers: Carlota Santana, Artistic Director; Alexandra Teaff, Administrative Assistant
Paid Staff: 3
Paid Artists: 12
Utilizes: Guest Artists; Guest Choreographers
Budget: $50,000 - $100,000
Income Sources: Private Foundations/Grants/Endowments; Business/Corporate Donations; Box Office; Government Grants; Individual Donations
Season: 52 Weeks

CAROL FONDA AND COMPANY/DANCE FORUM, INC.
111 Sullivan Street, Suite B, New York, NY 10012
(212) 431-3364
Founded: 1978
Arts Area: Modern
Status: Professional; Non-Profit
Type: Performing; Touring; Resident; Educational
Purpose: Performing arts series; Arts-in-Education projects; health and wellness projects
Management: Carol Fonda, Acting Managing Director
Officers: Dominick Attanasio, President/Phizer; Russ O'Haver, Vice President/Ernst & Young; Carol Fonda, Vice President/Artistic Director; Denise Mason, Finance Officer/Ernst & Young; Pat Lewis, Vice President/Citibank
Paid Staff: 1   **Volunteer Staff:** 3
Paid Artists: 6
Budget: $50,000 - $100,000

Income Sources: Private Foundations/Grants/Endowments; Business/Corporate Donations; Box Office; Individual Donations; Health & Education products
Annual Attendance: 3,000
Performance Facilities: Triplex; DIA Arts Center

CHARLES MOULTON DANCE COMPANY
285 Mott Street, #18A, New York, NY 10012
(212) 226-3616
    Arts Area: Modern; Tap
    Status: Professional; Non-Profit
    Type: Performing; Touring
    Purpose: To make art
    Paid Staff: 3 **Volunteer Staff:** 1
    Paid Artists: 7
    Budget: $50,000 - $100,000
    Income Sources: Private Foundations/Grants/Endowments; Business/Corporate Donations; Box Office; Government Grants; Individual Donations
    Season: 52 Weeks **Annual Attendance:** 2,000
    Performance Facilities: Performance Space 122

CHEN AND DANCERS
70 Mulberry Street, 2nd Floor, New York, NY 10013
(212) 349-0126
    Founded: 1978
    Arts Area: Modern
    Status: Professional; Non-Profit
    Type: Performing; Touring; Resident; Educational
    Purpose: Chen and Dancers is a professional touring dance company performing contemporary works rooted in an Asian-American heritage.
    Management: H.T. Chen, Artistic Director; Dian Dong, Associate Director; Osamu Uehara, Company Associate; David B. Cheng, Business Manager; Catherine M. Vaucher, Development Coordinator; Sumon Chin, School Administrator, AGC
    Officers: Chris Wu, President/Chairman
    Paid Staff: 14 **Volunteer Staff:** 2
    Paid Artists: 12
    Utilizes: Guest Choreographers
    Budget: $100,000 - $500,000
    Income Sources: Private Foundations/Grants/Endowments; Business/Corporate Donations; Box Office; Government Grants; Individual Donations
    Season: 52 Weeks **Annual Attendance:** 20,000
    Affiliations: APAP

CHINESE FOLK DANCE COMPANY
c/o NY Chinese Cultural Center, 90 West Broadway, #5A, New York, NY 10007
(212) 964-7903
FAX: (212) 732-2482
    Founded: 1973
    Arts Area: Ethnic; Folk
    Status: Professional; Non-Profit
    Type: Performing; Touring; Educational
    Purpose: To perform, present and commission traditional and contemporary dances in the Chinese idiom
    Management: Amy Chin, Executive Director
    Paid Staff: 2 **Volunteer Staff:** 1
    Paid Artists: 20
    Utilizes: Guest Artists
    Budget: $50,000 - $100,000
    Income Sources: Private Foundations/Grants/Endowments; Business/Corporate Donations; Box Office; Government Grants; Individual Donations; Tuition; Fees
    Season: 52 Weeks **Annual Attendance:** 22,000
    Performance Facilities: Triplex Performing Arts Center/Borough of Manhattan Community College

CODANCECO
47 West 73rd Street, New York, NY 10023
(516) 286-7939
    Founded: 1983
    Arts Area: Modern
    Status: Professional; Non-Profit
    Type: Performing; Touring; Resident
    Management: Nancy Duncan, Producing Director
    Paid Staff: 2

Paid Artists: 12
Utilizes: Guest Artists
Budget: $50,000 - $100,000
Income Sources: Private Foundations/Grants/Endowments; Business/Corporate Donations; Box Office; Government Grants; Individual Donations

COURANTE DANCE COMPANY
335 West 35th Street, 12th Floor, New York, NY 10001
(212) 695-3943
Founded: 1981
Arts Area: Historical
Status: Professional
Type: Performing; Touring; Educational
Purpose: To recreate dance from the 16th to 19th centuries; to provide a resource for theater and dance performance practice in historical dance style
Management: Janis Pforsich, Director
Officers: Janis Pforsich, President; Larry Gillaspie, Treasurer; Eleanor Siebold, Secretary
Utilizes: Special Technical Talent; Guest Conductors; Guest Musicians
Budget: $1,000 - $50,000
Income Sources: Private Foundations/Grants/Endowments; Box Office; Individual Donations
Affiliations: Society of Dance History Scholars

DAN WAGONER AND DANCERS
476 Broadway, New York, NY 10013
(212) 334-1880
FAX: (212) 941-1071
Founded: 1969
Arts Area: Modern
Status: Professional; Non-Profit
Type: Performing; Touring; Resident; Educational
Purpose: To maintain Dan Wagoner's dance company; to facilitate the making of new works and the performance of the repertory of Dan Wagoner
Management: Dan Wagoner, Artistic Director; Renee Aarons, Administrative Director; Karen Kloster, Company Manager; Laura Marlow, Development Associate
Officers: Russell Piccione, President; Grace Goodman, Vice President; Edward Henry, Treasurer; Essie Borden, Secretary
Paid Staff: 4 **Volunteer Staff:** 12
Paid Artists: 9
Utilizes: Special Technical Talent; Guest Artists; Guest Accompanists
Budget: $100,000 - $500,000
Income Sources: Private Foundations/Grants/Endowments; Business/Corporate Donations; Box Office; Government Grants; Individual Donations
Season: 52 Weeks **Annual Attendance:** 15,000

DANCE - JUNE LEWIS AND COMPANY
48 West 21st Street, New York, NY 10010
(212) 741-3044
Founded: 1968
Arts Area: Modern
Status: Professional
Type: Performing; Touring; Resident; Educational
Management: Mel Leifer, Publicity Manager; June Lewis, Artistic Director
Paid Artists: 11

DANCE COLLECTIVE
463 West Street, 512A, New York, NY 10014
(212) 624-4275
FAX: (718) 398-9898
Founded: 1974
Arts Area: Modern
Status: Professional; Non-Profit
Type: Performing; Touring
Management: Carol Nolte, Artistic Director; Deborah Demast, Assistant Director
Officers: Allyn Freeman, Chairman, Board of Directors; Stanley Alpert, Attorney
Paid Staff: 1 **Volunteer Staff:** 4
Paid Artists: 6
Budget: $1,000 - $50,000
Income Sources: Private Foundations/Grants/Endowments; Box Office; Individual Donations
Season: September - June

DANCE THEATRE OF HARLEM
466 West 152nd Street, New York, NY 10031
(212) 690-2800
> **Founded:** 1969
> **Arts Area:** Ballet
> **Status:** Professional; Non-Profit
> **Type:** Performing; Touring; Educational
> **Purpose:** To provide creative and educational opportunities for youngsters while maintaining a professional dance company
> **Management:** Arthur Mitchell, Artistic Director; Robert Taylor, Executive Director; Amy Wynn, Director of Administration
> **Officers:** Shahara Ahmad-Llewellyn, Chair; Della Baeza, Gordon Davis, Vice Chairs; Arthur Mitchell, President; Kenneth Ross, Treasurer; Ponchita Pierce, Secretary
> **Paid Staff:** 51   **Volunteer Staff:** 1
> **Paid Artists:** 52
> **Utilizes:** Special Technical Talent; Guest Conductors; Guest Choreographers
> **Budget:** $5,000,000 - $10,000,000
> **Income Sources:** Private Foundations/Grants/Endowments; Business/Corporate Donations; Box Office; Government Grants; Individual Donations; Performance Fees; Tuition
> **Season:** March - April
> **Annual Attendance:** 21,000

DANCE THEATRE WORKSHOP
219 West 19th Street, New York, NY 10011
(212) 691-0173
> **Founded:** 1965
> **Arts Area:** Modern
> **Status:** Professional; Non-Profit
> **Type:** Performing
> **Purpose:** To identify and nurture the most provocative and visionary independent artists at work in the contemporary arena of dance, performance, theatre, music and allied arts
> **Management:** David R. White, Artistic Director/Producer; Laura Shandlemyer, Associate Producer; Gail Goldstein, Assistant Producer
> **Officers:** Bessie Schoenberg, Chairman; Carol Brice Buchanan, Secretary of Development
> **Paid Staff:** 25   **Volunteer Staff:** 5
> **Budget:** $1,000,000 - $5,000,000
> **Income Sources:** Private Foundations/Grants/Endowments; Business/Corporate Donations; Box Office; Government Grants; Individual Donations
> **Season:** August - June   **Annual Attendance:** 25,000
> **Performance Facilities:** Bessie Schoenberg Theater

DANCE 2000: THE FELICE LESSER DANCE THEATER
484 West 43rd Street, #4J, New York, NY 10036
(212) 594-3388
> **Founded:** 1975
> **Arts Area:** Modern; Ballet
> **Status:** Professional; Non-Profit
> **Type:** Performing; Touring; Resident; Educational
> **Purpose:** To engage in the creation of new dance works; To perform, teach and tour
> **Management:** Felice Lesser, Artistic Director
> **Utilizes:** Special Technical Talent; Guest Artists; Composers; Fine Artists
> **Budget:** $1,000 - $50,000
> **Income Sources:** Private Foundations/Grants/Endowments; Business/Corporate Donations; Box Office; Individual Donations

DANCEBRAZIL
c/o Capoeira Foundation Inc., 104 Franklin Street, New York, NY 10013
(212) 274-9737
FAX: (212) 925-0369
> **Arts Area:** Modern; Ethnic; Folk
> **Status:** Professional; Non-Profit
> **Type:** Performing; Touring; Resident; Educational; Sponsoring
> **Purpose:** To produce, perform and preserve traditional and contemporary Brazilian and Afro-Brazilian dance and music; to explore, educate and innovate within the context of a culturally specific art form so that an African-based tradition is renewed and maintained, new audiences are created and linkages among differing communities are built
> **Management:** Jelon Viera, Artistic Director; Nem Brito, Associate Artistic Director
> **Budget:** $100,000 - $500,000

Income Sources: Private Foundations/Grants/Endowments; Business/Corporate Donations; Box Office; Government Grants; Individual Donations

DANCELLINGTON, INC.
PO Box 20346, Parkwest Finance Station, New York, NY 10025
(212) 724-5562
Founded: 1982
Arts Area: Modern; Ballet; Jazz; Ethnic; Tap
Status: Professional; Non-Profit; Commercial
Type: Performing; Touring; Educational
Purpose: To preserve tap dance heritage and its place in American history; to present the development of tap dance combining other dance forms
Management: Mercedes Ellington, Artistic Director; Ilona Copen, Advisory Coimmittee Chair; Florio Roettger, Financial Advisor; Rosemary Joyce, Public Relations/Grant Producer
Officers: Mercedes Ellington, President; Ruth B. Boatwright, Vice President; Denise Batts, Secretary
Volunteer Staff: 4
Non-Paid Artists: 16
Utilizes: Special Technical Talent; Guest Artists; Guest Choreographers; Grant Writers
Budget: $1,000 - $50,000
Income Sources: Private Foundations/Grants/Endowments; Business/Corporate Donations; Box Office; Government Grants; Individual Donations
Season: 52 Weeks

DANCING IN THE KITCHEN SERIES
c/o Haleakala Inc., 512 West 19th Street, New York, NY 10011
(212) 255-5793
FAX: (212) 645-4258
Arts Area: Modern
Status: Professional; Non-Profit
Type: Performing; Resident; Educational; Sponsoring
Purpose: To identify and nurture artists whose distinguished voices contribute to the development of the field; to reflect a diversity of artists from a vast landscape of cultural perspectives, exploring their own issues of personal and cultural identity through their work
Management: Lauren Amazeen, Executive Director; JoAnn Jansen, Dance Curator
Officers: Paula Cooper, Chairman of the Board
Income Sources: Private Foundations/Grants/Endowments; Business/Corporate Donations; Box Office; Government Grants; Individual Donations
Performance Facilities: The Kitchen

DANCING IN THE STREETS, INC.
131 Varick Street, Suite 903, New York, NY 10013
(212) 989-6830
FAX: (212) 727-2535
Arts Area: Modern; Ethnic; Folk
Status: Professional; Non-Profit
Type: Producing
Purpose: To make performing arts recognized as a public art form, drawing attention to unusual architecture and natural settings; to bring the work of innovative artists to new audiences
Management: Elise Bernhardt, Executive Director/Producer
Budget: $100,000 - $500,000
Income Sources: Private Foundations/Grants/Endowments; Business/Corporate Donations; Government Grants; Individual Donations

DANSE MIRAGE, INC./ELINOR COLEMAN DANCE EMSEMBLE
153 Mercer Street, 2nd Floor, New York, NY 10012-3239
(212) 226-5767
FAX: (212) 219-0601
Founded: 1982
Arts Area: Modern; Jazz
Status: Professional
Type: Performing; Touring; Educational; Sponsoring
Management: Donna M. Bost, Managing Director
Officers: Elinor Coleman, President/Artistic Director
Paid Staff: 3   **Volunteer Staff:** 2
Paid Artists: 10
Budget: $100,000 - $500,000
Income Sources: Private Foundations/Grants/Endowments; Business/Corporate Donations; Individual Donations
Season: September - July

THE DANSPACE PROJECT, INC.
St. Mark's Church, Second Avenue and Tenth Street, New York, NY 10003
(212) 674-8112
FAX: (212) 529-2318
Founded: 1974
Arts Area: Modern; Experimental; Postmodern
Status: Professional; Non-Profit
Type: Performing; Artists Services
Purpose: To present new choreography by emerging and seasoned artists
Management: Laurie Uprichard, Executive Director
Officers: Penelope Dannenberg, President; Elizabeth Berger, Vice President; Elizabeth Rectanus, Bebe Miller, Co-Treasurers; Pamela Auchincloss, Secretary
Paid Staff: 7   **Volunteer Staff:** 20
Paid Artists: 50
Utilizes: Guest Artists; Guest Choreographers
Budget: $100,000 - $500,000
Income Sources: Private Foundations/Grants/Endowments; Business/Corporate Donations; Box Office; Government Grants; Individual Donations
Season: September - June   **Annual Attendance:** 9,000
Performance Facilities: Sanctuary Performace Space at St. Mark's Church

DAVID GORDON/PICK UP COMPANY
104 Franklin, New York, NY 10013
(212) 431-0447
FAX: (212) 431-0425
Founded: 1978
Arts Area: Modern; Theater
Status: Professional; Non-Profit
Type: Performing; Touring; Resident
Purpose: To produce and promote the work of David Gordon
Management: June Poster, Managing Director
Officers: Arlene Shuler, Chairperson; Michael Brill, Vice Chairperson; Michael Remer, Secretary
Paid Staff: 2   **Volunteer Staff:** 1
Paid Artists: 15
Budget: $100,000 - $500,000
Income Sources: Private Foundations/Grants/Endowments; Business/Corporate Donations; Box Office; Government Grants; Individual Donations
Affiliations: Dance USA; APAP; WAAA

DAVID PARSONS DANCE COMPANY
476 Broadway, New York, NY 10013
(212) 941-1038
FAX: (212) 941-1071
Founded: 1985
Arts Area: Modern; Ballet
Status: Professional
Type: Performing; Touring; Resident; Educational
Purpose: To create and perform modern dance; to educate and experiment
Management: Sheldon Soffer, Management; David Parsons, Artistic Director; Gray Montague, Executive Director
Paid Staff: 3
Paid Artists: 8
Utilizes: Guest Artists
Budget: $500,000 - $1,000,000
Income Sources: Private Foundations/Grants/Endowments; Business/Corporate Donations; Box Office; Government Grants; Individual Donations
Season: 52 Weeks   **Annual Attendance:** 180,000

DINOSAUR DANCE COMPANY
211 West 61st Street, 4th Floor, New York, NY 10023
(212) 315-3616
Founded: 1968
Arts Area: Modern
Status: Professional; Non-Profit
Type: Performing; Touring
Purpose: Modern dance performances, self-produced, and touring
Management: Michael Mao, Artistic Director; Joseph Richards, Manager Director
Officers: Elizabeth Mallinckroot, President; Michael Klein, Treasurer

Paid Staff: 4   **Volunteer Staff:** 15
Paid Artists: 15
Utilizes: Special Technical Talent; Guest Artists
Budget: $100,000 - $500,000
Income Sources: Private Foundations/Grants/Endowments; Box Office; Government Grants; Individual Donations
Season: March - May - September - November
Performance Facilities: Studio Workshop

THE DONALD BYRD DANCE FOUNDATION, INC.
59 Franklin Street, New York, NY 10013
(212) 431-7362
FAX: (212) 431-3025
Founded: 1984
Arts Area: Modern; Ballet; Jazz
Status: Professional
Type: Performing; Touring; Resident; Educational
Purpose: To introduce dance to as wide an audience as possible
Management: Donald Byrd, Artistic Director; Dee Warfield, Administrative Director; Fabio Pacciucci, Development Director
Officers: Donald Byrd, President; Andrea Reese, Treasurer; Clarence Clark, Secretary
Paid Staff: 3   **Volunteer Staff:** 2
Paid Artists: 14
Utilizes: Special Technical Talent; Guest Artists; Guest Choreographers
Budget: $100,000 - $500,000
Income Sources: Private Foundations/Grants/Endowments; Business/Corporate Donations; Box Office; Government Grants; Individual Donations
Season: September - March
Annual Attendance: 20,000

DOUG ELKINS DANCE COMPANY
PO Box 951, New York, NY 10011
(212) 228-2071
Founded: 1987
Arts Area: Modern; Street Styles; House Styles
Status: Professional; Non-Profit
Type: Performing; Educational
Purpose: To create and present the work of Doug Elkins; to teach all levels and ages
Management: Doug Elkins, Artistic Director; Jane Weiner, Company Manager; Lisa Nicks, Financial Director; Cathy Zimmerman, Booking
Paid Staff: 4
Paid Artists: 9
Utilizes: Guest Artists
Budget: $50,000 - $100,000
Income Sources: Private Foundations/Grants/Endowments; Box Office; Government Grants; Individual Donations
Season: September - August
Annual Attendance: 10,000

DOUGLAS DUNN AND DANCERS
c/o Rio Grande Union, Inc., 541 Broadway, New York, NY 10012
(212) 966-6999
FAX: (212) 274-1804
Founded: 1976
Arts Area: Modern
Status: Professional; Non-Profit
Type: Performing; Touring; Educational
Purpose: To produce and promote the works of contemporary choreographer Douglas Dunn
Management: Elizabeth Powers, Manager; Jessica Baker, Booking Representative-Pentacle
Officers: Christopher Sweet, Amy Lamphere, Anne Bradner, Douglas Dunn, Directors
Paid Staff: 2
Paid Artists: 8
Utilizes: Special Technical Talent
Budget: $100,000 - $500,000
Income Sources: Private Foundations/Grants/Endowments; Business/Corporate Donations; Box Office; Government Grants; Individual Donations; Presenter Commissions
Season: 52 Weeks
Annual Attendance: 10,000
Affiliations: Pentacle/Danceworks, Inc.

EDITH STEPHEN ELECTRIC CURRENTS
55 Bethune Street, 630 A, New York, NY 10014
(212) 989-2250
Founded: 1980
Arts Area: Modern
Status: Professional
Type: Performing; Touring
Purpose: To perform throughout the United States and Europe giving multimedia programs combining dance with film, sculpture, new music and visuals
Management: Ben Jennings, Company Manager
Officers: Lee Wallace, President Board of Directors; Lucille Jason, Treasurer; Elaine Shipman, Secretary
Paid Staff: 3
Paid Artists: 6 **Non-Paid Artists:** 1
Utilizes: Special Technical Talent
Budget: $50,000 - $100,000
Income Sources: Private Foundations/Grants/Endowments; Box Office; Government Grants; Individual Donations
Season: 52 Weeks
Annual Attendance: 5,000
Affiliations: American Dance Guild; Foundation for the Advancement of Dance; American Dance Guild
Performance Facilities: Dance Connection

EDWARD VILLELLA AND DANCERS
316 West 82nd Street, 1R, New York, NY 10024
(914) 462-7384
FAX: (914) 462-1858
Founded: 1976
Arts Area: Ballet
Status: Professional
Type: Performing; Touring; Resident; Educational
Purpose: To illuminate the art of ballet
Management: Marcia Preiss, Management
Paid Artists: 5
Budget: $1,000 - $50,000
Income Sources: Fees
Season: 52 Weeks

EIKO AND KOMA
c/o Foundation for Independent Artists, 104 Franklin Street, New York, NY 10013
(212) 226-2000
FAX: (212) 925-0369
Arts Area: Contemporary
Status: Professional; Non-Profit
Type: Performing; Touring; Resident; Educational
Purpose: To perform the theater choreography of Eiko and Koma
Management: Eiko and Koma Otake, Artistic Directors/Choreographers
Budget: $100,000 - $500,000
Income Sources: Business/Corporate Donations; Government Grants; Touring Income; Fees

ELEO POMARE DANCE COMPANY
325 West 16th Street, New York, NY 10011
(212) 924-4628
Founded: 1958
Arts Area: Modern
Status: Professional; Non-Profit
Type: Performing; Touring; Resident; Educational
Management: Eleo Pomare, Company Manager
Paid Staff: 3
Paid Artists: 20
Season: 52 Weeks

ELISA MONTE DANCE COMPANY
39 Great Jones Street, New York, NY 10012
(212) 533-2226
FAX: (212) 254-4071
Founded: 1981
Arts Area: Modern
Status: Professional; Non-Profit
Type: Performing; Touring; Educational

Purpose: To advance and enrich the art of dance through the presentation of the innovative choreography and outreach activities of Elisa Monte
Management: Bernard G. Schmidt, Managing Director
Officers: Elisa Monte, President; David Brown, Treasurer; Nathalie Berliet, Chair
Paid Staff: 2   **Volunteer Staff:** 2
Paid Artists: 9
Budget: $100,000 - $500,000
Income Sources: Private Foundations/Grants/Endowments; Business/Corporate Donations; Box Office; Government Grants; Individual Donations
Season: 52 Weeks   **Annual Attendance:** 30,000
Affiliations: Dance USA
Performance Facilities: The Joyce Theater

ERICK HAWKINS DANCE COMPANY
38 East 19th Street, 8th Floor, New York, NY 10003
(212) 777-7355
Founded: 1952
Arts Area: Modern
Status: Professional; Non-Profit
Type: Performing; Touring; Educational
Purpose: To perform the choreography of Erick Hawkins with an annual home season in New York City; to tour
Management: Erick Hawkins, Artistic Director; Robert Engstrom, President; Michael Wright, Executive Director; Beverly Wright, Booking Management
Officers: Michael Levin, Chairman of the Board
Paid Staff: 5   **Volunteer Staff:** 1
Paid Artists: 24
Utilizes: Special Technical Talent; Commissioned Music
Budget: $500,000 - $1,000,000
Income Sources: Private Foundations/Grants/Endowments; Business/Corporate Donations; Box Office; Government Grants; Individual Donations; Touring Fees; School Tuition
Season: 52 Weeks   **Annual Attendance:** 40,000
Affiliations: APAP

ERNESTA CORVINO'S DANCE CIRCLE COMPANY
c/o DanceCor, Inc., 451 West 50th Street, New York, NY 10019
(212) 582-0571
Founded: 1981
Arts Area: Ballet
Status: Professional; Non-Profit
Type: Performing
Purpose: To provide the public with high quality and affordable dance performances as well as workshops and lecture demonstrations
Management: Ernesta Corvino, Director; Andra Corvino, Ballet Mistress; Gail S. Block, Manager
Officers: Ernesta Corvino, President; Andra Corvino, Vice President; Robert E. Lynn, Treasurer/Secretary
Budget: $1,000 - $50,000
Income Sources: Box Office; Individual Donations
Performance Facilities: Marymount Manhattan Theatre

EUGENE JAMES DANCE COMPANY
GPO 2504, New York, NY 10116
(212) 564-1026
Founded: 1967
Arts Area: Modern; Ethnic
Status: Professional; Non-Profit
Type: Performing; Touring; Resident
Purpose: To extend the contributions of Afro-American rhythms in dance
Management: Richard Williams, Manager; Eugene James, Artistic Director
Volunteer Staff: 3
Paid Artists: 8
Budget: $1,000 - $50,000
Income Sources: Box Office; Individual Donations
Season: September - May

FELD BALLETS/NY
The Lawrence A. Wien Center for Dance & Theatre, 890 Broadway, New York, NY 10003
(212) 777-7710
FAX: (212) 353-0936
Founded: 1974

Arts Area: Ballet
Status: Professional; Non-Profit
Type: Performing; Touring; Resident; Educational
Purpose: To perform the works of Eliot Feld that span his twenty-five years of choreography; the company tours both domestically and abroad and performs at the Joyce Theatre approximately six weeks a year and tours for approximately 10 weeks a year
Management: Eliot Feld, Director/Choreographer; Susan Spier, Director of Media and Public Relations; Eugene Lowery, Booking Manager; Susan J. Kirschner, Director of Finance; Roz Black, Director of Development; Zetta Zaka, Company Manager; Patrice Thomas, Production Manager
Officers: Eliot Feld, President; Cora Cahan, Vice President; Bernard Gersten, Treasurer; Peter L. Felcher Esq., Secretary
Paid Staff: 12   **Volunteer Staff:** 1
Paid Artists: 22
Budget: $1,000,000 - $5,000,000
Income Sources: Private Foundations/Grants/Endowments; Business/Corporate Donations; Box Office; Government Grants; Individual Donations; Sponsor Fees
Season: 52 Weeks
Annual Attendance: 21,000
Affiliations: AGMA
Performance Facilities: Joyce Theater

14TH STREET DANCE CENTER AT EDUCATIONAL ALLIANCE
197 East Broadway, New York, NY 10002
(212) 673-2207
Arts Area: Modern; Mime; Ballet; Jazz; Ethnic; Folk
Status: Non-Profit
Type: Sponsoring; Presenting
Purpose: To present contemporary music and dance at affordable prices
Management: Oceola Bragg, Executive/Artistic Director
Officers: Bradley Nance, Chairman of the Board
Budget: $100,000 - $500,000
Income Sources: Private Foundations/Grants/Endowments; Business/Corporate Donations; Box Office; Government Grants; Individual Donations
Performance Facilities: Theater at Educational Alliance

ICE THEATER OF NEW YORK, INC.
Sky Rink, 450 West 33rd Street, 16th Floor, New York, NY 10001
(212) 239-4320
FAX: (212) 239-4327
Arts Area: Modern
Status: Professional; Non-Profit
Type: Performing; Touring; Educational
Purpose: To build an artistic repertory of ice skating performance pieces; to provide an environment in which professional skaters from various backgrounds can collaborate with choreographers, musicians and visual artists to create and perform new works
Management: Moira North, Director; Rob McBrien, Artistic Director
Officers: William Candee III, Chairman
Budget: $100,000 - $500,000
Income Sources: Private Foundations/Grants/Endowments; Business/Corporate Donations; Box Office; Government Grants; Individual Donations
Performance Facilities: Sky Rink

JANIS BRENNER AND DANCERS
356 East 89th Street, 5A, New York, NY 10128
(212) 534-3227
Founded: 1987
Arts Area: Modern
Status: Professional; Non-Profit
Type: Performing; Touring; Educational
Purpose: To perform the work of Janis Brenner; to conduct teaching workshops in technique, improvisation, composition, repertory and voice
Management: Brenda Sale Artists Managment
Paid Artists: 6
Utilizes: Special Technical Talent; Guest Composers; Designers
Budget: $1,000 - $50,000
Income Sources: Private Foundations/Grants/Endowments; Business/Corporate Donations; Box Office; Individual Donations

JENNIFER MULLER-THE WORKS
131 West 24th Street, New York, NY 10011
(212) 691-3803
FAX: (212) 206-6630
Founded: 1970
Arts Area: Modern
Status: Professional; Non-Profit
Type: Performing; Touring; Resident
Management: Lauren Barnes, Executive Director; Jennifer Muller, Artistic Director
Paid Staff: 2 **Volunteer Staff:** 1
Paid Artists: 10
Utilizes: Guest Artists
Budget: $100,000 - $500,000
Income Sources: Private Foundations/Grants/Endowments; Business/Corporate Donations; Box Office; Government Grants; Individual Donations
Season: 52 Weeks

JOAN MILLER'S DANCE PLAYERS
1380 Riverside Drive, New York, NY 10033
(212) 568-8854
Founded: 1969
Arts Area: Modern; Ballet; Jazz; Ethnic
Status: Professional
Type: Performing; Touring
Purpose: Joan Miller's Dance Players are primarily a multi-ethnic performing company but are excellently qualified to teach a wide range of dance-related activities.
Management: Joan Miller, Artistic Director/Choreographer; Margaret Hanks, Company Manager
Officers: Samuel Coleman, President of the Board; Susan Skovronek, Vice President; Michael Flanigan, Treasurer; Davis Roberts, Secretary
Paid Staff: 3 **Volunteer Staff:** 5
Paid Artists: 15 **Non-Paid Artists:** 5
Utilizes: Special Technical Talent; Guest Artists
Budget: $1,000 - $50,000
Income Sources: Private Foundations/Grants/Endowments; Business/Corporate Donations; Box Office; Government Grants; Individual Donations
Season: October - June **Annual Attendance:** 9,000
Affiliations: DTW

JOFFREY BALLET
130 West 56th Street, New York, NY 10019
(212) 265-7300
FAX: (212) 397-1786
West Coast Operations Office: 14819 Magnolia Boulevard, Suite 202, Sherman Oaks, CA 91403; (818) 986-4503
Founded: 1956
Arts Area: Ballet
Status: Professional; Non-Profit
Type: Performing; Touring; Resident; Educational; Sponsoring
Management: Gerald Arpino, Artistic Director; C.C. Conner, Acting Executive Director; Roberta Stewart, West Coast Representative
Officers: Michael Tennebaum, Chairman
Paid Staff: 39 **Volunteer Staff:** 10
Paid Artists: 51
Utilizes: Special Technical Talent; Guest Choreographers
Budget: $5,000,000 - $10,000,000
Income Sources: Private Foundations/Grants/Endowments; Business/Corporate Donations; Box Office; Government Grants; Individual Donations
Annual Attendance: 250,000
Performance Facilities: City Center

THE JOFFREY II DANCERS
130 West 56th Street, New York, NY 10019
(212) 265-7300
Arts Area: Ballet
Status: Professional; Non-Profit
Type: Performing; Educational
Management: Jeremy Blanton, Artistic Director
Paid Artists: 10
Budget: $100,000 - $500,000

Income Sources: Private Foundations/Grants/Endowments; Business/Corporate Donations; Individual Donations
Season: September - May
Affiliations: Joffrey Ballet

JOSE LIMON DANCE COMPANY
622 Broadway, 5th Floor, New York, NY 10012
(212) 777-3353
FAX: (212) 777-4764
Founded: 1968
Arts Area: Modern
Status: Professional; Non-Profit
Type: Performing; Touring; Resident
Management: Carla Maxwell, Artistic Director
Paid Staff: 3
Paid Artists: 14
Utilizes: Special Technical Talent; Guest Artists; Guest Choreographers
Budget: $100,000 - $500,000
Income Sources: Private Foundations/Grants/Endowments; Business/Corporate Donations; Box Office; Government Grants; Individual Donations
Season: 52 Weeks

JUILLIARD DANCE ENSEMBLE
The Juilliard School, 60 Lincoln Center Plaza, New York, NY 10023
(212) 799-5000
Founded: 1951
Arts Area: Modern; Ballet; Jazz; Ethnic; Tap
Status: Non-Professional; Non-Profit
Type: Performing; Resident
Purpose: Training company
Management: Benjamin Jarkarvy, Artistic Director; Martha Hill, Artistic Director Emeritus
Non-Paid Artists: 30
Utilizes: Guest Artists
Season: November - March
Performance Facilities: Juilliard Theater

K2 DANCE AND ARTS COMPANY, INC.
336 East 5th Street, New York, NY 10003
(718) 852-5944
Founded: 1981
Arts Area: Modern
Status: Professional
Type: Performing; Educational
Purpose: To develop cultural awareness in the community through dance performances
Officers: Diane Roberts, Publicist; Penny Ward, Board Director; Kay Nishikawa, Artistic Director
Paid Staff: 2   **Volunteer Staff:** 2
Paid Artists: 8
Utilizes: Guest Artists
Budget: $1,000 - $50,000
Income Sources: Box Office; Individual Donations
Season: Fall; Winter   **Annual Attendance:** 1,000

KAZUKO HIRABAYASHI DANCE THEATRE
330 Broome Street, New York, NY 10002
(212) 966-6414
Founded: 1971
Arts Area: Modern
Status: Professional; Non-Profit
Type: Performing; Touring; Educational
Purpose: Combining her Japanese heritage, Eastern philosophy and artistic grounding, with a firm base in classical and modern dance, Kazuko Hirabayashi creates her own strikingly beautiful dance pieces. Performances to the public are offered, as well as educational programs.
Officers: Kazuko Hirabayashi, President; Robert Swinton, Vice President
Non-Paid Artists: 10
Budget: $1,000 - $50,000
Annual Attendance: 1,500
Performance Facilities: Kazuko Hirabayashi Dance Theatre

KEI TAKEI'S MOVING EARTH (MOVING EARTH INC.)
28 Vesey Street, #2200, New York, NY 10007
(212) 459-4383
FAX: (212) 732-3926
Founded: 1969
Arts Area: Modern
Status: Professional
Type: Performing; Touring
Purpose: To perform the internationally acclaimed, award-winning choreography of Kei Takei
Management: Laz Brezer, Executive Director
Officers: Kei Takei, Chairwoman; Louise Roberts, President; Maldwyn Pate, Vice President; Lawrence Brezer, Secretary/Treasurer
Paid Staff: 3   **Volunteer Staff:** 12
Paid Artists: 18   **Non-Paid Artists:** 8
Budget: $100,000 - $500,000
Income Sources: Private Foundations/Grants/Endowments; Business/Corporate Donations; Box Office; Government Grants; Individual Donations
Season: 52 Weeks   **Annual Attendance:** 100,000

KENNETH KING AND DANCERS
c/o Transmedia Kinetrics Coalition Inc., 104 Franklin, New York, NY 10013
(212) 226-2000; (212) 925-6917
FAX: (212) 925-0369
Arts Area: Contemporary
Status: Professional; Non-Profit
Type: Performing; Touring; Resident; Educational
Purpose: To perform the work and choreography of Kenneth King
Management: Kenneth King, Manager/Choreographer
Budget: $50,000 - $100,000
Income Sources: Business/Corporate Donations; Government Grants; Individual Donations; Touring Fees

LABAN/BARTENIEFF INSTITUTE OF MOVEMENT STUDIES
11 East Fourth Street, 3rd Floor, New York, NY 10003-6902
(212) 477-4299
FAX: (212) 477-3702
Founded: 1978
Arts Area: Modern; Mime; Ballet; Body Therapy; Movement Analysis
Status: Professional; Non-Professional; Non-Profit
Type: Performing; Educational; Sponsoring
Purpose: To teach Labon movement analysis, Bartenieff fundamentals and movement dance theatre and health
Management: Martha Eddy, Executive Director; Janis Pforsich, Certificate Director; Cheryl Clark, Programming Director
Officers: Frank Didero, Chair; Riccardo Gondolfo, Treasurer; Dorit Dyke, Vice President of Promotion; Karen Bradley, Vice President of Education
Paid Staff: 3
Utilizes: Guest Artists
Budget: $100,000 - $500,000
Income Sources: Private Foundations/Grants/Endowments; Business/Corporate Donations; Box Office; Government Grants; Individual Donations; Tuition
Season: September - July
Affiliations: NASD; Emergency Fund for Student Dancers; DTW: ADTA; International Movement Therapists Association; National Dance Association; International Association for Dance Medicine and Science

LAR LUBOVITCH DANCE COMPANY
15-17 West 18th Street, 5th Floor, New York, NY 10011-4601
(212) 242-0633
FAX: (212) 691-8315
Founded: 1968
Arts Area: Modern
Status: Professional; Non-Profit
Type: Performing; Touring; Educational
Purpose: The creation, performance and teaching of contemporary dance throughout the United States and the world
Management: Dick Caples, Executive Director; Lar Lubovitch, Artistic Director
Paid Staff: 5
Paid Artists: 16
Utilizes: Guest Artists
Budget: $1,000,000 - $5,000,000
Income Sources: Private Foundations/Grants/Endowments; Business/Corporate Donations; Box Office; Government Grants; Individual Donations

Season: 52 Weeks **Annual Attendance:** 100,000
Affiliations: Dance USA; APAP
Performance Facilities: City Center Theater

LARRY RICHARDSON DANCE FOUNDATION
40 Park Avenue, New York, NY 10016
(212) 685-5972
Founded: 1967
Arts Area: Modern; Mime; Ballet; Jazz; Ethnic
Status: Professional; Non-Profit
Type: Performing; Resident; Educational; Sponsoring
Purpose: To foster interest in and create a new audience for dance and the allied performing arts in the community
Management: Larry Richardson, Artistic Director; J. Antony Siciliano, Administrative Director
Officers: John Afton, Counsel
Paid Staff: 4
Paid Artists: 8
Utilizes: Special Technical Talent; Guest Artists
Income Sources: Box Office
Season: 52 Weeks
Performance Facilities: Larry Richardson's Dance Gallery

LAURA DEAN DANCERS AND MUSICIANS
260 West Broadway, New York, NY 10013
(212) 941-7746
Founded: 1976
Arts Area: Modern
Status: Professional; Non-Profit
Type: Performing; Touring; Educational
Purpose: This internationally acclaimed company presents the works of choreographer/composer Laura Dean.
Management: Laura Dean, Artistic Director; Michael Feibish, Managing Director; Mary Rindfleisch, Company Manager
Officers: Charles Burger, Laura Dean, Fran Kaufman, W. McNeil Lowry, Elaine Malsin
Paid Staff: 3 **Volunteer Staff:** 1
Paid Artists: 17
Utilizes: Special Technical Talent
Budget: $500,000 - $1,000,000
Income Sources: Private Foundations/Grants/Endowments; Business/Corporate Donations; Box Office; Government Grants; Individual Donations
Season: 52 Weeks

LES BALLETS TROCKADERO DE MONTE CARLO
130 West 56 Street, New York, NY 10019
(212) 757-8060
Founded: 1973
Arts Area: Ballet
Status: Professional; Non-Profit
Type: Performing; Touring
Purpose: Ballet parody
Management: Sheldon Soffer Management
Paid Artists: 12
Utilizes: Guest Artists
Budget: $500,000 - $1,000,000
Income Sources: Box Office; Individual Donations
Season: 52 Weeks

LUCINDA CHILDS DANCE COMPANY
541 Broadway, New York, NY 10012
(212) 431-7599
Founded: 1973
Arts Area: Modern
Status: Professional; Non-Profit
Type: Performing; Touring; Resident; Educational
Purpose: To create and perform works by Lucinda Childs
Management: Lucinda Childs, Artistic Director
Officers: Lucinda Childs, President
Paid Staff: 3
Paid Artists: 10
Utilizes: Special Technical Talent
Budget: $100,000 - $500,000

Income Sources: Private Foundations/Grants/Endowments; Business/Corporate Donations; Government Grants; Individual Donations
Season: July - June **Annual Attendance:** 5,000
Affiliations: Dance USA; APAP; WAAA

LUIS RIVERA SPANISH DANCE COMPANY
232 East 26th Street, New York, NY 10010
(212) 689-0921
Founded: 1970
Arts Area: Ethnic; Folk
Status: Professional; Non-Profit; Commercial
Type: Performing; Touring; Educational
Purpose: To further the knowledge and appreciation of Spanish dance
Management: Luis Rivera, Artistic Director
Officers: Robert P. Luzell, President; Maura G. Luzell, Secretary/Treasurer; Ruth Ontiveros, Dale Goodwin, Directors
Paid Artists: 6
Utilizes: Special Technical Talent; Guest Artists
Income Sources: Box Office; Government Grants; Individual Donations

MANHATTAN BALLET FOUNDATION
61 West 62nd Street, New York, NY 10023
(212) 315-4478
Founded: 1985
Arts Area: Ballet; Contemporary
Status: Professional; Non-Profit
Type: Performing; Touring
Management: Charla Genn, Artistic Director; Paul Croitoroo, Executive Director; Karollyn Philip, Director of Development
Paid Staff: 3
Paid Artists: 16
Utilizes: Guest Artists
Budget: $100,000 - $500,000
Income Sources: Box Office; Individual Donations
Season: 52 Weeks

MARK DE GARMO AND DANCERS
179 East Third Street, #24, New York, NY 10009-7754
(212) 353-1351
FAX: (212) 353-1351
Founded: 1982
Arts Area: Modern
Status: Professional
Type: Performing; Touring; Resident; Educational
Purpose: To develop and perform the original choreography of Mark DeGarmo
Management: Jan Michael Hanvik, Manager
Paid Staff: 1 **Volunteer Staff:** 2
Paid Artists: 6
Budget: $50,000 - $100,000
Income Sources: Private Foundations/Grants/Endowments; Business/Corporate Donations; Box Office; Government Grants; Individual Donations
Season: 52 Weeks
Affiliations: Dance USA

MARK MORRIS DANCE GROUP
225 Lafayette Street, Suite 504, New York, NY 10012
(212) 219-3660
FAX: (212) 219-3960
Founded: 1980
Arts Area: Modern
Status: Professional; Non-Profit
Type: Performing; Touring
Purpose: To create and perform the works of Mark Morris
Management: Mark Morris, Artistic Director; Barry Alterman, General Director; Nancy Umanoff, Managing Director
Paid Staff: 9 **Volunteer Staff:** 2
Paid Artists: 17
Utilizes: Special Technical Talent; Guest Conductors; Guest Artists
Budget: $1,000,000 - $5,000,000

Income Sources: Private Foundations/Grants/Endowments; Business/Corporate Donations; Box Office; Government Grants; Individual Donations

MARTHA GRAHAM DANCE COMPANY

316 East 63rd Street, New York, NY 10021
(212) 832-9166
FAX: (212) 223-0351
  Founded: 1926
  Arts Area: Modern
  Status: Professional; Non-Profit
  Type: Performing; Touring; Educational
  Purpose: To perform the original works of Martha Graham
  Management: Ron Protas and Linda Hooks, Artistic Directors; Russ Alley, Executive Director; James M. Johnson, Director of Operations
  Paid Staff: 12
  Paid Artists: 30
  Utilizes: Guest Conductors
  Budget: $1,000,000 - $5,000,000
  Income Sources: Private Foundations/Grants/Endowments; Business/Corporate Donations; Box Office; Government Grants; Individual Donations
  Season: 52 Weeks

MARY ANTHONY DANCE THEATRE-PHOENIX

736 Broadway, New York, NY 10003
(212) 674-8191
  Founded: 1956
  Arts Area: Modern
  Status: Professional; Non-Profit
  Type: Performing; Touring; Educational
  Purpose: To present modern dance through performances, lecture-demonstrations and technique classes
  Management: Mary Anthony, Artistic Director
  Officers: Mary Anthony, President
  Paid Staff: 6   **Volunteer Staff:** 15
  Paid Artists: 12
  Budget: $50,000 - $100,000
  Income Sources: Private Foundations/Grants/Endowments; Business/Corporate Donations; Box Office; Government Grants; Individual Donations

MERCE CUNNINGHAM DANCE COMPANY

55 Bethune Street, New York, NY 10014
(212) 255-8240
FAX: (212) 633-2453
  Founded: 1964
  Arts Area: Modern
  Status: Professional; Non-Profit
  Type: Performing; Touring; Educational
  Purpose: To develop understanding and public interest in the field of dance through performances, dance instruction and videotapes
  Management: Merce Cunningham, Artistic Director; Art Becofsky, Executive Director
  Officers: Daniel Wolf, Chairman; Allan G. Sperling, Vice Chairman; Candace Krugman Beinecke, Treasurer; David Vaughan, Secretary/Archivist
  Paid Staff: 36
  Paid Artists: 27
  Utilizes: Special Technical Talent; Guest Artists
  Budget: $1,000,000 - $5,000,000
  Income Sources: Private Foundations/Grants/Endowments; Business/Corporate Donations; Box Office; Government Grants; Individual Donations
  Season: 52 Weeks
  Affiliations: AGMA; NASD; Dance USA
  Performance Facilities: Merce Cunningham Studio

MEREDITH MONK - THE HOUSE FOUNDATION FOR THE ARTS

131 Varick Street, Suite 901, New York, NY 10013
(212) 206-1440
  Founded: 1968
  Arts Area: Modern
  Status: Professional; Non-Profit
  Type: Performing; Touring; Educational

Purpose: Meredith Monk is an internationally renowned composer, director, singer, choreographer and filmmaker. The House Foundation for the Arts administrates her companies and activities.
Management: Meredith Monk, Artistic Director; Barbara Dufty, Managing Director; Sue Latham, Company Manager
Officers: Micki Wesson, President
Paid Staff: 4
Budget: $500,000 - $1,000,000
Income Sources: Private Foundations/Grants/Endowments; Business/Corporate Donations; Box Office; Government Grants; Individual Donations
Season: 52 Weeks
Affiliations: APAP; MAAA

MIMI GARRARD DANCE COMPANY
155 Wooster Street, New York, NY 10012
(212) 674-6868
Founded: 1972
Arts Area: Modern
Status: Professional; Non-Profit
Type: Performing; Touring; Resident
Purpose: To present original, professional dance theatre productions to the public and offer classes, and workshops for participants of all ages
Management: Liz Rodgers, Booking Manager
Officers: James Seawright, Secretary/Treasurer
Paid Staff: 1
Paid Artists: 8
Utilizes: Guest Artists
Budget: $1,000 - $50,000
Income Sources: Private Foundations/Grants/Endowments; Business/Corporate Donations; Box Office; Government Grants; Individual Donations
Season: September - June
Affiliations: DTW
Performance Facilities: Mimi Garrard Dance Company

MOMIX
130 West 56th Street, New York, NY 10019
(203) 868-7454
FAX: (203) 868-2317
Founded: 1980
Arts Area: Modern; Dancer Illusionists
Status: Professional; Commercial
Type: Performing; Touring
Purpose: Dance theatre
Management: Scheldon-Soffer Management; Moses Pendleton, Artistic Director
Paid Staff: 3
Paid Artists: 10
Utilizes: Guest Artists
Budget: $100,000 - $500,000
Income Sources: Box Office
Season: September - July

MULTIGRAVITATIONAL AERODANCE GROUP
234 East 23rd Street, New York, NY 10010
(212) 696-5274; (212) 255-8166
FAX: (212) 633-1128
Founded: 1971
Arts Area: Modern
Status: Professional; Non-Profit
Type: Performing; Touring
Purpose: The Multigravitational Aerodance Group is involved in the choreographic exploration of aerial dance/theatre. Aerodance performs on various suspended sculptural sets allowing the dancers to move through 360 degrees in space.
Management: Barbara Salz, Administrative Director
Officers: Dr. Kenneth L. Mathis, President; Catherine L. Woodman, Secretary
Paid Staff: 1   **Volunteer Staff:** 4
Paid Artists: 4
Utilizes: Special Technical Talent; Guest Artists
Budget: $1,000 - $50,000
Income Sources: Private Foundations/Grants/Endowments; Business/Corporate Donations; Box Office; Government Grants; Individual Donations
Season: 52 Weeks   **Annual Attendance:** 50,000
Performance Facilities: The Sirovich Center

THE NANETTE BEARDEN CONTEMPORARY DANCE THEATRE
357 Canal Street, New York, NY 10013
(212) 966-6828
> **Founded:** 1976
> **Arts Area:** Modern; Ballet; Jazz
> **Status:** Professional; Non-Profit
> **Type:** Performing; Resident
> **Purpose:** A choreographers collective, founded in 1976, their works are examined and performed, uniting modern and ballet
> **Management:** Nanette Bearden, Artistic Director; Walter Rutledge, Assistant Artistic Director
> **Paid Staff:** 4
> **Paid Artists:** 12
> **Utilizes:** Guest Artists; Guest Choreographers
> **Budget:** $100,000 - $500,000
> **Income Sources:** Private Foundations/Grants/Endowments; Business/Corporate Donations; Box Office; Government Grants; Individual Donations
> **Season:** 52 Weeks

NATIONAL DANCE INSTITUTE
594 Broadway, Room 805, New York, NY 10012
(212) 226-0083
FAX: (212) 226-0761
> **Founded:** 1976
> **Arts Area:** Modern; Jazz
> **Status:** Non-Profit
> **Type:** Performing; Educational
> **Purpose:** To make the arts, through the media of dance, a foundation of children's education; to reach children who otherwise would not have the opportunity to be involved in the arts
> **Management:** Jacques d'Amboise, Artistic Director/Choreographer; Barbara Vogdes, Executive Director
> **Officers:** Robert D. Krinsky, Acting Chairman
> **Paid Staff:** 15
> **Utilizes:** Special Technical Talent; Guest Conductors; Guest Artists; Guest Choreographers
> **Budget:** $1,000,000 - $5,000,000
> **Income Sources:** Private Foundations/Grants/Endowments; Business/Corporate Donations; Box Office; Government Grants; Individual Donations
> **Season:** September - June
> **Annual Attendance:** 10,000

NETA PULVERMACHER AND DANCERS
39 Claremont Avenue, #41, New York, NY 10027
(212) 316-3888
> **Founded:** 1987
> **Arts Area:** Modern; Ballet
> **Status:** Professional
> **Type:** Performing; Touring; Resident; Educational; Sponsoring
> **Purpose:** To bring contemporary performance arts to the public through performances
> **Management:** Circum Arts Foundation
> **Officers:** Neta Pulvermacher, President; Kate Foley, Treasurer/Secretary; Paul Hendrix, Vice President
> **Paid Staff:** 1   **Volunteer Staff:** 2
> **Paid Artists:** 12   **Non-Paid Artists:** 2
> **Utilizes:** Guest Choreographers
> **Budget:** $1,000 - $50,000
> **Income Sources:** Private Foundations/Grants/Endowments; Business/Corporate Donations; Box Office; Government Grants; Individual Donations
> **Annual Attendance:** 15,000
> **Affiliations:** DTW; Circum Arts

THE NEW BALLET SCHOOL
The Lawrence A. Wien Center for Dance and Theatre, 890 Broadway, New York, NY 10003
(212) 777-7710
FAX: (212) 353-0936
> **Founded:** 1978
> **Arts Area:** Ballet
> **Status:** Professional; Non-Profit
> **Type:** Educational
> **Purpose:** To provide tuition-free professional ballet training to gifted New York City Public School children; to reflect the variety of NYC's racial and ethnic population long absent from ballet schools and stages

Management: Eliot Feld, Founder and Director; Katherine Moore, Administrative Director; Elizabeth Barrow, Faculty Co-ordinator; Lynn Muller, Administrative Coordinator
Officers: Feld Ballets/NY
Paid Staff: 14   **Volunteer Staff:** 1
Utilizes: Special Technical Talent
Budget: $1,000,000 - $5,000,000
Income Sources: Private Foundations/Grants/Endowments; Business/Corporate Donations; Government Grants; Individual Donations
Affiliations: New York City Board of Education

NEW DANCE GROUP STUDIO INC.
254 West 47th Street, New York, NY 10036
(212) 719-2733
    Founded: 1932
    Arts Area: Modern; Ballet; Jazz; Ethnic
    Status: Professional; Non-Profit
    Type: Performing; Educational
    Purpose: To foster the art of dance through a wide range of classes, scholarships, rehearsal space and performance
    Management: Rick Schussel, Artistic/Executive Director
    Paid Staff: 6
    Budget: $100,000 - $500,000
    Income Sources: Private Foundations/Grants/Endowments; Business/Corporate Donations; Government Grants
    Season: 52 Weeks

THE NEW YORK BAROQUE DANCE COMPANY
280 Riverside Drive, #5H, New York, NY 10025
(212) 662-8829
    Founded: 1976
    Arts Area: Historical
    Status: Professional
    Type: Performing; Touring; Resident; Educational
    Purpose: To revive the dances of the 18th century with a sense of spontaneity and scholarship and educate the public and the dance field
    Officers: Catherine Turocy, Artistic Director; James Richman, Music Director
    Paid Staff: 2   **Volunteer Staff:** 2
    Paid Artists: 14   **Non-Paid Artists:** 2
    Utilizes: Special Technical Talent; Guest Directors; Guest Choreographers
    Budget: $100,000 - $500,000
    Income Sources: Private Foundations/Grants/Endowments; Business/Corporate Donations; Box Office; Government Grants; Individual Donations

NEW YORK CITY BALLET
20 Lincoln Center, New York, NY 10023
(212) 877-4700
    Founded: 1948
    Arts Area: Ballet
    Status: Professional; Non-Profit
    Type: Performing; Touring; Resident; Educational
    Management: Patricia Turk, General Director; Jerome Robbins, Ballet Master-In-Chief; Peter Martins, Ballet Master-in-Chief/Artistic Director; Lincoln Kirstein, Director Emeritus
    Officers: Orville H. Schell, Paul A. Allaire, Co-Chairmans; Gillian Attfield, President/Chief Executive Officer; Marvin A. Asnes, Treasurer
    Paid Staff: 45   **Volunteer Staff:** 400
    Paid Artists: 185
    Utilizes: Special Technical Talent
    Budget: Over 10,000,000
    Income Sources: Private Foundations/Grants/Endowments; Business/Corporate Donations; Box Office; Government Grants
    Season: November - April - February - June   **Annual Attendance:** 420,000
    Affiliations: School of American Ballet
    Performance Facilities: New York State Theater

NIKOLAIS AND MURRAY LOUIS DANCE COMPANY
375 West Broadway, New York, NY 10012
(212) 226-7700
FAX: (212) 226-0442
    Founded: 1953
    Arts Area: Modern
    Status: Professional; Non-Profit

Type: Performing; Touring; Resident; Educational
Purpose: To present the choreographic work of Murray Louis and Alwin Nikolais and to display their aesthetics of dance
Management: Ian McColl, Director of Development/Company Manager
Officers: Murray Louis, Alwin Nikolais, Co-Artistic Directors
Paid Staff: 4
Paid Artists: 11
Budget: $500,000 - $1,000,000
Income Sources: Private Foundations/Grants/Endowments; Business/Corporate Donations; Box Office; Government Grants; Individual Donations
Season: 52 Weeks
Affiliations: APAP; Dance USA; AAA

PAUL TAYLOR DANCE COMPANY
552 Broadway, New York, NY 10012
(212) 431-5562
FAX: (212) 966-5673
Founded: 1966
Arts Area: Modern
Status: Professional; Non-Profit
Type: Performing; Touring; Resident
Purpose: To promote interest in dance, allow creation of new dance works and present them to broad audiences
Management: Paul Taylor, Director; Ross Kramberg, Executive Director
Paid Staff: 8
Paid Artists: 20
Utilizes: Special Technical Talent
Budget: $1,000,000 - $5,000,000
Income Sources: Private Foundations/Grants/Endowments; Business/Corporate Donations; Box Office; Government Grants; Individual Donations
Season: 42 weeks
Performance Facilities: City Center Theatre

PEARL LANG DANCE COMPANY AND FOUNDATION
382 Central Park West, New York, NY 10025
(212) 866-2680
Founded: 1954
Arts Area: Modern; Ethnic
Status: Professional; Non-Profit
Type: Performing; Touring; Educational
Management: Pearl Lang, Artistic Director; Lois Schaffer, General Manager
Paid Artists: 12
Utilizes: Guest Artists
Budget: $100,000 - $500,000
Income Sources: Private Foundations/Grants/Endowments

PERFORMANCE SPACE 122 INC.
150 First Avenue, New York, NY 10009
(212) 477-5829
FAX: (212) 353-1315
Arts Area: Modern; Mime; Ballet; Jazz; Ethnic; Folk
Status: Professional; Non-Profit
Type: Sponsoring
Purpose: To be a not-for-profit arts center serving the New York City dance and performing community
Management: Mark Russell, Director; Dominick Balletta, Managing Director
Budget: $500,000 - $1,000,000
Income Sources: Private Foundations/Grants/Endowments; Business/Corporate Donations; Box Office; Government Grants; Individual Donations
Performance Facilities: Performing Space 122

PERIDANCE ENSEMBLE
132 Fourth Avenue, 2nd Floor, New York, NY 10003
(212) 505-0886
Founded: 1985
Arts Area: Modern; Ballet
Status: Professional; Non-Profit
Type: Performing; Touring
Management: Igal Perry, Artistic Director

Paid Artists: 15
Budget: $1,000 - $50,000
Income Sources: Private Foundations/Grants/Endowments; Business/Corporate Donations; Box Office; Government Grants; Individual Donations
Season: November - Ferbruary

PHYLLIS LAMHUT DANCE COMPANY
225 West 71st Street, #31, New York, NY 10023
(212) 799-9048
Founded: 1970
Arts Area: Modern
Status: Professional
Type: Performing; Touring; Resident; Educational
Purpose: To present the work of Phyllis Lamhut, Choreographer
Management: Mrs. A.M. Sutton, Manager
Officers: Jon Garness, President; Ruth Scherer, Vice President; Ruth Gravert, Secretary/Treasurer
Volunteer Staff: 1
Paid Artists: 3
Utilizes: Special Technical Talent; Guest Conductors; Guest Artists
Budget: $1,000 - $50,000
Income Sources: Private Foundations/Grants/Endowments; Business/Corporate Donations; Box Office; Government Grants; Individual Donations
Annual Attendance: 2,000

POLISH AMERICAN FOLK DANCE COMPANY
58 West 58th Street, New York, NY 10019
(212) 753-0450
FAX: (212) 935-3706
Founded: 1948
Arts Area: Folk
Status: Non-Professional; Non-Profit
Type: Performing; Touring
Purpose: To preserve and present the culture of Poland
Management: Stanley Pelc, Artistic Director
Paid Staff: 1
Paid Artists: 48
Budget: $1,000 - $50,000
Income Sources: Private Foundations/Grants/Endowments; Business/Corporate Donations; Box Office; Government Grants; Individual Donations
Season: 52 Weeks

POOH KAYE/ECCENTRIC MOTIONS INC.
99 Vandam Street, New York, NY 10013
(212) 691-9522
Arts Area: Experimental Dance
Status: Professional; Non-Profit
Type: Performing; Touring; Educational
Purpose: To produce dance and films for public performance and distribution; to conduct educational seminars on movement and film language
Management: Pooh Kaye, Artistic Director
Budget: $50,000 - $100,000
Income Sources: Government Grants; Fees

RALPH LEMON COMPANY
PO Box 143, New York, NY 10011
(212) 675-8394
Arts Area: Modern
Status: Professional; Non-Profit
Type: Performing; Touring; Resident; Educational
Purpose: To present the work of choreographer Ralph Lemon through performances, workshops and lecture demonstrations
Management: Ralph Lemon, Artistic Director; Heide Sackerlotzky, Management
Officers: Norton Owen, Chairman of the Board
Budget: $100,000 - $500,000
Income Sources: Private Foundations/Grants/Endowments; Business/Corporate Donations; Box Office; Government Grants; Individual Donations

RISA JAROSLOW AND DANCERS
65 Greene Street, New York, NY 10012
(212) 941-9358
FAX: (212) 475-3278
   Arts Area: Modern
   Status: Professional; Non-Profit
   Type: Performing; Touring; Resident; Educational
   Purpose: To bring new dance and music to as wide an audience as possible; to reveal the essence of human relationships through dance
   Management: Risa Jaroslow, Artistic Director; Beverly Wright and Associates, Booking Agents
   Budget: $50,000 - $100,000
   Income Sources: Private Foundations/Grants/Endowments; Business/Corporate Donations; Box Office; Government Grants; Individual Donations
   Performance Facilities: University Settlement

ROSALIND NEWMAN AND DANCERS
124 Chambers Street, New York, NY 10007
(212) 962-1327
   Founded: 1977
   Arts Area: Modern
   Status: Professional; Non-Profit
   Type: Performing; Touring; Educational
   Purpose: To perform the choreography of Rosalind Newman
   Paid Artists: 8   **Non-Paid Artists:** 4
   Income Sources: Private Foundations/Grants/Endowments; Business/Corporate Donations; Box Office; Government Grants; Individual Donations

SAEKO OCHINOHE AND COMPANY, INC.
159 West 53rd Street, New York, NY 10019
(212) 757-2531
FAX: (212) 757-3614
   Founded: 1970
   Arts Area: Modern; Ethnic
   Status: Professional; Non-Profit
   Type: Performing; Touring; Educational
   Purpose: To present multicultural dance programs of the highest quality to all walks of life while showing inter-ethnic harmony
   Management: Saeko Ichinohe, Executive Director; Mariko Hirata, Assistant to Director
   Officers: Miki Tatum, Chairman of the Board; Saeko Ichinohe, President; Jane Berenbeim, Treasurer; Elizabeth Massey, Secretary
   Paid Staff: 1   **Volunteer Staff:** 5
   Paid Artists: 7
   Utilizes: Special Technical Talent; Guest Artists
   Budget: $1,000 - $50,000
   Income Sources: Private Foundations/Grants/Endowments; Business/Corporate Donations; Box Office; Government Grants; Individual Donations
   Annual Attendance: 10,000

SCHOOL OF HARD KNOCKS
201 East Fourth Street, New York, NY 10009
(212) 533-9473
FAX: (212) 260-5382
   Arts Area: Post-Modern
   Status: Non-Profit
   Type: Performing; Touring
   Purpose: To produce the works of Yoshiko Chuma and other members of the School of Hard Knocks
   Management: Yoshiko Chuma, Artistic Director; Carolyn Palmer, Manager
   Budget: $1,000 - $50,000
   Income Sources: Private Foundations/Grants/Endowments; Business/Corporate Donations; Box Office; Government Grants; Individual Donations

SOLARIS DANCE THEATRE
264 West 19th Street, Room 53, New York, NY 10011
(212) 741-0778
FAX: (212) 242-2201
   Founded: 1976
   Arts Area: Modern; Ethnic; Folk
   Status: Professional; Non-Profit

Type: Performing; Touring; Resident; Educational
Purpose: To create experimental dance theatre through the workshop process and through cross-cultural performance; to create bonds with people otherwise unrecognized in our society
Paid Staff: 5   **Volunteer Staff:** 10
Paid Artists: 15
Utilizes: Special Technical Talent; Guest Artists
Budget: $100,000 - $500,000
Income Sources: Private Foundations/Grants/Endowments; Business/Corporate Donations; Box Office; Government Grants; Individual Donations
Season: September - June   **Annual Attendance:** 15,000

THE SOLOMONS COMPANY-DANCE
889 Broadway, New York, NY 10003
(212) 477-1321
Founded: 1972
Arts Area: Modern
Status: Non-Profit
Type: Performing; Touring; Educational
Purpose: Presentation of experimental pure-motion dances and environmental dance events accessible to public audiences
Management: Gus Solomons, Jr., Artistic Director; Toby Twining, Musical Director; Pentacle, Fiscal Management CircumArts Administrative Representation
Paid Staff: 2
Paid Artists: 8
Budget: $50,000 - $100,000
Income Sources: Box Office; Government Grants; Individual Donations
Season: 52 Weeks

SPANISH THEATRE REPERTORY CO., LTD.
138 East 27th Street, New York, NY 10016
(212) 889-2850
FAX: (212) 686-3732
Founded: 1968
Arts Area: Spanish Classical
Status: Professional; Non-Profit
Type: Performing; Touring; Resident; Educational; Sponsoring
Purpose: To create and showcase the best of Hispanic theatre forms, including dance
Management: Rene Buch, Artistic Director; Gilberto Zaldivar, Producer; Robert Weber Federico, Associate Producer
Officers: Gilberto Zaldivar, President; Rene Buch, Vice President; Robert Weber Federico, Secretary/Treasurer
Paid Staff: 12
Paid Artists: 25
Utilizes: Special Technical Talent; Guest Artists; Guest Directors; Guest Choreographers
Budget: $1,000,000 - $5,000,000
Income Sources: Private Foundations/Grants/Endowments; Business/Corporate Donations; Box Office; Government Grants; Individual Donations
Annual Attendance: 40,000
Performance Facilities: Gramercy Arts Theatre

STEPHEN PETRONIO DANCE COMPANY
95 St. Mark's Place, Suite 10, New York, NY 10009
(212) 473-1660
FAX: (212) 477-3471
Arts Area: Modern
Status: Professional; Non-Profit
Type: Performing; Touring
Management: Stephen Petronio, Artistic Director; Janet Stapleton, Managing Director
Budget: $100,000 - $500,000
Income Sources: Private Foundations/Grants/Endowments; Business/Corporate Donations; Government Grants; Individual Donations

SUSAN MARSHALL & COMPANY
c/o Downtown Art Co., 280 Broadway, Room 412, New York, NY 10007-1896
(212) 732-1201
FAX: (212) 732-1297
Founded: 1983
Arts Area: Modern
Status: Professional; Non-Profit
Type: Performing; Touring
Purpose: To support the creation, development and performance of the works of choreographer Susan Marshall

Management: Downtown Art Co., Ryan Gilliam, Management Services; Rena Shagen Associates, Booking Services
Paid Staff: 8
Paid Artists: 8
Budget: $100,000 - $500,000
Income Sources: Private Foundations/Grants/Endowments; Business/Corporate Donations; Government Grants; Individual Donations
Season: 52 Weeks
Affiliations: Dance USA

THEATRE OF THE RIVERSIDE CHURCH
490 River Drive, New York, NY 10027
(212) 864-2929
Founded: 1978
Status: Professional; Non-Profit
Type: Performing; Educational
Purpose: To present a yearly dance festival
Management: Shellie Bransford, General Manager
Budget: $50,000 - $100,000
Income Sources: Business/Corporate Donations; Box Office; Government Grants; Individual Donations
Season: 52 Weeks
Performance Facilities: Theatre of the Riverside Church

TOKUNAGA DANCE COMPANY
1 Sheridan Square, New York, NY 10014
(212) 929-8937
Founded: 1974
Arts Area: Modern; Ballet; Ethnic
Status: Professional; Non-Profit
Type: Performing; Touring; Educational
Purpose: To educate and entertain audiences through various cultural and historical aspects of dance
Officers: Robert Asahina, Chairman; Emiko Tokunaga, President; Elaine Tokunaga, Treasurer; Donna Quon, Secretary
Paid Staff: 3   **Volunteer Staff:** 4
Paid Artists: 7
Utilizes: Special Technical Talent
Budget: $50,000 - $100,000
Income Sources: Private Foundations/Grants/Endowments; Business/Corporate Donations; Box Office; Government Grants; Individual Donations
Season: 52 Weeks   **Annual Attendance:** 50,000

TRISHA BROWN COMPANY
225 Lafayette Street, New York, NY 10012
(212) 334-9374
Founded: 1964
Arts Area: Modern
Status: Professional; Non-Profit
Type: Performing; Touring; Resident; Educational
Purpose: Trisha Brown has been recognized as seminal in contemporary dance and for the past 16 years has created a repertory known for its structural rigor and supple kineticism.
Management: Lawrence C. Zucker, Executive Director; Johanna C. Foley, Company Administrator
Officers: Robert Rauschenberg, Chairman; Sylvia Mazzola, Vice Chairman; Trisha Brown, President; Fredericka Hunter, Secretary
Paid Staff: 5
Paid Artists: 13
Utilizes: Guest Artists
Budget: $500,000 - $1,000,000
Income Sources: Private Foundations/Grants/Endowments; Business/Corporate Donations; Box Office; Government Grants; Individual Donations
Annual Attendance: 1,000,000
Performance Facilities: City Center Theatre

TWYLA THARP DANCE FOUNDATION
c/o MPL Productions 170 West 74th Street, New York, NY 10023
(212) 874-3990
FAX: (212) 874-8605
Founded: 1970
Arts Area: Modern; Ballet; Jazz
Status: Professional; Non-Profit
Type: Performing; Touring
Purpose: The making and performance of dance works

Management: Pam Strahl, Office Manager; Penny Curry, Manager for Twyla Tharp and TTDF; Diana Estigarribia, Office Assistant; Shelley Washington, Ballet Mistress
Paid Staff: 4
Income Sources: Private Foundations/Grants/Endowments; Business/Corporate Donations; Box Office; Government Grants; Individual Donations

URBAN BUSH WOMEN
c/o St. Marks Church, Tenth Street and Second Avenue, New York, NY 10003
(212) 777-4425
FAX: (212) 529-2318
Arts Area: Modern; Ethnic
Status: Non-Professional
Type: Performing; Touring
Purpose: To realize a creative vision continuously enriched by the folklore and religious traditions of Africans throughout the diaspora; through movement, live music, a cappella vocalizations, and the drama and wit of the spoken word, Urban Bush Women·explores the struggle, growth, transformation, and survival of the human spirit
Management: Laurie Uprichard, Managing Director; Jawole Willa Jo Zollar, Artistic Director; Rhoda Cerritelli, Administative Director
Officers: Jawole Willa Jo Zollar, Chairman of the Board
Budget: $500,000 - $1,000,000
Income Sources: Private Foundations/Grants/Endowments; Business/Corporate Donations; Government Grants; Individual Donations; Earned Income; Fees
Season: 52 Weeks

VICTORIA MARKS PERFORMANCE COMPANY
c/o Terra Moto Inc., 47-49 King Street, Suite 10, New York, NY 10014
(212) 255-7738
Arts Area: Modern
Status: Professional; Non-Profit
Type: Performing; Touring; Resident; Educational
Purpose: To provide a creative vehicle for the choreography of Victoria Marks; to bring the arts to diverse communities and educational situations
Management: Victoria Marks
Budget: $50,000 - $100,000
Income Sources: Private Foundations/Grants/Endowments; Box Office; Government Grants; Individual Donations

WORLD MUSIC INSTITUTE INC.
49 West 27th Street, Ste 810, New York, NY 10001
(212) 545-7536
FAX: (212) 889-2771
Arts Area: Ethnic; Folk
Status: Non-Profit
Type: Touring
Purpose: To present traditional & contemporary music and dance from around the world
Management: Robert H. Browning, Executive and Artistic Director; Eileen Macholl, Administrative Director
Officers: Daisy Paradis, Chair
Budget: $500,000 - $1,000,000
Income Sources: Private Foundations/Grants/Endowments; Business/Corporate Donations; Box Office; Government Grants; Individual Donations
Season: 52 Weeks

ZE'EVA COHEN AND DANCERS
c/o Pentacle Management, 104 Franklin Street, New York, NY 10013
(212) 226-2000
FAX: (212) 925-0369
Founded: 1972
Arts Area: Modern
Status: Professional; Non-Profit
Type: Performing; Touring; Resident
Management: Ze'Eva Cohen, Artistic Director
Paid Staff: 4
Paid Artists: 15
Utilizes: Guest Artists
Budget: $1,000 - $50,000
Income Sources: Private Foundations/Grants/Endowments; Business/Corporate Donations; Box Office; Government Grants; Individual Donations
Season: 52 Weeks

INSTRUMENTAL MUSIC

AEOLIAN CHAMBER PLAYERS
173 Riverside Drive, New York, NY 10024
(212) 595-4688
FAX: (212) 724-5283
Founded: 1961
Arts Area: Chamber
Status: Professional
Type: Performing; Touring; Resident
Purpose: The performance of a broad repertoire with music from the classical to the contemporary
Management: Joanne Rile Artists Management
Officers: Lewis Kaplan, President
Paid Staff: 2 **Volunteer Staff:** 2
Paid Artists: 4
Utilizes: Guest Artists
Budget: $1,000 - $50,000
Income Sources: Private Foundations/Grants/Endowments; Business/Corporate Donations; Box Office; Government Grants; Individual Donations
Season: 52 Weeks **Annual Attendance:** 15,000
Affiliations: NEA; NYSCA; Bowdoin Summer Music Festival

AFFILIATE ARTISTS INC.
37 West 65th Street, New York, NY 10023
(212) 580-2000
Arts Area: Soloists
Status: Professional; Non-Profit
Type: Resident; Educational; Sponsoring
Purpose: To help develop the careers of the nation's most promising young performing artists; to help develop audiences for the arts throughout the country; to develop corporate and foundational support for the arts
Management: Richard C. Clark, President/Artistic Director; Joseph Chart, Director of Programs/and Development
Budget: $1,000,000 - $5,000,000
Income Sources: Private Foundations/Grants/Endowments; Business/Corporate Donations; Government Grants

AMERICAN COMPOSERS ORCHESTRA
37 West 65th Street, New York, NY 10023
(212) 496-5330
FAX: (212) 580-1356
Founded: 1976
Arts Area: Symphony; Orchestra
Status: Professional; Non-Profit
Type: Performing
Purpose: The ACO's purpose is to discover, produce and present the widest possible spectrum of American repertoire, past and present, in performances of the highest quality, thereby focusing national awareness and support of American composers and their music.
Management: Jesse Rosen, Executive Director; Dennis Russell Davies, Music Director
Officers: Francis Thorne, President
Paid Staff: 4
Paid Artists: 80
Utilizes: Guest Conductors; Guest Artists
Budget: $500,000 - $1,000,000
Income Sources: Private Foundations/Grants/Endowments; Business/Corporate Donations; Box Office; Government Grants; Individual Donations
Season: September - June
Affiliations: ASOL
Performance Facilities: Carnegie Hall

AMERICAN SYMPHONY ORCHESTRA
850 Seventh Avenue, Suite 1106, New York, NY 10019
(212) 581-1365
Founded: 1962
Arts Area: Symphony; Orchestra; Ensemble
Status: Professional; Non-Profit
Type: Performing
Purpose: American Symphony Orchestra is the only self-governing orchestra in the United States with a subscription series at Carnegie Hall. It is also a resource organization providing musical service to communities nurturing young artists.
Management: Eugene Carr, Executive Director
Paid Staff: 2

Non-Paid Artists: 8
Utilizes: Guest Conductors; Guest Artists
Budget: $1,000,000 - $5,000,000
Income Sources: Private Foundations/Grants/Endowments; Business/Corporate Donations; Box Office; Government Grants; Individual Donations
Season: October - July
Performance Facilities: Carnegie Hall

AMERICAN TAP DANCE ORCHESTRA
170 Mercer Street, New York, NY 10012
(212) 925-3980
Founded: 1986
Arts Area: Rhythm, Jazz and Tap Dance
Status: Professional; Non-Profit
Type: Performing; Touring; Educational
Purpose: To celebrate, preserve and perpetuate one of America's few indigenous art forms, tap dance
Management: Siegel Artist Management; Liz Silverstein, Ethel Siegel, Jane Lawrence Curtiss
Officers: Brenda Bufalino, Founder/Artistic Director; Tony Waag, Executive Director; Barbara Duffy, Dance Captain; Lurea Herman, Company Manager
Paid Staff: 3   **Volunteer Staff:** 10
Utilizes: Special Technical Talent; Guest Artists
Budget: $100,000 - $500,000
Income Sources: Private Foundations/Grants/Endowments; Business/Corporate Donations; Box Office; Government Grants; Individual Donations
Performance Facilities: Woodpeckers Tap Dance Center

THE ASSOCIATION FOR THE ADVANCEMENT OF CREATIVE MUSICIANS, NEW YORK CHAPTER
PO Box 187, Times Square Station, New York, NY 10108
(212) 594-7121
Arts Area: Ensemble
Status: Professional; Non-Profit
Type: Performing
Purpose: To provide a forum for composers and performers to perform their own original music
Management: Richard Abrams
Income Sources: Government Grants

THE BLOOMINGDALE HOUSE OF MUSIC
323 West 108th Street, New York, NY 10025
(212) 663-6021
Founded: 1964
Arts Area: Orchestra; Chamber; Ensemble; Ethnic; Folk; Electronic & Live Electronic
Status: Professional; Non-Profit
Type: Performing; Educational; Sponsoring
Purpose: To promote, foster and develop the love of and interest for the musical arts
Management: Lawrence Davis, Executive Director
Paid Staff: 8
Paid Artists: 50
Budget: $500,000 - $1,000,000
Income Sources: Private Foundations/Grants/Endowments; Business/Corporate Donations; Government Grants; Individual Donations
Season: 52 Weeks
Affiliations: NGCSA

CARNEGIE CHAMBER PLAYERS
514 West 110th Street, Suite 41, New York, NY 10025
(212) 666-6740
Arts Area: Chamber; Ensemble
Status: Professional; Non-Profit
Type: Performing; Touring; Resident; Educational
Purpose: To promote chamber music in a mixed string and woodwind ensemble, commissioning new works as well as performing a traditional chamber music repertoire
Management: Richard Goldsmith, Yari Bond, Artistic Directors
Budget: $1,000 - $50,000
Income Sources: Private Foundations/Grants/Endowments; Business/Corporate Donations; Box Office; Government Grants; Individual Donations
Performance Facilities: Montshire Science Museum, Norwich VT; Therneaur School, Tenafly NJ

CHAMBER MUSIC AMERICA
545 Eighth Avenue, New York, NY 10018
(212) 244-2772
FAX: (212) 244-2776
Founded: 1977
Arts Area: Chamber
Status: Professional; Non-Profit
Type: Educational; Service Organization
Purpose: To promote professional chamber music and to make chamber music a vital part of American cultural life
Management: Dean K. Stein, Executive Director
Officers: Richard Bogomolny, Chairman; Paul Katz, President
Paid Staff: 8
Budget: $500,000 - $1,000,000
Income Sources: Private Foundations/Grants/Endowments; Business/Corporate Donations; Government Grants; Individual Donations

THE CHAMBER MUSIC SOCIETY OF LINCOLN CENTER
70 Lincoln Center Plaza, New York, NY 10023
(212) 875-5775
FAX: (212) 875-5799
Founded: 1969
Arts Area: Chamber; Ensemble; Instrumental Group
Status: Professional; Non-Profit
Type: Performing; Touring; Resident; Educational
Purpose: To present chamber music concerts
Management: David Shifrin, Artistic Director; Charles Kargacos, Executive Director
Officers: Laurence Dow Lorett, Chairman; Henry S. Ziegler, Vice Chairman; Mrs. John D. Coffin, President; Donaldson C. Pillsbury, Secretary; Donald Schnabel, Treasurer
Paid Staff: 11   **Volunteer Staff:** 8
Paid Artists: 18
Utilizes: Guest Artists
Budget: $1,000,000 - $5,000,000
Income Sources: Private Foundations/Grants/Endowments; Business/Corporate Donations; Box Office; Government Grants; Individual Donations
Season: October - May
Annual Attendance: 80,000
Performance Facilities: Alice Tully Hall

CHELSEA CHAMBER ENSEMBLE
c/o Timothy Malosh, 69 West End Avenue, Apt. 1-F, New York, NY 10025
(212) 222-3472
Arts Area: Chamber; Ensemble
Status: Professional; Non-Profit
Type: Performing; Touring; Resident; Educational
Purpose: To present unusual music from the past; to commission new works by American composers
Management: Timothy Malosh, Marc Goldberg, David Jolley, Artistic Directors
Officers: Theodore W. Volck, Chairman of the Board
Budget: $1,000 - $50,000
Income Sources: Private Foundations/Grants/Endowments; Business/Corporate Donations; Box Office; Government Grants; Individual Donations
Performance Facilities: Weill Recital Hall, Carnegie Hall

THE CHINESE MUSIC ENSEMBLE OF NEW YORK, INC.
149 Canal Street, New York, NY 10002
(212) 925-6110
Founded: 1961
Arts Area: Ensemble; Ethnic; Folk
Status: Semi-Professional; Non-Profit
Type: Performing; Touring; Educational
Purpose: To promote Chinese music in the United States
Officers: Yu-chiung Teng, Director; Terence Yeh and Oiman Chan, Associate Directors
Paid Staff: 3   **Volunteer Staff:** 12
Paid Artists: 45
Budget: $50,000 - $100,000
Income Sources: Private Foundations/Grants/Endowments; Business/Corporate Donations; Box Office; Government Grants; Individual Donations
Season: 52 Weeks
Annual Attendance: 9,000

CITY SYMPHONY ORCHESTRA OF NEW YORK, INC.
311 West 34th Street, New York, NY 10001
(212) 947-3362
FAX: (212) 465-2367
Arts Area: Symphony; Chamber
Status: Professional; Non-Profit
Type: Performing
Purpose: To present young performers at the major concert halls in New York City; to present performances and music by artists of different ethnic backgrounds
Management: David Eaton, Artistic Director; Leonid Fleishaker, Personnel Contractor
Officers: Chung Hwan Kwak, Chairman of the Board; David Eaton, President
Budget: $100,000 - $500,000
Income Sources: Private Foundations/Grants/Endowments; Business/Corporate Donations; Box Office; Government Grants; Individual Donations
Performance Facilities: Carnegie Hall; Alice Tully Hall

THE CLASSICAL QUARTET
225 West 99th Street, New York, NY 10025
(212) 222-2700
Founded: 1979
Arts Area: Chamber; Ensemble
Status: Professional
Type: Performing; Touring; Resident; Educational
Purpose: The Classical Quartet was founded to present masterpieces of the Classic Era, string quartets of Haydn, Mozart, Beethoven and their contemporaries, on period instruments.
Management: Beverly Simmons, Artist Representative
Officers: Nancy Wilson, President; David Miller, Treasurer
Volunteer Staff: 2
Paid Artists: 4
Utilizes: Guest Artists
Budget: $1,000 - $50,000
Income Sources: Box Office; Government Grants; Individual Donations
Season: 52 Weeks
Performance Facilities: Saint Michael's Church

CONCORDIA
330 Seventh Avenue, 21st Floor, New York, NY 10001
(212) 967-1290
FAX: (212) 629-0508
Founded: 1984
Arts Area: Orchestra; Chamber
Status: Professional; Non-Profit
Type: Performing; Educational
Purpose: A unique and adventurous fifty piece orchestra dedicated to breaking down the barriers between jazz and classical music by presenting innovative concerts combining American Symphonic masterpieces, orchestral jazz, and commissioned premieres
Management: Maria Alsop, Artistic Director/Conductor; Leslie Stifelman, Executive Director
Officers: Tomio Taki, Chairman/Board of Directors; Joel Hirschtritt, President/Board of Directors
Paid Staff: 4   **Volunteer Staff:** 15
Utilizes: Guest Artists
Budget: $100,000 - $500,000
Income Sources: Private Foundations/Grants/Endowments; Business/Corporate Donations; Box Office; Government Grants; Individual Donations
Season: October - June
Annual Attendance: 4,000
Performance Facilities: Alice Tully Hall, Lincoln Center

CONTINUUM (THE PERFORMERS' COMMITTEE INC.)
333 West End Avenue, 16C, New York, NY 10023
(212) 873-3258
Founded: 1966
Arts Area: Orchestra; Chamber; Ensemble; Instrumental Group; Vocal
Status: Professional
Type: Performing; Touring; Educational
Purpose: To promote 20th century music through annual concert series in New York; to tour in the U.S. and abroad; to educate through mini-residences and recordings
Management: Cheryl Seltzer and Joel Sachs, Co-Directors

Officers: Cheryl Seltzer, President; Joel Sachs, Vice President
Paid Staff: 1
Paid Artists: 50
Budget: $100,000 - $500,000
Income Sources: Private Foundations/Grants/Endowments; Business/Corporate Donations; Box Office; Government Grants; Individual Donations; Performance Fees
Season: September - June
Performance Facilities: Alice Tully Hall

COSMOPOLITAN SYMPHONY ORCHESTRA
PO Box 1045, Ansonia Station, New York, NY 10023
(212) 873-7784
Founded: 1964
Arts Area: Symphony
Status: Non-Profit
Type: Performing; Educational
Purpose: To give young professional conductors, instrumentalists and soloists an opportunity to make New York appearances; to create a new audience
Management: Rita Asen, Managing Director; Simon Asen, Founder
Officers: Martin Snyder, Vice President
Volunteer Staff: 4
Paid Artists: 8   **Non-Paid Artists:** 45
Utilizes: Guest Conductors; Guest Artists
Budget: $1,000 - $50,000
Income Sources: Private Foundations/Grants/Endowments; Business/Corporate Donations; Individual Donations
Season: November - May
Performance Facilities: Town Hall

DA CAPO CHAMBER PLAYERS, INCORPORATED
215 West 90th Street, New York, NY 10024
(212) 873-1065
FAX: (212) 873-1065
Arts Area: Chamber
Status: Professional
Type: Performing; Touring; Resident; Educational
Purpose: To perform a repertoire of the music of today, including scores of commissioned works, often featured with traditional repertoire selections
Management: John Gingrich Management, Inc.
Paid Artists: 5
Utilizes: Guest Artists
Budget: $50,000 - $100,000
Income Sources: Private Foundations/Grants/Endowments; Business/Corporate Donations; Box Office; Government Grants; Individual Donations
Annual Attendance: 2,765
Performance Facilities: Merkin Concert Hall; Kathryn Bache Miller Theatre; 92nd Street Y

THE DOCTORS' ORCHESTRAL SOCIETY OF NEW YORK
201 East 19th Street, New York, NY 10003
(212) 477-1660
FAX: (212) 477-1888
Founded: 1938
Arts Area: Symphony; Orchestra
Status: Non-Professional; Non-Profit
Type: Performing; Educational
Purpose: To perform the great music of the world for our own education and enjoyment and to bring this music to our community for their enjoyment and education; the group also works with the public school system of New York City
Management: Philip Traugott, Music Director
Officers: Dr. Harvey Salomon, President; Dr. Pauline Hecht, Vice President; Dr. Edward Bowe; Dr. David Tiersten, Treasurers
Volunteer Staff: 5
Non-Paid Artists: 5
Utilizes: Guest Artists
Budget: $1,000 - $50,000
Income Sources: Business/Corporate Donations; Individual Donations
Season: September - June
Annual Attendance: 2,000
Performance Facilities: Stuyvesant High School Auditorium

DOWNTOWN MUSIC PRODUCTIONS
310 East 12th Street, New York, NY 10003
(212) 477-1594
FAX: (212) 477-5567
  Arts Area: Orchestra; Chamber; Instrumental Group; Adult/Children's Operatic
  Status: Professional; Non-Profit
  Type: Performing; Educational
  Purpose: To produce music programs that heighten our consciousness on the possibility of meaningful communication through art; the organization has been a recipient of the 1992 Mayor's Special Arts Award in music, the American Composer's Alliance Laurel Leaf Award for fostering and encouraging American music and the 1990 ASCAP/Chamber Music America Award for adventuresome programming.
  Management: Mimi Stern-Wolfe, Artistic Director/Conductor/Pianist
  Budget: $100,000 - $500,000
  Income Sources: Private Foundations/Grants/Endowments; Business/Corporate Donations; Government Grants; Individual Donations

EARLY MUSIC AMERICA, INC.
30 West 26th Street, Suite 1001, New York, NY 10015
(212) 366-5643
FAX: (212) 366-5265
  Arts Area: Early Music
  Status: Non-Profit
  Type: Service Organization
  Purpose: To expand the audiences for early music in North America; to foster an appreciation for early American music among our listeners
  Management: Daniel Nimetz, Executive Director; Thomas F. Kelly, President
  Budget: $100,000 - $500,000
  Income Sources: Private Foundations/Grants/Endowments; Business/Corporate Donations; Government Grants; Membership Dues

EXPERIMENTAL INTERMEDIA FOUNDATION
224 Centre Street, New York, NY 10013
(212) 431-5127
FAX: (212) 431-4486
  Founded: 1968
  Arts Area: Chamber; Ensemble; Instrumental Group; Electronic & Live Electronic; Video; Film
  Status: Non-Profit
  Type: Performing; Educational; Sponsoring
  Purpose: To provide a forum for experimental music and intermedia
  Management: Phill Niblock, Director; Mary Jane Leach, Associate Director
  Officers: Arthur Stidfole, President; Mary Jane Leach, Treasurer
  Paid Staff: 4   **Volunteer Staff:** 5
  Paid Artists: 30
  Utilizes: Special Technical Talent; Guest Artists
  Budget: $100,000 - $500,000
  Income Sources: Private Foundations/Grants/Endowments; Business/Corporate Donations; Box Office; Government Grants; Individual Donations
  Season: 52 Weeks
  Annual Attendance: 2,000

FLUTE FORCE
124 West 72 Street, Suite #5C, New York, NY 10023
(212) 873-0272
  Founded: 1981
  Arts Area: Chamber; Ensemble; Instrumental Group
  Status: Professional
  Type: Performing; Touring; Educational
  Purpose: To further the knowledge of the flute and its repertiore through performance and lectures
  Management: Simonds Management
  Officers: Rie Schmidt, Artistic Director; Gretchen Pusch, Executive Director
  Volunteer Staff: 4
  Paid Artists: 4
  Utilizes: Guest Artists
  Budget: $1,000 - $50,000
  Income Sources: Private Foundations/Grants/Endowments; Business/Corporate Donations; Box Office; Government Grants; Individual Donations
  Season: 52 Weeks

HIGHLIGHTS IN JAZZ
7 Peter Copper Road, New York, NY 10010
(212) 982-3697
Founded: 1973
Arts Area: Jazz
Status: Professional
Type: Performing
Purpose: To perform in an 8-concert series at Pace University, NY, with all-star assemblages
Management: Jack Kleinsinger, Producer; Sid Trommer, Development Director
Officers: Jack Kleinsinger, President; Arnold Jay Smith, James Bartow, Harriet Wasser and Sid Trommer, Board Members; Richard Kalty, Treasurer
Paid Staff: 2   **Volunteer Staff:** 5
Paid Artists: 100
Utilizes: Guest Artists
Budget: $50,000 - $100,000
Income Sources: Private Foundations/Grants/Endowments; Business/Corporate Donations; Box Office; Government Grants; Individual Donations; Fundraising
Season: October - May   **Annual Attendance:** 5,700
Affiliations: New Jersey Symphony Orchestra
Performance Facilities: Pace University Theatre

HORIZON CONCERTS INC.
475 Riverside Drive, Suite 249, New York, NY 10115
(212) 563-6885
FAX: (212) 563-6885
Arts Area: Ensemble; Instrumental Group
Status: Professional; Non-Profit
Type: Performing; Educational
Purpose: To bring free, classical-music concerts to people deprived of the opportunity to hear live performances including the elderly, AIDS hospices, homeless shelters, Alzheimer clinics and underprivileged youth
Management: Clive Lythgoe, Executive Director/Music Director
Officers: Joan T. Ades, President of the Board
Budget: $100,000 - $500,000
Income Sources: Private Foundations/Grants/Endowments; Business/Corporate Donations; Government Grants; Individual Donations

JUPITER SYMPHONY
155 West 68th Street, New York, NY 10023
(212) 799-1259
Founded: 1979
Arts Area: Symphony; Orchestra; Chamber; Instrumental Group
Status: Professional; Non-Profit
Type: Performing; Touring; Resident; Educational; Sponsoring
Purpose: To interest young people in music at a most crucial time of their lives
Management: Harry Beall Management
Officers: Jens Nygaard, Conductor/Artistic Director; Carole Mertz, Director of Development
Budget: $100,000 - $500,000
Income Sources: Private Foundations/Grants/Endowments; Business/Corporate Donations; Box Office; Government Grants; Individual Donations
Season: 52 Weeks

THE LITTLE ORCHESTRA SOCIETY OF NEW YORK
220 West 42nd Street, 18th Floor, New York, NY 10036
(212) 704-2100
FAX: (212) 704-4037
Founded: 1947
Arts Area: Orchestra
Status: Non-Profit
Type: Performing
Purpose: To provide unique adventures in the world's finest music for concert-goers of all ages
Officers: John Kordel, Managing Director
Paid Staff: 5
Utilizes: Special Technical Talent; Guest Conductors; Guest Artists; Guest Directors
Budget: $500,000 - $1,000,000
Income Sources: Private Foundations/Grants/Endowments; Business/Corporate Donations; Box Office; Government Grants; Individual Donations
Season: September - August
Affiliations: ASOL

Performance Facilities: Avery Fisher Hall; Alice Tully Hall; Bruno Walter Auditorium; Greek Orthodox Cathedral of the Holy Trinity

MEET THE COMPOSER INC.
2112 Broadway, Suite 505, New York, NY 10023
(212) 787-3601
FAX: (212) 787-3745
Arts Area: Symphony; Orchestra; Chamber; Ensemble; Ethnic; Folk; Instrumental Group; Electronic & Live Electronic; Band
Status: Non-Profit
Type: Grant-giving
Purpose: To foster the creation, performance and recording of music by American composers; to expand audience fields
Management: John Duffy, Director/President
Budget: $1,000,000 - $5,000,000
Income Sources: Private Foundations/Grants/Endowments; Business/Corporate Donations; Box Office; Government Grants; Individual Donations
Performance Facilities: Springfield Symphony Hall

MOZART FESTIVAL ORCHESTRA
33 Greenwich Avenue, New York, NY 10014
(212) 675-9127
Founded: 1960
Arts Area: Symphony; Orchestra
Status: Professional; Non-Profit
Type: Performing
Purpose: To present idiomatic performances of music of all styles and periods emphasizing the 18th century; to enlarge repertory; to sponsor lectures, publications, exhibitions, and young artists
Management: Baird Hastings, Conductor
Officers: Baird Hastings, Treasurer; Louise Hastings, Secretary
Paid Artists: 20
Utilizes: Guest Directors
Budget: $1,000 - $50,000
Income Sources: Private Foundations/Grants/Endowments; Box Office; Individual Donations
Season: February - May   **Annual Attendance:** 1,200
Performance Facilities: Main Hall, First Presbyterian Church

MUSIC BEFORE 1800, INC.
Corpus Christi Church, 529 West 121st Street, New York, NY 10027
(212) 666-0675
Founded: 1975
Arts Area: Chamber
Status: Professional
Type: Performing; Sponsoring
Purpose: To present performances of vocal and instrumental chamber music before 1800
Officers: Louise Basbas, President/Executive Director
Paid Staff: 3   **Volunteer Staff:** 10
Paid Artists: 60
Budget: $50,000 - $100,000
Income Sources: Private Foundations/Grants/Endowments; Business/Corporate Donations; Box Office; Government Grants; Individual Donations
Season: September - May   **Annual Attendance:** 2,500
Affiliations: CMA; EMA
Performance Facilities: Corpus Christi Church

MUSICA DE CAMARA, INC.
1215 Fifth Avenue, Apt. 1-B, New York, NY 10029
(212) 410-5612
Arts Area: Orchestra; Chamber; Ensemble; Solo; Baroque Orchestra
Status: Professional; Non-Profit
Type: Performing; Touring; Educational
Purpose: To promote classical instrumental singers and composers of Puerto Rican and Hispanic background
Management: Eva de la O, Executive Director
Officers: Tonio Burgos, Chairman; Carlotta Madura, Anita Soto, Myrna Riveria, Michael Nieves, Board Members
Budget: $1,000 - $50,000
Income Sources: Private Foundations/Grants/Endowments; Business/Corporate Donations; Government Grants
Performance Facilities: Merkin Concert Hall

NATIONAL ORCHESTRAL ASSOCIATION INC.
475 Riverside Drive, Suite 249, New York, NY 10115
(212) 870-2009
FAX: (212) 870-2129
    Arts Area: Orchestra; Chamber
    Status: Non-Profit
    Type: Educational
    Officers: Frances Kennedy, President
    Performance Facilities: Carnegie Hall

NEW MUSIC CONSORT, INC.
498 West End Avenue, #1B, New York, NY 10024
(212) 362-0962
    Arts Area: Chamber; 20th Century
    Status: Professional; Non-Profit
    Type: Performing; Touring; Educational
    Purpose: To present a wide variety of music of 20th century performers on the highest interpretive level; to encourage audience awareness of 20th century chamber music through performances and lecture demonstrations
    Management: Madeline Shapiro and Claire Heldrich, Artistic Directors
    Budget: $50,000 - $100,000

THE NEW SONG QUINTET (PROJECT)
New Song Foundation Inc., 510 West 112th Street, New York, NY 10025
(212) 866-3827
    Founded: 1979
    Arts Area: Ethnic; Folk; Instrumental Group; Children's Music
    Status: Professional; Non-Profit
    Type: Performing; Touring; Educational; Workshops
    Purpose: To promote multi-cultural understanding through music performances and workshops for all ages and communities; to give children insight into, and to elicit their participation in, songwriting and creativity; to provide musical experiences for special communities including seniors, intergenerational groups, the psychiatric community and the developmentally and physically disabled community
    Management: Mike Glick, Artistic Director; The New Music Foundation
    Officers: Alan Diamond, Treasurer
    Volunteer Staff: 1
    Paid Artists: 6
    Budget: $50,000 - $100,000
    Income Sources: Private Foundations/Grants/Endowments; Box Office
    Season: 52 Weeks
    Affiliations: New York Foundation for the Arts

NEW YORK CHAMBER ENSEMBLE
475 Riverside Drive, Suite 621, New York, NY 10115-0621
(212) 870-2439
FAX: (212) 870-2192
    Founded: 1987
    Arts Area: Ensemble
    Status: Professional; Non-Profit
    Type: Performing; Touring
    Purpose: To perform a 15-member, mixed ensemble repertoire, usually requiring a conductor
    Management: Donna Zajonc Management, Ann Arbor, MI
    Officers: Peter Morris Dixon, President; Kathleen Byrum, Vice President; Charles L. Marshall Jr., Secretary; Howard W. Connaughton, Treasurer
    Paid Staff: 1
    Paid Artists: 40
    Utilizes: Guest Artists
    Budget: $50,000 - $100,000
    Income Sources: Private Foundations/Grants/Endowments; Business/Corporate Donations; Box Office; Government Grants; Individual Donations
    Season: Fall - Spring   **Annual Attendance:** 6,000
    Performance Facilities: Florence Gould Hall

NEW YORK CONSORT OF VIOLS
201 West 86th Street, New York, NY 10024
(212) 580-9787
    Arts Area: Chamber
    Status: Professional; Non-Profit

Type: Performing; Touring; Educational
Purpose: To perform the vast repertoire of music for viols from the Renaissance and baroque periods; to encourage the composition of new works for viols
Management: Judith Davidoff, Artistic Director
Budget: $1,000 - $50,000
Income Sources: Private Foundations/Grants/Endowments; Business/Corporate Donations; Box Office; Government Grants; Individual Donations
Season: 52 Weeks

NEW YORK HARP ENSEMBLE
140 West End Avenue, Suite 3K, New York, NY 10023
(212) 799-5989
FAX: (212) 799-5989
Founded: 1970
Arts Area: Chamber
Status: Professional; Non-Profit
Type: Performing; Touring; Resident; Educational
Purpose: To play concerts worldwide; to perform new contemporary compositions for four harps; to provide master classes and participate in recordings and television
Management: Dr. Aristid von Wurtzler, Music Director; Metropolitan Artists Management
Officers: Dr. Aristid von Wurtzler, President
Paid Staff: 2   **Volunteer Staff:** 6
Paid Artists: 5
Budget: $1,000 - $50,000
Income Sources: Private Foundations/Grants/Endowments; Individual Donations
Season: 52 Weeks

NEW YORK NEW MUSIC ENSEMBLE
48 Horatio Street, New York, NY 10014
(212) 633-6260
Founded: 1976
Arts Area: Chamber; Ensemble; Instrumental Group; Electronic & Live Electronic; Contemporary; 20th Century
Status: Professional
Type: Performing; Touring; Educational
Purpose: To crusade for contemporary music; to support new composers by performing significant contemporary works; to play experimental avant garde mixtures of music, electronics, theatre and music
Officers: Jayn Rosenfeld, Executive Director/Flutist; Daniel Druckman, Treasurer/Percussionist/Tour Manager; Jean Kopperud, Tour Manager/Clarinetist; Christopher Finckel, Repertory Research/Cellist/Conductor; James Winn, Composer Liaison/Pianist; Linda Quan, Schedule Coordinator/Violinist; Robert Black, Tour Research/Conductor
Paid Staff: 2   **Volunteer Staff:** 7
Paid Artists: 7
Utilizes: Special Technical Talent; Guest Conductors; Guest Artists; Guest Directors
Budget: $50,000 - $100,000
Income Sources: Private Foundations/Grants/Endowments; Business/Corporate Donations; Box Office; Government Grants; Individual Donations
Season: October - May   **Annual Attendance:** 2,500

NEW YORK PHILHARMONIC
65th Street at Broadway, New York, NY 10023
(212) 875-5700
FAX: (212) 875-5929
Founded: 1842
Arts Area: Symphony; Orchestra; Chamber
Status: Professional
Type: Performing; Touring; Resident; Educational
Management: Deborah Borda, Managing Director; Edward Sermier, Controller; Allison Vulgamore, General Manager; Elizabeth Ostrow, Music Administrator
Officers: Stephen Stamas, Chairman; H. Frederick Krimendahl II, President
Paid Staff: 60   **Volunteer Staff:** 375
Paid Artists: 106
Utilizes: Guest Conductors; Guest Artists
Budget: Over 10,000,000
Income Sources: Private Foundations/Grants/Endowments; Business/Corporate Donations; Box Office; Government Grants; Individual Donations
Season: 52 Weeks
Affiliations: ASOL
Performance Facilities: Avery Fisher Hall

NEW YORK PHILOMUSICA CHAMBER ENSEMBLE
105 West 73rd Street, #4C, New York, NY 10023
(212) 580-9933
> **Arts Area:** Chamber; Ensemble
> **Status:** Professional; Non-Profit
> **Type:** Performing; Recording
> **Purpose:** To perform and record the music written from 1750 to the present for wind, strings and piano, with guest soloists
> **Management:** Robert Johnson, Artistic Director
> **Officers:** George Plimpton, President of the Board
> **Utilizes:** Guest Artists
> **Budget:** $100,000 - $500,000
> **Income Sources:** Private Foundations/Grants/Endowments; Business/Corporate Donations; Box Office; Government Grants; Individual Donations
> **Performance Facilities:** American Concert Hall; Alice Tully Hall

NEW YORK POPS ORCHESTRA
ICM Artists, Ltd., 40 West 57th Street, 16th Floor, New York, NY 10019
(212) 556-6871
FAX: (212) 556-6877
> **Founded:** 1983
> **Arts Area:** Symphony
> **Status:** Professional; Non-Profit
> **Type:** Performing; Touring
> **Purpose:** The New York Pops was founded to fill the void that has existed between highbrow classical tastes and top-10 rock with emphasis on light classical selections as well as contemporary works of merit.
> **Management:** Skitch Henderson, Founder/Music Director; Peter Lane, Executive Director; Dick Corrado, Agent
> **Paid Artists:** 95
> **Utilizes:** Guest Conductors; Guest Artists
> **Income Sources:** Business/Corporate Donations; Box Office; Individual Donations
> **Season:** October - May   **Annual Attendance:** 30,000
> **Performance Facilities:** Carnegie Hall

NEW YORK YOUTH SYMPHONY
Carnegie Hall, Suite 504, 881 Seventh Avenue, New York, NY 10019
(212) 581-5933
> **Founded:** 1963
> **Arts Area:** Symphony; Chamber
> **Status:** Non-Professional; Non-Profit
> **Type:** Performing; Educational; Sponsoring
> **Purpose:** New York Youth Symphony is established as the premier orchestra in metropolitan New York offering a unique learning experience and musical showcase for the gifted, young orchestral musician, conductor, soloist and composer. Composed of 135 of the most talented musicians aged 12 to 22 from the Tri-State Area, representing every racial, ethnic and economic background.
> **Management:** Barry Goldberg, Executive Director; Samuel Wong, Music Director; Jonathan David, Manager of Operations
> **Officers:** Leslie J. Garfield, Chairman; Theodore L. Kesselman, President; Robert L. Poster, Vice President; Benson J. Chapman, Treasurer
> **Paid Staff:** 3
> **Non-Paid Artists:** 135
> **Utilizes:** Guest Artists
> **Budget:** $100,000 - $500,000
> **Income Sources:** Private Foundations/Grants/Endowments; Business/Corporate Donations; Government Grants; Individual Donations; Fund-raising
> **Season: September - May**   **Annual Attendance:** 10,000
> **Performance Facilities:** Carnegie Hall

NEW YORK'S ENSEMBLE FOR EARLY MUSIC
217 West 71 Street, New York, NY 10023
(212) 749-6600
FAX: (212) 316-7404
> **Founded:** 1974
> **Arts Area:** Ensemble; Medieval Music; Drama
> **Status:** Professional; Non-Profit
> **Type:** Performing; Touring; Resident
> **Purpose:** To present authentic performances of medieval music and music drama
> **Management:** Fredrick Renz, Director; Carl K. Steffes, Managing Director; Kerby Lovallo, Hillyer International Tour Management

Officers: Lawrence M. Addington, Treasurer; Myles Astor, Diane Cochrane, Janice Haggerty and Edwin David Robertson, Board Members
Paid Staff: 2
Paid Artists: 30
Budget: $100,000 - $500,000
Income Sources: Private Foundations/Grants/Endowments; Business/Corporate Donations; Box Office; Government Grants; Individual Donations
Season: October - May
Annual Attendance: 10,000
Affiliations: Early Music America
Performance Facilities: Cathedral of Saint John the Divine

NORTH/SOUTH CONSONANCE, INC.
PO Box 698, Cathedral Station, New York, NY 10025-0698
(518) 274-4956
FAX: (518) 274-4956
Founded: 1980
Arts Area: Chamber; Ensemble; Instrumental Group; Electronic & Live Electronic; New Music
Status: Professional; Non-Profit
Type: Performing; Touring; Resident; Educational
Purpose: To promote and perform the music of living composers with emphasis placed on music from the Americas
Officers: Max Lifchitz, Director; Laura Ellis, President
Volunteer Staff: 2
Paid Artists: 12
Utilizes: Special Technical Talent; Guest Conductors; Guest Artists
Budget: $1,000 - $50,000
Income Sources: Private Foundations/Grants/Endowments; Business/Corporate Donations; Box Office; Government Grants; Individual Donations
Season: October - June
Annual Attendance: 2,000
Affiliations: CMA
Performance Facilities: Merkin Hall; Weil Recital Hall

ODYSSEY CHAMBER PLAYERS, INC.
PO Box 1607, Cathedral Station, New York, NY 10025
(212) 496-7071
FAX: (508) 291-0087
Arts Area: Chamber
Status: Professional; Non-Profit
Type: Performing
Purpose: To perform works featuring between six and 20 winds
Management: H. Robert Reynolds, Artistic Advisor; Maury Okun, Executive Director
Budget: $1,000 - $50,000
Income Sources: Private Foundations/Grants/Endowments; Business/Corporate Donations; Box Office; Government Grants; Individual Donations
Performance Facilities: Brooklyn Music School; Madison Avenue Presbyterian Church

ORCHESTRA OF ST. LUKE'S
130 West 42nd Street, New York, NY 10036
(212) 840-7470
FAX: (212) 840-7585
Founded: 1974
Arts Area: Orchestra; Chamber; Ensemble
Status: Professional; Non-Profit
Type: Performing
Management: Michael Feldman, Artistic Director; Marianne C. Lockwood, Executive Director; Curt Sharp, General Manager; Susannah Halston, Director of Marketing and Development; Rosalyn Bindman, Education Director
Officers: M. Bernard Aidinoff, Chairman; Michael Feldman, President; Marianne C. Lockwood, Vice President/Secretary; Steven Leifer, Treasurer
Paid Staff: 10   **Volunteer Staff:** 15
Paid Artists: 300
Utilizes: Guest Conductors; Guest Artists; Guest Directors
Budget: $1,000,000 - $5,000,000
Income Sources: Private Foundations/Grants/Endowments; Business/Corporate Donations; Box Office; Government Grants; Individual Donations
Season: October - May
Annual Attendance: 100,000

Affiliations: St. Luke's Chamber Ensemble
Performance Facilities: Merkin Concert Hall; Carnegie Hall; Caramoor Music Festival; Avery Fisher Hall

ORPHEUS CHAMBER ORCHESTRA, INC.
490 Riverside Drive, New York, NY 10027
(212) 678-1700
FAX: (212) 678-1717
    Arts Area: Orchestra; Chamber
    Status: Professional; Non-Profit
    Type: Performing; Touring
    Purpose: To allow members to work in collaboration on the selection and interpretation of pieces
    Management: Julian Fifer, Executive Director/President; Norma Hurlburt, Vice President/General Manager
    Officers: Fred Rubenstein, Chairman of the Board
    Budget: $1,000,000 - $5,000,000
    Income Sources: Private Foundations/Grants/Endowments; Business/Corporate Donations; Box Office; Government Grants; Individual Donations
    Performance Facilities: Carnegie Hall

QUINTET OF THE AMERICAS
134 Bowery, New York, NY 10013
(212) 431-8786
FAX: (212) 966-0954
    Founded: 1976
    Arts Area: Chamber; Ethnic
    Status: Professional; Non-Profit
    Type: Performing; Touring; Resident; Educational
    Purpose: To present chamber music and contemporary music especially from North and South America
    Officers: Barbara Oldham, President; Matt Sullivan, Vice President; Tom Novak, Treasurer; Christopher Jepperson, Secretary
    Paid Artists: 5
    Utilizes: Guest Artists
    Budget: $1,000 - $50,000
    Income Sources: Private Foundations/Grants/Endowments; Business/Corporate Donations; Box Office; Government Grants; Individual Donations
    Season: 52 Weeks
    Performance Facilities: Center for Inter-American Relations

THE RIVERSIDE SYMPHONY
258 Riverside Drive, #7C, New York, NY 10025
(212) 864-4197
FAX: (212) 864-9795
    Arts Area: Symphony; Orchestra
    Status: Professional; Non-Profit
    Type: Performing; Resident; Educational
    Purpose: To present new and less-familiar work; to present emerging artists; to produce American music
    Management: Anthony Korf, Artistic Director; George Rothman, Conductor/Music Director; Elaine Carroll, Administrative Director
    Budget: $100,000 - $500,000
    Income Sources: Private Foundations/Grants/Endowments; Business/Corporate Donations; Box Office; Government Grants; Individual Donations
    Performance Facilities: Kathyrn Bache Miller Theatre, Columbia University; Alice Tully Hall

ROULETTE INTERMEDIUM, INC.
228 West Broadway, New York, NY 10013
(212) 219-8242
FAX: (212) 219-8773
    Arts Area: Chamber; Ensemble; Ethnic; Folk; Instrumental Group; Electronic & Live Electronic; Band
    Status: Non-Profit
    Type: Presenting
    Purpose: To be a presenting organization and facility for innovative composers and musicians through its concert series, commissions and recording distribution services; to support a broad range of new music by young established artists
    Management: Jim Staley, Program Director; David Weinstein, Projects Director; Suzanne Youngerman, Managing Director
    Officers: Jim Staley, President
    Budget: $100,000 - $500,000
    Income Sources: Private Foundations/Grants/Endowments; Business/Corporate Donations; Box Office; Government Grants; Individual Donations
    Performance Facilities: Roul

SAINT LUKES CHAMBER ENSEMBLE, INC.
130 West 42nd Street, Suite 804, New York, NY 10036
(212) 840-7470
FAX: (212) 840-7585
Arts Area: Orchestra; Chamber
Status: Non-Profit
Type: Performing; Touring; Educational; Sponsoring
Purpose: Encompasses three performing divisions; St. Luke's Chamber Ensemble; Orchestra of St. Luke's; Children's Free Opera and Dance of New York
Management: Michael Feldman, Artistic Director; Marriane C. Lockwood, Executive Director
Officers: M. Bernard Aidinoff, Chairman of the Board
Budget: $1,000,000 - $5,000,000
Income Sources: Private Foundations/Grants/Endowments; Business/Corporate Donations; Box Office; Government Grants; Individual Donations
Performance Facilities: Avery Fisher Hall; Merkin Concert Hall; Brooklyn Academy of Music; Triplex Theatre; Town Hall

SATURDAY BRASS QUNITET
c/o St. Michael's Episcopal Church, 225 West 99th Street, New York, NY 10025
(212) 222-2700
Arts Area: Chamber
Status: Professional; Non-Profit
Type: Performing; Touring; Resident; Educational
Purpose: To present classics of the brass chamber genre; to solicit and perform new selections for brass
Budget: $50,000 - $100,000
Income Sources: Private Foundations/Grants/Endowments; Business/Corporate Donations; Box Office; Government Grants; Individual Donations

SPECULUM MUSICAE, INC.
127 West 96th Street, #16H, New York, NY 10025
(212) 865-9028
Arts Area: Chamber; Ensemble
Status: Professional; Non-Profit
Type: Performing; Touring; Resident; Educational; Sponsoring
Purpose: To devote its performances and recordings to high quality interpretations of a broad range of new music and older "classics" of the 20th century
Management: Amy Frawley, Adminstrative Director; Eric Bartlett, President
Budget: $50,000 - $100,000
Income Sources: Private Foundations/Grants/Endowments; Business/Corporate Donations; Box Office; Government Grants; Individual Donations
Performance Facilities: Merkin Concert Hall

SYLVAN WINDS, INCORPORATED
246 West 38th Street, New York, NY 10018
FAX: (212) 944-9082
Arts Area: Chamber; Ensemble; Instrumental Group
Status: Professional; Non-Profit
Type: Performing; Touring; Educational
Purpose: Since its formation in 1976, Sylvan Winds has devoted itself exclusively to the performance of chamber music for wind instruments.
Management: Steve Elmer, Executive Director; Svjetlana Kabalin, Artistic Director
Officers: Florence Reif Richman, President of the Board
Budget: $50,000 - $100,000
Income Sources: Private Foundations/Grants/Endowments; Business/Corporate Donations; Box Office; Government Grants; Individual Donations
Performance Facilities: Weill Recital Hall at Carnegie Hall; Merkin Concert Hall at Abraham Goodman House

SYMPHONY FOR UNITED NATIONS
205 West End Avenue, Suite 21C, New York, NY 10023
(212) 873-2872
FAX: (212) 874-7720
Founded: 1974
Arts Area: Symphony; Chamber; Ensemble; Ethnic; Folk
Status: Professional; Semi-Professional; Non-Profit
Type: Performing; Touring; Educational; Sponsoring
Purpose: To produce concerts and festivals around issues of human and global concern
Management: Joseph Eger, Conductor
Officers: Joseph Eger, President; Dr. Ruth Mack, Vice President; Diane Siewering, Secretary

Paid Staff: 4 **Volunteer Staff:** 22
Utilizes: Special Technical Talent; Guest Conductors; Guest Artists; Guest Directors
Budget: $100,000 - $500,000
Income Sources: Private Foundations/Grants/Endowments; Business/Corporate Donations; Box Office; Government Grants; Individual Donations
Season: 52 Weeks

TISCH CENTER FOR THE ARTS
1395 Lexington Avenue, New York, NY 10128
(212) 415-5740
FAX: (212) 415-5738
Arts Area: Orchestra; Chamber; Ensemble; Pops; Theatre; Jazz
Status: Non-Profit
Type: Performing; Educational
Management: Omus Hirshbein, Vice Chairman; Raymond Grant, Director; Jacqueline Taylor, Managing Director
Paid Staff: 8
Utilizes: Special Technical Talent; Guest Conductors; Guest Artists; Guest Directors
Budget: $1,000,000 - $5,000,000
Income Sources: Private Foundations/Grants/Endowments; Business/Corporate Donations; Box Office; Government Grants; Individual Donations
Season: September - July
Performance Facilities: Kaufmann Concert Hall

WAVERLY CONSORT, INC.
305 Riverside Drive, 5#, New York, NY 10025
(212) 666-1260
FAX: (212) 666-1559
Arts Area: Ensemble
Status: Professional; Non-Profit
Type: Performing; Touring
Purpose: To present early music to the public in NY and throughout the country
Management: Michael Jaffee, Artistic Director
Budget: $50,000 - $100,000
Income Sources: Private Foundations/Grants/Endowments; Business/Corporate Donations; Box Office; Government Grants; Individual Donations

VOCAL MUSIC

AFTER DINNER OPERA COMPANY
23 Stuyvesant Street, New York, NY 10003
(212) 477-6212
Founded: 1949
Arts Area: Lyric Opera
Status: Professional; Non-Profit
Type: Performing; Touring; Educational
Purpose: To perform opera, promote American composers and performers and educate the public in opera
Management: Richard Flusser, Administrative Director; Beth Flusser, Production Manager; Elizabeth Mozza, Producer; Conrad Strausser, Musical Director
Officers: Roslyn Borkow, President
Paid Staff: 4 **Volunteer Staff:** 6
Paid Artists: 20
Utilizes: Special Technical Talent; Guest Artists; Guest Directors
Budget: $50,000 - $100,000
Income Sources: Private Foundations/Grants/Endowments; Business/Corporate Donations; Box Office; Government Grants
Season: September - June
Annual Attendance: 10,000
Performance Facilities: Lincoln Center for the Performing Arts; Queensborough Community College

AMATO OPERA THEATRE
319 Bowery, New York, NY 10003
(212) 228-8200
Founded: 1948
Arts Area: Grand Opera; Light Opera
Status: Professional; Semi-Professional; Non-Profit
Type: Performing
Officers: Anthony Amato, President; Sally Amato, Treasurer
Volunteer Staff: 10

Non-Paid Artists: 100
Utilizes: Special Technical Talent; Guest Conductors; Guest Artists
Budget: $50,000 - $100,000
Income Sources: Private Foundations/Grants/Endowments; Business/Corporate Donations; Box Office; Government Grants; Individual Donations
Season: September - May
Annual Attendance: 8,500

AMERICAN CHAMBER OPERA COMPANY, INC.
657 West 161st Street, #3F, New York, NY 10032
(212) 781-0857
Founded: 1983
Arts Area: Chamber Opera
Status: Professional; Non-Profit
Type: Performing
Purpose: To present American and other chamber operas in full productions emphasizing musical and dramatic values
Management: Raquel Rossman, Production Manager; George Zarr, Stage Manager
Officers: Douglas Anderson, Executive Director; Laura Greenberg, Artistic Director; Giboney Whyte, Managing Director
Paid Staff: 5   **Volunteer Staff:** 15
Paid Artists: 95
Utilizes: Special Technical Talent; Guest Conductors; Guest Artists; Guest Directors
Budget: $1,000 - $50,000
Income Sources: Private Foundations/Grants/Endowments; Business/Corporate Donations; Box Office; Government Grants; Individual Donations
Season: October - May   **Annual Attendance:** 1,500
Performance Facilities: Marymount Manhattan Theatre

ASSOCIATION FOR THE FURTHERMENT OF BEL CANTO
11 Riverside Drive, New York, NY 10023
(212) 877-1595
Founded: 1968
Status: Professional; Non-Profit
Type: Performing; Resident
Purpose: To present productions of Bel Canto, Italian and French Opera pieces
Management: Stefan Zucker, General Manager/Artistic Director
Paid Staff: 3   **Volunteer Staff:** 5
Paid Artists: 100   **Non-Paid Artists:** 5
Utilizes: Special Technical Talent; Guest Conductors; Guest Artists; Guest Directors
Budget: $50,000 - $100,000
Income Sources: Business/Corporate Donations; Box Office; Individual Donations
Season: 52 Weeks
Performance Facilities: Merkin Concert Hall; Casa Italiana, Columbia University

CENTER FOR CONTEMPORARY OPERA
Gracie Station, PO Box 1350, New York, NY 10028-0010
(212) 308-6728
FAX: (212) 308-6744
Founded: 1982
Arts Area: Lyric Opera
Status: Professional; Non-Profit
Type: Performing
Management: Richard Marshall, Director
Paid Staff: 1
Utilizes: Special Technical Talent; Guest Artists; Guest Directors
Budget: $50,000 - $100,000
Income Sources: Private Foundations/Grants/Endowments; Business/Corporate Donations; Box Office; Government Grants; Individual Donations
Season: October - June
Affiliations: NOA; Operaliner

CONCERT ROYAL, INC.
280 Riverside Drive, Suite 5H, New York, NY 10025
(212) 662-8829
FAX: (212) 662-8829
Arts Area: Baroque Opera; Ballet; Orchestra
Status: Professional; Non-Profit
Type: Performing; Touring
Purpose: To perform baroque and classical music on original instruments with a strong vocal and dance component

Management: James Richman, Artistic Director/Conductor; Suzanne Konowitz, General Manager
Budget: $100,000 - $500,000
Income Sources: Private Foundations/Grants/Endowments; Business/Corporate Donations; Box Office; Government Grants; Individual Donations
Performance Facilities: Merkin Concert Hall; Florence Gould Hall

GOODMAN CHAMBER CHOIR
145 Fourth Avenue, New York, NY 10003
(212) 254-1717
Founded: 1984
Arts Area: Choral
Status: Professional; Non-Profit
Type: Performing; Touring
Purpose: To employ American and Russian emigres for performances of choral music
Budget: $1,000 - $50,000
Income Sources: Private Foundations/Grants/Endowments; Business/Corporate Donations; Box Office; Government Grants; Individual Donations
Season: September - June   **Annual Attendance:** 10,000

GREGG SMITH SINGERS, INC.
171 West 71st Street, New York, NY 10023
(212) 874-2990
Arts Area: Choral
Status: Professional; Non-Profit
Type: Performing; Touring; Resident; Educational
Purpose: To lead the way in establishing the rightful place of American choral music
Management: Gregg Smith, Music Director; Walter Gould, Booking Manager
Budget: $100,000 - $500,000
Income Sources: Private Foundations/Grants/Endowments; Business/Corporate Donations; Box Office; Government Grants; Individual Donations

I CANTORI DI NEW YORK
PO Box 4156, New York, NY 10185-0035
Founded: 1983
Arts Area: Choral
Status: Semi-Professional
Type: Performing
Purpose: To present a wide variety of choral music, juxtaposing contemporary and the past
Utilizes: Guest Artists
Budget: $1,000 - $50,000
Income Sources: Private Foundations/Grants/Endowments; Business/Corporate Donations; Box Office; Individual Donations
Season: September - May   **Annual Attendance:** 1,500

JUILLIARD OPERA CENTER
The Juilliard School, 60 Lincoln Center Plaza, New York, NY 10023-6588
(212) 799-5000
FAX: (212) 724-0263
Founded: 1969
Arts Area: Grand Opera; Lyric Opera; Light Opera
Status: Non-Professional; Non-Profit; Training
Type: Performing; Educational
Purpose: To provide training for post-graduate, pre-professional opera singers
Management: Frank Corsaro, Artistic Director
Officers: Joseph W. Polisi, President, The Juilliard School
Paid Staff: 20
Non-Paid Artists: 20
Utilizes: Special Technical Talent; Guest Conductors; Guest Directors
Budget: $100,000 - $500,000
Income Sources: The Juilliard School
Season: December - April   **Annual Attendance:** 8,000
Affiliations: The Juilliard School
Performance Facilities: Juilliard Theater

L'OPERA FRANCAIS DE NEW YORK
515 West 111th Street, Suite 3F, New York, NY 10025
(212) 678-0548
Founded: 1988

Arts Area: Lyric Opera
Status: Professional
Type: Performing
Purpose: To bring French lyric opera to American audiences
Management: Yves Abel, Susan Mebroin, Artistic Directors; Melanie Smith, General Manager; Ron Jamini, Administrative Assistant; Caroline Criscuolo, Development
Officers: Yves Abel, President; Susan Melvora, Vice President; Melanie Smith, Secretary
Paid Staff: 4 **Volunteer Staff:** 2
Paid Artists: 120
Utilizes: Special Technical Talent; Guest Artists; Guest Directors
Budget: $100,000 - $500,000
Income Sources: Private Foundations/Grants/Endowments; Business/Corporate Donations; Box Office; Individual Donations
Season: February - June **Annual Attendance:** 3,000
Affiliations: French Institute; Alliance Francaise
Performance Facilities: Florence Gould Hall

LIEDERKRANZ OPERA THEATRE
6 East 87th, New York, NY 10128
(212) 534-0880
Founded: 1960
Arts Area: Grand Opera; Lyric Opera; Light Opera; Operetta
Status: Professional
Type: Performing
Purpose: To foster a performance outlet for young singers
Management: John Balme, Music Director
Officers: Hans Hachmann, President
Paid Staff: 1
Paid Artists: 40
Utilizes: Guest Artists; Guest Directors
Budget: $1,000 - $50,000
Income Sources: Private Foundations/Grants/Endowments; Box Office
Season: September - May **Annual Attendance:** 2,500
Performance Facilities: Liederkranz Building

LIGHT OPERA OF MANHATTAN
316 East 91st Street, New York, NY 10028
(212) 831-2000; (212) 222-9192
FAX: (212) 864-6682
Founded: 1969
Arts Area: Light Opera; Operetta; Musical Theatre
Status: Professional; Non-Profit
Type: Performing
Purpose: To promote the continued performance and appreciation of a nearly-forgotten art form, the operetta
Management: Steven M. Levy, Producer; Elaine Malbin, Artistic Director
Officers: Patricia Greenwald, Chairman; Jean Dairymple, President; Steven Levy, Secretary; Reed Simmons, Treasurer
Paid Staff: 3 **Volunteer Staff:** 12
Paid Artists: 33
Utilizes: Guest Conductors; Guest Directors
Budget: $500,000 - $1,000,000
Income Sources: Private Foundations/Grants/Endowments; Business/Corporate Donations; Box Office; Government Grants; Individual Donations
Season: 52 Weeks **Annual Attendance:** 30,000
Performance Facilities: Playhouse 91

MEASURED BREATHS THEATRE COMPANY
193 Spring Street, #3R, New York, NY 10012
(212) 334-8402
Founded: 1989
Arts Area: Lyric Opera; Theatre
Status: Professional; Commercial
Type: Performing
Purpose: To create and revive all forms of operatic musical theatre in order to strengthen the dramatic basis of museum theatre
Management: Robert Press, Artistic Director
Utilizes: Special Technical Talent; Guest Conductors; Guest Artists
Budget: $1,000 - $50,000
Income Sources: Box Office; Individual Donations
Season: 52 Weeks **Annual Attendance:** 600

THE METROPOLITAN GREEK CHORALE
PO Box 2690, New York, NY 10185
(212) 475-3394; (212) 874-4482
Founded: 1965
Arts Area: Choral; Ethnic
Status: Semi-Professional; Non-Professional; Non-Profit
Type: Performing
Purpose: To present fine performances of traditional Greek music, as well as contemporary Greek and Greek-American composers
Officers: George Haikalis, President; Elaine Scurtis, Vice President; Frances Bishop, Secretary; Jerry Kolaitis, Treasurer
Volunteer Staff: 12
Non-Paid Artists: 35
Utilizes: Guest Artists
Budget: $1,000 - $50,000
Income Sources: Private Foundations/Grants/Endowments; Business/Corporate Donations; Box Office; Government Grants; Individual Donations
Season: October - June   **Annual Attendance:** 700
Performance Facilities: Merkin Hall; Alice Tully Hall

METROPOLITAN OPERA
Lincoln Center, New York, NY 10023
(212) 799-3100
Founded: 1883
Arts Area: Grand Opera
Status: Professional; Non-Profit
Type: Performing; Touring; Resident
Purpose: To produce and present opera performances in New York, on tour and through broadcasts of live performances throughout the United States and Canada
Management: Joseph Volpe, General Director; James Levine, Artistic Director
Officers: Mrs. Gilbert W. Humphrey, Honorary Chairman of the Board; James S. Marcus, Chairman; Bruce Crawford, President; Wilbur Daniels, Chairman, Executive Committee; Alton E. Peters, Robert L.B. Tobin, Vice Presidents; Ray J. Groves, Treasurer/Secretary
Utilizes: Special Technical Talent; Guest Conductors; Guest Artists; Guest Directors
Budget: Over 10,000,000
Income Sources: Private Foundations/Grants/Endowments; Business/Corporate Donations; Box Office; Government Grants; Individual Donations
Season: September - April
Affiliations: OA
Performance Facilities: Metropolitan Opera House

MUSIC-THEATRE GROUP, INC.
29 Bethune Street, New York, NY 10014
(212) 924-3108
FAX: (212) 255-1981
Founded: 1971
Arts Area: Music Theatre
Status: Professional; Non-Profit
Type: Performing; Touring
Purpose: To commission, develop and produce innovative music theatre
Management: Diane Wondisford, Managing Director; Lyn Austin, CEO/Producing Director
Officers: Lyn Austin, President; Lynda Sturner Traum, Vice President; Charles Houerith Jr., Secretary; Bernard Rosenberg, Treasurer; Rosita Sarnoff, Chair
Paid Staff: 4   **Volunteer Staff:** 2
Paid Artists: 75
Utilizes: Special Technical Talent; Guest Conductors; Guest Artists; Guest Directors
Budget: $500,000 - $1,000,000
Income Sources: Private Foundations/Grants/Endowments; Business/Corporate Donations; Box Office; Government Grants; Individual Donations; Touring
Season: September - May   **Annual Attendance:** 15,000
Affiliations: OA; TCG; ART/NY

MUSICA SACRA
165 West 86th Street, New York, NY 10024
(212) 874-3104
FAX: (212) 874-7815
Founded: 1973
Arts Area: Choral
Status: Professional

Type: Performing
Purpose: To perform choral works spanning the ages
Management: Elizabeth Bond, General Manager
Officers: Jonathan Prinz, President; Jen T. Farrah, Robert F. Langley, Robert Brauer, Vice Presidents; Barbara G. Landau, Secretary; Gerald W. Richman, Treasurer
Paid Staff: 2
Paid Artists: 120
Utilizes: Guest Artists
Budget: $500,000 - $1,000,000
Income Sources: Private Foundations/Grants/Endowments; Business/Corporate Donations; Box Office; Government Grants; Individual Donations
Season: September - April
Performance Facilities: Lincoln Center; Carnegie Hall

NEW AMSTERDAM SINGERS
PO Box 373, Cathedral Station, New York, NY 10025
(212) 662-6523
Founded: 1968
Arts Area: Choral
Status: Non-Professional
Type: Performing
Purpose: To perform and promote choral music
Management: Clara Longstreth, Music Director; Wendy S. Fay, Manager
Officers: Joanne Cossa, President; Carol O' Connor, Vice President; Paul Pausekian, Treasurer; Paula Franklin, Secretary
Paid Staff: 4 **Volunteer Staff:** 10
Non-Paid Artists: 70
Utilizes: Guest Artists
Budget: $50,000 - $100,000
Income Sources: Private Foundations/Grants/Endowments; Business/Corporate Donations; Box Office; Government Grants; Individual Donations
Season: October - June **Annual Attendance:** 800

NEW YORK CHORAL SOCIETY
165 West 57th Street, New York, NY 10019
(212) 624-0027
Founded: 1958
Arts Area: Choral
Status: Non-Professional; Non-Profit
Type: Performing; Touring
Purpose: To present choral masterpieces and lesser-known works in Carnegie Hall
Officers: David Nickols, President; Joanne Lawson, Treasurer; Pam Reich, Vice President; Lisa Guida, President Elect
Volunteer Staff: 14
Paid Artists: 2 **Non-Paid Artists:** 180
Utilizes: Special Technical Talent; Guest Conductors; Guest Artists; Contract Orchestras
Budget: $100,000 - $500,000
Income Sources: Private Foundations/Grants/Endowments; Business/Corporate Donations; Box Office; Government Grants; Individual Donations; Perfomance Fees
Season: September - May **Annual Attendance:** 10,000
Performance Facilities: Carnegie Hall; Lincoln Center

NEW YORK CITY OPERA
20 Lincoln Center, New York, NY 10023
(212) 870-5600
FAX: (212) 724-1120
Founded: 1944
Arts Area: Grand Opera; Musical Theatre
Status: Professional
Type: Performing; Touring; Resident; Educational
Purpose: To produce grand opera; to develop and present young American singers; to present opera as theater
Management: Christopher A. Keene, General Director
Officers: Robert W. Wilson, Chairman; Martin J. Oppenheimer, Vice Chairman
Paid Staff: 70 **Volunteer Staff:** 50
Paid Artists: 450
Utilizes: Special Technical Talent; Guest Conductors; Guest Artists; Guest Directors
Budget: Over 10,000,000
Income Sources: Private Foundations/Grants/Endowments; Business/Corporate Donations; Box Office; Government Grants; Individual Donations
Season: July - November **Annual Attendance:** 350,000

Affiliations: OA
Performance Facilities: New York State Theater

NEW YORK CITY OPERA NATIONAL COMPANY
211 West 61st Street, 6th Floor, New York, NY 10023
(212) 399-6409
FAX: (212) 399-6414
Founded: 1979
Arts Area: Grand Opera; Lyric Opera
Status: Professional; Non-Profit
Type: Performing; Touring
Purpose: To take top-quality, fully-staged orchestra performances of standard repertory operas to relatively isolated areas; to provide young singers with valuable performing experience
Management: Christopher Keene, General Director; Nancy Kelly, Administrative Director; Joseph Colaneri, Music Director
Officers: Robert W. Wilson, Chairman; Martin J. Oppenheimer, Vice Chairman
Paid Staff: 3 **Volunteer Staff:** 2
Paid Artists: 70
Utilizes: Special Technical Talent; Guest Artists; Guest Directors
Budget: $1,000,000 - $5,000,000
Income Sources: Private Foundations/Grants/Endowments; Business/Corporate Donations; Government Grants; Performance Fees
Season: January - April **Annual Attendance:** 100,000

THE NEW YORK CONCERT SINGERS
401 East 80th Street, New York, NY 10021
(212) 879-4412
Founded: 1988
Arts Area: Choral; Vocal Chamber Music
Status: Professional
Type: Performing; Educational
Purpose: To present choral and vocal chamber programs
Officers: Judith Clurman, Chair; Marcia Klugman, Vice Chair/Treasurer; Lola Terch Gold, Secretary
Paid Staff: 1 **Volunteer Staff:** 3
Utilizes: Guest Artists
Budget: $1,000 - $50,000
Income Sources: Private Foundations/Grants/Endowments; Box Office; Individual Donations
Season: 52 Weeks **Annual Attendance:** 600
Performance Facilities: Mertan Hall; Lincoln Center

NEW YORK GILBERT AND SULLIVAN PLAYERS
251 West 91st Street #4C, New York, NY 10024
(212) 769-1000
Founded: 1974
Arts Area: Operetta; Musical Theatre
Status: Professional
Type: Performing; Touring; Resident; Educational
Purpose: To promote and produce works of Gilbert and Sullivan, as well as related works using orchestras and small ensembles
Management: Albert Bergeret, Artistic Director/General Manager
Officers: Charles Pye, President; Albert Bergeret, Vice President; Ivy Reale, Secretary; John Behonet, Treasurer
Paid Staff: 1 **Volunteer Staff:** 1
Paid Artists: 80
Utilizes: Guest Artists
Budget: $100,000 - $500,000
Income Sources: Private Foundations/Grants/Endowments; Business/Corporate Donations; Box Office; Government Grants; Individual Donations
Season: 52 Weeks **Annual Attendance:** 20,000
Affiliations: AEA; AFM

OPERA EBONY
2109 Broadway, New York, NY 10023
(212) 874-7245
FAX: (212) 580-2920
Founded: 1973
Arts Area: Grand Opera; Ethnic; Folk; 20th Century Works
Status: Professional; Non-Profit

Type: Performing; Touring; Educational
Purpose: To promote and discover singers, directors, composers, technicians and choreographers
Management: Wayne Sanders, Music Director; Benjamin Matthews, Artistic Director; Mohammed Hatim, Special Projects Director
Officers: Ibraham Abdul-Malek, Chairman; Garnald King, Vice President; Clarie Stanton, Secretary
Paid Staff: 6 **Volunteer Staff:** 15
Utilizes: Special Technical Talent; Guest Conductors; Guest Artists; Guest Directors
Budget: $1,000,000 - $5,000,000
Income Sources: Private Foundations/Grants/Endowments; Business/Corporate Donations; Box Office; Government Grants; Individual Donations
Season: September - July **Annual Attendance:** 8,000
Affiliations: The American Music Center; OA
Performance Facilities: Aaron Davis Hall

OPERA NORTHEAST
530 East 89th Street, New York, NY 10128
(212) 472-2168
Founded: 1972
Arts Area: Grand Opera; Operetta
Status: Professional; Non-Profit
Type: Performing; Touring; Educational
Purpose: Build a first-class touring organization to produce and present authentic classical lyric theatre
Management: Donald Westwood, Artistic Director; Ronald Forsmo, David Seatter, Managing Directors
Paid Staff: 5
Paid Artists: 200
Utilizes: Special Technical Talent; Guest Conductors; Guest Artists; Guest Directors
Budget: $500,000 - $1,000,000
Income Sources: Private Foundations/Grants/Endowments; Business/Corporate Donations; Box Office; Government Grants; Individual Donations
Season: 52 Weeks **Annual Attendance:** 150,000

OPERA ORCHESTRA OF NEW YORK
239 West 72nd Street, Suite 2R, New York, NY 10023-2734
(212) 799-1982
Founded: 1971
Arts Area: Grand Opera; Lyric Opera
Status: Professional; Non-Profit
Type: Performing; Sponsoring
Purpose: To bring rarely heard or little-known operas to the public
Management: Eve Queler, Music Director; Yvonne Altmann, Director of Development; Alix Barthelmes, Manager
Paid Staff: 3 **Volunteer Staff:** 4
Paid Artists: 140
Utilizes: Guest Artists
Budget: $500,000 - $1,000,000
Income Sources: Private Foundations/Grants/Endowments; Business/Corporate Donations; Box Office; Government Grants; Individual Donations
Season: November - May **Annual Attendance:** 15,000
Performance Facilities: Carnegie Hall

ORATORIO SOCIETY OF NEW YORK
881 Seventh Avenue, Carnegie Hall, #504, New York, NY 10019
(212) 247-4199
Founded: 1873
Arts Area: Choral
Status: Non-Professional; Non-Profit
Type: Performing; Touring; Resident; Educational
Purpose: To bring the people of Greater New York seldom-done, good oratorio music and to offer a platform for promising young artists
Officers: Joseph W. Brinkley, Chairman; Ellen L. Blair, President; Evelyn Arcudi and Janet Plucknett, Vice Presidents
Paid Staff: 2 **Volunteer Staff:** 3
Non-Paid Artists: 200
Utilizes: Guest Conductors; Guest Artists
Budget: $100,000 - $500,000
Income Sources: Private Foundations/Grants/Endowments; Business/Corporate Donations; Box Office; Government Grants; Individual Donations
Season: September - June **Annual Attendance:** 10,000
Performance Facilities: Carnegie Hall

PALA OPERA ASSOCIATION
7 West 81st Street, New York, NY 10024
(212) 769-8760
FAX: (212) 769-8760
Founded: 1989
Arts Area: Grand Opera; Opera/Theater Combinations
Status: Professional
Type: Performing
Purpose: To present high-calibre, ascendent-star artists in an elegant, professional situation, with full orchestra and chorus, where they will be heard by critics and discerning, paying audiences
Management: Elizabeth Moxley Falk, Producer/Artistic Director; Timothy Lindberg, Music Director; Richard Woitach, Chief Music Consultant; Phillip Gossett, Bel Canto Enbellishments
Officers: Lee Falk, President of Parent Organization: Provincetown Academy of the Living Arts; Elizabeth Moxley Falk, Richard Woitach, Vice Presidents P.A.L.A.
Utilizes: Guest Artists
Budget: $100,000 - $500,000
Income Sources: Private Foundations/Grants/Endowments; Business/Corporate Donations; Box Office; Individual Donations
Season: October - June **Annual Attendance:** 2,000
Affiliations: OA; NOA

POMERIUM MUSICES, INCORPORATED
945 West End Avenue, #1C, New York, NY 10025
(212) 316-3953
FAX: (215) 247-4323
Arts Area: Choral; Renaissance
Status: Professional; Non-Profit
Type: Performing; Touring
Purpose: A 13-member a cappella ensemble dedicated to performing the music written for virtuoso chapel choirs in the 15th and 16th centuries
Management: Alexander Blachly, Artistic Director
Budget: $50,000 - $100,000
Income Sources: Private Foundations/Grants/Endowments; Box Office; Government Grants; Individual Donations

PRO MUSICIS FOUNDATION, INC.
140 West 79th Street, Suite 9F, New York, NY 10024
(212) 787-0993
FAX: (212) 362-0352
Founded: 1965
Arts Area: Recital
Status: Professional; Non-Profit; Community Service
Type: Performing; Sponsoring
Purpose: To encourage career development for emerging recitalists through recitals in major concert halls; to perform community service through recitals in various institutions
Officers: Fr. Eugene Merlet, President; John E. Haag, Executive Director
Paid Staff: 1 **Volunteer Staff:** 3
Budget: $100,000 - $500,000
Income Sources: Private Foundations/Grants/Endowments; Business/Corporate Donations; Box Office; Government Grants; Individual Donations
Season: January - May **Annual Attendance:** 3,000
Performance Facilities: Weill Hall, New York; Jordan Hall, Boston

THE SAINT THOMAS CHOIR OF MEN AND BOYS
Saint Thomas Church, Fifth Avenue, 1 West 53rd Street, New York, NY 10019
(212) 757-7013
Founded: 1919
Arts Area: Choral
Status: Professional; Non-Profit
Type: Performing; Touring; Resident
Purpose: To provide Anglican music of the highest standards for Saint Thomas Church Fifth Avenue; to give a concert series each season and to record; to tour domestically and overseas
Management: Saint Thomas Church Fifth Avenue; Karen Mc Farlane Artists, Inc.
Officers: Gerre Hancock, Director; Phelicia Wingfield, Music Administrator; Lee Whitley, Marketing Consultant
Paid Staff: 3 **Volunteer Staff:** 50
Paid Artists: 32
Utilizes: Special Technical Talent; Guest Artists; Guest Directors
Budget: $50,000 - $100,000

Income Sources: Private Foundations/Grants/Endowments; Business/Corporate Donations; Box Office; Individual Donations
Season: September - June **Annual Attendance:** 6,000
Performance Facilities: Saint Thomas Church

THEATRE ROCOCO
Empire State Building, Suite 3304, New York, NY 10118
(212) 971-9702
Founded: 1969
Arts Area: 18th Century Opera
Status: Professional
Type: Performing; Touring; Educational
Purpose: To perform opera of the 18th century
Management: Jeannette Ferrell, General Manager; Janet Poland, Producer
Officers: Fritz Maraffi, Musical Director
Paid Staff: 2 **Volunteer Staff:** 3
Paid Artists: 29
Utilizes: Guest Artists; Guest Musicians
Budget: $50,000 - $100,000
Income Sources: Box Office; Touring Fees Worldwide
Season: October - April

TOURING CONCERT OPERA COMPANY
228 East 80th Street, New York, NY 10021
(212) 988-2542
Founded: 1971
Arts Area: Grand Opera
Status: Professional; Non-Profit
Type: Performing; Touring; Educational
Purpose: To bring live, fully professional grand opera to areas where it is less frequently seen and heard; to give young professional artists another outlet for their talents
Management: Ramon Alsina, Company Representative
Officers: Ramon Alsina, President/Treasurer; Anne de Figols, Vice President/Secretary
Paid Staff: 3 **Volunteer Staff:** 7
Paid Artists: 20
Utilizes: Special Technical Talent; Guest Conductors; Guest Artists; Guest Directors; Guest Choreographers
Budget: $1,000 - $50,000
Income Sources: Private Foundations/Grants/Endowments; Business/Corporate Donations; Box Office; Government Grants; Individual Donations
Season: 52 Weeks

VILLAGE LIGHT OPERA GROUP
PO Box 143, Village Station, New York, NY 10014
(212) 243-6281
Founded: 1934
Arts Area: Light Opera; Operetta; Musical Theatre
Status: Non-Professional; Non-Profit
Type: Performing; Educational
Purpose: To provide high-quality lyric theatre experiences in all phases of production and performance for interested amateurs at the lowest possible ticket prices
Volunteer Staff: 50
Paid Artists: 24
Budget: $50,000 - $100,000
Income Sources: Business/Corporate Donations; Box Office; Individual Donations; Rentals
Season: November - and April
Annual Attendance: 5,000
Performance Facilities: Haft Theatre, Fashion Institute of Technology

WESTERN WIND VOCAL ENSEMBLE, INC.
263 West 86th Street, New York, NY 10024
(212) 873-2848
FAX: (212) 873-2849
Founded: 1969
Arts Area: Ensemble
Status: Professional
Type: Performing; Touring; Resident; Educational
Purpose: To bring to the public the beauty of vocal music through performance, recording, radio and workshops
Management: William Zukof, Executive Director; Margaret O'Brien, Administrator
Officers: Hazel Toennies, Treasurer; David Freund, Chairman; Diane Cochrane, President

Paid Staff: 2
Paid Artists: 6
Utilizes: Guest Artists
Budget: $100,000 - $500,000
Income Sources: Private Foundations/Grants/Endowments; Business/Corporate Donations; Box Office; Government Grants; Individual Donations
Season: 52 Weeks
Affiliations: AFTRA; CMA; ACDA

THEATRE

ABOUTFACE THEATRE COMPANY
442 West 42nd Street, New York, NY 10036
(212) 268-9638
Founded: 1984
Arts Area: Professional; Musical; Theatrical Group
Status: Professional; Non-Profit
Type: Resident; Sponsoring
Purpose: To generate, develop and produce original new plays exploring American mythology and idealogy
Management: Sean Burke, Artistic Director; Allison Jones, Managing Director; Martin Fluger, Resident Director; Michael Herz, General Manager; Ron O'Conner, Barry Rowell, Ralph Lewis, Development
Officers: Julie Tibbetts, Chair; Kerry Mackenzie, Michael Mejias, April Cowin, Cheryl Davis-Counsel, Thomas G. Dunn
Volunteer Staff: 40
Utilizes: Special Technical Talent
Budget: $50,000 - $100,000
Income Sources: Private Foundations/Grants/Endowments; Business/Corporate Donations; Box Office; Government Grants; Individual Donations
Season: September - June
Annual Attendance: 5,000
Affiliations: ART/NY; New York Foundation for the Arts
Performance Facilities: Nat Horne Theatre and Studios

THE ACTING COMPANY
PO Box 898, Times Square Station, New York, NY 10108
(212) 564-3510
FAX: (212) 714-2643
Founded: 1972
Arts Area: Professional
Status: Professional; Non-Profit
Type: Performing; Touring; Resident; Educational
Purpose: The Company is dedicated to the development of classical repertory actors and a national audience for the theatre.
Management: Margot Harley, Executive Producer; Zelda Fichandler, Artistic Director
Officers: Edgar Lansbury, Chairman/President; Margot Harley, Carol Crowley, Vice Presidents; John McDonald, Earl Weiner, Secretaries; Martha L. Jay, Secretary/Treasurer
Paid Staff: 22   **Volunteer Staff:** 3
Paid Artists: 29
Utilizes: Special Technical Talent; Guest Directors
Budget: $1,000,000 - $5,000,000
Income Sources: Private Foundations/Grants/Endowments; Business/Corporate Donations; Box Office; Government Grants; Individual Donations
Season: July - May   **Annual Attendance:** 150,000

THE ACTING STUDIO, INC./NEW THEATRE ALLIANCE/CHELSEA REPERTORY COMPANY
29 East 19th Street, 4th Floor, New York, NY 10003
(212) 228-2700
Founded: 1983
Arts Area: Theatrical Group; School
Status: Professional; Semi-Professional
Type: Performing; Resident; Educational
Purpose: To serve as a training institution; to develop new scripts; to provide a resident theatre company
Management: James Price, Artistic Director; John Grabowski, Associate Director
Paid Staff: 3   **Volunteer Staff:** 30
Budget: $50,000 - $100,000
Income Sources: Box Office; Tuition
Season: 52 Weeks
Annual Attendance: 1,500

ACTORS' ALLIANCE INC. (AAI)
JAF PO Box 7370, New York, NY 10116-4630
(718) 768-6110
 Founded: 1976
 Arts Area: Professional
 Status: Professional; Non-Profit
 Type: Performing; Touring; Resident
 Purpose: To produce classical, contemporary and new plays explored and developed by a resident company of theatre artists
 Management: Melanie Sutherland, Artistic Director
 Volunteer Staff: 9
 Non-Paid Artists: 8
 Utilizes: Special Technical Talent; Guest Artists; Guest Directors
 Budget: $1,000 - $50,000
 Income Sources: Private Foundations/Grants/Endowments; Business/Corporate Donations; Box Office; Government Grants; Individual Donations
 Season: September - June

ACTORS STUDIO
432 West 44th Street, New York, NY 1947
(212) 757-0870
 Founded: 1947
 Arts Area: Professional
 Status: Professional; Non-Profit
 Type: Resident
 Purpose: Theater workshop of professional actors
 Management: Ellen Burstyn, Artistic Director; Frank Corsaro, Artistic Director
 Officers: Paul Newman, President
 Paid Staff: 5   **Volunteer Staff:** 100
 Budget: $100,000 - $500,000
 Income Sources: Private Foundations/Grants/Endowments; Business/Corporate Donations; Government Grants; Individual Donations
 Season: October - May
 Performance Facilities: Actors Studio

AMAS REPERTORY THEATRE
450 West 42nd Street, New York, NY 10036
(212) 563-2565
 Founded: 1967
 Arts Area: Professional; Summer Stock; Musical; Folk
 Status: Professional; Non-Profit
 Type: Performing; Touring; Resident; Educational; Sponsoring
 Purpose: To provide a starting place for new American theatrical pieces in a multi-racial environment which instills creative professionalism
 Management: Rosetta LeNoire, Founder/Artistic Director; Gary Halcott, Business Manager/Administrator; Stephen Schaffer, Administrator
 Officers: Don Ellwood, Chairman; Rosetta LeNoire, President; Catherine McDonald, Secretary; Daisy Haynes, Treasurer
 Paid Staff: 3   **Volunteer Staff:** 20
 Paid Artists: 10   **Non-Paid Artists:** 5
 Utilizes: Special Technical Talent; Guest Artists; Guest Directors
 Income Sources: Private Foundations/Grants/Endowments; Business/Corporate Donations; Box Office; Government Grants; Individual Donations
 Season: 52 Weeks
 Annual Attendance: 10,000

AMERICAN CENTER FOR STANISLAVSKI THEATRE ART, INC.
485 Park Avenue, New York, NY 10022
(212) 755-5120
 Founded: 1964
 Arts Area: Professional
 Status: Professional; Non-Profit
 Type: Performing; Touring; Educational
 Purpose: To bring Stanislavski's method of Physical Actions, his ultimate acting technique, solution to spontaneity to the American theatre
 Management: Sonia Moore, Artistic Director; Thalia White, Executive Director; Marie Lou Catalano, Development Consultant
 Officers: Sonia Moore, President; Edward Katz, Acting Chairman
 Paid Staff: 4   **Volunteer Staff:** 1
 Non-Paid Artists: 15

Utilizes: Special Technical Talent; Guest Directors
Budget: $50,000 - $100,000
Income Sources: Business/Corporate Donations; Box Office; Individual Donations; Student Tuition
Season: 52 Weeks
Annual Attendance: 1,000
Affiliations: ART/NY
Performance Facilities: Trinity Presbyterian Church

THE AMERICAN ENSEMBLE COMPANY
PO Box 972, Peck Slip Station, New York, NY 10272
(212) 571-7594
Founded: 1967
Arts Area: Professional; Musical; Theatrical Group
Status: Professional; Non-Profit
Type: Performing; Touring; Resident; Educational
Purpose: Production of plays and musicals of literary merit and development of a working ensemble of actors, directors, designers, and writers
Management: Robert Petito, Artistic Director; Robert Dominguez, General Manager
Paid Staff: 1   **Volunteer Staff:** 8
Utilizes: Special Technical Talent; Guest Directors
Budget: $1,000 - $50,000
Income Sources: Business/Corporate Donations; Box Office; Individual Donations
Season: September - June   **Annual Attendance:** 8,000

THE AMERICAN PLACE THEATRE
111 West 46th Street, New York, NY 10036
(212) 840-2960
FAX: (212) 391-4019
Founded: 1963
Arts Area: Theatrical Group
Status: Professional; Non-Profit
Type: Performing
Purpose: To produce new plays by living American writers
Management: Wynn Handman, Director; Dara Hershman, General Manager
Officers: Wynn Handman, Acting Board Chairman
Paid Staff: 6
Utilizes: Special Technical Talent; Guest Artists; Guest Directors
Budget: $500,000 - $1,000,000
Income Sources: Private Foundations/Grants/Endowments; Business/Corporate Donations; Box Office; Government Grants; Individual Donations
Season: September - June   **Affiliations:** AEA
Performance Facilities: Main Stage; Subplot Theatre; First Floor Theatre

AMERICAN THEATRE OF ACTORS
314 West 54th Street, New York, NY 10019
(212) 581-3044
Founded: 1977
Arts Area: Theatrical Group
Status: Professional; Non-Profit
Type: Performing
Purpose: To help develop new playwrights, actors and directors; to produce new plays
Management: James Jennings, Artistic Director; James Lynn, Technical Director; David Lipsky, Press Agent
Officers: James Jennings, President; Jane Culley, Vice President; William Kirksey, Treasurer; James Bernet, Secretary
Paid Staff: 1   **Volunteer Staff:** 3
Utilizes: Guest Artists; Guest Directors
Income Sources: Private Foundations/Grants/Endowments; Business/Corporate Donations; Box Office; Individual Donations; Rentals; Rehearsals
Season: 52 Weeks

BLACK SPECTRUM
119-07 Merrick Boulevard, New York, NY 11434
(718) 723-1800
FAX: (718) 723-1806
Founded: 1970
Arts Area: Professional; Musical; Dinner; Theatrical Group
Status: Professional; Non-Profit
Type: Performing; Touring; Educational
Purpose: To present Black classical and contemporary works of social significance

Management: Carl Clay, Founder/Producer
Paid Staff: 6   **Volunteer Staff:** 50
Utilizes: Special Technical Talent; Guest Artists; Guest Directors
Budget: $100,000 - $500,000
Income Sources: Private Foundations/Grants/Endowments; Business/Corporate Donations; Box Office; Government Grants
Season: October - June   **Annual Attendance:** 4,000

BOND STREET THEATRE COALITION
2 Bond Street, New York, NY 10012
(212) 254-4614; (518) 678-3332
FAX: (212) 254-4614; (212) 678-3332
Founded: 1975
Arts Area: Professional; Theatrical Group; Artists' Colony
Status: Professional; Non-Profit
Type: Performing; Touring; Sponsoring; Artists' Colony
Purpose: To create new theatre works using a physical and imagistic vocabulary, illuminating politically relevant themes to a broad range of audiences
Management: Joanna Sherman, Artistic Director; Patrick Sciarratta, Producing Director; Mariella Bisson, Director of Development; Michael McGuigan, Associate Director; Brad Beckman, Marketing Director
Officers: Patrick Sciarratta, President; Joanna Sherman, Vice President; Linda Sweet, Secretary; Lisa Brill, Treasurer
Paid Staff: 5   **Volunteer Staff:** 6
Paid Artists: 8
Utilizes: Special Technical Talent; Guest Artists; Guest Directors; Guest Choreographers, Composers
Budget: $100,000 - $500,000
Income Sources: Private Foundations/Grants/Endowments; Business/Corporate Donations; Box Office; Government Grants; Individual Donations; Performance Fees
Season: 52 Weeks   **Annual Attendance:** 15,000
Affiliations: ART/NY
Performance Facilities: Interarts Theatre

BROADWAY TOMORROW, INC.
191 Claremont Avenue, Suite 53, New York, NY 10027
(212) 864-4736
Founded: 1983
Arts Area: Musical
Status: Professional; Non-Profit
Type: Performing
Purpose: To nurture new musicals
Management: Elyse Curtis, Artistic Director; Ellie Serena, Literary Manager; Norman Curtis, Musical Director
Officers: Elyse Curtis, President; Gene Liberty, Vice President; Norman Curtis, Secretary/Treasurer
Volunteer Staff: 6
Paid Artists: 10
Utilizes: Special Technical Talent; Guest Conductors; Guest Artists; Guest Directors
Budget: $1,000 - $50,000
Income Sources: Private Foundations/Grants/Endowments; Business/Corporate Donations; Box Office; Government Grants; Individual Donations
Season: Fall; Spring
Performance Facilities: Phipps Plaza Theatre

CHICAGO CITY LIMITS
351 East 74th Street, New York, NY 10021
(212) 772-8707
Founded: 1977
Arts Area: Professional
Status: Professional; Commercial
Type: Performing; Touring; Resident; Educational
Purpose: Chicago City Limits presents satirical comedy revues which incorporate audience suggestions into an evening of comedy, improvisation and song.
Management: Paul Zuckerman, Artistic Director; Andrea Olin-Gomes, Touring Manager
Paid Staff: 4
Paid Artists: 12
Utilizes: Guest Artists
Budget: $100,000 - $500,000
Income Sources: Box Office; Touring Fees
Season: 52 Weeks   **Annual Attendance:** 20,000
Performance Facilities: Jan Hus Theatre

CIRCLE IN THE SQUARE
1633 Broadway, New York, NY 10019
(212) 307-2700
FAX: (212) 581-6371
> **Founded:** 1951
> **Arts Area:** Professional
> **Status:** Professional; Non-Profit
> **Type:** Performing
> **Purpose:** To produce classics, rarely-done works that deserve a second look, and new plays
> **Management:** Theodore Mann, Artistic Director; Robert A. Buckley, Managing Director
> **Officers:** John C. Russell, Chairman of the Board
> **Paid Staff:** 14
> **Paid Artists:** 80
> **Utilizes:** Special Technical Talent; Guest Artists; Guest Directors
> **Budget:** $1,000,000 - $5,000,000
> **Income Sources:** Private Foundations/Grants/Endowments; Business/Corporate Donations; Box Office; Government Grants; Individual Donations
> **Season:** 52 Weeks
> **Affiliations:** LORT; TCG; League of American Theatres and Producers
> **Performance Facilities:** Circle In The Square

CIRCLE REPERTORY THEATRE COMPANY
161 Avenue of the Americas, 4th Floor, New York, NY 10013
(212) 691-3210
FAX: (212) 675-8098
> **Founded:** 1969
> **Arts Area:** Professional
> **Status:** Professional; Non-Profit
> **Type:** Performing; Resident
> **Purpose:** A resident theatre company producing professional theatre with an emphasis on new American plays
> **Management:** Tanya Berezin, Artistic Director; Abigail Evans, Managing Director; Meredith Freeman, General Manager; Mark S. Romant, Associate Artistic Director
> **Officers:** John Lack, Chairman; Priscilla Morgan, Secretary; Duane Wilder, Treasurer; Elaine Bond
> **Paid Staff:** 18
> **Utilizes:** Special Technical Talent; Guest Artists; Guest Directors
> **Budget:** $1,000,000 - $5,000,000
> **Income Sources:** Private Foundations/Grants/Endowments; Business/Corporate Donations; Box Office; Government Grants; Individual Donations
> **Season:** September - May
> **Annual Attendance:** 50,000
> **Performance Facilities:** Circle Repertory Theatre

CREATION PRODUCTION COMPANY
127 Greene Street, New York, NY 10012
(212) 674-5593
> **Founded:** 1977
> **Arts Area:** Theatrical Group
> **Status:** Professional; Non-Profit
> **Type:** Performing; Touring; Educational
> **Purpose:** Experimental theatre
> **Management:** Anne Hemenway, Director; Jennifer McDowall, Managing Director; Susan Mosakowski, Matthew Maguire, Co-Artistic Directors
> **Paid Staff:** 3
> **Paid Artists:** 30
> **Budget:** $100,000 - $500,000
> **Income Sources:** Private Foundations/Grants/Endowments; Business/Corporate Donations; Box Office; Government Grants; Individual Donations
> **Season:** 52 Weeks
> **Annual Attendance:** 3,500

CREATIVE ARTS TEAM
715 Broadway, 5th Floor, New York University, New York, NY 10003
(212) 998-7380
FAX: (212) 995-4151
> **Founded:** 1974
> **Arts Area:** Professional; Theatrical Group
> **Status:** Professional; Non-Profit
> **Type:** Performing; Touring; Resident; Educational

Management: Lynda Zimmerman, Executive Director; Jim Mirrione, Playwright-in-Residence; Dr. Leslie White, Managing Director; Mark Riherd, Program Director
Paid Staff: 70
Paid Artists: 50
Budget: $500,000 - $1,000,000
Income Sources: Private Foundations/Grants/Endowments; Business/Corporate Donations; Government Grants; Individual Donations
Season: September - July
Annual Attendance: 40,000
Affiliations: NYSCA; TCG; New York University

CSC REPERTORY
136 East 13th Street, New York, NY 10003
(212) 677-4210
FAX: (212) 477-7504
Founded: 1967
Arts Area: Professional; Theatrical Group
Status: Professional; Non-Profit
Type: Performing; Resident
Purpose: To produce classics with a relevance to today's audience
Management: David Esbjornson, Artistic Director; Patricia Taylor, Managing Director; Kelley Voorhees, Company Manager; Jeffrey Berzon, Production Manager
Officers: Turner P. Smith, President; Donald S. Donovan, Vice President
Paid Staff: 5   **Volunteer Staff:** 4
Utilizes: Special Technical Talent; Guest Directors
Budget: $500,000 - $1,000,000
Income Sources: Private Foundations/Grants/Endowments; Business/Corporate Donations; Box Office; Government Grants; Individual Donations
Season: October - March
Affiliations: AEA
Performance Facilities: CSC Repertory

DON QUIJOTE CHILDREN'S THEATRE
250 West 65th Street, New York, NY 10023
(212) 496-8009
Founded: 1972
Arts Area: Professional; Musical; Theatrical Group; Puppet
Status: Professional; Non-Profit
Type: Performing; Touring; Resident; Educational
Purpose: To provide inspirational, entertaining, educational theatre for children
Management: Oswaldo Pradere, Artistic Director; Stefanie Scott, Resident Director; Jim Finn, Administrator; Wendy Samuel, Administrative Assistant
Officers: Martha Bograd, President; Estrellita Brodsky, Vice President; Oswaldo Pradere, Treasurer; Karen Cooke, Secretary
Paid Staff: 3   **Volunteer Staff:** 2
Paid Artists: 25
Budget: $50,000 - $100,000
Income Sources: Private Foundations/Grants/Endowments; Business/Corporate Donations; Box Office; Government Grants; Individual Donations
Season: 52 Weeks
Annual Attendance: 45,000

DOWLING ENTERTAINMENT CORPORATION
226 West 47th Street, Suite 700, New York, NY 10036
(212) 719-3090
FAX: (212) 719-2987
Founded: 1984
Arts Area: Professional
Status: Professional; Commercial
Type: Performing
Purpose: Business management
Management: Doreen Chila, Office Manager
Officers: Kevin Dowling, President; Carol Prugh, Vice President
Paid Staff: 3
Income Sources: Box Office
Season: 52 Weeks
Performance Facilities: The Cherry Lane Theatre

DOWNTOWN ART CO., INC.
280 Broadway, Room 412, New York, NY 10007-1896
(212) 732-1201
FAX: (212) 732-1297
Founded: 1987
Arts Area: Professional; Theatrical Group
Status: Professional; Non-Profit
Type: Performing; Touring; Sponsoring
Purpose: To support the creation, development and presentation of comtemporary performance works
Management: Ryan Gilliam, Artistic Director; Cliff Scott, Producing Director; Dan Hurlin, Dan Froot, Artistic Associates
Officers: Cliff Scott, President; Ryan Gilliam, Vice President/Treasurer; Dan Hurlin, Secretary
Paid Staff: 6   **Volunteer Staff:** 1
Paid Artists: 25
Utilizes: Special Technical Talent; Guest Artists
Budget: $100,000 - $500,000
Income Sources: Private Foundations/Grants/Endowments; Box Office; Government Grants; Individual Donations
Season: September - June   **Annual Attendance:** 5,000
Affiliations: National Association of Artists; ART/NY

ECCENTRIC CIRCLES THEATRE
400 West 43rd Street, Suite 4N, New York, NY 10036
(212) 564-3798
Founded: 1979
Arts Area: Professional; Theatrical Group
Status: Non-Profit
Type: Performing
Purpose: To produce original works, one-act and full-length plays
Management: Rosemary Hopkins, Paula Kay Pierce, Artistic Directors; Maryanne Mongoni, Production Manager
Paid Staff: 3   **Volunteer Staff:** 5
Budget: $1,000 - $50,000
Income Sources: Private Foundations/Grants/Endowments; Business/Corporate Donations; Box Office; Individual Donations
Season: 52 Weeks   **Annual Attendance:** 2,500
Affiliations: ART/NY

EN GARDE ARTS, INC.
225 Rector Place, Suite 3A, New York, NY 10280
(212) 941-9793
FAX: (212) 274-8123
Arts Area: Professional
Status: Professional; Non-Profit
Type: Performing
Purpose: To commission artists to create theatrical productions inspired by architecturally, historically or socially significant sites; the only site specific theatre in the country
Management: Anne Hamburger, Producer; Ron Aja, Managing Director; Mary McBride, Director of Development
Budget: $100,000 - $500,000
Income Sources: Private Foundations/Grants/Endowments; Business/Corporate Donations; Box Office; Government Grants; Individual Donations
Season: 52 Weeks

THE ENSEMBLE STUDIO THEATRE
549 West 52nd Street, New York, NY 10019
(212) 247-4982
FAX: (212) 664-0041
Arts Area: Professional; Theatrical Group
Status: Non-Profit
Type: Performing
Purpose: To nurture and develop the American theatre artist
Management: Curt Dempster, Artistic Director
Budget: $500,000 - $1,000,000
Income Sources: Private Foundations/Grants/Endowments; Business/Corporate Donations; Box Office; Government Grants; Individual Donations
Performance Facilities: The Ensemble Studio Theatre

THE FIJI COMPANY
47 Great Jones Street, New York, NY 10012
(212) 966-0284
Founded: 1972

Arts Area: Professional; Theatrical Group
Status: Professional; Non-Profit
Type: Performing; Touring; Resident; Educational
Purpose: Created out of a desire to incorporate the visual arts (dance, film, video and theater) into a multimedia show questioning the syntax of global theater
Management: Ping Chong, Artistic Director; Joe Jeffcoat, Managing Director
Paid Staff: 4   **Volunteer Staff:** 3
Paid Artists: 55
Utilizes: Special Technical Talent; Guest Artists
Budget: $100,000 - $500,000
Income Sources: Private Foundations/Grants/Endowments; Business/Corporate Donations; Box Office; Government Grants; Individual Donations
Season: July - July   **Annual Attendance:** 25,000
Affiliations: TCG; ART/NY

FREDERICK DOUGLASS CREATIVE ARTS CENTER, INC.
168 West 46th Street, New York, NY 10036
(212) 944-9870
Founded: 1971
Arts Area: Theatrical Group; Literary
Status: Professional; Non-Profit
Type: Resident
Purpose: A writers development group with a performance component
Management: Fred Hudson, Artistic Director; Yvonne Hudson, Executive Administrator
Utilizes: Special Technical Talent; Guest Artists; Guest Directors
Budget: $100,000 - $500,000
Income Sources: Private Foundations/Grants/Endowments; Business/Corporate Donations; Box Office; Government Grants; Individual Donations
Season: September - June

GAY PERFORMANCES COMPANY
PO Box 1647, Old Chelsea Station, New York, NY 10011
(212) 595-1445
Founded: 1987
Arts Area: Professional; Theatrical Group
Status: Professional; Non-Profit
Type: Performing
Purpose: To present positive images of gay people and to counteract the negative stereotypes of gay people prevalent in society at large; to represent the lives and experiences of women and all the minorities in the gay community
Management: Don Barrington, Founder
Utilizes: Special Technical Talent; Volunteer Artists
Budget: $1,000 - $50,000
Income Sources: Government Grants; Individual Donations
Season: May - October
Performance Facilities: Gay Community Center

THE GLINES
240 West 44th Street, New York, NY 10036
(212) 354-8899
Founded: 1976
Arts Area: Theatrical Group
Status: Non-Profit
Type: Performing; Resident
Purpose: To promote positive gay images and dispel negative stereotyping
Management: John Glines, Artistic Director
Officers: John Glines, President/Treasurer; Steve Carpenter, Vice President; Ralph DeMarco, Secretary; Tom Cannon, Kathleen Mary, Mark Hostetter, Richard Glatfelter, Dr. Harry Clarke Noyes, Board of Directors
Paid Staff: 3   **Volunteer Staff:** 20
Paid Artists: 12
Budget: $100,000 - $500,000
Income Sources: Box Office; Individual Donations
Annual Attendance: 12,000
Performance Facilities: Courtyard Playhouse

HARLEM ARTISTS' DEVELOPMENT LEAGUE ESPECIALLY FOR YOU (HADLEY PLAYERS)
207 West 133rd Street, New York, NY 10030
(212) 368-9314
Arts Area: Professional; Community; Theatrical Group
Status: Professional; Semi-Professional; Non-Profit

Type: Performing; Resident; Educational
Purpose: To present professional theatre in the Harlem community at affordable prices; to train aspiring artists in acting, speech, and dance
Management: Gertrude Jeannette, Artistic Director; Ajene Washington, Business/Company Manager; Murphree Johnson, Secretary/Treasurer; Louise Mike, Training Supervisor; Dr. Nathan A. Wright, Chairman of the Board
Volunteer Staff: 15
Non-Paid Artists: 25
Utilizes: Special Technical Talent; Guest Artists; Guest Directors
Budget: $1,000 - $50,000
Income Sources: Private Foundations/Grants/Endowments; Box Office; Individual Donations
Season: September 15 - June 30   **Annual Attendance:** 4,026
Affiliations: Community Service Council of Greater Harlem
Performance Facilities: Saint Philips Church

HISPANIC ORGANIZATION OF LATIN ACTORS (HOLA)
250 West 65th Street, New York, NY 10023
(212) 595-8286
FAX: (212) 799-6718
Founded: 1977
Arts Area: Professional; Community; Theatrical Group
Status: Non-Profit
Type: Arts Service Organization
Purpose: Advocacy-training, workshops and referrals
Management: Francisco G. Rivela, Executive Director; Manny Alfaro, Managing Director
Officers: Elsie C. Stark, President/Chairman of the Board; Arnaldo Melendez, Arnold E. Rivera, Board Members
Paid Staff: 3   **Volunteer Staff:** 4
Utilizes: Special Technical Talent; Guest Directors
Budget: $50,000 - $100,000
Income Sources: Private Foundations/Grants/Endowments; Business/Corporate Donations; Government Grants; Individual Donations

HUDSON GUILD THEATRE
441 West 26th Street, New York, NY 10001
(212) 760-9816; (212) 760-9800
Founded: 1973
Arts Area: Professional; Theatrical Group
Status: Professional; Non-Profit
Type: Performing
Management: Geoffrey Sherman, Producing Director; James Abar, Associate Director; Steve Ramay, Literary Manager; Laura Fowler, Business Manager
Officers: Emily Meschter, Board Chairperson
Paid Staff: 59   **Volunteer Staff:** 5
Paid Artists: 50
Utilizes: Special Technical Talent; Guest Artists; Guest Directors
Budget: $100,000 - $500,000
Income Sources: Private Foundations/Grants/Endowments; Business/Corporate Donations; Box Office; Government Grants; Individual Donations
Season: September - June
Annual Attendance: 22,000
Performance Facilities: Strasser Auditorium

IGLOO, THE THEATRICAL GROUP
225 East Fourth Street, Apt. 6, New York, NY 10009
(212) 460-9055
Founded: 1985
Arts Area: Professional; Musical; Theatrical Group
Status: Professional; Non-Profit
Type: Performing; Resident
Purpose: Based on ensemble participation in the acting design, direction and choice of productions, Igloo is dedicated to new and rarely done works.
Management: Maria Taribassi, Chris Peditto and Paul Peditto, Artistic Directors
Officers: Chris Peditto, President; Maria Tirabassi, Treasurer; Dan Piburn, Secretary
Paid Staff: 2
Non-Paid Artists: 10
Utilizes: Guest Artists; Guest Directors
Budget: $1,000 - $50,000
Income Sources: Private Foundations/Grants/Endowments; Business/Corporate Donations; Box Office; Individual Donations

Season: May - April
Annual Attendance: 12,000

INTERNATIONAL ARTS RELATIONS DBA INTAR HISPANIC AMERICAN ARTS CENTER
420 West 42nd Street, New York, NY 10036
(212) 695-6135
FAX: (212) 268-0102
Founded: 1966
Arts Area: Professional
Status: Professional; Non-Profit
Type: Performing
Purpose: To identify, develop and present the work of Hispanic-American theatre artists and multi-cultural visual artists, as well as to introduce outstanding works by internationally respected Latin artists to American audiences
Management: May Ferra, Artistic Director; Eva Brune, Managing Director
Officers: Stanley Stairs, Chairman; Richard Ramirez, Tony Bechara, Co-Vice Presidents; Paul Vidich, Treasurer; Jane Stanicki, Secretary
Paid Staff: 13   **Volunteer Staff:** 8
Paid Artists: 32
Utilizes: Special Technical Talent; Guest Artists; Guest Directors
Budget: $100,000 - $500,000
Income Sources: Private Foundations/Grants/Endowments; Business/Corporate Donations; Box Office; Government Grants; Individual Donations
Season: October - June   **Annual Attendance:** 10,000
Affiliations: TCG; ART/NY

INTERNATIONAL FESTIVAL OF PUPPETRY
c/o Jim Henson Foundation, 117 East 69th Street, New York, NY 10021
(212) 794-2400
FAX: (212) 570-1147
Arts Area: Puppet
Status: Non-Profit
Type: Sponsoring
Purpose: To bring a sampling of the best of international puppetry performers to American audiences
Management: Leslee Asch, Executive Director
Budget: $500,000 - $1,000,000
Income Sources: Private Foundations/Grants/Endowments; Business/Corporate Donations; Box Office; Government Grants; Individual Donations
Performance Facilities: Joseph Papp Public

IRISH ARTS CENTRE THEATRE
553 West 51st Street, New York, NY 10019
(212) 757-3318
Founded: 1972
Arts Area: Professional
Status: Professional; Non-Profit
Type: Performing; Resident
Purpose: To preserve, celebrate and develop Irish culture in America by producing Classic Irish, New Irish and Irish-American plays
Management: Nye Heron, Artistic Director; Marianne Delaney, Executive Director
Officers: Jim Sheridan, Chairman of the Board
Paid Staff: 3   **Volunteer Staff:** 6
Paid Artists: 200   **Non-Paid Artists:** 30
Utilizes: Guest Artists
Budget: $500,000 - $1,000,000
Income Sources: Private Foundations/Grants/Endowments; Business/Corporate Donations; Box Office; Government Grants; Individual Donations
Season: 52 Weeks   **Annual Attendance:** 20,000
Performance Facilities: Irish Arts Center Theatre

JAM AND COMPANY
331 West 38th Street, #5, New York, NY 10018
(212) 714-2263
Founded: 1985
Arts Area: Theatrical Group
Status: Semi-Professional
Type: Performing
Management: John Amudd, Artistic Director
Paid Staff: 13   **Volunteer Staff:** 1

Budget: $1,000 - $50,000
Income Sources: Private Foundations/Grants/Endowments; Box Office; Individual Donations

JEAN COCTEAU REPERTORY
330 Bowery, New York, NY 10012
(212) 677-0060
Founded: 1971
Arts Area: Professional; Theatrical Group
Status: Professional; Non-Profit
Type: Performing; Resident; Educational
Purpose: Cocteau Repertory is committed to presenting the classics of world literature in an innovative light. We are also dedicated to a resident company working rotating repertory.
Management: Robert Hupp, Artistic Director; Scott Shattuck, Managing Director
Officers: Albert Podell, President; Robert Berend, Alan Goldman, Co-Chairmans; Barbara Udell, Treasurer; Susan Fawcett, Secretary
Paid Staff: 7   **Volunteer Staff:** 4
Paid Artists: 16   **Non-Paid Artists:** 10
Utilizes: Guest Directors; Guest Designers
Budget: $100,000 - $500,000
Income Sources: Private Foundations/Grants/Endowments; Business/Corporate Donations; Box Office; Government Grants; Individual Donations
Season: August - May   **Annual Attendance:** 21,000
Affiliations: TCG; ART/NY
Performance Facilities: Bouwerie Lane Theatre

JEWISH REPERTORY THEATRE
344 East 14th Street, New York, NY 10003
(212) 674-7200
Arts Area: Professional
Status: Professional; Non-Profit
Type: Performing
Purpose: To present plays, in English, relating to the Jewish experience
Management: Rau Avni, Artistic Director
Paid Staff: 6
Paid Artists: 50
Budget: $100,000 - $500,000
Income Sources: Private Foundations/Grants/Endowments; Business/Corporate Donations; Box Office; Government Grants; Individual Donations
Season: September - July   **Annual Attendance:** 14,000
Affiliations: AEA
Performance Facilities: Jewish Repertory Theatre

LA MAMA EXPERIMENTAL THEATRE CLUB
74A East Fourth Street, New York, NY 10003
(212) 475-7710
FAX: (212) 254-7597
Founded: 1961
Arts Area: Theatrical Group; Multi-Art
Status: Professional; Non-Profit
Type: Performing; Producing
Purpose: To further the playwright and all aspects of the theater
Management: Ellen Stewart, Founder/Artistic Director; Meryl Vladimer, Executive Director
Utilizes: Special Technical Talent; Guest Artists; Guest Directors
Budget: $500,000 - $1,000,000
Income Sources: Private Foundations/Grants/Endowments; Business/Corporate Donations; Box Office; Government Grants; Individual Donations
Season: September - July
Performance Facilities: La Mama Experimental Theatre

THE LAMB'S THEATRE COMPANY LTD.
130 West 44th Street, New York, NY 10036
(212) 997-0210
Founded: 1980
Arts Area: Professional
Status: Professional; Non-Profit
Type: Performing; Touring; Educational
Purpose: To develop and present the work of new American theatre artists hoping to offer positive solutions to modern ethical problems

Management: Carolyn Rossi-Copeland, Producing Director; Clark Cameron, Production Manager; Carl H. Jaynes, Administrative Coordinator; Larry Staroff, Box Office Treasurer
Officers: Kendyl K. Monroe, Chairman; Patricia McCorkle, Secretary; Reverend David Best
Paid Staff: 11
Paid Artists: 45
Utilizes: Guest Directors
Budget: $100,000 - $500,000
Income Sources: Private Foundations/Grants/Endowments; Business/Corporate Donations; Box Office; Government Grants; Individual Donations
Season: August - June   **Annual Attendance:** 67,500
Affiliations: TCG, ART/NY
Performance Facilities: Lamb's Theatre; Lamb's Little Theatre

LATIN AMERICAN THEATRE ENSEMBLE
PO Box 18, Radio City Station, New York, NY 10019
(212) 246-7478
Founded: 1970
Arts Area: Professional; Theatrical Group
Status: Professional; Non-Profit
Type: Performing; Touring; Resident; Educational
Purpose: Our purpose is to expand the theatre movement to the Spanish and English communities.
Management: Margarita Toirac, Executive Director; Mario Pena, Founder
Officers: Mario Pena, President; Tania Robles-Pena, Secretary; Guillermo Fernandez, Treaurer
Paid Staff: 2   **Volunteer Staff:** 10
Paid Artists: 20
Utilizes: Guest Artists; Guest Directors
Budget: $1,000 - $50,000
Income Sources: Business/Corporate Donations; Box Office; Government Grants; Individual Donations
Season: 52 Weeks
Annual Attendance: 4,000

LINCOLN CENTER THEATER
150 West 65th Street, New York, NY 10023
(212) 362-7600
FAX: (212) 873-0761
Founded: 1985
Arts Area: Professional; Theatrical Group
Status: Professional; Non-Profit
Type: Performing
Management: Hattie Jutagin, Director of Development; Jeffrey Hamlin, Production Manager; Stephen Callahan, General Manager; Bernard Gernstein, Executive Producer
Paid Staff: 33
Utilizes: Special Technical Talent; Guest Artists; Guest Directors
Budget: Over 10,000,000
Income Sources: Private Foundations/Grants/Endowments; Business/Corporate Donations; Box Office; Government Grants; Individual Donations
Season: September - June
Performance Facilities: Vivian Beaumont Theater; Mitzi E. Newhouse Theater

THE LIVING THEATRE, INC.
272 East Third Street, New York, NY 10009
(212) 979-0601
FAX: (212) 865-3234
Founded: 1947
Arts Area: Theatrical Group
Status: Non-Profit
Type: Performing; Touring; Resident; Educational
Purpose: To create socially relevant theatre to be performed by an artistic ensemble of the highest calibre
Management: Hanon Reznikov, Executive Director; Judith Malina, Artistic Director; Joanie Fritz, Managing Director; Isha Manna Beck, Managing Associate
Officers: Hanon Reznikov, President, Board of Directors
Paid Staff: 4
Paid Artists: 20
Utilizes: Guest Conductors; Guest Artists; Guest Directors
Budget: $100,000 - $500,000
Income Sources: Private Foundations/Grants/Endowments; Business/Corporate Donations; Box Office; Government Grants; Individual Donations
Season: September - June   **Annual Attendance:** 16,000
Affiliations: ART/NY; TCG

MABOU MINES
150 First Avenue, New York, NY 10009
(212) 473-0559
FAX: (212) 473-2410
   Founded: 1969
   Arts Area: Professional; Theatrical Group
   Status: Professional; Non-Profit
   Type: Performing; Touring; Educational
   Purpose: This is a four-member, producing collective dedicated to the creation of original work.
   Management: Allison Astor, Company Manager
   Officers: Terry O'Reilly, President
   Paid Staff: 4   **Volunteer Staff:** 3
   Paid Artists: 10
   Utilizes: Special Technical Talent; Guest Artists; Guest Directors
   Budget: $500,000 - $1,000,000
   Income Sources: Private Foundations/Grants/Endowments; Business/Corporate Donations; Box Office; Government Grants; Individual Donations
   Season: September - June
   Annual Attendance: 20,000
   Affiliations: TCG; ART/NY
   Performance Facilities: Mabou Mines/Suite

MANHATTAN THEATRE CLUB
453 West 16th Street, New York, NY 10011
(212) 645-5590
   Founded: 1970
   Arts Area: Professional
   Status: Non-Profit
   Type: Performing
   Purpose: To encourage, develop, and present important new theatrical work providing insights to life, culture, and conflict by American and international writers
   Management: Lynne Meadow, Artistic Director; Barry Grove, Managing Director; Victoria B. Bailey, General Manager
   Paid Staff: 25   **Volunteer Staff:** 12
   Paid Artists: 46
   Utilizes: Guest Artists; Guest Directors
   Budget: $1,000,000 - $5,000,000
   Income Sources: Private Foundations/Grants/Endowments; Business/Corporate Donations; Box Office; Government Grants; Individual Donations
   Season: September - July   **Annual Attendance:** 60,000
   Affiliations: TCG; ART/NY; FEDAPT

MIRROR REPERTORY COMPANY
50 East 96th Street, New York, NY 10028
(212) 427-7393
   Founded: 1982
   Arts Area: Professional; Theatrical Group
   Status: Professional; Non-Profit
   Type: Performing; Resident; Educational
   Management: Sabra Jones, Artistic Director; Weiler/Miller Associates, Managing Directors; Shirley Herz Associates, Press Representative
   Officers: Robert Treat, Chairman of the Board
   Paid Staff: 5
   Utilizes: Guest Artists; Guest Directors
   Budget: $1,000,000 - $5,000,000
   Income Sources: Private Foundations/Grants/Endowments; Business/Corporate Donations; Box Office; Government Grants; Individual Donations
   Season: January - May
   Affiliations: AEA
   Performance Facilities: Mirror Repertory Theater

MUSIC THEATRE GROUP AT LENOX ARTS CENTER
29 Bethune Street, New York, NY 10014
(413) 298-5122
   Founded: 1970
   Arts Area: Professional; Theatrical Group; Musical Theatre
   Status: Professional; Non-Profit
   Type: Performing; Touring

Purpose: Exclusively engaged in and dedicated to the creation of new musical theatre works with distinctive focus on developing new forms and artists through unique combinations of music, theatre, dance and visual arts
Management: Lyn Austin, Producing Director; Diane Wondisford, General Director; Jessica Balboni, Development
Officers: Rosita Sarnoff, Chairman; Lynda Sturher-Traum, Vice Chairman; Lyn Austin, President; Charles Hollerith, Jr., Secretary; Bernard Rosenberg, Treasurer
Paid Staff: 9   **Volunteer Staff:** 10
Paid Artists: 150
Utilizes: Special Technical Talent; Guest Conductors; Guest Artists
Budget: $1,000,000 - $5,000,000
Income Sources: Private Foundations/Grants/Endowments; Business/Corporate Donations; Box Office; Government Grants; Individual Donations
Season: November - May   **Annual Attendance:** 52,000
Affiliations: AEA; TCG; ART/NY

MUSICAL THEATRE WORKS
440 Lafayette Street, New York, NY 10003
(212) 677-0040
Founded: 1983
Arts Area: Professional; Musical; Theatrical Group
Status: Professional; Non-Profit
Type: Performing; Resident
Purpose: To develop and produce new works for the American musical theatre
Management: Anthony Stimack, Artistic Director; Marilyn Stimack, General Manager; Mike Teel, Managing Director
Paid Staff: 6
Utilizes: Special Technical Talent; Guest Artists; Guest Directors
Budget: $100,000 - $500,000
Income Sources: Private Foundations/Grants/Endowments; Business/Corporate Donations; Box Office; Government Grants; Individual Donations
Season: 52 Weeks
Affiliations: AEA; TCG; ART/NY

NAT HORNE MUSICAL THEATRE
440 West 42nd Street, New York, NY 10036
(212) 268-4125
Founded: 1973
Arts Area: Professional; Musical
Status: Professional; Non-Profit
Type: Performing
Purpose: To provide actors with training in the American musical theater
Management: Rick Pool, Artistic Director
Budget: $100,000 - $500,000
Income Sources: Private Foundations/Grants/Endowments; Business/Corporate Donations; Box Office; Government Grants; Individual Donations
Season: 52 Weeks   **Annual Attendance:** 20,000
Affiliations: AEA; ART/NY; Theater Development Fund
Performance Facilities: Nat Horne Musical Theatre

NATIONAL BLACK THEATRE
2033 Fifth Avenue, New York, NY 10035
(212) 427-5615; (212) 722-3800
FAX: (212) 926-1571
Founded: 1968
Arts Area: Theatrical Group
Status: Professional; Non-Profit
Type: Performing; Touring; Resident
Purpose: To instill human dignity and respect by broadening the availability, appreciation and unity of Black Theatre and workshops
Management: Barbara Ann Teer, Founder/CEO; Shirley Faison, Executive Director; Tunde Samuel, Performing Program Director; Ade Faison, Action Arts Director; Nabi Faison, Rental Program Director
Officers: Dr. Eugene Callender, Chairman; Julietta Velma Banks, Secretary/Treasurer; Jim Haughton, Martin Leaf, Jerry Lewis, Basil Patterson, William Strickland, Barbara Ann Teer
Paid Staff: 9
Paid Artists: 50
Utilizes: Guest Artists; Guest Directors
Budget: $100,000 - $500,000
Income Sources: Private Foundations/Grants/Endowments; Business/Corporate Donations; Box Office; Government Grants; Individual Donations
Season: November - October
Performance Facilities: National Black Institute of Communication Through Theatre Arts

NATIONAL BLACK TOURING CIRCUIT
466 Grand Street, New York, NY 10002
(212) 598-0400
Founded: 1974
Arts Area: Professional; Theatrical Group
Status: Professional; Non-Profit
Type: Performing; Touring; Resident; Educational
Purpose: To make existing Black theatre productions available to a larger audience by touring to colleges, Black art centers, community organizations and resident professional theatres
Management: Woodie King, Jr., Producer; Herman LeVern Jones, Gloria Mitchell, Associate Producers
Officers: Majorie Moon, Chair; Shaneille Perry, Vantile Whitfield, Gloria Mitchell, Board Members
Paid Staff: 3   **Volunteer Staff:** 3
Utilizes: Special Technical Talent; Guest Artists; Guest Directors
Budget: $50,000 - $100,000
Income Sources: Private Foundations/Grants/Endowments; Business/Corporate Donations; Box Office; Government Grants
Season: 52 Weeks   **Annual Attendance:** 10,000
Affiliations: New Federal Theatre
Performance Facilities: Henry Street Settlement

NATIONAL IMPROVISATIONAL THEATRE
223 Eighth Avenue, New York, NY 10011
(212) 243-7224
FAX: (212) 366-4312
Founded: 1984
Arts Area: Professional; Theatrical Group
Status: Non-Profit
Type: Performing; Educational
Purpose: To take art improvisation to it highest potential
Management: Christopher Smith, Executive Director; Tamara Wilcox-Smith, Artistic Director; Robert Martin, Vice President of Public Relations; Eva Mahoney, Vice President of Operations
Paid Staff: 6   **Volunteer Staff:** 20
Non-Paid Artists: 30
Budget: $100,000 - $500,000
Income Sources: Business/Corporate Donations; Box Office; Individual Donations; Sale of Services
Season: September - July

NATIONAL SHAKESPEARE COMPANY
414 West 51st Street, New York, NY 10019
(212) 265-1340
Founded: 1963
Arts Area: Professional
Status: Professional
Type: Performing; Touring
Purpose: To nurture and develop the performing arts in America by bringing professional, live theatre to its communities
Management: Elaine Sulka, Artistic Director; Michael Cooper, Executive Director; Tom Rice, General Manager
Paid Staff: 5
Paid Artists: 15
Budget: $500,000 - $1,000,000
Income Sources: Business/Corporate Donations; Box Office; Individual Donations
Season: 52 Weeks   **Annual Attendance:** 100,000
Performance Facilities: The Cubiculo

NEGRO ENSEMBLE COMPANY
155 West 46th Street, Suite 409, New York, NY 10036
(212) 575-5860
Founded: 1967
Arts Area: Theatrical Group
Status: Professional; Non-Profit
Type: Performing; Touring
Purpose: To perform plays that are about Black people and their experiences
Management: Douglas Turner Ward, Artistic Director; Leon B. Denmark, Managing Director
Utilizes: Special Technical Talent; Guest Artists; Guest Directors
Budget: $50,000 - $100,000
Income Sources: Private Foundations/Grants/Endowments; Business/Corporate Donations; Box Office; Government Grants; Individual Donations
Season: September - May
Performance Facilities: Theatre Four

NEW DRAMATISTS
424 West 44th Street, New York, NY 10036
(212) 757-6960
> **Founded:** 1949
> **Arts Area:** Theatrical Group
> **Status:** Semi-Professional; Non-Profit
> **Type:** Resident; Educational
> **Purpose:** To the development of playwrights and plays
> **Management:** Elana Greenfield, Director of Artistic; Jana Jevnikar, Director of Finance; Paul Slee, Director of Development
> **Officers:** Isabelle Robins-Konecky, Board Chairman
> **Paid Staff:** 3
> **Budget:** $100,000 - $500,000
> **Income Sources:** Private Foundations/Grants/Endowments; Business/Corporate Donations; Government Grants; Individual Donations
> **Season:** 52 Weeks
> **Affiliations:** AEA
> **Performance Facilities:** New Dramatists Theater

NEW FEDERAL THEATRE
466 Grand Street, New York, NY 10002
(212) 598-0400
> **Founded:** 1970
> **Arts Area:** Theatrical Group
> **Status:** Professional; Non-Profit
> **Type:** Performing; Resident
> **Purpose:** To present new works and unknown works while allowing known and unknown actors and directors the chance to work together
> **Management:** Woodie King Jr., Producing Director; Linda Herring, Managing Director
> **Officers:** Woodie King Jr., President; Linda Herring, Treasurer; Maritza Myers, Secretary; Leon Gildin, Chairman of the Board
> **Paid Staff:** 8 **Volunteer Staff:** 2
> **Utilizes:** Special Technical Talent; Guest Artists; Guest Directors
> **Budget:** $100,000 - $500,000
> **Income Sources:** Private Foundations/Grants/Endowments; Business/Corporate Donations; Box Office; Government Grants; Individual Donations
> **Season:** September - June **Annual Attendance:** 10,000
> **Affiliations:** AEA; ART/NY; TCG
> **Performance Facilities:** Henry Street Settlement; New Federal Theater

THE NEW RAFT THEATER COMPANY
450 West 42nd Street, Suite 2J, New York, NY 10036
(212) 967-7079
FAX: (212) 268-5501
> **Founded:** 1976
> **Arts Area:** Professional; Musical; Theatrical Group
> **Status:** Professional; Non-Profit
> **Type:** Performing
> **Purpose:** To find and develop original plays and musicals
> **Management:** Avi Ber Hoffman, Artistic Director; Mary Ellen Ashley, Associate Producer
> **Officers:** Eric Krebs, Executive Director; Avi Ber Hoffman, Artistic Director
> **Volunteer Staff:** 10
> **Budget:** $1,000 - $50,000
> **Income Sources:** Private Foundations/Grants/Endowments; Business/Corporate Donations; Box Office; Government Grants; Individual Donations
> **Season:** 52 Weeks
> **Performance Facilities:** Houseman Theatre Complex

NEW YORK SHAKESPEARE FESTIVAL
425 Lafayette Street, Joseph Papp Public Theater, New York, NY 10003
(212) 598-7150
> **Founded:** 1954
> **Arts Area:** Professional
> **Status:** Professional; Non-Profit
> **Type:** Performing
> **Purpose:** Operated in the belief that a theater with the highest professional standards can attract and should be made available to a broadly based public. From this guiding principal has emerged a contemporary theater of extraordinary range and quality, rooted in the classics with more American plays as its primary focus.

Management: Joseph Papp, Founder; JoAnne Akalaitis, Artistic Director; Jason Steven Cohen, Producing Director; Rosemarie Tichler, Associate Artistic Director; Bruce Campbell, Press Representative
Officers: Robert W. Pittman, Chairman; Larry F. Condon, Joan K. Davidson, H. Scott Higgins, Judith Peabody, Vice Presidents; Stanley H. Lowell, Secretary/Treasurer
Paid Staff: 150
Paid Artists: 450
Utilizes: Special Technical Talent; Guest Conductors; Guest Artists; Guest Directors
Budget: Over 10,000,000
Income Sources: Private Foundations/Grants/Endowments; Business/Corporate Donations; Box Office; Government Grants; Individual Donations
Season: 52 Weeks
Performance Facilities: Joseph Papp Public Theater; Delacorte Theater

NEW YORK THEATRE WORKSHOP
220 West 42nd Street, 18th Floor, New York, NY 10036
(212) 302-7737
Founded: 1983
Arts Area: Professional
Status: Professional; Non-Profit
Type: Performing
Purpose: To present new plays that are inventive in style and form, and to present new directors
Management: Nancy Kassak-Diekmann, Managing Director; James C. Nicola, Artistic Director
Officers: Stephen Graham, Founding Trustee; Elizabeth Williams, Chairman; Alison Clarkson, Vice Chairman; Dena M. Steele, Treasurer; Elliot Brown, Secretary
Paid Staff: 10   **Volunteer Staff:** 4
Paid Artists: 35
Utilizes: Guest Artists; Guest Directors
Budget: $500,000 - $1,000,000
Income Sources: Private Foundations/Grants/Endowments; Business/Corporate Donations; Box Office; Government Grants; Individual Donations
Season: October - May   **Annual Attendance:** 5,000
Affiliations: AEA; TCG; ART/NY
Performance Facilities: New York Theatre Workshop

OHIO THEATRE
66 Wooster, New York, NY 10012
(212) 966-4844
Founded: 1977
Arts Area: Professional; Theatrical Group
Status: Professional
Type: Performing; Sponsoring
Purpose: To present experimental theatre
Management: Robert Lyons, Artistic Director
Paid Staff: 1   **Volunteer Staff:** 4
Utilizes: Guest Artists; Guest Directors; Resident Company
Budget: $1,000 - $50,000
Income Sources: Box Office; Rentals
Season: September - July
Affiliations: Downtown Theatre Coalition
Performance Facilities: Ohio Theatre

ONTOLOGICAL-HYSTERIC THEATRE, INC.
260 West Broadway, New York, NY 10013
(212) 941-8911
FAX: (212) 334-5149
Arts Area: Professional
Status: Professional; Non-Profit
Type: Performing
Purpose: To produce and present the works of playwright/director/designer Richard Foreman
Management: Richard Foreman, Artistic Director; Susan Latham, Administrator
Budget: $100,000 - $500,000
Income Sources: Private Foundations/Grants/Endowments; Business/Corporate Donations; Box Office; Government Grants; Individual Donations
Performance Facilities: Ontological at St. Mark's Theater

THE OPEN BOOK
525 West End Avenue, 12E, New York, NY 10024-3207
(212) 362-0329
Founded: 1975

Arts Area: Professional; Theatrical Group; Authors Reading Series
Status: Professional; Non-Profit
Type: Performing; Touring; Resident
Purpose: To present the best of all genres of literature—prose, poetry, drama and nonfiction—in readers theatre format with emphasis on work bypassed by commercial theatre
Management: Marvin Kaye, Artistic Director; Nancy Temple, Public Relations Director; Pat Costello, Director of Development
Officers: Bill Bonham, Chief Executive Officer; Saralee Kaye, Chief Financial Officer; Jay Broad, Mary Higgins Clark, Mario Fratti, Rev. Kathleen La Camera, Marc Lewis, Beverly Penberthy, Eugenia Rawls, Board
Volunteer Staff: 3
Utilizes: Guest Artists
Budget: $1,000 - $50,000
Income Sources: Private Foundations/Grants/Endowments; Business/Corporate Donations; Box Office; Government Grants; Individual Donations
Season: Spring; Fall **Annual Attendance:** 400
Affiliations: AEA
Performance Facilities: Bruno Walter Auditorium; Lincoln Center 2; The Amsterdam Room

THE OPEN EYE: NEW STAGINGS
270 West 89th Street, New York, NY 10024
(212) 769-4141
FAX: (212) 595-0336
Founded: 1972
Arts Area: Professional; Theatrical Group
Status: Professional; Non-Profit
Type: Performing; Touring; Educational
Purpose: Presents productions of new and rare plays, plays geared for family audiences and provides playwrights the opportunity to develop new works through the New Stagings Lab
Management: Jean Erdman, Founding Director; Amie Brockway, Artistic Director; Adrienne Brockway, Production Manager/Business Manager
Officers: Stephen Graham, Chairman; Joan Stein, Vice President; Elliot Brown, Secretary
Paid Staff: 3 **Volunteer Staff:** 5
Paid Artists: 35
Utilizes: Special Technical Talent; Guest Artists; Guest Directors
Budget: $100,000 - $500,000
Income Sources: Private Foundations/Grants/Endowments; Business/Corporate Donations; Box Office; Government Grants; Individual Donations
Season: September - June **Annual Attendance:** 65,000
Affiliations: TCG; ART/NY; ASSITEJ
Performance Facilities: The Open Eye: New Stagings

OTRABANDA COMPANY
345 East Fifth Street, New York, NY 10003
(212) 420-9090
Arts Area: Experimental Theatre Dance
Status: Professional; Non-Profit
Type: Performing; Touring
Purpose: To create works which attempt to blur the distinction between theater and dance
Management: Roger Barb, Artistic Director; Rachelle Bornstein, Manager
Budget: $1,000 - $50,000
Income Sources: Private Foundations/Grants/Endowments; Government Grants
Season: 52 Weeks
Performance Facilities: Downtown Arts; Public School 122

PAN ASIAN REPERTORY THEATRE
423 West 46th Street, New York, NY 10036
(212) 245-2660
Mailing Address: 47 Great Jones Street, New York, NY 10012
Founded: 1977
Arts Area: Professional; Theatrical Group
Status: Professional; Non-Profit
Type: Performing; Touring; Resident; Educational
Purpose: To produce, under the highest artistic standards, new plays from the Asian-American experience, adaptations of world classics and American premieres of Asian masterworks
Management: Tisa Chang, Artistic/Producing Manager; Russell Murphy, Business Manager; Marjorie Hebard, Development Associate
Officers: Tisa Chang, President; Jeff Chin, Chairman; Muzaffar Chishti, Vice Chairman; Bonnie Crown, Secretary; Thomas Ruppel, Treasurer
Paid Staff: 4 **Volunteer Staff:** 50

Paid Artists: 150
Utilizes: Guest Artists; Guest Directors
Budget: $100,000 - $500,000
Income Sources: Private Foundations/Grants/Endowments; Business/Corporate Donations; Box Office; Government Grants; Individual Donations
Season: October - June
Annual Attendance: 14,000
Affiliations: TCG: ART/NY
Performance Facilities: Playhouse 46

THE PAPER BAG PLAYERS
50 Riverside Drive, New York, NY 10024
(212) 362-0431
Founded: 1958
Arts Area: Professional; Theatrical Group
Status: Professional; Non-Profit
Type: Performing; Touring; Resident; Educational
Purpose: To create a contemporary theatre for children with shows based on a child's everyday experiences and perceptions of the world
Management: Judith Liss, Administrator; Judith Martin, Director
Officers: Susan Patricof, President; Marjorie Federbush, Vice President
Paid Staff: 4   **Volunteer Staff:** 1
Paid Artists: 9
Budget: $500,000 - $1,000,000
Income Sources: Private Foundations/Grants/Endowments; Business/Corporate Donations; Box Office; Government Grants; Individual Donations
Season: 52 Weeks
Annual Attendance: 150,000

THE PEARL THEATRE COMPANY
125 West 22nd Street, New York, NY 10011
(212) 645-7708
FAX: (212) 645-7709
Founded: 1982
Arts Area: Professional; Theatrical Group
Status: Professional; Non-Profit
Type: Performing; Resident; Educational
Purpose: To present a full-range repertory strongly rooted in the classics with a resident acting company, guest artists and theatre staff
Management: Shepard Sobel, Artistic Director; Mary Harpster, General Manager; Joanne Camp, Artistic Associate; Larry Auld, Director of Development
Officers: Kenneth J. Rotman, President; Alice Teirstein, Secretary; Walter Fekula, Treasurer
Paid Staff: 3   **Volunteer Staff:** 1
Utilizes: Guest Artists; Guest Directors
Budget: $100,000 - $500,000
Income Sources: Private Foundations/Grants/Endowments; Business/Corporate Donations; Box Office; Government Grants; Individual Donations
Season: November - April   **Annual Attendance:** 5,000
Affiliations: ART/NY; TCG; AEA

PLAYWRIGHTS HORIZONS
416 West 42nd Street, New York, NY 10036
(212) 564-1235
Founded: 1971
Arts Area: Professional
Status: Professional; Non-Profit
Type: Performing; Educational
Purpose: Dedicated to the development of American playwrights, composers and lyricists, Playwrights Horizons also offers internship opportunities and training programs.
Management: Don Scardino, Artistic Director; Paul S. Daniels, Executive Director
Paid Staff: 30
Paid Artists: 150
Utilizes: Special Technical Talent; Guest Artists; Guest Directors
Budget: $1,000,000 - $5,000,000
Income Sources: Private Foundations/Grants/Endowments; Business/Corporate Donations; Box Office; Government Grants; Individual Donations
Season: October - June   **Annual Attendance:** 25,000

Affiliations: AEA; ART/NY; New York University
Performance Facilities: Mainstage Theatre; Studio Theatre

PRIMARY STAGES COMPANY
584 Ninth Avenue, New York, NY 10036
(212) 333-7471
> **Founded:** 1983
> **Arts Area:** Professional; Theatrical Group
> **Status:** Professional; Non-Profit
> **Type:** Performing
> **Purpose:** To identify and produce the best new American plays
> **Management:** Casey Childs, Artistic Director; Janet Reed, Associate Artistic Director; Anne Binhorn, Director of Public Relations; Seth Gordon, Literary Manager; Gina Gionfriddo, Casting Director
> **Utilizes:** Special Technical Talent; Guest Artists; Guest Directors
> **Budget:** $100,000 - $500,000
> **Income Sources:** Private Foundations/Grants/Endowments; Business/Corporate Donations; Box Office; Individual Donations
> **Season:** September - June
> **Performance Facilities:** 45th Street Theatre; William Redfield Theatre

PROCESS STUDIO THEATRE
257 Church Street, New York, NY 10007
(212) 226-1124
> **Founded:** 1977
> **Arts Area:** Professional; Musical; Theatrical Group
> **Status:** Professional; Non-Profit
> **Type:** Performing; Touring; Resident; Educational; Sponsoring; Outreach
> **Purpose:** To promote new works and artists; home for professional artists
> **Management:** Bonnie Loren, Artistic Director; Anthony Sandkamp, Technical Director
> **Utilizes:** Special Technical Talent; Guest Conductors; Guest Artists; Guest Directors
> **Income Sources:** Private Foundations/Grants/Endowments; Box Office; Individual Donations
> **Season:** 52 Weeks

PUERTO RICAN TRAVELING THEATRE COMPANY
141 West 94th Street, New York, NY 10025
(212) 354-1293
> **Founded:** 1967
> **Arts Area:** Professional
> **Status:** Professional; Non-Profit
> **Type:** Performing; Touring; Educational
> **Purpose:** To present bilingual plays; to conduct workshops for financially underprivileged youth; to provide training for new playwrights
> **Management:** Miriam Colon, Artistic Director; Michael Palma, Managing Director
> **Utilizes:** Special Technical Talent; Guest Artists; Guest Directors
> **Budget:** $500,000 - $1,000,000
> **Income Sources:** Private Foundations/Grants/Endowments; Business/Corporate Donations; Box Office; Government Grants; Individual Donations
> **Season:** January - August
> **Annual Attendance:** 25,000
> **Performance Facilities:** Puerto Rican Travelling Theatre

QUAIGH THEATRE
205 West 89th Street, New York, NY 10024
(212) 787-0862
> **Founded:** 1971
> **Arts Area:** Theatrical Group
> **Status:** Professional; Non-Profit
> **Type:** Performing; Resident
> **Purpose:** Quaigh is a playwrights theatre presenting four new, full-length plays and, roughly, 60 one-act plays each season.
> **Management:** Will Liebenson, Artistic Director; Judith Robin, Executive Director
> **Officers:** Albert Brower, Chairman; Jane Wolf, Secretary
> **Paid Staff:** 2   **Volunteer Staff:** 10
> **Paid Artists:** 50   **Non-Paid Artists:** 100
> **Budget:** $100,000 - $500,000
> **Income Sources:** Private Foundations/Grants/Endowments; Business/Corporate Donations; Box Office; Government Grants; Individual Donations
> **Season:** October - June
> **Affiliations:** TCG; ART/NY

RIDGE THEATER
141 Ridge Street, Suite 8, New York, NY 10002
(212) 674-5485
    Arts Area: Professional
    Status: Non-Profit
    Type: Performing
    Purpose: To explore the boundaries of opera and theater
    Management: Bob McGrath, Artistic Director
    Officers: Laurie Olinder, President of the Board
    Budget: $50,000 - $100,000
    Income Sources: Private Foundations/Grants/Endowments; Business/Corporate Donations; Box Office; Government Grants; Individual Donations

THE RIDICULOUS THEATRICAL COMPANY
1 Sheridan Square, New York, NY 10014-3505
(212) 989-6524
    Founded: 1967
    Arts Area: Professional
    Status: Professional; Non-Profit
    Type: Performing; Resident
    Purpose: With Everett Quinton as artistic director, the company synthesizes wit, parody, vaudeville, farce, melodrama and satire, giving reckless immediacy to classical stagecraft.
    Management: Everett Quinton, Artistic Director; Steven Asher, General Manager
    Officers: Elaine Friedman, Bruce Donnell, Nancy Scerbo, Ross Anesin, Board of Directors; Walter Gidaly, Attorney
    Paid Staff: 7
    Paid Artists: 12
    Budget: $500,000 - $1,000,000
    Income Sources: Private Foundations/Grants/Endowments; Business/Corporate Donations; Box Office; Government Grants; Individual Donations
    Annual Attendance: 25,000
    Performance Facilities: The Theatre at 1 Sheridan Square

RIVERSIDE SHAKESPEARE COMPANY
Shakespeare Center, 165 West 86th Street, New York, NY 10024
(212) 369-2273
FAX: (212) 410-6663
    Founded: 1976
    Arts Area: Professional; Theatrical Group
    Status: Professional
    Type: Performing; Touring; Resident; Educational
    Purpose: To bring the classics to life making them accessible to the public in a way unique to the demands of the context of modern theater
    Management: Gus Kaikkonen, Artistic Director; Ann Harvey, Executive Director; Robert Mooney, Academy Director
    Officers: Judith C. Radash, Chairman; John Pfisterer, Treasurer
    Paid Staff: 5   **Volunteer Staff:** 10
    Paid Artists: 36
    Utilizes: Special Technical Talent; Guest Artists; Guest Directors
    Budget: $100,000 - $500,000
    Income Sources: Private Foundations/Grants/Endowments; Business/Corporate Donations; Box Office; Government Grants; Individual Donations
    Season: 52 Weeks
    Annual Attendance: 7,000

ROGER FURMAN THEATRE
60 East 42nd Street, Suite 1336, New York, NY 10017
(212) 599-1922
FAX: (212) 599-2414
    Founded: 1964
    Arts Area: Professional; Theatrical Group
    Status: Professional; Non-Profit
    Type: Performing; Touring; Resident; Educational
    Purpose: Roger Furman Theatre has established a fine reputation for contributing to the cultural pluralism of New York City by presenting quality and professional Black theatrical productions.
    Management: Voza Rivers, Executive Director
    Paid Staff: 3   **Volunteer Staff:** 10
    Paid Artists: 30   **Non-Paid Artists:** 5
    Utilizes: Special Technical Talent; Guest Artists; Guest Directors
    Budget: $1,000 - $50,000

Income Sources: Business/Corporate Donations; Box Office; Government Grants; Individual Donations
Season: September - June
Affiliations: NEA; Department of Cultural Affairs
Performance Facilities: Roger Furman Theater; B Smiths Rooftop Cafe

ROUNDABOUT THEATRE COMPANY
1530 Broadway, New York, NY 10036
(212) 719-9393; (212) 869-8400
FAX: (212) 869-8817
Founded: 1965
Arts Area: Professional; Theatrical Group
Status: Professional; Non-Profit
Type: Performing; Resident
Purpose: Resident theatre institution emphasizing the production of revivals of ancient and modern classics
Management: Todd Haimes, Producing Director; Ellen Richard, General Manager
Officers: Christian C. Yegen, Chairman of the Board
Paid Staff: 75 **Volunteer Staff:** 15
Paid Artists: 80
Utilizes: Special Technical Talent; Guest Artists; Guest Directors
Budget: $1,000,000 - $5,000,000
Income Sources: Private Foundations/Grants/Endowments; Business/Corporate Donations; Box Office; Government Grants; Individual Donations
Season: 52 Weeks **Annual Attendance:** 150,000
Affiliations: AEA; LORT; SSDC

SAINT BART'S PLAYHOUSE
109 East 50th Street, New York, NY 10022
(212) 751-1616
Founded: 1927
Arts Area: Musical; Theatrical Group; Revival
Status: Semi-Professional; Non-Profit
Type: Performing; Resident; Educational
Paid Staff: 5 **Volunteer Staff:** 16
Paid Artists: 5 **Non-Paid Artists:** 75
Utilizes: Special Technical Talent; Guest Directors
Budget: $100,000 - $500,000
Income Sources: Business/Corporate Donations; Box Office; Individual Donations
Season: September - May **Annual Attendance:** 10,000
Affiliations: TCG
Performance Facilities: Saint Bartholomew's Community House

SALT AND PEPPER MIME COMPANY, INC.
320 East 90th, #1B, New York, NY 10128
(212) 262-4989
Founded: 1978
Arts Area: Professional; Musical; Community; Theatrical Group; Drama; Variety; Children's
Status: Professional; Non-Profit
Type: Performing; Touring; Educational
Purpose: To preserve the art of mime and vaudeville through performing, exhibitions and workshops
Management: Scottie Davis, Artistic Manager/Producer; Chuck Wise, Director; Mark Pearce, Resident Playwright
Officers: Houston Brummit, President; Marian Straw, Secretary; Tim Taylor, Treasurer
Paid Staff: 1 **Volunteer Staff:** 2
Paid Artists: 6
Utilizes: Special Technical Talent; Guest Artists; Guest Directors
Budget: $1,000 - $50,000
Income Sources: Private Foundations/Grants/Endowments; Box Office; Government Grants; Individual Donations
Season: January - October **Annual Attendance:** 4,000
Affiliations: ART/NY; Westside Arts Coalition
Performance Facilities: Lincoln Square Theatre; Studio Theatre

THE SECOND STAGE THEATRE
2162 Broadway, New York, NY 10022
(212) 787-8302; (212) 873-6103
FAX: (212) 877-9886
Mailing Address: PO Box 1807, Ansonia Station, NY 10023
Founded: 1979
Arts Area: Professional; Theatrical Group
Status: Professional; Non-Profit

Type: Performing
Purpose: To produce plays of the recent past which we feel deserve a second production; to produce world and New York premieres by emerging authors, with emphasis on women authors and authors of color
Management: Carole Rothman, Artistic Director; Carol Fishman, Associate Producer; Suzanne Davidson, Producing Director
Paid Staff: 16
Utilizes: Guest Artists; Guest Directors
Budget: $500,000 - $1,000,000
Income Sources: Private Foundations/Grants/Endowments; Business/Corporate Donations; Box Office; Government Grants; Individual Donations
Season: October - June **Annual Attendance:** 16,000

SEVENTH SIGN THEATRE COMPANY, INC.
PO Box 20467, Park West Finance, New York, NY 10025
(212) 666-3955
Founded: 1979
Arts Area: Theatrical Group
Status: Professional; Non-Profit
Type: Performing; Educational
Purpose: To produce theatre of quality at low box office prices; to present literate plays, both classical and contemporary
Management: Donna Niemann, Artistic Director; Emma Nicole, Producing Director; Kim T. Sharp, Artistic Associate; Lila Gaynes Vornchuck, Treasurer
Officers: Donna Niemann, President; Emma Nicole, Vice President; Lila Vornchuck, Treasurer/Secretary
Volunteer Staff: 6
Non-Paid Artists: 20
Utilizes: Special Technical Talent; Guest Artists; Guest Directors
Budget: $1,000 - $50,000
Income Sources: Box Office; Government Grants; Individual Donations
Season: September - May **Annual Attendance:** 1,000
Performance Facilities: Good Shepherd Church

THE SHADOW BOX THEATRE
325 West End Avenue, New York, NY 10023
(212) 877-7356
FAX: (212) 724-0767
Arts Area: Musical; Folk; Puppet
Status: Professional; Non-Profit
Type: Performing; Touring; Resident; Educational; Sponsoring
Purpose: To serve inner city disadvantaged children with a high quality art-in-education program
Management: Sandra Robbins, Executive Director; Michael Royce, Managing Director
Paid Staff: 3 **Volunteer Staff:** 5
Paid Artists: 10
Budget: $100,000 - $500,000
Income Sources: Private Foundations/Grants/Endowments; Business/Corporate Donations; Box Office; Government Grants; Individual Donations
Season: September - May **Annual Attendance:** 40,000

SKYSAVER PRODUCTIONS
5 East Third Street, New York, NY 10003
(212) 677-3190
Season: 52 Weeks

SOUPSTONE PROJECT
309 East Fifth Street, Suite 19, New York, NY 10003
(212) 473-7584
Founded: 1985
Arts Area: Professional; Theatrical Group
Status: Professional
Type: Performing
Purpose: To expand the constituency of theatergoers through free, trilingually-accessible productions of new American works
Management: Neile Weissman, Director/Literary Manager
Paid Staff: 1
Paid Artists: 45
Budget: $1,000 - $50,000
Income Sources: Private Foundations/Grants/Endowments; Business/Corporate Donations; Government Grants; Individual Donations
Season: 52 Weeks **Annual Attendance:** 2,400
Performance Facilities: Henry Street Settlement; Louis Abrons Art Center

SPANISH THEATRE REPERTORY COMPANY
138 East 27th Street, New York, NY 10016
(212) 889-2850
FAX: (212) 686-3732
Founded: 1969
Arts Area: Professional; Musical; Community; Theatrical Group
Status: Professional
Type: Performing
Purpose: To fulfill the need for professional Spanish-language theatre and to promote the rich heritage of the Hispanic culture
Management: Gilbert Zaldivar, Producer; Robert Federico, Associate Producer; Ellen Jacobs, Press Agent
Officers: Gilbert Zaldivar, President; Rene Buch, Vice President; Robert Federico, Financial Secretary
Paid Staff: 25
Utilizes: Guest Artists; Guest Directors
Budget: $1,000,000 - $5,000,000
Income Sources: Private Foundations/Grants/Endowments; Business/Corporate Donations; Box Office; Government Grants; Individual Donations
Season: 52 Weeks   **Annual Attendance:** 40,000
Affiliations: TCG; AAA; ART/NY
Performance Facilities: Gramercy Arts Theatre; Equitable Tower Auditorium

STAGEWRIGHTS, INC.
PO Box 4745, Rockefeller Center Station, New York, NY 10185-0041
(212) 768-8964
Founded: 1983
Arts Area: Theatrical Group
Status: Semi-Professional; Non-Profit
Type: Writer's Theatre
Purpose: Script development
Officers: Tom Ross; Uwe Taubert; John Albanese
Volunteer Staff: 25
Non-Paid Artists: 100
Utilizes: Guest Directors
Budget: $1,000 - $50,000
Income Sources: Private Foundations/Grants/Endowments; Business/Corporate Donations; Individual Donations
Season: 52 Weeks

TALKING BAND
PO Box 293, Prince Street Station, New York, NY 10012
(212) 295-0371
Arts Area: Professional; Theatrical Group
Status: Professional; Non-Profit
Type: Performing; Touring
Purpose: To create and perform n ew works for the theater
Management: Paul Zinet, Artistic Director
Officers: J. Anthony Sheldon, President of the Board
Budget: $50,000 - $100,000
Income Sources: Private Foundations/Grants/Endowments; Business/Corporate Donations; Box Office; Government Grants; Individual Donations

THEATER FOR THE NEW CITY
155-57 First Avenue, New York, NY 10003
(212) 254-1109
Founded: 1970
Arts Area: Professional; Theatrical Group
Status: Professional; Non-Profit
Type: Performing; Touring
Purpose: Dedicated to the creation and performance of new theater of new writers; to produce 30 to 40 new works each year with our annual free summer street-theater tour
Management: George Bartenieff, Executive Director; Crystal Field, Artistic Directors
Paid Staff: 9
Paid Artists: 700
Utilizes: Special Technical Talent; Guest Artists; Guest Directors
Budget: $500,000 - $1,000,000
Income Sources: Private Foundations/Grants/Endowments; Business/Corporate Donations; Box Office; Government Grants; Individual Donations
Season: August - July   **Annual Attendance:** 50,000
Affiliations: ART/NY; TCG; AAA

THEATRE DU GRAND-GUIGNOL® DE PARIS (GRAND-GUIGNOL® THEATRE OF PARIS)
310 East 70th Street, New York, NY 10021
(212) 861-1813
  Founded: 1896
  Arts Area: Professional
  Status: Professional; National Theatre of Montmartre
  Type: Performing; Touring; Resident
  Purpose: World's largest theatre specializing in grotesquery, the macabre, shock, terror, and earthy laughter
  Management: Ministry of Culture
  Officers: Barry Alan Richmond, Director-General
  Paid Artists: 15
  Utilizes: Special Technical Talent; Guest Artists; Guest Directors
  Budget: $1,000,000 - $5,000,000
  Income Sources: Private Foundations/Grants/Endowments; Box Office; Government Grants; Other State Entities
  Season: 52 Weeks
  Affiliations: State Theatre of the Republic of Montmartre

THEATRE FOR A NEW AUDIENCE
154 Christopher Street, Suite 36, New York, NY 10014-2839
(212) 229-2819
  Founded: 1979
  Arts Area: Professional; Theatrical Group
  Status: Professional; Non-Profit
  Type: Performing; Educational
  Purpose: To produce plays of poetic imagination; to build a diverse theatre audience
  Management: Jeffrey Horowitz, Artistic/Production Director; Lisa A. Lacroce, General Manager; Margie Salvante, Education Director; Kristin Ebbert, Development Associate; Patrick Scully, Production Manager
  Officers: Daryl D. Smith, Chairman; Jeffrey Horowitz, President; Adelaide Kent, Treasurer; Larry Loeb, Secretary
  Paid Staff: 15
  Paid Artists: 35
  Budget: $500,000 - $1,000,000
  Income Sources: Private Foundations/Grants/Endowments; Business/Corporate Donations; Box Office; Government Grants; Individual Donations
  Season: January - April   **Annual Attendance:** 12,000
  Affiliations: TCG
  Performance Facilities: Theatre at Saint Clement's Church

THEATRE OFF PARK
224 Waverly Place, New York, NY 10014
(212) 627-2556
  Founded: 1975
  Arts Area: Professional; Musical; Theatrical Group
  Status: Professional; Non-Profit
  Type: Educational
  Purpose: To produce new works as well as focus on neglected or unproduced works by established writers
  Management: Albert Harris, Artistic Director
  Paid Staff: 3   **Volunteer Staff:** 10
  Paid Artists: 75
  Utilizes: Special Technical Talent; Guest Artists; Guest Directors
  Budget: $100,000 - $500,000
  Income Sources: Private Foundations/Grants/Endowments; Business/Corporate Donations; Box Office; Government Grants; Individual Donations
  Season: October - June   **Annual Attendance:** 12,000
  Affiliations: AEA; ART/NY
  Performance Facilities: Theatre Off Park

THEATREMOVES, INC./RAJECKAS AND INTRAUB MOVEMENT THEATER
PO Box 1333, New York, NY 10009
(212) 529-8068
  Arts Area: Professional; Community; Theatrical Group; Movement Theatre
  Status: Professional; Non-Profit
  Type: Performing; Touring; Educational
  Purpose: To increase public exposure to movement theatre as a viable art form
  Management: Neil Intraub, Paul Rajeckas, Co-Artistic Directors
  Budget: $50,000 - $100,000
  Income Sources: Private Foundations/Grants/Endowments; Business/Corporate Donations; Government Grants; Individual Donations; Performance Fees

THEATREWORKS/USA
890 Broadway, New York, NY 10003
(212) 926-4100
FAX: (212) 353-1632
Founded: 1961
Arts Area: Professional; Musical; Folk; Theatrical Group; Puppet
Status: Professional; Non-Profit
Type: Performing; Touring; Resident; Educational; Sponsoring
Purpose: Theatreworks/USA, a nonprofit organization and America's largest theatre creating, producing, and touring plays for young audiences, has presented more than 27,000 performances to well over 22 million young people in schools, art centers, museums and theatres, in 49 states.
Management: Charles Hull, Managing Director; Jay Harnick, Artistic Director
Officers: Robert Wood, Chairman of the Board; Jay Harnick, President; Charles Hull, Vice President/Treasurer; David Dretzin, Secretary
Paid Staff: 15
Paid Artists: 145
Utilizes: Guest Artists; Guest Directors; Composers; Lyricists; Writers
Budget: $1,000,000 - $5,000,000
Income Sources: Private Foundations/Grants/Endowments; Business/Corporate Donations; Box Office; Government Grants; Individual Donations
Season: September - August   **Annual Attendance:** 2,000,000
Performance Facilities: Town Hall; Promenade Theatre; Variety Arts Theatre

THUNDER BAY ENSEMBLE
350 Central Park West, Apt. 14H, New York, NY 10025
(212) 749-2262
Season: 52 Weeks

UBU REPERTORY THEATER
15 West 28th Street, New York, NY 10001
(212) 679-7540
FAX: (212) 679-2033
Founded: 1982
Arts Area: Professional
Status: Professional; Non-Profit
Type: Performing
Purpose: To present French language playwrights in translation to American audiences
Management: Francoise Kourilsky, Artistic Director; Kevin Duffy, Acting Literary Manager; Ingrid Nyeboe, Administrator; Anna Morrone, Marketing Director
Officers: Jacques Bouhet, Chairman
Paid Staff: 5   **Volunteer Staff:** 2
Paid Artists: 100
Utilizes: Special Technical Talent; Guest Conductors; Guest Artists; Guest Directors
Budget: $500,000 - $1,000,000
Income Sources: Private Foundations/Grants/Endowments; Business/Corporate Donations; Box Office; Government Grants; Individual Donations
Season: September - June   **Annual Attendance:** 10,000
Affiliations: TCG

VINEYARD THEATRE
108 East 15th Street, New York, NY 10003-9689
(212) 353-3366
FAX: (212) 353-3803
Founded: 1981
Arts Area: Professional; Musical; Theatrical Group
Status: Professional; Non-Profit
Type: Performing
Purpose: To develop new plays and musical theatre
Management: Douglas Aibel, Artistic Director; Barbara Zinn Krieger, Executive Director; Jon Nakagawa, Managing Director
Paid Staff: 3   **Volunteer Staff:** 2
Utilizes: Guest Artists; Guest Directors
Budget: $500,000 - $1,000,000
Income Sources: Private Foundations/Grants/Endowments; Business/Corporate Donations; Box Office; Government Grants; Individual Donations
Season: 52 Weeks   **Annual Attendance:** 10,000
Affiliations: TCG, OA

WESTBETH THEATRE CENTER
151 Bank Street, New York, NY 10014
(212) 691-2272
FAX: (212) 924-7185
> **Founded:** 1977
> **Arts Area:** Professional
> **Status:** Professional; Non-Profit
> **Purpose:** To develop new plays and musicals
> **Management:** Arnold Engelman, Producing Director; Anne Rothschild, Administrative Assistant; Steven Bloom, Literary Manager
> **Paid Staff:** 4   **Volunteer Staff:** 2
> **Budget:** $100,000 - $500,000
> **Income Sources:** Private Foundations/Grants/Endowments; Business/Corporate Donations; Box Office; Government Grants; Individual Donations
> **Season:** 52 Weeks

WESTSIDE COMMUNITY REPERTORY
252 West 81st Street, New York, NY 10024
(212) 874-7290
> **Founded:** 1969
> **Arts Area:** Professional; Theatrical Group
> **Status:** Semi-Professional; Non-Profit
> **Type:** Performing; Resident
> **Purpose:** To perform classics and provide a less expensive alternative to Broadway in the process
> **Management:** Allen Schroeter, Artistic Director
> **Paid Staff:** 5   **Volunteer Staff:** 5
> **Paid Artists:** 5   **Non-Paid Artists:** 20
> **Budget:** $1,000 - $50,000
> **Income Sources:** Private Foundations/Grants/Endowments; Box Office; Government Grants; Individual Donations
> **Season:** 52 Weeks
> **Annual Attendance:** 3,500
> **Affiliations:** ART/NY; Westside Arts Coalition

WHITE BIRD PRODUCTIONS, INC.
PO Box 20233, Columbus Circle Station, New York, NY 10023
(718) 788-5984
> **Founded:** 1989
> **Arts Area:** Professional; Theatrical Group
> **Status:** Professional; Non-Profit
> **Type:** Performing; Touring; Educational
> **Purpose:** To assist in the development of theatrical pieces that generally or specifically address an environmental theme
> **Management:** Kathryn Dickinson, Artistic Director; Liz Loftus, Associate Artistic Director; John Istel, Dramaturge; Christina Denzinger, Literary Manager
> **Volunteer Staff:** 4
> **Utilizes:** Guest Artists; Guest Directors
> **Budget:** $1,000 - $50,000
> **Income Sources:** Box Office; Government Grants; Individual Donations
> **Season:** 52 Weeks

WOMEN'S INTERART CENTER
549 West 52nd Street, New York, NY 10019
(212) 246-1050
> **Founded:** 1971
> **Arts Area:** Professional; Theatrical Group
> **Status:** Professional; Non-Profit
> **Type:** Performing
> **Purpose:** Committed to exploring all areas of theatrical expression while emphasizing the presentation of new playwrights
> **Management:** Margot Lewitin, Artistic Director; Jean Rowan, Dramaturge; Susan Waring Morris, Development Director
> **Officers:** Bill Perlman, Board Chairman
> **Paid Staff:** 3
> **Utilizes:** Special Technical Talent; Guest Artists; Guest Directors
> **Budget:** $100,000 - $500,000
> **Income Sources:** Private Foundations/Grants/Endowments; Business/Corporate Donations; Box Office; Government Grants; Individual Donations
> **Season:** 52 Weeks
> **Affiliations:** AEA
> **Performance Facilities:** Interart Theater

WOMEN'S PROJECT AND PRODUCTIONS
7 West 63rd Street, New York, NY 10023
(212) 873-3040
FAX: (212) 873-3788
> **Founded:** 1978
> **Arts Area:** Professional; Theatrical Group
> **Status:** Professional; Non-Profit
> **Type:** Performing; Resident; Educational; Sponsoring
> **Purpose:** To promote and develop the work of women playwrights and directors in the theatre by creating opportunities for them to work
> **Management:** Julia Miles, Artistic Director; Liz Diamond, Artistic Associate; Jennifer Greenfield, Managing Director
> **Officers:** Julia Miles, President; Pat Schoenfeld, Chairperson; Billie Allen, Treasurer; Helene Kaplan, Secretary
> **Paid Staff:** 9
> **Utilizes:** Special Technical Talent; Guest Artists; Guest Directors; Playwrights
> **Budget:** $500,000 - $1,000,000
> **Income Sources:** Private Foundations/Grants/Endowments; Business/Corporate Donations; Box Office; Government Grants; Individual Donations
> **Season:** October - June   **Annual Attendance:** 5,000
> **Affiliations:** TCG; ART/NY

THE WOOSTER GROUP
PO Box 654, Canal Street Station, New York, NY 10013
(212) 966-9796; (212) 966-3651
FAX: (212) 226-6576
> **Founded:** 1967
> **Arts Area:** Theatrical Group
> **Status:** Non-Profit
> **Type:** Performing; Touring; Resident; Sponsoring
> **Purpose:** A collective of artists working together on collaborative projects over long periods of time
> **Management:** Elizabeth LeCompte, Artistic Director; Andrea Most, Administrative Director
> **Officers:** Peyton Smith, President; Kate Valk, Secretary
> **Paid Staff:** 8   **Volunteer Staff:** 4
> **Paid Artists:** 17
> **Budget:** $500,000 - $1,000,000
> **Income Sources:** Private Foundations/Grants/Endowments; Business/Corporate Donations; Box Office; Government Grants; Individual Donations
> **Season:** 52 Weeks
> **Affiliations:** TCG
> **Performance Facilities:** The Performing Garage

THE WORKING THEATRE COMPANY, INC.
400 West 40th Street, New York, NY 10018
(212) 967-5464
> **Arts Area:** Professional
> **Status:** Professional; Non-Profit
> **Type:** Performing; Educational
> **Purpose:** America's only professional theatre company dedicated to producing new plays of cultural diversities that reflect the issues and concerns that working people face in the modern world
> **Management:** Bill Mitchelson, Artistic Director; Honour Molloy, Development Director
> **Officers:** Larry Beers, Chairman
> **Budget:** $100,000 - $500,000
> **Income Sources:** Private Foundations/Grants/Endowments; Business/Corporate Donations; Box Office; Government Grants; Individual Donations

WPA THEATRE
519 West 23rd Street, New York, NY 10011
(212) 206-0523
FAX: (212) 637-7154
> **Founded:** 1977
> **Arts Area:** Professional
> **Status:** Professional; Non-Profit
> **Type:** Performing
> **Purpose:** The WPA Theatre is dedicated to the creation of a new American repertory theatre based on realistic writing, acting and design.
> **Management:** Kyle Renick, Artistic Director; Donna Lieberman, Managing Director
> **Paid Staff:** 6
> **Paid Artists:** 60
> **Budget:** $500,000 - $1,000,000

Income Sources: Private Foundations/Grants/Endowments; Business/Corporate Donations; Box Office; Government Grants; Individual Donations
Season: October - June
Annual Attendance: 13,000
Affiliations: ART/NY; TCG
Performance Facilities: Chelsea Playhouse

THE YORK THEATRE COMPANY
2 East 90th Street, New York, NY 10128
(212) 534-5366
FAX: (212) 222-9458
Founded: 1969
Arts Area: Professional; Musical; Theatrical Group
Status: Professional; Non-Profit
Type: Performing
Purpose: A professional equity off-off-Broadway company dedicated to presenting great classical works as well as revivals and/or premieres of unusual, avant-garde musicals
Management: Janet Hayes Walker, Producing Director; Molly Pickering Grose, Managing Director; Charles Dodsley Walker, Business Manager; Sarah Tod Smith, Technical Director
Officers: W. David McCoy, Chairman of the Board
Paid Staff: 8 **Volunteer Staff:** 6
Paid Artists: 36
Utilizes: Special Technical Talent; Guest Conductors; Guest Artists; Guest Directors
Budget: $100,000 - $500,000
Income Sources: Private Foundations/Grants/Endowments; Business/Corporate Donations; Box Office; Individual Donations
Season: October - June **Annual Attendance:** 7,500
Affiliations: AEA

PERFORMING SERIES

AMERICAN LANDMARK FESTIVALS
26 Wall Street, Federal Hall National Monmument, New York, NY 10005
(212) 866-2086
FAX: (212) 264-3186
Founded: 1973
Arts Area: Dance; Vocal Music; Instrumental Music; Theater; Festivals; Lyric Opera; Grand Opera
Status: Professional
Type: Performing
Purpose: To combine performances with exceptional historic settings
Officers: Francis L. Heilbut, President
Utilizes: Special Technical Talent; Guest Conductors; Guest Artists; Guest Directors
Income Sources: Individual Donations
Season: 52 Weeks **Annual Attendance:** 100,000

BANG ON A CAN, INC.
222 East Fifth Street, #16, New York, NY 10003
(212) 777-8442
FAX: (212) 777-8442
Founded: 1987
Arts Area: Festivals
Status: Professional; Non-Profit
Type: Performing
Purpose: To present new music by young and emerging composers
Management: Rebecca A. Sayles, Executive Director
Officers: Michael Gordon, David Lang, Julia Wolfe, Artistic Directors
Paid Staff: 1
Budget: $100,000 - $500,000
Income Sources: Private Foundations/Grants/Endowments; Business/Corporate Donations; Box Office; Government Grants; Individual Donations
Season: May **Annual Attendance:** 3,000

CHILDREN'S FREE OPERA AND DANCE
130 West 42nd Street, New York, NY 10036
(212) 840-7470
FAX: (212) 840-7585
Founded: 1976
Arts Area: Dance; Theater; Opera; Music

Status: Professional; Non-Profit
Type: Performing; Educational
Purpose: Educational
Management: Michael Feldman, Artistic Director; Marianne C. Lockwood, Executive Director; Curt Sharp, General Manager; Susannah Halston, Director of Marketing/Development; Rosalyn Bindman, Education Director
Officers: M. Bernar Aidinoff, Chairman; Michael Feldman, President; Marianne C. Lockwood, Vice President; Steven Leifer, Treasurer
Paid Staff: 10   **Volunteer Staff:** 15
Paid Artists: 60
Utilizes: Special Technical Talent; Guest Conductors; Guest Artists; Guest Directors
Budget: $100,000 - $500,000
Income Sources: Private Foundations/Grants/Endowments; Business/Corporate Donations; Government Grants; Individual Donations
Season: October - May   **Annual Attendance:** 60,000
Affiliations: Orchestra of Saint Luke's
Performance Facilities: Town Hall; Brooklyn Academy of Music; State University of New York at Purchase; Lehman Center Triplex Theatre

CITY CENTER OF MUSIC AND DRAMA
70 Lincoln Central Plaza, 4th Floor, New York, NY 10023-6580
(212) 870-4266
Founded: 1943
Arts Area: Dance; Vocal Music; Instrumental Music; Theater
Status: Professional; Non-Profit
Type: Performing; Touring; Educational
Purpose: To provide opera, ballet and drama so that everyone, regardless of income, can see and hear great works
Management: Carla Hunter, Controller
Officers: Martin J. Oppenheimer, Chairman; Gillian Attfield, Vice Chairman
Paid Staff: 12   **Volunteer Staff:** 2
Utilizes: Guest Conductors; Guest Artists; Guest Directors
Budget: Over 10,000,000
Income Sources: Private Foundations/Grants/Endowments; Business/Corporate Donations; Box Office; Government Grants; Individual Donations
Season: 52 Weeks   **Annual Attendance:** 801,000
Performance Facilities: New York State Theater

FOOLS COMPANY, INC.: THE INTERNATIONAL OFFESTIVAL
358 West 44th Street, New York, NY 10036-5426
(212) 307-6000
Founded: 1970
Arts Area: Theater; Festivals
Status: Professional; Non-Profit
Type: Performing; Educational
Purpose: To produce a theatre arts festival and other works and workshops in the performing arts
Management: Jill Russell, Executive Director; Martin Russell, Associate Executive Director; Susan Cline, Executive Administrator
Officers: James Wertheim, President; Marcus Bicknell, Vice President; Joseph Benitez, Secretary/Treasurer
Paid Staff: 5   **Volunteer Staff:** 12
Utilizes: Guest Artists
Budget: $1,000 - $50,000
Income Sources: Private Foundations/Grants/Endowments; Business/Corporate Donations; Box Office; Government Grants; Individual Donations
Season: April - June   **Annual Attendance:** 3,000
Performance Facilities: John Houseman Theatre Studio

JAZZMOBILE INCORPORATED
154 West 127th Street, New York, NY 10027
(212) 866-4900
FAX: (212) 866-3613
Arts Area: Instrumental Music; Jazz
Status: Professional; Non-Profit
Type: Performing; Touring; Resident; Educational
Purpose: To preserve, propogate and present jazz--America's classical music--by all means possible
Management: David Bailey, Executive Director; Dr. Anita Batisti, Development Director
Officers: Dr. George Butler, Chairman of the Board
Budget: $500,000 - $1,000,000
Income Sources: Private Foundations/Grants/Endowments; Business/Corporate Donations; Box Office; Government Grants; Individual Donations; Earned Income

KOHAV THEATRE FOUNDATION
118 Riverside Drive, New York, NY 10024
(212) 877-1667
Founded: 1959
Arts Area: Theater
Status: Professional; Non-Profit
Type: Performing
Management: Hava Kohav Beller, Director; Kathleen Greene, Production Assistant; Herbert C. Kantor, Counsel
Paid Staff: 1 **Volunteer Staff:** 1
Utilizes: Special Technical Talent; Guest Artists
Income Sources: Private Foundations/Grants/Endowments; Government Grants; Individual Donations

LINCOLN CENTER OUT-OF-DOORS
c/o Lincoln Center for the Performing Arts, 70 Lincoln Center Plza., New York, NY 10023
(212) 875-5000
FAX: (212) 875-5145
Arts Area: Dance; Vocal Music; Instrumental Music; Theater
Status: Professional; Non-Profit
Type: Sponsoring
Management: Jenneth Webster, Associate Director - Programming
Paid Staff: 24
Paid Artists: 600
Utilizes: Guest Artists
Budget: $100,000 - $500,000
Income Sources: Private Foundations/Grants/Endowments; Business/Corporate Donations; Box Office; Government Grants; Individual Donations
Season: August - September
Annual Attendance: 300,000
Performance Facilities: Lincoln Center North Plaza, Damrosch Park Bandshell

LINCOLN CENTER'S MOSTLY MOZART FESTIVAL
70 Lincoln Center Plaza, 9th Floor, New York, NY 10023
(212) 875-5000
Founded: 1966
Arts Area: Instrumental Music
Status: Professional; Non-Profit
Type: Sponsoring
Purpose: A major summer festival in New York where the focus of the programing is on Mozart and music of that period
Management: Gerard Schwarz, Music Director; W.W. Lockwood Jr., Festival Director; Frederick W. Noonan, Associate Director; Michele A. Balm, Production Coordinator
Paid Staff: 6
Paid Artists: 150
Utilizes: Guest Conductors; Guest Artists
Budget: $1,000,000 - $5,000,000
Income Sources: Private Foundations/Grants/Endowments; Business/Corporate Donations; Box Office; Government Grants; Individual Donations
Season: July - August **Annual Attendance:** 105,000
Performance Facilities: Avery Fisher Hall

METROPOLITAN MUSEUM CONCERTS AND LECTURES
1000 5th Avenue and 82nd Street, New York, NY 10028
(212) 879-5500
FAX: (212) 570-3973
Founded: 1954
Arts Area: Vocal Music; Instrumental Music; Festivals
Status: Professional
Type: Sponsoring
Purpose: To sense a vital function as one of the major presenting organizations in New York City and reflect the museum's charter in promoting education and cultural events which reflect the museum's holdings
Management: Hilde Annik Limondjian, Program Administrator
Paid Staff: 50
Budget: $1,000,000 - $5,000,000
Income Sources: Box Office; Government Grants
Season: October - May
Annual Attendance: 200,000
Affiliations: AAM
Performance Facilities: Grace Rainey Rogers Auditorium; Velez Blanco Patio

THE NEW YORK INTERNATIONAL FESTIVAL OF THE ARTS
386 Park Avenue South, Suite 2000, New York, NY 10016
(212) 679-5200
FAX: (212) 679-5677
Founded: 1986
Arts Area: Festivals
Status: Professional; Non-Profit
Type: Sponsoring
Purpose: To encourage international friendships; to demonstrate why New York City is considered to be the cultural capital; to promote tourism and its positive economic role
Management: Claudia E. Keenan, Director of Public Affairs
Officers: Martin E. Segal, Chairman; Frank A. Bennack, George B. Munroe, Vice Chairmen; Gordon J. Davis, Treasurer; Diane M. Coffey, Secretary
Paid Staff: 5
Utilizes: Music, Dance, Theatre Companies
Budget: $500,000 - $1,000,000
Income Sources: Private Foundations/Grants/Endowments; Business/Corporate Donations; Individual Donations
Season: June **Annual Attendance:** 95,000

PRESENTATIONS OF THE ELAINE KAUFMAN CULTURAL CENTER
129 West 67th Street, New York, NY 10023
(212) 362-8060; (212) 362-8719
FAX: (212) 874-7865
Arts Area: Vocal Music; Instrumental Music; Festivals
Status: Professional
Type: Educational; Sponsoring
Management: Andrew Berger, Concert Director
Officers: Lewis Kruger, Chairman
Utilizes: Guest Artists
Income Sources: Private Foundations/Grants/Endowments; Business/Corporate Donations; Box Office; Government Grants; Individual Donations
Season: September - May
Performance Facilities: Merkin Concert Hall

THE YARD
890 Broadway, New York, NY 10003
(212) 228-0911; (508) 645-9662
Founded: 1973
Arts Area: Dance; Instrumental Music; Theater
Status: Professional; Non-Profit
Type: Performing; Touring; Resident; Educational
Purpose: To support the growth and development of professional choreographers through residency programs and other services
Management: Patricia N. Nanon, Director
Officers: Patricia N. Nanon, President; Polly Siwek, Vice President; David Washburn, Secretary; Joseph S. Iseman, Treasurer
Paid Staff: 4 **Volunteer Staff:** 2
Paid Artists: 25
Utilizes: Guest Artists
Budget: $100,000 - $500,000
Income Sources: Private Foundations/Grants/Endowments; Business/Corporate Donations; Box Office; Government Grants; Individual Donations
Season: May - September **Annual Attendance:** 2,000
Performance Facilities: Barn Theater, Chilmark, MA

FACILITY

AMBASSADOR THEATRE
215 West 49th Street, New York, NY 10019
(212) 239-6200
FAX: (212) 944-4136
Type of Facility: Theatre House
Type of Stage: Proscenium **Orchestra Pit**
Seating Capacity: 1,125
Year Built: 1921 **Architect:** Herbert J. Krapp
Year Remodeled: 1956

Contact for Rental: Peter Entin;   (212) 944-3700
Manager: Shubert Organization

AMERICAN PLACE THEATRE
111 West 46th Street, New York, NY 10036
(212) 840-2960
FAX: (212) 391-4019
Type of Facility: Theatre House
Type of Stage: Flexible
Seating Capacity: 299
Year Built: 1971   **Architect:** Richard D. Kaplan
Manager: Sara Hershman
Resident Groups: The American Place Theatre

APOLLO THEATRE
253 West 125th Street, New York, NY 10027
(212) 661-3344
FAX: (212) 749-2743
Type of Facility: Concert Hall; Theatre House
Facility Originally: Vaudeville
Type of Stage: Modified Apron Proscenium
Stage Dimensions: 68'6"Wx37'6"D; 37'6"Wx28'2"H proscenium opening
Seating Capacity: 1,500
Year Built: 1914   **Architect:** George Kiester
Year Remodeled: 1987   **Architect:** LeGendre Johnson McNeil   **Cost:** $16,900,000
Contact for Rental: Oliver Sutton;   (212) 661-3344

BELASCO THEATRE
111 West 44th Street, New York, NY 10036
(212) 239-6200
Type of Facility: Theatre House
Type of Stage: Proscenium
Seating Capacity: 1,018
Year Built: 1907   **Architect:** George Kiester
Year Remodeled: 1953
Contact for Rental: Peter Entin;   (212) 239-6200
Manager: Shubert Organization

BMCC/TRIPLEX PERFORMING ARTS CENTER
199 Chambers Street, New York, NY 10007
(212) 618-1900
FAX: (212) 732-2482
Type of Facility: Theatre Complex; Concert Hall; Auditorium; Studio Performance; Environmental; Performance Center; Off Broadway; Theatre House; Multi-Purpose
Facility Originally: School
Type of Stage: Proscenium; 3/4 Arena; Environmental
Stage Dimensions: 3 spaces: A - 46'x37'x19'; B - 28'x39'x18'; C - 24'x26'x18'   **Orchestra Pit**
Seating Capacity: A - 930; B - 280; C - 99
Contact for Rental: Joel Bassin;   (212) 618-1900

BOOTH THEATRE
222 West 45th Street, New York, NY 10036
(212) 239-6200
Type of Facility: Theatre House
Type of Stage: Proscenium   **Orchestra Pit**
Seating Capacity: 783
Year Remodeled: 1913   **Architect:** Henry B. Herts
Contact for Rental: Philip Smith;   (212) 239-6200
Manager: Shubert Organization
Orchestra pit available upon request

BROADHURST THEATRE
235 West 44th Street, New York, NY 10035
(212) 239-6200
Type of Facility: Theatre House
Type of Stage: Proscenium   **Orchestra Pit**
Seating Capacity: 1,157
Year Built: 1917   **Architect:** Herbert J. Krapp

Contact for Rental: Peter Entin or Philip Smith;   (212) 239-6200
Manager: Shubert Organization

BROADWAY THEATRE
1681 Broadway, New York, NY 10019
(212) 239-6200
> **Type of Facility:** Theatre House
> **Type of Stage:** Proscenium   **Orchestra Pit**
> **Seating Capacity:** 1,765
> **Year Built:** 1924   **Architect:** Eugene DeRosa
> **Year Remodeled:** 1942
> **Contact for Rental:** Peter Entin;   (212) 239-6200
> **Manager:** Shubert Organization

BROOKS ATKINSON THEATRE
256 West 47th Street, New York, NY 10036
(212) 719-4099
> **Type of Facility:** Theatre House
> **Type of Stage:** Proscenium
> **Seating Capacity:** 1,086
> **Year Built:** 1926
> **Contact for Rental:** Peter Russell;   (212) 730-8200
> **Manager:** The Nederlander Organization

CARNEGIE HALL
154 West 57th Street, New York, NY 10019
(212) 903-9600
FAX: (212) 581-6539
> **Type of Facility:** Concert Hall
> **Type of Stage:** Proscenium
> **Seating Capacity:** Main Hall - 2,804, Recital Hall - 268
> **Year Built:** 1891   **Architect:** William Burnett Tuthill   **Cost:** $1,000,000
> **Year Remodeled:** 1986   **Architect:** James S. Polshek & Partners   **Cost:** $60,000,000
> **Contact for Rental:** Gilda Weissberger;   (212) 903-9710

CIRCLE IN THE SQUARE INC.
1633 Broadway, New York, NY 10019
(212) 307-2700
FAX: (212) 581-6371
> **Type of Facility:** Theatre House
> **Type of Stage:** 3/4 Arena
> **Seating Capacity:** 750
> **Year Built:** 1951
> **Contact for Rental:** Robert Buckley;   (212) 307-2700

CITY CENTER
131 West 55th Street, New York, NY 10019-5390
(212) 247-0430
FAX: (212) 246-9778
> **Founded:** 1943
> **Type of Facility:** Theatre Complex; Concert Hall; Auditorium; Studio Performance; Performance Center; Office Space
> **Facility Originally:** Masonic Hall; Shriner's "Mecca Temple"
> **Type of Stage:** Proscenium
> **Stage Dimensions:** 38'H proscenium; 45'Wx43'Dx60' to grid stage   **Orchestra Pit**
> **Seating Capacity:** 2,684
> **Year Built:** 1923
> **Year Remodeled:** 1988   **Architect:** Rothzeid, Kaiserman, Thompson & Bee
> **Acoustical Consultant:** Sound Associates
> **Contact for Rental:** Peter Clark, Theater Manager;   (212) 247-0430
> **Resident Groups:** Joffrey Ballet; Alvin Ailey Dance Theater; Paul Taylor Dance Company; Merce Cunningham Dance Company; Lar Lubovitch Dance Company; Martha Graham Dance; Trisha Brown Dance
> *City Center contains Stage I, Stage II and City Center Theater.*

CITY CENTER - CITY CENTER STAGE I
131 West 55th Street, New York, NY 10019-5390
(212) 247-0430
FAX: (212) 246-9778
> **Type of Facility:** Black Box

Type of Stage: Flexible
Stage Dimensions: 40'x50'
Seating Capacity: 299
Contact for Rental: Peter Clark

CITY CENTER - CITY CENTER STAGE II
131 West 55th Street, New York, NY 10019-5390
(212) 247-0430
FAX: (212) 246-9778
Type of Facility: Black Box
Type of Stage: Flexible
Stage Dimensions: 45'x60'
Seating Capacity: 150
Contact for Rental: Peter Clark

CITY CENTER - CITY CENTER THEATRE
131 West 55th Street, New York, NY 10019-5390
(212) 247-0430
FAX: (212) 246-9778
Type of Facility: Theatre House
Facility Originally: Meeting Hall; Movie House
Type of Stage: Proscenium
Stage Dimensions: 45'Wx60'D   **Orchestra Pit**
Seating Capacity: 2,731
Year Built: 1923
Year Remodeled: 1986   **Architect:** Fred Lebensohl, Bernard Rothzeid
Contact for Rental: Peter Clark

CORT THEATRE
138 West 48th Street, New York, NY 10036
(212) 239-6200
FAX: (212) 239-5134
Type of Facility: Theatre House
Type of Stage: Proscenium   **Orchestra Pit**
Seating Capacity: 1,089
Year Built: 1912   **Architect:** Edward B. Corey
Contact for Rental: Philip Smith;   (212) 944-3710
Manager: Shubert Organization

CSC REPERTORY LTD.
136 East 13th Street, New York, NY 10003
(212) 677-4210
FAX: (212) 477-7504
Founded: 1967
Type of Facility: Theatre House
Facility Originally: Movie House
Type of Stage: 3/4 Arena
Stage Dimensions: 30'x30'
Seating Capacity: 180
Year Built: 1890
Year Remodeled: 1974
Contact for Rental: Patricia Taylor, Manager;   (212) 677-4210
Resident Groups: CSC Repertory Ltd.
For resident company to perform classics

DANCE THEATER WORKSHOP'S BESSIE SCHONBERG THEATRE
219 West 19th Street, New York, NY 10011
(212) 691-6500
FAX: (212) 633-1974
Founded: 1960
Type of Facility: Loft; Black Box Proscenium Style
Facility Originally: Business Facility
Type of Stage: Proscenium; Black Box Proscenium style
Stage Dimensions: 26'x32' with wings; 26'x48' without wings
Seating Capacity: 100
Contact for Rental: Laura Schandelmeier, Phil Sandstrom, Production Managers;   (212) 691-6500
Manager: David R. White, Executive Director;   (212) 691-6500
31'x35' rehearsal studio is available for rent.

DELACORTE THEATRE IN CENTRAL PARK
81st Street at Central Park West, New York, NY 10003
(212) 861-7277
   Type of Facility: Amphitheater
   Type of Stage: Thrust
   Seating Capacity: 1,936
   Year Built: 1962   **Architect:** Eldon Elder
   Year Remodeled: 1977   **Architect:** Giorgio Cavaglieri
   Performance facility of the New York Shakespeare Festival. Contact address is: 425 Lafayette Street, New York, NY 10003

EDEN'S EXPRESSWAY
537 Broadway, New York, NY 10012
(212) 925-0880
   Type of Facility: Studio Performance; Multi-Purpose; Loft
   Facility Originally: Business Facility
   Type of Stage: Flexible
   Stage Dimensions: 35'x45'x11'
   Seating Capacity: 100
   Year Built: 1974   **Architect:** Jorge Abrosini   **Cost:** $50,000
   Year Remodeled: 1977   **Architect:** Tod Miller   **Cost:** $16,000
   Contact for Rental: Frances Alenikoff, Director;   (516) 324-1833
   Resident Groups: Frances Alenikoff Dance Theater; T'ai Chi (Maggie Newman)
   Ongoing renovations; available for rehearsals and workshops

EISNER-LUBIN AUDITORIUM
566 LaGuardia Place, New York, NY 10012
(212) 998-4909
FAX: (212) 995-4094
   Type of Facility: Theatre Complex; Concert Hall; Auditorium; Multi-Purpose
   Type of Stage: Platform
   Stage Dimensions: 17'x27'6"x13'6"
   Seating Capacity: 726
   Year Built: 1959
   Acoustical Consultant: Steve Freytag
   Contact for Rental: Jonathan Ross, Operations Scheduling;   (212) 998-4909
   Located at Loeb Student Center, New York University; groups renting must be non-profit organizations

ENSEMBLE STUDIO THEATRE
549 West 52nd Street, New York, NY 10019
(212) 247-4982
   Type of Facility: Studio Performance
   Facility Originally: Warehouse
   Type of Stage: Flexible
   Seating Capacity: 100
   Acoustical Consultant: Kert Lundell

ETHEL BARRYMORE THEATRE
243 West 47th Street, New York, NY 10036
(212) 239-6200
   Type of Facility: Theatre House
   Type of Stage: Proscenium
   Orchestra Pit
   Seating Capacity: 1,096
   Year Built: 1928
   Architect: Herbert J. Krapp
   Contact for Rental: Philip Smith;   (212) 944-3710
   Manager: Shubert Organization

EUGENE O'NEILL THEATER
230 West 49th Street, New York, NY 10019
(212) 239-6200
   Type of Facility: Theatre House
   Type of Stage: Proscenium
   Orchestra Pit
   Seating Capacity: 1,101

Year Built: 1925   Architect: Herbert J. Krapp
Contact for Rental: Jujamcyn Theaters;   (212) 840-8181

46TH STREET THEATRE
226 West 46th Street, New York, NY 10036
(212) 221-1211
    Type of Facility: Theatre House
    Type of Stage: Proscenium
    Seating Capacity: 1,338
    Year Built: 1924   Architect: Herbert J. Krapp
    Contact for Rental: Peter Russell;   (212) 730-8200
    Manager: The Nederlander Organization

GERSHWIN THEATRE
222 West 51st Street, New York, NY 10019
(212) 586-6510
    Type of Facility: Theatre House
    Type of Stage: Proscenium
    Seating Capacity: 1,933
    Year Built: 1972
    Architect: Ralph Alswang   Cost: $9,000,000
    Contact for Rental: Leo Cohen;   (212) 262-2400
    Manager: The Nederlander Organization;   (212) 262-2400

GRAMERCY ARTS THEATER
138 East 27th Street, New York, NY 10016
(212) 889-2850
    Type of Facility: Off Broadway; Theatre House
    Facility Originally: Private Residence
    Type of Stage: Proscenium; Platform
    Stage Dimensions: 20'x25'
    Seating Capacity: 153
    Year Built: 1850
    Year Remodeled: 1972   Architect: Leslie Cortese   Cost: $20,000
    Manager: Gilberto Zaldivar
    Resident Groups: Spanish Theater Repertory Company

H.B. PLAYWRIGHTS FOUNDATION THEATRE HOUSE
124 South Bank Street, New York, NY 10014
(212) 989-6540
    Type of Facility: Auditorium; Theatre House
    Facility Originally: Garage
    Type of Stage: Flexible
    Stage Dimensions: 18'x32'
    Seating Capacity: 100
    Year Remodeled: 1964   Architect: V. Gruen
    Acoustical Consultant: V. Gruen
    Manager: Glen Paris, Artistic Director;   (212) 989-6540
    Resident Groups: H.B. Playwrights Foundation

HELEN HAYES THEATRE
240 West 44th Street, New York, NY 10036
(212) 944-9450; (212) 944-9457
FAX: (212) 302-3584
    Type of Facility: Theatre House
    Type of Stage: Proscenium
    Stage Dimensions: 28'Wx28'D; 28'Wx17'10"H proscenium opening
    Seating Capacity: 565
    Year Built: 1912
    Year Remodeled: 1980
    Contact for Rental: Susan Myerberg;   (212) 944-9457
    Built in 1912 by Winthrop Ames as the Little Theatre, it became the Helen Hayes Theatre in 1983. It is the smallest theatre on Broadway and is independently owned by the Little Theatre Company.

IMPERIAL THEATRE
249 West 45th Street, New York, NY 10036
(212) 944-3700
    Type of Facility: Theatre House

Type of Stage: Proscenium   **Orchestra Pit**
Seating Capacity: 1,452
Year Built: 1923   **Architect:** Herbert J. Krapp
Contact for Rental: Philip Smith;   (212) 944-3710
Manager: Shubert Organization

JOHN GOLDEN THEATRE
252 West 45th Street, New York, NY 10036
(212) 944-3700
Type of Facility: Theatre House
Type of Stage: Proscenium
Orchestra Pit
Seating Capacity: 805
Year Built: 1927   **Architect:** Herbert J. Krapp
Contact for Rental: ;   (212) 944-3710
Manager: Shubert Organization

THE JOSEPH PAPP PUBLIC THEATER
425 Lafayette Street, New York, NY 10003
(212) 598-7100
FAX: (212) 598-7199
Type of Facility: Performance Center
Year Built: 1860
Year Remodeled: 1970   **Architect:** Giorgio Caraglieri   **Cost:** $700,000
Acoustical Consultant: Christopher Jaffe
Resident Groups: New York Shakespeare Festival
Converted into a theater in 1970 Seating Capacity: Anspacher Theater - 275; Little Film Theater - 91; LuEsther Hall - 240; Martinson Hall - 240; Shiva Theater - 90

THE JOYCE THEATER
175 Eighth Avenue, New York, NY 10011
(212) 691-9740
FAX: (212) 727-3658
Founded: 1981
Type of Facility: Performance Center; Theatre House; Dance Theater
Type of Stage: Proscenium
Stage Dimensions: 43'x35'x21'
Seating Capacity: 472
Year Built: 1981   **Architect:** Hugh Hardy of Hardy, Holzman, Pfeiffer   **Cost:** $4,000,000
Acoustical Consultant: Chris Jaffe, Jaffe Acoustics
Contact for Rental: Martin Wechsler;   (212) 691-9740
Resident Groups: Feld Ballets/NY; Pilobolus

KAUFMANN CONCERT HALL
1395 Lexington Avenue, New York, NY 10028
(212) 415-5740
FAX: (212) 415-5738
Type of Facility: Concert Hall; Auditorium; Theatre House
Type of Stage: Proscenium
Stage Dimensions: 35'x30'x23'6"
Seating Capacity: 916
Year Built: 1929
Year Remodeled: 1977
Contact for Rental: Valerie Simmons;   (212) 415-5740
Manager: Raymond T. Grant;   (212) 415-5740
Resident Groups: New York Chamber Symphony

KAZUKO HIRABAYASHI DANCE THEATRE
330 Broome Street, New York, NY 10002
(212) 966-6414
Type of Facility: Studio Performance; Loft
Facility Originally: School
Type of Stage: Flexible
Stage Dimensions: 32'x38'
Seating Capacity: 100
Year Built: 1979   **Cost:** $10,000
Contact for Rental: Robert Swinston;   (212) 966-6414

THE LAMB'S THEATRE
130 West 44th Street, New York, NY 10036
(212) 997-0210
FAX: (212) 997-1082
   Type of Facility: Studio Performance; Off Broadway; Theatre House; Room
   Facility Originally: Lamb's Club, Men's Theatre Organization
   Type of Stage: Flexible; Proscenium
   Stage Dimensions: Mainstage 26'x23'x27'6"; Little Theatre 23'x23'x12'
   Seating Capacity: Main Theatre - 349, Little Theatre - 99
   Year Built: 1902   **Architect:** Stanford White
   Year Remodeled: 1974
   Contact for Rental: Carl H. Jaynes, Facilities Manager;   (212) 997-0210
   Resident Groups: Lamb's Theatre Company

LEHMAN CENTER FOR THE PERFORMING ARTS
Bedford Park Boulevard, West, New York, NY 10468
(212) 960-8232
FAX: (212) 960-8935
   Type of Facility: Theatre Complex; Concert Hall; Auditorium; Outdoor (Concert); Theatre House; Amphitheater
   Type of Stage: Proscenium
   Stage Dimensions: Concert Hall - 60'x30'; Theatre - 35'4"x26'6"   **Orchestra Pit**
   Seating Capacity: Concert Hall - 2,300; Theatre - 500
   Year Built: 1980   **Architect:** David Todd/Jan Pokorny
   Contact for Rental: Jack Globenfelt;   (212) 960-8232
   Resident Groups: Aeolian Chamber Players

LINCOLN CENTER FOR THE PERFORMING ARTS
140 West 65th Street, New York, NY 10023
(212) 877-1800
FAX: (212) 874-2659
   Type of Facility: Theatre Complex; Performance Center
   Lincoln Center contains Alice Tully Hall, Avery Fisher Hall, Juilliard Opera Theatre, Juillard School Drama Workshop, Metropolitan Opera House, Mitzi E. Newhouse Theater, New York Public Library   Auditorium, New York State Theater, Paul Recital Hall and Vivian Beaumont Theater. See separate listings for additional information.

LINCOLN CENTER FOR THE PERFORMING ARTS - ALICE TULLY HALL
1941 Broadway, New York, NY 10023
(212) 875-5000
   Type of Facility: Concert Hall
   Type of Stage: Proscenium
   Stage Dimensions: 50'Wx21'6"D   **Orchestra Pit**
   Seating Capacity: 1,096
   Year Built: 1969   **Architect:** Pietro Belluschi, Helge Westermann
   Acoustical Consultant: Heinrich Keilholz
   Contact for Rental: Delmar Hendricks;   (212) 580-8700
   Manager: John Fleming
   Resident Groups: Chamber Music Society of Lincoln Center; Film Society of Lincoln Center

LINCOLN CENTER FOR THE PERFORMING ARTS - AVERY FISHER HALL
Broadway and 65th Street, New York, NY 10023
(212) 875-5000
FAX: (212) 875-5011
   Type of Facility: Concert Hall
   Type of Stage: Concert Shell
   Stage Dimensions: 45'x68'x40'4"
   Seating Capacity: 2,738
   Year Built: 1962   **Architect:** Harrison & Abramovitz
   Contact for Rental: Delmar Hendricks;   (212) 580-8700
   Manager: John Fleming
   Resident Groups: New York Philharmonic

LINCOLN CENTER FOR THE PERFORMING ARTS - THE JUILLIARD OPERA CENTER
60 Lincoln Center Plaza, New York, NY 10023
(212) 799-5000
FAX: (212) 724-0263
   Type of Facility: Theatre House
   Type of Stage: Proscenium
   Orchestra Pit

Seating Capacity: 1,026
Year Built: 1969   **Architect:** Pietro Belluschi
Acoustical Consultant: Heinrich Keilholz
Manager: Rick Harold

LINCOLN CENTER FOR THE PERFORMING ARTS - THE JUILLIARD SCHOOL DRAMA WORKSHOP
60 Lincoln Center Plaza, New York, NY 10023
(212) 799-5000
FAX: (212) 875-8437
    Type of Facility: Theatre House
    Type of Stage: Flexible
    Seating Capacity: 206
    Year Built: 1969   **Architect:** Pietro Belluschi
    Acoustical Consultant: Heinrich Keilholz
    Manager: Katherine Hood

LINCOLN CENTER FOR THE PERFORMING ARTS - METROPOLITAN OPERA HOUSE
30 Lincoln Center Plaza, New York, NY 10023
(212) 799-3100
FAX: (212) 874-2659
    Type of Facility: Opera House
    Seating Capacity: Auditorium - 3,788; Liszt Hall - 144
    Year Built: 1966   **Architect:** Wallace K. Harrison   **Cost:** $46,900,000
    Acoustical Consultant: Vilhelm L. Jordan and Dr. Cyril Harris
    Contact for Rental: Bruce Crawford;   (212) 799-3100
    Resident Groups: Metropolitan Opera

LINCOLN CENTER FOR THE PERFORMING ARTS - MITZI E. NEWHOUSE THEATER
150 West 65th Street, New York, NY 10023
(212) 362-7600
FAX: (212) 873-0761
    Type of Facility: Theatre House
    Type of Stage: Thrust
    Stage Dimensions: 25'x35'
    Seating Capacity: 280
    Year Built: 1965   **Architect:** Eero Saarinen

LINCOLN CENTER FOR THE PERFORMING ARTS - NEW YORK PUBLIC LIBRARY AUDITORIUM
40 Lincoln Center Plaza, New York, NY 10023
(212) 870-5500
    Type of Facility: Auditorium
    Type of Stage: Platform
    Stage Dimensions: 14'x36'
    Seating Capacity: 212
    Year Built: 1965
    Architect: Skidmore, Owings & Merrill
    Cost: $8,000,000
    Contact for Rental: Richard M. Buck;   (212) 870-1613
    Free concerts and events daily. The Heckscher Oval Theater is in the children's section.

LINCOLN CENTER FOR THE PERFORMING ARTS - NEW YORK STATE THEATER
20 Lincoln Center Plaza, New York, NY 10023
(212) 870-5500
FAX: (212) 870-4285
    Type of Facility: Theatre House
    Type of Stage: Proscenium   **Orchestra Pit**
    Seating Capacity: 2,737
    Year Built: 1964
    Architect: Philip Johnson
    Manager: Mitchell Brower;   (212) 870-5505
    Resident Groups: New York City Ballet; New York City Opera

LINCOLN CENTER FOR THE PERFORMING ARTS - PAUL RECITAL HALL
60 Lincoln Center Plaza, New York, NY 10023
(212) 799-5000
FAX: (212) 724-0263
    Type of Facility: Concert Hall
    Seating Capacity: 278

Year Built: 1969
Architect: Pietro Belluschi
Acoustical Consultant: Heinrich Keilholz
Manager: Ed Fleischman

LINCOLN CENTER FOR THE PERFORMING ARTS - VIVIAN BEAUMONT THEATER
150 West 65th Street, New York, NY 10023
(212) 362-7600
    Type of Facility: Theatre House
    Type of Stage: Thrust
    Stage Dimensions: 40'x90'
    Seating Capacity: 1,089
    Year Built: 1965 **Architect:** Eero Saarinen
    Contact for Rental: Steve Callahan; (212) 362-7600

LONGACRE THEATRE
220 West 48th Street, New York, NY 10036
(212) 239-6200
    Type of Facility: Theatre House
    Type of Stage: Proscenium **Orchestra Pit**
    Seating Capacity: 1,096
    Year Built: 1913 **Architect:** Henry B. Herts
    Contact for Rental: Philip Smith; (212) 944-3710
    Manager: Shubert Organization

LUCILLE LORTEL THEATRE
121 Christopher Street, New York, NY 10014
(212) 924-2817
    Type of Facility: Off Broadway
    Type of Stage: Thrust; Proscenium
    Stage Dimensions: 28'x30'
    Seating Capacity: 299
    Year Built: 1950
    Contact for Rental: Ben Sprecher; (212) 924-2817

LUNT-FONTANNE THEATRE
205 West 46th Street, New York, NY 10036
(212) 575-9200
    Type of Facility: Theatre House
    Type of Stage: Proscenium
    Seating Capacity: 1,478
    Year Built: 1910 **Architect:** Carrere & Hastings
    Contact for Rental:
    Manager: The Nederlander Organization

LYCEUM THEATRE
149 West 45th Street, New York, NY 10036
(212) 239-6200
    Type of Facility: Theatre House
    Type of Stage: Proscenium **Orchestra Pit**
    Seating Capacity: 924
    Year Built: 1903 **Architect:** Herts & Tallent
    Contact for Rental: Philip Smith; (212) 944-3710
    Manager: Shubert Organization

MADISON SQUARE GARDEN
Pennsylvania Plaza, New York, NY 10001
(212) 456-6000
    Type of Facility: Concert Hall; Auditorium; Performance Center; Theatre House; Arena; Multi-Purpose
    Type of Stage: Thrust; Flexible; 3/4 Arena; Arena
    Seating Capacity: Arena - 20,000; The Paramount - 5,000
    Year Built: 1968 **Architect:** Charles Luckman Associates **Cost:** $50,000,000
    Contact for Rental: Booking Department; (212) 563-8000
    Resident Groups: New York Knicks; New York Rangers

MAJESTIC THEATRE
245 West 44th Street, New York, NY 10036
(212) 239-6200
> **Type of Facility:** Theatre House
> **Type of Stage:** Proscenium   **Orchestra Pit**
> **Seating Capacity:** 1,655
> **Year Built:** 1927   **Architect:** Herbert J. Krapp
> **Contact for Rental:** Philip Smith;   (212) 944-3710
> **Manager:** Shubert Organization

MANHATTAN THEATRE CLUB
453 West 16th Street, New York, NY 10011
(212) 645-5590
FAX: (212) 691-9106
> **Type of Facility:** Multi-Purpose; Room
> **Facility Originally:** Meeting Hall; Movie House
> **Type of Stage:** Experimental Space
> **Year Remodeled:** 1986   **Architect:** Superstructures
> **Contact for Rental:** Production Office;   (212) 645-5590
> **Resident Groups:** Manhattan Theatre Club

MARQUIS
211 West 45th Street, New York, NY 10036
(212) 382-0100
> **Type of Facility:** Theatre House
> **Type of Stage:** Proscenium
> **Seating Capacity:** 1,617
> **Year Built:** 1986
> **Contact for Rental:** Peter Russell;   (212) 730-8200
> **Manager:** The Nederlander Organization

MARTIN BECK THEATER
302 West 45th Street, New York, NY 10036
(212) 239-6200
> **Type of Facility:** Theatre House
> **Type of Stage:** Proscenium   **Orchestra Pit**
> **Seating Capacity:** 1,302
> **Year Built:** 1924   **Architect:** G. Albert Lansburg
> **Contact for Rental:** Jujamcyn Theaters;   (212) 840-8181

MARYMOUNT MANHATTAN COLLEGE - MARYMOUNT MANHATTAN THEATRE
221 East 71st Street, New York, NY 10021
(212) 517-0475
FAX: (212) 517-0413
> **Type of Facility:** Off Broadway; Theatre House
> **Type of Stage:** Proscenium
> **Stage Dimensions:** 30'x30' unmasked and 12' apron   **Orchestra Pit**
> **Seating Capacity:** 249
> **Year Built:** 1975   **Architect:** Evans & Delehanty
> **Acoustical Consultant:** Steven Wolf
> **Contact for Rental:** Mary Fleischer, Managing Director;   (212) 517-0475
> **Resident Groups:** Dramatists Guild; American Chamber Opera; Martha Graham Ensemble

MERCE CUNNINGHAM DANCE STUDIO
55 Bethune Street, New York, NY 10014
(212) 691-9751
FAX: (212) 633-2453
> **Type of Facility:** Studio Performance
> **Stage Dimensions:** 52'x45'
> **Seating Capacity:** 150
> **Year Remodeled:** 1971   **Architect:** Justin Hanshell   **Cost:** $25,000
> **Acoustical Consultant:** Nicole Werner
> **Contact for Rental:** Alice Hepern;   (212) 691-9751
> **Resident Groups:** Merce Cunningham Dance Company

MERKIN CONCERT HALL AT ELAINE KAUFMAN CONCERT CENTER
129 West 67th Street, New York, NY 10023
(212) 362-8060
FAX: (212) 874-7865
    Type of Facility: Performance Center
    Facility Originally: School
    Type of Stage: Proscenium
    Stage Dimensions: 57'Wx22'D, stage 35'W at back
    Seating Capacity: 457
    Year Built: 1978   **Architect:** Ashok M. Bhavnani
    Acoustical Consultant: Peter George
    Contact for Rental: Linda Gel;   (212) 362-8060
    Resident Groups: Mendelssohn String Quartet; Music Today
    Contains the Ann Goodman Recital Hall, which has a seating capacity of 125

MINETTA LANE THEATRE
18 Minetta Lane, New York, NY 10012-1207
(212) 420-8000
    Type of Facility: Off Broadway; Theatre House
    Facility Originally: Factory
    Type of Stage: Platform
    Seating Capacity: 399
    Year Built: 1984   **Cost:** $2,000,000
    Contact for Rental: Alan Schuster, Managing Director;   (212) 460-0990

MINSKOFF THEATRE
200 West 45th Street, New York, NY 10036
(212) 869-0550
    Type of Facility: Theatre House
    Type of Stage: Proscenium   **Orchestra Pit**
    Seating Capacity: 1,621
    Year Built: 1972
    Architect: Kahn & Jacobs
    Contact for Rental: Peter Russell;   (212) 730-8200
    Manager: The Nederlander Organization

MUSIC BOX
239 West 45th Street, New York, NY 10036
(212) 239-6200
    Type of Facility: Theatre House
    Type of Stage: Proscenium   **Orchestra Pit**
    Seating Capacity: 1,010
    Year Built: 1921   **Architect:** C. Howard Crane
    Contact for Rental: Sherman Gross;   (212) 239-6200
    Manager: Shubert Organization

NEDERLANDER THEATRE
208 West 41st Street, New York, NY 10036
(212) 921-8000; (212) 262-2400
    Type of Facility: Theatre House
    Type of Stage: Proscenium   **Orchestra Pit**
    Seating Capacity: 1,206
    Year Built: 1921   **Architect:** William N. Smith
    Contact for Rental: Leo Cohen
    Manager: The Nederlander Organization

NEIL SIMON THEATRE
250 West 52nd Street, New York, NY 10019
(212) 757-8646
    Type of Facility: Theatre House
    Type of Stage: Proscenium
    Orchestra Pit
    Seating Capacity: 1,334
    Year Built: 1927   **Architect:** Herbert J. Krapp   **Cost:** $800,000
    Contact for Rental:
    Manager: The Nederlander Organization

NEW DRAMATISTS
424 West 44th Street, New York, NY 10036
(212) 757-6960
FAX: (212) 265-4738
    Founded: 1949
    Type of Facility: Studio Performance; Multi-Purpose; Black Box
    Facility Originally: Church
    Seating Capacity: Theatre 1 - 90; Theatre 2 - 60
    Contact for Rental: (212) 757-6960
    Resident Groups: New Dramatists

THE OPEN EYE: NEW STAGINGS
270 West 89th Street, New York, NY 10024
(212) 769-4141
    Founded: 1972
    Type of Facility: Theatre House
    Facility Originally: Bowling Alley
    Type of Stage: Modified Apron Proscenium
    Stage Dimensions: 25'Wx30'D
    Seating Capacity: 105
    Year Built: 1927
    Year Remodeled: 1987 **Architect:** Mitchell Kurtz **Cost:** $350,000
    Contact for Rental: Adrienne Brockway; (212) 769-4141
    Resident Groups: The Open Eye: New Stagings

ORPHEUM THEATRE
126 Second Avenue, New York, NY 10003
(212) 477-2477
    Type of Facility: Off Broadway; Theatre House
    Facility Originally: Orpheum Concert Gardens
    Type of Stage: Proscenium
    Stage Dimensions: 26'Dx24'W
    Seating Capacity: 349
    Year Built: 1902
    Year Remodeled: 1979
    Contact for Rental: Alan Schuster; (212) 420-8000

PACE DOWNTOWN THEATER
1 Pace Plaza, New York, NY 10038
(212) 346-1715
FAX: (212) 346-1933
    Type of Facility: Theatre Complex; Concert Hall; Performance Center; Theatre House; Multi-Purpose
    Type of Stage: Proscenium
    Stage Dimensions: 60'x40'
    Seating Capacity: 659
    Year Built: 1970
    Contact for Rental: Jillian Panfel; (212) 346-1398
    Resident Groups: Eiko & Koma

PALACE THEATRE
1564 Broadway, New York, NY 10036
(212) 730-8200
    Type of Facility: Theatre House
    Facility Originally: Vaudeville
    Type of Stage: Proscenium **Orchestra Pit**
    Seating Capacity: 1,723
    Year Built: 1913 **Architect:** Kirchoff & Rose
    Year Remodeled: 1966 **Architect:** McNamara **Cost:** $288,000
    Contact for Rental: Leo Cohen; (212) 730-8200
    Manager: The Nederlander Organization; (212) 242-2400

PERFORMING GARAGE
33 Wooster Street, New York, NY 10013
(212) 966-3651
FAX: (212) 226-6576
    Founded: 1972
    Type of Facility: Multi-Purpose; Room
    Facility Originally: Machine Shop

Type of Stage: Flexible
Seating Capacity: 220
Year Built: 1958
Year Remodeled: 1962   **Architect:** Jerry N. Rojo   **Cost:** $45,000
Manager: Andrea Most;   (212) 966-9796
Resident Groups: The Wooster Group

PLYMOUTH THEATRE
236 West 45th Street, New York, NY 10036
(212) 239-6200
Type of Facility: Theatre House
Type of Stage: Proscenium   **Orchestra Pit**
Seating Capacity: 1,082
Year Built: 1917
Architect: Herbert J. Krapp
Contact for Rental: Philip Smith;   (212) 944-3710
Manager: Shubert Organization;   (212) 944-3700

PROMENADE THEATRE
2162 Broadway, New York, NY 10023
(212) 924-2817
Type of Facility: Theatre House
Type of Stage: Proscenium
Stage Dimensions: 40'W proscenium opening
Seating Capacity: 299
Contact for Rental: Ben Sprecher;   (212) 580-3777

PROVINCETOWN PLAYHOUSE
133 McDougal, New York, NY 10014
(212) 477-5048
Type of Facility: Theatre House
Type of Stage: Proscenium
Seating Capacity: 175
Contact for Rental: Arthur Cantor, Inc.;   (212) 496-5710

RADIO CITY MUSIC HALL
1260 Avenue of the Americas, New York, NY 10020
(212) 632-4000
Type of Facility: Theatre Complex; Concert Hall; Auditorium; Studio Performance; Theatre House; Opera House
Type of Stage: Proscenium
Stage Dimensions: 144'Wx80'D   **Orchestra Pit**
Seating Capacity: 6,000
Year Built: 1932   **Architect:** Raymond Hood   **Cost:** $250,000,000
Year Remodeled: 1980
Acoustical Consultant: Donald Deskey
Contact for Rental: Nancy De Sotto;   (212) 632-4000
Resident Groups: The Rockettes; Radio City Music Hall Orchestra
Radio City Music Hall has been designated a National Historic Landmark. The indicated original construction cost shown above constitutes the original construction cost of the Music Hall plus the cost for construction of the remaining buildings in the complex built concurrently. These buildings, along with subsequent additions over the years, are now known as Rockefeller Center.

ROYALE THEATRE
242 West 45th Street, New York, NY 10036
(212) 239-6200
Type of Facility: Theatre House
Type of Stage: Proscenium   **Orchestra Pit**
Seating Capacity: 1,058
Year Built: 1927   **Architect:** Herbert J. Krapp
Contact for Rental: Philip Smith;   (212) 944-3710

SAINT CLEMENT'S CHURCH
423 West 46th Street, New York, NY 10036
(212) 246-7277
FAX: (212) 246-7278
Type of Facility: Concert Hall; Auditorium; Off Broadway; Theatre House; Church Sanctuary
Facility Originally: Church
Type of Stage: Thrust; Flexible

Stage Dimensions: 45'x45'
Seating Capacity: 151
Year Built: 1830
Year Remodeled: 1989
Contact for Rental: Douglas Williams;   (212) 246-7277
Resident Groups: Theatre for a New Audience; Pan-Asian Repertory

SAINT JAMES THEATER
246 West 44th Street, New York, NY 10036
(212) 239-6200
Type of Facility: Theatre House
Type of Stage: Proscenium   **Orchestra Pit**
Seating Capacity: 1,644
Year Built: 1927   **Architect:** Warren and Wetmore
Contact for Rental: Jujamcyn Theaters;   (212) 840-8181

SHUBERT THEATRE
225 West 45th Street, New York, NY 10036
(212) 239-6200
Type of Facility: Theatre House
Type of Stage: Proscenium   **Orchestra Pit**
Seating Capacity: 1,483
Year Built: 1913   **Architect:** Henry B. Harris
Contact for Rental: Philip Smith;   (212) 944-3710
Manager: Shubert Organization;   (212) 944-3700

SOHO REP
524 West 57th Street, Building 533/1, New York, NY 10019
(212) 977-5955
Founded: 1974
Type of Facility: Theatre House; Off-Broadway
Type of Stage: Flexible
Stage Dimensions: 22'x28'
Seating Capacity: 75
Year Remodeled: 1991   **Architect:** Martin Holub
Contact for Rental: Julian Webber

STEVE MCGRAW'S
158 West 72nd Street, New York, NY 10023
(212) 595-7400
Founded: 1989
Type of Facility: Cabaret Theatre
Facility Originally: Small Supper Club
Type of Stage: Proscenium; Platform
Stage Dimensions: 19'Wx10'D
Seating Capacity: 135
Year Built: 1980
Year Remodeled: 1988   **Architect:** Al D'Avanzo   **Cost:** $400,000
Contact for Rental: Nancy McGraw;   (212) 595-7400
Resident Groups: Forever Plaid
Available for rental on a limited basis

SULLIVAN STREET PLAYHOUSE
181 Sullivan Street, New York, NY 10012
(212) 674-3838
Type of Facility: Off Broadway; Theatre House
Facility Originally: Nightclub
Type of Stage: 3/4 Arena
Seating Capacity: 155
Year Built: 1895
Year Remodeled: 1922
Contact for Rental: Jules Field;   (212) 674-3838
Resident Groups: The Fantasticks

THE SUPPER CLUB
240 West 47th Street, New York, NY 10036
(212) 921-1940
Type of Facility: Supper Club

Facility Originally: Edison Hotel Ballroom
Type of Stage: Flexible
Stage Dimensions: 44'x56'
Seating Capacity: 450
Year Built: 1960   **Architect:** Gehron & Seltzer
Year Remodeled: 1991   **Architect:** Robert Couturier
Contact for Rental: Lionel Casseroux, Armando Rivera;   (212) 921-1940
Manager: Rick Wahlstedt, General Manager

UNIVERSITY SETTLEMENT
184 Eldridge Street, New York, NY 10002
(212) 674-9120, ext. 183
FAX: (212) 475-3278
Type of Facility: Studio Performance; Multi-Purpose; Room
Type of Stage: Flexible
Stage Dimensions: 1,900 square feet studio space (no obstructions)
Seating Capacity: 120
Contact for Rental: Jeff Lependorf;   (212) 674-9120, ext. 183

VILLAGE GATE
160 Bleecker Street, New York, NY 10012
(212) 475-5120
FAX: (212) 982-3490
Type of Facility: Theatre Complex; Concert Hall; Performance Center; Off Broadway; Theatre House; Multi-Purpose;
Room
Facility Originally: Hotel & Meeting Rooms
Type of Stage: Thrust; Flexible; 3/4 Arena
Seating Capacity: 855
Year Built: 1898
Year Remodeled: 1972   **Architect:** Max Vogel
Manager: Arthur D'Lugoff
Available for rent

VIRGINIA THEATER
245 West 52nd Street, New York, NY 10019
(212) 840-8181
Type of Facility: Theatre House
Type of Stage: Proscenium
Orchestra Pit
Seating Capacity: 1,260
Year Built: 1925   **Architect:** Crane, Franzheim & Bettis
Contact for Rental: Jujamcyn Theaters;   (212) 840-8181

WALTER KERR THEATRE
219 West 48th Street, New York, NY 10036
Type of Facility: Theatre House
Type of Stage: Proscenium   **Orchestra Pit**
Seating Capacity: 954
Year Built: 1921   **Architect:** Herbert J. Krapp
Contact for Rental: Jujamcyn Theaters;   (212) 840-8181

WESTBETH THEATRE CENTER
151 Bank Street, New York, NY 10014
(212) 691-2272
Type of Facility: Theatre Complex; Performance Center; Off Broadway; Theatre House
Facility Originally: Bell Labs Sound Stage
Year Built: 1900
Year Remodeled: 1977   **Architect:** David Chapman   **Cost:** $150,000
Contact for Rental: Arnold Engelman;   (212) 691-2272
*The Theatre Center contains the Big Room, Second Floor Theatre and Studio Theatre. See separate listings for additional
information.*

WESTBETH THEATRE CENTER - BIG ROOM
151 Bank Street, New York, NY 10014
(212) 691-2272
Type of Facility: Theatre House
Type of Stage: Proscenium
Stage Dimensions: 32'x48'

Seating Capacity: 125
Contact for Rental: Arnold Engelman;   (212) 691-2272

WESTBETH THEATRE CENTER - SECOND FLOOR THEATRE
151 Bank Street, New York, NY 10014
(212) 691-2272
    Type of Facility: Theatre House
    Type of Stage: Proscenium
    Stage Dimensions: 22'x30'
    Seating Capacity: 70
    Contact for Rental: Arnold Engelman;   (212) 691-2272

WESTBETH THEATRE CENTER - STUDIO THEATRE
151 Bank Street, New York, NY 10014
(212) 691-2272
    Type of Facility: Theatre House
    Type of Stage: Proscenium
    Stage Dimensions: 25'x30'
    Seating Capacity: 90
    Contact for Rental: Arnold Engelman;   (212) 691-2272

WESTSIDE ARTS THEATRE
407 West 43rd Street, New York, NY 10036
(212) 315-2302; (212) 315-2244
FAX: (212) 315-2307
    Founded: 1991
    Type of Facility: Theatre Complex; Performance Center; Off-Broadway; Two-Stage Theatre Complex
    Facility Originally: Church
    Type of Stage: Thrust; Proscenium
    Stage Dimensions: Stage 1 (modified thrust) - 40'x18'; Stage 2 - 40'x26'6"
    Seating Capacity: 299; 250
    Year Built: 1889   **Architect:** Henry F. Kilburn   **Cost:** $25,000
    Year Remodeled: 1991   **Architect:** Roger Morgan Studios, Designer   **Cost:** $1,200,000
    Acoustical Consultant: Masque Sound; Jaffe Acoustics
    Contact for Rental: Terry Byrne;   (212) 315-2302
    Manager: Peter Askin, Director;   (212) 315-2302
    Built originally as the Second Baptist Church, the building, remodeled as a theatre in 1973, became the Westside Theatre
    in 1991 after extensive restoration.

WINTER GARDEN THEATRE
1634 Broadway, New York, NY 10019
(212) 239-6200
    Type of Facility: Theatre House
    Type of Stage: Proscenium   **Orchestra Pit**
    Seating Capacity: 1,503
    Year Built: 1911
    Architect: William A. Swasey
    Contact for Rental: Philip Smith;   (212) 944-3710
    Manager: Shubert Organization

North Greece

PERFORMING SERIES

GREECE PERFORMING ARTS SOCIETY
PO Box 300, North Greece, NY 14515
(716) 227-5953
    Founded: 1972
    Arts Area: Vocal Music; Instrumental Music; Theater
    Status: Non-Profit
    Type: Sponsoring
    Purpose: To foster the development, in the community of Greece, of an appreciation for artistic and cultural activities,
    GPAS sponsors the Greece Symphony Orchestra, Greece Community Orchestra and Greece Choral Society & GPAS Sum-
    mer Theatre
    Management: William Coons, Program Coordinator
    Officers: Joanne Dennstedt, President; William Coons, Treasurer; Carol Coons, Secretary
    Paid Staff: 2   **Volunteer Staff:** 25
    Paid Artists: 7

Utilizes: Guest Artists
Budget: $1,000 - $50,000
Income Sources: Business/Corporate Donations; Box Office; Government Grants; Individual Donations

---
North Tonawanda
PERFORMING SERIES

HERSHELL CARROUSEL FACTORY MUSEUM
180 Thompson Street, PO Box 672, North Tonawanda, NY 14120
(716) 693-1885
Founded: 1983
Arts Area: Dance; Vocal Music; Instrumental Music; Theater; Festivals
Status: Professional; Semi-Professional; Non-Profit
Type: Sponsoring; Museum
Purpose: Family-oriented entertainment in a carousel museum setting
Management: Elizabeth Brick, Director; Trent Turlock, Education Coordinator
Officers: Raphaelle A. Proefrock, President; Douglas A. Bathke, Vice President; Albert Baked, Secretary; Philip Lockman, Treasurer
Paid Staff: 4   **Volunteer Staff:** 70
Paid Artists: 12   **Non-Paid Artists:** 10
Budget: $1,000 - $50,000
Income Sources: Private Foundations/Grants/Endowments; Box Office
Season: June - September   **Annual Attendance:** 2,000
Affiliations: New York State Council of Arts

Northport
DANCE

POSEY DANCE EDUCATION SERVICE
PO Box 254, Northport, NY 11768
(516) 757-2700; (212) 966-8658
Founded: 1953
Arts Area: Modern; Ballet; Jazz
Status: Professional; Non-Profit
Type: Performing; Touring; Educational
Purpose: Education
Management: Elsa Posey, Artistic Director; Donna Brady, Managing Director
Paid Artists: 12
Utilizes: Guest Artists; Guest Choreographers
Budget: $50,000 - $100,000
Income Sources: Private Foundations/Grants/Endowments; Business/Corporate Donations; Box Office; Government Grants; Individual Donations
Season: September - June   **Annual Attendance:** 1,400
Affiliations: American Dance Guild

FACILITY

POSEY SCHOOL OF DANCE
57 Main Street, PO Box 254, Northport, NY 11768
(516) 757-2700
Founded: 1953
Type of Facility: Studio Performance
Facility Originally: Meeting Hall; Ballroom
Type of Stage: 3/4 Arena
Stage Dimensions: 20'x25'
Seating Capacity: 125
Year Built: 1891
Year Remodeled: 1992   **Architect:** Bob Ruege   **Cost:** $4,000
Contact for Rental: Elsa Posey, Director;   (516) 757-2700
Resident Groups: Posey Dance Company; Posey School of Dance

Nyack

DANCE

DEBRA WEISS DANCE COMPANY
51 Summit Street, Nyack, NY 10960
(914) 353-3860
> **Founded:** 1983
> **Arts Area:** Modern; Ethnic; Historical Dance Drama
> **Status:** Professional; Non-Profit
> **Type:** Performing; Touring; Resident; Educational
> **Management:** Debra Weiss, Artistic Director/President
> **Officers:** Eric Bender, Treasurer
> **Paid Staff:** 1   **Volunteer Staff:** 4
> **Paid Artists:** 4
> **Utilizes:** Guest Artists
> **Budget:** $1,000 - $50,000
> **Income Sources:** Private Foundations/Grants/Endowments; Business/Corporate Donations; Box Office; Government Grants; Individual Donations
> **Season:** 52 Weeks   **Annual Attendance:** 8,000

THEATRE

ELMWOOD PLAYHOUSE
16 Park Street, Nyack, NY 10960
(914) 353-1313
> **Founded:** 1946
> **Arts Area:** Community
> **Status:** Non-Professional; Non-Profit
> **Type:** Performing; Educational
> **Officers:** Maggie Klappas, President; Candy Pittari, Vice President
> **Budget:** $50,000 - $100,000
> **Income Sources:** Box Office; Individual Donations
> **Season:** September - June   **Annual Attendance:** 8,000
> **Affiliations:** Art Council of Rockland County
> **Performance Facilities:** Elmwood Playhouse

Ogdensburg

THEATRE

OGDENSBURG COMMAND PERFORMANCES
PO Box 322, Ogdensburg, NY 13669
(315) 393-2323
> **Founded:** 1962
> **Arts Area:** Professional; Musical
> **Status:** Non-Profit
> **Type:** Sponsoring
> **Purpose:** To present drama, music, and other theatrical productions for the stimulation, inspiration, and enjoyment of the citizens of Ogdensburg and the surrounding North Country Area
> **Officers:** Sally Palao, President; Mary Jane Wilson, Executive Vice President; Cynthia Wilson, Administrative Vice President; Terry Rhinehold, Recording Secretary; Nancy Siegel, Corresponding Secretary; Betty Simms, Treasurer
> **Volunteer Staff:** 60
> **Utilizes:** Guest Artists
> **Budget:** $50,000 - $100,000
> **Income Sources:** Private Foundations/Grants/Endowments; Business/Corporate Donations; Box Office; Government Grants; Individual Donations
> **Season:** October - May   **Annual Attendance:** 4,000
> **Performance Facilities:** George Hall Auditorium, Ogdensburg Free Academy

---
Old Forge

FACILITY

ARTS CENTER/OLD FORGE
Route 28, Old Forge, NY 13420
> **Founded:** 1952

Type of Facility: Multi-Purpose
Facility Originally: Warehouse
Type of Stage: No stage-concrete floor
Seating Capacity: 250
Year Remodeled: 1974

Oneonta

INSTRUMENTAL MUSIC

CATSKILL SYMPHONY ORCHESTRA
PO Box 14, Oneonta, NY 13820
(607) 432-6670
> **Founded:** 1972
> **Arts Area:** Symphony; Orchestra
> **Status:** Professional; Non-Profit
> **Type:** Performing; Educational
> **Purpose:** To bring quality music to the immediate and outlying areas of central New York State
> **Management:** Deborah Wolfanger, General Manager; Charles England, Personnel Manager
> **Officers:** Ciara Markuson, President; Rita Brown, Vice President; Allan Cleinman, Treasurer; Mary Ann Mazarak, Secretary
> **Paid Staff:** 4
> **Paid Artists:** 75   **Non-Paid Artists:** 7
> **Utilizes:** Guest Artists
> **Budget:** $100,000 - $500,000
> **Income Sources:** Private Foundations/Grants/Endowments; Business/Corporate Donations; Box Office; Government Grants; Individual Donations
> **Season:** September - April   **Annual Attendance:** 2,000
> **Performance Facilities:** Hunt Union, State University of New York-Oneonta

PERFORMING SERIES

FESTIVAL OF THE ARTS
248 Main Street, Upper Catskill Community Council of the Arts, Oneonta, NY 13820
(607) 432-2070
> **Founded:** 1969
> **Arts Area:** Dance; Vocal Music; Instrumental Music; Theater; Festivals
> **Status:** Professional; Non-Profit
> **Type:** Educational; Sponsoring
> **Management:** Pamela Cooley, Director
> **Paid Staff:** 5   **Volunteer Staff:** 125
> **Paid Artists:** 300
> **Utilizes:** Guest Conductors; Guest Artists
> **Budget:** $50,000 - $100,000
> **Income Sources:** Private Foundations/Grants/Endowments; Business/Corporate Donations; Box Office; Government Grants; Individual Donations
> **Season:** September - July   **Annual Attendance:** 10,000
> **Affiliations:** State University of New York-Oneonta
> **Performance Facilities:** Slade Auditorium; Anderson Theater

UPPER CATSKILL COMMUNITY COUNCIL OF THE ARTS
248 Main Street, Oneonta, NY 13820
(607) 432-2070
> **Founded:** 1970
> **Arts Area:** Dance; Vocal Music; Theater
> **Status:** Professional; Non-Professional; Non-Profit
> **Type:** Educational; Sponsoring
> **Purpose:** As a community service arts agency, we sponsor community performances and coordinate elementary and secondary school performances
> **Management:** Pamela Cooley, Executive Director; Elissa Kane, Associate Director
> **Officers:** Katherine Dailey, President; Margaret Hathaway, Vice President
> **Paid Staff:** 4   **Volunteer Staff:** 75
> **Utilizes:** Guest Artists
> **Budget:** $100,000 - $500,000
> **Income Sources:** Private Foundations/Grants/Endowments; Business/Corporate Donations; Box Office; Government Grants; Individual Donations
> **Season:** 52 Weeks

Ossining

DANCE

WESTCHESTER BALLET COMPANY
2 Dale Avenue, Ossining, NY 10562
(914) 941-4532
Founded: 1954
Arts Area: Ballet
Status: Professional; Semi-Professional; Non-Professional; Non-Profit
Type: Performing; Educational
Purpose: To provide high-quality ballet training; to be an integral part of the community
Management: Jean Logrea, Artistic Director
Officers: Beth Fritz Logrea, President; Dennis Cole, Vice President; Jane Truebig, Secretary; Jaime Rich, Treasurer
Volunteer Staff: 20
Paid Artists: 8   **Non-Paid Artists:** 70
Utilizes: Special Technical Talent; Guest Artists
Budget: $1,000 - $50,000
Income Sources: Private Foundations/Grants/Endowments; Business/Corporate Donations; Box Office; Individual Donations
Season: September - May   **Annual Attendance:** 2,000
Performance Facilities: Marymount College, Tarrytown

Oyster Bay

DANCE

OYSTER BAY CONTEMPORARY BALLET
PO Box 374, Oyster Bay, NY 11771
(516) 549-0025
Founded: 1981
Arts Area: Ballet; Jazz
Status: Professional; Non-Profit
Type: Performing
Purpose: Contemporary Ballet Company was formed by a group of dedicated dance professionals motivated by the strong belief in dance as a creative performing art. Its primary goal is to communicate this interest in dance and to widen appreciation among the audiences of Long Island.
Management: Regina Collins, Artistic Director; Diane Bellas, General Manager
Officers: Regina Collins, President; Diane Bellas, Secretary
Paid Artists: 9
Budget: $1,000 - $50,000
Income Sources: Box Office; Government Grants; Individual Donations
Season: May - August   **Annual Attendance:** 3,000

Pawling

DANCE

JOSE MOLINA BAILES ESPANOLES
Arthur Shafman International Limited, PO Box 352, Pawling, NY 12564
(914) 855-3005
FAX: (914) 855-3167
Founded: 1962
Arts Area: Ethnic
Status: Professional; Commercial
Type: Performing; Touring
Purpose: To present American audiences with the best of all styles of Spanish dance
Management: Arthur Shafman, International Limited; Jose Molina, Artistic Director
Paid Staff: 1
Paid Artists: 8
Utilizes: Guest Artists
Budget: $100,000 - $500,000
Income Sources: Box Office
Season: September - June

THEATRE FANTASTIQUE
c/o Arthur Shafman International Ltd., PO Box 352, Pawling, NY 12564
(914) 855-3005
FAX: (914) 855-3167
    Founded: 1984
    Arts Area: Mime
    Status: Professional; Commercial
    Type: Performing; Touring; Resident; Educational; Sponsoring
    Management: Richard Zachary, Director
    Officers: Arthur Shafman, President
    Paid Staff: 4
    Paid Artists: 5
    Utilizes: Special Technical Talent
    Budget: $100,000 - $500,000
    Income Sources: Box Office; Performance Fees
    Season: September - April   **Annual Attendance:** 125,000

THEATRE

IMAGO, THE THEATRE MASK ENSEMBLE
PO Box 352, Pawling, NY 12564
(914) 855-3005
FAX: (914) 855-3167
    Founded: 1981
    Arts Area: Professional; Summer Stock; Community; Theatrical Group
    Status: Professional
    Type: Performing; Touring; Resident; Educational
    Purpose: To present their special art form to audiences
    Management: Carol Uselman, Jerry Mouwad, Artistic Directors
    Officers: Arthur Shafman, President
    Utilizes: Special Technical Talent
    Budget: $100,000 - $500,000
    Income Sources: Private Foundations/Grants/Endowments; Business/Corporate Donations; Box Office; Government Grants; Individual Donations; Earned Fees
    Annual Attendance: 200,000
    Affiliations: Westaff Touring Program; North Carolina Touring Program; Arts Midwest; Performing Arts Touring Program of Oregon

PERFORMING SERIES

PAWLING CONCERT SERIES
300 Route 22, Pawling, NY 12564
(914) 855-3100
    Founded: 1973
    Arts Area: Vocal Music; Instrumental Music
    Status: Non-Profit
    Type: Sponsoring; Presenting
    Purpose: To bring excellent quality live classical, folk and jazz music to the area
    Budget: $1,000 - $50,000
    Income Sources: Private Foundations/Grants/Endowments; Individual Donations
    Season: October - May   **Annual Attendance:** 1,200

Pearl River

DANCE

PAT CANNON FOOT AND FIDDLE DANCE COMPANY
164 Prospect Place, Pearl River, NY 10965
(914) 735-8951
FAX: (914) 735-1431
    Founded: 1981
    Arts Area: Tap; Clogging
    Status: Professional; Non-Profit
    Type: Performing; Touring; Resident; Educational
    Purpose: To present a blend of clogging, square dance and tap dance; to perform folk material with tap technique
    Officers: Pat Cannon, Artistic Director
    Volunteer Staff: 2

Non-Paid Artists: 12
Budget: $100,000 - $500,000
Income Sources: Private Foundations/Grants/Endowments; Contracted Services
Season: 52 Weeks

Peekskill

FACILITY

PARAMOUNT CENTER FOR THE ARTS
1008 Brown Street, Peekskill, NY 10990
(914) 739-2333
Founded: 1980
Type of Facility: Performance Center
Facility Originally: Movie House
Type of Stage: Proscenium
Stage Dimensions: 40'Wx36'D
Seating Capacity: 1,025
Year Built: 1930   **Architect:** Rapp & Rapp
Year Remodeled: 1986   **Architect:** Battaglia & Seckler   **Cost:** $100,000
Contact for Rental: Mark Hough;   (914) 739-2333
Resident Groups: Orpheus Chamber Orchestra; Taghkanic Chorale; Philharmonia Virtuosi

Penn Yan

PERFORMING SERIES

YATES PERFORMING ARTS SERIES
PO Box 503, Penn Yan, NY 14527
(315) 536-2095
Founded: 1972
Arts Area: Dance; Vocal Music; Instrumental Music; Festivals; Lyric Opera
Status: Professional; Non-Professional; Non-Profit
Type: Performing; Touring
Purpose: To supply entertainment to the residents of Yates County
Officers: Sylvia Eisenhart, President; Emily Seager, Vice President; Linda Dofy, Secretary; Engelke Heggis, Treasurer
Volunteer Staff: 25
Paid Artists: 5
Budget: $1,000 - $50,000
Income Sources: Business/Corporate Donations; Box Office; Government Grants; Individual Donations; Season Tickets
Season: September - May   **Annual Attendance:** 2,000
Performance Facilities: Penn Yan Academy

Plainview

PERFORMING SERIES

UNITED JEWISH YS OF LONG ISLAND
55 Manetto Hill Road, Plainview, NY 11803
(516) 938-4600
FAX: (516) 938-3006
Founded: 1973
Arts Area: Dance; Vocal Music; Instrumental Music; Theater; Festivals; Lyric Opera
Status: Professional; Non-Profit
Type: Performing; Sponsoring
Purpose: International Jewish Arts Festival of Long Island and the Grand Performance Series provide unique cultural experiences unattainable elsewhere on Long Island
Management: Rea Jacobs, Director, Cultural Arts
Officers: Arthur M. Katz, President; Sidney N. Soloman, Chairman of the Board; Alfred W. Levy, Chairman of the Executive Board; Kenneth J. Gabel, Executive Vice President; Martin Eglow, Vice President
Paid Staff: 12   **Volunteer Staff:** 500
Paid Artists: 105
Utilizes: Special Technical Talent; Guest Conductors; Guest Artists
Budget: $500,000 - $1,000,000
Income Sources: Private Foundations/Grants/Endowments; Business/Corporate Donations; Box Office; Government Grants; Individual Donations; Rentals

Season: September - April   **Annual Attendance:** 45,000
Affiliations: ISPAA; APAP

Port Jefferson

THEATRE

THEATRE THREE PRODUCTIONS
412 Main Street, PO Box 512, Port Jefferson, NY 11777
(516) 928-9202
Founded: 1969
Arts Area: Professional; Musical; Theatrical Group
Status: Professional; Non-Profit
Type: Performing; Touring; Resident; Educational
Purpose: To produce the finest in professional theatre on central Long Island and Suffolk County in Port Jefferson
Management: Bradlee Bing, Executive Artistic Director; Jeffrey Sanzel, Associate Artistic Director
Paid Staff: 9   **Volunteer Staff:** 4
Paid Artists: 100
Utilizes: Special Technical Talent; Guest Artists; Guest Directors
Budget: $500,000 - $1,000,000
Income Sources: Private Foundations/Grants/Endowments; Business/Corporate Donations; Box Office; Government Grants; Individual Donations
Season: July - June   **Annual Attendance:** 70,000
Affiliations: Port Jefferson Arts Council

FACILITY

THEATRE THREE PRODUCTIONS - MAINSTAGE
412 Main Street, PO Box 512, Port Jefferson, NY 11777
(516) 928-9202
Type of Facility: Theatre House
Facility Originally: Vaudeville
Type of Stage: Thrust
Seating Capacity: 473
Year Built: 1875
Contact for Rental: Sharon Greenstone;   (516) 928-9202
A $3,000,000 renovation beginning in 1992.

THEATRE THREE PRODUCTIONS - SECOND STAGE
412 Main Street, PO Box 512, Port Jefferson, NY 11777
(516) 928-9202
Type of Facility: Theatre House
Type of Stage: 3/4 Arena
Seating Capacity: 154
Year Remodeled: 1987   **Cost:** $100,000
Contact for Rental: Sharon Greenstone;   (516) 928-9202
A $3,000,000 renovation beginning in 1992

Poughkeepsie

DANCE

POUGHKEEPSIE CIVIC BALLET
6 Raymond Avenue, Poughkeepsie, NY 12603
(914) 452-3055
Founded: 1968
Arts Area: Ballet; Jazz
Status: Non-Profit
Type: Resident
Management: Roya Curie, Artistic Director
Paid Artists: 10
Income Sources: Box Office; Individual Donations
Season: 52 Weeks
Performance Facilities: Marist College Theater

INSTRUMENTAL MUSIC

HUDSON VALLEY PHILHARMONIC
129 North Water Street, PO Box 191, Poughkeepsie, NY 12602
(914) 454-1222
Founded: 1959
Arts Area: Symphony; Orchestra; Chamber
Status: Professional
Type: Performing; Resident; Sponsoring
Purpose: To sponsor and support a professional symphony orchestra which will present performances of the highest artistic quality and promote the musical growth of the region
Management: Randall Fleischer, Musical Director; Babette Schmidt, General Manager
Officers: Hamilton Meserve, President; Henry Peters, Vice President; Andrea Simon, Treasurer; Ziva Dahl, Secretary
Paid Staff: 8   **Volunteer Staff:** 2
Paid Artists: 80
Utilizes: Guest Artists
Budget: $500,000 - $1,000,000
Income Sources: Private Foundations/Grants/Endowments; Business/Corporate Donations; Box Office; Government Grants; Individual Donations
Season: September - May   **Annual Attendance:** 200,000
Affiliations: ASOL; ASCAP; BMI
Performance Facilities: Ulster Performing Arts Center; Bardavon 1869 Opera House; Paramount Theatre, Vassar College

THEATRE

NEW DAY REPERTORY COMPANY, INC.
12 Vassar Street, PO Box 269, Poughkeepsie, NY 12601
(914) 485-7399
Founded: 1963
Arts Area: Professional; Community
Status: Professional; Non-Profit
Type: Performing; Touring; Resident; Educational
Purpose: To promote the arts and culture through theatre; to enhance the quality of life and leisure for all within our sphere, regardless of race or creed
Management: Rodney K. Douglas, Producer/Artistic Director
Officers: Noel Tepper, Chairman; Janet Nicodemus, Treasurer; Rodney K. Douglas, President; Olive Douglas, Vice President
Paid Staff: 3   **Volunteer Staff:** 3
Utilizes: Guest Artists; Guest Directors
Budget: $100,000 - $500,000
Income Sources: Private Foundations/Grants/Endowments; Business/Corporate Donations; Box Office; Government Grants; Individual Donations; Fund-raising
Season: 52 Weeks   **Annual Attendance:** 15,000
Performance Facilities: Vassar Institute Theatre

FACILITY

BARDAVON 1869 OPERA HOUSE
35 Market Street, Poughkeepsie, NY 12601
(914) 473-5288
FAX: (914) 473-4259
Founded: 1976
Type of Facility: Concert Hall; Auditorium; Performance Center; Theatre House; Opera House
Type of Stage: Proscenium
Stage Dimensions: 34'Wx24'D and thrust   **Orchestra Pit**
Seating Capacity: 944
Year Built: 1869   **Architect:** James S. Post   **Cost:** $50,000
Year Remodeled: 1976   **Cost:** $1,600,000
Contact for Rental: Lucia S. Edgcomb, Managing Director, Theatre Operations;   (914) 473-5288
Manager: Barbara Hauptman, Executive Director;   (914) 473-5288
Resident Groups: Hudson Valley Philharmonic
Box Office (914) 473-2072

MID-HUDSON CIVIC CENTER
14 Civic Center Plaza, Poughkeepsie, NY 12601
(914) 454-9800
FAX: (914) 454-5877
Type of Facility: Concert Hall; Auditorium; Civic Center; Multi-Purpose

Type of Stage: Proscenium
Stage Dimensions: 70'x32'
Seating Capacity: 3,050
Year Built: 1976
Contact for Rental: Cathy Vodrazka;   (914) 454-9800

Purchase

FACILITY

STATE UNIVERSITY OF NEW YORK-PURCHASE - PERFORMING ARTS CENTER
735 Anderson Hill Road, Purchase, NY 10577
(914) 251-6222
   Type of Facility: Performance Center
   Year Built: 1978   **Architect:** Edward Larabee Barnes   **Cost:** $35,000,000
   Acoustical Consultant: Bolt, Beranek & Newman
   Contact for Rental: Steve Grober;   (914) 253-5949
   Resident Groups: State University of New York-Purchase Music, Theater and Dance Departments
   The Performing Arts Center contains Theaters A, B, C and D. See separate listings for additional information.

STATE UNIVERSITY OF NEW YORK-PURCHASE - THEATER A
735 Anderson Hill Road, Purchase, NY 10577
(914) 251-6222
   Type of Facility: Concert Hall; Theatre House
   Type of Stage: Thrust; Flexible; Proscenium; Hydraulic Lift Stage
   Stage Dimensions: 9"Dx76'3"H; 53'10"H proscenium opening
   Orchestra Pit
   Seating Capacity: 1,372
   Year Built: 1978
   Contact for Rental: Steve Grober;   (914) 253-5949

STATE UNIVERSITY OF NEW YORK-PURCHASE - THEATRE B
735 Anderson Hill Road, Purchase, NY 10577
(914) 251-6222
   Type of Facility: Concert Hall; Theatre House
   Type of Stage: Proscenium; Hydraulic Lift Stage
   Stage Dimensions: 95'7"Wx43'10"Dx68'H; 54'9"Wx28'H proscenium opening
   Orchestra Pit
   Seating Capacity: 673
   Year Built: 1978
   Contact for Rental: Steve Grober;   (914) 253-5949

STATE UNIVERSITY OF NEW YORK-PURCHASE - THEATRE C
735 Anderson Hill Road, Purchase, NY 10577
(914) 251-6222
   Type of Facility: Concert Hall; Theatre House
   Type of Stage: Proscenium
   Stage Dimensions: 3'11"Dx67'6"H; 44'8"Wx30'H proscenium opening
   Seating Capacity: 476
   Year Built: 1978
   Contact for Rental: Steve Grober;   (914) 253-5949

STATE UNIVERSITY OF NEW YORK-PURCHASE - THEATRE D
735 Anderson Hill Road, Purchase, NY 10577
(914) 251-6222
   Type of Facility: Theatre House
   Type of Stage: Flexible
   Stage Dimensions: 82'8"Dx34'H
   Seating Capacity: 500
   Year Built: 1978
   Contact for Rental: Steve Grober;   (914) 253-5949

Rego Park

INSTRUMENTAL MUSIC

QUEENS SYMPHONY ORCHESTRA
99-11 Queens Boulevard, Rego Park, NY 11374
(718) 275-5000
FAX: (718) 261-5224
Founded: 1953
Arts Area: Symphony
Status: Professional; Non-Profit
Type: Performing
Management: Ellen Young, Executive Director; John Harmon, Box Office Manager
Paid Staff: 7   **Volunteer Staff:** 7
Paid Artists: 78
Utilizes: Guest Conductors; Guest Artists; Guest Directors
Budget: $500,000 - $1,000,000
Income Sources: Private Foundations/Grants/Endowments; Business/Corporate Donations; Box Office; Government Grants; Individual Donations
Season: October - August   **Annual Attendance:** 125,000
Affiliations: ASOL
Performance Facilities: Colden Center for the Arts, Queens College

---

Rochester

DANCE

GARTH FAGAN DANCE
50 Chestnut Street, Rochester, NY 14604
(716) 454-3260
FAX: (716) 454-6191
Founded: 1970
Arts Area: Modern; Ethnic
Status: Professional; Non-Profit
Type: Performing; Touring; Resident; Educational
Purpose: A modern dance company that is highly competitive on a national level. The original choreography by Garth Fagan offers a blend of modern dance and Black culture.
Management: Garth Fagan, Founder/Artistic Director; Cynthia C. Wassell, General Manager
Officers: Garth Fagan, President; Nancy D. Peck Esq., Chair of the Board; Deborah Runner Esq., Vice Chair of the Board; Jesse Dudley, Joseph Bonvissoto, Vice Chairs; Patricia D. Baker, Treasurer; Philip Silver, Secretary
Paid Staff: 6
Paid Artists: 17
Budget: $1,000,000 - $5,000,000
Income Sources: Private Foundations/Grants/Endowments; Business/Corporate Donations; Box Office; Government Grants; Individual Donations
Annual Attendance: 5,000
Performance Facilities: Nazareth Arts Center

INSTRUMENTAL MUSIC

GREECE SYMPHONY ORCHESTRA
950 East Avenue, Rochester, NY 14607
(716) 473-6711
Founded: 1968
Arts Area: Orchestra
Status: Semi-Professional; Non-Profit
Type: Performing; Sponsoring
Purpose: To enhance the cultural life of Greece and the surrounding area through free concerts and other performances; to sponsor young artists competition through local schools
Management: David Fetler, Director
Non-Paid Artists: 65
Utilizes: Guest Artists
Budget: $1,000 - $50,000
Income Sources: Government Grants; Individual Donations
Season: October - May   **Annual Attendance:** 1,000
Affiliations: Greece (NY) Performing Arts Society

ROCHESTER CHAMBER ORCHESTRA
950 East Avenue, Rochester, NY 14607
(716) 473-6711
> **Founded:** 1964
> **Arts Area:** Orchestra
> **Status:** Professional; Non-Profit
> **Type:** Performing; Sponsoring
> **Purpose:** To offer the Rochester community an outstanding music repertoire from the 17th century to the present for chamber orchestra; to present newly commissioned works
> **Management:** David Fetler, Director
> **Officers:** Betty Allman, President
> **Volunteer Staff:** 16
> **Paid Artists:** 40
> **Utilizes:** Guest Artists
> **Budget:** $1,000 - $50,000
> **Income Sources:** Business/Corporate Donations; Box Office; Government Grants; Individual Donations
> **Season:** October - May   **Annual Attendance:** 44,000
> **Performance Facilities:** Asbury First Methodist Church

ROCHESTER PHILHARMONIC ORCHESTRA
108 East Avenue, Rochester, NY 14604
(716) 454-2620
> **Founded:** 1922
> **Arts Area:** Symphony
> **Status:** Professional; Non-Profit
> **Type:** Performing; Sponsoring
> **Purpose:** Presentation of Rochester Philharmonic Orchestra and other events for the area community
> **Officers:** Carl J. Atkins, President/Chief Executive Officer
> **Paid Staff:** 30   **Volunteer Staff:** 1,000
> **Utilizes:** Guest Conductors; Guest Artists
> **Budget:** $5,000,000 - $10,000,000
> **Income Sources:** Private Foundations/Grants/Endowments; Business/Corporate Donations; Box Office; Government Grants; Individual Donations
> **Season:** 52 Weeks   **Annual Attendance:** 250,000
> **Performance Facilities:** Eastman Theatre; Finger Lakes Performing Arts Center

THEATRE

GEVA THEATRE
75 Woodbury Boulevard, Rochester, NY 14607
(716) 232-1366
FAX: (716) 232-4031
> **Founded:** 1973
> **Arts Area:** Professional; Musical; Theatrical Group
> **Status:** Professional; Non-Profit
> **Type:** Performing; Resident; Educational
> **Management:** Howard Millman, Producing Director; Anthony Zerbe, Artistic Director; Ann Patrice Carrigan, Literary Director; Timothy Shields, Managing Director
> **Officers:** Linda Cornell Weinstein, Chairman
> **Paid Staff:** 50
> **Paid Artists:** 70
> **Utilizes:** Special Technical Talent; Guest Artists; Guest Directors
> **Budget:** $1,000,000 - $5,000,000
> **Income Sources:** Private Foundations/Grants/Endowments; Business/Corporate Donations; Box Office; Government Grants; Individual Donations
> **Season:** September - July   **Annual Attendance:** 120,000
> **Affiliations:** TCG; AAA; LORT
> **Performance Facilities:** Richard Pine Theatre; Elaine Wilson Theatre

THEATRE ON THE RIDGE
200 Ridge Road West, Building 28, Rochester, NY 14652-3211
(716) 477-7519
FAX: (716) 477-8041
> **Arts Area:** Professional; Musical; Dinner; Community
> **Status:** Professional; Commercial
> **Type:** Performing; Resident; Sponsoring
> **Purpose:** To provide entertainment to Eastman Kodak Company and the local community
> **Management:** David R. Dunn, Manager

Paid Staff: 7   **Volunteer Staff:** 1,000
Utilizes: Guest Artists
Income Sources: Business/Corporate Donations; Box Office
Season: 52 Weeks

PERFORMING SERIES

KODACTORS
200 Ridge Road West, Rochester, NY 14652-3211
(716) 722-2402
FAX: (716) 477-8041
Founded: 1956
Arts Area: Dance; Vocal Music; Instrumental Music; Theater
Status: Non-Professional
Type: Performing
Purpose: To provide cultural outlet for members of Eastman Kodak Company, their families and friends
Management: Philip E. Roy, Artistic Director; Mary Agnes Alrutz-Roy, Musical Director; Kimm Leuhm Wesley, Dance Director
Volunteer Staff: 5
Non-Paid Artists: 25
Utilizes: Special Technical Talent
Budget: $1,000 - $50,000
Income Sources: Business/Corporate Donations; Box Office
Season: September - June   **Annual Attendance:** 10,000
Performance Facilities: Eastman Kodak Recreation Center Auditorium

NAZARETH COLLEGE ARTS CENTER
Nazareth College, 4245 East Avenue, Rochester, NY 14618-3790
(716) 586-2483
FAX: (716) 586-1284
Founded: 1967
Arts Area: Dance; Vocal Music; Instrumental Music; Theater
Status: Professional; Non-Profit
Type: Performing; Sponsoring
Purpose: To present a subscription series of professional performing artists and organizations for the benefit of Nazareth students and the community of Rochester
Management: Joseph F. Baranowski, Director of Programs; Dr. David M. Ferrell, Director
Officers: Fred E. Strauss, Chairman of the Board; Dr. Rose Marie Beston, President of the College
Paid Staff: 7   **Volunteer Staff:** 50
Utilizes: Guest Artists
Budget: $100,000 - $500,000
Income Sources: Box Office; Government Grants
Season: September - May   **Annual Attendance:** 15,000
Affiliations: APAP
Performance Facilities: Nazareth College Arts Center

THE QUARTET PROGRAM
1163 East Avenue, Rochester, NY 14607
(716) 274-1592
Founded: 1970
Arts Area: Instrumental Music
Status: Professional; Non-Profit
Type: Performing; Resident; Educational; Sponsoring
Officers: Charles Castleman, Artistic Director; Joseph Cunningham, Board Chairman
Paid Staff: 2
Non-Paid Artists: 42
Utilizes: Guest Artists
Budget: $100,000 - $500,000
Income Sources: Private Foundations/Grants/Endowments; Business/Corporate Donations; Box Office; Government Grants; Individual Donations
Season: June - August   **Annual Attendance:** 1,500
Performance Facilities: Fireman Performance Arts Center

UNIVERSITY OF ROCHESTER THEATRE PROGRAM
107 Todd Union, Rochester, NY 14627
(716) 275-4088
Founded: 1968
Arts Area: Theater

Status: Semi-Professional; Non-Profit
Type: Performing; Resident; Educational
Purpose: To provide a classical, contemporary and modern series of plays combined with a professional training program taught by the members of our company
Management: Maxim Kunin, Production Manager; Mervyn Willis, Artistic Director
Paid Staff: 4   **Volunteer Staff:** 160
Paid Artists: 16   **Non-Paid Artists:** 4
Utilizes: Special Technical Talent; Guest Artists; Guest Directors
Budget: $100,000 - $500,000
Income Sources: Box Office; Government Grants; Individual Donations
Season: September - May   **Annual Attendance:** 5,500
Performance Facilities: Black Box Theatre

FACILITY

AUDITORIUM CENTER
875 East Main Street, Rochester, NY 14605-2789
(716) 271-3250
FAX: (716) 423-9539
   Founded: 1989
   Type of Facility: Theatre Complex; Concert Hall; Auditorium; Performance Center; Off Broadway; Theatre House; Opera House
   Type of Stage: Proscenium
   Stage Dimensions: 96'Wx42'D   **Orchestra Pit**
   Seating Capacity: 2,541
   Year Built: 1929
   Contact for Rental: Daniel Black;   (716) 271-3250

EASTMAN SCHOOL OF MUSIC - KILBOURN HALL
26 Gibbs Street, Rochester, NY 14604
(716) 274-1110
   Type of Facility: Concert Hall
   Type of Stage: Proscenium   **Orchestra Pit**
   Seating Capacity: 459
   Year Built: 1921
   Year Remodeled: 1976
   Manager: Andrew E. Green
   Resident Groups: Eastman School of Music

NAZARETH COLLEGE - NAZARETH ARTS CENTER
4245 East Avenue, Rochester, NY 14618
(716) 586-2483
   Type of Facility: Theatre Complex; Concert Hall; Auditorium; Performance Center
   Type of Stage: Thrust
   Seating Capacity: 1,153
   Year Built: 1967   **Architect:** Giffels & Rossetti   **Cost:** $4,000,000
   Contact for Rental: Terry Meyer, Assistant Director;   (716) 586-2483
   Resident Groups: Nazareth College Theatre League

PYRAMID ARTS CENTER
274 North Goodman Street, Rochester, NY 14607
(716) 461-2222
FAX: (716) 442-2870
   Type of Facility: Theatre Complex; Auditorium; Studio Performance; Multi-Purpose
   Facility Originally: Warehouse
   Type of Stage: Flexible
   Seating Capacity: 200
   Year Remodeled: 1989
   Contact for Rental: Fredric Wagner;   (716) 461-2222

UNIVERSITY OF ROCHESTER-RIVER CAMPUS - STRONG AUDITORIUM
Rochester, NY 14627
(716) 275-2330
   Type of Facility: Auditorium
   Type of Stage: Proscenium   **Orchestra Pit**
   Seating Capacity: 1,100
   Year Built: 1921
   Manager: Brian Sickels

Resident Groups: University Music Groups
Limited availability

Rockaway Park

DANCE

THE PHYLLIS ROSE DANCE COMPANY
102-00 Shore Front Parkway, Suite 10P, Rockaway Park, NY 11694
(718) 474-1672; (914) 245-7163
Founded: 1969
Arts Area: Modern; Jazz; Ethnic; Folk; Novelty; Theatre
Status: Professional; Non-Profit
Type: Performing; Resident; Educational; Sponsoring
Purpose: To bring high quality multi-cultural dance and movement programs to audiences of all ages, with a special focus on young audiences
Management: Dance Vectors, Inc.; Phyllis Rose, Company Director; Phyllis Cohn, Agent/Program Coordinator
Officers: Phyllis Rose, President; Ivy Rosen, Secretary; Susan Cherniak, Treasurer
Paid Staff: 20 **Volunteer Staff:** 2
Paid Artists: 13
Utilizes: Special Technical Talent; Guest Artists; Guest Choreographers
Budget: $1,000 - $50,000
Income Sources: Business/Corporate Donations; Box Office; Government Grants; Individual Donations; Touring
Season: September 1 - June 30 **Annual Attendance:** 200
Performance Facilities: The Intimate Space Dance Theater

Rome

FACILITY

CAPITOL CIVIC CENTER
218 Liberty Plaza, Rome, NY 13440
(315) 337-6277
Type of Facility: Theatre House
Type of Stage: Proscenium
Stage Dimensions: 22'x4' **Orchestra Pit**
Seating Capacity: 1,750
Year Built: 1928 **Architect:** Lempert
Contact for Rental: Joseph Ferlo
Resident Groups: Summerstock Theatre

Rosendale

DANCE

THE VANAVER CARAVAN
140A Mountain Road, Rosendale, NY 12472
(914) 658-9748
FAX: (914) 255-3202
Founded: 1972
Arts Area: Modern; Ethnic; Folk
Status: Professional; Non-Profit
Type: Performing; Touring; Educational
Management: Arthur Shafman International Ltd., Tour Direction
Officers: Livia Vanaver; Julien Studley; Eileen Channer; Elizabeth Murphy; Joseph Esposito
Paid Staff: 3 **Volunteer Staff:** 10
Paid Artists: 14
Utilizes: Special Technical Talent; Guest Artists
Budget: $100,000 - $500,000
Income Sources: Private Foundations/Grants/Endowments; Business/Corporate Donations; Box Office; Government Grants; Individual Donations; Performance Fees
Annual Attendance: 50,000

Rye Brook

DANCE

DANCE SOLOS, INC.
Hillandale Road, Rye Brook, NY 10573
    Arts Area: Modern
    Status: Professional; Non-Profit
    Type: Performing; Touring; Resident; Educational
    Purpose: To educate and disseminate the art of solo dancing; to keep alive the art of the great solo dancers
    Management: Annabelle Gamson, Artistic Director; Sheldon Soffer, Booking Manager
    Officers: Annabelle Gamson, President; Arnold Gamson, Secretary
    Budget: $50,000 - $100,000
    Income Sources: Private Foundations/Grants/Endowments; Box Office; Government Grants; Individual Donations
    Performance Facilities: St. Mark's Church; Joyce Theater; Dance Theater Workshop

---
Salem

THEATRE

METTAWEE THEATRE COMPANY
RD #3, Salem, NY 12865
(518) 854-9357
    Arts Area: Professional
    Status: Professional; Non-Profit
    Type: Performing; Touring
    Purpose: To present original theatre works which incorporate masks, larger than life figures and live music in adaptions of myths and legends from many different cultures
    Management: Ralph Lee, Artistic Director; Casey Compton, Managing Director
    Officers: Stephanie Gallas, President
    Budget: $50,000 - $100,000
    Income Sources: Private Foundations/Grants/Endowments; Business/Corporate Donations; Box Office; Government Grants; Individual Donations

---
Saranac Lake

PERFORMING SERIES

ADIRONDACK FESTIVAL OF AMERICAN MUSIC
c/o Gregg Smith Singers, PO Box 562, Saranac Lake, NY 12983
(518) 891-1057
    Arts Area: Vocal Music; Instrumental Music; Choral
    Status: Professional; Non-Profit
    Type: Performing; Educational
    Purpose: To present a program focusing on American music--past and present, as well as some traditional repertoire
    Management: Gregg Smith, Artistic Director; Linda Ferriera, Director of Vocal Workshop
    Officers: Frank Manley, Chairman of the Board
    Budget: $50,000 - $100,000
    Income Sources: Private Foundations/Grants/Endowments; Business/Corporate Donations; Box Office; Government Grants; Individual Donations
    Season: 52 Weeks
    Performance Facilities: Town Hall

Saratoga Springs

PERFORMING SERIES

SARATOGA PERFORMING ARTS CENTER
Saratoga Spa State Park, Saratoga Springs, NY 12866
(518) 584-9330
FAX: (518) 584-0809
    Founded: 1966
    Arts Area: Dance; Vocal Music; Instrumental Music; Theater; Grand Opera
    Status: Professional; Non-Profit
    Type: Performing; Educational; Sponsoring

Officers: Mrs. Cornelius Vanderbilt Whitney, Honorary Chairman; Charles V. Wait, Chairman; Herbert A. Chesbrough, President; Mrs. Walter M. Jeffords Jr., Secretary; Harold N. Langlitz, Treasurer
Paid Staff: 14   **Volunteer Staff:** 600
Paid Artists: 625
Utilizes: Special Technical Talent; Guest Conductors; Guest Artists; Guest Directors
Budget: $5,000,000 - $10,000,000
Income Sources: Private Foundations/Grants/Endowments; Business/Corporate Donations; Box Office; Government Grants; Individual Donations
Season: June - September
Affiliations: IAAM; New York Performing Arts Association

FACILITY

SARATOGA PERFORMING ARTS CENTER
Saratoga Springs, NY 12866
(518) 584-9330
    Type of Facility: Performance Center
    Year Built: 1966   **Architect:** Vollmer Associates   **Cost:** $4,000,000
    Acoustical Consultant: Paul S. Veneklasen
    Resident Groups: Summer only: New York City Ballet; Philadelphia Orchestra
    The Performing Arts Center contains the Amphitheatre and the Little Theatre. See separate listings for additional information.

SARATOGA PERFORMING ARTS CENTER - AMPHITHEATRE
Saratoga Springs, NY 12866
(518) 584-9330
FAX: (518) 584-0809
    Founded: 1966
    Type of Facility: Amphitheater
    Type of Stage: Proscenium
    Stage Dimensions: 80'Wx60'D   **Orchestra Pit**
    Seating Capacity: 5,100 indoor; Additional lawn seating
    Year Built: 1965   **Architect:** Vollmer Associates   **Cost:** $4,000,000

SARATOGA PERFORMING ARTS CENTER - LITTLE THEATRE
Saratoga Springs, NY 12866
(518) 584-9330
    Type of Facility: Theatre House
    Facility Originally: Lecture Hall
    Type of Stage: Proscenium
    Stage Dimensions: 40'Wx30'D
    Seating Capacity: 500
    Year Built: 1930

Scarsdale

THEATRE

GREENVILLE COMMUNITY THEATER
PO Box 291, Scarsdale, NY 10583
(914) 472-0389
    Founded: 1964
    Arts Area: Community
    Status: Non-Profit
    Type: Performing
    Purpose: To provide quality theatrical entertainment through two major productions each year and approximately eight one-act workshops
    Management: Board of Directors
    Officers: Valerie Gehn, President; Barbara Evans, Vice-President; Marie Lee, Corresponding Secretary; Nancy Smith, Recording Secretary; Al Gehn, Treasurer
    Volunteer Staff: 110
    Utilizes: Special Technical Talent
    Budget: $1,000 - $50,000
    Income Sources: Business/Corporate Donations; Box Office; Individual Donations
    Season: September - June   **Annual Attendance:** 2,000
    Affiliations: NYSCA
    Performance Facilities: Edgemont High School Auditorium

Schenectady

VOCAL MUSIC

SCHENECTADY LIGHT OPERA COMPANY
PO Box 1006, Schenectady, NY 12301
(518) 393-5732; (518) 374-9566
>**Founded:** 1926
>**Arts Area:** Light Opera; Broadway Musicals
>**Status:** Non-Profit
>**Type:** Performing
>**Purpose:** To present Light Opera and Broadway Musicals
>**Management:** Peter Codella, Business Manager
>**Officers:** Joseph Agostine, President; Della Gilman, Secretary; Michael Jegabbi, Treasurer
>**Volunteer Staff:** 200
>**Budget:** $50,000 - $100,000
>**Income Sources:** Box Office; Individual Donations
>**Season:** October - May   **Annual Attendance:** 9,000
>**Affiliations:** NYSCA

THEATRE

THE SCHENECTADY CIVIC PLAYERS
12 South Church Street, Schenectady, NY 12305
(518) 382-2081
>**Founded:** 1928
>**Arts Area:** Community
>**Status:** Non-Professional; Non-Profit
>**Type:** Performing; Resident
>**Purpose:** Continuation of long tradition of providing non-profit community theatre
>**Volunteer Staff:** 131
>**Budget:** $1,000 - $50,000
>**Income Sources:** Business/Corporate Donations; Box Office; Government Grants
>**Season:** September - June
>**Annual Attendance:** 6,000
>**Affiliations:** New York State Community Theatre Association, New York State Theater Festival Association

FACILITY

PROCTOR'S THEATRE
432 State Street, Schenectady, NY 12305
(518) 382-3884
>**Type of Facility:** Concert Hall; Auditorium; Off Broadway; Theatre House; Opera House
>**Facility Originally:** Vaudeville
>**Type of Stage:** Proscenium
>**Stage Dimensions:** 35'x47'   **Orchestra Pit**
>**Seating Capacity:** 2,700
>**Year Built:** 1926   **Architect:** Thomas Lamb   **Cost:** $1,500,000
>**Year Remodeled:** 1979
>**Acoustical Consultant:** Jaffe Acoustics
>**Contact for Rental:** Jacqueline E. Mosher;   (518) 382-3884

THE SCHENECTADY CIVIC PLAYERS, INC.
12 South Church Street, Schenectady, NY 12305
(518) 382-2081
>**Founded:** 1928
>**Type of Facility:** Theatre House
>**Facility Originally:** Shrine Temple
>**Type of Stage:** Proscenium
>**Stage Dimensions:** 19'Wx26'Dx60'H
>**Seating Capacity:** 267
>**Year Built:** 1868
>**Year Remodeled:** 1961   **Architect:** Sarkis Parkell

Sea Cliff

INSTRUMENTAL MUSIC

THE SEA CLIFF CHAMBER PLAYERS
PO Box 311, Sea Cliff, NY 11579
(516) 671-6263
FAX: (561) 671-6514
Founded: 1970
Arts Area: Orchestra; Chamber
Status: Professional; Non-Profit
Type: Performing; Touring
Purpose: To produce quality chamber music concerts on Long Island featuring a chamber ensemble, chamber orchestra, and the Long Island Mozart Festival
Management: Herbert Sucoff, Executive Director; Barbara Speer, Musical Director
Officers: David Sterling, President; Sam Goldman, Vice President; Harry F. Lavo, Treasurer; David A. Black, Treasurer
Paid Staff: 6 **Volunteer Staff:** 80
Paid Artists: 62
Utilizes: Guest Artists
Budget: $100,000 - $500,000
Income Sources: Private Foundations/Grants/Endowments; Business/Corporate Donations; Box Office; Government Grants; Individual Donations
Season: October - May
Annual Attendance: 30,000
Performance Facilities: The Sea Cliff School; Tilles Center; Planting Fields Arboretum; Northport School; Rockville Center School; Staller Center

---
Skaneateles

PERFORMING SERIES

SKANEATELES FESTIVAL
PO Box 385, Skaneateles, NY 13152
(315) 685-7418
FAX: (315) 685-0744
Founded: 1980
Arts Area: Festivals
Status: Professional; Non-Profit
Type: Performing; Educational
Purpose: To present live chamber music concerts featuring nationally recognized musicians during the last four weeks of summer
Management: Claire Howard, General Manager; Robert Weirich, Music Director
Officers: Andrea Latchem, President; Judith Lauerons, Vice President; Karen Pardee, Treasurer; Mary Ellen Casey, Secretary
Paid Staff: 2
Paid Artists: 80
Utilizes: Guest Conductors; Guest Artists
Budget: $50,000 - $100,000
Income Sources: Private Foundations/Grants/Endowments; Business/Corporate Donations; Box Office; Government Grants; Individual Donations
Season: August - September **Annual Attendance:** 5,000

South Nyack

DANCE

HUMAN ARMS
19 Division Avenue, South Nyack, NY 10960
(914) 358-0489
Founded: 1985
Arts Area: Modern; Jazz
Status: Professional; Non-Profit
Type: Performing; Touring; Educational
Purpose: To present dramatic works that examine contradictions that appear in our most intimate thoughts and in the society that surrounds these thoughts, and to encourage and guide children to express themselves creatively through dance
Management: Harry Streep, Artistic Director; Frank Ferrucci, Cyro Baptista, Pentacle Management
Officers: John Rothman, Chairman

Paid Artists: 7
Utilizes: Guest Artists
Budget: $1,000 - $50,000
Income Sources: Business/Corporate Donations; Box Office; Individual Donations
Season: 52 Weeks

South Salem

VOCAL MUSIC

THE NEW YORK VIRTUOSO SINGERS
Cove Road, South Salem, NY 10590
(914) 763-3453
Founded: 1988
Arts Area: Choral
Status: Professional; Non-Profit
Type: Performing
Purpose: To perform chamber choral works from all periods with a special emphasis on 20th century repertoire; to commission, perform and record premieres
Paid Staff: 2
Paid Artists: 16
Utilizes: Guest Artists
Budget: $1,000 - $50,000
Income Sources: Private Foundations/Grants/Endowments; Business/Corporate Donations; Box Office; Government Grants; Individual Donations
Season: September - June   **Annual Attendance:** 550
Performance Facilities: Merkin Concert Hall

Southampton

FACILITY

LONG ISLAND UNIVERSITY - FINE ARTS THEATRE
Southampton Campus, Montauk Highway, Southampton, NY 11968
(516) 283-4000
Type of Facility: Concert Hall; Auditorium; Theatre House
Type of Stage: Thrust; Proscenium
Stage Dimensions: 50'Wx48'D, 18' of depth beyond proscenium
Seating Capacity: 440
Year Built: 1966   **Architect:** A. Alverez
Contact for Rental: Tim Bishop, Provost;   (516) 283-4000
Manager: Jon Fraser, Associate Dean

Staten Island

FACILITY

SNUG HARBOR CULTURAL CENTER
1000 Richmond Terrace, Staten Island, NY 10301
(718) 448-2500
FAX: (718) 442-8534
Type of Facility: Concert Hall; Outdoor (Concert)
Facility Originally: Church
Type of Stage: Platform
Stage Dimensions: Platform - 30'x50'; Chapel - 10'x40'
Seating Capacity: 210
Year Built: 1856   **Architect:** James Salmon
Year Remodeled: 1984   **Architect:** Gibson-Bauer Associates
Contact for Rental: Brian Rehr, Performing Arts Director;   (718) 448-2500

VETERANS MEMORIAL HALL
1000 Richmond Terrace, Staten Island, NY 10301
(718) 448-2500
FAX: (718) 442-8534
Type of Facility: Concert Hall
Facility Originally: Church

Type of Stage: Platform
Stage Dimensions: 35'Wx12'D
Seating Capacity: 200
Year Built: 1856
Year Remodeled: 1985
Acoustical Consultant: Jaffe
Contact for Rental: Kim D. Sio;   (718) 448-2500

WILLIAMSON THEATRE
715 Ocean Terrace, Staten Island, NY 10301
(718) 390-7725
Founded: 1968
Type of Facility: Auditorium; Performance Center; Theatre House; Multi-Purpose
Type of Stage: Proscenium   **Orchestra Pit**
Seating Capacity: 900
Contact for Rental: D. Zarrilli or C. Brandifino;   (718) 390-7948

Stony Brook

DANCE

LONG ISLAND DANCE COMPANY
1320 Stony Brook Road, Stony Brook, NY 11790
(516) 751-2195
Founded: 1969
Arts Area: Modern; Ballet; Jazz
Status: Professional; Non-Profit
Type: Performing; Touring; Resident
Purpose: To promote the awareness of dance and its varied styles
Management: Sandra Jemal, Artistic Director
Paid Artists: 16
Utilizes: Guest Artists
Budget: $1,000 - $50,000
Income Sources: Private Foundations/Grants/Endowments; Business/Corporate Donations; Box Office; Government Grants; Individual Donations
Season: 52 Weeks

PERFORMING SERIES

BACH ARIA FESTIVAL AND INSTITUTE
PO Box 997, Stony Brook, NY 11790
(516) 632-7239
FAX: (516) 632-6252
Founded: 1981
Arts Area: Vocal Music; Instrumental Music; Festivals; Baroque Opera
Status: Professional; Non-Profit
Type: Performing; Educational
Purpose: To provide professional training and concertizing based on cantata literature of J.S. Bach; to study and present other literature
Management: Carol K. Baron, Executive Director
Paid Staff: 2   **Volunteer Staff:** 30
Paid Artists: 50
Utilizes: Guest Artists; Fellows of Insitute
Budget: $100,000 - $500,000
Income Sources: Private Foundations/Grants/Endowments; Business/Corporate Donations; Box Office; Government Grants; Individual Donations
Season: June   **Annual Attendance:** 3,000
Affiliations: SUNY Stony Brook
Performance Facilities: Staller Center for the Arts; Chelsea Mansion; Cathedral of Saint John the Divine

Stony Point

THEATRE

PENGUIN REPERTORY COMPANY
Crickettown Road, Stony Point, NY 10980
Founded: 1977

Arts Area: Professional
Status: Professional; Non-Profit
Type: Performing
Purpose: To mount new plays, giving new playwrights opportunities; to stage "tried and true" works
Management: Joe Brancato, Artistic Director; Andrew Horn, Executive Director
Officers: Annabelle Goldschmidt, President; Francine Newman McCarthy, Vice President; Catherine Grassi, Secretary/Treasurer
Paid Staff: 4 **Volunteer Staff:** 2
Utilizes: Guest Artists; Guest Directors
Budget: $100,000 - $500,000
Income Sources: Private Foundations/Grants/Endowments; Business/Corporate Donations; Box Office; Government Grants; Individual Donations
Season: October - August
Affiliations: AEA; SSDC

Sunnyside

INSTRUMENTAL MUSIC

ROSEWOOD CHAMBER ENSEMBLE, INC.
43-31 39th Street, Sunnyside, NY 11104
(718) 729-4614
    Founded: 1980
    Arts Area: Chamber; Ensemble
    Status: Professional; Non-Profit
    Type: Performing; Educational
    Purpose: To bring good classical music to the community; to provide musical education for the young
    Officers: Ruth Javna, Chairman; Bridie Race, Secretary; Al Friedman, Treasurer; Karla Moc and David Moore, Co-Artistic Directors; Chris Bianchi, Vice Chair
    Paid Staff: 1 **Volunteer Staff:** 10
    Paid Artists: 20
    Utilizes: Guest Artists
    Budget: $1,000 - $50,000
    Income Sources: Business/Corporate Donations; Box Office; Government Grants; Individual Donations
    Season: November - April
    Annual Attendance: 700

THEATRE

THALIA SPANISH THEATRE
41-17 Greenpoint Avenue, Sunnyside, NY 11104
(718) 729-3880
    Founded: 1969
    Arts Area: Professional; Musical; Community; Theatrical Group
    Status: Professional; Non-Profit
    Type: Performing; Touring; Resident
    Purpose: To present to the Hispanic communities of New York City, productions of the highest artistic quality and professionalism
    Management: Silvia Brito, Artistic/Executive Director; Kathryn A. Giaimo, Administrative Director; Felix Arocho, Marketing Director; Guillermo Escudero, Technical Director
    Officers: Anna Harrsch, Chairperson/Treasurer; Silvia Brito, President; Emilio C. Cueto, Vice President; Ruth Diez, Secretary
    Paid Staff: 4 **Volunteer Staff:** 4
    Paid Artists: 40
    Utilizes: Special Technical Talent; Guest Artists; Guest Directors
    Budget: $100,000 - $500,000
    Income Sources: Private Foundations/Grants/Endowments; Business/Corporate Donations; Box Office; Government Grants; Individual Donations
    Season: 52 Weeks
    Annual Attendance: 9,000
    Affiliations: ART/NY; AHA; TCG; Flushing Council on Culture and the Arts; Arts and Business Council; Queens Council on the Arts
    Performance Facilities: Thalia Theatre

Syracuse

INSTRUMENTAL MUSIC

SYRACUSE SOCIETY FOR NEW MUSIC
312 Crawford Avenue, Syracuse, NY 13224
(315) 446-5733
> **Founded:** 1971
> **Arts Area:** Chamber; Electronic & Live Electronic; Chamber Opera; Jazz; New Music
> **Status:** Professional; Non-Profit
> **Type:** Performing; Touring; Resident; Educational; Sponsoring
> **Purpose:** To present new music, commission new works and take new music into the public schools
> **Officers:** Harris Lindenfield, President; Ann Sitsbee and Daniel Godfrey, Vice Presidents; Steven Stuckey and Neva Pilgrim, Program Advisor
> **Volunteer Staff:** 6
> **Paid Artists:** 175
> **Utilizes:** Guest Artists
> **Budget:** $50,000 - $100,000
> **Income Sources:** Private Foundations/Grants/Endowments; Business/Corporate Donations; Box Office; Government Grants; Individual Donations; Benefits
> **Season:** September - April; July-August   **Annual Attendance:** 10,000
> **Performance Facilities:** Syracuse University; Crouse College; Everson Muesum

SYRACUSE SYMPHONY ORCHESTRA
411 Montgomery Street, Syracuse, NY 13203
(315) 424-8222
FAX: (315) 424-1131
> **Founded:** 1960
> **Arts Area:** Symphony; Orchestra; Chamber
> **Status:** Professional; Non-Profit
> **Type:** Performing; Touring; Resident; Educational
> **Purpose:** To maintain and further develop a resident, professional symphony orchestra; to produce musical performances of the highest artistic quality; to fulfill the cultural, educational and entertainment needs of the central and northern New York communities we serve
> **Management:** Melvin A. Eggers, President/Executive Director; Kazuyoshi Akiyama, Music Director/Conductor; Fabio Mechetti, Associate Conductor; Richard Decker, Orchestra Manager; Susan Schwartz, Director of Marketing/Public Relations
> **Paid Staff:** 25   **Volunteer Staff:** 700
> **Paid Artists:** 86
> **Utilizes:** Special Technical Talent; Guest Conductors; Guest Artists
> **Budget:** $1,000,000 - $5,000,000
> **Income Sources:** Private Foundations/Grants/Endowments; Business/Corporate Donations; Box Office; Government Grants; Individual Donations
> **Season:** 52 Weeks   **Annual Attendance:** 210,000
> **Affiliations:** ASOL; APAP
> **Performance Facilities:** John H. Mulroy Civic Center

SYRACUSE SYMPHONY YOUTH ORCHESTRA
411 Montogomery Street, Syracuse, NY 13203
(315) 424-8222
FAX: (315) 424-1131
> **Founded:** 1961
> **Arts Area:** Symphony; Orchestra
> **Status:** Non-Professional; Non-Profit
> **Type:** Performing; Touring; Resident; Educational
> **Management:** Ernest Muzquiz, Conductor
> **Officers:** Dr. Arthur Rosenbaum, Chairman
> **Paid Staff:** 1   **Volunteer Staff:** 10
> **Non-Paid Artists:** 80
> **Utilizes:** Guest Artists
> **Budget:** $1,000 - $50,000
> **Income Sources:** Private Foundations/Grants/Endowments; Box Office; Individual Donations
> **Season:** September - May   **Annual Attendance:** 5,000
> **Affiliations:** ASOL (Youth Orchestra Division); Syracuse Symphony Orchestra
> **Performance Facilities:** H.W. Smith Elementary School

VOCAL MUSIC

SYRACUSE OPERA COMPANY
100 East Washington Street, PO Box 6904, Syracuse, NY 13217-6904
(315) 475-5915
> **Founded:** 1973
> **Arts Area:** Grand Opera; Lyric Opera; Light Opera; Operetta
> **Status:** Professional; Non-Profit
> **Type:** Performing; Touring; Resident; Educational
> **Purpose:** To produce high-quality opera productions using talented, young American artists from the central New York region; to provide quality opera productions outside the central New York region
> **Management:** Julie Richards, General Director; Richard McKee, Artistic Director
> **Paid Staff:** 11   **Volunteer Staff:** 4
> **Paid Artists:** 75   **Non-Paid Artists:** 20
> **Utilizes:** Special Technical Talent; Guest Conductors; Guest Artists; Guest Directors
> **Budget:** $500,000 - $1,000,000
> **Income Sources:** Private Foundations/Grants/Endowments; Business/Corporate Donations; Box Office; Government Grants; Individual Donations
> **Season:** October - May   **Annual Attendance:** 33,500
> **Affiliations:** OA; NYSCA
> **Performance Facilities:** Crouse-Hinds Concert Theater

THEATRE

SYRACUSE STAGE
820 East Genesee, Syracuse, NY 13210
(315) 443-4008
FAX: (315) 443-9846
> **Founded:** 1974
> **Arts Area:** Professional; Theatrical Group
> **Status:** Professional; Non-Profit
> **Type:** Performing; Touring; Educational
> **Purpose:** Through the artistry of the playwrights, directors, designers and actors, Syracuse Stage seeks to enrich the lives of Central New York theater-goers and to challenge their perceptions of the world.
> **Management:** James A. Clark, Producing Director; Tazewell Thompson, Artistic Director; Diana C. Coles, Administrative Director; Don Buschmann, Production Manager
> **Officers:** Joan Green, Chairman; Lucius Kempton, President; Louis Marcoccia, Treasurer; Sandra Townes, Secretary
> **Paid Staff:** 40
> **Paid Artists:** 75
> **Utilizes:** Guest Artists; Guest Directors
> **Budget:** $1,000,000 - $5,000,000
> **Income Sources:** Private Foundations/Grants/Endowments; Business/Corporate Donations; Box Office; Government Grants; Individual Donations
> **Season:** October - May   **Annual Attendance:** 100,000
> **Affiliations:** TCG; LORT; AEA
> **Performance Facilities:** The John D. Archbold Theatre

PERFORMING SERIES

CULTURAL RESOURCES COUNCIL OF SYRACUSE AND ONONDAGA COUNTY
411 Montgomery Street, Syracuse, NY 13202
(315) 435-2155
> **Founded:** 1968
> **Arts Area:** Dance; Theater; Festivals
> **Status:** Professional; Non-Profit
> **Type:** Performing
> **Purpose:** To identify, coordinate, promote and present all the performing arts to serve a 10-county central New York area
> **Management:** Jerold Reichard, Executive Directorn
> **Officers:** Wallace Conkling, President; Susan Connelly, Vice President; Jay Jackler CPA, Treasurer
> **Paid Staff:** 22   **Volunteer Staff:** 150
> **Paid Artists:** 250   **Non-Paid Artists:** 2
> **Utilizes:** Special Technical Talent; Guest Artists; Guest Directors
> **Income Sources:** Private Foundations/Grants/Endowments; Business/Corporate Donations; Box Office; Government Grants; Individual Donations
> **Annual Attendance:** 350,000
> **Affiliations:** ISPAA
> **Performance Facilities:** Civic Center of Ononadaga County

FACILITY

CIVIC CENTER OF ONONDAGA COUNTY
411 Montgomery Street, Syracuse, NY 13202
(315) 425-2155
> **Type of Facility:** Performance Center; Civic Center
> **Year Built:** 1976 **Architect:** McAfee Malo Afflect Lebensold Nichol **Cost:** $23,000,000
> **Acoustical Consultant:** ARTEC
> **Contact for Rental:** Robert Oliver; (315) 425-2155
> **Resident Groups:** Syracuse Symphony Orchestra; Opera Theater of Syracuse; Syracuse Ballet Theater
> *The Civic Center contains Bevard Community Room, Carrier Theater and Crouse-Hinds Concert Theater. See separate listings for additional information.*

CIVIC CENTER OF ONONDAGA COUNTY - BEVARD COMMUNITY ROOM
411 Montgomery Street, Syracuse, NY 13202
(315) 425-2155
> **Type of Facility:** Black Box
> **Type of Stage:** Flexible
> **Stage Dimensions:** 60'Wx40'Dx24'H
> **Seating Capacity:** 200
> **Year Built:** 1976
> **Contact for Rental:** Robert Oliver; (315) 425-2155

CIVIC CENTER OF ONONDAGA COUNTY - CARRIER THEATER
411 Montgomery Street, Syracuse, NY 13202
(315) 425-2155
> **Type of Facility:** Studio Performance
> **Type of Stage:** Flexible
> **Stage Dimensions:** 27'x57'x25'
> **Seating Capacity:** 463
> **Year Built:** 1976
> **Contact for Rental:** Robert Oliver; (315) 425-2155

CIVIC CENTER OF ONONDAGA COUNTY - CROUSE-HINDS CONCERT THEATER
411 Montgomery Street, Syracuse, NY 13202
(315) 425-2155
> **Type of Facility:** Concert Hall; Theatre House
> **Type of Stage:** Proscenium
> **Stage Dimensions:** 110'Wx50'Dx85'H; 60'Wx40'H proscenium opening **Orchestra Pit**
> **Seating Capacity:** 2,117
> **Year Built:** 1976
> **Contact for Rental:** Robert Oliver; (315) 425-2155
> *Two separate lifts - 60'Wx14'D and 60'Wx10'D*

SYRACUSE AREA LANDMARK THEATRE
362 South Salina Street, Syracuse, NY 13202
(315) 475-7979
FAX: (315) 475-7993
> **Founded:** 1975
> **Type of Facility:** Theatre Complex; Concert Hall; Auditorium; Off Broadway; Theatre House; Opera House; Multi-Purpose; Movie House
> **Facility Originally:** Movie House
> **Type of Stage:** Proscenium
> **Stage Dimensions:** 30'x50' **Orchestra Pit**
> **Seating Capacity:** 2,922
> **Year Built:** 1928 **Architect:** Thomas Lamb **Cost:** $2,000,000
> **Year Remodeled:** 1975 **Cost:** $1,000,000
> **Contact for Rental:** Frank M. Malfitano; (315) 475-7979

Tarrytown

DANCE

BALLET THEATRE OF WESTCHESTER
62 Main Street, Tarrytown, NY 10591
(914) 631-6878
> **Arts Area:** Ballet

Status: Professional
Type: Performing; Touring; Resident
Management: Claire Kelley, Artistic Director; Carmen Williams, Administrative Director
Income Sources: Box Office; Individual Donations
Performance Facilities: Master School Auditorium

FACILITY

LYNDHURST
635 South Broadway, Tarrytown, NY 10591
(914) 631-0046
FAX: (914) 631-6825
  Type of Facility: Outdoor (Concert)
  Type of Stage: Proscenium
  Seating Capacity: Tent - 1,000; Outdoors - 4,000
  Manager: Susanne Pandrich, Director
  Resident Groups: Sunset Serenades

Ticonderoga

PERFORMING SERIES

TICONDEROGA FESTIVAL GUILD, INC.
PO Box 125, 324 Champlain Avenue, Ticonderoga, NY 12883
(518) 545-6716
  Founded: 1980
  Arts Area: Festivals
  Status: Non-Profit
  Type: Performing
  Purpose: To bring cultural events to an area rural in nature, where the performing arts are at a premium
  Management: Sharon P. Ofner, Executive Director
  Officers: Mark Johnson, President; Thomas Latrell, First Vice President; Richard Cunningham, Second Vice President; Michael Corsi, Treasurer; Carolyn Malaney, Secretary
  Paid Staff: 1   **Volunteer Staff:** 20
  Income Sources: Private Foundations/Grants/Endowments; Business/Corporate Donations; Box Office; Government Grants; Individual Donations
  Season: July - August   **Annual Attendance:** 3,500

Troy

INSTRUMENTAL MUSIC

TROY CHROMATICS CONCERTS, INC.
PO Box 1574, Troy, NY 12181
(518) 235-3000
  Founded: 1895
  Arts Area: Symphony; Chamber; Ensemble; Soloists
  Status: Non-Profit
  Type: Sponsoring
  Purpose: To provide world class artists and programs to the capital region of New York state
  Officers: Michael A. Nofac, President
  Budget: $50,000 - $100,000
  Income Sources: Private Foundations/Grants/Endowments; Business/Corporate Donations; Box Office; Government Grants; Individual Donations
  Season: October - May   **Annual Attendance:** 5,000
  Performance Facilities: Troy Savings Bank Music Hall

FACILITY

RENSSELAER NEWMAN FOUNDATION CHAPEL AND CULTURAL CENTER
2125 Burdett Avenue, Troy, NY 12180
(518) 274-7793
  Type of Facility: Theatre Complex; Concert Hall; Auditorium; Outdoor (Concert); Performance Center; Multi-Purpose
  Type of Stage: Thrust; Flexible; Platform
  Stage Dimensions: 80'x80'

Seating Capacity: 400
Year Built: 1967   **Architect:** Peter Levatich   **Cost:** $500,000
Contact for Rental: William McQuiston, Director;   (518) 274-7793
Resident Groups: Rensselaer Theater Company; Electronic-Video Arts At RPI; RPI Ensembles; Religion and the Arts
Festival; Literary Arts At RPI; Visiting Artists Series; RPI Youth Theater Workshop

TROY ARENA
689 Burden Avenue, PO Box 97, Troy, NY 12181
(518) 273-8400
Type of Facility: Civic Center; Arena; Multi-Purpose
Type of Stage: Arena
Stage Dimensions: 40'Wx60'D
Seating Capacity: 4,000
Year Built: 1945
Contact for Rental: Ted Bayly;   (518) 273-8400

TROY - HAYNER CULTURAL CENTER
301 West Main Street, Troy, NY 45373
(513) 339-0457
Founded: 1976
Type of Facility: Outdoor (Concert); Community Cultural Center
Facility Originally: Historic Mansion
Type of Stage: Ballroom
Stage Dimensions: 20'x20' floor space
Seating Capacity: 115
Year Built: 1914
Architect: Leonard B. Willeke
Contact for Rental: Martha Stone;   (513) 339-0457

TROY SAVINGS BANK MUSIC HALL
State and Second Streets, Troy, NY 12180
(518) 273-0038
FAX: (518) 274-7762
Mailing Address: 88 Fourth Street, Troy, NY 12180
Founded: 1875
Type of Facility: Concert Hall
Facility Originally: Concert Hall
Type of Stage: Thrust; Apron is curved; stage is slighty raised
Stage Dimensions: 68'Wx21'D
Seating Capacity: 1,200
Year Built: 1875
Architect: George Brown Post   **Cost:** $500,000
Contact for Rental: Mitchell A. Gordon;   (518) 273-0038

Uniondale

INSTRUMENTAL MUSIC

NASSAU SYMPHONY SOCIETY, INC.
185 California Avenue, Uniondale, NY 11553-1131
(516) 481-3196
FAX: (516) 481-3382
Arts Area: Symphony
Status: Professional; Non-Profit
Type: Performing; Educational
Purpose: To perform symphonic music of the highest quality for residents of all ages on Long Island
Management: Sherry Smolev, Executive Director
Officers: Robert Buescher, Chairman of the Board
Budget: $500,000 - $1,000,000
Income Sources: Private Foundations/Grants/Endowments; Business/Corporate Donations; Box Office; Government
Grants; Individual Donations
Performance Facilities: John Cranford Adams Playhouse, Hofstra University

---
Utica

PERFORMING SERIES

MUNSON-WILLIAMS-PROCTOR INSTITUTE PERFORMING ARTS DIVISION
310 Genesee Street, Utica, NY 13502
(315) 797-0055
FAX: (315) 797-5608
> **Founded:** 1932
> **Arts Area:** Dance; Vocal Music; Instrumental Music; Theater; Festivals; Lyric Opera; Grand Opera; Jazz; Folk; Children's; Film
> **Status:** Professional; Non-Profit
> **Type:** Performing; Educational; Sponsoring
> **Purpose:** To provide exemplary programs and educational opportunites in the performing and cinematic arts, setting a national standard for artistic achievement.
> **Officers:** Milton J. Bloch, President; George J. Trudeau, Director of Performing Arts
> **Paid Staff:** 5   **Volunteer Staff:** 30
> **Paid Artists:** 200
> **Utilizes:** Guest Artists
> **Budget:** $500,000 - $1,000,000
> **Income Sources:** Private Foundations/Grants/Endowments; Business/Corporate Donations; Box Office; Government Grants; Individual Donations; Program Advertising
> **Annual Attendance:** 30,000
> **Affiliations:** ISPAA; BOMI; ASOL; NEP; APAP
> **Performance Facilities:** Stanley Performing Arts Center; Museum of Art Auditorium and Sculpture Court; Festival Tent

FACILITY

STANLEY PERFORMING ARTS CENTER
259 Genesee Street, Utica, NY 13501
(315) 724-5919
FAX: (315) 732-8468
> **Type of Facility:** Concert Hall; Auditorium; Theatre House
> **Facility Originally:** Movie House
> **Type of Stage:** Proscenium
> **Stage Dimensions:** 57'Wx30'D   **Orchestra Pit**
> **Seating Capacity:** 2,945
> **Year Built:** 1928   **Architect:** Thomas Lamb   **Cost:** $1,500,000
> **Year Remodeled:** 1992   **Architect:** Alesia and Crewell   **Cost:** $4,000,000
> **Acoustical Consultant:** Jacek Figwer
> **Contact for Rental:** John Faust;   (315) 724-5919
> **Resident Groups:** Broadway Theatre League (touring shows); Great Artists Series; Utica Symphony Orchestra

UTICA MEMORIAL AUDITORIUM
400 Oriskany Street, Utica, NY 13502
(315) 738-0164
> **Type of Facility:** Auditorium; Multi-Purpose
> **Type of Stage:** Flexible
> **Stage Dimensions:** 44'x56'
> **Seating Capacity:** 6,000
> **Year Built:** 1960   **Architect:** Gehron and Seltzer
> **Year Remodeled:** 1986
> **Contact for Rental:** Murray Sislen
> **Resident Groups:** Utica Devils Hockey Team

Watertown

DANCE

1000 ISLANDS FESTIVAL BALLET COMPANY, INC.
PO Box 513, Watertown, NY 13601
(315) 782-2566
> **Founded:** 1985
> **Arts Area:** Ballet
> **Status:** Semi-Professional; Non-Profit
> **Type:** Performing; Touring; Educational; Sponsoring
> **Purpose:** To provide educational and performance opportunities for students and the community

Management: Jean Spear, Artistic Director
Officers: Mark Gebo, Attorney; Charles Hamlin, Comptroller; Patricia Johnson, Secretary/Treasurer; Beverly Youngs, Public Relations
Paid Staff: 1 **Volunteer Staff:** 15
Utilizes: Special Technical Talent; Guest Artists
Budget: $1,000 - $50,000
Income Sources: Private Foundations/Grants/Endowments; Box Office; Individual Donations
Season: September - May **Annual Attendance:** 8,000
Performance Facilities: Dulles State Office Building

THEATRE

WATERTOWN LYRIC THEATER PRODUCTIONS
1333 Holcomb Street, Watertown, NY 13601
(315) 788-6492
Founded: 1972
Arts Area: Musical; Community; Theatrical Group
Status: Non-Professional; Non-Profit
Type: Performing; Educational
Purpose: To present live theatre to the community using local talent and provide the youth of the community an education in musical theatre
Officers: Michael Bajjaly, President; William Boulter, Vice President; Barbara Flynn, Secretary; Daniel Davis, Treasurer
Volunteer Staff: 75
Non-Paid Artists: 300
Utilizes: Special Technical Talent
Budget: $1,000 - $50,000
Income Sources: Box Office; Individual Donations
Season: 52 Weeks **Annual Attendance:** 3,000
Performance Facilities: State Office Building Auditorium

FACILITY

NEW YORK STATE OFFICE OF GENERAL SERVICES
317 Washington Street, Dulles State Building, Watertown, NY 13601
(315) 785-2451
Type of Facility: Theatre Complex; Concert Hall; Auditorium; Performance Center; Theatre House; Multi-Purpose
Type of Stage: Proscenium
Stage Dimensions: 20'x60'x30' **Orchestra Pit**
Seating Capacity: 795
Year Built: 1972 **Architect:** Sargeant, Webster Cronshaw and Folley
Contact for Rental: Gerald F. Casey; (315) 785-2451
Resident Groups: Watertown Lyric Theater; Watertown Little Theater; Third Wave Productions

---

Westbury

PERFORMING SERIES

WESTBURY MUSIC FAIR
960 Brush Hollow Road, Westbury, NY 11590
(516) 333-7228
FAX: (516) 333-7991
Founded: 1956
Arts Area: Dance; Vocal Music; Instrumental Music; Theater
Status: Professional; Commercial
Type: Performing
Purpose: To provide the best entertainment in all areas of entertainment to metropolitan New York
Management: Dana F.X. Amendola, General Manager
Paid Staff: 100
Utilizes: Special Technical Talent; Guest Conductors; Guest Artists
Budget: $100,000 - $500,000
Income Sources: Box Office
Season: February - December

FACILITY

WESTBURY MUSIC FAIR
960 Brush Hollow Road, Westbury, NY 11590
(516) 333-7228
    Type of Facility: Performance Center; Theatre House; Arena
    Type of Stage: Arena; In-the-round Capability
    Stage Dimensions: 30' diameter **Orchestra Pit**
    Seating Capacity: 2,932
    Year Built: 1965 **Architect:** Hassinger & Schwamm **Cost:** $1,500,000
    Acoustical Consultant: Kevin Hickson
    Contact for Rental: Laurel Kramer; (516) 333-2101
    Management reserves the right to permit rentals for specific purposes.

Westfield

THEATRE

DAS PUPPENSPIEL PUPPET THEATER, INC.
1 1/2 East Main Street, Westfield, NY 14787-1319
(716) 326-2611
FAX: (716) 326-6625
    Founded: 1974
    Arts Area: Professional; Theatrical Group; Puppet
    Status: Professional; Non-Profit
    Type: Performing; Touring; Educational
    Management: Kevin Kuhlman, Managing Director
    Paid Staff: 2 **Volunteer Staff:** 1
    Paid Artists: 6 **Non-Paid Artists:** 1
    Utilizes: Guest Directors
    Budget: $100,000 - $500,000
    Income Sources: Private Foundations/Grants/Endowments; Business/Corporate Donations; Box Office; Government Grants; Individual Donations
    Season: October - August **Annual Attendance:** 65,000
    Affiliations: UNIMA; Puppeteers of America; Children's Theatre Association of America

White Plains

VOCAL MUSIC

WESTCHESTER CHORAL SOCIETY, INC.
Box 94, White Plains, NY 10604
(914) 693-2453
    Founded: 1942
    Arts Area: Choral
    Status: Non-Professional; Non-Profit
    Type: Performing; Resident
    Purpose: To promote appreciation of fine music in the community
    Management: Lyndon Woodside, Music Director; David Ralph, Accompanist; Shirley Rubenstein, Administration
    Officers: David Issacs, President; Irving Shepard, Treasurer
    Paid Staff: 3 **Volunteer Staff:** 20
    Utilizes: Guest Artists
    Budget: $1,000 - $50,000
    Income Sources: Private Foundations/Grants/Endowments; Business/Corporate Donations; Box Office; Government Grants; Individual Donations
    Season: August **Annual Attendance:** 1,000
    Performance Facilities: SUNY Purchase

THEATRE

THE STREET THEATER
228 Fisher Avenue, White Plains, NY 10606
(914) 761-3307
FAX: (914) 422-2340
    Founded: 1970
    Arts Area: Professional; Theatrical Group
    Status: Semi-Professional; Non-Profit

Type: Performing; Touring; Educational
Purpose: Committed to educational programs dealing with social issues; to support a touring youth company
Management: Gray Smith, Artistic Director
Paid Staff: 2
Utilizes: Special Technical Talent; Guest Artists; Guest Directors
Budget: $100,000 - $500,000
Income Sources: Private Foundations/Grants/Endowments; Business/Corporate Donations; Box Office; Government Grants; Individual Donations
Season: 52 Weeks
Affiliations: AEA

TRAVELING PLAYHOUSE
104 Northampton Drive, White Plains, NY 10603
(914) 946-5289
Founded: 1948
Arts Area: Professional; Summer Stock
Status: Professional; Non-Profit
Type: Performing; Touring; Resident; Educational
Purpose: To present a repertory of plays for children 6-12 years of age by adult professional actors
Management: Kay Rockefeller, Director; Ken Rockefeller, Producer; Franklin Birt, Production Manager; Richard Kinter, Resident Author/Composer
Paid Staff: 6
Paid Artists: 30
Budget: $100,000 - $500,000
Income Sources: Box Office
Season: 52 Weeks
Affiliations: AATA; AEA
Performance Facilities: Kaufmann Auditorium; Symphony Space

Woodside

DANCE

TOMOV FOLK DANCE ENSEMBLE
66-12 48th Street, Woodside, NY 11377
Founded: 1974
Arts Area: Folk
Status: Semi-Professional; Non-Profit
Type: Performing; Touring; Educational
Purpose: To showcase the folk music, dance and songs of the Balkans
Management: Folkdance Foundation, Inc. (Parent Organization)
Officers: George Tomov, President/Artistic Director
Volunteer Staff: 20
Paid Artists: 40
Utilizes: Guest Artists; Guest Choreographers
Budget: $1,000 - $50,000
Income Sources: Private Foundations/Grants/Endowments; Business/Corporate Donations; Box Office; Government Grants; Individual Donations
Season: 52 Weeks

Woodstock

INSTRUMENTAL MUSIC

MAVERICK CONCERTS, INC.
PO Box 102, Woodstock, NY 12498
(914) 679-8217
Arts Area: Chamber
Status: Professional; Non-Profit
Type: Performing
Purpose: To provide Sunday afternoon chamber-music concerts during the summer; Maverick Concerts is the oldest chamber music session in the United States and is about to celebrate its 78th season
Management: Vincent Wagner, Artistic Director
Officers: Gerald Widoff, Chairman of the Board
Budget: $1,000 - $50,000

Income Sources: Private Foundations/Grants/Endowments; Business/Corporate Donations; Box Office; Government Grants; Individual Donations
Performance Facilities: Maverick Concert Hall

THEATRE

COMMON STAGE THEATRE COMPANY, INC.
PO Box 1028, Woodstock, NY 12498
(914) 679-9256
> **Founded:** 1989
> **Arts Area:** Theatrical Group; Women Playwrights Only
> **Status:** Semi-Professional; Non-Profit
> **Purpose:** To develop and produce plays by women
> **Officers:** Gloria Dickler, Kathi Wood, Co-Artistic Directors; Joseph Schwarz, Managing Director
> **Volunteer Staff:** 15
> **Paid Artists:** 10   **Non-Paid Artists:** 10
> **Utilizes:** Special Technical Talent; Guest Artists
> **Budget:** $1,000 - $50,000
> **Income Sources:** Private Foundations/Grants/Endowments; Business/Corporate Donations; Box Office; Individual Donations
> **Season:** May - June; September-October   **Annual Attendance:** 800

FACILITY

MAVERICK CONCERT HALL
PO Box 102, Woodstock, NY 12498
(914) 679-8217
> **Founded:** 1915
> **Type of Facility:** Concert Hall; Outdoor (Concert)
> **Type of Stage:** Platform
> **Stage Dimensions:** 20'x12'
> **Seating Capacity:** Inside-270; Outside-150
> **Year Built:** 1916
> **Year Remodeled:** 1977   **Architect:** Leonhard T. Hartman   **Cost:** $59,000
> **Acoustical Consultant:** Edgar Villchiure
> **Contact for Rental:** Vincent Wagner;   (914) 338-3074

Yonkers

PERFORMING SERIES

MANCHESTER MUSIC FESTIVAL
93 Franklin Avenue, Yonkers, NY 10705
(914) 965-5533
> **Founded:** 1974
> **Arts Area:** Vocal Music; Instrumental Music; Festivals
> **Status:** Non-Profit
> **Type:** Performing; Educational
> **Purpose:** School for gifted instrumentalists; festival concerts
> **Management:** Michael Rudiakov, Director; Ariel Rudiakov, Assistant
> **Paid Staff:** 10   **Volunteer Staff:** 16
> **Paid Artists:** 10
> **Utilizes:** Guest Artists
> **Budget:** $100,000 - $500,000
> **Income Sources:** Private Foundations/Grants/Endowments; Business/Corporate Donations; Box Office; Government Grants; Individual Donations
> **Season:** July - August   **Annual Attendance:** 1,000
> **Performance Facilities:** Southern Vermont Arts Center

Yorktown Heights

DANCE

DANCE THEATRE IN WESTCHESTER
1974 Commerce Street, Yorktown Heights, NY 10598
(914) 245-2940
> **Founded:** 1979

Arts Area: Modern; Ballet; Jazz
Status: Professional; Non-Profit
Type: Performing; Touring; Resident
Purpose: Regional Dance Company
Management: Rose-Marie Menes, Artistic Director
Officers: Bernard Werner, President Board of Directors
Paid Staff: 4 **Volunteer Staff:** 10
Paid Artists: 11 **Non-Paid Artists:** 6
Utilizes: Guest Artists; Guest Choreographers
Budget: $50,000 - $100,000
Income Sources: Private Foundations/Grants/Endowments; Business/Corporate Donations; Box Office; Individual Donations
Season: September - May **Annual Attendance:** 10,000

VOCAL MUSIC

THE TAGHKANIC CHORALE
PO Box 144, Yorktown Heights, NY 10598
(914) 621-1240
Founded: 1967
Arts Area: Choral
Status: Semi-Professional; Non-Profit
Type: Performing; Educational
Purpose: Preparation and performance of choral works with emphasis on quality and authenticity
Management: Johannes Somary, Music Director
Officers: Sallye Adams, President; Virgina Perunko, Vice President; Ed Falcone, Secretary; Eileen Donnelly, Treasurer
Paid Staff: 2 **Volunteer Staff:** 40
Paid Artists: 75 **Non-Paid Artists:** 100
Utilizes: Special Technical Talent; Guest Artists
Budget: $1,000 - $50,000
Income Sources: Private Foundations/Grants/Endowments; Business/Corporate Donations; Box Office; Government Grants; Individual Donations
Season: September - June **Annual Attendance:** 2,000
Affiliations: CA

NORTH CAROLINA

Asheville

INSTRUMENTAL MUSIC

HOWARD HANGER JAZZ FANTASY
31 Park Avenue, Asheville, NC 28801
(704) 254-6265
Founded: 1966
Arts Area: Ensemble; Electronic & Live Electronic
Status: Professional
Type: Performing; Touring; Educational
Purpose: To perform new age and traditional jazz and to introduce jazz to children ages 6-12
Management: Howard Hanger, Musical Director
Budget: $50,000 - $100,000

THEATRE

PISGAH PLAYERS
One University Heights, Asheville, NC 28804
(704) 251-6580
Founded: 1988
Arts Area: Theatrical Group
Status: Non-Professional; Non-Profit
Type: Performing; Touring; Sponsoring
Purpose: To produce original contemporary scripts and reinterpret the classics
Management: David B. Hopes, Jade Parsons, Directors
Volunteer Staff: 8
Non-Paid Artists: 70
Utilizes: Special Technical Talent; Guest Artists; Guest Directors
Budget: $1,000 - $50,000
Income Sources: Private Foundations/Grants/Endowments; Box Office; Individual Donations
Season: 52 Weeks   **Annual Attendance:** 1,000
Affiliations: University of North Carolina at Asheville Creative Writing Department

SMOKY MOUNTAIN REPERTORY THEATRE
26 South Lexington Street, Asheville, NC 28801
(704) 252-9661
Founded: 1981
Arts Area: Professional; Folk; Theatrical Group
Status: Semi-Professional; Non-Profit
Type: Performing; Touring; Resident; Educational
Purpose: To produce new works and new adaptations with a particular focus on works of regional significance
Management: H. Byron Ballard, Managing Director; Joe Fioccola, Business Manager; M. Michael Hyatt, Technical Director; Vivienne Conjura, Youth Director
Officers: M. Michael Hyatt, President; Anne Monteath Hyatt, Vice President; H. Byron Ballard, Secretary
Paid Staff: 1   **Volunteer Staff:** 3
Paid Artists: 25   **Non-Paid Artists:** 10
Utilizes: Special Technical Talent
Budget: $1,000 - $50,000
Income Sources: Private Foundations/Grants/Endowments; Business/Corporate Donations; Box Office; Individual Donations
Season: 52 Weeks
Performance Facilities: First Artists Studio-Theater

PERFORMING SERIES

ASHEVILLE CHAMBER MUSIC SERIES
PO Box 1003, Asheville, NC 28802
(704) 669-6141
Founded: 1952
Arts Area: Instrumental Music
Status: Non-Professional; Non-Profit
Type: Performing
Purpose: To provide chamber music concerts
Officers: Dr. Harold Rotman, President; Philip Walker, Vice President; Perien Gray, Secretary; J. H. Wynn, Treasurer

Volunteer Staff: 15
Utilizes: Guest Artists
Budget: $1,000 - $50,000
Income Sources: Private Foundations/Grants/Endowments; Box Office; Individual Donations
Season: October - March   **Annual Attendance:** 720
Affiliations: CMA

FACILITY

ASHEVILLE CIVIC CENTER
87 Haywood Street, Asheville, NC 28801
(704) 259-5736
Type of Facility: Auditorium
Type of Stage: Proscenium
Stage Dimensions: 40'x70'; working stage - 32'x50'   **Orchestra Pit**
Seating Capacity: 2,357
Year Built: 1936
Year Remodeled: 1974   **Architect:** Wood & Cort, PA   **Cost:** $125,000
Contact for Rental: William J. Murphy;   (704) 259-5736

Banner Elk

FACILITY

LEES MCRAE COLLEGE - HAYES AUDITORIUM
Main Street, Banner Elk, NC 28604
(704) 898-8748
FAX: (704) 898-8711
Type of Facility: Concert Hall; Auditorium
Type of Stage: Thrust; Proscenium
Seating Capacity: 815
Year Built: 1973
Contact for Rental: Roy D. Krege;   (704) 898-8748
Resident Groups: Lees McRae College Summer Theatre Forum

Boone

PERFORMING SERIES

AN APPALACHIAN SUMMER
c/o Office of Cultural Affairs, ASU, 801 Rivers Street, Boone, NC 28608
(704) 262-6084
FAX: (704) 262-2848
Arts Area: Dance; Vocal Music; Instrumental Music; Theater
Status: Professional; Non-Profit
Type: Performing; Touring; Resident; Educational; Sponsoring
Purpose: To enrich the lives of people in northwestern North Carolina and the surrounding region through music, theater, dance and art
Management: Gil Morgenstern, Artistic Director; H. Perry Mixter, Director of Cultural Affairs
Officers: Arnold and Muriel Rosen, Broyhill Family Foundation, Martin and Doris Rosen, Contributors
Budget: $100,000 - $500,000
Income Sources: Private Foundations/Grants/Endowments; Business/Corporate Donations; Box Office; Government Grants; Individual Donations
Season: 52 Weeks
Performance Facilities: Farthing Auditorium

HORN IN THE WEST
PO Box 295, Boone, NC 28607
(704) 264-2120
Founded: 1952
Arts Area: Dance; Vocal Music; Theater; Festivals
Status: Professional; Non-Profit
Type: Performing; Educational
Purpose: To relive the past, focusing mainly on the revolutionary war period and the early settlers' struggles with the Indians
Management: Curtis Smalling, General Manager/ Museum Director; Sharon Fairweather, Public Relations
Paid Staff: 80   **Volunteer Staff:** 12

Paid Artists: 50
Income Sources: Private Foundations/Grants/Endowments; Business/Corporate Donations; Box Office; Government Grants; Individual Donations
Season: June - August
Affiliations: Southern Appalachian Historical Association
Performance Facilities: Horn In The West

FACILITY

FARTHING AUDITORIUM
Rivers Street, ASU, Boone, NC 28608
(704) 262-6372
FAX: (704) 262-2848
    Founded: 1975
    Type of Facility: Auditorium
    Type of Stage: Proscenium
    Stage Dimensions: 56'x44'   **Orchestra Pit**
    Seating Capacity: 1,800
    Year Built: 1975   **Architect:** Fred W. Butner and Associates   **Cost:** $2,300,000
    Contact for Rental: Gregory Williams;   (704) 262-6372

Brevard

FACILITY

BREVARD MUSIC CENTER - STRAUS AUDITORIUM
Probart Street, PO Box 592, Brevard, NC 28712
(704) 884-2011
FAX: (704) 884-2036
    Type of Facility: Concert Hall; Auditorium
    Facility Originally: Recreation Hall; Gymnasium
    Type of Stage: Proscenium
    Stage Dimensions: 25'Wx15'D
    Seating Capacity: 300
    Year Built: 1927
    Contact for Rental: Bill Boggs;   (704) 884-2011

BREVARD MUSIC CENTER - WHITTINGTON-PFOHL AUDITORIUM
Probart Street, PO Box 592, Brevard, NC 28712
(704) 884-2011
FAX: (704) 884-2036
    Type of Facility: Concert Hall; Auditorium; Opera House
    Type of Stage: Proscenium
    Stage Dimensions: 50'Wx35'D   **Orchestra Pit**
    Seating Capacity: 1,647
    Year Built: 1964   **Architect:** Six Associates   **Cost:** $225,000
    Year Remodeled: 1983   **Architect:** Alfred F. Platt   **Cost:** $220,000
    Contact for Rental: Bill Boggs;   (704) 884-2011
    Resident Groups: Brevard Music Center Orchestra; Transylvania Symphony Orchestra; Transylvania Youth Orchestra; Wind Ensemble; Brevard Music Center Opera Workshop

Cameron

INSTRUMENTAL MUSIC

MOORE COMMUNITY BAND
Route 1, PO Box 98, Cameron, NC 28326
(919) 245-7267
    Founded: 1984
    Arts Area: Band
    Status: Non-Profit
    Type: Performing; Resident
    Purpose: Provide opportunity to play and perform good band literature; to support local civic and community programs
    Management: David Sieberling, Director
    Officers: Jay Phillips, President; Elouise Whitesell, Secretary; Dorothy Verney, Treasurer
    Volunteer Staff: 8
    Paid Artists: 6   **Non-Paid Artists:** 35

Utilizes: Guest Conductors; Guest Artists; Guest Directors
Budget: $1,000 - $50,000
Income Sources: Business/Corporate Donations; Box Office; Individual Donations
Season: 52 Weeks **Annual Attendance:** 1,200
Affiliations: Sandhills Arts Council
Performance Facilities: Performing Arts Center

Camp Lejeune

FACILITY

CAMP THEATER
Building 19, Camp Lejeune, NC 28542
(919) 451-1759
FAX: (919) 451-1879
Type of Facility: Theatre House
Type of Stage: Proscenium
Stage Dimensions: 45'x45' **Orchestra Pit**
Seating Capacity: 1,585
Year Built: 1942 **Architect:** Carr & J.E. Greiner Company
Contact for Rental: Ray Herbert

Carrboro

THEATRE

ARTSCENTER
300-G East Main Street, Carrboro, NC 27510
(919) 942-2041
Founded: 1973
Arts Area: Professional; Musical; Community; Theatrical Group
Status: Professional; Non-Professional; Non-Profit
Type: Performing; Touring; Resident; Educational; Sponsoring
Purpose: To produce and present a balanced selection of community and professional performing arts groups, offering opportunities for participation in all aspects of theatre art; Visual arts gallery and art school are included
Management: Mary H. Ruth, Operations Manager; Eileen Helton, General Manager
Officers: Fred Good, Chairman; Hank Straus, Chairman-Elect; Tyler Vermylia, Secretary; Gina DeVine, Treasurer
Paid Staff: 10 **Volunteer Staff:** 2
Utilizes: Special Technical Talent; Guest Artists; Guest Directors
Budget: $100,000 - $500,000
Income Sources: Private Foundations/Grants/Endowments; Business/Corporate Donations; Box Office; Government Grants; Individual Donations
Season: 52 Weeks **Annual Attendance:** 15,000
Performance Facilities: Earl Wynn Theatre

TOUCH
PO Box 631, Carrboro, NC 27510
(919) 968-1721
Founded: 1976
Arts Area: Professional; Theatrical Group
Status: Professional; Non-Profit
Type: Performing; Touring; Educational
Purpose: Tour, perform original mime theatre for adults and children: "It's all right to laugh out loud."
Management: Patricia Towne, Secretary
Officers: Jef, President; Patricia Towne, Secretary; Laurie Wolf, Sheila Kerrigan, Jef, Co-Artistic Directors
Paid Staff: 1
Paid Artists: 6
Utilizes: Special Technical Talent; Guest Artists; Guest Directors
Budget: $100,000 - $500,000
Income Sources: Private Foundations/Grants/Endowments; Business/Corporate Donations; Box Office; Government Grants; Individual Donations
Season: September - May
Affiliations: North Carolina Theatre Conference; SETC; ROOTS; NMTA

FACILITY

THE ARTSCENTER
300-G East Main Street, Carrboro, NC 27510
(919) 929-2787
Founded: 1974
Type of Facility: Theatre Complex; Concert Hall; Auditorium; Studio Performance; Performance Center; Theatre House; Multi-Purpose; Visual And Performing Arts Classrooms
Facility Originally: Grocery Store
Type of Stage: Greek; 3/4 Arena
Stage Dimensions: 16'x24'
Seating Capacity: 350
Year Built: 1968
Year Remodeled: 1986   **Architect:** Lucy Carol Davis Associates   **Cost:** $1,000,000
Contact for Rental: Mary Ruth;   (919) 929-2787
Manager: Eileen Helton;   (919) 929-2787
Resident Groups: Transactors Improv Company; New Plays Rising; The Children's Tap Compnay
The facility is available for non-arts events only

Chapel Hill

THEATRE

PLAYMAKERS REPERTORY COMPANY
Graham Memorial Building, CB# 3235, Chapel Hill, NC 27599
(919) 962-1122
FAX: (919) 962-4069
Founded: 1976
Arts Area: Professional; Theatrical Group
Status: Professional
Type: Performing; Educational
Purpose: Provide professional training for promising actors who work with a LORT professional company
Management: Milly S. Barranger, Executive Producer; David Hammond, Artistic Director; Mary Robin Wells, Administrative Director
Paid Staff: 42   **Volunteer Staff:** 82
Paid Artists: 35   **Non-Paid Artists:** 7
Utilizes: Special Technical Talent; Guest Artists; Guest Directors
Budget: $500,000 - $1,000,000
Income Sources: Private Foundations/Grants/Endowments; Business/Corporate Donations; Box Office; Government Grants; Individual Donations
Season: September - May   **Annual Attendance:** 50,000
Affiliations: LORT; TCG
Performance Facilities: Paul Green Theatre

PERFORMING SERIES

INSTITUTE OF OUTDOOR DRAMA
CB 32-40 Nations Bank Plaza, UNC, Chapel Hill, NC 27599-3240
(919) 962-1328
Founded: 1963
Arts Area: Theater; Outdoor
Status: Non-Profit
Type: Educational; Sponsoring
Purpose: Research and advisory agency of University of North Carolina, sponsors regional auditions annually for performers and technicians in outdoor dramas; hosts management conference annually; conducts feasibility studies; assists established dramas
Management: Scott J. Parker, Director
Paid Staff: 5
Utilizes: Special Technical Talent; Guest Artists
Budget: $50,000 - $100,000
Income Sources: Government Grants; Individual Donations; Fees

Charlotte

DANCE

CHARLOTTE CITY BALLET
8612 Monroe Road, Charlotte, NC 28212
(704) 536-0615
>**Founded:** 1986
>**Arts Area:** Ballet
>**Status:** Semi-Professional; Non-Profit
>**Type:** Performing; Resident
>**Purpose:** To give professionals and pre-professionals an outlet and bring the art of ballet to the community
>**Management:** Claudia Folts-Mercure, Artistic Director
>**Paid Artists:** 4   **Non-Paid Artists:** 16
>**Utilizes:** Guest Artists; Guest Choreographers
>**Budget:** $1,000 - $50,000
>**Income Sources:** Private Foundations/Grants/Endowments; Business/Corporate Donations; Box Office; Government Grants; Individual Donations
>**Season:** October - March
>**Affiliations:** Charlotte Ballet Association

NORTH CAROLINA DANCE THEATER
800 North College Street, Charlotte, NC 28202
(704) 372-0101
FAX: (704) 375-0260
>**Founded:** 1970
>**Arts Area:** Modern; Ballet
>**Status:** Professional; Non-Profit
>**Type:** Performing; Touring
>**Purpose:** To present the art of dance and dancers doing choreographers' work
>**Management:** Nyrna Saturn Gatty, Executive Director
>**Officers:** Guy A. Wilson, President; Elisabeth Hair, Vice President
>**Paid Staff:** 9
>**Paid Artists:** 16
>**Utilizes:** Guest Artists; Guest Choreographers
>**Budget:** $1,000,000 - $5,000,000
>**Income Sources:** Private Foundations/Grants/Endowments; Business/Corporate Donations; Box Office; Government Grants; Individual Donations
>**Season:** September - June   **Annual Attendance:** 70,000
>**Affiliations:** North Carolina School of the Arts
>**Performance Facilities:** North Carolina Blumenthal Performing Arts Center

INSTRUMENTAL MUSIC

CAROLINA PRO MUSICA
PO Box 32022, Charlotte, NC 28232
(704) 334-3468
>**Founded:** 1977
>**Arts Area:** Chamber; Ensemble; Choral
>**Status:** Professional; Non-Profit
>**Type:** Performing; Touring; Educational; Sponsoring
>**Purpose:** To perform music primarily written before 1800 in an historically-correct style, using period instruments
>**Management:** Karen Hite Jacob, Artistic Director; Edward Ferrell, Research; Susan Shoemaker, Technician
>**Paid Staff:** 3   **Volunteer Staff:** 10
>**Paid Artists:** 10
>**Utilizes:** Special Technical Talent; Guest Artists
>**Budget:** $1,000 - $50,000
>**Income Sources:** Private Foundations/Grants/Endowments; Business/Corporate Donations; Box Office; Individual Donations
>**Season:** October - March   **Annual Attendance:** 450
>**Affiliations:** Early Music America
>**Performance Facilities:** Historic 1892 Chapel

CHAMBER MUSIC OF CHARLOTTE
2114 Amboy Court, Charlotte, NC 28205
(704) 535-3024
>**Founded:** 1977
>**Arts Area:** Chamber

Status: Professional; Semi-Professional; Non-Profit
Type: Performing; Educational
Purpose: To encourage composition, performance and enjoyment of chamber music
Officers: Lisa Spring, President; Jeff Bernard, Vice President; Linda Whitener, Secretary; Linda Hess, Treasurer
Volunteer Staff: 5
Paid Artists: 60 **Non-Paid Artists:** 15
Budget: $1,000 - $50,000
Income Sources: Private Foundations/Grants/Endowments; Business/Corporate Donations; Box Office; Government Grants; Individual Donations
Season: 52 Weeks **Annual Attendance:** 17,000

CHARLOTTE SYMPHONY ORCHESTRA SOCIETY
1415 South Church Street, Suite S, Charlotte, NC 28203
(704) 332-6136
FAX: (704) 332-1963
Founded: 1932
Arts Area: Symphony; Orchestra; Chamber; Ensemble
Status: Professional; Non-Profit
Type: Performing; Touring; Resident; Educational
Purpose: To bring the rewards of great music to the citizens of Charlotte and the surrounding region by presenting a professional symphony orchestra and its ensembles in a full range of musical performances of artistic excellence
Management: Sally Meanor, Interim Executive Director; Leo B. Driehuys, Music Director
Officers: James Worrell, President; Fred Figge, Secretary/Treasurer
Paid Staff: 12 **Volunteer Staff:** 700
Paid Artists: 90
Utilizes: Guest Conductors; Guest Artists
Budget: $1,000,000 - $5,000,000
Income Sources: Private Foundations/Grants/Endowments; Business/Corporate Donations; Box Office; Government Grants; Individual Donations
Season: September - July **Annual Attendance:** 190,000
Affiliations: ASOL; Association of Symphony Orchestras of North Carolina; Arts Advocates of North Carolina
Performance Facilities: Ovens Auditorium; Dana Auditorium

VOCAL MUSIC

CHARLOTTE CHORAL SOCIETY
345 North College Street, #407, Charlotte, NC 28202
(704) 374-1564
Founded: 1953
Arts Area: Choral
Status: Non-Profit
Type: Performing
Purpose: To provide a wide range of quality productions to a varied audience
Management: Vince DeLap, Executive Director; Keri Blocker, Development Director; Lynda Shuler, Administrative Assistant
Officers: Thomas Schaumburg, Chairman; Pam Summey, President
Paid Staff: 7
Utilizes: Special Technical Talent; Guest Conductors; Guest Artists; Guest Directors
Budget: $100,000 - $500,000
Income Sources: Private Foundations/Grants/Endowments; Business/Corporate Donations; Box Office; Individual Donations
Season: 52 Weeks **Annual Attendance:** 30,000
Affiliations: Arts and Science Council
Performance Facilities: Ovens Auditorium; Spirit Square

OPERA CAROLINA
345 North College Street, Charlotte, NC 28202
(704) 332-7177
Founded: 1948
Arts Area: Grand Opera; Lyric Opera; Light Opera; Operetta
Status: Professional; Non-Profit
Type: Performing; Touring; Resident; Educational
Purpose: To provide the highest quality of professional opera, in season and touring form; to provide educational and community programs throughout the region; to encourage and develop talent
Management: James W.Wright, Chief Executive Officer
Officers: Woodrow E. Nail, Chairman
Paid Staff: 11 **Volunteer Staff:** 100
Paid Artists: 115 **Non-Paid Artists:** 20
Utilizes: Special Technical Talent; Guest Conductors; Guest Artists; Guest Directors

Budget: $1,000,000 - $5,000,000
Income Sources: Private Foundations/Grants/Endowments; Business/Corporate Donations; Box Office; Government Grants; Individual Donations
Season: October - May
Affiliations: OA; COS; NOA
Performance Facilities: Ovens Auditorium

ORATORIO SINGERS OF CHARLOTTE
345 North College Street, Suite 408, Charlotte, NC 28202
(704) 332-8151
FAX: (704) 332-3627
Founded: 1951
Arts Area: Choral
Status: Semi-Professional; Non-Profit
Type: Performing; Touring; Educational
Purpose: To provide choral training for church directors and provide excellent choral (classical) music for the Piedmont area
Management: Gregory A. Siberman, Executive Director
Officers: Kathryn C. Preyer, President; Carol F. Innes, Vice President; Sally Pierce Hall, President-Elect; Lynn Seals De-Jaco, Treasurer; Carolyn Wells Kibler, Secretary
Paid Staff: 2
Paid Artists: 3
Utilizes: Guest Artists
Budget: $100,000 - $500,000
Income Sources: Private Foundations/Grants/Endowments; Business/Corporate Donations; Box Office; Government Grants; Individual Donations
Season: September - May   **Annual Attendance:** 10,000
Affiliations: CA; Arts and Science Council
Performance Facilities: Calvary Church; Performing Arts Center

THEATRE

CENTRAL PIEDMONT COMMUNITY THEATRE
Kings Drive at Elizabeth Avenue, Charlotte, NC 28212
(704) 342-6568
FAX: (704) 342-5934
Founded: 1974
Arts Area: Musical; Theatrical Group
Status: Semi-Professional
Type: Performing; Educational
Purpose: To provide training to students entering professional theatre and provide quality community entertainment
Management: Tom Vance, Producer/Director; Tom Hollis, Director
Officers: Gene Bryant, Chairman
Paid Staff: 6
Paid Artists: 40   **Non-Paid Artists:** 40
Utilizes: Special Technical Talent; Guest Artists; Guest Directors
Budget: $100,000 - $500,000
Income Sources: Box Office
Season: June - August   **Annual Attendance:** 27,000
Affiliations: North Carolina Theatre Conference; SETC
Performance Facilities: Pease Auditorium

CHARLOTTE REPERTORY THEATRE
345 North College Street, Charlotte, NC 28202
(704) 375-4796
FAX: (704) 375-9462
Founded: 1976
Arts Area: Professional; Theatrical Group
Status: Professional; Non-Profit
Type: Performing; Resident
Purpose: To present contemporary plays, to develop and present new works, and revive the classics of modern drama
Management: Keith T. Martin, Managing Director
Officers: Muriel W. Helms, President; Buddy LeTourneau, President-Elect; Tate K. Sterrett, Secretary; Rick Fujita, Treasurer
Paid Staff: 8   **Volunteer Staff:** 2
Paid Artists: 86
Utilizes: Special Technical Talent; Guest Artists; Guest Directors
Budget: $500,000 - $1,000,000

Income Sources: Private Foundations/Grants/Endowments; Business/Corporate Donations; Box Office; Government Grants; Individual Donations
Season: September - June   **Annual Attendance:** 32,500
Affiliations: AEA
Performance Facilities: Spirit Square Center for the arts; North Carolina Blumenthal Performing Arts Center; Jewish Community Center

THEATRE CHARLOTTE
501 Queens Road, Charlotte, NC 28207
(704) 376-3777; (704) 334-9128
FAX: (704) 347-5216
    Founded: 1927
    Arts Area: Community; Theatrical Group
    Status: Non-Profit
    Type: Performing; Educational
    Purpose: To provide an opportunity to community members to attend or participate in an avocational theatre experience
    Management: Denise Malloy Hubbard, Executive Director
    Officers: Terry Shook, President
    Paid Staff: 4
    Utilizes: Special Technical Talent; Guest Directors
    Budget: $100,000 - $500,000
    Income Sources: Private Foundations/Grants/Endowments; Business/Corporate Donations; Box Office; Individual Donations
    Season: 52 Weeks   **Annual Attendance:** 12,465
    Affiliations: Auxiliary and First Nighters

FACILITY

CENTRAL PIEDMONT COMMUNITY COLLEGE - SUMMER THEATRE
Box 35009, Charlotte, NC 28235
(704) 342-6568
    Type of Facility: Theatre Complex; Auditorium
    Type of Stage: Proscenium
    Stage Dimensions: 40'Wx29'D   **Orchestra Pit**
    Seating Capacity: 439
    Year Built: 1969   **Architect:** J.N. Pease   **Cost:** $1,500,000
    Contact for Rental: Central Piedmont Community College;   (704) 342-6950
    Resident Groups: Central Piedmont Community College Theatre; Central Piedmont Community College Summer Theatre

NORTH CAROLINA BLUMENTHAL PERFORMING ARTS CENTER
130 North Tryon Street, Charlotte, NC 28202
(704) 333-4686
FAX: (704) 376-2289
    Founded: 1992
    Type of Facility: Theatre Complex; Performance Center
    Type of Stage: Proscenium
    Stage Dimensions: Belk Theatre - 55'x54'; Booth Playhouse - 40'x37'
    Orchestra Pit
    Seating Capacity: Belk - 2,100; Booth - 440
    Year Built: 1992   **Architect:** Cesar Pelli & Associates
    Contact for Rental: Drew Murphy;   (704) 333-4686
    Resident Groups: Charlotte Symphony; Opera Carolina; Community Concerts; North Carolina Dance Theater; Charlotte Repertory Theater; Charollotte Choral Society; Oratorio Singers of Charlotte

OVENS AUDITORIUM
2700 East Independence Boulevard, Charlotte, NC 28205
(704) 372-3600
FAX: (704) 372-3620
    Type of Facility: Auditorium
    Type of Stage: Proscenium
    Stage Dimensions: 100'Wx50'D   **Orchestra Pit**
    Seating Capacity: 2,603
    Acoustical Consultant: Carey Heintz
    Contact for Rental: Hubert J. McLendon;   (704) 372-3600

SPIRIT SQUARE CENTER FOR THE ARTS
345 North College Street, Charlotte, NC 28202
(704) 372-9664
FAX: (704) 377-9808
Founded: 1976
Type of Facility: Concert Hall; Studio Performance; Theatre House; Multi-Purpose; Visual Art Galleries; Studio Spaces
Facility Originally: Church; Education Building; Print Shop
Type of Stage: Thrust; Proscenium
Seating Capacity: Hall 1 - 692; Hall 2 - 180; Hall 3 - 110 (Flexible)
Year Built: 1909   **Architect:** J.M. McMichael
Year Remodeled: 1989   **Architect:** Middleton-McMillan   **Cost:** $6,500,000
Contact for Rental: Lesa Delahunty;   (704) 372-9664
Resident Groups: Charlotte Repertory Theatre; Opera Carolina; Oratorio Singers Choral Society

Cullowhee

INSTRUMENTAL MUSIC

SMOKY MOUNTAIN BRITISH BRASS
PO Box 2438, Cullowhee, NC 28723
(704) 293-9312
Founded: 1981
Arts Area: Chamber; Band
Status: Semi-Professional
Type: Performing; Touring; Educational
Purpose: To perform quality brass band music of all eras and artists
Management: Bert Wiley, General Manager
Paid Staff: 2   **Volunteer Staff:** 28
Utilizes: Guest Conductors
Budget: $1,000 - $50,000
Income Sources: Private Foundations/Grants/Endowments; Business/Corporate Donations; Box Office; Government Grants; Individual Donations
Season: 52 Weeks   **Annual Attendance:** 15,000

Durham

DANCE

THE AFRICAN-AMERICAN DANCE ENSEMBLE
804 Berkeley Street, Durham, NC 27701
(919) 560-2720
Founded: 1983
Arts Area: Ethnic
Status: Semi-Professional; Non-Profit
Type: Performing; Touring; Resident; Educational
Purpose: The African-American Dance Ensemble is dedicated to sharing and preserving the finest dance and music of the African and Afro-American tradition as a cultural resource for all people.
Management: Pamela D. Martin, Company Manager; Chuck Davis, Artistic Director; Khalid Saleem, Musical Director
Officers: Joseph T. Hughes Jr., Board Chairman
Paid Staff: 1   **Volunteer Staff:** 10
Paid Artists: 18
Utilizes: Special Technical Talent; Guest Artists
Budget: $100,000 - $500,000
Income Sources: Private Foundations/Grants/Endowments
Season: 52 Weeks
Affiliations: American Dance Festival

AMERICAN DANCE FESTIVAL
PO Box 6097, College Station, Durham, NC 27708
(919) 684-6402
FAX: (919) 684-5459
Founded: 1934
Arts Area: Modern
Status: Professional; Non-Profit
Type: Educational; Sponsoring

Purpose: To encourage and support the creation of our dance heritage by established and emerging choreographers; to provide a sound scientific/aesthetic professional education; to assist in the enlargement of a national and international American modern dance audience
Management: Charles Reinhart, Director; Stephanie Reinhart, Associate Director; Art Waber, Operations Manager
Officers: Carlton Midytte, Chairperson; Judith Sagan, Secretary
Paid Staff: 75 **Volunteer Staff:** 350
Paid Artists: 150
Utilizes: Guest Artists
Budget: $1,000,000 - $5,000,000
Income Sources: Private Foundations/Grants/Endowments; Business/Corporate Donations; Box Office; Government Grants; Individual Donations
Season: June - July **Annual Attendance:** 25,000
Affiliations: Duke University
Performance Facilities: Page Auditorium; Reynolds Industries Theatre

NEW PERFORMING DANCE COMPANY
120 Morris Street, Durham, NC 27701
(919) 560-2732
Founded: 1975
Arts Area: Modern
Status: Professional; Non-Profit
Type: Performing; Touring
Purpose: To promote the art form of modern dance by regular production and performance of original choreography
Management: Linda Stier, Administrative Director; Lee Wenger, Artistic Director
Officers: Mary Ellen Taylor, President Board of Directors
Paid Staff: 6 **Volunteer Staff:** 1
Paid Artists: 5 **Non-Paid Artists:** 1
Utilizes: Special Technical Talent
Budget: $1,000 - $50,000
Income Sources: Box Office; Government Grants; Individual Donations
Season: September - June **Annual Attendance:** 2,000
Affiliations: Durham Arts Council

INSTRUMENTAL MUSIC

CHAMBER ARTS SOCIETY
PO Box 22146, Duke Station, Durham, NC 27706
(919) 684-5578
FAX: (919) 684-3200
Founded: 1945
Arts Area: Chamber
Status: Non-Profit
Type: Sponsoring
Purpose: To provide five or six chamber music concerts a year of the highest possible quality, with an emphasis on string quartet
Management: Ruth M. Blum, Director; Susan Coon, Ex Officio, Director of Office of Cultural Affairs
Paid Staff: 3 **Volunteer Staff:** 8
Paid Artists: 20
Utilizes: Guest Artists
Budget: $1,000 - $50,000
Income Sources: Private Foundations/Grants/Endowments; Box Office; Individual Donations
Season: September - April
Affiliations: Duke University, Office of Cultural Affairs
Performance Facilities: Bryan Center

VOCAL MUSIC

DURHAM CIVIC CHORAL SOCIETY
120 Morris Street, Durham, NC 27701
(919) 560-2733
Arts Area: Choral
Status: Non-Professional; Non-Profit
Type: Performing
Management: Susan L. Van Wyck, Membership Chair
Officers: Judy Via, President; Ken Hoover, Vice President; Kate Goldstucker, Secretary; Mary Ann Dotson, Treasurer; Barbara NamKoong, Librarian; Joan Wall, Historian
Paid Staff: 1
Paid Artists: 2 **Non-Paid Artists:** 154
Utilizes: Guest Artists

Budget: $50,000 - $100,000
Income Sources: Private Foundations/Grants/Endowments; Business/Corporate Donations; Box Office; Individual Donations
Season: September - May   **Annual Attendance:** 2,100
Performance Facilities: Duke University Chapel; Baldwin Auditorium, Duke University

TRIANGLE OPERA THEATER
120 Morris Street, Durham, NC 27701
(919) 560-2741
FAX: (919) 560-2704
Founded: 1985
Arts Area: Grand Opera; Lyric Opera; Light Opera
Status: Non-Profit
Type: Performing
Purpose: To present and perform opera in the Raleigh-Durham-Chapel Hill area
Management: Sara Elizabeth J. Hyre, Manager; Scott Tilley, Music Director
Officers: Kenneth Susiska, Chair; Wes Neuman, Vice Chair; Sara Armentrout, Secretary; Steven Largent, Treasurer
Paid Staff: 2   **Volunteer Staff:** 20
Paid Artists: 75   **Non-Paid Artists:** 20
Utilizes: Special Technical Talent; Guest Artists
Budget: $100,000 - $500,000
Income Sources: Private Foundations/Grants/Endowments; Business/Corporate Donations; Box Office; Individual Donations
Season: October - June   **Annual Attendance:** 7,500
Affiliations: OA
Performance Facilities: Pace Auditorium/Duke University; Brighthead Square

Eden

THEATRE

CHILDREN'S THEATRE OF EDEN
PO Box 547, Eden, NC 27288
(919) 342-2536
Founded: 1971
Arts Area: Professional; Musical; Folk; Theatrical Group; Puppet
Status: Non-Profit
Type: Sponsoring
Purpose: Provide professional plays to all Eden city school children free of charge
Officers: Susan Pace, President; Clayton Nations, Treasurer
Volunteer Staff: 15
Paid Artists: 35
Budget: $1,000 - $50,000
Income Sources: Private Foundations/Grants/Endowments; Business/Corporate Donations
Season: September - May   **Annual Attendance:** 2,500
Performance Facilities: High School Auditorium

Elkin

INSTRUMENTAL MUSIC

ELKIN BIG BAND
116 East Main Street, Elkin, NC 28621
(919) 835-2621
Founded: 1982
Arts Area: Band
Status: Non-Profit
Type: Performing
Purpose: To present the big band sounds for both public and private functions
Management: Larry Irwin, Organizer/Leader
Volunteer Staff: 16
Income Sources: Private Foundations/Grants/Endowments

Season: 52 Weeks   **Annual Attendance:** 700
Affiliations: Foot Hills Arts Council

Fayetteville

INSTRUMENTAL MUSIC

CUMBERLAND COUNTY FRIENDS OF THE ORCHESTRA
1624 Ireland Drive, Fayetteville, NC 28304
(919) 484-8121
> **Founded:** 1980
> **Arts Area:** Orchestra
> **Status:** Non-Profit
> **Type:** Educational; Sponsoring
> **Purpose:** To maintain a community support group for the Cumberland County School Orchestra Program, lending volunteer hours and financial aid where needed to maintain excellence in the program
> **Management:** Janice Swoope, Orchestra Coordinator
> **Officers:** Mrs. David J. Phleeger, President; Rita Warren, Secretary; Lynn Gloyeski, Treasurer
> **Utilizes:** Guest Artists; Guest Directors
> **Budget:** $1,000 - $50,000
> **Income Sources:** Private Foundations/Grants/Endowments; Business/Corporate Donations; Individual Donations
> **Season:** 52 Weeks   **Annual Attendance:** 5,000

HIGHLAND BRITISH BRASS BAND ASSOCIATION
2405 Morganton Road, Fayetteville, NC 28303
(919) 484-0281
> **Founded:** 1980
> **Arts Area:** Band
> **Status:** Semi-Professional; Non-Profit
> **Type:** Performing
> **Purpose:** To provide a suitable outlet for musically talented adults who are interested in promoting good band music in the British Brass Band format for the instruction and edification of the general public
> **Officers:** Robert Downing, Chairman, Board of Directors
> **Utilizes:** Guest Conductors; Guest Artists
> **Budget:** $1,000 - $50,000
> **Income Sources:** Private Foundations/Grants/Endowments; Business/Corporate Donations; Box Office; Government Grants; Individual Donations
> **Season:** 52 Weeks
> **Affiliations:** Arts Council of Fayetteville and Cumberland County
> **Performance Facilities:** Methodist College

THEATRE

CAPE FEAR REGIONAL THEATRE
1209 Hay Street, Fayetteville, NC 28305
(919) 323-4234
FAX: (919) 323-0898
> **Founded:** 1962
> **Arts Area:** Professional; Musical; Community; Puppet; Drama
> **Status:** Semi-Professional; Non-Profit
> **Type:** Performing
> **Purpose:** To present a regional theatre program that incorporates a diverse selection of plays which will appeal to a wide selection of potential theatre-goers in the Cape Fear Region
> **Management:** Bo Thorp, Artistic Director; Deborah Martin-Mintz, Associate Director
> **Officers:** Steven Tussey, President of the Board; Bill Bowman, Vice President; Gina Keel, Secretary; Charlie Johnson, Treasurer
> **Paid Staff:** 9   **Volunteer Staff:** 100
> **Paid Artists:** 1
> **Utilizes:** Special Technical Talent; Guest Conductors; Guest Artists; Guest Directors; Choreographers; Designers
> **Budget:** $100,000 - $500,000
> **Income Sources:** Private Foundations/Grants/Endowments; Business/Corporate Donations; Box Office; Government Grants; Individual Donations
> **Season:** September - June   **Annual Attendance:** 1,156,500
> **Affiliations:** North Carolina Theatre Conference; SETC; Arts Council

FACILITY

CUMBERLAND COUNTY CIVIC CENTER
Highway 301 South, Fayetteville, NC 28306
(919) 323-5088
FAX: (919) 323-2742
    Type of Facility: Theatre Complex; Auditorium; Arena; Multi-Purpose
    Type of Stage: Flexible; Proscenium; Platform
    Stage Dimensions: 64'x40'
    Orchestra Pit
    Seating Capacity: Arena - 6,300; Auditorium - 2,439
    Contact for Rental: Kendall Wall, Danny Lucas;   (919) 323-5088
    Manager: Wilson Roger

Flat Rock

THEATRE

FLAT ROCK PLAYHOUSE
Thomas Wolfe Drive, Flat Rock, NC 28731
(704) 693-0731
FAX: (704) 693-6795
    Founded: 1937
    Arts Area: Professional; Summer Stock; Musical; Theatrical Group
    Status: Professional; Non-Profit; Commercial
    Type: Performing; Touring; Resident; Educational; Sponsoring
    Purpose: To present a 16-week summer stock season in conjunction with The Vagabond School of Drama Workshops; to tour North Carolina schools throughout the year
    Management: Robin R. Farquhar, Executive/Artistic Director
    Officers: Albert Gooch, President of Board of Trustees
    Paid Staff: 60   **Volunteer Staff:** 4
    Paid Artists: 25   **Non-Paid Artists:** 20
    Utilizes: Special Technical Talent; Guest Artists; Guest Directors
    Budget: $500,000 - $1,000,000
    Income Sources: Private Foundations/Grants/Endowments; Business/Corporate Donations; Box Office; Government Grants; Individual Donations
    Season: May - September   **Annual Attendance:** 60,000
    Affiliations: AEA; SETC
    Performance Facilities: Flat Rock Playhouse

Gastonia

THEATRE

LITTLE THEATRE OF GASTONIA
238 South Clay Street, Gastonia, NC 28052
(704) 865-0160
    Founded: 1950
    Arts Area: Musical; Community
    Status: Non-Professional; Non-Profit
    Type: Performing; Educational
    Purpose: To provide entertainment and instruction in theatre arts and sciences
    Management: Carolyn E. Sanders, Administrator
    Officers: Locke Bell, President; Sherry Abernathy, Vice President; Eleanor Wixson, Secretary; Betty C. Blume, Treasurer
    Paid Staff: 1   **Volunteer Staff:** 20
    Non-Paid Artists: 50
    Utilizes: Special Technical Talent
    Budget: $50,000 - $100,000
    Income Sources: Private Foundations/Grants/Endowments; Business/Corporate Donations; Box Office; Government Grants; Individual Donations
    Season: September - July   **Annual Attendance:** 9,000
    Affiliations: United Arts & Science Council of Gastonia; North Carolina Theatre Conference; SETC
    Performance Facilities: The Little Theatre of Gastonia

Greensboro

DANCE

JOHN GAMBLE/JAN VAN DYKE DANCE COMPANY
306 Aberdeen Terrace, Greensboro, NC 27403
(919) 370-4819
  Founded: 1989
  Arts Area: Modern
  Status: Professional; Non-Profit
  Type: Performing; Touring
  Management: Darlene Errett, Administrative Assistant
  Officers: John Gamble, Jan Van Dyke, Artistic Directors
  Paid Staff: 1   **Volunteer Staff:** 2
  Paid Artists: 12
  Budget: $1,000 - $50,000
  Income Sources: Private Foundations/Grants/Endowments; Box Office; Government Grants; Individual Donations
  Season: 52 Weeks   **Annual Attendance:** 2,500
  Affiliations: University of North Carolina-Greensboro
  Performance Facilities: University of North Carolina-Greensboro Dance Theatre

INSTRUMENTAL MUSIC

BEL CANTO COMPANY
PO Box 10752, Greensboro, NC 27404
  Founded: 1983
  Arts Area: Ensemble
  Status: Semi-Professional
  Type: Performing
  Purpose: Dedicated to the highest performance standards of choral literature of all historical periods
  Management: David Pegg, Music Director/Conductor
  Officers: Alice Isaacson, Chairman; Sarah Warmath, Vice Chairman; Linda Shaban, Secretary; Lauren Search, Treasurer
  Paid Staff: 2   **Volunteer Staff:** 18
  Paid Artists: 2   **Non-Paid Artists:** 18
  Utilizes: Special Technical Talent; Guest Artists
  Budget: $1,000 - $50,000
  Income Sources: Private Foundations/Grants/Endowments; Business/Corporate Donations; Box Office; Individual Donations
  Season: September - May
  Annual Attendance: 1,200
  Affiliations: Greensboro Parks and Recreation
  Performance Facilities: Dana Auditorium

GREENSBORO CONCERT BAND
200 North Davie Street, Greensboro, NC 27401
(919) 373-2549
FAX: (919) 373-2060
  Founded: 1977
  Arts Area: Band
  Status: Non-Professional
  Type: Performing
  Purpose: To share musical understanding through serious practice and the real enthusiasm, pleasure, and sense of accomplishment in public performance
  Management: Lynn H. Donovan, Executive Director; Charles Murph, Conductor
  Officers: Stuart Fitzpatrick, President; Gary Anderson, Vice President; Ninette Humbler, Recording Secretary; Shirley Vann, Correspondence Secretary; John Morck, Treasurer; Linda Deese, Librarian
  Paid Staff: 2   **Volunteer Staff:** 20
  Paid Artists: 2   **Non-Paid Artists:** 75
  Utilizes: Guest Conductors; Guest Artists
  Budget: $1,000 - $50,000
  Income Sources: Private Foundations/Grants/Endowments; Business/Corporate Donations; Box Office; Individual Donations
  Season: September - July
  Annual Attendance: 6,500

>**Affiliations:** City of Greensboro; The Music Center
>**Performance Facilities:** Dana Auditorium

GREENSBORO SYMPHONY ORCHESTRA
200 North Davie Street, PO Box 20303, Greensboro, NC 27420
(919) 333-7490
>**Founded:** 1977
>**Arts Area:** Orchestra
>**Status:** Professional
>**Type:** Performing
>**Purpose:** To strive seriously for the highest quality of performance, with the ultimate goal of attaining a truly professional sound, the love of playing orchestral literature remaining the prime factor for participation
>**Management:** Barry Auman, Music Director
>**Officers:** Robert Lavietas, President; Erik Salzwedel, Librarian
>**Utilizes:** Guest Conductors; Guest Artists
>**Budget:** $500,000 - $1,000,000
>**Income Sources:** Private Foundations/Grants/Endowments; Business/Corporate Donations; Box Office; Government Grants; Individual Donations
>**Season:** September - May
>**Annual Attendance:** 2,900
>**Affiliations:** City of Greensboro
>**Performance Facilities:** War Memorial Auditorium

VOCAL MUSIC

CHORAL SOCIETY OF GREENSBORO
200 North Davie Street, Greensboro, NC 27401
(919) 373-2549
FAX: (919) 373-2060
>**Founded:** 1984
>**Arts Area:** Choral
>**Status:** Non-Professional
>**Type:** Performing
>**Purpose:** To share musical understanding through serious practice and the real pleasure, enthusiasm, sense of accomplishment and quality musicianship in public performance
>**Management:** William Carroll, Conductor; Lynn H. Donovan, Executive Director
>**Officers:** Peggy Clapper, President; Tom Wright, Vice President; Jennifer Blevins, Recording Secretary; Kathy Riffe, Correspondence Secretary; Lucy Amaxopulus, Treasurer; Sandra Schaller, Librarian
>**Paid Staff:** 2 **Volunteer Staff:** 25
>**Paid Artists:** 2 **Non-Paid Artists:** 200
>**Utilizes:** Guest Conductors; Guest Artists
>**Budget:** $1,000 - $50,000
>**Income Sources:** Private Foundations/Grants/Endowments; Business/Corporate Donations; Box Office; Individual Donations
>**Season:** September - May
>**Annual Attendance:** 6,500
>**Affiliations:** City of Greensboro; The Music Center
>**Performance Facilities:** Dana Auditorium

GREENSBORO OPERA COMPANY
1828 Banking Street, Greensboro, NC 27408
(919) 273-9472
>**Founded:** 1981
>**Arts Area:** Grand Opera
>**Status:** Professional; Non-Profit
>**Type:** Performing; Educational; Sponsoring
>**Purpose:** To serve and enrich the cultural life of Greensboro and the surrounding area through the development and promotion of a program of quality operas and opera education
>**Management:** Mary C. Eubanks, Administrator
>**Officers:** Ann Snyder, President
>**Paid Staff:** 1 **Volunteer Staff:** 50
>**Utilizes:** Special Technical Talent; Guest Artists
>**Budget:** $100,000 - $500,000
>**Income Sources:** Private Foundations/Grants/Endowments; Business/Corporate Donations; Box Office; Individual Donations
>**Season:** November
>**Annual Attendance:** 4,500
>**Affiliations:** OA; COS
>**Performance Facilities:** War Memorial Auditorium; Carolina Theatre

THEATRE

COMMUNITY THEATRE OF GREENSBORO
200 North Davie Street, Greensboro, NC 27401
(919) 333-7470; (919) 333-7445
>**Arts Area:** Musical; Dinner; Community; Theatrical Group
>**Status:** Non-Professional; Non-Profit
>**Type:** Performing; Resident; Educational
>**Purpose:** To provide an outlet in the community whereby persons may participate avocationally in a live theatrical experience of high calibre, both as talent and audience under professional guidance
>**Management:** Mitchel Sommers, Executive Director; Pauline Cobrda, Business Manager; Darleen Callaghan, Administrative Assistant
>**Officers:** Pamela Murphy, President Board of Trustees; Doug Anderson, Vice President; Stephen Wilkowski, Secretary; Dennis Duquette, Treasurer
>**Paid Staff:** 3   **Volunteer Staff:** 10
>**Paid Artists:** 50   **Non-Paid Artists:** 200
>**Utilizes:** Special Technical Talent; Guest Artists; Guest Directors
>**Budget:** $100,000 - $500,000
>**Income Sources:** Private Foundations/Grants/Endowments; Business/Corporate Donations; Box Office; Government Grants; Individual Donations
>**Season:** October - June   **Annual Attendance:** 15,000
>**Affiliations:** United Arts Council of Greensboro; SETC; North Carolina State Arts Council
>**Performance Facilities:** Carolina Theatre; Town Hall; Coliseum; Weaver Education Center

GREENSBORO CHILDREN'S THEATRE
200 North Davie Street, Greensboro, NC 27401
(919) 373-2026
>**Founded:** 1971
>**Arts Area:** Musical; Community; Theatrical Group
>**Status:** Non-Professional; Non-Profit
>**Type:** Performing
>**Purpose:** To perform three shows throughout the year by and for children
>**Management:** Barbara Britton, Director
>**Paid Staff:** 3   **Volunteer Staff:** 20
>**Non-Paid Artists:** 100
>**Utilizes:** Guest Directors
>**Budget:** $1,000 - $50,000
>**Income Sources:** Box Office; Government Grants; Individual Donations
>**Season:** November - May   **Annual Attendance:** 3,000
>**Affiliations:** SETC
>**Performance Facilities:** Town Hall; Greensboro Coliseum Complex

LIVESTOCK PLAYERS MUSICAL THEATRE
200 North Davie Street, Greensboro, NC 27401
(919) 373-2026
>**Founded:** 1971
>**Arts Area:** Musical; Dinner; Community; Theatrical Group
>**Status:** Non-Professional; Non-Profit
>**Type:** Performing
>**Purpose:** To perform six musicals throughout the year
>**Management:** Barbara Britton, Director
>**Paid Staff:** 10
>**Non-Paid Artists:** 200
>**Utilizes:** Guest Conductors; Guest Directors
>**Budget:** $1,000 - $50,000
>**Income Sources:** Box Office; Government Grants; Individual Donations
>**Season:** 52 Weeks   **Annual Attendance:** 10,000
>**Affiliations:** SETC
>**Performance Facilities:** Carolina Theatre

PERFORMING SERIES

EASTERN MUSIC FESTIVAL
200 North Davie Street, Greensboro, NC 27401
(919) 333-7450
FAX: (919) 333-7454
>**Founded:** 1961
>**Arts Area:** Symphony; Orchestra; Chamber

Status: Professional; Non-Profit
Type: Performing; Educational
Purpose: To provide six weeks of intensive music study to 200 gifted young musicians from the U.S. and abroad; to provide a high-level music series for the southeast region
Management: Walter W. Heid, Executive Director; Sheldon Morgenstern, Music Director; Juanita Lawson-Haith, Development/Marketing; Dianne Lyle, Business Manager; Janis Nilsen, Admissions Director; Renee Ward, Artistic Administrator
Officers: Dr. Gerald Truesdale, President; William Bearding, James Bethel, Pamela Allen, Thorns Craven and Sue Starr, Vice Presidents; Nancye Tothill, Secretary; Kenneth Dimmock, Treasurer; Howard Covington, Past President
Paid Staff: 10   **Volunteer Staff:** 120
Paid Artists: 100
Utilizes: Guest Conductors; Guest Artists
Budget: $1,000,000 - $5,000,000
Income Sources: Private Foundations/Grants/Endowments; Business/Corporate Donations; Box Office; Government Grants; Individual Donations; Tuition
Season: June - August   **Annual Attendance:** 60,000
Affiliations: BMI; ASCAP

FACILITY

AYCOCK AUDITORIUM
University of North Carolina at Greensboro, Greensboro, NC 27412
(919) 334-5800
FAX: (919) 334-3008
    Type of Facility: Auditorium
    Type of Stage: Proscenium
    Orchestra Pit
    Seating Capacity: 2,300

THE CAROLINA THEATRE
310 South Greene Street, Greensboro, NC 27401
(919) 333-2605; (919) 333-2600
    Type of Facility: Concert Hall; Auditorium; Performance Center; Theatre House
    Facility Originally: Vaudeville
    Type of Stage: Flexible; Proscenium
    Stage Dimensions: 30'x40'x35'
    Orchestra Pit
    Seating Capacity: 1,139
    Year Built: 1927   **Architect:** J.H. DeSibour   **Cost:** $500,000
    Year Remodeled: 1981   **Architect:** Ken Bell   **Cost:** $200,000
    Contact for Rental: Brian Gray;   (919) 333-2600
    Manager: Kathy Worrell
    Resident Groups: Livestock Players Musical Theatre; Community Theatre of Greensboro; Greensboro Civic Ballet; Greensboro Symphony Orchestra

GREENSBORO WAR MEMORIAL AUDITORIUM
1921 West Lee Street, Greensboro, NC 27403
(919) 373-7400
    Type of Facility: Auditorium
    Type of Stage: Proscenium
    Stage Dimensions: 95'Wx46'D
    Orchestra Pit
    Seating Capacity: 2,414
    Year Built: 1959
    Architect: McMinn, Norfleet & Wicker
    Cost: $3,000,000
    Contact for Rental: Andrea Turner;   (919) 373-7400
    Manager: James Evans;   (918) 373-7400

Greenville

INSTRUMENTAL MUSIC

SUMMER STRINGS ON THE MEHERRIN
303 South Elm Street, Greenville, NC 27858
(919) 752-2542
    Founded: 1972

Arts Area: Chamber; Ensemble
Status: Non-Profit
Type: Performing; Resident; Educational
Purpose: Summer Strings On The Meherrin offers a three-week program for 12 to 18-year-old bowed string players to improve their musicianship and techniques and to present chamber music concerts
Management: Paul Topper, Musical Director; James Chamblee, Chowan College Officer
Officers: John R. Kernodle Jr., President; Thaddeus A. Adams III, Howard E. Covington Jr., Robert C. Ketner, Rollin J. McCrory; Angela Seawell, Secretary
Paid Staff: 4
Paid Artists: 4
Utilizes: Guest Artists
Budget: $1,000 - $50,000
Income Sources: Private Foundations/Grants/Endowments; Tuition
Season: July - August   **Annual Attendance:** 500
Affiliations: Chowan College
Performance Facilities: Daniels Hall, Chowan College

FACILITY

HENDRIX THEATRE
c/o Mendenhall Student Center, Greenville, NC 27858-4353
(919) 757-4702
FAX: (919) 757-4778
Founded: 1973
Type of Facility: Concert Hall; Auditorium; Performance Center; Theatre House
Type of Stage: Proscenium
Stage Dimensions: 22'Dx50'W
Seating Capacity: 760
Year Built: 1974   **Architect:** Carter Williams
Contact for Rental: Central Reservations Office;   (919) 757-4731

WRIGHT AUDITORIUM
East Carolina University, Campus Circle, Greenville, NC 27858-4353
(919) 757-6269; (919) 757-6290
FAX: (919) 757-4778
Founded: 1927
Type of Facility: Concert Hall; Auditorium; Performance Center; Theatre House
Type of Stage: Proscenium
Stage Dimensions: 70'x18' apron; 40'Wx25'D stage   **Orchestra Pit**
Seating Capacity: 1,510
Year Remodeled: 1986   **Architect:** J.N. Pease   **Cost:** $4,000,000
Acoustical Consultant: Rein Pirn
Contact for Rental: Central Reservations Office;   (919) 757-4731

Hickory

THEATRE

HICKORY COMMUNITY THEATRE
30 Third Street, NW, Hickory, NC 28601
(704) 327-3855
Founded: 1949
Arts Area: Musical; Community; Dramatic
Status: Non-Professional; Non-Profit
Type: Performing; Touring; Resident; Educational
Purpose: To provide quality theatre performances for the benefit of the community and for the involvement of local talent
Management: Pamela Sinclair, Executive Director; Dana Biehler, Executive Secretary; Aaron Lewis, Technical Director; John Coffey, Musical Director; Charles E. Jeffers, Artistic Director
Officers: Vivienne Stafford, President; Allen Finley, Vice President; Rae Hunsucker, Secretary; G. Rudy Wright, Treasurer
Paid Staff: 4   **Volunteer Staff:** 650
Non-Paid Artists: 250
Utilizes: Special Technical Talent; Guest Artists; Guest Directors
Budget: $100,000 - $500,000
Income Sources: Private Foundations/Grants/Endowments; Business/Corporate Donations; Box Office; Government Grants; Individual Donations
Season: September - July   **Annual Attendance:** 16,000
Affiliations: Catawba County Council for the Arts; North Carolina Theatre Conference; SETC
Performance Facilities: Old City Hall

YOUTHEATRE
810 8th Street NE, Hickory, NC 28601
(704) 327-8081
Founded: 1976
Arts Area: Community; Theatrical Group
Status: Professional; Semi-Professional; Commercial
Type: Performing; Touring; Educational; Sponsoring
Purpose: To provide a forum for young people's creative expression through study and performance
Management: Sylvia B. Hoffmire, Owner/Executive Director
Paid Staff: 3
Utilizes: Special Technical Talent; Guest Artists; Guest Directors
Budget: $1,000 - $50,000
Income Sources: Private Foundations/Grants/Endowments; Business/Corporate Donations; Box Office; Government Grants
Season: September - May
Affiliations: Catawba County Council for the Arts

High Point

THEATRE

HIGH POINT COMMUNITY THEATRE
305 North Main Street, Suite 205, High Point, NC 27260
(919) 882-2542
FAX: (919) 889-2298
Founded: 1976
Arts Area: Community; Theatrical Group
Status: Non-Professional; Non-Profit
Type: Performing
Purpose: To foster community involvement in the performing arts and provide quality entertainment to the citizens of our area
Management: Jennifer Blevins, Executive Director
Officers: Elizabeth Koonce, President; Katherine Grigg, Vice President; Carol Traen, Secretary; Sharon Janesick, Treasurer
Paid Staff: 9   **Volunteer Staff:** 100
Non-Paid Artists: 100
Utilizes: Special Technical Talent; Guest Conductors; Guest Directors
Budget: $50,000 - $100,000
Income Sources: Private Foundations/Grants/Endowments; Business/Corporate Donations; Box Office; Individual Donations
Season: September - May   **Annual Attendance:** 5,000
Affiliations: High Point Arts Council
Performance Facilities: High Point Theatre and Exhibition Center

PERFORMING SERIES

HIGH POINT THEATRE AND EXHIBITION CENTER
220 East Commerce Street, High Point, NC 27260
(919) 883-3401
Founded: 1975
Arts Area: Dance; Vocal Music; Theater; Festivals
Status: Professional; Non-Profit
Type: Performing; Touring; Resident; Educational; Sponsoring
Purpose: To provide quality experiences in the performing arts for the community as entertainment and as education
Management: Steve Willis, Theatre Director
Paid Staff: 5   **Volunteer Staff:** 300
Utilizes: Special Technical Talent; Guest Artists
Budget: $100,000 - $500,000
Income Sources: Private Foundations/Grants/Endowments; Box Office; Government Grants
Season: September - May   **Annual Attendance:** 68,000
Affiliations: APAP; SAF

THE NORTH CAROLINA SHAKESPEARE FESTIVAL
305 North Main Street, PO Box 6066, High Point, NC 27262
(919) 841-2273
Founded: 1977
Arts Area: Theater
Status: Professional; Non-Profit

Type: Performing; Touring; Resident; Educational
Purpose: NCSF seeks to serve the cultural and educational needs of North Carolina audiences through traditional and non-traditional staging of the plays of Shakespeare and other classic playwrights.
Management: Lou Rackoff, Artistic Director; Gian Paul Morelli, Marketing/Public Relatons Director; Pedro Silva, Producer
Officers: William DiPaolo, Chairman of the Board; Kay Philipps, Vice Chairman
Paid Staff: 9
Paid Artists: 60
Utilizes: Guest Artists; Guest Directors
Budget: $500,000 - $1,000,000
Income Sources: Private Foundations/Grants/Endowments; Business/Corporate Donations; Box Office; Government Grants; Individual Donations; Booking Fees
Season: July - September   **Annual Attendance:** 1,300
Affiliations: The North Carolina School of the Arts; The Arts Councils of High Point
Performance Facilities: High Point Theatre

FACILITY

HIGH POINT THEATRE AND EXHIBITION CENTER
220 East Commerce Avenue, High Point, NC 27260
(919) 883-3401
FAX: (919) 883-3419
Founded: 1975
Type of Facility: Theatre Complex; Concert Hall; Auditorium; Performance Center; Civic Center; Multi-Purpose
Type of Stage: Proscenium
Stage Dimensions: 65'x40'x35'   **Orchestra Pit**
Seating Capacity: 967
Year Built: 1975   **Architect:** Six Associates   **Cost:** $2,000,000
Contact for Rental: Steve Willis;   (919) 887-3109
Resident Groups: North Carolina Shakespeare Festival

Highlands

PERFORMING SERIES

HIGHLANDS CHAMBER MUSIC FESTIVAL
PO Box 1702, Highlands, NC 28741
(704) 526-4904
Founded: 1982
Arts Area: Vocal Music; Instrumental Music; Festivals
Status: Professional
Type: Performing; Touring; Resident; Educational; Sponsoring
Purpose: To promote the performance and appreciation of chamber music
Management: Dean F. Zuch, Festival Manager; Lucas Drew, Artistic Director
Officers: Alanson G. Charles, President & CEO; Joanna Rainey, Vice President/Artistic Affairs; Dr. Louis Reynaud, Vice President/Administrative Affairs; Dr. Thomas A. Garman, Secretary; Stephen L. Lucas, Treasurer; Dr. Lucas Drew, Artistic Director
Paid Staff: 2   **Volunteer Staff:** 15
Paid Artists: 22
Utilizes: Guest Artists
Budget: $50,000 - $100,000
Income Sources: Private Foundations/Grants/Endowments; Business/Corporate Donations; Box Office; Government Grants; Individual Donations
Season: July - August   **Annual Attendance:** 1,550
Affiliations: CMA; Macon County Cultural Arts Council
Performance Facilities: Great Hall, Episcopal Church of the Incarnation

FACILITY

HIGHLANDS PLAYHOUSE
PO Box 896, Highlands, NC 28741
(704) 526-2695
Type of Facility: Theatre House
Facility Originally: School
Type of Stage: Proscenium
Seating Capacity: 200
Year Built: 1932
Manager: A.W. Staub, Producer

Resident Groups: Highlands Playhouse
Converted into a theater in 1960

Lincolnton

PERFORMING SERIES

LINCOLN ARTS COUNCIL
PO Box 45, Lincolnton, NC 28093
(704) 732-9044
Founded: 1973
Arts Area: Instrumental Music; Festivals
Status: Non-Profit
Type: Performing; Educational; Sponsoring
Purpose: To develop, promote and foster all forms of art by arranging and offering exhibits, lectures, demonstrations, classes and performances, etc. in the field of creative arts
Management: Lea Evelyn Tatich, Director; Amy Crump, Office Asssistant
Officers: Madeline Elmore, President; Kenneth Brown, First Vice President; beverly McAdams, Second Vice President
Paid Staff: 2   **Volunteer Staff:** 100
Budget: $50,000 - $100,000
Income Sources: Business/Corporate Donations; Box Office; Government Grants; Individual Donations
Annual Attendance: 1,200
Affiliations: North Carolina Association of Arts Councils; North Carolina Arts Council
Performance Facilities: Lincoln Citizens Center; Lincoln Cultural Center

---
Lumberton

INSTRUMENTAL MUSIC

TRINKLE BRASS WORKS
803 West 24th Street, Lumberton, NC 28358
(919) 671-4556
Founded: 1977
Arts Area: Chamber; Ensemble; Instrumental Group
Status: Professional; Non-Profit
Type: Performing; Touring; Resident; Educational
Purpose: Established in 1977 to provide art centers, universities and schools with concerts and lecture-recitals in brass and percussion chamber music. Concerts include performances on Renaissance, Baroque and modern instruments.
Officers: Steven Trinkle, President; Genie Burkett, Vice President; Dr. Alan Kalkor, Secretary; Joel Gordon, Treasurer
Volunteer Staff: 4
Paid Artists: 4
Utilizes: Special Technical Talent; Guest Artists
Budget: $1,000 - $50,000
Income Sources: Private Foundations/Grants/Endowments; Business/Corporate Donations; Government Grants; Individual Donations
Season: 52 Weeks
Annual Attendance: 5,000
Affiliations: Wisconsin Arts Board

Manteo

PERFORMING SERIES

ROANOKE ISLAND HISTORICAL ASSOCIATION INC.
PO Box 40, Manteo, NC 27954
(919) 473-2127
FAX: (919) 473-6000
Founded: 1932
Arts Area: Dance; Theater
Status: Professional; Non-Profit
Type: Performing
Purpose: Non-profit, educational and historical corporation dedicated to commemorating Sir Walter Raleigh, Virginia Dare and English colonists from 1584-1587
Management: Robert Knowles, General Manager
Officers: Thomas L. White Jr., Chairman; Casher Evans, Vice Chairman; Mollie A. Fearing, Secretary; Ellen Newbold, Treasurer

Paid Staff: 50 **Volunteer Staff:** 25
Paid Artists: 125
Budget: $500,000 - $1,000,000
Income Sources: Business/Corporate Donations; Box Office; Government Grants; Individual Donations
Season: June - August **Annual Attendance:** 75,000
Affiliations: Institute of Outdoor Drama; SETC
Performance Facilities: Waterside Theatre

Marion

THEATRE

FOOTHILLS COMMUNITY THEATRE
24 South Main, PO Box 1387, Marion, NC 28752
(704) 652-8610
Founded: 1972
Arts Area: Community
Status: Non-Professional; Non-Profit
Type: Performing
Purpose: Provide opportunity for participation in performing arts and to help in advancement of culture plus entertainment of our community
Management: Sandra Epperson, Artistic Director
Officers: Sandi McCarter, President; Pat Reel, Vice President; Bebe Ragaz, Secretary; Nancy Greenlee, Treasurer
Paid Staff: 2 **Volunteer Staff:** 3
Utilizes: Special Technical Talent; Guest Conductors; Guest Artists; Guest Directors
Budget: $1,000 - $50,000
Income Sources: Private Foundations/Grants/Endowments; Business/Corporate Donations; Box Office; Government Grants
Season: October - May **Annual Attendance:** 3,570
Affiliations: McDowell Arts and Craft Association
Performance Facilities: McDowell East Junior High; McDowell Technical College

Mars Hill

THEATRE

SOUTHERN APPALACHIAN REPERTORY THEATRE
PO Box 620, Mars Hill, NC 28754
(704) 689-1384
FAX: (704) 689-1474
Founded: 1975
Arts Area: Professional; Summer Stock; Musical; Community
Status: Professional; Non-Profit
Type: Performing; Touring; Resident
Purpose: To present quality theatre, including drama that portrays the life and traditions of the Appalachian region and to encourage the writing and production of new plays; We invite new scripts each year and choose five for the annual Southern Applachian Playwrights Conference in January. One of the five is produced in the summer season with 29 premieres produced in an 18 year history.
Management: James W. Thomas, Artistic Director; Jan W. Blalock, Assistant Managing Director/Business Manager; John T. Oertling, Managing Director
Paid Staff: 6 **Volunteer Staff:** 5
Paid Artists: 45 **Non-Paid Artists:** 25
Utilizes: Special Technical Talent; Guest Artists; Guest Directors
Budget: $50,000 - $100,000
Income Sources: Private Foundations/Grants/Endowments; Box Office; Government Grants; Individual Donations
Season: June - August
Annual Attendance: 8,000
Affiliations: Mars Hill College
Performance Facilities: Owen Theatre

FACILITY

MOORE AUDITORIUM
Mars Hill College, Marshall Highway, Mars Hill, NC 28754
(704) 689-1260
FAX: (704) 689-1474
Founded: 1856

Type of Facility: Concert Hall; Auditorium; Performance Center; Theatre House; Multi-Purpose
Type of Stage: Proscenium
Stage Dimensions: 80'x35'
Orchestra Pit
Seating Capacity: 1,750
Year Built: 1965
Year Remodeled: 1987
Contact for Rental: David Hartley;   (704) 689-1260

Marshville

INSTRUMENTAL MUSIC

UNION SYMPHONY ORCHESTRA
Route 2, Box 248A, Marshville, NC 28103
(800) 438-4129
Founded: 1986
Arts Area: Symphony; Orchestra; Chamber; Ensemble; Instrumental Group
Status: Non-Profit
Type: Performing; Touring; Educational
Purpose: USO is a Union County civic and educational organization which practices and performs music in central North Carolina and South Carolina.
Management: David Lowry, Conductor
Non-Paid Artists: 35
Budget: $1,000 - $50,000
Income Sources: Private Foundations/Grants/Endowments; Individual Donations
Season: September - April
Performance Facilities: Austin Auditorium

Mooresville

THEATRE

MOORESVILLE COMMUNITY THEATRE
PO Box 194, Mooresville, NC 28115
(704) 664-5254
Founded: 1973
Arts Area: Community; Theatrical Group
Status: Non-Professional; Non-Profit
Type: Performing
Purpose: To bring the opportunity of live theatre to the Mooresville area
Officers: Clayton Miller, President; Larry Gambill, Vice President; Clayton Miller, Secretary/Treasurer; Agnes Neel, Finance Chairman
Volunteer Staff: 2
Non-Paid Artists: 12
Budget: $1,000 - $50,000
Income Sources: Business/Corporate Donations; Box Office; Individual Donations
Season: October - May   **Annual Attendance:** 800
Affiliations: Kedell Arts Council

Mount Airy

PERFORMING SERIES

SURRY ARTS COUNCIL
PO Box 141, Mount Airy, NC 27030
(919) 786-7998
FAX: (919) 786-9822
Founded: 1968
Arts Area: Musical
Status: Non-Profit
Type: Educational; Sponsoring
Purpose: To give encouragement and direction in the arts through classroom instruction, workshops and performances to the children and adults of Surry County
Management: Tanya Reese, Executive Director
Paid Staff: 2

Utilizes: Guest Conductors; Guest Artists; Guest Directors
Budget: $50,000 - $100,000
Income Sources: Business/Corporate Donations; Box Office; Government Grants; Individual Donations
Season: September - May   **Annual Attendance:** 1,650
Performance Facilities: Andy Griffith Playhouse; Mount Airy Fine Arts Center

FACILITY

MOUNT AIRY FINE ARTS CENTER/ANDY GRIFFITH PLAYHOUSE
218 Rockford Street, Mount Airy, NC 27030
(919) 786-7998
FAX: (919) 986-9822
Type of Facility: Auditorium
Facility Originally: School
Type of Stage: Proscenium
Seating Capacity: 300
Contact for Rental: Tanya Rees;   (919) 786-7998
Converted into an auditorium in 1967

Murfreesboro

FACILITY

CHOWAN COLLEGE - MCDOWELL COLUMNS AUDITORIUM
Jones Drive, Murfreesboro, NC 27855
(919) 398-4101
FAX: (919) 398-1190
Type of Facility: Auditorium
Facility Originally: School
Type of Stage: Thrust
Stage Dimensions: 60'x40'
Seating Capacity: 600
Year Built: 1912
Year Remodeled: 1983   **Cost:** $40,000
Contact for Rental: Director of Special Programs;   (919) 398-4101

New Bern

DANCE

ATLANTIC DANCE THEATRE
262 Shoreline Drive, New Bern, NC 28562
(919) 636-1760
Founded: 1985
Arts Area: Modern; Ballet
Status: Non-Profit
Type: Performing; Touring; Resident
Utilizes: Guest Artists
Budget: $1,000 - $50,000
Income Sources: Business/Corporate Donations; Box Office; Government Grants

Pembroke

FACILITY

PEMBROKE STATE UNIVERSITY - GIVENS PERFORMING ARTS CENTER
Pembroke, NC 28372
(919) 521-4214
Type of Facility: Concert Hall; Auditorium; Performance Center; Theatre House
Type of Stage: Thrust; Proscenium
Stage Dimensions: 64'Wx35'D
Orchestra Pit
Seating Capacity: 1,688
Year Built: 1975   **Architect:** Hayes & Howell   **Cost:** $1,800,000
Acoustical Consultant: Jaffe Acoustics
Contact for Rental: William Biddle;   (919) 521-6287

Resident Groups: Pembroke State University Performing Arts Groups
Only non-profit organizations may use the facility

Pittsboro

VOCAL MUSIC

CHAPEL HILL-CARRBORO COMMUNITY CHORUS
164 Fearrington Post, Pittsboro, NC 27312
(919) 542-1602
> **Founded:** 1980
> **Arts Area:** Choral
> **Status:** Non-Professional; Non-Profit
> **Type:** Performing; Educational
> **Purpose:** To develop arts appreciation in the area, and to provide a cultural resource for all citizens in the area
> **Officers:** Henry Castner, President; Steve Lockwood, Vice-President; Judy Purvis, Treasurer; Carl L. Stam, Conductor; Bonnie Olsen, Secretary; Cornelia Johnson, Librarian
> **Volunteer Staff:** 2
> **Paid Artists:** 5   **Non-Paid Artists:** 70
> **Budget:** $1,000 - $50,000
> **Income Sources:** Business/Corporate Donations; Government Grants; Individual Donations; Contributions at Concerts
> **Season:** September - April
> **Annual Attendance:** 750

Raleigh

INSTRUMENTAL MUSIC

NORTH CAROLINA SYMPHONY
2 South Street, Raleigh, NC 27601
(919) 733-2750
FAX: (919) 733-9920
> **Founded:** 1932
> **Arts Area:** Symphony; Orchestra; Chamber; Ensemble
> **Status:** Professional; Non-Profit
> **Type:** Performing; Touring; Resident; Educational; Sponsoring
> **Purpose:** To bring live orchestral music to the citizens of North Carolina; to provide music education to the school children of the state
> **Management:** Banks C. Talley, Jr., Executive Director; Gerhardt Zimmermann, Music Director/Conductor; Hiram B. Black, General Manager
> **Officers:** R. Horace Johnson, Chairman; William Kress, Vice Chairman; Mrs. Johnny Bryant, Secretary; J. Richard Futrell Jr., Treasurer
> **Paid Staff:** 20
> **Paid Artists:** 68
> **Utilizes:** Guest Conductors; Guest Artists
> **Budget:** $1,000,000 - $5,000,000
> **Income Sources:** Private Foundations/Grants/Endowments; Business/Corporate Donations; Box Office; Government Grants; Individual Donations
> **Season:** September - June
> **Affiliations:** ASOL

VOCAL MUSIC

NATIONAL OPERA COMPANY
Box 12800, Raleigh, NC 27605
(919) 890-6082
FAX: (919) 890-6095
> **Founded:** 1948
> **Arts Area:** Lyric Opera; Light Opera; Operetta
> **Status:** Professional; Non-Profit
> **Type:** Performing; Touring; Educational
> **Purpose:** To introduce art form to students; to give experience to young singers; to perform in a language the audience understands
> **Management:** Don Wilder, Artistic Director/Conductor
> **Officers:** J.A. Goodmon, President; David Witherspoon, Vice President; Louise Stephenson, Secretary; John Brennan, Treasurer
> **Paid Staff:** 4

Paid Artists: 12
Utilizes: Special Technical Talent; Guest Artists; Guest Directors
Budget: $100,000 - $500,000
Income Sources: Private Foundations/Grants/Endowments
Season: September - May

RALEIGH BOYCHOIR
1329 Ridge Road, Raleigh, NC 27607
(919) 881-9259
Mailing Address: PO Box 12481, Raleigh, NC 27605
Founded: 1968
Arts Area: Choral
Status: Semi-Professional
Type: Performing; Touring; Resident; Educational
Purpose: To give 8 to 15-year-old boys an opportunity to perform some of the world's great choral music
Management: Thomas E. Sibley, Founder/Director; Terry L. Poe, Associate Director/Accompanist; Betsy Hood, Pat Simms, Administrative Coordinators
Officers: Gene Brown, President; Donald and Candy Teeter, Vice Presidents; Betty Warren, Secretary; Dwight Davis, Treasurer; Gail Black, President Elect
Paid Staff: 3   **Volunteer Staff:** 40
Utilizes: Special Technical Talent; Guest Artists
Budget: $50,000 - $100,000
Income Sources: Private Foundations/Grants/Endowments; Business/Corporate Donations; Individual Donations
Season: July - June   **Annual Attendance:** 9,000

THEATRE

THE NORTH CAROLINA THEATRE
One East South Street, Raleigh, NC 27601
(919) 755-6916
Founded: 1983
Arts Area: Professional; Musical; Theatrical Group
Status: Professional
Type: Performing
Purpose: To provide Broadway-quality professional theatre at an affordable price as well as provide available employ-ment to theatre artists and craftsmen
Management: De Ann S. Jones, Executive Director
Officers: Dianne Davidian, Chairman, Board of Directors; K.D. Kennedy Jr., Vice Chairman
Paid Staff: 7   **Volunteer Staff:** 65
Paid Artists: 215
Utilizes: Guest Artists; Guest Directors
Budget: $500,000 - $1,000,000
Income Sources: Private Foundations/Grants/Endowments; Business/Corporate Donations; Box Office; Government Grants; Individual Donations
Season: April - November   **Annual Attendance:** 75,000

SIDE BY SIDE
PO Box 19416, Raleigh, NC 27619
(919) 829-2003
Founded: 1981
Arts Area: Musical; Dinner; Community; Folk
Status: Semi-Professional; Non-Profit
Type: Performing
Purpose: To entertain
Management: Paul B. Conway, Director
Paid Artists: 5
Budget: $1,000 - $50,000
Income Sources: Box Office; Individual Donations
Season: 52 Weeks   **Annual Attendance:** 1,600

THEATRE IN THE PARK
107 Pullen Road, Raleigh, NC 27605
(919) 831-6936
FAX: (919) 831-9475
Founded: 1972
Arts Area: Musical; Community; Theatrical Group
Status: Non-Professional; Non-Profit
Type: Performing; Touring; Resident; Educational; Sponsoring

Purpose: Theatre In The Park is a non-profit community theatre established to provide the Greater Raleigh community with the very best in live theatre, and to provide a training ground for young actors and actresses.
Management: Ira David Wood, III, Executive Director; Alan Reet, General Manager; Bruce Laks, Office Manager; Peter Girvin, Technical Director
Officers: Bill Parmelee, President; G. Troy Page, Vice President; Camille Patterson, Secretary; Johy Taylor, Treasurer
Paid Staff: 6
Utilizes: Guest Directors
Budget: $100,000 - $500,000
Income Sources: Private Foundations/Grants/Endowments; Business/Corporate Donations; Box Office; Government Grants; Individual Donations
Season: 52 Weeks   **Annual Attendance:** 30,000
Affiliations: AATA; North Carolina Community Theatre
Performance Facilities: Theatre In The Park

PERFORMING SERIES

ARTSPLOSURE
300/200 Parham Street, Raleigh, NC 27312
(919) 831-6221
Founded: 1980
Arts Area: Dance; Vocal Music; Instrumental Music; Theater; Festivals
Status: Non-Profit
Type: Performing; Festivals
Purpose: To produce annual arts festivals for Raleigh and Walce Communities
Management: Debra Karp, Executive Director
Officers: Miller Sigmon, President
Paid Staff: 3   **Volunteer Staff:** 150
Paid Artists: 200
Budget: $100,000 - $500,000
Income Sources: Private Foundations/Grants/Endowments; Business/Corporate Donations; Box Office; Government Grants; Individual Donations
Season: September - June   **Annual Attendance:** 100,000

UNITED ARTISTS OF RALEIGH AND WAKE COUNTY
201 East Dazie Street, Raleigh, NC 27605
(919) 839-1498
FAX: (919) 839-6002
Founded: 1962
Status: Non-Profit
Type: Educational; Sponsoring
Purpose: Develops and supports cultural programs for all Wake County citizens
Management: Robert Bush, Executive Director
Officers: Michael Lowder, President; Travis Tracy, President-Elect; Joy Cook, Secretary; Mike Whitley, Treasurer
Paid Staff: 3   **Volunteer Staff:** 40
Paid Artists: 75
Utilizes: Guest Conductors; Guest Artists
Budget: $100,000 - $500,000
Income Sources: Private Foundations/Grants/Endowments; Business/Corporate Donations; Government Grants; Individual Donations
Season: 52 Weeks

FACILITY

RALEIGH CIVIC CENTER
500 Fayetteville Street Mall, Raleigh, NC 27601
(919) 831-6011
FAX: (919) 831-6013
Type of Facility: Civic Center
Year Built: 1977   **Architect:** Haskins Rice Savage & Pierce; A.G. Odell   **Cost:** $19,000,000
Contact for Rental: Holly Kreuz;   (919) 831-6011
Raleigh Civic Center contains the Arena and Theatre. See separate listings for further information.

RALEIGH CIVIC CENTER - ARENA
500 Fayetteville Street Mall, Raleigh, NC 27601
(919) 831-6011
FAX: (919) 831-6013
Type of Facility: Concert Hall; Civic Center; Arena
Type of Stage: Platform

Seating Capacity: 4,000
Year Built: 1977   Architect: Haskins Rice Savage & Pierce; A.G. Odell   Cost: $18,000,000
Contact for Rental: Holly Kreuz;   (919) 831-6011

RALEIGH CIVIC CENTER - THEATRE
500 Fayetteville Street Mall, Raleigh, NC 27601
(919) 831-6011
FAX: (919) 831-6013
Type of Facility: Concert Hall; Theatre House
Type of Stage: Proscenium
Stage Dimensions: 0'Wx30'H proscenium opening
Orchestra Pit
Seating Capacity: 2,300
Year Built: 1932
Year Remodeled: 1977   Architect: Haskins Rice Savage & Pierce; A.G. Odell   Cost: $1,000,000
Contact for Rental: Holly Kreuz;   (919) 831-6011
Resident Groups: North Carolina Symphony; North Carolina Theatre
The Theatre was remodeled at the time of the Arena construction.

RALEIGH LITTLE THEATRE
301 Pogue Street, PO Box 5637, Raleigh, NC 27650
(919) 821-4579
FAX: (919) 821-7961
Type of Facility: Studio Performance; Theatre House; Amphitheater
Type of Stage: Proscenium
Stage Dimensions: 46'x36'
Orchestra Pit
Seating Capacity: Main Stage - 268; Studio Stage - 150
Year Built: 1938
Contact for Rental: Managing Director;   (919) 821-4579
Resident Groups: Raleigh Little Theatre

THEATRE IN THE PARK
107 Pullen Road, Raleigh, NC 27605
(919) 831-6936
FAX: (919) 831-9475
Founded: 1973
Type of Facility: Theatre House
Facility Originally: National Guard Armory
Type of Stage: Flexible
Stage Dimensions: 30'x60'
Seating Capacity: 300
Year Built: 1937
Year Remodeled: 1985   Architect: Envirotech, Phillip Safriet   Cost: $163,000
Acoustical Consultant: Gene Brantley
Contact for Rental: Allen Reep;   (919) 831-6936
Manager: Allen Reep, General Manager;   (919) 831-6936

Roanoke Rapids

THEATRE

ROANOKE VALLEY PLAYERS
PO Box 729, Roanoke Rapids, NC 27870
(919) 535-4161
Founded: 1965
Arts Area: Community; Theatrical Group
Status: Non-Profit
Type: Performing; Educational
Purpose: As the Drama Division of the Roanoke Valley Arts Council, to promote the theatrical arts in Roanoke Valley.
Management: Jim Ivey, Manager
Paid Staff: 1   Volunteer Staff: 150
Paid Artists: 5   Non-Paid Artists: 150
Utilizes: Special Technical Talent; Guest Artists; Guest Directors
Budget: $1,000 - $50,000
Income Sources: Private Foundations/Grants/Endowments; Business/Corporate Donations; Box Office; Government Grants; Individual Donations
Season: 52 Weeks

Annual Attendance: 3,500
Affiliations: Roanoke Valley Arts Council; North Carolina Theatre Conference
Performance Facilities: Canal Arts Center

Salisbury

INSTRUMENTAL MUSIC

SALISBURY SYMPHONY ORCHESTRA
PO Box 4264, Salisbury, NC 28144
(704) 637-4314
>**Founded:** 1966
>**Arts Area:** Symphony; Orchestra
>**Status:** Professional; Non-Profit
>**Type:** Performing; Educational
>**Purpose:** To perform symphonic music and to increase the musical knowledge and appreciation in the area; to present four full concerts a year, including a free concert for young people
>**Management:** Missy Shives, General Manager; David Hagy, Conductor/Music Director
>**Officers:** Jim Norman, President; Richard Harris, Vice President; Laura Rusher, Secretary; Chester zumBrunnen, Treasurer
>**Paid Staff:** 2
>**Paid Artists:** 67 **Non-Paid Artists:** 4
>**Utilizes:** Guest Artists
>**Budget:** $100,000 - $500,000
>**Income Sources:** Private Foundations/Grants/Endowments; Business/Corporate Donations; Box Office; Government Grants; Individual Donations
>**Season:** 52 Weeks
>Annual Attendance: 2,500
>**Affiliations:** The United Arts Council of Rowan; ASOL; Association of Symphony Orchestras of North Carolina; Arts Advocates of North Carolina
>**Performance Facilities:** Keppel Auditorium, Catawba College

THEATRE

PIEDMONT PLAYERS THEATRE
PO Box 762, Salisbury, NC 28145-0762
(704) 633-5471
>**Founded:** 1961
>**Arts Area:** Community; Theatrical Group
>**Status:** Non-Professional; Non-Profit
>**Type:** Performing
>**Purpose:** To entertain the community
>**Management:** Brenda C. Bouser, Executive Assistant
>**Officers:** Kevin Eddinger, President; B. Douglas Robinson, Vice President; Kay Weden, Secretary; Gunnar Fromen, Treasurer
>**Paid Staff:** 1 **Volunteer Staff:** 100
>**Utilizes:** Special Technical Talent; Guest Conductors; Guest Artists
>**Budget:** $100,000 - $500,000
>**Income Sources:** Business/Corporate Donations; Box Office; Government Grants; Individual Donations
>**Season:** September - July
>**Annual Attendance:** 10,000
>**Performance Facilities:** Catawba College's Hendrick Theatre

PERFORMING SERIES

ROWAN COMMUNITY CONCERT ASSOCIATION
PO Box 4234, Salisbury, NC 28145-4234
(704) 636-5861
>**Founded:** 1981
>**Arts Area:** Dance; Vocal Music; Instrumental Music
>**Status:** Professional
>**Type:** Sponsoring
>**Purpose:** To bring the best music to the area by means of a non-profit organization; to foster and encourage public appreciation of music
>**Officers:** Richard Miller, President; Susan Eldridge, Vice President
>**Utilizes:** Guest Artists
>**Budget:** $1,000 - $50,000

Income Sources: Box Office; Government Grants
Season: Fall - Spring
Affiliations: Community Concerts, New York
Performance Facilities: Keppel Auditorium

FACILITY

COLLEGE COMMUNITY CENTER
Catawba College, Salisbury, NC 28144
(704) 637-4417
FAX: (704) 637-4304
    Founded: 1925
    Type of Facility: Theatre Complex; Auditorium; Theatre House
    Type of Stage: Thrust; Proscenium
    Stage Dimensions: Keppel Auditorium - 42'x60'; Hedrick Theatre - 45'x40'
    Orchestra Pit
    Seating Capacity: Keppel Auditorium - 1,500; Hedrick Theatre - 251
    Year Built: 1966   **Architect:** John Ramsay
    Contact for Rental: Hoyt McCachren;   (704) 637-4417
    Resident Groups: School of Performing Arts

Sanford

THEATRE

TEMPLE THEATRE COMPANY
120 Carthage Street, PO Box 1391, Sanford, NC 27330
(919) 774-4512
    Founded: 1925
    Arts Area: Professional; Musical; Community
    Status: Semi-Professional; Non-Profit
    Type: Performing; Educational; Sponsoring
    Purpose: To provide experiences in live theatre and performing arts for our audiences' entertainment; to provide the opportunity for artistic involvement in live theatre and performing arts for anyone wishing to participate
    Management: Tim Morrissey, Artistic Director; Bill Freeman, Technical Director; Sheila Brewer, Office Manager; Corinna Wicker, Box Office Manager
    Officers: Jim Stevens, President; Joe Raulerson, Vice President; Mary Ellen Bowen, Secretary; Ted Havens, Treasurer
    Paid Staff: 4   **Volunteer Staff:** 25
    Paid Artists: 20   **Non-Paid Artists:** 60
    Utilizes: Special Technical Talent; Guest Artists; Guest Directors
    Budget: $100,000 - $500,000
    Income Sources: Private Foundations/Grants/Endowments; Business/Corporate Donations; Box Office; Government Grants; Individual Donations
    Season: 52 Weeks
    Annual Attendance: 19,000
    Affiliations: SETC; North Carolina Theatre Conference
    Performance Facilities: Temple Theatre

FACILITY

TEMPLE THEATRE COMPANY INC.
PO Box 1391, 120 Carthage Street, Sanford, NC 27331-1391
(919) 774-4512
    Founded: 1981
    Type of Facility: Auditorium; Performance Center; Theatre House
    Facility Originally: Vaudeville
    Type of Stage: Proscenium
    Stage Dimensions: 27'x42'   **Orchestra Pit**
    Seating Capacity: 339
    Year Built: 1925   **Cost:** $40,000
    Year Remodeled: 1984   **Architect:** Frank DeStefano   **Cost:** $500,000
    Contact for Rental: Tim Morrissey;   (919) 774-4512

Southern Pines

THEATRE

SANDHILLS LITTLE THEATRE
250 NW Broad Street, Southern Pines, NC 28387
(919) 692-3799
> **Founded:** 1981
> **Arts Area:** Community
> **Status:** Non-Professional; Non-Profit
> **Type:** Performing; Resident; Sponsoring
> **Purpose:** To please our audiences
> **Management:** Paula Reeder, Administrator
> **Officers:** Sandy Tuten, President; Edd Sechrist, Vice President; Bernice Vernon, Secretary; Howard Stevens, Treasurer
> **Paid Staff:** 1
> **Non-Paid Artists:** 200
> **Utilizes:** Special Technical Talent; Guest Directors
> **Budget:** $1,000 - $50,000
> **Income Sources:** Box Office; Individual Donations
> **Season:** September - June   **Annual Attendance:** 10,000
> **Affiliations:** NETC; SETC
> **Performance Facilities:** Performing Arts Center

FACILITY

PERFORMING ARTS CENTER
250 NW Broad Street, PO Box 405, Southern Pines, NC 28388
(919) 692-4356; (919) 692-3611
> **Type of Facility:** Multi-Purpose
> **Type of Stage:** Platform
> **Stage Dimensions:** 20'x40'
> **Seating Capacity:** 369
> **Year Built:** 1898
> **Year Remodeled:** 1985   **Cost:** $280,000
> **Contact for Rental:** Stuart Fulghum

Statesville

THEATRE

STATESVILLE COMMUNITY THEATRE
PO Box 1702, Statesville, NC 28677
(704) 871-2743
> **Founded:** 1958
> **Arts Area:** Community
> **Status:** Non-Profit
> **Type:** Performing; Educational
> **Purpose:** To provide entertainment; to encourage public appreciation of drama, experimental theatre, and individual artistic expression; to present music theatre productions
> **Officers:** David Farris, President; Nathan Sisk, Vice President
> **Volunteer Staff:** 8
> **Non-Paid Artists:** 30
> **Budget:** $1,000 - $50,000
> **Income Sources:** Box Office; Individual Donations
> **Season:** 52 Weeks   **Annual Attendance:** 1,800
> **Performance Facilities:** Landmark Theater

Tryon

INSTRUMENTAL MUSIC

PADDYWHACK
Route 2, PO Box 60, Tryon, NC 28782
(704) 894-8091
> **Founded:** 1978
> **Arts Area:** Ensemble; Ethnic; Folk; Band
> **Status:** Semi-Professional

Type: Performing; Touring; Educational
Purpose: To play and promote the popular music of the 16th-19th centuries
Officers: Claude Graves, Owner/Booking; Richard Beard, Historian/Arranger
Volunteer Staff: 6
Paid Artists: 6
Utilizes: Guest Artists
Budget: $1,000 - $50,000
Income Sources: Box Office
Season: 52 Weeks
Affiliations: Schiele Museum

FACILITY

TRYON FINE ARTS CENTER
208 Melrose Avenue, Tryon, NC 28782
(704) 859-8322
Type of Facility: Theatre Complex; Concert Hall; Auditorium; Multi-Purpose
Type of Stage: Proscenium
Stage Dimensions: 31'x26'
Seating Capacity: 315
Year Built: 1968   **Architect:** Benkert   **Cost:** $300,000
Acoustical Consultant: Robert Cook
Contact for Rental: Sylvia Brink;   (704) 859-8322
Resident Groups: Tryon Little Theatre; Tryon Concert Association; Tryon Community Chorus; Tryon Youth Center; Tryon Painter and Sculpters; Tryon Film Club; Tryon Crafts; Carolina Camera Club

Valdese

THEATRE

OLD COLONY PLAYERS
PO Box 112, Valdese, NC 28690
(704) 874-0176
Founded: 1967
Arts Area: Professional; Musical; Dinner; Community; Theatrical Group; Choral Society
Status: Professional; Non-Profit
Type: Performing; Touring; Resident; Educational
Purpose: To produce the historical outdoor drama "From This Day Forward" annually; to produce Dicken's "A Christmas Carol" annually; to produce other dramas, engage in outreach activities, and sponser workshops and cultural events.
Management: Martin R. Rice, General Manager
Officers: Kenneth Newcomb, President Board of Directors; Doug Setzer, Vice President Board of Directors; Charles Moseley, Treasurer; Louise Barrett, Secretary
Paid Staff: 2
Paid Artists: 54
Utilizes: Special Technical Talent; Guest Conductors; Guest Directors
Budget: $50,000 - $100,000
Income Sources: Private Foundations/Grants/Endowments; Business/Corporate Donations; Box Office; Government Grants; Individual Donations
Season: 52 Weeks   **Annual Attendance:** 3,500
Affiliations: SETC; North Carolina Theatre Conference; North Carolina Association of Professional Theatres; Burke County Chamber of Commerce; Burke Arts Council
Performance Facilities: Old Colony Players Amphitheater; Old Rock School, Valdese

Wilkesboro

PERFORMING SERIES

JOHN A. WALKER EVENTS, INC.
Collegiate Drive, PO Box 120, Wilkesboro, NC 28697
(919) 651-8666
FAX: (919) 651-8749
Founded: 1985
Arts Area: Dance; Vocal Music; Instrumental Music; Theater; Festivals
Status: Non-Profit
Type: Performing; Touring; Resident; Educational; Sponsoring
Officers: Arnold Lakey, President
Paid Staff: 7   **Volunteer Staff:** 20

Budget: $100,000 - $500,000
Income Sources: Business/Corporate Donations; Box Office; Government Grants; Individual Donations
Season: 52 Weeks
Annual Attendance: 32,000
Affiliations: APAP; North Carolina Arts Council
Performance Facilities: John A. Walker Community Center

FACILITY

JOHN A. WALKER COMMUNITY CENTER
Wilkes Community College, Collegiate Drive, Wilkesboro, NC 28697
(919) 651-8666
FAX: (919) 651-8749
    Founded: 1985
    Type of Facility: Auditorium; Outdoor (Concert); Civic Center
    Type of Stage: Proscenium
    Stage Dimensions: 33'Dx80'W add 16' from curtain; 21Hx42'W proscenium opening
    Orchestra Pit
    Seating Capacity: 1,131
    Year Built: 1985   **Cost:** $2,000,000
    Contact for Rental: Kathy Thomas; (919) 651-8666

Williamston

THEATRE

MARTIN COMMUNITY PLAYERS
Watts Street, Williamston, NC 27892
(919) 792-6104
    Founded: 1974
    Arts Area: Musical; Community; Theatrical Group
    Status: Non-Professional; Non-Profit
    Type: Performing; Resident
    Purpose: To bring theatre to all the citizens in the county, mainly through the schools, with one selected offering per year
    Management: Allan Osborne, Artistic Director
    Officers: Cynthia Veneris, President; Stan Crowe, Vice President; Janie Griffin, Treasurer; Lucy Weaver, Secretary
    Paid Staff: 1   **Volunteer Staff:** 100
    Paid Artists: 10
    Budget: $1,000 - $50,000
    Income Sources: Private Foundations/Grants/Endowments; Business/Corporate Donations; Box Office; Government Grants; Individual Donations
    Season: September - June
    Annual Attendance: 3,000
    Performance Facilities: Martin County Auditorium

Wilmington

INSTRUMENTAL MUSIC

WILMINGTON SYMPHONY ORCHESTRA
601 South College Road, Wilmington, NC 28403
(919) 791-9262
    Founded: 1970
    Arts Area: Symphony
    Status: Non-Professional; Non-Profit
    Type: Performing; Educational
    Purpose: To act as a local cultural resource and educational institution
    Management: Joanne Riesz, General Manager
    Officers: Dr. Clayton Callaway, President, Board of Directors; Dr. Ruth Funk, Vice President, Board of Directors
    Paid Staff: 2   **Volunteer Staff:** 20
    Paid Artists: 5   **Non-Paid Artists:** 60
    Utilizes: Guest Artists
    Budget: $50,000 - $100,000
    Income Sources: Private Foundations/Grants/Endowments; Business/Corporate Donations; Box Office; Government Grants; Individual Donations
    Season: September - May   **Annual Attendance:** 4,000

Affiliations: ASOL; Association of Symphony Orchestras of North Carolina
Performance Facilities: Kenan Auditorium

THEATRE

OPERA HOUSE THEATRE COMPANY
306 Nun Street, Wilmington, NC 28401
(919) 762-4234
Founded: 1985
Arts Area: Professional; Summer Stock; Musical; Theatrical Group
Status: Professional
Type: Performing; Educational
Purpose: To produce and promote high quality, professional theatre and to make theatre available for all audiences; to train and develop the talents of actors, technicians amd musicians
Management: Lou Criscuolo, Executive Director/Founder; Mary James Morgan, Company Manager; Beverly S. Skinner, Assistant Company Manager
Officers: Diane F. Green, President; Guy Ferreri, Vice President; Rebecca Rhine, Secretary/Treasurer
Paid Staff: 4 **Volunteer Staff:** 1
Paid Artists: 15 **Non-Paid Artists:** 20
Utilizes: Special Technical Talent; Guest Conductors; Guest Artists; Guest Directors
Budget: $100,000 - $500,000
Income Sources: Private Foundations/Grants/Endowments; Business/Corporate Donations; Box Office; Government Grants; Individual Donations
Season: 52 Weeks **Annual Attendance:** 7,500
Performance Facilities: Thalian Hall Center for the Performing Arts

PERFORMING SERIES

NORTH CAROLINA JAZZ FESTIVAL
1924 South 16th Street, Wilmington, NC 28401
(919) 762-5207
Founded: 1980
Arts Area: Festivals
Status: Non-Profit
Type: Sponsoring
Purpose: To promote traditional jazz to the general public
Officers: Dr. Harry Van Velsor, President; A.R. Harold, Vice President; Ren Williamson, Treasurer
Volunteer Staff: 20
Paid Artists: 12
Utilizes: Guest Artists
Budget: $1,000 - $50,000
Income Sources: Box Office
Annual Attendance: 1,000
Affiliations: American Federation of Jazz Societies
Performance Facilities: Wilmington Hilton

FACILITY

THALIAN HALL - THALIAN HALL CENTER FOR THE PERFORMING ARTS
310 Chestnut Street, PO Box 371, Wilmington, NC 28402
(919) 343-3660
Founded: 1963
Type of Facility: Theatre Complex; Concert Hall; Auditorium; Studio Performance; Performance Center; Theatre House; Arena; Multi-Purpose
Facility Originally: Opera House
Type of Stage: Flexible; Proscenium; Mainstage; Studio Theater; Ballroom
Stage Dimensions: 32'Wx30'D; 32Wx20'H proscenium opening **Orchestra Pit**
Seating Capacity: Mainstage - 750; Studio Theatre - 140; Ballroom - 250
Year Built: 1858 **Architect:** John Montague Trimble **Cost:** $17,000
Year Remodeled: 1990 **Architect:** Hanbury Evans/Ligon Flynn; Peter George Theatre Consultant
Cost: $5,000,000
Acoustical Consultant: Peter George Theatre Consultants
Contact for Rental: Tony Rivenbark, Executive Director; (919) 343-3660
Resident Groups: Opera House Theatre Company; Thalian Association Community Theatre; Tapestry Theatre Company; Willis Richarim Players; Playwrights Producing Company

UNIVERSITY OF NORTH CAROLINA-WILMINGTON - SARAH GRAHAM KENAN MEMORIAL AUDITORIUM
PO Box 3725, Wilmington, NC 28401
(919) 791-9695; (800) 732-3643
>**Type of Facility:** Theatre House
>**Type of Stage:** Proscenium
>**Stage Dimensions:** 16'x40'x30'   **Orchestra Pit**
>**Seating Capacity:** 982
>**Year Built:** 1970
>**Contact for Rental:** Don Hawley

Wilson

INSTRUMENTAL MUSIC

WILSON SYMPHONY
West Lee Street, Wilson, NC 27893
(919) 399-6300
>**Founded:** 1985
>**Arts Area:** Symphony
>**Status:** Non-Profit
>**Type:** Performing
>**Purpose:** Community orchestra for non-professionals
>**Management:** Virginia Whitehurst, Director
>**Officers:** Dr. Harold Ladwig, President; Harlee Lyon, Vice President
>**Utilizes:** Guest Artists
>**Budget:** $1,000 - $50,000
>**Income Sources:** Box Office; Government Grants
>**Season:** August - May
>**Affiliations:** Arts Council of Wilson

Winston-Salem

INSTRUMENTAL MUSIC

WINSTON-SALEM SYMPHONY ASSOCIATION
610 Coliseum Drive, Winston-Salem, NC 27106
(919) 725-1035
>**Founded:** 1947
>**Arts Area:** Symphony; Orchestra; Chamber; Ensemble
>**Status:** Professional; Non-Profit
>**Type:** Performing; Resident; Educational
>**Purpose:** To present the finest in symphonic and choral literature; to provide the best in music education for the children of Winston-Salem and Forsythe County
>**Management:** Christine Belcik-Griffith, Executive Director; Peter Perret, Music Director
>**Officers:** Angela Peterson, Guild President
>**Paid Staff:** 9   **Volunteer Staff:** 250
>**Paid Artists:** 81
>**Utilizes:** Guest Conductors; Guest Artists
>**Budget:** $500,000 - $1,000,000
>**Income Sources:** Private Foundations/Grants/Endowments; Business/Corporate Donations; Box Office; Government Grants; Individual Donations
>**Season:** September - July
>**Annual Attendance:** 70,000
>**Affiliations:** ASOL; BMI; ASCAP; Association of Symphony Orchestras of North Carolina
>**Performance Facilities:** Roger L. Stevens Center for the Performing Arts

VOCAL MUSIC

PIEDMONT OPERA THEATRE
610 Coliseum Drive, Winston-Salem, NC 27106
(919) 725-2022
>**Founded:** 1978
>**Arts Area:** Grand Opera; Lyric Opera; Light Opera; Operetta
>**Status:** Professional; Non-Profit
>**Type:** Performing; Resident; Educational
>**Purpose:** To increase knowledge of the opera art form, produce high quality opera and provide educational opportunities for the furtherance of opera

Management: Norman Johnson, General Director; Carollee Harman, Administrator
Officers: Clyde W. Fitzgerald Jr., President; Lynne Hart, Executive Vice President; Vicky Auchincloss, Vice President of Patronage; Loy McGill, Vice President of Marketing; Dr. William McCall Jr., Vice President of Corporate Sponsorship; Sharon Reed, Vice President of Special Projects; Margaret Kolb, Vice President of Education; Timothy K. Cahill, Secretary; N. Broughton Correll III, Treasurer
Paid Staff: 2   **Volunteer Staff:** 30
Paid Artists: 100
Utilizes: Special Technical Talent; Guest Artists; Guest Directors
Budget: $100,000 - $500,000
Income Sources: Private Foundations/Grants/Endowments; Business/Corporate Donations; Box Office; Government Grants; Individual Donations
Season: September; - April   **Annual Attendance:** 6,500
Affiliations: OA; COS; NOA; Arts Council, Inc./Winston-Salem
Performance Facilities: Roger L. Stevens Center for the Performing Arts

THEATRE

CHILDREN'S THEATRE BOARD, INC.
610 Coliseum Drive, Winston-Salem, NC 27106
(919) 725-4531
> **Founded:** 1940
> **Arts Area:** Theatrical Group
> **Status:** Professional; Non-Profit
> **Type:** Performing; Educational; Sponsoring
> **Purpose:** Children's Theatre Board (CTB) provides opportunities for students, educators and families to experience and participate in the performing arts. CTB offers multidisciplinary, culturally diverse programs to foster sensitivity and acceptance of others. Our programs are accessible and entertaining, our vision is to reach young people through experimental learning.
> **Management:** Pat Land, Executive Director; Jennifer Lewis, Director of Marketing and Development
> **Officers:** Mary Harper, President; Libby Noah, President-Elect; Leslie Madigan, Treasurer; Ernestine Worley, Treasurer-Elect; Janet Bondurant, Immediate Past President
> **Paid Staff:** 2   **Volunteer Staff:** 60
> **Paid Artists:** 120
> **Utilizes:** Special Technical Talent
> **Budget:** $100,000 - $500,000
> **Income Sources:** Private Foundations/Grants/Endowments; Business/Corporate Donations; Box Office; Government Grants; Individual Donations
> **Season:** September - May   **Annual Attendance:** 45,000
> **Performance Facilities:** The Arts Council Theatre; W-S/FC Schools; Reynolds Auditorium

THE LITTLE THEATRE OF WINSTON-SALEM
610 Coliseum Drive, Winston-Salem, NC 27106
(919) 725-4001·
> **Founded:** 1935
> **Arts Area:** Community
> **Status:** Non-Professional; Non-Profit
> **Type:** Performing; Educational
> **Purpose:** To provide for all within the community an avenue for education and development in all aspects of theatrical arts and to provide entertainment for the community by offering a series of well-staged performances of live theatre
> **Management:** Roger A. Richardson, Managing Producer
> **Officers:** Eva Wu, President of the Board
> **Paid Staff:** 7   **Volunteer Staff:** 200
> **Non-Paid Artists:** 100
> **Utilizes:** Special Technical Talent; Guest Directors
> **Budget:** $100,000 - $500,000
> **Income Sources:** Business/Corporate Donations; Box Office; Individual Donations
> **Season:** 52 Weeks   **Annual Attendance:** 20,000
> **Affiliations:** Winston-Salem Arts Council
> **Performance Facilities:** Hanes Community Center; Arts Council Theatre

NORTH CAROLINA BLACK REPERTORY COMPANY
610 Coliseum Drive, PO Box 2793, Winston-Salem, NC 27102
(919) 723-7907
> **Founded:** 1979
> **Arts Area:** Professional; Musical; Theatrical Group
> **Status:** Professional; Non-Profit
> **Type:** Performing; Touring; Resident; Educational; Sponsoring
> **Purpose:** The professional production of plays and musicals with a repertoire of renowned and original works having universal and ethnic (African-American) themes

Management: Larry Leon Hamlin, Founder/Executive/Artistic Director; Nathan Ross Freeman, Resident Playwright; Chena Sulley, Administrative Assistant
Officers: Will T. Jenkins, President; Irvin Hodges, Vice President; Warren Leggett, Treasurer
Paid Staff: 3   **Volunteer Staff:** 500
Paid Artists: 70
Utilizes: Special Technical Talent; Guest Artists; Guest Directors
Budget: $100,000 - $500,000
Income Sources: Private Foundations/Grants/Endowments; Business/Corporate Donations; Box Office; Government Grants; Individual Donations
Season: September - June
Annual Attendance: 8,000
Performance Facilities: Winston-Salem Arts Council Theatre

FACILITY

THE ARTS COUNCIL THEATRE
610 Coliseum Drive, Winston-Salem, NC 27106
(919) 724-6776
FAX: (919) 724-0490
   Founded: 1958
   Type of Facility: Auditorium; Theatre House; Multi-Purpose
   Type of Stage: Proscenium
   Stage Dimensions: 32'x28'   **Orchestra Pit**
   Seating Capacity: 541
   Year Built: 1958   **Architect:** Larson & Larson   **Cost:** $1,000,000
   Year Remodeled: 1980   **Architect:** Arthur Cotton Moore Associates   **Cost:** $1,000,000
   Contact for Rental: Russell J. Wicker, Manager;   (919) 724-6776
   Manager: Russell J. Wicker;   (919) 724-6776
   Resident Groups: The Little Theatre of Winston-Salem; Children's Theatre; North Carolina Black Repertory Company
   Live theatre; films; assemblies

THE NORTH CAROLINA SCHOOL OF THE ARTS - ROGER L. STEVENS CENTER FOR THE PERFORMING ARTS
405 West Fourth Street, Winston-Salem, NC 27101
(919) 721-1654
   Type of Facility: Concert Hall; Theatre House; Opera House
   Facility Originally: Movie House
   Type of Stage: Proscenium
   Stage Dimensions: 82'Wx44'D; 42'Wx30'H proscenium opening   **Orchestra Pit**
   Seating Capacity: 1,380
   Year Built: 1929   **Architect:** Johnson & Brannan Architects   **Cost:** $1,000,000
   Year Remodeled: 1983   **Architect:** Newman Calloway Johnson Winfree   **Cost:** $10,300,000
   Acoustical Consultant: Peter George and Glenn White
   Contact for Rental: Steve Davis, Executive Director;   (919) 726-6320
   Resident Groups: North Carolina School of the Arts; Winston-Salem Symphony; Piedmont Opera Company

REYNOLDS MEMORIAL AUDITORIUM
301 North Hawthorne Road, Winston-Salem, NC 27104
(919) 727-2180
   Type of Facility: Concert Hall; Auditorium; Theatre House; Opera House
   Type of Stage: Proscenium
   Stage Dimensions: 66'Wx36'Dx27'H
   Orchestra Pit
   Seating Capacity: 1,922
   Year Built: 1923
   Year Remodeled: 1963
   Contact for Rental: Terry Hicks, Manager;   (919) 727-2260
   Manager: Terry Hicks;   (919) 727-2260
   Resident Groups: Winston-Salem Symphony Society

Yadkinville

THEATRE

YADKIN PLAYERS/YADKIN YOUTH THEATRE
108 East Elm Street, PO Box 667, Yadkinville, NC 27055
(919) 679-2941
   Founded: 1974
   Arts Area: Community

Status: Non-Profit
Type: Performing; Touring; Educational
Management: Nancy Davis, Executive Director
Officers: Gray Renegar, Chairman
Paid Staff: 1
Non-Paid Artists: 80
Utilizes: Guest Artists; Guest Directors
Budget: $1,000 - $50,000
Income Sources: Private Foundations/Grants/Endowments; Business/Corporate Donations; Box Office; Government Grants; Individual Donations
Season: October - May
Annual Attendance: 3,000

Yanceyville

FACILITY

CASWELL COUNTY CIVIC CENTER
Intersection of Highway 158 & Highway 62, PO Box 609, Yanceyville, NC 27379
(919) 694-4591
FAX: (919) 694-5154
    Type of Facility: Auditorium; Civic Center; Multi-Purpose
    Type of Stage: Thrust; Proscenium
    Stage Dimensions: 45'Wx30'D and a 14' apron
    Seating Capacity: 1,000
    Year Built: 1979   **Architect:** Smart & Isley   **Cost:** $1,200,000
    Contact for Rental: H Lee Fowlkes, Director;   (919) 694-4591

NORTH DAKOTA

Bismarck

INSTRUMENTAL MUSIC

BISMARCK-MANDAN ORCHESTRAL ASSOCIATION
216 North Sixth Street, Bismarck, ND 58501
(701) 258-8345
Founded: 1975
Arts Area: Symphony; Orchestra; Instrumental Group
Status: Non-Profit
Type: Performing
Purpose: To present an ensemble chamber-music series
Management: Susan Lundberg-Dehoff, Executive Director; Thomas Wellin, Music Director
Officers: Troy Vredanburg, President; Joanne Pearson, Secretary; James Collins, Vice President/Treasurer
Paid Staff: 2 **Volunteer Staff:** 1
Paid Artists: 3 **Non-Paid Artists:** 60
Utilizes: Guest Artists
Budget: $100,000 - $500,000
Income Sources: Private Foundations/Grants/Endowments; Business/Corporate Donations; Box Office; Government Grants; Individual Donations
Season: September - April **Annual Attendance:** 3,500
Performance Facilities: Bismarck City Auditorium

FACILITY

BISMARCK CIVIC CENTER - ARENA
201 North Sixth Street, PO Box 1075, Bismarck, ND 58502
(701) 222-6487
FAX: (701) 222-6599
Type of Facility: Civic Center; Arena; Multi-Purpose
Type of Stage: Arena
Seating Capacity: 8,500
Year Built: 1969 **Cost:** $2,500,000
Contact for Rental: Paul Johnson; (701) 222-6487

BISMARCK CIVIC CENTER - BISMARCK CITY AUDITORIUM
201 North Sixth Street, Bismarck, ND 58502
(701) 222-6487
FAX: (701) 222-6599
Type of Facility: Concert Hall; Auditorium; Theatre House; Opera House
Type of Stage: Proscenium
Stage Dimensions: 54'Wx29'7"D **Orchestra Pit**
Seating Capacity: 1,074
Year Built: 1914 **Cost:** $46,000
Year Remodeled: 1987 **Architect:** Jiran
Contact for Rental: Paul Johnson; (701) 222-6487
Resident Groups: Bismarck-Mandan Orchestra; Bismarck-Mandan Concerts; Dakota Stage Limited; University of Mary Theater Department

Devils Lake

INSTRUMENTAL MUSIC

DEVILS LAKE COMMUNITY ORCHESTRA
828 Fifth Street, PO Box 151, Devils Lake, ND 58301
(701) 662-8353
Founded: 1980
Arts Area: Orchestra; Chamber
Status: Non-Profit
Type: Performing; Educational
Purpose: To provide orchestral music for the Devils Lake area
Management: Russell Pearson, Music Director
Officers: Curtis Sinness, President; Agnes Christianson, Secretary; Reuben Schnaidt, Treasurer
Volunteer Staff: 6

Non-Paid Artists: 48
Budget: $1,000 - $50,000
Income Sources: Business/Corporate Donations; Box Office; Government Grants; Individual Donations
Season: November - March   **Annual Attendance:** 1,200
Affiliations: NEA; Lake Region Arts Council
Performance Facilities: Ramsey County Memorial Building

Fargo

DANCE

RED RIVER DANCE AND PERFORMING COMPANY
824 Main Avenue PO Box 283, Fargo, ND 58107
(701) 280-2289; (701) 280-0004
   Founded: 1979
   Arts Area: Ballet; Jazz; Tap
   Status: Professional; Non-Profit
   Type: Performing; Touring; Resident; Educational
   Purpose: A non-profit tax exempt arts and educational organization as well as a professional, regional dance company with an established season and educational programming and touring history
   Management: Kathryn and Eddie Gasper, Co-Artistic Directors; Sandra Lee, Business Manager; Linda Christman, Director of Touring; Lois Neys, Business Assistant
   Officers: Ellen Cromwell-Cecrle, President; Katie Oppegard, Treasurer; Joel Charon, Secretary
   Paid Staff: 3
   Paid Artists: 8   **Non-Paid Artists:** 7
   Utilizes: Special Technical Talent; Guest Conductors; Guest Artists; Guest Choreographers
   Budget: $100,000 - $500,000
   Income Sources: Private Foundations/Grants/Endowments; Business/Corporate Donations; Box Office; Government Grants; Individual Donations
   Season: September - May   **Annual Attendance:** 20,000
   Performance Facilities: North Dakota State University; Reineke Fine Arts Council

INSTRUMENTAL MUSIC

FARGO-MOORHEAD ORCHESTRAL ASSOCIATION
PO Box 1753, Fargo, ND 58107
(218) 233-8397
FAX: (218) 236-1845
   Founded: 1931
   Arts Area: Symphony; Orchestra; Chamber; Ensemble; Instrumental Group
   Status: Semi-Professional; Non-Profit
   Type: Performing; Resident
   Purpose: To provide quality symphonic music to the Fargo-Moorhead area
   Management: Mark D. Madson, Manager; Joel N. Revzen, Music Director
   Officers: Howard Dahl, President; Mary Stahl, Vice President; Gen Eidem, Secretary; Allan Severson, Treasurer
   Paid Staff: 6
   Paid Artists: 85
   Utilizes: Special Technical Talent; Guest Conductors; Guest Artists
   Budget: $1,000,000 - $5,000,000
   Income Sources: Private Foundations/Grants/Endowments; Business/Corporate Donations; Box Office; Government Grants; Individual Donations
   Season: September - April   **Annual Attendance:** 11,500
   Affiliations: ASOL
   Performance Facilities: Concordia College Memorial Auditorium

FARGO-MOORHEAD SYMPHONY ORCHESTRA
PO Box 1753, Fargo, ND 58107
(218) 233-8397
FAX: (218) 236-1846
   Founded: 1931
   Arts Area: Symphony; Orchestra; Chamber; Ensemble; Instrumental Group
   Status: Semi-Professional; Non-Profit
   Type: Performing; Resident
   Purpose: To provide quality symphonic music to the Fargo-Moorhead area
   Management: Mark D. Madson, Manager; Joel Revzen, Music Director
   Officers: Howard Dahl, President; Mary Staahl, Vice President; Gen Eidem, Secretary; Allan Severson, Treasurer
   Paid Staff: 3
   Paid Artists: 95

Utilizes: Special Technical Talent; Guest Conductors; Guest Artists
Budget: $100,000 - $500,000
Income Sources: Private Foundations/Grants/Endowments; Business/Corporate Donations; Box Office; Government Grants; Individual Donations
Season: September - April   **Annual Attendance:** 11,500
Affiliations: ASOL
Performance Facilities: Concordia Memorial Auditorium

VOCAL MUSIC

FARGO-MOORHEAD CIVIC OPERA COMPANY
806 NP Avenue, Fargo, ND 58102
(701) 239-4558
> **Founded:** 1968
> **Arts Area:** Grand Opera; Lyric Opera; Light Opera; Operetta
> **Status:** Professional; Non-Profit
> **Type:** Performing; Touring; Educational
> **Purpose:** To produce three different operas a year, performing each usually three times
> **Management:** David Martin, Artistic Director; Jill M. Johnson-Danielson, Exective Director
> **Officers:** Winnie Stadter, President; Dr. George O'Neill, Vice President; Ruth Swenson, Secretary; Dr. Grey McCarthy, Treasurer
> **Paid Staff:** 4   **Volunteer Staff:** 12
> **Paid Artists:** 50   **Non-Paid Artists:** 45
> **Utilizes:** Special Technical Talent; Guest Artists; Guest Directors
> **Budget:** $100,000 - $500,000
> **Income Sources:** Private Foundations/Grants/Endowments; Business/Corporate Donations; Box Office; Government Grants; Individual Donations; Fundraising
> **Season:** October - May   **Annual Attendance:** 5,000
> **Affiliations:** OA

THEATRE

FARGO-MOORHEAD COMMUNITY THEATRE
333 South Fourth Street, Fargo, ND 58107
(701) 235-1901
> **Founded:** 1946
> **Arts Area:** Community
> **Status:** Non-Profit
> **Type:** Resident
> **Purpose:** To provide quality avocational theatre opportunities to the cities of Fargo and Moorhead, as well as the region
> **Management:** Bruce E. Tinker, Artistic Director; Richard J. Jordan, Finance Director
> **Officers:** Pamela Anderson, President; Timothy Hill, Vice President; Perry Score, Treasurer; Gerry Emery, Secretary; Richard Burns, Member at Large
> **Paid Staff:** 9   **Volunteer Staff:** 300
> **Paid Artists:** 6   **Non-Paid Artists:** 175
> **Utilizes:** Special Technical Talent; Guest Conductors; Guest Artists; Guest Directors
> **Budget:** $100,000 - $500,000
> **Income Sources:** Private Foundations/Grants/Endowments; Business/Corporate Donations; Box Office; Individual Donations; Charitable Gaming
> **Season:** September - June   **Annual Attendance:** 20,000
> **Affiliations:** NACT; NDAA; ACT; Lake Agassiz Arts Council; North Dakota Community Theatre Association; Minnesota Association of Community Theaters; Fargo Chamber of Commerce; Minnesota Citizens for the Arts
> **Performance Facilities:** Emma K. Herbst Playhouse

LITTLE COUNTRY THEATRE
12th Avenue North and West College Street, Fargo, ND 58105
(701) 237-7784
> **Founded:** 1914
> **Arts Area:** Theatrical Group
> **Status:** Non-Profit
> **Type:** Educational
> **Purpose:** To produce theatrical productions reflecting a high degree of professionalism; to develop artists in the theatre as well as responsive audiences
> **Management:** Don Stowell Jr., Director, Division of Fine Arts; Don Larew, Artistic Director; M. Joy Erickson, Managing Director
> **Paid Staff:** 11
> **Non-Paid Artists:** 50
> **Utilizes:** Special Technical Talent; Guest Artists
> **Budget:** $1,000 - $50,000

Income Sources: Box Office; Individual Donations; Student Government Fees
Season: September - May   **Annual Attendance:** 4,000
Affiliations: ACTF; USITT
Performance Facilities: Askanase Auditorium; Walsh Studio Theatre

FACILITY

FESTIVAL CONCERT HALL
North Dakota State University, Fargo, ND 58105
(701) 237-8241
FAX: (701) 237-8043
Founded: 1982
Type of Facility: Concert Hall
Type of Stage: Proscenium
Stage Dimensions: 50'x40'   **Orchestra Pit**
Seating Capacity: 997
Year Built: 1982   **Architect:** Foss Associates
Contact for Rental: William Blain;   (701) 237-8241

Fort Totten

THEATRE

FORT TOTTEN LITTLE THEATRE
PO Box 97, Fort Totten, ND 58335
(701) 766-4473
Founded: 1962
Arts Area: Musical; Community; Theatrical Group
Status: Semi-Professional; Non-Professional; Non-Profit
Type: Performing; Resident
Purpose: Provide an opportunity for talented people to have theatre experience; attract tourists to a state historic site; entertainment for the citizens of rural areas
Management: Carol Leevers, Jane Traynor, Community Relations; John Traynor, Attorney; Chuck Jerome, Advanced Ticket Drive; Armin Hanson, Publicity
Officers: Carol Leevers, President; Jane Traynor, Vice President; Dean Petska, Treasurer/Secretary; Judy Ryan, Artistic Director
Paid Staff: 12   **Volunteer Staff:** 60
Non-Paid Artists: 20
Utilizes: Special Technical Talent
Budget: $1,000 - $50,000
Income Sources: Private Foundations/Grants/Endowments; Box Office
Season: July - August   **Annual Attendance:** 6,000
Affiliations: North Dakota Council of Arts; Council of Lake Region
Performance Facilities: Cavalry Square, Historic Site

Grafton

DANCE

POLISH NATIONAL ALLIANCE DANCERS
c/o Sandy Schuster, Rural Route 3, PO Box 107, Grafton, ND 58237
(701) 352-3483
Founded: 1940
Arts Area: Ethnic; Folk
Status: Non-Professional; Non-Profit
Type: Performing
Purpose: To preserve authentic Polish folk dances which are native to residents of Northeast North Dakota
Management: Sandy Schuster, Dance Director
Utilizes: Guest Artists; Guest Directors; Guest Choreographers
Budget: $1,000 - $50,000
Income Sources: Individual Donations
Season: April - November

Grand Forks

FACILITY

UNIVERSITY OF NORTH DAKOTA - CHESTER FRITZ AUDITORIUM
University Station, PO Box 8282, Grand Forks, ND 58202
(701) 777-3076
Type of Facility: Concert Hall; Auditorium
Type of Stage: Thrust; Proscenium
Stage Dimensions: 90'Wx35'D; 90'Wx35'H proscenium opening   **Orchestra Pit**
Seating Capacity: 2,386
Year Built: 1972   **Architect:** Wells Denbrook Adams   **Cost:** $3,500,000
Acoustical Consultant: Coffeen & Associates
Contact for Rental: Truman Reed;   (701) 777-3076
Resident Groups: Grand Fork Symphony

Milton

THEATRE

THE LITTLE STAR THEATRE ASSOCIATION
PO Box 47, Milton, ND 58260
(701) 496-3353
Founded: 1985
Arts Area: Community
Status: Non-Profit
Type: Touring; Resident; Sponsoring
Purpose: To make available theatre arts (acting, directing and so forth) to the people of a rural community
Management: Peggy Gross, Director
Officers: Harlan Hanson, President; Carol Goodman, Secretary/Treasurer
Volunteer Staff: 25
Paid Artists: 2
Budget: $1,000 - $50,000
Income Sources: Private Foundations/Grants/Endowments; Box Office; Individual Donations
Season: April - November   **Annual Attendance:** 1,500
Affiliations: Milton Community Betterment Organization
Performance Facilities: The Little Star Theatre

Minot

INSTRUMENTAL MUSIC

INTERNATIONAL MUSIC CAMP
1725 11th Street, SW, Minot, ND 58701
(701) 838-8472
FAX: (701) 838-8472
Founded: 1956
Arts Area: Symphony; Orchestra; Chamber; Ensemble; Instrumental Group; Electronic & Live Electronic; Band
Status: Professional; Semi-Professional; Non-Professional; Non-Profit
Type: Performing; Resident; Educational
Purpose: To develop a greater appreciation among students of all nations through their mutual interest in the arts
Management: Joseph T. Alme, Camp Director
Officers: Vernon Gerig, President; Clifford Grubb, Vice President; Roy Johnson, Secretary; Carter Lehmann, Treasurer
Paid Staff: 50
Paid Artists: 150
Utilizes: Special Technical Talent; Guest Conductors; Guest Artists
Budget: $100,000 - $500,000
Income Sources: Private Foundations/Grants/Endowments; Business/Corporate Donations; Government Grants; Individual Donations
Season: June - July   **Annual Attendance:** 3,000

MINOT SYMPHONY ASSOCIATION
PO Box 461, Minot, ND 58702
(701) 839-8844
Founded: 1965
Arts Area: Symphony; Orchestra
Status: Professional; Non-Profit

Type: Performing; Resident
Purpose: To foster and perpetuate the Minot Symphony Orchestra, a college-community orchestra
Management: Sylvia Kerian, Manager; Dr. Daniel Hornstein, Conductor
Officers: Richard White, President; Dr. Selmer Moen, Treasurer
Paid Staff: 1 **Volunteer Staff:** 4
Paid Artists: 65
Utilizes: Guest Artists
Budget: $50,000 - $100,000
Income Sources: Private Foundations/Grants/Endowments; Business/Corporate Donations; Box Office; Government Grants; Individual Donations
Season: September - May
Annual Attendance: 3,000
Affiliations: North Dakota Council of Arts; Minot Area Council of Arts; North Dakota Arts Alliance; ASOL; NEA
Performance Facilities: McFarland Auditorium

VOCAL MUSIC

MINOT CHAMBER CHORALE
PO Box 1855, Minot, ND 58701
(701) 857-3837
Founded: 1973
Arts Area: Choral
Status: Semi-Professional; Non-Professional; Non-Profit
Type: Performing; Touring; Educational
Purpose: To bring the finest in choral literature to the north central area of North Dakota
Management: Sandra Starr, Executive Director/Conductor
Officers: Charles Weiser, President; Kenneth Starr, Vice President; Mary Muhlbradt, Secretary; Doug Freeman, Treasurer
Paid Staff: 4 **Volunteer Staff:** 42
Paid Artists: 2 **Non-Paid Artists:** 42
Utilizes: Special Technical Talent; Guest Artists; Guest Composers
Budget: $1,000 - $50,000
Income Sources: Private Foundations/Grants/Endowments; Business/Corporate Donations; Box Office; Government Grants; Individual Donations
Season: September - May
Annual Attendance: 1,200
Affiliations: Minot Area Council of the Arts

MINOT COMMUNITY OPERA
PO Box 2012, Minot, ND 58702
(701) 839-5341; (701) 857-3269
Founded: 1976
Arts Area: Grand Opera; Lyric Opera; Light Opera
Status: Non-Profit
Type: Performing; Resident; Educational
Purpose: To bring the highest quality opera to Minot; to educate, develop and encourage regional talent
Management: Julianne Walling, General Director
Officers: Linda Luedke, President; Jan Clark, Public Relations
Paid Staff: 1 **Volunteer Staff:** 20
Paid Artists: 5
Utilizes: Guest Artists; Guest Directors
Budget: $1,000 - $50,000
Income Sources: Business/Corporate Donations; Box Office; Government Grants; Individual Donations
Annual Attendance: 900
Affiliations: Minot State University
Performance Facilities: Minot State Auditorium; McFarland Auditorium, Minot State University

THEATRE

MOUSE RIVER PLAYERS
PO Box 1101, Minot, ND 58702
(701) 838-3939
Founded: 1972
Arts Area: Musical; Dinner; Community; Theatrical Group; Puppet
Status: Non-Professional; Non-Profit
Type: Performing; Touring; Educational

Purpose: Community theatre to promote adult education and provide theatre arts to surrounding communities children's educational performing arts
Management: Sandra Karnack, Resident Director
Officers: Ken Haarstad, President; Shirley Olson, Vice President; Lori Garnes, Secretary; Jerry Jorgenson, Treasurer
Paid Staff: 4   **Volunteer Staff:** 1
Non-Paid Artists: 187
Utilizes: Special Technical Talent; Guest Artists
Budget: $50,000 - $100,000
Income Sources: Private Foundations/Grants/Endowments; Business/Corporate Donations; Box Office; Government Grants; Individual Donations
Season: 52 Weeks
Annual Attendance: 11,400
Affiliations: Minot Area Council on the Arts; North Dakota Community Theatre Association
Performance Facilities: Minot Holiday Inn

Moorhead

THEATRE

GOOSEBERRY PARK PLAYERS
500 Center Avenue, POP Box 779, Moorhead, ND 56560
(701) 235-3534; (218) 299-5340
   Founded: 1984
   Arts Area: Theatrical Group
   Status: Non-Profit
   Type: Performing
   Purpose: Provide a summer outdoor theatre for and by children for family entertainment providing a fun, educational experience for young people
   Management: Ann and John Vandermaten, Directors
   Officers: Ann Vandermaten, President
   Paid Staff: 6   **Volunteer Staff:** 20
   Utilizes: Special Technical Talent
   Budget: $1,000 - $50,000
   Income Sources: Private Foundations/Grants/Endowments; Business/Corporate Donations; Box Office; Individual Donations
   Season: May - August
   Annual Attendance: 1,000
   Affiliations: Moorhead Parks and Recreational Department

Park River

THEATRE

PARK RIVER COMMUNITY THEATRE
PO Box 4, Park River, ND 58270
(701) 284-7221, ext. X285
   Founded: 1984
   Arts Area: Musical; Dinner; Community; Theatrical Group
   Status: Non-Professional; Non-Profit
   Type: Performing; Educational; Sponsoring
   Purpose: Provide community theatre productions for the citizens of Park River and arts involvement for the youth of the city and surrounding area
   Officers: Ray Alkofer, President; Darla Sheldon, Vice President; Tony Klienjan, Secretary; Peggy Seboe, Treasurer
   Volunteer Staff: 10
   Utilizes: Special Technical Talent; Guest Directors
   Budget: $1,000 - $50,000
   Income Sources: Private Foundations/Grants/Endowments; Business/Corporate Donations; Box Office; Government Grants; Individual Donations
   Season: 52 Weeks   **Annual Attendance:** 1,000
   Affiliations: North Dakota Community Theatre Association
   Performance Facilities: Park River City Hall

OHIO

Akron

DANCE

OHIO BALLET
354 East Market Street, Akron, OH 44325
(216) 375-7900
> **Founded:** 1968
> **Arts Area:** Ballet
> **Status:** Professional; Non-Profit
> **Type:** Performing; Touring
> **Purpose:** To produce and perform the ballets of Heinz Poll, master works of major and emerging choreographers of our time
> **Management:** Jack R. Lemmon, General Manager; Heinz Poll, Artistic Director; Thomas R. Skelton, Barbara S. Schubert, Associate Directors
> **Officers:** Jon R. Kelly, President
> **Paid Staff:** 15 **Volunteer Staff:** 4
> **Paid Artists:** 18
> **Utilizes:** Guest Choreographers
> **Budget:** $1,000,000 - $5,000,000
> **Income Sources:** Private Foundations/Grants/Endowments; Business/Corporate Donations; Box Office; Government Grants; Individual Donations
> **Season:** July - June **Annual Attendance:** 120,000
> **Affiliations:** Dance USA
> **Performance Facilities:** E.J. Thomas Hall; Akron Ohio Theater, Playhouse Square Center

INSTRUMENTAL MUSIC

AKRON SYMPHONY ORCHESTRA
17 North Broadway, Akron, OH 44308
(216) 535-8131
FAX: (216) 535-7302
> **Founded:** 1951
> **Arts Area:** Symphony; Orchestra; Chamber; Ensemble
> **Status:** Professional; Non-Profit
> **Type:** Performing; Educational
> **Purpose:** To provide the community with the finest quality symphonic and choral music; to educate the local public with respect to classical and contemporary music; and to extend special support to worthy local individual artists and projects
> **Management:** Connie F. Linsler, General Manager; Maureen Horrigan, Director of Marketing and Public Relations
> **Paid Staff:** 7 **Volunteer Staff:** 160
> **Paid Artists:** 95
> **Utilizes:** Guest Conductors; Guest Artists
> **Budget:** $500,000 - $1,000,000
> **Income Sources:** Private Foundations/Grants/Endowments; Business/Corporate Donations; Box Office; Government Grants; Individual Donations
> **Season:** September - May **Annual Attendance:** 60,000
> **Affiliations:** ASOL; OOOO
> **Performance Facilities:** E.J. Thomas Hall

AKRON YOUTH SYMPHONY
17 North Broadway, Akron, OH 44308
(216) 535-8131
FAX: (216) 535-7302
> **Founded:** 1954
> **Arts Area:** Symphony; Orchestra; Chamber; Ensemble
> **Status:** Non-Professional; Non-Profit
> **Type:** Performing; Educational; Sponsoring
> **Management:** Eric Benjamin, Music Director/Conductor
> **Non-Paid Artists:** 75
> **Season:** September - May **Annual Attendance:** 2,700
> **Affiliations:** Akron Symphony Orchestra; ASOL (Youth Orchestra Division)
> **Performance Facilities:** E.J. Thomas Hall

MUSIC FROM STAN HYWET
714 North Portage Path, Akron, OH 44303
(216) 836-5533; (216) 672-3114
> **Founded:** 1982
> **Arts Area:** Chamber
> **Status:** Non-Profit
> **Type:** Sponsoring
> **Purpose:** To showcase the great wealth of musical talent in northeast Ohio; to promote Stan Hywet Hall, a manor house and its tradition of music
> **Management:** Lola Rothmann, Concert Chair
> **Officers:** Bruce F. Rothmann MD, President; John E. Perry, Vice President; Robert L. Henke, Treasurer; Duane L. Isham Esq., Secretary; Diana Truyell, Recording Secretary
> **Volunteer Staff:** 17
> **Utilizes:** Guest Artists
> **Budget:** $1,000 - $50,000
> **Income Sources:** Private Foundations/Grants/Endowments; Business/Corporate Donations; Box Office; Government Grants; Individual Donations
> **Season:** September - May **Annual Attendance:** 900
> **Performance Facilities:** Music Room at Stan Hywet Hall

THEATRE

CAROUSEL DINNER THEATRE
1275 East Waterloo, Akron, OH 44306
(216) 724-9855; (800) 362-4100
> **Founded:** 1973
> **Arts Area:** Professional; Musical; Dinner
> **Status:** Professional
> **Type:** Performing
> **Purpose:** To provide professional musical theatre and Las Vegas entertainers to guests of America's largest professional dinner theatre
> **Management:** Scott Griffith, Executive Producer/Owner; Marc A. Resnik, Associate Producer
> **Paid Staff:** 26
> **Paid Artists:** 25
> **Utilizes:** Special Technical Talent; Guest Artists; Guest Directors
> **Budget:** $1,000,000 - $5,000,000
> **Income Sources:** Box Office
> **Season:** 52 Weeks **Annual Attendance:** 175,000
> **Affiliations:** ADTA; AEA
> **Performance Facilities:** Carousel Dinner Theatre

PERFORMING SERIES

E.J. THOMAS HALL
198 Hill Street, Akron, OH 44325
(216) 972-7595
> **Founded:** 1973
> **Arts Area:** Dance; Vocal Music; Instrumental Music; Theater; Festivals; Lyric Opera; Grand Opera
> **Status:** Professional; Non-Profit
> **Type:** Performing; Educational; Sponsoring
> **Purpose:** To present a varied program to community
> **Management:** Dan Dahl, Managing Director
> **Paid Staff:** 11 **Volunteer Staff:** 120
> **Utilizes:** Guest Conductors; Guest Artists; Guest Directors
> **Budget:** $1,000,000 - $5,000,000
> **Income Sources:** Private Foundations/Grants/Endowments; Business/Corporate Donations; Box Office; Government Grants; Individual Donations
> **Season:** 52 Weeks
> **Affiliations:** IAAM; ISPAA; APAP
> **Performance Facilities:** E.J. Thomas Hall

GREATER AKRON MUSICAL ASSOCIATION
17 North Broadway, Akron, OH 44308
(216) 535-8131
FAX: (216) 535-7302
> **Founded:** 1950
> **Arts Area:** Vocal Music; Instrumental Music
> **Status:** Professional; Non-Profit

Type: Performing; Educational
Purpose: To provide the Greater Akron Area with the finest quality symphonic and choral music and related fine arts; to educate the local public with respect to classical and contemporary music
Management: Alan Balter, Music Director/Conductor; Eric Benjamin, Conductor/Youth Symphony; Connie F. Linsler, General Manager
Officers: Wayne Knabel, President; Ellen Otto, Executive Vice President
Paid Staff: 10
Paid Artists: 95
Utilizes: Guest Conductors; Guest Artists
Budget: $500,000 - $1,000,000
Income Sources: Private Foundations/Grants/Endowments; Business/Corporate Donations; Box Office; Government Grants; Individual Donations
Season: September - May **Annual Attendance:** 140,000
Performance Facilities: E.J. Thomas Hall

FACILITY

AKRON CIVIC THEATRE
182 South Main Street, Akron, OH 44308
(216) 535-3179
Type of Facility: Auditorium; Performance Center; Theatre House; Opera House
Facility Originally: Movie House
Type of Stage: Proscenium
Orchestra Pit
Seating Capacity: 2,668
Year Built: 1929 **Architect:** John Eberson **Cost:** $2,000,000
Year Remodeled: 1982 **Architect:** John Eberson
Acoustical Consultant: Ronald Rasmussen
Contact for Rental: Tammy Kaylor; (216) 535-3179
Manager: Lynn Dudnick; (216) 535-3179

CAROUSEL DINNER THEATRE
1275 East Waterloo, PO0Box 7530, Akron, OH 44306
(216) 724-9855
FAX: (216) 724-9855
Type of Facility: Theatre House; Arena; Dinner Theatre
Facility Originally: Supermarket
Type of Stage: Arena
Stage Dimensions: 20'x24' **Orchestra Pit**
Seating Capacity: 518
Year Remodeled: 1973 **Cost:** $100,000
Contact for Rental: Virginia Kancler; (216) 272-9855
Resident Groups: Carousel Dinner Theatre

E.J. THOMAS PERFORMING ARTS HALL
University Avenue and Hill Streets, The University of Akron, Akron, OH 44325-0501
(216) 972-7595
FAX: (216) 972-6571
Founded: 1973
Type of Facility: Concert Hall; Auditorium; Performance Center; Theatre House; Opera House; Multi-Purpose
Type of Stage: Proscenium
Stage Dimensions: 60'x55' **Orchestra Pit**
Seating Capacity: 2,969
Year Built: 1973 **Architect:** Caudill Rowlett Scott **Cost:** $13,900,000
Acoustical Consultant: Vern Knudsen
Contact for Rental: Cynthia Hollis; (216) 972-7595
Manager: Dan Dahl, Managing Director; (216) 972-7595
Resident Groups: Akron Symphony; Ohio Ballet; Tuesday Musical Society; Children's Concert Society

Ashland

INSTRUMENTAL MUSIC

ASHLAND SYMPHONY ORCHESTRA
PO Box 13, Ashland, OH 44805
(419) 289-5115
Founded: 1970
Arts Area: Symphony; Orchestra

Status: Semi-Professional; Non-Profit
Type: Performing; Educational
Purpose: To provide symphonic orchestra programs for people of all ages in Ashland and the surrounding area
Management: James E. Thomas, General Manager; Albert George Schram, Music Director/Conductor
Officers: Dr. John W. Fraas, President, Board of Directors
Paid Staff: 3   **Volunteer Staff:** 350
Paid Artists: 87   **Non-Paid Artists:** 35
Utilizes: Guest Artists
Budget: $50,000 - $100,000
Income Sources: Private Foundations/Grants/Endowments; Business/Corporate Donations; Box Office; Individual Donations
Season: September - June   **Annual Attendance:** 4,500
Affiliations: OOOO
Performance Facilities: Hugo Young Theatre

Ashtabula

INSTRUMENTAL MUSIC

THE ASHTABULA CHAMBER ORCHESTRA
3325 West 13th Street, Ashtabula, OH 44004
(216) 964-3322
Founded: 1982
Arts Area: Orchestra; Chamber
Status: Non-Professional; Non-Profit
Type: Performing; Resident
Purpose: To educate the people of the area in all types of stringed music; to provide string ensemble music for public enjoyment; to encourage young people on strings
Management: Michael Gelfand, Music Director
Officers: Brad Stevenson, President; Carol Quirke, Vice President; Eleanor Stevenson, Secretary/Treasurer
Paid Staff: 1
Non-Paid Artists: 35
Utilizes: Special Technical Talent; Guest Conductors; Guest Artists; Guest Directors
Budget: $1,000 - $50,000
Income Sources: Private Foundations/Grants/Endowments; Business/Corporate Donations; Box Office; Individual Donations
Season: 52 Weeks   **Annual Attendance:** 850
Affiliations: Kent State University, Ashtabula Campus
Performance Facilities: Kent State University Auditorium, Ashtabula Campus

FACILITY

ASHTABULA ARTS CENTER
2928 West 13th Street, Ashtabula, OH 44004
(216) 964-3396
Founded: 1953
Type of Facility: Outdoor (Concert); Environmental; Performance Center; Theatre House; Multi-Purpose
Facility Originally: Private Residence
Type of Stage: Proscenium
Stage Dimensions: 70'x30'
Seating Capacity: 235
Year Built: 1975   **Architect:** Fred Toguchi   **Cost:** $167,000
Year Remodeled: 1987   **Architect:** John George   **Cost:** $367,000
Resident Groups: GB Repertory

Athens

FACILITY

ATHENS MEMORIAL AUDITORIUM
Athens, OH 45701
(614) 593-1761
FAX: (614) 593-0047
Type of Facility: Auditorium
Type of Stage: Proscenium   **Orchestra Pit**
Seating Capacity: 2,200
Year Built: 1928   **Architect:** Howell & Thomas   **Cost:** $349,000

Year Remodeled: 1974   **Architect:** Gronsow & Guss   **Cost:** $90,000
Contact for Rental: Gretchen Stephens;   (614) 593-1761
Resident Groups: Ohio University Symphony Orchestra

OHIO UNIVERSITY - PATIO THEATER
307 Kantner Hall, School of Theater, Athens, OH 45701
(614) 593-4818
Type of Facility: Theatre House
Type of Stage: Proscenium
Seating Capacity: 300
Contact for Rental: Lonny Fraze;   (614) 593-4850
Manager: William F. Condee
Resident Groups: Ohio University Theater; Ohio Valley Summer Theater

OHIO UNIVERSITY - SCHOOL OF MUSIC
Athens, OH 45701
(614) 593-4244
Type of Facility: Auditorium
Seating Capacity: 198
Year Built: 1970
Architect: Joe Baker
Contact for Rental: Harold Robinson;   (614) 593-4246
Resident Groups: Music School Organizations

Barberton

THEATRE

MAGICAL THEATRE COMPANY
565 West Tuscarawas Avenue, Barberton, OH 44203
(216) 848-3708
Founded: 1973
Arts Area: Theatrical Group
Status: Professional; Non-Profit
Type: Performing; Touring; Resident; Educational; Sponsoring
Management: Graham Whitehead, Ph.D., Artistic Director; Nancy Steimel-Sistek, Executive Director
Officers: JeriLynn Ferguson, President; Kevin McQuaide, Vice President; Frank Heckel, Treasurer; Donna Early, Secretary
Paid Staff: 6   **Volunteer Staff:** 30
Paid Artists: 9   **Non-Paid Artists:** 15
Utilizes: Special Technical Talent; Guest Artists; Guest Directors
Budget: $100,000 - $500,000
Income Sources: Private Foundations/Grants/Endowments; Business/Corporate Donations; Box Office; Individual Donations
Season: 52 Weeks   **Annual Attendance:** 63,000
Affiliations: OTA

FACILITY

MAGICAL THEATRE COMPANY
565 West Tuscarawas Avenue, Barberton, OH 44203
(216) 848-3708
Type of Facility: Auditorium; Theatre House
Facility Originally: Movie House
Type of Stage: Proscenium
Stage Dimensions: 28'x26'
Seating Capacity: 380
Year Built: 1919
Year Remodeled: 1985   **Architect:** Curtis & Rassmussen
Cost: $120,000
Acoustical Consultant: Reid Woodbury
Resident Groups: Magical Theatre Company
Phase II of remodeling plan underway

Bay Village

THEATRE

HUNTINGTON THEATRE
28601 Lake Road, Bay Village, OH 44140
(216) 871-8333
    Founded: 1958
    Arts Area: Musical; Community; Theatrical Group
    Status: Non-Professional; Non-Profit
    Type: Performing; Educational
    Purpose: Community theatre
    Officers: J.B. Binns, President; T. Meyrose, Vice President; A. Clark, Secretary/Treasurer
    Volunteer Staff: 100
    Paid Artists: 3   **Non-Paid Artists:** 100
    Utilizes: Special Technical Talent; Guest Directors
    Budget: $1,000 - $50,000
    Income Sources: Business/Corporate Donations; Box Office; Individual Donations
    Season: May - January
    Performance Facilities: Huntington Playhouse

FACILITY

HUNTINGTON PLAYHOUSE
28601 Lake Road, Bay Village, OH 44140
(216) 871-8333
    Type of Facility: Theatre Complex; Auditorium
    Type of Stage: Proscenium   **Seating Capacity:** 248
    Year Built: 1971   **Cost:** $250,000
    Contact for Rental: Mr. Melrose or Mr. Clark;   (216) 521-1525
    Manager: Mr. Melrose;   (216) 344-7700
    Resident Groups: Huntington Theatre

Beachwood

INSTRUMENTAL MUSIC

SUBURBAN SYMPHONY ORCHESTRA
PO Box 22653, Beachwood, OH 44122
(216) 449-2389
    Founded: 1954
    Arts Area: Symphony; Orchestra
    Status: Professional; Semi-Professional; Non-Professional; Non-Profit
    Type: Performing
    Purpose: To provide accomplished professional and non-professional musicians with the opportunity to perform in a symphony orchestra, and to perform five free symphonic concerts per season
    Management: Martin Kessler, Music Director; Paul Pride, General Manager
    Officers: Ethel Epstein, President; Allan Scherl, Vice President; Connie West, Secretary; Harlan Meinwald, Treasurer
    Paid Staff: 2   **Volunteer Staff:** 10
    Paid Artists: 15   **Non-Paid Artists:** 70
    Utilizes: Guest Conductors; Guest Artists
    Budget: $1,000 - $50,000
    Income Sources: Private Foundations/Grants/Endowments; Business/Corporate Donations; Government Grants; Individual Donations
    Season: September - May   **Annual Attendance:** 4,000
    Performance Facilities: Beachwood High School Auditorium

Berea

FACILITY

BALDWIN WALLACE COLLEGE - KULAS MUSICAL ARTS CONCERT HALL
96 Front Street, Berea, OH 44017
(216) 826-2375
    Type of Facility: Concert Hall
    Facility Originally: School

Type of Stage: Platform
Orchestra Pit
Seating Capacity: 650
Year Built: 1912
Year Remodeled: 1958
Manager: William R. Carlson;   (216) 826-2376
Resident Groups: Conservatory-Ohio Chamber Orchestra

Bowling Green

INSTRUMENTAL

VENTI DA CAMERA
Bowling Green State University, Bowling Green, OH 43403
(419) 372-2955
Founded: 1965
Arts Area: Chamber; Woodwind Quintet
Status: Professional
Type: Performing; Touring; Resident; Educational
Purpose: To perform works for wind quintet and other ensembles using these instruments in various combinations, offering a wide range of repertoire for a wide range of audiences
Management: College of Musical Arts, Bowling Green State University Ensemble Members - John Bently, Oboe/Correspondent; Judith Bentley, Flute; Edward Marks, Clarinet; Robert Moore, Bassoon; Herbert Spencer, Horn
Paid Artists: 5
Budget: $1,000 - $50,000
Season: September - May
Affiliations: Bowling Green State University College of Music
Performance Facilities: Bryan Recital Hall

THEATRE

THE HURON PLAYHOUSE
Bowling Green State University, Theatre Department, Bowling Green, OH 43403
(419) 372-2523
Founded: 1949
Arts Area: Summer Stock; Musical
Status: Non-Professional; Non-Profit
Type: Performing; Educational
Purpose: To provide a unique educational theatre experience for company members; to extend services of Bowling Green State University; to provide live theatre to a large area
Management: Dr. Allen Kepke, Chairman, Theatre Department
Officers: Dr. P.J. Olscamp, President; Dr. E. Clark, Vice President; Dr. Ralph Townsend, Interim Dean, Arts and Sciences
Paid Staff: 20
Paid Artists: 30
Utilizes: Special Technical Talent; Guest Conductors; Guest Directors
Budget: $100,000 - $500,000
Income Sources: Box Office; University Subsidies
Season: June - August   **Annual Attendance:** 15,000
Affiliations: North Central Ohio Arts Council
Performance Facilities: McCormick Junior High School Auditorium, Huron

Brecksville

THEATRE

BRECKSVILLE LITTLE THEATRE
PO Box 41131, Brecksville, OH 44141
(216) 526-4477
Founded: 1941
Arts Area: Musical; Community; Theatrical Group
Status: Non-Professional; Non-Profit
Type: Performing; Resident; Educational
Purpose: To present good theatre; to provide an opportunity to perform
Officers: Georgia Maresh, President; Ruth Wheaton, Vice President; Jan Futhey, Secretary; Ann Leopold, Treasurer
Volunteer Staff: 45
Non-Paid Artists: 100

Utilizes: Special Technical Talent; Guest Conductors; Guest Artists; Guest Directors
Budget: $1,000 - $50,000
Income Sources: Business/Corporate Donations; Box Office; Individual Donations
Season: September - June   **Annual Attendance:** 2,500
Performance Facilities: Old Towne Hall, Brecksville Square

THEATER ON THE SQUARE
47 Public Square, PO Box 41002, Brecksville, OH 44141
(216) 526-6245
Founded: 1975
Arts Area: Community
Status: Semi-Professional; Non-Profit
Type: Performing; Educational
Purpose: To mount a variety of shows as a community theater and to educate area youth
Management: Marlene Kalnitzky, Managing Director
Paid Staff: 3   **Volunteer Staff:** 18
Utilizes: Guest Directors
Budget: $1,000 - $50,000
Income Sources: Private Foundations/Grants/Endowments; Business/Corporate Donations; Box Office; Government Grants; Individual Donations
Season: April - September   **Annual Attendance:** 2,500
Affiliations: OAC
Performance Facilities: Old Towne Hall

FACILITY

BRECKSVILLE LITTLE THEATRE
49 Public Square, Brecksville, OH 44141
(216) 526-4477
Type of Facility: Auditorium; Theatre House; Civic Center; Multi-Purpose
Facility Originally: Meeting Hall; Movie House
Type of Stage: Proscenium
Stage Dimensions: 16'x31'
Seating Capacity: 144
Contact for Rental: City of Brecksville;   (216) 526-4351
Resident Groups: Brecksville Little Theatre; Brecksville Senior Citizens; Theatre On The Square

Cambridge

PERFORMING SERIES

CAMBRIDGE CONCERT ASSOCIATION
63041 Ridgewood Drive, Cambridge, OH 43725
(614) 432-7371; (614) 439-7735
Founded: 1936
Arts Area: Dance; Vocal Music; Instrumental Music; Lyric Opera
Status: Non-Profit
Type: Sponsoring
Purpose: To make available to the community, on a membership basis, high quality artistic talents and entertainment
Officers: David Carroll, Chairman
Volunteer Staff: 37
Paid Artists: 4
Utilizes: Guest Artists
Budget: $1,000 - $50,000
Income Sources: Private Foundations/Grants/Endowments; Business/Corporate Donations; Box Office; Government Grants; Individual Donations
Season: September - May   **Annual Attendance:** 2,600
Affiliations: ORACLE
Performance Facilities: Vergari's State Theater

FACILITY

SCOTTISH RITE AUDITORIUM
941 Wheeling Avenue, Cambridge, OH 43725
(614) 432-4346
Type of Facility: Theatre House
Type of Stage: Flexible; Proscenium

Stage Dimensions: 39'x26'
Orchestra Pit
Seating Capacity: 955
Year Built: 1937   **Cost:** $900,000
Year Remodeled: 1975   **Architect:** Higgins Construction Company   **Cost:** $100,000
Available for rent

Canton

DANCE

CANTON BALLET
1001 North Market Avenue, Canton, OH 44702
(216) 455-7220
Founded: 1965
Arts Area: Ballet
Status: Non-Professional; Non-Profit
Type: Performing; Touring; Resident; Educational
Purpose: To offer progressive levels of dance training of the highest quality and provide performance opportunities for dancers
Management: Cassandra Crowley, Artistic Director; Kris Furlan, General Manager; Deborah Sherrod, Administrative Assistant
Officers: Christine Wilkof, President; Catherine Di Maio, Past President; Christine Trudeau, Vice President; Paul Stolic, Treasurer
Paid Staff: 12   **Volunteer Staff:** 3
Non-Paid Artists: 17
Utilizes: Special Technical Talent; Guest Artists
Budget: $100,000 - $500,000
Income Sources: Private Foundations/Grants/Endowments; Business/Corporate Donations; Box Office; Government Grants; Individual Donations
Season: September - June   **Annual Attendance:** 22,000
Affiliations: Regional Dance America; Ohio Citizens Committee for the Arts; NARB; Ohio Dance
Performance Facilities: Palace Theatre

INSTRUMENTAL MUSIC

CANTON SYMPHONY ORCHESTRA
1001 North Market Avenue, Canton, OH 44702
(216) 452-3434
FAX: (216) 452-4429
Founded: 1937
Arts Area: Symphony; Orchestra; Chamber; Ensemble
Status: Professional; Non-Profit
Type: Performing
Purpose: To maintain an orchestra of the highest quality as a cultural and educational resource and to bring the enjoyment and enrichment of great music to increasing numbers of citizens in northeastern Ohio
Management: Linda V. Moorhouse, Executive Director
Officers: Sheila M. Markley, President
Paid Staff: 4
Paid Artists: 80
Utilizes: Guest Conductors; Guest Artists
Budget: $500,000 - $1,000,000
Income Sources: Private Foundations/Grants/Endowments; Business/Corporate Donations; Box Office; Government Grants; Individual Donations
Season: October - May   **Annual Attendance:** 101,000
Affiliations: ASOL
Performance Facilities: William E. Umstattd Performing Arts Hall

CANTON YOUTH SYMPHONY
1001 North Market Avenue, Canton, OH 44702
(216) 452-3434
FAX: (216) 452-4429
Founded: 1962
Arts Area: Symphony; Orchestra
Status: Non-Professional; Non-Profit
Type: Performing; Educational; Sponsoring
Management: Linda V. Moorhouse, Manager; Janna Hymes, Conductor
Volunteer Staff: 6

Non-Paid Artists: 60
Budget: $1,000 - $50,000
Season: September - May   **Annual Attendance:** 1,000
Affiliations: ASOL (Youth Orchestra Division); Canton Symphony Orchestra
Performance Facilities: Fine and Professional Arts Building, Kent State University

THEATRE

PLAYERS GUILD OF CANTON
1001 North Market Street, Canton, OH 44702
(216) 453-7619
Founded: 1932
Arts Area: Community
Status: Non-Professional; Non-Profit
Type: Performing
Purpose: A charitable and educational institution which produces and exhibits plays and provides instruction of the theatre arts for the purpose of fostering and advancing education in and appreciation of the theatre by and among the people of the Greater Canton Area
Management: Lisa Alter, General Manager; Rick Lombardo, Artistic Director; Donald E. Keith, Technical Director/Designer; Deanna Kuebel, Administrative Associate; William Fry, Youth Theatre Director
Officers: Beve Carver, President; William Strohmenger, First Vice President; Frank Ianni, Second Vice President; Janet Barry, Secretary; Carolyn Brothers, Treasurer
Paid Staff: 6
Utilizes: Guest Artists; Guest Directors
Budget: $500,000 - $1,000,000
Income Sources: Box Office
Season: August - June   **Annual Attendance:** 39,000
Affiliations: ATA; Ohio Community Theatre Alliance

FACILITY

PALACE THEATRE
605 Market Avenue North, Canton, OH 44702-1016
(216) 454-8172
Type of Facility: Multi-Purpose
Facility Originally: Vaudeville
Type of Stage: Proscenium
Stage Dimensions: 52'Wx27'D
Orchestra Pit
Seating Capacity: 1,500
Year Built: 1926   **Architect:** John Eberson   **Cost:** $1,000,000
Year Remodeled: 1987   **Architect:** Lawrence Dykes Bower & Clancy   **Cost:** $1,200,000
Contact for Rental: Bea W. Constantino;   (216) 454-8172
Resident Groups: Canton Ballet Company; North Canton Theatre Guild
The Palace is a member of the League of Historic American Theatres

PLAYERS GUILD OF CANTON
1001 North Market Street, Canton, OH 44702
(216) 453-7619
Type of Facility: Cultural Center
Type of Stage: Proscenium
Stage Dimensions: 56'6"Wx22'Hx40'D   **Orchestra Pit**
Seating Capacity: 496
Year Built: 1971   **Architect:** Lawrence Dykes Bower & Clancy   **Cost:** $9,000,000
Contact for Rental: (216) 453-7619
Manager: Lisa Atler

Chagrin Falls

THEATRE

CHAGRIN VALLEY LITTLE THEATRE
40 River Street, Chagrin Falls, OH 44022
(216) 247-8955
Founded: 1930
Arts Area: Theatrical Group
Status: Non-Professional; Non-Profit
Type: Performing

Purpose: Community theater
Management: Rollin DeVere, Business Manager
Officers: Craig Kasper, President
Paid Staff: 3   **Volunteer Staff:** 30
Non-Paid Artists: 150
Budget: $50,000 - $100,000
Income Sources: Private Foundations/Grants/Endowments; Box Office; Individual Donations
Season: 52 Weeks   **Annual Attendance:** 22,000

Cincinnati

DANCE

CINCINNATI BALLET
1216 Central Parkway, Cincinnati, OH 45210
(513) 621-5219
FAX: (513) 621-4844
Founded: 1966
Arts Area: Ballet
Status: Professional
Type: Performing; Touring; Resident; Educational
Purpose: To perform an extensive ballet repertoire in both Cincinnati and Knoxville
Management: Paul Stuhlreyer, Executive Producer; Nigel Burgoine, Artistic Director; Michael Dennison, Operations Director
Officers: Blanche Maier, Chairman; Charles MacDonell, President
Paid Staff: 16   **Volunteer Staff:** 500
Paid Artists: 51
Utilizes: Guest Directors; Guest Choreographers
Budget: $1,000,000 - $5,000,000
Income Sources: Private Foundations/Grants/Endowments; Business/Corporate Donations; Box Office; Government Grants; Individual Donations
Season: August - May   **Annual Attendance:** 45,000
Affiliations: Dance USA; Ohio Dance; NAA
Performance Facilities: Music Hall

CONTEMPORARY DANCE THEATER
2728 Vine Street, PO Box 19220, Cincinnati, OH 45219
(513) 751-2800
Founded: 1972
Arts Area: Modern; Mime; Jazz; Ethnic
Status: Professional; Non-Profit
Type: Performing; Touring; Resident; Educational; Sponsoring
Purpose: To promote the art of dance; provide educational demonstrations and performances for the community and provide dance instruction; to present and produce dance
Management: Jefferson James, Artistic Director; Kathy Valin, Publicity Director; Dennis Reed, Technical Director
Officers: Janelle Montgomery, President; Bea Rose, Vice President; Edna Rosenberg, Secretary; Steve Schwartz, Treasurer
Paid Staff: 4   **Volunteer Staff:** 15
Paid Artists: 20
Utilizes: Guest Artists; Guest Choreographers
Budget: $100,000 - $500,000
Income Sources: Private Foundations/Grants/Endowments; Business/Corporate Donations; Box Office; Government Grants; Individual Donations; Benefits
Season: September - July   **Annual Attendance:** 30,000
Affiliations: Ohio Dance; Cincinnati Commission of the Arts; Dance Action
Performance Facilities: The Dance Hall

INSTRUMENTAL MUSIC

CINCINNATI POPS ORCHESTRA
1241 Elm Street, Cincinnati, OH 45210
(513) 621-1919
Founded: 1977
Arts Area: Pops
Status: Professional; Non-Profit
Type: Performing; Touring
Management: Erich Kunzel, Conductor; Steven Monder, Executive Director
Paid Artists: 98
Utilizes: Guest Artists

Season: 52 Weeks
Affiliations: Cincinnati Symphony Orchestra
Performance Facilities: Music Hall

CINCINNATI SYMPHONY
1241 Elm Street, Cincinnati, OH 45210
(513) 621-1919
FAX: (513) 621-2132
Founded: 1895
Arts Area: Symphony; Orchestra; Chamber; Ensemble
Status: Professional; Non-Profit
Type: Performing; Touring; Resident; Educational
Purpose: To provide an orchestra of such high quality that it is an aesthetic joy, is patronized to the capacity of our facility, is a source of civic pride and community reputation and is tailored to the character of our city
Management: Steven Monder, Executive Director; Jesus Lopez-Cobos, Music Director; Jeffrey Alexander, Manager; Dianne Cooper, Marketing Director; Donald Auberger, Financial Director; Kenneth Goode, Development Director
Officers: Clement L. Buenger, President; Stephen P. Donovan, Vice-President; Harold Poe, Treasurer; Patricia Bryan, Secretary
Paid Staff: 43   **Volunteer Staff:** 600
Paid Artists: 98
Utilizes: Guest Conductors; Guest Artists
Budget: Over 10,000,000
Income Sources: Private Foundations/Grants/Endowments; Business/Corporate Donations; Box Office; Government Grants; Individual Donations; Fund-raising
Season: 52 Weeks
Affiliations: ASOL; OOOO; AFM; Cincinnati Fine Arts Fund
Performance Facilities: Music Hall; Riverbend

CINCINNATI YOUTH SYMPHONY ORCHESTRA
8529 Morning Calm Drive, Cincinnati, OH 45221
(513) 474-9719
Founded: 1965
Arts Area: Symphony; Orchestra; Chamber
Status: Non-Professional; Non-Profit
Type: Performing; Educational; Sponsoring
Purpose: To provide an experience that augments the educational opportunities available in public school programs, afford an opportunity to perform with other talented student musicians as well as performing in concert with the Cincinnati Symphony, and to provide knowledge that students can take with them to their respective school programs
Management: H. Teri Murai, Music Director/Conductor; Mack Richardson, Manager/Assistant Conductor
Paid Staff: 2   **Volunteer Staff:** 16
Non-Paid Artists: 85
Budget: $1,000 - $50,000
Income Sources: Business/Corporate Donations; Box Office; Individual Donations
Season: September - May   **Annual Attendance:** 5,000
Affiliations: ASOL (Youth Orchestra Division)
Performance Facilities: Corbett Auditorium, University of Cincinnati

VOCAL MUSIC

CINCINNATI BOYCHOIR
8315 Firshade Terrace, Cincinnati, OH 45239
(513) 385-7276
Founded: 1965
Arts Area: Choral
Status: Non-Profit
Type: Performing; Touring; Resident; Educational
Purpose: The Cincinnati Boychoir was formed in 1965 to give boys with unchanged voices an educational and performing experience and to encourage singing through the voice change.
Management: Randall Wolfe, Director; Barry Mersmann, Program Manager
Officers: Randall Wolfe, President
Paid Staff: 2   **Volunteer Staff:** 8
Paid Artists: 3   **Non-Paid Artists:** 110
Utilizes: Guest Conductors
Budget: $50,000 - $100,000
Income Sources: Private Foundations/Grants/Endowments; Business/Corporate Donations; Box Office; Individual Donations
Season: September - June

CINCINNATI OPERA
1241 Elm Street, Cincinnati, OH 45220
(513) 621-1919
> **Founded:** 1920
> **Arts Area:** Grand Opera; Lyric Opera; Operetta
> **Status:** Professional; Non-Profit
> **Type:** Performing
> **Purpose:** To present opera to Cincinnati and the Tri-State Area
> **Management:** James de Blasis, Artistic Director; Paul A. Stuhlreyer III, Managing Director
> **Officers:** Kingston Fletcher, Chairman; Ellen G. van der Horst, President
> **Paid Staff:** 11   **Volunteer Staff:** 22
> **Paid Artists:** 247
> **Utilizes:** Special Technical Talent; Guest Conductors; Guest Artists; Guest Directors
> **Budget:** $1,000,000 - $5,000,000
> **Income Sources:** Private Foundations/Grants/Endowments; Business/Corporate Donations; Box Office; Government Grants; Individual Donations
> **Season:** June - July   **Annual Attendance:** 30,000
> **Affiliations:** OA
> **Performance Facilities:** Music Hall

VOCAL ARTS ENSEMBLE OF CINCINNATI
PO Box 8904, Cincinnati, OH 45208
(513) 483-5888
FAX: (513) 556-2698
> **Founded:** 1979
> **Arts Area:** Choral
> **Status:** Professional; Non-Profit
> **Type:** Performing; Touring; Educational
> **Purpose:** To present choral music
> **Management:** Lindsay Zierolf, Manager; Kathy Wall, Box Office/Ticket Sales; Nancy Nolan, Marketing; Vicki Ross, Publicity; Richard Weinberg, Development; Earl Rivers, Music Director/Conductor; Mary Bramlage, Librarian
> **Officers:** James R. Cumming, President; Lisa Vorst, Treasurer; Amy Hill, Secretary
> **Paid Staff:** 4   **Volunteer Staff:** 6
> **Paid Artists:** 26
> **Utilizes:** Guest Conductors; Guest Artists; Guest Composers
> **Budget:** $50,000 - $100,000
> **Income Sources:** Private Foundations/Grants/Endowments; Business/Corporate Donations; Box Office; Government Grants; Individual Donations
> **Season:** October - June   **Annual Attendance:** 18,000
> **Affiliations:** CA

THEATRE

ARTREACH TOURING THEATRE
3074 Madison Road, Cincinnati, OH 45209
(513) 871-2300
FAX: (513) 871-2501
> **Founded:** 1976
> **Purpose:** To provide quality, theatrical presentations to family audiences in schools and theatres across the nation
> **Management:** Kathryn Schultz Miller, Artistic Director; Dahns Schwarz, Production Manager; Andi Guess, Business Manager; Selley Weisheit, Tour Coordinator
> **Officers:** Barry Miller, President; Bob Bonini, Chairman; Cindy Piccano, Treasurer; Janis Flanagan, Secretary
> **Paid Staff:** 5   **Volunteer Staff:** 1
> **Paid Artists:** 13
> **Utilizes:** Special Technical Talent; Guest Artists; Guest Directors
> **Budget:** $100,000 - $500,000
> **Income Sources:** Private Foundations/Grants/Endowments; Government Grants
> **Season:** September - May   **Annual Attendance:** 300,000
> **Affiliations:** TCG; APAP; AATE; Arts Midwest

CINCINNATI PLAYHOUSE IN THE PARK
962 Mount Adams Circle, Cincinnati, OH 45202
(513) 345-2242
FAX: (513) 345-2254
> **Founded:** 1960
> **Arts Area:** Professional
> **Status:** Professional; Non-Profit

Type: Performing; Resident
Purpose: To bring the highest quality of professional theatre to the Greater Cincinnati Area and to contribute to the growth and development of American theatre
Management: Edward Stern, Producing Artistic Director; Buzz Ward, Executive Director
Officers: James M. Edwards, President; Howard Tomb, Vice President; Alberta Marsh, Secretary; Martin Wade, Treasurer
Paid Staff: 60
Paid Artists: 150
Utilizes: Special Technical Talent; Guest Artists; Guest Directors
Budget: $1,000,000 - $5,000,000
Income Sources: Private Foundations/Grants/Endowments; Business/Corporate Donations; Box Office; Government Grants; Individual Donations
Season: September - August   **Annual Attendance:** 240,000
Affiliations: LORT; TCG
Performance Facilities: Cincinnati Playhouse, Thompson Shelterhouse; Robert S. Marx

INTUITION THEATRE COMPANY
4735 Winton Road, Cincinnati, OH 45232
(513) 541-1257
FAX: (513) 542-7858
Founded: 1981
Arts Area: Theatrical Group; MIME
Status: Professional; Non-Profit
Type: Performing; Touring; Resident
Purpose: To perform original theatre for children and adults using mime, movement, clown, improvisation and music
Management: The Talent Center; Connie Gregory
Paid Staff: 4   **Volunteer Staff:** 2
Paid Artists: 3
Utilizes: Special Technical Talent
Budget: $1,000 - $50,000
Income Sources: Private Foundations/Grants/Endowments; Business/Corporate Donations; Box Office; Government Grants; Individual Donations
Season: September - July
Annual Attendance: 100,000
Affiliations: National Mime Association

MADCAP PRODUCTIONS
1630 First Avenue, Cincinnati, OH 45205
(513) 921-5965
Founded: 1984
Arts Area: Puppet
Status: Professional; Non-Profit
Type: Performing; Touring; Educational
Purpose: To present educational theatre experiences and further the art of puppet theatre
Management: Jerry Handorf, Art Director
Officers: Jerry Handorf, President; Lisa Hall, Vice President
Paid Staff: 4
Paid Artists: 6
Utilizes: Special Technical Talent
Budget: $1,000 - $50,000
Income Sources: Private Foundations/Grants/Endowments; Business/Corporate Donations; Box Office
Season: 52 Weeks

MARIEMONT PLAYERS
4101 Walton Creek Road, Cincinnati, OH 45227
(513) 561-9775
Founded: 1937
Arts Area: Community; Theatrical Group
Status: Non-Professional; Non-Profit
Type: Performing
Purpose: To produce plays for the enjoyment of area audiences
Officers: Kathy Biel-Morgan, President; Pam Lux, Secretary; Rick Pender, Treasurer
Budget: $1,000 - $50,000
Income Sources: Private Foundations/Grants/Endowments; Business/Corporate Donations; Box Office; Individual Donations
Season: 52 Weeks
Affiliations: AACT-Cincinnati; Ohio Community Theatre Alliance
Performance Facilities: Walton Creek Playhouse

STAGECRAFTERS
1580 Summit Road, Cincinnati, OH 45237
(513) 761-7500
Founded: 1952
Arts Area: Community
Status: Non-Professional
Type: Performing; Resident
Purpose: For people who are interested in theatre and perform for the community
Management: Board of Directors
Officers: Bernard Berg, Chairperson; Marcella Valin, Vice President/Production; Saranne Funk, Secretary; Ethel Youngerman, Treasurer; Gittee Bortz, Vice President/Administration
Volunteer Staff: 50
Non-Paid Artists: 25
Utilizes: Special Technical Talent; Guest Directors
Budget: $1,000 - $50,000
Income Sources: Box Office; Individual Donations
Season: September - April   **Annual Attendance:** 2,400
Affiliations: AACT; Ohio Community Theatre Alliance
Performance Facilities: Jewish Community Center

PERFORMING SERIES

ARTS CONSORTIUM STUDIO THEATRE
1515 Linn Street, Cincinnati, OH 45214
(513) 381-0645
Founded: 1980
Arts Area: Dance; Vocal Music; Instrumental Music; Theater; Festivals; Photography; Visual Arts
Status: Non-Profit
Type: Performing; Resident; Educational
Purpose: To celebrate, advance and preserve African-American culture and achievment through art, history and education
Management: Candace Roseman, Arts and Education Director; Ernest Britton, Executive Director; Jerry Denges, Administrative Director
Paid Staff: 1   **Volunteer Staff:** 10
Non-Paid Artists: 75
Utilizes: Special Technical Talent; Guest Artists; Guest Directors
Budget: $1,000 - $50,000
Income Sources: Private Foundations/Grants/Endowments; Box Office; Individual Donations
Season: September - June   **Annual Attendance:** 3,000
Performance Facilities: Arts Consortium Studio Theatre

CINCINNATI MAY FESTIVAL
1241 Elm Street, Cincinnati, OH 45210
(513) 621-1919
Founded: 1873
Arts Area: Vocal Music; Instrumental Music; Festivals
Status: Professional; Non-Profit
Type: Performing; Resident; Sponsoring
Purpose: Cincinnati May Festival presents, as the oldest continuing choral festival in the Western Hemisphere, an exciting repertoire of choral and orchestral music featuring the May Festival Chorus, world-renowned guest soloists and conductors and the Cincinnati Symphony Orchestra.
Management: James Conlon, May Festival Music Director; Robert Porco, May Festival Chorus Director; Steven Monder, Executive Director; Jeffrey Alexander, Manager; Vera Menner, Director of Marketing/Development
Officers: Mary Margret Rochford, Chairman; Alice Sweet, Vice Chairman; Ruthy Korelitz, Secretary
Paid Staff: 3   **Volunteer Staff:** 100
Paid Artists: 20   **Non-Paid Artists:** 200
Utilizes: Guest Conductors; Guest Artists
Budget: $500,000 - $1,000,000
Income Sources: Private Foundations/Grants/Endowments; Business/Corporate Donations; Box Office; Government Grants; Individual Donations
Season: May   **Annual Attendance:** 13,000
Affiliations: Cincinnati Symphony Orchestra
Performance Facilities: Music Hall; Cathedral Basillica of the Assumption

CINCINNATI MUSIC HALL ASSOCIATION
1243 Elm Street, Cincinnati, OH 45210
(513) 621-1919
FAX: (513) 621-5390
Founded: 1878

Arts Area: Dance; Vocal Music; Instrumental Music; Theater; Festivals; Lyric Opera; Grand Opera
Status: Non-Profit
Type: Performing; Touring; Resident; Educational
Purpose: Concert and performance hall
Management: David Curry, General Manager; Joe Dopkins, Manager; Tom Bockenstette, Manager
Officers: Dudley S. Taft, President
Paid Staff: 15   **Volunteer Staff:** 20
Budget: $1,000,000 - $5,000,000
Income Sources: Private Foundations/Grants/Endowments; Business/Corporate Donations; Government Grants; Individual Donations; Rentals
Season: 52 Weeks   **Annual Attendance:** 700,000
Performance Facilities: Music Hall

RIVERBEND-CINCINNATI SYMPHONY AND POPS ORCHESTRA CONCERTS
1241 Elm Street, Cincinnati, OH 45210
(513) 621-1919
FAX: (513) 621-2132
Founded: 1984
Arts Area: Vocal Music; Instrumental Music
Status: Professional; Non-Profit
Type: Sponsoring
Management: Jesus Lopez-Cobos, CSO Music Director; Erich Kunzel, POPS Conductor; Cincinnati Symphony Orchestra
Utilizes: Guest Conductors; Guest Artists
Income Sources: Business/Corporate Donations; Box Office
Season: June - August   **Annual Attendance:** 100,000
Performance Facilities: Riverbend Music Center

FACILITY

CINCINNATI JEWISH COMMUNITY CENTER
1580 Summit Road, Cincinnati, OH 45237-1999
(513) 761-7500
FAX: (513) 761-0084
Type of Facility: Civic Center
Type of Stage: Proscenium
Seating Capacity: 800
Year Built: 1958
Year Remodeled: 1986   **Architect:** Richard Lemker   **Cost:** $100,000
Acoustical Consultant: Richard Lemker & Associates
Contact for Rental: Anna Geottleman;   (513) 761-7500
Manager: Marie Wolfson
Resident Groups: Center Stage; Just Us Kids; Spotlight; Stagecrafters; Senior Adult Theater

CINCINNATI MUSIC HALL
1243 Elm Street, Cincinnati, OH 45210
(513) 621-1919
Founded: 1878
Type of Facility: Concert Hall; Auditorium; Multi-Purpose
Type of Stage: Proscenium
Stage Dimensions: 50'Wx48'D; 50'Wx39'H proscenium opening   **Orchestra Pit**
Seating Capacity: 3,357
Year Built: 1878   **Architect:** Hannaford & Proctor   **Cost:** $325,000
Year Remodeled: 1970   **Architect:** Schatz Associates   **Cost:** $10,000,000
Contact for Rental: David Curry;   (513) 621-1919
Resident Groups: Cincinnati Symphony Orchestra; Cincinnati Opera; Cincinnati Ballet Company; Cincinnati May Festival; Cincinnati Pops Orchestra
Music Hall was designated a National Historic Landmark in 1975.

CINCINNATI PLAYHOUSE - ROBERT S. MARX THEATRE
962 Mount Adams Circle, Eden Park, Cincinnati, OH 45202
(513) 345-2242
FAX: (513) 345-2254
Founded: 1960
Type of Facility: Theatre House
Type of Stage: Thrust; Symmetrical Thrust
Stage Dimensions: 35'Wx60'D
Seating Capacity: 629

Year Built: 1968   **Architect:** Hardy Holzman Pfeiffer Associates   **Cost:** $1,000,000
Acoustical Consultant: Robert A. Hansen Associates

CINCINNATI PLAYHOUSE - THOMPSON SHELTERHOUSE
962 Mount Adams Circle, Eden Park, Cincinnati, OH 45202
(513) 345-2242
FAX: (513) 345-2254
Founded: 1960
Type of Facility: Theatre House
Facility Originally: Meeting Hall
Type of Stage: Thrust
Stage Dimensions: 18'Wx24'D
Seating Capacity: 219
Year Built: 1874
Year Remodeled: 1980   **Architect:** Architects Team Associates   **Cost:** $100,000

RIVERBEND MUSIC CENTER
6295 Kellogg Avenue, Cincinnati, OH 45230
(513) 232-5882
FAX: (513) 232-7577
Founded: 1983
Type of Facility: Outdoor (Concert); Performance Center; Amphitheater
Type of Stage: Proscenium
Stage Dimensions: 70'x62'   **Orchestra Pit**
Seating Capacity: Pavilion-6,000; On Lawn-12,000
Year Built: 1983   **Architect:** Michael Graves   **Cost:** $15,000,000
Acoustical Consultant: Jaffe Acoustics
Resident Groups: Cincinnati Symphony Orchestra

SHOWBOAT MAJESTIC
Foot of Broadway at the Public Landing, Cincinnati, OH 45203
(513) 475-5803
Mailing Address: c/o Cincinnati Recreation Commission, 644 Linn Street, Cincinnati, OH 45203
Founded: 1923
Type of Facility: Showboat
Type of Stage: Proscenium
Stage Dimensions: 17'9"Wx14'5"Dx12'H; 6'D apron
Seating Capacity: 233
Year Built: 1923   **Architect:** Tom Reynolds
Year Remodeled: 1967
Manager: Tim Perrino;   (513) 241-6550
The Showboat is on the National Register of Historic Places.

UNIVERSITY OF CINCINNATI - CORBETT AUDITORIUM
Corbett Center for the Performing Arts, College Conservatory of Music, Cincinnati, OH 45221-0003
(513) 556-9430
Type of Facility: Concert Hall; Theatre House
Type of Stage: Modified Apron Proscenium
Stage Dimensions: 53'8"Wx30'D with 16'8" apron; hydraulic orchestra pit lift   **Orchestra Pit**
Seating Capacity: 743
Year Built: 1967
Contact for Rental: Martha Crabtree

UNIVERSITY OF CINCINNATI - CORBETT CENTER FOR THE PERFORMING ARTS
College Conservatory of Music, Cincinnati, OH 45221-0003
(513) 556-9430
Type of Facility: Theatre Complex
Year Built: 1967   **Architect:** Edward Schulte
Year Remodeled: 1972   **Architect:** Pistler Brown Architection   **Cost:** $4,000,000
Contact for Rental: Martha Crabtree
Manager: John Mcdonagh
Resident Groups: Philharmonia Orchestra; Concert Orchestra; Opera and Musical Theater & Drama Series; Hot Summer
Nights
*Corbett Center for the Performing Arts contains Corbett Auditorium, Patricia Corbett Theater and Watson Hall. See
separate listings for further information. Limited availability.*

UNIVERSITY OF CINCINNATI - PATRICIA CORBETT THEATER
Corbett Center for the Performing Arts, College Conservatory of Music, Cincinnati, OH 45221-0003
(513) 556-9430
    Type of Facility: Concert Hall; Theatre House
    Type of Stage: Proscenium
    Stage Dimensions: 44'1"Wx34'2"D   **Orchestra Pit**
    Seating Capacity: 400
    Year Built: 1967
    Contact for Rental: Martha Crabtree

UNIVERSITY OF CINCINNATI - WATSON HALL
Corbett Center for the Performing Arts, College Conservatory of Music, Cincinnati, OH 45221-0003
(513) 556-9430
    Type of Facility: Recital Hall
    Type of Stage: Platform
    Seating Capacity: 140
    Year Built: 1967
    Contact for Rental: Martha Crabtree

WALTON CREEK PLAYHOUSE
4101 Walton Creek Road, Cincinnati, OH 45227
(513) 561-9775
    Type of Facility: Auditorium; Theatre House; Room
    Facility Originally: School
    Type of Stage: Proscenium
    Seating Capacity: 120
    Year Built: 1861
    Year Remodeled: 1960
    Contact for Rental: Elemor Shepard;   (513) 561-7688
    Resident Groups: Mariemont Players

WESTWOOD TOWN HALL
3017 Harrison Avenue, Cincinnati, OH 45213
(513) 662-9109
    Type of Facility: Theatre Complex; Auditorium; Civic Center; Multi-Purpose
    Facility Originally: Town Hall
    Type of Stage: Proscenium; 3/4 Arena
    Stage Dimensions: 53'Wx25'Dx30'H
    Seating Capacity: 250
    Year Built: 1888   **Architect:** Charles Crapsey/William Brown
    Contact for Rental: Director;   (513) 662-9109
    Manager: Mike Thomas
    Resident Groups: Cincinnati Civic Orchestra; The Drama Workshop; The Footlighters; Cincinnati Young People's Theatre; Womens Theatre of Cincinnati; Continental Round Dancers

Cleveland

DANCE

CLEVELAND SAN JOSE BALLET
One Playhouse Square, #330, Cleveland, OH 44115
(216) 621-2260
FAX: (216) 566-0752
    Founded: 1976
    Arts Area: Ballet
    Status: Professional; Non-Profit
    Type: Performing; Touring; Resident; Educational; Sponsoring
    Purpose: Dedicated to creating quality ballet
    Management: Dennis Nahat, Artistic Director; David Oakland, General Manager
    Paid Staff: 25
    Paid Artists: 37
    Utilizes: Special Technical Talent; Guest Artists; Guest Choreographers
    Budget: $5,000,000 - $10,000,000
    Income Sources: Private Foundations/Grants/Endowments; Business/Corporate Donations; Box Office; Government Grants; Individual Donations
    Season: October - May   **Annual Attendance:** 120,000

Affiliations: Dance USA; USITT; BOMI
Performance Facilities: State Theatre; Playhouse Square Center

DANCECLEVELAND
1148 Euclid Avenue, 3rd Floor, Cleveland, OH 44115
(216) 861-2213
Founded: 1956
Arts Area: Modern; Mime; Ballet; Jazz; Folk
Status: Non-Profit
Type: Educational; Sponsoring
Purpose: DANCECLEVELAND was formed to foster an appreciation of and interest in dance in the Greater Cleveland Area through education and concert programming, the presentation of an annual concert series, dance education and dance/movement therapy programs.
Management: Stephanie Brown, Executive Director; Craig Rich, Marketing Director
Officers: Jeffrey S. Glazer, President; Lucinda Lavelli, Vice President, Programming; Ann Sethness, Vice President, Contributed Revenues; Jeffrey Linton, Vice President, Earned Revenues; Tom Leib, Secretary/Treasurer; Sheila Fox, Vice President, Trustees
Paid Staff: 5 **Volunteer Staff:** 35
Paid Artists: 124
Utilizes: Guest Artists
Budget: $100,000 - $500,000
Income Sources: Private Foundations/Grants/Endowments; Business/Corporate Donations; Box Office; Government Grants; Individual Donations
Season: October - July **Annual Attendance:** 22,500
Affiliations: OAC; NEA; ORACLE; APAP; ISPAA; Arts Midwest; Dance USA; Arts Presenters; Ohio Dance
Performance Facilities: Ohio Theatre; Playhouse Square Center; Beck Center for the Cultural Arts

SAINT SAVA FREE SERBIAN ORTHODOX CHURCH
2151 West Wallings, Cleveland, OH 44147
(216) 524-5991
Founded: 1982
Arts Area: Ethnic; Folk
Status: Non-Professional; Non-Profit
Type: Performing; Touring; Resident; Educational
Purpose: To encourage and perpetuate our Serbian music, dance, language, culture and heritage, and to have fun doing it
Management: Dragica Zamiska, Director
Volunteer Staff: 4
Budget: $1,000 - $50,000
Income Sources: Individual Donations
Season: September - July
Affiliations: Saint Sava Free Serbian Orthodox Church; School Congregation; Cleveland Area Arts Council

INSTRUMENTAL MUSIC

THE CHINA MUSIC PROJECT
334 Claymore Boulevard, Cleveland, OH 44143-1730
(216) 531-2188
Founded: 1980
Arts Area: Orchestra; Chamber; Ensemble; Ethnic; Instrumental Group
Status: Professional; Non-Profit
Type: Performing; Touring; Resident; Educational; Sponsoring
Purpose: To bring traditional Chinese music and information about it to the American public through performances, lectures, demonstrations, radio and TV broadcasts
Management: Marjorie Ann Ciarlillo, Director
Officers: Dr. K. Laurence Chang, Chairman of the Board
Utilizes: Guest Artists
Budget: $1,000 - $50,000
Income Sources: Private Foundations/Grants/Endowments; Business/Corporate Donations
Season: 52 Weeks

CLEVELAND CHAMBER MUSIC SOCIETY
2316 Belvoir Boulevard, Cleveland, OH 44121
(216) 531-7094
Founded: 1950
Arts Area: Chamber; Ensemble
Status: Non-Profit
Type: Sponsoring
Purpose: To promote chamber music through presentation of the best available works and through the commissioning of new works

Officers: Toni Miller, President; David A. Richardson, First Vice President; John Boatright, Second Vice President; Lois Rose, Third Vice President
Paid Staff: 1   **Volunteer Staff:** 18
Paid Artists: 45
Utilizes: Guest Artists
Budget: $50,000 - $100,000
Income Sources: Private Foundations/Grants/Endowments; Box Office; Individual Donations
Season: September - May   **Annual Attendance:** 3,500

CLEVELAND JAZZ ORCHESTRA
PO Box 360140, Cleveland, OH 44136
(216) 572-2562
Founded: 1985
Arts Area: Ensemble; Instrumental Group; Band
Status: Professional; Non-Profit
Type: Performing; Resident; Educational; Sponsoring
Purpose: To establish Cleveland Jazz Orchestra in Northeast Ohio; to enhance availability and quality of jazz; to assist in educating young musicians; to encourage involvement and training of minority musicians
Officers: Gary Scott, President; Kris Lutz, Secretary; Joseph Mikelonis, Treasurer
Volunteer Staff: 10
Paid Artists: 18
Utilizes: Guest Artists
Budget: $1,000 - $50,000
Income Sources: Private Foundations/Grants/Endowments; Business/Corporate Donations; Box Office; Government Grants; Individual Donations
Season: 52 Weeks
Affiliations: Cuyahoga Community College; Northeast Ohio Jazz Society; Cleveland Playhouse

CLEVELAND ORCHESTRA
11001 Euclid Avenue, Cleveland, OH 44106
(216) 231-7300
FAX: (216) 231-0202
Founded: 1918
Arts Area: Symphony; Orchestra; Ensemble
Status: Professional; Non-Profit
Type: Performing; Touring; Resident; Educational; Sponsoring
Management: Thomas W. Morris, Executive Director; Christoph von Dohnanyi, Music Director; Nancy Bell Cue, Manager
Paid Staff: 60
Paid Artists: 110
Utilizes: Guest Conductors; Guest Artists
Budget: Over 10,000,000
Income Sources: Private Foundations/Grants/Endowments; Business/Corporate Donations; Box Office; Individual Donations
Season: September - May
Affiliations: ASOL; OOOO
Performance Facilities: Severance Hall; Blossom Music Center

CLEVELAND PHILHARMONIC ORCHESTRA
8702 Bessemer Avenue, PO Box 16251, Cleveland, OH 44116
(216) 341-7474
Founded: 1938
Arts Area: Symphony; Orchestra
Status: Semi-Professional; Non-Profit
Type: Performing; Resident; Sponsoring
Purpose: To provide quality performances at modest ticket prices; to be a training orchestra for aspiring musicians; and to provide technical education for musicians
Management: Martha Hamilton, General Manager; William B. Slocum, Music Director/Conductor
Officers: James Roosa, President; Stanley Lasky and Kris Pasternak, Vice Presidents; Susan Reusser, Secretary; Philip Melaragno, Treasurer
Paid Staff: 2   **Volunteer Staff:** 3
Non-Paid Artists: 60
Utilizes: Guest Conductors; Guest Artists
Budget: $1,000 - $50,000
Income Sources: Private Foundations/Grants/Endowments; Business/Corporate Donations; Box Office; Government Grants; Individual Donations
Season: September - May   **Annual Attendance:** 3,000

Affiliations: ASOL; Saint Vincent Quadrangle Association
Performance Facilities: Cuyahoga Community College

OHIO CHAMBER ORCHESTRA
PO Box 14886, Cleveland, OH 44114
(216) 781-4466
Founded: 1972
Arts Area: Symphony; Orchestra; Chamber; Ensemble
Status: Professional
Type: Performing; Touring; Resident
Purpose: To perform at the highest artistic level possible programs specialiozing in literatire written specifically for chamber orchestra in appropriate (intimate) settings, featuring soloists of local and international standing
Management: Eugenia L. Epperson, Executive Director
Officers: Paul R. Bunker, President; William Steffee MD, Chairman Executive Committee; Robert H. Jackson, Executive Vice Chairman; James E. Wilcosky, Treasurer; Martha Vail, Secretary; Norma Glazer, President of Ohio Chamber Orchestra Council
Paid Staff: 7
Paid Artists: 75
Utilizes: Guest Conductors; Guest Artists
Budget: $500,000 - $1,000,000
Income Sources: Private Foundations/Grants/Endowments; Business/Corporate Donations; Box Office; Government Grants; Individual Donations
Season: October - May   **Annual Attendance:** 14,000
Performance Facilities: The Cleveland Play House

UNIVERSITY CIRCLE CHAMBER ORCHESTRA
Music Department, Case Western Reserve University, Cleveland, OH 44106
(216) 368-2400
Arts Area: Symphony; Orchestra; Chamber; Ensemble; Instrumental Group
Status: Non-Professional; Non-Profit
Type: Performing; Resident; Educational
Purpose: A community orchestra open to both university students and interested amateurs, performing stimulating repertoire in an enjoyable yet intense atmosphere
Management: Music Department, Case Western Reserve University
Officers: Rando Laycock, Music Director
Paid Staff: 2
Non-Paid Artists: 18
Utilizes: Guest Artists
Budget: $1,000 - $50,000
Income Sources: Private Foundations/Grants/Endowments; Individual Donations
Season: August - May
Affiliations: Case Western Reserve University
Performance Facilities: Harkness Chapel

VOCAL MUSIC

CLEVELAND OPERA
1422 Euclid Avenue, Suite 1052, Cleveland, OH 44115-2001
(216) 575-0903
FAX: (216) 575-1918
Founded: 1976
Arts Area: Grand Opera; Lyric Opera; Light Opera
Status: Professional; Non-Profit
Type: Performing; Touring; Resident; Educational
Purpose: To bring outstanding presentations of opera to the people of Northern Ohio; create the opportunity to develop operatic and dramatic skills of local artists; to make opera accessible to the broadest possible spectrum of the community and region
Management: David Bamberger, General Manager/Artistic Director
Paid Staff: 55   **Volunteer Staff:** 250
Paid Artists: 300   **Non-Paid Artists:** 6
Utilizes: Special Technical Talent; Guest Conductors; Guest Artists; Guest Directors
Budget: $1,000,000 - $5,000,000
Income Sources: Private Foundations/Grants/Endowments; Business/Corporate Donations; Box Office; Government Grants; Individual Donations
Season: October - May   **Annual Attendance:** 62,000
Affiliations: OA
Performance Facilities: State Theatre, Playhouse Square Center

THE CLEVELAND ORCHESTRA CHORUS
11001 Euclid Avenue, Cleveland, OH 44106
(216) 231-7300
FAX: (216) 231-0202
Founded: 1952
Arts Area: Choral; Concert Opera; Pops
Status: Non-Professional; Non-Profit
Type: Performing; Touring; Resident
Purpose: To assist the Cleveland Orchestra in performing choral-orchestral works
Management: Gareth Morrell, Director of Choruses; Nancy Gage, Coordinator of Choruses; Eleanor Kushnick, Librarian; Joela Jones, Accompanist/Soloist; Betty Meyers, Donald Shelhorn, Assitant Accompanists
Officers: Margaret B. Robinson, Chair; The Cleveland Orchestra Chorus Operating Committee
Paid Staff: 6
Non-Paid Artists: 170
Utilizes: Guest Conductors; Guest Artists
Income Sources: Private Foundations/Grants/Endowments
Season: September - August   **Annual Attendance:** 100,000
Performance Facilities: Severence Hall; Blossom Music Center

LYRIC OPERA CLEVELAND
PO Box 06198, Cleveland, OH 44106
(216) 231-2484
Founded: 1973
Arts Area: Lyric Opera; Light Opera; Operetta; Musical Theatre
Status: Professional; Non-Profit
Type: Performing; Resident; Educational; Sponsoring
Purpose: To utilize talented artists from the North in music theatre productions
Management: Michael McConnell, Executive Director; Kristen Manthey, Artistic Administrator; Joe Wochna, Marketing/Development Assistant; Amy Capwell, Administrative Assistant; Stephen Szabo, Business Manager
Officers: Richard C. Gordon, President Board of Trustees; Becky Elliot, President Guild
Utilizes: Special Technical Talent; Guest Conductors; Guest Directors
Budget: $100,000 - $500,000
Income Sources: Private Foundations/Grants/Endowments; Business/Corporate Donations; Box Office; Government Grants; Individual Donations
Season: July - August   **Annual Attendance:** 5,000
Affiliations: OA
Performance Facilities: Cleveland Institute Of Music

NEW CLEVELAND OPERA COMPANY
1422 Euclid Avenue, #1052, Cleveland, OH 44115-2001
(216) 575-0903
Founded: 1976
Arts Area: Grand Opera; Lyric Opera; Light Opera; Operetta
Status: Professional; Non-Profit
Type: Resident
Management: David Bamberger, General Director; Carola Bamberger, Associate Director
Officers: Dr. Clyde L. Nash Jr. MD, President; Oliver F. Emerson, Chairman; John N. Lauer, Derek R. Mumford and Frederick C. Tyler Jr., Vice Presidents; Ronald H. Bell DDS, Secretary; Charles W. Hall, Treasurer
Paid Staff: 15   **Volunteer Staff:** 1
Utilizes: Special Technical Talent; Guest Conductors; Guest Artists; Guest Directors
Budget: $1,000,000 - $5,000,000
Income Sources: Private Foundations/Grants/Endowments; Business/Corporate Donations; Box Office; Government Grants; Individual Donations
Season: October - May
Affiliations: OA
Performance Facilities: State Theatre; Playhouse Square Center

THEATRE

THE CLEVELAND PLAY HOUSE
8500 Euclid Avenue, Cleveland, OH 44106
(216) 795-7010
FAX: (216) 795-7005
Founded: 1916
Arts Area: Professional
Status: Professional; Non-Profit
Type: Performing; Educational

Purpose: To provide the experience of a complete performing arts environment through its varied repertoire of classical and contemporary theatre, facilities and the continuance of young people's theatre training
Management: Dean R. Gladden, Managing Director; Will Rhys, Artistic Director
Officers: George D. Kirkham, Chairman; Richard H. Hahn, President; Harold Fallon, Joseph Gorman, William Jones, Frances Pendleton, Claiborne Rankin, Vice Presidents
Paid Staff: 80
Utilizes: Special Technical Talent; Guest Artists; Guest Directors
Budget: $5,000,000 - $10,000,000
Income Sources: Private Foundations/Grants/Endowments; Business/Corporate Donations; Box Office; Government Grants; Individual Donations
Season: September - May   **Annual Attendance:** 165,000
Affiliations: LORT; TCG; OAC
Performance Facilities: Bolton Theatre; Drury Theatre; Brooks Theatre

CLEVELAND PUBLIC THEATRE
6415 Detroit Avenue, Cleveland, OH 44102
(216) 631-2727
FAX: (216) 523-1440
Founded: 1981
Arts Area: Musical; Community; Folk; Theatrical Group; Puppet; Performance Art
Status: Semi-Professional; Non-Profit
Type: Performing; Touring; Resident; Educational; Sponsoring
Purpose: To provide access to theatre to nontraditional audiences and provide opportunities for artists in the Greater Cleveland Area
Management: James A. Levin, Executive Director; Linda Eisenstein, Development Director; Kevin Beaney, Administrative Director
Officers: William Grulich, President, Board of Trustees; Beverly Wykoff, Secretary; David Ellison, Treasurer
Paid Staff: 10   **Volunteer Staff:** 40
Paid Artists: 50   **Non-Paid Artists:** 80
Utilizes: Special Technical Talent; Guest Artists; Guest Directors
Budget: $100,000 - $500,000
Income Sources: Private Foundations/Grants/Endowments; Business/Corporate Donations; Box Office; Government Grants; Individual Donations
Season: 52 Weeks   **Annual Attendance:** 12,000
Affiliations: OTA; TCG

FAIRMOUNT THEATRE OF THE DEAF
8500 Euclid Avenue, Cleveland, OH 44106
(216) 229-2838
Founded: 1975
Arts Area: Theatrical Group; Sign Language Translators
Status: Professional; Non-Profit
Type: Performing; Touring; Resident; Educational
Purpose: FTD accepts the unique responsibility for providing theatrical and educational performances and workshops for deaf, hearing impaired and hearing people.
Management: Michael G. Regnier, Acting Executive Director; Shanny Mow, Artistic Director
Officers: Jonathan K. Wise, President
Paid Staff: 4   **Volunteer Staff:** 6
Paid Artists: 10
Utilizes: Special Technical Talent; Guest Artists; Guest Directors; SIGN LANGUAGE TRANSLATORS
Budget: $100,000 - $500,000
Income Sources: Private Foundations/Grants/Endowments; Business/Corporate Donations; Box Office; Government Grants; Individual Donations
Season: September - May   **Annual Attendance:** 40,000
Performance Facilities: Cleveland Play House

KARAMU HOUSE
2355 East 89th Street, Cleveland, OH 44106-9990
(216) 795-7070
Founded: 1915
Arts Area: Community
Status: Semi-Professional; Non-Profit
Type: Performing; Touring; Resident
Purpose: To continue the history of rich commitment and dedication to the arts community which has made Karamu House a very important resource in the arts
Management: Margaret Ford-Taylor, Executive Director; Jeff Gruszewski, Program Director
Officers: Lyman Phillips, President; William Robertson, First Vice President; Rev. Marvin McMikle, Second Vice President; Andrew Jackson, Third Vice President; Helen Forbes, Secretary; David Richards, Treasurer
Paid Staff: 7   **Volunteer Staff:** 100

Paid Artists: 12
Utilizes: Special Technical Talent; Guest Artists; Guest Directors
Budget: $100,000 - $500,000
Income Sources: Private Foundations/Grants/Endowments; Business/Corporate Donations; Box Office; Government Grants; Individual Donations
Season: September - June   **Annual Attendance:** 30,000
Affiliations: AATA
Performance Facilities: Karamu House Performing Arts Theatre

PLAYHOUSE SQUARE FOUNDATION
1501 Euclid Avenue, Cleveland, OH 44115
(216) 771-4444
FAX: (216) 771-0217
Founded: 1970
Arts Area: Professional; Musical; Community; Theatrical Group
Status: Professional; Non-Profit
Type: Performing; Touring; Resident; Educational
Purpose: Renovate and operate the three theatres of the Playhouse Square Center
Management: John H. Hemsath, Director of Theatre Operations; Robert J. Rody, Technical Director; Gina Vernaci, Director of Programming; Richard Hyer, Director of Marketing; William Hilyard, Director of Development
Officers: Art J. Falco, President
Paid Staff: 150   **Volunteer Staff:** 1,200
Utilizes: Special Technical Talent; Guest Conductors; Guest Artists; Guest Directors
Budget: $5,000,000 - $10,000,000
Income Sources: Private Foundations/Grants/Endowments; Business/Corporate Donations; Box Office; Government Grants; Individual Donations
Season: 52 Weeks   **Annual Attendance:** 700,000
Affiliations: League of Historic American Theatres; APAP; IAAM; APAC
Performance Facilities: Palace, State and Ohio theatres

PERFORMING SERIES

ART SONG FESTIVAL
c/o The Cleveland Insitute of Music, 11021 East Boulevard, Cleveland, OH 44106
(216) 791-5000, ext. 299
FAX: (216) 791-3063
Founded: 1985
Arts Area: Vocal Music; Instrumental Music; Festivals
Status: Professional; Non-Profit
Type: Performing; Resident; Educational
Purpose: To further collaborative aspects of art song; two singer/pianist master teams offer master classes to participant teams; master recitals and team finale recitals at culmination of festival week
Management: George Vassos, Artistic Director; Karen Knowlton, Executive Director; Sara Smith, Assistant Administrator
Officers: Ralph Drake, Beverly Page and Enid Politzer, Committee Members
Paid Staff: 3   **Volunteer Staff:** 3
Paid Artists: 4   **Non-Paid Artists:** 20
Utilizes: Guest Artists
Budget: $50,000 - $100,000
Income Sources: Private Foundations/Grants/Endowments; Business/Corporate Donations; Box Office; Government Grants; Individual Donations
Season: May   **Annual Attendance:** 1,500
Affiliations: The Cleveland Institute of Music
Performance Facilities: Kulas Recital Hall; Le Pavillon at CIM

THE CLEVELAND MUSEUM OF ART CONCERTS
11150 East Boulevard, Cleveland, OH 44106
(216) 421-7340
FAX: (216) 421-0411
Founded: 1916
Arts Area: Vocal Music; Instrumental Music
Status: Non-Profit
Type: Educational; Sponsoring
Management: Karel Paukert, Chief Curator of Musical Arts; Bruce Shewitz, Associate Curator of Musical Arts
Paid Staff: 3   **Volunteer Staff:** 10
Utilizes: Guest Artists
Income Sources: Private Foundations/Grants/Endowments; Box Office; Individual Donations
Season: 52 Weeks   **Annual Attendance:** 15,000
Performance Facilities: Gartner Auditorium

GREAT LAKES THEATER FESTIVAL
1501 Euclid Avenue, Suite 250, Cleveland, OH 44115
(216) 241-5490
Founded: 1962
Arts Area: Professional
Status: Professional; Non-Profit
Type: Performing; Educational
Purpose: Produce theater with the emphasis on world classics, especially Shakespeare and nonclassical works that contribute significantly to the American theater
Management: Gerald Freedman, Artistic Director; Mary Bill, Managing Director; Phil Crosby, Marketing Director; Bill Rudman, Special Projects Directors; Ann Gardbler, Development Director
Officers: William MacDonald III, Chairman; Mary Ann Jorgenson, Co-Chair; John E. Katzenmeyer, President
Paid Staff: 13 **Volunteer Staff:** 100
Paid Artists: 100
Utilizes: Special Technical Talent; Guest Artists; Guest Directors
Budget: $1,000,000 - $5,000,000
Income Sources: Private Foundations/Grants/Endowments; Business/Corporate Donations; Box Office; Government Grants; Individual Donations
Season: MayandJune - September **Annual Attendance:** 50,000
Affiliations: LORT; AAA
Performance Facilities: Ohio Theatre, Playhouse Square Center

TRI-C JAZZFEST
2900 Community College Avenue, Theatre 11, Cleveland, OH 44115
(216) 987-4444
FAX: (216) 987-4404
Founded: 1980
Arts Area: Vocal Music; Festivals
Status: Non-Profit
Type: Performing; Educational
Purpose: To provide a major event in jazz education for high school and college students, permitting aspiring high school and college jazz musicians to improve their skills and techniques in jazz through instruction by leading jazz educators and artists; to bring together outstanding jazz artists, educators and high school and college students in planned and shared educational and musical experiences
Management: Dr. Thomas Horning, Director; Susan Stone, Education Events Coordinator; Max Dehn, Booking Coordinator; Terri Pontremolli, Special Projects; Cliffie Jones, Office Manager
Paid Staff: 5 **Volunteer Staff:** 50
Paid Artists: 20 **Non-Paid Artists:** 20
Utilizes: Special Technical Talent; Guest Conductors; Guest Artists; Guest Directors
Budget: $100,000 - $500,000
Income Sources: Private Foundations/Grants/Endowments; Business/Corporate Donations; Box Office; Government Grants; Individual Donations
Season: April **Annual Attendance:** 15,000
Affiliations: IAJE
Performance Facilities: College Campus Auditorium; Severance Hall; State Theatre at Playhouse Square

FACILITY

CASE WESTERN RESERVE UNIVERSITY - ELDRED HALL
219099 Euclid Avenue, Cleveland, OH 44106-7077
(216) 368-2858
FAX: (216) 368-5184
Type of Facility: Theatre House
Type of Stage: Proscenium
Stage Dimensions: 17'x27'x31'
Seating Capacity: 152
Year Built: 1897
Year Remodeled: 1938 **Cost:** $35,000
Manager: John M. Orlock, Artistic Director
Originally converted in 1920 at a cost of $11,000

THE CLEVELAND INSTITUTE OF MUSIC - KULAS HALL
11021 East Boulevard, Cleveland, OH 44106
(216) 791-5165
FAX: (216) 791-3063
Type of Facility: Concert Hall; Auditorium; Opera House
Type of Stage: Proscenium

Stage Dimensions: 45'Wx26'D; add 10'D with pit cover in place
Orchestra Pit
Seating Capacity: 540
Year Built: 1960   **Architect:** Shaffer, Flynn, Williams   **Cost:** $3,000,000
Contact for Rental: Laurie Wright;   (216) 791-5165
Resident Groups: Cleveland Baroque Soloists; Canterbury Trio; Cleveland Institute of Music Symphony Orchestra; Chamber Orchestra; Opera Ensemble; Case Western Reserve University Wind Ensemble; Jazz Ensemble; University Chorale and Chamber Choir
Available for rent on a very limited basis

THE CLEVELAND MUSEUM OF ART - GARTNER AUDITORIUM
11150 East Boulevard, Cleveland, OH 44106
(216) 421-7340, ext. 284
FAX: (216) 421-0411
Type of Facility: Concert Hall; Auditorium
Type of Stage: Platform
Stage Dimensions: 67'Wx18'D
Seating Capacity: 765
Year Built: 1971   **Architect:** Marcel Breuer
Resident Groups: Department of Musical Arts: Karel Paukert, Chief Curator/Organist-in-Residence; Bruce Shewitz, Associate Curator
Presents a performing-arts series of 80 concerts each season

THE CLEVELAND PLAY HOUSE
8500 Euclid Avenue, Cleveland, OH 44106
(216) 795-7010
FAX: (216) 795-7005
Type of Facility: Theatre Complex; Performance Center
Year Built: 1927   **Architect:** Francis Draz   **Cost:** $250,000
Year Remodeled: 1984   **Architect:** Philip Johnson   **Cost:** $15,000,000
Contact for Rental: Carl Ritenour, Facilities Coordinator;   (216) 795-7010
The Cleveland Play House contains the Boulton, Brooks and Drury Theatres. See separate listings for further information. 1984 addition added the Boulton Theatre & support facilities for the Center.

THE CLEVELAND PLAY HOUSE - BOULTON THEATRE
8500 Euclid Avenue, Cleveland, OH 44106
(216) 795-7010
FAX: (216) 795-7005
Type of Facility: Theatre House
Type of Stage: Proscenium
Stage Dimensions: 42'Wx40'D; 42'Wx28'H proscenium opening   **Orchestra Pit**
Seating Capacity: 612
Year Built: 1984   **Architect:** Philip Johnson
Contact for Rental: Carl Ritenour, Facilities Coordinator;   (216) 795-7010

THE CLEVELAND PLAY HOUSE - BROOKS THEATRE
8500 Euclid Avenue, Cleveland, OH 44106
(216) 795-7010
FAX: (216) 795-7005
Type of Facility: Theatre House
Type of Stage: Proscenium
Stage Dimensions: 20'Wx26'D; 20'Wx14'H proscenium opening
Seating Capacity: 160
Year Built: 1927
Contact for Rental: Carl Ritenour, Facilities Coordinator;   (216) 795-7010

THE CLEVELAND PLAY HOUSE - DRURY THEATRE
8500 Euclid Avenue, Cleveland, OH 44106
(216) 795-7010
FAX: (216) 795-7005
Type of Facility: Theatre House
Type of Stage: Proscenium
Stage Dimensions: 30'Wx40'D; 30'Wx28'H proscenium opening   **Orchestra Pit**
Seating Capacity: 499
Year Built: 1927
Contact for Rental: Carl Ritenour, Facilities Coordinator;   (216) 795-7010

CLEVELAND PUBLIC THEATRE
6415 Detroit Avenue, Cleveland, OH 44102
(216) 631-2727
FAX: (216) 523-1440
> **Founded:** 1982
> **Type of Facility:** Studio Performance; Environmental; Theatre House; Arena; Multi-Purpose; Loft
> **Facility Originally:** Ballroom; Warehouse
> **Type of Stage:** Flexible; Environmental; Arena
> **Seating Capacity:** 171
> **Year Built:** 1910
> **Year Remodeled:** 1986
> **Contact for Rental:** James A. Levin; (216) 523-1600; (216) 631-2727
> **Resident Groups:** Cleveland Public Theatre
> *Theatre, performance art, music and mixed-media events*

KARAMU HOUSE PERFORMING ARTS THEATRE
2355 East 89th Street, Cleveland, OH 44106
(216) 795-7070
> **Type of Facility:** Outdoor (Concert); Theatre House; Amphitheater
> **Year Built:** 1949   **Architect:** Francis Draz   **Cost:** $600,000
> **Contact for Rental:** Thelma McKinley, Registrar; (216) 795-7070
> **Manager:** Jeff Gruszewski

KARAMU HOUSE PERFORMING ARTS THEATRE - AMPHITHEATRE
2355 East 89th Street, Cleveland, OH 44106
(216) 795-7070
FAX: (216) 795-7070
> **Type of Facility:** Outdoor (Concert); Amphitheater
> **Type of Stage:** Proscenium; Environmental
> **Stage Dimensions:** 17'9"x32'x32'
> **Seating Capacity:** 400
> **Year Built:** 1949
> **Contact for Rental:** Thelma McKinley, Registrar; (216) 795-7070
> **Manager:** Jeff Gruszewski

KARAMU HOUSE PERFORMING ARTS THEATRE - ARENA
2355 East 89th Street, Cleveland, OH 44106
(216) 795-7070
> **Type of Facility:** Arena
> **Type of Stage:** Arena
> **Stage Dimensions:** 13'6"x45'
> **Seating Capacity:** 125
> **Year Built:** 1949
> **Contact for Rental:** Thelma McKinley, Registrar; (216) 795-7070
> **Manager:** Jeff Gruszewski

KARAMU HOUSE PERFORMING ARTS THEATRE - PROSCENIUM
2355 East 89th Street, Cleveland, OH 44106
(216) 795-7070
FAX: (216) 795-7070
> **Type of Facility:** Theatre House
> **Type of Stage:** Proscenium
> **Stage Dimensions:** 40'x60'
> **Seating Capacity:** 200
> **Year Built:** 1949
> **Contact for Rental:** Thelma McKinley, Registrar; (216) 795-7070
> **Manager:** Jeff Gruszewski

PLAYHOUSE SQUARE CENTER
1501 Euclid Avenue, Cleveland, OH 44115
(216) 771-4444
> **Type of Facility:** Theatre Complex; Performance Center
> **Acoustical Consultant:** Jaffe Acoustics
> **Contact for Rental:** John Hemsath; (216) 771-4444
> **Resident Groups:** Cleveland Ballet; Cleveland Opera; Great Lakes Theatre Festival; Dance Cleveland; Ohio Ballet; Playhouse Square Center Productions
> *Playhouse Square Center contains the Ohio, Palace and State Theatres. See separate listings for further information.*

PLAYHOUSE SQUARE CENTER - OHIO THEATRE
1519 Euclid Avenue, Cleveland, OH 44115
(216) 771-4444
>   **Type of Facility:** Concert Hall; Auditorium; Studio Performance; Theatre House; Opera House
>   **Facility Originally:** Vaudeville
>   **Type of Stage:** Proscenium
>   **Stage Dimensions:** 70'Wx40'D; 41'Wx28'H proscenium opening   **Orchestra Pit**
>   **Seating Capacity:** 1,035
>   **Year Built:** 1921   **Architect:** Thomas Lamb
>   **Year Remodeled:** 1982   **Architect:** van Dijk Johnson & Partners   **Cost:** $4,000,000
>   **Acoustical Consultant:** Jaffe Acoustics
>   **Contact for Rental:** John Hemsath
>   **Resident Groups:** Great Lakes Theatre Festival; DANCECLEVELAND
>   *The Theatre is a National Historic Landmark.*

PLAYHOUSE SQUARE CENTER - PALACE THEATRE
1519 Euclid Avenue, Cleveland, OH 44115
(216) 771-4444
>   **Type of Facility:** Concert Hall; Auditorium; Studio Performance; Theatre House; Opera House
>   **Facility Originally:** Vaudeville
>   **Type of Stage:** Proscenium; Hydraulic Lift Stage
>   **Stage Dimensions:** 90'Wx38'D; 55'Wx35'H proscenium opening   **Orchestra Pit**
>   **Seating Capacity:** 2,800
>   **Year Built:** 1922   **Architect:** Rapp & Rapp
>   **Architect:** van Dijk Johnson & Partners   **Cost:** $8,000,000
>   **Acoustical Consultant:** Jaffe Acoustics
>   *The Theatre is a National Historic Landmark.*

PLAYHOUSE SQUARE CENTER - STATE THEATRE
1519 Euclid Avenue, Cleveland, OH 44115
(216) 771-4444
>   **Type of Facility:** Concert Hall; Auditorium; Studio Performance; Theatre House; Opera House
>   **Facility Originally:** Vaudeville
>   **Type of Stage:** Proscenium
>   **Stage Dimensions:** 110'Wx65'D; 55'Wx34'H proscenium opening   **Orchestra Pit**
>   **Seating Capacity:** 3,098
>   **Year Built:** 1921   **Architect:** Thomas Lamb
>   **Year Remodeled:** 1984   **Architect:** van Dijk Johnson & Partners   **Cost:** $12,000,000
>   **Acoustical Consultant:** Jaffe Acoustics
>   **Contact for Rental:** John Hemsath
>   **Resident Groups:** Cleveland Opera; San Jose Cleveland Ballet
>   *The Theatre is a National Historic Landmark.*

SEVERANCE HALL
11001 Euclid, Cleveland, OH 44106
(216) 231-7300
FAX: (216) 231-0202
>   **Type of Facility:** Auditorium
>   **Type of Stage:** Proscenium   **Orchestra Pit**
>   **Seating Capacity:** 2,046
>   **Year Built:** 1931
>   **Contact for Rental:** Cherilyn Byers;   (216) 231-7300
>   **Manager:** Peter Karas;   (216) 231-7300
>   **Resident Groups:** Cleveland Orchestra

Cleveland Heights

DANCE

SHALHEVET INTERNATIONAL FOLK ENSEMBLE
2140 Lee Road, Suite 218, Cleveland Heights, OH 44118
(216) 932-3455
>   **Founded:** 1968
>   **Arts Area:** Ethnic; Folk
>   **Status:** Professional
>   **Type:** Performing; Touring; Resident; Educational

Purpose: To preserve and promote folklore dance and music from around the world in which the Jewish people have lived; to foster an appreciation of all people; to promote an understanding of our nation's cultural diversity
Management: Clara A. Amster, Executive Director; Daniel M. Ducoff, Artistic Director
Officers: Daniel Ducoff, President; Paul Kantor, Vice President; Stuart Meyer, Treasurer; Clara Amster, Secretary
Paid Staff: 1   **Volunteer Staff:** 20
Paid Artists: 20
Utilizes: Special Technical Talent; Guest Artists; Guest Choreographers
Budget: $1,000 - $50,000
Income Sources: Private Foundations/Grants/Endowments; Business/Corporate Donations; Box Office; Individual Donations
Season: 52 Weeks   **Annual Attendance:** 10,000
Performance Facilities: Blance R. Halle Theatre

INSTRUMENTAL MUSIC

THE CLEVELAND OCTET
1510 Crest Road, Cleveland Heights, OH 44121
(216) 381-9031
FAX: (216) 291-0502
Founded: 1977
Arts Area: Chamber; Ensemble
Status: Professional; Non-Profit
Type: Performing; Touring
Purpose: To present and perform rarely performed masterpieces for ensembles of six to eight players
Management: Columbia Artist Management, NY Sheldon Division
Officers: Erich Eichhorn, Founder and Director
Volunteer Staff: 1
Paid Artists: 8
Utilizes: Guest Artists
Income Sources: Private Foundations/Grants/Endowments; Box Office; Individual Donations
Season: September - May
Affiliations: ORACLE; Cleveland Museum of Art; Cleveland Orchestra
Performance Facilities: Cleveland Museum of Art

HEIGHTS CHAMBER ORCHESTRA
3165 Monmouth Road, Cleveland Heights, OH 44118
(216) 321-4259
Founded: 1983
Arts Area: Symphony; Orchestra
Status: Non-Profit
Type: Performing
Purpose: Community orchestra and extension of music education in the public and private schools
Management: Gino Raffaeli, Concert Master; John Fioritto, Conductor
Volunteer Staff: 1
Paid Artists: 4   **Non-Paid Artists:** 52
Budget: $1,000 - $50,000
Income Sources: Government Grants; Individual Donations
Season: September - May   **Annual Attendance:** 1,500
Affiliations: Cleveland Heights Board of Education; Cleveland Heights Parks and Recreation Department
Performance Facilities: Performing Arts Center, Cleveland Heights High School

SHAKER SYMPHONY ORCHESTRA
2843 Edgehill Road, Cleveland Heights, OH 44118
(216) 321-3704
Founded: 1938
Arts Area: Symphony; Orchestra
Status: Non-Professional; Non-Profit
Type: Performing
Purpose: Opportunity for amateurs to perform 5-6 times in concert
Management: Dr. Henry Schackne, Manager
Budget: $1,000 - $50,000
Income Sources: Private Foundations/Grants/Endowments; Individual Donations

THEATRE

DOBAMA THEATRE
1846 Coventry Road, Cleveland Heights, OH 44118
(216) 932-6838
Founded: 1959

Arts Area: Theatrical Group
Status: Non-Professional; Non-Profit
Type: Performing; Resident; Educational
Purpose: Produce five plays not yet available to Cleveland Heights audiences; encourage new American playwrights by offering staged readings and full world premiere productions of their work; encourage creative expression in children through annual Marilyn Biarchi Kids Playwriting Festival
Management: Jean Cummins, Literary Manager; Owen Kelly, Public Relations Director; Joyce Casey, Artistic and Managing Director; Deborah Bradlin, Development Director; Ron Newell, Technical Director; Dave Morris, House Manager
Officers: Jewish Community Center of Cleveland Board of Directors
Volunteer Staff: 10
Non-Paid Artists: 70
Budget: $50,000 - $100,000
Income Sources: Private Foundations/Grants/Endowments; Business/Corporate Donations; Box Office; Government Grants; Individual Donations
Season: September - June   **Annual Attendance:** 7,000
Affiliations: OTA

PERFORMING SERIES

JEWISH COMMUNITY CENTER OF CLEVELAND
3505 Mayfield Road, Cleveland Heights, OH 44118
(216) 382-4000
FAX: (216) 382-5401
Arts Area: Dance; Theater; Visual Arts
Status: Professional; Non-Professional; Non-Profit
Type: Performing; Resident; Educational
Purpose: To provide opportunities through the arts for persons of all ages to explore and strengthen Jewish identity, arts expertise, and human-relation skills toward more effective living in our diverse, democratic society
Management: David Kleinman, Executive Director; Michael J. Peterman, President
Utilizes: Guest Conductors; Guest Artists; Guest Directors
Income Sources: Box Office; Individual Donations
Affiliations: National Jewish Welfare Board; United Torch; Jewish Community Center
Performance Facilities: Blanche R. Halle Theater

PARK ARTS FESTIVAL - SUMMER SEASON
Lee and Superior Roads, Cleveland Heights, OH 44118
(216) 291-5796
FAX: (216) 291-2064
Founded: 1938
Arts Area: Dance; Vocal Music; Instrumental Music; Theater; Festivals; Visual Arts
Status: Professional; Non-Profit
Type: Sponsoring
Management: Janet Herman-Barlow, General Manager; B.D. Thomas, Operations Manager
Paid Staff: 50
Paid Artists: 200
Utilizes: Guest Conductors; Guest Artists; Guest Directors
Budget: $100,000 - $500,000
Income Sources: Private Foundations/Grants/Endowments; Business/Corporate Donations; Box Office; Government Grants; Individual Donations
Season: June - September   **Annual Attendance:** 100,000
Affiliations: OAC
Performance Facilities: Evans Amphitheatre; Evans Alma Theater

SHALHAVET
2140 Lee Road, Suite 218, Cleveland Heights, OH 44118
(216) 932-3455
Management: Clara Amster, Executive Director
Budget: $1,000 - $50,000

FACILITY

DOBAMA THEATRE
1846 Coventry Road, Cleveland Heights, OH 44118
(216) 932-6838
Type of Facility: Theatre House
Facility Originally: Bowling Alley
Type of Stage: Thrust
Stage Dimensions: 13'x24'x16'

Seating Capacity: 200
Year Built: 1920
Year Remodeled: 1968
Converted into a theatre in 1968

Columbus

DANCE

BALLET METROPOLITAN
322 Mount Vernon Avenue, Columbus, OH 43215
(614) 224-1672
 Founded: 1974
 Arts Area: Ballet
 Status: Professional; Non-Profit
 Type: Performing; Touring; Resident; Educational; Sponsoring
 Purpose: To maintain a resident professional ballet company; to develop a repertoire encompassing a range of classical and contemporary work; to provide educational audience development services to the community; to build a dance academy which provides professional training and vocational instruction
 Management: John McFall, Artistic Director; Xandra Auderhalt, Dance Academy Administrator; Mary K. Bailey, Executive Director
 Officers: Nancy Strause, Chairman of the Board; Jeff Rich, Executive Officer
 Paid Staff: 20 **Volunteer Staff:** 5
 Paid Artists: 25
 Utilizes: Special Technical Talent; Guest Artists
 Budget: $1,000,000 - $5,000,000
 Income Sources: Private Foundations/Grants/Endowments; Business/Corporate Donations; Box Office; Government Grants; Individual Donations
 Season: August - April **Annual Attendance:** 100,000
 Affiliations: NARB; Dance USA
 Performance Facilities: Ohio Theatre

PERFORMING ARTS PROGRAMS IN DANCE
Wexner Center for the Arts, North High Street at 15th Avenue, Columbus, OH 43210
(614) 292-0330
FAX: (614) 292-3369
 Arts Area: Modern; Mime; Ballet; Jazz; Ethnic; Folk
 Status: Professional; Non-Profit
 Type: Performing; Touring; Resident; Educational; Sponsoring
 Purpose: To present the best in contemporary arts
 Management: William Cook, Acting Director; Adrienne Bosworth, Director of Communications
 Budget: $100,000 - $500,000
 Income Sources: Private Foundations/Grants/Endowments; Business/Corporate Donations; Box Office; Government Grants; Individual Donations
 Performance Facilities: Mershon Auditorium

STUART PIMSLER DANCE & THEATER
61 Jefferson Avenue, Columbus, OH 43215
(614) 461-0132
 Founded: 1978
 Arts Area: Modern
 Status: Professional
 Type: Performing
 Purpose: To present performance work that comments on contemporary issues
 Management: William Powell, Company Administrator; Stuart Pimsler
 Officers: Elizabeth Bank, President; Katherine Burman, Secretary; Sue Haidle, Treasurer
 Paid Staff: 1 **Volunteer Staff:** 3
 Paid Artists: 6
 Utilizes: Special Technical Talent; Guest Artists; Guest Directors
 Budget: $100,000 - $500,000
 Income Sources: Private Foundations/Grants/Endowments; Business/Corporate Donations; Individual Donations
 Season: September - June
 Affiliations: Ohio Dance; APAP; Alliance for Dance and Movement Arts

UNIVERSITY DANCE COMPANY
Dance Dept., Ohio State University, 1813 North High Street, Columbus, OH 43210
(614) 292-7977
 Founded: 1968

Arts Area: Modern
Status: Semi-Professional; Non-Profit
Type: Performing; Touring; Resident; Educational
Purpose: University Dance Company functions as a professional training ground for selected dance majors working towards a professional career in dance and performance.
Management: Rosalind Pierson, Director; Vera Blaine, Chair, Department of Dance
Paid Staff: 4
Paid Artists: 7   **Non-Paid Artists:** 20
Utilizes: Special Technical Talent; Guest Conductors; Guest Artists
Budget: $1,000 - $50,000
Income Sources: Private Foundations/Grants/Endowments; Business/Corporate Donations; Box Office
Season: September - June   **Annual Attendance:** 12,000
Affiliations: National Association of School of Dance; American College Dance Festival Association
Performance Facilities: Sullivan Theatre

WORTHINGTON CIVIC BALLET AND JAZZ NORTH DANCE COMPANIES
7029 Huntley Road, Suite G, Columbus, OH 43229
(614) 888-7471
Founded: 1963
Arts Area: Ballet; Jazz
Status: Professional; Semi-Professional; Non-Profit
Type: Performing; Touring; Educational
Purpose: Worthington Civic Ballet, a student-civic company, presents yearly performances of "The Nutcracker" as well as spring concerts and "Jazz North" artists-in-schools tours throughout central Ohio.
Management: Barbara Burrows, Director/Choreographer
Officers: Barbara Burrows, President; Duard Farquhar, Vice President; Robert Albright, Secretary
Paid Staff: 12   **Volunteer Staff:** 15
Paid Artists: 6   **Non-Paid Artists:** 20
Utilizes: Special Technical Talent; Guest Artists; Guest Directors
Budget: $100,000 - $500,000
Income Sources: Private Foundations/Grants/Endowments; Business/Corporate Donations; Box Office; Individual Donations
Season: 52 Weeks   **Annual Attendance:** 24,000
Performance Facilities: Battelle Auditorium; Ohio Theatre; Worthington High School

INSTRUMENTAL MUSIC

COLUMBUS SYMPHONY ORCHESTRA
55 East State Street, Columbus, OH 43215
(614) 224-5281
FAX: (614) 224-7273
Founded: 1952
Arts Area: Symphony; Orchestra; Chamber; Ensemble
Status: Professional
Type: Performing; Educational; Sponsoring
Purpose: To foster, promote, and increase musical knowledge of the public by educational activities and presenting performances of music
Management: Stephen Vann, Executive Director; Susan Rosenstock, Orchestra Manager
Officers: John Kane, Chairman; Ronald Pizzuti, First Vice Chairman; Peter Frenzer and Paula B. Brothers, Vice Chairmen; John Josephson, Secretary; David Lauer, Treasurer
Paid Staff: 24   **Volunteer Staff:** 1,500
Paid Artists: 125
Utilizes: Special Technical Talent; Guest Conductors; Guest Artists
Budget: $5,000,000 - $10,000,000
Income Sources: Private Foundations/Grants/Endowments; Business/Corporate Donations; Box Office; Government Grants; Individual Donations
Season: September - August   **Annual Attendance:** 250,000
Affiliations: ASOL
Performance Facilities: Ohio Theatre; Mershon Auditorium

COLUMBUS SYMPHONY YOUTH ORCHESTRA
55 East State Street, Columbus, OH 43215
(614) 224-5281
FAX: (614) 234-7273
Founded: 1955
Arts Area: Symphony; Orchestra; Chamber
Status: Non-Professional; Non-Profit
Type: Performing; Touring; Educational

Purpose: To provide the highest quality educational and performance experiences for central Ohio's most gifted instrumentalists
Management: Peter Stafford Wilson, Music Director/Conductor
Officers: Linda Odronic, Chairman; Harold Scharp, Vice Chairman; Linda Hampton, Secretary; Becky Stains, Treasurer
Paid Staff: 4   **Volunteer Staff:** 15
Non-Paid Artists: 250
Utilizes: Guest Artists
Budget: $50,000 - $100,000
Income Sources: Box Office
Season: November - May   **Annual Attendance:** 5,000
Affiliations: ASOL (Youth Orchestra Division); Columbus Symphony Orchestra
Performance Facilities: Weigel Hall, Ohio State University

THE JAZZ ARTS GROUP OF COLUMBUS
709 College Avenue, Columbus, OH 43209
(614) 231-7836
FAX: (614) 235-9744
Founded: 1972
Arts Area: Orchestra; Jazz
Status: Professional; Non-Profit
Type: Performing; Touring; Resident; Educational
Purpose: To present and perform America's only indigenous art form
Management: Ray Eubanks, General Manager/Artistic Director; Margaret Barr, Operations; Mitch Swain, Marketing/Development; Andy Houser, Box Office
Officers: Jim Brock, President; Bob Ackerman, Vice President; Mark Shary, Treasurer; Ethel Shapiro, Secretary
Volunteer Staff: 25
Utilizes: Guest Artists
Budget: $1,000,000 - $5,000,000
Income Sources: Private Foundations/Grants/Endowments; Business/Corporate Donations; Box Office; Government Grants; Individual Donations
Season: 52 Weeks   **Annual Attendance:** 305,000
Affiliations: City of Columbus Music in the Air
Performance Facilities: Batelle Auditorium; Palace Theatre

PRO MUSICA CHAMBER ORCHESTRA OF COLUMBUS
444 East Broad Street, Columbus, OH 43215
(614) 464-0066
FAX: (614) 464-4141
Arts Area: Symphony; Orchestra; Chamber
Status: Professional; Non-Profit
Type: Performing; Touring
Purpose: To establish a partnership with the audience in order to understand and fulfill audience needs for a variety of entertaining and enlightening musical performances as well as educational experiences
Management: Francis Little, General Manager; Dr. Timothy Russell, Music Director/Conductor
Paid Staff: 5   **Volunteer Staff:** 15
Utilizes: Guest Conductors; Guest Artists
Income Sources: Private Foundations/Grants/Endowments; Business/Corporate Donations; Box Office; Individual Donations
Season: October - July
Performance Facilities: Weigel Hall; Riverfront Amphitheatre

VOCAL MUSIC

COLUMBUS SYMPHONY CHORUS
c/o Columbus Symphony Orchestra Inc., 55 East State Street, Columbus, OH 43215
(614) 224-5281
FAX: (614) 224-7273
Arts Area: Choral
Status: Non-Professional; Non-Profit
Type: Performing; Resident; Educational
Purpose: To educate and inform the public about great music
Management: Ron Jenkins, Conductor; Lois Zook, Assistant to Conductor
Officers: John Kane, Chairman of the Board
Budget: $1,000 - $50,000
Income Sources: Private Foundations/Grants/Endowments; Business/Corporate Donations; Box Office; Government Grants; Individual Donations
Season: 52 Weeks
Performance Facilities: Ohio Theatre

OPERA/COLUMBUS
177 Naghten Street, Columbus, OH 43215
(614) 461-8101
FAX: (614) 461-0806
Founded: 1980
Arts Area: Grand Opera
Status: Professional; Non-Profit
Type: Performing; Educational
Purpose: Opera/Columbus shall produce high-quality, professional opera and make it easily accessible to the diverse audience in the central Ohio area while also providing educational and audience-building outreach programs, growing into a regional producing company of national stature. Opera/Columbus shall engage established artists of national and international prominence, all the while maintaining the fiscal stability necessary to achieve its artistic goals.
Management: William F. Russell, General Director; Barb Seckler, Director of Marketing; Michael Ranney, Director of Development; Ned Snyder, Business Manager; Alice Hunt, Office Manager
Officers: Sheldon Taft, President; Walt Holway and Irma Cooper, Vice Presidents; Lois Chope, Secretary; Molly Morris, Past President
Paid Staff: 10   **Volunteer Staff:** 2
Paid Artists: 100
Utilizes: Special Technical Talent; Guest Conductors; Guest Artists; Guest Directors
Budget: $1,000,000 - $5,000,000
Income Sources: Private Foundations/Grants/Endowments; Business/Corporate Donations; Box Office; Government Grants; Individual Donations
Season: October - May   **Annual Attendance:** 25,000
Affiliations: OA
Performance Facilities: Palace Theatre

THEATRE

ACTORS' SUMMER THEATRE COMPANY
1000 City Park, Columbus, OH 43206
(614) 444-6888
Founded: 1982
Arts Area: Summer Stock; Musical; Community; Theatrical Group
Status: Semi-Professional; Non-Profit
Type: Performing; Touring; Resident; Educational
Purpose: Free, outdoor, public theatre company which aims to make quality theatre with an emphasis on entertaining productions of Shakespeare, accessible to the entire area
Management: Patricia B. Ellson, Artistic Director; Scott Skiles, Designer/Technical Director
Officers: Howard Hamilton, President
Paid Staff: 3   **Volunteer Staff:** 2
Paid Artists: 35   **Non-Paid Artists:** 100
Utilizes: Special Technical Talent; Guest Conductors; Guest Artists; Guest Directors
Budget: $100,000 - $500,000
Income Sources: Private Foundations/Grants/Endowments; Business/Corporate Donations; Box Office; Government Grants; Individual Donations
Season: June - September   **Annual Attendance:** 30,000
Performance Facilities: Schiller Park Amphitheatre

PLAYERS THEATRE COLUMBUS
77 South High Street, Columbus, OH 43215
(614) 644-5300
FAX: (614) 621-2338
Mailing Address: PO Box 18185, Columbus, OH 43218-0185
Founded: 1923
Arts Area: Professional
Status: Professional; Non-Profit
Type: Performing; Touring; Resident; Educational
Purpose: Committed to providing a wide range of high quality theatrical productions and programs to Central Ohio audiences, young and old
Management: Ed Graczyk, Artistic Director; Jean Ann Klaus, Managing Director; Steven C. Anderson, Associate Artistic Director; Lenore P. Kaler, Marketing Director; P. Susan Sharrock, Public Relations Manager; John York, Carol Dultigg, Production Managers
Officers: Charles R. Martin, President-Board of Directors; Kenneth Warren, Executive Vice President; Tanny Crane, Secretary; Robert G. Jones, Treasurer; Joel Teaford, Vice President
Paid Staff: 45   **Volunteer Staff:** 1,800
Paid Artists: 120

Utilizes: Special Technical Talent; Guest Conductors; Guest Artists; Guest Directors
Budget: Over 10,000,000
Income Sources: Private Foundations/Grants/Endowments; Business/Corporate Donations; Box Office; Government Grants; Individual Donations
Season: September - June
Annual Attendance: 125,000
Affiliations: LORT; OTA; AEA; USA; TCG; Cols Area Chamber of Commerce; Greater Columbus Commercial Visitor Bureau
Performance Facilities: Vern Riffe Center for Government and the Arts; Capitol Theatre; Studio One Theatre; Studio Two Theatre

THE REALITY THEATRE
736 North Pearl Street, Columbus, OH 43215
(614) 294-7541
Founded: 1985
Arts Area: Theatrical Group
Status: Semi-Professional; Non-Profit
Type: Performing; Resident
Purpose: Primarily dedicated to the development of experimental plays and also the presentation of original scripts written by Ohio playwrights
Management: Frank A. Barnhart, Producer/Artistic Director; Daneta Shepherd, Producer/Artistic Director
Paid Staff: 16   **Volunteer Staff:** 10
Paid Artists: 16
Utilizes: Guest Artists; Guest Directors
Budget: $50,000 - $100,000
Income Sources: Private Foundations/Grants/Endowments; Business/Corporate Donations; Box Office; Government Grants; Individual Donations
Season: 52 Weeks
Annual Attendance: 6,000

STROLLERS STUDENT THEATRICS
1739 North High Street, Ohio Union, Box 36, Columbus, OH 43201
(614) 292-6061
Founded: 1892
Arts Area: Musical; Community; Theatrical Group
Status: Non-Professional; Non-Profit
Type: Performing
Purpose: To provide the students of Ohio State University and members of the community with the opportunity to participate in all aspects of the performing arts
Officers: Kyle Grube, President; Sandy Hugill, Vice President; Stacey Feldman, Recording Secretary; Keith Davis, Corresponding Secretary; Katy Beachy, Treasurer
Budget: $1,000 - $50,000
Income Sources: Box Office
Season: September - May

PERFORMING SERIES

COLUMBUS ARTS FESTIVAL
55 East State Street, Columbus, OH 43215
(614) 224-2606
Founded: 1961
Arts Area: Dance; Vocal Music; Instrumental Music; Festivals
Status: Professional; Non-Professional; Non-Profit
Type: Performing; Festival
Purpose: To present an annual arts festival
Management: Rod Reiner, General Manager; Vikki Shultz, Fesitval Assistant
Officers: Ray Hanley, President
Paid Staff: 2   **Volunteer Staff:** 35
Budget: $500,000 - $1,000,000
Income Sources: Business/Corporate Donations; Earned Income
Season: June   **Annual Attendance:** 500,000
Affiliations: Greater Columbus Arts Council

FACILITY

DAVIS DISCOVERY CENTER - AGNES JEFFREY SHEDD THEATRE
549 Franklin Avenue, Columbus, OH 43215
(614) 645-7469
Type of Facility: Theatre House

Type of Stage: Proscenium
Stage Dimensions: 42'Wx30'Dx30'H; 42'Wx12'H proscenium opening   **Orchestra Pit**
Seating Capacity: 350
Year Built: 1976   **Architect:** Feinknoff, Maclore & Shappa
Contact for Rental: Jack Zimmerman;   (614) 645-6639
Limited availability on theatre rental

DAVIS DISCOVERY CENTER - HENRY VAN FLEET THEATRE
549 Franklin Avenue, Columbus, OH 43215
(614) 645-7469
Type of Facility: Black Box
Type of Stage: Flexible
Stage Dimensions: 28'Wx21'Dx16'H
Seating Capacity: 199
Year Remodeled: 1976   **Architect:** Feinknoff, Maclore & Shappa
Contact for Rental: Jack Zimmerman;   (614) 645-6639

JEWISH COMMUNITY CENTER OF CLEVELAND - BLANCHE R. HALLE THEATER
3505 Mayfield Road, Columbus, OH 44118
(216) 382-4000
Type of Facility: Cultural Center
Orchestra Pit
Seating Capacity: 275
Year Built: 1960
Manager: Dorothy Silver

MARTIN LUTHER KING JR. PERFORMING AND CULTURAL ARTS COMPLEX
867 Mt. Vernon Avenue, Columbus, OH 43203
(614) 252-5464
FAX: (614) 252-3807
Founded: 1985
Type of Facility: Performance Center; Multi-Purpose
Facility Originally: Vaudeville; Ballroom
Type of Stage: Proscenium
Stage Dimensions: 19'11"Dx50'10"W apron to proscenium
Seating Capacity: 444
Year Built: 1926   **Architect:** Samuel Plato   **Cost:** $125,000
Year Remodeled: 1986   **Architect:** Moody Nolan and Associates
Acoustical Consultant: Howard Newman
Contact for Rental: Joe Barrett;   (614) 252-5464
Resident Groups: Center Stage Theatre; Imani Theatre Folk

OHIO STATE UNIVERSITY - STADIUM II THEATRE
1089 Drake Union, 1849 Cannon Drive, Columbus, OH 43210
(614) 292-5821
Type of Facility: Theatre Complex; Studio Performance; Theatre House
Type of Stage: Thrust; Platform; 3/4 Arena
Stage Dimensions: 29'x24'
Seating Capacity: 250
Year Built: 1972
Year Remodeled: 1987
Contact for Rental: (614) 252-5821
Resident Groups: Ohio State University Theatre Company

OHIO STATE UNIVERSITY - THURBER THEATRE
1089 Drake Union, 1849 Cannon Drive, Columbus, OH 43210
(614) 292-5821
Type of Facility: Theatre Complex; Auditorium; Theatre House
Type of Stage: Proscenium
Stage Dimensions: 36'x30'
Orchestra Pit
Seating Capacity: 600
Year Built: 1972
Year Remodeled: 1986
Available for rent

OHIO THEATRE
55 East State Street, Columbus, OH 43215-4264
(614) 469-1045
FAX: (614) 224-7461
Founded: 1927
Type of Facility: Concert Hall; Auditorium; Studio Performance; Performance Center; Theatre House; Multi-Purpose
Facility Originally: Movie House
Type of Stage: Proscenium
Stage Dimensions: 47'4x62'
Orchestra Pit
Seating Capacity: 2,897
Year Built: 1927   **Architect:** Thomas W. Lamb   **Cost:** $865,000
Year Remodeled: 1984   **Architect:** Hardy Holzman Pfeiffer Associates   **Cost:** $6,000,000
Acoustical Consultant: Peter George Associates
Contact for Rental: Douglas F. Kridler or Debra Rosental;   (614) 469-1045
Resident Groups: Columbus Symphony Orchestra; BalletMet; Columbus Theatrical Association; Columbus Association for the Performing Arts (CAPA)

PALACE THEATRE
34 West Broad Street, Columbus, OH 43215-4264
(614) 469-1045
FAX: (614) 224-7461
Founded: 1926
Type of Facility: Concert Hall; Auditorium; Performance Center; Theatre House; Opera House; Multi-Purpose
Facility Originally: Vaudeville; Movie House
Type of Stage: Proscenium
Stage Dimensions: 47'8"x35'
Orchestra Pit
Seating Capacity: 2,827
Year Built: 1926   **Architect:** Thomas W. Lamb   **Cost:** $3,000,000
Year Remodeled: 1980   **Architect:** Bohm-NBBJ   **Cost:** $2,000,000
Contact for Rental: Douglas F. Kridler or Debra Rosenthal;   (614) 469-1045
Resident Groups: Opera/Columbus; Jazz Arts Group; Columbus Theatrical Association (producer of Broadway plays); CAPA

PLAYERS THEATRE COLUMBUS
Vern Riffe Center for Government & the Arts, 77 High Street South, Columbus, OH 43215
(614) 644-5300
Type of Facility: Theatre Complex
Facility Originally: Private Residence
Year Remodeled: 1976   **Architect:** Feinknoff Maclore & Shappa   **Cost:** $1,000,000
Contact for Rental: John H. York;   (614) 644-5300
Resident Groups: Players Theatre Columbus
The Players Theatre contains the Agnes Jeffrey Shedd Theatre and the Henry Van Fleet Theatre. Limited availability on theatre rental

VETERANS MEMORIAL
300 West Broad Street, Columbus, OH 43215
(614) 221-4341
FAX: (614) 221-8422
Type of Facility: Multi-Purpose
Type of Stage: Proscenium
Stage Dimensions: 182'Wx32'D; 72'Wx27'H proscenium opening
Orchestra Pit
Seating Capacity: 3,944
Year Built: 1955   **Architect:** Associate Architects   **Cost:** $6,000,000
Contact for Rental: Richard P. Nolan, Melody A. Stevens;   (614) 221-4341

WEXNER CENTER FOR THE ARTS/MERSHON AUDITORIUM
30 West 15th Avenue, Columbus, OH 43210
(614) 292-5785
Type of Facility: Concert Hall; Auditorium
Type of Stage: Proscenium
Stage Dimensions: 42'x100'x63'9"
Orchestra Pit

Seating Capacity: 3,058
Year Built: 1957
Acoustical Consultant: Jeff McMahon
Contact for Rental: Claudia Bonham; (614) 292-5785
Manager: Charles Helm, Director, Performing Arts; (614) 292-5785

Cuyahoga Falls

DANCE

CUYAHOGA VALLEY YOUTH BALLET
1853 Joan of Arc Circle, PO Box 3131, Cuyahoga Falls, OH 44223
(216) 928-4027
  Founded: 1975
  Arts Area: Modern; Ballet
  Status: Non-Professional; Non-Profit
  Type: Performing; Resident; Educational
  Purpose: To provide performing experience for talented young dancers, educating them in the realities of professional ballet; to educate area children and families in the appreciation of ballet as an art form at affordable prices
  Management: Nan Klinger, Artistic Director
  Officers: Tom Hardy, President; Andrea Kok, Vice President; Gail Noble, Recording Secretary; Bernadette Harris, Corresponding Secretary; David Sarver, Treasurer
  Volunteer Staff: 33
  Non-Paid Artists: 33
  Utilizes: Guest Artists; Guest Choreographers
  Budget: $1,000 - $50,000
  Income Sources: Private Foundations/Grants/Endowments; Business/Corporate Donations; Box Office; Individual Donations
  Affiliations: OAC
  Performance Facilities: Akron Civic Theatre; E.J. Thomas Hall

FACILITY

BLOSSOM MUSIC CENTER
1145 West Steels Corners Road, Cuyahoga Falls, OH 44223
(216) 231-7300
  Type of Facility: Outdoor (Concert); Amphitheater
  Type of Stage: Proscenium
  Stage Dimensions: 71'x49' **Orchestra Pit**
  Seating Capacity: Pavilion - 5,281; Lawn - 13,500
  Year Built: 1968 **Architect:** Peter van Dijk **Cost:** $9,113,230
  Acoustical Consultant: Jaffe Acoustics
  Contact for Rental: Alan J. DeZon; (216) 920-8040
  Resident Groups: Cleveland Orchestra
  To promote and present approximately 60 events during an 18-week summer season ranging from classical to rock 'n roll

Dayton

DANCE

DANCE THEATRE DAYTON
1306 East Fifth Street, Dayton, OH 45402
(513) 223-9228
  Arts Area: Ballet
  Status: Professional; Non-Profit
  Type: Performing
  Management: Deborah DeRado, Artistic Director
  Paid Artists: 17
  Income Sources: Box Office; Individual Donations
  Performance Facilities: Victory Theater

DAYTON BALLET
140 North Main Street, Dayton, OH 45402
(513) 449-5060
FAX: (513) 461-8353
  Founded: 1937
  Arts Area: Ballet; Contemporary

Status: Non-Profit
Type: Performing
Purpose: To present professional dance; to train professional dancers; to aid the growth and development of dance
Management: James R. Albright, General Manager; James Clouser, Artistic Director/Choreographer; Dermot Burke, Executive Director
Officers: R. Daniel Sadlier, President; Daniel W. Duval, Chairman of the Board
Paid Staff: 19   **Volunteer Staff:** 10
Paid Artists: 17   **Non-Paid Artists:** 25
Utilizes: Special Technical Talent; Guest Choreographers
Budget: $100,000 - $500,000
Income Sources: Private Foundations/Grants/Endowments; Business/Corporate Donations; Box Office; Government Grants; Individual Donations
Season: October - April   **Annual Attendance:** 48,000
Affiliations: APAP; Ohio Dance; ORACLE
Performance Facilities: Victoria Theatre

DAYTON CONTEMPORARY DANCE COMPANY
126 North Main Street, Suite 200, Dayton, OH 45402
(513) 223-3232
FAX: (513) 223-6156
Founded: 1968
Arts Area: Modern; Ballet; Jazz; Ethnic; Folk; Contemporary
Status: Professional; Non-Profit
Type: Performing; Touring; Resident
Management: Jeraldyne Blunden, Artistic Director; Hal Andress, Managing Director; Kevin Ward, Associate Artistic Director; Debbie Blunden-Diggs, Director, 2nd Company; Mark Coldiron, Production Manager; Karen Clark, Stage Manager; Lowell Mathwich, Tour Manager; Dawn Wood, Rehearsal Mistress
Officers: Stanley Earley, Chairman of the Board of Trustees
Paid Staff: 11   **Volunteer Staff:** 10
Paid Artists: 15   **Non-Paid Artists:** 12
Utilizes: Special Technical Talent; Guest Artists; Guest Choreographers
Budget: $100,000 - $500,000
Income Sources: Private Foundations/Grants/Endowments; Business/Corporate Donations; Box Office; Government Grants; Individual Donations; Performance Fees
Season: August - May   **Annual Attendance:** 32,000
Affiliations: American Dance Festival
Performance Facilities: The Victory Theatre

INSTRUMENTAL MUSIC

DAYTON PHILHARMONIC ORCHESTRA ASSOCIATION
Memorial Hall, 125 East First Street, Dayton, OH 45422
(513) 224-3521
FAX: (513) 223-9189
Founded: 1933
Arts Area: Symphony; Orchestra; Chamber
Status: Professional; Non-Profit
Type: Performing; Resident; Educational; Sponsoring
Purpose: To maintain and foster a professional symphonic orchestra of the highest possible quality and provide live concerts for pleasure and cultural enhancement
Management: John E. Bauser, Executive Director; Isaiah Jackson, Music Director
Officers: James Vanvleck, President; Mrs. Steve Mason, Vice President; Mrs. William McCormick, Secretary; John Hazelton, Treasurer
Paid Staff: 7   **Volunteer Staff:** 1
Paid Artists: 102
Utilizes: Guest Conductors; Guest Artists
Budget: $1,000,000 - $5,000,000
Income Sources: Private Foundations/Grants/Endowments; Business/Corporate Donations; Box Office; Government Grants; Individual Donations
Season: September - May
Affiliations: ASOL; AAA; ACA; OOOO; OCCA
Performance Facilities: Montgomery County's Memorial Hall; Dayton Convention and Exhibition Center

DAYTON PHILHARMONIC YOUTH ORCHESTRA
Memorial Hall, 125 East First Street, Dayton, OH 45402
(513) 224-3521
FAX: (513) 223-9189
Founded: 1982
Arts Area: Symphony; Orchestra

Status: Non-Professional; Non-Profit
Type: Performing; Educational
Purpose: To give aspiring young musicians of the Dayton area an opportunity to work together studying challenging orchestral music; to attempt to strengthen and expand the musical skills, knowledge, talent and experience through the study of the symphonic orchestral literature
Management: Dr. William J. Steinhort, Conductor/Music Director; Sonia Goldfarb, Operations Manager, Dayton Philharmonic Orchestra; Xiao-Guang Zhu, Conductor, Junior String Orchestra
Paid Staff: 1   **Volunteer Staff:** 180
Non-Paid Artists: 90
Utilizes: Guest Artists
Budget: $1,000 - $50,000
Season: September - July   **Annual Attendance:** 16,000
Affiliations: ASOL (Youth Orchestra Division); Ohio Music Club; Dayton Philharmonic Orchestra
Performance Facilities: Concert Hall, Wright State University

THE TOP BRASS QUARTET
PO Box 9327, Dayton, OH 45409
(513) 253-5812
Founded: 1979
Arts Area: Chamber; Instrumental Group
Status: Professional
Type: Performing; Touring; Recording
Purpose: Nationwide performance in a wide variety of settings
Management: Scott Bridges, Management Director; David Coleman, Internal Manager; Norlan Bewley, Artistic Manager
Paid Staff: 3
Paid Artists: 5
Utilizes: Guest Artists
Season: 52 Weeks
Annual Attendance: 50,000

VOCAL MUSIC

DAYTON OPERA ASSOCIATION
Memorial Hall, 125 East First Street, Dayton, OH 45402
(513) 228-0662; (513) 228-0287
FAX: (513) 228-9612
Founded: 1960
Arts Area: Grand Opera; Operetta; Musical Theatre
Status: Professional; Non-Profit
Type: Performing; Resident; Educational
Purpose: To increase appreciation for opera through education; to present and promote opera of high quality to the Dayton region as well as present balanced programs; to utilize international artists; to encourage local and regional artistic development
Management: Jane Nelson, General Director
Paid Staff: 4   **Volunteer Staff:** 325
Paid Artists: 150   **Non-Paid Artists:** 30
Utilizes: Special Technical Talent; Guest Conductors; Guest Artists; Guest Directors
Budget: $1,000,000 - $5,000,000
Income Sources: Private Foundations/Grants/Endowments; Business/Corporate Donations; Box Office; Government Grants; Individual Donations
Season: October - May
Annual Attendance: 20,000
Affiliations: OA; AAA; Dayton Performing Arts Fund
Performance Facilities: Montgomery County's Memorial Hall

THEATRE

THE CREEKSIDE PLAYERS
636 Superior Avenue, Dayton, OH 45407
(513) 228-2012
Founded: 1978
Arts Area: Community
Status: Non-Professional; Non-Profit
Type: Performing

Purpose: To develop, present, and promote Black Theatre as an important art form, using dramatic art as the medium to convey the African and African-American experience
Management: Ray Alexander, Artistic Director; Nancy Gibson, Administrative Assistant
Officers: Leo A. Lucas, Treasurer
Volunteer Staff: 7
Non-Paid Artists: 10
Utilizes: Guest Directors
Budget: $1,000 - $50,000
Income Sources: Private Foundations/Grants/Endowments; Box Office; Individual Donations
Season: October - July
Annual Attendance: 3,000

DAYTON PLAYHOUSE
1301 East Siebenthaler Avenue, Dayton, OH 45414
(513) 277-0144
Founded: 1959
Arts Area: Musical; Community; Theatrical Group
Status: Non-Professional; Non-Profit
Type: Performing
Management: Jim Payne, Managing Director
Officers: Noel Vaughn, Chairman; John Riley, Treasurer
Paid Staff: 7 **Volunteer Staff:** 650
Utilizes: Special Technical Talent; Guest Artists; Guest Directors
Budget: $100,000 - $500,000
Income Sources: Private Foundations/Grants/Endowments; Business/Corporate Donations; Box Office; Government Grants; Individual Donations
Season: 52 Weeks   **Annual Attendance:** 13,500
Affiliations: ACT; OCTA
Performance Facilities: Dayton Playhouse

PERFORMING SERIES

THE UNIVERSITY OF DAYTON ARTS SERIES
Dayton, OH 45469-0619
(513) 229-2787
FAX: (513) 229-4000
Founded: 1961
Arts Area: Dance; Vocal Music; Instrumental Music; Theater
Status: Professional; Non-Profit
Type: Performing; Sponsoring
Purpose: To provide a performing arts series presenting the variety of the arts to campus and community
Management: Maureen Cronin Masters, Directors
Paid Staff: 2 **Volunteer Staff:** 18
Paid Artists: 10
Utilizes: Special Technical Talent; Guest Artists
Budget: $1,000 - $50,000
Income Sources: Private Foundations/Grants/Endowments; Box Office; Government Grants; Individual Donations
Season: September - April   **Annual Attendance:** 5,000
Affiliations: APAP
Performance Facilities: Boll Theatre

FACILITY

DAYTON CONVENTION AND EXHIBITION CENTER
22 Dave Hall Plaza, East 5th Street, Dayton, OH 45402
(513) 443-4700
FAX: (513) 443-4711
Type of Facility: Civic Center
Type of Stage: In-the-round Capability
Seating Capacity: 674
Year Built: 1973   **Architect:** DeVeau-Kleski   **Cost:** $6,000,000
Contact for Rental: Manager;   (513) 443-4700

DAYTON PLAYHOUSE
1301 East Siebenthaler Avenue, Dayton, OH 45414
(513) 222-7000
FAX: (513) 277-9539
Type of Facility: Auditorium; Theatre House

Type of Stage: Thrust; Flexible; Proscenium; 3/4 Arena; Arena
Stage Dimensions: 39'x28'
Seating Capacity: 210
Year Built: 1988

MONTGOMERY COUNTY'S MEMORIAL HALL
125 East First Street, Dayton, OH 45422
(513) 225-5898
FAX: (513) 225-4922
Type of Facility: Concert Hall; Auditorium; Theatre House; Opera House
Facility Originally: Meeting Hall; Veteran's Memorial
Type of Stage: Proscenium
Stage Dimensions: 73'6"Wx36'71/2"D; 58'Wx26'H proscenium opening   Orchestra Pit
Seating Capacity: 2,501 Year Built: 1910
Year Remodeled: 1990
Acoustical Consultant: Sound Force
Contact for Rental: Betty Rice;   (513) 225-5898
Manager: Carol Cleavenger, Director of Cultural Facilities and Affairs
Resident Groups: Dayton Philharmonic Orchestra; Dayton Opera

Euclid

DANCE

THE TOM EVERT DANCE COMPANY
Shore Cultural Centre, 291 East 222 Street, Euclid, OH 44123
(216) 261-3654
Founded: 1986
Arts Area: Modern
Status: Professional; Non-Profit
Type: Performing; Touring; Resident; Educational; Special Events
Purpose: To create choreography and perform it in concerts; to serve as an educational resource
Management: Tom Evert, Artistic Director; Marcia Unger, Administrative Assistant; Susana Evert, Marketing Director; Lawrence L. Evert Jr., Bookings
Officers: Dennis Sutcliff, Chairman; Timothy Evert, President; Thomas R. Hawn, Treasurer; Hugh McKay, Secretary
Paid Staff: 3   Volunteer Staff: 2
Paid Artists: 6   Non-Paid Artists: 1
Utilizes: Special Technical Talent; Guest Artists; Original Music Scores
Budget: $100,000 - $500,000
Income Sources: Private Foundations/Grants/Endowments; Business/Corporate Donations; Box Office; Government Grants; Individual Donations; Benefits and Fundraisers
Season: 52 Weeks   Annual Attendance: 20,000
Affiliations: APAP; Arts Midwest; Arts Presenters Network; Ohio Dance; Ohio Citizens Committee for the Arts
Performance Facilities: Cleveland Playhouse

Fostoria

THEATRE

FOSTORIA FOOTLIGHTERS
PO Box 542, Fostoria, OH 44830
(419) 435-7501
Founded: 1959
Arts Area: Musical; Community; Theatrical Group
Status: Non-Professional; Non-Profit
Type: Performing; Resident; Educational
Officers: Ann Duffield, President; Jackie Bodart, Vice President; Douglas F. Bland, Secretary; C. Browning Payne, Treasurer
Volunteer Staff: 12
Non-Paid Artists: 100
Utilizes: Guest Artists; Guest Directors
Budget: $1,000 - $50,000
Income Sources: Business/Corporate Donations; Box Office; Individual Donations

Season: September - May   **Annual Attendance:** 4,000
Affiliations: Ohio Community Theatre Alliance
Performance Facilities: Fostoria Footlighters

FACILITY

FOSTORIA FOOTLIGHTERS, INC.
PO Box 542, Fostoria, OH 44830
(419) 435-7501
    Type of Facility: Theatre House
    Facility Originally: Church
    Type of Stage: Thrust; Proscenium
    Stage Dimensions: 30'x30'
    Seating Capacity: 180
    Year Built: 1885   **Cost:** $18,000
    Year Remodeled: 1972   **Cost:** $8,000
    Contact for Rental: Donald Shoub;   (419) 435-1063
    Manager: Joanne Love;   (419) 435-0337
    Resident Groups: Fostoria Footlighters

Gates Mills

INSTRUMENTAL MUSIC

CROATIAN TAMBURITZA ORCHESTRA OF CLEVELAND
6974 Gates Road, Gates Mills, OH 44040-9646
(216) 442-0231
    Founded: 1953
    Arts Area: Orchestra; Ethnic; Folk; Instrumental Group
    Status: Semi-Professional; Non-Profit
    Type: Performing; Touring; Educational
    Purpose: To preserve and perpetuate the art of playing the national folk instrument of Croatia (the tamburitza) as well as Croatia's classical/semi-classical and folk music
    Management: Nick S. Babic, Manager/Musical Director
    Officers: Rudy Ujcich, President; Linda Fuduric, Treasurer
    Volunteer Staff: 20
    Non-Paid Artists: 20
    Utilizes: Special Technical Talent
    Budget: $1,000 - $50,000
    Income Sources: Private Foundations/Grants/Endowments; Business/Corporate Donations; Individual Donations
    Season: 52 Weeks
    Annual Attendance: 10,000

Granville

DANCE

ZIVILI: DANCES AND MUSIC OF THE SOUTH SLAVS
1753 Loudon Street, Granville, OH 43023
(614) 855-7805
FAX: (614) 587-1690
    Founded: 1973
    Arts Area: Ethnic
    Status: Professional; Non-Profit
    Type: Performing; Touring; Educational
    Purpose: To preserve the dance, music and song of the Croations, Slovenians, Serbs, Bosnians and Montenegrins
    Management: Robert M. Gewald, Booking Agent; Melissa P. Obenauf, Executive Director
    Officers: Sue P. Glander, President; Diane M. Lease, President-Elect; Constance Leal, Treasurer

Paid Staff: 9　**Volunteer Staff:** 1
Paid Artists: 28
Utilizes: Special Technical Talent; Guest Choreographers
Budget: $100,000 - $500,000
Income Sources: Private Foundations/Grants/Endowments; Business/Corporate Donations; Box Office; Government Grants; Individual Donations
Season: September - May　**Annual Attendance:** 50,000
Performance Facilities: Palace Theatre

Kent

THEATRE

PORTHOUSE THEATRE COMPANY
PO Box 5190, Kent, OH 44242-0001
(216) 672-3884
　　　Founded: 1968
　　　Arts Area: Professional; Summer Stock; Musical; Theatrical Group
　　　Status: Professional; Semi-Professional; Non-Profit
　　　Type: Performing; Educational
　　　Management: Raynette Halvorsen Smith, Producing Director; David Colwell, Managing Director; Eric Barr, Interim Artistic Director
　　　Officers: Jay Thomas, President; Bryan Williams, Secretary; Maria Mastromatteo, Treasurer
　　　Paid Staff: 3
　　　Paid Artists: 50
　　　Utilizes: Special Technical Talent; Guest Conductors; Guest Artists; Guest Directors
　　　Budget: $100,000 - $500,000
　　　Income Sources: Private Foundations/Grants/Endowments; Business/Corporate Donations; Box Office; Government Grants; Individual Donations; Kent State University
　　　Season: June 19 - August 16　**Annual Attendance:** 8,000
　　　Affiliations: Kent State University
　　　Performance Facilities: Porthouse Theatre of Blossom Music Center

Lakeside

INSTRUMENTAL MUSIC

LAKESIDE SYMPHONY
236 Walnut Avenue, Lakeside, OH 43440
(419) 798-4461
　　　Founded: 1925
　　　Arts Area: Symphony; Orchestra; Chamber
　　　Status: Professional; Non-Profit
　　　Type: Performing; Resident; Educational
　　　Purpose: To provide a resident orchestra at Lakeside on a professional level for part of the summer season
　　　Management: Philip L. Zimmerman, Executive Director; Robert L. Conquist, Musical Director; Barbara J. Sauvey, Manager
　　　Officers: Lary L. Faris, President; Kenneth J. Erb, Vice President; Lucille Smith, Secretary; Neil L. Allen, Treasurer
　　　Paid Staff: 3　**Volunteer Staff:** 20
　　　Paid Artists: 60
　　　Utilizes: Guest Artists
　　　Budget: $50,000 - $100,000
　　　Income Sources: Individual Donations
　　　Season: August 1 - August 28　**Annual Attendance:** 10,000
　　　Performance Facilities: Hoover Auditorium

PERFORMING SERIES

THE LAKESIDE ASSOCIATION
236 Walnut Avenue, Lakeside, OH 43440
(419) 798-4461
FAX: (419) 798-5033
　　　Founded: 1873
　　　Arts Area: Dance; Vocal Music; Instrumental Music; Theater

Status: Professional; Non-Profit; Commercial
Type: Sponsoring
Purpose: To establish and maintain schools, conferences, institutes, lecture courses and other means of aesthetic culture
Management: Philip Zimmerman, Executive Director
Paid Staff: 100 **Volunteer Staff:** 1
Utilizes: Guest Conductors; Guest Artists
Budget: $1,000,000 - $5,000,000
Income Sources: Individual Donations
Season: June - September **Annual Attendance:** 44,000
Performance Facilities: Auditorium

Lakewood

THEATRE

THE BECK CENTER FOR THE CULTURAL ARTS
17801 Detroit Avenue, Lakewood, OH 44107
(216) 521-2540
Founded: 1930
Arts Area: Musical; Community
Status: Non-Professional
Type: Performing; Touring; Resident; Educational
Purpose: The Beck Center is one of only two comprehensive cultural arts organizations in the state.
Management: Scott Spencer, Acting Artistic Director; Andrea Krist, Managing Director; Stuart Mendel, Director of Development; Linda Sackett, Director of Education; Don McBride, Production and Design
Officers: Rosemary Corcoran, President; Brian King, Vice President; Marjorie Wiess, Treasurer
Paid Staff: 78 **Volunteer Staff:** 300
Non-Paid Artists: 200
Utilizes: Special Technical Talent; Guest Conductors; Guest Artists; Guest Directors
Budget: $1,000,000 - $5,000,000
Income Sources: Private Foundations/Grants/Endowments; Business/Corporate Donations; Box Office; Government Grants; Individual Donations
Season: September - June
Annual Attendance: 60,000

FACILITY

KENNETH C. BECK CENTER FOR THE PERFORMING ARTS
17801 Detroit Avenue, Lakewood, OH 44107
(216) 521-2540
Type of Facility: Auditorium
Type of Stage: Proscenium
Seating Capacity: 500
Year Built: 1976 **Architect:** Fred Toguchi **Cost:** $1,500,000
Contact for Rental: Manager; (216) 521-2540

Lancaster

VOCAL MUSIC

THE LANCASTER CHORALE
PO Box 251, Lancaster, OH 43130
(614) 569-4306
Founded: 1985
Arts Area: Choral
Status: Professional
Type: Performing; Touring
Purpose: To bring the highest quality choral art to Lancaster in a subscription series and to record and tour

Officers: Cathy Tolbert, President Board of Directors
Paid Staff: 3
Paid Artists: 32
Utilizes: Guest Artists
Budget: $1,000 - $50,000
Income Sources: Private Foundations/Grants/Endowments; Business/Corporate Donations; Box Office; Government Grants; Individual Donations
Season: November - July
Affiliations: CA

PERFORMING SERIES

CAMEO CONCERTS, INC.
127 West Wheeling Street, PO Box 1452, Lancaster, OH 43130
(614) 687-4808
FAX: (614) 654-4626
Founded: 1980
Status: Non-Profit
Type: Educational; Sponsoring
Purpose: To promote and foster an appreciation of classical musicl; to organize concerts and other programs in the community which feature classical music; to sponsor dramas and other theatrical productions, films, lectures, art exhibits, choreographic presentations and other events which serve to enrich the cultural climate of the community
Management: Eleanor Hood and Barbara Hunzicker, Co-Directors; Jim Bletzacker, Site Manager; Gary Sheldon, Music Director; Steve Rosenberg, Orchestra Manager
Officers: Don Wendel Jr, President; Jim Carpenter, Vice President; Connie Leitnaker, Secretary; Bob Wolfinger, Financial Director
Paid Staff: 1   **Volunteer Staff:** 30
Paid Artists: 473
Utilizes: Special Technical Talent; Guest Conductors; Guest Artists; Guest Directors
Budget: $100,000 - $500,000
Income Sources: Private Foundations/Grants/Endowments; Business/Corporate Donations; Box Office; Government Grants; Individual Donations
Season: July - August   **Annual Attendance:** 45,000

Lima

INSTRUMENTAL MUSIC

LIMA SYMPHONY ORCHESTRA
PO Box 1651, Lima, OH 45802
(419) 222-5701
Founded: 1953
Arts Area: Symphony; Orchestra; Chamber
Status: Semi-Professional; Non-Profit
Type: Performing; Educational; Sponsoring
Purpose: To promote the musical knowledge and appreciation of the public by organizing and presenting performances of live music (symphonic, chamber, opera and others)
Management: Leslie Vining, Executive Director; Joseph Firszt, Music Director/Conductor; Anita Sims Skinner, Personnel Manager
Officers: Victor Marone, President; James Chiles, First Vice President; Anita Hayes, Treasurer
Paid Staff: 4
Paid Artists: 80
Utilizes: Guest Conductors; Guest Artists; Guest Directors
Budget: $100,000 - $500,000
Income Sources: Private Foundations/Grants/Endowments; Business/Corporate Donations; Box Office; Government Grants; Individual Donations
Season: September - April   **Annual Attendance:** 20,000
Affiliations: ASOL
Performance Facilities: Veterans Memorial Civic and Convention Center

PERFORMING SERIES

COUNCIL FOR THE ARTS OF GREATER LIMA
120 East Elm Street, Lima, OH 45801
(419) 222-1096
Founded: 1966
Arts Area: Dance; Vocal Music; Instrumental Music; Theater; Festivals; Lyric Opera
Status: Non-Profit

Type: Educational; Sponsoring
Purpose: To promote, encourage, foster, develop, increase, advance, and diffuse knowledge, respect, understanding, taste, and public appreciation in the fields of literature, science, and the arts to benefit the people of Lima
Management: Diane Peterson, Executive Director; Cheryl Krouse, Assistant Director; Rebecca Elberfeld-Hoge, Development Director; Nora Davis, Office Manager
Officers: Richard Seitz, President; Neil Winget, Vice President; Starr Cook, Financial Officer; Mary Ann Sadlier, Secretary
Paid Staff: 4
Paid Artists: 250
Budget: $100,000 - $500,000
Income Sources: Private Foundations/Grants/Endowments; Business/Corporate Donations; Box Office; Government Grants; Individual Donations
Season: 52 Weeks   **Annual Attendance:** 125,000
Performance Facilities: Civic Center

FACILITY

VETERANS MEMORIAL CIVIC AND CONVENTION CENTER
7 Public Square, Lima, OH 45801
(419) 224-5222
Founded: 1984
Type of Facility: Theatre Complex; Multi-Purpose
Type of Stage: Proscenium
Stage Dimensions: 60'x40'   **Orchestra Pit**
Seating Capacity: 1,767
Year Built: 1984   **Architect:** Sasaki Associates, Inc.   **Cost:** $10,000,000
Acoustical Consultant: Bolt, Beranek & Newman
Contact for Rental: Jane L. Riggs or Roger Lammers;   (419) 224-5222
Manager: Florian Smith
Veterans Memorial Convention and Civic Center contains the Crouse Performance Hall, Exhibition Hall and meeting rooms. See separate listing for further information on Crouse Performance Hall.

VETERANS MEMORIAL CIVIC AND CONVENTION CENTER - CROUSE PERFORMANCE HALL
7 Public Square, Lima, OH 45801
(419) 224-5222
Type of Facility: Concert Hall; Theatre House
Type of Stage: Proscenium
Stage Dimensions: 60'Wx40'D   **Orchestra Pit**
Seating Capacity: 1,771
Year Built: 1984
Contact for Rental: Florian Smith;   (419) 224-5222
Resident Groups: Lima Symphony Orchestra; Lima Area Concert Band; Lima Civic Chorus

Lorain

FACILITY

PALACE CIVIC CENTER
Broadway at 6th Street, Lorain, OH 44052
(216) 245-2323
Type of Facility: Performance Center; Multi-Purpose
Facility Originally: Vaudeville; Movie House
Type of Stage: Proscenium
Stage Dimensions: 40'x50'x26'   **Orchestra Pit**
Seating Capacity: 1,399
Year Built: 1928
Year Remodeled: 1977   **Cost:** $500,000
Contact for Rental: John R. Handyside;   (216) 245-2323

Loveland

INSTRUMENTAL MUSIC

OHIO VALLEY BRASS QUINTET
156 Buckboard Lane, Loveland, OH 45140
(513) 722-1855
Founded: 1982

Arts Area: Chamber; Instrumental Group
Status: Professional
Type: Performing; Educational
Purpose: To provide a fine musical experience as part of any occasion for which brass ensemble music is appropriate
Management: Stephen E. Heimlich, Managing Director
Volunteer Staff: 2
Paid Artists: 5
Budget: $1,000 - $50,000
Income Sources: Private Foundations/Grants/Endowments; Business/Corporate Donations
Season: 52 Weeks

Lyndhurst

DANCE

GRANDINELE LITHUANIAN FOLK DANCERS
1620 Curry Drive, Lyndhurst, OH 44124
(216) 442-8674
Founded: 1953
Arts Area: Ethnic
Status: Non-Professional; Non-Profit
Type: Performing; Touring
Purpose: To promote folk art
Volunteer Staff: 3
Non-Paid Artists: 43
Budget: $1,000 - $50,000
Income Sources: Private Foundations/Grants/Endowments; Business/Corporate Donations; Box Office; Individual Donations
Season: September 15 - June 15   **Annual Attendance:** 5,000

Mansfield

INSTRUMENTAL MUSIC

MANSFIELD SYMPHONY SOCIETY, INC.
142 Park Avenue West, Mansfield, OH 44902
(419) 524-5927
Founded: 1930
Arts Area: Symphony; Orchestra; Ensemble
Status: Professional; Non-Profit
Type: Performing; Touring; Educational
Purpose: To present symphony concerts mainly from symphony repertoire including educational and pops programming
Management: Dr. Thomas J. Carto, General Manager; Jeff Holland Cook, Music Director/Conductor; Janet E. Keeler, Development Director
Officers: William McIntyre, President; Jeanne Alexander, Vice President; J. Brad Preston, Secretary; Dan Scurci, Treasurer
Paid Staff: 8   **Volunteer Staff:** 15
Paid Artists: 120
Utilizes: Guest Conductors; Guest Artists
Budget: $100,000 - $500,000
Income Sources: Private Foundations/Grants/Endowments; Business/Corporate Donations; Box Office; Government Grants; Individual Donations
Season: September - May   **Annual Attendance:** 18,000
Affiliations: ASOL; ORACLE; OCCA
Performance Facilities: Renaissance Theater

THEATRE

MANSFIELD PLAYHOUSE
95 East Third Street, Mansfield, OH 44902
(419) 522-8140
Founded: 1929
Arts Area: Musical; Community; Theatrical Group
Status: Non-Professional
Type: Performing; Touring; Resident; Educational
Purpose: To provide entertainment and to encourage the advancement of theatre art in all its branches

Management: Lisa Plant, Artistic Director; Cliff Mears, Business Manager; Gary Simmons, Building Manager; Kathy Maxwell, Secretary/Box Office Manager
Officers: Sondra Asher, President; Lynda Smith, Treasurer; Cliff Mears, Business Manager; Doug Wertz, First Vice President; Maggie Paul, Second Vice President; Gene White, Secretary; Steve Zigmund, Assistant Secretary
Paid Staff: 30   **Volunteer Staff:** 70
Paid Artists: 7
Utilizes: Special Technical Talent; Guest Conductors; Guest Artists; Guest Directors; Guest Musicians
Budget: $100,000 - $500,000
Income Sources: Private Foundations/Grants/Endowments; Business/Corporate Donations; Box Office; Government Grants; Individual Donations
Season: September - June   **Annual Attendance:** 12,000
Affiliations: OTA; OAC; Ohio Community Theatre Alliance

THE RENAISSANCE THEATRE
138 Park Avenue West, Mansfield, OH 44902
(419) 522-2726
Founded: 1979
Arts Area: Professional; Community
Status: Professional; Semi-Professional; Non-Profit; Commercial
Type: Performing; Educational; Sponsoring
Purpose: To operate a community and regional entertainment, cultural, educational and civic center; to preserve and restore the Renaissance Theatre
Management: Tony Miller, Executive Director; Joan Gemzer, Operations Manager; Aaron Ferguson, Technical Director
Paid Staff: 9   **Volunteer Staff:** 350
Utilizes: Special Technical Talent; Guest Conductors; Guest Artists; Guest Directors
Budget: $500,000 - $1,000,000
Income Sources: Private Foundations/Grants/Endowments; Business/Corporate Donations; Box Office; Government Grants; Individual Donations
Season: 52 Weeks   **Annual Attendance:** 125,000
Affiliations: APAP; ORACLE; OTA
Performance Facilities: Renaissance Theatre

FACILITY

CENTRAL PARK BANDSHELL
Mansfield City Square, Mansfield, OH 44902
(419) 755-9819
Type of Facility: Outdoor (Concert); Amphitheater
Type of Stage: Concert Shell
Stage Dimensions: 20'x20'
Seating Capacity: 100
Year Built: 1977   **Architect:** Tim Alexander
Contact for Rental: Park Office
Rental available at no charge

Marietta

INSTRUMENTAL MUSIC

MARIETTA COLLEGE/CIVIC SYMPHONETTE
Department of Music, Marietta College, Marietta, OH 45750
(614) 374-4688
Founded: 1963
Arts Area: Symphony; Orchestra
Status: Non-Professional; Non-Profit
Type: Performing
Purpose: To provide playing experience for students, faculty, and community; to provide the community with an opportunity to hear symphonic music
Management: H. Dean Cummings, Conductor/Manager
Paid Staff: 3
Paid Artists: 8
Utilizes: Guest Artists
Budget: $1,000 - $50,000
Income Sources: Private Foundations/Grants/Endowments
Season: August - May   **Annual Attendance:** 2,000
Affiliations: ASOL; OOOO

Marion

THEATRE

MARION COMMUNITY THEATER
PO Box 981, Marion, OH 43302
(614) 383-2101
>**Founded:** 1963
>**Arts Area:** Musical; Theatrical Group
>**Status:** Non-Professional; Non-Profit
>**Type:** Performing; Educational
>**Purpose:** To stimulate, promote and develop interest in the dramatic arts by operation of a permanent theatre
>**Management:** Val Freeman, Tim McGhee, Kevin Orth, Directors
>**Officers:** Tim McGhee, President; Kathy Heberding, Secretary
>**Volunteer Staff:** 25
>**Non-Paid Artists:** 90
>**Budget:** $50,000 - $100,000
>**Income Sources:** Private Foundations/Grants/Endowments; Business/Corporate Donations; Box Office; Individual Donations
>**Season:** September - June   **Annual Attendance:** 8,000
>**Affiliations:** Ohio Concerned Citizens for the Arts; FACT
>**Performance Facilities:** Palace Theatre

FACILITY

PALACE THEATRE
276 West Center Street, Marion, OH 43302
(614) 383-2101
>**Type of Facility:** Performance Center
>**Type of Stage:** Thrust; Flexible; Proscenium
>**Stage Dimensions:** 49'8"Wx30'D   **Orchestra Pit**
>**Seating Capacity:** 1,431
>**Year Built:** 1928   **Architect:** John Eberson   **Cost:** $500,000
>**Year Remodeled:** 1976   **Architect:** Burris Edwards Lockwood   **Cost:** $550,000
>**Contact for Rental:** Errol Selsby, Managing Director;   (614) 383-2101
>**Resident Groups:** Marion Community Theatre; Marion Concert Association; Marion Travel & Adventure Series; Marion Community Band
>*The Palace Cultural Arts Association manages the theatre*

Mayfield Heights

INSTRUMENTAL MUSIC

THE SHAKER SYMPHONY ORCHESTRA
5910 Mayflower Avenue, Mayfield Heights, OH 44124
(216) 461-7149
>**Founded:** 1938
>**Arts Area:** Symphony; Orchestra
>**Status:** Non-Professional; Non-Profit
>**Type:** Performing; Resident
>**Purpose:** For the weekly meeting and classical music playing by non-professionals of all ages and backgrounds for public free concerts
>**Management:** Henry Schakne, Business Manager
>**Officers:** Dr. J. Werner Kiwi, President; Debbie Horn, Secretary; Bernard Biederman, Treasurer
>**Paid Staff:** 1   **Volunteer Staff:** 9
>**Non-Paid Artists:** 2
>**Utilizes:** Guest Artists
>**Budget:** $1,000 - $50,000
>**Income Sources:** Business/Corporate Donations; Individual Donations
>**Season:** September - May   **Annual Attendance:** 1,500
>**Performance Facilities:** Orange High School Auditorium

Mentor

INSTRUMENTAL MUSIC

THE HERITAGE BRASS QUINTET
6231 Dawson Boulevard, Mentor, OH 44060
(216) 257-4678
>**Founded:** 1981
>**Arts Area:** Ensemble
>**Status:** Professional; Non-Profit
>**Type:** Performing; Touring; Resident; Educational
>**Purpose:** To develop awareness and to give performances of brass quintet literature at the highest level
>**Management:** Erik S. Svoboda, Manager
>**Paid Staff:** 1
>**Paid Artists:** 5
>**Budget:** $1,000 - $50,000
>**Income Sources:** Private Foundations/Grants/Endowments; Business/Corporate Donations; Box Office; Individual Donations

---
New Philadelphia

INSTRUMENTAL MUSIC

TUSCARAWAS PHILHARMONIC
PO Box 406, New Philadelphia, OH 44663
(216) 477-6153
>**Founded:** 1935
>**Arts Area:** Symphony; Orchestra
>**Status:** Semi-Professional; Non-Profit
>**Type:** Performing
>**Purpose:** To bring musical enjoyment to young and old, and improve cultural aspects of the community
>**Management:** Margery Kent Henke, Music Director/Conductor; Robert L. Henke, General Manager
>**Officers:** Melanie Winn, President; Paul Hurd, Vice President; Janice Cosenza, Secretary; Peggy Bears, Treasurer
>**Paid Staff:** 2
>**Paid Artists:** 25   **Non-Paid Artists:** 35
>**Utilizes:** Guest Artists
>**Budget:** $1,000 - $50,000
>**Income Sources:** Private Foundations/Grants/Endowments; Business/Corporate Donations; Box Office; Government Grants; Individual Donations
>**Season:** October - May   **Annual Attendance:** 3,500
>**Performance Facilities:** Dover High School

PERFORMING SERIES

OHIO OUTDOOR HISTORICAL DRAMA ASSOCIATION
PO Box 450, New Philadelphia, OH 44633
(216) 364-5111
>**Founded:** 1967
>**Arts Area:** Musical
>**Status:** Non-Profit
>**Type:** Educational; Sponsoring
>**Purpose:** To produce Paul Green's original outdoor drama, "Trumpet in the Land"
>**Management:** Margaret M. Bonamico, Producer
>**Officers:** Jim Stoll, President; James E. King, Vice President; Rhonda Leeper, Secretary; Todd Turner, Treasurer
>**Paid Staff:** 3   **Volunteer Staff:** 1
>**Paid Artists:** 70
>**Utilizes:** Special Technical Talent; Guest Directors
>**Budget:** $100,000 - $500,000
>**Income Sources:** Private Foundations/Grants/Endowments; Business/Corporate Donations; Box Office; Government Grants; Individual Donations
>**Season:** June - September   **Annual Attendance:** 30,000
>**Affiliations:** AEA
>**Performance Facilities:** Schoenbrunn Amphitheatre

FACILITY

SCHOENBRUNN AMPHITHEATRE
PO Box 450, New Philadelphia, OH 44663
(216) 339-1132; (216) 364-5111
Type of Facility: Amphitheater
Type of Stage: Proscenium
Stage Dimensions: 60'Wx30'D
Seating Capacity: 1,600
Year Built: 1969 **Architect:** Don M. Hisaka   **Cost:** $725,000
Contact for Rental: Manager;   (216) 339-1132

TUSCARAWAS CAMPUS OF KENT STATE UNIVERSITY - AUDITORIUM
University Drive, NE, New Philadelphia, OH 44663
(216) 339-3391
Type of Facility: Auditorium; Film & Lecture Hall
Type of Stage: Proscenium
Seating Capacity: 300
Year Built: 1968 **Architect:** Marr Knapp Crawfis
Year Remodeled: 1971 **Architect:** Marr Knapp Crawfis
Contact for Rental: Tuscarawas Campus of Kent State University;   (216) 339-3391

Niles

FACILITY

TRUMBULL NEW THEATRE
5883 Youngstown-Warren Road, Niles, OH 44446
(216) 652-1103
Type of Facility: Theatre House
Type of Stage: Thrust
Stage Dimensions: 38'Wx30'D
Seating Capacity: 186
Year Built: 1957 **Architect:** Thomas A. Schroth   **Cost:** $50,000
Year Remodeled: 1977 **Cost:** $100,000
Contact for Rental: Manager;   (216) 652-1103

Norwalk

THEATRE

TOWNE AND COUNTRY PLAYERS
55 East Main Street, PO Box 551, Norwalk, OH 44857
(419) 668-1641
Founded: 1966
Arts Area: Musical; Dinner; Community; Theatrical Group
Status: Semi-Professional; Non-Profit
Type: Performing
Purpose: Clean family programs
Management: Ronn Koerper, Executive Director
Officers: Cheryl Gfell, President
Paid Staff: 15 **Volunteer Staff:** 75
Paid Artists: 3 **Non-Paid Artists:** 2
Utilizes: Special Technical Talent; Guest Artists
Budget: $100,000 - $500,000
Income Sources: Private Foundations/Grants/Endowments; Business/Corporate Donations; Box Office;
Individual Donations
Season: 52 Weeks **Annual Attendance:** 50,000

FACILITY

TOWNE AND COUNTRY PLAYERS
55 East Main Street, PO Box 551, Norwalk, OH 44857
(419) 668-1641
Type of Facility: Theatre House
Type of Stage: Proscenium
Stage Dimensions: 30'x25' **Orchestra Pit**

Seating Capacity: 900
Year Built: 1941
Year Remodeled: 1986
Contact for Rental: Ronn Koerper;   (419) 668-1641

Novelty

FACILITY

FAIRMOUNT FINE ARTS CENTER
8400 Fairmount Road, PO Box 80, Novelty, OH 44072
(216) 338-3171
    Type of Facility: Film & Lecture Hall
    Type of Stage: Rehearsal Studio
    Year Built: 1970   **Cost:** $150,000
    Contact for Rental: Marsha Carl;   (216) 338-3171
    Resident Groups: Fairmount Spanish Dancers; Fairmount Dancin' Jazz Company; Fairmount Junior Spanish Dancers
    Studio rental and meetings

Oberlin

INSTRUMENTAL MUSIC

OBERLIN BAROQUE ENSEMBLE
Conservatory of Music, Oberlin College, Oberlin, OH 44074
(216) 338-3171
    Founded: 1973
    Arts Area: Chamber; Ensemble; Instrumental Group
    Status: Professional
    Type: Performing; Touring; Resident; Educational
    Purpose: An ensemble dedicated to performing 17th and 18th-century music on original instruments
    Management: Kathie Stewart
    Paid Staff: 1
    Paid Artists: 4
    Utilizes: Guest Artists
    Budget: $1,000 - $50,000
    Income Sources: Private Foundations/Grants/Endowments; Box Office
    Season: September - July   **Annual Attendance:** 2,000
    Affiliations: Oberlin College Conservatory of Music
    Performance Facilities: Oberlin Conservatory

VOCAL MUSIC

OBERLIN COMMUNITY CHAMBER SINGERS
PO Box 0354, Oberlin, OH 44074
(216) 774-2226
    Founded: 1966
    Arts Area: Choral
    Status: Non-Profit
    Type: Performing; Touring; Educational
    Purpose: To bring together excellent musicians to learn and perform a wide variety of quality choral repertoire; to specialize in music by female or black composers; to provide staged programs as well as others
    Management: Fran Baumann, Concert Manager; Carol Longsworth, Music Director
    Officers: Sharon Morgan, President; Brian Schieferstein, Vice President; Doug Fox, Secretary; Marion Drummond, Treasurer
    Paid Staff: 2   **Volunteer Staff:** 20
    Paid Artists: 2   **Non-Paid Artists:** 22
    Utilizes: Guest Artists; Guest Directors
    Budget: $1,000 - $50,000
    Income Sources: Private Foundations/Grants/Endowments; Business/Corporate Donations; Box Office; Government Grants; Individual Donations
    Season: September - June   **Annual Attendance:** 1,000

Oxford

INSTRUMENTAL MUSIC

MIAMI WIND QUINTET
Department of Music, Miami University, Oxford, OH 45056
(513) 529-1809, ext. 3014
FAX: (513) 529-3841
Founded: 1985
Arts Area: Chamber; Instrumental Group
Status: Professional
Type: Performing; Touring; Resident; Educational
Purpose: Perform chamber music for winds and assist young wind players
Management: Cathy McVey, Director of Audience Development
Paid Staff: 1
Paid Artists: 5
Utilizes: Guest Artists
Budget: $1,000 - $50,000
Income Sources: Private Foundations/Grants/Endowments
Season: August - May   **Annual Attendance:** 7,000
Affiliations: Miami University
Performance Facilities: Souers Recital Hall, Miami University

---

Parma Heights

FACILITY

CUYAHOGA COMMUNITY COLLEGE - WESTERN CAMPUS THEATRE
11000 Pleasant Valley, Parma Heights, OH 44130
(216) 842-7773
Type of Facility: Theatre Complex
Type of Stage: Proscenium
Stage Dimensions: 20'x40'x40'
Orchestra Pit
Seating Capacity: 476
Year Built: 1975
Architect: Caudill Rowlett Scott; Lipaj Woyer & Tomsick
Cost: $2,000,000
Contact for Rental: Kathy Moskin;   (216) 987-5051
Manager: Michael Stone
Resident Groups: Western Campus Theatre; Cleveland Philharmonic

---

Shaker Heights

INSTRUMENTAL MUSIC

CLEVELAND BAROQUE SOLOISTS
268 Bratemahl Place, Shaker Heights, OH 44120
(216) 751-5327; (216) 268-1729
Founded: 1972
Arts Area: Chamber; VOCAL
Status: Professional; Non-Profit
Type: Performing; Touring; Resident; Educational
Purpose: To present a wide variety of vocal works and instrumental works on historically appropriate instruments
Management: Beverly Simmons, Artists Manager; Doris Ornstein, Director
Paid Staff: 1
Paid Artists: 5
Utilizes: Guest Artists
Budget: $1,000 - $50,000
Income Sources: Box Office
Season: 52 Weeks   **Annual Attendance:** 8,000
Affiliations: Cleveland Institute of Music; Case Western Reserve University
Performance Facilities: Cleveland Institute of Music Concert Hall; Harkness Chapel

HOTFOOT QUARTET
3712 Traynham Road, Shaker Heights, OH 44122
(216) 991-4911
Founded: 1978
Arts Area: Ensemble; Folk; Band
Status: Professional
Type: Performing, Touring; Educational
Purpose: To perform modern and traditional Bluegrass music
Management: Robert Frank, Business Manager
Officers: Quartet members - Robert Frank, Guitarist; Roland Kausen, Mandolin; Ron Jarvis, Bass; John Saunders, Banjo
Paid Artists: 4
Budget: $1,000 - $50,000
Income Sources: Box Office
Season: 52 Weeks

THEATRE

UNITARIAN PLAYERS
21600 Shaker Boulevard, Shaker Heights, OH 44122
(216) 751-0715
Founded: 1955
Arts Area: Community
Status: Non-Professional; Non-Profit
Type: Performing
Purpose: To provide a vehicle of expression for cast and crew as well as entertainment for a thoughtful audience
Management: Board of Directors
Officers: Benham Bates, President; Dale Clark, Secretary; Carol Bates, Treasurer
Volunteer Staff: 50
Budget: $1,000 - $50,000
Income Sources: Box Office
Season: September - June   **Annual Attendance:** 800

FACILITY

UNITARIAN PLAYERS
21600 Shaker Boulevard, Shaker Heights, OH 44122
(216) 751-2320
Type of Facility: Auditorium; Multi-Purpose
Facility Originally: Church; Meeting Hall; Movie House
Type of Stage: Proscenium
Stage Dimensions: 30'Wx24'D
Seating Capacity: 120
Year Built: 1955   **Architect:** Philip Small
Year Remodeled: 1985
Contact for Rental: Carol Gibson;   (216) 751-2320
Resident Groups: Unitarian Players

Springfield

INSTRUMENTAL MUSIC

SPRINGFIELD SYMPHONY ORCHESTRA
PO Box 1374, Springfield, OH 45501
(513) 325-8100
Founded: 1944
Arts Area: Symphony; Chamber
Status: Professional; Non-Profit
Type: Performing; Sponsoring
Purpose: To provide the best in symphonic music to the entire community and music education to young people
Management: Gregory Anthes, Executive Director
Officers: Maxine E. Harris, President
Paid Staff: 2
Paid Artists: 86
Utilizes: Guest Conductors; Guest Artists
Budget: $100,000 - $500,000
Income Sources: Private Foundations/Grants/Endowments; Business/Corporate Donations; Box Office; Government Grants; Individual Donations

Season: October - April   Annual Attendance: 6,800
Affiliations: ASOL
Performance Facilities: North Auditorium

VOCAL MUSIC

OHIO LYRIC THEATRE
PO Box 432, Springfield, OH 45501
(513) 323-7755
Founded: 1962
Arts Area: Lyric Opera; Light Opera; Choral; Musical Theatre
Status: Semi-Professional; Non-Profit
Type: Performing; Touring; Educational; Sponsoring
Purpose: To produce and promote quality vocal music/musical theatre experiences in order to progress cultural enrichment and the appreciation of lyric theater and vocal music presentations
Management: Cindy Needles, General Manager
Officers: Kathleen Wilkins, President; Trudi Byrd, Vice President; Marilyn Engle, Secretary; Linda Berger, Treasurer
Paid Staff: 1
Utilizes: Special Technical Talent; Guest Conductors; Guest Artists; Guest Directors
Budget: $1,000 - $50,000
Income Sources: Private Foundations/Grants/Endowments; Business/Corporate Donations; Box Office; Government Grants; Individual Donations
Season: 52 Weeks   Annual Attendance: 10,000
Affiliations: Springfield Arts Council; OAC; NOA; COS
Performance Facilities: Veteran's Park Amphitheater; Kuss Auditorium

PERFORMING SERIES

WITTENBERG UNIVERSITY - WITTENBERG SERIES
PO Box 720, Springfield, OH 45501
(513) 327-6231
FAX: (513) 327-6340
Founded: 1845
Arts Area: Dance; Vocal Music; Instrumental Music; Theater; Grand Opera
Status: Non-Profit
Type: Educational; Sponsoring
Purpose: To enrich the cultural life of the Springfield and Wittenberg and to fulfill the University's mission
Management: Gwen Scheffel, Series Coordinator
Paid Staff: 1   Volunteer Staff: 9
Utilizes: Guest Artists
Budget: $50,000 - $100,000
Income Sources: Private Foundations/Grants/Endowments; Business/Corporate Donations; Individual Donations; University Funding
Season: September - June
Performance Facilities: Weaver Chapel; Student Center; HPERC-Gym 2

Sylvania

FACILITY

FRANCISCAN LIFE CENTER
6832 Convent Boulevard, Sylvania, OH 43560
(419) 885-1547
FAX: (419) 882-2981
Founded: 1981
Type of Facility: Theatre Complex; Auditorium; Multi-Purpose
Type of Stage: Flexible; Proscenium
Seating Capacity: 872
Year Built: 1981   Architect: Angel, Mull and Associates   Cost: $8,000,000
Contact for Rental: Patricia Zajac;   (419) 885-1547
Resident Groups: Toledo Repertoire Theatre; Toledo Symphony Mainly Mozart Series

---
Toledo

DANCE

THE TOLEDO BALLET SCHOOL
Franklin Park Mall Shopping Center, Toledo, OH 43623
(419) 471-0049
> **Founded:** 1958
> **Arts Area:** Ballet; Jazz
> **Status:** Professional; Semi-Professional; Non-Professional; Non-Profit
> **Type:** Performing; Touring; Resident; Educational; Sponsoring
> **Purpose:** To provide performing opportunities for area dancers, quality dance to the community, dance scholarships and dance education
> **Management:** Marie Bollinger Vogt, Artistic Director/Founder; Jack Jones Jr., Business Manager; Roger L. Benham Jr., Assistant Business Manager
> **Officers:** James Bugert, President; Dan Jenks, III, Mrs. D.L. Schwartz, Mrs. John P. Stockwell, Vice Presidents; Mrs. Duane Schooley, Mrs. W.E. Willie, Secretaries; Michael L. DeBacker, Treasurer
> **Volunteer Staff:** 50
> **Paid Artists:** 41 **Non-Paid Artists:** 23
> **Utilizes:** Guest Conductors; Guest Artists
> **Budget:** $100,000 - $500,000
> **Income Sources:** Private Foundations/Grants/Endowments; Business/Corporate Donations; Box Office; Government Grants; Individual Donations
> **Season:** September - June **Annual Attendance:** 15,000
> **Affiliations:** Ohio Dance
> **Performance Facilities:** Lourdes Auditorium; Masonic Auditorium

INSTRUMENTAL MUSIC

BRAVADO STRING QUARTET
2619 Sherbrooke Road, Toledo, OH 43606
(419) 471-9751
> **Founded:** 1980
> **Arts Area:** Chamber; Ensemble; Instrumental Group
> **Status:** Semi-Professional
> **Type:** Performing; Resident
> **Purpose:** To perform at various public and private functions throughout northwest Ohio and southeast Michigan
> **Management:** Risa Sindel, Manager
> **Budget:** $1,000 - $50,000
> **Income Sources:** Business/Corporate Donations
> **Season:** 52 Weeks

TOLEDO JAZZ SOCIETY
1700 North Reynolds Road, Toledo, OH 43615
(419) 531-9935
> **Founded:** 1980
> **Arts Area:** Orchestra; Ensemble; Band
> **Status:** Professional; Non-Profit
> **Type:** Performing; Resident; Educational; Sponsoring
> **Purpose:** To promote the performance and preservation of the jazz art form through educational programs, concerts, lectures, and the fostering of the Toledo Jazz Orchestra
> **Officers:** Bart Polot, President; Richard Shell, Vice President; Joan DiRondo, Secretary; Susan Gilmore, Treasurer
> **Volunteer Staff:** 10
> **Paid Artists:** 82
> **Utilizes:** Guest Artists
> **Budget:** $50,000 - $100,000
> **Income Sources:** Private Foundations/Grants/Endowments; Business/Corporate Donations; Box Office; Government Grants; Individual Donations
> **Season:** 52 Weeks **Annual Attendance:** 37,400
> **Affiliations:** APAP; Arts Midwest
> **Performance Facilities:** The Embers

THE TOLEDO SYMPHONY
One Stranahan Square, Toledo, OH 43604
(419) 241-1272
FAX: (419) 321-6890
> **Founded:** 1943
> **Arts Area:** Symphony; Orchestra; Chamber; Ensemble; Instrumental Group

Status: Professional; Non-Profit
Type: Performing; Touring; Educational
Purpose: To furnish performances of the highest artistic caliber to the widest possible audience; to conduct public service and education functions
Management: Robert Bell, Managing Director; Andrew Massey, Music Director; John Hancock, Orchestra Manager
Officers: Robert Lanigan, President, Board of Trustees
Paid Staff: 13
Paid Artists: 17
Utilizes: Guest Conductors; Guest Artists
Budget: $1,000,000 - $5,000,000
Income Sources: Private Foundations/Grants/Endowments; Business/Corporate Donations; Box Office; Government Grants; Individual Donations
Season: September - May
Performance Facilities: Toledo Museum of Art Peristyle

VOCAL MUSIC

TOLEDO OPERA
1700 North Reynolds Road, Toledo, OH 43615
(419) 531-5511
FAX: (419) 531-7196
Founded: 1959
Arts Area: Grand Opera; Lyric Opera; Light Opera
Status: Professional; Non-Profit
Type: Performing; Touring; Educational
Purpose: To present opera and works of an operatic nature to the communities of northwestern Ohio and southern Michigan; to conduct widespread community outreach programs and offer educational apprenticeship programs through the schools
Management: James Meena, Artistic Director; Joan Eckermann, Company/Education Coordinator
Officers: Marina Lury, President; Jon W. Klotz, First Vice President; Joseph M. Colturi, Eugene R. Wos, Sam Boteck Jr., Worth W. Wilson, Vice Presidents; Orval Seydlitz, Mark K. Hemsatch, Treasurers; Lyman F. Spitzer, Secretary
Paid Staff: 4
Paid Artists: 75   **Non-Paid Artists:** 50
Utilizes: Special Technical Talent; Guest Conductors; Guest Artists; Guest Directors
Budget: $100,000 - $500,000
Income Sources: Private Foundations/Grants/Endowments; Business/Corporate Donations; Box Office; Government Grants; Individual Donations
Season: October - May   **Annual Attendance:** 7,500
Affiliations: OA; AGMA; IATSE; AFM
Performance Facilities: Toledo Masonic Auditorium

THEATRE

THE TOLEDO REP
16 Tenth Street, Toledo, OH 43624
(419) 243-7335
Founded: 1933
Arts Area: Theatrical Group
Status: Semi-Professional; Non-Profit
Type: Performing; Educational
Purpose: To entertain, educate, and provide services to the Greater Toledo Area and surrounding communities
Management: Matthew Parent, Producing Artistic Director
Officers: Douglas Braun, Chairman of the Board; Michael Calabrese, President; Carlane Miller, Second Vice President
Paid Staff: 8   **Volunteer Staff:** 25
Utilizes: Special Technical Talent; Guest Conductors; Guest Artists; Guest Directors
Budget: $100,000 - $500,000
Income Sources: Private Foundations/Grants/Endowments; Business/Corporate Donations; Box Office; Government Grants; Individual Donations
Season: September - June   **Annual Attendance:** 35,000
Affiliations: Ohio Concerned Citizens for the Arts

PERFORMING SERIES

THE TOLEDO MUSEUM OF ART
2445 Monroe Street, Box 1013, Toledo, OH 43697
(419) 255-8000
Founded: 1901
Arts Area: Dance; Vocal Music; Instrumental Music; Theater; Lyric Opera

Status: Non-Profit
Type: Performing; Educational; Sponsoring
Purpose: To present the finest local, national and international performing artists
Management: Joyce E. Smar, Manager of Performing Arts; Annette Baker, Performing Arts Assistant; Ann Mather, Coordinator of Ticketing Services
Paid Staff: 8   **Volunteer Staff:** 80
Paid Artists: 5   **Non-Paid Artists:** 40
Utilizes: Guest Artists
Budget: $100,000 - $500,000
Income Sources: Private Foundations/Grants/Endowments; Business/Corporate Donations; Box Office; Government Grants; Individual Donations
Season: September - May   **Annual Attendance:** 60,000
Affiliations: APAP; BOMI; ISPAA; League of Historical American Theaters
Performance Facilities: Peristyle; Great Gallery; Little Theatre

FACILITY

OHIO THEATRE
3114 Lagrange Street, Toledo, OH 43608
(419) 241-6785
    Founded: 1976
    Type of Facility: Concert Hall; Auditorium; Theatre House; Multi-Purpose
    Facility Originally: Vaudeville; Movie House
    Type of Stage: Thrust
    Stage Dimensions: 40'x60'
    Seating Capacity: 975
    Year Built: 1921
    Contact for Rental: Roxanne Stone;   (419) 241-6785

TOLEDO MASONIC AUDITORIUM
4645 Heather Downs Boulevard, Toledo, OH 43614
(419) 381-8851
    Type of Facility: Concert Hall; Auditorium; Theatre House; Opera House
    Type of Stage: Proscenium; Hydraulic Lift Stage
    Stage Dimensions: 48'x60'   **Orchestra Pit**
    Seating Capacity: 2,520
    Year Built: 1969
    Contact for Rental: Penny Marks;   (419) 381-8851

THE TOLEDO MUSEUM OF ART - PERISTYLE
2445 Monroe Street, Box 1013, Toledo, OH 43697
(419) 255-8000
FAX: (419) 255-8534
    Type of Facility: Museum
    Type of Stage: Proscenium
    Stage Dimensions: 45'Wx35'D   **Orchestra Pit**
    Seating Capacity: 1,752
    Year Built: 1933   **Architect:** E.B. Green & Son   **Cost:** $1,000,000
    Acoustical Consultant: Clifford Swan
    Contact for Rental: Manager of Performing Arts;   (419) 255-8000
    Resident Groups: Toledo Symphony; Toledo Choral Society
    Available for rental to non-profit groups only

Upper Arlington

PERFORMING SERIES

UPPER ARLINGTON CULTURAL ARTS COMMISSION
3600 Tremont Road, Upper Arlington, OH 43220
(614) 457-5080, ext. 324
FAX: (614) 457-6620
    Founded: 1972
    Arts Area: Dance; Vocal Music; Instrumental Music; Theater; Festivals; Lyric Opera
    Status: Non-Profit
    Type: Sponsoring
    Purpose: To encourage, promote and provide cultural activities and opportunities for the enrichment of the lives of the community
    Management: Doris T. Nelson, Arts Manager

Officers: Jan Schmidt, Chairman; William C. Lamneck, Vice Chairman
Paid Staff: 1 **Volunteer Staff:** 16
Paid Artists: 300
Utilizes: Guest Conductors; Guest Artists
Budget: $50,000 - $100,000
Income Sources: Private Foundations/Grants/Endowments; Business/Corporate Donations; Box Office; Government Grants
Annual Attendance: 7,000
Performance Facilities: Upper Arlington Municipal Center

Warren

INSTRUMENTAL MUSIC

THE JAZZ REVIVAL ORCHESTRA
2252 Wilson NE, Warren, OH 44483
(216) 372-1933
Founded: 1985
Arts Area: Ensemble; Instrumental Group
Status: Semi-Professional; Non-Profit
Type: Performing; Educational
Purpose: To educate and entertain
Officers: Dennis Reynolds, Chairman; Rich Rollo, President; Mike Kamuf, Vice President; John Veneskey, Secretary/Treasurer
Volunteer Staff: 4
Paid Artists: 17
Utilizes: Guest Artists
Budget: $1,000 - $50,000
Income Sources: Box Office; Government Grants; Individual Donations
Season: 52 Weeks

PERFORMING SERIES

WARREN CIVIC MUSIC ASSOCIATION
PO Box 1052, 837 Trumbull SE, Warren, OH 44484
(216) 369-5670
Founded: 1937
Arts Area: Dance; Vocal Music; Instrumental Music; Theater; Lyric Opera; Grand Opera
Status: Professional; Semi-Professional; Non-Profit
Type: Performing; Educational; Sponsoring
Purpose: To build and maintain a permanent concert audience in Warren and surrounding areas; to cultivate interest in music and encourage the performance of music by qualified artists
Officers: Robert I. Lowry, President; Mrs. Kenneth C. Gibson, George F. Gilbert, K. Robert Matheny and William E. Mottice, Vice Presidents; Phillip R. Meigs, Treasurer; David R. Vogt, Assistant Treasurer; Carole Menelle, Secretary; Jeannette Dietz, Membership
Volunteer Staff: 15
Budget: $50,000 - $100,000
Income Sources: Private Foundations/Grants/Endowments; Business/Corporate Donations; Box Office; Government Grants; Individual Donations
Season: September - April **Annual Attendance:** 10,000
Affiliations: Ohio Arts Council
Performance Facilities: W.D. Packard Music Hall and Convention Center

West Liberty

THEATRE

MAD RIVER THEATER WORKS
105 1/2 North Detroit Street, West Liberty, OH 43357
(513) 465-6751
Founded: 1978
Arts Area: Professional; Musical; Theatrical Group
Status: Professional; Non-Profit
Type: Performing; Touring; Resident; Educational
Purpose: To preserve the rich heritage of the Midwest by collecting stories and crafting them into plays that depict life around the turn of the century, all adapted from true stories
Management: Jeff Hooper, Producing Director; Margaret A. Heinlen, Administrative Director

Officers: Shelley Wammes, Chair; Joyce Woodruff, Vice Chair; Bill Montgomey, Secretary
Paid Staff: 3   **Volunteer Staff:** 60
Paid Artists: 20
Utilizes: Special Technical Talent; Guest Artists; Guest Directors
Budget: $100,000 - $500,000
Income Sources: Private Foundations/Grants/Endowments; Business/Corporate Donations; Box Office; Government Grants; Individual Donations
Season: 52 Weeks   **Annual Attendance:** 65,000
Affiliations: TCG

Westerville

INSTRUMENTAL MUSIC

WESTERVILLE CIVIC SYMPHONY
170 West Park Street, Westerville, OH 43081
(614) 895-1102
> **Founded:** 1982
> **Arts Area:** Symphony; Orchestra; Ensemble
> **Status:** Non-Professional; Non-Profit
> **Type:** Performing; Educational
> **Purpose:** A non-profit, charitable corporation functioning as an aesthetic, educational and cultural resource, presenting performances primarily of symphonic music; an artistic outlet for amateur and semi-professional musicians
> **Management:** Jeanne Earhart, Business Manager
> **Officers:** Donna Kerr, President, Board of Trustees; John Gale, Vice President; Lyle Barkhymer, Secretary; Michael Howard, Treasurer
> **Paid Staff:** 2
> **Paid Artists:** 20   **Non-Paid Artists:** 50
> **Utilizes:** Guest Artists
> **Budget:** $1,000 - $50,000
> **Income Sources:** Private Foundations/Grants/Endowments; Business/Corporate Donations; Box Office; Government Grants; Individual Donations
> **Season:** September - July   **Annual Attendance:** 2,400
> **Performance Facilities:** Cowan Hall, Otterbein College

FACILITY

COWAN HALL
30 Grove Street, Westerville, OH 43081
(614) 898-1657
FAX: (614) 898-1898
> **Founded:** 1959
> **Type of Facility:** Theatre Complex; Concert Hall; Auditorium; Theatre House; Multi-Purpose
> **Type of Stage:** Proscenium
> **Stage Dimensions:** 44'2"Wx30'Dx20'H
> **Seating Capacity:** 1,120
> **Year Built:** 1959
> **Contact for Rental:** Jeanne Augustus;   (614) 898-1657
> **Resident Groups:** Otterbein College - various groups

Wooster

INSTRUMENTAL MUSIC

WOOSTER SYMPHONY ORCHESTRA
College of Wooster, Music Department, Wooster, OH 44691
(216) 263-2047
> **Founded:** 1915
> **Arts Area:** Symphony; Orchestra
> **Status:** Non-Professional
> **Type:** Performing; Resident
> **Purpose:** To bring live orchestral repertoire to the community
> **Paid Staff:** 2
> **Paid Artists:** 12   **Non-Paid Artists:** 48
> **Utilizes:** Guest Artists
> **Budget:** $1,000 - $50,000
> **Income Sources:** Box Office; Individual Donations

Season: November - April **Annual Attendance:** 3,800
Affiliations: College of Wooster
Performance Facilities: McGaw Chapel

Yellow Springs

INSTRUMENTAL MUSIC

CHAMBER MUSIC IN YELLOW SPRINGS, INC.
Box 448, Yellow Springs, OH 45387
(513) 767-1458
FAX: (513) 767-9350
Founded: 1983
Arts Area: Chamber
Status: Professional; Non-Profit
Type: Sponsoring
Purpose: To present high quality professional chamber music performances
Officers: Bruce Bradtmiller, President; Ruth Bunt, Vice President; Barbara Mann, Secretary; Kenneth Tregillus, Treasurer
Paid Artists: 6
Utilizes: Guest Artists
Budget: $1,000 - $50,000
Income Sources: Private Foundations/Grants/Endowments; Business/Corporate Donations; Box Office; Government Grants; Individual Donations
Season: October - April **Annual Attendance:** 900
Performance Facilities: First Presbyterian Church

THE EARLY MUSIC CENTER
242 Northwood Drive, Yellow Springs, OH 45387
(513) 767-8181
Founded: 1979
Arts Area: Chamber; Instrumental Group
Status: Professional; Non-Profit
Type: Performing; Touring; Resident; Educational; Sponsoring
Purpose: To perform and encourage the performance of music written before 1750
Management: Patricia Olds, Director
Paid Staff: 1 **Volunteer Staff:** 1
Paid Artists: 4
Utilizes: Guest Artists **Budget:** $1,000 - $50,000
Income Sources: Private Foundations/Grants/Endowments; Business/Corporate Donations; Box Office; Government Grants; Individual Donations
Season: 52 Weeks **Annual Attendance:** 10,000

Youngstown

DANCE

BALLET WESTERN RESERVE
1361 Fifth Avenue, Youngstown, OH 44504
(216) 744-1934
Founded: 1962
Arts Area: Modern; Ballet; Jazz
Status: Non-Professional; Non-Profit
Type: Performing; Educational
Purpose: To promote interest in ballet, modern dance and jazz, arrange performances and prepare students for performance and professional dance careers
Management: Anita Lin O'Donnell, Director; Kathy DuBois, Office Manager
Officers: Alan Goldberg and Sara Kennedy, Co-Presidents; James Kennedy, First Vice President; Charlene Pastoro, Second Vice President; Patti Keenan, Secretary; Kathy DuBois, Treasurer
Paid Staff: 7 **Volunteer Staff:** 25
Utilizes: Special Technical Talent; Guest Artists; Guest Choreographers
Budget: $100,000 - $500,000
Income Sources: Private Foundations/Grants/Endowments; Business/Corporate Donations; Box Office; Individual Donations
Season: September - July **Annual Attendance:** 15,000
Performance Facilities: Youngstown State University; Powers Auditorium; Stambaugh Auditorium; Penn State University

INSTRUMENTAL MUSIC

YOUNGSTOWN SYMPHONY ORCHESTRA
260 Federal Plaza West, Youngstown, OH 44503
(216) 744-4269
> **Founded:** 1931
> **Arts Area:** Symphony
> **Status:** Professional; Non-Profit
> **Type:** Performing; Resident; Educational
> **Management:** Patricia C. Syak, General Manager
> **Paid Staff:** 10
> **Paid Artists:** 85   **Non-Paid Artists:** 150
> **Utilizes:** Special Technical Talent; Guest Conductors; Guest Artists; Guest Directors
> **Budget:** $1,000,000 - $5,000,000
> **Income Sources:** Private Foundations/Grants/Endowments; Business/Corporate Donations; Box Office; Government Grants; Individual Donations
> **Season:** September - May   **Annual Attendance:** 50,000
> **Affiliations:** ASOL; OOOO
> **Performance Facilities:** Youngstown Symphony Center, Edward W. Powers Auditorium

VOCAL MUSIC

YOUNGSTOWN MUSICA SACRA
323 Wick Avenue, Youngstown, OH 44503
(216) 743-3175
> **Founded:** 1980
> **Arts Area:** Choral
> **Status:** Semi-Professional
> **Type:** Performing; Resident
> **Purpose:** To perform masterpieces of sacred choral literature in liturgical and concert settings
> **Management:** Dr. Ronald L. Gould, Daniel W. Laginua, Co-Conductors
> **Utilizes:** Guest Artists
> **Budget:** $1,000 - $50,000
> **Income Sources:** Private Foundations/Grants/Endowments; Individual Donations
> **Season:** October - May

FACILITY

STAMBAUGH AUDITORIUM
Monday Musical Club Inc., 1000 Fifth Avenue, Youngstown, OH 44504-1603
(216) 743-2617
> **Founded:** 1896
> **Type of Facility:** Concert Hall; Auditorium; Lecture Room; Ballroom
> **Type of Stage:** Proscenium
> **Stage Dimensions:** 60'Wx27'   **Orchestra Pit**
> **Seating Capacity:** 2,535
> **Year Built:** 1925   **Architect:** Harvey Wiley Corbett   **Cost:** $1,500,000
> **Contact for Rental:** Barbara J. Armstrong;   (216) 747-5175
> *For the enjoyment, pleasure, entertainment, and education of the community of Youngstown and the contigous area.*

THE YOUNGSTOWN PLAYHOUSE
600 Playhouse Lane, Youngstown, OH 44511
(216) 788-8739
FAX: (216) 788-1208
> **Type of Facility:** Theatre Complex; Auditorium; Studio Performance; Environmental; Performance Center; Arena; Multi-Purpose; Room; Loft
> **Type of Stage:** Flexible; Proscenium; Arena
> **Stage Dimensions:** 34'Wx36'D; 34'Wx18'H proscenium opening   **Orchestra Pit**
> **Seating Capacity:** Auditorium - 624; Arena - 120
> **Year Built:** 1959   **Architect:** Jones & Buchanon
> **Contact for Rental:** Charles H. Reed;   (216) 788-8739
> **Resident Groups:** Youngstown Community Theatre; Youngstown Youth Theatre

YOUNGSTOWN STATE UNIVERSITY - BLISS RECITAL HALL
410 Wick Avenue, Youngstown, OH 44555
(216) 742-3636
> **Type of Facility:** Concert Hall; Multi-Purpose
> **Type of Stage:** Greek

Stage Dimensions: 60'Wx35'D
Seating Capacity: 250
Year Built: 1977 **Architect:** Caudill Rowlett Scott **Cost:** $2,600,000
Acoustical Consultant: Caudill Rowlett Scott
Contact for Rental: Rocco Mediate; (216) 742-3115

YOUNGSTOWN STATE UNIVERSITY - FORD THEATRE
410 Wick Avenue, Youngstown, OH 44555
(216) 742-3625
FAX: (216) 742-3499
Type of Facility: Auditorium; Performance Center; Theatre House
Type of Stage: Proscenium
Stage Dimensions: 36'Wx28'D
Orchestra Pit
Seating Capacity: 425
Year Built: 1973 **Architect:** Caudill Rowlett Scott **Cost:** $6,000,000
Contact for Rental: Rocco A. Mediate; (216) 742-3115
Resident Groups: Youngstown State University Theatre

YOUNGSTOWN STATE UNIVERSITY - SPOTLIGHT ARENA THEATRE
410 Wick Avenue, Youngstown, OH 44555
(216) 742-3625
Type of Facility: Studio Performance; Arena
Type of Stage: Flexible; 3/4 Arena; Arena
Stage Dimensions: 16'x21'
Seating Capacity: 200
Year Built: 1973 **Architect:** Caudill Rowlett Scott **Cost:** $6,000,000
Contact for Rental: Rocco A. Mediate; (216) 742-3115
Resident Groups: Youngstown State University Theatre

YOUNGSTOWN SYMPHONY CENTER - POWERS AUDITORIUM
260 Federal Plaza West, Youngstown, OH 44503
(216) 744-4269
FAX: (216) 744-1441
Type of Facility: Auditorium
Type of Stage: Proscenium
Orchestra Pit
Seating Capacity: 2,351
Year Built: 1930 **Cost:** $1,500,000
Year Remodeled: 1969 **Architect:** Damon, Worley, Cady, Kirk **Cost:** $1,000,000
Acoustical Consultant: Christopher Jaffe
Contact for Rental: Patricia Syak
Resident Groups: Youngstown Symphony Orchestra; Youngstown Symphony Chorus; Youngstown Symphony Youth Orchestra; Junior League Town Hall Lecture Series; Youngstown State University Lectures

Zanesville

INSTRUMENTAL MUSIC

ZANESVILLE CHAMBER ORCHESTRA
1102 South Slope Bay, Zanesville, OH 43761
(614) 453-4925
Founded: 1982
Arts Area: Chamber
Status: Semi-Professional; Non-Profit
Type: Performing; Educational; Sponsoring
Purpose: To promote music for string orchestra and string chamber ensemble
Management: Renee Shaw, Executive Director
Paid Staff: 1 **Volunteer Staff:** 3
Non-Paid Artists: 15
Utilizes: Guest Artists
Budget: $1,000 - $50,000
Income Sources: Private Foundations/Grants/Endowments; Business/Corporate Donations; Box Office; Individual Donations
Season: 52 Weeks **Annual Attendance:** 400
Performance Facilities: Zanesville Art Center

FACILITY

ZANESVILLE ART CENTER
620 Military Road, Zanesville, OH 43701
(614) 452-0741
Type of Facility: Auditorium
Facility Originally: Private Residence
Type of Stage: Platform
Stage Dimensions: 18'x22'
Seating Capacity: 125
Year Remodeled: 1985   **Architect:** Richard Dittmar & Associates   **Cost:** $400,000
Contact for Rental: Mrs. Joseph Howell;   (614) 452-0741
Resident Groups: Thursday Music Club; Junior Music Club; Beaux Arts Club

OKLAHOMA

Ada

FACILITY

EAST CENTRAL UNIVERSITY - DOROTHY I. SUMMERS THEATER
Ada, OK 74820-6899
(405) 332-8000
> **Type of Facility:** Theatre Complex; Concert Hall; Auditorium; Performance Center; Theatre House;
> Multi-Purpose
> **Type of Stage:** Proscenium
> **Seating Capacity:** 600
> **Contact for Rental:** Dr. Bob Payne;   (405) 332-8000

Alva

FACILITY

ALVA MEMORIAL AUDITORIUM
14th and Flynn, Alva, OK 73717
(405) 327-4823
> **Type of Facility:** Auditorium
> **Type of Stage:** Platform
> **Seating Capacity:** 900
> **Year Built:** 1956   **Architect:** Dow Gumerson   **Cost:** $200,000
> **Contact for Rental:** Lynn Hoskins;   (405) 327-4823

ALVA PUBLIC LIBRARY AUDITORIUM
504 Seventh, Alva, OK 73717
(405) 327-1833
> **Type of Facility:** Auditorium
> **Facility Originally:** Library
> **Seating Capacity:** 150
> **Year Remodeled:** 1963   **Architect:** Lawrence & Fletcher   **Cost:** $350,000
> **Contact for Rental:** Larry Thorne;   (405) 327-1833
> *Promotion of the arts*

Ardmore

THEATRE

ARDMORE LITTLE THEATRE
PO Box 245, Ardmore, OK 73402
(405) 223-6387
> **Founded:** 1955
> **Arts Area:** Community
> **Status:** Non-Profit
> **Type:** Performing
> **Purpose:** To provide live theatre to Ardmore and the surrounding communities and act as a local showcase for talent
> **Management:** Board of Directors elected by membership
> **Officers:** Charles Tate, President; Lil Williams, Vice President; Carla Reasoner, Secretary; Joel Wellnitz, Treasurer
> **Volunteer Staff:** 20
> **Non-Paid Artists:** 150
> **Utilizes:** Special Technical Talent; Guest Directors
> **Budget:** $1,000 - $50,000
> **Income Sources:** Business/Corporate Donations; Box Office; Government Grants; Individual Donations
> **Season:** September - April
> **Annual Attendance:** 4,000
> **Affiliations:** Oklahoma Community Theatre Association; SWTC
> **Performance Facilities:** Charles B. Goddard Center

FACILITY

CHARLES B. GODDARD CENTER
First Avenue and D Street SW, Ardmore, OK 73401
(405) 226-0909
>**Type of Facility:** Theatre Complex; Concert Hall; Performance Center; Civic Center
>**Type of Stage:** Proscenium
>**Stage Dimensions:** 50'x54'x36'
>**Seating Capacity:** 350
>**Year Built:** 1970   **Architect:** Flood-Isenberg-Hann   **Cost:** $1,040,000
>**Year Remodeled:** 1986   **Architect:** Isenberg-Hann   **Cost:** $290,000
>**Contact for Rental:** Mort Halmilton; Becky Jones;   (405) 226-0909
>**Resident Groups:** Ardmore Little Theatre

Bartlesville

DANCE

BARTLESVILLE CIVIC BALLET
PO Box 921, Bartlesville, OK 74005
(918) 336-4746
>**Founded:** 1970
>**Arts Area:** Ballet
>**Status:** Non-Professional; Non-Profit
>**Type:** Performing; Resident
>**Purpose:** To offer youngsters the opportunity to perform ballet for the community
>**Management:** Charlotte Lyke, Artistic Director
>**Officers:** Glenn E. Davis, President; William J. Carter, Executive Vice President; Phil Blender, Treasurer
>**Non-Paid Artists:** 25
>**Utilizes:** Guest Artists; Guest Choreographers
>**Budget:** $50,000 - $100,000
>**Income Sources:** Private Foundations/Grants/Endowments; Business/Corporate Donations; Box Office; Individual Donations
>**Season:** Fall - Spring   **Annual Attendance:** 4,000
>**Performance Facilities:** Bartlesville Community Center

INSTRUMENTAL MUSIC

BARTLESVILLE SYMPHONY ORCHESTRA
PO Box 263, Bartlesville, OK 74005
(918) 333-8287
>**Founded:** 1957
>**Arts Area:** Symphony; Orchestra
>**Status:** Non-Professional; Non-Profit
>**Type:** Resident
>**Purpose:** To provide symphonic musical experiences both for community musicians and community audiences
>**Management:** Lauren Green, Music Director/Conductor/Manager
>**Officers:** Mark Roberts, President; Beverly Taverner, David Laurin, Vice Presidents
>**Paid Staff:** 2   **Volunteer Staff:** 30
>**Paid Artists:** 1   **Non-Paid Artists:** 50
>**Utilizes:** Special Technical Talent; Guest Conductors; Guest Artists
>**Budget:** $100,000 - $500,000
>**Income Sources:** Private Foundations/Grants/Endowments; Business/Corporate Donations; Box Office; Government Grants; Individual Donations
>**Season:** September - May   **Annual Attendance:** 7,000
>**Performance Facilities:** Bartlesville Community Center

PERFORMING SERIES

OK MOZART INTERNATIONAL FESTIVAL
500 Southeast Dewey, Bartlesville, OK 74003
(918) 336-9900
FAX: (918) 662-1527
>**Mailing Address:** PO Box 2344, Bartlesville, OK 74005
>**Founded:** 1985
>**Arts Area:** Dance; Vocal Music; Instrumental Music; Festivals; Grand Opera
>**Status:** Professional; Non-Profit
>**Type:** Sponsoring

Management: Nan Buhlinger, Artistic Administrator; Ransom Wilson, Artistic Director; Linda Cubbage, General Manager
Paid Staff: 3   **Volunteer Staff:** 400
Paid Artists: 40
Utilizes: Guest Conductors; Guest Artists
Budget: $100,000 - $500,000
Income Sources: Private Foundations/Grants/Endowments; Business/Corporate Donations; Box Office; Government Grants; Individual Donations
Season: June - July   **Annual Attendance:** 8,000
Affiliations: APAP; Oklahoma State Arts Council
Performance Facilities: Bartlesville Community Center

FACILITY

BARTLESVILLE COMMUNITY CENTER
300 East Adams Boulevard, Bartlesville, OK 74003
(918) 337-2787
Type of Facility: Theatre Complex; Concert Hall; Studio Performance; Performance Center; Civic Center; Multi-Purpose
Type of Stage: Proscenium
Stage Dimensions: 60'Wx46'D; 18' and 30' wing space   **Orchestra Pit**
Seating Capacity: 1,735
Year Built: 1982   **Architect:** William Wesley Peters; Taliesin Associated Architects   **Cost:** $13,500,000
Acoustical Consultant: Vern C. Plane
Contact for Rental: Pat Johnson;   (918) 337-2787
Manager: Allan Longacre
Resident Groups: Bartlesville Theater Guild; Bartlesville Symphony Orchestra; Bartlesville Civic Ballet

Bristow

FACILITY

AMERICAN LEGION
121 West Eighth Street, Bristow, OK 74010
Type of Facility: Concert Hall; Auditorium; Performance Center; Multi-Purpose
Facility Originally: Meeting Hall; Ballroom; Movie House
Type of Stage: Proscenium
Stage Dimensions: 49'Dx24'6"D
Seating Capacity: 5,000
Contact for Rental: Bobbie Lloyd, Bob Burris;   (918) 367-9767
Resident Groups: Bristow Arts and Humanities
Performing arts; dance; concerts; banquets

KLINGENSMITH PARK AMPHITHEATRE
110 West Seventh Street, Bristow, OK 74010
(918) 367-2237
Type of Facility: Outdoor (Concert); Amphitheater
Type of Stage: Proscenium
Seating Capacity: 5,000
Year Built: 1934
Year Remodeled: 1987
Contact for Rental: Tony Elias, Mayor;   (918) 367-2237
Resident Groups: Bristow Community Players

Clinton

DANCE

WESTERN OKLAHOMA BALLET THEATRE
700 Avant, Clinton, OK 73601
(405) 323-5954
Founded: 1977
Arts Area: Modern; Ballet
Status: Non-Professional; Non-Profit
Type: Performing; Educational
Purpose: To foster and promote dance in western Oklahoma
Management: Penny Askew, Artistic Director
Officers: Marian Tisdal, President; Susie Simon, Vice President; Cindi Delay, Secretary; Don Askew, Treasurer
Volunteer Staff: 2

Non-Paid Artists: 9
Utilizes: Guest Artists; Guest Choreographers
Budget: $1,000 - $50,000
Income Sources: Business/Corporate Donations; Box Office; Government Grants; Individual Donations
Season: 52 Weeks   **Annual Attendance:** 2,500
Affiliations: Regional Dance America; Southwestern Regional Ballet Association
Performance Facilities: Southwestern Oklahoma State University Fine Arts Center

Enid

INSTRUMENTAL MUSIC

ENID-PHILLIPS SYMPHONY ORCHESTRA
301 West Maine, Suite 15, Enid, OK 73701
(405) 237-9646
> **Founded:** 1906
> **Arts Area:** Symphony; Orchestra
> **Status:** Professional; Non-Profit
> **Type:** Performing; Educational
> **Management:** Douglas Newell, Artostic Director; Eleanor Hornbaker, Administrative Associate
> **Officers:** Maye Adele Kirtley, President, Enid Phillips Symphony Association
> **Paid Staff:** 1   **Volunteer Staff:** 4
> **Paid Artists:** 65
> **Utilizes:** Guest Conductors; Guest Artists
> **Budget:** $50,000 - $100,000
> **Income Sources:** Private Foundations/Grants/Endowments; Business/Corporate Donations; Box Office; Government Grants; Individual Donations
> **Season:** September - May   **Annual Attendance:** 9,500
> **Affiliations:** ASOL
> **Performance Facilities:** Eugene S. Briggs Auditorium

Lawton

INSTRUMENTAL MUSIC

LAWTON PHILHARMONIC ORCHESTRA
PO Box 1473, Lawton, OK 73502
(405) 248-2001
> **Founded:** 1962
> **Arts Area:** Symphony; Orchestra
> **Status:** Professional; Non-Profit
> **Type:** Performing; Touring; Resident; Educational; Sponsoring
> **Purpose:** To educate the public and provide entertainment for the Lawton community
> **Management:** Carlana N. Sitch, General Manager; Whittie Rainwater, Assistant Manager
> **Paid Staff:** 3   **Volunteer Staff:** 250
> **Paid Artists:** 75
> **Utilizes:** Guest Conductors; Guest Artists
> **Budget:** $100,000 - $500,000
> **Income Sources:** Private Foundations/Grants/Endowments; Business/Corporate Donations; Box Office; Government Grants; Individual Donations; Fund-raising
> **Season:** October - June   **Annual Attendance:** 15,000
> **Affiliations:** ASOL
> **Performance Facilities:** McMahon Memorial Auditorium

VOCAL MUSIC

AMERICAN CHORAL DIRECTORS ASSOCIATION
PO Box 6310, Lawton, OK 73506
(405) 355-8161
FAX: (405) 248-1465
> **Arts Area:** Choral
> **Status:** Non-Profit
> **Type:** Educational
> **Purpose:** To provide information to members
> **Management:** Dr. Gene Brooks, Executive Director; John Haberlen, President
> **Income Sources:** Government Grants
> **Season:** 52 Weeks

FACILITY

CAMERON UNIVERSITY, THEATRE ARTS DEPARTMENT
2800 West Gore Boulevard, Lawton, OK 73505
(405) 536-2346
Type of Facility: Auditorium; Studio Performance; Theatre House
Type of Stage: Flexible; Proscenium
Seating Capacity: 432
Acoustical Consultant: Scott Hofmann
Contact for Rental: Scott Hofmann;   (405) 581-2428

MCMAHON MEMORIAL AUDITORIUM
801 Ferris, PO Box 522, Lawton, OK 73502
(405) 581-3470
FAX: (405) 248-0243
Founded: 1954
Type of Facility: Auditorium
Type of Stage: Proscenium
Stage Dimensions: 92'Wx40'D   **Orchestra Pit**
Seating Capacity: 1,525
Year Built: 1954   **Architect:** Paul Harris
Year Remodeled: 1991   **Architect:** Philip Burk   **Cost:** $900,000
Acoustical Consultant: C.P. Boner & Associates
Contact for Rental: Jim McCarthy;   (405) 581-3470
Manager: Ann Weisman;   (405) 581-3470
Resident Groups: Lawton Philharmonic Society; Lawton Community Concerts; Lawton Arts and Humanities Council;
Miss Lawton Pageant

Muskogee

THEATRE

MUSKOGEE LITTLE THEATRE
329 East Cincinnati, PO Box 964, Muskogee, OK 74402
(918) 683-5332
Founded: 1972
Arts Area: Community
Status: Non-Profit
Type: Performing
Purpose: To foster interest and support of dramatic arts in the community; to design programs and activities to encourage
involvement of community members in the study of dramatic arts; to produce and perform plays benefiting the community
and surroundings
Officers: Bob Crandell, President; Janice Ward, Vice President; Nancy Williams, Secretary; David King,
Treasurer
Volunteer Staff: 200
Non-Paid Artists: 75
Budget: $1,000 - $50,000
Income Sources: Business/Corporate Donations; Box Office; Individual Donations
Season: September - July   **Annual Attendance:** 2,500
Affiliations: Oklahoma Community Theatre Association
Performance Facilities: Muskogee Little Theatre

FACILITY

MUSKOGEE LITTLE THEATRE
Cincinnati and D, Muskogee, OK 74402-0964
(918) 683-5332
Type of Facility: Concert Hall; Auditorium; Performance Center; Theatre House
Type of Stage: Proscenium
Stage Dimensions: 36'Wx12'D
Seating Capacity: 114
Year Built: 1962
Year Remodeled: 1972
Contact for Rental: Marjorie Szabo, Treasurer;   (918) 682-3257

Norman

DANCE

OKLAHOMA FESTIVAL BALLET
563 Elm Avenue, Room 209, Norman, OK 73019
(405) 325-4021
FAX: (405) 325-5322
> **Arts Area:** Ballet
> **Status:** Semi-Professional
> **Type:** Performing; Touring; Resident; Educational
> **Purpose:** To perform an eclectic repertoire using a classical ballet of young dancers
> **Officers:** Mary Margaret Holt, Director; Dennis Poole, Ballet Master; Kathleen Burnett, Rehearsal Assistant; Max Burnett, Manager; Scott Simmons, Technical Director
> **Paid Staff:** 5 **Volunteer Staff:** 2
> **Paid Artists:** 16
> **Budget:** $50,000 - $100,000
> **Income Sources:** Private Foundations/Grants/Endowments; Box Office; Government Grants; Individual Donations
> **Season:** August - May
> **Annual Attendance:** 20,000
> **Affiliations:** University of Oklahoma
> **Performance Facilities:** Rupel Jones Theatre

VOCAL MUSIC

CIMARRON CIRCUIT OPERA COMPANY
PO Box 1085, Norman, OK 73070
(405) 364-8962
> **Founded:** 1975
> **Arts Area:** Grand Opera; Lyric Opera; Light Opera; Children's Opera
> **Status:** Professional; Non-Profit
> **Type:** Performing; Touring; Sponsoring
> **Purpose:** To provide training and experience for young singers in Oklahoma and take opera to areas of Oklahoma where residents would not normally have access to opera performances
> **Management:** Thomas Carey, Artistic Director; Lisa Anderson, Musical Director; Alan Parker, Technical Director
> **Officers:** Stan Williams, President; Mike Abraham, Vice President; Mary McCord, Secretary; Rodney Evans, Treasurer
> **Paid Staff:** 6 **Volunteer Staff:** 15
> **Paid Artists:** 30 **Non-Paid Artists:** 5
> **Utilizes:** Guest Artists; Guest Directors
> **Budget:** $50,000 - $100,000
> **Income Sources:** Private Foundations/Grants/Endowments; Business/Corporate Donations; Box Office; Government Grants; Individual Donations; Fundraising
> **Season:** September - April **Annual Attendance:** 25,000
> **Affiliations:** COS; MAAA

PERFORMING SERIES

JAZZ IN JUNE, INC.
PO Box 2405, Norman, OK 73070
(405) 325-3388
> **Founded:** 1985
> **Arts Area:** Vocal Music; Instrumental Music
> **Status:** Professional; Semi-Professional
> **Type:** Performing
> **Purpose:** To present a jazz festival for Oklahoma residents
> **Management:** Phoebe Morales, Executive Director of the Norman Arts and Humanities Council
> **Volunteer Staff:** 20
> **Paid Artists:** 25
> **Utilizes:** Special Technical Talent; Guest Conductors; Guest Artists; Guest Directors
> **Budget:** $1,000 - $50,000
> **Income Sources:** Business/Corporate Donations; Box Office; Government Grants; Individual Donations
> **Season:** June **Annual Attendance:** 5,000
> **Affiliations:** AFM

FACILITY

THE SOONER THEATRE OF NORMAN, INC.
PO Box 6565, 101 East Main, Norman, OK 73070
(405) 321-9600
    Founded: 1976
    Type of Facility: Concert Hall; Auditorium; Performance Center; Theatre House; Opera House; Civic Center
    Facility Originally: Vaudeville; Movie House
    Type of Stage: Proscenium
    Stage Dimensions: 29'Dx45'W; 25'5"Dx25'W playing area **Orchestra Pit**
    Seating Capacity: 687
    Year Built: 1929 **Architect:** Harold Gimeno **Cost:** $200,000
    Year Remodeled: 1982 **Cost:** $150,000
    Contact for Rental: Kym E. Bracken; (405) 321-9600
    Resident Groups: Stone Soup Theatre; Cimarron Circuit Opera Company; Norman Ballet Company

UNIVERSITY OF OKLAHOMA THEATRE
563 Elm Street, Norman, OK 73019
(405) 325-4021
    Type of Facility: Theatre Complex; Studio Performance; Performance Center
    Type of Stage: Thrust; Flexible; Proscenium; Arena
    Stage Dimensions: 40'Wx20'Hx47'D with a 45' deep thrust **Orchestra Pit**
    Seating Capacity: 668
    Year Built: 1965 **Architect:** A. Blaine Imel **Cost:** $1,500,000
    Contact for Rental: Dr. Gregory Kunesh, Director; (405) 325-4021
    Resident Groups: Oklahoma Festival Ballet; Modern Dance Repertory; University Theatre; Southwest Repertory Theatre

---

Oklahoma City

DANCE

BALLET OKLAHOMA
7421 North Classen, Oklahoma City, OK 73116
(405) 843-9898
FAX: (405) 843-9894
    Founded: 1972
    Arts Area: Ballet; Jazz
    Status: Professional
    Type: Performing; Touring; Resident; Educational; Sponsoring
    Purpose: Professional resident ballet company and ballet school
    Management: Bryan Pitts, Artistic Director; Gail Beals, General Manager
    Officers: Michael Laird, President, Board of Trustees
    Paid Staff: 10
    Paid Artists: 21
    Utilizes: Special Technical Talent; Guest Artists; Guest Choreographers
    Budget: $1,000,000 - $5,000,000
    Income Sources: Private Foundations/Grants/Endowments; Business/Corporate Donations; Box Office; Government Grants; Individual Donations
    Season: September - April **Annual Attendance:** 40,000
    Performance Facilities: Civic Center

PRAIRIE DANCE THEATRE
2100 NE 52nd, Oklahoma City, OK 73111
(405) 842-5235
    Founded: 1978
    Arts Area: Modern; Ethnic; Folk
    Status: Professional; Non-Profit
    Type: Performing; Touring; Resident; Educational
    Purpose: To present modern dance performances with Southwestern USA themes
    Management: Peter Shumway, Manager; Beth Shumway, Artistic Director; Cynthia Longley, Public Relations
    Officers: Vicky Galloway, President; Pat Hughes, Vice President; Keesa Crouch, Secretary/Treasurer
    Paid Staff: 1 **Volunteer Staff:** 10
    Paid Artists: 6
    Utilizes: Special Technical Talent; Guest Artists; Guest Directors; Guest Choreographers
    Budget: $50,000 - $100,000
    Income Sources: Private Foundations/Grants/Endowments; Business/Corporate Donations; Box Office; Individual Donations
    Season: September - May **Annual Attendance:** 2,000

Affiliations: Kirpatrick Center Museum; MidAmerica Dance Network
Performance Facilities: Kirpatrick Centre

INSTRUMENTAL MUSIC

GO FOR BAROQUE
PO Box 20178, Oklahoma City, OK 73120
(405) 840-0278
Founded: 1982
Arts Area: Chamber; Ensemble
Status: Professional
Type: Performing; Touring; Educational
Purpose: Formal Baroque Concerts, Young People's Concerts
Management: Peggy Green Payne
Paid Artists: 8
Budget: $1,000 - $50,000
Income Sources: Private Foundations/Grants/Endowments; Business/Corporate Donations
Season: 52 Weeks

OKLAHOMA CITY PHILHARMONIC ORCHESTRA
428 West California, Suite 210, Oklahoma City, OK 73102
(405) 232-7575
FAX: (405) 232-4353
Founded: 1988
Arts Area: Symphony; Orchestra
Status: Professional; Non-Profit
Type: Performing; Resident
Purpose: To perform orchestral, classical and popular music; to entertain and educate; to enhance cultural environment of the city and the state
Management: Joel Levine, Music Director/Conductor; Alan D. Valentine, General Manager; Eddie Walker, Operations Manager
Officers: Paul Reed, President of Board of Directors; Jane Harlow, President-Elect; Al Dearmon, Vice President; Harrison Levy, Treasurer; Priscilla Braun, Secretary
Paid Staff: 11
Paid Artists: 85
Utilizes: Special Technical Talent; Guest Conductors; Guest Artists
Budget: $1,000,000 - $5,000,000
Income Sources: Private Foundations/Grants/Endowments; Business/Corporate Donations; Box Office; Government Grants; Individual Donations; Fee Engagements
Season: September - May **Annual Attendance:** 105,000
Affiliations: ASOL; Allied Arts of Oklahoma City
Performance Facilities: Civic Center Music Hall

VOCAL MUSIC

OKLAHOMA OPERA AND MUSIC THEATER COMPANY
Oklahoma City University, 2501 North Blackwelder, Oklahoma City, OK 73106
(405) 521-5315
FAX: (405) 521-5264
Founded: 1904
Arts Area: Grand Opera; Lyric Opera; Light Opera; Operetta; Choral
Status: Non-Professional; Non-Profit
Type: Performing; Educational
Purpose: To provide high quality performances for the general public; to provide a professional forum in which students can develop their talents
Management: Cheryl L. Zrnic, General Director
Paid Staff: 5 **Volunteer Staff:** 50
Paid Artists: 4
Utilizes: Special Technical Talent; Guest Directors
Budget: $50,000 - $100,000
Income Sources: Private Foundations/Grants/Endowments; Business/Corporate Donations; Box Office; Government Grants; Individual Donations
Season: October - April **Annual Attendance:** 10,000
Affiliations: Oklahoma City University
Performance Facilities: Kirkpatrick Theater

THEATRE

JEWEL BOX THEATRE
3700 North Walker, Oklahoma City, OK 73118
(405) 521-1786
Founded: 1957
Arts Area: Community
Status: Non-Professional
Type: Performing
Purpose: Continuing excellence in theatre
Management: Charles Tweed, Production Director
Officers: Pat Tweed, Chairman of Board of Advisors; Neta Unger, Co-Chairman
Paid Staff: 1   **Volunteer Staff:** 50
Budget: $50,000 - $100,000
Income Sources: Business/Corporate Donations; Box Office; Individual Donations
Season: August - May
Affiliations: ACTA; Oklahoma Community Theatre Association; Southwest Repertory Theatre Association
Performance Facilities: Jewel Box Theatre

LYRIC THEATRE OF OKLAHOMA
2501 North Blackwelder, Oklahoma City, OK 73106
(405) 528-3636
Founded: 1962
Arts Area: Musical
Status: Professional; Non-Profit
Type: Performing; Resident
Purpose: To provide a professional atmosphere for trained young artists; an extension of the University of Oklahoma Drama Department
Management: Gayle Pearson, Producing Manager
Paid Staff: 3
Utilizes: Special Technical Talent; Guest Artists; Guest Directors
Budget: $500,000 - $1,000,000
Income Sources: Private Foundations/Grants/Endowments; Business/Corporate Donations; Box Office; Government Grants; Individual Donations
Season: June - August
Affiliations: U/RTA
Performance Facilities: Kirkpatrick Auditorium, Oklahoma City University

OKLAHOMA COMMUNITY THEATRE ASSOCIATION
200 North Harvey, Suite 902, Oklahoma City, OK 73102
(405) 235-9508
Founded: 1969
Arts Area: Community
Status: Non-Professional; Non-Profit
Type: State Theatre Association
Purpose: To encourage excellence in community theatre throughout the state of Oklahoma
Management: Anthony Klatt, Administrative Coordinator
Officers: Mary S. Patterson, President; Charles Hair, President-Elect
Paid Staff: 1   **Volunteer Staff:** 18
Utilizes: Special Technical Talent; Guest Conductors; Guest Artists; Guest Directors
Budget: $100,000 - $500,000
Income Sources: Private Foundations/Grants/Endowments; Business/Corporate Donations; Box Office; Government Grants; Individual Donations
Affiliations: SWTC; AACT

FACILITY

CIVIC CENTER MUSIC HALL
201 Channing Square, Suite 100, Oklahoma City, OK 73102
(405) 297-2584
Founded: 1937
Type of Facility: Theatre Complex; Concert Hall; Auditorium; Performance Center; Civic Center; Multi-Purpose
Facility Originally: Arena   **Type of Stage:** Proscenium
Stage Dimensions: 69'10"Wx48'D   **Orchestra Pit**
Seating Capacity: 3,200
Year Built: 1937   **Architect:** J.O. Parr
Year Remodeled: 1967   **Architect:** Turnbull & Mills
Contact for Rental: Tom Anderson;   (405) 297-2584
Resident Groups: Oklahoma City Philharmonic Orchestra; Ballet Oklahoma; Canterbury Choral Society

OKLAHOMA CITY UNIVERSITY
2501 North Blackwelder, Oklahoma City, OK 73106
(405) 521-5315
    Type of Facility: Performance Center
    Year Built: 1929 **Architect:** Seminoff-Bowman-Bowdie **Cost:** $1,000,000
    Year Remodeled: 1969 **Architect:** Seminoff-Bowman-Bowdie **Cost:** $250,000
    Contact for Rental: Nina Anderson; (405) 521-5316
    Resident Groups: Sinfonia of Mid-America Lyric Theater; American Spirit Dancers; Civic Music Association
    Oklahoma City University contains Burg Theatre and Kirkpatrick Auditorium. See separate listings for additional information.

OKLAHOMA CITY UNIVERSITY - BURG THEATRE
2501 North Blackwelder, Oklahoma City, OK 73106
(405) 521-5315
    Type of Facility: Theatre House
    Type of Stage: Proscenium **Orchestra Pit**
    Seating Capacity: 300
    Year Built: 1929
    Year Remodeled: 1969
    Contact for Rental: Nina Anderson; (405) 521-5316

OKLAHOMA CITY UNIVERSITY - KIRKPATRICK AUDITORIUM
2501 North Blackwelder, Oklahoma City, OK 73106
(405) 521-5315
    Type of Facility: Auditorium
    Type of Stage: 3/4 Arena
    Seating Capacity: 1,119
    Year Built: 1929
    Year Remodeled: 1969
    Contact for Rental: Nina Anderson; (405) 521-5316

OKLAHOMA CITY ZOO AMPHITHEATRE
2101 NE 50th, Oklahoma City, OK 73111
(405) 424-3344
    Type of Facility: Concert Hall; Outdoor (Concert); Environmental; Amphitheater; Multi-Purpose
    Type of Stage: Greek; Proscenium
    Stage Dimensions: 60'Wx40'D
    Seating Capacity: 9,000
    Year Built: 1936
    Architect: Civilian Conservation Corps
    Contact for Rental: Donna Chain; (405) 424-3344
    Updating facility yearly

Ponca City

THEATRE

PONCA PLAYHOUSE
516 East Grand, Ponca City, OK 74601
(405) 765-7786; (405) 765-5360
    Mailing Address: PO Box 1414, Ponca City, OK 74602
    Founded: 1959
    Arts Area: Musical; Community; Theatrical Group
    Status: Non-Professional; Non-Profit; Commercial
    Type: Performing; Touring; Resident
    Purpose: To provide the interested area amateur with the opportunity to participate in the process of producing live theatre for a discriminating audience
    Officers: Jerry Hughes, President; Iris Ballou, Secretary; Tom Cawley, Vice President
    Paid Staff: 4 **Volunteer Staff:** 20
    Paid Artists: 2
    Utilizes: Special Technical Talent; Guest Artists; Guest Directors
    Budget: $50,000 - $100,000
    Income Sources: Business/Corporate Donations; Box Office; Individual Donations
    Season: September - May **Annual Attendance:** 10,000
    Affiliations: AACT; Oklahoma Community Theatre Association; SWTC

FACILITY

PONCA PLAYHOUSE
516 East Grand, Ponca City, OK 74601
(508) 765-7786
> **Type of Facility:** Theatre House
> **Type of Stage:** Proscenium
> **Stage Dimensions:** 30'Wx20'H proscenium opening   **Orchestra Pit**
> **Seating Capacity:** 412
> **Year Built:** 1927
> **Contact for Rental:** John A. Robinson;   (405) 765-7786
> **Resident Groups:** Ponca Playhouse

Tahlequah

THEATRE

CHEROKEE NATIONAL HISTORICAL SOCIETY
PO Box 515, Tahlequah, OK 74465
(918) 456-6007
> **Founded:** 1964
> **Arts Area:** Theatrical Group
> **Status:** Professional; Non-Profit
> **Type:** Resident; Educational
> **Purpose:** The Cherokee National Historical Society seeks to preserve the history and traditions of the Cherokee Indian tribe and to educate the public concerning the Cherokee story through the presentation of the "Trail of Tears" drama and other endeavors.
> **Management:** Tom Mooney, Acting Executive Director
> **Officers:** Gary Chapman, President; Wilma Mankiller, Vice President
> **Paid Staff:** 10
> **Paid Artists:** 80
> **Utilizes:** Special Technical Talent
> **Budget:** $100,000 - $500,000
> **Income Sources:** Private Foundations/Grants/Endowments; Business/Corporate Donations; Box Office; Government Grants; Individual Donations
> **Season:** June - August   **Annual Attendance:** 30,000
> **Affiliations:** Outdoor Drama Association
> **Performance Facilities:** Cherokee Heritage Center Amphitheater

FACILITY

CHEROKEE HERITAGE CENTER AMPHITHEATER
Willis Road, PO Box 515, Tahlequah, OK 74465
(918) 456-6007
> **Type of Facility:** Amphitheater
> **Type of Stage:** Greek
> **Seating Capacity:** 1,800
> **Year Built:** 1969   **Architect:** Charles Chief Boyd   **Cost:** $400,000
> **Contact for Rental:** Lisa Finley, Director of Marketing;   (918) 456-6007
> **Resident Groups:** Trail of Tears

Tulsa

DANCE

TULSA BALLET THEATRE
4512 South Peoria, Tulsa, OK 74105
(918) 749-6030
FAX: (918) 749-0532
> **Founded:** 1956
> **Arts Area:** Ballet
> **Status:** Professional; Non-Profit
> **Type:** Performing; Touring
> **Purpose:** The understanding of ballet and its related arts through the establishment of a ballet company which is part of the cultural life of Tulsa and its environs
> **Management:** Roman Jasinski, Artistic Director; Connie Cronley, General Manager

Officers: Hannah Robson, President; Donald F. Marlar, Chairman of the Board; Larry Chambers, Executive Vice President; Jack Kelley, Vice President/ Long Range Planning; Bob Morgan, Vice President/ Finance and Budget; Mary Barnes, Edward Taylor, Vice Presidents at Large; Ginny Creveling, Vice President/ Development; Aubyn Howe, Vice President/ Research and Development of Fundraising; Bonnie Henke, Parliamentarian; Elizabeth Rainey, Corresponding Secretary; Jim Burdett, Treasurer; Patty Floyd, Recording Secretary
Paid Staff: 11
Paid Artists: 28
Utilizes: Special Technical Talent; Guest Conductors; Guest Artists; Guest Directors; Guest Choreographers
Budget: $1,000,000 - $5,000,000
Income Sources: Private Foundations/Grants/Endowments; Business/Corporate Donations; Box Office; Government Grants; Individual Donations
Season: September - May   **Annual Attendance:** 101,000
Affiliations: NARB; Dance USA
Performance Facilities: Chapman Music Hall; Tulsa Performing Arts Center

INSTRUMENTAL MUSIC

CONCERTIME
3936 East 38th, Tulsa, OK 74135-2406
(918) 742-4087
Founded: 1954
Arts Area: Chamber
Status: Professional; Non-Profit
Type: Performing; Educational
Purpose: We introduced chamber music to Tulsa and, because of our efforts, interest has been increased. Our continuing purpose is to cultivate future audiences for chamber music.
Management: Robert Heckman, Manager
Officers: Deborah Pinkerton, President; Dr. John K. Major, Vice President; Bathany Kolmar, Secretary; Dr. Richard W. Ekdahl, Treasurer
Paid Staff: 1   **Volunteer Staff:** 27
Paid Artists: 4
Utilizes: Guest Artists
Budget: $1,000 - $50,000
Income Sources: Private Foundations/Grants/Endowments; Box Office; Government Grants; Individual Donations
Season: October - April   **Annual Attendance:** 1,600
Affiliations: CMA
Performance Facilities: John H. Williams Theater, Tulsa Performing Arts Center

TULSA PHILHARMONIC
2901 South Harvard Avenue, Suite A, Tulsa, OK 74114-6100
(918) 584-2533
FAX: (918) 747-7496
Founded: 1947
Arts Area: Symphony; Orchestra; Chamber; Ensemble
Status: Professional; Non-Profit
Type: Performing; Touring; Resident; Educational; Sponsoring
Purpose: Live symphony music
Management: Stepehen Boyd, Executive Director; William Schmieding, Orchestra Manager; Virginia Will, Business Manager
Officers: Henry Will, Chairman; Sally Minshall, Vice Chairman; Betty Clark, President
Paid Staff: 15   **Volunteer Staff:** 1
Paid Artists: 80
Utilizes: Guest Conductors; Guest Artists
Budget: $1,000,000 - $5,000,000
Income Sources: Private Foundations/Grants/Endowments; Business/Corporate Donations; Box Office; Government Grants; Individual Donations
Season: September - May   **Annual Attendance:** 100,000
Affiliations: ASOL
Performance Facilities: Tulsa Performing Arts Center

TULSA YOUTH SYMPHONY ORCHESTRA
2901 South Harvard, Tulsa, OK 74114
(918) 747-7473
FAX: (918) 747-7496
Founded: 1963
Arts Area: Symphony; Orchestra; Chamber
Status: Non-Professional; Non-Profit
Type: Performing; Touring; Educational

Purpose: Tulsa Youth Symphony Orchestra aims to encourage and develop students' musical abilities through rehearsal, concert performance and regular contact with professional musicians, offering training and performance opportunities unavailable at any single educational institution.
Management: Ronald Wheeler, Conductor/Administrator; Catherine Venable, Administrative Assistant; Christopher Henry, Librarian
Officers: Rebecca Robinson, President; Neema Drew, Treasurer
Paid Staff: 3
Non-Paid Artists: 85
Utilizes: Guest Conductors; Guest Artists
Budget: $1,000 - $50,000
Income Sources: Business/Corporate Donations; Individual Donations; Fundraising
Season: September - May **Annual Attendance:** 4,000
Affiliations: ASOL (Youth Orchestra Division); Tulsa Philharmonic; Junior Division of the Tulsa Philharmonic Society, Inc.
Performance Facilities: Union High School Performing Arts Center; Tulsa Performing Arts Center

VOCAL MUSIC

TULSA OPERA
1610 South Boulder, Tulsa, OK 74119
(918) 582-4035
Founded: 1948
Arts Area: Grand Opera
Status: Professional; Non-Profit
Type: Performing; Sponsoring
Purpose: To present music/opera theater of the finest quality for a diverse audience drawn from a four-state region (OK, KS, AR, MI); to encourage musical talents, composers, lyricists and related artists through scholarships and opportunities; to develop an awareness of, and appreciation for opera through extensive educational programs
Management: Myrna Smart Ruffner, Executive Director; Cheryl L. Zrnic, Managing Director; Nicholas Muni, Artistic Director
Officers: Hilliary Kito, President; Scott Graham, Chairman of the Board; Jim Dodd, Vice President; Marilyn Strange, Secretary; Edgar Sandeton, Treasurer
Paid Staff: 10 **Volunteer Staff:** 25
Paid Artists: 40 **Non-Paid Artists:** 75
Utilizes: Special Technical Talent; Guest Conductors; Guest Artists; Guest Directors
Budget: $1,000,000 - $5,000,000
Income Sources: Private Foundations/Grants/Endowments; Business/Corporate Donations; Box Office; Government Grants; Individual Donations
Season: November - May **Annual Attendance:** 20,000
Affiliations: OA; AAA; Arts and Humanities Council of Tulsa
Performance Facilities: Chapman Music Hall

THEATRE

AMERICAN THEATRE COMPANY
1820 South Boulder Place, Tulsa, OK 74119
(918) 747-9494
Founded: 1970
Arts Area: Theatrical Group
Status: Professional; Non-Profit
Type: Performing
Management: Kitty Roberts, Producing Artistic Director; Laurie Bryant, Education Director
Paid Staff: 4 **Volunteer Staff:** 30
Paid Artists: 20
Utilizes: Special Technical Talent
Budget: $100,000 - $500,000
Income Sources: Private Foundations/Grants/Endowments; Business/Corporate Donations; Box Office; Government Grants; Individual Donations
Season: 52 Weeks **Annual Attendance:** 22,000
Affiliations: TCG; Arts and Humanities Council of Tulsa
Performance Facilities: The Williams Theatre

THEATRE TULSA
207 North Main, Tulsa, OK 74103
(918) 587-8402
Founded: 1922
Arts Area: Community; Theatrical Group
Status: Non-Professional; Non-Profit
Type: Performing; Touring; Resident; Educational; Sponsoring

Purpose: To provide entertainment, education, and enrichment to any and all sections of the community through participation in and enjoyment of the theatre arts
Management: Wayne G. Campbell, President/Chief Operating Officer; Kelly Jackson, Office Manager
Officers: Wayne Campbell, President/Chief Operating Officer; Jim Holloman, Chairman of the Board; Brent Curry, Treasurer; Ed Behnken, Vice President of Fund-raising; Pat Hanford, Vice President of Production; Kirby Lehman, Secretary
Paid Staff: 3   **Volunteer Staff:** 300
Paid Artists: 20   **Non-Paid Artists:** 100
Utilizes: Special Technical Talent; Guest Conductors; Guest Artists; Guest Directors
Budget: $100,000 - $500,000
Income Sources: Private Foundations/Grants/Endowments; Business/Corporate Donations; Box Office; Government Grants; Individual Donations
Season: July - June   **Annual Attendance:** 40,000
Affiliations: Oklahoma Community Theatre Association; State Arts Council of Oklahoma
Performance Facilities: Performing Arts Center

FACILITY

A.D.A.M.S. THEATRE
1511 South Delaware, Tulsa, OK 74104
(918) 835-5843
> **Type of Facility:** Performance Center; Off Broadway
> **Type of Stage:** Proscenium
> **Stage Dimensions:** 24'x30'
> **Seating Capacity:** 383
> **Year Built:** 1932
> **Year Remodeled:** 1992   **Architect:** John Morrison
> **Contact for Rental:** Ruth Davis;   (918) 742-3267
> **Resident Groups:** Actors, Dancers and Musicians Society

BRADY THEATRE
105 West Brady, Tulsa, OK 74103
(918) 582-5239
FAX: (918) 587-9531
> **Type of Facility:** Concert Hall; Theatre House
> **Facility Originally:** Vaudeville
> **Type of Stage:** Proscenium
> **Stage Dimensions:** 65'Wx37'D; 50'Wx20'H proscenium opening   **Orchestra Pit**
> **Seating Capacity:** 2,800
> **Year Built:** 1914
> **Year Remodeled:** 1985
> **Acoustical Consultant:** Peking Sound
> **Contact for Rental:** Joe Trotter;   (918) 582-5239
> **Resident Groups:** Oklahoma Symphony; Tulsa Pops Orchestra

TULSA PERFORMING ARTS CENTER
110 East Second Street, Tulsa, OK 74103-3212
(918) 596-7122
FAX: (918) 596-7144
> **Founded:** 1977
> **Type of Facility:** Theatre Complex; Concert Hall; Studio Performance; Performance Center; Multi-Purpose
> **Type of Stage:** Proscenium
> **Stage Dimensions:** 94'Wx51'Dx85'H   **Orchestra Pit**
> **Seating Capacity:** 2,345
> **Year Built:** 1977   **Architect:** Minoru Yamasaki & Associates   **Cost:** $19,000,000
> **Acoustical Consultant:** Bolt, Beranek & Newman
> **Contact for Rental:** John E. Scott;   (918) 596-7122
> **Resident Groups:** Tulsa Opera; Tulsa Philharmonic Orchestra; Tulsa Ballet Theatre; Theatre Tulsa; American Theatre Company; Tulsa Town Hall Lecture Series; Tulsa Summer Stage
> *The Tulsa Performing Arts Center also contains the Chapman Music Hall, John H. Williams Theatre, Studio I and Studio II. See separate listings for additional information.*

TULSA PERFORMING ARTS CENTER - CHAPMAN MUSIC HALL
110 East Second Street, Tulsa, OK 74103-3204
(918) 596-7122
FAX: (918) 596-7144
> **Founded:** 1977
> **Type of Facility:** Concert Hall
> **Type of Stage:** Proscenium

Stage Dimensions: 60'W'x34"H   **Orchestra Pit**
Seating Capacity: 2,450
Year Built: 1977   **Architect:** Minoru Yamasaki   **Cost:** $22,000,000
Acoustical Consultant: Warren Houtz
Contact for Rental: John E. Scott;   (918) 596-7122

TULSA PERFORMING ARTS CENTER - JOHN H. WILLIAMS THEATRE
110 East Second Street, Tulsa, OK 74103-3212
(918) 596-7122
FAX: (918) 596-7144
Type of Facility: Theatre Complex
Type of Stage: Proscenium
Stage Dimensions: 38'Wx22'H   **Orchestra Pit**
Seating Capacity: 429
Year Built: 1977   **Architect:** Minoru Yamasaki   **Cost:** $22,000,000
Acoustical Consultant: Warren Houtz
Contact for Rental: John E. Scott;   (918) 596-7122

TULSA PERFORMING ARTS CENTER - STUDIO I
110 East Second Street, Tulsa, OK 74103-3212
(918) 596-7122
FAX: (918) 596-7144
Founded: 1977
Type of Facility: Studio Performance
Type of Stage: Flexible
Stage Dimensions: 60'x36'
Seating Capacity: 288
Year Built: 1977   **Architect:** Minoru Yamasaki   **Cost:** $22,000,000
Acoustical Consultant: Warren Houtz
Contact for Rental: John E. Scott;   (918) 596-7122

TULSA PERFORMING ARTS CENTER - STUDIO II
110 East Second Street, Tulsa, OK 74103-3212
(918) 596-7122
FAX: (918) 596-7144
Founded: 1977
Type of Facility: Studio Performance
Type of Stage: Flexible
Stage Dimensions: 52'x52'
Seating Capacity: 200
Year Built: 1977   **Architect:** Minoru Yamasaki   **Cost:** $22,000,000
Acoustical Consultant: Warren Houtz
Contact for Rental: John E. Scott;   (918) 596-7122

UNIVERSITY OF TULSA - KENDALL HALL
600 South College, Tulsa, OK 74104
(918) 592-6000
Founded: 1884
Type of Facility: Multi-Purpose
Type of Stage: Flexible
Orchestra Pit
Seating Capacity: 400
Year Built: 1975   **Architect:** McCune McCune & Associates   **Cost:** $3,500,000
Acoustical Consultant: C.P. Boner & Associates
Contact for Rental: David Cook;   (918) 631-2566
Resident Groups: Tulsa University Theatre Department

UNIVERSITY OF TULSA - TYRRELL HALL
600 South College, Tulsa, OK 74114
(918) 631-2000
Type of Facility: Concert Hall
Facility Originally: Meeting Hall; Movie House
Type of Stage: Proscenium
Seating Capacity: 131
Year Remodeled: 1974   **Architect:** McCune McCune & Associates   **Cost:** $400,000
Manager: Ronald Predl

Weatherford

FACILITY

SOUTHWESTERN OKLAHOMA STATE UNIVERSITY - FINE ARTS CENTER
Department of Music, 100 Campus Drive, Weatherford, OK 73096
(405) 772-6611
FAX: (405) 774-3795
Type of Facility: Concert Hall; Auditorium; Multi-Purpose
Type of Stage: Proscenium
Stage Dimensions: 64'Wx40'D, 49'10"Wx22'H proscenium opening   **Orchestra Pit**
Seating Capacity: 1,465
Year Built: 1984   **Architect:** RGDG   **Cost:** $2,500,000
Contact for Rental: Joe B. Thompson;   (405) 774-3705

Woodward

THEATRE

WOODWARD ARTS AND THEATRE COUNCIL
818 Main, Woodward, OK 73802
(405) 256-7120
Founded: 1981
Arts Area: Musical; Community; Theatrical Group
Status: Non-Profit
Type: Performing; Sponsoring
Purpose: To encourage and correlate activities dedicated to the promotion of the cultural arts of Woodward and neighboring areas and to own, manage, and operate the Woodward Arts Theatre
Management: E.J. Mann, Manager
Officers: Laverne Phillips, President; Larry Kelley, Vice President; Leonard Hart, Secretary/Treasurer
Paid Staff: 1   **Volunteer Staff:** 1
Utilizes: Special Technical Talent; Guest Artists
Budget: $1,000 - $50,000
Income Sources: Private Foundations/Grants/Endowments; Business/Corporate Donations; Box Office; Government Grants; Individual Donations
Season: July - June   **Annual Attendance:** 5,000
Affiliations: State Arts Council of Oklahoma

OREGON

Albany

PERFORMING SERIES

CITY OF ALBANY PARKS AND RECREATION DEPARTMENT
433 SW Fourth Avenue, Albany, OR 97321
Founded: 1983
Arts Area: Vocal Music; Instrumental Music; Festivals
Status: Non-Profit
Type: Sponsoring
Purpose: To present a free summer outdoor concert series "River Rhythms", plus a six concert childrens performing arts series
Management: Dave Clark, Director; Sherry Halligan, Program Coordinator
Paid Staff: 6
Utilizes: Special Technical Talent; Guest Artists
Budget: $50,000 - $100,000
Income Sources: Private Foundations/Grants/Endowments; Business/Corporate Donations
Season: July - August; September-May **Annual Attendance:** 53,200

Ashland

INSTRUMENTAL MUSIC

CHAMBER MUSIC CONCERTS
SOSC, 1250 Siskiyou Boulevard, Ashland, OR 97520
(503) 552-6333
FAX: (503) 552-6380
Founded: 1984
Arts Area: Chamber
Status: Professional; Non-Profit
Type: Performing
Purpose: To bring excellence in chamber music performances to the southern Oregon community
Management: Dr. Gregory Fowler, Founder/Director; Lesley Pohl, Assistant
Paid Staff: 1 **Volunteer Staff:** 12
Paid Artists: 20
Utilizes: Guest Artists
Budget: $1,000 - $50,000
Income Sources: Private Foundations/Grants/Endowments; Business/Corporate Donations; Box Office; Individual Donations
Season: October - May **Annual Attendance:** 2,500
Performance Facilities: SOSC Music Building Recital Hall

VOCAL MUSIC

ROQUE OPERA
1250 Siskiyou Boulevard, Music Hall 107, Ashland, OR 97520
(508) 552-6400
Founded: 1978
Arts Area: Grand Opera; Light Opera; Operetta
Status: Non-Profit
Type: Performing; Touring
Management: Marcia Von Furstenberg, Managing Director
Officers: Judith Audley, President; Ron Kramer, Vice President; Tim Cusick, Treasurer
Paid Staff: 1 **Volunteer Staff:** 60
Paid Artists: 100
Utilizes: Special Technical Talent; Guest Conductors; Guest Artists; Guest Directors
Budget: $50,000 - $100,000
Income Sources: Private Foundations/Grants/Endowments; Business/Corporate Donations; Box Office; Individual Donations
Season: August - January **Annual Attendance:** 10,000
Performance Facilities: Oregon Shakespeare Festival Theatres; Cabaret Theatre; Dorothy Stolp Theatre

THEATRE

ACTORS' THEATER OF ASHLAND
295 East Main, Suite 5, Ashland, OR 97520
(503) 482-9659
>**Founded:** 1982
>**Arts Area:** Professional; Musical; Community; Folk; Theatrical Group; Puppet
>**Status:** Semi-Professional; Non-Profit
>**Type:** Performing; Touring; Educational
>**Purpose:** To encourage local playwrights and composers through production of their works; to challenge the status quo through public demonstration of freedom of the imagination; to strive to increase awareness of the ecology, politics and social issues; to entertain
>**Management:** Michael O'Rourke, Artistic Director, Actors' Workshop; Alison Grant, Artistic Director, Young Actors' Workshop
>**Officers:** Elliot Reinert, President
>**Paid Staff:** 2   **Volunteer Staff:** 3
>**Paid Artists:** 10   **Non-Paid Artists:** 20
>**Utilizes:** Special Technical Talent; Guest Artists; Guest Directors
>**Budget:** $1,000 - $50,000
>**Income Sources:** Business/Corporate Donations; Box Office; Individual Donations
>**Season:** 52 Weeks   **Annual Attendance:** 4,000
>**Affiliations:** Oregon Theatre Association

OREGON SHAKESPEAREAN FESTIVAL ASSOCIATION
15 South Pioneer, Ashland, OR 97520
(503) 482-2111
>**Founded:** 1935
>**Arts Area:** Professional
>**Status:** Professional; Non-Profit
>**Type:** Performing; Touring; Resident; Educational
>**Purpose:** Production of professional performances of the plays of Shakespeare and other works of high literary quality in a rotating repertory system
>**Management:** Henry Woronicz, Artistic Director; William Patton, Executive Director; Paul Nicholson, General Manager
>**Officers:** William R. Moffat, President; John Hassen, Vice President; Patricia Romeo, Secretary; Robert Rasmussen, Treasurer
>**Paid Staff:** 281   **Volunteer Staff:** 800
>**Paid Artists:** 84
>**Utilizes:** Special Technical Talent; Guest Directors
>**Budget:** $5,000,000 - $10,000,000
>**Income Sources:** Private Foundations/Grants/Endowments; Business/Corporate Donations; Box Office; Government Grants; Individual Donations
>**Season:** February - October   **Annual Attendance:** 360,000
>**Affiliations:** AEA; ATA; U/RTA; TCG
>**Performance Facilities:** Angus Bowmer Theatre; Black Swan Theatre; Elizabethan Stage

QUARTZ THEATRE
392 Taylor, Ashland, OR 97520
(513) 482-8119
>**Founded:** 1976
>**Arts Area:** Theatrical Group
>**Status:** Non-Profit
>**Type:** Performing
>**Purpose:** Playwright development
>**Management:** Robert Spira, Artistic Director
>**Budget:** $1,000 - $50,000
>**Income Sources:** Box Office
>**Season:** 52 Weeks

STUDIO X PLAYHOUSE
208 Oak Street, Ashland, OR 89502
(503) 488-2011
>**Founded:** 1988
>**Arts Area:** Theatrical Group
>**Status:** Semi-Professional; Non-Profit
>**Type:** Performing; Resident
>**Purpose:** To produce all types of theatre--classic, contemporary and new

Management: Jim Funk, Artistic Director
Paid Staff: 1   **Volunteer Staff:** 10
Non-Paid Artists: 10
Utilizes: Guest Directors
Budget: $1,000 - $50,000
Income Sources: Private Foundations/Grants/Endowments; Box Office; Government Grants; Individual Donations
Season: 52 Weeks   **Annual Attendance:** 6,000

PERFORMING SERIES

ASHLAND FOLK MUSIC CLUB
PO Box 63, Ashland, OR 97520
(503) 488-1561
Founded: 1984
Arts Area: Dance; Vocal Music; Instrumental Music
Status: Non-Profit
Type: Performing; Sponsoring
Purpose: To perpetuate folk traditions; to bring the best in folk music to the area
Management: Nancy Spencer, Coordinator
Volunteer Staff: 4
Utilizes: Guest Artists
Budget: $1,000 - $50,000
Income Sources: Box Office; Individual Donations
Season: 52 Weeks   **Annual Attendance:** 600
Performance Facilities: Carpenter Hall

FACILITY

OREGON SHAKESPEARE FESTIVAL - ANGUS BOWMER THEATRE
15 South Pioneer, Ashland, OR 97520
(503) 482-2111
Type of Facility: Theatre Complex; Theatre House
Type of Stage: Open-end Modified Thrust
Orchestra Pit
Seating Capacity: 601
Year Built: 1970   **Architect:** Kirk Wallace McKinley   **Cost:** $2,500,000
Acoustical Consultant: Robin M. Towne Associates
Contact for Rental: Paul Nicholson;   (503) 482-2111
Resident Groups: Oregon Shakespeare Festival
Shares backstage space with Elizabethan Stage

OREGON SHAKESPEARE FESTIVAL - BLACK SWAN THEATRE
15 South Pioneer, Ashland, OR 97520
(503) 482-2111
Type of Facility: Theatre Complex; Theatre House
Facility Originally: Garage
Type of Stage: 3/4 Arena
Seating Capacity: 140
Year Remodeled: 1977   **Cost:** $127,000
Contact for Rental: Paul Nicholson;   (503) 482-2111
Resident Groups: Oregon Shakespeare Festival

OREGON SHAKESPEARE FESTIVAL - ELIZABETHAN STAGE
15 South Pioneer, Ashland, OR 97520
(503) 482-2111
Type of Facility: Theatre Complex; Outdoor (Concert); Amphitheater
Type of Stage: Environmental; Elizabethan-style with Modified Thrust
Seating Capacity: 1,194
Year Built: 1959   **Architect:** Jack Edson   **Cost:** $425,000
Year Remodeled: 1992   **Architect:** Treffinger, Walz & MacLeod   **Cost:** $7,500,000
Contact for Rental: Paul Nicholson;   (503) 482-2111
Resident Groups: Oregon Shakespeare Festival
America's first Elizabethan Stage, it shares backstage space with the Angus Bowmer Theatre.

Astoria

DANCE

LITTLE BALLET THEATRE
3432 Franklin, Astoria, OR 97103
(503) 325-3961
Founded: 1978
Arts Area: Ballet
Status: Non-Professional; Non-Profit
Type: Performing; Educational
Purpose: To provide exposure to ballet to all people in the North Coast area of Oregon
Management: Jeanne Maddox Fastabend, Artistic Director
Officers: Terri Johnson, President; Wendy Page, Vice President; Tina Ames, Secretary; Linda Dugan, Treasurer
Volunteer Staff: 55
Paid Artists: 2   **Non-Paid Artists:** 100
Utilizes: Guest Artists
Budget: $1,000 - $50,000
Income Sources: Private Foundations/Grants/Endowments; Business/Corporate Donations; Box Office; Individual Donations
Season: October - December   **Annual Attendance:** 1,800
Performance Facilities: Astoria High School Auditorium

Bend

THEATRE

COMMUNITY THEATRE OF THE CASCADES
148 NW Greenwood, Bend, OR 97701
(503) 389-0803
Founded: 1978
Arts Area: Musical; Community; Theatrical Group
Status: Non-Professional; Non-Profit
Type: Performing
Purpose: To provide quality live theatre for the community
Management: Barbara Matlick, Business Manager
Officers: Zelia Nauer, Chairman; Barbara Jordan, Secretary
Paid Staff: 1   **Volunteer Staff:** 100
Non-Paid Artists: 50
Utilizes: Special Technical Talent
Budget: $1,000 - $50,000
Income Sources: Business/Corporate Donations; Box Office; Individual Donations
Season: July - June   **Annual Attendance:** 10,000
Affiliations: Oregon Theatre Association

Cannon Beach

FACILITY

COASTER THEATER
108 North Hemlock, PO Box 643, Cannon Beach, OR 97110
(503) 436-1242
Type of Facility: Concert Hall; Auditorium; Studio Performance; Performance Center; Off Broadway; Theatre House; Multi-Purpose
Facility Originally: Skating Rink
Type of Stage: Flexible; Proscenium; Platform
Stage Dimensions: 30'x35'
Seating Capacity: 200
Year Built: 1920
Year Remodeled: 1972   **Architect:** Ray Watkins
Contact for Rental: Stephen A. Diehl;   (503) 436-1242
Resident Groups: Coaster Theater Players

Cave Junction

INSTRUMENTAL MUSIC

SISKIYOU BAROQUE ENSEMBLE
9345 Takilma Road, Cave Junction, OR 97523
(503) 592-2681
Founded: 1982
Arts Area: Ensemble
Status: Professional
Type: Performing
Purpose: To offer original instrument performances of 17th and 18th-century vocal and instrumental chamber music to residents of the Siskiyou Bioregion
Management: James Rich, Musical Director
Volunteer Staff: 1
Paid Artists: 7
Utilizes: Guest Artists
Budget: $1,000 - $50,000
Income Sources: Box Office; Individual Donations
Season: Fall - Spring   **Annual Attendance:** 700
Performance Facilities: Barnstormers' Theater, Grants Pass; Carpenter Hall, Ashland

---
Coos Bay

PERFORMING SERIES

OREGON COAST MUSIC ASSOCIATION
PO Box 663, Coos Bay, OR 97420
(503) 267-0938
Founded: 1988
Arts Area: Instrumental Music; Festivals
Status: Non-Profit
Type: Educational; Sponsoring
Purpose: To present an annual classical music festival and year round musical and educational activities
Management: Crystal Landucci, General Manager; Linda Kissinger, Office Manager
Officers: Kim Thompson, Board President; Kay Snelgrove, Treasurer
Paid Staff: 2   **Volunteer Staff:** 20
Paid Artists: 120   **Non-Paid Artists:** 5
Utilizes: Guest Artists
Budget: $50,000 - $100,000
Income Sources: Private Foundations/Grants/Endowments; Business/Corporate Donations; Box Office; Government Grants; Individual Donations
Season: October - July   **Annual Attendance:** 8,000
Performance Facilities: Marshfield Auditorium

Corvallis

INSTRUMENTAL MUSIC

FRIENDS OF CHAMBER MUSIC
3904 NW Clarence Circus, Corvallis, OR 97330
(503) 757-0086
FAX: (503) 967-8902
Founded: 1958
Arts Area: Chamber
Status: Non-Professional; Non-Profit
Type: Sponsoring
Purpose: To present the highest quality chamber music
Officers: Carole Orloff, Chair; John Morris, Vice Chair; Jean Nath, Secretary; Stefan Bloomfield, Treasurer
Paid Artists: 6
Utilizes: Guest Artists
Budget: $1,000 - $50,000
Income Sources: Business/Corporate Donations; Box Office; Individual Donations
Season: September - May   **Annual Attendance:** 3,000
Performance Facilities: Laseus Stewart Center

FACILITY

LA SELLS STEWART CENTER
Oregon State University, Corvallis, OR 97331-3102
(503) 737-2402
FAX: (503) 737-3187
Founded: 1981
Type of Facility: Concert Hall
Type of Stage: Flexible
Stage Dimensions: 53'8"x43'4"x26'   **Orchestra Pit**
Seating Capacity: 1,200
Year Built: 1981   **Cost:** $4,500,000
Contact for Rental: Sylvia Moore;   (503) 737-2402

OREGON STATE UNIVERSITY - GILL COLISEUM
15th and Jefferson, Corvallis, OR 97331
(503) 737-2547
Type of Facility: Basketball Gymnasium
Type of Stage: Proscenium
Stage Dimensions: 4'x8' up to 24'x44', can be made larger if needed
Seating Capacity: 15,000
Year Built: 1949
Year Remodeled: 1986   **Cost:** $1,700,000
Contact for Rental: Sylvia Moore;   (503) 737-2402
Manager: Bob Herndon

OREGON STATE UNIVERSITY - MILAN AUDITORIUM
26th and Campus Way, Corvallis, OR 97331
(503) 737-0123
Type of Facility: Auditorium
Type of Stage: Platform
Seating Capacity: 750
Year Built: 1952
Contact for Rental: Beth Dyer;   (503) 737-2181

Eugene

DANCE

EUGENE BALLET COMPANY
PO Box 11200, Eugene, OR 97440
(503) 485-3992
Founded: 1978
Arts Area: Ballet
Status: Professional; Non-Profit
Type: Performing; Touring; Resident; Sponsoring
Management: Toni Pimble, Artistic Director; Riley Grannan, Managing Director; Robert Dwan, Development Director; Eloise Zenger, Financial Manager; Tamara Richey, Marketing Director
Officers: Janet Reed, President; Larry Hedberg, Vice President; Margaret Leonard, Secretary; Kenneth Kohnen, Treasurer
Paid Staff: 5   **Volunteer Staff:** 5
Paid Artists: 20   **Non-Paid Artists:** 3
Utilizes: Guest Conductors
Budget: $100,000 - $500,000
Income Sources: Private Foundations/Grants/Endowments; Business/Corporate Donations; Box Office; Government Grants; Individual Donations
Season: September - April   **Annual Attendance:** 40,000
Performance Facilities: Hult Center for the Performing Arts

INSTRUMENTAL MUSIC

EMERALD CHAMBER PLAYERS
3080 Potter, Eugene, OR 97405
(503) 344-0483
Founded: 1962
Arts Area: Orchestra; Chamber; Ensemble; Instrumental Group
Status: Non-Professional; Non-Profit
Type: Performing

Purpose: To afford amateurs opportunities to play chamber music for themselves and for others
Management: Orval Etter, Convener
Income Sources: Private Foundations/Grants/Endowments; Government Grants; Individual Donations
Season: 52 Weeks **Annual Attendance:** 2,000

EUGENE SYMPHONY
45 West Broadway, #201, Eugene, OR 97401
(503) 687-9487
FAX: (503) 687-0527
Founded: 1966
Arts Area: Symphony; Orchestra
Status: Semi-Professional; Non-Profit
Type: Performing; Resident
Purpose: To produce music of the highest professional quality for the enjoyment of a diverse public
Management: Michael Anderson, Interim Executive Director
Officers: John C. Watkinson, President; Georgianne Beaudet, Vice President; Ted Scherer, Secretary; Robert Fenstermacher, Treasurer
Paid Staff: 10 **Volunteer Staff:** 15
Paid Artists: 85
Utilizes: Guest Conductors; Guest Artists
Budget: $100,000 - $500,000
Income Sources: Private Foundations/Grants/Endowments; Business/Corporate Donations; Box Office; Government Grants; Individual Donations
Season: September - May **Annual Attendance:** 40,150
Affiliations: ASCAP; ASOL
Performance Facilities: Hult Center for the Performing Arts

OREGON MOZART PLAYERS
541 Willametta Street, Suite 308, Eugene, OR 97401
(503) 345-6648
Founded: 1982
Arts Area: Orchestra; Chamber
Status: Professional; Non-Profit
Type: Performing; Touring; Resident; Educational
Purpose: To play chamber orchestra music and provide an opportunity for talented, local musicians to perform as soloists as members of the orchestra, and in chamber ensembles
Management: Jeffrey Eaton, General Manager
Officers: Jim Dotson, President; Sharon Schuman, Vice President; Russell Donnelly, Secretary/Treasurer
Paid Staff: 1 **Volunteer Staff:** 2
Paid Artists: 35
Utilizes: Special Technical Talent; Guest Conductors; Guest Artists
Budget: $100,000 - $500,000
Income Sources: Private Foundations/Grants/Endowments; Business/Corporate Donations; Box Office; Government Grants; Individual Donations; Special Events
Season: September - May **Annual Attendance:** 6,000
Performance Facilities: Hult Center For The Performing Arts; Beall Concert Hall, University of Oregon

VOCAL MUSIC

EUGENE OPERA
PO Box 11200, Eugene, OR 97440
(503) 485-3985
FAX: (503) 683-3783
Founded: 1976
Arts Area: Grand Opera; Lyric Opera; Light Opera; Operetta
Status: Professional; Non-Profit
Type: Performing; Educational
Purpose: To produce opera
Management: James Toland, Artistic Director
Officers: Alan Evans, Board President
Paid Staff: 5 **Volunteer Staff:** 4
Utilizes: Special Technical Talent; Guest Conductors; Guest Artists; Guest Directors
Budget: $100,000 - $500,000
Income Sources: Private Foundations/Grants/Endowments; Business/Corporate Donations; Box Office; Government Grants; Individual Donations
Season: December - April **Annual Attendance:** 14,000
Affiliations: OA; COS
Performance Facilities: Hult Center for the Performing Arts

THEATRE

MAINSTAGE THEATRE COMPANY
996 Willamette Street, Eugene, OR 97401
(503) 683-4368
Founded: 1979
Arts Area: Professional; Musical; Dinner; Community; Theatrical Group
Status: Semi-Professional; Non-Professional; Non-Profit
Type: Performing
Purpose: To offer a wide range of experiences for participants and audiences both in a community theatre and in a professional theater atmosphere
Management: Jim Roberts, Producer/Executive Director; Joe Zingo, Artistic Director
Officers: Joe Zingo, Chairperson
Paid Staff: 2 **Volunteer Staff:** 12
Paid Artists: 24 **Non-Paid Artists:** 100
Budget: $50,000 - $100,000
Income Sources: Business/Corporate Donations; Box Office; Individual Donations
Season: 52 Weeks **Annual Attendance:** 15,200
Performance Facilities: Downtown Cabaret; Eugene Downtown Mall

OREGON FANTASY THEATRE
820 East 36th Street, Eugene, OR 97405
(503) 686-1574
Founded: 1978
Arts Area: Musical; Community; Theatrical Group; Puppet
Status: Professional; Non-Professional; Commercial
Type: Performing; Touring; Educational
Purpose: Produce and perform puppet shows with combination live actors, marionettes, hand puppets, shadows and masks
Management: Celeste Rose, Director
Paid Staff: 1 **Volunteer Staff:** 10
Paid Artists: 3 **Non-Paid Artists:** 3
Utilizes: Special Technical Talent; Guest Artists
Budget: $1,000 - $50,000
Income Sources: Box Office
Season: 52 Weeks **Annual Attendance:** 2,000
Affiliations: Puppeteers of America
Performance Facilities: Hult Center for the Performing Arts

PERFORMING SERIES

CHAMBER MUSIC SERIES
University of Oregon, Eugene, OR 97403
(503) 346-5678
FAX: (503) 346-5669
Founded: 1968
Arts Area: Dance; Vocal Music; Instrumental Music; Festivals
Status: Non-Profit
Type: Performing; Touring; Educational
Purpose: To present classical chamber music concerts
Management: Stephen Stone, Manager
Paid Staff: 2
Budget: $1,000 - $50,000
Income Sources: Private Foundations/Grants/Endowments; Business/Corporate Donations; Box Office; Individual Donations
Season: October - May **Annual Attendance:** 3,800
Performance Facilities: Beall Concert Hall

OREGON BACH FESTIVAL
University of Oregon, School of Music, Eugene, OR 97403
(503) 346-5666
FAX: (503) 346-5669
Founded: 1970
Arts Area: Vocal Music; Instrumental Music; Festivals
Status: Professional; Non-Profit
Type: Performing; Resident; Educational
Purpose: To create for performers, audience and the community at large an artistic experience that elevates the human spirit through excellence in performance
Utilizes: Special Technical Talent; Guest Conductors; Guest Artists

Budget: $1,000,000 - $5,000,000
Income Sources: Private Foundations/Grants/Endowments; Business/Corporate Donations; Box Office; Government Grants; Individual Donations
Season: June - July   **Annual Attendance:** 31,000
Performance Facilities: University of Oregon School of Music; Beall Concert Hall; Hult Center for Performing Arts; Silva Concert Hall; Soreng Theatre

FACILITY

HULT CENTER FOR THE PERFORMING ARTS
One Eugene Centre, Eugene, OR 97401
(503) 687-5087
> **Type of Facility:** Theatre Complex; Performance Center
> **Year Built:** 1982   **Architect:** Hardy Holzman Pfeiffer Associates
> **Acoustical Consultant:** Jaffe Acoustics
> **Contact for Rental:** Karm Hagedorn;   (503) 687-5087
> *Hult Center for the Performing Arts contains Silva Concert Hall and Soreng Theatre. See separate listings for further information.*

HULT CENTER FOR THE PERFORMING ARTS - SILVA CONCERT HALL
One Eugene Centre, Eugene, OR 97401
(503) 687-5087
> **Type of Facility:** Concert Hall; Performance Center; Opera House; Multi-Purpose
> **Type of Stage:** Proscenium
> **Stage Dimensions:** 113'Wx50'D; 57'10"W proscenium opening   **Orchestra Pit**
> **Seating Capacity:** 2,504
> **Year Built:** 1982
> **Contact for Rental:** Karm Hagedorn;   (503) 687-5087
> **Resident Groups:** Eugene Symphony; Eugene Ballet; Eugene Festival of Musical Theater; Oregon Bach Festival

HULT CENTER FOR THE PERFORMING ARTS - SORENG THEATRE
One Eugene Centre, Eugene, OR 97401
(503) 687-5087
> **Type of Facility:** Concert Hall; Theatre House
> **Type of Stage:** Proscenium
> **Stage Dimensions:** 55'Wx30'D; 55'W proscenium opening   **Orchestra Pit**
> **Seating Capacity:** 500
> **Year Built:** 1982
> **Contact for Rental:** Karm Hagedorn;   (503) 687-5087
> **Resident Groups:** Oregon Mozart Players; Hult Children's Series

UNIVERSITY OF OREGON - BEALL CONCERT HALL
Eugene, OR 97403
(503) 686-5678
> **Type of Facility:** Concert Hall; Auditorium
> **Type of Stage:** Platform
> **Stage Dimensions:** 50'Wx35'D
> **Seating Capacity:** 550
> **Year Built:** 1921   **Architect:** Ellis Lawrence
> **Year Remodeled:** 1973   **Architect:** John Amundsen   **Cost:** $100,000
> **Contact for Rental:** Manager;   (503) 686-5678

Forest Grove

INSTRUMENTAL MUSIC

PACIFIC UNIVERSITY COMMUNITY ORCHESTRA
Pacific University, Music Department, Forest Grove, OR 97116
(503) 357-6151
> **Founded:** 1849
> **Arts Area:** Orchestra; Chamber
> **Status:** Non-Professional; Non-Profit
> **Type:** Performing; Resident; Educational
> **Purpose:** Educational training for music students and music outlet for members of the community
> **Management:** Craig Gibson, Conductor
> **Paid Staff:** 1
> **Paid Artists:** 50
> **Utilizes:** Guest Artists

Budget: $1,000 - $50,000
Season: September - May   Annual Attendance: 1,000
Performance Facilities: University Center

FACILITY

PACIFIC UNIVERSITY - TOM MILES THEATRE
2043 College Way, Forest Grove, OR 97116
(503) 359-2200
Type of Facility: Multi-Purpose; Room
Facility Originally: Meeting Hall; Movie House
Type of Stage: Proscenium
Stage Dimensions: 10'x20'x20'
Seating Capacity: 350
Year Built: 1962
Contact for Rental: Ed Collier;   (503) 359-2200

THEATRE IN THE GROVE
2028 Pacific Avenue, PO Box 263, Forest Grove, OR 97116
(503) 359-5349
Founded: 1970
Type of Facility: Auditorium; Theatre House
Facility Originally: Movie House
Type of Stage: Thrust; Flexible; Proscenium; revolving center stage
Stage Dimensions: 20'x30'x30'   Orchestra Pit
Seating Capacity: 350
Year Built: 1910
Year Remodeled: 1992   Architect: Dave Giulletti   Cost: $200,000
Contact for Rental: Jeff Zimmerman, Manager;   (503) 359-5349
Manager: Jeff Zimmerman
Resident Groups: Theatre in the Grove

Lake Oswego

INSTRUMENTAL MUSIC

PORTLAND FESTIVAL SYMPHONY
PO Box 359, Lake Oswego, OR 97034
(503) 636-8769
Founded: 1986
Arts Area: Symphony
Status: Professional
Type: Performing
Purpose: To provide free concerts (to promote symphonic music) to large audiences in cooperation with the City Park Bureau
Management: Lajos Balogh, Music Director/Conductor
Volunteer Staff: 15
Paid Artists: 72
Utilizes: Guest Conductors; Guest Artists
Budget: $1,000 - $50,000
Income Sources: Private Foundations/Grants/Endowments; Business/Corporate Donations; Government Grants; Individual Donations
Annual Attendance: 20,000
Performance Facilities: Washington Park

THEATRE

LAKEWOOD THEATRE COMPANY
368 South State Street, PO Box 274, Lake Oswego, OR 97034
(503) 635-3901
Founded: 1952
Arts Area: Musical; Community; Theatrical Group
Status: Non-Professional; Non-Profit
Type: Performing; Resident; Educational; Sponsoring
Purpose: Training for actors, actresses, directors and technical people for personal and/or professional enjoyment
Management: Andrew Edwards, Executive Director; Kay Vega, Executive Producer
Officers: Paul Graham, President
Paid Staff: 5   Volunteer Staff: 2

Paid Artists: 100   **Non-Paid Artists:** 50
Utilizes: Special Technical Talent; Guest Conductors; Guest Artists; Guest Directors
Budget: $100,000 - $500,000
Income Sources: Private Foundations/Grants/Endowments; Business/Corporate Donations; Box Office; Individual Donations
Season: 52 Weeks   **Annual Attendance:** 25,000
Affiliations: Oregon Theatre Association; Oregon Advocates for the Arts; Portland Area Theatre Alliance

McMinnville

THEATRE

GALLERY THEATRE OF OREGON
Second and Ford Streets, McMinnville, OR 97128
(503) 472-2227
Founded: 1968
Arts Area: Musical; Community
Status: Non-Profit
Type: Performing; Educational
Purpose: Provide center for the performing arts in Yamhill County
Management: Corby Wright, Managing Director
Officers: Chris Browne, President of the Board; Carol Burnett, Vice President; Barbara Knutson, Secretary; Jim Capps, Treasurer
Volunteer Staff: 20
Non-Paid Artists: 150
Utilizes: Special Technical Talent; Guest Artists; Guest Directors
Budget: $100,000 - $500,000
Income Sources: Private Foundations/Grants/Endowments; Business/Corporate Donations; Box Office; Government Grants; Individual Donations
Season: 52 Weeks   **Annual Attendance:** 30,000

Medford

DANCE

MEDFORD CIVIC BALLET
9 Hawthorne Street, Medford, OR 97502
(503) 772-1362
Founded: 1982
Arts Area: Ballet
Status: Non-Profit
Type: Performing
Purpose: To excel in dance and dance education
Management: Mary Cowden Snyder, Artistic Director
Officers: Bonnie McKinley, Chairperson
Paid Staff: 3   **Volunteer Staff:** 20
Paid Artists: 3   **Non-Paid Artists:** 20
Utilizes: Guest Artists
Budget: $1,000 - $50,000
Income Sources: Private Foundations/Grants/Endowments; Business/Corporate Donations; Box Office; Individual Donations
Season: September - July   **Annual Attendance:** 10,000

PERFORMING SERIES

BRITT FESTIVALS
PO Box 1124, Medford, OR 97501
(503) 779-0847
FAX: (503) 776-3712
Founded: 1963
Arts Area: Dance; Vocal Music; Instrumental Music; Theater; Festivals
Status: Professional; Non-Profit
Type: Performing; Touring; Resident; Educational; Sponsoring
Management: Ron Mellne, General Manager; Chris Sackett, Productions Manager; Stacey Stover, Marketing; Debbie Whipple, Financial Manager; Barbara Frenna, Box Office Manager
Officers: Diane Christopher, President; Gary Lovre, Vice President; Diane Somers, Vice President; Lois Thorson, Treasurer; Margaret Cutler, Secretary

Paid Staff: 15 Volunteer Staff: 500
Paid Artists: 240
Utilizes: Guest Conductors; Guest Artists; Guest Directors
Budget: $500,000 - $1,000,000
Income Sources: Private Foundations/Grants/Endowments; Business/Corporate Donations; Box Office; Government Grants; Individual Donations
Season: June - September Annual Attendance: 51,000
Performance Facilities: The Britt Gardens

FACILITY

CRATERIAN THEATRE
23 South Central Avenue, Medford, OR 97501
(503) 779-8195
Founded: 1924
Type of Facility: Performance Center; Theatre House; Multi-Purpose
Facility Originally: Vaudeville; Movie House
Type of Stage: Thrust; Proscenium; Stage is elevated 4' from main floor
Stage Dimensions: 32'x35' Orchestra Pit
Seating Capacity: 650
Year Built: 1924 Architect: Frank Clark Cost: $176,000
Contact for Rental: Teresa Collins Ley; (503) 779-8195

Monmouth
FACILITY

WESTERN OREGON STATE COLLEGE
345 Monmouth Avenue, Monmouth, OR 97361
(503) 838-8462
Type of Facility: Theatre Complex; Auditorium; Studio Performance; Recital Hall
Type of Stage: Flexible; Proscenium; Platform; Environmental; 3/4 Arena with on-stage seating
Stage Dimensions: 52'x30' Orchestra Pit
Seating Capacity: 619
Year Built: 1976 Architect: Payne and Setticase Cost: $2,000,000
Contact for Rental: (503) 838-8462
Resident Groups: Western Oregon State College Theatre

North Bend
THEATRE

DOLPHIN PLAYERS
2540 Union, North Bend, OR 97459
(503) 756-7088
Founded: 1980
Arts Area: Musical; Dinner; Community; Theatrical Group
Status: Non-Professional; Non-Profit
Type: Performing; Resident; Educational; Sponsoring
Purpose: To present quality theater productions in an intimate setting
Officers: Alice Carlson, President; Mark Thimm, Vice President; Clara Radcliffe, Secretary; Mable Hayes, Treasurer
Volunteer Staff: 3
Non-Paid Artists: 50
Budget: $1,000 - $50,000
Income Sources: Business/Corporate Donations; Box Office; Individual Donations
Season: 52 Weeks

Portland
DANCE

THE CONTEMPORARY DANCE SEASON
c/o Portland State University, PO Box 751, Portland, OR 90207
(503) 725-3131
FAX: (503) 725-4882
Arts Area: Modern

Status: Professional; Non-Profit
Type: Educational; Presenting
Purpose: To present contemporary dance and dance education of the highest quality
Management: Carolyn Altman, Managing Director
Budget: $100,000 - $500,000
Income Sources: Private Foundations/Grants/Endowments; Business/Corporate Donations; Box Office; Government Grants; Individual Donations
Performance Facilities: Lincoln Hall

METRO DANCERS
6433 NE Tillamook, Portland, OR 97213
(503) 282-5061
Founded: 1979
Arts Area: Modern; Ballet
Status: Non-Professional; Non-Profit
Type: Performing
Purpose: Arts should be accessible to everyone.
Management: Nancy Y. Thompson, Artistic Director
Non-Paid Artists: 20
Utilizes: Guest Artists
Budget: $1,000 - $50,000
Income Sources: Government Grants
Season: April - October
Affiliations: Regional Dance Association/Pacific

OREGON BALLET THEATRE
1120 SW Tenth Avenue, Portland, OR 97205
(503) 227-0977
FAX: (503) 227-4186
Founded: 1989
Arts Area: Modern; Ballet; Jazz
Status: Professional; Non-Profit
Type: Performing; Touring; Resident; Educational; Sponsoring
Purpose: To offer the highest quality professional ballet to the people of Oregon, the Pacific Northwest and the U.S.; to entertain and educate audiences, and to encourage the creative talents of dancers, choreographers, composers and musicians
Management: James Canfield, Artistic Director; Dennis Spaight, Associate Director/Resident Choreographer; Niel De Ponte, Music Director
Officers: Ken Lewis, Chairman; Scott Howard, Secretary; Tracy Montgomery, Treasurer
Paid Staff: 67   **Volunteer Staff:** 135
Paid Artists: 25
Utilizes: Guest Artists; Guest Choreographers
Budget: $1,000,000 - $5,000,000
Income Sources: Private Foundations/Grants/Endowments; Business/Corporate Donations; Box Office; Government Grants; Individual Donations
Season: October - May   **Annual Attendance:** 76,000
Affiliations: WESTAF; WAA; Dance USA; Portland Arts Alliance
Performance Facilities: Portland Civic Auditorium

INSTRUMENTAL MUSIC

CHAMBER MUSIC NORTHWEST
522 SW Fifth Avenue, Suite 725, Portland, OR 97204
(503) 233-3202
Founded: 1971
Arts Area: Chamber; Ensemble
Status: Professional; Non-Profit
Type: Performing
Purpose: To present an annual summer music festival (five weeks/25 concerts) with world renowned performers in residence
Management: Linda Magee, Executive Director; David Shifrin, Music Director; Marte Lamb, Operations Director; Katherine King, Business Manager
Officers: Anne Munch, President; Sharon Van Sickle, Vice President; Jeffrey Grayson, Secretary; Robert Steinberg, Treasurer
Paid Staff: 14
Paid Artists: 43
Utilizes: Guest Artists
Budget: $100,000 - $500,000
Income Sources: Private Foundations/Grants/Endowments; Business/Corporate Donations; Box Office; Government Grants; Individual Donations

Season: June - July   **Annual Attendance:** 14,000
Affiliations: CMA
Performance Facilities: Reed College Commons; Catlin Gabel School's Cabell Center

THE CHAMBER MUSIC SOCIETY OF OREGON
1935 NE 59th Avenue, Portland, OR 97213
(503) 287-2175
>**Founded:** 1973
>**Arts Area:** Orchestra; Chamber; Ensemble; Instrumental Group
>**Status:** Non-Professional; Non-Profit
>**Type:** Performing; Resident; Educational
>**Purpose:** To promote music in our schools for its value in teaching children how to learn
>**Officers:** Patricia Ann Haim, President; Dr. Floyd Grant Jackson, Vice President; Beatrice Matin, Secretary; John B. Gould, Treasurer; Hazel M. DeLorenzo, Executive Director
>**Volunteer Staff:** 25
>**Utilizes:** Special Technical Talent; Guest Artists
>**Budget:** $1,000 - $50,000
>**Income Sources:** Private Foundations/Grants/Endowments; Business/Corporate Donations; Individual Donations; Fees from Summer Music Day Camp
>**Season:** 52 Weeks   **Annual Attendance:** 12,000
>**Performance Facilities:** St. Philip Neri Church; Hood River Middle School

OREGON SYMPHONY ORCHESTRA
711 SW Alder, Suite 200, Portland, OR 97205
(503) 228-4294
>**Founded:** 1896
>**Arts Area:** Symphony; Orchestra
>**Status:** Non-Profit
>**Type:** Performing; Sponsoring
>**Purpose:** To provide concerts of the highest quality orchestral music for the people of Oregon and the Northwest
>**Management:** Don Roth, Managing Director
>**Officers:** William Scott, Chairman of the Board
>**Paid Staff:** 23   **Volunteer Staff:** 1
>**Paid Artists:** 88
>**Utilizes:** Special Technical Talent; Guest Conductors; Guest Artists
>**Budget:** $5,000,000 - $10,000,000
>**Income Sources:** Private Foundations/Grants/Endowments; Business/Corporate Donations; Box Office; Government Grants; Individual Donations
>**Season:** August - June   **Annual Attendance:** 300,000
>**Affiliations:** ASOL; AFM
>**Performance Facilities:** Arlene Schnitzer Concert Hall

PORTLAND YOUTH PHILHARMONIC ASSOCIATION
1119 SW Park Avenue, Portland, OR 97205
(503) 223-5939
FAX: (503) 223-5003
>**Founded:** 1924
>**Arts Area:** Symphony; Orchestra; Ensemble
>**Status:** Non-Professional; Non-Profit
>**Type:** Performing; Touring; Resident; Educational
>**Purpose:** It is the purpose of the Portland Youth Philharmonic to maintain the finest possible resident youth orchestra in order to inspire, train and educate young people in the performance and appreciation of symphonic music and to provide a cultural asset to the community.
>**Management:** Jacob Avshalomov, Conductor/Musical Director; Janet Fry, General Manager; Maria Yolz, Secretary/Receptionist
>**Officers:** Ernestine Oringdulph, President; Kathy Froom, Wayne Landsreck, Doug McCaslin, Richard Wouldridge, Vice Presidents; Charles Kobin, Corporate Secretary; Catherine Freedman, Recording Secretary; Kathy Whilteman Johnson, Treasurer
>**Paid Staff:** 3   **Volunteer Staff:** 400
>**Paid Artists:** 2   **Non-Paid Artists:** 206
>**Utilizes:** Guest Artists
>**Budget:** $100,000 - $500,000
>**Income Sources:** Private Foundations/Grants/Endowments; Business/Corporate Donations; Box Office; Government Grants; Individual Donations
>**Season:** September - June   **Annual Attendance:** 43,000
>**Affiliations:** ASOL (Youth Orchestra Division)
>**Performance Facilities:** Arlene Schnitzer Concert Hall; Civic Auditorium

VIRTUOSI DELLA ROSA, INC.
1501 SE Holly Street, Portland, OR 97214
(503) 236-8678
> **Founded:** 1985
> **Arts Area:** Chamber; Contemporary; Multimedia
> **Status:** Professional; Non-Profit
> **Type:** Performing; Touring; Educational; Sponsoring
> **Purpose:** To perform new music with excellence and with particular attention to women, minorities and Northwest composers
> **Management:** Judith Bokor, Founder/Director; Scott Kritzer, Co-Director; George Anne Ries, Assistant Director
> **Officers:** Elizabeth Booker, President; Brian Wagner, Vice President; Ronald Kogen, Treasurer; Sara Mahler, Steve Prince
> **Volunteer Staff:** 3
> **Paid Artists:** 15
> **Utilizes:** Guest Artists
> **Budget:** $1,000 - $50,000
> **Income Sources:** Private Foundations/Grants/Endowments; Business/Corporate Donations; Box Office; Government Grants; Individual Donations; Fundraising
> **Season:** September - June   **Annual Attendance:** 1,500

VOCAL MUSIC

OREGON REPERTORY SINGERS
PO Box 894, Portland, OR 97207
(503) 227-3929
> **Founded:** 1974
> **Arts Area:** Choral
> **Status:** Non-Profit
> **Type:** Performing
> **Purpose:** ORS contributes to the cultural community through performances in Portland, tours outside the metropolitan area, educational programs and special projects of an edifying nature.
> **Management:** Richard Seeley, Artistic Director; Richard Brown, Administration
> **Paid Staff:** 1   **Volunteer Staff:** 3
> **Paid Artists:** 30   **Non-Paid Artists:** 50
> **Utilizes:** Guest Artists
> **Budget:** $1,000 - $50,000
> **Income Sources:** Private Foundations/Grants/Endowments; Business/Corporate Donations; Box Office; Government Grants; Individual Donations
> **Season:** September - June   **Annual Attendance:** 4,000
> **Performance Facilities:** Agnes Flanagan Chapel, Lewis and Clark College

PORTLAND OPERA
1516 SW Alder, Portland, OR 97201
(503) 241-1407
FAX: (503) 241-4212
> **Founded:** 1964
> **Arts Area:** Grand Opera; Lyric Opera; Light Opera; Operetta
> **Status:** Professional; Non-Profit
> **Type:** Performing; Touring; Resident
> **Management:** Robert Bailey, General Director
> **Paid Staff:** 22   **Volunteer Staff:** 100
> **Paid Artists:** 200   **Non-Paid Artists:** 50
> **Utilizes:** Special Technical Talent; Guest Conductors; Guest Artists; Guest Directors; Guest Designers; Guest Soloists
> **Budget:** $1,000,000 - $5,000,000
> **Income Sources:** Private Foundations/Grants/Endowments; Business/Corporate Donations; Box Office; Government Grants; Individual Donations; Set & Costume Rentals
> **Season:** September - June   **Annual Attendance:** 55,000
> **Affiliations:** OA
> **Performance Facilities:** Portland Civic Auditorium

PORTLAND SYMPHONIC CHOIR
PO Box 1517, Portland, OR 97207
(503) 223-1217
> **Founded:** 1946
> **Arts Area:** Choral
> **Status:** Non-Professional; Non-Profit
> **Type:** Performing
> **Purpose:** To provide an opportunity for talented singers to perform music representing the widest spectrum of choral literature

Management: Board of Directors
Officers: Ralph Nelson, President; Robert Morrison, Vice President; Jan Sapinski, Secretary; Karen Shepard, Treasurer
Paid Staff: 3 **Volunteer Staff:** 30
Paid Artists: 45
Utilizes: Guest Conductors; Guest Artists
Budget: $50,000 - $100,000
Income Sources: Private Foundations/Grants/Endowments; Business/Corporate Donations; Box Office; Government Grants; Individual Donations
Season: September - May **Annual Attendance:** 5,500
Affiliations: Oregon Symphony
Performance Facilities: First United Methodist Church

THEATRE

PORTLAND BLACK REPERTORY
PO Box 8655, Portland, OR 97207-8655
(503) 287-3959
Founded: 1978
Arts Area: Community; Theatrical Group
Status: Semi-Professional; Non-Profit
Type: Performing; Touring; Resident; Educational; Sponsoring; Equity Company
Purpose: To produce excellent quality live theatre utilizing the skills and talents of local artists and to present and preserve the rich culture of African-Americans; Its aim is to produce an annual season of classic and superior contemporary plays acted, directed and designed at a standard of excellence comparable to that of the nation's leading professional companies.
Management: Rosemary Allen, Producing Artistic Director; Patrick Stewart, Resident Designer; Eugene Hughes, Manager
Officers: Rosemary Allen, President; Lonnie Nettles, Secretary; LeCheryl Cooper, Treasurer
Utilizes: Special Technical Talent; Guest Directors
Budget: $50,000 - $100,000
Income Sources: Private Foundations/Grants/Endowments; Business/Corporate Donations; Box Office; Individual Donations
Season: September - May **Annual Attendance:** 7,000
Affiliations: Oregon Advocates for the Arts; Portland Theater Alliance; Oregon Association of Minority Entrepreneurs

PERFORMING SERIES

ARTS CELEBRATION/ARTQUAKE FESTIVAL
720 SW Washington, Suite 100, Portland, OR 97205
(503) 227-2787
Founded: 1977
Arts Area: Dance; Vocal Music; Instrumental Music; Theater; Festivals
Status: Professional; Non-Profit
Type: Sponsoring
Purpose: Annual arts showcase of local, regional companies, artists and performers
Management: Keri Hoops, Executive Director
Officers: Stuart Tiecher, President; Don Vallaster, Vice President; Patsy Ferman, Secretary; Trudy Thatcher, Treasurer
Paid Staff: 2
Paid Artists: 600
Utilizes: Special Technical Talent; Guest Conductors; Guest Artists; Guest Directors
Budget: $100,000 - $500,000
Income Sources: Private Foundations/Grants/Endowments; Business/Corporate Donations; Box Office; Government Grants; Individual Donations
Season: May - September **Annual Attendance:** 300,000
Performance Facilities: Portland Performing Arts Center; Outdoor Festival

FACILITY

ARLENE SCHNITZER CONCERT HALL
SW Broadway at Main Street, Portland, OR 97201
(503) 248-4335
FAX: (503) 274-7490
Type of Facility: Concert Hall
Type of Stage: Proscenium
Stage Dimensions: 54'x32'x34' **Orchestra Pit**
Seating Capacity: 2,776
Year Built: 1928 **Architect:** Rapp & Rapp
Year Remodeled: 1984 **Architect:** Broome Oringdulph O'Toole Rudolph & Associates; ELS Design Group
Cost: $10,000,000
Acoustical Consultant: R. Lawrence Kirkegaard & Associates

Contact for Rental: Booking Manager;   (503) 248-4335
Resident Groups: Oregon Symphony Orchestra; Portland Youth Philharmonic

COMMUNITY MUSIC CENTER - DAVID CAMPBELL RECITAL HALL
3350 SE Francis, Portland, OR 97202
(530) 823-3177
   Type of Facility: Auditorium
   Facility Originally: Fire Station
   Type of Stage: Thrust; Platform
   Stage Dimensions: 16'x26'
   Seating Capacity: 110
   Year Built: 1912
   Year Remodeled: 1969   **Architect:** Robert Oringdulph   **Cost:** $80,000
   Contact for Rental: Charles Farmer;   (530) 823-3177

ECHO THEATRE
1515 SE 37th Avenue, Portland, OR 97214
(503) 231-1232
   Founded: 1983
   Type of Facility: Concert Hall; Studio Performance; Environmental; Performance Center; Theatre House; Multi-Purpose;
   Room
   Facility Originally: Movie House
   Type of Stage: Flexible; Proscenium; Dance Theatre
   Stage Dimensions: 42'Wx36'D
   Seating Capacity: 185
   Year Built: 1910
   Year Remodeled: 1983   **Architect:** Aaron Faegre   **Cost:** $24,000
   Acoustical Consultant: Aron Faegre
   Contact for Rental: Office Manager;   (503) 231-1232
   Resident Groups: Do Jump Movement Theatre

NEW ROSE THEATRE
904 SW Main Street, Portland, OR 97205
(503) 222-2487
   Type of Facility: Theatre House
   Facility Originally: Business Facility
   Type of Stage: 3/4 Arena
   Stage Dimensions: 22'x25'
   Seating Capacity: 119
   Resident Groups: New Rose Theatre Company

PORTLAND CENTER FOR THE PERFORMING ARTS - PORTLAND CIVIC AUDITORIUM
222 SW Clay Street, Portland, OR 97201
(503) 248-4335
   Type of Facility: Auditorium
   Type of Stage: Proscenium
   Stage Dimensions: 30'x60'x42'   **Orchestra Pit**
   Seating Capacity: 3,000
   Year Built: 1917   **Architect:** A.J. Doyle
   Year Remodeled: 1968   **Architect:** Stanton Boles Maguire & Church   **Cost:** $3,900,000
   Contact for Rental: Lori Leyba, Booking Manager;   (503) 248-4335
   Resident Groups: Portland Opera; Oregon Symphony

REED COLLEGE - REED THEATRE
Portland, OR 97202
(503) 771-1112, ext. X357
   Type of Facility: Theatre House
   Facility Originally: Warehouse
   Type of Stage: Flexible
   Stage Dimensions: 40'x80'
   Seating Capacity: 150
   Year Built: 1972   **Architect:** Robert Oringdulph   **Cost:** $140,000
   Year Remodeled: 1979

WILSON CENTER FOR THE PERFORMING ARTS
1111 SW 10th, Portland, OR 97205
(503) 223-6281
   Type of Facility: Performance Center

Facility Originally: Business Facility
Type of Stage: Arena
Stage Dimensions: 20'x40'
Seating Capacity: 110
Year Built: 1973   **Architect:** Stanton Boles Maguire & Church   **Cost:** $56,231
Year Remodeled: 1977   **Architect:** Stanton Boles Maguire & Church   **Cost:** $2,693
Contact for Rental: YWCA;   (503) 223-6281
Manager: Artists Repertory Theatre;   (503) 242-2420
Resident Groups: Artists Repertory Theatre

Roseburg

INSTRUMENTAL MUSIC

UMPQUA SYMPHONY ASSOCIATION
PO Box 241, Roseburg, OR 97470
(503) 672-6104
> **Founded:** 1955
> **Arts Area:** Symphony; Orchestra; Chamber; Ensemble; Instrumental Group
> **Status:** Non-Profit
> **Type:** Sponsoring
> **Purpose:** To bring classical music and dance to the local community
> **Management:** Bob Robbins, Production Director
> **Officers:** David Jones, President; Anita Daily, Vice President
> **Volunteer Staff:** 15
> **Utilizes:** Guest Artists
> **Budget:** $1,000 - $50,000
> **Income Sources:** Private Foundations/Grants/Endowments; Business/Corporate Donations; Box Office; Individual Donations
> **Season:** October - May   **Annual Attendance:** 2,400
> **Performance Facilities:** Umpqua Community College Auditorium

Saint Benedict

PERFORMING SERIES

ABBEY BACH FESTIVAL
Mount Angel Abbey, Saint Benedict, OR 97373
(503) 845-3321
FAX: (503) 845-3594
> **Founded:** 1972
> **Arts Area:** Vocal Music; Instrumental Music
> **Status:** Professional; Semi-Professional
> **Type:** Performing
> **Officers:** Abbot Peter Ebere OSB, President; Father Bruno Becker OSB, Executive Director
> **Volunteer Staff:** 20
> **Paid Artists:** 15
> **Utilizes:** Guest Artists
> **Budget:** $1,000 - $50,000
> **Income Sources:** Box Office; Individual Donations
> **Season:** July   **Annual Attendance:** 1,500
> **Performance Facilities:** Damian Center

Salem

INSTRUMENTAL MUSIC

CAMERATA MUSICA
714 Tillman Avenue SE, Salem, OR 97302
(503) 364-8263
> **Founded:** 1976
> **Arts Area:** Chamber; Instrumental Group
> **Status:** Professional; Non-Professional; Non-Profit
> **Type:** Performing; Sponsoring
> **Purpose:** Camerata Musica presents a series of six chamber music concerts each season at the Salem Public Library. All of the concerts are open to the public without charge.

Management: Lydia Woods, Program Coordinator
Officers: Miriam Bednarz, President; Lydia Woods, Vice President; Dorothy Boardman, Secretary; Kelly Woods, Treasurer
Volunteer Staff: 10
Paid Artists: 12   **Non-Paid Artists:** 12
Utilizes: Special Technical Talent
Budget: $1,000 - $50,000
Income Sources: Private Foundations/Grants/Endowments; Business/Corporate Donations; Individual Donations
Season: October - May   **Annual Attendance:** 1,600
Performance Facilities: Salem Public Library Lecture Hall

OREGON SYMPHONY ASSOCIATION
161 High Street SE, Suite 230, Salem, OR 97301
(503) 364-0149
Founded: 1955
Arts Area: Symphony; Orchestra
Status: Non-Profit
Type: Sponsoring
Purpose: To use corporate funds exclusively for literary, benevolent, educational and cultural purposes by one or more of the following means: sponsor and promote public orchestral group or individual performances in the city of Salem and promote community interest
Management: N. Andrew Toney, Executive Director
Officers: Elaine K. Young, President; Gregor Strum MD, Vice President; Charles Weyant, Secretary; Jack Donovan, Treasurer; Ron Kelemen, Member-at-Large
Paid Staff: 1
Budget: $100,000 - $500,000
Income Sources: Business/Corporate Donations; Box Office; Individual Donations; Fund-raising
Season: September - May   **Annual Attendance:** 10,000
Affiliations: ASOL; Mid-Valley Arts Council
Performance Facilities: Smith Auditorium, Willamette University

WHEATLAND CHAMBER PLAYERS
7390 Wheatland Road, Salem, OR 97303-3451
(503) 393-6950
Founded: 1980
Arts Area: Chamber; Ethnic; Folk; Instrumental Group
Status: Professional; Non-Profit
Type: Performing; Resident; Educational
Purpose: To exhibit good classical and folk music
Management: Ralph Cater, Director
Officers: E. Bengingheim, Judith Dwyer, Norvada Smedley, Victor Palmerson, Del Giglio, Ralph Cater
Budget: $1,000 - $50,000
Income Sources: Individual Donations
Season: October - May
Annual Attendance: 2,000
Affiliations: American String Teachers Association

THEATRE

SALEM THEATER OF PERFORMING ARTS
191 High Street NE, Salem, OR 97301
(503) 588-7002
Founded: 1980
Arts Area: Musical; Community; Theatrical Group
Status: Non-Professional; Non-Profit
Type: Performing; Educational
Purpose: We present a variety of entertainment events and allow participation by all persons, whether experienced or not. We are incorporated as a non-profit educational group, and present productions, classes and manage a theatre facility which is open to other organizations.
Management: Dorothy Gahlsdorf, Theatre Manager; Bill Smith, Technical Director
Officers: Gary Esgate, President; Dan Nelson, Vice President; Diane Fredricks, Secretary; Eloise Smith, Treasurer
Volunteer Staff: 3
Utilizes: Guest Directors
Budget: $1,000 - $50,000
Income Sources: Private Foundations/Grants/Endowments; Business/Corporate Donations; Box Office; Individual Donations
Affiliations: Oregon Theatre Association
Performance Facilities: Grand Theatre

Seaside

FACILITY

SEASIDE CIVIC AND CONVENTION CENTER
415 First Avenue, Seaside, OR 97138
(503) 738-8585
FAX: (503) 738-0198
    Type of Facility: Civic Center
    Type of Stage: Proscenium
    Seating Capacity: 1,350
    Year Built: 1971   **Architect:** Brown Brown & Grider   **Cost:** $500,000
    Year Remodeled: 1992   **Architect:** HDN   **Cost:** $2,000,000
    Contact for Rental: Betty Wilson;   (503) 738-8585
    Manager: Les McNary;   (503) 738-8585

The Dalles

THEATRE

THE MASQUERADERS
7440 Mill Creek Road, The Dalles, OR 97058
(503) 298-4644
    Founded: 1965
    Arts Area: Musical; Dinner; Community; Theatrical Group
    Status: Non-Profit
    Type: Performing; Educational; Sponsoring
    Purpose: To provide the community with various performing arts presentations using a variety of formats; to provide community services and scholarships
    Officers: Paula Richmond, President; Robert Carsner, Vice President; Adrienne Stacher, Secretary
    Volunteer Staff: 10
    Non-Paid Artists: 50
    Utilizes: Special Technical Talent
    Budget: $1,000 - $50,000
    Income Sources: Box Office
    Season: September - May   **Annual Attendance:** 2,000

PENNSYLVANIA

Allentown

INSTRUMENTAL MUSIC

ALLENTOWN SYMPHONY ASSOCIATION
Symphony Hall, 23 North Sixth Street, Allentown, PA 18101
(215) 432-7961
FAX: (215) 432-6009
Founded: 1950
Arts Area: Symphony; Orchestra; Performing Arts; Comedians
Status: Non-Profit
Type: Performing; Educational
Purpose: To promote cultural values by providing high quality symphonic music and performing arts events, with broad community appeal, and education concerning them, in Allentown's historic Symphony Hall
Management: Anna Maria Marzullo, Music Director
Officers: Lona Farr, President; Judge James Knoll Gardner, First Vice President; Julian Lewis, Third Vice President; Reed Steele, Secretary; Barbara McGovern, Treasurer; Boyd Kreglow, Assistant Treasurer
Paid Staff: 6
Paid Artists: 80
Utilizes: Special Technical Talent; Guest Artists
Budget: $500,000 - $1,000,000
Income Sources: Private Foundations/Grants/Endowments; Business/Corporate Donations; Box Office; Government Grants; Individual Donations
Season: September - May
Annual Attendance: 100,000
Affiliations: ASOL; Association of Pennsylvania Orchestras; Lehigh Valley Arts Council; ASCAP; Preservation Pennsylvania; Allentown Chamber of Commerce; Allentown Cultural Alliance; Allentown Arts Commission
Performance Facilities: Symphony Hall

IMPROVISATIONALMUSICCO, INC.
908 North Penn Street, Allentown, PA 18102
(215) 820-9017
FAX: (215) 820-9017
Arts Area: Ethnic; Instrumental Group; New Music
Status: Professional; Non-Profit
Type: Educational; Presenting
Purpose: To expose people in eastern Pennsylvania to new music; to support the performers of that music, both American and foreign
Management: Pamela Fearing-Hassey, Executive Director
Officers: Gary Hassay, President; Donald Lehr, Hope Carr, Vice Presidents
Budget: $1,000 - $50,000
Income Sources: Private Foundations/Grants/Endowments; Business/Corporate Donations; Box Office; Government Grants; Individual Donations
Performance Facilities: Open Space Gallery

THEATRE

PENNSYLVANIA STAGE COMPANY
837 Linden Street, Allentown, PA 18101
(215) 434-6110
Founded: 1979
Arts Area: Professional; Theatrical Group
Status: Professional; Non-Profit
Type: Performing; Touring; Resident; Educational
Management: Ellen Baker-Baltz, Managing Director; Charles Richter, Artistic Director; Rosanne Damico, Marketing/Public Relations
Officers: Nancy Orr, Board President
Paid Staff: 14
Utilizes: Special Technical Talent; Guest Artists; Guest Directors
Income Sources: Private Foundations/Grants/Endowments; Business/Corporate Donations; Box Office; Government Grants; Individual Donations
Season: October - June
Affiliations: AEA; LORT
Performance Facilities: Pennsylvania Stage Company Theater

PERFORMING SERIES

ALLENTOWN COMMUNITY CONCERT ASSOCIATION
3736 Broadway, Allentown, PA 18104
(215) 432-9143
    Founded: 1927
    Arts Area: Dance; Vocal Music; Instrumental Music
    Status: Non-Profit
    Type: Educational; Sponsoring
    Purpose: To present four annual concerts with varied programs; membership is open to the public during the annual campaign
    Management: Agnus Balluit, Executive Director
    Officers: William Lazenberg, President
    Volunteer Staff: 2
    Paid Artists: 4
    Utilizes: Guest Artists
    Affiliations: Community Concerts

FACILITY

SYMPHONY HALL
23 North Sixth Street, Allentown, PA 18103
(215) 432-7961
    Type of Facility: Concert Hall
    Facility Originally: Vaudeville
    Type of Stage: Proscenium
    Stage Dimensions: 70'Wx45'D; 36'Wx38'H proscenium opening   **Orchestra Pit**
    Seating Capacity: 1,465
    Year Built: 1890
    Contact for Rental: Charles Kalan;   (215) 770-1932
    Resident Groups: Allentown Symphony
    Major renovation planned with Benjamin Walbert, Architect. Check for availability.

Altoona

DANCE

ALLEGHENY BALLET COMPANY
PO Box 369, Altoona, PA 16603
(814) 941-9944
    Arts Area: Ballet
    Status: Semi-Professional; Non-Profit
    Type: Performing; Resident
    Management: Deborah Anthony, Artistic Director; Marjorie Lantz, Business Manager
    Paid Artists: 8
    Income Sources: Box Office; Individual Donations
    Performance Facilities: Mishler Theatre

PERFORMING SERIES

BLAIR COUNTY CIVIC MUSIC ASSOCIATION
PO Box 6Q, Altoona, PA 16602
(814) 943-9951
    Founded: 1944
    Arts Area: Dance; Vocal Music; Instrumental Music; Theater; Grand Opera
    Status: Professional; Non-Profit
    Type: Presenting
    Purpose: To bring the best of the performing arts to Blair County at an affordable fee for our league of subscribers
    Officers: Patricia Gilder, President; Charlotte Morris, First Vice President; Richard Russell, Second Vice President; Estrida McLaughlin, Third Vice President; Pauline Hoover, Recording Secretary; Jane Gable, Membership Secretary
    Volunteer Staff: 38
    Budget: $50,000 - $100,000
    Income Sources: Box Office
    Season: October - April   **Annual Attendance:** 7,500
    Performance Facilities: Roosevelt Junior High School Auditorium

FACILITY

MISHLER THEATRE
1208 12th Avenue, Altoona, PA 16601
(814) 944-9434
    Type of Facility: Theatre House
    Type of Stage: Proscenium **Orchestra Pit**
    Seating Capacity: 910
    Year Built: 1906
    Architect: Pietrolungo and Kimbell
    Cost: $118,000
    Contact for Rental: William B. Malloy; (814) 944-9434

Avoca

INSTRUMENTAL MUSIC

NORTHEASTERN PENNSYLVANIA PHILHARMONIC
PO Box 71, Avoca, PA 18641
(717) 342-0920
FAX: (717) 457-5901
    Founded: 1972
    Arts Area: Symphony; Orchestra
    Status: Professional; Non-Profit
    Type: Performing; Touring; Educational
    Purpose: To produce the highest quality symphony orchestra and chamber ensemble performances possible; to provide musical services; to maintain an organizational environment in which local and national talent serve as a cultural resource and source of pride
    Management: Jeth Mill, Executive Director; Hugh Keelan, Music Director/Conductor; Mary Walsh, Director of Operations; John Jablowski, Director of Development
    Officers: Larry Stetler, President; George Ginader, Wallace Stettler, Kathleen Graff, Vice Presidents; Jay Niskey, Treasurer; Otto Robinson, Assistant Treasurer; Joyce Lomma, Secretary
    Paid Staff: 6 **Volunteer Staff:** 3
    Paid Artists: 80
    Utilizes: Guest Conductors; Guest Artists
    Budget: $1,000,000 - $5,000,000
    Income Sources: Private Foundations/Grants/Endowments; Business/Corporate Donations; Box Office; Government Grants; Individual Donations
    Season: September - May **Annual Attendance:** 350,000
    Affiliations: ASOL; Citizens for the Arts in Pennsylvania
    Performance Facilities: Masonic Temple; Kirby Center for the Performing Arts

Bethlehem

DANCE

BALLET GUILD OF LEHIGH VALLEY
556 Main Street, Bethlehem, PA 18018
(215) 865-0353
    Founded: 1958
    Arts Area: Ballet
    Status: Semi-Professional; Non-Profit
    Type: Performing; Educational
    Management: Pat McAndrew, General Manager; Alexi Ramov, Artistic Director
    Officers: John L. Cleveland, President; Charlotte M. Fretz, Treasurer; Marjorie Heiberger, Secretary
    Paid Staff: 6 **Volunteer Staff:** 2
    Paid Artists: 3 **Non-Paid Artists:** 18
    Utilizes: Guest Artists; Guest Choreographers
    Budget: $100,000 - $500,000

Income Sources: Private Foundations/Grants/Endowments; Business/Corporate Donations; Box Office; Government Grants; Individual Donations
Season: 52 Weeks
Affiliations: Northeast Regional Association

INSTRUMENTAL MUSIC

CHAMBER MUSIC SOCIETY OF BETHLEHEM
PO Box 4208, Bethlehem, PA 18018
(215) 868-8702
    Founded: 1951
    Arts Area: Chamber
    Status: Non-Profit
    Type: Performing; Sponsoring
    Purpose: To provide chamber music and promote educational activities
    Management: H.F. Dienel, President; J.P. Allen, Vice President; E. Walakovits, Treasurer; M.J. Van DePutte, Secretary
    Volunteer Staff: 13
    Utilizes: Guest Artists
    Budget: $1,000 - $50,000
    Income Sources: Private Foundations/Grants/Endowments; Business/Corporate Donations; Box Office; Individual Donations
    Season: September - May   **Annual Attendance:** 2,000

THEATRE

TOUCHSTONE THEATRE
321-323 East Fourth Street, Bethlehem, PA 18015
(215) 867-1689
    Founded: 1981
    Arts Area: Professional; Musical; Folk; Theatrical Group
    Status: Professional; Non-Profit
    Type: Performing; Touring; Resident; Educational; Sponsoring
    Purpose: Dedicated to the creation and performance of original movement-inspired drama that enriches our diverse audiences with a voice at once personal and universal; Non-profit regional theatre dedicated to the creation and presentation of orignal and esemble drama; Serving our community and audiences of all ages and cultures, at home and on tour, by entertaining, illuminating, challenging and fostering international and intercultural collaborations
    Management: Bridget George, Producing Director; Eric Beatty, Esemble Manager; Billie P. Lindo, Marketing Director; Christina Lankay, Office Manager
    Officers: Richard E. Thulin, President Board of Trustees; Robert Davidson, Treasurer; Harold G. Black, Secretary
    Paid Staff: 8   **Volunteer Staff:** 30
    Paid Artists: 36
    Utilizes: Special Technical Talent; Guest Artists; Guest Directors
    Budget: $100,000 - $500,000
    Income Sources: Private Foundations/Grants/Endowments; Business/Corporate Donations; Box Office; Government Grants; Individual Donations; Touring
    Season: September - August   **Annual Attendance:** 60,000
    Affiliations: TCG; Theatre Association of Pennsylvania; National Mime Association
    Performance Facilities: Touchstone Theatre

FACILITY

TOUCHSTONE THEATRE
321-323 East Fourth Street, Bethlehem, PA 18015
(215) 867-1689; (215) 866-5279
    Type of Facility: Performance Center; Black Box
    Facility Originally: Fire Station
    Type of Stage: Platform
    Stage Dimensions: 18'1"Wx18'6"D
    Seating Capacity: 72
    Year Built: 1875
    Year Remodeled: 1987   **Architect:** Christine Uffler-Trumbell   **Cost:** $203,750
    Contact for Rental: Billie Lindo;   (215) 867-1689
    Resident Groups: Touchstone Ensemble

Bloomsburg

THEATRE

BLOOMSBURG THEATRE ENSEMBLE
226 Center Street, PO Box 66, Bloomsburg, PA 17815
(717) 784-5530
> **Founded:** 1978
> **Arts Area:** Professional; Theatrical Group
> **Status:** Professional; Non-Profit
> **Type:** Performing; Touring; Resident; Educational; Sponsoring
> **Purpose:** The resident professional ensemble lives and works in this rural region because, in the face of world events, we feel we need to be in a place where dialogue with an audience is possible, and the impact of our theatre on a community is positive and demonstrable.
> **Management:** Leigh Strimbeck, Ensemble Director; Stephen Loppick, Administrative Director
> **Officers:** Joe Petruncio, President; Shirley Alters, Secretary; Bill Frost, Treasurer
> **Paid Staff:** 10   **Volunteer Staff:** 1
> **Paid Artists:** 23
> **Utilizes:** Guest Artists; Guest Directors
> **Budget:** $100,000 - $500,000
> **Income Sources:** Private Foundations/Grants/Endowments; Business/Corporate Donations; Box Office; Government Grants; Individual Donations
> **Season:** September - May   **Annual Attendance:** 32,925
> **Affiliations:** TCG; Theatre Association of Pennsylvania
> **Performance Facilities:** Alvina Krause Theatre

FACILITY

BLOOMSBURG UNIVERSITY - CARVER HALL
Bloomsburg, PA 17815
(717) 389-4291
> **Type of Facility:** Auditorium
> **Type of Stage:** Proscenium
> **Seating Capacity:** 900
> **Year Built:** 1869
> **Year Remodeled:** 1900   **Architect:** Price Dickey
> **Acoustical Consultant:** Boyd Buckingham
> **Contact for Rental:** Tom Wright;   (717) 389-4291
> **Resident Groups:** Bloomsburg Players; Music Department groups
> *Small groups (comedians, simple plays, speakers)*

BLOOMSBURG UNIVERSITY - HAAS CENTER FOR THE ARTS
Bloomsburg, PA 17815
(717) 389-4291
> **Type of Facility:** Concert Hall; Auditorium; Theatre House; Road House
> **Type of Stage:** Proscenium
> **Stage Dimensions:** 60'Wx30'D   **Orchestra Pit**
> **Seating Capacity:** 1,900
> **Year Built:** 1968   **Architect:** Price Dickey   **Cost:** $1,500,000
> **Acoustical Consultant:** Dr. Jiri Tishi
> **Contact for Rental:** Tom Wright;   (717) 389-4291
> **Resident Groups:** Bloomsburg Players
> *Remodeling currently in progress*

Boiling Springs

THEATRE

ALLENBERRY PLAYHOUSE
PO Box 7, Boiling Springs, PA 17007
(717) 258-3211
FAX: (717) 258-1464
> **Founded:** 1949
> **Arts Area:** Professional; Theatrical Group
> **Status:** Professional; Commercial
> **Type:** Performing; Resident
> **Purpose:** Legitimate repertory equity theatre presenting shows April-November

Management: John J. Heinze, Producer
Paid Artists: 14
Budget: $100,000 - $500,000
Income Sources: Box Office
Season: April - November
Affiliations: AEA; SSDC
Performance Facilities: Allenberry Playhouse

Bradford

PERFORMING SERIES

BRADFORD CREATIVE AND PERFORMING ARTS CENTER, INC.
PO Box 153, Bradford, PA 16701
(814) 362-2522; (814) 362-1025
FAX: (814) 368-7040
Founded: 1984
Arts Area: Dance; Instrumental Music; Theater; Grand Opera
Status: Non-Profit
Type: Sponsoring
Purpose: To foster and promote the creative and performing arts
Officers: James D. Guelfi, President; Rosemary, Morici, Vice President; Patricia D. Vecellio, Treasurer; Sandra Lyter, Secretary; Olie Lowry, Corresponding Secretary
Volunteer Staff: 15
Paid Artists: 8
Utilizes: Guest Conductors; Guest Artists; Guest Directors
Budget: $100,000 - $500,000
Income Sources: Private Foundations/Grants/Endowments; Business/Corporate Donations; Box Office; Government Grants; Individual Donations
Season: 52 Weeks   **Annual Attendance:** 5,000
Affiliations: Pennsylvania Presenters; Citizens for the Arts in Pennsylvania; Pennsylvania Rural Association

---
Broomall

PERFORMING SERIES

CRS NATIONAL FESTIVAL FOR THE PERFORMING ARTS
724 Winchester Road, Broomall, PA 19008
(215) 544-5920
FAX: (215) 544-5921
Founded: 1981
Arts Area: Dance; Vocal Music; Instrumental Music; Festivals
Status: Professional; Semi-Professional; Non-Profit
Type: Performing; Touring; Resident; Educational
Purpose: To offer performers, composers, teachers, libraries, educational institutions, amateurs, devotees of music and prosepective sponsors cultural enrichment through vast musical sources
Management: Contemporary Record Society Artists Management
Volunteer Staff: 30
Utilizes: Special Technical Talent; Guest Conductors; Guest Artists; Guest Directors; Soloist; Composers
Budget: $1,000 - $50,000
Income Sources: Private Foundations/Grants/Endowments; Business/Corporate Donations; Government Grants; Individual Donations; Membership
Season: July
Affiliations: Contemporary Record Society

Chester

FACILITY

WIDENER UNIVERSITY-ALUMNI AUDITORIUM - BERT MUSTIN THEATRE
1 University Place, Chester, PA 19013
(215) 499-4000
Type of Facility: Concert Hall; Auditorium; Theatre House; Amphitheater; Multi-Purpose
Type of Stage: Proscenium
Stage Dimensions: 20'x36'x26'   **Orchestra Pit**
Seating Capacity: 425

Year Built: 1962
Acoustical Consultant: John Vanore, Widener University Music Director
Contact for Rental: Kristin McJunkins;   (215) 499-4400
Limited availability due to extensive use by university groups

---

Clarion

FACILITY

MARWICK - BOYD AUDITORIUM
Clarion University, Clarion, PA 16214
(814) 226-2449
FAX: (814) 226-2037
  Founded: 1812
  Type of Facility: Auditorium; Performance Center; Theatre House
  Type of Stage: Proscenium
  Stage Dimensions: 51'Wx30'Dx17'H   **Orchestra Pit**
  Seating Capacity: 1,500
  Year Built: 1972
  Contact for Rental: Carl Callenburg;   (814) 226-4167

Coraopolis

THEATRE

ROBERT MORRIS COLONIAL THEATER
Narrows Run Road, Coraopolis, PA 15108
(412) 262-8336
  Founded: 1967
  Arts Area: Community
  Status: Non-Professional; Non-Profit
  Type: Performing; Educational
  Purpose: To provide our Western Pennsylvania Community with a high standard of community theater in light summer fare and winter classics
  Management: Tom Gaydos, Managing Director
  Paid Staff: 3
  Utilizes: Special Technical Talent; Guest Directors
  Budget: $50,000 - $100,000
  Income Sources: Box Office; Individual Donations
  Season: February - November   **Annual Attendance:** 6,000
  Affiliations: TAP; ATHE; East Coast Theatre Conference

Devon

THEATRE

VALLEY FORGE MUSIC FAIR PRODUCTIONS, INC.
176 Swedesford Road, Devon, PA 19333
(215) 644-5004
FAX: (215) 647-6860
  Founded: 1955
  Arts Area: Professional
  Status: Professional
  Type: Touring; Sponsoring
  Purpose: One of a number of professional, commercial theatres operated and owned by Music Fair Group, Incorporated
  Management: James McCormick, Vice President/General Manager
  Officers: Rick Gross, President
  Paid Staff: 150
  Paid Artists: 250
  Utilizes: Special Technical Talent; Guest Conductors; Guest Artists; Guest Directors
  Budget: $5,000,000 - $10,000,000
  Income Sources: Box Office
  Season: March - December   **Annual Attendance:** 700,000
  Affiliations: Music Fair Group
  Performance Facilities: Valley Forge Music Fair

FACILITY

VALLEY FORGE MUSIC FAIR
7 Route 202, Devon, PA 19333
(215) 644-5004
Type of Facility: Performance Center; Theatre House; Arena
Type of Stage: Arena; In-the-round Capability
Stage Dimensions: 30' diameter   **Orchestra Pit**
Seating Capacity: 2932
Year Built: 1972   **Architect:** Hassinger & Schwamm   **Cost:** $2,500,000
Acoustical Consultant: Donald Pacitti
Contact for Rental: Barbara Abrahams;   (215) 644-5004
Manager: James McCormick
Management reserves the right to permit rentals only for specific purposes

Ephrata

VOCAL MUSIC

EPHRATA CLOISTER CHORUS
632 West Main Street, Ephrata, PA 17522
(717) 733-4811
FAX: (717) 733-4811
Founded: 1959
Arts Area: Choral
Status: Non-Profit
Type: Performing; Educational
Purpose: To interpret the Ephrata Cloister through music
Management: Barry L. Sawyer, Director
Officers: Betty Weidman, President; Janer Colodonato, Vice President; George Andrews, Secretary; Susan Miller, Treasurer
Paid Staff: 1   **Volunteer Staff:** 35
Utilizes: Guest Conductors; Guest Artists
Budget: $1,000 - $50,000
Income Sources: Private Foundations/Grants/Endowments; Box Office; Individual Donations
Season: 52 Weeks   **Annual Attendance:** 2,000
Performance Facilities: Ephrata Cloister

PERFORMING SERIES

VORSPIEL DRAMA EPHRATA CLOISTER ASSOCIATES
632 West Main Street, Ephrata, PA 17522
(717) 733-4811
FAX: (717) 733-4811
Founded: 1958
Arts Area: Musical
Status: Non-Profit
Type: Performing; Educational
Purpose: To interpret the Ephrata Cloister through musical, historical drama
Management: Board of Directors
Officers: Becky Weidman, President; Janet Colodonato, Vice President; George Andrews, Secretary; Susan Miller, Treasurer
Paid Staff: 8   **Volunteer Staff:** 75
Utilizes: Guest Artists
Budget: $100,000 - $500,000
Income Sources: Box Office; Individual Donations
Season: July - August   **Annual Attendance:** 2,200
Performance Facilities: Amphitheater, Ephrata Cloister

FACILITY

EPHRATA PERFORMING ARTS CENTER - EPHRATA COMMUNITY PARK
Cocalico Street, PO Box 173, Ephrata, PA 17522
(717) 738-0664; (717) 733-7966
Type of Facility: Theatre House; Amphitheater
Facility Originally: Barn
Type of Stage: 3/4 Arena
Stage Dimensions: 50'x25'   **Orchestra Pit**

Seating Capacity: 203
Year Built: 1913
Resident Groups: Summer Stock; Ephrata Performing Arts Center - Mainstage; Children's Theatre; Monday Series
Modified barn used in the summer for theatrical productions

Erie

INSTRUMENTAL MUSIC

ERIE PHILHARMONIC
1001 State Street, Suite 924, Erie, PA 16501-1878
(814) 455-1375
FAX: (814) 455-1377
    Founded: 1913
    Arts Area: Symphony; Orchestra
    Status: Non-Profit
    Type: Performing
    Purpose: To provide symphonic, pops and youth orchestra concerts, quality educational experiences for all ages, as well as leadership in the cultural life of Erie and the tri-state area
    Management: Eiji Oue, Music Director; Tony Beadle, Executive Director
    Officers: Wallace J. Knox, President; J. Gary Ramy, Executive Vice President; Charles Harris, Vice President of Marketing; M. Peter Scibetta, Vice President of Music; Douglas Murphy, Treasurer
    Paid Staff: 5
    Utilizes: Guest Conductors; Guest Artists
    Budget: $500,000 - $1,000,000
    Income Sources: Private Foundations/Grants/Endowments; Business/Corporate Donations; Box Office; Government Grants; Individual Donations
    Season: September - May   **Annual Attendance:** 20,869
    Performance Facilities: Warner Theatre

PERFORMING SERIES

ERIE CIVIC MUSIC ASSOCIATION
PO Box 143, Erie, PA 16512
(814) 864-0875
    Founded: 1928
    Arts Area: Vocal Music; Instrumental Music
    Status: Non-Profit
    Type: Sponsoring
    Purpose: We present the greatest international talent available at the most reasonable costs.
    Officers: Rodney Blystone Jr., President; John Brauns, Naomi Purchase, Vice Presidents; Beatrice Hansen, Secretary; Lois Blystone, Corresponding Secretary; Jerome Neidinger, Treasurer
    Volunteer Staff: 40
    Utilizes: Guest Artists
    Budget: $50,000 - $100,000
    Income Sources: Private Foundations/Grants/Endowments
    Season: September - May   **Annual Attendance:** 7,500
    Affiliations: Erie Area Fund for the Arts
    Performance Facilities: Warner Theatre

FACILITY

ERIE CIVIC CENTER
811 State Street, PO Box 6140, Erie, PA 16512
(814) 452-4857
    Type of Facility: Civic Center
    Contact for Rental: John "Casey" Wells; (814) 452-4857
    The Civic Center contains the L.J. Tullio Convention Hall and the Warner Theatre. See separate listings for additional information.

ERIE CIVIC CENTER - L.J. TULLIO CONVENTION HALL
811 State Street, PO Box 6140, Erie, PA 16512
(814) 452-4857
    Type of Facility: Concert Hall; Auditorium; Arena
    Type of Stage: Flexible; Platform
    Seating Capacity: 7,500
    Year Built: 1983   **Architect:** Heidt Evans Salata   **Cost:** $13,000,000

Contact for Rental: John "Casey" Wells; (814) 452-4857
Resident Groups: East Coast Hockey League - Erie Panthers

ERIE CIVIC CENTER - WARNER THEATRE
811 State Street, PO Box 6140, Erie, PA 16512
(814) 452-4857
Type of Facility: Concert Hall; Theatre House
Facility Originally: Movie House
Type of Stage: Proscenium
Stage Dimensions: 42'Wx28'D   Orchestra Pit
Seating Capacity: 2,506
Year Built: 1931   Architect: Rapp & Rapp
Contact for Rental: John "Casey" Wells; (814) 452-4857
Resident Groups: Erie Philharmonic Orchestra; Erie Civic Ballet; Erie Civic Music Association

---

Fayetteville

THEATRE

TOTEM POLE PLAYHOUSE
9555 Golf Course Road, PO Box 603, Fayetteville, PA 17222-0603
(717) 352-2164
Founded: 1954
Arts Area: Professional; Summer Stock
Status: Professional; Commercial
Type: Performing; Resident
Purpose: To provide the best in professional theater in our local area
Management: Sue Kocek, Managing Director; Carl Schurr, Producing Artistic Director
Officers: Carl Schurr, President/Treasurer; Sue Kocek, Secretary
Paid Staff: 75
Paid Artists: 14
Utilizes: Special Technical Talent; Guest Artists; Guest Directors
Budget: $100,000 - $500,000
Income Sources: Box Office
Season: May - September   Annual Attendance: 40,000
Affiliations: AEA
Performance Facilities: Totem Pole Playhouse

FACILITY

TOTEM POLE PLAYHOUSE
9555 Golf Course Road, Fayetteville, PA 17222
(717) 352-2164
Type of Facility: Theatre House
Type of Stage: Proscenium
Stage Dimensions: 28'Wx24'D
Seating Capacity: 453
Year Built: 1970   Architect: Noelker and Hull
Manager: Sue Kocek; (717) 352-2164
Resident Groups: Totem Pole Playhouse; Thunder Bird Ltd, Inc.

Glenside

DANCE

BODY LANGUAGE DANCE COMPANY
230 Clivedon Avenue, Glenside, PA 19128
(215) 886-9227
Founded: 1974
Arts Area: Modern
Status: Professional
Type: Performing; Touring; Resident; Educational
Purpose: To create and perform new forms of dance-theater
Officers: Ellen Forman, Director; Hettie Drummond, Secretary; Ellen Foody, Treasurer
Paid Staff: 1
Paid Artists: 8
Utilizes: Guest Artists; Guest Directors

Budget: $50,000 - $100,000
Income Sources: Private Foundations/Grants/Endowments; Business/Corporate Donations; Box Office; Government Grants; Individual Donations
Affiliations: Philadelphia Dance Alliance; Greater Philadelphia Clutural Alliance

Grantham

VOCAL MUSIC

GRANTHAM ORATORIO SOCIETY
Messiah College, Grantham, PA 17027
(717) 766-2511
    Founded: 1948
    Arts Area: Choral
    Status: Non-Professional; Non-Profit
    Type: Performing; Resident; Educational
    Purpose: To present choral works with orchestra
    Management: Dr. Ronald Sider, Conductor
    Officers: Rebecca Probst, President; Nancy Travitz, Secretary; Kenneth Stoessel, Treasurer
    Paid Staff: 1   **Volunteer Staff:** 5
    Paid Artists: 30   **Non-Paid Artists:** 150
    Utilizes: Guest Artists
    Budget: $1,000 - $50,000
    Income Sources: Business/Corporate Donations; Box Office; Individual Donations
    Season: January - April   **Annual Attendance:** 1,000
    Affiliations: Messiah College
    Performance Facilities: Eisenhower Auditorium

Greensburg

INSTRUMENTAL MUSIC

WESTMORELAND SYMPHONY ORCHESTRA
PO Box 1025, Greensburg, PA 15601
(412) 837-1850
FAX: (412) 836-6126
    Arts Area: Symphony; Orchestra; Ensemble
    Status: Semi-Professional; Non-Profit
    Type: Performing; Educational
    Purpose: To bring cultural enrichment through music to an ever-expanding segment of the community; to provide an enjoyable, inspirational and motivating experience
    Management: Kypros Markov, Music Director; Christel Horner, Manager
    Officers: Hugh M. Dempsey, President; John Foreman, Treaurer
    Budget: $100,000 - $500,000
    Income Sources: Private Foundations/Grants/Endowments; Business/Corporate Donations; Box Office; Government Grants
    Performance Facilities: Palace Theatre

Greenville

INSTRUMENTAL MUSIC

GREENVILLE SYMPHONY SOCIETY
PO Box 364, Greenville, PA 16125
(412) 588-2911
    Founded: 1927
    Arts Area: Symphony; Orchestra
    Status: Non-Profit
    Type: Performing
    Purpose: To educate in the field of music through performances
    Management: John H. Evans, Manager; Vicki Poe, Jamie Scott, Personnel Directors; Jean Sankey, Librarian
    Officers: Richard Szymkowski, President; Mark McGrath, Vice President/Grants Officer; Robert E. Davis, Treasurer
    Paid Staff: 1   **Volunteer Staff:** 20
    Paid Artists: 3
    Utilizes: Guest Artists
    Budget: $1,000 - $50,000

Income Sources: Private Foundations/Grants/Endowments; Business/Corporate Donations; Box Office; Government Grants; Individual Donations
Season: September - June   **Annual Attendance:** 7,700
Affiliations: Pennsylvania Council on the Arts
Performance Facilities: Passavant Memorial Center, Thiel College

FACILITY

THIEL COLLEGE - PASSAVANT MEMORIAL CENTER
Greenville, PA 16125
(412) 589-2125
Type of Facility: Auditorium
Type of Stage: Proscenium
Stage Dimensions: 70'Wx50'D
Seating Capacity: 2,000
Year Built: 1971
Architect: Brooks & Redfoot
Cost: $1,500,000
Contact for Rental: Susan Richards;   (412) 589-2125
Resident Groups: Greenville Symphony Orchestra; Thiel College Performing Arts; Greenville Community Performing Arts
Concerts; plays; ballet; community events

Harrisburg

INSTRUMENTAL MUSIC

HARRISBURG SYMPHONY ASSOCIATION
128 Locust Street, Harrisburg, PA 17101
(717) 232-8751
FAX: (717) 232-2921
Founded: 1930
Arts Area: Symphony; Orchestra
Status: Professional; Non-Profit
Type: Performing
Purpose: To bring symphonic music to central Pennsylvania
Management: Larry Newland, Music Director; Kathleen D. Ebner, Executive Director
Paid Staff: 5   **Volunteer Staff:** 3
Paid Artists: 80
Utilizes: Guest Artists
Budget: $500,000 - $1,000,000
Income Sources: Private Foundations/Grants/Endowments; Business/Corporate Donations; Box Office; Government Grants; Individual Donations; Fund-raising
Season: October - May   **Annual Attendance:** 12,000
Affiliations: ASOL; ASCAP
Performance Facilities: The Forum

HARRISBURG YOUTH SYMPHONY ORCHESTRA
128 Locust Street, Harrisburg, PA 17101
(717) 232-8751
FAX: (717) 232-2921
Arts Area: Symphony; Orchestra
Status: Non-Professional; Non-Profit
Type: Performing; Touring; Educational; Sponsoring
Purpose: To give young people an opportunity to play in an orchestra
Management: Dr. Ronald E. Schafer, Music Director/Conductor
Paid Staff: 3
Non-Paid Artists: 70
Budget: $1,000 - $50,000
Income Sources: Private Foundations/Grants/Endowments; Box Office; Government Grants
Season: October - May
Affiliations: ASOL (Youth Orchestra Division)
Performance Facilities: Susquehanna Township Middle School

THEATRE

HARRISBURG COMMUNITY THEATRE
513 Hurlock Street, Harrisburg, PA 17110
(717) 232-5501
Founded: 1926
Arts Area: Musical; Community; Theatrical Group
Status: Non-Professional; Non-Profit
Type: Performing; Educational
Purpose: To provide quality theatrical experiences, opportunities and education to the Capital Region
Management: Thomas G. Hostetter, Artistic Director; Kathy Lemke, Managing Director
Officers: David A. Schankweiler, President; George F. Grode, Vice President of Grants and Gifts; Michael L. Greenwald, Vice President of Audience Development; Sheri L. Phillips, Secretary; Michael S. Cover, Treasurer
Paid Staff: 8   **Volunteer Staff:** 400
Paid Artists: 5
Utilizes: Guest Artists; Guest Directors
Budget: $100,000 - $500,000
Income Sources: Private Foundations/Grants/Endowments; Business/Corporate Donations; Box Office; Government Grants; Individual Donations
Season: September - June   **Annual Attendance:** 21,000
Affiliations: Theatre Association of Pennsylvania; AACT

OPEN STAGE OF HARRISBURG
PO Box 3805, Harrisburg, PA 17105
(717) 652-7529
Founded: 1983
Arts Area: Professional
Status: Professional; Non-Profit
Type: Performing; Touring; Resident; Educational; Sponsoring
Purpose: To develop and support an ensemble of theatre artists for the purpose of presenting modern, contemporary and original dramatic literature in close relationship with its audiences; to provide educational opportunites through a school and outreach program
Management: Donald L. Alsedek, Artistic Director/Chief Executive Officer; Marianne M. Fischer, Managing Director; Anne L. Alsedek, Studio/School Director
Officers: Dennis W. Felty, President; Ruth Leventhal, Vice President; Jonathan Vipond III Esq., Treasurer; Dolly Holtzman, Secretary
Paid Staff: 2   **Volunteer Staff:** 10
Paid Artists: 30
Utilizes: Special Technical Talent; Guest Artists; Guest Directors
Budget: $50,000 - $100,000
Income Sources: Private Foundations/Grants/Endowments; Business/Corporate Donations; Box Office; Government Grants; Individual Donations
Season: October - June   **Annual Attendance:** 3,000
Affiliations: TCG; Citizens for the Arts in Pennsylvania; Theatre Association of Pennsylvania

PERFORMING SERIES

CENTRAL PENNSYLVANIA FRIENDS OF JAZZ, INC.
PO Box 10738, Harrisburg, PA 17105
(717) 540-1010
FAX: (717) 540-7735
Founded: 1980
Arts Area: Instrumental Music; Festivals
Status: Non-Profit
Type: Performing; Educational; Sponsoring
Purpose: To present, promote and preserve America's unique art form, jazz
Management: Steve Rudolph, Executive Director
Officers: Lee Swartz, President; Robert Hendershot, First Vice President; Keith Thomas, Second Vice President; Rosemary Barrett, Third Vice President; Don Senoi, Treasurer; John Bottonari, Secretary
Paid Staff: 1   **Volunteer Staff:** 25
Paid Artists: 90   **Non-Paid Artists:** 30
Utilizes: Guest Artists
Budget: $100,000 - $500,000
Income Sources: Private Foundations/Grants/Endowments; Business/Corporate Donations; Box Office; Government Grants; Individual Donations
Season: 52 Weeks   **Annual Attendance:** 5,000
Affiliations: Allied Arts Fund; Metro Arts of Central Pennsylvania

MARKET SQUARE CONCERTS
PO Box 1292, Harrisburg, PA 17108
(717) 697-6224
FAX: (717) 697-6430
   Arts Area: Chamber Music
   Status: Professional; Non-Profit
   Type: Educational; Presenting
   Purpose: To present a wide representation of solo and chamber music by distinguished artists, both established and emerging
   Management: Lucy Miller, Director
   Officers: Jason J. Litton, President
   Budget: $100,000 - $500,000
   Income Sources: Private Foundations/Grants/Endowments; Business/Corporate Donations; Box Office; Government Grants; Individual Donations
   Season: 52 Weeks
   Performance Facilities: Market Square Church; Rose Lehrman Art Center

FACILITY

FARM SHOW ARENA
2301 North Cameron Street, Harrisburg, PA 17110-9408
(717) 787-5373
   Type of Facility: Arena; Multi-Purpose
   Facility Originally: Business Facility
   Type of Stage: Flexible
   Stage Dimensions: 36'x72'
   Seating Capacity: 7,600
   Year Built: 1939
   Architect: Laurie & Green   **Cost:** $1,250,000
   Contact for Rental: Victoria Ritter;   (717) 787-5373

Hershey

PERFORMING SERIES

HERSHEY THEATRE
15 East Caracas Avenue, Hershey, PA 17033
(717) 534-3411
FAX: (717) 533-2882
   Founded: 1965
   Arts Area: Dance; Vocal Music; Instrumental Music; Theater; Grand Opera
   Status: Professional; Non-Profit
   Type: Touring; Sponsoring
   Purpose: To provide a variety of high quality live entertainment with emphasis on enhancing the cultural and educational opportunities in Central Pennsylvania
   Management: Susan R. Fowler, Executive Director
   Paid Staff: 35
   Paid Artists: 100
   Utilizes: Guest Artists
   Budget: $500,000 - $1,000,000
   Income Sources: Private Foundations/Grants/Endowments; Box Office
   Season: September - April   **Annual Attendance:** 50,000
   Performance Facilities: Hershey Theatre

FACILITY

HERSHEY THEATRE
15 East Caracas Avenue, Hershey, PA 17033
(717) 534-3411
   Type of Facility: Concert Hall; Auditorium; Theatre House
   Facility Originally: Vaudeville
   Type of Stage: Proscenium
   Stage Dimensions: 70'Wx44'6"D   **Orchestra Pit**
   Seating Capacity: 1,904
   Year Built: 1933
   Manager: Susan R. Fowler, Executive Director

Huntingdon Valley

VOCAL MUSIC

THE MARY GREEN SINGERS
990 Old Huntingdon Pike, Huntingdon Valley, PA 19006
(215) 572-5063
Founded: 1986
Arts Area: Choral
Status: Semi-Professional
Type: Performing; Touring; Educational
Officers: Mary Woodmansee Green, Music Director/Conductor
Paid Staff: 1
Budget: $100,000 - $500,000
Income Sources: Box Office; Individual Donations

Jennerstown

THEATRE

MOUNTAIN PLAYHOUSE
PO Box 54, Jennerstown, PA 15547
(814) 629-9201
Founded: 1939
Arts Area: Professional; Musical
Status: Professional; Commercial
Type: Resident; Educational
Management: Teresa M. Stoughton, Teresa A. Stoughton, Mary Louise Stoughton, Producing Directors
Paid Staff: 18
Paid Artists: 40
Utilizes: Guest Directors
Budget: $100,000 - $500,000
Income Sources: Box Office
Season: May - October   **Annual Attendance:** 35,000
Performance Facilities: Mountain Playhouse

FACILITY

MOUNTAIN PLAYHOUSE
PO Box 205, Jennerstown, PA 15547
(814) 629-9201
FAX: (814) 629-6221
Type of Facility: Theatre House
Type of Stage: Proscenium
Seating Capacity: 444
Year Built: 1939   **Architect:** James Stoughton   **Cost:** $4,000
Acoustical Consultant: R.A. Stoughton, Sr.
Original structure was converted to a theater in 1939.

Jim Thorpe

PERFORMING SERIES

LAUREL FESTIVAL OF THE ARTS
PO Box 206, Jim Thorpe, PA 18229
(717) 325-4439
Founded: 1990
Arts Area: Dance; Vocal Music; Instrumental Music; Festivals; Poetry
Status: Professional; Non-Profit
Type: Performing; Resident; Educational
Purpose: To bring together the finest performers to work together and present events to the public
Management: Marc Mostaroy, Artistic Director; Randall Perry, Weeknight Concerts; Herbert Thompson, Publicity; Barbara Loeffler, Marketing
Officers: Harry Hintz, Chairman; Peter Kern, Vice Chairman; Shirley Stermer, Treasurer
Paid Staff: 2   **Volunteer Staff:** 30
Paid Artists: 30
Utilizes: Guest Artists

Budget: $1,000 - $50,000
Income Sources: Private Foundations/Grants/Endowments; Business/Corporate Donations; Box Office; Government Grants; Individual Donations
Season: June   **Annual Attendance:** 1,500
Performance Facilities: Mauch Chunk Opera House

Johnstown

INSTRUMENTAL MUSIC

JOHNSTOWN SYMPHONY ORCHESTRA
215 Main Street, Johnstown, PA 15901
(814) 535-6738
  Founded: 1929
  Arts Area: Symphony; Orchestra; Chamber
  Status: Professional
  Type: Performing
  Purpose: To perform classical music to the greater Johnstown area
  Management: Anthony M. Blackner, Executive Director; Lawrence R. Samay, Business Manager; Helen Chiclot, Administrative Assistant; Istvan Jaray, Music Director
  Officers: James Richey, President; Mary DiFrancesco, Past President; Mary Borkow, President Elect; Carmela Bagistro, Secretary; Orlando Hanselman, Treasurer
  Paid Staff: 4   **Volunteer Staff:** 5
  Paid Artists: 75
  Utilizes: Guest Artists
  Budget: $100,000 - $500,000
  Income Sources: Private Foundations/Grants/Endowments; Business/Corporate Donations; Box Office; Government Grants; Individual Donations
  Season: October - May   **Annual Attendance:** 5,500
  Performance Facilities: Pasquerilla Performing Arts Center

Kennett Square

PERFORMING SERIES

LONGWOOD GARDENS
PO Box 501, Kennett Square, PA 19348
(215) 388-6741
  Founded: 1929
  Arts Area: Instrumental Music; Theater; Festivals
  Status: Non-Profit
  Type: Performing; Educational
  Management: Priscilla Johnson, Performing Arts Coordinator
  Paid Artists: 250   **Non-Paid Artists:** 50
  Budget: $1,000 - $50,000
  Income Sources: Private Foundations/Grants/Endowments; Box Office
  Season: 52 Weeks

FACILITY

OPEN AIR THEATRE
Longwood Gardens, PO Box 501, Kennett Square, PA 19348
(215) 388-6741
FAX: (215) 388-2078
  Type of Facility: Amphitheater
  Type of Stage: Trapezoidal
  Stage Dimensions: 75'Wx35'D
  Seating Capacity: 2,080
  Year Built: 1912   **Architect:** Pierre S. du Pont
  Year Remodeled: 1927
  Contact for Rental: Priscilla Johnson;   (215) 388-6741, ext. 451
  Resident Groups: The Savoy Company; Brandywiners; Kennett Symphony
  Dressing rooms and water curtain added in 1927 renovation

Kingston

DANCE

BALLET THEATRE PENNSYLVANIA
239 Schuyler Avenue, Kingston, PA 18704
(717) 283-9682
Founded: 1983
Arts Area: Modern; Ballet
Status: Professional; Non-Profit
Type: Performing; Touring; Resident; Educational
Management: Mary Hepner, Artistic/Executive Director
Paid Staff: 6   **Volunteer Staff:** 6
Paid Artists: 16   **Non-Paid Artists:** 12
Utilizes: Guest Artists; Guest Choreographers
Budget: $100,000 - $500,000
Income Sources: Private Foundations/Grants/Endowments; Business/Corporate Donations; Box Office; Government Grants; Individual Donations
Season: October - June
Performance Facilities: F.M. Kirby Center for the Performing Arts

Kutztown

PERFORMING SERIES

NEW ARTS PROGRAM
173 West Main Street, PO Box 82, Kutztown, PA 19530
(215) 683-6440
Founded: 1974
Arts Area: Dance; Literary; Visual; Performing
Status: Professional; Non-Profit
Type: Performing; Resident
Purpose: To present individual artists from the literary, performing and visual arts for two days of one-to-one consultations plus a collective consultation in a presentation/performance setting
Management: James F.L. Carroll, Director
Officers: James F.L. Carroll, President; Michael Kessler, Vice President; James F.L. Carroll, Treasurer; Joanne P. Carroll, Secretary
Paid Staff: 1   **Volunteer Staff:** 3
Budget: $50,000 - $100,000
Income Sources: Private Foundations/Grants/Endowments; Business/Corporate Donations; Box Office; Government Grants; Individual Donations
Season: September - July   **Annual Attendance:** 975
Performance Facilities: Saint Johns UCC

FACILITY

KUTZTOWN UNIVERSITY - SCHAEFFER AUDITORIUM
College Hill, Kutztown, PA 19530
(215) 683-4000
FAX: (215) 683-4671
Founded: 1867
Type of Facility: Concert Hall; Auditorium; Outdoor (Concert); Studio Performance; Theatre House; Opera House; Arena; Multi-Purpose; Room
Type of Stage: Proscenium; Arena
Stage Dimensions: 54'Wx40'D
Seating Capacity: 800
Contact for Rental: Kutztown University Foundation;   (215) 683-4118
Resident Groups: Theatre Department

Lancaster

THEATRE

FULTON OPERA HOUSE
12 North Prince Street, PO Box 1865, Lancaster, PA 17603
(717) 394-7133
Founded: 1963

Arts Area: Professional; Musical; Theatrical Group
Status: Professional; Non-Profit
Type: Performing; Touring; Educational
Management: Deidre W. Simmons, Executive Director; Kathleen A. Collins, Artistic Director; Barry Kornhauser, Education Director; Lettie Herbert, General Manager
Officers: L. Thomas Gemmil Jr., President; John W. Espenshade, M. Waldron Vail, Vice Presidents; John A. Church, Treasurer; Patricia J. Otto, Secretary
Paid Staff: 13   **Volunteer Staff:** 300
Paid Artists: 200
Utilizes: Special Technical Talent; Guest Artists; Guest Directors
Budget: $500,000 - $1,000,000
Income Sources: Private Foundations/Grants/Endowments; Business/Corporate Donations; Box Office; Government Grants; Individual Donations
Season: October - June   **Annual Attendance:** 130,000
Affiliations: TCG; AEA; League of Historic American Theaters; National Historic Theatres
Performance Facilities: Fulton Opera House

THE INDEPENDENT EYE
PO Box 8, Lancaster, PA 17603
(717) 393-9088
Founded: 1974
Arts Area: Professional; Theatrical Group
Status: Professional; Non-Profit
Type: Performing; Touring; Resident; Educational
Purpose: Avant-garde and experimental theatre showcasing new works
Management: Conrad Bishop, Producing Director; Elizabeth Fuller, Associate Producing Director
Officers: Robert Webber, Chair, Board of Trustees
Paid Staff: 2
Paid Artists: 8
Utilizes: Special Technical Talent; Guest Artists
Budget: $50,000 - $100,000
Income Sources: Private Foundations/Grants/Endowments; Business/Corporate Donations; Box Office; Government Grants; Individual Donations
Season: September - May   **Annual Attendance:** 10,000
Affiliations: TCG

FACILITY

FULTON OPERA HOUSE FOUNDATION
12 North Prince Street, Lancaster, PA 17603
(717) 394-7133
FAX: (717) 397-3780
Founded: 1963
Type of Facility: Theatre House; Opera House
Facility Originally: Meeting Hall; Built on foundations of historic jail
Type of Stage: Proscenium
Stage Dimensions: 33'Wx39'Dx28'H proscenium opening   **Orchestra Pit**
Seating Capacity: 909
Year Built: 1852   **Architect:** Samuel Sloane
Year Remodeled: 1904   **Architect:** C. Emlen Urban
Contact for Rental: Lettie Herbert;   (717) 394-7133
Resident Groups: Fulton Opera House Professional Theatre; Lancaster Opera Company; Lancaster Symphony Orchestra; Actors' Company of Pennsylvania

Lehigh Valley

INSTRUMENTAL MUSIC

LEHIGH VALLEY CHAMBER ORCHESTRA
PO Box 20641, Lehigh Valley, PA 18002-0641
(215) 770-9666
Founded: 1980
Arts Area: Orchestra
Status: Professional; Non-Profit
Type: Performing; Touring; Educational; Recording

Purpose: To nurture interest, support, and appreciation for classical music through performances of the highest standard of excellence; to enhance the quality of life in our community by fostering musical heritage by promoting contemporary American music, providing educational programming and presenting virtuoso performers of international stature; create and seek opportunities to enhance our reputation in the community, region and world of performing arts
Management: Llyena Boylan, Executive Director; Donald Spieth, Music Director
Officers: Clifford G. Vernick M.D., President; Michael Miller, Treasuer; John Rumsey, V.P. Development; Glenn Ossiander, V.P. Marketing; Robert Stanton, Secretary
Paid Staff: 4   **Volunteer Staff:** 40
Paid Artists: 50
Utilizes: Guest Artists
Budget: $100,000 - $500,000
Income Sources: Private Foundations/Grants/Endowments; Business/Corporate Donations; Box Office; Government Grants; Individual Donations
Season: September - June   **Annual Attendance:** 30,000
Affiliations: ASOL; Citizens for the Arts in Pennsylvania; The Association of Pennsylvania Orchestras
Performance Facilities: Dorothy & Dexter Baker Center for the Arts, Muhlenberg College, Allentown

Malvern

THEATRE

THE PEOPLE'S LIGHT AND THEATRE COMPANY
39 Conestoga Road, Malvern, PA 19355
(215) 647-1900
FAX: (215) 640-9521
Founded: 1974
Arts Area: Professional; Theatrical Group
Status: Professional; Non-Profit
Type: Performing; Resident; Educational
Purpose: To help unify a culturally diverse society by giving the community barrier-free access to drama that celebrates our joys, terrors and dreams as we struggle to live together in difficult times
Management: Danny S. Fruchter, Producing Director; Greg Rowe, Managing Director; Alda Cortese, Literary Manager; Mary Bashaw, Public Information Director; Abigail Adams, Associate Artistic Director; Wendy E. Worthington, Marketing Director
Officers: William F. Drake Jr., Board President; Carole Haas, Vice President; L. Frederick Sutherland, Treasurer; Paul H. Rohrkemper, Secretary
Paid Staff: 16
Paid Artists: 24
Utilizes: Special Technical Talent; Guest Artists; Guest Directors
Budget: $1,000,000 - $5,000,000
Income Sources: Private Foundations/Grants/Endowments; Business/Corporate Donations; Box Office; Government Grants; Individual Donations
Season: 52 Weeks   **Annual Attendance:** 60,000
Affiliations: AEA; LORT
Performance Facilities: The People's Light Theater - Mainstage and Steinbright Stage

Meadville

INSTRUMENTAL MUSIC

ALLEGHENY CIVIC SYMPHONY
Music Department, Allegheny College, Meadville, PA 16335
(814) 332-3356
Founded: 1957
Arts Area: Symphony
Status: Semi-Professional; Non-Profit
Type: Performing; Educational
Purpose: To give an opportunity for student artists to perform with area musicians; to present high quality performances to local audiences
Management: Robert Bond, Conductor
Non-Paid Artists: 60
Utilizes: Guest Artists
Season: September - June   **Annual Attendance:** 2,000
Affiliations: Allegheny College
Performance Facilities: Raymond P. Shafer Auditorium

Merion Station

PERFORMING SERIES

MOZART ON THE SQUARE
PO Box 237, Merion Station, PA 19066
(215) 668-1799
Founded: 1980
Arts Area: Festivals
Status: Non-Profit
Type: Performing
Purpose: To present chamber music concerts, mainly of music from the Classic and early Romantic eras
Officers: Carole F. Haas, President; David Crownover, Vice President; William H. Roberts, Treasurer; F. Otto Haas, Acting Secretary
Paid Staff: 2   **Volunteer Staff:** 15
Paid Artists: 80
Utilizes: Guest Artists
Budget: $50,000 - $100,000
Income Sources: Private Foundations/Grants/Endowments; Business/Corporate Donations; Box Office; Government Grants; Individual Donations
Season: May - June   **Annual Attendance:** 5,000
Performance Facilities: The Church of the Holy Trinity; Curtis Hall; BZ-BI Synagog

Mill Hall

FACILITY

MILLBROOK PLAYHOUSE
Country Club Lane, Mill Hall, PA 17751
(717) 748-8083
Type of Facility: Theatre House
Facility Originally: Barn
Type of Stage: Arena
Stage Dimensions: 12'x30'x20'
Seating Capacity: 300
Year Remodeled: 1963   **Architect:** Richard Swietzer   **Cost:** $15,000

Mount Gretna

THEATRE

GRETNA PRODUCTIONS
Mt. Gretna Playhouse, PO Box 578, Mount Gretna, PA 17064
(717) 964-3322
Founded: 1978
Arts Area: Professional; Theatrical Group
Status: Professional; Non-Profit
Type: Performing; Touring
Management: Robin Wray, Managing Director; Al Franklin, Producing Director
Officers: Wendy DiMatteo, President
Paid Staff: 7   **Volunteer Staff:** 40
Paid Artists: 20   **Non-Paid Artists:** 3
Utilizes: Special Technical Talent; Guest Artists; Guest Directors
Budget: $100,000 - $500,000
Income Sources: Private Foundations/Grants/Endowments; Business/Corporate Donations; Box Office; Government Grants; Individual Donations
Season: June - August   **Annual Attendance:** 20,000
Affiliations: LORT; AEA; Theatre Association of Pennsylvania; Metro Arts of Harrisburg
Performance Facilities: Mt. Gretna Playhouse

TIMBERS DINNER THEATER
Timber Road, Mount Gretna, PA 17064
(717) 964-3601
Arts Area: Musical; Dinner
Status: Professional; Commercial
Type: Performing
Management: John Briody, Owner

Paid Staff: 20
Paid Artists: 11
Income Sources: Box Office

PERFORMING SERIES

MUSIC AT GRETNA
PO Box 519, Mount Gretna, PA 17064
(717) 964-3836
Founded: 1975
Arts Area: Festivals
Status: Professional; Non-Profit
Type: Educational; Sponsoring; Producing
Management: Kathy Judd, Executive Director; Gail Nourse, Assistant Director
Officers: Carl Ellenberger Jr., Founder/Artistic Director; Charles V. Henry III, President
Paid Staff: 3   **Volunteer Staff:** 30
Paid Artists: 35
Utilizes: Guest Artists
Budget: $100,000 - $500,000
Income Sources: Private Foundations/Grants/Endowments; Business/Corporate Donations; Box Office; Government Grants; Individual Donations
Season: 52 Weeks   **Annual Attendance:** 15,000
Affiliations: Chautauqua Playhouse; Strand-Capitol Performance Hall

FACILITY

TIMBERS DINNER THEATER
Timber Road, Mount Gretna, PA 17064
(717) 964-3601
Type of Facility: Theatre House
Facility Originally: Restaurant
Type of Stage: Proscenium   **Orchestra Pit**
Seating Capacity: 500
Year Built: 1960   **Architect:** John Briody
Year Remodeled: 1976
Acoustical Consultant: John Briody
Manager: John Briody

Mountainhome

THEATRE

POCONO PLAYHOUSE
Playhouse Lane, Mountainhome, PA 18342
(717) 595-7456
Founded: 1947
Arts Area: Professional; Musical; Theatrical Group
Status: Professional; Commercial
Type: Performing; Educational
Management: Hubert Fryman, Owner/Producer; Donna McMicken, General Manager
Paid Staff: 5   **Volunteer Staff:** 30
Paid Artists: 250
Utilizes: Guest Directors
Income Sources: Box Office
Season: June - October
Performance Facilities: Pocono Playhouse

FACILITY

POCONO PLAYHOUSE
Playhouse Lane, Mountainhome, PA 18342
(717) 595-7456
FAX: (717) 595-7465
Founded: 1947
Type of Facility: Theatre House
Type of Stage: Proscenium
Seating Capacity: 497

Year Built: 1947
Resident Groups: Pocono Playhouse

Narberth

VOCAL MUSIC

SPRUCE STREET SINGERS
244 Woodbine Avenue, Narberth, PA 19072
(215) 667-1532
    Founded: 1985
    Arts Area: Choral
    Status: Non-Professional
    Type: Performing
    Purpose: To have fun; to make music; to raise monies for community causes in the Philadelphia area
    Management: David Hall, Musical Director
    Officers: John Simpson, President; Jim Rinier, Vice President; Ed Zacks, Treasurer
    Paid Staff: 1   **Volunteer Staff:** 7
    Non-Paid Artists: 32
    Utilizes: Guest Artists
    Budget: $1,000 - $50,000
    Income Sources: Business/Corporate Donations; Individual Donations; Fundraising
    Season: 52 Weeks
    Annual Attendance: 500
    Performance Facilities: Saint Luke and the Epiphany Episcopal Church

---
New Hope

THEATRE

BUCKS COUNTY PLAYHOUSE
70 South Main, PO Box 313, New Hope, PA 18938
(215) 862-2046
    Founded: 1939
    Arts Area: Professional; Musical; Theatrical Group
    Status: Professional; Commercial
    Type: Performing; Educational; Partial-Equity Season
    Management: Jade Curtain Ltd.: Hubert Fryman Jr., Associate Producer
    Paid Staff: 5   **Volunteer Staff:** 30
    Paid Artists: 250
    Utilizes: Guest Directors
    Income Sources: Box Office
    Season: June - October
    Performance Facilities: Bucks County Playhouse

FACILITY

BUCKS COUNTY PLAYHOUSE
70 South Main, PO Box 313, New Hope, PA 18938
(215) 862-2046
    Type of Facility: Theatre House
    Facility Originally: Paper Mill
    Type of Stage: Proscenium
    Stage Dimensions: 59'6"Wx27'D; 29'6"Wx18'H proscenium opening
    Seating Capacity: 453
    Year Remodeled: 1939
    Contact for Rental: Nancy Pflaumer, General Manager; (215) 862-2046
    Resident Groups: Bucks County Playhouse

New Wilmington

PERFORMING SERIES

CELEBRITY SERIES
Westminster College, Market Street, New Wilmington, PA 16172
(412) 946-7371
Founded: 1852
Arts Area: Dance; Instrumental Music; Theater; Grand Opera
Status: Non-Profit
Type: Educational; Sponsoring
Purpose: To present a variety of the Performing Arts for the campus and community
Management: Eugene Decaprio, Assistant Dean of the College, Director of the Celebrity Series; Maria McKee, Box Office Manager
Paid Staff: 11
Paid Artists: 7
Utilizes: Guest Artists
Budget: $50,000 - $100,000
Income Sources: Private Foundations/Grants/Endowments; Box Office; Government Grants
Season: September - May   **Annual Attendance:** 6,000
Affiliations: APAP
Performance Facilities: Will W. Orr Auditorium

FACILITY

WESTMINSTER COLLEGE - BEEGHLY THEATER
New Wilmington, PA 16172-0001
(412) 946-7241
Type of Facility: Auditorium; Theatre House
Type of Stage: Proscenium
Stage Dimensions: 36'Wx28'Dx16'H   **Orchestra Pit**
Seating Capacity: 300
Year Built: 1966   **Architect:** W.G. Eckles Company
Contact for Rental: Business Manager;   (412) 946-7140
Limited availability due to theatre department activities. Shallow orchestra pit

WESTMINSTER COLLEGE - WILL W. ORR AUDITORIUM
Market Street, New Wilmington, PA 16172
(412) 946-7371
Type of Facility: Concert Hall; Auditorium
Type of Stage: Proscenium
Stage Dimensions: 50'Wx38'Dx30'H
Seating Capacity: 1,756
Year Built: 1962   **Architect:** W.G. Eckels Company
Acoustical Consultant: Ed Simons & Company
Contact for Rental: Business Manager;   (412) 946-7140
Manager: Gene De Caprio;   (412) 946-7271

Philadelphia

DANCE

BALLET DES JEUNES
1447 Manoa Road, Philadelphia, PA 19151
(215) 473-2253
Founded: 1958
Arts Area: Modern; Ballet; Jazz
Status: Non-Professional; Non-Profit
Type: Performing; Touring
Purpose: To give gifted young performers the opportunity to develop talent
Management: Ursula Maleta, Artistic Director; Donna Tambussi, Co-Director
Non-Paid Artists: 30
Utilizes: Guest Artists; Guest Choreographers
Budget: $1,000 - $50,000
Income Sources: Private Foundations/Grants/Endowments; Box Office
Season: September - July

CONVERGENCE DANCERS & MUSICIANS
32 Strawberry Street, Philadelphia, PA 19106
(215) 627-3374
>**Founded:** 1989
>**Arts Area:** Modern
>**Status:** Professional
>**Type:** Performing; Touring; Educational
>**Purpose:** To develop and present collaborative contemporary dance and music
>**Management:** Janaea Rose Lyn, Anthony Scafide, Artistic Directors
>**Volunteer Staff:** 4
>**Paid Artists:** 14   **Non-Paid Artists:** 2
>**Utilizes:** Guest Artists; Guest Choreographers; Guest Composers
>**Budget:** $1,000 - $50,000
>**Income Sources:** Private Foundations/Grants/Endowments; Business/Corporate Donations; Box Office; Government Grants; Individual Donations
>**Season:** Fall; Spring   **Annual Attendance:** 1,000

DANCE AFFILIATES OF AMERICAN BALLET COMPETITION
910 Cherry Street, 4th Floor, Philadelphia, PA 19107
(215) 829-9800
FAX: (215) 829-0508
>**Arts Area:** Modern; Ballet; Jazz; Ethnic; Folk
>**Status:** Non-Profit
>**Type:** Sponsoring
>**Purpose:** To create an environment where the arts are a necessary and integral part of our lives so they may illuminate, enrich and civilize the human spirit
>**Management:** F. Randolph Swartz, Artistic Director; Virginia Villalon, Director of Development
>**Officers:** F. Randolph Swartz, President; Cheryl V. Shepherd, Chairman of the Board; Mikhail Korogodsky, Lolly LaGreca, Ira Lefton Esq., Marietta Nettl, Barbara Sandonato, Board Members
>**Paid Staff:** 4   **Volunteer Staff:** 1
>**Utilizes:** Guest Artists; Guest Choreographers
>**Budget:** $500,000 - $1,000,000
>**Income Sources:** Private Foundations/Grants/Endowments; Business/Corporate Donations; Box Office; Government Grants; Individual Donations
>**Season:** November - May   **Annual Attendance:** 20,000
>**Affiliations:** University of the Arts; Annenberg Center; Philadelphia Dance Alliance
>**Performance Facilities:** Annenberg Center; Drake Theatre

GROUP MOTION MULTI MEDIA DANCE THEATER
624 South Fourth Street, 3rd Floor, Philadelphia, PA 19147
(215) 928-1495
>**Founded:** 1971
>**Arts Area:** Modern
>**Status:** Professional; Semi-Professional; Non-Professional; Non-Profit
>**Type:** Performing; Resident; Educational; Sponsoring
>**Purpose:** To provide artistic and educational services in all phases of multimedia dance theatre in the forms of teaching and instructing, production and presentation of performances
>**Officers:** Brigitta Herrmann, President; Manfred Fischbeck, Secretary
>**Paid Staff:** 3   **Volunteer Staff:** 8
>**Paid Artists:** 8
>**Utilizes:** Special Technical Talent; Guest Artists
>**Budget:** $1,000 - $50,000
>**Income Sources:** Private Foundations/Grants/Endowments; Business/Corporate Donations; Box Office; Government Grants; Individual Donations
>**Season:** September - June
>**Affiliations:** Philadelphia Dance Alliance; Greater Philadelphia Cultural Alliance

PENNSYLVANIA BALLET
1101 South Broad Street, Philadelphia, PA 19147
(215) 551-7000
FAX: (215) 551-7224
>**Founded:** 1961
>**Arts Area:** Ballet
>**Status:** Professional; Non-Profit
>**Type:** Performing; Touring; Resident
>**Management:** Christopher D'Ambose, Artistic Director
>**Paid Staff:** 35
>**Paid Artists:** 36

Utilizes: Guest Artists; Guest Choreographers
Budget: $100,000 - $500,000
Income Sources: Private Foundations/Grants/Endowments; Business/Corporate Donations; Box Office; Government Grants; Individual Donations
Season: September - August
Affiliations: Milwaukee Ballet
Performance Facilities: Academy of Music; Merriam Theatre

PHILDANCE/PHILADELPHIA DANCE COMPANY
9 North Preston Street, Philadelphia, PA 19104
(215) 387-8200
   Founded: 1970
   Arts Area: Modern; Ballet; Jazz
   Status: Professional; Non-Profit
   Type: Performing; Touring; Resident; Educational
   Purpose: A professional dance company that also has instruction and training programs annually offering tuition-free instruction and performing opportunities to young dancers
   Management: Joan Myers Brown, Artistic/Executive Director; Blondell Reynolds, Managing Director; Gwen Coleman, General Manager; Shaw Concerts, Tour Representative
   Officers: Spencer Werthemier, Chairman; Beverly Harper, President; Don Haskin, Alton Knight, Vice Presidents; Geri Packman, Secretary
   Paid Staff: 7   **Volunteer Staff:** 4
   Paid Artists: 17
   Utilizes: Special Technical Talent; Guest Artists; Guest Choreographers
   Budget: $500,000 - $1,000,000
   Income Sources: Private Foundations/Grants/Endowments; Business/Corporate Donations; Box Office; Government Grants; Individual Donations; Fundraising Efforts
   Season: Fall - Spring   **Annual Attendance:** 50,000
   Affiliations: Dance USA; International Association for Blacks in Dance; Coalition of Afro-American Cultural Organizations; American Dance Guild; Greater Philadelphia Cultural Alliance; PDA; TAAC

ZERO MOVING DANCE COMPANY
3500 Lancaster Avenue, Philadelphia, PA 19104
(215) 243-0260
FAX: (215) 222-4038
   Founded: 1974
   Arts Area: Modern
   Status: Professional; Non-Profit
   Type: Performing; Touring; Educational
   Purpose: To present original works by founding artist Hellmut Gottschild and Artistic Director Karen Bamonte
   Management: Karen Bamonte, Artistic Director; Jane E. Brown, Executive Director
   Officers: Hellmut Gottschild, President
   Budget: $100,000 - $500,000
   Income Sources: Private Foundations/Grants/Endowments; Business/Corporate Donations; Box Office; Government Grants; Individual Donations
   Affiliations: Philadelphia Dance Alliance; Dance Theatre Worker; Greater Phildelphia Cultural Alliance; Dance USA
   Performance Facilities: Community Education Center

INSTRUMENTAL MUSIC

BALTIMORE CONSORT
8871 Norwood Avenue, Philadelphia, PA 19118-2710
(410) 889-5123; (215) 247-4323
FAX: (215) 247-4323
   Founded: 1980
   Arts Area: Chamber; Ensemble; Folk; Instrumental Group
   Status: Professional; Non-Profit
   Type: Performing; Touring; Resident; Educational
   Purpose: Performance of popular music from the 16th and 17th centuries
   Management: Joane Rile, Artist Management
   Officers: Franklin T. Caudill, Chairman
   Paid Staff: 2
   Paid Artists: 7
   Utilizes: Guest Artists
   Budget: $50,000 - $100,000
   Income Sources: Private Foundations/Grants/Endowments; Business/Corporate Donations; Box Office; Government Grants; Individual Donations

Season: September - May   **Annual Attendance:** 5,000
Affiliations: Walters Art Gallery

CHESTNUT BRASS COMPANY
PO Box 30165, Philadelphia, PA 19103
(215) 787-6792
   Founded: 1977
   Arts Area: Chamber; Ensemble; Instrumental Group
   Status: Professional; Non-Profit
   Type: Performing; Touring; Resident; Educational
   Purpose: To present to the public a historical view of brass instruments
   Management: Joanne Rile Management Company
   Officers: Marian Hesse, President; Jay Krush, Vice President; Bruce Barrie, Treasurer
   Budget: $100,000 - $500,000
   Income Sources: Private Foundations/Grants/Endowments; Government Grants; Individual Donations
   Season: 52 Weeks
   Affiliations: Greater Philadelphia Cultural Alliance; Temple University, Esther Boyle School

CONCERTO SOLOISTS
Walnut Street Theatre Building, Ninth and Walnut Streets, Philadelphia, PA 19107
(215) 574-3550
FAX: (215) 574-3598
   Founded: 1964
   Arts Area: Orchestra; Chamber; Ensemble; Instrumental Group
   Status: Non-Profit
   Type: Performing; Touring; Resident; Educational; Sponsor Produced
   Purpose: To be a part of the Philadelphia community and cultural institutions
   Management: Marc Mostovoy, Artistic/Music Director; Ken Wesler, General Manager; Kelli Marshall, Artistic Administrator
   Officers: Kenneth Jarin, President of Board; Otto Haas, Chairman of Board
   Utilizes: Guest Conductors; Guest Artists
   Budget: $1,000,000 - $5,000,000
   Income Sources: Private Foundations/Grants/Endowments; Business/Corporate Donations; Box Office; Government Grants; Individual Donations
   Season: October - May
   Affiliations: Greater Philadelphia Arts Council; Performing Arts League of Philadelphia; ASOL
   Performance Facilities: Walnut Street Theatre; Church of the Holy Trinity

MARLBORO SCHOOL OF MUSIC
135 South 18th Street, Philadelphia, PA 19103
(215) 569-4690
   Founded: 1951
   Arts Area: Chamber
   Status: Professional; Non-Profit
   Type: Performing; Educational
   Purpose: Professional school for advanced training in chamber music
   Management: Anthony P. Checchia, Manager
   Officers: Irving Moskovitz, Chairman; James H. Heineman, Phyllis J. Mills, Paul N. Olson, Vice Presidents; M. Todd Cooke, Treasurer
   Paid Staff: 7
   Non-Paid Artists: 70
   Budget: $500,000 - $1,000,000
   Income Sources: Private Foundations/Grants/Endowments; Business/Corporate Donations; Box Office; Government Grants; Individual Donations
   Season: June - August
   Performance Facilities: Marlboro College Concert Hall

PHILADELPHIA CHAMBER MUSIC SOCIETY
135 South 18th Street, Philadelphia, PA 19103
(215) 569-8587
FAX: (215) 569-9497
   Arts Area: Chamber
   Status: Professional; Non-Profit
   Type: Educational; Sponsoring; Presenting
   Purpose: To present a diverse roster of acclaimed artists and ensembles featuring both highly experienced and emerging performers

Management: Philip Maneval, Manager; Anthony P. Checchia, Museum Director
Officers: Jerry G. Rubenstein, Chairman of the Board; Anthony P. Checchia, President of the Board
Budget: $100,000 - $500,000
Income Sources: Private Foundations/Grants/Endowments; Business/Corporate Donations; Box Office; Government Grants; Individual Donations
Performance Facilities: Port of History Museum

PHILADELPHIA ORCHESTRA ASSOCIATION
1420 Locust Street, Philadelphia, PA 19102
(215) 893-1900
FAX: (215) 893-1948
Founded: 1900
Arts Area: Symphony; Orchestra
Status: Professional; Non-Profit
Type: Performing
Purpose: To maintain the preeminence of the Philadelphia Orchestra as one of Philadelphia's outstanding cultural assets and as one of the world's greatest orchestras
Management: Joseph H. Kluger, President/Chief Operating Officer; Joseph A. Horgan, Director of Finance; Judith Frankfurt, General Manager; Cathy Barbash, Orchestra Manager; Jean E. Brubaker, Director of Marketing; Diana Burgwyn, Director of Public Relations; Maria T. Giliotto, Director of Development; Phyllis Susen, Director of Education; Elizabeth Walker, Director of Volunteer Activities; Hugh F. Walsh Jr., Manager of the Academy of Music
Officers: Joseph Neubauer, Chairman of the Board/CEO
Paid Staff: 40
Paid Artists: 106
Utilizes: Guest Conductors; Guest Artists
Budget: Over 10,000,000
Income Sources: Private Foundations/Grants/Endowments; Business/Corporate Donations; Box Office; Government Grants; Individual Donations
Season: 52 Weeks   **Annual Attendance:** 775,000
Affiliations: ASOL
Performance Facilities: Academy of Music

PHILADELPHIA RENAISSANCE WIND BAND
739 North 25th Street, Philadelphia, PA 19130
(215) 235-8469
Founded: 1980
Arts Area: Chamber; Ensemble; Early Music
Status: Professional; Non-Profit
Type: Performing; Touring; Educational
Purpose: To perform Renaissance and early Baroque music on period instruments
Management: Siegel Artist Management; Ethel Siegel, Joan Kimball, Co-Directors; Liz Silverstein, Associate Director
Officers: William Gross, Chairman of the Board
Utilizes: Guest Artists
Budget: $50,000 - $100,000
Income Sources: Private Foundations/Grants/Endowments; Business/Corporate Donations; Box Office; Government Grants; Individual Donations
Season: September - April   **Annual Attendance:** 1,600
Affiliations: CMA; EMA

PHILADELPHIA YOUTH ORCHESTRA
PO Box 41810, Philadelphia, PA 19101
(215) 765-8485
Founded: 1939
Arts Area: Symphony; Orchestra; Chamber; Ensemble
Status: Non-Professional; Non-Profit
Type: Performing; Touring; Educational
Purpose: To promote, encourage and foster the study and practice of music by making available to deserving and talented youth opportunities for orchestra instruction and supervision of their work and to provide concerts for promoting musical art and its appreciation
Management: Joseph Primavera, Music Director/Conductor; Troy Peters, Assistant Conductor
Officers: Barbara Noseworthy, President
Paid Staff: 1   **Volunteer Staff:** 30
Non-Paid Artists: 105
Budget: $50,000 - $100,000
Income Sources: Private Foundations/Grants/Endowments; Business/Corporate Donations; Box Office; Government Grants; Individual Donations; Fund-raising
Season: September - May   **Annual Attendance:** 15,000

Affiliations: ASOL (Youth Orchestra Division); Greater Philadelphia Cultural Alliance
Performance Facilities: Academy of Music

RELACHE ENSEMBLE
c/o Relache, Inc., 11 South Strawberry Street, Philadelphia, PA 19106
(215) 574-8246
FAX: (215) 574-0253
Arts Area: Chamber; Ensemble; Instrumental Group; Electronic & Live Electronic; Contemporary Music
Status: Professional; Non-Profit
Type: Performing; Touring; Resident; Educational; Sponsoring
Purpose: To develop, produce and present works by living composers
Management: Joseph Franklin, Executive Artistic Director; Arthur Stidfole, Director of Planning and Development;
Laurel Wyckoff, Director of Educational Projects
Budget: $100,000 - $500,000
Income Sources: Private Foundations/Grants/Endowments; Business/Corporate Donations; Box Office; Government
Grants; Individual Donations
Performance Facilities: Mandell Theater

VOCAL MUSIC

CHORAL ARTS SOCIETY OF PHILADELPHIA
1420 Locust Street, Suite 220, Philadelphia, PA 19102
(215) 545-8634
Founded: 1982
Arts Area: Choral
Status: Semi-Professional; Non-Profit
Type: Performing; Touring; Educational
Purpose: To present a choral/symphonic repertoire from all periods of music
Management: Sean Deibler, Artistic Director; Michael Scolamiero, Executive Director
Paid Artists: 10   **Non-Paid Artists:** 140
Utilizes: Guest Artists
Budget: $100,000 - $500,000
Income Sources: Private Foundations/Grants/Endowments; Business/Corporate Donations; Box Office; Government
Grants; Individual Donations; Special Events
Season: December - May   **Annual Attendance:** 20,000
Performance Facilities: Mann Music Center; Academy of Music

CHORUS AMERICA
2111 Sansom Street, Philadelphia, PA 19103
(215) 563-2430
FAX: (215) 563-2431
Founded: 1977
Arts Area: Choral
Status: Non-Profit
Purpose: To promote the high quality and artistic growth of vocal ensembles; to stimulate further development of remu-
neration for singers; to encourage greater understanding, appreciation and enjoyment of choral music by all segments of
society
Officers: Robert Page, President; Marshall A. Rutter Esq., Vice President
Paid Staff: 5
Income Sources: Private Foundations/Grants/Endowments; Business/Corporate Donations; Government Grants;
Individual Donations

LITTLE LYRIC OPERA THEATRE
608 South Broad Street, Philadelphia, PA 19145
(215) 755-1288
Founded: 1987
Arts Area: Grand Opera; Lyric Opera
Status: Non-Profit
Type: Performing; Educational
Purpose: To provide repertoire experience for deserving amateur, professional and semi-professional singers
Management: A.C. Pugliese, President; Margaret Kastle, Vice President/Secretary; Maestro Carl Suppa, Musical Director
Utilizes: Guest Artists
Budget: $1,000 - $50,000
Income Sources: Box Office; Individual Donations
Season: September - May   **Annual Attendance:** 2,000

OPERA COMPANY OF PHILADELPHIA
Graham Building, 20th Floor, One Penn Square West, Philadelphia, PA 19102
(215) 981-1450; (215) 981-1454
FAX: (215) 981-1455
> **Founded:** 1975
> **Arts Area:** Grand Opera
> **Status:** Professional; Non-Profit
> **Type:** Performing
> **Purpose:** OCP presents original productions of classical opera literature featuring renowned artists and promising young singers. OCP also sponsors the world's largest voice competition--the Opera Company of Philadelphia/Luciano Pavarotti International Voice Competition.
> **Management:** Robert B. Driver, General Director; Catherine Welborn, Director of Marketing and Public Relations; Danielle Orlando, Artistic Administrator; Grey Nemeth, Competition Director
> **Officers:** John P. Mulroney, President; Mrs. H. Douglas Paxson, Chairman of the Board
> **Paid Staff:** 18 **Volunteer Staff:** 10
> **Paid Artists:** 163
> **Utilizes:** Special Technical Talent; Guest Conductors; Guest Artists; Guest Directors
> **Budget:** $1,000,000 - $5,000,000
> **Income Sources:** Private Foundations/Grants/Endowments; Business/Corporate Donations; Box Office; Government Grants; Individual Donations
> **Season:** October - May   **Annual Attendance:** 39,000
> **Affiliations:** OA; Greater Philadelphia Cultural Alliance
> **Performance Facilities:** Academy of Music

OPERA NORTH
6933 Ardley Street, Philadelphia, PA 19119
(215) 472-3111
> **Founded:** 1978
> **Arts Area:** Grand Opera; Light Opera
> **Status:** Professional; Non-Profit
> **Type:** Performing; Educational
> **Purpose:** Opera North was formed to provide additional opportunities in grand opera for previously unheralded minority talent, among others, in the Delaware Valley.
> **Management:** Darryl Hobson-Reynolds, Artistic Director
> **Officers:** Samuel R. Crosby, President
> **Paid Staff:** 2
> **Paid Artists:** 50
> **Utilizes:** Special Technical Talent; Guest Conductors; Guest Artists; Guest Directors
> **Budget:** $100,000 - $500,000
> **Income Sources:** Private Foundations/Grants/Endowments; Business/Corporate Donations; Box Office; Government Grants; Individual Donations; Fund-raising
> **Season:** 52 Weeks
> **Annual Attendance:** 15,000
> **Affiliations:** OA; Greater Philadelphia Cultural Alliance
> **Performance Facilities:** Academy of Music

THE PENNSYLVANIA OPERA THEATER
1217 Sanson Street, Philadelphia, PA 19107
(215) 440-9797
> **Founded:** 1975
> **Arts Area:** Lyric Opera
> **Status:** Professional; Non-Profit
> **Type:** Performing; Touring; Educational
> **Purpose:** To present high-quality productions which emphasize the theatrical as much as the musical elements; to present operas from all eras, sung in English; to commission new works of America opera; to broaden opera audiences through education and outreach
> **Management:** Barbara Silverstein, Artistic Director; Scott Kessler, Acting General Manager; Tonia Kimbrough, Director of Development and Marketing
> **Officers:** William L. Leonard, Chairman; Joyce S. Sando, Vice Chairman
> **Paid Staff:** 9 **Volunteer Staff:** 50
> **Paid Artists:** 75 **Non-Paid Artists:** 5
> **Utilizes:** Special Technical Talent; Guest Conductors; Guest Artists; Guest Directors
> **Budget:** $1,000,000 - $5,000,000
> **Income Sources:** Private Foundations/Grants/Endowments; Business/Corporate Donations; Box Office; Government Grants; Individual Donations; Fund-raising
> **Season:** October - May   **Annual Attendance:** 10,000
> **Affiliations:** OA; COS
> **Performance Facilities:** Merriam Theatre

THE PHILADELPHIA SINGERS
1700 Walnut Street, Suite 510, Philadelphia, PA 19103
(215) 732-3370
FAX: (215) 732-8288
Founded: 1972
Arts Area: Choral
Status: Professional
Type: Performing
Management: Oliver Bass, Executive Director; David Hayes, Artistic Director; Janice Bryson, Director of Development; Deborah Fleischman, Director of Marketing; Kenneth Landis, Administrative Director
Officers: Edith Reinhardt, Chairman of the Board; Alexis Barron, President of Board; Samuel Rudofker, Vice President; F. Hastings Griffin Esq., Secretary; James K. Abel, Treasurer
Paid Staff: 6   **Volunteer Staff:** 3
Paid Artists: 75
Utilizes: Guest Artists
Budget: $500,000 - $1,000,000
Income Sources: Private Foundations/Grants/Endowments; Business/Corporate Donations; Box Office; Government Grants; Individual Donations
Season: October - April   **Annual Attendance:** 30,000
Performance Facilities: Academy of Music; Church of the Holy Trinity; St. Clement's Church

THEATRE

BUSHFIRE THEATRE OF PERFORMING ARTS
228 South 52nd Street & Locust, Philadelphia, PA 19139
(215) 747-9230
Founded: 1976
Arts Area: Professional; Musical; Theatrical Group
Status: Professional; Non-Profit
Type: Performing; Educational
Management: Al Simpkins, Artistic Director; Verlina Dawson, Executive Director
Paid Staff: 5   **Volunteer Staff:** 4
Paid Artists: 50
Utilizes: Special Technical Talent; Guest Artists; Guest Directors
Budget: $100,000 - $500,000
Income Sources: Private Foundations/Grants/Endowments; Business/Corporate Donations; Box Office; Government Grants; Individual Donations
Season: October - May
Affiliations: AEA
Performance Facilities: Bushfire Theatre of Performing Arts; Writers Workshop; Sassy's Salt Peanut Cafe; Artists' Hut

GERMANTOWN THEATRE GUILD
4821 Germantown Avenue, Philadelphia, PA 19144
(215) 842-0658
Founded: 1933
Arts Area: Professional; Theatrical Group
Status: Professional; Non-Profit
Type: Performing; Touring; Educational; Sponsoring
Management: Katherine Minehart, Artistic Director; Darla Max, Executive Assistant
Officers: Michael Carr, President; John Jordan, Secretary/Treasurer
Paid Staff: 2   **Volunteer Staff:** 10
Paid Artists: 15
Utilizes: Guest Artists; Guest Directors
Budget: $50,000 - $100,000
Income Sources: Private Foundations/Grants/Endowments; Business/Corporate Donations; Box Office; Individual Donations; Touring
Season: Fall - Spring   **Annual Attendance:** 30,000
Affiliations: Theatre Alliance of Pennsylvania; Greater Philadelphia Cultural Alliance; Citizens for the Performing Arts in Pennsylvania; Performing Arts League of Philadelphia

MOVEMENT THEATRE INTERNATIONAL
3700 Chestnut Street, Philadelphia, PA 19104
(215) 382-0600
FAX: (215) 382-0627
Arts Area: Professional; Mime; Clown
Status: Non-Profit
Type: Performing; Educational; Sponsoring

Purpose: To support and increase awareness and understanding of performing artists who originate and perform their own work
Management: Michael A. Pedretti, Director; Sylvia Purnell, Development Officer; Beth Case, Administrative Assistant
Officers: Bob Krutsick, Chair; Judy Wicks, Prentice Cole, Vice Chairs; Oliver Franklin, Secretary
Paid Staff: 8
Paid Artists: 100
Budget: $500,000 - $1,000,000
Income Sources: Private Foundations/Grants/Endowments; Business/Corporate Donations; Box Office; Government Grants; Individual Donations; Tours
Season: January - August   **Annual Attendance:** 18,000
Affiliations: NMTA; PALP; Greater Philadelphia Cultural Alliance; Dance USA
Performance Facilities: MTI Tabernacle Theatre

NEW FREEDOM THEATRE
1346 North Broad Street, Philadelphia, PA 19121
(215) 765-2793
Management: John E. Allen, Founder; Robert E. Leslie, General Manager; A. Warren Merrick, Development Director
Officers: Lorenna Marshall, Chairman of the Board; Robert E. Baker and H. Theodore Roudford, Vice Chairmen; Steven Sanders, Secretary

PHILADELPHIA DRAMA GUILD
100 North 17th Street, Robert Morris Building, Philadelphia, PA 19103
(215) 563-7530
Founded: 1970
Arts Area: Professional; Theatrical Group
Status: Professional; Non-Profit
Type: Performing; Educational
Purpose: To deliver an ongoing program of professional theatre employing the highest standards in acting, directing and design; to make the theatre-going experience integral in the lives of our young people; to provide an alternative to the mass media's homogenization of our culture
Management: Mary B. Robinson, Artistic Director; Daniel L. Schay, Executive Director; Scott Robinson, Marketing Director
Officers: Carl A. Posse, Chairman of the Board
Paid Staff: 20
Utilizes: Special Technical Talent; Guest Artists; Guest Directors
Budget: $1,000,000 - $5,000,000
Income Sources: Private Foundations/Grants/Endowments; Business/Corporate Donations; Box Office; Government Grants; Individual Donations
Season: October - May
Affiliations: AEA; LORT
Performance Facilities: Zellerbach Theater

PHILADELPHIA FESTIVAL THEATRE FOR NEW PLAYS
3900 Chestnut Street, Philadelphia, PA 19104
(215) 222-5000
Founded: 1981
Arts Area: Professional; Theatrical Group
Status: Professional; Non-Profit
Type: Performing
Purpose: To produce only new plays by contemporary playwrights
Management: Carol Rocamora, Artistic/Producing Director; Michael Hollinger, Literary Manager; Hilary Missan, Casting Director
Officers: Eleanor Tarbox, Board President
Paid Staff: 5
Utilizes: Special Technical Talent; Guest Artists; Guest Directors
Budget: $500,000 - $1,000,000
Income Sources: Private Foundations/Grants/Endowments; Business/Corporate Donations; Box Office; Government Grants; Individual Donations
Season: October - June
Affiliations: AEA; LORT
Performance Facilities: Harold Prince Theater

THE PHILADELPHIA THEATRE COMPANY
The Bourse Building, 21 South Fifth Street, Philadelphia, PA 19106
(215) 592-8333
Founded: 1981
Arts Area: Professional; Theatrical Group
Status: Professional; Non-Profit
Type: Performing; Resident

Management: Sarah Garonzik, Producing Artistic Director; Ada Coppock, General Manager
Officers: Monika Krug, Board President
Paid Staff: 12
Income Sources: Private Foundations/Grants/Endowments; Business/Corporate Donations; Box Office; Government Grants; Individual Donations
Season: September - June
Affiliations: AEA
Performance Facilities: Plays and Players Theater

SOCIETY HILL PLAYHOUSE
507 South Eighth Street, Philadelphia, PA 19147
(215) 923-0210
Founded: 1959
Arts Area: Professional; Theatrical Group
Status: Professional; Non-Profit
Type: Performing; Touring; Educational
Purpose: Dedicated to sharing the magic of theater with its audience, presenting the best of contemporary European and American writers
Management: Jay Kogan, Artistic Director; Deen Kogan, Managing Director; Walter Vail, Director of Play Development
Paid Staff: 6
Utilizes: Special Technical Talent; Guest Artists; Guest Directors
Budget: $100,000 - $500,000
Income Sources: Private Foundations/Grants/Endowments; Business/Corporate Donations; Box Office; Government Grants; Individual Donations
Season: 52 Weeks
Affiliations: AEA; SPT; TCG; Theatre Association of Pennsylvania; AAA
Performance Facilities: Society Hill Playhouse

WALNUT STREET THEATRE COMPANY
Ninth and Walnut Streets, Philadelphia, PA 19107
(215) 574-3550
FAX: (215) 574-3598
Founded: 1982
Arts Area: Professional; Musical; Theatrical Group
Status: Professional; Non-Profit
Type: Performing; Resident; Educational
Purpose: Committed to developing the art form of theatre in the Delaware Valley, developing audiences for the theatre and sponsoring and training local artists and technicians, Walnut Street Theatre Company believes that as the art form prospers and grows in Philadelphia, it creates an exciting environment which builds on its own successes.
Management: Bernard Havard, Executive Director; Ken Wesler, General Manager
Officers: John D. Graham, Board President
Paid Staff: 110   **Volunteer Staff:** 210
Paid Artists: 144
Utilizes: Special Technical Talent; Guest Artists; Guest Directors
Budget: $1,000,000 - $5,000,000
Income Sources: Private Foundations/Grants/Endowments; Business/Corporate Donations; Box Office; Government Grants; Individual Donations
Season: October - April   **Annual Attendance:** 195,000
Affiliations: Greater Philadelphia Cultural Alliance; Philadelphia Chamber of Commerce
Performance Facilities: The Walnut Street Theatre

THE WILMA THEATER
2030 Sansom Street, Philadelphia, PA 19103-4417
(215) 963-0249
FAX: (215) 963-0377
Founded: 1973
Arts Area: Professional
Status: Professional
Type: Performing
Purpose: To produce innovative theatre of the highest artistic quality from international and contemporary American repertoires
Management: W. Courtenay Wilson, Managing Director; Florence Zeller, Director of Development; Frank Wood, Director of Marketing; Larry Kenney, Business Manager; Ian Goldstein, Audience Services Manager; Blanka Zizka, Jiri Zizka, Co-Artistic/Producing Directors; Roy Gray, Technical Director; Janet E. Finegar, Literary Manager
Paid Staff: 13
Paid Artists: 6
Utilizes: Special Technical Talent; Guest Directors
Budget: $500,000 - $1,000,000

Income Sources: Private Foundations/Grants/Endowments; Business/Corporate Donations; Box Office; Government Grants; Individual Donations
Season: September - June   **Annual Attendance:** 23,000
Affiliations: TCG

PERFORMING SERIES

AMERICAN MUSIC THEATER FESTIVAL
2005 Market Street-1 Commerce Square, 18th Floor, Philadelphia, PA 19103
(215) 851-6450
Founded: 1983
Arts Area: Festivals; Musical Theater
Status: Non-Profit
Type: Sponsoring
Purpose: A national festival exclusively dedicated to the development of music theatre in all its forms: contemporary, drama, comedy
Management: Donna Powell, General Manager; Marjorie Samoff, Producing Director; Eric Salzman, Artistic Director
Officers: Nichand Sherman, President
Paid Staff: 60   **Volunteer Staff:** 50
Paid Artists: 100
Utilizes: Special Technical Talent; Guest Conductors; Guest Artists; Guest Directors
Budget: $1,000,000 - $5,000,000
Income Sources: Private Foundations/Grants/Endowments; Business/Corporate Donations; Box Office; Government Grants; Individual Donations
Season: September - October   **Annual Attendance:** 30,000

BACH FESTIVAL OF PHILADELPHIA
8419 Germantown Road, Philadelphia, PA 19118
(215) 247-4070
FAX: (215) 247-4070
Founded: 1976
Arts Area: Vocal Music; Instrumental Music; Festivals
Status: Professional; Non-Profit
Type: Educational; Presenting
Purpose: The Bach Festival of Philadelphia is dedicated to enriching the community through concerts and educational programs presented by some of the best Baroque interpreters in the world.
Management: Janice Fiore, Director; Robert Mikrut, Development Administrator
Officers: Allen Model, President; Edna Phillips, Chairman; George Reath, Vice President; Dr. Margaret Rappaport, Secretary
Paid Staff: 5   **Volunteer Staff:** 1
Utilizes: Special Technical Talent; Guest Conductors; Guest Artists; Guest Directors
Budget: $100,000 - $500,000
Income Sources: Private Foundations/Grants/Endowments; Business/Corporate Donations; Box Office; Government Grants; Individual Donations
Season: 52 Weeks
Affiliations: Greater Philadelphia Cultural Alliance
Performance Facilities: St. Paul's Episcopal Church; Unitarian Society of Germantown; Mother of Consolation Church; Bryn Mawr Church; Springside School

MANN MUSIC CENTER, INC.
52nd Street & Parkside Avenue, Fairmount Park, Philadelphia, PA
(215) 567-0707
FAX: (215) 567-0734
Executive Offices: 1617 John F. Kennedy Boulevard, Philadelphia, PA 19103
Founded: 1930 (as Robin Hood Dell)
Arts Area: Dance; Instrumental Music; Orchestra; Special Events
Status: Professional
Type: Performing
Purpose: To present the Philadelphia Orchestra in an 18-concert summer series--providing 10,000 free general-admission tickets for each concert; supported by individual and corporate memberships as well as government agencies
Management: Charles Dutoit, Artistic Director/Principal Conductor; Helen W. Martin, President/Chief Executive Officer
Officers: Bernard M. Guth, Chairman of the Board; Helen W. Martin, President
Paid Staff: 6
Utilizes: Guest Conductors; Guest Artists
Budget: $1,000,000 - $5,000,000
Income Sources: Private Foundations/Grants/Endowments; Business/Corporate Donations; Box Office; Government Grants; Individual Donations
Season: June - September

PRESIDENTIAL JAZZ WEEKEND
c/o African-American History Museum, 701 Arch Street, Philadelphia, PA 19106
(215) 574-0380
FAX: (215) 574-3110
   Founded: 1989
   Arts Area: Vocal Music; Instrumental Music; Festivals; Ethnic
   Status: Professional; Semi-Professional; Non-Profit
   Type: Performing; Educational; Sponsoring
   Purpose: To celebrate African-American classical music
   Management: Rhoda Blount, Jazz Live Director; Dr. Rowena Stewart, Museum Director
   Officers: Clarence Farmer, Chairman of the Board; Leslie Willis, Head of Public Relations
   Utilizes: Special Technical Talent; Guest Artists; Guest Directors
   Income Sources: Private Foundations/Grants/Endowments; Business/Corporate Donations; Box Office; Government
   Grants; Individual Donations
   Season: 52 Weeks
   Affiliations: Greater Philadelphia Cultural Alliance; AAM; Coalition of Afro-American Organizations

FACILITY

ACADEMY OF MUSIC
Broad and Locust Streets, Philadelphia, PA 19102
(215) 893-1935
FAX: (215) 545-4588
   Type of Facility: Concert Hall; Performance Center; Opera House
   Year Built: 1857
   Year Remodeled: 1987
   Contact for Rental: Hugh Walsh, Jr.;   (215) 893-1935
   A National Historic Landmark, the Academy of Music is the oldest operating opera house in the United States. The building contains the Hall and Main Auditorium. See separate listings for additional information.

ACADEMY OF MUSIC - HALL
Broad and Locust Streets, Philadelphia, PA 19102
(215) 893-1935
FAX: (215) 545-4588
   Type of Facility: Ballroom
   Type of Stage: Platform
   Seating Capacity: 480
   Contact for Rental: Hugh Walsh, Jr.;   (215) 893-1935

ACADEMY OF MUSIC - MAIN AUDITORIUM
Broad and Locust Streets, Philadelphia, PA 19102
(215) 893-1935
FAX: (215) 545-4588
   Type of Facility: Concert Hall; Theatre House; Opera House
   Type of Stage: Proscenium
   Stage Dimensions: 48'Wx70'D; 48'Wx34'H proscenium opening   **Orchestra Pit**
   Seating Capacity: 2,929
   Contact for Rental: Hugh Walsh, Jr.;   (215) 893-1935
   Resident Groups: Philadelphia Orchestra

CURTIS INSTITUTE - CURTIS HALL
1724 Locust Street, Philadelphia, PA 19103
(215) 893-5252
   Type of Facility: Auditorium
   Type of Stage: Proscenium
   Stage Dimensions: 15'x15'
   Seating Capacity: 235
   Year Built: 1927   **Architect:** E. Pederson   **Cost:** $305,000
   Manager: Dr. V. Sokoloff

FORREST THEATRE
1114 Walnut Street, Philadelphia, PA 19107
(212) 923-1515
   Type of Facility: Theatre House
   Type of Stage: Proscenium
   Stage Dimensions: 94'Wx39'D; 43'Wx30'H proscenium opening   **Orchestra Pit**
   Seating Capacity: 1,847

Contact for Rental: Peter Entin;   (212) 944-3700
Manager: Shubert Organization
Limited availability for rental

MANN MUSIC CENTER
1617 John F. Kennedy Boulevard, #850, Philadelphia, PA 19103
(215) 567-0707
FAX: (215) 567-0734
    Type of Facility: Outdoor (Concert); Amphitheater; Multi-Purpose
    Type of Stage: Proscenium
    Stage Dimensions: 71'Wx60'D   **Orchestra Pit**
    Seating Capacity: 4,639
    Year Built: 1976   **Architect:** MacFadyen and DeVido   **Cost:** $7,500,000
    Acoustical Consultant: Avram Melzer
    Resident Groups: Philadelphia Orchestra

MERRIAM THEATER
250 South Broad Street, Philadelphia, PA 19102
(215) 732-5997
FAX: (215) 732-1396
    Founded: 1918
    Type of Facility: Theatre House
    Facility Originally: Horticulture Center
    Type of Stage: Proscenium
    Stage Dimensions: 45'Wx25'H'42'7"D   **Orchestra Pit**
    Seating Capacity: 1,668
    Year Remodeled: 1987   **Architect:** Raphael Vilamil
    Contact for Rental: Mary Bensel;   (215) 732-5997
    Resident Groups: Pennsylvania Ballet; The Pennsylvania Opera Theater

PAINTED BRIDE
230 Vine Street, Philadelphia, PA 19104
(215) 925-9914
FAX: (215) 925-7402
    Founded: 1969
    Type of Facility: Performance Center; Theatre House; Visual Arts Gallery
    Facility Originally: Factory
    Type of Stage: Flexible
    Stage Dimensions: 30'x50'
    Seating Capacity: 300
    Year Remodeled: 1982
    Acoustical Consultant: Dan Araco
    Contact for Rental: Lenny Seidman;   (215) 925-9914
    Manager: Patricia Robinson;   (215) 925-9914

PHILADELPHIA CIVIC CENTER
34th Street and Civic Centre Boulevard, Philadelphia, PA 19104
(215) 823-5601
    Type of Facility: Civic Center
    Contact for Rental: James Reardon
    Philadelphia Civic Center contains the Convention Hall, Exhibition Halls and Pennsylvania Hall. See separate listings for additional information.

PHILADELPHIA CIVIC CENTER - CONVENTION HALL
34th Street and Civic Centre Boulevard, Philadelphia, PA 19104
(215) 823-5601
    Type of Facility: Auditorium
    Type of Stage: Flexible
    Seating Capacity: 11,000
    Year Built: 1930
    Year Remodeled: 1955
    Contact for Rental: James Reardon

PHILADELPHIA CIVIC CENTER - EXHIBITION HALLS
34th Street and Civic Centre Boulevard, Philadelphia, PA 19104
(215) 823-5601
    Type of Facility: Exhibition Hall
    Type of Stage: Flexible

Year Built: 1967
Contact for Rental: James Reardon
The five Exhibition Halls total 283,000 square feet.

PHILADELPHIA CIVIC CENTER - PENNSYLVANIA HALL
34th Street and Civic Centre Boulevard, Philadelphia, PA 19104
(215) 823-5601
    Type of Facility: Concert Hall; Auditorium
    Type of Stage: End Stage
    Stage Dimensions: 56'6"Wx45'Dx21'H
    Seating Capacity: 4,000
    Year Built: 1978
    Contact for Rental: James Reardon

SOCIETY HILL PLAYHOUSE
507 South Eighth Street, Philadelphia, PA 19147
(215) 923-0210
FAX: (215) 923-1789
    Founded: 1959
    Type of Facility: Studio Performance; Theatre House
    Facility Originally: Meeting Hall; Movie House
    Type of Stage: Proscenium
    Stage Dimensions: 24'Wx20'D
    Seating Capacity: 250
    Year Built: 1902
    Year Remodeled: 1984
    Contact for Rental: Deen Kogan;   (215) 923-0210
    Resident Groups: Society Hill Playhouse Company; Philadelphia Youth Theatre
The Playhouse also contains a 90-seat, black box theatre.

THE SPECTRUM
Pattison Place, Philadelphia, PA 19148
(215) 336-3600
    Type of Facility: Concert Hall; Auditorium; Arena; Multi-Purpose
    Type of Stage: Flexible
    Stage Dimensions: 60'x40'
    Seating Capacity: 19,500
    Year Built: 1967
    Contact for Rental: Roger Dixon, General Manager;   (215) 389-9530
    Resident Groups: Philadelphia Flyers ; Philadelphia '76ers

WALNUT STREET THEATRE
Ninth and Walnut Streets, Philadelphia, PA 19107
(215) 574-3550
FAX: (215) 574-3598
    Type of Facility: Theatre Complex; Concert Hall; Studio Performance; Performance Center; Theatre House
    Facility Originally: "New Circus" Equestrian Theatre
    Type of Stage: Flexible; Proscenium
    Seating Capacity: 1,052
    Year Built: 1809
    Year Remodeled: 1971   **Architect:** F. Brian Loving   **Cost:** $4,000,000
    Contact for Rental: Ken Wesler;   (215) 923-2055
    Resident Groups: Walnut Street Theatre Company; Concerto Soloists Chamber Orchestra
America's oldest theater, the building became Walnut Street Theatre—a legitimate theater—in 1812. Designated a National Historic Landmark in 1964, the building contains Mainstage, Studio Five and Studio Three. See separate listings for additional information.

WALNUT STREET THEATRE - MAINSTAGE
Ninth and Walnut Streets, Philadelphia, PA 19107
(215) 574-3550
    Type of Facility: Theatre House
    Type of Stage: Proscenium
    Stage Dimensions: 60'6"Wx41'D; 38'Wx24'H proscenium opening   **Orchestra Pit**
    Seating Capacity: 1,052
    Contact for Rental: Ken Wesler;   (215) 923-2055
    Resident Groups: Walnut Street Theatre Company

WALNUT STREET THEATRE - STUDIO 3
Ninth and Walnut Streets, Philadelphia, PA 19107
(215) 574-3550
Type of Facility: Studio Performance; Multi-Purpose
Type of Stage: Flexible
Stage Dimensions: 22'2"Wx43'D
Seating Capacity: 85
Contact for Rental: Ken Wesler;   (215) 923-2055

WALNUT STREET THEATRE - STUDIO 5
Ninth and Walnut Streets, Philadelphia, PA 19107
(215) 574-3550
Type of Facility: Theatre House
Type of Stage: Proscenium
Stage Dimensions: 21'11"Wx15'10"D; 10'5"H grid
Seating Capacity: 99
Contact for Rental: Ken Wesler;   (215) 923-2055

WILMA THEATER
2030 Sansom Street, Philadelphia, PA 19103
(215) 963-0249
Type of Facility: Black Box
Facility Originally: Factory
Type of Stage: Flexible
Stage Dimensions: 50'9"Dx37'W
Seating Capacity: 106
Year Remodeled: 1972
Resident Groups: The Wilma Theater

Pittsburgh

DANCE

DANCE ALLOY
4400 Forbes Avenue, Pittsburgh, PA 15213
(412) 621-6670
FAX: (412) 621-6671
Founded: 1976
Arts Area: Modern
Status: Professional; Non-Profit
Type: Performing; Touring; Educational
Purpose: To perform; to provide educational services
Management: Mark Taylor, Artistic Director; Marilyn M. Coleman, Managing Director
Paid Staff: 3
Non-Paid Artists: 6
Utilizes: Special Technical Talent; Guest Artists; Guest Choreographers
Budget: $1,000 - $50,000
Income Sources: Private Foundations/Grants/Endowments; Business/Corporate Donations; Box Office; Government Grants; Individual Donations
Season: October - March
Performance Facilities: Fulton Theatre

PITTSBURGH BALLET THEATRE
2900 Liberty Avenue, Pittsburgh, PA 15201
(412) 281-0360
FAX: (412) 281-9901
Founded: 1969
Arts Area: Ballet
Status: Professional; Non-Profit
Type: Performing; Touring; Resident; Educational
Purpose: To present quality professional ballet performances in Pittsburgh, regionally and nationally
Management: Steven B. Libman, Managing Director; Patricia Wilde, Artistic Director; Nancy Hrynkiw, Director of Marketing; Mary Ellen Miller, Director of Development
Officers: Eugene Barone, Chairman; Harry Weil, President
Paid Staff: 25   **Volunteer Staff:** 109

Paid Artists: 35
Utilizes: Guest Conductors; Guest Artists; Guest Choreographers
Budget: $5,000,000 - $10,000,000
Income Sources: Private Foundations/Grants/Endowments; Business/Corporate Donations; Box Office; Government Grants; Individual Donations
Season: October - April   **Annual Attendance:** 125,000
Affiliations: NEA; Dance USA
Performance Facilities: Benedum Center for the Performing Arts

PITTSBURGH DANCE COUNCIL INC.
719 Liberty Avenue, Pittsburgh, PA 15222
FAX: (412) 355-0413
Founded: 1969
Arts Area: Modern; Ballet; Ethnic; Folk
Status: Non-Profit
Type: Sponsoring; Presenting
Purpose: To invest in the research and development of new artists and educational projects
Management: Carolelinda Dickey, Executive Director
Officers: William Wycoff, President, Board of Directors
Paid Staff: 5
Utilizes: Special Technical Talent
Budget: $50,000 - $100,000
Income Sources: Private Foundations/Grants/Endowments; Business/Corporate Donations; Box Office; Government Grants; Individual Donations
Affiliations: Pittsburgh Cultural Trust
Performance Facilities: Benedum Center; Eddy Theater at Chatham College; Fulton Theater

INSTRUMENTAL MUSIC

DUQUESNE UNIVERSITY TAMBURITZANS
1801 Boulevard of the Allies, Pittsburgh, PA 15219
(412) 434-5185
FAX: (412) 434-5583
Founded: 1937
Arts Area: Ensemble; Ethnic; Folk
Status: Non-Professional; Non-Profit
Type: Performing; Touring
Purpose: To preserve and perpetuate Eastern European cultural heritage in the United States
Management: Paul G. Stafura, Managing Director
Paid Staff: 11
Non-Paid Artists: 40
Utilizes: Special Technical Talent
Budget: $100,000 - $500,000
Income Sources: Private Foundations/Grants/Endowments; Business/Corporate Donations; Box Office; Government Grants; Individual Donations
Season: September - June
Annual Attendance: 200,000
Affiliations: Duquesne University

PITTSBURGH CHAMBER MUSIC SOCIETY
4200 Fifth Avenue, Pittsburgh, PA 15260
(412) 624-4129
Founded: 1961
Arts Area: Chamber
Status: Professional; Non-Profit
Type: Sponsoring
Purpose: To present chamber music; to commission new works; outreach
Management: Joan Sher, Executive Director
Officers: Michael Kumer, President; Dale Hershey, Vice President; Jane MacLeod, Secretary; Marlee S. Myers, Treasurer
Paid Staff: 2
Utilizes: Guest Artists
Budget: $100,000 - $500,000
Income Sources: Private Foundations/Grants/Endowments; Business/Corporate Donations; Box Office; Government Grants; Individual Donations
Season: October - May
Annual Attendance: 5,000

Affiliations: CMA; PA Presenters
Performance Facilities: The Carnegie Music Hall

THE PITTSBURGH NEW MUSIC ENSEMBLE
Duquesne University School of Music, 600 Forbes Avenue, Pittsburgh, PA 15282
(412) 261-0554
FAX: (412) 434-5479
    Founded: 1975
    Arts Area: Chamber; Instrumental Group; Contemporary Chamber Ensemble
    Status: Professional; Non-Profit
    Type: Performing; Touring; Resident; Educational; Sponsoring
    Purpose: The Pittsburgh New Music Ensemble performs 20th century music, mostly American, providing a showcase for many live composers. Many of the works were written for the ensemble or commissioned.
    Management: Eva Tumiel-Kozak, Executive Director; David Stock, Conductor
    Officers: Michael Kumer, President; Joan Humphrey, Vice President; John C. Juback, Secretary; Jaime Brown, Treasurer
    Paid Staff: 1   **Volunteer Staff:** 5
    Paid Artists: 20
    Utilizes: Guest Conductors; Guest Artists
    Budget: $100,000 - $500,000
    Income Sources: Private Foundations/Grants/Endowments; Business/Corporate Donations; Box Office; Government Grants; Individual Donations
    Season: October - May   **Annual Attendance:** 8,400
    Affiliations: CMA
    Performance Facilities: Levy Hall at The Fulton Theatres

PITTSBURGH SYMPHONY ORCHESTRA
Heinz Hall, 600 Penn Avenue, Pittsburgh, PA 15222
(412) 392-4800
    Founded: 1926
    Arts Area: Symphony; Orchestra; Chamber
    Status: Non-Profit
    Type: Performing; Touring; Educational; Presenting
    Purpose: To strive for and attain the highest standards of artistic achievement
    Management: Gideon Toeplitz, Executive Vice President/Managing Director
    Officers: David W. Christopher, President; Gideon Toeplitz, Executive Vice President/Managing Director
    Paid Staff: 51
    Paid Artists: 102
    Utilizes: Guest Conductors; Guest Artists
    Budget: Over 10,000,000
    Income Sources: Private Foundations/Grants/Endowments; Business/Corporate Donations; Box Office; Government Grants; Individual Donations
    Season: 52 Weeks
    Annual Attendance: 500,000
    Affiliations: Pittsburgh Symphony Society
    Performance Facilities: Heinz Hall for the Performing Arts

PITTSBURGH YOUTH SYMPHONY ORCHESTRA ASSOCIATION, INC.
Heinz Hall, 600 Penn Avenue, Pittsburgh, PA 15222
(412) 392-4872
    Founded: 1954
    Arts Area: Symphony; Orchestra; Chamber; Ensemble
    Status: Non-Professional; Non-Profit
    Type: Performing; Touring; Resident; Educational; Sponsoring
    Purpose: To maintain a music and educational program designed to aid young people to attain solid positions in the music profession, be it in performance, symphony orchestra, or teaching
    Management: Barbara Yahr, Music Director; Willa Moriarity, Managing Director; Gina Zeglinski, Personnel Manager/Librarian; Cecelia Klaphake, Administrative Assistant
    Officers: Suzanne C. Ross, President; Mrs. William H. George, Executive Vice President; Evelyn B. Pearson, Secretary; John McElroy, Treasurer
    Paid Staff: 5   **Volunteer Staff:** 2
    Paid Artists: 6
    Utilizes: Guest Artists
    Budget: $100,000 - $500,000
    Income Sources: Private Foundations/Grants/Endowments; Business/Corporate Donations; Box Office; Individual Donations
    Season: September - June
    Annual Attendance: 10,000
    Affiliations: Pittsburgh Symphony Society
    Performance Facilities: Heinz Hall for the Performing Arts

RENAISSANCE AND BAROQUE SOCIETY OF PITTSBURGH
PO Box 10156, Pittsburgh, PA 15232
(412) 682-5253
Founded: 1969
Arts Area: Orchestra; Chamber; Early Music Presenter
Status: Professional
Type: Sponsoring
Purpose: To sponsor touring ensembles from the US and abroad who perform early music on period instruments
Officers: Russell W. Ayers III, President; Cynthia Elm, Vice President; Abigail McGuire, Secretary; Tod Pike, Treasurer
Utilizes: Guest Artists
Budget: $100,000 - $500,000
Income Sources: Private Foundations/Grants/Endowments; Business/Corporate Donations; Box Office; Government Grants; Individual Donations
Season: September - May **Annual Attendance:** 7,000
Performance Facilities: Synod Hall; Fulton Theatre; Carnegie Music Hall

RIVER CITY BRASS BAND
PO Box 6436, Pittsburgh, PA 15212
(412) 322-7222
FAX: (412) 322-6821
Founded: 1980
Arts Area: Band
Status: Professional; Non-Profit
Type: Performing; Touring; Resident
Purpose: To produce superior quality performances of brass band and brass ensemble music that appeals to a broad spectrum of the community
Management: Robert Bernat, President/Music Director; William Schlageter, Regional Concert Sales Manager; Milton Orkin, Contracted Performances Representative; Joseph Zuback, Personnel/Production Manager; Carl Jackson, Recording Manager
Officers: W. Keith Smith, Chairman; John C. Marous Jr., Vice Chairman; Robert Bernat, President; R. Daniel McMichael, Vice President; Richard M. Hays, Secretary; Jay C. Juliussen, Treasurer
Paid Staff: 10 **Volunteer Staff:** 95
Paid Artists: 29
Utilizes: Guest Conductors; Guest Artists
Budget: $1,000,000 - $5,000,000
Income Sources: Private Foundations/Grants/Endowments; Business/Corporate Donations; Box Office; Government Grants; Individual Donations; Sponsors
Season: September - April **Annual Attendance:** 125,000
Affiliations: APAP; American Concert Band
Performance Facilities: Carnegie Music Hall

VOCAL MUSIC

OPERA THEATER OF PITTSBURGH, INC.
PO Box 110108, Pittsburgh, PA 15232
(412) 521-5209; (412) 683-1967
Arts Area: Grand Opera; Children's Opera; Chamber Opera
Status: Professional; Non-Profit
Type: Performing; Touring; Educational
Purpose: To provide professional opera to areas outside the metropolitan centers; to introduce children to opera; to develop emerging professionals
Management: Gary Race, Artistic Director
Officers: Mildred Miller Posvar, President/Co-Founder; Henry Hoffstot, Chairman of the Board
Budget: $50,000 - $100,000
Income Sources: Private Foundations/Grants/Endowments; Business/Corporate Donations; Box Office; Government Grants; Individual Donations
Performance Facilities: The Carnegie Music Hall

PITTSBURGH BOYCHOIR, INC.
300 Mt. Lebanon Boulevard, Suite 315, Pittsburgh, PA 15234
(412) 343-7464
FAX: (412) 343-9281
Founded: 1986
Arts Area: Choral; Musical Theatre
Status: Semi-Professional; Non-Profit
Type: Performing; Touring; Educational
Purpose: To provide a choral training program for Pittsburgh youth with a goal of music excellence; to tour abroad
Management: J. Scot Franklin, Managing Director; Judith Phelps, Administrator

Officers: Roy L. Franklin, President; John Ferguson, Secretary; Thomas Funk, Treasurer; William S. Smith, Esquire; Mark Stahl, CPA
Paid Staff: 5   **Volunteer Staff:** 200
Paid Artists: 4   **Non-Paid Artists:** 105
Utilizes: Special Technical Talent; Guest Conductors; Guest Artists
Budget: $100,000 - $500,000
Income Sources: Private Foundations/Grants/Endowments; Business/Corporate Donations; Box Office; Individual Donations; Fundraisers; Sales
Season: August - June   **Annual Attendance:** 600
Affiliations: CA; ACDA; MENC; American Guild of Organists
Performance Facilities: Fulton Theatre; Heinz Chapel-University of Pittsburgh

PITTSBURGH CIVIC LIGHT OPERA
719 Liberty Avenue, Benedum Center, Pittsburgh, PA 15222
(412) 281-3973
FAX: (412) 281-5339
Founded: 1946
Arts Area: Light Opera; Operetta
Status: Professional; Non-Profit
Type: Performing; Educational
Purpose: To perpetuate, preserve and create musical, light opera and drama productions for the cultural and educational enrichment of our audiences, primarily in western Pennsylvania and, secondarily, the United States; ticket prices are set to enable maximum community participation
Management: Charles Gray, Executive Director/General Manager; Corinne Imbach, Director of Development
Paid Staff: 200   **Volunteer Staff:** 20
Paid Artists: 60
Utilizes: Special Technical Talent; Guest Artists; Guest Directors
Budget: $5,000,000 - $10,000,000
Income Sources: Private Foundations/Grants/Endowments; Business/Corporate Donations; Box Office; Government Grants; Individual Donations
Season: May - August   **Annual Attendance:** 165,000
Affiliations: Musical Theater Works; National Musical Theater Network

PITTSBURGH OPERA
711 Penn Avenue, 8th Floor, Pittsburgh, PA 15222
(412) 281-0912
FAX: (412) 281-4324
Founded: 1940
Arts Area: Grand Opera
Status: Professional; Non-Profit
Type: Performing
Purpose: To present grand operas
Management: Tito Capobianco, General Director
Officers: Vincent A. Sarni, Chairman; Thomas H. O'Brien, President; Tito Capobianco, Vice President
Paid Staff: 22
Utilizes: Special Technical Talent; Guest Conductors; Guest Artists; Guest Directors
Budget: $1,000,000 - $5,000,000
Income Sources: Private Foundations/Grants/Endowments; Business/Corporate Donations; Box Office; Government Grants; Individual Donations
Season: October - May   **Annual Attendance:** 55,400
Affiliations: OA
Performance Facilities: Benedum Center for the Performing Arts

RENAISSANCE CITY CHOIR
1432 Summit Street, Pittsburgh, PA 15221
(412) 242-5539
Founded: 1985
Arts Area: Choral
Status: Non-Professional; Non-Profit
Type: Performing
Management: Ed Burau, General Manager
Paid Staff: 1   **Volunteer Staff:** 4
Non-Paid Artists: 30
Utilizes: Guest Conductors; Guest Artists
Budget: $1,000 - $50,000
Income Sources: Private Foundations/Grants/Endowments; Business/Corporate Donations; Box Office; Individual Donations
Season: May - December   **Annual Attendance:** 1,000
Performance Facilities: Campbell Chapel/Chatham College

THEATRE

CITY THEATRE COMPANY
57 South 13th Street, Pittsburgh, PA 15203
(412) 431-4400
FAX: (412) 431-5535
Founded: 1974
Arts Area: Professional; Theatrical Group
Status: Professional; Non-Profit
Type: Performing; Resident; Educational
Purpose: To bring the richness and excitement of live theatre to a diverse public through the production of plays of relevant to contemporary American values and culture
Management: Marc Masterson, Producing Director
Officers: Robert M. Frankel, President; Thomas Hollander, Vice President; Jane Arkus, Secretary; Libby G. Fishman, Treasurer
Paid Staff: 20   **Volunteer Staff:** 2
Paid Artists: 50
Utilizes: Special Technical Talent; Guest Artists; Guest Directors
Budget: $500,000 - $1,000,000
Income Sources: Private Foundations/Grants/Endowments; Business/Corporate Donations; Box Office; Government Grants; Individual Donations
Season: October - May   **Annual Attendance:** 24,000
Affiliations: TCG
Performance Facilities: City Theatre

PITTSBURGH PUBLIC THEATER
Allegheny Square, Pittsburgh, PA 15212-5362
(412) 323-8200
Founded: 1974
Arts Area: Professional; Theatrical Group
Status: Professional; Non-Profit
Type: Performing; Educational
Purpose: To present the highest quality of professional theater in classical and modern genres to the Pittsburgh community
Management: William T. Gardner, Producing Director; Dan Fallon, Managing Director
Officers: Richard H. Daniel, Chairman
Paid Staff: 25
Utilizes: Special Technical Talent; Guest Artists; Guest Directors
Budget: $1,000,000 - $5,000,000
Income Sources: Private Foundations/Grants/Endowments; Business/Corporate Donations; Box Office; Government Grants; Individual Donations
Season: September - June
Affiliations: AEA; LORT
Performance Facilities: Theodore Hazlett Theatre

SALTWORKS
5001 Baum Boulevard, Pittsburgh, PA 15213
Founded: 1982
Arts Area: Professional; Theatrical Group
Status: Semi-Professional; Non-Profit
Type: Performing; Touring; Educational
Purpose: To perform plays for youth and families that address social issues
Management: Lynn George, Executive Director
Paid Staff: 6
Paid Artists: 5
Utilizes: Special Technical Talent; Guest Directors
Budget: $100,000 - $500,000
Income Sources: Private Foundations/Grants/Endowments; Business/Corporate Donations; Box Office; Individual Donations; Performance Fees
Season: 52 Weeks   **Annual Attendance:** 250

PERFORMING SERIES

LIVING MASTERS SUBSCRIPTION SERIES
c/o Manchester Craftsmen's Guild, 1815 Metropolitan Street, Pittsburgh, PA 15233
(412) 322-1773
FAX: (412) 321-2120
Arts Area: Jazz

Status: Professional; Non-Profit
Type: Educational; Presenting
Purpose: To present jazz as an art form and include educational and community activities
Management: Martin Jay Ashby, Director of Performing Arts; Jay Ashby, Music Educational Director
Officers: William Strickland Jr., Director
Budget: $100,000 - $500,000
Income Sources: Private Foundations/Grants/Endowments; Business/Corporate Donations; Box Office; Government Grants; Individual Donations
Performance Facilities: Manchester Craftmen's Guild Music Hall

THREE RIVERS SHAKESPEARE FESTIVAL
1617 Cathedral of Learning, University of Pittsburgh, Pittsburgh, PA 15260
(412) 624-1953
FAX: (412) 624-6338
    Founded: 1980
    Arts Area: Vocal Music; Theater
    Status: Professional; Non-Profit
    Type: Performing; Touring; Resident; Educational
    Purpose: To produce works of William Shakespeare and other classical dramatists in a manner accessible to the general public while maintaining high artistic standards
    Management: Attilio Favorini, Producing Director; Susan O'Connell, Publicity Director; Christine Frezza, Planning Administrator; Sharyn Redpath, Director of Outreach; Eileen Davin, Director of Finance; Cathy Focareta, Director of Group Sales; Ellen Kelson, Literay Manager
    Officers: Joseph Coogle Jr., Board President; Eric Springer, Vice Chairman/Board of Advisors
    Paid Staff: 20   **Volunteer Staff:** 10
    Paid Artists: 60   **Non-Paid Artists:** 10
    Utilizes: Special Technical Talent; Guest Artists; Guest Directors
    Budget: $5,000,000 - $10,000,000
    Income Sources: Private Foundations/Grants/Endowments; Business/Corporate Donations; Box Office; Government Grants; Individual Donations; University of Pittsburgh
    Season: May - August
    Annual Attendance: 40,000
    Affiliations: AEA; U/RTA
    Performance Facilities: Stephen Foster Memorial

FACILITY

BENEDUM CENTER
719 Liberty Avenue, Pittsburgh, PA 15222
(412) 456-2600
FAX: (412) 456-2645
    Founded: 1987
    Type of Facility: Concert Hall; Theatre House; Opera House
    Facility Originally: Movie Palace
    Type of Stage: Proscenium
    Stage Dimensions: 144'Wx78'D; 56'Wx36'6" proscenium opening   **Orchestra Pit**
    Seating Capacity: 2,887
    Year Built: 1928
    Year Remodeled: 1987   **Architect:** MacLachlin Cornelius & Filoni   **Cost:** $42,000,000
    Acoustical Consultant: Schultz
    Contact for Rental: Gene Ciavarra;   (412) 456-2600
    Manager: Michael Taormina;   (412) 456-2600
    Resident Groups: Pittsburgh Opera; Pittsburgh Ballet Theatre; Pittsburgh Civic Light Opera; Pittsburgh Dance Council
    Formerly the Stanley Theater, Benedum Center has the third-largest stage in the country.

THE CARNEGIE - LECTURE HALL
4400 Forbes Avenue, Pittsburgh, PA 15213
(412) 622-3360
FAX: (412) 622-3274
    Type of Facility: Film & Lecture Hall
    Type of Stage: Platform
    Stage Dimensions: 30'Wx11'D
    Seating Capacity: 617
    Year Built: 1895   **Architect:** Longfellow Alden & Harlow
    Contact for Rental: Eilene Dewalt, Special Events Coordinator;   (412) 622-3360
    Resident Groups: International Poetry Forum

THE CARNEGIE - MUSEUM OF ART THEATRE
4400 Forbes Avenue, Pittsburgh, PA 15213
(412) 622-3360
Type of Facility: Visual And Performing Arts Classrooms
Type of Stage: Platform
Stage Dimensions: 33'Wx9'D
Seating Capacity: 198
Year Built: 1974 **Architect:** Edward Larabee Barnes
Contact for Rental: Eilene Dewalt; (412) 622-3360
Resident Groups: The Carnegie Film and Video Series

THE CARNEGIE - MUSIC HALL
4400 Forbes Avenue, Pittsburgh, PA 15213
(412) 622-3360
Type of Facility: Concert Hall; Civic Center
Type of Stage: Concert Shell
Stage Dimensions: 66'3"Wx34'Dx51'H
Seating Capacity: 1,950
Year Built: 1895 **Architect:** Longfellow Alden & Harlow
Year Remodeled: 1907
Contact for Rental: Eilene Dewalt; (412) 622-3360
Resident Groups: River City Brass Band; Pittsburgh Chamber Music; Mendelssohn Choir; Bach Choir; Travel & Adventure Series; Man & Ideas Series; Carnegie Music Hall Philharmonic

HEINZ HALL FOR THE PERFORMING ARTS
600 Penn Avenue, Pittsburgh, PA 15222
(412) 392-4800
Type of Facility: Concert Hall; Studio Performance; Performance Center; Theatre House; Opera House; Multi-Purpose
Facility Originally: Vaudeville
Type of Stage: Proscenium
Stage Dimensions: 32'x54'x60'
Orchestra Pit
Seating Capacity: 2,847
Year Built: 1927 **Architect:** Rapp & Rapp
Year Remodeled: 1971 **Architect:** Stotz Hess McLachlin & Fosner **Cost:** $13,000,000
Acoustical Consultant: Dr. Heinrich Keilholz
Contact for Rental: Don Craig; (412) 392-4843
Resident Groups: Pittsburgh Symphony Orchestra; Pittsburgh Symphony Youth Orchestra; Mendelsohn Choir; Diet Coke Broadway Series

PITTSBURGH CIVIC ARENA
300 Auditorium Place, Pittsburgh, PA 15219
(412) 642-1800
Type of Facility: Civic Center
Type of Stage: Proscenium
Orchestra Pit
Seating Capacity: 15,000
Year Built: 1961 **Architect:** Deeter, Ritchey, Sippel **Cost:** $22,000,000
Contact for Rental: Booking Director; (412) 642-1800
Manager: Tim Murphy

Reading

INSTRUMENTAL MUSIC

READING SYMPHONY ORCHESTRA
147 North Fifth Street, Reading, PA 19601
(215) 373-7557
Founded: 1912
Arts Area: Symphony
Status: Professional
Type: Performing; Educational; Sponsoring
Purpose: To present the highest quality orchestral concerts possible in Berks County and the city of Reading
Management: Stuart B. Weiser, Executive Director
Officers: Robert S. Pollack, President; Thomas B. Souders, Vice President; Alice F. Friedman, Treasurer
Paid Staff: 2 **Volunteer Staff:** 1

Utilizes: Guest Conductors; Guest Artists
Budget: $100,000 - $500,000
Income Sources: Private Foundations/Grants/Endowments; Business/Corporate Donations; Box Office; Government Grants; Individual Donations
Season: October - April **Annual Attendance:** 15,000
Affiliations: ASOL
Performance Facilities: Rajah Theatre

THEATRE

READING COMMUNITY PLAYERS
11th and Buttonwood Street, PO Box 1032, Reading, PA 19604
(215) 375-9106
> **Founded:** 1920
> **Arts Area:** Community; Theatrical Group
> **Status:** Non-Professional; Non-Profit
> **Type:** Performing; Educational
> **Purpose:** To create and develop interest in the theatrical arts of the community
> **Management:** Terry Fullmer, Business Manager
> **Officers:** Hal Kremser, Treasurer
> **Volunteer Staff:** 114
> **Non-Paid Artists:** 114
> **Budget:** $1,000 - $50,000
> **Income Sources:** Private Foundations/Grants/Endowments; Business/Corporate Donations; Box Office; Government Grants
> **Season:** 52 Weeks

PERFORMING SERIES

HAAGE CONCERTS/HARRIS PRESENTS
435 Walnut Street, Reading, PA 19611
(215) 374-3161
> **Founded:** 1907
> **Arts Area:** Dance; Vocal Music; Instrumental Music; Theater
> **Status:** Professional
> **Type:** Sponsoring
> **Purpose:** To present classical and pops attractions of high quality featuring new and innovative groups, dance, mime, Renaissance and others
> **Management:** Louise M. Harris, Manager
> **Utilizes:** Guest Artists
> **Budget:** $50,000 - $100,000
> **Income Sources:** Box Office; Individual Donations
> **Season:** October - April
> **Performance Facilities:** Rajah Theatre

STAR SERIES OF READING
147 North Fifth Street, Reading, PA 19601
(215) 376-3395
FAX: (215) 376-3336
> **Founded:** 1970
> **Arts Area:** Dance; Vocal Music; Instrumental Music
> **Status:** Non-Profit
> **Type:** Sponsoring
> **Purpose:** Presentation of music and music-related performances of cultural value to the community, in the areas of classical music, jazz, dance, ethnic music, and others
> **Management:** Lawrence H. Passmore, Executive Director
> **Officers:** James A. Williamson, Jr., Chairman; Louise Dreisbach, Secretary; Patricia Moulton, Treasurer; Nicole Backenstoss, Artist Selection Chairman
> **Utilizes:** Guest Artists
> **Budget:** $50,000 - $100,000
> **Income Sources:** Private Foundations/Grants/Endowments; Box Office; Government Grants; Individual Donations
> **Season:** September - May
> **Affiliations:** Reading Musical Foundation
> **Performance Facilities:** Rajah Theatre; Albright Theatre

FACILITY

RAJAH THEATRE
136 North Sixth Street, Reading, PA 19601
(215) 375-0185
FAX: (215) 376-7821
    Type of Facility: Theatre Complex; Concert Hall; Auditorium; Theatre House
    Type of Stage: Proscenium   **Orchestra Pit**
    Seating Capacity: 2,040
    Year Remodeled: 1922
    Contact for Rental: Diane L. Lewis;   (215) 372-8936

Rose Valley

THEATRE

HEDGEROW THEATRE
64 West Rose Valley Road, Rose Valley, PA 19065
(215) 565-4211
    Founded: 1923
    Arts Area: Theatre Group
    Status: Professional; Non-Equity
    Type: Performing; Touring; Resident; Educational
    Purpose: To build an ensemble capable of presenting all types of theatre in repertory
    Management: Penelope Reed, Artistic Director; John Gallagher, General Manager; Gay Kuhn, Fiscal Director
    Officers: Patrick Horrigan, President; Janet Kelsey, Secretary/Treasurer
    Paid Staff: 15   **Volunteer Staff:** 70
    Paid Artists: 15   **Non-Paid Artists:** 70
    Utilizes: Special Technical Talent; Guest Artists; Guest Directors
    Budget: $100,000 - $500,000
    Income Sources: Private Foundations/Grants/Endowments; Business/Corporate Donations; Box Office; Government Grants; Individual Donations; Touring
    Season: 52 Weeks
    Performance Facilities: Hedgerow Theatre

Scranton

FACILITY

SCRANTON CULTURAL CENTER AT THE MASONIC TEMPLE
420 North Washington Avenue, Scranton, PA 18503
(717) 346-7369
FAX: (717) 346-7365
    Founded: 1927
    Type of Facility: Theatre Complex; Civic Center
    Type of Stage: Proscenium
    Stage Dimensions: 50'x31'
    Orchestra Pit
    Seating Capacity: 1,836
    Year Built: 1927   **Architect:** Raymond Hood   **Cost:** $3,000,000
    Contact for Rental: Colin Bissett;   (717) 346-7369
    Resident Groups: Northeastern Philharmonic Orchestra; Community Concerts; Broadway Theatre League

Slippery Rock

FACILITY

MILLER AUDITORIUM
Slippery Rock Unversity, Slippery Rock, PA 16057
(412) 738-2090
FAX: (412) 738-2098
    Founded: 1960
    Type of Facility: Auditorium
    Type of Stage: Proscenium
    Stage Dimensions: 65'x37' stage floor; 45'x13'9" proscenium opening
    Seating Capacity: 896

Year Built: 1960
Architect: Altenhof and Bown
Contact for Rental: Laurel Dagnon;   (412) 738-2027
Resident Groups: Slippery Rock University Department of Theatre

---

Somerset

PERFORMING SERIES

LAUREL ARTS, INC./THE PHILIP DRESSLER CENTER FOR THE ARTS
214 South Harrison Avenue, PO Box 414, Somerset, PA 15501-0414
(814) 443-2433
Founded: 1975
Arts Area: Dance; Vocal Music; Instrumental Music; Theater; Festivals; Multidisciplinary
Status: Professional; Non-Profit
Type: Performing; Touring; Resident; Educational; Sponsoring
Purpose: To promote, exhibit and preserve multidisciplinary art; to foster the creative process of individuals and groups; to provide cultural diversity an accessibility a broad scope of arts for people of all ages in Someset County
Management: Robert B. Locklin Jr., Executive Director; Lori M. Troy, Office Manager; Carol L. Ogle, Public Relations Director; Stephanie Williams, Dance Administrator; Terri Klink, Financial Recordkeeper
Officers: Lana Miller, President; Robert Spochart, Vice President; Bonne Gurzenda, Secretary; Eugene Hankinson, Treasurer; Dorothy Dressler, Director Emeritus
Paid Staff: 7   **Volunteer Staff:** 300
Paid Artists: 500
Utilizes: Special Technical Talent; Guest Artists
Budget: $100,000 - $500,000
Income Sources: Private Foundations/Grants/Endowments; Business/Corporate Donations; Box Office; Government Grants; Individual Donations
Season: 52 Weeks   **Annual Attendance:** 75,000

State College

DANCE

PENNSYLVANIA DANCE THEATRE
101 South Fraser Street, State College, PA 16801
(814) 237-2188
Founded: 1979
Arts Area: Modern
Status: Professional; Non-Profit
Type: Performing; Touring; Educational
Purpose: To offer audiences an overview of the mainstream as well as the cutting edge in modern dance
Management: Michael Casper, Managing Director; Annunciata Marino, Company Manager
Officers: Ann Van Kuren, Artistic Director
Paid Staff: 2   **Volunteer Staff:** 2
Paid Artists: 8   **Non-Paid Artists:** 1
Utilizes: Special Technical Talent; Guest Artists; Guest Choreographers
Budget: $100,000 - $500,000
Income Sources: Private Foundations/Grants/Endowments; Business/Corporate Donations; Box Office; Government Grants; Individual Donations
Season: September - July

PERFORMING SERIES

CENTRAL PENNSYLVANIA FESTIVAL OF THE ARTS
PO Box 1023, State College, PA 16804
(814) 237-3682
FAX: (814) 237-0708
Founded: 1967
Arts Area: Festivals
Status: Non-Profit
Type: Performing
Purpose: To produce an annual arts festival celebrating all the arts: performing, visual and literary
Management: Philip L. Walz, Executive Director; Katherine Talcott, Assistant Director
Officers: Linda J. Gall, President; Kenneth Thigpen, Vice President; Grace Pilato, Secretary; John Black, Treasurer
Paid Staff: 2   **Volunteer Staff:** 200

Paid Artists: 200   **Non-Paid Artists:** 400
Utilizes: Guest Artists
Budget: $100,000 - $500,000
Income Sources: Business/Corporate Donations; Government Grants; Individual Donations
Season: July   **Annual Attendance:** 250,000
Affiliations: APAP

Swarthmore

PERFORMING SERIES

SWARTHMORE MUSIC AND DANCE FESTIVAL
Swarthmore College, Swarthmore, PA 19081
(215) 328-8239
Founded: 1982
Arts Area: Dance; Vocal Music; Instrumental Music; Festivals
Status: Professional; Non-Professional; Non-Profit
Type: Resident; Educational; Sponsoring
Purpose: To present and interrelate top quality music and dance events to a wide audience
Management: Allison Herz, Executive Director; James Freeman, Artistic Director; Sharon Friedler, Artistic Director; Judy Lord, Administrative Assistant
Paid Staff: 4   **Volunteer Staff:** 3
Paid Artists: 30   **Non-Paid Artists:** 15
Utilizes: Guest Conductors; Guest Artists
Budget: $50,000 - $100,000
Income Sources: Private Foundations/Grants/Endowments; Business/Corporate Donations; Box Office; Government Grants; Individual Donations; Advertising
Season: September - November   **Annual Attendance:** 6,000
Affiliations: Pennsylvania Presenters
Performance Facilities: Lang Hall; Pearson Hall Theatre

Uniontown

FACILITY

STATE THEATRE CENTER FOR THE ARTS
27 East Main Street, Uniontown, PA 15401
(412) 439-1360
Founded: 1989
Facility Originally: Vaudeville; Movie House
Type of Stage: Proscenium
Stage Dimensions: 36'6"x28'   **Orchestra Pit**
Seating Capacity: 1,650
Year Built: 1921
Architect: Lamb
Contact for Rental: Kelly Johnson;   (412) 439-1360

University Park

THEATRE

PENNSYLVANIA CENTRE STAGE
213 Arts Building, University Park, PA 16802
(814) 863-0255
Founded: 1985
Arts Area: Professional; Theatrical Group
Status: Professional
Type: Performing; Educational
Purpose: Professional regional theatre on the Pennsylvania State University campus
Management: Travis DeCastro, Producing Director
Paid Staff: 10
Paid Artists: 75

Utilizes: Special Technical Talent; Guest Artists; Guest Directors
Budget: $500,000 - $1,000,000
Income Sources: Private Foundations/Grants/Endowments; Business/Corporate Donations; Box Office;
Individual Donations
Season: June - October
Annual Attendance: 30,000
Affiliations: TCG; U/RTA; Theatre Association of Pennsylvania
Performance Facilities: Playhouse Theatre; Pavilion Theatre

FACILITY

PENNSYLVANIA STATE UNIVERSITY - EISENHOWER AUDITORIUM
University Park, PA 16802
(814) 863-0388
> **Type of Facility:** Concert Hall; Auditorium; Performance Center; Theatre House
> **Type of Stage:** Proscenium
> **Stage Dimensions:** 104'Wx52'D   **Orchestra Pit**
> **Seating Capacity:** 2,599
> **Year Built:** 1974   **Architect:** Sanders and Bicksler   **Cost:** $6,700,000
> **Acoustical Consultant:** Bolt, Beranek & Newman
> **Contact for Rental:** Lisa Faust;   (814) 863-0388
> **Resident Groups:** Center for the Performing Arts/Artist Series; University Performing Ensembles; Independent Presenters

PENNSYLVANIA STATE UNIVERSITY - PAVILION THEATRE
137 Arts Building, University Park, PA 16802
(814) 863-0381
FAX: (814) 863-7327
> **Type of Facility:** Theatre House
> **Facility Originally:** Livestock Judging Facility
> **Type of Stage:** 3/4 Arena; Arena
> **Stage Dimensions:** 20'x32'
> **Seating Capacity:** 5318
> **Year Built:** 1914   **Architect:** Day & Klauder   **Cost:** $76,152
> **Year Remodeled:** 1992   **Architect:** Peno & Associates   **Cost:** $1,500,000
> **Acoustical Consultant:** Bolt, Beranek & Newman
> **Manager:** Lee Byron;   (814) 863-0381
> **Resident Groups:** Penn State University Resident Theatre Company; Department of Theatre Arts;
Pennsylvania Centre Stage

PENNSYLVANIA STATE UNIVERSITY - PLAYHOUSE THEATRE
137 Arts Building, University Park, PA 16802
(814) 863-0381
FAX: (814) 863-7327
> **Type of Facility:** Theatre House
> **Type of Stage:** Thrust; Proscenium
> **Stage Dimensions:** 90'x62'   **Orchestra Pit**
> **Seating Capacity:** 515
> **Year Built:** 1963   **Architect:** Eschbach Pullinger Stevens & Bruder   **Cost:** $1,835,030
> **Acoustical Consultant:** Bolt, Beranek & Newman
> **Manager:** Lee Byron;   (814) 863-0381
> **Resident Groups:** Penn State University Resident Theatre Company; Department of Theatre Arts;
Pennsylvania Centre Stage

PENNSYLVANIA STATE UNIVERSITY - SCHWAB AUDITORIUM
University Park, PA 16802
(814) 863-0388
> **Type of Facility:** Concert Hall; Auditorium; Performance Center; Theatre House
> **Type of Stage:** Proscenium
> **Stage Dimensions:** 42'Wx20'D
> **Seating Capacity:** 972
> **Year Built:** 1902   **Cost:** $155,863
> **Year Remodeled:** 1978   **Architect:** Office of Physical Plant   **Cost:** $1,305,811
> **Acoustical Consultant:** Howard Kingsbury
> **Contact for Rental:** Lisa Faust;   (814) 863-0388
> **Resident Groups:** Center for the Performing Arts/Artist Series; University Performing Ensembles; Independent Presenters

Wilkes-Barre

DANCE

WILKES-BARRE BALLET THEATRE
102-104 South Main Street, Wilkes-Barre, PA 18701
(717) 824-8602
Arts Area: Modern; Ballet
Status: Professional; Non-Profit
Type: Resident
Management: Mary Hepner, Artistic Director
Paid Staff: 6
Paid Artists: 9   **Non-Paid Artists:** 3
Utilizes: Special Technical Talent; Guest Artists
Budget: $100,000 - $500,000
Income Sources: Private Foundations/Grants/Endowments; Business/Corporate Donations; Box Office; Individual Donations
Season: October - June
Performance Facilities: F.M. Kirby Center for the Performing Arts

FACILITY

F.M. KIRBY CENTER FOR THE PERFORMING ARTS
71 Public Square, Wilkes-Barre, PA 18701
(717) 823-4599
FAX: (717) 823-4890
Founded: 1986
Type of Facility: Performance Center
Facility Originally: Movie House
Type of Stage: Proscenium
Stage Dimensions: 47'Wx26'6"D   **Orchestra Pit**
Seating Capacity: 1,800
Year Built: 1938
Year Remodeled: 1986   **Architect:** Eugene Ogozolet; Pyros & Sanderson   **Cost:** $3,500,000
Contact for Rental: Dennis Madden;   (717) 823-4599
Resident Groups: Wilkes-Barre Ballet Theatre; Northeastern Philharmonic Orchestra
Kirby Center, designated a National Historic Landmark, is a member theatre of the League of Historic American Theatres.

WILKES UNIVERSITY - DOROTHY DICKSON DARTE CENTER FOR THE PERFORMING ARTS
South Street, Wilkes-Barre, PA 18766
(717) 824-4651
Type of Facility: Theatre Complex; Concert Hall; Performance Center; Amphitheater
Type of Stage: Proscenium
Stage Dimensions: 30'x38'   **Orchestra Pit**
Seating Capacity: 500
Year Built: 1965
Architect: Lacy Atherton & Davis   **Cost:** $980,000
Contact for Rental: Bruce Phair;   (717) 824-4651
Resident Groups: Wilkes University Department of Music, Theatre and Dance
Community cultural events

Wind Gap

VOCAL MUSIC

SINGING BOYS OF PENNSYLVANIA
PO Box 206, Wind Gap, PA 18091
(215) 759-6002
FAX: (215) 759-6042
Arts Area: Choral; Ethnic; Folk
Status: Non-Professional; Non-Profit
Type: Performing; Touring; Resident; Educational; Sponsoring
Purpose: To provide audiences with a wide spectrum of repertoire covering five centuries of classical, sacred and secular music
Officers: Dr. K. Bernard Schade, Director
Paid Staff: 2   **Volunteer Staff:** 2

Non-Paid Artists: 26
Utilizes: Special Technical Talent; Guest Artists
Budget: $100,000 - $500,000
Income Sources: Private Foundations/Grants/Endowments; Business/Corporate Donations; Box Office; Government Grants; Individual Donations; Tuition
Season: 52 Weeks   **Annual Attendance:** 72,000

York

FACILITY

STRAND-CAPITOL PERFORMING ARTS CENTER - CAPITOL THEATRE
50 North George Street, York, PA 17401
(717) 846-1155
FAX: (717) 843-1208
   Type of Facility: Theatre House; Film & Lecture Hall
   Facility Originally: Vaudeville
   Type of Stage: Proscenium
   Seating Capacity: 718
   Year Built: 1917   **Architect:** Demp Wolf
   Year Remodeled: 1982   **Architect:** Hardy Holzman & Pfeiffer; Hamme Associates
   Contact for Rental: Clyde Lindsley;   (717) 846-1155
   Resident Groups: York Flicks (fine films)
   Stage being remodeled

STRAND-CAPITOL PERFORMING ARTS CENTER - STRAND THEATRE
50 North George Street, York, PA 17401
(717) 846-1155; (717) 846-1111
FAX: (717) 843-1208
   Type of Facility: Concert Hall; Theatre House; Opera House
   Facility Originally: Vaudeville
   Type of Stage: Proscenium
   Stage Dimensions: 61'Wx24'6"D; 37'4"Wx19'9"H proscenium opening   **Orchestra Pit**
   Seating Capacity: 1,214
   Year Built: 1925   **Architect:** Demp Wolf   **Cost:** $1,000,000
   Year Remodeled: 1980   **Architect:** Hardy Holzman & Pfeiffer   **Cost:** $1,600,000
   Contact for Rental: Clyde Lindsley;   (717) 846-1155
   Resident Groups: York Symphony Orchestra; Spring Garden Band; Performing Arts for Children; Dance A Story; Strand-Capitol Performing Arts Series

RHODE ISLAND

Barrington

DANCE

SHODA MOVING THEATRE (M.O.V.E. CO.)
110 Highland Anvenue, Barrington, RI 02806
(401) 245-6956
> **Founded:** 1974
> **Arts Area:** Modern; Mime; Movement Theatre
> **Status:** Professional; Non-Profit
> **Type:** Performing; Touring
> **Officers:** Kelli Wicke Davis, Artistic Director
> **Paid Artists:** 6
> **Budget:** $1,000 - $50,000
> **Income Sources:** Private Foundations/Grants/Endowments; Business/Corporate Donations; Box Office; Individual Donations

Bristol

PERFORMING SERIES

BLITHEWOLD GARDENS AND ARBORETUM "CONCERTS BY THE BAY"
101 Ferry Road, Route 114, Bristol, RI 02809-0716
(401) 253-2707
> **Founded:** 1978
> **Arts Area:** Vocal Music; Instrumental Music
> **Status:** Non-Profit
> **Type:** Performing
> **Purpose:** To carry on the tradition of live musical performances in this gracious home along the shores of the Narragansett Bay
> **Management:** Mark Zelonis, Executive Director; Harriet Linn, Special Events Coordinator; Joan Roth, Series Coordinator
> **Paid Staff:** 2   **Volunteer Staff:** 5
> **Utilizes:** Guest Artists
> **Budget:** $1,000 - $50,000
> **Income Sources:** Private Foundations/Grants/Endowments; Box Office
> **Season:** June - September   **Annual Attendance:** 1,000

Kingston

FACILITY

UNIVERSITY OF RHODE ISLAND FINE ARTS CENTER
Kingston, RI 02881
(401) 792-5921
> **Type of Facility:** Theatre Complex; Performance Center
> **Year Built:** 1970   **Architect:** Lester Millman
> **Contact for Rental:** Paula McGlasson;   (401) 792-2705
> **Resident Groups:** University of Rhode Island Department of Theatre
> *University of Rhode Island Fine Arts Center contains J Studio and Robert E. Will Theatre. See separate listings for further information.*

UNIVERSITY OF RHODE ISLAND FINE ARTS CENTER - J STUDIO
Kingston, RI 02881
(401) 792-5921
> **Type of Facility:** Studio Performance; Environmental; Black Box
> **Type of Stage:** Flexible; Environmental
> **Stage Dimensions:** 66'Wx88'Dx32'H
> **Seating Capacity:** 250
> **Year Built:** 1970
> **Contact for Rental:** Paula McGlasson;   (401) 792-2705

UNIVERSITY OF RHODE ISLAND FINE ARTS CENTER - ROBERT E. WILL THEATRE
Kingston, RI 02881
(401) 792-5921
FAX: (401) 792-5618
   Type of Facility: Theatre Complex; Concert Hall; Theatre House
   Type of Stage: Thrust; Proscenium
   Stage Dimensions: 50'Wx24'Hx45'D proscenium opening   **Orchestra Pit**
   Seating Capacity: 550
   Year Built: 1970
   Year Remodeled: 1992
   Contact for Rental: Paula McGlasson;   (401) 792-2705

Lincoln
DANCE

STATE BALLET OF RHODE ISLAND
Sherman Avenue, PO Box 155, Lincoln, RI 02865
(401) 334-2560
   Founded: 1960
   Arts Area: Ballet
   Status: Semi-Professional; Non-Profit
   Type: Performing; Touring; Resident; Educational
   Purpose: A training ground for future professional dancers as well as for future teachers and ballet lovers
   Management: Herci Marsden, Artistic Director; Ana Marsden Fox, General Manager
   Officers: Herci Marsden, Chairperson; Ana Mardsen Fox, Vice Chairperson/Treasurer; Marion Fattore, Recording Secretary
   Paid Staff: 2   **Volunteer Staff:** 50
   Paid Artists: 8   **Non-Paid Artists:** 50
   Utilizes: Special Technical Talent; Guest Artists; Guest Choreographers
   Budget: $1,000 - $50,000
   Income Sources: Private Foundations/Grants/Endowments; Business/Corporate Donations; Box Office; Individual Donations
   Season: 52 Weeks   **Annual Attendance:** 5,000
   Performance Facilities: Roberts Hall Theatre; Rhode Island College

Matunuck
THEATRE

THEATRE-BY-THE-SEA
364 Cards Pond Road, Matunuck, RI 02879
(401) 782-8587
FAX: (401) 783-9452
   Founded: 1933
   Arts Area: Professional; Summer Stock; Musical
   Status: Commercial
   Type: Performing; Resident
   Purpose: Summer theatre entertainment
   Management: Richard Ericson, Laura Harris, Lawrence Serre, Rolt Smith, Producers
   Paid Staff: 20
   Paid Artists: 40
   Utilizes: Special Technical Talent; Guest Conductors; Guest Artists; Guest Directors
   Income Sources: Box Office
   Season: June - September
   Performance Facilities: Theatre-by-the-Sea

Newport
DANCE

ISLAND MOVING COMPANY
3 Charles Street, Newport, RI 02840
(401) 847-4470
FAX: (401) 849-7718
   Founded: 1982

Arts Area: Modern; Ballet
Status: Professional; Non-Profit
Type: Performing; Touring; Resident; Educational
Purpose: To present new choreography; to educate a dance audience; to act as a training ground for dance
Management: Dominique Alfandre, Managing Director; Miki Ohlsen, Artistic Director
Officers: R. William Ohlsen, President; Jean Sanders, Treasurer; Teresa Ritter, Secretary
Paid Staff: 3   **Volunteer Staff:** 4
Paid Artists: 10   **Non-Paid Artists:** 2
Utilizes: Guest Artists; Guest Choreographers; Guest Musicians
Budget: $50,000 - $100,000
Income Sources: Private Foundations/Grants/Endowments; Business/Corporate Donations; Box Office; Government Grants; Individual Donations; Contracted Services
Season: October - August   **Annual Attendance:** 7,500
Affiliations: ACA
Performance Facilities: Rogers Auditorium; Bristol Community College; St. Georges School

THEATRE

THE RHODE ISLAND SHAKESPEARE THEATRE
PO Box 1126, Newport, RI 02840
(401) 849-7892
   Founded: 1971
   Arts Area: Theatrical Group
   Status: Semi-Professional; Non-Profit
   Type: Performing; Educational
   Purpose: TRIST serves as a pre-professional training ground for those with community theater experience who wish to increase their skills by working with an artistic director with professional experience.
   Management: Bob Colonna, Artistic Director; Maureen Collura, General Manager
   Officers: Mardi Sayer, Board President; Jan Prager, Vice President; Gloria Dunn, Secretary; Rick Meffert, Treasurer
   Paid Staff: 1
   Utilizes: Guest Artists; Guest Directors
   Budget: $50,000 - $100,000
   Income Sources: Private Foundations/Grants/Endowments; Business/Corporate Donations; Box Office; Individual Donations
   Season: January - August

PERFORMING SERIES

NEWPORT MUSIC FESTIVAL
PO Box 3300, Newport, RI 02840
(401) 846-1133
FAX: (401) 849-1857
   Founded: 1969
   Arts Area: Dance; Vocal Music; Instrumental Music; Festivals
   Status: Non-Profit
   Type: Performing; Sponsoring
   Purpose: The world-renowned Newport Music Festival performs little-known music of the Romantic era and sponsors the North American debuts of international artists.
   Management: Mark P. Malkovich, III, General Director
   Officers: Herbert B. Swope Jr., President
   Paid Staff: 5   **Volunteer Staff:** 150
   Paid Artists: 60
   Utilizes: Guest Artists
   Budget: $500,000 - $1,000,000
   Income Sources: Private Foundations/Grants/Endowments; Business/Corporate Donations; Box Office; Government Grants; Individual Donations
   Season: July   **Annual Attendance:** 20,000
   Performance Facilities: Fabled Mansions of Newport

North Providence

DANCE

FESTIVAL BALLET
5 Hennessey Avenue, North Providence, RI 02911
(401) 353-1129
   Founded: 1977

Arts Area: Ballet
Status: Professional; Non-Profit
Type: Performing; Touring; Resident
Purpose: To present the best works from the classical and contemporary repertoire
Management: Christine Hennessy, Artistic Director
Officers: Joan Abrams, President; Kerry Altman, Vice President; Henry Barney, Treasurer; Gail Higgins Fogarty, Secretary
Paid Staff: 2 **Volunteer Staff:** 5
Paid Artists: 8 **Non-Paid Artists:** 20
Utilizes: Special Technical Talent; Guest Artists; Guest Directors
Budget: $100,000 - $500,000
Income Sources: Private Foundations/Grants/Endowments; Business/Corporate Donations; Box Office; Government Grants; Individual Donations
Season: September - May **Annual Attendance:** 25,000
Performance Facilities: Providence Performing Arts Center

Pascoag

DANCE

AMERICAN BALLET
86 Main Street, Pascoag, RI 02859
(401) 568-0015; (401) 568-1680
Founded: 1984
Arts Area: Ballet
Status: Semi-Professional; Non-Profit
Type: Performing; Touring; Educational
Purpose: Non-profit educational and performance institution devoted to the highest standard in the art of classical ballet
Management: Patricia A. Christiansen, Artistic Director
Paid Staff: 4 **Volunteer Staff:** 6
Paid Artists: 10 **Non-Paid Artists:** 20
Utilizes: Special Technical Talent; Guest Artists
Budget: $50,000 - $100,000
Income Sources: Private Foundations/Grants/Endowments; Business/Corporate Donations; Box Office; Government Grants; Individual Donations
Season: September - August **Annual Attendance:** 4,000
Affiliations: NARB
Performance Facilities: Assembly Theatre

Providence

INSTRUMENTAL MUSIC

RHODE ISLAND PHILHARMONIC ORCHESTRA
222 Richmond Street, Providence, RI 02903
(401) 831-3123
Founded: 1945
Arts Area: Symphony
Status: Professional; Non-Profit
Type: Performing; Resident; Educational
Management: Karen R. Dobbs, Executive Director
Paid Staff: 6
Paid Artists: 80
Utilizes: Guest Conductors; Guest Artists
Budget: $1,000,000 - $5,000,000
Income Sources: Private Foundations/Grants/Endowments; Business/Corporate Donations; Box Office; Government Grants; Individual Donations
Season: October - May **Annual Attendance:** 150,000
Performance Facilities: Veterans Memorial Auditorium

YOUNG PEOPLES SYMPHONY OF RHODE ISLAND
131 Washington Street, Providence, RI 02903
(401) 421-0460
Founded: 1970
Arts Area: Symphony; Orchestra; Chamber
Status: Non-Profit
Type: Performing; Educational

Purpose: To provide music study and performance opportunity for all talented youngsters from an early age through college

Management: Dr. Joseph Conte, Music Director; Rose Tragar, Manager

Officers: Joseph Puleo, President

Paid Staff: 10 **Volunteer Staff:** 25

Utilizes: Guest Conductors; Guest Artists

Budget: $1,000 - $50,000

Income Sources: Private Foundations/Grants/Endowments; Business/Corporate Donations; Box Office; Individual Donations

Season: September - June **Annual Attendance:** 5,000

Performance Facilities: Veterans Memorial Auditorium

VOCAL MUSIC

RHODE ISLAND CIVIC CHORALE AND ORCHESTRA
334 Westminster Mall, Room #300, Providence, RI 02903
(401) 521-5670

Founded: 1958

Arts Area: Choral; Chamber

Status: Non-Profit

Type: Performing

Purpose: To present choral music at concerts and public performances; to promote musical concerts; to perform all other acts necessary and incidental to the maintenance, furtherance and encouragement of the musical and artistic knowledge, spirit and appreciation of the community

Management: Diana Cerwonka, Manager; Edward Markward, Music Director

Officers: Chester S. Labedz Jr., President; Roberta Padula, First Vice President; Margaret Gidley, Second Vice President; Herman Eschentacher, Third Vice President; David T. Riedel, Secretary; Walter Hope Jr., Treasurer; Joseph A. Goldkamp, Assistant Treasurer

Paid Staff: 2 **Volunteer Staff:** 130

Paid Artists: 45 **Non-Paid Artists:** 70

Utilizes: Guest Conductors; Guest Artists; Guest Directors

Budget: $50,000 - $100,000

Income Sources: Private Foundations/Grants/Endowments; Business/Corporate Donations; Box Office; Government Grants; Individual Donations

Season: September - May **Annual Attendance:** 1,200

Performance Facilities: Veterans Memorial Auditorium; Grace Church

THEATRE

ALIAS STAGE
120 Manton Avenue, Providence, RI 02909
(401) 831-2919

Founded: 1984

Arts Area: Professional

Status: Semi-Professional; Non-Profit

Type: Performing

Purpose: To develop new works which focus on a true expression of the world in which we live

Officers: Kate Stone, Chairperson; George Marcincavage, President; Daniel Welch, Treasurer; Steve Sookikian; Dan Devine, Ann Powers, Lucinda Powers, Board Members

Volunteer Staff: 26

Paid Artists: 30

Utilizes: Guest Artists; Guest Directors

Budget: $1,000 - $50,000

Income Sources: Business/Corporate Donations; Box Office; Fund-raising

Season: 52 Weeks **Annual Attendance:** 2,500

Performance Facilities: Building 1-A

BRIGHT LIGHTS THEATRE COMPANY
PO Box 3277, Providence, RI 02906
(401) 273-8982
FAX: (401) 273-8987

Founded: 1983

Arts Area: Theatrical Group

Status: Non-Profit

Type: Performing

Purpose: To present little-known works, classics and new plays while remaining an "open-shop" for artists in Rhode Island

Management: Elaine Raka, Artistic Director

Volunteer Staff: 20

Non-Paid Artists: 20

Utilizes: Guest Artists; Guest Directors
Budget: $1,000 - $50,000
Income Sources: Box Office; Government Grants; Individual Donations
Annual Attendance: 5,000

BROWN UNIVERSITY THEATRE
77 Waterman Street, Providence, RI 02912
(401) 863-2838
Founded: 1901
Arts Area: Summer Stock; Theatrical Group
Status: Non-Professional; Non-Profit
Type: Performing; Resident; Educational; Sponsoring
Purpose: To provide a balanced theatrical season (academic year and summer) for the university community and the Providence community, and to provide training for students
Management: John R. Lucas, Managing Director; John Emigh, Chairman
Paid Staff: 4
Non-Paid Artists: 200
Utilizes: Guest Directors
Budget: $1,000 - $50,000
Income Sources: Private Foundations/Grants/Endowments; Business/Corporate Donations; Box Office
Season: September - August   **Annual Attendance:** 20,000
Performance Facilities: Faunce House Theatre; Leeds Theatre

LOOKING GLASS THEATRE
50 Orchard Avenue, Providence, RI 02906
(401) 331-9080
Founded: 1965
Arts Area: Professional
Status: Professional; Non-Profit
Type: Touring; Educational; Sponsoring
Purpose: Looking Glass Theatre strives to enlighten and educate children and their families through audience participation, theater and follow-up workshops. LGT presents four new productions annually focusing on the classics and topical issues.
Management: Pat Clark, Managing Director; Diane Postoian, Artistic Director
Paid Staff: 3   **Volunteer Staff:** 25
Paid Artists: 30
Utilizes: Guest Artists; Guest Directors
Budget: $50,000 - $100,000
Income Sources: Private Foundations/Grants/Endowments; Business/Corporate Donations; Box Office; Government Grants; Individual Donations
Season: September - June   **Annual Attendance:** 50,000
Affiliations: TCG
Performance Facilities: Looking Glass Theatre

NEWGATE THEATER
134 Mathewson Street, Providence, RI 02903
(401) 421-9680
Founded: 1982
Status: Semi-Professional; Non-Profit
Type: Performing; Resident; Producing
Purpose: To create a theatrical community of social substance, important ideas and significant language; to produce theatre of visual beauty and power with a sense of excitement and spiritual renewal
Management: Alan Hawkridge, Artistic Director; Crista Crewdson, General Manager
Paid Staff: 1   **Volunteer Staff:** 25
Paid Artists: 22
Utilizes: Guest Artists; Guest Directors
Budget: $50,000 - $100,000
Income Sources: Box Office; Government Grants; Individual Donations
Season: September - June   **Annual Attendance:** 2,000
Affiliations: NETC

RITES AND REASON
Brown University, PO Box 1148, Providence, RI 02912
(401) 863-3558
Founded: 1970
Arts Area: Professional; Theatrical Group
Status: Professional; Non-Profit

Type: Performing; Touring; Resident; Educational
Purpose: Rites and Reasons is a developmental research theatre dedicated to producing new plays that celebrate and explore Afro-American history and culture.
Management: Elmo Terry-Morgan, Artistic Director; Karen Baxter, Managing Director; Rhett Jones, Research Director; Donna Mitchell, Administrative Director
Paid Staff: 5
Utilizes: Guest Artists; Guest Directors
Budget: $500,000 - $1,000,000
Income Sources: Private Foundations/Grants/Endowments; Box Office; Government Grants; Individual Donations
Season: February - May
Affiliations: AEA; U/RTA
Performance Facilities: Churchill House

TRINITY REPERTORY COMPANY
201 Washington Street, Providence, RI 02903
(401) 521-1100
Founded: 1964
Arts Area: Professional; Theatrical Group
Status: Professional; Non-Profit
Type: Performing; Touring; Educational
Purpose: To provide theatrical performances and educational services to Rhode Island and nearby New England audiences
Management: Richard Jenkins, Artistic Director; Dennis Conway, General Manager; Pamela Messore, Audience Development Director; Neal Baron, Assistant to Richard Jenkins; Kibbe Reilly, Director of Development
Officers: Sally T. Dowling, Chairman; Edward P. Grace, III, Vice Chairman; John M. Harpootian, Secretary; Harry A. Schult, Treasurer
Paid Staff: 50   **Volunteer Staff:** 600
Paid Artists: 50
Utilizes: Guest Artists; Guest Directors
Budget: $1,000,000 - $5,000,000
Income Sources: Private Foundations/Grants/Endowments; Business/Corporate Donations; Box Office; Government Grants; Individual Donations
Season: 52 Weeks   **Annual Attendance:** 170,000
Affiliations: LORT   **Performance Facilities:** Trinity Repertory Company

PERFORMING SERIES

FIRST NIGHT PROVIDENCE
c/o Shanon Tise Stormer & Assoc., 10 Donnace Street, Suite 1205, Providence, RI 02903
(401) 521-1166
FAX: (401) 273-5630
Arts Area: Dance; Vocal Music; Instrumental Music; Theater; Festivals
Status: Non-Profit
Type: Performing; Educational; Sponsoring
Management: Shanon Stormer, Director; Doris Stephens, Community Relations; Carolyn Ticil, Associate Director; Jan Matthews, Administrative Director
Paid Staff: 4   **Volunteer Staff:** 8
Paid Artists: 200
Budget: $100,000 - $500,000
Income Sources: Private Foundations/Grants/Endowments; Business/Corporate Donations; Box Office; Government Grants; Individual Donations
Season: New Years Eve   **Annual Attendance:** 50,000

PERFORMING ARTS ASSOCIATION
338 Rochambeau Avenue, Providence, RI 02906
(401) 331-0061
FAX: (401) 751-3227
Founded: 1954
Arts Area: Dance; Theater
Status: Professional; Non-Profit
Type: Sponsoring
Purpose: To present professional concerts
Management: Board of Directors
Officers: Mrs. Frederic W. Schwartz, President
Volunteer Staff: 5
Utilizes: Guest Artists
Income Sources: Box Office

Season: October - May
Performance Facilities: Veterans Memorial Auditorium: Providence Civic Center

FACILITY

PROVIDENCE CIVIC CENTER
One LaSalle Square, Providence, RI 02903
(401) 331-0700
    Type of Facility: Civic Center
    Seating Capacity: 13,000
    Year Built: 1971   **Architect:** Ellerbe Architects   **Cost:** $13,000,000
    Contact for Rental: Stephen M. Lombardi, Executive Director;   (401) 331-0700

PROVIDENCE PERFORMING ARTS CENTER
220 Weybosset Street, Providence, RI 02903
(401) 421-2997
    Type of Facility: Concert Hall; Performance Center; Theatre House; Opera House
    Type of Stage: Proscenium
    Stage Dimensions: 86'Wx28'6"D(left); 31'6"D(right); 52'Wx33'6"H proscenium opening   **Orchestra Pit**
    Seating Capacity: 3,198
    Year Built: 1928   **Architect:** Rapp & Rapp   **Cost:** $2,500,000
    Acoustical Consultant: P.M.A. Engineering
    Contact for Rental: Norbertt Mongeon;   (401) 421-2997
    Manager: Alan Chille
    Resident Groups: Rhode Island Philharmonic Orchestra; Festival Ballet

TRINITY ARTS CENTER
55 Locust Street, Providence, RI 02906
(401) 751-6480
    Type of Facility: Auditorium
    Facility Originally: Church; School
    Type of Stage: Proscenium
    Stage Dimensions: 35'Wx22'D   **Orchestra Pit**
    Seating Capacity: 400

VETERANS MEMORIAL AUDITORIUM
Brownell Street and Park Streets, Providence, RI 02903
(401) 277-1467; (401) 277-3150
FAX: (401) 277-1466
    Mailing Address: PO Box 28345, Providence, RI 02908
    Founded: 1950
    Type of Facility: Concert Hall
    Type of Stage: Proscenium
    Stage Dimensions: 85'Wx40'D   **Orchestra Pit**
    Seating Capacity: 2,118
    Year Built: 1928   **Architect:** Osgood & Osgood   **Cost:** $1,800,000
    Year Remodeled: 1990   **Architect:** Robert Haig Associates   **Cost:** $5,500,000
    Acoustical Consultant: Chris Blair
    Contact for Rental: Jack Lafond, Director;   (401) 277-1467
    Resident Groups: Rhode Island Philharmonic Orchestra

Warwick

THEATRE

WARWICK PLAYERS
PO Box 545, Warwick, RI 02889
(401) 738-2000, ext. 372
    Founded: 1974
    Arts Area: Theatrical Group
    Status: Non-Professional; Non-Profit
    Type: Performing
    Purpose: To provide the community with quality comedies, dramas and musicals
    Officers: Armand Leroux, Vice President; Maria Toxi, Recording Secretary; Patricia Renaud, Correspondence Secretary; Diana Addessi, Treasurer
    Paid Staff: 1
    Budget: $1,000 - $50,000
    Income Sources: Private Foundations/Grants/Endowments; Business/Corporate Donations; Box Office

Season: October - May   **Annual Attendance:** 1,500
Affiliations: Warwick Consortium For The Arts and Humanities; AACT, Rhode Island
Performance Facilities: Warwick City Hall

Westerly

VOCAL MUSIC

CHORUS OF WESTERLY
16 High Street, PO Box 132, Westerly, RI 02891
(401) 596-8663
Founded: 1959
Arts Area: Choral
Status: Non-Professional; Non-Profit
Type: Performing; Educational; Sponsoring
Purpose: To present fine choral and orchestral music; to promote interest in choral singing and choral music appreciation
Management: Susan Bosworth, Manager
Officers: Dr. Douglas Rayner, President; Jill Blanchette, Katie Utter and Jane Gencarelli, Vice Presidents; Bailey Blandette, Treasurer; Dr. Nora Spens, Recording Secretary; Anne Utter, Cooresponding Secretary
Paid Staff: 2   **Volunteer Staff:** 10
Paid Artists: 101   **Non-Paid Artists:** 180
Utilizes: Special Technical Talent; Guest Artists; Guest Directors
Budget: $100,000 - $500,000
Income Sources: Private Foundations/Grants/Endowments; Business/Corporate Donations; Box Office; Government Grants; Individual Donations; Fundraising Events
Season: November - June   **Annual Attendance:** 36,000
Affiliations: CA
Performance Facilities: Chorus of Westerly Performance Hall

SOUTH CAROLINA

Abbeville

FACILITY

THE ABBEVILLE OPERA HOUSE
Court Square, PO Box 247, Abbeville, SC 29620
(803) 459-2157
FAX: (803) 459-9266
Founded: 1908
Type of Facility: Theatre House; Opera House
Type of Stage: Proscenium   **Orchestra Pit**
Seating Capacity: 300
Year Built: 1908
Year Remodeled: 1968
Contact for Rental: Kathy Genevie;   (803) 459-2157
Manager: Michael Genevie;   (803) 459-5338
Resident Groups: Summer Stock

Aiken

DANCE

AIKEN CIVIC BALLET COMPANY
142 Greenville Street, Aiken, SC 29801
(803) 648-5771
Founded: 1972
Arts Area: Modern; Ballet; Jazz
Status: Semi-Professional; Non-Professional; Non-Profit
Type: Touring; Resident; Educational
Purpose: To further dance in the immediate area
Management: Carl Crosby, Artistic Director
Officers: Mary Lou Wallace, President; Mary Jo Wilson, Secretary; Helen Kelly, Costume Chairman
Volunteer Staff: 12
Paid Artists: 3
Utilizes: Guest Artists; Guest Directors; Guest Choreographers
Budget: $1,000 - $50,000
Income Sources: Box Office; Individual Donations
Season: September - May   **Annual Attendance:** 500
Performance Facilities: Etherredge Center, University of South Carolina

THEATRE

AIKEN COMMUNITY PLAYHOUSE
PO Box 125, Aiken, SC 29802
(803) 648-1438
Founded: 1953
Arts Area: Community
Status: Non-Profit
Type: Performing
Purpose: To allow people of the community to act in and produce plays of the legitimate theatre and to encourage public appreciation of the theatre arts
Management: Board of Directors
Officers: David Howard, President; Marcia Harris, First Vice President; Elaine Schmidt, Second Vice President
Budget: $1,000 - $50,000
Income Sources: Business/Corporate Donations; Box Office; Individual Donations
Season: 52 Weeks   **Annual Attendance:** 3,500
Affiliations: South Carolina Theatre Association
Performance Facilities: Aiken Community Playhouse

FACILITY

ETHERREDGE CENTER - UNIVERSITY OF SOUTH CAROLINA AT AIKEN
171 University Parkway, Aiken, SC 29803
(803) 641-3328
Founded: 1986
Type of Facility: Theatre Complex; Concert Hall; Auditorium; Studio Performance; Performance Center; Multi-Purpose
Type of Stage: Thrust; Proscenium
Stage Dimensions: 38'x24'   **Orchestra Pit**
Seating Capacity: 687
Year Built: 1985   **Architect:** Alexander Moorman   **Cost:** $3,000,000
Acoustical Consultant: George Izenhaur
Contact for Rental: Marti Costantino;   (803) 641-3328
Resident Groups: University of South Carolina, Aiken: Players; Band; Choral Society; Faculty

---

Anderson

THEATRE

THE SOUTH CAROLINA THEATRE COMPANY
PO Box 331, Anderson, SC 29622-0331
(803) 224-7648
Founded: 1965
Arts Area: Professional; Theatrical Group
Status: Professional
Type: Performing; Touring; Resident; Educational
Purpose: To provide continued employment for actors; to bring Shakespeare and classics to students at colleges, universities and high schools in 30 states
Management: Milton A. Dickson, Producer/Director; A. Alexander, Casting Director/New York, NY
Paid Staff: 2
Paid Artists: 43
Utilizes: Guest Artists
Budget: $100,000 - $500,000
Income Sources: Box Office
Season: 52 Weeks
Performance Facilities: Play Box Theatre

Beaufort

PERFORMING SERIES

THE BYRNE MILLER DANCE THEATRE, INC.
2400 Wilson Drive, PO Box 1667, Beaufort, SC 29901
(803) 524-9148
Founded: 1971
Arts Area: Dance; Mime; Movement Theatre
Status: Professional; Non-Profit
Type: Educational; Sponsoring
Purpose: To present a wide variety of excellent dance and related movement, both to our concert audience and to students in our schools
Management: Byrne Miller, Director; Mary Whisonant, Assistant Director
Officers: Lillian Nilsson, President; William Cochrane, Vice President; Byrne Miller, Secretary; David Harper, Treasurer
Volunteer Staff: 15
Paid Artists: 4
Utilizes: Special Technical Talent; Guest Artists
Budget: $1,000 - $50,000
Income Sources: Private Foundations/Grants/Endowments; Business/Corporate Donations; Box Office; Government Grants; Individual Donations; Fundraising
Season: October - May   **Annual Attendance:** 3,500
Affiliations: APAP
Performance Facilities: Lasseter Theatre; Marine Corps Air Station

FACILITY

UNIVERSITY OF SOUTH CAROLINA BEAUFORT ARTS CENTER
800 Carteret, Beaufort, SC 29902
(803) 521-4156
FAX: (803) 521-4199; (803) 521-4198
> **Facility Originally:** School
> **Type of Stage:** Proscenium
> **Seating Capacity:** 472
> **Year Remodeled:** 1991   **Architect:** Denziger
> **Contact for Rental:** John P. Blair Jr.;   (803) 521-4156
> **Resident Groups:** Rafael Sabatini Players; Beaufort Little Theatre; Beaufort Chamber Orchestra

Charleston

DANCE

THE CHARLESTON BALLET
354 1/2 King Street, PO Box 262, Charleston, SC 29401
(803) 722-8779
> **Founded:** 1959
> **Arts Area:** Modern; Ballet; Jazz
> **Status:** Professional; Non-Profit
> **Type:** Performing; Touring; Educational; Sponsoring
> **Purpose:** To present dance of the highest quality to the Charleston Area and to provide training and performance opportunities for talented area dancers
> **Management:** Don and Patricia Cantwell, Artistic Directors; Jill Eathorne Bahr, Resident Choreographer; Kim Brantingham, Company Manager
> **Officers:** Courtney Quattlebaum, President; Linda Helmly, Vice President; Andrea Crappa-Hurley, Treasurer; Bradford Marshall, Secretary
> **Paid Staff:** 4   **Volunteer Staff:** 25
> **Paid Artists:** 18   **Non-Paid Artists:** 10
> **Utilizes:** Guest Artists; Guest Choreographers
> **Budget:** $100,000 - $500,000
> **Income Sources:** Private Foundations/Grants/Endowments; Business/Corporate Donations; Box Office; Government Grants; Individual Donations
> **Season:** September - June   **Annual Attendance:** 25,000
> **Affiliations:** NARB; SERBA
> **Performance Facilities:** Gaillard Municipal Auditorium

ROBERT IVEY BALLET
1632 Ashley Hall Road, Charleston, SC 29407
(803) 556-1343
> **Founded:** 1977
> **Arts Area:** Modern; Ballet; Jazz; Guest Choreographers
> **Status:** Semi-Professional; Non-Profit
> **Type:** Resident
> **Management:** Robert Ivey, Artistic Director
> **Officers:** Sandra Cook, Assistant to Director; Nancy Barnwell, President of Board
> **Non-Paid Artists:** 30
> **Utilizes:** Guest Artists; Guest Choreographers
> **Budget:** $50,000 - $100,000
> **Income Sources:** Private Foundations/Grants/Endowments; Business/Corporate Donations; Box Office; Government Grants; Individual Donations
> **Season:** September - May   **Annual Attendance:** 20,000
> **Affiliations:** College of Charleston
> **Performance Facilities:** Emmett Robinson Theatre; School of the Arts; College of Charleston

INSTRUMENTAL MUSIC

CHARLESTON SYMPHONY ORCHESTRA
14 George Street, Charleston, SC 29401
(803) 723-7528
FAX: (803) 722-3463
> **Founded:** 1936
> **Arts Area:** Symphony; Orchestra; Chamber; Ensemble
> **Status:** Professional; Non-Profit

Type: Performing; Touring; Resident; Educational
Purpose: To provide quality musical performances to the citizens of our state and to educate children using smaller orchestra and ensembles
Management: Darrell G. Edwards, Executive Director; David Stahl, Music Director/Conductor
Officers: Marianne P. Mead, President; Burton Schools, Vice President of Development; Edward H. Sparkman, Treasurer; Laura Hewitt, Secretary
Paid Staff: 7 **Volunteer Staff:** 20
Paid Artists: 89
Utilizes: Guest Conductors; Guest Artists
Budget: $1,000,000 - $5,000,000
Income Sources: Private Foundations/Grants/Endowments; Business/Corporate Donations; Box Office; Government Grants; Individual Donations
Season: September - May **Annual Attendance:** 30,000
Affiliations: Charleston Symphony League; Singers Guild
Performance Facilities: Gaillard Municipal Auditorium

THEATRE

FOOTLIGHT PLAYERS
20 Queen Street, PO Box 62, Charleston, SC 29402
(803) 722-7521
Founded: 1931
Arts Area: Musical; Community; Theatrical Group
Status: Non-Professional; Non-Profit
Type: Performing; Resident
Purpose: As a community theatre, to produce plays, to be a means of self-expression for the community through amateur theatre, and to hold classes in drama and allied subjects
Management: Mrs. Kit Lyons, General Manager; Richard Heffner, Designer/Technical Director; Dorothy D'Anna, Artistic Director
Officers: Vic Brandt, President; Dr. A. Bert Pruitt, First Vice President; Edward DiResta, Second Vice President; Ms. Suzanne Kaiser, Secretary; Mr. Hasell Barton, Treasurer
Paid Staff: 2 **Volunteer Staff:** 150
Non-Paid Artists: 100
Utilizes: Guest Directors
Budget: $100,000 - $500,000
Income Sources: Private Foundations/Grants/Endowments; Business/Corporate Donations; Box Office; Government Grants; Individual Donations
Season: September - May **Annual Attendance:** 12,000
Affiliations: South Carolina Theatre Association; Charleston Area Arts Council; Southeastern Theatre Conference; American Association of Community Theatres
Performance Facilities: Footlight Players Theatre

PERFORMING SERIES

SPOLETO FESTIVAL USA
PO Box 157, Charleston, SC 29402
(803) 722-2764
Founded: 1976
Arts Area: Dance; Vocal Music; Instrumental Music; Theater; Festivals; Lyric Opera; Grand Opera
Status: Professional; Semi-Professional; Non-Profit
Type: Performing; Educational; Sponsoring
Purpose: The Festival presents opera, dance, theater, symphonic and chamber music, jazz and visual arts exhibits of the highest quality. It also serves as an educational environment for young artists and arts administrators.
Management: Gian Carlo Menotti, Artistic Director; Marcus L. Overton, Executive Director; Carmen Kovens, Director of Operations; Betty Kunreuther, Director of Finance; Constance M. Baldwin, Acting Director of Development
Officers: Homer C. Burrows, Chairman; Giancarla Berti, President; Charles S. Way, Chairman Emeritus
Paid Staff: 16 **Volunteer Staff:** 300
Paid Artists: 350
Utilizes: Special Technical Talent; Guest Conductors; Guest Artists; Guest Directors
Budget: $1,000,000 - $5,000,000
Income Sources: Private Foundations/Grants/Endowments; Business/Corporate Donations; Box Office; Government Grants; Individual Donations
Season: May - June
Annual Attendance: 80,000
Affiliations: OA; Dance USA; TCG; NIMT; AAA
Performance Facilities: Gaillard Municipal Auditorium; Dock Street Theater; Garden Theater

FACILITY

DOCK STREET THEATRE
135 Church Street, Charleston, SC 29401
(803) 720-3968
> **Type of Facility:** Theatre House
> **Facility Originally:** Hotel & Meeting Rooms
> **Type of Stage:** Proscenium
> **Stage Dimensions:** 33'8"Wx33'3"D; 33'8"Wx17'6"H proscenium opening   **Orchestra Pit**
> **Seating Capacity:** 463
> **Year Built:** 1736
> **Year Remodeled:** 1937   **Architect:** Albert Simons   **Cost:** $400,000
> **Contact for Rental:** Lorraine Adrahamfon, Curator;   (803) 724-7308
> **Resident Groups:** Spoleto Festival USA; Charleston Symphony; Events, Inc.; Amazing Stage; Moja Arts Festival; Department of Special Facilities, Charleston; Piccolo Spoleto Festival; Sherry Grace Productions; Charleston Theatre Works; Chopstick Theatre; Professional Theatre
> *The original 1736 structure is no longer standing. Using various documentation, a conjectural reconstruction was completed in 1937.*

FOOTLIGHT PLAYERS THEATRE
20 Queen Street, PO Box 62, Charleston, SC 29401
(803) 722-7521
> **Founded:** 1931
> **Type of Facility:** Theatre House
> **Facility Originally:** Warehouse
> **Type of Stage:** Proscenium
> **Stage Dimensions:** 40'Wx33'D
> **Seating Capacity:** 285
> **Year Built:** 1840
> **Year Remodeled:** 1941
> **Contact for Rental:** Kit Lyons, General Manager;   (803) 722-7521
> **Resident Groups:** Footlight Players

GAILLARD MUNICIPAL AUDITORIUM
77 Calhoun Street, Charleston, SC 29403
(803) 577-7400
> **Type of Facility:** Theatre Complex; Concert Hall; Auditorium; Multi-Purpose
> **Type of Stage:** Proscenium
> **Stage Dimensions:** 80'Wx50'Dx65'H   **Orchestra Pit**
> **Seating Capacity:** 2,734
> **Year Built:** 1968   **Architect:** Lucas & Stubbs   **Cost:** $6,000,000
> **Contact for Rental:** Cam Patterson;   (803) 577-7400

Columbia

DANCE

COLUMBIA CITY BALLET
PO Box 11898, Columbia, SC 29211
(803) 799-7605
FAX: (803) 799-7928
> **Founded:** 1960
> **Arts Area:** Ballet
> **Status:** Semi-Professional; Non-Profit
> **Type:** Performing; Touring; Resident; Educational
> **Purpose:** To present the art of dance to Columbia and its surrounding communities; to contribute to the cultural and educational lives of audiences, dancers, and students
> **Management:** William Starrett, Artistic Director
> **Officers:** Lyles Glenn, President; Bill Timmerman, Treasurer; Karen Schulze, Secretary
> **Paid Staff:** 5
> **Paid Artists:** 12   **Non-Paid Artists:** 35
> **Utilizes:** Special Technical Talent; Guest Artists; Guest Choreographers; Guest Instructors
> **Budget:** $100,000 - $500,000
> **Income Sources:** Private Foundations/Grants/Endowments; Business/Corporate Donations; Box Office; Government Grants; Individual Donations
> **Season:** September - April   **Annual Attendance:** 35,000
> **Performance Facilities:** Koger Center for the Arts

INSTRUMENTAL MUSIC

COLUMBIA YOUTH ORCHESTRA
PO Box 5703, Columbia, SC 29250
(803) 771-7937
> **Arts Area:** Symphony; Orchestra
> **Status:** Non-Professional; Non-Profit
> **Type:** Performing; Educational
> **Management:** Judith Lawrence, General Manager; Robert Kemsley, Resident Conductor
> **Paid Staff:** 2   **Volunteer Staff:** 50
> **Non-Paid Artists:** 100
> **Season:** September - April   **Annual Attendance:** 2,000
> **Affiliations:** ASOL(Youth Orchestra Division); South Carolina Philharmonic
> **Performance Facilities:** Booker T. Washington Hall; Frazier Hall, University of South Carolina

SOUTH CAROLINA PHILHARMONIC AND CHAMBER ORCHESTRAS
PO Box 5703, Columbia, SC 29250
(803) 771-7937
> **Founded:** 1964
> **Arts Area:** Symphony; Orchestra; Chamber
> **Status:** Professional; Non-Profit
> **Type:** Performing; Touring; Educational; Sponsoring
> **Purpose:** To present symphony orchestra performances; sponsOr educational programs
> **Management:** Mark Huber, Executive Director; Catherine Comet, Artistic Advisor
> **Officers:** Frank Brown, President
> **Paid Staff:** 9   **Volunteer Staff:** 200
> **Paid Artists:** 90
> **Utilizes:** Special Technical Talent; Guest Conductors; Guest Artists
> **Budget:** $500,000 - $1,000,000
> **Income Sources:** Private Foundations/Grants/Endowments; Business/Corporate Donations; Box Office; Government Grants; Individual Donations
> **Season:** November - April   **Annual Attendance:** 15,000
> **Affiliations:** ASOL
> **Performance Facilities:** Richland Township Auditorium; Keenan Theatre; Koger Center

THEATRE

COLUMBIA STAGE SOCIETY AT TOWN THEATRE
1012 Sumter Street, Columbia, SC 29201
(803) 799-2510
> **Founded:** 1919
> **Arts Area:** Community; Theatrical Group
> **Status:** Non-Professional; Non-Profit
> **Type:** Performing; Educational
> **Purpose:** The advancement in the community, both city and state, of the experimental arts of the little theatre, including spoken drama, pantomime, music, musical drama, and promotion of such literary and artistic objects as will foster and develop the cultural aspects of our community life
> **Management:** W. J. Arvay, Manager; Emmalee E. Robbins, Director; John W.K. Young, Technical Director; Ann B. Fogle, Assistant Manager
> **Officers:** Robert R. Russell Jr., President; E. Warner Wells, Vice President; Thomas P. Monahan, Treasurer; David M. Dunlap, Secretary
> **Paid Staff:** 4   **Volunteer Staff:** 500
> **Utilizes:** Guest Conductors; Guest Artists
> **Budget:** $100,000 - $500,000
> **Income Sources:** Private Foundations/Grants/Endowments; Business/Corporate Donations; Box Office; Government Grants; Individual Donations
> **Season:** August - June   **Annual Attendance:** 26,000
> **Affiliations:** South Carolina Theatre Association
> **Performance Facilities:** The Town Theatre

TRUSTUS
529 Lady Street, PO Box 11721, Columbia, SC 29211
(803) 254-9732
> **Founded:** 1985
> **Arts Area:** Professional
> **Status:** Professional; Non-Profit
> **Type:** Performing; Resident; Educational
> **Purpose:** To bring to the area a professional theatre dedicated to new works, plays of literary and artistic merit, and quality mainstream theatre in an environment that allows us to reach a broad spectrum of patrons

Management: Jim Thigpen, Artistic Director; Kay Thigpen, Producing Director; Steve Levine, Box Office Manager; Brian Riley, Technical Director
Officers: Robert Howard, President; Len Marini, Vice President; Sam Wilkins, Secretary; Kay Thigpen, Treasurer
Paid Staff: 9   **Volunteer Staff:** 25
Paid Artists: 65
Utilizes: Special Technical Talent; Guest Artists; Guest Directors
Budget: $100,000 - $500,000
Income Sources: Private Foundations/Grants/Endowments; Business/Corporate Donations; Box Office; Government Grants; Individual Donations
Season: 52 Weeks   **Annual Attendance:** 11,000
Affiliations: TCG; South Carolina Theatre Association

FACILITY

KOGER CENTER FOR THE ARTS
University of South Carolina, Columbia, SC 29208
(803) 777-7500
FAX: (803) 777-5774
Founded: 1989
Type of Facility: Concert Hall; Auditorium; Theatre House; Opera House; Multi-Purpose
Type of Stage: Proscenium   **Orchestra Pit**
Seating Capacity: 2,236
Year Built: 1989   **Architect:** GMH and Associates   **Cost:** $15,000,000
Acoustical Consultant: Chris Jaffe
Contact for Rental: Ron Pearson;   (803) 777-7500
Resident Groups: South Carolina Philharmonic; Columbia City Ballet; University of South Carolina: Symphony; Chamber; Orchestra; Opera; Mastersingers

UNIVERSITY OF SOUTH CAROLINA - DRAYTON HALL THEATRE
Green and Sumter Streets, Columbia, SC 29208
(803) 777-4288
Type of Facility: Theatre Complex; Concert Hall; Auditorium; Theatre House
Type of Stage: Proscenium
Stage Dimensions: 36'Wx22'D   **Orchestra Pit**
Seating Capacity: 400
Year Built: 1890
Year Remodeled: 1987
Acoustical Consultant: Elbin Cleveland
Contact for Rental: Carol DuPree, Business Manager;   (803) 777-5863
Resident Groups: University Mainstage Productions; University of South Carolina Departments of Music, Theatre and Speech; University of South Carolina Dance Company; The Puppet Regime
For theatrical or musical productions

UNIVERSITY OF SOUTH CAROLINA - LONGSTREET THEATRE
Green and Sumter Streets, Columbia, SC 29208
(803) 777-4288
Type of Facility: Theatre Complex; Theatre House; Arena; Multi-Purpose
Facility Originally: Church
Type of Stage: Thrust; Arena
Stage Dimensions: 28' Diameter Circle
Seating Capacity: 312
Year Built: 1855
Year Remodeled: 1972   **Architect:** George Izenour
Acoustical Consultant: George Izenour
Contact for Rental: Carol DuPree, Business Manager;   (803) 777-5863
Resident Groups: University of South Carolina Department of Theatre and Speech; University of South Carolina Dance Company; The Puppet Regime

Conway

FACILITY

UNIVERSITY OF SOUTH CAROLINA-COASTAL CAROLINA COLLEGE - LITTLE THEATRE
Conway, SC 29526
(803) 347-3161
Type of Facility: Concert Hall; Auditorium; Studio Performance; Theatre House; Multi-Purpose; Room
Type of Stage: Proscenium; Environmental; Arena

Stage Dimensions: 20'x30'
Seating Capacity: 125
Contact for Rental: Thomas E. Jones, Director;   (803) 349-2510
Manager: Dr. Mallard, Chairman of Theatre Dept.;   (803) 349-2442
Resident Groups: Upstage Company

UNIVERSITY OF SOUTH CAROLINA-COASTAL CAROLINA COLLEGE -
WHEELWRIGHT PERFORMING ARTS CENTER
Conway, SC 29526
(803) 347-3161
Type of Facility: Concert Hall; Auditorium; Studio Performance; Performance Center; Theatre House
Type of Stage: Proscenium
Stage Dimensions: 40'x40'   Orchestra Pit
Seating Capacity: 817
Year Built: 1981   Architect: Riddle & Wilkes   Cost: $3,500,000
Contact for Rental: Thomas E. Jones, Director;   (803) 349-2510
Manager: Dr. Mallard, Chairman of Theatre Dept.;   (803) 349-2442
Resident Groups: Coastal Carolina Theatre; Coastal Carolina Choir

Georgetown

THEATRE

SWAMP FOX PLAYERS
PO Box 911, Georgetown, SC 29442
(803) 527-2924
Founded: 1971
Arts Area: Community
Status: Non-Professional; Non-Profit
Type: Performing; Resident
Purpose: To develop a cultural center for the area; to bring dramatic presentations to the citizens of this region
Officers: Ruth Buck, President; Mark Brown, Vice President; Lyn Going-Smith, Secretary; Nina Morris,
Treasurer
Volunteer Staff: 11
Non-Paid Artists: 60
Utilizes: Guest Artists
Budget: $1,000 - $50,000
Income Sources: Box Office
Performance Facilities: The Strand Theatre

FACILITY

THE STRAND THEATRE
710 Front Street, PO Box 911, Georgetown, SC 29442
(803) 527-2297
Type of Facility: Theatre House
Type of Stage: Platform
Seating Capacity: 200
Year Built: 1937
Contact for Rental: Abe Fogel;   (803) 546-7800
Resident Groups: Swamp Fox Players
Member, League of Historic American Theatres; National Register of Historic Places

Greenville

DANCE

CAROLINA BALLET THEATRE
872 Woodruff Road, Greenville, SC 29607
(803) 297-1635
Founded: 1974
Arts Area: Ballet
Status: Non-Professional; Non-Profit
Type: Performing
Management: Barbara Selvey, Artistic Director
Officers: Cindy DeLoache, Chairman
Paid Artists: 3   Non-Paid Artists: 20

Utilizes: Guest Artists; Guest Choreographers
Budget: $50,000 - $100,000
Income Sources: Private Foundations/Grants/Endowments; Business/Corporate Donations; Box Office; Individual Donations
Season: October - June
Performance Facilities: Peace Center

INSTRUMENTAL MUSIC

GREENVILLE SYMPHONY ASSOCIATION
Magill Music Hall, PO Box 10002, Greenville, SC 29603
(803) 232-0344
FAX: (803) 240-3113
Founded: 1948
Arts Area: Symphony; Chamber; Ensemble; Pops
Status: Semi-Professional; Non-Profit
Type: Performing; Resident; Educational
Purpose: To provide the community with the finest possible musical education and entertainment
Management: Patricia G. Quarles, Office Manager; Julie Greer, Operations Manager; David Sz. Pollitt, Conductor; Joel E. Keller, General Manager; Edith K. Diver, Ticket Manager; Susan Bocook, Librarian
Officers: Edward H. Stall Jr., President; Mrs. David E. Mills, First Vice President; Robert T. Thompson Sr., Second Vice President; Mrs. R. J. Stephenson III, Secretary; William J. Rothfuss, Treasurer
Paid Staff: 6 **Volunteer Staff:** 304
Paid Artists: 90
Utilizes: Guest Artists
Budget: $1,000,000 - $5,000,000
Income Sources: Private Foundations/Grants/Endowments; Business/Corporate Donations; Box Office; Government Grants; Individual Donations
Season: September - April **Annual Attendance:** 23,000
Affiliations: ASOL; ASCAP; BMI
Performance Facilities: Peace Center for the Performing Arts

VOCAL MUSIC

THE GREENVILLE CHORALE
c/o Dr. Bingham Vick Jr., Furman University, Greenville, SC 29613
(803) 294-2161; (803) 242-0890
Founded: 1961
Arts Area: Choral
Status: Semi-Professional; Non-Profit
Type: Performing; Resident
Purpose: To provide opportunities for professional and amateur singers to study and perform choral/orchestral literature by classical and contemporary composers; to continue to add challenging choral/orchestral works to the repertoire; to provide the community with opportunities to hear professional performances of great music
Management: Bingham Vick, Jr., Director/Primary Administrator
Officers: Maurice Brown, President; M. Gordon Howle, Martha A. Vaughn, Shirley L. Duncan, Vice Presidents; Ann Keith, Secretary; L.W. Brummer, Treasurer
Paid Staff: 4 **Volunteer Staff:** 15
Paid Artists: 12 **Non-Paid Artists:** 190
Utilizes: Special Technical Talent; Guest Conductors; Guest Artists
Budget: $50,000 - $100,000
Income Sources: Private Foundations/Grants/Endowments; Business/Corporate Donations; Box Office; Government Grants; Individual Donations
Season: September - May **Annual Attendance:** 6,000
Affiliations: ASCAP; ACDA; CA
Performance Facilities: Peace Center for the Performing Arts; McAlister Auditorium-Furman University

FACILITY

FURMAN UNIVERSITY - MCALISTER AUDITORIUM
Greenville, SC 29613
(803) 294-2124
Type of Facility: Concert Hall; Auditorium; Opera House; Multi-Purpose
Type of Stage: Proscenium
Stage Dimensions: 80'x65'x60' **Orchestra Pit**
Seating Capacity: 1,922
Year Built: 1962 **Architect:** Perry, Dean & Stewart
Contact for Rental: Eric R. Harrell; (803) 294-2124
Resident Groups: Furman University Music Department; Furman Presents; Greenville Civic Chorale

GREENVILLE MEMORIAL AUDITORIUM
401 East North Street, Greenville, SC 29601
(803) 241-3800
    Type of Facility: Concert Hall; Theatre House; Arena; Multi-Purpose
    Type of Stage: Flexible
    Seating Capacity: 6,200
    Year Built: 1959   **Architect:** Cunningham and Walker   **Cost:** $2,100,000
    Contact for Rental: Clifford Gray
    Contains a 25,000 square foot exhibit hall

Greenwood

FACILITY

GREENWOOD CIVIC CENTER
PO Box 3008, Greenwood, SC 29648
(803) 223-3395
    Type of Facility: Concert Hall; Theatre House; Arena; Multi-Purpose
    Type of Stage: Flexible
    Seating Capacity: 4,800
    Year Built: 1979   **Architect:** Greenwood Associates   **Cost:** $4,000,000
    Contact for Rental: Gary Craigo;   (803) 223-3395

Hartsville

THEATRE

HARTSVILLE COMMUNITY PLAYERS
PO Box 1192, Hartsville, SC 29550
(803) 332-5721
    Founded: 1970
    Arts Area: Musical; Community
    Status: Non-Profit
    Type: Performing
    Officers: Vicki Price, President; Harry Wallace Sr., Vice President; Liz Taylor, Secretary; Cliff McBride, Treasurer
    Volunteer Staff: 12
    Non-Paid Artists: 100
    Utilizes: Guest Artists; Guest Directors
    Budget: $1,000 - $50,000
    Income Sources: Business/Corporate Donations; Box Office; Individual Donations
    Season: October - March   **Annual Attendance:** 125
    Performance Facilities: Center Theater

FACILITY

CENTER THEATER
212 North Fifth Street, Hartsville, SC 29550
(803) 332-5721
    Founded: 1936
    Type of Facility: Concert Hall; Auditorium; Performance Center; Off Broadway; Opera House
    Facility Originally: Movie House/Civic Auditorium
    Type of Stage: Proscenium
    Stage Dimensions: 34'Wx20'3"H proscenium opening; 34'Hx64/74'Wx29'7"D stage   **Orchestra Pit**
    Seating Capacity: 861
    Year Built: 1936   **Architect:** Lafaye and Lafaye
    Year Remodeled: 1969   **Architect:** Clark and McCall, AIA   **Cost:** $175,000
    Contact for Rental: J. Lamar Caldwell Jr.;   (803) 332-5721
    Resident Groups: Hartsville Community Players

Myrtle Beach

FACILITY

CONVENTION CENTER
21st Avenue North and Oak Street, Myrtle Beach, SC 29577
(803) 448-7166
FAX: (803) 448-7448
    Type of Facility: Auditorium; Arena
    Year Built: 1967 **Architect:** Riddle & Wilkes
    Contact for Rental: Steve Jones; (803) 448-7166
    Manager: Mani Costa
    Convention Center contains the Auditorium and Exhibit Hall. See separate listings for further information.

CONVENTION CENTER - AUDITORIUM
21st Avenue North and Oak Street, Myrtle Beach, SC 29577
(803) 448-7166
FAX: (803) 448-7448
    Type of Stage: Proscenium
    Stage Dimensions: 65'Wx65'D; 48'Wx20'H proscenium opening
    Seating Capacity: 2,100
    Year Built: 1967
    Contact for Rental: Steve Jones; (803) 448-7166
    Manager: Mani Costa

CONVENTION CENTER - EXHIBIT HALL
21st Avenue North and Oak Street, Myrtle Beach, SC 29577
(803) 448-7166
FAX: (803) 448-7448
    Type of Facility: Exhibition Hall
    Type of Stage: Arena
    Stage Dimensions: 42'Wx20'D
    Seating Capacity: 2,550
    Year Built: 1977
    Contact for Rental: Steve Jones; (803) 448-7166
    Manager: Mani Costa

Newberry

THEATRE

NEWBERRY COLLEGE THEATRE
Newberry College, Newberry, SC 29108
(803) 276-5010
    Founded: 1856
    Arts Area: Musical; Dinner; Theatrical Group
    Status: College
    Type: Performing; Educational
    Purpose: To provide a quality performing arts program in a liberal arts college environment
    Officers: Sidney C. Pitts, Director of Theatre/Coordinator of Performing Arts/Chair, Department of Theatre; Rupert Gaddy, Technical Director
    Paid Staff: 3 **Volunteer Staff:** 45
    Utilizes: Special Technical Talent; Guest Artists; Guest Directors
    Budget: $1,000 - $50,000
    Income Sources: Business/Corporate Donations; Box Office; Individual Donations
    Season: September - May **Annual Attendance:** 1,500
    Affiliations: SETC

Rock Hill

FACILITY

WINTHROP COLLEGE - JAMES F. BYRNES AUDITORIUM
Rock Hill, SC 29733
(803) 323-2196
    Type of Facility: Auditorium

Type of Stage: Proscenium   **Orchestra Pit**
Seating Capacity: 3,496
Year Built: 1939   **Architect:** James B. Urquhart   **Cost:** $1,000,000
Contact for Rental: Joynes Center;   (803) 323-2196
Under renovation; not available for use

Spartanburg

FACILITY

SPARTANBURG MEMORIAL AUDITORIUM
385 North Church Street, PO Box 1410, Spartanburg, SC 29304
(803) 582-8107
FAX: (803) 583-9850
 Type of Facility: Civic Center
 Year Built: 1951
 Year Remodeled: 1986   **Architect:** Ned Lustig   **Cost:** $3,000,000
 Acoustical Consultant: Atlee Pettit
 Contact for Rental: Steve Jones;   (803) 582-8107
 Spartanburg Memorial Auditorium contains the Arena and Theatre. See separate listings for additional information.

SPARTANBURG MEMORIAL AUDITORIUM - ARENA
385 North Church Road, PO Box 1410, Spartanburg, SC 29304
(803) 582-8107
 Type of Facility: Arena
 Type of Stage: Platform
 Stage Dimensions: 100'Wx100'D
 Seating Capacity: 3,500
 Year Built: 1951
 Year Remodeled: 1986
 Acoustical Consultant: Atlee Pettit
 Contact for Rental: Steve Jones;   (803) 582-8107

SPARTANBURG MEMORIAL AUDITORIUM - THEATRE
385 North Church Street, PO Box 1410, Spartanburg, SC 29304
(803) 582-8107
FAX: (803) 583-9850
 Type of Facility: Auditorium
 Type of Stage: Proscenium
 Stage Dimensions: 55'Wx35'D; 55'Wx28'H proscenium opening; add 18'D with pit inserts   **Orchestra Pit**
 Seating Capacity: 3,406
 Year Built: 1951
 Year Remodeled: 1986
 Acoustical Consultant: Atlee Pettit
 Contact for Rental: Steve Jones;   (803) 582-8107

Sumter

FACILITY

SUMTER COUNTY CULTURAL CENTER
135 Haynsworth, Sumter, SC 29150
(803) 775-1455
 Founded: 1987
 Type of Facility: Concert Hall; Auditorium; Theatre House; Multi-Purpose; Gallery
 Facility Originally: School
 Type of Stage: Proscenium
 Stage Dimensions: 47'x26'   **Orchestra Pit**
 Seating Capacity: 1,017
 Year Built: 1929   **Architect:** James, DuRant, Mathews and Shelley
 Year Remodeled: 1986   **Architect:** James, DuRant, Matthews and Shelley   **Cost:** $3,700,000
 Contact for Rental: Director;   (803) 775-1455

SOUTH DAKOTA

Aberdeen

INSTRUMENTAL MUSIC

ABERDEEN UNIVERSITY CIVIC SYMPHONY
Northern State College, Aberdeen, SD 57401
(605) 622-2519
>**Founded:** 1920
>**Arts Area:** Symphony; Orchestra; Ensemble
>**Status:** Non-Professional; Non-Profit
>**Type:** Performing; Resident; Educational
>**Purpose:** To study and perform literature for orchestra; to provide opportunity for music students to become acquainted with standard literature
>**Management:** Joseph E. Koob, II, Conductor
>**Paid Staff:** 1
>**Paid Artists:** 20   **Non-Paid Artists:** 50
>**Utilizes:** Guest Artists
>**Budget:** $1,000 - $50,000
>**Income Sources:** Private Foundations/Grants/Endowments; Government Grants; Individual Donations
>**Season:** September - June   **Annual Attendance:** 3,000
>**Performance Facilities:** Johnson Fine Arts Center

THEATRE

ABERDEEN COMMUNITY THEATRE (ACT 2)
PO Box 813, Aberdeen, SD 57401
(605) 225-6273
>**Founded:** 1979
>**Arts Area:** Musical; Dinner; Community; Theatrical Group
>**Status:** Non-Professional; Non-Profit
>**Type:** Performing; Educational; Sponsoring
>**Purpose:** To educate, entertain and further the performing arts through local involvement
>**Management:** James L. Walker, Artistic/Managing Director
>**Officers:** Rory King, President; Merry Coleman, Vice President; Sherri Rawstern, Secretary; Rosemary Walker, Treasurer
>**Paid Staff:** 1   **Volunteer Staff:** 1
>**Non-Paid Artists:** 50
>**Utilizes:** Guest Directors
>**Budget:** $50,000 - $100,000
>**Income Sources:** Private Foundations/Grants/Endowments; Business/Corporate Donations; Box Office; Government Grants; Individual Donations
>**Season:** April - November   **Annual Attendance:** 8,000
>**Affiliations:** AACT; South Dakota Theatre Association

Armour

THEATRE

ARMOUR STAR HAM PLAYERS
921 Main, Armour, SD 57313
(605) 724-2370
>**Founded:** 1976
>**Arts Area:** Community
>**Status:** Non-Professional; Non-Profit
>**Type:** Resident; Educational; Sponsoring
>**Purpose:** Provide live theatre for the community and sponsor art groups
>**Officers:** Carter Wiese, President; Kim Krull, Vice President; Cheri Altenburg, Secretary; Marjory Hartman, Treasurer
>**Utilizes:** Special Technical Talent
>**Budget:** $1,000 - $50,000
>**Income Sources:** Box Office
>**Season:** June - September   **Annual Attendance:** 700

Brookings

INSTRUMENTAL MUSIC

BROOKINGS CHAMBER MUSIC SOCIETY
Music Department, South Dakota State University, Brookings, Brookings, SD 57007
(605) 688-5187
> **Founded:** 1982
> **Arts Area:** Orchestra; Chamber; Ensemble; Instrumental Group
> **Status:** Non-Profit
> **Type:** Performing; Educational; Sponsoring
> **Purpose:** To bring outstanding artists and ensembles to the Brookings area and South Dakota State University
> **Management:** John F. Colson, Program Coordinator
> **Officers:** Barbara Fishback, President; Warren Hatfield, Vice President; Joan Tabor, Secretary; Norma Linn, Treasurer
> **Volunteer Staff:** 15
> **Paid Artists:** 35
> **Utilizes:** Guest Artists
> **Budget:** $1,000 - $50,000
> **Income Sources:** Private Foundations/Grants/Endowments; Business/Corporate Donations; Box Office; Government Grants; Individual Donations
> **Season:** October - April   **Annual Attendance:** 2,000
> **Affiliations:** South Dakota State University
> **Performance Facilities:** Peterson Recital Hall

SOUTH DAKOTA STATE UNIVERSITY CIVIC SYMPHONY
Music Department, South Dakota State University, Brookings, SD 57007
(605) 688-5187
> **Founded:** 1966
> **Arts Area:** Symphony; Orchestra
> **Status:** Non-Professional; Non-Profit
> **Type:** Performing; Educational
> **Purpose:** To perform symphonic literature from the Baroque through contemporary periods; to highlight outstanding soloists
> **Management:** John F. Colson, Music Director/Conductor
> **Paid Staff:** 1
> **Paid Artists:** 20   **Non-Paid Artists:** 50
> **Utilizes:** Guest Artists
> **Budget:** $1,000 - $50,000
> **Income Sources:** Private Foundations/Grants/Endowments; Business/Corporate Donations; Government Grants; Individual Donations
> **Season:** October - April   **Annual Attendance:** 6,000
> **Affiliations:** South Dakota State University
> **Performance Facilities:** Peterson Recital Hall

FACILITY

SOUTH DAKOTA ART MUSEUM
PO Box 2250, Brookings, SD 57007
(605) 688-5423
> **Type of Facility:** Multi-Purpose
> **Type of Stage:** Thrust
> **Seating Capacity:** 147
> **Year Built:** 1969   **Architect:** Howard Parezo   **Cost:** $500,000
> **Manager:** Joseph M. Stuart
> **Resident Groups:** University Theatre

De Smet

PERFORMING SERIES

LAURA INGALLS WILDER PAGEANT SOCIETY
PO Box 154, De Smet, SD 57231
(605) 688-5423
> **Founded:** 1971
> **Arts Area:** Theater
> **Status:** Non-Profit
> **Type:** Performing

Purpose: An outdoor pageant that depicts The Little Town on the Prairie books by Laura Ingalls Wilder, the site of the pageant is across the road from the Ingalls homestead site
Management: Portia Potvin, Managing Director
Officers: Arnold Poppen, President; Norma Dannenbring, Secretary/Treasurer
Volunteer Staff: 12
Budget: $1,000 - $50,000
Income Sources: Box Office; Individual Donations
Season: June - July **Annual Attendance:** 10,000

Dell Rapids

THEATRE

OLD OPERA HOUSE PLAYERS
PO Box 163, Dell Rapids, SD 57022
(605) 428-3260
Founded: 1976
Arts Area: Community
Status: Non-Professional; Non-Profit
Type: Performing; Resident
Purpose: To support community theatre; to train young actors
Officers: Phyllis Rydberg, President; Richard Fitzgerald, Vice President; Dale Nighbert, Treasurer; Angie Sward, Secretary
Volunteer Staff: 15
Budget: $1,000 - $50,000
Income Sources: Box Office
Season: June - August **Annual Attendance:** 600
Performance Facilities: The Hayloft Theater

Huron

INSTRUMENTAL MUSIC

HURON MUNICIPAL BAND
PO Box 1387, Huron, SD 57350
(605) 352-8561
Founded: 1885
Arts Area: Band
Status: Semi-Professional
Type: Performing
Purpose: To provide the community with live band music for patriotic and civic functions and summer concerts
Officers: Clarke Christiansen, President; Ted Peterman, Secretary; Randall Lampe, Treasurer
Paid Artists: 32
Budget: $1,000 - $50,000
Income Sources: Government Grants
Season: Memorial Day - August **Annual Attendance:** 10,000
Performance Facilities: Band Shell, City Park

Lennox

INSTRUMENTAL MUSIC

LENNOX MUNICIPAL BAND
c/o Lennox Independent Newspaper, Lennox, SD 57039
(605) 647-2284
Founded: 1883
Arts Area: Band
Status: Non-Professional; Non-Profit
Type: Performing
Purpose: To provide band music for civic and municipal events in and around Lennox; to provide weekly concerts in the park during the summer season
Management: William Hoffman, Director
Officers: Sharla West, President; Marion Smith, Vice President; Betty Barnett, Secretary; Nancy Straatmeyer, Treasurer
Paid Staff: 1
Non-Paid Artists: 35
Utilizes: Guest Artists

Budget: $1,000 - $50,000
Season: June - August   **Annual Attendance:** 1,000
Performance Facilities: Jacobs Memorial Band Shell, City Park

---

Madison

PERFORMING SERIES

MADISON AREA ARTS COUNCIL
PO Box 147, Madison, SD 57042
(605) 256-5270
    Founded: 1968
    Arts Area: Dance; Vocal Music; Instrumental Music; Theater; Festivals
    Status: Non-Profit
    Type: Educational; Sponsoring
    Purpose: Promote an appreciation of the arts; sponsor activities in the arts; and provide opportunities for instruction in the arts for members of the community
    Management: Eve Fisher, Arts Coordinator
    Officers: Katherine Presuhn, President; Mollie Freier, Vice President; Nancy Sabbe, Secretary; Keith Knutson, Treasurer
    Paid Staff: 1   **Volunteer Staff:** 17
    Utilizes: Guest Artists; Guest Directors
    Budget: $1,000 - $50,000
    Income Sources: Private Foundations/Grants/Endowments; Business/Corporate Donations; Box Office; Government Grants; Individual Donations
    Season: September - May   **Annual Attendance:** 2,000
    Affiliations: South Dakota Arts Council; Community Arts Council Network; South Dakota Alliance
    Performance Facilities: Dakota Prairie Playhouse

Mitchell

INSTRUMENTAL MUSIC

MITCHELL MUNICIPAL BAND
1509 Bridle Drive, Mitchell, SD 57301
(605) 996-5467
    Founded: 1900
    Arts Area: Band
    Status: Professional
    Type: Performing
    Purpose: Free summer family entertainment and city affairs
    Management: Joseph F. Pekas, Director
    Officers: Arnold Braught, President; Bernice Sellars, Secretary/Treasurer
    Paid Staff: 2
    Paid Artists: 35
    Budget: $1,000 - $50,000
    Season: May - August   **Annual Attendance:** 50,000
    Affiliations: AFM
    Performance Facilities: Band Shell

Pierre

INSTRUMENTAL MUSIC

CAPITAL CITY BAND
1005 West Elizabeth, Pierre, SD 57501
(605) 224-1343
FAX: (605) 224-1343
    Founded: 1900
    Arts Area: Band
    Status: Non-Professional; Non-Profit
    Type: Performing; Touring
    Purpose: Provide weekly summer band concerts in city parks and make special appearances
    Management: Terry C. Anderson, Director
    Paid Staff: 1
    Non-Paid Artists: 53
    Utilizes: Guest Directors

Budget: $1,000 - $50,000
Income Sources: Government Grants
Season: June - August   **Annual Attendance:** 10,000
Affiliations: American Association of Concert Bands

THEATRE

PIERRE PLAYERS
109 South Pierre Street, PO Box 933, Pierre, SD 57501
(605) 224-9709
    Founded: 1968
    Arts Area: Community
    Status: Non-Professional; Non-Profit
    Type: Performing
    Purpose: Providing quality theatre to the people of Central South Dakota; Pierre Players gives them an appreciation of legitimate theatre and provides an opportunity to take part in the active production
    Management: Don Boyd, Manager
    Officers: Bob Brancel, President; Kathy Valnes, Vice President; Darlene Gage, Secretary; John Clauson, Treasurer
    Paid Staff: 1   **Volunteer Staff:** 100
    Non-Paid Artists: 100
    Utilizes: Special Technical Talent; Guest Directors
    Budget: $50,000 - $100,000
    Income Sources: Business/Corporate Donations; Box Office; Individual Donations
    Season: 52 Weeks   **Annual Attendance:** 8,000

Rapid City

INSTRUMENTAL MUSIC

BLACK HILLS SYMPHONY ORCHESTRA
PO Box 2246, Rapid City, SD 57709
(605) 348-4676
    Founded: 1931
    Arts Area: Symphony; Orchestra
    Status: Non-Profit
    Type: Performing; Resident; Educational
    Purpose: To encourage understanding and appreciation of music in the area and to provide opportunities to area musicians to develop and express talent through performance and training
    Management: Lowell Holmgren, Executive Director; Jack Knowles, Conductor; Coral White, Concert Master
    Officers: Jo Anne Messerli, President, Board of Directors; Steve Montgomery, First Vice President; Linda Zazula, Secretary; Craig Grotenhouse, Treasurer
    Paid Staff: 3
    Paid Artists: 75   **Non-Paid Artists:** 10
    Utilizes: Guest Artists
    Budget: $100,000 - $500,000
    Income Sources: Private Foundations/Grants/Endowments; Business/Corporate Donations; Box Office; Government Grants; Individual Donations
    Season: October - April   **Annual Attendance:** 5,500
    Performance Facilities: Rushmore Plaza Civic Center Theater

THEATRE

BLACK HILLS COMMUNITY THEATRE
713 Seventh Street, Rapid City, SD 57701
(605) 394-1786
    Founded: 1968
    Arts Area: Community
    Status: Non-Profit
    Type: Performing
    Purpose: To provide quality theatrical entertainment utilizing talent from the community
    Management: Merritt Olsen, Manager
    Officers: Angie McKie, President; Tim Pittman, Treasurer; Wayne Gilbert, Secretary
    Paid Staff: 2   **Volunteer Staff:** 25
    Paid Artists: 15   **Non-Paid Artists:** 150
    Budget: $50,000 - $100,000
    Income Sources: Business/Corporate Donations; Box Office; Government Grants; Individual Donations
    Season: September - May   **Annual Attendance:** 6,000
    Affiliations: South Dakota Arts Council; Allied Arts Fund

BLACK HILLS PLAYHOUSE
PO Box 2513, Rapid City, SD 57709
(605) 255-4242
    Founded: 1946
    Arts Area: Summer Stock; Theatrical Group
    Status: Professional; Semi-Professional; Non-Profit
    Type: Performing; Resident; Educational
    Purpose: To provide high quality performances for its theater audience and to provide intensive professional training for theater students
    Management: Jan D. Swank, Managing Artistic Director; Jill Swank, Business Manager
    Officers: Kay Snyder, President; Tim Case, Vice President; Clara Clay, Secretary; Patrick Burchill, Treasurer
    Paid Staff: 65
    Utilizes: Special Technical Talent; Guest Artists; Guest Directors; Students
    Budget: $100,000 - $500,000
    Income Sources: Private Foundations/Grants/Endowments; Business/Corporate Donations; Box Office; Government Grants; Individual Donations
    Season: June - August   **Annual Attendance:** 20,000
    Performance Facilities: Black Hills Playhouse (Custer State Park)

FACILITY

RUSHMORE PLAZA CIVIC CENTER
444 Mount Rushmore Road North, Rapid City, SD 57701
(605) 394-4115
FAX: (605) 394-4119
    Founded: 1977
    Type of Facility: Concert Hall; Theatre House; Civic Center; Arena; Multi-Purpose
    Type of Stage: Proscenium
    Stage Dimensions: 43'Dx55' proscenium opening; 68' to grid   **Orchestra Pit**
    Seating Capacity: 1,774
    Year Built: 1977   **Architect:** Spitznagel   **Cost:** $10,000,000
    Contact for Rental: (605) 394-4119
    Manager: Kevin Buntrock;   (605) 394-4115
    Resident Groups: Black Hills Symphony; Rapid City Concert Association; Black Hills Dance Theatre
    Rushmore Plaza Civic Center also contains an 11,200 seat Arena and 150,000 square foot Convention Auditorium.

Sioux Falls

DANCE

CIVIC DANCE ASSOCIATION
PO Box 646, Sioux Falls, SD 57101
(605) 335-8913
    Founded: 1970
    Arts Area: Modern; Ballet; Jazz
    Status: Non-Profit
    Type: Performing; Touring; Resident; Educational; Sponsoring
    Purpose: To bring professional dance to our city
    Officers: Terri Bowden, President; Gary Wirt, Vice President; Karen Johnson, Secretary; J.D. Thompson, Treasurer
    Volunteer Staff: 8
    Budget: $1,000 - $50,000
    Income Sources: Private Foundations/Grants/Endowments; Business/Corporate Donations; Box Office; Government Grants; Individual Donations
    Season: Spring - Fall

INSTRUMENTAL MUSIC

SIOUX FALLS MUNICIPAL BAND
City Hall, Sioux Falls, SD 57102
(605) 339-7290
    Founded: 1919
    Arts Area: Instrumental Group; Band
    Status: Semi-Professional; Non-Profit
    Type: Performing
    Purpose: To provide free concerts of band music to the citizens of our community

Management: Dr. Bruce T. Ammann, Conductor
Officers: Craig Alberty, President
Paid Staff: 3
Paid Artists: 50
Utilizes: Guest Conductors; Guest Artists
Budget: $50,000 - $100,000
Income Sources: Private Foundations/Grants/Endowments; Business/Corporate Donations; Individual Donations
Season: October - August   **Annual Attendance:** 40,000

SOUTH DAKOTA SYMPHONY
300 Norh Dakota, Suite 405, Sioux Falls, SD 57102
(605) 335-7933
    Founded: 1922
    Arts Area: Symphony; Orchestra; Chamber; Ensemble
    Status: Professional; Non-Profit
    Type: Performing; Touring; Resident; Educational
    Purpose: Providing the highest quality orchestral music to the people of the Northern Plains, the South Dakota Symphony takes leadership in enhancing the cultural environment of the region, developing an understanding and interest in the people of the state for fine artistic expression.
    Management: Marti A. Baumert, Executive Director; Henry Charles Smith, Music Director
    Officers: Ron Williamson, President
    Paid Staff: 5   **Volunteer Staff:** 150
    Paid Artists: 85
    Utilizes: Guest Artists; Guest Directors
    Budget: $500,000 - $1,000,000
    Income Sources: Private Foundations/Grants/Endowments; Business/Corporate Donations; Box Office; Government Grants; Individual Donations
    Season: September - May   **Annual Attendance:** 67,000
    Affiliations: ASOL
    Performance Facilities: Sioux Falls Coliseum

VOCAL MUSIC

SIOUX FALLS MASTER SINGERS
PO Box 1753, Sioux Falls, SD 57101
(605) 368-2390
    Founded: 1984
    Arts Area: Light Opera; Choral; Ethnic; Folk
    Status: Non-Profit
    Type: Performing; Educational
    Purpose: To perform quality choral literature to a regional audience of all ages
    Management: Jamesina McLeod, Business Manager; Alan Stanza, Music Director
    Officers: Diane Hohn, President; Elmer Tursan, Secretary/Treasurer
    Paid Staff: 1   **Volunteer Staff:** 25
    Non-Paid Artists: 30
    Utilizes: Guest Artists
    Budget: $1,000 - $50,000
    Income Sources: Private Foundations/Grants/Endowments; Business/Corporate Donations; Box Office; Government Grants; Individual Donations
    Season: October - April   **Annual Attendance:** 2,500

THEATRE

THE BARN THEATER
Rural Route 3, PO Box 126, Sioux Falls, SD 57106
(605) 339-1263
    Founded: 1978
    Arts Area: Summer Stock; Theatrical Group
    Status: Semi-Professional
    Type: Performing; Resident
    Purpose: To provide wholesome summer entertainment and an outlet for actors who wish to perform
    Management: Delores Cullen, Owner/Producer; James Connor, Director
    Paid Staff: 2
    Utilizes: Special Technical Talent; Guest Directors
    Budget: $1,000 - $50,000

Income Sources: Box Office
Season: June - August **Annual Attendance:** 2,200

SIOUX FALLS COMMUNITY PLAYHOUSE
315 North Phillips, PO Box 600, Sioux Falls, SD 57101
(605) 336-7418
    Founded: 1931
    Arts Area: Community
    Status: Non-Profit
    Type: Performing; Touring; Resident; Educational; Sponsoring
    Purpose: To provide the community and area with an opportunity to experience live theatre at a variety of participatory levels
    Management: Ron Ziegler, Managing Director
    Paid Staff: 5 **Volunteer Staff:** 500
    Paid Artists: 5 **Non-Paid Artists:** 150
    Budget: $100,000 - $500,000
    Income Sources: Private Foundations/Grants/Endowments; Business/Corporate Donations; Box Office; Government Grants; Individual Donations
    Season: 52 Weeks **Annual Attendance:** 25,000
    Affiliations: AACT; South Dakota Arts Council
    Performance Facilities: Sioux Falls Community Playhouse

FACILITY

SIOUX FALLS COLISEUM
600 East Seventh Street, Sioux Falls, SD 57102
(605) 339-7196
    Type of Facility: Theatre Complex; Auditorium; Theatre House
    Type of Stage: Proscenium
    Stage Dimensions: 60'x40'x35' **Orchestra Pit**
    Seating Capacity: 1,933
    Year Built: 1917
    Year Remodeled: 1972 **Architect:** Kock **Cost:** $168,000
    Contact for Rental: Kenn Friesen; (605) 339-7060
    Resident Groups: Sioux Falls Symphony; Community Concerts Association

SIOUX FALLS COMMUNITY PLAYHOUSE
315 North Phillips, PO Box 600, Sioux Falls, SD 57101
(605) 336-7418
FAX: (605) 336-2243
    Type of Facility: Theatre Complex
    Facility Originally: Vaudeville
    Type of Stage: Proscenium
    Stage Dimensions: 53'Wx32'D **Orchestra Pit**
    Seating Capacity: 692
    Year Built: 1913 **Architect:** Solari Brothers
    Year Remodeled: 1984 **Architect:** Spitznagel Partners **Cost:** $800,000
    Contact for Rental: Bob Wyant, Business Manager; (605) 336-7418
    Manager: Ron Ziegler; (605) 336-7418
    Resident Groups: Sioux Falls Community Playhouse

Spearfish

THEATRE

MATTHEWS OPERA HOUSE SOCIETY
PO Box 874, Spearfish, SD 57783-0874
(605) 642-7973
    Founded: 1987
    Arts Area: Musical; Community; Theatrical Group
    Status: Non-Professional; Non-Profit
    Type: Performing; Educational
    Purpose: To provide opportunities for people with talent and interest in theatre to work together; to continue Opera House restoration efforts
    Management: Julie Bulat, Arts Coordinator
    Officers: Sandy Sorlie, President; Brian McNeill, Treasurer
    Paid Staff: 1
    Utilizes: Special Technical Talent

Budget: $1,000 - $50,000
Income Sources: Box Office; Government Grants; Individual Donations
Performance Facilities: Senior High Theatre; Matthews Opera House

FACILITY

MATTHEWS OPERA HOUSE
PO Box 874, Spearfish, SD 57783
(605) 642-7973
    Founded: 1910
    Type of Facility: Performance Center; Theatre House; Opera House
    Facility Originally: Vaudeville; Movie House
    Type of Stage: Proscenium; Platform
    Stage Dimensions: 16'x26'
    Seating Capacity: 250
    Year Built: 1910
    Year Remodeled: 1989   **Architect:** James McDonald; Herb AsLesen   **Cost:** $500,000
    Contact for Rental: Julie Bulat;   (605) 642-7973

Vermillion

FACILITY

UNIVERSITY OF SOUTH DAKOTA - SLAGLE AUDITORIUM
414 East Clark, Vermillion, SD 57069
(605) 677-5481
    Type of Facility: Concert Hall
    Facility Originally: School
    Type of Stage: Proscenium   **Orchestra Pit**
    Seating Capacity: 2,400
    Year Built: 1924
    Contact for Rental: College of Fine Arts;   (605) 677-5481
    Manager: Wayne S. Knutsen

UNIVERSITY OF SOUTH DAKOTA - WARREN M. LEE CENTER FOR THE FINE ARTS
414 East Clark, Vermillion, SD 57069
(605) 677-5481
    Type of Facility: Theatre Complex; Performance Center; Multi-Purpose
    Seating Capacity: Theatre I - 470
    Year Built: 1974   **Architect:** The Spitznagel Partners   **Cost:** $3,500,000
    Acoustical Consultant: Richard Borgen
    Contact for Rental: Cheryl Feight;   (605) 677-5481
    Manager: Wayne S. Knutsen
    Resident Groups: University of South Dakota Departments of Music, Art and Theater

Wagner

INSTRUMENTAL MUSIC

YANKTON AREA SUMMER BAND
Rural Route 1, PO Box 133, Wagner, SD 57380-9627
(605) 384-3355
FAX: (605) 384-3156
    Founded: 1982
    Arts Area: Band
    Status: Semi-Professional; Non-Profit
    Type: Performing
    Purpose: Providing summer band concerts, each concert is directed by a member of the band who is an area band director.
    Management: Chuck Stastny, Band Manager
    Paid Staff: 11
    Non-Paid Artists: 80
    Utilizes: Special Technical Talent
    Budget: $1,000 - $50,000
    Income Sources: Private Foundations/Grants/Endowments; Business/Corporate Donations; Individual Donations
    Season: June - July   **Annual Attendance:** 3,000

Affiliations: Yankton Department of Parks and Recreation; Yankton Area Arts Association
Performance Facilities: Riverside Park

Watertown

INSTRUMENTAL MUSIC

WATERTOWN MUNICIPAL BAND
1015 North Park, Watertown, SD 57201
(605) 886-3216
    Founded: 1930
    Arts Area: Band
    Status: Semi-Professional; Non-Profit
    Type: Performing
    Purpose: To provide summer concerts in the park for area residents
    Management: Douglas R. Carpenter, Director
    Officers: Leonard Timmerman, Treasurer
    Paid Staff: 2
    Paid Artists: 45
    Utilizes: Guest Directors
    Budget: $1,000 - $50,000
    Income Sources: Government Grants
    Season: May - August   **Annual Attendance:** 8,000
    Performance Facilities: Wenger Showmobile

THEATRE

TOWN PLAYERS
5 South Broadway, Watertown, SD 57201
(605) 882-2076
    Founded: 1940
    Arts Area: Musical; Community; Theatrical Group
    Status: Non-Professional; Non-Profit
    Type: Performing; Touring; Resident
    Purpose: To promote interest in and appreciation of the dramatic arts
    Management: Renee Carey, Manager
    Paid Staff: 1   **Volunteer Staff:** 20
    Paid Artists: 14   **Non-Paid Artists:** 45
    Utilizes: Special Technical Talent; Guest Conductors; Guest Artists; Guest Directors
    Budget: $1,000 - $50,000
    Income Sources: Private Foundations/Grants/Endowments; Box Office; Individual Donations
    Season: September - April   **Annual Attendance:** 5,000

Webster

INSTRUMENTAL MUSIC

WEBSTER COMMUNITY EDUCATION
102 East Ninth Avenue, Webster, SD 57274
(605) 345-4653
    Founded: 1983
    Arts Area: Ensemble; Band
    Status: Non-Professional; Non-Profit
    Type: Performing; Resident; Educational
    Purpose: To provide an opportunity for members of the community (youth and adult) to gather to present performances in various mediums of the performing arts
    Management: Barbara Ohleen, Community Education Director
    Volunteer Staff: 3
    Non-Paid Artists: 50
    Budget: $1,000 - $50,000
    Annual Attendance: 300

TENNESSEE

Alcoa

FACILITY

SMOKY MOUNTAIN PASSION PLAY
366 Glascock Street, Alcoa, TN 37701-2439
(615) 448-2244
Type of Facility: Amphitheater
Type of Stage: Greek
Stage Dimensions: 80'x45'
Seating Capacity: 2,000
Year Built: 1973
Architect: Lindsay-Maples
Cost: $350,000
Contact for Rental: Charles Reese;   (615) 984-4111
Resident Groups: Smoky Mountain Passion Play Company

Austin

INSTRUMENTAL MUSIC

CREATIVE OPPORTUNITY ORCHESTRA
PO Box 3215, Austin, TN 78764
(512) 448-3485
Arts Area: Ensemble; Jazz; New Music
Status: Professional; Non-Profit
Type: Performing; Touring; Resident; Educational
Purpose: To create a performing composers' forum for the evolution of new jazz music
Management: Tina Marsh, Artistic Director
Budget: $100,000 - $500,000
Income Sources: Private Foundations/Grants/Endowments; Business/Corporate Donations; Box Office; Government Grants; Individual Donations

---

Bristol

THEATRE

THEATER BRISTOL
512 State Street, Bristol, TN 37620
(615) 968-4977
Founded: 1965
Arts Area: Musical; Community; Theatrical Group
Status: Non-Professional; Non-Profit
Type: Performing; Resident; Educational; Sponsoring
Purpose: To provide quality entertainment and educational programs for children and adults, offering complete seasons for both
Management: Cathy De Caterina, Executive Director; Libby Everett, Business Manager; Robert Dean, Producing Director
Officers: Debbie Curry, President, Board of Directors; William H. Thompson, First Vice President; Michael E. Riley, Second Vice President; Lettie Jackson, Treasurer
Paid Staff: 6   **Volunteer Staff:** 400
Paid Artists: 25   **Non-Paid Artists:** 300
Utilizes: Special Technical Talent; Guest Conductors; Guest Directors
Budget: $100,000 - $500,000
Income Sources: Business/Corporate Donations; Box Office; Government Grants; Individual Donations
Season: February - November
Annual Attendance: 35,000
Performance Facilities: The Paramount Center for the Arts

Chattanooga

DANCE

CHATTANOOGA BALLET
PO Box 6175, Chattanooga, TN 37401
(615) 755-4672
> **Founded:** 1976
> **Arts Area:** Modern; Ballet; Jazz
> **Status:** Non-Profit
> **Type:** Performing; Touring; Resident; Educational; Sponsoring
> **Purpose:** We are a producing and presenting ballet company and school
> **Management:** Robert Willie, Artistic Director; Karen Smith, School Director; Frank Hay, Ballet Master
> **Officers:** William Montague, Board President; John Phillips, Vice President; Sally Wall, Secretary;
> Lynn Pfannkuche, Treasurer
> **Paid Staff:** 4 **Volunteer Staff:** 11
> **Paid Artists:** 3 **Non-Paid Artists:** 11
> **Utilizes:** Special Technical Talent; Guest Artists; Guest Directors
> **Budget:** $50,000 - $100,000
> **Income Sources:** Private Foundations/Grants/Endowments; Business/Corporate Donations; Box Office; Government
> Grants; Individual Donations
> **Season:** December - June
> **Affiliations:** SERBA; Allied Arts of Greater Chattanooga
> **Performance Facilities:** Fine Arts Center, University of Tennessee-Chattanooga; Tivoli Theater

VOCAL MUSIC

CHATTANOOGA BOYS CHOIR
1206 Market Street, #27 Freight Depot, Chattanooga, TN 37402
(615) 265-3030
FAX: (615) 265-3030
> **Founded:** 1954
> **Arts Area:** Choral
> **Status:** Professional; Non-Profit
> **Type:** Performing; Touring
> **Purpose:** To teach boys the love and appreciation of good music through a comprehensive training program
> **Management:** Alkahest Agency
> **Officers:** Phyllis Brewer, Administrator; Everett O'Neal, Conductor
> **Paid Staff:** 1 **Volunteer Staff:** 30
> **Paid Artists:** 7 **Non-Paid Artists:** 45
> **Utilizes:** Guest Artists
> **Budget:** $100,000 - $500,000
> **Income Sources:** Private Foundations/Grants/Endowments; Business/Corporate Donations; Box Office; Government
> Grants; Individual Donations
> **Season:** September - June **Annual Attendance:** 25,000

CHATTANOOGA SYMPHONY AND OPERA ASSOCIATION
630 Chestnut Street, Chattanooga, TN 37402
(615) 267-8583
> **Founded:** Symphony - 1933; Opera - 1944
> **Arts Area:** Grand Opera; Lyric Opera; Light Opera; Operetta; Symphony
> **Status:** Professional; Non-Profit
> **Type:** Performing; Touring; Educational
> **Management:** Donald L. Andrews, Managing Director
> **Officers:** Thomas C. Hardy, President
> **Paid Staff:** 7 **Volunteer Staff:** 1
> **Paid Artists:** 95 **Non-Paid Artists:** 40
> **Utilizes:** Special Technical Talent; Guest Conductors; Guest Artists; Guest Directors
> **Budget:** $1,000,000 - $5,000,000
> **Income Sources:** Private Foundations/Grants/Endowments; Business/Corporate Donations; Box Office; Government
> Grants; Individual Donations
> **Season:** September - May **Annual Attendance:** 100,000
> **Affiliations:** Tennesseans for the Arts; OA; ASOL
> **Performance Facilities:** Tivoli Theatre

FACILITY

ROLAND HAYES CONCERT HALL
University of Tennessee, 615 McCallie Avenue/ FAC #324, Chattanooga, TN 37403
(615) 755-4371
FAX: (615) 755-5249
  Founded: 1980
  Type of Facility: Theatre Complex; Concert Hall; Studio Performance; Performance Center
  Type of Stage: Thrust; Proscenium
  Stage Dimensions: 45'x42'; 17'x2' wings   **Orchestra Pit**
  Seating Capacity: 505
  Year Built: 1980   **Architect:** Derthick & Henley, Architects   **Cost:** $7,000,000
  Acoustical Consultant: Stephen M. Sessler, Newcomb & Boyd
  Contact for Rental: Ken Kapelinski;   (615) 755-4371
  Resident Groups: University of Tennessee: Theatre Department; Music Department; Visual Arts Department

TIVOLI THEATRE
709 Broad Street, Chattanooga, TN 37402
(615) 757-5042
FAX: (615) 757-5326
  Founded: 1921
  Type of Facility: Concert Hall; Performance Center; Theatre House
  Facility Originally: Vaudeville
  Type of Stage: Proscenium
  Stage Dimensions: 43'Dx46'Wx26'H   **Orchestra Pit**
  Seating Capacity: 1,700
  Year Built: 1921   **Architect:** Rapp & Rapp   **Cost:** $700,000
  Year Remodeled: 1989   **Architect:** Selmon T. Franklin   **Cost:** $6,500,000
  Contact for Rental: David E. Johnson;   (615) 757-5050
  The Tivoli Theatre is a National Historic Landmark.

Clarksville

THEATRE

ROXY THEATER
100 Franklin Street, Clarksville, TN 37040
(615) 645-7699
  Founded: 1983
  Arts Area: Professional; Musical; Community; Theatrical Group
  Status: Non-Profit
  Type: Performing; Educational
  Purpose: To promote and produce the visual and performing arts
  Management: Tom Thayer, General Manager; John McDonald, Artistic Director
  Officers: Tom Thayer, President; Cinders Murdock-Vaughan, Vice President; Linda Ellis, Secretary;
  Jean J. Faust, Treasurer
  Paid Staff: 3   **Volunteer Staff:** 5
  Non-Paid Artists: 2
  Utilizes: Guest Artists; Guest Directors
  Budget: $50,000 - $100,000
  Income Sources: Private Foundations/Grants/Endowments; Business/Corporate Donations; Box Office; Government
  Grants; Individual Donations
  Season: 52 Weeks   **Annual Attendance:** 7,500

Cleveland

THEATRE

CLEVELAND CREATIVE ARTS GUILD
PO Box 395, Cleveland, TN 37364
(615) 478-3114
  Founded: 1965
  Arts Area: Dinner; Community
  Status: Non-Profit
  Type: Performing; Educational
  Purpose: Working to provide creative opportunity and to enrich the cultural life of the community

Officers: Gaye Ogle, President; Julia Penney, First Vice President; Dale Dotson, Second Vice President; Pat McCracken, Secretary; Gaye Ogle, Treasurer
Volunteer Staff: 50
Utilizes: Guest Artists
Budget: $1,000 - $50,000
Income Sources: Box Office; Individual Donations
Season: 52 Weeks   **Annual Attendance:** 1,600
Affiliations: Tennesseans for the Arts

Crossville

THEATRE

CUMBERLAND COUNTY PLAYHOUSE
Highway 70, PO Box 484, Crossville, TN 38557
(615) 484-5000
Founded: 1965
Arts Area: Professional; Theatrical Group
Status: Professional; Non-Profit
Type: Performing; Touring; Resident; Educational; Sponsoring
Purpose: To provide cultural enrichment for the area
Management: Jim Crabtree, Producing Director; Mary Crabtree, Consulting Producer
Officers: Steven Douglas, Chairman; Bill Startup, First Vice Chairman; L.A. Ezell, Second Vice Chairman; Stan Bise, Secretary
Paid Staff: 14   **Volunteer Staff:** 10
Paid Artists: 13   **Non-Paid Artists:** 65
Utilizes: Guest Artists; Guest Directors
Budget: $500,000 - $1,000,000
Income Sources: Private Foundations/Grants/Endowments; Business/Corporate Donations; Box Office; Government Grants; Individual Donations
Season: March - November   **Annual Attendance:** 70,000
Affiliations: TCG
Performance Facilities: Cumberland County Playhouse

Franklin

THEATRE

PULL-TIGHT PLAYERS
Second Avenue South, PO Box 105, Franklin, TN 37064
(615) 790-6782
Founded: 1968
Arts Area: Community; Theatrical Group
Status: Non-Professional; Non-Profit
Type: Performing; Resident
Purpose: To bring quality community theatre to the Williamson County Area
Officers: Iain MacPherson, President; Roz Highfill, Vice President; Steve Evans, Secretary; John Emberton, Treasurer
Non-Paid Artists: 60
Utilizes: Guest Artists; Guest Directors
Budget: $1,000 - $50,000
Income Sources: Private Foundations/Grants/Endowments; Business/Corporate Donations; Box Office
Season: 52 Weeks   **Annual Attendance:** 3,000

Germantown

THEATRE

POPLAR PIKE PLAYHOUSE
7653 Old Poplar Pike, Germantown, TN 38138
(901) 755-7775
FAX: (901) 756-2356
Founded: 1976
Arts Area: Musical; Community; Theatrical Group
Status: Non-Profit
Type: Performing; Educational
Purpose: Basically an educational theatre housed at Germantown High School

Management: Frank Bluestein, Managing Director; Robin McDurmott, Assistant Managing Director/Musical Director; Almeda Zent, Scenic Artist; Norma Early and Brenda Bluestein, Costumes; Staci Martin, Box Office
Paid Staff: 5   **Volunteer Staff:** 20
Non-Paid Artists: 20
Utilizes: Special Technical Talent; Guest Conductors; Guest Artists; Guest Directors
Budget: $50,000 - $100,000
Income Sources: Private Foundations/Grants/Endowments; Business/Corporate Donations; Box Office; Government Grants; Individual Donations
Season: September - May   **Annual Attendance:** 5,000
Affiliations: Tennessee Theater Association

Jackson

INSTRUMENTAL MUSIC

JACKSON SYMPHONY ASSOCIATION
1903 North Highland, Suite 4, Jackson, TN 38303-3429
(901) 427-6440
  Mailing Address: PO Box 3429, Jackson, TN 38303
  Founded: 1961
  Arts Area: Symphony; Orchestra
  Status: Semi-Professional
  Type: Performing; Touring; Resident; Educational
  Purpose: To support a performing orchestra of increasing quality for Jackson and its surrounding area; to promote the preservation of our musical heritage and audience exposure to the finer aspects of that heritage by providing programs that are attractive and entertaining
  Management: Dr. Jordan Tang, Music Director; Karen Lenard, Administrative Assistant
  Officers: Larry Dooley, President; Mary Jane McWherter, Secretary
  Paid Staff: 3
  Paid Artists: 70   **Non-Paid Artists:** 1
  Utilizes: Guest Artists
  Budget: $100,000 - $500,000
  Income Sources: Private Foundations/Grants/Endowments; Business/Corporate Donations; Box Office; Government Grants; Individual Donations
  Season: September - May   **Annual Attendance:** 25,000
  Affiliations: ASOL
  Performance Facilities: The Jackson Civic Center

THEATRE

JACKSON RECREATION CHILDREN'S THEATRE
400 South Highland, Jackson, TN 38301
(901) 423-0075
  Founded: 1974
  Arts Area: Musical; Dinner; Community
  Status: Non-Professional
  Type: Performing
  Purpose: Provide training to young people interested in the performing arts; provide entertainment to children and adults and encourage them to be patrons of the arts
  Management: Pat Gilliland-Alford, Director
  Volunteer Staff: 2
  Non-Paid Artists: 100
  Budget: $1,000 - $50,000
  Income Sources: Box Office
  Annual Attendance: 3,000
  Affiliations: Jackson Recreation and Parks; Jackson Theatre Guild
  Performance Facilities: Jackson Civic Center, Little Theatre

JACKSON THEATRE GUILD
PO Box 7041, Jackson, TN 38308
(901) 422-2484
  Founded: 1966
  Arts Area: Musical; Community; Theatrical Group
  Status: Non-Profit
  Type: Performing; Resident; Educational
  Purpose: To provide live theatre and performance education in the area
  Management: Scott Conley, Artistic Director; Melody Pierce, Business Manager
  Officers: Emily Canter, President; Phillip Collins, Vice President; Brian Kurt, Secretary; Roxanne Rhoads, Treasurer

Paid Staff: 1
Paid Artists: 1
Utilizes: Special Technical Talent; Guest Artists; Guest Directors
Budget: $50,000 - $100,000
Income Sources: Private Foundations/Grants/Endowments; Business/Corporate Donations; Box Office; Government Grants; Individual Donations
Season: 52 Weeks
Affiliations: Jackson Arts Council

FACILITY

JACKSON CIVIC CENTER
400 South Highland Avenue, Jackson, TN 38301
(901) 423-9404
Type of Facility: Concert Hall; Civic Center; Multi-Purpose
Type of Stage: Proscenium
Stage Dimensions: 150'Wx50'D   **Orchestra Pit**
Seating Capacity: 2,200
Year Built: 1973   **Architect:** W.C. Harris   **Cost:** $5,000,000
Acoustical Consultant: Burris-Meyer
Contact for Rental: Jerry Gist, Executive Director;   (901) 423-9404

LAMBUTH COLLEGE - LAMBUTH THEATRE
Department of Theatre, 705 Lamburth Boulevard, Jackson, TN 38301
(901) 425-2500, ext. 235
FAX: (901) 423-1990
Type of Facility: Theatre Complex
Facility Originally: Recreation Hall; Gymnasium
Type of Stage: Proscenium
Stage Dimensions: 35'Wx28'D
Seating Capacity: 250
Year Built: 1945
Year Remodeled: 1972
Contact for Rental: Jesse Byron

Johnson City

DANCE

TENNESSEE ASSOCIATION OF DANCE
PO Box 2432, Johnson City, TN 37605
(615) 929-1129
Founded: 1971
Arts Area: Modern; Ballet; Jazz; Tap
Status: Professional; Non-Professional; Non-Profit
Type: Educational
Purpose: To unite people in the state of Tennessee with interest in the advancement of dance in all its forms; to upgrade training programs; to promote dance opportunities and appreciation
Management: Judith Woodruff, Executive Coordinator
Officers: Jane Fabian, President
Volunteer Staff: 13
Utilizes: Guest Artists
Budget: $1,000 - $50,000
Income Sources: Private Foundations/Grants/Endowments; Box Office; Government Grants; Individual Donations
Annual Attendance: 200
Performance Facilities: Middle Tennessee State University

VOCAL MUSIC

JOHNSON CITY CIVIC CHORALE
Eastern Tennessee State University, PO Box 24427, Johnson City, TN 37614
(615) 753-2722
Founded: 1975
Arts Area: Choral
Status: Non-Professional; Non-Profit
Type: Performing; Touring; Resident
Purpose: To enhance the musical life of the community; to provide a musical outlet for talented area singers through performance of great choral music

Management: Robert LaPella, Musical Director/Conductor
Officers: Dr. James Odum, President
Volunteer Staff: 5
Non-Paid Artists: 3
Budget: $1,000 - $50,000
Income Sources: Private Foundations/Grants/Endowments; Business/Corporate Donations; Individual Donations
Season: September - May   **Annual Attendance:** 1,600
Performance Facilities: Munsey Memorial Methodist Church; Gilbreath Auditorium

THEATRE

THE ROAD COMPANY
PO Box 5278 EKS, Johnson City, TN 37603
(615) 926-7726
Founded: 1976
Arts Area: Professional; Theatrical Group
Status: Professional; Non-Profit
Type: Performing; Touring; Resident
Purpose: Dedicated to the production of new theatre which reflects the concerns and interests of the community in which we live and work, TRC is a touring theatre based in Johnson City serving the Upper Tennessee Valley, the southern mountains from the East Coast to the Mississippi River.
Management: Robert H. Leonard, Artistic Director; Nancy Fischman, Development Director; Eugene Wolf, Christine Murdock, Laurene Scalf, Senior Ensemble Members; Emily Green, Projects Director; Ailene Watterson, Administrative Assistant
Officers: Constance Douglas, President; Ignacy Fonberg, Vice President; Nancy Fischman, Treasurer
Paid Staff: 4   **Volunteer Staff:** 25
Paid Artists: 6
Utilizes: Guest Artists; Guest Directors
Budget: $100,000 - $500,000
Income Sources: Private Foundations/Grants/Endowments; Business/Corporate Donations; Box Office; Government Grants; Individual Donations
Season: September - June   **Annual Attendance:** 6,000
Affiliations: TCG; Johnson City Arts Council; Alternate ROOTS
Performance Facilities: Beeson Hall/Johnson City

Jonesborough

THEATRE

JONESBOROUGH REPERTORY THEATRE
125 1/2 Main Street, Jonesborough, TN 37659
(615) 282-2876
Founded: 1970
Arts Area: Community; Theatrical Group
Status: Non-Professional; Non-Profit
Type: Performing; Resident
Purpose: To bring live theatre to the area
Officers: Mylene Starr, President; Fred Bechelhimer, Treasurer
Volunteer Staff: 12
Non-Paid Artists: 25
Budget: $1,000 - $50,000
Income Sources: Box Office; Individual Donations
Season: April - November   **Annual Attendance:** 4,000
Affiliations: Arts Council

Kingsport

INSTRUMENTAL MUSIC

KINGSPORT SYMPHONY ORCHESTRA
1200 East Center Street, Kingsport, TN 37660
(615) 372-8423
Founded: 1947
Arts Area: Symphony; Orchestra; Chamber; Ensemble; Instrumental Group
Status: Semi-Professional; Non-Professional; Non-Profit
Type: Performing; Resident; Educational; Sponsoring
Purpose: To provide orchestral concerts to the public and educational and entertainment-oriented programs

Management: Mr. David Itkin, Music Director; Barbara Gerwe, General Manager; Mrs. Jolly Hill, Librarian
Officers: Alice Barlow, President; Charles Norrell, First Vice President; Louise Ammons, Second Vice President; Ann Bacon, Secretary; Mrs. Charles Eberhart, Treasurer
Paid Staff: 4   **Volunteer Staff:** 2
Paid Artists: 13   **Non-Paid Artists:** 60
Utilizes: Special Technical Talent; Guest Conductors; Guest Artists
Budget: $100,000 - $500,000
Income Sources: Private Foundations/Grants/Endowments; Business/Corporate Donations; Box Office; Government Grants; Individual Donations
Season: September - May   **Annual Attendance:** 8,500
Affiliations: ASOL; Kingsport Fine Arts Center
Performance Facilities: Eastmen Employee Center

Knoxville

DANCE

THE KNOXVILLE BALLET COMPANY
PO Box 10305, Knoxville, TN 37939-0305
(615) 966-7654
Founded: 1973
Arts Area: Modern; Ballet; Jazz
Status: Semi-Professional; Non-Profit
Type: Educational; Sponsoring
Purpose: To raise the calibre of dance in this area through public performances; to build technically proficient dancers through the use of professional teachers, choreographers, and performers brought in by the company
Management: Irma Witt O'Fallon, Artistic Director
Officers: Samuel A. Shipman, President
Volunteer Staff: 13
Paid Artists: 3   **Non-Paid Artists:** 24
Utilizes: Special Technical Talent; Guest Conductors; Guest Artists; Guest Choreographers
Budget: $1,000 - $50,000
Income Sources: Private Foundations/Grants/Endowments; Business/Corporate Donations; Box Office; Government Grants; Individual Donations
Season: September - May   **Annual Attendance:** 1,500

KNOXVILLE METROPOLITAN DANCE THEATRE
201 Sherway Road, Knoxville, TN 37922
(615) 691-2671
Founded: 1982
Arts Area: Modern; Ballet; Jazz
Status: Non-Professional; Non-Profit
Type: Performing
Purpose: To promote an appreciation of dance in many forms
Management: Sondra Nanney, Administrative Director
Volunteer Staff: 5
Non-Paid Artists: 30
Budget: $1,000 - $50,000
Income Sources: Box Office; Individual Donations
Season: September - May
Affiliations: Tennessee Association of Dance

NEW REPERTORY DANCE COMPANY
Alumni Gym Dance Program, Knoxville, TN 37996
(615) 974-2169
Founded: 1973
Arts Area: Modern; Ballet; Jazz
Status: Semi-Professional
Type: Performing; Educational
Purpose: To train college dancers in the art of performing; to provide quality dance concerts to the university community
Management: Barbara B. Mason, Director
Paid Staff: 4
Utilizes: Special Technical Talent; Guest Artists
Budget: $1,000 - $50,000
Income Sources: Business/Corporate Donations; Box Office; Individual Donations
Season: September - May   **Annual Attendance:** 1,800
Affiliations: University of Tennessee-Knoxville
Performance Facilities: Clarence Brown Theatre

TENNESSEE CHILDREN'S DANCE ENSEMBLE
4216 Sutherland Avenue, Knoxville, TN 37919
(615) 588-8842
> **Founded:** 1981
> **Arts Area:** Modern
> **Status:** Professional; Non-Profit
> **Type:** Performing; Touring; Resident; Educational
> **Purpose:** To perform professionally using the medium of modern dance and, in so doing, show that children can achieve the same artistic excellence as a professional adult company
> **Management:** Judy Robinson, Administrative Coordinator
> **Officers:** Laura Kress, President; Fran Shea, Vice President; Deborah Wallace, Secretary; Louise Josephson, Treasurer
> **Paid Staff:** 4   **Volunteer Staff:** 24
> **Paid Artists:** 26
> **Utilizes:** Special Technical Talent; Guest Artists; Guest Choreographers
> **Budget:** $100,000 - $500,000
> **Income Sources:** Private Foundations/Grants/Endowments; Business/Corporate Donations; Box Office; Government Grants; Individual Donations
> **Season:** 52 Weeks   **Annual Attendance:** 200,000
> **Performance Facilities:** Concert Stage

INSTRUMENTAL MUSIC

KNOXVILLE SYMPHONY ORCHESTRA
708 Gay Street, Knoxville, TN 37902
(615) 523-1178
FAX: (615) 546-3766
> **Founded:** 1935
> **Arts Area:** Symphony; Orchestra
> **Status:** Professional; Non-Profit
> **Type:** Performing; Touring; Educational
> **Purpose:** To maintain a symphony orchestra for the entertainment and education of the east Tennessee region
> **Management:** Constance Harrison, Executive Director; Martha Weaver, Director of Development
> **Officers:** Jame L. Clayton, President; Mrs. E.E. Duncan, Vice President
> **Paid Staff:** 9
> **Paid Artists:** 85
> **Utilizes:** Guest Conductors; Guest Artists
> **Budget:** $1,000,000 - $5,000,000
> **Income Sources:** Private Foundations/Grants/Endowments; Business/Corporate Donations; Box Office; Government Grants; Individual Donations
> **Season:** September - May   **Annual Attendance:** 50,000
> **Performance Facilities:** Tennessee Theatre

KNOXVILLE SYMPHONY YOUTH ORCHESTRA
708 Gay Street, Knoxville, TN 37902
(615) 523-1178
> **Founded:** 1974
> **Arts Area:** Symphony; Orchestra
> **Status:** Non-Professional; Non-Profit
> **Type:** Performing; Educational
> **Purpose:** To give young people a chance to learn symphonic music, to rehearse in an organized setting and to perform in a symphony orchestra
> **Management:** Barbara Adamick, Manager; Sande MacMorran, Music Director/Conductor
> **Paid Staff:** 1   **Volunteer Staff:** 3
> **Non-Paid Artists:** 60
> **Budget:** $1,000 - $50,000
> **Income Sources:** Box Office; Individual Donations
> **Season:** September - April   **Annual Attendance:** 1,000
> **Affiliations:** ASOL (Youth Orchestra Division); Knoxville Symphony
> **Performance Facilities:** University of Tennessee Music Hall

VOCAL MUSIC

KNOXVILLE OPERA COMPANY
602 South Gay Street, Suite 700, Knoxville, TN 37902
(615) 524-0795
> **Founded:** 1976
> **Arts Area:** Grand Opera; Lyric Opera; Light Opera; Musical Theatre
> **Status:** Professional; Non-Profit

Type: Performing; Sponsoring
Purpose: To produce opera and musical theatre performances on with current standards; to provide performance opportunities for developing American artists; to develop an appreciation for the art form through a program of opera education
Management: Robert Lyall, General Director; Ann Broadhead, Business Manager; Don Townsend, Production Manager
Officers: Joseph De Leese, President; Sammie Lynn Puett, President-Elect; Fuad Mishu, Secretary; Ruth Love, Treasurer
Paid Staff: 6
Paid Artists: 150   **Non-Paid Artists:** 160
Utilizes: Special Technical Talent; Guest Artists; Guest Directors
Budget: $500,000 - $1,000,000
Income Sources: Private Foundations/Grants/Endowments; Business/Corporate Donations; Box Office; Government Grants; Individual Donations
Season: 52 Weeks   **Annual Attendance:** 15,000
Affiliations: OA
Performance Facilities: Civic Auditorium

THEATRE

CARPET BAG THEATRE
3018 East Fifth Avenue, Knoxville, TN 37914
(615) 522-2801
Founded: 1970
Arts Area: Professional
Status: Professional; Non-Profit
Type: Touring
Purpose: Dedicated to the production of new work, the ensemble creates new scripts through improvisation and collaboration. CBT is comprised of writers, actors, dancers, musicians and is known for its performances, workshops and other activities.
Management: Linda Parris-Bailey, Executive Director/Producer; Jeff Cody, Business Director/Technical Director
Paid Staff: 1   **Volunteer Staff:** 3
Paid Artists: 5
Utilizes: Special Technical Talent; Guest Artists; Guest Directors
Budget: $1,000 - $50,000
Income Sources: Government Grants; Individual Donations
Season: September - February; November-June   **Annual Attendance:** 150,000
Affiliations: Alternate ROOTS; Black Theatre Alliance

CLARENCE BROWN THEATRE COMPANY
University of Tennessee, 1714 Andy Holt Avenue, PO Box 8450, Knoxville, TN 37996
(615) 974-3447
Founded: 1974
Arts Area: Professional; Theatrical Group
Status: Professional; Non-Profit
Type: Performing; Touring; Resident
Management: Margaret Ferguson, General Manager; Dennis E. Perkins, Company Manager
Paid Staff: 18
Paid Artists: 35
Utilizes: Guest Artists; Guest Directors
Budget: $100,000 - $500,000
Income Sources: Business/Corporate Donations; Box Office; Individual Donations
Season: October - April   **Annual Attendance:** 20,000
Affiliations: LORT; TCG; Knoxville Arts Council; University of Tennessee
Performance Facilities: Clarence Brown Theatre

THEATER KNOXVILLE
c/o The Bijou Theater, PO Box 1746, Knoxville, TN 37901
(615) 523-4211
Founded: 1976
Arts Area: Community
Status: Non-Professional; Non-Profit
Type: Performing; Touring; Educational
Purpose: To provide quality shows using actors and technical persons from the community
Officers: Rusty Young, President; Gerry Diftler, Vice President; Debbie Feldman, Secretary; Wendie Wilson, Treasurer
Volunteer Staff: 15
Utilizes: Special Technical Talent
Budget: $1,000 - $50,000
Income Sources: Private Foundations/Grants/Endowments; Box Office; Individual Donations
Season: September - August   **Annual Attendance:** 6,000
Performance Facilities: The Bijou Theater

PERFORMING SERIES

THE ARTS COUNCIL OF GREATER KNOXVILLE
PO Box 2506, Knoxville, TN 37901
(615) 523-7543
FAX: (615) 523-7312
Founded: 1976
Arts Area: Festivals
Status: Non-Profit
Type: Educational
Purpose: To promote the importance of a rich cultural life to the vitality and economic well-being of the Knoxville region; this is accomplished through public advocacy, programs and the support of the cultural institution
Management: Sandy Garber, Executive Director
Officers: Jerry Becker, President; Mary Lynn Majors, President Elect/Vice President; Donald Wright, Treasurer; Linda Underwood, Secretary; Bill Hays, Vice President Special Projects; Katherine Bell, Vice President Community Service
Paid Staff: 7   **Volunteer Staff:** 3
Budget: $100,000 - $500,000
Income Sources: Private Foundations/Grants/Endowments; Business/Corporate Donations; Box Office; Government Grants; Individual Donations; Fundraising

FACILITY

BIJOU THEATRE CENTER
803 South Gay Street, Knoxville, TN 37901
(615) 523-4211
FAX: (615) 524-0821
Founded: 1980
Type of Facility: Theatre House
Facility Originally: Vaudeville
Type of Stage: Proscenium
Stage Dimensions: 35'x30'
Seating Capacity: 750
Year Built: 1908
Year Remodeled: 1980
Contact for Rental: Stephen F. Krempasky;   (615) 523-4211
Resident Groups: Knoxsville Chamber Orchestra; Appalachian Ballet; Young Pianist Series

KNOXVILLE CIVIC AUDITORIUM AND COLISEUM - AUDITORIUM
500 East Church Avenue, Knoxville, TN 37901
(615) 544-5399
FAX: (615) 544-5386
Type of Facility: Auditorium
Type of Stage: Proscenium
Stage Dimensions: 108'Wx54'D; 60'Wx27'H proscenium opening   **Orchestra Pit**
Seating Capacity: 2,534
Year Built: 1961   **Architect:** McCarty Holsaple   **Cost:** $5,400,000
Year Remodeled: 1987   **Architect:** McCarty Holsaple   **Cost:** $1,500,000
Contact for Rental: Paul C. Sherbakoff, Manager;   (615) 544-5399
Manager: Paul C. Sherbakoff;   (615) 544-5399

TENNESSEE THEATER
604 South Gay Street, Knoxville, TN 37902
(615) 525-2250
FAX: (615) 523-3954
Type of Facility: Performance Center; Theatre House; Opera House
Type of Stage: Proscenium
Stage Dimensions: 54'Dx26'H   **Orchestra Pit**
Seating Capacity: 1,515
Year Built: 1928   **Architect:** Graven & Mayger   **Cost:** $1,200,000
Year Remodeled: 1982   **Architect:** Ron Childrif & Associates   **Cost:** $1,500,000
Acoustical Consultant: Coffeen & Associates
Contact for Rental: Robert Frost;   (615) 525-2250

UNIVERSITY OF TENNESSEE MUSIC HALL
1741 Volunteer Boulevard, Knoxville, TN 37996-2600
(615) 974-5110
Founded: 1965
Type of Facility: Concert Hall; Auditorium; Multi-Purpose

Type of Stage: Proscenium
Stage Dimensions: 43'x33'   **Orchestra Pit**
Seating Capacity: 573
Year Built: 1965
Architect: Barber & McMurray
Contact for Rental: W. Harvey Smeltzer;   (615) 974-5110
Resident Groups: Knoxville Symphony Orchestra; Knoxville Opera Company
The Tennessee Theater is on the National Register of Historic Places.

Lebanon

FACILITY

CUMBERLAND UNIVERSITY AUDITORIUM
South Greenwood Street, Lebanon, TN 37087
(615) 444-2562
FAX: (615) 444-2569
Type of Facility: Auditorium
Year Built: 1920
Architect: Beaty Gresham
Manager: Mike Wiggington

Maryville

DANCE

APPALACHIAN BALLET COMPANY
215 West Broadway, Maryville, TN 37801
(615) 982-8463
Founded: 1972
Arts Area: Ballet
Status: Semi-Professional; Non-Profit
Type: Performing; Touring; Resident; Educational
Purpose: To promote excellence in dance
Management: Cheryl Van Metre, Artistic Director; Katharine Dorner, Company Manager
Officers: Aleta Ledendecker, Chairman; Greg Walters, Vice Chairman; Jane Tolhurst, Fundraising Chairman;
Tanya Prine, Special Events Chairman
Paid Staff: 7
Paid Artists: 6   **Non-Paid Artists:** 32
Utilizes: Special Technical Talent; Guest Artists
Budget: $50,000 - $100,000
Income Sources: Private Foundations/Grants/Endowments; Business/Corporate Donations; Box Office; Government
Grants; Individual Donations
Season: September - May   **Annual Attendance:** 20,000
Performance Facilities: Knoxville Civic Auditorium; Tennessee Theater

FACILITY

MARYVILLE COLLEGE
Maryville, TN 37801
(615) 981-8000
FAX: (615) 983-0581
Type of Facility: Concert Hall; Auditorium; Theatre House
Type of Stage: Thrust; Proscenium; Platform   **Orchestra Pit**
Seating Capacity: Auditorium - 1,200; Theatre - 450; Recital Hall - 250
Year Built: 1950   **Architect:** Schweiken and Elting
Year Remodeled: 1956
Contact for Rental: Office of Conferences and Special Programs;   (615) 981-8117
Resident Groups: Maryville College: Community Wind Ensemble; Community Chorus; Theatre; Concert Choir; Jazz
Band; Maryville-Alcoa College Community Orchestra

Memphis

INSTRUMENTAL MUSIC

MEMPHIS SYMPHONY
3100 Walnut Grove Road, Suite 501, Memphis, TN 38111
(901) 324-3627
FAX: (901) 324-3698
  Founded: 1952
  Arts Area: Symphony; Orchestra; Chamber
  Status: Professional; Non-Profit
  Type: Performing; Educational; Sponsoring
  Management: Alan Balter, Music Director/Conductor; Michael Maxwell, Executive Director; Mark Salvage,
  Director of Operations; Ron Jewell, Marketing Director
  Paid Staff: 14
  Paid Artists: 80
  Utilizes: Guest Conductors; Guest Artists
  Budget: $1,000,000 - $5,000,000
  Income Sources: Private Foundations/Grants/Endowments; Business/Corporate Donations; Box Office; Government
  Grants; Individual Donations
  Season: October - May   **Annual Attendance:** 300,000
  Affiliations: ASOL; Memphis Arts Council
  Performance Facilities: Vincent deFrank Hall, Memphis Convention Center Complex

MEMPHIS YOUTH SYMPHONY ORCHESTRA
3100 Walnut Grove Road, Suite 402, Memphis, TN 38111
(901) 324-3627
  Arts Area: Symphony; Orchestra
  Status: Non-Professional; Non-Profit
  Type: Performing; Educational
  Management: Rita Garrigan, Manager
  Non-Paid Artists: 60
  Income Sources: Business/Corporate Donations; Box Office; Government Grants; Individual Donations
  Season: October - May
  Affiliations: ASOL (Youth Orchestra Division)
  Performance Facilities: Harding Academy; Ridgeway High School

ROSCOE'S SURPRISE ORCHESTRA
PO Box 41824, Memphis, TN 38174
(901) 725-4147
  Founded: 1981
  Arts Area: Orchestra; Chamber; Ensemble; Ethnic; Instrumental Group; Electronic & Live Electronic
  Status: Professional; Non-Profit
  Type: Performing; Touring; Educational; Sponsoring
  Purpose: To perform and promote music of the 20th century and, whenever possible, the music of living composers and
  produce concerts
  Management: John Boatner, Executive Director
  Officers: Karin English, Chairman; Floyd Deal, Secretary; Alfred Rudd, Treasurer
  Paid Staff: 1   **Volunteer Staff:** 5
  Paid Artists: 95
  Utilizes: Special Technical Talent; Guest Conductors; Guest Artists; Guest Directors
  Budget: $1,000 - $50,000
  Income Sources: Private Foundations/Grants/Endowments; Business/Corporate Donations; Box Office; Government
  Grants; Individual Donations
  Season: 52 Weeks   **Annual Attendance:** 2,095
  Affiliations: Memphis Arts Council; CMA

VOCAL MUSIC

THE GARY BEARD CHORALE
40 East Parkway South, Memphis, TN 38104
(901) 458-1652
FAX: (901) 458-0145
  Arts Area: Grand Opera; Lyric Opera; Operetta; Choral
  Status: Professional
  Type: Performing; Touring; Resident
  Purpose: To return the professional chorale to prominence, excelling in the great choral literature and quality performances
  Officers: Gary Beard, Director/Conductor; Chris Nemec, Associate Director/Conductor/Accompanist

Paid Staff: 2
Paid Artists: 23
Utilizes: Guest Artists
Budget: $1,000 - $50,000
Income Sources: Private Foundations/Grants/Endowments; Box Office; Individual Donations
Season: 52 Weeks **Annual Attendance:** 30,000
Affiliations: Community Concerts
Performance Facilities: Lindenwood Christian Church Sanctuary

OPERA MEMPHIS
Memphis State University, South Campus, Memphis, TN 38152
(901) 678-2706
FAX: (901) 678-3506
Founded: 1956
Arts Area: Grand Opera; Music; Theatre
Status: Professional; Non-Profit
Type: Performing; Touring
Purpose: To present high-quality opera performances for regional audiences
Management: Robert Driver, General/Artistic Director; Bert Adler-Wolss, Executive Director; Michael Ching, Artistic Director
Officers: Willis H. Willie, Chairman, Board of Trustees; James P. Gates, First Vice President; Hugh M. Stephens Jr., Treasurer; Martin H. Hawssenberg, Secretary; Sheila Zancor, Opera Guild President
Paid Staff: 8
Utilizes: Special Technical Talent; Guest Artists; Guest Directors
Budget: $500,000 - $1,000,000
Income Sources: Private Foundations/Grants/Endowments; Business/Corporate Donations; Box Office; Government Grants; Individual Donations
Season: October - February **Annual Attendance:** 37,000
Affiliations: OA; COS; AAA; Tennesseans for the Arts
Performance Facilities: Orpheum Theatre

THEATRE

CIRCUIT PLAYHOUSE
51 South Cooper, Memphis, TN 38104
(901) 725-0776
FAX: (901) 272-7530
Founded: 1969
Arts Area: Professional; Theatrical Group
Status: Professional
Type: Performing; Resident
Purpose: To produce live theatrical productions in a two-theater complex, as well as new plays, off-Broadway and Broadway offerings
Management: Jackie Nichols, Executive Director; Elizabeth Howard, Administrative Director; Kay Zimmerman, Artistic Director; Chuck Britt, Technical Director
Officers: William Clark, President; Nino Shipp, Past President/First Vice President; Gene Katz, Second Vice President; David Williams, Secretary; Pat Bogan, Treasurer
Paid Staff: 20 **Volunteer Staff:** 6
Paid Artists: 15 **Non-Paid Artists:** 80
Utilizes: Special Technical Talent; Guest Artists; Guest Directors
Budget: $100,000 - $500,000
Income Sources: Private Foundations/Grants/Endowments; Business/Corporate Donations; Box Office; Government Grants; Individual Donations
Season: 52 Weeks **Annual Attendance:** 40,000
Affiliations: SETC; TCG; Tennessee Theatre Association; Playhouse on the Square
Performance Facilities: Circuit Playhouse

MEMPHIS CHILDREN'S THEATRE
2599 Avery Avenue, Memphis, TN 38112
(901) 452-3968
Founded: 1948
Arts Area: Community
Status: Non-Profit
Type: Performing; Educational
Purpose: Memphis Children's Theatre uses children, ages 5-18, and involves them in all aspects of theatre
Management: Lisa M. Sikes, Theatre Director; Ken Lightfoot, Theatre Coordinator
Officers: Brian Ford, Chairman of Support Group; Ashley Bugg, Children Committee President
Paid Staff: 5 **Volunteer Staff:** 27
Paid Artists: 7 **Non-Paid Artists:** 6

Utilizes: Special Technical Talent; Guest Artists; Guest Directors
Budget: $100,000 - $500,000
Income Sources: Private Foundations/Grants/Endowments; Business/Corporate Donations; Government Grants; Individual Donations
Season: 52 Weeks   **Annual Attendance:** 10,000
Affiliations: American Children's Theatre Association; Tennessee Theatre Association; Southeastern Theatre Conference

PLAYHOUSE ON THE SQUARE
51 South Cooper Street, Memphis, TN 38104
(901) 725-0776
Founded: 1968
Arts Area: Professional; Theatrical Group
Status: Professional; Non-Profit
Type: Performing; Touring; Resident; Educational
Purpose: To produce live theatrical productions in a two-theatre complex, as well as new plays, off-Broadway and Broadway productions
Management: Jackie Nichols, Executive Director; Elizabeth Howard, Administrative Director; Patty McNaulty, Public Relations Director
Officers: William Clark, President; Randall Reagan, Vice President; Pat Bogan, Secretary; Gene Katz, Treasurer
Paid Staff: 10   **Volunteer Staff:** 6
Paid Artists: 12
Utilizes: Special Technical Talent; Guest Artists; Guest Directors
Income Sources: Private Foundations/Grants/Endowments; Business/Corporate Donations; Box Office; Government Grants; Individual Donations
Season: September - July
Affiliations: TCG; Circuit Playhouse
Performance Facilities: Playhouse On The Square

THEATRE MEMPHIS
630 Perkins Extended, Memphis, TN 38117-4799
(901) 682-8323
Mailing: PO Box 240117, Memphis, TN 38124
Founded: 1919
Arts Area: Community; Theatrical Group
Status: Non-Professional; Non-Profit
Type: Performing
Purpose: To provide interested persons with the opportunity to see theatrical productions and provide the opportunity to act in and/or assist with the production of plays
Management: Brad Watson, Director of Marketing; Diane M. Jahnke, Subscription and Ticketing Director; Dr. Jim Seemann, Scenic Designer/Production Manager
Officers: Sherwood Lohrey, President; Jim Cairns, General Manager
Paid Staff: 14   **Volunteer Staff:** 500
Paid Artists: 5   **Non-Paid Artists:** 200
Utilizes: Guest Artists; Guest Directors
Budget: $500,000 - $1,000,000
Income Sources: Private Foundations/Grants/Endowments; Business/Corporate Donations; Box Office; Government Grants; Individual Donations
Season: September - June   **Annual Attendance:** 80,000
Affiliations: ACT; SETC; Tennessee Theatre Association; Memphis Arts Council; Tennessee Arts Commission
Performance Facilities: Theatre Memphis

PERFORMING SERIES

MEMPHIS IN MAY INTERNATIONAL FESTIVAL
245 Wagner Place, Suite 220, Memphis, TN 38103
(901) 525-4611
Founded: 1976
Arts Area: Dance; Vocal Music; Instrumental Music; Theater; Festivals
Status: Non-Profit
Type: Educational; Sponsoring
Management: Cynthia Ham, Executive Director; Davis Tillman, Artistic Director; Deanie Parker, Marketing Director
Officers: Harry Miller, President; Joyce Blackmon, President-Elect; Tom Jones, Secretary; John Presley, Treasurer
Paid Staff: 12   **Volunteer Staff:** 2,200
Utilizes: Guest Artists
Budget: $1,000,000 - $5,000,000
Income Sources: Business/Corporate Donations; Box Office; Government Grants; Individual Donations
Season: May - June   **Annual Attendance:** 1,000,000

FACILITY

MEMPHIS CHILDREN'S THEATRE
2599 Avery Avenue, Memphis, TN 38112
(901) 452-3968
> **Type of Facility:** Theatre House
> **Type of Stage:** Proscenium
> **Seating Capacity:** 200
> **Year Built:** 1982   **Architect:** Awsumb Waye Watson   **Cost:** $250,000
> **Acoustical Consultant:** Gott
> **Contact for Rental:** Lisa Sikes;   (901) 452-3968

MEMPHIS COOK CONVENTION CENTER COMPLEX
255 North Main Street, Memphis, TN 38103
(901) 576-1200
FAX: (901) 576-1212
> **Type of Facility:** Auditorium; Civic Center
> **Year Built:** 1924   **Architect:** George Awsumb   **Cost:** $800,000
> **Year Remodeled:** 1958   **Architect:** Haglund & Venable   **Cost:** $4,500,000
> **Contact for Rental:** Betty Ball;   (901) 576-1200
> **Manager:** David E. Greer
> **Resident Groups:** Memphis Orchestral Society; Memphis Symphony Orchestra; Beethoven Club
> *Memphis Convention Center Complex contains Dixon-Myers Hall and Vincent DeFrank Hall. See separate listings for further information.*

MEMPHIS COOK CONVENTION CENTER COMPLEX - DIXON-MYERS HALL
255 North Main Street, Memphis, TN 38103
(901) 576-1200
> **Type of Facility:** Auditorium
> **Type of Stage:** Proscenium; Hydraulic Lift Stage
> **Stage Dimensions:** 72'9"Wx32'D; add 8'D with pit at stage level   **Orchestra Pit**
> **Seating Capacity:** 4,361
> **Year Remodeled:** 1974   **Architect:** Haglund & Venable
> **Contact for Rental:** Betty Ball;   (901) 576-1200
> **Manager:** David E. Greer
> *Shares stage with Vincent DeFrank Hall, spaces cannot be used concurrently*

MEMPHIS COOK CONVENTION CENTER COMPLEX - VINCENT DEFRANK HALL
255 North Main Street, Memphis, TN 38103
(901) 576-1200
> **Type of Facility:** Concert Hall
> **Type of Stage:** Proscenium
> **Stage Dimensions:** 69'Wx32'Hx32'D   **Orchestra Pit**
> **Seating Capacity:** 2,424
> **Year Remodeled:** 1974   **Architect:** Haglund & Venable
> **Contact for Rental:** Betty Ball;   (901) 576-1200
> **Manager:** David E. Greer
> *Shares stage with Dixon-Meyers Hall, spaces cannot be used concurrently*

ORPHEUM THEATRE
203 South Main Street, PO Box 3370, Memphis, TN 38173
(901) 525-7800
FAX: (901) 526-0829
> **Founded:** 1928
> **Type of Facility:** Concert Hall; Performance Center; Off Broadway; Theatre House; Opera House
> **Facility Originally:** Vaudeville
> **Type of Stage:** Proscenium   **Orchestra Pit**
> **Seating Capacity:** 2,300
> **Year Built:** 1928   **Architect:** Rapp & Rapp   **Cost:** $1,600,000
> **Year Remodeled:** 1982   **Architect:** Awsumb & Williamson   **Cost:** $4,500,000
> **Contact for Rental:** Donna Darwin;   (901) 525-7800
> **Resident Groups:** Opera Memphis; Memphis Concert Band

THEATRE MEMPHIS
630 Perkins Extended, Memphis, TN 38117-4799
(901) 682-8323
FAX: (901) 763-4096
> **Type of Facility:** Studio Performance; Theatre House

Type of Stage: Flexible; Proscenium
Stage Dimensions: Mainstage - 65'x50'x25'   **Orchestra Pit**
Seating Capacity: Mainstage - 435; Little Theatre - 100
Year Built: 1975   **Architect:** Wells Awsumb   **Cost:** $1,500,000
Acoustical Consultant: Bolt, Beranek & Newman
Contact for Rental: James Cairns;   (901) 682-8323
Resident Groups: Show Wagon Troop
Theatrical performances; meetings; shows

Milligan College

FACILITY

MILLIGAN COLLEGE - DERTHICK THEATRE
Milligan College, TN 37682
(615) 461-8705
Type of Facility: Theatre House
Type of Stage: Thrust; Proscenium
Seating Capacity: 150
Year Remodeled: 1975
Contact for Rental: (615) 461-8705

MILLIGAN COLLEGE - SEEGER CHAPEL CONCERT HALL
Milligan College, TN 37682
(615) 929-0116
Type of Facility: Concert Hall
Type of Stage: Proscenium
Stage Dimensions: 25'x50'x30'   **Orchestra Pit**
Seating Capacity: 1,196
Year Built: 1966   **Architect:** E. Rawls   **Cost:** $1,800,000
Contact for Rental: Ruth Loving;   (615) 561-8720
Resident Groups: Milligan College Concert Choir; Milligan College Chorale; Milligan College Chamber Singers

Morristown

THEATRE

MORRISTOWN THEATRE GUILD
314 South Hill Street, Morristown, TN 37814
(615) 586-9260
Founded: 1934
Arts Area: Musical; Dinner; Community
Status: Non-Professional; Non-Profit
Type: Performing; Educational
Purpose: Exposure to and participation in live theatre; educational training for school-age children
Management: David Horton, Artistic Director
Officers: Linda Dietrich, Chairman; Randy Turner, Vice Chairman; Sue Carey, Secretary; George Haggard, Treasurer
Paid Staff: 1   **Volunteer Staff:** 30
Non-Paid Artists: 50
Budget: $1,000 - $50,000
Income Sources: Business/Corporate Donations; Box Office; Individual Donations
Season: September - May   **Annual Attendance:** 3,000
Affiliations: Tennessee Theatre Association
Performance Facilities: Theatre Guild

FACILITY

THEATRE GUILD
314 South Hill Street, Morristown, TN 37814
(615) 586-9260
Type of Facility: Theatre House
Facility Originally: Church
Type of Stage: Thrust
Stage Dimensions: 40'x140'
Seating Capacity: 125
Year Built: 1881

Year Remodeled: 1981   Cost: $6,000
Contact for Rental: Linda Dietrich, Chairman;   (615) 587-2164

Nashville

DANCE

NASHVILLE BALLET
2976 Sidco Drive, Nashville, TN 37204-3715
(615) 244-7233
FAX: (615) 242-1741
Founded: 1986
Arts Area: Ballet
Status: Professional; Non-Profit
Type: Performing; Touring; Educational
Purpose: To present both classical and modern ballet in a manner that entertains and educates our audiences; to foster a love of dance in the community through education of both pre-professionals and the general audience
Management: Edward Myers, Artistic Director; Terrance L. Demas, Managing Director; Jane Fabian, School Administrator
Officers: Dudley Richter, President; Elizabeth Nichols, Vice President; Don Shriver, Treasurer; John Stein, Secretary
Paid Staff: 14
Paid Artists: 28   **Non-Paid Artists:** 8
Utilizes: Special Technical Talent; Guest Conductors; Guest Choreographers; Composers; Designers; Educators
Budget: $1,000,000 - $5,000,000
Income Sources: Private Foundations/Grants/Endowments; Business/Corporate Donations; Box Office; Government Grants; Individual Donations; Concessions; Touring; Video
Season: September - June   **Annual Attendance:** 18,322
Performance Facilities: Tennessee Performing Arts Center

NASHVILLE CONTEMPORARY BALLET COMPANY
PO Box 50580, Nashville, TN 37205
(615) 352-8078
Founded: 1984
Arts Area: Ballet; Jazz
Status: Semi-Professional; Non-Profit
Type: Performing
Purpose: To provide a performing outlet for Middle Tennessee young people/artists with professional/ semi-professional quality
Management: Jan Brooks, Artistic Director
Officers: Wanda Lenk Walters, President; Michael Childers, Daryle Tallent, Treasurers; Marci Fairhead, Secretary
Paid Staff: 1   **Volunteer Staff:** 3
Non-Paid Artists: 12
Utilizes: Guest Artists
Budget: $1,000 - $50,000
Income Sources: Private Foundations/Grants/Endowments; Business/Corporate Donations; Government Grants; Individual Donations
Season: September - July   **Annual Attendance:** 2,000
Affiliations: Dance Alliance

TENNESSEE DANCE THEATRE
PO Box 121884, Nashville, TN 37212
(615) 255-9533; (615) 248-3262
Founded: 1983
Arts Area: Modern
Status: Professional; Non-Profit
Type: Performing; Touring; Resident
Purpose: To cultivate, promote, foster and develop the love, understanding and appreciation of the art of dance in Tennessee
Management: Linda Mason, Executive Director; Susan Sanders, Managing Director
Officers: Lind Mason, President; Suzanne Shambaugh, Secretary
Paid Staff: 1   **Volunteer Staff:** 2
Paid Artists: 6
Utilizes: Special Technical Talent; Guest Artists
Budget: $100,000 - $500,000
Income Sources: Private Foundations/Grants/Endowments; Business/Corporate Donations; Box Office; Government Grants; Individual Donations

Season: October - June   **Annual Attendance:** 4,000
Affiliations: Metro Division of Parks and Recreation

INSTRUMENTAL MUSIC

NASHVILLE SYMPHONY ASSOCIATION
208 23rd Avenue North, Nashville, TN 37203
(615) 329-3033
FAX: (615) 329-2304
> **Founded:** 1946
> **Arts Area:** Symphony; Orchestra; Chamber
> **Status:** Professional
> **Type:** Performing
> **Purpose:** Dedicated to enhancing the quality of life in Nashville and the surrounding communities by providing opportunities for all citizens to enjoy live performances of symphonic music in its various forms
> **Management:** Steven Greil, Executive Director; Beth Zeitlin, Director of Public Relations; Laura Lonergan, Controller/Financial Director; Kim Carpenter, Director of Development
> **Officers:** Susan R. Russell, Chairman; Larry Larkin, Vice Chairman; Mary Neil Price, Secretary; Bill Hawkins, Treasurer
> **Paid Staff:** 28
> **Paid Artists:** 82
> **Utilizes:** Special Technical Talent; Guest Conductors; Guest Artists
> **Budget:** $1,000,000 - $5,000,000
> **Income Sources:** Private Foundations/Grants/Endowments; Business/Corporate Donations; Box Office; Government Grants; Individual Donations
> **Season:** September - August   **Annual Attendance:** 250,000
> **Affiliations:** ASOL; AAA; ASCAP; BMI
> **Performance Facilities:** Tennessee Performing Arts Center; War Memorial Auditorium

NASHVILLE YOUTH SYMPHONY
2400 Blakemore Avenue, Nashville, TN 37212
(615) 322-7651
> **Founded:** 1947
> **Arts Area:** Symphony; Orchestra
> **Status:** Non-Professional; Non-Profit
> **Type:** Performing; Touring; Educational; Sponsoring
> **Management:** Emelyne Bingham, Manager/Conductor
> **Paid Staff:** 4   **Volunteer Staff:** 20
> **Non-Paid Artists:** 160
> **Utilizes:** Guest Artists
> **Budget:** $50,000 - $100,000
> **Income Sources:** Private Foundations/Grants/Endowments; Box Office; Individual Donations
> **Season:** August - May   **Annual Attendance:** 2,500
> **Affiliations:** ASOL (Youth Orchestra Division)
> **Performance Facilities:** War Memorial Auditorium; Cohn High School Auditorium; Blair School of Music Recital Hall

VOCAL MUSIC

NASHVILLE OPERA
1900 Belmont Boulevard, Fidelity Hall 402, Nashville, TN 37212
(615) 292-5710
FAX: (615) 292-0549
> **Founded:** 1981
> **Arts Area:** Grand Opera; Lyric Opera; Light Opera
> **Status:** Professional; Non-Profit
> **Type:** Performing; Educational
> **Purpose:** To present operatic productions to middle Tennesseans
> **Management:** Kyle Ridout, General Director; Leanne Porter, Executive Assistant
> **Paid Staff:** 2   **Volunteer Staff:** 10
> **Paid Artists:** 120
> **Utilizes:** Special Technical Talent; Guest Conductors; Guest Artists; Guest Directors
> **Budget:** $500,000 - $1,000,000
> **Income Sources:** Private Foundations/Grants/Endowments; Business/Corporate Donations; Box Office; Government Grants; Individual Donations
> **Season:** 52 Weeks   **Annual Attendance:** 7,500
> **Affiliations:** OA
> **Performance Facilities:** Tennessee Performing Arts Center

THEATRE

ACTORS PLAYHOUSE OF NASHVILLE
2318 West End Avenue, Nashville, TN 37203
(615) 327-0049
>**Arts Area:** Professional; Theatrical Group
>**Status:** Semi-Professional; Non-Profit
>**Type:** Performing
>**Purpose:** Specializes in off-Broadway plays to contemporary playwrights to present plays not routinely seen in the Nashville area
>**Management:** Dennis Ewing, Artistic Director/Co-Founder; Janet Claire, Producing Director/Co-Founder
>**Officers:** Janet Claire, President of Board; Dennis Ewing, Vice President of Board
>**Paid Staff:** 4
>**Utilizes:** Special Technical Talent; Guest Directors
>**Budget:** $1,000 - $50,000
>**Income Sources:** Box Office
>**Season:** 52 Weeks   **Annual Attendance:** 10,000
>**Performance Facilities:** Actors Playhouse of Nashville

CHAFFIN'S BARN - A DINNER THEATRE
8204 Highway 100, Nashville, TN 37221
(615) 646-9977
>**Founded:** 1967
>**Arts Area:** Professional; Musical; Dinner
>**Status:** Professional
>**Type:** Performing
>**Purpose:** Package price for buffet dining and professional theatre productions produced by staff directors utilizing professional, non-equity performers
>**Management:** John P. Chaffin and Dianne Chaffin, Managers
>**Officers:** John P. Chaffin, President; Dianne Chaffin, Secretary
>**Paid Staff:** 15
>**Paid Artists:** 120
>**Utilizes:** Guest Directors
>**Budget:** $100,000 - $500,000
>**Income Sources:** Box Office
>**Season:** 52 Weeks   **Annual Attendance:** 32,000
>**Performance Facilities:** Chaffin's Barn

NASHVILLE ACADEMY THEATRE
724 Second Avenue South, Nashville, TN 37210
(615) 254-9103
>**Founded:** 1931
>**Arts Area:** Professional; Theatrical Group
>**Status:** Professional; Non-Profit
>**Type:** Performing; Resident; Educational
>**Purpose:** To contribute to the cultural development of young people by providing them with the finest in professional theatre for young audiences
>**Management:** Scot Copeland, Artistic Director; Jean Johnson, Financial Administration
>**Officers:** Dr. Helen Brown, Chair; Dorothy Wright, Vice Chair; Beth Alexander, Secretary; Mary Jones, Treasurer; John Lehman, Chair-Elect
>**Paid Staff:** 9   **Volunteer Staff:** 30
>**Paid Artists:** 24
>**Utilizes:** Special Technical Talent; Guest Artists; Guest Directors
>**Budget:** $100,000 - $500,000
>**Income Sources:** Private Foundations/Grants/Endowments; Business/Corporate Donations; Box Office; Government Grants; Individual Donations
>**Season:** September - May   **Annual Attendance:** 72,050

TENNESSEE REPERTORY THEATRE
427 Chestnut Street, Nashville, TN 37203
(615) 244-4878
FAX: (615) 244-1232
>**Founded:** 1985
>**Arts Area:** Professional; Theatrical Group
>**Status:** Professional
>**Type:** Performing; Resident
>**Purpose:** To present quality, professional theatre in a full season of plays as a resident company at the Tennessee Performing Arts Center

Management: Brian J. Laczko, Managing Director; Mac Pirkle, Artistic Director; Jennifer Orth, Company Manager; Edie Crane, Director of Public Relations/Marketing; Sherry R. Ridlon, Director of Audience Development; Don Jones, Associate Artistic Director; Donna J. Gillroy, Director of Development
Officers: Nicky Weaver, President, Board of Trustees; John O. Bovender Jr., President-Elect; Mac Pirkle, Trustee
Paid Staff: 5   **Volunteer Staff:** 12
Utilizes: Guest Conductors; Guest Artists; Guest Directors
Budget: $1,000,000 - $5,000,000
Income Sources: Private Foundations/Grants/Endowments; Business/Corporate Donations; Box Office; Government Grants; Individual Donations
Season: October - June   **Annual Attendance:** 35,000
Affiliations: AEA; LORT
Performance Facilities: James K. Polk Theater, Tennessee Performing Arts Center

WEST END DRAMA MINISTRIES
2200 West End Avenue, Nashville, TN 37203
(615) 321-8500
Founded: 1976
Arts Area: Theatrical Group
Status: Non-Profit
Type: Resident; Educational
Purpose: To develop community through dramatic projects that not only enhance performance skills but tell the Gospel through dramatic media
Management: Ken Nelson, Chairman; Alice Swason, Assistant Director; Don Marler, Director of Music
Paid Staff: 1   **Volunteer Staff:** 30
Paid Artists: 4   **Non-Paid Artists:** 50
Utilizes: Special Technical Talent; Guest Directors
Budget: $1,000 - $50,000
Income Sources: Private Foundations/Grants/Endowments; Individual Donations
Season: 52 Weeks   **Annual Attendance:** 2,000

PERFORMING SERIES

TENNESSEE PERFORMING ARTS CENTER MANAGEMENT CORPORATION
505 Deaderick Street, Nashville, TN 32719
(615) 741-7985
FAX: (615) 741-1266
Founded: 1977
Arts Area: Dance; Vocal Music; Instrumental Music; Theater
Status: Non-Profit
Type: Educational; Sponsoring
Purpose: To present touring groups; to operate educational programs; to coordinate constituent programs
Officers: James Randolph, President
Paid Staff: 47   **Volunteer Staff:** 30
Utilizes: Guest Artists
Budget: $1,000,000 - $5,000,000
Income Sources: Private Foundations/Grants/Endowments; Business/Corporate Donations; Box Office; Government Grants; Individual Donations
Season: 52 Weeks   **Annual Attendance:** 500,000
Affiliations: APAP; IAAM
Performance Facilities: Tennessee Performing Arts Center

FACILITY

CHAFFIN'S BARN
8204 Highway 100, Nashville, TN 37221
(615) 646-9977
Founded: 1967
Type of Facility: Dinner Theatre
Type of Stage: Arena; Arena has in-the-round capability
Stage Dimensions: 16'x16'
Seating Capacity: 300
Year Built: 1966   **Cost:** $100,000
Year Remodeled: 1986   **Cost:** $250,000
Contact for Rental: John P. Chaffin;   (615) 646-9977
Resident Groups: Chaffin's Barn - A Dinner Theatre
Conventions; groups; private functions

GRAND OLE OPRY HOUSE
2804 Opryland Drive, Nashville, TN 37214
(615) 889-7502
    Type of Facility: Opera House
    Type of Stage: Thrust
    Stage Dimensions: 75'Wx80'D   **Orchestra Pit**
    Seating Capacity: 4,424
    Year Built: 1974   **Architect:** Welton Becket   **Cost:** $25,000,000
    Contact for Rental: Jerry Stobel;   (615) 889-7502
    Manager: Hal Derm, General Manager

LANGFORD AUDITORIUM
Garland Avenue, Nashville, TN 37232
(615) 322-2170
    Founded: 1978
    Type of Facility: Auditorium
    Type of Stage: Platform
    Stage Dimensions: 30'x50'W curved lip
    Seating Capacity: 1,200
    Year Built: 1978
    Acoustical Consultant: Steven Durr
    Contact for Rental: Betty King;   (615) 343-3365

NASHVILLE CONVENTION CENTER
601 Commerce Street, Nashville, TN 37203
(615) 259-7900
    Type of Facility: Civic Center; Multi-Purpose; Room; Exhibition Hall
    Type of Stage: Flexible
    Seating Capacity: 5,300
    Year Built: 1987   **Architect:** Yearwood Johnson & Crabtree   **Cost:** $45,500,000
    Contact for Rental: Judy McCoy, Acting Managing Director;   (615) 742-2000
    Nashville Convention Center also contains 22 meeting rooms

TENNESSEE PERFORMING ARTS CENTER
505 Deaderick Street, Nashville, TN 37219
(615) 741-7975
    Type of Facility: Theatre Complex; Concert Hall; Theatre House; Multi-Purpose
    Year Built: 1980   **Architect:** Taylor & Crabtree   **Cost:** $42,000,000
    Acoustical Consultant: Bolt, Beranek & Newman
    Contact for Rental: Tom Baker;   (615) 741-7975
    Resident Groups: Nashville Symphony Orchestra; Tennessee Repertory Theatre; Nashville City Ballet; Circle Players; Nashville Opera Association; Friends of Music Chamber Music Series
    Tennessee Performing Arts Center contains Andrew Jackson Hall, Andrew Johnson Theatre and James K. Polk Theatre. See individual listings for additional information. TPAC is a mixed-use development encompassing three performing-arts halls, a museum and an office tower.

TENNESSEE PERFORMING ARTS CENTER - ANDREW JACKSON HALL
505 Deaderick Street, Nashville, TN 37219
(615) 741-7975
FAX: (615) 741-1266
    Type of Facility: Concert Hall; Performance Center
    Type of Stage: Proscenium
    Stage Dimensions: 130'6"Wx53'D; 57'x35' proscenium opening   **Orchestra Pit**
    Seating Capacity: 2,398
    Year Built: 1980   **Architect:** Taylor and Crabtree
    Acoustical Consultant: Bolt Beranek & Newman - original; Jaffe Acoustics - current
    Contact for Rental: Sherri Rheinhardt, Sales Manager;   (615) 741-7975
    Manager: James L. Randolph, President/Chief Executive Officer;   (615) 741-7975
    Resident Groups: Nashville Symphony; Nashville Opera Association; Tennessee Performing Arts Center's Broadway Series
    A museum and office tower are included in the building as well as the three theaters.

TENNESSEE PERFORMING ARTS CENTER - ANDREW JOHNSON THEATER
505 Deaderick Street, Nashville, TN 37219
(615) 741-7975
FAX: (615) 741-1266
    Type of Facility: Studio Performance; Performance Center; Multi-Purpose
    Type of Stage: Flexible

Stage Dimensions: 59'6"Wx52'D
Seating Capacity: 300
Year Built: 1980 **Architect:** Taylor and Crabtree
Contact for Rental: Sherri Rheinhardt, Sales Manager;   (615) 741-7975
Manager: James L. Randolph, President/Chief Executive Officer;   (615) 741-7975
Resident Groups: Circle Players

TENNESSEE PERFORMING ARTS CENTER - JAMES K. POLK THEATER
505 Deaderick Street, Nashville, TN 37219
(615) 741-7975
FAX: (615) 741-1266
Type of Facility: Performance Center; Theatre House
Type of Stage: Thrust; Proscenium
Stage Dimensions: 90'Wx50'D; 47'x27'6" proscenium opening   **Orchestra Pit**
Seating Capacity: 1,010
Year Built: 1980 **Architect:** Taylor and Crabtree
Contact for Rental: Sherri Rheinhardt, Sales Manager;   (615) 741-7975
Manager: James L. Randolph, President/Chief Executive Officer;   (615) 741-7975
Resident Groups: Tennessee Repertory Theatre; Nashville Ballet; Friends of Music Chamber Music Series
The Polk Theater includes two vomitories

Oak Ridge

INSTRUMENTAL MUSIC

OAK RIDGE SYMPHONY ORCHESTRA
PO Box 4271, Oak Ridge, TN 37831
(615) 483-5569
Founded: 1942
Arts Area: Symphony; Orchestra
Status: Semi-Professional; Non-Profit
Type: Performing; Educational
Purpose: To provide quality music to the community and serve as an outlet for gifted performers
Management: John D. Welsh, Music Director/Conductor; Rosemary Ahmad, Choral Director; C. Anne Brackins, Office Administrator; Robert Adamcik, Operations Manager
Officers: Sydney Ball, President; Ernest Silver, Secretary; Amy Hagemeyer, Treasurer
Paid Staff: 4
Paid Artists: 40   **Non-Paid Artists:** 35
Utilizes: Special Technical Talent; Guest Conductors; Guest Artists
Budget: $100,000 - $500,000
Income Sources: Private Foundations/Grants/Endowments; Business/Corporate Donations; Box Office; Government Grants; Individual Donations
Season: October - May   **Annual Attendance:** 8,000
Affiliations: ASOL; Tennesseans for the Arts
Performance Facilities: Oak Ridge High School Auditorium

THEATRE

OAK RIDGE COMMUNITY PLAYHOUSE
PO Box 5705, Oak Ridge, TN 37831-5705
(615) 482-9999
Founded: 1943
Arts Area: Community
Status: Non-Profit
Type: Performing
Purpose: To offer quality, varied theatre to the community and maintain volunteer status
Management: Ron McIntyre, Founder/Artistic Director; Patti Rogers-Copeland, General Manager; Bradley E. Brown, Public Relations Director
Officers: Nathan E. Way, President, Board of Directors; Reeva Abraham, Vice President; Harold Clark, Secretary; Jeff Backus, Treasurer
Paid Staff: 5
Paid Artists: 6   **Non-Paid Artists:** 300
Utilizes: Special Technical Talent; Guest Directors

Budget: $100,000 - $500,000
Income Sources: Private Foundations/Grants/Endowments; Business/Corporate Donations; Box Office;
Individual Donations
Season: 52 Weeks   **Annual Attendance:** 20,000
Affiliations: ACT; SETC; TTA; Knoxville Area Theatre Coalition, Arts Council of Oak Ridge, Greater Knoxville Area
Arts Council
Performance Facilities: Oak Ridge Playhouse in Jackson Square

PERFORMING SERIES

OAK RIDGE CIVIC MUSIC ASSOCIATION
PO Box 4271, Oak Ridge, TN 37831-4271
(615) 483-5569
Founded: 1944
Arts Area: Vocal Music; Instrumental Music; Chamber Series
Status: Professional; Non-Professional; Non-Profit
Type: Performing; Educational; Sponsoring
Purpose: To bring quality music to the community and to encourage the youth of the community to appreciate good music
Management: Robert Adamcik, Operations Manager; John Welsh, Orchestra Conductor; Rosemary Ahmad,
Chorus Conductor
Officers: Sidney Boll, President
Paid Staff: 3
Paid Artists: 16   **Non-Paid Artists:** 50
Utilizes: Guest Artists
Budget: $100,000 - $500,000
Income Sources: Private Foundations/Grants/Endowments; Business/Corporate Donations; Box Office; Government
Grants; Individual Donations
Season: October - June
Annual Attendance: 7,000
Performance Facilities: Oak Ridge High School Auditorium

FACILITY

OAK RIDGE COMMUNITY PLAYHOUSE
PO Box 5705, Oak Ridge, TN 37831
(615) 482-9999
Founded: 1942
Type of Facility: Theatre House
Facility Originally: Movie House
Type of Stage: Proscenium
Stage Dimensions: 32'x40'
Seating Capacity: 344
Contact for Rental: Patti Lynn Rogers-Copeland;   (615) 482-9999
Resident Groups: Oak Ridge Community Playhouse; Oak Ridge Junior Playhouse

Sewanee

INSTRUMENTAL MUSIC

SEWANEE SUMMER MUSIC CENTER
University of the South, Sewanee, TN 37375
(615) 598-5931
Founded: 1957
Arts Area: Symphony; Chamber; Ensemble
Status: Non-Profit
Type: Performing; Educational
Management: Martha McCrory, Director
Volunteer Staff: 6
Utilizes: Guest Conductors; Guest Artists
Budget: $100,000 - $500,000
Income Sources: Box Office; Government Grants; Individual Donations
Season: June 27 - August 2
Performance Facilities: Guerry Auditorium

Tullahoma

FACILITY

SOUTH JACKSON CIVIC CENTER
Corner of South Jackson and Decherd Streets, Tullahoma, TN 37388
(615) 455-5321
  Founded: 1978
  Type of Facility: Concert Hall; Auditorium; Performance Center; Theatre House; Civic Center; Multi-Purpose; Room; Rehearsal Hall
  Facility Originally: School
  Type of Stage: Proscenium
  Stage Dimensions: 48'x36'
  Seating Capacity: 450
  Year Built: 1922
  Year Remodeled: 1978
  Contact for Rental: Emma Lee Cowan; (615) 455-3991
  Resident Groups: Community Playhouse

Woodbury

THEATRE

CANNON COMMUNITY PLAYHOUSE
PO Box 404, Woodbury, TN 37190
(615) 563-5206
  Founded: 1979
  Arts Area: Community
  Status: Non-Professional; Non-Profit
  Type: Performing; Educational; Sponsoring
  Purpose: Theatre productions and theatre arts education
  Officers: Darryl T. Deason, President; Drunell Higgins, Vice President; E.L. Richards, Secretary/Treasurer
  Volunteer Staff: 200
  Non-Paid Artists: 65
  Utilizes: Special Technical Talent; Guest Artists
  Budget: $1,000 - $50,000
  Income Sources: Private Foundations/Grants/Endowments; Business/Corporate Donations; Box Office; Government Grants; Individual Donations
  Season: March - November   **Annual Attendance:** 3,000
  Affiliations: Tennessee Theatre Association

TEXAS

Abilene

INSTRUMENTAL MUSIC

ABILENE PHILHARMONIC ASSOCIATION
310 North Willis, Suite 108, Abilene, TX 79603
(915) 677-6710
Founded: 1950
Arts Area: Symphony; Orchestra
Status: Professional; Non-Profit
Type: Performing; Educational
Purpose: To present to the people of Abilene and the surrounding area the opportunity to hear the best in symphonic literature
Management: George Yaeger, Music Director/Conductor; Ed Allcorn, Manager/Librarian; Susan Saver, Executive Secretary
Officers: Tom Boecking, President; Dick Tarpley, First Vice President; David Watson, Second Vice President; Susan King, Third Vice President; Harriet Connor, Fourth Vice President; Jane Bell, Secretary
Paid Staff: 3   **Volunteer Staff:** 180
Paid Artists: 70
Utilizes: Guest Conductors; Guest Artists
Budget: $100,000 - $500,000
Income Sources: Private Foundations/Grants/Endowments; Business/Corporate Donations; Box Office; Government Grants; Individual Donations
Season: September - April   **Annual Attendance:** 18,000
Affiliations: ASOL
Performance Facilities: Abilene Civic Center

FACILITY

ABILENE CIVIC CENTER
1100 North Sixth Street, PO Box 60, Abilene, TX 79604
(915) 676-6211
FAX: (915) 676-6343
Type of Facility: Theatre Complex; Concert Hall; Auditorium; Performance Center; Theatre House; Civic Center; Multi-Purpose
Type of Stage: Proscenium   **Orchestra Pit**
Year Built: 1970
Contact for Rental: Tim Stephens;   (915) 676-6211
The Civic Center contains the Exhibit Hall and Theater. See separate listings for additional information.

ABILENE CIVIC CENTER - EXHIBIT HALL
1100 North Sixth Street, PO Box 60, Abilene, TX 79604
(915) 676-6211
FAX: (915) 676-6343
Founded: 1970
Type of Facility: Concert Hall; Civic Center; Multi-Purpose
Type of Stage: Flexible; Portable
Stage Dimensions: Flexible
Year Built: 1970
Contact for Rental: Tim Stephens;   (915) 676-6211
Contains 20,000 square feet of exhibit space

ABILENE CIVIC CENTER - THEATER
1100 North Sixth Street, PO Box 60, Abilene, TX 79604
(915) 676-6211
FAX: (915) 676-6343
Type of Facility: Concert Hall; Auditorium; Theatre House; Civic Center
Type of Stage: Proscenium
Stage Dimensions: 60'Wx72'D   **Orchestra Pit**
Seating Capacity: 2,150
Year Built: 1970
Contact for Rental: Tim Stephens;   (915) 676-6211
Resident Groups: Abilene Philharmonic Orchestra

Addison

THEATRE

ADDISON CENTRE THEATRE
15650 Addison Road, Addison, TX 75248
(214) 934-3913
>**Founded:** 1976
>**Arts Area:** Theatrical Group
>**Status:** Professional; Non-Profit
>**Type:** Performing; Touring; Educational; Sponsoring
>**Management:** David Minton, Executive Director; Kelly Cotten, Artistic Director
>**Paid Staff:** 3
>**Paid Artists:** 200
>**Utilizes:** Guest Directors
>**Budget:** $100,000 - $500,000
>**Income Sources:** Private Foundations/Grants/Endowments; Business/Corporate Donations; Box Office; Government Grants; Individual Donations
>**Season:** 52 Weeks   **Annual Attendance:** 6,000
>**Performance Facilities:** Addison Centre Theatre

Albany

THEATRE

FORT GRIFFIN FANDANGLE ASSOCIATION
PO Box 185, Albany, TX 76430
(817) 762-2525
>**Founded:** 1938
>**Arts Area:** Theatrical Group
>**Status:** Non-Professional; Non-Profit
>**Type:** Performing
>**Purpose:** Historical narration accompanied by song and dance
>**Management:** Board of Directors
>**Officers:** Watt R. Matthews, President; John Matthews, Vice President; K.C. Jones, Vice President/Treasurer; Louann George, Executive Secretary
>**Paid Staff:** 6
>**Non-Paid Artists:** 250
>**Utilizes:** Special Technical Talent
>**Budget:** $50,000 - $100,000
>**Income Sources:** Box Office; Individual Donations
>**Season:** June   **Annual Attendance:** 10,000
>**Performance Facilities:** Fort Griffin Fandangle Outdoor Theatre

FACILITY

THE AZTEC
c/o Albany Chamber of Commerce, PO Box 185, Albany, TX 76430
(915) 762-2525
>**Type of Facility:** Theatre House
>**Facility Originally:** Movie House
>**Type of Stage:** Thrust
>**Stage Dimensions:** 30'x30'   **Orchestra Pit**
>**Seating Capacity:** 250
>**Year Built:** 1927
>**Year Remodeled:** 1991   **Architect:** Bill Booziotis & Associates
>**Contact for Rental:** Sally Stapp;   (915) 762-2525
>*Musical theatre, organizational performances and meetings; due to open in summer 1993*

FORT GRIFFIN FANDANGLE OUTDOOR THEATRE
PO Box 155, Albany, TX 76430
(915) 762-2525; (915) 762-3642
>**Type of Facility:** Amphitheater
>**Type of Stage:** Greek
>**Seating Capacity:** 1,650
>**Year Built:** 1955   **Architect:** Robert Nail
>**Manager:** Marge Bray
>*Hosts annual original song and dance contest during last two weekends in June, since 1937.*

OLD JAIL ART CENTER
Route 1, PO Box 1, Albany, TX 76430
(915) 762-2269
> **Type of Facility:** Studio Performance; Civic Center; Room; Art Museum; Research Library
> **Type of Stage:** Platform
> **Stage Dimensions:** 28'x28'
> **Seating Capacity:** 150
> **Year Built:** 1877   **Architect:** John Thomas   **Cost:** $9,500
> **Year Remodeled:** 1979   **Architect:** Arthur Weinman, AIA   **Cost:** $700,000
> **Acoustical Consultant:** Arthur Weinman
> **Contact for Rental:** Joan Farmer;   (915) 762-2269

Amarillo

DANCE

LONE STAR BALLET, INC.
1,000 South Polk, Amarillo, TX 79101
(806) 372-2463
FAX: (806) 373-3909
> **Founded:** 1976
> **Arts Area:** Ballet
> **Status:** Non-Profit
> **Type:** Performing; Touring; Resident; Educational; Sponsoring
> **Purpose:** To present ballet both as a sponsoring and performing company to citizens of this area which includes five states
> **Management:** Neil Hess, Artistic Director; Juana Ree Forrester, Administrative Secretary; Kathy McAfee, Wardrobe Mistress
> **Officers:** C. Mac Douglas, President; R. Michael Isley, Vice President; Jayne Brainard, Secretary; A. Dale Williams, Treasurer
> **Paid Staff:** 3
> **Paid Artists:** 24
> **Utilizes:** Special Technical Talent; Guest Artists
> **Budget:** $100,000 - $500,000
> **Income Sources:** Private Foundations/Grants/Endowments; Business/Corporate Donations; Box Office; Government Grants; Individual Donations
> **Season:** October - April   **Annual Attendance:** 17,200
> **Affiliations:** MAAA
> **Performance Facilities:** Amarillo Civic Center

INSTRUMENTAL MUSIC

AMARILLO SYMPHONY
PO Box 2552, Amarillo, TX 79105
(806) 376-8782
> **Founded:** 1924
> **Arts Area:** Symphony; Orchestra; Chamber; Ensemble
> **Status:** Professional; Non-Profit
> **Type:** Performing; Educational
> **Purpose:** To educate and stimulate appreciation of music in the Texas Panhandle
> **Management:** Cheryl C. Cox, Executive Director; James Setapen, Music Director
> **Officers:** Don Patterson, President; C.C. Burgess, Vice President; Celine Freeman, Secretary; Joe Street, Treasurer
> **Paid Staff:** 11
> **Paid Artists:** 85
> **Utilizes:** Guest Conductors; Guest Artists
> **Budget:** $500,000 - $1,000,000
> **Income Sources:** Private Foundations/Grants/Endowments; Business/Corporate Donations; Box Office; Government Grants; Individual Donations; Fund-raising; Guild Support
> **Season:** September - May
> Annual Attendance: 19,000
> **Affiliations:** ASOL
> **Performance Facilities:** Amarillo Civic Center

FACILITY

AMARILLO CIVIC CENTER
401 South Buchanan, Amarillo, TX 79101
(806) 378-4297
> **Type of Facility:** Civic Center

Year Built: 1969
Year Remodeled: 1978
Contact for Rental: Operations Manager; (806) 378-4297
Resident Groups: Amarillo Symphony
The Civic Center contains the Arena and Music Hall. See separate listings for additional information.

AMARILLO CIVIC CENTER - ARENA
401 South Buchanan, Amarillo, TX 79101
(806) 378-4297
FAX: (806) 378-4234
Type of Facility: Arena
Type of Stage: Flexible; Arena
Seating Capacity: 7,600
Year Built: 1969
Year Remodeled: 1978
Contact for Rental: Operations Manager; (806) 378-4297

AMARILLO CIVIC CENTER - MUSIC HALL
401 South Buchanan, Amarillo, TX 79101
(806) 378-4297
FAX: (806) 378-4234
Type of Facility: Auditorium
Type of Stage: Proscenium   Orchestra Pit
Seating Capacity: 2,400
Year Built: 1969
Year Remodeled: 1978
Contact for Rental: Operations Manager; (806) 378-4297
Resident Groups: Amarillo Symphony

Arlington

VOCAL MUSIC

ARLINGTON OPERA ASSOCIATION
6103 Cool Springs Drive, Arlington, TX 76017
(817) 483-5022
FAX: (817) 277-7126
Founded: 1985
Arts Area: Lyric Opera; Light Opera; Operetta
Status: Professional; Non-Profit
Type: Performing; Resident; Educational
Purpose: To produce at least two operas per year and to promote interest in and appreciation of opera
Management: Karen Earnest, General Director; Gehlin Menti, Artistic Director
Officers: Dr. Frank Bendiks, President; Mike Yaw, Vice President; Rosemary Biel, Secretary; Dr. Dorothy Brooks, Treasurer
Paid Staff: 2   Volunteer Staff: 10
Paid Artists: 37   Non-Paid Artists: 20
Utilizes: Special Technical Talent; Guest Artists; Guest Directors
Budget: $1,000 - $50,000
Income Sources: Private Foundations/Grants/Endowments; Business/Corporate Donations; Box Office; Individual Donations
Season: April - July   Annual Attendance: 750
Affiliations: Arts Council of Fort Worth and Tarrant County; Arlington Arts Council
Performance Facilities: Arlington Community Center

THEATRE

THEATRE ARLINGTON
305 West Main Street, Arlington, TX 76010
(817) 275-7661
Founded: 1973
Arts Area: Community; Theatrical Group
Status: Semi-Professional; Non-Profit
Type: Performing; Resident; Educational
Management: Penny Patrick, Managing/Producing Director; J. Kathryn "Judy" Rehders, Assistant Director
Paid Staff: 8   Volunteer Staff: 95
Paid Artists: 10   Non-Paid Artists: 400
Utilizes: Special Technical Talent; Guest Artists; Guest Directors

Budget: $100,000 - $500,000
Income Sources: Private Foundations/Grants/Endowments; Business/Corporate Donations; Box Office;
Individual Donations
Season: September - August   **Annual Attendance:** 25,000
Affiliations: Texas Nonprofit Theatre
Performance Facilities: Theatre Arlington

FACILITY

THEATRE ARLINGTON
305 West Main Street, Arlington, TX 76010
(817) 275-7661
Type of Facility: Performance Center
Facility Originally: Church
Type of Stage: Proscenium
Stage Dimensions: 28'Wx26'D; 28'Wx27'H proscenium opening
Seating Capacity: 134
Year Built: 1951
Year Remodeled: 1980   **Architect:** Mike Smith   **Cost:** $200,000
Contact for Rental: Judy Rehder;   (817) 275-7661
Resident Groups: Theatre Arlington; Creative Arts Theatre
Theatre has limited availability for rental

UNIVERSITY OF TEXAS AT ARLINGTON - MAINSTAGE THEATER
Arlington, TX 76019
(817) 273-2011
Type of Facility: Theatre House
Type of Stage: Flexible; Proscenium   **Orchestra Pit**
Seating Capacity: 450
Year Built: 1970
Contact for Rental: Dennis Maher;   (817) 273-2650

UNIVERSITY OF TEXAS AT ARLINGTON - STUDIO THEATER
Arlington, TX 76019
(817) 273-2011
Type of Facility: Studio Performance; Black Box
Type of Stage: Flexible; Arena
Seating Capacity: 250
Year Built: 1970
Contact for Rental: Dennis Maher;   (817) 273-2650

Austin

DANCE

BALLET AUSTIN
3002 Guadalupe, Austin, TX 78705
(512) 476-9051
FAX: (512) 472-3073
Founded: 1956
Arts Area: Ballet
Status: Professional; Non-Profit
Type: Performing; Touring
Management: Lambros Lambrou, Artistic Director; Mitchell Gordon, General Manager
Paid Artists: 14
Utilizes: Guest Artists; Guest Choreographers
Budget: $100,000 - $500,000
Income Sources: Private Foundations/Grants/Endowments; Box Office; Individual Donations
Season: September - March
Performance Facilities: Performing Arts Center, University of Texas at Austin; Paramount Theatre for the Performing
Arts

DANCE UMBRELLA
PO Box 1352, Austin, TX 78701
(512) 322-0227
Founded: 1977
Arts Area: Modern; Mime; Ballet; Jazz; Ethnic; Folk; New Dance; Performance
Status: Professional; Semi-Professional; Non-Professional; Non-Profit

Type: Educational; Sponsoring; Producing
Purpose: To foster the growth of the dance community of Austin and surrounding areas
Management: Phyllis Slattery, Executive Director
Officers: Sharon Vasquez, President; Livia Baskin, Vice President/Treasurer; Robin Coiley, Secretary
Paid Staff: 1   **Volunteer Staff:** 5
Paid Artists: 35
Utilizes: Special Technical Talent; Guest Artists
Budget: $100,000 - $500,000
Income Sources: Private Foundations/Grants/Endowments; Business/Corporate Donations; Box Office; Government Grants; Individual Donations; Member Dues
Season: 52 Weeks   **Annual Attendance:** 12,000
Affiliations: National Performance Network
Performance Facilities: Synergy Studio

DEBORAH HAY DANCE COMPANY
1007 Lorrain, Austin, TX 78703
(512) 472-0763
Founded: 1980
Arts Area: Modern; New Dance
Status: Professional; Non-Profit
Type: Performing; Touring
Purpose: To foster, support and preserve the creation and performance of the highest quality contemporary dance works by Deborah Hay
Officers: Johanna Smith, President; Claudia Boles, Treasurer
Paid Artists: 1
Utilizes: Guest Composers
Budget: $1,000 - $50,000
Income Sources: Government Grants; Individual Donations
Season: January - May

SHARIR DANCE COMPANY
PO Box 339, Austin, TX 78767
(512) 458-8158
Founded: 1982
Arts Area: Modern; Post-Modern
Status: Professional
Type: Performing; Touring; Resident; Sponsoring
Purpose: To produce, promote and present new dance, art and music
Management: Carol Smith Adams, Managing Director; Amarante Lucero, Production Manager; Yacov Sharir, Founder/Artistic Director
Officers: Margaret Perry, President; Beverly Reeve, Vice President; Kim Weidman, Secretary; Chris Adams, Treasurer
Paid Staff: 4   **Volunteer Staff:** 3
Paid Artists: 13
Utilizes: Guest Artists
Budget: $100,000 - $500,000
Income Sources: Private Foundations/Grants/Endowments; Business/Corporate Donations; Box Office; Government Grants; Individual Donations
Season: September - May   **Annual Attendance:** 7,500
Affiliations: University of Texas

INSTRUMENTAL MUSIC

AUSTIN CHAMBER MUSIC CENTER
4925 Strass Drive, Austin, TX 78731
(512) 454-7562
Founded: 1981
Arts Area: Chamber
Status: Professional; Non-Profit
Type: Performing; Educational; Sponsoring
Purpose: To foster the love and knowledge of chamber music through education and performance
Officers: Felicity Coltman, Director; Fiona Otten, President; Hugh Sparks, Vice President of Programs; Kathy Thatcher, Secretary; Ora Shay, Treasurer
Volunteer Staff: 3
Paid Artists: 20
Utilizes: Guest Artists
Budget: $1,000 - $50,000
Income Sources: Private Foundations/Grants/Endowments; Business/Corporate Donations; Box Office; Government Grants; Individual Donations
Season: September - June   **Annual Attendance:** 1,000

THE AUSTIN SYMPHONY ORCHESTRA SOCIETY
1101 Red River, Austin, TX 78701
(512) 476-6064
FAX: (512) 476-6242
>**Founded:** 1911
>**Arts Area:** Symphony; Orchestra; Chamber; Ensemble; Ethnic; Folk; Band
>**Status:** Professional
>**Type:** Performing; Touring; Resident; Educational; Sponsoring
>**Purpose:** To provide live symphonic music for the citizens of Austin and central Texas
>**Management:** Kenneth Caswell, Executive Director; Rusty Buckner, Technical Director; Diana Eblen, Director of Educational Programs; Barbara Uhlaender, Assistant to Executive Director; David Ray, Production Manager
>**Officers:** Mrs. D.J. Shibley Jr., President; George More, Executive Vice President
>**Paid Staff:** 8
>**Paid Artists:** 120
>**Utilizes:** Guest Conductors; Guest Artists
>**Budget:** $1,000,000 - $5,000,000
>**Income Sources:** Private Foundations/Grants/Endowments; Business/Corporate Donations; Box Office; Government Grants; Individual Donations
>**Affiliations:** ASOL
>**Performance Facilities:** University of Texas Theater for the Performing Arts

VOCAL MUSIC

THE AUSTIN LYRIC OPERA
PO Box 984, Austin, TX 78767
(512) 472-5927
FAX: (512) 472-4143
>**Founded:** 1985
>**Arts Area:** Grand Opera; Lyric Opera
>**Status:** Professional; Non-Profit
>**Type:** Performing; Educational
>**Purpose:** To promote and support opera; to foster public awareness of opera as a fine art; to provide opportunities
>**Management:** Joseph McClain, General Director; Jeannie Lynch, Business Manager; Molly Brownie, Marketing/Development; Sam Smith, Administrative Assistant
>**Officers:** Bryce Jordan, Chairman; Joanne Christian, President
>**Paid Staff:** 4   **Volunteer Staff:** 20
>**Utilizes:** Special Technical Talent; Guest Conductors; Guest Artists; Guest Directors
>**Budget:** $500,000 - $1,000,000
>**Income Sources:** Private Foundations/Grants/Endowments; Business/Corporate Donations; Box Office; Individual Donations
>**Season:** October - May
>**Affiliations:** COS

THEATRE

GENESIUS PLAYERS
6307 Wild Street, Austin, TX 78757
(512) 452-1775
>**Founded:** 1976
>**Arts Area:** Theatrical Group
>**Status:** Non-Profit
>**Type:** Performing; Touring; Educational
>**Management:** Wanda Van Stone-Pierce, Executive Producer
>**Officers:** Wanda Van Stone-Pierce, President; April Hayner, Vice President; Cary Smith, Secretary/Treasurer
>**Volunteer Staff:** 4
>**Utilizes:** Special Technical Talent; Guest Artists; Guest Directors
>**Budget:** $1,000 - $50,000
>**Income Sources:** Private Foundations/Grants/Endowments; Business/Corporate Donations; Box Office; Government Grants; Individual Donations
>**Affiliations:** Austin Circle of Theatres

PROJECT INTERACT - ZACHARY SCOTT THEATRE CENTER
1510 Toomey Road, Austin, TX 78704
(512) 476-0594
FAX: (512) 476-0314
>**Founded:** 1977
>**Arts Area:** Professional; Theatrical Group
>**Status:** Professional

Type: Performing; Touring; Educational
Purpose: To present the best of classical and contemporary scripts as well as original works for youth using a multicultural company
Management: Jeff Frank, Artistic Director; Alex B. Alford, Business Manager
Officers: Karen R. Campbell, President; John Whisenhunt, Vice President; Kit Webster. Treasurer; Wade Porter, Secretary
Paid Staff: 2
Paid Artists: 18
Utilizes: Special Technical Talent; Guest Artists
Budget: $100,000 - $500,000
Income Sources: Private Foundations/Grants/Endowments; Business/Corporate Donations; Box Office; Government Grants; Individual Donations; Support Organization
Season: September - May   **Annual Attendance:** 75,000
Affiliations: TCG; AATE; Theatre in Disability; Austin Circle of Theatres
Performance Facilities: ZSTC Arena; ZSTC Kleberg

VORTEX REPERTORY COMPANY
1921 East Ben White, Austin, TX 78741
(512) 448-2299
Founded: 1988
Arts Area: Professional; Theatrical Group
Status: Professional; Non-Profit
Type: Performing; Touring; Resident; Educational; Sponsoring
Purpose: To produce and present cutting-edge theatre and performance art
Management: Steve Bacher, Managing Director; Bonnie Cullum, Artistic Director
Paid Staff: 2   **Volunteer Staff:** 2
Paid Artists: 100   **Non-Paid Artists:** 200
Utilizes: Special Technical Talent; Guest Artists; Guest Directors
Budget: $100,000 - $500,000
Income Sources: Private Foundations/Grants/Endowments; Business/Corporate Donations; Box Office; Government Grants; Individual Donations
Season: October - September   **Annual Attendance:** 6,000
Performance Facilities: Vortex Performance Cafe

PERFORMING SERIES

BLACK ARTS ALLIANCE
1157 Navasota, Austin, TX 78702
(512) 477-9660
Founded: 1981
Arts Area: Dance; Vocal Music; Theater
Status: Professional; Non-Profit; Commercial Art
Type: Performing; Educational; Sponsoring
Purpose: Featuring the Black artist of Central Texas and touring artist from around the nation, we are a multi-disciplinary arts organization dedicated to the promotion of artists in the Central Texas Region.
Management: Michele Bocknite, Director; Trina McKenzie, Publicist; Karol McMary, Clerical Assistant
Officers: Pam Hart, President; Rudy Greene, Vice President
Paid Staff: 3   **Volunteer Staff:** 2
Paid Artists: 50   **Non-Paid Artists:** 20
Utilizes: Special Technical Talent; Guest Conductors; Guest Artists; Guest Directors
Budget: $50,000 - $100,000
Income Sources: Private Foundations/Grants/Endowments; Business/Corporate Donations; Box Office; Government Grants; Individual Donations
Season: 52 Weeks
Affiliations: ISPAA; Texas Performing Network

FACILITY

LESTER E. PALMER AUDITORIUM
400 South First Street, Austin, TX 78704
(512) 476-5461
FAX: (512) 404-4416
Founded: 1958
Type of Facility: Auditorium
Type of Stage: Modified Apron Proscenium
Stage Dimensions: 100'Wx50'D; 68'Wx26'H proscenium opening   **Orchestra Pit**
Seating Capacity: Configurations of 3,000, 4,300 or 6,000 seats
Year Built: 1958   **Architect:** Wolf Jesson & Associates   **Cost:** $3,200,000
Year Remodeled: 1986   **Architect:** Walker Doty Freeman   **Cost:** $3,000,000
Acoustical Consultant: C.P. Boner & Associates

Contact for Rental: Raylene Brookshire;   (512) 476-5461
Includes City Coliseum, a 2000-seat arena with 40'x60' maximum size portable stage

PARAMOUNT THEATER FOR THE PERFORMING ARTS
713 Congress Avenue, Austin, TX 78767
(512) 472-2901
Type of Facility: Theatre House
Facility Originally: Vaudeville
Type of Stage: Proscenium
Stage Dimensions: 30'x33'   **Orchestra Pit**
Seating Capacity: 1,332
Year Built: 1915   **Architect:** Eberson Fugard & Knapp
Year Remodeled: 1979   **Architect:** Bell Klein & Hoffman
Contact for Rental: Paul Beutel;   (512) 472-2901
Presenting and producing performing arts including dance, music, theatre

UNIVERSITY OF TEXAS AT AUSTIN - B. IDEN PAYNE THEATRE
Winship Drama Building, Austin, TX 78712
(512) 471-5793
Type of Facility: Performance Center
Type of Stage: Proscenium   **Orchestra Pit**
Seating Capacity: 500
Year Built: 1963
Year Remodeled: 1976
Contact for Rental: Sharon Vasquez
Resident Groups: Dance Repertory
Rarely available for rent

UNIVERSITY OF TEXAS AT AUSTIN - THEATRE ROOM
Winship Drama Building, Austin, TX 78712
(512) 471-5793
Type of Facility: Performance Center; Room
Type of Stage: Flexible; In-the-round Capability
Stage Dimensions: 60'x60'
Seating Capacity: 250
Year Built: 1963
Year Remodeled: 1976
Contact for Rental: Sharon Vasquez
Rarely available for rent

UNIVERSITY OF TEXAS AT AUSTIN PERFORMING ARTS CENTER
23rd and East Campus Drive, PO Box 7818, Austin, TX 78713
(512) 471-2787
Type of Facility: Theatre Complex; Performance Center
Year Built: 1981   **Architect:** Fisher & Spillman   **Cost:** $44,000,000
Acoustical Consultant: C.P. Boner & Associates
Contact for Rental: Pebbles Wadsworth
The Performing Arts Center contains the Bass Concert Hall, Bates Recital Hall and the McCullough Theatre . See separate listings for additional information.

UNIVERSITY OF TEXAS AT AUSTIN PERFORMING ARTS CENTER - THE BASS CONCERT HALL
23rd and East Campus Drive, PO Box 7818, Austin, TX 78713
(512) 471-2787
Type of Facility: Concert Hall; Performance Center; Off Broadway; Opera House
Type of Stage: Proscenium
Stage Dimensions: 52'Wx32'H proscenium opening   **Orchestra Pit**
Seating Capacity: 3,000
Contact for Rental: Pebbles Wadsworth

UNIVERSITY OF TEXAS AT AUSTIN PERFORMING ARTS CENTER - BATES RECITAL HALL
23rd and East Campus Drive, PO Box 7818, Austin, TX 78713
(512) 471-2787
Type of Facility: Auditorium; Performance Center; Organ Concert Hall
Type of Stage: Platform
Stage Dimensions: 25'Wx8'D
Seating Capacity: 700
Contact for Rental: Pebbles Wadsworth;   (512) 471-2787
Contains a Viser-Rowland Tracker Organ

UNIVERSIFY OF TEXAS AT AUSTIN PERFORMING ARTS CENTER - THE MCCULLOUGH THEATRE
23rd and East Campus Drive, PO Box 7818, Austin, TX 78713
(512) 471-2787
    Type of Facility: Performance Center; Opera House
    Type of Stage: Proscenium
    Stage Dimensions: 30'Wx36'D; 30'Wx18'H proscenium opening   **Orchestra Pit**
    Seating Capacity: 400
    Contact for Rental: Pebbles Wadsworth; (512) 471-2787

Bastrop

THEATRE

OLD BASTROP OPERA HOUSE
711 Spring, PO Box 691, Bastrop, TX 78602
(512) 321-6283
    Founded: 1889
    Arts Area: Summer Stock; Musical; Dinner; Community; Theatrical Group
    Status: Semi-Professional; Non-Professional; Non-Profit
    Type: Performing; Sponsoring
    Purpose: To use the restored opera house as a performing arts center for theatre, dance and music
    Management: Chester Eitze, Executive Director
    Officers: Henry Gideon, President
    Paid Staff: 1   **Volunteer Staff:** 15
    Paid Artists: 10
    Utilizes: Special Technical Talent; Guest Artists; Guest Directors
    Budget: $50,000 - $100,000
    Income Sources: Private Foundations/Grants/Endowments; Business/Corporate Donations; Box Office; Individual Donations
    Season: May - January   **Annual Attendance:** 8,000
    Performance Facilities: Old Bastrop Opera House

FACILITY

OLD BASTROP OPERA HOUSE
711 Spring, PO Box 691, Bastrop, TX 78602
(512) 321-6283
    Type of Facility: Concert Hall; Auditorium; Performance Center; Theatre House; Opera House; Reception/Party Hall
    Facility Originally: Meeting Hall; Vaudeville; Movie House
    Type of Stage: Thrust; Proscenium
    Stage Dimensions: 24'Wx28'Dx14'H
    Seating Capacity: 300
    Year Built: 1889   **Architect:** Dave Green & P.O. Elzner   **Cost:** $15,000
    Year Remodeled: 1979   **Cost:** $50,000
    Contact for Rental: Chester Eitze; (512) 321-6283
    Resident Groups: Bastrop Community Chorus; Bastrop Chamber Singers; Bastrop Community Orchestra; Bastrop Children's Chorus; Bastrop Children's Theatre Program

Beaumont

DANCE

BEAUMONT BALLET THEATRE
4555 Calder, Beaumont, TX 77706
(409) 892-4441
    Founded: 1978
    Arts Area: Ballet; Jazz
    Status: Non-Professional; Non-Profit
    Type: Performing; Educational
    Purpose: Educate and train qualified students in the art of dance; encourage and develop public appreciation of dance and ballet
    Management: Bonnie Cokinos, Artistic Director
    Officers: Jimmie P. Cokinos, President; Pat Walker, Vice President; Mildred Sohlinger, Secretary/Treasurer
    Volunteer Staff: 12
    Paid Artists: 2   **Non-Paid Artists:** 50
    Utilizes: Guest Artists; Guest Directors
    Budget: $1,000 - $50,000

Income Sources: Private Foundations/Grants/Endowments; Box Office; Individual Donations
Season: 52 Weeks   **Annual Attendance:** 3,000
Affiliations: SWRBA
Performance Facilities: Julie Rogers Theatre

BEAUMONT CIVIC BALLET
c/o Marsha Woody Academy of Dance, 3717 Calder, Beaumont, TX 77706
(409) 838-4397; (409) 892-2605
Founded: 1971
Arts Area: Ballet
Status: Non-Profit
Type: Performing
Purpose: To provide high-quality dance to our area; to develop dance-arts educational programs for all ages
Management: Marsha Woody, Founder/Director
Officers: Ron Cole, President; N. Edwards, Vice President
Paid Staff: 2   **Volunteer Staff:** 75
Utilizes: Guest Artists
Budget: $50,000 - $100,000
Income Sources: Private Foundations/Grants/Endowments; Business/Corporate Donations; Box Office; Government Grants; Individual Donations
Season: August - May   **Annual Attendance:** 13,000
Affiliations: Marsha Woody Academy
Performance Facilities: Julie Rogers Theatre

INSTRUMENTAL MUSIC

SYMPHONY OF SOUTHEAST TEXAS
PO Box 1047, Beaumont, TX 77704
(409) 835-7100
Founded: 1953
Arts Area: Symphony; Orchestra
Status: Semi-Professional; Non-Profit
Type: Performing; Resident
Purpose: Provide quality musical entertainment of all types for the people of Southeast Texas
Management: Kathy Clark, Business Manager
Officers: Brian Alter, President; Allison Golias, President-Elect; Jan Allred, First Vice President; Martha Hicks, Second Vice President; Elaine Verret, Secretary; Ed Aromi, Treasurer
Paid Staff: 1
Paid Artists: 5
Utilizes: Guest Artists
Budget: $100,000 - $500,000
Income Sources: Private Foundations/Grants/Endowments; Business/Corporate Donations; Box Office; Government Grants; Individual Donations
Season: September - March   **Annual Attendance:** 16,100
Affiliations: ASOL; ASCAP; BMI
Performance Facilities: Julie Rogers Theatre

VOCAL MUSIC

BEAUMONT CIVIC OPERA
1030 Harriott, Beaumont, TX 77705
(409) 833-2120
Founded: 1962
Arts Area: Grand Opera; Light Opera; Operetta; Musical Comedy
Status: Non-Profit
Type: Resident
Purpose: To bring quality musical productions to Southwest Texas and to give young artists performing opportunities
Officers: Matthew White, President; Delores Black, Business Manager; Charlene Kiker, BM Emeritus; Irma Silvernail, Treasurer
Volunteer Staff: 20
Utilizes: Special Technical Talent; Guest Artists; Guest Directors
Budget: $50,000 - $100,000
Income Sources: Private Foundations/Grants/Endowments; Business/Corporate Donations; Box Office; Government Grants; Individual Donations; Fundraising
Season: March
Annual Attendance: 24,000
Affiliations: OA
Performance Facilities: Julie Rogers Theatre

PERFORMING SERIES

BEAUMONT MUSIC COMMISSION
PO Box 3926, Beaumont, TX 77704
(409) 833-7832
>**Founded:** 1923
>**Arts Area:** Dance; Vocal Music; Instrumental Music
>**Status:** Non-Profit
>**Type:** Educational; Sponsoring
>**Purpose:** To present vocal and instrumental artists in recitals/concerts, small ensembles, small orchestras, dance groups, operas and musicals
>**Officers:** Mrs. Russell R. Phels, President; Naaman J. Woodland Jr., First Vice President/Chairman; Charlene Kiker, Second Vice President; J. Robert Madden, Third Vice President; Mrs. Irving Eisen, Fourth Vice President; Mary Frances Roach, Recording Secretary; Mrs. Edwin Gale, Assistant Recording Secretary; Murray Anderson, Treasurer
>**Utilizes:** Guest Artists
>**Budget:** $50,000 - $100,000
>**Income Sources:** Private Foundations/Grants/Endowments; Business/Corporate Donations; Box Office; Individual Donations
>**Season:** September - May
>**Annual Attendance:** 5,000
>**Performance Facilities:** Julie Rogers Theatre for the Performing Arts

YOUNG AUDIENCES OF BEAUMONT
PO Box 5346, Beaumont, TX 77726-5346
(409) 835-3884
>**Founded:** 1963
>**Arts Area:** Dance; Instrumental Music; Theater; Drama
>**Status:** Non-Profit
>**Type:** Performing; Educational
>**Purpose:** To provide school students an opportunity to listen to, and participate in, live performances by professional artists; To promote the arts in education
>**Management:** Helen Smith, Executive Assistant
>**Officers:** Carolyn Whaley, President; Becky Moss, Betsy Boyd, Vice Presidents; Cathy Ingraham, Secretary; Don Tantzen, Treasurer
>**Paid Staff:** 1
>**Paid Artists:** 6
>**Utilizes:** Guest Artists
>**Budget:** $1,000 - $50,000
>**Income Sources:** Private Foundations/Grants/Endowments; Business/Corporate Donations; Individual Donations
>**Season:** September - May

FACILITY

CIVIC CENTER COMPLEX - EXHIBIT HALL
701 Main Street, Beaumont, TX 77701
(409) 838-3435
FAX: (409) 838-3715
>**Type of Facility:** Exhibition Hall
>**Type of Stage:** Flexible
>**Stage Dimensions:** 130'x225'
>**Seating Capacity:** 6,500
>**Year Built:** 1979   **Architect:** Gruen & Associates
>**Contact for Rental:** Claudie Hawkins;   (409) 838-3435

CIVIC CENTER COMPLEX - THE JEFFERSON THEATRE
345 Fannin Street, Beaumont, TX 77701
(409) 838-3435
FAX: (409) 838-3715
>**Type of Facility:** Theatre House
>**Facility Originally:** Vaudeville
>**Type of Stage:** Proscenium
>**Stage Dimensions:** 40'Wx31'D   **Orchestra Pit**
>**Seating Capacity:** 1,500
>**Year Built:** 1927   **Architect:** Emil Weil
>**Year Remodeled:** 1987   **Architect:** David Hoffman
>**Contact for Rental:** Claudie Hawkins;   (409) 838-3435

Resident Groups: Beaumont Community Players
Restoration/remodeling is in progress

CIVIC CENTER COMPLEX - JULIE ROGERS THEATRE FOR THE PERFORMING ARTS
701 Main Street, Beaumont, TX 77701
(800) 782-3081
FAX: (409) 838-3715
 Type of Facility: Theatre Complex; Concert Hall; Auditorium; Performance Center; Theatre House
 Facility Originally: City Hall
 Type of Stage: Proscenium
 Stage Dimensions: 50'Wx34'9"D **Orchestra Pit**
 Seating Capacity: 1,695
 Year Built: 1922
 Year Remodeled: 1982 **Architect:** Milton Bell, Rex Goode **Cost:** $4,600,000
 Acoustical Consultant: Variable Acoustics
 Contact for Rental: Claudie Hawkins; (800) 782-3081
 Resident Groups: Beaumont Symphony Orchestra; Beaumont Civic Ballet; Beaumont Music Commission; Beaumont Ballet Theatre; Beaumont Civic Opera

LAMAR UNIVERSITY - LAMAR UNIVERSITY PROSCENIUM THEATRE
Beaumont, TX 77710
(409) 880-8037
 Type of Facility: Theatre House
 Type of Stage: Proscenium
 Stage Dimensions: 21'x48'x56' **Orchestra Pit**
 Seating Capacity: 520
 Year Built: 1960 **Architect:** Miller Mebane Pitts & Phelps
 Year Remodeled: 1982 **Architect:** Miller Mebane Pitts & Phelps
 Acoustical Consultant: James Miller
 Manager: Dr. Adonia Placette
 Resident Groups: Lamar Theatre

LAMAR UNIVERSITY - LAMAR UNIVERSITY STUDIO THEATRE
Beaumont, TX 77710
(409) 880-8037
 Type of Facility: Studio Performance
 Type of Stage: Flexible
 Stage Dimensions: 60'x60'
 Seating Capacity: 200
 Year Built: 1960 **Architect:** Miller Mebane Pitts & Phelps
 Year Remodeled: 1982 **Architect:** Miller Mebane Pitts & Phelps
 Acoustical Consultant: James Miller
 Manager: Dr. Adonia Placette
 Resident Groups: Lamar Theatre

Big Spring

PERFORMING SERIES

BIG SPRING CULTURAL AFFAIRS COUNCIL
215 West Third, Big Spring, TX 79720
(915) 263-7641
 Arts Area: Dance; Vocal Music; Instrumental Music; Theater
 Status: Non-Profit
 Type: Touring
 Purpose: To provide a balance of cultural activities for the community; to enrich our natural cultural resources locally, regionally, statewide, and nationally
 Management: Marae Brooks, Director
 Officers: Gloria Hopkins, Volunteer Chairman
 Paid Staff: 1
 Utilizes: Special Technical Talent; Guest Conductors; Guest Artists
 Budget: $1,000 - $50,000
 Income Sources: Private Foundations/Grants/Endowments; Business/Corporate Donations; Box Office; Government Grants; Individual Donations

FACILITY

HOWARD COLLEGE AT BIG SPRING - HOWARD COLLEGE AUDITORIUM
1001 Birdwell Lane, Big Spring, TX 79720
(915) 264-5000
> **Type of Facility:** Auditorium
> **Type of Stage:** Proscenium   **Orchestra Pit**
> **Seating Capacity:** 475
> **Year Built:** 1956
> **Contact for Rental:** President's Office;   (915) 264-5027

HOWARD COLLEGE AT BIG SPRING - HOWARD COLLEGE COLISEUM
1001 Birdwell Lane, Big Spring, TX 79720
(915) 264-5000
> **Type of Facility:** Multi-Purpose
> **Type of Stage:** Arena
> **Seating Capacity:** 5,000
> **Contact for Rental:** Auxiliary Services Director;   (915) 264-5051

Brenham

PERFORMING SERIES

ARTS COUNCIL OF WASHINGTON COUNTY
701 Milroy Drive, Brenham, TX 77833
(409) 836-3120
> **Founded:** 1981
> **Arts Area:** Vocal Music; Instrumental Music; Theater
> **Status:** Professional; Semi-Professional; Non-Professional; Non-Profit
> **Type:** Touring; Resident; Educational; Sponsoring
> **Purpose:** To promote the local arts in the community and to bring things to the community that cannot be locally provided
> **Officers:** Dr. Wilfred D. Dietrich, President; Ann Horton, Vice President; Linda Patterson, Secretary; Helen Harris, Treasurer
> **Volunteer Staff:** 21
> **Utilizes:** Special Technical Talent; Guest Conductors; Guest Artists; Guest Directors
> **Budget:** $1,000 - $50,000
> **Income Sources:** Private Foundations/Grants/Endowments; Business/Corporate Donations; Box Office; Individual Donations
> **Season:** 52 Weeks   **Annual Attendance:** 750
> **Affiliations:** TCA

Brownsville

THEATRE

CAMILLE PLAYERS
1 Dean Porter Park, Brownsville, TX 78520
(210) 542-8900
> **Founded:** 1964
> **Arts Area:** Musical; Community; CHILDREN'S THEATRE
> **Status:** Non-Professional; Non-Profit
> **Type:** Performing
> **Purpose:** To stimulate an interest in drama by the presentation of plays and the application of the arts necessary to such presentations using the talents of interested persons to accomplish this
> **Management:** Laurence Siegle, Artistic Director; Richard Moore, Executive Director
> **Officers:** Henri De Stefano, President; Nina Fisher, Operating Advertising Vice President; Thelma Taylor, Secretary; Nena Roser, Treasurer
> **Paid Staff:** 2   **Volunteer Staff:** 6
> **Budget:** $50,000 - $100,000
> **Income Sources:** Private Foundations/Grants/Endowments; Business/Corporate Donations; Box Office; Individual Donations
> **Season:** September - June   **Annual Attendance:** 9,000
> **Performance Facilities:** Camille Lightner Playhouse

FACILITY

CAMILLE LIGHTNER PLAYHOUSE
1 Dean Porter Park, Brownsville, TX 78520
(210) 542-8900
> **Type of Facility:** Theatre House
> **Type of Stage:** Thrust; Proscenium
> **Stage Dimensions:** 20'x48'x28'   **Orchestra Pit**
> **Seating Capacity:** 301
> **Year Built:** 1964   **Architect:** Robert E. Velten
> **Contact for Rental:** Dr. Laurence Siegle;   (512) 542-8900
> **Resident Groups:** Camille Players

Brownwood

FACILITY

BROWNWOOD COLISEUM
500 East Baker, Brownwood, TX 76804
(915) 646-3586
FAX: (915) 646-0938
> **Founded:** 1963
> **Type of Facility:** Theatre Complex; Civic Center; Arena; Multi-Purpose
> **Type of Stage:** Flexible; 3/4 Arena; Arena
> **Stage Dimensions:** 64'Wx32'D
> **Seating Capacity:** 3,500
> **Year Built:** 1963
> **Architect:** Frank C. Dill, AIA   **Cost:** $821,784
> **Contact for Rental:** David Withers;   (915) 646-3586

Bryan

INSTRUMENTAL MUSIC

BRAZOS VALLEY SYMPHONY ORCHESTRA
PO Box 3524, Bryan, TX 77805
(409) 774-2877
> **Arts Area:** Symphony; Orchestra; Chamber
> **Status:** Non-Professional
> **Type:** Performing
> **Purpose:** Provide an outlet for musicians in the area and entertainment for residents of the Brazos Valley
> **Management:** Jennifer Nelson, Manager; Franz Anton Krager, Music Director
> **Paid Staff:** 2
> **Paid Artists:** 3
> **Utilizes:** Guest Artists
> **Budget:** $100,000 - $500,000
> **Income Sources:** Private Foundations/Grants/Endowments; Business/Corporate Donations; Box Office; Individual Donations
> **Season:** August - May

PERFORMING SERIES

CITY OF BRYAN PARKS AND RECREATION
PO Box 1000, Bryan, TX 77805
(409) 361-3656
FAX: (409) 361-3885
> **Arts Area:** Dance; Vocal Music; Theater; Festivals
> **Status:** Non-Profit
> **Type:** Performing; Touring; Resident; Educational; Sponsoring
> **Purpose:** Provide quality entertainment to area residents
> **Management:** Sarah Cliver, Recreation Programmer
> **Paid Staff:** 2   **Volunteer Staff:** 20
> **Paid Artists:** 20   **Non-Paid Artists:** 10
> **Utilizes:** Special Technical Talent
> **Budget:** $1,000 - $50,000
> **Income Sources:** Government Grants
> **Season:** 52 Weeks

Canyon

PERFORMING SERIES

TEXAS - THE MUSICAL DRAMA
Palo Duro Canyon State Park, PO Box 268, Canyon, TX 79015
(806) 655-2181
FAX: (806) 655-7425
Founded: 1966
Arts Area: Dance; Vocal Music; Instrumental Music; Theater
Status: Professional; Non-Profit
Type: Performing; Educational
Purpose: To perpetuate the heritage of the area by presenting a historical drama about the 1880's settling of the Texas Panhandle
Management: Patty Bryant, Assistant Manager; Neil Hess, Director; Raymond Raillard, Manager; Monette Merriman, Office Manager; Joan Castleman, Bookkeeper; Katie Greer, Publicist
Officers: Lois Rice, President; Raymond Raillard, Executive Vice President; Mrs. Ralph Randel, Vice President; Carolyn Blackburn, Secretary; Don Maxvars, Treasurer
Paid Staff: 12
Paid Artists: 140
Utilizes: Special Technical Talent
Budget: $1,000,000 - $5,000,000
Income Sources: Private Foundations/Grants/Endowments; Business/Corporate Donations; Box Office; Individual Donations
Season: June - August   **Annual Attendance:** 100,000
Affiliations: Texas Panhandle Heritage Foundation, Inc.
Performance Facilities: Pioneer Amphitheatre

FACILITY

PIONEER AMPHITHEATRE
Palo Duro Canyon State Park, PO Box 268, Canyon, TX 79015
(806) 488-2421
Type of Facility: Amphitheater
Type of Stage: Thrust; Proscenium
Seating Capacity: 1,744
Year Built: 1964   **Architect:** Earl Parge   **Cost:** $500,000
Contact for Rental: Manager;   (806) 488-2421
Resident Groups: Texas - The Musical Drama

WEST TEXAS STATE UNIVERSITY - BRANDING IRON THEATER
Canyon, TX 79016
(806) 656-2000
Type of Facility: Theatre House
Type of Stage: Proscenium
Stage Dimensions: 16'x40'x28'   **Orchestra Pit**
Seating Capacity: 305
Year Built: 1959   **Architect:** Macon O. Carden   **Cost:** $180,000
Contact for Rental: Royal R. Brantley;   (806) 656-2811

Cisco

FACILITY

KENDRICK AMPHITHEATER
Route 2, PO Box 46, Cisco, TX 76437
(817) 629-8672
Type of Facility: Outdoor (Concert); Amphitheater; Multi-Purpose
Type of Stage: Flexible; Greek
Stage Dimensions: 365'W
Seating Capacity: 100,000
Year Built: 1965   **Architect:** J.H. Kendrick Family
Contact for Rental: Mrs. J.H. Kendrick or Phil Kendrick;   (817) 629-8672
Manager: J.H. Kendrick
The Amphitheater was specially constructed for the outdoor religious production of "The Life of Christ."

College Station

THEATRE

STAGECENTER
PO Box 9475, College Station, TX 77842
(409) 846-0287
>**Founded:** 1966
>**Arts Area:** Community
>**Status:** Non-Profit
>**Type:** Performing; Educational
>**Purpose:** To provide the community with an outlet for direct participation in theatre as actors/technicians and audience members
>**Management:** Winnie Nelson, Business Manager
>**Officers:** Sandy Siddall, President
>**Non-Paid Artists:** 50
>**Utilizes:** Special Technical Talent; Guest Directors
>**Budget:** $1,000 - $50,000
>**Income Sources:** Private Foundations/Grants/Endowments; Business/Corporate Donations; Box Office; Individual Donations
>**Season:** September - June   **Annual Attendance:** 3,000
>**Affiliations:** Arts Council of Brazos Valley

FACILITY

UNIVERSITY CENTER THEATRE COMPLEX AND CONFERENCE TOWER
Texas A&M University, College Station, TX 77840
(409) 845-8903
>**Type of Facility:** Theatre Complex; Auditorium; Performance Center; Theatre House; Multi-Purpose
>**Year Built:** 1973   **Architect:** JPJ Architects   **Cost:** $20,000,000
>**Contact for Rental:** Tom Baxter;   (409) 845-8903
>*The University Center contains the Theatre Complex in which the performance spaces of Rudder Auditorium, Rudder Forum and Rudder Theatre are found as well as the Conference Tower. See individual listings for additional information.*

UNIVERSITY CENTER THEATRE COMPLEX AND CONFERENCE TOWER - RUDDER AUDITORIUM
Texas A&M University, College Station, TX 77840
(409) 845-8903
>**Type of Facility:** Auditorium
>**Type of Stage:** Proscenium; Hydraulic Lift Stage
>**Stage Dimensions:** 126'Wx48'D; 60'Wx28'H proscenium opening   **Orchestra Pit**
>**Seating Capacity:** 2,500
>**Year Built:** 1973
>**Contact for Rental:** Tom Baxter;   (409) 845-8903

UNIVERSITY CENTER THEATRE COMPLEX AND CONFERENCE TOWER - RUDDER FORUM
Texas A&M University, College Station, TX 77840
(409) 845-8903
>**Type of Facility:** Studio Performance
>**Type of Stage:** Flexible; Platform
>**Seating Capacity:** 245
>**Year Built:** 1973
>**Contact for Rental:** Tom Baxter;   (409) 845-8903

UNIVERSITY CENTER THEATRE COMPLEX AND CONFERENCE TOWER - RUDDER THEATRE
Texas A&M University, College Station, TX 77840
(409) 845-8903
>**Type of Facility:** Theatre House
>**Type of Stage:** Proscenium
>**Stage Dimensions:** 77'Wx18'8"D; 47'Wx25'H proscenium opening
>**Seating Capacity:** 750
>**Year Built:** 1973
>**Contact for Rental:** Tom Baxter;   (409) 845-8903

Commerce
FACILITY

EAST TEXAS STATE UNIVERSITY - UNIVERSITY PLAYHOUSE STAGE
Performing Arts Center, Commerce, TX 75429
(903) 886-5337
    Type of Facility: Theatre House
    Type of Stage: Modified Apron Proscenium
    Stage Dimensions: 36'Wx40'D;36'Wx20'H proscenium opening;28' diameter turntable
    Seating Capacity: 304
    Year Built: 1976   **Architect:** Harper Kemp Clutts & Parker   **Cost:** $2,105,602
    Resident Groups: East Texas State University Theater Department
    Additionally, within the building is located a 40' square, Black Box theatre seating 110.

Coppell
VOCAL MUSIC

COPPELL COMMUNITY CHORUS
524 Leavalley Circle, Coppell, TX 75019
(214) 462-1090
    Founded: 1986
    Arts Area: Choral
    Status: Non-Professional; Non-Profit
    Type: Performing; Resident
    Purpose: Enjoyment of singing together in a group
    Management: Peggy Waldschmidt, Music Director
    Officers: Donna Knox, President
    Volunteer Staff: 6
    Paid Artists: 2
    Utilizes: Guest Directors
    Budget: $1,000 - $50,000
    Income Sources: Business/Corporate Donations; Box Office; Government Grants; Individual Donations
    Season: Fall - Spring   **Annual Attendance:** 200

Corpus Christi
DANCE

CORPUS CHRISTI BALLET
5610 Everhart, Corpus Christi, TX 78411
(512) 991-8521
FAX: (512) 991-8521
    Founded: 1972
    Arts Area: Ballet
    Status: Non-Professional; Non-Profit
    Type: Performing; Touring; Resident; Educational; Sponsoring
    Management: Cristina Stirling Munro, Director
    Paid Staff: 3   **Volunteer Staff:** 10
    Paid Artists: 15
    Utilizes: Guest Conductors; Guest Artists; Guest Choreographers
    Budget: $100,000 - $500,000
    Income Sources: Private Foundations/Grants/Endowments; Business/Corporate Donations; Box Office; Individual Donations
    Season: September - May
    Affiliations: Munro Ballet Studios
    Performance Facilities: Bayfront Plaza Auditorium

INSTRUMENTAL MUSIC

CORPUS CHRISTI CHAMBER MUSIC SOCIETY, INC.
4709 Curtis Clark, Corpus Christi, TX 78411
(512) 855-0264; (512) 886-1614
    Founded: 1982
    Arts Area: Chamber
    Status: Non-Profit

Type: Performing
Purpose: To bring world-class chamber music groups to our city
Management: Joan Allison, Vice President/Program Director
Officers: Michael Evans, President; Joan Allison, David Parker, Vice Presidents; Betty Allen, Secretary; Gretchen Perrin, Treasurer
Volunteer Staff: 25
Paid Artists: 15
Budget: $1,000 - $50,000
Income Sources: Private Foundations/Grants/Endowments; Business/Corporate Donations; Box Office; Government Grants; Individual Donations
Season: September - May   **Annual Attendance:** 2,500
Performance Facilities: Richardson Auditorium

CORPUS CHRISTI SYMPHONY
PO Box 495, Corpus Christi, TX 78403
(512) 882-4091
   Founded: 1945
   Arts Area: Symphony; Orchestra; Chamber; Ensemble
   Status: Semi-Professional; Non-Profit
   Type: Performing
   Management: Litta R. Kline, Executive Director/Manager
   Officers: Harold Gillispie, Chairman of the Board; Dr. Herbert Madalin, President; George Hodges, President Elect; Jace Hoffman, Vice President; Maxine Somers, Secretary
   Paid Staff: 3
   Utilizes: Special Technical Talent; Guest Conductors; Guest Artists; Guest Directors
   Budget: $100,000 - $500,000
   Income Sources: Private Foundations/Grants/Endowments; Business/Corporate Donations; Box Office; Government Grants; Individual Donations
   Season: October - April   **Annual Attendance:** 15,000
   Affiliations: ASOL
   Performance Facilities: Bayfront Plaza Auditorium

THEATRE

BILINGUAL THEATER COMPANY/SOUTH TEXAS PERFORMANCE CO.
4722 Everhart, Corpus Christi, TX 78411
(512) 993-8898
   Founded: 1980
   Arts Area: Theatrical Group
   Status: Professional; Non-Profit
   Type: Performing; Touring; Resident; Educational
   Purpose: To present bilingual/bicultural performances
   Management: Dr. Graciela P. Rosenberg, Managing Director; Dr. Joe Rosenberg, Artistic Director; Larry Bogus, Executive Director; John Daniels Jr., Theatre Manager; Jose Gayton, Financial Director; Christopher Lawrence, Publicity Director
   Officers: George Dunson, Chairman; Dr. Joe Rosenberg, President; Dr. Graciela P. Rosenberg, Vice President
   Paid Artists: 15
   Utilizes: Special Technical Talent; Guest Artists
   Budget: $100,000 - $500,000
   Income Sources: Private Foundations/Grants/Endowments; Business/Corporate Donations; Box Office; Government Grants; Individual Donations
   Season: July - June   **Annual Attendance:** 35,000

PERFORMING SERIES

CATHEDRAL CONCERT SERIES
620 Lipan, Corpus Christi, TX 78401
(512) 888-6520
FAX: (512) 882-9018
   Founded: 1985
   Arts Area: Vocal Music; Instrumental Music; Festivals
   Status: Professional; Semi-Professional; Non-Professional; Non-Profit
   Type: Performing; Touring; Resident
   Utilizes: Guest Conductors; Guest Artists; Guest Directors
   Budget: $1,000 - $50,000
   Income Sources: Private Foundations/Grants/Endowments; Business/Corporate Donations; Government Grants; Individual Donations
   Season: October - June   **Annual Attendance:** 5,000

TEXAS JAZZ FESTIVAL SOCIETY
403 North Shoreline Boulevard, Corpus Christi, TX 78403
(512) 883-4500
>**Founded:** 1969
>**Arts Area:** Vocal Music; Instrumental Music; Festivals
>**Status:** Professional; Non-Profit
>**Type:** Performing
>**Purpose:** Now in its 28th year of producing the annual Texas Jazz Festival, free of charge to the public, the Society promotes and preserves American jazz as a fine art.
>**Management:** Al Beto Garcia, Festival Originator
>**Officers:** Wanda Gregory, President; Eddie Olivares, Vice President; Kate Trevino, Secretary; Herb Hicks, Treasurer
>**Volunteer Staff:** 15
>**Utilizes:** Special Technical Talent; Guest Conductors; Guest Artists; Guest Directors
>**Budget:** $1,000 - $50,000
>**Income Sources:** Private Foundations/Grants/Endowments; Business/Corporate Donations; Government Grants; Individual Donations
>**Season:** 52 Weeks   **Annual Attendance:** 8,000
>**Performance Facilities:** Bayfront Plaza Convention Center

FACILITY

BAYFRONT PLAZA CONVENTION CENTER - AUDITORIUM
1901 North Shoreline Drive, Corpus Christi, TX 78401
(512) 883-8543
FAX: (512) 883-0788
>**Type of Facility:** Auditorium
>**Type of Stage:** Proscenium
>**Stage Dimensions:** 48'Wx40'D; 48'Wx25'H proscenium opening   **Orchestra Pit**
>**Seating Capacity:** 2,526
>**Year Built:** 1978   **Architect:** SHWC Architects; CRS Architects
>**Contact for Rental:** Terri Cardona;   (512) 883-8543
>**Resident Groups:** Corpus Christi Symphony; Munro Ballet

RICHARDSON AUDITORIUM
101 Baldwin Avenue, Corpus Christi, TX 78404
(512) 886-1243
FAX: (512) 886-1276
>**Type of Facility:** Auditorium; Theatre House
>**Type of Stage:** Proscenium
>**Stage Dimensions:** 55'Wx37'Dx24'H   **Orchestra Pit**
>**Seating Capacity:** 1,780
>**Year Built:** 1951   **Architect:** Brock & Anderson
>**Acoustical Consultant:** Boner & Associates
>**Contact for Rental:** Brad Gallaway;   (512) 886-1243
>**Resident Groups:** Corpus Christi Chamber Music Society; Corpus Christi Chorale; Corpus Christi Creative Arts Center

Corsicana

THEATRE

CORSICANA COMMUNITY PLAYHOUSE
119 West Sixth, Corsicana, TX 75110
(903) 872-5421
>**Founded:** 1971
>**Arts Area:** Community; Theatrical Group
>**Status:** Semi-Professional; Non-Profit
>**Type:** Performing; Touring
>**Purpose:** To provide quality theatrical performances to Corsicana and north and east Texas cities
>**Management:** Cranston Dodds, Resident Director
>**Officers:** Tom Hecker, President; David Ralston, Vice President; Mary Burson, Secretary; Steve Johnson, Treasurer
>**Paid Staff:** 5
>**Utilizes:** Guest Artists
>**Budget:** $100,000 - $500,000
>**Income Sources:** Private Foundations/Grants/Endowments; Business/Corporate Donations; Box Office; Government Grants; Individual Donations
>**Season:** February - December   **Annual Attendance:** 10,000

Affiliations: Texas Nonprofit Theatre
Performance Facilities: Warehouse Living Arts Center

FACILITY

WAREHOUSE LIVING ARTS CENTER
119 West Sixth, Corsicana, TX 75110
(903) 872-5421
> **Founded:** 1971
> **Type of Facility:** Theatre Complex; Theatre House
> **Facility Originally:** Warehouse
> **Type of Stage:** Thrust
> **Stage Dimensions:** 31'x41'
> **Seating Capacity:** 127
> **Year Built:** 1900
> **Year Remodeled:** 1980   **Architect:** Cranston Dodds   **Cost:** $250,000
> **Manager:** Cranston Dodds;   (903) 872-5421
> **Resident Groups:** Corsicana Community Playhouse

Crockett

FACILITY

DISCOVER HOUSTON COUNTY VISITORS CENTER - MUSEUM
303 South First, Crockett, TX 75835
(409) 544-9520
> **Mailing Address:** 629 North Fourth, Crockett, TX 75835
> **Founded:** 1983
> **Type of Facility:** Theatre Complex; Auditorium; Outdoor (Concert); Environmental; Civic Center; Arena; Multi-Purpose; Room
> **Facility Originally:** Business Facility; Railroad Depot
> **Type of Stage:** Platform; Environmental
> **Seating Capacity:** 250
> **Year Built:** 1909   **Architect:** International & Great Northern Railroad Company
> **Year Remodeled:** 1987   **Architect:** David Woodcock, AIA, RIBA   **Cost:** $75,000
> **Contact for Rental:** Eliza H. Bishop;   (409) 544-5304
> **Resident Groups:** Piney Woods Fine Arts Association
> *Restoration is expected to be completed in 1995.*

Dallas

DANCE

DALLAS BLACK DANCE THEATRE
2627 Flora Street, Dallas, TX 75201
(214) 871-2387
FAX: (214) 871-2842
> **Founded:** 1976
> **Arts Area:** Modern; Jazz; Ethnic
> **Status:** Non-Profit
> **Type:** Performing; Touring; Educational
> **Purpose:** To present ethnic dance as a truly meaningful art form
> **Management:** Ann M. Williams, Founder/Artistic Director; Venetta Drew, Executive Director
> **Officers:** Marvin Robinson, President
> **Paid Staff:** 4
> **Utilizes:** Guest Artists
> **Budget:** $50,000 - $100,000
> **Income Sources:** Private Foundations/Grants/Endowments; Business/Corporate Donations; Box Office; Government Grants; Individual Donations
> **Season:** August - May

DALLAS DANCE COUNCIL
PO Box 740511, Dallas, TX 75374-0511
(214) 713-2795
> **Founded:** 1974
> **Arts Area:** Modern; Ballet; Jazz; Ethnic; Folk
> **Status:** Semi-Professional; Non-Profit

Type: Educational; Sponsoring
Purpose: To support the art of dance, including ballet, modern, jazz, ethnic, post-modern, experimental and theatre dance; to represent the dance community, serving as a central information agency for all aspects of dance
Officers: Taura Hunter, President; JoAnn Robertson, Board Chairman
Budget: $1,000 - $50,000
Income Sources: Private Foundations/Grants/Endowments; Business/Corporate Donations; Government Grants; Individual Donations

DALLAS METROPOLITAN BALLET
6815 Hillcrest Avenue, Dallas, TX 75205
(214) 361-0278
Founded: 1964
Arts Area: Ballet
Status: Semi-Professional; Non-Profit
Type: Performing; Touring; Resident; Educational
Purpose: To develop an audience for dance; to develop dancers in the Dallas area and the Southwest
Management: Ann Etgen, Bill Atkinson, Artistic Directors; Board of Directors
Paid Staff: 3
Paid Artists: 4   **Non-Paid Artists:** 18
Utilizes: Special Technical Talent; Guest Artists; Guest Choreographers
Budget: $1,000 - $50,000
Income Sources: Private Foundations/Grants/Endowments; Business/Corporate Donations; Box Office; Government Grants; Individual Donations
Season: August - June   **Annual Attendance:** 15,000
Affiliations: NARB
Performance Facilities: McFarlin Auditorium; Southern Methodist University

INSTRUMENTAL MUSIC

DALLAS BACH SOCIETY
PO Box 140201, Dallas, TX 75214
(214) 827-2224
Founded: 1982
Arts Area: Orchestra; Chamber; Choral
Status: Professional; Semi-Professional; Non-Profit
Type: Performing; Sponsoring
Purpose: To produce and present Baroque music: to perform choral, instrumental, chamber and keyboard selections; to operate the Dallas Bach Orchestra and the Dallas Bach Choir
Management: Paul Riedo, Artistic Director; Angeline Churchill, General Manager
Officers: Mary Glerum, President; Betty Nadalini, Vice President
Volunteer Staff: 2
Paid Artists: 50   **Non-Paid Artists:** 20
Utilizes: Guest Artists
Budget: $100,000 - $500,000
Income Sources: Private Foundations/Grants/Endowments; Business/Corporate Donations; Box Office; Individual Donations
Season: September - May   **Annual Attendance:** 5,000
Affiliations: CA; International Bach Society
Performance Facilities: Dallas Museum of Art; Saint Thomas Aquinas Church

DALLAS CHAMBER ORCHESTRA
Sammons Center for the Arts, 3630 Harry Hines Boulevard, Suite 302, Dallas, TX 75219-3201
(214) 520-3121
FAX: (214) 522-9174
Founded: 1979
Arts Area: Orchestra; Chamber; Ensemble
Status: Professional; Non-Profit; Commercial
Type: Performing; Touring; Resident; Educational
Management: Jack Bunning, Executive Director; Ronald Neal, Music Director
Officers: Dan Chesnut, President; John Fesperman, Lyla O'Driscoll, Vice Presidents; Gordon Lindsey, Secretary; Bob Melvin, Treasurer
Paid Staff: 2   **Volunteer Staff:** 20
Paid Artists: 15
Utilizes: Guest Artists
Budget: $100,000 - $500,000
Income Sources: Private Foundations/Grants/Endowments; Business/Corporate Donations; Box Office; Government Grants; Individual Donations
Season: September - May   **Annual Attendance:** 15,000
Performance Facilities: Caruth Auditorium, Southern Methodist University

DALLAS CLASSIC GUITAR SOCIETY
PO Box 140724, Dallas, TX 75214
(214) 528-3733
Founded: 1979
Arts Area: Chamber; Ensemble; Ethnic; Folk
Status: Non-Profit
Type: Performing; Resident; Educational; Sponsoring
Purpose: To promote appreciation and understanding of classical guitar by increasing exposure to the instrument and its music
Management: Suzanne Davidson, General Manager
Officers: James R. Shaw, President; Christopher McGuire, Chairman, Advisory Board
Paid Staff: 2
Paid Artists: 50
Utilizes: Guest Artists
Budget: $100,000 - $500,000
Income Sources: Private Foundations/Grants/Endowments; Business/Corporate Donations; Box Office; Government Grants; Individual Donations
Season: September - April   **Annual Attendance:** 10,000
Affiliations: APAP; GFA
Performance Facilities: Majestic Theatre; Meyerson Symphony Center; Caruth Hall, Southern Methodist University; Music Hall at Fair Park

DALLAS SYMPHONY ASSOCIATION, INC.
2301 Flora Street, Suite 300, Dallas, TX 75201
(214) 871-4000
FAX: (214) 953-1218
Founded: 1900
Arts Area: Symphony
Status: Professional; Non-Profit
Type: Performing; Resident; Educational
Purpose: To manage the Dallas Symphony Orchestra; to secure additional funding as necessary over and above revenue
Management: Leonard D. Stone, Executive Director; Fred W. Hoster, General Manager; Victor Marshall, Music Administrator; Mark Melson, Director of Orchestra Operations
Officers: R.A. Freling, Chairman; Howard Haflam, President; Donald G. Reynolds, Vice President of Marketing; Darryl D. Pounds, Treasurer
Paid Staff: 50   **Volunteer Staff:** 5
Paid Artists: 45
Utilizes: Guest Conductors; Guest Artists
Budget: Over 10,000,000
Income Sources: Private Foundations/Grants/Endowments; Business/Corporate Donations; Box Office; Government Grants; Individual Donations
Season: 52 Weeks
Annual Attendance: 425,000
Affiliations: ASOL
Performance Facilities: Morton H. Meyerson Symphony Center

DALLAS SYMPHONY ORCHESTRA
2301 Flora Street, Dallas, TX 75201
(214) 871-4000
FAX: (214) 953-1218
Founded: 1900
Arts Area: Symphony; Orchestra
Status: Professional; Non-Profit
Type: Performing; Touring; Resident; Educational; Sponsoring
Purpose: DSO provides the Dallas community with the very best in musical performances and education as recognized by national and international standards, audience acclaim, and critical appraisal
Management: Leonard Stone, Executive Director; Eduardo Mata, Director of Music/Conductor; Douglas Kinzey, Director of Marketing; Warren Gould, Director of Development; Fred Hoster, General Manager; Mark Melson, Director of Orchestra Operations; Amy Groff, Director of Finance; Sydney Reid-Hedge, Director of Volunteers
Officers: Liener Temerlin, Chairman; William Schilling, President; Nancy Nelson, Secretary; Seymour Thum, Treasurer
Paid Staff: 34
Paid Artists: 93
Utilizes: Guest Conductors; Guest Artists
Budget: Over 10,000,000
Income Sources: Private Foundations/Grants/Endowments; Business/Corporate Donations; Box Office; Government Grants; Individual Donations
Season: 52 Weeks
Performance Facilities: Morton H. Meyerson Symphony Center

EARTHLY PLEASURES
9215 Forest Hills Boulevard, Dallas, TX 75218
(214) 327-6823
> **Founded:** 1978
> **Arts Area:** Instrumental Group
> **Status:** Semi-Professional
> **Type:** Performing
> **Purpose:** Performance of Renaissance and Medieval music on period instruments
> **Management:** David G. Barton, Director; Susan Barton, Assistant Director
> **Paid Artists:** 5
> **Budget:** $1,000 - $50,000
> **Income Sources:** Box Office **Season:** 52 Weeks

FINE ARTS CHAMBER PLAYERS
3630 Harry Hines Boulevard, Dallas, TX 75219
(214) 520-2219
FAX: (214) 522-9174
> **Founded:** 1980
> **Arts Area:** Chamber; Ensemble
> **Status:** Professional; Non-Profit
> **Type:** Performing; Educational
> **Purpose:** To provide high-quality, professional chamber ensemble concerts to Dallas citizens free of charge
> **Management:** Rogene Russell, Artistic Director
> **Officers:** David S. Nafziger, Board President; Natalie Nielson, Vice President; Fred Sims, Treasurer; Rebecca Hamilton, Secretary
> **Paid Staff:** 1 **Volunteer Staff:** 3
> **Paid Artists:** 34
> **Budget:** $50,000 - $100,000
> **Income Sources:** Private Foundations/Grants/Endowments; Business/Corporate Donations; Government Grants; Individual Donations
> **Season:** September - August **Annual Attendance:** 14,000
> **Performance Facilities:** Dallas Civic Garden Center; Dallas Museum of Art

GREATER DALLAS YOUTH ORCHESTRA ASSOCIATION
3630 Harry Hines, Dallas, TX 75219
(214) 528-7747
FAX: (214) 522-9174
> **Founded:** 1972
> **Arts Area:** Symphony; Orchestra; Ensemble
> **Status:** Non-Professional; Non-Profit
> **Type:** Performing; Resident; Educational
> **Purpose:** To provide ensemble training for serious student musicians in the Dallas Area
> **Management:** Carol Cobb, Executive Director
> **Officers:** Kevin Wiggins, President
> **Paid Staff:** 3
> **Paid Artists:** 4
> **Utilizes:** Guest Conductors; Guest Artists; Guest Directors
> **Budget:** $100,000 - $500,000
> **Income Sources:** Private Foundations/Grants/Endowments; Business/Corporate Donations; Box Office; Government Grants; Individual Donations; Tuition
> **Season:** September - May
> **Annual Attendance:** 14,200
> **Affiliations:** ASOL
> **Performance Facilities:** Morton H. Meyerson Symphony Center

VOICES OF CHANGE
310 Meadows Building, 5646 Milton, Dallas, TX 75206
(214) 987-0889
> **Founded:** 1975
> **Arts Area:** Chamber; Ensemble
> **Status:** Professional; Non-Profit
> **Type:** Performing; Touring; Resident; Educational
> **Purpose:** To present music of living composers and 20th-century "classics"; to present work through a seasonal series, monthly radio broadcasts, tours, recordings, commissionings and special-event concerts
> **Management:** Jo Boatright, Artistic Director
> **Officers:** Lydia Scheer, President; Ken Long, Vice President; John Lumsford, Secretary; Sylvia Elton, Treasurer
> **Paid Staff:** 2 **Volunteer Staff:** 25
> **Paid Artists:** 15

Utilizes: Special Technical Talent; Guest Conductors; Guest Artists
Budget: $100,000 - $500,000
Income Sources: Private Foundations/Grants/Endowments; Business/Corporate Donations; Box Office; Government Grants; Individual Donations; Benefit Promotions
Season: September - August
Annual Attendance: 5,000
Affiliations: CMA; Southern Methodist University; American Music Center; Meet the Composers; Texas Composers Forum
Performance Facilities: Caruth Auditorium, Southern Methodist University; Dallas Museum of Art; Greiner Middle School Academy; Morton Meyerson Center

VOCAL MUSIC

THE DALLAS OPERA
3102 Oak Lawn Avenue, Suite 430, Dallas, TX 75210
(214) 443-1043
FAX: (214) 443-1060
Founded: 1957
Arts Area: Grand Opera
Status: Professional; Non-Profit
Type: Performing; Educational; Sponsoring
Purpose: The Dallas Opera is an opera company committed to the presentation of opera at the international level. It enriches the community through performances of grand and chamber opera, operatic concerts, recitals and attendant education and community service programs.
Management: Plato Karayanis, General Director; Jonathon Pell, Artistic Administrator
Officers: Jim Erwin, President
Paid Staff: 28 **Volunteer Staff:** 800
Paid Artists: 262
Utilizes: Special Technical Talent; Guest Conductors; Guest Artists; Guest Directors
Budget: $5,000,000 - $10,000,000
Income Sources: Private Foundations/Grants/Endowments; Business/Corporate Donations; Box Office; Government Grants; Individual Donations
Season: October - May **Annual Attendance:** 116,400
Affiliations: OA; AAA; Texas Arts Alliance
Performance Facilities: Music Hall at Fair Park

DALLAS SYMPHONY CHORUS
c/o Dallas Symphony Association, 2301 Flora Street, Suite 300, Dallas, TX 75201
(214) 871-4000
FAX: (214) 953-1218
Arts Area: Lyric Opera; Light Opera; Operetta; Choral; Ethnic; Folk
Status: Non-Professional; Non-Profit
Type: Performing; Touring; Resident
Purpose: To support the Dallas Symphony Association by performing major choral works with the symphony
Management: Leann Binford, Chorus Representative
Officers: Paul Talbot, President
Budget: $1,000 - $50,000
Income Sources: Private Foundations/Grants/Endowments; Business/Corporate Donations; Government Grants; Individual Donations
Performance Facilities: Meyerson Symphony Center

THE LYRIC OPERA OF DALLAS
PO Box 12656, Dallas, TX 75225-0656
(214) 368-2183
Founded: 1982
Arts Area: Grand Opera; Lyric Opera; Light Opera; Operetta
Status: Professional; Non-Profit
Type: Performing; Resident; Educational
Purpose: To produce music theatre that is accessible and appealing to a wide audience and gives opportunities to new American talent
Management: Terry Hicklin, General Director; John Burrows, Artistic Director; LeAnn Binford, Managing Director; Elizabeth Daggerhart, Director of Box Office; Robert Hull, Development Counsel; Steven Friedlander, Producing Director/Lighting Designer
Officers: Donald G. Williamson, President; Robert M. Dickson, Eugene Coker, Vice Presidents; Mrs. Charles Blaylock, Secretary; Alice Worham Austin, Treasurer
Paid Staff: 5 **Volunteer Staff:** 65
Paid Artists: 118
Utilizes: Guest Conductors; Guest Artists; Guest Directors
Budget: $500,000 - $1,000,000

Income Sources: Private Foundations/Grants/Endowments; Business/Corporate Donations; Box Office; Government Grants; Individual Donations
Season: May - August
Annual Attendance: 12,000
Affiliations: OA
Performance Facilities: Plaza Theatre

TURTLE CREEK CHORALE
PO Box 190806, Dallas, TX 75219-0806
(214) 526-3214
FAX: (214) 522-9174
Founded: 1980
Arts Area: Choral
Status: Non-Professional; Non-Profit
Type: Performing
Purpose: To enhance the musical, educational and cultural life in Dallas and the state of Texas through the presentation of chorale music for men's voices
Management: Dr. Timothy Seelig, Artistic Director; Ann Albritton, Principal Accompanist; Antoine Spener, Assistant Accompanist; Jeannette Teel, Business Manager
Officers: Chet Flake, Chairman of the Board; A.G. Black, President; Dennis Plemmons, Vice President; Gary Williams, Secretary; Franklin Reed, Treasurer
Paid Staff: 2   **Volunteer Staff:** 10
Paid Artists: 10
Utilizes: Special Technical Talent; Guest Artists
Budget: $100,000 - $500,000
Income Sources: Private Foundations/Grants/Endowments; Business/Corporate Donations; Box Office; Government Grants; Individual Donations; Fund-raising
Season: October - August
Annual Attendance: 1,500
Performance Facilities: Meyerson Symphony Center

THEATRE

AFRO-AMERICAN PLAYERS
PO Box 36309, Dallas, TX 75235
(214) 399-0161
FAX: (214) 506-9030
Founded: 1971
Arts Area: Professional; Theatrical Group; Children's Theatre
Status: Professional; Non-Profit
Type: Performing; Touring; Resident; Educational
Purpose: To educate, entertain, and enlighten through theatre so that cross-cultural communication and interaction can occur
Management: Glodean Baker, Executive Director; Fred Gardner, Executive Producer
Paid Staff: 3   **Volunteer Staff:** 13
Paid Artists: 8
Utilizes: Special Technical Talent; Guest Artists; Guest Directors
Budget: $100,000 - $500,000
Income Sources: Private Foundations/Grants/Endowments; Business/Corporate Donations; Box Office; Government Grants; Individual Donations
Season: 52 Weeks
Annual Attendance: 100,000
Affiliations: STAGE; Black Theatre Network
Performance Facilities: Cultural Arts Center

CABBAGES AND KINGS
7732 Forest Lane, #224, Dallas, TX 75230
(214) 363-7292
FAX: (214) 867-7615
Founded: 1984
Arts Area: Professional; Theatrical Group
Status: Professional; Non-Profit
Type: Performing; Touring
Purpose: To entertain and enlighten children and their families; to present original plays based on stories and mythology and to relate them to present day situations
Management: Linda Comess, Founder/Artistic Director; Tricia Avery, Business Manager
Officers: Linda Comess, President; Hal Harris, Vice President; Leonard Comess, Secretary; Miriam Harris, Treasurer
Paid Staff: 2   **Volunteer Staff:** 2
Paid Artists: 28

Utilizes: Special Technical Talent; Guest Artists; Guest Directors
Budget: $50,000 - $100,000
Income Sources: Private Foundations/Grants/Endowments; Business/Corporate Donations; Box Office; Government Grants; Individual Donations
Season: 52 Weeks
Affiliations: AEA
Performance Facilities: Addison Centre Theatre

DALLAS CHILDREN'S THEATER
2215 Cedar Springs, Dallas, TX 75201
(214) 978-0110
Founded: 1984
Arts Area: Professional; Theatrical Group
Status: Non-Profit
Type: Performing; Touring; Educational
Purpose: To enrich the lives of children through the art of theater
Management: Robin Baker Flatt, Executive Director; Dennis Vincent; Executive Producer
Officers: Laurie Harrison, President; Melissa Deakins, Chairman of Executive Committee
Paid Staff: 4
Utilizes: Special Technical Talent; Guest Artists; Guest Directors
Budget: $100,000 - $500,000
Income Sources: Private Foundations/Grants/Endowments; Business/Corporate Donations; Box Office; Government Grants; Individual Donations
Season: September - July
Annual Attendance: 35,000
Affiliations: ASSITEJ
Performance Facilities: El Centro College, Crescent Theatre

DALLAS PUPPET THEATER
3018 Commerce, Dallas, TX 75229
(214) 939-0004
Founded: 1982
Arts Area: Professional; Puppet
Status: Professional; Non-Profit
Type: Performing; Touring; Resident; Educational; Sponsoring
Purpose: To provide a greater awareness of the art of puppetry in construction and performance
Management: James Smith, Founding Artistic Director; Michael Robinson, Technical Director
Paid Staff: 3   **Volunteer Staff:** 7
Utilizes: Special Technical Talent; Guest Artists; Guest Directors
Budget: $1,000 - $50,000
Income Sources: Private Foundations/Grants/Endowments; Business/Corporate Donations; Box Office; Government Grants; Individual Donations
Season: 52 Weeks   **Annual Attendance:** 60,000

DALLAS REPERTORY THEATRE
PO Box 12208, Dallas, TX 75225
(214) 692-5611
Founded: 1969
Arts Area: Professional; Theatrical Group
Status: Professional; Non-Profit
Type: Performing
Purpose: To promote, encourage and advance the performing arts in Dallas through the production of fine-quality, current Broadway plays and musicals
Management: Ed DeLatte, Founder
Officers: Charles McMullen, President; Jay MacAuley, Secretary/Treasurer
Paid Staff: 8   **Volunteer Staff:** 20
Paid Artists: 75   **Non-Paid Artists:** 250
Utilizes: Special Technical Talent; Guest Conductors
Budget: $500,000 - $1,000,000
Income Sources: Private Foundations/Grants/Endowments; Business/Corporate Donations; Box Office; Government Grants; Individual Donations
Season: September - August   **Annual Attendance:** 40,000
Affiliations: AEA; Texas Nonprofit Theatre
Performance Facilities: Crescent Theatre

DALLAS SUMMER MUSICALS
Music Hall at Fair Park, 909 First Avenue Parry, Dallas, TX 75210
(214) 565-1116
Arts Area: Professional; Musical

Status: Professional; Non-Profit
Type: Performing; Sponsoring
Purpose: To arouse public interest in good music; to educate the public in music appreciation and in one phase of the performing arts
Management: Tom Hughes, Producer/Manager
Utilizes: Special Technical Talent; Guest Artists; Guest Directors
Income Sources: Box Office
Performance Facilities: Music Hall at Fair Park

DALLAS THEATER CENTER
3636 Turtle Creek Boulevard, Dallas, TX 75219
(214) 526-8210
FAX: (214) 521-7666
  Founded: 1959
  Arts Area: Professional; Theatrical Group
  Status: Professional; Non-Profit
  Type: Performing; Resident; Educational
  Purpose: To provide a variety of artistically excellent professional theatre experiences representing a wide range of styles and periods
  Management: Richard Hamburger, Artistic Director; Jeff West, Managing Director
  Officers: Bess Enloe, Chairman; Richard Boysen, President
  Paid Staff: 78   **Volunteer Staff:** 14
  Paid Artists: 104
  Utilizes: Special Technical Talent; Guest Artists; Guest Directors
  Budget: $1,000,000 - $5,000,000
  Income Sources: Private Foundations/Grants/Endowments; Business/Corporate Donations; Box Office; Government Grants; Individual Donations
  Season: October - May   **Annual Attendance:** 136,229
  Affiliations: TCG; LORT; AAA
  Performance Facilities: Kalita Humphreys Theater; Arts District Theater

DRAMA CIRCLE THEATRE
2929 Mayhew, Dallas, TX 75228
(214) 270-9255
  Founded: 1971
  Arts Area: Theatrical Group
  Status: Semi-Professional; Non-Profit
  Type: Performing; Touring; Educational
  Purpose: To promote the theatre arts
  Management: Linda Boatman, Managing Director; Bill Green, Founder; Nan Truax, Co-Founder
  Volunteer Staff: 4
  Non-Paid Artists: 30
  Budget: $1,000 - $50,000
  Income Sources: Private Foundations/Grants/Endowments; Business/Corporate Donations; Box Office; Individual Donations
  Season: December - October
  Annual Attendance: 4,500

KATHY BURKS MARIONETTES
2979 Ladybird Lane, Dallas, TX 75229
(214) 353-9277
  Founded: 1971
  Arts Area: Professional; Theatrical Group; Puppet
  Status: Professional; Non-Profit
  Type: Performing; Resident; Educational
  Purpose: We do this for the perpetuation of the art of puppetry. We cover the spectrum of the art itself.
  Management: Kathy Burks, Artistic Director; Sarah Jayne Fiorello, Managing Director; Douglas Burks, Master Puppeteer/Co-Artistic Director; Beatrice Wolf, Composer/Lyricist
  Paid Staff: 7
  Paid Artists: 5
  Utilizes: Guest Artists
  Budget: $50,000 - $100,000
  Income Sources: Box Office
  Season: September - August
  Annual Attendance: 100,000
  Affiliations: Puppeteers of America; Lone Star Puppet Guild
  Performance Facilities: The Loft Puppet Theatre at Fairview Farms, Plano, TX

PEGASUS THEATRE
3916 Main Street, Dallas, TX 75226
(214) 821-6005
Founded: 1985
Arts Area: Professional; Musical; Theatrical Group
Status: Professional; Non-Profit
Type: Performing; Touring
Purpose: To produce new and original comedies
Management: Kurt Kleinmann, Artistic Director; Barbara Weinberger, General Manager
Officers: Pat Hadley, President; Becky Chavarria Chairez, Vice President; Billy Stone, Secretary; Jay Marshall, Treasurer
Paid Staff: 3 **Volunteer Staff:** 1
Paid Artists: 100
Utilizes: Special Technical Talent; Guest Artists; Guest Directors
Budget: $100,000 - $500,000
Income Sources: Private Foundations/Grants/Endowments; Business/Corporate Donations; Box Office; Government Grants; Individual Donations
Season: 52 Weeks **Annual Attendance:** 16,500
Affiliations: STAGE
Performance Facilities: Pegasus Theatre

POCKET SANDWICH THEATRE
5400 East Mockingbird, #119, Dallas, TX 75206
(214) 821-1860
Founded: 1980
Arts Area: Professional; Musical; Dinner
Status: Professional; Commercial
Type: Performing
Purpose: To present a variety of live theatre performances
Management: Rodney Dobbs, Owner/Technical Director; Joe Dickinson, Owner/Artistic Director
Paid Staff: 9
Paid Artists: 73
Utilizes: Special Technical Talent; Guest Artists; Guest Directors
Budget: $1,000 - $50,000
Income Sources: Box Office; Food Sales
Season: 52 Weeks **Annual Attendance:** 24,000
Performance Facilities: Pocket Sandwich Theatre

TEATRO HISPANO DE DALLAS
2204 Commerce, Dallas, TX 75201
(214) 741-6833
FAX: (214) 946-5820
Founded: 1985
Arts Area: Professional; Community; Theatrical Group
Status: Professional; Semi-Professional; Non-Profit
Type: Performing
Management: Cora Cardona, Artistic Director/Producer; Christie Hernandez, Executive Director
Officers: Vicki Meek, President; Donna Miller, Vice President
Paid Staff: 2 **Volunteer Staff:** 25
Paid Artists: 20
Utilizes: Special Technical Talent; Guest Artists; Guest Directors
Budget: $100,000 - $500,000
Income Sources: Private Foundations/Grants/Endowments; Business/Corporate Donations; Box Office; Government Grants; Individual Donations
Season: February - November **Annual Attendance:** 3,000
Performance Facilities: Teatro Dallas

THEATRE GEMINI
PO Box 191225, Dallas, TX 75219
(214) 521-6331
Founded: 1984
Arts Area: Community; Theatrical Group
Status: Non-Professional; Non-Profit
Type: Performing; Educational
Management: Craig Hess, General Manager
Volunteer Staff: 50
Non-Paid Artists: 60
Budget: $50,000 - $100,000

Income Sources: Private Foundations/Grants/Endowments; Business/Corporate Donations; Box Office; Individual Donations
Season: 52 Weeks   **Annual Attendance:** 2,500

THEATRE THREE
2800 Routh, Dallas, TX 75201
(214) 871-2933
FAX: (214) 871-3139
    Founded: 1961
    Arts Area: Professional; Musical
    Status: Professional; Non-Profit
    Type: Performing; Touring; Resident; Educational; Sponsoring
    Purpose: To provide professional theatre and related activities for the Dallas community
    Management: Jac Alder, Executive Producer; Norma Young, Artistic Director; Larry O'Dwyer, Associate Director
    Officers: David Wells, President; Greg Balew, Treasurer
    Paid Staff: 30   **Volunteer Staff:** 60
    Paid Artists: 60   **Non-Paid Artists:** 20
    Utilizes: Special Technical Talent; Guest Conductors; Guest Artists; Guest Directors
    Budget: $1,000,000 - $5,000,000
    Income Sources: Private Foundations/Grants/Endowments; Business/Corporate Donations; Box Office; Government Grants; Individual Donations
    Season: 52 Weeks   **Annual Attendance:** 61,600
    Affiliations: AEA; TCG

UNDERMAIN THEATRE
3202 Elm, Dallas, TX 75226
(214) 748-3082
    Founded: 1983
    Arts Area: Professional
    Status: Non-Profit
    Type: Performing
    Purpose: To focus on regional and national premieres of emotionally, intellectually and philosphically challanging work
    Management: Katherine Owens, Raphael Perry, Artistic Directors; Robert McVay, Technical Director; Sheila L. Sullivan, Marketing
    Utilizes: Special Technical Talent; Guest Directors
    Budget: $100,000 - $500,000
    Income Sources: Private Foundations/Grants/Endowments; Business/Corporate Donations; Box Office; Government Grants; Individual Donations
    Season: August - June   **Annual Attendance:** 5,000
    Affiliations: TCG; Texas Association of Performing Arts; AEA
    Performance Facilities: Undermain Theatre Basement

PERFORMING SERIES

CHAUTAUQUA SERIES
1928 Ross Avenue, Dallas, TX 75201
(214) 220-2727
    Founded: 1948
    Arts Area: Vocal Music; Instrumental Music; Theater
    Status: Non-Professional; Non-Profit
    Type: Performing; Sponsoring
    Purpose: To provide entertainment to the community Sunday evenings in summer
    Management: Ronald Kauffmann, Director of Music and Arts
    Paid Staff: 2
    Utilizes: Special Technical Talent; Guest Artists; Guest Directors
    Budget: $1,000 - $50,000
    Income Sources: Private Foundations/Grants/Endowments; Individual Donations
    Season: July - August   **Annual Attendance:** 4,500
    Performance Facilities: First United Methodist Church

DALLAS CHAMBER MUSIC SOCIETY
4808 Drexel Drive, Dallas, TX 75205
(214) 526-7301
    Founded: 1954
    Arts Area: Instrumental Music
    Status: Professional; Non-Profit
    Type: Performing; Sponsoring
    Purpose: To give chamber music concerts on the highest professional level at minimum cost to Dallas audiences
    Management: Dorothea Kelley, Manager; Celia Bingham, Assistant

Officers: Walter Brudno, President; Masha Porte, Vice President; Margaret Stevenson, Secretary; Mrs. Martin Anastasi, Membership Secretary; Mrs. Ray Entenman, Entertainment Secretary; Mrs. Karl Kahn, Treasurer
Paid Staff: 1 **Volunteer Staff:** 10
Paid Artists: 21
Utilizes: Guest Artists
Budget: $1,000 - $50,000
Income Sources: Private Foundations/Grants/Endowments; Box Office; Individual Donations
Season: October - April **Annual Attendance:** 2,800
Performance Facilities: Caruth Auditorium, Southern Methodist University

JUNIOR BLACK ACADEMY OF ARTS AND LETTERS
650 South Griffin, Dallas, TX 75202
(214) 658-7144; (214) 658-7147
FAX: (214) 658-7163
Founded: 1977
Arts Area: Dance; Vocal Music; Instrumental Music; Theater; Festivals
Status: Professional; Non-Profit
Type: Performing; Educational
Purpose: Designed to promote, foster, cultivate, perpetuate and preserve the arts and letters of Black Americans in the fine, literary and performing arts
Management: Curtis King, Founder and President; Gwen Hargrove, Facility Operations Manager; Ken Rowe, Developmental Manager; Gail Johnson, Membership Developer; Marilyn Clark, Publicist
Officers: Brooks Fitch, Chairman of the Board
Paid Staff: 7 **Volunteer Staff:** 150
Paid Artists: 100 **Non-Paid Artists:** 100
Utilizes: Special Technical Talent; Guest Conductors; Guest Artists; Guest Directors
Budget: $100,000 - $500,000
Income Sources: Private Foundations/Grants/Endowments; Business/Corporate Donations; Box Office; Government Grants; Individual Donations
Season: September - August

SHAKESPEARE FESTIVAL OF DALLAS
3630 Harry Hine Boulevard, Dallas, TX 75219
(214) 807-4046
Founded: 1972
Arts Area: Professional
Status: Professional; Non-Profit
Type: Performing; Educational
Management: Jeff West, Managing Director; Dale A.J. Rose, Artistic Director; Robert Glenn, Founder/Consulting Producer
Officers: Otto K. Wetzel, Chairman of the Board; Sherry Patterson, Secretary; Catherine Z. Smith, Treasurer
Paid Staff: 4 **Volunteer Staff:** 20
Paid Artists: 30 **Non-Paid Artists:** 10
Utilizes: Special Technical Talent; Guest Artists; Guest Directors
Budget: $100,000 - $500,000
Income Sources: Private Foundations/Grants/Endowments; Business/Corporate Donations; Government Grants; Individual Donations
Season: June - July **Annual Attendance:** 36,000
Performance Facilities: Fair Park Band Shell

TITAS - THE INTERNATIONAL THEATRICAL ARTS SOCIETY
3900 Lemmon Avenue, Suite 20, Dallas, TX 75219
(214) 528-5576
FAX: (214) 528-2617
Founded: 1982
Arts Area: Dance; Instrumental Music
Status: Non-Profit
Type: Sponsoring
Purpose: To present international cultural and educational programs
Management: Tom Adams, Executive Producer
Officers: Margie Reese, President
Paid Staff: 3 **Volunteer Staff:** 2
Utilizes: Guest Artists
Budget: $100,000 - $500,000
Income Sources: Private Foundations/Grants/Endowments; Business/Corporate Donations; Box Office; Government Grants; Individual Donations
Season: September - May
Annual Attendance: 69,000

Affiliations: ISPAA
Performance Facilities: McFarlin Auditorium, Southern Methodist University

FACILITY

BATH HOUSE CULTURAL CENTER
521 East Lawther Drive, Dallas, TX 75218
(214) 670-8749
    Type of Facility: Theatre House
    Facility Originally: Bathhouse
    Type of Stage: 3/4 Arena; In-the-round Capability
    Seating Capacity: 130
    Year Built: 1930
    Year Remodeled: 1981
    Contact for Rental: Teri Aguilar;   (214) 328-8428
    Resident Groups: The Gryphon Players; Actors Theatre of Dallas; Irregular Pearl; Actors Stock Company; New Horizon Theatre; Moving Collaborations; Dance Fusion
    To foster the growth, development and quality of multi-cultural arts within the City of Dallas

BIBLICAL ARTS CENTER
7500 Park Lane, Dallas, TX 75225
(214) 691-4661
FAX: (214) 691-4752
    Type of Facility: Auditorium; Multi-Purpose
    Facility Originally: Museum
    Type of Stage: Proscenium
    Stage Dimensions: 25'Wx25'6"D
    Seating Capacity: 350
    Year Built: 1981   **Architect:** Burson Hendricks & Wall   **Cost:** $1,200,000
    Acoustical Consultant: Variable Acoustics
    Contact for Rental: Ronnie L. Roese;   (214) 691-4661

DALLAS CONVENTION CENTER
650 South Griffin, Dallas, TX 75202
(214) 939-2700
    Type of Facility: Civic Center; Multi-Purpose
    Architect: George Dahl
    Contact for Rental: Gloria Medrano;   (214) 939-2700
    The Convention Center contains the Arena and Theater. See separate listings for additional information.

DALLAS CONVENTION CENTER - ARENA
650 South Griffin, Dallas, TX 75202
(214) 939-2700
    Type of Facility: Arena; Multi-Purpose
    Type of Stage: Flexible; Arena
    Seating Capacity: 9,816
    Year Built: 1958
    Acoustical Consultant: Jim Moxley
    Contact for Rental: Gloria Medrano;   (214) 939-2700

DALLAS CONVENTION CENTER - THEATER
650 South Griffin, Dallas, TX 75202
(214) 393-2700
    Type of Facility: Concert Hall; Auditorium; Theatre House; Multi-Purpose
    Type of Stage: Proscenium
    Stage Dimensions: 80'Wx45'5"D
    Orchestra Pit
    Seating Capacity: 1,770
    Year Built: 1957
    Contact for Rental: Gloria Medrano;   (214) 939-2700

DALLAS REPERTORY THEATRE
PO Box 12208, Dallas, TX 75225
(214) 358-3997
    Founded: 1969
    Type of Facility: Auditorium; Theatre House
    Facility Originally: Business Facility
    Type of Stage: Thrust

Stage Dimensions: 20'x30'
Seating Capacity: 215
Year Built: 1966 **Architect:** Harrell & Hamilton, OmniPlan Architects
Year Remodeled: 1984 **Architect:** Art Rogers **Cost:** $650,000
Resident Groups: Dallas Repertory Theatre
Ed DeLatte, Founder/Artistic Director

DALLAS THEATER CENTER - ARTS DISTRICT
2401 Flora Street, Dallas, TX 75204
(214) 922-0422
Type of Facility: Theatre House; Arena; Multi-Purpose
Type of Stage: Flexible
Seating Capacity: 500
Year Built: 1984
Contact for Rental: Donna Flippin; (214) 526-8210
Resident Groups: Dallas Theater Center

DALLAS THEATER CENTER - KALITA HUMPHREYS THEATER
3636 Turtle Creek Boulevard, Dallas, TX 75219
(214) 526-8210
Type of Facility: Theatre House
Type of Stage: Thrust
Seating Capacity: 466
Year Built: 1959 **Architect:** Frank Lloyd Wright **Cost:** $1,000,000
Contact for Rental: Donna Flippin; (214) 526-8210
Resident Groups: Dallas Theater Center

FAIR PARK BANDSHELL
Cullum Boulevard and Martin Luther King Drive, Dallas, TX 75226
(214) 421-8702
Type of Facility: Amphitheater
Type of Stage: Elizabethan
Seating Capacity: 3,792
Year Built: 1936 **Architect:** George Dahl
Year Remodeled: 1986 **Architect:** City of Dallas
Contact for Rental: Frank Wyatt; (214) 670-8402
Manager: Eddie Hueston, Executive General Manager; (214) 670-8463

MAJESTIC THEATRE
1925 Elm, Dallas, TX 75201-4516
(214) 880-0137
FAX: (214) 880-0097
Founded: 1921
Type of Facility: Concert Hall; Auditorium; Performance Center; Off Broadway; Theatre House; Opera House; Multi-Purpose
Facility Originally: Vaudeville
Type of Stage: Proscenium; Includes 12' apron
Stage Dimensions: 39'Wx28'D **Orchestra Pit**
Seating Capacity: 1,648
Year Built: 1921 **Architect:** John Eberson **Cost:** $2,000,000
Year Remodeled: 1983 **Architect:** The Oglesby Group **Cost:** $5,000,000
Acoustical Consultant: Jaffe Acoustics
Contact for Rental: David Boddie; (214) 880-0137
Resident Groups: Dallas Broadway Series (touring shows); Dallas Black Dance Theatre; Anita N. Martinez Ballet Folklorico; Dallas Classic Guitar Society; Ballet Dallas
Performances, meetings, conferences, banquet/party facilities

THE MORTON H. MEYERSON SYMPHONY CENTER - EUGENE MCDERMOTT CONCERT HALL
2301 Flora Street, PO Box 26207, Dallas, TX 75226
(214) 565-9100
Founded: 1989
Type of Facility: Concert Hall; Performance Center
Type of Stage: Platform
Stage Dimensions: 36'D; 60'W downstage, 41'W upstage
Seating Capacity: 2,200
Architect: I.M. Pei and Partners **Cost:** $85,000,000

Acoustical Consultant: ARTEC
Contact for Rental: City of Dallas;   (214) 565-9100
Resident Groups: Dallas Symphony Association

MUSIC HALL AT FAIR PARK
PO Box 150188, Dallas, TX 75315
(214) 565-1116
FAX: (214) 428-4526
    Type of Facility: Theatre House
    Type of Stage: Proscenium; Modified Apron Proscenium
    Stage Dimensions: 52'Wx42'D; 52'Wx30'H proscenium opening   **Orchestra Pit**
    Seating Capacity: 3,420
    Year Built: 1925
    Year Remodeled: 1972   **Architect:** JPJ Architects   **Cost:** $5,500,000
    Contact for Rental: Nancy Marshall;   (214) 565-1116
    Manager: Gary Surratt
    Resident Groups: The Dallas Opera; Dallas Summer Musicals

REUNION ARENA
777 Sports Street, Dallas, TX 75207
(214) 939-2770
    Type of Facility: Concert Hall; Performance Center; Arena
    Type of Stage: Arena
    Seating Capacity: 9,500
    Year Built: 1980   **Architect:** Harwood K. Smith & Partners   **Cost:** $27,000,000
    Acoustical Consultant: Don Moxley
    Contact for Rental: Will Caudell;   (214) 939-2770

SOUTH DALLAS CULTURAL CENTER
3400 South Fitzhugh, Dallas, TX 75210
(214) 670-0314
    Type of Facility: Auditorium; Theatre House; Multi-Purpose
    Type of Stage: In-the-round Capability
    Seating Capacity: 160
    Year Built: 1986   **Cost:** $1,500,000
    Contact for Rental: Sydney Davis, Technical Director;   (214) 670-0314
    Manager: Mittie Jordan, Director;   (214) 670-0314

SOUTHERN METHODIST UNIVERSITY - BOB HOPE THEATRE
Owen Fine Arts Center, Dallas, TX 75275
(214) 692-3383
FAX: (214) 692-4138
    Type of Facility: Theatre Complex; Theatre House
    Type of Stage: Proscenium
    Stage Dimensions: 42'Wx38'D   **Orchestra Pit**
    Seating Capacity: 392
    Year Built: 1968   **Architect:** George Dahl
    Acoustical Consultant: C.P. Boner & Associates
    Contact for Rental: Jim D'Asaro;   (214) 692-3383
    Resident Groups: SMU Theatre; SMU Dance; SMU Opera

SOUTHERN METHODIST UNIVERSITY - CARUTH AUDITORIUM
Owen Fine Arts Center, Dallas, TX 75275
(214) 692-2713
FAX: (214) 692-4138
    Type of Facility: Concert Hall
    Type of Stage: Arena
    Stage Dimensions: 63'Wx24'D
    Seating Capacity: 521
    Year Built: 1968   **Architect:** George Dahl
    Acoustical Consultant: C.P. Boner & Associates
    Contact for Rental: John Gibson;   (214) 692-2713
    Resident Groups: SMU Symphony; SMU Wind Ensemble; SMU Jazz Ensemble; Dallas Chamber Music Society; Voices of Change; Dallas Chamber Orchestra
    Recitals, instrumental concerts

SOUTHERN METHODIST UNIVERSITY - MARGO JONES THEATRE
Owen Fine Arts Center, Dallas, TX 75275
(214) 692-3383
FAX: (214) 692-4138
    Type of Facility: Arena
    Type of Stage: Flexible; Arena
    Stage Dimensions: 60'x60'
    Seating Capacity: 132
    Year Built: 1968 **Architect:** George Dahl
    Acoustical Consultant: C.P. Boner & Associates
    Contact for Rental: Jim D'Asaro; (214) 692-3383
    Resident Groups: SMU Theatre; SMU Dance

SOUTHERN METHODIST UNIVERSITY - MCFARLIN MEMORIAL AUDITORIUM
6400 Hillcrest Avenue, PO Box 152, Dallas, TX 75275
(214) 692-3129
FAX: (214) 692-4138
    Type of Facility: Auditorium
    Facility Originally: Convocation Hall
    Type of Stage: Proscenium
    Stage Dimensions: 47'6"Wx33'D; 46'6"Wx32'H proscenium opening **Orchestra Pit**
    Seating Capacity: 2,404
    Year Built: 1926 **Cost:** $500,000
    Year Remodeled: 1961 **Cost:** $900,000
    Contact for Rental: Jane Lane; (214) 692-3129

THANKS-GIVING SQUARE
Intresection of Bryan, Pacific and Ervay, PO Box 1777, Dallas, TX 75221
(214) 969-1977
    Type of Facility: Environmental; Performance Center
    Year Built: 1977 **Architect:** Philip Johnson **Cost:** $6,000,000
    Contact for Rental: Elizabeth Espersen, Executive Director; (214) 969-1977
    Thanks-Giving Square, built to express gratitude and praise to God, contains the Chapel of Thanksgiving, Courtyard and Hall of World Thanksgiving. See separate listings for additional information.

THANKS-GIVING SQUARE - CHAPEL OF THANKSGIVING
Intersection of Bryan, Pacific and Ervay, PO Box 1777, Dallas, TX 75221
(214) 969-1977
    Type of Facility: Chapel
    Type of Stage: Curved Ramp
    Stage Dimensions: 4'Wx100'L
    Seating Capacity: 100
    Year Built: 1977
    Contact for Rental: Elizabeth Espersen, Executive Director; (214) 969-1977

THANKS-GIVING SQUARE - COURTYARD AT THANKS-GIVING SQUARE
Intersection of Bryan, Pacific and Ervay, PO Box 1777, Dallas, TX 75221
(214) 969-1977
    Type of Facility: Outdoor Garden Courtyard
    Type of Stage: Patio & Elevated Bridge
    Stage Dimensions: Patio - 20'x24'; Bridge - 5'Wx80'L
    Seating Capacity: 500
    Year Built: 1977
    Contact for Rental: Elizabeth Espersen, Executive Director; (214) 969-1977

THANKS-GIVING SQUARE - HALL OF WORLD THANKSGIVING
Intersection of Byran, Pacific and Ervay, PO Box 1777, Dallas, TX 75221
(214) 969-1977
    Type of Facility: Multi-Purpose; Room
    Type of Stage: Flexible
    Seating Capacity: 125
    Year Built: 1977
    Contact for Rental: Elizabeth Espersen, Executive Director; (214) 969-1977

THEATRE THREE
2800 Routh, Dallas, TX 75201
(214) 871-2933; (214) 871-3139
    Type of Facility: Theatre House

Facility Originally: Meeting Hall; Movie House
Type of Stage: Arena
Stage Dimensions: 20'x26' plus alcove stages
Seating Capacity: 243
Year Built: 1969   **Architect:** Jac Alder   **Cost:** $60,000
Year Remodeled: 1986   **Architect:** RTKL; The Oglesby Group   **Cost:** $650,000
Acoustical Consultant: Jac Alder
Contact for Rental: Jack Alder;   (214) 871-2933

Denton

INSTRUMENTAL MUSIC

ONE O'CLOCK LAB BAND
North Texas State University Lab Bands, PO Box 5038, Denton, TX 76203
(817) 565-3743
   Founded: 1947
   Arts Area: Ensemble
   Status: Non-Profit
   Type: Performing; Touring; Educational
   Management: Neil Slater, Director/Professor of Music
   Non-Paid Artists: 21
   Income Sources: Box Office
   Season: 52 Weeks
   Affiliations: North Texas State University

THEATRE

BREAD AND CIRCUS THEATRE
1009 Bull Run, Denton, TX 76201
(817) 387-2408
   Founded: 1982
   Arts Area: Professional; Theatrical Group; Summer Stock; Community; Musical
   Status: Professional; Semi-Professional
   Type: Performing; Touring
   Purpose: To provide a fun theatrical experience for audiences of all ages through audience participation
   Management: Connie Whitt-Lambert, Managing Director
   Officers: Artistic Board - Jeannene Abney, Jim Wilson, John Evarts, Dennis Welch, Melinda Milstead, Kyla Haynes, Marth Kirkpatrick
   Paid Staff: 1   **Paid Artists:** 8
   Utilize: Special Technical Talent; Guest Artists
   Budget: $1,000 - $50,000
   Income Sources: Box Office
   Season: June - August   **Annual Attendance:** 3,500

DENTON COMMUNITY THEATRE
400 East Hickory, PO Box 1931, Denton, TX 76202
(817) 382-7014
   Founded: 1969
   Arts Area: Community; Theatrical Group
   Status: Non-Professional; Non-Profit
   Type: Performing; Educational
   Purpose: To provide artistic, educational experiences for participants and quality theatre for audiences
   Management: Julie Crawford Angelo, Executive Director
   Officers: Lindsay Keffer, President; Jeff Springer, Vice President; Terry Widmer, Development Secretary; Phil Diebel, Treasurer; Gayland Howell, Vice President of Membership; Michael Flanagan, Vice President of Production
   Paid Staff: 5   **Volunteer Staff:** 12
   Paid Artists: 4   **Non-Paid Artists:** 250
   Utilizes: Special Technical Talent; Guest Artists; Guest Directors
   Budget: $100,000 - $500,000
   Income Sources: Private Foundations/Grants/Endowments; Business/Corporate Donations; Box Office; Government Grants; Individual Donations; Membership; Special Events
   Season: 52 Weeks   **Annual Attendance:** 7,500
   Affiliations: ACT; SWTC; Texas Nonprofit Theatre
   Performance Facilities: Center for the Visual Arts

FACILITY

TEXAS WOMAN'S UNIVERSITY - REDBUD THEATRE
PO Box 23865, TWU Station, Denton, TX 76204
(817) 898-2500
FAX: (817) 898-3198
Type of Facility: Theatre Complex
Type of Stage: Proscenium
Stage Dimensions: 32'Wx16'H   **Orchestra Pit**
Seating Capacity: 332
Year Built: 1952
Year Remodeled: 1985   **Architect:** Glenn McFaddin   **Cost:** $150,000
Contact for Rental: Vice President for Academic Affairs;   (817) 898-3301
Manager: Charles Harrill
Resident Groups: TWU Theatre

UNIVERSITY OF NORTH TEXAS - CONCERT HALL
College of Music, Denton, TX 76203
(817) 565-2791
FAX: (817) 565-4919
Founded: 1890
Type of Facility: Concert Hall
Type of Stage: Proscenium
Seating Capacity: 714
Year Built: 1961   **Cost:** $1,000,000
Contact for Rental: Conference Management;   (817) 565-3628
Manager: M. Wade Kelley, Assistant to the Dean;   (817) 565-3707
Resident Groups: University Symphony; Symphonic Wind Ensemble; Chamber Orchestra; Concert Band; Chamber
Winds; A Cappella Choir; Grand Chorus; Men's and Women's Chorus Brass Choir

UNIVERSITY OF NORTH TEXAS - DEPARTMENT OF DANCE AND DRAMA
PO Box 13126, Denton, TX 76203-3126
(817) 565-2211
Type of Facility: Theatre Complex; Concert Hall; Auditorium; Studio Performance
Type of Stage: Flexible; Proscenium
Stage Dimensions: 44'x40'   **Orchestra Pit**
Seating Capacity: 500
Year Built: 1968   **Architect:** CRS Architects
Year Remodeled: 1987   **Cost:** $225,000
Acoustical Consultant: C.P. Boner & Associates
Contact for Rental: Ralph B. Culp, Chairman;   (817) 565-2211
Resident Groups: University of North Texas Department of Dance and Drama; School of Music
Total cost of Speech and Drama Building - $2,053,000

Edinburg

INSTRUMENTAL MUSIC

SOUTH TEXAS SYMPHONY ASSOCIATION
PO Box 2832, First City Tower 1305, Edinburg, TX 78502
(512) 630-5355
FAX: (512) 632-2352
Founded: 1976
Arts Area: Symphony; Chamber
Status: Semi-Professional; Non-Profit
Type: Performing; Resident; Educational
Purpose: The purpose of South Texas Symphony Association is to promote, encourage and support the performance of
symphonic music in South Texas.
Management: John Daugherty, Executive Director
Officers: Walter Passmore, President; Kathy Didieu, Vice President; Billy Joe Day, Treasurer; Marilyn Meyer,
Parliamentarian
Paid Staff: 2
Paid Artists: 70   **Non-Paid Artists:** 60
Utilizes: Special Technical Talent; Guest Artists
Budget: $100,000 - $500,000
Income Sources: Private Foundations/Grants/Endowments; Business/Corporate Donations; Box Office; Government
Grants; Individual Donations

Season: October - May   Annual Attendance: 6,500
Affiliations: ASOL; Pan American University
Performance Facilities: Pan American University Fine Arts Auditorium

FACILITY

UNIVERSITY OF TEXAS-PAN AMERICAN - FINE ARTS AUDITORIUM
Pan American University, Edinburg, TX 78539
(512) 381-3471
Type of Facility: Auditorium
Type of Stage: Proscenium   Orchestra Pit
Seating Capacity: 1,000
Year Built: 1967   Architect: Kenneth Bentsen
Contact for Rental: Manager;   (512) 381-3471
Resident Groups: University faculty and groups

UNIVERSITY OF TEXAS-PAN AMERICAN - THEATER
1201 West University Drive, Edinburg, TX 78539
(512) 381-3581
Type of Facility: Theatre Complex; Studio Performance; Environmental; Theatre House; Multi-Purpose; Black Box
Type of Stage: Thrust; Flexible
Seating Capacity: Thrust - 296; Black Box - 200
Year Built: 1984   Architect: SHSC   Cost: $8,000,000
Contact for Rental: Tom Grabowski;   (512) 381-3588
Manager: Linda Donahue, Managing Director;   (512) 381-3581
Resident Groups: Pan American University Theater

El Paso

DANCE

BALLET OF THE AMERICAS
PO Box 335, El Paso, TX 79968
(915) 533-2200
Founded: 1970
Arts Area: Ballet
Status: Professional; Non-Profit
Type: Performing; Touring; Resident
Purpose: Binational and bicultural ballet company
Management: Ingeborg Heuser, Artistic Director; James R. Osborne, Executive Director; Susan Merrill,
Development Director
Officers: Marlene Stewart, Chairman of the Board; Manuel Vargas, President of the Board
Paid Staff: 4
Utilizes: Guest Artists; Guest Choreographers
Budget: $500,000 - $1,000,000
Income Sources: Private Foundations/Grants/Endowments; Business/Corporate Donations; Box Office;
Individual Donations
Season: September - May

INTERNATIONAL BALLET FOLKLORICO
PO Box 3777, El Paso, TX 79923
(915) 566-5084
Arts Area: Modern; Jazz; Ethnic; Folk
Status: Semi-Professional; Non-Profit
Type: Performing; Educational
Purpose: To provide cultural entertainment to the community and surrounding areas; to preserve the cultural heritage of
the Southwest through dance
Management: Rosa Guerrico, Artistic Director; Oscar Hernandez, Jessica Bravo, Assistant Directors
Officers: Yolanda Delgado, President
Volunteer Staff: 28
Paid Artists: 18   Non-Paid Artists: 35
Budget: $1,000 - $50,000
Income Sources: Private Foundations/Grants/Endowments; Business/Corporate Donations; Box Office;
Individual Donations
Season: 52 Weeks   Annual Attendance: 400,000
Performance Facilities: Lower Valley YWCA

INSTRUMENTAL MUSIC

EL PASO PRO-MUSICA
1330 East Yandell, El Paso, TX 79902
(915) 532-9139
FAX: (915) 532-9199
Founded: 1977
Arts Area: Orchestra; Chamber; Ensemble
Status: Professional; Non-Profit
Type: Performing; Educational
Purpose: To promote musical and cultural development in El Pasoand environs by presenting choral and instrumental performances ranging from the Renaissance to the contemporary
Management: C.C. Leeper, Executive Director; Michelle Chapa, Office Manager; Dr. Jerry Forderhase, Artistic Director; Jana Tippen, Publicity Coordinator
Officers: Bryan McVeigh, Chairman of the Board/President; Lonnie Busby, President Elect; Russell Blanchard, Mary Ann Gum, Lynn Jacobson, Robert Rosen MD, Marlene Stewart, Nancy Wacker, Bobbie Young, Vice Presidents; Marion S. Becker MD, Secretary; William D. Tippin Jr., Treasurer
Paid Staff: 7 **Volunteer Staff:** 1
Paid Artists: 81
Utilizes: Guest Conductors; Guest Artists; Guest Directors
Budget: $100,000 - $500,000
Income Sources: Private Foundations/Grants/Endowments; Business/Corporate Donations; Box Office; Government Grants; Individual Donations
Season: October - May **Annual Attendance:** 15,000
Affiliations: CA

EL PASO SYMPHONY ORCHESTRA
PO Box 180, El Paso, TX 79942
(915) 532-3776
Founded: 1930
Arts Area: Symphony; Orchestra
Status: Professional; Non-Profit
Type: Performing; Educational; Sponsoring
Purpose: To promote symphonic music in the El Paso community
Management: Gay Brown, General Manager; Abraham Chavez Jr., Music Director/Conductor
Officers: Ann C. Brown, Chairman of the Board
Paid Staff: 4 **Volunteer Staff:** 400
Paid Artists: 85
Utilizes: Guest Conductors; Guest Artists
Budget: $500,000 - $1,000,000
Income Sources: Private Foundations/Grants/Endowments; Business/Corporate Donations; Box Office; Government Grants; Individual Donations
Season: September - April **Annual Attendance:** 35,000
Affiliations: ASOL; El Paso Arts Alliance; El Paso Arts Resource Board
Performance Facilities: El Paso Civic Center Theater

THEATRE

SOUTHWEST REPERTORY ORGANIZATION
1301 Texas Avenue, El Paso, TX 79901
(915) 533-1671
Founded: 1978
Arts Area: Musical; Community; Theatrical Group
Status: Non-Professional; Non-Profit
Type: Performing; Touring
Purpose: A community theatre providing a main season of contemporary dramas, musicals, comedies, a summer repertory of contemporary plays, and acting, directing and technical classes
Management: Ed Hamilton, Interim Executive/Artistic Director; Glen O. Brooks, Technical Director; Glenda Nevarez, Office Manager
Officers: Maryanne Phinney, President; Sarah Griffin, President of the Board; Mike Williams, Vice President
Paid Staff: 3 **Volunteer Staff:** 28
Paid Artists: 6
Utilizes: Guest Directors
Budget: $50,000 - $100,000
Income Sources: Private Foundations/Grants/Endowments; Business/Corporate Donations; Box Office; Government Grants; Individual Donations
Season: 52 Weeks **Annual Attendance:** 6,000

PERFORMING SERIES

VIVA EL PASO!
PO Box 31340, El Paso, TX 79931
(915) 565-6900
FAX: (915) 565-6999
> **Founded:** 1978
> **Arts Area:** Dance; Vocal Music; Theater; Ballet; FOLK
> **Status:** Professional; Non-Profit
> **Type:** Performing; Resident
> **Purpose:** VIVA EL PASO! is an outdoor drama with heavy dance emphasis which celebrates the Indian, Spanish, Mexican and Western American cultures that have blended during El Paso's history.
> **Management:** David D. Mills, Managing Director; Hector M. Serrano, Artistic Director
> **Officers:** Barbara Daughtry, President; Jan Drehr, Ruly Armendariz, Madge Zuloaga, Vice Presidents; Consuelo Forti, Secretary; Sheila Loudner, Treasurer
> **Paid Staff:** 12
> **Paid Artists:** 50   **Non-Paid Artists:** 7
> **Budget:** $500,000 - $1,000,000
> **Income Sources:** Private Foundations/Grants/Endowments; Business/Corporate Donations; Box Office; Government Grants; Individual Donations
> **Season:** June - September   **Annual Attendance:** 40,000
> **Affiliations:** Institute of Outdoor Drama
> **Performance Facilities:** McKelligon Canyon Amphitheater

FACILITY

CHAMIZAL NATIONAL MEMORIAL - THEATER
800 South San Marcial, PO Box 722, El Paso, TX 79905
(915) 532-7273
FAX: (915) 532-7240
> **Type of Facility:** Concert Hall; Auditorium; Outdoor (Concert); Theatre House; Amphitheater; Multi-Purpose
> **Type of Stage:** Flexible; Modified Thrust Proscenium
> **Stage Dimensions:** 60'Wx38'D; 60'Wx48'D with pit cover in place   **Orchestra Pit**
> **Seating Capacity:** 502; 446 in thrust configuration
> **Year Built:** 1973   **Architect:** George Izenour   **Cost:** $1,200,000
> **Acoustical Consultant:** George Izenour
> **Contact for Rental:** Manager
> **Resident Groups:** Siglo de Oro Drama Festival; Zarzuela Festival; Borden Folk Festival; Music Theatre El Paso; On Stage
> *Rentals are restricted to non-profit groups only*

EL PASO CIVIC CENTER - EXHIBITION HALL
1 Civic Center Plaza, El Paso, TX 79901-1187
(915) 534-0600
> **Type of Facility:** Auditorium; Performance Center; Theatre House; Civic Center; Arena
> **Type of Stage:** Proscenium; Platform
> **Stage Dimensions:** Platform - 60'Wx40'D; Proscenium - 30'x56'   **Orchestra Pit**
> **Seating Capacity:** Concert Hall - 6,000; Performance Theatre - 2,400
> **Year Built:** 1972
> **Contact for Rental:** Joyce Trujillo, Booking Manager;   (915) 534-0609

EL PASO CIVIC CENTER - THEATRE
1 Civic Center Plaza, El Paso, TX 79901
(915) 541-4920
> **Type of Facility:** Concert Hall; Performance Center; Theatre House
> **Type of Stage:** Proscenium
> **Stage Dimensions:** 56'Wx56'D   **Orchestra Pit**
> **Seating Capacity:** 2,548
> **Year Built:** 1974
> **Contact for Rental:** Manager;   (915) 541-4920

UNIVERSITY OF TEXAS AT EL PASO - MAIN PLAYHOUSE
500 West University, El Paso, TX 79968-0549
(915) 747-5146
> **Type of Facility:** Theatre House; University Playhouse
> **Type of Stage:** Thrust; Flexible; Proscenium
> **Stage Dimensions:** 80'Wx32'D, 46'W proscenium opening   **Orchestra Pit**
> **Seating Capacity:** 430

Year Built: 1974   **Architect:** Marmon & Mok Associates
Acoustical Consultant: Bolt, Beranek & Newman

Fort Hood

PERFORMING SERIES

FORT HOOD COMMUNITY MUSIC AND THEATER - FORT HOOD COMMUNITY PLAYERS
Building 2803, Fort Hood, TX 76544
(817) 287-6116
> **Founded:** 1950
> **Arts Area:** Dance; Vocal Music; Instrumental Music; Theater; Festivals
> **Status:** Non-Professional
> **Type:** Performing; Touring
> **Purpose:** To afford the opportunity to the military man, his family and the area residents to perform in shows, musicals and talent competitions (variety shows)
> **Management:** Jean Zavoina, Director Music/Theater; Roland Gagne, Music Director; Fred Baker, Technical Director; Tom Ross, Costumer
> **Paid Staff:** 11   **Volunteer Staff:** 25
> **Utilizes:** Guest Conductors; Guest Directors
> **Budget:** $1,000 - $50,000
> **Season:** 52 Weeks   **Annual Attendance:** 3,000

FACILITY

FORT HOOD MUSIC AND THEATER - THEATER #1
Building 134, Fort Hood, TX 76544-5056
(817) 287-6116
> **Type of Facility:** Concert Hall; Auditorium; Performance Center; Theatre House; Multi-Purpose
> **Facility Originally:** Movie House
> **Type of Stage:** Thrust; Proscenium
> **Stage Dimensions:** 34'Wx20'Dx18'H (flexible)
> **Seating Capacity:** 320
> **Year Built:** 1951
> **Architect:** United States Government
> **Contact for Rental:** Brent D. Pierson;   (817) 287-6116
> **Resident Groups:** Fort Hood Community Players; Fort Hood Silver Singers; Fort Hood Community Singers

Fort Worth

DANCE

BALLET CONCERTO
3803 Camp Bowie, Fort Worth, TX 76107
(817) 738-7915
> **Founded:** 1969
> **Arts Area:** Ballet
> **Status:** Non-Profit
> **Type:** Performing
> **Purpose:** Free and paid exposure to ballet through performances in public schools and concerts in other locations
> **Management:** Margo Dean, Artistic Director
> **Officers:** John Merrifield, President
> **Paid Staff:** 1   **Volunteer Staff:** 20
> **Paid Artists:** 3   **Non-Paid Artists:** 10
> **Utilizes:** Special Technical Talent; Guest Conductors; Guest Artists; Guest Directors
> **Budget:** $1,000 - $50,000
> **Income Sources:** Private Foundations/Grants/Endowments; Business/Corporate Donations; Box Office; Government Grants; Individual Donations
> **Season:** 52 Weeks   **Annual Attendance:** 5,000
> **Affiliations:** SWRBA

FORT WORTH BALLET COMPANY
6845 Green Oaks Road, Fort Worth, TX 76116
(817) 763-0207
FAX: (817) 763-0624
> **Founded:** 1964
> **Arts Area:** Ballet

Status: Professional; Non-Profit
Type: Performing; Touring; Resident; Educational
Purpose: High quality ballet
Management: Paul Mejia, Artistic Director; David Mallette, Executive Director
Paid Staff: 5
Paid Artists: 23
Utilizes: Special Technical Talent; Guest Artists
Budget: $1,000,000 - $5,000,000
Income Sources: Private Foundations/Grants/Endowments; Business/Corporate Donations; Box Office
Season: September - April
Performance Facilities: Tarrant County Convention Center

INSTRUMENTAL MUSIC

FORT WORTH SYMPHONY
4401 Trail Lake Drive, Fort Worth, TX 76109
(817) 921-2676
FAX: (817) 921-9795
Founded: 1925
Arts Area: Symphony; Orchestra; Chamber
Status: Professional; Non-Profit
Type: Performing; Touring
Purpose: To provide the leadership and financial support required to maintain a symphony orchestra of the first rank and to build an internationally-recognized chamber orchestra, both dedicated to artistic development and performances of superior quality
Management: Ann Koonsman, Executive Director; John Giordano, Music Director
Paid Staff: 16
Paid Artists: 90
Utilizes: Guest Conductors; Guest Artists
Budget: $500,000 - $1,000,000
Income Sources: Private Foundations/Grants/Endowments; Business/Corporate Donations; Box Office; Government Grants; Individual Donations
Season: September - May   Annual Attendance: 54,000
Affiliations: ASOL
Performance Facilities: Tarrant County Convention Center; Ed Landreth Auditorium, Texas Christian University

YOUTH ORCHESTRA OF GREATER FORT WORTH
Orchestra Hall, 4401 Trail Lake Drive, Fort Worth, TX 76109
(817) 923-3121
FAX: (817) 923-3174
Founded: 1965
Arts Area: Orchestra
Status: Non-Profit
Type: Performing; Touring; Educational
Purpose: To educate young musicians, ages 3 to 22
Management: Freda Wise, General Manager
Officers: Betty Landy, President; Jonathan Suder, Executive Vice President; Nancy Mitchell, June Wolff, Vice Presidents
Paid Staff: 4   Volunteer Staff: 3
Paid Artists: 22   Non-Paid Artists: 1
Utilizes: Guest Artists
Budget: $100,000 - $500,000
Income Sources: Private Foundations/Grants/Endowments; Business/Corporate Donations; Individual Donations; Tuition
Season: September - May   Annual Attendance: 5,000
Affiliations: ASOL
Performance Facilities: Orchestra Hall

VOCAL MUSIC

FORT WORTH OPERA ASSOCIATION
3505 West Lancaster, Fort Worth, TX 76107
(817) 731-0833; (817) 731-0200
FAX: (817) 731-0835
Founded: 1946
Arts Area: Grand Opera; Lyric Opera
Status: Professional; Non-Profit
Type: Performing; Resident; Educational
Purpose: To cultivate and promote understanding and love of opera
Management: William Walker, General Director; Leeanne Parma, Development Assistant
Officers: Dr. Jack S. Hardwick, President; Dr. Adelia Hale-Stanley, President, Opera Guild of Fort Worth

Paid Staff: 5   **Volunteer Staff:** 2
Paid Artists: 392
Utilizes: Special Technical Talent; Guest Conductors; Guest Artists; Guest Directors
Budget: $500,000 - $1,000,000
Income Sources: Private Foundations/Grants/Endowments; Business/Corporate Donations; Box Office; Government Grants; Individual Donations
Season: November - May   **Annual Attendance:** 22,000
Affiliations: OA; Arts Council of Fort Worth and Tarrant County
Performance Facilities: Tarrant County Convention Center

SCHOLA CANTORUM OF TEXAS
3505 West Lancaster, Fort Worth, TX 76107
(817) 737-5788
   Founded: 1962
   Arts Area: Choral
   Status: Semi-Professional; Non-Profit
   Type: Performing
   Purpose: To provide top quality choral music to the Metroplex; to provide a musical outlet for our singers
   Management: Gary Ebensberger, Director; Pamela Wood, Executive Director
   Officers: Shelby L. Adams, Board President; Steven O'Kelley, President-Elect
   Paid Staff: 3
   Non-Paid Artists: 60
   Utilizes: Special Technical Talent; Guest Artists
   Budget: $50,000 - $100,000
   Income Sources: Private Foundations/Grants/Endowments; Business/Corporate Donations; Box Office; Individual Donations
   Season: October - May   **Annual Attendance:** 3,800
   Performance Facilities: Kimbell Art Museum; Irons Recital Hall, University of Texas-Arlington; Ed Landreth Auditorium, Texas Christian University

THE TEXAS BOYS CHOIR
PO Box 100219, Fort Worth, TX 76185-0219
(817) 924-1482
FAX: (817) 926-9932
   Founded: 1946
   Arts Area: Choral; Folk
   Status: Professional; Non-Profit
   Type: Performing; Touring; Resident; Educational
   Purpose: To establish, create, organize, and manage a boys' choir and related educational activities and provide for the education and training of boys in the art of music and scholastic achievement
   Management: Jack Noble White, Executive Director; A.Z. Rowland, Jr., Business Manager
   Officers: Jeffrey B. King, Assistant Treasurer; A.Z. Rowland Jr., Ex-Officio/Business Manager; Jack Noble White, Ex-Officio/Executive Director; Michael D. Palmer, Immediate Past President; Billy B. Hill Jr., President; Michael C. Mason, President of Parents Club; Mrs. S. Keith Jackson Jr., Vice President of Administration; Derrell H. Boggs, Vice President of Dallas Affairs; Bruce A. Rockett, Vice President of Finance/Treasurer; John M. Thompson Jr., Vice President of Marketing/Public Relations; T. Pollard Rogers, Vice President of Program & President/"Friends"; Terry McGrath, Vice President of Property
   Paid Staff: 6
   Utilizes: Special Technical Talent; Guest Conductors; Guest Artists
   Budget: $500,000 - $1,000,000
   Income Sources: Private Foundations/Grants/Endowments; Business/Corporate Donations; Box Office; Individual Donations
   Season: August - June   **Annual Attendance:** 100,000
   Affiliations: Arts Council of Fort Worth

THE TEXAS GIRLS CHOIR
4449 Camp Bowie Boulevard, Fort Worth, TX 76107
(817) 732-8161
   Founded: 1962
   Arts Area: Choral; Ethnic; Folk
   Status: Non-Professional; Non-Profit
   Type: Performing; Touring; Educational
   Purpose: To develop little girls' lives through excellence in music; girls, ages 8-14, come from 30 different north Texas cities and participate in music and leadership training throughout the year
   Management: Shirley Carter, Founder/Executive Director; Debi Weir, Administrative Assistant/Handbell Director
   Paid Staff: 11   **Volunteer Staff:** 100
   Non-Paid Artists: 200
   Utilizes: Guest Artists

Budget: $100,000 - $500,000
Income Sources: Private Foundations/Grants/Endowments; Business/Corporate Donations; Box Office; Individual Donations
Season: October - May
Annual Attendance: 30,000

THEATRE

CASA MANANA MUSICALS INC.
3101 West Lancaster, Fort Worth, TX 76107
(817) 332-2272
FAX: (817) 332-5711
Founded: 1958
Arts Area: Professional; Summer Stock; Musical
Status: Non-Profit
Type: Performing; Touring; Resident; Educational
Purpose: To bring Broadway musicals to Fort Worth, with special appearances by stars; to produce plays for children and adults
Management: Van Kaplan, Producer/General Manager; Deborah Brown, Assistant Producer/Executive Director of Children's Playhouse
Officers: Kay Granger, Chairman of the Board; Michael Hyatt, President
Paid Staff: 24 **Volunteer Staff:** 82
Paid Artists: 100
Utilizes: Special Technical Talent; Guest Artists; Guest Directors
Budget: $1,000,000 - $5,000,000
Income Sources: Private Foundations/Grants/Endowments; Box Office; Individual Donations
Season: 52 Weeks **Annual Attendance:** 250,000
Performance Facilities: Casa Manana Theatre

CASA MANANA PLAYHOUSE
3101 West Lancaster, Fort Worth, TX 76107
(817) 332-9319
Founded: 1962
Arts Area: Professional; Musical
Status: Professional; Non-Profit
Type: Performing; Resident; Educational
Purpose: To present plays for children Fridays and Saturday with special weekday performances for local schools; to present Casa Kids, 15 children who provide free performances for area civic and non-profit organizations
Management: Van Kaplan, Executive Producer; Deborah Brown, Director of the Playhouse
Officers: Bob Bolen, Chairman; Ted B. Bevan, President; David Walker, Vice President, Finance and Budget; D'Ann Reed Dagen, Secretary
Paid Staff: 35
Paid Artists: 15
Utilizes: Guest Artists; Guest Directors
Budget: $100,000 - $500,000
Income Sources: Private Foundations/Grants/Endowments; Business/Corporate Donations; Box Office; Government Grants; Individual Donations
Season: September - May **Annual Attendance:** 130,000
Affiliations: ASSITEJ; AEA; AFM
Performance Facilities: Casa Manana Theatre

CIRCLE THEATRE, INC.
1227 West Magnolia Avenue, #520, Fort Worth, TX 76104
(817) 921-3040
FAX: (817) 923-6087
Founded: 1981
Arts Area: Theatrical Group
Status: Semi-Professional; Non-Profit
Type: Performing; Resident
Purpose: To produce original and contemporary theatre scripts not yet seen in Fort Worth
Management: Rose Pearson, Executive Director; Bill Newberry, Managing Director; Carlo Cuesta, Director of Public Relations/Marketing
Officers: Joan Kline, President; Robert I. Fenandez, Tom Gaffney, Vice Presidents; Kim Kirk, Sherry Jackson, Corresponding and Recording Secretaries; Marilyn Austin, Treasurer
Paid Staff: 4 **Volunteer Staff:** 50
Paid Artists: 75

Utilizes: Special Technical Talent; Guest Directors
Budget: $100,000 - $500,000
Income Sources: Private Foundations/Grants/Endowments; Business/Corporate Donations; Box Office; Government Grants; Individual Donations
Season: 52 Weeks   Annual Attendance: 10,000

FORT WORTH THEATRE
3505 West Lancaster, Fort Worth, TX 76107
(817) 738-7491
Founded: 1955
Arts Area: Theatrical Group
Status: Non-Professional; Non-Profit
Type: Performing; Resident
Purpose: To present quality theatre for Fort Worth; to provide an avocation for talented amateurs in all phases of production
Management: William Garber, Artistic Director; Brynn Bristol, Administrative Director
Officers: Gaylord Lummis, President
Paid Staff: 5   Volunteer Staff: 30
Utilizes: Guest Artists; Guest Directors
Budget: $50,000 - $100,000
Income Sources: Private Foundations/Grants/Endowments; Business/Corporate Donations; Box Office; Government Grants; Individual Donations
Season: 52 Weeks   Annual Attendance: 22,500
Performance Facilities: William Edrington Scott Theatre

HIP POCKET THEATRE
1627 Fairmount Avenue, Fort Worth, TX 76104
(817) 927-2833
Founded: 1977
Arts Area: Professional; Musical; Folk; Theatrical Group; Puppet
Status: Professional; Non-Profit
Type: Performing; Touring; Resident; Educational
Purpose: Showcase original works by regional playwrights and composers, as well as other works rarely performed in this area
Management: Diane Simons, Producer; Johnny Simons, Artistic Director; Holly Nelson Leach, General Manager
Officers: D. Lee Thomas, President; Carlela K. Vogel, President-Elect; Mary Kaye Juran, Secretary; Richard W. Chowning, Treasurer
Paid Staff: 3   Volunteer Staff: 3
Paid Artists: 23
Utilizes: Special Technical Talent; Guest Artists; Guest Directors
Budget: $100,000 - $500,000
Income Sources: Private Foundations/Grants/Endowments; Business/Corporate Donations; Box Office; Government Grants; Individual Donations
Season: June - November   Annual Attendance: 11,000
Affiliations: TCG
Performance Facilities: Oak Acres Amphitheatre

SOJOURNER TRUTH PLAYERS
6619 Forest Hill Drive, Fort Worth, TX 76140
(817) 483-7111
Founded: 1972
Arts Area: Theatrical Group
Status: Non-Professional; Non-Profit
Type: Performing; Touring; Educational; Sponsoring
Purpose: To provide arts entertainment to the community and provide training classes and quality instruction to children and adults
Management: Charlece Thomas-James, Producer
Officers: Mattie Peterson Compton, Chairperson
Paid Staff: 3   Volunteer Staff: 5
Paid Artists: 2   Non-Paid Artists: 25
Utilizes: Special Technical Talent; Guest Artists; Guest Directors
Budget: $50,000 - $100,000
Income Sources: Private Foundations/Grants/Endowments; Business/Corporate Donations; Box Office; Government Grants; Individual Donations
Season: August - June   Annual Attendance: 10,000
Affiliations: Texas Nonprofit Theatre; SWTC; Texas Assembly Arts Agency
Performance Facilities: Sojourner Truth Players Cultural Arts Center

STAGE WEST

312 Houston Street, PO Box 2587, Fort Worth, TX 76113
(817) 332-6265
Founded: 1979
Arts Area: Professional; Theatrical Group
Status: Professional; Non-Profit
Type: Performing
Purpose: To produce a variety of works with at least eight major productions a year including some musicals; to present theater works ranging from new to classical and contemporary.
Management: Jerry Russell, Artistic/Managing Director; James Covault, Associate Director; Sam Hatcher, Technical Director; Lu Ann Adamson, Business Manager; Buckley Sachs, Box Office Manager; Diane Anglim, Marketing Director
Officers: Jack L. Johnson, Board President; Jeff Davis, Vice President; Carol Stanford, Treasurer
Paid Staff: 7 **Volunteer Staff:** 1
Paid Artists: 60
Utilizes: Special Technical Talent; Guest Artists; Guest Directors
Budget: $100,000 - $500,000
Income Sources: Private Foundations/Grants/Endowments; Business/Corporate Donations; Box Office; Government Grants; Individual Donations
Season: October - September **Annual Attendance:** 30,000
Affiliations: AEA; SPT; TCG; Texas Nonprofit Theatre; Live Theatre League of Tarrant County; Arts Council of Fort Worth and Tarrant County
Performance Facilities: Stage West at the Caravan of Dreams Performing Arts Center

PERFORMING SERIES

CARAVAN OF DREAMS

312 Houston Street, Fort Worth, TX 76102
(817) 877-3000
Mailing Address: PO Box 886, Fort Worth, TX 76101
Founded: 1983
Arts Area: Dance; Vocal Music; Instrumental Music; Theater
Status: Professional; Commercial
Type: Sponsoring
Management: Mike Dunagan, Booking Manager; Ken Bergle, Technical Director
Utilizes: Guest Artists
Budget: $500,000 - $1,000,000
Income Sources: Box Office
Season: 52 Weeks
Performance Facilities: Caravan of Dreams

SHAKESPEARE-IN-THE-PARK

3113 South University, Suite 310, Fort Worth, TX 76109
(817) 923-6698
Founded: 1977
Arts Area: Theater; Festivals
Status: Professional; Non-Profit
Type: Performing; Touring
Purpose: To provide free Shakespeare-in-the-Park to the people of Fort Worth
Management: Michael Muller, Producing Director
Officers: Judy Harmon, President
Paid Staff: 2 **Volunteer Staff:** 1,500
Paid Artists: 60
Utilizes: Guest Directors
Budget: $100,000 - $500,000
Income Sources: Private Foundations/Grants/Endowments; Business/Corporate Donations; Box Office; Government Grants; Individual Donations
Season: June - July; November - December **Annual Attendance:** 43,000
Affiliations: Texas Christian University; City of Fort Worth
Performance Facilities: The Trinity Park Playhouse; Southwest United States Tour

VAN CLIBURN FOUNDATION

2525 Ridgmar Boulevard, Fort Worth, TX 76116
(817) 738-6536
FAX: (817) 738-6534
Founded: 1961
Arts Area: Vocal Music; Instrumental Music
Status: Professional; Non-Profit
Type: Performing; Touring; Educational; Sponsoring

Purpose: To produce the Van Cliburn International Piano Competition and to produce the Cliburn Concert Series
Management: Richard Rodzinski, Executive Director
Officers: Susan Tilley, Chairman
Paid Staff: 9
Paid Artists: 12
Utilizes: Guest Artists
Budget: $100,000 - $500,000
Income Sources: Private Foundations/Grants/Endowments; Business/Corporate Donations; Box Office; Government Grants; Individual Donations
Season: September - May   **Annual Attendance:** 5,000
Affiliations: Texas Arts Council; ASOL; APAP; ISPAA
Performance Facilities: Kimbell Art Museum; Ed Landreth Auditorium, Texas Christian University

FACILITY

CARAVAN OF DREAMS
312 Houston Street, Fort Worth, TX 76102
(817) 877-3000
FAX: (817) 877-3752
    Type of Facility: Performance Center; Multi-Purpose
    Type of Stage: Thrust; Proscenium; 3/4 Arena
    Seating Capacity: Theater - 212; Jazz Club - 300
    Year Built: 1983   **Architect:** Margaret Augustine
    Contact for Rental: Rob Hansen;   (817) 877-3000
    Manager: Jerry Thompson
    Resident Groups: Theatre of All Possibilities Stage West
    Also used a a jazz recording studio; live radio broadcasts Tuesdays

CASA MANANA THEATRE
3101 West Lancaster, Fort Worth, TX 76107
(817) 332-9319
FAX: (817) 332-5711
    Type of Facility: Theatre House
    Type of Stage: In-the-round Capability
    Stage Dimensions: 28'x34'   **Orchestra Pit**
    Seating Capacity: 1,816
    Year Built: 1958   **Architect:** R. Buckminster Fuller   **Cost:** $500,000
    Acoustical Consultant: Ricky Pratt
    Contact for Rental: Candice Nickelson, Assistant General Manager;   (817) 332-9319
    Manager: Bud Franks
    Resident Groups: Casa Manana Musicals, Inc.
    Only limited rental possible

FORT WORTH/TARRANT COUNTY CONVENTION CENTER - CONVENTION CENTER THEATER
1111 Houston Street, Fort Worth, TX 76102
(817) 884-2222
FAX: (817) 884-2323
    Type of Facility: Auditorium
    Type of Stage: Proscenium
    Stage Dimensions: 30'x65'x50'   **Orchestra Pit**
    Seating Capacity: 3,054
    Year Built: 1968   **Architect:** The Associated Convention Center Architects
    Acoustical Consultant: Tracor
    Contact for Rental: Helen Crawford, Booking Manager;   (817) 884-2222
    Manager: Jimmy Earl
    Resident Groups: Fort Worth Symphony; Fort Worth Ballet; Texas Boys Choir; Fort Worth Opera Association
    Total construction cost of Tarrant County Convention Center was $20,000,000 in 1968.

OAK ACRES AMPHITHEATRE
1627 Fairmont Avenue, Fort Worth, TX 76104
(817) 927-2833
    Type of Facility: Amphitheater
    Type of Stage: Environmental
    Seating Capacity: 200
    Year Built: 1979   **Cost:** $500
    Contact for Rental: James Quave;   (817) 927-2833
    Resident Groups: Hip Pocket Theater
    Available for rental November through April

SOUTHWESTERN BAPTIST THEOLOGICAL SEMINARY - REYNOLDS AUDITORIUM
PO Box 22000, Fort Worth, TX 76122
(817) 923-1921
Type of Facility: Concert Hall; Auditorium; Studio Performance
Type of Stage: Proscenium
Seating Capacity: 500
Year Built: 1926   Architect: Preston Geren   Cost: $150,000
Year Remodeled: 1961   Cost: $500,000
Contact for Rental: Dr. David Music;   (817) 923-1921

TEXAS CHRISTIAN UNIVERSITY - ED LANDRETH AUDITORIUM
School of Fine Arts, PO Box 32928, Fort Worth, TX 76129
(817) 921-7625
FAX: (817) 921-7333
Type of Facility: Theatre House
Type of Stage: Proscenium
Stage Dimensions: 35'x40'
Seating Capacity: 218
Year Built: 1949   Architect: Hedrick Geren Peblich
Manager: Vince Pankey

TEXAS WESLEYAN COLLEGE - TEXAS WESLEYAN FINE ARTS AUDITORIUM
Rosedale and Wesleyan, PO Box 50010, Fort Worth, TX 76105
(817) 531-4443
Type of Facility: Auditorium
Facility Originally: Church
Type of Stage: Proscenium; Modified Thrust
Stage Dimensions: 20'x30'   Orchestra Pit
Seating Capacity: 750
Year Built: 1923
Year Remodeled: 1962
Contact for Rental: J. Allen Brown;   (817) 531-4443
Resident Groups: Texas Wesleyan College Theatre Department

WILLIAM EDRINGTON SCOTT THEATRE
3505 West Lancaster, Fort Worth, TX 76107
(817) 738-1938
Type of Facility: Theatre House
Type of Stage: Thrust; Proscenium   Orchestra Pit
Seating Capacity: 493
Year Built: 1966   Architect: Joseph Pelich   Cost: $1,250,000
Contact for Rental: William Garber;   (817) 738-1938
Resident Groups: Fort Worth Theatre

Galveston

PERFORMING SERIES

THE GRAND 1894 OPERA HOUSE
2020 Post Office Street, Galveston, TX 77550
(409) 763-7173
FAX: (409) 763-1068
Founded: 1974
Arts Area: Dance; Vocal Music; Instrumental Music; Theater; Lyric Opera; Grand Opera; Meetings; Parties; Workshops
Status: Professional; Non-Professional; Non-Profit
Type: Performing; Touring; Resident; Educational; Sponsoring; Presenting
Purpose: To present professional performing arts in a restored, historic structure and to maintain that structure; to serve the Galveston and the Greater Houston areas
Management: Maureen M. Patton, Executive Director; William C. Lindstrom, Stage Manager
Paid Staff: 9   Volunteer Staff: 350
Utilizes: Guest Artists
Budget: $500,000 - $1,000,000
Income Sources: Private Foundations/Grants/Endowments; Business/Corporate Donations; Box Office; Government Grants; Individual Donations; Rentals
Season: September - May   Annual Attendance: 29,000
Affiliations: APAP; League of Historic American Theatres; Southwest Performing Arts Presenters
Performance Facilities: The Grand 1894 Opera House

FACILITY

GRAND 1894 OPERA HOUSE
2020 Postoffice Street, Galveston, TX 77550
(409) 763-7173
FAX: (409) 763-1068
    Type of Facility: Concert Hall; Performance Center; Theatre House; Opera House; Multi-Purpose
    Type of Stage: Proscenium
    Stage Dimensions: 27'Hx38'Wx36'D **Orchestra Pit**
    Seating Capacity: 1,000
    Year Built: 1894 **Architect:** Frank Cox **Cost:** $100,000
    Year Remodeled: 1986 **Architect:** Killis P. Almond, AIA **Cost:** $7,000,000
    Contact for Rental: Maureen M. Patton, Director; (409) 763-7173
    Resident Groups: Galveston Symphony Orchestra; Galveston Ballet

MOODY CIVIC CENTER - EXHIBITION HALL
2100 Seawall Boulevard, Galveston, TX 77550
(409) 762-9608
FAX: (406) 762-8911
    Type of Facility: Multi-Purpose
    Type of Stage: Platform
    Stage Dimensions: 90'Wx200'D
    Seating Capacity: 2,000
    Year Built: 1956
    Year Remodeled: 1981 **Architect:** Louis Oliver
    Contact for Rental: Anthony Martinez, Joe Romero; (409) 762-9608

Garland

INSTRUMENTAL MUSIC

DALLAS BRASS
4321 Clemson Drive, Garland, TX 75042
(214) 276-7114
    Founded: 1982
    Arts Area: Ensemble; Instrumental Group
    Status: Professional; Commercial
    Type: Performing; Touring; Resident; Educational
    Purpose: To strive to bridge the musical gaps from classical to pop
    Management: Michael Levin, Director; Wiss Rudd, Booking Coordinator
    Paid Staff: 3 **Volunteer Staff:** 25
    Paid Artists: 8
    Utilizes: Guest Artists
    Income Sources: Box Office
    Season: 52 Weeks

GARLAND SYMPHONY ORCHESTRA
1721 Reserve, Garland, TX 75042
(214) 553-1223
FAX: (214) 533-0081
    Founded: 1978
    Arts Area: Symphony; Orchestra
    Status: Professional; Non-Profit
    Type: Performing; Educational
    Purpose: To present the finest concerts possible consistent with financial integrity
    Management: Robert Carter Austin, Music Director; Richard Stieber, Assistant General Manager
    Officers: George and Lee Ann Christ, Co-Presidents; Tom and Peggy Jenkins, Co-Presidents Elect; Duane Blakely, Secretary; Douglas Taylor, Treasurer
    Paid Staff: 2
    Paid Artists: 75
    Utilizes: Guest Conductors; Guest Artists
    Budget: $100,000 - $500,000
    Income Sources: Private Foundations/Grants/Endowments; Business/Corporate Donations; Box Office; Individual Donations
    Season: October - April **Annual Attendance:** 9,000
    Performance Facilities: Garland Performing Arts Center

TEXAS BAROQUE ENSEMBLE
2221 Royal Crest Drive, Garland, TX 75043
(214) 278-2458
FAX: (214) 278-2458
  Founded: 1980
  Arts Area: Chamber; Ensemble; Choir
  Status: Professional; Non-Profit
  Type: Performing; Touring; Resident; Educational
  Purpose: The Texas Baroque Ensemble focuses on performing music written before 1800 with the music being played on the original instruments for which the music was written.
  Management: Susan Ferre, Musical Director/Administrator; Rosemary Heffley, Development Director; Eileen Rees, Membership
  Officers: Brooks Morris II; Eileen Rees; Charles Lang; Susan Ferre; Rosemary Heffley; Ed Rodriguez; Jean Rodriguez
  Volunteer Staff: 3
  Paid Artists: 50
  Utilizes: Special Technical Talent
  Budget: $1,000 - $50,000
  Income Sources: Private Foundations/Grants/Endowments; Business/Corporate Donations; Box Office; Government Grants; Individual Donations
  Season: 52 Weeks   **Annual Attendance:** 3,000
  Affiliations: Early Music at Round Top
  Performance Facilities: Perkins Chapel, Southern Methodist University; Saint Stephen Presbyterian Church; Round Top Festival Institute; San Fernando Cathedral, San Antonio; Catholic Cathedral, Guadalupe

THEATRE

GARLAND CIVIC THEATRE
PO Box 461252, Garland, TX 75046
(214) 349-1331
FAX: (214) 553-0081
  Founded: 1967
  Arts Area: Musical; Theatrical Group
  Status: Semi-Professional; Non-Profit
  Type: Performing; Resident
  Purpose: To provide quality entertainment for our audiences, provide a space for performers in the community, and to advance theatre in general
  Management: James Weir, Producing Director; Linda White, Administrative Assistant; Dwight Swanson, Technical Director
  Officers: Holt Irby, President; Steve Chaffin, Vice President; Marilyn Schwartz, Secretary; Anne Bond, Treasurer; Michelle Tucker, Vice President of Development
  Paid Staff: 2   **Volunteer Staff:** 3
  Budget: $100,000 - $500,000
  Income Sources: Private Foundations/Grants/Endowments; Business/Corporate Donations; Box Office; Government Grants; Individual Donations
  Season: September - June   **Annual Attendance:** 10,000
  Affiliations: Texas Nonprofit Theatre; TCG
  Performance Facilities: Garland Center For the Performing Arts

PERFORMING SERIES

GARLAND SUMMER MUSICALS
P.O. Box 462049, Garland, TX 75046-2049
(214) 205-2780
  Founded: 1983
  Arts Area: Dance; Vocal Music; Instrumental Music
  Status: Semi-Professional; Non-Profit
  Type: Sponsoring
  Purpose: Committed to the community to present the highest quality productions and continue a tradition of excellence in family entertainment
  Management: Patty Granville, Producer; Buff Shurr, Director
  Paid Staff: 6
  Utilizes: Special Technical Talent; Guest Artists
  Budget: $50,000 - $100,000
  Income Sources: Business/Corporate Donations; Box Office
  Season: June - July
  Affiliations: AEA
  Performance Facilities: Garland Center for the Performing Arts

FACILITY

GARLAND CENTER FOR THE PERFORMING ARTS
PO Box 469002, Garland, TX 75046-9002
(214) 205-2780
    Type of Facility: Theatre Complex
    Year Built: 1982   **Architect:** Harper, Kemp, Clutts & Parker   **Cost:** $3,500,000
    Contact for Rental: Patty Granville;   (214) 205-2780
    Resident Groups: Garland Civic Theater; Garland Symphony Orchestra; Garland Summer Musicals

GARLAND CENTER FOR THE PERFORMING ARTS - THEATER #1
PO Box 469002, Garland, TX 75046-9002
(214) 205-2780
    Type of Facility: Theatre House
    Type of Stage: Proscenium
    Seating Capacity: 195
    Year Built: 1982
    Contact for Rental: Patty Granville;   (214) 205-2780

GARLAND CENTER FOR THE PERFORMING ARTS - THEATER #2
PO Box 469002, Garland, TX 75046-9002
(214) 205-2780
    Type of Facility: Theatre House
    Type of Stage: Proscenium
    Stage Dimensions: 40'x35'   **Orchestra Pit**
    Seating Capacity: 719
    Year Built: 1982
    Contact for Rental: Patty Granville;   (214) 205-2780

Granbury

THEATRE

GRANBURY OPERA HOUSE
116 East Pearl Street, PO Box 297, Granbury, TX 76048
(817) 573-9191
    Founded: 1974
    Arts Area: Year-round Stock
    Status: Non-Profit
    Type: Performing; Educational
    Management: Joann Miller, Manager
    Paid Staff: 15
    Utilizes: Guest Artists
    Budget: $50,000 - $100,000
    Income Sources: Box Office; Individual Donations
    Season: 52 Weeks
    Performance Facilities: Granbury Opera House

FACILITY

GRANBURY OPERA HOUSE
116 East Pearl Street, PO Box 297, Granbury, TX 76048
(817) 573-9191
    Type of Facility: Opera House
    Type of Stage: Proscenium
    Stage Dimensions: 26'x18'   **Orchestra Pit**
    Seating Capacity: 303
    Year Built: 1886   **Cost:** $2,500
    Year Remodeled: 1974   **Architect:** Ed Beran   **Cost:** $250,000
    Manager: Joanne Miller, Managing Director
    Resident Groups: Granbury Opera House Company

Harlingen

FACILITY

HARLINGEN CULTURAL ARTS CENTER - AUDITORIUM
576 '76 Drive, PO Box 609, Harlingen, TX 78551
(210) 423-9736
   Type of Facility: Multi-Purpose
   Type of Stage: Proscenium
   Stage Dimensions: 30'Wx16'D
   Seating Capacity: 150
   Year Built: 1986   **Cost:** $260,000
   Contact for Rental: Cultural Arts Center Office;   (512) 423-9736
   The Cultural Arts Center also contains a 50-seat Studio Theatre and a 30-seat Studio Theatre. Cost referenced above is the total construction cost for the Center.

Houston

DANCE

ALLEGRO BALLET OF HOUSTON
1801 Dairy Ashford, Suite 130, Houston, TX 77077
(713) 496-4670
   Arts Area: Modern; Ballet; Jazz; Ethnic
   Status: Semi-Professional; Non-Profit
   Type: Performing; Resident; Educational
   Purpose: To offer a performing outlet for gifted dancers by presenting them in concerts both at home and abroad in a classical and contemporary repertoire
   Management: Peggy Girouard, Glenda Brown, Directors; Vanessa Brown, Associate Director/Manager
   Officers: Ray Cashman, President; Jeff Love, Vice President; Pamela Penny, Secretary; John Niemann, Treasurer; James Crownover, Chairman of the Board
   Paid Staff: 3   **Volunteer Staff:** 4
   Paid Artists: 2   **Non-Paid Artists:** 15
   Utilizes: Special Technical Talent; Guest Artists; Guest Choreographers
   Budget: $1,000 - $50,000
   Income Sources: Private Foundations/Grants/Endowments; Business/Corporate Donations; Box Office; Individual Donations; Fund-raising
   Season: September - June   **Annual Attendance:** 10,000
   Affiliations: SWRBA; Regional Dance America
   Performance Facilities: Jones Hall, Wortham; Mitchell Pavillion, Woodland; Episcopal High School Auditorium

CHRYSALIS REPERTORY DANCE COMPANY
10006 Briar Rose, Houston, TX 77042
(713) 522-6557
   Founded: 1983
   Arts Area: Modern; Post-Modern; Performance Art
   Status: Professional; Non-Profit
   Type: Performing; Touring; Resident; Educational; Sponsoring
   Purpose: To present innovative, quality dance to enhance Houston and other communities where we perfrom
   Management: Christine Lidvall, Linda Phenix, Co-Directors
   Officers: Elizabeth Jones-Boswell, President; Daniel Platt, Vice President/Treasurer; Flora Yeh, Secretary
   Paid Staff: 2
   Paid Artists: 7
   Utilizes: Special Technical Talent; Guest Artists; Guest Choreographers
   Budget: $50,000 - $100,000
   Income Sources: Private Foundations/Grants/Endowments; Business/Corporate Donations; Box Office; Government Grants; Individual Donations
   Season: September - May   **Annual Attendance:** 10,000
   Affiliations: Texas Arts Council; Houston Dance Coalition
   Performance Facilities: Heinen Theatre, Houston Community College; Kaplan Theatre; Jewish Community Center

CITY BALLET OF HOUSTON
9902 Long Point, Houston, TX 77055
(713) 468-8708
FAX: (713) 468-8708
   Founded: 1958
   Arts Area: Ballet

Status: Non-Profit
Type: Performing
Purpose: To serve as a training ground for young dancers and as a showcase for choreographers, both local and well-established; to offer presentations of high-quality performances at low ticket cost
Management: Margo and Dennis Marshall, Co-Artistic Directors; Victoria Vittum, Resident Choreographer; Frederic Franklin, Artistic Advisor; Jennifer Mettar, Stage Director
Officers: James DeVault, President, Board of Directors; Tom Shoffner, Vice President
Paid Staff: 2 **Volunteer Staff:** 2
Paid Artists: 4 **Non-Paid Artists:** 30
Utilizes: Guest Artists; Guest Choreographers
Budget: $100,000 - $500,000
Income Sources: Private Foundations/Grants/Endowments; Business/Corporate Donations; Box Office; Individual Donations
Season: September - May **Annual Attendance:** 5,000
Affiliations: NARB; SWRBA
Performance Facilities: Galveston Grand Opera House; Music Hall; Scottish Rite Temple

CLEAR LAKE METROPOLITAN BALLET
PO Box 580466, Houston, TX 77258
(713) 338-1615
Founded: 1976
Arts Area: Ballet
Status: Semi-Professional; Non-Profit
Type: Performing
Management: Lynette Mason-Hale, Artistic Director
Paid Staff: 1 **Volunteer Staff:** 25
Paid Artists: 6 **Non-Paid Artists:** 20
Utilizes: Guest Artists
Budget: $1,000 - $50,000
Income Sources: Private Foundations/Grants/Endowments; Box Office; Individual Donations
Season: September - May **Annual Attendance:** 8,000
Affiliations: Southwest Regional Ballet Association
Performance Facilities: University of Houston at CLear Lake

THE DELIA STEWART DANCE COMPANY
1202 Calumet Street, Houston, TX 77004
(713) 522-6375
Founded: 1981
Arts Area: Jazz
Status: Semi-Professional; Non-Profit
Type: Performing; Touring; Resident; Educational
Purpose: To foster the art of musical theater concert jazz dance; to provide an opportunity to educate the community about this art form and establish in Houston an internationally-recognized concert jazz dance company
Management: Delia Stewart, Director; Julie Stewart, Associate Director; Michelle Smith, Administrator
Officers: John Burris, President; Floyd Robinson Jr., Secretary
Paid Staff: 4
Paid Artists: 4 **Non-Paid Artists:** 8
Utilizes: Guest Artists
Budget: $100,000 - $500,000
Income Sources: Private Foundations/Grants/Endowments; Business/Corporate Donations; Individual Donations
Season: 52 Weeks **Annual Attendance:** 10,000
Affiliations: CACH; Houston Coalition

DISCOVERY DANCE GROUP AND TRAINING CENTER
6427 Atwell, Houston, TX 77006
(713) 667-3416
Founded: 1963
Arts Area: Modern; Ballet; Jazz; Ethnic
Status: Professional; Non-Profit
Type: Performing; Touring; Educational
Purpose: To provide an outlet for talented dancers and further educate them in performance techniques and to perpetuate the unique Camille Long Hill technique and method
Management: Camille Long Hill, Artistic Director/Managing Director; Pam Stockman, Associate Artistic/Managing Director
Officers: Alice Lanza, President; Martha Owen, First Vice President; Shelley Johnson, Secretary; Gary Lynn McGregor, Treasurer
Paid Staff: 4 **Volunteer Staff:** 4
Paid Artists: 10 **Non-Paid Artists:** 6
Utilizes: Guest Artists

Budget: $50,000 - $100,000
Income Sources: Private Foundations/Grants/Endowments; Business/Corporate Donations; Box Office; Individual Donations
Season: September - August

HOUSTON BALLET
1916 West Gray, PO Box 130487, Houston, TX 77219-0487
(713) 523-6300
    Arts Area: Ballet
    Status: Professional; Non-Profit
    Type: Performing; Touring; Resident; Educational
    Paid Staff: 35
    Paid Artists: 46
    Budget: $5,000,000 - $10,000,000
    Income Sources: Private Foundations/Grants/Endowments; Business/Corporate Donations; Box Office; Government Grants; Individual Donations
    Season: September - June
    Affiliations: Dance USA; National Corporate Fund for Dance
    Performance Facilities: Jesse H. Jones Hall for the Performing Arts

JOAN KARFF'S NEW DANCE
5443 Parsley Group, Houston, TX 77096
(713) 721-2316
    Founded: 1979
    Arts Area: Modern
    Status: Semi-Professional; Non-Profit
    Type: Performing; Educational
    Purpose: To provide modern dance works of quality and to collaborate with other local artists
    Management: Joan Karff, Director
    Officers: Paula Friedlander, President
    Paid Staff: 1
    Paid Artists: 8
    Utilizes: Special Technical Talent; Guest Artists
    Budget: $1,000 - $50,000
    Income Sources: Private Foundations/Grants/Endowments; Business/Corporate Donations; Box Office; Government Grants; Individual Donations
    Season: September - May   **Annual Attendance:** 1,500
    Performance Facilities: Saint John's School Theatre; Jewish Center Theatre

SEVERAL DANCERS CORE
2332 Bissonnet, Houston, TX 77005
(713) 520-5530
FAX: (713) 524-4036
    Founded: 1980
    Arts Area: Modern
    Status: Professional; Non-Profit
    Type: Performing; Touring; Presenting
    Purpose: To provide quality dance to the public and to provide an outlet for choreographers and dancers to present their work
    Management: Sue Schroeder, Kathy Russell, Co-Artistic/Executive Directors; Rebecca Leary Safon, Development Coordinator/Community Liason; Deborah Schultz , Erica Yoder, Projects Coordinators
    Officers: Sue Schroeder, President; Kathy Russell, Secretary/Treasurer
    Paid Staff: 2   **Volunteer Staff:** 5
    Paid Artists: 4
    Utilizes: Special Technical Talent; Guest Artists; Guest Choreographers
    Budget: $100,000 - $500,000
    Income Sources: Private Foundations/Grants/Endowments; Business/Corporate Donations; Box Office; Government Grants; Individual Donations
    Season: September - May   **Annual Attendance:** 5,000
    Affiliations: Several Dancers Core of Atlanta

SOCIETY FOR THE PERFORMING ARTS
615 Louisiana, Houston, TX 77002
(713) 227-5134
FAX: (713) 223-8301
    Arts Area: Modern; Mime; Ballet; Jazz; Ethnic; Folk
    Status: Professional; Non-Profit
    Type: Sponsoring

Purpose: To present the world's greatest in performing arts, whether dance, music or theatre
Management: Toby Mattox, Executive Director
Officers: John M. Kirksey, Chairman of the Board
Income Sources: Private Foundations/Grants/Endowments; Business/Corporate Donations; Box Office; Government Grants; Individual Donations
Performance Facilities: Jones Hall; Wortham Theatre Center

SOUTHWEST JAZZ BALLET COMPANY
720 1/2 Pinemont, Houston, TX 77018
(713) 694-6114
FAX: (713) 686-4868
   Founded: 1979
   Arts Area: Ballet; Jazz
   Status: Professional; Non-Profit; Commercial
   Type: Performing; Touring; Educational
   Purpose: America through song and dance
   Management: Rita Brosh, Artistic Director; Pamela Eden, Musical Coordinator
   Officers: G. R. DeFillipe, President/Chief Executive Officer
   Paid Staff: 16   **Volunteer Staff:** 40
   Paid Artists: 14   **Non-Paid Artists:** 25
   Utilizes: Special Technical Talent; Guest Conductors; Guest Artists; Guest Directors
   Budget: $500,000 - $1,000,000
   Income Sources: Private Foundations/Grants/Endowments; Business/Corporate Donations; Box Office; Government Grants; Individual Donations
   Season: 52 Weeks   **Annual Attendance:** 400,000

INSTRUMENTAL MUSIC

CLEAR LAKE SYMPHONY
PO Box 890582, Houston, TX 77289-0582
(713) 534-7610; (713) 251-9210
   Founded: 1976
   Arts Area: Symphony; Orchestra
   Status: Non-Professional; Non-Profit
   Type: Performing
   Purpose: To provide the community with a source of live symphonic music and provide the performers with an outlet for their talents
   Officers: Roje Yap, President; Melodie Cunningham, Secretary
   Paid Staff: 1   **Volunteer Staff:** 55
   Paid Artists: 2   **Non-Paid Artists:** 6
   Utilizes: Guest Artists
   Budget: $1,000 - $50,000
   Income Sources: Private Foundations/Grants/Endowments; Business/Corporate Donations; Box Office; Individual Donations
   Season: October - June   **Annual Attendance:** 2,500
   Affiliations: NSOL
   Performance Facilities: Bayou Auditorium

HOUSTON CIVIC SYMPHONY ORCHESTRA
University of Houston School of Music, Houston, TX 77204-4893
(713) 747-0018
   Founded: 1967
   Arts Area: Symphony; Orchestra; Chamber
   Status: Semi-Professional; Non-Profit
   Type: Performing
   Purpose: To provide a playing and performance opportunity for professional and non-professional musicians who earn the major portion of their livelihood outside full-time, professional music performances
   Management: Oscar Wehmanen, Director of Performances; Marlene Ballard, Manager of Personnel; Bruce Leon, Librarian; Joe Munsteri, Director of Funding; Dan Sloan, Director of Sound Recording
   Officers: Kathy Hannah, President; Nancy Francis, Vice President; John Snyder, Secretary; Greg Nelson, Treasurer
   Volunteer Staff: 13
   Non-Paid Artists: 65
   Utilizes: Guest Directors
   Budget: $1,000 - $50,000
   Income Sources: Private Foundations/Grants/Endowments; Business/Corporate Donations; Individual Donations
   Season: September - May   **Annual Attendance:** 2,000
   Affiliations: University of Houston
   Performance Facilities: Cullen Hall, University of Houston

HOUSTON FRIENDS OF MUSIC
c/o Shepperd School of Music, Rice University, PO Box 1892, Houston, TX 77251
(713) 285-5400
>**Founded:** 1959
>**Arts Area:** Chamber; Ensemble; Instrumental Group
>**Status:** Professional; Non-Profit
>**Type:** Performing; Sponsoring
>**Purpose:** The Houston Friends of Music is a non-profit organization dedicated to the presentation of chamber ensembles with national and international reputations and development of new audiences.
>**Management:** Alicia D. Less, Administrative Director
>**Volunteer Staff:** 25
>**Utilizes:** Guest Artists
>**Budget:** $50,000 - $100,000
>**Income Sources:** Private Foundations/Grants/Endowments; Business/Corporate Donations; Box Office; Government Grants; Individual Donations
>**Season:** September - May **Annual Attendance:** 5,000
>**Affiliations:** Shepherd School of Music
>**Performance Facilities:** Seude Concert Hall

HOUSTON HARPSICHORD SOCIETY
PO Box 271193, Houston, TX 77277
(713) 977-4581
>**Founded:** 1968
>**Arts Area:** Chamber; Ensemble; Ethnic; Folk; Dance
>**Status:** Professional; Non-Profit
>**Type:** Educational; Sponsoring
>**Purpose:** To perform early music, especially works arranged for harpsichord
>**Management:** Becky Lao, President/Executive Director
>**Officers:** Becky Lao, President; Dr. Maritza Mascarenhas, Vice President; Lola Norton, Secretary; Robert Thomas, Treasurer
>**Paid Artists:** 50 **Non-Paid Artists:** 8
>**Utilizes:** Guest Artists
>**Budget:** $1,000 - $50,000
>**Income Sources:** Private Foundations/Grants/Endowments; Business/Corporate Donations; Box Office; Government Grants; Individual Donations
>**Season:** September - June **Annual Attendance:** 2,000

HOUSTON SYMPHONY
615 Louisiana, Houston, TX 77002
(713) 224-4240
>**Founded:** 1913
>**Arts Area:** Orchestra; Chamber; Ensemble; Ethnic; Folk
>**Status:** Professional; Non-Profit
>**Type:** Performing; Touring; Resident; Educational
>**Purpose:** To provide a musical organization committed to fulfilling Houston's need for outstanding cultural entertainment and music education; to present works consistently at the highest level of performance quality
>**Management:** David Wax, Executive Director
>**Officers:** Jane McDavid, Chairman
>**Paid Staff:** 32 **Volunteer Staff:** 2
>**Paid Artists:** 150
>**Utilizes:** Special Technical Talent; Guest Conductors; Guest Artists; Guest Directors
>**Budget:** $5,000,000 - $10,000,000
>**Income Sources:** Private Foundations/Grants/Endowments; Business/Corporate Donations; Box Office; Government Grants; Individual Donations
>**Season:** June - May
>**Performance Facilities:** Jesse H. Jones Hall for the Performing Arts

VOCAL MUSIC

HOUSTON GRAND OPERA
510 Preston, Houston, TX 77002-1594
(713) 546-0200
FAX: (713) 247-0906
>**Founded:** 1955
>**Arts Area:** Grand Opera; Lyric Opera; Light Opera; Operetta; Musical Theatre
>**Status:** Professional; Non-Profit
>**Type:** Performing; Touring; Resident; Educational

Purpose: To produce opera of consistent excellence offering nontraditional and innovative works; to develop new forms, new artists and new audiences; In addition, Houston Grand Opera must direct itself toward becoming accessible to all segments of the greater community.
Management: David Gockley, General Director; John DeMain, Music Director; Dolores Johnson, Managing Director; James Ireland, Producing Director; Krista Rimple, Community Programs Director
Officers: Constantine S. Nicandros, President; Harris Masterson III, Honorary Chairman; John M. Seidl, Chairman of the Board; Mrs. Oscar S. Wyatt Jr., Vice Chairman; David Gockley, Executive Vice President
Paid Staff: 110
Paid Artists: 600
Utilizes: Special Technical Talent; Guest Conductors; Guest Artists; Guest Directors
Budget: Over 10,000,000
Income Sources: Private Foundations/Grants/Endowments; Business/Corporate Donations; Box Office; Government Grants; Individual Donations
Season: October - July
Annual Attendance: 200,000
Affiliations: OA
Performance Facilities: Wortham Theater Center

HOUSTON SYMPHONY CHORUS
615 Louisiana, Houston, TX 77002
(713) 224-4240
FAX: (713) 222-7024
Founded: 1946
Arts Area: Choral
Status: Non-Professional; Non-Profit
Type: Performing; Resident
Management: Dr. Charles Hausmann, Director; Marilyn Dyess, Chorus Manager; Scott Holshouser, Accompanist; Betsy Weber, Assistant Director
Paid Staff: 5 **Volunteer Staff:** 1
Non-Paid Artists: 170
Utilizes: Guest Conductors; Guest Artists
Budget: $50,000 - $100,000
Season: 52 Weeks
Affiliations: CA
Performance Facilities: Jesse H. Jones Hall for the Performing Arts

THE RUMBLE SEAT FOUR QUARTET
PO Box 25348, Houston, TX 77265
(713) 522-3805
Founded: 1984
Arts Area: Barbershop Quartet
Status: Semi-Professional
Type: Performing
Purpose: Preserve and encourage barbershop quartet singing
Management: Richard A. Mills, Agent
Paid Staff: 1
Paid Artists: 4
Budget: $1,000 - $50,000
Income Sources: Box Office
Season: 52 Weeks
Affiliations: SPEBSQSA

TEXAS OPERA THEATER
510 Preston, Suite 500, Houston, TX 77002
(713) 546-0290
FAX: (713) 247-0906
Founded: 1973
Arts Area: Grand Opera; Lyric Opera; Light Opera; Operetta
Status: Non-Profit
Type: Performing; Touring; Resident; Educational
Purpose: To nurture the careers of young American artists
Management: David Gockley, General Director
Paid Staff: 9
Paid Artists: 7
Utilizes: Special Technical Talent; Guest Conductors; Guest Artists; Guest Directors
Budget: $500,000 - $1,000,000
Income Sources: Private Foundations/Grants/Endowments; Business/Corporate Donations; Box Office; Government Grants; Individual Donations

Season: September - May
Annual Attendance: 75,000

THEATRE

A.D. PLAYERS
2710 West Alabama, Houston, TX 77098
(713) 526-2721
    Founded: 1967
    Arts Area: Professional; Theatrical Group
    Status: Semi-Professional; Non-Profit
    Type: Performing; Touring; Resident; Educational
    Purpose: To provide a full season of Christian theatrical productions to the Houston audience; to send touring repertory and concert productions nationally and internationally
    Management: Jeannette Clift George, Artistic Director/Co-Manager; Doug Gettyl, Production Manager
    Officers: Jim Hunt, Chairman, Board of Directors
    Paid Staff: 4
    Paid Artists: 19
    Utilizes: Special Technical Talent; Guest Artists; Guest Directors
    Budget: $100,000 - $500,000
    Income Sources: Private Foundations/Grants/Endowments; Business/Corporate Donations; Box Office; Individual Donations
    Season: 52 Weeks
    Annual Attendance: 15,000
    Affiliations: Texas Nonprofit Theatre; TCG; Houston Theatre Association; Cultural Arts Council of Houston
    Performance Facilities: Grace Theatre

ALLEY THEATRE
615 Texas Avenue, Houston, TX 77002
(713) 228-9341
FAX: (713) 222-6542
    Founded: 1947
    Arts Area: Professional; Theatrical Group
    Status: Professional; Non-Profit
    Type: Performing; Touring; Resident; Educational; Sponsoring
    Purpose: To promote the performance of theatrical literature
    Management: Gregory Boyd, Artistic Director; Stephen J. Albert, Executive Director
    Officers: Meredith J. Long, Chairman; T. William Porter, President
    Paid Staff: 140   **Volunteer Staff:** 1,000
    Paid Artists: 100
    Utilizes: Special Technical Talent; Guest Artists; Guest Directors
    Budget: $5,000,000 - $10,000,000
    Income Sources: Private Foundations/Grants/Endowments; Business/Corporate Donations; Box Office; Government Grants; Individual Donations
    Season: September - August
    Annual Attendance: 500,000
    Affiliations: LORT; AEA; USA; SSDC
    Performance Facilities: Alley Theatre

CHANNING PLAYERS
PO Box 631363, Houston, TX 77263
(713) 785-9492
    Founded: 1955
    Arts Area: Community
    Status: Non-Profit
    Type: Performing; Educational
    Purpose: To produce quality plays
    Management: Janis Halliday, Artistic Director; Donald Williams, Technical Director
    Officers: Martha Raymond, President; Janis Halliday, Vice President; Anthony Addison, Secretary; Linda Stern, Treasurer
    Volunteer Staff: 50
    Non-Paid Artists: 50
    Utilizes: Special Technical Talent
    Budget: $1,000 - $50,000
    Income Sources: Private Foundations/Grants/Endowments; Business/Corporate Donations; Box Office; Individual Donations
    Season: October - June   **Annual Attendance:** 1,500
    Affiliations: Cultural Arts Council of Houston; Texas Nonprofit Theatre

THE ENSEMBLE
3535 Main, Houston, TX 77002
(713) 520-0055; (713) 520-0063
Founded: 1976
Arts Area: Theatrical Group
Status: Professional; Non-Profit
Type: Performing; Touring; Resident; Educational
Purpose: To provide professional Black theatre to the city of Houston
Management: Eileen Morris, Artistic Director
Paid Staff: 10   **Volunteer Staff:** 25
Paid Artists: 50
Utilizes: Special Technical Talent; Guest Artists; Guest Directors
Budget: $100,000 - $500,000
Income Sources: Private Foundations/Grants/Endowments; Business/Corporate Donations; Box Office;
Individual Donations
Season: September - August   **Annual Attendance:** 25,000
Performance Facilities: The Ensemble Theatre

MAIN STREET THEATER
2540 Times Boulevard, Houston, TX 77005
(713) 524-6706
Founded: 1975
Arts Area: Theatrical Group
Status: Professional; Semi-Professional; Non-Professional
Type: Performing; Touring; Resident
Management: Rebecca Greene Udden, Artistic Director; Patti Bean, Production Manager
Officers: Susan Imle, President; David Cooney Jr., Vice President; Victoria Benson, Secretary; Jack S. Blanton, Jr.,
Treasurer
Paid Staff: 5   **Volunteer Staff:** 15
Paid Artists: 45
Budget: $100,000 - $500,000
Income Sources: Private Foundations/Grants/Endowments; Business/Corporate Donations; Box Office;
Individual Donations
Season: 52 Weeks

STAGES REPERTORY THEATRE
3201 Allen Parkway, #101, Houston, TX 77019
(713) 527-0240
FAX: (713) 527-8669
Founded: 1978
Arts Area: Professional; Theatrical Group
Status: Professional; Non-Profit
Type: Performing; Touring; Resident; Educational; Sponsoring
Purpose: To produce plays that challenge a developing artistic company, being of social value to the community and setting a standard of excellence deserving of audience and critical acclaim
Management: Peter Bennett, Artistic Director
Officers: Anne Wright, President; Mimi Kilgore, Chair
Paid Staff: 18   **Volunteer Staff:** 250
Paid Artists: 65
Utilizes: Special Technical Talent; Guest Artists; Guest Directors
Budget: $500,000 - $1,000,000
Income Sources: Private Foundations/Grants/Endowments; Business/Corporate Donations; Box Office; Government
Grants; Individual Donations
Season: 52 Weeks   **Annual Attendance:** 65,000
Affiliations: TCG

TALENTO BILINGUE DE HOUSTON
PO Box 230326, Houston, TX 77223-0326
(713) 921-5093
Founded: 1976
Arts Area: Musical; Community; Theatrical Group
Status: Non-Profit
Type: Performing; Touring; Educational; Sponsoring
Purpose: Non-profit educational and cultural organization
Management: Richard E. Reyes, Artistic/Project Director; Fernando Gonzales, Manager; Rodney Becerra,
Technical Director; Jim Bratton, Publicity
Officers: Peter Garcia, President; Jim Bratton, Vice President; Manuel Barrera, Secretary/Treasurer
Paid Staff: 3   **Volunteer Staff:** 2

Paid Artists: 10   Non-Paid Artists: 40
Utilizes: Guest Artists; Guest Directors
Budget: $50,000 - $100,000
Income Sources: Private Foundations/Grants/Endowments; Business/Corporate Donations; Box Office; Government Grants; Individual Donations
Season: 52 Weeks
Annual Attendance: 12,000

THEATRE ON WHEELS
PO Box 440056, Houston, TX 77244
(713) 493-5500
Founded: 1979
Arts Area: Theater
Status: Semi-Professional; Non-Profit
Type: Performing; Touring; Resident; Educational; Sponsoring
Purpose: To reach as many school age students with our quality children's theatre repertoire and after-school dramatic instruction for kids in grades K - 12
Management: Ellen Baltz, Founder/Executive Director; Cari Skain, Events Coordinator; Cindy Wigginton, Public Relations and Education Director; Terry McManigle, Associate Administrator
Officers: Jan Norris, Chairman; Ellen B. Baltz, President; Dow Heard, Vice President; Diane Sturgess, Treasurer
Paid Staff: 4   Volunteer Staff: 2
Paid Artists: 9   Non-Paid Artists: 15
Utilizes: Special Technical Talent; Guest Artists; Guest Directors
Budget: $100,000 - $500,000
Income Sources: Private Foundations/Grants/Endowments; Business/Corporate Donations; Box Office; Government Grants; Individual Donations
Season: 52 Weeks
Affiliations: AATY; Cultural Arts Council of Houston; SWTC

THEATRE SUBURBIA
1410 West 43rd, Houston, TX 77018
(713) 682-3525
Founded: 1960
Arts Area: Theatrical Group
Status: Non-Professional; Non-Profit
Type: Performing
Purpose: To provide quality entertainment for the general public with a wide variety of plays ranging from light comedy to heavy drama, being noted for producing top quality original scripts
Management: C.R. Glover, Box Office; Keith Ross, Technical Director; Melissa Merten, Back Stage Coordinator
Officers: Doris Merten, President; Sherah Bates, Vice President; Bette Ann Ross, Secretary; Carolyn Montgomery, Treasurer
Paid Staff: 1   Volunteer Staff: 30
Paid Artists: 20
Utilizes: Guest Directors
Budget: $1,000 - $50,000
Income Sources: Private Foundations/Grants/Endowments; Business/Corporate Donations; Box Office; Individual Donations
Season: 52 Weeks
Annual Attendance: 12,000
Performance Facilities: Theatre Suburbia

THEATRE UNDER THE STARS
4235 San Felipe, Houston, TX 77002
(713) 622-1626
FAX: (713) 622-0025
Arts Area: Professional; Musical; Theatrical Group
Status: Professional; Non-Profit
Type: Performing; Touring; Educational
Purpose: To present light opera regionally and on tour; to operate a school for future artists; to foster the creation of new works of musical theatre
Management: Frank M. Young, Executive Director/Founder; John Holly, Producing Director; Cissy Segall, Managing Director; Vivian Flynn, General Manager
Officers: Dennis Irvine, President of the Board
Budget: Over 10,000,000
Income Sources: Private Foundations/Grants/Endowments; Business/Corporate Donations; Box Office; Government Grants; Individual Donations
Performance Facilities: The Music Hall

PERFORMING SERIES

THE HOUSTON INTERNATIONAL FESTIVAL
1100 Louisania, Suite 1275, Houston, TX 77002
(713) 654-8808
FAX: (713) 654-1719
> **Founded:** 1966
> **Arts Area:** Dance; Vocal Music; Instrumental Music; Festivals
> **Status:** Professional; Non-Profit
> **Type:** Educational; Sponsoring
> **Purpose:** To sponsor a 10-day cultural celebration in an urban setting, focusing on a different country every year
> **Management:** Dr. James Austin, President and COO
> **Paid Staff:** 10   **Volunteer Staff:** 4
> **Paid Artists:** 2
> **Utilizes:** Guest Artists
> **Budget:** $1,000,000 - $5,000,000
> **Income Sources:** Private Foundations/Grants/Endowments; Business/Corporate Donations; Box Office
> **Season:** Spring
> **Annual Attendance:** 1,000,000
> **Affiliations:** Cultural Arts Council of Houston; Houston Convention and Visitors Center

HOUSTON SHAKESPEARE FESTIVAL
University of Houston, Drama Department, Houston, TX 77204-5071
(713) 743-3003
> **Founded:** 1975
> **Arts Area:** Theater; Festivals
> **Status:** Professional; Non-Profit
> **Type:** Performing
> **Purpose:** To provide free classical theater to the citizens of Houston and the surrounding area
> **Management:** Sidney L. Berger, Producing Director; Suzanne Phillips, Associate Producer; Roxanne Collins, Business Manager
> **Paid Staff:** 4   **Volunteer Staff:** 100
> **Paid Artists:** 35
> **Utilizes:** Guest Artists; Guest Directors
> **Budget:** $100,000 - $500,000
> **Income Sources:** Private Foundations/Grants/Endowments; Business/Corporate Donations; Government Grants; Individual Donations
> **Season:** July - September
> **Annual Attendance:** 25,000
> **Affiliations:** University of Houston
> **Performance Facilities:** Miller Outdoor Theatre

JEWISH COMMUNITY CENTER OF HOUSTON
5601 South Braeswood, Houston, TX 77096
(713) 729-3200
FAX: (713) 551-7223
> **Founded:** 1935
> **Arts Area:** Dance; Vocal Music; Instrumental Music; Theater; Festivals
> **Status:** Non-Profit
> **Type:** Performing; Educational; Sponsoring
> **Purpose:** To provide education and leisure time activities, and recreational services to the southwest Houston community; to promote an appreciation of theatre
> **Management:** Jerry Wische, Executive Director; Gerry Buncher, Assistant Executive Director; David J. Marco, Director of Performing Arts
> **Officers:** Linda Walters, President
> **Paid Staff:** 120   **Volunteer Staff:** 100
> **Paid Artists:** 125   **Non-Paid Artists:** 50
> **Utilizes:** Special Technical Talent; Guest Artists; Guest Directors
> **Budget:** $100,000 - $500,000
> **Income Sources:** Private Foundations/Grants/Endowments; Business/Corporate Donations; Box Office; Government Grants; Individual Donations
> **Season:** 52 Weeks
> **Annual Attendance:** 35,000
> **Affiliations:** Texas Nonprofit Theatre; National Council of Jewish Theatres
> **Performance Facilities:** Jewish Community Center - Kaplan Theatre, Joe Frank Theater of the Arts

FACILITY

ALLEY THEATRE
615 Texas Avenue, Houston, TX 77002
(713) 228-9341
FAX: (713) 222-6542
Founded: 1947
Type of Facility: Theatre Complex
Type of Stage: Arena; Modified Thrust
Seating Capacity: Large Stage - 824; Arena Stage - 296
Year Built: 1968   **Architect:** Ulrich Franzen   **Cost:** $6,500,000
Contact for Rental: Zannie Voss;   (713) 228-9341
Manager: Stephen J. Albert;   (713) 228-9341
Resident Groups: Alley Theatre
The Alley Theatre contains the Hugo V. Neuhaus Arena Stage and Large Stage. See separate listings for additional information.

ALLEY THEATRE - HUGO V. NEUHAUS ARENA STAGE
615 Texas Avenue, Houston, TX 77002
(713) 228-9341
FAX: (713) 222-6542
Founded: 1947
Type of Facility: Theatre House; Arena
Type of Stage: Arena
Stage Dimensions: 30'x30'
Seating Capacity: 296
Year Built: 1968   **Architect:** Ulrich Franzen   **Cost:** $6,500,000
Contact for Rental: Zannie Voss;   (713) 228-9341
Manager: Stephen J. Albert;   (713) 228-9341

ALLEY THEATRE - LARGE STAGE
615 Texas Avenue, Houston, TX 77002
(713) 228-9341
FAX: (713) 222-6542
Founded: 1947
Type of Facility: Theatre House
Type of Stage: Modified Thrust
Stage Dimensions: 36'Dx20'W, widening to 38'W upstage
Seating Capacity: 824
Year Built: 1968   **Architect:** Ulrich Franzen   **Cost:** $6,500,000
Contact for Rental: Zannie Voss;   (713) 228-9341
Manager: Stephen J. Albert;   (713) 228-9341

HOUSTON CIVIC CENTER
PO Box 61649, Houston, TX 77208
(713) 247-1000
Type of Facility: Theatre Complex; Performance Center; Civic Center
Year Built: 1938
George R. Brown Convention Center, Gus Wortham Theater Center, Jesse H. Jones Hall for the Performing Arts, The Music Hall and Sam Houston Coliseum comprise Houston Civic Center. See separate listings for further information.

HOUSTON CIVIC CENTER-GEORGE R. BROWN CONVENTION CENTER
1001 Convention Center Boulevard, Houston, TX 77010
(713) 853-8000
FAX: (713) 853-8090
Type of Facility: Convention Center
Year Built: 1987   **Architect:** Convention Center Architects   **Cost:** $175,000,000
Manager: Melanie Meeks;   (713) 853-8039
George R. Brown Convention Center is part of Houston Civic Center and contains a Ballroom, Exhibition Hall and General Assembly Hall. See separate listings for further information. Rental purpose and contacts are as follows: Public Show Rentals, Melvina Chapman (713) 853-8020; Corporate Meetings, Jennifer Hanson (713) 855-8042; Conventions, Melanie Meeks, (713) 853-8039. This center is rarely used for performance, musical or theatrical events.

HOUSTON CIVIC CENTER-GEORGE R. BROWN CONVENTION CENTER - BALLROOM
1001 Convention Center Boulevard, Houston, TX 77010
(713) 853-8000
Type of Facility: Multi-Purpose; Room; Chamber Hall
Type of Stage: Flexible

Seating Capacity: 4,500
Manager: Melanie Meeks;   (713) 853-8039

HOUSTON CIVIC CENTER-GEORGE R. BROWN CONVENTION CENTER - EXHIBITION HALL
1001 Convention Center Boulevard, Houston, TX 77010
(713) 853-8000
    Type of Facility: Multi-Purpose; Room
    Type of Stage: Flexible
    Stage Dimensions: 87 sections, 6'x8' each
    Year Built: 1987
    Manager: Melanie Meeks;   (713) 853-8039
    The Exhibition Hall contains 470,500 square feet of usable floor area.

HOUSTON CIVIC CENTER-GEORGE R. BROWN CONVENTION CENTER - GENERAL ASSEMBLY HALL
1001 Convention Center Boulevard, Houston, TX 77010
(713) 853-8000
    Type of Facility: Concert Hall; Auditorium; Theatre House; Multi-Purpose
    Type of Stage: Flexible
    Stage Dimensions: 76'Wx70'D
    Seating Capacity: 3,600 - 3 sections of 1,200 seats each
    Manager: Melanie Meeks;   (713) 853-8039

HOUSTON CIVIC CENTER-GUS WORTHAM THEATER CENTER
510 Preston, Houston, TX 77002
(713) 237-1439
FAX: (713) 237-9313
    Founded: 1987
    Type of Facility: Theatre Complex; Concert Hall; Performance Center; Opera House
    Type of Stage: Proscenium   **Orchestra Pit**
    Seating Capacity: 2,174; 1,066
    Year Built: 1987   **Architect:** Morris-Aubrey Architects   **Cost:** $74,000,000
    Acoustical Consultant: Jaffe Acoustics
    Contact for Rental: Leslie Watson;   (713) 237-1439
    Manager: Robyn Williams
    Resident Groups: Houston Grand Opera; Houston Ballet
    The Gus Wortham Theater Center, part of Houston Civic Center, contains Alice & George Brown Theater and Lilly & Roy Cullen Theater. See separate listings for additional information.

HOUSTON CIVIC CENTER-GUS WORTHAM THEATER CENTER - ALICE AND GEORGE BROWN THEATER
510 Preston, Houston, TX 77002
(713) 237-1439
FAX: (713) 237-9313
    Type of Facility: Concert Hall; Theatre House; Opera House
    Type of Stage: Proscenium; Hydraulic Lift Stage
    Stage Dimensions: 52'Wx65'6"D
    Orchestra Pit
    Seating Capacity: 2,176
    Year Built: 1987
    Acoustical Consultant: Jaffe Acoustics
    Contact for Rental: Leslie Watson;   (713) 237-1439
    Manager: Robyn Williams;   (713) 237-1439
    Resident Groups: Houston Grand Opera; Houston Ballet

HOUSTON CIVIC CENTER-GUS WORTHAM THEATER CENTER - LILLY AND ROY CULLEN THEATER
510 Preston, Houston, TX 77002
(713) 237-1439
FAX: (713) 237-9313
    Type of Facility: Concert Hall; Theatre House
    Type of Stage: Proscenium; Hydraulic Lift Stage
    Stage Dimensions: 38'Wx51'D
    Orchestra Pit
    Seating Capacity: 1,101
    Year Built: 1987
    Acoustical Consultant: Jaffe Acoustics
    Contact for Rental: Leslie Watson;   (713) 237-1439
    Manager: Robyn Williams;   (713) 237-1439

HOUSTON CIVIC CENTER - JESSE H. JONES HALL FOR THE PERFORMING ARTS
615 Louisiana, PO Box 61469, Houston, TX 77208
(713) 227-3974
   Type of Facility: Concert Hall; Auditorium; Theatre House
   Type of Stage: Proscenium
   Stage Dimensions: 60'Wx36'D; 60'Wx32'H proscenium opening
   Orchestra Pit
   Seating Capacity: 3,001
   Year Built: 1966   **Architect:** CRS Architects   **Cost:** $9,000,000
   Contact for Rental: Donna Barrett;   (713) 227-3974
   Manager: Vivian Montejano;   (713) 227-3974
   Jones Hall is part of the Houston Civic Center.

HOUSTON CIVIC CENTER - THE MUSIC HALL
810 Bagby, PO Box 61649, Houston, TX 77208
(713) 247-2592
   Type of Facility: Auditorium; Theatre House
   Type of Stage: Proscenium
   Stage Dimensions: 50'Wx36'Dx27'H
   Seating Capacity: 3,010
   Year Built: 1938
   Contact for Rental: John Thomas;   (713) 247-2697
   Resident Groups: Theatre Under the Stars

HOUSTON CIVIC CENTER - SAM HOUSTON COLISEUM
810 Bagby, PO Box 61649, Houston, TX 77208
(713) 237-1439
   Type of Facility: Performance Center; Arena; Multi-Purpose
   Type of Stage: Arena
   Stage Dimensions: 230'x91'
   Seating Capacity: Permanent - 8,806; Portable - add 2,400
   Year Built: 1938
   Contact for Rental: Tracy Johnson;   (713) 237-1439
   Part of Houston Civic Center

JEWISH COMMUNITY CENTER - JOE FRANK THEATRE
5601 South Braeswood, Houston, TX 77096
(713) 729-3200
FAX: (713) 551-7223
   Founded: 1984
   Type of Facility: Environmental; Multi-Purpose; Room
   Facility Originally: Meeting Hall; Movie House
   Type of Stage: Flexible
   Stage Dimensions: 27'Wx45'D
   Seating Capacity: 125
   Year Built: 1984   **Cost:** $150,000
   Contact for Rental: David J. Marco;   (713) 729-3200, ext. 275
   Performances, lectures, meetings, demonstrations

JEWISH COMMUNITY CENTER - KAPLAN THEATRE
5601 South Braeswood, Houston, TX 77096
(713) 729-3200
FAX: (713) 551-7223
   Founded: 1970
   Type of Facility: Theatre Complex; Performance Center; Theatre House
   Type of Stage: Thrust; Proscenium
   Stage Dimensions: 40'Wx32'D
   Seating Capacity: 318
   Year Built: 1970   **Cost:** $400,000
   Contact for Rental: David J. Marco;   (713) 729-3200, ext. 275
   Performances, lectures, demonstrations

MILLER OUTDOOR THEATRE
Hermann Park, PO Box 1562, Houston, TX 77251
(713) 520-3291
   Type of Facility: Outdoor (Concert); Performance Center
   Type of Stage: Proscenium
   Stage Dimensions: 58'Wx40'D

Orchestra Pit
Seating Capacity: Permanent - 1,583; Hillside - 12,000
Year Built: 1968   **Architect:** Eugene Werlin & Associates   **Cost:** $1,300,000
Year Remodeled: 1986   **Architect:** 3D/International   **Cost:** $1,700,000
Contact for Rental: Robert Forshaw;   (713) 520-1391

RICE UNIVERSITY - HAMMAN HALL
PO Box 1892, Houston, TX 77251
(713) 527-4027
Type of Facility: Theatre House
Type of Stage: Proscenium
Stage Dimensions: 42'Wx45'D
Seating Capacity: 506
Year Built: 1957   **Architect:** Harvin C. Moore
Year Remodeled: 1967
Contact for Rental: Neil Haven;   (713) 527-4027
Resident Groups: Rice Players; Rice Chorales

STAGES REPERTORY THEATRE
3201 Allen Parkway, #101, Houston, TX 77019
(713) 527-0240
Type of Facility: Theatre Complex; Studio Performance; Performance Center; Off Broadway; Theatre House; Arena; Multi-Purpose; Room
Facility Originally: Engraving Plant
Type of Stage: Thrust; Flexible; Platform; 3/4 Arena; Arena
Stage Dimensions: Arena - 20'x30'; Thrust - 20'x20'
Seating Capacity: Arena - 248; Thrust - 191
Year Built: 1929
Year Remodeled: 1984   **Architect:** W.O. Neuhaus & Associates   **Cost:** $660,000
Acoustical Consultant: John F. Bos
Contact for Rental: James Gladwin;   (713) 527-0240
Manager: Peter Bennett, Artistic Director;   (713) 527-0240
Resident Groups: Stages Repertory Theatre

THEATRE SUBURBIA
1410 West 43rd, Houston, TX 77018
(713) 682-3525
Founded: 1961
Type of Facility: Theatre House
Facility Originally: Business Facility
Type of Stage: Flexible
Seating Capacity: 110
Year Remodeled: 1986   **Architect:** Brian Wycoff   **Cost:** $2,000
Resident Groups: Theatre Suburbia

Huntsville

FACILITY

SAM HOUSTON STATE UNIVERSITY THEATRE AND DANCE DIVISION
Theatre and Dance Division, Avenue H at 17th Street, Huntsville, TX 77341
(409) 294-1329
FAX: (409) 294-1598
Type of Facility: Theatre Complex; Auditorium; Performance Center
Year Built: 1976   **Architect:** Calhoun Tungate & Jackson   **Cost:** $3,500,000
Acoustical Consultant: Variable Acoustics
Manager: Dr. James R. Miller;   (409) 294-1329
Resident Groups: Drama Department
The facility contains the Main Stage Theatre and Studio Theatre. See separate listings for further information.

SAM HOUSTON STATE UNIVERSITY THEATRE AND DANCE DIVISION - MAIN STAGE THEATRE
Drama Center, Avenue I at 17th Street, Huntsville, TX 77341
(409) 294-1329
Type of Facility: Auditorium; Theatre House
Type of Stage: Proscenium
Stage Dimensions: 20'x54'4"x38'8"   **Orchestra Pit**
Seating Capacity: 495
Year Built: 1976

SAM HOUSTON STATE UNIVERSITY THEATRE AND DANCE DIVISION - STUDIO THEATRE
Theatre and Dance Division, Avenue H at 17th Street, Huntsville, TX 77341
(409) 294-1329
FAX: (409) 294-1598
>**Type of Facility:** Black Box
>**Type of Stage:** Flexible
>**Seating Capacity:** 120
>**Year Built:** 1976
>**Manager:** Dr. James R. Miller;   (409) 294-1329

Ingram

THEATRE

SMITH-RITCH POINT THEATRE
PO Box 176, Highway 39, Ingram, TX 78025
(210) 367-5121
>**Founded:** 1959
>**Arts Area:** Community
>**Status:** Non-Professional; Non-Profit
>**Type:** Performing; Touring; Educational
>**Purpose:** Dedicated to the visual and performing arts
>**Management:** Susan Balentine, Theatre Director; Lane Tait, Executive Director; Douglas Balentine, Technical Director
>**Paid Staff:** 20
>**Paid Artists:** 3
>**Utilizes:** Guest Conductors; Guest Artists; Guest Directors
>**Budget:** $50,000 - $100,000
>**Income Sources:** Private Foundations/Grants/Endowments; Business/Corporate Donations; Box Office; Government Grants; Individual Donations
>**Season:** June - August
>**Affiliations:** Texas Nonprofit Theatre; Texas Educators Theatre Association
>**Performance Facilities:** Smith-Ritch Point Theater

PERFORMING SERIES

HILL COUNTRY ARTS FOUNDATION
Highway 39, PO Box 176, Ingram, TX 78025
(210) 367-5121
>**Founded:** 1958
>**Arts Area:** Dance; Vocal Music; Instrumental Music; Theater
>**Status:** Non-Profit
>**Type:** Performing; Educational
>**Purpose:** To promote the visual and performing arts
>**Management:** Lane Tait, Executive Director; Susan Balentine, Theatre Director
>**Officers:** J. Tom Graham, President of Board of Directors
>**Paid Staff:** 5   **Volunteer Staff:** 150
>**Paid Artists:** 30   **Non-Paid Artists:** 75
>**Utilizes:** Special Technical Talent; Guest Conductors; Guest Directors
>**Budget:** $100,000 - $500,000
>**Income Sources:** Private Foundations/Grants/Endowments; Business/Corporate Donations; Box Office; Government Grants; Individual Donations
>**Season:** 52 Weeks   **Annual Attendance:** 23,000
>**Affiliations:** AACT; Texas Nonprofit Theatre
>**Performance Facilities:** Outdoor Amphitheatre

Irving

DANCE

IRVING BALLET COMPANY
3900 Acapulco, Irving, TX 75062
(214) 717-3926
>**Founded:** 1982
>**Arts Area:** Ballet; Jazz
>**Status:** Semi-Professional
>**Type:** Performing
>**Purpose:** To expand ballet audiences in the Irving area and establish a permanent base for future dance audiences

Management: Dale Riley, Artistic Director
Officers: Laurita Wilkinson, President; Bud Tatum, Vice President; Janine Philips, Secretary; Barbara Cardwell, Treasurer
Volunteer Staff: 20
Paid Artists: 6   **Non-Paid Artists:** 25
Utilizes: Guest Artists; Guest Directors; Guest Choreographers
Budget: $1,000 - $50,000
Income Sources: Private Foundations/Grants/Endowments; Business/Corporate Donations; Box Office
Season: December - May   **Annual Attendance:** 4,000
Affiliations: Irving Symphony; Cultural Affairs Council
Performance Facilities: Irving Arts Center

INSTRUMENTAL MUSIC

IRVING SYMPHONY ORCHESTRA
3501 North MacArthur Boulevard, Suite 406, Irving, TX 75062
(214) 257-1210
    Founded: 1962
    Arts Area: Symphony; Orchestra
    Status: Non-Profit
    Type: Performing
    Purpose: To provide outstanding music to Irving and surrounding communities
    Management: Hector Guzman, Music Director/Conductor; Marguerite Korkmas, Executive Director
    Officers: Donald J. Schiller, President; Ron Drew, President-Elect; Norman McMurray, Vice President of Administration; Nelda Bailey, Secretary; Pam Carroll, Treasurer
    Paid Staff: 1
    Paid Artists: 5
    Utilizes: Guest Artists
    Budget: $100,000 - $500,000
    Income Sources: Private Foundations/Grants/Endowments; Business/Corporate Donations; Box Office; Individual Donations
    Season: October - May
    Performance Facilities: Irving Arts Center; Carpenter Hall

THEATRE

IRVING COMMUNITY THEATER
3333 North MacArthur Boulevard, Suite 300, Irving, TX 75060
(214) 252-7558
    Arts Area: Musical; Community; Theatrical Group
    Status: Non-Professional; Non-Profit
    Type: Performing; Resident
    Purpose: For the literary, educational, and cultural advancement of the citizens of Irving and outlying areas
    Officers: Mary Bongfeldt, President; Steve Crozier, Treasurer
    Utilizes: Guest Directors
    Budget: $1,000 - $50,000
    Income Sources: Private Foundations/Grants/Endowments; Business/Corporate Donations; Box Office; Individual Donations
    Season: 52 Weeks   **Annual Attendance:** 5,000
    Affiliations: Cultural Affairs Council
    Performance Facilities: Irving Center for Cultural Arts

PERFORMING SERIES

IRVING COMMUNITY CONCERT ASSOCIATION
PO Box 154336, Irving, TX 75015
(214) 252-3838
    Founded: 1956
    Arts Area: Dance; Vocal Music; Instrumental Music; Theater
    Status: Non-Profit
    Type: Sponsoring
    Officers: Dotty Verett, President; Mary Higbie, Vice President
    Volunteer Staff: 30
    Utilizes: Guest Artists
    Budget: $1,000 - $50,000
    Income Sources: Business/Corporate Donations; Box Office; Government Grants; Individual Donations
    Season: October - April
    Affiliations: Community Concerts

FACILITY

IRVING ARTS CENTER
3333 North MacArthur Boulevard, Suite 300, Irving, TX 75062
(214) 252-7558
FAX: (214) 570-4962
> **Type of Facility:** Theatre Complex; Concert Hall; Performance Center; Theatre House
> **Type of Stage:** Proscenium **Orchestra Pit**
> **Seating Capacity:** Dupree Theatre - 256; Carpenter Theatre - 712
> **Year Built:** 1990 **Architect:** F & S Partners **Cost:** $7,200,000
> **Contact for Rental:** George Cook; (214) 252-7558
> **Manager:** Robert O. Cloutier; (214) 252-7558
> *The Irving Arts Center contains two theatres.*

Kerrville

PERFORMING SERIES

KERRVILLE FESTIVALS
Quiet Valley Ranch, PO Box 1466, Kerrville, TX 78029
(210) 257-3600
> **Founded:** 1972
> **Arts Area:** Dance; Vocal Music; Instrumental Music; Theater; Festivals
> **Status:** Professional; Commercial
> **Type:** Performing
> **Purpose:** To provide music festivals, workshops and recordings presenting regional and national performers with an emphasis on song writers and acoustic musicians
> **Management:** Rod Kennedy, Producer
> **Officers:** Rod Kennedy, President
> **Paid Staff:** 3 **Volunteer Staff:** 350
> **Paid Artists:** 150 **Non-Paid Artists:** 40
> **Utilizes:** Special Technical Talent; Guest Artists
> **Budget:** $100,000 - $500,000
> **Income Sources:** Box Office; Advertising; Commercial Sponsors
> **Season:** May - September **Annual Attendance:** 30,000
> **Affiliations:** Texas Festivals Association; Texas Music Association
> **Performance Facilities:** Festival Outdoor Theater

KERRVILLE PERFORMING ARTS SOCIETY
PO Box 1884, Kerrville, TX 78029
(210) 257-4600
> **Founded:** 1983
> **Arts Area:** Vocal Music; Instrumental Music; Festivals; Lyric Opera; Grand Opera
> **Status:** Non-Profit
> **Type:** Performing
> **Purpose:** Provide classical and popular music
> **Officers:** Arney Davis, President; Hubert Palmer, President-Elect; Nancy Neal, Treasurer
> **Volunteer Staff:** 25
> **Non-Paid Artists:** 12
> **Utilizes:** Special Technical Talent; Guest Conductors; Guest Artists; Guest Directors
> **Budget:** $50,000 - $100,000
> **Income Sources:** Private Foundations/Grants/Endowments; Business/Corporate Donations; Box Office; Government Grants; Individual Donations
> **Season:** 52 Weeks **Annual Attendance:** 6,000
> **Performance Facilities:** City Auditorium

FACILITY

FESTIVAL OUTDOOR THEATER
Quiet Valley Ranch, PO Box 1466, Kerrville, TX 78029
(210) 257-3600
> **Type of Facility:** Outdoor (Concert); Amphitheater
> **Type of Stage:** Proscenium; Environmental
> **Stage Dimensions:** 26'x46'
> **Seating Capacity:** 5,000
> **Year Built:** 1974 **Architect:** Rod Kennedy **Cost:** $26,000
> **Year Remodeled:** 1981 **Architect:** Rod Kennedy **Cost:** $21,000
> **Acoustical Consultant:** Spectratech

Contact for Rental: Rod Kennedy;   (512) 257-3600
Resident Groups: Kerrville Folk Festival; Kerrville Wine and Music Festival

---

Killeen

THEATRE

VIVE LES ARTS THEATRE
3401 South W.S. Young Drive, Killeen, TX 76547
(817) 526-9090
    Founded: 1976
    Arts Area: Professional; Musical; Community; Theatrical Group
    Status: Professional; Non-Professional; Non-Profit
    Type: Performing; Touring; Sponsoring
    Purpose: To develop and maintain cultural and artistic activities in the Killeen, Harker Heights, Fort Hood and Copperas Cove areas
    Management: Ron Hannemann, Managing/Artistic Director
    Officers: Jetty and Grady Monaghan, Chairmen
    Paid Staff: 1   **Volunteer Staff:** 150
    Utilizes: Special Technical Talent; Guest Conductors; Guest Artists
    Budget: $50,000 - $100,000
    Income Sources: Private Foundations/Grants/Endowments; Business/Corporate Donations; Box Office; Government Grants; Individual Donations
    Season: 52 Weeks   **Annual Attendance:** 6,500
    Affiliations: Texas Commission on the Arts; NALAA
    Performance Facilities: Vive Les Arts Center for the Arts

FACILITY

VIVE LES ARTS SOCIETE AND THEATRE
2501 SW Young Drive, PO Box 3401, Killeen, TX 76547
(817) 526-4599
    Type of Facility: Theatre Complex; Concert Hall; Auditorium; Performance Center; Theatre House; Multi-Purpose
    Type of Stage: Thrust; Proscenium
    Stage Dimensions: 30'Wx32'D
    Orchestra Pit
    Seating Capacity: 400
    Year Built: 1987   **Architect:** Paul E. Burns & Associates   **Cost:** $1,500,000
    Acoustical Consultant: Variable Acoustics
    Contact for Rental: Ron Hannemann;   (817) 526-9090

Laredo

INSTRUMENTAL MUSIC

LAREDO PHILHARMONIC ORCHESTRA
518 Flightline, Laredo, TX 78040
(210) 727-8886
    Founded: 1980
    Arts Area: Symphony; Orchestra; Chamber
    Status: Professional; Non-Profit
    Type: Performing; Touring; Resident; Educational
    Purpose: Cultural enrichment of the Laredo Area
    Management: Robert W. Muir, General Manager
    Officers: Julia Watson Jones, President; James E. Moore, Vice President; Amber Yeary, Secretary; Tanya K. Rose, Treasurer
    Paid Staff: 4   **Volunteer Staff:** 75
    Paid Artists: 75
    Budget: $100,000 - $500,000
    Income Sources: Private Foundations/Grants/Endowments; Business/Corporate Donations; Box Office; Individual Donations
    Season: September - May   **Annual Attendance:** 15,000
    Performance Facilities: Laredo Civic Center

Longview

INSTRUMENTAL MUSIC

LONGVIEW SYMPHONY ORCHESTRA
PO Box 1825, Longview, TX 75606
(903) 236-9739
> **Founded:** 1968
> **Arts Area:** Symphony; Orchestra
> **Status:** Semi-Professional; Non-Profit
> **Type:** Performing; Resident; Educational
> **Purpose:** To present orchestral music of the highest calibre, performed in the most capable manner, as an alternative music medium to the citizens of east Texas
> **Management:** Tonu Kalam, Conductor/Music Director; Sally Bommarito, Business Manager
> **Officers:** W.H. Throckmorton, President; Richard Miller, Vice President; Mrs. Robert Rigby, Secretary; Richard Wade, Treasurer
> **Paid Staff:** 1   **Volunteer Staff:** 33
> **Paid Artists:** 65
> **Utilizes:** Guest Conductors; Guest Artists
> **Budget:** $100,000 - $500,000
> **Income Sources:** Private Foundations/Grants/Endowments; Business/Corporate Donations; Box Office; Government Grants; Individual Donations
> **Season:** September - April   **Annual Attendance:** 4,500
> **Performance Facilities:** T.G. Field Auditorium

Lubbock

INSTRUMENTAL MUSIC

LUBBOCK SYMPHONY ORCHESTRA
916 Main Street, Suite 442, Lubbock, TX 79401
(806) 762-4707
FAX: (806) 762-5776
> **Founded:** 1942
> **Arts Area:** Symphony; Orchestra; Chamber; Ensemble
> **Status:** Professional; Non-Profit
> **Type:** Performing; Educational
> **Purpose:** To bring symphonic music to Lubbock and to enrich the quality of life and music of the Lubbock Area
> **Management:** Jim Regan, Executive Director; Gurer Aykal, Music Director/Conductor
> **Paid Staff:** 3   **Volunteer Staff:** 400
> **Paid Artists:** 76
> **Utilizes:** Guest Conductors; Guest Artists
> **Budget:** $100,000 - $500,000
> **Income Sources:** Private Foundations/Grants/Endowments; Business/Corporate Donations; Box Office; Individual Donations
> **Season:** September - June   **Annual Attendance:** 22,000
> **Affiliations:** ASOL; ASCAP
> **Performance Facilities:** Lubbock Memorial Civic Center; Lubbock Municipal Auditorium

PERFORMING SERIES

UNIVERSITY CENTER CULTURAL EVENTS
University Center, Texas Tech University, Lubbock, TX 79409
(806) 742-3621
> **Founded:** 1925
> **Arts Area:** Dance; Vocal Music; Instrumental Music; Theater; Lyric Opera
> **Status:** Professional; Non-Profit
> **Type:** Educational; Sponsoring
> **Purpose:** To add to the educational experience of Texas Tech students and the quality of life in the Lubbock area
> **Management:** Jennifer Lampe, Activites Spec. I; Mary Donahue, Activities Spec. IV
> **Paid Staff:** 3
> **Utilizes:** Guest Artists
> **Budget:** $100,000 - $500,000
> **Income Sources:** Box Office; Government Grants; Student Service Fees
> **Season:** September - April
> **Affiliations:** NACA; APAP
> **Performance Facilities:** Allen Theatre

FACILITY

LUBBOCK MEMORIAL CIVIC CENTER
1501 Sixth Street, Lubbock, TX 79401
(806) 762-6411
FAX: (806) 765-5803
    Type of Facility: Civic Center
    Type of Stage: Platform
    Year Built: 1977   **Architect:** The Architect Group
    Contact for Rental: (806) 762-6411
    Manager: Sandy Baker
    Lubbock Memorial Civic Center contains the Banquet Hall, Coliseum, Exhibit Hall, Municipal Auditorium and Theater.
    See separate listings for further information.

LUBBOCK MEMORIAL CIVIC CENTER - BANQUET HALL
1501 Sixth Street, Lubbock, TX 79401
(806) 762-6411
    Type of Facility: Performance Center; Multi-Purpose; Reception/party Hall
    Type of Stage: Proscenium
    Stage Dimensions: 30'Wx16'D
    Seating Capacity: 1,300
    Year Built: 1977
    Contact for Rental: (806) 762-6411
    Manager: Sandy Baker
    The entire Hall covers 14,105 square feet.

LUBBOCK MEMORIAL CIVIC CENTER - COLISEUM
Fourth and Boston, Lubbock, TX 79457
(806) 762-6411
FAX: (806) 765-5803
    Type of Facility: Performance Center; Arena; Multi-Purpose
    Type of Stage: Arena
    Seating Capacity: Reserved-7,510; Festival-10,500
    Year Built: 1977
    Contact for Rental: Sandy Baker;   (806) 762-6411

LUBBOCK MEMORIAL CIVIC CENTER - EXHIBIT HALL
1501 Sixth Street, Lubbock, TX 79457
(806) 762-6411
FAX: (806) 765-5803
    Type of Facility: Multi-Purpose; Exhibition Hall
    Type of Stage: Platform
    Seating Capacity: 400
    Year Built: 1977
    Contact for Rental: (806) 762-6411
    Manager: Sandy Baker
    The Exhibit Hall contains 30,000 square feet

LUBBOCK MEMORIAL CIVIC CENTER - MUNICIPAL AUDITORIUM
Fourth and Boston, Lubbock, TX 79457
(806) 762-6411
FAX: (806) 765-5803
    Type of Facility: Auditorium; Performance Center; Multi-Purpose
    Type of Stage: Proscenium
    Stage Dimensions: 100'Wx50'D   **Orchestra Pit**
    Seating Capacity: 3,015
    Year Built: 1977
    Contact for Rental: (806) 762-6411
    Manager: Sandy Baker

LUBBOCK MEMORIAL CIVIC CENTER - THEATER
1501 Sixth Street, Lubbock, TX 79457
(806) 762-6411
    Type of Facility: Theatre House
    Type of Stage: Proscenium
    Stage Dimensions: 80'Wx40'D   **Orchestra Pit**
    Seating Capacity: 1,422
    Year Built: 1977

Contact for Rental: (806) 762-6411
Manager: Vick Barker
Resident Groups: Lubbock Symphony Orchestra; Ballet Lubbock; Lubbock Summer Repertory

TEXAS TECH UNIVERSITY CENTER - ALLEN THEATRE
15th and Boston, Box 42031, Lubbock, TX 79409
(806) 742-3636
FAX: (806) 742-1974
Type of Facility: Theatre House; Multi-Purpose
Type of Stage: Proscenium
Stage Dimensions: 102'Wx60'D   **Orchestra Pit**
Seating Capacity: 1,006
Year Built: 1951   **Architect:** Atcheson & Atkinson
Year Remodeled: 1974   **Architect:** Atcheson & Atkinson
Contact for Rental: Bill Branan, Theatre Coordinator

TEXAS TECH UNIVERSITY CENTER - MUSIC BUILDING
15th and Boston, Box 42033, Lubbock, TX 79409
(806) 742-2270
Type of Facility: Concert Hall; Auditorium
Type of Stage: Proscenium; Platform
Orchestra Pit
Seating Capacity: Hall I - 1,000; Hall II - 600
Year Built: 1976   **Architect:** Architects III   **Cost:** $5,500,000
Acoustical Consultant: C.P. Boner & Associates
Contact for Rental: Wayne Hobbs

Marshall

INSTRUMENTAL MUSIC

MARSHALL SYMPHONY ORCHESTRA
PO Box 421, Marshall, TX 75671
(903) 935-4484
Founded: 1952
Arts Area: Symphony; Orchestra
Status: Semi-Professional; Non-Profit
Type: Performing
Purpose: To allow local musicians to perform with a core of professional musicians for an audience composed of local and area lovers of symphonic music
Management: Leonard Kacenjar, Artistic Director/Conductor; Jim Bob McMillan, Management Consultant; Mona Collins, Bookkeeper
Officers: Mrs. Sam B. Hall Jr., President, Marshall Symphony Society
Paid Staff: 3   **Volunteer Staff:** 35
Paid Artists: 50   **Non-Paid Artists:** 15
Utilizes: Special Technical Talent; Guest Conductors; Guest Artists
Budget: $50,000 - $100,000
Income Sources: Private Foundations/Grants/Endowments; Business/Corporate Donations; Box Office; Individual Donations
Season: October - May   **Annual Attendance:** 2,000
Affiliations: Marshall Regional Arts Council; Texas Association of Symphony Orchestras
Performance Facilities: Marshall Theater at the Civic Center

PERFORMING SERIES

MARSHALL REGIONAL ARTS COUNCIL
2501 East End Boulevard, PO Box C, Marshall, TX 75670
(903) 935-4484
FAX: (903) 938-3531
Founded: 1979
Arts Area: Dance; Vocal Music; Instrumental Music; Theater; Festivals; Grand Opera
Status: Professional; Non-Profit
Type: Educational; Sponsoring
Purpose: To encourage and support the arts in East Texas
Management: Jim Bob McMillan, Executive Director
Officers: Sandy Toussaint, President
Paid Staff: 2   **Volunteer Staff:** 10
Paid Artists: 300

Utilizes: Special Technical Talent; Guest Artists
Budget: $100,000 - $500,000
Income Sources: Private Foundations/Grants/Endowments; Business/Corporate Donations; Box Office; Government Grants; Individual Donations
Season: October - May   **Annual Attendance:** 6,000
Affiliations: APAP; NALAA; Texas Arts Council; Country Music Association
Performance Facilities: Marshall Theater at the Civic Center

FACILITY

MARSHALL CIVIC CENTER
2501 East End Boulevard South, Marshall, TX 75670
(903) 935-4472
Type of Facility: Civic Center
Year Built: 1984   **Architect:** George Rodgers   **Cost:** $3,700,000
Acoustical Consultant: C.P. Boner & Associates
Contact for Rental: Manager;   (903) 935-4472
Resident Groups: Marshall Parks and Recreation Department; Marshall Regional Arts Council
Marshall Civic Center contains the Marshall Theater at the Civic Center. See separate listing for further information.

MARSHALL THEATER AT THE CIVIC CENTER
2501 East End Boulevard South, Marshall, TX 75670
(903) 935-4472
Type of Facility: Concert Hall; Auditorium; Performance Center; Theatre House; Opera House
Type of Stage: Proscenium
Stage Dimensions: 62'Wx58'D   **Orchestra Pit**
Seating Capacity: 1,608
Year Built: 1984
Contact for Rental: Manager;   (903) 935-4472

McAllen

DANCE

RIO GRANDE VALLEY BALLET
205 Pecan Boulevard, McAllen, TX 78501
(210) 682-2721
Founded: 1973
Arts Area: Ballet; Jazz; Ethnic; Folk
Status: Semi-Professional; Non-Profit
Type: Performing; Touring; Resident; Educational; Sponsoring
Purpose: To present top-quality Mexican Folkloric, Spanish and Flamenco; to produce the "Nutcracker" and other classic ballets to paying audiences in Rio Grande Valley; to hold "Nutcracker" matinees for schools in the Valley; to present 16 one-hour concerts at the Texas State Fair in Dallas each October
Management: Mr. Doria Avila, Artistic Director/Executive Director; Rosemary Tatum, Executive Secretary; Deborah Martin, Director of Development and Community Support/Public School Coordinator
Officers: Rosemary Tatum, President/Treasurer; Mr. Doria Avila, Vice President
Paid Staff: 1   **Volunteer Staff:** 15
Paid Artists: 12   **Non-Paid Artists:** 60
Utilizes: Special Technical Talent; Guest Artists; Guest Choreographers
Budget: $100,000 - $500,000
Income Sources: Private Foundations/Grants/Endowments; Business/Corporate Donations; Box Office; Government Grants; Individual Donations
Season: September - May   **Annual Attendance:** 38,000
Performance Facilities: Mc Allen Civic Center; Harlingen Municipal Auditorium

INSTRUMENTAL MUSIC

VALLEY SYMPHONY ORCHESTRA & CHORALE AND VALLEY SINFONETTE
PO Box 2832, McAllen, TX 78502
(210) 381-8682
FAX: (210) 632-2352
Founded: 1952
Arts Area: Symphony; Orchestra; Chamber
Status: Non-Profit
Type: Educational
Management: John D. Daugherty, Executive Director
Officers: Walter Passmore, President

Paid Staff: 2
Paid Artists: 70
Utilizes: Guest Artists
Budget: $100,000 - $500,000
Income Sources: Private Foundations/Grants/Endowments; Business/Corporate Donations; Box Office; Government Grants; Individual Donations; Runout Concert Contracts
Season: September - May   **Annual Attendance:** 5,000
Affiliations: University of Texas-Pan American
Performance Facilities: UTPA Fine Arts Auditorium; McAllen Civic Center

PERFORMING SERIES

MCALLEN PERFORMING ARTS, INC.
10 North Broadway, McAllen, TX 78501
(210) 631-2545
FAX: (210) 631-8571
Arts Area: Vocal Music; Theater; Broadway Musicals
Status: Professional; Non-Profit
Type: Performing; Touring
Purpose: To provide the public with professional touring theatre productions and entertainment not available through local agencies
Management: Genevia Crow, Executive Director
Paid Staff: 1   **Volunteer Staff:** 12
Paid Artists: 5
Budget: $100,000 - $500,000
Income Sources: Box Office
Season: November - March   **Annual Attendance:** 1,300
Performance Facilities: McAllen Civic Center

RIO GRANDE VALLEY INTERNATIONAL MUSIC FESTIVAL
PO Box 2315, McAllen, TX 78502
(210) 686-1456
Founded: 1960
Arts Area: Dance; Vocal Music; Instrumental Music; Festivals; Grand Opera
Status: Non-Profit
Type: Performing; Touring; Educational; Presenting
Purpose: To present a major symphony orchestra annually, in varied concerts for students and adults, with emphasis on education of young listeners; by experiencing highly artistic musical performances, lives of area residents are culturally enriched
Officers: Dean R. Canty PhD, Chairman; Joy Judin, Vice Chairman; Carol Edrington, Secretary/Treasurer; Mildred Erhart, Financial Secretary
Volunteer Staff: 93
Paid Artists: 55   **Non-Paid Artists:** 14
Utilizes: Special Technical Talent; Guest Artists
Budget: $100,000 - $500,000
Income Sources: Private Foundations/Grants/Endowments; Business/Corporate Donations; Box Office; Government Grants; Individual Donations
Season: February   **Annual Attendance:** 12,669
Performance Facilities: McAllen International Civic Center; Rowe School Auditorium; SPI Convention Center

Mesquite

INSTRUMENTAL MUSIC

MESQUITE COMMUNITY BAND
1525 Springbrook Drive, Mesquite, TX 75149
(214) 289-6365
Founded: 1986
Arts Area: Band
Status: Non-Professional; Non-Profit
Type: Performing
Purpose: The purpose of the Mesquite Community Band is to contribute to the musical environment of the areas it serves.
Management: Elton Polk, Conductor
Volunteer Staff: 10
Non-Paid Artists: 70
Budget: $1,000 - $50,000
Income Sources: Private Foundations/Grants/Endowments; Business/Corporate Donations; Individual Donations
Season: 52 Weeks

THEATRE

MESQUITE COMMUNITY THEATRE
PO Box 850-918, Mesquite, TX 75185-0918
(214) 270-3309
>**Founded:** 1983
Arts Area: Professional; Community; Theatrical Group
Status: Semi-Professional; Non-Profit
Type: Performing
Purpose: To have good, live theatre for the Mesquite Community
Officers: John Nichols, Chairperson
Volunteer Staff: 10
Utilizes: Special Technical Talent; Guest Artists; Guest Directors
Budget: $1,000 - $50,000
Income Sources: Private Foundations/Grants/Endowments; Business/Corporate Donations; Box Office; Government Grants; Individual Donations
Season: February - October
Performance Facilities: East Ridge Park Christian Church

Midland

INSTRUMENTAL MUSIC

MIDLAND-ODESSA SYMPHONY AND CHORALE, INC.
3100 LaForce Boulevard, PO Box 6266, Midland, TX 79711
(915) 563-0921
>**Founded:** 1962
Arts Area: Symphony; Orchestra; Chamber; Ensemble
Status: Non-Profit
Type: Performing; Educational
Purpose: To provide symphonic, choral and chamber music for the people of the Permian Basin
Management: Don Th. Jaeger, Music Director; Philip D. West, General Manager
Officers: Jerry Caddel, President
Paid Staff: 6
Paid Artists: 80   **Non-Paid Artists:** 100
Utilizes: Guest Conductors; Guest Artists
Budget: $500,000 - $1,000,000
Income Sources: Private Foundations/Grants/Endowments; Business/Corporate Donations; Box Office; Government Grants; Individual Donations
Season: August - June
Affiliations: ASOL
Performance Facilities: Lee Auditorium; Barham Junior High School Auditorium

Nacogdoches

THEATRE

LAMP-LITE THEATER
PO Box 630466, Nacogdoches, TX 75936
(409) 564-8300
>**Founded:** 1971
Arts Area: Musical; Community
Status: Non-Professional; Non-Profit
Type: Performing; Touring; Educational
Purpose: To bring high-quality live theatre to the east Texas area; to offer a vital creative experience to actors and other artists
Officers: Dr. Tom Nall, President; Hazel Abernathy, Vice President; Diana Haney, Treasurer; Anne Hurst, Secretary
Volunteer Staff: 60
Non-Paid Artists: 120
Budget: $1,000 - $50,000
Income Sources: Private Foundations/Grants/Endowments; Business/Corporate Donations; Box Office; Individual Donations
Season: 52 Weeks
Affiliations: Texas Nonprofit Theatre
Performance Facilities: Lamp-Lite Theater

Odessa

THEATRE

GLOBE OF THE GREAT SOUTHWEST
2308 Shakespeare Road, Odessa, TX 79761
(915) 332-1586
Founded: 1958
Arts Area: Professional; Community; Theatrical Group
Status: Non-Profit
Type: Performing; Educational
Purpose: To provide Shakespearean and classical plays that are educational; to present contemporary and religious plays and musicals; to sponsor a touring program for schools and universities; to present an annual Shakespeare Festival; to advance the enjoyment, appreciation and study of great literature; to make available the Globe Building and grounds to the community for all the arts and a convention center for the cultural and business affairs of the area
Management: Clay Francell, Executive Director; Myrtle Crane, Box Office Manager
Officers: Sue McLelland, Chairman; Mike Gieb, Vice Chairman; Shawn Watson, Secretary; Frances Dunn, Treasurer
Paid Staff: 3 **Volunteer Staff:** 5
Paid Artists: 5 **Non-Paid Artists:** 15
Utilizes: Special Technical Talent; Guest Artists; Guest Directors
Budget: $100,000 - $500,000
Income Sources: Private Foundations/Grants/Endowments; Business/Corporate Donations; Box Office; Government Grants; Individual Donations
Season: 52 Weeks **Annual Attendance:** 11,000
Affiliations: Fine Arts Society of Texas; Texas Arts Council; Odessa Cultural Council
Performance Facilities: Globe of the Great Southwest

PERMIAN PLAYHOUSE OF ODESSA INC.
310 West 42nd, PO Box 13374, Odessa, TX 79768
(915) 362-2329
Founded: 1939
Arts Area: Community; Theatrical Group
Status: Non-Professional; Non-Profit
Type: Performing; Touring; Educational
Management: Coy L. Sharp, Artistic Director; Carla Bryant, Business Manager
Paid Staff: 6 **Volunteer Staff:** 442
Non-Paid Artists: 157
Utilizes: Special Technical Talent; Guest Conductors; Guest Artists; Guest Directors
Budget: $100,000 - $500,000
Income Sources: Private Foundations/Grants/Endowments; Business/Corporate Donations; Box Office; Government Grants; Individual Donations
Season: September - June **Annual Attendance:** 12,280
Affiliations: AACT; SWTC; Texas Nonprofit Theater

FACILITY

GLOBE OF THE GREAT SOUTHWEST
2308 Shakespeare Road, Odessa, TX 79761
(915) 332-1586
Type of Facility: Theatre House
Type of Stage: Elizabethan
Stage Dimensions: 36'x60'
Orchestra Pit
Seating Capacity: 410
Year Built: 1958 **Architect:** J. Ellsworth Powell
Acoustical Consultant: J. Ellsworth Powell
Contact for Rental: Clay Francell; (915) 332-1586

Orange

FACILITY

LUTCHER THEATER
707 West Main Street, Orange, TX 77630
(409) 886-5535
FAX: (409) 886-5537
Founded: 1980

Type of Facility: Theatre Complex; Concert Hall; Auditorium; Performance Center; Theatre House
Facility Originally: Nightclub
Type of Stage: Proscenium
Stage Dimensions: 45'Wx35'D   **Orchestra Pit**
Seating Capacity: 1,494
Year Built: 1979   **Architect:** Page Southerland Page   **Cost:** $8,000,000
Acoustical Consultant: Charles Boner, Boner Associates, Inc.
Contact for Rental: James Clark;   (409) 886-5535

Palestine

FACILITY

PALESTINE CIVIC CENTER COMPLEX
Highway 287-19N, Palestine, TX 75801
(903) 723-3014; (903) 729-6066
FAX: (903) 729-2083
   Type of Facility: Auditorium; Civic Center; Multi-Purpose
   Type of Stage: Proscenium
   Stage Dimensions: 52'Wx19'10"D
   Seating Capacity: 1,375
   Year Built: 1981   **Architect:** Ted Moffitt   **Cost:** $1,500,000
   Contact for Rental: Palestine Chamber of Commerce;   (903) 723-3014
   Manager: Susan Mervish

Pampa

DANCE

PAMPA CIVIC BALLET
315 North Nelson, Pampa, TX 79065
(806) 669-6361
   Founded: 1972
   Arts Area: Ballet
   Status: Non-Professional; Non-Profit
   Type: Performing; Resident; Educational; Sponsoring
   Purpose: To encourage the more gifted and dedicated dancers in the area and to offer them a performance opportunity
   Management: Jeanne M. Willingham, Artistic Director
   Officers: Mary Wilson, President; Iris Day, Vice President; Linda Holt, Secretary; Michael Epps, Treasurer; Ruth Riehart, Company Representative
   Volunteer Staff: 1
   Non-Paid Artists: 20
   Utilizes: Special Technical Talent; Guest Artists; Guest Directors; Guest Choreographers
   Budget: $1,000 - $50,000
   Income Sources: Business/Corporate Donations; Box Office; Individual Donations
   Season: September - June   **Annual Attendance:** 1,600
   Affiliations: Texas Arts Alliance
   Performance Facilities: M.K. Brown Auditorium

FACILITY

M.K. BROWN AUDITORIUM
1100 West Coronado Drive, Pampa, TX 79065
(806) 669-5790
FAX: (806) 669-5712
   Type of Facility: Civic Center
   Seating Capacity: 700
   Year Built: 1972
   Architect: Brasher, Gayetter & Repier
   Cost: $1,200,000
   Contact for Rental: Seleta Chance;   (806) 669-5790

Paris
FACILITY

PARIS JUNIOR COLLEGE
2400 Clarksville, Paris, TX 75460
(903) 785-7661
FAX: (903) 784-9370
Founded: 1924
Type of Facility: Auditorium
Type of Stage: Proscenium
Seating Capacity: 350
Year Built: 1939 **Architect:** Bill Lightfoot
Year Remodeled: 1975 **Architect:** B.P. Denney **Cost:** $140,000
Contact for Rental: Kenneth Webb; (903) 784-9433
Manager: Ray E. Karrer
Resident Groups: Le Troupe

Pasadena
FACILITY

SLOCOMB AUDITORIUM
8060 Spencer Highway, Pasadena, TX 77501
(713) 476-1829
Founded: 1965
Type of Facility: Theatre Complex; Concert Hall; Auditorium; Theatre House
Type of Stage: Proscenium
Stage Dimensions: 47'10" at arch; 22'Hx37'D
Seating Capacity: 1,003
Year Built: 1965 **Architect:** Burleson and Associates
Year Remodeled: 1992 **Architect:** P.B.R. Architects **Cost:** $1,000,000
Contact for Rental: Debbie Wade; (713) 476-1863
Resident Groups: Theatre San Jacinto; San Jacinto College School of Music

---
Plano
THEATRE

PLANO REPERTORY THEATRE
1028 East 15th Place, Plano, TX 75074
(214) 422-7460
Founded: 1975
Arts Area: Musical; Community; Theatrical Group
Status: Non-Professional; Non-Profit
Type: Performing; Educational
Volunteer Staff: 30
Non-Paid Artists: 100
Utilizes: Guest Directors
Budget: $50,000 - $100,000
Income Sources: Private Foundations/Grants/Endowments; Business/Corporate Donations; Box Office; Government Grants; Individual Donations
Season: 52 Weeks **Annual Attendance:** 9,000
Affiliations: Cultural Arts Council of Plano
Performance Facilities: PRT Art Centre Theatre

Rockport
THEATRE

REPERTORY THEATER OF AMERICA
PO Box 1296, Rockport, TX 78382
(512) 729-6274
Founded: 1967
Arts Area: Professional; Dinner
Status: Professional

Type: Performing; Touring
Purpose: To provide quality professional theatre to schools, colleges, clubs, and community organizations
Management: Drexel H. Riley, Director
Paid Staff: 4
Paid Artists: 12
Utilizes: Guest Directors
Budget: $100,000 - $500,000
Income Sources: Sponser Fees
Season: September - May
Affiliations: NACA

Round Top

PERFORMING SERIES

FESTIVAL AT ROUND TOP/INTERNATIONAL FESTIVAL-INSTITUTE AT ROUND TOP
Festival Institute, PO Drawer 89, Round Top, TX 78954
(409) 249-3129
FAX: (409) 249-3100
Founded: 1971
Arts Area: Instrumental Music; Festivals
Status: Professional; Non-Profit
Type: Performing; Educational
Purpose: To conduct an intensive educational institute for young artists of demonstrated ability in the performaing arts, with particular emphasis on music; to conduct festivals, workshops, and symposia; to commission the composition and production of new music and works of art for the education of the public and the training of young artists
Management: James Dick, Founder/Artistic Director; Richard Royall, Managing Director; Alain Declert, Director of Information; Lamar Lentz, Curator; Charles Reeves, Office Manager
Paid Staff: 6 **Volunteer Staff:** 20
Paid Artists: 25
Utilizes: Guest Conductors; Guest Artists
Budget: $100,000 - $500,000
Income Sources: Private Foundations/Grants/Endowments; Business/Corporate Donations; Box Office; Government Grants; Individual Donations
Season: May - August **Annual Attendance:** 12,000
Performance Facilities: Festival Concert Hall; Menke Conference Center; W.L. Clayton House

FACILITY

INTERNATIONAL FESTIVAL-INSTITUTE AT ROUND TOP - FESTIVAL CONCERT HALL
State Highway 237 and Jaster Road, Round Top, TX 78954
(409) 249-3129
FAX: (409) 249-3100
Founded: 1981
Type of Facility: Concert Hall; Auditorium; Performance Center
Type of Stage: Flexible; Proscenium; Platform
Stage Dimensions: 70'x50'
Orchestra Pit
Seating Capacity: 1,200
Year Built: 1981 **Architect:** Edward Mattingly, Dale Norton and James Dick **Cost:** $3,000,000
Acoustical Consultant: Boner Associates
Contact for Rental: Alain G. Declert; (409) 249-3086
Festival-Institute is a center for intensive studies in classical music May-August. It is a conference center and site of monthly benefit concerts during the rest of the year.

San Angelo

INSTRUMENTAL MUSIC

SAN ANGELO SYMPHONY ORCHESTRA AND CHORALE
PO Box 5922, San Angelo, TX 76902
(915) 658-5877
Founded: 1948
Arts Area: Symphony
Status: Professional; Non-Professional; Non-Profit
Type: Performing
Purpose: To promote cultural advancement and interest in the field of symphonic music in San Angelo and the vicinity

Management: Gene Chartier Smith, Music Director/Conductor; Tim Young, Manager
Officers: Tom Ridgway, President; Juanita Baker, Secretary; George Randall, Treasurer
Paid Staff: 3 **Volunteer Staff:** 45
Paid Artists: 100 **Non-Paid Artists:** 140
Utilizes: Special Technical Talent; Guest Artists
Budget: $100,000 - $500,000
Income Sources: Private Foundations/Grants/Endowments; Business/Corporate Donations; Box Office; Government Grants; Individual Donations
Season: October - July **Annual Attendance:** 25,000
Affiliations: BMI; ASCAP; ASOL
Performance Facilities: City Auditorium

VOCAL MUSIC

TWIN MOUNTAIN TONESMEN
PO Box 2711, San Angelo, TX 76902
(915) 949-0608
Founded: 1979
Arts Area: Barbershop Quartet
Status: Non-Professional; Non-Profit
Type: Performing; Resident
Purpose: As members of the National Society of Barbershop Singing, we perform this type of music around our area and in contests
Management: Mark E. Clark, Assistant Director
Officers: Laylan Bratcher, President; Nolen Mears, Executive Vice Presidents; John Parker, Secretary; Bob Gordon, Treasurer; Lanny Kiest, Program Director
Volunteer Staff: 10
Non-Paid Artists: 38
Utilizes: Guest Artists
Budget: $1,000 - $50,000
Income Sources: Private Foundations/Grants/Endowments; Box Office
Season: 52 Weeks **Annual Attendance:** 1,500
Affiliations: Cultural Affairs Council; SPEBSQSA
Performance Facilities: City Auditorium

FACILITY

ANGELO STATE UNIVERSITY - AUDITORIUM
2601 West Avenue North, San Angelo, TX 76909
(915) 942-2021
Type of Facility: Auditorium
Type of Stage: Proscenium
Orchestra Pit
Seating Capacity: 450
Year Built: 1950 **Architect:** Lovett & Sellars
Year Remodeled: 1974 **Architect:** Lovett & Sellars **Cost:** $300,000
Manager: Dr. Raymond E. Carver

ANGELO STATE UNIVERSITY - MODULAR THEATRE
2601 West Avenue North, San Angelo, TX 76909
(915) 942-2021
Type of Facility: Modular Theatre
Type of Stage: Flexible
Seating Capacity: 300
Year Built: 1975 **Architect:** Chakos Zentner Marks
Acoustical Consultant: Jules Fisher
Manager: Dr. Raymond E. Carver; (915) 942-2146

SAN ANGELO CITY AUDITORIUM
500 Rio Concho Drive, San Angelo, TX 76903
(915) 653-9577
FAX: (915) 658-1110
Type of Facility: Auditorium
Type of Stage: Proscenium
Stage Dimensions: 35'x40' **Orchestra Pit**
Seating Capacity: 1,577
Year Built: 1929
Year Remodeled: 1982 **Architect:** Barbutti **Cost:** $1,200,000
Acoustical Consultant: C.P. Boner & Associates

Contact for Rental: John L. Braswell;   (915) 653-9577
Manager: Michael McEnrue;   (915) 653-9577
Resident Groups: San Angelo Symphony; San Angelo Civic Ballet

San Antonio

DANCE

GUADALUPE FOLK DANCE COMPANY
c/o Guadalupe Cultural Arts Center, 1300 Guadalupe Street, San Antonio, TX 78207
(210) 271-3151
FAX: (210) 271-3480
   Arts Area: Modern; Folk
   Status: Non-Profit
   Type: Resident
   Purpose: To perform two major theatrical dance productions per year with functions interspersed throughout the year
   Management: Pedro Rodriguez, Executive Director
   Officers: Maria Elena Torralva, Chairman of the Board
   Income Sources: Private Foundations/Grants/Endowments; Business/Corporate Donations; Box Office; Government Grants; Individual Donations
   Season: 52 Weeks
   Performance Facilities: Guadalupe Theater

SAN ANTONIO BALLET
212 East Mulberry, San Antonio, TX 78212
(210) 736-5144
   Founded: 1970
   Arts Area: Ballet
   Status: Professional; Non-Profit
   Type: Performing; Educational
   Purpose: To promote the art of dance through performances and educational programs and provide for the professional development of gifted dancers
   Management: Vladimir Marek, Artistic Director; Nancy Smith, Administration Director
   Officers: Dr. D. Ford Nielsen, President; Nancy Smith, Vice President/Treasurer; Vladimir Marek, Secretary
   Paid Staff: 2
   Non-Paid Artists: 20
   Budget: $50,000 - $100,000
   Income Sources: Private Foundations/Grants/Endowments; Business/Corporate Donations; Individual Donations
   Season: 52 Weeks

INSTRUMENTAL MUSIC

SAN ANTONIO CHAMBER MUSIC SOCIETY
PO Box 12702, San Antonio, TX 78212
   Founded: 1938
   Arts Area: Orchestra; Chamber; Ensemble; Instrumental Group
   Status: Non-Profit
   Type: Sponsoring
   Purpose: To present five to six chamber music concerts per year
   Officers: Lyle Donaldson, President; Robert Persellin, Artists Committee
   Volunteer Staff: 25
   Utilizes: Guest Artists
   Budget: $1,000 - $50,000
   Income Sources: Private Foundations/Grants/Endowments; Business/Corporate Donations; Box Office; Individual Donations
   Season: September - May   **Annual Attendance:** 4,200

SAN ANTONIO SYMPHONY
222 East Houstin Street, Suite 200, San Antonio, TX 78205
(210) 225-6161
FAX: (210) 554-1008
   Founded: 1939
   Arts Area: Symphony; Orchestra
   Status: Professional; Non-Profit
   Type: Performing; Educational
   Purpose: To meet selected cultural, educational and entertainment needs of the South Texas Community by providing the highest possible quality professional symphony presenting orchestral music

Management: Christopher Wilkins, Music Director Designate; David Mairs, Resident Conductor; Jorge Ramirez, Director of Marketing/Public Relations; Stephanie Cavanaugh, Finance Director
Officers: Rick Lester, President
Paid Staff: 10
Paid Artists: 81
Utilizes: Guest Conductors; Guest Artists
Budget: $1,000,000 - $5,000,000
Income Sources: Private Foundations/Grants/Endowments; Business/Corporate Donations; Box Office; Government Grants; Individual Donations
Season: September - June   **Annual Attendance:** 156,000
Affiliations: ASOL
Performance Facilities: Lila Cockrell Theatre, San Antonio Convention Center; Laurie Auditorium, Trinity University

VOCAL MUSIC

TEXAS BACH CHOIR
504 Avenue E, San Antonio, TX 78215
(210) 824-6597
Founded: 1976
Arts Area: Choral
Status: Semi-Professional; Non-Profit
Type: Performing; Touring; Resident
Purpose: To perform classical sacred choral music from all periods, specializing in Baroque
Management: Daniel Long, Musical Director; John Moore, Accompanist; Samantha A. Beer, Administrator
Officers: Loula Gregg, President
Paid Staff: 3
Paid Artists: 12   **Non-Paid Artists:** 36
Utilizes: Special Technical Talent; Guest Artists
Budget: $1,000 - $50,000
Income Sources: Private Foundations/Grants/Endowments; Business/Corporate Donations; Box Office; Government Grants; Individual Donations
Season: September - May   **Annual Attendance:** 2,500
Affiliations: CA

THEATRE

GUADALUPE CULTURAL ARTS CENTER
1300 Guadalupe Street, San Antonio, TX 78207
(210) 271-3151
FAX: (210) 271-3480
Arts Area: Professional; Musical; Community; Folk; Puppet; Multi-Cultural Events
Status: Non-Profit
Type: Performing; Touring; Resident; Educational; Sponsoring; Presenting
Purpose: To present and promote Mexican-American arts; to facilitate a deeper understanding and appreciation of Latino and Native American cultures and their respective artistic expressions
Management: Pedro Rodriguez, Executive Director
Officers: Maria Elena Torralva, Chairman of the Board
Budget: $1,000,000 - $5,000,000
Income Sources: Private Foundations/Grants/Endowments; Business/Corporate Donations; Box Office; Government Grants; Individual Donations
Performance Facilities: Guadalupe Theater

JUMP-START PERFORMANCE COMPANY
1035 South Alamo, San Antonio, TX 78210
(210) 227-5867
Founded: 1985
Arts Area: Professional; Community; Theatrical Group
Status: Semi-Professional
Type: Performing; Touring; Resident; Educational; Sponsoring; Commissioning
Purpose: Jump-Start Performance Company (JSPC) was founded by a group of diverse artists to encourage and promote new ideas in performance
Management: Steve Bailey, Artistic Director; Sterling Houston, Administrator; Max Parrilla, Technical Director
Officers: Dennis Poplin, President; Cathy Pollock, Secretary
Paid Staff: 3   **Volunteer Staff:** 10
Paid Artists: 200
Utilizes: Guest Artists; Guest Directors
Budget: $50,000 - $100,000

Income Sources: Private Foundations/Grants/Endowments; Box Office; Government Grants; Individual Donations; Tuition; Sponsor Fees
Season: September - June   **Annual Attendance:** 6,000
Affiliations: AACT; ROOTS
Performance Facilities: Jump-Start Theater

SAN ANTONIO LITTLE THEATRE
800 West Ashby, San Antonio, TX 78212
(210) 735-6922
FAX: (210) 734-2651
   Founded: 1912
   Arts Area: Community
   Status: Non-Profit
   Type: Performing; Educational
   Purpose: Literary and educational community theatre
   Management: Francis Elborne, Managing Artistic Director; Steve Hernandez, Office Manager
   Officers: Dora Hauser, President, Board of Directors; John Thuman, Vice President; Richard Taylor, Treasurer
   Paid Staff: 6
   Utilizes: Guest Directors
   Budget: $100,000 - $500,000
   Income Sources: Private Foundations/Grants/Endowments; Business/Corporate Donations; Box Office; Individual Donations
   Season: September - August
   Affiliations: Texas Nonprofit Theatre

24TH STREET EXPERIMENT
411 SW 24th Street, San Antonio, TX 78207
(210) 435-2103
   Founded: 1981
   Arts Area: Professional; Musical; Community
   Status: Professional; Non-Profit
   Type: Performing; Touring; Resident; Educational
   Purpose: To provide professional, quality, experimental, musical and children's theatre to San Antonio and Texas, and to provide jobs for local theatre artists
   Management: Richard Slocum, Artistic Director; Kevin Lechler, General Manager
   Officers: Anna Hoelting, President, Board of Directors; Tina Cantu-Navarro, Vice President; Charles A. Schmidt, Secretary/Treasurer
   Paid Staff: 4
   Paid Artists: 20
   Budget: $50,000 - $100,000
   Income Sources: Private Foundations/Grants/Endowments; Business/Corporate Donations; Box Office; Government Grants; Individual Donations
   Season: October - September   **Annual Attendance:** 40,000
   Affiliations: Our Lady of the Lake University
   Performance Facilities: Theatre West Thiry Auditorium

PERFORMING SERIES

ARTS SAN ANTONIO!
217 East Travis, San Antonio, TX 78205
(210) 226-2891
FAX: (210) 226-1981
   Founded: 1981
   Arts Area: Dance; Vocal Music; Instrumental Music; Theater; Festivals; Lyric Opera; Grand Opera
   Status: Professional; Non-Profit
   Type: Performing
   Purpose: To provide a versatile program of the performing arts, including local, regional, national and international talent
   Management: Frank Villani, Acting General Manager
   Officers: Jon Wood, President; Elaine Dagen Bela, Chairman; Bobby Duncan, Treasurer
   Paid Staff: 4   **Volunteer Staff:** 3
   Paid Artists: 120
   Utilizes: Special Technical Talent; Guest Conductors; Guest Artists; Guest Directors
   Budget: $1,000,000 - $5,000,000
   Income Sources: Private Foundations/Grants/Endowments; Business/Corporate Donations; Box Office; Government Grants; Individual Donations
   Season: 52 Weeks   **Annual Attendance:** 30,000

SAN ANTONIO PERFORMING ARTS ASSOCIATION
110 Broadway, Suite 320, San Antonio, TX 78205
(210) 224-8187
Founded: 1978
Arts Area: Dance; Vocal Music; Instrumental Music; Theater; Festivals
Status: Non-Profit
Type: Sponsoring
Purpose: To present the most outstanding national and international music, dance and theatre year-round in San Antonio
Management: Margaret K. Stanley, Executive Director
Officers: Timothy L. Austin, Chairman; Woody York, President
Paid Staff: 8
Utilizes: Guest Artists
Budget: $1,000,000 - $5,000,000
Income Sources: Private Foundations/Grants/Endowments; Business/Corporate Donations; Box Office; Government Grants; Individual Donations
Season: 52 Weeks   **Annual Attendance:** 30,000
Affiliations: TCA; NEA; City of San Antonio

FACILITY

ARNESON RIVER THEATRE
418 Villita Street, San Antonio, TX 78205
(210) 299-8610
FAX: (210) 299-8444
Founded: 1940
Type of Facility: Outdoor (Concert)
Type of Stage: Greek
Stage Dimensions: 630 square feet
Seating Capacity: 800
Year Built: 1939   **Architect:** Robert Hugmann
Year Remodeled: 1988   **Architect:** Milton Babbitt   **Cost:** $290,000
Acoustical Consultant: Variable Acoustics
Contact for Rental: ;   (210) 299-8610
Resident Groups: Fiesta Noche Del Rio; Fiesta Flamenca

BEETHOVEN HALL - SAN JOSE CONVENTION CENTER
200 East Market, San Antonio, TX 78205
(210) 299-8500
FAX: (210) 223-1495
Type of Facility: Concert Hall
Type of Stage: Proscenium
Stage Dimensions: 32'Wx41'6"D; 32'Wx21'H proscenium opening
Seating Capacity: 640
Year Built: 1895
Year Remodeled: 1981
Contact for Rental: Martha Wood;   (210) 299-8500
Originally built by Mannerchor, a German immigrants' vocal group

MUNICIPAL AUDITORIUM
100 Auditorium Circle, San Antonio, TX 78205
(210) 299-8500
Type of Facility: Auditorium
Type of Stage: Proscenium
Stage Dimensions: 120'Wx54'D; 76'Wx37'H proscenium opening   **Orchestra Pit**
Seating Capacity: 5,000
Year Built: 1926
Year Remodeled: 1985   **Architect:** Phelps Garza Simmons & Baumberger   **Cost:** $13,500,000
Contact for Rental: Martha Wood;   (210) 299-8500
Original Auditorium burned in 1979. It was rebuilt on the same site and was reopened in 1985.

SAN ANTONIO CONVENTION CENTER
200 East Market Street, San Antonio, TX 78205
(210) 299-8500
Type of Facility: Theatre Complex; Theatre House; Civic Center; Arena; Multi-Purpose
Type of Stage: Proscenium; Arena
Seating Capacity: Theatre - 2,540; Arena - 15,500

Year Built: 1968
Year Remodeled: 1986   **Cost:** $32,000,000
Contact for Rental: Martha Wood, Charlotte Winans;   (210) 299-8500
Manager: Yolanda Jensen, Facilities Manager
The San Antonio Convention Center contains the Lila Cockrell Theatre. See separate listing for further information.

SAN ANTONIO CONVENTION CENTER - LILA COCKRELL THEATRE
200 East Market Street, San Antonio, TX 78205
(210) 299-8500
> **Type of Facility:** Theatre Complex; Concert Hall; Performance Center; Off Broadway; Theatre House; Opera House; Multi-Purpose; Room; Loft
> **Type of Stage:** Proscenium
> **Stage Dimensions:** 55'5"Wx60'D; 55'5"Wx30'H proscenium opening   **Orchestra Pit**
> **Seating Capacity:** 2,541
> **Year Built:** 1968
> **Year Remodeled:** 1986
> **Contact for Rental:** Martha Wood or Charlotte Winans;   (210) 299-8500

TRINITY UNIVERSITY - DEPARTMENT OF SPEECH AND DRAMA
715 Stadium Drive, San Antonio, TX 78284
(210) 736-8511
FAX: (210) 736-7305
> **Type of Facility:** Theatre Complex
> **Type of Stage:** Thrust; Flexible; Proscenium; Black Box
> **Seating Capacity:** Theater I - 235; Attic II - 110; Cafe - 80
> **Year Built:** 1966   **Architect:** O'Neil Ford   **Cost:** $1,250,000
> **Acoustical Consultant:** O'Neil Ford

TRINITY UNIVERSITY - LAURIE AUDITORIUM
San Antonio, TX 78212
(210) 736-8119
FAX: (210) 736-8100
> **Type of Facility:** Concert Hall; Auditorium
> **Type of Stage:** Flexible; Proscenium
> **Stage Dimensions:** 78'Wx24'D   **Orchestra Pit**
> **Seating Capacity:** 2,965
> **Year Built:** 1971   **Architect:** Ford, Powell & Carson   **Cost:** $7,000,000
> **Acoustical Consultant:** Jaffe Acoustics
> **Contact for Rental:** John McFadden;   (210) 736-8119
> *No rock or rap shows*

San Benito

THEATRE

DAWSON THEATRE GUILD
925 East Stenger, San Benito, TX 78586
(210) 399-5321
> **Founded:** 1984
> **Arts Area:** Dinner; Community
> **Status:** Non-Professional; Non-Profit
> **Type:** Performing; Touring; Educational
> **Purpose:** Enhance cultural and theatrical offerings in the Lower Rio Grande Valley
> **Officers:** Ivan Baker, President; Arlene Hushen, Velma de los Santon, Vice Presidents; Mickey Boland, Treasurer
> **Volunteer Staff:** 3
> **Non-Paid Artists:** 50
> **Utilizes:** Guest Artists; Guest Directors
> **Budget:** $1,000 - $50,000
> **Income Sources:** Private Foundations/Grants/Endowments; Business/Corporate Donations; Box Office; Individual Donations
> **Season:** 52 Weeks   **Annual Attendance:** 4,000
> **Affiliations:** Texas Nonprofit Theater
> **Performance Facilities:** South Padre Island Hilton; San Benito Auditorium

---
Seguin

FACILITY

JACKSON AUDITORIUM
1000 West Court, Seguin, TX 78155
(210) 372-8180
FAX: (210) 372-8096
    Founded: 1986
    Type of Facility: Auditorium
    Type of Stage: Proscenium
    Stage Dimensions: 45'x22' proscenium opening   **Orchestra Pit**
    Seating Capacity: 1,050
    Year Built: 1986   **Architect:** Marmon Mok   **Cost:** $3,000,000
    Contact for Rental: Susan Rinn;   (210) 372-8180

Sherman

INSTRUMENTAL MUSIC

SHERMAN SYMPHONY ORCHESTRA
Austin College, Suite 61592, Sherman, TX 75091
(903) 813-2251
    Founded: 1966
    Arts Area: Symphony; Orchestra
    Status: Non-Professional; Non-Profit
    Type: Performing; Educational; Sponsoring
    Purpose: To provide concert performances of standard orchestral repertoire for area audiences, with guest appearances of nationally-known concert soloists
    Management: Dan Dominick, Conductor
    Paid Staff: 5   **Volunteer Staff:** 9
    Paid Artists: 4   **Non-Paid Artists:** 2
    Utilizes: Guest Artists
    Budget: $1,000 - $50,000
    Income Sources: Private Foundations/Grants/Endowments; Business/Corporate Donations; Government Grants; Individual Donations
    Season: September - May   **Annual Attendance:** 4,000
    Performance Facilities: Wynne Chapel

PERFORMING SERIES

COMMUNITY SERIES, INC.
61602 Austin College, PO Box 1177, Sherman, TX 75091-1177
(903) 813-2472
FAX: (903) 813-3199
    Founded: 1967
    Arts Area: Dance; Vocal Music; Instrumental Music; Theater; Lyric Opera; Grand Opera
    Status: Professional
    Type: Educational; Sponsoring
    Purpose: To bring to the Sherman-Denison area the best of a diversity of music, dance and drama and to offer some events in residency and in the schools
    Management: Bruce G. Lunkley, Manager; Susan Brown, Assistant Manager
    Officers: Dr. A.J. Carlson, President; Janie Whitten, Vice President
    Paid Staff: 2   **Volunteer Staff:** 34
    Paid Artists: 60
    Utilizes: Guest Conductors; Guest Artists
    Budget: $50,000 - $100,000
    Income Sources: Private Foundations/Grants/Endowments; Business/Corporate Donations; Box Office; Individual Donations
    Season: September - May   **Annual Attendance:** 7,000
    Affiliations: APAP; Southwest Arts Presenters Association
    Performance Facilities: Wynne Chapel; Richardson Center; Ida Green Theatre

---
Sonora
PERFORMING SERIES

THE OUTDOOR DRAMA GROUP ASSOCIATION
PO Box 1196, Sonora, TX 76950
(915) 387-3105
Founded: 1987
Arts Area: Folk
Status: Non-Profit
Type: Performing; Educational
Purpose: To plan for and create an outdoor drama depicting the heritage of Sutton County as a means of promoting tourism in order to enhance the economy
Management: Jimmy Cahill, Coordinator
Volunteer Staff: 10
Non-Paid Artists: 100
Utilizes: Guest Artists
Budget: $1,000 - $50,000
Income Sources: Business/Corporate Donations; Box Office; Individual Donations
Season: June - August **Annual Attendance:** 2,000
Performance Facilities: Caverns of Sonora

Temple
THEATRE

TEMPLE CIVIC THEATRE
2413 South 13th Street, Temple, TX 76504
(817) 778-4751
Founded: 1965
Arts Area: Community; Theatrical Group
Status: Non-Professional; Non-Profit
Type: Performing; Educational
Purpose: To promote the development of theatre arts in the community and to offer a creative outlet for the talents of the community
Management: C. Suzanne Hudson-Smith, Artistic/Managing Director; Roger Daniels, Technical Director
Officers: Dick Sweeden, President; Jody Donaldson, Vice President; Deborah Ellis, Secretary; Bill Stokes, Treasurer
Paid Staff: 3 **Volunteer Staff:** 200
Utilizes: Guest Directors
Budget: $100,000 - $500,000
Income Sources: Private Foundations/Grants/Endowments; Business/Corporate Donations; Box Office; Individual Donations
Season: 52 Weeks **Annual Attendance:** 17,000
Affiliations: TNT; SWTC

PERFORMING SERIES

CULTURAL ACTIVITIES CENTER
3011 North Third Street, Temple, TX 76501
(817) 773-9926
Founded: 1958
Arts Area: Dance; Vocal Music; Theater; Festivals; Grand Opera
Status: Professional; Semi-Professional; Non-Professional; Non-Profit
Type: Performing; Touring; Resident; Educational; Sponsoring
Purpose: The Cultural Activities Center is a creative and performing arts center that also serves as the community arts council for Temple and the surrounding area.
Management: Larry Scottfield, Executive Director; Deloris Rosen, Business Manager; Richard Phillips, Operations Manager/Technical Director; Helen Kwiatkowski, Visual Arts Director
Officers: Robert Mason, President; Marilyn Hoster, President-Elect; Marianne String Fellow, Vice President; Allan Walters, Treasurer
Paid Staff: 7
Utilizes: Guest Conductors; Guest Artists
Budget: $100,000 - $500,000
Income Sources: Private Foundations/Grants/Endowments; Business/Corporate Donations; Box Office; Government Grants; Individual Donations
Season: September - May **Annual Attendance:** 30,000
Affiliations: APAP; NALAA; ACA; Texas Arts Council

FACILITY

CULTURAL ACTIVITIES CENTER
3011 North Third Street, Temple, TX 76501
(817) 773-9926
> **Type of Facility:** Theatre House; Multi-Purpose; Room
> **Type of Stage:** Proscenium
> **Stage Dimensions:** 40'Wx30'D   **Orchestra Pit**
> **Seating Capacity:** 489
> **Year Built:** 1978   **Architect:** Rucker & Chamlee   **Cost:** $1,200,000
> **Year Remodeled:** 1984   **Architect:** Bill Chamlee   **Cost:** $300,000
> **Contact for Rental:** Richard Phillips, Technical Director;   (817) 773-9926
> **Manager:** Larry Scofield, Executive Director

TEMPLE CIVIC THEATRE
2413 South 13th Street, PO Box 3732, Temple, TX 76501
(817) 778-4751
> **Type of Facility:** Theatre House; Loft
> **Type of Stage:** Thrust; 3/4 Arena
> **Stage Dimensions:** 24'x18'   **Orchestra Pit**
> **Seating Capacity:** 249
> **Year Built:** 1977   **Architect:** Charles Voelter   **Cost:** $235,000
> **Acoustical Consultant:** C.P. Boner & Associates
> **Contact for Rental:** C. Suzanne Hudson-Smith;   (817) 778-4751

Texarkana

FACILITY

PEROT THEATRE
221 Main Street, Texarkana, TX 75501
(903) 792-8681
> **Type of Facility:** Performance Center
> **Facility Originally:** Vaudeville
> **Type of Stage:** Proscenium
> **Stage Dimensions:** 68'9"Wx30'D; 43'3"Wx25"H proscenium opening   **Orchestra Pit**
> **Seating Capacity:** 1,606
> **Year Built:** 1924   **Architect:** Emil Weil   **Cost:** $300,000
> **Year Remodeled:** 1981   **Architect:** Bell Klein Hoffman   **Cost:** $1,900,000
> **Acoustical Consultant:** David McCandless, Jr.
> **Contact for Rental:** Texarkana Regional Arts and Humanities Council;   (214) 792-8681
> **Manager:** Charles R. Rogers
> **Resident Groups:** Perot Theatre Series
> *The Perot Theatre, originally the Saenger Theatre, has been designated a National Historic Landmark. Cary Grant's last appearance was on the stage at the Perot Theatre.*

Tyler

INSTRUMENTAL MUSIC

EAST TEXAS SYMPHONY ORCHESTRA
911 South Broadway, Tyler, TX 75701
(903) 592-1427
> **Founded:** 1936
> **Arts Area:** Symphony; Orchestra
> **Status:** Professional; Semi-Professional
> **Type:** Performing
> **Purpose:** To bring quality orchestral music to the East Texas area
> **Management:** Lloyd Roesch, Executive Director
> **Officers:** Andrew Morawski, President
> **Paid Staff:** 3
> **Paid Artists:** 70
> **Utilizes:** Guest Conductors; Guest Artists
> **Budget:** $100,000 - $500,000
> **Income Sources:** Private Foundations/Grants/Endowments; Business/Corporate Donations; Box Office; Government Grants; Individual Donations
> **Season:** October - April   **Annual Attendance:** 15,000

Affiliations: ASOL
Performance Facilities: Caldwell Auditorium

Victoria

PERFORMING SERIES

VICTORIA BACH FESTIVAL ASSOCIATION
PO Box 3522, Victoria, TX 77903
(512) 575-1375
Founded: 1976
Arts Area: Vocal Music; Instrumental Music; Festivals
Status: Professional; Semi-Professional; Non-Professional; Non-Profit
Type: Performing; Educational; Sponsoring
Purpose: To sponsor and promote a three to five-day festival featuring symphonic, chamber and choral works, with strong emphasis on the Baroque period
Management: Craig Johnson, Artistic Director/Conductor
Officers: Dorothy L. Welton, President; Ann V. Herbst, First Vice President; James Reinhardt, Second Vice President; Myrna L. Wallace, Secretary; E.P. Mixon, Treasurer
Volunteer Staff: 18
Paid Artists: 39
Utilizes: Guest Artists
Budget: $1,000 - $50,000
Income Sources: Private Foundations/Grants/Endowments; Business/Corporate Donations; Box Office; Government Grants; Individual Donations; Auctions; Benefit Concerts
Season: May   **Annual Attendance:** 700
Performance Facilities: First United Methodist Church

Waco

THEATRE

HIPPODROME THEATRE
724 Austin Avenue, Waco, TX 76701
(817) 752-9797
Founded: 1980
Arts Area: Professional; Musical; Theatrical Group; Puppet
Status: Non-Profit
Type: Performing; Touring; Sponsoring
Purpose: To present professional touring theatre, dance, and music groups to the Waco area and to provide a fully-equipped performing arts center for use by local performing groups
Management: Mary L. Isham, Managing Director
Officers: Brenda Marwitz, Chairman; Don Mayfield Jr., Vice Chairman; Susan Diebolt, Secretary; Derral Parks, Treasurer
Paid Staff: 3
Utilizes: Special Technical Talent; Guest Artists
Budget: $100,000 - $500,000
Income Sources: Private Foundations/Grants/Endowments; Business/Corporate Donations; Box Office; Government Grants; Individual Donations
Season: September - May
Performance Facilities: Hippodrome

FACILITY

HIPPODROME
724 Austin Avenue, Waco, TX 76701
(817) 752-9797
Founded: 1981
Type of Facility: Theatre House
Facility Originally: Vaudeville
Type of Stage: Proscenium
Stage Dimensions: 30'Wx25'D   **Orchestra Pit**
Seating Capacity: 955
Year Built: 1914
Year Remodeled: 1986   **Architect:** Bell & Hoffman   **Cost:** $2,200,000
Contact for Rental: Shelli Wright, Interim Managing Director;   (817) 752-9797

WACO CONVENTION CENTER
100 Washington Avenue, PO Box 2570, Waco, TX 76703
(817) 750-5810
> **Type of Facility:** Multi-Purpose; Room
> **Year Built:** 1971   **Architect:** Bennett Carnahan   **Cost:** $3,000,000
> **Year Remodeled:** 1988   **Architect:** Dudley Bailey Jezek & Rose   **Cost:** $2,500,000
> **Contact for Rental:** Emory Oney
> *Waco Convention Center contains Chisholm Hall and 12 other rooms. See separate listing for further information.*

WACO CONVENTION CENTER - CHISHOLM HALL
100 Washington Avenue, PO Box 2570, Waco, TX 76703
(817) 750-5810
FAX: (817) 750-5801
> **Type of Facility:** Multi-Purpose
> **Type of Stage:** Flexible; Platform
> **Stage Dimensions:** 60'Wx24'D
> **Seating Capacity:** 4,000
> **Contact for Rental:** Emory Oney

Wichita Falls

DANCE

WICHITA FALLS BALLET THEATRE
3412 Buchanan, Wichita Falls, TX 76308-1825
(817) 322-2552; (817) 322-5538
> **Founded:** 1963
> **Arts Area:** Modern; Ballet
> **Status:** Semi-Professional; Non-Profit
> **Type:** Performing; Touring; Resident
> **Purpose:** To foster the art of dance through ballet
> **Management:** Gari Boehm, Patricia Thornton, Co-Artistic Directors
> **Officers:** Joy Williams, President of the Board
> **Paid Artists:** 2   **Non-Paid Artists:** 18
> **Utilizes:** Special Technical Talent; Guest Artists
> **Budget:** $50,000 - $100,000
> **Income Sources:** Private Foundations/Grants/Endowments; Business/Corporate Donations; Box Office;
> Individual Donations
> **Season:** September - May
> **Affiliations:** SWRBA
> **Performance Facilities:** Memorial Auditorium

INSTRUMENTAL MUSIC

WICHITA FALLS SYMPHONY ORCHESTRA
30005 Garnett, Parker Square, Wichita Falls, TX 76308
(817) 322-4489
FAX: (817) 322-4480
> **Founded:** 1946
> **Arts Area:** Symphony; Orchestra
> **Status:** Non-Profit
> **Type:** Performing
> **Purpose:** To provide for our community symphonic music of the highest quality, serving as an educational organization
> for the youth of our area
> **Management:** Alex Rouggieri, Manager; Theodore Plute, Music Director/Conductor
> **Officers:** Dr. Grant Huse Wagner M.D., President
> **Paid Staff:** 2
> **Utilizes:** Guest Artists
> **Budget:** $100,000 - $500,000
> **Income Sources:** Business/Corporate Donations; Box Office; Individual Donations
> **Season:** October - May   **Annual Attendance:** 8,000
> **Performance Facilities:** Memorial Auditorium

THEATRE

WICHITA FALLS BACKDOOR PLAYERS
501 Indiana, PO Box 896, Wichita Falls, TX 76307
(817) 322-5000
>**Founded:** 1971
>**Arts Area:** Musical; Dinner; Community; Theatrical Group
>**Status:** Non-Profit
>**Type:** Performing
>**Purpose:** Producing theatre group that encourages participation from anyone interested in any aspect of theatre regardless of experience
>**Management:** Gare Brundidge, Managing Director; Linda Bates, Business Manager
>**Officers:** Linda Frischer, President; Rick Taylor, First Vice President; Jeanne Meharg, Second Vice President; Suzanne Russell, Secretary; Nona Bailey, Treasurer
>**Paid Staff:** 4
>**Non-Paid Artists:** 250
>**Utilizes:** Special Technical Talent; Guest Artists; Guest Directors
>**Budget:** $100,000 - $500,000
>**Income Sources:** Private Foundations/Grants/Endowments; Box Office; Individual Donations
>**Season:** 52 Weeks   **Annual Attendance:** 16,000

FACILITY

MEMORIAL AUDITORIUM
1300 Seventh Street, Wichita Falls, TX 76307
(817) 761-7974
>**Founded:** 1927
>**Type of Facility:** Auditorium
>**Type of Stage:** Proscenium
>**Stage Dimensions:** 60'Wx42'D   **Orchestra Pit**
>**Seating Capacity:** 2,717
>**Year Built:** 1927   **Architect:** Voelker & Dixon   **Cost:** $700,000
>**Year Remodeled:** 1963   **Architect:** Pardue Reed & Dice
>**Acoustical Consultant:** C.P. Boner & Associates
>**Contact for Rental:** Donald M. Burkman;   (817) 761-7974
>**Resident Groups:** Wichita Falls Ballet Theatre; Wichita Falls Symphony Orchestra

The Woodlands

FACILITY

CYNTHIA WOODS MITCHELL PAVILION
2005 Lake Robbins Drive, The Woodlands, TX 77380
(713) 363-3300
FAX: (713) 364-3011
>**Founded:** 1990
>**Type of Facility:** Amphitheater
>**Type of Stage:** Proscenium
>**Stage Dimensions:** 50'x60'   **Orchestra Pit**
>**Seating Capacity:** 10,000
>**Year Built:** 1990   **Architect:** Abe Sustaita   **Cost:** $9,000,000
>**Resident Groups:** Houston Symphony

UTAH

American Fork

DANCE

UTAH REGIONAL BALLET
88 North, 350 West, PO Box 321, American Fork, UT 84003
(801) 768-8859; (801) 756-8091
Arts Area: Ballet
Status: Professional; Non-Profit
Type: Performing; Touring
Management: Jacqueline Coolidge, Artistic Director; Stoh Harston, Executive Director
Officers: Carol Clarke, Chairman of the Board
Paid Artists: 20
Budget: $100,000 - $500,000
Income Sources: Box Office; Individual Donations
Season: September - May
Performance Facilities: De Jong Concert Hall, BYU

Cedar City

PERFORMING SERIES

UTAH SHAKESPEAREAN FESTIVAL
351 West Center, Cedar City, UT 84720
(801) 596-7880; (801) 586-7878
Founded: 1961
Arts Area: Theater
Status: Semi-Professional; Non-Profit
Type: Performing; Resident; Educational
Purpose: Repertory performance of six Shakespearean and classic works each summer
Management: Fred C. Adams, Executive Producer; R. Scott Phillips, Managing Director; Cameron Harvey, Producing Artistic Director; Douglas N. Cook, Producing Artistic Director; Roger Bean, Marketing Director
Paid Staff: 52   **Volunteer Staff:** 100
Paid Artists: 200
Utilizes: Special Technical Talent; Guest Artists; Guest Directors
Budget: $1,000,000 - $5,000,000
Income Sources: Private Foundations/Grants/Endowments; Business/Corporate Donations; Box Office; Government Grants; Individual Donations
Season: June - September   **Annual Attendance:** 125,000
Affiliations: ATA; URTA; TCG
Performance Facilities: Adams Memorial Shakespearean Theatre; Randall L. Jones Theatre

---

Farmington

FACILITY

LAGOON OPERA HOUSE
375 North Highway 91, Farmington, UT 84025
(801) 451-0101
Type of Facility: Theatre House
Type of Stage: Proscenium
Stage Dimensions: 25'Wx35'D   **Orchestra Pit**
Seating Capacity: 300
Year Built: 1968   **Cost:** $375,000
Acoustical Consultant: Tim Leishman
Contact for Rental: Ron Van Woerden;   (801) 451-0101
Meetings; small theatrical offerings. Opera House is only open during summer months, June-August.

Logan

INSTRUMENTAL MUSIC

THE CHAMBER MUSIC SOCIETY OF LOGAN, INC.
PO Box 3620, Logan, UT 84321
(801) 752-5867
Founded: 1981
Arts Area: Chamber
Status: Non-Profit
Type: Sponsoring
Purpose: To present chamber music concerts
Officers: Howard Carlisle, Chair; L. Grant Reese, Past Chair; Andrew Keller, Treasurer; Melva Wiebe, Secretary
Volunteer Staff: 12
Paid Artists: 34
Budget: $1,000 - $50,000
Income Sources: Private Foundations/Grants/Endowments; Business/Corporate Donations; Box Office; Government Grants; Individual Donations
Season: October - April   **Annual Attendance:** 1,100
Performance Facilities: Harrison Auditorium

FACILITY

LYRIC THEATRE
28 West Center, Logan, UT 84321
(801) 750-1500
Type of Facility: Theatre House
Type of Stage: Proscenium
Stage Dimensions: 21'Wx25'D; 21'Wx25'H proscenium opening
Seating Capacity: 388
Year Built: 1913
Contact for Rental: Arlene Hoggan;   (801) 750-3040
Resident Groups: Old Repertory Company

UTAH STATE UNIVERSITY - CHASE FINE ARTS CENTER
Logan, UT 84322
(801) 750-3040
Type of Facility: Theatre Complex; Concert Hall; Theatre House
Year Built: 1966   **Architect:** Burtch W. Beall   **Cost:** $2,500,000
Acoustical Consultant: L.K. Levine
Contact for Rental: Arlene Hoggan, Scheduling Clerk;   (801) 750-3040
Chase Fine Arts Center contains Kent Concert Hall and Morgan Theatre. See separate listings for further information.

UTAH STATE UNIVERSITY - KENT CONCERT HALL
Chase Fine Arts Center, Logan, UT 84322
(801) 750-3040
Type of Facility: Concert Hall
Type of Stage: Proscenium
Stage Dimensions: 72'Wx33'D; 72'Wx20'H proscenium opening   **Orchestra Pit**
Seating Capacity: 2,183
Year Built: 1966
Contact for Rental: Arlene Hoggan, Scheduling Clerk;   (801) 750-3040

UTAH STATE UNIVERSITY - MORGAN THEATRE
Chase Fine Arts Center, Logan, UT 84322
(801) 750-3040
Type of Facility: Theatre House
Type of Stage: Modified Thrust
Stage Dimensions: 63'Wx26'D; 63'Wx25'H proscenium opening; 25'D thrust   **Orchestra Pit**
Seating Capacity: 711
Year Built: 1966
Contact for Rental: Arlene Hoggan, Scheduling Clerk;   (801) 750-3040

Manti
PERFORMING SERIES

MORMON MIRACLE PAGEANT
PO Box O, Manti, UT 84642
(801) 835-2333
> **Founded:** 1967
> **Arts Area:** Theater
> **Status:** Non-Professional; Non-Profit
> **Type:** Performing; Resident
> **Purpose:** Portrayal of Latter-Day Saints' religious history as it relates to national events
> **Management:** Macksene Rux, Artistic Director
> **Officers:** Lee R. Barton, Chairman
> **Utilizes:** Guest Directors
> **Income Sources:** Individual Donations
> **Season:** July
> **Performance Facilities:** Manti Temple Grounds Amphitheatre

FACILITY

MANTI TEMPLE GROUNDS AMPHITHEATRE
Manti, UT 84642
(801) 835-3000
> **Type of Facility:** Amphitheatre
> **Stage Dimensions:** 300'x100'
> **Seating Capacity:** 18,000
> **Year Built:** 1885
> **Manager:** Lee R. Barton
> **Resident Groups:** Mormon Miracle Pageant

Ogden
FACILITY

DEE EVENTS CENTER
4450 Harrison Boulevard, Ogden, UT 84408
(801) 626-6666
> **Type of Facility:** Arena; Multi-Purpose
> **Type of Stage:** Flexible; Arena
> **Seating Capacity:** 11,615 permanent; 500 portable
> **Year Built:** 1977 **Cost:** $13,500,000
> **Contact for Rental:** Lou Johnson, Manager/Director; (801) 626-7001

VAL A. BROWNING CENTER FOR THE PERFORMING ARTS
Weber State University, Ogden, UT 84408-1901
(801) 626-7000
FAX: (801) 626-6811
> **Founded:** 1965
> **Type of Facility:** Theatre Complex; Concert Hall; Auditorium; Outdoor (Concert); Studio Performance; Performance Center; Amphitheater; Civic Center; Multi-Purpose
> **Type of Stage:** Flexible; Proscenium; Amphitheatre
> **Stage Dimensions:** 60'x50'; 35'x45'; 40'x40' flexible **Orchestra Pit**
> **Seating Capacity:** 1800; 330; 200; 200
> **Year Built:** 1964
> **Contact for Rental:** Scott Jensen; (801) 626-7000
> **Resident Groups:** Utah Musical Theatre; Webster State University Performing Arts Department

---
Orem
DANCE

CLOG AMERICA
PO Box 903, Orem, UT 84057
(801) 225-6450
> **Founded:** 1970

Arts Area: Folk
Status: Semi-Professional; Commercial
Type: Performing; Touring; Educational
Purpose: To promote clogging workshops, festivals, tours and performances throughout the USA and abroad
Management: Dennis H. Cobia, Director; D. Bryan Steele, Co-Director
Paid Staff: 1   **Volunteer Staff:** 20
Paid Artists: 150   **Non-Paid Artists:** 1,500
Budget: $1,000 - $50,000
Income Sources: Individual Donations
Season: 52 Weeks   **Annual Attendance:** 7,000
Affiliations: Utah Arts Council; National Clogging Leaders Organization
Performance Facilities: Scera Shell Amphitheatre

Payson

THEATRE

PLAYMAKERS CHILDREN'S ACADEMY OF THEATRE ARTS
PO Box 182, Payson, UT 84651
(801) 465-2752
Founded: 1984
Arts Area: Musical; Community; Theatrical Group; Children's
Status: Non-Professional; Non-Profit
Type: Performing; Resident; Educational
Purpose: To give children a hands-on experience with as many aspects of theatre as possible
Officers: Marilyn Crawford, President; Rose Cope, Vice President; Coco Hardle, Secretary; Valerie Massey, Treasurer; Delcia Hill, Publicity
Paid Staff: 4
Paid Artists: 2
Utilizes: Special Technical Talent; Guest Directors
Budget: $1,000 - $50,000
Income Sources: Private Foundations/Grants/Endowments; Business/Corporate Donations; Box Office; Government Grants
Season: June - August   **Annual Attendance:** 800

Provo

INSTRUMENTAL MUSIC

UTAH CLASSICAL GUITAR SOCIETY
1466 East 920 South, Provo, UT 84606
Founded: 1984
Arts Area: Chamber
Status: Non-Profit
Type: Performing
Purpose: To promote the study and performance of classical guitar music in Utah
Management: James Mahood, President; David Norton, Program Director; Stephen Hanka, Secretary
Volunteer Staff: 5
Paid Artists: 2   **Non-Paid Artists:** 5
Utilizes: Guest Artists
Budget: $1,000 - $50,000
Income Sources: Government Grants; Individual Donations
Season: September - June   **Annual Attendance:** 500
Performance Facilities: First Presbyterian Church, Salt Lake City

UTAH VALLEY SYMPHONY
461 East 2875 North, Provo, UT 84604
(801) 377-6995
Founded: 1958
Arts Area: Symphony
Status: Non-Professional; Non-Profit
Type: Performing; Resident; Educational
Purpose: To bring fine music to the Utah Valley and afford a musical outlet for the musicians of Utah County
Management: Beverly D. Dunford, Business Manager
Officers: Dr. Willard V. Loveridge, Board President; Dr. Duane Davis, Cornelia Madsen, Rhoda Vaun Young, Vice Presidents; Helen Robinson, Treasurer; Joyce Hooker, Secretary
Volunteer Staff: 23

Utilizes: Guest Conductors; Guest Artists
Budget: $1,000 - $50,000
Income Sources: Box Office; Individual Donations
Season: September - April   **Annual Attendance:** 7,200
Performance Facilities: Provo LDS Tabernacle

UTAH VALLEY YOUTH SYMPHONY
PO Box 1235, Provo, UT 84603
(708) 244-2258
FAX: (708) 244-8283
Founded: 1958
Arts Area: Symphony; Orchestra; Chamber
Status: Non-Profit
Type: Performing; Touring; Educational
Purpose: To educate
Management: Brent E. Taylor, Executive Director; Britton E. Davis, Music Director
Officers: A. Harold Goodman, President
Paid Staff: 10
Utilizes: Guest Conductors; Guest Artists
Budget: $1,000 - $50,000
Income Sources: Private Foundations/Grants/Endowments; Business/Corporate Donations; Government Grants
Season: September - May   **Annual Attendance:** 5,000
Affiliations: ASOL
Performance Facilities: Symphony Hall

THEATRE

PROVO THEATRE COMPANY
3319 North University Avenue, Suite 200, Provo, UT 84604
(801) 224-3543
FAX: (801) 375-3865
Founded: 1986
Arts Area: Theatrical Group
Status: Semi-Professional; Non-Profit
Type: Performing
Purpose: High quality community theatre, focused on education, exposure and audience entertainment
Management: Charles L. Frost, Artistic Director; Richard L. Hill, Business Manager
Officers: Charles L. Frost, President; Shawn Moon, Vice President
Paid Staff: 10   **Volunteer Staff:** 65
Paid Artists: 20   **Non-Paid Artists:** 60
Utilizes: Special Technical Talent; Guest Conductors; Guest Artists; Guest Directors
Budget: $50,000 - $100,000
Income Sources: Private Foundations/Grants/Endowments; Business/Corporate Donations; Box Office; Government Grants; Individual Donations
Season: July - March   **Annual Attendance:** 15,000
Affiliations: ACTA; ATA

PERFORMING SERIES

BRIGHAM YOUNG UNIVERSITY - UNIVERSITY CONCERTS
Harris Fine Arts Center, E316, Provo, UT 84602
(801) 378-6340
FAX: (801) 378-5973
Founded: 1875
Arts Area: Dance; Vocal Music; Instrumental Music; Theater; Grand Opera
Status: Professional; Semi-Professional; Non-Profit
Type: Performing; Touring; Educational; Sponsoring
Purpose: A varied production and concert season in support of academic programs in music, dance and theatre
Management: Paul Duerden, Concert Manager
Officers: K. Newell Dayley, Chairman
Paid Staff: 8   **Volunteer Staff:** 15
Paid Artists: 15
Utilizes: Special Technical Talent; Guest Conductors; Guest Artists; Guest Directors
Budget: $100,000 - $500,000
Income Sources: Private Foundations/Grants/Endowments; Box Office; Individual Donations
Season: 52 Weeks   **Annual Attendance:** 150,000
Affiliations: APAP; WAAA
Performance Facilities: Harris Fine Arts Center, Brigham Young University

FACILITY

BRIGHAM YOUNG UNIVERSITY - HARRIS FINE ARTS CENTER
Provo, UT 84602
(801) 378-2818
FAX: (801) 378-4730
> **Type of Facility:** Cultural Center
> **Type of Stage:** Flexible; Proscenium; Arena
> **Year Built:** 1964   **Architect:** William Pereira & James Langenheim
> *Seating Capacity: Concert Hall - 1,450; Drama Theatre - 600; Recital Hall - 425; Experimental Theatre - 325; Music Theatre - 200; Arena Theatre - 150*

Saint George

INSTRUMENTAL MUSIC

SOUTHWEST SYMPHONY ORCHESTRA
2961 Jacob Hamblin Drive, Saint George, UT 84770
(801) 673-6290
> **Founded:** 1980
> **Arts Area:** Symphony; Orchestra
> **Status:** Non-Professional; Non-Profit
> **Type:** Performing; Resident; Educational
> **Purpose:** To provide symphony concerts in the community, offer youth instruction programs and foster and develop a youth symphony
> **Management:** Linda Sappington, General Manager
> **Volunteer Staff:** 16
> **Paid Artists:** 1   **Non-Paid Artists:** 65
> **Utilizes:** Guest Artists
> **Budget:** $1,000 - $50,000
> **Income Sources:** Business/Corporate Donations; Box Office; Government Grants; Individual Donations
> **Season:** September1 - June1   **Annual Attendance:** 6,000
> **Performance Facilities:** Dixie Center Proscenium Stage

FACILITY

DIXIE COLLEGE - DIXIE CENTER
425 South 700 East, Saint George, UT 84770
(801) 628-3121
> **Type of Facility:** Concert Hall; Auditorium; Performance Center; Theatre House; Civic Center; Arena; Room; Basketball Arena
> **Type of Stage:** Proscenium; Arena
> **Stage Dimensions:** 56'x45' - play area   **Orchestra Pit**
> **Seating Capacity:** 1,200
> **Year Built:** 1986   **Architect:** Les Stoker
> **Acoustical Consultant:** Milo Hughes
> **Contact for Rental:** Pam Hilton;   (801) 628-7003
> **Manager:** Randy Lowell;   (801) 628-7003
> **Resident Groups:** Southwest Symphony; College Band; Jazz Ensemble; Southern Utah Dance Theatre
> *Dixie Center contains the Proscenium Stage. See separate listing for additional information regarding Theatre/Auditorium; Convention Hall.*

DIXIE COLLEGE - DIXIE CENTER PROSCENIUM STAGE
225 South 700 East, Saint George, UT 84770
(801) 628-3121
> **Type of Facility:** Theatre House
> **Type of Stage:** Proscenium
> **Seating Capacity:** 1,200
> **Year Built:** 1986
> **Contact for Rental:** Sherm Bennett;   (801) 628-3121

DIXIE COLLEGE FINE ARTS CENTER
225 South 700 East, Saint George, UT 84770
(801) 628-3121
> **Type of Facility:** Performance Center
> **Year Built:** 1963   **Architect:** Rowe Smith
> **Contact for Rental:** C. Paul Andersen;   (801) 673-4811

Resident Groups: Pioneer Courthouse Players; Southwest Symphony; Dixie College Theatre Productions; Jazz Ensemble; Southern Utah Dance Theatre; Dixie College Band
The Fine Arts Center contains the Arena Theatre and Proscenium Theatre. See separate listings for additional information.

DIXIE COLLEGE FINE ARTS CENTER - ARENA THEATRE
225 South 700 East, Saint George, UT 84770
(801) 628-3121
    Type of Facility: Theatre House
    Type of Stage: Arena
    Seating Capacity: 200
    Year Built: 1963
    Contact for Rental: C. Paul Andersen; (801) 673-4811

DIXIE COLLEGE FINE ARTS CENTER - PROSCENIUM THEATRE
225 South 700 East, Saint George, UT 84770
(801) 628-3121
    Type of Facility: Theatre House
    Type of Stage: Proscenium
    Seating Capacity: 512
    Year Built: 1963
    Contact for Rental: C. Paul Andersen; (801) 673-4811

Salt Lake City

DANCE

BALLET WEST
50 West 200 South, Salt Lake City, UT 84101
(801) 524-8300
    Founded: 1963
    Arts Area: Ballet
    Status: Professional
    Type: Performing; Touring; Resident; Educational
    Purpose: To present ballet performances of high quality
    Management: John Hart, CBE, Artistic Director; Susan Barrell, Executive Director; Kenneth O. Hill, President
    Officers: Richard Kieffer, Chairman; Fredric Reed, Vice Chairman; Kevin Bischoff, Secretary; Lynne Wilhelmsen, Treasurer
    Paid Staff: 28
    Paid Artists: 39   **Non-Paid Artists:** 6
    Utilizes: Special Technical Talent; Guest Conductors; Guest Artists; Guest Choreographers
    Budget: $1,000,000 - $5,000,000
    Income Sources: Private Foundations/Grants/Endowments; Business/Corporate Donations; Box Office; Government Grants; Individual Donations
    Season: June - April   **Annual Attendance:** 130,000
    Affiliations: Dance USA; WAAA; APAP
    Performance Facilities: Capitol Theatre

EASTERN ARTS ETHNIC DANCE COMPANY
PO Box 526362, Salt Lake City, UT 84152
(801) 487-9208; (801) 485-5824
    Founded: 1977
    Arts Area: Ethnic
    Status: Professional; Non-Profit
    Type: Performing; Educational; Sponsoring
    Purpose: To present the highest quality of authentic Eastern ethnic dance and dance masters
    Officers: Katherine St. John, Dance Director; Lloyd Miller, Music Director
    Paid Staff: 2   **Volunteer Staff:** 2
    Paid Artists: 8   **Non-Paid Artists:** 10
    Utilizes: Guest Artists
    Budget: $1,000 - $50,000
    Income Sources: Private Foundations/Grants/Endowments; Business/Corporate Donations; Government Grants; Individual Donations; Workshops; Arts Products Sales
    Season: October - August   **Annual Attendance:** 250,000
    Affiliations: WAAA; Society for Ethno-Musicology; Middle East Studies Association; Society for Dance Ethnology

REPERTORY DANCE THEATRE
PO Box 510427, Salt Lake City, UT 84151-0427
(801) 534-6345
FAX: (801) 534-6344
    Founded: 1966
    Arts Area: Modern
    Status: Professional
    Type: Performing; Touring; Resident; Educational; Sponsoring
    Purpose: To preserve old choreographies; nurturing new works and commissioning dances committed to presenting works from the full spectrum of modern dance
    Management: Kathy Johnson, General Manager; Linda C. Smith, Artistic Director; Amy Sawyer, Director of Development; Liz McClane, Booking Director; Vickie Hutter, Publicist
    Officers: Ralph Sawyer, President; B. Murphy, Vice President; John Harrington, Secretary; Carol Horton, Treasurer
    Paid Staff: 5   **Volunteer Staff:** 10
    Paid Artists: 11
    Utilizes: Guest Artists
    Budget: $100,000 - $500,000
    Income Sources: Private Foundations/Grants/Endowments; Business/Corporate Donations; Box Office; Government Grants; Individual Donations
    Season: September - August   **Annual Attendance:** 10,000
    Performance Facilities: Capitol Theatre; Local Festival Auditorium

RIRIE-WOODBURY DANCE COMPANY
200 South 50 West, Salt Lake City, UT 84101
(801) 328-1062
FAX: (801) 359-3504
    Founded: 1963
    Arts Area: Modern
    Status: Professional; Non-Profit
    Type: Performing; Touring; Resident; Educational; Sponsoring
    Management: Joan Woodbury, Shirley Ririe, Artistic and Co-Directors; Francis McGovern, Executive Director
    Officers: Kathy Black, Office Manager; Jena Thompson, Outreach/Marketing Director; Greg Gielmann, Company Manager
    Paid Staff: 6   **Volunteer Staff:** 20
    Paid Artists: 9
    Utilizes: Special Technical Talent; Guest Conductors; Guest Artists; Guest Directors; Guest Choreographers
    Income Sources: Private Foundations/Grants/Endowments; Business/Corporate Donations; Box Office; Government Grants; Individual Donations
    Season: Fall - Spring   **Annual Attendance:** 2,000
    Performance Facilities: Capital Theatre

INSTRUMENTAL MUSIC

CHAMBER MUSIC SOCIETY OF SALT LAKE CITY
PO Box 58825, Salt Lake City, TN
(801) 583-9264
    Founded: 1966
    Arts Area: Chamber
    Status: Non-Profit
    Type: Sponsoring
    Purpose: To present an annual series of recitals by world-class chamber music ensembles
    Officers: Gwen Hovey, President; Carter Foss, Vice President; Paul Griffin, Treasurer; Kathleen Rice, Secretary
    Volunteer Staff: 20
    Utilizes: Guest Artists
    Income Sources: Private Foundations/Grants/Endowments; Individual Donations; Membership Fees
    Season: November - May
    Performance Facilities: Museum of Fine Arts, University of Utah

GRANITE YOUTH SYMPHONY
340 East 3545 South, Salt Lake City, UT 84115
(801) 268-8542
FAX: (801) 263-6128
    Founded: 1957
    Arts Area: Symphony; Orchestra; Instrumental Group
    Status: Non-Profit
    Type: Performing; Touring; Educational
    Purpose: Study and performance of standard symphonic literature

Management: Ellis C. Worthen, PhD Staff Associate, Music Education, Granite School District
Paid Staff: 4
Paid Artists: 1
Utilizes: Guest Conductors; Guest Artists
Budget: $1,000 - $50,000
Season: September - July   **Annual Attendance:** 10,000
Affiliations: Granite School District

UTAH SYMPHONY
123 West South Temple, Salt Lake City, UT 84101
(801) 533-5626
FAX: (801) 521-6634
Founded: 1940
Arts Area: Symphony
Status: Professional; Non-Profit
Type: Performing; Educational
Purpose: To maintain a symphony orchestra capable of providing performances of the highest possible quality; to provide performance opportunities for skilled professional musicians; to foster musical education for persons of all ages
Management: Joseph Silverstein, Music Director; Robert Henderson, Associate Conductor; Paul L. Chummers, Executive Director
Officers: Ken Knight, Chairman of the Board
Paid Staff: 20
Paid Artists: 85
Utilizes: Guest Conductors; Guest Artists; Guest Directors
Budget: $5,000,000 - $10,000,000
Income Sources: Private Foundations/Grants/Endowments; Business/Corporate Donations; Box Office; Government Grants; Individual Donations
Season: 52 Weeks   **Annual Attendance:** 450,000
Affiliations: ASOL; AAA
Performance Facilities: Symphony Hall

UTAH YOUTH SYMPHONY
204 Gardner Hall, University Of Utah, Salt Lake City, UT 84112
(801) 485-5252
Founded: 1959
Arts Area: Symphony
Status: Non-Professional; Non-Profit
Type: Performing
Purpose: To rehearse and perform original master works from the orchestral repertoire under professional leadership
Management: Barbara Ann Scowcroft, Music Director
Officers: Lynn Larson, President
Paid Staff: 1   **Volunteer Staff:** 10
Non-Paid Artists: 85
Utilizes: Guest Artists
Budget: $1,000 - $50,000
Income Sources: Business/Corporate Donations; Individual Donations
Season: September - June   **Annual Attendance:** 1,500
Performance Facilities: 200 Gardner Hall

VOCAL MUSIC

MORMON TABERNACLE CHOIR
50 East North Temple Street, Salt Lake City, UT 84150
(801) 531-3221
Founded: 1847
Arts Area: Choral
Status: Non-Professional; Non-Profit
Type: Performing; Touring; Resident
Purpose: To serve as a public relations organization of The Church of Jesus Christ of Latter-day Saints performing in Salt Lake City and on tours, both national and international; to represent the Latter-day Saints Church and, at times, the United States of America
Management: Jerold D. Ottley, Director; Donald Ripplinger, Associate Director; Richard Elliott, John Longhurst, Clay Christiansen, Organists
Officers: Wendell M. Smoot, President; Udell Poulsen, Manager; Herold Gregory, Adminisrative Assistant
Paid Staff: 5   **Volunteer Staff:** 15
Non-Paid Artists: 325
Utilizes: Guest Conductors; Guest Artists
Income Sources: Private Foundations/Grants/Endowments; Business/Corporate Donations; Individual Donations
Season: 52 Weeks

Affiliations: Utah Symphony; Church of Jesus Christ of Latter-day Saints
Performance Facilities: Mormon Tabernacle

ORATORIO SOCIETY OF UTAH
PO Box 11714, Salt Lake City, UT 84147
(801) 943-3416
Founded: 1915
Arts Area: Choral
Status: Semi-Professional; Non-Profit
Type: Performing; Touring
Purpose: Oratorio music and cultural exchanges to other countries
Officers: Richard G. Horak, President
Volunteer Staff: 20
Paid Artists: 20   **Non-Paid Artists:** 250
Utilizes: Guest Conductors; Guest Artists
Budget: $50,000 - $100,000
Income Sources: Private Foundations/Grants/Endowments; Business/Corporate Donations; Box Office; Government Grants; Individual Donations
Season: 52 Weeks   **Annual Attendance:** 10,000

SALT LAKE OPERA THEATRE
44 West Broadway, Suite 807-S, Salt Lake City, UT 84101
(801) 965-4147
Arts Area: Grand Opera; Lyric Opera; Light Opera; Operetta; Choral
Status: Semi-Professional; Non-Profit
Type: Performing; Touring
Purpose: To serve the community with quality opera and light opera at reasonable prices; to provide a launching opportunity for aspiring artists
Management: Robert Zabriskie, General Director; Robert Van Wagenen, Assistant; Columb Robinson, Artistic Director
Officers: Guy Curtis, Orchestra Manager; Brian Johnson, Orchestra Contract Manager; Beverly Zabriskie, Secretary
Volunteer Staff: 6
Non-Paid Artists: 90
Utilizes: Special Technical Talent; Guest Artists; Guest Directors
Budget: $1,000 - $50,000
Income Sources: Private Foundations/Grants/Endowments; Business/Corporate Donations; Box Office; Government Grants; Individual Donations
Season: September - June   **Annual Attendance:** 3,000
Performance Facilities: Kingbury Hall; Judge Memorial Auditorium

SALT LAKE SYMPHONIC CHOIR
PO Box 45, Salt Lake City, UT 84110
(801) 466-8701
Founded: 1959
Arts Area: Choral
Status: Professional; Non-Profit
Type: Performing; Touring
Purpose: To present choral concerts throughout the world, "a choral adventure from Bach to rock"
Management: Richard M. Taggart, Manager; George Welch, Choral Director
Officers: Richard M. Taggart, President; Greg Bettinson, Vice President; Bethne Hickcox, Secretary
Budget: $1,000 - $50,000
Income Sources: Private Foundations/Grants/Endowments; Business/Corporate Donations; Box Office; Government Grants; Individual Donations
Season: September - May

UTAH OPERA COMPANY
50 West 200 South, Salt Lake City, UT 84101
(801) 534-0842
FAX: (801) 359-3504
Founded: 1978
Arts Area: Grand Opera; Light Opera
Status: Professional; Non-Profit
Type: Performing; Resident; Educational
Purpose: To present quality productions of standard opera repertoire for the community and as an educational enterprise
Management: Leslie Peterson, Director of Operations; Anne Ewers, General Director; Lynn Jemison-Renner, Music Administration
Officers: David T. Mortensen, Chairman
Paid Staff: 10   **Volunteer Staff:** 2
Paid Artists: 100   **Non-Paid Artists:** 30
Utilizes: Special Technical Talent; Guest Conductors; Guest Artists; Guest Directors

Budget: $1,000,000 - $5,000,000
Income Sources: Private Foundations/Grants/Endowments; Business/Corporate Donations; Box Office; Government Grants; Individual Donations
Season: October - May   **Annual Attendance:** 30,000
Affiliations: OA; AAA; Utah Arts Council; Salt Lake City Arts Council
Performance Facilities: Capitol Theatre

THEATRE

PIONEER THEATRE COMPANY
University of Utah, Salt Lake City, UT 84112
(801) 581-7118
FAX: (801) 581-5472
    Founded: 1962
    Arts Area: Professional; Theatrical Group
    Status: Professional; Non-Profit
    Type: Performing; Educational
    Purpose: Committed to quality professional theater for Utah and the northwestern United States
    Management: Charles Morey, Artistic Director; Christopher Lino, Managing Director; Susan Koles, Audience Development Director
    Paid Staff: 20
    Utilizes: Special Technical Talent; Guest Artists; Guest Directors
    Budget: $1,000,000 - $5,000,000
    Income Sources: Private Foundations/Grants/Endowments; Business/Corporate Donations; Box Office; Government Grants; Individual Donations
    Season: September - May
    Affiliations: AEA; LORT
    Performance Facilities: Pioneer Memorial Theater

THE SALT LAKE ACTING COMPANY
168 West 500 North, Salt Lake City, UT 84103
(801) 363-0526
FAX: (801) 363-8681
    Founded: 1977
    Arts Area: Professional; Theatrical Group
    Status: Professional; Non-Profit
    Type: Performing
    Purpose: To present a unique and innovative repertoire of plays and regional premieres to the city; to support new works and develop a community of artists; to make a contribution to the American professional theater
    Management: Edward J. Gryska, Producing Artistic Director; Victoria Panella, Managing Director
    Paid Staff: 8
    Paid Artists: 70
    Utilizes: Guest Artists; Guest Directors
    Budget: $500,000 - $1,000,000
    Income Sources: Private Foundations/Grants/Endowments; Business/Corporate Donations; Box Office; Government Grants; Individual Donations
    Season: September - July
    Annual Attendance: 25,000
    Affiliations: TCG
    Performance Facilities: The Salt Lake Acting Company Theater

SUNDANCE INSTITUTE
PO Box 16450, Salt Lake City, UT 84116
(801) 328-3456
FAX: (801) 575-5175
    Founded: 1981
    Arts Area: Professional; Film
    Status: Professional; Non-Profit
    Type: Educational
    Purpose: To support the development of emerging filmmakers; to exhibit new, independent dramatic and documentary films
    Management: Nicole Guillemet, Director of Administration; Geoff Gilmore, Program Director; Michelle Satter, Director of Feature Film Programming
    Officers: Robert Redford, President; Gary Beer, Executive Vice President
    Paid Staff: 7   **Volunteer Staff:** 50
    Budget: $1,000,000 - $5,000,000

Income Sources: Private Foundations/Grants/Endowments; Business/Corporate Donations; Box Office; Government Grants; Individual Donations
Season: 52 Weeks

PERFORMING SERIES

THE GINA BACHAUER INTERNATIONAL PIANO FOUNDATION
PO Box 11664, #5 Triad Center, Suite 515, Salt Lake City, UT 84147
(801) 521-9200
FAX: (801) 521-9202
Founded: 1976
Arts Area: Instrumental Music; Festivals
Status: Non-Profit
Type: Performing; Educational; Sponsoring
Purpose: To further the pianistic art by holding international piano competitions, solo recitals and educational sessions; to enrich the community and build an artistic and educational environment for musicians and non-musicians alike
Management: Andrea Barnes, General Manager; Paul Pollei, Artistic Director/Founder
Officers: Robert W. Mendenhall, Chairman; Arlene Darger, Vice Chairman; Kent M. Acomb, Treasurer; Linda Babcock, Secretary; Andrea Barnes, Ex-Officio Member
Paid Staff: 3   **Volunteer Staff:** 3
Utilizes: Guest Artists
Budget: $100,000 - $500,000
Income Sources: Private Foundations/Grants/Endowments; Business/Corporate Donations; Box Office; Government Grants; Individual Donations
Performance Facilities: Symphony Hall; Salt Lake City Assembly Hall; Temple Square

FACILITY

CAPITOL THEATRE
48 West Second South, Salt Lake City, UT 84101
(801) 534-6660
FAX: (801) 538-2272
Type of Facility: Theatre House; Opera House
Type of Stage: Proscenium
Stage Dimensions: 100'Wx48'D; 43'6"Wx40'3"H proscenium opening   **Orchestra Pit**
Seating Capacity: 1927
Year Built: 1913   **Architect:** G. Albert Lansburg
Year Remodeled: 1978   **Architect:** Steven T. Baird   **Cost:** $5,000,000
Contact for Rental: Marion Iwasaki;   (801) 534-6364
Resident Groups: Ballet West; Utah Opera Company; Ririe-Woodbury Company

SYMPHONY HALL
123 West South Temple, Salt Lake City, UT 84101
(801) 534-6660
Type of Facility: Concert Hall
Type of Stage: Proscenium
Stage Dimensions: 72'Wx36'D; 72'Wx36'H proscenium opening
Seating Capacity: 2,801
Year Built: 1976   **Architect:** FFKR/Architects   **Cost:** $12,000,000
Acoustical Consultant: Dr. Cyril Harris
Contact for Rental: Marion Vigio;   (801) 534-6364
Manager: Samuel Driggs
Resident Groups: Utah Symphony Orchestra

UNIVERSITY OF UTAH - KINGSBURY HALL
Salt Lake City, Salt Lake City, UT 84112
(801) 581-6261
Type of Facility: Concert Hall; Auditorium; Theatre House; Opera House
Type of Stage: Greek; Proscenium; Platform
Stage Dimensions: 46'x59'x29'   **Orchestra Pit**
Seating Capacity: 1,917
Year Built: 1929   **Architect:** Raymond Evans
Contact for Rental: Linda Christenson;   (801) 581-6261
Resident Groups: University of Utah Music Department Ensembles; University of Utah Ballet and Modern Dance Companies

---

Sundance

THEATRE

THE SUNDANCE CHILDREN'S THEATRE
Rural Route 3, PO Box 624-D, Sundance, UT 84604
(801) 225-4107
FAX: (801) 225-3096
      Founded: 1990
      Arts Area: Professional; Theatrical Group
      Status: Professional; Semi-Professional; Non-Profit
      Type: Performing; Touring
      Purpose: To develop and produce new plays for young audiences
      Management: David Kirk Chambers, Managing Director; Jerry Parch, Artistic Director
      Paid Staff: 2
      Utilizes: Guest Artists; Guest Directors
      Budget: $100,000 - $500,000
      Income Sources: Private Foundations/Grants/Endowments; Business/Corporate Donations; Box Office; Government Grants; Individual Donations
      Season: June - October   **Annual Attendance:** 30,000

VERMONT

Barre

VOCAL MUSIC

VERMONT OPERA THEATER
PO Box 1030, Barre, VT 05641
(802) 223-5801
   Arts Area: Lyric Opera; Light Opera; Operetta
   Status: Semi-Professional; Non-Profit
   Type: Performing; Educational
   Officers: Naomi Flanders, President; Ken Carter, Vice President; Ellen Pitkin, Treasurer; Debbie Quick, Secretary; Mark W. Hall, Artistic Director
   Budget: $1,000 - $50,000
   Income Sources: Business/Corporate Donations; Box Office; Government Grants; Individual Donations

FACILITY

BARRE OPERA HOUSE
12 North Main Street, PO Box 583, Barre, VT 05641
(802) 476-8188
   Type of Facility: Concert Hall; Theatre House; Opera House
   Type of Stage: Proscenium
   Stage Dimensions: 59'Wx34'D; 35'Wx22'H proscenium opening   **Orchestra Pit**
   Seating Capacity: 434
   Year Built: 1899   **Architect:** Charles Adams
   Year Remodeled: 1984   **Architect:** Robert Burley   **Cost:** $500,000
   Contact for Rental: Don Hirsch;   (802) 476-8188
   Resident Groups: Vermont Opera Theatre; Vermont Philharmonic Orchestra; Vermont Symphony Orchestra; Barre Players; Centerstage Company
   The Opera House has been designated a National Historic Landmark and is a member theatre of the League of Historic American Theatres.

Bennington

THEATRE

OLDCASTLE THEATRE COMPANY
PO Box 1555, Bennington, VT 05201
(802) 447-0564
   Founded: 1972
   Arts Area: Professional; Musical; Theatrical Group
   Status: Professional; Non-Profit
   Type: Performing; Touring; Resident; Educational; Sponsoring
   Purpose: Full-time professional theatre currently in residence at Southern Vermont College in Bennington
   Management: Eric Peterson, Producing Director; Shelli DuBoff, Richard Howe, Associate Artistic Directors; Deborah Woodward, General Manager
   Officers: Thomas Steffen, Board President
   Paid Staff: 6   **Volunteer Staff:** 30
   Utilizes: Guest Artists; Guest Directors
   Budget: $100,000 - $500,000
   Income Sources: Private Foundations/Grants/Endowments; Business/Corporate Donations; Box Office; Government Grants; Individual Donations
   Season: 52 Weeks   **Annual Attendance:** 10,000
   Performance Facilities: Southern Vermont College Theatre

Brattleboro

VOCAL MUSIC

BLANCHE MOYSE CHORALE
15 Walnut Street, Brattleboro, VT 05301
(802) 257-4523
   Founded: 1976
   Arts Area: Choral

Status: Non-Professional; Non-Profit
Type: Performing; Touring; Resident
Purpose: To perform the music of J.S. Bach as the resident choral ensemble of the New England Bach Festival; to tour with programs of a cappella works from all periods
Management: Blanche Honegger Moyse, Conductor; Zon Eastes, Manager
Officers: Beth-Ann Betz, President
Paid Staff: 1 **Volunteer Staff:** 2
Non-Paid Artists: 36
Budget: $1,000 - $50,000
Income Sources: Private Foundations/Grants/Endowments; Business/Corporate Donations; Box Office; Individual Donations
Season: 52 Weeks **Annual Attendance:** 5,000
Performance Facilities: Persons Auditorium, Marlboro College; First Baptist Church

THEATRE

NATIONAL MARIONETTE THEATRE
82 Putney Road, Bratleboro, VT 05301
(802) 257-3090
Founded: 1968
Arts Area: Professional; Theatrical Group; Puppet
Status: Professional; Non-Profit
Type: Performing; Touring
Management: David Syrotiak, Artistic Director
Paid Staff: 6 **Volunteer Staff:** 15
Paid Artists: 6
Utilizes: Special Technical Talent
Budget: $100,000 - $500,000
Income Sources: Private Foundations/Grants/Endowments; Business/Corporate Donations; Box Office
Season: September - May
Affiliations: APAP; NECA; New England Arts Foundation

PERFORMING SERIES

BRATTLEBORO MUSIC CENTER
15 Walnut Street, Brattleboro, VT 05301
(802) 257-4523
Founded: 1952
Arts Area: Vocal Music; Instrumental Music; Festivals
Status: Non-Profit
Type: Performing; Sponsoring
Management: Zon Eastes, Managing Director
Paid Staff: 4 **Volunteer Staff:** 10
Paid Artists: 100 **Non-Paid Artists:** 100
Utilizes: Guest Artists
Budget: $100,000 - $500,000
Income Sources: Private Foundations/Grants/Endowments; Box Office; Government Grants; Individual Donations
Season: September - June **Annual Attendance:** 12,000

Burlington

DANCE

VERMONT BALLET THEATRE
PO Box 5069, Burlington, VT 05402
(802) 862-6466
Founded: 1985
Arts Area: Ballet
Status: Professional; Non-Profit
Type: Performing; Touring; Educational
Purpose: A company of ten professional dancers performing classical and contemporary repertory in concerts with lecture demonstrations throughout the Northeast
Management: Angela Whitehill, Artistic Director; James Whitehill, Technical Director; William Noble, Director, Public Relations; Arthur Leeth, Ballet Master
Officers: Ralph Carbo, President; Rena Chernick, Vice President; Carolyn Singer, Secretary; Kathy Brunovski, Treasurer
Paid Staff: 2 **Volunteer Staff:** 2
Paid Artists: 10
Utilizes: Guest Choreographers

Budget: $1,000 - $50,000
Income Sources: Private Foundations/Grants/Endowments; Business/Corporate Donations; Box Office; Government Grants; Individual Donations
Season: April - November

INSTRUMENTAL MUSIC

HEXAGON
c/o Melvin Kaplan Inc., 115 College Street, Burlington, VT 05401
FAX: (802) 658-6089
    Arts Area: Chamber; Ensemble
    Status: Professional
    Type: Performing
    Purpose: An ensemble of five winds and piano that performs masterworks from Mozart to Poulenc as well as new compositions for wind and piano combinations
    Management: Melvin Kaplan, Manager
    Income Sources: Box Office; Government Grants
    Season: 52 Weeks

LA FAMILLE BEAUDOIN - FAMILY GROUP
14 Lyman Avenue, Burlington, VT 05401
(802) 862-5076
    Founded: 1972
    Arts Area: Ethnic
    Status: Non-Professional
    Type: Performing
    Purpose: To promote and perpetuate French Canadian folklore music
    Management: Wilfred J. Beaudoin, Leader
    Paid Artists: 5
    Income Sources: Private Foundations/Grants/Endowments
    Season: April - October
    Affiliations: Vermont Council of the Arts

VERMONT SYMPHONY ORCHESTRA
2 Church Street, Burlington, VT 05401
(802) 864-5741
    Founded: 1934
    Arts Area: Symphony; Ensemble
    Status: Professional; Non-Profit
    Type: Performing; Touring; Educational
    Purpose: To provide high quality live classical music to all the areas of the state
    Management: Thomas Philion, General Manager; Frances Combs, Office Manager; Natalie Nevert, Marketing and Production Coordinator; Kate Tamarkin, Music Director
    Officers: Wayne Granquist, President
    Paid Staff: 4
    Paid Artists: 65
    Utilizes: Guest Artists
    Budget: $500,000 - $1,000,000
    Income Sources: Private Foundations/Grants/Endowments; Business/Corporate Donations; Box Office; Government Grants; Individual Donations
    Season: 52 Weeks   **Annual Attendance:** 60,000
    Affiliations: ASCAP; BMI
    Performance Facilities: Flynn Theatre

VERMONT YOUTH ORCHESTRA
PO Box 905, Burlington, VT 05402
(802) 862-6732
    Founded: 1964
    Arts Area: Symphony; Orchestra
    Status: Non-Professional; Non-Profit
    Type: Performing; Educational
    Purpose: To bring music to young people, especially classical
    Management: Carolyn Long, Manager; David Dworkin, Music Director/Conductor
    Officers: Burlington Friends of Music
    Paid Staff: 2   **Volunteer Staff:** 10
    Non-Paid Artists: 85
    Utilizes: Guest Conductors
    Budget: $1,000 - $50,000

Income Sources: Private Foundations/Grants/Endowments; Business/Corporate Donations; Box Office; Government Grants; Individual Donations
Season: August - May   **Annual Attendance:** 4,000
Affiliations: ASOL (Youth Orchestra Division)
Performance Facilities: Flynn Theatre

PERFORMING SERIES

DISCOVER JAZZ FESTIVAL
153 Main Street, Burlington, VT 05401
(802) 863-7992
   Founded: 1983
   Arts Area: Vocal Music; Instrumental Music; Festivals
   Status: Non-Profit
   Type: Performing; Educational; Sponsoring
   Purpose: To offer the widest possible diversity of jazz
   Management: James P. Swift, Director
   Officers: Andrea Rogers, Director Flynn Theatre for the Performing Arts; Susan Green, Burlington City Arts
   Budget: $50,000 - $100,000
   Income Sources: Private Foundations/Grants/Endowments; Business/Corporate Donations; Box Office; Government Grants; Individual Donations
   Season: June   **Annual Attendance:** 25,000
   Affiliations: Burlington City Arts; Flynn Theatre

VERMONT MOZART FESTIVAL
PO Box 512, Burlington, VT 05402
(802) 862-7352
   Founded: 1973
   Arts Area: Vocal Music; Instrumental Music; Festivals
   Status: Professional; Non-Profit
   Type: Performing
   Purpose: To provide high-quality chamber music to Vermont in various picturesque settings
   Management: Joy Facos, Manager; Mary Madigan, General Manager; Rhoda Rowell, Assistant Manager
   Paid Staff: 2   **Volunteer Staff:** 400
   Paid Artists: 75
   Utilizes: Special Technical Talent; Guest Conductors; Guest Artists; Guest Directors
   Budget: $100,000 - $500,000
   Income Sources: Private Foundations/Grants/Endowments; Business/Corporate Donations; Box Office; Government Grants; Individual Donations
   Season: July - March   **Annual Attendance:** 16,000
   Affiliations: Greater Burlington Performing Arts Council

FACILITY

BURLINGTON MEMORIAL AUDITORIUM
250 Main Street, Burlington, VT 05401
(802) 864-6044
   Type of Facility: Concert Hall; Auditorium; Studio Performance; Performance Center; Multi-Purpose; Loft; Multi-Purpose Building
   Type of Stage: Proscenium; Gymnasium
   Seating Capacity: 2,500
   Year Built: 1928
   Contact for Rental: (802) 864-6044

FLYNN THEATRE FOR THE PERFORMING ARTS
153 Main Street, Burlington, VT 05401-8402
(802) 863-8778
   Type of Facility: Concert Hall; Performance Center; Theatre House; Multi-Purpose
   Facility Originally: Vaudeville; Movie House
   Type of Stage: Proscenium
   Stage Dimensions: 85'Wx24'D; 48'Wx29'H proscenium opening   **Orchestra Pit**
   Seating Capacity: 1,454
   Year Built: 1930   **Architect:** Mowll & Rand
   Year Remodeled: 1989   **Architect:** Wiemann & Camphere, Ashok Bhaunani, Roland Batten   **Cost:** $2,000,000
   Contact for Rental: Philip Bither;   (802) 863-8778
   Manager: Andrea Rogers, Executive Director;   (802) 863-8778
   Resident Groups: Lyric Theatre; Vermont Symphony Orchestra; Vermont Youth Orchestra; Flynn Theatre Presentations

UNIVERSITY OF VERMONT - RECITAL HALL
Music Building, Redstone Campus - South Prospect Street, Burlington, VT 05405
(802) 656-3040
> **Type of Facility:** Concert Hall
> **Type of Stage:** Concert Stage
> **Stage Dimensions:** 40'x36'x26'
> **Seating Capacity:** 300
> **Year Built:** 1974   **Architect:** Burlington Associates   **Cost:** $1,400,000
> **Acoustical Consultant:** Bolt, Beranek & Newman
> **Manager:** Jane Ambrose
> **Resident Groups:** University Music Department student and faculty ensembles; Lane Series

Craftsbury

INSTRUMENTAL MUSIC

CRAFTSBURY CHAMBER PLAYERS
PO Box 37, Craftsbury, VT 05826
(802) 586-2822
> **Founded:** 1966
> **Arts Area:** Chamber
> **Status:** Non-Profit
> **Type:** Performing; Touring; Educational
> **Purpose:** To present a variety of chamber music to a wide section of audiences in northern Vermont
> **Management:** Mary Anthony Cox, Executive Director
> **Officers:** Morrow Decker, President; Andrea Brightenback, Secretary
> **Paid Staff:** 3   **Volunteer Staff:** 50
> **Utilizes:** Guest Artists
> **Budget:** $1,000 - $50,000
> **Income Sources:** Private Foundations/Grants/Endowments; Business/Corporate Donations; Box Office; Individual Donations
> **Season:** July - August   **Annual Attendance:** 2,550
> **Affiliations:** Vermont Council on the Arts; Vermont Touring Artists Registry
> **Performance Facilities:** Hardwick Town House; Alumni Auditorium, Champlain College, Burlington; Recital Hall, Redstone Campus, University of Vermont, Burlington

Dorset

THEATRE

AMERICAN THEATRE WORKS, INC.
PO Box 519, Dorset, VT 05251
(802) 867-2223
FAX: (802) 867-0144
> **Founded:** 1976
> **Arts Area:** Professional; Summer Stock
> **Status:** Professional; Non-Profit
> **Type:** Performing; Resident; Educational; Publishing
> **Purpose:** Summer production season of five plays; writers' colony; youth theatre program; publisher of national theatre directories
> **Management:** Jill Charles, Artistic Director; John Nassivera, Producing Director; C. Barrack Evans, Managing Director; Gene Sirotof, Publications Manager
> **Officers:** Sally Brown, President of Board of Trustees; Paul Wheeler Jr., Vice President; Michael Scelsi, Treasurer; Dr. Maxine Bernstein, Secretary
> **Paid Staff:** 15
> **Paid Artists:** 30
> **Utilizes:** Special Technical Talent; Guest Artists
> **Budget:** $100,000 - $500,000
> **Income Sources:** Private Foundations/Grants/Endowments; Business/Corporate Donations; Box Office; Government Grants; Individual Donations; Publications Sales
> **Season:** June - September   **Annual Attendance:** 14,000
> **Affiliations:** TCG
> **Performance Facilities:** Dorset Playhouse

PERFORMING SERIES

DORSET THEATRE FESTIVAL
PO Box 519, Dorset, VT 05251
(802) 867-2223
        Founded: 1960
        Arts Area: Theater
        Status: Professional; Non-Profit
        Type: Performing
        Management: Jill Charles, Artistic Director; John Nassicera, Producing Director
        Paid Staff: 6   **Volunteer Staff:** 21
        Paid Artists: 50
        Utilizes: Guest Artists; Guest Directors
        Budget: $100,000 - $500,000
        Income Sources: Private Foundations/Grants/Endowments; Business/Corporate Donations; Box Office; Government Grants; Individual Donations
        Season: June - September   **Annual Attendance:** 14,000
        Affiliations: TCG
        Performance Facilities: Dorset Playhouse

Manchester

PERFORMING SERIES

FESTIVAL OF THE ARTS
Southern Vermont Arts Center/West Coast, Manchester, VT 05254
(802) 362-1405
        Founded: 1929
        Arts Area: Vocal Music; Instrumental Music; Festivals
        Status: Professional; Non-Profit
        Type: Sponsoring
        Management: Christopher Madkour, Executive Director
        Paid Staff: 9   **Volunteer Staff:** 150
        Paid Artists: 5
        Utilizes: Guest Artists
        Budget: $50,000 - $100,000
        Income Sources: Private Foundations/Grants/Endowments; Business/Corporate Donations; Box Office; Government Grants; Individual Donations
        Season: August
        Performance Facilities: Southern Vermont Arts Center

MANCHESTER MUSIC FESTIVAL
PO Box 735, Manchester, VT 05254
(802) 362-1956
        Founded: 1975
        Arts Area: Instrumental Music; Grand Opera; Classical; Chamber
        Status: Non-Professional; Non-Profit
        Type: Performing; Touring; Educational
        Purpose: To educate young artists toward a professional career
        Management: Carol Glenn, Eugene List, Founders; Michael Rudiakov, Director
        Paid Staff: 20
        Non-Paid Artists: 6
        Utilizes: Guest Conductors; Guest Artists
        Budget: $1,000 - $50,000
        Income Sources: Government Grants; Individual Donations
        Season: June - August   **Annual Attendance:** 2,000
        Performance Facilities: The Louise Arkell Pavilion

Marlboro

PERFORMING SERIES

MARLBORO MUSIC FESTIVAL
Marlboro, VT 05344
(802) 254-2394
FAX: (802) 254-4307
        Founded: 1951

Arts Area: Instrumental Music
Status: Professional; Non-Profit
Type: Performing; Touring; Resident; Educational; Sponsoring
Purpose: Artistic development of younger musicians with older, more experienced musicians
Management: Frank Saloman, Anthony Checchia, Administrators
Paid Staff: 20   **Volunteer Staff:** 5
Non-Paid Artists: 75
Utilizes: Guest Artists; Guest Directors
Budget: $500,000 - $1,000,000
Income Sources: Private Foundations/Grants/Endowments; Business/Corporate Donations; Box Office; Government Grants; Individual Donations
Season: July - August   **Annual Attendance:** 11,000
Performance Facilities: Persons Auditorium

Middlebury

THEATRE

POTOMAC THEATRE PROJECT
4 Nedde Lane, Middlebury, VT 05753
(802) 388-3318
Founded: 1977
Arts Area: Professional; Theatrical Group
Status: Professional; Non-Profit
Type: Performing; Resident; Educational
Purpose: To produce new works of a highly theatrical nature; to have a substantial involvement with professional theatre training
Management: Cheryl Faraone, James Petosa, Richard Romagnoli, Directors
Officers: Ellen Schaplowsky, Board Chairperson
Paid Staff: 3   **Volunteer Staff:** 10
Paid Artists: 12   **Non-Paid Artists:** 15
Utilizes: Guest Artists
Budget: $50,000 - $100,000
Income Sources: Private Foundations/Grants/Endowments; Business/Corporate Donations; Box Office; Government Grants; Individual Donations
Affiliations: ART/NY; Vermont Council on the Arts
Performance Facilities: Hall of Nations

FACILITY

MIDDLEBURY COLLEGE - WRIGHT THEATRE
Middlebury, VT 05753
(802) 388-3711, ext. 5601
Founded: 1800
Type of Facility: Theatre House
Type of Stage: Proscenium With Forestage
Stage Dimensions: 28'Wx14'H; 48'D from forestage to upstage wall   **Orchestra Pit**
Seating Capacity: 375
Year Built: 1958   **Architect:** Edward Cole   **Cost:** $700,000
Acoustical Consultant: Bolt, Beranek & Newman

Montpelier

INSTRUMENTAL MUSIC

BANJO DAN AND THE MID-NITE PLOWBOYS
25 Kent Street, Montpelier, VT 05602
(802) 229-5733
Founded: 1972
Arts Area: Folk
Status: Professional   **Type:** Performing
Purpose: We are a professional band, 4 or 5 pieces, playing bluegrass music in concerts, festivals and schools.
Management: Dan Lindner, Band Leader/Booking Agent

THEATRE

MONTPELIER THEATRE GUILD
33 Clarendon Avenue, Montpelier, VT 05602
(802) 223-5392
> **Founded:** 1922
> **Arts Area:** Musical; Community
> **Status:** Non-Professional; Non-Profit
> **Type:** Performing
> **Purpose:** To advance the appreciation of theatrical arts by providing good theatre in all its forms
> **Management:** Board of Directors
> **Officers:** George Kleine, President; Brian Stone, Vice President; James Catone, Corresponding Secretary; Ann Monte, Recording Secretary; Olga Wackerman, Treasurer
> **Volunteer Staff:** 100
> **Non-Paid Artists:** 100
> **Budget:** $1,000 - $50,000
> **Income Sources:** Box Office
> **Season:** November - April   **Annual Attendance:** 1,500
> **Performance Facilities:** Union School Auditorium

Norwich

VOCAL MUSIC

OPERA NORTH
PO Box 83, Norwich, VT 05055
(802) 649-3750
> **Founded:** 1980
> **Arts Area:** Grand Opera; Lyric Opera; Light Opera; Operetta
> **Status:** Professional; Non-Professional; Non-Profit
> **Type:** Performing; Touring; Educational
> **Purpose:** To create opera and musical theatre productions of professional orientation and quality, primarily in northern New England; to develop the artistic resources of the region through training and performance; to work in and with related arts disciplines
> **Management:** Board of Directors
> **Officers:** Nancy Saccani, President; Flo Klausner, Producer; Louis Burkot, Artistic Director; George Klausner, Treasurer
> **Paid Artists:** 40   **Non-Paid Artists:** 25
> **Utilizes:** Special Technical Talent; Guest Artists
> **Budget:** $50,000 - $100,000
> **Income Sources:** Private Foundations/Grants/Endowments; Business/Corporate Donations; Box Office; Individual Donations
> **Season:** July - January   **Annual Attendance:** 3,000
> **Performance Facilities:** Lebanon Opera House

Pittsfield

THEATRE

GREEN MOUNTAIN GUILD
PO Box 659, Pittsfield, VT 05762
(802) 746-8320
> **Founded:** 1971
> **Arts Area:** Professional; Summer Stock; Musical; Theatre for Children
> **Status:** Professional
> **Type:** Performing; Touring; Resident
> **Purpose:** To develop and promote excellence in the performing arts in Northern New England
> **Management:** Marjorie O'Neill-Butler, Program Coordinator/Managing Director; Robert O'Neill-Butler, Artistic Director; Jay Berkow, Associate Artistic Director
> **Officers:** Robert O'Neill-Butler, President; Jonathan Huberth, Vice President; Marjorie O'Neill-Butler, Secretary/Treasurer
> **Paid Staff:** 3   **Volunteer Staff:** 2
> **Paid Artists:** 30   **Non-Paid Artists:** 3
> **Utilizes:** Guest Directors
> **Income Sources:** Box Office; Individual Donations
> **Season:** March - December   **Annual Attendance:** 10,000
> **Affiliations:** NETC; Vermont Council on the Arts; New England Touring Foundation
> **Performance Facilities:** Killington Playhouse, Killington

---
Putney

PERFORMING SERIES

YELLOW BARN MUSIC FESTIVAL
Rural Delivery 2, Box 371, Putney, VT 05346
(802) 387-6637
>**Founded:** 1969
>**Arts Area:** Instrumental Music; Festivals
>**Status:** Non-Profit
>**Type:** Performing; Educational
>**Purpose:** To provide a professional training institute and performance festival for gifted young chamber artists
>**Management:** Tova Malin, Executive Director; David Wells and Janet Wells, Artistic Directors; Maury McNaughton, Administrator
>**Officers:** Hanz Vitzthum, Chair
>**Paid Staff:** 10
>**Paid Artists:** 20   **Non-Paid Artists:** 50
>**Utilizes:** Guest Conductors; Guest Artists
>**Budget:** $100,000 - $500,000
>**Income Sources:** Private Foundations/Grants/Endowments; Business/Corporate Donations; Box Office; Government Grants; Individual Donations; Fundraising
>**Season:** July - August   **Annual Attendance:** 4,000

FACILITY

YELLOW BARN
Rural Delivery 2, Box 371, Putney, VT 05346
(802) 387-6637
>**Type of Facility:** Barn
>**Type of Stage:** Platform
>**Seating Capacity:** 150

Randolph

FACILITY

CHANDLER MUSIC HALL AND CULTURAL CENTER
71-73 Main Street, Randolph, VT 05060
(802) 728-9878
>**Founded:** 1907
>**Type of Facility:** Theatre Complex; Concert Hall; Performance Center; Theatre House; Opera House; Civic Center; Art Gallery; Cultural Center
>**Facility Originally:** Music Hall
>**Type of Stage:** Proscenium
>**Stage Dimensions:** 31'6"x19'4" proscenium opening   **Orchestra Pit**
>**Seating Capacity:** 625
>**Year Built:** 1907   **Architect:** Ernest H. Boyden   **Cost:** $31,500
>**Year Remodeled:** 1972   **Cost:** $250,000
>**Contact for Rental:** Francis Hartigan;   (802) 728-3849
>**Resident Groups:** Chandler Players; Randolph Singers

Rutland

PERFORMING SERIES

KILLINGTON MUSIC FESTIVAL
PO Box 386, Rutland, VT 05702
(802) 773-4003
>**Founded:** 1982
>**Arts Area:** Instrumental Music
>**Status:** Non-Profit
>**Type:** Performing; Educational
>**Purpose:** To present summer chamber concert series and operate a summer school for aspiring musicians
>**Paid Staff:** 1
>**Paid Artists:** 10
>**Utilizes:** Guest Directors
>**Budget:** $100,000 - $500,000

Income Sources: Private Foundations/Grants/Endowments; Business/Corporate Donations; Box Office; Government Grants; Individual Donations
Season: July - August   **Annual Attendance:** 2,000

Saint Johnsbury

DANCE

CATAMOUNT FILM AND ARTS COMPANY
PO Box 324, Saint Johnsbury, VT 05819
(802) 748-2600
    Founded: 1975
    Arts Area: Modern; Mime; Ballet; Jazz; Ethnic; Folk
    Status: Professional; Non-Profit
    Type: Performing; Educational
    Purpose: Catamount is a community-based multidisciplinary presenter
    Management: Phil Reynolds, Executive Director
    Paid Staff: 9   **Volunteer Staff:** 20
    Budget: $100,000 - $500,000
    Income Sources: Private Foundations/Grants/Endowments; Business/Corporate Donations; Box Office; Government Grants; Individual Donations; Concessions; Rental Income
    Season: 52 Weeks   **Annual Attendance:** 25,000

Thetford Center

VOCAL MUSIC

THROUGH THE OPERA GLASS
Rural Route 1, Box 7, Tucker Hill Road, Thetford Center, VT 05075
(802) 785-4559; (800) 932-7396
    Founded: 1987
    Arts Area: Grand Opera; Lyric Opera; Light Opera; Operetta; Musical Theatre
    Status: Professional
    Type: Performing; Touring; Resident; Educational; Produce-it-Yourself Programs
    Purpose: To tour thematic excerpted opera programs, including collaborations; to make these unique thematic programs available to other performing groups in "produce-it-yourself" packages
    Management: Caren Calafati Showerman, Managing Director
    Paid Staff: 2
    Paid Artists: 12
    Utilizes: Guest Artists; Collaborations
    Budget: $50,000 - $100,000
    Income Sources: Private Foundations/Grants/Endowments; Box Office; Individual Presenters; Budget
    Season: 52 Weeks
    Affiliations: Vermont Council on the Arts; New Hampshire Council on the Arts; Massachusetts Cultural Council

---

Tunbridge

DANCE

ED LARKIN OLD-TIME CONTRA DANCERS
c/o Swayze, RFD, PO Box 131B, Tunbridge, VT 05077
(802) 889-5584
    Founded: 1956
    Arts Area: Ethnic
    Status: Semi-Professional; Non-Professional; Non-Profit
    Type: Performing; Touring; Educational
    Purpose: To perform authentic Vermont-style contradances and quadrilles as they were done in the 1930s and earlier with traditional music and antique costumes
    Officers: Carl Martin, President; George Cushman, Vice President; Dorothy Swayze, Secretary; Wayne Martin, Treasurer
    Volunteer Staff: 25
    Non-Paid Artists: 37
    Income Sources: Individual Donations
    Season: 52 Weeks
    Affiliations: Vermont Council on the Arts

Wells River

VOCAL MUSIC

NORTH COUNTRY CHORUS
65 Main Street, Wells River, VT 05081
(802) 757-2325
Founded: 1948
Arts Area: Choral
Status: Semi-Professional; Non-Profit
Type: Performing; Touring; Resident
Purpose: The enriching of the musical life of residents of the North Country Area through participation in a singing group whose membership is open to all who love to sing
Management: Mary Whitney Rowe, Conductor; Jean Anderson, Pianist
Officers: Joan M. Blankinship, President; Edith Emery, Vice President; Margaret Eastman, Secretary; Amy Jarrell, Treasurer
Paid Staff: 1
Paid Artists: 6
Utilizes: Special Technical Talent; Guest Artists; Guest Directors
Budget: $1,000 - $50,000
Income Sources: Private Foundations/Grants/Endowments; Business/Corporate Donations; Box Office; Government Grants; Individual Donations
Season: 52 Weeks

VIRGINIA

Abingdon

THEATRE

BARTER THEATRE - STATE THEATRE OF VIRGINIA
Main Street, PO Box 867, Abingdon, VA 24210
(703) 628-2281
FAX: (703) 628-4551
   Founded: 1933
   Arts Area: Professional
   Status: Professional; Non-Profit
   Type: Performing; Touring; Resident; Educational
   Purpose: To perform the best in classical and contemporary theatre for residents and visitors to our region
   Management: Rex Partington, Artistic Director/Producer
   Officers: Fillmore McPherson, President; Frank Defrience Jr., Vice President/Treasurer; James P. Jones, Secretary
   Paid Staff: 25
   Paid Artists: 50
   Utilizes: Guest Artists; Guest Directors
   Budget: $1,000,000 - $5,000,000
   Income Sources: Private Foundations/Grants/Endowments; Business/Corporate Donations; Box Office; Government Grants; Individual Donations
   Season: April - October   **Annual Attendance:** 75,000
   Affiliations: AEA; LORT; TCG
   Performance Facilities: Barter Playhouse; Barter Theatre House

FACILITY

BARTER PLAYHOUSE
Main Street, PO Box 867, Abingdon, VA 24210
(703) 628-2281
   Type of Facility: Theatre House
   Facility Originally: Church
   Type of Stage: 3/4 Arena
   Seating Capacity: 138
   Year Built: 1833
   Year Remodeled: 1978
   Contact for Rental: (703) 628-2281
   Resident Groups: Barter Theatre

BARTER THEATRE HOUSE
Main Street, PO Box 867, Abingdon, VA 24210
(703) 628-3991
   Type of Facility: Theatre House
   Facility Originally: Church
   Type of Stage: Proscenium   **Orchestra Pit**
   Seating Capacity: 394
   Year Built: 1833
   Contact for Rental: Pearl Hayter;   (703) 628-2281
   Resident Groups: Barter Theatre
   Converted into a theatre in 1933

Alexandria

THEATRE

AMERICAN SHOWCASE THEATRE COMPANY
1822 Duke Street, Alexandria, VA 22314
(703) 548-9044
FAX: (703) 548-9089
   Founded: 1984
   Arts Area: Professional; Theatrical Group
   Status: Professional; Non-Profit
   Type: Performing; Touring; Educational
   Purpose: To offer a season of mainstage productions, staged readings and new-play development, as well as acting classes

Management: Sherry Brown, Director of Management Resources; Carolyn Griffin, Producing Director
Officers: Trudy B. Levy Esq., President; Thomas P. Hartnett Esq., Vice President; Barbara Berschler Esq., Treasurer; Louise Rosenbaum, Secretary
Paid Staff: 2 **Volunteer Staff:** 3
Utilizes: Guest Directors
Budget: $100,000 - $500,000
Income Sources: Private Foundations/Grants/Endowments; Business/Corporate Donations; Box Office; Government Grants; Individual Donations
Season: September - June **Annual Attendance:** 4,000
Affiliations: TGC; League of Washington Theatres; Alexandria Chamber of Commerce; Cultural Alliance of Greater Washington; King Street Metro Enterprise Team

Annandale

INSTRUMENTAL MUSIC

FAIRFAX SYMPHONY ORCHESTRA
PO Box 1300, Annandale, VA 22003
(703) 642-7200
FAX: (703) 642-7205
Founded: 1957
Arts Area: Symphony; Orchestra; Chamber; Ensemble; Instrumental Group
Status: Professional; Non-Profit
Type: Performing; Touring; Resident; Educational
Management: Mark W. Ohnmacht, Executive Director
Officers: Fredrick G. Hutchinson Jr., President; Paul H. Geithner Jr., Immediate Past President
Paid Staff: 4 **Volunteer Staff:** 10
Paid Artists: 90
Utilizes: Guest Artists
Budget: $500,000 - $1,000,000
Income Sources: Private Foundations/Grants/Endowments; Business/Corporate Donations; Box Office; Government Grants; Individual Donations
Season: October - July **Annual Attendance:** 75,000
Performance Facilities: George Mason University

PERFORMING SERIES

INTERNATIONAL CHILDREN'S FESTIVAL
4022 Hummer Road, Annandale, VA 22003
(703) 642-0862
FAX: (703) 642-1773
Founded: 1971
Arts Area: Dance; Vocal Music; Instrumental Music; Theater; Festivals
Status: Professional; Non-Profit
Type: Performing; Resident; Sponsoring
Management: Toni Winters McMahon, President/Chief Operating Officer; Kathy Sears, Program Director
Officers: John P. Stenbit, Chairman
Paid Staff: 6 **Volunteer Staff:** 1,250
Paid Artists: 40
Utilizes: Special Technical Talent; Guest Artists
Budget: $100,000 - $500,000
Income Sources: Private Foundations/Grants/Endowments; Business/Corporate Donations; Box Office; Government Grants; Individual Donations
Annual Attendance: 35,000
Affiliations: Fairfax County Council of the Arts
Performance Facilities: Wolf Trap Farm Park for the Performing Arts

Arlington

DANCE

ARLINGTON DANCE THEATRE
2700 South Lang Street, Arlington, VA 22204
(703) 548-1017
Founded: 1956
Arts Area: Modern; Ballet; Jazz
Status: Semi-Professional; Non-Profit

Type: Performing; Educational
Purpose: Dedicated to excellence in the performance and teaching of dance
Management: Robens Siegel, Artistic Director; Judy Rhodes, Director, Children's Program and Apprentice Company
Officers: M.J. Boster, President; Robin Shallant, Vice President; Kathy Cagel, Secretary; Julia Blackburn, Treasurer
Volunteer Staff: 21
Non-Paid Artists: 16
Utilizes: Special Technical Talent; Guest Artists
Budget: $50,000 - $100,000
Income Sources: Private Foundations/Grants/Endowments; Business/Corporate Donations; Box Office; Government Grants; Individual Donations
Season: September - July   **Annual Attendance:** 2,000
Affiliations: Arlington County Cultural Affairs Office
Performance Facilities: Thomas Jefferson Community Theatre

INSTRUMENTAL MUSIC

HESPERUS
3706 North 17th Street, Arlington, VA 22207
(703) 525-7550
Arts Area: Chamber; Folk; Early Music; Classical
Status: Professional; Non-Profit
Type: Touring; Resident
Purpose: To trace the cultural parallels between the Old World and the New World
Management: Scott Reiss, Artistic Director; Tina Chancey, Producing Director
Budget: $100,000 - $500,000
Income Sources: Private Foundations/Grants/Endowments; Business/Corporate Donations; Box Office; Government Grants; Individual Donations; Fees
Performance Facilities: Smithsonian Institute - National Museum of American History

TWENTIETH CENTURY CONSORI
828 South Wakefield Street, Arlington, VA 22204
(703) 920-9727
Arts Area: Chamber
Status: Professional; Non-Profit
Type: Performing; Touring; Resident; Educational
Purpose: To provide the best in 20th-century classical music
Management: Christopher Kendall, Artistic Director
Budget: $1,000 - $50,000
Income Sources: Private Foundations/Grants/Endowments; Business/Corporate Donations; Box Office; Government Grants; Individual Donations
Performance Facilities: Hirshorn Museum

VOCAL MUSIC

OPERA THEATRE OF NORTHERN VIRGINIA
2700 South Lang Street, Arlington, VA 22206
(703) 739-2918
Founded: 1961
Arts Area: Grand Opera; Light Opera
Status: Professional; Non-Profit
Type: Performing; Resident
Purpose: To provide affordable opera in English to the northern Virginia and Greater Metropolitan Washington Area; to sponsor educational programs and performances geared to young audiences; to provide stage experience emphasizing utilization of local talent
Management: John Edward Niles, Artistic Director/Conductor
Officers: Virginia D. Marrin, Vice President, Production
Paid Staff: 1   **Volunteer Staff:** 25
Paid Artists: 100
Utilizes: Special Technical Talent; Guest Artists; Guest Directors
Budget: $50,000 - $100,000
Income Sources: Private Foundations/Grants/Endowments; Business/Corporate Donations; Box Office; Government Grants; Individual Donations; Fundraising
Season: December - April   **Annual Attendance:** 7,000
Affiliations: OA; Cultural Alliance of Greater Washington
Performance Facilities: Thomas Jefferson Community Theatre

PERFORMING SERIES

OFFICE OF CULTURAL AFFAIRS
2700 South Lang Street, Arlington, VA 22206
(703) 358-6960
>**Arts Area:** Dance; Vocal Music; Instrumental Music; Theater; Festivals; Grand Opera
>**Status:** Non-Profit
>**Type:** Performing; Educational; Sponsoring
>**Purpose:** To create and maintain an environment within Arlington County that is conducive to the development of the arts
>**Management:** Norma Kaplan, Supervisor
>**Paid Staff:** 14
>**Paid Artists:** 100   **Non-Paid Artists:** 100
>**Utilizes:** Special Technical Talent; Guest Conductors; Guest Artists; Guest Directors
>**Budget:** $100,000 - $500,000
>**Income Sources:** Private Foundations/Grants/Endowments; Government Grants
>**Season:** 52 Weeks
>**Affiliations:** NALAA

Blacksburg

FACILITY

BURRUSS AUDITORIUM
Virginia Technical Campus, 225 Squires Center, Blacksburg, VA 24061-0138
(703) 231-5431
FAX: (703) 231-5430
>**Founded:** 1936
>**Type of Facility:** Auditorium
>**Facility Originally:** Meeting Hall; School
>**Type of Stage:** Proscenium
>**Stage Dimensions:** 58'Wx17'6"H   **Orchestra Pit**
>**Seating Capacity:** 2,960
>**Year Built:** 1936
>**Year Remodeled:** 1985   **Cost:** $1,200,000
>**Acoustical Consultant:** Acentech
>**Contact for Rental:** UUSA Events Planning;   (703) 231-5005

Bristol

DANCE

BRISTOL BALLET COMPANY
628 Cumberland Street, Bristol, VA 24201
(703) 466-2401
>**Founded:** 1959
>**Arts Area:** Ballet
>**Status:** Non-Profit
>**Type:** Performing
>**Purpose:** To promote, encourage and sustain community interest in the art of ballet; to contribute to the cultural progress and entertainment of the community and the larger Tri-cities Area
>**Management:** Mary Anne Snyder-Sowers, Artistic Director; Nancy Peoples, Production Director
>**Officers:** Sam Crockett, President; Rita Hairston, Vice President; Lee Duncan, Recording Secretary; Nancy Peoples, Treasurer
>**Paid Staff:** 4   **Volunteer Staff:** 27
>**Non-Paid Artists:** 15
>**Utilizes:** Guest Artists; Guest Choreographers
>**Budget:** $50,000 - $100,000
>**Income Sources:** Private Foundations/Grants/Endowments; Business/Corporate Donations; Box Office; Government Grants; Individual Donations
>**Season:** September - August   **Annual Attendance:** 6,000
>**Affiliations:** SERBA; Tennessee Arts Commission; Virginia Commission for the Arts
>**Performance Facilities:** Paramount Center

Charlottesville

INSTRUMENTAL MUSIC

TUESDAY EVENING CONCERT SERIES
112 Old Cabell Hall, University of Virginia, Charlottesville, VA 22903
(804) 924-3600
FAX: (804) 982-2002
> **Founded:** 1948
> **Arts Area:** Chamber; Ensemble; Soloists
> **Status:** Professional; Non-Profit
> **Type:** Sponsoring
> **Purpose:** To sponsor an annual series of six chamber concerts
> **Management:** Karen Pellon, Manager
> **Officers:** Lilli Meier, President; Collins Beagle, Vice President; Jean Minehart, Treasurer
> **Paid Staff:** 1   **Volunteer Staff:** 25
> **Utilizes:** Guest Artists
> **Budget:** $50,000 - $100,000
> **Income Sources:** Private Foundations/Grants/Endowments; Business/Corporate Donations; Box Office; Government Grants; Individual Donations
> **Season:** September - April   **Annual Attendance:** 4,000
> **Affiliations:** University of Virginia
> **Performance Facilities:** Cabell Hall Auditorium, University of Virginia

THEATRE

OFFSTAGE THEATRE
PO Box 131, Charlottesville, VA 22902
(804) 295-7249
> **Founded:** 1989
> **Arts Area:** Professional; Theatrical Group; Independent Theatre
> **Status:** Semi-Professional; Non-Profit
> **Type:** Performing; Touring; Resident; Educational
> **Purpose:** Dedicated to producing high-quality, new plays in low-cost, nontraditional theatre environments
> **Management:** Tom Coash, Doug Grissom, Co-Artistic Directors; John Quinn, Resident Director;
> Amy Lowenstein, Public Relations Director
> **Officers:** Tom Coash, President; Doug Grissom, Vice President; John Quinn, Treasurer; Amy Lowenstein, Secretary
> **Paid Staff:** 2   **Volunteer Staff:** 20
> **Paid Artists:** 15
> **Utilizes:** Guest Artists; Guest Directors
> **Budget:** $1,000 - $50,000
> **Income Sources:** Business/Corporate Donations; Box Office; Individual Donations
> **Season:** 52 Weeks   **Annual Attendance:** 10,000

Fairfax

DANCE

JANE FRANKLIN AND DANCERS
10723 West Drive, #304, Fairfax, VA 22030
(703) 591-1893
> **Founded:** 1983
> **Arts Area:** Modern
> **Status:** Professional; Non-Profit
> **Type:** Performing; Touring; Educational
> **Purpose:** To present dance and live music with pieces featuring voice and text
> **Management:** Jane Franklin, Artistic Director; Carol Coteus, Administrative Assistant
> **Paid Staff:** 1   **Volunteer Staff:** 8
> **Paid Artists:** 5   **Non-Paid Artists:** 3
> **Utilizes:** Guest Artists
> **Budget:** $1,000 - $50,000
> **Income Sources:** Private Foundations/Grants/Endowments; Box Office
> **Season:** 52 Weeks

FACILITY

GEORGE MASON UNIVERSITY CENTER FOR THE ARTS
4400 University Drive, Fairfax, VA 22030
(703) 993-8877
FAX: (703) 993-8883
>   **Founded:** 1990
>   **Type of Facility:** Theatre Complex; Concert Hall; Studio Performance; Theatre House; Opera House; Multi-Purpose
>   **Type of Stage:** Thrust; Flexible; Proscenium
>   **Stage Dimensions:** Concert Hall - 52'x40'   **Orchestra Pit**
>   **Seating Capacity:** Concert Hall - 1,935
>   **Year Built:** 1990   **Architect:** General - McGuire Group; Concert Hall - Izenour Associates   **Cost:** $12,000,000
>   **Acoustical Consultant:** Izenour Associates
>   **Contact for Rental:** Director of Operations;   (703) 993-8877

Fort Eustis

FACILITY

FORT EUSTIS MUSIC AND VIDEO CENTER
ATZF-PRC-MT BUILDING 224, Fort Eustis, VA 23604-5109
(804) 878-5031
>   **Type of Facility:** Studio Performance; Environmental; Performance Center; Civic Center; Multi-Purpose
>   **Facility Originally:** Library; Recreation Hall/gymnasium
>   **Year Built:** 1950   **Architect:** U.S. Army Corps of Engineers
>   **Year Remodeled:** 1976   **Architect:** U.S. Army Corps of Engineers
>   **Manager:** Mike Hassell
>   **Resident Groups:** Soldier Theatre
>   *Fort Eustis Music and Video Center contains the Jacobs Theatre and Soldier Theatre. See separate listings for further information.*

FORT EUSTIS MUSIC AND VIDEO CENTER - JACOBS THEATRE
ATZF-PRC-MT BUILDING 224, Fort Eustis, VA 23604-5109
(804) 878-5031
>   **Type of Facility:** Studio Performance
>   **Type of Stage:** Modified Apron Proscenium
>   **Stage Dimensions:** 48'Wx48'D, includes 12'D apron past proscenium
>   **Seating Capacity:** 1,000
>   **Contact for Rental:** Mike Hassell;   (804) 878-5031

FORT EUSTIS MUSIC AND VIDEO CENTER - SOLDIER THEATRE
ATZF-PRC-MT BUILDING 224, Fort Eustis, VA 23604-5109
(804) 878-5031
>   **Type of Facility:** Studio Performance; Multi-Purpose
>   **Type of Stage:** Platform
>   **Stage Dimensions:** 36'Wx28'Dx16'H
>   **Seating Capacity:** 800
>   **Contact for Rental:** Mike Hassell;   (804) 878-5031

Fredericksburg

PERFORMING SERIES

FREDERICKSBURG CHAMBER MUSIC FESTIVAL
PO Box 7816, Fredericksburg, VA 22404
(703) 371-4805
>   **Founded:** 1988
>   **Arts Area:** Vocal Music; Instrumental Music
>   **Status:** Non-Profit
>   **Type:** Performing; Educational
>   **Purpose:** To present the finest in performing arts to Fredericksburg and the surrounding area at reasonable prices
>   **Management:** David R. Freeman, Chairman; Edward Bennan, President of the Board; Mary Triola, Festival Coordinator; Heidi Lehwalder, Artistic Director
>   **Volunteer Staff:** 50
>   **Paid Artists:** 13

Utilizes: Guest Conductors; Guest Artists
Budget: $50,000 - $100,000
Income Sources: Private Foundations/Grants/Endowments; Business/Corporate Donations; Box Office; Individual Donations
Season: June
Performance Facilities: Dodd Auditorium, Mary Washington College; St. George Episcopal Church

Hampton

DANCE

HAMPTON ROADS CIVIC BALLET
4607 Victoria Boulevard, Hampton, VA 23669
(804) 722-8216
Founded: 1959
Arts Area: Ballet
Status: Non-Profit
Type: Performing; Resident; Educational
Purpose: To bring live ballet to our area at affordable prices; to provide training for young dancers hoping to become professionals
Management: Muriel Evans, Director; Lisa Schultz, Ballet Mistress
Officers: Mark Watson, President; Melissa Berry, Vice President; Diane Nusbaum, Secretary; Debbie Scott, Treasurer
Utilizes: Guest Artists
Budget: $1,000 - $50,000
Income Sources: Box Office; Individual Donations
Annual Attendance: 2,000

PERFORMING SERIES

HAMPTON ARTS COMMISSION
4205 Victoria Boulevard, Hampton, VA 23669
(804) 722-2787
FAX: (804) 727-1152
Founded: 1987
Arts Area: Dance; Vocal Music; Instrumental Music; Theater
Status: Professional
Type: Performing; Educational; Sponsoring
Purpose: To present and promote the finest in the performing and visual arts
Management: Michael P. Curry, Director
Officers: Nancy B. Adams, Chair
Paid Staff: 3   **Volunteer Staff:** 12
Paid Artists: 8
Utilizes: Guest Artists
Budget: $100,000 - $500,000
Income Sources: Box Office; Government Grants
Season: September - May   **Annual Attendance:** 30,000
Affiliations: APAP
Performance Facilities: Ogden Hall

FACILITY

HAMPTON COLISEUM
PO Box 7309, Hampton, VA 23666
(804) 838-5650
FAX: (804) 838-2595
Type of Facility: Arena
Type of Stage: Proscenium
Stage Dimensions: 80'Wx40'H
Seating Capacity: 10,953; 13,800
Year Built: 1969   **Architect:** A.G. Odell   **Cost:** $8,500,000
Contact for Rental: Andrew G. Greenwell;   (804) 838-5650
Manager: Andrew D. Greenwell;   (804) 838-5650

Hanover

THEATRE

BARKSDALE THEATRE
PO Box 7, Hanover, VA 23069
(804) 730-4860
    Founded: 1953
    Arts Area: Professional; Musical; Dinner; Theatrical Group
    Status: Professional; Non-Profit
    Type: Performing; Touring
    Purpose: To offer excellent theatre
    Management: David Kilgore, Muriel McAvley, Artistic Directors/Co-Owners; Nancy Kilgore, Co-Owner; Katherine Tracy, General Manager; Cynthia Theaksto, Director of Audience Relations and Group Sales; Jacqueline O'Conner, Box Office Manager
    Paid Staff: 5   **Volunteer Staff:** 15
    Utilizes: Special Technical Talent; Guest Artists; Guest Directors
    Budget: $50,000 - $100,000
    Income Sources: Private Foundations/Grants/Endowments; Business/Corporate Donations; Box Office; Government Grants; Individual Donations
    Season: 52 Weeks   **Annual Attendance:** 30,000
    Affiliations: Actor's Studio

Harrisonburg

FACILITY

WILSON HALL AUDITORIUM
James Madison University, Harrisonburg, VA 22807
(703) 568-6754
FAX: (703) 568-6920
    Founded: 1930
    Type of Facility: Auditorium; Theatre House
    Type of Stage: Thrust; Proscenium
    Stage Dimensions: 34'x35' proscenium opening   **Orchestra Pit**
    Seating Capacity: 1,347
    Year Built: 1930   **Architect:** Charles M. Robinson   **Cost:** $250,000
    Year Remodeled: 1987   **Architect:** McClintock and Associates   **Cost:** $900,000
    Contact for Rental: Connie Kerlin, Programming;   (703) 568-6330

Hot Springs

PERFORMING SERIES

GARTH NEWEL MUSIC CENTER
Route 220, Hot Springs, VA 24445
(703) 839-5018
FAX: (703) 839-3154
    Founded: 1975
    Arts Area: Vocal Music; Instrumental Music; Festivals
    Status: Professional; Non-Profit; Student Program
    Type: Performing; Touring; Resident; Educational
    Purpose: To promote and perform chamber music
    Management: Luca and Arlene Di Cecco, Directors
    Officers: H.H. Ingalls, President; Luca Di Cecco, Executive Vice President; Thomas Roberts, Treasurer; Arlene Di Cecco, Secretary
    Paid Staff: 6   **Volunteer Staff:** 10
    Paid Artists: 12
    Utilizes: Guest Conductors; Guest Artists
    Budget: $100,000 - $500,000
    Income Sources: Private Foundations/Grants/Endowments; Business/Corporate Donations; Box Office; Government Grants; Individual Donations
    Season: July - September   **Annual Attendance:** 5,000
    Performance Facilities: Herter Hall

Leesburg

PERFORMING SERIES

BLUEMONT CONCERT SERIES
PO Box 208, Leesburg, VA 22075-0208
  Arts Area: Festivals; Traditional; Variety
  Status: Non-Profit
  Type: Educational; Sponsoring
  Purpose: To provide a wide variety of high-quality events for the community
  Management: Pete H. Dunning, President
  Paid Staff: 3   **Volunteer Staff:** 400
  Paid Artists: 400
  Utilizes: Special Technical Talent
  Budget: $100,000 - $500,000
  Income Sources: Private Foundations/Grants/Endowments; Business/Corporate Donations; Box Office; Government Grants; Individual Donations
  Season: 52 Weeks   **Annual Attendance:** 150,000

Lexington

INSTRUMENTAL MUSIC

WASHINGTON AND LEE UNIVERSITY CONCERT GUILD
Washington and Lee University, Lexington, VA 24450
(703) 463-8855
  Arts Area: Chamber
  Status: Professional; Non-Profit
  Type: Educational; Sponsoring
  Management: Timothy Gaylord, Music Department
  Budget: $1,000 - $50,000
  Season: October - March
  Performance Facilities: Lenfest Centre

THEATRE

LIME KILN ARTS INCORPORATED
PO Box 663, Lexington, VA 24450
(703) 463-7088
  Arts Area: Professional; Summer Stock; Musical; Folk; Theatrical Group
  Status: Professional; Non-Profit
  Type: Performing; Touring; Resident; Educational; Sponsoring
  Purpose: To promote and preserve the tradition of the southern Appalachian Mountains and explore their myths and potential
  Management: Don Baker, Artistic Director; Ken Sheck, Manager
  Officers: Bob Martis, President
  Budget: $500,000 - $1,000,000
  Income Sources: Private Foundations/Grants/Endowments; Business/Corporate Donations; Box Office; Government Grants; Individual Donations
  Performance Facilities: Lime Kiln Theater

Lynchburg

FACILITY

LYNCHBURG FINE ARTS CENTER
1815 Thomson Drive, Lynchburg, VA 24501
(804) 846-8451
  Type of Facility: Concert Hall; Theatre House
  Type of Stage: Proscenium
  Orchestra Pit
  Seating Capacity: 510
  Year Built: 1962   **Architect:** Carl Cress
  Contact for Rental: (804) 846-8451
  Manager: Kathleen Bowne, Contact Person
  Resident Groups: Women's Group
  Also contains the Dillard and Lounge Visual Arts Galleries

Martinsville

VOCAL MUSIC

MARTINSVILLE-HENRY COUNTY FESTIVAL OF OPERA
South College Street, PO Box 406, Martinsville, VA 24112
(703) 632-5861
Founded: 1977
Arts Area: Grand Opera; Lyric Opera; Light Opera; Operetta; Choral
Status: Professional; Non-Profit
Type: Performing; Touring; Resident; Educational
Purpose: To bring live professional opera to the region on a regular basis
Management: Priscilla Gordon, Artistic Director; Alberto Figols, Managing Director; Floyd Sharp,
Musical Director
Volunteer Staff: 6
Paid Artists: 12
Utilizes: Special Technical Talent; Guest Conductors; Guest Artists; Guest Directors
Budget: $1,000 - $50,000
Income Sources: Private Foundations/Grants/Endowments; Business/Corporate Donations; Box Office; Government
Grants; Individual Donations
Season: April - December
Affiliations: Touring Concert Opera Company

McLean

FACILITY

ALDEN THEATRE
1234 Ingleside Avenue, McLean, VA 22101
(703) 790-0123
FAX: (703) 556-0547
Founded: 1975
Type of Facility: Theatre Complex
Type of Stage: Proscenium
Stage Dimensions: 28'x35'   **Orchestra Pit**
Seating Capacity: 424
Year Built: 1975
Year Remodeled: 1988   **Architect:** Cooper-Lecky
Contact for Rental: Clare Kiley;   (703) 790-0123

Middletown

THEATRE

WAYSIDE THEATRE
7853 Main Street, Middletown, VA 22645
(703) 869-1776
FAX: (703) 869-1782
Founded: 1962
Arts Area: Professional
Status: Professional; Non-Profit
Type: Performing; Touring; Resident
Purpose: To produce the best contemporary English-American theatre for the entertainment and education of the citizens
of northern Virginia
Management: Christopher Owens, Artistic Director; Donna Johnson, General Manager; Kay Parker, Box Office Manager;
Sharon Gochenauer, Administrative Assistant; John Ervin, Technical Director
Officers: Nick Nerangis, President of the Board; Ian Williams, Vice President; Richard Helm, Treasurer; Diane Collis,
Secretary
Paid Staff: 8   **Volunteer Staff:** 3
Paid Artists: 30
Utilizes: Special Technical Talent; Guest Directors; Organization Contracts
Budget: $100,000 - $500,000
Income Sources: Private Foundations/Grants/Endowments; Business/Corporate Donations; Box Office; Government
Grants; Individual Donations
Season: May - December   **Annual Attendance:** 22,000

Newport News

VOCAL MUSIC

VIRGINIA CHORAL SOCIETY
Warwick Station, PO Box 1131, Newport News, VA 23601
(804) 851-9114
Founded: 1931
Arts Area: Choral
Status: Non-Profit
Type: Performing
Purpose: To bring to the community an appreciation and enjoyment of fine music
Management: Gary Lewis, Artistic Director; Oliver Douberly, Assistant Artistic Director;
Constance J. O'Sullivan, Marketing Director
Officers: Jean Putnam, President; Barbara Sardella, Vice President; Kay Stewart, Corresponding Secretary;
Katherine Bradshaw, Recording Secretary; Michael Martin, Treasurer; Phyllis Wharton, Archivist
Paid Staff: 1　**Volunteer Staff:** 23
Paid Artists: 2　**Non-Paid Artists:** 90
Utilizes: Guest Artists
Budget: $1,000 - $50,000
Income Sources: Private Foundations/Grants/Endowments; Business/Corporate Donations; Box Office; Government
Grants; Individual Donations
Season: December - May　**Annual Attendance:** 4,600

Norfolk

DANCE

VIRGINIA BALLET THEATRE
134-136 West Onley Road, Norfolk, VA 23510
(804) 622-4822
Founded: 1961
Arts Area: Ballet
Status: Non-Professional; Non-Profit
Type: Performing; Resident
Management: Frank and Janina Bove, Artistic Directors
Non-Paid Artists: 40
Utilizes: Guest Artists
Budget: $1,000 - $50,000
Income Sources: Private Foundations/Grants/Endowments; Business/Corporate Donations; Box Office; Government
Grants; Individual Donations
Season: May - December

INSTRUMENTAL MUSIC

NORFOLK CHAMBER CONSORT
5511 Willow Grove Court, Norfolk, VA 23505
(804) 440-1803
FAX: (804) 440-0080
Founded: 1969
Arts Area: Chamber
Status: Professional
Type: Performing
Purpose: To present known and unknown works from the vast repertoire of chamber music from 1600 to the present,
with a concentration on chamber music for mixed winds, strings, and voice
Management: Allen Shaffer, F. Gerard Errante, Co-Directors
Utilizes: Special Technical Talent; Guest Conductors; Guest Artists
Budget: $1,000 - $50,000
Income Sources: Business/Corporate Donations; Box Office; Government Grants; Individual Donations
Annual Attendance: 1,000
Performance Facilities: Chrysler Museum Theater; Chandler Recital Hall, Old Dominion University

THE VIRGINIA SYMPHONY
PO Box 26, Norfolk, VA 23501
(804) 623-8590
FAX: (804) 623-7068
Founded: 1920

Arts Area: Symphony; Orchestra; Chamber
Status: Professional; Non-Profit
Type: Performing; Touring; Educational
Purpose: To support an orchestra of the highest artistic excellence and reputation; to provide enjoyment, education, enrichment, inspiration and pride for the citizens of Hampton Roads and the Commonwealth of Virginia; to bring recognition and credit to the entire region
Management: Benjamin Greene, Executive Director; Joann Falletta, Music Director; Skitch Henderson, Principal Pops Conductor
Officers: Asa Shield Jr., President of Board of Directors
Paid Staff: 12   **Volunteer Staff:** 500
Paid Artists: 81
Utilizes: Guest Conductors; Guest Artists
Budget: $1,000,000 - $5,000,000
Income Sources: Private Foundations/Grants/Endowments; Business/Corporate Donations; Box Office; Government Grants; Individual Donations
Season: September - June   **Annual Attendance:** 100,000
Affiliations: ASOL
Performance Facilities: Chrysler Hall; Pavilion Theatre; Ogden Hall

VOCAL MUSIC

CANTATA CHORUS OF NORFOLK
560 West Olney Road, Norfolk, VA 23507
(804) 627-5665
Founded: 1960
Arts Area: Choral
Status: Semi-Professional; Non-Profit
Type: Performing
Purpose: To present major choral works as near to the composer's concept and instrumentation as possible
Management: Grover J. Oberle, Director; Dr. Allen Shaffer, Assistant Director
Paid Staff: 1   **Volunteer Staff:** 6
Paid Artists: 40   **Non-Paid Artists:** 60
Utilizes: Special Technical Talent; Guest Conductors; Guest Artists
Budget: $1,000 - $50,000
Income Sources: Business/Corporate Donations; Individual Donations
Season: September - May   **Annual Attendance:** 2,000

I. SHERMAN GREENE CHORALE, INC.
PO Box 1071, Norfolk, VA 23501
(804) 467-8971
Arts Area: Choral
Status: Semi-Professional
Type: Performing; Touring; Resident; Educational
Purpose: To promote and render quality performances of choral works of the great masters and music by black composers
Officers: Harry Scott, President; Lynn Briley, Vice President; Emogene Mc Artis, Secretary; Zenobia Pendleton, Treasurer; Carl Haywood, Conductor
Paid Staff: 4   **Volunteer Staff:** 14
Paid Artists: 1   **Non-Paid Artists:** 45
Utilizes: Guest Artists; Guest Directors
Budget: $1,000 - $50,000
Income Sources: Private Foundations/Grants/Endowments; Business/Corporate Donations; Box Office; Government Grants; Individual Donations
Season: October - May   **Annual Attendance:** 1,900
Affiliations: Cultural Alliance
Performance Facilities: Booker T. Washington High School Auditorium; Grace Episcopal Church

VIRGINIA OPERA
PO Box 2580, Norfolk, VA 23501
(804) 853-7567; (804) 623-1223
FAX: (804) 853-9162
Founded: 1974
Arts Area: Grand Opera
Status: Professional; Non-Profit
Type: Performing; Touring; Educational
Management: Peter Mark, General/Artistic Director; Ken Freeman, General Manager; George Glander, Production Manager; Virginia Thumm, Developing Director; Lisa Jardanhazy, Marketing Director

Paid Staff: 36   **Volunteer Staff:** 24
Paid Artists: 105   **Non-Paid Artists:** 12
Utilizes: Special Technical Talent; Guest Conductors; Guest Artists; Guest Directors
Budget: $1,000,000 - $5,000,000
Income Sources: Private Foundations/Grants/Endowments; Business/Corporate Donations; Box Office; Government
Grants; Individual Donations; Fund-raising
Season: September - April   **Annual Attendance:** 40,000
Affiliations: Cultural Arts Alliance of Greater Hampton Roads; OA; AAA

THEATRE

GENERIC THEATRE
912 West 21st Street, Norfolk, VA 23517
(804) 441-2160
> **Founded:** 1982
> **Arts Area:** Community; Theatrical Group
> **Status:** Non-Profit
> **Type:** Performing; Producing
> **Purpose:** To produce new plays; to produce adult-orientated black-box theatre at dirt-cheap prices
> **Management:** Elmwood Robinson, Technical Director; Bob Nelson, Artistic Director
> **Paid Staff:** 4   **Volunteer Staff:** 4
> **Non-Paid Artists:** 36
> **Utilizes:** Special Technical Talent; Guest Directors
> **Budget:** $50,000 - $100,000
> **Season:** September - May   **Annual Attendance:** 5,000
> **Affiliations:** City of Norfolk Parks and Recreation Department
> **Performance Facilities:** Generic Theatre

LITTLE THEATRE OF NORFOLK
801 Claremont Avenue, Norfolk, VA 23507
(804) 627-8551
> **Founded:** 1926
> **Arts Area:** Community
> **Status:** Non-Profit
> **Type:** Performing
> **Purpose:** To provide excellent amateur theatre with commercial box office attractions, giving all non-professional artists a
> chance to use their talents
> **Officers:** E.H. Strawbridge, Past President; Marguerite Burgess, Secretary; Eunice Pittman, Treasurer
> **Budget:** $1,000 - $50,000
> **Income Sources:** Box Office
> **Season:** September - June   **Annual Attendance:** 4,000
> **Performance Facilities:** Little Theatre of Norfolk

VIRGINIA STAGE COMPANY
PO Box 3770, Norfolk, VA 23514
(804) 627-6988; (804) 627-1234
FAX: (804) 628-5958
> **Founded:** 1980
> **Arts Area:** Professional; Theatrical Group
> **Status:** Professional; Non-Profit
> **Type:** Performing; Resident; Educational; Sponsoring
> **Purpose:** To serve Hampton Roads through the production of theatrical art of the highest quality; to produce plays of
> language and literacy; to reaffirm the theatre's place in the age of electronic media and choose work which is uniquely
> stage-worthy
> **Management:** Tom Gardner, Artistic Director; Kathleen Bateson-Glass, Executive Director
> **Officers:** Sidney N. Askew Jr., President, Board of Trustees; Patrick M. Barberrich, Vice President/Treasurer;
> Van Van der Meer, Vice President of Administration; Denver Hicks, Vice President of Development
> **Paid Staff:** 35   **Volunteer Staff:** 100
> **Paid Artists:** 40
> **Utilizes:** Special Technical Talent; Guest Artists; Guest Directors
> **Budget:** $1,000,000 - $5,000,000
> **Income Sources:** Private Foundations/Grants/Endowments; Business/Corporate Donations; Box Office; Government
> Grants; Individual Donations
> **Season:** October - March   **Annual Attendance:** 45,000
> **Affiliations:** LORT; TCG
> **Performance Facilities:** Wells Theatre

FACILITY

GENERIE THEATER
912 West 21st Street, Norfolk, VA 23517
(804) 441-2160
    Type of Facility: Studio Performance; Multi-Purpose
    Facility Originally: Warehouse
    Type of Stage: Flexible
    Stage Dimensions: 28'x56'
    Seating Capacity: 120
    Contact for Rental: Bob Nelson; (804) 441-2160
    Resident Groups: Generic Theatre
    The original warehouse was converted into a theatre space by the city of Norfolk in 1983.

LITTLE THEATRE OF NORFOLK
801 Claremont Avenue, Norfolk, VA 23508
(804) 627-8551
    Founded: 1926
    Type of Facility: Theatre House
    Type of Stage: Proscenium
    Seating Capacity: 224
    Year Built: 1950

NORFOLK SCOPE CULTURAL AND CONVENTION CENTER
Scope Plaza, 201 East Brambleton Avenue, Norfolk, VA 23501
(804) 441-2764
    Type of Facility: Civic Center
    Seating Capacity: 11,584
    Year Built: 1971   **Architect:** Williams, Tazewell & Associates   **Cost:** $35,000,000
    Acoustical Consultant: Bolt, Beranek and Newman
    SCOPE contains the Arena and Chrysler Hall. See separate listings for additional information.

NORFOLK SCOPE CULTURAL AND CONVENTION CENTER - ARENA
Scope Plaza, 201 East Brambleton Avenue, Norfolk, VA 23501
(804) 441-2764
    Type of Facility: Arena
    Type of Stage: Platform; Arena
    Stage Dimensions: 36'x60'x48'
    Seating Capacity: 11500
    Year Built: 1971   **Architect:** Williams, Tazewell & Associates   **Cost:** $35,000,000
    Contact for Rental: John Rhamstine, Cynthia Carter West; (804) 441-2764
    Manager: W.H. "Bill" Luther; (804) 441-2764
    Resident Groups: Hampton Roads Admirals - ECHL Hockey Team

NORFOLK SCOPE CULTURAL AND CONVENTION CENTER - CHRYSLER HALL
Scope Plaza, 201 East Brambleton Avenue, Norfolk, VA 23501
(804) 441-2764
    Founded: 1971
    Type of Facility: Theatre House
    Type of Stage: Proscenium
    Stage Dimensions: 31'x159'x43' **Orchestra Pit**
    Seating Capacity: 2,461
    Year Built: 1971
    Contact for Rental: John Ramstine, Cynthia Carter West; (804) 441-2764
    Manager: W.H. "Bill" Carter; (804) 441-2764
    Resident Groups: The Virginia Symphony

WELLS THEATRE
Monticello Avenue and Tazewell Street, Norfolk, VA 23514
(804) 627-6988
    Type of Facility: Theatre House
    Facility Originally: Vaudeville
    Type of Stage: Proscenium
    Seating Capacity: 677
    Year Built: 1913
    Year Remodeled: 1987 **Architect:** Hanbury Evans Newill & Vlattas **Cost:** $3,850,000
    Contact for Rental: Cynthia Carter; (804) 444-2764, ext. 253

Resident Groups: Virginia Stage Company
The Wells Theatre has been designated a National Historic Landmark.

Petersburg

DANCE

PETERSBURG BALLET
44 Goodwich Avenue, Petersburg, VA 23805
(804) 733-9998
Founded: 1984
Arts Area: Ballet; Jazz
Status: Semi-Professional; Non-Profit
Type: Performing; Touring; Resident
Purpose: To allow area students the opportunity to perform and dance with the company
Management: Gloria F. Dance, Artistic Director; Evelia Emiliani, President; Ann Taylor, Vice President; Donna Yeatts, Secretary; Dr. Christopher Egan, Treasurer
Non-Paid Artists: 24
Utilizes: Guest Artists
Budget: $1,000 - $50,000
Income Sources: Private Foundations/Grants/Endowments; Business/Corporate Donations; Box Office; Government Grants; Individual Donations
Season: 52 Weeks

Radford

FACILITY

RADFORD UNIVERSITY THEATRE
Norwood Street, PO Box 6969, Radford, VA 24142
(703) 831-5207
FAX: (703) 831-6313
Type of Facility: Theatre Complex; Performance Center
Type of Stage: Thrust; Proscenium
Stage Dimensions: 58'Wx30'Dx21'H   **Orchestra Pit**
Seating Capacity: 483
Year Built: 1972   **Architect:** Thompson & Payne   **Cost:** $1,000,000
Resident Groups: Radford University Theatre Department

Reston

FACILITY

RESTON COMMUNITY CENTER THEATRE
2310 Colts Neck Road, Reston, VA 22091
(703) 476-4500; (703) 476-1111
FAX: (703) 476-8617
Type of Facility: Theatre House
Type of Stage: Proscenium
Stage Dimensions: 32'Wx28'D   **Orchestra Pit**
Seating Capacity: 300
Year Built: 1979
Year Remodeled: 1986   **Architect:** Kinetic Artistry   **Cost:** $25,000
Contact for Rental: Leila H. El-Bisi;   (703) 476-4500
Resident Groups: Community organizations; regularly-scheduled children's theatre; international film series

Richmond

DANCE

THE CONCERT BALLET OF VIRGINIA
103 East Main Street, Richmond, VA 23219
(804) 780-1279; (804) 644-5991
Founded: 1976

Arts Area: Modern; Ballet; Jazz
Status: Non-Professional; Non-Profit; Commercial
Type: Performing; Touring; Educational
Purpose: To provide a regular season of classical and contemporary innovative dance programming for the Richmond area along with statewide performances for the public as well as civic, educational and social organizations
Management: Robert Watkins, Director; Scott Boyer, Associate Director; Mrs. Thomas C. Rennie, Executive Assistant; deVeaux Riddick, Technical Director
Officers: Mrs. James St. Germain, President; Pat Morris, Vice President; Jill Melichar, Public Relations
Volunteer Staff: 40
Paid Artists: 5   **Non-Paid Artists:** 15
Utilizes: Guest Conductors; Guest Artists; Guest Choreographers
Budget: $50,000 - $100,000
Income Sources: Private Foundations/Grants/Endowments; Business/Corporate Donations; Box Office; Individual Donations
Season: 52 Weeks   **Annual Attendance:** 15,000
Affiliations: Sacred Dance Guild
Performance Facilities: The Woman's Club Auditorium; Blackwell Auditorium, Randolph Macon College; Alberarle High School Auditorium; Dogwood Dell Amphitheatre

EZIBU MUNTU AFRICAN DANCE COMPANY
PO Box 62, Richmond, VA 23201
(804) 264-3965
Founded: 1973
Arts Area: Ethnic; Folk
Status: Professional
Type: Performing; Touring; Educational
Purpose: To communicate the richness of a variety of African cultures and customs through dance, rhythm, and song in an exciting, energetic and colorful manner
Management: Janine Bell, General Manager; C. Rene Taylor, Business Manager; Faye Walker, Artistic Director; Kurt Patterson, Drum Captain
Officers: Janine Bell, President; Faye Walker, Secretary; C. Rene Taylor, Treasurer
Paid Staff: 4   **Volunteer Staff:** 2
Paid Artists: 12
Utilizes: Guest Artists; Guest Directors
Budget: $1,000 - $50,000
Income Sources: Private Foundations/Grants/Endowments; Business/Corporate Donations; Individual Donations
Season: 52 Weeks
Annual Attendance: 13,000

RICHMOND BALLET - THE STATE BALLET OF VIRGINIA
614 North Lombardy Street, Richmond, VA 23220
(804) 359-0906
FAX: (804) 355-4640
Founded: 1957
Arts Area: Ballet
Status: Professional; Non-Profit
Type: Performing; Touring; Resident; Educational
Purpose: To preserve the tradition of classical ballet; to perform works of this century and to create new works
Management: Stoner Winslett, Artistic Director; Dwight Bowes, Managing Director
Paid Staff: 31   **Volunteer Staff:** 5
Paid Artists: 22
Utilizes: Guest Conductors; Guest Artists; Guest Choreographers
Budget: $1,000,000 - $5,000,000
Income Sources: Private Foundations/Grants/Endowments; Business/Corporate Donations; Box Office; Government Grants; Individual Donations
Season: November - April
Annual Attendance: 55,000
Performance Facilities: The Mosque; Carpenter Center for the Performing Arts

INSTRUMENTAL MUSIC

RICHMOND SYMPHONY
The Berkshire, 300 West Franklin Street, Richmond, VA 23220
(804) 788-4717
FAX: (804) 788-1541
Founded: 1956

Arts Area: Symphony; Orchestra; Chamber
Status: Professional; Non-Profit
Type: Performing; Touring; Educational
Management: Catherine Wichterman, Executive Director; George Manahan, Music Director/Conductor
Paid Staff: 19
Paid Artists: 90
Utilizes: Guest Conductors; Guest Artists
Budget: $1,000,000 - $5,000,000
Income Sources: Private Foundations/Grants/Endowments; Business/Corporate Donations; Box Office; Government Grants; Individual Donations; Fund-raising
Season: September - June
Annual Attendance: 140,000
Affiliations: ASOL
Performance Facilities: The Mosque; Carpenter Center for the Performing Arts; Virginia Commonwealth University Performing Arts Center

ROXBURY CHAMBER PLAYERS
6207 Dustin Drive, Richmond, VA 23226
(804) 288-5935
Arts Area: Chamber
Status: Professional; Non-Profit
Type: Performing; Touring
Purpose: To perform repertory from baroque to modern utilizing visiting composers, guest artists, lecture concerts and student concerts
Management: David Niethamer, Artistic Director
Budget: $1,000 - $50,000
Income Sources: Private Foundations/Grants/Endowments; Business/Corporate Donations; Box Office; Government Grants; Individual Donations

THEATRE

THEATRE IV
114 West Broad Street, Richmond, VA 23220
(804) 783-1688
FAX: (804) 775-2325
Founded: 1975
Arts Area: Professional; Theatrical Group
Status: Professional; Non-Profit
Type: Performing; Touring; Resident; Educational
Purpose: To create professional, exciting and innovative theatrical productions of the highest calibre
Management: Bruce C. Miller, Artistic Director; Phil Whiteway, Managing Director
Paid Staff: 16
Utilizes: Special Technical Talent; Guest Artists; Guest Directors
Budget: $1,000,000 - $5,000,000
Income Sources: Private Foundations/Grants/Endowments; Business/Corporate Donations; Box Office; Government Grants; Individual Donations
Season: October - May
Affiliations: TCG
Performance Facilities: The Empire Theatre; The Little Theatre

THEATRE VIRGINIA
2800 Grove Avenue, Richmond, VA 23221
(804) 367-0840
Founded: 1955
Arts Area: Professional
Status: Professional; Non-Profit
Type: Performing; Resident
Management: William Gregg, Artistic Director; Paul Tyler, General Manager
Paid Staff: 25   **Volunteer Staff:** 250
Paid Artists: 75
Utilizes: Special Technical Talent; Guest Artists; Guest Directors
Budget: $1,000,000 - $5,000,000
Income Sources: Private Foundations/Grants/Endowments; Business/Corporate Donations; Box Office; Government Grants; Individual Donations
Season: September - May
Annual Attendance: 90,000
Affiliations: LORT; AEA; SSDC

FACILITY

CARPENTER CENTER FOR THE PERFORMING ARTS
600 East Grace Street, Richmond, VA 23219
(804) 782-3930
FAX: (804) 649-7402
 Type of Facility: Concert Hall; Performance Center; Theatre House; Room
 Type of Stage: Proscenium
 Stage Dimensions: 46'Wx35'D
 Orchestra Pit
 Seating Capacity: 2,033
 Year Built: 1928 **Architect:** John Eberson **Cost:** $1,000,000
 Year Remodeled: 1983 **Cost:** $7,000,000
 Contact for Rental: Sue Bahen
 Resident Groups: Richmond Ballet; Richmond Symphony; Virginia Opera Association

THE EMPIRE THEATRE COMPLEX
114 West Broad Street, Richmond, VA 23220
(804) 344-8040
FAX: (804) 775-2325
 Type of Facility: Theatre Complex
 Year Built: 1911
 Contact for Rental: Phil Whiteway; (804) 783-1688
 Resident Groups: Theater IV
 The Empire Theatre Complex contains the Empire Stage and the Litte Theatre Stage. See separate listings for additional
 information.

THE EMPIRE THEATRE COMPLEX - EMPIRE STAGE
118 West Broad Street, Richmond, VA 23220
(804) 344-8040
FAX: (804) 775-2325
 Type of Facility: Theatre House
 Type of Stage: Proscenium
 Stage Dimensions: 58'Wx31'6"D
 Seating Capacity: 604
 Year Built: 1911
 Contact for Rental: Phil Whiteway; (804) 783-1688
 Resident Groups: Theater IV

THE EMPIRE THEATRE COMPLEX - LITTLE THEATRE STAGE
114 West Broad Street, Richmond, VA 23220
(804) 783-1688
FAX: (804) 775-2325
 Type of Facility: Studio Performance
 Facility Originally: Vaudeville
 Type of Stage: Proscenium
 Stage Dimensions: 25'x14'
 Orchestra Pit
 Seating Capacity: 80
 Year Built: 1911
 Year Remodeled: 1990 **Architect:** Bond, Comet, Westmoreland & Galusha
 Cost: $2,300,000
 Contact for Rental: Mr. L. Moore; (804) 344-8048
 Manager: Phil Whiteway; (804) 783-1688
 Resident Groups: Theatre IV; Gilpin Stage Company

UNIVERSITY OF RICHMOND - JAMES L. CAMP MEMORIAL THEATRE
Richmond, VA 23173
(804) 289-8263
 Type of Facility: Auditorium; Theatre House
 Type of Stage: Proscenium
 Stage Dimensions: 34'3"Wx25'H
 Orchestra Pit
 Seating Capacity: 686
 Year Built: 1967
 Resident Groups: University Players

Roanoke

INSTRUMENTAL MUSIC

ROANOKE SYMPHONY SOCIETY
PO Box 2433, Roanoke, VA 24010
(703) 343-6221
FAX: (703) 343-3954
>**Arts Area:** Symphony
>**Status:** Professional; Non-Profit
>**Type:** Performing; Touring; Educational
>**Purpose:** To perform the highest quality symphonic music for the largest possible audiences throughout the region
>**Management:** Victoria Bond, Music Director; Margarite Fourcoy, Executive Director
>**Officers:** Heidi Krisch, President
>**Budget:** $1,000,000 - $5,000,000
>**Income Sources:** Private Foundations/Grants/Endowments; Business/Corporate Donations; Box Office; Government Grants; Individual Donations
>**Performance Facilities:** Roanoke Civic Center

ROANOKE VALLEY CHAMBER MUSIC SOCIETY
PO Box 8041, Roanoke, VA 24014
(703) 774-2899
>**Founded:** 1980
>**Arts Area:** Chamber
>**Status:** Professional; Non-Profit
>**Type:** Educational; Sponsoring
>**Purpose:** To present professionally-performed chamber-music concerts; to sponsor educational functions; to create an awareness of music and especially chamber music
>**Management:** Ann-Marie W. Horner, President/Executive Director
>**Paid Staff:** 1
>**Utilizes:** Guest Artists
>**Budget:** $1,000 - $50,000
>**Income Sources:** Private Foundations/Grants/Endowments; Business/Corporate Donations; Box Office; Individual Donations
>**Season:** Fall - Spring   **Annual Attendance:** 1,500
>**Affiliations:** CMA
>**Performance Facilities:** Olin Theater, Roanoke College

VOCAL MUSIC

OPERA ROANOKE
111 West Campbell Avenue, Roanoke, VA 24011
(703) 982-2742
FAX: (703) 343-3954
>**Founded:** 1977
>**Arts Area:** Grand Opera; Light Opera; Operetta
>**Status:** Professional
>**Type:** Performing; Resident
>**Purpose:** To produce professional opera in southwestern Virginia
>**Management:** Judith Clark, Executive Director; Victoria Band, Artistic Director
>**Officers:** J. Tyler Pugh, President; Joseph Logan III, Vice President; Michael Quinn, Treasurer; Carol Danielsen, Secretary; Cynthia Dillon, Vice President Friends of the Opera
>**Paid Staff:** 5
>**Utilizes:** Guest Artists; Guest Directors
>**Budget:** $100,000 - $500,000
>**Income Sources:** Business/Corporate Donations; Box Office; Government Grants; Individual Donations
>**Season:** 52 Weeks   **Annual Attendance:** 1,600
>**Affiliations:** OA
>**Performance Facilities:** Mill Mountain Theatre; Olin Theatre

THEATRE

MILL MOUNTAIN THEATRE COMPANY
One Market Square SE, Second Floor, Roanoke, VA 24011-1437
(703) 342-5730
FAX: (703) 224-1238
>**Founded:** 1964
>**Arts Area:** Professional; Musical; Theatrical Group

Status: Professional; Non-Profit
Type: Performing; Resident; Educational
Purpose: Professional production of musicals, dramas and comedies with particular emphasis on the production and development of original works
Management: Jere Lee Hodgin, Executive/Artistic Director; James L. Ayers, Business Manager; Judy Graham, Director of Marketing/Development
Officers: Michael Warner, President; E.R. Feinour, Vice President; Robert Fishburn, Senior Vice President; Ann Hammersley, Secretary; Sandra Light, Treasurer
Paid Staff: 24 **Volunteer Staff:** 1
Paid Artists: 95 **Non-Paid Artists:** 50
Utilizes: Guest Artists; Guest Directors
Budget: $1,000,000 - $5,000,000
Income Sources: Private Foundations/Grants/Endowments; Business/Corporate Donations; Box Office; Government Grants; Individual Donations
Season: 52 Weeks **Annual Attendance:** 50,000
Affiliations: TCG; New Dramatists; SETC; Theatre Council of Virginia
Performance Facilities: Mill Mountain Theatre; Mainstage; Theatre B

FACILITY

MILL MOUNTAIN THEATRE
One Market Square, Second Floor, Roanoke, VA 24011-1437
(703) 342-5730
FAX: (703) 224-1238
　　Founded: 1964
　　Type of Facility: Theatre Complex
　　Type of Stage: Greek; Proscenium; Alternate stage - Black Box
　　Stage Dimensions: 35'Wx35'D
　　Orchestra Pit
　　Seating Capacity: Main Stage - 411; Alternate Stage - 125
　　Year Built: 1983 **Architect:** Hayes, Seay, Mattern & Mattern **Cost:** $1,400,000
　　Acoustical Consultant: Systems Design
　　Contact for Rental: Mona Black;　(703) 345-5730
　　Resident Groups: Mill Mountain Theatre Company
　　Primarily for the in-house production of live, professional theatre

ROANOKE CIVIC CENTER
710 Williamson Road, NE, Roanoke, VA 24016
(703) 981-2241
FAX: (703) 981-2748
　　Type of Facility: Theatre House; Civic Center; Arena; Multi-Purpose
　　Type of Stage: Proscenium
　　Stage Dimensions: 66'x105'x55'
　　Orchestra Pit
　　Seating Capacity: 2,475
　　Year Built: 1971 **Architect:** Associated Architects & Engineers **Cost:** $14,800,000
　　Acoustical Consultant: Bolt, Beranek & Newman
　　Contact for Rental: B.E. Chapman;　(703) 981-2241
　　Resident Groups: Roanoke Symphony Orchestra

Salem

FACILITY

SALEM CIVIC CENTER
PO Box 886, Salem, VA 24153
(703) 981-2241
　　Type of Facility: Concert Hall; Civic Center; Arena
　　Type of Stage: Flexible
　　Seating Capacity: 8,000
　　Year Built: 1967 **Architect:** Wells and Meagher
　　Contact for Rental: Manager;　(703) 375-3004

Sweet Briar

FACILITY

SWEET BRIAR COLLEGE - BABCOCK AUDITORIUM
Sweet Briar, VA 24595
(804) 381-6123
    Type of Facility: Concert Hall; Auditorium
    Type of Stage: Proscenium
    Stage Dimensions: 55'x50'x28'   **Orchestra Pit**
    Seating Capacity: 652
    Year Built: 1961   **Architect:** Clark, Nexson and Owen
    Acoustical Consultant: Harold Burris-Meyer
    Contact for Rental: Thomas N. Connors; (804) 381-6200
    Resident Groups: Student theatre and dance groups
    In addition to Babcock Auditorium, the building also contains a small, black box theatre.

Vienna

PERFORMING SERIES

WOLF TRAP FARM FOUNDATION
1624 Trap Road, Vienna, VA 22182
(703) 255-1900
    Founded: 1971
    Arts Area: Dance; Vocal Music; Instrumental Music; Theater; Lyric Opera
    Status: Professional; Non-Profit
    Type: Educational; Sponsoring
    Purpose: To expose people of all ages to every aspect of the performing arts; to increase understanding and
    appreciation of the role the performing arts has in community life
    Management: Matthew Hessburg, Director, Public Affairs and Communications; Paulann Doane,
    Director of Special Events
    Officers: Charles A. Walters Jr., Vice President/Finance Officer; Ann McPherson McKee,
    Vice President of Program and Production
    Paid Staff: 40
    Utilizes: Special Technical Talent; Guest Conductors; Guest Artists; Guest Directors
    Budget: $5,000,000 - $10,000,000
    Income Sources: Private Foundations/Grants/Endowments; Business/Corporate Donations; Box Office; Government
    Grants; Individual Donations
    Season: June - August; October - May   **Annual Attendance:** 420,000
    Performance Facilities: Filene Center; The Barns

FACILITY

WOLF TRAP FARM PARK FOR THE PERFORMING ARTS
1624 Trap Road, Vienna, VA 22180
(703) 255-1900
    Type of Facility: Outdoor Theatre
    Type of Stage: Proscenium
    Seating Capacity: 900
    Year Built: 1977   **Architect:** Thomas J. Madigan   **Cost:** $71,000
    Manager: Vistoria Rapaport; (703) 938-8463

Virginia Beach

FACILITY

VIRGINIA BEACH PAVILION CONVENTION CENTER
1000 19th Street, Virginia Beach, VA 23458
(804) 428-8000
FAX: (804) 422-8860
    Type of Facility: Civic Center; Convention Center
    Year Built: 1980   **Architect:** Walsh Ashet Dill   **Cost:** $20,000,000
    Acoustical Consultant: Coffeen & Anderson
    Contact for Rental: Bill Holland; (804) 428-8000
    The Convention Center contains the Exhibit Hall and Pavilion Theater. See separate listings for additional information.

VIRGINIA BEACH PAVILION CONVENTION CENTER - EXHIBIT HALL
1000 19th Street, Virginia Beach, VA 23458
(804) 428-8000
FAX: (804) 422-8860
    Type of Facility: Exhibition Hall
    Type of Stage: Flexible
    Year Built: 1980
    Contact for Rental: Bill Holland;   (804) 428-8000
    The Exhibit Hall contains 57,200 square feet of usable floor area.

VIRGINIA BEACH PAVILION CONVENTION CENTER - PAVILION THEATER
1000 19th Street, Virginia Beach, VA 23458
(804) 428-8000
FAX: (804) 422-8860
    Type of Facility: Concert Hall; Theatre House; Opera House
    Type of Stage: Proscenium
    Stage Dimensions: 55'Wx47'6"D; 46'7"Wx24'H proscenium opening   **Orchestra Pit**
    Seating Capacity: 1,000
    Year Built: 1980
    Contact for Rental: Bill Holland;   (804) 428-8000

Williamsburg

DANCE

THE INSTITUTE FOR DANCE, INC.
PO Box 1568, Williamsburg, VA 23187
(804) 229-1717
    Founded: 1978
    Arts Area: Ballet; Jazz; Ethnic; Folk; Tap
    Status: Non-Profit
    Type: Performing; Educational
    Purpose: To promote the art of dance
    Management: Heidi S. Robitshek, Director
    Officers: Anne Hamrick, President; Paul Kershner, Vice President; Irving H. Robitshek, Secretary/Treasurer
    Paid Staff: 7   **Volunteer Staff:** 100
    Utilizes: Special Technical Talent; Guest Artists; Guest Choreographers
    Budget: $100,000 - $500,000
    Income Sources: Business/Corporate Donations; Box Office; Government Grants; Individual Donations
    Season: 52 Weeks   **Annual Attendance:** 7,000
    Performance Facilities: Phi Beta Kappa Memorial Hall, The College of William and Mary

PERFORMING SERIES

VIRGINIA SHAKESPEARE FESTIVAL
College of William and Mary, PO Box 8795, Williamsburg, VA 23187-8795
(804) 221-2660
FAX: (804) 221-1773
    Founded: 1978
    Arts Area: Theater; Festivals
    Status: Professional; Non-Profit
    Type: Performing; Educational
    Purpose: To perform quality Shakespeare in a classical manner
    Management: Jerry H. Bledsoe, Executive Director
    Volunteer Staff: 10
    Paid Artists: 50   **Non-Paid Artists:** 20
    Utilizes: Special Technical Talent; Guest Artists; Guest Directors
    Budget: $50,000 - $100,000
    Income Sources: Private Foundations/Grants/Endowments; Business/Corporate Donations; Box Office; Government Grants; Individual Donations
    Season: July - August   **Annual Attendance:** 10,000
    Affiliations: The College of William and Mary
    Performance Facilities: Phi Beta Kappa Memorial Hall, The College of William and Mary

Woodstock

PERFORMING SERIES

SHENANDOAH VALLEY MUSIC FESTIVAL
PO Box 12, Woodstock, VA 22664
(703) 459-3396

Founded: 1963
Arts Area: Dance; Vocal Music; Instrumental Music; Festivals; Lyric Opera; Grand Opera
Status: Non-Profit
Type: Sponsoring
Purpose: To foster, promote, and increase the musical knowledge of the public by organizing and presenting programs chosen primarily from the literature of symphonic music, and incidentally from chamber music, opera, solo recitals, vocal chorus and dance; to present jazz, folk and others forms
Management: Melissa S. Deibert, Executive Director
Paid Staff: 3 **Volunteer Staff:** 50
Paid Artists: 125
Budget: $100,000 - $500,000
Income Sources: Private Foundations/Grants/Endowments; Business/Corporate Donations; Box Office; Government Grants; Individual Donations
Season: April - September **Annual Attendance:** 7,500
Affiliations: Shenandoah Arts Council
Performance Facilities: Orkney Springs Pavilion

WASHINGTON

Aberdeen

FACILITY

BISHOP CENTER FOR PERFORMING ARTS
1610 E.P. Smith Drive, Aberdeen, WA 98520
(206) 533-0177
FAX: (206) 532-6716
Founded: 1974
Type of Facility: Concert Hall; Performance Center
Type of Stage: Thrust; Proscenium
Stage Dimensions: 40'x60'   **Orchestra Pit**
Seating Capacity: 500
Year Built: 1974
Architect: Sneet & Lundgren
Cost: $1,000,000
Contact for Rental: C. Wellington;   (206) 532-9020
Resident Groups: Grays Harbor Symphony; Elks National Band; Hume Street Jazz Band

---

Bellevue

PERFORMING SERIES

BELLEVUE PARKS AND RECREATION DEPARTMENT - BELLEVUE JAZZ FESTIVAL
PO Box 90012, Bellevue, WA 98009-9012
(206) 451-4106
FAX: (206) 451-7259
Founded: 1976
Arts Area: Vocal Music; Instrumental Music; Festivals
Status: Professional; Non-Profit
Type: Performing; Sponsoring
Purpose: To present the oldest jazz festival in the Pacific Northwest featuring 100 professionals, Northwest-resident jazz musicians and vocalists performing all aspects of jazz
Management: Mick Mellor, Festival Director
Paid Staff: 2   **Volunteer Staff:** 30
Paid Artists: 100
Utilizes: Guest Artists
Budget: $1,000 - $50,000
Income Sources: Private Foundations/Grants/Endowments; Box Office; Government Grants; City of Bellevue
Season: July   **Annual Attendance:** 8,000
Affiliations: BMI
Performance Facilities: Bellevue Community College

Bellingham

FACILITY

MORCA FOUNDATION OF THE DANCE
1349 Franklin, Bellingham, WA 98225
(206) 676-1864
Type of Facility: Studio Performance
Facility Originally: Church
Type of Stage: Greek; 3/4 Arena
Stage Dimensions: 18'x20'
Seating Capacity: 65
Year Built: 1902
Year Remodeled: 1979
Contact for Rental: Ted Morca;   (206) 676-1864

Resident Groups: Morca Dance Theatre
Concerts, Lectures, Music Recitals

MOUNT BAKER THEATRE
106 North Commercial, Bellingham, WA 98225
(206) 734-6080
FAX: (206) 671-0114
Founded: 1927
Type of Facility: Performance Center; Film House
Facility Originally: Vaudeville; Movie House
Type of Stage: Proscenium
Stage Dimensions: 26'Dx42'W   **Orchestra Pit**
Seating Capacity: 1,500
Year Built: 1927
Architect: R.C. Reamer
Contact for Rental: Ruth Shaw, General Manager;   (206) 734-6080
Resident Groups: Whatcom Symphony Orchestra

WESTERN WASHINGTON UNIVERSITY - CONCERT HALL
Performing Arts Center, Bellingham, WA 98225
(206) 676-3866
FAX: (206) 676-3028
Type of Facility: Concert Hall
Type of Stage: Concert Stage
Seating Capacity: 711
Year Built: 1973
Architect: Henry Klein & Associates
Cost: $2,053,321
Acoustical Consultant: Jaffe Acoustics
Contact for Rental:
Manager: Robert Sylvester

WESTERN WASHINGTON UNIVERSITY - EXPERIMENTAL THEATER
Performing Arts Center, Bellingham, WA 98225
(206) 676-3876
Type of Facility: Performance Center
Type of Stage: Flexible
Stage Dimensions: 16'x38'x25'
Year Built: 1978   **Architect:** Henry Klein & Associates
Manager: Tom Ward

WESTERN WASHINGTON UNIVERSITY - MAIN STAGE
Performing Arts Center, Bellingham, WA 98225
(206) 676-3866
FAX: (206) 676-3028
Type of Facility: Auditorium
Facility Originally: School
Type of Stage: Proscenium
Stage Dimensions: 40'Wx35'D   **Orchestra Pit**
Seating Capacity: 1,130
Year Built: 1952   **Cost:** $1,250,000
Year Remodeled: 1973
Contact for Rental: Robert Sylvester, Dean, College of Fine and Performing Arts;   (206) 676-3866

WESTERN WASHINGTON UNIVERSITY - OLD MAIN THEATER
High Street, Bellingham, WA 98225
(206) 676-3866
Type of Facility: Auditorium
Facility Originally: Recreation Hall; Gymnasium
Type of Stage: Thrust
Stage Dimensions: 11'6"x32'x31'
Seating Capacity: 300
Year Built: 1960
Year Remodeled: 1974
Architect: Henry Klein & Associates
Contact for Rental: Robert Sylvester, Manager;   (206) 676-3866

Bremerton

DANCE

PENINSULA DANCE THEATRE
515 Chester Avenue, Bremerton, WA 98310
(206) 377-6214
Arts Area: Ballet
Status: Professional; Non-Profit
Type: Performing; Resident
Management: Lawan Morrison, Artistic Director
Paid Artists: 15
Income Sources: Box Office; Individual Donations
Performance Facilities: Win Graulund Performing Arts Center

INSTRUMENTAL MUSIC

BREMERTON SYMPHONY ASSOCIATION
PO Box 996, Bremerton, WA 98310
(206) 373-1722
Founded: 1942
Arts Area: Symphony; Orchestra; Ensemble
Status: Non-Professional; Non-Profit
Type: Performing; Resident; Educational
Purpose: To provide musical outlets for qualified performers and quality performances for interested audiences
Officers: Al Dillan, President; Fran Reh, First Vice President; Jan Cisler, Second Vice President; Stephen Chertok, Secretary; Jeffrey Smith, Treasurer
Volunteer Staff: 8
Paid Artists: 5   **Non-Paid Artists:** 60
Utilizes: Special Technical Talent; Guest Artists
Budget: $50,000 - $100,000
Income Sources: Business/Corporate Donations; Box Office; Government Grants; Individual Donations
Season: September - June   **Annual Attendance:** 5,000
Affiliations: ASOL
Performance Facilities: Sylvan Way Baptist Church

THEATRE

COMMUNITY THEATRE
599 Lebo Boulevard, Bremerton, WA 98310
(206) 373-5152
Founded: 1945
Arts Area: Musical; Community; Theatrical Group
Status: Non-Professional; Non-Profit
Type: Performing
Management: Robert Montgomery, Business Manager
Officers: Bruce Hankins, President; Betty Bell, Secretary; Robert Montgomery, Treasurer
Volunteer Staff: 10
Non-Paid Artists: 35
Utilizes: Special Technical Talent; Guest Conductors; Guest Artists; Guest Directors
Budget: $1,000 - $50,000
Income Sources: Business/Corporate Donations; Box Office; Individual Donations
Season: September - June   **Annual Attendance:** 10,000

FACILITY

COMMUNITY THEATRE
599 Lebo Boulevard, Bremerton, WA 98310
(206) 373-5152
Founded: 1947
Type of Facility: Auditorium; Theatre House
Type of Stage: Proscenium
Stage Dimensions: 65'Wx25'D, 30'Wx15'H proscenium opening   **Orchestra Pit**
Seating Capacity: 192
Year Built: 1976   **Architect:** Anderson Associates   **Cost:** $350,000
Contact for Rental: Shirley Chase, Office Manager;   (206) 373-5152
Availability limited

Centralia
FACILITY

CENTRALIA COLLEGE - CORBET THEATRE
600 West Locust, Centralia, WA 98531
(206) 723-9391
FAX: (206) 753-3404
    Type of Facility: Performance Center
    Type of Stage: Thrust; Proscenium
    Stage Dimensions: 40'x28' **Orchestra Pit**
    Seating Capacity: 170
    Year Built: 1972 **Cost:** $600,000
    Contact for Rental: Helen Lucier; (206) 736-9391, ext. 218
    Manager: Philip R. Wickstrom

Chelan
PERFORMING SERIES

LAKE CHELAN BACH FESTIVAL
PO Box 554, Chelan, WA 98816
(509) 687-3918
    Founded: 1982
    Arts Area: Vocal Music; Instrumental Music; Lyric Opera
    Status: Professional; Non-Professional; Non-Profit
    Type: Performing; Educational
    Purpose: To foster the classical arts
    Volunteer Staff: 42
    Paid Artists: 8 **Non-Paid Artists:** 40
    Utilizes: Guest Artists
    Budget: $1,000 - $50,000
    Income Sources: Private Foundations/Grants/Endowments; Business/Corporate Donations; Box Office; Individual Donations
    Season: July **Annual Attendance:** 5,000

Edmonds
DANCE

OLYMPIC BALLET THEATRE
700 Main Street, Anderson Cultural Center, Edmonds, WA 98020
(206) 774-7570
    Founded: 1981
    Arts Area: Ballet
    Status: Semi-Professional; Non-Profit
    Type: Resident
    Purpose: To create high-quality dance; to provide training and performance opportunities for pre-professional dancers
    Management: John and Helena Wilkins, Artistic Directors
    Officers: Dave Railsback
    Paid Staff: 12
    Non-Paid Artists: 21
    Utilizes: Special Technical Talent; Guest Artists
    Budget: $50,000 - $100,000
    Income Sources: Private Foundations/Grants/Endowments; Business/Corporate Donations; Box Office; Government Grants; Individual Donations
    Season: September - June
    Affiliations: PRBA
    Performance Facilities: Puget Sound Theatre

INSTRUMENTAL MUSIC

CASCADE SYMPHONY ORCHESTRA
PO Box 550, Edmonds, WA 98026
(206) 778-4737
    Founded: 1962
    Arts Area: Symphony; Orchestra; Chamber; Ensemble

Status: Semi-Professional; Non-Professional
Type: Performing; Resident; Sponsoring
Purpose: To perform symphonic literature ranging from baroque to contemporary
Management: Ropen Shakarian, Conductor
Officers: David Earling, President; Philip Elvrum, Vice President; Alice Dawson, Recording Secretary; Judith Bogataj, Corresponding Secretary; Gail Hankinson, Treasurer
Paid Staff: 1 **Volunteer Staff:** 19
Utilizes: Guest Conductors; Guest Artists
Budget: $1,000 - $50,000
Income Sources: Private Foundations/Grants/Endowments; Business/Corporate Donations; Box Office; Individual Donations
Season: October - April **Annual Attendance:** 3,000
Affiliations: ASOL; BMI; ASCAP; AFM
Performance Facilities: Puget Sound Christian College

Everett

FACILITY

EVERETT CIVIC AUDITORIUM
2415 Colby Avenue, Everett, WA 98201
(206) 339-4298
Type of Facility: Auditorium
Type of Stage: Thrust
Stage Dimensions: 50'Wx58'D **Orchestra Pit**
Seating Capacity: 1,565; 1,506 with orchestra pit
Year Built: 1939 **Architect:** Earl W. Morrison
Year Remodeled: 1979 **Architect:** Bryant Butterfield & Frets **Cost:** $1,300,000
Acoustical Consultant: Towne Richards and Chaudibre
Contact for Rental: Nola Deierling; (206) 339-4280
Manager: W.D. Williamson, Technical Manager; (206) 339-4280

Fort Lewis

PERFORMING SERIES

ENTERTAINMENT BRANCH, CRD
Building 2410, Fort Lewis, WA 98433
(206) 967-3044
Founded: 1950
Arts Area: Dance; Vocal Music; Instrumental Music; Theater
Status: Semi-Professional; Non-Profit
Type: Performing; Educational
Purpose: To provide diverse and comprehensive performing arts-related activities for the soldier, his family, the Fort Lewis community and for interested individuals in the surrounding civilian community
Management: Howard A. Hoadley, Entertainment Director; William C. Strock, David V. Wright, Theatre Specialists; Leona M. Hay, Administrative Assistant
Paid Staff: 4 **Volunteer Staff:** 12
Utilizes: Special Technical Talent; Guest Artists; Guest Directors
Income Sources: Box Office; Government Grants
Season: October - June **Annual Attendance:** 5,000
Performance Facilities: Chinook Center for the Performing Arts

FACILITY

CENTURION PLAYHOUSE
Building 5300, Music & Theatre Branch, Fort Lewis, WA 98433
(206) 968-3402
Type of Facility: Theatre House
Type of Stage: Flexible
Stage Dimensions: 60'x100' **Orchestra Pit**
Seating Capacity: 200

THE CHINOOK THEATRE FOR THE PERFORMING ARTS
F Street, Fort Lewis, WA 98433-5000
(206) 967-5636
Type of Facility: Performance Center; Theatre House

Facility Originally: Recreation Hall; Gymnasium
Type of Stage: Thrust; Proscenium
Stage Dimensions: 36'x17'6"x28'; 36'W proscenium opening   **Orchestra Pit**
Seating Capacity: 100
Year Built: 1940
Year Remodeled: 1977
Contact for Rental: Howard Hoadley;   (206) 967-3044

Friday Harbor

THEATRE

SAN JUAN COMMUNITY THEATRE AND ARTS CENTER
100 Second Street, Friday Harbor, WA 98250
(206) 378-3210
Founded: 1989
Arts Area: Community
Status: Non-Professional; Non-Profit
Type: Performing; Educational; Sponsoring
Purpose: To maintain a center for performing and visual arts for the island community
Management: Douglas Scott, Executive Director
Officers: Shirley Neilson, President of the Board
Paid Staff: 3   **Volunteer Staff:** 70
Income Sources: Box Office; Individual Donations
Season: 52 Weeks   **Annual Attendance:** 16,000

Gig Harbor

THEATRE

THE PERFORMANCE CIRCLE
6615 38th Avenue NW, Gig Harbor, WA 98335
(206) 851-7529
Founded: 1976
Arts Area: Musical; Theatrical Group
Status: Semi-Professional; Non-Profit
Type: Performing; Touring; Educational
Purpose: To promote theatre arts and cultural enrichment through performances as well as educational workshops and classes
Management: Kathleen L. McGilliard, Artistic Director/Founder; Shirley M. Coffin, Managing Director; Milt Boyd, Technical Director
Officers: Jill Johnson, President; Kris Quinn, Vice President; Ruth Peacock, Treasurer; Melinda Wilson, Secretary; John O'Melveny, Immediate Past President
Paid Staff: 3   **Volunteer Staff:** 50
Utilizes: Special Technical Talent; Guest Artists; Guest Directors
Budget: $100,000 - $500,000
Income Sources: Private Foundations/Grants/Endowments; Business/Corporate Donations; Box Office; Individual Donations
Season: 52 Weeks

Hoquiam

FACILITY

7TH STREET THEATRE
313 Seventh Street, Hoquiam, WA 98550
(206) 532-0302; (206) 532-6058
Founded: 1928
Type of Facility: Auditorium; Theatre House
Facility Originally: Vaudeville; Movie House
Type of Stage: Proscenium   **Orchestra Pit**
Seating Capacity: 1,106
Year Built: 1928   **Cost:** $175,000
Year Remodeled: 1992   **Architect:** Andring and Gozart   **Cost:** $2,000,000
Contact for Rental: Patricia C. Stevenson;   (206) 532-6058

Longview

THEATRE

COLUMBIA THEATRE FOR THE PERFORMING ARTS
1231 Vandercook Way, Longview, WA 98632
(206) 423-1011
>**Arts Area:** Musical; Community; Theatrical Group
Status: Non-Profit
Type: Performing; Sponsoring
Purpose: Facility is used by a variety of groups to present and produce events
Management: James Murphy, General Manager
Paid Staff: 2   **Volunteer Staff:** 6
Budget: $100,000 - $500,000
Income Sources: Private Foundations/Grants/Endowments; Business/Corporate Donations; Box Office; Government Grants; Individual Donations
Season: September - July   **Annual Attendance:** 30,000

FACILITY

MCCLELLAND ARTS CENTER
951 Delaware, Longview, WA 98632
(206) 577-3356
>**Founded:** 1974
Type of Facility: Theatre Complex; Concert Hall; Auditorium; Outdoor (Concert); Multi-Purpose
Type of Stage: Flexible
Seating Capacity: 515
Year Built: 1974   **Architect:** Robert and Shaw   **Cost:** $200,000
Contact for Rental: Phyllis L. Sayles;   (206) 577-3356

Lynnwood

DANCE

ANACRUSIS MODERN TAP DANCE
c/o The FAME Agency, 19003 52nd Avenue West, Lynnwood, WA 98036
(206) 670-3890
FAX: (206) 670-3890
>**Founded:** 1986
Arts Area: Tap
Status: Professional; Non-Profit
Type: Performing; Touring; Educational
Purpose: To create tap dance that is strikingly visual, in which movement in space and percussive footwork are equal partners
Management: Thomas M. Ries, Owner, The FAME Agency
Officers: Cheryl Johnson, Anthony Peters, Artistic Directors
Paid Staff: 1
Paid Artists: 6   **Non-Paid Artists:** 2
Utilizes: Special Technical Talent; Guest Artists; Guest Choreographers
Budget: $50,000 - $100,000
Income Sources: Private Foundations/Grants/Endowments; Business/Corporate Donations; Box Office; Government Grants; Individual Donations
Season: September - June
Affiliations: National Tap Dance Association

Mt. Vernon

FACILITY

LINCOLN THEATRE CENTRE
712 South First Street, Mt. Vernon, WA 98273
(206) 336-2858
FAX: (206) 336-2929
>**Founded:** 1987
Type of Facility: Concert Hall; Auditorium; Performance Center; Theatre House
Facility Originally: Vaudeville; Movie House
Type of Stage: Flexible; Proscenium; Platform

Stage Dimensions: Main - 13'x24'; Platform - 16'x20'   **Orchestra Pit**
Year Built: 1926   **Cost:** $2,000,000

Oak Harbor

FACILITY

WHIDBEY PLAYHOUSE
1094 Midway Boulevard, Oak Harbor, WA 98277
(206) 679-2237
> **Founded:** 1966
> **Type of Facility:** Theatre House
> **Facility Originally:** Church
> **Type of Stage:** Proscenium
> **Stage Dimensions:** 15'x40'
> **Seating Capacity:** 138

Olympia

INSTRUMENTAL MUSIC

OLYMPIA SYMPHONY ORCHESTRA
PO Box 7635, Olympia, WA 98507
(206) 753-0074
> **Founded:** 1970
> **Arts Area:** Symphony; Orchestra
> **Status:** Professional; Non-Profit
> **Type:** Performing; Educational
> **Purpose:** To encourage the growth and development of the symphony orchestra and maintain the orchestra; to promote musical and cultural entertainment in diverse forms; to provide the musicians of Thurston County and its surrounding areas with the opportunity to play in a symphony
> **Management:** Cynthia Morrison, General Manager; Ian Edlund, Music Director/Conductor
> **Paid Staff:** 1
> **Paid Artists:** 80
> **Budget:** $50,000 - $100,000
> **Income Sources:** Private Foundations/Grants/Endowments; Business/Corporate Donations; Box Office; Government Grants; Individual Donations
> **Season:** October - March   **Annual Attendance:** 3,500
> **Affiliations:** ASOL
> **Performance Facilities:** Washington Center for the Performing Arts

FACILITY

WASHINGTON CENTER FOR THE PERFORMING ARTS
512 Washington Street SE, Olympia, WA 98501
(206) 753-8585
FAX: (206) 754-1177
> **Founded:** 1985
> **Type of Facility:** Performance Center
> **Facility Originally:** Movie House
> **Type of Stage:** Proscenium; Black Box
> **Stage Dimensions:** Black Box - 54'x48'; 45'Wx35'6"Hx35'1"D proscenium opening   **Orchestra Pit**
> **Seating Capacity:** Proscenium - 982; Black Box - 125
> **Year Built:** 1924
> **Year Remodeled:** 1985   **Cost:** $5,000,000
> **Contact for Rental:** Ruth Palmerlee, Operations Manager;   (206) 753-8585

Richland

INSTRUMENTAL MUSIC

MID-COLUMBIA SYMPHONY
PO Box 65, Richland, WA 99352
(509) 735-7356
> **Founded:** 1945
> **Arts Area:** Symphony; Orchestra

Status: Non-Professional; Non-Profit
Type: Performing; Resident; Educational
Purpose: To promote music education, interest and appreciation through the presentation of concerts, lectures, and other activities
Officers: Richard Romanelli, President; Kathy Dempsey, Vice President; Jim O'Brien, Secretary; Sid Gire, Treasurer
Paid Staff: 6   **Volunteer Staff:** 2
Paid Artists: 5
Utilizes: Guest Artists
Budget: $100,000 - $500,000
Income Sources: Private Foundations/Grants/Endowments; Business/Corporate Donations; Box Office; Individual Donations
Season: October - May   **Annual Attendance:** 5,000
Affiliations: ASOL
Performance Facilities: Richland High School Auditorium

Seattle

DANCE

CO-MOTION DANCE
PO Box 20025, Seattle, WA 98102
(206) 382-0626
> **Founded:** 1979
> **Arts Area:** Modern
> **Status:** Professional; Non-Profit
> **Type:** Performing; Touring; Educational; Sponsoring
> **Purpose:** To develop a diverse and informed audience for professional modern dance
> **Management:** Jane Hyde Walsh, Executive Director
> **Officers:** Paula Swenson, President; Jesse Jaramillo, Vice President; Barron Aoyama, Treasurer; Mary Lou McCollum, Secretary
> **Paid Staff:** 1   **Volunteer Staff:** 2
> **Paid Artists:** 12
> **Utilizes:** Special Technical Talent; Guest Artists; Guest Choreographers
> **Budget:** $50,000 - $100,000
> **Income Sources:** Private Foundations/Grants/Endowments; Business/Corporate Donations; Box Office; Government Grants; Individual Donations
> **Season:** July - March   **Annual Attendance:** 35,000

FILIPINIANA ARTS AND CULTURAL CENTER
569 North 166th Street, Seattle, WA 98133
(206) 542-7245
> **Founded:** 1970
> **Arts Area:** Ethnic
> **Status:** Semi-Professional; Non-Profit
> **Type:** Performing; Touring; Resident; Educational; Sponsoring
> **Purpose:** To preserve, promote and enhance the Filipino people's cultural heritage
> **Management:** Roger Del Rosario, Director
> **Officers:** Roger Del Rosario, President; Mencho Santos, Vice President; Marilyn Sanchez, Secretary/Treasurer; John Urrotia, Auditor
> **Utilizes:** Special Technical Talent; Guest Artists; Guest Choreographers
> **Budget:** $1,000 - $50,000
> **Income Sources:** Private Foundations/Grants/Endowments; Business/Corporate Donations; Box Office; Government Grants; Individual Donations
> **Season:** 52 Weeks
> **Annual Attendance:** 5,000

MEANY HALL FOR THE PERFORMING ARTS
University of Washington, AB-10, Seattle, WA 98195
(206) 543-4882
FAX: (206) 685-2759
> **Arts Area:** Modern; Mime; Ballet; Jazz; Ethnic
> **Status:** Non-Profit
> **Type:** Sponsoring; Presenting
> **Management:** Matthew Krashan, Director; Deborah Fishler, Director of Business and Finance; John Idstrom, Director of Development; Jan Steadman, Director of Marketing and Public Relations
> **Officers:** Robert Frayn Jr., Board Chair; John Nesholm, Vice Chair; Jo Allen Patton, Secretary/Treasurer; Frances J. Carr; Professor Ernest Henley

Paid Staff: 15
Utilizes: Guest Conductors; Guest Artists; Guest Directors; Guest Choreographers
Budget: $1,000,000 - $5,000,000
Income Sources: Private Foundations/Grants/Endowments; Business/Corporate Donations; Box Office; Government Grants; Individual Donations
Season: 52 Weeks **Annual Attendance:** 130,000
Affiliations: University of Washington
Performance Facilities: Meany Hall

NEW PERFORMANCE SERIES/NORTHWEST NEW WORKS
c/o On the Boards, 153 14th Avenue, Seattle, WA 98122
(206) 325-7901
FAX: (206) 325-7903
Arts Area: Modern
Status: Professional; Non-Profit
Type: Commissioning; Presenting
Purpose: To intoduce audiences and artists to a wide variety of performances from around the world; to support the development of contemporary artists in the Northwest
Management: Mark Murphy, Programming Director; Andrea Wagner, Managing Director
Budget: $100,000 - $500,000
Income Sources: Private Foundations/Grants/Endowments; Business/Corporate Donations; Box Office; Government Grants; Individual Donations
Affiliations: Washington Hall Performance Gallery

OCHEAMI
PO Box 31635, Seattle, WA 98103-1635
(206) 329-8876
Founded: 1978
Arts Area: Ethnic
Status: Professional; Non-Profit
Type: Performing; Touring; Educational
Purpose: To promote cultural enrichment in the form of traditional African music and dance
Management: Kofi Anang, Artistic Director; Cecilia Anang, Manager
Paid Staff: 2 **Volunteer Staff:** 4
Paid Artists: 4
Utilizes: Guest Artists; Guest Choreographers
Budget: $1,000 - $50,000
Income Sources: Private Foundations/Grants/Endowments; Business/Corporate Donations; Box Office; Government Grants; Individual Donations
Season: 52 Weeks

PACIFIC NORTHWEST BALLET
4649 Sunnyside Avenue North, Seattle, WA 98103
(206) 547-5900
Founded: 1972
Arts Area: Ballet
Status: Professional; Non-Profit
Type: Performing; Touring; Resident
Purpose: To maintain a professional ballet company and school
Management: Kent Stowell, Francia Russell, Artistic Directors
Officers: Arthur Jacobus, President/Chief Executive Officer; Susan Brotman, Chairperson
Paid Staff: 300 **Volunteer Staff:** 200
Paid Artists: 81
Utilizes: Special Technical Talent; Guest Choreographers
Budget: $5,000,000 - $10,000,000
Income Sources: Private Foundations/Grants/Endowments; Business/Corporate Donations; Box Office; Government Grants; Individual Donations
Season: October - June **Annual Attendance:** 200,000
Affiliations: Dance USA; AAA; Washington State Arts Alliance
Performance Facilities: Seattle Center Opera House

RADOST FOLK EMSEMBLE
PO Box 31295, Seattle, WA 98103
Founded: 1975
Arts Area: Ethnic
Status: Semi-Professional; Non-Profit
Type: Performing; Touring; Educational; Sponsoring
Purpose: To present and preserve the ethnic dance and music of Eastern Europe and America
Management: Glenn Nielsen, Artistic Director; Karen Powell, Producing Director; Scott Nagel, General Manager

Officers: Karen Powell; Mario Isely; Jill Lole; Scott Nagel; Glenn Nielsen; Jill Johnson
Paid Staff: 1 **Volunteer Staff:** 4
Utilizes: Special Technical Talent; Guest Artists; Guest Choreographers
Budget: $50,000 - $100,000
Income Sources: Private Foundations/Grants/Endowments; Business/Corporate Donations; Box Office; Government Grants; Individual Donations
Season: October - July **Annual Attendance:** 30,000

WORLD DANCE SERIES
c/o University of Washington, AB-10, Seattle, WA 98195
(206) 543-4880
FAX: (206) 685-2759
Arts Area: Modern; Ballet; Jazz; Ethnic
Status: Professional; Non-Profit
Type: Performing; Touring; Educational
Purpose: To bring world-class performers to the Seattle community via the University of Washington
Management: Matt Krashan, Director; Jan Steadman, Director of Marketing and Public Relations
Budget: $100,000 - $500,000
Income Sources: Private Foundations/Grants/Endowments; Business/Corporate Donations; Box Office; Government Grants; Individual Donations
Performance Facilities: Meany Theater

INSTRUMENTAL MUSIC

EARLY MUSIC GUILD OF SEATTLE
1605 12th Avenue, Suite 19, Seattle, WA 98122
(206) 325-7066
Founded: 1977
Arts Area: Chamber; Early Music
Status: Professional; Non-Profit
Type: Educational; Sponsoring
Purpose: To present an international series of six concerts by touring ensembles each year
Management: Maria Caldwell, Executive Director
Paid Staff: 1 **Volunteer Staff:** 2
Utilizes: Guest Artists
Budget: $100,000 - $500,000
Income Sources: Private Foundations/Grants/Endowments; Business/Corporate Donations; Box Office; Government Grants; Individual Donations
Season: October - May **Annual Attendance:** 5,000

NORTHWEST CHAMBER ORCHESTRA
1305 Fourth Avenue, #522, Seattle, WA 98101
(206) 343-0445
Founded: 1973
Arts Area: Orchestra; Chamber
Status: Professional; Non-Profit
Type: Performing; Touring; Resident; Educational
Purpose: To bring chamber repertoire to our community and provide employment opportunities for professional musicians; to present educational programs through young people's concerts and workshops
Management: Sandra Schwab, Managing Director; Sidney Harth, Principal Director
Officers: Jeannette Privat, President; Corinne Campbell, Vice President; Phillip LeDuc, Vice President; Kathryn Battuello, Secretary; Pamela Hughes, Treasurer
Paid Staff: 4 **Volunteer Staff:** 20
Paid Artists: 15
Utilizes: Guest Conductors; Guest Artists
Budget: $100,000 - $500,000
Income Sources: Private Foundations/Grants/Endowments; Business/Corporate Donations; Box Office; Government Grants; Individual Donations
Season: September - May **Annual Attendance:** 8,000
Affiliations: AFM
Performance Facilities: Kane Hall, University of Washington

PHILADELPHIA STRING QUARTET
PO Box 45776, Seattle, WA 98145
(206) 527-8839
Founded: 1960
Arts Area: Chamber
Status: Professional; Non-Profit
Type: Performing; Touring; Educational; Sponsoring

Purpose: To perform string quartets; to produce the Olympic Music Festival
Management: Alan Iglitzin, Executive Director
Paid Staff: 3   **Volunteer Staff:** 60
Paid Artists: 4
Utilizes: Guest Artists
Budget: $100,000 - $500,000
Income Sources: Private Foundations/Grants/Endowments; Business/Corporate Donations; Box Office; Government Grants; Individual Donations
Season: 52 Weeks   **Annual Attendance:** 25,000

PUGET SOUND CHAMBER MUSIC SOCIETY
93 Pike Street, #315, Seattle, WA 98101
(206) 622-1393
Arts Area: Chamber
Status: Non-Profit
Type: Presenting
Purpose: To present a chamber music festival of the highest quality
Management: Kyle Siebrecht, Executive Director
Officers: Stuart Rolfe, President of the Board
Budget: $100,000 - $500,000
Income Sources: Private Foundations/Grants/Endowments; Business/Corporate Donations; Box Office; Government Grants; Individual Donations

SEATTLE CHAMBER MUSIC FESTIVAL
2618 Eastlake Avenue East, Seattle, WA 98102
(206) 328-5606
Founded: 1982
Arts Area: Chamber
Status: Professional; Non-Profit
Type: Performing
Purpose: To present twelve chamber-music concerts of the highest artistry during a four-week summer series
Management: Toby Saks, Artistic Director; Cheryl Swab, Executive Director
Officers: Alan Morgan, President; Bill Cohn, Ruth Gerberding, Vice Presidents; Helen Gurvich, Secretary; Bill Cobb, Treasurer
Paid Staff: 4   **Volunteer Staff:** 50
Paid Artists: 31
Utilizes: Guest Artists
Budget: $100,000 - $500,000
Income Sources: Private Foundations/Grants/Endowments; Business/Corporate Donations; Box Office; Government Grants; Individual Donations
Season: June - July   **Annual Attendance:** 4,800
Performance Facilities: Lakeside School; Saint Nicholas Hall

SEATTLE SYMPHONY ORCHESTRA
305 Harrison Street, Seattle, WA 98109
(206) 443-4740
Founded: 1903
Arts Area: Symphony; Orchestra; Chamber; Ensemble; Instrumental Group
Status: Professional; Non-Profit
Type: Performing; Resident; Educational
Purpose: To present classical music concerts and special events throughout the Puget Sound region for people of all ages
Management: Gerard Schwarz, Music Director/Conductor
Officers: Ron Woodard, Chairman of the Board; Mary Ann Champion, President
Paid Staff: 34   **Volunteer Staff:** 5
Paid Artists: 84
Utilizes: Special Technical Talent; Guest Conductors; Guest Artists
Budget: $5,000,000 - $10,000,000
Income Sources: Private Foundations/Grants/Endowments; Business/Corporate Donations; Box Office; Government Grants; Individual Donations
Season: September - July   **Annual Attendance:** 180,000
Affiliations: ASOL; Corporate Council for the Arts
Performance Facilities: Seattle Center Opera House; Moore Theatre

SEATTLE YOUTH SYMPHONY ORCHESTRA
11065 Fifth NE, Suite E, Seattle, WA 98125
(206) 362-2300
Founded: 1942
Arts Area: Symphony; Orchestra
Status: Non-Profit

Type: Performing; Educational
Purpose: To perform and promote an appreciation of good music
Management: Ruben Gurevich, Conductor/Musical Director; Davis B. Fox, Executive Director
Officers: Joyce Brewster, President
Paid Staff: 20
Paid Artists: 3
Utilizes: Guest Artists
Budget: $100,000 - $500,000
Income Sources: Private Foundations/Grants/Endowments; Business/Corporate Donations; Box Office; Government Grants; Individual Donations
Season: September - May   **Annual Attendance:** 6,700
Affiliations: ASCAP; BMI
Performance Facilities: Seattle Center Opera House

VOCAL MUSIC

CIVIC LIGHT OPERA
PO Box 75672, Northgate Station, Seattle, WA 98125
(206) 363-2809
Founded: 1978
Arts Area: Light Opera; Musical Theatre
Status: Semi-Professional; Non-Profit
Type: Performing; Resident
Purpose: To introduce the community to musical productions; to give actors, directors, and other artists practical experience and exposure
Management: Susan Jensen, Publicity; Elma Badten, Finance
Officers: Julia Quinton, President; Wadad Saba, Vice President; Stella Warnick, Secretary; Alma Badten, Treasurer
Paid Staff: 2   **Volunteer Staff:** 50
Utilizes: Guest Conductors; Guest Artists; Guest Directors
Budget: $100,000 - $500,000
Income Sources: Box Office; Individual Donations
Season: October - June   **Annual Attendance:** 14,000
Performance Facilities: Jane Addams Auditorium

ORCHESTRA SEATTLE/SEATTLE CHAMBER SINGERS
1305 Fourth Avenue, Suite 402, Seattle, WA 98101
(206) 682-5208
Founded: 1969
Arts Area: Choral; Folk; Baroque Opera; Symphonic Works
Status: Semi-Professional; Non-Profit
Type: Performing; Resident
Purpose: To enrich the quality of life in the Pacific Northwest by musical performance; to introduce audiences to rarely-heard works and to perform new works by Northwest composers
Management: Daniel Peterson, Managing Director; Ron Haight, Production Manager; George Shangrow, Music Director
Officers: Paula Rimmer, President; Dennis Purvine, Treasurer
Paid Staff: 8   **Volunteer Staff:** 3
Paid Artists: 80   **Non-Paid Artists:** 120
Utilizes: Special Technical Talent; Guest Conductors; Guest Artists; Guest Directors
Budget: $100,000 - $500,000
Income Sources: Private Foundations/Grants/Endowments; Business/Corporate Donations; Box Office; Government Grants; Individual Donations
Season: August - May   **Annual Attendance:** 8,000
Affiliations: KING-FM; Western Pianos; University Unitarian Church
Performance Facilities: University Unitarian Church; Kane and Meany Halls, University of Washington

SEATTLE MEN'S CHORUS
PO Box 20146, Seattle, WA 98102
(206) 323-0750
FAX: (206) 323-9425
Founded: 1979
Arts Area: Choral
Status: Non-Professional; Non-Profit
Type: Performing; Touring
Management: Dennis Coleman, Conductor; Debra Berend, Executive Director
Officers: John Rochford, President
Paid Staff: 8   **Volunteer Staff:** 7
Non-Paid Artists: 125
Utilizes: Guest Artists

Budget: $500,000 - $1,000,000
Income Sources: Private Foundations/Grants/Endowments; Business/Corporate Donations; Box Office; Government Grants; Individual Donations
Season: September - June **Annual Attendance:** 12,000
Performance Facilities: Meany Hall, University of Washington; Seattle Opera House

SEATTLE OPERA ASSOCIATION
1020 John Street, Seattle, WA 98109
(206) 389-7600
FAX: (206) 389-7651
Founded: 1964
Arts Area: Grand Opera
Status: Non-Profit
Type: Performing; Educational
Purpose: To promote and present grand opera
Management: Speight Jenkins, General Director; Gary Tribble, Finance Director; Kathy Magiera, Administrative Director; Melanie Ross, Production Director; Linda Prather, Marketing Director
Officers: Richard S. Twiss, President; Beverly Brazeau, Assistant President; Sylvia Black, Secretary; Jack Irwin, Treasurer; Lawrence W. Clarkson, Chairman
Paid Staff: 75 **Volunteer Staff:** 150
Paid Artists: 300
Utilizes: Special Technical Talent; Guest Conductors; Guest Artists; Guest Directors
Budget: Over 10,000,000
Income Sources: Private Foundations/Grants/Endowments; Business/Corporate Donations; Box Office; Government Grants; Individual Donations
Season: 52 Weeks **Annual Attendance:** 100,000
Affiliations: OA
Performance Facilities: Seattle Opera House

THEATRE

ALICE B THEATRE
1100 East Pike, Third Floor, Seattle, WA 98122
(206) 322-5742
Arts Area: Professional
Status: Professional; Non-Profit
Type: Performing; Touring; Educational
Purpose: To present professional-quality theatrical and cultural events that are racially and culturally diverse and have gender parity; to offer the productions in a spirit of creativity, integrity, social responsiblity, adventure and excellence
Management: Christopher, Managing Director; Susan Finque, Rick Ranklin, Artistic Directors
Officers: Mark Miller, President of the Board
Budget: $100,000 - $500,000
Income Sources: Private Foundations/Grants/Endowments; Business/Corporate Donations; Box Office; Government Grants; Individual Donations
Performance Facilities: Pioneer Square Theater; Broadway Performance Hall; Theater Off Jackson

BATHHOUSE THEATRE
7312 West Greenlake Drive North, Seattle, WA 98103
(206) 524-3608
FAX: (206) 527-1942
Founded: 1970
Arts Area: Professional; Theatrical Group
Status: Professional; Non-Profit
Type: Performing; Touring; Resident
Purpose: To develop the full potential of a permanent resident theatre company; to make excellent theatre accessible to the broadest possible public
Management: Arne Zaslove, Artistic Director; Steven Lerian, Managing Director
Officers: Kathleen Southwick, Board President; Donald W. Rowe, Vice President; Joy Jackson, Secretary; Bob Kaplan, Treasurer
Paid Staff: 16
Paid Artists: 30
Utilizes: Guest Directors
Budget: $1,000,000 - $5,000,000
Income Sources: Private Foundations/Grants/Endowments; Business/Corporate Donations; Box Office; Government Grants; Individual Donations
Season: January - December **Annual Attendance:** 74,000
Affiliations: TCG; AEA; SPTA
Performance Facilities: Bathhouse Theatre

A CONTEMPORARY THEATRE
100 West Roy Street, Seattle, WA 98119
(206) 285-3220
> **Founded:** 1965
> **Arts Area:** Theatrical Group
> **Status:** Professional; Non-Profit
> **Type:** Resident
> **Purpose:** To present the best contemporary theater and the most important plays
> **Management:** Jeff Steitzer, Artistic Director; Susan Trapnell Moritz, Managing Director; Philip G. Schermer, Producing Manager; Gregory A. Falls, Founding Director; Barry Allar, Public Relations Director
> **Officers:** Douglass E. Norberg, President Board of Directors
> **Paid Staff:** 30
> **Utilizes:** Special Technical Talent; Guest Artists; Guest Directors
> **Budget:** $1,000,000 - $5,000,000
> **Income Sources:** Private Foundations/Grants/Endowments; Business/Corporate Donations; Box Office; Government Grants; Individual Donations
> **Season:** May - January   **Annual Attendance:** 100,000
> **Affiliations:** AEA; LORT; AAA; Washington State Arts Alliance
> **Performance Facilities:** A Contemporary Theatre

THE EMPTY SPACE THEATRE
PO Box 1748, Seattle, WA 98111-1748
(206) 587-3737
> **Founded:** 1970
> **Arts Area:** Professional; Musical; Theatrical Group
> **Status:** Professional; Non-Profit
> **Type:** Performing; Resident; Educational
> **Management:** Kurt Beattie, Artistic Director; Melissa Hines, Managing Director
> **Paid Staff:** 20
> **Utilizes:** Special Technical Talent; Guest Artists; Guest Directors
> **Income Sources:** Business/Corporate Donations; Box Office; Individual Donations
> **Season:** September - May
> **Affiliations:** AEA
> **Performance Facilities:** Empty Space Theatre

THE GROUP THEATRE COMPANY
3940 Brooklyn Avenue NE, Seattle, WA 98105
(206) 545-4969
> **Founded:** 1978
> **Arts Area:** Professional; Musical; Theatrical Group
> **Status:** Professional; Non-Profit
> **Type:** Performing; Touring
> **Management:** Ruben Sierra, Founding Artistic Director; Tim Bond, Artistic Director; Paul O'Connell, Producing Director
> **Paid Staff:** 14
> **Paid Artists:** 150
> **Utilizes:** Guest Artists; Guest Directors
> **Budget:** $500,000 - $1,000,000
> **Income Sources:** Private Foundations/Grants/Endowments; Business/Corporate Donations; Box Office; Government Grants; Individual Donations
> **Season:** September - July   **Annual Attendance:** 45,000
> **Affiliations:** TCG; AEA
> **Performance Facilities:** The Ethnic Theatre

INTIMAN THEATRE COMPANY
PO Box 19760, Seattle, WA 98109
(206) 626-0775
FAX: (206) 626-0778
> **Arts Area:** Theatrical Group
> **Season:** 52 Weeks

THE NEW CITY THEATER
1634 11th Avenue, Seattle, WA 98122
(206) 323-6801
FAX: (206) 328-4683
> **Founded:** 1982
> **Arts Area:** Professional; Theatrical Group
> **Status:** Professional; Non-Profit
> **Type:** Performing; Resident

Purpose: Dedicated to research and development in the contemporary arts
Management: John Kazanjian, Artistic Director; Alan Horton, Theater Manager
Paid Staff: 3   **Volunteer Staff:** 6
Paid Artists: 85
Utilizes: Guest Directors
Budget: $100,000 - $500,000
Income Sources: Private Foundations/Grants/Endowments; Business/Corporate Donations; Box Office; Government Grants; Individual Donations
Season: September - May
Affiliations: TCG
Performance Facilities: The New City Theatre

NW PUPPET CENTER
6615 Dayton Avenue North, Seattle, WA 98103
(206) 782-3955
FAX: (206) 783-0851
Founded: 1985
Arts Area: Puppet
Status: Professional; Non-Profit
Type: Performing; Touring; Resident; Educational; Sponsoring
Purpose: To present and produce quality professional puppet theatre
Management: Stephen Carter, Chris Carter, Executive Co-Directors
Officers: Barbara Sand, Joan Weiss, Board Co-Chairs; Iris Okimoto-Nielson, Secretary; Jim Thwing, Treasurer
Paid Staff: 5   **Volunteer Staff:** 65
Paid Artists: 15   **Non-Paid Artists:** 2
Utilizes: Guest Artists
Budget: $100,000 - $500,000
Income Sources: Private Foundations/Grants/Endowments; Business/Corporate Donations; Box Office; Government Grants; Individual Donations
Season: October - June   **Annual Attendance:** 65,000
Affiliations: Puppeteers of America; UNIMA

SEATTLE CHILDREN'S THEATRE
305 Harrison, Seattle, WA 98109
(206) 443-0807
FAX: (206) 443-0442
Founded: 1975
Arts Area: Professional; Theatrical Group
Status: Professional; Non-Profit
Type: Performing; Touring; Resident; Educational
Purpose: To produce professional theater for the young with appeal to people of all ages; to provide theater education and theater arts training; to develop scripts and musical scores for new theater works and young audiences
Management: Linda Hartzell, Artistic Director; Thomas Pechar, Managing Director
Officers: Craig Schuman, Board President; Roberta Katz, First Vice President; Diane Kuenster, Second Vice President; Eve Alvord, Secretary; Jim Williams, Treasurer
Paid Staff: 36
Paid Artists: 120
Utilizes: Special Technical Talent; Guest Artists; Guest Directors
Budget: $1,000,000 - $5,000,000
Income Sources: Private Foundations/Grants/Endowments; Business/Corporate Donations; Box Office; Government Grants; Individual Donations
Season: September - July   **Annual Attendance:** 160,000
Affiliations: TCG; AATE; AAA; Equity
Performance Facilities: PONCHO Theatre; Charlotte Martin Theatre (opening Fall, 1993)

SEATTLE MIME THEATRE
915 East Pine Street, #419, Seattle, WA 98122
(206) 324-8788
Founded: 1977
Arts Area: Theatrical Group
Status: Non-Profit
Type: Performing; Touring; Educational
Purpose: To present physical/visual theatre
Management: Beth Amsbany, General Manager; David Lieberman, Artists' Representative
Officers: Bruce L. Wylie, President; Richard L. Davidson, Secretary; Elizabeth Roth, Treasurer
Paid Staff: 1
Paid Artists: 3
Utilizes: Guest Artists; Guest Directors
Budget: $100,000 - $500,000

Income Sources: Private Foundations/Grants/Endowments; Business/Corporate Donations; Box Office; Government Grants; Individual Donations
Season: 52 Weeks

SEATTLE REPERTORY THEATRE
155 Mercer Street, Seattle, WA 98109
(206) 443-2210
FAX: (206) 443-2379
Founded: 1963
Arts Area: Professional; Theatrical Group
Status: Professional; Non-Profit
Type: Performing; Resident
Purpose: To provide professional live theatre productions and educational services for the Pacific Northwest community
Management: Daniel Sullivan, Artistic Director; Benjamin Moore, Managing Director; Douglas Hughes, Associate Artistic Director
Officers: Stanley D. Savage, Chairman of the Board; Ann Ramsay-Jenkins, President of the Board
Paid Staff: 350
Paid Artists: 200
Utilizes: Special Technical Talent; Guest Conductors; Guest Artists; Guest Directors
Budget: $5,000,000 - $10,000,000
Income Sources: Private Foundations/Grants/Endowments; Business/Corporate Donations; Box Office; Government Grants; Individual Donations
Season: October - May
Annual Attendance: 242,000
Affiliations: AEA; LORT
Performance Facilities: Bagley Wright Theatre

TAPROOT THEATRE COMPANY
204 North 85th Street, Seattle, WA 98103
(206) 781-9705
Founded: 1976
Arts Area: Professional; Dinner; Theatrical Group
Status: Semi-Professional; Non-Profit
Type: Performing; Touring; Resident
Purpose: To preserve the integrity of Christian values and perspectives, maintaining excellence through diverse production activities
Management: Scott Nolte, Producing Artistic Director
Officers: M.B. Jewell, Board President; Scott Nolte, Vice President; Daniel Ichinaga, Secretary; Sharon Morrison, Treasurer
Paid Staff: 14   **Volunteer Staff:** 30
Paid Artists: 25   **Non-Paid Artists:** 10
Utilizes: Guest Artists; Guest Directors
Budget: $100,000 - $500,000
Income Sources: Private Foundations/Grants/Endowments; Business/Corporate Donations; Box Office; Individual Donations
Season: 52 Weeks
Annual Attendance: 110,000
Affiliations: Seattle Chamber of Commerce; TCG; USITT

PERFORMING SERIES

BUMBERSHOOT, THE SEATTLE ARTS FESTIVAL
PO Box 9750, Seattle, WA 98109-0750
(206) 622-5123
FAX: (206) 622-5154
Founded: 1971
Arts Area: Dance; Vocal Music; Instrumental Music; Theater; Festival; Literary; Visual
Status: Non-Profit
Type: Performing
Purpose: To produce a four-day art festival featuring all genres of the arts; to produce an affordable, high-quality festival
Management: One Reel, Producer
Paid Staff: 20   **Volunteer Staff:** 300
Utilizes: Guest Artists
Budget: $1,000,000 - $5,000,000
Income Sources: Private Foundations/Grants/Endowments; Business/Corporate Donations; Box Office
Season: September   **Annual Attendance:** 250,000
Performance Facilities: Seattle Center

LADIES MUSICAL CLUB (LMC)
Cobb Building, 1305 Fourth Avenue, Suite 500, Seattle, WA 98101
(206) 622-6882
> **Founded:** 1891
> **Arts Area:** Vocal Music; Instrumental Music
> **Status:** Professional; Semi-Professional; Non-Profit
> **Type:** Performing; Resident; Educational; Sponsoring
> **Purpose:** To grant scholarships to deserving music students; to sponsor a yearly International Artists Series; to foster music among its members and the community
> **Officers:** Helen Holtzclaw, President; Peggy Bardarson, Vice President; Leone Turner, Recording Secretary; Eleanor Gozinsky, Corresponding Secretary; Kathleen Dow, Treasurer; Phyllis Mines, Concert Manager
> **Utilizes:** Special Technical Talent; Guest Artists
> **Budget:** $100,000 - $500,000
> **Income Sources:** Private Foundations/Grants/Endowments; Business/Corporate Donations; Box Office; Government Grants; Individual Donations
> **Season:** September - May   **Annual Attendance:** 10,000
> **Performance Facilities:** Meany Hall, University of Washington; Seattle Public Library; Museum of History and Industry

NORTHWEST FOLKLIFE
305 Harrison Street, Seattle, WA 98109-4695
(206) 684-7300
FAX: (206) 684-7190
> **Founded:** 1971
> **Arts Area:** Festivals
> **Status:** Professional; Semi-Professional; Non-Professional; Non-Profit
> **Type:** Performing; Touring; Educational; Sponsoring
> **Purpose:** To preserve and present ethnic and traditional arts; to foster understanding of different cultures
> **Management:** Scott Nagel, Executive Director; Paul de Barros, Program Director; Annie Jamison, Producing Director; Dana Giddings, Public Affairs Director
> **Officers:** Vivian Williams, President; Anthony Butler, Vice President; Frank Hungate, Treasurer
> **Paid Staff:** 8   **Volunteer Staff:** 800
> **Paid Artists:** 100   **Non-Paid Artists:** 6,000
> **Budget:** $500,000 - $1,000,000
> **Income Sources:** Private Foundations/Grants/Endowments; Business/Corporate Donations; Box Office; Government Grants; Individual Donations
> **Season:** Memorial Day Weekend   **Annual Attendance:** 200,000
> **Performance Facilities:** Seattle Center

PACIFIC NORTHWEST FESTIVAL
Seattle Opera, 1020 John Street, PO Box 9248, Seattle, WA 98109
(206) 389-7699
FAX: (206) 389-7651
> **Founded:** 1975
> **Arts Area:** Grand Opera
> **Status:** Professional; Non-Profit
> **Type:** Performing; Resident; Sponsoring
> **Management:** Speight Jenkins, General Director
> **Officers:** Richard Twiss, President
> **Paid Staff:** 60   **Volunteer Staff:** 150
> **Paid Artists:** 30
> **Utilizes:** Guest Conductors; Guest Artists
> **Budget:** $1,000,000 - $5,000,000
> **Income Sources:** Private Foundations/Grants/Endowments; Business/Corporate Donations; Box Office; Government Grants; Individual Donations
> **Season:** August   **Annual Attendance:** 20,000
> **Affiliations:** Seattle Symphony; Seattle Opera
> **Performance Facilities:** Seattle Opera House

SEATTLE INTERNATIONAL CHILDREN'S FESTIVAL
305 Harrison Street, Seattle, WA 98109
(206) 684-7338
FAX: (206) 684-7342
> **Founded:** 1987
> **Arts Area:** Festivals
> **Status:** Professional; Non-Profit
> **Type:** Performing; Educational
> **Purpose:** To provide an international performing-arts festival for children

Management: Marilyn Raichle, Festival Director; Mary Machala, Projects Director; Cathy Palmer, Director of Education
Officers: Karla Steel, President of the Board; Gerald Hendin, Marcia Garrett, Vice Presidents; Susan Vergara, Secretary; Timothy Dawes, Treasurer
Paid Staff: 8 **Volunteer Staff:** 230
Paid Artists: 160
Utilizes: Guest Artists
Budget: $100,000 - $500,000
Income Sources: Private Foundations/Grants/Endowments; Business/Corporate Donations; Box Office; Government Grants; Individual Donations
Season: May
Annual Attendance: 70,000
Affiliations: WAAA; ASSITEJ; USA
Performance Facilities: Seattle Center

UPSTAGE!
PO Box 7094, Seattle, WA 98133
(206) 743-4240; (206) 363-3306
Founded: 1991
Arts Area: Theater
Status: Semi-Professional; Non-Profit
Type: Touring; Educational
Purpose: Upstage! is dedicated to engaging the mind, emotions, and conscience through artistically and culturally diverse productions for youths and adults.
Officers: Richard Reuther, President; Robert Sibson, Vice President; Gayle Record, Secretary; Ralph Eatom, Treasurer
Utilizes: Special Technical Talent; Guest Conductors; Guest Artists; Guest Directors
Budget: $1,000 - $50,000
Season: September - May
Affiliations: Washington Community Theatre Association; Snohomish County Arts Community

FACILITY

A CONTEMPORARY THEATRE
100 West Roy Street, Seattle, WA 98119
(206) 285-3220
FAX: (206) 298-3100
Founded: 1965
Type of Facility: Theatre House
Facility Originally: Meeting Hall; Movie House
Type of Stage: Thrust
Stage Dimensions: 16'x20'x36'
Seating Capacity: 423
Year Built: 1913
Year Remodeled: 1965 **Architect:** Hewitt-Daly **Cost:** $100,000
Contact for Rental: Jim Verdery; (206) 285-3220

ALICE B THEATRE
1100 East Pike, Third Floor, Seattle, WA 98122
(206) 322-5742
Type of Facility: Studio
Type of Stage: Thrust
Seating Capacity: 150
Year Built: 1991
Contact for Rental: Christopher Malarkey; (206) 322-5742

BAGLEY WRIGHT THEATRE
305 Harrison, Seattle, WA 98109
(206) 625-4254
Type of Facility: Theatre House
Type of Stage: Proscenium
Stage Dimensions: 90'Wx45'D, 44'Wx24'H proscenium opening **Orchestra Pit**
Seating Capacity: 864
Year Built: 1983 **Architect:** The NBBJ Group **Cost:** $10,000,000
Acoustical Consultant: Purcell Noppe & Associates
Contact for Rental: Margaret Wetter; (206) 625-4254
Resident Groups: The Seattle Repertory Theatre

BATHHOUSE THEATRE
7312 West Greenlake Drive North, Seattle, WA 98103
(206) 524-3608
FAX: (206) 527-1942
Founded: 1970
Type of Facility: Theatre House
Facility Originally: Bathhouse
Type of Stage: Thrust
Stage Dimensions: 13'x29'x20'
Seating Capacity: 174
Year Built: 1927 **Cost:** $26,000
Year Remodeled: 1970 **Architect:** Arne Bystrom **Cost:** $20,000
Resident Groups: Bathhouse Theatre Company

MEANY HALL
University of Washington, Seattle, WA 98195
(206) 543-4882
FAX: (206) 685-2759
Founded: 1974
Type of Facility: Concert Hall; Performance Center; Theatre House; Opera House
Type of Stage: Proscenium
Stage Dimensions: 130'Wx55'D **Orchestra Pit**
Seating Capacity: 1,210
Year Built: 1974 **Architect:** Kirk Wallace and Hatch **Cost:** $10,000,000
Acoustical Consultant: Paul Vaneklausen
Contact for Rental: Sue Stark; (206) 543-4882

SEATTLE CENTER ARENA
305 Harrison, Seattle, WA 98109
(206) 684-7202
FAX: (206) 684-7234
Type of Facility: Arena
Facility Originally: Ice Arena
Type of Stage: Flexible
Seating Capacity: 6,100
Year Built: 1927
Year Remodeled: 1976 **Cost:** $500,000
Contact for Rental: Margaret Wetter; (206) 684-7202
Manager: Virginia Anderson; (206) 684-7342
Resident Groups: Seattle Thunderbirds - WHL Hockey Team

SEATTLE CENTER COLISEUM
305 Harrison, Seattle, WA 98109
(206) 684-7202
FAX: (206) 684-7342
Founded: 1962
Type of Facility: Arena
Type of Stage: Flexible
Seating Capacity: 15,000
Year Built: 1962
Year Remodeled: 1976 **Cost:** $750,000
Contact for Rental: Margaret Wetter; (206) 684-7202
Manager: Virginia Anderson, Director; (206) 684-7330
Resident Groups: Seattle Super Sonics - NBA Basketball Team; Seattle Thunderbirds - WHL Hockey Team

SEATTLE CENTER OPERA HOUSE
305 Harrison, Seattle, WA 98109
(206) 625-4254
Type of Facility: Opera House
Facility Originally: Vaudeville
Type of Stage: Proscenium
Stage Dimensions: 70'x108' **Orchestra Pit**
Seating Capacity: 3,099
Year Built: 1927 **Cost:** $4,000,000
Year Remodeled: 1976 **Cost:** $1,500,000
Contact for Rental: Margaret Wetter; (206) 684-7202
Manager: Virginia Anderson, Director; (206) 684-7330

Resident Groups: Seattle Opera Association; Seattle Symphony Orchestra; Pacific Northwest Ballet; Seattle Youth Symphony; World Cavalcade (Film Travelogues)

SEATTLE PUBLIC LIBRARY-DOWNTOWN LIBRARY
1000 Fourth Avenue, Seattle, WA 98104
(206) 386-4636
FAX: (206) 386-4685
    Type of Facility: Auditorium; Multi-Purpose
    Type of Stage: Proscenium
    Seating Capacity: 200
    Contact for Rental: Ray Serebrin; (206) 386-4660
    Rental is free of charge.

Sedro-Woolley

INSTRUMENTAL MUSIC

WESTWOOD WIND QUARTET
2235 Willida Lane, Sedro-Woolley, WA 98284
(206) 856-4779
FAX: (206) 856-4989
    Founded: 1959
    Arts Area: Chamber; Ensemble; Instrumental Group
    Status: Professional
    Type: Performing; Touring; Educational; Recording
    Management: Artists' Alliance Management
    Officers: Peter Christ, Leader
    Volunteer Staff: 2
    Budget: $1,000 - $50,000
    Income Sources: Private Foundations/Grants/Endowments; Business/Corporate Donations; Box Office; Individual Donations
    Season: 52 Weeks

Sequim

DANCE

PERFORMING COMPANY OF PIONEER DANCE ARTS
503 North Sequim Avenue, PO Box 238, Sequim, WA 98382
(206) 683-3693
    Founded: 1976
    Arts Area: Modern; Ballet; Jazz; Ethnic; Tap
    Status: Non-Professional; Non-Profit
    Type: Performing; Resident; Educational; Sponsoring
    Purpose: To raise dance-art awareness in the north Olympic Peninsula
    Management: Kathleen H. Moore, Director; Gloria Price, Secretary; Judy Lynn, Treasurer
    Officers: Judy Reandeau, President; Beverly Hendrickson, Vice President; Gloria Price, Secretary; Judy Lynn, Treasurer
    Paid Staff: 3 **Volunteer Staff:** 12
    Paid Artists: 2 **Non-Paid Artists:** 100
    Utilizes: Guest Artists; Guest Choreographers
    Budget: $1,000 - $50,000
    Income Sources: Business/Corporate Donations; Box Office; Government Grants; Individual Donations
    Annual Attendance: 1,600
    Performance Facilities: Port Angeles High School Auditorium

Spokane

DANCE

SPOKANE BALLET
1427 West Dean, Spokane, WA 99201
(509) 327-4049
    Founded: 1980
    Arts Area: Ballet
    Status: Professional; Non-Profit
    Type: Performing; Touring; Resident; Educational

Purpose: To maintain and further a professional ballet company and school in eastern Washington, providing home seasons, educational programs and concert touring
Management: Robert C. Herold PhD, Executive Director; Susan Hales, Assistant Executive Director; Jane Grovijahn, General Manager; Julie E. Stocker, Company Manager
Officers: Diane Kane, President of Board of Directors; Maryann Sanger, President-Elect; David Mattson, Vice President; Judi Kyle, Secretary
Paid Staff: 17   **Volunteer Staff:** 45
Paid Artists: 10
Utilizes: Special Technical Talent; Guest Artists; Guest Choreographers
Budget: $100,000 - $500,000
Income Sources: Private Foundations/Grants/Endowments; Business/Corporate Donations; Box Office; Government Grants; Individual Donations
Season: August - May   **Annual Attendance:** 38,100
Affiliations: Eastern Washington University
Performance Facilities: Spokane Opera House

INSTRUMENTAL MUSIC

SPOKANE SYMPHONY ORCHESTRA
621 West Mallon, Suite 203, Spokane, WA 99201
(509) 326-3136
Arts Area: Symphony; Orchestra; Chamber
Status: Professional; Non-Profit
Type: Performing; Touring; Resident; Educational; Sponsoring
Purpose: The Spokane Symphony Orchestra exists to provide orchestral music in its many forms to meet the cultural needs of Spokane and the inland northwest region. It seeks to provide the highest quality musical product of which it is able within a sound economic framework that ensures its continuance.
Management: Richard Early, Executive Director; Vakhpang Jordania, Music Director
Officers: Donald Hart, President
Paid Staff: 15   **Volunteer Staff:** 4
Paid Artists: 75
Utilizes: Special Technical Talent; Guest Conductors; Guest Artists; Guest Directors
Budget: $1,000,000 - $5,000,000
Income Sources: Private Foundations/Grants/Endowments; Business/Corporate Donations; Box Office; Government Grants; Individual Donations
Season: September - May   **Annual Attendance:** 122,000
Performance Facilities: Spokane Opera House

THEATRE

SPOKANE CIVIC THEATRE
1020 Howard, PO Box 5222, Spokane, WA 99205
(509) 325-1413
Founded: 1947
Arts Area: Community; Theatrical Group
Status: Non-Professional; Non-Profit
Type: Performing; Educational
Purpose: To offer residents the opportunity to participate (on-stage, backstage and as members of the audience) in the art of theatre; to promote the development of new plays
Management: John (Jack) G. Phillips, Executive Producer
Paid Staff: 9   **Volunteer Staff:** 2,000
Paid Artists: 20   **Non-Paid Artists:** 150
Utilizes: Special Technical Talent; Guest Conductors; Guest Artists; Guest Directors
Budget: $100,000 - $500,000
Income Sources: Private Foundations/Grants/Endowments; Business/Corporate Donations; Box Office; Government Grants; Individual Donations
Season: October - June   **Annual Attendance:** 45,000
Affiliations: ACT; Washington State Arts Commission; Washington Arts Alliance
Performance Facilities: Spokane Civic Theatres

SPOKANE INTERPLAYERS ENSEMBLE
174 South Howard Street, Spokane, WA 99204
(509) 455-7529
Founded: 1980
Arts Area: Professional; Theatrical Group
Status: Professional; Non-Profit
Type: Performing; Resident; Educational
Purpose: To establish, maintain and nurture a non-profit, resident, professional theatre company performing an annual season of plays chosen from contemporary, classic and original works

Management: Robert A. Welch, Producing Artistic Director; Joan Welch, Artistic Director; Mary Cravens, Office Manager; Dave Zack, Clark-White & Associates, Marketing/Public Relations
Officers: Geoff Praeger, President; Don Moeller, Vice President; Robert Clausen, Secretary; Shirley Cornelius, Treasurer
Paid Staff: 8   **Volunteer Staff:** 250
Paid Artists: 52
Utilizes: Guest Directors
Budget: $100,000 - $500,000
Income Sources: Private Foundations/Grants/Endowments; Business/Corporate Donations; Box Office; Government Grants; Individual Donations
Season: October - June   **Annual Attendance:** 34,000
Affiliations: TCG; Arts Alliance of Washington
Performance Facilities: Spokane Interplayers Ensemble Theatre

PERFORMING SERIES

PINESONG/SPOKANE FALLS COMMUNITY COLLEGE
3410 West Fort George Wright Drive, MS 3020, Spokane, WA 99204-2052
(509) 533-3800
FAX: (509) 533-3433
    Founded: 1986
    Arts Area: Festivals
    Status: Non-Profit
    Type: Sponsoring
    Purpose: To present a multi-cultural festival featuring arts, music and hands-on participation
    Management: Nancy Lindberg, Festival Manager; John Thompson, Festival Director
    Paid Staff: 2   **Volunteer Staff:** 100
    Paid Artists: 50
    Utilizes: Special Technical Talent; Guest Artists
    Budget: $1,000 - $50,000
    Income Sources: Private Foundations/Grants/Endowments; Business/Corporate Donations; Box Office; Government Grants
    Season: June   **Annual Attendance:** 12,000

FACILITY

GONZAGA UNIVERSITY - GENE RUSSELL THEATRE
Spokane, WA 99258-0001
(509) 328-4220, ext. 3257
    Type of Facility: Theatre House
    Facility Originally: Recreation Hall; Gymnasium
    Type of Stage: Thrust; Flexible
    Stage Dimensions: 50'x60'
    Seating Capacity: 225
    Year Remodeled: 1968   **Cost:** $25,000
    Contact for Rental: Dr. Tim Soulis, Director;   (509) 328-4220, ext. 3257

THE METROPOLITAN PERFORMING ARTS CENTER
901 West Sprague, Spokane, WA 99204
(509) 455-6500
FAX: (509) 459-0898
    Founded: 1988
    Type of Facility: Concert Hall; Auditorium; Studio Performance; Performance Center; Theatre House; Opera House
    Facility Originally: Vaudeville; Movie House
    Type of Stage: Thrust
    Stage Dimensions: 32'Wx24'D   **Orchestra Pit**
    Seating Capacity: 760
    Year Built: 1915
    Year Remodeled: 1988   **Architect:** Bill Arsenault   **Cost:** $2,000,000
    Contact for Rental: Michael Smith;   (509) 455-7811
    Resident Groups: Uptown Opera; Spokane Symphony; Spokane String Quartet; Allegro Theatre Ballet

SPOKANE COLISEUM
1101 North Howard, Spokane, WA 99201
(509) 353-6500
FAX: (509) 353-6511
    Type of Facility: Arena; Multi-Purpose
    Type of Stage: Arena
    Seating Capacity: 7,200 reserved; 8,500 festival seating

Year Built: 1953   Cost: $3,000,000
Contact for Rental: Events Supervisor;   (509) 353-6500

SPOKANE CONVENTION CENTER
1101 North Howard, Spokane, WA 99201
(509) 353-6500
FAX: (509) 353-6511
Seating Capacity: Concert - 5,000; Theatre - 4,000; Banquet - 3,200
Contact for Rental: Events Supervisor;   (509) 353-6500

SPOKANE OPERA HOUSE
334 West Spokane Falls Boulevard, Spokane, WA 99201
(509) 353-6500
FAX: (509) 353-6511
Type of Facility: Concert Hall; Auditorium; Opera House
Facility Originally: Auditorium
Type of Stage: Proscenium
Stage Dimensions: 150'Wx59"D; 67'Wx27'H proscenium opening   Orchestra Pit
Seating Capacity: 2,700
Year Built: 1974   Architect: WMFL   Cost: $9,000,000
Acoustical Consultant: Purcell-Noppe
Contact for Rental: Kevin Twohig;   (509) 353-6500
Resident Groups: Spokane Symphony; G & B Presents
Curved-edge pit lift adds 16'D at center line raised to stage level

---

Tacoma

DANCE

BALLETACOMA
508 Sixth Avenue, Tacoma, WA 98402
(206) 272-9631
Founded: 1955
Arts Area: Ballet
Status: Semi-Professional
Type: Performing
Purpose: To provide quality, fully-staged classical ballets for the southern Puget Sound area
Management: Nikki Smith, Executive Director
Officers: John Hodder, Chairman
Paid Staff: 4   Volunteer Staff: 2
Paid Artists: 3   Non-Paid Artists: 20
Utilizes: Guest Artists; Guest Choreographers
Budget: $100,000 - $500,000
Income Sources: Private Foundations/Grants/Endowments; Business/Corporate Donations; Box Office; Government Grants; Individual Donations
Season: October - May   Annual Attendance: 12,000
Affiliations: NARB; PRBA
Performance Facilities: Pantages Theater

JO EMERY DANCE COMPANY
2315 Sixth Avenue, Tacoma, WA 98403
(206) 627-8272
Arts Area: Jazz
Status: Professional; Non-Profit
Type: Performing
Management: Jo Emery, Artistic Director
Paid Artists: 8
Utilizes: Guest Choreographers
Budget: $1,000 - $50,000
Income Sources: Private Foundations/Grants/Endowments; Business/Corporate Donations; Box Office; Government Grants; Individual Donations
Season: 52 Weeks

TACOMA PERFORMING DANCE COMPANY
2315 Sixth Avenue, Tacoma, WA 98407
(206) 759-0782
Founded: 1967

Arts Area: Modern; Ballet; Jazz
Status: Semi-Professional; Non-Profit
Type: Performing; Touring; Resident
Management: Jo Emery, Director
Utilizes: Guest Artists; Guest Directors
Budget: $1,000 - $50,000
Income Sources: Private Foundations/Grants/Endowments; Box Office; Government Grants
Season: September - June
Performance Facilities: Pantages Centre

INSTRUMENTAL MUSIC

TACOMA CONCERT BAND
717 San Juan Avenue, Tacoma, WA 98466
(206) 564-4954
Founded: 1981
Arts Area: Band
Status: Non-Profit
Type: Performing
Purpose: To present band concerts throughout the year in Tacoma and the surrounding area
Management: Robert C. Musser, Conductor/Musical Director
Volunteer Staff: 1
Non-Paid Artists: 60
Utilizes: Guest Conductors; Guest Artists
Budget: $1,000 - $50,000
Income Sources: Box Office; Individual Donations
Season: September - April   **Annual Attendance:** 5,000
Affiliations: University of Puget Sound
Performance Facilities: Pantages Centre

TACOMA PHILHARMONIC
901 Broadway, Tacoma, WA 98402
Founded: 1936
Arts Area: Symphony; Chamber; Soloists of Classical Music
Status: Professional; Non-Profit
Type: Presenting
Purpose: To present classical music concerts, offering the community a six-series season
Management: Kathryn O. Galbraith, Executive Director
Paid Staff: 2
Utilizes: Guest Artists
Budget: $100,000 - $500,000
Income Sources: Private Foundations/Grants/Endowments; Business/Corporate Donations; Box Office; Government Grants; Individual Donations
Season: August - May   **Annual Attendance:** 6,000
Performance Facilities: Pantages Theatre

TACOMA SYMPHONY ORCHESTRA
PO Box 19, Tacoma, WA 98401
(206) 272-7264
Founded: 1959
Arts Area: Symphony; Orchestra
Status: Professional; Non-Profit
Type: Performing
Purpose: To provide affordable classical music to the community
Management: Carlene Garner, Executive Director; Edward Seferian, Musical Director; Hollie Seibert, Office Manager
Officers: Thomas Park, President; Parker Geesen, Vice President; Landon Brazier, Treasurer
Paid Staff: 3
Paid Artists: 75   **Non-Paid Artists:** 10
Utilizes: Guest Conductors; Guest Artists
Budget: $100,000 - $500,000
Income Sources: Private Foundations/Grants/Endowments; Business/Corporate Donations; Box Office; Government Grants; Individual Donations
Season: October - April
Annual Attendance: 20,000
Affiliations: ASOL
Performance Facilities: Pantages Theatre

TACOMA YOUTH SYMPHONY
PO Box 660, Tacoma, WA 98401
(206) 627-2792
FAX: (206) 591-2013
Founded: 1962
Arts Area: Symphony; Orchestra; Chamber; Ensemble
Status: Non-Professional; Non-Profit
Type: Performing; Educational
Purpose: To provide leadership by competent conductors and coaches; to educate and inspire youth musicians from seven to 21 years of age; to work for excellence in the performance of symphonic literature
Management: Shirley M. Getzin, Executive Director
Officers: James Billingsley MD, President; Patricia Borgen, First Vice President; George Fong, Second Vice President; Kaye Adkins, Third Vice President; Dagny Sollie, Treasurer; Rodney Ray, Past President
Paid Staff: 4
Non-Paid Artists: 285
Utilizes: Guest Artists
Budget: $100,000 - $500,000
Income Sources: Private Foundations/Grants/Endowments; Business/Corporate Donations; Box Office; Government Grants; Individual Donations; Fund-raising
Season: September - May   **Annual Attendance:** 21,000
Affiliations: ASOL (Youth Orchestra Division)
Performance Facilities: Pantages Centre

VOCAL MUSIC

ORPHEUS MALE CHORUS OF TACOMA
PO Box 1222, Tacoma, WA 98401
(206) 582-4435
Founded: 1903
Arts Area: Choral
Status: Non-Professional; Non-Profit
Type: Performing
Purpose: To cultivate and develop refined musical numbers and present them to our audiences; to further music appreciation
Management: Peter Herpst, Conductor; Vern Anderson, Assistant Conductor; David Abbott, Financial Secretary; Frank O. Boers, Auditor; Vicki Lynn Day, Accompanist
Officers: Bill Zimmerman, President; David Abbott, Financial; Larry Palbert, Recording Secretary; Hal Mortland, Treasurer; Ray Wall, Assistant Financial Secretary
Paid Staff: 2   **Volunteer Staff:** 15
Paid Artists: 2   **Non-Paid Artists:** 40
Utilizes: Special Technical Talent; Guest Artists
Budget: $1,000 - $50,000
Income Sources: Business/Corporate Donations; Box Office; Individual Donations
Season: February - May; September - December
Annual Attendance: 600
Performance Facilities: First United Methodist Church

TACOMA OPERA ASSOCIATION
PO Box 7468, Tacoma, WA 98407
(206) 627-7789
Founded: 1968
Arts Area: Light Opera
Status: Professional
Type: Performing
Purpose: To produce light opera in English for patrons in the South Puget Sound region
Management: Anne W. Farrell, Executive Director; Hans Wolf, Artistic Director
Officers: Bob Slaton, President; William Ryberg, Priscilla Bosch, Vice Presidents; John Hodder, Treasurer; Mickey Kramer, Secretary
Paid Staff: 3   **Volunteer Staff:** 2
Paid Artists: 100   **Non-Paid Artists:** 100
Utilizes: Special Technical Talent; Guest Conductors; Guest Artists; Guest Directors
Budget: $100,000 - $500,000
Income Sources: Private Foundations/Grants/Endowments; Business/Corporate Donations; Box Office; Government Grants; Individual Donations; Opera Guilds
Season: October - March
Annual Attendance: 7,000
Performance Facilities: Pantages Theater; Railto Theater

THEATRE

TACOMA ACTORS GUILD
1323 South Yakima, Tacoma, WA 98405
(206) 272-3107
Founded: 1978
Arts Area: Professional; Theatrical Group
Status: Professional; Non-Profit
Type: Performing; Resident
Purpose: To provide quality theatre that entertains and enriches the south Puget Sound community and engages that community in a dynamic partnership that explores challenging dramatic literature
Management: Kate Haas, Managing Director; Bruce K. Sevy, Artistic Director
Paid Staff: 20   **Volunteer Staff:** 100
Paid Artists: 85
Utilizes: Special Technical Talent; Guest Artists; Guest Directors
Budget: $1,000,000 - $5,000,000
Income Sources: Private Foundations/Grants/Endowments; Business/Corporate Donations; Box Office; Government Grants; Individual Donations; Benefit Events
Season: October - May   **Annual Attendance:** 37,000
Affiliations: TCG
Performance Facilities: Tacoma Actors Guild

Toledo

INSTRUMENTAL MUSIC

WASHINGTON BLUEGRASS ASSOCIATION
PO Box 490, Toledo, WA 98591
(206) 864-2074
Founded: 1982
Arts Area: Ethnic; Folk; Instrumental Group; Band; Acoustic Bluegrass
Status: Non-Profit
Type: Educational; Sponsoring
Purpose: To perform at concerts throughout the year
Officers: Earla Harding, President; Sue Murphy, Secretary/Treasurer
Volunteer Staff: 100
Utilizes: Special Technical Talent; Guest Artists
Budget: $1,000 - $50,000
Income Sources: Individual Donations; Dues
Season: 52 Weeks   **Annual Attendance:** 5,000
Affiliations: BMI
Performance Facilities: Toledo High School Grounds

Vancouver

THEATRE

OLD SLOCUM HOUSE THEATRE COMPANY
605 Esther Street, Vancouver, WA 98660
Founded: 1969
Arts Area: Musical; Community
Status: Non-Profit
Type: Resident
Purpose: To restore the Slocum House Theatre; to produce 19th-century plays
Management: Board of Directors
Officers: Hermine Guthie Decker, President; Mike Heywood, Vice President; Ruby Lloyd, Secretary
Budget: $1,000 - $50,000
Season: 52 Weeks

FACILITY

COLUMBIA ARTS CENTER
400 West Evergreen Boulevard, Vancouver, WA 98660
(206) 693-0351
FAX: (206) 643-0794
Type of Facility: Cultural Center
Facility Originally: Church

Type of Stage: Platform
Stage Dimensions: 26'6"Wx33'D
Seating Capacity: 220
Year Built: 1912   **Architect:** William Tobey
Year Remodeled: 1983   **Architect:** Dolle/Swatash   **Cost:** $350,000
Contact for Rental: Ralph Welsh;   (206) 693-0351

Walla Walla

INSTRUMENTAL MUSIC

WALLA WALLA SYMPHONY
PO Box 92, Walla Walla, WA 99362
(509) 529-8020
Founded: 1906
Arts Area: Symphony; Orchestra
Status: Non-Professional; Non-Profit
Type: Performing
Purpose: To promote the tradition of great symphonic music; to bring high-quality performances to all segments of the community, including children
Management: Sharon Thompson, Manager; Linda Desmond, Assistant Manager
Officers: Michael de Grasse, President; Dina Baker, Vice President; Jane Drabeck, Secretary; Albert Marshall, Treasurer
Paid Staff: 4
Paid Artists: 13   **Non-Paid Artists:** 40
Utilizes: Guest Conductors; Guest Artists
Budget: $100,000 - $500,000
Income Sources: Private Foundations/Grants/Endowments; Business/Corporate Donations; Box Office; Government Grants; Individual Donations
Season: October - May   **Annual Attendance:** 6,000
Performance Facilities: Cordiner Hall

FACILITY

WHITMAN COLLEGE - CORDINER HALL
Walla Walla, WA 99362
(509) 527-5111
Type of Facility: Concert Hall
Type of Stage: Proscenium
Year Built: 1968   **Cost:** $1,600,000
Contact for Rental: Gayle Worthington;   (509) 527-5111
Resident Groups: Walla Walla Symphony Orchestra; Community Concerts; Walla Walla School District

---

Wenatchee

DANCE

CHILDREN'S BALLET THEATRE
PO Box 2053, Wenatchee, WA 98801
(509) 663-4056
Founded: 1985
Arts Area: Ballet; Multi-Media Productions
Status: Semi-Professional; Non-Profit
Type: Performing; Touring; Resident
Purpose: Children's Ballet Theatre is an outgrowth of Wenatchee Civic Ballet, which was the first company of its kind to be incorporated in the Pacific Northwest. It has brought the finest professional artists to north-central Washington for the past fifteen years.
Management: Joan Shelton-Mason, Director
Officers: Betty Jean Gibson, Chairman of the Board; Lillian Auwerter, Secretary; Joan Shelton-Mason, Founder/Director
Volunteer Staff: 50
Utilizes: Special Technical Talent; Guest Artists; Guest Choreographers; 0
Budget: $1,000 - $50,000
Income Sources: Private Foundations/Grants/Endowments; Business/Corporate Donations; Box Office; Government Grants; Individual Donations
Season: September - June   **Annual Attendance:** 5,000

Yakima

INSTRUMENTAL MUSIC

YAKIMA SYMPHONY ORCHESTRA
PO Box 307, Yakima, WA 98907
(509) 248-1414
FAX: (509) 457-0980
Founded: 1971
Arts Area: Symphony; Orchestra
Status: Professional; Non-Profit
Type: Performing; Educational
Purpose: To perform and promote symphonic music
Management: Sarah S. Marley, Manager; Brooke Creswell, Music Director
Officers: John Bloxom Jr., President; Carmela Newstead, First Vice President; Bruce Willis, Second Vice President; Darrell Blue, Treasurer; Priscilla Wyckoff, Secretary; Gayle Scholl, Member at Large
Paid Staff: 4
Paid Artists: 60
Utilizes: Guest Conductors; Guest Artists
Budget: $100,000 - $500,000
Income Sources: Private Foundations/Grants/Endowments; Business/Corporate Donations; Box Office; Government Grants; Individual Donations
Season: October - April   **Annual Attendance:** 4,500
Affiliations: ASOL
Performance Facilities: Capitol Theatre

YAKIMA YOUTH ORCHESTRA
PO Box 307, Yakima, WA 98907
(509) 248-1414
Arts Area: Symphony; Orchestra; Chamber
Status: Non-Professional; Non-Profit
Type: Performing; Educational
Management: Dennis Clauss, Conductor
Non-Paid Artists: 20
Season: September - May   **Annual Attendance:** 300
Affiliations: Yakima Symphony Orchestra

FACILITY

CAPITAL THEATRE
19 South Third Street, PO Box 102, Yakima, WA 98907
(509) 575-6267
Type of Facility: Theatre House
Facility Originally: Vaudeville
Type of Stage: Proscenium
Stage Dimensions: 90'Wx38'D; 30'Hx30'W proscenium opening   **Orchestra Pit**
Seating Capacity: 1,505
Year Built: 1920   **Architect:** B. Marcus Priteca
Year Remodeled: 1978   **Architect:** William Paddock   **Cost:** $4,200,000
Contact for Rental: Steven J. Caffery;   (509) 575-6267
The Capital Theatre is a National Historic Landmark.

WEST VIRGINIA

Beckley

THEATRE

THEATRE WEST VIRGINIA, INC.
PO Box 1205, Beckley, WV 25801
(304) 256-6800; (800) 666-9142
FAX: (304) 256-6807
    Founded: 1955
    Arts Area: Professional; Theatrical Group; Puppet
    Status: Professional
    Type: Performing; Touring; Educational; Sponsoring
    Purpose: To provide theatre of the highest quality to community and state residents as well as tourists
    Management: Susan Landis, Acting General Manager; John Arnold, Artistic Director; Carrie Sandersturner, Development Director; Marina Hunley, Sales Director; Gayle Bowling, Administrative Assistant
    Officers: Susan Landis, President; Blair Friar, President-Elect; John Rust, Vice President; Judy Harrah, Secretary; Arnold Graybeat, Treasurer
    Paid Staff: 5 **Volunteer Staff:** 50
    Paid Artists: 50
    Utilizes: Guest Artists; Guest Directors
    Budget: $500,000 - $1,000,000
    Income Sources: Private Foundations/Grants/Endowments; Business/Corporate Donations; Box Office; Government Grants; Individual Donations
    Season: 52 Weeks **Annual Attendance:** 140,000

FACILITY

CLIFFSIDE AMPHITHEATRE OF WEST VIRGINIA
PO Box 1205, Beckley, WV 25801
(304) 253-8131
FAX: (304) 256-6807
    Type of Facility: Outdoor (Concert); Amphitheater
    Type of Stage: Proscenium
    Stage Dimensions: 60'x45'
    Orchestra Pit
    Seating Capacity: 1,200
    Year Built: 1961 **Cost:** $250,000
    Year Remodeled: 1991
    Contact for Rental: Robert Shreue, Executive Director; (304) 256-6803
    Resident Groups: Hatfields & McCoys; Broadway Musical Repertory; Stonewall - Old Blue Light

Buckhannon

FACILITY

WEST VIRGINIA WESLEYAN COLLEGE - ATKINSON AUDITORIUM
59 College Avenue, Buckhannon, WV 26201
(304) 473-8000, ext. 8044
    Type of Facility: Auditorium
    Facility Originally: Chapel
    Type of Stage: Proscenium
    Stage Dimensions: 32'Wx24'D
    Seating Capacity: 500
    Year Built: 1920
    Year Remodeled: 1977
    Contact for Rental: (304) 473-8258
    Resident Groups: West Virginia Wesleyan College Theatre

Charles Town

FACILITY

THE OLD OPERA HOUSE COMPANY
204 North George Street, Charles Town, WV 25414
(304) 725-4420
Founded: 1973
Type of Facility: Opera House
Type of Stage: Proscenium
Stage Dimensions: 42'Wx24'D   **Orchestra Pit**
Seating Capacity: 336
Year Built: 1910   **Architect:** T.A. Mullett   **Cost:** $50,000
Year Remodeled: 1979   **Cost:** $400,000
Contact for Rental: Hubert Rolling, Manager;   (304) 725-4420
Manager: Hubert Rolling;   (304) 725-4420
Resident Groups: Old Opera House Theatre Company
Available for concerts or two-night runs. We also do a full season consisting of three plays, two musicals and a children's show.

Charleston

DANCE

APPALACHIAN YOUTH JAZZ-BALLET COMPANY
PO Box 575, Charleston, WV 25301
(304) 343-1076
Founded: 1982
Arts Area: Ballet; Jazz
Status: Non-Profit
Type: Performing; Touring; Educational
Purpose: To provide talented aspiring dancers liaisons between classroom and the professional stage; to enrich the community through concerts and lecture demonstrations; to provide inspiration to youngsters in the audience
Management: Nina Denton, Artistic Director
Officers: Ricklin Brown, President; John Breed, Vice President; Catherine Halloran, Secretary; Carol Velasquez, Treasurer
Volunteer Staff: 2
Non-Paid Artists: 2
Utilizes: Guest Artists; Guest Choreographers
Budget: $1,000 - $50,000
Income Sources: Private Foundations/Grants/Endowments; Business/Corporate Donations; Box Office; Individual Donations
Season: September - June   **Annual Attendance:** 15,000
Affiliations: Washington Community Education
Performance Facilities: Charleston Civic Center; Municipal Auditorium

CHARLESTON BALLET
822 Virginia Street East, Charleston, WV 25301
(304) 342-6541
Founded: 1956
Arts Area: Modern; Ballet; Folk
Status: Semi-Professional; Non-Profit
Type: Performing; Touring
Purpose: To present ballet concerts for professional and talented young dancers
Management: Kim R. Pauley, Director/Choreographer
Officers: Mary Lou Lewis, MD, President; Jerry Howard, Vice President; Jean McCune, Secretary; Kim R. Pauley, Treasurer
Paid Staff: 2   **Volunteer Staff:** 10
Paid Artists: 15   **Non-Paid Artists:** 20
Utilizes: Special Technical Talent; Guest Artists; Guest Choreographers
Budget: $50,000 - $100,000
Income Sources: Private Foundations/Grants/Endowments; Business/Corporate Donations; Box Office; Government Grants; Individual Donations
Season: 52 Weeks

INSTRUMENTAL MUSIC

CHARLESTON CHAMBER MUSIC SOCIETY
PO Box 641, Charleston, WV 25323
(304) 344-5389
>**Founded:** 1941
>**Arts Area:** Chamber; Ensemble
>**Status:** Non-Profit
>**Type:** Performing; Sponsoring
>**Purpose:** To bring outstanding chamber-music ensembles to Charleston
>**Management:** N. David Stern, Executive Director
>**Paid Staff:** 1 **Volunteer Staff:** 25
>**Paid Artists:** 6
>**Utilizes:** Guest Artists
>**Budget:** $1,000 - $50,000
>**Income Sources:** Private Foundations/Grants/Endowments; Business/Corporate Donations; Box Office; Government Grants; Individual Donations
>**Season:** October - May **Annual Attendance:** 2,500
>**Affiliations:** APAP; CMA
>**Performance Facilities:** Christ Church United Methodist

LILLIPUT ORCHESTRA
16 Terrace Road, Charleston, WV 25314
(304) 346-6095
>**Founded:** 1979
>**Arts Area:** Symphony; Orchestra; Chamber; Opera
>**Status:** Professional
>**Type:** Performing; Touring; Educational
>**Purpose:** To bring symphonic music and opera to West Virginians and others
>**Management:** Suzanne Riggio, General Manager
>**Officers:** Robert Bobst, President
>**Volunteer Staff:** 1
>**Paid Artists:** 40
>**Utilizes:** Guest Artists
>**Budget:** $1,000 - $50,000
>**Income Sources:** Private Foundations/Grants/Endowments; Business/Corporate Donations; Box Office; Government Grants; Individual Donations
>**Season:** August - June **Annual Attendance:** 10,000

MONTCLAIRE STRING QUARTET
c/o West Virginia Symphony Orchestra, PO Box 2292, Charleston, WV 25328
(304) 342-0151
FAX: (304) 342-0152
>**Founded:** 1982
>**Arts Area:** Symphony; Chamber; Ensemble; Instrumental Group
>**Status:** Professional
>**Type:** Performing; Touring; Resident; Educational; Sponsoring
>**Purpose:** To present the highest quality string quartet repertoire throughout the state of West Virginia; to provide leadership in the West Virginia Symphony Orchestra; to present educational programs in West Virginia schools
>**Management:** Shirley Furry, Executive Director; Thomas Conlin, Artistic Director; Emily Papadopoulos, Director of Development
>**Officers:** John L. McClaugherty, President; Patrick Bond, Vice President of Development
>**Utilizes:** Guest Artists
>**Budget:** $1,000,000 - $5,000,000
>**Income Sources:** Private Foundations/Grants/Endowments; Business/Corporate Donations; Box Office; Government Grants; Individual Donations
>**Season:** September - May
>**Performance Facilities:** St. Matthew's Episcopal Church

WEST VIRGINIA SYMPHONY
1210 Virginia Street East, Charleston, WV 25301
(304) 342-0151
FAX: (304) 342-0152
>**Arts Area:** Symphony; Ensemble
>**Status:** Professional
>**Type:** Performing

Purpose: To present classical music concerts and education throughout the state of West Virginia
Management: Shirley A. Furry, Executive Director
Officers: John L. McClaugherty, President
Volunteer Staff: 7
Non-Paid Artists: 85
Utilizes: Special Technical Talent; Guest Artists
Budget: $1,000,000 - $5,000,000
Income Sources: Private Foundations/Grants/Endowments; Business/Corporate Donations; Box Office; Government Grants; Individual Donations
Season: September - May **Annual Attendance:** 42,500
Affiliations: ASOL
Performance Facilities: Municipal Auditorium

VOCAL MUSIC

CHARLESTON AREA COMMUNITY CHOIR
PO Box 20253, Charleston, WV 25302
(304) 342-3183
Founded: 1976
Arts Area: Choral; Ethnic; Folk
Status: Professional; Semi-Professional; Non-Professional; Non-Profit
Type: Performing; Touring; Resident; Educational; Sponsoring
Purpose: To stimulate composition of original works; to illustrate meaningful application of various musical instruments in accompanying vocal groups; to identify and analyze Black religious music
Management: Ethel Caffie-Austin, Director; Barbara Rowell, Executive Secretary/Business Manager
Officers: Elston Canada, President
Volunteer Staff: 75
Non-Paid Artists: 8
Utilizes: Special Technical Talent; Guest Artists; Guest Directors
Budget: $1,000 - $50,000
Income Sources: Private Foundations/Grants/Endowments; Box Office; Government Grants; Individual Donations
Season: 52 Weeks
Performance Facilities: Charleston Cultural Center

CHARLESTON CIVIC CHORUS
PO Box 2014, Charleston, WV 25327-2014
(304) 747-4944
Founded: 1952
Arts Area: Choral
Status: Non-Professional; Non-Profit
Type: Performing; Resident
Purpose: To perform high-quality choral classics as well as some lighter fare
Management: J. Truman Dalton, Music Director
Officers: Judith Arnold, President; Thomas Llewellyn, Vice President; Evan Buck, Treasurer
Paid Staff: 2
Utilizes: Guest Artists
Budget: $1,000 - $50,000
Income Sources: Business/Corporate Donations; Government Grants; Individual Donations
Season: September - May **Annual Attendance:** 600
Performance Facilities: The Baptist Temple

CHARLESTON LIGHT OPERA GUILD
PO Box 1762, Charleston, WV 25326
(304) 342-9312
Founded: 1949
Arts Area: Light Opera
Status: Non-Profit
Type: Performing
Purpose: To present musical comedy
Officers: Horace Emery, President; Tim Harper, Vice President; Emma Jean Thomas, Secretary; Bill Rogers, Treasurer
Paid Artists: 3
Utilizes: Special Technical Talent
Budget: $50,000 - $100,000
Income Sources: Private Foundations/Grants/Endowments; Business/Corporate Donations; Box Office; Government Grants; Individual Donations
Season: 52 Weeks **Annual Attendance:** 10,000
Performance Facilities: Charleston Civic Center - Little Theater

THEATRE

KANAWHA PLAYERS
5315 MacCorkle Avenue, SE, Charleston, WV 25304
(304) 925-5051
Founded: 1922
Arts Area: Dinner; Community; Theatrical Group
Status: Non-Professional; Non-Profit
Type: Performing; Touring; Educational
Management: Kathie M. Frank, Company Administrator; Betsy Stuart, Historian
Officers: Stephen E. Kawash, President
Paid Staff: 1   **Volunteer Staff:** 30
Paid Artists: 5   **Non-Paid Artists:** 175
Utilizes: Special Technical Talent; Guest Artists; Guest Directors
Budget: $50,000 - $100,000
Income Sources: Private Foundations/Grants/Endowments; Business/Corporate Donations; Box Office;
Individual Donations
Season: September - June   **Annual Attendance:** 6,500
Affiliations: Arts Advocacy of West Virginia
Performance Facilities: Charleston Civic Center - Little Theatre

FACILITY

CHARLESTON CIVIC CENTER
200 Civic Center Drive, Charleston, WV 25301
(304) 345-1500
FAX: (304) 357-7432
Type of Facility: Civic Center
Type of Stage: Proscenium
Stage Dimensions: 38'Wx30'D
Seating Capacity: 750
Year Built: 1959
Contact for Rental: John Robertson;   (304) 345-1500
The Charleston Civic Center contains the Coliseum, Little Theater and Municipal Auditorium. See separate listings for further information.

CHARLESTON CIVIC CENTER - COLISEUM
200 Civic Center Drive, Charleston, WV 25301
(304) 345-1500
FAX: (304) 357-7435
Type of Facility: Concert Hall; Performance Center; Multi-Purpose
Type of Stage: Flexible
Seating Capacity: 3,500
Contact for Rental: John Robertson;   (304) 345-1500

CHARLESTON CIVIC CENTER - LITTLE THEATER
200 Civic Center Drive, Charleston, WV 25301
(304) 345-1500
FAX: (304) 357-7435
Type of Facility: Auditorium; Multi-Purpose
Type of Stage: Proscenium
Stage Dimensions: 34'Wx30'D; 50'H to grid   **Orchestra Pit**
Seating Capacity: 750
Year Built: 1959
Contact for Rental: John Robertson;   (304) 345-1500

CHARLESTON CIVIC CENTER - MUNICIPAL AUDITORIUM
200 Civic Center Drive, Charleston, WV 25301
(304) 345-1500
FAX: (304) 357-7432
Type of Facility: Auditorium
Type of Stage: Proscenium
Stage Dimensions: 62'Wx35'D; 50'H to grid; 40 fly lines
Orchestra Pit
Seating Capacity: 3,483
Contact for Rental: John Robertson;   (304) 345-1500

GEARY AUDITORIUM
2300 MacCorkle Avenue, SE, Charleston, WV 25304-1099
(304) 357-4807
FAX: (304) 357-4915
   Type of Facility: Auditorium
   Type of Stage: Proscenium
   Stage Dimensions: 38'4"Wx25'4"D
   Seating Capacity: 1,000
   Year Built: 1947
   Contact for Rental: Diane Stockholm;   (304) 357-4807
   Resident Groups: Capital Events; University of Charleston Conservatory

WEST VIRGINIA STATE COLLEGE CAPITOL CENTER
123 Summers Street, Charleston, WV 25301
(304) 342-6522
   Type of Facility: Theatre House
   Facility Originally: Vaudeville
   Type of Stage: Modified Apron Proscenium
   Stage Dimensions: 48'Wx24'D; 30'Wx22'H proscenium opening   **Orchestra Pit**
   Seating Capacity: 1,132
   Year Built: 1912
   Year Remodeled: 1984   **Architect:** Paul D. Marshall & Associates   **Cost:** $650,000
   Contact for Rental: Laura McCullough;   (304) 342-6522
   The Theater is a National Historic Landmark constantly undergoing renovation.

Fairmont

INSTRUMENTAL MUSIC

FAIRMONT CHAMBER MUSIC SOCIETY, INC.
1109 Alexander Place, Fairmont, WV 26554
(304) 363-1326
   Arts Area: Chamber
   Status: Professional; Non-Profit
   Type: Sponsoring
   Purpose: To present classical chamber music in northern West Virginia
   Officers: John Ashton, President; D.J. Romino II, Vice President; Ruth Brooks, Secretary; Nancy Hussey,
   Treasurer
   Volunteer Staff: 15
   Paid Artists: 13
   Utilizes: Guest Artists
   Budget: $1,000 - $50,000
   Income Sources: Private Foundations/Grants/Endowments; Box Office; Government Grants; Individual Donations
   Season: September - May   **Annual Attendance:** 600
   Performance Facilities: Christ Episcopal Church

Huntington

INSTRUMENTAL MUSIC

HUNTINGTON CHAMBER ORCHESTRA
800 Fifth Avenue, Huntington, WV 25701
(304) 525-0670
   Founded: 1970
   Arts Area: Orchestra; Chamber
   Status: Professional; Non-Profit
   Type: Performing; Resident
   Purpose: To perform the finest music written for chamber orchestras
   Management: George Beter, Manager; Paul W. Whear, Music Director
   Officers: Leland Thornburg, President; Kay Wildman, Secretary; Morris Kuntz, Treasurer
   Paid Staff: 2   **Volunteer Staff:** 50
   Paid Artists: 42
   Utilizes: Guest Artists
   Budget: $1,000 - $50,000
   Income Sources: Private Foundations/Grants/Endowments; Business/Corporate Donations; Box Office; Government
   Grants; Individual Donations
   Season: October - May   **Annual Attendance:** 2,400

Affiliations: ASOL
Performance Facilities: Huntington Galleries

PERFORMING SERIES

MARSHALL ARTISTS SERIES
Marshall University, 400 Hal Greek Boulevard, Huntington, WV 25701
(304) 696-6656
>   **Founded:** 1936
>   **Arts Area:** Dance; Vocal Music; Instrumental Music; Theater; Lyric Opera; Grand Opera
>   **Status:** Non-Profit
>   **Type:** Educational; Sponsoring
>   **Purpose:** To aid, promote and contribute to the educational and cultural life of Marshall University and the surrounding area
>   **Management:** Celeste Winters-Nunley, Manager; Anne S. Moncer, Administrative Assistant
>   **Officers:** J. Wade Gilley, President
>   **Paid Staff:** 2   **Volunteer Staff:** 30
>   **Budget:** $100,000 - $500,000
>   **Income Sources:** Private Foundations/Grants/Endowments; Business/Corporate Donations; Box Office; Government Grants; Individual Donations
>   **Season:** September - May   **Annual Attendance:** 14,000
>   **Affiliations:** Marshall University
>   **Performance Facilities:** Keith-Albee Theatre

FACILITY

THE HUNTINGTON CIVIC CENTRE
1 Civic Center Plaza, Huntington, WV 25727
>   **Type of Facility:** Civic Center
>   **Type of Stage:** Wenger
>   **Stage Dimensions:** 60'x40'x4'
>   **Seating Capacity:** 8,500
>   **Year Built:** 1976
>   **Contact for Rental:** Maria DiGabriele;   (304) 696-5990

HUNTINGTON MUSEUM OF ART - AMPHITHEATRE
Park Hills, Huntington, WV 25701
(304) 529-2701
>   **Type of Facility:** Amphitheater
>   **Type of Stage:** Environmental
>   **Stage Dimensions:** 60'Wx30'D
>   **Seating Capacity:** 750
>   **Year Built:** 1976   **Architect:** Dean
>   **Contact for Rental:** James Lawhorn;   (304) 529-2701

HUNTINGTON MUSEUM OF ART - AUDITORIUM
Park Hills, Huntington, WV 25701
(304) 529-2701
>   **Type of Facility:** Auditorium
>   **Type of Stage:** Proscenium
>   **Stage Dimensions:** 34'Wx19'D
>   **Seating Capacity:** 300
>   **Year Built:** 1972   **Architect:** Walter Gropius
>   **Contact for Rental:** James Lawhorn;   (304) 529-2701
>   **Resident Groups:** Community Players

KEITH-ALBEE THEATRE
925 Fourth Avenue, Huntington, WV 25720
(304) 525-8311
>   **Type of Facility:** Theatre House
>   **Type of Stage:** Proscenium
>   **Stage Dimensions:** 47'Wx27'D   **Orchestra Pit**
>   **Seating Capacity:** 1,800
>   **Year Built:** 1928   **Architect:** Thomas W. Lamb   **Cost:** $2,000,000
>   **Year Remodeled:** 1976   **Architect:** Mel Glatz   **Cost:** $250,000
>   **Contact for Rental:** Manager;   (304) 525-8311

MARSHALL UNIVERSITY - JOAN C. EDWARDS PLAYHOUSE
400 Halgreer Boulevard, Huntington, WV 25755-2242
(304) 696-2787
　　Type of Facility: Auditorium
　　Type of Stage: Proscenium
　　Stage Dimensions: 52'Wx27'D
　　Seating Capacity: 650
　　Year Built: 1907
　　Year Remodeled: 1964
　　Contact for Rental: James Morris Smith;　(304) 696-7514
　　Resident Groups: Marshall University Performing Arts groups

MARSHALL UNIVERSITY - SMITH RECITAL HALL
400 Halgreer, Huntington, WV 25755-2242
(304) 696-3117
　　Type of Facility: Concert Hall
　　Type of Stage: Proscenium
　　Stage Dimensions: 57'Wx30'D
　　Seating Capacity: 650
　　Year Built: 1907
　　Year Remodeled: 1964
　　Contact for Rental: James Morris Smith;　(304) 696-2514
　　Resident Groups: Marshall University Performing Arts groups

Institute

FACILITY

WEST VIRGINIA STATE COLLEGE - F.S. BELCHER THEATRE
Fine Arts Building, Institute, WV 25112
(304) 766-3186
　　Type of Facility: Auditorium; Studio Performance; Theatre House
　　Type of Stage: Proscenium
　　Stage Dimensions: 30'x32'x35'　**Orchestra Pit**
　　Seating Capacity: 355
　　Year Built: 1965　**Architect:** C.E. Sillings　**Cost:** $1,700,000
　　Contact for Rental: David Wohl;　(304) 766-3186
　　Resident Groups: West Virginia State College Players

Keyser

THEATRE

APPLE ALLEY PLAYERS
PO Box 144, Keyser, WV 26726
(304) 788-1105
　　Founded: 1980
　　Arts Area: Community
　　Status: Non-Profit
　　Type: Resident; Sponsoring
　　Purpose: To provide quality theatre for the surrounding area
　　Officers: Annette Favara, President; Bob Shadler, Vice President; Alexa Fazenbaker, Secretary; Sandy Shadler, Treasurer
　　Volunteer Staff: 20
　　Paid Artists: 6
　　Utilizes: Special Technical Talent
　　Budget: $1,000 - $50,000
　　Income Sources: Business/Corporate Donations; Box Office; Government Grants; Individual Donations
　　Annual Attendance: 25,000
　　Performance Facilities: McKee Art Center, Potomac State College

---
Lewisburg

THEATRE

THE GREENBRIER VALLEY THEATRE
PO Box 494, Lewisburg, WV 24901
(304) 645-3838; (304) 645-1354
> **Founded:** 1966
> **Arts Area:** Summer Stock; Musical
> **Status:** Non-Professional
> **Type:** Performing; Touring; Educational
> **Purpose:** To provide a vehicle for bringing live, professional-quality theatre experiences to our community; to explore all practical means of encouraging the performing arts and artists in our area
> **Management:** Cathey Crowell Sawyer, Artistic Director; Kit Stauton, Managing Producer
> **Officers:** Greg Johnson, President; Rita Hassen, Secretary; Jack Hewitt, Treasurer
> **Volunteer Staff:** 40
> **Utilizes:** Guest Directors
> **Budget:** $50,000 - $100,000
> **Income Sources:** Private Foundations/Grants/Endowments; Business/Corporate Donations; Box Office; Individual Donations
> **Season:** 52 Weeks   **Annual Attendance:** 4,000
> **Performance Facilities:** The Barn

FACILITY

CARNEGIE HALL, INC.
105 Church Street, Lewisburg, WV 24901
(304) 645-7917
> **Founded:** 1983
> **Type of Facility:** Concert Hall; Auditorium; Performance Center; Multi-Purpose; Cultural/Educational Center
> **Facility Originally:** School
> **Type of Stage:** Proscenium
> **Stage Dimensions:** 31'x23'3"
> **Seating Capacity:** 500
> **Year Built:** 1902   **Architect:** W.G. McDowell   **Cost:** $33,000
> **Year Remodeled:** 1992   **Architect:** Paul Marshall
> **Acoustical Consultant:** Mary Leb
> **Contact for Rental:** Lynn Creamer;   (304) 645-7917

Morgantown

FACILITY

WEST VIRGINIA UNIVERSITY CREATIVE ARTS CENTER
PO Box 6111, Morgantown, WV 26505-6111
(304) 293-4841
> **Type of Facility:** Performance Center
> **Architect:** Alex Manhood
> **Acoustical Consultant:** Bolt, Beranek & Newman
> **Contact for Rental:** Mark Oreskovich;   (304) 293-4642, ext. 105
> **Resident Groups:** West Virginia University Divisions of Music and Theater; University Symphony Orchestra; University Jazz, Percussion and Wind Ensembles; University Concert Band; University Chorus
> *West Virginia University Creative Arts Center contains the Choral Recital Hall, Classroom Theatre, Concert Theatre, Opera Theatre and Studio Theater. See separate listings for additional information.*

WEST VIRGINIA UNIVERSITY CREATIVE ARTS CENTER - CHORAL RECITAL HALL
PO Box 6111, Morgantown, WV 26505-6111
(304) 293-4841
> **Type of Facility:** Concert Hall
> **Type of Stage:** Platform

Stage Dimensions: 40'Wx20'D
Seating Capacity: 150
Contact for Rental: Mark Oreskovich; (304) 293-4642, ext. 105

WEST VIRGINIA UNIVERSITY CREATIVE ARTS CENTER - CLASSROOM THEATRE
PO Box 6111, Morgantown, WV 26505-6111
(304) 293-4841
    Type of Facility: Theatre House; Room
    Type of Stage: Proscenium
    Stage Dimensions: 40'Wx25'D
    Seating Capacity: 50
    Contact for Rental: Mark Oreskovich; (304) 293-4642, ext. 105
    Used as a laboratory and experimental theater for students

WEST VIRGINIA UNIVERSITY CREATIVE ARTS CENTER - CONCERT THEATRE
PO Box 6111, Morgantown, WV 26505-6111
(304) 293-4841
    Type of Facility: Concert Hall; Theatre House; Opera House
    Type of Stage: Proscenium
    Stage Dimensions: 58'Wx40'D
    Orchestra Pit
    Seating Capacity: 1,500
    Contact for Rental: Mark Oreskovich; (304) 293-4642, ext. 105

WEST VIRGINIA UNIVERSITY CREATIVE ARTS CENTER - OPERA THEATRE
PO Box 6111, Morgantown, WV 26505-6111
(304) 293-4841
    Type of Facility: Theatre House; Opera House; Black Box
    Type of Stage: Flexible
    Seating Capacity: 150
    Contact for Rental: Mark Oreskovich; (304) 293-4642, ext. 105

WEST VIRGINIA UNIVERSITY CREATIVE ARTS CENTER - STUDIO THEATER
PO Box 6111, Morgantown, WV 26505-6111
(304) 293-4841
    Type of Facility: Theatre House; Black Box
    Type of Stage: Flexible
    Seating Capacity: 250
    Contact for Rental: Mark Oreskovich; (304) 293-4642, ext. 105

Oak Hill

PERFORMING SERIES

FAYETTE COUNTY FINE ARTS COUNCIL
1147 Country Club Road, Oak Hill, WV 25901
(304) 469-6517
    Founded: 1974
    Arts Area: Dance; Vocal Music; Theater
    Status: Non-Profit
    Type: Sponsoring
    Purpose: To provide fine-arts programs to an area which is culturally and economically deprived
    Officers: Betty M. Steen, Guy O. Baker, Co-Chairmen; Nancy Boyd, Secretary; Nancy Hannabass, Treasurer; Carolyn Hill, Historian
    Volunteer Staff: 10
    Utilizes: Special Technical Talent; Guest Artists
    Budget: $1,000 - $50,000
    Income Sources: Business/Corporate Donations; Box Office; Government Grants; Individual Donations
    Season: September - May
    Annual Attendance: 1,000
    Performance Facilities: Fayette High School; Oak Hill High School

---
Parkersburg

DANCE

PARKERSBURG WHEELING BALLET COMPANY
PO Box 4204, Parkersburg, WV 26104
(304) 428-2010
Founded: 1982
Arts Area: Ballet
Status: Professional; Non-Profit
Type: Performing; Touring; Educational; Sponsoring
Management: N. Gunter, Artistic Director; S. Gunter, Choreographer; D. Dix, Marketing Director; T. Forster, Development Director
Officers: Tom Wiseman, President; D. Dix, Vice President; S. LeMasters, Secretary; S. Stout, Treasurer
Paid Staff: 2 **Volunteer Staff:** 9
Paid Artists: 2 **Non-Paid Artists:** 40
Utilizes: Special Technical Talent; Guest Artists
Budget: $1,000 - $50,000
Income Sources: Business/Corporate Donations; Box Office; Government Grants; Individual Donations
Season: 52 Weeks
Annual Attendance: 40,000

Wheeling

INSTRUMENTAL MUSIC

WHEELING SYMPHONY
Hawley Building, Wheeling, WV 26003
(304) 232-6191
FAX: (304) 233-2679
Founded: 1929
Arts Area: Symphony; Orchestra
Status: Professional; Non-Profit
Type: Performing; Touring; Resident; Educational
Purpose: To provide balanced and diversified musical programs which broaden audience appreciation and improve the quality of life in our area
Management: Laura Willumsen, Executive Director
Officers: Joan C. Stamp, President
Paid Staff: 8
Paid Artists: 78
Utilizes: Guest Artists
Budget: $500,000 - $1,000,000
Income Sources: Private Foundations/Grants/Endowments; Business/Corporate Donations; Box Office; Government Grants; Individual Donations; Special Projects; Fund-raising
Season: 52 Weeks **Annual Attendance:** 40,000
Affiliations: ASOL; ASCAP; BMI
Performance Facilities: Capitol Music Hall

PERFORMING SERIES

OGLEBAY INSTITUTE
Oglebay Park, Wheeling, WV 26003
Founded: 1930
Arts Area: Dance; Instrumental Music; Theater; Lyric Opera
Status: Professional; Non-Profit
Type: Performing; Touring; Educational
Utilizes: Guest Artists
Budget: $1,000 - $50,000
Income Sources: Private Foundations/Grants/Endowments; Business/Corporate Donations; Box Office; Government Grants; Individual Donations
Season: October - May

FACILITY

CAPITOL MUSIC HALL
1015 Main Street, Wheeling, WV 26003
(304) 232-1170
FAX: (304) 234-0067
> **Type of Facility:** Concert Hall; Theatre House; Opera House
> **Type of Stage:** Proscenium
> **Stage Dimensions:** 72'Wx35'D; 44'W proscenium opening   **Orchestra Pit**
> **Seating Capacity:** 2,500
> **Year Built:** 1928
> **Year Remodeled:** 1977
> **Contact for Rental:** Paula Anderson
> **Resident Groups:** Wheeling Symphony; Music Hall Players; Jamboree USA

WHEELING CIVIC CENTER
14th Street, #2, Wheeling, WV 26003
(304) 233-7000
> **Type of Facility:** Arena; Multi-Purpose
> **Type of Stage:** Flexible
> **Seating Capacity:** Concert - 7,700; Festival - 9,800
> **Year Built:** 1977
> **Contact for Rental:** Dennis Magruder;   (304) 233-7000

WISCONSIN

Appleton

THEATRE

APPLETON WEST THEATRE
610 North Badger Avenue, Appleton, WI 54912
(414) 832-6259
Arts Area: Theatrical Group
Status: Non-Profit
Type: Educational
Management: Roger Danielson, Manager
Paid Staff: 4
Utilizes: Special Technical Talent; Guest Conductors; Guest Artists; Guest Directors
Budget: $1,000 - $50,000
Income Sources: Private Foundations/Grants/Endowments; Business/Corporate Donations; Box Office; Government Grants
Season: September - June   **Annual Attendance:** 50,000
Performance Facilities: Appleton West Community Auditorium

FACILITY

LAWRENCE UNIVERSITY - MUSIC-DRAMA CENTER
420 East College Avenue, Appleton, WI 54912
(414) 832-7000
Type of Facility: Concert Hall
Facility Originally: School
Type of Stage: Flexible   **Orchestra Pit**
Seating Capacity: 250
Year Built: 1958   **Architect:** Frank C. Shattuck Associates   **Cost:** $1,250,000
Acoustical Consultant: Bolt, Beranek & Newman
Contact for Rental: Conservatory Business Office, Lawrence University

Beloit

PERFORMING SERIES

BELOIT COLLEGE PERFORMING ARTS SERIES
700 College Street, Beloit, WI 53511
(608) 363-2577
FAX: (608) 363-2718
Arts Area: Dance; Vocal Music; Instrumental Music; Theater; Jazz
Status: Professional; Non-Profit
Management: William F. Faust, Events Coordinator
Paid Staff: 1
Utilizes: Guest Artists
Budget: $1,000 - $50,000
Income Sources: Private Foundations/Grants/Endowments; Box Office; Government Grants
Season: September - April   **Annual Attendance:** 650
Affiliations: Beloit College
Performance Facilities: Eaton Chapel

Eagle River

PERFORMING SERIES

HEADWATERS COUNCIL, PERFORMING ARTS
Box 1481, Eagle River, WI 54521
(715) 479-3131
FAX: (715) 479-1015
Founded: 1982
Arts Area: Dance; Vocal Music; Instrumental Music; Theater
Status: Non-Profit
Type: Performing

Purpose: To bring quality entertainment to our community, located in a rather remote area of Wisconsin
Officers: Sharon Nielsen, President; Robert Schroeter, Vice President; Deborah Heehn, Secretary; Mary Schwaiger, Treasurer
Volunteer Staff: 20
Utilizes: Guest Artists
Budget: $1,000 - $50,000
Income Sources: Business/Corporate Donations; Government Grants; Individual Donations
Season: October - May   **Annual Attendance:** 2,400
Performance Facilities: Northland Pines High School

FACILITY

NORTHLAND PINES HIGH SCHOOL
Eagle River, PO Box 1269, Eagle River, WI 54521
(715) 479-4473
Type of Facility: Auditorium
Type of Stage: Proscenium
Stage Dimensions: 40'Wx28'D
Seating Capacity: 500
Contact for Rental: Northland Pines High School;   (715) 479-4473
Resident Groups: Headwaters Council Performing Arts

Eau Claire

THEATRE

CHIPPEWA VALLEY THEATRE GUILD
316 Eau Claire Street, Eau Claire, WI 54701
(715) 832-7529
Founded: 1982
Arts Area: Community
Status: Non-Profit
Type: Performing; Educational
Purpose: To bring quality theatre productions to our area, as well as allowing community members to perform in a theatrical production
Officers: Susan Frederick, President; Lynn Weber, Vice President
Volunteer Staff: 50
Paid Artists: 3
Utilizes: Special Technical Talent; Guest Conductors; Guest Directors
Budget: $1,000 - $50,000
Income Sources: Private Foundations/Grants/Endowments; Business/Corporate Donations; Box Office; Individual Donations
Season: September - May   **Annual Attendance:** 5,000
Affiliations: Eau Claire Parks and Recreation
Performance Facilities: The State Regional Arts Center

PERFORMING SERIES

UNIVERSITY ARTISTS SERIES
Davies Center 133, University of Wisconsin, Eau Claire, WI 54702
(715) 836-4805
Arts Area: Dance; Vocal Music; Instrumental Music; Theater
Status: Non-Profit
Type: Performing; Educational
Purpose: To provide students and area citizens with opportunities to see and hear professional orchestras, solo artists, dance and opera
Management: Beatrice Foley, Performing Arts Director
Paid Staff: 8
Utilizes: Guest Conductors; Guest Artists; Guest Directors
Budget: $50,000 - $100,000
Income Sources: Box Office; Government Grants
Season: September - April   **Annual Attendance:** 9,400
Affiliations: APAP; NACA
Performance Facilities: University Arena, Fine Arts Center

FACILITY

W.L. ZORN ARENA
Garfield Avenue, Eau Claire, WI 54702-4004
(715) 836-4805
FAX: (715) 836-5030
> **Type of Facility:** Arena
> **Type of Stage:** Platform
> **Stage Dimensions:** 44'x48'
> **Seating Capacity:** 3,307
> **Year Built:** 1953
> **Contact for Rental:** Karen Stuber;   (715) 836-3881

Egg Harbor

PERFORMING SERIES

BIRCH CREEK MUSIC CENTER
PO Box 230, Egg Harbor, WI 54209
(414) 868-3763
> **Founded:** 1976
> **Arts Area:** Instrumental Music; Festivals
> **Status:** Professional; Non-Professional; Non-Profit
> **Type:** Performing; Resident; Educational
> **Purpose:** To present a summer concert series; to train young professionals and music students
> **Management:** James Dutton, Executive Director; Fran Dutton, Manager
> **Officers:** James Dutton, President; Duane Feurer, Vice President; Fran Dutton, Treasurer; Paul Dickinson, Secretary; Lois Deanne, Richard Stolley, and Bill White
> **Paid Staff:** 21   **Volunteer Staff:** 10
> **Paid Artists:** 35   **Non-Paid Artists:** 60
> **Utilizes:** Guest Artists
> **Budget:** $100,000 - $500,000
> **Income Sources:** Private Foundations/Grants/Endowments; Business/Corporate Donations; Box Office; Individual Donations
> **Season:** June - August   **Annual Attendance:** 7,500

FACILITY

BIRCH CREEK MUSIC CENTER
PO Box 230, Egg Harbor, WI 54209
(414) 868-3763
> **Founded:** 1976
> **Type of Facility:** Concert Hall; Performance Center
> **Facility Originally:** Barn
> **Type of Stage:** Thrust
> **Stage Dimensions:** 30'x30'
> **Seating Capacity:** 375
> *Summer music workshops*

Elm Grove

THEATRE

SUNSET PLAYHOUSE
800 Elm Grove Road, Elm Grove, WI 53122
(414) 782-4430
> **Founded:** 1953
> **Arts Area:** Community; Theatrical Group
> **Status:** Non-Professional; Non-Profit
> **Type:** Performing; Open Auditions
> **Purpose:** To introduce as many new people as possible to live entertainment
> **Management:** Tom Somerville, Artistic Director; John Kleis, Technical Director
> **Income Sources:** Box Office
> **Performance Facilities:** Sunset Playhouse

Ephraim

PERFORMING SERIES

PENINSULA FESTIVAL
PO Box 340, Ephraim, WI 54211
(414) 854-4060
    Founded: 1953
    Arts Area: Instrumental Music; Festivals
    Status: Professional; Non-Profit
    Type: Performing; Educational
    Purpose: To perform quality music in a casual atmosphere and promote young, new artists
    Management: Sharon Grutzmacher, General Manager
    Officers: Virginia Terhune, Chairman
    Paid Staff: 1 **Volunteer Staff:** 100
    Paid Artists: 55
    Utilizes: Guest Conductors; Guest Artists
    Budget: $100,000 - $500,000
    Income Sources: Private Foundations/Grants/Endowments; Business/Corporate Donations; Box Office; Government Grants; Individual Donations
    Season: August **Annual Attendance:** 7,500
    Affiliations: ASOL
    Performance Facilities: Door Community Auditorium

Fish Creek

THEATRE

THE PENINSULA PLAYERS
W4351 Peninsula Players Road, Fish Creek, WI 54212-9799
(414) 868-3287
FAX: (414) 868-3288
    Founded: 1935
    Arts Area: Professional; Summer Stock; Theatrical Group
    Status: Professional; Non-Profit
    Type: Performing; Resident; Educational
    Purpose: As America's oldest professional resident summer theatre, our purpose is to present the latest of Broadway fare.
    Management: Tom Birmingham, General Manager; James B. McKenzie, Executive Producer
    Budget: $100,000 - $500,000
    Income Sources: Private Foundations/Grants/Endowments; Business/Corporate Donations; Box Office; Individual Donations
    Season: June - October **Annual Attendance:** 33,000
    Affiliations: CORST; AEA
    Performance Facilities: Theatre in a Garden; Open Air Pavilion

---
Fond du Lac

INSTRUMENTAL MUSIC

FOND DU LAC SYMPHONIC BAND
536 East Tenth Street, PO Box 1779, Fond du Lac, WI 54916-1779
(414) 922-5703
    Founded: 1898
    Arts Area: Band
    Status: Semi-Professional; Non-Profit
    Type: Performing; Touring
    Purpose: To provide quality musical entertainment for our area and beyond; to enhance the image of the concert band as a performing medium; to provide a sophisticated performing opportunity for adult instrumentalists
    Management: Raymond C. Wifler, Music Director; Mary A. Arthur, Manager; Mary Liz Julka, Treasurer; Bruce Zabel, Equipment Manager; Joan Perry, Librarian
    Officers: Kathy Nachtwey, President; James Neujahr, Vice President; Tess Flaherty, Secretary
    Paid Staff: 5
    Paid Artists: 50 **Non-Paid Artists:** 20
    Utilizes: Guest Conductors; Guest Artists
    Budget: $1,000 - $50,000
    Income Sources: Private Foundations/Grants/Endowments; Business/Corporate Donations; Box Office; Government Grants; Individual Donations

Season: 52 Weeks   **Annual Attendance:** 10,000
Affiliations: Association of Concert Bands; AFM

Green Bay

INSTRUMENTAL MUSIC

GREEN BAY SYMPHONY ORCHESTRA
115 South Jefferson Street, Green Bay, WI 54301
(414) 435-3465
FAX: (414) 435-3465
  Founded: 1914
  Arts Area: Symphony; Orchestra; Chamber
  Status: Non-Profit
  Type: Performing; Educational
  Purpose: To maintain an orchestra of the highest quality possible within our means to enhance the cultural reputation of the area; to provide the youth of the community the opportunity to develop their musical abilities
  Management: Dr. James Bankhead, Executive Director
  Officers: Frederick L. Schmidt, President; David Schanke, Vice President; Rick Nuetzel, Treasurer
  Paid Staff: 4
  Paid Artists: 8   **Non-Paid Artists:** 75
  Utilizes: Guest Artists
  Budget: $500,000 - $1,000,000
  Income Sources: Private Foundations/Grants/Endowments; Business/Corporate Donations; Box Office; Government Grants; Individual Donations
  Season: October - May   **Annual Attendance:** 1,522
  Affiliations: ASOL; AWSO
  Performance Facilities: Weidner Center for The Performing Arts

FACILITY

WEIDNER CENTER FOR THE PERFORMING ARTS
2420 Nicolet Drive, Green Bay, WI 54311
(414) 465-2726
FAX: (414) 465-2619
  Founded: 1992
  Type of Facility: Theatre Complex; Concert Hall; Multi-Purpose
  Type of Stage: Flexible; Proscenium
  Orchestra Pit
  Seating Capacity: 2,040; 220; 90
  Year Built: 1992   **Architect:** Beckley Myers   **Cost:** $16,000,000
  Acoustical Consultant: Chris Jaffe and Associates
  Contact for Rental: Sid McQueen, Director;   (414) 465-2726

Green Lake

PERFORMING SERIES

GREEN LAKE FESTIVAL OF MUSIC
PO Box 569, Green Lake, WI 54941
(414) 748-9398
  Founded: 1979
  Arts Area: Vocal Music; Instrumental Music; Festivals
  Status: Professional; Semi-Professional; Non-Professional; Non-Profit
  Type: Performing; Touring; Resident; Educational; Sponsoring
  Purpose: The Green Lake Festival of Music is a non-profit corporation founded for cultural enrichment through the creation, promotion and public performance of the musical arts
  Management: Douglas Morris, Executive/Artistic Director; Marie Deitrich, Administrative Director
  Paid Staff: 2
  Paid Artists: 50   **Non-Paid Artists:** 130
  Utilizes: Guest Conductors; Guest Artists
  Budget: $50,000 - $100,000

Income Sources: Private Foundations/Grants/Endowments; Business/Corporate Donations; Box Office; Government Grants; Individual Donations
Season: June - August   **Annual Attendance:** 2,500

Hudson

FACILITY

PHIPPS CENTER FOR THE ARTS
109 Locust Street, Hudson, WI 54016
(715) 386-2305
    Founded: 1980
    Type of Facility: Concert Hall; Studio Performance; Performance Center; Theatre House; Multi-Purpose; Art Galleries & Studios
    Facility Originally: Meeting Hall; Movie House
    Type of Stage: Proscenium; Black Box
    Stage Dimensions: 87'Wx34'D; 17'Hx36'W proscenium opening   **Orchestra Pit**
    Seating Capacity: Proscenium - 241; Black Box - 125
    Year Built: 1983   **Architect:** BWBR Architects   **Cost:** $2,500,000
    Year Remodeled: 1992   **Architect:** KKE Architects   **Cost:** $4,000,000
    Acoustical Consultant: William H.O. Kroll
    Contact for Rental: General Manager;   (715) 386-2305
    Manager: John H. Potter;   (715) 386-2305
    Resident Groups: The Phipps Center for the Arts Drama Council; Children's Theatre Council; Music Council; Visual Arts Council; The Phipps Center Oratorio Society; The Western Wisconsin Photographic Club; The Phipps Festival Chorus

Kenosha

INSTRUMENTAL MUSIC

KENOSHA SYMPHONY ASSOCIATION, INC.
4917 68th Street, Kenosha, WI 53142
(414) 654-9080
FAX: (414) 654-9080
    Founded: 1941
    Arts Area: Symphony; Orchestra; Chamber
    Status: Professional; Semi-Professional; Non-Professional; Non-Profit
    Type: Performing; Educational
    Purpose: To provide a symphony orchestra in a community setting
    Management: Deborah Dunlap Ruffolo, General Manager
    Officers: Kathleen Braun, President; John Mongreig, First Vice President; Bill Kuessow, Second Vice President; Sharon Bailey, Secretary; Keith Bell, Treasurer
    Paid Staff: 1
    Paid Artists: 4
    Utilizes: Guest Artists
    Budget: $100,000 - $500,000
    Income Sources: Private Foundations/Grants/Endowments; Business/Corporate Donations; Box Office; Individual Donations
    Season: October - May
    Annual Attendance: 7,000
    Affiliations: Kenosha Unified Schools
    Performance Facilities: Reuther Auditorium

Kohler

PERFORMING SERIES

KOHLER FOUNDATION, INC.
104 Orchard Road, Kohler, WI 53044
(414) 458-1972
    Founded: 1940
    Arts Area: Dance; Vocal Music; Instrumental Music; Theater
    Status: Non-Profit
    Type: Performing
    Purpose: To provide cultural opportunities for the benefit of the community
    Management: Eleaner A. Jung, Executive Director

Paid Staff: 3
Paid Artists: 4
Budget: $1,000 - $50,000
Income Sources: Private Foundations/Grants/Endowments; Box Office
Season: September - April   **Annual Attendance:** 3,200
Performance Facilities: Kohler Memorial Theater

La Crosse

INSTRUMENTAL MUSIC

LA CROSSE SYMPHONY ORCHESTRA
815 South Ninth Street, La Crosse, WI 54601
(608) 791-0491
FAX: (608) 791-0367
Founded: 1938
Arts Area: Symphony; Orchestra; Ensemble; Instrumental Group
Status: Semi-Professional; Non-Profit
Type: Performing
Management: Marcee H. Peplinski, Manager
Officers: Kim Kress, President; Bill Schrum, Vice President; Brian Elder, Treasurer
Paid Staff: 3
Paid Artists: 53   **Non-Paid Artists:** 8
Utilizes: Special Technical Talent; Guest Artists
Budget: $100,000 - $500,000
Income Sources: Private Foundations/Grants/Endowments; Business/Corporate Donations; Box Office; Government Grants; Individual Donations
Season: October - May   **Annual Attendance:** 15,000
Affiliations: ASOL; AWSO
Performance Facilities: Viterbo College Fine Arts Center

VOCAL MUSIC

THE LA CROSSE BOYCHOIR
PO Box 186, 815 South Ninth Street, La Crosse, WI 54602
(608) 784-0040, ext. 476
Founded: 1974
Arts Area: Choral
Status: Professional; Non-Profit
Type: Performing; Touring
Purpose: To encourage, select and train boys from the La Crosse area in choral activities; to develop an appreciation for music and teach self-discipline and social responsibility; to develop a boychoir as a cultural asset; to arrange, sponsor and support musical engagements and other events
Management: Daniel Johnson-Wilmot, Founder/Director; Judy Stafslien, Accompanist
Officers: Ann Arlt, President; Roger Grant, First Vice President; Lynn Blakeley, Second Vice President; Ronald Pugh, Treasurer; Cynthia Vileth, Secretary
Paid Staff: 3   **Volunteer Staff:** 13
Utilizes: Guest Artists
Budget: $50,000 - $100,000
Income Sources: Private Foundations/Grants/Endowments; Business/Corporate Donations; Box Office; Government Grants; Individual Donations
Season: August - May   **Annual Attendance:** 5,000
Performance Facilities: Viterbo College Fine Arts Center

PERFORMING SERIES

GREAT RIVER FESTIVAL OF ARTS
119 King Street, La Crosse, WI 54601
(608) 785-1434
Founded: 1960
Arts Area: Dance; Vocal Music; Instrumental Music; Festivals
Status: Professional; Non-Profit
Type: Sponsoring
Management: Kathy Fitchuk, Administrator
Paid Staff: 1   **Volunteer Staff:** 1,500
Paid Artists: 100
Utilizes: Guest Artists
Budget: $50,000 - $100,000

Income Sources: Private Foundations/Grants/Endowments; Box Office; Individual Donations
Season: July - August   **Annual Attendance:** 28,500
Performance Facilities: Great River Festival of Arts

FACILITY

LA CROSSE CENTER
300 Harborview Plaza, La Crosse, WI 54601
(608) 789-7400
    Type of Facility: Auditorium; Civic Center; Arena
    Type of Stage: Flexible; Proscenium
    Stage Dimensions: 40'x60'
    Seating Capacity: 8,000
    Year Built: 1980   **Architect:** HRS Associates   **Cost:** $10,000,000
    Contact for Rental: (608) 782-4500
    Manager: Glen Walinski

Ladysmith

DANCE

LYNN DANCE COMPANY
W8555 Deertail Road, Ladysmith, WI 54848
(715) 532-6863
    Founded: 1976
    Arts Area: Modern
    Status: Professional
    Type: Performing; Resident; Educational
    Purpose: Development of the Chalicestream Dance Center for dance performance and teaching; dance development
    Management: Barry Lynn, Michael Doran
    Paid Staff: 2
    Paid Artists: 2
    Utilizes: Guest Artists
    Budget: $1,000 - $50,000
    Income Sources: Box Office; Individual Donations; Teaching
    Season: February - August
    Performance Facilities: Chalicestream Dance Center

Madison

DANCE

KANOPY DANCE THEATRE
315 North Henry Street, Madison, WI 53703
(608) 255-2211
    Founded: 1978
    Arts Area: Modern; Jazz
    Status: Professional
    Type: Performing; Touring; Resident; Educational; Sponsoring
    Purpose: To maintain a full-time dance company and teaching studio, present concerts, conduct residencies and teach classes
    Management: Elizabeth Ogden, Associate Director; Christine Stevens, Artistic Director; Mary Beth Heydt, General Clerical
    Officers: Deirdre Wilson Garton, President; David Egger, Secretary; Colin Jefcoate, Treasurer
    Paid Staff: 3   **Volunteer Staff:** 1
    Paid Artists: 10
    Utilizes: Special Technical Talent; Guest Conductors; Guest Artists; Guest Directors
    Budget: $50,000 - $100,000
    Income Sources: Private Foundations/Grants/Endowments; Business/Corporate Donations; Box Office; Government Grants; Individual Donations
    Season: September - May   **Annual Attendance:** 5,000
    Affiliations: Wisconsin Dance Council
    Performance Facilities: Kanopy Studio; Wisconsin Union Theatre

M.M. COLBERT
1321 East Johnson Street, Madison, WI 53703
(608) 257-9807
> **Founded:** 1980
> **Arts Area:** Modern; Ballet; Jazz
> **Status:** Non-Profit
> **Type:** Performing
> **Purpose:** To present original modern ballets in collaboration with other living artists
> **Management:** M. M. Colbert, Director/Choreographer
> **Officers:** Nancy Idaka Sheran, Chairperson, Board of Directors
> **Utilizes:** Special Technical Talent; Guest Artists
> **Budget:** $1,000 - $50,000
> **Income Sources:** Private Foundations/Grants/Endowments; Business/Corporate Donations; Box Office; Government Grants; Individual Donations
> **Annual Attendance:** 2,000

MADISON SCOTTISH COUNTRY DANCERS
2404 Fox Avenue, Madison, WI 53711
(608) 238-1227
> **Founded:** 1977
> **Arts Area:** Ethnic
> **Status:** Non-Professional; Non-Profit
> **Type:** Performing; Educational
> **Purpose:** To perform, teach, and promote Scottish country dancing and its music
> **Management:** Norma Briggs and Chuck Snowdon, Teachers
> **Officers:** Priscilla Arsove, Chair; Nancy McClements, Secretary
> **Volunteer Staff:** 2
> **Non-Paid Artists:** 60
> **Utilizes:** Guest Artists
> **Budget:** $1,000 - $50,000
> **Income Sources:** Business/Corporate Donations; Box Office; Government Grants; Individual Donations
> **Season:** 52 Weeks **Annual Attendance:** 3,000
> **Affiliations:** Royal Scottish Country Dance Society (Scotland)
> **Performance Facilities:** University of Wisconsin; Memorial Union

MELROSE MOTION COMPANY
1050 University Avenue, Madison, WI 53706
(608) 262-0382
> **Founded:** 1985
> **Arts Area:** Modern
> **Status:** Professional; Non-Profit
> **Type:** Performing; Touring
> **Purpose:** To present works by Claudia Melrose and selected guest artists; to create and maintain high standards for dance in the Midwest; to educate and build audiences; to create a strong reputation for dance in the Midwest; to bring quality modern dance to the largest public eye possible
> **Management:** Claudia Melrose, Director; Tim Glenn, Assistant
> **Paid Staff:** 1 **Volunteer Staff:** 10
> **Paid Artists:** 10 **Non-Paid Artists:** 1
> **Utilizes:** Special Technical Talent; Guest Artists
> **Budget:** $1,000 - $50,000
> **Income Sources:** Private Foundations/Grants/Endowments; Business/Corporate Donations; Box Office; Government Grants; Individual Donations
> **Season:** October - April **Annual Attendance:** 5,000
> **Affiliations:** University of Wisconsin-Madison

TAP-IT DANCING AND THEATRICAL COMPANY, LTD.
1957 Winnebago Street, Madison, WI 53704
(608) 244-2938
> **Founded:** 1985
> **Arts Area:** Jazz; Tap; Theater
> **Status:** Professional; Non-Profit
> **Type:** Performing; Touring; Educational; Sponsoring
> **Purpose:** To promote professional tap dance; to bring quality tap artists to the Midwest; to sponsor educational workshops and tap dance demonstrations; Tap-It creates and produces new theatre works; all productions speak to all socioeconomic backrounds
> **Management:** Donna Peckett, Danielle Dresden, Associate Directors
> **Officers:** Felicia Roberts, President; Valerie Hodgson, Vice President; Jane Denny, Secretary; Bob Queen, Treasurer
> **Paid Staff:** 2 **Volunteer Staff:** 3

Paid Artists: 10   Non-Paid Artists: 4
Utilizes: Special Technical Talent; Guest Artists
Budget: $1,000 - $50,000
Income Sources: Private Foundations/Grants/Endowments; Business/Corporate Donations; Box Office; Government Grants; Individual Donations
Season: 52 Weeks

WILLOW...A DANCE CONCERN
122 State Street, Lower Level, Madison, WI 53703
(608) 251-5233
Founded: 1975
Arts Area: Modern
Status: Non-Profit
Type: Performing
Purpose: To promote dance as a performing art and form of personal expression
Management: Phyllis Sanfilippo, Director
Volunteer Staff: 2
Non-Paid Artists: 5
Utilizes: Special Technical Talent; Guest Artists
Budget: $1,000 - $50,000
Income Sources: Private Foundations/Grants/Endowments; Business/Corporate Donations; Box Office; Government Grants; Individual Donations
Season: 52 Weeks   Annual Attendance: 1,000

INSTRUMENTAL MUSIC

MADISON JAZZ SOCIETY
PO Box 8866, Madison, WI 53708-8866
(608) 233-2702
Founded: 1984
Arts Area: Instrumental Group
Status: Non-Profit
Type: Sponsoring
Purpose: To promote the performance and education of jazz in the Madison area
Utilizes: Guest Artists
Budget: $1,000 - $50,000
Income Sources: Private Foundations/Grants/Endowments; Box Office; Individual Donations
Annual Attendance: 1,300

MADISON MUSIC COLLECTIVE
PO Box 2096, Madison, WI 53701-2096
(608) 241-4631
Founded: 1985
Arts Area: Ensemble; Instrumental Group; Electronic & Live Electronic; Improvised Music
Status: Non-Profit
Type: Educational; Sponsoring
Purpose: To support improvised music in the Madison Dane County Wisconsin area.
Officers: Joan Wildman, President; Dave Stoler, Vice President; Bill Grahm, Secretary; Don Breitenbach, Treasurer; Marilyn Fisher, Member at Large
Volunteer Staff: 10
Paid Artists: 50
Utilizes: Local and Regional Artists   Budget: $1,000 - $50,000
Income Sources: Private Foundations/Grants/Endowments; Business/Corporate Donations; Government Grants; Individual Donations
Season: 52 Weeks   Annual Attendance: 1,000
Affiliations: IAJE

MADISON SYMPHONY ORCHESTRA
211 North Carroll Street, Madison, WI 53703
(608) 257-3734
FAX: (608) 258-2315
Founded: 1926
Arts Area: Symphony
Status: Semi-Professional
Type: Performing; Educational
Management: Robert R. Palmer, General Manager
Officers: Marian Bolz, President
Paid Staff: 4
Paid Artists: 80

Utilizes: Guest Conductors; Guest Artists
Budget: $500,000 - $1,000,000
Income Sources: Private Foundations/Grants/Endowments; Business/Corporate Donations; Box Office; Government Grants; Individual Donations
Season: September - May   **Annual Attendance:** 16,000
Performance Facilities: Oscar Mayer Theatre

WISCONSIN CHAMBER ORCHESTRA
22 North Carroll Street, Suite 104, Madison, WI 53703
(608) 257-0638
FAX: (608) 257-0611
Founded: 1962
Arts Area: Orchestra; Chamber
Status: Professional; Non-Profit
Type: Performing
Purpose: To perform musical works
Management: Samuel Woodward, Executive Director; David Lewis Crosby, Artistic Director
Officers: Bob Mohelnitzky, President of Board; Susan Schmitz, Vice President; Joe Boucher, Treasurer; Stuart Sears, Secretary
Paid Staff: 4
Paid Artists: 40
Utilizes: Guest Conductors; Guest Artists
Budget: $100,000 - $500,000
Income Sources: Private Foundations/Grants/Endowments; Business/Corporate Donations; Box Office; Government Grants; Individual Donations
Season: 52 Weeks   **Annual Attendance:** 127,000
Performance Facilities: Capitol Square; First Congregational Church; Oscar Mayer Theatre

WISCONSIN YOUTH SYMPHONY ORCHESTRAS
1621 C Humanities Building, 455 North Park Street, Madison, WI 53706
(608) 263-3320
FAX: (608) 262-2150
Founded: 1966
Arts Area: Orchestra
Status: Non-Profit
Type: Performing; Touring; Educational
Purpose: To meet the symphonic needs of the musically-talented youth of southern Wisconsin
Management: James R. Smith, Music Director; Kenneth Strmiska, Manager
Officers: Steve Rosing, President
Paid Staff: 10
Utilizes: Special Technical Talent
Budget: $50,000 - $100,000
Income Sources: Private Foundations/Grants/Endowments; Business/Corporate Donations; Government Grants; Individual Donations
Season: September - May   **Annual Attendance:** 10,000
Performance Facilities: Mills Concert Hall, University of Wisconsin

VOCAL MUSIC

THE FESTIVAL CHOIR
PO Box 44634, Madison, WI 53744
(608) 849-9672
Founded: 1972
Arts Area: Operetta; Choral; Folk; A Cappella; Instrumental
Status: Semi-Professional; Non-Profit
Type: Performing; Touring
Purpose: To perform an ever-growing repertoire of choral works, drawn from classical literature, traditional carols, madrigals and contemporary compositions, for audiences worldwide
Management: David Lewis Crosby, Music Director/Conductor; Becky C. Olson, General Manager
Officers: Paul Cleven, President; Sarah Stoltz, Vice President/Secretary; June Johnson, Treasurer
Paid Staff: 2
Non-Paid Artists: 45
Utilizes: Guest Artists
Budget: $1,000 - $50,000
Income Sources: Private Foundations/Grants/Endowments; Business/Corporate Donations; Individual Donations
Season: September - April   **Annual Attendance:** 3,000
Performance Facilities: Madison Civic Center

THE MADISON BOYCHOIR
PO Box 326, Madison, WI 53701
(608) 256-5709
Founded: 1971
Arts Area: Choral
Status: Professional; Non-Profit
Type: Performing; Touring; Resident; Educational
Purpose: To encourage, select and train boys from the Madison area in choral activities; to develop an appreciation for music and to teach self-discipline and social responsibility; to be a cultural asset to the community, cooperating with other music groups in performances
Management: Gregory Dennis, Director; Margaret hadley, Accompanist; Ellen Seuferer, General Manager
Paid Staff: 4
Utilizes: Guest Artists
Budget: $100,000 - $500,000
Income Sources: Private Foundations/Grants/Endowments; Business/Corporate Donations; Box Office; Government Grants; Individual Donations
Season: June - May   **Annual Attendance:** 12,000

MADISON OPERA
458 Charles Lane, Madison, WI 53711
(608) 238-8085
Founded: 1962
Arts Area: Grand Opera; Light Opera
Status: Semi-Professional; Non-Profit
Type: Performing; Educational
Purpose: To bring quality opera, locally produced, to the city of Madison with sponsorship and support of the Madison Opera Guild
Management: Ann Stanke, Opera Manager; Robert Palmer, Manager, Madison Civic Music Association
Officers: Jack Poulson, President; Thomas Travers, Vice President; Mary Jane Woerpel, Secretary; C. George Extrom, Treasurer
Paid Staff: 1   **Volunteer Staff:** 38
Paid Artists: 75   **Non-Paid Artists:** 75
Utilizes: Special Technical Talent; Guest Artists; Guest Directors
Budget: $100,000 - $500,000
Income Sources: Private Foundations/Grants/Endowments; Business/Corporate Donations; Box Office; Government Grants; Individual Donations
Season: September - April   **Annual Attendance:** 5,000
Affiliations: OA; OGI
Performance Facilities: Oscar Mayer Theatre

OPERA FOR THE YOUNG
c/o James Tucker, 2914 Robin Court, Madison, WI 53711
(608) 274-3138
Founded: 1965
Arts Area: Lyric Opera; Light Opera
Status: Semi-Professional; Non-Profit
Type: Performing; Touring; Educational
Purpose: Touring of abridged opera productions (fully staged and performed in English) to schools throughout Wisconsin and northern Illinois
Management: James Tucker, Executive Director
Officers: Rachelle Richards, President; Susanna Herro, Vice President; Jane Ferris, Secretary; Mary Stroud, Treasurer
Volunteer Staff: 3
Paid Artists: 9
Budget: $50,000 - $100,000
Income Sources: Business/Corporate Donations; Box Office; Government Grants; Individual Donations
Season: September - May   **Annual Attendance:** 12,000

THEATRE

BROOM STREET THEATER
1119 Williamson Street, Madison, WI 53703
(608) 244-8338
Founded: 1969
Arts Area: Professional; Theatrical Group
Status: Professional; Non-Profit
Type: Performing

Purpose: Produces eight original plays by Madison playwrights per year. The shows are directed or supervised by the playwrights. Our work is highly visual and physical. We are one of the oldest experimental theaters in the United States, and occasionally tour.
Management: Joel Gersmann, Artistic Director; Gary Cleven, Technical Director
Officers: Rod Clark, Chairperson; Kurt Meyer, Acting Chairperson/Vice Chairperson; Tracy Will, Treasurer
Paid Staff: 3 **Volunteer Staff:** 25
Paid Artists: 64 **Non-Paid Artists:** 150
Budget: $50,000 - $100,000
Income Sources: Private Foundations/Grants/Endowments; Business/Corporate Donations; Box Office; Government Grants; Individual Donations
Season: 52 Weeks **Annual Attendance:** 6,000

MADISON REPERTORY THEATRE
122 State Street, Suite 201, Madison, WI 53703
(608) 256-0029
> **Founded:** 1969
> **Arts Area:** Professional
> **Status:** Professional
> **Type:** Performing; Resident
> **Management:** Joseph Hanreddy, Artistic Director; Vick Stewart, Managing Director
> **Officers:** Beth Korth, President
> **Paid Staff:** 8 **Volunteer Staff:** 20
> **Utilizes:** Guest Artists; Guest Directors
> **Budget:** $1,000,000 - $5,000,000
> **Income Sources:** Private Foundations/Grants/Endowments; Business/Corporate Donations; Box Office; Government Grants; Individual Donations
> **Season:** July - May **Annual Attendance:** 33,000
> **Affiliations:** TCG
> **Performance Facilities:** Madison Civic Center

MADISON THEATRE GUILD
2410 Monroe Street, Madison, WI 53711
(608) 238-9322
> **Founded:** 1946
> **Arts Area:** Community; Theatrical Group
> **Status:** Non-Profit
> **Type:** Performing; Educational
> **Purpose:** To provide education and recreation through theatrical production
> **Management:** Robby Sonzogi, Costume Shop Manager
> **Officers:** Jay Rath, President; Carol Pierick, Treasurer
> **Paid Staff:** 4 **Volunteer Staff:** 15
> **Non-Paid Artists:** 150
> **Utilizes:** Special Technical Talent; Guest Directors
> **Budget:** $50,000 - $100,000
> **Income Sources:** Private Foundations/Grants/Endowments; Business/Corporate Donations; Box Office; Government Grants; Individual Donations
> **Season:** September - May **Annual Attendance:** 8,000
> **Affiliations:** Wisconsin Theatre Association
> **Performance Facilities:** McDaniels Auditorium

WISCONSIN UNION THEATER
800 Langdon Street, Madison, WI 53706-1495
(608) 262-2202
FAX: (608) 262-5487
> **Founded:** 1939
> **Arts Area:** Professional; Musical; Community; Folk; Theatrical Group
> **Status:** Non-Profit
> **Type:** Sponsoring
> **Purpose:** Cultural, entertainment and educational programming for university and community audiences
> **Management:** Michael Goldberg, Director; Rauel LaBreche, Operations Manager
> **Paid Staff:** 10 **Volunteer Staff:** 40
> **Paid Artists:** 60
> **Utilizes:** Special Technical Talent; Guest Artists
> **Budget:** $100,000 - $500,000
> **Income Sources:** Box Office; Government Grants
> **Season:** September - May **Annual Attendance:** 200,000
> **Affiliations:** APAP
> **Performance Facilities:** Wisconsin Union Theater

FACILITY

MADISON CIVIC CENTER
211 State Street, Madison, WI 53703
(608) 266-6550
>**Type of Facility:** Theatre Complex; Civic Center; Multi-Purpose
>**Year Built:** 1980
>**Architect:** Hardy, Holtzman & Pfeiffer
>**Contact for Rental:** Rudy Lienau;   (608) 266-6550
>**Resident Groups:** Madison Art Center; Madison Symphony Orchestra; CTM, Inc.; The Rep
>*Madison Civic Center contains the Isthmus Playhouse and Oscar Mayer Theatre. See separate listings for further information.*

MADISON CIVIC CENTER - ISTHMUS PLAYHOUSE
211 State Street, Madison, WI 53703
(608) 266-6550
>**Type of Facility:** Auditorium; Performance Center; Theatre House
>**Type of Stage:** Thrust
>**Stage Dimensions:** 30'x18'; 20'x24' proscenium opening
>**Seating Capacity:** 343
>**Year Built:** 1979   **Architect:** Hardy Holzman & Pfeiffer
>**Acoustical Consultant:** Jaffe Acoustics
>**Contact for Rental:** Rudy Lienau;   (608) 266-6550
>**Resident Groups:** CTM, Inc.; Madison Repertory Theater

MADISON CIVIC CENTER - OSCAR MAYER THEATRE
211 State Street, Madison, WI 53703
(608) 266-6550
>**Type of Facility:** Auditorium; Theatre House; Multi-Purpose
>**Facility Originally:** Vaudeville; Movie House
>**Type of Stage:** Proscenium
>**Stage Dimensions:** 42'Dx80'W; 56' proscenium opening   **Orchestra Pit**
>**Seating Capacity:** 2,225
>**Year Built:** 1928   **Architect:** Rapp & Rapp
>**Year Remodeled:** 1980   **Architect:** Hardy Holzman & Pfeiffer   **Cost:** $9,000,000
>**Acoustical Consultant:** Jaffe Acoustics
>**Contact for Rental:** Rudy Lienau;   (608) 266-6550
>**Resident Groups:** Madison Civic Music Association

Manitowoc

FACILITY

SILVER LAKE COLLEGE
2406 South Alverno Road, Manitowoc, WI 54220
(414) 684-6691
>**Type of Facility:** Concert Hall; Performance Center; Theatre House
>**Facility Originally:** Church
>**Type of Stage:** Proscenium; Platform
>**Seating Capacity:** 380
>**Year Built:** 1960
>**Acoustical Consultant:** L. Brey
>**Resident Groups:** Silver Lake College Concert Band; Jazz Band; Madrigal Singers; Concert Choir; Recorder Ensemble; String Ensemble; Women's Choir
>*Concerts; Recitals; Lectures*

Marshfield

INSTRUMENTAL MUSIC

MARSHFIELD-WOOD COMMUNITY SYMPHONY
2000 West Fifth Street, Marshfield, WI 54449
(715) 387-1147
FAX: (715) 389-6539
>**Founded:** 1965
>**Arts Area:** Symphony; Orchestra
>**Status:** Non-Profit

Type: Performing; Educational
Purpose: To present the best music possible for the least possible cost
Management: Robert I. Biederwolf, Conductor
Officers: Sarah Hanson, President, Friends of the Orchestra
Paid Staff: 1   **Volunteer Staff:** 20
Utilizes: Guest Artists
Budget: $1,000 - $50,000
Income Sources: Private Foundations/Grants/Endowments; Business/Corporate Donations; Box Office; Government Grants; Individual Donations
Season: October - May   **Annual Attendance:** 1,800
Affiliations: ASOL
Performance Facilities: Fine Arts Building Theatre

PERFORMING SERIES

UNIVERSITY OF WISCONSIN LECTURES AND FINE ARTS SERIES
200 West 5th Street, Marshfield, WI 54449
(715) 387-1147
Founded: 1962
Arts Area: Dance; Vocal Music; Instrumental Music; Theater
Status: Non-Profit
Type: Educational; Sponsoring
Purpose: Provide performances and lectures for the University and the community
Management: Robert I. Biederwolf, Professor of Music
Paid Staff: 1
Paid Artists: 20
Utilizes: Guest Artists
Budget: $1,000 - $50,000
Income Sources: Private Foundations/Grants/Endowments; Business/Corporate Donations; Box Office; Government Grants; Individual Donations
Season: August - May
Performance Facilities: University of Wisconsin Center Theater

Menasha

INSTRUMENTAL MUSIC

FOX VALLEY SYMPHONY
1800 Appleton Road, Menasha, WI 54952
(414) 731-3385
Founded: 1966
Arts Area: Symphony
Status: Non-Profit
Type: Performing; Resident; Educational; Sponsoring
Purpose: To provide symphonic music for all; to sponsor youth orchestras
Management: Patricia D. Rodgers, General Manager
Officers: Robert Young, President, Fox Valley Symphony Association; Jeanette Kranzusch, President, Symphony League
Paid Staff: 2
Paid Artists: 2
Utilizes: Guest Conductors; Guest Artists
Budget: $100,000 - $500,000
Income Sources: Private Foundations/Grants/Endowments; Business/Corporate Donations; Box Office; Government Grants; Individual Donations
Season: September - May   **Annual Attendance:** 8,000
Affiliations: ASOL; AWSO; Fox Valley Arts Alliance
Performance Facilities: Pickard Auditorium; Lawrence University Chapel

PERFORMING SERIES

UNIVERSITY OF WISCONSIN CENTER - FOX VALLEY
1478 Midway Road, Menasha, WI 54952
(414) 832-2600
Arts Area: Dance; Vocal Music; Instrumental Music; Theater
Status: Non-Profit
Type: Performing; Educational
Paid Staff: 1
Budget: $1,000 - $50,000

Income Sources: Private Foundations/Grants/Endowments; Box Office; Student Fees
Season: September - May
Annual Attendance: 1,500
Performance Facilities: Fine Arts Theatre

Menomonie

THEATRE

GREENWOOD PLAYERS CHILDREN'S THEATER
314 11th Street, Menomonie, WI 54751
(715) 235-6650
Founded: 1981
Arts Area: THEATRE
Status: Semi-Professional; Non-Profit
Type: Performing; Touring; Resident; Educational
Purpose: To create original plays based on folk tales using improvisation
Management: Marion Lang, Artistic Director; Nancy Blake, Program Coordinator
Officers: William O'Neill, President; Jane B. Hoyt, Treasurer
Paid Staff: 4
Paid Artists: 10
Budget: $50,000 - $100,000
Income Sources: Private Foundations/Grants/Endowments; Business/Corporate Donations; Box Office; Government Grants; Individual Donations
Season: 52 Weeks
Annual Attendance: 4,000
Affiliations: Educational Outreach
Performance Facilities: Mabel Tainter Theater

MABEL TAINTER MEMORIAL THEATER
205 Main Street, Menomonie, WI 54751
(715) 235-9726
Founded: 1890
Arts Area: Professional; Musical; Community; Folk
Status: Non-Profit
Type: Sponsoring
Purpose: Historic 1890's theater with a performing arts season
Management: Maggie Foote, Executive Director
Paid Staff: 8   **Volunteer Staff:** 15
Utilizes: Guest Artists
Budget: $100,000 - $500,000
Income Sources: Private Foundations/Grants/Endowments; Business/Corporate Donations; Box Office; Government Grants; Individual Donations
Season: 52 Weeks   **Annual Attendance:** 10,800
Affiliations: League of Historic American Theaters
Performance Facilities: Mabel Tainter Memorial Theater

FACILITY

MABEL TAINTER MEMORIAL THEATER BUILDING
205 Main Street, PO Box 250, Menomonie, WI 54751
(715) 235-9726, ext. 0001
Type of Facility: Concert Hall; Auditorium; Performance Center; Theatre House; Opera House; Civic Center; Multi-Purpose
Facility Originally: Library; Church; Meeting Hall; Movie House
Type of Stage: Thrust; Proscenium
Stage Dimensions: 26'1/2"x20'x14'H   **Orchestra Pit**
Seating Capacity: 313
Year Built: 1889   **Architect:** Harvey Ellis, L. S. Buffington Company   **Cost:** $125,000
Year Remodeled: 1966   **Architect:** DeNardo Studios   **Cost:** $80,000
Contact for Rental: Maggie Foote, Executive Director;   (715) 235-9726
Resident Groups: Greenwood Players Children's Theater

Middleton

DANCE

MESOGHIOS DANCE TROUP
3813 South Meadow Drive, Middleton, WI 53562
(608) 831-4485
Founded: 1978
Arts Area: Ethnic; Folk
Status: Semi-Professional; Non-Profit
Type: Performing; Educational
Purpose: Performance of Greek, Turkish and Russian ethnic and folk dances, and presentation and description of Greek and Turkish ethnic dress, decoration and custom
Management: Vicky Knoedler, Artistic Director
Officers: Craig Schreiner, President; Vicky Knoedler, President-Elect; William Knoedler, Secretary/Treasurer
Volunteer Staff: 1
Non-Paid Artists: 15
Utilizes: Guest Artists; Guest Choreographers
Budget: $1,000 - $50,000
Income Sources: Private Foundations/Grants/Endowments; Box Office; Government Grants; Individual Donations
Season: 52 Weeks   **Annual Attendance:** 5,000

Milwaukee

DANCE

BAUER CONTEMPORARY BALLET
727 North Milwaukee Street, Milwaukee, WI 53202
(414) 276-3180
Founded: 1974
Arts Area: Modern; Ballet; Jazz; Tap
Status: Professional; Non-Profit
Type: Performing; Touring; Resident; Educational
Purpose: To move toward becoming a repertory company performing new works from various choreographers
Management: Susie Bauer, Artistic Director; Richard Rovito, Executive Director
Officers: Polly Morris, President; Ray Vogel, Vice President; Michael Williams, Treasurer; Eddie Jackson; Sally Ann Mesich
Paid Staff: 2   **Volunteer Staff:** 2
Paid Artists: 8
Utilizes: Guest Choreographers
Budget: $100,000 - $500,000
Income Sources: Private Foundations/Grants/Endowments; Business/Corporate Donations; Box Office; Government Grants; Individual Donations
Season: 52 Weeks   **Annual Attendance:** 1,000
Affiliations: United Performing Arts Fund
Performance Facilities: Bauer Contemporary Ballet Studio Theatre

BETTY SALAMUN'S DANCECIRCUS
404 South Seventh Street, 2nd Floor, Milwaukee, WI 53204
(414) 272-6683
Founded: 1975
Arts Area: Modern; Folk
Status: Professional; Non-Profit
Type: Performing; Touring; Educational
Purpose: To encourage advancement of the fine arts
Management: Betty Salamun, Artistic Director; Gordon Reistad, Compny Manager
Officers: Susan Mingesz, Board President; David H.B. Drake, Controller
Paid Staff: 3
Utilizes: Guest Artists; Guest Choreographers
Budget: $50,000 - $100,000
Income Sources: Private Foundations/Grants/Endowments; Business/Corporate Donations; Box Office; Government Grants; Individual Donations; Classes
Season: 52 Weeks   **Annual Attendance:** 30,000

DANCECIRCUS LIMITED
404 South Seventh Street, 2nd Floor, Milwaukee, WI 53204
(414) 272-6683
Founded: 1975

Arts Area: Modern; Arts/Environment
Status: Professional
Type: Performing; Touring; Resident; Educational; Sponsoring
Purpose: Professional touring modern dance company emphasizing environmental programs in concert and outreach programs and a diverse modern dance repertoire concert
Management: Betty Salamun, Artistic Director; Gordon Reistad, Company Manager
Officers: Susan Mingesz, President; Terry Rice, Treasurer; Becky Skulrolsky, Secretary
Paid Staff: 3   **Volunteer Staff:** 1
Paid Artists: 6
Utilizes: Special Technical Talent; Guest Artists; Guest Choreographers; Poets, Visual Artists, Composers
Budget: $50,000 - $100,000
Income Sources: Private Foundations/Grants/Endowments; Business/Corporate Donations; Box Office; Government Grants; Individual Donations
Season: 52 Weeks   **Annual Attendance:** 30,000

MILWAUKEE BALLET
504 West National Avenue, Milwaukee, WI 53204
(414) 643-7677
FAX: (414) 649-4066
Founded: 1970
Arts Area: Ballet
Status: Professional; Non-Profit
Type: Performing; Touring; Resident; Educational
Purpose: To blend volunteer support, artistic direction, and professional management to create, nurture, and preserve a nationally recognized, resident ballet company performing classical, contemporary and new works on a scale which evokes support sufficient to endure
Management: Dane LaFontsee, Artistic Director; Basil Thompson, Ballet Master Regisseur
Officers: Gary Keller, President/Chief Executive Officer
Paid Staff: 29   **Volunteer Staff:** 650
Paid Artists: 60
Utilizes: Special Technical Talent; Guest Artists
Budget: $1,000,000 - $5,000,000
Income Sources: Private Foundations/Grants/Endowments; Business/Corporate Donations; Box Office; Government Grants; Individual Donations
Season: September - May   **Annual Attendance:** 86,000
Affiliations: Arts Midwest, Wisconsin Citizens for the Arts
Performance Facilities: Uihlein Hall; Milwaukee Performing Arts Center

INSTRUMENTAL MUSIC

EARLY MUSIC NOW
PO Box 71303, Milwaukee, WI 53211-1303
(414) 225-3113
FAX: (414) 278-0335
Founded: 1986
Arts Area: Early Music
Status: Non-Profit
Type: Educational; Sponsoring
Purpose: To enrich and expand Milwaukee's musical offerings by presenting historically informed performances and educational experiences by recognized artists and ensembles who specialize in music before 1800
Officers: Ralph Bielenberg, President; Eric Duncan, Vice President; Jean Neal, Secretary; JoAnn Husslein, Treasurer; Thallis Hoyt Drake, Founder
Volunteer Staff: 25
Utilizes: Guest Artists
Budget: $1,000 - $50,000
Income Sources: Private Foundations/Grants/Endowments; Box Office; Individual Donations
Season: September - May   **Annual Attendance:** 1,500
Performance Facilities: Public Library Hall

MILWAUKEE CHAMBER ORCHESTRA
929 North Water Street, Milwaukee, WI 53202
(414) 347-1564
Founded: 1974
Arts Area: Orchestra; Chamber
Status: Professional
Type: Performing

Purpose: To present six to ten concerts annually, encompassing chamber orchestra repertoire from Baroque to 20th century
Management: Lisa A. Froemming, Managing Director; Stephen Colburn, Music Director
Officers: Herbert M. Swick, MD, President; Joseph F. Ahern, Marlene Stocking, Vice Presidents; Thomas Wakefield, Treasurer
Paid Staff: 2   **Volunteer Staff:** 4
Paid Artists: 60
Utilizes: Guest Conductors; Guest Artists
Budget: $100,000 - $500,000
Income Sources: Private Foundations/Grants/Endowments; Business/Corporate Donations; Box Office; Government Grants; Individual Donations
Season: September - June   **Annual Attendance:** 4,000
Performance Facilities: Vogel Hall, Milwaukee County Performing Arts Center

MILWAUKEE SYMPHONY ORCHESTRA
330 East Kilbourn Avenue, Suite 900, Milwaukee, WI 53202
(414) 291-6010
FAX: (414) 291-7610
Founded: 1959
Arts Area: Symphony; Orchestra
Status: Professional; Non-Profit
Type: Performing; Touring; Educational
Management: Gary L. Good, Executive Director
Officers: Michael J. Schmitz, President
Paid Artists: 95
Budget: Over 10,000,000
Income Sources: Private Foundations/Grants/Endowments; Business/Corporate Donations; Box Office; Government Grants; Individual Donations
Season: September - July
Performance Facilities: Performing Arts Center; Uihlein Hall

MILWAUKEE YOUTH SYMPHONY ORCHESTRA
929 North Water Street, Milwaukee, WI 53202
(414) 272-8540
Founded: 1956
Arts Area: Symphony; Orchestra; Chamber; Ensemble
Status: Non-Professional; Non-Profit; Youth Orchestra
Type: Performing; Educational
Management: Frances S. Richman, Managing Director; Susan M. Chandler, Music Coordinator; Margery Deutsch, Music Director/Senior Symphony
Officers: Wilson D. Perry, President
Paid Staff: 15
Utilizes: Guest Conductors; Guest Artists
Budget: $100,000 - $500,000
Income Sources: Private Foundations/Grants/Endowments; Business/Corporate Donations; Box Office; Government Grants; Individual Donations; Student Fees
Season: September - May
Annual Attendance: 10,000
Affiliations: ASOL
Performance Facilities: Uihlein Hall

PRESENT MUSIC, INCORPORATED
1840 North Farwell, Suite 301, Milwaukee, WI 53202
(414) 271-0711
Founded: 1983
Arts Area: Chamber; Ensemble; Instrumental Group
Status: Professional; Non-Profit
Type: Performing; Touring; Resident; Educational; Recording
Purpose: To broaden public appreciation of music with an emphasis on small ensemble productions of contemporary concert music in a manner that is engaging, provocative and fun
Management: Kevin Stalheim, Artistic Director; Daniel Petry, Managing Director
Officers: Timothy C. Frautschi, President; James Chenevert, Secretary
Utilizes: Guest Artists
Budget: $100,000 - $500,000
Income Sources: Private Foundations/Grants/Endowments; Business/Corporate Donations; Box Office; Government Grants; Individual Donations
Season: September - May
Affiliations: NPN; Art Reach Milwaukee

VOCAL MUSIC

THE BACH CHAMBER CHOIR AND ORCHESTRA
PO Box 14503, Milwaukee, WI 53214
(414) 228-7468
> **Founded:** 1970
> **Arts Area:** Choral
> **Status:** Semi-Professional; Non-Profit
> **Type:** Performing
> **Purpose:** To promote chamber music and choral music to the public through performance
> **Management:** Steven L. Joyal, Music Director; Liz Joyal, General Manager
> **Officers:** Carol Kennedy, President; Ed Eurich, Vice President; Patricia P. Radzin, Secretary; Ellen Chesak Ball, Treasurer
> **Paid Staff:** 2   **Volunteer Staff:** 11
> **Non-Paid Artists:** 45
> **Utilizes:** Guest Artists
> **Budget:** $1,000 - $50,000
> **Income Sources:** Private Foundations/Grants/Endowments; Business/Corporate Donations; Box Office; Individual Donations
> **Season:** 52 Weeks   **Annual Attendance:** 1,000

BEL CANTO CHORUS OF MILWAUKEE
828 North Broadway, #510, Milwaukee, WI 53202
(414) 272-7950
> **Founded:** 1945
> **Arts Area:** Choral
> **Status:** Semi-Professional; Non-Profit
> **Type:** Performing; Touring
> **Purpose:** To present to the citizens of Milwaukee and Southeastern Wisconsin the great choral literature for chorus and orchestra
> **Management:** Kathleen Asta, General Manager; Richard Hynson, Musical Director
> **Paid Staff:** 2
> **Paid Artists:** 10   **Non-Paid Artists:** 150
> **Utilizes:** Guest Conductors; Guest Artists
> **Budget:** $100,000 - $500,000
> **Income Sources:** Private Foundations/Grants/Endowments; Business/Corporate Donations; Box Office; Government Grants; Individual Donations
> **Season:** September - June   **Annual Attendance:** 10,000
> **Affiliations:** CA; United Performing Arts Fund
> **Performance Facilities:** Performing Arts Center; Pabst Theater

FLORENTINE OPERA COMPANY
750 North Lincoln Memorial Drive, Milwaukee, WI 53202
(414) 273-1474
FAX: (414) 273-2480
> **Founded:** 1933
> **Arts Area:** Grand Opera
> **Status:** Professional; Non-Profit
> **Type:** Performing; Touring; Educational
> **Purpose:** Production of Grand Opera in the state of Wisconsin
> **Management:** Dennis Hanthorn, General Manager; Joseph Rescigno, Artistic Director
> **Officers:** George T. Jacobi, President
> **Paid Staff:** 8
> **Paid Artists:** 285
> **Utilizes:** Special Technical Talent; Guest Conductors; Guest Artists; Guest Directors
> **Budget:** $1,000,000 - $5,000,000
> **Income Sources:** Private Foundations/Grants/Endowments; Business/Corporate Donations; Box Office; Government Grants; Individual Donations
> **Season:** November - May   **Annual Attendance:** 32,000
> **Affiliations:** OA; United Performing Arts Foundation
> **Performance Facilities:** Milwaukee Performing Arts Center; Pabst Theater

MILWAUKEE OPERA COMPANY
820 East Knapp Street, Milwaukee, WI 53202
(414) 276-2244; (414) 961-1474
> **Founded:** 1966
> **Arts Area:** Grand Opera; Light Opera; Operetta
> **Status:** Professional; Non-Profit
> **Type:** Performing; Educational

Purpose: To develop and showcase local and regional artists; to develop audiences for Milwaukee arts groups; to present opera and musical theatre at moderate prices
Management: Josephine Busalacchi, Executive Director/Founder
Paid Staff: 4 **Volunteer Staff:** 4
Paid Artists: 100
Utilizes: Guest Artists
Budget: $50,000 - $100,000
Income Sources: Private Foundations/Grants/Endowments; Business/Corporate Donations; Box Office; Government Grants; Individual Donations
Season: 52 Weeks **Annual Attendance:** 25,000
Performance Facilities: Pabst Theatre; Milwaukee Performing Arts Center; Lincoln Center for the Arts

SKYLIGHT COMIC OPERA LIMITED
813 North Jefferson Street, Milwaukee, WI 53202
(414) 271-9580
FAX: (414) 271-8896
Founded: 1959
Arts Area: Grand Opera; Lyric Opera; Light Opera; Operetta; Musical Theatre
Status: Professional; Non-Profit
Type: Performing; Resident; Educational; Sponsoring
Purpose: To present musical theater in southeastern Wisconsin; to make the productions the best possible
Management: Chas Rader-Shieber, Artistic Director; Richard Carsey, Music Director
Officers: Byron Foster, President; Linda Rieke, Vice President of Finance
Paid Staff: 9
Paid Artists: 230
Utilizes: Special Technical Talent; Guest Conductors; Guest Artists; Guest Directors
Budget: $1,000,000 - $5,000,000
Income Sources: Private Foundations/Grants/Endowments; Business/Corporate Donations; Box Office; Government Grants; Individual Donations; Fund-raising
Season: September - May; July; August **Annual Attendance:** 42,000
Affiliations: OA; Arts, Inc; AAA
Performance Facilities: Skylight Theatre

THEATRE

ACACIA THEATRE
924 East Juneau Avenue, Suite 227, Milwaukee, WI 53202-2748
(414) 223-4996
Founded: 1980
Arts Area: Theatrical Group
Status: Semi-Professional; Non-Profit
Type: Touring; Resident; Educational
Purpose: To produce plays of various kinds on a regular basis with a Christian world view
Management: Jon Layton, Artistic Director; Jeffrey Bohmann, Marketing Director
Officers: David Stubbs, President; Jane Domach, Secretary; Randy Peterson, Treasurer
Paid Staff: 2 **Volunteer Staff:** 90
Paid Artists: 5 **Non-Paid Artists:** 10
Utilizes: Special Technical Talent; Guest Artists; Guest Directors
Budget: $100,000 - $500,000
Income Sources: Private Foundations/Grants/Endowments; Business/Corporate Donations; Box Office; Individual Donations
Season: October - August **Annual Attendance:** 43,000

THE GREAT AMERICAN CHILDREN'S THEATRE COMPANY
PO Box 92123, Milwaukee, WI 53202
(414) 276-4230
FAX: (414) 276-2214
Founded: 1975
Arts Area: Professional
Status: Professional; Non-Profit
Type: Performing; Touring; Educational; Sponsoring
Purpose: To provide quality theatre for young audiences
Management: Teri Solomon Mitze, Producer; Annie Jurczyk, Managing Director
Officers: Paul Medved, President; Danita Medved, Vice President of Development; Thomas Balgeman, Secretary/Treasurer
Paid Staff: 3 **Volunteer Staff:** 100
Paid Artists: 1
Utilizes: Special Technical Talent; Guest Artists
Budget: $1,000,000 - $5,000,000

Income Sources: Private Foundations/Grants/Endowments; Business/Corporate Donations; Box Office; Individual Donations
Season: September - May   **Annual Attendance:** 70,000
Performance Facilities: Pabst Theatre

MILWAUKEE CHAMBER THEATRE
152 West Wisconsin Avenue, Suite 731, Milwaukee, WI 53203
(414) 276-8842
FAX: (414) 276-8842
Founded: 1979
Arts Area: Theatrical Group
Status: Professional; Non-Profit
Type: Performing; Touring; Resident
Purpose: To produce professional quality shows of a classical and neoclassical nature, highlighting the season with an annual Shaw Festival (George Bernard) in May and June
Management: Carla Slawson, General Manager; Montgomery Davis, Artistic Director; Sharon Middleton, Subscription Manager
Officers: Richard Moake, President; Mary Ann Gerlack, Vice President; Richard Meadows, Secretary; Philip Crump, Treasurer
Paid Staff: 3   **Volunteer Staff:** 4
Paid Artists: 35   **Non-Paid Artists:** 10
Utilizes: Guest Artists; Guest Directors
Budget: $100,000 - $500,000
Income Sources: Private Foundations/Grants/Endowments; Business/Corporate Donations; Box Office; Government Grants; Individual Donations
Season: October - June   **Annual Attendance:** 12,500
Affiliations: TCG
Performance Facilities: Stiemke Theatre; Helfaer Theatre

MILWAUKEE PUBLIC THEATRE
PO Box 07147, Milwaukee, WI 53207
(414) 271-8484
Founded: 1973
Arts Area: Professional; Musical; Theatrical Group; Puppet
Status: Professional
Type: Performing; Touring; Resident; Educational; Sponsoring
Purpose: Creation and presentation of theatre, performance, video, and celebrations/festivals
Management: Mike Moynihan, Barbara Leigh, Co-Founders; Melinda Boyd, Production Manager
Officers: Paul Sardry, President; Win Quirmbach, Keith Roberts, Vice Presidents; Lon Frederick, Treasurer
Paid Staff: 20   **Volunteer Staff:** 30
Paid Artists: 15   **Non-Paid Artists:** 5
Utilizes: Special Technical Talent; Guest Artists; Guest Directors
Budget: $100,000 - $500,000
Income Sources: Private Foundations/Grants/Endowments; Business/Corporate Donations; Box Office; Government Grants; Individual Donations
Season: February - December
Annual Attendance: 49,000
Affiliations: TCG; WTA; MACA

MILWAUKEE REPERTORY THEATER
108 East Wells, Milwaukee, WI 53202
(414) 273-7121
Founded: 1954
Arts Area: Professional; Theatrical Group
Status: Professional; Non-Profit
Type: Performing; Resident; Educational
Purpose: Devoted to the creation of theatrical experiences that explore and illuminate the human condition
Management: John Dillon, Artistic Director; Sarah O'Conner, Managing Director; Cindy Moran, Public Relations
Officers: Vincent L. Martin, Board President
Paid Staff: 15
Utilizes: Special Technical Talent; Guest Artists; Guest Directors
Budget: $1,000,000 - $5,000,000
Income Sources: Private Foundations/Grants/Endowments; Business/Corporate Donations; Box Office; Government Grants; Individual Donations
Season: October - June
Affiliations: AEA; LORT
Performance Facilities: Milwaukee Repertory Theater

NEXT ACT THEATRE
PO Box 394, Milwaukee, WI 53201
(414) 278-7780
> **Founded:** 1990
> **Arts Area:** Professional; Theatrical Group
> **Status:** Professional; Non-Profit
> **Type:** Performing
> **Purpose:** Professional equity company producing engaging intimate and exciting adventures in theatrical presentation of classical and contemporary drama
> **Management:** David Cecsarini, Producing Director; Charles Kakuk, General Manager
> **Officers:** Catherine Anderson, Acting President
> **Paid Staff:** 3
> **Utilizes:** Guest Artists; Guest Directors
> **Budget:** $100,000 - $500,000
> **Income Sources:** Private Foundations/Grants/Endowments; Business/Corporate Donations; Box Office; Government Grants; Individual Donations
> **Season:** September - May   **Annual Attendance:** 8,000
> **Affiliations:** Wisconsin Professional Community Theatre Association
> **Performance Facilities:** Milwaukee Repertory Theater; Stimeke theater

THEATRE X
PO Box 92206, Milwaukee, WI 53202
(414) 278-0555
FAX: (414) 278-8233
> **Founded:** 1969
> **Arts Area:** Professional; Theatrical Group
> **Status:** Professional; Non-Profit
> **Type:** Performing; Touring; Sponsoring
> **Purpose:** Theatre X is an ensemble devoted to theatrical research and development
> **Management:** John Schneider, Wes Savick, Co-Artistic Directors; Pam Percy, Managing Director
> **Officers:** Leonard Sobczak, President; John Ogden, Vice President; William Fox, Secretary
> **Paid Staff:** 1
> **Paid Artists:** 7
> **Utilizes:** Special Technical Talent; Guest Artists; Guest Directors
> **Budget:** $100,000 - $500,000
> **Income Sources:** Private Foundations/Grants/Endowments; Business/Corporate Donations; Box Office; Government Grants; Individual Donations
> **Season:** September - June   **Annual Attendance:** 5,000
> **Affiliations:** TCG

PERFORMING SERIES

ARTIST SERIES AT THE PABST
144 East Wells Street, Milwaukee, WI 53202
(414) 226-8802
FAX: (414) 286-2793
> **Arts Area:** Instrumental Music; Classical Music
> **Status:** Non-Profit
> **Type:** Performing
> **Purpose:** To present fine chamber music to the city of Milwaukee
> **Management:** Joan Lounsbery, Executive Director; Lynn Lucius, General Manager
> **Officers:** Dennis Conta, President of the Board
> **Budget:** $100,000 - $500,000
> **Income Sources:** Private Foundations/Grants/Endowments; Business/Corporate Donations; Box Office; Government Grants; Individual Donations
> **Performance Facilities:** Pabst Theatre

FACILITY

ALVERNO COLLEGE
Pitman Theatre, 3401 South 39th Street, PO Box 343922, Milwaukee, WI 53234-3922
(414) 382-6151
> **Founded:** 1944
> **Type of Facility:** Auditorium; Theatre House; Recital Hall (three facilities)
> **Type of Stage:** Proscenium
> **Stage Dimensions:** 39'x42'   **Orchestra Pit**
> **Seating Capacity:** 930; 360; 175
> **Contact for Rental:** Erick Hoffman;   (414) 382-6151

BLATZ TEMPLE OF MUSIC - WASHINGTON PARK BANDSHELL
4420 West Vliet Street, Milwaukee, WI 53208
(414) 278-4389
FAX: (414) 933-4104
> **Type of Facility:** Outdoor (Concert); Video Studio
> **Type of Stage:** Concert Shell
> **Seating Capacity:** 12,000
> **Year Built:** 1938
> **Resident Groups:** Washington Park Temple of Music
> *Available for rent*

MILWAUKEE AREA TECHNICAL COLLEGE - COOLEY AUDITORIUM
700 West State Street, Milwaukee, WI 53233-1443
(414) 278-6600
FAX: (414) 271-2195
> **Type of Facility:** Auditorium; Loft
> **Type of Stage:** Proscenium
> **Stage Dimensions:** 40'Wx35'D   **Orchestra Pit**
> **Seating Capacity:** 1,800
> **Year Built:** 1918
> **Year Remodeled:** 1977   **Cost:** $90,000
> **Contact for Rental:** Ruby Collier;   (414) 278-6223
> **Manager:** Dale S. Shively;   (414) 278-6310
> **Resident Groups:** Milwaukee Civic Band; Milwaukee Civic Orchestra; M & W Productions
> *Theatre, Dance, Audio Visual Presentations*

MILWAUKEE PERFORMING ARTS CENTER
929 North Water Street, Milwaukee, WI 53202
(414) 273-7121
FAX: (414) 273-5480
> **Type of Facility:** Theatre Complex; Concert Hall; Performance Center; Amphitheater; Multi-Purpose
> **Type of Stage:** Proscenium; Platform; 3/4 Arena; Environmental   **Orchestra Pit**
> **Seating Capacity:** Uihleen - 2,301; Vogel- 486; Wehr - 500
> **Year Built:** 1969   **Architect:** Harry Weese & Associates   **Cost:** $12,500,000
> **Acoustical Consultant:** Bolt, Beranek & Newman
> **Contact for Rental:** Joe Ahern;   (414) 273-7121
> **Manager:** Michael T. Stirdivant;   (414) 273-7121
> **Resident Groups:** Milwaukee Symphony Orchestra; Milwaukee Ballet; Florentine Opera; Bel Canto Chorus; First Stage Milwaukee Theater for Children; Milwaukee Youth Symphony Orchestra
> *Milwaukee Performing Arts Center contains The Uihleen, Vogel and Wehr Theatres.*

PABST THEATER
144 East Wells Street, Milwaukee, WI 53202
(414) 278-3665
FAX: (414) 278-2154
> **Founded:** 1895
> **Type of Facility:** Concert Hall; Theatre House; Opera House
> **Type of Stage:** Proscenium
> **Stage Dimensions:** 72'Wx38'D; 35' proscenium opening   **Orchestra Pit**
> **Seating Capacity:** 1,400
> **Year Built:** 1895   **Architect:** Otto Strack   **Cost:** $600,000
> **Year Remodeled:** 1976   **Architect:** Mark F. Pfaller II   **Cost:** $2,500,000
> **Contact for Rental:** Charlane O'Rourke;   (414) 278-3665
> **Manager:** Philip Proctor;   (414) 278-3665
> **Resident Groups:** Bel Canto Chorus; Artist Series at the Pabst; Great Artists Series; Milwaukee Theater Festival; Kennan Forum on International Affairs

SKYLIGHT OPERA THEATRE
813 North Jefferson Street, Milwaukee, WI 53202
(414) 271-9580
FAX: (414) 271-8896
> **Type of Facility:** Theatre House; Opera House; Room
> **Facility Originally:** Garage
> **Type of Stage:** Flexible; Platform; 3/4 Arena
> **Stage Dimensions:** 12'x24' Expandable   **Orchestra Pit**
> **Seating Capacity:** 249
> **Year Built:** 1918
> **Year Remodeled:** 1981   **Architect:** Wenzler & Associates   **Cost:** $250,000

Contact for Rental: John VandeWalle, Artistic Administrator; (414) 271-9580
Resident Groups: Skylight Opera Theatre

Monona

DANCE

WISCONSIN DANCE ENSEMBLE
6332 Monona Drive, Monona, WI 53716
(608) 221-4535
Founded: 1977
Arts Area: Ballet
Status: Semi-Professional; Non-Profit
Type: Performing; Resident; Educational
Purpose: To perform and teach the art of ballet for young dancers and young audiences
Management: Jo Jean Retrum, Director
Paid Staff: 3 **Volunteer Staff:** 4
Paid Artists: 6 **Non-Paid Artists:** 200
Utilizes: Guest Artists
Budget: $1,000 - $50,000
Income Sources: Private Foundations/Grants/Endowments; Business/Corporate Donations; Box Office; Government Grants; Individual Donations
Season: 52 Weeks **Annual Attendance:** 25,000
Affiliations: Regional Dance America
Performance Facilities: Madison Civic Center; Wisconsin Union Theatre

Mount Horeb

VOCAL MUSIC

SONG OF NORWAY FESTIVAL
PO Box 132, Mount Horeb, WI 53572
(608) 437-4600
Founded: 1966
Arts Area: Operetta
Status: Non-Professional; Non-Profit
Type: Performing; Educational
Purpose: To present Forrest and Wright's operetta "Song of Norway" and other Norwegian/American-related material as an annual summer educational and entertainment offering in south central Wisconsin
Officers: Michael Mudrey, President; Orville Phillips, Vice President; Joanne Hall, Secretary; Valonne Eckel, Treasurer
Paid Staff: 7 **Volunteer Staff:** 20
Paid Artists: 45 **Non-Paid Artists:** 70
Utilizes: Special Technical Talent
Budget: $1,000 - $50,000
Income Sources: Private Foundations/Grants/Endowments; Business/Corporate Donations; Box Office; Government Grants; Individual Donations
Season: June - July **Annual Attendance:** 3,000

Oshkosh

INSTRUMENTAL MUSIC

OSHKOSH SYMPHONY ORCHESTRA
PO Box 522, Oshkosh, WI 54902
(414) 233-7510
Founded: 1940
Arts Area: Symphony; Orchestra
Status: Semi-Professional
Type: Performing
Management: Rebecca Spurlock, Business Manager
Officers: David Hayford, President
Paid Staff: 2
Paid Artists: 4
Utilizes: Guest Artists

Budget: $100,000 - $500,000
Income Sources: Private Foundations/Grants/Endowments; Business/Corporate Donations; Box Office; Individual Donations
Season: October - May
Annual Attendance: 5,000
Affiliations: AWSO; ASOL
Performance Facilities: Osh Kosh Civic Auditorium

FACILITY

GRAND OPERA HOUSE
100 High Avenue, PO Box 1004, Oshkosh, WI 54902
(414) 424-2355
Type of Facility: Opera House
Type of Stage: Proscenium
Stage Dimensions: 30'x30'   **Orchestra Pit**
Seating Capacity: 730
Year Built: 1883   **Architect:** William Waters
Year Remodeled: 1986   **Architect:** Robert Yarbro   **Cost:** $3,400,000
Contact for Rental: Mark A. Nerenhausen;   (414) 424-2355

Platteville

PERFORMING SERIES

UNIVERSITY OF WISCONSIN - PLATTEVILLE PERFORMING ARTS SERIES
One University Plaza, Platteville, WI 53818
(608) 342-1495
FAX: (608) 342-1478
Founded: 1959
Arts Area: Dance; Vocal Music; Instrumental Music; Theater; Festivals; Lyric Opera; Grand Opera
Status: Non-Profit
Type: Educational; Sponsoring
Purpose: To provide a well balanced performing arts series to our students and our community
Management: John Mominee, Director; Jim Waite, Coordinator/Programming; Susan Berggren, Coordinator/Fine Arts
Paid Staff: 3   **Volunteer Staff:** 10
Utilizes: Guest Artists
Budget: $50,000 - $100,000
Income Sources: Private Foundations/Grants/Endowments; Box Office; Government Grants; Individual Donations
Season: September - May
Annual Attendance: 4,200
Affiliations: University of Wisconsin
Performance Facilities: Center for the Arts Concert Hall

FACILITY

CENTER FOR THE ARTS - UNIVERSITY OF WISCONSIN, PLATTEVILLE
One University Plaza, Platteville, WI 53818
(608) 342-1398
FAX: (608) 342-1478
Founded: 1866
Type of Facility: Concert Hall; Theatre House
Type of Stage: Flexible; Proscenium
Stage Dimensions: Concert Hall - 55'4"x48'6"; Theatre - 24'x36'   **Orchestra Pit**
Seating Capacity: Concert Hall - 600; Theatre - 300
Year Built: 1983
Architect: Bill Wenzler
Cost: $5,200,000
Acoustical Consultant: Artel
Contact for Rental: Director, Center for the Arts;   (608) 342-1398
Resident Groups: Theatre Department; Music Department; SAB Performing Arts Series

Portage

THEATRE

PORTAGE AREA COMMUNITY THEATRE
PO Box 263, Portage, WI 53901
(608) 742-6942
Founded: 1971
Arts Area: Community; Theatrical Group
Status: Non-Professional; Non-Profit
Type: Performing
Purpose: To promote, encourage and increase the public's knowledge and appreciation of the arts, especially theatre, and to provide an outlet for the above
Management: Board of Directors
Officers: Pat Madoni, President; Lisa Piekarski, Vice President; Fran Malone, Secretary/Registered Agent; Hans Jensen, Treasurer
Volunteer Staff: 100
Non-Paid Artists: 300
Budget: $1,000 - $50,000
Income Sources: Box Office; Individual Donations
Season: September - June   **Annual Attendance:** 4,500
Affiliations: Wisconsin Theatre Association; Wisconsin Council on the Arts

Racine

INSTRUMENTAL MUSIC

RACINE SYMPHONY ORCHESTRA
PO Box 1751, Racine, WI 53401
(414) 636-9285
Founded: 1931
Arts Area: Symphony; Orchestra
Status: Semi-Professional; Non-Professional
Type: Performing
Purpose: To supply the community of Racine with its own symphony orchestra and provide an outlet for good local talent, non-professional and semi-professional
Management: Mildred Schroth, Executive Secretary/Administrative Coordinator; Carol Wallace, General Manager
Officers: Janet Tidwell, President; Charlene Melzer, Vice President; James Cook, Past President; Barbara Namowicz, Treasurer
Paid Staff: 3   **Volunteer Staff:** 21
Paid Artists: 70
Utilizes: Special Technical Talent; Guest Conductors; Guest Artists; Guest Directors
Budget: $100,000 - $500,000
Income Sources: Private Foundations/Grants/Endowments; Business/Corporate Donations; Box Office; Individual Donations
Season: 52 Weeks   **Annual Attendance:** 40,000
Affiliations: Racine Arts Council   **Performance Facilities:** Racine-on-the-Lake Festival Hall

Ripon

PERFORMING SERIES

RIPON COLLEGE/CAESTECKER FINE ARTS SERIES
300 Seward Street, PO Box 248, Ripon, WI 54971
(414) 748-8112
FAX: (414) 748-9262
Arts Area: Dance; Vocal Music; Instrumental Music; Theater
Status: Non-Profit
Type: Sponsoring
Purpose: To present four to five performing and visual artists, representing diverse backgrounds and arts areas each season for the college and surrounding Ripon community
Management: Stacy Shrode, Director of Student Activities
Budget: $1,000 - $50,000
Income Sources: Private Foundations/Grants/Endowments; Box Office
Season: September - April   **Annual Attendance:** 1,200
Performance Facilities: Memorial Hall Gym; Benstead Theater; Demmer Recital Hall

FACILITY

RIPON COLLEGE - DEMMER RECITAL HALL
Rodman Arts Center, 300 Seward Street, Box 248, Ripon, WI 54971
(414) 748-8120
    Type of Facility: Performance Center
    Type of Stage: Platform
    Stage Dimensions: 65'x40'
    Seating Capacity: 286
    Year Built: 1972 **Architect:** Shattuck & Stewart **Cost:** $2,500,000
    Acoustical Consultant: Bolt, Beranek & Neumann
    Contact for Rental: Cal Wolff, Director of Conferences; (414) 748-8137
    Manager: Raymond Stahura
    Resident Groups: Ripon College Music Department (Demmer); Ripon College Drama Department; Ripon College Dance Company (Benstead Theater)

Shawano

THEATRE

SHAWANO COUNTY ARTS COUNCIL
PO Box 213, Shawano, WI 54166
(715) 526-2525
    Founded: 1967
    Arts Area: Musical; Community; Folk; Theatrical Group
    Status: Non-Profit
    Type: Resident; Sponsoring
    Officers: Dolly Danbury, President; Deb Lonick, Vice President; Jaquee Salzman, Treasurer
    Paid Staff: 1 **Volunteer Staff:** 50
    Budget: $50,000 - $100,000
    Income Sources: Private Foundations/Grants/Endowments; Business/Corporate Donations; Box Office; Government Grants; Individual Donations
    Season: 52 Weeks **Annual Attendance:** 10,000
    Performance Facilities: Mielke Theatre

Sheboygan

INSTRUMENTAL MUSIC

SHEBOYGAN SYMPHONY ORCHESTRA
901 Superior Avenue, Room 344, Sheboygan, WI 53081
(414) 452-1985
    Founded: 1918
    Arts Area: Symphony; Orchestra
    Status: Semi-Professional; Non-Profit
    Type: Performing; Educational
    Management: Arnold W. Gesch, General Manager
    Officers: Barbara G. Bossewitz, President; Karl Grube, Vice President; Lee Robinson, Treasurer
    Paid Staff: 2 **Volunteer Staff:** 6
    Paid Artists: 4 **Non-Paid Artists:** 70
    Utilizes: Guest Conductors; Guest Artists
    Budget: $50,000 - $100,000
    Income Sources: Private Foundations/Grants/Endowments; Business/Corporate Donations; Box Office; Individual Donations
    Season: September - May **Annual Attendance:** 5,000
    Performance Facilities: Kohler Memorial Auditorium

THEATRE

SHEBOYGAN COMMUNITY PLAYERS
607 South Water Street, Sheboygan, WI 53081
(414) 459-3779
    Founded: 1934
    Arts Area: Community; Theatrical Group
    Status: Non-Professional; Non-Profit
    Type: Performing; Resident; Educational

Purpose: The advancement of and involvement in quality community theatre from the classical to contemporary, that afford entertainment and education for both audience and participants
Management: Ralph Maffongelli, Director of Theatre; Steven Stauber, Business Manager; Marty Kooi, Technical Director
Officers: Liz Kohlbeck, President; Wally Waldhart, First Vice President; Valerie Black, Second Vice President; Harold Lang, Secretary; Bob Travis, Treasurer
Paid Staff: 2   **Volunteer Staff:** 300
Budget: $100,000 - $500,000
Income Sources: Business/Corporate Donations; Box Office; Individual Donations; Concessions/Program Advertising
Season: September - May   **Annual Attendance:** 18,000
Performance Facilities: Leslie W. Johnson Theatre; Horace Mann Middle School

FACILITY

FINE ARTS THEATRE
One University Drive, Sheboygan, WI 53081
(414) 459-6600
>**Type of Facility:** Auditorium; Theatre House
>**Type of Stage:** Thrust
>**Stage Dimensions:** 40'x36'   **Orchestra Pit**
>**Seating Capacity:** 400
>**Year Built:** 1970   **Architect:** Bray   **Cost:** $700,000
>**Year Remodeled:** 1986   **Architect:** Bray   **Cost:** $556,000
>**Contact for Rental:** Tom Mortenson;   (414) 459-6600
>**Manager:** Bruce Browne
>**Resident Groups:** UWS Players

JOHN MICHAEL KOHLER ARTS CENTER
608 New York Avenue, Sheboygan, WI 53081
(414) 458-6144
>**Type of Facility:** Theatre Complex; Concert Hall; Performance Center; Multi-Purpose
>**Type of Stage:** Thrust
>**Stage Dimensions:** 22'x38'   **Seating Capacity:** 162
>**Year Built:** 1970   **Architect:** Eugene Wasserman   **Cost:** $750,000
>**Contact for Rental:** Mary Jo Ballschmider;   (414) 458-6144

Spring Green

THEATRE

AMERICAN PLAYERS THEATRE
Route 3, Spring Green, WI 53588
(608) 588-7401
>**Founded:** 1980
>**Arts Area:** Professional; Theatrical Group
>**Status:** Professional; Non-Profit
>**Type:** Performing; Touring; Resident; Educational
>**Management:** Sheldon Wilner, Managing Director; David Frank, Associate Director; Kathryn Long, Artistic Director
>**Utilizes:** Special Technical Talent; Guest Artists; Guest Directors
>**Budget:** $1,000,000 - $5,000,000
>**Income Sources:** Private Foundations/Grants/Endowments; Business/Corporate Donations; Box Office; Government Grants; Individual Donations
>**Season:** June - October
>**Affiliations:** TCG; AEA
>**Performance Facilities:** American Players Theater

Stevens Point

INSTRUMENTAL MUSIC

CENTRAL WISCONSIN SYMPHONY ORCHESTRA
PO Box 65, Stevens Point, WI 54481
(715) 344-1420
>**Founded:** 1947
>**Arts Area:** Symphony; Orchestra
>**Status:** Non-Professional; Non-Profit
>**Type:** Performing; Resident
>**Purpose:** To promote the appreciation and enjoyment of orchestral literature through live performance

Management: Jodi Engum Kryshak, Manager
Officers: Ed Wotruba, President; Jennifer Burton, Vice President; Jeff Peterson, Treasurer; Nancy Mattowitz, Secretary
Paid Staff: 3   **Volunteer Staff:** 1
Paid Artists: 75
Utilizes: Special Technical Talent; Guest Conductors; Guest Artists; Community Members; Students
Budget: $100,000 - $500,000
Income Sources: Private Foundations/Grants/Endowments; Business/Corporate Donations; Box Office; Government Grants; Individual Donations
Season: October - May   **Annual Attendance:** 7,000
Performance Facilities: Sentry Theater

Superior

FACILITY

UNIVERSITY OF WISCONSIN-SUPERIOR - PAUL E. HOLDEN FINE AND APPLIED ARTS CENTER
Superior, WI 54880
(715) 394-8369
    Type of Facility: Theatre Complex; Multi-Purpose
    Type of Stage: Flexible
    Stage Dimensions: 50'x85'   **Orchestra Pit**
    Seating Capacity: 350
    Year Built: 1973   **Architect:** Larson, Playter & Smith   **Cost:** $5,000,000
    Contact for Rental: William Stock;   (715) 394-8269

Wales

THEATRE

REED MARIONETTES, INC.
700 Llambaris Pass, Wales, WI 53183
(414) 968-3277
    Founded: 1950
    Arts Area: Professional; Puppet
    Status: Professional
    Type: Performing; Touring
    Purpose: A professional touring company presenting colorful, entertaining and faithful versions of children's classics, combining the best of the arts of puppetry and theatre
    Management: Robin Reed, Managing Director
    Officers: Robin Reed, President
    Paid Staff: 3
    Paid Artists: 3
    Utilizes: Special Technical Talent
    Budget: $1,000 - $50,000
    Income Sources: Box Office
    Season: 52 Weeks   **Annual Attendance:** 80,000
    Affiliations: Puppeteers of America; Wisconsin Puppetry Guild

Waukesha

INSTRUMENTAL MUSIC

WAUKESHA SYMPHONY
PO Box 531, Waukesha, WI 53187
(414) 547-1858
    Founded: 1947
    Arts Area: Symphony; Orchestra
    Status: Semi-Professional; Non-Profit
    Type: Performing; Resident
    Purpose: To play classical music for the Waukesha area
    Management: Diane M. Bennett, General Manager
    Officers: Tom Derse, President; Sandy Stuckmann, Executive Vice President; Jane Darling, Senior Vice President; Jeannine Gabel, Secretary; Jim Wilkie, Treasurer
    Paid Staff: 1
    Paid Artists: 85
    Utilizes: Guest Artists

Budget: $100,000 - $500,000
Income Sources: Private Foundations/Grants/Endowments; Business/Corporate Donations; Box Office; Individual Donations
Season: October - May   **Annual Attendance:** 5,000
Affiliations: ASOL; AWSO
Performance Facilities: Shattuck Auditorium

THEATRE

WAUKESHA CIVIC THEATRE
506 North Washington, Waukesha, WI 53188
(414) 547-4911
Founded: 1957
Arts Area: Musical; Community; Theatrical Group
Status: Semi-Professional; Non-Professional; Non-Profit
Type: Performing; Educational
Purpose: To stimulate an interest in drama, offer theatre opportunities and promote theatre as an educational tool
Management: Betsey Folsom, Managing Director; Pat Trecker, Development Director
Officers: Tim Hawley, President; Robb Moodie, Vice President; Debra Zibrel, Secretary; Brad Sebena, Treasurer
Paid Staff: 2   **Volunteer Staff:** 200
Paid Artists: 1   **Non-Paid Artists:** 80
Utilizes: Guest Directors
Budget: $50,000 - $100,000
Income Sources: Private Foundations/Grants/Endowments; Business/Corporate Donations; Box Office; Government Grants; Individual Donations
Season: 52 Weeks   **Annual Attendance:** 7,000
Affiliations: ATA; AACT

FACILITY

WAUKESHA CIVIC THEATRE
506 North Washington, Waukesha, WI 53188
(414) 547-4911
Type of Facility: Theatre House
Facility Originally: Church
Type of Stage: Thrust
Stage Dimensions: 17'x38'
Seating Capacity: 136
Year Built: 1950
Year Remodeled: 1964
Resident Groups: Waukesha Civic Theatre

Waupacu

PERFORMING SERIES

WAUPACA FINE ARTS FESTIVAL
Box 55, Waupacu, WI 54981
(715) 258-3054
Founded: 1962
Arts Area: Dance; Vocal Music; Instrumental Music; Theater
Status: Non-Profit
Type: Performing
Purpose: Encouragement of active participation of musicians, artists and listeners/viewers of all the fine arts
Officers: Gerald Knoepfel, Chairman; Charles Spanhauer, Co-Chairman; Blanche Fanik, Treasurer
Volunteer Staff: 50
Paid Artists: 50   **Non-Paid Artists:** 300
Utilizes: Guest Artists
Budget: $1,000 - $50,000
Income Sources: Business/Corporate Donations; Box Office; Individual Donations
Season: October - June
Affiliations: Wisconsin Art Council
Performance Facilities: High School Auditorium

WYOMING

Casper

INSTRUMENTAL MUSIC

CASPER CHAMBER MUSIC SOCIETY
PO Box 2899, Casper, WY 82602
(307) 234-7127
    Founded: 1983
    Arts Area: Chamber
    Status: Semi-Professional; Non-Profit
    Type: Performing
    Purpose: To provide high-calibre performing opportunities to local and regional chamber ensembles
    Officers: Inge N. Kutchins, President; Judy Vernon, Vice President; Adrienne Bonnet, Secretary; Louis C. Rognstad, Treasurer; Janet Ahlquist, Jo Jackson and Albert V. Metz, Board-at-Large
    Paid Artists: 17
    Utilizes: Guest Artists
    Budget: $1,000 - $50,000
    Income Sources: Private Foundations/Grants/Endowments; Business/Corporate Donations; Box Office; Individual Donations
    Season: October - April **Annual Attendance:** 550
    Performance Facilities: Aley Fine Arts Hall, Casper College

CASPER SYMPHONY ORCHESTRA
PO Box 667, Casper, WY 82602
(307) 266-1478
    Founded: 1950
    Arts Area: Symphony; Orchestra
    Status: Professional; Non-Profit
    Type: Performing; Touring; Educational
    Purpose: To enrich the cultural lives of audiences; to expand the musical horizons of children; to provide an outlet for the creative talents of area musicians and for an expanding audience
    Management: Christopher Boor, General Adminstrator; Curtis Peacock, Music Director/Conductor
    Paid Staff: 4 **Volunteer Staff:** 10
    Paid Artists: 72 **Non-Paid Artists:** 2
    Utilizes: Guest Artists
    Budget: $100,000 - $500,000
    Income Sources: Private Foundations/Grants/Endowments; Business/Corporate Donations; Box Office; Government Grants; Individual Donations; Fund-raising
    Season: September - May **Annual Attendance:** 10,000
    Affiliations: Casper Chamber of Commerce; Wyoming Council on the Arts; NEA; ASOL; Wyoming Advocates for Cultural Development
    Performance Facilities: John F. Welsh Auditorium; Natrona County High School

FACILITY

CASPER COLLEGE - DURHAM HALL
125 College Drive, Casper, WY 82601
(307) 268-2606
    Type of Facility: Concert Hall; Studio Performance; Performance Center
    Type of Stage: Platform
    Seating Capacity: 309
    Year Built: 1968 **Architect:** Henry Therkildson **Cost:** $600,000
    Contact for Rental: Jan Delgarno; (307) 268-2606
    Resident Groups: Casper College - Jazz Ensemble; Percussion Ensemble; Concert Band; Chamber Orchestra; String Ensemble
    Also hosts student recitals, jazz combos and contemporary singers

CASPER EVENTS CENTER
1 Events Center Drive, PO Box K10, Casper, WY 82602
(307) 235-8441
FAX: (307) 235-8445
    Type of Facility: Concert Hall; Theatre House; Arena; Multi-Purpose
    Type of Stage: Flexible; Platform
    Seating Capacity: 10,452

Year Built: 1982   **Architect:** Gorder South Group   **Cost:** $22,000,000
Contact for Rental: Max L. Torbert, General Manager;   (307) 235-8441

Cheyenne

INSTRUMENTAL MUSIC

CHEYENNE SYMPHONY ORCHESTRA
PO Box 851, Cheyenne, WY 82003
(307) 778-8561
  Founded: 1954
  Arts Area: Symphony; Orchestra; Chamber
  Status: Professional; Non-Profit
  Type: Performing; Educational
  Purpose: To present high-quality professional symphonic music to the widest possible audience with emphasis on educational outreach
  Management: Betty Flood, Executive Director
  Officers: Renee Middleton, President; Larry Wolfe, President-Elect
  Paid Staff: 3
  Paid Artists: 110
  Utilizes: Guest Conductors; Guest Artists
  Budget: $100,000 - $500,000
  Income Sources: Private Foundations/Grants/Endowments; Business/Corporate Donations; Box Office; Government Grants; Individual Donations
  Season: September - May   **Annual Attendance:** 9,028
  Affiliations: ASOL; Symphony and Choral Society of Cheyenne
  Performance Facilities: Cheyenne Civic Center

THEATRE

CHEYENNE LITTLE THEATRE PLAYERS
2706 East Pershing Boulevard, PO Box 1086, Cheyenne, WY 82001
(307) 638-6543
  Founded: 1930
  Arts Area: Musical; Dinner; Community
  Status: Non-Professional; Non-Profit
  Type: Performing; Educational
  Purpose: To provide entertainment and education through theatre to residents of southeastern Wyoming; to promote creativity and excellence among volunteers
  Management: Patrick Brien, Managing Director
  Officers: Rick Flood, President; Barbara Dorr, President-Elect; Marlyn Salley, Secretary; Vicki Lewis, Treasurer
  Paid Staff: 2   **Volunteer Staff:** 250
  Paid Artists: 2   **Non-Paid Artists:** 100
  Utilizes: Guest Artists; Guest Directors
  Budget: $100,000 - $500,000
  Income Sources: Private Foundations/Grants/Endowments; Business/Corporate Donations; Box Office; Government Grants; Individual Donations
  Season: 52 Weeks   **Annual Attendance:** 12,000
  Affiliations: AACT
  Performance Facilities: Mary Godfrey Playhouse; Atlas Theatre

PERFORMING SERIES

WYOMING ARTS COUNCIL
2320 Capitol Avenue, Cheyenne, WY 82002
(307) 777-7742
FAX: (307) 777-5499
  Founded: 1967
  Arts Area: Dance; Vocal Music; Instrumental Music; Theater; Festivals; Lyric Opera; Grand Opera
  Status: Non-Profit
  Type: Educational; Sponsoring
  Purpose: To promote visual, literary and performing arts in Wyoming
  Management: Rita Moxey, Acting Director of Community Services; Renee Bovee, Performing Arts Coordinator; Wendy Bredehoft, AIE Coordinator
  Officers: Jo Campbell, Chairman
  Paid Staff: 7   **Volunteer Staff:** 2
  Budget: $100,000 - $500,000

Income Sources: Private Foundations/Grants/Endowments; Government Grants
Affiliations: WSAF; NASSA; NALAA; WAAA

FACILITY

CHEYENNE CIVIC CENTER
2101 O'Neil Avenue, Cheyenne, WY 82001
(307) 637-6364
FAX: (307) 637-6454
  Founded: 1981
  Type of Facility: Concert Hall; Auditorium; Performance Center; Off Broadway; Theatre House; Civic Center
  Type of Stage: Proscenium
  Stage Dimensions: 60'Wx40'D   **Orchestra Pit**
  Seating Capacity: 1,496
  Year Built: 1981   **Architect:** Ira Blackwell Architects   **Cost:** $4,200,000
  Contact for Rental: Dru Rohla;   (307) 637-6364
  Resident Groups: Cheyenne Symphony Orchestra

Laramie

PERFORMING SERIES

WESTERN ARTS MUSIC FESTIVAL
University of Wyoming, Department of Music, PO Box 3037, Laramie, WY 82071-3037
(307) 766-5242
  Founded: 1972
  Arts Area: Vocal Music; Instrumental Music; Festivals; Lyric Opera
  Status: Professional; Non-Profit
  Type: Performing; Touring; Resident; Educational
  Purpose: To bring quality music to the public during the summer months
  Management: Fredrick Gersten, Chairman of the Music Department
  Paid Staff: 1   **Volunteer Staff:** 10
  Paid Artists: 15
  Utilizes: Guest Artists
  Budget: $1,000 - $50,000
  Income Sources: Private Foundations/Grants/Endowments; Business/Corporate Donations; Government Grants; Individual Donations
  Season: June - July   **Annual Attendance:** 4,850
  Affiliations: Wyoming Council of the Arts
  Performance Facilities: The Fine Arts Council Hall, University of Wyoming; Saint Mary's Cathedral

FACILITY

UNIVERSITY OF WYOMING - ARENA AUDITORIUM
PO Box 3254, Laramie, WY 82071
(307) 766-1121
  Type of Facility: Auditorium; Arena
  Type of Stage: Flexible; Platform   **Stage Dimensions:** 60'Wx40'D
  Seating Capacity: 15,000
  Year Built: 1982
  Contact for Rental: Terri Howes;   (307) 766-4091

UNIVERSITY OF WYOMING - ARTS AND SCIENCES AUDITORIUM
PO Box 3254, Laramie, WY 82071
(307) 766-1121
  Type of Facility: Concert Hall; Auditorium; Theatre House
  Type of Stage: Proscenium   **Stage Dimensions:** 48'Wx32'D
  Seating Capacity: 1,996
  Year Built: 1945
  Contact for Rental: Violet Baker;   (307) 766-4388
  Resident Groups: University of Wyoming Music and Theater Departments

UNIVERSITY OF WYOMING - FINE ARTS CONCERT HALL
PO Box 3037, Laramie, WY 82071
(307) 766-6250
  Type of Facility: Concert Hall
  Type of Stage: Proscenium
  Seating Capacity: 700

Year Built: 1976
Contact for Rental: Frederick Gersten; (307) 766-5242
Resident Groups: University of Wyoming Music Department

Moose

DANCE

THE LAUBINS
PO Box 4, Moose, WY 83012
(307) 733-2690
Founded: 1948
Arts Area: Ethnic
Status: Professional
Type: Performing; Touring; Resident; Educational
Purpose: To introduce Native American dancing (Plains and Woodlands) as a fine art; to bring about a better under-standing of Indian dancing
Management: Reginald K. and Gladys Laubin, Directors
Paid Artists: 2
Income Sources: Box Office
Annual Attendance: 10,000

Sheridan

THEATRE

SHERIDAN CIVIC THEATRE GUILD
PO Box 1, Sheridan, WY 82801
(307) 672-9886
Founded: 1953
Arts Area: Musical; Community; Theatrical Group
Status: Non-Profit
Type: Performing; Resident
Purpose: To foster community theatre in the area; to involve community members in all aspects of theatre; to entertain
Management: Judi O'Neal, Manager
Officers: Tim Lervick, President; Sam Yorks, Vice President; Sarah Olson, Secretary; Marilyn Palmer, Treasurer
Paid Staff: 1
Utilizes: Special Technical Talent; Guest Conductors
Budget: $1,000 - $50,000
Income Sources: Private Foundations/Grants/Endowments; Business/Corporate Donations; Box Office; Government Grants; Individual Donations
Season: September - May   **Annual Attendance:** 2,000
Performance Facilities: Carriage House Theatre

FACILITY

WYO THEATER, INC.
42 North Main Street, Sheridan, WY 82801
(307) 672-9083
Founded: 1923
Type of Facility: Concert Hall; Auditorium; Performance Center; Theatre House; Multi-Purpose
Facility Originally: Vaudeville
Type of Stage: Thrust; Proscenium
Stage Dimensions: 33'x20'; 6'thrust
Seating Capacity: 487
Year Built: 1923
Year Remodeled: 1989   **Architect:** Tim Belton, Malone, Belton Architects   **Cost:** $1,400,000
Acoustical Consultant: David Adams Associates
Contact for Rental: Sophie S. Pelissier;   (307) 672-9083
Resident Groups: WYO Theater, Inc.

Teton Village

PERFORMING SERIES

GRAND TETON MUSIC FESTIVAL
PO Box 490, Teton Village, WY 83025
(307) 733-1128
Founded: 1962
Arts Area: Vocal Music; Instrumental Music; Festivals
Status: Professional; Non-Profit
Type: Performing; Sponsoring
Purpose: To establish a resident ensemble of like-minded artists to perform in small ensembles in a superb symphony orchestra; to bring the musical resources of a great metropolis to the northern Rocky Mountain region for the summer season
Management: Ling Tung, Music Director
Officers: William D. Weiss, President
Paid Staff: 15   **Volunteer Staff:** 45
Paid Artists: 175
Utilizes: Guest Conductors
Budget: $1,000,000 - $5,000,000
Income Sources: Private Foundations/Grants/Endowments; Business/Corporate Donations; Box Office; Government Grants; Individual Donations
Season: June - August   **Annual Attendance:** 17,000
Performance Facilities: Walk Festival Hall

PUERTO RICO

Corozal

DANCE

GUATEQUE FOLKLORIC BALLET OF PUERTO RICO
HC-01, PO Box 6894, Corozal, PR 00783
(809) 859-8601; (809) 787-3837
   Arts Area: Ethnic; Folk
   Status: Non-Professional; Non-Profit
   Type: Performing; Educational; Touring
   Purpose: To promote and preserve the culture of Puerto Rico and to expose other people to its culture
   Management: Joachim Nieres; Luz Esther Ortiz, Secretary; Orlando Gonzalez, Public Relations
   Budget: $1,000 - $50,000
   Income Sources: Box Office; Government Grants; Individual Donations; Touring Fees

San Juan

DANCE

BALLETS DE SAN JUAN
PO Box S-5713, San Juan, PR 00901
(809) 725-9140; (809) 721-3257
FAX: (809) 721-3257
   Arts Area: Ballet
   Status: Professional; Non-Profit
   Type: Performing; Touring
   Purpose: To develop professional ballet dancers and choreographers in Puerto Rico
   Management: Ana Garcia, Director; Nydia Fernandez, Administrative Assistant
   Officers: Ana Garcia, Director; Jaime Suarez, President, Friends of Ballets de San Juan
   Paid Staff: 6   **Volunteer Staff:** 3
   Paid Artists: 12   **Non-Paid Artists:** 12
   Utilizes: Special Technical Talent; Guest Artists; Guest Conductors; Guest Choreographers
   Income Sources: Private Foundations/Grants/Endowments; Business/Corporate Donations; Box Office; Government Grants; Individual Donations
   Budget: $100,000 - $500,000
   Season: August-June   **Annual Attendance:** 12,000
   Performance Facilities: Bellas Artes Center

THEATRE

TEATRO DEL SERENTA INC.
PO Box 5122, Puerta de Tierra Station, San Juan, PR 00906
(809) 723-1403; (809) 725-9494
FAX: (809) 723-1403
   Founded: 1963
   Arts Area: Professional; Theatrical Group
   Status: Professional; Non-Profit
   Type: Performing; Educational; Touring
   Purpose: To perform and develop national and international theater of the highest quality for Puerto Rico
   Management: Alexis Gueits, General Manager; Belein Rios, Public Relations; Idalia Perez-Garay, Artistic Director; Jose Felix Gomez, Associate Artistic Director
   Officers: Jaime S. Ramirez, President; Israel Rodriguez, Director; Flora Perez-Garay, Director; Mamel Portela, Treasurer
   Utilizes: Special Technical Talent; Guest Artists; Guest Directors
   Budget: $100,000 - $500,000
   Income Sources: Private Foundations/Grants/Endowments; Business/Corporate Donations; Box Office; Government Grants; Individual Donations
   Season: 52 Weeks   **Annual Attendance:** 30,000
   Performance Facilities: Center for Performing Arts-Theater Hall, University of Puerto Rico

Santurce

DANCE

BALLET CONCIERTO DE PUERTO RICO
PO Box 13245, Santurce, PR 00908-3245
(809) 724-7023
FAX: (809) 725-5642

Arts Area: Modern; Ballet
Status: Professional; Non-Profit
Type: Performing; Educational; Touring; Resident; Sponsoring
Purpose: To teach the people of Puerto Rico about ballet and dancing
Management: Lolita San Miguel, Artistic Director; Julie Montes, Administration
Officers: Carlos Ivan Berrios, Chairman of the Board
Income Sources: Private Foundations/Grants/Endowments; Business/Corporate Donations; Box Office; Government Grants; Individual Donations
Performance Facilities: Centro de Bellas Artes

VIRGIN ISLANDS

Charlotte Amalie

FACILITY

REICHHOLD CENTER FOR THE ARTS
2 John Brews Bay, Charlotte Amalie, VI 00802-9990
(809) 774-8475
FAX: (809) 774-4482
 Type of Facility: Performance Center; Multi-Purpose
 Type of Stage: Proscenium
 Stage Dimensions: 48'Wx26'Dx38'6"H; 48'Wx26'H proscenium opening
 Seating Capacity: 1,196
 Year Built: 1978
 Contact for Rental: Maysen Gore; (809) 774-8475
 Resident Groups: Caribbean Dance Company

DANCE INDEX

ABHINAYA DANCE COMPANY, 75
ACADEMY OF CREATIVE DANCE AND ELIZABETH MANDEVILLE DANCE COMPANY, 234
AFRICAN-AMERICAN DANCE ENSEMBLE, THE, 1052
AFRICAN DANCE FESTIVAL FOR KANKOURAN WEST AFRICAN DANCE CO., 297
AGNES DE MILLE DANCE THEATER, 908
AIKEN CIVIC BALLET COMPANY, 1255
AJDE! FOLK DANCE ENSEMBLE, 270
AKASHA AND COMPANY, 422
ALBANO BALLET COMPANY, 262
ALEXANDRA BALLET COMPANY, 743
ALLEGHENY BALLET COMPANY, 1194
ALLEGRO BALLET OF HOUSTON, 1354
ALLNATIONS DANCE COMPANY, 908
ALPHA-OMEGA THEATRICAL DANCE COMPANY, 909
ALVIN AILEY AMERICAN DANCE THEATER, 909
ALVIN AILEY REPERTORY ENSEMBLE, 909
AMAN INTERNATIONAL MUSIC AND DANCE COMPANY, 100
AMERICAN AUTHENTIC JAZZ DANCE THEATRE, 910
AMERICAN BALLET, 1248
AMERICAN BALLET THEATRE, 910
AMERICAN BALLROOM THEATER COMPANY INC., 910
AMERICAN DANCE FESTIVAL, 1052
AMERICAN DANCE MACHINE, THE, 815
AMERICAN FESTIVAL BALLET, 411
AMERICAN INTERNATIONAL DANCE THEATRE, INC., 910
AMERICAN MIME THEATRE, THE, 911
AMERICAN YOUTH BALLET, 531
AMERICAN YOUTH BALLET COMPANY, 597
AMHERST BALLET THEATRE COMPANY, 601
ANACRUSIS MODERN TAP DANCE, 1451
ANCHORAGE CONCERT ASSOCIATION INC., 13
ANCHORAGE FOLK DANCE CONSORTIUM, 13
ANDAHAZY BALLET COMPANY, 723
ANJANI'S KATHAK DANCE OF INDIA, 215
ANN ARBOR BALLET THEATRE, 657
ANN ARBOR CIVIC BALLET, 657
ANNABELLA GONZALEZ DANCE THEATER, INC., 911
APPALACHIAN BALLET COMPANY, 1288
APPALACHIAN YOUTH JAZZ-BALLET COMPANY, 1476
ARLINGTON DANCE THEATRE, 1422
ART BRIDGMAN/MYRNA PACKER, 911
ART OF BLACK DANCE AND MUSIC, 643
ASIAN AMERICAN DANCE PERFORMANCES, 161
ASIAN AMERICAN DANCE THEATRE, 911
ATLANTA BALLET, THE, 377
ATHENS BALLET, 376
ATLANTIC DANCE THEATRE, 1067
AUGUSTA BALLET COMPANY, 387
AURORA DANCE ARTS, 223
AVAZ INTERNATIONAL DANCE THEATRE, 203
AVODAH DANCE ENSEMBLE, 822
BAILES FLAMENCOS, 162
BALLET ALASKA, 13
BALLET ARIZONA, 28
BALLET ARKANSAS, 48
BALLET AUSTIN, 1307
BALLET CHICAGO, 422
BALLET COLBERT, 795
BALLET CONCERTO, 1343
BALLET CONCERTO COMPANY OF MIAMI, 339
BALLET CONCIERTO DE PUERTO RICO, 1526
BALLET CULTURAL AZTECA, 691
BALLET DENVER, 234
BALLET DES JEUNES, 1215
BALLET ETUDES, 329
BALLET FLORIDA, 372
BALLET FOLKLORICO OF EAST CHICAGO, INDIANA, 487
BALLET GUILD OF LEHIGH VALLEY, 1195
BALLET HISPANICO OF NEW YORK, 912
BALLET IOWA, 522
BALLET IOWA ASSOCIATION, 522
BALLET MANHATTAN FOUNDATION, INC., 912
BALLET METROPOLITAN, 1121

BALLET MISSISSIPPI, 734
BALLET MONTMARTRE, THE, 72
BALLET OF THE AMERICAS, 1340
BALLET OKLAHOMA, 1163
BALLET PACIFICA, 95,
BALLET SPECTACULAR/INTERNATIONAL CULTURAL EXCHANGE, INC., 340
BALLET THEATRE OF ANNAPOLIS, 585
BALLET THEATRE OF WESTCHESTER, 1033
BALLET THEATRE PENNSYLVANIA, 1209
BALLET WEST, 1401
BALLET WESTERN RESERVE, 1152
BALLETACOMA, 1468
BALLETS DE SAN JUAN, 1525
BALTIMORE DANCE THEATRE, 586
BARBARA FELDMAN AND DANCERS, 270
BARTLESVILLE CIVIC BALLET, 1158
BATON ROUGE BALLET THEATRE, 555
BATTERY DANCE COMPANY, 912
BAUER CONTEMPORARY BALLET, 1503
BAY AREA REPERTORY DANCE THEATRE (BARD), 59
BEACON DANCE COMPANY, 391
BEAUMONT BALLET THEATRE, 1312
BEAUMONT CIVIC BALLET, 1313
BEBE MILLER COMPANY, 912
BERKELEY CITY BALLET, 59
BETHUNE THEATREDANSE, 100
BETTY SALAMUN'S DANCECIRCUS, 1503
BEVERLY BLOSSOM AND COMPANY, 869
BILL T. JONES/ARNIE ZANE AND COMPANY, 913
BODY LANGUAGE DANCE COMPANY, 1202
BOSTON BALLET COMPANY, 604
BOSTON BALLET II, 605
BOSTON FLAMENCO BALLET, 617
BRISTOL BALLET COMPANY, 1424
BROOKLYN CENTER FOR THE PERFORMING ARTS AT BROOKLYN COLLEGE, 869
BRUCE KING FOUNDATION FOR AMERICAN DANCE, 913
CALIFORNIA BALLET COMPANY, 152
CANTON BALLET, 1099
CAPITOL BALLET COMPANY, 297
CARLOTA SANTANA SPANISH DANCE COMPANY, 913
CAROL FONDA AND COMPANY/DANCE FORUM, INC., 913
CAROLINA BALLET THEATRE, 1262
CATAMOUNT FILM AND ARTS COMPANY, 1418
CHARLES MOORE - DANCES AND DRUMS OF AFRICA, 870
CHARLES MOULTON DANCE COMPANY, 914
CHARLESTON BALLET, 1476
CHARLESTON BALLET, THE, 1257
CHARLOTTE CITY BALLET, 1048
CHATTANOOGA BALLET, 1278
CHEN AND DANCERS, 914
CHHANDAM CHITRESH DAS DANCE COMPANY, 151
CHICAGO DANCE COALITION, 422
CHICAGO MOVING COMPANY, 423
CHILDREN'S BALLET THEATRE, 1472
CHILDREN'S DANCE THEATRE OF NEW MILFORD, 275
CINCINNATI BALLET, 1101
CITY BALLET OF HOUSTON, 1354
CITY CELEBRATION, INC., 162
CIVIC DANCE ASSOCIATION, 1272
CHINESE FOLK DANCE COMPANY, 914
CHRYSALIS REPERTORY DANCE COMPANY, 1354
CLEAR LAKE METROPOLITAN BALLET, 1355
CLEO PARKER ROBINSON DANCE ENSEMBLE, 234
CLEVELAND SAN JOSE BALLET, 1108
CLOG AMERICA, 1397
CODANCECO, 914
COLORADO BALLET, 234
COLORADO SPRINGS DANCE THEATRE, 229
COLUMBIA CITY BALLET, 1259
CO-MOTION DANCE, 1453
CO'MOTION DANCE THEATER, 507
CONCERT BALLET OF VIRGINIA, THE, 1435
CONCERT DANCE THEATRE, 211

INSTRUMENTAL MUSIC

VOCAL MUSIC

AFTER DINNER OPERA COMPANY, 952
ALASKA LIGHT OPERA THEATRE, 14
ALBUQUERQUE CIVIC LIGHT OPERA, 849
ALBUQUERQUE OPERA THEATRE - OPERA SOUTHWEST, 849
AMATO OPERA THEATRE, 952
AMERICAN BOYCHOIR SCHOOL, 833
AMERICAN CHAMBER OPERA COMPANY, INC., 953
AMERICAN CHORAL DIRECTORS ASSOCIATION, 1160
ANCHORAGE CONCERT CHORUS, 14
ANCHORAGE OPERA COMPANY, 15
ANNAPOLIS OPERA, 585
ARIZONA OPERA COMPANY, 37
ARLINGTON OPERA ASSOCIATION, 1306
ARS MUSICA CHORALE AND ORCHESTRA, 832
ASSOCIATION FOR THE FURTHERMENT OF BEL CANTO, 953
ATLANTA BACH CHOIR, 379
ATLANTA OPERA, THE, 379
ATLANTA SYMPHONY CHORUS, 379
AUGUSTA OPERA ASSOCIATION, 388
AURORA SINGERS, 224
AUSTIN LYRIC OPERA, THE, 1309
B SHARP MUSIC CLUB OF NEW ORLEANS, THE, 564
BACH CHAMBER CHOIR AND ORCHESTRA, THE, 1506
BALTIMORE CHORAL ARTS SOCIETY, 588
BALTIMORE MEN'S CHORUS, 588
BALTIMORE OPERA COMPANY, 588
BALTIMORE SYMPHONY CHORUS, 589
BATON ROUGE GILBERT AND SULLIVAN SOCIETY, 555
BATON ROUGE OPERA, 555
BEAUMONT CIVIC OPERA, 1313
BEL CANTO CHORUS OF MILWAUKEE, 1506
BERKELEY OPERA, 60
BERKSHIRE CHORAL INSTITUTE, 642
BERKSHIRE LYRIC THEATRE, 639
BERKSHIRE OPERA COMPANY, INC., 630
BIRMINGHAM OPERA THEATER, 2
BLANCHE MOYSE CHORALE, 1409
BOISE MASTER CHORALE, 412
BOISE OPERA, 412
BOSTON LYRIC OPERA COMPANY, 609
BOSTON OPERA ASSOCIATION, 609
BRAINTREE CHORAL SOCIETY, 616
BRONX OPERA COMPANY, 868
CANTATA ACADEMY, 672
CANTATA CHORUS OF NORFOLK, 1432
CENTER FOR CONTEMPORARY OPERA, 953
CENTRAL CITY OPERA, 236
CHAMBER OPERA CHICAGO, 429
CHAPEL HILL-CARRBORO COMMUNITY CHORUS, 1068
CHARLESTON AREA COMMUNITY CHOIR, 1478
CHARLESTON CIVIC CHORUS, 1478
CHARLESTON LIGHT OPERA GUILD, 1478
CHARLOTTE CHORAL SOCIETY, 1049
CHATTANOOGA BOYS CHOIR, 1278
CHATTANOOGA OPERA ASSOCIATION, 1278
CHATTANOOGA SYMPHONY AND OPERA ASSOCIATION, 1278
CHAUTAUQUA OPERA, 881
CHERRY CREEK CHORALE, 243
CHICAGO CHILDREN'S CHOIR, 429
CHICAGO OPERA THEATER, 430
CHICAGO SYMPHONY CHORUS, 430
CHILDREN'S OPERA THEATER, 592
CHORAL ART SOCIETY OF NEW JERSEY, THE, 845
CHORAL ARTS SOCIETY OF PHILADELPHIA, 1220
CHORAL ARTS SOCIETY OF WASHINGTON, 302
CHORAL GUILD OF ATLANTA, 379
CHORAL SOCIETY OF GREENSBORO, 1058
CHORAL SOCIETY OF PENSACOLA, 353
CHORAL SOCIETY OF THE PALM BEACHES, INC., THE, 352
CHORUS AMERICA, 1220
CHORUS OF WESTERLY, 1253
CIMARRON CIRCUIT OPERA COMPANY, 1162
CINCINNATI BOYCHOIR, 1102
CINCINNATI OPERA, 1103

CIVIC LIGHT OPERA, 1457
CLARION CHAMBER CHORALE, 789
CLEVELAND OPERA, 1111
CLEVELAND ORCHESTRA CHORUS, THE, 1112
COLLEGE LIGHT OPERA COMPANY, 627
COLORADO CHILDREN'S CHORALE, 237
COLORADO SPRINGS CHORALE, 230
COLUMBUS SYMPHONY CHORUS, 1123
COMIC OPERA GUILD, 658
COMMONWEALTH OPERA, 637
COMMUNITY OPERA, INCORPORATED, 838
CONCERT ROYAL, INC., 953
CONCORD SINGERS OF NEW ULM, THE, 720
CONNECTICUT CHORAL ARTISTS, INC., 268
CONNECTICUT GRAND OPERA, 280
CONNECTICUT OPERA, 263
COPPELL COMMUNITY CHORUS, 1320
DALE WARLAND SINGERS, 710
DALLAS OPERA, THE, 1327
DALLAS SYMPHONY CHORUS, 1327
DAYTON OPERA ASSOCIATION, 1130
DELAWARE SINGERS, THE, 293
DELAWARE VALLEY OPERA, 907
DENVER CHAMBER CHOIR, THE, 237
DES MOINES METRO OPERA, 518
DESERT OPERA THEATRE, 137
DETROIT SYMPHONY CHORALE, 695
DETROIT SYMPHONY CHORUS, 696
DIABLO LIGHT OPERA COMPANY, 216
DIAMOND STATE CHORUS OF SWEET ADELINES INTERNATIONAL, 291
DIE MEISTERSINGERS, 790
DISTRICT CURATORS, INC., 302
DORIAN OPERA THEATRE, 513
DURANGO CHORAL SOCIETY, 243
DURHAM CIVIC CHORAL SOCIETY, 1053
EPHRATA CLOISTER CHORUS, 1200
EUGENE OPERA, 1179
FAIRBANKS CHORAL SOCIETY, CHILDREN'S CHOIR AND CHORUS!, 18
FAIRBANKS LIGHT OPERA THEATRE, 19
FARGO-MOORHEAD CIVIC OPERA COMPANY, 1085
FESTIVAL CHOIR, THE, 1497
FINE ARTS CHORALE, 645
FLORENTINE OPERA COMPANY, 1506
FLORIDA LYRIC OPERA, 357
FLORIDA STATE OPERA AT FLORIDA STATE UNIVERSITY, 365
FORT LAUDERDALE OPERA, 323
FORT WORTH OPERA ASSOCIATION, 1344
FRIEDRICH SCHORR MEMORIAL PERFORMANCE PRIZE IN VOICE, 655
FULLERTON CIVIC LIGHT OPERA, 83
GARDEN STATE PHILHARMONIC CHORUS, 839
GARY BEARD CHORALE, THE, 1289
GLACIER CHORALE, 776
GLEN ELLYN CHILDREN'S CHORUS, 457
GOLD COAST OPERA, 355
GOODMAN CHAMBER CHOIR, 954
GRANTHAM ORATORIO SOCIETY, 1203
GREATER BUFFALO OPERA COMPANY, 877
GREATER MIAMI OPERA ASSOCIATION, THE, 342
GREATER NEW BRITAIN OPERA ASSOCIATION, 268
GREELEY CHORALE, THE, 248
GREENSBORO OPERA COMPANY, 1058
GREENVILLE CHORALE, THE, 1263
GREENWICH CHORAL SOCIETY, 261
GREGG SMITH SINGERS, INC., 954
GUILD OPERA COMPANY, INC., 106
GULF COAST OPERA THEATRE, 731
HARTFORD CHORALE, INC., THE, 255
HAWAII ECUMENICAL CHORALE, 404
HAWAII OPERA THEATRE, 405
HEARTLAND MEN'S CHORUS, 746
HELENA YOUTH CHOIRS, INC., 773

THEATRE

PERFORMING SERIES

ABBEY BACH FESTIVAL, 1190
ADIRONDACK FESTIVAL OF AMERICAN MUSIC, 1024
AFRICAN-AMERICAN CULTURAL CENTER, 878
ALABAMA SHAKESPEARE FESTIVAL, 10
ALFRED UNIVERSITY, 862
ALLENTOWN COMMUNITY CONCERT ASSOCIATION, 1194
AMATEUR MUSICAL CLUB OF PEORIA, INC., 468
AMERICAN ARTISTS SERIES, 663
AMERICAN LANDMARK FESTIVALS, 990
AMERICAN MUSIC THEATER FESTIVAL, 1225
AMERICAN MUSIC THEATER GROUP, 264
AMERICAN STAGE FESTIVAL, 809
AMES INTERNATIONAL ORCHESTRA FESTIVAL ASSOCIATION, 507
ANCHORAGE FESTIVAL OF MUSIC, 15
ANN ARBOR SUMMER FESTIVAL, 659
APPALACHIAN SUMMER, AN, 1044
APPEL FARM ARTS AND MUSIC CENTER, 819
ARCADY MUSIC SOCIETY, 575
ARIZONA MINI-CONCERTS, 39
ARMSTRONG CHAMBER CONCERTS, INC., 285
ART SONG FESTIVAL, 1114
ARTIST SERIES AT THE PABST, 1509
ARTPARK, 904
ARTS AT ARGONNE, 419
ARTS CELEBRATION/ARTQUAKE FESTIVAL, 1188
ARTS CONSORTIUM STUDIO THEATRE, 1105
ARTS COUNCIL OF GREATER KNOXVILLE, THE, 1287
ARTS COUNCIL OF WASHINGTON COUNTY, 1316
ARTS SAN ANTONIO!, 1385
ARTSPLOSURE, 1070
ASHEVILLE CHAMBER MUSIC SERIES, 1043
ASHLAND FOLK MUSIC CLUB, 1175
ASPEN MUSIC FESTIVAL AND SCHOOL, 221
ASSEMBLY HALL, 421
ATLANTA JAZZ FESTIVAL, 383
ATLANTIC CENTER FOR THE ARTS, 346
AUDITORIUM THEATRE COUNCIL, 443
BACH ARIA FESTIVAL AND INSTITUTE, 1029
BACH DANCING AND DYNAMITE SOCIETY GROUP, 78
BACH FESTIVAL OF PHILADELPHIA, 1225
BANG ON A CAN, INC., 990
BAR HARBOR MUSIC FESTIVAL, 575
BARGEMUSIC LTD., 874
BATES DANCE FESTIVAL, 577
BAY CHAMBER CONCERTS, 576
BAY VIEW MUSIC FESITVAL, 662
BEAUMONT MUSIC COMMISSION, 1314
BEETHOVEN FESTIVAL, 905
BELLEVUE PARKS AND RECREATION DEPARTMENT - BELLEVUE JAZZ FESTIVAL, 1445
BELOIT COLLEGE PERFORMING ARTS SERIES, 1487
BERKELEY SHAKESPEARE FESTIVAL, 62
BERKSHIRE HILLS MUSIC AND DANCE ASSOCIATION, 278
BERKSHIRE THEATRE FESTIVAL, 647
BG-WC ARTS COMMISSION, 540
BIG SPRING CULTURAL AFFAIRS COUNCIL, 1315
BING CONCERTS, 114
BINGHAMTON SUMMER MUSIC FESTIVAL, INC., 866
BIRCH CREEK MUSIC CENTER, 1489
BIRMINGHAM FESTIVAL OF ARTS ASSOCIATION, 3
BLACK ARTS ALLIANCE, 1310
BLACK MUSIC SOCIETY OF MISSOURI, 760
BLAIR COUNTY CIVIC MUSIC ASSOCIATION, 1194
BLITHEWOLD GARDENS AND ARBORETUM "CONCERTS BY THE BAY", 1245
BLUEMONT CONCERT SERIES, 1429
BOSTON EARLY MUSIC FESTIVAL AND EXHIBITION, INC., 612
BOULDER FOLK AND BLUEGRASS ASSOCIATION, 226
BRADFORD CREATIVE AND PERFORMING ARTS CENTER, INC., 1198
BRANDEIS SUMMER MUSIC FESTIVAL, 648
BRATTLEBORO MUSIC CENTER, 1410
BRECKENRIDGE MUSIC INSTITUTE, 228

BRIGHAM YOUNG UNIVERSITY - UNIVERSITY CONCERTS, 1399
BRITT FESTIVALS, 1183
BROADWAY THEATRE LEAGUE OF THE QUAD-CITIES, 512
BROOKLYN ACADEMY OF MUSIC, 874
BUMBERSHOOT, THE SEATTLE ARTS FESTIVAL, 1461
BYRNE MILLER DANCE THEATRE, INC., THE, 12
CABRILLO MUSIC FESTIVAL, 56
CALDWELL FINE ARTS SERIES, 413
CAMBRIDGE CONCERT ASSOCIATION, 1098
CAMEO CONCERTS, INC., 1136
CANDLELIGHT CONCERT SOCIETY, INC., 593
CAPE AND ISLANDS CHAMBER MUSIC FESTIVAL, THE, 638
CARAMOOR CENTER FOR MUSIC AND THE ARTS, 901
CARAVAN OF DREAMS, 1348
CARLETON COLLEGE CONCERT SERIES, 720
CARMEL BACH FESTIVAL, 69
CASA DE UNIDAS, 670
CASTLE HILL FESTIVAL, 629
CATHEDRAL CONCERT SERIES, 1321
CELEBRATE BROOKLYN FESTIVAL, 875
CELEBRITY SERIES, 1215
CELEBRITY SERIES OF BOSTON, INC., 612
CENTRAL FLORIDA CULTURAL ENDEAVORS, 321
CENTRAL PENNSYLVANIA FESTIVAL OF THE ARTS, 1239
CENTRAL PENNSYLVANIA FRIENDS OF JAZZ, INC., 1205
CHAMBER ARTS NORTH, 688
CHAMBER MUSIC/LA FESTIVAL, 114
CHAMBER MUSIC SERIES, 1180
CHARLES RIVER CREATIVE ARTS PROGRAM, 625
CHAUTAUQUA INSTITUTION, 881
CHAUTAUQUA SERIES, 1332
CHEBOYGAN AREA ARTS COUNCIL, 664
CHILDREN'S FREE OPERA AND DANCE, 990
CINCINNATI MAY FESTIVAL, 1105
CINCINNATI MUSIC HALL ASSOCIATION, 1105
CITICORP SUMMERFEST, 760
CITY CELEBRATION ARTS, 178
CITY CENTER OF MUSIC AND DRAMA, 991
CITY OF ALBANY PARKS AND RECREATION DEPARTMENT, 1173
CITY OF BRYAN PARKS AND RECREATION, 1317
CITY OF LOS ANGELES CULTURAL AFFAIRS DEPARTMENT, 115
CLEVELAND MUSEUM OF ART CONCERTS, THE, 1114
CLOWES MEMORIAL HALL, 497
COLGATE UNIVERSITY CONCERT SERIES, 894
COLORADO COUNCIL ON THE ARTS, 239
COLORADO DANCE FESTIVAL, 226
COLORADO MUSIC FESTIVAL, 226
COLORADO OPERA FESTIVAL, 230
COLORADO SHAKESPEARE FESTIVAL, 227
COLORADO STATE UNIVERSITY - OFFICE OF CULTURAL PROGRAMS, 246
COLUMBIA FESTIVAL, INC., 594
COLUMBUS ARTS FESTIVAL, 1125
COMMUNITY ARTS AND MUSIC ASSOCIATION OF SANTA BARBARA, 195
COMMUNITY PLAYERS, INC., 1388
COMMUNITY SERIES, INC., 1388
CONCERTS-AT-THE-COMMON (HARVARD UNITARIAN CHURCH), 650
CONNECTICUT EARLY MUSIC FESTIVAL, 274
CONNETICUT COLLEGE CONCERT AND ARTIST SERIES, 274
COOPERSTOWN CONCERT SERIES, INC., 883
CORNING-PAINTED POST CIVIC MUSIC ASSOCIATION, 884
COUNCIL FOR THE ARTS OF GREATER LIMA, 1136
COUNTY OF WESTCHESTER - PARKS, RECREATION AND CONSERVATION - PERFORMING ARTS, 896
CROCKER ART MUSEUM, 149
CROOKED TREE ARTS COUNCIL, 688
CRS NATIONAL FESTIVAL FOR THE PERFORMING ARTS, 1198
CRYSTAL BALLROOM CONCERT ASSOCIATION, 444
CULTURAL ACTIVITIES CENTER, 1389

L'ENSEMBLE, 860
LEVITT PAVILION FOR THE PERFOMING ARTS, 289
LIED CENTER FOR PERFORMING ARTS, THE, 786
LINCOLN ARTS COUNCIL, 1064
LINCOLN CENTER OUT-OF-DOORS, 992
LINCOLN CENTER'S MOSTLY MOZART FESTIVAL, 992
LINCOLN FRIENDS OF CHAMBER MUSIC, 787
LIONEL HAMPTON, CHEVRON JAZZ FESTIVAL, 415
LIVELY ARTS AT STANFORD UNIVERSITY, THE, 204
LIVING MASTERS SUBSCRIPTION SERIES, 1234
LONGWOOD GARDENS, 1208
LOS ANGELES COUNTY MUSEUM OF ART: MUSIC
    PROGRAMS, 116
LOS ANGELES FESTIVAL, 116
MACHIAS BAY CHAMBER CONCERTS, INC., 578
MACPHAIL CENTER FOR THE ARTS, 716
MADISON AREA ARTS COUNCIL, 1270
MAINE FESTIVAL, THE, 582
MAMOU CAJUN MUSIC FESTIVAL ASSOCIATION, 561
MANCHESTER MUSIC FESTIVAL, 1040, 1414
MANHATTAN ARTS COUNCIL, 530
MANN MUSIC CENTER, INC., 1225
MARKET SQUARE CONCERTS, 1206
MARLBORO MUSIC FESTIVAL, 1414
MARSHALL ARTISTS SERIES, 1481
MARSHALL REGIONAL ARTS COUNCIL, 1374
MARYLAND HANDEL FESTIVAL, 593
MATEEL COMMUNITY CENTER, INC., 144
MCALLEN PERFORMING ARTS, INC., 1376
MEADOW BROOK MUSIC FESTIVAL, 690
MEMPHIS IN MAY INTERNATIONAL FESTIVAL, 1291
MENDOCINO MUSIC FESTIVAL ASSOCIATION, 122
MESSIAH FESTIVAL OF MUSIC, 529
METROPOLITAN MUSEUM CONCERTS AND LECTURES, 992
MICHIGAN BACH FESTIVAL, 666
MICHIGAN RENAISSANCE FESTIVAL, 663
MID-ATLANTIC CENTER FOR THE ARTS, 817
MIDLAND COMMUNITY CONCERT SOCIETY, 685
MIDSUMMER MOZART, 179
MINNESOTA ORCHESTRA, 717
MOHAWK TRAIL CONCERTS, 643
MONADNOCK MUSIC, 811
MONTEREY JAZZ FESTIVAL, 126
MONTREUX ATLANTA MUSIC FESTIVAL, 384
MONTREUX DETROIT JAZZ FESTIVAL - DETROIT
    RENAISSANCE FOUNDATION, 670
MOORHEAD STATE UNIVERSITY, 719
MORMON MIRACLE PAGEANT, 1397
MOUNT DESERT FESTIVAL OF CHAMBER MUSIC, 579
MOZART ON THE SQUARE, 1212
MULE BARN THEATRE OF TARKIO COLLEGE, 766
MULTI-CULTURAL MUSIC AND ART FOUNDATION OF
    NORTHRIDGE, 129
MUNICIPAL THEATER ASSOCIATION OF SAINT LOUIS, 761
MUNSON-WILLIAMS-PROCTOR INSTITUTE PERFORMING
    ARTS DIVISION, 1036
MURRAY CIVIC MUSIC ASSOCIATION, 551
MUSIC AT GRETNA, 1213
MUSIC CENTER OF LOS ANGELES COUNTY, THE, 116
MUSIC FESTIVAL OF ARKANSAS, 45
MUSIC FROM BEAR VALLEY, 58
MUSIC FROM SALEM, 880
MUSIC HALL ARTIST SERIES, 353
MUSIC IN THE MOUNTAINS, 127
MUSIC IN THE MOUNTAINS, FESTIVAL OF MUSIC AT
    PURGATORY, 243
MUSIC MOUNTAIN, 260
MUSIC THEATRE OF WICHITA, 536
MUSICORDA SUMMER STRING PROGRAM AND
    FESTIVAL, THE, 644
NAPERVILLE-NORTH CENTRAL COLLEGE PERFORMING
    ARTS ASSOCIATION, 464
NATIONAL BLACK ARTS FESTIVAL, 384
NATIONAL GALLERY OF ART/CONCERT SERIES, 308
NAZARETH COLLEGE ARTS CENTER, 1021
NEVADA SYMPHONY ORCHESTRA, 797
NEW ARTS PROGRAM, 1209
NEW BRUNSWICK CULTURAL CENTER, INC., 829

NEW HAMPSHIRE MUSIC FESTIVAL, 803
NEW MUSIK DIRECTIONS, 573
NEW ORLEANS JAZZ AND HERITAGE FESTIVAL, 566
NEW YEAR'S FEST, 682
NEW YORK INTERNATIONAL FESTIVAL OF THE
    ARTS, THE, 993
NEWBURYPORT FAMILY YMCA, 635
NEWPORT MUSIC FESTIVAL, 1247
NORFOLK CHAMBER MUSIC FESTIVAL - YALE SUMMER
    SCHOOL OF MUSIC, 276
NORTH AMERICAN NEW MUSIC FESTIVAL, 879
NORTH CAROLINA JAZZ FESTIVAL, 1077
NORTH CAROLINA SHAKESPEARE FESTIVAL, THE, 1062
NORTH CENTRAL ARKANSAS CONCERT ASSOCIATION, 47
NORTH COUNTRY CENTER FOR THE ARTS, 807
NORTHEAST LOUISIANA UNIVERSITY CONCERTS, 562
NORTHROP DANCE SERIES, 717
NORTHWEST FOLKLIFE, 1462
NORTHWEST MISSOURI STATE UNIVERSITY PERFORMING
    ARTS SERIES, 751
OAK RIDGE CIVIC MUSIC ASSOCIATION, 1300
OAKLAND JAZZ ALLIANCE, 133
OCCIDENTAL COLLEGE ARTIST SERIES, 117
OFFICE OF CULTURAL AFFAIRS, 1424
OFFICE OF PUBLIC EVENTS, 140
OGLEBAY INSTITUTE, 1485
OHIO OUTDOOR HISTORICAL DRAMA ASSOCIATION, 1141
OJAI FESTIVALS, 134
OK MOZART INTERNATIONAL FESTIVAL, 1158
OLD TIMERS CONCERT, 778
OPERA FESTIVAL OF NEW JERSEY, 835
ORANGE COAST COLLEGE, 73
OREGON BACH FESTIVAL, 1180
OREGON COAST MUSIC ASSOCIATION, 1177
OUTDOOR DRAMA GROUP ASSOCIATION, THE, 1389
PACIFIC NORTHWEST FESTIVAL, 1462
PACT-RUTH ECKERD HALL AT THE BAUMGARDNER
    PERFORMING ARTS CENTER, 318
PARADISE AREA ARTS COUNCIL, 139
PARK ARTS FESTIVAL - SUMMER SEASON, 1120
PAUL MASSON SUMMER SERIES, 201
PAWLING CONCERT SERIES, 1014
PENINSULA FESTIVAL, 1490
PERFORMING ARTS ASSOCIATION, 1251
PERFORMING ARTS PRESENTATIONS, 146
PERFORMING ARTS SERIES OF MOUNTAIN HOME, 415
PIERRE MONTEUX SCHOOL, THE, 577
PINESONG/SPOKANE FALLS COMMUNITY COLLEGE, 1467
PLAYBOY JAZZ FESTIVAL, 65
PLYMOUTH MUSIC SERIES OF MINNESOTA, 717
PORTLAND PERFORMING ARTS CENTER, INC., 583
PRESCOTT PARK ARTS FESTIVAL, 813
PRESENTATIONS OF THE ELAINE KAUFMAN CULTURAL
    CENTER, 993
PRESIDENTIAL JAZZ WEEKEND, 1226
PRINCESS THEATRE, 25
PRO MUSICA, INC., 677
PTG-FLORIDA, INC./PARKER PLAYHOUSE, 324
QUAD CITY ARTS, 471
QUARTET PROGRAM, THE, 1021
QRS ARTS FOUNDATION, 879
RAMONA HILLSIDE PLAYERS, 86
RAMONA PAGEANT ASSOCIATION, 86
RAVINIA FESTIVAL, 459
REDLANDS BOWL SUMMER MUSIC FESTIVAL, 143
REDLANDS SYMPHONY ASSOCIATION, 143
REED WHIPPLE CULTURAL ARTS CENTER, 797
REGIONAL CENTER FOR THE ARTS, 216
REIF ARTS COUNCIL, THE, 705
RIO GRANDE VALLEY INTERNATIONAL MUSIC
    FESTIVAL, 1376
RIPON COLLEGE/CAESTECKER FINE ARTS SERIES, 1513
RIVERBEND-CINCINNATI SYMPHONY AND POPS
    ORCHESTRA CONCERTS, 1106
ROANOKE ISLAND HISTORICAL ASSOCIATION INC., 1064
ROCKY RIDGE MUSIC CENTER, 787
ROWAN COMMUNITY CONCERT ASSOCIATION, 1072
RUSSIAN RIVER JAZZ FESTIVAL, INC., 85

FACILITY INDEX

GENERAL INDEX

CHAMBER OPERA CHICAGO, 429
CHAMBER ORCHESTRA OF ALBUQUERQUE, 848
CHAMIZAL NATIONAL MEMORIAL - THEATER, 1342
CHAMPAIGN-URBANA SYMPHONY, 421
CHANDLER CENTER FOR THE ARTS, 25
CHANDLER MUSIC HALL AND CULTURAL CENTER, 1417
CHANGING SCENE THEATER, 238, 240
CHANHASSEN DINNER THEATRE, 701
CHANNING PLAYERS, 1360
CHANTICLEER, 511
CHANTICLEER STRING QUARTET, 501
CHANUTE COMMUNITY THEATRE, 525
CHAPEL HILL-CARRBORO COMMUNITY CHORUS, 1068
CHARLES B. GODDARD CENTER, 1158
CHARLES IVES CENTER - PAVILION, 258
CHARLES MOORE - DANCES AND DRUMS OF AFRICA, 870
CHARLES MOULTON DANCE COMPANY, 914
CHARLES RIVER CREATIVE ARTS PROGRAM, 625
CHARLESTON AREA COMMUNITY CHOIR, 1478
CHARLESTON BALLET, 1476
CHARLESTON BALLET, THE, 1257
CHARLESTON CHAMBER MUSIC SOCIETY, 1477
CHARLESTON CIVIC CENTER, 1479
CHARLESTON CIVIC CENTER - COLISEUM, 1479
CHARLESTON CIVIC CENTER - LITTLE THEATER, 1479
CHARLESTON CIVIC CENTER - MUNICIPAL AUDITORIUM, 1479
CHARLESTON CIVIC CHORUS, 1478
CHARLESTON LIGHT OPERA GUILD, 1478
CHARLESTON SYMPHONY ORCHESTRA, 1257
CHARLESTOWN WORKING THEATER, 622
CHARLIE PARKER MEMORIAL FOUNDATION, 745
CHARLIN JAZZ SOCIETY, INC., 299
CHARLOTTE CHORAL SOCIETY, 1049
CHARLOTTE CITY BALLET, 1048
CHARLOTTE COUNTY MEMORIAL AUDITORIUM, 356
CHARLOTTE PLAYERS, 356
CHARLOTTE REPERTORY THEATRE, 1050
CHARLOTTE SYMPHONY ORCHESTRA SOCIETY, 1049
CHATTANOOGA BALLET, 1278
CHATTANOOGA BOYS CHOIR, 1278
CHATTANOOGA OPERA ASSOCIATION, 1278
CHATTANOOGA SYMPHONY AND OPERA ASSOCIATION, 1278
CHAUTAUQUA INSTITUTION, 881
CHAUTAUQUA INSTITUTION - AMPHITHEATER, 882
CHAUTAUQUA INSTITUTION - NORTON HALL, 882
CHAUTAUQUA OPERA, 881
CHAUTAUQUA SERIES, 1332
CHAUTAUQUA SYMPHONY ORCHESTRA, 881
CHEBOYGAN AREA ARTS COUNCIL, 664
CHEBOYGAN OPERA HOUSE - CITY HALL, 665
CHELSEA CHAMBER ENSEMBLE, 940
CHEN AND DANCERS, 914
CHEROKEE HERITAGE CENTER AMPHITHEATER, 1167
CHEROKEE NATIONAL HISTORICAL SOCIETY, 1167
CHERRY COUNTY PLAYHOUSE, 687
CHERRY CREEK CHORALE, 243
CHESHIRE COMMUNITY THEATRE, 257
CHESTNUT BRASS COMPANY, 1218
CHEYENNE CIVIC CENTER, 1521
CHEYENNE LITTLE THEATRE PLAYERS, 1520
CHEYENNE SYMPHONY ORCHESTRA, 1520
CHHANDAM CHITRESH DAS DANCE COMPANY, 151
CHICAGO ACTORS ENSEMBLE, 434
CHICAGO BAR ASSOCIATION SYMPHONY ORCHESTRA, 426
CHICAGO BRASS QUINTET, 426
CHICAGO CHAMBER ORCHESTRA, THE, 426
CHICAGO CHILDREN'S CHOIR, 429
CHICAGO CITY LIMITS, 965
CHICAGO CITY THEATRE COMPANY, 434
CHICAGO DANCE COALITION, 422
CHICAGO DRAMATISTS WORKSHOP, 434
CHICAGO MEDIEVAL PLAYERS, THE, 435
CHICAGO MOVING COMPANY, 423
CHICAGO OPERA THEATER, 430
CHICAGO PHILHARMONIA, 427
CHICAGO SINFONIETTA, 470

CHICAGO STRING ENSEMBLE, 427
CHICAGO SYMPHONY CHORUS, 430
CHICAGO SYMPHONY ORCHESTRA, 427
CHICAGO THEATRE COMPANY, THE, 435
CHICAGO YOUTH SYMPHONY, 428
CHILD'S PLAY THEATRE COMPANY, 703
CHILD'S PLAY TOURING THEATRE, 435
CHILDREN'S BALLET THEATRE, 1472
CHILDREN'S DANCE THEATRE OF NEW MILFORD, 275
CHILDREN'S FREE OPERA AND DANCE, 990
CHILDREN'S OPERA THEATER, 592
CHILDREN'S THEATER ASSOCIATION, 590
CHILDREN'S THEATER COMPANY, THE, 712
CHILDREN'S THEATRE BOARD, INC., 1079
CHILDREN'S THEATRE COMPANY, THE, 718
CHILDREN'S THEATRE OF EDEN, 1054
CHILKAT CENTER FOR THE ARTS, 20
CHINA MUSIC PROJECT, THE, 1109
CHINESE CLASSICAL ORCHESTRA, THE, 479
CHINESE FOLK DANCE COMPANY, 914
CHINESE MUSIC EDUCATIONAL PROGRAM, 479
CHINESE MUSIC ENSEMBLE OF NEW YORK, INC., THE, 940
CHINESE MUSIC SOCIETY OF NORTH AMERICA, 479
CHINOOK THEATRE FOR THE PERFORMING ARTS, THE, 1449
CHIPPEWA VALLEY THEATRE GUILD, 1488
CHORAL ART SOCIETY OF NEW JERSEY, THE, 845
CHORAL ARTS SOCIETY OF PHILADELPHIA, 1220
CHORAL ARTS SOCIETY OF WASHINGTON, 302
CHORAL GUILD OF ATLANTA, 379
CHORAL SOCIETY OF GREENSBORO, 1058
CHORAL SOCIETY OF PENSACOLA, 353
CHORAL SOCIETY OF THE PALM BEACHES, INC., THE, 352
CHORUS AMERICA, 1220
CHORUS OF WESTERLY, 1253
CHOWAN COLLEGE - MCDOWELL COLUMNS AUDITORIUM, 1067
CHRISTIAN ARTS AUDITORIUM, 481
CHRYSALIS REPERTORY DANCE COMPANY, 1354
CIMARRON CIRCUIT OPERA COMPANY, 1162
CINCINNATI BALLET, 1101
CINCINNATI BOYCHOIR, 1102
CINCINNATI JEWISH COMMUNITY CENTER, 1106
CINCINNATI MAY FESTIVAL, 1105
CINCINNATI MUSIC HALL, 1106
CINCINNATI MUSIC HALL ASSOCIATION, 1105
CINCINNATI OPERA, 1103
CINCINNATI PLAYHOUSE - ROBERT S. MARX THEATRE, 1106
CINCINNATI PLAYHOUSE - THOMPSON SHELTERHOUSE, 1107
CINCINNATI PLAYHOUSE IN THE PARK, 1103
CINCINNATI POPS ORCHESTRA, 1101
CINCINNATI SYMPHONY, 1102
CINCINNATI YOUTH SYMPHONY ORCHESTRA, 1102
CIRCA '21 DINNER PLAYHOUSE, 470
CIRCLE IN THE SQUARE, 966
CIRCLE IN THE SQUARE INC., 995
CIRCLE REPERTORY THEATRE COMPANY, 966
CIRCLE THEATRE, INC., 790, 1346
CIRCUIT PLAYHOUSE, 1290
CIRCUS ARTS FOUNDATION OF MISSOURI, 758
CITIARTS THEATRE, 71
CITICORP SUMMERFEST, 760
CITY AUDITORIUM, 231
CITY BALLET OF HOUSTON, 1354
CITY CELEBRATION, INC., 162
CITY CELEBRATION ARTS, 178
CITY CENTER, 995
CITY CENTER - CITY CENTER STAGE I, 995
CITY CENTER - CITY CENTER STAGE II, 996
CITY CENTER - CITY CENTER THEATRE, 996
CITY CENTER OF MUSIC AND DRAMA, 991
CITY LIT THEATER COMPANY, 436
CITY OF ALBANY PARKS AND RECREATION DEPARTMENT, 1173
CITY OF BRYAN PARKS AND RECREATION, 1317
CITY OF GRAND HAVEN COMMUNITY CENTER, 673

HENRY J. KAISER CONVENTION CENTER - ARENA, 133
HENRY J. KAISER CONVENTION CENTER - CALVIN
  SIMMONS THEATRE, 133
HERITAGE ARTISTS, 883
HERITAGE BRASS QUINTET, THE, 1141
HERITAGE DAYS, 787
HERITAGE SQUARE MUSIC HALL, 247
HERSHELL CARROUSEL FACTORY MUSEUM, 1010
HERSHEY THEATRE, 1206
HESPERUS, 1423
HESSTON PERFORMING ARTS SERIES, 527
HEXAGON, 1411
HEYMANN PERFORMING ARTS AND CONVENTION
  CENTER, 558
HIBBING COLLEGE - COMMUNITY BAND, 705
HICKORY COMMUNITY THEATRE, 1061
HIGH POINT COMMUNITY THEATRE, 1062
HIGH POINT THEATRE AND EXHIBITION
  CENTER, 1062, 1063
HIGHFIELD THEATRE, 627
HIGHLAND BRITISH BRASS BAND ASSOCIATION, 1055
HIGHLANDS CHAMBER MUSIC FESTIVAL, 1063
HIGHLANDS PLAYHOUSE, 1063
HIGHLIGHTS IN JAZZ, 944
HILL COUNTRY ARTS FOUNDATION, 1368
HILO COMMUNITY PLAYERS, 401
HINGHAM CIVIC MUSIC THEATRE, 629
HINGHAM HIGH SCHOOL - AUDITORIUM, 629
HIP POCKET THEATRE, 1347
HIPPODROME, 328, 1391
HIPPODROME STATE THEATRE, 328
HIPPODROME THEATRE, 1391
HIRSCH MEMORIAL COLISEUM, 571
HIS IMAGE, SACRED DANCE, 317
HIS MAJESTIE'S CLERKES, 453
HISPANIC ORGANIZATION OF LATIN ACTORS (HOLA), 970
HISTORIC IRONWOOD THEATRE, 679
HISTORY MAKING PRODUCTIONS, 649
HOBSON MEMORIAL UNION - PROGRAM BOARD, 700
HOLE IN THE WALL THEATRE, 269
HOLLYWOOD BOWL, 89
HOLLYWOOD BOWL SUMMER FESTIVAL, 115
HOLLYWOOD PALLADIUM, 89
HOLLYWOOD PLAYHOUSE, 329
HOLLYWOOD THEATER COMPANY, 207
HOMEMADE JAM, 773
HONOLULU CHILDREN'S OPERA CHORUS, 405
HONOLULU SYMPHONY SOCIETY, 403
HONOLULU THEATRE FOR YOUTH, 405
HOPE COLLEGE ORCHESTRA AND SYMPHONETTE, 677
HOPE COLLEGE THEATRE DEPARTMENT, 678
HOPE MARTIN THEATRE, 521
HOPKINS CENTER SUMMER, 806
HORACE A. MOSES BUILDING, 650
HORACE BUSHNELL MEMORIAL HALL, 265
HORIZON CONCERTS INC., 944
HORIZONS THEATRE, 305
HORN IN THE WEST, 1044
HORSE CAVE THEATRE, 544
HOT SPRINGS CONVENTION AND VISITORS' BUREAU, 47
HOTFOOT QUARTET, 1145
HOUGHTON COLLEGE - WESLEY CHAPEL, 897
HOUGHTON COLLEGE ARTIST SERIES, 896
HOUSTON BALLET, 1356
HOUSTON CIVIC CENTER, 1364
HOUSTON CIVIC CENTER-GEORGE R. BROWN
  CONVENTION CENTER, 1364
HOUSTON CIVIC CENTER-GEORGE R. BROWN
  CONVENTION CENTER - BALLROOM, 1364
HOUSTON CIVIC CENTER-GEORGE R. BROWN
  CONVENTION CENTER - EXHIBITION HALL, 1365
HOUSTON CIVIC CENTER-GEORGE R. BROWN
  CONVENTION CENTER - GENERAL ASSEMBLY
  HALL, 1365
HOUSTON CIVIC CENTER-GUS WORTHAM THEATER
  CENTER, 1365
HOUSTON CIVIC CENTER-GUS WORTHAM THEATER
  CENTER - ALICE AND GEORGE BROWN THEATER, 1365

HOUSTON CIVIC CENTER-GUS WORTHAM THEATER
  CENTER - LILLY AND ROY CULLEN THEATER, 1365
HOUSTON CIVIC CENTER - JESSE H. JONES HALL FOR THE
  PERFORMING ARTS, 1366
HOUSTON CIVIC CENTER - THE MUSIC HALL, 1366
HOUSTON CIVIC CENTER - SAM HOUSTON COLISEUM, 1366
HOUSTON CIVIC SYMPHONY ORCHESTRA, 1357
HOUSTON FINE ARTS CENTER, 241
HOUSTON FRIENDS OF MUSIC, 1358
HOUSTON GRAND OPERA, 1358
HOUSTON HARPSICHORD SOCIETY, 1358
HOUSTON INTERNATIONAL FESTIVAL, THE, 1363
HOUSTON SHAKESPEARE FESTIVAL, 1363
HOUSTON SYMPHONY, 1358
HOUSTON SYMPHONY CHORUS, 1359
HOWARD COLLEGE AT BIG SPRING - HOWARD COLLEGE
  AUDITORIUM, 1316
HOWARD COLLEGE AT BIG SPRING - HOWARD COLLEGE
  COLISEUM, 1316
HOWARD HANGER JAZZ FANTASY, 1043
HUBBARD STREET DANCE COMPANY, 423
HUDSON GUILD THEATRE, 970
HUDSON THEATRE, 213
HUDSON VALLEY PHILHARMONIC, 1017
HULT CENTER FOR THE PERFORMING ARTS, 1181
HULT CENTER FOR THE PERFORMING ARTS - SILVA
  CONCERT HALL, 1181
HULT CENTER FOR THE PERFORMING ARTS - SORENG
  THEATRE, 1181
HUMAN ARMS, 1027
HUMBOLDT STATE UNIVERSITY, 56
HUMBOLDT STATE UNIVERSITY - EAST GYMNASIUM, 57
HUMBOLDT STATE UNIVERSITY - FULKERSON RECITAL
  HALL, 57
HUMBOLDT STATE UNIVERSITY - JOHN VAN DUZER
  THEATRE, 57
HUMBOLDT STATE UNIVERSITY - KATE BUCHANAN
  ROOM, 57
HUNGARIAN OPERA WORKSHOP, 430
HUNTINGTON BEACH PLAYHOUSE, 89
HUNTINGTON CHAMBER ORCHESTRA, 1480
HUNTINGTON CIVIC CENTRE, THE, 1481
HUNTINGTON MUSEUM OF ART - AMPHITHEATRE, 1481
HUNTINGTON MUSEUM OF ART - AUDITORIUM, 1481
HUNTINGTON PARK CIVIC THEATRE, 90
HUNTINGTON PLAYHOUSE, 1096
HUNTINGTON THEATRE, 1096
HUNTINGTON THEATRE COMPANY, 611
HUNTSVILLE CIVIC BALLET, 5
HUNTSVILLE LITTLE THEATRE, 7
HUNTSVILLE OPERA THEATER, 6
HUNTSVILLE SYMPHONY ORCHESTRA, 6
HUNTSVILLE YOUTH ORCHESTRA, 6
HURON MUNICIPAL BAND, 1269
HURON PLAYHOUSE, THE, 1097
HUTCHINSON SYMPHONY, 528
I CANTORI DI NEW YORK, 954
I. SHERMAN GREENE CHORALE, INC., 1432
ICE THEATER OF NEW YORK, INC., 922
IDAHO FALLS SYMPHONY, 413
IDAHO REPERTORY THEATRE COMPANY, 414
IDAHO SHAKESPEARE FESTIVAL, 412
IDAHO STATE UNIVERSITY - FRAZIER AUDITORIUM, 416
IDAHO STATE UNIVERSITY - GORANSON HALL, 416
IDAHO STATE UNIVERSITY - POWELL LITTLE THEATRE, 416
IDAHO THEATER FOR YOUTH, 412
IDYLLWILD SCHOOL OF MUSIC AND THE ARTS, 90
IGLOO, THE THEATRICAL GROUP, 970
IL PICCOLO TEATRO DELL'OPERA, INC., 871
ILLINOIS CHAMBER SYMPHONY, 473
ILLINOIS PHILHARMONIC ORCHESTRA ASSOCIATION, 466
ILLINOIS SHAKESPEARE FESTIVAL, 464
ILLINOIS THEATRE CENTER, 466, 467
ILLINOIS WESLEYAN SCHOOL OF DRAMA - MCPHERSON
  HALL, 421
ILLINOIS WESLEYAN UNIVERSITY - WESTBROOK
  AUDITORIUM, 421
ILLUSION THEATER, 713

UP WITH PEOPLE, 37
UPPER ARLINGTON CULTURAL ARTS COMMISSION, 1149
UPPER CATSKILL COMMUNITY COUNCIL OF THE
  ARTS, 1012
UPSALA COLLEGE - WORKSHOP 90 THEATER, 818
UPSTAGE!, 1463
URBAN BUSH WOMEN, 937
USA INTERNATIONAL BALLET COMPETITION, 736
UTAH CLASSICAL GUITAR SOCIETY, 1398
UTAH OPERA COMPANY, 1404
UTAH REGIONAL BALLET, 1395
UTAH SHAKESPEAREAN FESTIVAL, 1395
UTAH STATE UNIVERSITY - CHASE FINE ARTS
  CENTER, 1396
UTAH STATE UNIVERSITY - KENT CONCERT HALL, 1396
UTAH STATE UNIVERSITY - MORGAN THEATRE, 1396
UTAH SYMPHONY, 1403
UTAH VALLEY SYMPHONY, 1398
UTAH VALLEY YOUTH SYMPHONY, 1399
UTAH YOUTH SYMPHONY, 1403
UTICA MEMORIAL AUDITORIUM, 1036
VAL A. BROWNING CENTER FOR THE PERFORMING
  ARTS, 1397
VALDOSTA STATE COLLEGE - SAWYER THEATRE, 400
VALDOSTA STATE COLLEGE - WHITEHEAD
  AUDITORIUM, 400
VALENCIA COMMUNITY COLLEGE - BLACK BOX
  THEATRE, 351
VALENCIA COMMUNITY COLLEGE - PERFORMING ARTS
  CENTER, 351
VALENTINA OUMANSKY DRAMATIC DANCE
  FOUNDATION, 103
VALLEY COMMUNITY THEATER, 418
VALLEY FORGE MUSIC FAIR, 1200
VALLEY FORGE MUSIC FAIR PRODUCTIONS, INC., 1199
VALLEY LIGHT OPERA, 601
VALLEY PERFORMING ARTS, 22
VALLEY SYMPHONY ORCHESTRA & CHORALE AND
  VALLEY SINFONETTE, 1375
VAN CLIBURN FOUNDATION, 1348
VAN WEZEL AUDITORIUM, 364
VANAVER CARAVAN, THE, 1023
VANDERBURGH AUDITORIUM CONVENTION
  CENTER, 489
VAUDEVILLE PALACE, 358
VEERA WIBAUX MIME THEATRE, 178
VENETIAN THEATRE, 901
VENICE COMMUNITY CENTER, 371
VENICE LITTLE THEATRE, THE, 370
VENTI DA CAMERA, 1097
VENTURA COUNTY SYMPHONY ASSOCIATION, 213
VERMONT BALLET THEATRE, 1410
VERMONT MOZART FESTIVAL, 1412
VERMONT OPERA THEATER, 1409
VERMONT SYMPHONY ORCHESTRA, 1411
VERMONT YOUTH ORCHESTRA, 1411
VERO BEACH THEATRE GUILD, 371
VETERANS MEMORIAL, 1127
VETERAN'S MEMORIAL AUDITORIUM, 75
VETERANS MEMORIAL AUDITORIUM, 1252
VETERANS MEMORIAL CIVIC AND CONVENTION
  CENTER, 1137
VETERANS MEMORIAL CIVIC AND CONVENTION CENTER -
  CROUSE PERFORMANCE HALL, 1137
VETERANS MEMORIAL HALL, 1028
VETERANS' MEMORIAL THEATRE, 76
VICTOR VALLEY COLLEGE PERFORMING ARTS
  CENTER, 214
VICTORIA BACH FESTIVAL ASSOCIATION, 1391
VICTORIA MARKS PERFORMANCE COMPANY, 937
VICTORIAN THEATRE, 239, 242
VICTORY GARDENS THEATER, 443, 448
VICTORY PARK AUDITORIUM, 347
VICTORY THEATRE, 67
VIGILANTE THEATRE COMPANY, 771
VIKLARBO CHAMBER EMSEMBLE, 105
VILLA JULIA COLLEGE - INSCAPE THEATRE, 598
VILLA MONTALVO CENTER FOR THE ARTS, 202

VILLA MONTALVO CENTER FOR THE ARTS - CARRIAGE
  HOUSE THEATRE, 202
VILLA MONTALVO CENTER FOR THE ARTS - LILIAN
  FONTAINE GARDEN THEATRE, 202
VILLAGE BACH FESTIVAL, 664
VILLAGE GATE, 1008
VILLAGE LIGHT OPERA GROUP, 961
VILLAGE PLAYERS, 783
VILLAGE PLAYERS, THE, 347
VILLAGE PLAYERS (OAK PARK-RIVER FOREST CIVIC
  THEATRE, INC.), 465
VINCENNES UNIVERSITY SUMMER THEATRE, 505
VINEYARD THEATRE, 987
VIRGINIA BALLET THEATRE, 1431
VIRGINIA BEACH PAVILION CONVENTION CENTER, 1441
VIRGINIA BEACH PAVILION CONVENTION CENTER -
  EXHIBIT HALL, 1442
VIRGINIA BEACH PAVILION CONVENTION CENTER -
  PAVILION THEATER, 1442
VIRGINIA CHORAL SOCIETY, 1431
VIRGINIA OPERA, 1432
VIRGINIA SHAKESPEARE FESTIVAL, 1442
VIRGINIA STAGE COMPANY, 1433
VIRGINIA SYMPHONY, THE, 1431
VIRGINIA THEATER, 1008
VIRTUOSI DELLA ROSA, INC., 1187
VISALIA CONVENTION CENTER - EXHIBIT HALL, 214
VISALIA CONVENTION CENTER - L.J. WILLIAMS
  THEATRE, 214
VISALIA CONVENTION CENTER - ROTARY THEATRE, 215
VIVA EL PASO!, 1342
VIVE LES ARTS SOCIETE AND THEATRE, 1371
VIVE LES ARTS THEATRE, 1371
VOCAL ARTS ENSEMBLE OF CINCINNATI, 1103
VOICES OF CHANGE, 1326
VON BRAUN CIVIC CENTER, 7
VON BRAUN CIVIC CENTER - ARENA, 7
VON BRAUN CIVIC CENTER - CONCERT HALL, 7
VON BRAUN CIVIC CENTER - EXHIBIT HALL, 7
VON BRAUN CIVIC CENTER - PLAYHOUSE, 8
VORSPIEL DRAMA EPHRATA CLOISTER ASSOCIATES, 1200
VORTEX REPERTORY COMPANY, 1310
WACO CONVENTION CENTER, 1392
WACO CONVENTION CENTER - CHISHOLM HALL, 1392
WADSWORTH AUDITORIUM, 892
WAIMEA COMMUNITY THEATRE, 408
WALDORF COMMUNITY ARTISTS SERIES, 516
WALKER ART CENTER, 716
WALLA WALLA SYMPHONY, 1472
WALLINGFORD SYMPHONY ORCHESTRA, 284
WALNUT STREET THEATRE, 1228
WALNUT STREET THEATRE - MAINSTAGE, 1228
WALNUT STREET THEATRE - STUDIO FIVE, 1229
WALNUT STREET THEATRE - STUDIO THREE, 1229
WALNUT STREET THEATRE COMPANY, 1224
WALTER KERR THEATRE, 1008
WALTON CREEK PLAYHOUSE, 1108
WANG CENTER FOR THE PERFORMING ARTS, THE, 616
WAR MEMORIAL AUDITORIUM, 325
WAREHOUSE LIVING ARTS CENTER, 1323
WARNER THEATRE, 313
WARNOR'S THEATER, 82
WARREN CIVIC MUSIC ASSOCIATION, 1150
WARREN PERFORMING ARTS CENTER, 498
WARREN PERFORMING ARTS CENTER - ESCH
  AUDITORIUM, 498
WARREN PERFORMING ARTS CENTER - STUDIO
  THEATER, 498
WARREN SYMPHONY ORCHESTRA, 696
WARTBURG COLLEGE - NEUMANN AUDITORIUM, 522
WARTBURG COLLEGE ARTISTS SERIES, 522
WARWICK PLAYERS, 1252
WASHINGTON AND LEE UNIVERSITY CONCERT GUILD,
  1429
WASHINGTON BACH CONSORT, 303
WASHINGTON BALLET, THE, 298
WASHINGTON BLUEGRASS ASSOCIATION, 1471
WASHINGTON CENTER FOR THE PERFORMING ARTS, 1452